SELAH!

Harmony Commentary of the Four Gospels
(with connotations on historical and relevant social, moral, religious, and political issues)

The King James or Authorized Version of the Bible, the Fourth Edition of 1769

The above edition of the 1611 Authorized Version was published in 1769
under the supervision of Dr. Benjamin Blayney (1728-1801).
This is the King James Bible that is popularly used today.

By Missionary Henry R. Pike, Ph.D.

AMBASSADOR INTERNATIONAL
GREENVILLE, SOUTH CAROLINA & BELFAST, NORTHERN IRELAND

www.ambassador-international.com

Selah!

Harmony Commentary of the Four Gospels

Printed in the United States of America

Selah! ISBN: 978-1-62020-040-7
Selah! (ebook) ISBN: 978-1-62020-041-4

Scripture quotations are from the King James Version (Authorized Version), fourth edition, 1769.

Cover Photos
Top: Scenes in the land of Israel
Bottom: Sea of Galilee

AMBASSADOR INTERNATIONAL
Emerald House
427 Wade Hampton Blvd.
Greenville, SC 29609, USA
www.ambassador-international.com

AMBASSADOR BOOKS
The Mount
2 Woodstock Link
Belfast, BT6 8DD, Northern Ireland, UK
www.ambassador-international.com

The colophon is a trademark of Ambassador

Welcome to *Selah! Harmony Commentary of the Four Gospels.*

This book is also available as an ebook from amazon.com and bn.com.

CONDENSED TABLE OF CONTENTS

DEDICATION

We live, work, die, and leave our memories behind. This book is given as a lasting memory to our four children and six grandchildren. The latter gave us a new outlook on life and a better understanding of our failures and successes as young parents. The crowns of this old couple, still happy sweethearts after fifty-eight years of marriage, are Timothy, Jeremy, Christy, Cody, Caroline, and Nicholas. All of us leave behind a composite of memories. Both sadness and joy are the life companions of all men. They are part of the time woven fabric of human existence. The legacy of genuine Christians should be that of Prov. 10:7, "The memory of the just *is* blessed." Beloved children and greatly beloved grandchildren, meet "Mom and Dad" and "Papa and Nana" in heaven when your earthly days have ended. You know the way; He is Jesus Christ, the Son of the living God. How joyful when we reach the end of life and find that everything God has done, be it ever so dark and mysterious, will bring eternal thanksgiving from our lips and honor to His Name. Keep remembering that *true* Christians see the future in the present!

ACKNOWLEDGEMENTS

During the years spent in building this harmony commentary, we have passed through one storm after another. Our oldest son incurred a major heart attack from which he never fully recovered. My wife suffered a massive stroke while we were out of state in meetings. She is a genuine miracle in view of the enormity of this monster malady, brain surgery, and her amazing recovery to this moment. Prior to these things, my second son fell ill with leukemia in Johannesburg, South Africa. He also miraculously survived the ravages of this deadly disease. I have passed through eight surgeries and am now, at the ripe old age of eighty, confined to a wheelchair for the remainder of my earthly days. These ills of human life have driven us deeper into God's loving arms. It was out of this stormy background that *Selah! Harmony Commentary of the Four Gospels* was born. The tears of God's children are the diamonds that make heaven shine.

Many people have helped to make this book possible. Giants of the faith, some of them now in heaven enjoying God forever, from whose works I have drawn, are given the salute of Christ. These pages would never have been written had my Sunday school teacher, the late Mrs. Ruth Gifford, not led me to the Savior in 1946. Among my numerous helpers are the following:

First, is my precious wife of fifty-eight years, Addien, who supports me in everything, along with our sons, David, Timothy, Phillip, and daughter, Rosemary. My grandsons, Timmy, Jeremy, and Cody, often rescued me from those confounding computer problems. Standing up front among our helpers are Bill and Mary Chappell. Mary spent many hours typing and assisting with layout designs. Bill drove me back and forth to the doctors amid my various illnesses while this work was being written. Our long list of helpers includes Chris Taylor, Kenny Waldrop, Luke and Katelyn Bundy, Frankie Tye, Janice Morgan, Sam Clark, Eddie Ledford, Grace Heimendinger, Tommy Kyser, Bonnie Links, Jerald Manley, Donna Kagel, Tony and Daisy Fowler, Lee Lawrence, Judy Gilbert, Eulala and Chuck Fletcher, Victoria Ralph, Brownie Rogers, Ron Thompson, Kenny Layne, Jan Hall, and Julie McCrum. Thanks also to Joan Cosby, Daniel and Debbie O'Renick, Chuck Garrett, Vaughan Thandroyan, Johnny Campbell, Pastor James Mills, and Bronston Baptist Church along with Freedom Baptist Church, and pastor Ed Parton gave financially to the publication of this book. Kenny O'Dell, Alex Wheeler, Dr. Chrissy Heise, and Mike and Sharlotte McGary also helped. Dean Wilson, Ron Widner, Fred and Pat Chapman, Timothy Green, Bill and Frances Mosley, Kevin Anderson, and Dr. Sarah White deserve a salute of gratitude. Dawn and Kevin Deuter, Howard Gough, Dr. Leigh Anne Randall, and Marie Hunter, all of them in far off Australia, perused many pages. Anne Smith's work was a great blessing despite many "long distance collect" phone calls! Peter and Ruth Thomas read hundreds of pages, made corrections, and offered many timely suggestions. Sherman Dye, Tony Miller, and Sam Lowry gave me wise counsel regarding printing requirements. Some have chosen to be anonymous.

Sandra King, our Australian daughter, while helping nurse my wife out of a stroke, did hours of manuscript reading. Daniel Black, a helpful friend rescued the whole effort from being lost in computer mayhem and laid out the final format. Neva Huff did a comprehensive perusal of this work.

Lastly, Professor Stan Eby and Rebecca Weier, assisted in many ways. Other Christians shared in building this harmony commentary. After fourteen years of labor, I cannot remember all my helpers. Happily, God knows their names and addresses. For all who made this book possible, the Bible has a unique message recorded in Heb. 6:10. *Thank you!*

HOW TO USE THIS HARMONY COMMENTARY

The miracle of Christ's coming into the world resulted in a different style of historical religious literature. Though all Scripture was given by inspiration of the Holy Spirit, the four gospels are the crown of all biblical writings. A reliable harmony of these gospels is the first tool necessary in studying the life of Christ. One cannot properly understand the record of His earthly years without this resource. Nahum Tatian, a heretical Gnostic who lived for a time in Syria, composed the most ancient harmony known. Shortly after A.D. 150, he wrote a *Diatessaron,* meaning "a harmony in four parts." Being a Gnostic, he doctored his work, leaving out references to the deity of Christ. None of it survived the ravages of time, but other ancient writers mentioned it in their writings. Over the centuries, hundreds of harmonies were produced, often taking varying approaches to the Master's life and work. The *Selah! Harmony Commentary of the Four Gospels* is another attempt to harmonize (as far as possible) the records of Jesus' life. This book has two major differences; first, it contains a massive commentary, and second, the author holds to the absolute inspiration of the four gospels as well as the entire canon of Holy Scripture. As explained later, God did not intend that all four gospels be totally harmonized. If so, we could dispense of three and use just one. The following briefly explains the methodology, literary tools, and techniques employed in producing this work.

● **Text:** The *Authorized* or *King James Version,* fourth edition of 1769.

● **Authors' names attached to the four gospels:** It is incorrect to think that the names of the gospels prove that these men wrote them. Several centuries before names were added, the belief existed that Matthew, Mark, Luke, and John wrote these documents. Their names were later attached at the heading of each book. Consequently, in time, the Holy Spirit, not men, vindicated their authorship.

● **The length of His ministry:** This has been determined by the number of Passover celebrations the Savior attended. The author understands that the feast of John 5:1 has reference to this great annual event in Hebrew history. I have reckoned the length of His ministry, beginning at His baptism with four successive Passovers following. Writers have used this approach for centuries. This is discussed at the beginning of Section 52, footnotes a, b, and c. The author *conjectures* that Christ died at approximately thirty-four years old. His early years were in the reign of King Herod the Great. He was reasonably somewhere under two years old when Herod slaughtered the infants and Joseph fled to Egypt with his family. Shortly after Herod's death in 4 B.C., they returned to the land of Israel.

● **Disclaimer:** British spellings remain as they are. For example the word "fullness" is spelt as "fulness," the style used in the Scripture texts. Errors in quotations and some spellings (unless of serious nature) taken from the documentation sources have been retained as originally printed. A few quoted misspellings are tagged by the grammatical tool "sic." Having read hundreds of books over the years, the author drew some of this work from a rusty memory and cannot now precisely document them. Quotations from an author are not my endorsement of all his theological beliefs. Citations from John Gill, F. W. Farrar, John Lightfoot, Adam Clarke, A. T. Robertson, Joachim Jeremias, and Alfred Edersheim illustrate this. The Soncino Edition of the *Babylonian Talmud,* the works of Josephus, Joseph Klausner, George Foot-Moore, Will Durant, and all other pseudo, or non-Christian sources are used for historical purposes, not theological. Doctor C. I. Scofield's comments in his footnotes at John 5:3; Mk. 11:26; Acts 8:37; Col. 2:2; and 1 John 5:7 reflect that he was slightly poisoned by German higher criticism.

● **Quotation marks, capitalization, and font styles:** Quotation marks are inserted throughout the text of the four gospels. They help the reader to determine "who" is saying, "what" in the biblical passages. Capitalizations are used in the Footnotes-Commentaries when they speak of the "Holy Spirit," and the "Word of God," whether it is Christ the Word, or the Scriptures. Pronominal mentions of God, Jesus, and the Holy Spirit are also in the uppercase. No punctuation marks exist in biblical manuscripts, including the Textus Receptus. Translators added these later. All words spoken by Satan and demons are in a heavy Gothic font to reflect their malevolent intentions toward God, man, and creation.

● **Color system:** All of Christ's Words are in red letters. This idea originated in 1899 with a German immigrant, Dr. Steven Klopsch, and was used in the first edition of the *Christian Herald Magazine.* Old Testament quotations or allusions in the four gospels and selected mentions of Jesus as the Messiah are set in dove gray backgrounds with a dark letter font. The three times that God spoke audibly to Christ are shaded in gray with red font. The four Passovers Jesus attended during His ministry are set in a gray background. His entry into Jerusalem on Palm Sunday and the major events to His ascension are shaded in gray or typed in heavy red or black font. These two colors are used in some chapter and Section headings. Italics, gray backgrounds, or heavy black and red fonts emphasize certain words and subjects. Peter's three denials, Pilate's five innocent verdicts, Jesus' seven sayings from the cross, and the five different mentions of the Great Commission are all set in a gray background with red letters.

- **Many repetitions and helps:** Four histories, written about the same Man, contain numerous repetitions. *This work has hundreds of these.* Repetitions are not that painful, unless they become tautological. The gospels reveal that Jesus repeated Himself; even decades after His ascension (compare Matt. 13:9 with Rev. 2:7, 11, 17, and 29). Portions of the Footnotes-Commentary in one Section may be repeated in another Section. I reasoned it best to reiterate many things, instead of continually sending the readers back and forth through this work by using the *ibid* back-reference tool. The hundreds of cross references, many doublets, triplets, and quadruplicates will make this work difficult for some. Most references are identified by "See Section . . .", "Note . . .", or "Refer to Section . . .", and so forth. Frequent mention is made of the "learned academicians," "great scholars," and "experts." These terms point mostly to the *unsaved* religious intellectuals who think they are qualified to translate and censure the Bible, a book in which they do not believe in the first place. Nothing rude is intended by these descriptive terms. Across the top of each Section is a long narrow Information Box briefly stating what is in that particular Section. The twenty chapters in this harmony commentary vary in length due to their contents.

- **Finding paragraphs easily:** Most Footnotes-Commentary headings have numerous sub-paragraphs. These are marked by **2p-**, **3p-**, meaning second and third paragraphs. This literary tool will aid readers to locate quickly the desired sub-paragraphs under any of the Footnotes-Commentary headings. Some of these paragraphs are independent thoughts not connected with previous subjects.

- **Departures and styles used:** Frequently, I have bypassed some of the standard methodology used in literary presentations. The *ibid* notation, referring to a text or book previously quoted, has been excluded. I chose to repeat the book title and author's name. This will save the astute much reader time in backtracking through hundreds of pages to locate the original source. Technical theological terms have been avoided as far as possible. The grammatical tools, *i.e., cit., e.g., op., cf.,* ampersand *(&)* except in book titles and the ellipsis, are used sparingly. The old term *passim* meaning "here and there," is found in a few places. Symbols such as ▶, ◙, and ●, along with the asterisk identify or connect specific topics. Not every statement is documented. Such acute preciseness would require many extra pages and lay an unnecessary burden upon the readers. Academicians have the tendency to over-document their works, believing this demonstrates their great knowledge and vast research capabilities. Too much of this is a nuisance for the average reader. I have sought to mitigate this boredom. Devotional, exegetical, homiletical, and historical methodologies with literal and allegorical hermeneutics have been used. The Supplements attached to Section 23 and Section 38 are without Footnotes-Commentary.

- **A one-volume work:** Every verse in the four gospels is in the twenty chapters of this work with hundreds of references and comments. Explanatory words are indicated by brackets within the Scripture texts and by inverted commas after the texts. The two longest Sections are The Sermon on the Mount, Sections 44–47, and the Olivet Discourse, in Section 163 with its parallels in Mk. 13 and Lk. 21. Chapters 1 and 8 are divided into four parts for precise explanations. Ancient Hebrew customs and manners are frequently explained. The genealogies of Christ are given from five slightly different angels in Chapter 3. They reveal that He was from the Hebrew nation; their promised Messiah. There are eight Appendices to expand specific topics, a General Subject Index, and a Selected Bibliography.

- **The world's most hated Man:** Theological liberalism with its cavalier attitude presents Jesus as another "nice guy" religious figure. He is unsaved mankind's most despised person because He is the world's only Savior. Never in the past two thousand years has the Son of God been so publicly ridiculed and blasphemed as He is today. *The da Vinci Code* and *The Lost Gospel According to Judas Iscariot* scandalized His perfect character. Islam fiercely hates His death and resurrection. He is maligned by the educational, political, and entertainment systems. Both the History and National Geographic television channels present Him as an ignorant Jew, trying to find His purpose in life. "Experts" are summoned from America's hellhole seminaries to decide whether He arose from the dead! To pray publicly in His divine Name may insult the godless and bring litigation. Cultural and spiritual corruption is poisoning America. In this book, sin and Satan are described as they are. I have sought to "speak the truth in love" (Eph. 4:15), while at the same time "tell the truth" without varnishing sin and its disastrous results in the bodies and souls of men. Unsaved theological academicians are slouched into a no-such-thing-as-sin posture. They pander to a Hollywood-style Jesus. The "religious best sellers" avoid controversial issues and are "always positive." Naming sin, its effects, damnation, and hell are taboo. We shun habitual negativity, yet negatives are part of life. God gave Ten Commandments. (They have now become "The Ten Suggestions.") Eight of these are negative and two are positive. Jesus was sorely abstract when confronting religious hypocrites. This book has negatives when dealing with apostasy and sin. We hold that all that is *truly* noble, good, and lofty in civilization is the fruit of Christ's appearing among men.

If a genuine Christian seeks to live according to Scripture, he is "politically incorrect." He is branded as a "fundamentalist" or "the religious right." Dealing biblically with abortion, adultery, fornication, sodomy, same sex marriages, heresy, radical Islam, apostasy, false religions, and corrupt politics is hate crime language. Satanic tolerance is the god that rules American society. The confused masses are conditioned to be nice to sin and the Devil. "Hell" and "damnation" preached from the pulpit are insultingly inappropriate. Yet, the habitual use of these two words in the public domain is acceptable. The humanistic tolerance of today is not the highest expression of freedom. The vice of human indecision has turned millions of Christians into cowards. It is the seedbed of anarchy toward God. Men have enthroned themselves in their hearts. Immoral moralists have recast decency into a dirt mold. They connive to silence those who oppose their evil, believe in Christ, and stand for purity and right. Supporting wickedness is an act of individual cowardice. Once Americans believed that every man had the right to his opinion. Today, every man's opinion is right! Where are the responsibilities and absolutes that are required of every man? Everything is fluid, relevant, and compatible. Men protest, "We have our rights!" Yes, even the right to go to hell. Sound reasoning is enslaved by passions and the "will of the people." Animals do not practice what some do in the name of "civil liberties." In public functions, traditional prayer is being replaced by a "moment of silence." A man can almost marry his cow with court approval and possibly government tax support. Are "America's freedoms" licenses to future doom?

● **Rejecting ecumenical pluralism.** This work contains no ecumenical "inter-faith" appeal. Apostasy is rejected because Scripture teaches it is wrong. Cults, sects, religions, denominations, philosophies, educators, academicians, theologians, and politicians who oppose foundational Bible teachings are the enemies of God and men. We are not "one global family." Sin has divided humanity beyond repair; all need Jesus Christ. Man is not the measure of all things. He is a failure without the Savior. An apologetic stance upholds the major doctrines of Scripture. Calvinism, Arminianism, and academic infidelity are demonic departures from sound biblical doctrine. I have sought to mitigate my judicial opinions with Christian candor and calm. If describing Satan and his imps for what they are is unchristian, then this book is unchristian. Contemplating heaven or hell and the destiny of men, demands brutal honesty. Thus, it has been impossible to write in a total dispassionate style. In spiritual matters, most people prefer a sweet lie to the bitter truth. A Christian who disbelieves the total inspiration of Scripture cannot be trusted very far with spiritual issues. Soon, he will miss the mark, for he has no infallible guide. Education without Christ and God's Word makes unsaved religious men clever devils.

● **Personal experiences and other points:** Selected events from my Christian life are included to enhance particular subjects. Comments that are relevant in today's social, economic, political, moral, and spiritual crises will frequently appear. Some of these are repeated later in other Sections. Questions regarding chronology are touched upon several times. A few Hebrew and Greek words are used for clarification not correction. King Herod died in 4 B.C. Christ was born shortly before this date. About the first five or six years of our Savior's life lapsed back into the B.C. era of King Herod. As mentioned, it is assumed that Jesus died at thirty-four years of age in about A.D. 30. Thus, His death was approximately forty years before the destruction of Jerusalem in A.D. 70. Accuracy, without pretending to know all the answers, let alone the questions, has been the prime goal. No work of man is infallible, but genuine effort should be expended to make it the best that he can produce. In a book this large, so extended, and intricate, the author could not escape all errata. Over time, some will find problems, inadvertent inaccuracies, errors, and questions that need answering. My conjectures are given as possibilities, not facts. Most of these appear in italics. I have prayed for heavenly help from the start to finish. Now, I ask all readers for patience and pardon where necessary. The world crowns success; the Lord of heaven crowns faithfulness. To wear the diadem of His approval is the highest honor for any *true* Christian.

In the Bible, God established all divine doctrine that He wants us to know. It is found nowhere else. The history of this afterward is the story of divine preservation. Intermittently, this work carries an appeal to prepare for eternity. The gospel brings life and immortality into the darkness of sin for all who receive Christ as personal Lord and Savior. At death, we step through one door and enter another called eternity. *This cannot be spent!* The prudent person will ponder this inevitable fact and hurry to Jesus, the Son of God, for forgiveness of sins and the gift of eternal life. ***Selah!* "Think of that."**

DETAILED TABLE OF CONTENTS

Section introductions identified by ***** *at end of sentence:*

Appearing at Jordan for baptism, the third silent period of eighteen years ends. His public
ministry begins by depicting in baptism how His work would end some three years later.

*Section introductions identified by * at end of sentence:*

*Section introductions identified by * at end of sentence:*

CHAPTER 10

The days of the Passion Week of Jesus before His death are highlighted in gray below.

CHAPTER 14

*Section introductions identified by * at end of sentence:*

*Section introductions identified by * at end of sentence:*

From His early morning resurrection to the Emmaus road surprise later that afternoon

The brief history of Jesus giving the Great Commission five different times at five different places

●Which of these two occurred first?

It seems impossible to determine which of the two above mentions of the Commission came first. The author's order for the Third and Fourth placement is a *conjecture*. They may be reversed with no violence being done to the Scripture texts. This is a question of the right chronology for these two events and not one of divine inspiration.

The Son of God, Jesus the Messiah, returns to the Father

+++++++++++++++++++++++++++++++++

VERSE FINDER FOR EVERY PASSAGE IN THE FOUR GOSPELS

John

Acts

AUTHOR'S INTRODUCTION

The King James Version of the Bible and related subjects

Matthew's book is considered to be the first written and therefore, the oldest of the four gospels. In this harmony commentary, the other three are harmonized (as closely as possible) with his record and not that of Mark. Their histories give portions of the life of Christ but hardly all of it. At times, their entries in the four narratives are not in any particular chronological order, while at other times they are. Variations of subject matter reveal the absence of personal collaboration. The four gospels are brief, informal, yet dramatic and powerful. Infidel critics consider them inartistic, nonconforming, and disjointed. These opinions demonstrate that "The natural man receiveth not the things of the Spirit of God: for they are foolishness unto him: neither can he know *them*, because they are spiritually discerned" (1 Cor. 2:14). For example, writing by divine compulsion, not human choice, or genius, Matthew recorded a deed of Christ at one place in his history, while Mark or Luke penned it at another; yet God directed each one in what He wanted written about the life of His Son and where He wanted it placed in their books. In all such cases, the events, themselves were of greater importance than the order in which they occurred. Examples of how the four writers often placed the same events into different chronological slots are listed just before Section 29 under the heading *"From This Point Forward."* Due to the unique style in which God had the gospels written, it is impossible to build one complete unitary harmony of all four. If this were done, we could dismiss three of them and use only one. The Holy Spirit purposely inhibited this. We have four gospels; they are similar yet different. God arranged it this way so those who study the life of Christ have a broader view of His Son. Because the beauty of Christ's life transcends all of earth's mortals, to record a brief part of it in absolute accuracy is an accomplishment of grace that excels all literary innovations.

Divine authority directed all four evangelists in what they wrote regardless of where they may have gotten it; whether from memory, the testimony of others, or straight from God. Similarities in vocabulary, sentence constructions are normal, since they all wrote on the life of Christ. Skeptic theologians tell us that John penned his gospel as a "helpful supplement" to the other three in an attempt to fill in the gaps they left. John wrote as the Holy Spirit directed. He recorded many things not given by the other three evangelists. Whatever his work did or did not do for the other three is a matter of individual understanding. All four gospels intermittently supplement one another, even though the human authors wrote independently. For a discussion of "when" the gospels were written, see *Appendix Seven*. A German literary critic, Gottlob Storr (died 1805), popularized the myth that Mark wrote his gospel first; then Matthew and Luke borrowed, swapped, and chopped all they could from him. Needing more material, they went to a mythical source. No one knows where this was or what became of it. Unbelieving theologians named this nonexistent thing "Q" or "logia." It was another academic delusion hatched by the unsaved "literary authorities" who reject an inspired Bible.

The surly conjectures of "greatly learned minds" that toyed with the Scripture originated in Europe among unregenerate "religionists." These men disdained a Bible that is trustworthy and demoted Christ to the rank of world thinkers and philosophers. Rationalism, whether it is the German, British, or American variety, has never been the friend of Christ, God's Word, or the souls of men. It purports to believe in God, on the one hand, yet discredits His Word, and ballyhoos divine inspiration on the other. How troubling to hear great ministers stand and struggle to explain to their congregations why dozens of verses and hundreds of *serious* words have been dropped out of the "easier to understand versions" they use. The next several paragraphs briefly relate the story of unsaved religionists, who attempted to critique the four gospels. Beginning with the premise that the Scriptures were fabricated, the message of the inspired four gospels flew in the face of the "superior learning" of these professional infidels. Frustrated by the darkness of their unconverted souls, early critics of Scripture named their inability to understand how God gave the first three gospels, "the synoptic problem." This pseudo science was the offspring of Old Testament higher criticism. Called "innovations in philosophy," higher criticism originated with Satan. He planted it into the minds of two Catholics, Richard Simon (died 1712), and Jean Astruc (died 1766). It was another product of the grossly dark Enlightenment Period in Europe.

A German rationalist, Johann Griesbach (born 1812), created and popularized the "synoptic problem" beast. He may have adopted this heresy from the Platonist infected Augustine, *presently* listed as one of the famed "canonized doctors of the Roman Catholic Church." As usual, liberal conservatives in Britain and America embraced Herr Griesbach's textual corruption in order to appear "scholarly and academic." Though fiercely censured by some of the divines of his day for tampering with and changing Scripture, he was unmoved. Griesbach denied the deity of Christ, the Holy Trinity, and was among the first German translators who changed the Received Text of the New Testament. Unitarians poured their patronage upon him after he removed 1 John 5:7 from his new text published in 1806. (Most of the "better modern day translations" have also removed this, or dropped it to a footnote.) His rejection of various Scriptures and dark comments about Christ are brushed aside by many "great scholars" of today. His verse tampering and blasphemies are still hailed in theological classrooms as truth. Fragments of his soul's darkness also came from G. E. Lessing, an agnostic philosopher and poet (died 1781). In an essay written in 1778 and published after his death, Lessing wrote that the four evangelists were "human historians," meaning God had nothing to do with their writings. Such are the irreverent liberties that proud learning, cloaked in religion, dares to take with the Holy Bible.

Dr. Griesbach echoed the same falsehood when he wrote that portions of the gospels were "sheer fabrication" and "worthless fables." For a comprehensive article on "Professor" Griesbach, the handmaid of the "synoptic problem" myth, see the *Biblical, Theological, and Ecclesiastical Cyclopaedia,* vol. lll, pages 1008-1010, by M'Clintock and Strong. Beware of apologists for an uninspired Bible, who describe those upholding divine inspiration as, "Always assaulting the person not the problem." It is like opposing sin but never the Devil, who is the father of sin. Something is seriously wrong with men who use this rebuttal and then defend the "specialists" who delete hundreds of *serious* words and many verses from their new translations. Griesbach and his kind were not faceless theologians with good intentions; they were men who rejected the Christ of the Scriptures and the Scriptures of Christ.

Years after Griesbach's death (1812), a female German religionist, Dr. Eta Linnemann, a retired professor of the New Testament at the infamous Philipps University, Marburg, Germany, had something to say. She unleashed a barrage of stinging comments about "synoptic problem" invention, and "the science of historical criticism." For years, she had poisoned the minds of hundreds of students with the lies of Griesbach's historical criticism and the "synoptic problem" fable. Then something wonderful happened: Professor Linnemann was saved by the grace of God! The three main books she wrote after her rejection of liberal theological heresy were, *Historical Criticism of the Bible,* then, *Is There a Synoptic Problem?* and lastly, *Biblical Criticism on Trial: How Scientific is Scientific Theology?* They pungently expose the rottenness of historical-critical theology. On pages 209-210 of the second work, she states that the problem with the people who defend and teach these untruths is that they need to be saved! Linnemann wrote on page 210, "A decisive conversion to Jesus breaks the bonds of historical-critical theology." This is the cure for those who have ingested the poison of infidel textual criticism. Academic rejection and opposition to the reliability of Scripture are always the same: it is a sin problem in the human heart. Degradation of the Savior reveals that men are aliens to the miracle of the new birth.

Dr. Linnemann candidly stated that those who teach this theological system are unsaved. It is striking that personal testimonies of God's saving grace in the lives of these critics cannot be found in their writings. It is what these people do not say that is deeply troublesome. Where is any mention of personal conversion and the urgent, pressing need to bring men to Christ? *It is anti-academic and highly insulting to their superior learning to write such things.* Salvation, rarely mentioned, is always in dubious language. From Preface to Conclusion, there is no statement that the author was a born again Christian; that he wanted to share with every reader the joy of this marvelous wonder. A few ecumenically infected liberal conservatives feebly mention salvation couched in such terms as "inter-faith," "building bridges," "the work of the kingdom," "Christian world view," and the "catholicity of the church." Plain Bible language, such as "saved," "born again," "redeemed by the blood of the Lamb," written in forthright, unblushing terms are foreign to their writings. Divinely unenlightened scholarship with its scientific tools of Scriptural scrutiny, yet void of the new birth, has always had a terrible problem with the miracle of personal salvation. It is a subject they neglect, reject, mitigate, hate, or reinterpret into an ecumenical labyrinth of spiritual or political human rights nothingness.

As charming and "greatly educated" as some of these people are, they cannot be trusted with eternal matters as laid down in Holy Scripture. Their rejection of an inspired Bible did not spring from arrogance; it originated in their unregenerate hearts. Darkness was their guide: it failed them in life and death. Paul described these people as, "Professing themselves to be wise, they became fools" (Rom. 1:22). At the end of life's road, standing face-to-face with God, the Devil, and death they will be exposed as the enemies of Christ, the Bible, and humankind. These religionists and their predecessors have tampered with the four gospels for centuries. Inspiration of Scripture is repugnant and offends their mental superiority. They are praised as textual critics, yet they are deathly off in Christology (the doctrine of Christ) and soteriology (the doctrine of salvation). Anyone erring in these chief doctrines of Scripture is off more or less everywhere else in his faith. To be wrong about Jesus, the only Savior is eternal death!

After lecturing to a group of theological students at Stellenbosch University in Cape Province, South Africa, an elderly Dutch professor told me he "felt intimidated," when certain Christians in his class spoke about being saved. He expressed stern dissatisfaction with what they were saying. His basic problem was obvious: this mannerly and courteous gentleman did not know Jesus Christ as personal Lord and Savior. It offended and terrified him when others spoke of their joy in salvation. (Christless eyes are blind to eternal matters.) This same problem confronts all liberal-heretical theological scholarship. Unconverted men and women do not have the Holy Spirit and therefore, cannot understand the divine meaning of Holy Scripture (Rom. 8:9b). Some may find a moral or historical lesson here and there; others are ultra-qualified in the semantics of the original languages, philology, morphology, ancient customs, history, geography, and so forth; but the mega-thrust of God's Bible is beyond their comprehension. Their intellectual prowess fails at life's most critical issue: salvation from sin, or its eternal consequences. Like the professor mentioned above, they are terrified when confronted with the biblical dogmatic of Christ or hell. A brilliantly trained mind is useless to God when one is a spiritual zero in Jesus Christ.

"Scholars" who announce that the four gospels have hundreds of inaccuracies, contradictions, anachronisms, interpolations, and redactions are wrong. Booksellers hail them before the Christian public as "great men and women who have made classic contributions to the cause of Christ." What good are their contributions if their lives end in hell? Those who deny that Jesus Christ is the Son of God and Savior of men will die in their sins and awake in the home of the damned, unless they are saved. America is bombarded with the garbage from the National Geographic channel calling into question just about everything the Bible says Jesus did. His death for our sins is perverted into a mistake and His resurrection doubted or flatly denies. The Word of God that these people have changed, altered, dropped verses from, reworked, adjusted, reinterpreted, rejected, and glossed, will judge them at the end (John 12:48). If the four gospels are riddled with mistakes, then the following twenty-three books of the New Testament rest on an insecure foundation. Theology is the queen of all sciences; her heartbeat is the story of Jesus; she stands or falls on Him. If Her Majesty is without a sure foundation, then she becomes, at best, a slick dressed, perfumed street woman, deceiving those who trust her. Despite every machination of the Devil and his friends against the four gospels, they remain the only infallible histories of the life of Christ.

In the 1700s, Dr. Nathaniel Lardner, a British Presbyterian (who turned Independent) gave the English world the most unanswerable defense of the four gospels ever written up to that time. It is a work without equal in its extent and accuracy of thorough investigation. The original seventeen-volume opus stood on the side of divine inspiration as a bulwark against the voices of the unsaved critics of that era. They are entitled, *The Credibility of the Gospel History.* His basic writings were reprinted into ten volumes under the inclusive name, *The Works of Nathaniel Lardner.* To this hour, they remain a premier bastion of truth that theological liberalism and false textual criticism cannot undo. Lardner's work impeccably proves the *historical* trustworthiness of the gospels. He wrote as European rationalists were beginning to flaunt their unbelief, slowly convincing the West that the Bible is not an inspired, trustworthy document. The failure of later Christian teachers to oppose this assault on the credibility of the gospels has put the fox in command of the church henhouse.

In 1864, Simon Greenleaf, a leading founder of Harvard Law School, published his epochal work, *The Testimony of the Evangelists Examined by the Rules of Evidence Administered in Courts of Justice* (better known as *The Testimony of the Evangelists*). After years of research, Greenleaf affirmed from a strict legal perspective the veracity of the four gospels and the fact of Jesus' death, burial, and resurrection. His "juridical apologetics" on behalf of the life of Christ stands as a stone mountain before the infidel critics and religious skeptics. Men like Greenleaf soundly refute the disdain of the unsaved academicians that Bible believers are rustic, ignorant, and gullible. Such champions of eternal truth deserve our salute of thanks. However, beyond the apologetics of good men, it remains true that we have been instructed to "walk by faith, not by sight" (2 Cor. 5:7). With this, God is well pleased (Heb. 11:6).

A prevailing ignorance regarding the reliability of the four gospels and the continuing need for an updated edition of the *Authorized Version* is the intrepid handmaid who has delivered into the hands of the English-reading church the tidal wave of "new and easier to understand" versions. This ignorance directs many Christians to use a translation that has (for example) deleted "begotten" from John 3:16, along with dozens of complete verses and *serious* words. Various footnotes or marginal comments in these "better translations" continually read, "Some manuscripts omit." We have yet to find one margin or footnote that reads, "Some manuscripts do not omit." The psychological impression from "Some manuscripts omit," or "The most ancient authorities omit," is that they are more interested in telling us what is omitted instead of what is not. I do not decry the use of side marginal readings or footnote comments and similar but alternate readings. "Alternate" does not mean error or mistake; rather, it refers to a text that the translators think may say it better. The original version of the *Authorized Bible*, printed in 1611, has thousands of side marginal alternative readings or vertical footnotes. These are mostly explanatory comments or comparative readings. One example of the side notes in the first edition of the *KJV Bible* is Luke 17:36. The side comment states, "This 36th verse is wanting in most of the Greek copies." Critics point to this as "proof" of mistakes. They should point out that this *exact* same passage is recorded in Matt. 24:40 with no side note attached! A comment at John 4:46, explains what a "noble man" was in ancient days. Lastly, a side comment defines what a talent was worth in Matt. 18:24. It is not the footnoting in the "new and better translations" that we question; rather, what some of them infer, say, or worse, do not say. This is not a matter of respecting the opinions of "good men," "searching for truth," or learning to "disagree agreeably about the Bible." It goes far deeper than courteous clichés.

A man who denies the reliability of Holy Scripture, the deity of Christ, and the fact of heaven and hell is not *finally* a "good man." Worse, if he is involved in the arduous task of Bible translating, he could be an enemy postured in the right place. Herein, we find the most serious of all issues because on it hangs the salvation of souls. Those who blatantly alter the inspired writings of Matthew, Mark, Luke, and John, are opposing God. He gave us these four gospels as the infallible record of His Son's earthly life.

Expunging dozens of entire passages and scores of *important* words is extracting, not translating. Translating a document into another language may involve one word taking the place of others. (See symbol ● below.) In other cases, several words may replace one. It just works that way. For example, the single Greek word *"tetelestai"* is translated by three English words, "It is finished" in John 19:30. Does this negate the providence of God in keeping His Word pure? Word condensation, grammatical adjustments, parsing, cultural idioms, syntax, and morphology with its intricate details are part of the package. Rejecting hundreds of *major* words and dozens of verses is not part of the package. Scores of these are relegated to diminutive or obscure footnotes that are meaningless to the average reader. Pastor David H. Sorenson in *Touch Not The Unclean Thing,* pages 236-237, documented that as many as seventeen entire passages have been dropped from one of the "better translations." If a professional linguist-translator proficient in the Russian language received a twenty-line document to translate from Russian into English, and he ended his work by removing the last twelve sentences from the document, he would be sued or fired for incompetence. This is precisely what most modern translations have done. The final twelve verses in the book of Mark (and many others) are the classic example of this. The record of Jesus' earthly life as written in the four gospels is correct, including Mk. 16:9-20. It cannot be partially right and partially wrong. Many translators believe they are both. This is demonstrated in their translations and defensive comments afterward as they try to explain why they have left out so much. Regardless of what Erasmus, Wycliffe, Tyndale, Coverdale, the *Great Bible, Geneva,* or the *Bishops' Bible,* and the *Latin Vulgate* say or anyone else did or did not do, the Lord of heaven has preserved His Word for mankind. Inspiration guaranteed preservation. Divine inspiration originally gave God's Word, while divine preservation has kept it over the centuries. Inspiration does not mean that every event written in the Bible has heavenly approval. God did not approve David's adultery with Bathsheba, though He recorded it by the Holy Spirit. The differences between the Pilgrim's *Geneva Bible* (when dealing with doctrine) and the *Authorized Version* are like the differences between light gray and lighter gray. ●An example of word changes, as mentioned above, occurred over a hundred years ago in the African country of Sudan. Linguists struggled with the pagan language of a northern tribe. These people had no word for "snow," found some twenty-four times in our English Bible. One of the missionaries asked the tribal elders what was the whitest thing they knew or had ever seen. An old man responded "The inside of a coconut." Thus, the word "snow" was changed to read, "The inside of a coconut." This is true Bible translating. It carries God's Word from English into another language understood by a particular people.

God has not left mankind in limbo regarding His beloved Son. He is exactly what the four gospels have presented Him to be: the eternal, only begotten Son of the Living God, virgin-born among men, gloriously mysterious, and wonderfully manifested. He is the promised Messiah of Israel; the sinless One who is the perfect and final atonement on the cross for the sins of all mankind. He arose bodily, triumphant over death, the grave, and hell, then ascended to the Father's right hand. This Divine Person is the world's only hope of forgiveness. Not to know Him as personal Lord and Savior is to live in spiritual darkness and ultimately in eternity's everlasting conscious death, known as the lake of fire (1 John 5:12 with Matt. 25:41 and Rev. 20:15). It is true that some translators feebly confess to the above. When they remove vital words and passages from the gospels and other parts of the New Testament that teach these truths, they deny what they confess. It is like "The voice of Jacob, but the hands of Esau" (Gen. 27:22).

Beware of "Spirit filled Christians" who support any translation on the market, regardless. The conspiratorial-infiltration theory is used by certain champions of the *King James Bible* to prove just about anything is a lame duck. The general conclusion that the *Revised Standard Version* (or whatever version) is just as good or superior to the *Authorized Version* is ridiculous. The unread, and thus uninformed, are left with a "draw the lucky ticket" approach to the question of "Which Bible should I use?" It becomes a toss-up, "Heads this new version, or tails that one." Authors often advise students to cross-reference as many of the new translations as possible. This is supposed to give them a "firm grasp on the meaning of a particular passage." How can a student cross-reference from most of the new translations? Where can he find the hundreds of missing words and verses to cross-reference them? *Surely, not in the Sinaitic, Alexandrian, or Vatican Codices!* Where did the Christians of yesteryear get their "grasp" on verse meanings, and then bring millions to Christ? They lived centuries before the flood of "new and easier to understand Bibles" swept over the church. Have we missed something or did they miss nothing?

No *sensible* believer could object to an improved edition of our present day *King James Bible*. Its numerous archaic (old) words need updating. A few from the long list are *asswaged, bakemeats, holpen, brigandine, chapmen, collops, concupiscence, cracknel, emerods, habergeon, neesing, higgaion, meteyard, ringstraked, sith, champaign, agone, piss, pisseth, ensamples,* and *quaternion*. This Bible has hundreds of verb endings, such as, "deck-eth," "form-eth," "teach-eth," that need updating. (There is a strange teaching that the Bible itself will define these terms into present day English!) Every mention of the Holy Spirit should be capitalized. Yet not all of its old English words are outdated. The usage of the pronominal forms "thee," "thou," and "thine," illustrate this. They make clear distinction in English between singular and plural pronouns. The translators of the *KJV Bible* did not use "thee," "thou," and "thine" because they were standard English. They sought to be true to the singular and plural form of this pronoun. Most of the new translations have dropped the pronominal distinctions under the explanation of "easier to read and understand." The words "thee" and "thou" are a lofty way to sing and pray when addressing supreme deity. Most men praying in English still employ these noble biblical terms. Italicized words are inserted in the *KJV Bible* to clarify a sentence. An example of this is 1 John 2:23. They were not inserted into the text to suggest, "erroneous wording." Such a claim reflects the mental paucity of those who posture this theory. The italicized words in the *Authorized Version* are also missing in most of the "better translations." All the above have nothing to do with divine inspiration; rather, they pertain to spelling, punctuation, pronunciation, clarity, and so forth.

The first edition of the *KJV Bible* has the spellings and grammar of that era. In the original 1611 edition "believest" is spelled "beleeuset" (John 11:26); "believe" is "beleeue" (Acts 16:31). My facsimile copy of the first *Authorized Version* has hundreds of these ancient spellings. "John" is "Iohn," "impossible" is "vnpossible," "daughters" is "doughters," "months" is "moneths," "loved" is "loued," and "have everlasting" is "haue euerlasting." These words are not wrong but spellings have changed over the past four hundred years. Updated English orthography corrects this. Those who boast they "preach from the original 1611 version" would have a hard time reading one, as illustrated by the spellings above. Our *KJV Bible* of today is an edition of the 1611 original. It was printed in 1769 at Oxford University Press. A British clergyman-linguist, Dr. Benjamin Blayney (died 1801), was paid £5000 by Oxford Press for his labors in this task. For a little history on Blayney and his work, see the *Biblical, Theological, and Ecclesiastical Cyclopaedia*, vol. I. pages 562-563, by M'Clintock and Strong. In Blayney's 1769 edition, the following entries were deleted from the front pages of the first 1611 Bible: "The Bookes called Apocrypha all fourteen of them; An Almanacke for xxxxix. Yeeres" (sic); the lengthy "To The Reader" instructions; and a table entitled "Thefe to be obferued for Holy dayes, and none other." One is troubled when examining this table for observing "Holy dayes." (Note, in reading the above entries that the English letter "s" is often printed as "f.") On the page for February 1, of the original *KJV,* the "holy day" to be observed is the "Purification of Mary." The event recorded in Lk. 2:21-24, was taken by the Papal system and turned into something unscriptural. To this day, the Roman Church observes this practice, calling it, "The feast of the purification of the blessed virgin Mary, commonly called Candlemas-day." It is listed in the Roman Catholic schedules of yearly events. By inserting it into the Preface of the *original KJV Bible,* we see Romanism slightly emerging from the Anglican translators. Both Testaments in the original 1611 had marginal references to the apocrypha. These were all historical references, *not doctrinal*. It is no more than Paul quoting three heathen writers in Acts 17:28; 1 Cor. 15:32-33; and Titus 1:12 to get across a point. By 1769, (some one hundred and fifty-eight years after the original 1611 version) God's providence moved men to sift from His Word the unnecessary preliminaries that were part of the first *KJV Bible*.

Other changes in the 1769 edition had to do with spelling, typeset adjustments, italics added to make meanings clearer, correction in some footnotes and references, and proofreader's oversights. An example of needed spelling changes is found in two separate editions of the *1611 KJV Bible*. One was named the *"He Bible,"* and the other the *"She Bible."* This is because one of them printed the term "she went" in Ruth 3:15, as "he went," and the other, as "she went." (The correct reading is "she.") A sampling of some changes made in the 1769 edition of the four gospels is as follows. Matt. 27:22 was changed to read, "Pilate saith," instead of "Pilate said." Mark. 6:7 reads in the 1611 version, "he calleth." It was altered to read, "he called." Lk. 11:16 was adjusted from "other" to "others." Lastly, John 11:34 now states, "They said unto him," instead of "They say unto him." The translators of the original 1611 Bible stated in the Preface of their work that a continual update of language was needed. Enemies of the *King James Version* have flaunted these things for decades, trying to prove that holy preservation of Scripture is impossible. For the exact number of editions (not versions) that followed the first *KJV Bible*, including printings of the New Testament, and the orthographical adjustments made in these, see the *Historical Catalogue of Printed Editions of the English Bible 1525-1961* by A. S. Herbert. The British and Foreign Bible Society of London & New York published this work in 1968. Again, all the above has nothing to do with inspiration but grammatical preferences, font set, (such as it was in those days) typographical, and proofreader's oversights. These are easily corrected in time.

It stands true that if Paul, the apostle, gave us a new edition of the *KJV Bible*, some unread, ill-informed Christian (defending God!) would condemn it. This was seen at the appearing of the *New King James Bible* some years ago. Shortly after its release, a howl of protest went up. Among other *valid* objections, on the inside cover critics found a "pagan satanic emblem known as the 'triqueta.'" Thomas Nelson Publishers claimed it was "an ancient emblem for the Trinity." Because this "configuration of evil" was on the front of the *NKJV Bible*, it was hailed as the Devil's work. The people who raised this uproar seemed to have missed the fact that on the very first page of the original version of the *1611 King James Bible*, there is also an ancient occult emblem! In my copy, at the middle bottom of page 1, is depicted a pelican tearing open her breast to feed her young with blood. One pagan version of this emblem states that a serpent bit the chicks; however, they were saved by drinking their mother's blood. I have yet to hear one person who upholds the *Authorized Version* (as I do) mention this or even attempt to explain it (*away*)! If the *New King James Version* has a "serpent coiled inside its cover," can we say the original *King James Version* also has one on its first page? Honesty would be the best rule. Could it be that the layout artist of the first page of the *1611 Version* was ignorant of what this pelican figure originally meant? Can we allow the same for whoever used the triqueta on the *NKJV Bible*? Must we invent another secret conspiracy? For documentation, see *Symbols of the Church*, page 15, edited by Carroll E. Whittemore and *Dictionary of Symbolism. Cultural Icons and the Meanings Behind Them*, page 261, by Hans Biedermann, translated by James J. Hulbert. On this same page in Biedermann's work, we read how the pelican is part of the Scottish Freemasonry rite known as "Society of the Rosey Cross," symbolizing "purification." This esoteric secret society originated in Germany in the early 1600s. Prior to this, the Papal Church had books called "bestiaries" that spoke of the lower creatures and contained hymns. A line in one of these read, "O merciful pelican, Lord Jesus." Here, the Catholic Church referred to the Son of God as a pelican, an emblem rooted deeply in occult history. The Papal theological doctor, Thomas Aquinas (died A.D. 1274), saw in the pelican feeding her blood to the young a picture of the Catholic mass! Does this mean that the emblem of a pelican in the first edition of the *KJV Bible* also signifies the same untruth? As stated above, could this have been an oversight or ignorance?

The well read *honest* Christian knows there are difficulties in the *Authorized Version* of the Bible. However, difficulties do not constitute errors, contradictions, or mistakes. Synonyms and adjectives often prove tough for the best of translators. English orthography that deals with letters and spelling has greatly changed since the year 1611. Some words and punctuations need uniformity. This is shown in Section 62, by the symbol ▶ in Matt. 11:8. Note also Section 12, third paragraph of footnote g. Sentences should start with caps, never lowercase. Upper and lower cases are not inspired. All prima-facie problems with any biblical text have their origin in human reasoning, never in the work of the Holy Spirit. Diligent study, the blessing of the Holy Spirit, and proper research, in our little work for God and men may serve to correct *some* of this mortal frailty. Of course, the "specialists," tell us the opposite. In their thinking, Scriptures are wrong because they were never inspired to start with. If they were, it was somehow lost over the centuries. Now, they are correcting them. It is an undeniable fact that none of the so-called "textual variants" (if left to stand as the critics see them) in either the Old or New Testament affects a single minor or major doctrine of the Christian faith. Liberal-conservatives make this confession as they try to explain the mess, they have gotten themselves into with God and His Word. The calamity of a translator, who disdains inspiration and becomes an interpreter of Scripture, is unspeakable.

The modern day charity rule for religious correctness, which prevails among authors, publishing houses, and booksellers, that requires us to keep silent on clear points where God has spoken, is treason to the Trinity! This be-nice-to-the-Devil policy only delays a battle that will eventually come.

In about A.D. 68 Paul wrote Timothy, "All Scripture is given by inspiration of God" (2 Tim. 3:16). In using "all," he referred to "all" of the Hebrew Tanakh or Old Testament. The *completed* New Testament canon did not exist at that time. Paul did not say, "Timothy, remember that everything in the original Old Testament manuscripts is inspired of God." By A.D. 68, these manuscripts had worn out and vanished from the scene. In this sense, there are no "originals" today of either Testament. Paul could only have referred to copies, of copies, of copies, that were available to Timothy, and those who had taught him from childhood. Paul informed Timothy (and all subsequent readers) that these "copies of copies of copies" of Scripture were (still) "all inspired of God." How is this possible when these copies of copies, were written hundreds of years after the originals had perished? Did divine preservation have anything to do with it? The Scriptures were still "sharper than any two-edged sword," centuries *after* the originals were written (Heb. 4:12). Is this be because God "keepeth truth forever" (Ps. 146:6)?

To say, "We do not know how the original Scriptures were inspired," is learned ignorance. God breathed life one time into His written Word when it was originally transmitted to the human authors. Peter wrote that the Word of God "liveth and abideth for ever" (1 Peter 1:23). Like Paul, Peter also first had the Old Testament in mind. This implanted life is eternal and that into which it was breathed (the Scriptures) continues eternally. Divine imbuement into God's Word did not wear out, rub out, play out, or fade out; it was forever. Nor did the Holy Spirit re-inspire the *KJV Bible* (or any Bible, for that matter) as some claim. The assertion of re-inspiration of Scripture is a confession that original inspiration was not everlasting. Jehovah's sovereign providence (control and guidance in the process of history) preserved and vouchsafed the Scriptures to this present day, though they are before us as a copy of a copy, and of another copy, hundreds of years later. Paul asserted this fact to Timothy regarding the inspiration of Scriptures he had known as a child. These copies of copies *retained* the inherent power to make him wise unto salvation (2 Tim. 3:15). On the other side of this impasse, we have the liberal conservatives. These "scholars" believe that God saved His Word from extinction by their "scientific" approach to Bible translating that has its origin with religious infidels in Europe. The assertion that European academicians, who deny the Person and work of Christ, have restored the true biblical text is scandalous. Those English and American "scholars" who gave verbal assent to the basic doctrines of the Christian faith, and then believe they were saved by infant baptism, are also wrong. It was from *their* fragmented, and expunged, patched-up "original text" that most of the new translations have come to us. Are we so gullible as to believe that "record breaking sales" qualify them as the most reliable translations on the market?

Inspiration of Scripture does not mean that God locked the human authors into a robot mode, subdued, and excluded their intellects, social customs, use of favorite words, and education from being drawn upon as they wrote. For example, Matthew, a converted tax superintendent, was a man who handled large sums of money. Hence, he used more monetary terms in his book than any of the other gospel writers. Luke, a physician, used over four hundred Greek medical words in his two books that are not found in the other three gospels. The Holy Spirit used saved men as they were, often drawing from their individual vocabularies, but still directed what they wrote. It is here that the quasi-liberal conservatives, both translators and their defenders, draw back in horror. They cannot believe the Bible was somehow inspired when originally written. Now, only these "authorities" can figure out what is God's Word while using the Devil's methodology to do this. Historically, this methodology was named "higher criticism" and "synoptic problem." A German rationalist, Dr. Johann Eichhorn (died 1827) supposedly coined the term "higher criticism." This is a "style of literary analysis that investigates the origin of biblical texts." From the start, this "science" has postulated that there is no such thing as total divine inspiration; it is hostile to the supernatural. Whether it is "higher criticism," "radical criticism," "form criticism," or whatever, all have their origin in a satanic approach to God's Word. "Higher criticism" is the academic assault on the first five books of the Old Testament. The "synoptic problem" is the same attack on the four gospels in the New Testament. Robert D. Wilson in *Is Higher Criticism Scholarly?* has forever answered these critics.

When European "academicians" completed their lobotomy of Scripture, British theologians received it with joy. In America, religious infidels such as Walter Rauschenbusch, the apostate Baptist, Harry E. Fosdick, Bishop Pike, and Nels Ferre, also welcomed their academic poison. Over the following centuries, demon spirits kept alive and perpetuated this Antichrist critique of Scripture. Their purpose is to deceive men regarding the reliability of the Bible, thus blinding them to their individual need for the Savior. Regarding inspiration, the liberal neoconservatives are saying it is irrational to believe that a translation into a language that did not exist in the days of Christ could define the correct meanings of documents written half a world away in a completely different language. Their public confession is that they do not believe in the preservation of original doctrine through sovereign providence. Is it irrational to believe that God has preserved the meaning of His Word for Adam's race? If not, humanity gropes in awful darkness regarding spiritual matters. Our hope for truth from God is not found in the machinations of those using the wretched art of historical-critical theology. (By no means am I saying that all Bible translators are of this ilk.) Has God preserved His Word for man or was it muddled up along the way? The prattle that German, British, and American theologians, who denied the deity of Christ, the fact of sin, and salvation, gave us the correct science for translating Scripture is an abomination. How odd that these "experts" could never find themselves in need of Jesus Christ as personal Lord and Savior.

Westcott and Hort were two Englishmen, who in 1881 completed their "Neutral Text that restored the New Testament Greek text." Those who defend the "any version will do" philosophy remind us that both Westcott and Hort "believed in the deity of Christ, the atonement and His resurrection from the dead" and that "they were not fundamental Baptists." The truth is, they were not fundamentalist anything. Of course, they confessed to the deity of Christ, atonement, and resurrection. I have heard the Pope, and his bishops confess the same things. Westcott-Hort defenders do not seem to know that this confession has been part of the doctrinal code of the Anglican Church from its beginning. Anglicans from the time of King James 1 (and before) to this present day confess many of the basics of the Christian faith in their creeds. The fact that the *King James Version* is the official Bible of the Anglican and Mormon Church and often used by Romans Catholics means nothing. (These people also eat food, sleep in beds, and wear clothes.) The great question is "How are Anglicans, Mormons, Catholics, and Orthodox people taught to be saved?" It is always by baptism, "Holy Communion," and a system of works and rituals. Neither the *KJV* nor any other half-decent version of the Bible teaches such untruths. Yes, Westcott, Hort and their kind confessed some of the foundations of the faith. *How they understood partaking of eternal life as laid out in these doctrines of truth is another matter.* At this point, the hammer of divine truth falls on every religion operating under the umbrella of Christianity. For a review of what Westcott and Hort believed, see *Life and Letters of Brooke Foss Westcott,* (2 vols.) by his son, Arthur Westcott. Refer to vol. 1, page 99, 214, 239, and vol. 2, page 69. On one occasion while visiting a monastery at Leicestershire, England, Westcott saw the place where Catholics knelt to a sculpture of Mary holding the dead body of Jesus. He wrote of this experience in *Life and Letters . . .* vol. 1, page 81, these revealing words, "Had I been alone I could have knelt there for hours." Hort's record of religious infamy is no better. In *Life and Letters of A. F. Hort,* (2 vols.), also written by his son, Dr. Hort stated, "I have been persuaded for many years that Mary-worship and Jesus-worship have much in common in their causes and their results" (vol. 1, page 76). These were the men who produced the so-called "Neutral Text." Mary worship is blasphemy, a violation of God's Word, and an insult to the precious mother of Jesus. Regarding *unjustly* critiquing others out of malice, see Section 1, Part 4, fifth paragraph of footnote j.

I spent seventeen years working as a missionary in Australia among Roman Catholics, Anglicans, and others. It is an undisputable fact that most Anglicans believe that their sins are remitted when they were sprinkled as infants. Official church dogma states that this puts them into the body of Christ, bringing personal justification. The unsaved condition of the *average* Church of England or Anglican Church communicant was observed thousands of times during our work across the Queensland diocese and into the Northern Territory. Westcott and Hort, like all good Anglicans (including the Presbyterian King James I and his diversity of translators) were sprinkled as babies and later taught that this placed them into eternal life, thus making them Christians. Baptismal regeneration has always been part of Anglican Church doctrine. It has deceived millions of people into believing that they are Christians. Sprinkling water on the heads of babies or burying adults under water has never secured remission of sins.

One irate Australian Anglican rector (pastor) threatened me with a lawsuit because two of his church members were saved and then scripturally baptized as believers by immersion. No "church ritual" makes anyone a Christian anymore than going into a barn makes one a cow. Only Christ saves, and He is not received into one's life by baptism, communion, or any church ritual. Salvation is acquired exclusively by faith. My copy of the Church of England or Anglican *Book of Common Prayer* (first written in 1548) bristles with flashes of Catholic rituals. Page 264 states that "water and the Holy Ghost" put infants "into Christ's holy church" (which is *their* church, of course). All the Anglican clergy are required to agree with these statements of faith. Roman Catholics burned alive Thomas Cramer and Nicholas Ridley, who assisted in preparing the Anglican *Book of Common Prayer*. So much for the Papal Church!

The *Thirty-Nine Articles*, that summarize the dogmatic tenets of the Anglican Church became official by an act of Parliament in 1566 under the rule of Queen Elizabeth 1. This was thirty-seven years before James I took the throne in 1603. These *Articles* dogmatically teach salvation by infant baptism. This has not changed in over four hundred years. The Anglican practice of the "Holy Eucharist" (Lord's Supper) is similar to the mass of the Roman Catholic Church in the dress and antics of the officiating priests. For the most part, Anglicans are not taught the Bible doctrine of personal salvation acquired only through repentance and faith in Christ. Catechized in their articles of faith, they believe that eternal life begins when one is sprinkled as an infant or adult. There are infrequent exceptions to the above Anglican Church dogma. In missionary work across Australia and South Africa, I also met Church of England or Anglican ministers and parishioners who gave powerful testimony of the saving grace of God in their lives. They vehemently rejected the falsehood of salvation by sprinkling. Many of these people left "their church" where this heinous error was taught. I remember an Australian, who had worked in the Anglican Church for twenty years. Les was saved in Melbourne and shared the wonderful news with his rector (pastor) and fellow Anglicans. He was summarily expelled from the Anglican Church, for "heresy."

Over the centuries, countless Church of England communicants have found Christ as personal Lord and Savior, *apart* from the rituals of their church. Many of these have made timeless contributions to the cause of Christ. I have quoted several of them in this work who would disagree with me on the textual issue of the Bible. I saw in Australia that if saved Anglicans became too noisy in witnessing for Jesus, the hierarchy ostracized them as troublemakers. The pseudo baptismal practice described above was the religious heritage of B. F. Westcott and F. J. A. Hort, the two men who played the major role in producing "the true Greek text of the New Testament." Defenders of the new versions never mention the above facts about the Anglican Church, or they mitigate them. To do otherwise would weaken their defense of Westcott and Hort as *spiritually* qualified translators. Westcott, in his popular work, *The Gospel According to St. John,* the 1954 edition, vol. I, page 272, wrote in the footnotes that John 12:13 and 19:12 were "false readings." By what authority does this "scholar" decide which verses are "false" and, which are not? He sweeps other verses away as "glosses." On page 257, Westcott wrote that baptism is "the new birth." Millions of devout church people confess the deity of Christ, then claim baptism and communion as the means of salvation. This is the chief heresy among many larger "churches" today.

On the other hand, translators who deny Christ's deity like the German critics did, are evil regardless of how well educated they are. In time, they will "bring upon themselves swift destruction" (2 Peter 2:1-3). Peter's words apply to all men without exception. Jesus said, "Without me ye can do nothing." (John 15:5). This is either true or false. In Section 159, we read the Savior's fearful condemnation upon the super religionists of His day. To write what the skeptics have said about the Son of God and the Bible is not attacking character. Nor is it "unchristian," "belligerent," "vindictive," or "unloving." John admonished the elect lady and her children not to allow into their houses those who deny "the doctrine of Christ" (2 John 10-11). Did God inspire him to write this, or is it spurious? Is it valid today or not?

A Unitarian minister, Dr. G. V. Vance, served on the translating team with Westcott and Hort! Despite a majority vote that he could not participate, Dean Arthur Stanley, Westcott, Hort, and Bishop Thirlwall said if Vance were dismissed, they would not serve. *He was not dismissed, and they stayed on.* Stanley's sympathies with popery, Unitarianism, and German liberal criticisms of Scripture are well known. All Unitarians reflect the ancient demon spirit of Gnosticism-Arianism and vehemently deny the deity of Christ. Paul was not instructing Titus to be vindictive to believers on the island of Crete when he wrote, "A man that is an heretick after the first and second admonition reject" (Titus 3:10).

Does it mean *not* to reject him? Are there times among Christians for these things to be done? Mitigating the truth about these "learned scholars" by writing that they were "Christians according to their times and were reputable translators" is untrue. People are saved only by the grace of God regardless of what "time" in history it is. Unsaved men serving in the church are spiritual zombies in God's work.

An army of "educated" skeptics who denied the final authority of inspired Scripture, the deity of Christ, and personal salvation, came amass out of the (dark) Enlightenment and Rationalist Movement of the seventeenth and eighteenth centuries. These evil men turned religious Europe on its head. Some of the fathers of the theological travesties to emerge in this era were Schleiermacher, Leibntiz, Wolff, Lessing, Semler, Grotius, Wetstein, Griesbach, Strauss, and Feuerbach. Their legacy over the decades has spiritually crippled the minds of thousands, especially young ministerial students. Multitudes have believed their myths about Christ and God's Word. Regarding the four gospels, men like Griesbach and his textual clones bequeathed a masterpiece "doctrines of demons" (1 Tim. 4:1-2). It destroys faith in biblical trustworthiness and discredits Jesus Christ the major theme of the gospels. These men did not "illuminate the four gospels," they assaulted them. Translators who use their methods are wrong. It is like taking your medicine from a spoon into which someone has spat. Knowingly supporting or defending those who slander our Savior is sin. God will attend to the people who defame His truth (Ps. 50:22).

The informed Christian public can rest assured that if another "ancient manuscript" is found in an Egyptian sand dune or a trash bucket in a Greek monastery with Genesis 1 and John 3:16 missing, in time, this will serve as proof that these "pericopes" were not a part of the original Scripture. Such discoveries have become the basis for dropping verses out of the "new and better translations." If enough of these "ancient manuscripts" are discovered we may end up with another *Good as New Version* like the one produced by a defunct Baptist minister in England, John Hinson. It attacks family values, reeks with secularism, oozes with sex, and vulgarizes the names of various biblical characters. Britain's head of the Anglican Church, Dr. Rowan Williams, a religious infidel, said it was dedicated to "establishing peace, justice, dignity, and rights for all." The Preface reads like a call for political activism from Marx's, *Communist Manifesto,* or the godless American Civil Liberties Union (ACLU).

Thousands have been saved by faith in the (so-called) "spurious readings," "latter additions," "anachronisms," "verse drop-outs," and that bottomless pit of "textual variants." This tells thinking Christians that they are genuine. Redemption from sin and hell is not received by believing in the *Three Little Pigs* or *Old Mother Goose.* Only God's Word, anointed by the Holy Spirit, brings the new birth; not genuine "spurious readings." The Scripture forever retains its inherent power to convict and "beget" into God's family all who believe (James 1:18). I have used the so-called "spurious readings" to win men to Christ. Thus, how can they be "spurious?" Some charge us of being "Seventh Day Adventist" in defending the *KJV.* Oddly, these same objectors defend the virgin birth. Could we respond that they are "Roman Catholics?" The any-version-will-do-contenders believe that the KJV Bible has more errors than the Koran. They flip a coin and pick a Bible for one is as good as the other, they think!

In 1970, while teaching at a family camp in North Queensland, Australia, a Yugoslav immigrant, who spoke and understood English, was saved. The Scripture used to show him that Christ is the Son of God was Acts 8:37. (This middle-aged man drowned in a fishing accident some months later.) How ironic that he found Christ by believing in the critics "spurious passage" of Acts 8:37. According to the "best authorities and new translations," this passage should be scrapped. Regardless, the sword of the Spirit is still the Word of God, including Acts 8:37. The *Scofield Reference Bible*, page 1160, center footnote h, also popularized the myth that this is a questionable verse. When men are saved by believing "spurious verses," they are not "spurious." They are God's Word and the infidel critics are wrong.

I cannot resolve all the problems, we, who uphold the *KJV,* face. The Roman Catholic, Desiderius Erasmus, who primarily gave us the Received Text (from which the *KJV* mostly came), was a shadowy figure who ran with the hares and hounds. He fiercely criticized many of the practices of the Papal Church but never left it. His first edition of the Received Text was dedicated to Pope XI. This does not make him a bad man, but it does qualify him as being a theological ignoramus. Those who present him as an angel from heaven should research what he said about communion! Erasmus published some five editions of the Received Text; Robert Stephanus, four; Theodore Beza and the Eliziver family also sponsored several editions. Various changes were made in the later editions such as the removal of 1 John 5:7. (Muslim websites bristle with hatred for 1 John 5:7, along with liberal conservatives who so eloquently explain it away.) There are some minor different readings in the *Wycliffe Bible* of 1380, against certain verses in the first *King James Version* of 1611. Many translations of Scripture into other languages were not derived from the Received Text, and untold thousands have come to Christ through these translations. Several examples of these are the major Spanish, French, Dutch, and Afrikaans's translations. Many people have been saved and blessed by preaching from some of the "new versions." This reveals that enough of God's Word remains in them for men to come to Christ. Yet, why should a Christian settle for a second or third best Bible? Pieces of good bread are in the garbage can, but who wants to eat there? The good in some new translations is not worth the bad that go with the exchange.

The conspiratorial aspect attached to the *KJV Bible* has a little merit at intervals in history. The Gunpowder Plot to kill King James 1 and members of Parliament was the work of five Roman Catholics and a Jesuit missionary, John Gerard. However, the "conspiracy" theory cannot be used for every problem we face. Extreme defenders of the *Authorized Version* have not intelligently responded to most of these difficulties. Some have twisted history to read in their favor. Others tell us that in time most of the world will be reading the English language and therefore, will understand the *King James Bible*! Such absurd statements turn thinking people away from our cause. Despite the kingly sin, chaos, in-fighting, political intrigue, murder plots and so on, God took the reigns of British history, overruled the wrath of man, and used the old rascal King James 1 and his translators (good and bad) to give us the *Authorized Version of the Bible*. Its effect is unprecedented in English literary history, excelling even the works of Shakespeare. Without it, men would have never heard Handel's *The Messiah*, or read Bunyan's *Pilgrim's Progress*.

This *Author's Introduction* does not hint, intimate, or state that those who use the "new and easier to understand translations" are evil people. Such rhetoric reflects a twisted character. It is just as true that not all the *KJV* advocates have their wings either. Listening to *some* of them, one could believe they may have horns instead! I have ministered in churches where the "any version will do" mentality exists. Confusion reigns among those in the congregation who are trying to follow the reading in some of the "better translations," against the *Authorized Version*. Often, the verse differences are shocking. Words or entire passages are missing from many of the "easier to understand versions." Some versions add words not found in any extant Greek text. In the dawn of antiquity, before the written Word of God was given, the Lord communicated His intentions by discourse with Adam and his early posterity. This was in a language they all knew. Later, divinely spoken Words were uttered to the patriarchs, prophets, and others. Lastly, over the centuries, beginning with Moses, God gradually gave His written Word. Often speaking a dim message from nature, God *finally* deals with men from the Scripture, anointed by the Holy Spirit. The results this produces reveal they are from God. Supernatural inspiration is the foundation of written biblical revelation. Informed Christians will not apologize for this or minimize its importance.

The Holy Bible, especially the four gospels, demonstrates to the *individual,* that in Jesus Christ is solved the problem of religion, history, philosophy, education, morals, politics, and the reconciliation of man to God in eternal joy. All enduring good that exists is found in the Son of God. Apart from Him, the helpless New World Order, Global Ecumenism, United Nations, and the International Community stagger on in awful darkness. Ever groping, never grasping; searching without finding; looking without seeing; having without keeping until their arrival in hell. Jim Elliot, a missionary martyred for his faith wrote, "He is no fool who gives up that which he cannot keep to gain that which he cannot lose." Without God's Word and the Holy Spirit, the greatest minds on earth are dysfunctional to the *true religion* from heaven and divine things of eternal worth. The good they have given in the arts, and sciences are thankfully used; however, they have failed humanity at its greatest need: preparing them for true life, death, and eternity!

There will never be, nor can we expect any clearer revelation or higher religious attainment than what we find in the Son of God as recorded by Matthew, Mark, Luke, and John. His earthly story is infallibly true. It is no marvel the four gospels continue to be the object of scorn, envy, and fierce hatred. Every device of men and devils is set to pull them down. Yet, they remain! The infidel historian, Will Durant, wrote of the gospels and Jesus Christ these surprising words: "That a few simple men should in one generation have invented so powerful and appealing a personality, so lofty and ethic and so inspiring a vision of human brotherhood would be a miracle far more incredible than any recorded in the Gospel." See Durant's, *Story of Civilization*, vol. 3, page 553-554. Beams of eternal truth infrequently shine, even from God's enemies! In 1852, Dr. W. T. Hamilton pastor of the Government Street Church, in Mobile, Alabama, wrote in *The Friend of Moses,* page 143, "The Bible is from God. It is the one sole light that heaven has vouchsafed to illumine our path to life's close." On this, we children of weakness securely hang our helpless souls and our hope of heaven when the sun of earth's little while has forever set.

Selah! "Think of that."

The author: Henry Randall Pike.
Greenville, SC USA. 2012.

CHAPTER 1
(Presented in Four Parts)

JESUS CHRIST IS THE ETERNAL WORD AND GOD THE CREATOR. TRUE LIFE AND LIGHT CAME THROUGH HIM. THE WITNESS OF JOHN THE BAPTIST. MESSIAH'S REJECTION, GLORY, FULLNESS, GRACE, AND TRUTH. HE IS THE REVEALER OF GOD. LOOKING BACK YEARS LATER, THE APOSTLE JOHN REMEMBERS THE GLORY OF HIS SAVIOR.

Time: From the dateless past into earth's time

The Son of God pre-existed before time. Two of His Names were Memra and Logos. His deity, work in creation, and the life–light He gives to men.

Nothing is known concerning the original recipients of this book, except that they lived outside the land of Israel and were unfamiliar with various Hebrew cities, villages, landmarks, and customs. The people to whom this work was addressed were not Jewish. This is reflected in John explaining geographical locations and various Hebrew customs for the readers. His preeminent reason for writing is stated in Section 202, John 20:30-31. Clearly, he wanted his readers to believe that Jesus was the Messiah and thus be saved. This book has become a standard for Christians around the world. John, the brother of James, was one of the original twelve apostles. He distinguishes himself by the title, "that disciple whom Jesus loved." He was the human instrument through whom God gave this great work that glorifies the deity of Christ. He was inspired to write more about Jesus' theology than Jesus' biography.

Matt.	Mk.	Lk.	John 1:1-5—*Place of writing unknown.*
			1 In the beginning [a] was the Word,[b] and the Word was with God, and the Word was God.[c] **2** The same was in the beginning with God. **3** All things were made[d] by him; and without him was not any thing made that was made. **4** In him was life; and the life was the light[e] of men. **5** And the light shineth in darkness; [of sin] and the darkness comprehended it not [could not put the light out]. (Verse 6 cont. in Section 1, Part 2.)

Footnotes-Commentary

[a] **The beginning.** "Arche." Beginning, origin, the dateless past. No other written cosmogony, regardless, ever mentions the origin of things. They all started with something already in existence and then speculate how this evolved into its presence form. See *The Defenders Study Bible*, footnote "1:1 created," page 3 for more on these thoughts. The Bible begins with the Triune God the first source or cause of all things. Prior to this He had always been, even forever, without beginning, dwelling in eternity past (Isa. 57:15). In Gen. 1:1, the Hebrew Name for God, "Elohim," is a *plural* noun denoting (among other things) several Persons in One, or One who is several Persons. This is a grammatical peculiarity, a cryptic suggestion of the Trinity. The word "Person," does not give us the full truth yet it is the best single word that expresses the connection between the Father, Son, and Holy Spirit. It cannot be used in the sense in which we apply "person" to John or Peter. Thus, our employment of it regarding the Holy Trinity is only an inadequate but acceptable expression. The undivided essence of the Godhead belongs equally to all Three. God is not Three and One, but Three in One. Despite the fierce monotheism of the Jews, "Elohim" was their chief word for God. It is translated different ways in Scripture and given various applications, even to pagan idols. Heathen Canaanite tribes were infamous for their religious misusages of the Name "Elohim." When they applied it apart from God, it may not connote its uniplural structure. Nevertheless, this plurality shadows the inclusiveness of the Godhead. Non-Christian Hebrew linguists and anti-Trinitarians struggle to explain away the uniplural factor; it is too suggestive of the Trinity, something they fiercely hate. The "Sacred Name" cults also distort this truth. Rejecting "God" as the proper English noun for the Almighty, they teach that "God" is only a title and claim to have "discovered and restored the original Hebrew designations for deity." Some of these cults require their followers to use "Elohim" in order to be saved. Others have produced their own Bible, which they claim has correctly translated God's true Name. They have assaulted the Name of Jesus or "Yeshua," saying that this pronunciation is a conspiracy to hide His correct Name ("Yahshua"). Naturally, only *they* know how to enunciate God's holy Name! The myth that the noun "Yeshua" is pagan in origin reveals their desperation to prove falsity. After the Tower of Babel, the scattered multitudes distorted the Almighty's Name, attaching it to their thousands of

deities in numerous corrupt linguistic forms. This reveals His true Name existed *before* they did. God has forever been three eternal, co-equal Persons: Father, Son, and Holy Spirit. It is indeed astounding that Elohim is both masculine and feminine in the Hebrew language, each being a part of the other. This reflects the dominion of God over all mortals. The priests of the old Greek Orthodox Church wear a long well groomed beard and beautiful flowing gown. This is intended to demonstrate that Elohim is sovereign over all, whether male or female!

2p-The Holy Trinity. As stated above, in the Bible's first verse the Name of God is a plural construction. "In the beginning God ["Elohim," plural] created ["bara," singular] the heaven and the earth (Gen. 1:1). The plural noun is followed by a singular verb. This reveals that a plural unity singularly produced creation! Three Persons were One, and One Person was three, and they made all things! John begins his gospel by introducing his original readers to "the Word," who was with God when time began and is declared to be God. Verse 3 affirms that He ["the Word"] made all things, while Eph. 3:9 declares that God "created all things by Jesus Christ." See also Heb. 1:2b with Col. 1:14-17. Later, John wrote in his gospel that this Word or Person, who was in the beginning and shared in the creation, became flesh or a man (John 1:14; Gal. 4:4; Heb. 2:14; and Phil. 2:7-8). This Person is Jesus Christ; not a Christianized Gnostic spirit, for John *both* saw and touched Him (1 John 1:1 with Lk. 24:36-39).

3p-Paul, in 1 Tim. 3:16 affirms that God was manifested in the flesh: hence, the conclusion that this Word is God, and was revealed in the Person of Jesus Christ. Jehovah claims to be the only Savior in Isa. 43:11. He is called "our Saviour" in Titus 1:3, 2:10, and 3:4, while Christ is called "our Saviour" in the same book (1:4). There either are two distinct "Saviours" or they are the same Person. In addition, present in that dateless past of Gen. 1:1 was the Holy Spirit. He also participated in the work of creation (Gen. 1:2; Job 26:13; Ps. 104:30). As the Father and Son are "eternal," so is the Spirit (Heb. 9:14). God called Himself "the first and the last" in the Old Testament (Isa. 41:4, 44:6, 48:12). Yet in the New Testament, Christ "the Word" claimed to be "the first and the last" (Rev. 1:8, 11, 22:13). *Clearly, they are both the same.* The eternal relationships within the Godhead cannot be understood by natural reasoning. He who is wrong on Christology is wrong more or less everywhere in his theology and spiritual life. Beware of any interpretation placed upon 1 Tim. 3:16 that change its obvious meaning. Academicians who teach that Jesus Christ is the product of a religious intellectual evolution or pagan philosophies are wrong. Our Lord postulated that He was both divine and that unique Messianic Person. This was the major issue in His ministry, trials before the Sanhedrin, and death on the cross. The Jews clearly understood His claim of equality with God and flew into a rage, plotting to kill Him. Note this in Section 123, John 10:30-31 and Section 181, Matt. 26:63-64, with relative footnotes. It is not much different today with those who despise the glorious supremacy and deity of Jesus Christ. For a review of His ineffable equality with God, see Section 175, footnote p; and Section 197, footnote i.

(b) The Word or Logos. This idiom is peculiar to John. It reflects that He (Jesus) was also the earthly spokesman for the Holy Trinity; He, the "Word," spoke for them (Heb. 1:2). The term "Word" is derived from the Greek "logos." Among other things, "logos" was the name for a major part of Gnostic beliefs. Gnosticism was an ancient religion that originated in the satanic philosophies of paganism. Heathen Greeks such as Plato, the ex-wrestling champion in the Isthmian games, had developed distorted notions of a one true God. Gnostics adhering to pieces of Plato's philosophy believed this one God could be reached or united with by "knowledge. Gnosticism colored by Platonic ideology became something of a salvation by knowledge. In this context, the devotees of Gnosticism spoke of a particular or unique logos. Men could move upward and find union with the one true God through this created force, spirit, or thing. Later, heretics such as the Ebionites taught that this logos-spirit came upon Jesus at His baptism and He became "a Son of God." The Jehovah's Witness Bible, *The New World Translation*, reflects the same untruth at John 1:1. It reads that Christ is "a son of God." Some pagans referred to this "spirit-son-force" as a plurality of "good demons" assisting those seeking religious truths. This horrific belief was resident among the idolatrous people at Athens. They described Paul's gospel as "a setter forth of strange gods" or "demons" (Acts 17:18). John's use of logos is not a "Christianized version" of pagan philosophy or Platonism packaged in Christianity. Refer to footnote c below for a brief discussion of this subject.

2p-The pagan Greek philosopher, Heraclitus (born 535 B.C.) allegedly penned the earliest known mention of logos among heathens. By 300 B.C., fellow pagans such as Socrates, Plato, Zeno, and Aristotle used this term in their schools or academies of dialogue. Later, a Hellenized (Greek influenced) Jew, dwelling at Alexandria, Egypt, named Philo (died about A.D. 50) mentioned logos hundreds of times in his writings. He employed a Hebrew form of heathenism in his works. The so-called philosophers of those ages were esoteric, demon-possessed mystics squandering in wine, women, song, sodomy, and worshiping at satanic altars. They were immoral moralists, personified examples of all that was savage, disgusting, vile, and vain. Whatever scraps of truth about God and His Son, (the true "Logos") Heraclitus, his student Plato, and other pagan philosophers embraced, it came from the works of Moses, other extant Old Testament books, and Jewish believers of those days. They had many previous contacts with the *valid* traditions and Holy Scriptures of true God-fearing Jews. Hence, the fragmented divine truths found in pagan writings, especially those of Plato (died 347 B.C.). These scraps of divine doctrine in the mouths of ancient heathens, to this day are as "gold in a swine's snout" (Prov. 11:22). God's truths laid down in Old Testament Scripture were distorted by the evil genius of these men (especially the Greeks) too proud in their blindness to give credit to the only true and living God amid their millions of idols. In Paul's day pagan Greeks still sought "wisdom" or "philosophy" (1 Cor. 1:22). Someone said, "Philosophy is what you study when you want to increase your ignorance." The great apostle to the Gentiles called these people "fools" in Rom. 1:22.

3p-The Bible doctrine of the Logos as penned by John owes nothing to pagan sources as the unsaved critics affirm. He took nothing from Plato, the man who prohibited his students from "touching beans," or Socrates that molester of Athens' youth, or any heathen writer. He wrote as the Spirit of God directed him. The history of secular philosophy is the history of unsaved, spiritually blinded, pseudo academicians working to replace life's instructions found in God's Word with their own dark wisdom and Antichrist philosophy. To this day, all *secular* philosophies emanating from the institutions of "higher learning" traduce the teachings of Holy Scripture. They build on the quicksand of rejecting Jesus Christ and opposition to the Bible. This academic arsenic ran over into every sector of western education. It is often referred to as "relevant theology" or "humanism."

4p-The "learned minds" of secular education oppose the divine truism, "The fear of the LORD is the beginning of knowledge and wisdom" (Prov. 1:7 with 9:10). It threatens them, for the greatest mentalities apart from the Son of God are finally spiritual blackouts at the end of life! To the believer, Christ becomes true "wisdom, and righteousness, and sanctification, and redemption" (1 Cor. 1:30). "In whom are hid all the treasures of wisdom and knowledge" (Col. 2:3). For more on pagan philosophers plagiarizing God's Word see *The Christian Tradition*, vol. 1, pages 28-36, by Jaroslav Pelikan; *Clarke's Commentary*, vol. v, pages 511-515, 522; *Gill's Commentary*, vol. 7, pages xii-xiii, and 737-739; and the brilliant work by Theophilus Gale, *The Court of the Gentiles*, published in 1676. Secular historians have fiercely ridiculed Gale's work to this present day! This is because he aptly demonstrated that the philosophies of heathen Gentiles were distortions of various Bible truths. Sir Walter Raleigh printed his five-volume opus, *History of the World* in 1614. In Part 1, Book 1, chapters 6 and 7 he affirms categorically that heathen writers got their opinions of God from the Jewish Scriptures. Newman in *A Manual of Church History,* vol. one, page 239 wrote, "All that is pure and noble in Greek literature was stolen from the Old Testament. Socrates and Plato derived their ideas from God and Moses." Hence, the vitriolic bitterness vented via the internet by Christ haters who accuse the biblical authors of borrowing doctrines and practices from pagans. It was the opposite. Pagans stole from the original ancient Scriptures, and then distorted divine truths to agree with their shameful idolatrous beliefs and antics. A dispassionate examination of the teachings and lives of the famed philosophers of antiquity demonstrates that they were mentally sick, utterly corrupt in morals, and wickedly irregular in conduct. It was from the lofty instructions and high morals of the Christian religion alone that *true* philosophy and genuine philosophers sprang. Prior to this, all ancient philosophies were a cesspool of filth, evil, Devil worship, and darkness. In the secular world of education, these teachings are a standard for wisdom and learning today!

5p-Targums. Several centuries before Christ, Jewish scribes began to interpret their Scriptures into Aramaic for the benefit of the younger generations of Jews not so familiar with the Hebrew language. Gradually, this became a normal part of synagogue service. These expositional interpretations were called "targums," meaning, "To translate and explain." Amid the Scripture readings accompanied with verbal interpretations, something called "Memra" or "Word" emerged in synagogue theology. When a particular Scripture mentioned God's Name (YHWH) twice, then one of these was often substituted with the noun Memra. This replaced YHWH. In time, this glorious Memra was identified as Israel's Messiah, who was also the same as God. See numbers 1 and 2 below. Gen. 15:6 illustrates this: "And he (Abraham) believed in the YHWH (Memra substituted here) and he (YHWH or the LORD) counted it to him (Abraham) for righteousness." The nearest thing to the Hebrew Memra (in the Greek language) was logos, for both meant "Word." John was as familiar with this Greek term as he was with fishing! He was not weaving the Gnostic logos (with its satanic origins) into the Christian faith. This is academic nonsense. He translated the Aramaic Memra by the word logos, which was the best Greek noun to convey his message.

6p-Below, numbers 1 through 6 reveals that the ancient Jewish Memra is the same Person as John's Logos or Messiah. He is the Son of Jehovah God. John's Logos was not the knowledge or "spirit of good demons" of the heathen Gnostics. To confuse the two is to toy with blasphemy. On targums, see *Commentary of the New Testament . . . ,* vol. 3, pages 239-241, by John Lightfoot, and *Smith's Dictionary of the Bible,* vol. iv, pages 3395-3423. What the scribe-rabbis targumized *orally,* taught or later wrote about the Memra, John applied portions of this to Jesus the Messiah. He was the true Logos. John was presenting Jesus Christ as the "Memra-Logos" mentioned so frequently in the synagogue targums. Whenever pious Jews read his book, they instantly understood what he was affirming. Listed below are eight ancient beliefs about the Memra of the Hebrew Scriptures. With great skill, John is inspired to apply each of these to Jesus of Nazareth, Israel's Messiah. This glorious fact is for both Jews and Gentiles, who have studied his book for almost two thousand years. The apostle John understood the Memra was the same as God according to his words in John 1:1b. Note below how he associated Memra with Almighty God.

1. Memra was God's agent in creation (John 1:2-3, 4a).
2. Memra was God's source of enlightenment to His own people Israel (John 1:4b, 9).
3. Memra was God's agent for physical and spiritual salvation (John 1:12-13).
4. Memra was God's way of becoming visible in flesh without men dying (John 1:14, 18).

5. Memra was God's channel of sending messages and revelations to men about Himself. He would speak for God to His people (John 1:1, 8:25-27; 12:48-50; 17:8). See also John 1:18, footnote 1 under Part 4.

6. Lastly, the Memra reflected the glory of God (John 1:14b with 17:4).

7p-See the article under "MEMRA" in *The Jewish Encyclopedia*, vol. 8, pages 464-465. Alfred Edersheim discusses the Memra in *Life and Times of Jesus the Messiah*, Appendix 2, pages 931-934.

8p-Messiah in ancient Jewish theology. Dr. Sigmund Mowinckel in, *He that cometh. The Messiah Concept in the Old Testament & Later Judaism,* pages 280-345 gives a coverage of this subject. However, like the liberal academicians, the late Norwegian professor fell on his face trying hard to explain this subject while not believing in the inspiration of Scripture. Men who write prolifically about the Messiah and do not believe the entire account of His life as recorded in the four gospels are like exotic fish that cannot swim. They just hang there.

(c) Clement of Alexandra (died A.D. 215) held that Plato's works were inspired because they contained *portions* of truth. He and his predecessors at the "Alexandrian school" *over stressed* the allegorical method of biblical interpretation. Hundreds of Old Testament verses and events were twisted into foreshadowing things they could never mean. The balanced use of the literal historical exegesis was missing. The hermeneutical rule is that there must be balance between these two methods of interpretation. From the "educators and teachers" at the school of Alexandria, Egypt, came a mixture of pagan philosophies, Stoicism, speculative expositions of Scripture, and a firm *disbelief* of divine inspiration. The "church father," Origin (died A.D. 254), presided over this ecumenical den for several decades after the demise of Saccas. Like other church fathers, he underwent great persecution for his heresies. These included "soul sleep," "salvation by baptism," an early form of "universalism," a denial of the history of Genesis. Origin when so far as to state that Jesus' encounter with Satan was a legend. Famed for his allegorical exegesis of Scripture, yet he could not handle the literal temptations of his humanity and thus castrated himself to avoid sinning! In time, a heretic named Arius (died A.D. 336) seized by the quasi-Gnostic philosophy, created great consternation among true believers. Their counterparts exist today in the liberal institutions of divinity, various churches, "Christian cults," and seminaries of the West. They deny, change, or redefine the deity of Jesus Christ. They were blind to the fact that our Lord's deity is indissolubly linked to God in both Testaments as seen in Isa. 7:14 with Matt. 1:21-23. God calls Jesus "God" in Heb. 1:8. There is only one "Almighty God," revealed in Scripture, and He addressed Himself to Abraham as such (Gen. 17:1). Over two thousand years later, the Lord Jesus Christ claimed to be "the Almighty" when He spoke to the elderly apostle John on the island of Patmos (Rev. 1:8). It is obvious that both of these are the same Person. Paul's statement that "The head of Christ *is* God" (1 Cor. 11:3) has contextual reference to His submission to human death and how God honored that by raising Him from the dead. The one true God eternally exists as three distinct Persons: the Father, Son, and Holy Spirit. The undivided essence of the Godhead belongs equally to each. Among the church fathers, some defended the deity of Christ and other eternal truths, yet denied the inspiration Scripture, meaning they had no foundation for what they professed to believe. *All the fathers whose writings are extant held that men were saved by infant baptism and partaking of communion!* It is not much different today. One may believe the truths of Holy Scripture with all his heart. However, if he is off on *how to be saved* from sin and hell, better had he never been born.

2p-Platonic heresy not taught in the New Testament. Enemies of Christianity have perpetuated the lie that the Scriptures teach various forms of pagan Greek philosophy. Religious and secular critics, denying the complete inspiration of Scripture, the deity of Christ, and the eternal suffering of the damned, continually use this appeal to the ignorant masses. A wise man once said, "A lie goes around the world seven times while truth is putting her boots on." We discover why this is so in 2 Cor. 4:4 and 1 John 5:19.

(d) All three divine Persons co-shared equally in the creation. In the process of human history, pagans distorted and perverted the doctrine of the Trinity along with all major truths of God. Unitarians, Universalists, Christiadelphians, Christian Science, Jehovah's Witness, Muslims, Judaism, various cults, and persons have vehemently denied the triune nature of God. Over the centuries mentally deranged, pseudo "Christians" executed men for not believing in the Holy Trinity. Both John Calvin of Geneva and King James I of England were guilty of this crime. The Trinity is not a myth borrowed by Christians from the dark religions of pagan neighbors, as blasphemers delight to proclaim. It is the exact opposite. Pagans inspired by demon spirits produced counterfeits, not only of the Holy Trinity but also of things of God and Christ, thousands of years before our Lord was born. Satan and his angels from the beginning foresaw the plan of God for the ages. They worked insidiously to duplicate it in thousands of ways through the religious channels of heathenism pouring across the earth from the Tower of Babel. For more on this awful thought, see Section 9, second and third paragraphs under footnote i. The heathen mythological character, Orpheus, who supposedly lived before 500 B.C., wrote of something resembling the Holy Trinity. John Gill in his *Commentary,* vol. 1, page 3 documents this. Citing from an older source called *Universal History,* vol. 1, page 33, Gill states that Orpheus wrote, "All things were made by one Godhead of three names . . ." This ancient text shows that pagans had scraps of original God given truth. Over the centuries, these were blended into idolatrous doctrines and practices. Heathen religions reflected their lost knowledge of the Memra true and living God!

The famed pagan, Pliny the Elder, (born A.D. 23), "the man who knew everything," also toyed with the Hebrew belief of the one, true, living God. His massive encyclopedia, *Natural History* touches on this and other subjects.

2p-Evolution originated in paganism. It is education's biggest lie, teaching that nothing produced something, which has resulted in everything. Darwinism purports to explain the cause of all things by means of the natural, while rejecting the supernatural. The word "creation" is being replaced, while the term "intelligent design" serves as a substitute without mentioning God. On the other hand, theistic evolution, or gap theory creationism, which affirms that God employed long time periods (millions of years) to create all things, is a blatant compromise of truth. Men, who refuse to believe what the Scriptures state, usually embrace these fables. Great men such as James Orr and Augustus Strong struggled to reconcile the record of Genesis 1 with uniformitarianism's mythical geological timetables. The *Scofield Reference Bible*, page 4, footnote 2, also allows for the possibility of theistic evolution. Both atheistic and theistic evolution defies God, contradicts His Word, and should be classified as doctrines of demons (1 Tim. 4:1-2). God stated twice that those who deny His existence are "fools" (Ps. 14:1; 53:1). On the day of His resurrection, Christ said that men who are "slow to believe" the Old Testament Scriptures are also fools (Lk. 24:25). Churches, seminaries, and institutions of education across America are full of these "fools," postured in positions of authority. They graduate annually into the public domain an army of academic atheists. These continue to propagate their "superior" but dark learning into the minds of others. Hence, we discover the meaning of 2 Cor. 4:4 and 1 John 5:19. This is why the Western World has gone mad against God, Jesus Christ, morality, and things that are obviously right. For a powerful work dealing with evolution, see *The God-Haters: Angry Atheists, Shallow Scholars, Silly Scientists, Pagan Preachers, and Embattled Evolutions Declare War on Christians,* by Dr. Don Boys. For comments on the war between faith and science, see Section 91, third paragraph of footnote d.

3p-Christian orthodoxy defended and shamed at the Council of Nicaea. In A.D. 325, Emperor Constantine called for a gathering of churches in his domain to defend the deity of Christ against the heresy known as Arianism. This teaching degraded Jesus to a created being unequal with God. The ecumenical collection of the emperor's churches drew up the Nicene Creed. It was a collective affirmation of basic Christian theology regarding the Holy Trinity. After this meeting, those who did not accept these Bible truths were arrested, tortured, imprisoned, and some were put to death! The "great Christian Constantine" had hundreds killed *after* his profession of Christ, including his wife and son. Men, who defend the fundamentals of the faith, then kill those who do not, deny the very truths they supposedly uphold. *True* Christianity does not operate this way. *Nowhere in the New Testament did the early believers have their opponents beaten, tortured, banished, or executed.* "Christian apologists" for these crimes assure us it was "the spirit of that age." However, the Lord Jesus said murder is the work of the Devil (John 8:44). It remains true that all murder is killing but not all killing is murder. Over the course of church history, religious fanatics slaughtering their opponents in the name of God and quoting verses from the Bible, fall guilty under the first category. They were cold-blooded murderers! For several of the "great defenders of the Christian faith" and the treatment they meted out to those who disagreed with them, see Section 14, numbers 1 through 8, under footnote f.

(e) "The light of men." Sin slammed the whole of creation into the abyss of spiritual, moral, and intellectual darkness. God gave Adam's fallen race "light" and sure hope in the Person of His Son. (This hope was prefigured over the Old Testament millenniums before the Savior was born in Bethlehem.) In Lk. 2:32, He is called a light for the Gentiles. Therefore, His salvation was not an exclusively Jewish thing. Standing in the temple He announced to the people and the woman taken in adultery, "I am the light of the world." In His divine authority to speak forgiveness, the darkness of the woman's sins vanished in the light of His love (John 8:11-12). John 1:5 is suggestive of Gen. 1:2-3, hence shaded in gray signifying an Old Testament citation.

2p-The Talmud asks the question in tractate, Sanhedrin 99a, "When will Messiah come?" Then it answers, "When darkness cover[s] these people [Israel]." At Bethlehem's manger, God turned on the Light of the world for Israel and all mankind. The rabbis taught that the temple, Torah Law, and Messiah were the only lights for mankind. Yet when Messiah came, they bitterly rejected Him. To Nicodemus (who came to Him by night) our Lord said that by coming to Him men would find light. See Section 30, John 3:2, 19-21 for the story. To a man born blind Christ declared, "I am the light of the world" (John 9:1, 5). Many pottery lamps were excavated from Jewish burial grounds at Gezer (1 Kings 9:15-17) on which were inscribed the words, "The light of Messiah shines for all [Jews]." See also John 12:35-36; Eph. 5:8, 14; and Col. 1:13. When Christ entered the land of Zebulon, the lights came on! Seven hundred years prior Isaiah had written that the people residing there in spiritual darkness, saw "great light." See Section 38, Matt. 4:16, footnote o. John 1:9 says that Jesus brings illumination to every man born into the world.

3p-Verse 5. "Shineth in darkness." Seemingly a reference to Gen. 1:3 and partly cited in 2 Cor. 4:6.

4p-Verse 5. "Comprehended it not." The compounded Greek word "katalambano," used here carries the idea to "stop or hold down." A degenerate unsaved world did not welcome the divine light that came with the birth of Christ. Years later, John, looking back as he wrote, declares that sin, and Satan could not "comprehend," "stop or hold down," Jesus Christ the Word of God. Rather, He overcame them on the cross and in His resurrection (Col. 2:14-17). *Every effort by men and devils to extinguish His eternal light has failed.* It continues to shines with the same authority and power for all who receive Him as personal Lord and Savior (John 1:12).

Jesus Christ and John the Baptist, the God-sent witness of the Light. He is the only true spiritual Light for mankind throughout the world.

Matt.	Mk.	Lk.	John 1:6-9—*Place of writing unknown.*
			6 There was a man sent from God, whose name *was* John. **7** The same came for a witness, to bear witness[f] of the Light, that all *men* through him might believe. **8** He was not that Light, but *was sent* to bear witness of that Light. **9** *That* was the true Light, which lighteth every man that cometh into the world. (Verse 10 cont. in Section 1, Part 3.)

Footnotes-Commentary

[f] **John, the witness of Christ the Light.** The term "John the Baptist" is found some nineteen times in this gospel. In Lk. 7:20 it is translated "John Baptist." Hebrew sages taught that the physical Elijah of their history would literally return to Israel *before* the appearing of Messiah. For details on this, see *Appendix Four*. Among other things, he would be preeminently the forerunner and prepare the way for Israel's King. John the Baptist emphatically denied being the *literal physical* Elijah. However, he was Elijah in the spiritual sense. For explanation of this, see Section 105, Matt. 17:10-13, footnote m. John's ministry was to prepare a people for the coming Messiah by giving faithful witness of Him (John 5:31-35). He did this as see seen in Lk. 1:17. John, looking back as he wrote, informs his readers that the Baptist preached that men should believe in Christ, the light that brings salvation and *true* life. For twenty-one things John the Baptist did and preached, see Section 21, Part 4, footnote q.

2p-**Verse 9. "Lighteth every man."** John's striking statement that Christ the Messiah lights "every man" that comes into the world is a revelation! He did not say "every man who is one of the elect." Paul's *first* appeal to the pagans at Lystra, was to point them to the wonders of creation. Then, he explained that this was the handiwork of the One and only living God (Acts 14:15 and Ps. 146:6). As a missionary serving in Africa, the author has done exactly the same thing in attempting to introduce the true and living God to the pagan natives. Below are several verses explaining why the heathens will stand before God "without excuse" (Rom. 1:20). All men have been offered degrees of enlightenment. Some by nature, some by conscience, and others by Bible revelation. Concerning the truth of *every man* being touched by the light of Christ through whatever channel, see Ps. 19:1-4; Acts 14:16-17; Rom. 2:14-15; 10:18; Col. 1:6; and Titus 2:11. In John 3:19-21 we read that they mostly rejected this heavenly appeal.

3p-**Are heathens lost?** For a clear explanation regarding the plight of pagans and God's truths being originally known by them, see *Eternity in Their Hearts*, by Don Richardson. An outstanding work dealing with this question is *The Discovery of Genesis: How the Truths of Genesis Were Found Hidden in the Chinese Language,* by G. H. Kang and Ethel R. Nelson. This book skillfully demonstrates that within the Chinese language (dating back some five thousand years) can be found various characters that, when broken down into component parts, speak of the creation of man and woman, the Garden of Eden, marriage, the temptation, fall, death, Noah's flood, Tower of Babel, hell, and other Bible truths. They were known long before Moses existed. The ancient Chinese received these truths from their ancestors who were scattered from the Tower of Babel in Gen. 11:1-9. *The Deluge Story in Stone*, by Byron Nelson, confirms the fragmented knowledge of God among the earliest pagan tribes of the world. For their idolatrous corruption of this divine knowledge, see Section 1, Part 4, third paragraph under footnote j.

4p-**Satanic perversions.** Adam and original human posterity knew the full truth about God, sin, and His Son, our Savior. With the dispersion of the human race from Babel (mentioned above), these truths were gradually perverted over the centuries through idolatry. In time, God finally gave them "up" and "up" and lastly "over" to their sins (Rom. 1:18, 24, 26, and 28). For more on God turning the incorrigible pagan nations loose to their own sins, see Deut. 32:8 with Acts 14:16. The unspeakable moral perversions of ancient heathen religions were condemned in Lev. 18. Their decline into occult practices is seen in Deut. 18:9-14. *These verse were commanded to Israel long after the Torah Law was given at Mr. Sinai.* Sacrifices offered by pagans to their deities were actually offered to Satan and demons (Deut. 32:16-17; Lev. 17:7; and Ps. 106:35-38). An idol within itself is nothing (1 Cor. 8:4). However, they often became dwelling places for evil spirits (Lev. 17:7; Deut. 7:25-26; 12:29-31; and 1 Cor. 10:20). God warned Israel, "And there shall cleave nought of the cursed thing to thine hand . . ." (Deut. 13:17). For evil brought into the home of unsuspecting Christians, see Section 20, paragraphs two through five of footnote l.

5p-**Light offered to every man.** Before His ascension, Jesus commanded His followers to take the saving gospel to "every creature" (Mk. 16:15), and "all nations," meaning the masses (Matt. 28:19 with Lk. 24:47-48). The Savior's commission also included discipleship, teaching, and believer's baptism. Contextually, only men filled with the Holy Spirit can finally do this work. For more on this, see Section 206, Acts 1:8, footnote e. The first Christians fulfilled the *original* Great Commission to their generation and before the destruction of Jerusalem in A.D. 70. See Section 163, footnote f, third paragraph of number 16, for a discussion as to how this was accomplished.

Jesus Christ was unknown by the world and rejected by His people. Nevertheless, all who receive Him and believe on His Name are born of God.* Man has no work-part in the divine miracle of saving grace.

See Section 30 and all of footnote e for an explanation of what "born of God" or "new birth" meant to the Jewish people before, during, and after the time of Nicodemus. It was a term well known.

Matt.	Mk.	Lk.	John 1:10-13—*Place of writing unknown.*
			10 He was in the world, and the world was made by him, and the world knew him not. **11** He came unto his own, and his own received him not.**(g)** **12** But as many as received him, to them gave he power to become the sons of God, *even* to them that believe**(h)** on his name: **13** Which were born, not of blood, nor of the will of the flesh, nor of the will of man, but of God.**(i)** (Verse 14 cont. in Section 1, Part 4.)

Footnotes-Commentary

(g) The unwanted Messiah. The majority of His own Jewish people rejected Him (Matt. 12:14; 23:27-37; Lk. 19:14; John 5:15-16). The religious leaders of Israel attempted to kill the Lord Jesus on various occasions. See Section 52, John 5:16, footnote l, and Section 124, John 11:8, footnote g. In Ex. 4:22 the nation of Israel is called God's son, even His firstborn. Christ is called the "firstborn of every creature" or "prototokos" in Col. 1:15. The meaning is that because He is deity and God, He was first to rise from the dead in a glorified body never to die again. He is therefore, preeminent or first above all things. Jesus Christ is not one of these things, but the creator of them all! With the coming of Messiah, and Israel's deliberate rejection of Him, and His atoning death on the cross, adoption of sons to God was offered freely to *all* nations without distinction. The worst of Gentile pagan outcasts were now invited to Christ for salvation, forgiveness, and peace with God. A few days before His death, our Lord taught this hated truth to the Jews in Section 153, footnote k. They understood Him and were greatly offended.

(h) Faith in Christ is not an intellectual or historical faith. Rather, it is produced out of God's Word working in the heart (Rom. 10:17). Acts 17:4 and 5 reveal that some will exercise this God-given faith while others will not. (This has nothing to do with works, rather how salvation does work.) Before the foundation of the world, God ordained to eternal life all who would believe in His Son (Acts 13:48). The elect are those who believe and the non-elect are those who (finally) will not. Super Calvinist John Gerstner talks about God electing sinners without dependence on their foreseen faith, that "God does not foresee" any faith in depraved sinners except as He bestows it on those He unconditionally elects. The theology that God only sees what He bestows on anyone is wrong. Reversed, this means He cannot see what He did not bestow. God foresees all things, good and bad. By His sovereign choice, He determined to save all who will believe on the Lord Jesus Christ. To depict this as "sinner's merit" is absurd. *It works this way because God makes it work this way.* The God of the Calvinist with His ineffable sovereignty damned billions to eternal hell (before the foundation of the world), and honorably brings others to eternal life. This debauchery of truth includes billions of infants who are not of the elect and will suffer the pangs of torment forever! Like Arminianism, it is a hideous untruth that shames the grace of God. Grace is not a license to promote sin and doctrinal heresy. It firmly opposes both while offering *true* salvation to "all men" (Titus 2:11).

2p-Read the words of a "leading Reformed scholar" in the third paragraph of footnote i below. No one seems to understand God like these people do for they are His elect. Their hermeneutics are beyond mortal challenge. Only they correctly interpret Romans chapter 11. Those who disagree are, "antinomian," "Arminian," "fundamentalist," or "dispensationalists." Regarding their arch-heresy of "baby faith" as was taught by Luther, Calvin, various Reformed, and Presbyterian Churches, see Section 150, second paragraph of footnote f. This is so radical that certain Calvinistic Baptist Churches have backed off from it in horror.

3p-Infralapsarianism, sublapsarianism, and supralapsarianism. Men meddling with the sovereign decrees of God invented these philosophical terms. They fain to explain God's predestinations of humanity, with each school assuring us they are right. Briefly, infralapsarianism holds that in the mind of God, the fall preceded the decrees to election and reprobation. Sublapsarianism declares that after the fall, God decreed the election or non-election of individual men to salvation. Loosely, supralapsarianism states that God determined to save some and permit others to be damned before He decided to permit the fall. These speculations are examples of puny men invading the inscrutable mind of God to discover His secret councils. Such learned verbiage may tickle the ears of seminary students, and exhibit the professor's great learning, but avails nothing to men dying without Christ. Paul affirmed, "For who hath known the mind of the Lord, that he may instruct him?" (1 Cor. 2:16). It is written, "Canst thou by searching find out God?" (Job 11:7). Who can picture the missionary apostle giving a discourse on the above topics to the somber nine members of Athens Supreme Court on Mars Hill or the educated pagans at Corinth?

The average church congregation needs more than loquacious prattle and presumed theological solutions to rescue them from hell. Ministers and Christians must learn to weep with those that weep (Rom. 12:15). If God elected so many for heaven before the foundation of the world, then we may do nothing to rescue them. He will bring them into eternal life regardless of what anyone does or does not do. Thus, the Great Commission is a mockery. Paul praying for Israel to be saved is absurd (Rom. 10:1). Jesus weeping twice over Jerusalem for rejecting Him is ignorance (Matt. 23:37 and Lk. 19:41-44), since God ordained their refusal in eternity past.

4p-Verses 12. In this passage, John writes only about the origin of the new birth not its reception. He tells us here where it does come from. Salvation is received by believing and receiving Jesus the Messiah.

5p-Verse 13. The human mind, enlightened by God's Word, and the Holy Spirit, hears, understands, and then can freely exercise divinely given faith or refuse to do so. This is how God planned it. In these words, John contradicts the standard Jewish notion of who was a son or child of God. In strict Hebrew thinking, one became a child of Jehovah by physical birth into the family of Abraham. This was referred to as "born of water." See Section 30, all of footnote f for explanation. Gentiles could also become Jews by proselytism. This included obeying the tradition of the elders, the Torah Law, and various other formalities. Though salvation is mentioned in the law and across the Old Testament, many Jews missed it in their mad pursuit of legalism, oral traditions, and stress on outward purity. John opposed these traditions when he wrote that any man who receives (or believes on Christ the Messiah) would be spiritually born anew. For salvation in the Old Testament, see Section 30, footnote h, with Section 144, footnote i. Those across the Old Testament, who trusted Christ yet to come, were saved just as well as those who trusted Him *after* He came. John's firm conclusion was that Hebrew "flesh and blood" cannot give eternal life. Salvation is a spiritual miracle that changes the person (soul) inside the physical body. It is unrelated in its origin, reception, and results to anything the flesh can produce. Below, verse 13 lays down three negatives and one positive regarding the subject of being born again. *Below he tells us where it does not come from. In verse 12, he tells us where it does come from:*

1. **First negative. It is *not* hereditary.** The new birth is not received by physical genetics through family bloodlines. The Jews had a curious belief that more or less allowed for this. See Section 30, first paragraph of footnote f for other details on the statement "born of water."

2. **Second negative. It is *not* received by human endeavor.** Good deeds are described in this verse as "the will of the flesh." See Rom. 7:18 for what the flesh contains, and Gal. 5:19-21 for the works it produces. On the Jewish usage of the expression "flesh and blood," see Section 103, number 3 under footnote f. Human merits produced by "the will of man" within the confines of Moses' Law, or apart from it, will not save a soul from sin and hell. Over the centuries, intellectual and religious ingenuity has concocted innumerable ways to have sins forgiven. All have failed. Only when the Word of God and the Holy Spirit activates the free will of man can it respond acceptably to the Almighty or reject what He offers. God arranged it this way. Human interference into this divine plan has resulted in unspeakable error, sorrow, and destruction. See first through the third paragraphs of footnote l below for examples of this.

3. **Third negative. The new birth is *not* an ideal acquired by the choice of man.** Man deciding when he wants to be saved does not alone bring regeneration. The teaching that our *personal choice* is all that God requires for men to secure the new birth is false. As previously stated, a "freewill" or "ability to choose" (that God has given to every normal man), when awakened by the Holy Spirit, may respond to the gospel or may not. *God makes it work this way and Rom. 9:16 now makes sense.* The term "freewill" is found in the Scripture some seventeen times. Ezra 7:13 gives us a classic example of the meaning of this word. If man has no "free will," then the "freewill offerings" of the Old Testament are senseless (Lev. 22:18). Martin Luther's work, *Bondage of the Will,* only added mud to the water. In his catechisms, he wrote that baptism and communion were necessary for salvation. Refer to Section 203, eighth paragraph of footnote d for Luther's theological travesty. John 5:40 is clear that men can reject God's invitation to life even when offered by His Son. The Savior, choosing individuals as recorded in John 15:16, speaks of service, not salvation. The context of this verse refers to "fruit bearing" (which follows salvation), and not eternal life, which is received prior. God kidnaps no one to heaven, not even the "elected" Calvinists responding to "irresistible grace," and the "effectual call." Nor does He allow Arminians to get in by virtue of "their choice" and its "good works." Men are saved by grace, or they are not saved. Confirmed reprobates ordain themselves by their own stubbornness to hell (2 Peter 2:1). This is because they ultimately, "turn the grace of God [offered to them, Titus 2:11] into lasciviousness" (Jude 4). God has ordained (or decreed) that all who repent (Acts 17:30), and believe on the Lord Jesus (Acts 16:31), have secured eternal life. These are the elect whom He foreknew would be saved. *After* conversion, the saved are predestinated to be conformed to the image of His Son, which is a lifetime process (Rom. 8:29). Thus, Acts 13:48 makes sense when it reads, "And as many [in Paul's synagogue audience] as were ordained to eternal life believed." That is, their faith or belief in Christ revealed the previous ordination to eternal life established by God in the dateless past of eternity. They were part of those known only to Him, who

would believe in His dear son. The Holy Spirit forced no one in Paul's audience to believe or not believe in Christ. Those who did instantly became members of the vast elect of all ages. This is not God complying with man's choice; rather, it is man being enabled by grace to do the predetermined will of God, thus complying with His choice.

4. **The one positive.** The two words, "of God," reveal that the new birth has its origin in God. It is His gift received through faith in the finished work of Christ's atonement and resurrection. It is absurd to teach that men are saved, then have faith or believe in Christ. The rule is that they repent, believe, and are saved. This pattern is seen in Acts 18:8. Galatians. 3:26 states that one becomes a child of God "by faith," but not before faith. In the Greek New Testament, "faith" and "belief" mean the same. John's first wrote to bring his readers to salvation through believing that Jesus was the Christ, the Son of God (John 20:30-31). For more on these things, see Section 25, fourth and fifth paragraphs of footnote d.

(i) **Verse 13**. **"Not of . . . nor of . . . but of God."** There is a heavenly birth received in this life when one is saved by the grace of God. It brings a new life that mortal flesh did not generate. It is strictly "of God." In His program of things, God has established that men, upon hearing the gospel, accompanied by the Holy Spirit's illumination, will be given the ability to repent and believe to salvation (Acts 5:31; Rom. 2:4 with Acts 11:18). When convicted of their sins men are granted "space" or "time" to repent and believe (Rev. 2:20-21 with 9:20-21). This determination of God has nothing to do with a work of the human will but entirely His sovereign choice in arranging things this way. Going too far into these mysteries results in extremes, blasphemous interpretations, and horrendous forms of soteriology. Men like A. W. Pink (died 1952) invaded the forbidden realms of God's eternal counsels. His book, *The Sovereignty of God*, makes the Almighty a monster and Adam's children His helpless prey. An Australian "bushman" after reading Pink's book, took a kangaroo rifle and shot his brains out by pulling the trigger with his toe. A suicide note read, "I am not one of God's elect. Life means nothing."

2p-Killing one another. Will Durant in *The Story of Civilization,* vol. 7, page 190, wrote of early British Presbyterians and Puritans, who requested Parliament in 1648, to "Legislate life imprisonment for all who continued to teach Catholic, Arminian, Baptist, or Quaker views." By law, only Calvin's elite doctrine could be taught! Durant mentioned the divisions among Puritans and their requirements for men to adhere to "strict Calvinism." This theological infamy descended like a dark cloud over thousands. He wrote, "Some thinking themselves damned [by God's decree] went about the streets groaning in anticipation of their eternal doom. The thunderbolts of God seemed always to hang over the heads of men." Inspired by Satan the church in power used the sword of the state to enforce her beliefs. John Calvin did this at Geneva, seeking to silence or drive out all opposition to his Reformed doctrines. The Anabaptist divided into four groups: Swiss, German/Austrian, Dutch, and Hutterites. In Europe, splinter groups of Anabaptists (the crazy German Münsterites) went wild. Among the most radical were those who "danced in the Spirit" spoke in tongues, and fell into contortions and trances. One Anabaptist sectarian group, called "rationalists," denied the Trinity. Baptist historian Thomas Armitage in *A History of Baptist*, 1:350, records one of the decrees established by "the great Reformers" against *all* Anabaptists true and false. It reads, "On the 7th of March, 1526, the Council of Zurich decreed that those who baptize any person who had been previously christened, should, if condemned, be drowned without mercy." Murdering people in the name of a doctrine, sacred wall, hill, valley, building, fountain, rock, cave, creed, shrine, and so forth is religious insanity. Over early history, the ruling Anglican, Reformed, and Catholic churches *armed with the sword of the state,* sought to kill all, good, and bad, who would not comply with their beliefs. People of highly passionate religious and political persuasions, unchecked by *rightly divided Scripture* are history's greatest tyrants. There have been thousands of these monsters.

3p-Mummified in theological error. The spiritually blinding effects of Calvinism flashes from the words of Dr. Jay Adams in *Competent to Counsel,* page 70. He wrote,, "As a reformed Christian, the writer believes that counselors must not tell any unsaved counselee that Christ died for him. No man knows except Christ himself who are His elect for whom He died." When the Philippian jailer inquired of the missionaries, "Sirs, what must I do to be saved?" (Acts 16:30), why did they not respond, "We cannot answer this, for you may not be one of the elect." Yet the jailer was saved and "rejoiced, believing in God with all his house" (verse 34). One muses how "infants" could have Scripture explained to them (verse 32), and rejoice as water was poured or sprinkled on their tiny heads in baptism? Did this awaken the heresy of "baby faith" slumbering in their souls? Adam's words reveal a "professional theologian" who knows nothing about the biblical history of bringing men to Christ. May God spare anyone from going to Adams for "competent counseling." His statement flies in the face of world missions and true biblical evangelism. For more of his "evangelical" travesties, see Section 68, third paragraph of footnote e. *It should be pointed out that not all Calvinists are ignorant to the truth of soul winning as Jay Adams.* The author has many friends of Reformed persuasions who work day and night bringing men to Christ. Refer to Section 62, fifth paragraph of footnote h for the names of some outstanding Reformed Christians, who won thousands to the Savior. These great people are among the warmhearted true saints of God. They are not part of that icy "ordained elect," frozen stiff before the foundation of the world, and soundly mummified in theological error.

Jesus Christ's incarnate glory is remembered by John the author. John the Baptist had faithfully witnessed of His preeminence, fullness, grace, truth, and intimacy with God. Jesus revealed the Father by His words and works.

Matt.	Mk.	Lk.	John 1:14-18—*Place of writing unknown.*
			14 And the Word was made flesh,(j) and dwelt among us, (and we beheld his glory, the glory as of the only begotten of the Father,) full of grace and truth. **15** John [the Baptist] bare witness of him, and cried, saying, "This was he of whom I spake, 'He that cometh after me is preferred before me: for he was before me.'" **16** "And of his fulness have all we received, and grace for grace. **17** "For the law was given by Moses, *but* grace and truth came by Jesus Christ.(k) **18** "No man hath seen God(l) at any time; the only begotten Son, which is in the bosom of the Father, he hath declared(m) *him*."(n) (Verse 19 cont. in Section 24.)

Footnotes-Commentary

(j) **"Made flesh."** With this, John speaks of the virgin birth of Christ whereby He took on a body of human flesh through Mary His mother (Heb. 10:5). See Section 12, Matt. 1:18, footnote b, for a brief discussion of the pagan perversions of the virgin birth and other basic truths of Scripture. Beholding His glory occurred hundreds of times before the apostles, but especially in the latter months of Christ's ministry when John and several others experienced the Mount of Transfiguration miracle (Matt. 17:1-9). They also beheld His glory in the post-resurrection period just before His ascension. Paul affirms that the incarnation is without controversy (1 Tim. 3:16). It is a divine mystery that is above (not against) human intellect. Some worthy expositors see a prediction of the incarnation in Ezek. 1:26 with "the appearance of a man" above God's throne. Whosoever attacks the truth that Jesus was God in the flesh, tears the most important page from all history. Blend 1 Tim. 3:16 with Rom. 1:3; Phil. 2:5-11; 2 Tim. 2:8; and Heb. 2:14-16 for more on the incarnation.

2p-We must not kid ourselves into thinking that we may mentally comprehend the incarnation. Men who try this play silly games. Neither the nature of Christ nor His deity will be understood by mortal mind. Any unbiased inspection of the life of Christ and His character will suffice to show that He cannot be classified *solely* with mankind, though He was man. When He said, "I am from above" (John 8:23), He set Himself as peculiarly different from all mortals. He was the supernatural manifested in its highest grade and order, yet in human form. When He declared to the Jews, "I and my Father are one" (John 10:30), He made Himself very God, standing in the flesh of very man. Godless men cannot bear this highest truth of earth's history. They continually discredit this glorious fact.

3p-**Demonic imitations.** Darkened heathen poets and historians produced flamboyant stories of their gods and goddesses coming to earth incarnate and dwelling among men and women. What did such contrivances as Jupiter, Juno, Venus, Mars, Vulcan, and others accomplish? They were all hideous monsters of lust, envy, murder, destruction, rape, and sexual perversions that defy description. These heathen fables were invented by the nations scattered at the Tower of Babel. Paul preached in Acts 14:16 that God suffered these rebellious masses to "walk in their own ways." Paganism invented thousands of satanic mimes to discredit the future coming at Bethlehem of the living God in the flesh. Contrast the life and works of Christ with those of the pagan gods "dwelling in the flesh" among men. It is as heaven set against hell. In these verses, John, the former fisherman, penned the *true* account of God visiting the earth via human form in opposition to shocking pagan fables of that era. The heathen distortions of the only true religion have now been made respectable and acceptable. Atheistic cultural anthropologists and sociologists assisted by the national media and secular education present these heathen perversions as the original sources of the Christian faith. For a response to this, refer to Section 1, Part 2, third through fifth paragraphs of footnote f. *Christians should reject all suspected or known artifacts or objects having their origin in paganism.* They must have no place in their homes, businesses, or personal adornment. This unknown and overlooked subject is continued in Section 20, second through sixth paragraphs of footnote 1.

4p-**An old infidel academic response.** In 1922, Thomas Inman released a work called *Ancient Pagan and Modern Christian Symbolism.* This book credits the origin of *all* Christian doctrine to the innumerable pagan religions and heathen myths of history. The late Dr. Inman wrote on page 3 these words of learned ignorance, "The religion of Christ has been adulterated by Paganism." The agnostic physicist, Dr. Charles Panati, published in 1996 his unique addition to the parade of Bible ridicule. It is entitled *Sacred Origins of Profound Things.* For Dr. Panati's paganising the Lord's Supper, refer to Section 174, second paragraph of footnote b. This "expert in origins" is confident that he has traced the countless events of Scripture back into the bosom of folklore, myth, and heathenism. Those who deny the existence of God, and the historical reliability of Holy Scripture must then invent a rebuttal to these things. Men like Inman and Panati believe they have done this. See paragraph three above.

5p-Christians must remember. Every *true* believer should regularly call to mind where he came from, then what he is doing, and where he is going. Had it not been for divine grace, many of us would be in that army of atheists, critics, false cults, and the religious and political hypocrites who oppose God, Jesus Christ, and the Bible. Peter called on believers to remember the "time past" of their lives (1 Peter 4:3-5). Isaiah said to look into the "hole of the pit" from which God rescued us (Isa. 51:1). Considering what we have been and what God has made us now, we knell in thankful humility. For more on this subject, refer to Section 14, fourth paragraph of footnote f.

(k) Prevalent at this time was the fundamental synagogue teaching that grace and truth came by the Law of Moses and tradition of the elders. John reverses this. Grace and truth come only through Memra-Logos, Jesus the eternal Word of God. Note Section 1, Part 1, footnote b for explanation of the Memra-Logos. For salvation in the Old Testament, see Section 30, fourth paragraph of footnote h, with Section 144, footnote i.

(l) Seeing God. The idea in this statement is that no man living in human flesh has seen with the mortal eye the *absoluteness* of God Almighty. Humanity could not bear the sight. Moses desired to see God's face and glory, however, his request was summarily refused because no man could do this and live (Ex. 33:18, 20). Over two thousand years before Christ was born, Job knew in the future at the resurrection he would "see God" (Job 19:25-26). A thousand years before Christ came, David wrote, "As for me, I will behold thy face in righteousness: I shall be satisfied, when I awake, with thy likeness" (Ps. 17:15). When Philip inquired about seeing the Father, Christ responded, "He that hath seen me hath seen the Father" (John 14:9-11; John 12:45; and 1 John 4:12). In the Old Testament, God appeared to men in various forms as seen in Gen. 18:1; Ex. 3:1-14; Josh. 5:13; and Dan. 10:1-9. The glorious felicity of God's total magnificence was veiled behind the flesh of Christ. Philip did not yet know this truth. A glimpse of holy brilliance on the Mount of Transfiguration dazzled the apostles (Mk. 9:2-8). Years later, John, on Patmos, again in the presence of Jesus' glory, dropped as a dead man (Rev. 1:17).

2p-The only true God exists in unspeakable divine Light. It is inaccessible to human mortality. Man may enter this glorious bliss in heaven to come only through possessing Jesus Christ as personal Lord and Savior. *There is no other way to God!* Within Christ's physical frame dwelt, the absolute fullness of the Godhead bodily (Col. 2:9). Bethlehem's manger was the supreme and only example of God coming to earth in a human form to walk among men. Finally, when His plan for the ages has reached its consummation, then, all the redeemed "shall see his face" (Rev. 22:4). And they "shall be like him" (1 John 3:2).

3p-"In the bosom" was an eastern expression. For other comments on this, see Section 131, Lk. 16:23, footnote e, and Section 172, John 13:23, footnote g. The person sitting closest to the host was considered to be "in his bosom" or of such intimacy that he shared the heart of the master of the feast. They were as one. This closeness is mentioned in the Talmud tractates, Ta'anith 11a, which states that the "bosom is the same as the soul," and in Yevamoth 63b, it speaks of a "good wife." In the dateless past, Christ as the Son lay in the bosom of His Father. From all eternity, they shared a unity and indissoluble oneness that mortal words cannot describe. As man, He lay in the womb of a virgin and acquired a human frame; picturing His death, He immersed Himself under water in baptism and rose again; as death's conqueror, He was laid in a borrowed tomb but gave it back a few days later. Verse 18 signifies that Jesus was both God and the Son. As such, they perfectly shared, in essence, and infinity, the knowledge of all things that have been or that ever would be.

4p-As perfect and True Man, Christ was called the Son of man. As perfect and True Deity, He was called God. He is both the Son of God and God the Son. *Scripture never deifies Christ's humanity nor does it humanize His deity*. It remains true that because God is who He is, He is what He is. This union of humanity with deity is indissoluble and indefinable. Rejecting this on the grounds of "mysterious" is unacceptable. Intellectual efforts to explain these things are futile, for he who defines God explains God away.

(m) The Son declares the Father. The writer of Hebrews states that God has spoken to us by His Son (Heb. 1:1-2). Therefore, what the Savior said was God speaking through Him. While on earth, the Lord Jesus was Jehovah's exclusive spokesperson. In His incarnation, He had knowledge of God as no other mortal did. His frame of humanity did not hinder His impeccable intimacy with the Father. None of the great leaders, prophets, and sages of Israel knew God, as Christ did while He walked among men. Christ's knowledge of His Father was infinite. He was impeccably equal with Him, being of the same divine spiritual essence. He was totally acquainted with His sovereign counsels and qualified to give the perfect public revelation of Him. *There were times during His incarnation when He chose not to use His omniscience*. This seriously important subject is explained in Section 163, Mk. 13:32, fourth paragraph of footnote v. The Savior uniquely declared (revealed) to men the true and living God. *Those who reject Jesus Christ and deny His deity and atonement will never know God*. In Section 162, John 12:44-45, the Savior stated that when men saw Him, they were seeing God in action, though veiled in a physical body.

2p-To the Jews Jesus said, "My doctrine [teaching] is not mine, but his [God's] that sent me" (John 7:16). He only taught what God told Him to teach. See Section 19, third and fourth paragraphs of footnote c, for how God taught Jesus "morning by morning." Christ was unprecedented in His public revelation of the Father. Hundreds of years before His birth, the rabbis taught that Messiah alone could thoroughly reveal God. The incontrovertible conclusion is that only through Christ can God be rightly known. This truth is fiercely despised. *In time, America's hate crime laws will be used against Christians to silence the message of Jesus Christ, the world's only Savior.*

3p-Our Lord's exclusive authority to reveal God is stated in Section 63, Matt. 11:27, footnote f; Section 115, Lk. 10:22; Col. 2:9; and 1 John 5:20. Near the end of His ministry, in the upper room, the night before His cross, He spoke again of these things (John 14:6-9). His statement in John 12:45, "He that seeth me seeth him [God] that sent me" is most profound! *Only those who see God in Christ can see God and Christ.*

4p-Natural Theology. Popularized in the eighteenth century, this term is supposed to distinguish the knowledge of God drawn from nature as different from that found in the divine revelation of Holy Scriptures. Many of America's founding fathers were deists who relied on Natural Theology, holding that the complex constitution and operation of all things proved the existence of God. They did not need, nor did they want, the established and inspired revelation. No rational mind doubts that God's fingerprints are impressed upon everything. However, this alone will not bring lost souls to a saving knowledge of Christ. In Ps. 19, David, in poetic language, sees (as it were) God in the heavens above and over the earth beneath; yet, he concludes his marvelous thesis with "The law of the LORD *is* perfect, converting [saving] the soul: the testimony of the LORD *is* sure, making wise the simple" (verse 7). The Torah Law, the prophets, and all inspired writers of the Old Testament pointed with one finger to the coming Messiah, the Savior of men, Jesus Christ, God's Son. For more on wide diversity of early American beliefs regarding the Bible, God, and the Savior, see Section 155, fifth paragraph of footnote g.

5p-Nature good but not good enough. With all its wonders, yet being impersonal, nature is unable to communicate the gospel with clear understanding, leading men to forgiveness of sins and eternal life. See paragraph four above. However, nature has practical and often humorous lessons. A few of these are, never step down into water to check its depth, never shop for groceries when you are hungry, and never slap a man in the face when he is chewing tobacco! Though nature exercises some into deep spiritual or practical musing, it cannot explain the cross, and why Christ died there. The gospel *exclusively* remains the "power of God unto salvation to everyone that believes" (Rom. 1:16). Men are "born again" by the Word of God and the Holy Spirit (1 Peter 1:23 with James 1:18). Created nature is God standing in the background, while Christ is God standing in the foreground offering salvation from sin and sure hope for eternity.

6p-Any book will do, except one. The above paragraph about nature, reveals that mankind *must* have a trustworthy frame of reference to which he can appeal regarding moral and religious matters. God has given this in the Holy Bible. Herein, we discover the reason for local, national, and world hatred of this Book. In hard-line Islamic nations, people are put to death for reading the Bible. Why? They are not imprisoned, beaten, and even executed for reading a newspaper, magazine, billboard or watching television. *Why is the Bible such a threat to these killer religionists?* In America, we can still freely read the Koran or any religious literature and no one cuts our throats or beats us half to death in a public arena. To be caught with a Bible in certain Muslim lands means death! The vicious hatred for this book demonstrates that it is a different; there is something supernatural about its Words. Because deranged and demon-possessed persons often use the Bible to justify their actions, demonstrates that Satan seeks to discredit its teachings. Such people reflect the mind of the English Quaker, Thomas Paine (died 1809) who wrote, *The Age of Reason. An Interpretation of True and Fabulous Theology.* He, rejected the inerrancy of God's Word and looked to the marvels of nature for guidance. One of his favorite quips was, "My religion is to do good." Read what Isa. 64:6; John 15:5; and Rom. 3:12 states about men doing good apart from Christ as personal Lord and Savior. Pain's arguments against Scripture and the personal true God were a rehash of those parroted by the atheistic, intellectual elite of that era. Hailed as a revolutionary hero, Thomas Pain lived like a fool and died like one. For further comments on these "great Americans fools," see Section 115, the third paragraph of footnote e. Section 155, fifth paragraph of footnote g, discusses the question of *who* originally made this country great.

7p-Hollywood and the Bible. Hollywood, another of America's entertainment off ramps to hell delights in presenting a debauched Christianity. The "preacher" is always a whiskey drinking, gun-slinging parson, who will fight, curse, and commit adultery with the other man's wife. He is a scoundrel with his collar on backwards, and a boot propped on a bar rail. Unsaved scriptwriters, producers, and actors create this garbage. Rarely is the other side ever given. They have poisoned the minds of millions regarding divine things. If wickedness suddenly vanished from the earth, Hollywood would go broke! There would be nothing left to make their trash films about to corrupt minds, blaspheme God and morals, and degrade the good things in life. These people are described in Isa. 5:20 and Mal. 3:15. For more on the general hatred of the Bible, see Section 21, Part 5, the fifth paragraph of footnote i.

(n) Verses 15-18. These are the words of John the Baptist, not John the writer. They reveal his insight into the mystical glorious union of the Father with the Son. Refer to Section 21, Part 4, footnote q, for twenty-one things that John the Baptist did and said during his ministry while preparing a people for Jesus, the coming Messiah.

CHAPTER 2

THE GOSPEL ACCORDING TO LUKE AND TO WHOM IT WAS SENT.

Time: The history in Luke's gospel covers about thirty-four years.

Many orderly accounts had been written about Christian beliefs. Eyewitnesses and ministers of God's Word from the beginning delivered the facts to Luke the inspired historian. With his perfect understanding of the Savior's life, He reconfirms what Theophilus had been taught about Jesus.

Matt.	Mk.	Lk. 1:1-4—*Place of writing unknown.*
		1 Forasmuch as many[a] have taken in hand to set forth in order a declaration of those things which are most surely believed[b] [about Christ] among us, 2 Even as they delivered them unto us, which from the beginning were eyewitnesses,[c] and ministers of the Word; 3 It seemed good to me also, having had perfect understanding of all things from the very first,[d] to write unto thee in order, most excellent Theophilus,[e] 4 That thou mightest know the certainty[f] of those things, wherein thou hast been instructed.[g] (Verse 5 cont. in Section 8.)

Footnotes-Commentary

[a] **Many books had been written.** Men, good and bad, whose lives greatly affected human history usually have numerous books written about them. This is more so of Christ than any person. How many books were written in Luke's day we cannot know, but certainly, there were more than two. (He was not speaking of the accounts written by Matthew and Mark because "many" can hardly mean two.) With thousands of believers scattered over the known world of that era, and one can safely conjecture that there were hundreds of "declarations" (or "orderly narratives") written about the Lord Jesus. These writings covered the civilized world and were found wherever people could read. Because Luke was familiar with *many* of these works, he could make this statement. In addition, what did these written "declarations," proclaim? They proclaimed, "Those things which are most surely believed among us." There were numerous heretical writings also in circulation. Luke knew the difference.

[b] For over two thousand years, God's people have "believed" and loved the "things" about Jesus. The narrative of His birth, with its awe and tenderness, the amazing story of His life and deeds stand unparalleled in human literature. His doctrines, miracles, love for sinners, sufferings, and death for mankind cause trembling hearts to bow in silent reverence, being overwhelmed with thankfulness. The sinless life, triumphant resurrection, glorious ascension to heaven, and much more were the "things most surely believed among us." *All the good ever known to mortal man is found in the Son of God!* Of such marvelous things, "many" of the ancients wrote in the days of Luke.

[c] **Correct documentation validates a historical work.** Luke's history was thoroughly documented, for his sources were those who "from the beginning [of Christ's ministry] were eyewitnesses and ministers of the Word." Among these witnesses must have been some of the twelve apostles of Christ. Most of them were living as Luke, under heavenly inspiration, gathered information from eyewitnesses and those who had ministered God's Word. Surely, the Christians of that day knew whether the things regarding Jesus were true or not. They had witnessed His marvelous life and works from "the beginning" to the end. Now, fully convinced, they went forth as "ministers of the Word" to preach what they had both seen and heard. Scoffers of today cannot be more reliable witnesses of Jesus than those who lived with Him. "Eyewitnesses" are people who convince men in a court of law. From the Greek medical word "autoptes," we have our English term "autopsy" meaning, "To see or witness." It is perfectly translated "eyewitnesses." All Luke's compilations were guided by the Holy Spirit and thus inerrant.

[d] As sound as the other books may have been, God directed Luke to write his own contribution to this ocean of Jesus literature. Inspiration led him to pen "the very first" acts in the drama of Christ's entrance into the world, things with which he was familiar with from their beginning. He begins by explaining to Theophilus his purpose in writing. Next, he records the circumstance of the birth of John the Baptist, Messiah's forerunner. The Spirit of God directed Luke to use his own powers of intellect to investigate what was the truth about Jesus Christ, and the Spirit continually presided over his faculties to keep him from error. He claims to have fullness of knowledge about his subject before he wrote (a sure mark of inspiration). The "order" does not refer to a rigid form of single chronological progression throughout the book. Rather, it speaks of the order in which he received the sure information about Christ. Luke states that he interviewed those who "delivered" to him information about Jesus (verse 2). However, he wrote his record under the direction of the Holy Spirit after ascertaining the facts.

[e] **Who was Theophilus?** The word means "friend of God." It was a common Jewish name but also found among the pagan Gentiles. If it was originally a heathen given name it would be defined as "a friend of god" in the

lowercase, as it had reference to a pagan deity. "Most excellent" was a title of political respect. It reflects that Theophilus was a person of high social rank and honor. Later, Paul used precisely the same title as he respectfully addressed the Roman governor Festus (Acts 26:25). See its usage further in Acts 23:26 and 24:3, where in the latter passage, it is translated "noble." It is similar to the title "Your Excellency." Whoever he was, he had previously embraced the gospel and was saved. Now, he was the "friend of God" through faith in Christ. Luke wrote that Theophilus had received prior instruction concerning the life of Christ. He had been "catechized" or had received earlier teaching from someone else regarding the Savior. Who this was that supported the faith of Theophilus, we cannot know. Such study classes surely occurred countless thousand of time over the course of early church history.

(f) **You can know for sure.** Though a believer, Theophilus, well known to Luke, in the early days of his faith needed verification ("That thou mightest know the certainty") of what he had previously been "catechized" or taught concerning Christ. In that age, as it is today, the world was full of religions, each competing against the other, and all of them claiming to have the truth. Luke's book was originally intended for one man. However, God in His sovereign providence has used this work to bless and bring untold thousands to the saving knowledge of Christ. The wise man will learn from Theophilus' desire to labor hard and long, if necessary, to ascertain the certainty of those doctrines on which he hangs the salvation of his soul.

(g) **Theophilus had a record of the first sixty-odd years of church history.** Later, Luke resumes his story in the book of Acts. There he picks up where he left off in his first letter. Acts continues with further information for Theophilus (Acts 1:1). By connecting the beginning of Acts with the end of Luke, one has a unique timeline-history of Christ's life and the early church. The book of Luke began about one year before Jesus' birth with the announcement of John's conception (Lk. 1:11-14). It ends on the day of Christ's ascension (Lk. 24:50-53). The Acts of the Apostles picks up the history here and ends about three decades later with Paul under house arrest in Rome, Italy (Acts 28:16, 30-31). Thus joined, *both letters* lay before us some sixty consecutive or unbroken years of the first Christian history. Dr. Luke wrote his second letter (Acts) to Theophilus not many years *before* the destruction of Jerusalem in A.D. 70. He cherished these letters from Luke and kept them as prized possessions. They were perceived to be from God and accepted by believers as being equal with the Hebrew Old Testament Scriptures.

2p-**An early canon of Scripture?** Church councils did *not decide* which books written in the apostolic era were inspired. They recognized those that had been used centuries prior by early Christians. The first mention of a collection of New Testament writings is in 2 Peter 3:16. Peter's words, written about A.D. 66, affirm that there existed other writings called "the other scriptures." This term was applied exclusively to the inspired writings. He classified Paul's letters with these. During Peter's lifetime, believers recognized and collected certain Holy Books, including Paul's letters. Long before the third century, the New Testament Scriptures were gathered, used, and revered as being "holy." The church fathers also drew up various lists of New Testament writings. Constantine's Council of Nicaea (A.D. 325) did not establish the deity of Christ nor which books were of God. (A year after his "conversion to Christianity" the "Christian emperor" had his wife, and son killed!) Neither the first Council of Nicaea (A.D. 325) nor any church assembly settled these issues. Christ's deity had always been, and God recorded it forever in Scripture. Church councils accepting or rejecting various books or doctrines of Scripture are plain old religious vanity. Men who denied immediate personal salvation supervised these meetings. They taught that rituals, creeds, communion, baptism, and so forth gave forgiveness of sins and eternal life. Those who disagreed were, over time, persecuted, imprisoned, banished, or put to death. Historically, several events led to an early canonizing of the New Testament. First, was the rise of cults, sects, and countless heresies. These things could only be countered by the rightly divided infallible truth that the Holy Spirit has penned in Scripture. Word of mouth was no longer sufficient. Second, the fierce persecutions that fell upon Christians, with political and religious tyrants destroying their copies of Scripture, drove them to gather and guard the written Word of God. This reveals the early necessity for a settled New Testament canon of inspired writings. Because we do not have the exact date when canonization occurred, means nothing. Correct dates cannot save our souls from hell! *God's Son can.*

3p-**When did Rom. 10:9 become valid?** Later, famed infidels such as David Strauss (died 1874), Joseph E. Renan (died 1892), Rudolph Bultmann (died 1976), and others called into question just about everything recorded in the four gospels, including their origin. Like the humanist philosopher, Albert Schweitzer (died 1965), they rejected the supernatural events of Scripture and the resurrection of Christ. For more on religious skeptics, see Section 195, footnote g. Jehovah's Witnesses, Islam, and various cults vehemently oppose this foundational doctrine of the Christian faith. The first believers did not understand Jesus' resurrection, thus did not know to believe in it. See Section 196, John 20:9 and attached side and bottom notes. *After* Pentecost, they all understood. Since then, Rom. 10:9 is necessary for anyone to be saved. As the older skeptics passed into eternity, Satan raised up others to continue their legacy of unbelief in Christ's deity, resurrection, and the reliability of Scripture. Luke's letters are especially the target of human impudence because he wrote with "perfect understanding" about Jesus' life, death, burial, and resurrection. See *Author's Introduction* for a brief advocacy upholding God's Word against theological infidels dressed in the garments of religion, who spent their lives courteously maligning the Savior and the Bible.

CHAPTER 3

MATTHEW'S RECORD TRACES JESUS FAMILY LINE FROM ABRAHAM DOWN TO JOSEPH AND MARY. THIS CHAPTER CONTAINS FOUR SECTIONS THAT SHOW THE TWO HUMAN GENEALOGIES OF CHRIST. HIS PHYSICAL ANCESTRY IS TRACED THROUGH BOTH TESTAMENTS.

Paul warns in Titus 3:9, "But avoid foolish questions and genealogies." There are two genealogies in the New Testament: those of Matthew and Luke. Both are God-inspired and laid down in Scripture for our instruction. We are not afraid to trust them amid the clamor of unbelieving "professional theologians." Ancient Jewish legends and rabbinical conjectures about the ancestry of Messiah are wildly exaggerated. This shows how far these people departed from the teaching of their Tanakh (Old Testament) regarding this subject. When men refuse or spurn the inspired statements of God's Word, they inevitably turn to myths and fables, then distort these in ten thousand ways to prove what Scripture says cannot be possible. Both Jews and Gentiles stand guilty before God of this awful sin. The Messiah's true ancestry is recorded in the pages of the Bible. Though often written in piece-meal form, with gaps, cultural styles, and missing names, it is, nonetheless, the record attested by the Holy Spirit. Chapter 3 covers this subject, demonstrating that Jesus of Nazareth is the biblically promised Messiah-Savior of Israel and the world. How sad that the great people of Israel are still waiting for their Messiah to come, when He did that some two thousand years ago at Bethlehem's manger. Even worse, His death for their sins remains reinterpreted, ignored, cursed, fableized, bitterly rejected, or courteously pushed aside to this hour.

....

Time: *Matthew's genealogy from Abraham down to Jesus covers about two thousand years. Luke's genealogy from Adam to Mary embraces a period of at least six thousand years. In 1650, the Anglican Archbishop Ussher set the date of creation at "October 22, 4004 B.C." This error, widely popularized by the Scofield Reference Bible, has resulted in all sorts of imaginary eschatological date setting. The Reece Chronological Bible, page 1, sets the creation at 3976 B.C. No man knows when the Holy Trinity began their work of creating. One cannot set a date when mortal time did not exist. Among those believers who work hard to prove that the biblical teachings of creation as recorded in Genesis chapter 1 are trustworthy, some have gone to extremes forcing everything into an unbroken chronology. Their reason for this is to prove the seven-thousand-year theory of earth's history. It is undoubtedly this old, but reasonably older without stepping over into the messy mud of theistic evolution. The "year day theory" postulated from 2 Peter 3:8, is a citation from Psa. 90:4. It is another lacerated interpretation of Holy Scripture pushed by eschatologists. Taking the seven days of creation and turning them into a thousand years each, then seeking to demonstrate from this that the world will only continue this long, is wrong. (Try this on Matt. 12:40!) According to this schedule, we are already behind time! Nor does this support Daniel 9:24-27. It is true that certain verses such as Lev. 25:8. Num. 14:34, Isa. 32:10 and others use this method of chronology. However, to apply this to the return of Christ for His church, when no man knows the moment of the blessed event is incorrect. Peter's statement teaches that God exists outside the realm of time, not that one day is equal to a thousand years. The latter part of this passage, "a thousand years as one day" is never used. Applying this to their seven thousand years myth would take us back to Adam in the garden! The "year day" fallacy was employed by William Miller to launch the Seventh Day Adventist cult and is popular among many genuine Bible believing Christians.

Fellow Jews read Matthew's words that Jesus descended from Abraham and David and is Israel's Messiah. Beginning with Abraham, he moved down to Jesus' virgin birth and earthly parents. He shows that Joseph cannot be His physical father.

Matthew's genealogy or family tree of Christ is recorded in Section 5, Matt. 1:1-17. Thousands of young converts have opened their Bibles to this first chapter of the New Testament only to be confounded at what they see. Why does the New Testament begin with a long, hard-to-pronounce list of some forty-two names? The answer is that Matthew, the converted (former) publican, wrote *first* but not exclusively to fellow Jews, who were unsaved. To his Hebrew compatriots, he demonstrated in this chapter that Jesus of Nazareth was indeed the promised Messiah of their Old Testament. He did this in typical Jewish fashion by first presenting Messiah's family tree for them to consider. Matthew begins, "The book of the generation [ancestry] of . . ." This introductory style was standard in ancient Hebrew genealogical writings. For example, Moses had written in the Old Testament about fifteen hundred years prior to Matthew, "the book of the generations [ancestry] of Adam" (Gen. 5:1). As the first genealogy of the Old Testament presented the created man (Adam), who plunged humanity in the curse of sin, it is fitting that the first genealogy of the New Testament presents the God-man (Jesus Christ) who saves humanity from the curse of Adam's transgression. Informed Hebrews expected their Messiah to enter the world as a physical descendent of Abraham, founder of their nation; and David, their most illustrious king. See Section 9, Lk. 1:32, footnote g. Orthodox Jews would not believe that Jesus was the Messiah, unless it could be documented from genealogical records that His human ancestry descended from these two celebrated personages. Matthew established the Messianic credibility of Jesus of Nazareth. Further comments on this are found in Section 119, John 7:42, footnote t.

It is frequently repeated in this work that Israel's Messiah, or the promised seed, *must* come into the world through **Abraham** (Gal. 3:16 with Heb. 2:16), his son **Isaac** (Gen. 21:10-12), then **Jacob**, the son of Isaac (Gen. 35:10-12). Next, Messiah's ancestry would be through Jacob's son **Judah** (Ps. 78: 68; Heb. 7:14; with Rev. 5:5), then via **King David** (Ps. 89:3-4; John 7:42; Acts 13:22-23; and 2 Tim. 2:8). Lastly, **Mary** was the human vehicle in which was formed the physical house wherein dwelt God the Son, as the Son of man while He lived in this world (Lk. 2:7-20). Note Section 7 for diagram illustrations of this. It is also emphasized that the Name "Christ" in the New Testament always means the "anointed one," or "Messiah." This Christ-Messiah is that eminent Person so dramatically portrayed in Dan. 9:25-26 and earlier in Ps. 2:7-12. In verse 1, Matthew begins the first chapter[a] with the "generations" or ancestry of Jesus. Next, he directs his readers to revert over a thousand years earlier to David, then, another thousand years back to Abraham, the federal head of the Hebrew nation. He unites Jesus in His birth with these two famed heroes of Israel. Jewish readers looking back saw Messiah-David-Abraham. "Son of" carried several meanings such as a literal son, grandson, close friend, disciple, or even a deceased person.

The vast temple archives at Jerusalem contained thousands of Jewish family records, genealogies, and documents. For example, the historian Josephus, who served for years as a priest in the temple, wrote of these archives. Josephus also stated that copies of the "holy books" (Old Testament Scriptures) were secured in these archives. See his Dissertation 4, Part 1. This repository of temple records is explained in *Smith's Dictionary of the Bible,* vol. II, page 1307. All records were public property and lasted until the destruction of Jerusalem in A.D. 70. Matthew wrote his book before this date. He could have been led of God to use these records in compiling his ancestry because nine Jewish names in his family tree *cannot* be found anywhere in Old Testament genealogies. The missing names range from Abiud through Jacob (Matt. 1:13-15). Earlier, Matthew omitted the names Ahaziah, Joash, Amaziah found between Joram and Uzziah (Section 5, Matt. 1:8-9). This is further explained in the center column of Section 6. Regarding the question of when the four gospels were written, see *Appendix Seven*.

The presentation of Jesus as the Messiah had to be accurate and communicate incontrovertible facts. Zealous Jews, curious about whether or not Jesus was the promised Messiah of Israel, surely scrutinized Matthew's genealogy. Here, we meet a question, "Where did Matthew obtain the names in his family tree if he did not copy them from the existing Old Testament records?" There are several possibilities but one surety. He could have received them directly from the Holy Spirit, who inspired him to write. He may have (as mentioned above) been divinely led to copy his list of names from the temple family records. These would have been filed under "Joseph of Nazareth son of Jacob" (Matt. 1:16). *Where* Matthew obtained his genealogical list is of no single importance. *How* he got it is. Matthew wrote his entire book inspired of God, regardless of the source. That is the one surety. Commentaries on Matthew chapter 1 make too much noise about the "problems, difficulties, and contradictions" contained in this ancestral list. It was a common practice of the ancients to leave certain names out of genealogical listings in order to connect persons of the greatest importance. Matthew. 1:1 clearly illustrates this. Jewish scribes would write a great-grandfather as being the actual father (1 Sam. 9:1). Names with different spellings but applicable to a single person were common. This was not explained but accepted, as seen in Ezra 10:23. For different names given the same person, see numbers 43 and 56 under Matthew's listing in Section 6.

Certain "scholars" when faced with the "problems" in these genealogies academically decided they could not be inspired. Ancient history informs us that there was no objection to either Matthew or Luke's genealogies in the first century. An article in the *Biblical, Theological, and Ecclesiastical Cyclopaedia,* vol. III, page 772, by M'Clintock and Strong, mentions this overlooked fact. It was not until the days of Julius Africanus, a "Christian writer" (A.D. 160-240?), that hostile critics questioned these lists. Had some flaw or contradiction existed, the early Christ-rejecting Jews and pagan apologists would have raised their voices in fierce opposition. This is especially true of Matthew and his book. Many fellow

Jews knew he had been one of their own but defected to the cursed Romans as a tax collector. Worse, he then became a follower of Jesus of Nazareth, whom their religious leaders had crucified as an impostor. Early pagan writers also attacked certain Christian beliefs but never found fault with these genealogies. Had they contained contradictions, opponents to Christianity would have questioned their reliability. These two genealogies presented no problem to those who lived closest to the time they were written. Centuries later, "learned textual critics" of French and German origin passed their rationalistic unbelief onto British and American "scholars" who also questioned the genuineness of these genealogies.

The inclusion of four female names in Messiah's tree is most extraordinary! It reveals that Matthew wrote under more than Jewish literary compulsion. Rarely were women included in Hebrew genealogies. Notice some famed females *not* mentioned. Where is Sarah, the mother of Isaac, and beautiful Rebekah, riding to her wedding on a camel? Missing from Matthew's list is Rachel and her envy Leah, along with Zilpah, who started history's first maternity race. Why are only females of shame and infamy mentioned in this list? In Matt. 1:3-6, we meet Thamar, guilty of incest (Gen. 38:13-18); Rahab, a Gentile harlot (Josh. 2:1); Ruth, from a pagan background (Ruth 1:1-4); and Bathsheba, guilty of adultery (2 Sam. 11:1-5). Their names are highlighted in black font in Section 5, under Matthew's genealogy. Good women rarely make history, while bad ones do. Conversely, the four women in Matthew's ancestry became monuments of saving grace, and are supreme examples of God's forgiveness and restoration into normal life. Luke mentions no females in his genealogy of our Savior.

Some of the men in Matthew's list also lived notoriously wicked lives, as bad or worse than the four women mentioned. Examples of these are Roboam (Rehoboam), Manasses (Manasseh) and Amon. For the difference in name spellings and doublets, see Section 6, footnote a. Matthew shows that God's saving grace reaches both Jews and Gentiles in the lowest of sin and transplants them into the spiritual family (line) of Christ. For Jesus' spiritual family, refer to Section 69, Matt. 12:46-50, footnotes d and e.

During the earthly life of Christ, but especially after His ascension, rumors became rife that He had been born of fornication. See John 8:41 for the Jewish slander regarding His birth. Matthew would have been familiar with this defamation. He resolved these rumors for every concerned Hebrew reader. Gentiles and unsaved "academicians," not understanding the Jewish style in which he wrote the family tree of Jesus the Messiah, call it into question. The former publican-tax and collector demonstrated that Joseph was *not* Jesus' father by listing King Jeconiah (also called Jehoiachin, Jechoniah, and Coniah) among the men who descended from King David's family line (Section 5, Matt. 1:11-12). Informed Jews knew the divine prohibition recorded in Jer. 22:24-30 and 36:30-31 in which Jehovah cursed *all* male descendants of Jeconiah (spelled Jechonias in Matt. 1:11). God declared that *none* of them would ever sit on King David's throne. Because Joseph the carpenter was a son of King Jechoniah (some eleven generations later), he too was banned from the throne by the curse of God as well as *all* of his four sons by Mary (Matt. 13:54-56). If Jesus was Joseph's biological son, then the curse applied to Him as well. However, before His birth, the angel told Mary that her Son *would* sit on King David's throne (Lk. 1:31-33). The prophet Isaiah wrote some seven hundred years earlier of this promised future enthronement of the Messiah (Isa. 9:6-7). Because God was the Father of Christ's physical body, and Christ was virgin-born, our Lord bypassed the Jechoniah curse that ran through His stepfather's ancestry. Christ alone is qualified as King David's descendant through King Jechoniah to sit on David's throne and rule.[b] Matthew's three groupings in Section 5, Matt. 1:17 are questioned by "religious scholarship." He wrote that from Abraham to David are fourteen generations; from David until the carrying away into Babylon, fourteen; and from the carrying away into Babylon unto Christ are fourteen generations.[c] Strict numerical accuracy was not considered necessary when employing this writing method. In these verses, we see a Jew writing to fellow Jews in a literary style *their* culture comprehended. It was customary for Hebrew (and even some pagan writers) to reduce names and events by leaving some out of the fixed sets of numbers. This way, they were more easily remembered. The technique of reducing things into fixed groups of numbers was a literary tool used, to sum up, what had just been written. Hebrew readers understood that he was giving a summation of Christ's family tree by grouping memorial persons or events that permanently influenced their history. Below are the three divisions used by Matthew.

The First division begins with Abraham, father of the nation, and ends with the words, "to David" (Israel's greatest king). All pious Jews were familiar with these two famed personages in their history.

The Second division commences with "from David until the carrying away into Babylon." Babylon was the most infamous calamity in all Hebrew history up to that time. These fierce people destroyed both the city and most of the temple in 586 B.C.

The Third division of Matthew begins with "from the carrying away into Babylon unto Christ" (or Messiah). The Jesus of Nazareth that Matthew presented as the Messiah was well known in the minds of both friends and foes of that era. He needed no introduction. Two historical persons, Abraham and David, with the Babylonian catastrophe, were selected by Matthew to present to his Jewish readers a directory, by which they could recall the most profound events in Israel's past. His guideposts were (1) Abraham, (2) David, (3) Babylonian captivity, and (4) Messiah. No other individuals or events in Jewish history *before* the destruction of Jerusalem and the temple in A.D. 70 had such profound impact on Israel as Abraham, David, the Babylon captivity, and Christ-Messiah. Matthew used these four dramatic markers as a literary tool for dividing Hebrew history into easy-to-understand sections.

The missing names in the three guide divisions of verse 17 reveal that Matthew was not inspired to pen mathematical exactness by listing each person. He wrote the family tree of Jesus in the accepted traditional style that his Hebrew countrymen understood. The ex-publican wanted Jews to know that Jesus was their Messiah, the One who had changed his life. The Savior's family tree breathes with Hebraisms that fellow Jews instantly understood.

Many decades after the ascension, the fact that Jesus of Nazareth was popularly known as Israel's Messiah and King lived in the thoughts of future generations of Jews. His claim to be King even troubled certain Gentile rulers over the known world of those times. Roman emperors such as Vespasian, Domitian, and Trajan hunted down and killed all Jews associated with the household of David. They feared the Messiah would somehow return through them and reassert His kingship over Israel. This would create insurmountable problems for the Roman Empire. See documentation in *The Works of Nathaniel Lardner,* vol. 1, pages 154-155; and Section 183, second paragraph of footnote q. Charles Ludwig's work, *Ludwig's Handbook of New Testament Rulers & Cities,* page 84, gives details on the arrests and treatment of our Lord's physical family relations during the rule of Domitian (died A.D. 96). He also records the story of the arrest of Jude's grandsons and their response to the pagan imperial tyrant.

Various Reference Bibles state that Matthew presented Jesus as the King of Israel, then give elaborate outlines to that end. This misses the point. He is spoken of as King only nine times in Matthew's work. In the Gospel of John, He is the King sixteen times! Using this measure, John presented Jesus as King, not Matthew. The critical theme of Matthew's book was *first* to inform all Jewish readers that Jesus of Nazareth was their Messiah. No Hebrew could be their King, unless it was impeccably shown that he was first the promised Messiah. Matthew did this in his gospel. Kingship was not the issue; it was Messiahship. Regarding the Jew's attempt to crown Christ King of Israel, note John's comments in Section 94, second and third paragraphs under footnote a. He fled the crowds refusing to be Israel's Sovereign at that time (John 6:15). Being in Herod Antipas' jurisdiction had nothing to do with it. Israel did not "reject His kingdom offer,"[d] instead, they rejected Him as their Messiah-Savior and King.

Footnotes-Commentary

[a] Chapter and verse division was not *fully* accomplished throughout the entire Scriptures until A.D. 1560. Paul's use of the term "the second Psalm" (Acts 13:33) hardly proves the Old Testament had chapter and verse divisions in his day. Instead, it reveals that Israel's ancient hymnbook, the Psalms, had long been divided into sections for singing as modern day hymnbooks have numbered pages. Jews used the twenty-two letters of their alphabet in place of numeric digits. The second Psalm was numbered by the character (ב) "beth," the second letter of the Hebrew alphabet. It is equivalent to our number 2. For more on this subject see Section 59, footnote t.

[b] Refer to Section 9, Lk. 1:32, footnote g; Section 39, and all of footnote a, for comments on the two aspects of the kingdom of God and Messiah's rule. Some expositors attempt to spiritualize *every* mention of David's throne and Israel's kingdom. Various verses do fit that scenario but hardly all of them.

[c] For those who require the exact number of fourteen names in each column, see *Barnes' Notes, The Gospels,* page 4 for an excellent response to this error.

[d] **"The kingdom offer myth."** This is an eschatological fable. Note Section 39, the third paragraph of footnote a, and Section 207, footnote b for comments on the kingdom, kingship, and eternal priesthood of Christ.

Luke's record traces Christ's line from Joseph back to Adam. Joseph's name replaced Mary's in the list. Luke informed Theophilus that the record of Messiah's forerunner, virgin birth, life, death, and resurrection are historical facts.

Matthew gave the family line of the Lord Jesus through His stepfather, Joseph, while Luke records the ancestry of Mary, His mother (Lk. 3:23-38). Whoever Theophilus was, to whom Luke addressed his work, it is sensible to believe that he understood the style in which the story was transmitted to him. Otherwise, Luke's presentation of the genealogy of Jesus would have been unintelligible. Before writing the genealogy of Mary, Luke explains in detail the background events that led up to the miraculous birth of Christ (Lk. 1:26-56 with 2:1-16). As a trained physician (Col. 4:14), he believed Jesus was born of a virgin. In 1882, William K. Hobart produced a surprising work called *The Medical Language of St. Luke.* He convincingly shows how Luke used hundreds of medical words in the Greek text in both of his books. Only one thoroughly familiar with medical language of that day could have accomplished such a feat. Matthew begins his family line with Abraham and descends to Jesus. Luke begins his genealogy immediately after our Lord's baptism. He starts with Joseph, the "supposed" father of Christ (Lk. 3:23), and then moves backward to Adam, the first man created by God (Lk. 3:38). Luke presented the fact that Jesus was divine as well as human. On the other hand, Matthew's narrative reveals how God overruled the Jechoniah curse and sent Israel, her promised Messiah-Savior and King.

The Savior's humanity and deity are reflected in Luke's genealogy, while His Messiahship is prominent in Matthew's family tree. Christ was perfect God and perfect man. See Section 1, Part 4, footnote j, for more on the incarnation, and Section 7, for tracing His family ancestry. Luke's words in Lk. 3:23 are perplexing to some. It states, "Joseph, which was the son of Heli," and then traces Heli's ancestry back to Adam. We cannot believe that Luke was tracing the pedigree of Joseph back to Adam! To write to Theophilus that Joseph came from Adam would have been absurd! Did not every man on earth come from Adam, even Theophilus himself? Unless one is familiar with the Jewish literary styles of this era, he would interpret this to mean that Luke was penning the family line of Joseph of Nazareth, and not of Mary. He lists Joseph and moves through the family line, "Heli-Matthat-Levi-Melchi" and so on, back to Adam the first man. This enigma can be resolved. Ancient Hebrews would not customarily begin or end a genealogy with the name of a woman. It was the accepted practice to substitute the husband's name at the beginning or ending of a family tree for the name of his wife. If a woman had no husband, a close male relative was selected. This is obvious in Luke's genealogy for he wrote, "Joseph (his name replaces Mary's) which was the son of Heli." Technically, Joseph was the son-in-law of Heli. Matthew wrote that Joseph's father was named "Jacob" (Matt. 1:16) and *not* "Heli." The name difference in Luke's record reveals that his original source was Jewish in its literary style. He was inspired to copy it as he found it. For explanation of this name difference, see Section 5, the second paragraph of footnote d.

If the above-mentioned custom had not dictated that a female name should not begin a genealogy, then Lk. 3:23 would have read, "Mary, the daughter of Heli." Theophilus must have understood this Jewish custom, for Luke did not explain it to him. In view of what Luke had just written about the virgin birth of Christ (Lk. 1:26-37 with 2:1-20), it is clear in beginning Mary's family tree, why he uses the words, "Jesus . . . *as was supposed* the son of Joseph." It was the normal "supposition" among the residents of Nazareth, family, and friends that Joseph was the (physical) father of Christ (John 1:45). None of them would have believed in the virgin birth anyway. Mary's genealogy must begin with her husband's name replacing hers. The believing physician had just written in Lk. 3:22 regarding God's Words spoken at Christ's baptism, "Thou art my beloved Son." How can it be held that suddenly Luke sets out in the next verse to prove that Joseph is Jesus' father? Did Jesus have two fathers? To present Christ as *both* the son of Joseph and the Son of God would have been ridiculous to Theophilus. Luke's statement is accurate according to the literary style and times in which it was written. The repetition in Luke's long list of names, "which was *the son* of,"[a] used some seventy-five times, affirms that he was inspired to copy from existing genealogies. These records were a strict Jewish compilation. As explained, had Theophilus been unfamiliar with Jewish genealogical styles, Luke would have explained these to his friend.

Luke included the name "Cainan" in his list from Shem to Abraham (Section 5, Lk. 3:36). This name cannot be found in the two identical Old Testament lists of Gen. 11:10-26 and 1 Chron. 1:24-27. (The fact that the *Septuagint Version* of the Old Testament has the name Cainan means nothing). For reasons not given, the authors of the Genesis and 1 Chronicles records were inspired to leave "Cainan" out, while Luke was inspired to write it in Mary's family tree. God wrote it that way, and it is wise to leave it there (Deut. 29:29 with Prov. 25:2). Often, the same name occurred several times in these lists, as seen in Section 6, footnote a. Dropping certain names from genealogical lists became the standard practice. However, the Bible's first genealogy in Genesis 5 seems to be an exception to this rule. Millenniums later Jude 14 stated, "Enoch also, the seventh from Adam." Jude used the numeric seven, which reflects, he had counted the names in Moses' record, and noted Enoch was seventh in the list (Gen. 5:18).

Cainan's name missing in Old Testament genealogies between Gen. 11:13 and 14, but recorded in Luke in 3:36 has caused great concern. Certain creationists run amuck as they try to justify their scheme of unbroken Hebrew genealogies. Creationists have made a timeless contribution in demonstrating the Genesis record is thoroughly reliable in every detail. Then, when faced with "Cainan," some of them use the liberal, higher critical handling of inspired Scripture. Among their ranks, we read and hear that the name "Cainan" is "an error that crept into the sacred text." Their explanations are loaded with "if," "maybe," "could be," "scribal slips," "copyist oversights," "probably," "the earliest copies," "it seems," "added later," and the rest. (It reads like certain Reformed Christians trying to justify the imaginary covenant that God made with Adam in the garden.) They must have complete genealogies in the Old Testament in order to fit God's program for the world into a concrete seven thousand-year eschatological plan. However, such genealogies do not exist, and therefore, it will not fit.

Equally, in error are those Christians, who allow *countless* thousands of years between Adam and Abraham. This is a revised version of the theistic evolution fable mixed with *secular* geology-archaeology. "Authorities," who feel they have discovered the date of Adam's creation at about A.D. 4000, like the famous Archbishop Ussher, have aimed at nothing and hit it. For Ussher's date setting, see the second italicized paragraph under the main heading in Section 3, and Section 13, the third paragraph of footnote g. God has not given us concrete dates for creation, human history, end times, and most other events. The prudent Christian will leave it there. It is wrong to inject into Holy Scripture conjectural chronological assumptions, and then present them as established traditional truth.

Summarizing Matthew and Luke's genealogies, all male descendants from Joseph of Nazareth were forbidden to sit on the throne of David due to a previous curse upon these descendants by Jehovah God. Centuries later, God bypassed His own curse by sending Jesus into the family of Joseph, who was a descendent of King David. He did this through Joseph's wife Mary, also of David's family line, who gave birth to Christ while she was a virgin. Being thus born, Jesus could *not* have been the son of Joseph and, therefore, not of Joseph's cursed ancestry. Because Mary and Joseph were *both* direct descendants from the line of David, their virgin-born Son was fully qualified for the throne. Thus, the stepson of Joseph, Jesus the Messiah, could legally sit on King David's throne and reign as the angel had promised Mary prior to His birth (Lk. 1:31-33). Luke reaffirmed the continuing validity of this promise by penning her genealogy years *after* Jesus' ascension. It had not been canceled out. Through His mother (not under the Jechoniah curse but a descendent from David), Christ was born into the royal line of King David (Rom. 1:3 with Matt. 22:42). He was called "the son of David"[b] during His earthly ministry and years afterward (Matt. 9:27; 12:23; 15:22; 21:9, 15; Acts 2:25-31; 13:22-23, 34-37; Rom. 1:3; 2 Tim. 2:8; Rev. 5:5; and 22:16). "Son of David" was the preeminent Messianic title among the ancient Jews. In tracing Christ's ancestry through Mary[c] back to Adam (Lk. 3:38), Luke shows that He was also the Son of God in a human frame (verse 38). Through His physical body, He somehow shared in the feelings of mankind's infirmities caused by Adam's transgression (Isa. 53:3 with Heb. 4:14-15). Because He is the only Savior of men, Jesus of Nazareth, the virgin-born Son of the living God, is hated by the unsaved world.[d]

Footnotes-Commentary

(a) **"The son."** Translators inserted these two words to give systematic rhythm in reading Luke's genealogy in English. The *Authorized* or *King James Version* of the Bible has all such translator's helps printed in italics. This literary tool instantly informs the reader that these italicized additions were not in the Received Text manuscripts from which the *Authorized Version* was mostly translated. At this writing, most of the new versions of the Bible in English (except the *New King James Version*) have dismissed these invaluable signposts in rightly dividing and understanding God's Word. Ill-informed critics, hostile to the *Authorized Version*, propagate the falsity that italics are for identifying contradictions in verse translations. They are for clarification in reading any of the Scriptures.

(b) "Son of David." Matthew used this title some eight times, as he wrote to fellow Jews. For Christ's Messianic titles with explanations, see *Christology of the Old Testament*, by E. W. Hengstenberg, a Kregel reprint from the 1847 edition. *The Messiah Texts*, by Raphel Patai, is a helpful work for the historical background of this subject. The article "MESSIAH" in *The Jewish Encyclopedia*, pages 505–512, lists a few of the Messianic titles of the Jesus while denying He is Israel's Messiah. For more on His divine Names or titles, see Section 7, and Section 66, Matt. 12:23, footnote b. The Name "I AM," as a designation of Christ putting Him equal with God, is further discussed in Section 95, footnote i.

(c) For the names in Mary's family line, see right-hand vertical column, Section 6, with the footnotes.

(d) Modern day skeptic "theological scholarship" denies the ancient historicity of the coming Israel's Messiah. These infidels tell us that Messiah was a *later invention* of oppressed Jews and was introduced into their eschatology during the age of the latter prophets! See *Appendix Three* for many predictions of Messiah coming into the world. Today, religious Jews have sharp disagreements among themselves about the nature of Messiah, the Messianic age, rebuilding the temple and so forth. For more on this, see Section 161, third paragraph of footnote l. Orthodox rabbis have located in Isaiah many (often imaginary) things Messiah will do when He finally arrives. Several are:

1. He will reestablish the Sanhedrin (Isa. 1:26). The reinstitution of the Sanhedrin at Tiberius on October 14, 2004 means nothing. *Messiah is to build it.* No one involved in this project can trace his lineage back to Aaron. It was another effort of radical Jews to do something God will never allow.
2. Once Messiah is crowned king, world leaders will look to Him for guidance (Isa. 2:4).
3. The whole world will worship the one true and living God (Isa. 2:17).
4. Messiah must descend from King David and King Solomon's family lines (1 Chron. 22:8-10).
5. He will put down all evil (Isa. 11:4).
6. The entire world will have the knowledge of true and living God (Isa. 11:9).
7. All members of Israel will be gathered back into their ancestral homeland (Isa. 11:12).
8. Death will vanish forever (Isa. 25:8).

2p-The great Jewish people have missed everything of eternal value by rejecting Jesus of Nazareth as their Messiah and Savior. Many of them state openly that they do not need supernatural salvation from sin, that sincere repentance and good deeds are sufficient to obtain forgiveness. The claim of Islam and all the Christ rejecting religions is be saved by good deeds. Christ's death on the cross for our sins is to them a joke, accident, or myth.

3p-Liberal ecumenism and Billy Graham. In today's "glorious ecumenical age," the absolutes of the Bible are reinterpreted. Some churches no longer openly reject Jesus as the Son of God, and sole Savior of men. Instead, men lovingly strip Him of His deity, uniqueness, and eternal atonement on the cross. Worse, His triumphant resurrection from the dead is questioned or reinterpreted. He is *reduced* to another "great" historical religious figure. Islam is the classical example of this treatment of our Savior. Others assert some of the basics, yet believe that men may be saved apart from Christ. This awful lie prevails in the extreme ecumenical movements as they ditch the *fundamental* doctrines of the Christian faith to "have oneness and fellowship." World famous evangelist, Billy Graham, admits to apostate ecumenism. In his book *Just As I Am,* he wrote on page 375, "My goal I always made clear, was not to preach against Catholic beliefs or to proselytize people who were already committed to Christ within the Catholic Church . . ." Graham's after evangelism tactics sent his converts back into spiritual darkness. John Wesley called this "putting live chicks under a dead hen." The millions slaughtered by the Catholic Church, the untold number of children molested by priests, and preeminently, Rome's false teaching about salvation scream that Graham was wrong. Thousand have been saved through his plain gospel preaching. Yet, what does he tell them to do after salvation? His gospel pulls lost souls out of the poison of false religions, then, his ecumenism throws them back in. For Graham's shocking comments on infant baptism, see Section 30, fourth paragraph of footnote f.

4p-Over the course of church history, men have added religious works, such as baptism and the Lord's Supper, to the *complete* atonement of Christ. For an example of this, see Martin Luther's startling comments on these subject recorded in Section 203, eighth and ninth paragraphs under footnote d.

5p-All world religions except Christianity have a common fatal denominator: none of them has a Savior, who paid for their sins, conquered the dark grave, arose, and lives forever more. They all grope in awful religious darkness, falsely hoping they can do enough goodness to acquire forgiveness and be saved at the end of life.

6p-Scripture states, "He that hath the Son hath life; *and* he that hath not the Son of God hath not life" (1 John 5:12). In other words, it is Christ or hell! One acquires the Son of God into his life by repentance and faith in His finished work on the cross and resurrection. This is the saving gospel (Rom. 1:16). The will to repent or change one's mind about sin and believe the gospel is the work of God gendered by His Word and the Holy Spirit in man's heart. His grace allows man to respond or reject the gospel. The term "free grace" is a contradiction. Grace is free because it is grace. *A gift has to be received.* God forces no one into forgiveness and salvation, not even the elect.

A comparison of Matthew's record with that of Luke.

Matthew began with Abraham and moved forward to Mary and Joseph. Luke begins with Heli, the father of Mary, and goes past Abraham back to Adam. Ancestral heads are boxed in gray with red letters. The four infamous female names in Matthew's family line are in dark font as seen in verses 3-6 below.

Place of writing unknown.

Matt. 1: 1–14	Mk.	Lk. 3:23–31	John
1 The book of the generation [ancestry] of Jesus Christ,[(a)] the son of David, the son of Abraham. 2 **Abraham** begat Isaac; and Isaac begat Jacob; and Jacob begat Judas and his brethren; 3 And Judas begat Pha-res and Za-ra of **Tha-mar;** and Pha-res begat Es-rom; and Es-rom begat A-ram; 4 And A-ram begat A-min-a-dab; and A-min-a-dab begat Na-as-son; and Na-as-son begat Sal-mon;[(b)] 5 And Sal-mon begat Bo-oz of **Ra-chab**; and Bo-oz begat O-bed of **Ruth;** and O-bed begat Jesse; 6 And Jesse[(c)] begat **David** the king; and David the king begat Solomon of her **[Bathsheba]** *that had been the wife* of U-ri-as; 7 And Solomon begat Ro-bo-am; and Ro-bo-am begat A-bi-a; and A-bi-a begat A-sa; 8 And A-sa begat Jos-a-phat; and Jos-a-phat begat Jo-ram; and Jo-ram begat O-zi-as; 9 And O-zi-as begat Jo-a-tham; and Jo-a-tham begat A-chaz; and A-chaz begat Ez-e-ki-as; 10 And Ez-e-ki-as begat Ma-nas-ses; and Ma-nas-ses begat Amon; and Amon begat Jo-si-as; 11 And Jo-si-as begat Jech-o-ni-as and his brethren, about the time they were carried away to Babylon: 12 And after they were brought to Babylon, Jech-o-ni-as begat Sa-la-thi-el; and Sa-la-thi-el begat Zo-rob-a-bel; 13 And Zo-rob-a-bel begat A-bi-ud; and A-bi-ud begat E-li-a-kim; and E-li-a-kim begat A-zor; 14 And A-zor begat Sa-doc; and Sa-doc		23 And **Jesus** himself began to be about thirty years of age, being (as was supposed) the son of Joseph, which was *the son* of He-li, 24 Which was *the son* of Mat-that, which was *the son* of Levi, which was *the son* of Mel-chi, which was *the son* of Jan-na, which was *the son* of Joseph, 25 Which was *the son* of Mat-ta-thi-as, which was *the son* of Amos, which was *the son* of Na-um, which was *the son* of Es-li, which was *the son* of Nag-ge, 26 Which was *the son* of Ma-ath, which was *the son* of Mat-ta-thi-as, which was *the son* of Sem-e-i, which was *the son* of Joseph, which was *the son* of Juda, 27 Which was *the son* of Jo-an-na, which was *the son* of Rhe-sa, which was *the son* of Zo-rob-a-bel, which was *the son* of Sa-la-thi-el, which was *the son* of Ne-ri, 28 Which was *the son* of Mel-chi, which was *the son* of Ad-di, which was *the son* of Co-sam, which was *the son* of El-mo-dam, which was *the son* of Er, 29 Which was *the son* of Jo-se, which was *the son* of E-li-e-zer, which was *the son* of Jo-rim, which was *the son* of Mat-that, which was *the son* of Levi, 30 Which was *the son* of Simeon, which was *the son* of Juda, which was *the son* of Joseph, which was *the son* of Jo-nan, which was *the son* of E-li-a-kim, 31 Which was *the son* of Me-le-a, which was *the son* of Me-nan, which	

Matt. 1:14–17	Mk.	Lk. 3:31–38	John

Matt. 1:14–17

begat A-chim; and A-chim begat E-li-ud; **15** And E-li-ud begat E-le-a-zar; and E-le-a-zar begat Mat-than; and Mat-than begat Jacob; **16** And Jacob begat Joseph the husband of Mary, of whom was born Jesus, who is called Christ.[d] **17** So all the generations from Abraham to David *are* fourteen generations; and from David until the carrying away into Babylon *are* fourteen generations; and from the carrying away into Babylon unto **Christ** *are* fourteen generations. (Verse 18 cont. in Section 12.)

Footnotes–Commentary

[a] Matthew begins by presenting to his Jewish readers the seed of Abraham and heir of David's throne, Jesus Christ. "Christ" *always* means "Messiah" in the New Testament, the "anointed one." See footnote d below for more on this subject.

[b] Salmon was a famed prince in the tribe of Judah. He is reputed to have founded Bethlehem, where later Jesus was born. In 1 Chron. 2:11 his name is spelled "Salma."

[c] In the Talmud tractate, Berachoth 29a, "Messiah" or "Mashiach" (spelled differently in the sources) is also called the "Son of Jessie," who was father of King David. Isaiah 11:1 is a popular rabbinical prophecy of the Messiah. He is described as a "rod" and "Branch out of Jesse" (spelled "Jesse" in Scriptures). These titles had reference to His Hebrew family lineage. Matthew and Luke's ancestry chart of Messiah is in Section 6.

[d] This confirms that Jesus was recognized as "Christ" or "Messiah." He is identified as "Christ" at least five hundred fifty-five times in the New Testament. Our Lord told the Samaritan woman and Caiaphas that He was the Messiah (John 4:25-26 with Matt. 26:63-64.).

2p-In verse 16 above, Mary's father-in-law is called "Jacob," yet Luke wrote that the Joseph's father was "Heli" (Lk. 3:23). Like hundreds of others, these were two different names for the same man. Mary's father was called "Jacob" and "Heli." Moses' father-in-law was both "Reuel" and "Jethro" (Ex. 2:18 with 3:1). Some of the apostles had several different names. See Section 57, numbers 1, 6, 8, and 10 under footnote m.

Lk. 3:31–38

was *the son* of Mat-ta-tha, which was *the son* of Nathan, which was *the son* of **David**, **32** Which was *the son* of Jesse, which was *the son* of O-bed, which was *the son* of Bo-oz, which was *the son* of Sal-mon, which was *the son* of Na-as-son, **33** Which was *the son* of A-min-a-dab, which was *the son* of A-ram, which was *the son* of Es-rom, which was *the son* of Pha-res, which was *the son* of Juda, **34** Which was *the son* of Jacob, which was *the son* of Isaac, which was *the son* of **Abraham**, which was *the son* of Tha-ra, which was *the son* of Na-chor, **35** Which was *the son* of Sa-ruch, which was *the son* of Ra-gau, which was *the son* of Pha-lec, which was *the son* of He-ber, which was *the son* of Sa-la, **36** Which was *the son* of Ca-i-nan,[a] which was *the son* of Ar-phax-ad, which was *the son* of Sem, which was *the son* of No-e, which was *the son* of La-mech, **37** Which was *the son* of Ma-thu-sa-la, which was *the son* of E-noch, which was *the son* of Ja-red, which was *the son* of Ma-le-le-el, which was *the son* of Ca-i-nan, **38** Which was *the son* of E-nos, which was *the son* of Seth, which was *the son* of **Adam**, which was *the son*[b] of God. (Next chap., Lk. 4:1, cont. in Section 23.)

Footnotes–Commentary

[a] See Section 6, footnote a.

[b] By creation not regeneration. See Section 1, Part 3, and John 1:12, footnote h, for how men become the sons of God. Note also Luke's ancestry chart of Messiah under the right-hand vertical column in Section 6. Refer to Sections 4 and 7 for more on His genealogy.

Various names and historical events in Christ's two family genealogies.

Places of writing unknown.

JOSEPH'S TREE: Matthew, for the benefit of his Jewish readers, traces the Messiah from Abraham down to King David; then through David's son Solomon to Joseph, the foster-father of Christ. *He gives the royal or kingly line.*	MARY'S TREE: Luke traces the Messiah from Adam to Abraham to David, through David's son Nathan down to Heli, Mary's father. True to custom, Joseph's name is substituted for Mary's in Luke's record. *He gives the priestly line.*

Matt. 1:1-7		Lk. 3:38-30
1. ---	Matthew does not include in his listing the genealogy from Adam down to Terah or Thara, the father of Abraham (Gen. 11:26). Hence, in his chart the names for numbers 1 through 20 are absent. Luke, however, has recorded the missing names as seen in numbers 1 to 20 of his work.	1. Adam
2. ---		2. Seth
3. ---		3. E-nos
4. ---		4. Ca-i-nan
5. ---		5. Ma-le-le-el
6. ---		6. Ja-red
7. ---	**Luke's list has been purposely reversed to start with Adam and work down to Heli, the father of Mary.** For a brief but sound explanation why certain names were dropped from genealogies, see *How Old Is the Earth,* pages 21–37, by Dr. A. J. White. The boxes shaded in gray in both columns, starting with number 21, are to identify Abraham in both trees as the head of the Hebrew nation, and David through whom Christ-Messiah came into the world. Matthew traced the family line down to Joseph, the foster-father of Jesus. Luke traced his list to Joseph, but his (Joseph's) name replaced Mary's in the family tree. Correctly then, Luke ends his genealogy with Mary, the mother of Jesus. Both writers conclude with Christ the Messiah of Israel and Savior of men.	7. E-noch
8. ---		8. Ma-thu-sa-la
9. ---		9. La-mech
10. ---		10. No-e
11. ---		11. Sem
12. ---		12. Ar-phax-ad
13. ---		13. Ca-i-nan[a]
14. ---		14. Sa-la
15. ---		15. He-ber
16. ---		16. Pha-lec
17. ---		17. Ra-gau
18. ---		18. Sa-ruch
19. ---		19. Na-chor
20. ---		20. Tha-ra
21. Abraham ▶	It states in Heb. 2:16, that Jesus "Took on *him* the seed of Abraham," meaning His body physically came through Abraham's family line via Mary. Thus, He is called both "The son of Abraham and David" (Matt. 1:1). Refer to Section 5, footnote a and Section 158, footnote e. From Abraham to David, their genealogies are identical. Persons in Matthew's kingly line intermarried with persons in Luke's priestly line. The first high priest, Aaron, enacted this merger when he wedded Elisheba, a daughter of Judah in the kingly line (Ex. 6:23). Joseph, of royal lineage married Mary, who was in the priestly line. For more on this, see Section 13, the third paragraph of footnote g.	21. Abraham
22. Isaac		22. Isaac
23. Jacob		23. Jacob
24. Judas		24. Juda
25. Pha-res		25. Pha-res
26. Es-rom		26. Es-rom
27. A-ram		27. A-ram
28. A-min-a-dab		28. A-min-a-dab
29. Na-as-son		29. Na-as-son
30. Sal-mon		30. Sal-mon
31. Bo-oz		31. Bo-oz
32. O-bed		32. O-bed
33. Jesse		33. Jesse
34. David		34. David
35. Solomon ▶	▶At number 35 in both lists, two different sons of David are introduced. In Matthew's tree, it is Solomon; in Luke's, it is Nathan. Both were sons of Bathsheba by David (2 Sam. 5:14; 1 Chron. 3:5; and 14:4). Joseph, Jesus' foster-father, descended from King Solomon's line, and Mary from Nathan's. Both came from David's ancestry. He was the *first* king in Israel from the tribe of Judah to sit on the throne (Rev. 5:5).	35. Nathan ◀
36. Ro-bo-am		36. Mat-ta-tha
37. Abia-Abijah		37. Me-nan
38. ---		38. Me-le-a
39. ---		39. E-li-a-kim
40. Asa		40. Jo-nan

Matt. 1:8–16		Lk. 3:30–23
41. Jo-sa-phat	*For explanation of why the verse numbers in Luke are ▶ reversed, see the top of previous page in the right side upper box titled **Mary's Tree**.*	**41.** Joseph
42. Jo-ram		**42.** Juda
43. O-zias▶	◀Ozias was also Uzziah in 2 Kings 15:13, and Azariah in 2 Chron 22:6. ●Matthew is inspired to leave out three men who were kings between Ozias and Joatham. Their names are in italics. In Section 5, Matt. 1:13-15, he included in his list nine persons found nowhere in the Old Testament. Below in Matthew's list, these nine names run from Abiud, number 62, to Jacob in number 76. Some believe these nine persons lived *after* the Old Testament canon was closed.	**43.** Simeon
44. *Jo-ash*●		**44.** Levi
45. *Am-a-ziah*		**45.** Mat-that
46. *Uz-ziah*		**46.** Jo-rim
47. Jo-a-tham		**47.** E-li-e-zer
48. A-chaz		**48.** Jo-se
49. Ez-e-ki-as		**49.** Er
50. Ma-nas-ses		**50.** El-mo-dam
51. A-mon		**51.** Co-sam
52. Jo-sias▶	◀After Josias, three other kings not listed in Matthew's tree ruled. These are in italics. These were in the lineage of Christ but not listed by Matthew. Who ruled and the exact times are not always clear as the records were written for original readers over two-thousand years ago! They would have understood where we do not.	**52.** Ad-di
53. *Jehoahaz*		**53.** Mel-chi
54. *Jehoiakim*		**54.** Ne-ri
55. *Zedekiah*		**55.** ---
56. Jechonias**	**God had cursed **King Jechonias** and his male posterity for their sins (Jer. 36:30-31). He was also known as Coniah, Jechoniah, and Jehoiachin (Jer. 22:24-30 with Matt. 1:12). None of their male progeny from any future generation could be king and sit on David's throne.[b] Joseph was a son of Jechonias' line approximately twelve generations later. Therefore, if Joseph was the physical father of Jesus, then Jesus could not sit on the throne, being in the cursed line. However, the angel told Mary that Christ *would* reign on David's throne forever (Lk. 1:31-33). God bypassed the Jehoiakim-Jechoniah curse through the virgin birth of His Son. By Joseph's marriage to Mary, she was brought into David's kingly ancestry. Thus, her son (Joseph's stepson, Jesus) became rightful heir to the throne of David. The curse was circumvented, and Christ is the true heir to David's throne. See Information Box at the top of the next page for other details.	**56.** Sa-la-thi-el
57. Sa-la-th-iel		**57.** Zo-rob-a-bel
58. Zo-rob-a-bel		**58.** ---
59. ---		**59.** Rhe-sa
60. ---		**60.** Jo-an-na[c]
61. ---		**61.** Juda
62. A-bi-ud		**62.** Joseph
63. E-l-iakim		**63.** Sem-e-i
64.—		**64.** Mat-ta-thi-as
65.—		**65.** Ma-ath
66. ---		**66.** Nag-ge
67. ---		**67.** Es-li
68. A-zor		**68.** Na-um
69. ---		**69.** Amos
70. ---		**70.** Mat-ta-thi-as
71. Sa-doc	Not all the various names of individuals are listed in Scripture. Persons in both Testaments often carried several different names. There was nothing abnormal about this social practice. For example, Luke gives Zorobabel as the son of Salathiel (Lk. 3:27). In the Hebrew text, he was the son of Pedaiah (1 Chron. 3:19). They were the same person. Names missing, spelled differently, or applied in curious places mean these family lists were written according to the custom of that day and understood by those who read them. See paragraph above by the two asterisks for one person with several different names.	**71.** Joseph
72. A-chim		**72.** Jan-na
73. Eli-ud		**73.** Mel-chi
74. El-e-azar		**74.** Levi
75. Mat-than		**75.** Mat-that
76. Jacob (or Heli)		**76.** He-li[d] (or Jacob)
77. Joseph		**77.** Joseph-[Mary■]
78. Jesus◀		**78. Jesus**◀
(Matthew's tree ended)		(Luke's tree ended)
	▶"Jesus the supposed[e] son of Joseph" Lk. 3:23.	■ For explanation of why Joseph's name replaced Mary's in this list, see second and third paragraphs of Section 4.

25

Luke's genealogy is Jewish in style. As previously explained, Hebrew scribes would not customarily begin or end a family tree with a woman's name. Instead, they would use the name of her husband or a near relative. As already mentioned, Mary's tree ended with Joseph's name in her place, as illustrated in number 77 above. *We have no way to determine exactly how many names were left out of both genealogical lists.* Neither do we need to know. The chief purpose of the names in the two family records above is explained in Sections 3 and 4. For an exhaustive article dealing with Bible genealogies and the family line of Christ from different aspects, see *A Dictionary of the Bible*, pages 121-141, the 1906 edition, by James Hastings. Like all Bible dictionaries, the validity of any article by a "contributing authority," depends on whether or not he wrote as a saved man or a religious skeptic who rejected the absolute inspiration of all Scriptures. In 2007, Magnus Zetterholm, of Sweden, edited *The Messiah in early Judaism and Christianity*. It is a masterpiece of liberal unbelief in the trustworthiness of God's Word, skillfully calling into question things of major importance the Bible says about the Son of God. How dangerous when unsaved men and women take it upon themselves to write of Jesus Christ, as though He was just another figure to rise in the process of religious history (Prov. 1:20-33). There are thousands searching for God, who read this academic tripe and find no help or hope as they seek peace over their sins. They are eaten up by doubt in the truth of Holy Scripture. At God's final judgment there will be awful answering required of those "scholars" who have discredited our Savior, whether it was done out of sincere ignorance or deliberate intentions. He is the Person Scripture declares Him to be, the promised Messiah of Israel, God's only begotten Son, and mankind's sole hope of forgiven sin, and eternal life. Because this is true, Jesus Christ is hated and despised by the world in general.

Footnotes-Commentary

(a) **"Cainan."** Number 13 in Luke's list. I have hypothetically counted this name as though it were in the genealogy given by Moses in Gen. 11:10-26. This addition is only for purposes of trying to harmonize. (It should be returned to its place afterward.) For reasons unrevealed to us, Moses was inspired to leave this name "Cainan" out of his listing. This is no cause for alarm. Biblical genealogies are replete with gaps created by dropping out certain names. It was the normal way of writing them. For illustrations of this, see the paragraphs in the center column of the previous page. Note in Ezra 7:2 where the writer was inspired to leave out some six generations for brevity. We find in Ezra 7 an incomplete genealogy of Ezra back to Aaron, the first high priest. It contains seventeen generations. However, this list cannot cover a period of over one thousand years from Aaron down to Ezra's journey back to Jerusalem. The "Seraiah" of Ezra 7:1 was the high priest who was killed by King Nebuchadnezzar during the fall of Jerusalem over one hundred years prior (2 Kings 25:18-21). In the Ezra text, his name is used to signify a line of descendents; in this case six of them. The six missing names in Ezra fit between Azariah and Meraioth. They are added later in 1 Chron. 6:1-15. The events recorded in Ezra occurred about one hundred and twenty years after the death of Seraiah. These are not "discrepancies" but peculiar marks of Holy Spirit supervision. Luke's inspired addition of the name "Cainan" to his list would not have upset his friend Theophilus in the least, should he have compared it with Moses' record in (what is now) Gen. 11:10-26.

2p-Several names are repeated in Luke's list. Two are named Juda in numbers 24 and 61, two are named Mattathias in 64 and 70, and there are the four different Josephs in numbers 41, 62, 71, and 77. There are two Cainans in numbers 4 and 13, one who lived before Noah's flood and one afterwards. Note Section 57, where several of the apostles also had different names. Spelling differences, especially in proper names and geographical locations mean nothing as this has always been the rule in translating ancient as well as modern documents. The differences in Scripture names have nothing to do with inspiration; they are a matter of translation and the use of other spellings. King Jechonias listed under number 56 in the left hand vertical column on the previous page has several different spellings of his name, yet they all refer to the same person. In *Clarke's Commentary*, vol. 1, page 157-158 there is a vertical list of dozens of names spelled differently in the Bible. Such spelling differences should be corrected and made uniform. It is to be remembered that God can write on a crooked wall as well as a straight line. Numerous women mentioned in Scripture were given male names! Eight of these are listed in *Dake's Annotated Bible*, vertical left column, page 348. For more on different spellings in Scripture, note Section 12, third paragraph of footnote g.

3p-The Septuagint Version and the Samaritan Pentateuch. Neither of these ancient copies of Scripture are considered in the Cainan problem. They are not the inspired Word of God and thus are left to be read for comparative and historical value. *The Septuagint and Samaritan Pentateuch should not be used to settle doctrinal issues.* They should be classified with the heathen poets cited by Paul in Acts 17:28; 1 Cor. 15:32-33; and Titus 1:12. He quoted these for historical purposes. It is amusing to read where "conservatives," "Bible believers," and "creationists," run over themselves writing about "interpolations," "scribal additions," and "oversights," as they try to resolve the Cainan question. God has written some things that do not fit our modern day understanding. Could He have deliberately given us the "Cainan problem" (as well as others) to reveal our behavior toward the eternal inspiration of His Word? If so, some people are in big trouble.

(b) Zedekiah, who also sat on David's throne, was not the father of Jechoniah. He was Jechoniah's uncle and had fostered him. See 1 Chron. 3:16; 2 Chron. 36:9-11; and Jer. 37:1. His *original* name Mattaniah was changed to

Zedekiah (2 Kings 24:17). Note marginal readings in these passages. For an explanation, see *Commentary on the Old Testament,* by Keil & Delitzsch, vol. 3, pages 359 and 720. Was this a satanic attempt to circumvent the curse God had placed on Jechoniah's family line by an uncle being made king? If so, it was a miserable failure. For Jesus on David's throne, see Section 9, footnote g.

(c) Masculine, meaning John.

(d) **Heli was Mary's father.** In the mid 1600s, John Lightfoot produced *A Commentary on the New Testament from the Talmud and Hebracia.* (From here forward, this work is abbreviated as *A Commentary on the New Testament . . .,* Lightfoot quoted from an uncensored version of the Jerusalem Talmud. One particular tractate he cites defames Mary, the mother of Jesus, and then refers to her as "the daughter of Heli." See vol. 1, page iii–v, and vol. 3, pages 54-55 of his commentary. The rabbis who wrote these slanders over 1500 years ago knew very well that Heli was indeed Mary's father! So did Luke when he penned Mary's family tree. The "greatly learned" critics (of course) know otherwise. See Section 4 for an explanation of Luke's genealogy of Mary.

2p-**The *Talmud* and Jesus.** For a clear presentation of what both the Jerusalem and Babylonian Talmud say about Jesus, His mother, and the gospel, see *The Talmud: What It Is and What It Knows About Jesus and His Followers,* by Bernhard Pick, published in 1887, and *The Talmud Unmasked,* by I. B. Prataitis, published in 1892. Prataitis was a Papal priest who lived in Russia and vehemently opposed the Jews. His work is void of spiritual truth but is of historical merit. It was taken from an unexpunged text of the Talmud and is invaluable for research. In 1631, by order of the Jewish leaders at Petrikau, Poland, all references to Jesus Christ were to be removed from every copy of the Talmud. This was due to a fierce persecution the Roman Catholic Church had unleashed against the Jews. An English clergyman penned the following: "The name of Jesus occurs some twenty times only in the unexpurgated editions of the Talmud, the last of which appeared at Amsterdam in 1645. The allusions to Him are characterized by intense hatred, disguised by fear. Christians are usually called–partly, no doubt, to conceal the allusions to them—'pupils of Balaam,' 'Minim' [heretics-Christians], 'Gentiles,' 'Nazarenes.' Our blessed Lord is called 'that man,' 'he whom we may not name,' 'Ha-Notzri,' [the Nazarene], 'the fool,' 'the hung,' 'Absalom,' 'Ben-Stada,' [and] 'Ben Pandera.' He is reported to have learned magic in Egypt, was a seducer of the people, and was first stoned, then hung [crucified] as a blasphemer." On Jesus learning magic, see *The Life of Christ,* page 737, by Dr. F. W. Farrar, published in London, in 1883. Farrar shows how the worst of blasphemies are attached to the Names "Ben-Stada" and "Ben-Pandera" when referring to the Lord Jesus. On pages 756-759, he has included in his work an excellent evaluation of the Talmud with rare insights into some of its problems and devices. Dr. Farrar wrote that in the Talmud we find "some beautiful illustrations, and a considerable number of just moral sentiments, which sometimes rise to the dignity of noble thought." However, he warns that all its good qualities are buried in an "almost immeasurable rubbish heap." Some of this "rubbish" is recorded in the next paragraph below. This harmony commentary draws from the Babylonian Talmud in places where it speaks of the Lord Jesus, Bible doctrine, history, characters, events, rabbinical philosophy, customs, and manners.

3p-**Talmudic rubbish.** It is untrue that the Old Testament is the supreme book of Orthodox Judaism. Rather, it is the Talmud. The older, uncensored editions of the Talmud are disturbing with their traducing comments about Jesus Christ. In various tractates or sections, the Talmud vibrates with hatred of Gentiles and Christians. Mary, the mother of Jesus is called a harlot in the Talmud tractate, Sanhedrin 106a. The Talmud reeks with sickening statements about sodomy, adultery and other immoral subjects. For example, in the Soncino edition, we read in tractate, Yebamoth 63a that, "Adam had sexual relations with all the animals in the Garden of Eden." Tractate Baba Mezia 59b states that God intervenes in a rabbinical argument and He (God!) was defeated by the rabbis' answer! "Sexual relations with a girl less than three is (sic) nothing," according to tractate, Kethuboth 11b. For other shocking Talmudic declarations, see tractates Sanhedrin 55b with 58b; Baba Kama 37b with 38a; Erubin 21b; and Gittim 57a. The tractate Abodah Zarah 17a says that Christianity is worse than incest, while Yevamoth 103b reads, "Eve copulated with the serpent." *Jewish apologists struggle hard to explain (away) these vicious statements in their writings.* Those who deny these facts are either unread in the Talmud or deceivers. Others, honest enough to admit that these horrendous words are there, argue that they are the work of "anti–Semites," or "haters of Israel," added later to their Talmud. The old Hebrew Talmud contains everything from gold to garbage.

4p-For a brief explanation of the Jerusalem and Babylonian Talmud, refer to Section 89, number three, under footnote c. For an updated look at Christ-bashing in Hebrew literature, see *Jesus in the Talmud,* by Peter Schafer. For a work published in 1994 by a well-known professor at the Hebrew University, Israel Shahak, see *Jewish History, Jewish Religion.* Shahak confirms the hatred and racism found in the Talmud. Regarding "Christian leaders" who were Jew haters, see Section 14, the list of popular names under footnote f.

5p-Like radical Muslims trying to cover up the murderous statements recorded in their Koran (while swearing to blot Israel from the earth), similarly the Talmud, in places, has poison for Christians and demeans portions of New Testament history. Both the Talmud and Koran reek with intermittent hatred and curses of doom on all who are not of their religion. This has historically always been the infallible hallmark of a false cult or religion, condemning to hell all not of their persuasion. Eternal life, forgiveness of sins, and the *true religion of God* is not found in a sect, cult, church, group, organization, secret society, movement, ritual, ordinance, pact, club, or anything else. It is found only and exclusively in Jesus Christ, the promised Messiah and Savior of men (Acts 4:12 with 1 John 5:12 and 20). Religions that beat, torture, frighten, and force others into their faith are evil. Men who do this serve the Devil, not God. All hatred (except for Satan and sin) is from hell, and those who practice it will go there.

6p-A second Messiah? After the ascension of Christ, Jewish rabbis *invented* various fables regarding a second Messiah. These appeared in written form during the seventh and eighth century A.D. Yet, the origin of this mythical Messianic figure is found centuries earlier in the Talmud tractate, Sukkah 52a. There are several variations of the story. Tradition says that he was to appear *before* Messiah ben [son of] David. (The real Messiah of Israel was Jesus Christ, who appeared at Bethlehem's manger.) This imaginary character was named "Messiah ben [son of] Joseph" or "son of Ephraim." According to Jewish myth, this Messiah would die in a battle at Jerusalem against the heathen armies of Gog and Magog, led by a powerful Antichrist called Armilius. (Oddly, his dead body was to remain in a street. With this in mind, see Rev. 11:8.) Early Christians dogmatically affirmed that Isaiah chapter 53 was fulfilled by Jesus Christ. Hence, the rabbinical invention of the "son of Joseph Messiah" who, in his death, they claimed, met the requirements of Isaiah. These Jews struggled to escape from Jesus Christ of Nazareth, who is the obvious meaning of this great prophetic chapter in their Old Testament or Tanakh.

7p-Another explanation of Isa. 53. Rabbi Rashi (died A.D. 1105) created his own unique perversion of Isa. 53, stating that its personal pronouns spoke of the sufferings of Israel for her sins and not Jesus the Christian's Messiah! Many Jewish apologists over the years have adopted Rashi's distortions to explain away the obvious meaning of Isaiah's predictions. (For an exact opposite comment also from Rashi, see Section 12, third paragraph of footnote f.) They did not realize that "Messiah ben [son of] David" was Jesus (the foster-son of Joseph, the carpenter), their true Messiah and King. Some Christian Jews see in these two titles for Messiah, an unconscious depiction of Jesus suffering as did Joseph in Egypt, and Jesus the Messiah born from the lineage of King David. It is true that the sorrows Christ experienced in His earthly ministry were pre-shadowed in the life of Joseph: rejected by his brothers and suffering as an innocent man in the land of Egypt. Further, Christ was born of the seed of David according to the flesh (Rom. 1:3). This simply meant that Jesus was Messiah, and He entered the world by physical birth from Mary through the family line of King David. Other details on the various Messiahs invented by troubled rabbis may be found in Section 161, footnote l. George Foot-Moore in his two-volume work on *Judaism,* Part VII, pages 323-376, gives much information about the expected Jewish Messiah. The old *Jewish Encyclopedia,* pages 118-120, carries a good article with clear explanations regarding the mythical Antichrist named Armilius. For a review of the history of the Antichrist or false Messiah in ancient Jewish eschatology, see *Appendix Eight.* For a detailed but repetitive look at the biblical ancestry of Jesus Christ, the true Messiah, from Abraham, the federal head of Israel down to Mary His mother, see Sections 3, 4, 5, and 7.

8p-For the opinion of a late non-Christian Jew on the two Messiahs, see Joseph Klausner's book, *The Messianic Idea in Israel,* pages 480-501. The famed liberal theologians, S.R. Driver and A. Neubauer in their work, *The Suffering Servant of Isaiah according to the Jewish Interpreters*, made numerous mentions of the two imaginary Messiahs invented by the rabbis that would appear in Israel. Raphael Patai in his book, *The Messiah Texts*, devotes all of chapters 16 and 17 to sweeping coverage of the mythical Armilius. Dr. Patai writes as a non-Christian Hebrew. Like Klausner, his historical information and documentation are helpful. His theological interpretations of our Savior are appalling. According to the infallible witness of the Old Testament, which is corroborated by the New Testament, there is only *one* Messiah and Savior of mankind. He is Jesus of Nazareth, the Son of the living God. For more on the two Messiahs myth, see Section 161, third paragraph under footnote l.

9p-Messiah in the Dead Sea scrolls and early literature. "Scholars" searching ancient literature to determine if Jesus was the true Messiah of Israel are chasing the wind. Whatever good the archives of pre-and post- Christian literature contains, none of them came by divine inspiration. Because of this, they cannot point us with absolute certainty to that *authentic* Messianic Person and the highest reason for His coming to earth. The numerous Messiahs portrayed in extra-biblical writings demonstrate that the real Messiah was coming or had come. The exaggerations and claims of these writers were distorted opinions concerning the genuine Savior of Israel. Searching for Messiah in ancient writings is an impossible task. Holy Scripture is the *only* trustworthy source where men may discover God's Anointed One, Jesus of Nazareth, our only hope of salvation.

(e) "Supposed son of Joseph" by whom? Luke wrote of general public opinion with which he was familiar. It was natural for Joseph to refer to Jesus as his son. Family, friends, and the people of Nazareth where Jesus grew up did the same (John 1:45 with 6:42). (What would they have thought had Joseph, and Mary told them the whole story of Jesus' birth?) Refer to Section 9, footnote h, for further details on this. Over the centuries, "supposition" has become a battering ram in the hands of ill-informed, anti-God public opinion, false cults, and religions. They struggle to change a "supposition" into a "fact," with the intention of making Joseph the natural father of Jesus. The import of all such infamy is to deny His deity by attempting to make a man His human father. Regardless, of the noise of religious skeptics, and their kind, Scripture reveals Him as the eternal Son of the true and living God. Review Section 1, Part 1, second and third paragraphs of footnote a for more on His deity.

Synopsis of our Lord's physical ancestry traced through some one hundred Scriptures, with several of His unique Names and titles. Key figures and important points are highlighted in red.

1.

> The three patriarchs of the nation of Israel.
> Abraham.   Isaac.   Jacob.
> Gen. 12:1-5   Gen. 25:19   Gen. 25:20-26

2.

> Jacob's 12 sons.
> Gen. 49:1-28

> Judah is the key figure of Jacob's twelve sons.
> Ex. 49:8-10

3.

> **Messiah through Jacob's fourth son.**
>
> | | |
> |---|---|
> | Reuben | Dan |
> | Simeon | Gad |
> | Levi | Asher |
> | Judah | Naphtali |
> | Zebulun | Joseph |
> | Issachar | Benjamin |
>
> **Israel's twelve tribes**

Jesus is all of the following Persons.

(For other names and titles, see Section 25, footnote a)

1. The Old and New Testament Son of God: Ps. 2:7, 12. Parts of Ps. 2 are cited in the New Testament three times (Acts 13:33; and Heb. 1:5; 5:5). Each quote is applied to a different work of Christ. Other verses that speak of the Son of God are Prov. 30:4; Isa. 9:6; Hosea 11:1; with Matt. 2:13-15; 16:13-17; 26:62-64; Lk. 1:35; 8:28; John 3:16; and 11:27. See Section 14, footnote f for *today's* Jewish opinion of Jesus.

2. The Prophet like unto Moses: Deut. 18:15 with John 1:21, 45; 6:14; and 7:40. In Acts 3:22-26, Peter said that this prophet spoken of by Moses was Christ.

3. The Son or seed of Abraham: Matt. 1:1; John 8:56; Gal. 3:16; and Heb. 2:16.

4. The Son or seed of David: Matt. 1:1; 9:27; 12:23; 22:41-42; 2 Tim. 2:8; and John 7:42. Rabbinical tradition said, "Whoever rears a boy is called his father." Gossip reported that Jesus was "born of fornication." In Section 120, John 8:19 with verse 41, the Jews threw this old slander at our Lord a few months before His death on the cross. See also Section 6, footnotes d, and e, and Section 9, footnote j.

5. The Son of Man: Matt. 16:13; Mk. 9:31; Lk. 19:10. For details on the Son of Man title that was used of Christ, see Section 103, footnote b.

6. The Messiah or Christ: Matt. 16:13-16; 26:62-64; with Mk. 14:61-62; John 1:41; 4:25-26; 7:40-43; 10:22-25; 11:27; Acts 9:20; 17:3-4; and 18:28. See Section 5, Matt. 1:1, footnote a .

7. The King of the Jews (or Israel): Matt. 2:1-2; John 12:12-13; Lk. 23:1-3; John 19:19-20; 1 Tim. 1:17; and 6:15. See Section 9, footnote g, and Section 189, footnote f.

8. The only Savior of Mankind: This exclusive trait of the Lord Jesus is hated by evil men more than any other. Liberal ecumenism clamors for a universal religion that all mankind may embrace. With these people, sin is a myth and hell is a joke. It rejects or reinterprets the basic doctrines of the Christian faith. Others talk about Jesus but deny He is received *solely* by repentance and faith as personal Lord and Savior. Matt. 1:21; Lk. 2:11; 19:10; John 3:16; Acts 4:12; 5:31; 1 Tim. 2:5; 1 John 5:12; and Rev. 5:8-10.

4.

> **Messiah from David who was a descendent of Judah.**
>
> Gen. 49:10; Ps. 78:68, 70; Ps. 89:3-4, 34-37; 132:10-11; Isa. 11:1; Jer. 23:5-6; 30:9. Acts 2:29-36; 13:22-23; Heb. 7:14; Rev. 5:5; and 22:16; See also Ps. 132:17; Ezek. 34:23-24 Hosea 3:5; Matt. 22:41-42; Lk. 1:32, 69; John 7:42; Rom. 1:1-3; and 2 Tim. 2:8. They read that Jesus Christ came via King David.

5.

> **Mary and Joseph were also from David's family line.**
>
> Matt. 1:6, 16, 20; Lk. 2:4; 3:31; John 6:42; and Gal. 4:4. The book of Hebrews speaks of Jesus' physical body. God prepared this for Him in Mary. In Heb. 10:7 we read that He came in this body to do the will of God. We read in Heb. 10:10, that His physical body was offered as the one accepted sacrifice for our sins. With this, see John 6:51; Rom. 9:5, 1 Peter 2:24; and 4:1.

CHAPTER 4

AN ELDERLY HEBREW PRIEST MEETS THE ANGEL GABRIEL IN THE TEMPLE.* HE RECEIVES AN AMAZING MESSAGE FROM GOD ABOUT THE BIRTH OF JOHN. LATER, HIS WIFE MIRACULOUSLY CONCEIVES.

Time: The above events took several weeks.

The rabbis held that with the end of Malachi's revelation, Israel had not heard from God in four centuries, and that the Holy Spirit had departed from the nation. Gabriel's message to Zacharias broke this curse. It is of deep interest that the first words from the angelic messenger to this priest were "fear not," signifying that new hope was in store for God's people, Israel. How sad for the great nation of Israel that most of them rejected Jesus Christ the Son of God, as their Messiah. See footnote f below. For John's birth, see Section 11.

Matt.	Mk.	Lk. 1:5-18—Jerusalem's temple and Judaea	John
		Zacharias busy in the temple	
		5 There was in the days of Herod,[a] the king of Judaea, a certain priest named Zacharias, of the course of Abia:[b] and his wife *was* of the daughters of Aaron, and her name *was* Elisabeth.	
		6 And they were both righteous before God, walking in all the commandments and ordinances of the Lord blameless.	
		7 And they had no child,[c] because that Elisabeth was barren, and they both were *now* well stricken in years.	
		8 And it came to pass, that while he executed the priest's office before God in the order of his course,	
		9 According to the custom of the priest's office, his lot was to burn incense[d] when he went into the temple of the Lord.	
		10 And the whole multitude of the people were praying without at the time of incense.	
		Zacharias sees an angel	
		11 And there appeared unto him an angel of the Lord standing on the right side [e] of the altar of incense.	
		12 And when Zacharias saw *him*, he was troubled, and fear fell upon him.	
		13 But the angel said unto him, "Fear not, Zacharias: for thy prayer is heard;[f] and thy wife Elisabeth shall bear thee a son, and thou shalt call his name John.	
		14 "And thou shalt have joy and gladness; and many shall rejoice at his birth.	
		15 "For he shall be great in the sight of the Lord, and shall drink neither wine nor strong drink; and he shall be filled with the Holy Ghost, even from his mother's womb.[g]	
		16 "And many of the children of Israel shall he turn to the Lord their God.	
		17 "And he shall go before him in the spirit and power of E-li–as, [Elijah] to[h] **'turn the hearts of the fathers to the children,'**[i] and the disobedient to the wisdom of the just; to make ready a people prepared for the Lord."	
		Zacharias cannot believe	
		18 And Zacharias said unto the angel, "Whereby shall I know this? for I am an old man, and my wife well stricken in years."	

Matt.	Mk.	Lk. 1:18-25—*Jerusalem's temple and Judaea*	John
		Zacharias struck dumb	
		19 And the angel answering said unto him, "I am Gabriel, that stand in the presence of God; and am sent to speak unto thee, and to shew thee these glad tidings.	
		20 "And, behold, thou shalt be dumb, and not able to speak, until the day that these things shall be performed, because thou believest not[j] my words, which shall be fulfilled in their season."	
		Zacharias returns home	
		21 And the people waited for Zacharias, and marvelled that he tarried so long in the temple.	
		22 And when he came out, he could not speak unto them: and they perceived that he had seen a vision in the temple: for he beckoned unto them, and remained speechless.[k]	
		23 And it came to pass, that, as soon as the days of his ministration [service] were accomplished, he departed to his own house. (in Judaea)	
		A miraculous conception	
		24 And after those days his wife Elisabeth conceived, and hid[l] herself five months, saying,	
		25 "Thus hath the Lord dealt with me in the days wherein he looked on *me*, to take away my reproach among men."[m] (Verse 26 cont. in Section 9.)	

Footnotes-Commentary

[a] **King Herod.** The history of Herod the Great, as King of Judaea reads like a horror story. His father, Antipater, was an Edomite from the descendants of Esau (Gen. 36). They lived in the desert regions some forty miles south of Jerusalem. To make matters worse, Antipater married a Gentile of Arab descent, and from this union came a baby boy to whom they gave a Greek name, "Herod," meaning "Son of the hero." In the eyes of the Jewish people, he was handicapped from the start by having non-Hebrew parents and a cursed pagan name. In addition, he was to be King of the Jews! With the conquest of Jerusalem and Judaea by the Romans in 63 B.C., Antipater was appointed by Rome as ruler in Israel. After a span of intrigue, subversion, lies, bribery, and bloodshed, his son Herod was appointed "King of the Jews" by the Roman Senate in 40 B.C. Herod ruled Judea for about thirty-six years, during which time he oversaw many construction projects. He was responsible for the vast enlargement and remodeling of the magnificent temple so often frequented by the Savior. His work on the temple is briefly mentioned in the Talmud tractate, Sukkah 51b and at length in Josephus' *Antiquities,* Book 15, all of chapter 11. Even though Herod converted to the Jewish religion, he, nevertheless, was looked upon as a hated half-breed Gentile. During his years of infamy, he married ten wives, two of them his nieces; murdered Mariamne, his favorite wife; had affairs with his own slaves; executed his sons; and twice attempted to commit suicide. He reigned at the time of Jesus' birth and died shortly afterwards.

2p-Paranoid with power, Herod killed thousands of children and tried to murder baby Jesus upon hearing that He was born "King of the Jews" (Matt. 2:2). He fathered children who cast a dark shadow of infamy over much of New Testament background history. Suffering from a lack of breath, thighs rotting with gangrene, maggots, corruption, and failing kidneys, he went into a cursing, raging coma. A few days afterwards, nearing seventy years of age, Herod died in Jericho in 4 B.C. For an exhaustive work on Herod, see *The Life and Times of Herod the Great,* by Steward Perowne, reprinted by Hodder & Stoughton, 1956. In the revised and updated version of James Ussher's, *The Annals of the World,* by Larry and Marion Pierce, pages 779-784, there is a graphic account of King Herod's last days, death and extravagant funeral. Does the pomp and pageantry of funerary for the bodies of wicked men on earth intensify the sufferings of their souls in hell below?

[b] **"Of Abia."** A thousand years before Christ during the reign of King David, the priests and Levites became so numerous that there was hardly room to minister about the altar of God in the tabernacle. To solve this problem, David divided them into twenty-four groups or courses (1 Chron. 24:1, 10 and 18). Zacharias was a priest serving in the course or group of Abia ("Abijah" in Hebrew) which was number eight in the order of the twenty-four working groups. Each course served only twice a year at the temple. See *The Temple its Ministry and Services,* by Alfred Edersheim, pages 86-91, for detailed information.

2p-Verse 6. "Both righteous before God." This was not like the Pharisees, who were righteous before men. Nor does this mean that they were "made righteous by keeping the law," for the great missionary wrote that "no man is justified [made righteous] by the law in the sight of God" (Gal. 3:11 with Rom. 9:30–32). Like a *minority* of persons over the Old Testament period, this elderly couple was "justified or made righteous" by faith in the promised Messiah to come. Paul made it clear that only by faith in Christ are men "justified from all things, from which ye could not be justified by the Law of Moses" (Acts 13:38–39). Their "walking in all the commandments and ordinances of the Lord blameless" was not the *source* of their righteousness or justification but the *evidence* of it. They were "blameless" (verse 6) but not "sinless," for we read in verse 20 that Zacharias was punished for his sin of unbelief in the angelic message. For salvation in the Old Testament, see Section 30, all of footnote h, and Section 144, footnote i. Paul wrote, "I do not frustrate the grace of God: for if righteousness *come* by the law, then Christ [Messiah] is dead in vain" (Gal. 2:21). In addition, nowhere in this text or its context does Paul give the slightest hint that he was speaking *only* of the ceremonial law. *Jesus Christ alone is made unto us, "wisdom, and righteousness, and sanctification, and redemption"* (1 Cor. 1:30). God does *not* have different ways of salvation.

(c) **Without children.** The anxiety of the Hebrews to have children was intense. To be childless was counted life's greatest disaster for the ancients. It produced a cloud of sadness that continually lingered in the home and over the soul. Jewish men looked with contempt upon women who could not bear children. The Talmud tractate, Berakhoth 5a, stated that "childlessness" was a punishment for sin! However, Zacharias and Elisabeth knew this ancient Jewish belief did *not* apply to their manner of living (verse 6). Old and worn, they sat together in solemn loneliness, frustrated over years of unanswered prayers for children (Deut. 7:14). Their sun of hope was setting. Jehovah God had other plans! "For a small moment have I forsaken thee; but with great mercies will I gather thee" (Isa. 54:7). "He maketh the barren woman to keep house, *and to be* a joyful mother of children. Praise ye the LORD" (Ps. 113:9). See footnote f below.

2p-Past retirement age? The Torah Law required a priest to begin service at the age of thirty and continue until he reached fifty (Num. 4:3, 30, 35). Apparently, due to the heavy workload, the starting age was lowered to twenty-five years (Num. 8:24). In the time of King David, it was dropped again to the age of twenty (1 Chron. 23:24). However, the law called for automatic retirement at fifty (Num. 4:3, 23). Zacharias was past fifty, being "well stricken in age" (verse 7). Why was this old man was still serving at the temple? Was he working some sort of overtime or was it his choice to serve past the fixed age of retirement?

(d) **"Burn incense."** Only once in a priest's lifetime was the privilege of burning incense in the Holy Place afforded. The lot cast in the meeting room beneath the vast temple structure early that morning had marked Zacharias for this highest honor. The Law of Moses required incense to be burned twice a day (Ex. 30:7-8). It consisted of several aromatic ingredients, "stacte, onycha and galbanum" (Ex. 30:34), with pure frankincense added, and could be used only in the temple. The smell produced as the incense was sprinkled on the hot coals of the altar of incense was peculiarly pleasant and ascended upward. A tinkling bell sounded as Zacharias stepped into the Holy Place with incense. This signaled to the people standing outside that the time of "very silent prayer" had begun in the temple. The book of Luke begins in the temple and ends in the temple (Lk. 24:53).

2p-Verse 9. "Went into the temple of the Lord." With this statement, we find the *first mention* of the Hebrew temple at Jerusalem, in the New Testament. Our Savior frequented this place many times during His life and ministry. Every pious Jew over the known world was familiar with it. Millions made the pilgrimages here to observe the seven feasts or celebrations of Jehovah God. The magnificent structure with its abundance of gold and glory was demolished and burnt in A.D. 70 by the mighty Roman army. This calamity is described at length in Section 163. In the Jewish Talmud, tractate Middoth, one finds a comprehensive description of this building. With all its glory and grandeur, the temple vanished from history and the church of the redeemed became the permanent and eternal temple abode for Almighty God. For a thorough review of the Hebrew temple, its services, and functions, see the *Biblical, Theological, and Ecclesiastical Cyclopaedia*, vol. x, pages 250-266, by M'Clintock and Strong. The subject of an alleged rebuilt Jewish temple is discussed in Section 134, paragraphs three through five of footnote d, and Section 163, fifth paragraph of footnote i.

(e) **A sign of sudden death.** Jewish tradition alleged that if a priest on duty "saw an angel standing by the right side of the altar," he would instantly die! Hence, great "fear fell upon" Zacharias. The angel was Gabriel (verse 19) meaning "man of God." His message, however, was one of hope and good cheer. Leaving Zacharias, he went to Mary next (Lk. 1:26-27). For further discussion of the "right side" in Jewish and divine thinking, see Section 166, footnote d and Section 205, second paragraph of footnote e.

(f) **"Fear not."** This term and its equivalents are found in Scripture three hundred sixty-six times. For western culture this could mean we have a "fear not" for every day of the year, including leap year. The aged couple's prayers and dreams of having children had seemingly been dashed. Time and physical decay had slowly shut the door of hope. Zacharias was overwhelmed at what fell upon his ears: "thy prayer is heard; and Elisabeth thy wife shall bear thee a son." See footnote c above. Over ten years later, the angel of God announced to a Roman army officer, Cornelius, the grand news of his prayers being answered (Acts 10:31). Who says God does not answer prayer according to His will and time? Since the book of Malachi was written about 450–400 B.C., this was the *first spoken message* sent from heaven to a Jew in over four hundred years. And what a message it was! That son, would, in time, introduce the Messiah to the nation of Israel.

(g) **"He shall be great."** Drinking no wine or strong drink had reference to John being a Nazarite. For more on the Nazarites, see Section 105, footnote l. Great men have always refused to fill their stomachs with strong drink, seeking rather to have their souls filled with the Holy Spirit (Eph. 3:16, 5:18).

2p-The Spirit filled unborn babe. In a unique and peculiar sense, John was Spirit filled *before* physical birth. This is beyond human explanation, but true. Both his father and mother were Spirit filled people as seen in Lk. 1:41, and 1:67. For the Spirit in the Old Testament, see Section 10, second paragraph, footnote b. John's entire ministry was under the power of the Holy Spirit, yet he did no miracle and died as a lonely martyr under the hand of Herod Antipas. See Section 92 for details on John's murder. These facts hardly comply with the claims of the "Spirit-filled supermen" seen and heard on national television. Those who tell us the Holy Spirit was something of an unknown entity during this period of history have missed the mark. In view of what is said of John in this passage, compare it with Jer. 1:5 for an interesting parallel. The old priest knew what the angel meant by being filled with the Holy Spirit. See the angelic announcement to Mary about the mystical work of the Holy Spirit in her body to produce a physical house in which Jesus dwelt. For this, refer to Section 9, Lk. 1:35, footnote i.

(h) For centuries, the scribes had taught that the *literal Elijah* of their Old Testament would appear before Messiah came to prepare His way. This was based on Isa. 40:1–8 and Mal. 4:5–6. Joseph Klausner's, *The Messianic Idea in Israel*, pages 454–457, has various details on the appearing of Elijah. Many of the rabbinical claims for their returned Elijah are so absurd they do not deserve to be written. Others were sane and according to the predictions of Old Testament Scripture. For example, it was believed that Messiah's forerunner would have a "double portion" of God's Spirit on his ministry. This belief was based on a rabbinical interpretation of 2 Kings 2:9. John was Spirit-filled from his mother's womb as mentioned in footnote g above. For the details on the supposed reappearing of the real Old Testament Elijah among the Jews, see *Appendix Four*. To this day, at the Passover (seder) meal, his invisible presence is welcomed in every devout Hebrew home with a large glass of wine placed in the middle of the table. At circumcision, the chair on which the "Sandaq" or godfather sat holding the child is called the "Chair of Elijah." Some Jews believe the prophet appears and embraces the little one in his arms during the ceremony.

(i) **No return of Elijah is found here. The double fulfillment?** This Old Testament quotation from Mal. 4:5–6 was a common expression among the Jews. It referred to renewing broken family ties, then making a fresh start together. Through the preaching of John the Baptist, some of the Jews were ready to receive their soon-coming Messiah and Savior. And when He appeared, they followed Him. It is interesting that the angel spoke this partial quotation from Mal. 4:6 to the aged priest. *He then applied it to the ministry of John the Baptist, not Elijah.* John's ministry prepared a people for a true relationship with one another and with God through Jesus the Messiah, who is indeed "the wisdom of the just." For our Lord's opinion about John, see Section 105, Matt. 17:10–13, and relevant footnotes. The angel of God knew of whom the passage spoke. *Hyper* dispensationalists force this passage to speak of a "returned Elijah," thousands of years in the future preaching in a great tribulation period. They must do this for they have *guessed* that one of the unnamed witnesses in Rev. 11:3 is the Elijah of the Old Testament. The only passage they can find to prove this is Mal. 4:5–6! And here they must extract a "double fulfillment" to demonstrate their point. That sort of hermeneutic will not work with thinking Christians. Gabriel quoted from Malachi, and then applied it to John the Baptist, and that settled it. For more on this, see Section 21, Part 1, second and third paragraphs, under footnote f. It is clear in Section 11, Lk. 1:77, footnote n that John preached salvation to his audiences. They put faith in Christ, who was soon to appear.

2p-From Gabriel's use of Scripture in Lk. 1:17, we learn that even the angels of heaven (including the Devil) know God's Word and recite it at will. Note Section 23, Matt. 4:6, footnote f, with James 2:19. Chronologically, this was the *first* Old Testament verse recorded in the New Testament Scriptures.

(j) Here, is a curious statement: a man, who prayed many years for a child, did not believe, yet had his prayers answered. *There are some things God will do whether we believe or not!*

(k) Talking to angels was hardly an everyday experience. If he had not been struck dumb, Zacharias would still have been speechless. Stunned and confounded, the old man staggered out before the wondering crowds. According to Section 11, Lk. 1:62–64, footnote c, he was both dumb and deaf: Scripture tells us "they made signs" to Zacharias, affirming that he could not hear.

(l) **"Hid herself."** A Hebrew woman carrying a child dedicated to the Nazarite vow (as was John) would "hide herself" (or stay indoors) for as long as possible, lest in some public place, she should contact any form of proscribed defilement that would render her unborn child unclean. Elisabeth believed and practiced this ancient national custom. See Num. 6:2–21 for the Nazarite vow. The Talmud tractate, Yevamoth 42a has dozens of restrictions for women to follow before marriage, in remarriage, during pregnancy and afterwards. Some of these customs included "hiding" or "withdrawing" from the public for a time. There is nothing mystic about this action.

(m) See footnote c above for explanation.

33

CHAPTER 5

GABRIEL STARTLES MARY WITH ASTOUNDING NEWS. HE ANNOUNCES THE BIRTH OF JESUS THE MESSIAH AND SAVIOR. SHE GOES TO ELISABETH AND SHARES HER STORY. JOHN THE BAPTIST IS BORN. AFTER A DIVINE DREAM, JOSEPH BELIEVES IN THE VIRGIN BIRTH.

Time: The above events took approximately six months.

The angel that appeared to Zacharias in the temple at Jerusalem, now stands before Mary at Nazareth to make another startling announcement.

Matt.	Mk.	Lk. 1:26-38—*At Nazareth in Galilee*	John
		Gabriel's message	
		26 And in the sixth month[(a)] the angel Gabriel was sent from God unto a city of Galilee,[(b)] named Nazareth,	
		27 To a virgin espoused [engaged] to a man whose name was Joseph, of the house of David; and the virgin's name *was* Mary.[(c)]	
		28 And the angel came in unto her, and said, "Hail,[(d)] *thou that art* highly favoured, the Lord *is* with thee: blessed *art* thou among[(e)] women."	
		29 And when she saw *him*, she was troubled at his saying, and cast in her mind what manner of salutation this should be.	
		30 And the angel said unto her, "Fear not, Mary: for thou hast found favour with God.	
		31 "And, behold, thou shalt conceive in thy womb,[(f)] and bring forth a son, and shalt call his name JESUS.	
		32 "He shall be great, and shall be called the Son of the Highest: and the Lord God shall give unto him the throne[(g)] of his father David:	
		33 "And he shall reign over the house of Jacob for ever; and of his kingdom there shall be no end."	
		Mary's question answered	
		34 Then said Mary unto the angel, "How shall this be,[(h)] seeing I know not a man?"	
		35 And the angel answered and said unto her, "The Holy Ghost shall come upon thee,[(i)] and the power of the Highest shall overshadow thee: therefore also that holy thing[(j)] which shall be born of thee shall be called the Son of God.	
		36 "And, behold, thy cousin Elisabeth, she hath also conceived a son in her old age: and this is the sixth month with her, who was called barren. [(k)]	
		The source of this miracle	
		37 "For with God nothing shall be impossible."	
		Mary's willingness to be used of God for this task	
		38 And Mary said,[(l)] "Behold the handmaid of the Lord; be it unto me according to thy word." And the angel departed from her.[(m)] (Verse 39 cont. in Section 10.)	

Footnotes-Commentary

(a) The only sensible meaning is six months after Elisabeth's conception. See Section 10, footnote j.

(b) **Galilean garbage.** In rabbinical circles, the lowest contempt was held for anything associated with Galilee. The common insult "Galilean fool," was heard daily over the land. By the standards of Jews living in Judaea, the people of Galilee were stupid, unlearned, and so ignorant they were unable to speak "proper" Hebrew. See Section 181, Mk. 14:70, concerning the Galilean Peter and his accent problem. Our Lord chose eleven of His apostles from backward Galilee. See Section 57, second paragraph of footnote f for other details on the twelve apostles. Nazareth was especially singled out as a city having nothing acceptable to the leaders of religion in Judaea (John 1:46). Here, God found humble Mary and Joseph, the carpenter. He chose this wonderful pair dwelling in despised Nazareth for mankind's most honorable task: the rearing of His beloved Son (1 Cor. 1:26-27).

(c) **Mary means "bitter."** The etymology of the name also suggests "rebellion." However, the grace of God turns bitter into sweet. There are six different women named Mary in the New Testament:

1. **Mary, the mother of Jesus.** The context is always clear when it speaks of this Mary. See Lk. 1:27 as an example. Refer to Section 12, footnote k for a review of the fables and insults attached to Mary, Jesus' mother, by the Roman Catholic Church.

2. **Mary, Magdalene.** See Lk. 8:2 with 24:10. She is the one "out of whom went seven demons." Unfailing in love and loyalty to her Savior, she supported His ministry (Lk. 8:2-3), was present at the cross (John 19:25), went to the tomb (John 20:1), and was first to see the resurrected Lord (John 20:14-18).

3. **Mary, the sister of Lazarus.** The one who anointed Jesus prior to His death and resurrection. See Matt. 26:7; Lk. 10:39-42 with John chapters 11 and 12:3.

4. **Mary, the wife of Cleophas, mother of James the Less, and sister of Jesus' mother.** Note, Matt. 27:56 with Mk. 15:40. The hypothesis exists that her name should be translated "Mari," and not "bitter," as that of her sister in number 1 above. This would explain two females in the same family with the same name. Such was not uncommon. We meet her first by name at the crucifixion of Jesus (John 19:25). Oddly, some Jewish women had male names as seen in Num. 36:11 with the name "Noah."

5. **Mary, the mother of John Mark.** See Acts 12:12. She is also called sister to Barnabas (Col. 4:10). Her house at Jerusalem was open for believers to gather and pray (Acts 12:12-17). Her son, Mark, accompanied Paul on his first missionary journey, but turned back for some unknown reason (Acts 13:5, 13). Years later, he was listed among Paul's helpers (Col. 4:10).

6. **Mary, a helper of missionary Paul.** See Rom 16:6.

(d) This was a standard form of respect or courteous social greeting similar to our "hello." There is nothing sacred in these words. The Roman Catholic Church and others have perverted this greeting into a magical formula for many things, including the forgiveness of sins. See Section 12, third, fourth, and fifth paragraphs of footnote k for an example of this abominable use of Scripture.

(e) The angel said "among," not "above," women. See Section 10, first paragraph under footnote g for Mary's need of salvation like any other mortal. Salvation is the very life of God in the very soul of man. It is forever!

2p-Verse 30. "Thou hast found favour with God." *Mary did not possess gifts of grace and dispense them to all who secured her pleasure.* See footnote l below and Section 10 footnote g for more on these thoughts.

(f) At this point, Mary did not associate herself with the virgin of Isa. 7:14. It is untrue that all deeply religious Jewish virgins prayed to be the one mentioned in the Isaiah text. Overzealous Christians invented this myth. Alfred Edersheim wrote that the earlier rabbis did not interpret this text as applicable to the birth of their coming Messiah. See *The Life and Times of Jesus the Messiah,* by Edersheim, Appendix 9, for a list of 456 Old Testament verses applied to the Hebrew Messiah by ancient Jewish teachers. The famed Isa. 7:14 is missing from this list. However, on pages 125-126, Edersheim wrote about the supernatural being attached to Messiah's birth. Most Jewish academics deny that Isa. 7:14 was a prediction of the Messiah. (What else could they say and keep their jobs?) Nevertheless, it would be credulous to think this was the consensus of every Hebrew rabbi before Christ was born. No doubt, many of them knew that this passage spoke of the coming Messiah. It was the Jew, Matthew, who was first in the New Testament record to give Isa. 7:14 its correct interpretation and application. At the beginning of his book, he explained the true meaning of this verse to his fellow Hebrew readers (Section 12, Matt. 1:22-23). Since Matthew wrote some years after these events were history, his careful but brief explanation of Messiah's virgin birth suggests it was still a problem among some of the Jewish people. He was inspired to give them the truth of the matter in a concise written form. By this time, the Jews in general had heard the story of Mary and the virgin birth. Now, they could read the facts of how it happened, penned by one of their own.

(g) **Throne of his father David.** A thousand years before, God had promised King David that Israel's future Messiah, descending from his family line, would sit on his throne and rule forever over his (David's) kingdom (2 Sam. 7:13-16; Ps. 89:3-4, 34-37; and Ps. 132:10-11). Speaking to Mary, the angel Gabriel reaffirmed this. Two lines of prophetic truth about Messiah are blended here. He will be born of a virgin and of the ancestry of King David. The writer of Hebrews quoted from 2 Sam. 7:14 and applied the passage in Heb. 1:5 as speaking of Christ. Jesus "was made of the seed [ancestry] of David according to the flesh" (Rom. 1:3). Paul preached years later in the synagogue at Antioch, "Of this man's [David] seed hath God according to *his* promise raised unto Israel a Saviour, Jesus" (Acts 13:23). On the day of Pentecost, Peter said that Christ was now seated on David's throne (Acts 2:29-33). This is understood as being a heavenly thing that has been operative for almost two thousand years. For a discussion of Christ, presently serving as heaven's only and eternal high priest and King, see Section 207, footnote b.

This hardly changes His future and *glorified* kingship over redeemed Israel and the church, when all things become one in Him.

2p-Verse 33. "The House of Jacob." This is the literal nation of Israel. Has it become a spiritual thing? Erring covenant theology holds that the church began during the Old Testament period. A Dutchman, named R. B. Kuiper (died 1966) wrote in *The Glorious Body of Christ,* page 22, that Adam and Eve "constituted the first Christian church." Another Dutchman, Abraham Kuyper (died 1920) popularized the myth of "salvation slumbering in the souls of the elect." In summary, covenant theology teaches that the promises God made to Abraham, Isaac, Jacob, Israel, and King David are to be spiritualized, and transferred to the New Testament church. They failed to understand that the throne of David is *both* a future literal throne and presently a spiritual one on which Christ now sits in heaven. For the kingship of Christ, refer to Section 183, footnotes q and r. For His ascension and work at God's right hand, see Section 158, footnote d, with Section 207, footnote b. Conversely, *extreme* dispensational eschatology teaches that the church consists only of those saved between the resurrection of Christ, or the Day of Pentecost, and the calling out of the church. Some go so far as to affirm that believers who died before the Day of Pentecost and those who are "saved after the rapture" are not a part of God's Church. Absurd exegetical radicalism has gripped both fields of thought. Filling in the slots that God has left blank is risky business. Regarding spiritual Israel or the "Israel of God," see Section 74, second and third paragraphs of footnote e.

3p-Israel, the church in the Old Testament and spiritualizing geography? Were the geographical promises given to Abraham and his descendents fulfilled when Joshua divided the land to Israel (Josh. 21:43–45)? Here, we read, "There failed not ought of any good thing which the LORD had spoken unto the house of Israel; all came to pass" (verse 45). *In view of what God said centuries later, this can only mean "all" up to that time.* Hundreds of years after the words recorded in the book of Joshua, we read the prophet Jeremiah declaring that Israel would yet have their land as a future possession (Jer. 7:7; 11:1–5; 25:5; 30:1–3; and 35:15). Further, the weeping prophet penned God's personal assurance that He would never forget the nation of Israel. "Thus saith the LORD, which giveth the sun for a light by day, *and* the ordinances of the moon and of the stars for a light by night, which divideth the sea when the waves thereof roar; The LORD of hosts *is* his name. If those ordinances depart from before me, saith the LORD, *then* the seed of Israel also shall cease from being a nation before me for ever. Thus saith the LORD; If heaven above can be measured, and the foundations of the earth searched out beneath, I will also cast off all the seed of Israel for all that they have done, saith the LORD." (Jer. 31:35–37). If God is forever through with Israel, then according to the Scriptures above, all of creation must slowly stop! Over seven hundred years after Joshua, the prophet Micah was still waiting for the fulfillment of God's promises to Israel (Micah 7:20). Zacharias, the father of John the Baptist, looked for the promises in his day (Lk. 1:72). Spiritualizing *everything* God promised Israel and giving it to the church is mishandling Holy Scripture.

4p-Can some of Israel's promises be applied to the church? Some of God's promises to physical Israel are realized in Abraham's *spiritual* seed, which is the church. This is not true with all of them. The church is a "spiritual Israel," and "Abraham's seed," but she is not physical Israel. Covenant theologians have *invented* all sorts of doctrines starting with Adam, with whom (they say) God made a covenant of works. This myth is also called the Edenic covenant. In this agreement, works would have saved Adam from sin, had he obeyed God! There is not one shred of evidence or even the slightest hint of such a covenant found anywhere in the Bible. It is built on forcing Scripture to say something to fit an earlier error. Before the imaginary covenant with Adam, there was a covenant of redemption made before the world was created. In this *invented* covenant, God elected so many to eternal life and all others to damnation. Scripture is clear that salvation was planned in the dateless past. To insert into this that God chose some and damned others is a ghastly perversion. Lastly, the proponents of this philosophy bring in the covenant of grace. By dragging God's sovereign grace into this theological mess, they can prove just about anything. According to Louis Berkhof, one Kaspar Olevianus (died 1587) was the man who invented this teaching. See Berkhof's *Systematic Theology*, 1941 edition, page 221, for more on this issue.

5p-On the other side, *radical* dispensationalists have invented just as many imaginary doctrines as have reformed or covenant theologians, and in some cases more. They have different gospels for different periods of time, and have distorted salvation by grace into a system of salvation by works under the law, and over literalized many verses of Scripture. Refer to Section 39, footnotes a and g for details on the two different aspects of the kingdom.

(h) Mary's first words in Scripture. Here, she confessed her virginity before an angel of God. Had this not been the case, she would have been terrified at making such a false claim before this mighty visitor from heaven. See footnote j below. Out of pure innocence, she sincerely questioned God's plan at that time, not understanding any of the future implications of Gabriel's words. For example, who, including Mary herself, would believe that a virgin could give birth to a child? For her own immediate family to accept that she was with Child under such miraculous conditions would have been a joke! Who would believe such a fairy tale? We need no stimulation to imagine the vicious gossip that surrounded the sudden pregnancy of Mary. In time, she, Joseph and Jesus would feel the bitter sting of many scandalous tongues. Note this in Section 120, John 8:19, 41, footnote t. See Section 6, footnote e for comments on Joseph being called Jesus' father. Blasphemers claim that Mary was guilty of adultery. For Mary's second words spoken, see footnote l below. Her final words are recorded in Section 27, footnote g (John 2:5).

(i) The physical anatomy of the Lord Jesus Christ was the work of the Holy Spirit in its conception. See footnote j below. In Judaism, the true religion was prepared for mankind, while in heathenism, mankind was prepared for the true religion. Within Mary, a human form was conceived and molded to receive that divine Person, known later as "Jesus Christ of Nazareth." How this mysterious and glorious conception took place, we are not told. See footnote l below for further comment on *when* this event might have occurred.

2p-Did Jewish writers use pagan myths? Centuries before the angel visited Mary and announced God's plan for her to bring Israel's Messiah into the world, thousands of heathen myths were in vogue about virgin-born gods. Decades ago, Sigmund Mowinckel published his work, *He That Cometh. The Messiah Concept in the Old Testament and Later Judaism.* Like all "theological specialists" who do not believe in the inspiration of Scripture, Mowinckel tried to build a case for Isaiah's use of heathen myths. We know that Isa. 9:6 is a well-known Messianic prediction. On pages 113, 115-116 of his book, we read that the pagan distortions of virgin-born gods who would be saviors of their worshippers were rationalized and adopted by Isaiah. Mowinckel states that Isaiah does not write about Messiah but rather a prince in Israel. This is more academic unbelief in the inspiration of the Bible from one who purported to be a Bible teacher. Unsaved religious writers have employed various literary stratagems to discredit the virgin birth of Christ. They practice unbridled imaginations within the domain of pagan history. This embellished their literary works, attaching to them mystic powers and events.

3p-The late Christian Hebrew, Alfred Edersheim, disagreed with Mowinckel, the former professor of theology at Oslo University in Norway. In his *Life and Times of Jesus the Messiah,* Appendix 9, pages 993-994, he affirmed that the verses in Isa. 9 were employed by ancient rabbis in their targums as referring to Israel's Messiah. For meaning of "targums," see Section 1, Part 1, fifth paragraph of footnote b. As previously explained, heathen religions of that era and thousands of years prior were rife with fables about gods, goddesses, virgin-born and resurrected saviors. The Devil, foreseeing the coming Messiah-Savior, produced these lies in a frantic effort to turn humanity from the true and living Savior of Adam's fallen race. Thousands of "learned academicians" still point to these demonic diversions as proof of the "Jesus myth." Concerning pagan reproductions of biblical truths, their origins and continuing impact today, see Section 1, Part 4, third paragraph of footnote j.

(j) **"That holy thing."** The human side or physical body of Christ, which at this point was yet to be, was described as being a "holy thing." Christ's humanity was free from any taint of original sin that all mankind carries by natural descent from Adam. In 1 John 1:1, Christ is again referred to in the neuter gender "That." Jesus was the Perfect God and became the Perfect Man in His incarnation and life. See Section 1, Part 1, footnotes a and b for more on this subject. The divine nature of Christ did not come from Mary, only the human nature. Christ's God-divinity was from everlasting without beginning. In Heb. 10:5-7, we read that David in Ps. 40:6-8, prophesied the physical body of Christ a thousand years in advance.

(k) **"Elisabeth . . . hath . . . conceived."** Hearing Gabriel's announcement about her cousin Elisabeth, Mary was inspired with great confidence and faith. It seemed as impossible for Elisabeth to bare a child at her age, as it was for Mary to conceive under the conditions spoken by the angel. Now, both were true. The statement in Lk. 1:36 that Elisabeth was Mary's cousin (or relative) hardly prevents Mary being of the tribe of Judah. Section 8 and Lk. 1:5 states that Elisabeth was from the tribe of Levi. Some hold that because Mary was a "cousin" or "kindred" of Elisabeth means that she descended from the tribe of Levi and not from the Judah. The Torah Law that forbade intermarrying among tribes had to do only with preserving the inheritance of each tribe. Levites had no inheritance. This law was not applicable to them; they lost nothing regardless of what Hebrew tribe they married into.

2p-Paul called all Israel his "kinsmen according to the flesh" (Rom. 9:3). In the days of Christ, laxity among the Hebrews regarding the Law of Moses was common. For the wickedness of the Jews in this era, see Section 67, fourth paragraph of footnote b. We *conjecture* that Elisabeth was from the tribe of Levi on her father's side and from the tribe of Judah on her mother's side. For the priests and Levites, their intermarriages, polygamy, abrogation of Torah Law, see *Jerusalem in the Time of Jesus,* pages 96, 105-107, 160-176, and 343, by Joachim Jeremias.

(l) **"Handmaid," meaning a "female slave."** This is the second utterance spoken by Mary recorded in Scripture. The idea here is not that of harsh servitude (as some think) but of joyful submission to the will of God. See footnote h above for her first words. After sincerely questioning the will of God in verse 34, she now offers herself in trusting obedience to do His bidding. Some believe it was at this point of Mary's yielding to God's newly announced plan for her life that the conception of Jesus' physical body took place. In Lk. 1:45 Elisabeth praised Mary for believing what God had said. Little did this sweetest flower growing in despised Nazareth know what this surrender would bring into her life. When her Son was forty days old, the aged Simeon warned Mary that Jesus would cause a "sword to pierce her own soul" (Lk. 2:34-35), meaning His Words and deeds would unsettle her to no end. Several years later, hanging on the cross, Jesus committed His mother into the hands of a trusted apostle. Refer to Section 190, John 19:25-27, footnote m, and Section 207, Acts. 1:14, footnote g for more on Mary.

(m) Swift to do God's business, holy angels never linger. Upon completion of their tasks, they vanished as suddenly as they appeared. See Section 14, Lk. 2:9, footnote c.

Mary hurriedly travels some fifty miles south of Nazareth to share her amazing news with the elderly Elisabeth.

Matt.	Mk.	Lk. 1:39-56—*In the hill country of Judaea*	John
		Elisabeth's song of praise **39** And Mary arose in those days, and went into the hill country with haste, into a city of Juda; **40** And entered into the house of Zacharias, and saluted Elisabeth. **41** And it came to pass, that, when Elisabeth heard the salutation of Mary, the babe leaped in her womb;[a] and Elisabeth was filled with the Holy Ghost:[b] **42** And she spake out with a loud voice, and said, "Blessed *art* thou among women, and blessed *is* the fruit of thy womb.[c] **43** "And whence *is* this to me, that the mother of my Lord[d] should come to me? **44** "For, lo, as soon as the voice of thy salutation sounded in mine ears, the babe leaped in my womb for joy. **45** "And blessed *is* she that believed:[e] for there shall be a performance of those things which were told her from the Lord." *Mary's song of praise* **46** And Mary said,[f] "My soul doth magnify the Lord, **47** "And my spirit hath rejoiced in God my Saviour.[g] **48** "For he hath regarded the low estate[h] of his handmaiden: for, behold, from henceforth all generations shall call me blessed. **49** "For he that is mighty hath done to me great things; and holy *is* his name. **50** "And his mercy *is* on them that fear him from generation to generation. **51** "He hath shewed strength with his arm; he hath scattered the proud in the imagination of their hearts. **52** "He hath put down the mighty from *their* seats, and exalted them of low degree. **53** "He hath filled the hungry with good things; and the rich he hath sent empty away. **54** "He hath holpen [helped] his servant Israel, in remembrance of *his* mercy; **55** "As he spake to our fathers, to Abraham,[i] and to his seed for ever." *Mary returns to Nazareth* **56** And Mary abode with her about three months,[j] and returned to her own house.[k] (Verse 57 cont. in Section 11.)	

Footnotes–Commentary

(a) Medical science has confirmed the old rabbinical belief that an unborn child could hear voices and sounds and relate to them while in the womb. Apparently, this is the suggestion here. It was believed the fetus could sing, pray, dance, and even sin. The Jewish idea that an unborn child might commit sin is reflected in the disciples' question as seen in Section 121, John 9:2, footnote b. They inquired "Master, who did sin, this man, or his parents, that he was born blind?" This reveals they were the product of standard rabbinical theology. The first recorded act of John was to leap at the sound of the voice of Mary, the mother of Christ. Therefore, he heard the voice from his mother's womb! Some thirty years later, this very Christ would become the absolute object of John's life and ministry.

(b) **The Holy Spirit before Pentecost.** Every attempt to explain this away is senseless. It means just what it says. Both mother and baby were acquainted with the Holy Spirit. John was Spirit-filled before he was born, as stated in Section 8, Lk. 1:15, footnote g. How this relates to the doctrine of original sin, I do not know! People were filled with the Spirit, in whatever measure, long before the Pentecost of Acts 2. It was in the power of the indwelling Holy Spirit that Elisabeth uttered her song of praise (verses 41-45). She was a saved woman.

2p-**Did the Holy Spirit indwell Old Testament believers?** The teaching that He only came upon men for specific purposes but never indwelt them is wrong. This erroneous pneumatology springs from *radical* dispensationalism. *The Spirit was omnipresent but not always openly prominent across Old Testament history.* In the first book of the Bible, the Holy Spirit assisted in the creation (Gen. 1:2). Later, God warned the wicked antediluvian world that His "Spirit would not always strive with man" (Gen. 6:3). Can this mean that the Holy Spirit accompanied the preaching of Enoch and Noah (Jude 14-15 with 2 Peter 2:5)? A pagan Egyptian king discerned that the Holy Spirit was *dwelling in* Joseph (Gen. 41:38). The Spirit was *in* Joshua the son of Nun (Num. 27:18). Jehovah declared that He had *filled* Bezaleel with His Spirit thus giving him unique gifts for his work in the field of metallurgy (Ex. 31:1-3). At other times, the Spirit came or moved upon various persons energizing them for special tasks. This is seen in the seventy elders of Israel upon whom the Spirit of God came, empowering them to prophesy (Num. 11:25-26). The Holy Spirit came upon Othniel (Judges 3:10), Gideon (Judges 6:34), Jephthah (Judges 11:29), and various others, filling them with might to accomplish God's purposes for special occasions. They could not correctly do the service of God without Him. Micah was full of power by the Spirit of the LORD, to "declare unto the people their sins" (Micah 3:8). Stubborn Israel, "provoked [resisted] God's Spirit" in the wilderness (Ps. 95:8, 9 with Isa. 63:10). This is a profound statement when we remember that as Moses led millions of Hebrews through this dense area, and that they resisted the Holy Spirit. We later read in the New Testament that God preached the gospel to Israel during this forty-year journey and they refused to have faith in His preaching (Heb. 3:17 and 4:1-2). In 1 Cor. 10:4 it is clear that "Christ followed" Israel during their long wilderness trek. He was present among the nation in some unique way that is not explained. Peter wrote that the Spirit was *in* the Old Testament prophets (1 Peter 1:11). Surely, this must mean all of them. In Ps. 51:11-12, David requested in prayer that the Holy Spirit not be taken from him after his sin with Bathsheba. This is understood when we remember that the Jews believed that great sin in one's life would drive the Spirit of God away. Basis rabbinical teaching held that God's Spirit had left Israel after their gross sins resulted in the final Babylonian captivity in 586 B.C. Refer to Section 25, footnote c, for more details on this teaching. It is incorrect that we have a *missing* Holy Spirit in the Old Testament era. He was there from the beginning, omnipresent but not prominent during that era. His time of *full public action* came later, on the day of Pentecost and forward. It has been said that God worked with men over the Old Testament, Christ across the New Testament, and the Holy Spirit works today. See *Knowing the Holy Spirit Through the Old Testament*, by Christopher J. H. Wright for more on this subject. A too ridged form of dispensationalism is the mother of the erroneous teaching that the Holy Spirit was generally absent across Old Testament history, and that He indwelt no one. Note the last sentence of footnote 3p below for a reference on this.

3p-**The Holy Spirit after Pentecost.** With atonement provided for mankind, the Spirit entered the world on the day of Pentecost in a universal and unprecedented dimension (Acts 2). No longer does He move and work among *selected* persons to ensure that the will of God is done in bringing the Savior into the world. Now, humanity is His field. At Pentecost, He took full indwelling among all true believers as He had done with individuals during the Old Testament period. However, now He is building them into the spiritual temple that is the church, of which Christ is the head. In the early New Testament, it was known as the kingdom, but gradually this term gave way to the word "church." No such entity as the church existed in Old Testament history. The Spirit's first work today is to convict the hearts of "whosoever will" from among both Jews and Gentiles and to "testify" of Christ's salvation. The statement in John 7:39, that "the Holy Ghost was not yet given," had reference to how He was "given" in full power at Pentecost. (It must be remembered that John wrote this long after that great Pentecost was over, while looking back on history.) That the Spirit of God was something of an unknown entity in the Old Testament is a serious error. Conversely, to hold that He was as active as is seen later in the book of Acts and forward is equally incorrect. Across Old Testament history, the Holy Spirit moved, *indwelt,* and worked among believers in a variety of ways. In a unique but higher sense, He does the same today, while living permanently in the inner man, also called both heart and soul (Eph. 3:16; Gal. 4:6; with 2 Cor. 1:22). See Section 10, the second paragraph, footnote b for the work of the Holy Spirit *before* the birth of Christ and across Old Testament history.

(c) According to the words of Elisabeth, Mary had already conceived the physical body of the Lord Jesus *before* visiting her. The Holy Spirit had revealed Mary's miraculous conception to this saintly old woman. She pronounced a typical Jewish blessing upon the unborn Child. Jews had a peculiar saying that the six measures of barley that Boaz gave to Ruth (3:15) signified that she would be blessed with six great blessings, one of them being the Messiah, who would spring from her family line. They also taught that Israel's Messiah would have six blessings bestowed upon Him. These are listed in Isa. 11:2, which the rabbis held was a Messianic prophecy.

(d) **"My Lord."** Elisabeth understood far more than the brief text relates. She was the *first* person in the New

Testament to call Christ "my Lord" (1 Cor. 12:3 with Phil. 2:9-11). How did she know the babe carried in Mary's body would house the Lord of the Old Testament? See footnote c above. For a summary review of the incarnation, see Section 1, Part 1, footnote a.

(e) How puzzling that youthful and inexperienced Mary believed the angel's message, while the elder Zacharias, who had walked with God for decades, did not! Can over familiarity within the spiritual realm breed faithlessness? Note in Lk. 1:45, where Elisabeth instantly affirmed that it would happen. Apparently, Elisabeth had a higher faith in God than did her aged priestly husband at that time. *Often, quiet good women live higher and closer to God than men.*

(f) **"My soul doth magnify the Lord."** All genuine praise to God must flow from a redeemed soul indwelt by the Holy Spirit. Thus, Mary uttered this amazing deluge of scriptural adoration to her Lord. Beginning with verse 46 and going through verse 55, she cites directly or generally, many passages from the Jewish Tanakh or Old Testament in a great outburst of praise. They are as follows: verse 46 from Ps. 34:3; verse 47 from Ps. 35:9; verse 48 from 1 Sam. 1:11; verse 49 from Ps. 111:9; verse 50 from Ps. 103:17; verse 51 from Ps. 89:10-11; verse 52 from Job 5:11; verse 53 from Ps. 107:9; verse 54 from Ps. 98:3; verse 55 from Gen. 17:7; and Micah 7:20. Our Lord's mother, even as a young woman, was well versed in the Hebrew Scriptures. Mary's words resemble Hannah's song of praise given over a thousand years before at the dedication of her son Samuel (1 Sam. 2:1-10).

(g) **"God my Saviour."** The mother of Christ needed salvation like any other person. Note Section 9, footnote e. She called God her Saviour. The inference is clear that she was *already* a saved person and knew it. Paul called God "our Saviour" in Titus 1:3, 2:10 and 3:4. Then he referred to Christ as "our Saviour" in Titus 1:4. Peter called God "our Saviour" in 2 Peter 1:1, and Jude called God "our Saviour" in Jude 25. The process whereby Mary came to understand that her Son was the Messiah-Savior sent from heaven developed gradually in her heart over time. The last picture of Mary in Scripture is in the upper room on the day of Jesus' ascension to heaven. She is seen in prayer with the other disciples, along with the four half-brothers of Christ (Acts 1:14). For Jesus' family, see Section 91, Matt. 13:55-56. Corrupt religion has distorted Mary's place in God's plan of redemption. Refer to Section 12, all of footnote k for more on this subject.

2p-**"Blessed."** The word signifies to be "happy" because of a special honor. Thus, the little flower of Nazareth is still remembered over two thousand years later as the woman honored by God to conceive and bear the human house in which His Son would dwell during His earthly tenure. For comments on several of the wild extremes and false honors that have been placed upon Mary, see Section 12, footnote k.

(h) This reflects Joseph and Mary's deep poverty. Note what Mary's son James wrote years later regarding this subject (James 2:5). God passed by the rich and famous and pitched His tent of Messianic blessings over this good man and his young wife, a virgin dwelling in Nazareth. See Section 17, Matt. 2:11, footnote l, for a question regarding this wonderful couple's financial need. On their poverty, see Section 16, footnote d.

(i) **Our fathers and Abraham.** Mary, like all pious Jews was familiar with the covenant God had made with Abraham and the nation of Israel some two thousand years before (Gen. 12:1-3, 7; 13:14-16; 15:18-21, and all of Gen. 17 with 22:17-18). She had been taught this from the chair of the rabbis in the local synagogue. A short time later, Zacharias the father of John the Baptist said similar things in Spirit filled praises to God. See Section 11, Lk. 1:73, footnote k. Note Mary quoting many passages from the Old Testament in footnote f above.

(j) This apparently means that Mary tarried with Elisabeth until after the birth of John the Baptist. Add the six months in Lk. 1:26, to the three months mentioned here in Lk. 1:56. Refer also to Section 9, footnote a. "Returned to her own house" affirms that Mary went back to Nazareth. It was at this time that Joseph discovered her condition and was shocked into dismay. This was by visible observation of Mary, already showing her pregnancy.

2p-There was a rule among the Jews, that a divorced woman or a widow must wait three months before remarriage to ensure she was not with child by her former mate. As mentioned previously the Talmud tractate, Yevamoth, is filled with all sorts of bewildering instructions regarding who can marry whom, childbirth, and other directives. We cannot understand how the three months' waiting period would have been applicable to youthful Mary, who had never been married nor had carnal dealings with any man.

(k) **"Her own house."** This was the house of her father, "Heli," also called "Jacob," under whose authority she lived. Refer to Section 5, second paragraph of footnote d, and Section 6, first paragraph of footnote d for more on Mary's father. What did the family say when Mary physically showed her pregnancy? Who would have believed her story anyhow? A painful silence falls over these human questions: God refuses to speak about them. Is it because we mortals realize the answers, having lived among fellow humans and thus know our reactions toward such assumed terrible issues? O the wonderful mercy and grace of God showered upon us creatures of earth's little while. Of His goodness, it is written, "*It is of* the LORD'S mercies that we are not consumed, because his compassions fail not. *They are* new every morning: great *is* thy faithfulness" (Lam. 3:22-23).

2p-What did the quiet conversation between these two women involve? Amid it all, the wheels of God's sovereign counsel went into motion. At the end of this divine road, a virgin would embrace in her bosom a tiny Babe, who was the salvation of mankind. Surely, the quiet carpenter Joseph, stood by in wondering awe.

The birth of John the Baptist and related phenomena.

Matt.	Mk.	Lk. 1:57-77—*In the hill country of Judaea*	John
		John's circumcision, naming, and wonderment **57** Now Elisabeth's full time came that she should be delivered; and she brought forth a son. **58** And her neighbors and her cousins heard how the Lord had shewed great mercy upon her; and they rejoiced with her. **59** And it came to pass, that on the eighth day they came to circumcise[a] the child; and they called him Zacharias, after the name of his father. **60** And his mother answered and said, "Not *so*; but he shall be called John.[b] **61** And they said unto her, "There is none of thy kindred that is called by this name." **62** And they made signs[c] to his father, how he would have him called. **63** And he asked for a writing table, and wrote,[d] saying, "His name is John." And they marvelled all. ***Zacharias regains his speech after some nine months*** **64** And his mouth was opened immediately, and his tongue *loosed*, and he spake, and praised God. **65** And fear came on all that dwelt round about them: and all these sayings were noised [reported] abroad throughout all the hill country of Judaea. **66** And all they that heard *them* laid *them* up in their hearts, saying, "What manner of child shall this be!" And the hand[e] of the Lord was with him. ***Prophecies relating to John and Jesus*** **67** And his father Zacharias was filled[f] with the Holy Ghost, and prophesied,[g] saying, **68** "Blessed *be* the Lord God[h] of Israel; for he hath visited and redeemed his people, **69** "And hath raised up an horn[i] of salvation for us in the house of his servant David; **70** "As he spake by the mouth of his holy prophets, which have been since the world began:[j] **71** "That we should be saved from our enemies, and from the hand of all that hate us; **72** "To perform the mercy *promised* to our fathers, and to remember his holy covenant; **73** "The oath which he sware to our father Abraham,[k] **74** "That he would grant unto us, that we being delivered out of the hand of our enemies[l] might serve him without fear, **75** "In holiness and righteousness before him, all the days of our life. **76** "And thou, child, shalt be called the prophet of the Highest: for thou shalt go before the face of the Lord[m] to prepare his ways; **77** "To give knowledge of salvation unto his people by the remission of their sins,[n]	

Matt.	Mk.	Lk. 1:78-80—*In the hill country of Judaea*	John
		78 "Through the tender mercy of our God; whereby the dayspring[o] from on high hath visited us, 79 "To give light to them that sit in darkness and *in* the shadow of death, to guide our feet into the way of peace." ***John's seclusion from society*** 80 And the child grew, and waxed strong in spirit, and was in the deserts[p] till the day of his shewing[q] unto Israel. (Next chap., Lk. 2:1, cont. in Section 13.)	

Footnotes-Commentary

(a) Jewish tradition called for family and friends to gather each night from the time of a boy's birth until his circumcision. The rite was performed on the eighth day (Gen. 17:12; Lev. 12:3; and Phil. 3:5). It marked the child's official initiation into the Hebrew nation, and God's covenant made with Abraham. It was normally performed in the morning when the stomach was empty to prevent excess bleeding. Usually, the child was named at this time. Traditional naming was not commanded in the law. It was based upon Abraham's name change at the time of his circumcision (Gen. 17:5, 10). Almost anyone capable of the task, except a Gentile, could perform the operation; even a woman. Usually, it was the duty of the father. Zacharias, however, could not circumcise his infant son, for he was *both* deaf and dumb and therefore, unable to pronounce the blessing that always accompanied this ceremony. See *Gill's Commentary*, vol. 7, page 514, for a reproduction of the blessing articulated by the father over his son at circumcision. Male infants dying at birth were circumcised over their graves! Traditional circumcision was necessary to enter God's covenant with Israel. A Jew was considered an apostate who would not do this. The finer details and traditions of ancient Jewish circumcision are replete with superstitions and would fill several pages.

(b) Elisabeth broke with the Hebrew custom of passing on family names and declared, "He shall be called John." Her husband had previously informed her by writing that the angel, when he appeared in the temple, had already assigned this name to their child (Lk. 1:13).

(c) Here, we discover that he had been struck *both* deaf and dumb by the angel. This fact was not recorded in Lk. 1:20. Hence, sign language was employed in communicating with him.

(d) Surely, the old priest wrote in the Hebrew language. "John" means "God is gracious." The amazing circumstances of John's birth, the visit of the angel, the promise of a son in old age, the judgment on Zacharias, the stunning miracle of his speech and hearing being instantly restored at the circumcision of his son; all of these shook family and friends with an awful reverence of divine Majesty.

2p-A great stir. The hill country of Judaea rumbled with whisperings as everyone was convinced that God was with this strange child in a most extraordinary manner. Word spread everywhere about this baby. The presence of Jehovah was peculiarly upon him. Some thirty years later, this same child would again shake the country when he suddenly appeared as Messiah's forerunner, fearlessly preaching with God's mighty power still upon his life. Section 21 is divided into four parts, with each one describing a different aspect of John's public ministry.

(e) **"The hand of the Lord."** This was a Jewish expression applied to John. It meant that the Holy Spirit was with him. The rabbis interpreted 1 Chron. 28:19 and other passages in this manner. See also Ezek. 1:3 and 3:14, 22. Pagan Egyptians in Moses' day spoke similarly of God's power (Ex. 8:19). Jesus used a like term when referring to the Holy Spirit as "the finger of God." See Section 66, Lk. 11:20, footnote g.

(f) The Spirit of God supervised the whole drama, preparing the way for the births of John and the Lord Jesus. This is seen in Lk. 1:35, and 1:41. For the Holy Spirit in the Old Testament, see Section 10, Lk. 1:41, footnote b. This text demonstrates that men were filled with the Spirit of God, long before the day of Pentecost.

(g) Zacharias' predictions contain profound insight into the plan of God. He spoke as he was empowered by the Holy Ghost. See Micah 3:8 with 2 Peter 1:21. Later, Simon Peter said that *all* the prophets pointed to Christ (Acts 10:43). Refer to footnote j below for more on this thought.

(h) To **"bless God"** is not to invoke a blessing or wish of goodness on Him, for He is the source of all true blessings and good things. There is none greater than He. God needs no blessing, being the Creator, who is blessed forevermore. To "bless God" is to praise Him for His sure mercies graciously bestowed. It was an ancient form of opening prayer or praising God for His kindness (1 Chron. 16:36; 2 Chron. 6:4; Ps. 41:13; and 72:18). In some church circles, this has become preacher's slang. It is both irreverent and highly profane.

(i) **"Horn of Salvation."** This poetic expression referred to Messiah-Christ, who shortly was to enter the world through the family of King David by Mary, as illustrated in Section 7. The Talmud uses the same words in describing the Messiah in tractate, Pesachim 117b. The horn is to the beast what the arm is to man; the source of strength, defense, and protection. The Son of God is Israel's Messiah, the "Horn" of all who are saved. He is strength, defense, and protection for those redeemed by His precious blood.

(j) **"Since the world began."** Zacharias was surely familiar with the Old Testament predictions of the coming Messiah, beginning with the first one in Gen. 3:15. The old priest knew very well that God had His witnesses from the beginning of the world. See a similar statement by Peter in Acts 3:21. For details on God's *eternal witness* of Himself, refer to Section 1, Part 2, footnote f. When men longer witness of God, the heavens above step into their pulpits and preach! It is written, "The heavens declare the glory of God; and the firmament sheweth his handywork" (Ps. 19:1). Again, we read in Ps. 8:3-4, "When I consider the heavens, the work of thy fingers, the moon and the stars, which thou hast ordained; what is man, that thou art mindful of him?" The work of the Holy Spirit at creation and in the Old Testament has been noted in Section 10, footnote b. His grand work is to reveal Christ to the hearts and minds of men that they might believe on Him to everlasting life.

(k) **"The oath to Abraham."** This affirms that the covenant with Abraham was not yet completely fulfilled; there was more to come. Like Mary, he, too, associated the coming Messiah with the covenant God had made with Abraham some two thousand years before. See Lk. 1:55 for Mary's confession of the same things and her profound use of numerous verses from the Old Testament. Both Zacharias and Mary were aware that the Messiah was to come to the nation of Israel, because God had promised Him as part of the covenant with Abraham. See Gen. 22:15-18 and compare it with Paul's interpretation in Gal. 3:16 of the word "seed" as meaning Christ or the Messiah. It was the message and actions of Jesus that confounded all observers, as He did not conduct Himself as the rabbis had taught their Messiah would.

(l) **"The hand of our enemies."** The predictions made here speak of a physical and political deliverance only. This is seen in the words "all the days of our life" (verses 74 and 75). Rescue from the rule of heathen, Roman bondage was the heart's cry of every pious Jew. It was spoken of as "deliverance, redemption, and salvation." All such expressions, when used in this sense, had *nothing* to do with the salvation of the soul from sin. See footnotes n and o below.

2p-For some four hundred years, the physical salvation that Messiah would bring to Israel was the salvation taught in the synagogues. The disciples understood salvation this way, and it explains in part why they did not originally understand the death of Messiah on the cross. This is discussed in Sections 104, 105, 107, and 141.

(m) **"Go before."** Here, Zacharias presents John as the forerunner of Christ. This reveals the old priest knew some of God's plan, which had been revealed to him by the Holy Spirit.

(n) **"Knowledge of salvation."** The assurance of eternal life only comes *after* sins have been remitted or forgiven, which occurs at the time of the new birth. Both John and Jesus made it abundantly clear how people receive salvation and the remission of their sins: through the "dayspring from on high," the Lord Jesus Himself. It is grossly incorrect that John and Jesus came offering *only* a literal political kingdom to Israel and no more. However, it was true that Israel was looking for a temporal salvation from the yoke of Gentile and Roman rule. The Son of God came *first* to provide everlasting atonement for the sins of mankind and to establish the *spiritual side* of His kingdom, known later as the church. See Section 39, footnotes a and g for an explanation of the kingdom.

(o) **"Dayspring."** Verses 78 and 79 are Messianic predictions. "Dayspring" is one of His ancient Names, while verse 79 speaks of the *major works* He would accomplish in Israel ("give light and peace"). For centuries, the nation of Israel had deemed itself to be sitting in darkness and the very shadow of death; her only hope was for the coming Messiah to direct her feet into His peace. The word "dayspring" refers to the "rising of the sun" as predicted in Mal. 4:2 and Isa. 9:1-2. It was a rabbinical title for the Messiah. Zacharias interprets the passages from Isaiah as applying to the Lord Jesus. For some four hundred years before the birth of Jesus, the rabbis also held that these verses in Malachi and Isaiah pointed to that Messianic Person. The synagogue interpreted the "BRANCH" in Isa. 11:1; Jer. 23:5; Zech. 3:8, and 6:12 as being similar or sometimes equivalent to the term "dayspring," (Messiah) as used by Zacharias.

(p) **"Deserts."** This does not signify a hot, dry, sandy area with no life or vegetation, but rather a secluded area away from public intercourse. We read that John's parents lived "in the hill country . . . of Juda" (Lk. 1:39). God's sovereignty arranged for John to grow up in this environment, thus preventing the Messiah's forerunner from being defiled by the corrupted Jewish religious system of that day. *Being the son of a priest, he should have entered the temple priesthood.* When John stepped out to preach, he was clean from the doctrinal and moral corruptions of the common Judaism of that day. To identify John as a member of the Essene sectarian group of this time, because he grew up in the desert, is wrong. John lived a monastic type of life because God directed him to do so, not because he took the Essene oath of celibacy. Members of the Essene community abstained from meat, yet John ate locusts and wild honey. Men who do not hold to the inspiration of Scripture can convince themselves to believe just about anything. Unbelief in the authority of God's Word is the source of their foolish statements.

2p-Thus, these two boys of heavenly destiny later grew up through the passing years; one in the lonely, desert hills of Judaea after his old parents had died, leaving him, no doubt, at an early age. Meanwhile, Jesus was laboring in a carpenter's shop at Nazareth, that city of exceeding wickedness. Both were waiting for their "shewing unto the nation of Israel." Forever John and Jesus changed the course of world history.

(q) **"His shewing [revealing] unto Israel."** Why must John be shown to Israel? They must know that he was the fulfillment of Mal. 4:5-6. Later, we read that the "word of God came to John in the wilderness" and called him to begin publicly his ministry (Lk. 3:2).

2p-Some two thousand years before John the Baptist, the same "word of the LORD" came to Abraham. It was on this occasion that he was saved and declared righteous through faith in the gospel that God explained (Gen. 15:1-7; Rom. 4:1-3; with Gal. 3:6 and 8). He was divinely chosen to become the federal head of the Hebrew nation. This was some 430 years *before* the Law of Moses was given (Gal. 3:17). Thus, we can better understand our Savior's comment that "Abraham rejoiced to see my day" (John 8:56). This same "word of the LORD" also spoke to Joel 1:1; Jonah 1:1; Micah 1:1; Zeph. 1:1; and Mal. 1:1. There are numerous places in the Old Testament where this subject is mentioned. For a brief explanation of Jesus, the eternal "word of the LORD," co-equal with the Father, and joint participant in the creation, see Section 1, Part 1, footnote b. The Bible's final picture of "The Word of God," is dramatically presented in Rev. 19:11-13. God used Abraham's nation to give us the Savior. He is of the "seed of Abraham" (Heb. 2:16). Chapter 3 of this harmony presents the family line of Christ from five slightly different angles.

3p-Hatred for Israel. International despite for these people is an established fact. History reeks with the stench of kings, potentates, nations, armies, organizations, religions, and individuals from various walks of life that have cursed the "wandering Jew." The religion of Islam swears to obliterate Israel from the face of the earth! So-called "Christian icons" of centuries past have mouthed their poison rancor upon the Hebrew people. Refer to Section 14, all under the third paragraph of footnote f, for some of their names. Standing in the shadows is the first cause of all racism, that invisible spirit person, called the Devil or Satan. Assisted by millions of demons, he has produced and directed all the malice for Israel and countless others over the ages. World contempt for Israel stems from the fact that she gave us the Savior. Ironically, on the other hand, there are Jews that curse the Savior their nation gave the world! All haters are blind to the source of their sin (2 Cor. 4:4). At the end of a two-thousand year old road beginning with Abraham, down to Bethlehem's manger, the great miracle of all time occurred. A Hebrew virgin from Nazareth, named Mary, by miraculous conception gave humankind the Savior, Jesus the Son of God. Herein is the reason for the global contempt for Israel and Jesus. What has been said above about Christ can be said of no other religious figure in world history. This is because of who He is and what He did for the human race on the cross and in His resurrection. If the French or Spanish had given us the Savior, the world would hate the French and Spanish! Hatred for the Son of God is universally prolific (John 7:7 with 8:23). Section 14, the sixth paragraph under footnote f, speaks of Jews, who hide behind the word "racism" to do their dirty work.

4p-Hatred for Jesus Christ. Opposite to the above, numerous Jews equally hate Jesus of Nazareth. As the world in general vomits at Israel, so many Israelis join in the anthem of hell and vent their wrath upon the Savior. While parts of unsaved humanity wish a total demise for all Jews, many Israelis in turn fiercely denounce Christ and Christianity. (Not *every* Jew and Gentile despises Jesus of Nazareth, the Savior of men.) Among His enemies are those who give Him a salute of courtesy but totally reject His claims on their lives. Their "superior education" or "experience" has taught them better! For others, His atoning death on the cross is a joke, and His resurrection from the grave is a "pagan myth palmed off on ignorant Christians." Then we have both Jews and Gentiles, who fly into fits of rage, cursing, swearing, and blaspheming at the mention of His Holy Name. In Australia, an elderly Hebrew tool sharpener spat at me for speaking to him about Jesus the Messiah. While talking over the phone to a rabbi in Brooklyn, New York, I courteously told him I was a Christian, and was calling to acquire information about ancient Hebrew culture. He went into a screaming rage, slamming the phone down. However, not all Jews or Gentiles act in this manner, only those who are mentally or religiously deranged. For information on how staunch Jews treat those of their number that come to the saving knowledge of "Yeshua ha'Mashiach," see Section 146, footnote o. The internet reeks with websites that defame, slander, or cleverly explain away our Savior as a "Christian superstition." Some of these drip with venom and oppose Jesus Christ in awful blasphemy. Both spiritually blinded Jews and Devil inspired Gentiles are behind these Antichrist websites. Happily, there is no respect of persons or racism with God (Rom. 2:11). He has written, "For there is no difference between the Jew and the Greek [Gentile]: for the same Lord over all is rich unto all that call upon him" (Rom. 10:12). *Men who reject God's Son, reject God (John 5:22-23).* Millions viciously oppose this fact. Regardless of race, religion, education, national origin, creed or color, all Christ rejecters have their destiny guaranteed (Rev. 20:15).

5p-The day of acknowledgement is coming. As sure as the sun shines, the time is coming, be it near or a thousand years ahead, when every mortal that has ever lived, will bow their knees and confess that "Jesus Christ is Lord of all" (Phil. 2:9-11). It is repeated over this work, that *because He is the world's only Savior, He is therefore, the world's most hated man.* Reader, are you among the hate-mongers? Is your heart guilty over unbelief and sin? Do you want help? If so, God reaches out to save and bless you with total forgiveness and a new life. Receive Christ by simple faith as your personal Lord and Savior. It is written in the Bible, "For whosoever shall call upon the name of the Lord shall be saved" (Rom. 10:13). "Now *is* the accepted time; behold, now *is* the day of salvation" (2 Cor. 6:2). A thief dying on a Roman cross called upon Jesus Christ for mercy and was granted a home in paradise (Lk. 23:42-43.) *Most of us are not much better and the same Savior waits to forgive us as well.*

Joseph's tormenting dilemma and the angel in his dream.*

After the angelic explanation regarding Mary's condition, Joseph then understood and believed.

Matt. 1:18-25—*At Nazareth in Galilee*	Mk.	Lk.	John
Matthew explains Joseph's problem to his readers **18** Now the birth of Jesus Christ was on this wise: When as his mother Mary was espoused[a] [engaged] to Joseph, before they came together, she was found with child[b] of the Holy Ghost. **19** Then Joseph her [promised] husband, being a just *man*, and not willing to make her a publick example, was minded to put her away privily.[c] ***An angel appears in his first dream and solves Joseph's distress*** [d] **20** But while he thought on these things, behold, the angel of the Lord appeared unto him in a dream, saying, "Joseph, thou son of David, fear not to take unto thee Mary [for] thy wife: for that which is conceived in her is of the Holy Ghost. **21** "And she shall bring forth a son, and thou shalt call his name JESUS:[e] for he shall save his people from their sins." ***Matthew looking back interprets Isa 7:14 as applying to Mary and Jesus*** **22** Now all this was done, that it might be fulfilled which was spoken of the Lord by the prophet, saying, **23** "Behold, a virgin[f] shall be with child, and shall bring forth a son, and they shall call his name Em-man-u-el,"[g] which being interpreted[h] is, "God with us." ***Joseph's obedience*** **24** Then Joseph being raised from sleep did[i] as the angel of the Lord had bidden him, and took unto him [Mary for] his wife: **25** And knew her not[j] till she had brought forth her firstborn son: and he called[k] his name JESUS. (Next chap., Matt. 2:1, cont. in Section 17.)			

Footnotes-Commentary

(a) **"Espoused."** Also known as "betrothal," it was an official form of engagement employed by ancient Jews and others. The Hebrew word "kuddushin" meant, in this case, "setting aside" a particular woman for a particular man. The espousal lasted for about one year after the signing of a formal contract by the two parties and before the actual nuptials of marriage. The contract was called "ketubbah." *The Encyclopedia of Judaism,* page 413 reads, "This form of marriage agreement can be dated back to the fourth century." A copy of an ancient "ketubbah" was found buried, and completely preserved in the dry sand of southern Egypt. Though not officially married during this period, they were, nevertheless, called husband and wife and in a state of pending wedlock, though living separately. Infidelity on the part of either person during this time was considered worse than adultery after a marriage. See third paragraph below. Under the Law of Moses, adultery incurred the death penalty in the form of stoning, burning, beheading, or strangling. Due to personal corruption and willful neglect of the Jewish religious leaders, these punishments were not enforced in the days of Christ. For explanation of this, see Section 67, fourth paragraph, footnote b. The Talmud tractate, Sanhedrin 7, outlines the penalties for adultery. Originally, a bill of divorce, adultery, or death would break the espousal or marriage contract. This divorce bill is mentioned in Deut. 24:1, 3. In Torah Law divorces, the marriage bond was considered completely dissolved with the previous mate being called "former" (Deut. 24:4). This is seen in the fact that the woman was forbidden to return to her first husband if the second or third husband had divorced her (Deut. 24:4). Jehovah, not Moses, gave this commandment.

2p-A short review concerning the pagan myths of the "perpetual virginity" ascribed to Mary is given in footnote k below. For further information and cross references to the heathen fables of virgin-born gods, see second paragraph of footnote g below.

3p-**Break wedlock.** Joseph could not bear the thought of Mary being guilty of adultery. God had declared over five hundred years prior in Ezek. 16:38, that those who commit adultery "break wedlock." Six verses prior to Ezek. 16:38, in verse 32 it states that the "break" occurred with adultery. This was valid during the espousal period or after the consummation of a marriage. Like all pious Jews, Joseph would have been familiar with this. He intended to put Mary away quietly by issuing her a "writing of divorcement" which would dissolve the betrothal contract. In the Old Testament, God represents Himself as putting away (divorcing) the nation of Israel, His spiritual wife, by issuing her a bill or certificate of divorce (Isa. 50:1). She had committed adultery with pagan idols and severed her union with Jehovah. Jeremiah the prophet employed the same marital symbolism between God and Israel, because of the nation's spiritual adultery in going after (serving) other gods (Jer. 3:8-10). Many of the idolatrous rituals involved physical adultery with the pagan priests and priestesses. The book of Hosea is a strong condemnation of adultery. Almost six hundred years later, Christ said that the sin of adultery still broke the union between married men and women. Refer to Section 137, Matt. 19:9, footnote g for His Words. See footnote c below. *God has forgiven and restored millions guilty of this sin.* In Jewish culture, after marriage, a person could still be referred to as an "espoused" wife or husband (Lk. 2:5). Section 45, footnote i has further details on this subject.

(b) **"Found [or seen to be] with child."** It was visibly obvious that she was pregnant. Pagan mythology of this era and for thousands of years previous reeked with bizarre stories of saviors and gods coming to earth and women conceiving children by them. Frequently, the women, supposedly conceiving by these heathen gods were called virgins! Their monstrous children were called "sons of the gods." Satan created this history-long scenario through pagan religions to imitate, mock, and discredit the *true* virgin birth of Christ that was to come. Matthew's Jewish readers had heard these heathen fables countless times. Consequently, Matthew explains the details, divine source, and miracle of Mary's conception. It was a work of the "Holy Spirit" or the "Ruach HaKodesh," a familiar term in the Hebrew Tanakh or Old Testament (Isa. 63:11). The Jews believed that the Holy Spirit was a creator. This is mentioned in their Scriptures (Job 26:13, 33:4 with Ps. 104:30).

2p-Verse 19. Matthew was inspired to write that Joseph was a "just man." About three decades later, the wife of Governor Pilate warned her husband with similar words about Jesus. She wrote that He was a "just man," and admonished him to do Christ no harm. Shortly after this, Pilate said almost the exact words about Jesus (Matt. 27:19 and 24). How did the heathen governor and his wife know this of our Lord?

3p-When Matthew wrote his book (a few years *after* the ascension of Christ), haters of Christianity had spread rumors that Mary conceived Jesus out of wedlock by Joseph or someone else. Others relegated her story of a virgin birth to the realm of pagan myths. Later, Celsus, a Christ hating philosopher wrote that Jesus' father was a Roman soldier who was later named Panthera. See Section 137, first paragraph of footnote d for details. Matthew wrote with some of these *earlier* lies in mind, knowing that many of his readers had heard and believed them.

(c) **"Privily." Without involving public attention and the Sanhedrin.** The Mosaic Law called for death in the case of adultery (Deut 22:23-24 with Lev. 20:10). According to this law, Mary, if guilty of the crime, was to have been stoned publicly in a most ignominious manner. However, at this time in history, Israel had fallen into a state of decadence, sin, and law breaking. Christ told the religious leaders that none of them kept the Law of Moses (John 7:19). Joseph, a "good man," was overwhelmed and sought to divorce Mary quietly, thinking she was guilty. Her innocence justified Joseph's actions in not laying a formal charge of adultery before the Sanhedrin. Honest Jews reading Matthew's words would have felt a note of tender sympathy for both Joseph and Mary.

(d) **His first dream.** This good man had three other heavenly visitations in the form of dreams. See Section 18, Matthew 2:13, 19, and 22 for more on this. Matthew wrote of the angel's visit during Joseph's sleep and the explanation given to him about Mary. Jews deeply believed in dreams and angelic visitations. Though rejecting all pagan myths about gods and women, they could accept that the Spirit of God (Ruach-Elohim) of their Old Testament could perform such a miracle if Jehovah so decreed. We can readily believe that Mary *tried* to explain the whole story to Joseph; however, like any other man, he would find it impossible to believe her story. Now, by divine intervention, he understood the truth about his beloved Mary! Who could imagine the thoughts that raged like a storm in his heart before the angel's comforting explanation (verses 19-21)? He instantly believed!

(e) **Jesus is "Yeshua" in Hebrew.** In time, this glorious Name, "Yeshua," has become the object of hatred among certain Jews. In their contempt for our Savior, they deliberately altered the Name into the term "Yeshu," dropping off the last letter (that is, instead of "Ye-shoo'-ah" it became "Yeh-shoo"). Thus, "Yeshu" was created as a dreadful expletive intended to conjure all sorts of infamy upon Jesus Christ in a coded form. Other Christ-hating Jews understand this. *Many younger Israelis use the word today without knowing its etymology and intent.* This calumny is found three times in the Talmud tractate, Sanhedrin 43a. It reveals a slanderous usage of Jesus' Name that was in vogue several centuries after His ascension. For the blasphemies against Christ found in the Babylonian Talmud, see Section 6, footnotes d and e, and Section 18, second paragraph of footnote i.

2p-As mentioned above in footnote b, by the time Matthew had written his book, some years after the ascension of Christ, Jews everywhere had heard of "Jesus, the Savior of men." This was the gospel message carried throughout the known world of the first century (Col. 1:5-6). At the time of Matthew's writing, the message of salvation was no longer that of a political "salvation from the Romans," rather, it had become a spiritual reality in

"Jesus saving his people from their sin" (Matt. 1:21 with Acts 4:12). Many of Matthew's readers had heard this very message proclaimed. All informed Jews knew of the promise of their Messiah (the "BRANCH") in Jer. 23:5-6 and numerous other Old Testament references. In the Talmud tractate, Sanhedrin 90a, Israel is called the "vine of God's planting." With this title in mind, note Isa. 61:3.

(f) Further information regarding heathen fables of virgin-born gods is in footnote b above. For the benefit of fellow Jewish readers, Matthew quoted their Tanakh or Hebrew scrolls, from Isa. 7:14. He clearly stated that this prediction was fulfilled in Mary and Jesus, her son. This would have had a profound effect on all of his readers, curious to know the truth about Jesus of Nazareth. After all, He had turned their nation upside down! At His death, the veil of their temple rent in two pieces and it could not be restored despite frantic efforts on the part of the Sanhedrin and priesthood. News of this spread to Jews over the habitable earth of those days, for it had permanently spoiled their temple rituals. Many conflicting stories about Mary and Jesus were in circulation. Several centuries later, hostile Hebrew writers called her a "hairdresser." This was a term of scandalous contempt and used for a woman who was an adulteress. Matthew had just written a genealogical tree in chapter 1. In this, he showed that Christ met the Messianic requirement by coming into the world through the family line of Abraham and King David. See Section 5, left vertical column and relative footnotes, and all of Section 7 for details. He demonstrated for his Hebrew readers that Jesus, the son of Mary, was that unique Messianic Person. The debate about whether or not Mary was a virgin at the birth of Christ was revived with the release of the *Revised Standard Version of the Bible* in 1946. A footnote on page 1 of the New Testament reads, "Other ancient authorities read, 'Joseph, to whom was betrothed the virgin Mary was the father of Jesus, who is called Christ.' " This lie was based on the corrupted Sinaitic Codex. The historical origins of the fallacy of "perpetual virginity" of Mary are given in footnote k below.

2p-Sigmund Mowinckel, in his work, *He that cometh. The Messiah Concept in the Old Testament & and Later Judaism,* wrote on page 111 regarding Isa. 7:14, "That a direct Christological interpretation is out of the question. Isaiah cannot here be referring to the birth of Jesus more than seven hundred years later." Matthew disagrees with the Professor Mowinckel. The former publican interpreted and applied Isa. 7:14 to the birth of Jesus Christ as seen in verses 22-23 given above. The historical fact that pagans in religious festivals, rites, and parades evoked a deity to accompany them, and used the term "Immanuel" (in whatever language) or "God with us," means ignorantly they abused the Name of God. The author has heard African pagan savages call out for their ancestor spirits to assist them in various undertakings. There is an oceanic difference between invoking the Name of the true and living God to bless and assist in a task or duty to that of demonic entities. The myths of heathen antiquity that "supernatural women" would bring forth savior-sons, were mimes of Satan, designed to mock humble Mary and Mighty Jesus, yet-to-be-born. Isaiah, in predicting the virgin birth of God's Son, did not borrow this from pagans. He was inspired by the Holy Spirit to write. Matthew wrote the facts for fellow Jews (and us) to read and believe.

3p-How interesting that over a thousand years *after* the birth of Christ, the most famed of all medieval Jewish Bible commentators, who viciously opposed the Lord Jesus, Rabbi Rashi (died 1105), wrote of Isa. 7:14 these words, "Behold the *'almah* shall conceive and bear a son and shall call his name *Immanu'el.'* This means that our creator will be with us. And this is the sign: the one who will conceive is a girl (*na'arah*) who never in her life has had intercourse with any man. Upon this one shall the Holy Spirit have power." Cited from Dr. David H. Stern's work, *Jewish New Testament Commentary* pages 6-7. Though it seems many of the earliest rabbis missed this truth, it is notable that some of the later ones did not. However, they still rejected Jesus as their Messiah.

(g) The first Old Testament passage quoted in Matthew. Matthew cites this from Isa. 7:14. It states that Jesus of Nazareth was God in human flesh. See footnotes h and j below. Matthew makes about one hundred twenty-nine quotations or allusions to the Jewish Old Testament in his book directly or indirectly. He alludes to persons, places, or events. Chronologically, Lk. 1:17 is the first Old Testament verse quoted in the New Testament. For a thorough look into the birth of our Savior, see *The Virgin Birth,* by J. G. Machen. Some may find Robert Gromachi's work, *The Virgin Birth (Doctrine of Deity)* shorter in content and easier to understand.

2p-Virgin born saviors among pagan religions. An explanation of this predominant belief of heathen religions thousands of years before the birth of Jesus is given in Section 9, second paragraph of footnote i. For a comprehensive look into heathenism and its duplications of Christianity, see *Early Gentile Christianity and its Hellenistic Background,* by Arthur D. Nock. (Nock wrote as a non-believer in Jesus Christ and the Scripture.) His spiritual conclusions are disastrous, but his documentation is enlightening. This shows again, how far in advance Satan imitated, in thousands of perverted forms, the truth of Christ and Scripture. Across the ancient world, the coming of God's Son was besmirched by heathen fabrications. From the beginning, the Devil mimed Cain's murder of Abel in pagan mythology. In Greek mythology, Heracles was purported to be virgin-born and called "savior," "only begotten," and the "prince of peace." In Egypt, a satanic god called "Krst," meaning the "anointed one," duplicated Christ. He was (supposedly) virgin-born, taught in a heathen temple at twelve years of age, was baptized in a river, performed miracles, and walked on water. Krst was supposedly crucified between two thieves, buried and rose again. Asia also had many satanic saviors. Zoroaster was allegedly virgin-born, baptized, tempted in the wilderness, and healed the blind. His followers celebrated a sacred meal called "the word was made flesh." In far away India, a young teacher emerged named "Krishna." The appearing of a star marked his acclaimed virgin birth. Skeptics tell us that the word "Krishna" is the origin for the Name "Christ." *It is stressed again; these demonic counterfeits of the real thing were designed to divert men from the true and living God and the salvation of His Son, Jesus Christ. Christ hating academics and atheists cringe at the above truth for it spells their ultimate doom!*

3p-Spelling differences. The spelling of "Emmanuel" in Matt. 1:23 differ from the spelling in Isa. 7:14, which is "Immanuel," though both refer to the Savior. This has nothing to do with inspiration of Scripture but is the result of the translator's choice in a letter and word sounds. Refer to Section 6, second paragraph of footnote a, for more on this subject. Another example is in the word "Zion" in Isa. 28:16. Centuries later, in 1 Peter 2:6 it has been written as "Sion." Both words refer to the same place.

(h) "Emmanuel." Matthew interprets this name for his readers as "God with us." Every educated Jew would have known this. Those not familiar with the Hebrew language also read Matthew's book, later written in Greek. This means that Mary's baby was God in human flesh, virgin–born without an earthly father. The Jews taught Messiah or the Memra, would be like God. See Section 1, Part 1, paragraph 6, under footnote b.

(i) Matthew explained that Joseph obeyed the instructions given him by the angel in verses 20 and 21.

(j) This statement affirms that Joseph had no sexual relationship with Mary until *after* the birth of Christ. Matthew, the writer, could have only known this by divine revelation. See verse 20 for the source of her pregnancy. Based on Isa. 9:6, "For unto us a child is born, unto us a son is given," some commentators believe that the body was formed first, and then the Son took up abode within this divinely created human house. *The conception of Christ's human body is stated in Scripture but not explained.* Prudence dictates that we leave it there. On the Lord Jesus being called Mary's "firstborn," see Section 13, second paragraph, footnote f for explanation. This word "firstborn" only makes sense if others were born afterwards.

(k) The myth of perpetual virginity and related subjects. Early religious fanatics such as Origen, Clement, and Cyril of Alexandria introduced this ancient infamy into the church. See second paragraph of footnote g above for a brief survey of this old pagan belief. Later, it was embellished by that doctrinal chameleon, Augustine (died A.D. 430) when he added his distortions to the myth. Then the supporters of the Papal system hurry off into the darkness of "tradition" to justify their misrepresentation of Mary. I once heard a priest quote Paul's words where he commanded the churches to obey the "traditions" he had taught them (2 Thess. 2:15 and 3:6). Then, he affirmed that all bishops and Popes over the centuries spoke with the same successive apostolic authority as Paul, for God had transferred His power to them. The conclusion of this untruth is that we are to obey Catholic prelates! Next, he quoted the writings of the doctrinally disarrayed church fathers as proof that Papal tradition regarding "perpetual virginity" was a valid doctrine. (Pagan religions had their virgin born gods thousands of years earlier!) Many Anglican, Orthodox Churches, and cults have deified Mary. Note paragraph three below. Only when men turn their hearts solely to Jesus Christ, humanity's exclusive Savior, will they find forgiveness and eternal life. He is received by faith, not through Mary or anyone else. Salvation is not found in the ritualistic traditions, customs, gilded crosses, baptisms, the Eucharist, catechisms, confirmations, pompous parades, ceremonies, colorful gowns, displays, folded hands, burning incense pots, pious words, and written prayers. Scripture declares, "By grace are ye saved through faith; and that not of yourselves: *it is* the gift of God" (Eph. 2:8). Fables of Mary answering prayers have steered thousands from simple saving faith in Jesus Christ. She has become something of a goddess! *The exclusive glory belonging uniquely to Christ has been taken from Him and given to her.* Years ago, I stood in the back of a Catholic Church building in Ingham, Queensland, Australia. Dozens came and knelt before statues of Joseph and Mary. I inquired of an Italian taxi driver what he was doing. He humbly replied, "I pray to them for forgiveness of my sins." These people are looking in the wrong place for the right thing. As long as they continue doing this, *true* forgiveness will never be found. They need Jesus, not Joseph and Mary.

2p–Mary's other children. New Testament Scripture and the Catholic Bible *both* teach that Joseph and Mary had at least six children after Jesus was born (Matt. 13:55-56). Like all pious Jews, Jesus' half-brothers devoutly attended the temple services and would have been known. As members of Jesus' earthly family, they had a unique notoriety throughout the land. Later, Roman emperors sought to kill the family members of Christ in their fear of His kingship being reclaimed. For more on this, see Section 183, second paragraph of footnote q. One thinks of Jesus' grandparents on both sides, aunties, uncles, cousins, and so forth.

3p–Mary, bringing men to Jesus. A Papal doctrine called the "Immaculate Conception" teaches that Mary was without sin from the beginning. This myth was publicly announced by Pope Pius IX announced in 1854. Devout Catholics tell us that Mary is the path that leads us to Christ. The publication *Christian News*, February 2, 1997, carried a short article, which stated, "She [Mary] was to become her son's faithful coworker for the salvation of the human race." Adding to this gross untruth, in 1950, the Roman Church via Pope Pius XII declared that Mary was taken body and soul into heaven! In 1965, she was named "the mother of the church." The lie that Mary is a "Co-Redemptrix" is the highest of blasphemies, and degrades the Son of God. Nowhere does the Bible teach that Mary assists Christ in saving lost souls. The prattle about "Mary smiling upon men" and "the rosary will bring us God's favor" is satanic. Mary cannot answer prayer nor command Jesus to do certain favors for those who pray to her. To call Mary, "the spouse of the Holy Spirit" is an abomination. Refer to Section 10, Lk. 1:47, footnote g where Mary confessed that God was her Savior. Only sinners need a Savior. The *New Catholic Edition of the Holy Bible*, 1953, reads in the footnote on page 198, that Mary was sinless! On page 1 Pope Leo XIII grants an "indulgence of 300 days" to those who read it daily for at least a quarter of an hour. This means three-hundred days less to suffer in the *nonexistent* Roman Catholic purgatory.

4p-"**You must pray to Mary!**" While in America on furlough in 1973, the author learned that, his first cousin was dying with cancer. Driving to his home early one Monday morning, I was greeted at the door by his wife. I went in, sat at the dining room table with my cousin, and announced the purpose of my visit. In the next hour, I poured my heart out to James, explaining the gospel and his need to trust Christ as Lord and Savior. His Roman Catholic wife became furious and pounded on the table. She continually interjected, interrupted, and interfered. Her violent complaint was, "James must pray to the virgin Mary and ask her to lead him to Jesus Christ for salvation." After some ten minutes, her husband ordered, "Shut up!" This female Devil, trying to hinder a soul from coming to Christ, ran into the kitchen, slamming the door. Acts 13:6-11 described her well. Trembling from weakness, my dying cousin leaned over the table, and poured his heart out to God. *He was instantly saved!* James passed into eternity several days later. It is the exclusive work of the Holy Spirit to bring men to Christ, after being enlightened by the gospel. That best of good mothers, Mary, has nothing to do with the salvation of mankind. No one is redeemed from their sin by praying the stations of the cross, carrying a Rosary, wearing the scapular, and other religious paraphernalia. Mary is not the "Queen of heaven" or the "Queen of the apostles." This sacrilegious fable has produced "Christianized" female idolatry and deceived thousands of honest Catholic people.

5p-**Mary, a mediator for Jesus?** There is not one scrap of evidence for this anywhere within the pages of Holy Scripture, not even the Roman Catholic Bible, except for its doctored footnotes. In Section 68, Lk. 11:27-28, the Lord Jesus rebuked a woman in His audience who publicly spoke praises to Mary, His mother. She, chosen by God to be the human vehicle, in which the body of Christ was formed, is now in heaven because she also trusted her Son as personal Lord and Savior. Scripture is emphatic that only Jesus Christ can mediate between God and men. The Bible declares, "For *there is* one God, and one mediator between God and men, the man Christ Jesus" (1 Tim. 2:5). Mary cannot mediate anything. The thousands of stories about statues and Madonna's crying, apparitions, and appearances of the mother of Christ, are demonic materializations designed to plunge devout and pious Catholics deeper into spiritual darkness. The Roman system claims to be the only valid church. *This indelibly marks it as a false religion deceiving those who follow it.* See the eleventh paragraph below for more on this untruth. The redemption of mankind was to be effected through a mediator who should unite in himself both the human and divine natures, in order that He might reconcile man to God and God to man. Jesus Christ alone is this mediator.

6p-**Church fathers and heretical radicalism.** *The true fathers of the church were James, John, Peter, Andrew, Paul, and so forth.* One can prove just about anything from the writings of the later fathers. On one page, they put down great Bible truths; on the next, they penned the exact opposite! Clement, Ignatius, Tertullian, Origen, Papias, Irenarus, Augustine, and Justin Martyr are prime examples of this. Origen taught that all men would finally be saved, including Satan! Over the years, liberal theologians, as well as "conservatives," have esteemed the writings of these men as almost sacred. The church fathers gradually mixed Greek pagan philosophy with Holy Scripture. Borrowing practices from mystic religions, they boasted an authority that God intended no mortal to wield. As they laid their good-bad theology upon the common people, slowly, their authority became singularly sacred. Only those *they* baptized or administered communion to could be saved. This lie was the embryo that later grew into the unbloody mass of the Roman Catholic Church. A church father named Tertullian was the first early writer to call ministers "priests." For more on Tertullian's poison, see Section 138, seventh paragraph of footnote a.

7p-**The results of the father's heresies–sacerdotalism.** From their abuse of baptism and communion came "sacerdotalism," or the belief that ministers of religion were the only intermediaries between God and man. Because of their office as bishops or ministers, they claimed to possess extraordinary authority from God. This was a precursor for the Papal system that later came out of Emperor Constantine's state church. With it appeared the curse of confessional, mass, and indulgences. Reinterpreting basic Bible doctrines, the fathers mystified, overly allegorized, distorted, and corrupted some of these truths. Others, they left unchanged! *Many of them actually died as martyrs for their heresies.* For centuries, religious historians and theologians have tried almost everything at the bar of the church fathers. And much of it has proven wanting! The value of their writings is in the historical data and the Scriptures they quoted from the existing New Testament canon of their day. This helps determine what Scriptures were known and used in those times. See *Unholy Hands on the Bible, an Examination of Six Major New Versions* (two volumes of three), by Jay P. Green Sr., for more details. There is no soteriological worth in the fathers' writings. They held that baptism and communion saved men from their sins! Some were so radical in baptizing that adults stripped naked and stood in the water! This assured that all of their sins were washed away! Afterward, they could not bathe for seven days! Emperor Constantine was baptized this way shortly before he died.

8p-**Modern day heretics.** The famed Dr. Robert Schuller preached to thousands in the Crystal Cathedral, at Garden Grove, CA, the following lie, "Sin is not what shatters our relationship to God [but it is] that we do not esteem ourselves enough. In the Crystal Cathedral, therefore, let the word sin be banished." He continued his defense of the Devil's lie with, "Christ was not drawing a profound moral compass in the Sermon on the Mount; he was just giving us a set of 'be (happy)' attitudes." For documentation of this myth regarding sin and salvation, see *No Place for Truth. Whatever Happened to Evangelical Theology?* by Dr. David F. Wells, page 175. Schuller's denial of sin and its consequences started with Satan and Eve in the Garden of Eden (Gen. 3:1-6). Water is sprinkled on the heads of scores of children standing on the stage of the Chrystal Cathedral. They are assured that this brings them into a right relationship with God. *Robert Schuller has now retired, and the church has gone into bankruptcy. Christians must pray that these poor deceived people will come to the saving knowledge of Jesus Christ.*

9p-From the Fathers to Catholicism. The church fathers invented a blue eyed, blond-haired Mary. They painted her in their chapels and later built her into stained glass windows when their corrupt theology finally evolved into full-blown Roman Catholic dogma. Today these windows are almost worshiped. The fathers' depictions of Mary reveals their historical and ethnic ignorance. She was a Hebrew, with dark skin, brown eyes, and black hair. And in her early teens when Gabriel came with his astounding message about the virgin birth of Jesus.

10p-Child abuse and the Inquisitions. The horrific revelations of child abuse by hundreds of priests are not marks of infallibility. Papal apologists sweat it out, trying to cover up or tone down these facts. Only the tip of this shameful iceberg has surfaced. Any church infected with these crimes, and having a violent murderous history, is not a church but a synagogue of Satan (Rev. 2:9). In their present push to gather all churches "back home to Rome," Catholic historians have rewritten their history, seeking to put a benevolent face on their bloody past. Papal defenders tell us that the excesses of the Spanish Inquisition were due to the state and not the instructions of the Popes. They lie because the Popes held supreme authority over every office of the state. Orders for the Inquisition came from them. Every inquisitor, regardless of his station in life, was a Catholic. In the old work, subtitled *History of the Inquisition in Spain*, vol. ii, page 114, by Henry Charles Lea, we read, "The [Catholic] church taught the punishing of heresy with burning 'to be an act so eminently pious that it accorded an indulgence to anyone who would contribute wood to the pile.'" This meant that anyone, who placed wood at the feet of those being burnt to death for not being Catholics, would receive special grace from God! Lea wrote of maids being violated, men with their feet burnt to the bone, and wives, husbands, fathers, mothers, and children dying screaming as the fires consumed their bodies. (Shades of John Calvin's Geneva in years to come!) For more of the horrific details, see Lea's, *A History of the Inquisition of the Middle Ages,* 1906, in three volumes. Lea was an American historian, who died 1909. The work, *Medieval Heresy and the Inquisition; The Spanish Inquisition,* by Author Stanley Turberville, documents the barbarity of the Papal system. The rebuttal, "That was done in the past, and it is not relevant today" is wrong. Has God cancelled judgment? At the Council of Torlouse in A.D. 1229, the Catholic Church unleashed a pogrom of murder. People were killed for possessing a Bible, goods confiscated, and houses burnt. Others were imprisoned and tortured. The "infallible Popes" cannot remove the blood of millions slaughtered by their church.

11p-The testimonies of others. Dr. W. E. H. Lecky (died 1901), was an Irish historian, turned atheist. He penned the unvarnished truth about religious persecutions. In *History of the Rise and Influence of the Spirit of Rationalism in Europe,* vol. 2, pages 40-45, he wrote, "The church of Rome has shed more innocent blood than any other institution that has ever existed among mankind." The vain pomp, the gowns, crosses, colors, priests, inquisitors, and their horrible instruments of torture were inventions of Satan. The methods of torture, and death inflicted by the monsters of the Roman Catholic Church fill volumes. In *History of European Morals,* vol. ii, page 331, Lecky wrote of priests and Popes, who, over several hundred years, were guilty of "adultery, incest, one with seventeen illegitimate children in a village, another with seventy concubines, and another with sixty-five illegitimate children." In present days, *The Times* of London, July 22, 2009, reported the abuse of 450 children by Catholic priests in the archdiocese of Dublin. Like the Mormon Church, her record of oppression, involvement in political intrigue and overthrow, harlotry, paramours, and the bastard sons of certain Popes, is sickening. And this system claims "infallibility" as "God's true church" to which men must belong in order to be saved. What a monstrous lie! For more on the machinations of Romanism, see *Vows of Secret. The Abuse of Power in the Papacy of John Paul 1I*, by Jason Berry and Gerald Remmer, and Section 95, footnote r. The impudence of priests claiming to absolve sins is among the highest abominations of religion. For an example of this, see Section 13, fourth paragraph of footnote f.

12p-Atheistic stupidity and sharing the guilt. Catholicism is not alone in religious murder. Many of the crusaders, Reformers, Puritans, violent splinter groups of the Anabaptists in Europe, "Protestants," Presbyterians, Anglicans, Puritans, and others are guilty before God. Both Roman Catholics and "Protestants" slaughtered each other and thousands of others "in the name of Christ." *Men who do these deeds serve Satan not God.* Atheist Christopher Hitchens (Christopher means "Christ-bearer"), has written about "Christian religions," and the atrocities they have committed. He blamed all earth's troubles (except dandruff and stinky feet) on Christians. *The world's mass killers, Lenin, Stalin, Mao, Pol Pot and others have all been atheists, just like Hitchens was!* Atheists are unable to distinguish between insane religious zealots, political tyrants murdering their opponents, and the beauty of *true* biblical Christianity. Hitchens proudly blasphemed God in his writings and public debates. This all ended with his death in December 2011. *Now, he knows better!* For more on the various kinds of God and Christ rejecters inside and outside the church, see Section 194, second paragraph of footnote d. The Devil has stationed his people in strategic places to discredit the Savior. Born again, *true* Christians are the minority and will always be (Matt. 7:14).

CHAPTER 6

EMPEROR CAESAR AUGUSTUS ISSUES A DECREE. THE GOVERNOR OF SYRIA PROBLEM. JESUS THE SAVIOR IS BORN AT BETHLEHEM.* HIS FIRST VISITORS APPEAR. HE IS CIRCUMCISED AND TAKEN INTO THE TEMPLE AT FORTY DAYS OLD. SIMEON AND ANNA APPEAR.

Time: The above events took several months

Jesus, the promised Messiah of Israel and Savior of men is born.

*The Lord Jesus was born without the inherit sin of Adam, yet with the potential to be tempted in His human frame. This miracle is beyond explanation and presented no problem to the Holy Trinity. See main heading Section 23 for other comments. Adam was created sinless by the act of God. Man did not beget him. The Son of God was born sinless, yet still in the form of man. The Holy Spirit begot his body. As the first Adam disobeyed God to the wreck and ruin of the human race, so the last Adam obeyed God to the bringing of forgiveness and salvation to all who will repent and believe in Him (Rom. 5:17-19).

Matt.	Mk.	Lk. 2:1-7—*From Nazareth to Bethlehem in Judaea*	John
		Why Joseph and Mary went to Bethlehem **1** And it came to pass in those days,[a] that there went out a decree from Caesar Augustus,[b] that all the world[c] should be taxed. **2** (*And* this taxing was first made when Cy-re-ni-us was governor[d] of Syria.) **3** And all went to be taxed, every one into his own city. **4** And Joseph also went up from Galilee, out of the city of Nazareth, into Judaea, unto the city of David, which is called Bethlehem; (because he was of the house and lineage of David:)[e] **5** To be taxed with Mary his espoused wife, being great with child. ***No room for the Savior*** **6** And so it was, that, while they were there, the days were accomplished that she should be delivered. **7** And she brought forth her firstborn son,[f] and wrapped him in swaddling clothes, and laid him in a manger; because there was no room for them in the inn.[g] (Verse 8 cont. in Section 14.)	

Footnotes-Commentary

[a] **"In those days"** indicates that Luke wrote his book some years later, looking back on the past.

[b] Caesar Augustus, who died in A.D. 14, was the nephew of Julius Caesar. He adopted the name "Augustus" (meaning "honorable"), as a compliment to his self-assumed greatness. He changed the name of the month Sextilis to Augustus (or August) in his own honor, which is still used in our present day calendars. He ruled from 27 B.C. to A.D. 14, which would be into the early teenage years of Jesus. Charles Ludwig wrote of Augustus, "He had sandy hair, merging brows, an odd–shaped head, and penetrating eyes. He suffered from a kind of ringworm that caused his skin to itch; [and] had gallstones." He was also crippled in his left leg and walked with a limp. See Ludwig's work *Rulers of the New Testament Times*, page 27–33. Little did this heathen maniac realize it, but God used him to fulfill Holy Scripture in bringing Mary to Bethlehem. *Here, we see God's sovereign rule in world history.* While she and Joseph were there, the prophecy of Micah 5:2 was fulfilled about seven hundred years *after* it was written.

[c] **"All the world should be taxed."** This meant the all the world under the domination of Rome. In other references, it means the entire habitable world, as in Mk. 16:15 and John 3:16. "Taxed," refers to a government enrollment in which names, occupations and addresses of Roman subjects were listed as well as their birthplace. The purpose of this enrollment was to levy taxes upon all persons under the fist of Caesar's might. There is no reason to change "taxing" into "enrollment" for the taxing began with the listing of thousands of names. Hence, both occurred at the same time. It was a registering for taxation to follow. The Jews were exempt from service in the Roman army but were obligated to pay taxes. *This was the only government taxing in world history that has fallen out to the good of the human race.* Later, the leaders of the Jewish religion tried to entangle the Lord Jesus in a tax evasion plot, which backfired in their faces. Note this in Section 155.

2p-For decades, infidel skeptics have attacked Luke's words about this taxation. There is a powerful and unanswerable defense of this historical event recorded in *The Works of Nathaniel Lardner*, vol. 1, pages 260-345. Dr. Larnder's old work, like a new broom, swept into oblivion the wordy dust and trash of the religious skeptics who spend their lives trying to prove errors in the Bible.

(d) "Cyrenius was governor." This statement has caused tremendous stir for years, the difficulty supposedly being that Cyrenius was not the governor of Syria until some twelve or fifteen years after the birth of Christ. Infidel critics would do well to leave God's Word alone, since all the information regarding Cyrenius and every other Roman governor is not available and will never be. Surely, Doctor Luke was in a better position to know the facts than modern day "scholars" living some two thousand years later. Since the original recipient of the book, Theophilus, was a political official of some high rank, he could easily have checked Luke's assertion to affirm its authenticity. Because Luke wrote by inspiration, his claim is historically accurate. The error lies in the *sources used by the critics* to disclaim Luke's words. The missionary doctor had written with "perfect understanding of all things from the very first" (Lk. 1:3). The overwhelming majority of commentaries call Luke's words into question. Originally, an infidel German critic put this untruth in print, and the masses simply accepted it without considering this an attack on God's Word. True scholarship does point out the "mistakes and errors in Scripture."

2p-The work of Professor William Ramsay is rarely cited regarding this issue. Is it because Dr. Ramsay, who was a *skeptic infidel*, later found the Lord Jesus as personal Savior and worked tirelessly proving his fellow critics wrong? Dr. H. C. Thiessen wrote concerning this textual problem, "Ramsay shows that the inscription at Tibur proved this man [Quirinius or Cyrenius] twice governed Syria under Augustus, and that Josephus referred to the one of them and Luke to the other." See *Introduction to the New Testament,* page 154, by H. C. Thiessen. Even though this historical fact has been engraved in stone and preserved for almost two millennia, infidel critics, possessed by their "academic superiority," are obsessed with trying to prove the Bible wrong. For a brief work demonstrating the New Testament's historical reliability, see *History and Christianity* by J. W. Montgomery. In 1860, George Rawlinson produced an apologetic work entitled, *Historical Evidences of the Truth of the Scripture Records.* In the field of Scripture apologetics, no work has ever been written like that of Nathaniel Lardner (born in 1684), who, in a most profound way, proves the trustworthiness of the four gospels beyond honest refutation. His seventeen-volume opus, entitled *The Credibility of the Gospel History,* was produced between 1727 and 1757. See *Author's Introduction* for more on this subject.

(e) The trip from Nazareth to Bethlehem, traveling on the eastern side of Jordan, was about seventy miles one way. Normally, it would take at least three days. Mary, "great with child," found it seriously difficult at best. She either walked or rode on the back of an animal or on a wagon. Verse 3 unequivocally demonstrates that Joseph was originally from Bethlehem. It is called "his own city," and he must have known the little village quite well, with perhaps some of his family members or acquaintances still living there.

2p-"The lineage of David." Numerous Old Testament passages affirm that Messiah would come into the world through the family of King David. This carried great weight religiously with every pious Jew well informed by his Old Testament. Not only, Christ's foster-father, but His mother, as well, descended from the Davidic line. See verse 5 in the following paragraph. Over twenty years later, Paul, preaching in the synagogue at Antioch of Pisidia, affirmed to his congregation the *fact* that Jesus of Nazareth descended from the line of King David (Acts 13:22-23). Every informed and sensitive Jew understood exactly what Paul was saying, for this was necessary for Messianic credibility. Israel's Messiah had to be from the line of David. For a sweeping examination tracing Christ from Abraham to David to Mary, refer to Sections 6 and 7.

3p-Verse 5. Mary's family line. The controversy over whether or not Mary was of David's lineage is put down by a brilliant comment from Samuel J. Andrews. In 1899, he penned in *The Life of our Lord Upon Earth,* page 59, these pungent words, "As his [Joseph's] wife, she became a true member of David's family." Marriage to Joseph automatically counted her as being part of his family line, which was that of King David. The words, "To be taxed with . . ." include Mary in the taxing. Thus, she was also counted as being from the village of Bethlehem.

4p-"Espoused wife." Though Joseph was already legally married to her, Mary was still called "espoused." This was another ancient Hebrew social customs that westerners find difficult to understand.

(f) "She brought forth." God comes to earth in human form! Refer to Section 1, Part 4, John 1:14, footnote j for more on this amazing fact of history and Satan's age-long madness to counterfeit it through pagan idolatry. Regarding this truth, Augustus Neander wrote, "The extraordinary circumstance of the birth of Christ . . . served as portents of the greatest event in the world's history." See *The Life of Jesus Christ,* page 33, by Neander. This "greatest event" was the atonement for the salvation of men and His resurrection from the dead. From His place in eternity, God projected himself into the limits of human time that we might join Him forever in heaven some day.

2p-"Her firstborn." The obvious meaning is that Mary had other children of which the Lord Jesus was the one born first. *This single passage explodes the myth of perpetual virginity for the mother of Christ.* The same word is used in Section 12, Matt. 1:25, footnote j. Again, Catholic apologists annotate, twist, change, pervert, and corrupt this statement for it exposes more of their false teaching. For the names of Jesus' four half-brothers and the mention of at least two half-sisters, refer to Section 91, Matt. 13:55-56, footnotes e and f. For the early attitude of His half-brothers toward His Messianic claims and work, note Section 111, John 7:5, footnote b. Tradition, gossip, fear, hearsay, and religious imaginations unchecked by Scripture have invented countless errors, and then convinced the ignorant, religiously inclined masses that they are divine truth. In the 16th century, the Papal Church *reintroduced* the Mary myth, announcing that the other children in Joseph and Mary's family belonged to Joseph by a previous marriage. See Section 18, footnote a; Section 28, footnote b; and Section 69, footnote b. For a penetrating look into the teachings of the Roman Catholic Church, see *Secrets of Romanism* by the converted Italian and ex-priest, Joseph Zacchello. Dr. Loraine Boettner's work, *Roman Catholicism,* is a standard classic on this subject. For the last mention of Jesus' human family in the New Testament, refer to Section 207, Acts 1:14. The final mention of Joseph, Jesus' step-father in Scripture is in Section 95, John 6:42. This was about seven months before the cross.

3p-Origin of the first Pope. With the death of Constantine (who in a unique sense was the first Pope) in A.D. 337, he left behind a network of churches whose bishops were state-government orientated puppets. The bishops (pastors) at Rome became bold in their claim of universal jurisdiction over all churches. Robert A. Baker tells us in *A Summary of Christian History*, page 73, that a religious prelate named Leo I was called the first pope ("father") of the church. Andrew Miller, in *Miller's Church History,* pages 297-298, plays down Leo's claim to have ascended to the chair of St. Peter and tells us to make allowances for "the character [spirit] of the times." This "spirit" possessed Bishop Leo. He announced that Peter had been the first bishop of Rome and had authority to rule all Christendom. With the rise of Emperor Valentinian III, the die was cast. He declared that no one could do anything contrary to the "venerable pope of the Eternal City." Next, was the lie that there must be on earth an infallible religious authority to interpret the Scriptures and guide the church. Roman bishops (later called "Popes" or "fathers") appointed themselves and their successors to this mythical position. The fraudulent claim purported by Valentinian III, spread across the world of that era. *Thousands of Christians refused these heresies and were put to death.* For more on the Roman Church and its barbaric history, see Section 12, paragraphs ten through twelve under footnote k.

4p-Kiss Peter's toe and peep at the Pope. In May 1966, while preaching in Rome, Italy, the author visited the Vatican. There stood a giant black statue of "Saint Peter." Hundreds of people were in line waiting to kiss his toe. This act granted them less time of suffering in purgatory after death! At the airport was a peep machine. Inside was a photo of the Pope with a promise that all who looked at him would have "500 years reduced" from their appointed time in purgatory. It cost .50 cents in American coinage for each peep! A converted ex-priest told me that while serving in the Roman Church, a pregnant nun came to the confessional. He told her, "Say three Hail Mary's and God would forgive you." Millions *trust* these lies for the forgiveness of their sins. What blasphemy when mortal man thinks, he acts in the stead of God and can grant forgiveness! Millions of sincere people in this religious system are fulfilling the frightful passage, "There is a way that seemeth right unto a man; but the end thereof *are* the ways of death" (Prov. 16:25). For factual reading regarding priests who were saved and left the Roman Church, see *Far From Rome, Near to God: Testimonies of Fifty Converted Roman Catholic Priests,* edited by Richard Bennett and Martin Buckingham. For more on the dark errors of the Papal machine, see Section 95, John 6:52, footnote r.

5p-Christianized paganism. Mother and child or Madonna. Sacredotalism. Emperor Constantine ordered all pagans to submit to Christian baptism (sprinkling). Thousands of unsaved heathens (escaping death) obeyed. They brought countless pagan religious practices and mysterious rites into the Emperor's state churches. The existing worship of mother and child or Madonna was one of them. Many of these rites remain in churches to this day, still practiced in revised editions. Gradually, the curse of sacredotalism, which goes hand in hand with dead formal religion, ruled. Soon, many ceased to worship Jesus Christ in Spirit and truth. Among the pagan practices brought into the body of believers was that of Mariolatry. Millenniums before these events transpired at Rome, ancient Babylon had been saturated with the worship of the female goddess. She had become a Babylonian deity with her son in arms. (This originated in Egypt with the worship of Isis, called the "Queen of heaven," and "Mother of God." Afterward, it spread to Babylon.) The veneration of mother and child spread over the heathen world. Ancient Germans worshiped her as the virgin Hertha, with a son. Scandinavians called her Dias; Egyptians, Isis. In India, it was Devaki and son Krishna. Asia had Cybele, early pagan Rome had Fortuna both with sons. Mexico, Central, and South America have all yielded figures of this idolatry from their ancient ruins. The cruel Aztecs had their own mother goddess, called Tlazolteotl, who reigned over filth and virtue. She became pregnant and bore Huitzilopochtli, chief god of all men. Museums across the world have many depictions of pagan women holding a baby. In 1966, the author of this book saw in the Louvre Museum at Paris, a massive stature of Isis nursing her infant son. It was dated two thousand years before Christ. The Papal and Orthodox churches have presented this paganism for centuries in modified forms to their parishioners. Today the Catholic Church calls Mary "the mother of God" and "Queen of heaven" just as the heathens of ancient Egypt did Isis thousands of years ago! As stated, it was brought into churches by pagans in the days of Constantine's state church, and developed into "Christian worship." An atheistic medical doctor, Thomas Inman, in *Ancient Pagan and Modern Christian Symbolism,* published 1912, gave a historical coverage of these things. In spiritual blindness, Inman accredited all doctrines of Scripture to heathenism, stripping Christ of His deity, and atoning sacrifice. This has been the fate of millions over the centuries; good with history, but doomed without Jesus Christ the greatest figure in world history.

6p-Mary, the mediator? As with ancient pagans, the Papal Church teaches that a woman is a mediator or mediatrix and that men must pray to her. Her name is Mary. There is not one verse in the Roman Catholic Bible that even suggests this doctrine. It is a demonic revision of ancient heathenism. It was no accident that an early Babylonian goddess was also called "Mylitta," or "Mediatrix." The hundreds of materializations of Mary are demonic apparitions, created by evil spirits to deceive people. Millions of sincere Catholics make pilgrimages to various Marian shrines, seeking miracles of healing and answers to prayer from Mary. Shrines built at these sites attract the superstitious and biblically untaught masses. In some places, horrible satanic apparitions also appear! These evil beings terrorize the worshippers by keeping them in the bondage of superstition. Any miracle that occurs by praying to Mary, or making her promises, is the work of demons, not God! For satanic miracles, see Matt. 7:21–23; Rev. 13:14, 16:14, and 19:20. It is high blasphemy to pray to Mary to save one's soul, bless life, protect children, provide needs, and unite us to the Holy Spirit. The Son of God, Jesus Christ, is degraded and reduced to a back seat driver by this heresy. Mariology is idolatry. Across the Bible, God hates and has cursed all forms of idolatry and idolaters. The final mention of this sin is Rev. 21:8. It declares, "idolaters . . . shall have their part in the lake which burneth with fire and brimstone." It is mentioned again that the earmark of every false religion, cult, sect, fellowship, and denomination is their claim to be God's only voice of truth on earth, that all others are wrong. The Catholic Church and hundreds of others teach this untruth. Jesus Christ alone is the way to God (John 14:6). He is received into one's life by simple faith, apart from the mass, creeds, churches, religions, ceremonies, baptisms, confessions, rituals, and anything else. *Those who teach Him in truth are right; those who do not are wrong.*

7p-"Manger." Places of confinement for domestic beasts are not clean, refreshing, and beautiful. The colorful pictures and Christmas cards of the manger scene fail to portray what the place was like where Jesus was born and how it smelled! It was amid such surroundings that the Son of God entered the human race as a baby.

(g) "No room." Thousands of travelers packed the roads, byways, and lanes, moving to their respective cities and villages for registration. From their home at Nazareth, in the mountains of Zabulon, Joseph, the village carpenter, and Mary, "great with Child," made their way along the winter roads. Upon arrival at Bethlehem, he found no place for Mary at the local inn or tavern. Finally, a crude form of covering was secured in a shelter used for domestic animals, possibly a cave. Upon the birth of our Savior, He was washed, wrapped in swaddling (long strips of linen cloth), and laid in one of the mangers or feeding troughs used for livestock. (These same types of "swaddles" were used for binding up dead bodies!) Years later, Christ's dead body was swaddled again in His burial, but He gave these up also in His resurrection. See John 20:5-7. A Hebrew midwife assisted in the birth of Christ, as this was standard Jewish practice. Older women did this work. Rabbinical law allowed midwives to travel and work on the Sabbath day. The Savior of men was born in the poorest of surroundings (2 Cor. 8:9).

2p-While the masters of Jewish religion pillowed their heads under a peaceful Jerusalem night sky, mumbling a final prayer for "Messiah's soon appearing," their long-awaited King breathed out His first cry amid the lowing of cattle and bleating of sheep. With this infant sob, Israel's Messiah entered into the world that would hate and kill him. Years later, He gave His *final* earthly cry hanging on a Roman cross, dying for the sins of mankind. Ah! What were the first words and thoughts of Joseph and Mary as they looked wonderingly upon that helpless little boy? The eternal God of heaven, wrapped in flesh, is held in the rough hands of a quiet carpenter from Nazareth. He nurses at the bosom of His youthful mother. It was the dawn of world redemption. "The Sun of righteousness" had risen with healing in His wings (Mal. 4:2). The "desire of the nations" had come (Haggai 2:7). And it happened in a cow-barn near little, unimportant Bethlehem. When kings were born, the whole realm would ring with joy. When the Messiah came, earth held her breath and waited in silence before her Creator.

3p-The error of date setting. For an exhaustive, but difficult to read examination into the time of Jesus' birth and various other Scripture dates, see *Handbook of Biblical Chronology*, pages 279-328, by Jack Finegan. For a massive volume covering all the periods of Bible chronology, see *The Annals of the World,* by Archbishop James Ussher (revised and updated by Larry and Marion Pierce, first printing October 2003). Ussher's amazing book is thrown off balance by his *exact* date settings before Abraham was born. Such chronology is impossible. Numerous reference Bibles, borrowing his *assumed* dates for Adam's creation down, have built a complex guesswork chronology, and then printed it as established history. Millions have believed this error and teach it as truth.

4p-The astute Presbyterian minister, Oswald T. Allis (died 1973) gave a terse response to Ussher's incorrect chronology for the dawn of human history. In his work, *The Five Books of Moses*, page 298, Allis wrote, "to insist on the acceptance of that [Ussher's] chronology is to place a stumbling block in the way of those who sincerely desire to accept the Book of Genesis as historically reliable." Allis affirms that the Genesis record of creation cannot be squeezed into a seven-thousand-year mold. It is from this kind of exegesis, mixed with an extreme form of dispensationalism, that the "pick a date" for the return of the Lord Jesus cults were born. From this error, thousands of well meaning but misguided Christians have attempted to determine the day of Jesus' appearing. They are always wrong. Later, in Matt. 16:1 we see that the Pharisees and Sadducees were also date setters. They wanted positive signs that would prove when the materialistic kingdom on earth would be established. Refer to Section 100, Matt. 16:1-4, footnotes a and b for details regarding these predictors of the end time and Jesus' response to their foolishness. *Appendix Eight* also deals with the issue of end time date setters and sign watchers.

History's greatest announcement made to lowly shepherds. The Savior of men is born. He is "Christ [Messiah] the Lord."

Matt.	Mk.	Lk. 2:8-20—*Near Bethlehem*	John
		Humble shepherds hear the glad news first **8** And there were in the same country[a] shepherds[b] abiding in the field, keeping watch over their flock by night. **9** And, lo, the angel of the Lord came upon them, and the glory of the Lord shone round about them: and they were sore [greatly] afraid.[c] **10** And the angel said unto them, "Fear not: for, behold, I bring you[d] good tidings of great joy, which shall be to all people. **11** "For unto you is born[e] this day in the city of David a Saviour, which is Christ [Messiah] the Lord. **12** "And this *shall be* a sign unto you; Ye shall find the babe wrapped in swaddling clothes, [strips of swathing cloth] lying in a manger." ***All heaven bursts into praise*** **13** And suddenly there was with the angel a multitude of the heavenly host praising God, and saying, **14** "Glory to God in the highest and on earth peace,[f] good will toward men." ***The shepherds hurry to find Jesus the Messiah*** **15** And it came to pass, as the angels were gone away from them into heaven, the shepherds said one to another, "Let us now go even unto Bethlehem, and see this thing which is come to pass, which the Lord hath made known unto us." **16** And they came with haste, and found Mary,[g] and Joseph, and the babe lying in a manger. ***The first evangelists*** **17** And when they had seen *it*, they made known abroad the saying which was told them concerning this child. **18** And all they that heard *it* wondered at those things which were told them by the shepherds. **19** But Mary kept all these things, and pondered *them* in her heart.[h] **20** And the shepherds returned, glorifying and praising[i] God for all the things that they had heard and seen, as it was told unto them. (Verse 21 cont. in Section 15.)	

Footnotes-Commentary

[a] The fields near Bethlehem (meaning "house of bread") were famed for rich pastures and attracted shepherds far and near. Here, a thousand years before, David had kept his father's sheep (1 Sam. 17:15). In a stable-shelter near Bethlehem, the "living bread of God sent down from heaven" to dwell among men (John 6:51). R. C. Foster wrote that an early believer named Justin Martyr, who was born in Israel and died in A.D. 166, wrote that Jesus was born in a cave near the village of Bethlehem, which served as a shelter for domestic animals. See Foster's *Studies in the Life of Christ*, page 29. Dean F. W. Farrar, in his work *The Life of Christ,* page 4, also wrote of the same thing. Because Martyr was one of the infamous church fathers, many true conservatives are skeptical of his statement. For comments on these men, see Section 12, sixth paragraph of footnote k.

[b] **"Shepherds."** Elite Jews frowned upon those involved in sheep herding. They were considered commoners and unclean. Their work was looked upon as menial, even vile, and embarrassing. The Talmud tractate, Berchoroth 35b said shepherds were "ignorant people." Baba Kama 94b stated that it was "difficult for them to repent." How marvelous that God chose common persons of this nature and first revealed to them that Messiah had come. The announcement that millions of pious Hebrews longed to hear was made to "unclean men," who found it impossible to get to the temple regularly for ritual cleansing. For more on shepherds, see footnote d below.

2p-Jewish tradition held that the *first* sign of the Messiah's appearing on earth would be near Bethlehem. Further, that He would be revealed at "the tower of the flock" (Migdal Eder) which was located on the road near to the small town. This was a popular haunt for shepherds and their flocks. It should be noted that the word "shepherds" is in the plural form. Verse 9 states the "angel came upon them." Only one shepherd tended a flock. Can this mean that numerous shepherds had gathered on some occasion, and suddenly heard the heavenly herald? Was the supposed cave of His birth located near this "tower of the flock," or was it at the tower, which was abandoned at this time in history? See footnote a above. This was based on Micah's prophecy as recorded in Micah 4:8 with 5:2. Curiously, all lambs born within this area were selected for the Passover sacrifice at the temple in Jerusalem, according to the Talmud tractate, Baba Kama 80a. Further, the rabbis had decreed that the lambs and sheep at this location were to remain there all year long and could *not* shift to other areas for better grazing. Hence, all the prattle about sheep not being in the fields on a "cold, wintry night" falls on its face. See *Life and Times of Jesus the Messiah,* pages 131-32, and Appendix 7 for Alfred Edersheim's explanation of these interesting matters.

(c) **"Sore afraid."** The *greatest* of men throughout the Bible were terror-struck by the visible presence of angelic beings: hence, these shepherds were smitten with fear. Angels played a leading role in the entrance of both John the Baptist and Jesus into the world. They appeared to Zacharias, Section 8, Lk. 1:11; to Mary, Section 9, Lk. 1:26-27; to Joseph, Section 12, Matt. 1:20; to the shepherds in Lk. 2:8-9 above; and to the wise men, who also literally heard them. Refer for this to Section 17, Matt. 2:12.

(d) **"I bring you."** Poor despised shepherds, often looked down upon by society, were chosen of God to first hear history's greatest announcement! The angel's words, "a Saviour, which is Christ the Lord" struck them with awe and overpowering amazement. These simple men of toil knew very well that "Christ" meant Israel's promised Messiah. Suddenly, they hear the news that millions have longed to hear, "The Messiah of Israel has come!" Such a glorious proclamation stunned these men of humble occupation. Tiny sparrows often get the best of crumbs!

(e) **"Born this day."** Some understand this to mean that our Lord was born in the daytime, not at night. The Jewish day actually began at sundown, and though it was dark, it was called the beginning of a new day. This may be what Luke was writing in this passage. Regardless, it is no marvel that Scripture declares, "Thanks be unto God for his unspeakable gift" (2 Cor. 9:15). Here, "the grace of God that bringeth salvation hath appeared to all men" (Titus 2:11). A child is born almost every heartbeat, but that was the most wonderful birth that had ever occurred. Many glorious wonders accompanied it. A mystery of holy awe surrounds this event. The eternal God of heaven who does not slumber (Ps. 121:3), slept His first human night in an ox manger at Bethlehem! With no badge of royalty, He was wrapped in swaddling cloths. He carries none of the world's honor. O the condescending of grace to rescue perishing sinners. "How unsearchable *are* his judgments, and his ways are past finding out!" (Rom. 11:33).

2p-**"Messiah."** These shepherds instantly understood what this meant! See Section 5, Matt. 1:1, footnotes a, and d with footnote b above. The writer of Hebrews says when Christ was born, all the angels of God were commanded to "worship him" (Heb. 1:6). Did this angelic worship service occur during the heavenly praises recorded in Lk. 2:13-14? It is noted that the angel applied three title-Names to the virgin-born infant. He was called "Savior," then "Christ" or "Messiah," and lastly "Lord" or "Jehovah God." He was recognized as both God and man even at His birth. Charles Wesley put it beautifully in the words, "Pleased as man with men to dwell."

3p-**Isa. 9:6.** This is one of the most profound predictions about the coming Messiah-Savior. He is a Child and Son. God's government will rest upon Him. He will be called "Counsellor, The mighty God, The everlasting Father, The Prince of Peace." Clearly, Mary's baby became these things to every mortal who reaches out to Him in faith. This is possible because He is, in fact, The Mighty God of heaven. Liberal theologians debate this last Name of Messiah by reminding us that Isaiah used it as the custom of the easterners did in those days. It was employed to accredit or describe the mighty attributes of kings and great rulers of that era and had no meaning of deity. Rationalists work overtime to set aside the deity of Jesus of Nazareth, the Son of God. For a gigantic dissertation on Isa. 9:6-7, see the work on this subject, *Christology of the Old Testament,* pages 193-199, by E. W. Hengstenberg. Refer also to Section 1, Part 1 footnotes a, b, and c for more on the deity of Christ. For the astounding angelic predictions concerning the Lord Jesus, see Section 9, Lk. 1:32, footnote g.

4p-**His first clothing.** These words mean "swathing bands," similar to those used to bind a wound or wrap the dead. The term does not mean "rags" as popularly believed. Angelic messengers gave a sign whereby the shepherds could identify the promised Messiah: "Ye shall find the babe wrapped in swaddling clothes, lying in a manger." The King of Israel, the Lord of the universe, had been born in a cow stable. Amazed and terrified, the shepherds hastened to Bethlehem to see this great sight, their Messiah! How contrary to what the rabbis had taught.

(f) **"Peace on earth."** Modern day Jewish rabbis quickly point to this passage as proof Jesus was *not* the promised Messiah. "For," they say, "he has brought neither peace on earth nor good will to men." Our Hebrew friends seem to miss continually the words in Lk. 12:51-52. Here, the Lord Jesus said that He had not come to bring world peace! May all Jewish readers understand that the peace Jesus the Messiah brings is *personal* peace in the human heart regarding sin, its terrible guilt, and the blessed assurance of forgiveness. The Messiah of Israel gives *individual* "peace on earth," as well as "justice and good will toward men." Christ did not come to convert nations or ethnic groups. He came to save individuals from their sin and hell, giving them new life and hope. It is clear in Rev. 5:9 that people are saved "out of every kindred, and tongue, and people, and nation." Jews and Gentiles, alike, receive these gifts when they accept by faith Jesus of Nazareth as personal Lord and Savior.

2p-Religious Jews make the mistake of judging Jesus Christ by twentieth-century Judaism rather than first-century Judaism. *The Jews of that era knew He was their Messiah and rejected Him.* The question is not, "Is Jesus of Nazareth the Messiah of present day Judaism?" Rather, it should be, "Is He the Messiah according to the predictions of the Hebrew Scriptures?" Judaism today is vastly different from the Judaism of Jesus' day. Those who teach that Judaism is the father of Christianity are wrong! At best, we could say that Judaism is Christianity's fellow, but never its father. Today, Judaism is greatly fragmented. Their views of the Messiah range from the sublime to the absurd. Reformed Jews do not believe in any Messiah! Many Hebrews simply could not care less. The multiple opinions on the Messiah as expressed by Jews today reflect their deep confusion. The great question that hangs like a sword over their heads is, "Did Jesus fulfill the criteria of their Tanakh (Bible) that qualified Him to be the Messiah of Israel?" Any *honest Jew* who searches the Tanakh and compares his findings with the four gospels will discover that Jesus *is* their promised Messiah. The only excuse left for our Hebrew friends is the old cliché, "The New Testament documents are unreliable." If so, then neither is the Jewish Tanakh on which the gospels are based.

3p-"Christian" tyrants. We fail to realize how *painfully difficult* it is for devout Jews to confess freely that "Yeshua ha-Notzri," or "Jesus of Nazareth" is the Messiah of Israel. One primary reason is that the Hebrew people have suffered unspeakably at the hands of so-called "Christians" in centuries past. The examples listed below are to assure every unsaved Jew, who reads these lines, that some of us *do* understand their plight and seek to bring them to Jesus, their Messiah, and Savior. The "Christians" listed below understood nothing of what the Scriptures taught about the coming of Christ into the world through the Jewish nation, and why He died on the cross. The following quotations ring with the anti-Semitic lie, "Get even with the dirty Jews for killing Jesus." For the explanation of who killed the Savior, see Section 153, footnote f. Below, read the words of famed "Christian" Jew haters of the past, who are oddly, hailed as "great men of the faith." These words are not signs of human error and youthful ignorance. They are the fruits of venomous satanic hate. Certain historians struggle to cover up or mitigate these savage words from "Christian tyrants." The next eight sub headings deal with this and related subjects over parts of church history.

1. **Constantine and the Council of Nicaea were fiercely anti-Jewish.** This meeting of churches convened in A.D. 325 under the direction of Emperor Constantine. He "theoretically" converted to Christianity in A.D. 312, after seeing the sign of a cross in the sky! His reign marked the union of the church with the state. Pagans no longer persecuted Christians; instead, they joined them! One year after the council, Constantine had his eldest son killed by "cold poison," and his wife Fausta, "suffocated in an overheated bath." Civil law and the point of the sword enforced decisions made at church meetings. The "Christian Emperor" used intimidation, persecution, arrests, prisons, torture, and death. *Jews were fiercely hated.* The state-church of the Roman Empire gradually became a bloody tyrant. (The Roman Catholic Church came out of these unholy union years later.) *True* Christians, by the thousands, fled the emperor's ecumenical monster. Within this fleeing "Pilgrim Church," God's truths were cherished and handed down from one generation to the other. The church fathers before this era and during it began to express hatred for the Jews. Ignatius, Justin Martyr, Origen of Alexandria, Peter the venerable (called "the meekest of men") and others were guilty. Some of the details are given below. Refer to *The Roots of Christian Anti-Semitism,* by Malcolm Hay for the shocking survey. For other details on the mentally unstable Constantine, see *Constantine's Sword: The Church and the Jews: A History,* by James Carroll.

2. **Augustine, a "Christian lawyer-bishop,"** (died A.D. 430), wrote of the Jews, "Slay them with a two-edged sword, so that there should be none to oppose your word!" See his *Confessions* 12:14 and *City of God* 18:46. He is a "canoninzed saint of the Roman Church," and people may pray to him! Canonization is a high honor given by the Papal system. The Pope canonized him in A.D. 1303. He was also donned the patron saint of brewers, printers, theologians, and sore eyes! Oddly, a convert to Orthodox Judaism, Dr. Paula Fredriksen, of Boston University, published a work called, *Augustine and the Jews.* She portrays him as a fatherly protector of the Hebrew people who influenced others to shield Israel. The raw truth is that this ex-lawyer from Hippo, like the other church fathers, was a Jew hater. He vacillated from Bible truth to bizarre forms of theological extremes and radicalism. For extended comments on the brilliant but erratic Saint Augustine, refer to Section 135, fourth paragraph of footnote e. For a shocking critique of the doctrinal perversions of Augustine, see *Calvinistic Paths Retraced,* by Samuel Fisk, pages 95-152.

3. **John Calvin,** (died in 1564), was no better. In *A Response to Questions and Objections of a Certain Jew,* pages 22-23, he wrote, "[The Jews] deserve to be oppressed and die without measure or end, and that they die in their misery without the pity of anyone." Nice words from the "world's greatest theologian."

4. **The Roman Catholic Church** has a bloody record of murdering thousands of Jews. The insane Emperor Constantine popularized the pseudo "sign of the cross." It has become an emblem of infamy to Israel, especially those learned in their history. During her inquisitions, the Roman Church murdered millions of Jews and Gentiles, who would not kiss the cross and confess loyalty to the papacy. Professor David

Kertzer (a pen name), published in 2001 the amazing book, *The Popes Against the Jews: The Vatican's role in the Rise of Modern Anti-Semitism*. This book shows how the Catholic Church, because of its historical campaign of hatred against Jews, helped make the Holocaust possible. An earlier book by Dr. Kertzer, *The Kidnapping of Edgardo Mortara*, told the factual story of how a six-year-old Hebrew child was kidnapped by Vatican thugs, taken to Rome, and reared by the Pope to become a priest. This revelation caused an international stir and fueled anti-papal sentiments among thousands of readers. Kertzer's works are not anti-Catholic but factual and impeccably documented. Later, history also revealed that officials in the Roman Church secretly aided Jew hating Nazi war criminals in escaping to South America at the end of World War II. (American intelligence services did the same!) The Papacy and its thugs covered up the "Odessa plot" for decades. See *The Real Odessa: How Peron Brought the Nazi War criminals to Argentina*, released in 2002, by Uki Goni, for the details. This work produced a tremendous upheaval in governments and churches.

5. **Martin Luther** (died A.D. 1546) fiercely hated the Jews. Marius Baar, in *The Unholy War*, page 121, records some of Luther's vitriolic words: "The Jews deserve the most severe penalties. Their synagogues should be leveled, [and] their homes destroyed, they should be exiled into tents like gypsies. Their religious writings should be taken from them. All professions should be closed to them. Only the hardest and coarsest work should be permitted them. Rich Jews should have their fortunes confiscated, and their money used to support Jews, who are willing to be converted." Luther concluded his tirade of racial hatred with this policy: "If these measures are unsuccessful, the Christian princes [magistrates] should have the duty of driving the Jews from their lands as they would rabid dogs." Luther's confusion regarding Israel is reflected in another statement, where he wrote, "we should love Jews, and bring them to Christ!" Kill or convert is anti-Christian. Hitler used Luther's vitriolic words to inflame the German people during his rise to power and later to justify his genocide of millions of Hebrews. Luther's work, *On the Jews and Their Lies,* reeks with hatred for these people. For his shocking opinion of communion and baptism, see Section 203, the eighth paragraph of footnote d.

6. **John Chrysostom** (died A.D. 420), the renowned Christian preacher referred to as the "golden voice one," was fiercely anti-Semitic. Some of his words about the Jewish people are anything but "golden." Edward H. Flannery records these in *The Anguish of the Jews*, pages 48–49. As with Luther, mentioned above, during World War II, the Nazi Party also used Chrysostom's writings to legitimize their slaughter of Jews. Chrysostom's objection that "the Jews killed Jesus" is theological ignorance. Jaroslav Pelikan, in his work, *The Christian Tradition*, vol. 1, page 25, cites him as saying of communion, "the Lord being sacrificed and laid upon the altar and the priest standing and praying over the victim." The Jew-hater Chrysostom (like Augustine) is listed as a "Doctor of the Roman Catholic Church." How "great men" failed to understand that Christ's death was not the work of the Jews, the Romans, and Pilate, so much as it was the plan of God for man's redemption, is odd. How they did not see their sins as the first cause of Jesus' death, and rejoice that He died for them, is troubling. Did they even understand why Jesus went to the cross in the first place? This is a terrible, lingering, unanswered question hanging over church history. Just as bad was their dogma on how one partakes of the atonement of Christ and salvation. To John Chrysostom and his kind, it was by sprinkling water on their heads and partaking of communion.

7. **The crusaders.** The word means, "The war of the cross." They lived during the eleventh through the thirteenth centuries. The crusaders were murderous, Roman Catholic zealots who lost their minds over a piece of real estate, named Jerusalem! Pope Urban II launched the first crusade in about 1095. They murdered Jews by the thousands, often herding them into the synagogues and burning them alive while marching about the inferno singing, "Christ, we adore thee." See Michael L. Brown's work, *Our Hands Are Stained with Blood: The Tragic Story of the "Church" and the Jewish People,* pages 88–97. Brown points out that *true* Christians had no part in these barbaric deeds committed in the Name of Jesus Christ. His deductions are correct. All Jewish readers should understand that such horrific deeds were the work of men possessed by the Devil; not *true* Christians. Adolf Hitler and Henry Ford stand up front, as some of history's most notorious Hebrew-haters. Islam has sworn to exterminate Israel. Behind this hatred is Satan, who seeks vengeance on the nation that gave us Jesus, the Savior of mankind.

8. **Thomas Aquinas.** Richard Wurmbrand, in his book *Christ on the Jewish Road*, page 42, quoting from another source, stated that this famed doctor of the Papal Church said, "The Jew is the enemy of Jesus." In this, the "greatly learned" Aquinas reflected his zero understanding of Holy Scripture.

4p-The people listed above were ignorant of God's *chief purpose* for Israel, which was to send His Son into the world to be the Savior of men. Their words and deeds often smacked of a religious insanity. They talked and performed like monsters when dealing with the Jews. An evil psychotic intent and spiritual aberration gripped them. On the other hand, there are times a Christian finds it necessary to weigh the words and actions of others regarding their behavior. However, his thumb should not be on the scales. *True* Christians must not measure the actions of others by themselves, or how they act, but rather by God's Word, rightly divided. "Christians," filled with hatred for those who do not agree with them on every *tiny point,* will later find that their hatred bites like a serpent. Standing in the forest, we only see a few trees. Outside, we see many of them. God help us as, we help ourselves to keep the outside look right, before stepping inside with judgment. Note also, Section 19, sixth paragraph of footnote c.

5p–For a dispassionate examination of the Reformers in general, and the heinous crimes they committed in the Name of God and truth, see Leonard Verduin's work, *The Reformers and Their Stepchildren.* The Calvin Foundation of Grand Rapids, Michigan, originally sponsored this work. It was a literary attempt to wash the blood of innocents from their hands, received by doctrinal inheritance from their Calvinistic ancestors. Some Calvinists hate Verduin's work and have attempted to dismantle it by lies and innuendos. Various "heroes of Christianity" have acted like animals in dealing with fellow humans, especially Jews. Their conduct is foreign to the teachings of the New Testament. Satan is mirrored in the Reformers as they imprisoned, tortured, and murdered many people (including Jews) in order to establish their church at Geneva. It is not how much of the Bible someone quotes, or the good things he fights for, but whether he demonstrates the truth of Scripture in *daily* practical life and conduct. Those who do not are the enemies of Christ and His gospel. May all Hebrews, who read these lines, understand that such persons do not represent *true* Christianity. In hating Israel, any nationality or religion, they are walking in darkness. Jesus of Nazareth is the "Mashiach," or "Messiah," and mankind's only Savior. He is the Prince of Peace as predicted in the Hebrew Tanakh (Isa. 9:6)! *On the other hand, Jews who hate Jesus Christ are equally guilty.*

6p-Double minded. A sharp double-mindedness exists among some of the Jewish people. If one exposes their evils, he is instantly branded "anti-Semitic." These protectors of Hebrew sins are as guilty as their persecutors listed above. Both Jews and Gentiles need the redeeming grace of God, found only in Jesus the Messiah. He alone makes the beautiful and eternal difference in life and conduct. Many Christians are living on the smell of an empty perfume bottle as they imagine their way into heaven. Those saved by grace, obedient to Holy Scripture, will not make statements of vitriolic hatred toward Jews or any person. The men listed above, with many others, had something seriously wrong with their hearts! Many books on church history, seminary lectures, and general Christian teaching often do not tell the truth about the men listed under the third paragraph of footnote f above. It is silenced in order to maintain "ecclesiastical myths" and whitewashing those who carried hatred in their hearts for others. Atheist Karen Armstrong, in *A History of God,* pages 77-78, wrote this stinging word, "Christianity makes a song and dance about creeds and beliefs." Regarding unbelieving Jews, who persecute their fellow Hebrews for trusting Christ, refer to Section 146, footnote o. Jehovah calls all Jews to "B'rith chadashah" (repent of sin) and trust "Yeshua ha'Mashiach" (Jesus the Messiah). God's new covenant for Israel and all men is recorded in the Hebrew Bible (Tanakh), in Jer. 31:31-33. Rabbi Paul explained its meaning and application in Heb. 8:7-13 and 9:1-28.

(g) Found Mary. Searching diligently nearby caves and shelters, these wide-eyed shepherds found the Messiah. Albeit, He was not arrayed in the purple and scarlet of royalty or crowned with gold; rather, this helpless infant, their King, is cuddled in the bosom of His young mother, or sleeping and cradled in the fodder of oxen. Upon departing this awesome scene, they spread the news, not only across the hill country of Judaea, but also in the regions about Bethlehem and Jerusalem. As with the birth of John, again the countryside vibrates with rumors of another strange babe and the amazing events surrounding his birth. Who would believe that Israel's King and Messiah had come to earth in such contemptible conditions and amid such base surroundings? This was hardly compatible with the rabbinical Messianic theology sounded out every Sabbath from the synagogue chair.

(h) Mary's youthful reflections. She begins to look back, put together, and compare the odd events that led to the birth of her Son. *Good mothers are the best natural historians of their children, from conception through birth, and especially the early years.* Mary "pondered" in her heart. The word "pondered" carries the idea of setting things side by side for comparison. Surveying it all, she knew that these events were acts of God. Mary, Joseph, and a few others understood there was a virgin birth, that it was a singular miracle, but had no idea concerning the destiny of that precious baby. For the shocking religious abuse of Mary, Jesus' mother, see Section 13, footnote f.

(i) "Glorifying and praising God." *Angles in heaven and men on earth celebrated the birth of Christ. Why should not we?* Pagans may spoil such events, we do not! Simple and unlearned, the shepherds praised Jehovah over what had transpired. The unfathomable depths of His counsel moved into fulfillment. The foundations of the deep had been broken up. The "desire of the nations" was at hand (Hag. 2:7). The first chapter in the eternal redemption of mankind was opened. The dawning light of the Son that faintly shone from Bethlehem's barn had been predicted some seven hundred years prior in Isa. 60:1-4. Soon, His beams of hope, forgiveness, and salvation would flood across the masses of lost humanity. The "base things of the world" God continually chooses to carry first the glad tidings (1 Cor. 1:28). Of the fantastic wonders surrounding the birth of Jesus, nothing was seen on the surface of human society save that ripple in the manger and witness of the shepherds. Some of earth's greatest events had very humble beginnings. The morning after, the world went on with its business of earthly things, each one taken up with his interest and projects. That darling infant, virgin-born, was God in human flesh (1 Tim. 3:16). He committed Himself in helplessness to the hands of Joseph, the quite carpenter, and young Mary. How incredible that the salvation of men should hang on such a slender thread as the feeble heartbeat of an infant sleeping in an ox manger, somewhere in Israel's smallest village (Micah 5:2). Thus, are the amazing ways of God!

Circumcising and naming of baby Jesus.

Matt.	Mk.	Lk. 2:21—At *Bethlehem*	John
		21 And when eight days were accomplished for the circumcising of the child,[a] his name was called JESUS, which was so named of the angel before he was conceived in the womb.[b] (Verse 22 cont. in Section 16.)	

Footnotes-Commentary

[a] **Circumcision.** Technically, this verse is not an Old Testament quote. It refers to an act performed in obedience to Lev. 12:3 in the Torah Law. The practice of circumcision for the Jews started with Abraham some two thousand years earlier in Gen. 17:9-14, or some four hundred years before the Torah Law was given to Moses and Israel (Gal. 3:17). It was a mark carried in the flesh of every Jewish male to remind him daily of his covenant relation with Jehovah God. Gen. 17:14 reads that every male without it would be "cut off" from Israel or killed. This was because they had broken God's covenant. During the long and difficult sojourn of Israel in Egypt, the Jews had become lax in keeping this rite handed down from Abraham, Isaac, and Jacob. Breaking this command of God concerning Gershom was so serious that it almost cost Moses his life as seen in Ex. 4:24-26. He was saved from God's judgment by the actions of Zipporah, his wife. In John 7:22, Jesus confirmed that circumcision was not originally of Moses, but given to the fathers or founding heads of Israel, Abraham being the origin of the nation.

2p-The circumcision of baby Jesus probably took place somewhere in Bethlehem. It was *before* the trip to the temple for Mary's purification (Section 16). In this rite, He was "made like unto his [Hebrew] brethren" and became a physical member of the covenant nation of Israel (Heb. 2:16, 17). On this occasion of circumcision, His blood was first shed. Beth Moore, in her book *Jesus the One and Only*, pages 39-43, sees in Christ's circumcision a shadow of future redemption provided on the cross for mankind (Eph. 1:7 with Titus 2:14). For further comments on Jewish circumcision, see Section 11, Luke 1:59, footnote a. For the naming of this child before birth, see Section 12, Matt. 1:21, footnote e, footnote b below. In the context of verse 21 above, apparently the pronoun "they" in Matt. 1:23 refers to Joseph and Mary. If this is correct, *when* "they" called Jesus by the glorious Name "EMMANUEL," is unknown. Compare this with Isa. 7:14, where the wording suggests that Mary was the first to use this Name for her Son. Refer to Section 14, footnotes h and I, for further details on this subject.

[b] The rabbis taught that God had named six persons before they were born. These were Isaac, Ishmael, Moses, Solomon, Josiah, and the Messiah. The angel announced to the shepherds that Mary's baby was "a Saviour, which is Christ [Messiah] the Lord" (Lk. 2:11). See Section 5, Matt. 1:1, footnotes a and d, for more on Jesus the Messiah. This "Saviour-Christ-Messiah" was named "JESUS" when only eight days old at His circumcision. See footnote a above. Thus, we have JESUS, the Savior, Christ, and Messiah; all three in One. The name "Jesus" is derived from the ancient name "Joshua" and at best means, "God is salvation." Jewish teachers affirmed that Israel's *(political)* salvation would come from their Messiah. The conclusion from the meaning of His Name is that Jesus of Nazareth, the virgin-born Son of Mary, is the promised Messiah of Israel, the only hope of *spiritual salvation*. He was "Emmanuel" or "God with us."

2p-Jesus Christ, alone, saves men from their sins and prepares them for eternity because He is the true God-Man from heaven. Just as some chemical elements combine with certain other elements, not with all of them, so man was the only being with whom God is somehow compatible. God did not become an animal, fowl, or some other form of lower life. In the Person of Christ, He became one of our human order of beings, yet without sin. The fact that God became man, mysteriously reflects a uniqueness in sinful man that attracted His attention. Our sin violently offended His holiness, yet touched His loving compassion. That tiny babe, crying loudly at the pain of circumcision, set up a signpost that pointed to the agony of His death on the cross for the sins of humankind.

3p-After receiving life through His death and resurrection, the Bible offers many promises of hope for the Christian. These should not be taken to radical extremes resulting in disappointment, injury, or death. God's promise to save us from fire and drowning (Isa. 43:2), is usually fulfilled by our staying away from dangerous fires and uncertain waters. Only fools test water's depth by stepping in or the fire's heat by pushing a hand into its flame. The actions of common sense could be some of the greatest miracles in the Christian life. If not, then we trust in simple faith the Lord of heaven to attend to those things beyond our understanding and practical reactions. For more on this, see over looked subject, see Section 46, footnote q.

4p-The sinless humanity of Christ. The big question is, "Did Jesus inherit a sinful nature from Mary His mother?" He came in a human frame, subject to temptation, but lived victorious in the power of the Holy Spirit, and God's Word, thus, He was unable to commit sin. See *The Virgin Birth of Christ*, by James Orr, page 197 for an attempted explanation of this divine phenomenon. With the essential elements of human nature, the Savior could still say to the wrangling Jews a few months before His death on the cross, "Which of you convinceth me of sin?" (John 8:46). Over the centuries, wicked men have raged at this sinless claim of Christ.

The infant Messiah-Savior is taken into the temple for the first time.
Two elderly people appear and speak to Joseph and Mary.

Matt.	Mk.	Lk. 2:22-38—*In the temple at Jerusalem*	John
		Joseph and Mary obey the Mosaic Law **22** And when the days of her purification according to the law[a] of Moses were accomplished, they brought him to Jerusalem, to present *him* to the Lord;[b] **23** (As it is written in the law of the Lord,[c] **"Every male that openeth the womb shall be called holy to the Lord;"**) **24** And to offer a sacrifice according to that which is said in the law of the Lord,[d] **"A pair of turtledoves, or two young pigeons."** *Brief introduction of Simeon:* *led by the Holy Spirit he enters the temple* **25** And, behold, there was a man in Jerusalem, whose name *was* Simeon;[e] and the same man *was* just and devout, waiting for the consolation of Israel: and the Holy Ghost[f] was upon him. **26** And it was revealed unto him by the Holy Ghost, that he should not see death, before he had seen the Lord's Christ. **27** And he came by the Spirit into the temple: and when the parents brought in the child Jesus, to do for him after the custom of the law, *Simeon's amazing prophecy* **28** Then took he him up in his arms, and blessed God, and said,[g] **29** "Lord, now lettest thou thy servant depart in peace, according to thy word: **30** "For mine eyes have seen thy salvation, **31** "Which thou hast prepared before the face of all people; **32** "A light to lighten the Gentiles, and the glory of thy people Israel." *Joseph and Mary are amazed* **33** And Joseph and his mother marvelled[h] at those things which were spoken of him. *Simeon warns Mary* *of strange and troubling days because of this Child* **34** And Simeon blessed[i] them, and said unto Mary his mother, "Behold, this *child* is set for the fall and rising again of many in Israel; and for a sign which shall be spoken against; **35** "(Yea, a sword shall pierce through thy own soul also,) that the thoughts[j] of many hearts may be revealed." *Brief introduction of Anna* **36** And there was one Anna,[k] a prophetess, the daughter of Phanuel, of the tribe of Aser: she was of a great age, and had lived with an husband seven years from her virginity; **37** And she *was* a widow of about fourscore and four years, which departed not from the temple, but served *God* with fastings and prayers night and day. *Anna enters, gives thanks, and tells others of Jesus* **38** And she coming in that instant gave thanks likewise unto the Lord, and spake of him [Jesus] to all them that looked[l] for redemption in	

Matt.	Mk.	Lk. 2:38-40—*From Jerusalem to Nazareth*	John
		Jerusalem. ***They return to Nazareth: the physical growth of Jesus*** **39** And when they had performed all things according to the law of the Lord, they returned into[m] <mark>**Galilee, to their own city Nazareth.**</mark> **40** And the child grew, and waxed strong in spirit, filled with wisdom: and the grace of God was upon him.[n] (Verse 41 cont. in Section 20.)	

Footnotes-Commentary

[a] Joseph and Mary's quickness to obey God's commands is reflected in these verses and in Lk. 2:39 above and in Lk. 2:41. Joseph's plans to bypass the Law of Moses in the case of his beloved Mary when first suspecting her of adultery have been noted in Section 12, Matt. 1:19, footnote c. His actions were totally justified because Mary was innocent. Now, this wonderful couple brings the Lord of the temple into the temple of the Lord. The baby Jesus was forty days old. See footnote b below.

[b] **"To present him to the Lord."** Verses 23 and 24 record their observance of two different parts of the Torah Law. First, the redemption of the firstborn, and second, the purification of a mother after childbirth. The ceremony regarding the firstborn son was designed to remind the Hebrew people of their ancestor's deliverance from slavery in Egypt. At the end of ten horrible plagues upon the Egyptians, the death angel killed the firstborn son of every Egyptian throughout the entire nation. In this ceremony of the law, the Jews would dedicate every firstborn son of theirs to the service of Jehovah God. In reversal, God would allow them to redeem the boy back to themselves for a payment of five shekels, which is about 32 cents (Num. 18:16). Joseph paid this amount to the attending priest to keep baby Jesus as his own. The officiating priest would take the infant, wave him back and forth over his head, and recite a benediction. The carpenter from Nazareth loved that infant, as if He were his son; he redeemed Him as his firstborn and labored with his hands to provide food, clothing, and shelter for that blessed Child. Thus, it was only natural that Scripture would speak of Jesus as "the son of Joseph" (John 1:45), though, in fact, He was not. Refer to Section 6, footnote e for further details on this thought. Mary's purification was according to Lev. 12:1-8 and took place in the Women's Court of the temple forty days after the birth of a son. See third paragraph of footnote d below. She and Joseph traveled the few miles from Bethlehem northward to Jerusalem's temple for this occasion. Doubtless, these rules often served as a great burden to the people of Israel. Hence, they were often called "a yoke" by those saved from them (Acts 15:10 with Gal. 5:1).

2p-Today, Orthodox Jewish women, having no temple, immerse ("mikveh") themselves in water in observance of ancient Torah Law. According to Lev. 12:1-6, the time of purification for a mother following the birth of a female child was eighty days. This was double the time for a male child. The Jewish teachers reckoned that because a woman brought sin into the world, all succeeding females shared twice in Eve's guilt. Therefore, double time was required for the mother of the female child to be purified, and fit again for public and social contact. The guilt of the first woman, Eve, is also reflected in the ancient Jewish custom of having a woman lead the funeral procession to the burial site. See this illustrated in the death of the widow's son at Nain in Section 61, Lk. 7:12, all of footnote b.

[c] Luke quotes this from selected portions of Ex. 13:2, 12, and 15. Theophilus, the original recipient of this book, obviously understood much of the Jewish Law and its requirements, for Luke gave no detailed or pedant explanation to this friend.

[d] **Doves and pigeons.** Cited from Lev. 12:8. This offering was reserved for the poorest in Israel and reveals the economic status of Joseph. It was for the poverty-stricken class of Hebrews, since it allowed for the smallest offering in the Levitical category. Our Lord sanctified the state of *honest* poverty by passing through it and later preaching the gospel to the poor. In this Jewish ritual, Mary would lay her hands on the pigeons, and the officiating priest would wring one bird's neck at the southwest side of the altar and offer it as a sin offering. He would then present the other as a whole burnt offering. Mary would stand at the far gate of the Women's Court or treasury called the Nicanor gate. The priest would lightly sprinkle her with the blood of the first dove. Joseph, holding baby Jesus, stood nearby watching the ceremony. For Jesus and His mother, it was necessary to pass through these rites, or according to rabbinical rules, they would have been barred from both the temple and synagogues of the land.

2p-Cunningham Geikie in *The Life and Words of Christ*, page 159, points out an ironic note. The pigeons Joseph purchased for this humble offering were obtained from the "shops for selling doves" that were built on the Mount of Olives and owned by Annas, at that time the high priest of Israel. He sold each pair for one piece of gold! For more on the religious crook Annas, see Section 21, Part 1, number 6 under footnote b.

3p-Only Mary was ritually unclean according to the law; however, there were cases when the father also chose to undergo a bathing or baptism (mikveh) in water. This seems to have been the kind of purification that Paul later undertook for himself in Acts 21:22-27. He did this, *not* to demonstrate that he was under the law, but to show that he would become all things to all men that he might win some to Christ (1 Cor. 9:20-23.) Even to this present time, sensitive and pious Jews often immerse themselves in a "mikveh" (baptism) on Friday afternoon in order to be ritually pure before the beginning of the Sabbath. Today, many Orthodox Jewish women, after childbirth, lower themselves into water as a way of observing this ancient ritual. Technically, in the sight of God it only amounts to getting wet and carries no merit of forgiveness or salvation.

(e) **"Simeon."** There were many men named Simeon in Jerusalem at this time. Some older writers have conjectured that this Simeon was the son of Hillel, one of Israel's most distinguished teachers of the law and a president of the Sanhedrin for many years. How beautiful is the sight of aged men of faith and piety, hair whitened by the passing of many seasons, faces lined from age, yet still led of the Holy Ghost, patiently waiting, for the moment, when they shall "see the Lord's Christ." Aged Simeon's joy arrived that day when he stepped into the Women's Court of Jerusalem's temple, found his way through the crowds, and drew near the semi-circled steps that led up to the Nicanor gate. The "consolation" and "comfort" spoken of by Isaiah were, according to the rabbis, names for their coming Messiah (Isa. 40:1, 49:13, 52:9). With these verses from Isaiah, see 2 Cor. 1:3-4 with Phil. 2:1 footnote f below.

2p-**"Just and devout."** He was just in all his dealings with men, and devout in his heart toward God. It takes both virtues to demonstrate true faith in God. Some men are just but not devout. Others are devout but not just. There are some whose religion is simply being good and honest, but they do not know Christ as Lord and Savior.

(f) Again, we meet with the Holy Spirit of God. He was "upon" Simeon, led him to the temple, and assured him that before death, he would see Christ the Messiah. See Section 10, the second paragraph, footnote b, for comments on the Holy Spirit in the Old Testament era and long before Pentecost.

(g) Shocked, Joseph and young Mary had the infant swept from their arms by this strange old man. Oh, the glory of that moment as he pressed to his bosom the Messiah of Israel. What must this aged saint have felt? Simeon burst into a song of glorious praise, no doubt dancing about with the Child cuddled in his breast. What must the hundreds of onlookers standing nearby have thought? Joseph and Mary stood dumbfounded and speechless at the scene. A proverb states, "Old eyes in the ways of God see clearer than those of youth who are not!" For more on their reactions, see footnote h below.

2p-Verses 28-32 contain the prophetic words of Simeon. At a sublime moment in the past, God had promised that death would not take him away until his eyes had seen heaven's salvation (verses 29-30). This forty-day-old infant was the "salvation" of "all people," and "a light to lighten the Gentiles" (verses 31-32). The ancients interpreted the "light" in Ps. 43:3 as a Name for their coming Messiah. Perhaps Simeon had Isa. 52:10 in mind when he spoke of "seeing" the Messiah, and Isa. 42:6 with 49:6 as predictions referring to the conversion of Gentiles. No man is ready to die until, by the eye of faith, he has received the Lord's Christ. The synagogue taught that the Jewish Messiah was "the glory of Israel" (verse 32), and the temple was "the light of the world." Thirty years later, Christ standing in this same Women's Court or treasury declared, "I am the light of the world" (John 8:1-2, 12).

(h) **"Marvelled."** The blessed couple stood transfixed in holy awe and amazement. They understood little or nothing of what had transpired before their eyes and in their ears. This would come later.

(i) **"Blessed them."** This was a typical Jewish custom. The elderly Simeon, standing in the Court of Women, raised both hands to heaven and called on the "God of Abraham, Isaac and Jacob" to bless this special pair, a Galilean carpenter and his young wife. Suddenly, Simeon directed his predictions to Mary. He informed her that this Child would cause the following to happen:

1. **Many Jews in Israel will "fall,"** and many will "rise," because of Jesus. In this, Simeon referred to the Messianic passage in Isa. 8:14-15. Those who receive Him as the promised Messiah will "rise" to new life, and those who reject Him "fall" to damnation. See with this, Section 153, Matt. 21:42-44, Section 159, Matt. 23:33 and 1 Peter 2:4-8.

2. **He will be a "sign which shall be spoken against."** This may refer to the Messianic prophecy in Isa. 11:10-12 and to the sign of His resurrection from the dead. See all under main heading Section 67 for more on Jesus and signs. The Sanhedrin paid the Roman guards to lie about the sign of Jesus' rising from the dead (Matt. 28:11-15). Simeon warned Mary of the deadly opposition her Child would receive. We wonder what she thought.

3. **The "sword" piercing Mary's soul** speaks of the heartache she suffered until the total truth of her Son's work and mission on earth was understood. Mary became acquainted with great sorrow, as did her Son (Isa. 53:3). Because of the humanly impossible circumstances of Jesus' birth, she became the object of scandalous shame and carried in her heart (as any loving mother would) the pain such things can produce. The sight of Him dying on a pagan Roman cross was the chief sword that pierced her soul to its hilt. This is explained in Section 190, John 19:25-27, footnote j. Over the course of His ministry, many of His woes became hers. It is true with all good mothers. Refer to Section 12, Matt. 1:18, footnote b

(j) This expression must be connected with the latter portion of verse 34, which reads that Jesus will be "for a sign which shall be spoken against." The unique Person and work of Christ have for centuries drawn from the hearts of men their true thoughts and feelings. Millions have shown how violently they hate His virgin birth, sinless life, and perfect holiness. His precious blood shed to atone for the sins of humanity is, to this moment, openly cursed and trampled underfoot by the godless. Others, silently in their hearts, hold contempt for the Christ of heaven, or they courteously neglect His claims. On the other hand, having been saved by His grace, millions have loved Him even to the point of joyfully laying down their lives for His Name's sake. *Nothing so brings out the true thoughts of men as to tell them about the Lord Jesus, God's beloved Son, who died for their sins.* The author has seen these reactions from men and women thousands of times. Simeon's prophecy remains valid to this very hour.

(k) Anna was a "prophetess." At certain times, the Holy Spirit empowered her to prophesy. This occurred time by time in Israel. Prophets did not always predict the future, often they dealt with the present. Their prime role was to speak for God, whatever He had put in their hearts to say. Old Anna was of the "tribe of Aser" (or Asher in Ex. 1:1, 4), proving that this tribe was *not* totally lost in the Assyrian captivity some seven hundred years prior (2 Kings 17). This further exposes the genealogical errors of the British Israelite or Anglo-Israel cult. The tribe of Asher had settled in Galilee (Josh. 19:24-31), a place the religious hierarchy of Jerusalem deemed unfit to produce a prophet. The term "great age" (verse 36) means, "stricken in years" (Lk. 1:7). Anna had been married for seven years and then a widow for fourscore and four years (or eighty-four) a combined total of ninety-one years. Assuming she married at the age of fourteen (most Jewish girls were married by this time), she would have been about one hundred five years old when she encountered baby Jesus in the temple.

2p-It was the high mark of piety for the aged to spend much time in the temple compound in prayer and fasting. From the time of Moses' tabernacle down to Herod's temple, women, both good and bad, assembled at the door of God's house for prayer and religious devotions. Note this in 1 Sam. 2:22; and Ex. 38:8 with John 8:1-4. Near the end of His life, Jesus described the temple as the "house of prayer" in Lk. 19:45-48. The Sanhedrin often provided sustenance and shelter for aged saints who frequented the temple to spend time in prayer. The text reads that she "departed not from the temple" (verse 37).

(l) "Looked for redemption." This affirms that some among Israel were looking for some kind of deliverance or redemption at this time. It is true that Jewish opinion varied on this as on everything else, yet there was a uniform Messianic expectation among many of the Jews. In this Section, we meet two of them. Appearing on the scene just as Simeon lifted his voice in praise to God, Anna instantly knew who this Child was. Hastily departing from the temple precincts, she searched out those whom she knew were also looking for redemption in Jerusalem. Possibly, Anna was thinking of Isa. 52:9 as she spoke these words. This suggests there was a prevailing expectancy among some that Messiah was soon to appear. This expectancy is reflected in Section 17, footnotes c and d. What grand news as she spoke of Jesus to all who were looking for the Messiah. Anna knew this babe in the arms of old Simeon was Messiah the Prince of Israel. Probably, the redemption she spoke of, upon sight of the baby, was the hope of Israel's liberation from Gentile domination and oppression. This hope of *political deliverance* was also referred to as "waiting for the kingdom of God" (Mk. 15:43 with Lk. 17:20, and Section 11, Lk. 1:74, footnote l). The Talmud in tractate, Shabbath 138b speaks of "redemption when Messiah shall appear." *For the greater part, at this time in the Jewish mind redemption consisted of Messiah establishing a physical, material kingdom on earth.* Only a few understood the fact of *personal salvation* from sin and eternal life in Christ through the death of their Messiah, Jesus of Nazareth. Jewish literature reveals that such things as "charity, repentance, and observance of the ceremonial laws" would bring about Messianic redemption in this era. The Talmud tractate, Baba Bathra 10a states this very thing. However, many other pious acts were required, as it seemed that each rabbi had a different opinion about Messiah's salvation for Israel. For coverage of the subject of ancient Jewish redemption, see *The Messianic Idea in Israel*, Chapter IV, by the late Joseph Klausner, a non-Christian, Lithuanian Hebrew. Klausner also fathered the shameful book, *Jesus of Nazareth*, in which he called into question most major doctrines of the New Testament and wrote great injustices of Jesus of Nazareth. He concluded his comedy with these silly words, "Jesus became a Christian." However, it was a bad day for Klausner's blasphemy when the Christian Jew, Richard Wurmbrand answered him in the apologetic, *The Jews and Jesus of Nazareth. Anti-Klausner.*

2p-"Law of the Lord." There is no difference between the "Law of the Lord" and the "Law of Moses." The numerous law cults struggle to demonstrate this in order to prove their Sabbath worship.

3p-For salvation under the Old Testament, note Section 30, second paragraph of footnote h. For the Hebrew materialistic conception of their earthly kingdom, see Section 39, footnotes a and g. At Pentecost, the true redemption provided by His atonement on the cross was fully understood by all believing Jews. How people were saved during the ministry of Christ is explained in Section 144, footnote i.

(m) "Nazareth" is shaded in gray, being a prediction from the Old Testament. Refer to Section 18, Matt. 2:23, footnote h and i for this prediction and how Matthew found it in the Old Testament Scriptures. Among the people of Galilee, Jesus spent most of His life and the days of His public ministry. After Joseph and Mary returned to Nazareth, we hear almost nothing of the Savior until He is twelve years old. In verse 40, Luke informs Theophilus that Messiah grew physically, mentally, and spiritually during these silent years. The physical body of Jesus did not come to maturity at once, but came by degrees as with all normal children. Christ began His life as a helpless Child, subject to all of humanity's weaknesses, frailties and conditions, yet, He was perfect in and through all of them.

2p-The early years of Christ, in the home with Joseph and Mary, have drawn deep from the imaginations of sculptors, poets, and artists. Within this holy periphery, one's thoughts run rampant amid the grand scenes of Jewish devotion and religious piety. We reverently ask, "What was His favorite toy?" "When did Jesus learn to walk?" "What word did this Holy Child speak first?" and, "What games did He and Joseph play?" The questions are endless as we struggle to pick a piece here or there from these silent years of Jesus, seeking to discover if He was as we are. Long before He could attend the synagogue school, see Joseph and Mary bowing their heads in prayer with their "little boy." Ah! Behold that scene. There is Mary, that special mother, the first teacher, by actions and words of her divine Son. Then, brothers and sisters are born into this family (Matt. 13:55). Such events always bring great changes. The trips to Jerusalem and the observance of Israel's annual feasts at the temple capture our imaginations. We picture carpenter Joseph carrying his tithes some ninety miles south down to the temple. Surely, that lad dancing, jumping, playing, skipping, tossing stones, always full of "little boy's questions," tagged along in every footstep of His foster-father. Both angels and devils beheld those scenes with great wonder! Concerning the expression about Jesus being the "Son of Joseph," see Section 6, footnote e.

(n) Grace upon him. Only the Holy Spirit could have revealed such things to Luke, who wrote these comments years later. Not only was the grace of God upon the Child Jesus, but later New Testament revelation makes it clear that He is the fountain head and source of God's saving grace (John 1:17; 2 Cor. 13:14; and 2 Tim. 2:1). *When men have Christ as Lord and Savior, they are in God's grace.* Otherwise, they are not! See Section 19 for a comparative look at Lk. 2:39-40 with Matt. 2:23.

2p-Jewish schools in the days of Jesus. Understanding that the early years of our Savior's life were often disrupted by fleeing to Egypt, and then later returning to the land of Israel, we will look briefly into the education of Jewish children. No ancient nation on earth, of which anything is known, more deliberately set children in their midst as did Israel. One old rabbi once said, "The world only exists by the breath of little children." The Hebrew was sure that of all things on earth, a child was dearest to Jehovah God. These things being so, it is obvious that the education of children was highest on the list of national priorities. It is written in the Talmud, tractate Sabbath 119b. "Every town in which there are no school children shall be destroyed." In this same tractate, various rabbis cast their opinions as to why Jerusalem was destroyed in A.D. 70. Amazingly, one Jewish teacher named Hamuna wrote, "Jerusalem was destroyed because they neglected [the education of] school children." It was said of ancient Jerusalem that four hundred and eighty synagogues stood within the city and that each one had a school. If there was no synagogue, the children were instructed in the home of their teacher. According to Josephus, the origin of children being taught the Torah Law was traced back to Moses. See this in his *Antiquities of the Jews,* Book 4:8. 12, line 211 and *Against Apion* 2.26, line 204. The age for beginning school ranged between five and seven years. Teachers were paid by taxes levied from the residents of the particular city. Jewish teachers must be of the highest moral and religious character, and should never discourage the children. During the summer months, school did not meet between 10 a.m. and 3 p.m. due to the scorching heat. The Sanhedrin ruled that in any area where there were twenty-five boys, a schoolmaster was to be appointed. If forty boys were present, the master must be given an assistant; and if there were fifty boys, two masters must be appointed to the work. The only textbook was the Holy Scriptures. Most education was reduced to memorizing, and like all ancients, the Jews read everything aloud.

3p-The first day of school. This was a time of high excitement in the Jewish home. The boy was wakened early, before dawn, when it was still dark. After bathing, he was dressed in a gown with fringes. At the rising of the sun, he was taken to the synagogue or teacher's house, by his father or a wise friend of the family, if the father was not available. At the synagogue, he was placed in front of a reading desk upon which he saw a parchment roll with the Scripture of Ex. 20: 2-26 recorded. The teacher read this aloud to all present then gave a clear explanation. Next, the boy was given a slate with the twenty-two letters of the Hebrew alphabet written on it in pure honey! The children would lick these from off the slate according to the verses in Ezek. 3:1-3. Each child must memorize a text from the Scriptures that began with the first letter of his name and ended with the last letter of his name. After this powerful lesson, the children were given sweet cakes to eat, each having a verse from the law inscribed on them. Such simple but profound ceremonies impressed into the minds of these precious children the authority of God's Word to Israel. By the time of Christ, this authority had almost vanished from the nation. Nevertheless, with all this, it remained true that the home was considered the foundation of all education for pious Jews.

4p-How far our Savior advanced into the Hebrew system of education we are not told. It is sure that Joseph and Mary were devout in rearing their children for the honor of the God of Israel, and in obedience to the Torah Law. There is a curious text in John 7:15 which says of Jesus, "How knoweth this man letters, having never learned?" This referred to the two theological schools of Jerusalem, that of Hillel and Shammai. Jesus studied with neither of these and was usually in conflict with most of their teachings. Much of the above information is from the book, *Education Ideals in the Ancient World,* by the Scottish theologian, William Barclay (died 1978). He was excellent in Bible background, customs, and manners of the ancients. Yet, he was a theological zero who denied the virgin birth, deity, miracles of Christ, *personal* salvation, and other fundamentals of Scripture. Outside Holy Scripture, Barclay was a classic writer: inside God's Word, he was a hopeless failure.

CHAPTER 7
FOREIGNERS SEARCHING FOR A JEWISH KING TROUBLE JERUSALEM.*
THE FLIGHT TO EGYPT AND RETURN TO GALILEE. THE SECOND
SILENT PERIOD BEGINS AT THE AGE OF TWELVE AS THEY
LEAVE THE TEMPLE AND RETURN HOME TO NAZARETH.

Time: The above events took approximately ten years

Strange men appear from the East. Herod's deceptive reaction. The infant King is found and worshiped. Warned of God in a dream the wise men flee.

*The population of Jerusalem at this time was about 400,000. Word spread across the city that curious men from a far eastern country had appeared and were inquiring where they might find the newly born King of the Jews. Hundreds of Israelites pondered the greatest question, "Has Messiah come?"

Matt. 2:1-12—*Jerusalem and Bethlehem*	Mk.	Lk.	John
Foreign visitors and their stirring question			
1 Now when Jesus was born in Bethlehem of Judaea(a) in the days of Herod(b) the king, behold, there came wise men from the east(c) to Jerusalem,			
2 Saying, "Where is he that is born King of the Jews?(d) for we have seen his star in the east, and are come to worship him."(e)			
All Jerusalem is troubled			
3 When Herod the king had heard *these things*, he was troubled,(f) and all Jerusalem with him.			
4 And when he had gathered all the chief priests and scribes of the people together,(g) he demanded of them where Christ should be born.			
5 And they said unto him, "In Bethlehem of Judaea: for thus it is written by the prophet,(h)			
6 'And thou Bethlehem, in the land of Juda, art not the least among the princes of Juda: for out of thee shall come a Governor, that shall rule my people Israel.'"			
King Herod's deceit			
7 Then Herod, when he had privily called the wise men, enquired of them diligently what time the star appeared.			
8 And he sent them to Bethlehem, and said, "Go and search diligently for the young child; and when ye have found *him*, bring me word again, that I may come and worship him also."(i)			
Wise men greatly rejoice as they follow the wonderful star that led them to Jesus			
9 When they had heard the king, they departed; and, lo, the star, which they saw in the east, went before them, till it came and stood over where the young child was.			
10 When they saw the star,(j) they rejoiced with exceeding great joy.			
They worship and give: returning home another way			
11 And when they were come into the house,(k) they saw the young child with Mary his mother, and fell down, and worshipped him: and when they had opened their treasures, they presented unto him gifts; gold, and frankincense, and myrrh.(l)			
12 And being warned of God in a dream(m) that they should not return			

Matt. 2:12—*Jerusalem and Bethlehem*	Mk.	Lk.	John
to Herod, they departed into their own country another way.[n] (Verse 13 cont. in Section 18.)			

Footnotes-Commentary

[a] **"Bethlehem of Judaea."** It was thus called to distinguish it from the village Bethlehem in the land of Zebulon (Josh. 19:15). Apparently, some of Matthew's original Hebrew readers needed to know the difference; however, this could also suggest the wide circulation of his book among Jews in many foreign lands.

[b] **Anno Domini and Herod.** It has been established that King Herod the Great died in 4 B.C. Our present calendar is off by several years. A Catholic monk, Dionysius Exiguus invented the "Anno Domini" or A.D. calculation. In A.D. 525, he employed this term trying to compute the date of Easter for the Roman Catholic Church. He named this "the year of grace." Then, Exiguus inserted into his work the lines "Anno Domini," ("year of our Lord"). Hence, a Roman Catholic is the source for our popular but incorrect dating symbol A.D. The Pope's monk made a mistake of several years in attempting to determine the date of Easter. Contrary to popular opinion, the letters A.D. had nothing to do with Jesus' death. For brief details about Exiguus, see *A History of Early Medieval Europe 476-911*, pages 52-53, 111, 177, 265, by Margaret Deanesly. For further information on this subject, refer to the exhaustive work, *Anno Domini: The Origins of the Christian Era*, by Georges Declercq.

2p-Since King Herod died in 4 B.C., it is certain from Scripture that Christ was born shortly *before* his death. We read that the angel told Joseph to return to Israel with Mary and Jesus because Herod was dead (Matt. 2:19-20). Thus, our Lord's birth date drops back into the latter part of the B.C. era of chronology. See article in *Davies Harmony of the Gospels*, Appendix One, for a good discussion. Harold W. Hoehner in his little book *Chronological Aspects of the Life of Christ*, pages 11-27, gives a technical investigation into these things, citing various sources, but reaches few conclusions about anything. Christ haters, atheists, religious infidels, and certain "Christian" writers now employ the term C. E., meaning "Common Era." They seek either to avoid offense that may come by using His precious Name or to appear "scholarly." Others knock themselves out trying to be "academically" correct. They write long dissertations on Shepherds and sheep not being in the fields during the winter season in Israel, thus altering the time of His birth to another season of the year. On the fallacy of this, see Section 14, footnotes a and b.

[c] **"The east."** Jews firmly believed that inspired prophets and sages living in the eastern kingdom were of the posterity of Abraham and his concubine, Keturah, whom he married after the death of Sarah (Gen. 25:1-4 with 1 Chron. 1:32-33). Whoever these wise men were and whatever their number, it is sure they had retained the Old Testament Scriptures pursuant to the final dispersion of Israel in 586 B.C. At the time of the first Jewish return to the land of Israel, (536 B.C.) more Israelites remained in Babylon than returned under the leadership of Zerubbabel. According to the computations listed in Ezra 2, fewer than fifty thousand Jews returned to Jerusalem with Zerubbabel. Contained in Hebrew Scriptures, available in the eastern kingdoms, were promises concerning the coming King of the Jews, including the explicit prediction found in Num. 24:17. This prediction fixed Messiah's appearing with a star in Israel (or Jacob).

2p-Within Orthodox Judaism today, some understand this star to be the Messiah Himself! See footnote j below. The "wise men" were convinced that they would find the King of the Jews in the land of Israel and traveled hundreds of miles westward to see Him. Surely, they were the "kings" mentioned in Isa. 60:3 who were to visit the Messiah at His rising or physical appearing among men. The only two places they could have acquired such supernatural knowledge was from God and His inspired Old Testament. They seem to have been of Jewish stock from the Babylonian captivity. It is true that the word "Magi" (translated "wise men") was also used in an evil sense in some ancient writings. When Matthew wrote his letter, this could not have been the *absolute* case. He would never have used this occult identification in trying to convince fellow Jews that Jesus was their Messiah and King. Such tactics would have defeated his purpose in writing. These men had researched the Old Testament Scriptures in their native land and discovered that a Messiah–Savior was coming to the nation and land of Israel. *Somehow,* they saw the star in far off Babylon, instantly knew its significance, and it led them to Jerusalem.

[d] **"King of the Jews."** Where did these wise men acquire the knowledge that this babe was to be "born King of the Jews," in the land of Israel? It came from the predictions of Hebrew Holy Scripture as stated in footnote c above. Ancient writers, such as Tacitus, Suetonius, and Josephus mention that over the known world, a strange belief prevailed that a great king would appear in the land of Israel. Many held that someday, He would rule the world. (Some allege that Tacitus and others copied their information from Josephus. If this were so, would that make it untrue? Rather, it would seem to validate what Josephus wrote.) Could this widespread consciousness of some coming event have been the sovereign providence of God preparing the hearts of men? Greeks, Romans, and Persians all believed that the appearing and sudden disappearing of heavenly bodies, especially stars, hailed the births and deaths of great men. At the birth of Christ, there appeared phenomena so remarkable that a single star literally moved across the lower heavens above the earth's surface to point out the house where the Savior could be found. Shakespeare reflected this ancient premonition in astronomical signs at births and deaths of great men when

he wrote in *Julius Caesar* (II. ii), "The heavens themselves blaze forth the death of princes." Either Jesus was born "King of the Jews" or He was not. It was predicted centuries before that He would rule or be Governor over Israel (Isa. 9:6). Thus, He will be both King and Governor. See also Section 9, footnote g, and associated references for a discussion of Jesus' ruling over Israel or the church during the present dispensation. The claim that He is never called "the king of the church" is wrong. According to 1 Tim. 1:17, 1:7; Rev. 17:14; and 19:16, He is King and Lord over everything. To believe this does not include the church is unacceptable.

2p-**"His star."** Why did they specifically call this phenomenon of astronomy "His star," and associate it with the grand title "the King of the Jews?" They were familiar with the Jews' religion and *some* of their Scriptures and knew a Hebrew King was coming into the world. Refer to footnote j below for more on this subject.

(e) **"Are come to worship him."** Hundreds of miles across the hot and killing desert sands are a long way to go to worship a newborn Child. There is more in this brief statement than meets the casual eye. At the birth of the Lord Jesus, *all* the angels of God worshiped Him (Heb. 1:6). Later, in the beginning of Christ's ministry, the Devil sought to steal this worship for himself (Lk. 4:7-8). Here, men from the East bow before God in human flesh. See footnote k below. Some writers portray these men in bad light because they are called "magi." They had enough genuine spiritual discernment to seek, with all their hearts the infant Son of God. Upon finding Him, they fell upon their knees in loving worship and lavished the Christ Child with their rich treasures. Such divine perception and undaunted faith are not from men involved in the occult. See footnote j below for details on the guiding star.

(f) **The whole city troubled.** One can imagine the tremendous stir these eastern strangers caused as they rode with their vast caravans and camel trains into Jerusalem. At this time, the city had an estimated population of some four hundred thousand people. Their piercing question about "the King of the Jews" and their expressed desire to "worship Him," was reported to King Herod. This threw him into raging jealousy. The Roman Empire had crowned him "King of the Jews." Who was this intruder to his domain? Why had no one from the east come to worship him? He had lived a life of criminal success and utter misery. Now, as a wicked old man, entrapped in the jaws of his own savagery, he became fiercely inflamed by the question of these curious strangers, who, unannounced, rode into his domain. It seems apparent they understood each other's language, although being from vastly different cultures and countries. Did the wise men speak Greek or Hebrew, or was Aramaic employed in their conversations with the people of Jerusalem and King Herod himself? The Scriptures they had read in the land of Babylon, foretelling Christ's birth were written in the Hebrew language. "Scholars" who deem these wise men to be a company of occult ignoramuses reflect their own ignorance. What did aged Simeon and Anna think when they heard of these men from the east asking for Messiah the King? Their earlier story is in Section 16.

2p-Some thirty years later, and several days before His death, the Lord Jesus again troubled Jerusalem; the entire city was stirred as He rode in on the back of a donkey. See this in Section 148, Matt. 21:10, footnote j.

(g) Herod summoned the Hebrew Sanhedrin and demanded of them the place where *their* King would be born. This passage reveals that King Herod knew the Jewish Scriptures predicted future events of this nature, and that he did not doubt these predictions. The Sanhedrin pointed him to the *exact* place in their Old Testament Scriptures where Messiah their true King would appear. One wonders why these sages of Israel did not also go and seek Him. Some thirty years later, these Hebrew religionists, or their successors, were greatly confused regarding the actual birthplace of Messiah. They bickered among themselves, and with Nicodemus over this (John 7:41-43, footnote s).

(h) **Quoted from Micah 5:2.** With this verse, note Section 14, footnotes a and b. Various writers point out that this quotation from Micah reads the same way in the ancient Jewish *Targum of Jonathan* written some years before the birth of Christ. This reveals that the correct meaning and understanding of the passage had not changed over the centuries. Matthew wrote as a saved Jew, who believed in this particular Targumistic explanation of Micah 5:2. For the meaning and explanation of targums, refer to Section 1, Part 1, and fifth paragraph under footnote b.

2p-**"Rule my people Israel."** It seems wrong to interpret this to mean that Christ would only be "Governor" and rule over the church, His spiritual kingdom. On the rule of Christ, refer to Section 9, Lk. 1:32, footnote g, and Section 39, footnotes a and g.

(i) **"That I may worship him also."** This was Herod's pretext to the departing wise men. Demonic cunning echoes from these terrible words. Having come from a faraway land in the east, the wise men were apparently ignorant of the bloody record of this tyrant. Innocently they trusted this inhuman monster and moved forth under the guidance of the star. Some trusted writers believe that it moved several feet above the earth! God intervened and saved them from the vengeance of Herod, who did not intend to worship the infant King (verse 12).

2p-**Verse 9. They saw the star in the east.** The same thing is recorded in verse 2. How amazing! These men lived hundreds of miles east of Jerusalem and the land of Israel. Yet, they saw the star appear eastward from where they abode. Thus, the astronomical wonder moved from its eastward position across the heavens, over their heads, and traveled due west leading them to Jerusalem. Apparently, the wise men did not possess a copy of the book of Micah in which the prophecy of Jesus' birthplace was written. If so, they would have gone straight to Bethlehem instead of Jerusalem. See footnote h above.

3p-**The star led them to the house and "stood" over it.** This means what it says, and it happened at night.

(j) **"The star."** Predicted in Num. 24:17, where it tells of a star [Messiah] that would come (rise) out of Jacob or Israel. The mystic Hebrew book called *Zohar* also spoke of a heavenly body appearing at Messiah's birth. However, Moses had written of it *earlier* in the Number's text just given. See footnote c above. Many present day Orthodox Jews look upon this "star" as a prediction associated with the "coming Messiah." How sad that these people are two millennia late! Note Section 14, and all of footnote f, for comments on modern day Jewish opinion of Jesus of Nazareth, the Messiah of Israel. The absolute faith of the wise men in what this star signified is reflected in the words, "They rejoiced with exceeding great joy" upon sight of the heavenly wonder. To object that this star, the birth of Christ, and the coming of the wise men are unrelated because they are not written in a strict chronological order is wrong. There were hundreds of events in the life of Christ that neither Matthew, Mark, Luke, nor John were inspired to write about. Matthew's silence regarding the finer details of these wonderful events is because God did not inspire him to write of them. Millions today follow "sport stars" but fail to find the one that leads to Jesus.

(k) **"Into the house."** The amazing natal star led them to Jesus, but they did not find a babe in a manger. Rather, according to Matthew, it was in a "house" that "they saw the young child." The Lord Jesus was not a helpless infant, but was already more than a few months old when the wise men appeared. It may be that Messiah was not in Bethlehem but some other place. No doubt, Joseph moved his family from the stable to a house shortly after Jesus' birth. In any case, God has not given the details but has chosen to leave gaps in the wonderful story. *These men were the first Gentiles to worship the Son of God, even as a little boy.* See footnote e above. They recognized Him as God and alone worthy of human homage! Herod, later seeking revenge, ordered all males "from two years old and under" to be slain. Jesus fell into this age category and was quickly taken to Egypt. He was somewhere reasonably under the two years limit imposed by the tyrant King Herod. Thus, He was not a helpless babe as commonly depicted in the manger scenes, when the great men from the east arrived.

(l) For two thousand years, the imaginations of millions have played with the gifts of these wise men. Such emblems as deity, humanity, sinlessness, life, death, burial, and resurrection have been seen in the gold, frankincense, and myrrh. One writer saw in them the three divisions of the human race as found in Shem, Ham, and Japheth (Gen. 10:32)! The following gifts were brought as presents for the youthful King.

1. **Gold** is the most valuable metal known to mankind. There is a prophecy in Isa. 60:6 that speak of eastern people coming to worship Messiah and gold is among their gifts. Being a very heavy metal, it would have taken more than three men riding camels to cart these goods across the Great Syrian Desert.

2. **Frankincense** was a resin extracted from certain shrubs and trees. It was exported from the Middle East to different parts of the known world, thus making it very costly. It was used in the worship of God. The prescription for its mixture and usage in God's service is recorded in Ex. 30:34-38. Those who made imitations of this were put to death. It seems to picture prayer, intercession, and worship in the Old Testament. Note Lev. 2:1, 2, 15 and 16 where it was used in presenting the "sweet savour" offerings.

3. **Myrrh** was extracted from a bush and used to make perfume, cosmetics, oil, and a chief substance employed in preparing dead bodies. It was one of the ingredients used in the embalming to combat the smell of decaying human flesh. John 19:39 tells us it was placed upon the body of the Lord Jesus. Paul's preaching in the synagogue at Antioch of Syria, years after the resurrection of Jesus, stated, His flesh saw no corruption" (Acts 13:37). This was not due to the presence of myrrh. Jesus rose victorious over death and decay by the power of the Holy Spirit (Rom. 8:11). Some Ancient Egyptian texts speak of it being used in the burying of their kings and high officials. The Song of Solomon mentions this pleasant smelling essence more than any book in the Bible. It is associated with the most invigorating of odors or smells, always precious and enjoyed. *The Illustrated Bible Dictionary,* Part 2, p. 1110, shows a wall painting from ancient Egypt of women wearing "head cones" from which sweet oil dripped into their hair! One ponders what *poor* Joseph and Mary did with these immensely rich treasures, especially the gold. See Section 10, Lk. 1:48, footnote h for mention of their humble economic state.

(m) **"Warned of God in a dream."** The heavenly revelation to these men confirms that they were *not* "occult magicians." God clearly condemned every form of occult involvement (Deut. 18:9-14). *This was given long after the Torah Law had been received by Israel.* God spoke to them in a dream, warning them to flee from the enraged Herod. They instantly understood this message and were swift to obey. Jehovah also spoke to Joseph in exactly the same fashion on several occasions, saving his life as well (Matt. 1:20; 2:13, 19 and 23). Both Joseph and the wise men knew the true and living God and clearly understood when He communicated to them. During such times, sleep was more blessed than waking! Refer to Section 12, footnote d for Joseph's dreams, and Section 18, Matt. 2:13, footnote a, for more on Joseph "the dreamer."

(n) **"Another way."** Herod's soldiers were stationed on all main roads leading east. The "wise men" avoided arrest by taking another, but longer route home. We have no way of knowing which road they took. One can imagine the great stir they caused, when, upon their return home, they announced the Savior of the world and King of the Jews had been born! When they did not return, Herod's insane rage was vented. Seeking to kill the youthful Savior, he slew thousands of children. See Section 18, footnote d for the awful details.

Joseph and Mary, with baby Jesus flee to Egypt. King Herod kills the children in Judaea. This commences the first silent* period in Jesus' life. A few years later Herod dies in 4 B.C. The family returns to the land of Israel. This begins the second silence** until He is twelve years old.

*See second paragraph of footnote f below for more on this first time period. **For the second silent period in Jesus' life, see footnote g below. The third time span of eighteen years is mentioned in Section 20 footnote j. It concludes in Section 22, footnote b with His baptism by John.*

Matt. 2:13-23—*Bethlehem, Egypt, Judaea and Nazareth*	Mk.	Lk.	John
Joseph's second dream; his swift flight to Egypt 13 And when they were departed, behold, the angel of the Lord appeareth to Joseph in a dream,(a) saying, "Arise, and take the young child and his mother, and flee into Egypt, and be thou there until I bring thee word: for Herod will seek the young child to destroy him." 14 When he arose, he took the young child and his mother by night, and departed into Egypt:(b) 15 And was there until the death of Herod: that it might be fulfilled which was spoken of the Lord by the prophet, saying,(c) **"Out of Egypt have I called my son."** *Herod rages in anger* 16 Then Herod, when he saw that he was mocked of the wise men, was exceeding wroth, and sent forth, and slew(d) all the children that were in Bethlehem, and in all the coasts [borders] thereof, from two years old and under, according to the time which he had diligently enquired of the wise men. 17 Then was fulfilled that which was spoken by Jeremy [Jeremiah] the prophet, saying,(e) 18 **"In Rama was there a voice heard, lamentation, and weeping, and great mourning, Rachel weeping for her children, and would not be comforted, because they are not."** *Joseph's third dream; his return to Israel* 19 But when Herod was dead, behold, an angel of the Lord appeareth in a dream to Joseph in Egypt, 20 Saying, "Arise, and take the young child and his mother, and go into the land of Israel: for they are dead which sought the young child's life." 21 And he arose, and took the young child and his mother, and came into the land of Israel. *Joseph's fourth dream; his fear upon arriving in Judaea* 22 But when he heard that Ar-che-la-us(f) did reign in Judaea in the room of his father Herod, he was afraid to go thither: notwithstanding, being warned of God in a dream, he turned aside into the parts of Galilee: *Back in Nazareth again: Scripture fulfilled* 23 And he came(g) and dwelt in a city called Nazareth: that it might be fulfilled which was spoken by the prophets,(h) **"He shall be called a Nazarene."**(i) (Next chap., Matt. 3:1, cont. in Section 21, Part 1.)			

Footnotes-Commentary

(a) **Joseph's dreams.** How wonderfully close to God, this carpenter from Galilee must have lived to have such intimacy with the Lord of Heaven. Not one word spoken by Joseph is recorded in Scripture, yet we note that his life was engaged in *doing* the will of God, instantly, silently, without hesitation or question. This practical attitude of faith is reflected in the book that was later written by his son, James. Perhaps the boy took a lesson from his quiet, faithful father. See Section 17, Matt. 2:12, footnote m, for other comments on Joseph's dreams and the wise men from the east. A *worthless* old legend states that he died young. Refer to Section 28, footnote b for more on this.

2p-**"By night."** This reveals the good common sense of Joseph, in being seriously cautious, as all roads in Judaea would have been guarded. We can believe that hundreds of parents fled the slaughter of children to protect their little ones. Joseph would have wisely taken the "back trails" to lead his family out of the domain of the insane King Herod. In this action, we learn that it is both right and righteous that Christians should employ good reasoning and practical actions in their service for God and men. Missionary Paul, when trapped in the city of Damascus, escaped arrest and death by going over the wall in a basket at night (Acts 9:22-25 and 2 Cor. 11:32-33).

(b) Thousands of Jews had been living in Egypt since the days of Jeremiah and the Babylonian captivity (Jer. 43). The large seaport city of Alexandria had a powerful Jewish community whose influence reached even to Caesar's palace in Rome. At the time Joseph fled "by night," Egypt was a Roman province *not* under King Herod's personal jurisdiction. Here, they would have felt safe from the rage of this insane tyrant. For details about Herod, see Section 8, footnote a. In Alexandria, a bustling city of great enterprise, Joseph could have easily found employment. It is remarkable that our Lord found a haven in the land where the children of Israel once suffered so much under the Egyptian rulers. The land that had been a house of bondage and groaning for Israel of old now served as a place of refuge for Israel's newly born King. Over the years, Christ haters have pointed to Jesus' stay in Egypt as the time in which He learned occult magic. Some fifteen hundred years before His birth, we read of genuine black magic being practiced in an effort to refute the authority of Moses. Yet, in every case, the power of God conquered these satanic miracles (Ex. 7:10-13; 8:16-19; and 9:11). People who scorn Jesus of Nazareth often claim that the secret of His supernatural deeds had its origin in the demonic magic of ancient Egypt. Consider Christ's response to the Pharisees, who had accused Him of using satanic powers when healing a man born blind and dumb in Section 66, Matt. 12:22-32. Read John 8:44 for the origin of their malicious conclusions and hatred for the Savior. It is wonderfully odd that some fifteen hundred years prior, Moses also miraculously escaped death from the king, and fled Egypt (Ex. 2:1-10). In Deut. 18:15-18, Moses prophesied centuries in advance that he and Christ would have similar experiences.

(c) **"Out of Egypt."** Found in Hosea. 11:1. A needless fuss is made of this passage. Matthew shows his Jewish readers that when their Messiah, as a Child, was brought out of Egypt, that this event had been previously shadowed in a particular Old Testament prophecy. The prophecy was Hosea 11:1. It *first* pointed back to the Jews leaving Egypt in the great exodus traveling to their promised land. In Ex. 4:22, God called the nation of Israel His son. Matthew applies the Exodus text to Hosea 11:1 and says it points to the Lord Jesus departing Egypt and returning to the land of Israel. God "called" His *greatest* Son out of Egypt when He instructed the carpenter Joseph to return to Israel with Jesus (Matt. 2:19-21). Joseph's obedience to the angel of the Lord fulfilled the imagery shadowed in the Hosea verse. See footnote f below for comments on their return to the land of Israel.

(d) **Slaughter of the children.** The wise men did not return to Jerusalem as King Herod had requested. Thus, he flew into a rage and ordered the death of all infants "from two years old and under" at Bethlehem and the surrounding districts ("borders"). After all, a helpless infant somewhere out yonder was threatening "King Herod the Great," whose entire career was red with the blood of those he had murdered. On his insanity, see Section 8, Lk. 1:5, footnote a. "Scholars" who question the validity of this event because Josephus and other contemporary writers made no mention of it simply show their scholarly ignorance. During a recent national television program aired on the Discovery Channel, an infidel "expert" (professor at a famed theological institution) said, "Matthew had confused Herod's murder of his two sons with the killing of these infants." (Therefore, according to the professor, Matthew's muddled reporting was an honest mistake!) The infallible Words of Holy Scripture mean nothing to these "learned authorities" unless they are corroborated by *external secular* evidence. What foolishness! Even then, it is merely an academic brain exercise. They reject a totally inspired and trustworthy Bible. In their superior thinking, Jesus Christ was just another figure in history, that is, if He lived at all! In their folly, they blazingly call Scripture into question by pointing fingers of doubt at such events as recorded by Matthew. Unless Bible history can be corroborated by extra biblical evidence, they assume the Bible is wrong! Section 163 demonstrates how Josephus' history buttresses in detail, parts of the Olivet Discourse. The biblical record is true whether archaeology, Josephus, or anyone else agrees with it. For more on this, see Section 42, second paragraph of footnote i. Someone said, "The absolute dates of archaeology last about twenty years and then die!"

2p-Secular history does indeed make mention of Herod's murder of the innocents. James Ussher (died 1656) in his massive work *The Annals of the World*, pages 780-781, quotes from an ancient source that mentions Herod's crime. His words read, "[Emperor] Augustus heard of the edict of Herod, by which all the children who were two years old or under were ordered to be killed. When Augustus learned that one of Herod's sons was also killed because of this edict, he said that 'It was better to be Herod's sow, than his son.' "

3p-Verse 16. "Two years old and under." This phrase indicates that our Lord was less than two years old, but likely more than one, when Herod went on his murderous rampage.

(e) Quoted from Jer. 31:15. The context of this passage reveals that the prophet Jeremiah (or Jeremy) was describing the sorrowful departure of the Jews and their families into Babylonian captivity. This was after the destruction of Jerusalem and its temple in 586 B.C. The captives were forced to assemble at a place called Rama (by Rachel's tomb), which was near Bethlehem. Here, the fierce soldiers of Babylon had massacred thousands of Jews, including many children. The wails and groans of these ancient captives in their helplessness depicted the aftermath of Herod's brutal murders some five hundred years later. In Jer. 31:15, Rachel is represented *symbolically* as weeping again for the destruction of Jewish children. In the context of Matthew's words, Rachel's crying is caused by King Herod killing the little ones. Matthew applies this passage, as though Rachel had risen from her nearby tomb and wept for a second time over the slaughter of her descendents. The beautiful imagery deeply expresses the unspeakable sorrow of those mothers whose children had been murdered by Herod. Incredibly, this ruthless tyrant died a horrible death shortly after slaughtering the innocent children; however, he met none of them in hell!

2p-Verse 21. The pseudo "Palestine state." Who owns the land of Israel? Over three thousand years ago, divine inspiration called it, "the land of Israel" (1 Sam. 13:19). God had earlier given it to the descendents of Abraham, namely, the Hebrew nation (Gen. 15:18-21). Its borders as laid out in Numbers 34 have nothing to do with "tribal tradition." Jehovah God was the surveyor and drew up the plat. Linguistically the name "Palestine," comes from the word "Plesheth," which in the Bible is translated as "Philistine." The root of this word means "moving or migratory." Originally, it had reference to Gentile people called Philistines, who "moved" or "migrated" into this land from the sea. They were neither Arabs nor Muslims and did not speak Arabic. These Philistine pagans had no connection, ethnic, linguistic, or historical with Arabia or Arabs. Historically, there has never been people called "Palestinians," nor was there originally a land named "Palestine." There is no Palestinian language; all of them speak Arabic. Yasser Arafat, founder of the terrorist body, the "Palestinian Liberation Organization" (PLO) was an Egyptian by birth. No one has ever been born a Palestinian for no such country exists. After many bloody wars with the Jews, the Roman Emperor Hadrian (died A.D. 340) renamed the land "Provincia Syria Palaestina." Hence, the word "Palestine." In an effort to blot out Israel, he colonized it with Gentiles from other countries. The name "Falastin" as used by Muslims and Arabs today is not an Arabic word. It is the Arabic pronunciation of the Latin term "Palaestina" coined by Hadrian. The United Nations, Islam, and other Jew haters politicized the "land of Israel" and turned it into the "Palestinian" fable. The book, *The Palestinian Right to Israel,* by Alex Grobman impeccably demonstrates who owns this land. His work on *Nations United: how the United Nations is Undermining Israel, and the West* exposes world hatred for Israel and America. Radical Islam, in a covert effort to steal the land that God originally gave to Israel, took a word from pagan history, invented a myth, and called it "Palestine" or the "Palestinian State." For more on this, refer to Section 18, second paragraph of footnote e, and Section 163, the fifth paragraph of footnote s. As normal, the secular media has persuaded the world to believe this travesty.

(f) **"Archelaus did reign in Judaea."** Herod the Great had previously executed his elder son, Antipater. Then he altered his will at Jericho in 4 B.C. just before his death. In his revised will, Herod bequeathed the kingdom of Judaea, Idumea, and Samaria to his other son Archelaus. He had the bloodthirsty disposition of his father. Shortly after coming to power, his soldiers invaded a Passover celebration and killed some three thousand Jews at Jerusalem in one day! Many of these died within the temple precincts! News of this slaughter spread to far away Egypt. Hence, we understand the cause of Joseph's fears upon re-entering Judaea. Archelaus' crimes kept the country in a constant uproar. In A.D. 6, Emperor Augustus removed him as "King of the Jews." Joseph's return to Israel had to be *before* his banishment to Gaul (France). For more on these dates refer to Section 17, footnote b.

2p-Christ's first silent period was in Egypt. A curtain of quietness falls over these youthful years while the young Christ dwelt in Egypt. Not knowing exactly how long Joseph and his family abode there, it is estimated that Jesus was approximately seven to eight years old when He was brought back into the land of Israel. This *assumption* would allow for six more years before He turned twelve, attended the Passover, and conversed with the doctors of the Torah Law in the temple. With the banishment of Archelaus, the long-time prophecy of Gen. 49:10 was fulfilled. *Now,* there was no pagan king ruling over Israel, and no heathen sceptre swayed over Judah and the Jews. For a short time, the position of a new ruler was vacant. Little did anyone know that during this vacancy "Shiloh" had come, albeit out of Egypt, with His foster-father and mother. Though a small Boy dwelling in the home of a poor carpenter, and yet uncrowned when Archelaus was deposed in 6 B.C., Jesus the true Shiloh (a title for "Messiah") held the sway of Israel and creation in His little hands! He will yet rule the new world in righteousness and might. For details on the two-fold nature of His kingdom, see Section 39, footnotes a and g.

3p-Finally, after the tumultuous rule of five previous governors, the Roman Senate appointed Pilate as the governor or procurator (not king) over Judea in about A.D. 26. For more on Pilate's demise and death, note Section 21, Part 1, number 2 under footnote b.

4p-"Into the parts of Galilee." The word "Galilee" means "circle or circuit." In Matthew 2:22 we find the first New Testament mention of this area. The Savior did most of His preaching, teaching, and miracles in this province. All of His apostles, except Judas the traitor came from Galilee. It was composed of two sections, Upper and Lower Galilee, which covered an area of roughly fifty miles from north to south, and thirty miles from east to west. The Upper region was more mountainous and rugged, while Lower Galilee consisted of mostly rolling hills and beautiful farmlands. Nazareth, the hometown (not birthplace) of Joseph, Mary and our Savior was situated in the middle lower part of the province. It stood adjacent to the Plain of Esdraelon on the west, and the infamous Valley of Jezreel located in a southeasterly direction. A famed place called Armageddon (Rev. 16:16) is located a few miles southward across a shallow valley from the village of Nazareth. Oddly, Nazareth was built on a hill with a sharp precipice (probably for security) just outside one of its city walls. Refer to this in Section 38, Lk. 4:28-29 where the angered synagogue mob attempted to kill the Savior by casting Him headlong into this deep ravine.

(g) **Back to the land of Israel. His second silent period begins.** Obeying the angel's message (Matt. 2:19-20), Joseph and family returned to Israel. This began the second silent time in Jesus' life. Upon hearing that Archelaus now ruled in Judaea, he "turned aside" into Galilee. It is noted that when Joseph went into Egypt, the Lord Jesus was referred to as a "young child" (verses 13, 14). Later, when departing Egypt, the Savior was still a "young child" (verses 20, 21). After learning of Archelaus' control in the place of his late father, Joseph gathered his family and hurried to Nazareth in Galilee, where he and Mary had previously lived. Galilee was not under the jurisdiction of Archelaus. (In footnote f above it is noted that Archelaus was deposed in A.D. 6.) Little did Joseph realize that in this move, he was fulfilling a series of prophecies given by the sages centuries earlier. Matthew knew what to write to fellow Jews. He was inspired to use the history they understood. See Section 3 for comments on Messiah's genealogy written by Matthew for fellow Hebrews.

(h) **Matthew's quotation.** In citing different Old Testament prophets, Matthew was inspired to select appropriate words from several verses and blend them together to make one definite point: the Scripture foretold that Messiah would live at Nazareth and consequently, be called "a Nazarene." See Section 19, footnotes a, and b for more on this subject. At least nineteen times in the four gospels the Lord Jesus is called by this title. Demons addressed Him as "Jesus of Nazareth," and "the Holy One of God" (Mk. 1:24 with Lk. 4:34). The rowdy crowds informed blind Bartimaeus that "Jesus of Nazareth passeth by" (Lk. 18:37-38), whereupon he instantly responded "Jesus, thou son of David, have mercy on me" (verse 38). "Son of David" was the classic title for Israel's promised Messiah. Refer to Section 4, footnote b, and Section 66, footnote b, for more on this grand designation for the Savior. Later, blind Bartimaeus *knew* Jesus was the Messiah of Israel and said so. Note details of this in Section 143, Mk. 10:47, footnote d. To this day, "the Son of David" remains the most universal appellation used by Orthodox Jews for their Messiah, our Savior. Even the pagan Roman governor Pilate affirmed that Jesus was from Nazareth and King of the Jews. He wrote this title in the three major languages of that day. For more on the signboard attached above the cross, see Section 189, John 19:19, footnote e.

2p-We do not know *exactly* from which of the "prophets" (plural) Matthew drew his conclusions. Nor do we need to know. It seems that he used Isa. 11:1, which predicted a ("netzer") or "Branch" would grow out of Jesse. In Micah 5:1-2, Christ is here called a "rod" or sprout of David at Bethlehem. Matthew surely noted that in Jer. 23:5, 33:15; Zech. 3:8, and 6:12, a ("tzemach") or "sprout" would appear in Israel, and this was Messiah. The rabbis understood these words to have reference to their Messiah and gave a wide variety of interpretations. They interpreted the "abominable branch" of Isa. 14:19 as having reference to a malefactor who was hanged on a cross. How marvelous that Jesus hanged between two of them. Matthew blended the two words "netzer," and "tzemach," into *one specific* meaning—Jesus of Nazareth the Messiah of Israel. Matthew and his Hebrew readers understood, and that was sufficient. He was pointing out to his Jewish people the reason Jesus was called "a Nazarene." This was because He grew up (as a beautiful sprouting branch) in the city called Nazareth. This is Matthew's fifth quotation from the Old Testament. As with the previous quotations, he demonstrated that Christ fulfilled other Old Testament prophecies and was Israel's Messiah. See Section 14, footnote f, for the modern day Jewish opinions of Jesus.

(i) **"Called a Nazarene."** As mentioned in footnote h above, Matthew is inspired to select various words from a series of Old Testament passages and blend them together to build this Name for Jesus. The objections about this passage not being found anywhere in the Old Testament, but a later interpolation, is more liberal unbelief. We do not need thirty verses of Scripture stating that Jesus was called "Nazarene" by family, foes, and disciples to believe this declaration. Matthew wrote his book looking back on history, therefore, it was true whether we have a written record of it or not. About twenty years later Dr. Luke affirmed that believers in Christ were known as "the sect of the Nazarenes" by their enemies (Acts 24:5). Refer to Section 19 for a side-by-side comparison of Matt. 2:23 with Lk. 2:39-40. See Section 19, footnotes a, and b for more of the so-called "Nazarene problem" in Matt. 2:23.

2p-In the Talmud, Jesus Christ is referred to seven times as "Ben Stada," a slanderous name associated with sedition, witchcraft, and idolatry. In the footnote 12 of the tractate, Sanhedrin 67a, another Hebrew writer refers to the Savior as "Jesus of Nazareth." David H. Stern in *Jewish New Testament Commentary,* page 15, wrote that in other Talmud tractates, He is called "Yeshu HaNotzri" or "Jesus of Nazareth." For the blasphemous usage of "Yeshu," by Christ hating Jews and Gentiles, see the comments in Section 12, footnote e.

73

A brief view of the first few years of Jesus' life at Nazareth and Jerusalem.*

The passages listed below were also given in Sections 16 and 18. They are repeated here in parallel columns with explanatory footnotes to demonstrate that they speak of different times in the early life of Jesus of Nazareth, the Christ or Messiah of Israel. God did not give us any of the fine details of these earlier years in the life of His Son. Perhaps this was because many earthly human parents could not handle the wonderful story in view of the frequent difficulties they experience in rearing their children.

From Jerusalem to Nazareth

Matt. 2:23	Mk.	Luke 2:39–40	John
23 And he came and dwelt in a city called Nazareth:[a] that it might be fulfilled which was spoken by the prophets,[b] **"He shall be called a Nazarene."**		39 And when they had performed all things according to the law of the Lord, they returned into Galilee, to their own city Nazareth.[a] 40 And the child grew, and waxed strong in spirit, filled with wisdom: and the grace of God was upon him.[c]	
In the verse above Matthew wrote of Joseph, Mary, and Jesus settling at Nazareth after returning from Egypt upon the death of King Herod. Jesus was approximately seven to eight years old. See Section 17, footnotes b and k. Matthew did not record the circumcision or events in the temple as Luke did.		In the verses above Luke wrote of Joseph, Mary, and Jesus' return to Galilee after the events in the temple with Simeon and Anna. This occurred when Jesus was an infant only forty days old. See Section 16, footnote b. Luke did not record the flight into Egypt and related events as Matthew did.	

Footnotes–Commentary

[a] Jesus grew up at Nazareth to fulfill the Old Testament prophecy. See Section 16, footnote m. As an adult, He moved from Nazareth after His rejection in the synagogue, and went to Capernaum some twenty–five miles away. This fulfilled another Old Testament prediction as seen in Section 38, Matt. 4:13-16 with Isa. 9:1-2. For more on Nazareth, refer to Section 18, Matt. 2:23, footnote g, footnote b below. Near the latter part of His ministry, the Lord Jesus pronounced a horrible curse upon Capernaum. This is given in Section 63, Matt. 11:23, footnote b.

[b] **Was Jesus called a "Nazarene?"** Matthew's citation, as such, is not found in the Old Testament. It was a summation of selected words taken from specific Old Testament verses. When blended, they state that Jesus would grow up at Nazareth. For more on this inspired method of using Old Testament passages, see Section 18, footnotes h and i. Scripture says, Jesus was called a "Nazarene." No further record is needed to confirm this. Matthew does not name any of the prophets from which he drew his conclusions. It is noticed that the word "prophets" is in the plural form. That his original Hebrew readers understood what he was writing, is seen in that he gave no further explanation. In footnote h of the previous Section 18, Matthew's free quotation was built by inspiration as he was led to draw words from such Old Testament verses as Isa. 11:1; Jer. 23:5; 33:15; Zech. 3:8, and 6:12. The men of Ephraim were called "Ephraimites" (Judges 12:4-5), and Peter of Galilee, was called a "Galilean" (Mk. 14:70). The prophets foresaw hundreds of years in advance, where Christ would grow up and collectively dubbed Him "a Nazarene." For more details of this predictive forecast, see Section 18, footnote g; Section 16, footnote m; and footnote a above. The word "Nazarene," meaning "a branch," or perhaps "germ" (something small like the town of Nazareth) was ascribed to the Lord Jesus. Usage of this term spread over the known world of that era, see Section 18, footnote i. It became a contemptuous appellation for early Christians and was used in far away Rome, Italy (Acts 28:22). They were slanderously called, "the sect of the Nazarenes" in Acts 24:5.

[c] A similar statement was made of little Samuel in 1 Sam. 2:26. This was a common way of expressing the welfare of a child. Jehovah communicated to His Son gradually and in proportion to the increase of His mental rationale. Verse 40 reveals that Christ assumed a physical body like ours, which does not come into full maturity at once, but by degrees. However, the amazing difference was that He lived without sin or sinning.

2p-His early childhood days. We live without remembering many experiences from our earliest years. Similarly, little is written of our Savior about the first years of His life. Is this so because God is trying to show us that His beloved Son has, likewise, traced our steps through those times? As we have been, so He was. Every tear, every bump and pain Jesus the child *somehow* felt in His youthful frame, as we have. How amazing that the pains and frustrations we cannot remember, the Son of God quietly lived through all of them! He has been touched with the feelings of our infirmities over all of our lives, from those early formative years to the present (Heb. 4:15).

3p-How Jesus learned as a human. The predictions in Isa. 50:4-6 (set in the context of Messianic prophecy) informs us *how* Jesus the Messiah, as a human, learned from the "morning by morning" teaching received from His Father. Because of His continual communication with God, later as a twelve-year-old lad, He confounded the learned doctors of the law with His questions and answers. See this in Section 20, Lk. 2:46-47, footnote f. Countless pages have been written by "scholars" who have tried to explain how Christ learned as a growing boy. The predictions in Isa. 50:4-6 (set in the context of Messianic prophecy) affirm unequivocally that it was God, who taught Jesus. This settles the question for everyone except the "greatly learned scholars." Everything must be subjected to their infallible scrutiny. If secular evidence cannot be found that corroborates Scripture, then Scripture is rejected. This is the reasoning of unconverted men who fain to interpret Holy Scripture. Luke indicates that the process of Jesus' learning was a progressive experience when he used the term "waxed strong in spirit." His was a physical humanity developing perfectly, unimpeded by hereditary faults, or the gradual and numerous acquired defects of sin. This was the only instance in human history of such a physical growth. Both sin and Satan assaulted the humanity of our Lord, but neither tainted it in the slightest. He was *both* perfect God and perfect man, yet His physical frame developed and grew as any normal child. Thus, the above verses from Isaiah tell us how Jesus, as a human, learned "from morning by morning," as the Father taught Him. As a twelve-year old lad, He confounded the doctors of the law with His questions and answers (Section 20: Lk. 2:46-47, footnote f). It would have been obvious to all spiritually minded observers that this lad had the grace of God upon Him and was full of truth. As Barnabas saw the grace of God upon the new converts at Antioch (Acts 11:23), so grace shined from the early life of our Lord. Family, friends, and the people of Nazareth noted His wonderful features. This attitude changed when He preached His *first* sermon in their synagogue years later. See the main heading of Section 38 and footnotes for this event.

4p-During His ministry Christ "learned" from God through the things He suffered as a human (Heb. 5:8), and by self-humbling (Phil. 2:8). Neither physical suffering nor self-humbling suggests sin; rather, these are normal processes of any man in whose life God is working. Note Luke's remarks about the similar growth of John the Baptist in Lk. 1:80. No one can understand, much less explain, the incarnation of Christ. Those who demand that *everything* be explained before they believe, often arrive early in hell. See Section 1, Part 1, third paragraph of footnote a, footnote d, and Section 1, Part 4, second and third paragraphs under footnote j for more on the unfathomable subject of incarnation. Difficult statements in Scripture that are not explained are still true and must be believed. The Lutheran, Dietrich Bonhoeffer, would not do this. Gaining fame by intensive studies and travels abroad, he lived in Germany under the Nazi regime. He was arrested in 1943, for his part in the assassination plot of Hitler and was hanged at the age of thirty-nine. Hailed today as a "Christian evangelical full of warm-hearted piety," Bonhoeffer's words tell us differently. His books reflect neo-orthodox existentialism, religious humanism, and the lies of Karl Barth. He called into question the virgin birth of Christ in *The Cost of Discipleship,* page 215. He denied the resurrection, questioned biblical inspiration, and dissembled personal salvation. He held to both infant and adult baptismal regeneration, and believed that the Genesis record of creation was scientifically naïve and full of myths. Some of His declarations of unbelief are in, *No Rusty Swords,* page 318, *The Communion of the Saints,* page 20, *Testimony to Freedom,* page 50-56, and *Creation and the Fall,* pages 318–319. Certain statements are like a precursor to liberation theology and situation ethics. Men void of personal salvation are the most dangerous people on earth when they become professional theologians. They say a thousand beautiful things about mankind but cannot instruct anyone concerning the way of salvation. Great humanitarian words do not redeem us from hell. It remains true that those who die without Jesus Christ as personal Savior die damned. We do not know the condition of Bonhoeffer's soul at his execution in 1945. Some of his theology, documented above, leaves one trembling.

5p-In 1861, Dr. Horace Bushnell, a Congregational minister, wrote a unique treatise on the humanity of Christ, entitled *The Character of Jesus, Forbidding His Possible Classification with Men.* Every devout, God-fearing Christian should read this thought-provoking classic. It will answer many questions regarding the humanity of our Lord. However, not all of Bushnell's writings are of this extraordinary quality. Amazingly, he was a skeptic who was dubbed "the father of American theological liberalism." For an explanation of how flashes of truth can come from a man like Bushnell, see Section 124, John 11:49-52, first and second paragraphs of footnote v.

6p-Marking iniquities. Beware of those who continually *specialize* in pointing out the evils of others. Every one of us struggles with temptations and sins. The deeds and heresies of such men as Calvin, Luther, Augustine, and the like, are mentioned because they lived and died in these. It was not a one-time thing done in the vanity of youthful inexperience. Habitual witch hunters are psychologically sick. See Section 14, fourth paragraph of footnote f for advice in dealing with these things. Regarding the biblical balance for *true* Christians to follow, note Section 54, third paragraph of footnote h. *If God marked petty faults, none would stand (Ps. 130:3).*

Twelve-year-old Jesus attends Passover. His wisdom amazes the doctors of the Torah Law. A frantic search takes place. Joseph and Mary are puzzled by His conduct. On returning to Nazareth the third silent period* in His life begins.

Regarding the first and second silent periods in our Lord's life and ministry, refer to main heading Section 18. See footnote j below for the third strange silence in the life of Christ.

Matt.	Mk.	Lk. 2:41-52—At Jerusalem and Nazareth	John
		Joseph and Mary keep the annual Passover **41** Now his parents[a] went to Jerusalem every year at the feast of the passover.[b] **42** And when he was twelve years[c] old, they went up to Jerusalem after the custom of the feast. ***He deliberately stays behind*** **43** And when they had fulfilled the days,[d] as they returned, the child Jesus tarried behind in Jerusalem; and Joseph and his mother knew not *of it.* ***Frantically, Joseph and Mary seek for Jesus*** **44** But they, supposing him to have been in the company, went a day's journey; and they sought him among *their* kinsfolk and acquaintance. **45** And when they found him not, they turned back again to Jerusalem, seeking him.[e] ***The surprising discovery after three days of agony*** **46** And it came to pass, that after three days they found him in the temple, sitting in the midst of the doctors, both hearing them, and asking them questions.[f] **47** And all that heard him were astonished at his understanding and answers. ***The mother's question*** **48** And when they saw him, they were amazed: and his mother said unto him, "Son, why hast thou thus dealt with us? behold, thy father[g] and I have sought thee sorrowing." ***The boy's puzzling answer*** **49** And he said unto them, "How is it that ye sought me? wist ye not that I must be about my Father's business?"[h] **50** And they understood not[i] the saying which he spake unto them. ***Home at Nazareth: Mary's heart filled with questions*** **51** And he went down with them, and came to Nazareth,[j] and was subject unto them: but his mother kept all these sayings in her heart. ***The wonderful child before God and men*** **52** And Jesus increased in wisdom and stature, and in favour with God and man. [k-l] (Next chap., Lk. 3:1, cont. in Section 21, Part 1)	

Footnotes-Commentary

(a) **"His parents."** This was the socially courteous form of identification for the dear couple who reared our Lord. Joseph was obliged to go to Jerusalem three times a year, as were all Jewish males who were heads of households, to observe the celebrations of Passover, Pentecost and Tabernacles (Deut. 16:16). It is noteworthy that the word "parents" is plural in this text, signifying that Mary went with her husband and family. This sterling example of keeping Passover reflected their devotion as pious Jews. It should serve to instruct all parents regarding the spiritual welfare of their children. Women were not required to attend these feasts, yet we see Mary by her husband's side making the three-day journey (ninety miles one-way) from Nazareth to Jerusalem and back again. We catch a glimpse of her voluntary loyalty in the Jewish religion and respect for the ordinances of God in the

Torah Law of Israel. All this, when she was not obliged to attend the event. By this time (as Jesus was twelve years of age) a number of other children had also been born into their family (Matt. 13:55-56).

(b) For some curious reason, many commentators tell us that this was the *first* time our Lord went up to Jerusalem to observe the Passover. The opposite is true. We may rest assured that Joseph and Mary took their beloved sons and daughters, from the earliest age, to the highest celebrations in the Jewish religion. Amid these events recalling Israel's glorious history, Joseph must have carefully explained the ancient significance couched in these Hebrew rituals of joy and worship. What a lasting impression the sight of that majestic temple, the marvel of its robed priests, linen-clad musicians, its sacrifices and offerings, its manifold functions, its gold and silver gildings, and much more, had upon the hearts of Jewish children. Who can fathom the emotion of the Boy Jesus as he beheld these things, knowing His destiny in this city and among these people? Someday, He would be the *final* Passover Lamb (1 Cor. 5:7)! See Section 29, John 2:13, footnote a, with footnote d below, for a description of the Passover.

2p-Three feasts mentioned. The seven annual celebrations God gave to Israel are listed in Lev. 23:1-44. Of these seven, three are mentioned in the four gospels. They are *Passover,* spoken of several times (John 2:13), the *Feast of Unleavened Bread* that immediately followed the Passover (Matt. 26:17), and the *Feast of Tabernacles* (John 7:2). Lastly, John 10:22 speaks of the *Feast of Dedication*, which was not commanded in the Law of Moses. For details on this different Jewish celebration not found in the Torah Law, see Section 123, John 10:22, footnote a.

(c) **The age of twelve years.** This was a critical time in the life of any Hebrew boy. According to Jewish legend, it was at the age of twelve that Moses left the house of Pharaoh's daughter, Samuel heard the voice of God calling him, Solomon gave his first great judgment that marked him as a man of wisdom, and the boy king Josiah began his sweeping reforms. All devout Jews, including Joseph and Mary, firmly believed these rabbinical teachings. At twelve years, each Jewish lad was to begin learning a trade for his own future support. With this, see Mk. 6:3 where Christ is called a "carpenter." He was also emancipated from the authority of his parents and became answerable to God alone for His Words and deeds.

2p-The age of thirteen years. This was the time when every Jewish boy became a "son of the law," or "ben-hat-torah," hence, the present day "bar-mitzvah" or "son of the commandment." This was all done with a formal ceremony. *Our Lord's experience at this time was not the ancient Hebrew bar-mitzvah.* The Talmud reads that a Jewish boy upon reaching the age of thirteen years and one day is obligated to keep the commandments of the Torah Law. See tractates, Yoma 82a and Maba Metziah 96a. After the bar-mitzvah ritual held in the hometown synagogue, the boy was considered a full-grown man. He would then wear the phylacteries and was presented by His father in the local synagogue on the Sabbath as a man in Israel. Some think Jesus did not wear these objects of the Hebrew religion. It is sure that our Lord passed through these basic Jewish ceremonies (whatever they totally were, is unknown) in the synagogue at Nazareth when He was thirteen. In recent years, many non-orthodox synagogues have a ceremony for girls known as "bat-mitzvah" ("daughter of the commandment"), which occurs on a Friday or Saturday afternoon. Often, it is held on a Sunday night. For a thorough discussion of this, see Rabbi Wayne Dosick's work, *Living Judaism. The Complete Guide to Jewish Belief, Tradition & Practice,* pages 293-295. Liberal theologians, struggle to explain away this event in the life of Christ by telling us "twelve years of age actually meant something else, more like seventeen or eighteen years." For example of this ridiculous statement, see *The Teaching of Jesus*, page 48, by the late notorious liberal theologian, T. W. Manson.

(d) **A total of eight days.** One day was for killing the lamb in observing the Passover, the other seven days were for the Feast of Unleavened Bread (Lev. 23:4-8). Another observation of these Jewish celebrations is found in Section 167, Lk. 22:1, footnote a. By this time in history, the Jews had blended both celebrations, Passover and Unleavened Bread. They were often spoken of as one. There were several weeks of preparations and preliminaries *before* the actual Passover day began. This is discussed in Section 146, John 11:55, footnote a. One ponder what our Lord, as a Child would have been thinking as He stood with His foster-father in the temple, watching hundreds of Passover lambs being killed. The Passover sacrifice was the only sacrifice in which the worshiper was personally involved in slaying the animal after laying hands on its head. Joseph would have done this. Jesus would have known His destiny as the Lamb of God (John 1:29). For how He learned as He grew, see Section 19, footnote c.

(e) **Turned back seeking him.** Who can describe the mental anguish this grand couple experienced as they discovered Jesus was not with their traveling company! Critics have rashly conjectured that verses 43-45 suggest a lack of diligence on the part of Joseph and Mary toward the Christ Child. However, once the customs of the pilgrims traveling to Jerusalem for the annual feasts are understood, this myth vanishes. Men and women walked in separate groups, men with men and women with women. Sometimes the children kept company with their fathers and at other times, they went with their mothers. Joseph, not seeing the boy Jesus in the men's company, would have naturally assumed He was with His mother. Mary, not seeing Him, thought He was with Joseph. At the campsite that night, both discovered He was missing from the vast company among which they traveled. Since all roads were literally packed with festive pilgrims now returning to their homes far and near, Joseph and Mary hurried to Jerusalem, meeting the oncoming traffic of thousands of Jews. The distraught couple surely inquired for their "missing Boy" at every stopping place along the way. Three anxiety-filled days and nights later, they found their

Child. Looking ahead we see another anxiety filled three day and nights; this same Child, now a man, would lay physically dead in a borrowed tomb! On both occasions, He emerged triumphant over it all. See footnote g below.

2p-Verse 46. "After three days." For this, see *Appendix One*, sub heading *A "fourth day" resurrection.*

(f) Lessons from the law. Where He slept and ate during these three days and nights we cannot know. Amid the feast days, it was a standard practice for the scribes or teachers of the Scripture to hold instructional classes in the Torah Law for the benefit of the pilgrims coming to Jerusalem. These continued for several weeks and were often carried over into the Feast of Unleavened Bread. Many lingered in the city for these lessons. Any Jew, young or old, could freely attend these lectures and ask questions on various points of which he was unsure or confused. Thus, the physical presence of the twelve-year-old Child did not signal anything extraordinary. Rather, it was His powerful articulations, framed in pure humility, and deep respect for His elders that electrified with wonder all present. How touching when we note that the Christ Child quietly heard the doctors of the law express themselves; we do not read of any arguing or debate over various legal points. He was not teaching them as some have conjectured. This would have been highly offensive for a child to instruct his religious peers in Jewish society. (Later, in His ministry as an adult, this all changed.) Few children today reflect the priceless virtues of quietness and honor for the hoary head of the aged. Hundreds of Jews and many curious spectators from different parts of the known world were present at these sessions. Edersheim wrote of these lectures at the temple in his *Life and Times of Jesus the Messiah*, pages 171-172. It was one of these "Jewish Bible studies" that the twelve-year-old Savior attended. Passing through the crowded temple, frantically racing into the dozens of rooms, inquiring of every person along the way, Mary rips open a door. To her shock, she faced the stern-looking Jewish doctors of law sitting in half-circle formation on the floor with her Son postured cross-legged in their midst! Every eye fell upon her and Joseph. See in imagination that precious Boy, so innocent, pure, and holy, sitting among the wisest sages of Israel.

2p-Verse 47. Astonished at Him. A. T. Robinson, in *Word Pictures of the New Testament*, page 34, wrote these lines regarding the word "astonished." "Joseph and Mary were 'struck out' by what they saw and heard." He continued, "Even they had not realized the power in this wonderful Boy. Parents often fail to perceive the wealth of nature in their children." *Gill's Commentary*, vol. 7, page 533, informs us that the leading doctors of the Sanhedrin *at this time* were "Hillel (called "the second Moses"), Shammai, Rabban Simeon (the son of Hillel), Rabbi Judah, Jonathan ben Uzziel, and Jonathan ben Zaccai." Geikie, conjectures in *The Life and Words of Christ,* page 158-159, that Nicodemus and Joseph of Arimathea were both present, along with Annas, who some twenty years later pursued the death of Jesus at His trial before the Sanhedrin. Refer to this in Section 180, John 18:13, footnote p. Whoever these rabbis were at this point in history, all present were stunned at this marvelous Child so full of grace, who with a clear, calm face and beaming eyes, answered their every question with profundity and clarity. His powerful and terse elucidation with perfect exactness of each point of the Torah Law deeply stirred their souls! There was nothing pert, rude, or forward in His conduct. The great doctors of the Torah Law were not offended that this Lad knew God's Word better than they did! The Lad asked searching questions, which they had never heard before. "What an amazing Child!" Surely, this was the consent of everyone present. About twenty-two years later, as a man, Jesus again stood before some of this same Hebrew hierarchy. This time they condemned Him and agreed on His death.

(g) His first recorded words. After three days and nights of frantic searching the packed streets of Jerusalem, young Mary, anxious as any good mother would be, cried out, "Son, why hast thou thus dealt with us? Behold thy father and I have sought thee sorrowing." The people sat stunned at this rude intrusion! Here, the sword old Simeon had spoken of first pierced her young soul. This is recorded in Section 16, Lk. 2:35, number 3 under footnote i. "Wist ye not?" or "Don't you know?" The answer of this little Boy seems to be a polite attempt to correct Mary as to who His Father was. It was kind, yet lofty, and must have fallen troublingly into Mary's heart. She did not yet comprehend His holy mission. His reply was strange. "Does it," she likely mused, "have some meaning that corresponds with His divine conception, His mysterious birth, or the visit of that angel who spoke of His birth?" (Who among the redeemed that follow Christ have not also asked in times of awful darkness, "Lord, why?")

2p-Puzzling things. Mary carried in her bosom a thousand questions about this wonderful Boy. The angel had called Him "that holy thing" (Lk. 1:35), and she had watched Him during these twelve years of celestial childhood. Suddenly, He speaks a dark enigma about things she cannot fathom. Was He saying that His presence amid the doctors of the law was part of His Father's work? Some twenty-two years later, the night before the morning of the cross, Jesus *again* mentions the business of His Father when he prayed, "I have finished the work which thou gavest me to do" (John 17:4). We wonder of the conversations that would have followed as Mary and Joseph, taking the hand of their Son, led Him through the bustling busy temple compound, out of the Eastern Gate, eastward across the Jordan River, and up the north road to their home at Nazareth. What did they say to that Child and what did He say to them? The holy silence over these events stirs the deep imagination of our poor hearts.

(h) The first recorded Words in Scripture spoken by the Lord Jesus. Shaded in gray for this seems to be the beginning of Ps. 40:8 as it was gradually fulfilled by the Savior. At this early age, He understood that God was His Father, and that He was commissioned to do His business, which began in the temple, His house. This place (with its offerings and sacrifices, architecture and furniture), pointed with a thousand fingers to the wisdom of God in sending

His Son to die for the sins of all mankind. All of Ps. 22 is a prediction of the death of Christ on the cross someone thousand years in advance. (*Appendix Three* contains a list of forty-two Old Testament predictions, all fulfilled by the Lord Jesus during His life and ministry.) According to Ps. 22:9-10, Christ in embryonic form, somehow knew God from His mother's womb. Prior to the incarnation, He and the Father shared perfect, absolute, and eternal fellowship together. Note Section 178, John 17:5, footnote g, and Section 1, Part 1, second paragraph of footnote a, for more on these glorious but deeply mysterious thoughts.

(i) **"They understood not."** *Here is another clear statement that reveals that neither Joseph nor Mary, at this time, understood the life their Child was to live and the end He was to meet.* See footnote g above. Later, it would all be clear, however, time moves slowly when troubling questions concerning our children are not answered. Joseph and Mary must have felt a strange but growing distance between themselves and this wonderful Lad. Perhaps it started here in the temple with His response about "My Father." Surely, both would have know that He was referring to someone higher, even greater than good Joseph, His loving foster-father. The mystery of His human and divine natures and His relation to the Father in heaven was drawing on Him more and more. Geikie penned these words of practical wisdom about this precious Child, "If ever there was a son, who might have been expected to claim his independence it was He, and yet, to sanctify and enforce filial obedience forever, He lived on, under their humble roof, exemplary in the implicit and far-reaching obedience of a Jewish youth to His parents." See Cunningham Geikie, *The Life and Words of Christ,* page 160.

(j) **The third silent period.** Nothing concrete is known of the Messiah Child for some eighteen years after this temple experience. Here, the third shade of silence is drawn over His life. Section 91, Mk. 6:3, footnote d, informs us that Jesus became a carpenter during this time and was addressed as such by His friends. (It is curious that some commentators consider this as a term of ridicule or sarcasm, and not reality.) As He grew, year by year, we can believe that a strange loneliness rose in His soul that somehow made Him different from others. Not one evil thought or impure word lodged itself in His mind or came from His mouth (1 Peter 2:22). This Child was to become "a tender plant, and as a root out of dry ground" (Isa. 53:2). He gradually felt the isolation, which in later years during His ministry became so extreme, for how could perfect sinlessness ever be at home in a sin cursed world? We cannot but bare our heads as we dare to ask, "When did He become a man of sorrows and acquainted with grief?" The details of these early years were so sacred that God refused to have them put on paper!

2p-**Divine childhood.** Verse 52 is a marvelous statement concerning the youthful Son of God. In His childhood, everyone loved Him. He was a celestial flower planted by Jehovah, so lovely and beautiful that heaven and earth smiled together on Him. As a rose unfolds itself to charm the hearts of men, behold, this Child's early life sent forth a scented fragrance wafted from other worlds: all those nearby caught the pleasant odor and were amazed at Him. The notion here is almost that of an earthly, yet superhuman youthfulness embodied in this small Lad, still a wonderful, adorable Child. Year after year passed and found Him at His daily toil, because His "hour was not yet come." He always displayed gentle patience, transparent blamelessness of conduct, natural and active goodness; in tender love, He found the ready favor of all about Him. He was loved and honored; but half veiled in the mysterious light of His perfect manhood, there was a kindling of original divinity. As such, the years passed quietly away; time pushed Him slowly forward into the ministry, fierce conflict with men and devils, and finally, the awful cross, its work made efficacious by His glorious resurrection to all who believe!

(k) **God and man.** As this Little Boy grew into youth and early manhood, we muse about those silent years. Surely, both Joseph and Mary had many private hours of conversation about that strange Lad. Luke wrote that He found "favour with [both] God and man." This affirms that the citizens of little Nazareth and God in heaven blessed this beautiful Child of wonder. Of those formative years, playmates and close friends, we read nothing. Later, the people that loved Jesus as a child, sought to kill Him as a man. Refer to Section 38, Lk. 4:15-30 for the story.

2p-**The third silent period ended.** The chronology of eighteen years was concluded when He, as a thirty-year-old adult, appeared for baptism in the River Jordan. Note Section 22, footnote b for this event.

(l) **Efforts to discredit Christ.** The *New Testament Apocryphal Gospels,* prove the truths of the four gospels by quoting from them. Their wild stories about Jesus as a child demonstrate their falsity. Other hostile works depict Him becoming a magician during His few years in Egypt; hence, His later ability to perform miraculous deeds. See Section 6, footnotes d and e for several quotes regarding the Lord Jesus found in the Talmud. For more Talmudic slanders about Christ using magic, note tractate, Sanhedrin 107b. Other books that specialize in Jesus bashing are, *Jesus Christ in the Talmud, Midrash, Zohar, and the Liturgy of the Synagogue* by "great Lutheran scholar," Gustav Dalman, pages 45-50, and *Jesus* by Joseph Klausner, pages 27-28 and 49-51. For a sneaky approach to this sacrilege, see *Christianity in the Talmud* by R. T. Hereford, pages 50-62. Possibly, the most blasphemous volume ever written to defame the Son of God was the *Toledot-Jeshu (Book of the Life of Jesus)*. Having its origin in a second-century oral tradition, this scurrilous sixth-century book drips with venom for the Messiah. It says that Mary was raped by a Roman soldier and gave birth to Jesus. One cannot doubt that it originated with the early Jews, who hated Jesus of Nazareth and sought to discredit Him. Dalman's work mentioned above, has a section titled *Jesus Christ in the Talmud,* by Heinrich Liable. With demonic mentality, Dr. Liable wrote on page 11, "he [Jesus] was born out of wedlock." Continuing he said, "Jesus was a bastard and Mary an adulteress." This entire section by Liable reeks with blasphemy from page 1 to the end of page 39. Liable's words reflect the attitude of the scribes and Pharisees in the gospels toward Jesus the Savior-Messiah of Israel. A British blasphemer, and fierce Christ hater, George W. Foote, revived the old *Toledot-Jeshu* lie and printed his version of it in 1885. Foote spent his life defaming Jesus Christ, was imprisoned for blasphemy by a British court, suffered a nervous breakdown and died in 1891. Note, Ps. 9:17 describe Christ haters like Foote.

2p-Satanic literature, objects, and practices. According to Acts 19:18-19; Eph. 4:27, and 6:11, certain books and things of evil nature as listed above, should not be in Christian homes. For example, the demonic work the *Sixth and Seventh Books of Moses*, is notorious for the destructive and deadly influence it has upon the lives of those who have practiced the occult crafts and formulas written in its pages. Satanic images, plaques, literature, engravings, Voodoo drums, idols, *evil* videos, and filthy home movies have no place in the dwellings of believers. Television must be carefully guarded. Tattooing originated in paganism as heathens marked their bodies to signify the demon(s) they served. Often, these cuttings were mixed with colors. Members of the Church of Body Modification butcher their physical bodies to have spiritual experiences. Eyeball tattooing, male and female genital cuttings, nipple splitting, slicing the tongue to resemble snakes and so on. *God condemns these things (1 Cor. 6:19-20).* For more on this, see Section 50, second paragraph of footnote g and Section 54, third paragraph of footnote h.

3p-Evil brought into homes. Bringing satanic objects into our homes is forbidden. In South Africa, the author knew a wealthy farmer whose wife traveled into the Orient. She purchased a costly jade idol of Buddha. Returning to their farm, she placed this object in her lounge (living room). Within two days, dreadful things fell upon this family. The main barn burned, costing thousands of rands or dollars worth of equipment loss. The oldest son fell off a roof and was almost killed. The wife was mangled in a horrific truck wreck. A plague of grasshoppers (something unheard of) wiped out their crops. A strange fever almost killed her husband. Over the ensuing months, their livestock died by the dozens for no apparent reason. The pet dog was found hanging by its neck in a fence.

4p-The curse. Detecting something evil in these calamities, the African farm hands fled the property in terror. An elderly Dutch missionary was called to help this embattled couple. After hearing of the situation, he ordered the idol to be smashed and burned (Acts 19:17-20). The distraught family (who were Christians) repented of this act of ignorance in bringing an idol into their dwelling. They called upon God to forgive their ignorance, and to cleanse their home of the devil's curse (Ps. 38:18; Prov. 28:13; with 1 John 1:9). It was broken! This family had learned a hard lesson about bringing satanic objects onto their property. Offerings for the sin of ignorance in Lev. 4 and Num. 15, always point to the Savior. He is our perfect atonement when we sin ignorantly. These people had unknowingly given place to the Devil by setting up a demonic idol in their home (Eph. 4:27). For further explanation of this mystery, see Section 1, Part 2, fourth paragraph of footnote f.

5p-Forbidden in the Old Testament. The Torah Law of Israel forbade Jews to bring satanic relics into their dwellings (Deut. 7:25-26). *After* the law was given other commands given years later, sternly condemned having contact with or practicing any form of the occult (Deut 18:9-14). Scripture forbids the entire occult system. "Have no fellowship with the unfruitful works of darkness, but rather reprove [expose] them" (Eph. 5:11), and "Abstain from all appearance of evil" (1 Thess. 5:22). In Scripture, Christ and early Christians are seen in conflict with the kingdom of the Devil. This does not imply any defect in the perfect atonement of Christ. However, it booms like thunder regarding our *fellowship* with God and His Son (1 John 1:3), with fellow believers (1 John 1:7), and fighting the spiritual life-long warfare (Eph. 6:10-18). This is not to be saved, but because we are saved. Those Christians who relegate this spiritual conflict with evil to the first apostles only are seriously in error.

6p-Voodoo. Haiti is a land ensnared by this demonic religion. African slaves brought Voodooism into Haiti decades ago. With it came the antics, signs, signals, acts, offerings, libations, dancing rituals, and trappings of Satan. For example, one of their chief ceremonies begins with a Roman Catholic prayer, and three drums commence gradually to beat faster and harder. Then, a pagan priest draws symbols in the dust and pours out offerings to the spirits. Devotees dance madly about a tree; some are slammed to the ground in awful convulsions when the great mother spirit, "Erzuli," suddenly possesses them. These people consider it an honor to be "ridden" or "captured" by a spirit or Loa. In these heathen ceremonies, participants often become possessed by spirits and are the prisoners of Satan. Only the Lord Jesus can set these captives free from this deep spiritual bondage. While serving in South Africa, I was called to the home of a man who "went wild at midnight." His wife and two daughters were at wits end. Doctors could not help. His prized grandfather clock would strike only at midnight. With that, he went wild, raving, cursing, and smashing the furniture. This clock was willed to him as a boy, by his neighbor, who was a witch. Ironically, she had died at midnight! Dragging it into a field across the street, he soaked it with petrol. It would not burn! After smashing it with a sledgehammer, he knelt and asked God to remove any bondage it had brought into his life. Eerily, as we moved across the street to his house, it struck a final midnight gong, suddenly burst into flames, and burnt! With this, the curse vanished from his home.

7p-For more on the satanic encroachment upon the lives of believers, see Part 1, Section 4, third paragraph of footnote j. As stated in footnote l above, this is designed by the powers of darkness to ultimately discredit the Lord Jesus Christ, and ruin the testimony of Christians.

CHAPTER 8
(Presented in Four Parts)

JOHN THE BAPTIST APPEARS. THE NATION OF ISRAEL IS SHAKEN.* JESUS' BAPTISM, TEMPTATION, EARLY DISCIPLES, AND FIRST MIRACLE. A SHORT VISIT TO CAPERNAUM BEFORE PASSOVER. HOW INSPIRATION DIRECTED THE FOUR GOSPELS TO BE WRITTEN.

Time: It is conjectured that the above events spanned some six to eight months.

John the Baptist's call, prophetic mission, audience, and oddities.

With John's appearing the four-hundred years of silence since the messages of Malachi had been given, ended. At last, Israel had another prophetic voice calling her back to God. John preached some six months before baptizing Christ. Later, he ministered another twelve months, was then imprisoned at the infamous castle of Machaerus on the eastern side of the Dead Sea for about one year. Afterward, he was executed by Herod Antipas. For details on Antipas, see number 3 under footnote b below, and Section 92 for information on John's murder. During his incarceration, he maintained contact with his disciples and Jesus. See Matt. 11:2-3 for details.

Desert area of Judaea and Jordan

Matt. 3:1–3	Mk. 1:1–3	Lk. 3:1–5	John
1 In those days[a]	1 The beginning[a] of the gospel of Jesus Christ, the Son of God;	1 Now in the fifteenth year of the reign of Tiberius Caesar,[b] Pontius Pilate	
being governor of Judaea, and Herod being tetrarch [ruler of a fourth part*] of Galilee, and his brother Philip tetrarch* of I-tu-rae-a and of the region of Trach-o-ni-tis, and Ly- sa-ni-as the tetrarch* of Ab-i-le-ne, 2 Annas and Caiaphas being the high priests, the word of God came unto John the son of Zacharias in the wilderness.			
came John the Baptist, preaching in the wilderness of Judaea, 2 And saying, "Repent[c] ye: for the kingdom of heaven is at hand."		3 And he came into all the country about Jordan, preaching the baptism of repentance[c] for the remission of sins;	
John in prophecy 3 For this is he that was spoken[d] of by the prophet Esaias, [Isaiah] saying,[e]	*John in prophecy* 2 As it is written[d] in the prophets,	*John in prophecy* 4 As it is written[d] in the book of the words of Esaias [Isaiah] the prophet, saying,[e]	
	"Behold, I send my messenger before thy face, which shall prepare thy way before thee."		
"The voice of one crying in the wilderness, 'Prepare ye the way of the Lord, make his paths straight.'"	3 "The voice of one crying in the wilderness, 'Prepare ye the way of the Lord, make his paths straight.'"	"The voice of one crying in the wilderness, 'Prepare ye the way of the Lord, make his paths straight. 5 "Every valley shall be	

81

Matt. 3:4-6	Mk. 1:4-6	Lk. 3:5-6	John
		filled, and every mountain and hill shall be brought low; and the crooked *shall* be made straight, and the rough ways shall be made smooth; 6 And all flesh shall see the salvation of God.'" (Verse 7 cont. in Section 21, Part 2.)	
John's peculiar style 4 ►And the same John had his raiment of camel's hair, and a leathern girdle about his loins;[f] and his meat was locusts and wild honey.			
	◄Mark places this same statement in verse 6 below. Luke does not mention John's raiment.		
	John's audience and work 4 John did baptize in the wilderness, and preach the baptism of repentance for the remission of sins.		
John's audience and work 5 Then went out to him Jerusalem, and all Judaea, and all the region round about Jordan,	5 And there went out unto him all the land of Judaea,		
	and they of Jerusalem,		
6 And were baptized of him in Jordan, confessing[g] their sins. (Verse 7 cont. in Section 21, Part 2.)	and were all baptized of him in the river of Jordan, confessing[g] their sins.		
	6 ►And John was clothed with camel's hair, and with a girdle of a skin about his loins; and he did eat locusts and wild honey;[h] (Verse 7 cont. in Section 21, Part 4.)	*◄Matthew places this same statement in verse 4 above. Each of the four evangelists wrote as the Holy Spirit directed them. Hence, their placements are often in different locations.*	

Footnotes-Commentary

(a) **"The beginning of the gospel of Jesus Christ."** This brief prologue to Mark's book is the welcome spiritual sunrise after the long, dark night. The Law of Moses, and every prophetic forecast regarding the coming of Christ was poised, waiting for fulfillment. It began with the appearing of John the Baptist, the Messiah's forerunner. More than four hundred years had passed since the prophetic voice of Malachi became silent. Mark symbolically tells his readers that the gospel sun rose and beamed its warm rays of new hope over Adam's fallen race with the appearing of John. The word "gospel" means "good news," and the term used here refers to the news that Christ, the promised Messiah, *has* come, lived, died, and risen to save men from sin. (Mark wrote looking back on this divine history.) He informs his original readers that a grand and glorious hope was introduced with the ministry of the Baptist. He is careful to base his claim on the sure predictions of the Old Testament Scripture. John the Baptist was the man whose "voice" had fulfilled the prophecy given by Malachi so long ago (Mal. 3:1). Mark does not mean that this "good news gospel" had never been preached before. Paul tells us that God had preached it to Abraham some two thousand years earlier (Gal. 3:8). God used Abraham as the supreme model of one who was saved by faith and concludes that this is how all men are to be saved today (Rom. 4:1-5). Hebrews 4:1-2 emphatically states that God had preached the gospel to the millions of Jews in the wilderness, and they rejected it. One need only look at the grand array of Old Testament saints listed across Hebrews 11 to understand that people *were* saved during Old Testament history. For more on this subject, see Section 144, footnote i. They put faith in Christ, who was yet to come, as we put faith in Him, who has already come. See Section 10, footnote b for more on the salvation of men and the work of the Holy Spirit over Old Testament history. During the ministry of Christ, people who put faith in Him were saved even though at the time they did not understand the full implications of His life and how it would end. The entire picture came into focus on the day of Pentecost.

2p-"The Son of God." In these words, Mark was distinguishing for his Gentile readers, between the demonic heathen fables of gods and their sons appearing on earth. This is explained in Section 103, the third paragraph of foot note b. Mark shows that God's plan of redemption, prefigured and preached over the Old Testament (and by which many were saved), had now stepped onto the stage. And it was in the Person of Jesus Christ the Son of the true and living God! In time, this gospel would reach out to all humanity. With the appearing of John from the wilderness of Judaea, Christ, the Savior of the world would be introduced. About three and a half years later, this gospel was historically accomplished in the death, burial, and resurrection of the Messiah. What had been prefigured across the Old Testament was performed; shadow became substance in the Lord Jesus. God's "good news" was no longer accessible to particular persons in history past, especially the Jews. With the preaching of John, the gospel flower fully blossomed. Mark presented John the Baptist as the *first* to proclaim that the promised Messiah of the Old Testament was at hand. He begins his book by explaining how John came, preached, introduced, and baptized Christ, the One who made the saving gospel a reality for all. After penning his story of the life of Christ, Mark concluded with the gospel's literal realization in the death, burial, and resurrection of God's Son. Lastly, he records the Great Commission of Christ to take this "good news" to every creature and baptize those who believe it (Mk. 16:15-16). Note Section 23, Matt. 4:3, third paragraph of footnote c for comments on the phrase "the Son of God." For a survey of what John did and preached, see this Section 21, Part 4, footnote q.

(b) For the benefit of Theophilus, the original recipient of this letter (Lk.1:3), Luke was inspired to list the names of five political rulers and two religious leaders of the past. Theophilus must have had some historical knowledge of each person. In these names, Luke roots in world history the appearing of the Baptist. It was a solid fact. None of the other three gospel writers listed such impeccable political-religious data. Luke's fastidiousness was necessary that Theophilus might know the absolute certainty of those things wherein he had been instructed. Further, he could have checked the credibility of Luke's claims concerning these Roman and Hebrew personalities. Luke even designated the territory and/or office of each one. For comprehensive details regarding Herod the Great and his sons, see *A History of the Jewish People in the Time of Jesus Christ,* vol. ii, pages 1-43, by Emil Schurer. The following provides information regarding each of the persons listed by Luke in chapter 3:1-2.

1. **Tiberius Caesar** was the third Roman emperor, ruling from A.D. 14 to 37. The word "Tiberius" means "the son of Tiber," and was a popular pagan name. For the alleged meaning of the *title* "Caesar," see Section 155, footnote c. In his later years, he became a debauched, power-mad murderer, given over to lewdness, visual pornography, and sexual acts with infants too revolting to write on paper. Tiberius ruled when Christ was crucified. Charles Ludwig wrote that Tiberius did not believe in the resurrection of Christ, "because the Roman Senate had not voted on Jesus as being divine." See *Ludwig's Handbook of New Testament Rulers & Cities,* page 22. Luke wrote that the "word of God" came to John in the fifteenth year of the reign of Tiberius, (Lk. 3:1-2) which would be exactly A.D. 29. Tiberius' name was later applied to both a city and the Sea of Galilee (John 6:1; 6:23; and 21:1). One more political wretch of the Roman Empire, Tiberius died in his seventy-ninth year. His decease is shrouded in mystery.

2. **Pontius Pilate** was appointed the sixth governor or procurator, of Idumea (Edom), Judaea and Samaria. He ruled from A.D. 26 to 36. His name means "javelin." For the meaning of the *title* "Pontius," see Section 183, footnote a. Pilate's decade of rule was filled with turmoil and bloodshed. A few years after the death of Jesus, he was recalled to Rome to answer for his irresponsible actions and was banished. Amazingly, Ethiopia's Coptic Church honors him annually on June 25 as a martyred saint! This is because Pilate washed his hands and said that he was "innocent of the blood of this just person" (Matt. 27:24). The Greek Church holds that his wife, Claudia Procula, a proselyte to the Jewish synagogue, later became a Christian. Note her surprising and accurate description of Jesus ("just man") in Matt. 27:19 and Pilate's affirmation of this fact a few moments afterward in verse 24. Years later, Paul wrote in 1 Tim. 6:13 that Christ had witnessed to Governor Pilate. Thus, the ill-fated Roman politician, Pilate, had his opportunity to be saved! A *legend* has it that he committed suicide in A.D. 36 somewhere near Lake Lucerne in Switzerland. Today, a section of this Swiss lake is "off limits" to tourists because of the awful phenomena and ghostly apparitions that occur there during the night hours. Some believe that these terrible materializations are satanically connected with Pilate's suicide. For an excellent article on Pilate, see the *Biblical, Theological, Ecclesiastical Cyclopaedia,* vol. viii, pages 199-204, by M'Clintock and Strong. Alfred Edersheim in *Life and Times of Jesus the Messiah,* page 972 gives a list of all the governors appointed to rule Judea until the destruction of Jerusalem in A.D. 70.

3. **Herod Antipas the tetrarch.** "Tetrarch" means "ruler of a fourth part," and Herod probably means "hero." Oddly, the name Antipas carries something of a double meaning, "for all, against all." Herod, also called Antipas, was a son of Herod the Great, who died in 4 B.C. See Section 8, Lk. 1:5, footnote a

for comments on King Herod the Great. Antipas' mother was Malthace, a Samaritan. He ruled in Galilee and Peraea from 4 B.C. to A.D. 39. History condemned Antipas when he stole Herodias, his half-brother Philip's wife (who was also his niece), and eloped with her. Later, the two had John the Baptist murdered (Mk. 6:17-29), with Herodias playing chief instigator in his death. It was Antipas whom Christ dubbed "that fox" in Lk. 13:32, and whose steward's wife, Joanna, supported Jesus' ministry (Lk. 8:3). Herod Antipas and "his men of war" mocked Jesus the night of His trial (Lk. 23:6-12). Antipas' name is united with that of Pilate in the death of Jesus in the apostles' prayer (Acts 4:24-30). One year after the death of Emperor Tiberius, in A.D. 37, the egotistical Herod Antipas, at the behest of his wretched wife, traveled to Rome. Their intentions were to request of the new emperor, Caligula, the title of "king" for Antipas and a crown. Caligula, however, had received a false tip-off that they were involved in a conspiracy. He flew into a rage and banished both Antipas and his wife. Refer to Josephus' *Antiquities,* Book 18:7. 1-2, lines 240-256 for details. They spent the rest of their lives in foreign exile and dire poverty. The twist of the story is that Herod was banished a few years after he and his men of war mocked the Lord Jesus. As reported above, Herodias his wife had been the chief instigator in the death of John the Baptist. There was an old legend that in her latter days, she fell through ice and her head was sliced off. It is also noteworthy that both Matt. 14:9 and Mk. 6:14 referred to Herod as "king." (Some hold his enemies gave him this title sarcastically.) This indicates that these two books were written *after* news of Herod's failure to procure the royal title had spread over the world of that era. Apparently, Antipas' kingly aspirations had become something of a public joke by the time Matthew and Mark penned their gospels. For a thorough study on Antipas, see *Herod Antipas: A Contemporary of Jesus Christ,* by H.W. Hoehner, pages 203-212, 331-333, and 340-342.

4. **Philip II** was also a son of Herod the Great. (He is not to be confused with his half brother, Philip I.) The name means "lover of horses." Philip II ruled the vast regions of Ituraea and Trachonitis from A.D. 4 to 34. Apparently, he lived a quiet life and was known for his moderation. Josephus wrote briefly of him in *Antiquities,* Book 18: 4. 6, lines 106 and 107. He built the city of Paneas, (or Panias) known in Scripture as Caesarea Philippi, where Peter made his famed confession in Matt. 16:13-17. Philip advanced the pagan fame of the city of Bethsaida by renaming it Julia, in honor of Emperor Augustus' daughter. Coins have been found with his image struck on them. His notoriety is found in the fact that he married Herodias, (mentioned above) a daughter of his half-brother Aristobulus (therefore, his niece and granddaughter of his father, Herod the Great!). Note Section 92, footnote f, for comments on Herodias. From this incestuous and adulterous union came a child named Salome, the dancer at a drunken party that resulted in the murder of the Baptist. Philip died at Julias-Bethsaida in A.D. 34. Refer to the *Biblical, Theological, and Ecclesiastical Cyclopaedia,* vol. viii, page 89, by M'Clintock and Strong for continued details on these matters.

5. **Lysanias** was not a son of Herod the Great. His name seems to mean, "Expel sorrow." Little is known of him except that his name has been found in some ancient inscriptions. History records that Emperor Claudius took away his rulership in A.D. 42. Josephus wrote briefly of him in *Antiquities,* Book 19:5. 1, lines 274- 277, and Book 20:7. 1, lines 137-140.

6. **Annas, Caiaphas and the rotted-out Jewish religion.** Annas means "humble." The name Caiaphas signifies "vomit." This was a father-in-law and son-in-law criminal conspiracy. At this time, financial corruption and power status controlled the office. For more on this, see Section 29, John 2:14, footnote b. It was Annas who originated the abomination of leasing booth sites within the temple compound to public vendors. Christ drove them out on two occasions; thus, Annas' hatred for Him. Now, a combination of father-in-law and son-in-law presided over the nation and temple. According to the Jewish law, only one high priest at a time could serve the nation of Israel, and the office was held for life. The sacred office was used by Annas and Caiaphas in a subversive manner to the financial advantage of both. H. Wayne House, in his work *Chronological and Background Charts of the New Testament,* pages 70-71, gives a list of the Jewish high priests from 350 B.C., until A.D. 70. Apart from trying to justify the non-existent "synoptic problem" myth (pages 88-93), Dr. House has given us a helpful book in this effort. For more on Annas, Caiaphas, and the Jewish priesthood, see *Appendix Five.*

7. **The high priests.** Luke's use of the plural "priests" is historically correct because during this time *both* men were using the office for financial and religious advantage. His openness in putting down these facts is obvious. For example, had John the Baptist not began to preach "in the fifteenth year of the reign of Tiberius," or had Herod, Philip, Pilate, and the others not done the things Luke had written, then his words would have been instantly detected as untrue by Theophilus. Are Bible believers expected to surrender their faith in God and His Word because centuries later some educated religionist slithers from his den in a university department of theology and ventures to sneer publicly at what his wicked soul hopes are not true? Their guilt is only heightened by their brazen attack on God's Word, clustered in wordy pretensions to have unique knowledge of the "facts." Accurate history and theology blush in the

presence of these learned infidels. Meanwhile, the infallible record of Dr. Luke endures. He set A.D. 29 as the year that John the Baptist began his ministry and that settled it.

2p-Hebrew religion, rotten to the core. The Jewish sages set down numerous signs supposedly proving *when* their Messiah would come to save Israel and set up His political kingdom. None of these pointed to His second advent, for they had never heard of such a thing! Rabbis wrote in the Talmud that in the day Messiah appears [to establish His earthly kingdom] sin would be rampant within Israel: "corn and costly wine, governments corrupt, disrespect of elders would prevail among children, and the synagogues would become brothels." According to the Talmud tractate Kethuboth 105a there were "349 synagogues" in Jerusalem when it was destroyed in A.D. 70. However, this sounds like a typical Jewish exaggeration. Regardless, see Talmud tractates, Yoma 9b, Sanhedrin 97a and 98a for rabbinical condemnation of the sins of Israel at this time. When Christ called these Jews "wicked and adulterous," morals had dropped so low that the "bitter water test" had been discontinued. This had been given by God, through which those guilty of adultery would be detected. See Num. 5:11-31 for the strange instructions of this test. This discontinuance was made official by Rabbi Jochanan ben Zacchai because Israel had been nicknamed "an adulterous race of people." Everyone listening knew what Jesus meant when He called them "an evil and adulterous generation." Josephus was a contemporary with some of these people or at least their children. He wrote scathing remarks about their moral and spiritual decadence. Such words as, "For that time was fruitful among the Jews in all sorts of wickedness, so that they left no evil deed undone; nor was there any new form of wickedness which anyone could invent if he wished to do so. Thus, they were all corrupt in both their public and private life, and they vied with each other over who should excel in impiety toward God and injustice to men. The more powerful oppressed the common people, and the common people eagerly sought to destroy the more powerful . . ." See *Introduction to the Gospel Records*, by William Nast, page 145, printed in 1866. Today's pious talk by certain Jews, claiming, "the temple was a place of learning the truth of God and to receive instructions from the noble rabbis and teachers of the law" is a joke. The above quotations, by those who lived during this era belie this claim. Jesus told the Jews that none of them had kept the law (John 7:19). God allowed these religious hypocrites to be destroyed in the horrific destruction of A.D. 70 at the hands of the vicious pagan Roman armies. For more on this, refer to Section 176, footnote t. Also, read Christ's fierce denunciations of the Jews in Section 159.

3p-Lk. 3:2. "The Word of God." The grand title, "The Word of God," whether it applies to Christ, the voice of God, or Holy Scripture is always written in uppercase. This rule is employed in all commentary notes used in this work. See explanation of headings, quotation marks, and capitalization, under *HOW TO USE THIS HARMONY COMMENTARY* for further explanation.

(c) **Matt. 3:2. "Repent"** was the clarion call that introduced the kingdom preached by John and Jesus. This word informs men as to how this kingdom may be entered. See footnote g below for confession of sin. Our Lord's kingdom was very different from the one expected by the religious Jews. This is explained in Section 39, footnote a; and Section 134, footnotes b and c. In verse 3, "Esaias" is a Greek style of writing the name "Isaiah."

(d) **"Spoken by the prophet Isaiah."** All three gospel writers base their claims on the authority of Old Testament Scriptures, which were spoken and written by Isaiah. This is Mark's first Old Testament quotation. He used the plural "prophets," as Isaiah was counted as one of the greatest among them. His quote comes from Mal. 3:1. His second quotation, in verse 3, is from Isa. 40:3. They are blended together for they speak of John the Baptist, our Lord's forerunner. All four gospel writers cited scores of verses from the Old Testament as they presented their inspired versions of the life of Christ.

(e) Matthew quotes from Isa. 40:3, while Mark cites verse 3 from the same passage. Luke also quotes from Isa. 40:3-5 then in verse 6 he cites from the latter part of Isa. 52:10. In doing this, he joined several lines from different Old Testament passages and blends them into one passage. This was a common method used among New Testament personalities, speakers, and writers. The aged Simeon quoted this verse when he first set his eyes on the infant Messiah, the salvation of mankind (Lk. 2:30). Revelation 1:7 predicts a time coming when "every eye shall see him." This includes the Roman soldiers that pierced His hands and feet (Ps. 22:16). There is a strong indication that all four of these men were converted at the cross. Refer to Section 192, footnote b for the moving story and their united confession of Christ.

2p-John the Baptist preached, "Prepare ye the way of the Lord, make his paths straight." A marching king escorted by his armies sent ahead messengers (forerunners) whose duty was to proclaim his approach and prepare the way. They were to remove obstructions, make roads and paths straight, level hills, and raise valleys. John the Baptist did these things in the spiritual sense as he made ready a people for Israel's coming Messiah (Lk. 1:17). Matthew's quotation from Isaiah fits the customs of that day and was understood by his Jewish readers. Nothing miraculous is intended here in the use of these geological terms. It is written in the Talmud tractate, Eiruvin 43b, "Messiah could not appear before Elijah had arrived." As stated, John was the predicted Elijah of the Old Testament. He stepped into the scene *before* the Savior, and prepared the way for Him to appear before the nation Israel. Refer to Section 21, Part 4, footnotes m and q for more on this thought. Sadly, over time, the leadership of Israel and the Hebrew people in general rejected their promised Messiah-Savior. For confirmation of this, see Section 153, main heading, footnote k.

(f) **Camel's hair and locusts.** The poorest people of the land wove camel's hair into coarse cloth. A leather waistband was also part of their adornment. The Torah Law in Lev. 11:21-22, lists four types of locusts that were fit for human consumption. Poorer class Bedouins eat them to this day. The Talmud lays down technical rules for preparation of locust before consuming them. These guidelines are in tractates, Chullin 65a and 66a. Wild honey means just what it implied, being the product of bees in the more desolate areas of the land. All the above suggests poverty and hardship living.

2p-John's apparel had similarities with that of Israel's greatest prophet, Elijah. This is why many Jews mistook John for the Old Testament prophet called the Tishbite. However, John denied being the *real* Elijah of the Old Testament, who, according to the rabbis, was to return *physically* to Israel to prepare for Messiah. This denial raised the question among the Jews: how could Jesus be their Messiah since Elijah had not first come to prepare the way for Him? With this denial, the religious leaders soon turned against John as he defended Christ and presented Him as Israel's true Messiah. Their opposition grew more hostile. The rabbis had taught for centuries that the *real* Tishbite would appear and prepare Israel for her Messiah. They failed to see that John fulfilled this role. These facts of Jewish history cannot be avoided by appealing that "John was only a type of Elijah; the real Elijah is yet to come in person during the tribulation period." An Orthodox Jew living in the time of Christ would not have believed such a myth, for they had never heard of a "tribulation period" to come over two thousand years in the future. Men who have struggled with Rev. 11:3-11 invented the earthly return of the real Elijah. These verses are anything but clear on this interpretation. Hermeneutical exactness and exegetical certainty are gravely missing on a moot point such as this. In church history, thousands of guesses have been postured regarding this mystery. Who these two men are no one knows, not even the end time gurus. *Appendix Eight* carries a review of the various speculations of those trying to figure out what God has not specifically said and absolutely will not allow.

3p-The disciples put the question to Christ, "Why then say the scribes that Elias [Elijah] must first come?" This inquiry reveals they believed the teaching of the rabbis on this point. Messiah responded by affirming that Elijah would first come and restore the nation of Israel. He agreed that this rabbinical teaching was correct up to this point. (The restoring of all things referred to the preparation of a people out of Israel, who were ready for the Messiah when He came. It had nothing to do with a glorified millennial reign of Christ several thousand years later.) The Savior continued, "But I say unto you, That Elias [Elijah] is come already, and they [the Jews] knew him not." This conversation between Jesus and His disciples concluded with a ring of finality: "Then the disciples understood that he spake unto them of John the Baptist." This is explained in Matt. 17:10-13. *Here, is a definite declaration that the prophecies of Malachi regarding the coming of Elijah were fulfilled in the ministry of John the Baptist.* See all of Section 8, footnote i for further comments on this point. Only by forcing these verses by appealing to extreme typology can commentators and preachers wrest out of them a "Second coming of Elijah." Sensational preaching is not necessarily biblical preaching. Consider some of the similarities between the Baptist and Elijah:

1. Both were anointed with the same Spirit and power. See 2 Kings 2:9 with Lk. 1:17.
2. Both wore similar garments and lived simple lives. See 2 Kings 1:8 with Matt. 3:4 and Mk. 1:6.
3. Both were fearless preachers and rebuked kings. See 1 Kings 18:16-19 with Matt. 14:3-4.
4. Both had trouble with discouragement. See 1 Kings 19:4 with Matt. 11:1-6.
5. Both had a great impact on the nation of Israel. See 1 Kings 18:25-41 with Lk. 1:16.

4p-Verse 4, "Baptism for remission of sin." See Section 203, first and second paragraph of footnote d.

5p-Verse 5. "Then went out to him." Thousands flocked to hear John. Many of them believed his message about the coming Messiah, confessed their sins and were baptized. Among the number were some men who later became the first disciples of the Lord Jesus (Acts 1:21-22). See Section 21, Part 3, paragraphs one and two of footnote l for the requirements John had laid down before he would baptize.

(g) **"Confessing."** This word also carries the meaning to "confess publicly." The idea is that the baptismal candidate *openly* confessed he was a repenting sinner who believed in Christ to come, the people standing along the banks heard this. He was publicly and verbally agreeing with God's verdict about him through the preaching of John. God through John's powerful preaching called for repentance and confession before water baptism. *And this He got!* Who can read into this scene an infant being thus baptized after confessing his sins? In Jewish thinking, sin was first a violation of their Torah Law (1 John 3:4). None of this makes any sense if one brings infants and small untaught children into the story. For an explanation of the Jewish idea of repentance, refer to Section 50, Matt. 9:13, footnote h. For repentance as John and Jesus preached it, see footnote c above.

(h) As slightly mentioned in the first paragraph of footnote f above, this was typical dress and food for the poorer classes of people. There is nothing here to be spiritualized or allegorized. It means just what it says. Locusts were gutted, washed, and roasted over an open fire for food. This practice is continued across parts of Africa to this day. John eating locusts affirms that he was not of the Essenes sect as they abstained from all meats, both domestic and wild. For continued information on this ancient split off from the Jewish religion, see under heading, *Did Christ quote the Talmud or Essenes in the Sermon on the Mount,* located just before Section 44.

John's preaching to Israel's religious leaders. Fruitful repentance from sin proves salvation. Avoid God's judgment and the damnation of hell fire.

Desert areas of Judaea and Jordan

Matt. 3:7-10	Mk.	Lk. 3:7-9	John
His response to the masses **7** But when he saw many of the Pharisees and Sadducees come to his baptism, he said unto them,[(i)] "O generation of vipers, who hath warned you to flee from the wrath to come? **8** "Bring forth therefore fruits meet for repentance: **9** "And think not to say within yourselves, 'We have Abraham[(j)] to *our* father:' for I say unto you, ►that God is able of these stones to raise up children unto Abraham. *Good fruit or fire* **10** "And now also the axe is laid unto the root of the trees: therefore every tree which bringeth not forth good fruit is hewn down, and cast into the fire."[(k)] (Verse 11 cont. in Section 21, Part 4.) ► *When Matthew's verse 9 is compared to Luke's verse 8, we note that one carries the uppercase, the other does not. For explanation of the grammatical difference, see, Section 62, and the notation at the end of Matthew 11:8. In the original version of the KJV 1611 Bible, both verses are in the lowercase. Whether a word begins with upper or lowercase has nothing to do with divine inspiration. It pertains rather to English grammar. As pointed out, the early biblical manuscripts had no punctuation marks, yet they were inspired of God (2 Tim. 3:16-17 with 2 Peter 1:21).*		*His response to the masses* **7** Then said he to the multitude[(i)] that came forth to be baptized of him, "O generation of vipers, who hath warned you to flee from the wrath to come? **8** "Bring forth therefore fruits worthy of repentance, and begin not to say within yourselves, 'We have Abraham[(j)] to *our* father:' for I say unto you, ►**T**hat God is able of these stones to raise up children unto Abraham. *Good fruit or fire* **9** "And now also the axe is laid unto the root of the trees: every tree therefore which bringeth not forth good fruit is hewn down, and cast into the fire."[(k)] (Verse 10 cont. in Section 21, Part 3.)	

Footnotes–Commentary

[(i)] **"He said unto them."** Contextually, these scathing words were addressed to the Pharisees and Sadducees, who prided themselves on being super-righteous and superior to all men. The "multitudes" were also included in his rebuke. Near the close of His ministry, our Lord fiercely condemned these men with the sure fate of eternal hell and the destruction of their city, temple, and all of its ceremonies and traditions in which they trusted. This occurred in A.D. 70. See Section 159, Matt. 23:1-39 where Jesus announces their doom again two days before His death.

2p-Verse 8. "Fruits meet for repentance." Here, we meet the ingredients that signal grace has done its work through faith. They are called "fruits." For the fruits that John the Baptist required of his converts before baptism, see the next Section 21, Part 3, all of footnote l. The history of Christianity and American politics is stained by those in authority who tell us, "God has called them" to serve. Thus, they are worthy of our vote and voice. Many of these are the fruitless charlatans. When caught in their sin, they quote the verse, "For *there is* not a just man upon the earth, that doeth good, and sinneth not" (Eccles. 7:20). "Christian" and political hypocrites use this passage as a "backup" for their next sin session. Across America, an earthquake of "evangelical leaders and pastors," as well as "presidents, presidential candidates, senators, congressional representatives, governors, advisors, and politicians" have had their secret sins were uncovered. One governor was running a prostitution ring! Those who live as though they are above God's moral law are fools. Instead of resigning office when exposed, work to get their lives in order, they continue to "serve the people" they have deceived. Meanwhile, they gives billions to our enemies who have sworn to kill us! And they will too, for a politician is someone who will lay down *your* life for his country. The *average* American believes that their religious and political leaders should be of the highest integrity and moral character. Aesop, the Greek fabulist wrote, "We hang petty thieves, and appoint the great ones to public office." *"God bless America," has almost become swear words to men who really know God and America!*

3p-A dose of their own medicine. Barnyard journalists excavate every bad deed of saints and sinners, even if it is a hundred years old, and these are "breaking news." O for a media outlet that exposed *only* the sins of journalists, network anchors, talk-show hosts, executives, and so on. The rats would run for their holes! *Instead of freedom of the press, we might enjoy freedom from the press for a while.* Christ's salvation lived daily, ultimately produces people who can better serve God, the media, and country. Historically, *true* Christians are the minority and minority votes never win. "The majority vote flop" is discussed in Section 101, fifth paragraph of footnote b.

4p-Sinning saints. "Born again believers" who defend sin and godlessness are sheep in wolf's clothing! The philosophy that "Christians" can lie, cheat, steal, live in immorality, then (sort of) "say a little prayer, and it's alright," is religious madness. God corrects, "Sinning saints" (Ps. 50:22). For explanation of this, see Section 46, eleventh paragraph of footnote g. Those who continue in evil refusing to repent bring down the chastisement of God.

5p-What the unsaved world really hates. It is something far more than *true* fundamentalist Christians. They compare us to the right-wing Mormon radicals like Glen Beck, maniacs like Warren Jeffs, Timothy Mcveigh, David Koresh, white supremacist, skinheads, militant Islam, neo-Nazi racists, Ku Klux clan, New Black Panthers, and the alleged crimes of the infamous Hephzibah House at Winona Lake-Warsaw, Indiana. *First, wicked men hate the Bible and the unique Savior it presents. Second, they fiercely resent what it teaches about their sin and hell.* (Some of the above quacks even quote the Bible to justify their heinous statements, deeds, and crimes!) Certain magistrates have singled out Christian parents who endeavor to rear their children according to biblical instructions. No judge or jury can bring up children, but *good parents* can. Being good parents is the toughest job in the world, especially if they have mean kids. They must learn to stand up to these little monsters, smack their tails when necessary, and say, "No." Sadly, not all parents have moral character. Some are dead beats, dope heads, adulterers, whoremongers, loiters, drunkards, welfare thieves, and child-beaters. Several years ago, I sat in a parking when suddenly a young woman raced out a shop door with two men in hot pursuit. She was shoplifting. Her little daughter stood crying. Without family members willing to help, in such cases *honest* magistrates and courts are needed. Honest, is italicized because the Devil possesses some of those who wear the black robe of justice. The Pennsylvania juvenile court judge, Mark Ciavarella, who sent scores of teenagers to incarceration for financial kickbacks, illustrates this. His sentence to twenty-eight years in prison reveals there is still justice in our legal system. On the other hand, in California, an alleged gay judge strikes down the law that banned same sex marriages. See Section 155, fourth paragraph of footnote g for more on this travesty. *True magistrates who judge according to the law and do not make their laws are God's gift to orderly society.* The late Dr. Benjamin Spock's lunacy about children is in Section 96, first paragraph of footnote l. Christian parents often mistakenly claim Prov. 22:6 as a sure-fire promise for child rearing. This error is corrected in Section 149, fourth paragraph of footnote g. For a terse response to the despisers of *true* fundamentalism, see Dr. Don Boys' work, *The God Haters*. Boys gives them a dose of their own medicine!

 (j) All devout Jews firmly believed that their heritage as physical descendants of Abraham gave them special favor with God, above all people on earth. They were the only children of God's kingdom. This superstitious plea did not satisfy John. He demanded they repent of their sins and believe on Jesus Christ the Messiah, whom he announced would soon appear. John's message and deeds are explained in Section 21, Part 4, footnote q. The first fruit of genuine Jewish repentance would be to receive Jesus of Nazareth, their promised Messiah.

2p-"Of these Stones." Some understand this to refer to the Gentiles, who worshiped countless images of wood and stone. It may suggest God's power to give life to the heathen, who was spiritually stone dead. Regardless of what these words may mean, in time, millions of Gentiles would come to the saving knowledge of Christ. See Section 38, footnote k for Jesus' *first* public intimation that Gentiles would be brought into His kingdom.

 (k) Because they rejected Messiah, their destiny was the ax of judgment and the fires of hell. See Section 72, Lk. 13:5, footnote f for other comments on this. For the rabbinical teaching on repentance, see Section 50, Matt. 9:13, footnote h. Christ said, "The children of the kingdom" would be cast into outer darkness. With this, note Section 60, Matt. 8:11-12 and comments in the Information Box at the end of the Scripture verses. The rabbis believed that hell was where evil spirits were imprisoned and called it "outer darkness." They held that all Jews who rejected the Torah Law, and the oral teachings, and all Gentiles would so be cast into this "outer darkness."

2p-God's ax of wrath struck Israel in A.D. 70. Over a million Jews were killed. Jesus spoke of this in Section 163. See also Josephus, *Wars of the Jews*, Books 5 and 6. John pointed to the lifeless stones along Jordan to illustrate Israel's doom. Still, God was ready to save all who would repent and believe in the Messiah. Most refused.

John explains the fruits of true repentance to a variety of inquirers. He describes the wonderful effects this will produce in their personal lives.

Desert area of Judaea and Jordan

Matt.	Mk.	Lk. 3:10–14	John
		The people's question is answered	
		10 And the people asked him, saying, "What shall we do then?" (to escape this coming judgment)	
		11 He answereth and saith unto them,[(1)] "He that hath two coats, let him impart to him that hath none; and he that hath meat, [food] let him do likewise."	
		The publicans' question is answered	
		12 Then came also publicans [tax collectors] to be baptized, and said unto him, "Master, what shall we do?"	
		13 And he said unto them, "Exact no more than that which is appointed you."	
		The soldiers' question is answered	
		14 And the soldiers likewise demanded of him, saying, "And what shall we do?" And he said unto them, "Do violence to no man, neither accuse *any* falsely; and be content with your wages." (Verse 15 cont. in Section 21, Part 4.)	

Footnotes-Commentary

[(1)] The country was aflame as thousands came to John for baptism! The fiery preacher, filled with the Spirit from his mother's womb, demanded an inward change in their lives that would be seen in outward practices, or "fruits" of conduct. Such are the results of real repentance. See Section 50, Matt. 9:13, footnote h, for comments on the Jewish understanding of repentance. Those who could *not* manifest these "fruits" outwardly were destined for the "fire" (Matt. 3:10). Below are some of John's requirements before baptizing any person:

1. Prosperous persons were required to share their food and raiment with those who had none (verse 11).
2. Hated tax collectors were to repent of their ill practices of thieving and fraud and take *only* what was due (verses 12–13). Note that John did not say they should stop collecting taxes.
3. Tough, overbearing Roman soldiers were commanded to repent of their ill treatment of the citizenry, false accusations, and grumbling over wages (verse 14). At one time, Roman soldiers were paid in salt, a precious commodity in that era. Hence, our expression "He's not worth his salt." Our English word "salary" has it origin in the word "salt," revealing its ancient origin in Roman times.

2p-Surely, there were more sins among the people than these! Apparently, this three-fold demand embraced the whole gamut of their personal wickedness. John dealt with the religious leaders of Israel and demanded repentance from all of them. He looked for outward proof of an inward change before he would give his witness to the baptism of anyone. This man had been acquainted with the Holy Spirit from his mother's womb! He preached with power and authority. He looked for external, practical deeds that would demonstrate genuine inward repentance and change in the lives of those requesting baptism. Objections that "repentance is a work and cannot be prerequisite to eternal life" are like the general who said, "I must hurry and catch up with the army for I am their leader." They are behind the truth, not marching with it.

3p-Those who teach a repentless salvation "turn the grace of God into lasciviousness" (Jude 4). Not only did the Baptist call for repentance from sin, but he also demanded that men confess their sins as well. This was indeed a new thing for the religious Jews, as well as the pagan Gentiles in his audience. In Matt. 3:6, personal confession of sin is a required prerequisite to water baptism. Section 21, Part 1 and Lk. 3:3 reveal that baptism exhibited the truth that sins had *already been remitted*. Baptism exhibits this fact. John's converts were people who had been forgiven by trusting the coming Christ as their Messiah. On salvation before the cross, see Section 144, footnote i. Paul's words in 2 Cor. 7:10 reveal that repentance occurs before salvation. He told King Agrippa that specific works accompanied genuine repentance (Acts 26:20). John's converts demonstrated, by baptism, the fact that forgiveness had been *previously* received.

4p-**Did John baptize babies?** Again, how can infant baptism fit into this scenario? The great Adam Clarke wrote in his *Commentary*, vol. 5, page 347, that the people who flocked to John's baptism brought "their little children also with them to be baptized." Clarke did not explain how little children repented and believed which was his requirement *before* baptism in water. See the next Section, footnote q, for twenty-one things John preached.

Part of John's message about the soon coming Messiah. Twenty-one things the forerunner of Jesus the Messiah did and preached.

Desert area of Judaea and Jordan

Matt. 3:11-12	Mk. 1:7-8	Lk. 3:15-18	John
		Has the Messiah come? 15 And as the people were in expectation, and all men mused in their hearts of John, whether he were the Christ, [Messiah] or not;[(m)]	
	Messiah is coming soon: what He will do 7 And preached, saying,	***Messiah is coming soon: what He will do*** 16 John answered, saying unto *them* all,	
Messiah is coming soon: what He will do 11 "I indeed baptize[(n)] you with water unto repentance: but he that cometh after me is mightier than I,		"I indeed baptize[(n)] you with water;	
	"There cometh one mightier than I after me, the latchet of	but one mightier than I cometh, the latchet of	
whose shoes I am not worthy to bear:	whose shoes I am not worthy to stoop down and unloose. 8 "I indeed have baptized you with water:	whose shoes I am not worthy to unloose:	
he shall baptize you with the Holy Ghost,[(o)] and *with* fire:	but he shall baptize you with the Holy Ghost."[(o)] (Verse 9 cont. in Section 22.)	he shall baptize you with the Holy Ghost[(o)] and with fire:	
12 "Whose fan[(p)] *is* in his hand, and he will throughly purge his floor, and gather his wheat into the garner; but he will burn up the chaff with unquenchable fire." (Verse 13 cont. in Section 22.)		17 "Whose fan[(p)] *is* in his hand, and he will throughly purge his floor, and will gather the wheat into his garner; but the chaff he will burn with fire unquenchable." ***John preached things not recorded in Scripture*** 18 And many other things[(q)] in his exhortation preached he unto the people. (Verse 19 cont. in Section 22.)	

Footnotes-Commentary

[(m)] **Is He Christ or not?** John did prepare a people for the coming Christ-Messiah. For centuries, theological liberals have denied that the people of Israel were looking for their promised Messiah (or Christ) during this era of history. Their basic objection is that there is no genuine evidence that Jesus ever made this claim. The root problem with religious skeptics is that a Bible, inspired of God and trustworthy, is too much for them. This single passage answers their wicked unbelief. Even though Jewish expectations greatly varied, nevertheless, they were looking for the Messiah. How could they be in expectation and muse in their hearts about whether John was their Messiah or not if they had been ignorant of or uninterested in their Messiah's coming? With the sudden appearing of John and shortly afterwards of Jesus, the people of Israel and others were shaken into a fresh, burning Messianic consciousness. This awareness is seen in John 1:20; 4:25-26; 6:14; 7:25-26, 40-44; 9:22; 10:24-25; and 12:42. It was heard in the early stages of Christ's ministry from the mouths of demons as noted in Section 40, Lk. 4:34, footnote d. At the end of His life, the Messianic awareness came from the lips of the high priest during Jesus' trial (Matt. 26:63-64). The angel had announced to Mary exactly who her baby would be before He was conceived (Lk. 1:31-33). Matthew informs his Jewish readers, "the conception and birth of Jesus Christ [Messiah] was on this wise" (Matt. 1:18). He was saying, "Here's how our Messiah was born," affirming that Jesus' birth was *different*. Even the maniac Herod inquired of the Jewish priests and scribes "where Christ (Messiah) should be born" (Matt. 2:4). Not one of them responded, "O king, you have made some mistake. We are not looking for any Messiah to come!" Instead, they instantly pointed to the Old Testament prediction stating the precise place of His birth (Matt. 2:5-6). For a recent work dealing with Christ, Israel's Messiah, as predicted in the Old Testament, see *Jesus the Messiah,* by Herbert W. Bateman, Darrell L. Bock and Gordon H. Johnstone.

(n) **John's baptism.** Our Lord's baptism was unique. It is explained in Section 22, first and second paragraph of footnote c. Water baptism by total immersion had been common in Israel for several hundred years before the appearing of John. The verb "baptizo" means, "immerse," or "dip" into something (Lk. 16:24). Gentile proselytes into the Jewish religion were (among other things) baptized *only* by immersion before acceptance into Judaism. This proselyte self-immersion was called "mikvah" among Orthodox Jews. For ritual cleansing, pious Jewish women practice mikvah immersion, along with brides and bridegrooms. Devout Hebrew males also self immerse under the waters for religious purposes. Mikvah pools are common in many Jewish homes, often resembling a small swimming pool. *In Hebrew history, there has never existed such a thing as a "sprinkling water" mikvah.* Present day pools contain two hundred gallons of rainwater, kept at the chest level, with access by a series of steps. The mikvah ritual could be accomplished only by immersion. Nor was John's baptism part of "washings" (or "baptisms") under the Law of Moses (Heb. 9:10). John did not derive immersion by modifying the Jewish proselyte ritual. His baptism was not that of the future church, which depicted the Savior's death, burial, and resurrection. At this time, few understood the death of Christ on the cross. These "few" included Anna, Simeon and unnamed others who were probably dead by the time Christ was crucified. For several days after the cross, Christ's disciples adamantly refused to believe that He had risen, even though they trusted that He was their Messiah. Refer to Section 196, John 20:9 and attached side and bottom notes regarding their ignorance of His resurrection. He spent forty days and nights performing many signs and wonders, convincing them, He was alive (Acts 1:3). Regarding how people were saved by grace before the cross and resurrection, see Section 64, footnote k, and Section 144, footnote i.

2p-**Getting ready for baptism.** Hebrew baptism for proselytes into Judaism was a serious event. Months before the actual ritual there were intense studies in the Torah Law and the customs of the Hebrew people. Permission had to be given by the religious authorities for any baptism to take place. See the Jews questioning John the Baptist over this in Section 24, footnote e. The person being baptized had to cut their nails, and make a fresh profession of faith in the Torah Law in the presence of specific persons called "fathers of baptism." The candidate undressed and stood with arms outstretched at a horizontal level. Next, he would give testimony to his conversion into Judaism. Upon hearing the names called of those men (usually three in number) who were witnesses giving attestation to his baptism, he would then immerse himself by squatting slowly down into the water until totally covered. No one was allowed to touch him or her. (Women were baptized in seclusion and assisted by the wives of the rabbis who were the witnesses.) This rising *up out* of the water from the squatting position, clearly explains the baptism of Christ where it reads, "And Jesus, when he was baptized, went up straightway out of the water" (Matt. 3:16). This means that He stood again after baptism to regain upright posture. The Lord Jesus did *not* undergo traditional Jewish proselyte baptism, for He was not a proselyte of Judaism. For the meaning of His baptism, see Section 22, footnote b.

3p-**Baptist who abuse John's baptism.** Among immersionists within the Baptist camp, some ran amuck with the subject of John's baptism. In 1887, Dr. J. R. Graves published a book entitled *John's Baptism.* Graves purported that John started the first Baptist Church and baptized Jesus, a Baptist! He attempted to prove the Baptist Church had been present since John, and that it is the only spiritual "authority" of God on earth. (Shades of false claims of Roman Catholicism!) This teaching gave gradual rise to a sectarian philosophy commonly known as "Landmarkism" and "Baptist Bride ecclesiology." As with all religious heresies and sectarianism, the finer details of their teachings differ from one group to another. Baptist historian, James E. McGoldrick in his work *Baptist Successionism: A Critical Question in Baptist History*, gives a sound response to the "Baptist Bride" error. In some places, Dr. McGoldrick confuses *basic* Bible doctrines adamantly adhered to by ancient Christians, with a particular denominational name. In this, he overlooks that amid these different groups where those who guarded foundational Scriptural truths and kept these from mitigation and corruption. Equally absurd is the teaching that water baptism brings salvation or puts one into God's kingdom. This was the position of many of the so-called Reformers, who brought this error out of the Papal system, then revised it to fit their theology. In summary, John baptized *only* those whose outward conduct manifested an inward change. His candidates both repented of and confessed their sins *before* baptism. How can helpless infants repent of their sins and believe on the Lord Jesus Christ? Amid the falsity of "baby faith" propagated by those infected with revised editions of Roman Catholic dogma, millions have died damned. They were sprinkled as infants and assured this gave salvation. For more on the fable of "baby faith," see Section 150, the second paragraph of footnote f. During the middle ages a small group of the more ritualistic Roman Catholics actually baptized by immersion! This was banned by order of the Pope. Regardless, immersion also avails nothing, unless the candidate has first been saved by the grace of God. *How amazing are the voices resounding from certain Reformed circles telling us that Jesus' forerunner should be called "John the Presbyterian because he sprinkled his converts."* Alas! The shameless levels some go to in order to justify doctrinal error, then alter Holy Scripture to fit the error without impunity of conscience. Soon, we may be reading about "Peter the Methodist," "Paul the Baptist." or "Andrew the Roman Catholic," all being more senseless distortions from "theologians" trying to prove something from nothing.

4p-Was Christian baptism borrowed from Jews and pagans? Some commentators write that because the early Christians came out of the Judaism of Jesus' time, Christian baptism was originally a Jewish pagan-practice! No informed person would deny that the church has taken many good things from the synagogue. However, to write that Christian baptism was originally Jewish-pagan is more "academic" hot air. Believer's baptism (by immersion under water) faintly resembles the various washing of ancient Judaism. *Yet in purpose and meaning, there is no similarity whatsoever.* No ancient Hebrew priest, proselyte, or mikveh bather was ever immersed to picture the death, burial, and resurrection of Jesus Christ. Thousands of baptisms practiced by heathens as they dipped under water or sprinkled themselves for outward ritual cleansings are documented in history. Yet, not one of these depicted anything pointing to the Savior. It is scurrilous teaching that proper Christian baptism was borrowed from Jews and pagans. When Christ gave the Great Commission, His Hebrew disciples understood the mode of baptism perfectly, but none of them linked the *reason* for believer's baptism with their vain religious history. All of this was perfectly understood with the coming of the Holy Spirit in His fulness at Pentecost. For He would then "teach them all things, and bring all things to their remembrance" (John 14:26).

5p-"Why did John baptize?" The angel Gabriel previously stated that part of John's work was "to prepare a people for the Lord" (Lk. 1:17). And this he did! See footnote q, below, for what John preached in preparing the masses for Christ. Every person who believed his message (that Jesus was the promised Messiah, the Lamb of God, who would take away the sin of the world) and became a penitent, fruit-bearing confessor, John baptized. He refused to baptize any who had not believed and whose lives were void of the fruits of repentance. Note his profound words in Section 32, John 3:36 about believing in Christ. After baptism, they were considered part of the people John was preparing for the coming Messiah or Christ. This is why John baptized.

6p-In the days of John the Baptist, no one was "baptized into" any church. The church (which would be purchased with Christ's blood, Acts 20:28) did *not* exist at this time, even though there were *true* believers. The Holy Spirit puts men into Christ (or His body), not water baptism (l Cor. 12:13 with Gal. 3:27). Saved believers existed at this time as they had throughout the Old Testament era. These pre-church converts of John, along with *all* the earlier saints, were finally reconciled to God on the cross (Col. 1:19-22). At Pentecost, they were all blended by the Holy Spirit into "one body" (Eph. 4:4) in Christ (Eph. 2:11-21 and 3:6). On this occasion, all Old Testament saints were made "perfect" *with* the then-existing New Testament saints (Heb. 11:40). This "one body" became primarily known (among other things) as the church. All Old Testament persons had to be in Christ to be saved. The name "church," as seen across Acts and the epistles, was gradually adopted and applied to this new community of believers. Jesus used the word "church" in preparing His apostles for this future Pentecostal entity (Matt. 16:18 and Matt. 18:17). Stephen's use of the same word in Acts 7:38 had nothing to do with the newly formed body that began at Pentecost. Contextually, he was referring to the called-out nation of Israel as an "assembly" of people. To make the "house of Moses" the same as the "house of Christ" (or the church) is faulty exegesis (Heb. 3:5-6). "Moses' house" was the nation of Israel, a mixture of a *few* saved people amid millions of stubborn, law-breaking Jews. See Heb. 4:1-2, where they rejected the preaching of the gospel, and Ps. 95:8-9 where they "provoked" the Holy Spirit. Isaiah reflecting back on Israel in the wilderness wrote, "They rebelled, and vexed his [God's] Holy Spirit" (Isa. 63:10). Oddly, some see Israel as the Old Testament Church, with male circumcision of its infants pointing to infant baptism in the New Testament and the Passover becoming the Lord's Supper! For Israel being the church and circumcision pointing to infant baptism, refer to Section 138, third through ninth paragraphs under footnote a.

7p-Approximately, two years after the death of John the Baptist, Peter said in the upper room that among those present were some who had been followers of Christ, "Beginning from the baptism of John" (Acts 1:21-22). Peter identified each person baptized by John as a follower of Jesus the Messiah. Multitudes of others not baptized by him (John) were also included as His followers (John 4:1-2). When Messiah appeared on the scene *most* of John's disciples gradually left him and followed the Savior (John 3:30). With the coming of the Holy Spirit at Pentecost, they *all* perfectly understood Messiah's death, burial, and resurrection. With this, their faith in Him as Israel's Messiah culminated in the glorious gospel truth (John 14:26). Refer to Section 144, footnote i for more on this thought. Some twenty years later, Paul found several defective converts of John's ministry in far-away Ephesus (Acts 19:1-7). Apollos, is usually blamed for this. For another explanation, see Section 51, Matt. 9:14, footnote a.

(o) John foresaw the unusual events that would occur on the day of Pentecost in Acts 2, almost four years away, when believers were baptized by the Holy Spirit into the body, or Christ's Church. John was no stranger to the Holy Spirit. From his mother's womb, he was acquainted with the Third Person of the Holy Trinity, and his parents were Spirit-filled people as seen in Section 8, Lk. 1:15, footnote g. His statement about baptism with the Holy Ghost and fire is of concern to many. To interpret the "fire" as being hellfire is erroneous. Beyond doubt, Matt. 3:10, 12, and Lk. 3:9 and 17 do speak of the torments of hell. John could not have had in mind the destruction of Jerusalem in A.D. 70 when speaking of the baptism with fire, for he said that those who are baptized with the Spirit would, likewise, be baptized with fire. Here, he was speaking of the Pentecost that occurred in Acts 2, in which the Spirit of God, like fire, fell on all believers present. Peter, looking back on these things said the same a few years later in Acts 10:15, 17. As already stated, the Holy Spirit blended these saints into the existing company of Jewish believers and this group became known as "Christ's one body." With this, He instantly illuminated them to understand perfectly the gospel, Messiah's death, burial, and resurrection. At Pentecost, He empowered them to preach the gospel to Jews and Gentile proselytes from some nineteen different countries of the world. They miraculously did this in languages never previously learned. See John 16:13; Acts 2:5-11; and Lk. 1:41, footnote b for more details on this amazing event. Some think the "fire" of Matt. 3:11 is the convicting and purifying work of the Holy Spirit at conversion. His words "the wrath to come," in Matt. 3:7 may have had reference to Jerusalem's doom A.D. 70.

(p) Jewish harvesters carried hand-fans that were used on threshing floors to separate the wheat and barley kernels from the chaff and trash. The Baptist, in using this well-known symbol, pointed to the Word of God, which the coming Messiah used like a hand-fan to separate the good from the bad in Israel. Specifically, the chaff probably represented the oral or Mishna law of the Jews that they had superimposed upon the Torah Law and prophets. See Section 52, footnote h; Section 89, footnote c; and Section 96, footnote d for explanation of these laws in Israel. The "unquenchable fire" surely had reference to eternal hell in the lake of fire. Matthew used the term "burn up" while Luke did not. Protagonists of annihilation see in the words "burn up," proof of their heresy. Literal chaff burns up but that to which it points is entirely different. If annihilation is taught here, we wonder why the fire is "unquenchable" in its content and duration.

(q) **"Many other things John preached."** Numerous commentaries, textbooks, and annotated Bibles tell us that John preached *only* to the nation of Israel. His message was to offer them their long-looked-for physical kingdom and King. These claims have seriously missed the purpose of John's ministry and message. His "shewing unto Israel" (Lk. 1:80), was not an exclusive event "for the Jew only." Not only did John preach to Israel, his ministry embraced a "whosoever will" audience. Some of John's converts to Christ were present in the upper room during the selection of an apostle to replace Judas. Matthias, who replaced Judas the traitor, was apparently a convert of John the Baptist (Acts 1:21-26). See Section 21, Part 3, first and second paragraphs of footnote l for how John dealt with unconverted Jews and Gentiles (Roman soldiers) who requested to be baptized. Below is a list of things John preached and did. Some of these have previously been touched mentioned.

1. Gabriel said that John would not drink strong drink, that he would be filled with the Holy Ghost from his mother's womb, and that his preaching would turn many Jews to the Lord their God, see Lk. 1:15-17. John the Baptist foresaw the day of Pentecost in Acts 2. This is the meaning of Matt. 3:11, footnote o above. For the Holy Spirit across the Old Testament, see Section 10, the second paragraph, footnote b.

2. John warned about a horrible place of fire that men should flee from (Lk. 3:7-9). This was not the destruction of Jerusalem in A.D. 70.

3. John preached that the "kingdom of God was at hand" and every person (who was saved) pressed into it (Lk. 16:16). Nowhere did he preach a withdrawal of the kingdom and its return over two thousand years later. This is serious eschatological error. It is another product of *radical* dispensationalism. Such teaching cannot be found in the first sixteen hundred years of Christianity. The Jews rejected Jesus as their Messiah and not a kingdom offer. For more on this, see Section 39, footnotes a and g.

4. John preached, had converts, and baptized them while at Anon (John 3:23). This town was several miles west of the Jordan River in the vile country of Samaria. He would have had few Jews in his audience at this place. Samaritan soil was cursed and hated by pious Jews.

5. John was the forerunner of Christ and prepared His way by winning converts who would follow the Savior when He came (Lk. 1:76 with Acts 1:21-23).

6. John gave knowledge of salvation to the people through the remission or forgiveness of their sins as they confessed Christ, the Messiah (Lk. 1:77).

7. John gave light (by preaching) to those who were in darkness and the shadow of death and guided their feet into peace (Lk. 1:79). What a wonderful thing to be said of any preacher of God!

8. He was sent from God to bear witness of the Light, which was Christ. He did this so that men would believe in the Lord Jesus, God's spiritual illumination for the awful darkness of sin (John 1:6-9).

9. John preached Christ as the "Lamb of God" which "taketh away the sin of the world." Therefore, he knew of Jesus' atoning death on the cross for *all* mankind (John 1:29).

10. He said in highly symbolic language that Christ was the bridegroom and would, in time, secure His bride (that is, have all the saved with Him in heaven at last). John greatly rejoiced over the sure prospect of this eternal consummation of all believers with their Lord when the plan of God for men is completed (John 3:29). It is noted that the church is referred to as a "new man" (not woman) in Eph. 2:15 and a "perfect man" in Eph. 4:13. In the New Testament, the church is not a *literal* feminine entity. Paul's words in 2 Cor. 11:2 do not have reference to the church or body of Christ. Rather, he was jealous over his converts at Corinth and wanted to present them to Christ, as a pure bride would be given to her husband. The statement in Rev. 21:2, where John saw "the holy city coming down from God out of heaven" cannot mean the church. The apostle was saying that the new Jerusalem was adorned or covered with jewels, as ancient brides were for their husbands (Isa. 49:18 with 61:10). In this chapter of Revelation, John is carried away in the Spirit to a great and high mountain and then shown the home of the saints, a city of overwhelming beauty descending from God (Rev. 21:9-10). One of the seven angels informs him that this city is the bride, "the Lamb's wife." The idea seems to be that because the saved of all ages will live here (Rev. 21:24) this glorious place will also be called "the bride or wife of Christ" because it is her home. Many weird doctrines have been built on Jesus Christ having the body of a woman, which is supposed to be His bride or church. This contortion of biblical typology will not hold up under Scriptural scrutiny. Similarly, the Song of Solomon has been used in the field of typology to prove just about anything. Whatever conclusion one may reach in this difficult area, it is sure that our Lord and Savior does not have a man's head and a woman's body (the church), not even in typology. It is sure that He does not marry a literal city (Rev. 19:7, 9). That dazzling final Jerusalem at the end of the Bible has no sin (Rev. 21:27). Above all, God and the Lamb will be there (Heb. 12:22 with Rev. 21:23). The bride inviting people to Christ (Rev. 22:17) speaks of those who were married to Him (in a spiritual sense) at conversion (Rom. 7:4). This is a "great mystery" and remains so to this hour (Eph. 4:32).

11. The Baptist decreased while Jesus increased (John 3:30).

12. John preached that Christ was "from above," that He spoke only "what He had seen and heard" from God in heaven and that "no man received His testimony" ("No" here is a comparative term for "few." Some did believe and are mentioned in verse 33.) He preached in John 3:33, that those who received Jesus' testimony "set to their seal" (it was confirmed in their hearts), that He was the Messiah Savior; that He did not receive the Spirit in a limited measure; and that God loved Him and had given Him all authority. This reveals the deep spiritual insight of John into the plan of God and Christ (John 3:31-35).

13. John the Baptist spoke one of the most profound claims recorded in the Bible. It has won millions to a saving knowledge of Christ (John 3:36).

14. John witnessed to the truth, which was Christ-Messiah (John 5:33 with John 14:6).

15. He condemned stealing and adultery and was martyred for it (Mk. 6:17-28).

16. He demanded that people repent of their sins before he would baptize them (Matt. 3:2 with Acts 13:24).

17. He preached hellfire and damnation (Matt. 3:10), the Holy Spirit (Mk. 1:7-8) and many other things not recorded in Scripture (Lk. 3:18). His message was not a "one way street" sermon for the Jews only.

18. He publicly rejected the traditional Jewish appeal that being a descendant of Abraham was sufficient before God to save one's soul (Matt. 3:9).

19. He taught his converts to fast and pray (Matt. 9:14; Lk. 5:33; and 11:1).

20. Later, Jesus commended John, amid great doubt and suffering, as being the greatest man ever born of women. Further, that the law and the prophets were until (or ended with) his appearing, and that he was the promised Elijah of the Old Testament (Matt. 11:7-15; 17:10-13; with Mal. 4:5-6).

21. Shortly before the death of Christ, the Jews admitted that, even though John did no miracle, everything he had told them about Messiah was true (John 10:41). This is the *final* mention in the four gospels of John the Baptist. What a way to step from the stage of human life! His enemies are compelled to confess that he preached the truth and used no astounding miracles to prove anything. Here, is a clear testimony that ministers of the Scripture do not need to use the sensational Hollywood approach to win lost souls to Christ. If Holy Spirit anointed preaching and teaching God's Word will not bring men to confession and/or conversion, then one had better leave them to the Lord of heaven. Let Him deal with them. Obtaining confessions by gimmicks, toys, steak house vouchers, promises of healing and prosperity, clown shows, parachute jumps, chasing greased pigs, smacking the pastor's face with a chocolate pie, or a thousand other contrivances will not get God's work done. Surely, some things may be used to bring men in, but only Jesus Christ saves through the work of the Holy Spirit and the Word of God. Lost souls are not easily won to Christ; it is a battle with the forces of sin and darkness all the way. Satan does not quickly give up his children to the joy of sins forgiven and eternal life. See an example of the Devil trying to prevent the salvation of an unsaved politician in Acts 13:6-12.

About thirty years old, the Savior begins His public ministry by baptism. Heaven opens, the Holy Spirit descends, and God the Father speaks* audibly.

*See comments under footnote f and g below for the astounding details of how God spoke to His Son.

Jordan River

Matt. 3:13–17	Mk. 1:9–11	Lk. 3:19–22	John
		John imprisoned **19** But Herod the te-trarch, [ruler of a fourth part] being reproved by him [John] for Herodias his brother Philip's wife, and for all the evils which Herod had done, **20** Added yet this above all, that he shut up John in prison.(a)	
John's question **13** Then cometh Jesus from Galilee to Jordan	**John baptizes Jesus** **9** And it came to pass in those days, that Jesus came from Nazareth of Galilee,(b)		

unto John, to be baptized of him.
14 But John forbade(c) him, saying, "I have need to be baptized of thee, and comest thou to me?"

The Savior's answer
15 And Jesus answering said unto him, "Suffer [let] *it to be so* now: for thus it becometh us to fulfill all righteousness." Then he [John] suffered [baptized] him.

Matt. 3:13–17	Mk. 1:9–11	Lk. 3:19–22	John
		Others baptized with Christ **21** Now when all the people were baptized, it came to pass, that Jesus also being baptized, and	
16 And Jesus, when he was baptized,	and was baptized of John in Jordan.	praying,(d)	
Jesus saw the Holy Spirit come down went up straightway	*Jesus saw the Holy Spirit come down* **10** And straightway coming up		
out of the water: and, lo,	out of the water, he saw	*Jesus saw the Holy Spirit come down*	
the heavens were opened(e) **unto him, and he saw the Spirit of God descending like a dove,**	**the heavens opened,**(e) **and the Spirit like a dove descending**	**the heaven was opened,**(e) **22 And the Holy Ghost descended in a bodily shape like a dove**	
and lighting upon him:	**upon him:**	**upon him,**	
God speaks audibly from heaven **17** And lo a voice(f) from heaven, saying,	*God speaks audibly from heaven* **11** And there came a voice(f) from heaven, *saying,*	*God speaks audibly from heaven* and a voice(f) came from heaven, which said,	

95

Matt. 3:17	Mk. 1:11	Lk. 3:22	John
"This is my beloved Son, in whom I am well pleased."(g) ▼ (Next chap., Matt. 4:1, cont. in Section 23.)	"Thou art my beloved Son, in whom I am well pleased."(g) (Verse 12 cont. in Section 23.)	"Thou art my beloved Son; in thee I am well pleased."(g) (Verse 23 cont. in Section 5.)	

▲Christ went from His baptism in Jordan, into the temptation on a wilderness mountaintop some few miles west of Jericho. Some believe that the temptation occurred in the region of Mt. Sinai, which was in a southerly direction many miles from Bethabara, Jordan. This seems incorrect in view of the great distance and time involved in walking to this location. See further comments in the Information Box just before footnotes in Section 23. John knew who Jesus was when he baptized Him (John 1:32-34).

Footnotes-Commentary

(a) These two verses do not fit the chronology of Christ's baptism as recorded by Matthew. This harmony commentary holds Matthew's work as the first gospel written. Luke is inspired to put these two verses here even though the events mentioned in them did not occur until much later. He did this in order to show in advance *how* the ministry of John the Baptist ended. Chronologically, John was not thrown into prison until many months after the baptism and temptation of Christ. Jesus did not start His on-the-road ministry until after Herod Antipas imprisoned John. Luke penned certain events in the life of Christ but did not place them in an established chronological order. This reflects that he wrote under divine inspiration and not self-choice or impulse. The unsaved "experts" frown at such, being blind to spiritual things and the work of the Holy Spirit. For more on the sad travesty of religious infidels critiquing Scripture, which they do not believe, refer to the *Author's Introduction.*

(b) **The third silent period ended by His baptism.** Our Lord walked a round-trip of about ninety miles from Nazareth in Galilee, to Bethabara, Jordan, to begin his ministry by baptism. In this act, He pictured to all observers, especially the Devil, *how* His ministry would conclude some three years by the cross and the resurrection. Long afterwards, the apostle John wrote, "This is he that came by water and blood …" (1 John 5:6). Thus, His water baptism now depicted His blood on the cross yet to come. See footnote a above. The Father's declaration, "Thou art my beloved Son," instantly caught Satan's attention. Satan and demons were terrified at the appearing of Jesus, the promised Messiah (James 2:19).

2p-**"Baptized of John," Mk. 1:9.** Did John speak a verbal sanction over Christ as He lowered Himself under the water? If so, we do not know what he said. In Jewish proselyte baptisms, a witness from the Sanhedrin spoke an audible attestation of each baptism. John did not use the formula of the church given several years later in Matt. 28:19. From heaven, God spoke His formal approval upon Jesus' baptism, "This is my beloved Son, in whom I am well pleased." *Such a divine proclamation has never been said of any religious leader in all world history.*

(c) John requested to be excused from the baptism of Christ, possibly because he thought the onlookers might believe he was greater than Christ, or he sensed his great unworthiness (John 3:30).

2p-**"You baptize me."** John spoke these words because he had never been baptized! His request that Christ witness His baptism is noteworthy. Christ began His ministry, depicting in baptism how His ministry would end some three and a half years later, by death, burial, and resurrection. This He exhibited by lowering Himself beneath the water and lifting Himself "up out" of it. In this act, John by being the human witness, and Jesus by baptism, *both* visibly signified that the only way "all righteousness" may be "fulfilled" in the souls of men is through Christ's death, burial, and resurrection. And this is received by faith. For Jewish baptisms, see Section 21, Part 4, footnote n. Christ did not take away our sins in baptism. He took them away on the cross. His baptism pictured that.

3p-**Baptism poured from a seashell!** Paintings that depict John pouring water from a seashell upon the Savior's head are meaningless. *What can this symbolize?* Pouring or sprinkling was *later* brought into the churches and distorted into the instrument of salvation by the church fathers and their successors. Others were immersed and taught that this secured the forgiveness of sins. Long before John appeared, various heathen religions immersed their members under water for cleansing, while others sprinkled the initiates. Neither pouring, infusion, immersion, nor sprinkling achieves anything concerning eternal life. It only gets the participants wet, some more than others.

4p-The Jewish "Christian" theologian, Augustus Neander (died 1850), wrote that Christ's baptism was a "rite of consecration to his theocratic reign." See Neander's *The Life of Jesus Christ,* pages 100-101. On pages 69-70 of the same work, he calls it our Lord's "Messianic baptism." However, ancient Hebrew literature is silent about Messiah being baptized. For the purpose in Jesus' baptism, see the 2p- above. As a Lutheran, and holding to infant baptism, this is the best Neander could get out of Jesus' baptism in the Jordan River. Neither Christ's nor Christian baptism is a "rite of consecration" for anything. Christian baptism is a simple act of loving obedience to the final earthly command of the Savior. It is to be performed *only* by those who have been saved. In this, the individual manifests that he has previously partaken by faith, of the death, burial, and resurrection of Christ. At the moment of salvation the newly born again soul is spiritually baptized *into* Christ's body or the true church (1 Cor. 12:13 with

Gal. 3:27). God accomplishes this miracle by the indwelling Holy Spirit (Eph. 3:16). Afterward, the same convert is physically "baptized *with* Christ" in water. In Rom. 6:4, it states that we are "buried with him by baptism into [His] death." The cycle is: first, the Holy Spirit puts the newly saved believer *into* Christ; second, he is then put *with* Christ under water (a figure of burial) in believer's baptism. Peter said baptism gives "The answer of a good conscience toward God" (1 Peter 3:21). How can infants have a good conscience toward God? Regarding the grand myth of "baby faith," see Section 150, second paragraph of footnote f. For more on the subject of baptism, see Section 203, paragraphs one through five of footnote d.

5p-Only dead men are buried! Burial is not accomplished by a handful of earth sprinkled or poured over a corpse. Interment of a dead body among the Jews involved a complete enclosure in whatever substance. Regarding baptismal distortion carried from the Papal Church into the Reformation, see documentation regarding Martin Luther, in Section 203, the eighth paragraph of footnote d. For other comments on the church fathers and their soteriological travesties in handling Scripture, see Section 12, sixth paragraph of footnote k, with Section 135, fourth paragraph of footnote e, and Section 138, seventh paragraph of footnote a.

6p-Dr. John Lightfoot, an Anglican theologian (died 1675) was sprinkled as an infant and called it "baptism." Yet he wrote that the Jews "plunged the whole body into [under] water" when they baptized. He stated that this signified "the most cruel kind of death," and it supposedly made "some women barren." However, the Jews have continued this practice over the centuries. See Lightfoot's *Commentary of the New Testament . . . ,* vol. 2, page 269.

(d) **"And praying."** Luke gives this beautiful detail not found in the other three gospels. Jesus prayed during His baptism, and the Spirit came upon Him as "the oil of gladness," in fulfillment of Ps. 45:7 and Isa. 61:1. John testified that the Spirit was not given to Christ "by measure" (John 3:34). Luke wrote that He was "full of the Holy Ghost" (Lk. 4:1). The Savior remained so the rest of His ministry. His death, resurrection, and ascension were in the power of the Spirit (Heb. 9:14 and 1 Peter 3:18 with Acts 1:2). One can communicate with God everywhere, which includes in his heart or even standing in a river (1 Tim. 2:8).

(e) **Heaven opened and the Spirit descended.** In a gray background as the fulfillment of Isa. 11:1-2. In Luke 3:21 it speaks of "all the people being baptized" on this occasion. *Gill's Commentary,* vol. 7, page 27, states that in the ancient Jewish book of mysticism called *Zohar,* there is the story that a dove would light upon the head of the Messiah, and He would receive glory from this dove. The *Zohar* is attributed to Moses de Leon of Spain in the A.D. 1200s. This is a collection of mystical teachings from the Torah with mentions of the Messiah. Years *after* Christ's ascension a dove became associated with the Messiah by the rabbis. Even though this was late, one can believe that its *original* source was earlier, even from the pages of the Christian New Testament. Various rabbis sought to change some of the Messianic statements recorded in the pages of the New Testament.

(f) **"A voice from heaven."** Long before the close of the Old Testament, the Jews had stories about voices from heaven. One in particular, the "bat(h) kol," was the "daughter of a voice." It was supposedly operative long before the birth of Christ. The rabbis believed they saw this in Gen. 22:11, where a voice from heaven spoke to Abraham. There would be nothing demeaning to Matthew's Jewish readers when he informs them that God spoke to Christ from heaven. They knew the rabbinical teaching that God spoke audibly to the prophets of their Old Testament.

(g) **The first record of God speaking audibly in the New Testament.** The three times God audibly spoke to the Son in the gospels are highlighted in red font in this work. These three are as follows in chronological order.

1. **First,** He spoke to Jesus at the *beginning* of His ministry, during His baptism as recorded above.
2. **Second,** near the *middle* of His ministry, God spoke to His Son from heaven as Moses and Elijah conversed with Him about His death on the cross. See Section 105, Matt. 17:5, footnote g, for the record of when God spoke on the Mount of Transfiguration.
3. **Third,** the Father spoke to Christ audibly at the *end* of His ministry the day before His death, affirming that He would glorify His Name as never before. This was done when He provided the perfect atonement for the sins of mankind. Refer to Section 161, John 12:28, footnote g.

2p-In Section 25, John 1:33, we have the record of a time when God spoke in some unknown manner to John the Baptist concerning how he could recognize the true Messiah. This message to John is also highlighted in red.

3p-Earlier in Section 5 it was noted that Luke 3:23 speaks of Jesus being "about thirty years" of age at His baptism. Great speculation has fallen upon this passage because of the word "thirty." This was the age when Levitical priests commenced their work (Num. 4:3). It was lowered to twenty-five a short time later (Num. 8:24-25). Some five hundred years afterwards, during the rule of King David, it was lowered to twenty (1 Chron 23:24-27). Jesus' baptism did not induct Him into the office of the high priest or anything else. His priesthood was *not* after that of Levi, but rather of Melchisedec, and is forever (Ps. 110:4 with Heb. 5:5-10). After thirty years of dwelling in human flesh, God was pleased with His Son, and said so from heaven! He had passed through the helpless stages of infancy and early childhood, the turmoil and frustrations of teenage years, and now into young manhood. Still, He was the perfect man in whom the Father was well pleased. Here, God did not "appoint Jesus as Messiah." He affirmed that He was such. The blasphemous Jewish Ebionite cult held that a spirit came upon Christ at baptism, thus making Him a prophet and a Messiah.

Section 23: The first recorded encounter of the Lord Jesus with the kingdom of darkness.

The temptation* of the Savior shortly after His baptism.

Though He was that unique divine Person, Jesus chose to function at the level of His humanity during these days. The last two temptations are left as they appear in Scripture. In the Supplement following this Section, they are adjusted and then re-harmonized. John was not inspired to write of these events in his record of the life of Christ.

On a wilderness mountain probably near Jericho

Matt. 4:1-6	Mk. 1:12-13a	Lk. 4:1-7	John
1 Then was Jesus led[a] up of the Spirit into the wilderness to be tempted of the devil.	**12** And immediately the Spirit driveth[a] him into the wilderness. **13a** And he was there in the wilderness forty days, tempted of Satan; and was with the wild beasts; (Verse 13b cont. bottom of next page.)	**1** And Jesus being full of the Holy Ghost returned from Jordan, and was led[a] by the Spirit into the wilderness, **2** Being forty days tempted of the devil.	
2 And when he had fasted[b] forty days and forty nights, he was afterward an hungered.		And in those days he did eat nothing:[b] and when they were ended, he afterward hungered.	
First temptation **3** And when the tempter[c] came to him, he said, **"If thou be the Son of God, command that these stones be made bread."**	◄*All the words of Satan and demons are in this heavy Gothic font style.*	*First temptation* **3** And the devil[c] said unto him, **"If thou be the Son of God, command this stone that it be made bread."**	
The Savior's response **4** But he answered and said, "It is written,[d] 'Man shall not live by bread alone, but by every Word that proceedeth out of the mouth of God.'"		*The Savior's response* **4** And Jesus answered him, saying, "It is written,[d] 'That man shall not live by bread alone, but by every Word of God.'"	
Second temptation recorded by Matthew: the pinnacle[e] **5** Then the devil taketh him up into the holy city, and setteth him on a pinnacle of the temple, **6** And saith unto him,[f] **"If thou be the Son of God, cast thyself down: for it is written,[g] 'He shall give his angels charge concerning thee: and in their hands they shall bear thee up, lest at any time thou dash thy foot against a stone.'"**	**Explanatory comments** ◄*A comparative reading of Matthew's record in verse 5, with that of Luke in verse 5, reveals that his order given for the last two temptations is reversed from that of Matthew. See footnote e below for comments. Also, note the harmonized Supplement of these verses in the next Section. In this, the footnotes in Matthew's record of the last two temptations are rearranged to match those in the record of Luke on the same subject. This adjustment is only for the purpose of harmonization of the events.*	*Second temptation record by Luke: the high mountain[i]* **5** And the devil, taking him up into an high mountain, showed unto him all the kingdoms of the world in a moment of time. **6** And the devil said unto him, **"All this power will I give thee,[j] and the glory of them: for that is delivered unto me; and to whomsoever I will I give it. 7 "If thou therefore wilt worship me,[k] all shall be thine."**	

Matt. 4:7-11	Mk. 1:13b	Lk. 4:8-13	John
The Savior's response **7** Jesus said unto him, "It is written again,[h] 'Thou shalt not tempt the Lord thy God.' " ▶	◄ *In these Words the Savior claimed to be both Lord and God. For comments on His equality with God, see Section 1, footnotes a and b. Refer also to Section 179, footnote e for more on this high and noble subject.*	*The Savior's response* **8** And Jesus answered and said unto him, "Get thee behind me, Satan: for it is written,[l] 'Thou shalt worship the Lord thy God, and him only shalt thou serve.'"[m]	
Third temptation recorded by Matthew: the mountain[i] **8** Again, the devil taketh him up into an exceeding high mountain, and showeth him all the kingdoms of the world, and the glory of them; **9** And saith unto him, **"All these things(j) will I give thee if thou wilt fall down and worship me."**[k]		*Third temptation recorded by Luke: the pinnacle*[e] **9** And he brought him to Jerusalem, and set him on a pinnacle of the temple, and said unto him,[f] **"If thou be the Son of God, cast thyself down from hence:** **10** **"For it is written,**[g] **'He shall give his angels charge over thee, to keep thee:'** **11** **"And 'in** *their* **hands they shall bear thee up, lest at any time thou dash thy foot against a stone.'"**	
The Savior's response **10** Then saith Jesus unto him, "Get thee hence, Satan: for it is written,[l] 'Thou shalt worship the Lord thy God, and him only shalt thou serve.'"[m]		*The Savior's response* **12** And Jesus answering said unto him, "It is said,[h] 'Thou shalt not tempt the Lord thy God.'"	
Satan leaves Him for a short time: angels appear to assist the Lord Jesus **11** Then the devil leaveth him, and, behold, angels came and ministered[n] unto him. (Verse 12 cont. in Section 33.)	**13b** and the angels ministered[n] unto him. (Verse 14 cont. in Section 33.)	*Satan leaves Him for a short time* **13** And when the devil had ended all the temptation, he departed from him for a season.[o] (Verse 14 cont. in Section 33.)	

The forty days temptation proved that Christ could not, and therefore, did not sin. As a human, somehow, the satanic temptation struck at Him in a way we cannot comprehend. Ravaged by hunger, Satan ordered Him to create bread, let angels keep Him safe, and take world domination. He rejected all three appeals by drawing power from God's Word and the indwelling Holy Spirit. By these, He thwarted the Devil. However, His human frame was weakened and exhausted. We do not know, nor can we understand, what kind of appeal that creating bread, jumping from the pinnacle of the temple, and having world authority made to the Savior, for God did not tell us in Scripture. After this ended, He returned to Bethabara where John was baptizing and was present in the crowds gathered to hear the confrontation between John and those Jews sent from Jerusalem. Note that John 1:26 reads, "standeth one [Jesus] among you." They questioned him regarding who he was and where he had gotten authority to baptize, since only the Sanhedrin could grant this right. Neither John nor Christ's disciples had their permission. Hence, the religious leadership at Jerusalem became greatly upset.

Footnotes–Commentary

(a) Temptation casts its awful shadow over the Son of God's humanity. Matthew and Luke wrote that the Spirit "led" Jesus. Mark wrote that He was "driven" by the Spirit into the wilderness (Mk. 1:12). Mark was speaking of His humanity under the Holy Spirit's perfect control. The Spirit leading Jesus into this reveals that the initiative for His temptations was divine and not diabolical. The noun "Devil" ("diabolos") means "adversary" or "slanderer," *the real Devil*. This dramatic history occurred in an uninhabited and fierce wilderness, still today a wild area with ferocious animals. Kenneth Wuest gives a brief but awesome description of it in his *Wuest's Word Studies* 1:26. For other details, refer to footnote k below. From this, we understand why angels ministered to Him. The *first* act of Messiah, following the baptismal depiction of His future death, burial, and resurrection, was to engage in fierce combat with Satan in this awful "wilderness." In his unceasing trek of "going to and fro in the earth, and from walking up and down in it" (Job 1:7, 2:2), the Devil made his journey to the banks of Jordan. He too heard God's announcement from heaven regarding the beloved Son. Lucifer's wicked heart erupted into jealous rage. Here, the enmity announced in Eden of old, now moves itself into hostile motion as the serpent strikes at the "seed of the woman" (Gen. 3:15). These recorded events literally occurred. Jesus was not engaged in a mental struggle or inner conflict. Satan materialized into a visible form. He appeared visibly and spoke audibly to the Son of God. This was no vision, allegory, dream, or word picture; it was horrific reality. Two eternal causes and destinies clashed.

2p-With this confrontation, all of good and all of evil stand opposed to each other. John had preached that "the kingdom of heaven" was at hand. He had baptized the King; in this act, the saving gospel was couched in symbolic imagery. Satan wanted the King of this new kingdom to be destroyed. In years past, his mad pawn, Herod, had failed to eliminate Jesus in helpless infancy. Here, at the outset of His ministry, the Prince of darkness seeks to extinguish the Prince of Light by vicious, concerted attacks upon His thoroughly impoverished humanity. How this was possible we do not know, but it was! (For Satan's chiefest of temptations, we must wait until *after* the forty days: by then Messiah was totally exhausted and physically helpless.) Lk. 4:2 makes it clear that Satan assailed Christ with countless temptations during the *entire* forty days and nights. What these were we do not know. Through this period, He was "in all points tempted as we are" (Heb. 4:15). Not until the conclusion of this period did the Devil attack the Son of God with the final three major assaults.

3p-**"In all points as we are."** What is implied in this statement? We must not assume that every temptation that comes upon mankind also befell the Savior. Men are tempted today in the space age by stratagems unheard of in the days of Christ on earth. Somehow, in His human frame, the Master felt the full blow of sin's powers, in its totality, and succumbed to none of them. No man since Jesus' time here on the mount, has been tempted to turn stones to bread or jump from the temple. The human Jesus felt temptation's sting in His body *without* its awful mental fantasies and fiercely wicked seductions that make their appeals to our fallen nature. *Never for one moment did the Lord Jesus entertain or long to obey any of the thousands of temptations that fell upon His humanity.* Here, is the difference between our Lord and us. To be tempted is not sin: yielding to the temptation is.

4p-**All are tempted.** It is impossible to live in this world and escape all temptations. In olden times holy men fled to caves, castles, and all human activities seeking to avoid the enticements to sin. They were unsuccessful for they carried in their hearts the very fountainhead of evil. All normal families are dysfunctional in some way or another; even the very best of them. None escapes this dilemma. We all carry the poison of sin in our bodies and minds but the joy of its forgiveness in our hearts. Only in heaven will we be free from all sin and its sorrows.

(b) **Christ's fasting was not like that of the Jews.** They fasted across a single day or many days, but gorged themselves with food and drink during all night hours, if they desired. The canons of the ancient Hebrews decreed that one fasting might commence eating at sunset and cease at cock crowing. "Fasting" is mentioned in the Talmud 112 Times. Dr. Lee I. Levine in his excellent work, *The Ancient Synagogue. The First Thousand Years,* page 393 writes, "Meals were also held there [in the synagogues] just prior to a public fast." He mentioned how some of the Jews ate "even to excess" on these occasions. Luke is diligent to point out this was not the case with Jesus: "And in those days He did eat nothing" (Lk. 4:2). Moses, the giver of the law, fasted forty days and nights (Deut. 9:9). Elijah, the restorer of the law at Carmel and chief of all prophets, likewise, fasted (1 Kings 19:8). Now He, in whom both the law and all the prophets run to find fulfillment, also fasts. Neither Moses nor Elijah had been so fiercely assailed by the Devil, as was Messiah. His work was to accomplish the fulfillment of *all* the Law of Moses, with its types and shadows, and of *every* article of prophecy pertaining to His life and work in securing atonement for mankind. For more on this, see Section 52, John 5:46-47, footnote z, with Acts 10:43. No marvel that Lucifer, the fallen angel, was so determined to destroy the human Christ. He must fatally bruise the seed of the woman or his kingdom of darkness was doomed.

(c) **"And when the tempter came to him, he said."** Here, we have Satan speaking audibly to Jesus. The historicity of Satan is graphically set forth in Holy Scripture. Children of the Devil usually deny the reality of the Devil. Paul wrote that the believer's intense conflict was "not against flesh and blood, but against principalities, against powers, against the rulers of the darkness of this world, against spiritual wickedness in high *places*" (Eph. 6:12). The nonmaterial or spiritual substance of Satan and his demons is reflected in the words, "The prince of the power of the air" (Eph. 2:2). Satan is said to be "the god of this world" (2 Cor. 4:4), the one who "deceiveth the whole world" (Rev. 12:9). Only those saved by the grace of God, found in the Lord Jesus Christ, are delivered from the everlasting doom of his dominion and the eternal damnation of his deceit. John touched on the dark mystery of evil powers when he wrote of three unclean spirits issuing out of the mouth of the dragon, the beast, and the false prophet as being "spirits of devils' [demons] (Rev. 16:13-14). As spiritual persons, they operate above the laws of natural science, being both invisible and incorporeal. However, they can materialize or take on various forms when such antics are conducive to their cause. In their strange nature, they are amoral, evil, depraved, filthy, vile, hideous, and sinful beyond explanation. Hence, certain demons are called "unclean" (Matt. 10:1; Mk. 1:27; with Rev. 16:13). and "foul spirits" (Rev. 18:2). Their workings on human beings are clear in Scripture and obvious to those who have had to deal with them. They produce in their victims a mental derangement, physical distortions, craving for sin, spiritual darkness, and (with some) a vicious, wild, anti-God character that is terrifying and horrible. Many of the fruits of these wicked entities are so gross and abominable that one dare not put them into human script or language.

2p-The term "demon," carries the etymology of "intelligence," or "knowing." Having observed the actions and conduct of all humanity from the fall of Adam, they are familiar with all nationalities, languages, habits, customs, antics, and deeds from the best to the worst. There seems to be nothing they do not know and are terrified at the mention of the true and living God (James 2:19), and His Son the Lord Jesus (Mk. 1:24). They are old father time's greatest practitioners in deceit and damnation. Satan and his spirits assist *some* to live well, noble, clean upright lives; even honorable and religious, as long as they do not receive Jesus Christ as personal Lord and Savior. Others, they slowly pull into the awful pits of human depravity. Both groups, dying without Christ, will be eternally damned in hell. Satan and demons figure in the moral collapse of millions who yield to gross carnality and sexual sins, so rampant on every side today (2 Tim. 3:1-9 with Rev. 9:20-21). *Every form of opposition to God, the Holy Bible, and the salvation of Jesus Christ, finally has its origin in Satan and demons!* The shocking decisions made by America's judicial systems are sounding the distant death knell for this country. The drive to cripple and finally abolish Christianity, ban prayer, and the message of the Bible, take parental authority and control from parents and put it into the hands of the state is part of the plot. The work of legalizing sins that have been abominations from the beginning of time is fathered by the Devil. Our Lord clashed with this same Devil during His days of awful temptation and over the course of His earthly ministry. Moreover, this is what *true* Christians face, more or less, every day of their lives. By the atoning death of Christ, His resurrection and ascension, with loving obedience, and moral self discipline in the application of Bible truth, we can be "more than conquerors" over this hateful foe (Rom. 8:37-39). God has prepared a place for Satan and his associates; it is described in Matt. 25:41; Rev. 20:10; and 20:15. Cults operating as "Christians" strongly deny these facts. These denials signal an alert for all believers to never support their heresy or bid them Gods speed (2 John 10-11). The word "house" in this verse refers to personal dwellings, not the house churches of that time in history. Heretics would not be mixing within the assemblies of believers. John, the writer of this command dwelt at Ephesus. When the Gnostic heretic, Cerinthus entered the public bath, the apostle John fled for fear that the roof would fall on such a blasphemer.

3p-"The Son of God." This was an echo from His baptism some forty days prior as seen in Matt. 3:17. Satan was present on that occasion. *Why did this so disturb the wicked one and his demons?* Note Section 40, Mk. 1:24 with James 2:19 for the answer. Some three years later it was made clear during the trial of Jesus, by the high priest, that this was one of the divine designations for the promised Messiah or Son of David, and Savior of Israel (Section 181, Matt. 26:63-64, footnote h). While hanging on the cross, this title was hurled into His face, by the pretenders of Jewish religion. It was done in a blasphemous manner (Section 190, Matt. 27:40-43). Hence, the scornful ridicule of Satan and his people in their shameful usage of this blessed prophetic Name. The wicked one knew this Man was God in flesh, the seed of Abraham, and that royal Person from David's family line, the Messiah, and Savior of mankind. (See chapter 3 for His family line.) He understood that Christ had come to destroy his rule of Adam's race through sin and death (Heb. 2:14-16 with 1 John 3:8). In footnote g below, the Devil quotes from Scripture. He is familiar with the Word of God and distorts its truths through his children and false religions to deceive and ultimately damn the souls of those who believe them. Both God's men and the Devil's people use the Bible to proclaim their messages. One is the bright herald of truth while the other is of the dark cloud of lies.

4p-**"Turn these stones to bread."** This was a real event. Satan materialized in a visible form, verbally spoke these words, and Christ audibly heard them. Matthew wrote "stones" plural, while Luke used the singular. It was both. Physically devastated from forty days of unbroken fasting, Satan made his strong appeal to our Lord's starved human frame. *Stones in this district resemble loaves of baked bread in both color and size. They are there to this day!* The Devil displayed one of these before Christ. At the weak points in our humanity, the serpent hisses with a great appeal. A low degree of physical health may afford our adversary opportunities of doing us great mischief.

(d) **"It is written"** was a common rabbinical preface for Scripture citations. Here, Jesus cites from Deut. 8:3. (In the four gospels we find at least eighty-seven Old Testament quotations on the lips of Jesus, not to mention the numerous allusions to people, places and events.) Jesus' quotation was in the context of Israel at the end of their forty years in the great wilderness, designed to *teach* them that they cannot live by bread alone. They had previously rejected God's Word, refusing to live by it. Now, fifteen hundred years later, God's Son applies this section of Jewish history to Himself, the King of the Jews. He too had been called out of Egypt with His stepfather and mother similarly as Israel had (Matt. 2:19-21). Christ *proved* that God's Word could fortify and sustain the soul, even if the flesh faints for material sustenance. With His human frame at its lowest, weakened by the long fast, and with every fiber screaming for bread, the Messiah refused in His broken condition to succumb to a seemingly harmless suggestion of Satan. The physical body of Christ now learns obedience by the things it suffers (Heb. 5:8). Israel in the wilderness never learned this lesson. Their King and Messiah in the wilderness did.

(e) **A pinnacle of the temple.** The order of the temptations as given by Matthew is not that given by Luke. Matthew lists the visit to the temple as the second temptation, whereas Luke puts it third or last. *See the supplement at the end of this Section for a side-by-side verse harmony.* The purpose of this history was not to give the exact chronology of the events. Rather, they were inspired to relate *only* the amazing facts of the story. Which occurred first is of no importance. This air flight to the "holy city" and temple's pinnacle literally occurred. The distance from the supposed temptation site near Jericho to the temple in Jerusalem is some nine miles. What a scene, Satan and Messiah traveling through the atmosphere and landing on this lofty pinnacle! Years later, from this same temple site, the Jews hurled James, the half-brother of Christ, to his death. Josephus the historian, who had served as a priest in this temple, informs us that the height was so great that one glance downward would cause a man to become dizzy. It was some six hundred feet to the valley below. Refer to John Lightfoot's *Commentary on the New Testament . . . ,* vol. 2, pages 85-86 for details. Satan had fallen from heaven's holy temple in the dateless past. This was beheld by the Son of God (Isa. 14:12, Lk. 10:18). Now, the Devil plots to watch the Son of God fall from earth's holy temple.

(f) **"And saith unto him."** Look! Satan speaks *audibly* and he quotes from God's Word! See footnote g for his Old Testament citation to the Son of God.

(g) Satan recited Ps. 91:11-12. Now, the prince of darkness resorts to Scripture to demonstrate that his request is valid. Had not Christ also cited from the Old Testament? See footnote d above for the citation given by the Lord Jesus. Here, we see the Devil is familiar with the Holy Scriptures and will use them (though they be twisted, perverted, and misapplied) to his own advantage, if possible. Refer to Section 200, the second paragraph of footnote c for further explanation of this.

2p-Knowing that his selection from a Psalm referred to the coming Messiah, Satan made a second appeal to the human side of the God-Man. Cunningly, he leaves out the clause "to keep thee in all thy ways." The essence of his proposal is one that can be heard a thousand times daily from the mouths of his emissaries: "See, here is a Scripture that proves hell is not eternal, or you must believe this or that." Every cult operating under the guise of Christianity parrots this pitch of the Devil into the ears of their prospective converts. As God, Christ could have thrown Himself into the valley below and survived unharmed. As man, He would have killed Himself, for He would be neglecting the ordinary means of safety while at the same time expecting God to save Him physically. As the *perfect man*, He would have none of Satan's heavy appeals to lay claim on His humanity, even those adorned with quotations from the Old Testament. Across Scripture, we find Satan speaking *audibly* three times as follows:

1. In Gen. 3:1. He became the first *textual critic* in world history by casting doubt upon the Word of God to Eve. In Satan's first recorded words in Scripture, he **accused God to man.**

2. In Job 1:6-12 and 2:2-5. He spoke a second time and **accused man to God.**

3. In the above passages of this Section, he spoke audibly and **accused the God-Man.**

3p-In the first book of the Bible, the Devil is the great accuser. At the end of the ages in the final book of the Bible, he is described by heaven's great voice as the accuser of the saints, day and night before God (Rev. 12:9-10). False accusations are a prime tool of Satan to create doubt and agony in the minds of men. Millions of Christians not understanding the fullness of Christ's atonement to forgive and blot out all their sins live in torment of the past. See Section 35, footnote i and the illustration of what God's forgiveness does to our sins. It is the prize possession of every saved soul. It is wickedly strange how clearly we can see our faults and those of others yet loose sight of Christ's precious blood that forever washes them away (1 John 1:2). Which one of us at judgment will be pointing a finger and saying, "Lord you know what he did?" There, every born again believer will be praising Jesus for what He did on the cross to take our sins and guilt away.

[h] Messiah cites His rebuttal from Deut. 6:16. Here, the contextual setting is that of Jehovah warning Israel, upon settling into the land of Canaan, not to forget Him who had delivered them from bondage in the land of Egypt. Continue to fear and serve God, and flee from the gods of the pagans into whose land you go was the content of His warnings. All idolatry is a form of Devil worship through the medium of demons (1 Cor. 10:19-21). Hence, to worship and serve idols is to worship and serve Satan. For Israel to do this knowingly and deliberately would be to tempt God to destroy them. Note the horrific penalty under the Torah Law for Devil-idol worship (Deut. 17:1-7). God's promises of mercy and protection do not extend to those who want only to provoke Him, and trifle with His promised help. Satan's corruption of Holy Scripture, in attempting to persuade Christ to leap from the lofty pinnacle, was met and defeated by Messiah's obedience and application of rightly divided Scripture to the situation.

2p-The lesson here is that man should not put himself into precarious situations of foolishness and danger, and then expect God to jump from heaven and save his skin when he has knowingly defied the laws of nature and common sense. Satan had just dared the *human* Son of God to leap from the temple pinnacle because (he suggested) His Father would come to His rescue! Men dare not tempt God to save them from sure calamity when they have played the fool and willfully entered into that, which is forbidden.

[i] **"Exceeding high mountain."** The highest elevation in the Holy Land is Mount Hermon, located north of the Sea of Galilee. It towers some nine thousand feet upward. From its melting snows, both Galilee and Jordan are supplied with water. Was this the "high mountain" or was it some other? What a spectacle, the Devil and Christ moving through the air to this high location!

[j] **"All these things."** Exhibiting his pseudo-rule (John 14:30; 16:11; 2 Cor. 4:4; Eph. 2:2) over the nations of this world, Satan, in a flash of dark brilliance, paraded their pomp and splendor before the weakened humanity of Messiah. *Satan offers Messiah the kingdom without the cross!* What a lie and it is still propagated by certain men today. God's Word again foiled this devilish panorama, though humanely desirable but fictitious and delusive. The physically spent Messiah wielded the Sword of Truth against history's longest-running liar (John 8:44). At this time, only the Old Testament existed, yet it was sufficient to repel this monster from outer space.

[k] **"Worship me." Satan's grand lie.** The conflict of earth's ages has been, "Who will mankind finally worship, God or Satan?" Rightly, all worship belongs to the true and living God. Satan thwarted this exclusive honor as millions worship him to the damnation of their souls (Matt. 25:41 with Rev. 20:10). Every appeal of the Devil to the Son of God was hurled at His devastated, weakened, and helpless physical frame. It was in His body of humanity that Christ received and defeated each temptation by use of God's Word as written in the Old Testament (Eph. 6:17). On this mountain, the prince of darkness attempted to steal the majesty of worship, which belongs to Jehovah God alone. Such an act was horrid blasphemy at its height. Note 1 Cor. 15:23-24 speaks of a time, yet *future,* when the Son shall deliver up the kingdoms of this world to the Father. They will be His in that day, when all redeemed creation bows before the Son and worships Him forever (Rev. 5:13-14). Refer to footnote f above for more on this thought. In God's time, Satan will confess, "Christ is Lord of all" (Phil. 2:9-11).

[l] Our Lord continually reverted to the Jewish Old Testament Scriptures. They were His final authority in matters of eternal value. Was the Son of God mistaken in trusting Holy Scripture? It was the very Word of God, reliable and trustworthy in every aspect. He resorted to this repeatedly. Whatever the critics may say, it put Satan to flight! Could this be one of the reasons they so resent a and oppose a *reliable* Bible? The next passage, Deut. 6:14, issues a warning against Devil worship in the form of idolatry.

[m] Cited from Deut. 6:13 blended with 10:20. In God's plan for salvation of mankind, there is no room for the ecumenical mixed pot of gods, goddesses, pagan religions, false and heretical doctrines, and cooperating with the Devil and sin in general. Only through Jesus Christ can men reach the Lord God of heaven (John 14:6).

[n] **"Angels came."** Had they not ministered to the helpless, exhausted physical body of Christ, He would have died. Perhaps they also protected their weakened Creator Lord from "the wild beasts" that Mark alone wrote about (Mk. 1:13). The first Adam in the Garden of Eden knowingly sinned amid surroundings that were perfect, with all lower creatures tame and gentle. The second Adam was victorious amid a creation wrecked by sin. Surrounded by fierce beastly creatures, both carnivorous and bloodthirsty, Christ as a man emerged triumphant. The night before the morning of the cross, angels again attend to Jesus as He struggled in Gethsemane in lonely prayer. Refer to Lk. 22:43 for this dramatic event.

[o] **"Satan departed for a season."** Defeated, the prince of this world departed from Christ for a season. A "season" normally has reference to several months. In the days ahead, he inspired the religious leadership of Israel with a fresh hatred for Messiah. Satan directed their schemes designed to bring about His physical destruction, but they continually failed. The night before the morning of the cross, he came on the scene again in the upper room. Messiah triumphantly announced to His apostles that the Devil, who was approaching, had nothing (could find no sin) in Him. Refer to Section 175, John 14:30, footnote r. Refer also to Heb. 4:15. However, Satan did find lodging in the soul of Judas. This awful fact is discussed in Section 147, Lk. 22:3, footnote a, with Section 172, John 13:26-27, footnote i. For a survey of Satan and demons, see first and second paragraphs under footnote c above.

Matthew and Luke's records of the temptations compared.*

In this Supplement, the last two temptations as recorded by Luke are adjusted in the right hand column to harmonize with the record of Matthew in the left column. God did not tell us why He inspired Luke to write his last two events in a different order from Matthew. It reveals that Luke did not copy from Matthew. The rearrangement presented in this Supplement is only for comparative study. Luke's record should be left as it was originally written.

Matt. 4:1–6	Mk. 1:12–13a	Lk. 4:1–4, Lk. 4: 9–11	John
1 Then was Jesus led up of the Spirit into the wilderness to be tempted of the devil.	**12** And immediately the Spirit driveth him into the wilderness. **13a** And he was there in the wilderness forty days, tempted of Satan; and was with the wild beasts; (Verse 13 cont. on next page.)	**1** And Jesus being full of Holy Ghost returned from Jordan, and was led by the Spirit into the wilderness, **2** Being forty days tempted of the devil.	
2 And when he had fasted forty days and forty nights, he was afterward an hungered.		And in those days he did eat nothing: and when they were ended, he afterward hungered.	
The first temptation **3** And when the tempter came to him, he said, **"If thou be the Son of God, command that these stones be made bread."** **4** But he answered and said, **"It is written, 'Man shall not live by bread alone, but by every Word that proceedeth out of the mouth of God.'"**	◄ *All the words of Satan and demons are in a heavy Gothic font throughout this work. They know all languages and can talk through the mouths of their captives. For more on these things, see Matt. 8:29 with Mk. 3:11-12. This is further illustrated in Section 20, the second and third paragraphs of footnote l.*	*The first temptation* **3** And the devil said unto him, **"If thou be the Son of God, command this stone that it be made bread."** **4** And Jesus answered him, saying, **"It is written, That 'man shall not live by bread alone, but by every Word of God.'"** (Verse 5 cont. on next page by symbol ►.)	
The second temptation **5** Then the devil taketh him up into the holy city, and setteth him on a pinnacle of the temple, **6** And saith unto him, **"If thou be the Son of God, cast thyself down:**		*The third temptation* Lk. 4:9–11 ►**9** And he brought him to Jerusalem, and set him on a pinnacle of the temple, and said unto him, **"If thou be the Son of God, cast thyself down from hence:**	
The Devil quotes Scripture from the Old Testament **for it is written 'He shall give his angels charge concerning thee:' and 'in *their* hands**		*The Devil quotes Scripture from the Old Testament* **10 "For it is written, 'He shall give his angels charge over thee, to keep thee:** **11 And 'in *their* hands**	

Matt. 4:6–11	Mk. 1:13b cont.	Lk. 4:11–13, Lk. 4:5–8	John
they shall bear thee up, lest at any time thou dash thy foot against a stone.'" 7 Jesus said unto him, "It is written again, 'Thou shalt not tempt the Lord thy God.'"▶		they shall bear thee up, lest at any time thou dash thy foot against a stone.'" 12 And Jesus answering said unto him, "It is said, 'Thou shalt not tempt the Lord thy God.'" 13 And when the devil had ended all the temptation, he departed from him for a season. (Verse 14 cont. in Section 33.)	
	◄ *In these Words the Savior claimed to be both Lord and God. See Section 1, Part 1, footnote a for more on this great doctrine of the faith.*	***The second temptation*** Lk. 4:5–8	
The third temptation 8 Again, the devil taketh him up into an exceeding high mountain, and sheweth him all the kingdoms of the world, and the glory of them; 9 And saith unto him, **"All these things**	*See sub heading in italics after Luke 4:4 on previous page for Lk. 4:9.*	◄5 And the devil, taking him up into an high mountain, shewed unto him all the kingdoms of the world in a moment of time. 6 And the devil said unto him, **"All this power will I give thee, and the glory of them: for that is delivered unto me; and to whomsoever I will I give it.** 7 **"If thou therefore wilt worship me, all shall be thine."**	
will I give thee, if thou wilt fall down and worship me." 10 Then saith Jesus unto him, "Get thee hence, Satan: for it is written, 'Thou shalt worship the Lord thy God, and him only shalt thou serve.'" 11 Then the devil leaveth him, and, behold, angels came and ministered unto him. (Verse 12 cont. in Section 33.)	13b and the angels ministered unto him. (Verse 14 cont. in Section 33.)	8 And Jesus answered and said unto him, "Get thee behind me, Satan: for it is written, 'Thou shalt worship the Lord thy God, and him only shalt thou serve.'" (See verse 9 on the previous page by symbol ▶.)	

No Footnotes–Commentary in Supplements

Hebrew authorities interrogate John the Baptist regarding His right to baptize. Christ standing unnoticed among the people listened to their debate.

Matt.	Mk.	Lk.	John 1:19–28—*At Bethabara, Jordan*
			John's response to the questions of the Jews
			19 And this is the record of John, when the Jews sent[a] priests and Levites from Jerusalem to ask him, "Who art thou?"
			20 And he confessed, and denied not; but confessed, "I am not the Christ." [or Messiah]
			21 And they asked him, "What then? Art thou Elias?"[b] (Elijah). And he saith, "I am not." "Art thou that prophet?"[c] And he answered, "No."
			22 Then said they unto him, "Who art thou? that we may give an answer to them that sent us. What sayest thou of thyself?"
			John knew he was fulfilling Scripture
			23 He said,[d] "I *am* 'the voice of one crying in the wilderness, "Make straight the way of the Lord," ' as said the prophet E-sa-ias." (Isaiah).
			24 And they which were sent were of the Pharisees.
			25 And they asked him, and said unto him, "Why baptizest thou then,[e] if thou be not that Christ, nor Elias, [Elijah] neither that prophet?"
			26 John answered them, saying, "I baptize with water: but there standeth[f] one among you, whom ye know not;
			27 "He it is, who coming after me is preferred before me, whose shoe's latchet I am not worthy to unloose."
			28 These things were done in Bethabara[g] beyond Jordan, where John was baptizing. (Verse 29 cont. in Section 25.)

Footnotes–Commentary

[a]Almost two years later, the Lord Jesus mentioned the Jews sending messengers to John the Baptist and questioning him (John 5:33). Christ *always* means Messiah ("Mashiach" or the "anointed One") in the New Testament Scriptures. In this query put to John by the Sanhedrin's agents from Jerusalem, it strictly referred to Israel's coming King.

2p-See Section 151, footnote a, where much *later* the Jews asked Jesus where He received authority to do His works and claim to be the Messiah. For this question to be asked and John to deny he was their Messiah affirms that they were indeed at that time looking for the Messiah. Refer to Section 16, footnote l, for two elderly Jews, who were looking for their Messiah and found Him as an infant in the temple. They were Simeon and Anna. This Hebrew national expectation was based on various Old Testament passages along with rabbinical conjectures and extra biblical writings known as the Apocrypha and Pseudepigrapha. These books produced a wide diversity of thought among the Jews about their coming Messiah. In different periods of Jewish history, Messiah had various Names, duties, and honors; often, these seriously contradicted each other. Joseph Klausner's work, *The Messianic Idea in Israel*, Part III, page 405 gives coverage of this, while at the same time denying Jesus was the real Messiah, who suffered and died for our sins. Nevertheless, there existed at the time of His birth a small group who knew He was coming, and what He would do as the Messiah and Savior of Israel.

3p-John the Baptist in the above verses denied that he was either their promised Messiah or their Old Testament Elijah. He did this because the Jews were looking for the *actual* Old Testament prophet to reappear physically on the scene. See footnote b below. In this expectation, they were seriously wrong. All this happened decades *before* Rev. 11:3-12 was written. In these ten verses of the Revelation, some believe they see a "Second coming of Elijah" to earth. Note footnote b below.

[b] **"Are you Elijah?"** The Jew's interrogation of John is mentioned later by Christ, in Section 52, John 5:31-35. For centuries, the synagogue had taught that the *physical* Elijah of the Old Testament would reappear *before* Messiah came and restore all things in Israel. They believed that amid terrible days of national judgment and calamity, Elijah would arrive and set the stage for Israel's King Messiah. This is further mentioned in footnote c

below. Hence, some observers mused that John the Baptist's rugged appearance and powerful message reminded them of Elijah of the Old Testament; that God had at last sent him to Israel. The rabbis located verses that predicted the appearing of Elijah, such as Mal. 3:1-3; 4:5-6; and Isa. 40:1-9. This belief was common knowledge in the days of Christ. Alfred Edersheim lists in *Appendix Eight* of his work, *The Life and Times of Jesus the Messiah*, many of the outlandish deeds and exaggerations the rabbis accredited to their coming Elijah. The Talmud also has numerous references to the coming of Elijah prior to the Messiah. See tractates, Eiruvin 43b and Pesachin 13a. Every devout Jew, as well as the apostles, believed the teachings of the rabbis concerning the literal reappearing of their most famed Old Testament prophet. This is reflected in their question recorded in Section 105, Matt. 17:10 and Mk. 9:11. For a review of the coming Elijah and his duties as *conjectured* by the ancient rabbis, see *Appendix Four*.

(c) **"Are you that prophet?"** Some Jews believed that the prediction made by Moses in Deut. 18:15 referred to a coming prophet, similar to Moses, who would appear in the days just before Messiah. He, along, with Elijah would turn Israel back to God. Others believed the prediction of Moses spoke of the Messiah. Among the crowds, some surmised that possibly, John was that prophet. However, Peter several years later at Pentecost quoted the passage from Deut. 18:15, and interpreted it as being fulfilled in the Lord Jesus (Acts 3:22-26). Peter believed that Moses spoke of Messiah in Deut. 18:15. Therefore, this could not have reference to some unknown prophet working in cooperation with Elijah as rabbinical superstition had conjectured.

(d) John the Baptist, familiar with Old Testament Scriptures, cites this portion from Isa. 40:3 and applied it to himself. He understood that his ministry would fulfill this prediction. If John had been an impostor, he could have claimed to have been whoever Israel was looking for and gathered a large following under this pretentious banner. However, he was only "a voice" pointing men to Jesus of Nazareth, the Messiah, who would soon make a public appearance on the banks of the Jordan and later in the temple at Jerusalem. In the temple, Jesus would present Himself publicly during the Passover for the *first* time as the promised Messiah of Israel. Refer to Section 29 for this event. "Make straight the way of the Lord," (verse 23) was an ancient expression for having all things ready and orderly in view of the soon arrival of a king or some notable person of great authority. It should be noted that in Isa. 40:3, the word "Lord" is spelt with uppercase, "LORD." This was an exclusive Old Testament designation used for Jehovah God, alone. *John Baptist thus calls Jesus "LORD" or "Jehovah."*

(e) **Permission to baptize.** It was a firm rule in Israel that all who baptized within the nation must secure permission from the Sanhedrin. This required three magistrates, or doctors of the Torah Law to be present for the occasion. It was believed that only Messiah and His forerunner, Elijah, did *not* need their permission. Neither Christ nor John had the official sanction to witness baptisms. Therefore, the Levites interrogated John as to the source of his authority to baptize in Israel. Hence, the stir over their baptisms, as some were thinking, John was possibly the promised forerunner, Elijah. John's denial of being Elijah simply meant he was not the *real* flesh and blood Elijah of the Old Testament they were looking for (John 1:21). Later, Jesus said that John *was* indeed the Elijah of this prophecy. His disciples then understood that He was speaking of John the Baptist (Matt. 17:11-13).

(f) This reveals that Jesus was in the midst of this group, listening to their conversation. Over a year later, Christ referred to John's clash with the delegation from Jerusalem. He said that John had given witness to the truth and was like a "burning and shining light" (John 5:35). Surprisingly, Jesus even said that the religious leaders (at least some of them) believed John "for a season" (Section 52, John 5:31-36). This early joy soon faded into hatred for Christ. He denounced their hypocrisy, oral commands, and accused them of being enemies to the people, and children of the Devil (John 8:44). The words "children of the Devil," were not an expression used friendly debate. *He meant it!*

(g) **"Bethabara."** Among other things, it has been translated as "ferry crossing," which was a place of water. It was located about twenty miles east of Jerusalem at a tributary on the southern end of the Jordan River. Christ visited here often with his disciples, as suggested in John 10:40. John also baptized at "Aenon near to Salim, because there was much water there" (John 3:23). Why did the forerunner of Jesus baptize in "much water" if (as some teach) he poured it on his converts' heads out of a seashell? See Section 22, Matt. 3:14, third paragraph of footnote c for further comments. It is interesting that Aenon was located within hostile Samaria a few miles west of Jordan. This contradicts the myth that John preached *only* to Israel and offered them a literal, material kingdom. See what John preached in Section 21, Part 4, footnote q. No loyal Hebrew would accept a cursed Samaritan within the ranks of Israel, unless they became a proselyte. All Samaritans were considered demon possessed by the Jews (John 8:48). The hard-line Jews often discriminated even against Samaritan proselytes to Israel! Racism was supposedly forbidden in Israel, though their rancor toward all Gentiles was known over the world of that era. Such actions reflected the deep hatred of the Jews toward those not of their nationality and religion. It remains valid to this day, that millions of individuals hate all men not of their culture, race, and beliefs.

2p-There is a vast difference in pointing out the error, lies, and deception of false religions and hating men because they are not what we are. The sinless Son of God continually struggled with the evil religious leaders of Israel but did not condone hating them. Paul the apostle was persecuted day and night for opposing wrong and preaching Christ, truth, and right (Acts 20:17-38). For sincerity in a false religion and the horrible things, it leads men to do, see Section 95, sixth paragraph of footnote r.

John the Baptist identifies Jesus as the Lamb sacrifice for the sin of the world and the "Son of God," Israel's Messiah. How he knew these things in advance.

Matt.	Mk.	Lk.	John 1:29-34—At Bethabara, Jordan
			All hail the "Lamb of God" **29** The next day John seeth Jesus coming unto him, and saith, "Behold the Lamb of God, **(a)** which taketh away the sin of the world. **30** "This is he of whom I said, 'After me cometh a man which is preferred before me: for he was before me.' **31** "And I knew him not: but that he should be made manifest to Israel, therefore am I come baptizing with water." **32** And John bare record, saying, "I saw the Spirit descending from heaven like a dove, and it abode upon him. ***How John was to identify the Messiah*** **33** "And I knew him not: but he [God] that sent me to baptize with water, the same said unto me, 'Upon whom thou shalt see the Spirit descending,**(b)** and remaining on him, the same is he which baptizeth with the Holy Ghost.' **(c)** **34** "And I saw, [the Spirit descend on Him] and bare record [witness] that this is the Son of God." **(d)** (Verse 35 cont. in Section 26.)

Footnotes-Commentary

(a) "The lamb of God." The statement "next day," had reference to John's confrontation with the Jewish inquisitors sent from Jerusalem. John's father, the aged Zacharias, a priest serving in the temple, had surely familiarized his son with the temple's services and functions before his death. See the Lord Jesus approaching His great forerunner: John bursts forth with the marvelous acclamation by which he identifies the final and greatest work of Christ. He spoke of the saving gospel to be factually accomplished some three years later in the death, burial, and resurrection. He had previously quoted from Isa. 40:3 and applied it to himself as Messiah's forerunner. From where did he get this information? No doubt, it was by divine revelation. In this herald, the Baptist moved forward through the book of Isaiah and identified Jesus with the "lamb to the slaughter" in Isa. 53:7. John the Baptist had been dead about one and a half years before Christ died on the cross. His death was for "The sin of the world" but only appropriated by those in the world who believe on Him. Their sins are taken away forever!

2p-The Jewish doctors of the law taught that one of Elijah's great works was to bring to Israel the good news of the coming of their Messiah. *This, John had just done in these very words!* The rabbis also taught that the continual morning and evening sacrifice of the lamb pointed to the everlasting efficacy of the blood. However, they failed to understand that the blood of their sacrificial lambs pointed to Messiah's atonement. Not only does the blood of Christ carry eternal efficacy across all ages of time, but also in the eternity of heaven, the precious blood of the lamb, (still) newly slain, continues in eternal worth and receives endless praises, "for ever and ever" (Rev. 5:6-13). John spoke the gospel, briefly, but it fell onto the deaf ears of the Israelites. Sadly, the *majority* of them did not yet understand his message. In their synagogue theology, Israel's Messiah, the King of the Jews, would destroy the pagan Romans. The *only* "world" in Jewish eschatology was a political-material world in which Israel would rule under King Messiah. Most of them did not know that He was the Lamb of God dying for the sins of the world (both Jews and Gentiles). Refer to Section 21, Part 4, Lk. 3:18, footnote q for a listing of what John did and preached.

Names and titles for the Savior recorded in John chapter 1. Some are doublets.

1. **The Word.** John 1:1. Refer to Section 1, Part 1, footnote b for explanation of this term.
2. **The Light.** John 1: 4 - 5, 7, 8 - 9. Refer to Section 1, Part 1, footnote e for explanation.
3. **The Word, the only begotten of the Father.** John 1:14. Refer to Section 1, Part, 1, footnote b for the meaning of the term "Word," and number 5 below for "only begotten."
4. **Jesus Christ.** John 1:17. For the meaning of the name "Jesus," see Section 12, footnote e. Christ always means "Messiah," the promised Savior of Israel. Refer to Section 5, left hand vertical column, footnotes a, c and d for explanation. Note also Section 34, John 4:25-26, footnotes k and l for the Samaritan woman's confession of the coming Messiah and His admission to being that divine Person.
5. **The Only begotten Son.** John 1:18. "Monogenes" ("only begotten"), means "unique," "none like it." Some new translations have omitted this critical word. It is the same as in number three above.
6. **The Christ (Messiah).** John 1:20. Same as in number 4 above.

7. **The Lord.** John 1:23. Here, "Lord" is applied to Jesus. This was taken from Isa. 40:3 where the prophet used the term "LORD" (all uppercase) that had strict reference to Jehovah God.

8. **That Christ (Messiah).** John 1:25. See number 4 above.

9. **Jesus, the Lamb of God.** John 1:29. This was John the Baptist's *exclusive* identification of the Lord Jesus as the sacrifice for mankind's sin.

10. **The Son of God.** John 1:34. See Section 103, Matt. 16:16, footnotes e and f, with footnote d below.

11. **The Lamb of God.** John 1:36.

12. **Rabbi (Master).** John 1:38. For explanation of this title, refer to Section 30, footnote d.

13. **Messias the Christ.** John 1:41. Follow references by number 4 above for the meaning.

14. **Jesus.** John 1: 42. Follow references by number 4 above for the meaning.

15. **Jesus.** John 1: 43. Follow references by number 4 above for the meaning.

16. **Jesus of Nazareth, the son of Joseph.** John 1:45. Refer to Section 6, footnote e for this term.

17. **Jesus.** John 1:47. Follow references by number 4 above for the meaning.

18. **Jesus.** John 1:48. Follow references by number 4 above for the meaning.

19. **Rabbi, Son of God, King of Israel.** John 1:49. For the meaning of rabbi, see Section 30 at number 12 above. For meaning of the term "Son of God," see number 10 above and footnote d below. For His public recognition as the King of the Jews by both friends and foes, refer to Section 17, footnote d; Section 26 footnote i; and Section 189, footnote e. Some stress that Jesus was never called the "King of the church." This is "pot luck" theology. In Rev. 15:3, our Savior is identified as the "King of the saints." According to Paul's letters, the saints and the church are the same (Eph. 1:1 with Phil. 1:1). To change the saints (mentioned thirteen times in the book of Revelation) into "Jews during the tribulation" is a mistake. Saints are saints, regardless of what age they lived. The emphasis on what Christ was *never* called in Scripture can be taken to extremes. Building a biblical doctrine on silence is a poor foundation.

20. **Jesus.** John 1:50. Refer to number 4 above for meaning.

21. **The Son of man.** John 1:51. Note Section 26, footnote k for several cross-references to the explanation of this peculiar term. Refer to Section 7 for more on His Names and titles.

3p-Verse 31. "Manifest to Israel." The idea here is that before the Savior lowered Himself under the waters of Jordan, John, the divinely illuminated attester of His baptism, verbally introduced Him as Israel's Messiah to the thousands present. Prior to this, John and Jesus were total strangers to each other. John's claim that this Person was Messiah was confirmed when he saw the Holy Spirit descend upon the Lord Jesus (verse 32).

(b) Before the baptism of Christ, God had communicated to John that he would *know* Israel's Messiah when he witnessed His baptism. When this communication took place, we are not told. The Baptist would *see* the Spirit descending and remaining upon the Messiah. Although the two men were relatives, apparently they had not met to this time. Jesus lived far north in Galilee, and John grew up in the southern wilderness of Judaea. John literally saw the Holy Ghost, *like* a dove, descending upon God's beloved Son. Clearly, at the baptism of Christ (some forty days prior to these words), John recognized Him by the sign of the Spirit coming upon Him. In verse 33, he declared that this experience and knowledge came from God; that he saw it happen just as God had revealed it to him.

(c) Here, God speaks to John the Baptist. Israel believed at this stage in history that the Holy Spirit had forsaken their nation and temple upon the deaths of their three final prophets, Haggai, Zachariah and Malachi. The rabbis maintained that with the death of Malachi, the Spirit of God had departed from Israel, especially the temple. The sages taught that only Messiah at his coming would impart the Holy Spirit to Israel again. This is precisely what John stated in this passage: "the same is he which baptizeth with the Holy Ghost." Surely, the oldest and wisest of Jews standing about understood the meaning of what he said. In this, we see *another* identification of Jesus as the Messiah. For the Holy Spirit across Old Testament history, see Section 10, the second paragraph, footnote b.

(d) "This is the Son of God." Again, we meet this sacred term. John knew exactly what he was doing in using this title. Jesus of Nazareth was the promised Messiah of Israel. That Satan and his demons understood the meaning of this term is demonstrated in Section 55, Mk. 3:11-12, footnote d. Here, the emissaries of darkness spoke audibly one of His Messianic titles. It is true that the term "Son of God" has designations in Scripture apart from that of Israel's Messiah. However, in the case of Jesus of Nazareth, it was employed as the distinctive appellation of the One to whom it belonged in a unique, exclusive sense (Lk. 1:32-33). Connect this "Son of God" statement of the Baptist with that of John the writer in Section 202, John 20:30-31, for the effect of this title on his original Jewish readers. Note what this title signaled to the terrified disciples in Section 94, Matt. 14:33, footnote j. See the confession of a Gentile from Ethiopia in Acts 8:36-38. It is similar to the term "Son of David." Both make direct reference to Israel's Messiah. Peter's words, "Thou art the Christ [Messiah], the Son of the living God" meant the same thing (Matt. 16:16). This description given by Peter some three decades later is recorded in 2 Peter 1:17-18.

2p-Heathen distortions of the Son of God and other truths. As previously stated, the *origin* of heathen religions is traced to that post-flood world, beginning at the Tower of Babel. Some ancient legends, traditions, and historians believe it began among the rebellious pre-flood citizens of Noah's day. Human rebels of those ages past perverted the known truths about the Trinity, virgin birth, incarnation, the only begotten Son of God, heaven, hell, Christ's atonement, resurrection, and other eternal doctrines (Rom. 1:19-32). The Devil and demons used heathen philosophies, priests, religions, and idolatry to do this. *All religious mythology, regardless of how bizarre or rudimentary it is, had its beginning in some original divine truth.* In the writings, *The Works of Nathaniel Lardner,* vol. 6, pages 371-391, Jewish and heathen perversions of the Christian faith are explained. Alexander Hislop, in a heavily documented work, *The Two Babylons,* also deals with many of these things. Some of his sources are no longer available. In places, he goes to extremes to prove a point; however, his work remains invaluable in this field of research. In 1997, Ralph Woodrow greatly corrected some of Hislop's errors in, *The Babylon Connection.* Many writers miss the *total* demonic origin and purpose of all idolatry. See Section 20 and all seven paragraphs under footnote l for more on this. The most authoritative work on the pagan corruption of truth is, *The Court of the Gentiles,* by Theophilus Gale, printed in 1676. It is the magna cum laude of research demonstrating the origin of heathen religions and their Antichrist meanings. For infidel academia's attacks on Gale' work, see Section 1, Part 1, fourth paragraph of footnote b. Paul makes it clear in 1 Cor. 10:19-21 that all idolatry is demon worship. For more on this, see Section 1, Part 4, third and fourth paragraphs of footnote j. John's public witness of the "Lamb of God" (verse 29), and "the Son of God' (verse 34), sent shock waves into the bastions of satanic paganism and the hypocritical Jewish religion.

3p-Heathen distortions of Holy Scripture. After the human race dispersed from the Tower of Babel, they created worldwide idolatry with millions of gods and goddesses. Later, heathens plagiarized the early books of the Jewish Old Testament and mingled these infallible teachings with their mythology. God's truths are still distorted by pagans in secular education and liberal theological institutions. Satan's purpose is to deviate men from Christ and damn their souls at death. This is the razor's edge in all religion and theology.

4p-Heathen and Christian distortions of repentance. Certain heathen religions required bizarre forms of repentance as they worshiped their idols. Often, this worship included self-inflicted mutilation and torture that proved genuine repentance. See modern day examples of this in Section 104, first paragraph of footnote e. Reformed teaching that only *after* men are saved can they genuinely repent is grossly false. See this in Section 1, Part 3, footnotes h and i. The rich man suffering in hell pled concerning his five brothers alive on earth, "If one went unto them from the dead, they will repent" (Section 131, Lk. 16:30). If repentance follows salvation he would have shouted, "Father Abraham, get my brothers saved so they can repent afterwards and then not come to this place." Many Calvinists work hard to convert others to "predestination" instead of to Christ. Splitting churches, dividing long-time friends, and forcing out those who disagree are part of the package. Some even steal church buildings paid for by others not of their persuasion. Everything is tested against *their* newly discovered "Doctrine of free grace." As ancient heathens distorted the truth about repentance, so have these people. *The good news is that not all Calvinists are thus poisoned.* The famed Calvinist, R. C. Sproul was honest enough to write about Reformed doctrine that "Augustine, Aquinas, Luther, Calvin, and Edwards could all be wrong." See *Chosen by God,* pages 15-16. This is a great man's confession!

5p-Arminianism, the opposite heresy. A counter to the above began with a Dutch Reform minister; Jacob Arminius (died 1609). Parts of his doctrine was wrong and even radical. A major place where he differed from sound Bible teachers of later years was that he believed that men did not need to fall, but it was still possible to lose salvation if they did! *He held to the error that man was depraved but his will was not.* Both Calvinism and Arminianism are poison because they shame the great doctrine of eternal soteriology. Every heresy, to gain acceptance, must have fragments of truth. Dr. Arthur T. Pierson (died 1911), was a Presbyterian by training. Pierson, who like Albert Barnes, was kicked out of the Presbyterian Church for opposing the limited atonement myth. Both men braved the fierce opposition of fellow Calvinists. Pierson penned a truth that many (but not all) Presbyterians deny, change, or run from. He stated in his 1905 work, *The Believer's Life: Its Past, Present, and Future Tenses,* pages 25–30, that "the sovereign will of God and the freedom of man" are both found in Scripture. Pierson further states, "Thus the last great invitation in God's Book is an appeal to the will." (Rev. 22:17).

6p-"God is in control." This term was also used among pagan priests who would assure their fellows that "the gods were in control" of all things. What does it mean for Christians? Was God in control as communism murdered millions? Was He in control when Hitler slaughtered the Jews? Where was God when abortion clinics across America, funded by tax dollars, killed over eighty million unborn babies? The sovereignty of God does not mean that He ordained these heinous crimes, or that they were committed with His approval. Men have free will and can choose not to exercise the freedom of moral choice. God knew from the beginning every act of humankind, but He is not the author of all their actions. Neither does He *make* men do right. All mentally responsible persons are the cause of their deeds by choosing to do them; often, their actions are inspired by the Devil. Intermittently, the Almighty chooses to interfere with the plans of men to adjust human and natural events for divine reasons. Intrusion into the forbidden zone of where time and eternity meet is calamitous. Those who daringly trespass, manifest a strange spiritual and mental imbalance of God's sovereignty. Their ridged dogmatism does not bring lost souls to Christ. While they enjoy, "in deep humility, being one of the elect," family members and friends slip off into hell. Refer to Section 29, third paragraph of footnote j for more on this. Ours is the Christ from heaven. Him we love and serve until death takes us from this life. *Every man is a prospect for heaven until he or God shows us different.*

Christ meets several men from Galilee, who later became His first disciples.* Leaving Bethabara, He travels northward returning to Galilee. He finds Philip, who also became a follower. Philip in turn tells Nathanael of Jesus. The two meet.

For our Lord's next recorded meeting with Peter, Andrew, James, and John, refer to Section 39.

Matt.	Mk.	Lk.	John 1:35-50—*Leaves Bethabara*
			John points his disciples to Jesus: they visit with Him
			35 Again the next day after John stood, and two of his disciples;
			36 And looking upon Jesus[(a)] as he walked, he saith, "Behold the Lamb of God!"
			37 And the two[(b)] disciples heard him speak, and they followed Jesus.
			38 Then Jesus turned, and saw them following,[(c)] and saith unto them, "What seek ye?" They said unto him, "Rabbi,[(d)] (which is to say, being interpreted, Master,) where dwellest thou?"
			39 He saith unto them, "Come and see." They came and saw where he dwelt, and abode with him that day: for it was about the tenth hour.[(e)] (4 p.m.)
			Andrew finds Peter and introduces
			him to Messiah: His strange prediction upon Simon Peter
			40 One of the two which heard John *speak*, and followed him, was Andrew, Simon Peter's brother.
			41 He first findeth his own brother Simon, and saith unto him, **"We have found the Messias," which is, being interpreted, the "Christ." (or Messiah)**
			42 And he brought him to Jesus.[(f)] And when Jesus beheld him, he said, "Thou art Simon the son of Jona: thou shalt be called Cephas," which is by interpretation, "A stone."
			Philip follows Jesus and finds Nathanael
			43 The day following Jesus would go forth [travel] into Galilee,[(g)] and findeth Philip, and saith unto him, "Follow me."
			44 Now Philip was of Bethsaida, the city of Andrew and Peter. **45** Philip[(h)] findeth Nathanael, and saith unto him, **"We have found him, of whom Moses in the law, and the prophets, did write, Jesus of Nazareth, the son of Joseph."**
			Sarcastic sincerity
			46 And Nathanael said unto him, "Can there any good thing come out of Nazareth?" Philip saith unto him, "Come and see."
			47 Jesus saw Nathanael coming to him, and saith of him, "Behold an Israelite indeed, in whom is no guile!"
			48 Nathanael saith unto him, "Whence knowest thou me?" Jesus answered and said unto him, "Before that Philip called thee, when thou wast under the fig tree, I saw thee."
			Nathanael confesses
			the Lord Jesus as the Messiah and Israel's king
			49 Nathanael answered and saith unto him, **"Rabbi, thou art the Son of God; thou art the King of Israel."**[(i)]
			50 Jesus answered and said unto him, "Because I said unto thee, 'I saw thee under the fig tree,' believest thou? thou shalt see greater things than these."

Matt.	Mk	Lk	John 1:51—*Leaves Bethabara*
			Messiah's promise to Nathanael
			51 And he saith unto him, "Verily, verily, I say unto you, Hereafter ye shall see heaven open, and the angels of God ascending and descending[j] upon the Son of man."[k] (Next chap., John 2:1, cont. in Section 27.)

Footnotes-Commentary

[a] **"Looking upon Jesus."** Only as believers do this by faith will they gradually discover His beauty. Behold, the wonder all ye saints, the eternal God has become a helpless infant, nursing the bosom of a maid from wicked Nazareth. Look at Him, the Little Boy King playing with the tools in his foster-father's carpenter shop. Contemplate His life, works, Words, and finally, His death for our sins. See Him rising to live forever and the terrible grave, at last, conquered. What matchless excellences wait for all those who will "look upon Jesus," the Son of God. The greatest of all "looks" is that one which by repentance and faith *secures* salvation to weary men (Isa. 45:22).

2p-"As he walked." What a curious statement. All normal men walk with their two legs! Does this suggest there was something unusual about the walk of our Lord? In what way did John associate the steps of Jesus with that of a lamb walking? More is here than meets the casual eye. Later, John wrote that we "ought to walk as he walked" (1 John 2:6). The author of this work has sat thousands of times on church stages and platforms waiting to be called up to teach or preach. He has noticed on numerous occasions the stance of those speakers before him. Men who stood solid on both feet usually had something to say. Those who did not were a bore. Their words were like a sprinkling of water on the audience; they soon evaporated.

[b] **"Saw two disciples."** According to verse 40, one of these was Andrew. The other was probably John, whose design was to conceal his name. See John 13:23; 19:26; 20:2; and 21:7, 20-24. Writing some years later, John, looking back, rejoiced to remember himself as that disciple "whom Jesus loved."

[c] **"Then Jesus turned, and saw them following."** With these epochal words, we are introduced to the *early* beginnings of the mighty spiritual kingdom or church of the Lord Jesus Christ. No movement in human history ever began in such obscurity, as did Christianity. How insignificant was that *first* meeting of the Messiah with five men: Andrew, Peter, Philip, Nathanael, and John. It was this same John, so meek that he shrank from using his name as he penned his story. See note b above. The record here is trivial. One could almost feel the inspired writer purposely avoided the details that human inquisitiveness scrambles to find. No fanfare, trumpet blasts, or sober formal call into the sacred office of apostleship, all such vanities are missing in these meager lines. Earthly glory and pomp have no stage here. We read *only* of a shy acquaintance. Andrew and John had walked some ninety miles south from Capernaum to the baptismal location in Jordan, to hear John the Baptist. However, he pointed them to Christ instead. Now, they desired to know more of this mysterious Man of whom the preaching Baptist had said so much.

2p-Where do you dwell? Upon observation of them "following Him," Jesus turned and inquired, "What seek ye?" Wishing not to hinder Him in the line of duty, they respond, "Master where dwellest thou?" or, "May we discourse with you after this day of busy service is done?" To their joy, the Lord replied, "Come and see." Perhaps they believed their King would lead them to a royal palace for the night. Instead, they were stunned to discover that He had no place to lay His head! Previous conversation with the Baptist had stirred in their hearts a desire to see this One whose way John was preparing. Now, they are invited into His *borrowed* dwelling place for a night and then into His great heart. In time, He will enter theirs. Here, the infant New Testament Church, the new kingdom of God, was laid in its cradle. The earliest buds of what would later be called the Christian faith would silently come forth through this babe. With this marvelous Child, the Church of the Living God was conceived, being mostly called the kingdom of God in the gospels. It would be fully born some three years later on the Day of Pentecost. This is not to decry the fact that people were saved across the Old Testament, even from the beginning of time. For the Holy Spirit and the new birth during Old Testament history, see Section 10, the second paragraph of footnote b, and Section 30, second paragraph of footnote h. At Pentecost, *all* believers of *all* ages became the total church. There has never been such a thing as a Jewish church and a separate body of believers called the Gentile church. Nor will there ever be! Paul tells us that there "*is* one body" (Eph. 4:4).

[d] **"Rabbi." John explains certain words for his readers.** It is noteworthy that he interpreted this word for his original readers. He did this a second and third time in verses 41 and 42. He wrote not only to fellow Jews but also to *anyone*, even those who could not understand certain inspired Hebrew words. For the benefit of his non-Jewish readers, John interpreted specific Hebrew words several other times in his book. See John 19:17 and 20:16. We should learn from this that some biblical words need fuller explanation. For more on this, see the second paragraph of footnote f below.

[e] The rabbis taught that Messiah would dwell in high royal splendor. Wherever our Lord was staying during this short time at Bethabara, these two men were shocked. They did not ask in order to know His address to visit Him on other occasions. Verse 43 reads that He *departed from that place* the next day. They found no palace or united Israel ready to overthrow the Roman Empire. Foxes had their holes and the birds their nests, but the glorious

King of Israel had no place (of His own) to lay His head. See Section 87, Matt 8:20, footnote c. The "tenth hour" is about 4:00 p.m. John specifically pinpointed certain times in his book (John 4:6, 52; 11:9; and 19:14). Apparently, these men spent the night with Jesus. What an experience! Our Lord's state of abject poverty must have shocked these fishermen from Galilee. "Was this how the King of Israel lives?" was a question that surely troubled their minds. See footnote c above. The next morning, Andrew emerged from that experience, convinced that Jesus of Nazareth was indeed the Messiah of Israel. He found his brother Peter and brought him to meet the Messiah.

2p-**Verse 41. "We have found."** Shaded in gray. This affirms Andrew was informed about this Messianic Person and had prior knowledge of His coming. Though not a direct quote from the Old Testament, nevertheless, it is a concise version of many promises to Israel about their coming Messiah or anointed One. Andrew called Jesus "Messiah." This Old Testament Name is used in Ps. 2:2 and Dan. 9:25-26. Refer to Section 5, footnotes a, c and d, for more on Jesus the Messiah of Old Testament prophecy.

(f) **"Brought him to Jesus."** Perhaps a million sermons have been mis-preached from this text! It has nothing to do with Andrew actually leading his brother Peter to a *saving* knowledge of Christ. Rather, it has reference to a formal introduction of the two men. How can this mean that Peter trusted Christ as his Savior, when some two years later, while in Caesarea Philippi, Peter violently opposed the death of Christ on the cross? Jesus even called him "Satan" and sharply rebuked Peter for his unbelief in the cross and His resurrection which was yet to be (Matt. 16:21-23). Saved men do not deny the atonement of the cross and the resurrection of Christ! At *this time* of introduction, Peter was an unsaved man but was seriously interested in his brother's new friend whom he had introduced as "the Messiah." Like all pious Jews, Peter and the others (at this time) believed synagogue theology regarding Israel's Messiah, was greatly defective. Now, in genuine prophetic power, the Son of God announced that this rough and tough fisherman would, in time, become "a stone" (something solid and dependable) in His great kingdom and church. And this he surely did! See more on this thought in Section 43, footnote h for comments on the possible time of Peter's true conversion.

2p-**The interpretation, "A stone."** John the writer interprets for his original readers the meaning of "Cephas." The words, "which is by interpretation, 'A stone,'" are from the apostle John, not Jesus. For more on John giving the interpretation of specific words to his original readers, see Section 188, footnote e. Note also, footnote d above.

3p-**Changing the message of the Bible.** With the flood of same sex marriages, attacks on the traditional home and families, corruption in politics, apostasy in religion, and decaying of morals, the Devil's crowd works hard to change the Bible's condemnation of their sins: they fiercely hate this. America's leading networks have their "consultants" to explain that the Bible is "Subject to public interpretation like all historical documents." Spiritually blind these unsaved "experts" struggle to change the warnings of Scripture. God's destruction of Sodom and Gomorrah, the judgments of Christ on wicked cities and people are made to mean something else. For more on these abominations, see Section 155, fourth paragraph of footnote g and Section 21, Part 2, fifth paragraph of footnote i.

(g) The journey from Bethabara (John 1:28), traveling northward on the eastern side of the Jordan River to the lower eastern border of Galilee, was about fifty miles. hard to change the Bible's condemnation of their sins: they fiercely hate this. America's leading networks have their consultants to explain that the Bible is "Subject to public interpretation like all historical documents."

(h) See footnotes b, and c above, and Section 57, footnotes l and m for further details regarding the twelve. The highlighted portion of this verse reveals that Philip knew Messiah was predicted in both the Law of Moses and the prophets. How he tied the coming Messiah with Joseph is not clear. Later, Jesus said almost the same thing to the Sanhedrin (Section 52, John 5:45-47, footnotes y and z). The five men are:

1. **Peter**. He is the best known of the twelve apostles. Jesus looks into his heart and pronounces the better side of his character, which still lay dormant. Peter will, in time, become "A stone" (verse 42). A long and difficult road was traveled before Messiah's prediction would become reality in Peter's life.

2. **Andrew.** The brother of Peter (Matt. 4:18). He is mentioned some thirteen times in Scripture.

3. **John.** Apparently, Andrew and John were already followers of the Baptist. No doubt, they had listened intently to John's thunderous sermons, his withering exposure of the hypocrisy of Israel's religious leadership, and his refusal to baptize those who produced no fruits of real repentance. Straightforward preaching has often attracted practical common people who want to hear God's truth.

4. **Philip.** John informs his readers that Philip was of the same city as the brothers Andrew and Simon Peter. Philip was a pure Greek name, common for Jews, who lived among the Greek people. His confession to Nathanael, that he had found the One of whom Moses and the prophets wrote, is interesting. He calls this Person "Jesus of Nazareth, the son of Joseph." See Section 6, footnote e. His words reveal that he was a product of the synagogue where it was taught that Moses and the prophets spoke of a coming Messiah. Referring to Jesus as "the son of Joseph" was socially ethical. This suggests that Philip was acquainted with Joseph, the stepfather of Jesus. The rabbis said, "Whoso rears a son, the same is his father." See this in Section 7, number 4. It was only natural for Joseph to be described as

such. Philip's description of the two was according to Jewish custom. Over-anxious conservatives panic at this statement, being unaware of Jewish culture. It has *nothing* to do with the virgin birth of Jesus.

5. **Nathanael.** As Andrew had found Peter, so Philip now finds his friend, Nathanael and seeks to introduce him to Jesus. Nathanael was from Cana of Galilee (John 21:2). He reveals that he was the product of Jewish-Jerusalem propaganda, which affirms that nothing of any spiritual worth could come from Galilee or any of its cities. At the urging of Philip, he came to "see" Jesus. As Christ had pronounced a future prediction upon Peter, so He now speaks of a present quality of Nathanael. To his surprise, the Lord exclaimed, "Behold an Israelite indeed, in whom is no guile" (verse 47). Amazed, Nathanael responds, "Whence knowest thou me?" Christ announced that He had seen him sitting under a fig tree, *before* Philip came his way. (verse 48). The Jews taught that to read the Scriptures and pray under a fig tree would bring special blessing and hasten the appearing of Israel's Messiah. F. W. Farrar wrote of this in his *Life of Christ*, pages 118-119. A curious verse in the Talmud tractate, Berachoth 57a reads, "If one sees a fig tree in his dream, his learning will be preserved in him." When Philip approached his friend, he was sitting under a fig tree reading. Gathering from the conversation, it appears, he was reading from Gen. 28:12-17. These verses relate the story of Jacob's dream of the ladder to heaven filled with angels. Concerning this dream, the ancient rabbis held that the ladder in this story was (among other things) their Messiah accompanied by angels coming down to Israel. Being stunned at the foresight of the Man standing before him, Nathanael exclaimed, "Rabbi, thou art the Son of God; thou art the King of Israel." Note Section 23, Matt. 4:3, second paragraph of footnote c for the term "Son of God." Here, we meet the second recorded confession that Jesus is the King of Israel. First, wise men from the east had uttered a similar claim some thirty years earlier. See Section 17, Matt. 2:2, footnote d. Nathanael's statement reveals that among the Hebrews, some were aware that their King was coming. In verse 51, Jesus confessed that He was the ladder that Jacob dreamed about and that Nathanael would, at a future time, see God's angels moving upon Him. He had just read of this in Jacob's dream. Unlike Jacob who had the dream, Nathanael was an Israelite in whom was no Jacob (guile). See footnote j below for more on this.

2p-Thus, we have a tiny sketch of five men who would become some of the earliest apostles and how they *first* believed in Jesus as Israel's Messiah. They were the embryo of the future Church of the Living God. Their minds had been fouled by the synagogues' continual preaching of a political Messiah "coming to destroy the Romans" and rule the world, with Israel being the prime of all nations. Rabbinical theology had *no* place for Israel's Messiah dying on a cross for the sins of the world. This was impossible in their thinking, if not blasphemous! In years to come, Isaiah 53 would be laced with Hebrew nationalistic and political interpretations. Centuries after Christ, Jewish rabbis declared the pronouns "he" and "him," in Isa. 53, had reference *only* to the nation of Israel suffering for her sins and not a person! They knew that Jesus had fulfilled and filled full these prophetic forecasts.

3p-The first apostles' faith in Jesus as the Messiah (at this time) embraced Him as the King of Israel and world ruler. At this point, they did not understand the cross and eternal blood atonement for man's sins. It is correct that a *few* maverick ancient rabbis intimated from their Old Testament sketchy fragments of a personal atonement from sin by their Messiah. Yet, these were distorted by rabbinical extremes and carnal perversions. However, the overwhelming majority believed otherwise. Jews worldwide have shared this fallacious belief. This is because of the ancient and false rabbinical interpretation of original sin, the fall of man, the need for personal redemption, and their entrapment in the oral law. All these doctrinal distortions, from early days to the present, were vastly different from what was later taught in the New Testament. For the modern day Jewish opinion of Jesus Christ, see Section 14, footnote f. After this adventure with Jesus, these men returned to Galilee and resumed their occupations. At this point, none of them followed the Messiah "full-time," to use a modern term. This came later.

(i) "Rabbi," "the Son of God," and "the King of Israel." Shaded in gray because of the Messianic connotations. What a confession! Nathanael applied these divine titles to Jesus. He had prior knowledge of the coming Messiah and was acquainted with some of His unique names. *He declared explicitly that God had a Son!* Nathanael's confession was similar to that of Peter's spoken later in Section 103, Matt. 16:16, footnote f. Both men affirmed that Jesus was Israel's promised Messiah. However, He was not performing as the rabbis had taught.

(j) We have no record of when this curious prediction took place in the life of Nathanael. However, we know it did, for the Lord Jesus said it would! Because it is not recorded in the four gospels hardly means it did not occur. Countless, thousands of things happened to all of these men but only a brief history is given in Holy Scripture.

(k) "The Son of man." On this title, see Section 103, footnote b; and Section 161, fifth paragraph of footnote l. For a discussion of the Lord Jesus as Perfect Man and Perfect God, see Section 1, Part 1, footnotes a and b, and with this Section 1, Part 4, first and second paragraphs under footnote j.

Entering Galilee, Jesus attends a wedding at Cana. He performs His first miracle by turning water into wine. The disciples believed on Him.

Matt.	Mk.	Lk.	John 2:1-11—*At Cana of Galilee*
			Invited to a wedding **1** And the third day[a] there was a marriage in Cana of Galilee;[b] and the mother of Jesus was there:[c] **2** And both Jesus was called, and his disciples, to the marriage. **3** And when they wanted wine, the mother of Jesus saith unto him, "They have no wine."[d] *His strange response to Mary and her reaction* **4** Jesus saith unto her, "Woman,[e] what have I to do with thee? mine hour is not yet come."[f] **5** His mother saith unto the servants, "Whatsoever he saith unto you, do *it*."[g] *Obedience brings great blessing* **6** And there were set there six waterpots of stone,[h] after the manner of the purifying of the Jews, containing two or three firkins apiece. [one firkin approx. nine gallons] **7** Jesus saith unto them, [the servants] "Fill the waterpots with water."[i] And they filled them up to the brim. **8** And he saith unto them, "Draw out now, and bear unto the governor[j] of the feast." And they bare *it*. **9** When the ruler of the feast had tasted the water that was made wine,[k] and knew not whence it was: (but the servants which drew the water knew;) the governor of the feast called the bridegroom, **10** And saith unto him, "Every man at the beginning doth set forth good wine; and when men have well drunk,[l] [consumed the good wine] then that which is worse: [is served] *but* thou hast kept the good wine until now." *His Messianic glory revealed: the disciples believed on Him* **11** This beginning of miracles[m] did Jesus in Cana of Galilee, and manifested forth his glory; and his disciples believed on him.[n] (Verse 12 cont. in Section 28.)

Footnotes-Commentary

(a) **Jesus a Mormon polygamist at Cana?** Apparently, "the third day" after the Savior had departed from Jordan, returning north to Galilee to start His ministry The Mormon cult (Church of Jesus Christ of Latter Day Saints) affirms that during this wedding Jesus married *both* Mary and Martha and had children by them! This is an attempt to justify polygamy as propounded by their sex-crazed founders Joseph Smith, Brigham Young, and others. Due to Federal laws against polygamy, the cult was *forced to alter* its teaching on the subject, just as they did regarding black people. When confronted with this, well-programmed Mormons will respond: "Our church has no official position on whether or not Jesus was married," or "someone received a new revelation from God." For "Jesus the polygamist," see the Mormon textbook *Journal and Discourses*, by Orson Hyde, vol. 4, pages 259-260, where this lie about the Savior is recorded. Bruce McConkie (died 1985) was a member of the Quorum of the Twelve Apostles of this system. He wrote, "Obviously the holy practice [plural marriages] will commence again after the second coming of the Son of man and the establishing of the millennial" (*Mormon Doctrine*, page 578). Spencer Kimball (died in 1985), the Twelfth President of the Mormon Church, wrote that Satan is the father of the teaching that men are saved by grace alone (*Miracle of Forgiveness*, page 206). The theology of Joseph Smith (died 1844) recorded in, *Teachings of the Prophet Joseph Smith,* page 345 reads, "We have imagined that God was God from all eternity. I will refute that idea and take away the veil, so that you may see." Apparently, Joe had never read Ps. 90:1-2 or Isa. 57:15. Joseph Smith wrote that there is no salvation outside the Mormon Church. Refer to *Mormon Doctrine*, page 670 for this statement. In the Mormon work, *Documentary History of the Church*, vol. 6, pages 319-321,

Smith's arrogance is reflected in this statement, "The whole earth shall bear me witness that I, like the towering rock in the midst of the ocean, which has withstood the mighty surges of the warring waves for centuries, am impregnable . . . combat errors of ages; I meet the violence of the mobs; I cope with illegal proceedings from executive authority; I cut the Gordian knot of power, and I solve the mathematical problems of universities, with truth -diamond truth; and God is my right-hand man." These are the words of an egotistical religious maniac. For a shocking exposure of this "sex oozing" religion from the viewpoint of a former insider, see *Mormonism, Mama & Me* by Thelma Greer. On pages 16-17, she documents how they teach that Jesus and the Devil are spiritual brothers! "Both were sexually sired and born in heaven." This is blasphemy of the highest sort! Fritz Ridenour, lays out a thorough examination of this cult in his work, *So What's the Difference,* pages 130-146. His book has an excellent array of documentation dealing with Mormon beliefs from every possible angle on pages 241-245. Better Christian bookstores and the internet are loaded with documentaries exposing this counterfeit religion pretending to be a Christian organization. To determine the truth and worth of any church, one should thoroughly check the history of its founders, their character, morals, and doctrinal beliefs regarding the Person and work of Jesus Christ. *On these grounds, the Church of Jesus Christ of Latter Day Saints is revealed to be a cult of the Devil.* That "religion has no bearing on a person's character" is a fable propagated by the New Age cults. This lie turns men from the teachings of the Bible regarding the depravity and sinfulness of Adam's race, and their need for personal salvation. From conception to death, all humanity is fouled by sin. There are no exemptions to this fiercely hated biblical truth.

2p-Mormon sex god and sex heaven! Recent revelations of polygamist sanctuaries in the western United States where children are beaten, molested, raped, impregnated, and women are used as sex slaves are but the tip of the iceberg. Apologists for the cult rush forward to announce that their church "banned polygamy" years ago, only make fools of themselves with those who know the truth about the Mormon religion. The heinous Mormon teaching that is part of their *present* theology, which declares that God is like a man living on a star in space having babies by His spiritual wives, reflects the sex madness of those who founded this religion. The defenders of Mormon blasphemy hesitate to tell the American public that every Mormon, who makes it into *their* heaven, will spend eternity with his thousands of spiritual wives having babies. As with Islam, so it is with Mormonism; heaven will be a sex paradise with everyone getting their share forever. The god of these people is not the *true* and living God, nor is their heaven the one revealed in Holy Scripture. For more on this, see Section 41, fifth paragraph of footnote h.

(b) **"Cana of Galilee."** For the benefit of his original readers, John distinguishes between the two cities named Cana. The particular Cana mentioned here was located about seven miles north of Nazareth. Only the apostle John mentions it. A second Cana (spelled "Kanah"), was situated even further north in the region belonging to the tribe of Asher (Josh. 19:28). Here, is another indication that some of John's original readers were unfamiliar with the geography of Israel. Nathanael was from the Cana in Galilee (John 21:2).

(c) Mary was already present at the wedding ("was there"). A line of thought in early history says that Mary was a relative of the family involved in the marriage. The word "called" means invited. Hence, Jesus and his first disciples (at least Andrew, Peter, John, Philip, and Nathanael) had received a formal invitation to attend. He joined His mother already present. The men following Jesus at this point were not yet "apostles," in the full meaning of the term, but only "disciples." Jewish weddings commonly lasted for one week or more. Christ partook in this wedding feast similar to the one recorded in Matt. 22:1-14. It was believed among the Jews that those attending a marriage were reflecting kindness, concern, and beneficence toward the wedded pair and their families. It was a high demonstration of social courtesy and concern for others. Invited guests were all issued special robes prior to the occasion. These were worn to the wedding and served as the correct identification for entrance into the feast after sunset (Matt. 22:11-12). The Savior's presence at this event manifested His pure character and concern being amiable toward the appeals and invitations of others. He bore testimony to the institution of marriage as honorable and herein teaches us to "rejoice with those that rejoice." Woe be to marriages that do not invite the Son of God as the honored guest to observe, approve, and bless every action and festivity. On this occasion, the Savior was about to perform His *first* miracle and thereby manifest the earliest beams of His glory as Israel's Messiah.

(d) **"They have no wine."** This was a calamity for the joyous event. The thought is that because of the failure to plan ahead by the host family (and not through intemperance and debauchery) the existing supply was exhausted. This was due to the large number of guests present. It would disgrace the host family with deep shame, and the joy of the wedding feast would not proceed with credit and happy honor. The bad situation afforded Mary's appeal to her Son, which was loaded with sacred suggestions. Why did she turn to Jesus at this desperately embarrassing moment? Did she perhaps remember the angel's promise of her Son's greatness (Lk. 1:31-32)? Though He had worked no previous miracle, did she somehow know something? The normal and customary appeal for more wine would have been given to the servants in command of this function and *never* to a woman, especially a guest. The Papal Church teaches that this proves men should always go to Mary first with their problems and she, in turn, will take them to Jesus for resolve. This is a sheer error without one shred of support in Scripture.

(e) For centuries, westerners, not understanding the culture of eastern life, have read this reply of Christ to His mother with horror! There is *nothing* rude or discourteous in our Lord's response. "Woman" comes from the Greek word "gune." It was the most respectful address spoken to one of the opposite gender. No man ever to walk the face of this earth practiced perfect courtesy as Jesus Christ did. He used the same formal address to the Syrophoenician woman (Matt. 15:28), the Samaritan woman (John 4:21), weeping Mary Magdalene (John 20:15), and to His mother as He hung upon the cross (John 19:26). Even angels from heaven employed the term "woman," when speaking to Mary Magdalene (John 20:13). Was Paul disrespectful when he used the term "wife" of believing women (1 Cor. 7:16)? Among pagan Greeks this was considered an accepted form of social respect.

(f) **"Mine hour is not yet come."** This expression was used by Jesus of Himself and by John, who employed it the same way across his book. They have direct reference to the "hour" or "time" when He was nailed on the cross to die for the sins of the world. The usage of this term may be traced starting with John 2:4 through John 7:30, 8:20, 12:23, 27, and 13:1. Lastly, it is found in Matt. 26:18 in Jesus' Words, "My time is at hand." In John 17:1, He said that His hour *had* arrived. Our Lord prayed this shortly before His arrest in the garden and crucifixion the following morning. This was the greatest hour in human history: sin and death would be conquered for all who trust Christ as personal Savior. Over the four gospels, the Lord Jesus mentioned His death and resurrection some fifty-four times, yet His closest disciples and twelve apostles did not understand this until forty days after His resurrection (Acts 1:3).

(g) **The final words of Mary the mother of Jesus recorded in Scripture.** They reflect a mother's trusting confidence in her Son to handle the crisis. This has nothing to do with the myth of Mary serving as a mediatrix between Christ and men. Years before, her *first* recorded statement in the Bible was shadowed in sincere question and spoken to the angel Gabriel. This is recorded in Section 9, Lk. 1:34, footnote h. For other comments on Mary, the mass, and the horrific abuses of Christian doctrines by the Papal Church, see Section 95, all of footnote r.

(h) **"Waterpots of stone."** This wedding was held in a deeply pious Jewish home. Ancient writings often mention such vessels being filled with fresh water. They were used in the ceremonial cleansings commanded in the oral law. Six pots also suggest that a large crowd had assembled. All deeply religious Jews were enslaved to the wicked "tradition of the elders." Because of this, they were habitually entangled in washings of countless sorts. (Not *all* the oral traditions were evil, but they were classified as such because they became a channel for salvation. Anything offered as a substitute for Christ's salvation is wicked, regardless of how good it is.) Purification was the prime requirement of the rabbis as they taught and expounded these oral laws from the synagogue chairs. Scrupulous and intense washing of hands, feet, faces, pots, pans, tables, doors, windows, walkways, door latches, beds, vessels, and so on were continually practiced. See Matt. 15:1–20 and the parallel of Mk. 7:1–23 for our Lord's fierce condemnation of these practices invented by the ancient teachers of Israel and used to supplant the Word of God. They are known as the Talmud, which consists of the "Mishna" ("text") and "Gemara" ("commentary") or "oral traditional law." See Section 52, footnote h; Section 89, footnote c; and Section 96, footnote d for comments on these thousands of man-made traditions. One "firkin" was about nine gallons. The six pots would hold well over one hundred gallons of wine. This great amount of drink points to a large crowd. These pots had been emptied from their first filling of several ferkins. Later, an empty waterpot eventually brought the Samaritan woman to Christ (John 4:28). Now, empty waterpots at the wedding become the grounds for our Lord's first Messianic miracle.

(i) No one questioned the Master's command. It took some lengthy, diligent effort for the servants to secure over a hundred gallons of water from the household well, spring, or drinking vessels then carry this amount to the pots. Next, they poured them full to the brim. *True* servants obey without questioning their Lord's instructions.

(j) **"Governor" or "ruler."** The exact equivalent to our present day "master of ceremonies."

(k) **What kind of wine?** For almost two thousand years, controversy has raged over the "kind" of wine Jesus created. It is disgusting to hear ministers of God's Word equating the various levels of intoxication that fermented wine produces with the joy of the Holy Spirit or serving Christ. This statement is the childish of ignorance. Such a spurious relation has never existed. Linking the second fruit of the Spirit to some form of mild drunkenness is repugnant (Gal. 5:22). The same Holy Spirit condemned this sin in other Scriptures. Men are barred from heaven because of it (1 Cor. 6:9-10 with Gal. 5:21). Among certain Reformed Christians, some Messianic Jewish, and other Gentile believers, the use of intoxicating beverages, especially wine, is spoken of in proud, if not boastful language. That the use of intoxicating wine diluted with water was necessary due to the bad drinking water in the days of Christ is more nonsense. When men feel a bit "tipsy" and this is equated with the power and joy of the Holy Ghost, it is evident that they are not familiar with the work of the Spirit. God did not make intoxicating beverage the emblem of those spiritual blessings that ensure peace and promote hope in the hearts of believers. To hold that the sinless Messiah from heaven approved such a state of things and point to the wedding at Cana as proof, is devilish thinking. It is alarming how many younger Reformed people and others look upon a beer, glass of wine, or a toddy as a "symbol of Christian liberty and self-control." This is just as popular as their "deep discussion about the elect and their predestination." While these "elected saints" are blowing the heads of their beers, and sipping wine, their loved ones ("not of the elect" of course) are dropping off into hell. *Someone is going to answer for this before God!* For an outstanding work on wine and drinking, see *ANCIENT WINE & THE BIBLE* . . . by David R. Brumbelow.

2p-"Controlled drinking." The call for "temperance or moderation" in drinking alcoholic beverage is absurd. Why not "temperance" when fondling the body of a strange woman, not one's wife? Why not "moderation" in stealing cash from the register? Who would require the "sipping saints" to "be moderate" when they read pornography, tell dirty jokes, or slander their neighbors? Drunkenness *is* classified with such gross sins as adultery, idolatry and so on. In former days, the manufacture, sale, and transportation of alcohol for consumption was banned in America from 1920-1933. This was known as "prohibition." In March 1933, President Franklin D. Roosevelt signed a repeal of prohibition. With this, the liquid Devil flowed over this land, as the pockets of gangsters and murderers were filled with blood money. Even governments have found it necessary to legislate ages for drinking of alcoholic beverages due to the havoc it plays in the lives of youth. Certain "born again Christians" will argue one to the floor that "moderate" drinking is the plan of God for believers. Only a sick mind can imagine the pure Son of God from heaven drinking a cold beer or sipping a glass of Old Crow whiskey and drawing on a cigarette before retiring at night. Wine has greater control on *many* Christians than the Holy Spirit does. One of the toughest jobs for pastors today is getting church members "unhooked" from their controlled, social, and private drinking. Though most of them would never get drunk, they are as addicted to moderate drinking as the "soaks" sleeping in the alleys are to non-moderation. Both groups are deceived (Prov. 20:1). This is seen in the terrible struggle many have trying to break the habit of temperate drinking that they "always keep under control." It binds just like the curse of compulsive drinking and literal drunkenness. *This problem would be solved if churches had it stated in their constitutions that the use of alcoholic beverages for consumption is forbidden for all persons seeking membership.*

3p-"*Wine that maketh glad (or cheers) the heart of man*" (Ps. 104:15). *This verse* does not refer to a happy and acceptable level of intoxication as some claim. In places, the expression "wine that maketh glad the heart of man," does speak of drunkenness (1 Sam. 25:36). However, in other verses, such an interpretation is impossible. For example, see Judges 9:13, where Scripture states, "wine . . . cheereth God and man." Who would dare intimate that this means the Almighty was in a low state of "acceptable" intoxication from the use of wine? A statement of this nature would be blasphemy! Albert Barnes wrote in 1832, "The common wine of Judea was the pure juice of the grape, without any mixture of alcohol, and was harmless." See *Barnes' Notes on the New Testament*, page 195. Barnes further points out how the ancients frequently spoke of "good wine" as that which was *free* from intoxication. The ancient custom of diluting intoxicating wine with water cannot apply to this event as explained in footnote l below. This diluting of strong drink with water to prevent drunkenness is mentioned in the *Jewish Encyclopedia,* vol. 12, page 533, 1901 edition. The Talmud also speaks of this practice in tractates, Shabbath 77a and Pesahim 108b. Josephus, who lived over two thousand years ago, stated in *Antiquities*, Book 2:5. 2, line 64 that the liquid from freshly squeezed grapes was called "wine." Thus, "wine" also speaks of non–intoxicating drink. It is incorrect that "wine" in ancient history and the Bible always means an alcoholic beverage. This error has caused great harm among weaker and untaught Christians. Secular history reveals that there were two different grape and other fruit beverages known by the ancients. Though both were called wine, they were radically opposite in substance, content, and effect. Americans and westerners in general understand the word "wine" to mean wine with the serpent's sting (or intoxication) in every drop. This was not so with the ancients or in the Scriptures. Wine across the entire Bible is a generic term meaning a variety of things from liquids to syrups, and even jellies. In the Old Testament, there are some eleven different Hebrew words translated by our *one* English word wine. See *Young's Analytical Concordance*, page 1058, for details. For a definitive exposure of alcoholic wine, see *Bible Wines or Laws of Fermentation and Wines of the Ancients* by William Patton, written in 1871. The work, *WINE. The Biblical Imperative: Total Abstinence,* by Dr. R. Teachout is excellent reading on this subject. No better coverage of wine in the Bible will be found than in the old *Temperance Bible-Commentary* by F. R. Lees and D. Burns, printed in 1894.

4p-Satanists infiltrating churches. In South Africa, two former Devil worshippers were saved. Both told in public meetings how in secret and intense training sessions, hand picked Satanists (especially beautiful young girls and handsome younger men) were assigned to infiltrate selected churches, create scandal and confusion, then vanish. The intent was to destroy the witness of these soul winning congregations. Their tools of destruction were sex, dope, money, tobacco, and "controlled drinking." The vehicles used to spread the gossip across the church body were the fickle teens and disgruntled elderly people! These covert Satan worshippers knew that undisciplined Christians, who were "moderate drinkers and smokers," were vulnerable targets for spiritual subversion. Those who justify their "moderate" and "temperate drinking," would do well to consider these awful words. Satan knows things about the wine-sipping and tobacco-puffing saints that they seemingly do not know about themselves. These two former Devil worshippers sternly warned us about purchasing occult jewelry, rings, pendants, necklaces charms, and other objects that were made by these people, and prayed over in the name of Lucifer. They were dedicated to demons to curse and bring bondage upon those who wore them or brought them into their homes! Tattoos with demonic emblems were a special delight to Satanists. For other details on these dark phenomena this, see Section 20, second through fifth paragraphs of footnote l, and Section 88, second paragraph of footnote e.

(l) **"Well drunk"** is seized upon to prove that after the guests at a wedding were half intoxicated, the servants rolled out a worse or lesser grade of wine to be consume. Consequently, due to their partly inebriated mental state, they would not know the difference! Who could imagine the Lord of Glory would set before hundreds of thirsty Jews about one hundred gallons of fermented wine with the design that they complete their half-drunken conditions into full-blown stupors? It was not the Savior, who made this statement, but the master of ceremonies or ruler-governor of the feast. He was speaking for himself, not for the Messiah. However, he confessed that the wine drawn from the waterpots was "good wine." This was a term of contrast and set against "old wine," which was of high alcoholic content. Whatever was originally in those waterpots before they were emptied is *not* the question. The question is, what did the Son of God turned the water into that the servants poured in the vessels after they were emptied. Despite what beer loving Baptists say, it was not "drinks on the house" or "roll out the barrel." *Strong church leadership standing against these things and a properly written constitution would correct this curse.*

2p-Demonstrating He was the sovereign creator, Christ bypassed the process of grape growing, which took some five years (Lev. 19:23-25), with the necessary elements of rain and sun, the long, hard season of harvesting and then pressing out the juice. He instantly created fresh, delicious "pure blood of the grape" which, under normal circumstances, could be extracted only at the winepress by crushing the clusters (Gen. 49:11 with Deut. 32:14). It was called "good wine" (or "new"), and in this case was void of fermentation (Isa. 65:8 with Prov. 3:9-10). In some passages, "new wine" is associated with intoxicating drink *after* it was mixed with other wines (Joel 1:5.) At this wedding, it was deemed "good wine" by the master of ceremonies, who tasted it.

(m) First miracle of Jesus. With a wonder that amazed everyone present, the Lord Jesus publicly exhibited His glory in performing this fantastic act. All drinking water was kept in covered vessels and was separate from those containers that held household water used for purifying as stated in the oral law. There was no possible means of a deception, craft, or covert mixture. The governor and servants were all convinced! According to custom, he was the first to taste its quality. *This wine was made from water and not from the product of any grape or fruit. Thus, it could not have been intoxicating!* What did the guests say and what did Mary and Joseph think after seeing Jesus "their Son" perform this miracle? Some things are too sacred to write about!

2p-The hundreds of guests present carried the news of this wonder across Galilee and other places as they returned home. Everyone was talking about "Jesus the son of Joseph," and His strange power. With this miracle, He publicly revealed that He was indeed the promised Messiah. It was here that John (the writer of this book) first beheld His glory as the only begotten of the Father (John 1:14). What cautious, guarded whisperings were exchanged between those early disciples as they softly followed behind their amazing Master. A few days later, He would again exhibit His glorious Messianic power at the upcoming Passover in Jerusalem. This is explained in Section 29, footnotes a, and j. Surely, many of the Jews present at the wedding had also attended the Passover. They carried home the news of this strange Person and His supernatural deeds. It was shared with every listening ear during the one day of Passover and the seven days Unleavened Bread. Note Section 29, second paragraph of footnote d, and Section 30, footnote d for further details on His wonderful deeds before the crowds gathered in the temple for the great Passover event. Friends and foes alike blazed his fame across the land of Israel and abroad..

3p-"Manifested forth His glory." One wishes that more details were given regarding this profound statement. His divine glory was briefly unveiled. This deeply affected His few disciples; they instantly "believed on Him." For the meaning of this, see footnote n below. News spread among the guests about what had taken place. Everyone wanted to see this miracle-working carpenter from Nazareth, and we are sure they did!

4p-Moderate drinking? When Christ turned the water to wine did that signal His approval of the "moderate drinking?" See second paragraph of footnote k above. The pious talk about "drinking in moderation" is tantamount to moderate smoking, adultery, stealing, lying, and the rest. The church is troubled with "sipping saints," who do not have the convictions of a goat regarding their private and public testimonies. As stated, they are just as addicted to "moderate drinking" as others are to their literal drunkenness. And thousands of these people would die before getting physically intoxicated. Baptist "controlled drinkers" trot out the British preacher, Charles Spurgeon as the prime example of a saint who was a controlled drinker and smoker. *Let all born again, beer burping, wine slurping Baptists, and other believers, know that every drunkard in hell and the millions on their way started their journey with the first drink.* On John Calvin's wine boozing, see Section 162, second paragraph of footnote c. For Spurgeon smoking cigars to the "glory of God," but later giving it up, see Section 135, fifth paragraph of footnote e.

(n) "Believed on him" as what? At this point, Jesus' public ministry had been about six months in length. His few disciples now believed more deeply than they had at Bethabara, that this Man was the promised Messiah of Israel. See their meeting the Savior on that occasion in Section 26, John 1:35-50. However, He was not performing as the rabbis had taught. He had not challenged the rule of Rome over Israel. His kingdom was not like the one that the rabbis had predicted. He was wonderful, but so different from what they expected. The truth of His death for sin and resurrection from the dead was yet unknown to these men. That would come later. See Peter's objections to His death, so violently expressed some few months after the wedding at Cana. Jesus sharply rebuked him for this. See Section 104, Matt. 16:21-23, footnote d. Note also Andrew's previous Messianic admission concerning Jesus to his brother Peter in John 1:42, and Nathanael's statement in this regard (John 1:49).

2p-Concerning the disciples and others believing in Christ for salvation, see Section 144, footnote i. On Resurrection Day, His disciples still did not understand about His death. Refer to John 20:9 with attendant side and bottom notes. John wrote this looking back, after Jesus had ascended to heaven. For more on this subject from the two men walking the Emmaus road on resurrection day, refer to Section 200, Lk. 24:21, footnote f.

Jesus, His mother, half-brothers, and first disciples return to Capernaum* after the Cana wedding. Shortly, they travel back to Jerusalem some ninety miles south for the upcoming Passover celebration.

Having grown up in Nazareth (Matt. 2:23 and Lk. 2:39-40), our Lord later moved His base of operations to the city of Capernaum. This was about twenty-five miles away on the upper northwest shores of Lake Galilee. He did so to fulfill Old Testament prophecy. For this, see Section 38, Matt. 4:13-15, footnote n, with Isa. 9:1-2. The earthly life of Christ was planned and predicted in the Old Testament. He was led or directed by the Holy Spirit in fulfilling every requirement of these prophecies. See Appendix Three for a sweeping review of this subject.

Matt.	Mk.	Lk.	John 2:12 —*A brief stay at Capernaum*
			12 After this he went down to Capernaum,[a] he, and his mother,[b] and his brethren, [half-brothers] and his disciples: and they continued there not many days.[c] (Verse 13 cont. in Section 29.)

Footnotes-Commentary

[a] This was a brief stay. The Savior planned to attend the upcoming Passover celebration at the temple in Jerusalem. It is now late March or early April. From Capernaum, traveling southward on the eastern side of the Jordan River, this trip by foot required some three days' journey, being about ninety miles. Rabbinical rules required pilgrims attending the Passover to appear at the temple several weeks in advance. See the Talmud, tractate Shabbath 19a. This was necessary in order to be purified from all defilement and thus ready for the greatest annual celebration in Hebrew history. For more on this, note Section 146, John 11:55 with Num. 9:1-14. The text reads that Jesus, and His disciples did not continue or stay many days at Capernaum. Apparently, our Lord's family had witnessed the uproar He created at this Passover. They were present on this occasion, and it is certain they heard of it. According to Lk. 2:41, the family of Christ had previously attended this great national celebration *together*. The Law of Moses required mandatory attendance at each Passover for all males who were heads of each Jewish family (Ex. 23:17 with Deut. 16:16). See Section 29, John 2:13, footnote a, for a description of the Passover. According to the wording of John 2:12-13, Jesus' mother, and His half-brothers also went to Jerusalem for this grand occasion. They surely heard of or witnessed the stir. He caused among the religious leaders in purging the temple.

[b] Here, we read of our Lord's half-brothers, who are later named in Scripture (Matt 13:55). Where was Joseph the foster-father of Jesus? John did not tell us on this occasion, therefore, we cannot know. However, we read that Joseph was alive and known by the religious leaders about six months *before* the cross, according to the words of the Jews (John 6:42).

[c] **"Not many days"** is an expression signifying "haste" or "urgency." This reveals the promptness of Jesus to get to Jerusalem and publicly reveal Himself for the first time as Israel's Messiah. He would do this during the Passover celebration. This is discussed in the next Section. From the moment of this disclosure of Himself as Messiah, He was in continual conflict with the religious elite of the nation and many of the Hebrew people.

2p-A new kingdom. During the final days of His ministry, Jesus warned the Jews in advance that God's kingdom would be taken from them and given to the Gentiles. This seriously important lesson contained in the Parable of the Vineyard Workers is recorded in Section 153, footnote m. Was this kingdom one of substance, material, and human politics, or was it a spiritual thing finding its gradual fulfillment in the church? Since Pentecost in Acts chapter 2, it has been the latter not the former. For a discussion of this question and the impossibility of spiritualizing all of Israel's promises and giving them to the church, see Section 9, footnote g. Nevertheless, there will yet be a *glorified* kingdom of God on this earth, where all things are new and without sin. For other comments on this unique rule of Christ, see Section 171, fourth and fifth paragraphs of footnote b. It will be something never known to men and angels. *Extreme* dispensationalists work hard trying to make "the kingdom of God" and "the kingdom of heaven" different entities. Section 39, footnote a carries an explanation of the kingdom and demonstrates by an illustration under footnote g that the terms "saved," "the kingdom of God," "the kingdom of heaven," and "eternal life" were identical in the teaching of Christ.

4p-The liberal's kingdom. The left-leaning, literalist-hating, neo evangelicals, who claim to believe the Scriptures, while denying their inspiration, talk so pleasantly about how one enters God's kingdom. Now, we hear that "the kingdom is inclusive and not exclusive of all men." And that "God welcomes all and rejects none." This is blatantly untrue. Smooth talking "love only clergymen" do not explain the rest of the story. God's love welcomes and receives all who will repent of their sins and trust Jesus Christ as personal Lord and Savior. Repentance from sin, wrought by the conviction of the Holy Spirit, is not a part of their theological portfolio. A church full of unconverted members is a curse to society and a tool of the Devil. Only saved people are in the spiritual kingdom or true church (Col. 1:13). All others are excluded, regardless. For Jesus' demand that men repent of their sins, see Section 72, Lk. 13:5, footnote f. Refer also to Section 65, second paragraph of footnote h for more on this despised doctrine. The untruth that "God rejects none" is refuted in Matt. 7:21-23 and Rev. 20:15.

FROM THIS POINT FORWARD

In Section 29, the Lord Jesus made His *first public* appearance as Israel's Messiah, during the annual Passover celebration at Jerusalem. This resulted in serious conflict with the religious leaders, and continued over the course of His ministry. After the Passover in John 2:13, the ensuing pages usher us into the heart of His ministry as recorded in the four gospels. Across this harmony commentary, some verses in the four gospels have been taken out of their fixed location sequence as found in the *King James* or *Authorized Version* and fitted into different places. This is necessary in trying to harmonize the life of Christ (as far as possible), without doing violence to the sacred texts. After harmonization, the adjusted passages have been returned to their original context.

A comprehensive, unbroken harmony of everything in the four gospels is impossible because of the diverse literary styles in which the Holy Spirit inspired them to be written. This diversity in writing and placement of the material is briefly seen on the next page. God designed this peculiar order to prevent four exact copies of the gospels from being made. If the works of Matthew, Mark, Luke, and John all reported the same things, in similar chronological orders, and with duplicated wording, we would have three too many gospels. To inhibit a quadruplicating of these four books, God had them written in a unique and different literary style. Consequently, only a partial harmonization is possible. Nevertheless, believers have four history books about the life of Christ to study instead of one. The *Selah! Harmony Commentary of the Four Gospels* has been produced with this divine uniqueness continually in mind.

The seven examples on the next page illustrate how the four gospel writers were inspired to place various events at different time sequences as they wrote their histories; nevertheless, all were true. In the forty-day period between the resurrection and ascension, Jesus appeared to believers at least eleven times and in eleven different places. These are covered in Sections 195–207. Each time He took on a varying form. However, in these different manifestations, it was always the *same* risen Christ. He is thus similarly presented across the four gospels.

In 1972, the author of this work saw a massive diamond at the "Great Hole" in Kimberly, South Africa. Different angles were cut into its precious substance. Each sparkled in diverse colors with a singular brilliance of its own, yet they all were part of that one gemstone. This is how the Son of God, the Messiah of Israel, shines to us from the works of Matthew, Mark, Luke, and John. It is because of this united variety that a total harmony of the four gospels, or forcing things to fit where God has not originally placed them, becomes dangerous. By attempting to arrange every one of the 3,799 verses of the gospels chronologically, the impact contained in certain events, in the location or context where God set them, would be lost. The Holy Spirit placed these as He saw fit; the prudent man will leave this alone. No man is truly wise apart from Jesus Christ. The Bible says, "He is made unto us wisdom" (1 Cor. 1:30). The world's most educated people are ignoramuses without the source of all genuine and lasting wisdom, which is the Son of God. Many are offended at this truth, but at the end of life, they will see the folly of their ways, usually too late. In Christ alone "are hidden all the treasure of wisdom and knowledge" (Col. 23:3). To know Him as personal Lord and Savior is the first step into life's *true* wisdom and knowledge.

Rarely, did ancient secular or religious writers produce their works in a straightforward, unbroken time-line style. In places, the four evangelists reported the same events within the same time period, while in others; they grouped their information in a different chronological order. Yet, God directed all four men in the formatting of their books. Nothing was done by chance, personal choice, human genius, or borrowing from other sources. Not one of the four evangelists copied from the other. As written in the *Author's Introduction* and other places across this work, their books were written independently.

On the next page are seven examples from an earlier period of Christ's Galilean ministry. This sampling will let the reader see what has been explained above regarding how God had the story of His Son put into writing. He rarely does things the way men do. The mixed order outlined on the next page reflects that the four authors were directed by divine authority as they wrote and not by human talents or known literary standards. The Holy Spirit has never written anything the way men would, though He has used men to write! These high truths the *unsaved* religious academicians cannot, and will never, understand. Scripture declares, "the world by [it's] wisdom knew not God" (1 Cor. 1:21). Jesus said the world hated Him (John 7:7). Christians should be the most honorable, moral, and upright people on earth. *Sadly, many of them are not.* A day of reckoning is coming for those who bring shame and reproach on the cause of Jesus Christ and the things of God (1 Peter 4:17-18). It may be soon or a thousand years off, nevertheless it is coming and all of us who carry the name "Christian" will be fully alive and there.

1. Matthew placed the Sermon on the Mount *before* the calling of the twelve.

2. Mark *omitted* the Sermon on the Mount but wrote of the calling of the twelve.

3. Luke placed the Sermon on the Plain* (called Sermon on the Mount in Matthew) *after* the calling of the twelve.

4. Matthew's order in writing the following events in the life of Christ.
   a. Sermon on the Mount, Matt. 5:1-8:1. Not the same as Luke's.
   b. Healing of the leper, Matt. 8:2-4.
   c. Healing of the centurion's servant, Matt. 8:5-13.
   d. Healing of Peter's mother-in-law, Matt. 8:14-17.
   e. Calling of the twelve apostles, Matt. 10:1-11:1.

5. Mark's different order in writing about these same events.
   a. Healing of Peter's mother-in-law, Mk. 1:29-31.
   b. Healing of the leper, Mk. 1:40-45.
   c. He omits the healing of the centurion's servant.
   d. He omits the Sermon on the Mount.
   e. Calling of the twelve apostles, Mk. 6:7-13.

6. Luke's arrangement of these events differed from both Matthew and Mark.
   a. Healing of Peter's mother-in-law, Lk. 4:38-39.
   b. Healing of the leper, Lk. 5:12-15.
   c. Calling of the twelve apostles, Lk. 6:12-16.
   d. Sermon on the Plain,* in Lk. 6:20-49 is called the Sermon on the Mount in Matthew. Luke's record of the sermon is not the same as Matthew's record. Luke wrote of a later time when Jesus only gave portions of the original message as seen in Matthew. For explanation, see asterisk under main heading of Section 58.

7. John was not inspired to write about any of the above events. This demonstrates he was directed by God in what to pen and did not copy from the other evangelists. Each man obeyed the Lord in *what* he wrote and *where* he placed it in his work.

The above diversity in placing these various events recorded in the four gospels has nothing to do with a "synoptic problem." There is no problem of this nature nor has there ever been. Unsaved German theological skeptics who disdain inspiration of the Bible invented this myth. For another example of how the Holy Spirit put the events of Scripture together, see the table of our Savior's parables found just before Section 73. The wide variety in the placement of the events listed above demonstrates *again* that the writers did not copy from each other. Rather, God directed what they penned and where He wanted it placed in their individual writings. Divine inspiration never wrote as natural men would. It continually reflects God's glorious but mysterious sovereignty in giving His Word to the human race. It is ours to believe this or refuse it. Rejection of God's way of doing things, in time, produces spiritually darkened minds. These same people try to make Holy Scripture fit the secular styles and literary methods of human composition. However, they will not fit! It is at this point the conflict begins. God either gave His Word to mankind and has preserved it over the tumultuous ages of time, or He has not. The *Author's Introduction* discusses this subject in detail.

*Luke's version of Matthew's Sermon on the Mount is called the "Sermon on the Plain" in this Harmony Commentary. Though somewhat alike, they are basically different. Luke did not borrow, copy, or take from Matthew's work what he wanted and then invent his own sermon. He wrote under divine inspiration. The likenesses and differences are because the Holy Spirit had them written this way. Skeptics disdain such things because the Bible is not written like *they* think it should be. If a literary document does not agree with their "superior learning," it is rejected or laid aside as unworthy of intellectual consideration. Since "God does not exist," everything about Him must be explained away! This includes creation, revelation, and salvation, which embraces all there is.

CHAPTER 9

THE FIRST PASSOVER IN JESUS' PUBLIC MINISTRY. HE WORKS MIRACLES AND PURGES THE TEMPLE. EVENTS UP UNTIL THE SECOND PASSOVER TWELVE MONTHS LATER. A BREAK OFF GROUP FROM THE DISCIPLES OF JOHN THE BAPTIST SIDES AGAINST THE SAVIOR.

Time: The above events covered about one year

All Israel was represented at the temple celebration. Christ reveals Himself as that Messianic Person. The Jews required a sign* to prove His claim. This encounter commenced His life long conflict with the religious leaders of Israel. In a unique sense, it continues to this present day.

*For the second time when the religious leaders demanded a Messianic sign of Him, refer to the main heading of Section 67. The scribes and Pharisees wanted a third sign from Christ as seen in Section 100. For His cleansing the temple a second and final time, and the clash with the Jews just before His death, see main heading of Section 150.

Matt.	Mk.	Lk.	John 2:13–25—*The temple at Jerusalem*
			His Father's house desecrated: He purged it of evil
			13 And the Jews' passover was at hand, and Jesus went up to Jerusalem, [a] *(His first Passover as Israel's promised Messiah. Next in John 5:1.)*
			14 And found in the temple those that sold oxen and sheep and doves, and the changers of money sitting: [b]
			15 And when he had made a scourge of small cords, he drove them all out of the temple, and the sheep, and the oxen; and poured out the changers' money, and overthrew the tables;
			16 And said unto them that sold doves, "Take these things hence; make not my Father's house an house [c] of merchandise."
			17 And his disciples remembered that it was written, [d] **"The zeal of thine house hath eaten me up."**
			The Jews require a sign: His strange answer
			18 Then answered the Jews and said unto him, "What sign [e] shewest thou unto us, seeing that thou doest these things?"
			19 Jesus answered and said unto them, [f] **"Destroy this temple, and in three days I will raise it up."** *(For explanation of three days, see Appendix One.)*
			20 Then said the Jews, "Forty and six years was this temple in building, and wilt thou rear it up in three days?" [g]
			21 But he spake of the temple of his body. [h]
			They remember later: no miracles for the fickle crowds
			22 When therefore he was risen from the dead, his disciples remembered that he had said this unto them; and they believed the Scripture, and the word which Jesus had said. [i]
			23 Now when he was in Jerusalem at the passover, in the feast *day,* many believed [j] in his name, when they saw the miracles which he did.
			A flash of His deity: only
			God could know all men and what was in them
			24 But Jesus did not commit himself unto them, because he knew all *men,*
			25 And needed not that any should testify of man: for he knew what was in man. [k] (Next chap., John 3:1, cont. in Section 30.)

Footnotes-Commentary

[a] **Passover.** Highlighted in gray for its importance in calculating Jesus' public ministry. The annual Passover

is critical in determining this question. During this particular Passover, the Lord Jesus presented Himself for the first time as the Messiah of Israel, fulfilling specific Old Testament predictions. See the second paragraph of footnote d below. Matthew, Mark, and Luke say nothing concerning the four Passovers that occurred between our Lord's baptism and death, except the last one. John wrote of all four in the following passages:

1. **John 2:23.** The first one attended *in His ministry* and explained in this Section. This was not the first Passover He attended as seen in Section 20, Lk. 2:41-42, footnotes a, b, and c. Pious and loyal Jews, with their families, attended every annual Passover celebration if it were humanly possible.

2. **John 5:1.** Whether or not the "feast of the Jews" mentioned in this text is a Passover is discussed in Section 52, footnote b. It is held to be that in this harmony commentary.

3. **John 6:4.** See Section 93, footnote e for a discussion of this third Passover Feast in the ministry of Jesus, which apparently He did not attend.

4. **John 11:55, 56; 12:1, 12; 13:1; 18:28, 39; and 19:14.** This was His fourth and final Passover. On this occasion, Christ fulfilled each of the various Passover prophecies and became the Lamb of God, dying on the cross to take away the sin of the world (John 1:29; 1 Peter 1:19-21; with Rev. 5:6-14). For a list of many Old Testament predictions regarding the death of Christ, spanning a period of some six thousand years, see *Appendix Three.*

2p-Passover means, "Passing or stepping over." It was one of the seven annual national celebrations of Israel as recorded in Lev. 23. It occurred in late March or early April and was the oldest of Jewish festivals, having its origin with the deliverance of Israel from Egypt (Ex. 12:6; Lev. 23:5; with Num. 9:3-5; 28:16). The New Testament reveals that it reflected Christ and redemption by His blood from sin's slavery and death (Ex. 12:13; 1 Cor. 5:7). On the evening before the celebration, the head of the family would search the house with a lighted candle for any vestige of leaven and remove it (Ex. 12:15). Rabbis pointed to Zeph. 1:12 for proof of this custom. Some sources tell us that deeply religious Jews would start purging leaven from their premises several weeks in advance. Dr. Cunningham Geikie, in his brilliant work, *The Life and Words of Christ,* page 150, gives an excellent description of Jewish preparation during this time. He wrote, "The purification of the house, however, was by no means all. Vessels of any kind, to be used at the feasts, were cleansed with prescribed rites, in a settled mode. Metal dishes, after being scoured, must be first dipped in boiling water—in a pot used for no other purpose—and then into cold. Iron vessels must be made red hot, and washed in the same way. Iron motors, for crushing grain for baking, were filled with red coals, until a thread tied outside was burned through. Wooden vessels after being wetted were rubbed with a red-hot stone. No clay dish could be used at all if not quite new, and it had to first be dipped thrice in running water, and consecrated by a special prayer. Personal purity was as strictly enforced. Everyone had to cut his hair and nails, and take a bath."

3p-Jew have a book that lays out the order for their modern day Passover. It is called the Haggadah. Christens, see various symbolism in the foods eaten at the Passover. First, *the lamb*, which pointed to Christ our salvation from sin. Second, three pieces of *the matzot* or unleavened bread, pointed to purity in life after conversion to Christ. Third, *the maror* or bitter herbs, spoke of Egypt's sorrows in making mortar without straw and sin's terrible consequences from which believers have been delivered. The Hebrew Passover is the world's oldest continually observed feast. It has been celebrated by Israel for over three thousand years.

4p-In the days of Jesus, the Passover was a spectacle to behold! It was a time of great joy among the Jewish people and not of sadness, as some Christians wrongly believe. Many *saved Jews* still celebrate Passover today, because it points them to Jesus of Nazareth, their precious Messiah. High with excitement and with great piety, Hebrews, as well as thousands of strangers and Gentiles, ascended to Jerusalem and the temple for this grand occasion. Bands of Jewish pilgrims coming from afar would sing and chant Ps. 122 as they neared the city. Thousands of makeshift camps dotted the terrain about Jerusalem, and every house in the city was open "free of charge" to fellow Jewish visitors from afar. Tourists from the known world were almost omni-present beholding the wonders of the Passover. In the work of Josephus, there is a footnote stating that up to three million, people converged upon the city during this festive event (*Wars of the Jews,* Book 6:9, footnote c.) Merchants, traders, hawkers, peddlers, all eagerly seeking to sell or barter their wares, flooded Judaea and Jerusalem. Beggars stationed themselves near all gates leading into the city and temple. Old friends renewed their acquaintance, happy children played their joyful games, as the elderly gathered to swap tales and speak of the fortunes and misfortunes of their beloved Israel. Wide-eyed tourists gasped at the colorful pageantry displayed before them. The pagan Castle of Antonio towering to the north of the temple structure had several thousand extra soldiers on duty. They served as an emergency peacekeeping force during the festivities. The Roman governor Pilate, Herod Antipas, and other dignitaries were usually present. Pilate kept himself within or near the castle area. Herod Antipas had quarters on the other side of the city. Their presence was an act of political correctness because the Romans and Jews fiercely hated each other. For a Roman soldier who was an exception to this hate rule, see asterisk under main heading of Section 60, footnote b. During His crucifixion, other centurions also confessed Christ as "the Son of God." Refer to Section 192, Matt. 27:54, footnote b for details on this wonderful conversion of other pagans.

5p-During this event, the Song of Solomon was read publicly. Passover being a one day event, it was immediately followed by the seven day Feast of Unleavened Bread. Thus, the two celebrations were "blurred together" and considered one. This is why each is often called by the name of the other. Josephus referred to it as "the feast for eight days," in *Antiquities,* Book 2:15. 1, line 317. Passover officially started on the fourteenth day of the Hebrew month Nisan (March-April), supposedly the day God led Israel out of Egypt. During the Babylonian captivity, Nisan was called Abib, but it had been known earlier by this name as far back as the days of Moses. With the exodus from Egypt, Nisan–Abib became the first month of the Jewish religious year and remains so to this present time (Ex. 13:4; 34:18; Num. 9:3-5; and 28:16).

6p-Thousands of lambs were corralled near the north side sheep gate. These were purchased by those offering sacrifices. See Section 14, footnote b, for the source of these animals. With a background of threefold blast from silver trumpets, amid the joyful responsive singing between the people and temple choristers, the ceremony was most impressive. The officiating priests would be chanting Ps. 81 amid their duties. This religious pomp took place in the temple proper, near the altar as the groups moved forward in three different companies. Each person brought his lamb, laid hands on the animal's head, and then slew it before the temple priest. The priest poured its blood into a basin. Next he instantly flayed, gutted, washed the carcass and gave it back to the worshiper within one minute! (The skin went to the priest as a payment for his services.) The flesh was eaten later that evening during the Passover supper as seen in Lk. 22:15 with John 13:1-2. A single lamb served a "company," which was usually not fewer than ten but not more than twenty people. This took place between the sun's decline and its disappearance on the fourteenth of Nisan. One estimate was that over two million lambs were offered at each Passover. See Josephus' *Wars of the Jews*, Book 2:14. 3, footnote b, and Book 6:9. 3, footnote c. This figure gives some idea of the number of people present for this occasion. Joachim Jeremias, in his helpful work, *Jerusalem in the Time of Jesus*, pages 78, 101 gives interesting details, but is off on his population numbers for Jerusalem. The temple floor was smoothly paved and sloped in selected directions so that the blood spilled from the thousands of sacrifices could be easily washed away. The main channel that carried it out of the temple was near the altar. From here, it flowed via an underground tunnel down to the valley of Kidron situated outside the east wall of the city. Jewish gardeners purchased this for fertilizer after it had dried. To use it without payment was considered high sacrilege. For further information on this, see the Talmud tractate, Yoma 58b. (It is of interest that today's Ashkenazi Jews do not eat lamb flesh at their Passovers because there is no temple where it can be slaughtered.)

7p-During the Passover and seven days of Unleavened Bread that followed, Jerusalem became something of a gigantic flea market or world emporium. A place called the Lower New Town was like a giant bazaar. It was a long street, packed with hundreds of stalls, booths, and shops. It bustled with thousands of shoppers and curious on-lookers milling about. Such goods as clothing, jewelry, exotic ointments, children's trinkets, spices, herbs, pastry, and bakements of every sort, dried foods, meats, cheese, fruits, fish, fowls, footwear, amazing articles of glass, brass and ironwork, wheat, dried herbs, woodcarvings, and wine were there. The requirements for accommodation, sanitation, solid fresh food, fruits, vegetables, spices, all sorts of drink, and hundreds of other items during Passover were incredible. Even a bridge of false teeth was discovered in one of the archaeological sites at this location in the ancient city! The tables of the infamous money changers lined the entrances into the city and the Court of the Gentiles adjacent to the temple compound. Hundreds of extra priests and Levites served overtime during the Passover. Christ made His way into this packed temple, knowing that fellow Jews from over the known world were present. Into this atmosphere, He stepped forward to present Himself, for the first time *publicly,* as the promised Messiah of Israel. *Devout Jews believed their Messiah would appear during a Passover. This was later denied after the resurrection of Chris by the rabbis.* Little did they know that Messiah stood unnoticed amid the crowds, ready to make His first dramatic appearance to the people He came to save. For a colorful picture of the splendor and glory of the ancient Passover restored some six hundred years before Christ, see 2 Chron. 35:1-19. *The Feasts of the Lord*, by K. Howard and M. Rosenthal, contains a brief but beautiful explanation of Israel's seven annual celebrations.

(b) Money changers. Rabbinical law forbade bringing foreign coins into the temple precincts for they carried impressions of heathen gods, goddesses, or rulers. The money merchants would exchange all foreign currency for Jewish monetary forms acceptable to the temple officials. A service fee of 5% or more was levied for *each* coin exchange. Devout Jews traveling hundreds of miles to observe the celebration could not bring their sacrificial lambs or food such distances. They exchanged their foreign money for that which was usable, and thus purchased personal goods, the needed lambs and other items at the sheep market, located on the northeastern side of the city, with the gate bearing this name (John 5:1-2).

2p-In the days of Christ, merchandising in the temple had become a corrupt business. It was under the strict control of Annas, the high priest, and his son–in–law, Caiaphas. (Both were called "high priests" in Lk. 3:2, because they filled the office simultaneously through political and religious corruption.) They leased various sites across the temple courtyards and porches for vendors and business enterprises. Tickets were sold to secure sites for trade. Common Israelis hated this practice but were helpless against the prestige and power of Annas and his bands of thieving priests. For a fascinating review of temple activities, see *The Temple its Ministry and Services*, by Alfred Edersheim, and the fact-packed work *Jerusalem in the Time of Jesus*, by Joachim Jeremias.

(c) **"An house of merchandise."** The sight of God's House being used as a hub of commercial enterprise disturbed Christ. Shouting merchants calling all to purchase their wares, the smell of animal droppings, and the general commotion of the scene; extortion, lying, and theft practiced upon the helpless people moved the Son of God to holy anger! He had viewed these evils on many previous occasions, but His presence at this Passover was to begin His public ministry as Israel's Messiah. The situation was explosive. The whisperings of honest, pious Jews, who faithfully came to the temple to offer sacrifices and worship God, had reached its peak. Hatred smoldered in the hearts of the common people over this abuse. They wanted something done! To loyal Jews beholding the deeds of this stranger in their beloved temple, it was an act of noble loyalty to Jehovah God, and something long overdue. Eighteen years before, Christ had sat in this very place and conversed with the doctors of the law, but as a Child only twelve years of age, He could do nothing. This event is recorded in Section 20. Now, thirty years old, Israel's Messiah would begin His "Father's business." God starts His work by purifying the things He will use. In this act, Christ placed Himself in direct antagonism to the Sanhedrin and the high priests because they had made merchandising in God's house possible. The Savior charged the Jewish hierarchy with religious profanity in misusing God's Temple as a center for *personal* business. It would be wrong to think the Sanhedrin did not immediately go into consultation about this Man from Galilee, who had challenged them. They were furious! Shortly, after this they were plotting to kill Him.

(d) **"Zeal" will eat a man up**! Cited from Ps. 69:9. Its consuming power must be mitigated by correct knowledge resulting in appropriate action. After weaving a small, whip-like instrument, the Lord Jesus, in a mighty show of righteous indignation over the desecration of His Father's House, burst upon the scene. According to Jewish law, only the temple police could bring any staff or rod into the court area. Our Lord's handmade scourge was a violation of temple rules. With a ringing voice of authority, He overturned the receptacles of the frightened money changers. They scrambled for bouncing, rolling coins across the marble floors in the Court of the Gentiles. Falling upon the greedy merchants, Christ "drove them all out of the temple." Large flocks of sheep and droves of cattle, hobbled behind makeshift fences, suddenly stampeded as they madly bolted, ran, and slid through the temple gates and down the adjacent hills. The angered Lord ordered the bird merchants to "take these things hence." Tearing about they pushed, pulled, shoved, and carried their cages, coups, and pens beyond His piercing eyes. It was a miracle that no one was killed in the mayhem of that hour. The temple was packed with thousands attending the Passover. His majestic presence awed them with wonder. A divine thunderstorm had fallen upon the scene. One can almost see and hear the terrified mothers snatching up screaming children and the youth wide-eyed at the sight. The elderly are dumbfounded as this carpenter from Galilee defied the entire religious establishment. And He did this in the House of God. Instantly, every Jew present at that scene inquired, *"Who is this man?"*

2p-Looking back. John, writing years after these events, looks back and adds an inspired editorial comment to the whole spectacle. He wrote that suddenly Jesus' disciples (he, being one of them), amid the uproar, remembered a passage from the Old Testament, "The zeal of thine house hath eaten me up" (Ps. 69:9), and "remembered" well they did, because the entirety of this Psalm pointed to their coming Messiah! At this early point in His ministry, His disciples numbered about five. Stumbling back, they were wide-eyed and aghast at this performance of their newly found Teacher. The terrible uproar caused by the Savior instantly brought the temple police and members of the Sanhedrin upon the scene. They, too, had stood in dismay as Jesus purged God's House. Their question, "What sign showest thou unto us, seeing that thou doest these things?" clearly means they interpreted His actions as being intentionally Messianic. Jesus had manifested, before the rulers and the people, God's vindication of the temple's sanctity by purging it. *This was done to fulfill the prophecy written in Mal. 3:1-3.* Every learned Jew knew these verses predicted that when Messiah appeared in their temple, He would first busy Himself with purging it. Then He would work to purify individuals within the nation of Israel. The rabbis taught that Messiah would manifest Himself during their beloved Passover. The prophet Malachi, some four hundred years before, predicted this in these words: "But who may abide the day of his coming? and who shall stand when he appeareth? for he *is* like a refiner's fire, and like fuller's soap: And he shall sit *as* a refiner and purifier of silver: and he shall purify the sons of Levi, and purge them as gold and silver, that they may offer unto the LORD an offering in righteousness"(Mal. 3:2-3). Driver and Neubauer in their work, *The Suffering Servant of Isaiah according to the Jewish Interpreters,* page 373, quote from an ancient Rabbi ben Maimon, who affirms that this citation from Mal. 3 spoke of Israel's Messiah appearing in the temple. The non-Christian Jew, Joseph Klausner, in his book, *The Messianic Idea In Israel,* pages 214-215, sees in these verses Israel's Messiah. At this Passover, these passages find the beginning of their fulfillment in the actions of Jesus. His fearless deeds thundered in the ears of every devout Jew something like this, "Look, ye men of Israel, on this Passover day your Messiah has appeared in the temple of God." Nevertheless, the purveyors of Jewish religion could not "abide the day of his coming." There can be no doubt that many present here knew Him from prior contact, especially the pilgrims from Galilee and His hometown Nazareth. His own family members were there somewhere among the multitudes and soon heard of this uproar.

(e) **"Sign."** The words of John, "the Jews . . . said unto him," mean that the religious leaders immediately clashed with this young troublemaker from Nazareth. (One year later, on the next Passover there was another confrontation of Jesus with the Jews when He healed a man on the Sabbath. See this under the main heading at Section 52 and John 5:1-17.) Jewish mentality was enslaved by the signs' mania. This is reflected in the Talmud where various rabbis wrote of "signs of sin, of the heavens, of mischief, of maturity, of the zodiac," and numerous other things. For examples, see tractates, Shabbath 33a, 156a, and Sukkah 29a. Joseph Klausner in *The Messianic Idea in Israel,* pages 427-439, gives a lengthy description of the absurd signs the Jews looked for that allegedly proved the coming of Messiah. George Foot-Moore in, *Judaism,* vol. II-III, page 355, continues the same thought. The synagogue was the main channel for public teaching about signs and Messiah in the nation of Israel. He would appear and perform amazing wonders before the people. Hence, on this occasion, the religious leaders demand of Him an extraordinary sign or miracle. They wanted a super-Messianic wonder to convince them that He was their Messiah! For the four unique Messianic signs, the rabbis taught that only their real Messiah could produce, see asterisk under main heading in Section 48. In response to their demand for a special Messianic miracle, Jesus declared that His resurrection was the only sign they would get. It would be infallible evidence impossible to deny, showing that He was the Son of David, Israel's Messiah (Rom. 1:3-4). His reply, though not understood at that time, was remembered later. It was used against Him in court some three years afterwards. See footnote f below. The empty tomb remains to this day the *only* sign, given by the Son of God to every "evil and adulterous generation." It looms over all who love sin and hate righteousness. It is the infallible token of their pending and eternal doom! Christ lives forevermore. He will judge all men someday, regardless of how far in the future that may be.

2p-Signs demanded five times. The Jews called for signs from Jesus at least five different times during His ministry. Three of His apostles asked about signs two days before His death; making a total of six. These are:

1. In this present Section 29, John 2:18. For this, see footnote e above.
2. In Section 66, Lk. 11:16, with no details given in this case except Christ aligning them with Satan, the strong man.
3. Refer to Section 67, Matt. 12:38 with Lk. 11:29. See relative footnotes at these verses.
4. See this in Section 95, John 6:30. In this verse, the multitudes requested a miracle sign. See footnote g at this verse for more details.
5. At this time, they requested a sign, see Section 100, Matt. 16:1. Also, see footnotes on this passage.
6. Refer to Section 163, Matt. 24: 3 where three apostles asked for a sign. Lastly, during His Mount Olivet Discourse, Jesus warned that the false Christs or Messiahs would appear in Israel prior to the fall of Jerusalem in A.D. 70, and would perform (demonic) signs in their attempts to deceive. This affirms that the Jewish madness for Messiah to be a wonder-worker would still be alive in Israel forty years *after* Jesus had ascended to heaven. See Section 163, Matt. 24:24 footnote k for the false Messiahs of A.D. 70 who attempted to lead astray the elect or saved persons during this awful time of pending judgment.

(f) Shaded in gray, for here our Lord makes the *first verbal* mention recorded in the New Testament of His future death and resurrection. His Words were something of a commentary on what had been prefigured in the Old Testament centuries before (Jonah 1:17 with Matt. 12:40). No one in His audience understood *at that time* what He was saying, but it surely haunted them. About three years later the Jews brought it up during His mock trial in Matt. 26:61, and again as He hung on the cross (Matt. 27:40). The resurrection of Jesus Christ has sounded the death sentence for every religion and faith apart from Him! He alone rose from the stronghold of death and lives forevermore. No religion across world history can make such a claim as Bible Christianity: devils, cults, and wicked men hate His atoning death and resurrection from the bonds of death, and they struggle to explain it away. His statement, "rearing up the temple in three days," greatly puzzled the religious leaders. Some three years afterwards, they remembered His claim and went to Pilate for soldiers to guard the tomb. Refer to main heading under Section 194 for this deed. For needed comments regarding those "religious" groups who deny the final authority of Scripture, oppose clear biblical teaching, and cover up their record of heresy, murder, lying, and religious subversion, see Section 33, third paragraph of footnote c. Regarding the disaster of sincerity in religion without the saving knowledge of Jesus Christ, see Section 95, sixth paragraph of footnote r.

(g) Revealing their ignorance of Christ's response to their demand for a spectacular Messianic sign, they fall back only on a faulty calculation of how long their temple had been in building and equate this to His words. See Edersheim's *Life and Times of Jesus the Messiah*, footnote 24 on page 259, for details. Critics have pointed out that the calculation here was wrong. The Jews made the incorrect statement, not Jesus. Herod the Great began temple work in 20-19 B.C. This continued until A.D. 64 and stopped due to so many wars. The work was always intermittent due to troubles, wars, and conflicts that continually plagued the Jews, Jerusalem, and the temple.

(h) Looking back as he wrote, John specifically explained (for the benefit of his *original readers*) what Jesus meant by this curious saying. The Jews would destroy or kill His physical body, but it would be raised from the grave in three days. See footnote f above.

(i) **Hind sight better than foresight.** Some three years later, after Jesus' resurrection, these very disciples reflected back and remembered what their Lord had said! *Then*, His answer to the Jews made perfect sense to them (Lk. 24: 44-46). During His post resurrection appearances, He began gradually to open their hearts to understand correctly how the Old Testament spoke of Him. For their astounding unbelief on the resurrection morning, note Section 196, John 20:9, and attached side and bottom comments by the symbols ▶and ▫.

(j) "Many believed in his name" which was Messiah. This reveals that they interpreted His actions and miracles as proof that He was claiming to be that Messianic Person. It happened "when they saw the miracles he did." This informs us that following the request of the religious leaders to see Him produce a unique sign (which He rejected), Jesus afterwards moved among the crowds and performed numerous signs and wonders. However, what did the "many" believe in Him for? They could not have believed in His future death, burial, and resurrection. At *this point,* in the life of Christ, the Jewish people did not yet understand His death for the sins of the world. Their faith was simply a historical belief in His Name, "Messiah." This did not include His death on the cross. That would come later. These texts tell us that hundreds of the people (who were in the temple court) saw His miracles and believed that He was Messiah. They held that He would first appear in the temple and be "approved of God" by countless miracles (Acts 2:22). As already mentioned, the rabbis taught that Messiah would appear during the celebration of Passover. Suddenly, it was all happening before their very eyes. *There He stood!*

2p-Verse 24. "He knew all *men.*" Only God could know all men. Thus, another clear affirmation that Jesus of Nazareth was God dwelling in human flesh (1 Tim. 3:16). For John's record of the omniscience of Christ, see John 1:42, 47, 48; 4:29; 6:61, 64; 11:4; 13:11; and 21:17. When the Savior sovereignly *chose not to know* certain facts for a limited time, see Section 163, Mk. 13:32, third paragraph of footnote v. Concerning Christ's words that the Father was greater than Him, refer to Section 175, John 14:28, footnote p.

3p-Has divine sovereignty become a theological dumpster? The word "sovereign" is employed to escape difficulties, explain the unexplainable, and exonerate God of wrongdoing. Calvinists remind us, "God is sovereign," and they alone seem to understand what this means. Logically defining the Almighty, who has numbered the sand on the shores, counted and named the stars of heaven, and knows each hair on our heads, is illogical. Men living in time speak of eternity, where God dwells (Isa. 57:15) but they cannot define it. We, though dwelling in earth's limits, are unable to describe its immensity. *The Almighty exists by the necessity of His own being!* Years ago, a Dutch Reformed minister in South Africa said, "If God decided to rob a bank it would be alright because He is sovereign." However, divine sovereignty does not include bank robbery or damning billions because it is His "good pleasure." Often Isa. 45:7 is quoted as proof of their ignorance. It reads, "I [God] form the light, and create darkness: I make peace, and create evil. I the LORD do all these things." Whatever this finally teaches (and there are reasonable explanations) it cannot mean that God is the author of sin, moral evil, bank robbery or pre damning helpless billions. Such sentiments are abhorrent to the general strain of Scripture. *It is true that God may use sin, sinlessly in order to accomplish His purposes.* Divine sovereignty must not be used as justification for heretical teaching. Holy things are too high for us. It is better to leave them with Him who will always do right. God alone has the perfect standard and balance of holiness, love, justice, and mercy. His holiness required and demanded atonement for sin, and His love provided that atonement on the cross. Divine justice enacted is the revulsion of God's holiness against all wickedness. Calvary gloriously demonstrated this. The punishments He inflicts upon sin are not vindictive but vindicative! His infinite mind always acts in an absolutely perfect manner. His totality is so awesome that there is never a moment when we are not in His thoughts (Ps. 139:1-4, 6). Knowing so little of human life, we mortals dump upon God things that we have done, as though He did them. The following story illustrates this. A boy was given two dimes: one for Sunday school, and one for candy. He stumbled, and the coins rolled away. Finally, he recovered one, but the other fell into a deep crack. Looking up to heaven he said, "Well, Lord, there goes your dime because you allowed it to get lost." This is how we often do things and then point to divine sovereignty as a religious dumpster for our failures. Regarding what God "allows and lets," and how this is misused to justify our personal ineptness, see Section 137, fourth and fifth paragraphs of footnote d.

(k) No character references needed. Knowing the hearts of those surging upon Him in the temple courtyard, Jesus did not commit Himself to any of their Messianic questions or expectations. One wonders what they requested of Him. A few years later, He hid from the zealous Jews in Galilee, who attempted to force kingship upon Him. This passage is exceedingly difficult for those who believe that Christ offered Himself as their King, and they rejected Him. Read of this attempt to crown Jesus as king in Section 94, John 6:15, footnote a. See also footnote c above.

2p-Moving about the temple, He was surrounded by the excited multitudes. Many were filled with joy for His fearless opposition of the wicked priesthood. Others came to Him out of curiosity. Standing among the milling throngs, one old sage, a respected member of the Sanhedrin, listened to, and watched this young Galilean. He sensed a driving compulsion to converse with this stranger. Had Jesus not just presented Himself, both in the temple and on the Passover, as the Messiah? Knowing the unstable crowds, Messiah moved from them. However, there was one to whom Jesus did "commit" Himself. Under the shadows of the night, He would soon meet with a respected, elderly Pharisee named Nicodemus, a famed ruler of the Jews. Unlike most of his fellows in the religion of Israel, he was honest in heart, venerable in intentions, and sought to know the truth about Jesus the purported Messiah of Israel.

A concerned old man named Nicodemus visits Jesus at night. He was a member of Israel's Supreme Court. Their amazing discourse as recorded by John.

Matt.	Mk.	Lk.	John 3:1-18—*Jerusalem*
			Nicodemus' great confession
			1 There was a man of the Pharisees,[a] named Nicodemus, a ruler[b] of the Jews:
			2 The same came to Jesus by night,[c] and said unto him, "Rabbi, we know that thou art a teacher come from God: for no man can do these miracles[d] that thou doest, except God be with him."
			Jesus' response
			3 Jesus answered and said unto him, "Verily, verily, I say unto thee, Except a man be born again,[e] he cannot see the kingdom of God."
			Nicodemus' question
			4 Nicodemus saith unto him, "How can a man be born when he is old? can he enter the second time into his mother's womb, and be born?"
			Jesus' response
			5 Jesus answered, "Verily, verily, I say unto thee, Except a man be born of water[f] and *of* the Spirit, he cannot enter into the kingdom of God.
			6 "That which is born of the flesh is flesh; and that which is born of the Spirit is spirit.
			7 "Marvel not that I said unto thee, 'Ye must be born again.'
			8 "The wind bloweth where it listeth, and thou hearest the sound thereof, but canst not tell whence it cometh, and whither it goeth: so is every one that is born of the Spirit."[g]
			Nicodemus, the untaught teacher
			9 Nicodemus answered and said unto him, "How can these things be?"
			10 Jesus answered and said unto him, "Art thou a master[h] of Israel, and knowest not these things?
			11 "Verily, verily, I say unto thee, We speak that we do know, and testify that we have seen; and ye receive not our witness.
			12 "If I have told you earthly things, and ye believe not, how shall ye believe, if I tell you *of* heavenly things?
			13 "And no man hath ascended up to heaven, but he that came down from heaven, *even* the Son of man which is in heaven.[i]
			How to be born again illustrated and explained
			14 "And as Moses lifted up the serpent in the wilderness,[j] even so must the Son of man be lifted up:
			15 "That whosoever believeth in him should not perish, but have eternal life.
			16 "For God so loved the world, that he gave his only begotten[k] Son, that whosoever believeth in him should not perish, but have everlasting life.
			17 "For God sent not his Son into the world to condemn the world; but that the world through him might be saved.
			Two classes of people and why
			18 "He that believeth on him is not condemned: but he that believeth

Matt.	Mk.	Lk.	John 3:18-21— *Jerusalem*
			not is condemned already, because he hath not believed in the name of the only begotten Son of God. **19** "And this is the condemnation, that light is come into the world, and men loved darkness⁽ˡ⁾ rather than light, because their deeds were evil. **20** "For every one that doeth evil hateth the light, neither cometh to the light, lest his deeds should be reproved. *Nicodemus had come to the Light* **21** "But he that doeth truth cometh to the light, that his deeds may be made manifest, that they are wrought in God."⁽ᵐ⁾ (Verse 22 cont. in Section 31.)

Footnotes-Commentary

⁽ᵃ⁾ **The Pharisees.** They were the strictest religious sect among the Jews. Their origin was a few hundred years before our Lord's birth. Josephus, who had been one of their members, wrote in *Antiquities,* Book 17:2. 4, line 42 that they numbered about six thousand. In the days of Christ, they were mostly corrupt, yet oddly enough, considered theologically sound! Pharisees believed in the inspired writings of the whole Old Testament, in the coming of Israel's promised Messiah, in angels, spirits, resurrection of the dead and future judgment. Membership into their fraternity was hereditary, thus Paul said, "A Pharisee, and the son of a Pharisee" (Acts 23:6). They became the implacable enemies of Jesus because He refused to adhere to their traditions or oral law, often referred to as the Talmudic Mishna. See Section 52, footnote h, Section 89, footnote c, and Section 96, footnote d for explanation of the oral law. The Pharisees slowly vanished from the Jewish religious scene after the destruction of Jerusalem in A.D. 70. For a documented treatment of the Pharisees, see Joachim Jeremias, *Jerusalem in the Times of Jesus*, page 246-267. *The Jewish Encyclopedia,* pages 661–666 carries an excellent article on this subject, but denies the Pharisees were hypocrites, as the four gospels state. John never mentions the Sadducees, Herodians, or any other Jewish sect in his book. He wrote of the Pharisees at least twenty times.

2p-Among a sect of present day Messianic Jews, one group teaches that the Lord Jesus was a Pharisee obeying their scruples and traditions! See Section 45, footnote b, for more on this claim. Jesus said these lazy hypocrites would not "move one finger" to assist fellow Jews struggling under their overbearing oral traditions. Refer to Section 159, Matt. 23:4, footnote d, for our Lord's announcement of doom upon these hypocrites.

3p-The Talmud in tractate, Sotah 22b tells us there were seven types of Pharisees. Dr. Farrar in *The Life of Christ*, pages 571–572, also explains this subject. The *Biblical, Theological, and Ecclesiastical Cyclopaedia,* vol. iii, pages 66-74 has a comprehensive article on the seven kinds of Pharisees. An extra eighth group is also listed below.

1. **The "shikmi" or Shechemite" Pharisee.** They obeyed the law out of self-interest only.
2. **The "nikpi" or "stumbling" Pharisee.** He walked with exaggerated humility and pretended to be stumbling and knocking his feet together because he was so lowly, meek, and unworthy of God.
3. **The "kizai" or "bleeding" Pharisee.** Feigning meekness, these religious hypocrites would often go about with their eyes closed, so as not to lust after a woman. They were continually smashing into objects, falling down, and causing themselves to bleed.
4. **The "pestle" or "mortar" Pharisee.** These men would *literally* rub clay over their eyelids to prevent the possibility of sinning through the eye gates. Jesus may have referred to them in Section 47, Matt. 7:3-5, where he warned about things in the eyes that must be removed.
5. **The "What is my duty, and I will do it" Pharisee.** This group enjoyed making a noise about their good works so that others would see and hear them. We note our Lord rebuking these men in Section 46, Matt. 6:1-4 and accompanying footnotes. The rich young ruler may have been of this persuasion in view of his question to the Lord Jesus, "What lack I yet?" as seen in Matt. 19:20.
6. **The "timid" or "fearful" Pharisee.** He lived in fear of breaking some oral law or tradition of the elders.
7. **The "Pharisee from love."** Here we meet the *minority* body among these men. They served God and attempted to obey the great Torah Law out of love alone! Surely, Nicodemus and Joseph of Arimathaea belonged to this small band of Jewish religionists who wanted the truth and found it in Jesus of Nazareth, the Messiah. For more on Joseph, see second paragraph of footnote c below.
8. **Women Pharisees.** We are amazed that Lightfoot's *Commentary on the New Testament,* vol. 2, pages 67-70, carries numerous restrictions for females who were also called Pharisees!

4p-Out of the excited crowds at the Passover, it was Nicodemus, an elderly Pharisee, to whom our Lord committed Himself. Nicodemus was *not* the ordinary Hebrew or Pharisee. He was a noble man of candor, eminence, and dignity, towering above his fellows in piety and religious devotion. His designation "a man of the Pharisees" is similar to modern day descriptions, such as "He was a Presbyterian," or "a Baptist." John Gill wrote that some align him as the brother of the famed historian and military commander Josephus. A *worthless tradition* makes him the brother of Joseph of Arimathaea. However, all this is far-fetched due to the age of Nicodemus who was a member of the Sanhedrin. Nicodemus was reputed to have been one of the three richest men in Jerusalem, whose daughter was famed for her beauty, and the extraordinary wealth paid for her dowry. His tremendous wealth is suggested in Section 193, John 19:39-42, where he lavished on Jesus' burial necessities sufficient to inter two hundred bodies! He is probably mentioned in the Talmud tractates, Gittin 56a; Kethuboth 65a; and Ta'anith 20a; under the names "Boni," and "Nicodemus ben Girion." In the tractate, Sanhedrin 43a, he is said to have been a disciple of Jesus. For an interesting view into this, see *The Talmud: What It Is and What It Knows About Jesus and His Followers*, 1887 edition by Bernard Pick. Refer to Section 6, footnotes d and e, for blasphemous Talmudic quotations about Jesus and issues of morality. *The Jewish Encyclopedia*, pages 299-300, surprisingly, carries an excellent article on Nicodemus.

5p-Celebrated for his power in prayer and timidity, he was supposedly a professional well digger. (Each member of the Sanhedrin was required to pursue an honorable occupation.) Some eight months before the cross and after his nocturnal visit to Jesus, he appears in the Sanhedrin timidly trying to defend the Messiah (John 7:45-53). In time, Nicodemus became a *public* convert to Christ. This occurred after he had watched the crucifixion, and no doubt related it to the things spoken by Him some three years earlier in John 3:14-18. Thereafter, an ancient tradition related, he was finally expelled as a member of the Sanhedrin, deprived of all riches, almost beaten to death, and driven from Jerusalem. Later, his daughter was seen picking seeds from camel droppings in an effort to secure food for survival. Further, this ancient ecclesiastical *tradition* reports that Gamaliel, who was a relative to Nicodemus, took him in and later provided for his burial. For these traditions or stories about Nicodemus and their probable validity, see the *Biblical and Ecclesiastical Cyclopaedia*, by M'Clintock and Strong, vol. vii, pages 70-71; *Gill's Commentary*, vol. 7, pages 766-767; all of *People and History in Relation to the Messiah*, 1885 edition, by Alfred Edersheim; and *Hastings' Dictionary of the Bible*, 1906 edition, vol. III, pages 543-544. Dr. Josef Blinzler has given a brief but helpful article on Nicodemus in his definitive work, *The Trial of Jesus*, pages 96-97.

(b) "Nicodemus a ruler of the Jews." Meaning he was a member of the Sanhedrin, that august body of seventy-one elders who ruled the nation of Israel with absolute authority, yet time after time bowed to the commands of Rome. They were the Supreme Court for the nation. Each member wore a distinguished long brown robe. See *Appendix Five* for a detailed explanation of the Sanhedrin and other Hebrew bodies of this time. For Jesus' trial before the Jewish high court, see Section 181, footnote c. For a brief but helpful article on the Sanhedrin, see *The New Schaff-Herzog Encyclopedia of Religious Knowledge,* vol. X, 203-244. Jewish tradition about the Sanhedrin is found in the lengthy and difficult Talmud tractate, Sanhedrin. For a clear explanation of this group, see the helpful article in *The Words & Works of Jesus*, 557-561, by Dwight Pentecost.

(c) "By night." Over the centuries, men have made a great fuss out of this statement. Many have accused Nicodemus of cowardice. Actually, John the writer refers to a rabbinical rule that forbade members of the great Sanhedrin to be on the streets at night. See Talmud tractate, Berachoth 43b. Jews believed that demons prowled during the shades of evening and would attack those who walked the streets. One notorious night-spirit, known for attacking men was called "Lilth" and is mentioned in the Talmud tractates, Shabbath 109a and Baba Bathra 73b. The Talmud also states in, Sanhedrin 44a, that Jews should greet no one at night with their standard "Shalom" lest it be a demon. Others held that a scandal of suspicion might erupt against a member of the Sanhedrin if he were seen about the city after sunset. The early night hours were to be employed in the study of the law, not loitering on the streets. For a short but clear review of the ancient Hebrew beliefs regarding demons, see *The Life of Christ*, page 745-746 by F. W. Farrar. For Nicodemus to dare break the rules of the High Court and Jewish traditions and venture out during the night hours is indeed amazing! It reveals that he was *not* a coward but totally earnest in seeking an interview with the great teacher and miracle worker Who acted as though he was the Messiah.

2p-**"We know that thou art a teacher come from God."** This confession was often used in reference to the Messiah. For a staunch Sanhedrinist to acknowledge that the carpenter from Nazareth was "a teacher from God" is amazing! Jesus had trained in none of the theological institutions. See Section 119, John 7:15, footnote c for more on this thought. In both visiting Christ and making this confession, Nicodemus committed a major compromise of the Jewish religious rules. For the meaning of "teacher," see footnote h below. According to the rabbis, Messiah would be the greatest teacher and miracle worker. His use of the pronoun "we" is noteworthy. Who else within the Sanhedrin secretly believed this about Jesus? Most surely, Joseph of Arimathaea did (Lk. 23:50 with John 19:38-39). Further, Nicodemus' use of the title "Rabbi" in addressing Christ is not without warrant. Originally, it signified "greatness" and was the title of the highest respect only applied to the most honored teachers. In this case, it was worthily applied to Jesus, the greatest teacher ever to speak. Christ forbade his disciples from using this title, though it was proper for Him to do so (Matt. 23:8-10).

(d) "Rabbi" and "these miracles." This reference shows that Nicodemus had been present during the excitement of John 2:13-25, and had *seen* the *numerous* miracles performed by Jesus in the vast temple courts. However, when had he heard Jesus teach? Was it on this occasion or a previous one? Had he met Jesus before? It is of great interest that Nicodemus calls Christ "Rabbi" even though He had no formal rabbinical training. *The ancient Hebrews held that Messiah would be the greatest of all rabbis.* Christ is given this distinguished title some fourteen times in Scripture. For a unique view of the ancient rabbis, see *Jerusalem in the Time of Jesus,* Chapter X, by Joachim Jeremias. No doubt, Nicodemus heard the debate with Jesus among the leaders of religion (himself being one of them) and the Savior's response regarding the destruction of the temple. Like all faithful Jews, he too believed Messiah would appear during a Passover and fulfill Mal. 3:1-3. Refer to footnote k below for more on the shocked Nicodemus as he heard what Jesus said to him.

(e) **"Born again" or "new birth." The ancient Jewish understanding of the term.** This was a common idiom from antiquity and known among both pagans and Jews. *However, the Lord Jesus applied it in a unique and exclusive manner.* In traditional Hebrew thinking of this time, it signified seven things:

1. All Gentile proselytes into Judaism were said to have been "reborn" or a "newborn infant" following their baptism by self-immersion. An old rabbi wrote this very thing in the Talmud tractate, Yevamoth 22a. However, this baptism signified only an outward ritual cleansing from the defilement of heathendom and had nothing to do with conversion of the soul.
2. When a Jew married, he was said to have been "born again."
3. Rabbis who became the head of a theological academy were "born again."
4. The person crowned king was described as being "born again."
5. Slaves set free were "born again."
6. Youths upon completion of the bar-mitzvah were described as having been "born again." The modern day ritual of a bar-mitzvah is not that of the ancients.
7. One physically born into the family line of Abraham was counted as being "born again" in Jewish thinking. There was the popular superstition that racial descent from Abraham automatically brought God's blessings. John the Baptist had rejected this myth earlier (Section 21, Part 2, Matt. 3:9, footnote j). In some pagan religions, those who were baptized into the heathen rites were also considered "reborn" or "born again." See *The Origin of Paul's Religion,* by J.G. Machen, pages 230-231; and *Early Gentile Christianity and Its Hellenistic Background,* by Arthur. D. Nock, pages 61-67. See also *Infant Baptism in the First Four Centuries,* pages 32-35 by Joachim Jeremias, and *The Jewish Encyclopedia,* vol. 10, pages 220-221. This satanic precursor, later in the church taught that baptism saves and puts one into Christ.

2p-The Jews wrote in the Talmud of a proselyte as being a "newborn infant" in tractate, Yevamont 62a. In present Judaism, boys are responsible to follow the Torah Law at age of thirteen. Hebrew females enter bat-mitzvah at the age of twelve. Most Orthodox synagogues will not allow women to read publicly the Torah or lead in prayers. However, this custom is changing. The first mention of a bar mitzvah in the Talmud is supposedly in tractate, Baba Mezia 96a, though it is difficult to detect. Within the three geographical divisions of the present day Israel, the Ashkenazi (European Jews), Sephardic (Spain and Portugal), and Mizrahim (Asia and Caucasusian) customs greatly vary. For an example of this, see Section 29, footnote a, the last sentence of sixth paragraph.

2p-Because the term "born again" was well known by Hebrews and pagans, upon hearing Christ's say that *he* "must be born again," Nicodemus was puzzled. Knowing that he did not qualify for this "rebirth" as it was understood in his Jewish culture, he questioned Jesus. He did *not* inquire, "How can I be born again?" Instead, he asked something like this, "How can I be born again since I am old?" As an *old* man, he had previously met the criteria for the Jewish understanding of the new birth. Nicodemus was or had been married, which was a requirement for membership in the Sanhedrin (number 2 above). He was or had been the head of a theological academy (number 3 above). Years before as a boy of thirteen, Nicodemus had undergone the ceremony that later became bar mitzvah (number 6 above). Obviously, he did not qualify for numbers 1, 4 or 5. *What else could he do?* The Messiah's requirement for entrance into "the kingdom of God" was a "rebirth." Sadly, it was one that Nicodemus did *not* understand. Being a literalist Pharisee, he looked only for a physical or material kingdom to be established at Jerusalem with Messiah as its King ruling the world. This hope, all informed Jews knew and expected at this time. If anyone qualified for admission to God's kingdom, surely this elderly man did. Yet, the amazing miracle worker purporting be Israel's Messiah, now tells him otherwise. He must be "born again" or "from above." Without this, he will *never* "*see*" the kingdom, much less get into it! Doubtless, this dumbfounded Nicodemus. "Born again" in his thinking consisted of seven things, and none of them came from heaven. No marvel he blurted out the question "How can these things be?" This wonderful old man was ignorant that his Old Testament taught about this new birth. This is explained in footnote h below.

(f) **What does "born of water," mean?** Christian baptism, as later practiced by the church was unknown at this time. The first churches did not practice the ordinance until some three years later, *after* the Great Commission was given. When Jesus met with Nicodemus He was about six months in His ministry. The church as it would later be known in New Testament history did not exist at this time! *Christian baptism in the Name of the Trinity had never been heard of.* Therefore, Savior could not have referred to this future church ordinance in saying, "born of water."

He said this to Nicodemus some twenty years *before* the word "Christian" was even known (Acts 11:26). The old man sitting before the Lord Jesus could not have understood His words as having reference to "believer's baptism" as we use the term today. It did not exist. Water baptism is never expressed by the word "water" alone. It always has additional words to clarify the meaning. *Regeneration is never ascribed to water in Scripture.* Sometimes it is God (1 Peter 1:3). Sometimes the Son (1 John 2:29), and sometime it is the Holy Spirit (Titus 3:5). These Three do the work of regeneration via the Word of God (1 Peter 1:23). Nicodemus had never heard of the church, the Lord's Supper, and Christian baptism; these were future entities. In his mind, baptism (a covering with water) was for Gentile proselytes as they came into his Jewish religion, or something done by the priests ministering in the temple, who would immerse themselves for outward ritual cleansing (Heb. 9:6-10). Some Jews believed that to be "born into the family of Abraham" was tantamount to being "born of water." Baptism does not picture Jewish circumcision.

2p-Can "water" here mean Scripture? There are several verses that speak of God's Word cleansing His people (Ps. 119:9; John 15:3 and Eph. 5:26). On this basis, some hold that Jesus, here was speaking of the Scripture's inherit power to destroy sin in our lives and not literal water. Scripture is also spoken of as bringing the new birth (James 1:18). This is an excellent approach to John 3:5, but in view of how the ancient Jews understood the term "born of water," the author prefers their interpretation, finding it more fitting to the Jewish historical background of the story. For more on this, see paragraph four below.

3p-For a thorough discussion of Jewish uses of the word "water," see the work, *The Fourth Gospel*, by Dr. Hugo Odeberg, a Swedish liberal theologian. He wrote that water was also used as a symbol of the physical birth among the Jews (page 48). Odeberg's book is fouled by academic unbelief in the total inspiration of Scripture. Though helpful in its historical research, such works are worthless in pointing men to Christ and duties of the Christian life. Many Baptists and Pentecostals hold that it speaks of the water breaking in a woman just before childbirth. This sounds good but it hardly agrees with Hebrew beliefs at this time. See all under footnote e above.

4p-Nicodemus could only interpret the Words of Christ within the framework of his understanding of the term. That could not have included Christian baptism. Contextually, he inquired in verse 4 "how" he could be born again. Jesus answered his question in verse 5 by informing him that even though he had been born of water (that is, into the family of Abraham), unless he had the birth of the Holy Spirit, which comes from above, he would not "enter into the kingdom of God." (Jesus was saying it takes more than "being born of water," that is being a Jew, to be part of His new kingdom.) Nicodemus was called upon to make a distinction between his proud Jewish birth-heritage, what it commanded him to do, and what the Messiah required. No longer could he boast with fellow Pharisees, that "We be Abraham's seed, and were never in bondage to any man" (John 8:33). For Martin Luther's shocking confession about infant baptism, refer to Section 203, the eighth paragraph of footnote d. Luther's heresy lives today. Some fifty years ago, the associate editor of the *Lutheran Standard* interviewed Billy Graham. In the Oct. 10, 1961, edition, he was questioned about infant baptism. The famed evangelists said, "I believe that a miracle happens in those children, so that they are regenerated, that is made a Christian through infant baptism." To report this untruth is not flaunting hatred, but exposing vicious untruth. For Graham turning converts back into the Catholic Church, see Section 4, third paragraph of footnote d. *He has never retracted any of his anti-biblical statements. Graham was a great gospel preacher, but afterward he was a failure in not correctly instructing his news converts.*

5p-For the first time in his long life, Nicodemus heard that Jehovah God required something *totally* apart from being "born of water," or into the family of Abraham, with strict obedience to the law, both written and oral. Now, this grand old man hears that his proud Jewish birth, his works, prayers, and efforts to attain a place in God's kingdom are futile. He stands aghast! The young man who had purged the temple and performed great signs and wonders now informs him that to "enter" his lifelong dream of God's kingdom, he "must be born again." The Greek word translated "again" is "anothen" and also means "again from above." This signifies that the new birth has its *origin in heaven* and comes from there. All of Nicodemus' claims as a Hebrew and his devout life as a Pharisee suddenly became insufficient. *A heavenly birth is required.* Identifying Himself with the serpent of brass, the Lord Jesus then explained in John 3:16 how one is reborn or enters the true kingdom. In time, Nicodemus came into full understanding of the gospel truth contained in John 3:16. Scripture states that he went openly with Joseph to Governor Pilate, and begged Jesus' body to give it a royal burial. See John 19:38-42 for details.

6p-Verse 6. Flesh gives birth to flesh. As a thoroughbred Jew, Nicodemus trusted his physical or human descent from Abraham (with various Torah requirements) for entrance into God's kingdom, something Jesus clearly denied. *This is why Nicodemus and all Jews needed the new birth: because flesh and its best works could not save.* The finest pedigree of human flesh, be it Jew or Gentile, cannot produce the new birth in the soul of any man. That alone is the work of the gospel and Holy Spirit of God (1 Cor. 4:15 with 1 Peter 1:23).

(g) Verse 6. Spirit gives birth to spirit. In all history, the Holy Spirit has produced only one body of human flesh; that being the embryo within Mary in which the Lord Jesus incarnated Himself (Heb. 10:5). Jewish rabbis taught that the Spirit of God worked as did the wind: strange, powerful, invisible, and beyond the control of men. Christ drew Nicodemus into an analogy that he knew. This was to inform him that the new birth He required for entrance into God's *true* kingdom is received only by a sovereign work of Jehovah God through the Holy Spirit as He wields God's Word. Moreover, its basis is the death and resurrection of Christ. This marvelous gift is appropriated *only* in the heart of those who will believe. Christ used the word "believe" in several tenses at least six times in this short discourse with Nicodemus. The Hebrew word "ruach" meaning "wind or spirit," in the Greek is "pneuma," also "wind or spirit," with the context deciding which is meant. Nicodemus, a long-time master or teacher in Israel, knew this. The majestic sovereignty, workings, and effects of the wind are comparable to that of the Holy Spirit of God in producing the new birth in the soul of one who believes! No man can see the wind or discern its curious laws. However, its effects are visible and its sounds are audible. The changes produced by the wind are astounding. Some are terrifying, while others are gratifying. The convicted sinner is terrified at his fate, while the converted soul is gratified with the joys of salvation. It is so with the operations of the Holy Spirit in the lives of men. He, working through the Word of God, is the effecter of the new birth (1 Cor. 4:15 "begotten" with 1 Peter 1:22-23 "born again"). Later, John explained how one is born again, "Whosoever believeth that Jesus is the Christ [Messiah] is born of God" (1 John 5:1). This, in *essence,* is what Christ told Nicodemus. See footnote j below.

2p-Dr. Augustus Neander, in *The Life of Jesus Christ*, page 187, affirms that the birth of the Spirit is the birth that takes men "into a divine new life." He further wrote that the Master set before Nicodemus the "total opposition between the natural [or physical] life . . . and the new life [or spiritual] which God imparts." Scripture declares that this "life" is received when one trusts Christ as personal Lord and Savior and by no other way.

(h) **"Master of Israel."** The word "master" signified "the most revered doctor of the law;" one who expounded the Torah with the highest authority. Christ applied it to Nicodemus and accepted it for Himself. The word also means that Nicodemus was ranked among a *special class* of teachers such as those mentioned in Lk. 2:46. It is the same term he used in addressing Christ as "teacher come from God" (verse 2). It means the highest of all religious classes. He was, or had been, the head of a theological academy and a chief teacher among the greatest of Israel. He had instructed many in the things of God, but was ignorant of the new birth that Christ had just mentioned.

2p-**What circumcision pointed to in the New Testament.** Nicodemus should have understood what Jesus said about the new birth for it is mentioned in the Old Testament of which he was a teacher. In the Jewish Bible (Tanakh), God commanded Israel to be born again. Using spiritual language in Deut. 10:16 He said, "Circumcise therefore the foreskin of your heart and be no more stiffnecked." (It was the heart or inward person that needed circumcision not the outward flesh.) Later, in Deut 30:6, He foretold the results of the new birth, "And the LORD thy God will circumcise thine heart, and the heart of thy seed, to love the LORD thy God with all thine heart, and with all thy soul, that thou mayest live." The New Testament makes it clear that Jewish *outward circumcision* points to the *inward circumcision* or the new birth. Colossians 2:11 emphatically affirms that this operation is the work of the Holy Spirit, not the hand's of men. In Rom. 2:29, it is written that a *true* Jew or Gentile is one who has been circumcised in his heart, or saved. "Circumcision of the heart" is the equivalent of salvation of the soul. Making the rite of physical circumcision, as commanded in the Torah Law, compatible to baptism in the church is wrong. This distortion was brought into the church by the fathers and later embraced by the Roman Catholic system. They taught that it brought salvation to infants and adults. *Not all churches that practice infant baptism believe this error.* However, most of them do and herein is the danger. It is a substitute for repentance and faith in the finished work of Christ, which alone brings the new birth. With this, one is miraculously circumcised in his heart or born again.

3p-**New birth in the Old Testament.** At genuine conversion, the Holy Spirit lives in the saved soul (Eph. 3:16). Then, He begins to write the things of God upon the tables of the heart, the inward man, or soul. This is the opposite to Moses writing the commandments outwardly on tables of stone (2 Cor. 3:3 with Ex. 34:27-28 and Deut. 31:9). Grace works first inside and is then seen outside. Some five hundreds years *after* Moses, the prophet Jeremiah wrote of this heart change in Jer. 31:31-34. Centuries later, the author of Hebrews took Jeremiah's inspired words and applied them to salvation by the atoning sacrifice of Christ (Heb. 10:8-18). Salvation by faith *was* known across the Old Testament. God had preached the saving gospel to Israel during her forty-year trek through the wilderness (Heb. 3:17 with 4:2). Hebrews 4:2 is clear that they refused to believe it and thus "vexed his Holy Spirit" as written in Isa. 63:10. Moses knew the reproach of Christ even in pagan Egypt (Heb. 11:26). We read that the Rock that followed the children of Israel was Christ (1 Cor. 10:4). Peter declared at the first church council (at Jerusalem) in about A.D. 50, that "they" (the Old Testament saints) were "saved by grace" just as New Testament people were (Acts 15:11). Paul selects Abraham as the supreme model of how all people *must* be saved and made righteous in Rom. 4:1-5. He wrote that God preached the saving gospel to Abraham and that through this, he was made righteous (Gal. 3:6-8). The great apostle further declared that every saved person is counted as one of Abraham's seed or children (Gal. 3:29). James 2:23 reads, that through Abraham's faith "righteousness was imputed to him." In the Rom. 4 passages, David (who lived about one thousand years before Christ) is presented as an example of one who had been saved by faith in Christ, and received perfect imputed righteousness, apart from any works (Rom. 4:6-8). Peter said that *every* Old Testament prophet (forty-four of them) witnessed that faith in the Son of God saves a man from his sin (Acts 10:43). It is naive to hold that they all wrote this but did not know what they were writing. Peter affirmed these prophets *did understand* salvation, but were only questioning, "when" (or the time) Christ would come to die for the sins of mankind (1 Peter 1:9-12). See also Section 203, first and second paragraphs of footnote d.

4p-**Objections to salvation in the Old Testament?** The brilliant Baptist theologian, Augustus Strong wrote in his *Systematic Theology,* page 842, that the "Patriarchs . . . had no knowledge of Christ." *This is incorrect.* It is the product of *extreme* dispensationalism. Strong tells us that, "people in the Old Testament were saved by looking for a kingdom not a cross." What heresy! Men who bypass the cross have a dim vision of salvation. David prayed, "Restore the joy of His salvation" in Ps. 51:12. Only a saved person could make such a petition. About six centuries before Christ, the prophet Habakkuk declared, "The just (or righteous) shall live by his faith" (Hab. 2:4). That rule was valid for every saved person across the entire Old Testament era. Six hundred years later, this was the same rule of missionary Paul in Rom. 1:17; Gal. 3:11, and Heb. 10:38. In these three verses, he said they just were *still* to live by faith. Whether it is the Old or New Testament, it remains right that "without faith it is impossible to please him" (Heb. 11:6). Nicodemus, a master teacher of the Old Testament, should have known these things; but like thousands in the church of today, he was religiously ignorant and lost. Men stand, preach, and teach, yet many of them have never been circumcised in the heart, or born again. Circumcision today is the operation of grace performed by the Holy Spirit in the inward man. *Hebrew circumcision in the Old Testament has nothing to do with baptism in the New Testament.* See Section 138, fifth and sixth paragraphs under footnote a.

5p-Some seven hundred years before Christ was born, the millions behind the walls of ancient Nineveh heard the powerful preaching of Jonah. Thousands of them repented of their sins and believed in the true and living God (Jonah 3:5 with Matt. 12:41). Hebrews chapter 11 names sixteen persons saved during the Old Testament era. Among the number, we have the names of fourteen men and two women. This list of Old Testament saints spans a period of some three thousand years, starting with Abel and ending with Samuel. (In this listing, hundreds of others are mentioned by experience but not their names.) While preaching in His home town synagogue at Nazareth, the Savior informed His angry audience that the pagan Syrian, Naaman, also came to believe in the true and living God of Israel (Lk. 4:16, 27-28 with 2 Kings 5:14-15). The self-righteous Jews sought to kill Jesus for stating this truth.

6p-Verse 11. Our Lord's use of the plurals "we" and "ye" in this text has troubled some. Of whom was He speaking? It could not have been His few disciples, for His discourse with Nicodemus was surely in private. At this time in His ministry, the disciples were confused as to what Messiah was doing. Jesus here, associates Himself with many others who had previously given "witness" or "testimony" of Him. They are mentioned in Acts 10:43.

(i) **"No man hath ascended up to heaven, but he that cometh down from heaven."** Historically, both Enoch and Elijah were literally taken to heaven and seem to be exceptions to this fact (Gen. 5:23-24 with 2 Kings 2:1). In this statement, Jesus claims that His ascension would be unique; there would never be another like it. After providing atonement full and free for all men, and rising from the dead, He will return to the Father in heaven who had sent Him to earth. There He would take up His work as the only eternal high priest after the order of Melchisedec (Heb. 7:21). For other details on the Savior's ascension and His work at the Father's right hand, see Section 207, footnote b. In this statement, Jesus affirms absolute equality with God in heaven, while He was on earth! This is real omnipresence. Refer to Section 1, Part 1, John 1:1, footnotes a, and c, for more on Christ's equality with God. The Lord Jesus declares that no man has come down from heaven as He had with the divine commission to die for sins and rise from the grave. Cults teaching "soul sleep" seize upon this statement and from it affirm that the Lord Jesus is saying that no one goes to heaven at death. The Lord said that no man has ever ascended into heaven and returned to earth to tell men what it is like. In the Old Testament, God spoke from heaven to men; now, He has come down among men in the Person of Christ. The Son came down from that glorious place, and being equal with God, He alone has this sovereign authority to speak of such things. Christ is saying that He was *both* in heaven and on earth at the same time! Being equal with God, this amazing paradox was possible. These mysterious words must have stunned the elderly Nicodemus. Never had he heard such! *The young Man before him was claiming to be God in heaven and God on earth at the same time!* In John 10:30 the Lord Jesus later said, "I and my Father are one." For more on Christ's equality with God, see Section 175, footnote p and references.

(j) **"Lifted up."** Quoted from Num. 21:9. The scribes of the Torah Law taught that the brazen serpent pointed to their future Messiah. Nicodemus knew this. Now, Christ informs him that He, the Son of Man, will be lifted up as well. However, unlike the lifting up of Moses' serpent, which restored the smitten Jews only to physical health, Christ's lifting up will give everlasting life to all who believe, and they will never perish. The common expression "lifted up" was understood as referring to death by crucifixion. For further details, refer to Section 120, John 8:28, footnote o. Nicodemus knew this very well. As Moses' serpent was a sign to Israel, so the cross and Christ's atonement later became the sign of salvation to the spiritual "Israel of God" (Gal. 6:14-16).

2p-Jesus like a serpent? Our Lord depicted as a serpent in these words has troubled some Christians. This emblem demonstrates that He became *cursed* and *vile* when our sins were laid upon Him (Isa. 53:6 and 1 Peter 2:24 with 2 Cor. 5:21). As such, He bore the punishment of death. Nicodemus perceived that Jesus was presenting Himself to be the Messiah as symbolized in the brazen serpent of Israel's history. Yet, at this point, he did not understand the "lifted up" part of Jesus' message. In his Jewish thinking, Israel's Messiah could never be nailed to a cross and crucified. *That* would be impossible! Rather, He would be a conquering king, victorious over all foes.

(k) **"God so loved the world that he gave"** and **"only begotten."** *True love is an action not a feeling.* (Calvinism with its soteriological perversions affirms, "It is not the whole that world God loves but only the elect.") See Section 25, number 5 in listing under footnote a, for the unique meaning of "begotten." Here is the gospel in a thimble. Nicodemus must have been shaken to his soul at the instructions of Jesus. First, He claimed to be the "unique," "exclusive," "one and only" Son of God. Second, He stated that *God loved the world*, which was a concept that was impossible in Jewish thinking. In his mind, Jehovah loved only the Hebrew nation, for He had chosen them. All the Gentile nations were cursed of God and doomed for gehenna, unless they were proselyted into Israel. Apart from this, they would never share in Israel's earthly material kingdom. Now, he hears that God loves them all! Millions of lost souls have been saved through the teaching and preaching of this passage. One can well believe that Nicodemus' head must have been spinning by this time. Never had he heard such things as he did that night in his interview with the temple troublemaker. About three years later, these things spoken by Christ flashed again into his memory as he stood on Calvary's hill and watched this man die on the cross. Then it would all be different; he would put the whole picture together. He understood, believed, and was born from above as his Messiah had said. On that occasion, the wind of the Holy Spirit blew upon his soul, and he knew from whence it came! See all of footnote a above for further extra biblical details on Nicodemus' life.

2p-To object that Nicodemus was not saved because Scripture does not explicitly say this, is like arguing that Jesus or Paul never took a bath because Scripture does not say so. For more on this thoughtless form of objection, see asterisk under main heading in Section 40. The *American Declaration of Independence* reads, "We hold these truths to be *self evident*," meaning they need no written confirmation, since they are obviously true to men who can think. Scripture bristles with *many* of these beautiful "self evident truths," such as those that are mirrored in the life of Nicodemus. Those who so fiercely debate that "unless the Bible says *whatever,* it cannot be true," are unable to think very far. On the other side of the coin, this acceptable kind of common-sense reasoning may be distorted into the wildest of extremes to prove anything. The Catholic Church, for example, cannot prove many of its teachings from Scripture. Thus, it resorts to "tradition," the "apocryphal books," or some "Papal edict" for justification.

(l) He had broken Sanhedrin rules by coming to Christ at night, yet in this he proved that he did *not* love darkness. This wise old Pharisee sought spiritual light, and in time found it. Some three years later, he openly assisted in the burial of Jesus (Section 193, John 19:39 footnote i.) See footnotes b and c for more on this great man.

(m) Had not this "master of Israel" just demonstrated by coming to Messiah, that he was seeking light? In searching out the Lord Jesus, he showed that his deeds were being "wrought by God." See footnote l above. One's heart is touched with tears as we behold Jesus showing the utmost tenderness toward Nicodemus, an ensnared and struggling old man caught in the jaws of deadly self-righteous Phariseeism and the oral traditions of Israel. This grand old man longed for the kingdom to come. Despite his sincerity, he was wrong in his religious beliefs.

2p-There are millions of religious people and church members like Nicodemus; they stand in the same peril. Their only hope, also like that of Nicodemus, is found in John 3:16! It is not a matter of historically agreeing with this great text of truth; many do, but have never been saved from their sin. One must, at a deliberate point in time, when enlightened by the Holy Spirit and the Word of God, repent of their sin and exercise child-like faith in Christ as personal Lord and Savior: this brings salvation and eternal life. The mind or will to repent is given by God's grace; it may be accepted or refused by the individual (Rev. 2:21). This does not enhance or diminish grace; rather, it proves it is grace. Forgiveness and the new birth are *instantaneous* gifts of God, individually and personally received now in this life, and they last forever. All possibilities for eternal life vanish with physical death. The cessation of hope for forgiveness is solemnly expressed in the Scripture, "For to him that is joined to all the living, there is hope: for a living dog is better than a dead lion" (Eccles. 9:4). Death brings the end of all possibilities for human hope. Purgatory after death is an ancient pagan myth. In church history, it was a tool of terror used by the Roman Catholic Church to pry money from the poor and helpless. For more on the non-existent purgatory, see Section 45, second and third paragraphs under footnote g. *We mortals fail to remember that in eternity, there is no time, for it is endless; in time, there is no eternity, for time ends.*

3p-At the height of their wickedness, God pled with Israel, "Come now, and let us reason together, saith the LORD: though your sins be as scarlet, they shall be as white as snow; though they be red like crimson, they shall be as wool" (Isa. 1:18). What love and grace when He pleads with evil men to reckon with Him! In high symbolic language, our sins are depicted as being "scarlet" and "crimson." Double dipping, or dyeing garments and various animal skins in boiling hot metal vats achieved these colors. Thus, they were set, fixed, and permanent. There was a slight difference between "scarlet" and "crimson," made possible by adding a substance from the murex shellfish. White, over the ages, has been the emblem of purity and cleanliness. Wool speaks of that material from sheep, which had been purged of all dirt, grime, and spot, ready for human usage, being highly prized, costly, and continually sought after. It was adorned to show a different degree of social standing. Some see in this the new life that salvation brings. Divine forgiveness occurs when a lost person is saved, and it continues with him forever. There is no forgiveness in heaven for no sin is there (Rev. 21:27). All its citizens are perfect like Christ (1 John 3:2).

4p-Paul wrote in 2 Cor. 6:2 These words of good cheer for all who reach out to God, "Now is the accepted time; behold, today is the day of salvation." Religion without Christ is the number one curse of America and the world. God's salvation (apart from religion) meets the needs of the human heart, pardons all sins, saves the soul, enlightens the mind, and safely delivers the recipients thereof into heaven when physical life has ended.

Christ's disciples baptizing* in Judaea. John baptizing in Aenon.

See footnote c below for comments regarding two of the different places where John the Baptist baptized.

Matt.	Mk.	Lk.	John 3:22-24—*Judaea*
			22 After these things came Jesus and his disciples into the land of Judaea;[a] and there he tarried with them, and baptized.[b] **23** And John also was baptizing in Aenon near to Salim, because there was much water[c] there: and they came, and were baptized. **24** For John was not yet cast into prison.[d] (Verse 25 cont. in Section 32.)

Footnotes-Commentary

[a] The city of Jerusalem belonged to none of the twelve tribes. *The rabbis reasoned that Jerusalem belonged to all of Israel.* It was not counted as an exclusive possession of any Jewish tribe but was a separate entity within itself. Hence, upon exiting the Holy city one entered into another area or place in the land of Israel, which in this case would be Judaea. This passage informs us that Jesus, and His little band of disciples *went out* of Jerusalem and into the land of Judaea, *where* they continued baptizing until John was imprisoned. Our Lord's departure from the actual boundaries of Judaea did not occur until later in John 4:3-4, when He moved northward into Samaria.

[b] Section 33, John 4:2, footnote c, is clear that Jesus did not baptize. Here, a great question arises, "Why did Jesus have His disciples baptize His followers?" For a discussion of this question and relative inquiries, see Section 21, Part 4, Matt. 3:11, footnote n. Clearly, those who believed in Christ from John's preaching were saved and had everlasting life according to John 3:36. For a look into how people were saved *before* the cross, see Section 64, footnote k, and Section 144, footnote i.

[c] If John sprinkled his converts, why did he do so where there was "much water"? This text is explicit that he baptized in Aenon *because* of the large amount of water in that place. This was for correct baptism (which is by immersion) to be accomplished by all who had believed in Jesus as the Messiah. There is no other rational explanation of this statement; however, there are dozens of irrational ones. One Presbyterian minister said that people who baptize by immersion sin, for their candidates might catch pneumonia and die!

2p-John's message was for all who would listen. Why did John preach and baptize in the *Samaritan town* of Aenon if his message was for Israel only? Aenon was located some thirty miles north of Jerusalem and was not part of the land of Israel. For John, the Baptist's final words recorded in Scripture before his imprisonment, see Section 32, John 3:36, footnote e. The Jewish historian, Josephus, wrote many interesting things about John. See *The Works of Josephus,* Appendix Dissertation 1.

3p-Verse 23. "And they came, and were baptized." This touches deeply our imagination. Who were these "many," and what became of them? The word "many" is used by John some thirty times across his book. It never denotes a "few" or "small number." The idea here is that hundreds came and were baptized, showing outwardly their inward faith in Messiah. We ponder, "Did they continue to follow the Messiah?" As is was then so it is today. Over the centuries, millions have made professions of faith in Christ, then what? New converts must be instructed in the elementary duties of the faith and then into the deeper doctrines of Christianity. Grace saves us, but a life of works demonstrates that salvation for all who watch our lives. There is a mundane side to living by faith. The everyday responsibilities of work and living can became a heavy burden unless one keeps solid faith in the instructions of Holy Scripture, and their eyes on the cross and empty tomb. Slowly, time marches on and we move each day closer to the end of life and the beginning of eternity. A dairy famer once said, "The only bad thing about milking a cow is they don't stay milked!" The other side of the story is that if they did stay milked, he would soon be bankrupt. Thus, even the burdensome duties of life are necessary. We must not expect babes in Christ to be as we are in every detail. It is written, "Then shall the lambs feed after their manner" (Isa. 5:17). Adult sheep do not feed, as do their little ones. In time, they graduated from mother feeding and tail wagging. They need a higher food. We have been admonished, "And let us not be weary in well doing: for in due season we shall reap, if we faint not" (Gal. 6:9). Believers must not grow weary in well doing. Christ alone can give strength for the work, He bids us do. Even our Lord oft felt the pressure of time's brevity, and the necessity for doing promptly the work which God has given Him. On once occasion He said, "I must work the works of him that sent me, while it is day; the night cometh, when no man can work" (John 9:4). The tomorrow that men say never comes, is here today!

[d] **Christ *fully* began His public ministry when John the Baptist stepped from the scene.** Prior to this, He worked in a limited capacity. John, the writer, gave only this concise summation of the Baptist's confinement. He did not write briefly because he was attempting to "supplement" the other three gospels. Critics who reject the divine inspiration of God's Word invented this "supplement" myth. John wrote in this style because he was moved by the Holy Spirit to do so. For a harmonization of the verses that tell of John's later imprisonment, see Section 33.

John's testimony of the Lord Jesus given in symbolic words. He used the illustration of a Jewish wedding and the bridegroom's friend.

Matt.	Mk.	Lk.	John 3:25-36—Aenon
			John's disciples tangle with the Jews
			25 Then there arose a question between *some* of John's disciples and the Jews about purifying.
			26 And they came unto John, and said unto him, "Rabbi, he that was with thee beyond Jordan, to whom thou barest witness, behold, the same baptizeth, and all *men* come to him."**(a)**
			John responds to their question
			27 John answered and said, "A man can receive nothing, except it be given him from heaven.
			28 "Ye yourselves bear me witness, that I said, 'I am not the Christ, [Messiah] but that I am sent before him.'
			29 "He that hath the bride is the bridegroom: but the friend of the bridegroom,**(b)** which standeth and heareth him, rejoiceth greatly because of the bridegroom's voice: this my joy therefore is fulfilled.
			John exalts the Messiah-Savior
			30 "He must increase, but I *must* decrease.
			31 "He that cometh from above is above all: he that is of the earth is earthly, and speaketh of the earth: he that cometh from heaven is above all.
			32 "And what he hath seen and heard, that he testifieth; and no man receiveth his testimony.
			33 "He that hath received his testimony hath set to his seal**(c)** that God is true.
			34 "For he whom God hath sent speaketh the Words of God: for God giveth not the Spirit**(d)** by measure *unto him.*
			35 "The Father loveth the Son, and hath given all things into his hand.
			One of the great salvation texts in Scripture
			36 "He that believeth on the Son hath everlasting life: and he that believeth not the Son shall not see life; but the wrath of God abideth on him."**(e)** (Next chap., John 4:1, cont. in Section 33.)

Footnotes-Commentary

(a) The syntax of these passages reveals that the dispute between the religious leaders and John's disciples over purifying developed into a greater question that puzzled the Jews, "Why was Jesus baptizing more people than anyone else?" They were curious about why "all men" came to Christ for baptism ("all" is a euphemism for "many"). In the following passages, the Baptist proceeds to answer this enigma, pointing out that it was the plan of God for John to decrease and Christ the Messiah to increase. He was from heaven and above all. His glorious preeminence and superiority are mirrored in John slowly moving off the scene.

(b) **"Friend of the bridegroom."** These are symbolic terms. They have been sorely abused and have nothing to do with who is in the church or who is not. To imagine that he referred to the church in his use of the word "bride" is incorrect. The common expression "friend of the bridegroom" referred *only* to the person who attended and assisted the bridegroom during a Jewish wedding of that era. It is used in the Talmud in this sense in tractates, Berachoth 6b and Shabbath 114a. Today, he would be "the best man." The church, as *later* seen and defined in Paul's letters, was unknown at this point. For a look at Christ and the bride, see Section 21, number 10 under footnote q.

2p-Baptist bride radicalism. Among certain Baptists, there exists the sectarian teaching that John started the Baptist Church. He baptized Jesus and thus our Lord became a Baptist! From that time to the present there has existed an unbroken chain of Baptist Churches, which (of course) is the *true* Church of Christ! (All other saved people outside the Baptist Church are, at the best, somehow semi-Christians wandering about in ignorance.) Thus, the church is a Baptist bride! This teaching has its origin in the early 1800s with two Baptist ministers, Dr. J.R. Graves of Memphis, Tennessee, and Dr. J. M. Pendleton of Bowling Green, Kentucky. Prior to this, it was unknown in established church history! It is a theological pancake flop; a psychological response to the "Papal succession of the Catholic Church" and the hilarious "Church of Christ A.D. 33" signboards seen in the southern United States. Both Graves and Pendleton invented a Baptist response to these two heresies and then palmed it off on pastors in Baptist Churches across the southern United States. American missionaries, captives to this untruth, have carried this falsity around the world and created unnecessary problems among national converts.

3p-Decisional evangelism or easy believism. In many Baptist Churches across America today, people walk the isles during "revival meetings," shake the pastor's hand, fill out a card, and then told that they are Christians. Those without baptism are lowered under the water and become full-fledged *unsaved* church members! These religious rites within the liberal bent, social-club-style Baptist churches are a curse. The same game is played in other groups with a few alterations to their membership qualifications. It is another form of demonic deceit conning men, women, young people, and often children into hell when life is over. Religion without Christ is the trump card of Satan. It is played against humanity in the western world. No one is saved because of a "decision," "letting Jesus into their heart," or "raising their hand for prayer." Only when lost souls are faced with their sin, the damnation of hell, the cross, confronted with Almighty God, and His terms for forgiveness and eternal life will they be saved. For more on these thoughts, see Section 192, third paragraph of footnote g.

4p-For other details regarding the origin of this Baptist bride error, see the work *A History of the Baptists*, by R. G. Torbet, pages 281-282, 442. John said that he was "the friend of the bridegroom." According to eastern custom, this meant (as stated above) that he was the "best man" or "chief attendant" of the bridegroom. In verse 29, John reaffirmed that he was indeed the "chief attendant" of Christ, being His forerunner, the one who prepared His way and pointed thousands to Him. In this sense, John was truly His "best man." When Christ began His absolute public ministry, *after* John's imprisonment, the Baptist gradually faded from the scene (John 3:30). John's joy was complete as people flocked the Messiah. How many ministers today would vanish into obscurity, letting Christ have all the glory and honor? Everything spoken from verse 27 through verse 36 are the words of the Baptist. They reveal his insight into God's plan. Decades after John's death, his life, and work were spoken of in high esteem. Note this in such places as Acts 1:5, 22; 10:37; 11:16; 13:24; 18:25; and 19:4. See Christ's testimony of John *after* Herod Antipas murdered him in Section 52, John 5:33-35, numbers 1 through 3, under footnote w.

5p-Verse 30. "I must decrease." Great men have always had a small opinion of themselves and a big opinion of Christ and other. They joyfully give place to Him and others in the faith.

(c) "Set to his seal." Jesus' forerunner is not saying that no single person had ever received the testimony of Christ or that Israel as a whole rejected it. Verse 33 says that some did. In addition, each person who did receive His testimony had it confirmed in his heart (or "set to his seal") that it was God who sent Jesus the Messiah of Israel. The point is that more rejected the witness of the Savior than received it. Refer to John 1:12 with Rom. 15:7, and 1 John 5:20 for more on this thought. For an explanation of the Jewish understanding of "sealing," see Section 95, John 6:27, footnote d where it is used of God's absolute approval of Christ.

(d) "Giving the Spirit by measure" This rabbinical expression referred to the gifts of the Holy Ghost. The rabbinical understanding of "spiritual gifts" was based upon such verses as Ex. 28:3 and 31:1-6. They were different from those operative in the early churches. John states that the fullness of the Spirit came upon Christ at His baptism, and that grace, with all its gifts, became His as a man. Now He was prepared for His earthly ministry. Our Lord was "anointed with the oil of gladness [the Holy Spirit] above his fellows" by immeasurable unction (Ps. 45:7). From conception to ascension, His earthly life was under the calm direction of the Holy Spirit (Acts 10:38).

(e) John's final words before being imprisoned. If this is not John's personal confession of his life's message and preaching, then words mean nothing anymore. It refutes the error that he came and *only* "offered a kingdom to the Jewish people with Jesus as their King." This confession spoken by the Baptist has been used to lead thousands of lost souls to the saving knowledge of God's Son. In relation to this, note Section 25, John 1:29, footnote a. It is no accident that this was the last recorded statement (verse 27 through 36) of Jesus' forerunner *before* Herod Antipas imprisoned him. It is the truth of Acts 16:31 about twenty years in advance.

2p-A blessed farewell. What a marvelous way to step from the action of the ministry by proclaiming a clear confession of the only means whereby men can be saved from sin and hell! This is how John the Baptist ended his life's work. Looking back over the story, as he later wrote his book, John the ex-fisherman said of John the Baptist that he *did* "bear witness of that light" (John 1:8). He accomplished the greatest task on earth, faithfully witnessing of Christ. Few Christians possess the gift of oratory. Unable to speak with the charm of allegory, the beauty of metaphor, or the passion of simile, yet some of these continue to give all that mortality can give. Modest in victory, compassionate in judgment, these heroes of God are the *real* foot soldiers of the cross. Their life's theme and anthem is "Jesus, Jesus, Jesus!" Such are the lives that glorify God and will live forever.

3p-John's confusion during imprisonment. Section 62, deals with the suffering, frustration, and doubts of this great man while waiting execution at the hand's of Herod Antipas.

Hearing of John's imprisonment, Jesus leaves* Judaea for Galilee and travels north to Sychar, Samaria. The Pharisees are jealous of His work.

See asterisk under main heading of Section 21, Part 1, for length of John's ministry, and Section 92 for the details of his death. Matthew, Mark, and Luke were not inspired in the three verses listed below to write of our Lord's trip through Samaria and the events that occurred. They greatly condensed this part of Christ's ministry by writing only that He "departed into Galilee," "came into Galilee" and "returned to Galilee." John alone was inspired to give us this history of the wonderful things that took place as Jesus passed through Samaria while returning home to Galilee. See Sections 34–36 for His trip through Judaea, Samaria, and into Galilee.

Leaving Jerusalem-Judaea, He travels toward Galilee

Matt. 4:12	Mk. 1:14	Lk. 4:14	John 4:1-3
			1 When therefore the Lord knew how the Pharisees[a] had heard that Jesus made and baptized more disciples than John, **2** (Though Jesus himself baptized not,[c] but his disciples,)
12 Now when Jesus had heard[b] that John was cast into prison, he departed◄	**14** Now after that John was put in prison, Jesus came	**14** And Jesus	**3** He left Judaea, and departed◄ again
into Galilee;[d] (Verse 13 cont. in Section 38.)	into Galilee,[d] preaching the gospel of the kingdom of God, (Verse 15 cont. in Section 39.)	returned in the power of the Spirit into Galilee:[d] and there went out a fame of him through all the region round about.[e] (Verse 15 cont. in Section 38.)	into Galilee.[d] (Verse 4 cont. in Section 34.)

► With His departure from Judaea into Galilee, our Lord went straight north and passed into Samaria. He did not take the standard northward road on the east side of the Jordan River. See comments by the asterisk under main heading above. Spending several days at Sychar, Samaria, He leaves and then reenters Galilee as seen in Section 36.

Footnotes-Commentary

[a] In this text, John gives a second reason for Jesus departing Judaea and returning to Galilee. The Pharisees, with whom He had previously clashed in John 2:18-21, were raging over the swell of popularity on behalf of the carpenter. It haunted them that He had acted as though He was Israel's Messiah during the Passover. As Jesus had heard of John's arrest and imprisonment, the Pharisees had heard of Jesus' fame across the land. They were becoming dangerously hostile. Seeking to avoid unnecessary conflict, Christ moved homeward to Galilee, but en- route, He took the most hazardous road and passed over the Judean border into cursed Samaria.

[b] John the Baptist was held in high regard among the people, even by wicked Herod Antipas. See Section 92, all of footnote h. News of his arrest and imprisonment spread across the land. When our Lord "heard of this arrest," it was a signal for Him to return northward into His home province of Galilee. Apparently, He had not reentered Galilee since coming from Capernaum down to Jerusalem to present Himself as the Messiah at the Passover. For this Passover event and the uproar it caused, see Section 29, footnote a.

[c] **Jesus did not baptize.** That the disciples of Christ were baptizing seriously upset the Sanhedrin. One had to secure their special permission to "baptize legally" in Israel. Neither Jesus' disciples nor John the Baptist had this approval. Apart from this brief mention, we hear no more of Christ's disciples baptizing their converts. We may assume that those who became followers of Christ through the preaching of His disciples were baptized. At this

early point in our Lord's ministry, who were these preaching-baptizing disciples, unless they constituted the people gathered in during His tarrying in Judaea (John 3:22). No doubt, many were also converts of John and extensions of his work. Before this Judaean effort, Jesus had already met Andrew, Peter, John, Philip, and Nathanael, who after meeting the Messiah, returned to their fishing business on Lake Galilee some ninety miles north. Therefore, it seems they had nothing to do with this group of converts in Judaea. Note Section 26, footnote c for this original meeting. Our Lord had more baptized followers than we read about in the four gospels. As this took place during the early months of His ministry, it reveals that His impact upon the masses was great even at this early stage of His work. *Small statements that describe large events as these reveal that the four gospels are inspired for they only give brief accounts of the life of Christ.* Man would have never written it this way.

2p-For what were they baptized? These numerous converts of our Lord's disciples were baptized to show that they were believers and followers of Jesus the Messiah. The baptismal formula *as later used* by the church was unheard of at this time (Matt. 28:19-20). No one was immersed in the Name of the Father, the Son, and the Holy Spirit until after Pentecost. For the requirements laid down by John *before* anyone was baptized a disciple of the Lord Jesus, see Section 21, Part 3, footnote l. These demands show that an inward change was required and must be seen outwardly before baptism was granted. It is impossible to fit infants into these baptismal prerequisites. *It must be stressed that not all churches, which baptize infants and adults, do this for salvation.* However, those that do practice this untruth have swelled the ranks of the damned by deceiving both children and adults regarding the way whereby men become children of God. It has been pointed out that the church fathers introduced this pagan practice into the churches; later, the state church of Emperor Constantine forced infant baptism and sprinkling on the heathen masses under threat of death. This brought thousands of unconverted people into churches. Albert H. Newman wrote, "Pagans flowed into the churches, taking with them many of their pagan habits of life and thought so that by the time of Diocletian (died A.D. 385), the church was corrupt and worldly as never before." See *A Manual of Church History*, vol. 1, page 167. Newman also wrote that Constantine gave large amounts of money to all who would "convert to Christianity." See vol. 1, page 307. Later, the Roman Catholic Church came out of Constantine's ecumenical conglomerate became the religious terror of Europe, England, Ireland, and Scotland. Luther launched the Reformation (1517) and Calvin followed in about 1533. Both were infected by the false doctrines and practices of the Catholic Church. However, things did not start like this. John only baptized men who professed faith in the coming Messiah, and their lives demonstrated the fruits of this faith. The apostles and early churches did the same. This changed. For more on who caused this change, see Section 12, sixth and seventh paragraphs of footnote k.

3p-Negatives are a part of Christianity. Truth has both positives and negatives. The *truthful* comments in this book regarding the Catholic Church, various cults with their historical records of murder, political scandals, sex perversions, and false doctrines are directed at sins and heresies, *not* individuals. The ecumenical fallacy that as long as one is sincere in his religion, he is all right is notoriously negative and false. Refer to Section 95, sixth paragraph of, footnote r for an explanation of the "sincerity" plea. God has commanded us to take the saving gospel of Christ to mankind. Some will listen, and others will not. *It is wrong to be against any person trapped in a false religion, cult, immorality, political corruption, or whatever.* The lies that have ensnared them must be opposed and exposed. Without Christ, all men are equally blind concerning life, death, and eternity. Many believe hell is a "myth" and heaven is a "pie in the sky." Freethinkers and secularists declare that sin is the biggest fable since *Old Mother Goose,* and a soul is something on their shoes. The Bible they scorn teaches that heaven is a prepared place for prepared people. If men went to heaven without changed hearts, they would turn it into a hell of hate and evil. God distinguishes between being "good" and being "righteous." A righteous man may be good, but a good man (apart from Jesus Christ) can never be righteous. At salvation, divine righteousness is imparted freely to the convert. It justifies him forever before God (Rom. 3:21-24 with 2 Cor. 5:21). We can add nothing to make this gift of justification valid or effective. All humanitarian efforts benefit concerts, and sincere charitable deeds *apart* from Christ prove helpful for millions, but they cannot save us from hell. Christ is mankind's only Savior (Acts 4:12). By nature, men want to feel they have a part in their salvation and thus secure divine favor. It does not work that way! Divine truth has negatives and positives. Christians must stand for the right and against wrong. This is God's plan.

(d) For the approximate length of time Jesus spent in Judaea, between His baptism-temptation and return to Galilee through Samaria, see asterisk under main heading Section 35.

2p-Verse 14. "Power of the Spirit." His authority was obvious to the people. He was different. He had the power of God upon His Words, actions, and unique conduct. Mark records that Jesus preached the "gospel of the kingdom of God." There was no such thing as a postponed kingdom, put on the shelf for Jews, who would accept it over two thousand years later. The kingdom of God and Christ are the same, though manifested in two different forms. One is here now, and the other is yet to come. For explanation of this, see Section 39, footnotes a and g.

(e) This passage reveals how everyone was stirred who heard Jesus speak. This is another of the many texts confirming that the notoriety of Christ had spread over the land. Refer to Section 40, footnote g, and Section 42, footnote h for more on the fame of God's Son during His earthly ministry. For other examples of the powerful Words and commands of the Savior, see Section 87, footnote h; Section 124, footnote r; and Section 149, footnote c.

En route to Galilee,* He passes through Samaria and stops at a well near Sychar. Sending His few disciples into the city to buy food, Jesus meets a woman coming to draw water at the well where He sat. The Savior goes against rabbinical oral law by speaking to her and requesting water to drink.

*See asterisk under main heading Section 33 for more on Christ's departure from Judaea to Galilee.

Matt.	Mk.	Lk.	John 4:4-20—*At Sychar-Shechem*
			He asks a woman for water
			4 And he must needs go through Samaria.**(a)**
			5 Then cometh he to a city of Samaria, which is called Sychar,**(b)** near to the parcel of ground that Jacob gave to his son Joseph.**(c)**
			6 Now Jacob's well was there. Jesus therefore, being wearied with *his* journey, sat thus on the well: *and* it was about the sixth hour.**(d)** (12:00 noon)
			7 There cometh a woman of Samaria to draw water: Jesus saith unto her, "Give me to drink."**(e)**
			8 (For his disciples were gone away unto the city to buy meat.)
			She is offended: Jesus answers her question
			9 Then saith the woman of Samaria unto him, "How is it that thou, being a Jew, askest drink of me, which am a woman of Samaria? for the Jews have no dealings with the Samaritans."
			10 Jesus answered and said unto her, "If thou knewest the gift of God, and who it is that saith to thee, 'Give me to drink;' thou wouldest have asked of him, and he would have given thee living water."**(f)**
			She is puzzled over Jesus' Words. Another question
			11 The woman saith unto him, "Sir, thou hast nothing to draw with, and the well is deep: from whence then hast thou that living water?**(g)**
			12 "Art thou greater than our father Jacob, which gave us the well, and drank thereof himself, and his children, and his cattle?"
			Jesus responds
			13 Jesus answered and said unto her, "Whosoever drinketh of this water shall thirst again:
			14 "But whosoever drinketh of the water that I shall give him shall never thirst; but the water that I shall give him shall be in him a well of water springing up into everlasting life."
			She asked for the living water
			15 The woman saith unto him, "Sir, give me**(h)** this water, that I thirst not, neither come hither to draw."
			She must face her sins
			16 Jesus saith unto her, "Go, call thy husband, and come hither."
			17 The woman answered and said, "I have no husband." Jesus said unto her, "Thou hast well said, 'I have no husband:'
			18 "For thou hast had five husbands; and he whom thou now hast is not thy husband: in that saidst thou truly."
			She asks where to worship
			19 The woman saith unto him, "Sir, I perceive that thou art a prophet.**(i)**
			20 "Our fathers worshipped in this mountain; and ye [Jews] say, that in Jerusalem [at the temple] is the place where men ought to worship."

Matt.	Mk.	Lk.	John 4:21-27—At Sychar-Shechem
			Jesus responds: God can be found anywhere **21** Jesus saith unto her, "Woman, believe me, the hour cometh, when ye shall neither in this mountain, nor yet at Jerusalem, worship the Father. **22** "Ye worship ye know not what: we know what we worship: for salvation is of the Jews.⁽ʲ⁾ **23** "But the hour cometh, and now is, when the true worshippers shall worship the Father in spirit and in truth: for the Father seeketh such to worship him. **24** "God *is* a Spirit: and they that worship him must worship *him* in spirit and in truth." *"I am the Messiah"* **25** The woman saith unto him, **"I know that Messias cometh, which is called Christ: when he is come, he will tell us all things."**⁽ᵏ⁾ **26** Jesus saith unto her, "I that speak unto thee am *he*."⁽ˡ⁾ *The disciples return to the well: they are shocked at Jesus talking to a Samaritan woman* **27** And upon this came his disciples, and marvelled⁽ᵐ⁾ that he talked with the woman: yet no man said, "What seekest thou?" or, "Why talkest thou with her?" (Verse 28 cont. in Section 35.)

Footnotes-Commentary

⁽ᵃ⁾ **"Samaria."** At this time in history, the land of Israel was divided into three parts: Galilee, which lay to the north; Samaria, in the middle, and Judaea, located to the south. Galilee was under the rule of Herod Antipas. For details on this human monster refer to Section 21, Part 1, Lk. 3:1, number 3 under footnote b, and Section 92, footnote a. Both Samaria and Judaea were under Pilate. He was appointed governor or procurator by Emperor Tiberius in A.D. 26.

2p-The origin of the Samaritans is probably traced to the Assyrian conquest of the ten northern tribes of Israel in 722-721 B.C. (2 Kings 17:5-23). Most of the people from the northern kingdom were carried into Assyria. Those left to tend the land for their conquerors integrated with the pagans whom the Assyrian king transported into the area. In time, these Jews and pagans intermarried. From this union eventually came, more or less, the Samaritans. The descendants of these mixed people were not all idolaters. Zerubbabel refused to allow the Samaritans to join in the rebuilding of the temple at Jerusalem. After Samaria's conquest by the Greeks, Alexander the Great gave permission in 332 B.C. for a temple to be built on Mount Gerizim. This produced a complete estrangement between Jews and Samaritans. This temple existed for some two centuries and was destroyed in 128 B.C. by John Hyrcanus a Jewish governor and high priest. Samaritans would gather at this site for various rituals, worship, and reading the Torah Law that they greatly revered. Meeting at this place finds credence in the words of the woman at the well, "Our fathers worshiped in this mountain" (John 4:20). Thirty years after Jesus' conversation with the woman, Samaritans fleeing Roman persecution escaped to Mount Gerizim and fought off the opposing armies for a month until they ran out of water. The Roman siege on this stronghold resulted in the slaughter of some ten thousand men. They held that the first five books of the Jewish Old Testament were the exclusive Word of God, but corrupted portions of it to favor their position by declaring that Mount Gerizim was the place to worship, not Jerusalem. Samaritan extremism held that Noah's ark landed on Mount Gerizim and not the mountains of Ararat (Gen. 8:4). Establishing their own priesthood, building their cities, teaching their children, and marrying among themselves, the Samaritans became something of a formidable religious enemy to Israel. Samaritan belief in the coming Messiah is reflected in the words of the woman (John 4:25). To this day, the small community of Samaritans returns to this site of stone rubble (where once their temple stood) to worship!

3p-For a recent and comprehensive study on the literature of the Samaritans, see *Tradition Kept: The Literature of the Samaritans*, by Robert T. Anderson and Terry Giles. For a thorough examination of the Samaritans, see the older *Biblical, Theological, and Ecclesiastical Cyclopaedia*, vol. 9, pages 277-308.

4p-"He must needs go." This carries the meaning of "being bound." From the foundation of the world, Christ had an appointment with this sordid woman. His great heart was constrained by the Holy Spirit to travel this road en route to Galilee. All pious Jews avoided passing through any part of Samaria when going north into Galilee or beyond, because centuries of enmity existed between the Jews and Samaritans. (However, Jews would still do business and trade with these people!) Most Jews preferred traveling the longer route to Galilee by moving due east from Jerusalem, crossing the ford at Jordan and proceeding northward up the eastern banks. The bigoted rabbis, in their fierce hatred toward all Samaritans, had invented scores of dreadful and terrifying curses that would befall Jews, who dared set foot on Samaritan soil. The saying, "shake off the dust of your feet," originated with travelers doing just that, as they entered Judaea from Samaria or other Gentile lands. See Section 59, Matt. 10:14, footnote h with Acts 13:51 for other details. One can imagine the horror with which Christ's reluctant few disciples followed behind Him as He walked some twenty miles north of Jerusalem and crossed the well-marked border into the "cursed" land of Samaria.

(b) **"Sychar."** This was a more relevant name for ancient Shechem, for John says, "Which is called." Its etymology denotes "a lie or a drunkard," but more probably reflects Jewish hatred for the land and its people. The Jews were fond of imposing vicious names upon persons and places they disliked. Jewish variance toward these people was rooted deep in history. The *original* Samaritans were a mixed-breed nation, half Jew and half Gentile, who had been entangled with shocking forms of Devil worship through the mediums of pagan idolatry. Sychar was known by the Romans as Neapolis, meaning "new city." This is not the Neapolis of Acts 16:11.

(c) Jacob purchased one piece of ground from the children of Hamor and here Joseph's bones were buried after being extracted from Egypt (Gen. 33:19 with Josh. 24:32). He also took a piece of ground from the Amorite(s), who had stolen it from him. This he gave to his son Joseph (Gen. 48:22). Probably, these two pieces of real estate lay close together and became the parcel mentioned in John 4:5.

(d) **"Sixth hour."** Opinions differ about the meaning of this term. Some hold it refers to Jewish time or high noon, while others believe it is Roman time, in which days were reckoned from midnight to midnight. However, since the Jews always ate their large meal at the noon hour, and Christ had sent the disciples away to buy food, it seems to have been midday. Christ would not have walked the road to Sychar during the dark hours of the morning to arrive there at 6:00 am. No one did that due to the serious dangers involved. See Peter waiting for food to be prepared at the Jewish noon hour (Acts 10:9-10). Later, John used the Roman time system when writing about a particular aspect of the trial of Christ (Section 187, John 19:14, footnote i).

(e) **"Give me to drink."** It was strictly forbidden for a Jewish man to speak to a woman in public places. See the Talmud tractate, Berachoth 43b. The Talmud reeks with shocking words about Samaritan women, all of which mirror Jewish hatred for these people. See, for example, Talmud tractates, Nidah 31b, 32b, and Sanhedrin 101b. Few, if any, drew water during the merciless heat of midday. The climate is prohibitive: a converted Muslim Arab told the author of this in 1966, "The Syrian sun can kill from the 12:00 o'clock hour until the mid or lower afternoon." As the disciples made their way up the hill into the city, they passed this woman coming down with her waterpot balanced on her head. Having been brainwashed by the hate theology of their rabbis about the uncleanness of all Samaritans, especially women, the little band shuddered as she walked by.

2p-Verse 9. Approaching the well, she noted the stranger sitting on its low stone wall. He was a Jew! This was obvious by his dress, notably the fringes on his garment. Only Jews wore a white "tallit," or "fringes," while the Samaritans wore blue ones. These do not refer to the borders around the garments that were blue (Num. 15:37-40) but to the four corners, with something like a tassel hanging down from each one. For the Roman soldier's gambling over Christ's coat, some three years later, see Section 189, footnotes h and i. To the woman's shock, this male Jew looked into her face and spoke, "Give me to drink." She instantly responded by reminding Him of the fierce hatred that raged between Jews and Samaritans. Imperceptibly she felt there was something different about this Person. He was no ordinary Jew. He requested of her water to drink! This awakened a warm but cautious curiosity in her heart.

3p-One other time we have the record of Jesus asking for water. This was as He neared death on the cross. This was a fulfillment of prophecy (John 19:28).

(f) **"The gift of God" and "living water."** This has reference to the unfailing and eternal gift of the new birth. In the power of the Holy Spirit, Messiah introduced to her the greatest need of her life. (Later our Savior spoke similar Words in Section 95, John 6:35.) Moreover, He did so in terms of what she was involved in doing. In speaking with Nicodemus a few nights before in Jerusalem, Jesus had mentioned the "kingdom of God." In both cases, Jesus took their *immediate interest* and began to witness to them. To this base woman, at high noon in Samaria, Jesus introduced the "water of life" in the context of being thirsty. Here, again, by Word and action, Christ refutes the later erroneous teaching that He preached only to the Jews and offered them a kingdom and Himself as their King, but they rejected it. One may look for years, but he will never see a literal kingdom with Jews ruling the world in either of these grand discourses. (This is not to say that the kingdom will never finally exist, but it is to affirm that Christ offered neither Nicodemus nor this woman a physical, earthly kingdom.) For explanation of this kingdom, see Section 39, footnotes a and g. The Son of God carefully pleads with this poor woman regarding her *truest* need to believe in Him as the Messiah. And this she did at the well curb. Oddly, Nicodemus took some three years before professing openly his faith in Christ. Each of us comes to eternal life in God's own time and way.

(g) Void of spiritual understanding, she thinks only of physical water from Jacob's well. However, she was observant enough to note that Jesus had nothing with which to draw. Instantly, Messiah turns her attention to what

He has to offer. As in footnote f above, again our Lord declares that He will create within her innermost being (or soul) a "well of water springing up into everlasting life." This affirms that the salvation of Christ is never failing, always viable, continually sufficient, and is not temporary in its power to satisfy as the water from Jacob's well. Behold as the Lamb reaches out, seeking to lead this woman to fountains of living water.

2p-**"The well is deep."** Engineers have measured this well. It is about one hundred and fifty feet in depth, nine feet in diameter and cut out of solid rock. This reflects the skill of ancient masons in chiseling through stone.

(h) **"Sir, give me this water."** Now, enlightened by the Word of God spoken by our Lord, the woman asks for the water that would bring everlasting life. See footnote f above for explanation of this water that Christ alone can give. Refer to second paragraph of footnote l below for a discussion of when this woman was saved.

2p-**Verse 16. "Go, call thy husband."** It was a firm custom of the ancients for all business affairs to be enacted via the husband to the woman. First, she must understand her sin and repent. Courteously exposing her evil, Christ requests an interview with her husband. Upon hearing her confession, the Savior revealed to her His divine knowledge of human affairs with His assertion "thou hast had five husbands." Dr. Moses Gaster, in his work *The Samaritans: Their History, Doctrines, and Literature*, published in 1925, revealed that the Samaritans, like the Jews, could divorce, and remarry on the grounds of adultery. If so, we have firm insight regarding this woman's character. Either her five former husbands had died or were guilty of adultery, and she divorced them, or she was guilty of the sin, and they divorced her. The fact that she was living with a man in an adulterous relationship, not being lawfully married to him, suggests the latter. Hence, the Messiah deals with her sin. Stunned, she replies, "Sir, I perceive that thou art a prophet." As the prophets had supernaturally perceived the sins of the people to whom they were sent and pointed them out, so did Christ (Isa. 58:1 with Micah 3:8). Such confrontations signaled that they were being called to repent and turn back to God. The woman at the well understood exactly what Christ had said. For more on marriage and divorce, see Section 45, first and second paragraphs of footnote h, and Section 137, footnote g.

(i) Because the Words of Jesus proved Him to be a prophet, the woman perplexed by the age-long controversy, now seeks the truth from the "prophet" who sat before her.

2p-**Verse 20. "Our fathers worshipped in this mountain."** Again, we note the work of Moses Gaster, *The Samaritans. Their History, Doctrines and Literature*, page 42 reads, "The text of the Samaritan Pentateuch contains an additional tenth commandment, the Jewish ten being reckoned as nine; this tenth refers to the selection of Mount Gerizim as the Holy Mount and the place where the altar [of sacrifice] should be established." Hence, the origin of the strange inquiry of the woman to the Savior. She simply believed what their "doctored" Scriptures said. In verse 24 below, the Lord Jesus gave her the classical answer that continues valid to this moment.

3p-**Jews worship in Jerusalem.** No truth was more deeply rooted in the hearts of all pious Jews, then that Jerusalem and the temple was the only place for acceptable and divine worship of God. Centuries before, Daniel, a captive in far away Babylon turned his face to Jerusalem in prayer (Dan. 6:10-11). In the thousands of synagogues of the Diaspora, scattered over the known world, men would turn their faces to Jerusalem in holy prayer. The greatest longing of a devout Hebrew heart was for Messiah to come and restore the vanished glory of their earthly kingdom. Behold! See this Messiah, He has appeared and stands on cursed Samaritan soil, conversing with a despised woman of that land. O, the marvels of redeeming grace and the Son of God that brought it down to men.

(j) **"Salvation is of the Jews."** In answering her inquiry, Christ sided with Jerusalem and Israel. However, it hardly ended there. Our Lord proceeds to explain that her question is not as important as she, the Samaritans, and Jews had been led to believe. It was of no consequence at all, in view of what will soon transpire by an act of God. With the appearing of Jesus the Messiah, His life, death, burial, and resurrection, the old dispensation of both Samaritan and Jewish Law would pass away. Full atonement would soon be provided for whosoever will. Christ informs her that the worship of God, which had for so long been centralized into a single place would cease, and could be celebrated everywhere with God's acceptance in one place as well as another.

2p-**Verse 24. "God is a Spirit."** This hardly means that He is a non-entity! *Contextually* He was saying something like this, "God is a real spirit Person, who is everywhere at the same time or omnipresent, be it at Samaria or down the road in Jerusalem." We do not know nor can we explain the spiritual essence of God. However, we do know that it is not flesh, blood, and bones as we are. Nor is He the sun, moon, stars, an image of stone, metal, wind, sand, the fowls of the air or lower creatures. All such is the work of His creation. God is not mind, feelings, emotions, or thoughts. He has revealed Himself to mankind in the Person of Jesus Christ. All three divine Persons of the Godhead consist of ineffable and indescribable spiritual essence and are omnipresent or everywhere at the same time. Man also has a triune nature (or three parts) but different from the divine essence of the Holy Trinity. Christ is informing the Samaritan woman that God is to be worshiped in the Holy Spirit, and that He is not limited to any earthly temple. *He can be found anywhere.* John on Patmos illustrated this many years later in Rev. 1:9-10. Jesus the Messiah does not tell her there would henceforth be no worship of God, rather, that *true* worship of Him could be performed anywhere in the Holy Spirit. In addition, such worship would be apart from racial and national boundaries, temples, rituals, dogmas, creeds, candles, color, flow, and the bright pageantry of formal religion. Be it in a towering cathedral of London or a grass hut in Africa, *all men* redeemed by the blood of Christ, can find God wherever they are and worship Him in the Holy Spirit to the joy of their souls. *In heaven at last, we read that we "shall see his face" (Rev. 22:4).*

3p-The hypnotic power of empty rituals. Simplicity in the worship of God has been greatly replaced with ritualistic pomp and show. People glory in their illuminated cathedral ceilings, the colorful gowns of the officiating minister or priest, his physical antics, and pious words muttered from "the altar." Lent, the forty days of preparation leading to Easter, captivates millions. Some give up their golf, wine, beer, whiskey, and other *cherished things* during these days. Parishioners are enthralled as the minister speaks of our Lord's forty days fast, temptations, and so forth. Missing in this religious pageantry is the plea for unsaved men and women to repent of their sins and received Jesus Christ as personal Lord and Savior. Any ritual that does not finally point men to Christ for salvation is false and deceiving. Herein, is the curse of pompous church ceremonies without the Lamb of God. Genuine self denial for the Name of Christ is unconscious of itself, wist not that it's face shines but points other to Jesus. *It is uncanny how men are overcome by show, and shine, and lose sight of the old rugged cross and the empty tomb!*

(k) "I know Messiah is coming." Highlighted in gray because of its importance in history at this time. Both Samaritans and Jews were looking for Messiah to appear. The Samaritans had gathered this knowledge from the first five books of the Old Testament. Only these were held as inspired Scripture. The key passages in the Pentateuch for the coming Messiah are Gen. 49:10 and Num. 24:17. A notable feature of the Samaritan Messiah, believed by these people, was that He would "tell them all things." This included the history of their lives, the will of God, His plan for mankind, their political salvation, and how to worship Him acceptably. Further, they believed the entire world would be filled with the knowledge of God upon the appearing of the Messiah. At this point, suddenly the woman at the well was gripped with awe as it slowly dawned on her, "Is this Jew sitting before me the Messiah?" and "Has He not told me what we Samaritans believe Messiah will do when He appears?" Hence, her halting words, "I know that Messias cometh, which is called Christ: when he is come, he will tell us all things." However, the Messiah of the Samaritans was a mixed bag! He would be strictly a political person referred to as "Taeb," meaning "He who returns." He would restore all the Torah Law commanded and convert all people and Jews to the true religion found *only* in Samaria! As for the rabbis down south in Jerusalem, their Messiah would be a great fighter, and lead them into battle. Then He would die naturally after establishing world peace. One can see the bewildering descriptions of the Messiah of the ancients, each one trying to outdo the other. The New Testament is clear that the real Messiah is from the nation of Israel and Savior of the world.

(l) "I that speak unto thee am *he.*" Christ's reply reverberated like a thunderclap in her ears. For comments on the divine meaning of "I am," see Section 95, John 6:35, footnote i. Before her sat the promised Messiah of the Old Testament! This drawer of water was rocked like an earthquake! Flushed with joy and astonishment, she turned on a heel and raced through the steaming heat of that noon hour, uphill into the city. *She even forgot her waterpot!* Running through the gate, hands waving frantically, she shouts for all to hear, "I have found the Messiah! I have found the Messiah!" (To be correct, the Messiah had found her.) Never had Sychar heard such a proclamation. Had He not shown this truth some few weeks before at the temple in Jerusalem during the Passover? His claim amid the very elite of Jewish learning and sophistication had exploded like a bomb. He had emphatically said to the woman at the well that He was that divine Person.

2p-When did she believe? In verse 15, she asked for the everlasting water from Jesus. Infidel critics of Scripture are swift to point out that nowhere in the text does it say that she believed on the Savior. Later, in verse 42, the entire Samaritan community confessed that He was "the Saviour of the world." Surely, she was part of that citywide acclamation! Her conduct reflects that something glorious had taken place in her life. Men who have never been forgiven of their sins by the grace of God are good at picking holes in the lives of those who have. When Jesus affirmed that He was the Messiah, immediately her faith flowed into His acclaim, and she trusted Him with all of her heart. With this came instant forgiveness! How sad are the millions struggling in their churches amid rituals, prayers, confessionals, working for peace with God but never finding it. Men are saved the moment, they trust Jesus Christ the Son of God as personal Lord and Savior. This does not take decades of religious struggling. Upon hearing Jesus' confession, she trusted Him and became a child of God. *We never hear of her again!* So are the ways of God. One is raised up out of obscurity to do a work for heaven; when accomplished, they vanish from the scene.

(m) "His disciples marveled." Upon the disciples' arrival with food, she instantly left the well and returned to Sychar with her flaming announcement. They were stunned that their Lord was talking to a Samaritan woman! Such conduct was strictly forbidden to all moral Jews. We muse as to what kind of food they purchased, for the rabbis at Jerusalem had decreed that all Samaritan (and Gentile) eatables were unfit for human consumption. It was as though one ate swine's flesh to the Jews. See Lightfoot's *Commentary on the New Testament . . . ,* vol. 3, pages 274-278, for a good coverage on the subject of eating Samaritan food.

2p-Awe struck, the disciples were too fearful to ask their Master why He dared to speak to a Samaritan female. They had been horrified by His recent performance at the temple. Now, they are again shocked into speechlessness! "What will He do next?" was the thought that stormed their trembling hearts. If Peter was among this group of earliest disciples, at least on this occasion, he apparently kept his mouth shut!

Section 35: More wonderful events that occurred along the way as Jesus returned to Galilee.

Returning to the city, the woman announces Messiah has come! The disciples get a lesson on evangelism. After Jesus and His men spend two days with the Samaritans,* many believe He is the Savior of the world.

*The time from the baptism of Jesus (Section 22, Matt. 3:13) until His return to Galilee through Samaria (John 4:3) is crucial in calculating the early months of His ministry. Our Lord's statement in John 4:35, "Say not ye, 'There are yet four months, and then cometh harvest?'" throws light on this question. According to Lev. 23:5-7, 10, 11, 14, 15, the first fruits of barley harvest were always presented before God on the second day of the Passover week (though Passover lasted only one day), which fell in late March or early April. The wheat harvest followed about three weeks later. It has been noted that our Lord attended the Passover in John 2:13, then afterward made His journey into Samaria. While sitting on the well, He said that the harvest was four months off. He said this at Sychar, in either late November or early December. From that November-December forward, we calculate that the harvest of either barley or wheat was some four months off, which would fall close enough to the next Passover in late March or early April. Apparently, He lingered in Judaea for a short time after His baptism-temptation, and then returned to Galilee by way of Samaria, where He met the woman at the well. See Section 31, John 3:22, footnote a, for explanation of the statement, "After these things [meeting with Nicodemus] Jesus and his disciples came into the land of Judaea." Except for the short account in Section 33, John 4:1-3, silence covers this brief period of His life in Judaea before leaving for Samaria. See Section 33, John 4:1, footnote b, for the reason why He did not tarry in Judaea while His disciples were baptizing but left for Samaria.

Matt.	Mk.	Lk.	John 4:28-41—At Sychar-Shechem
			She hurries to the city with grand news
			28 The woman then left her waterpot,(a) and went her way into the city, and saith to the men,
			29 "Come, see a man, which told me all things that ever I did: is not this the Christ?"(b) [Messiah]
			30 Then they went out of the city, and came unto him.(c)
			A lesson on evangelism
			31 In the mean while his disciples prayed him, saying, "Master, eat."
			32 But he said unto them, "I have meat to eat that ye know not of."
			33 Therefore said the disciples one to another, "Hath any man brought him *ought* to eat?"
			34 Jesus saith unto them, "My meat is to do the will(d) of him that sent me, and to finish his work.
			35 "Say not ye, 'There are yet four months,(e) and *then* cometh harvest?' behold, I say unto you, Lift up your eyes, and look on the fields; for they are white already to harvest.(f)
			36 "And he that reapeth receiveth wages, and gathereth fruit unto life eternal: that both he that soweth and he that reapeth may rejoice together.(g)
			37 "And herein is that saying true, 'One soweth, and another reapeth.'(h)
			38 "I sent you to reap that whereon ye bestowed no labour: other men laboured, and ye are entered into their labours."
			Many Samaritans believed in Him because of the woman's testimony
			39 And many of the Samaritans of that city believed on him for the saying of the woman, which testified, "He told me all that ever I did."(i)
			40 So when the Samaritans were come unto him, they besought him that he would tarry with them: and he abode there two days.(j)
			Many more believed in Christ after hearing Him speak
			41 And many more believed because of his own word;

147

Matt.	Mk.	Lk	John 4:42—At Sychar-Shechem
			The skeptic Samaritans are convinced **42** And said unto the woman, "Now we believe, not because of thy saying: for we have heard *him* ourselves, and know that this is indeed the Christ, [Messiah] the Saviour of the world."**(k)** (Verse 43 cont. in Section 36.)

Footnotes-Commentary

(a) "Waterpot." Great speculation has developed over this vessel. Why did she leave it? Some believe that she purposely left it so Christ, and his disciples might have something with which to draw water and drink (John 4:11). From the viewpoint of the disciples, this would be impossible, in view of how grossly unclean they considered all Samaritans. Others conjecture that upon learning that the man on the well was the Messiah, in sheer joy, she raced to the city. Did she overlook it in her rush to go tell the city of Messiah? On the other hand, did she consider it a hindrance and purposely leave it behind? Whatever the reason, it sat there in mute testimony that something wonderfully drastic had happened in her life; she had in her heart a new well springing up into everlasting life. Bob Keyes, a late Texas pastor told me years ago, "She left the waterpot and took the well home instead!"

(b) "Is not this the Christ or Messiah?" Detecting the overwhelming earnestness of this *former* adulterer and inspired by holy zeal, the men of Sychar raced down that hill to see this great Man. At this time, the Samaritans counted themselves as the true Israel of God: thus, the Messiah would appear *only* to them. They considered the Israelites in Judaea, and Jerusalem were wicked impostors. The Jews of Judaea felt the same way about the Samaritans. However, the genuine Messiah had come to both. First, He came to the temple at Jerusalem where the Sanhedrin had rejected Him, and the fickle crowds clamored over His miracles; now He came to the woman of Samaria, and she received Him.

2p-This was her appeal to the men of her city. No explanation was needed, for all Samaritans understood what the term "Messiah" conveyed in their religious beliefs. With this, note Section 34, John 4:25, footnote k. Despite her notorious behavior and ill reputation, it strikes us that the men listened sincerely to her claim. Normally, most men would simply ridicule or laugh off such impossible religious exclamations, especially from a woman of this lewd sort. She was so changed that her male consorts were convinced. Her account of meeting Messiah was so plain, honest, and powerful that the milling crowds were also persuaded. Christ makes wonderful changes in those who trust Him in simple faith for the gift of eternal life. However, there were those among the number who would not accept her convincing testimony. See footnote k below.

(c) "And came unto him." The instant response of the crowds reveals that all of them understood the woman's words about "Messiah." They had been taught that some day this Person would appear. Now, they rushed down the hill from the city to investigate for themselves if He was there! Here again, the myth is exploded that no one in this era was really looking for that unique One predicted in Scripture. This is especially powerful when we remember that the Samaritans only used the first five books of the Old Testament, which were written by Moses. Thus, they found in these books God's promise of sending the "Anointed One," even the Messiah-Savior. For a look into what Moses wrote about the coming Messiah fifteen hundred years before His birth, see Section 52, John 5:46-47, footnotes y and z. *Appendix Three*, carries some forty prophecies about Christ, written hundreds and thousands of years in advance with Scripture references showing that He fulfilled them with exact precision. The entire hullabaloo by the infidel critics that the Pentateuch was written by a group of men over long periods of time is the united voice of satanic unbelief, not real biblical scholarship. Pointing to God's *two different* commands about the number of animals taken into the ark, variations in writing styles, Moses penning the obituary or record of his death and burial, demonstrates their ignorance of divine inspiration, and their rejection of God's Word. For a historical review of these "literary authorities," and their irreverent abuse of Scripture, see the *Author's Introduction*.

2p-Some believe that her appeal to "the men" refers only to the men with whom she had lived in adultery. This is more guesswork that is false. A gang of adulterers would not have invited the Savior into the city to spend several days with them! Rather, it refers to the people who habitually gathered about the city gates for business, buying, selling, trading, swapping, and exchanging of general talk and gossip. Like the Jews, Samaritan social custom forbade women to speak in public, unless by permission of father or husband. We are amazed at her boldness. The joy of sins forgiven and "the gift of God" offered by the Messiah were now hers. Moreover, it was manifested as "a well of water springing up into everlasting life" flowing from her soul. She arrested the attention of hundreds as they gathered in compelling curiosity to hear her story. The *living water* of eternal life washes away cruel social barriers! Eastern men can be quickly flushed into instant and uncontrollable mobs, filled with united passion over the slightest issue. Nevertheless, this was hardly the situation in the gate of Sychar. Hundreds of Samaritans hurried to shut down their businesses, ended their bartering, gathered friends and family and marched down the hill to see the Man sitting on the well. Whoever He was, He had made an amazing difference in the life of that ill-reputed drawer of water. They must see and hear Him for themselves.

(d) **"My meat (or food) is to do the will of God."** This was another common expression for dedication to a cause or person. As the men in the city were questioning the woman, down at the well, Christ's disciples were pressing Him to eat some of the food they had purchased. Their request was out of concern for His welfare. John penned that He was "wearied" because of the walk from Jerusalem that morning (verse 6). Messiah's answer puzzled them. What did He mean about having meat to eat that they did not know of? (Meat here is a synonym for food in general and not specifically eatable flesh.) Not understanding at this point the spiritual significance of their Lord's words, they could only assume that someone else had given Him food during their absence. Did they muse, "Was it that woman who gave our Lord food?"

(e) As Jesus spoke these Words, hundreds of Samaritans pressed through the gate of Sychar and made their way down the hill to the well. No doubt, their muffled but excited voices could be heard as they approached the man who had changed "that woman." We have here a beautiful piece of instruction given by Christ concerning soul winning. It was a living object lesson taught from a wellside as they all watched the Samaritans converging upon them. Apparently, one of the disciples had called their attention to the field of grain that lay westward before them in the long valley at the foot of Mount Gerizim. Further, one of them had commented that it was four months before it should be harvested. (That same valley is there to this day and still produces a vast harvest.) Upon hearing the comment that harvest was four months away, the Son of God points to the Samaritans approaching from the city. Multitudes of Samaritans were coming to hear His Words. Had He not just a short time before patiently sowed the seed into the heart of that dreaded woman? Already, it was bearing fruit, as those pitiful disciples were shocked to see that multitude of men being led by the woman straight to their Master. With this troop of lost souls in view, the Messiah announced that the fields were white unto harvest (see footnote f below). He urges that reaping must begin among them. This labor will be rewarded with wages from heaven. Some three years later, Philip entered a city eight about miles from Sychar and reaped a bountiful harvest from this earlier work of Christ. We read that great spiritual awakening fell over the land, bringing the joy Messiah had spoken of (Acts 8:5-12). Following Philip's evangelism, there were "churches throughout . . . Samaria" (Acts 9:31). We wonder, into which of these churches went the woman at the well, who in one day brought a whole city to Christ!

(f) **"White unto harvest"** This metaphor of Christ becomes even more acute when we remember that all Samaritan males wore long, flowing white garments. What a sight as they came down the path from the city! Oh, to see men as Jesus saw them! Note similar things spoken later by our Lord in Matt. 9:37-38.

(g) If the disciples would but learn that Messiah had come with the "gift of God" for all who believed, then they too could rejoice (1 Cor. 3:6-9 with 1 Thess. 2:19-20). However, witness about anything to the foul Samaritans was beyond their theological and moral comprehension. Later, Christ commanded them to go and preach in Samaria (Acts 1:8). See footnote h below for more on this blessed thought.

(h) **"One soweth and another reapeth,"** The source of this saying spoken here by our Lord, was possibly a blending of selected words from Lev. 26:16 and Micah 6:15. It was apparently a familiar expression. Over the ages, millions have been saved because of unknown witnesses who did the initial work of sowing, praying, and weeping for lost souls. In time, death swept them from life's drama without knowing of one convert to Christ resulting from their arduous and heartbreaking toil. At last, yonder in heaven's glory, *all* who shared, both known and unknown, will rejoice together. Note Section 165, footnote i for more on this glorious thought from a real life illustration.

2p-Verse 38. "I sent you to reap . . ." When and where this occurred, we are not told. Here, is another demonstration that we have only a small part of the life of Christ recorded in Scripture. If the whole story had been recorded, we would have hundreds of volumes to read and study. What God has given is sufficient for us to be saved, live a noble Christian life, and bring honor to God and assistance to our fellow men.

(i) **"He told me all that I ever did."** This was not an exaggeration as some assume. It was the absolute truth! John does not give the total conversation between Messiah and this woman. Only a small portion is recorded of the entire event. Christ exposed her sinful life, for this is exactly what she announced upon arrival at the city gates. As an act of grace, the sordid side of her checkered deeds is not recorded. Divine forgiveness of sin hurls them into the realm of eternal forgetfulness (Ps. 103:10-12 with Heb. 10:17). The Calvinistic jargon about God "not forgetting our sins" but "choosing not to remember them," is like the man who asked the difference between black and black. Two things are infinite, God and human stupidity! The prudent will leave their pardoned sins where God has put them. *Like last winter's snow, they cannot be found.*

(j) **"Two days."** Behold that wonderful sight, as the "cursed" Samaritans welcomed the Messiah into their homes. However, it was not so with the "religiously enlightened" Jews of Jerusalem. Most of them hated Him with fierce passion. With but little press of imagination, one can appreciate the sheer horror that gripped Jesus' disciples as their Master led them amid hundreds of Samaritans back up the hill and through the gates of Sychar. They were going to spend time among the most cursed and filthy people known to Jewish thinking! However, here amid this horrific situation was their grand opportunity to reap and gather fruit unto eternal life. It is of interest that the Samaritans entreated the Lord Jesus and gladly welcomed Him, though a Jew, into their city.

2p-News quickly spread to Jerusalem of our Lord's forbidden action by mixing with Samaritans. This is why the Jewish religious leaders later called Him a Samaritan (John 8:48), a loathing and slanderous term. Sadly, His conduct was not yet understood. One can see gentle Jesus meek and mild, patiently, lovingly struggling to teach these few disciples the chief purpose of His coming: "To seek and save that which was lost" (Lk. 19:10). It would yet take several years before these old-guard Hebrew men, imprisoned by the message of the synagogue regarding Messiah's work among men, could understand. Over one year later, the Lord Jesus added to their frustration, for when sending out the twelve apostles, He forbade them to "enter into any village of the Samaritans" (Matt. 10:5). All these seemingly conflicting actions and instructions finally blended into His death on the cross "for the sins of the whole world" (1 John 2:2). After most of His own Jewish people rejected His message of life, He turned to the Gentiles (John 5:40 and Matt. 21:43-45). Our Lord's final commission to His disciples was to take the gospel to "all nations" and "every creature." The Savior later gave the Great Commission five different times after His resurrection. These are listed in Sections 201, 203-206.

3p-Refer to Section 112, Lk. 9:52-56, footnote f, for another Samaritan village that later rejected Christ and the reaction from two of his apostles.

(k) Ancient skeptics. Among the crowd's gathering at the well were some that had rejected or were skeptical about the woman's testimony. After their personal investigation of the proposed Messiah and hearing His message, they were convinced. It was Christ's teaching that these skeptics "heard for themselves" that persuaded them (verse 42). He was "indeed the Christ [Messiah], the Saviour of the world." What a marvelous proclamation from these simple people! However, the custodians of the Jewish religion at Jerusalem had only hatred for all Samaritans. When Jesus finished His teaching, the Samaritans instantly understood that He was sent to bring salvation to the world. They approved of and trusted Him. (For a survey of Samaritan beliefs, see *The Theology of the Samaritans*, by J. MacDonald.)

2p-Jesus' message was clear. What our Lord taught these people is clear in the Scriptural record. He had come to provide eternal life to all men. How sad that certain theologians, evangelists, pastors, and Bible teachers have not yet learned what these poor Samaritans did. However, as it is today, so it was yesterday. For standing there, were the early disciples, blind at that time to the glorious fact of redemption for the world. Had not the learned Nicodemus, only a few days before stumbled over the same gospel? It remains true, for every age, that God requires all men, like the Samaritans of two thousand years ago, to believe His message to be saved (Rom. 10:17). With John 4:42, this unnamed drawer of water vanished from inspired sacred history. Her single work in witnessing for the Messiah is unparalleled in the whole of New Testament history! It will be a great joy to meet her in heaven someday. For other women who aided Christ, see main heading, Section 65, footnotes e, and h for details.

3p-Modern day skeptics. As doubters were among the ancient Samaritans, so it is today. Theological institutions across America are mostly in the hands of religious infidels. They have poisoned themselves as well as the minds of thousands of youthful students. Wolves now herd the sheep! An example is Professor Bart D. Ehrman, a "New Testament scholar" and "textual critic of early Christianity." He advertises himself as an "evangelical Christian, who is an agnostic." (Like the man who walked in opposite directions at the same time.) Ehrman apostatized from his "evangelical upbringing," renounced the reliability of Scripture, and the historical trustworthiness of the New Testament figure, Jesus Christ. He is so educated that he can tell you which verses of Scripture are right and, which are in error! A professor (of nonsense) at the University of North Carolina in Chapel Hill, he has debated on national TV, assuring us how wrong the Bible is. He even discusses whether Jesus rose from the dead! People like Ehrman are the friends of neither God, Christ, nor the souls of men. Imbued with their "superior knowledge" of the original languages, textual expertise, and early Christianity, they display their infidelity before millions. Having no Bible that is inspired and trustworthy, these "scholars" worship at the altars of their professional superiority. Brains are their gods as they arrogantly flaunt their heresies. The day is coming when they will curse their Antichrist intellect. Hope is found if they repent of their blasphemies and receive the Son of God as personal Lord and Savior. The internet "academicians" who boast of being "deconverted from Christ," and now preach atheism are called fools in the Bible (Ps. 14:1). They are like the court jester who assured his king, he could unring a bell. Ehrman and his kind will bow their knees someday to the Savior they have so "intelligently" maligned. At judgment, his *New York Times* listed bestseller, *Misquoting Jesus: The Story Behind Who Changed the Bible and Why* will testify against him. The root problem of these "experts" is described in 2 Cor. 4:4 and 1 Tim. 4:1-2. Their hope is recorded in Isa. 55:7 with 2 Tim. 2:26.

4p-Answering Dr. Ehrman. For a solid response to Ehrman (mentioned above) read the works of Dr. Timothy Paul Jones. His definitive writings demonstrate the satanic darkness that inspires Ehrman and his colleagues in Bible butchering. Jones dismantles the fables of the religious textual critics in his book, *Conspiracies and the Cross*. "Authorities" and "clergymen" who play scrabble with Scripture, "enjoy fellowship" with the enemies of the cross, and try so hard to be polite to Satan (who is the father of their lies) should look anew at the old rugged cross. *If they have been saved, then they need a fresh view of the Son of God dying for their sins, and beg forgiveness for their religious cupidity.* Jesus Christ clearly stated, "He that is not with me is against me; and he that gathereth not with me scattereth abroad" (Matt. 12:30). In plain English, Acts 4:12 and 1 John 5:12 affirmatively declare that it is Christ or hell, for all of us! *Which will it be for you, reader?*

Jesus departs from Sychar, Samaria, and reenters Galilee. He is welcomed by those Galileans who saw His miracles at Jerusalem during the recent Passover.

Matt.	Mk.	Lk.	John 4:43-45—Galilee
			43 Now after two days he departed thence, and went into Galilee. **44** For Jesus himself testified, that a prophet hath no honour in his own country.^(a) **45** Then when he was come into Galilee, the Galileans received him, having seen^(b) all the things that he did at Jerusalem at the feast: for they also went unto the feast.^(c) (Verse 46 cont. in Section 37.)

Footnotes-Commentary

^(a) News spread across the land that Christ, who claimed to be the promised Messiah at the recent Passover, had spent two days amid the vile Samaritans. This infuriated thousands of Jews living in Judaea and around Jerusalem. Because of this ill report, He testified that He had received no honor from most of His Hebrew people. Thus, upon leaving Sychar, He traveled northward to his home in Galilee. With the rumors flying, we now have another reason for Jesus' departure from Judaea. See Section 33, John 4:1, footnote a. His actions at the temple during the previous Passover had created great hostility from the leaders of the Jewish religion. Now, they had a juicy piece of gossip to use against this repugnant troublemaker: He had lived among Samaritans! A short time later, He would be rejected in His own home village and synagogue (Lk. 4:24). Our Lord repeated the same things about being rejected at home on that doleful occasion. Months afterwards, Jesus again used this expression on a return visit to Nazareth (Matt. 13:57, with Mk. 6:4). This is another example of Christ repeating Himself. Nevertheless, a group of every-day Jews had become sympathetic with the Savior as he fearlessly opposed the evil of their religious leaders. See second paragraph of footnote c below for more on this.

^(b) Among the pilgrims visiting Jerusalem during the recent Passover were many who had been attracted by Christ's miracles. Some of these were Galileans. They welcomed Him back to Galilee because of the miracles, they had seen Him perform in the temple (Section 29, John 2:23, footnote j). These were not the suspicious Jews, whom He later encountered in the Nazareth synagogue. Exactly, where He met these friendly Galileans is not stated, but apparently, it was not at Nazareth. His statement about rejection in His own country (verse 44) seems to refer to His upcoming rejection at the Nazareth synagogue a short time later. See main heading, Section 38 for an introduction to this sad story.

^(c) Jews from over the known world, as well as those residing nearby or in the land of Israel faithfully attended the Passover. See Section 29, John 2:13, footnote a, for a description of this grand event in Jewish history. The word "feast" refers more to a religious celebration than to a time of national eating and drinking. Passover only lasted one day followed by the Feast of Unleavened Bread, which lasted for seven days. By the time of Christ, the Jews had blurred the distinction between the Passover and Unleavened feast, which followed immediately afterwards. They often spoke of one as being the other. Refer to Section 167, Lk. 22:1, the second paragraph of footnote a for further explanation.

2p-Hypocrisy abhorred. The fierce rigidity about finer points of the law, and its observance came from a public display of self-righteousness among the Jews. The wickedness of Israel's religious leadership, the political and financial intrigues of the priests and high priests, the moral decadence in general had stained the entire system of Hebrew worship. The holy temple became something of a shopping mall of sin during the annual feast days. The religious leaders had reinterpreted or changed many of the commandments of Jehovah to comply with their carnal aspirations. Their oral law or tradition of the elders had been exalted about the written Word of God found in their Tanakh or Old Testament. Rules were made to be broken, and the great Torah Law was shamed and replaced with their pursuit for self-glory. At Passover, the most important national celebration in the history of Israel, an outward form of godliness was publicly displayed, meanwhile the scribes, Pharisees and other Jews continued in their godless conniving and deceit. The ordinary Jew was fed up with the religious hypocrisy that plagued their beloved temple but were helpless to bring about change. They were terrified of the Sanhedrin and their rabbis. For a review of the sordid condition of the nation during the ministry of Christ, refer to Section 21, Part, 1, the second paragraph of footnote b. The greatest foes of the Savior during His ministry were *most* of Israel's religious leaders. It is noted that many regular people in the early years of His ministry held sympathy with His teaching, for Scripture states, "The common people head him gladly" (Mk. 12:37). From the beginning of His ministry, the Savior exposed the wickedness of the religious men of Israel. For two of our Lord's scathing public denunciations of these charlatans and the terrible doom that was coming upon them about forty years later, see Sections 159 and 163. During the famous Sermon on the Mount, He again condemned the self-righteousness scribes and Pharisees before the people. Refer to this in Section 45, Matt. 5:20, footnote e.

In Galilee again, Jesus revisits Cana where He had recently turned water into wine. He performs a second miracle by healing a nobleman's son who was miles away.* This is the first recorded miracle in the New Testament of long distance healing performed by the Savior.

*See main heading of Section 60, footnotes i and j, for His next long distance miracle. Note Section 97, where Jesus delivered a little girl from evil spirits and was miles away from her bed.

Matt.	Mk.	Lk.	John 4:46–54—At Cana of Galilee
			Jesus meets the distraught nobleman: his pitiful plea
			46 So Jesus came again into Cana of Galilee, where he made the water wine.[a] And there was a certain nobleman,[b] [court official] whose son was sick at Capernaum.
			47 When he heard[c] that Jesus was come out of Judaea into Galilee, he went unto him, and besought him that he would come down, and heal his son: for he was at the point of death.
			Jews always required a sign: are you the same?
			48 Then said Jesus unto him, "Except ye see signs and wonders, ye will not believe."[d]
			49 The nobleman saith unto him, "Sir, come down ere my child die."
			He wants no sign but simply believed Jesus' Words
			50 Jesus saith unto him, "Go thy way; thy son liveth." And the man believed[e] the Word that Jesus had spoken unto him, and he went his way.
			51 And as he was now going down, his servants met him, and told *him,* saying, "Thy son liveth."
			52 Then inquired he of them the hour when he began to amend. And they said unto him, "Yesterday at the seventh hour [1:00 p.m.] the fever left him."[f]
			Everyone believed in the Lord Jesus Christ
			53 So the father knew that *it was* at the same hour, in the which Jesus said unto him, "Thy son liveth:" and himself believed, and his whole house.[g]
			54 This *is* again the second[h] miracle *that* Jesus did, when he was come out of Judaea into Galilee.[i] (Next chap., John 5:1, cont. in Section 52.)

Footnotes-Commentary

(a) See Section 27, John 2:11, footnote m for the details regarding this miracle.

(b) The word **"nobleman"** has reference to an officer or court official. This man, probably a Jew, was an official in the court of Herod Antipas, who was the ruler over Galilee and later the murderer of John the Baptist. See Section 92 for the details of John's murder. Antipas, currying favor with the Jews, sought to recruit them into various levels of service in his domain. Hundreds of Jews were in his employment. His vast military consisted of men from all over the country far and near; however, most of these were Gentiles. Being a son of King Herod the killer of infants, Antipas carried a dreadful family legacy. Note Section 18, footnotes d, e, and f, for King Herod's murders. Antipas' magnificent palace and court were located at Tiberias. Whoever this Jewish court dignitary was, he had heard about Jesus and His power to heal. Other persons in Herod Antipas' palace who came to know Christ were Joanna the wife of Chuza, Herod's steward in Lk. 8:3, and Manaen in Acts 13:1. The saving grace of God invades the darkest domains of sin and rescues *every* soul that believes in Christ. This nobleman was not likely the same person as Chuza, mentioned just above.

(c) **"When he heard."** Someone informed him that Jesus had re-entered Galilee. Surely, he had heard of the miracle at the wedding in Cana. By this time, word of His miracles at the recent Passover had spread over the land. With the good news that Christ was this close to Capernaum, there was hope for his dying son!

(d) It is the same today. Men always want to see something instead of believing. The world says, "Show me and

I'll believe." God says, "Believe, and in time I will show you." Christ's Words were a gentle rebuke to another sign-seeking Jew. Refer to Section 29, John 2:18, footnote e, for the Jew's *first* request of Jesus for a Messianic sign. In addition, note the answer He gave them!

(e) Amazingly, this broken, distraught father simply believed the statement of Jesus, even though the Savior refused to come to his house (verse 49-50). See Heb. 11:6. Christ healed the child long-distance, for at this moment He was at Cana, which was some twenty-five miles southwest of Capernaum.

(f) **"The fever left him."** This is the first recorded miracle of Christ healing a sickness and not being present with the patient. For the next, see Section 60, footnote j. The nobleman had walked through the night to return home, since Cana was almost a day's journey from Capernaum. Upon hearing the report of his servants regarding the exact time his son became well, he computed it was 1:00 o'clock the previous afternoon. This was the same time Jesus spoke healing for his son, who was many miles away at Capernaum. *Simple faith in the Word's of our Lord is not restricted by distance.* See footnote e above. Note the example of Jesus casting an evil spirit out of a little girl when she was several miles away. This is recorded in Section 97.

(g) A close-knit family, they all shared in the agony of the child's pending death. Now, they all "believe" that Jesus is the Messiah, the Son of God. This included the servants. The sickness of the child became the channel of salvation for the entire household. How often over the course of church history, has calamity turned men to the saving grace of God? Fanny J. Crosby, the famed hymn writer, who lost her eyesight as a newly born infant was used of the Lord all of her life. She later testified that her blindness was the channel that brought her into the eternal light and sight!

(h) **"The second miracle."** John is not reporting that these are the *only* two miracles of Jesus up to this point. Messiah had previously shaken the Jews by His miracles at the Passover down south at Jerusalem. Verse 54 reports His first miracle upon returning to Galilee at this time, but it was His second miracle performed in that *area* of the state. The first, was turning the water to wine at Cana, a city also in Galilee. This miracle is reported in Section 27. Note Section 38, footnote j, for comments on other unrecorded miracles performed by Jesus somewhere in the vicinity of Capernaum.

(i) **John's one year of silence.** This verse ends with Jesus back in Galilee after attending Passover (John 2:13), the discourse with Nicodemus (John 3), His stay in Sychar (John 4), and healing the nobleman's son John 4:46-54). Suddenly, and to our surprise in John 5:1 we now find the Lord Jesus back at Jerusalem to attend "a feast of the Jews." It is *conjectured* by the author that this passage speaks of the annual Passover. If correct, this means we have a silent period of about one year between the end of chapter 4 and the beginning of John 5:1. Here, is another one of the peculiar marks of inspiration. What John did not write about during this year, the other evangelists partially covered as they were led by the Holy Spirit to write their respective narratives of the life of Christ. The gap left by John is generally covered in Sections 38 to 52 of this harmony.

2p-Alfred Edersheim in his *Life and Times of Jesus the Messiah,* page 319 calls this "The unknown feast." See further comments on this in Section 52, footnote b. Matthew Henry, in his *Commentary on the Whole Bible,* volume 5, page 741, holds that it was the annual Passover celebration. The excellent Albert Barnes wrote, "Probably the Passover, though it is not certain." See *Barnes' Notes on the Gospels,* page 224. As explained above it is conjecture that this was a Passover celebration. If this is wrong, then the length of Jesus' public ministry is shortened to somewhere reasonably less than three years.

His first recorded preaching tour across Galilee is completed.* Jesus returns to Nazareth and speaks in the hometown synagogue. They attempt to kill Him.** He escapes and departs Nazareth for Capernaum and Lake Galilee.

*At least four other tours of Galilee are recorded apart from this one ,which apparently He made without any of His disciples. They are as follows: Section 39 for a second tour, Section 42 the third, Section 56 a fourth, and Section 65 for the fifth trip. . The number of disciples with Him on these last four mission trips varies. See Section 91 for His second preaching endeavor in the Nazareth synagogue and the outcome.** See a possible harmonized supplemented view of this tumultuous event in the next Section.

Nazareth / Capernaum and Sea of Galilee

(Matt. 4:13–16)	Mk.	Lk. 4:15–23	John
		15 And he taught in their synagogues, being glorified of all.	
		Tour ends at home: He reads Scripture in synagogue on the Sabbath day	
		16 And he came to Nazareth,[(a)] where he had been brought up:[(b)] and, as his custom was, he went into the synagogue on the sabbath day, and stood up for to read.[(c)]	
		17 And there was delivered unto him the book of the prophet Esaias. [Isaiah] And when he had opened the book, he found the place where it was written,	
		18 "The Spirit of the Lord *is* upon me, because he hath anointed[(d)] me to preach the gospel to the poor; he hath sent me to heal the brokenhearted, to preach deliverance to the captives, and recovering of sight to the blind, to set at liberty them that are bruised,	
		19 "To preach the acceptable year of the Lord."[(e)]	
		20 And he closed the book, and he gave *it* again to the minister, and sat down. And the eyes of all them that were in the synagogue were fastened on him.	
		21 And he began to say unto them,[(f)] "This day is this Scripture fulfilled in your ears."	
		22 And all bare him witness, and wondered at the gracious words which proceeded out of his mouth.[(g)] And they said, [among themselves] "Is not this Joseph's son?"[(h)]	
		23 And he said unto them, "Ye will surely say unto me this proverb,[(i)] 'Physician, heal thyself: whatsoever we have heard done in Capernaum,[(j)] do	

Matt. 4:13–16	Mk.	Lk. 4:23–30	John
		also here in thy country.' "	
		24 And he said, "Verily I say unto you, No prophet is accepted in his own country."	
		Two examples of past Jewish unbelief	
		25 "But I tell you of a truth, many widows were in Israel in the days of Elias, [Elijah] when the heaven was shut up three years and six months, when great famine was throughout all the land;	
		26 "But unto none of them was Elias [Elijah] sent, save unto Sarepta, [Zarephath] *a city* of Sidon, unto a woman *that was* a widow.	
		27 "And many lepers were in Israel in the time of Eliseus [Elisha] the prophet; and none of them was cleansed, saving Naaman the Syrian."	
		Enraged at His *lesson they attempt to kill Him*	
		28 And all they in the synagogue, when they heard these things, were filled with wrath,(k)	
		29 And rose up, and thrust him out of the city, and led him unto the brow of the hill whereon their city [Nazareth] was built, that they might cast him down headlong.(l)	
		He mysteriously escapes to Capernaum	
In going to Capernaum *He fulfills Old Testament prophecy*		**30** But he passing through the midst of them went his way,(m) ◄ (Verse 31 cont. in Section 40.)	

13 And leaving Nazareth, ◄ he came and dwelt in Capernaum, which is upon the sea coast, in the borders of Zabulon and Nephthalim:

14 That it might be fulfilled which was spoken by Esaias [Isaiah] the prophet, saying,(n)

15 "The land of Zabulon, and the land of Nephthalim, *by* the way of the sea, beyond Jordan, Galilee of the Gentiles;

16 "That the people which sat in darkness saw great light;(o) and to them which sat in the region and shadow of death light is sprung up." (Verse 17 cont. in Section 39.)

►Luke wrote that Christ "went his way" (verse 30). Matthew takes up the narrative in verse 13 with the words "And leaving Nazareth." He records how Jesus, by moving into Galilee, fulfilled another Old Testament prophecy. Again, Matthew demonstrated to his Jewish readers that Jesus was the Messiah of Israel as He fulfilled the meanings of numerous predictions in their Old Testament called the Tanakh or scrolls. The word "Tanakh" is an acronym based on the three sections of the Hebrew Bible. The first section is the "**T**orah" and speaks of its first five books, called "the Pentateuch." The second part is known as "the prophets" or **N**evim. Lastly, **K**ethuvim is the third section, which Jews call "the writings." From these three underlined letters, the word "Ta**nak**h" is derived.

155

Footnotes-Commentary

(a) **Verse 15, "Synagogues."** For a brief explanation of the Jewish synagogue, refer to Section 89, footnote c, footnote c below. A non-Christian Hebrew, Dr. Lee I. Levine produced a comprehensive study into this fascinating subject in, *The Ancient Synagogue. The First Thousand Years.* This work is a feast of learning for anyone interested in this topic. For other meticulous details on synagogue functions, see *A History of the Jewish People in the Time of Jesus Christ*, vol. II, Second Division, pages 80-83, by Emil Schurer. *Judaism*, vol. l, pages 296–307, by George Foot-Moore, also carries a short but unique explanation of the workings of the ancient synagogue.

2p-Some hold this was Jesus' first return to Nazareth since leaving for Bethabara, Jordan, months before when He was baptized by John. See Section 22, Mk. 1:9, footnote b. This may or may not be so. At this occasion upon His return to the Nazareth synagogue, the people were already familiar with a wave of miraculous works He had performed during some previous time at the city of Capernaum (Lk. 4:23). Luke 4:14 explicitly tell us that He had previously made a tour across Galilee and had received a large measure of acceptance among the people. The term, "being glorified of all" in verse 15 is indicative of this. Jesus' return to His hometown and the local synagogue was *after* this Galilean tour, which apparently included His unknown miracles at Capernaum. Hence, the congregation's knowledge of His great deeds performed in that city (verse 23). See footnote j below. This reveals that early in His ministry, the country was buzzing with news of this young man from Nazareth claiming to be Israel's Messiah. As Nazareth was about six miles from Cana, surely the people of Christ's home village had heard of His miracle in turning the water to wine. This had occurred some months prior. However, despite this the people of Nazareth were filled with skepticism, which swiftly turned into fierce hatred as they heard Him preach. A second visit of our Lord to Nazareth is recorded in Section 91. Some hold this was many months later in his ministry. See the supplement attached to the end of this Section for an alternate harmonized view of this question.

(b) **"Where he had been brought up."** Again, see Section 19, Lk. 2:39, footnote a.

(c) **"Stood up for to read."** Synagogue services at this time were normally held on Mondays and Thursdays, these being the normal market days when the country people came into the nearby towns. Then there were the regular Sabbath services, of which this was one. With the words "his custom was," the text is clear that our Lord had regularly attended His hometown synagogue. Having grown up at Nazareth and attended this synagogue from childhood days (boys normally began at the age of five years), He was often selected to participate as a "reader of Scripture" during the worship time. Stepping through the low-set door of the synagogue, the "chazzan," or "minister," saw Jesus and assigned Him a portion of Scripture to be read at that service. It was not uncommon for seven different persons to give selected readings from the law and the prophets during the morning Sabbath meeting. This order varied for the afternoon synagogue service, which ended before sundown. It was mandatory for those who read from the prophets to stand and pendantly articulate a minimum of three sentences. The minister carefully removed the scroll of Isaiah from the "chest" or "ark" set into the wall just behind the bema platform; and, signaling Jesus to come forward and read, placed it onto the reading desk. The congregation stood, and all eyes were fastened on Him! They had heard rumors of His miracles done at Capernaum, a large fishing town located some twenty miles away on the northwest edge of the Sea of Galilee. The skeptical crowd mused, "Will this self-asserted hometown 'Messiah' do any amazing works here?"

(d) Written in Isa. 61:1-2. **"Messiah" or "Christ" always means "the anointed One."** See Section 5, left column, footnote a, footnote g below. From Isaiah, the Lord Jesus read a seven hundred-year-old prophecy pointing to Himself. His gripping voice seized the attention of every ear in that synagogue. There He stood, the "Son of Joseph." In a few moments, He was explaining that these Scriptures pointed to Him, the Messiah of Israel, the true anointed One. The entire audience was shocked to no end at such an announcement from the lips of this hometown lad, a village carpenter.

(e) Standing on the bema platform at the far end of the synagogue, "the son of Joseph" slowly unrolled the parchment until He found a specific "place where it was written." He deliberately searched for a foreknown portion of Scripture. Upon locating this, He read only two verses! The audience was stunned, for according to rabbinical rules, at least three parts must be read. Passing the scroll back to the minister who returned it to the "chest," Christ moved to the left and was seated in the synagogue chair. All teachers sat as they taught. After reading, the individual assigned to this work would normally make his way back into the congregation and be seated. A Jew known as the "methurgeman" (interpreter) would then step to the platform and proceed to explain the reading in the Aramaic language. This was for the benefit of younger Jews, who were not carefully familiar with their parent Hebrew tongue. It was called targumizing. For more on this subject, see Section 1, Part 1, fifth paragraph of footnote b. Christ shocked the congregation by becoming *both* the reader, and the expositor of the two Scriptures.

(f) **The Savior's sermon.** Dr. Lee I. Levine's great work (mentioned in footnote a above) gives the following explanatory comments on page 157. "The New Testament makes it crystal clear that the sermon (the exposition of an idea that appears in the scriptural reading) was a recognized component of the Sabbath service. The verbal exegesis of the Scripture reading became central to Jewish worship." However, Jesus' sermon was different! It exploded like a thunderstorm upon the congregation! Every adult Jew present knew very well, that the two passages read from Isaiah spoke exclusively of the supernatural works to be done by their coming Messiah. Spellbound, they listened with tingling ears as "the son of Joseph," the boy who had grown up in their town, whom everyone knew, sat before them in the sacred synagogue chair, and proclaimed Himself the Messiah! "This day is this Scripture fulfilled in your ears," He declared. In essence, He was saying, "I am the Person these prophecies speak of. I am the anointed One from God. I am your Messiah and have done at Capernaum the miracles predicted by Isaiah." He had presented Himself as Messiah at the recent Passover at Jerusalem and was rejected. This was His claim to the Samaritan woman, and it was believed with great joy. Now, weeks later, before hundreds of friends, neighbors, and even family members, the young village carpenter again makes this astounding announcement. The dark clouds of Jewish unbelief and hatred quickly gathered.

(g) Christ's teaching proved that He was "anointed" with the Holy Spirit (as in the text He had just read predicted). Our Lord spoke with pungent, powerful sentences; each one anointed by the indwelling Holy Spirit. Refer to Section 22, Lk. 3:21-22, footnote e, for Messiah's *original* first and only anointing with the Spirit at His baptism. The terse and masterful authority of His diction, the grace from His lips, the loving firmness of His countenance, and the moving tones of divine sincerity captured the attention of every soul. The atmosphere was electric! Their minds churned with silent reasoning, "But this is Joseph's son. He has never learned letters or sat at the feet of our great rabbis. He never attended any theological academy. From whence does he receive this spiritual power to speak? Has the son of Joseph gone mad?" Among that vast congregation were many Jews, who had already heard whisperings of His fantastic miracles performed earlier at Capernaum (verse 23). Some of these had also seen His miracles at the Passover in Jerusalem (John 2:23). Despite their awe over His powerful anointing to speak, fierce resentment rose in their hearts as He continued. It would shortly erupt into open rejection and violence. See footnote l below for the battle that exploded in the synagogue at Nazareth that Sabbath morning.

(h) "**Is not this Joseph's son?**" The Jews said, "Whoever rears a boy is called his father." Refer to Section 7, number 4 in block. It was from a loving heart that Joseph referred to Jesus as his son. Neither he nor Mary at this point could dare relate the entire story of His birth. Read Section 14, Lk. 2:19, footnote h for more on this thought. As Jesus grew up at Nazareth, it was natural and normal for all to refer to Him as Joseph's son; none of them, at this time, knew the truth of His birth.

(i) **A well-known proverb.** From the viewpoint of our Lord's claim to be the Messiah, it meant that the people were thinking in their hearts, "We have heard of your miracles done at Capernaum. Now, perform further signs and wonders here, in your hometown, and prove that you are our Messiah. Do this and we will believe in you." See Section 37, John 4:48, footnote d for relevant comments.

(j) "**We have heard.**" This reveals that Jesus had previously been in Capernaum and had stirred the city with His mighty miracles. News of this had quickly spread to Nazareth. See footnote a above. At what time this occurred in His *earlier* ministry, we are not informed. His brief visit to Capernaum noted in John 2:12, does not seem to fit the time frame required for such broadly heralded miracles to be performed. It is certain that this happened *before* His return to the synagogue at Nazareth as recorded in Lk. 4:16, for everybody in town had heard of it.

(k) This response reveals that Christ knew the thoughts of their hearts. He set before them two examples from their well-known history. Both illustrations proved that the Jews had previously rejected God's man with God's message on other occasions. Because of this rejection, the genuine prophets of God turned to the Gentiles, who were ready to believe. These two case histories in Israel were as follows:

1. Elijah had turned from the stubborn Hebrews of his day and was sent by God to a Gentile woman (1 Kings 17:8-24).
2. Conversely, a heathen army officer, Naaman, was sent to Elisha (2 Kings 5:1-27). In these illustrations, a pagan Gentile and the heathen military officer found the true religion and the true God of heaven. The Jews sitting in that synagogue would shortly try to kill Jesus because of the Words He had spoken.

2p-"Kill Him." In the Nazareth synagogue, before angry, hard-line Jews, our Lord clearly intimates the fate of Israel due to their final rejection of Him and the calling of the Gentiles into His kingdom. Absolutely, nothing would be more grating to their ears than to be reminded that, as a nation, they had a woeful record of trampling truth underfoot and opposing the prophets God had sent to rescue them. The Savior mentioned this rejection later in Matt. 23:29-36. Everyone in the congregation understood what "the son of Joseph" was implying by these remarks taken from Hebrew history. Hence, their uncontrolled anger and open ferocity. "How dare this village upstart to preach such things in our beloved synagogue," were the thoughts of many. Strict rules regulated the conduct of Jews attending Sabbath service. They were to be clean, neatly dressed but with great simplicity, serious in mood, and refrain from all loud or boisterous talk. Any sort of physical conflict was forbidden in the "house of the congregation," as it was often called. We should remember that our Lord and His human family were all brought up in this place. It was part of His life as a Hebrew and member of the great nation of Israel. The calm serenity that had always prevailed in the Jewish synagogue exploded into a maddened riot. The congregation, highly incensed at Jesus' statements, leaped from their seats, and rushed forward to kill Him! He had seriously offended the citizens of His hometown. To give the unclean pagan Gentiles credit for anything was highly offensive.

(l) **"Cast him down headlong."** This was done prior to stoning a victim, in hope that his neck would break and instant death would ensue. The tranquility of that peaceful Nazareth synagogue turned into a scene of violence! Typical of incensed eastern fanatics, the Jews stormed the bema platform and seized Jesus. Pushing Him out of the synagogue, they forced Him to the nearby edge of a forty-foot precipice. Their evil intentions were to dash Him on the jagged stones below, then stone Him. Blinded by demonic rage, these angry Jews paid no attention to the laws of their rabbis who forbade creating a disturbance or taking life on the Sabbath day.

(m) **The mysterious escape.** This is the second recorded attempt on His life. The first was by Herod the Great. For comments on this, note the main heading under Section 18, Matt. 2:16, footnote d. How the Lord Jesus escaped from this second effort to kill Him by a synagogue mob is not explained. John 8:59 records a later event when our Savior hid Himself from the Jews at Jerusalem seeking to stone Him. It seems incorrect to hold that He used the same disguise as employed a few years later, following His resurrection, while on the road to Emmaus (Lk. 24:16).

2p-For another pending threat on the life of Christ and His apostles, see Section 93, footnote a. In this Section our Lord, avoiding the rage of Herod Antipas, took His disciples and crossed the sea. Below are four other examples of the hostility of the Jews against Jesus recorded only by John. The four below occurred at different times from those given above.

1. At the recent Passover (John 2:13-18).
2. By baptizing more converts than John (John 4:1-3).
3. By spending several days among the Samaritans. See Section 36, John 4:44, footnote a.
4. This outburst of anger was, of all places, in His hometown synagogue at Nazareth. Each time it was because He had performed great works and/or claimed to be their Messiah. Refer to Section 123, John 10:39, footnote j for another narrow escape near the close of His ministry.

(n) Quoted from Isa. 9:1-2. The rabbis interpreted these verses as pointing to their Messiah. Matthew applied these passages to Jesus, making them the same Person. Matthew's original Jewish readers would have instantly understood what he was presenting to them.

(o) **"Light"** was one of the numerous Names given by the rabbis to their coming Messiah (Isa. 60:1-3). See more on this Messianic title in Section 1, Part 1, footnote e. Pagan nations believed, as did the Hebrews, that death stood between them and the sun. Thus, it cast a long and dark shadow across the whole world. This is also mentioned in Job 3:5; Ps. 23:4; and Jer. 2:6. The ancient Jews taught that only Messiah could abolish the horrible shadow of death. This is a prediction of Gentiles coming to the Messiah. Matthew, in citing this passage from Isaiah, would capture the attention of every astute Jewish reader. Clearly, he was proving again from their Scriptures that Jesus of Nazareth was the Messiah of Israel and that Israel has rejected Him. Thus, He turned to the Gentiles.

2p-At the moment of salvation, Gentiles (and all men) are baptized by the Holy Spirit into the spiritual kingdom of God and Christ (Rom. 6:3; Gal. 3:27; and 1 Cor. 12:13). This kingdom is also called "house" in Heb 3:6, a "spiritual house" in 1 Peter 2:5, and a habitation of God through the Spirit" in Eph. 2:22. Of this, Adam Clark wrote, "That the calling of the Gentiles was made known by the prophets in different ages of the Jewish Church is exceedingly clear; but it certainly was not made known in that clear and precise manner in which it was now revealed by the Spirit unto the ministers of the New Testament: nor was it made known unto them at all, that the Gentiles should find salvation without coming under the yoke of the Mosaic law, and that Jews themselves should be freed from that yoke of bondage . . . That promise [God made] made to Abraham extended to the Gentiles, the apostle [Paul] has largely proved in his Epistle to the Romans . . ." See *Clark's Commentary*, vol. vi, page 444. For the Savior's warning about God's kingdom being taken from the Jews and given to believing Gentiles, see Section in 153, footnote k. This warning became a reality after the resurrection of Christ and continues to this day.

3p-Heaven and the kingdom. Adam Clarke's "Jewish Church in the Old Testament," is explained in Section 138, tenth paragraph of footnote a. For more on Gentiles being saved and coming into the spiritual kingdom or church, refer to Section 55, footnote i. The main heading of Section 140, fifth paragraph of footnote j carries a more detailed description of this spiritual entity that Christ died for (Eph. 5:25). Section 39, footnote a also has a concise explanation with a clear illustration under footnote g demonstrating that the "eternal life," "the kingdom of heaven," "kingdom of God," and "saved" all mean the same thing. *Radical* dispensationalists are the eschatological culprits who struggle to make all of these different entities. This fact does not deny a *glorified* kingdom of both saved Jews and Gentiles, all one in Christ, at a time yet to come in God's plan for a new earth. For centuries, writers have labored to explain this blessed era in eternity where time is unknown, and all is made new. At best, our efforts fall miserably short of adequately describing what God has prepared for them that love Him. Most things about heaven and eternity are not explained in Scripture. This is by divine choice. Like the lake of fire, these things are real, and not a mental state. This world is not a habitation that a wise man would desire to live in forever. The young and thoughtless think to find happiness here but time teaches them the vanity of their expectations. God calls on us to relinquish our delusive hopes of earthly good and turn to Jesus. For a refreshing attempt to inform Christians about their eternal home, void of carnal extremeness that often accompany such works, see Randy Alcorn's book, *Heaven*. Regarding "the third heaven" that Paul visited, see Section 156, second paragraph of footnote g.

A possible harmonized view of Jesus' two rejections at Nazareth.

Christ's conflict in the Nazareth synagogue as recorded in Section 38, Lk. 4:16-30, occurred during the earlier part of His second year of ministry. It is called His "first rejection at Nazareth." In Section 91, Matt. 13:54-58 and Mk. 6:1-6, we read of another return to Nazareth. This is called "the second rejection." Because Matthew and Mark's records were chronologically placed near the end of the third year of His ministry (notably after the raising of Jarius' daughter), they are thought to report a later and different occasion from that given by Luke. This supplement shows the obvious similarity of Words spoken during this "second rejection" with those of the "first one." Could the similarities of all three records speak of the same event with Luke alone being inspired to give the dramatic details of the story?

Matt. 13:54–55	Mk. 6:1–3	Lk. 4:15–22	John
		Tour ends at home: He reads Scripture on the Sabbath day **15** And he taught in their synagogues, being glorified of all.	
He returns home **54** And when he was come into his own country,	***He returns home*** **1** And he went out from thence, and came into his own country; and his disciples follow him. **2** And when the sabbath day was come,	**16** And he came to Nazareth, where he had been brought up: and, as his custom was, he went to the synagogue on the sabbath day, and stood up for to read.	

17 And there was delivered unto him the book [scroll] of the prophet Esaias. [Isaiah] And when he had opened the book, he found the place where it was written,

18 "The Spirit of the Lord *is* upon me, because he hath anointed me to preach the gospel to the poor; he hath sent me to heal the brokenhearted, to preach deliverance to the captives, and recovering of sight to the blind, to set at liberty them that are bruised,
19 To preach the acceptable year of the Lord."

20 And he closed the book, and he gave *it* again to the minister, and sat down. And the eyes of all them that were in the synagogue were fastened on him.

He applies the reading to Himself: the congregation is shocked

he taught them in their synagogue,	he began to teach in the synagogue:	**21** And he began to say unto them, "This day is this Scripture fulfilled in your ears." **22** And all bare him witness, and wondered at the gracious words which proceeded out of his mouth.	
insomuch that they were astonished, and said, "Whence hath this *man* this wisdom, and *these* mighty works?	and many hearing *him* were astonished, saying, "From whence hath this *man* these things? and what wisdom *is* this which is given unto him, that even such mighty works are wrought by his hands?		
The puzzling question **55** "Is not this the	***The puzzling question*** **3** "Is not this the	***The puzzling question*** And they said, "Is not this	

Matt. 13:55–58	Mk. 6:3–6a	Lk. 4:22–30	John
carpenter's son? is not his mother called Mary? and his brethren, James, and Joses, and Simon and Judas? **56** "And his sisters, are they not all with us? Whence then hath this *man* all these things?"	carpenter, the son of Mary, the brother of James, and Joses, and of Juda, and Simon? and are not his sisters here with us?"	Joseph's son" **23** And he said unto them,	

"Ye will surely say unto me this proverb, 'Physician, heal thyself:' whatsoever we have heard done in Capernaum, do also here in thy country.'"

Home folks angered **57** And they were offended in him. But Jesus said unto them, "A prophet is not without honour, save in his own country, and in his own house."	***Home folks angered*** And they were offended at him. **4** But Jesus said unto them, "A prophet is not without honour, but in his own country, and among his own kin, and in his own house."	***Home folks angered*** **24** And he said, "Verily I say unto you, No prophet is accepted in his own country. ***Two historical examples of Jewish unbelief***	

25 "But I tell you of a truth, many widows were in Israel in the days of Elias, [Elijah] when the heaven was shut up three years and six months, when great famine was throughout all the land;

26 "But unto none of them was Elias [Elijah] sent, save unto Sarepta, [Zarephath] *a city* of Sidon, unto a woman *that was* a widow.

27 "And many lepers were in Israel in the time of El-i-se-us [Elisha] the prophet; and none of them was cleansed, saving Naaman the Syrian."

Enraged at His lesson they attempt to kill Him: He escapes to Capernaum

28 And all they in the synagogue, when they heard these things, were filled with wrath,

29 And rose up, and thrust him out of the city, and led him unto the brow of the hill whereon their city [Nazareth] was built, that they might cast him down headlong.

30 But he passing through the midst of them went his way, (Verse 31 cont. in Section 40.)

58 And he did not many mighty works there because of their unbelief. (Next chap., Matt. 14:1 cont. in Section 92.)	**5** And he could there do no mighty work, save that he laid his hands upon a few sick folk, and healed *them*. **6a** And he marveled because of their unbelief. (Verse 6b cont. in Section 56.)	◄ *These two verses reveal the adamant unbelief that ruled the hearts of the Jews in Jesus' home town of Nazareth.*	

No Footnotes-Commentary in Supplements

Returning to Capernaum, He meets* Peter, Andrew, James, and John again.** They are called to follow Him in a second Galilean preaching tour. When this mission was over, they returned to fishing in Lake Galilee.

*This was not the first meeting of Jesus with these four fishermen. However, on this occasion they received the first call to follow Him. Their original contact with Christ is in Section 26, John 1:35-42 and it occurred at Bethabara shortly after Christ's baptism-temptation. That first meeting was at least six months before the one recorded in this Section. According to John's record, Christ did not call them to follow Him at their first meeting as He did on this occasion. Apparently, James was not present at that time, but he was in the second meeting as seen in the parallel accounts below. John recorded the first meeting at Bethabara some twenty miles east of Jerusalem. Matthew and Mark wrote about what happened later at the Sea of Galilee some fifty miles north of Bethabara. The words and actions given in Section 43, Lk. 5:1-11, are different from those recorded below. In Luke 5, we read of their second call, which was for total and unbroken service. See footnote g below and asterisk under main heading of Section 43. **It is noted in the main heading of Section 38 that the Lord Jesus apparently made His first tour of Galilee alone.*

By the shores of Galilee

Matt. 4:17-22	Mk. 1:15-20	Lk.	John
A summary of His message **17** From that time Jesus began to preach, and to say, "Repent: for the kingdom of heaven [a] is at hand."	*A summary of His message* **15** And saying, "The time is fulfilled, and the kingdom of God [a] is at hand: repent ye, and believe the gospel."		
Two fishermen are called **18** And Jesus, walking by the sea of Galilee, [b] saw two brethren, Simon called Peter, and Andrew his brother, casting a net into the sea: for they were fishers. [c]	*Two fishermen are called* **16** Now as he walked by the sea of Galilee, [b] he saw Simon and Andrew his brother casting a net into the sea: for they were fishers. [c]		
19 And he saith unto them, "Follow me, and I will make you fishers of men." [d]	**17** And Jesus said unto them, "Come ye after me, and I will make you to become fishers of men." [d]		
20 And they straightway left *their* nets, and followed him. [e]	**18** And straightway they forsook their nets, and followed him. [e]		
21 And going on from thence, he saw other two brethren, James *the son* of Zebedee, and John his brother, in a ship with Zebedee their father, mending their nets; [f]	**19** And when he had gone a little farther thence, he saw James the *son* of Zebedee, and John his brother, who also were in the ship mending their nets. [f]		
They instantly go with Him and he called them. **22** And they immediately left the ship and their father,	*They instantly go with Him* **20** And straightway he called them: and they left their father Zebedee in the ship with the hired servants, and went after him. [g]		
and followed him. [g]			
(Verse 23 cont. in Section 42.)	(Verse 21 cont. in Section 40.)		

Footnotes-Commentary

[a] See the illustration **FOUR IDENTICAL THINGS THE KINGDOM WAS IN MATT. 19:16-26**, located at the end of this Section. The "kingdom of heaven" and the "kingdom of God" as mentioned in the New Testament *are* synonymous terms. These terms are found about one hundred times, and for the most part, our Lord defines their meaning by the usage of various parables. The earlier basis for this is found in Dan. 2:44, where it reads that the "God of heaven will set up a kingdom." He could not have been speaking of Israel, for they had been a kingdom for

over five hundred years when this promise was made. A comparison of Matt. 4:17 with Mk. 1:15 above demonstrates this. The same is also true for Matt. 11:11 with Lk. 7:28; Matt. 13:11 with Mk. 4:11; Mk. 4:30 with Matt. 13:31; Matt. 5:3 with Lk. 6:20; and lastly Matt. 10:7-8 with Lk. 9:1-2. The words written by Matthew, "Repent ye: for the kingdom of heaven is at hand" (Matt. 3:2), are recorded by Mark as, "The time is fulfilled, and the kingdom of God is at hand: repent ye, and believe the gospel" (Mk. 1:15). *In each of these cases, clearly the two terms are used interchangeably, with the meaning being determined by the immediate context.* (The "gospel" *at that time* was the "good news" that Messiah would soon appear and that men should turn from their sins and put faith in Him.) Matthew's "kingdom of heaven" and Mark's "kingdom of God" are the same. Neither of these terms *as used here* refers to a literal, physical, material kingdom with Messiah ruling as Supreme Potentate and King over two thousand years in the future. The Jews were expecting a Messiah, who would break the yoke of Gentile bondage, a king clothed in earthly splendor and manifested in the pomp of victory over the pagan Romans. In time, Christ will establish Israel's literal kingdom with Himself as King ruling the world. *But for now,* the kingdom preached by John and Jesus was not the physical one of the rabbis. Scofield's statement that the gospel of the kingdom of heaven and the kingdom of God are different is incorrect. See page 1003, footnote 1 of his Bible, and footnote g below.

2p-Christ, John the Baptist, and others were speaking of the spiritual manifestation of the kingdom, which gradually unfolded into the church. In the early days, John preached that the kingdom was at hand (or very near). It began in embryo form with the appearing of Christ. Later in His ministry, the kingdom was spoken of as a *present entity* already among them (Matt. 12:28). A man entered it by being born again (John 3:3). Only by attaining the highest righteousness could one be part of the new kingdom. It is the righteousness of God in Christ, and received through faith (Matt. 5:20; Rom. 3:21-26; and 1 Cor. 1:30). Our Lord affirmed on the morning of His death before the Roman governor, that His "kingdom was not of this world" (John 18:36). The slickest hermeneutical and political juggling will not change the meaning of these words. The kingdom He was building *then* and *now* is not of this sin cursed world. *Even that glorious earthly kingdom yet to come will be in a world free from sin and its decay.*

3p-John did not offer of a "physical king" or "earthly kingdom" to the Jews. This teaching is primarily the work of an Anglican priest, Ethelbert Bullinger, born in 1837. Later, John Darby introduced it in England and America. The Presbyterian-Congregationalist, Lewis S. Chafer founded in 1924, what became the Dallas Theological Seminary. They embraced this new eschatology with open arms. Later, in 1909, the footnotes in the *Scofield Reference Bible,* presented it as established historical truth. The charts of Clarence Larkin, in his popular *Dispensational Truths,* perpetuated it to millions. Today, Dwight Pentecost, Hal Lindsey, and other "end time specialists" are vanguards for the "kingdom offer" myth. (See the asterisk under the main heading of Section 94, John 6:15, footnote a, where Christ fled when the people sought to make Him their earthly king.) The old *Biblical, Theological, and Ecclesiastical Cyclopaedia* by M'Clintock and Strong, printed in 1868 knows nothing of the seven dispensations of Darby and his successors! Refer to vol. II. pages 820–821 and article under the heading Dispensation. John the Baptist did not call upon the multitudes to receive a human king; rather, he demanded that they repent of their sins and put faith in Jesus the Messiah, soon to appear. Nor did he preach that if they accepted Jesus as their King-Messiah, He would immediately build them a literal kingdom on earth and a new temple in Jerusalem. We wonder what would have happened to the cross had the Jews received the Lord Jesus as their human King? Upon facing this question, the proponents of the "kingdom offer" suddenly become able Calvinists and plead the "sovereignty of God" to handle the impossible situation! Who can imagine Jesus or John preaching, "Repent you Jews, for your literal kingdom is still over two thousand years away." For a review of what John preached, see Section 21, Part 4, Lk. 3:18, footnote q. *The Jewish Encyclopedia*, pages 502–503 carries an interesting article on the kingdom and blames Christians for the literal kingdom of Israel being exchanged for a spiritual one. In Jewish thinking, their kingdom is identified with "Olam Ha-Ba" or the "World to come." For what "Olam Ha-Ba," meant to ancient Israel, see Section 82, footnote d. For more on the imagined "kingdom offer" myth, refer to Section 44, third paragraph under footnote e.

4p-"Pray for peace in Jerusalem." The literalistic-minded Jews did not understand the heart of John's gospel or good news. Gradually, it came into focus for those who trusted Christ. At the end of His earthly ministry, the Messiah marched to Calvary and died for the sins of the world. With full atonement accomplished, the faith of all who had trusted Him as their Messiah met its fulfillment in His death, burial, and resurrection. Shortly thereafter, on the day of Pentecost, the spiritual side of the new kingdom (or the church) *fully* stepped onto the stage of human history. This spiritual manifestation has nothing to do with the *literal* kingdom and Messiah sitting on David's throne. See all of Sections 3 and 7 for details of Christ's impeccable qualifications as the King of Israel. The present *spiritual* manifestation of the kingdom, which is the church, hardly discounts the future plans of God for the nation of Israel (Acts 1:6-7). It is the same today. The spiritual manifestation of the kingdom is indisputably seen in Section 153, Matt. 21:43, footnote k. After casting out demons, Christ said in Matt. 12:28 with Lk. 11:20, "The kingdom of God is come unto you." He was telling the crowds that the exorcism was visible proof that the kingdom had arrived! And He was referring to its spiritual manifestation. The literal kingdom is yet to be at a time known only to God. This future kingdom will not be built by anyone "praying for the peace of Jerusalem." (Ps. 122:6). This verse has become a magical omen among "end time" experts. We hear them preach, "When there is peace in Jerusalem, there

162

will be peace in the world." David wrote this of circumstances that existed in his day. It has never been a prophetic promise of world peace. In Ps. 122, verse 4, the [twelve] tribes go to the testimony of Israel, to give thanks unto the name of the LORD. In verse 9, he wrote of the "house of the LORD our God." The temple was not built when David wrote this Psalm! His son, Solomon, constructed it years later. He was speaking of the tabernacle, which was pitched at Jerusalem for a time. This portable place of worship was also called "the house of the LORD" and "the temple" as well (1 Sam. 1:3, 7-9). Decades later, Jewish pilgrims traveling to the real temple would chant and sing this Psalm. It has nothing to do with world peace. In Rom. 10:1, we are told what to pray for Israel.

5p-God is not through with Israel. Paul stated that God is *not* finished with Israel (Rom. 11:1-2). He wrote these inspired words some twenty-five years *after* Christ's ascension. One reading of God's profound words regarding the Hebrew people in Jer. 31:35-37, overwhelmingly affirms His eternal establishment of this nation. The ordinances of heaven and earth will cease before He forsakes them. Exactly, how He will work all these things out to His eternal glory is not stated in these verses. Wise men will not force their conjectures into these verses.

6p-Some teach that the kingdom of God or heaven is something manifested *within* the teachings and deeds of Christ, that it is a "state of mind." Seventh Day Adventists and Armstrongites hold that the kingdom exists only in heaven and in time will come down with the return of Christ and cover the earth. The proponents of the literal-*only* kingdom (who reject its *present* spiritual manifestation in the church) are traveling a dead-end eschatological street. The chief apologists of this myth wrote that good works saved men under the law, but grace redeemed them after the death of Christ! See *The Scofield Reference Bible,* page 1115, footnote 2 for this terrible error.

7p-End time enthusiasts have invented several kinds of salvation, one for Old Testament people, one for New Testament people, and another kind for "the tribulations saints." This is a slap in the face to the perfect and eternal atonement of Christ. What a shock for thousands when they discovered that *The New Scofield Study Bible,* copyrighted in 1967, page 1125 changed completely the meaning of the old footnote on page 1115. Since 1909 with the first edition of this Bible, millions have read this note, taught two kinds of salvation, and preached it as truth. Now, that has been changed without explanation. The editorial committee of *The New Scofield Bible* should be saluted for removing this heresy from the old *Scofield Study Bible* footnotes.

8p-Along with the above, these people have also created different gospels. Some tell us there are three, some four, and now five other gospels! For example, see *The Revelation Expounded*, page 173, by William Kelly, and *The Matthew Mysteries* by G. T. Whipple. The work by Whipple is a classic example of misinterpreting certain doctrines of God's Word due to a lack of understanding ancient Jewish social customs and the historical background of Scripture. Dr. W. H. Scroggie, in *A Guide to the Gospels*, pages 564-65, has a good summary of the kingdom subject, but he was a victim of the synoptic problem lie. For an example of *radical* dispensationalism, see *Things to Come*, Chapter XXVI, by Dwight Pentecost. Missionary John Wilkinson's work, *Israel My Glory*, written in 1888, is excellent reading except for his date setting of Christ's "soon" return. At this time, Wilkinson has been wrong over seventy years about the "soon" return of our Savior.

9p-A present reality. This new kingdom is revealed across the history of Acts in 8:12; 20:24-25; with 28:31 as being a present reality. Paul confirmed this in his letters. It is demonstrated in 1 Cor. 6:9-11; Col. 1:13; and 4:11. The Thessalonian converts to Christ were *already* "called . . . unto his kingdom and glory" (1 Thess. 2:12). In Rom. 14:17, Paul wrote, "For the kingdom of God is not meat and drink; but righteousness, and peace, and joy in the Holy Ghost." In 1 Cor. 15:50, we read that, "flesh and blood cannot inherit the kingdom of God." The present kingdom is not a literal, material entity; it is spiritual. *All* of the above passages speak of a spiritual kingdom that was present *then* and *there;* not one of brick, stone and concrete, built in the land of Israel. These verses cannot have reference to a kingdom that would come into being over two thousand years later! Paul wrote of the kingdom of Christ (or church) which (at our present time in world history) has existed for almost two millenniums. It will continue so until the Lord Jesus comes again and calls it up to meet Him in the air (1 Thess. 4:16-17). This does not dispel the fact of some kind of glorified rule of Christ on earth at a future date.

10p-The Jewish law in the millennium? Dwight Pentecost's wrote, "Positions in the kingdom will be determined by one's attitude toward the law and by one's practice of the law." See *The Words & Works of Jesus Christ,* page 177. In Pentecost's literal, material, earthly Jewish kingdom, he has the Torah Law operative as the standard for position and promotion. We wonder what would happen should one break any of the 613 Torah commandments? Would he receive the punishments ordered in the law during this kind of Hebrew kingdom? Surely, he would or the law would be broken. If so, there will be thousands of hospitals, emergency clinics, funerals homes, and graveyards in operation during this "thousand years of worldwide peace." For more on this, see Section 171, fourth and fifth paragraphs of footnote f.

(b) Since the time of Joshua, the Jews believed that the Sea of Galilee was free to all. Restrictions had been set by the Sanhedrin to regulate the fishing industry for the good of all. No food was as popular as fish for the Hebrews and their Gentile neighbors. The rabbis gave instructions about what kind of fish to eat and how to prepare them. (Lev. 11:9-12). Tons of dried and salted fish were also imported into the land of Israel from abroad.

(c) "For they were fishers." Christ always calls industrious persons of energy and labor to do His work.

Laziness has no place in Christian service. God's best servants are not amid the ranks of idlers or shiftless loiterers.

(d) **"Come ye after me."** The Son of God called them unto Himself. Men serving in the ministry who have not been "God called" to be *near* the Savior have almost ruined the heritage of our Lord. Unless one is inwardly moved and summoned by the Holy Spirit, he is actually an intruder, doing injury to the cause of Christ. The divine art of fishing for men is vanishing from the church today. One cannot become this as he could become a carpenter or merchant. College, seminary, gifted oratory, and academic superiority have never *finally* made any man a soul winner. Only as we follow Christ in simple faith over the course of human life will we become genuine fishers of men." To bring lost souls to the saving knowledge of Jesus is the greatest enterprise for Christians. Except in the cases of Peter, James, John, Andrew, and Matthew, we have no *details* regarding the individual selection of the remaining seven men. The names of all twelve and comments about some of them are recorded in Section 57.

(e) **"Followed him."** At this point, they followed Christ on a part-time basis, and intermittently returned to their occupations thus making a livelihood. Here, they made their first tour with Jesus. They only "left their nets," as seen in Matt. 4:20. Upon their second call to go with Christ, "they forsook all and followed him" (Lk. 5:11).

(f) As the asterisk at the heading of this section denotes, these men had previously met the Master. Their acquaintance with Jesus was far deeper than these few verses relate. See footnote g below.

(g) Men do not abandon personal property, source of income, and family ties to follow a stranger into the unknown. Jesus was no stranger to these fishermen. He had previously preached in Galilee, according to Matt. 4:13-16, and brought great light to the people *before* calling these four men. He had met them earlier at Bethabara, and they believed that He was Messiah. See footnote e above. The *final* call for full service came some six months later.

THE NEW SPIRITUAL KINGDOM (LATER KNOWN AS THE CHURCH) WAS CALLED FOUR DIFFERENT BUT SAME THINGS ACCORDING TO MATT. 19:16–26.

This discourse below reveals that "eternal life," "the kingdom of heaven," "the kingdom of God," and "saved," were synonymous in the teaching of Christ. Verses 18 and 19 are highlighted being Old Testament quotations.

---

16 And, behold, one came and said unto him, "Good Master, what good thing shall I do, that I may have eternal life?" **17** And he said unto him, "Why callest thou me good? *There is* none good but one, *that is*, God: but if thou wilt enter into life, keep the commandments." **18** He saith unto him, "Which?" Jesus said, "'Thou shalt do no murder,' 'Thou shalt not commit adultery,' 'Thou shalt not steal,' 'Thou shalt not bear false witness,' **19** 'Honour thy father and *thy* mother:' and, 'Thou shalt love thy neighbour as thyself.'" **20** The young man saith unto him, "All these things have I kept from my youth up: what lack I yet?" **21** Jesus said unto him, "If thou wilt be perfect, go *and* sell that thou hast, and give to the poor, and thou shalt have treasure in heaven: and come *and* follow me." **22** But when the young man heard that saying, he went away sorrowful: for he had great possessions. **23** Then said Jesus unto his disciples, "Verily I say unto you, That a rich man shall hardly enter into the kingdom of heaven. **24** "And again I say unto you, It is easier for a camel to go through the eye of a needle, than for a rich man to enter into the kingdom of God." **25** When the disciples heard *it*, they were exceedingly amazed, saying, "Who then can be saved?" **26** But Jesus beheld *them*, and said unto them, "With men this is impossible; but with God all things are possible." (Refer to Section 139 for the harmony on this chapter.)

In the above Information Box, we note four things. The highlighted words connected by the arrows conclusively exhibit that all four of these terms mean the same thing. They are:
1. **"eternal life"** in verse 16.
2. **"the kingdom of heaven"** in verse 23.
3. **"the kingdom of God"** in verse 24.
4. **"saved"** in verse 25.

The disciple's question (verse 25) connected salvation with "eternal life," the "kingdom(s)," and being "saved." Their understanding of salvation at that time was first a political deliverance from Gentile oppression. On the day of Pentecost, with the coming of the Spirit in His fullness, *everything* became clear. See Section 21, Part 4, footnote q, for John's preaching about the kingdom. The book of Acts covers approximately the first thirty years of church history. Acts 1:6-7 concurs that the literal kingdom of Israel, as inquired about by the eleven apostles, just before our Lord's ascension, is different from the spiritual kingdom of Christ, which is the church. As explained in footnote a, above the difference in the kingdom of God and kingdom of Heaven is non-existent.

His first recorded encounter with a demon-possessed* man. This was on the Sabbath day in a synagogue. The evil spirits** audibly confessed He was the Messiah or the Holy One of God and fled. Jesus' fame spreads everywhere.

*Over the past thirty years more "conservative commentators" are telling us there is no such thing as demon possession, "for," they say, "demons cannot possess a person." However, Matt. 4:24; 8:16; 12:22; with Acts 16:16 reads the exact opposite. "Possessed, "means to be "demonized." It is sure that those who oppose such realities have never had an encounter with one who has demons dwelling in their physical body. Because something is not found in scripture hardly means, it is non-existent. Neither is the noun "Bible" found in the English text of Holy Scripture, but that does not invalidate it from being a real Book. The popular objection that unless a specific word or term is found in Scripture, it cannot be authentic is ludicrous. See further comments on this objection in Section 30, second paragraph of footnote k.
**Three issues have gained notoriety for splitting churches. They are the tongues plague, over emphasis on demonology, and radical versions of Calvinism. ▶It is to be noted that all words spoken by Satan and demons are given in a heavy Gothic font style throughout this harmony commentary.

In the synagogue at Capernaum

Matt.	Mk. 1:21-27	Lk. 4:31-36	John
	He teaches on the Sabbath 21 And they went into Capernaum; and straightway on the sabbath[a] day he entered into the synagogue, and taught. 22 And they were astonished[b] at his doctrine: for he taught them as one that had authority, and not as the scribes.	*He teaches on the Sabbath* 31 And came down to Capernaum, a city of Galilee, and taught them on the sabbath[a] days. 32 And they were astonished[b] at his doctrine: for his word was with power.	
	Demons recognize Him and speak 23 And there was in their synagogue a man with an unclean spirit; and he cried[c] out, 24 ▶Saying, **"Let *us* alone; what have we to do with thee, thou Jesus of Nazareth? art thou come to destroy us? I know thee[d] who thou art, the Holy One of God."**	*Demons recognize Him and speak* 33 And in the synagogue there was a man, which had a spirit of an unclean devil, and cried[c] out with a loud voice, 34 ▶Saying, **"Let *us* alone; what have we to do with thee, *thou* Jesus of Nazareth? art thou come to destroy us? I know thee[d] who thou art; the Holy One of God."**	
	He silences and expels them 25 And Jesus rebuked him, saying, "Hold thy peace, and come out of him." 26 And when the unclean spirit had torn him, and cried with a loud voice, he came out of him.[e]	*He silences and expels them* 35 And Jesus rebuked him, saying, "Hold thy peace, and come out of him." And when the devil had thrown him in the midst, he came out of him,[e] and hurt him not.	
	The people are shocked 27 And they were all amazed, insomuch that they questioned among themselves, saying, "What thing is this? what new doctrine *is* this?[f] for with authority commandeth he even the unclean spirits, and they do obey him."	*The people are shocked* 36 And they were all amazed, and spake among themselves, saying, "What a Word *is* this![f] for with authority and power he commandeth the unclean spirits, and they come out."	

Matt.	Mk. 1:28	Lk. 4:37	John
	His notoriety spreads over Galilee **28** And immediately his fame spread abroad throughout all the region(g) round about Galilee. (Verse 29 cont. in Section 41.)	*His notoriety spreads over Galilee* **37** And the fame of him went out into every place of the country(g) round about. (Verse 38 cont. in Section 41.)	

Footnotes-Commentary

(a) By this time, the term **"Jesus of Nazareth"** was a household word across the vast city of Capernaum, over Galilee, and the regions beyond. Though "Jesus" was a common name among Jews, His was distinguished from all others! (Josephus mentions thirteen persons with this name in the Index of his work.) Thousands had heard Him speak on the Sabbath days in the synagogues throughout Galilee. It was the standard custom for the presiding synagogue officer to invite various persons of fame and reputation to address the people. This began after reciting the Shema and reading of selected Scriptures. Christ always took advantage of this opportunity and addressed the congregation. Refer to Section 38 where the Savior went into His hometown synagogue and a terrible row broke out because of His teaching the Scriptures.

(b) **"Astonished."** This word means, "To strike a person out of his senses." Several hundred years before Christ was born, the rabbis had decreed that when Israel's Messiah came, He would speak and teach as no other person in Jewish history. What He had read and predicted a few months before at the Nazareth synagogue was *again* being fulfilled. Refer to Section 38, Lk. 4:22, footnote g for this prediction. He unceasingly preached under the anointing of the Holy Spirit. The powerful teaching, preaching, and miracles of Christ continually astounded His congregations, even "striking them out of their senses." See Section 47, Matt. 7:28-29, footnotes m, and n, for the effects of His Sermon on the Mount. For further explanation of His profound Words and works that continually proved He was the Messiah, see asterisk under the main heading of Section 48.

(c) **The demon cried out.** Their words are typed in a curious font to illustrate that evil spirits can talk! This was an audible screech coming from the foul spirit through the vocal faculties of its prisoner. *Luke described it as a "loud voice."* This scene reflects the covert condition in some of today's churches that harbor men who are instruments in the Devil's hands. The demon-possessed fellow sitting amid the worshipers in the synagogue on the Sabbath day was participating in the service. This is literal history. The demon(s) instantly recognized Christ as He entered the building and audibly spoke out their hatred of Him. Every person in the synagogue heard that awful verbal exchange between heaven and hell. They were frozen in horror! Both Mark and Luke affirmed that the demon "cried out." The term signifies, they audibly "screeched and screamed." Mark calls him an "unclean spirit," while Luke uses the term "unclean devil." The term "unclean" signified that these satanic entities produced the grossest of shameless sins and filth in the bodies and lives of those in whom they have dwelt.

2p-In Section 88, Christ, and His preachers encounter two demonized men, running crazed and naked over the hills and through the cemetery. What inspires the unashamed public nakedness and gross revealing of human flesh, so common today? Could it still be demon spirits? In the old Torah Law of Israel, God laid down stringent laws regarding the sacredness of the human body in its naked form (Lev. 18: 1-30). If the Jewish Law called for respect and sanctity of the human anatomy, then what would grace require? See 1 Tim. 2:9-10 for a few timely suggestions. In the verses above, this poor fellow had been attending the local synagogue and had carried devils resident in his body into the house of God. It is no different today in many churches. Many *unsaved* church members serve as transportation for Satan and evil, at work, in the home, and church as well. The greatest problem with this problem is that many "highly trained" professional ministers, and pastors utterly reject such facts regarding the Devil and evil. They tell us that if these things do exist, they are in dark Africa or the jungles of South America.

3p-Beware of the "learned social anthropologists" and "professional theologians" who declare that Satan, demons, and angels have their origin in mythology and pagan superstitions. Then they inform us that these ancient fables were gradually incorporated into the Bible. The heathens had ten thousand perverted notions about these spiritual realities; however, that hardly negates the truth of Holy Scripture on this subject. For a good review of the subject of demonology, see the *Scofield Reference Bible,* page 1004, footnote 1.

(d) **"I know thee,"** growled the chief evil spirit through his prisoner's mouth. See verse 24 below for explanation. Every minion of Satan's dark world knows who Jesus Christ is! Instantly, the God-Man invoked His supreme authority and rebuked the foul beings. Their reaction was fierce. Note, the chief evil spirit (resident in the man) directed the *audible conversation* against Christ on behalf of his fellow demons. His confession was heard by everyone present; "What have *we* to do with thee," revealed there were numerous demons in his physical body.

2p-Verse 24. Note the change from singular to plural in the demon's confession of Jesus Christ. From "I" to "we" are his awful words. Usually a chief demon (in this case "I") is in command of the captive victim while the others ("we") are under his authority. Christ spoke His command to the one in command. With this, the others instantly obey (verse 26). When the leader came out, his cohorts left with him. This same verbal exchange from singular to plural is noted in the case of Legion. Refer to Section 88, number 3 under footnote b for this.

3p-Verse 25. Literally, He told them to "shut up," or "be muzzled and gagged." Christ rejected any testimony from foul spirits to His deity. This is mentioned again in Section 41, footnote s. They were joined together in their work of evil. All demon spirits *knew* Jesus was from Nazareth and said so! At least, they understood the meaning of Matt. 2:23, if "modern scholarship" never does! Section 18, footnotes h and i has an explanation of this. The devils had watched with terror every step of the way from His birth to His rejection at Nazareth, which launched Him into His great Galilean ministry. Further, they recognized Him as "the Holy One of God," or "Christ," Israel's promised Messiah with authority to confine them into eternal torment! Hence, their cry, "art thou come to destroy us?" Satan and his hordes know that judgment, and hell await them, and they, in terror loathe the thought of it. This hardly means annihilation or extinction as the cult's teach. It is *eternal* destruction according to Matt. 25:41; 2 Thess. 1:9; with Rev. 20:10. Such destruction does not speak of eternal nothingness in an unconscious ash heap. Even among so-called "conservatives" and "fundamentalists," there is a rampant denial of the reality and activities of evil spirits in this present age. To believe this is to conclude there is no eternal hell-lake of fire for the wicked. *The denial of one is the denial of the other.*

(e) "He came out of him." Slamming their captive to the synagogue floor, kicking, growling, and twisting in horrible convulsions, the demons made a last attempt to injure him physically. Howling and screaming through his vocal faculties, they reluctantly fled the poor man's torn body. The audience shocked and terrified at these sights, and sounds stepped back with a shudder. Never had they experienced a Sabbath service like that one! Mark calls this dark thing "the unclean spirit" (verse 26), while Luke calls him "the devil" (verse 35). The two are inseparable; for as is one, so is the other. Many of the Jews present *heard* the demons confess, "Jesus of Nazareth" was "the Holy One of God," or "the Messiah!" They instantly made the connection. In view of all this, see James 2:19, where we read, "the devils [demons] tremble" at the thought of the one true God.

(f) Neither Mark nor Luke explained the particular doctrine Christ taught on this occasion. Whatever it was, the people were amazed at His teaching. See other examples of this in Section 47, Matt. 7:28-29, footnotes n, and m. See also Section 119, John 7:45-46, footnote u, where the temple police, so amazed at Jesus' teaching, confessed, "Never man spake like this."

(g) His fame goes abroad. With this dramatic event in the large synagogue at Capernaum, the previous conflict in Nazareth, healing of the nobleman's son, turning water to wine at Cana, His miracles at the Passover in Jerusalem, and other things not recorded in Scripture, everyone soon heard of Jesus. The whole countryside vibrated with stories about this grand Person. His "fame" spread across the land and further abroad. Shortly, there would be a human tidal wave of popular curiosity. This brought hundreds of thousands to see and hear Him. He was soon known across the land even to regions beyond. His fame is described in Section 33, footnote e; Section 41, footnote d, Section 42, footnote h; and Section 55, footnote b.

2p-What the Jews were thinking. "Is this man our Messiah? Do not the demons confess Him thus? Why do our rabbis hate Him so?" Under the asterisk in Section 60, we note that the fame of Christ spread into the Roman military ranks, especially among those stationed in His home state or province of Galilee. A short time after this synagogue uproar, we read in Section 42, footnotes f and h that people were coming to Him from faraway Syria and other distant places. The walk from Syria's extreme southern border to Galilee would have taken several weeks one way. This reflects the widespread interest in Jesus of Nazareth, claiming to be Israel's Messiah. The fact that secular history of that era mostly fails to mention this phenomena in detail means nothing. Those who appeal to this "silence," appeal to the wind not to blow again!

3p-The day of reckoning is coming, It happens in the experiences of humankind that often persons of extraordinary merit, and ability remain for a time in obscurity. Then suddenly, the unsuspected greatness of their lives and characters rises like a new sun after the dark night. Thus, it was with Jesus of Nazareth as He told men of His kingdom. However, it should be distinctly understood, that the *true* kingdom of Christ was not a great visible organization, consisting of good men and bad, bound together by some ecclesiastical tie of religion. The entrance into Christ's kingdom is narrow and its way straight. So as then, it is the same today, the Son of God counts all who refused to submit to His saving gospel as enemies of His kingdom or church. Amid the masses, that outwardly fain to follow Christ today one finds a mixture of good and bad, wheat and tares. In God's time, this will be corrected though it seems to have been forgotten by divine justice. *All incorrigible religious hypocrites have a front seat reserved in hell.* True Christians are in this world but not of it. They seek to be honest, live peacefully amid a madden society of crime and wickedness. They love their neighbors regardless, pay their taxes, respect all men, but will not accept the animal conduct and the vicious deeds of godless society. The ploy of "human rights" has been taken into outrageous extremes, and *genuine* Christians refuse to comply with these extremes. They will not embrace sodomy as a healthy lifestyle, or same sex marriage as an acceptable alternative. Sin is still sin! It wages are eventually death (Rom. 6:23). We are troubled that so many seem to get away with their unspeakable atrocities. Honest thinking, tells men of sound reasoning (many of whom are not even Christians) that a day of reckoning must come. For more on these things, see the Parable of the Tares and Poisonous Seed in Section 77.

After the synagogue uproar, Jesus retires to Peter's house* and cures his mother-in-law on the Sabbath. Great multitudes come after sundown to be healed and delivered. Again, demons confess publicly that He is the Christ or Messiah, the Son of God.

*See Section 49, when Christ later re-entered Peter's house, where He found food, friends, and rest.

Capernaum

Matt. 8:14–16	Mk. 1:29–34	Lk. 4:38–40	John
A healing in Peter's house	*A healing in Peter's house*	*A healing in Peter's house*	
	29 And forthwith, when they were come out of the synagogue, they entered into the house(a) of Simon and Andrew, with James and John.	38 And he arose out of the synagogue, and entered into Simon's house(a)	
14 And when Jesus was come into Peter's house,(a)			
he saw his wife's mother laid, and sick of a fever.	30 But Simon's wife's mother lay sick of a fever, and anon [quickly] they tell him of her.	And Simon's wife's mother was taken with a great fever; and they besought him for her.	
15 And he touched(b) her hand,	31 And he came and took(b) her by the hand, and lifted her up;	39 And he stood(b) over her, and rebuked the	
and the fever left her: and she arose, and ministered unto them.	and immediately the fever left her, and she ministered unto them.	fever; and it left her: and immediately she arose and ministered unto them.	
The Sabbath is ended: great multitudes come	*The Sabbath is ended: great multitudes come*	*The Sabbath is ended: great multitudes come*	
16 When the even was come,(c) they	32 And at even, when the sun did set,(c) they	40 Now when the sun was setting,(c) all they that had any sick with divers [various] diseases	
brought unto him many (d)	brought unto him all(d) that were diseased, and them that were possessed with devils.	brought them(d) unto him;	
that were possessed with devils: and he cast out the spirits with	*Thousands at Peter's house*		
	33 And all the city [Capernaum] was gathered together at the door.(e)		
	34 And he	and he laid his hands on every one of them,	
his word,(f) and healed all that were sick:	healed many(f) that were sick of divers	and healed them.(f)	

Matt. 8:17	Mk. 1:34	Lk. 4: 41	John
	[various] diseases, and cast out many devils; *All the words of Satan and ▶ demons are in a heavy Gothic font style throughout this work.* ***Demons are forbidden to speak of His deity*** and suffered [permitted] not the devils to speak, because they knew[g] him. (Verse 35 cont. in Section 42.)	41 And devils also came out of many, crying out, and saying, **"Thou art Christ** [Messiah] **the Son of God."** ***Demons are forbidden to speak of His deity*** And he rebuking *them* suffered [permitted] them not to speak: for they knew[g] that he was Christ. (Messiah) (Verse 42 cont. in Section 42.)	
His deeds fulfilled Old Testament prophecy 17 That it might be fulfilled which was spoken by E-sa-ias [Isaiah] the prophet, saying, **"Himself took *our* infirmities, and bare *our* sicknesses."**[h] (Verse 18 cont. in Section 87.)			

Footnotes-Commentary

(a) The text reveals that this was Peter's house. Apparently, his mother-in-law lived with him and his wife. We note that Peter's wife was alive some twenty years later and was mentioned in 1 Cor. 9:5. It is odd to western culture that the New Testament says nothing about the children or families of the apostles, except Judas. The comments about Judas are recorded in Section 146, footnote h.

2p-According to Mk. 1:29, several others also shared Peter's house, one being his brother Andrew. (It is a wonderful grace when men open their homes to the Son of God and His people.) Earlier it was noted that both Peter and his brother Andrew lived in Bethsaida according to John 1:44. Probably, they moved their homes to Capernaum (located about three miles westward on the upper northern end of the sea) when their Lord moved there from Nazareth. See asterisk under the main heading of Section 28, for the reason *why* the Lord Jesus made this move.

3p-Verse 14. Peter a married man. This verse demonstrates that another teaching of the Roman Catholic Church is untrue. The papists claim Peter as the head of God's Church on earth and its first Vicar. It is forbidden for Catholic priests, bishops and popes to marry, yet Peter had a wife! Honest Catholic people all over the world are frustrated at this discovery, which reads the same in their Catholic Bible. They should also investigate the numerous anti-biblical teachings of their church, *especially the ones on how salvation and forgiveness of sins may be received.* Readers, who want a fair and thorough investigation into the teachings of the Roman Catholic Church, see the timeless classic, *Roman Catholicism* by Loraine Boettner. For comments on other serious Catholic theological errors regarding Mary the mother of Jesus, see Section 12, footnote j and k.

(b) **Several postures.** The three writers inform us that Christ touched her, took her by the hand, stood over her, rebuked the fever, and lifted her up. Luke the physician called it "a great [high] fever" in verse 38. At times Jesus healed those who were miles away by a spoken Word, as noted in John 4:50-53. Sometimes He touched and then healed, as in the case here. At other times, He did both, as in Section 48, and Lk. 5:12-13. Our Lord "rebuked" the fever as He had just rebuked the demon in the synagogue drama in Mk. 1:25. (Is there a connection or does this signal that even the viruses of infection recognized the Son of God's sovereign authority and must obey His command?) In John 17:2, Christ said that He had "power over all flesh." Refer to Section 40, Lk. 4:35, footnote e, for His supreme authority over these evil spirits of the Devil. Both the raging fever in the woman's body and demons of the dark nether world yielded instantly to His authority. The Messiah had all elements: natural, physical and supernatural, under His command. Even winds and waves obeyed His Word. He spoke peace to the raging waters of Lake Galilee, and they instantly obeyed His command (Mk. 4:39),

2p-All three writers record that the woman, once healed, "ministered unto them." Instantly, she arose from the hot fever and demonstrated her gratitude in the form of practical service, and joyfully ministering to her wonderful Healer and His friends, one of them being her son-in-law.

(c) **"When even was come."** These three parallel verses all mean that this particular Sabbath day had now ended at sunset. It was during the early night hours that many of these miracles took place. The deliverance of the demon-possessed man and the healing of Peter's mother-in-law had occurred earlier that day. They were deeds strictly forbidden by the rabbis on the Sabbath day. At sunset, the Sabbath day was over. The people, now free from breaking a rule of the Pharisees, came by the thousands to find Jesus and be healed and blessed. All that Sabbath afternoon, we imagine that every home in Capernaum buzzed with talk about Jesus, His Messianic claims and matching works. News of His supernatural deeds had spread over the city. Everyone was talking about the Man, who claimed to be Messiah, and His daring confrontation before the rulers of the synagogue that very Sabbath morning. Scores of homes and hearts scattered over the city, and country were filled with suffering, sickness, and sorrow. Suddenly, a door of hope had opened to them in Jesus of Nazareth. Had not the demons openly confessed Him as the promised Messiah? See this in Section 40, Mk. 1:24, footnote d. In addition, the people had heard this stirring confession! For centuries, the rabbis had taught the Jews, that their Messiah would come in fulfillment of Mal. 4:2. Now, "the sun of righteousness . . . with healing in his wings" had risen over Capernaum. It was too good to be true!

(d) **"Many that were possessed with devils."** These reveal the spiritual and moral decadence among the Hebrews at this time. Josephus wrote regarding the religious and social condition of the Jews during this era in history, "There was not a nation under heaven more wicked than they were." Quoted by Adam Clarke in his *Commentary*, vol. 5, page 104. Amid this dreadful atmosphere of prevailing sin and spiritual ruin, we picture thousands streaming to the door of Peter's house. From all parts and every direction, they came. There were mothers, fathers, widows, wives, children, and husbands. They were leading, bringing, carting, carrying, and pulling their loved ones to Jesus. Amid the crowds were tiny infants, the young, middle aged, the elderly, and feeble. Vast multitudes of both Jews and Gentiles thronged the city. There gathered the halt, maimed, blind, lame, and disease-ridden, thousands who were afflicted with miserable infirmities and tormented by demons of every description. Curious spectators and nosy meddlers were present along with the snarling, jealous leaders of Jewish religion. Hoards of broken, bent, and beaten humanity gathered in stirring waves, amid cries, groans, and pleadings for help. All pressed upon Peter's house reaching out to Jesus the Holy One of Israel. This sea of hurting humanity was symbolic of the whole world wrecked by Satan and sin. They were pushing, shoving, pressing, and scrambling to find Jesus. No day like this had ever dawned upon Capernaum. Later, in His ministry, our Lord pronounced horrible curses upon this very city that had seen and heard so much, but *finally* rejected Him as the Messiah. Refer to Section 63, Matt. 11:23, footnote b; and Section 113, Lk. 10:15, footnote o where He repeated this curse on Capernaum, which happened in A.D. 70 at the hands of the Romans. The later part of this verse reveals that "devils" and "spirits" are identical but called by different names in this case.

(e) Never had the door of any house in Israel had such a collection of suffering humanity gathered outside. All of them wanted to come in and meet Jesus of Nazareth, the carpenter calming to be Israel's Messiah. Refer to footnote h below for more on this thought.

(f) **"With his Word."** He healed them by verbal commands. This demonstrates that the mystic powers of disease and death knew Jesus Christ and instantly obeyed His spoken command. Only God had such authority! Note how these healings are described: Matthew says "all," while Mark says "many." Luke wrote that Jesus healed "them." The words in Lk. 4:40, that He "laid his hands on every one of them" for hours on end, is incredible! Such exerted labor among the countless thousands of restless, milling people was enough to wreck physically the average person.

(g) **"Because they knew him."** Radically liberal church ministers, infidel theologians, and skeptic religionists who deny Jesus was the Messiah-Savior struggle re-interpreting, re-applying, or explaining away the awful words that were spoken by Satan or his emissaries. It is chilling to write this warning, but in *such cases* one would be wiser to believe what demons said about Christ, rather than the "greatly learned" theological experts. In this event, the devils spoke more truth about Jesus of Nazareth than these people do. However, these super minds are not a single class in their blindness to eternal realities. For a powerful examination of the evil work of these unsaved religionists, see *Fabricating Jesus; How Modern Scholars Distort the Gospels,* by Craig A. Evans. It is also right that amid the backward, rustic, and ignorant, one often finds just as many fools. Knowing God and Christ is not achieved by vast learning or base ignorance. It is found when one, under conviction of the Holy Spirit and enlightened by the Word of God, repents of sin and trusts Jesus Christ in simple faith to forgive and save. Demons confessed Him as the "Christ" or "Messiah," "the Son of God," while the religious leaders of Israel refused to do so. What a paradox! Note Section 5, Matt. 1:1, footnote a, for earlier comments on Jesus the Messiah. It is of interest that in Lk. 4:41 the descriptions "Christ-Messiah" and "Son of God" are applied to the same Person. Yet, Jesus refused the testimony of devils even though they spoke the truth. Here, is another incontrovertible proof that dark spirits can speak audibly through the mouths of their victims. Such glorious words of truth confessed by the evil entity were applicable strictly to the Savior, but He rejected any confirmation of His deity from the malevolent agents of Satan. These demonic voices shrieked out this highest of confessions through the vocal cords and tongues of their captives. Those standing about who heard them speak were terrified at such things. Jewish exorcists, who "specialized" in casting out demons ("shedim" in Hebrew), employed various methods, some of which smacked of the occult. Josephus wrote of this in *Antiquities,* Book 8:2. 5, lines 47 through 49.

2p-Rabbinical teaching on this subject was mixed with pagan superstitions from Babylon, Egypt, Persia and other heathen nations. It grossly distorted the reality of Satan and wicked spirits. Jewish exorcists used foul-smelling roots pushed into the nostrils, believing the evil spirits could not stand the odor and would flee. Some would call on a higher or more powerful demon to expel the weaker ones. Some sought to capture the attention of the spirits by using brightly colored strips of cloth or loud noises, and then they proposed to chase them away. Pagan Hindus hoist colorful streamers on long poles to chase away bad demons and attract "good ones." Rabbinical ideas regarding foul spirits were wild and greatly varied. Some held that demons were the offspring of Adam and Eve by copulating with wicked spirits! There was a queen of demons, named "Lilith," and thousands of others who worked at selected times during the night, morning, midday, and afternoon. The king of evil spirits was Asmodai or Samael. This is obviously a distorted version of Satan. The rabbis held that demons watched the actions of all men waiting for any sin or error to be committed by which they might gain entrance, and that they could materialize, taking on all sorts of hideous forms and apparitions. (These last two beliefs are true.) Evil spirits would materialize and appear in various forms and shapes. Some were pleasing and others hideous. Such things as ashes about one's bed thwarted evil spirits at night. Washing hands and arms vigorously, the afterbirth of a black cat, various amulet, and reciting certain incantations like those (supposedly) used by King Solomon, along with other ridiculous devices and practices would keep them safe. Some of these absurd cures are recorded in the Talmud tractate, Berachoth 6a.

3p-For a later mention of scribes and Pharisees and their children practicing exorcism, see Section 66, Matt. 12:27, footnote f. History informs us that during this time the Jews had professional exorcists traveling across the land, claiming the ability to expel evil spirits. Years after this synagogue encounter, we read in Acts 19:13-17 about one of these teams in faraway Ephesus attempting to drive out demons and how it backfired. Alfred Edersheim in *Life and Times of Jesus the Messiah* has an interesting review of Jewish angelology and demonology in Appendix 13 of his work. Dr. F. W. Farrar in *Life of Christ,* pages 745-746, has a documented article on Jewish angelology and demonology. The late German historian T. K. Oesterreich was a total unbeliever in the historical reliability of God's Word and its truth. Over fifty years ago, he wrote *Possession, Demonical & Other.* This book is a sweeping coverage of the subject over the centuries past. Even though he was a thorough rationalist and skeptic, his excellent documentation belies his argument. It proves Oesterreich wrong, and his scholarly efforts to *reinterpret* (or explain away) factual history fly into his face.

4p-He is victor over all. Never had the Jews witnessed anything like the Lord Jesus confronting the forces of darkness. The carpenter from Nazareth spoke with such absolute and divine authority that the evil entities fled at His command. The text in Lk. 4:41 explains why this was so. It reads, "They knew that he was Christ" (or Messiah). Later, in His death, burial, and resurrection, the Savior conquered all sin, the Devil, and death, and rose triumphant as "the Lord of all" (Acts 10:36 with Phil. 2:9-11). The keys of hell and death are now in His hand (Rev. 1:18). He has "spoiled" (conquered) every foul intrigue of darkness (Col. 2:14-15).

(h) Christ taking sicknesses and infirmities. Both written and spoken by the prophet of God some seven hundred years prior in Isa 53:4. Matthew gives something of an interpretative citation of this verse. It was now fulfilled in Jesus of Nazareth. This was a general quotation from Isa. 53:4 set in the prophetic context of the death of Christ for our sins. This does *not* mean that the actual diseases of those He healed were transferred into His physical body. It is a serious error to teach that the Son of God was riddled with tuberculosis, cancer, aids, Alzheimer's and so on. Those who propagate this awful untruth speak sacrilegious things. "Faith healing" advocates use this verse to "prove" that Christ's atonement not only provides salvation for all who believe but also provides complete healing for every physical sickness in this life. These people tell us it is never the will of God for any child of His to be sick; that those believers who are ill have not "claimed their miracle of healing." In view of this heresy, we note that according to 2 Kings 13:14, the prophet Elisha died of a personal sickness! During his ministry, he had performed at least fourteen miracles! We wonder why one of the greatest prophets in the Old Testament did not claim his healing miracle instead of dying by a physical illness? Jacob wrestled with the Lord and walked with a limp the rest of his life (Gen. 32:31). On one occasion our Lord said, that sick people needed a doctor (Matt. 9:12). For more on this abused subject, see Section 147, third paragraph of footnote g, and Section 203, number 6 under footnote c.

2p-Centuries of church history have conclusively shown that the "faith healers" are fervent enthusiasts who add to the saving gospel a false dimension. Final and everlasting healing of all mortal ills will be the inheritance of every believer at the resurrection of the just. With this every physical body will be perfect, even like that of our Savior (Rom. 6:5 with 1 John 3:2). *It is in this sense that atonement-healing is provided for all believers in the salvation of Christ.* Seasoned and experienced Christians understand that God does choose to heal sick bodies at times, however, *mass* faith healing for all believers of all times is not taught in Scripture, or found over the course of church history. *It is a farce!* Only the Lord Jesus, in demonstrating that He was Israel's exclusive Messiah, performed healings for countless thousands of people. This is briefly discussed in Section 29, John 2:18, footnote e, and under main heading Section 48. After the ascension of Christ, the apostles and early believers continued to perform many signs, wonders and miracles for a time, but these gradually faded into the sunset of passing history with only intermittent local flares along the way. It has continued to this present moment. Carefully note the comments on this subject in Section 207, Mk. 16:20, footnote h.

3p-All genuine miracles of healing from the hand of God in this life are temporary. *Every person Christ healed and raised from the dead had to die again at the end of their earthly life.* The Lord Jesus' sympathy with sufferers was so real that He felt the weaknesses and sorrows of their pains in His human frame. He literally hurt for them as they languished in sufferings. He was acquainted with their grief by personal human touch, but His grief was not due to sin, for He was sinless. As sin is the *original* cause of all sickness and disease, Christ did bear *all* human infirmities and illnesses as He bore all our sins on the cross. A large false cult teaches that Satan bore part of the punishment for mankind's sins. The very notion is too horrible to contemplate! Jesus carried *all* of mankind's sins in His own body on the cross, including every physical illness and pain, they produce. We all share the death of Adam by physical birth. However, all who repent and believe share the life of Christ by the new birth. This heavenly birth is not an ideal, religious philosophy. or aspiration. It is a miracle of God given through Christ's atonement and substitutionary death for sins. He died for Adam's entire race. It is in this sense that He took all our bodily ailments, illnesses, woes, and sins and suffered their just punishment that we might be finally saved from this. In His triumphant resurrection, He became victorious over sin and *all* of its consequences be they, physical ailments, or whatever. For helpful reading on the "faith healing" cults, see *Divine Healing Today* by Richard Mayhue; *The Agony of Deceit,* edited by Michael Horton; and *A Different Gospel,* by D. R. McConnell. The subject of divine healing is continued in Section 207, starting at the second paragraph of footnote i.

4p-Among the four gospel writers, up to this point in the life of Christ, only Matthew quoted Isa. 53:4. The rabbis believed and taught that it spoke of their Messiah, who would bring physical healing to Israel. This citation was aimed *first* at Matthew's Jewish readers in an effort to show them that Jesus of Nazareth was their Messiah, who fulfilled another prediction from their Scriptures. See Section 7 for an explanation of His Hebrew lineage as Israel's Messiah. Had He not fulfilled numerous predictions from their Scriptures? Many of the Old Testament passages fulfilled by Christ were among those the rabbis taught that pointed to Messiah. Refer to *Appendix Three* for a list of Old Testament prophecies fulfilled by our Lord during His life on earth. He continually fulfilled the Messianic prophecies. He had previously read in His hometown synagogue as seen in Section 38, Lk. 4:17-21, footnotes e and f. On this occasion, He presented Himself as their Messiah. A terrible uproar followed and the Jews tried to kill Him. For Matthew's first Messianic quotation from the Old Testament applied to the Savior, see Section 12, footnote g. He either knew that Jesus was the Messiah, or he was playing games with his Jewish readers.

5p-**Body parts and the resurrection? Sex insane religions.** When discussing the subject of the resurrection of the dead, and so forth, people often put the question concerning transplanted human body parts. Thousands carry in their physical frames, organs from the anatomy of someone else. What will happen at the resurrection? Will a heart or lung suddenly be made new, then removed from one body and transferred to its original owner? This is answered in Phil. 3:21, where in the context or our Lord's return it is written, "he is able even to subdue all things unto himself." For those who trouble themselves with such questions we may rest confident that God Almighty can handle the situation. With this confidence read Jer. 32:27 with Matt. 19:26. We have no way of knowing but little regarding the glorified body of resurrected believers. God has not put it in His Word. Speculation about these things accomplishes nothing. If men's guesses are put forward as established biblical doctrine, then we have overstepped the divine limits that God has recorded in Scripture. The glorified body of saved Christians will be like the resurrected body of Jesus Christ; wonderful, heavenly, and beyond mortal tongue to describe. Let no child of God, who reads these lines fret about body parts when Jesus returns. He can handle it very well! For a brief mention of the blasphemous teaching of the Mormon Church regarding heaven and glorified bodies, see Section 53, the fifth paragraph of footnote k. Islam also carries bizarre stories of a sexual paradise with young women waiting for devout Muslims, who kill themselves for their cause. Perpetual fantasies of suicides, killings, hatred for all enemies, sex, sex, and more sex, reflect the frightful and inflamed carnal aspirations of the persons who founded these religions. For a piercing look into the Mormon cults and sects and their horrific sexual perversions, see *Under the Banner of Heaven*, by Jon Krakauer. It is obvious that he wrote as an unsaved man, ignorant of basic biblical theology when he described Joseph Smith as "A true religious genius." For comments on Smith and other religious crackpots, see Section 27, footnote a. However, Krakauer's historical facts about sex have shaken the flag ship of Mormonism, Brigham Young University. Ancient paganism also bleeds with perverted sex stories of their gods and goddesses. Any religion, regardless, that is based on sex perversion, and seeks to glorify this sin by making it a part of their heaven is false. Christ said empathically that there was no marriage in heaven. See Section 156 for a discussion on this subject and His Words in Matt. 22:30.

6p-**Great rejoicing filled old Capernaum.** Untold thousands flocked to see and hear Him. Many were healed and blessed while others inspired by Satan and the Pharisees gradually rejected His claims as Israel's Messiah and opposed His ministry. In time, they became His most incessant and bitter enemies. About forty years after the ascension of our Lord to heaven, Section 163 describes the judgment of God upon these people and their children. This came to pass in A.D. 70 at the hands of the cruel Roman army.

He leaves Capernaum for a third evangelistic trip across Galilee.* Simon Peter and other unnamed disciples travel with Jesus on this tour.** His fame attracts vast multitudes from every direction.

*Section 38, Lk. 4:15 may suggest that Jesus traveled alone on His first Galilean tour. For His second missionary effort over Galilee (with some of His disciples), see Section 39. This present Section 42 tells of His third mission; Section 56, the fourth; and Section 65 deals with the fifth trip over Galilee. In the four last tours, some or all of His disciples accompanied Him. He surely made trips without them. How many days or weeks these large evangelistic efforts required among so many people we do not know. At the conclusion of this third tour, the four disciples resumed their work of fishing. It is assumed that prior to the Sermon on the Mount, Christ returned to the seaside with thousands following Him. After preaching from Peter's boat, He called him and his partners into His service for a second time. We read in Lk. 5:11 that these four fishermen "forsook all, and followed Him." Then Christ led them and the multitudes to a mountain plateau somewhere away from Capernaum. Here, they heard the greatest masterpiece of divine instruction ever sounded in mortal ear. It has been entitled the Sermon on the Mount and is recorded in Sections 44-47 of this harmony commentary. **For the disciples' return from this third mission trip, see the main heading of Section 43.

Galilee

Matt. 4:23	Mk. 1:35–39	Lk. 4:42–44	John
	An early prayer vigil **35** And in the morning, rising up a great while before day, he went out, and departed into a solitary place, and there prayed.(a) **36** And Simon and they that were with him followed after him. **37** And when they had found him, they said unto him, "All *men* seek for thee."	*An early prayer vigil* **42** And when it was day, he departed and went into a desert place: and the people sought him, and came unto him, and stayed [restrained] him, that he should not depart from them.	
	He must preach God's Word in other places **38** And he said unto them, "Let us go into the next towns, that I may preach [the kingdom of God](b) there also: for therefore came I forth." **39** And he preached in their synagogues(d) throughout all Galilee,	*He must preach God's Word in other places* **43** And he said unto them, "I must preach the kingdom(b) of God to other cities also: for therefore am I sent." **44** And he preached in the synagogues(d) of Galilee. (Next chapter Lk. 5:1 cont. in Section 43.)	
23 And Jesus went about all Galilee,(c) teaching in their synagogues,(d) and preaching the gospel of the kingdom, and healing all manner of sickness and all			

173

Matt. 4:23-25	Mk.1: 39	Lk.	John
manner of disease(e) among the people. *His great fame* **24** And his fame went hroughout all Syria:(f) and they brought unto him all sick people that were taken with divers [various] diseases and torments, and those which were possessed with devils, and those which were lunatic,(g) [moonstruck] and those that had the palsy; [paralysis] and he healed them. *The massive scope of His following* **25 And there followed him great multitudes(h) of people from Galilee, and from Decapolis, and from Jerusalem, and from Judaea, and from beyond Jordan.**(i) (Next chap. Matt. 5:1 cont. in Section 44.)	and cast out devils. (Verse 40 cont. in Section 48.) ◄ *"Beyond Jordan" to the ancients also embraced, Babylon or Iraq, Iran or Persia, and even far away India.*		

Footnotes-Commentary

(a) **"And there prayed."** Though perfectly holy and without sin, the Son of God regarded the duty of *secret prayer* of highest importance. If our Lord sought God's face in the early hours of morning, how much more should we? See Section 22, Lk. 3:21, footnote d; Section 48, Lk. 5:16, footnote h; and Section 57, Lk. 6:12, footnote a for more on Jesus' prayer life. The believer who does not pray, does not live, he only exists.

(b) On "kingdom" read Section 39, Matt. 4:17, and all of footnote a for a detailed explanation of both aspects of this kingdom of God. Refer to Christ's statement that His "kingdom was not of this world," in Section 183, John 18:36, footnote q.

(c) **Cities in Galilee.** Josephus wrote that there were many cities in Galilee, not counting the small villages. He explained that "The cities lie here [in Galilee] very thick … and many villages … are everywhere so full of people, by the richness of their soil, that the least of them contain about fifteen thousand inhabitants." See Josephus *Wars of the Jews,* Book 3:3. 1-3, especially lines 41 through 43 for other details. Dr. Harold W. Hoehner in his excellent work, *Herod Antipas a Contemporary of Jesus Christ,* pages 52-54 and 291-295, quotes a source where Josephus states the population of Galilee was about three million. Most "scholars" disagree with him. However, we prefer the calculation of Josephus because he lived among the people in those ancient days. The critics lived two thousand years later. Concerning Josephus' writings, see Section 163, second through the fourth paragraphs under footnote c. For a short review of ancient Galilee, see *Galilee in the Time of Christ,* by Dr. Selah Merrill. This article is found in the *The Hebrew Student,* March 1883 edition, vol. 2, pages 219-220. It gives a survey of this part of the land of Israel and offers solid reasons why the population figures of Josephus can be trusted.

2p-Regarding Jesus' ministry to the people of Galilee, what He did during this time was later described by Peter, who traveled with Him (Acts 10:38). Undoubtedly, He sought to preach in *every* synagogue throughout all of Galilee (Lk. 4:15). The notoriety of Christ flooded the country. According to verse 24, His fame traveled into the far northern areas and went into Syria. Later, the first missionary church was established at Antioch, Syria. (Acts 11:19-26). Word had spread because of His first tour with His few early disciples as seen under main heading at Section 39. Now, He sets out on a third missionary endeavor across His home state or province of Galilee. These follow-up efforts stirred the people and nations far and near to come and hear this Man. See footnotes f and i below for more on this.

(d) For various details regarding the synagogue, see Section 38, footnote c, and Section 89, footnote c. Repeatedly, in the gospel narratives, we read of Jesus preaching in the synagogues of Galilee, healing the sick, and casting out demons. For more on this, see footnote h below. Always, He pressed forward to the next village, with His message of hope and forgiveness, snatching all willing souls from the clutches of Satan and evil spirits. Every informed person in the land knew of His fame. Israel was aflame with the question "Is He our Messiah?" For a classic study of the synagogue, see *The Ancient Synagogue: The First Thousand Years*, by Lee. I. Levine.

(e) "All manner of diseases." What a statement! There are thousands of sicknesses and diseases among the human race. Yet all diseases and devils were subject to Him. For an explanation of Christ dealing with sickness and disease, read Section 41, footnote h. On expelling demons out of their victims and their confessions of Him as the "Son of God," refer to Section 40, Matt. 1:23-24, footnotes c and d; and Section 41, Lk. 4:41, footnote g.

(f) The scope of His fame. Thousands were healed as the multitudes came to Him from faraway Syria and other places. The entire country and distant nations buzzed with talk of a Man, Who claimed to be Israel's Messiah. We can easily believe that these multitudes, upon returning home, carried the wonderful news of Jesus to their respective countries, cities, towns, and villages. To think otherwise would be wrong. Refer to second paragraph of footnote g below for an Old Testament prediction of the masses coming to Jesus. It should be noted that this text (verse 24) distinguishes between demon possession and genuine physical maladies. Beware of those who hastily lay every problem into the lap of Satan, and contrariwise those who disbelieve in his existence. *Both groups serve him quite well!* This text categorizes "divers diseases and torments," in sharp contrast to "possessed with devils." We should try to do the same. Note Section 41, footnote s, for more on demonic reaction toward the Lord Jesus and His reaction to their truthful confession of His deity.

(g) "Lunatic." The word means to be "moonstruck." The ancients had many superstitions about the moon and their folklore bristles with these stories. Nevertheless, it is a medically and spiritually *established fact* that satanic forces work more fiercely during the full moon than at other times. Mental institutions watch the calendar for the full moon and put their staff on special alert. During these periods, many patients become so violent that they must be put under physical restraint. Satanists meet *only* in secret covens during the full moon. The psalmist spoke of the moon smiting by night (Ps. 121:6). For a later usage of the word "lunatic" being applied to a little child, see Matt. 17:15. The work of Satan and his myriads of evil spirits among people during the different moon phases is a field of theology yet untapped. Experienced men muse if it ever should be.

2p-Verse 25. Jacob had predicted on his deathbed that when Shiloh or Messiah came, "unto him *shall* the gathering of the people *be*" (Gen. 49:10). In verse 25, we see a fulfillment of his prophecy. Christ rejecting Jews have struggled with the word "Shiloh" trying every strategy in the book of tricks to prove it does not speak of Jesus the Messiah. Joseph Klausner demonstrates this in his work, *The Messianic Idea in Israel,* Chapter III.

(h) Jesus and the crowds. In Gen. 49:10, Moses recorded Jacob's prophecy of "Shiloh," which was an ancient title for the Messiah. Jacob's prediction mentioned above was fulfilled many times during the ministry of the Lord Jesus. Thus, it is highlighted in gray as being prophetic. For a list of forty-two Old Testament prophecies concerning the Lord Jesus, see *Appendix Three.* Verse 25 reads that "great multitudes" followed him. Matthew lists the names of six different geographical locations that included a vast region, primarily located on the eastern side of Jordan, where the half tribe of Manassah dwelt (Josh. 13:29-32). The prophet Ezekiel predicted, "And thy renown went forth among the heathen" (16:14). Messiah attracted thousands from every direction.

2p-Meaning of Decapolis. The word means "ten cities." Refer to *Nelson's Illustrated Bible Dictionary,* page 292, for an ancient list copied from the Greek historian, Pliny the Elder, containing the names of these ten cities. Thousands of Greeks and other pagan Gentiles also lived in this land, dwelling amid half the tribe of Manasseh. For more on this region, note Section 88, footnote l. The raising of swine in Gergesenes, Decapolis, (which was forbidden by the Law of Moses) may have been the work of these heathen Gentiles. See Lev. 11:24-28 for the ruling of the Torah Law on this subject. For more on the swine in Gergesenes becoming demon possessed, see Section 88, footnote g. Thousands came from these ten cities to see and hear Christ. Many also came from the regions of the Far East. Again, we note the futility of the claim that John the Baptist, and our Lord preached only to the Jews. Christ did not offer them an instant political kingdom and Himself as their King. Note Section 39, footnotes a and g for comments on the type of kingdom expected at this time by the nation of Israel in general and the religious leaders, in particular. For the kingdom John the Baptist preached, refer to Section 21, Part 4, and first paragraph of footnote q.

3p-Most of the literature about the life of Christ has the common thought that He was relatively an unknown figure. This is ill founded. David Klinghoffer makes this mistake in his book *Why The Jews Rejected Jesus* page 47. He wrote, "Only fraction of the Jews alive at the time [of Christ] were aware of his existence. His public ministry lasted only a year or so, from the arrest of John the Baptist to the crucifixion." The opposite is true. Hoards of humanity from every direction found their way to the land of Israel to see and hear this Man. While on his missionary journeys, Paul went into far distant synagogues and freely preached Jesus, without giving any background explanation as to who He was, and what He had done. This is illustrated in Acts 13:26-43; 17:2-4; 18:4-

5; 19:8-10; and 20:21. Among the several million pilgrims attending Passover, many of them "sought for Jesus" (John 11:55-56). How had they heard about Him? The Greeks far away from home also at Passover had heard so much about Jesus that they requested to see Him (John 12:20-22). Where did these Greeks learn about Jesus of Nazareth? He was not an obscure figure touching only a few people. He was known in far away lands.

(i) Matthew makes a distinction between the regions of "Decapolis" with its ten cities (see second paragraph of footnote h above) and an area called "beyond Jordan." Countless thousands of people resided in these geographical regions, some of which reached as far eastward as Babylon and even into India. For over a hundred years certain "historians" and "academicians" have questioned that if Jesus were such a powerful and popular figure, why then is He not mentioned more in the extant literature of first and second century history? Religious critics such as H. S. Reimarus, David Strauss, and K. L. Schmidt have written profusely against the real historical Jesus. They have blasphemed Him from start to finish on the basis that there are "few" or "no" secular extant documents that verify the historicity of His life and miracles. These objections have been answered in *He Walked Among Us,* by Josh McDowell and Bill Wilson, pages 11–89, and also in *Ancient Evidence for the Life of Jesus*, by Gary R. Habermas. Both are apologetic documentaries presenting Christ as a real figure, who is correctly portrayed in the four gospels. The garble about "searching for the historical Jesus" would end if men would believe the inspired records of the four gospels. For a warning about *unjustly* critiquing others, see Section 1, Part 4, fifth paragraph of footnote j.

2p-**The Bible is sufficient.** The writings mentioned above, by McDowell, Wilson, and Habermas are very helpful. However, the Christian has the Bible, God's Word. Holy Scripture does not stand or fall on secular historical confirmation. It is not valid because some believe it and others do not. *It stands on its own infallibility and therefore, cannot fall.* See Section 18, footnote d for more on this. Faith that must be finally verified from extra biblical sources and paganism is false. God's Word does not become acceptable when men believe it or someone thinks they have proven it right. The Bible is trustworthy whether men believe it or not. The germ of damning doubt begins its death in a man's heart when he slowly with quiet distrust turns from the teaching of Scripture and requires confirmation of biblical accounts in *external* sources. This scenario is satanically designed to discredit God's Word and cunningly escort men from its message of truth and hope. The fierce hatred vented against this fact proves it is true. It is the old story of whether we believe what God has said in the Bible, trust Christ in simple faith, and are saved, or cast our lot with the millions traveling the broad way to eternal doom.

3p-**Some do and some do not.** Lee Strobel, an investigative journalist was a confirmed Hebrew atheist. His wife challenged him to prove that Jesus Christ was a phony. After seriously scrutinizing the Savior's life as recorded in the four gospels, the Man he sought to prove did not exist saved him! His life was radically changed. Because of his conversion, the public enemies of Christianity slander Strobel on the internet. For more on this, see Section 137, first paragraph of footnote d. Strobel looked for God and found Him. Others bargaining with God pray something like this, "Heal my child," or "give me that job, and I will believe." In 1955, while busy in door-to-door visitation, I met a veteran of the Second World War. He swore amid the heat of a bloody battle in the Philippines that he would be saved and live for Christ. Haggard, distraught, and wrecked by sin, his wife, and children gone, I pleaded with Charlie about his need for salvation and a new life. He continually responded, "Not now." Several years later, he fell dead with a heart attack! On the other side of the fence, Christianity also has its deserters or apostates. A modern day example is John W. Loftus, a defunct Baptist minister, "with three degrees." Celebrated for his knowledge in philosophy and religion, and "pastor of a church," he suddenly announced that he had become an atheist! *Like all dropouts of this nature, Loftus had never dropped in!* He is a fulfillment of the statement in 2 Peter 2:1. (Swiftness in this verse refers to *how* destruction comes not the time.) This ex-preacher now writes against the (nonexistent!) God and Savior he formerly pretended to represent. His best sellers are cannon fodder for the Devil's crowd to "prove" their trash. *Why I Became an Atheist,* by Loftus, is a blockbuster for those working to secure a front seat in hell. Two thousand years ago, Paul had a "Loftus" on one of his missionary teams; His name was "Demus" (2 Tim. 4:10). History has millions like Demus and Loftus. Despite their foolishness, God waits in love to forgive their defections from His Son, and restore them into fellowship. Happily, some few return. Sadly, most hardened by sin continue in their self willed blindness until death sweeps them away.

4p-**Two more illustrations.** For two further examples of infidel scholarship (mentioned above) and "conservatives," questioning the historical claims of Scripture, see Herod's massacre of the innocents in Section 18, Matt. 2:16, footnote d, and the governorship of Cyrenius in Section 13, Lk. 2:2, footnote d, for details.

5p-**A change is needed.** Men change their religions like changing their sox. Muslims leave Islam and go into "Christianity." *False* "Christians" leave Christianity and go to Islam. Some Jews become "Protestants," and some "Protestants" become Jews. Men changing religions, means one thing: men change religions. Millions have "tried" Christianity without Christ, God without the Bible, and forgiveness without the cross and new birth. It does not work! This is why that some of these drifters are a Baptist one day, a Catholic the next, and dead drunk in jail the next! *They need to be saved!* The author once met a young man who rejected God because his sister died! (Oddly, he had not believed in God while she was alive!) His problem, somehow, touches all of us. Men need the true religion that changes their evil hearts on the inside and conduct on the outside. This is realized only in Jesus Christ, the Son of God (Col. 1:13 and 2 Cor. 5:17). It is not copyrighted by any single church or religion, regardless of who they are.

The third Galilean tour completed. Peter and the other disciples resume fishing.* Below, Jesus returns to Lake Galilee, preaches from Peter's boat, performs an astounding fish miracle, and gives the four men their second call. Forsaking** all, they follow Him. Leading the crowds from the seashore to a high plateau, He seats Himself and gives the Sermon on the Mount. This timeless message is recorded in the next four Sections.***

*See main heading Section 42 for their second call. **Some harmonies attempt to blend the first call of the fishermen in Section 39, Matt. 4:19, with the record of Luke as given below. However, the events below do not seem to coincide with the first call of these men. What Luke wrote here occurred some six months after their first invitation to tour Galilee. Refer to Section 26, John 1:45, footnote h, for background information on the early disciples who later became apostles. Note Section 57, all under footnote g, for continued details about the twelve apostles. Later, in Section 108, Peter experienced another fish miracle when Jesus sent him to get their temple tax payment. ***James, the half-brother of Jesus, repeated altered quotations from this beautiful sermon in his book called the Epistle of James. These various quotes are listed with an explanation in Appendix Two.

Matt.	Mk.	Lk. 5:1–11—*Shores of Galilee*	John
		Preaching from Peter's boat 1 And it came to pass, that, as the people pressed upon him to hear the word of God, he stood by the lake of Gennesaret,[a] 2 And saw two ships standing by the lake: but the fishermen were gone out of them, and were washing *their* nets.[b] 3 And he entered into one of the ships, which was Simon's, and prayed [asked] him that he would thrust out a little from the land. And he sat down, and taught the people out of the ship.[c] *Peter is instructed to fish again: the great catch* 4 Now when he had left [finished] speaking, he said unto Simon, "Launch out into the deep, and let down your nets for a draught."[d] (catch) 5 And Simon answering said unto him, "Master, we have toiled all the night,[e] and have taken nothing: nevertheless at thy Word I will let down the net." 6 And when they had this done, they inclosed a great multitude of fishes:[f] and their net brake. (begin to tear) 7 And they beckoned unto *their* partners, which were in the other ship, that they should come and help them. And they came, and filled both the ships, so that they began to sink.[g] *Peter's conviction* 8 When Simon Peter saw *it*, he fell down at Jesus' knees, saying, "Depart from me; for I am a sinful man, O Lord."[h] 9 For he was astonished, and all that were with him, at the draught [catch] of the fishes which they had taken: *The sons of Zebedee were also amazed* 10 And so *was* also James, and John, the sons of Zebedee, which were partners with Simon.[i] And Jesus said unto Simon, "Fear not; from henceforth thou shalt catch men."[j] *A new assignment. Leaving all they follow Jesus* 11 And when they had brought their ships to land, they forsook all, and followed him.[k] (Verse 12 cont. in Section 48.)	

177

Footnotes-Commentary

(a) **"Gennesaret."** Josephus mentioned that at various times, there were as many as 230 fishing boats on this lake. Fishing was open to all. Yet certain restrictions had been laid down by the Sanhedrin for order and peace to all engaged in this occupation. The Talmud speaks of this in Baba Kama 80b and 81b. This vast body of water was also known as the Sea of Galilee. John alone uses the term "the Sea of Tiberias." (The name has several spellings in the sources.) See Section 21, Part 1 and number 1, under footnote b, for information on Emperor Tiberius. Gennesaret (or Chinnereth), meaning "garden of riches," was the more ancient name, as seen in Num. 34:11 and Deut. 3:17. Originally, Gennesaret applied to both the lake and a town bearing the name. After His resurrection, Jesus met seven of the apostles at this lake, who at the behest of Peter returned to their fishing (John 21:1-3). Despite the untold physical disadvantages that plagued these hoards of humanity, thousands "pressed upon Him" (verse 1). They wanted to see His miracles and to hear the Word of God as He spoke under the unction of the Holy Spirit (Isa. 61:1 with Acts 10:38). The crowds were deeply moved by His powerful preaching and miracles.

(b) **Washing nets** was a common practice. It removed the soil and rubble collected during usage. After the nets were washed, they were mended. A spiritual lesson reminds us that God uses clean things in correct order to catch the souls of men (Isa. 52:11 with 2 Cor. 7:1).

(c) **What a glorious sight!** The Son of God, the Redeemer of men, spoke from the edge of a peaceful lake, from the pulpit of a worn fishing boat to the thousands sitting and standing silently on the shore. Refer to Section 55, Mk. 3:9-10, footnote c, where on another occasion, He retreated to a boat to prevent being trampled by the crowds pressing upon Him. Later, in Section 73, Matt. 13:2 footnote c, He gave a series of parables from another boat anchored along the shores of Lake Galilee. Surely, His teaching had more effect amid such a scene than under the roof of the most costly and splendid church edifice that wealth and art could produce. Our blessed Lord sought not the conveniences for preaching as men do today. A ship, a tree, a roadside, a mountaintop, a valley, a wheat field, a street corner, a bedside, a river bank; wherever men were, single or in masses, *there* Christ preached and taught the message of forgiveness and hope. How different from many of today's church platforms where the minister sits in a thousand-dollar velvet chair, stands behind a two-thousand-dollar pulpit, preaches his sermons surrounded by a three-million-dollar edifice; and continually assures his congregation that "God is richly blessing them." Longtime parishioners have heard this pastoral propaganda line so much they now believe it to be true; however, paying for it is another story!

2p-Surroundings do not give effectiveness to God's Word; rather, it is the opposite. The author once preached for three days in the shabby, dilapidated barn of a wheat farmer in far western Queensland, Australia. The crowds sat on planks, bails of hay, or the dirt floor. Many were saved and blessed as the gospel of Christ, anointed by the Holy Spirit, gave grace, divine charm, and enhancement to the whole scene. In such times, the Word of God, not the carpets, costly furniture, and paint, or the lack of these things, enthralls people. Many pastors today spend hours each month showing visitors their building program, educational block, gorgeous facilities, and of course, their library. Strangely, a great number of them never attempt to show their visitors the Lord Jesus Christ. Why? *Alternatively, would this prove too difficult if not impossible?* The word's of the ancient prophet fall upon our ears, and we struggle to understand them when he wrote, "Behold, I and the children whom the LORD hath given me" (Isa. 8:18). The man of God, Isaiah, gloried in the right things. What did the great missionary Paul mean when he wished to be "cut off" from Christ that his fellow Jews might be saved (Rom. 9:1-4)? He wept that men were the enemies of the cross of Christ (Phil. 3:18). Jude, the half-brother of Jesus, reveals that compassion is what makes the difference in the lives of those who contend for the faith (Jude 22). Like our Lord in the verses above, real saints know the sky is their ceiling, the North and South Poles their boundaries, a listening ear, their pulpit, and every man a prospect for heaven. Surely, our buildings and grand facilities are appreciated, but these things do not finally bring lost souls to the saving knowledge of Christ. A candle loses nothing by lighting another candle. Rather, it gains a partner in the bright work of illumination.

(d) **"Let down your nets for a draught."** When the Lord Jesus had concluded His message, He instructed Peter to return to work. Such a command at first must have sounded ludicrous. How hard and melancholy their work had become. Some human occupations are more toilsome than others are and professional fishing is one of them. Yet, had Peter not sat in the shadow of his Lord, and heard His teaching to the people, standing along the shore? Although he was dog-tired after fishing hard all night, his heart was strangely moved to obey this apparently absurd command from the mouth of this wonderful Person. The wise Christian will obey whatever his Lord commands, regardless of how strange it may seem. *However, he had better be sure it came from his Lord first!*

(e) Night was the best time for catching fish as the heat of day drove them to the bottom of the lake. Peter and his companions had worked "all the night." They were physically worn out, fatigued, and totally exhausted. Yet the Master had spoken His command. Peter discerned that there was absolute sovereignty in the orders of Jesus. He had seen demons expelled, hundreds healed, and countless astonishing miracles, all at the beck of His command. Though weary in the body, Peter moved swiftly to do his Lord's bidding.

(f) **Net breaks.** Rarely, if ever, in Peter's experience as a professional fisherman, had he seen his net breaking because of too many fish! It was a miracle and demonstrated that Messiah was also the Lord of the sea and all its creatures. Refer to Section 108, Matt. 17:24-27, where Peter saw another miracle occur in the Sea of Galilee when Jesus sent him fishing to pay their temple tax.

(g) **Boat sinking.** Never had these men stood on a ship that was sinking because there were so many fish loaded onboard! Commercial fishing does not work like that! The vessels were heavy laden with tons of struggling, flopping fish. They were actually going down! The word "beckoned" means they gave some familiar hand signals to their partners, James and John, to "come and help." Apparently, they were too far away to be heard.

(h) What a confession coming from the boisterous, domineering Simon Peter! Eventually, the strongest of men will break under the load of his sin. *Was this the time of Peter's true conversion to Christ?* See Section 26, John 1:42, footnote f, for the famous misused verse where Peter was *not* saved. Falling at Jesus' knees, he openly confessed his sinfulness. "He that covereth his sins shall not proper: but whoso confesseth and forsaketh *them* shall have mercy" (Prov. 28:13). Had he not just heard the "Word of God" preached while sitting in the shadow of heaven's Majesty? We may be sure that the thousands standing along the shoreline of Lake Galilee were just as amazed at the fantastic catch of fishes. Leaving the scene, the crowds quickly spread the news of this miracle everywhere.

(i) **Verse 6.** The net split and the boat began to sink! What was the Messiah trying to show these men? Had their lives as commercial fishermen ended? They were to understand that from this time forward their common lot was to follow Jesus in full surrender, unencumbered by mundane but often necessary earthly duties. There should henceforth be no more returning to their nets and boats. However, during the days shortly after the death of Jesus, a distraught Peter, and others returned to Lake Galilee and their fishing one final time (John 21:1-3). Soon, the world would be their sea, the gospel their net, and lost souls of mankind the fish to be caught. Refer to footnote j below for continued comments on this thought.

(j) **"Thou shalt catch men."** The highest calling for mortal man is to follow the Lord Jesus over the course of life. How wonderful that the Master prefaced His instructions to the fractious Peter with "Fear not." *It remains the same today; nothing has changed.* See Section 39, Matt. 4:22, footnote g, where they had earlier left their fishing ship. *Now,* forsaking "all," they followed Christ into the greatest enterprise of life: winning souls for heaven (Prov. 11:30; Dan. 12:3; with James 5:20). The next event on their Lord's heavenly agenda was the beautiful Sermon on the Mount (in the next four sections). Here, we note these fishermen's farewell to their earthly vocation, which occurred on the day of their greatest commercial success. What became of those boatloads of fresh fish towed to the shore? Despairing over not understanding the death of Christ, they returned one more time to fishing.

2p-Peter's next great catch was several years later on the day of Pentecost when "about three thousand souls" came to Christ. The context of this story states that those who were baptized had *first* received the message that Peter preached (Acts 2:41 with James 1:18). *The Word of God mixed with the conviction of the Holy Spirit brings to believing men the new birth.* Now, he is a preacher-fisher. With this big catch, he was becoming a real "fisher of men," and Cephas "a stone." Christ had predicted this of Peter at their first meeting almost three years prior. Refer to Section 26, John 1:42, footnote f, for more on Peter, (a chip off the rock) who would later become "a stone."

(k) **"And followed him." This means cross bearing.** For going after Jesus to "catch men," see Section 39, footnote d. After the death of Christ, seven of His apostles returned to their fishing. Fishing all night they caught nothing. Then, Jesus met them early the next morning on the shores of Lake Galilee (Section 205). Over the centuries, millions have left all and followed Him. In time, some think their cross is too heavy and wish for an exchange. However, each one's cross is best for him! Who among us knows what the other man must bear? Could we handle his load? Years ago, I went into a restaurant in Fort Oglethorpe, Georgia, for lunch. The waitress was unusually helpful. I spoke to her about salvation. She quickly replied that she knew Christ as her Savior. After the meal, she handed me the bill. I was impressed to give her a large tip for such genuine service. Seeing the amount, she loudly broke out into tears; startled I replied, "Can I help you with something?" Three days earlier her husband had abandoned her and two small children for another woman. She had no money and was desperate. None of us knows what waits tomorrow. Many Christians untaught about cross bearing, chaff at the strange will of God emerging in their lives. Some become disillusioned, faithless, or bitter over life's hardships. Undisciplined imaginations whisper that God no longer cares. Next, is the Devil's biggest lie that an old sin is the cause of their distress. *It is odd that the man who carries the heaviest cross walks closest to Christ.* For the Savior's instructions about daily cross bearing, see Section 128, footnote d. Luke 9:23. This verse speaks of taking up the cross and following the Savior wherever; but what of those who lay it down? Reader, if your cross is unbearable and you have thrown it off, get on your knees and look again at Calvary. *Seeing Him by faith on His cross changes things!* John the Baptist, the "greatest man born of women," was broken by suffering in prison. Everything seemed against him but Christ took his side! Refer to this in Section 62, first and second paragraphs of footnote b for the beautiful story. Genuine informed Christians do not worship, pray to, or hold respect for two pieces of wood that form a cross. Rather, it is the Man, who died there, and rose from the grave that they love, follow, and serve.

SECTION 44 BEGINS THE SERMON ON THE MOUNT. LATER, THE SAVIOR REPEATED PARTS OF THIS SERMON MAKING CERTAIN ADJUSTMENTS FOR THE UNDERSTANDING OF HIS AUDIENCES.

As the surging sea of lost, sick, and suffering humanity flocked to the Messiah, He taught them by companies, which were continually coming and going. It is noted later in this harmony commentary how astute Jesus was in organizing the crowds (Mk. 6:39-40). One wave after another came and listened intently as He explained the amazing truths of His new kingdom, or as it was later called, the church. They were stunned as He taught, healed the sick, cast out devils, and openly defied the hypocritical religious leadership of Israel. When He finished a particular lesson, the congregation moved out and made way for the next body of waiting people.

The Sermon on the Mount was repeated to every new group coming before Christ at each setting. It was never spoken word-for-word to the audiences without any form of change or variation. The Savior uttered the same truths thousands of times, to different gatherings on various occasions. The four gospels reveal that rarely was every message Jesus preached, pedantic or like the one given before. It was impossible for the thousands waiting at great distances to hear or see Him. Therefore, His continual repetition of the same truths constituted the word differences found in the same lessons or sermons spoken at various times. These differences are obvious to the careful reader of the four gospels. Divine inspiration had parts of them recorded as they were originally spoken, and the four evangelists were directed to place them where God wanted each one located in their respective works. For more on these things, refer to the *Author's Introduction.*

As seen in the chart on the following page, parts of Matthew's record of this sermon are similar to those written by Luke, while comparisons also reflect differences. This harmony commentary seeks to show these things in an effort to respond to the criminal unbelief of the theological critics who shamelessly deny the inspiration of the Holy Scripture. This is the root of their problem coupled with the fact that they deny personal salvation. Some good men hold that Matthew's record of the Sermon on the Mount (chapters 5-7) is the same as that of Luke's record in 6:20-49. This work does not support that possibility. Matthew's total record consists of one hundred and eleven verses while Luke's has thirty. One should notice the likenesses as well as the differences between the two narratives, not only in this sermon but also in various other lessons given by the Lord Jesus and recorded in the four gospels.

Ministers frequently preach the same message to their changing congregations just as Jesus did. However, it is rare indeed, if not impossible, for the same sermon to be given with the exact wording as was previously used. Our Lord employed this same method of teaching people. (Jesus did not read His messages!) Luke's version of the Sermon on the Mount could have been the third, fourth or even the twentieth time it was repeated. Who knows? Matthew's book, being the first inspired gospel history, gives the original (or part of the original) message as Christ *first* delivered it. Both men wrote what the Holy Spirit directed them to write. The dissimilarities in the four records hardly banish inspiration from their pages or those of the New Testament. Rather, they confirm it. *"Selah!"* Either the Bible is an inspired, dependable, and totally trustworthy book, or it is not. Those who clamor for partial inspiration of Scripture are holding onto a rope that is rotted along the way. In time, it will break.

The columns on the next page reflect a number of the doublets or repetitions that were spoken by Jesus and recorded in Matthew's Sermon on the Mount, then also recorded by Luke. There can be no doubt that our Lord repeated many of these truths across His ministry. A look at Luke's record on the following page obviously demonstrates this. He shows us how Jesus' Words were slightly changed to accommodate the existing situation and need of the audience, and how they were often spoken at different times. It is to be remembered that Luke was inspired of the Holy Spirit to place his account of the life of Christ where he did. His reasons for this curious style are not given; therefore, we would do well to leave that alone. Unsaved "scholars and critics" have a picnic with these things because they do not and cannot understand that the ways of God as past finding out. As pointed out in this work, men who do not hold to the full inspiration of God's Word, regardless of how well they teach, preach, and write cannot be trusted very long for they have no infallible source from which to instruct others regarding life, death, and eternity. In spiritual matters, men must have sure and sound direction. The *final authority* for this is rightly divided Holy Scripture.

Appendix Two shows how James was also inspired to include selected and adjusted portions of The Sermon on the Mount and incorporate them into his book known as The General Epistle of James.

PORTIONS OF THE SERMON ON THE MOUNT ARE ALSO RECORDED IN LUKE'S GOSPEL. THIS DEMONSTRATES THAT JESUS REPEATED* HIMSELF WITH VARIATIONS OFTEN BEING USED. REFER TO THE PREVIOUS PAGE FOR AN EXPLANATION OF THE COLUMNS BELOW.

Matthew	Luke
Matt. 5:3–6	Lk. 6:20–21
Matt. 5:11–12	Lk. 6:22–23
Matt. 5:15	Lk. 11:33
Matt. 5:18	Lk. 16:17
Matt. 5:25–26	Lk. 12:58–59
Matt. 5:32	Lk. 16:18
Matt. 5:39–40	Lk. 6:29
Matt. 5:42	Lk. 6:30
Matt. 5:44	Lk. 6:27–28
Matt. 5:46–47	Lk. 6:32–33
Matt. 5:48	Lk. 6:36
Matt. 6:19–21	Lk. 12:33–34
Matt. 6:22–23	Lk. 11:34–36
Matt. 6:24	Lk. 16:13
Matt. 6:25–33	Lk. 12:22–31
Matt. 7:1–5	Lk. 6:37–42
Matt. 7:7–11	Lk. 11:9–13
Matt. 7:12	Lk. 6:31
Matt. 7:13	Lk. 13:24
Matt. 7:16–21	Lk. 6:43–46
Matt. 7:22–23	Lk. 13:25–27
Matt. 7:24–27	Lk. 6:47–49

*For further details on our Savior repeating Himself as illustrated above, see all by asterisk under the main heading of Section 58.

DID CHRIST QUOTE THE ORAL LAW, *TALMUD*, RABBIS, OR THE ESSENES IN HIS SERMON ON THE MOUNT, AND AT OTHER TIMES IN HIS MINISTRY? ARE ANY OF THESE QUOTES RECORDED IN THE FOUR GOSPELS?

Portions of this sermon had been in vogue centuries before Christ was born. Our Lord used *some* rabbinical sayings in this great discourse. Several of His statements are similar to those known among the sect of the Essenes, which broke off from Judaism in about 200 B.C. In reiterating these sayings, Christ approved some because they were truth; others He changed, amended, or outright rejected. Hostile critics have seized on our Lord's usage of selected ancient maxims, possibly certain word's of Hillel (died A.D. 10), a famed teacher and president of the Sanhedrin, and try to demonstrate that He was not original in His teaching. For an excellent article on Jesus and Hillel, see *The Life of Christ*, by F. W. Farrar, pages 738-741. "Christ's wisdom and Words," the skeptics say, "came from Hillel and others." In 2010, Rabbi Joseph Telushkin released, *Hillel: if Not Now, When?* He discusses how Jesus may have been influenced by Hillel. Some present-day radicals claim that Jesus was a Pharisee trying to bring reform to the Jewish people! Rabbi Abraham Geiger, a Hebrew reformer of Frankfort, Germany, (died 1874), popularized this myth. An example of Christ rejecting academia is the work by Professor Thomas Sheehan of Stanford University. In 1986, Random House published his book, *The First Coming: how the Kingdom of God Became Christianity.* Among other things, he denies the deity and resurrection of Christ, and wrote that Jesus came to "reform Judaism." Did Sheehan find his theological garbage in Rabbi Geiger's trash can? "Jesus quoting things similar to those of the rabbis," the critics assert, "proves his learning was derived from Israel's ancient teachers and not God." The conclusion of this is, if I quote three times from Plato, then Plato educated me! Such credulous judgments disparage the uniqueness of Christ. By portraying Him as a common person, dependent upon others, they undermine His divine Person and work. Worse, (some say) His death for our sins, burial, and resurrection was unnecessary. Others hold, He was a victim of political martyrdom. Muslims and other religious infidels teach that He did not die on the cross at all. Islam says that Judas Iscariot or Pilate may have died on the cross instead of Jesus! Some hold that atonement for sin was a cunning revision of some "pagan myth," added to the gospel narratives years *after* they were originally written. "Learned" critics claim that over anxious Christians trying to give "Jesus the man" a god-like status comparable with the Roman Caesars invented this myth. This tirade of hatred aimed at Christ has continued for two thousand years. *Conversely, it historically demonstrates (what His critics hate most), that He is that unique Person, God's Son and mankind's only Savior.*

Did Jesus quote from the Talmud and Hillel? The Jews did not commence the Talmud until about A.D. 250, and it was not *finally* completed until A.D. 500. Thus, it was chronologically impossible that Matthew, Mark, Luke, John, or Jesus borrowed anything from this source. The four evangelists were long in heaven before the rabbis started collecting their Talmudic writings. Whatever our Lord may have cited from any Talmudic *oral* source or written documents, He did so because it was the truth, or something that needed correction, or was applicable to a present situation. This applies to His few citations that may have come from Hillel, the grandfather of Gamaliel. Historically, the Christ hating rabbis were the culprits. Centuries later when compiling their Talmud, they cunningly plagiarized from the *closed canon* of the New Testament by inserting selected but altered portions of it into their work, along with their perverted stories about Christ. If Jesus did quote from Hillel, He did so because it was a presently needed truth and not because Hillel taught our Lord. Anything Christ said that resembled the Essenes (or anyone else) simply confirms that He was familiar with their sayings, approving some and disapproving others. He spoke the perfect truth! Not once did Jesus hesitate in uncertainty when dealing with things and people. He was never unsure. *Jesus was always right!*

When the Savior used well-known proverbs, old rabbinical sayings or whatever, He was hardly placing His approval on *everything* spoken or written by that person or persons. The four gospels carry several examples of Jesus using ancient proverbs in Section 38, Lk. 4:23, footnote i; and Section 46, Matt. 6:21, footnote j. In citing these terse maxims, He was making specific points in His teaching. Truth is truth regardless of its source; be it the Old Testament Scriptures, ancient Hebrew sages, Rabbi Hillel, a member of the Essenes or even Balaam's ass (Num. 22:28-29 with 2 Peter 2:15-16). The written document that Messiah approved was the Jewish Bible called the Tanakh (Old Testament). He tested all things against these infallible Scriptures. If they agreed with the Tanakh, they were right; if not, they were wrong. He said, "The Scripture cannot be broken" or "wrong" (John 10:35). That remains valid.

In 1930, the Hebrew writer Claude Joseph Montefiore published *Rabbinic Literature and Gospel Teaching.* He purports to show how our Lord borrowed most of His teachings from earlier Jewish writings. One can feel from reading its pages that the author was deeply sincere as he wrote; however, he was sincerely wrong! An advocate of "Liberal Judaism," Montefiore rejected Christ as Messiah and the New Testament as being inspired of God. He passed into eternity in 1938.

That the Essene communities are not mentioned in the New Testament means a lot of nothing. For several original articles on the Essenes, see Index page 909 in Josephus under heading Essenes for multiple listings. Albert H. Newman, in *A Manual of Church History,* vol. 1, pages 50-52 lays out a clear but short review of this ancient Jewish sect. There were thousands of religious sects and cults in those days that are unmentioned in Scripture. Rationalistic theologians inquire, "Why is there no mention of John the Baptist or Jesus with the Essenes?" Their question infers that the compilers of the four gospels intentionally left this out of their writings in order to conceal John's and Jesus' connection and learning from these people. Neither Christ nor John were Essenes. This cult ate no meat. It was strictly forbidden. Jesus ate the Passover lamb, and John consumed "locusts and wild honey." The gospels do not record every event in the life of Christ or for that matter, the *totality* of anything. They contain what God wanted us to know about the life of His Son. Some of the rabbinical sayings Messiah approved or disapproved are noted in Section 44, footnotes m, n, and q, and Section 46, footnotes g, j, k, and m. For an irrefutable response to the charge, that Jesus deliberately copied His teaching from the rabbis, Essenes, or others, see the *Biblical, Theological, and Ecclesiastical Cyclopaedia,* vol. ix, pages 571-573, by M'Clintock and Strong. Also note vol. x of this same work, pages 166-199, for a list of the ridiculous and blasphemous statements recorded in the Talmud. Several of these are mentioned in Section 6 of this harmony commentary, second and third paragraphs under footnote d.

Fragments of Essene teachings *may* be suggested in the Sermon on the Mount in Matt. 5:33-37, forbidding swearing, and Matt. 6:1-4, calling for humility and meekness. If Christ used these, it means that He approved such virtuous traits. It should be pointed out that these moral qualities were known and practiced long before the Essenes existed. In Matt. 6:26, where Jesus spoke of the "fowls of the air," we note a similar rabbinical admonition in the Talmud tractate, Kiddushin 82b. Matt. 7:12 gives Jesus' citation of the "Golden Rule." In the Talmud tractate, Sabbath 31a, we find the words of Hillel are almost identical. When we learn that the "Golden Rule" was known *before* Hillel was born, we then ask, "From whom did Hillel borrow it?" Refer to Section 47, footnote e for more on this. Whoever or whatever the Lord Jesus quoted makes no difference. If He saw it as truth that needed to be further propounded or something that needed correction, He did that. Debating that Christ drew His wise sayings and lessons *strictly* from human sources because He was an "unlettered carpenter," is academic childishness or predetermined hatred. Christ's Words in Matt. 7:1-5, condemning hasty judgments are similar to a teaching in the Talmud tractate, Sanhedrin 100a. As explained above, it was impossible that He cited this from the written Talmud. It was not completed until some five hundred years after His ascension. Those who appeal to the oral or traditional sayings of the Jews as being the source of our Lord's teachings are chasing the wind. In the first place, it is uncertain that these sayings *originated* as oral expressions with either the rabbis or Essenes. Many of them were in use before the synagogue or the Essene communities began. Some of these maxims were transposed from the existing Old Testament Scriptures.

For more on Christ and the oral law, see Section 45, footnote b. Section 96, footnotes b through f explains the tradition of the elders or oral law of the Jews. It is vital that the student of Scripture understands this subject and its impact on the lives of the Hebrew people during the ministry of Jesus. To this day, thousands of Orthodox Jews still struggle to live by these laws.

The ancient Orthodox Jewish boast (borrowed by skeptic theologians) that Matthew, Mark, Luke, and John copied parts of their books from the oral Talmud, and then put them into the mouth of Jesus is absurd. "Learned and scholarly" objections to the divine veracity of Holy Scripture and the deity of the Savior emanate from the dark minds of unsaved men and women who presume to explain things of eternal truth; things in which they do not believe in the first place. They degrade the Son of God and the trustworthiness of what the four evangelists were inspired to write. Lastly, their infidelity honors the Devil, the father of sin, and lays a stumbling block for many who seek to know about forgiveness and eternal life. Their Antichrist opinions are the religious prattle of unconverted persons who do not believe in the infallibility of the gospel records, or that Jesus of Nazareth was the unique Messiah of Israel, the Son of God, and *only* Savior of mankind. Peter described these people in 2 Peter 2:1-2.

THE SERMON ON THE MOUNT COMMENCES.

This was a real event in which Christ taught His disciples, the multitudes,* and Israel's religious leaders. It is not a collection of our Lord's sayings or so much a message on how to be saved.** Rather, it instructs believers on how to live as members of His new Kingdom or church after their conversion.

Time: Earlier part of Jesus' ministry before calling the twelve.

Nine beatitudes. Lessons concerning salt, light, city on a hill and a candle.

Some believe that our Lord's "Sermon in the Plain" recorded in Section 58, Lk. 6:20-49, is the same as Matthew's narrative, and they should be harmonized together. This work does not follow that possibility. It credits Luke's record as referring to a separate event that occurred months later in which Christ repeated parts of the original message recorded by Matthew, but added new thoughts. See asterisk under the main heading of Section 58 for details. The "great multitudes" at the end of Matt. 4:25, seem to refer to the same "multitudes"* of Matt. 5:1 below. With the intervening events as described in Section 43, the Sermon on the Mount followed the end of Matthew 4. Matthew placed this as occurring before our Lord chose the twelve apostles. Accepting Matthew's book as the first written of the four gospels, this harmony commentary mostly follows his chronology. **Christ gave an appeal to salvation at the end of this sermon, as seen in Section 47, Matt. 7:24-27, and relative footnotes.

Matt. 5:1-15—*On a mountain in Galilee*	Mk.	Lk.	John
Introduction			
1 And seeing the multitudes, he went up into a mountain:[a] and when he was set,[b] his disciples came unto him:[c]			
2 And he opened his mouth,[d] and taught [e] them, saying,			
Nine beatitudes addressed to believers in general			
3 "Blessed[f] *are* the poor in spirit: for theirs is the kingdom of heaven.[g]			
4 "Blessed[h] *are* they that mourn:[i] for they shall be comforted.			
5 "Blessed *are* the meek: for they shall inherit the earth.[j]			
6 "Blessed *are* they which do hunger and thirst[k] after righteousness: for they shall be filled.			
7 "Blessed *are* the merciful:[l] for they shall obtain mercy.			
8 "Blessed *are* the pure in heart:[m] for they shall see God.			
9 "Blessed *are* the peacemakers:[n] for they shall be called 'the children of God.'			
10 "Blessed *are* they which are persecuted[o] for righteousness' sake: for theirs is the kingdom of heaven.			
A unique beatitude addressed to His disciples and all believers			
11 "Blessed are ye, when *men* shall revile you, and persecute *you*, and shall say all manner of evil against you falsely, for my sake.			
12 "Rejoice,[p] and be exceeding glad: for great *is* your reward in heaven: for so persecuted they the prophets which were before you.			
THREE COMMON SIMILITUDES OF BELIEVERS			
1. Salt			
13 "Ye are the salt[q] of the earth: but if the salt have lost his savour, wherewith shall it be salted? it is thenceforth good for nothing, but to be cast out, and to be trodden under foot of men.			
2. Burning lights in a city on a hill			
14 "Ye are the light of the world.[r] A city that is set on an hill cannot be hid.			
3. Shining candle in a house			
15 "Neither do men light a candle,[s] and put it under a bushel, [container] but on a candlestick; [light holder] and it giveth light unto all that are in			

Matt. 5:15-16—*On a mountain in Galilee*	Mk.	Lk.	John
the house. **The believer's greatest honor and duty: glorifying God** **16** "Let your light so shine before men, that they may see your good works, and glorify[t] your Father which is in heaven."[u] (Verse 17 cont. in Section 45.)			

A primary lesson found in this sermon is that the Lord Jesus exposed the self-righteous practices of the scribes and Pharisees. See Section 45, footnote e for more on this subject. No wonder the vast multitudes were astounded that this young carpenter would dare to challenge their religious peers. The new kingdom and divine righteousness He spoke about was unknown to them. Its beautiful truths were missing in the Hebrew religion and their personal lives.

Footnotes–Commentary

[a] **"He went up into a mountain"** was the description used by Matthew (Matt. 5:1 with 8:1). Hence, this message has been named, "The Sermon on the Mount." Luke records similar words, but then affirms that Jesus' message was delivered "in the plain," or on a tabletop mountain site. He recorded part of this message in Section 58, Lk. 6:20-49. Both writers speak of the same message; however, it was preached at different times and different places. Critics imagine they see "contradictions" in this. Practical reasoning tells us that Jesus continually repeated Himself. Common sense teaches that this mountain was not a jagged, dangerous, life-threatening promontory or the vast multitudes could not have reached the Savior to hear Him speak. It was from a place amiable and accessible to the crowds that our Lord delivered this most profound discourse as the thousands came and went in groups to hear Him speak.

2p-Heaven's teacher of truth, hounded by false religion, found a flat mountaintop (plateau) for his pulpit. Note His recent boat pulpit in Section 43, Lk. 5:3, footnote c. Observe, that it was a common mountain, even unnamed. In this, Christ revealed that the Word of saving grace could be found anywhere except the dark bosom of satanic religion. Under the Law of Moses, men were commanded to meet God at a specific place (Deut. 12:4-7 with 16:6). Now, in Christ's new kingdom, men can pray, preach, teach, worship, and find their Lord *anywhere*. Note the following contrast: In giving the Torah Law, God came down in fearful manifestations (Ex. 19:16-25 and Heb. 12:18-21). On Mount Sinai, He spoke amid deafening thunders and terrifying flashes of lightning as Israel trembled in terror! Now, grace steps forward: Christ sat in calm posture and spoke Words that shook the soul, not the body. Upon giving of the Sinai Law, the Jews fell back in a shudder, but now they draw ever near to the feet of Jesus so calmly reposed. Grace brings the blessed difference and proffers peace to the human soul and mind. Paul wrote, as he contemplated the saving gospel of grace in contrast to the Ten Commandments on tables of stone, "For if that [the ten commandments written on the tables of stone] which is done away was glorious, much more that [the saving gospel in the heart] which remaineth is glorious" (2 Cor. 3:3,11). Observe what is "done away" with and what "remains" in these texts.

3p-Alexander MacLaren, the famed British preacher wrote in *Exposition of Holy Scripture*, vol. 6, page 98. the following, "The contrast between the savage desolation of the wilderness and the smiling beauty of the sunny slope symbolizes the contrast . . . in the genius of the two codes . . . There God came down in majesty, and the cloud hid Him from the people's gaze; here Jesus sits amidst His followers, God [is now] with us. The King proclaims the fundamental laws of His new kingdom."

4p-The Sermon on the Mount was not primarily intended to be a message on salvation, but rather instructions for His followers on how to live righteously as members of His new kingdom of church. The Jewish leaders of religion missed this great lesson. Our Lord lucidly described the Jews of *that generation* as both "wicked and adulterous." Note Section 100, footnote d, for a unique historical confirmation of the base vileness of Israel during this era. In their adamant sinful madness, they were rejecting Him, their Messiah, and His message of hope. This Sermon on the Mount was no different; they rejected it as well.

5p-For a curious note, see *Appendix Two* and a short list of the times James seemingly quoted from this sermon in the New Testament epistle bearing his name. Can this mean the book of Matthew was in circulation when James wrote his epistle? Was he inspired to copy selected parts from it or did the Holy Spirit recall these quotes to his memory as he wrote? Conjecture is sweet but fades in time. Truth is sweeter and lasts forever!

[b] **"When he was set."** Some four hundred years before this, the prophet Malachi predicted that when Messiah came, He would "sit as a refiner and purifier of silver" (Mal. 3:3). Now, we behold Him repeatedly fulfilling this divine forecast. Here, He sits to teach God's Word, which alone had the power to refine and purify the hearts of men. Sitting was the standard posture for public teachers among the Jews and ancients. Other examples of this are given in Section 73, Matt. 13:1-2; Acts 13:14; and 16:13.

[c] Not only disciples but also thousands flocked to see and hear Christ. Never had the nation of Israel been so stirred over the appearance of a Person asserting to be their Messiah. A continual deluge of people sought Jesus. The

religious leaders, fuming with jealously, were infuriated at this young carpenter from Nazareth.

(d) **"Opened his mouth."** And out came a pearl of great price! His lips opened and the creative glory of His mind poured out living precepts for men of all times. Christ's teaching excelled the foul philosophy of Plato and Socrates. To this very day, nothing has been settled by the debates and reasoning of "Greek thinkers," or "Roman orators," or "worldly wise philosophers." Their declarations are as unsure now as when they were spoken over two thousand years ago. Nothing they said or wrote has so compelled men to truth and righteousness as the Word's of Jesus Christ, the Son of God. Simple and wonderful, He came forth from God, telling us what to do, how to be saved and live. He was full of moral beauty and heavenly truth. He did not produce long arguments to show what was right. He had no clumsy rhetoric or silly exaggerations. He meekly preached, taught, and spoke, then, it seemed as though heaven and earth stood silent in reverential awe at such truth. Jesus was the most unworldly of all human beings. He had no desire for what life or the world gives. His was a lot of privations and sorrows. His joy was in the cross that stood before Him and the salvation of countless millions (Heb. 12:2). Sadly, some good men and women have wrongfully assumed that the great Sermon on the Mount was spoken only to His disciples (Matt. 5:1-2). However, at the conclusion of this message thousands were present (Matt. 7:28-29 with 8:1). *Extreme* dispensationalists have placed upon this message a "future, tribulation period, Jewish twist" that is banefully unjustified. The *Scofield Reference Bible*, in its footnotes on pages 999-1003, comes forth with its intrepid "twofold application" exegesis. The message Christ gave here is not, nor was it ever intended to be, "the divine constitution for the righteous government of the earth." Scofield's footnote on page 1002, stating that forgiveness and salvation under the Law of Moses was different from salvation under grace, is seriously incorrect. See footnote 2 on page 1115 of the *Scofield Reference Bible*, for his two different ways people were saved from their sin. Such deject soteriology has only confused the issues and mudded the waters for men seeking the truth.

2p-In giving this great message or sermon, who could imagine the Savior from heaven ranting and raving, so common with "evangelists" and "preachers" today. Several times over the course of His ministry we read that Jesus did "lift His voice" in a loud pitch; each one being for a special reason. John records these unique events in the following places:

1. In John 7:28, He "cried" in the temple to the thousands present at the Feast of Tabernacles when many adamantly refused to acknowledge Him as their Messiah.
2. On the same occasion of the Tabernacle celebration, He "cried" to the people gathered at the temple altar to "come to him" and drink the water of eternal life. Refer to John 7:37-38.
3. In John 12:44, Christ "cried" loudly to the multitudes, trying to tell them that those who had believed in Him had actually believed in God. His equality with the Father is reflected in this statement.
4. Lastly, the word "cried" is used in reference to our Lord's final scream at the end of His sufferings on the cross; here it was a triumphal cry. This is recorded in Mk. 15:37.

3p-There is a Greek word "krazo" which signifies to "scream out." It was employed by the mobs shouting for Christ to be crucified (Matt. 27:23). There was something so unique in Jesus' death cry that the Roman soldiers attending the crucifixion confessed, "Truly this man was the Son of God." Never did our Lord "lift up His voice" in the harsh, overbearing loudness so familiar in many pulpits today. *Jesus was not a screaming, shouting, preacher.* See Section 55, Matt. 12:18-19, footnote h for more on the meek and mild Jesus in preaching.

(e) **"Taught them."** Some things in this discourse were directed *only* to the disciples; other comments were for the multitudes in general. All commands were intended for His spiritual kingdom or church through all ages of human time. It is obvious that some of Jesus' Words were for the scribes and Pharisees. This message has blessed the lives of millions with renewed hope and fresh love for God and His service. Untold thousands of lost souls have been saved through the preaching of the Sermon on the Mount when mixed with the gospel. Here, we find the greatest collection of concise statements ever made on the general subject of the *true religion* and morals found only in the kingdom of Christ.

2p-In this discourse, the Messiah touches on some of the most elemental and yet persistent problems concerning our relation to God and fellow believers. We find here *some* of the highest ideals for living that the world has ever received. Yet, certain voices tell us, "These words are *not* valid for Christians today." Some teach, "They only become acceptable during the tribulation period." Sober minds inquire where such eschatological garble comes from. The answer is always the same. Men, who force Scripture to fit into a previously existing theory regarding the return of Christ, developed it in the matrix of an extremely too-literal interpretation of God's Word. Matthew, in writing these inspired Words, showed fellow Jews the *outcome and fruits* of saving grace in the lives of all who trust Jesus of Nazareth as the promised Messiah and Savior. The Savior demonstrated in this sermon that His teachings are superior to the *entire system* of Moses under which they and their religious leaders lived. No marvel, the audience was dumbfounded when He finished speaking. *The Sermon on the Mount does not teach that good works atone for sin as liberal theologians and ministers often preach.* However, it does teach that good works will be the natural outcome of true salvation.

3p-Certain dispensationalists run amuck with the kingdom in this sermon and across the four gospels as well.

Ethelbert Bullinger (died 1913) is an example of this regarding Christ's sermon given on this occasion. He wrote, "As the kingdom was rejected and is now held in abeyance, so likewise this discourse is in abeyance with all its commands, until the gospel of the kingdom is again proclaimed." See *The Companion Bible*, page 1316. This means that since the Jews rejected the kingdom offer, God then put this sermon on a shelf. We are to believe that it has remained there for over two thousand years! The *Scofield Reference Bible* has popularized the "kingdom offer" myth more than any book in the English language. Refer to page 1011, footnotes 1 and 2, for examples of this. It is an incorrect interpretation of Scripture. The Jews did not reject a kingdom offer. They rejected the Messiah their King because He did not work to overthrow the Romans, and He strongly opposed their rabbinical oral laws or traditions. These traditions are explained in Section 52, footnote h; Section 89, footnote c; and Section 96, footnote d. Not one of Matthew's *original readers* or Christ's *original hearers* would have understood the kingdom-rejected-and-then-postponed fable. See first paragraph of footnote d above for more on Dr. Scofield's extremes. For an explanation of the kingdom in *both* its spiritual and literal manifestation, refer to Section 39, footnotes a and g.

(f) **Happiness.** Beginning with Matt. 5:3, the following nine sayings of Jesus as recorded by Matthew have become known as the beatitudes. This term is derived from Latin and means "blessed" or "happy." In all nine beatitudes (verses 10 and 11 list two separate but connecting ones), the Greek word "makarios" corresponds to the Hebrew word "Asher." It is translated "blessed," which means "happy." *How regretful that we have not kept the word "happy" at the high and holy elevation where Christ placed it. "Happy" as used by Jesus has nothing to do with the "circumstances" in our lives but rather a work of grace in our hearts.* Things, power, money, fame, and success finally make no one truly happy. The popular, Alex Fadeev, wrote about the joys of communism, in a novel called *Happiness,* and then shot himself. I have known of Christians who also committed suicide! This is always because of sin in their lives, not dealt with and secretly entertained. The sin that kills communists like Fadeev, theological radicals, antichrist skeptics, all hypocrites, and others, also kills *disobedient believers* who stubbornly refuse to get right with God. Its wages has always been death unless pardoned by the Lord (Rom.6:23). How God deals with His rebellious children who return to sin is explained in Section 46, eleventh paragraph of footnote g.

2p-**"Blessed."** Jesus begins with this term so well known to every Jew in His congregation. When Israel had entered the promise land some 1,500 years prior, God pronounced "blessing" for their obedience to the law and a "curse" for disobedience (Deut. 28). This prominent event in Israel's history was remembered by every informed person listening to Christ speak. Six tribes of Israel went to the top of Mount Gerizim and six to the top of Mount Ebal; both were located in Samaria. When the priests with the ark of God stood in the valley between the two mounts, all Israel turned their faces toward Mount Gerizim. The Scripture from Deuteronomy that promised blessing would be loudly read, echoing across the valley for all to hear. Everyone shouted "Amen!" Then turning their faces to Mount Ebal, the curses for disobedience were loudly read. At the conclusion of this reading, all Israel shouted again in unison a hearty "Amen!" Concerning the abuse of this word by the Sacred Name cults, see Section 46, Matt. 6:13, paragraphs seven through ten of footnote g.

3p-As if to give a new and higher meaning to this historical event, the Messiah of Israel sits on a mountain plateau. He began by pronouncing a "blessing" on all who obey the message of His new kingdom. In a later version of the same message, Luke gives *both* the "blessing" and the "woe" or "curse" consequences for those who obey or disobey this message (Section 58, Lk. 6:26–28).

4p-**Verse 3**. **"Blessed *are* the poor in spirit."** Section 58, Lk. 6:20, records it as reading "Blessed be ye poor," leaving off the two words "in spirit." It is not one's purse or bank account that Jesus speaks of here. Adam's race is spiritually bankrupt, poverty-stricken, and unaware of its plight and destiny. Blessed indeed is the man who discovers within himself the need of Christ, and who has not been hypnotized by the allurements of this world, being continually drawn to its baited hooks. Yet, there is an ironic side to this lesson. The rich in this world rarely feel the hunger pains for forgiveness and grace. Most of them have their "little heaven" in this life, unaware of what is to come. In Christ's later version of this same sermon, He added this fearful injunction, "But woe unto you that are rich! For you have received your consolation," in Section 58, Lk. 6:24. It is the most blessed day of a man's life when he, stricken by sin, and dying in his spiritual estate, falls before the Lord Jesus and believes on Him for the priceless treasures of forgiveness and the new birth.

5p-The rabbis taught that happiness would be found in riches, honor, learning the Torah, obeying the oral law, and so on. Now, Israel's Messiah again contradicts the main-line theology of the synagogue. In the Jewish literal, material, and physical kingdom, wealth and power were the hallmarks of notoriety. Later, the disciples of Jesus were amazed at His Words to the rich young ruler to sell all (Matt. 19:21). Personal position in their literal, material kingdom was of the highest importance among the Jews. Read the conspiring of James and John with their mother to secure a top spot in this kingdom. Refer to this in the main heading in Section 142. In the Messiah's spiritual kingdom, poverty in spirit was the token of blessedness! He speaks of believers (even if they are rich), who have the humble, dependent attitude of poor people starving more and more for God. To those deeply sensitive to their spiritual poverty and unceasing need for God, Christ pronounced, "blessed!" *All His kingdom had was theirs.* The rabbis had many sayings that related to a humble or poor spirit. Here, Jesus used one of their maxims that were well known. Indeed, blessed are both the rich and poor who are tremblingly aware of the need of their souls. Jesus speaks of the happy humiliation of the human spirit as it reaches upward, thirsting and panting after the Almighty. Such an estate of one's soul is beautifully described in Ps. 42.

(g) **"Theirs is the kingdom of heaven."** Jesus refers to His new kingdom or church as it would be called later in history. Matthew, writing to fellow Jews, painstakingly sought to avoid offense by mostly substituting the word "heaven" for the sacred Name "God." The Name of God was so holy, that it must not be written or pronounced. Many Orthodox Jews use "kingdom of heaven," intentionally omitting the word "God," or spelling it as "G-d."

(h) Who are the "blessed" or "happy" people Jesus describes in this sermon? Can He possibly be referring to the Jewish nation some two thousand years in the future and their projected condition at that faraway period in history? Such a proposal is surely out of order. Christ was describing to the people gathered on the plateau how true life will be after they are converted to Him and serve in His great new kingdom. He was speaking about the spiritual kingdom that was already there, albeit in its earliest infant stages. This is the kingdom that suddenly became "at hand" with the ministry of John the Baptist and Christ's appearing and preaching. It was not something thousands of years ahead after the tribulation period. Such a faraway, future kingdom would have had absolutely no relevance to anyone listening to Him speak.

(i) **Verse 4. "Blessed *are* they that mourn."** Now, we meet those in Christ's new kingdom who sense their spiritual need as sin becomes ever exceedingly sinful before their eyes, and lost humanity perishes without the *true* riches of God. Such a vision fills their hearts with immense sorrow and a longing to bring others to Christ. More is to be learned amid pain and sorrow than dancing in the house of merriment and sport. God has said, "It is better to go to the house of mourning, than to go to the house of feasting" and "sorrow is better than laughter" (Eccles. 7:2-3). At the end of life's journey, *all* truly saved Christians will kiss the hand that wounded them along the way. There is a sinful mourning or "sorrow of this world" that tends to death (2 Cor. 7:10). Conversely, there is a wholesome mourning. In this, the grace of God works to produce unique wisdom, holiness and compassion. Those who reflect these good virtues in this life will at last be eternally comforted in the bliss of heaven.

(j) **Verse 5. "Blessed *are* the meek."** Here our Lord quotes from Ps. 37:11. The unsaved world cannot discern between cowardliness and humility. Did not the Princes of Persia confuse Daniel's meekness with cowardliness (Dan. 6)? They became food for hungry lions because of their fatal error. Meekness here is not a natural moral virtue but a gift of grace in one's life. Meek saints are those who can bear the flames of fierce provocation without being consumed by them. They have grace to remain silent, or they may return a soft answer that breaks the bones. The blessed meek will not allow the unjust shames being imposed on all sides to transport them into the realms of vengeance and indecencies of speech. They mirror Him, whose great heart was "meek and lowly." See Section 63, Matt. 11:29, footnote g, for Christ's usage of similar expressions heard in the synagogue rituals. *There is great joy in walking through this life with a little opinion of self and a big opinion of God and others!* The Lord has said, "I dwell in the high and holy *place*, with him also *that is* of a contrite and humble spirit' (Isa. 57:15).

2p-"They shall inherit the earth." The expression "shall inherit the earth" (or land) was a common, everyday term used by the rabbis for centuries. The Greek word for "earth" in this verse is "ge." It also means "land" in the New Testament. Jesus' teaching had roots in the Old Testament where God promised the land of Canaan and adjacent regions to the house of Israel. The Hebrews of our Savior's time understood it to mean that Messiah would establish His literal kingdom in Canaan, and Israel would share in it. This thought is also contained in the Talmud tractates, Sanhedrin 90a, and 98a. In these two texts, it speaks of the Jews inheriting "the land forever." In rabbinical teaching, this earthly Hebrew kingdom in Canaan pictured the blessedness of heaven. The Jews, hearing Jesus use *this* terminology, instantly understood His symbolism. He preached that every genuinely meek believer would forever enjoy the inherited glory of His new kingdom. Surely, this startled the scribes and Pharisees. He was saying His (spiritual) kingdom was *not* situated in the land of Canaan (Israel) or in Jerusalem as they had taught. It was something higher than an earthly thing and "not of this world" (John 18:36).

3p-Some see in this statement of Jesus the image of a future millennial reign on earth where saints will share in some kind of judgment. This is based on 1 Cor. 6:2 where Paul asserts that believers "shall judge the world," and 2 Tim. 2:12 which reads, "we shall also reign with *him*." Lastly, Rev. 5:10 says that the redeemed of all ages "shall reign on the earth." It is exceedingly difficult to spiritualize these statements when they all speak of a future event. Much of the problem is not in the fact of some kind of earthly rule of Christ, but rather in the odd interpretations that certain "end time specialists" have injected into it. *Trying to fill in the blanks that God has left in His Word, usually results in various forms of eschatological heresy.* On spiritualizing the kingdom, refer to Section 9, footnote g.

(k) **Verse 6. "Hunger and thirst after righteousness."** Some fall into deep consternation at the thought that being hungry and thirsty could bring blessing. However, our Lord does not refer to physical hunger and thirst. Messiah used the strongest of human symbolism (something known to all men) the acuteness of thirst and pangs of hunger. He appealed to their hearts. "Righteousness" here represents the results of conversion and all the spiritual blessings of Messiah's new kingdom and covenant. As the human body craves material food, so the soul of the redeemed hungers for the spiritual sustenance from God's Word. No happier mortal ever lived than the person who feeds from God's Book, walks in fellowship with the Father, Son, and Spirit, and prays for His blessings upon his life. Where are those who hunger and thirst for things eternal in today's Christian society? One man in hot passion will kill another over six inches of soil in a heated border dispute. There exists little passion for the prayer closet, pleading for a full measure of God's gifts and power. Jesus the Messiah declares that those who hunger and thirst as they serve in His kingdom will, at last, be filled in the blessedness of heaven forever.

[(l)] **Verse 7. "The merciful."** At no point in life do we better *imitate* God than by showing mercy. In nothing does God delight more than in bestowing mercy to the human race (Ex. 34:6 with 2 Peter 3:9). Mercy is more than meekness. Our exercise of mercy is the condition of our receiving it. As a rule, the Christ rejecting world gives to us as a mirror does the reflection of our own faces. Merciful Christians get more mercy from God as they give it from their hearts. A hand on the brother's throat who has fiercely wronged us will in time turn back to strangle its user. Dare we fail to remember, it was to us guilty, and wicked mortals that Jehovah showed the greatest of mercies in giving His Son to die for our sins? We must not only bear with patience our own afflictions, but it is our honorable duty to partake of the afflictions of our brethren (as far as possible) by putting on "the bowels of mercy" (Col. 3:12). We are to "weep with them that weep" (Rom. 12:15) and feel for those in "bonds" as "bound with them" (Heb. 13:3). Every blessing, temporal and spiritual, enjoyed by the Christian is from God's hand of mercy (James 1:17). Therefore, it behooves us to reflect God's mercy to others whom we meet over life's pathway, whether friend or foe. What mercies we evidence to fellow men, God will take care to show the same to us. Note other relevant verses that speak of these things in Ps. 18:25, 41:1; and Acts 20:35.

[(m)] **Verse 8. "The pure in heart."** Over the land of Israel, many times each day, one would see a venerable old rabbi swaying back and forth chanting the words, "Blessed are the pure," "Blessed are the pure," "Blessed are the pure." However, at every turn of the hand, they found themselves unclean by breaking another precept of the law or the oral tradition of the elders. To the shock of the crowds, Jesus attaches to the well known rabbinical saying another sentence, "In heart for they shall see God." Messiah's words here are appended to the well-known rabbinical prayer–chant, and no doubt, rattled the audience. In strong opposition to the Pharisees who labored only for *outward* purity while inwardly their hearts were corrupt, Jesus called for an inward change in the hearts (or souls) of men, otherwise they will never see God.

2p-*True* Christianity lives within the purity of one's heart in the Person of the indwelling Holy Spirit (Eph. 3:16). Only by the saving grace of God can any man have a pure heart. We are commanded to lift before God a heart that is pure (Ps. 24:4-5). Apart from being born again, and growing in grace and knowledge of our Savior, the heart of man is a cesspool of filth and corruption (Jer. 17:9). Later, in Section 96, Matt. 15:19, footnote m, the Savior listed some of the awful works of the unregenerate human heart. In contrast to this, see the fruits of the saved ("pure") heart in Section 58, Lk. 6:45, footnote t. Men, busy in today's religious systems, seek to correct external actions by countless rituals, baptisms, ceremonies, and devices. Christ alone purifies the source of sin and its filth by giving a new (circumcised) heart when one is saved by the grace of God (Col. 2:11 with 2 Cor. 5:17).

[(n)] **Verse 9. "Peacemakers."** Scripture teaches that all men are in a state of hostility toward God and each other because of their sin. Only when one is truly saved will this vicious hostility vanish. While God works to bring men into His eternal bliss and give them peace over their sins, so often there rages a war among even those who have been redeemed. *Within the ranks of the Church of Christ, peacemakers are sorely absent!* Troublemakers seem to be omnipresent. The psalmist wrote, "I am for peace: but when I speak, they are for war" (Ps. 120:7). Paul told the factious Corinthians, "God hath called us to peace" (1 Cor. 7:15). The peacemaker's work within the church is a thankless task. Frequently, he finds himself the target of enmity and receives many blows from both sides. One of the most difficult duties of the minister is to seek reconciliation of those who are at variance with one another. Making peace is an impossible task when saints walk in the flesh, pursuing carnal aspirations. If any Christian on earth deserves to be called "a child of God," surely it is those who toil at the most difficult task of making and keeping peace. Real peacemakers uniquely reflect the likeness of their Father in heaven, who did so much to bring us to peace in Christ. The Jews talked much about "peace making." They taught, "Peace was in the spirit of the rabbis" in Talmud tractate, Shabbath 63a, and every Jew, who made peace in this life, would have peace in the world to come. Christ contradicts the rabbis and proclaims that peacemaking is not an exclusive work of the Hebrew religionists: it is an art exercised by those in His kingdom.

[(o)] **Verse 10. "Persecuted."** Over the course of church history, millions of Christians have suffered persecution and joyfully laid down their lives for the testimony of Christ. Some of the persecutors have operated under the name of Christianity. These include the crusaders, the Roman Catholic Church in her barbaric inquisitions, John Calvin and his Reformers exterminating their enemies, are all historical examples along with many others. The deeds of these people shock our sense of right and morality. In recent decades, we have seen the horrors of communism murdering millions. Now, we behold the sheer barbarity of militant Islam towards those who believe in the Lord Jesus Christ. The documented reports of radical Muslims, killing their own children who profess Christianity reflects the lowest form of subhuman barbarity. Persecutions not only fall upon God's children from political and religious institutions but from individuals as well. Vicious rumors, gossip, and slanders of a thousand designs are like sharp arrows that pierce the hearts of the innocent. Often, these arrows of verbal poison have destroyed a good character, wrecked homes, marked little children, and taken lives. *The old adage, "If it's true, tell it," is wrong!* Many things that are true should never pass the lips of God's children into the ears of others. It is written, "Tell *it* not in Gath, publish *it* not in the streets of Askelon; lest the daughters of the Philistines rejoice" (2 Sam. 1:20). We must not give occasion for God's enemies to blaspheme His holy cause. For more on religious murder in the Name of God and Jesus Christ, see Section 142, second paragraph of footnote e.

2p-"Ye." The pronoun changes from "they," to His disciples sitting about, listening. Verse 12, warns them of the persecution from the religious leaders who murdered the old prophets. Pagans or Christ rejecting Jews put most of His apostles to death by various means.

3p-Verse 11-12. "Revile you." Jesus warns his congregation that all previous generations of God's prophets and servants have passed the way of public scorn and suffering. Their lot would be no different as they served in His new kingdom. Much of their future persecution came from the hands of the scribes, Pharisees and Sanhedrin. Messiah promised His rewards in heaven. Jewish teachers promised "good rewards" and "greater rewards" in this life for all Israelites faithful to the Torah, the oral law and the rabbis. See Talmud tractates, Baba Kama 38a and Berachoth 4a for more details on this thought.

4p-We are reviled for being quiet and harmless while others often rant and rave. Karl Marx described faith in God as a "crutch for weaklings!" The testimony of a good conscience saves one from personal misery in his sufferings for Christ. In heaven, at last, the reward of those who have borne under the pains of ridicule, scorn, and contempt will be great.

(p) Verse 12. "Rejoice" in your sufferings and persecutions. *What a statement!* When the Lord Jesus concluded this first part of His Sermon on the Mount, the multitudes were greatly moved. Never had they heard such. No rabbi from any synagogue or theological academy in Jerusalem spoke like this. Practically, everything Jesus preached in these nine beatitudes ran contrary to the popular philosophy and teaching of their religious leaders. He instructed them to "rejoice" in sufferings that would often be the results in their obeying His new commandments. This was something no rabbi could ever say. A sunrise of warm, cheerful hope began to dawn on those confused people as they sat and heard grace pouring from His lips. Their hearts mused in sober contemplation as they remembered that He claimed to be their Messiah.

(q) "Salt of the earth." Jesus did not tell His disciples that they were "the sugar of the earth." Woe be the Christian, who thinks and acts like this! *Men can live without sugar but not without salt.* Messiah drew from the two well-known similitudes of salt and light to teach His audience what all members of His kingdom-church should be. Jewish sages used these emblems continually. They are mentioned in the Talmud hundreds of times. The rabbis taught that salt symbolized the higher things such as the soul and the Scriptures; that it pictured God's covenant with Israel and illustrated the acuteness of the intellect. They rightly believed that the world could not survive without salt. Newborn babies were lightly rubbed with salt to build outward immunity and for cleansing immediately after childbirth (Ezek. 16:4). Every sacrifice was salted before going to the temple altar (Lev. 2:13 with Ezek. 43:24). This pointed to the eternal perpetuity of Christ's perfect atonement for our sins on the final altar of the cross.

2p-It is a historical fact that the salt of the land of Israel became savorless when exposed to extreme heat and vapors emitted from the soil. It was then thrown into the streets and lanes and used as a form of pavement on which men trod. It was also scattered over dunghills to mitigate corruption and eliminate odors. Jesus told his hearers that those who lived shoddy, halfway godly lives, void of power and divine influence, were useless (like savorless salt) to the kingdom of God. The rabbis also taught that all Jews obedient to the Torah Law were like salt before Jehovah. Christ took this and said that those who obeyed His teaching were also like salt, and glorified the Father in heaven. Jesus again employed salt, as an illustration, in Section 109, Mk. 9:49-50, footnote m, and Section 128, Lk. 14:34-35, footnotes i and j. He often repeated Himself on important points.

(r) "Ye are the light of the world." This symbol, pious Jews applied to themselves in general; the scribes, Pharisees, rabbis, and Sanhedrin, in particular. *Above all else, it was a title for their Messiah.* To the amazement of those present, the Savior now places it upon the members of His new kingdom! They are the illumination the dark world needs, not the wretched unsaved religionists of Israel, who, for the most part, were arch-hypocrites. See Phil 2:15 where Paul reiterates the same message. Could Paul have read this from the book of Matthew? With these instructions, our Lord used light to reveal the illuminating influence, pure conversation, and total honesty of those who are part of His kingdom. This simile described the real Christian life. There is no such thing as dirty or soiled light. Light was given from God for the good of all humankind; it brings warmth, life, and renewed hope to those who have groped in darkness. The Jews were taught that Jerusalem, the temple, the Torah Law, and Israel's Messiah were the "Light of the world." Here Christ *partly* contradicts this false theology.

2p-"City on a hill." Middle East cities were built on hills for security, protection, and visibility. In such locations, they could be seen for miles. Thus, the public conduct of all saints should, likewise, be clearly seen by all observers. The end purpose of our salt-effect and light shining is that our Father in heaven may be forever glorified. God is never so glorified and honored as when we bring lost souls to His Son, the Lord Jesus. Refer to footnote t below for more on honoring God.

⁽ˢ⁾ **Like a "candle" in its holder.** We learn here that the testimony of a *true* Christian is something high and sublime; that it is observed by friend and foe alike. No sane person ignites a candle and puts it under a basket to cover its illumination. *We cannot arrive at this lofty and sublime place without hardship and pain; for as the candle sends out its light, it consumes and burns itself down.* See footnote o above. If only we could remember that suffering wonderfully draws us from this world and carries us nearer to heaven. On the other hand, it places us in view of the wicked, and makes us a target of the malice and hatred of carnal men. It also inspires fresh hope to fellow believers. See Section 76, Mk. 4:21-22, footnotes a and b, where Jesus spoke later along these same lines.

⁽ᵗ⁾ The supreme purpose of all mortal life is to glorify our Father in heaven by honoring His Son. *The most God-dishonoring people on earth are those who dishonor the Lord Jesus Christ.*

⁽ᵘ⁾ **"Father in heaven."** Used by Jesus some eight times in this discourse. The Jews also continually used it. Critics enjoy putting the question, "And where is this heaven?" We reply, "It is where God wants it to be." For more on the Hebrew usage of the Word "Father" in reference to God, refer to Section 46, Matt. 6:9, second paragraph of footnote g. The Savior used the term "Father" some 17 times in this Sermon on the Mount. "Father in heaven" is recorded in the Talmud twenty-five times. For an example, see tractates, Berechoth 30a, 30b; Yoma 76a; and Sotah 10a, 12a, and 38b. It was a well-known term, having direct reference to the only true and living God in heaven as contrasted to the idols of the pagan nations sitting in heathen temples. This was well understood by all listening to the Master speak. It was a Jewish thing, heard every day and understood at the time Jesus used it. Among the ancient Hebrews, most of them did not understand the meaning of a living relationship with God by faith in His Son. *However, this was understood later.* To project our Lord's Words over two thousand years into the future and apply it to a Jewish remnant during the tribulation is irresponsible exegesis. In this Sermon on the Mount, it had nothing to do with "Jews turning to God for salvation during the tribulation period" and suddenly calling Him "our Father."

2p-Witnessing in the tribulation. Just as erroneous as the above, is the teaching that "millions will be saved during this time of tribulation." Two centuries ago, such doctrine would have been instantly rejected by *sound* churches. Dr. Thomas Ice, a proponent of this myth wrote in the September 2002 edition of *Midnight Call*, page 19 these words, "I believe Scripture indicates that millions of people will be saved during the Tribulation. We see in Revelation 7:9 a report of the apparent result of the evangelistic efforts of the 144,000 Jewish witnesses." Nowhere in this chapter is it suggested that this multitude of people owed their conversion to 144,000 Jews! This guess must be inserted into the story for the Holy Spirit did not put it there. *Extreme* dispensationalists tell us that these Jewish preachers will win millions to Jesus during this horrific time. This novel eschatology, allowing millions to be saved during the tribulation, was unheard of two hundred years ago! After two thousand years of history, the Christian Church has barely reached 50% of the world for Christ. Now, we are to believe that Jewish preachers will travel across the entire globe without the mark of the ruling beast and do this job in about three years! Presently, there are some 6900 multi bilingual people living on earth. The father of this teaching was basically John Nelson Darby, born 1800 in London, England. Later, the *Scofield Reference Bible* spread this error across the English reading world. Zealous "experts" have swallowed it without serious historical research, and comparative eschatological studies. They are geniuses at filling in the blank spaces that God has inspired in His Bible, and always make them agree with their previous eschatological beliefs. This approach is not necessarily wrong if the original beliefs are time proven, established, foundational biblical doctrines, not something invented several centuries earlier by enigmatic "end time specialists." Church history is littered with "Christians" who died horrible deaths, some of them for heretical and anti-biblical beliefs! The word "great" is found in the book of Revelation some seventy-one times. Nowhere does this book state that the last three and one-half years of the tribulation are to be called "great tribulation." This is another invention of the "end time specialists." Regardless, of the length of this time of world horror, all of it will be a universal nightmare, not just the latter part. (This takes into account the so-called peace treaty signed by the Antichrist and Israel!) The great problem for the 144,000 Jewish preachers from the twelve tribe of Israel is that there are no pure bloodlines existing for any of the tribes. Centuries of intermarriages and mixed marriages have obliterated positive Hebrew tribal identity. The only way to prove a Hebrew is from the tribe of Levi, Judah, or whatever is to perform a biological miracle. Even DNA could not help. For further comments on the 144,000 guessing game, refer to Section 166, third paragraph of footnote c.

3p-How odd to embrace a teaching that was unknown the first eighteen hundred years of church history, then suddenly, it became foundational and original Christian eschatology! Those who adamantly defend these things must backtrack over ancient church history, searching to find where some monk, church father, recluse, or religious misfit, who suggested such teachings. In time, they will locate some erratic "Christian" whose eschatology and soteriology was as bizarre as that of Brigham Young, Ellen G. White, or Charles Taze Russell.

4p-Who is your spiritual father? Scripture teaches there are two spiritual fathers; the Devil (John 8:44, Acts 13:10, 1 John 3:10), and God in heaven (Eph. 1:2). He becomes our *eternal* Father when we repent of our sins and trust His Son as personal Savior (Gal. 3:26 with Rom. 8:15-16). With this, by a miracle of grace, we are instantly made His children. The "fatherhood of God and brotherhood of men" by passes, the atoning death of Christ for our sins. For more on this ecumenical nightmare, see Section 175, fourth and fifth paragraphs of footnote e.

THE SERMON ON THE MOUNT CONTINUES—

Jesus came to fulfill the Torah Law and the Old Testament prophets. Six Mosaic commands, reconciliation, and one Roman Law contrasted* with His new kingdom commandments. He demonstrated the superiority of His teachings over Jewish and pagan laws.

For easy identification of the contrasts given by the Lord Jesus, they are numbered, underlined, and highlighted in red, and set under subject headings. They begin with No. 1 below on the subject of murder and continue throughout this entire Section.

Matt. 5:17-26—On a mountain in Galilee	Mk.	Lk.	John
A statement of profound fact though greatly misunderstood **17** "Think not that I am come to destroy[(a)] the law, [of Moses] or the prophets: I am not come to destroy, but to fulfill. **18** "For verily I say unto you, Till heaven and earth pass,[(b)] one jot or one tittle[(c)] shall in no wise pass from the law, till all be fulfilled. *The reproach of breaking His new kingdom commandments* **19** "Whosoever therefore shall break one of these least commandments, [that I will now give you] and shall teach men so,[(d)] he shall be called the least in the kingdom of heaven: but whosoever shall do and teach *them*, the same shall be called great in the kingdom of heaven. *Beware of the self-righteousness as seen in your religious leaders* **20** "For I say unto you, That except your righteousness shall exceed *the righteousness* of the scribes and Pharisees,[(e)] ye shall in no case enter into the kingdom of heaven. **Six Laws of Moses and one Roman Law contrasted with the commandments of Christ's new kingdom or church** **1. On murder** (Moses' Law stated) **21** "**Ye have heard** that it was said by them of old time,[(f)] 'Thou shalt not kill; and whosoever shall kill shall be in danger of the judgment:' (to be imposed by the Jewish courts as in Deut. 16:18-20). (Christ's New Kingdom Law states in verse 22) **22** "**But I say unto you,** That whosoever is angry with his brother without a cause shall be in danger of the judgment: [of God], and whosoever shall say to his brother, 'Raca,' [scoundrel] shall be in danger of the council: [punishment of the Sanhedrin] but whosoever shall say, 'Thou fool,' [cursed fool or idiot] shall be in danger of hell fire. **2. On reconciliation before offering a gift** (No quote from Moses. Christ's New Kingdom Law states in verses 23-24) **23** "**Therefore if thou bring thy gift to the altar,** and there rememberest that thy brother hath ought against thee; **24** Leave there thy gift before the altar, and go thy way; first be reconciled to thy brother, and then come and offer thy gift. **3. Roman Law** (Roman Law quoted. Christ's New Kingdom Law states in verse 26)[(g)] **25** "**Agree with thine adversary quickly, whiles thou art in the way with him;** lest at any time the adversary deliver thee to the judge, and the judge deliver thee to the officer, and thou be cast into prison. **26** "**Verily I say unto thee,** Thou shalt by no means come out thence, till thou hast paid the uttermost farthing." (Smallest coin about one-fourth of a penny.)			

Matt. 5:27–42—On a mountain in Galilee	Mk.	Lk.	John
4. On committing adultery (Moses' Law stated in verse 27) **27** <u>"Ye have heard that it was said by them of old time,**(h)** 'Thou shall not commit adultery:'**</u> (Christ's New Kingdom Law states in verses 28-30) **28 "But I say unto you,** That whosoever looketh on a woman to lust after her hath committed adultery with her already in his heart. *Adultery has its origin in the eyes: the hands initiate this sin* **29** "And if thy right eye offend thee, pluck it out, and cast *it* from thee: for it is profitable for thee that one of thy members should perish, and not *that* thy whole body should be cast into hell. **30** "And if thy right hand offend thee, cut it off, and cast *it* from thee: for it is profitable for thee that one of thy members should perish, and not *that* thy whole body should be cast into hell. **5. On divorce and remarriage** (Moses' Law stated) **31** <u>"It hath been said,"</u> 'Whosoever shall put away his wife, let him give her a writing of divorcement:'**(i)** (Christ's New Kingdom Law states in verse 32) **32 "But I say unto you,** That whosoever shall put away his wife, saving for the cause of fornication, causeth her to commit adultery: and whosoever shall marry her that is divorced committeth adultery. **6. On oaths or vows** (Moses' Law stated) **33** <u>"Again, ye have heard that it hath been said by them of old time,</u> 'Thou shalt not forswear [perjure] thyself, but shalt perform unto the Lord thine oaths:'**(j)** (Christ's New Kingdom Law states in verses 34–37) **34 "But I say unto you,** Swear not at all; neither by heaven; 'for it is God's throne:' **35** "Nor by 'the earth; for it is his footstool:' [and] 'neither by Jerusalem; for it is the city of the great King.' **36** "Neither shalt thou swear by thy head, because thou canst not make one hair white or black. **37** "But let your communication be, 'Yea,' 'yea;' [and] 'Nay,' 'nay:' for whatsoever is more than these cometh of evil. **7. On reconciliation** Moses' Law stated **38** <u>"Ye have heard</u> that it hath been said, 'An eye for an eye, and a tooth for a tooth:'**(k)** (Christ's New Kingdom Law states in verses 39-42) **39 "But I say** unto you, That ye resist not evil: but whosoever shall smite thee on thy right cheek, turn to him the other also. **40** "And if any man will sue thee at the law, and take away thy coat, let him have *thy* cloke also.**(l)** **41** "And whosoever shall compel thee to go a mile, go with him twain. **42** "Give to him that asketh thee, and from him that would borrow**(m)** of thee turn not thou away.			

Matt. 5:43-48—On a mountain in Galilee	Mk.	Lk.	John
8. On divine love and deed *(Moses' Law stated)* **43 "Ye have heard that it hath been said, 'Thou shalt love thy neighbour, and hate thine enemy.'[n]** *(Christ's New Kingdom Law states in verses 44-48)* **44 "But I say** unto you, Love your enemies, bless them that curse you, do good to them that hate you, and pray for them which despitefully use you, and persecute you; **45** "That ye may be [acting like] the children of your Father[o] which is in heaven: for he maketh his sun[p] to rise on the evil and on the good, and sendeth rain on the just and on the unjust. *Love all men, regardless* **46** "For if ye love them which love you, what reward have ye? do not even the publicans [tax collectors] the same? **47** "And if ye salute your brethren only, what do ye more *than others*? do not even the publicans [tax collectors do] so? *Grow up spiritually: reflect a God-likeness in your life* **48 "Be ye therefore perfect,**[q] [mature] even as [or because] your Father which is in heaven is perfect."[r] (Next chap. Matt. 6:1 cont. in Section 46.)			

Footnotes-Commentary

[a] **"Think not."** At this point, in the ministry of Christ, seemingly rumors had spread regarding His intentions. Among these were accusations that aroused fierce anger among the best-meaning Jews within Israel. Nothing so infuriated the people as the gossip, "He seeks to destroy Moses' Law, the temple, and rejects our prophets." Several of these charges were later laid against Jesus during His trial (Section 181, Matt. 26:61 with Mk. 14:57-58), and against Stephen shortly after our Lord's ascension (Acts 6:13-14). Over 25 years later, Paul was also falsely accused with the same lie (Acts 21:17-21). In the Sermon on the Mount, Christ explained His attitude toward Moses' Law and the Jewish prophets. In His affirmation, "think not that I am come to destroy," the Savior publicly denied any plot to abolish even the smallest scribal hooks and marks of the law or words of the prophets. Instead, He was trying to put to rest their thoughts about His intentions. *He came to fulfill, not destroy.* This is precisely what He did with each requirement of the Torah Law under which He was born and all prophetic statements that pointed to Him.

[b] **Living under or by the Jewish Law?** Every individual, religion, or cult clinging to the code of Moses (or selected parts of it) point to this verse as a proof text for their beliefs. Those entangled in religious legal heresy and/or heterodoxy when confronted with the Torah Law (which they feel they must keep or partly keep), shelter themselves in Matt. 5:17. Our Lord did not say that every jot and tittle of Moses' Law would stand *until* heaven and earth passed away. *Instead, He said that heaven and earth would not pass away until the Law of Moses was fulfilled.* The lesson is that it would be easier for heaven and earth to vanish than for one letter (jot or tittle) of Moses' Law not to be fulfilled. Luke makes it even clearer than Matthew does when he wrote Jesus' statement, "And it is easier for heaven and earth to pass, than one tittle of the law to fail." For explanation of Luke's words, note Section 130, Lk. 16:17, footnote p. *The meaning is not the length of time the law is to last, as some teach. Rather, it is the certainty that Christ would not fail to fulfill the entire code of Moses.* It is beyond dispute that He fulfilled the total Mosaic Law, all of its 613 precepts. Our Lord Jesus was born under the Torah Law and fulfilled all of its requirements and precepts, however they may have applied to Him (Gal. 4:4 with Lk. 24:44). *He was, is, and forever will be the only perfect Mosaic Law keeper by practical obedience.*

2p-Ancient rabbis divided the law into 613 parts. The Jewish physician Moses (Rambam) Maimonides (died A.D. 1204) is usually accredited with codifying Moses' Law into separate divisions. Others say this was the work of the Great synagogue of the days of Nehemiah, which is probably correct. The ancients calculated that there were 248 positive commands supposedly pointing to the parts of the human body; then 365 negative commands representing the days of the year. This harmony commentary has documented many of the wild statements made by the ancient rabbis and recorded in the Talmud. One horrific example is in tractate, Yebamoth 63a, which reads that Adam had sexual intercourse with all the animals of the garden! Are we to teach bestiality because some deranged rabbi wrote this Talmudic blasphemy? (Not all Talmudic quotes are of this nature.) The rabbis so hated Jesus Christ that they wrote in their Talmud, "he worshiped a brick and was sent to hell to be boiled in human excrement." See Section 6, second paragraph of footnote d, for other outlandish statements in the Jewish Talmud.

3p-A certain element among Messianic Jews teaches that even though Christ fulfilled the Torah Law, its 248 positive commands remain valid for all Gentile and Jewish believers today. This sect within believing Judaism holds that after salvation, men are freed from the condemnation of the 365 negative commands because they no longer condemn us. Our guide (they say) is now the 248 positive commandments; for these show how to live after being saved. Some teach that the entire will of God for believers is in the Torah Law, especially the Ten Commandments. Various Reformed theologians affirm similar things. To teach that these commandments embody everything the Christian needs to know as he lives for the glory of Christ is seriously incorrect, if not heretical. For example, will these Jews and their Gentile proselytes tell us which of the 248 positive commandments or any of the Torah Law, for that matter, teaches the following?

1. Soul winning and personal witnessing of Christ.
2. Believers' baptism by immersion.
3. The memorial of the Lord's Supper for the saved only.
4. Growing in grace after salvation.
5. Church planting, its functions, and authority, as set down especially in the letters of Paul.
6. Missionary outreach throughout the whole world.
7. Local church polity, officers, and government. (Some of these were modeled after the synagogue, which was established after the law was given.)
8. Separation (not isolation) from sin and the world as is laid down in the New Testament.
9. God's plan of eschatology and end time events. This does not men guessing and filling in the blanks that the Holy Spirit has inspired in this broad subject.
10. The priesthood of every born again believer.

4p-Where are any of the above things taught in the "good side of the Torah?" *They are laid down only in the pages of the New Testament canon and cannot be found in the code of Moses.* Believing Jews, seeking to find these teachings in the Torah, search in vain. Others are fiercely hostile to the word "Christian," found three times in the New Testament (Acts 11:26; 26:28; and 1 Peter 4:16). They tell us that it *only* means "a follower of Mashiah," or Messiah. ("Mashiah" is the Hebrew Name for Messiah and has variant spellings.) Their interpretation of the word "Christian" is monstrously incorrect. Worse, the genuine radicals with this sectarian body attempt to align the Name "Jesus" with the Greek god Zeus, being (they say) a corruption of the Name Jesus! Some Israeli believers despise the term "Christian Jew," as though it were a secret Gentile plot to rob them of their honorable Jewishness. This is an insult to the millions who have died as martyrs because they were "saved Christians." (Certain Muslims must love this distortion of the term "Christian," for they do the same thing.) Dr. Arnold Fruchtenbaum, a saved Russian Jew, put it this way, "Hebrew Christians align themselves with other believers in Christ, whether they are Jews or Gentiles. Nationally, they identify themselves with the Jewish people." See Frucktenbaum's work, *Jesus was a Jew,* pages 114–115 for the details. For more information on the Name Cults, and their distortions of the Names of God and Jesus, see Section 46, ninth paragraph of footnote g.

5p-Title and name "Christian." Conflict over the word "Christian," has divided many saved Jews into two different camps. One group calls themselves "Messianic Jews." Among this number are some who disdain the name-title "Christian" and try to relegate it to the scrap pile of ancient linguistic history, believing they are not *real* Jews if they use it. A second group among saved Jews who identify themselves as "Hebrew Christians," obviously know the truth on this issue and reflect it in the name they proudly embrace. Certain voices from these competing ideologies tell us, "all saved believers are obligated to live by the 248 positive commands of the Mosaic code." These people affirm that only the "death sentence for sinners has been nullified" within the Torah Law. To this, we respond, *where is this laid down or even intimated in the letters of the greatest rabbi who has ever been saved?* He was Rabbi Saul of Tarsus.

6p-Rabbi Saul told Timothy, the half-Jew-half-Gentile, who the law was made for in 1 Tim. 1:9-10. Who can imagine the great Torah Law *emptied* of its power to condemn and punish those who break any of its 613 precepts by act or neglect? Cannot both omission and commission break the Torah? We are hearing that all saved Gentile Christians must live by the positive instructions of Moses' code. This sect of Jewish law-keepers, the Seventh Day Adventists, and various Reformed believers teach "the law's power to punish those who break its commands has been nullified" for those who believe in the Christ or Messiah. We question what happens if one living under this "toothless Torah" (with its fierce ability to condemn and punish sin now stripped away) should commit adultery, steal, or take the blessed Name of God in vain? Have any Messianic Jews or other law keepers ever committed these sins? Perhaps Gentile believers exclusively commit these crimes. We know what happens to those in *saving grace* that fall into sin! The following New Testament commands for the church make it clear: 1 Cor. 5:9-13; Heb. 12:5-8; 1 John 5:15-17; with Rev. 3:19. It is called "the chastisement of God" on His disobedient children. For more on this, see Section 46, eleventh paragraph of footnote g. In the days of Moses, those who broke the Torah are described in Heb. 10:28. They "died without mercy." However, "this side of the law has been canceled out," so they tell us!

7p-If every saved Jew on earth desires to live under the Torah, eat kosher, observe the Passover with its beautiful seder meal, diligently keep the Sabbath (Col. 2:16-17), circumcise their sons (Gal. 5:6, 6:12) according to

Lev. 12:3 and so forth—wonderful! We respect our Hebrew brethren in the quest to maintain their Jewishness, but wonder whether some of them are more interested in being a Jew inwardly or outwardly (Rom. 2:28-29). For them, *both* are the ideal, if they first possess the inward born again Jewishness (circumcision of the heart). We Gentiles should not expect Hebrew believers in Christ to conform to all our ways. It is a beautiful and proper thing that many of them cling to their great national customs in an effort to witness to their fellows who are unsaved. However, let no Messianic Jew, be he ever so "learned" or "Jewish," demand that any part of the yoke of Moses' Law be laid upon the necks of their Gentile brothers who know better. This is because they are familiar with the examples in Acts 15 and the book of Galatians. We will *not* follow Hagar to the bondage of Mount Sinai but rather sweet Sarah to Jerusalem above, for she is the mother *of us all* (Gal. 4:21-31). All the talk about "the law under grace" is a contradiction of terms. It is like being saved *in* sin instead of *from* it. The Internet has many messages from "Messianic Jews" who claim that the Lord Jesus was a member of the Pharisees, and that He actually approved the tradition of the elders or oral law. Abraham Geiger, a rabbi who died in Berlin in 1874, originally popularized this myth. The *Biblical, Theological, and Ecclesiastical Cyclopaedia,* vol. ix, right-hand vertical column, page 572, carries a good coverage of this subject. Numerous website Jewish evangelists teach, "Paul never changed his religion or condemned it." No, he did not change it; he was saved by the grace of God and made a new creature in Jesus of Nazareth the Messiah. God changed it for him. Regarding Paul's opinion of life and servitude in his Hebrew religion *before* he was saved, read his words in Phil. 3:1-9. Pointing to Acts 21:17-26, where Paul took a vow and went into the temple with other Jews, as proof that he lived under the Mosaic' code is sheer guesswork. He was practicing here what he had written earlier in 1 Cor. 9:20-23, "becoming all things to all men to win some." Had Paul remained a Pharisaic Jew, bound in Hebrew traditions, seeking justification by legal works, and never met Christ on Damascus road, he would have died in his sins and dropped off into everlasting hell. *Jews as well as Gentiles need to be saved out of their false religions and vain empty traditions just as Paul was.* Religion is what man does for God; salvation is what God does for man.

8p-Scripture teaches that *in* Jesus the Messiah, "There is neither [racially] Jew nor Greek," but "all [are] one in Christ Jesus" (Gal. 3:28). The inward oneness (that comes with the new birth) does not include the ecumenical proponents who deny personal salvation and seek religious unity apart from God's saving grace. Believing Jews, who demand that all Gentile believers step under the positive commands of the Torah, who continually mix Torah works with saving grace as the means of salvation are wrong. See Paul's comment on this in Rom. 11:6. Positive or negative Torah rules and saving grace will not mix. *We are not saved by faith in Christ, plus keeping the positive laws of the Torah. Men are saved from sin and hell only through repentance and faith in the finished work of Jesus of Nazareth the sole Messiah and Savior of all men, be they Jew or Gentile.* Those who add to this truth pollute the saving gospel. Some of the extreme Messianic Jews poke fun at Gentile missionary efforts among unsaved Hebrews, make light of the new birth, and continually retranslate the *King James Version Bible* to fit their superior knowledge of Scripture. This is illustrated in their handling of Gal. 5:18: "But if ye be led of the Spirit, ye are not under the law." It is shocking when they affirm that this speaks of salvation by the law. The verse has to do with Christian service, not eternal life. Worse, they scorn believers for attending worship on Sunday instead of their beloved "Queen Sabbath." Holy Spirit leadership takes on various forms and actions where there is saving faith. It will become obvious in a new lifestyle of good works. Where there are congregations of born again believers, honestly seeking the Lord, in time, there will be scriptural based government and order, for true faith produces these things. It is no surprise that ancient Jewish religious traditions and laws influenced the infant and early churches in their developing stages, especially circumcision and law keeping. Like the synagogue, so the church's liturgy consisted of Scripture reading, prayers, singing, and expositions of the Scripture. As the synagogue met at appointed times, so did believers of the New Testament era. The government of the early church, in the hands of elders, reflected that of the ancient synagogue. However, in all of these similarities, there was a firm difference between Christ rejecting Judaism and Christ accepting Christianity. While staunch Judaism made the written code of Moses, its food and drink, staunch Christianity embraced the teachings of Christ and the inspired letters of the apostles as their guiding light through a dark world. By no means did they discount the Tanakh or Jewish Old Testament. They affirmed that the grace of the new covenant speaks better and higher things than the old covenant or law. For explanation of this new covenant, see Section 95, second paragraph of footnote u. See all under the fourth paragraph of footnote h, below for how correctly taught Christians uphold the great Torah Law.

9p-Jesus a Pharisee? As previously mentioned, some Jewish writers tell us that Jesus was a member of the Pharisees! Hence, the reason He quoted particular sayings, especially those of the famed Pharisee Rabbi Hillel, who died about A.D. 10. For more on Christ and Hillel, see Section 47, first paragraph of footnote e. On the absurdity of Jesus citing the Talmud, see the *Biblical, Theological, and Ecclesiastical Cyclopaedia*, vol. ix, pages 571-573, by M'Clintock and Strong. Further, we read that Christ, quoting *portions* of the Talmud, confirms that He was a Pharisee. (As explained, the Talmud was not compiled until centuries after the ascension of Christ.) The author of this harmony commentary has quoted the Talmud for over forty years, but is not, nor has he ever been a member of the Pharisees. (When Paul claimed to be the "chief of sinners" in 1 Tim. 1:15, twenty-five years after his conversion, did he mean that he was still the greatest of sinners. He was he using illustrative words.) Christ gave various altered quotations or similarities that found their way *centuries later* into the Talmud and other Jewish sources; however, He did this long before these collections of Hebrew writings were compiled. This reveals that some of His quotations were wise sayings that had previously existed and were in vogue hundreds of years prior, while others were "fresh from God." The Savior upheld the Pharisaic teachings *only* when they were right. He sharply condemned those that were wrong. To assert that this proves He was a Pharisee is more religious fanaticism from men who are still entangled in the ancient Hebrew law.

10p-Two days before the cross Christ instructed the people to obey the scribes and Pharisees when they "sat in Moses' seat," or taught the commands of the law (Matt 23:1-4). He told His audience to observe the teaching of God's Word, but disdain the evil works of their rabbinical teachers. How this reveals our Savior was a Pharisee is a mystery. Most of the religious leaders hated Him with incensed passion. The scribes and Pharisees continually sought to kill our Lord because He fearlessly condemned their sins and blind dedication to the oral laws or traditions and misrepresentation of Moses. Their hatred was not engendered because He failed to keep the Torah. Christ the Messiah *perfectly* kept the Torah, not because He was a Pharisee, but because He was a loyal Jew and the Messiah from heaven. For an easy-to-read look at present day Hebrew attitudes toward the law, Hebrew beliefs, Messiah, Gentiles, and Christianity, see *Living Judaism: The Complete Guide to Jewish Belief, Tradition & Practice.* An unsaved Jew, Rabbi Wayne Dosick, wrote this fair and excellent work.

11p-**More tradition than Scripture?** Within the Messianic community of saved Jews, some of their practices border more on Pharisaic legalism than God's Word. Various forms of dress and social actions reflect this. Some of these believers in Christ wear their black coats and hats, side curls ("payot"), and even the skull caps ("kippah"). Others will not eat fish and meat from the same plate. This has its origin in a superstition of the oral law, some believing that it would cause leprosy! It is mentioned in the Talmud tractate, Pesachim 76b. For details on these and other Hebrew myths, see *The Second Jewish Book of Why*, by Alfred J. Kolatch. (Gentiles entangled in legalism usually act worse than saved Jews do!) Many of these practices are rooted in superstition and not the Word of God. Placing anything on par with Scripture is wrong. The Holy Bible is the final authority. It is binding and absolute in all matters of faith and practice for Christian Jews and Gentiles. Correct Torah observance is not groping through the ancient customs developed by generations of unsaved rabbis as recorded in the Talmud. It is allowing the Holy Spirit to reveal, "Jesus the Messiah" in all Torah precepts. Many ancient Jews exalted their scribes and oral traditions above the Word of God as recorded in their Tanakh (Old Testament). In the Talmud tractate Eiruvin 21b, we read these awful words, "My son, be more careful in [observance of] the words of the scribes than in the words of the Torah, for in the laws of the Torah, there are positive and negative precepts, but, as to the laws of the scribes, who ever transgresses any of the enactments of the scribe incurs the penalty of death." This dark statement tramples God's Word and prefers the foolishness of unsaved rabbis. It is nothing short of blasphemy! Clinging to vain traditions entrenches ignorance and ignorance breeds more ignorance. In time, it becomes a chain almost unbreakable binding the minds of those who are its prisoners. This is illustrated in the next two paragraphs.

12p-**Sabbath keepers and their teachings.** Those contending *strictly* for Sabbath worship, while condemning those who do not, may find help in reading, *Sunday: The History of the Day of Rest and Worship in the Earliest Centuries of the Christian Church* by Willy Rordorf. Satanic cults advertise over the land that those who "keep Sunday and not the Sabbath will have the mark of the beast." Many of these notions about Sabbath keeping find their origin in the teachings of the deranged Ellen G. White, co-founder of the Seventh Day Adventist movement. White purported to have received special visions from God! The date for Christ's return was set at October 22, 1844. One sees her obsession with the Sabbath day in the work entitled *Earlier Writings*, pages 85-86. Her religious insanity is reflected in the book, *Patriarchs and Prophets*, page 357. In this, she wrote the following blasphemy, "The blood of the Lord Jesus Christ, while it was to release the repentant sinner from the condemnation of the law, was not to cancel sin." In harmony with White, Uriah Smith, an early Adventist wrote in 1877 this lie, "Christ did not make atonement when he shed his blood upon the cross." Cited from *Are the Gospel and the 1844 Theology Compatible?* page 17, written by Robert Brinsmead, a former Australian Adventist. Refer to Section 110, sixth paragraph of footnote k for Dr. Walter Martin's attempt to exonerate White of her heresies.

13p-White's visions and revelations from God were of demonic or mentally deranged origin. In 1860, she wrote, "I am just as dependent upon the Spirit of the Lord in relating or writing a vision, as in having the vision." See *Spiritual Gifts,* vol. 2, page 293. A perusal of the Adventist work, *Questions on Doctrine*, page 93, reveals that White claimed that the Holy Spirit gave her unique revelations. The Adventist publication, *Ministry Magazine* of Oct. 1981 said the following, "We believe the revelation and inspiration of both the Bible and Ellen G. White's writings to be of equal quality. The superintendence of the Holy Spirit was just as thorough in one case as in the other." She claimed to have received over three thousand inspired messages from God! Adventists embrace the false teaching of baptismal regeneration, though they dogmatically affirm salvation by grace. Professor P. G. Damsteegt, professor at Andrews University (the flagship for Adventist education) produced the book, *Seventh-day Adventist Believe . . . A Biblical Exposition of 27 Fundamental Doctrines.* On pages 182-184, 187 passim, we note such things as, "In baptism believers enter into the passion experience of our Lord," and "baptism unites the new believer to Christ." Damsteegt also wrote, "Through baptism the Lord adds the new disciples to the body of believers, His body, the church, then they are members of God's family." Damsteegt is wrong. Repentance from sin and faith puts one into the family of God, nothing else! The old Galatian controversy, with which the apostle Paul continually battled, and its dozens of offshoot heresies are alive and well today. This monster shows its ugly face via the numerous Sabbath day law cults. For continued comments on the Adventist sect, see Section 53, third paragraph of footnote k. Regarding sincerity in religion without biblical truth, see Section 95, sixth paragraph of footnote r.

14p-The Jewish Law in the Millennium? Dwight Pentecost wrote, "positions in the kingdom will be determined by one's attitude toward the law and by one's practice of the law" (*The Words & Works of Jesus Christ*, page 177). In Dr. Pentecost's literal, material, earthly Jewish kingdom, he has the Torah Law operative as the standard for position and promotion. We wonder what would happen should someone break any of the 613 Torah commandments in this kind of kingdom (James 2:10)? Would he be dealt the punishments ordered in the law? Surely, he would or the law would be broken. If so, there will be a lot of hospitals, emergency clinics, funeral homes, and graveyards in operation during this "thousand years of worldwide peace." A mythical material kingdom, well mixed with the Law of Moses in operation is an example of extreme *radical* dispensationalism.

(c) **"Jot and tittle."** This refers to tiny letters or ornamental marks (hooks) used in writing stylish Hebrew script. The "jot," or better "yod," was the smallest letter employed in written Hebrew. The "tittle" or "little horn-like hook" enhanced or ornamented the Hebrew texts. The fact that "jots and tittles" are never found in any English translation of the Old Testament today demonstrates the teachings of Christ are infinitely true. These scribal marks are not needed; indeed, they cannot be put into English translations of the Old Testament. This is because Yeshua or Jesus, fulfilled their *every valid* and minutest significance, regardless of what these may have been. Fanaticism ruled among the scribes over their Torah Law, and this was enhanced by wild fables and their oral traditions. They went so far as to preach that if one letter were changed the whole world would be destroyed. See Edersheim's interesting discussion of this in *Life and Times of Jesus the Messiah,* pages 370-371.

2p-All informed Jews listening to the Savior understood His terminology, for He spoke in conformity with what they knew. The Messiah often used the same language as the scribes in order to lay upon His listeners the absolute authority and trustworthiness of God's Word (in this case the Old Testament). He said that it was dependable in the minutest punctuation mark or scribal ornamentation. Jesus clearly informed the people that He had come to fulfill and fill-full even the smallest vowel points of their written law. In this strong statement, He denies any intention to destroy it. There is a vast difference between fulfilling the law and the prophets and destroying them. Our Lord fulfilled Isa. 7:14 but hardly destroyed it. Both its original prediction and later fulfillment remain for us to study and learn from Scripture. However, the prediction in Isa. 7:14 will never again be realized. The Holy Spirit, Christ, and Mary filled it full. This prophecy met its absolute consummation in the birth of our Lord. The verses in Lk. 24:44 and Acts 10:43 clearly reveal Christ's relationship to the law and prophets.

(d) **"Shall break one of these least commandments, and shall teach men so."** This is what the religious leaders did with the instructions of Christ. The Son of God was speaking of the new commandments (for His kingdom) He was giving at that time, including the smallest of them. These commands of Christ are still applicable and valid for His kingdom or church to this present moment. "Commandments" as mentioned here by Christ *does not* have reference back to the Law of Moses that He had mentioned in verse 17. It was Messiah's new commandments or sayings that He gave on that occasion. They became the *first* directives for His spiritual kingdom or church. Men were to do and teach these, *not* the Law of Moses, for death by violent means ended the lives of thousands who had transgressed certain commands of the Torah. (Keep in mind that in the days of Christ, the Jews had abandoned obedience to the capital crime laws of the Torah.) To transgress the least of Christ's new commandments for His church or kingdom is to incur a disgraced and shameful reputation, but to do and teach them brings praise and blessing. He re-emphasized this fact at the conclusion of His message by saying, "whosoever heareth these sayings of mine, [not the law] and doeth them" or "doeth them not" (Matt. 7:24, 26). Christ's "instructions" and "sayings" are called commandments in John 13:34 and 1 John 2:3-5. The admonition to "do his commandments" in Rev. 22:14 has nothing to do with the Ten Commandments; if so, then it must mean that we are saved (or have the right to the tree of life) by keeping them. The same is true of Rev. 14:12 where cults instantly see the words "keep the commandments of God" and force it to mean the Ten Commandments, regardless! His commands that we are instructed to keep as mentioned in Section 175, John 14:15 and 21, were explained a *few seconds later* (in the same breath) as being His "Words" and "sayings" in verses 23 and 24 of the same chapter. Exegetically, these verses cannot have reference to the Decalogue or to any part of Moses' Code. Law cults run riot in their *misuse* of these verses to prove their heresy.

2p-Not all New Testament commandments were from the Torah Law. Forcing the above interpretation upon *every* mention of "commandments," "my Words," "sayings," and so on is misusing Scripture to justify a false teaching. Paul informed the Corinthian believers that the things he wrote in his letters "were the commandments of God" (1 Cor. 14:37). The Pharisees gave "a commandment" to apprehend Christ in Section 146, John 11:57. Were these "commandments" parts of the Decalogue? Clearly, God has more commandments than those contained in the Decalogue. Paul wrote another group of converts: "For ye know what commandments we gave you by the Lord

Jesus" (1 Thess. 4:2). None of these speaks of the Ten Commandments or the Torah Law. Jesus commanded His apostles in Acts 1:2 and Matt. 28:18-20, but who is so naïve as to make these commands to mean the Jewish law? Peter used similar language when he wrote, "That ye may be mindful … of the commandments of us the apostles of the Lord and Savior" (2 Peter 3:2). To twist all of these to mean the Ten Commandments or the Torah is wrong. *The idea that the Decalogue occupied an exclusive and independent place in apostolic preaching and teaching and in the New Testament letters is grossly false.* The Scriptures of the New Testament do not make their appeal for good conduct and honorable behavior based strictly on Torah rules or commandments. Rather, their appeal is made on the foundation of the superior revelation of the will of God, in Jesus Christ, and the infallibility of the letters of the New Testament as just reflected in the quotations above. Christ does not send us back to the Torah for direction in living the Christian life. We love it, teach from it, and learn from it, while knowing that it is a signpost pointing to something better, even perfect. This is the closed canon of the New Testament.

3p-The erroneous teaching that the first missionaries of the New Testament history preached the Ten Commandments to bring men under conviction and to Christ is foreign to the history of Acts. In the book of Acts, we find recorded some forty examples of teaching, preaching, and witnessing for Christ. *Not one of them reveals the use of the Torah Law to bring men under conviction of their sin and to faith in Christ.* Men heard the gospel, were convicted by the Spirit of God, and saved through repentance and faith in Christ. Paul did not learn of his awful sinfulness while sitting at the feet of Gamaliel, the greatest of all Torah teachers; rather he was confronted with his wickedness when he met the Christ of the cross and empty tomb on the road to Damascus in Acts 9: 1-22.

(e) The scribes and Pharisees are doomed. Directing this pungent remark to the crowds gathered on the mountaintop plateau, Jesus tells them plainly, that, unless they have a righteousness (or holiness) superior to that of their religious peers, they will *not* be a part of His new kingdom. Later, He spoke a sharp parable to these very men "who trusted in themselves that they were righteous and despised others" (Lk. 18:9). The majority of Israel's religionists believed they became righteous, holy and justified by obedience to Moses' Law and their Mishna or oral traditions. Paul continually faced this problem, as seen in the book of Romans and Galatians (Rom. 9:30-32). In short, Christ declared that the spiritual practices of Israel, especially its religious leadership in seeking acceptance before God, were *not* part of the new kingdom He was establishing. Christ called for inner righteousness, not the outward falsity of the scribes and Pharisees. It is ironic that even though the Old Testament contained instructions and illustrations on how men could be saved, they were sorely missed or rejected by Israel's religious elite. In Section 30, footnote h, there was the Pharisee Nicodemus, a prime example of religion without God. For people being saved under the Old Testament and before Jesus' death on the cross, refer to Section 10, footnote b, and Section 144, footnote i. Messiah called upon His audience to ascertain that their holiness was acceptable in heaven, for without this "no man shall see God" (Heb. 12:14). Otherwise, they, like their religious leaders, would "in no case" enter this wonderful new kingdom. See the scathing remarks Christ addressed to the scribes and Pharisees in Section 159, Matt. 23. The multitudes sat stunned at such bold condemnation of their religious peers.

(f) Here, Jesus quoted the sixth commandment in the Decalogue from Ex. 20:13 and Deut. 5:17. His expression "Ye have heard," refers to the Jewish people who had heard the Scriptures read by the doctors of the law and various rabbis in their synagogues. Next, He lays down a sharp contrast in the Words, "But I say unto you." With this, Jesus begins a critical contrast. (The term "whosoever shall kill shall be in danger of the judgment" was a well-known scribal *addition*, for they are not found in the original commandment of God.) After explaining that He had come to fulfill the law and the prophets (verse 17), the Savior proceeded in verses 21 through 48 to illustrate that the commandments of His new kingdom were collectively superior to those of Moses of old. *He was not reinterpreting the Torah.* Such an act would have been scandalous to the Jews. Rather, in the first part of The Sermon on the Mount, He *contrasted* six different verses of Torah Law, part of an oral tradition (that later found its way into the Talmud-Mishna), and one Roman Law against His new kingdom commandments to demonstrate, which was superior. These contrasts are numbered, enlarged, and highlighted by red in the Scripture texts above.

2p-Verses 21. "Ye have heard." In Jesus' usage of these terms, He follows the exact rabbinical style in public teaching. By the expression, "Ye have heard," and "them of old time," He refers to what the crowds had been taught in the synagogues thousands of times. Christ has in mind Moses and the prophets. His *first* illustration eloquently revealed that the sixth commandment of Moses only touched men externally. Its purpose was to *inhibit* the physical act of murder. It did not reach the source of the crime, which is in the heart of man. Messiah's new command on this subject did what Moses' Law could not do; it pinpointed the place where murder originates.

3p-Verse 21. "Shall kill and shall be in danger of the judgment." This injunction was also a common saying and made reference to the "judgment" of God as it was established in Jewish courts (Deut. 16:18). Premeditated murder called for the death sentence, though this was neglected in the days of Christ. Attorney W. M. Chandler, in his work, *The Trial of Jesus*, pages 46-47, quotes from the famed Rabbi Maimonides, who listed 36 capital crimes in Moses' Law. Murder is *first* conceived in the human heart, and then performed; the command of Moses attempted to stop the act from being committed. Christ the Messiah gives His new kingdom rule regarding murder: "Whosoever is angry with his brother shall be in danger of judgment." Not one member of that august body of the seventy-one judges of the Sanhedrin would have ever tried a man for being angry with his brother! The kingdom law of Jesus revealed the cause, which was anger-hatred in the human heart. Even deeper, Christ's new command stated that if one called his brother "Raca" (a term of the highest insult among the Jews); he should be brought before the "council" or Sanhedrin for judicial action. *Never had the Jews heard such teachings as this!*

4p-Verse 22. "But I say unto you." Now, He makes a strong contrast; He sets His Word against the teachers of Israel, and He affirms that His teachings are greater and must be heeded above all else. Our Lord is not in conflict with the *correct* teachings of Moses and the prophets; rather, He is laying before them the commandments of His new kingdom. They are superior to anything taught in Israel. At this time in Jewish history, the scribes and Pharisees had canceled out the teachings of the Torah Law, in preference to their countless oral traditions. These traditions are discussed in Section 96.

5p-Verse 22. "That whosoever is angry with his brother without a cause." In the new kingdom of Christ, those who harbor malice and hateful resentment in their hearts toward their fellows were making themselves libel to the judgment of a law court. What an over-generalization in view of the ill feelings that exist in most churches between Christians. In the days of Christ on earth, those who carried spite, grudges, or hatred in their hearts, regardless of who they were became ready candidates for a justified lawsuit.

6p-Verse 22. "Raca." This term was tantamount to calling someone by the slanderous word "imbecile." The Jews counted it as a deadliest insult. Members of our Lord's kingdom or church are forbidden to use such derogatory terms. Referring to His followers of *that day,* Christ warned them that to employ slanderous and impudent language would justify their punishment by the Sanhedrin court of Israel.

7p-Verse 22. "Thou fool." This means one spiritually destitute, incorrigible, and totally reprobated. That it, a person who is beyond all hope. This is *not* the general use of the word as employed by Jesus in Matt. 23:17 or Paul as seen in 1 Cor. 4:10. The context is clear that this awful term was considered deadlier than the use of "Raca." It described the vilest of sinners worthy of damnation. It might be interpreted to mean, "You damned [to hell] idiot or empty headed fool!" Christ is saying that the punishment of gehenna or the lake of fire was worse than the punishments meted out by any law court or even the Sanhedrin. How appropriate was Christ's condemnation of the foul use of this word, because the religious leaders continually described the citizens of Galilee as "Galilean fools." Note this in Section 9, footnote b. Verbal abuse of a fellow Jew was considered a high social crime, especially calling one a "moros fool." The Talmud tractate, Baba Metzia 58b stated that one deserved gehenna fire for committing such offenses. This is amazing in view of how the Jewish religious leaders abused and blasphemed the Son of God during His trial, and as He hung dying on the cross.

8p-Abusive language. How dreadful that our Lord seems to declare that one way to murder a fellow is using foul, demeaning, and slanderous language. Words hit harder than a fist!

9p-Verse 22. "Hell fire" or "gehenna." This spoke of a terrible valley just south of Jerusalem where the most horrible rites of pagan idolatry were committed in history. These included burning to death tiny children as offerings to a demon god called Moloch. This was done under the deafening beat of drums called "toph," which muffled the screams of the dying innocents. In the days of Jesus, this valley, called gehenna, came to typify the eternal damnation of the wicked. It was the city dump for Jerusalem, and a public incinerator where fires smoldered or burned continually, even in the rainy seasons. Christ does not refer to the myth of annihilation in this awful statement. For more information on gehenna, see Section 59, footnote o. Christ continued in verses 23 through 26 showing how all heart anger and wicked mischief should be properly dealt with and corrected before the secret intent became public reality.

10p-In cases of premeditated murder, enraged, vengeful anger, hate, and slanderous name-calling among the Jews, the commands of Christ given here, and later in Paul's letters, tower above anything recorded in the Torah Law. *The Sanhedrin would have been thrown into total chaos if they had practiced their Torah Law according to the teaching of the carpenter from Nazareth!* Repeatedly, the people were astonished at the Word's of Jesus. In this Sermon on the Mount alone (not counting various other New Testament verses) the Son of God laid down for His children the grandest summary of moral and religious instructions the world has ever heard. They are miles higher than the Decalogue, in that they expose and forbid in a divine way, murder, adultery, swearing, hypocrisy, covetousness, and every wrong act. Christ's new commands embrace all saved believers and point first to the heart where sin originates and its evil actions are planned.

11p-Verses 23-24. Forgiveness the rabbinical style. These Words of Christ must have dumbfounded His audience in view of the rabbis' teaching on forgiveness. This is explained in Section 110, Matt. 18:21-22, footnotes h and i.

(g) Roman Law or Lex Romana. Here, our Lord quoted part of a Roman Law, apparently well known to His audience, for He did not explain its source to them. The legal code of the Roman Empire was called "The Twelve Tables" and venerated as their prime legal source. They were engraved in bronze tables and displayed at the Forum in Rome, Italy, supposedly dating back to 450 B.C. Albert Barnes mentions this particular law about one's adversary and court in his *Notes on the Four Gospels,* page 55, where he quotes from a much older source. "Adversary" does not necessarily mean one's hateful enemy. It also referred to a debtor-creditor situation and often to a personal wrangle between friends and neighbors. In such cases, the Roman Law ("Lex Romana") stated that if opposing parties settled their differences "on the way to court" the case was automatically dismissed. (It was held that the persons at odds should walk to court together and try to settle their differences.) In brief, the Roman Tablet affirmed something like this: "Get reconciled with him and avoid the terrible ordeal of court, prison, and its consequences." Christ's lesson is, "You cannot approach God in acceptance with animosity against a brother. Put things right with them, and then come before God with your gifts." He used this same thought later in Section 71, Lk. 12:58-59, footnote z. Will Durant in his classic *Story of Civilization*, vol. 3, pages 31-33, and gives a concise but terse description of the famed laws of Rome. On page 32, he wrote that often under this system "a magistrate would become the judge." The Savior spoke of the "judge" in verse 25.

2p-Verse 26. Purgatory? Those who find the Papal doctrine of purgatory in this statement have found what is not there, historically, contextually, exegetically or sensibly. This monstrous pagan teaching flies in the face of the perfect and complete atonement of Christ for the sins of mankind. The error of purgatory teaches that we are not fully justified by faith in the finished work of Christ, and that believers who died with unforgiven sins must go into this mythical place and complete their suffering for venial or smaller sins. What blasphemy! The only punishment inflicted *after death* is that of hell fire for those who die in their sins without Christ as personal Lord and Savior. No one is prayed out of hell! The Roman Catholic system as well as many Orthodox Churches fails to distinguish between Christ's suffering as the total and complete expiatory or penal offering for our sins and the chastisement of wayward believers in this life. The wild Tertullian and the clever Augustine believed in purgatory. The myth of purgatory is against the everlasting and all sufficient atonement of Christ. In a 1928 version of an old book, *The Catholic Dictionary*, page 704, column 2, we read this amazing admission of a Catholic writer, "We doubt if [Scripture] contains an explicit and direct reference to purgatory." With countless millions of dollars poured into this religious fraud annually, almost a hundred years ago, one of their own confessed that purgatory could not be found in their Bible! Those who struggle with 2 Tim. 1:16-18 trying to find biblical justification for this myth are wrong. For more on the pagan origin of purgatory, see the fourth paragraph below. In verses 25-26 of His message, Christ used a Roman citizen to illustrate His lesson. This person had paid his previous debt and would be released from prison. Jesus' congregation understood what He meant in the use of this illustration.

3p-Jewish purgatory! *The Biblical Theological, and Ecclesiastical Cyclopaedia*, vol. viii, page 798, by M'Clintock and Strong, carries an article reflecting how Judaism has its own version of a purgatory. This includes prayers for the souls of the dead uttered during the Feast of Tabernacles. These supplications are called "kiddish" in Hebrew, which means "sanctification." They are recited at "yahrzeit" (usually for a fee!) on the anniversary of the death of a loved one. This enlightening article quotes prayers offered for the deceased and reflects how deeply this pagan practice has filtered into the rituals of the Hebrew religion. Regardless of the church or religion, men can only believe in and practice such infamous deeds because of their abject ignorance or rejection of the *complete, final, and perfect atonement* of Christ on the cross for the sins of all men of all times. It is the highest abomination to teach that Jesus did not fully suffer and die for all sins regardless of what they are. There is no part we can play by suffering for the remainder of our sins to be forgiven. Christ did that almost two thousand years ago for all men of all times.

4p-The doctrine of purgatory was taken from pagan religions and made part of Catholic dogma. Rome celebrated an ancient heathen feast called "Sacrum Purgatorium." It was here the Papal Church introduced the myth of purgatory. Martin Luther defied the Roman system because of their selling indulgences on October 31, 1517. Among the issues was a call for Scriptural proof for the doctrine of this intermediary place that held the souls of the dead. It could not be found. Some twenty-nine years later, at the Council of Trent in 1546-1547, bishops of the Papal system agreed to add further books to their Bible. Among the *six books added* to the Catholic Bible was 2 Maccabees, a non-canonical, uninspired historical work. It was written during the inter-testament period and spoke of the pagan custom of "praying for the dead" in chapter 12:45. Catholic apologists struggling to prove the scriptural basis of purgatory now use this exact passage! The fearless Luther defied various heresies in the Catholic Church but retained their views of baptism and the Lord's Supper as being necessary for salvation. Refer to Section 203, the eighth paragraph of footnote d for this.

(h) Adultery. The seventh commandment and quoted from Ex. 20:14 and Deut. 5:18. The superiority of Christ's law over this citation from the Decalogue is profound. The problem of sin in the eye originates first in a wicked and wanton heart of man. The Lord declared that the sin of adultery begins in a man's eye and heart before it is committed with his body. Hence, the dangerous peril of lewd pictures and plays observed by those who desire to keep themselves pure. From inward lust to abandoned passion, with *the* intention to go after that which is not one's own, counts as the sin already committed in the mind of God. Therefore, set a guard at the impulses of thy heart. "Keep it with all diligence for out of it are the issues of life" (Prov. 4:23). What one thinks continually in the chambers of his heart, "so is he" before God (Prov. 23:7). Job had it right when he declared, "I made a covenant with mine eyes; why then should I think upon a maid?" (Job 31:1). Jesus teaches in His new kingdom that men are to control the source of their sin, thus preventing the sin from being committed. An ounce of prevention is still worth a pound of cure even in the kingdom of God. The Savior's words, "Whosoever looketh on a woman to lust after her" is a direct attack against the popular rabbinical saying, "If anyone sees a woman [in] which he is delighted withal above his wife, let him dismiss his wife and marry her." Lightfoot quotes this in his *Commentary on the New Testament . . . ,* pages 118-119. Peter warned believers about "Having eyes full of adultery" (2 Peter 2:14). The most prolific and popular sins in the world are adultery and fornication.

2p-Christ declares that His Word is preeminently superior to the seventh command of the Decalogue in dealing with the ever-present temptation of adultery. Go to the source of the sin and deal with it there. A heart change is commanded for all members of the Lord's kingdom. This new heart was predicted and offered to Israel as she was facing entrance into the Promised Land. In Deut. 10:16 and 30:6, God *foretold* a time when He would "circumcise the hearts of their children." He even preached the gospel to Israel while they tramped through the wilderness, but most of them refused to believe it (Heb. 4:1-2). *The inward circumcision that God required of Jews in the wilderness spoke of the new birth.* For explanation of this, see details in Section 30 footnote h. When a person is saved and made part of the new kingdom, he is then considered "a Jew inwardly and his heart circumcised," or he has been born again (Rom. 2:29 with Col. 2:11). Then the new kingdom commands of Christ are gradually "written in the fleshly tables of their hearts" by the Holy Spirit. Again, we must mention this glorious process called "growing in grace," and it covers a lifetime for the child of God. Mature Christians come to understand that "love is the fulfilling of the law" (Rom. 13:8-10).

3p-Believers do not direct their lives by that which was written on the tables of stone brought down from thundering Mount Sinai. If they did, there would be no local church witnessing and reaching out to a lost world, for the tables of stone command none of these graces. The final revelation of God laid down in the closed canon of the New Testament, especially the letters of Paul to the churches, contain the *completeness* of God's commands, instructions, words, and orders for His people. All the 613 precepts of the law acted as a schoolmaster to bring Jews to Christ. It was in this sense that the Torah Law "converted the soul" and "made wise the simple" by pointing men to the Savior, who was to come (Ps. 19:7). This is the reason that, in the book of Deuteronomy, over and over God called upon Israel to obey and direct their lives according to His law. This is why the prophets condemned the nation for abandoning and breaking the law. David praised God for the law throughout the entire Ps. 119 because it was this very law that pointed him to the saving knowledge of Christ, whom he knew was coming to die for our sins (Ps. 22) and rise from the dead (Ps. 16:9-11 with Acts 2:26-28). Understanding the plan of salvation in Christ as shadowed in the law, David rejoiced in its every precept, found delight in its instructions and directed his life by them. Paul affirmed precisely the same thing when he wrote that his faith did not make void the law but rather that his faith in Christ led him to "establish [defend and affirm] the law" (Rom. 3: 31). Paul was "under the law to Christ" (1 Cor. 9:21), meaning he was directed by the teachings and commandments of Christ the Messiah, not the Torah. Bible Christianity *establishes and affirms* the fulfilled Law of Moses in various ways. A few of these are:

1. It recognizes Christ as the central and supreme theme of all the law's rites and ceremonies; every Torah precept points more or less to Him (Lk. 24:44 with Col. 2:14-17).

2. Christ was born under it as a Jew (Gal. 4:4) and perfectly fulfilled its every demand and requirement, be they positive or negative commands (Matt 5:17 with John 5:45-47).

3. The Lord Jesus ended its rule over all who are truly saved. He then gave His superior teachings, which in a few years were united with those of the other New Testament letters. These *now* constitute the infallible guide for His new kingdom or church, as it was later known. At no place in the *entire New Testament* are we directed to live by the 248 positive commands of the Torah Law. This myth was also invented by rabbis and is used by the law cults, which do not understand or have tried to mix the saving grace of God in one's life with Torah Law commandments.

4. The divine righteousness that the law demanded has been freely imputed to all believers through the Lord Jesus Christ (Rom. 3:21; 4:6-7; 8:3-4; with 1 Cor. 1:30). The required righteousness of the Torah was, in fact, the very righteousness of God in Christ. Zacharias and Elizabeth walked in this blessed imputed righteousness of the law "blameless" before the Lord (Lk. 1:6). Both were saved, Spirit-filled believers in Messiah to come (Lk. 1:41 with 67). David rejoiced in the blessing of Christ's imputed righteousness a thousand years before Jesus was born (Ps. 32: 1 with Rom. 4:5-8). He prayed to God to "restore the joy of his salvation" when he had fallen into sin (Ps. 51:12). How could the joy of salvation be renewed if David was not saved? (The teaching that Old Testament people were not saved is wrong.) David, Solomon, the prophets, and many others praised God for the law. Their schoolmaster taught them about the coming Messiah and Savior. David called Jesus his "Lord" in Ps. 110:1. He made this statement by the Holy Spirit according to Section 158, Mk. 12:36. This is why the Old Testament saints blessed *both* God and His Law and rejoiced living by its precepts. *The wonderful Torah Law pointed them to eternal life and forgiveness of sins in the coming Messiah, Jesus of Nazareth.* When the complete New Testament teachings were given, these became God's final guide for believers.

5. Lastly, Bible Christianity establishes and upholds the Law of Moses by including *some* of its moral and spiritual principles within the canon of New Testament Scriptures from which the church finds its direction and guidelines. Selected portions from the law were integrated by the Holy Spirit into the New Testament Scripture. However, they were placed on a superior level of meaning than they had been in

their Old Testament context (Matt. 18:15-16; Rom. 13:8-10; 1 Cor. 9:8-11; Eph. 6:1-3; with Heb. 8:6). In all of these, a greater spiritual lesson is presented, not the formal letter of the law. The saying so frequently heard from those trying to follow the thunder and lightning from Mt. Sinai, "We don't live *under* the law but *in* it," hardly changes anything; rather, it makes it only worse according to the all-comprehensive threat of James 2:10-11. This declares what happens if a single commandment is broken! The half-brother of Jesus pointed to the supreme standard by which Christians are to live; he called it "the law of liberty" (James 2:12), which was obviously a contrast to the "bondage" or "yoke" of the Mosaic legislation (Acts 15:10 with Gal. 5:1). Earlier James had written that those who look into this particular "law of liberty" and *continue* in it are the blessed ones (James 1:25). And what is the "law of liberty" speaking of? Indisputably, this refers to the teachings and new commandments of the Lord Jesus (John 13:34-35, 1 John 2:7-8 with 2 John 4, 6). These later became part of the commandments of His inspired apostles as they wrote their letters of instruction to churches and individuals (1 Cor. 5:9-11; 16:1; with Phil. 2:12). Refer to *Appendix Seven* for more on this.

4p-A cursory reading of the infallible letters of the New Testament show that the writers were *progressively* laying down directions for the early churches to follow. We inquire, where did any of these writers instruct the churches to obey the commands of the Torah Law? *After* the death of the twelve apostles (John being the last one to die in about A.D. 100), these letters were collected and recognized as God's final instructions for the kingdom of Christ or the church throughout all succeeding ages. *This in no way negates* the Old Testament. In its pages, the New Testament is concealed, and in the New Testament, the Old Testament is revealed. The latter, points to the former and the former gives substance, meaning, and understanding to the latter. The book of Hebrews demonstrates this in a profound way. One could not understand Hebrews without the laws and instructions that had been written in the Old Testament book of Leviticus. Nowhere in the New Testament canon is there any intimation that the church is to use the Torah Law or the Ten Commandments as its supreme guide in the service of Christ, not even Eph. 6:1-3. The teaching that the Torah was given to Adam in the garden and later renewed at Sinai is built on silence. (One wonders with *whom* he would have been tempted to commit adultery, *what* he would have been tempted to steal, and *how* he honored his father and mother and so on.) The various people, tribes, and ethnic groups that lived from Adam to Moses had their own laws. The walls, pyramid paintings, and the code of Hammurabi reveal this. However, to affirm that they had the Ten Commandments defies good sense, even when "based" on 1 John 3:4; Rom. 5:13, 20 with 1 Cor. 15:56. The verses in Deut. 5:2-3 emphatically state that the "covenant" or "ten commandments" (Deut. 4:13 with 9:9), were *not known* to the fathers, Abraham, Isaac and Jacob. And they are called "fathers" in Deut. 1:8, 6:10, 26:3. How could they have had the Torah Law if it was not known to them? Like the *extreme* dispensationalists who distort God's Word to pieces to justify some microscopic unjustifiable teaching, the Jewish cults and Reformed doctrine of living by the Decalogue and its covenants are from imagination, not the pages of Holy Scripture. Rom. 3:20 emphatically declares, "for by the law is the knowledge of sin." This is quoted as proof that the Ten Commandments were from the very beginning, even for Adam and Eve. The argument goes, "that if there was no law to be broken, then sin has no basis to condemn." Is that so? What condemned the angels that sinned in the dateless past of eternity when the law did not exist (Jude 6). All sin is first an offense against the Thrice Holy God of heaven—law or no law, Ten Commandments or no Ten Commandments. God gave the law at Sinai in order that the sins of Israel might have a basis (when broken) to judge and punish all offenders (Rom. 5:20). It is written, "The strength of sin [to condemn] is the [broken] law" (1 Cor. 15:56).

5p-The Mosaic Law did not always exist. What God gave to Moses for Israel, engraved on tables of stone, and was not without beginning! As mentioned above, some affirm that it was given to Adam and his descendants. Paul disagrees with this verdict. The law covenant for the nation of Israel had a historical beginning, and that was at Sinai with Israel. It also had a historical fulfillment at the cross and empty tomb of Christ. The apostle wrote, "For until the law sin was in the world" (Rom. 5:13). He said, "The law entered that the offence might abound" (Rom. 5:20). In Gal. 3:19 we read that the law was added, "because of transgressions." The words "until the law," "the law entered," and "the law was added" are senseless if the code of Moses had always been. How could the great missionary write that the law was not until some 430 years after Abraham if it had always been (Gal. 3:17)? With the perfect atonement of Christ, a new pedagogue spoke to the conscience of the new covenant Christians. The tables of stones or the old pedagogue for Jews was dismissed from the scene (Gal. 3:24-25). The Son of God established a new covenant of grace; our grand teacher is the Holy Spirit, and our textbook is the closed canon of Holy Scripture. He now writes this upon our hearts not in the stones of Sinai. For explanation of this new covenant, see Section 95, second paragraph of footnote u.

6p-Matt. 5:29-30. "Right eye and right hand." Our Lord's instructions regarding the eye and hand were standard expressions used by the Jews to describe the main channels through which sin assails and so often conquers humanity. First, man's eyes and next his hands are the chief human instruments used to initiate adultery. Christ is not teaching bodily mutilation as was practiced by pagan religions and the deranged church father Origin, who had himself emasculated, thinking to control his passions. See *Sex Worship*, page 108, by C. Howard, printed in 1890 for the shocking story. Even if a man cut off both hands and removed both eyes, he could still lust! Many portraits of passion hang in the long hallways of human imagination. Here, the Lord Jesus used harsh but figurative language understood by every person in His audience. The lesson is clear: it is better to use the extreme measures of self-control than to experience the sinful passions of human nature and at the end of life suffer the pangs of eternal damnation. Later, in His ministry, the Savior again employed similar terms in Section 109, Mk. 9:43-48, footnote k. Which was the better way, the Mosaic command that said, "Do not commit adultery," or the Master's new command that checked the source of the sin, which is in the heart of man?

(i) **Divorce, Jewish style.** This was cited from Deut. 24:1 but embellished with standard rabbinical tradition. In this text, the word "uncleanness" speaks of "shame, disgrace, or nakedness." Whatever this meant, it did *not* mean adultery or fornication, and yet divorce was allowed for it. In Deut. 22:13-21 we meet the case of a man, who married a woman, who was accused of premarital sex; if it was proven, she was stoned according to Deut. 22:21. However, the mystery text of Deut. 24:1 allowed divorce for *whatever* "uncleanness" meant to the ancient Jews, and there was no death penalty attached to it. (The talk about "God allowing" and "God letting" various things happen is incorrect. If God let it happen, then He did it; if he allowed it to happen, then. He also did it. Obviously, God knows everything that will happen, but He is hardly the cause of it all.) *Man is a responsible creature and will answer for what he does.* It was the interpretation of the word "uncleanness" that brought about the irreparable division in the two theological schools at Jerusalem, that of Hillel and Shammai. For a review of divorce among the ancient Jews, see *The New Testament and Rabbinic Judaism,* pages 362-372, by David Daube.

2p-**The two schools differ.** At this time in New Testament history, there was a sharp difference of opinion among the Jews regarding the reasons for *acceptable* divorce. The two Jewish theological academies at Jerusalem were split on their interpretation of the subject. The School of Hillel allowed divorce for almost any reason. The stricter institution, the School of Shammai, allowed divorce and remarriage only for the sin of fornication. Fornication included a vast variety of sexual sins and perversions, such as adultery, incest, molestation, unlawful copulation and numerous others too unsavory to mention. Because of this division of opinion, many Jewish men held to the School of Hillel and thus divorced their wives for the most trivial reasons. Near the end of Jesus' ministry, the Pharisees questioned Him over these things. This event is recorded in Section 137, Matt. 19:3. They inquired of Him, "Is it lawful for a man to put away his wife for every cause?" Their question came out of the division among the Jews over the issue. *They were asking his opinion of the liberal Hillel's view on the subject as is seen in the word "every."* Divorce became official when the wife was given written notice, called "cutting off." There is an English translation of the ancient Jewish divorce bill in *Dake's Annotated Bible,* page 46 of the New Testament, footnote f in the left vertical column. The bill was written in twelve lines, signed by the husband, witnessed by three people, and delivered to the wife in a well known place near a river if possible. She would insert it into the temple public archives and was free to marry whom she pleased. However, she was publicly branded an "adulteress" even though she may have been innocent of the sin. This reveals the one-sided wickedness of many Jewish men in their treatment of women. The religion of Islam is also infamous for their foul treatment of women.

3p-The Talmud tractate, Gittim is filled with instructions regarding women and divorce. Jews during this era freely used both polygamy and divorce to satisfy their lusts. (Those who write that the Jews did not practice polygamy at this time should reread history.) Our Lord made it clear that fornication/adultery was the *only* grounds for divorce and remarriage in His new kingdom. Years afterward, Paul added another valid reason in 1 Cor. 7. For details on these verses, see the fifth paragraph below. Some six hundred years before Christ, God said in Ezek. 16:38, that adultery broke wedlock. What does breaking wedlock mean? Can it mean *not* breaking wedlock? Some hold that the command of Christ spoken in Matt. 5:32 applied *only* to Jews and therefore, it is not valid today. Since He was instructing the crowds on the mountain regarding the superiority of the commands in His new kingdom over the system of Moses and the old Jewish kingdom, this interpretation seems incorrect. Contextually, the word "whosoever" means what it says. As stated above, our Lord again commented on this subject in Section 137, Matt. 19:1-12, where in verse 8 Jesus makes it clear that "from the beginning." Divorce was *not* the original plan of God. (In Section 130, Lk.16:18, footnote q, there is a condensed version of Matthew's words given in response to the conversations taking place at that time with the Pharisees.) When man fell from his *original* state of innocence and sin ravaged humanity, God later permitted divorce and remarriage on the grounds of irreconcilable adultery.

4p-**"God hates divorce."** In Mal. 2:16, Jehovah declares that He "hates putting away." This must mean for the *wrong reasons,* for in Ezra 10, we are amazed to read that God commanded some one hundred and fourteen men to divorce their wives! The events in Malachi and those in the book of Ezra occurred within the same chronological period. The reason for these divorces was "mixed marriages" with heathen nations (Ezra 10:2-3, 11) which were a violation of the Torah Law (Ex. 34:12-16 with Deut. 7:3). Commentators, who object that the Hebrew verb "yasa," meaning to "go out," (as used in Ezra) does not mean divorce, are incorrect. It is the *same verb* used in Deut. 24:2 where "departed out" clearly speaks of divorce. This *one-time* historical event is not recorded in Holy Scripture to provide a license for easy divorce. Some hold that God took this sternest of measures to correct a problem that apparently affected the family line through which the Messiah was to be born. However, this seems impossible for according to the genealogical list in Matthew chapter 1, the family line of Christ had many evil people in it. Regardless of the reason, it is astounding to read this story in Ezra. We can quickly believe (though it is not mentioned) that God also ordered some type of "alimony" or "reparations" for these divorced women and their children in view of His many commands to protect the "fatherless, widows and children" found in the Torah Law (Ex. 22:22; Deut. 10:18; and Ps. 68:5). Pointing to this to justify divorcing an unbelieving or heathen mate contradicts the later instructions of Paul in 1 Cor. 7:12-13. These are explained in the fifth paragraph below.

5p-*No couple since Adam and Eve have been united in absolute sinless innocence as they were.* Whatever their union was as husband and wife, it occurred during a very brief sin-free period in the garden. God's *original* design in that primeval first marriage drastically changed when sin entered the world and the world was plunged into chaos—so much so "that the whole creation groaneth and travaileth in pain together until now" (Rom. 8:22). These changes later included His permitting for *exclusive* divorces. If God did this, then He was the originator of it. Years later, Paul wrote that desertion (or abandonment) of a believer by an unbeliever also presented grounds for divorce and remarriage (1 Cor. 7:13-16). In this chapter, with verse 27, Paul used the term "loosed," which means "divorce," not separation. Biblically, there are at least two acceptable reasons for divorce and remarriage: *irreconcilable* fornication-adultery and *irreconcilable* desertion. Speaking of women (and men) who commit adultery, God said that they "break wedlock" (Ezek. 16:38). Therefore, the marriage "lock" is broken by this demoralizing sin. Those who quote the passage "that it was not so from the beginning" need to realize that after sin entered creation nothing remained "so" from the beginning. No man or woman has ever lived as our first parents did in that wonderful beginning of all things. For comments regarding physical and mental abuse in marriage, see Section 137, fourth paragraph of footnote g. Under the Torah Law a man who divorced his wife scripturally, was called "her former husband" (Deut 24:4). "Former" means what it says. It cannot imply that he "had two living wives."

6p-What does Rom 7:1-10 mean? Here Paul used an illustration from marriage to show that any power or authority that has been canceled out is thereby void and of no consequence. He writes that we "are dead to the law" by the "body [or atoning death] of Christ." *He is saying that when a marriage is dissolved because of adultery, the "law" of the husband ruling over his former wife no longer exists.* She is freed from all previous marriage ties and the authority of her previous husband. He has no power or rule over her whatsoever, just as the law cannot rule the saved Christian, who is freed from it by the death (atonement) of Christ. Since the female in Paul's illustration was still alive, she was not divorced for adultery, for that was *supposed* to have brought the death penalty. (Being divorced unscripturally and thus illegally, this type of woman would be called an adulteress by the Jewish community if she remarried.) However, if this woman's former husband died, regardless of her reasons for the earlier divorce, she was freed from the marriage bond, just as believers are free from the law by the atoning death of Christ. It is noted that he did not say free from the 365 negative parts of the law. The apostle was not writing about one divorced on the terms God had laid down, for she would not have been described as an adulterer. She was loosed or freed to be married to whom she would because her divorce was legal. Therefore, in employing this illustration, Paul used only one side of the marriage picture, not the whole story. Those who tell us that this illustration teaches "no divorce for any reason" have loaded the apostle's words with more than he intended in using this example. Paul knew what both theological schools believed about divorce and remarriage. He was thoroughly acquainted with what the Torah Law taught, the tradition of the elders, and what God permitted.

7p-Look before you leap! Though the above is true, individuals considering divorce should be meticulously diligent to ascertain that their case is based *only* upon God's Word, total honesty, and is irreconcilable. Greater attention should be paid to what God clearly commands men to do, than what He may allow them to do. A command is binding and must be obeyed, while an allowance is optional. *Frequently, in remarriage, the options prove far worse than the commands!* Jesus said that the teachings of His new kingdom or the church, tower above the Law of Moses, and that He did not agree with the liberal School of Hillel on divorce. God's ideal is for marriage to last a lifetime. However, sin has ravaged this holy institution. In all such cases, people can rejoice that the blood of Christ removes all sin! For a comprehensive and clear explanation of this, see *Divorce and Remarriage* by Guy Duty.

(j) **Verses 33-37. Oaths and vows.** This passage is a blending of selected words from Lev. 19:12 and Deut. 23:23, and again distorted by rabbinical jargon. The Jews of this time were inflamed with oath making. As the context reveals, they swore by their heads, by both the gray and black hairs on their heads, and by heaven and earth and numerous other objects. Christ rebuked them for swearing by the gold plates attached to the temple walls, by the altar of sacrifice within the temple compound, and even by the temple itself (Matt. 23:16-22). The Talmud tractate, Shebhuoth is loaded with instructions regarding various oaths as employed by the ancient Jews. Some Hebrews swore by the prophets, some by the books of their Old Testament; others swore by their food, by camels flying, by birds, by ducks, by stones, by the objects of creation and so on. These vanities became a part of daily conversation. The warning given earlier by Solomon against hasty vows in Eccles. 5:1-2 had no effect. By the time of Christ, swearing and making vows had sunk into extravagant decadence. Deuteronomy 10:20 commands Jews to 'Swear by the name of God." This had strict reference to affirmations and oaths given in court or exclusively to the Lord of heaven, not the glib, trifling statements of men who know not the fear of God.

2p-"Swear not at all." This command speaks of the profane everyday conversation of the Jews, but not of judicial oaths taken in a court of justice. Our Savior took such an oath at His trial (Section 181, Matt. 26:63-64). Paul called upon God to witness his sincerity (Rom. 1:9 and Gal. 1:20). James tried to correct this ongoing sin among "the twelve tribes" because of the habitual swearing that prevailed among them (James 5:12). It is noteworthy that, in his admonition, James quotes the teachings of Jesus, his half–brother. Speaking against this sordid state of swearing and oath making among the scribes, Pharisees and Hebrews in general, Jesus preached in this great sermon that in His kingdom, there was a nobler way of communication. "But I say unto you … let your communication be, Yea, yea; Nay, nay: for whatsoever is more than these cometh of evil" (verse 37). *A man's word was his bond.* The common people were amazed. Doubtless, many of them rejoiced at the refreshing, pungent truths spoken by the Messiah. It was so different from the hypocritical rabbis who taught one thing but lived another.

3p-Verses 34 and parts of 35 are free or general quotations that our Lord takes from words found in Isa. 66:1. The latter part of verse 35 was taken from Ps. 48:2. The rabbis continually took certain words from passages and used them to build specific verses. Now, the Savior uses this same method of exegesis. It was a standard practice and certainly acceptable as long as the original meaning of Scripture was not altered. Ministers do the same thing today. See where Matthew was inspired to use this rabbinical technique in Section 18, Matt. 2:23, footnote i.

(k) Retaliation. Cited from various words found in Ex. 21:24; Lev. 24:20; and Deut. 19:21. This was not a direct part of the Ten Commandments or the Law of Moses but was built by blending several citations together from different pieces of the law. It was a saying of the rabbis and reflected their distortion of God's Word. In the context of these three verses, the lesson is clear: God is *controlling* revenge among the Jews, not commanding it. The Pharisees had turned it into a fierce command! However, Christ is referring to a specific practice of the Jews, which was sanctioned by their magistrates. It required reparations to be paid by the guilty. We notice that our Lord did not *repeal* it. The problem was, by this time in Jewish history, it had fallen out of the control of the appointed magistrates and was being practiced by any Jew, who sought to avenge himself. The scribes and Pharisees seized upon this law as grounds to satisfy *private* resentments and take revenge at their pleasure. Not infrequently, their revenge was executed with sheer ruthlessness. When our Lord instructed the people not to resist evil, He was speaking within the bounds of rationality and common sense. The general lesson is that we are not to resist or fight against those who hate or misuse us. (See this illustrated by the apostles and Paul in the following verses, Acts 5:40-41, 7:59-60, and 16:22-25.) However, this rule may be carried too far. Contrary to rabbinical instructions, Messiah forbids vengeful retaliation from those who are in His great kingdom.

2p-On the other hand, Christ does not teach that we are to sit back and see our families murdered, our homes plundered and destroyed, by not resisting evil men and their cruel intentions. Not to resist is impossible in such circumstances and would be cowardly and exceedingly sinful. Nor does He teach that it is criminal to salute the national flag, fight in defensive wars, and defend what we have honestly acquired and so on. False cults and devilized political organizations of the worst sort propagate such dark passivity to their deluded disciples. To His hearers, Jesus presents several illustrations. Smiting one's right cheek was the most grievous insult possible among the Jews (1 Kings 22:24 with Isa. 50:6). Jesus ordered that those in His kingdom were to "turn the other cheek" and accept this deed of high insult without any reprisal. This shocked His audience.

(l) Among the ancients two garments were worn, the inner and outer. To take one's outer garment or coat was counted a heinous crime. It was forbidden in the Law of Moses (Ex. 22:26-27). Jesus commanded that if this occurs, we are to offer meekly the remainder of our garments to the oppressor. Lastly, the Messiah commands that His followers are to be uninhibited in their giving. See Section 58, Lk. 6:29, footnote f, for more details on this subject.

2p-Verse 41. "Compel to go a mile." The word for "compel" is an old term and comes from the Persian language. It had reference to a particular function in their vast postal system. It spoke of a "courier" or "one being *forced* to carry something." Our Lord's lesson on "going the extra mile" pointed to the custom continually used by the Roman soldiers who were stationed in the land of Israel as occupation troops. They could instantly and publicly commandeer selected Jews into various forms of compulsory labor. At any moment, day or night, a single soldier could order any stranger to carry his cases, packs or whatever for a long distance. This is what the Roman soldiers did to Simon of Cyrene when they compelled him to bear the horizontal beam of Jesus' cross to the crucifixion site (Section 188, Matt. 27:32, footnote b). The Jews hated the Romans for this intrusive form of slave induction. It was a threat of compulsion that continually hung over their heads. Christ again stuns His audience by declaring that in His new kingdom, the rule is to go peaceably with your enforcer and if needed, carry his load the extra mile! He was gradually introducing them to the marvelous works of grace in the life of a believer.

(m) "Borrowing." The Son of God is speaking within the bounds of propriety and prudence. Nowhere did our Lord encourage laziness or support of the idle at the expense of the industrious. With each *genuine* case of apparent need, that addresses itself to us, we are commanded to consider if it is within our means to assist. If a poor and needy person of honest character and reputation wishes to borrow, we are to step forward with the aid at our disposal, never turning him away. A word from Holy Scripture regarding all such cases is noted in Heb. 13:1-2.

(n) "Love thy neighbor and hate thine enemy." This quotation, used by the rabbis, was apparently taken from parts of Lev. 19:18 and Ps. 139:21-22. It was another distortion of Scripture to justify their wickedness. *A "neighbor" in strict Jewish thinking was exclusively another Jew.* Gentiles were bitterly hated, though Hebrew merchants courted them in business enterprises. Many attending to the Master's message had heard countless times this rabbinical admonition from the synagogue chair. It was held by Orthodox Hebrews that if one saw a Gentile fall into the sea, he must not lift him out. All uncircumcised pagans were the enemies of God, and the Jews had been traditionally taught to hate them. The carpenter from Nazareth contradicts standard rabbinical theology.

2p-Verse 44. Here, we find the most sublime piece of morality ever given to humanity. Such a command seems unreasonable to unconverted men, who often reason from hatred and greed. Love is the theme of the kingdom that Christ came to establish among men who are saved by His precious blood. This single precept is sufficient proof of the genuineness of the gospel and the absolute truth of the Christian religion, lifting it above and beyond the religions of all times. As mentioned above, the Jews were taught to love *only* their own. All others were despised or outright hated. Later, our Lord gave the lesson of the Good Samaritan in another attempt to correct this wicked rabbinical view. Refer to Section 116, Lk. 10:25-37, for an explanation of this occasion. Over history, many "churches" and "religions" have murdered those who would not bow to their demands. The Papal Church, the bloody crusaders, many Reformers, lunatic branches of Anabaptists, and *hundreds* of others stand guilty. For more on this awful subject, see Section 48, footnote d and Section 68, fourth paragraph of footnote e.

(o) **"Act like you belong to God."** To conduct oneself in compliance with the commands of Christ, as laid down in these portions of the Sermon on the Mount, could only reflect a God-likeness rarely seen within the nation of Israel of that day. Sinners saluted and praised fellow sinners; the cut-throat publicans greeted one another, but the people of this new kingdom were commanded to love all men! The Jewish public verbal salute was "peace be unto you." *It was never spoken to anyone other than fellow Jews or true proselytes.* Christ commanded every person in His kingdom to express a more extensive and sincere benevolence toward all men. Prejudice had no place. Never had the multitudes heard such things. They had been well trained in the bigotry of their Jewish theological teachers.

(p) God mercifully shares His sun and rain with wicked men who live in rebellion to Him. The ancients wrote much about the need for sun and rain. The rabbis said that "rain is both for the righteous and wicked" in the Talmud tractate, Tannith 7a. There were sayings similar to these spoken by Christ written in the Jewish canons. Jesus affirms that this act of God's goodness should teach His followers to do good to those that hate them, as they witness these proofs of indiscriminate love and mercy from their Father in heaven. No rabbi had ever preached such things. Jesus' statement about the rain may be a general quotation from Ps. 147:8 or Jer. 5:24.

(q) **"Be ye perfect."** This too is a general quotation from Deut. 18:13. In the context, Christ speaks of God's benevolent kindness to mankind in general, not His divine perfection being commanded as a standard for them. The meaning has nothing to do with one becoming sinless or humanly perfect. Such a proposal for any mortal living in fallen humanity and a wicked world would be absurd in view of such verses as 1 Kings 8:46; Eccles. 7:20; with Isa. 42:19. The word *originally* was applied to a piece of ancient machinery that was *complete* in all its parts. Thus, each one functioned properly. The idea is that as we look to God, who is perfect and complete in every aspect, we are as His children to mature and be united in love; each one operating as smoothly as possible (1 Cor. 12:25-26). Christ, in applying this rule to His new kingdom required a unique completeness, where nothing is defective or wanting. Maturity (or growing in grace) *over time* is the expectation of the King of Glory for His children. *We must remember that God love us as we are, but in Christ see us for what we can be.*

(r) **Perfect, like God?** Those who know God as spiritual Father should reflect certain of His attributes in their lives especially love. No divine art practiced by Christians so imitates God as loving friends, neighbors, and enemies as well. In the context here, we see God sharing *His* rain and sun with all men, regardless. The love of men is to love those that love them. God's love is to love all. Many "Bible-believing churches" are defending the truth, preaching the gospel, yet dying because God's love is missing. (The author is not speaking of the unsaved world's estimation of love.) *Today, more dirty work is done in the "name of love" than at any time in church history.*

2p-"And followed him." On following Jesus, note Section 39, footnote d. However, over two years later, after the death of Christ, several of the apostles returned to their fishing again and were met by the Lord on the shores of Lake Galilee in John 21.

3p-A professor teaching courses for Ph.D. candidates at a Canadian university informed his students, "If anyone here is a Christian, I want you to know I'm going to bash it out of you before this year is over." *This fierce opposition to Christianity openly demonstrates that it is the only true religion or faith in the world, and is therefore, hated by unsaved men, false religions, and devils alike.* Certain levels of government, especially in the judiciary, are determined to stamp out all public usage of the Name of Jesus Christ. Most governments promote and honor sin, incompetence, and wickedness. A few will pay cheap lip service to Jesus Christ, real Christianity, and the Bible, especially during election time!

4p-When experiencing opposition, genuine Christians must remember that God's love is produced in their lives only by the work of the indwelling Holy Spirit (Gal. 5:22 with Rom. 5:5). Scripture warns, "the Spirit indeed is willing, but the flesh is weak" (Matt. 26:41). Read Jesus' convicting Words in John 13:34-35, and those of Paul in 1 Cor. 13:1-13. Good feelings are one thing but to love supremely our Father in heaven as well as our enemies is something different (1 Cor. 8:3). True Christian love, be it toward God or man, can only be spelled s-a-c-r-i-f-i-c-e. In living for Jesus, no other spelling is acceptable because of love's requirements upon our lives.

THE SERMON ON THE MOUNT CONTINUED—

Jesus explains the right attitudes in giving, prayer, fasting, and God's provision in His new kingdom. His followers are warned about twelve things.

Matt. 6:1-17—On a mountain in Galilee	Mk.	Lk.	John
A lesson on giving			
1 "Take heed that ye do not your alms[(a)] [good deeds] before men, to be seen of them: otherwise ye have no reward of your Father which is in heaven.			
2 "Therefore when thou doest *thine* alms, do not sound a trumpet[(b)] before thee, as the hypocrites do in the synagogues and in the streets, that they may have glory of men. Verily I say unto you, They have their reward.			
3 "But when thou doest alms, let not thy left hand know what thy right hand doeth:[(c)]			
4 "That thine alms may be in secret: and thy Father which seeth in secret himself shall reward thee openly.			
FIVE LESSONS ON PRAYER AND FASTING			
1. Avoid public show in prayer			
5 "And when thou prayest,[(d)] thou shalt not be as the hypocrites *are*: for they love to pray standing in the synagogues and in the corners of the streets, that they may be seen of men. Verily I say unto you, They have their reward.			
6 "But thou, when thou prayest, enter into thy closet, and when thou hast shut thy door, pray to thy Father which is in secret; and thy Father which seeth in secret shall reward thee openly.			
2. God is omniscient: He hears everything			
7 "But when ye pray, use not vain repetitions, as the heathen[(e)] [Gentiles] *do*: for they think that they shall be heard for their much speaking.			
8 "Be not ye therefore like unto them: for your Father knoweth what things ye have need of, before ye ask him."[(f)]			
3. A synagogue model prayer			
9 "After this manner therefore pray ye: Our Father[(g)] which art in heaven, Hallowed be thy name.			
10 Thy kingdom come. Thy will be done in earth, as *it is* in heaven.			
11 Give us this day our daily bread.			
12 "And forgive us our debts, as we forgive our debtors.			
13 And lead us not into temptation, but deliver us from evil: For thine is the kingdom, and the power, and the glory, for ever. Amen.			
4. Believers must forgive			
14 "For if ye forgive men their trespasses, your heavenly Father will also forgive you:			
15 "But if ye forgive not men their trespasses, neither will your Father forgive your trespasses.[(h)]			
5. Correct way to fast			
16 "Moreover when ye fast,[(i)] be not, as the hypocrites, of a sad countenance: for they disfigure their faces, that they may appear unto men to fast. Verily I say unto you, They have their reward.			
17 "But thou, when thou fastest, anoint thine head, and wash thy face;			

Matt. 6:18-34—On a mountain in Galilee	Mk.	Lk.	John
18 "That thou appear not unto men to fast, but unto thy Father which is in secret: and thy Father, which seeth in secret, shall reward thee openly.			

TWELVE WARNINGS TO BELIEVERS

1. Do not trust riches

19 "Lay not up for yourselves treasures upon earth, where moth and rust doth corrupt, and where thieves break through and steal:

20 "But lay up for yourselves treasures in heaven, where neither moth nor rust doth corrupt, and where thieves do not break through nor steal:

21 "For where your treasure is, there will you heart be also.[j]

2. Be single minded: put God first

22 "The light of the body is the eye: if therefore thine eye be single, [good] thy whole body shall be full of light.

23 "But if thine eye[k] be evil, [bad] thy whole body shall be full of darkness. If therefore the light that is in thee be darkness, how great *is* that darkness!

24 "No man can serve two masters: for either he will hate the one, and love the other; or else he will hold to the one, and despise the other. Ye cannot serve God and mammon.[l]

3. Be not tormentingly anxious about life's necessities

(See warning number 4 in next Section 47)

25 "Therefore I say unto you, Take no thought for your life, what ye shall eat, or what ye shall drink; nor yet for your body, what ye shall put on. Is not the life more than meat, and the body than raiment?

26 "Behold the fowls[m] of the air: for they sow not, neither do they reap, nor gather into barns; yet your heavenly Father feedeth them. Are ye not much better than they?

27 "Which of you by taking thought can add one cubit [18 inches] unto his stature?

28 "And why take ye thought for raiment? [clothing] Consider the lilies of the field, how they grow; they toil not, neither do they spin:

29 "And yet I say unto you, That even Solomon in all his glory was not arrayed like one of these.

30 "Wherefore, if God so clothe the grass[n] of the field, which to day is, and to morrow is cast into the oven, *shall he* not much more *clothe* you, O ye of little faith?

31 "Therefore take no thought, saying, 'What shall we eat?' or, 'What shall we drink?' or, 'Wherewithal shall we be clothed?'

32 "(For after all these things do the Gentiles[o] seek:) for your heavenly Father knoweth that ye have need of all these things.

Life's antidote for undue fret and worry

33 "But seek ye first the kingdom of God, and his righteousness; and all these things shall be added unto you.[p]

34 "Take therefore no thought for the morrow: for the morrow shall take thought for the things of itself.[q] Sufficient unto the day *is* the evil thereof."[r]

(Next chap. Matt. 7:1 cont. in, Section 47)

Footnotes–Commentary

[a] **"Alms"** is the same word for "righteousness," and means good deeds in action. In verses 1-4, the Messiah was again correcting an error, before the people, a common practice of the religious leaders of Israel. It has been

previously observed that the scribes and Pharisees sought righteousness (or to be holy) before God by the deeds of the Law of Moses and the oral traditions. This is discussed in Section 45, Matt. 5:20, footnote e. Alms had reference to "doing righteousness" or performing deeds to acquire divine favor. Charity (along with other things) was *one* of the highest means in the Jewish religion whereby one could do acts of righteousness, be blessed of God, forgiven and finally saved. In the above verse, Christ warns the people against doing alms like the scribes and Pharisees in order to try to obtain righteousness before God (Gal. 3:21). George Foot-Moore in his book *Judaism,* vols. II–III, pages 162-179, wrote at length about the great efforts of the Jews to do deeds of kindness, especially to the poor and needy. These acts made religious Jews acceptable before Jehovah God. The Savior's later Parable of the Good Samaritan, given to a doctor of the Torah Law, strongly illustrates this truth. Refer to Section 116, footnote j, for this story.

(b) **The sound of a trumpet.** Members of Christ's new kingdom were forbidden to make a public show when practicing acts of charity and giving to God. Sitting in the Women's Court of the temple were thirteen trumpet-shaped chests wherein the people dropped their monetary gifts or alms. There was one chest for each tribe of Israel and the thirteenth for charitable purposes only. See footnote c below for explanation of this extra collection box. Each chest was designated for a different purpose within the function of the Jewish religion. Some held that the scribes and Pharisees actually had young boys to blow a loud trumpet as they dropped in their offerings! (A similar practice was known among the Persians, when professional beggars blew a resounding trumpet blast upon receiving gifts of relief.) In India today, certain Hindu priests blow a trumpet for the people to see their beneficence. One can better believe that Christ pointed to the large, trumpet-shaped temple chests with which every person in His congregation would have been familiar, especially the scribes and Pharisees. Constructed of heavy metal, these chests had small openings at the top and were flared at the bottom. Most often "trumpet(s)" is the translation of the Hebrew word "shofar" (with various spellings), referring to a large ram's horn. Hypocritical Jews, especially the scribes and Pharisees, in giving their offerings would purposely slam their money into the small opening. As it trickled down into the flared metal neck of the chest, it created an overly loud clanking or jingling effect. This became known as "the sound of the trumpet" and attracted the attention of others standing in line to offer their gifts to God.

(c) Here, Jesus used a proverbial expression known during this period of Jewish history. Its meaning was that deeds of giving by those in Christ's new kingdom should be performed as covertly as possible; seeking to avoid public eyes. Giving to God without the attended praises of men, was highly approved by the more sincere and upright Jews. Located within the Women's Court of the temple compound was a chest called "The treasury of the silent." Here, pious Hebrews, abhorrent to public attention, quietly and secretly dropped their gifts, which were used only for education and aid of the poor in Israel. The rebuke of Christ was aimed at the corrupt leaders of religion who sought the praises of men and wanted notice as they gave. See footnote b above.

(d) **Praying to be seen of others.** As in much of the Sermon on the Mount, here again our Lord highlights another hypocritical custom of the religious leaders and their companions. It is *not* prayer that Christ condemns in verses 5-6: but rather, the public hypocrisy that had become a part of the Jewish religious system of that day. Jesus' statement that "they (the religious hypocrites) love to pray standing in the synagogues and the corners of streets that they may be seen of men" is the stroke of doom on insincerity in prayer. The scribes and Pharisees had become so vain that they would invoke a prayer upon virtually everything they met in the streets. They could be heard praying for a particular tree, a building, the site of some miracle, a beggar, a maimed person and so on. Such prayers were no more than big noises designed to capture the attention of those who were nearby. Both their posture (standing) and their prayers (deliberately loud) were odious to God in heaven because *both* were false. Christ warned His hearers against these acts of wickedness professionally practiced by their rabbis and ministers. *The Son of God does not condemn public prayer in this statement.* He teaches that those who become part of His new kingdom are to *first* resort to their heavenly Father in the chambers of secrecy. The prayer closet brings death to our talents and scholarly abilities. Good preaching affects men; prayer affects God. Once in that lonely closet, we may pour out both heart and soul, for God sees and hears both. When one first attends to prayer in this manner, he will have little difficulty with hypocrisy when praying openly and publicly.

(e) Now, Jesus forbids the members of His new kingdom to employ vain repetitions as they prayed. Pagans were infamous for their shouts, cries, loudness, physical antics, and continual repetitions as they prayed to demonic gods and goddesses. See 1 Kings 18:26-28 for a classical example of this. It was firmly believed by the heathen that one could attract the attention of a certain god or goddess and procure their favor by much loudness and clamor. Some of these pagan-like actions had appeared within the nation of Israel and among their spiritual leaders. The rabbis had formulated hundreds of prayers. Some had to be repeated as many as "eighteen times" before God would hear! Others were chanted, mumbled, or recited loudly by the scribes as they stood in the synagogues, on street corners, or walked along public ways. They believed that the one who prayed most was the one God heard. The holy art of prayer had been seriously cheapened and even paganized by these Jews. Later, He rebuked them for their "long prayers" made in public (Section 159, Matt. 23:14).

2p-Over the course of church history, men in agony and deep sorrow have poured out their hearts to God with groaning, tears, and pain. This is *not* what our Lord referred to in this statement. He does not condemn all repetitions, for He prayed the same thing three times in Gethsemane the night before His death (Section 179, Matt. 26:44). The greatest encouragement to prayer is the fact of God's omniscience, Christ our high priest at His right hand, and the intercessions of the Holy Spirit, Who dwells in our inner man (Eph. 3:16; Rom. 8:26-27; with 34). The Holy Trinity becomes involved when the children of Christ's kingdom-church pray! In holy prayer, we kiss the face of God; thus, it behooves our ears to listen to what our hearts and tongues say to the Father in heaven.

(f) God knows beforehand. What heartwarming words of good cheer these were to the people. The Messiah announced to them that God *knew* their needs *before* they asked. They had no valid reason to inform Him as the scribes and Pharisees did with their countless recitations and vain repetitions. God would hear and reward them openly for their faithfulness. This blessing was for those who were part of Christ's new kingdom.

(g) "The Lord's prayer." This highly *erroneous* title has been laid upon these verses. There is not a fiber of evidence that Christ intended this to become a "formula prayer" for His people throughout all the succeeding ages of church history. Sadly, on the other hand, pastors and ministers, especially in staunchly conservative-fundamentalist churches, continually explain away what Messiah taught His congregation in this prayer lesson. Many of them believe this prayer will be fulfilled several thousand years in the future, that Jews suffering in a tribulation period will be forced to pray this for their food. This is another wrong interpretation of God's Word and has no grounds whatsoever in these verses. Regardless, there can be no harm in children being taught this model prayer, *if* the meaning is explained repeatedly to them. *Almost every line of this model prayer was already well known. It was heard continually in the synagogue services.* Devout Jews believed that one should *never* offer prayer alone. All sincere Jews addressed God by this plural "our Father." It was their way of showing that all of God's followers (in Israel only) were mystically represented together in their supplications. No Hebrew would pray "My Father" though the term was used in their general conversation.

2p-Jews had been instructed to pray from the cradle and say, "Our Father, which art in heaven." This paternal Name of the Almighty was thoroughly known, for the Hebrew people had been taught by their rabbis that God was the Father of Israel (Deut. 32:6). He created all people, but in a unique sense He made Israel as His son, even as His firstborn son (Ex. 4:22). The Hebrews daily used "our Father" thousands of times in their prayers. It is found frequently in the Talmud. For a clear explanation of this, see *Judaism,* vols. II and III, pages 204-211, by George Foot-Moore. Later, the New Testament reveals in the writings of Paul, that only those who have trusted Christ as their personal Lord and Savior actually have God as their spiritual Father (Gal. 3:26). Those who reach the time of responsibility for their actions and choose sin are then classified as unsaved. Like the Pharisees, from that time forward they have Satan as their spiritual progenitor. Therefore "hallowed" is the *true* description of God's Name. This can never be said of any idol, god, or goddess. The Jewish scribes were loath, out of deep reverence and fear, to write God's Name as they recopied the worn out manuscripts. One of the rabbinical substitutes for this all-divine Name was "Our Father" as used here by our Savior. The audience of Jesus, being products of the synagogues and rabbis, were accustomed to the standard prayer forms in vogue and had heard the rabbis pray "Our Father" hundreds of times. Christ employed the normal Jewish expression by using the plural "Our Father" in His prayer. However, He lifted it to a higher plain than that of the synagogue and thereby sanctioned its usage for those who are part of His kingdom or church.

3p-Verse 10. "Thy kingdom come." *Not* to pray for the kingdom to come was considered among devout Jews as though one had not prayed. Pious Hebrews looking and longing for their earthly kingdom prayed these words day and night. With this supplication for their earthly kingdom to come, the Jews had attached a peculiar ritual of shouting out certain words and phrases while standing in the temple praying (Lk. 17:21). Later, Christ rebuked them for their hypocritical prayers, verbal chants and incantations for the kingdom to come in Section 134, Lk. 17:20-24, footnote c. In this rebuke, He was speaking of their material, physical kingdom, void of God and Himself as their Messiah, Savior, and King. The kingdom to be prayed for here was the spiritual manifestation of God's kingdom. It was later known as the church. *At this point, His new kingdom was already there as a real entity though in an infantile form.* It was introduced by John the Baptist, continued by Christ and His disciples and is still in this world in the presence of the church. Jesus was not teaching His congregation to pray for a literal, political, material kingdom to come to earth. Those that heard Jesus speak these words have been dead for almost two thousand years! His spiritual kingdom has come and is still here. All who have been born again are part of it.

4p-Verse 11. "Daily bread." It seems small to ask bread for just one day. Why not ask for a week, or month or much more? Here, the Savior is teaching continual dependence. Some *hyper* dispensationalist commentators assure us that this prayer for "daily bread" refers only to a Jewish remnant starving during the tribulation period! Such interpretations give great occasion for the enemies of Christ to ridicule. We question how many Hebrews in Jesus' audience would have understood *that* meaning of His Words. None of them at *that time* had ever heard of such terms as a tribulation period for Israel, the church, believer's baptism by immersion, the Lord's Supper, the Great Commission, and scores of other things that were yet to be.

5p-Verses 12. "Debtors and forgive." Ancient Jews believed that if they did *not* forgive their fellow Jews, neither would God forgive them. Christ does not reject this teaching. Rather, He affirms that it is also valid in His new kingdom. The Jew, Paul, later explained the source of our forgiveness in Eph. 1:7. The forgiveness here is first applicable to a saved man, but it is not restricted to him. For the rule on rabbinical teaching about forgiving only a *limited* number of times, see Section 110, Matt. 18:21-22, footnotes h and i.

6p-Verse 13. "Lead us not into temptation." These words requesting *not* to be led into evil and deliverance from temptation must be understood in the light of how the audience of Christ understood the terms. God does not subject us to sinful temptations and evil. This is clearly stated in James 1:13. The term translated "temptation" here meant a test or trial and not necessarily wickedness or sin. A prospective buyer will test or try the new car to determine something of its true worth, but he can hardly tempt it! Jews held that God alone could lead or steer them from temptations and, at last, bring them safely into His kingdom (James 1:13-16). They based this on God leading Israel through the wilderness to the Promised Land. A typical Jewish prayer for deliverance is mentioned in the Talmud tractate, Sanhedrin 64a. Jews continually prayed for God's deliverance from temptation and evil. The idea here is, "God, do not let us lead or take ourselves into evil temptations, but save us from them." Christ's kingdom was totally different from the one expected by carnal Israel. Jews the world over prayed for "Messiah's kingdom to come." Asking for God's will to be done, for daily bread, and for sins to be forgiven was part of ancient synagogue liturgy. It is noteworthy that the Messiah agrees with some of these common practices as He relates this beautiful model prayer.

7p-Verse 13. "Amen." In *concluding* this pattern for prayer, Jesus used the rabbinical benediction heard at the end of the temple rituals and synagogue services. The officiating rabbi would raise both hands and chant, "The kingdom is Thine." The congregation of worshipers would respond in soft unison, "Amen." It means, "So be it." One can quickly see how the Savior did not reject or condemn this accepted form of Jewish prayer. On the contrary, He approved it! It is sad that in many churches this beautiful prayer has been parroted so many times by a mass of mumbling, half-dead, and often unsaved church members that it is no more than a meaningless verbal ritual. Christ challenged many things in His Sermon on the Mount, but He left this prayer standing as usable for all men in His new kingdom. Some teach that this prayer will be valid only for the Jews "during the great tribulation period" of the future! Not one person in His audience would have understood such a meaning, not even the apostles, for at this point none of them had ever heard of "the great tribulation period." They did not yet understand His death, burial, and resurrection, much less the wild interpretations being laid upon Scripture today.

8p-Abuse of the word "Amen." Here is the first mention of this term in the four gospels. With it, we meet another attempt to discredit Jesus and the Holy Scripture. The Hebrew priest, firstly, used the word "amen" in Num. 5:12-31, where a wife accused of adultery was to pronounce it twice after interrogation. Also, it is usually the last thing uttered at the end of a solemn statement and is found in various Old Testament passages. It means, "So be it." In John 3:3 where our Lord says, "Verily, verily, I say unto thee," it also means "Amen and Amen." "Selah," comes from a Hebrew root word "calah," meaning to hang or measure (weigh) something to determine its value. The Talmud tractate Sabbath 119b states that the Jews believed if they shouted "Amen" loudly, it would move Jehovah to open the gates of paradise! Thus, "Amen" is an exclamation of confidence in what has been said. We should measure ourselves by Bible truth and then hang our trust upon it.

9p-"Amen" a pagan god? All Name Cults and their break away groups tell us that "Amen" was originally the name of an ancient Egyptian deity, "Amun" (with its variations). It crept into the biblical texts. How preposterous is the assertion that every time a Christian expresses agreement with an honorable and worthy statement by usage of "Amen," he is calling out the name of a pagan deity! We find dozens of variations of this word in heathen traditions in Egypt and other lands. (The Name Jesus is found in various forms within the histories of mythology.) Whether the name of this ancient heathen god is pronounced as "Amun," "Amen-Ra, king of the gods," or "Amen the sun," means nothing. To make the "amen" of Scripture to be the "Amun" of demonism because they have similar pronunciations is absurd. The Scared Name cult and the Hebrew Roots Movement pander to these untruths. Lew White is a famed Sabbath day cultist, who released the book, *Fossilized Customs*. Typical of cult literature it has some helpful truth but enough poison to damage untaught Christians. White pushes the lie that the name Jesus is of pagan origin! Name Cults boast that they alone know the correct names for God, which is Yahweh and Jesus, which is Yeshua (some use the spelling Yahushua). Their prime heresy is Sabbath keeping.

10p-Syrian, Canaanite, and Egyptian texts speak of "Amun," and the hymns, they sang to this demonic entity. This hardly negates the usage of the word "Amen" as found in Scripture. That heathen semantics developed a trinity from an idol in Egypt only further proves the Bible right. All the pagan conglomeration of gods and goddesses reveals that God's purposes were known from the beginning, and Satan sought to thwart or pervert them. Today, they enjoy the assistance of "anti-God scholarship" and of men who disdain the teachings of Scripture. Propagandists of this theological travesty should remember that this is one of the Names of our Savior. He called Himself, "The Amen, the faithful and true witness" (Rev. 3:14). Bible haters declare that Christ sought to imitate the heathen god "Amun" by using this word and thus giving legitimacy to His life and work! The demon spirits that inspired the making of "Amun" intended to duplicate and pervert the *coming* eternal Son of the Living God and

Savior of men. Here, again, is confirmation of what has been repeated in this harmony commentary: Satan, foreseeing God's plan of redemption through the birth, life, death, and resurrection of Christ, works to discredit this truth. Evil spirits inspired pagan priests, prophets, seers, and sages to distort and counterfeit practically everything concerning God's plan for the world. Those "experts in history" who go over the country lecturing on "The pagan Christs" will, at death know the difference! From the sunrise of antiquity, Satan has sought to discredit God's Word by besmirching, changing, altering, adding to, and taking from it. Agnostic Charles Panati in his *Extraordinary Origins of Everyday Things* gives some details regarding the usage of the word "Amen" on page 41. Earlier on pages 12-13, he explains how pagans had a version of the Lord's Supper a thousand years before Christ established it in the upper room!

11p-Verses 14-15. Forgive or forgive not and its consequences? Jesus refers to the petition back in verse 12. He presses this statement because the Jews were infamous in seeking revenge on their enemies. They carried grudges against one another for a lifetime. The Lord Jesus forbids this evil in His new kingdom. The lesson here is that we forgive men of their ills regardless of what they have done to us. *Our Lord is not teaching that our forgiving others, somehow procures God's forgiveness for us!* Christians, who harbor darkness in their hearts towards fellow believers, and refuse to forgive injuries done to them, will not receive God's forgiveness. Instead, the Father in heaven takes down the rod of chastisement and lays it upon the life of His stubborn, unforgiving child. This divine correction is dealt out often in severe measures. The penman of Ps. 119:67 declared, "Before I was afflicted I went astray: but now have I kept thy word." The New Testament echoes the same message in Heb. 12:5-14. Jesus was saying, "Be quick to forgive." If not, then God will not forgive. Instead of divine pardon, you will receive divine chastisement in the place of forgiveness. Seemingly, the "sin unto death" refers to believers who adamantly hold to their sins and refuse God's loving discipline upon their lives (1 John 5:16-17). How far one must go before this final drastic measure is taken, we do not know. In the Corinthian Church, there was a disciplinary system whereby unrepentant persons were (somehow) turned over to Satan for their physical bodies to be killed, but their spirits or souls would remain saved (1 Cor. 5:1-5). God told Israel of old that He would not "leave thee wholly unpunished" (Jer. 28:28, 30:11). Abusing communion may bring God's chastisement upon a believer in Christ (1 Cor. 11:28-30).

(h) "Trespass." This means a "willful violation" or "consciously stepping into" a forbidden zone. Sin allures, and then compels men to do this. Jesus later used this word in another form in Section 149, Mk. 11:26, footnote i.

(i) "Fasting." Again, the Savior spotlights the hypocrites in Jewish religion. They were great pretenders of piety! History relates that they would disfigure their faces and smear them with ashes and soot in order to appear before others as men of sincere piety and prayer. During their fasts, the Jews would neither bathe, anoint their heads with oil, nor don clean apparel; they believed this made them appear more spiritual before others! The Pharisees had endless rules for fasting and anointing the body and clothing but not their heads. They even used anointing oil that they superstitiously supposed would make their fasting more acceptable to God and useful in dealing with evil spirits. It was something like liquid magic! The rabbis when applying it to the physical bodies of the sick often pronounced a verbal incantation or charm. How different when Christ sent out His apostles to heal the sick and they would anoint them with oil without the rabbinical chants and mutterings. These healings were instantly affected by the power of God and not the oil. They used the common ordinary oils available but obtained the most extraordinary results! In the kingdom of Christ, His followers were to hide their fasting from public eyes by dressing and acting normal. Such would be precious and intimate times between them and the Father in heaven. Thus, their reward would be sure. The Pharisees who fasted on Monday, and Thursday were the chief culprits in the *abuse* of fasting.

(j) Where is your heart? Apparently, this was another common proverb of those days. For the use of another maxim, see Section 38, Lk. 4:23, footnote i. If God and His service are the greatest treasures in a man's life, it is sure that this individual's heart belongs to his Lord. He who gives his heart to the world robs God of it and snatches at the shadows of earthly goods that will finally mock his unbearable loss. Messiah warns his children, "Do not spend all of life's strength collecting the treasures of earth, but be sure that your chief goal is to prepare for eternal felicity." He told those in His new kingdom not to trust riches and temporal goods. What a contrast to the Pharisees' quest for gain and wealth. In the second paragraph of footnote l below, Jesus said they stole from widows!

(k) "Eyes, darkness and light." The rabbis spoke much of these things. The eye is to the body what the lamp is to the house. To the Jews, having a "good [or single] eye" meant being a generous person from within. Hence, great deeds of charity illuminated everything in the person's soul. On the other hand, having a "bad [or evil] eye" meant being selfish and wicked. In the context (verses 19-21), Messiah had just related the need to have the right treasure, for *there* will the heart abide. Christ declared that the person in His kingdom who clings to selfishness is full of darkness, and it is fearfully great. Slavery was common at this point in history. Note Section 96, Mk. 7:22, number 12, under footnote m, and Section 140, Matt 20:15, footnote i, for other mentions of the "evil eye." Every person listening to the Messiah understood His parable of a single slave trying to serve two masters. It was impossible! It is interesting that in Egypt and across the parts of the Middle East, there existed a pagan god called Mammon. See footnote l below. How stinging was our Lord's application that to serve money is equated to worshiping a heathen god! The rich Pharisees must have writhed under such preaching.

(l) **"Mammon."** This signified *anything* that one worshiped, money or otherwise. See comments in footnote k above. Among the Gentile pagans was Plutus, a heathen god of riches, who was worshiped by millions seeking to acquire wealth. Jesus' audience understood very well what He was saying, especially since the Jews at this time were notorious for greed and gain. The Talmud in tractate, Sotah 49a carries a scathing denunciation of the Jews' sins at this period in history. It concludes by affirming, "The face of that generation [of Jews in the days of Messiah] is like the face of a dog." This is striking when we remember that the Jews called all Gentiles dogs! With His warning about serving two masters, the Savior's discourse now touched the common human trait of worrying over the necessities of life. Jesus repeated this much later in Section 130, Lk. 16:13, footnote k.

2p-Messiah stressed this lesson (in verse 24) because among the crowds were those who labored under the terrible burden of financial pressures, but also because the Pharisees, who were listening, were thieves, devouring even the widows' houses. This lowest of sins is noted in Section 159, Lk. 20:47, footnote j. *They* indeed bowed before the god Mammon (exactly as the pagan Gentiles did), and perhaps their faces were like those of the dogs mentioned in the Talmud quotation given in the paragraph just above. Christ did *not* forbid diligent thought and preparation for securing food, clothing, and shelter. However, He warned, "Don't be over anxious" and "Never be like the Pharisees." Prudent men plan ahead (Prov. 27:12). Jesus was referring to overbearing worry, filled with anxiety. Men to whom God gave the sense to make money should have enough sense not to keep all of it.

(m) The rabbis taught the people of God's care over His creation, especially the lower creatures. "Fowls of the air" are mentioned in the Talmud tractate, Yevamoth 79a. The birds and fish were created to praise His Name according to Rosh HaShana 31a. He painted the flowers their gay colors. Some of the rabbis said blue was one of God's favorite colors, for this was the color of the "Throne of glory in heaven," according to Sotah 17a. Christ takes their words regarding God's care of His creation and gives them a new application: "Are ye not much better than they?" Jesus said that God observed a single sparrow falling to the ground; therefore, of how much greater worth is one of His children. *God attends the funerals of a thousand fallen sparrows every day!* See His concern for the fowls of heaven expressed in Section 59, Matt. 10:29, footnote p. These words expressing God's infinite care of the most insignificant things must have comforted many sitting in His congregation as they comfort us today.

(n) In this passage, Christ presents the familiar imagery of dried grass, stubble, or straw being used for fuel in Jewish ovens. Every female cook and fire builder of workable age instantly got the meaning! This was exclusively women's work. The total of Christ's sublime Words was, "If God covers with so much botanical glory the fading things of this world, which will soon be burnt to ashes in baking ovens, will He not take care of His children who are supremely precious in His sight?" The expression "O ye of little faith" was common among the rabbis. It is found in the Talmud tractates, Arachin 15a and Pesachim 118b.

(o) **"Gentiles."** Jesus selected pagans to illustrate His Words. He was telling His *Jewish audience* that heathens, who are so destitute of the doctrines of God and unacquainted with dependence upon the Almighty, make it their chief priority to worry, murder, pillage, and plunder to obtain the necessities of life. The contrast must have been shattering to the Jews, who boasted that they *alone* knew the true and living God and yet continually worried themselves sick about material goods as did their heathen neighbors. He was saying, "If they *really* knew the true God, would He not take care of them?" See Section 38, Lk. 4:25-28, footnote k, for an earlier example of Jesus inflaming His audience by comparing them with the Gentiles.

(p) **The first most important thing.** Our Savior instructs His audience and us to put the things of God and His kingdom *first* in our lives, and the temporal things will fall into place as He sees they should. The kingdom and righteousness that Christ's hearers had been seeking were those taught by the scribes and Pharisees. *Both* were unacceptable to God and had no place in Messiah's new kingdom. Every astute person in our Lord's congregation clearly understood. They were deeply stirred at its implications in their personal religious beliefs. *God's righteousness is imputed or given freely to those who trust Christ as Lord and Savior (Rom. 3:21-22 with 1 Cor. 1:30).* The scribes, Pharisees, and rabbis present on that occasion were shaken at His teaching. Thus, they were all condemned before God. In Section 45, Matt. 5:20, footnote e, Jesus explained what was wrong with the spiritual leadership of Israel; they were *self*-righteous bigots. Paul's later explained this in Rom. 9:31-32 and Rom. 10:3.

(q) "Don't be overly concerned about tomorrow; there is enough trouble today to keep you occupied." The expression in verse 34 has a parallel in the Talmud tractate, Sanhedrin 100b and other places in Jewish writings. This tractate reads in part, "Don't distress thyself with tomorrow for thou knowest not what a day may bring forth." Here, our Lord draws upon another synagogue lesson with which they were acquainted and approved its truth. See Section 45, footnotes j, k, n, and o, for areas where He disapproved of rabbinical traditions and teachings. Many Christians are haunted by the ghosts of next week and weary themselves living in the sorrow of tomorrow. A healthy trust in God does not exclude practical life with its duties. An ancient proverb affirms, "Tie your horse to a tree as tight as you can, then pray 'Lord, please take care of my horse for me.'" Do not pull tomorrow's clouds over today's joy.

(r) Jesus was saying something like this. "Each day is filled with troubles, trials, and temptations; obey, by practice from a heart of love, what I have taught you. By this you will learn how to handle one day at a time."

THE SERMON ON THE MOUNT CONCLUDED.

He ends the twelve warnings given to those who were in His new kingdom. Lastly, the Lord Jesus makes an appeal for men to trust His Word and be saved. This puts them on the right foundation.

Matt. 7:1-18—On a mountain in Galilee	Mk.	Lk.	John
4. Do not judge hastily			
1 "Judge not, that ye be not judged.**(a)**			
2 "For with what judgment ye judge, ye shall be judged: and with what measure ye mete, it shall be measured to you again.			
3 And why beholdest thou the mote [speck] that is in thy brother's eye,**(b)** but considerest not the beam [plank] that is in thine own eye?			
4 "Or how wilt thou say to thy brother, 'Let me pull out the mote**(c)** [speck] out of thine eye;' and, behold, a beam [plank] *is* in thine own eye?			
5 "Thou hypocrite, first cast [pull] out the beam [plank] out of thine own eye; and then shalt thou see clearly to cast [pull] out the mote out of thy brother's eye.			
5. Dispense sacred things wisely			
6 "Give not that which is holy unto the dogs, neither cast ye your pearls before swine, lest they trample them under their feet, and turn again and rend [tear] you.			
6. Good things for those who ask according to His will			
7 "Ask,**(d)** and it shall be given you; seek, and ye shall find; knock, and it shall be opened unto you:			
8 "For every one that asketh receiveth; and he that seeketh findeth; and to him that knocketh it shall be opened.			
9 "Or what man is there of you, whom if his son ask bread, will he give him a stone?			
10 "Or if he ask a fish, will he give him a serpent?			
11 "If ye then, being evil, know how to give good gifts unto your children, how much more shall your Father which is in heaven give good things to them that ask him?			
7. Treat others right			
12 "Therefore all things 'whatsoever ye would that men should do to you, do ye even so to them:'**(e)** for this is [sums up] the law and the prophets."			
8. Choose your road by where it ends			
13 "Enter ye in at the strait gate: for wide *is* the gate, and broad *is* the way,**(f)** that leadeth to destruction, and many there be which go in thereat:			
14 "Because strait *is* the gate, and narrow *is* the way, which leadeth unto life, and few there be that find it.			
9. Choose your spiritual leaders by their doctrinal fruits			
15 "Beware of false prophets, which come to you in sheep's clothing, but inwardly they are ravening wolves.**(g)**			
16 "Ye shall know them by their fruits. Do men gather grapes of thorns, or figs of thistles?**(h)**			
17 "Even so every good tree bringeth forth good fruit; but a corrupt tree bringeth forth evil [bad] fruit.			
18 "A good tree cannot bring forth evil [bad] fruit, neither *can* a corrupt tree bring forth good fruit.			

Matt. 7:19-29—On a mountain in Galilee	Mk.	Lk.	John
19 "Every tree that bringeth not forth good fruit is hewn down, and cast into the fire.			
20 "Wherefore by their fruits ye shall know them.(i)			
10. Those deceived by good works for salvation will hear, "I never knew you"			
21 "Not every one that saith unto me, 'Lord, Lord,'(j) shall enter into the kingdom of heaven; but he that doeth the will of my Father which is in heaven.			
22 "Many will say to me in that day, 'Lord, Lord, have we not prophesied in thy name? and in thy name have cast out devils? and in thy name done many wonderful works?'			
23 "And then will I profess unto them, I never knew you:(k) 'depart from me, ye that work iniquity.'			
11. Results of choosing right			
24 "Therefore whosoever heareth these sayings of mine, and doeth them,(l) I will liken him unto a wise man, which built his house upon a rock:			
25 "And the rain descended, and the floods came, and the winds blew, and beat upon that house; and it fell not: for it was founded upon a rock.			
12. Results of choosing wrong			
26 "And every one that heareth these sayings of mine, and doeth them not, shall be likened unto a foolish man, which built his house upon the sand:			
That horrible eternal fall			
27 "And the rain descended, and the floods came, and the winds blew, and beat upon that house; and it fell: and great was the fall of it."			
Effect of His sermon on the multitudes			
28 And it came to pass, when Jesus had ended these sayings, the people were astonished at his doctrine:(m)			
29 For he taught them as *one* having authority, and not as the scribes.(n) (Next chap. Matt. 8:1 cont. in Section 48.)			

Footnotes-Commentary

(a) **"Judge not."** Across the Sermon on the Mount, the Lord Jesus referred to the practices of the scribes, Pharisees and their companions in religion. Several of these places are Matt. 5:20, 43, 46; 6:2, 5, and 16; 7:5, 15. He directs these comments to their rash, hasty judgments of others. Our Lord was not speaking of properly constituted law courts, the necessary judgments of a father over his children, the church over its communicants and so on. Correct, needful laws and judgments to keep things orderly must restrict life. Without this, our corner of the world would be anarchy. His instructions were intended as a sharp reproof for the scribes and Pharisees present on the mount. Though the ancient Jews had beautiful laws forbidding rash judgments, yet they had become thoroughly criminal in committing forbidden deeds and issuing wrong judgments. Due to a secret, corrupt disposition of human nature, man endeavors to elevate himself above all others, wanting to believe that he is better or even perfect. From this foul nature, issues numerous evil surmising, rash judgments, arrogant decision, and dark condemnations. The Pharisees were infamous for this. The world and every man in it were judged by their apostate religion and hypocritical double standards. Woe be those who did not meet their pernicious requirements, especially keeping their oral law or traditions.

(b) Similar quotations abound in ancient Jewish literature. For illustrations of this, see the Talmud tractates, Kiddushin 24b; Kethuboth 32b; and 84d. In Matt. 7:3, our Lord lifted a wholesome expression from the sayings of the rabbis. He affirmed its truthfulness, but then in a unique manner reapplied its meaning to the scribes and Pharisees, who were guilty of this outrageous sin. John Gill lists numerous examples of this old Hebrew maxim in his *Gill's Commentary*, vol. 7, pages 67-68. The rabbis taught, "Samson walked after his eyes. Therefore, the Philistines put them out," that "Absalom lifted up his mind and the hair on his skull hanged him," and "as he lay with his father's ten concubines. Therefore, he was pierced with ten lances." The meaning found its way into another ancient proverb, "What the eye sows it also reaps." See Gal. 6:7 for Paul's general usage of this rabbinical saying, many years later, in his letter to the Galatian Churches.

(c) **"Mote."** In verse 4, our Lord, reflecting His knowledge as a carpenter, mentioned the "mote" that was a tiny speck of wood (sawdust), straw or stone. For Jesus being called a carpenter, see Section 91, Mk. 6:3.

2p-**"Beam"** spoke of a large plank, something like our present day two-by-fours used in the construction of frame buildings. Note Section 58, Lk. 6:41-42, footnote r, where Jesus later repeated this thought with minor changes. The Pharisees of old and many in this present hour scrutinize and dwell upon the smaller specks of fault seen in the lives of others. They gloried in every microscopic flaw and blew it a thousand times out of proportion. In their eyes lodged the "beams" of far greater sins. Their very lives were framed by pride, arrogance, vain opinions of themselves, total confidence in their own righteousness, vile hypocrisy, covetousness and numerous other iniquities. Their mortal sin was their vitriolic hatred for Jesus of Nazareth, the promised Messiah of Israel. Men past, present and future who conduct themselves as did these vipers of religion deserve the full damnation of hell (Section 159, Matt. 23:14). These strong Words from the lips of Christ again shook His audience to no end! Everyone present knew to *whom* He was referring, and His chief lesson to the people was, "Don't judge hastily like they do." In verse 4, Jesus relates to the ministers of the Jewish religion, who were forever trying to remove the "speck" or "mote" from their neighbor's life while their own eyes (or lives) were amassed with beams (or sins) of unspeakable dimension and substance.

3p-**"Dogs."** In verse 6, Christ uses strong language! "Holy" speaks of anything from God or dedicated to Him. This warning refers to scraps of meat that fell off the cutting tables during the preparation of various sacrifices offered to God on the temple altar. These meat scraps were swept up, thrown out of the city at day's end and eaten by dog packs, hence the origin of the term. This is also mentioned in the Talmud tractate, Nidah 31a. Messiah affirmed to His audience that the smallest part of *holy teachings* was not to be wasted on the scribes, Pharisees and their counterparts in hypocrisy. They were, in nature and character, as dogs scavenging the city dump of Jerusalem!

4p-**"Swine"** or "boars" running wild swarmed over the Jordan valley. If cornered, they would trample men to the ground, and with long razor-sharp tusks rip them to shreds. These two awful emblems pictured most of the religious leaders of Israel. A short time later, the Savior warned His disciples regarding these men in the words "Let them alone." This sharp command is found in Matt. 15:14. The members of His new kingdom were forbidden to give the holy things of God to the scribes, Pharisees, and those of their evil persuasion. If the Son of God appeared today amid the men of earth, He would pronounce the same shocking sentence upon the hypocrites hidden away in the church and the Christian faith. They are still "dogs" and "swine." One is struck by the strong language of meek and gentle Jesus when dealing with religious hypocrites of Israel. The unsaved world, sleeping so soundly in Lucifer's bosom, approves and cuddles any religion, just as long as it is a religion. They hate the Bible message of Christ's atonement by His precious blood, and His unique claim to be the only way to heaven. A foolish seaman ignores the sure signals of the lighthouse and secures his shipwreck and doom. *Jesus is heaven's only lighthouse.*

5p-Dogs and hogs are mentioned again in New Testament Scripture. See 2 Peter 2:22, where they are symbolic of apostate teachers, who having never been saved pervert and corrupt the doctrines of Christ. This is reflected across America, especially in the Mormon cult and its splinter groups. The Jehovah's Witnesses and the Mosaic Law sects drag their converts under the yoke of bondage while promising them freedom (Gal. 5:1 with Col. 2:14-17).

6p-**"Pearls."** The latter portion of verse 6 continues the above lesson regarding swine but now transfers it to pearls. Being precious "pearls," they picture holy things. In Section 84, footnotes a and d, the saved are depicted as the pearl of great price. The Greek word here for pearl is "margarites." This is the mother of our popular feminine names Margarita and Margaret. For a curious note on pearls and their use by the ancients, see Section 84, footnote c. The Master warns His followers not to waste God's jewels of divine truth on *incorrigible* hypocrites. They were comparable to "dogs" and "swine." *Both* were counted high abominations among the people of Israel. The rabbis habitually referred to "dogs" and "swine" in exposing the wickedness of their Gentile neighbors. (Oddly, the Jews were allowed to keep dogs if they were restrained or tied up! For other Hebrew usages of swine products, see Section 88, second paragraph of footnote g.) To the shock of those present, Christ *reversed* the terminology and now laid it upon these purveyors of apostate religion. How utterly amazed was Messiah's congregation, and how infuriated were the religious prelates that sat among them. The Son of God thus commanded, "Dispense of sacred things wisely." Church members who pay religious infidels to preach their distortions to them each Sunday could learn from this stern admonition. Woe be those who assist or support the damnation of their fellow men by such deeds (Ps. 1:1 with Acts 13:6-10). The stern words in Ezek. 33:6 warns of the serious fate of those who will not work to save the perishing from sure doom. On the other hand, Dan. 12:3 speaks of the blessedness of those who do.

(d) See this thought in Section 46, footnotes d, e, f, and g for Messiah's comments on prayer. Here, Jesus teaches on "How God answers prayer and His superior benevolence in specifically caring for His children's needs." He taught that our heavenly Father gives only those things *He considers* good for us, not what we consider good. For later comments on Christ and prayer, refer to Section 118, Lk. 11:1, footnote a.

(e) **The Golden Rule.** A rewording of Lev. 19:18, hence highlighted in gray. The origin of this beautiful title is lost in antiquity. Some older Jewish writers, who were fiercely opposed to Jesus the Messiah, claim that He borrowed this verse from the famed Hebrew teacher Hillel, who died in about A.D. 10. However, this is not the case. Ancient history affirms that this proverb was in use several hundred years *before* either Hillel or Christ was born! As stated above, it was actually a paraphrase of Lev. 19:18 that had been written by Moses about 1,500 years *before* the time of Jesus and Hillel. The *New Twentieth Century Encyclopedia of Religious Knowledge* by J. D. Douglas, pages 361–362, carries a good review of this subject. Rabbinical canons written *after* the law was given on Sinai contain various altered forms of this command. Some historians tell us that it was in vogue even among the heathens who (beyond doubt) plagiarized it from the works of Moses. On pagan writers taking quotes from the Old Testament Scriptures, see Section 1, Part 1, fourth paragraph of footnote b. *The New Schaff-Hertozg Encyclopedia of Religious Knowledge*, vol. xi, pages 255–264, has a comprehensive article on this subject along with the *Biblical, Theological, and Ecclesiastical Cyclopaedia*, vol. x, pages 166–190, by M'Clintock & Strong. Both sources give a clear explanation of this topic. For more on Christ and Hillel, see Section 45, ninth paragraph of footnote b.

2p-In stating His new kingdom version or commandment of this Golden Rule, our Lord approved another saying that was right within the teachings of the Jewish rabbis, though it did not originate with any of them. The final or sum total of all said in the Law of Moses, and the prophets was intended to bring men to a saving knowledge of Christ, then bring them to this rule of life. *The Golden Rule is the foundation of a moral, stable, and peaceful society.* Alas! Sin entered, and the Devil with his willing men have foiled and distorted the instructions of Holy Writ. Because Christ came and fulfilled *both* the law and the prophets, God has promised that all who know His Son as Lord and Savior will someday live in the perfect harmony of the Golden Rule (Rev. 21:4–8). Summarizing verse 12, Jesus declared to His kingdom members this simple but profound dictum, "Treat others right." See a parallel to this verse given later by the Savior in Section 58, Lk. 6:31, footnote h.

(f) **Verses 13–14. "Roads, ways and gates."** Hebrew canons (writings) were meticulous in describing the main roads of Israel, their *entrance*, measures, conditions, and *destination*. The beginning of a journey on a Jewish road in the land of Israel was often called "entering through the gate." It was a common question put to a traveler: "Where will your road end?" One can read of these things in the Talmud tractates, Mo'ed Katan 2a; Eiruvin 22b; and Rosh Hashana 18a. Tractates Baba Kama and Kethuboth have dozens of instructions about road travel for the Jews, some dealing with emergencies that might be encountered. Christ forcefully stresses these travelers' questions to His audience, and then applied them to the beginning and consummation of human life, especially where one's road will end. The only options are "destruction" (in the lake of fire forever) or "life" (in the presence of God forever). Surely, His listeners understood as He preached, "Choose the road by where it ends." At the end of most roads stood a gate or door for entrance into a city or house. This would allow entrance in or shut the traveler out. In this wording, Christ gave an appeal to anyone in His congregation to become part of His new kingdom by accepting Him, the right beginning, and ending. It is instructive that He said this near the end of the Sermon on the Mount.

(g) **Verse 15. "Wolves in sheep's clothing."** Jesus again referred to the ministers of Jewish religion. The expression "Wolves in sheep's clothing" was a choice maxim among the ancients. Here, it is used by the Messiah to describe the rabbis and their cohorts. Jesus required that all those listening should check the religious trees from which they received their theological food to assure that their fruits were compatible with their claims. A tree produces what it is. John the Baptist had preached the same, and many of Jesus' congregation remembered His Words. Men do not judge a tree by its bark, leaves, or blossoms but by its fruit. For the fruit of the tree is that with which they feed and satisfy themselves. The scribes and Pharisees sat in Moses' seat and expounded the law but were unsaved or uncircumcised in the heart. (This expression "Moses' seat" is explained in Section 159, Matt. 23:2, footnote b.) Their vileness manifested itself in their vicious hypocrisy. For more on this, see the scathing rebuke that Christ laid on the religious leaders months later in Section 96 over their oral law. At this point, the congregation of Christ was alarmed at what He had said about their scribes and rabbis. He, like the Baptist, went so far as to pronounce the sentence of hell fire upon those who produced poisoned fruit. Every sincere, faithful Jew who heard Jesus speak these fiery Words knew well that He preached a long overdue truth in Israel. The Master admonished His congregation, "Choose the right leaders who have the right fruits."

2p-Sheep in wolf's clothing! This scenario is more disgusting than the above. We can expect Satan's servants to mime God's people, but when God's people act like devils, it is enough to make angels weep.

(h) **Verse 16. "Thorns and thistles."** Jesus compared the fruit of the religious leaders to noxious plants. The Talmud tractate, Baba Bathra 156b forbade letting thistles grow in a garden, while tractate, Pesachim 49a forbade grafting various plants together. It names the thorn bush. It was counted a product of the Edenic curse and used by the Jews for fuel or fencing in livestock. When their sharpness was worn away, they were burned as firewood. Oddly, another Talmud passage in tractate, Shabbath 76a speaks of a weird occult practice of the Jews in dealing with a high fever. It instructs the one caring for the sick to "tie a white twisted thread to a thorn hedge" and speak various incantations! Certain superstitious and occult formulas given by the rabbis are listed in tractate, Shabbath 77b. The congregation understood our Lord's preaching and was amazed.

(i) **Verses 17–20. "Trees."** While preaching over the Holy Land in 1966, the author of this harmony commentary heard an ancient proverb used by an Arab Christian, who stated, "A gourd is known by its branches." Our Lord seems to have taken something like this old saying and reversed the meaning. Jesus preached that men do not judge a tree by its bark, leaves, flowers, or branches. These are only ornamental. The fruit is of service to man, and from this, he forms an opinion of the tree's value to his needs. In using the term "false prophets," Christ *first* referred to the scribes and Pharisees, who outwardly appeared righteous, but their fruit (or perverted doctrine from the Mishna oral law) was poison to the soul. For the meaning of the Mishna or Talmud, see Section 52, footnote h; Section 89, footnote c; and Section 96, footnote d.

2p-"Do the will." Can this mean that we are saved by what we do? John 6:29 tells us that the work God accepts from men is to believe on His Son, the Lord Jesus Christ, whom He sent into the world.

3p-As the final work of the tree is to produce fruit, so is the duty of saved Christians. It must be remembered that all fruit bearings are a seasonal function. No fruit tree on earth provides fresh fruit every day of the year. The psalmist wrote of the man who "bringeth forth his fruit in his season" (Ps. 1:1–3). The lesson here is that those who *never have a fruitful season* and whose lives continually produce foul fruit do not know God. The genuine believer's fruit is seasonally produced by the indwelling Holy Spirit (Gal. 5:22–25), and it is the fruit that "remains" to the glory of God (John 15:16). People whose lives are continually void of seasonal fruit bearing are destined for the fire (verse 19). Messiah's audience understood His cutting remarks as having direct reference to the religious leaders of Israel and all who believed them.

(j) **Verse 21. "Lord, Lord."** This term is derived from the Greek term "kurios." It carried several shades of meaning in the New Testament. The call "lord, lord" was daily heard across Israel. It was used of wives to husbands, of slaves toward their masters, of poor to the rich, of the employee to the employer. In the New Testament, it is used of the Lord Jesus in a *distinctive* manner, identifying Him with God in the Old Testament! Christ makes it clear that His Lordship is unique and totally apart from all others. He is not just another "lord" but that divine Person and Supreme Lord sent from heaven, the One to whom men will answer in judgment. The hinges of human history have turned on the Lordship of Christ. During this era, many of Israel's religious leaders professed to do great and wondrous works for the glory of God. They even boasted of passing on their miraculous powers, such as casting out demons, to their children. Our Lord spoke of this in Section 66, Matt. 12:27. However, Jesus warns that only those who do the will of God in heaven will see heaven. The *preeminent* will of God is that men believe on the Son, whom He sent to die for the sins of the world. This, the scribes, Pharisees and many of the Jews refused to do.

2p-In an awesome moment, the Lord reflected far ahead into the final judgment of the Father and solemnly warned the people that they will need more than obedience to the Mishna rules of the scribes to pass the inspection of that dreadful day. Otherwise, they will hear the most horrible words ever spoken: "Depart from me." What a terrible separation! What a fearful and devastating benediction on one's life: "Depart from me." The "Me" is the Son of God, the Messiah of Israel, the Prince of Peace, the healing of the nations, the forgiver of our sins, the Savior and Lord of glory. *Build, O reader, on the Rock of ages or your house is doomed!* What a horrible thing for men to cast out devils and at the end be cast with Satan in the lake of fire! In this, Christ intimated that they (the Pharisees and their children) were all in a league with Satan. See paragraph below for more on evil men expelling demons.

3p-The author of this harmony commentary saw an African witch doctor who "professed Christianity" expel demons from several patients. Instantly, the demons entered the witch doctor throwing him violently to the ground (usually backward) in horrible fits and convulsions. *It is in this sense only that false professors of religion may cast out a demon. It is a matter of Satan switching interest and location from one of his captives to another.* Better to have not been born than to hear these words: "I never knew you . . . depart from me!" In connection with this, see the dreadful fate of Rev. 20:15. Many are deceived by the wrong choice, and the results are unspeakably horrible.

(k) **Verse 23.** The latter part of this verse is a direct quotation from Ps. 6:8.

(l) **Verses 24–25.** These passages bring us to the conclusion of His Sermon on the Mount. Now, the Savior admonished all to *hear and obey,* and the results of their actions are illustrated by the building of two houses. He demonstrated His knowledge as a carpenter (see footnote c above). Jesus now compares those who hear and do His Word to wise men who build on a rock. The first house described by Jesus stands to the glory of God and joy of the builder. The storms of sin and Satan beat upon all such dwellings, but they stand because of the rock-sure foundation. It is written, "For other foundation can no man lay than that is laid, which is Jesus Christ" (1 Cor. 3:11).

2p-Verses 26–27. Fools hear not, neither obey; thus, they build on sand. The rabbis often referred to such metaphors in their synagogue lessons. Christ used here another familiar rabbinical similitude, but laced it to the eternal truth of the living God. The test of time pounds fiercely upon both structures. One of them falls, forever gone, with the Savior's woeful benediction, "great was the fall of it." The greatest of life's calamities is to die without the saving knowledge of the Lord Jesus Christ.

3p-Frequently entire villages in Israel vanished under the torrents of powerful rains and swelling oncoming floods. Hundreds in the audience of Christ instantly related to these illustrations. He warned them to "hear" what He had just preached and "do" it with all their hearts. (It remains true that "faith comes by hearing," Rom. 10:17.)

Choose Jesus' Words that He spoke as the right foundation. All who heeded would be saved forever and have part in His new kingdom. The countless thousands as well as the twelve apostles who heard the Sermon on the Mount were thunderstruck at His infallible claims and superior doctrines. The scribes and Pharisees were furious over His public denunciation of their shameless hypocrisy and evil deeds. Their united hatred for Him intensified. About two years later, it erupted into open vengeance at His trial and crucifixion. These events are considered in Sections 181-188.

(m) **"Astonished."** *No man in the whole of world history ever spoke like Christ.* The obvious meaning of this statement (uttered by the astonished people) who had just heard the earthshaking Sermon on the Mount was that Jesus did not teach like the rabbis. They always built their theology upon the sayings and instructions of previous rabbis. This style is seen throughout the Talmud. Christ departed from this method of teaching preaching. He spoke with authority given directly from the indwelling Holy Spirit of God. The Jews were smitten in conscience when they heard Him speak. This, the rabbis could not do. According to verse 28, the people instantly detected the difference! Months later, the temple police reported to the Pharisees the amazing speaking ability of the Savior (Section 119, John 7:46). Near the close of His ministry, the people were still astonished at His teaching. This is noted in Section 150, Mk. 11:18, footnote h. Other comments on the power and wonder of the Lord Jesus are by the asterisk under the main heading of Section 48.

(n) **"Not like the scribes."** The power of Christ's teaching astounded the people; no teacher in the history of Israel had ever preached or taught like Him. The Savior sitting on the mountain top demonstrated more authority than the religious leaders did standing in their plush synagogues or sitting in Moses' seat. They preached and taught like a naughty schoolboy fumbling through the lesson, demonstrating that he did not know his subject. Sadly, today many pulpits do no better, especially in many of the Methodists, Baptist, Presbyterians, and other churches that once stood like a mountain for God and right. The mumbling of clerics who have never been saved, or teachers whose hearts are void of the seriousness of God's work have done irreparable damage to the vineyard of the Lord. Tears and brokenness for men without Christ are considered as signs of weakness or shame. In parts of the deep south of the United States, ranting, raving, high stepping, wind-sucking preachers have mistaken noise and physical gymnastics for the power of God, and work of the Holy Spirit. This big carnal racket only serves to grieve Him and further hinder the mysterious working of the Spirit of God in the souls of men. God's ministers should be different; not in worldly wisdom, the car they drive, the suits they wear, the jokes they crack, or the house in which they live, but in divine power and authority. This alone will arrest the attention of those who are lost in sin and without eternal hope. The Presbyterian-Congregationalist evangelist, Charles G. Finny (died 1875) walked into a factory in New England, and dozens fell to their knees begging God for forgiveness! He was so anointed of God that sinners were smitten to the floor. Today "greatly learned theologians and authorities in church history," tell us that "Finney was the precursor for the wild charismatic movements" playing havoc on all sides. People say this because they know nothing of *genuine* spiritual awakening. The most timorous of *true* Christians, possessing the highest of academic credentials, and belonging to a dead denomination, still have enough respect and fear not to traduce God's amazing work. The Great Awakening in early America in the days of Edwards, Whitefield, Finney, and others was a sovereign act of God. Christless, formal religion will never understand these things because it is not of God.

2p-Whatever happened to the Holy Spirit? There is another side to this story. Where is conviction today in the best of churches? *This is the greatest problem we presently face.* Have we substituted the Spirit's work for "after glows, games, picnics, parties, outings, Bible studies, hikes, conferences, group discussions, in depth counseling" and so forth? Are we so dumb to think that a sermon prepared with perfect homiletics, exact exegesis, and pedant hermeneutics will bring men to salvation? Often pastors and church leaders make things happen in their services and youth meetings by manipulating the circumstances. The best of singing touches the mind and emotions; only the Word of God and Holy Spirit reaches the imprisoned soul (Heb. 4:12). Today's popular evangelists are "booked up for five years." This is a sure sign that "God is blessing their ministry," so we hear. (At this writing, former President Bill Clinton is booked up for fifteen years with speaking engagements!) For a brief review of the spiritual condition of the *average* "conservative," "fundamentalist," or "evangelical Bible believing church" in America, see Section 76, second and third paragraph of footnote f; Section 184, fourth paragraph of footnote f; and Section 192, the second and third paragraphs of footnote g. There are exceptions to these shames, but they are in the minority.

3p-Strange winds of change have slowly swept over many believers. Radical "end time experts" assure us that all this is according to Bible prophecy; that it must be. This fatalistic reasoning creates despair and a sense of hopelessness in the lives of untaught Christians. Thousands of seminary graduates are trained in parsing a sentence from their Greek New Testament, but they are unable to preach under the anointing of the Holy Spirit. They debate so eloquently the ingenious heresies of Calvinism or Arminianism, the partial inspiration of the Bible, but collapse under fierce persecution. Years ago, the author sat in the home of a "famed Baptist minister" in Texas, known as a "staunch defender of the faith." He whined and complained because his wife failed to buy chocolate ice cream for after dinner treat! We now have a generation of spiritual "softies" or "academic ice cubes," who will take up the mantel of God's work in years to come. Alas! Will this mess end as it started with the "church in thy house?"

Sermon over, He descends the mount. Entering an unnamed city, Jesus touches and heals a leper.* In this, He demonstrated what He had just preached: love and help all men as far as possible. Only Israel's Messiah could touch and heal a leper. Unable to stay in the city, He withdrew into the wilderness to pray.

*The Jews believed their Messiah could be identified by His extraordinary Words and works. Among the thousands of miracles, He performed, four were unprecedented in Israel's history. (1) Healing a leper, as illustrated below in footnotes a and b. (2) Exorcising one possessed with a dumb demon, discussed at asterisk in main heading of Section 66. (3) Restoring sight to one "born blind," as seen in Section 121. (4) Raising the dead after three days and nights was also an exclusive Messianic miracle. This last miracle was exhibited in the raising of Lazarus. See Section 124, second paragraph of footnote w.

A city somewhere in Galilee?

Matt. 8:1–4	Mk. 1:40–45	Lk. 5:12–15	John
Thousands follow Him **1** When he was come down from the mountain, great multitudes followed him.			
The leper's request **2** And, behold, there came a leper[a] and worshipped him, saying, "Lord, if thou wilt, thou canst make me clean."[b]	***The leper's request*** **40** And there came a leper[a] to him, beseeching him, and kneeling down to him, and saying unto him, "If thou wilt, thou canst make me clean."[b]	***The leper's request*** **12** And it came to pass, when he was in a certain city, behold a man full of leprosy:[a] who seeing Jesus fell on *his* face, and besought him, saying, "Lord, if thou wilt, thou canst make me clean."[b]	
The Savior's response **3** And Jesus put forth *his* hand, and touched[c] him, saying, "I will; be thou clean." And immediately his leprosy was cleansed.	***The Savior's response*** **41** And Jesus, moved with compassion, put forth *his* hand, and touched[c] him, and saith unto him, "I will; be thou clean." **42** And as soon as he had spoken, immediately the leprosy departed from him, and he was cleansed.	***The Savior's response*** **13** And he put forth *his* hand, and touched[c] him, saying, "I will: be thou clean." And immediately the leprosy departed from him.	
	His strange instructions **43** And he straitly charged him, and forthwith sent him away;	***His strange instructions*** **14** And he charged him	
His strange instructions **4** And Jesus saith unto him, "See thou tell[d] no man; but go thy way, shew thyself to the priest,[e] and offer the gift that Moses commanded, for a testimony[f] unto them." (Verse 5 cont. in Section 60.)	**44** And saith unto him, "See thou say[d] nothing to any man: but go thy way, shew thyself to the priest,[e] and offer for thy cleansing those things which Moses commanded, for a testimony[f] unto them."	to "tell[d] no man: but go, and shew thyself to the priest,[e] and offer for thy cleansing, according as Moses commanded, for a testimony[f] unto them."	
	The results of praise **45** But he went out, and	***The results of praise*** **15** But so much the more	

Matt.	Mk. 1:45	Lk. 5:15–16	John
	began to publish *it* much, and to blaze abroad the matter, insomuch that Jesus could no more openly enter into the city, but was without in desert places: and they[g] came to him from every quarter. (Next chap. Mk. 2:1 cont. in Section 49.)	went there a fame abroad of him: and great multitudes[g] came together to hear, and to be healed by him of their infirmities. *Withdrawing from men He seeks God in prayer* **16** And he withdrew himself into the wilderness, and prayed.[h] (Verse 17 cont. in Section 49.)	

Footnotes-Commentary

[a] **"There came a leper."** The Old Testament teaching about leprosy and its horrific toll on men well illustrates the New Testament teaching about sin. However, the paramount lesson here is that the Messiah physically healed a leper who we understand was already a believer in Him. No ancient disease afflicting the human race was more dreadful than leprosy. It was deemed by the Law of Moses a distemper so horrible that even garments, vessels and houses were infected by it (Lev. 14:1-57). Most victims wallowed for years in indescribable misery. Once diagnosed by the Hebrew priest at the temple, the subject rent his garments, placed a mask over his mouth, and exclaimed in the hearing of every approaching person, "unclean!" He then took his place in a filthy dwelling isolated from the rest of society. This was the leper's camp. The horrible disease imperceptibly increased over the years, slowly spreading throughout the victim's human frame. Ugly, blistering tumors appeared, eyebrows swelled, ears grew thick as fingers, and toe joints became inflamed. In time, these joints painlessly dropped from the body as nerve endings ceased their function. All Jewish doctors of medicine and rabbis stood helpless and terrified in the presence of leprosy. There was no cure for this living death. In time, the Jews concluded that only Israel's Messiah, when He came, could cure this dreaded curse. It was held that no person had ever been healed of leprosy *within* the nation of Israel since the giving of the complete law by Moses. (Miriam, the sister of Moses, was healed *before* the law came in its final form as recorded in the book of Deuteronomy. Her story is recorded in Num. 12:10-15. In 2 Kings 5, Naaman, a Gentile Syrian was healed of the disease.) Even though two chapters of the Law of Moses carried detailed rituals regarding the offerings of one who had been healed of the disease, these 116 verses had *never* been used in some 1,500 years of Hebrew history! What the Torah Law said about this disease is explained in Lev. 13-14. Many Jews in the days of Christ believed that *only* Messiah could heal one afflicted with this malady. See footnote e, below, for details on this thought.

[b] **"If thou wilt, thou canst make me clean."** The request of this dying man reveals that news had spread into the isolated leper camps about Jesus of Nazareth. He claimed to be the promised Messiah of Israel, who *could* cleanse a man of this loathsome disease. We are struck with amazement that this poor fellow sought the "will of Christ" in his healing! The frequent mystery of God's *sovereign will* for our lives is noticed here. Never is it true that God *always* answers prayer, regardless; even when "no" is the answer. There are times when healing is withheld, and the need is not supplied because of higher reasons. Most unanswered prayer will never be understood in this life. That greatest of missionaries suffered unspeakable pain from the thorn in his flesh and from cold, thirst, and hunger (2 Cor. 12:7-10; Phil. 4:12; and 2 Cor. 11:27). Our estimation of what we need is usually contrary to divine counsel.

2p-The subjected will of this poor leper, fouled by the most dreadful of diseases, is painfully convicting for most of us. He wanted only the will of Christ for his life, even if it involved dying as a miserable leper. The cheap and vulgar preaching of today that God lavishes His children with health, wealth, and *life long* material prosperity is a myth that has deceived millions and led to bitter disillusionment. Christians living in certain pagan lands, under communism, or militant Islam, continually suffer untold pain, often without food, clothing, or shelter. Most Christians in the world live in abject conditions because of oppressive governments, false religions, and hatred of the Bible and Jesus Christ. According to the prosperity cult preachers of America, these people are "not right with God." The hallmark of a genuine believer is not his house, car, bank account, or popularity, but how much he has suffered for the Savior and His gospel. That greatest of all missionaries wrote a cantankerous group of churches who continually wrangled over circumcision, law keeping, and Sabbaths, these stinging words: "From henceforth let no man trouble me: for I bear in my body the marks of the Lord Jesus" (Gal. 6:17). Paul could raise his garments and show the ugly scars on his body, received in the service of the gospel. How many famed prosperity preachers could say this and not be lying? We would like to see on national television their marks received in the work of God. In their twisted thinking, it is a three million-dollar mansion overlooking the ocean, custom tailored thousand-dollar suits, a fleet of imported cars, and best selling "Christian books."

3p-Here, is the first record of Christ healing a leper. No doubt, numerous others had been cured, yet the evangelists were not inspired to mention them. The healing of almost anything is suggested in Mk. 1:32-34 and Matt. 4:24. News that Jesus was actually healing men of this plague was impeccable evidence that He was the Messiah of Israel. See number 1 under asterisk in the main heading of the Section above. The entire nation was moved into wonderment concerning Jesus of Nazareth. Thousands mused, "Is this our Messiah for He heals lepers?"

(c) "Touched him." Coming down from the mount, the first thing Jesus did was to touch an infected man. Not only did His teaching greatly move the people, now His actions stun them! No devout Jew in his right mind would ever touch a leper! The reason for this is explained in Lev. 13:44-46 and Num. 5:2-3. Every man fell back in horror at the sight of one fouled by this cursed disease. Rabbinical oral law, later written in the Mishna (called "tradition of the elders" in Mk. 7:5), even prescribed the distance to keep from a leper when one was met on the road. The disciples and crowds were horrified as they saw Jesus "put forth his hand" and touch his rotting mortal flesh. See Section 61, Lk. 7:14, footnote d, for Christ also touching the dead, which was also forbidden in the Torah Law. None, however, saw the loving compassion of His great heart that moved Him to do so. Can we imagine the absolute amazement, the overflowing joy that poured upon that scene, when they beheld with their eyes as the dreaded, fatal disease instantly vanished, and the sick man's flesh became new? That moment reverberated with holy power and erupted into loud praises to God.

2p-**The strange statement of Lev. 13:3.** Here, the infected leper was pronounced "unclean," yet this verse affirms that one totally contagious was declared, "clean." The diagnostic reason for this was known to the officiating priests at that time, but God did not explain it any further. Lack of explanation hardly invalidates this inspired statement. It is another one of those things that the ancients understood, but we do not.

(d) "Tell no man." Such a command was like telling water it cannot be wet! In this restriction, our Lord attempted to tone down the vicious hatred that the scribes and Pharisees had spread over the nation and entire countryside about His ministry. The leaders of religion and members of the Sanhedrin became enraged as they beheld untold thousands flocking to Jesus. With each new miracle, the purveyors of Israel's religion became fiercer in their opposition to Him. What an astonishing enmity lies in the souls of unsaved religious men when they seek to destroy those who disagree with their political or religious creeds. One thinks of John Calvin and his bloody Reformers, torturing, banishing, and putting to death those who would not tow their line; the radical Anabaptist at Münster, and present day fundamentalist Islam. (For documentation on the left wing Anabaptist, see *Calvinistic Paths Retraced*, pages 131-132, by Samuel Fisk.) Such heinous deeds are the poison fruits of indescribable depravity. This fellow, full of unspeakable joy, accosted every person on the road to the temple. During the trip, some ninety miles south, he did not stop sharing with all who would listen, what Christ had done for him! Silence was impossible. It was *acceptable* disobedience. Fellow lepers, upon hearing this sought out Jesus by the hundreds. With the land ablaze that a leper had been healed, thousands surged out of their dwellings to see and hear Jesus. This unnamed city was packed with suffering, sick, and hurting humans, all crying for their Messiah. Several other times Jesus ordered silence about His work. See Matt. 9:30-31, Matt. 12:15-16, Matt. 16:20; Mk. 5:43, Mk. 7:36. In one case, Jesus ordered His convert to tell others of His great deeds. See Mk. 5:19-20 for the story.

2p-Our Lord also ordered this "no talk" policy on other occasions during His ministry. Refer to Mk. 5:43 and 7:36. It is noted that with the deliverance of the demoniac of the Gadarenes, the Savior commanded him to go home and tell his friends what Christ had done for him (Mk. 5:18-20). This miracle occurred in the region called Decapolis (ten cities) which was east of the Jordan River and inhabited mostly by Gentiles. Hence, the prohibition of Jesus concerning the religious leaders was unnecessary on this occasion.

(e) "Go to the priest." This command from Moses was based on Lev. 14:2. Christ *deliberately* instructed him to return to the temple in Jerusalem and present himself before the officiating priest as one "cured of leprosy." See footnote f below for more on this thought. The reason for this was far higher than the fulfillment of Moses' Law. Records were kept of every person who had been diagnosed with this incurable illness. It was a simple formality to check in the temple archives for the earlier diagnosis made by the priest on duty at that time. As expressed in footnote a above, *never* had a healed leper stood before a Jewish priest and requested the required ritual for *post-leprosy* cleansing as laid out in Lev. 14. Our Lord's Words, "but go, and show thyself to the priest," (Lk. 5:14), are loaded with meaning. The entire temple workforce on duty that day were amazed to hear that a *former* leper appeared at the Nicanor Gate and announced, "Jesus of Nazareth healed me." Here, was the irrefutable affirmation that this "troublemaker" was, in fact, Israel's long-looked-for Messiah. News spread in the temple and over the city, from menial servants busy at their lowly tasks to the high priest himself, everyone heard the amazing news! "A leper has been healed in Israel." This meant that Messiah had come! Driver and Neubauer in their work *The Suffering Servant of Isaiah According to the Jewish Interpreters,* page 7, list a curious quotation from the Babylonian Talmud. It said that Messiah was called (among other things) "the leprous one." This was, because "he had [exclusively] bore Israel's sicknesses," which included the curse of leprosy. David Stern wrote in his *Jewish New Testament Commentary,* page 34, the following: "By the first century, Judaism had developed a list of major signs the true Messiah could be expected to give as proof of his identity." One of these was healing a leper.

(f) **"For a testimony unto them."** Our Lord speaks of the priests ("them") who were on duty at the temple. For more on this, see footnote e above. Had He not recently disturbed these same Jewish prelates at the last Passover by asserting that He was the Messiah? This is recorded in Section 29, John 2:18, footnote e. At that time, was not the entire religious establishment thrown into an uproar because of Him? Now, what will they do? Here stands one, who according to their medical records is an incurable leper. However, behold, he dances with joy and praises God with a loud voice unashamedly before all. Something heavenly has happened to him. *He is healed!* Who performed this earthquake-like miracle? That village carpenter from Nazareth, the One, who months before had stood in the Nazareth synagogue and read the predictions from Isa. 61. This event is recorded in Lk. 4:18-19. It was on that occasion when He asserted to be Israel's Messiah, and that He had fulfilled the predictions of Isaiah.

(g) **"They came to him from every quarter."** What an over-generalization. This means that thousands came and were healed and carried the news of Christ back to their homes and respective countries.

(h) **"Into the wilderness, and prayed."** What did Christ do in view of the uncontrollable mob situation that had arisen across the city? The wild enthusiasm of the crowds upon hearing of the leper being healed spread like fire. He retired into a secluded place where human traffic was small and resorted again to the solace and comfort of communication with His Father in prayer. We must order our earthly affairs and toil so that servile labor, by which we procure the necessities of life, will not interfere or hinder our communion with God. When men are too busy to pray, something is seriously amiss. William Herberg, a Jewish philosopher, wrote words more applicable to believers than unbelievers. "We are surrounded on all sides by the wreckage of our great intellectual tradition. Instead of freedom, we have the all-engulfing whirl of pleasure and power; instead of order, we have the jungle wilderness of unrestrained self-indulgence." Quoted by Michael S. Horton in, *Made in America: The Shaping of Modern American Evangelism,* page 24.

2p-Paralyzed by prayerlessness. Divine prayer is relegated to nice words parroted in the "sanctuary" where all present may hear. Holy Ghost conviction of personal sin is vanishing. Hollywood techniques and popular evangelism, where men deal in and promote glamour instead of Christ, and professionals give seminars on how to "market the church" to the ungodly world, dominate much of the scene. The church has superimposed Hollywood upon itself because of her expertise in playacting. Preachers "have degrees" but no heat. Everyone is a doctor while the church is dying for a spiritual hospice nurse. Tears for the lost have dried up; they are a sign of weakness or embarrassment. We have entered the electronic era where invisible currents are frying brains. Too many power point presentations are replacing anointed preaching. Sports are more important then lost souls and God. Meanwhile, many of the sport "Star Professionals" are drunkards, whoremongers, liars, thieves, crooks, and dope heads. Marital infidelity is as popular as coffee and cake. Millions love Jerry Springer's trash, and clap their way into hell, while particular "politicians, preachers, Christians, athletes, entrepreneurs, teachers," and others enjoy their self approved sins and crimes, at least until they are caught! Human responsibility is almost a thing of the past. Everyone does what they want, regardless of how heinous it is and it has the God hating world's approval.

3p-Afraid of the answer? Are we afraid that we might get what God wills for us? Everything in life will eventually fade, save Christ and His infallible Word. *The Bible contains errors only because man's understanding of what is an error is erroneous!* Psychiatry, that cure-all panacea, the medical goddess of millions, is now on the couch reaching out for the help she has failed to give. Real prayer still moves the hand that moves the world. The Lordship of Christ is the hinge on which human history turns. Jesus, the perfect man found refuge and strength in the secret pavilion of an audience with God. The painful silence of this mysterious but holy event shouts so loudly that we are dumbstruck with guilt. *O what a tormenting silent voice to hear!* Trespassing into that forbidden prayer scene of Christ, we are shaken in mind and smitten in conscience. Its quietness offends us; its wordlessness makes us angry, and its refusal to tell us something drives a dagger of conviction into our haughty hearts. Some prayers dare not be recorded! This is one of them. Passages in the Bible (like Lk. 5:16 above) say more by saying nothing than they would by saying something. Their silence rends our hearts as a garment of ugly sackcloth.

4p-For His all-night prayer vigil *before* selecting the twelve apostles, see the main heading Section 57, Lk. 6:12 with footnote a. Who among prudent men would dare to *overly* comment on that dark night of bloody-sweat prayer prior to His awful cross, the next morning (Lk. 22:39-44)? These supreme examples must ignite our souls into the holy frame of calling on the Lord in prayer. Soon, it will be said of us as with the Psalmist, "The prayers of David the son of Jesse are ended" (Ps. 72:20). There will be no praying in heaven; it must be done *now* while we are on earth. Prayer is first the service of the heart that touches the heart of God.

Returning to the city, He re-enters Peter's house and preaches.* The roof is opened, and a paralytic is lowered before Jesus and healed. More conflict erupts with the leaders of the Jewish religion.

*See Section 41 for an earlier visit to Peter's house. Jesus was in and out of this home many times.

Capernaum

Matt. 9:1–2	Mk. 2:1–5	Lk. 5:17–20	John
He returns to Capernaum **1** And he entered into a ship, and passed over, and came into his own city.[a]			
	He returns to Capernaum **1** And again he entered into Capernaum[a] after *some* days; and it was noised that he was in the house.[b]		
		He returns to Capernaum **17** And it came to pass on a certain day, as he was teaching, that there were Pharisees and doctors of the law sitting by, which were come out of every town of Galilee, and Judaea, and Jerusalem:[d]	
	2 And straightway many were gathered together, insomuch that there was no room[c] to receive *them*, no, not so much as about the door: and he preached the word unto them.		
		and the power of the Lord was *present* to heal them.[e]	
The roof is raised **2** And, behold, they brought to him a man sick of the palsy, [paralysis] lying on a bed:[f] (mat)	*The roof is raised* **3** And they come unto him, bringing one sick of the palsy, [paralysis] which was borne [carried] of four.[f] (men)	*The roof is raised* **18** And, behold, men brought in a bed a man which was taken with a palsy: [paralysis] and they sought *means*[f] to bring him in, and to lay *him* before him. (Jesus)	
	4 And when they could not come nigh unto him for the press, they uncovered the roof where he was: and when they had broken *it* up, they let down[g] the bed [mat] wherein the sick of the palsy lay.	**19** And when they could not find by what *way* they might bring him in because of the multitude, they went upon the housetop, and let him down[g] through the tiling with *his* couch [mat] into the midst before Jesus.	
and Jesus seeing[h] their faith said unto the sick of the palsy; "Son, be of good cheer; thy sins be forgiven thee."[i]	**5** When Jesus saw[h] their faith, he said unto the sick of the palsy, "Son, thy sins be forgiven thee."[i]	**20** And when he saw[h] their faith, he said unto him, "Man, thy sins are forgiven thee."[i]	

Matt. 9:3-8	Mk. 2:6-12	Lk. 5:21-26	John
Religious leaders angered	*Religious leaders angered*	*Religious leaders angered*	
3 And, behold, certain of the scribes said within themselves,	6 But there were certain of the scribes sitting there, and reasoning in their hearts,	21 And the scribes and the Pharisees began to reason, saying,	
"This *man* blasphemeth."[(j)] ▶ *See Section 62, Matt. 11:8 for more on this upper and lower-case change.*	7 "Why doth this *man* thus speak blasphemies?[(j)] ◀who can forgive sins but God only?"	"Who is this which speaketh blasphemies?[(j)] Who can forgive sins, but God alone?"	
Jesus to responds to them	*Jesus responds to them*	*Jesus responds to them*	
4 And Jesus knowing their thoughts said, "Wherefore think ye evil in your hearts?	8 And immediately when Jesus perceived in his spirit that they so reasoned within themselves, he said unto them, "Why reason ye these things in your hearts?	22 But when Jesus perceived their thoughts, he answering said unto them, "What reason ye in your hearts?	
5 "For whether is easier, to say, '*Thy* sins be forgiven thee;' or to say, 'Arise, and walk?'[(k)]	9 "Whether is it easier to say to the sick of the palsy, '*Thy* sins be forgiven thee;' or to say, 'Arise, and take up thy bed, and walk?'[(k)]	23 "Whether is easier, to say, '*Thy* sins be forgiven thee;' or to say, 'Rise up and walk?'[(k)]	
6 "But that ye may know that the Son of man hath power on earth to forgive sins," (then saith he to the sick of the palsy,) (paralysis)	10 "But that ye may know that the Son of man hath power on earth to forgive sins," (he saith to the sick of the palsy,) (paralysis)	24 "But that ye may know that the Son of man hath power upon earth to forgive sins," (he said unto the sick of the palsy,) (paralysis)	
Jesus sends the man home	*Jesus sends the man home*	*Jesus sends the man home*	
"Arise, take up thy bed, [mat] and go unto thine house."[(l)]	11 "I say unto thee, Arise, and take up thy bed, [mat] and go thy way into thine house."[(l)]	"I say unto thee, Arise, and take up thy couch, [mat] and go into thine house."[(l)]	
7 And he arose,[(m)] and departed to his house.	12 And immediately he arose,[(m)] took up the bed, [mat] and went forth before them all;	25 And immediately he rose[(m)] up before them, and took up that whereon he lay, and departed to his own house, glorifying God.	
The crowds are shocked	*The crowds are shocked*	*The crowds are shocked*	
8 But when the multitude saw *it*, they marvelled, and glorified God,[(n)] which had given such power unto men. (Verse 9 cont. in Section 50.)	insomuch that they were all amazed, and glorified God,[(n)] saying, "We never saw it on this fashion."[(o)] (Verse 13 cont. in Section 50.)	26 And they were all amazed, and they glorified God,[(n)] and were filled with fear, saying, "We have seen strange things[(o)] to day." (Verse 27 cont. in Section 50.)	

Footnotes-Commentary

(a) **"His own city."** This reveals that Jesus had left Nazareth and was now settled somewhere in Capernaum. The previous Section 48, footnote g, reveals that the great crowds of people actually prevented Jesus from returning "openly" to Capernaum! He, therefore, retreated into a desert place until the crowds subsided, but even there they swamped Him with their needs. The above verse tells us that after some unknown period, He could reenter the city. However, the searching crowds soon discovered where He was and flocked around Him again.

(b) No doubt the house of Simon Peter, as seen in Lk. 4:38.

(c) **"No room."** Only a few weeks prior, Peter's house and the surrounding grounds was the scene of thousands packed together and standing on all sides seeking Jesus. Upon Messiah's return to Capernaum, news spread that He was again lodging with Simon Peter. For the second time in a few weeks, literally thousands of people filled the grounds and court area surrounding the house. Our Lord seized the opportunity of this "no room" situation and preached God's message to them.

(d) The presence of such an array of religious dignitaries from hundreds of towns and villages across the entire Holy Land raised great suspicion. Why were the bitter enemies of our Lord gathered at Peter's house to hear what Jesus said? His fame had so widely spread that these evil men united to catch Him in some word or deed wherewith they might have something to accuse Him. No doubt, this army of religionists had been sent by the Sanhedrin at Jerusalem to spy on our Lord. They were in for the shock of their lives!

(e) Dr. Luke alone penned the statement that God's healing power was present on that occasion. This reveals that the presence of wicked men does not necessarily curtail the work and might of God.

(f) Meanwhile, outside Peter's house, there was a tremendous stir among the restless crowds. Four men had brought a beloved friend to be healed by Jesus. The sea of humanity was so vast they could not push their way through the masses to the door or a window of the house to reach the Messiah. Someone among the group of four hits on the idea of making their way up to the flat top roof and letting the ill man down through the sealed trap door that gave access to and from the housetop. Seeing the couch was too large to fit through the opening, they began tearing a larger hole in the tiling. This would grant them access into the room below where Christ sat ministering. One cannot but wonder what Peter thought when he looked up and saw the ceiling of his house being literally torn open! The sick man, so weak and feeble, was unable to help himself. His friends determined that nothing would stop them, and brought him to Jesus. The author's Sunday school teacher, the late Mrs. Ruth Gifford, led him to a saving knowledge of the Lord Jesus Christ in 1946. Those who have helped us come to Christ are life's truest friends.

(g) **Raising the roof for Jesus.** The Jews had strict laws governing housetops or roofs (Deut. 22:8). Dead bodies might be placed there according to Talmud tractate, Shabbath 27b. Some retreated to the roof for prayer (Acts 10:9). Flat top houses were often used to store fruits and grain, as seen in Josh. 2:6 with Talmud tractate, Cullin 13a. When houses were built side by side, their roofs could be used for travel by stepping from one to the other. These were nicknamed "roof roads." They are mentioned in Section 163, Matt. 24:17, as a means of quick escape from pending danger. For more on the use of rooftops, see Section 59, Matt. 10:27, footnote n. Sitting in this packed room were the religious spies filled with hostile intent, ever ready to ensnare the Lord. One can well imagine the shock as the overhead trap door slowly raised, and faces began to appear in the opening. Jesus abruptly ended His discourse. Struggling to get the mat, to which the paralytic clung, through the opening, they began to rip out the material in order to make a larger hole. Soon, a pallet-couch, tied to ropes at the four corners, came slowly down. It was eased to the floor in the presence of the Messiah! Wide-eyed Jews, aghast with surprise, beheld in utter amazement the scene that appeared through the ceiling! The faces of the four men flushed with pitiful hope, the eyes of the paralytic turned upward to the great Messiah, who slowly rose and stood over him. One can believe that a hopeful silence fell over that packed room. *The Master had everything under control!*

(h) **Real faith can be seen.** It is progressively active, never passive. The Savior instantly *saw* the faith of the four men, reflected in their undaunted determination to lay their sick friend before Him, even if it required rending the roof open! The helpless paralytic manifested his faith in Jesus by his willingness to make this hazardous journey to the Master's feet. This is genuine faith shown through deeds as explained in James 2:14-26. It will always work this way.

(i) **"Thy sins be forgiven thee."** To the jolting shock of the doctors of law and Pharisees sitting all about, Christ opens His mouth and announces to the paralytic that his sins were forgiven (Lk. 5:20). Never had sweeter music fallen into his ears! Instantly, his sins vanished from the books of God in heaven. In addition, he knew it too! It must not be unnoticed that Christ, *first* dealt with his sins! Later, we hear our Lord making the same announcement, this time to a sinful woman Lk. 7:48. Men who seek help from God and secretly cling to their sins, refusing to repent will receive nothing of lasting value. It is written, "He that covereth his sins shall not prosper: but whoso confesseth and forsaketh *them* shall have mercy" (Prov. 28:13). King David, after his terrible sin with Bathsheba, and the awful aftermath, wrote in Psa. 38:18, "I will declare mine iniquity; I will be sorry for my sin." The man on the cot said nothing! Christ looked into his heart, saw deep remorse, and heard the silent plea for help.

And it was instantly given. It is striking how across the ministry of Christ, so many who were forgiven, healed, delivered, saved, and blessed said not one word! Can this suggest that the quiet language of a broken heart, sick of sin, and in need of help, is heard before the audible words of the tongue? See footnote k below.

(j) **Here comes religion.** Raging with hatred against Christ, these religious hypocrites reasoned in their minds, "Only God can forgive sins." However, they seemed to have forgotten that they had taught that when Israel's Messiah came, He would have absolute authority to pardon the Jews of their sins as well as heal the sick. See footnote k below.

(k) Christ challenged the *thoughts* of these spies, for He knew what was in their hearts. With the ability to read their thoughts, He demonstrated again that He was God. Instantly, He confronted them with a tough question. The essence of His challenge was, "Tell me, doctors of Israel, which is easier to say to this paralytic: your sins are forgiven or take up your bed and walk?" Not one member of their celebrated company would dare to speak either command. Since they all believed that their Messiah could *both* forgive sins and heal, He demonstrated these abilities for them to behold. The conclusion was inescapable: this Man is the Messiah.

(l) **"Go home!"** Turning to the paralytic lying helpless on his pallet, He commanded that he rise, roll up his bed and go home! (In Lk. 5:24 "bed" is translated "couch," which was another name for a floor pallet or mat.) The room was dramatically charged with God's power; everyone held their breath and gazed steadfastly down at the pitiful and unnamed man. All questioned, "Will he get up?"

(m) **What a miracle!** Instantly, new life and vigor surged through his deteriorated muscular structure; hands, arms, legs, feet, neck, shoulders, all responded. His wilted atrophy vanished. He easily and swiftly arose and took up his bed or mat. The stunned crowds moved backward, stumbling and falling over each other in the shock of the moment, as they made way for him to pass through. With a free hand waving, eyes bright, jumping, dancing, skipping, and in a loud voice, shouting praises to God, this former paralytic vanished amid the crowds and headed for home. One wonders what sort of reception there was when he who hours ago had been carried out like a dead man, now walks through the door filled with joy of sins forgiven and a healed body. Little wonder Luke wrote that he "departed to his own house, glorifying God" (Lk. 5:25). There was surely little sleep among the members of his family that night! We can well picture his four friends being there as chief cheerleaders amid the ocean of joy flooding that house. For another occasion of great joy over the works of Jesus, see Section 89, Mk. 5:42, footnote s. The streets of Capernaum rang with praises to God as the Messiah performed His mighty deeds.

(n) **They glorified God.** A roar of reverberating approval spontaneously exploded from the untold thousands as the fear of God fell upon that scene. News *again* spread everywhere of the amazing deeds of the Man, who was acting like Israel's promised Messiah. Meanwhile, the leaders of Jewish religion were infuriated as the multitudes lifted up their voices in thanks to God. Divine things make a deeper impression on the hearts of ordinary common people, far more than all the worldly wisdom of learned doctors and carnal unconverted theologians.

(o) **"Strange things." Unleashed nature is a stern teacher.** Again, the people were stunned as they heard the teaching and witnessed the works of Jesus the Messiah. Divine wonders are "strange phenomena" and should lead men into a deep reverential fear of the Almighty. Paul wrote that we have another teacher called "nature' (1 Cor. 11:14). Some of her lessons are fierce as she lashes out with floods, fires, earthquakes, and natural disasters causing great devastation and death. Regardless, in the face of these things, America continues making sin legally respectable. In the military, an insane Muslim psychiatrist, a terrorist murderer, slays innocent soldiers while shouting "Allah Akbar." Defense lawyers are trying to decide if he should plead insanity. God forewarned us, "Because sentence against an evil work is not executed speedily, therefore, the hearts of the sons of men is fully set in them to do evil" (Eccles. 8:11). Men and women in all stations of life have ruled out the Holy Bible, the infallible standard of right and wrong, by which to measure ourselves, find direction, guidance, and the favor of God. Meanwhile, the president of the United States, Barack Obama, pulls off his shoes, bows to the floor, and "offers prayers to Allah" in a Washington D.C. Mosque! Claiming to be "a Christian," He kneels amid people who fiercely deny Jesus Christ is the Son of God, and that He died on the cross for our sins. To whom did the president pray in such a hostile atmosphere? We are sure that it was not the God of the Holy Bible. The Lord of heaven will not always tolerate our vicious insults regardless of where they originate. *To whom would Americans pray should He arrange for nature to teach us some lessons bigger than those that hit Japan and Indonesia?* The major networks with their "political consultants" would spend weeks discussing the origin of such things. However, geology and not God Almighty would be their agenda. After all, we should not frighten little children or insult the humble atheists.

2p-**Can we blush anymore?** Shame for wrong and evil is vanishing. Biblical standards for morality and right are scorned, laughed at, and dismissed as antiquated in "our educated era." However, this is not new in history. Some five hundred years before Christ was born, the nation of Israel, a people particularly chosen by God to be His treasure, became so godless that He destroyed thousands of them. Among these rebel Jews, there was no longer any sting of conscience over their wickedness. The prophet inquired, "Were they ashamed when they had committed abomination?" He then answered His question, "nay, they were not at all ashamed, neither could they blush" (Jer. 6:15). Men often blush and regret their sins today, not because they are sorry, but because they were caught.

Leaving Peter's house, He calls a tax officer, Matthew-Levi, to follow Him. He leaves all for Jesus and prepares a great supper for his new Master. Jesus mingles with wicked sinners. The religious leaders are angered again, attacking Christ.

Capernaum

Matt. 9:9–12	Mk. 2:13–17	Lk. 5:27–31	John
	Seaside teaching **13** And he went forth again by the sea side; and all the multitude resorted unto him, and he taught them.		
Matthew **9** And as Jesus passed forth from thence,(a) he saw a man, named Matthew, sitting at the receipt of custom: [tax station] and he saith unto him, "Follow me." And he arose, and followed him.(b)	*Matthew also called Levi* **14** And as he passed by,(a) he saw Levi the *son* of Alphaeus sitting at the receipt of custom, [tax station] and said unto him, "Follow me." And he arose and followed him.(b)	*Matthew also called Levi* **27** And after these things he went forth,(a) and saw a publican, [tax collector] named Levi, sitting at the receipt of custom: [tax station] and he said unto him, "Follow me." **28** And he left all, rose up, and followed him.(b)	
A great feast given: many sinners are present **10** And it came to pass, as Jesus sat at meat in the house,(c) behold, many publicans [tax collectors] and sinners(d) came and sat down with him and his disciples.	*A great feast given: many sinners are present* **15** And it came to pass, that, as Jesus sat at meat in his house,(c) many publicans [tax collectors] and sinners(d) sat also together with Jesus and his disciples: for there were many, and they followed him.	*A great feast given: many sinners are present* **29** And Levi made him a great feast in his own house:(c) and there was a great company of publicans [tax collectors] and of others(d) that sat down with them.	
Religious leaders object because Jesus loved sinners **11** And when the Pharisees saw *it*, they said unto his disciples, "Why eateth(e) your Master with publicans [tax collectors*] and sinners?"	*Religious leaders object because Jesus loved sinners* **16** And when the scribes and Pharisees saw him eat with publicans and sinners, they said unto his disciples, "How is it that he eateth(e) and drinketh with publicans [tax collectors*] and sinners?"	*Religious leaders object because Jesus loved sinners* **30** But their scribes and Pharisees murmured against his disciples, saying, "Why do ye eat(e) and drink with publicans [tax collectors] and sinners?"	
Jesus' response **12** But when Jesus heard *that*, he said unto them, "They that be whole	*Jesus' response* **17** When Jesus heard *it*, he saith unto them, "They that are whole	*Jesus' response* **31** And Jesus answering said unto them, "They that are whole	

Matt. 9:12–13	Mk. 2:17	Lk. 5:31–32	John
need not a physician,[f] but they that are sick. **13** "But go ye and learn what *that* meaneth, 'I will have mercy, and not sacrifice:'[g] for I am not come to call the righteous, but sinners to repentance."[h] (Verse 14 cont. in Section 51.)	have no need of the physician,[f] but they that are sick: I came not to call the righteous, but sinners to repentance."[h] (Verse 18 cont. in Section 51.)	need not a physician;[f] but they that are sick. **32** "I came not to call the righteous, but sinners to repentance."[h] (Verse 33 cont. in Section 51.)	

Footnotes–Commentary

[a] **"As Jesus passed forth from thence."** That is, from Peter's house at Capernaum to the seaside, where, as Mark wrote, "the multitude resorted unto him, and he taught them" (Mk. 2:13).

[b] Numerous commentators have questioned, "how" Matthew (or Levi, as Mark and Luke call him) would have so suddenly "left all, risen up and followed Jesus." Every person in Capernaum had heard of Jesus by this time. All the synagogues in Galilee knew His voice and had witnessed His miracles. The healing of the leper, probably at the leper camp near the city, news of the paralyzed man at Peter's house, and news of hundreds of other miracles had spread into every ear. It is impossible to believe that Matthew had not often been among the people, watching with astonishment Christ's miracles and listening with awe to His preaching. This was not his first introduction to the Lord Jesus.

[c] **"In his own house."** Social contact with "the godless" was strictly forbidden by the religious leaders of Israel. It was unthinkable that Israel's Messiah would mix with the dregs of society as were gathered at Matthew-Levi's house. They were his (former) partners in crime. Hundreds of them were present. Mark. 2:15 reads, "for there were many," while Lk. 5:29 described them as "a great company of publicans and others." The noise, harsh loudness, and coarse conversation must have horrified the self-righteous scribes and Pharisees as they peeked in upon that rowdy scene. Matthew's heart yearned in compassion for all of them. He "threw" this great banquet in order to introduce his ex-companions in sin and tax thievery to the Messiah, who had so wonderfully changed his life. Had he not walked out of the Roman custom's office at Capernaum, leaving it all to follow Christ? Surely, this was a chief topic among his old cronies and friends across the country. They were deeply curious to know what had happened to him. And they were all there to hear the wonderful story, and meet this strange Man, Jesus of Nazareth.

[d] **"Publicans and sinners."** One of the strongest words for evil is used here. It means, "To be devoted or loyal to sin," thus causing one to "miss the mark." It had reference to the most notorious of sinners, the male and female scum of society. Of this sort were Matthew's friends. As a despised publican or tax farmer on the pay of the pagan Romans, every loyal Jew fiercely hated him. Alfred Edersheim informs us in *The Life and Times of Jesus the Messiah*, page 356, that the Talmud probably names five of Jesus' disciples. Matthew is among the list. Further, Edersheim wrote that there were two classes of publicans. First were the "gabbai," who were publicans in general, and second, the hated "mokhes," who were the ruthless customhouse (tax office) officials. Today we would call them "district managers" for the Internal Revenue Service (IRS). Of the latter group (mokhes) was Matthew-Levi. For this class, the Romans built custom stations or offices at the main road junctions, seaport docks and chief places wherever humanity traveled and congregated. They were located at the end of every bridge, at the mouth of rivers and larger streams that were navigable, by the seashores, often at the entering and exiting of city gates and amid the market places. Even some public baths and toilets had tax charges levied for their use! When one paid his dues at the booth, he was issued a "ticket" or "seal" by the customs official to present to the official yonder on the other side of the crossing as "proof of payment."

2p-The burden of Roman taxes was unbearable. They overlooked nothing from which to extract another coin for Caesar and the Senate. There were ground or land taxes, animal taxes, axle taxes, poll or head taxes, bridge taxes, and water taxes. Taxes were levied on grain, leather goods, dried foodstuffs, cloth and clothing, wood products and dried meats of every sort. The vicious income tax amounted to 1 percent, while the head money or poll tax was laid on all persons, bond, and free. In the case of men, it started at the age of fourteen and with women from age twelve. Along with these, there were harbor dues, town dues, and even road taxes. Standard products and goods as well as luxury items were taxed. The greedy publicans, seeking to pry more taxes from the common people, continually vexed travelers going almost anywhere. They were forced to unload their beasts of burden and open every bag and package while the publican freely rummaged through it all. There was no protection from such unscrupulous oppression. Matthew was not only a publican, but he was a "mokhes," the most ruthless and cruel of all Roman puppets. He was thus fiercely despised by his own Jewish people and counted a social outcast.

3p-As mentioned above, the term "sinners" as used here had reference to the scum of human existence: those whose sins were public, blatant, and obvious. Hundreds of them were present at this feast. The Son of God gladly went among these human dregs, calling them to repentance and seeking to convert them to Himself. Months prior, He had done the same thing in Samaria among the citizens of Sychar. Christians who dare to move among this class of people and work to bring them to Christ are rare today. Many churches are so self-righteous, "non-compromising, and fundamental" that they frequently give great sermons warning believers never to be seen amid sinners lest "you get a bad name." It should be noted that Jesus was given a bad Name, but it came from the religious hypocrites, not those He sought to save. See Sections 34 and 35 for Jesus in Samaria, again among the worst of sinners, and the outcome of this event.

(e) Eating with sinners. It was only natural that publicans from across the country should, upon receiving the invitation from Matthew, come to his house to meet the Man, who gave him a new life. Surely, all of them heard how their friend Matthew had "left his lucrative job to follow this preacher." Picture our Lord (and His disciples) reclining at a long table, around which are crowded the scum of society. Drunks, prostitutes, liars, thieves, whoremongers, murderers, robbers; every level of human wickedness was drawn by God's power to hear the moving Words of this wonderful Man. The Pharisees condemned *both* Jesus and His disciples for being present amid this scandalous gathering (Matt. 9:11; Mk. 2:16; and Lk. 5:30). Among these men were those whose lives were so debauched and enslaved by sin, that they could not free themselves from notorious companions and deeds. Only an act of God's grace can deliver them. *To expose men of rotten character when it is necessary is not wrong. It must be done for the protection of the innocent, the revealing of sin, and the presentation of the gospel as its cure.*

2p-Here, we see Jesus, the source of all grace, patiently but surely winning some of them to His way. He answers their questions, refutes their objections, and silences their arguments. The purest One moves among the vilest. *God is very high but he reaches very low!* Jesus, the "friend of sinners," was earnestly calling and compelling them to repentance. Amid the noise and clamor that always attended such a party, the kingdom of Satan suffered tremendous losses! Matthew was enjoying the great feast above all else. His friends were being saved as he had been! In the weeks that followed, everyone in Capernaum was talking about the big blast at Matthew's mansion. It should be noted that the expression used in Mk. 2:16, "Eateth and drinketh," was a common term used daily. Socially, it denoted friendship and familiarity not necessarily drunken revelry. The latter sense is how the Pharisees employed it in their efforts to slander Christ. Those "sipping saints" who attempt to depict our Lord pouring down flasks of wine and strong drink, eating like a pig, talking loudly, coarse and riotous among the crowds at Matthew's house, have seriously misrepresented the character of the Son of God. Are these drinking believers trying to justify their social sins by such terms? Refer to Section 27, footnotes k and l, for relevant comments on Christ turning the water into wine.

(f) "Sick people need a doctor." The faith healers have a dreadful struggle with this statement. Their only resort is to quote 2 Chron. 16:12 and Mk. 5:26 to defend their absurdities. Often, they retort with, "You pray for healing, and go to the doctor. That's not faith." See *Christianity in Crisis* and *Counterfeit Revival*, both by Hank Hannegraaff, for a thorough examination of the healthy-wealthy-healing cults. It is most instructive that Christ advised the sick to see a doctor. Physicians were hated and despised by the Jewish elite at this time. They were classified with common laborers and the lowest classes of society. Due to the continual meat diet of the priests, stomach ailments were rampant among the temple ministers. The Talmud in tractate, Kiddushin 82a, states, "The best doctors are destined for Gehenna" or the torments of hell. Trained physicians were continually on duty in the temple to attend to the scourge of foot ailments that seemed to plague the priests and Levites. They were required to work barefooted. This resulted in serious problems, especially during winter months as they were moving about on freezing cold stone floors. The Lord Jesus deliberately employed the metaphor of a Hebrew doctor attending to one physically ill to show the Jewish religionists that sinners must be brought to Him at all costs. As they hated doctors, so they have hated Him. There at Matthew's house, amid hundreds of spiritually ill sinners, the worst of society, Christ presented Himself as the Sovereign Physician of souls. Jesus, the "kind doctor from heaven," went to the terminally ill patients (Matthew's house was full of them) and ministered the medicine of forgiveness and eternal life to all who would listen and believe. See Section 41, Matt. 8:17, second paragraph of footnote h, for more on Christ healing the sick. *The Christian's response to sickness today is prayer, faith, and a good doctor!*

(g) Calling sinners to repentance. Quoted from blending selected words found in 1 Sam. 15:22 and Hosea 6:6. It was given in response to the charge of the Pharisees that Christ was mixing with sinners. Note Section 53, Matt. 12:7, footnote i, where Christ quoted this same verse on a later occasion. The meaning is that God takes more delight in showing mercy than in having a perfect animal sacrifice offered to His Name. The whole purpose of *all* sacrifices was to point in some way to the higher mercy of God, in giving Christ's blood to establish the new covenant of eternal redemption. For explanation of this new covenant, see Section 95, second paragraph of footnote u. When the heart of the offerer was filled with wickedness (which was the precise case with the Pharisees), their sacrifices became sacrilegious mockery. The self-righteous Pharisees drove away those who were smitten over their sinfulness and sought God's mercy and forgiveness. *True* religion always seeks to bring the dregs of humanity to the glorious saving knowledge of Christ. It feels no guilt as it dares to mingle with the worst of sinners in order to lead them out of their sin into forgiveness and eternal life. *Mixing with them in no way connotes partaking of their evil deeds.* The days of the unsaved coming to the church and being converted to Christ are just about over. From the start to the present, the church is to go out and bring men to a saving knowledge of Christ.

2p-Christianized prostitution and other acceptable sins? "Evangelism" that sins with sinners in order to "win them" is a sham. "Christian tattoos," "Christian strip tease," "Christian gay and lesbian clubs," "Christian rock bands," "Christian ballroom dancing," "Christian rap," and "Christian séances" are covert snake pits. They degrade the saving gospel of Christ by negating its firm requirement of repentance from sin *before* God will save the soul. This integration of sugar-coated evil into the Christian faith is contrary to historical Christianity and biblical teaching. Years ago, while sitting in a waiting room of an automotive repair garage in Alberton, South Africa, a young Dutch woman came in and sat down. I began to speak to her about Christ. Carroll quickly informed me that she was a "born again believer" and served her Lord. It sounded good until I inquired in what way she served. To my shock, she smilingly said, "I am in Christian prostitution." Further, she had just spent the night with a man in the hotel across the street, "collecting money for her congregation and witnessing for Jesus." Upon hearing the name of her church, I knew instantly why she was deceived into believing such lies as "Christian prostitution." Only a gospel according to the Devil could produce the twisted practices of that twenty-five-year-old woman. Despite my pleas, Carroll insisted what she and the other girls were doing was right, for "God had revealed it to them." This is an example of "Christianized sin" that rules in churches raised up by the Devil. A cross displayed on a church building does not mean that Christ is in the hearts of those sitting inside.

3p-False separation. Opposite to the above evils are "Bible believers" that isolate and insulate themselves from certain sections of the lost world under the pretext of "separation" or "militant fundamentalism." These people are just as guilty as the Christ-denying liberals are, and the churches that produced the young woman mentioned above who "served Jesus as prostitute." Some years ago, I heard a great Bible teacher say that he was invited to a Roman Catholic school to share his beliefs with the students; *there were no strings attached.* He declined on the basis that he "did not believe in this type of interaction." This good man's priorities were seriously fouled up. Surely, Satan was pleased with his "non-compromising," "Bible believing" decision. He even quoted two verses to prove he was right! This is not true biblical separation but ignorance, if not self-righteous hypocrisy. *Christ went to sinners; we are to do the same!* The old rebuttal is always thrown in our face, "What will people say if they see us going in or coming out of such places?" The answer is that they will say to us what the scribes and Pharisees said to Jesus. "Bible believers" who think they are so right that they may embarrass God by going to those without Christ are sick. This disease did not die out with the Pharisees. Some early Christians sold themselves in the slave markets of the Roman Empire in order to gain entrance into the homes of the rich. When there, they used this awful place of cruel slavery as a channel of witnessing for their Savior. Did God consider this a "compromise" of His Word?

4p-Debating in a room full of gamblers. Working as a missionary in Gladstone, Queensland, Australia, in the early 1960s, I often visited in the back room of a tailor shop at night and sat among gamblers, drunkards, and thieves as they played poker, cursed, swore, guzzled beer, and told their filthy stories. The shop owner, Bob Burgess (with whom I was friendly), invited me there on a particular Friday night to "talk to his friends about God." It was a set-up joke on me! Present was a ranting, raving, wild man named Jack Greatorex, who fiercely challenged me to debate him on the subject of communism. Everyone in that smoke-filled room stopped their card games, drinking, and loud talk. They listened to us verbally "fight it out" for over an hour. When it was finished, the men sitting at the tables gave a round of applause! Gossip spread over the entire village that the American missionary was "preaching to the men in Bob's back room." And what came out of that "interaction" with the toughest sinners in that Aussie town? Over two decades later (after working many years in Africa), I returned to Australia and found Bob Burgess, a wrinkled, trembling old man, sitting on the edge of his bed in a nursing home north of Brisbane. He was instantly led to a saving knowledge of Christ and died some nine months later. A week before His death, Bob told me that it all started because I visited that back room, debated, argued, and fought for Christ and right. It was during the heated debate that the Holy Spirit first spoke to his heart about salvation. According to *some* fundamentalists, I flatly compromised with sin by going into that foul smelling room. Following Christ's example, I did what was right, and it was ultimately blessed of the Lord. Had I not believed in "interaction with the lost," despite town gossip, Bob would be in hell today! I was the only "clergyman" in that village he would talk to about "religious matters."

5p-The author is not defending "ecumenical evangelism" that comforts the unholy in their sin and leaves the impression that any religion is right if one is sincere in what he believes. For an explanation of sincerity in religion without Christ, see Section 95, sixth paragraph of footnote r. Only as men go forth and seek the lost (where they are) will they "learn" the truth of Jesus' Words in Matt. 9:12-13. Next, they become involved in the arduous task of bringing sin-sick sinners to the Great Physician and Savior. Those who labor to lead unsaved men to Christ (regardless of the circumstances) are the *first* to understand that God *does* "have mercy," in preference to the elaborate and costly sacrifices from the hands of church hypocrites or steel hearted "Bible believing," bigots.

(h) **"Repentance."** For more on this subject, see Section 72, Lk. 13:5, footnote f. Someone said, "Repentance is man deciding with God against himself." However, the Jewish understanding of repentance and the forgiveness of sin (at this time in their history) was *not* the concept as later laid out in the pages of the New Testament. Nor was it the concept as preached by John the Baptist or our Lord. Briefly, in synagogue theology, Jewish repentance was something brought about and made acceptable to God by numerous and various good works. Then, *after* this good-work-produced repentance was accomplished, the penitent Jew believed he had secured divine forgiveness. It was like "buying repentance from God." The late non-Christian Jew Joseph Klausner, in his book *The Messianic Ideal in Israel*, pages 428-429, describes the Hebrew practice of repentance during this era in history as an endeavor to win favor with God. This was not the repentance required by their Messiah. For them, repentance and forgiveness were only for those who loved and adhered to the Law of Moses and were true Hebrews. Again, their Messiah acted contrary to the theology of the rabbis. Christ's very presence among these notorious sinners, both male and female, stunned the Pharisees. This acclaimed Messiah viewed all men, Jews and Gentiles, as potential prospects for His new kingdom. The religious leaders were alarmed that in His evangelism, *none* were rejected! He received *all* without distinction. Neither Jew nor Gentile was prohibited. Sinful humanity flocked to Him, just as they were, lost and without God or hope; His arms were open for all. To the shock of the religionists, amid this feast of wild sinners, in the home of a cursed publican, He reclined among the worst of Jews and Gentiles alike. He was ever busy calling them to repentance, the forgiveness of sins and eternal life. That is what He went to Matthew's house for.

2p-Part of the present day Jewish understanding of repentance is recorded in the Talmud, tractate Shabbath 32a. It reads, "Repentance and works of charity are man's intercessors before God's throne." However, Holy Scripture informs us that only one Person can intercede before God's throne for mankind. In the Hebrew language, He is called "Yeshua ha'Mashiach" or "Jesus the Messiah" (Rom. 8:34 with Heb. 7:25). Regarding man's works by which he might be saved, the Jewish Bible states, "our righteousnesses *are* as filthy rags" before God (Isa. 64:6). Why did the Hebrew people not believe and practice their own Scripture regarding these things?

3p-The lesson He had given to His disciples months previous at the Samaritan well, "sowing in view of reaping eternal wages," was being revealed before their eyes. For they were present with their Lord among that shady company of financial criminals gathered at Matthew's house. They were just as horrified as the Pharisees at what their Master was doing. The chief lesson remains clear: the saving gospel must be carried to the lost, wherever they are found. God saves sinners as they accept His call to repentance from their sin and put their faith in His beloved Son. He does not save those who *think* they may somehow get themselves good enough to be forgiven. Christ saves only lost sinners (Lk. 19:10 with 1 Tim. 1:15). In light of this, we now understand our Lord's teaching "for I am not come to call the righteous, but sinners to repentance" (Matt. 9:13). We can imagine the fierce anger of the religious leaders at Christ's conduct, witnessing among that motley, and wicked crowd at Matthew's house.

4p-Repentance no longer required? The teaching that "repentance is not necessary for salvation" is a gross error. No repentance before salvation is another doctrine that demons teach in their unceasing effort to water down the requirements of the saving gospel. It adds faulty converts into the local churches (1 Tim. 4:1-2). Raw Calvinism affirms that man can only repent *after* he has been saved! This reversal of divine truth is not the work of God. Everyone in eternity's hell realizes the need for sinners to repent, but too late, while some pulpits and congregations on earth are void of this realization. Read the horrific call for repentance from the city of the damned in Lk. 16:30. In Section 67, Matt. 12:41, the Savior affirmed that the people of Nineveh repented of their sin, under the preaching of Jonah. This was a blunder if repentance is not prerequisite to forgiveness and salvation. It is written in 2 Peter 3:9 that God "is not willing that any should perish, but that all should come to repentance." Only error can make this mean, "come to repentance after they are saved?" Paul said that God "commandeth all men every where to repent" (Acts 17:30). What shameless impudence to read this as, "commandeth all the elect to repent." For more on repentance and our Lord's demand for it, see Section 72, Lk. 13:5, footnote f, and Section 201, second and third paragraphs of footnote n. The Reformed doctrine that men cannot repent until after they are saved is a wolf in sheep's clothing. *It requires God do what He requires man to do after giving him the power to do it.*

5p-One as bad as the other. Arminianism, which teaches salvation partly by man's moral choice and partly by grace, is equally malevolent. Like Calvinism, it is replete with errors while mixed with fragments of truth. This distortion proclaims the joys of salvation for those who are saved, then poisons them with the horror of losing eternal life at the flick of a finger or slip of the tongue. Years ago while speaking to a soldier near Fort Knox, Kentucky, he informed me that he had been saved six times but was now lost again! With tears he pled, "I want to be saved the seventh time." I tried to show him from Scripture that Christ died *once* for mankind forever; that He would not come to earth and die the seventh time for him to be saved again. This young man from Chicago was so deceived by Arminianism that he could not comprehend the fact of Christ's everlasting, one time atonement for his sins. This doctrine is so dumb that it attempts to mix grace with works! Contrary wise, Calvinism is worse. It insults the full atonement of Christ by limiting it to a select group, while pre-damning all else including billions of helpless children. Alas! The fears and sorrows that these heretical twins have laid upon humankind are beyond description. Once they are brought into a church assembly and not *immediately* dealt with there will be serious trouble. For other comments on this subject, see Section 203, the eleventh paragraph of footnote d.

A break-off sect of John's disciples sides with the Pharisees against the Lord Jesus over the question of fasting and prayer. He responds with three illustrations of a bridegroom, cloth, and wineskin bottles.

Capernaum

Matt. 9:14-17	Mk. 2:18-22	Lk. 5:33-37	John
Their troubling question	*Their troubling question*	*Their troubling question*	
14 Then came to him the disciples of John,[a] saying, "Why do we and	18 And the disciples of John[a] and of the Pharisees used to fast: and they come and say unto him, "Why do the disciples of John and of the	33 And they[a] said unto him, "Why do the disciples of John fast often, and make prayers, and likewise	
the		*the disciples* of the Pharisees;	
Pharisees fast oft, but thy disciples fast not?"[b]	Pharisees fast, but thy disciples fast not?"[b]	but thine eat and drink?"[b]	
Jesus' three responses	*Jesus' three responses*	*Jesus' three responses*	
1. The bridegroom	1. The bridegroom	1. The bridegroom	
15 And Jesus said unto them, "Can the children [guests] of the bridechamber mourn, as long as the bridegroom is with them?[c]	19 And Jesus said unto them, "Can the children [guests] of the bridechamber fast, while the bridegroom is with them?[c] as long as they have the bridegroom with them, they cannot fast.	34 And he said unto them, "Can ye make the children [guests] of the bridechamber fast, while the bridegroom is with them?[c]	
but the days will come, when the bridegroom shall be taken from them, and then shall they fast.[d]	20 "But the days will come, when the bridegroom shall be taken away from them, and then shall they fast[d] in those days.	35 "But the days will come, when the bridegroom shall be taken away from them, and then shall they fast[d] in those days."	
		2. The old and new cloth	
		36 And he spake also a parable unto them;	
2. The old and new cloth	2. The old and new cloth	"No man putteth a	
16 "No man putteth a piece of new cloth unto an old garment, for that which is put in to fill it up taketh from the garment, and the rent is made worse.[e]	21 "No man also seweth a piece of new cloth on an old garment: else the new piece that filled it up taketh away from the old, and the rent is made worse.[e]	piece of a new garment upon an old; if otherwise, then both the new maketh a rent, and the piece that was *taken* out of the new agreeth not with the old.[e]	
3. The old and new bottles	3. The old and new bottles	3. The old and new bottles	
17 "Neither do men putteth new wine into old [skin] bottles: else the bottles break, and the	22 "And no man putteth new wine into old [skin] bottles: else the new wine burst the	37 "And no man putteth new wine into old [skin] bottles; else the new wine will burst the	

Matt. 9:17	Mk. 2:22	Lk. 5:37-39	John
wine runneth out, and the [skin] bottles⁽ᶠ⁾ perish: but they put new wine⁽ᵍ⁾ into new [skin] bottles, and both are preserved." (Verse 18 cont. in Section 89.)	bottles, and the wine is spilled, and the [skin] bottles⁽ᶠ⁾ will be marred: but new wine must be put into⁽ᵍ⁾ new [skin] bottles." (Verse 23 cont. in Section 53.)	bottles, and be spilled, and the [skin] bottles⁽ᶠ⁾ shall perish. **38** "But new wine must be put into⁽ᵍ⁾ new [skin] bottles; and both are preserved." ***The Jews had rejected Christ's teaching: their old wine or oral traditions were better than His new Words of salvation and forgiveness*** **39** "No man also having drunk old *wine* straightway desireth new: for he saith, 'The old is better.' "⁽ʰ⁾ (Next chap. Lk. 6:1 cont. in Section 53.)	

Footnotes-Commentary

⁽ᵃ⁾ **"Disciples of John."** At this time, John the Baptist had been in prison for many months but not yet put to death. See the asterisk under main heading of Section 21, Part 1, for details of his imprisonment and murder. Some of John's disciples were strongly attached to him and chose to imitate his peculiar austerity of life and habits, even after his imprisonment. Some of them had not abandoned the Baptist to follow wholly the Messiah, though many had. These loyal devotees maintained contact with John, who was in Herod's prison at Machaerus, in Moab on the eastern side of Jordan. They were a *sectarian group* that clung fast to the Baptist's peculiar lifestyle. Upon learning that Christ and His disciples had attended the feast at Matthew's house, they were greatly offended. It seems they had been questioned by the Pharisees regarding our Lord's presence at Matthew's party. This small sect-group staunchly agreed with the Pharisees on the custom of fasting and "separation from sinners." Hence, their conclusion that Christ had no business in such a place! The fasting referred to here was not that required in the Law of Moses but rather private, individual acts that were practiced by some of John's disciples, by the Pharisees, and their disciples. These fasts were part of "the tradition of the elders" as explained in Matt. 15:1-3.

2p-Normally, the Jews fasted twice a week on Mondays and Thursdays (Lk. 18:12). The Torah Law of Moses required fasting *only* on the Day of Atonement. See *The IVP Bible Background Commentary on the New Testament*, page 70, by C. S. Keener for details. The rabbis invented and then placed upon the people dozens of compulsory fasts. These were for rain, in times of war, disaster, famine, sickness, and countless other reasons. The question in verse 14 reveals that this breakaway group of John's disciples had joined with the Pharisees on the point of fasting and prayer. Being instigated by the Pharisees, they came and attacked the Lord Jesus on this issue. This factious sect continued for years in New Testament history. Over two decades later, Paul met twelve of them in far away Ephesus. They were still ignorant of God's plan for the salvation of men (Acts 19:1-7)! It is noted that the mighty Apollos had been influenced or taught by this separatist group. Aquila and Priscilla, the husband and wife team, took him aside, "and expounded unto him more perfectly the way of God" (Acts 18:24-2). We cannot but ponder, "Did John, sitting in prison know of these factions among his followers who had taken sides with the enemies of Jesus the Messiah?"

⁽ᵇ⁾ **"Thy disciples fast not."** The Sanhedrin had their spies everywhere watching Christ and His disciples in hopes of catching them in some conflict with *their* fabricated rules and oral laws of the Mishna. This conflict later came to a head in Section 96. It was obvious that the disciples of Christ were no longer joining with the standard fasts and associated prayers as practiced by the Jews. This was not a fast in the Jewish law, but more of the traditions and oral commands. There were heavy burdens placed upon the people. Note Matt. 23:4 with Lk. 11:46, for other mentions of burdens under which the people struggled.

⁽ᶜ⁾ Christ answered them from a well-known Jewish social custom. In using the word "bridegroom" Jesus refers to Himself, and by "the children of the bridechamber" (or guests), He speaks of His disciples. Months prior, John, their master, had acknowledged Christ as being the bridegroom; therefore, his (John's) followers ought to do the same. Further, John had also claimed to be a "friend of the bridegroom" and rejoiced at hearing Jesus' voice (or message). Since their master, John had stated that having the bridegroom present with them required feasting, not fasting, and joy instead of sadness, they should obey his teaching and abandon the man-made fasts, and dead legal prayers imposed on them by Jewish traditions. Hebrew wedding custom forbade fasting, mourning, or severe labor during wedding time, which normally lasted seven days. This was because the bridegroom was among them. Christ the "bridegroom," the Messiah, was, likewise, present with them; therefore, how rude and inappropriate it was to fast. See Section 32, John 3:29, footnote b, for an explanation of the use of the term "bridegroom."

(d) In conclusion, the Messiah told John's disciples that since He was there with them, it would be out of order to mourn and fast. Jewish history agrees with this. The Talmud in various places relates that marriage was a time of great joy and relaxation from particular duties. See Berachoth 6b, 11a and 16a for illustrations of this. Even though this was true, the Lord Jesus warned that the time was coming when He would be "taken away from them" at His ascension. Then they could weep, lament, and fast. Nevertheless, this long season of heaviness and sorrow would end when He would see them forever. An interesting note is that the ancient Hebrews taught all fasting would end during the earthly days of their Messiah. This is precisely what Jesus is trying to tell John's disciples. He, the Messiah, was there, so why fast. You can do that when He is gone!

(e) **"New cloth onto an "old garment."** Realizing that this sectarian element of John's disciples had not understood what He said, our Lord resorted to the use of two well-known illustrations in an attempt to clarify His teaching. First, He speaks of putting a piece of "new cloth" onto an "old garment." When washed, the new piece will shrink, thus tearing the old cloth and rendering it useless. Christ is telling them that the "old garment" represents the oral teaching, traditions, countless laws, and rules of the Jewish elders. These thousands of traditions *were not* contained in the Torah Law given by Moses but were additions to its original 613 precepts. Later, the rabbis divided these 613 into two different parts, called the negative and positive laws. For explanation of this, see Section 45, first and second paragraphs under footnote b. The endless restrictions about eating, drinking, walking, dressing, washing of tables, doors, pots, pans, steps, windows and thousands of other things were named the oral law or tradition of the elders. They are to this day still found in the Talmud-Mishna or oral law. By rigid practice of these burdensome "commandments of men," the Jews considered themselves righteous and acceptable before God.

2p-The piece of "new cloth" was the new kingdom teaching being introduced and spread by the Messiah and His disciples. His teaching was incompatible with the tradition of the elders. The two would never blend. It was either His doctrine or theirs. These sectarian disciples of John greatly needed this lesson, seeing they were still holding to this fasting-prayer custom of the scribes and rabbis. They were confused as to why the "new cloth" of Jesus' teaching would not blend with these rabbinical traditions of fasting. Christ explains the two are forever irreconcilable; for what He preached would *never* merge with the false religious practices of the Jews. There is no synthesis of the two, in time the faulty doctrinal garment will tear and the old theological bottle will break.

(f) **The Master and the Mishna.** Then Lord Jesus gives a second illustration for John's inquiring disciples to consider. Contrary to a popular but erroneous belief, Jesus was not speaking of *fermenting* wine inside a wine skin bottle. No skin, regardless of how "new" it was, could finally withstand the tremendous pressure of gas producing, fermenting wine. In time, the whole thing would "blow" or "explode." With this, both bottle and contents were lost. Jesus was speaking of a non-intoxicating liquid put inside new wineskins. This way, both were preserved. In this illustration, He again exposed the hopelessness of trying to unite His teaching as Israel's Messiah with the tradition of the elders (or Mishna law), as propagated by the scribes and Pharisees. See footnote e above. Moreover, this is what the sect of John's disciples was trying to do! "Old bottles" were actually animal skins that had been turned inside out and dried to hold liquids. In time, they had been stretched to their limit and would become dried and cracked. "New bottles" speak of fresh skins carefully prepared to receive and hold *fresh new liquids* free from the various additives that produced fermentation. See footnote g below. New bottles or skins do not break, being freshly pliable, soft, and flexible: thus, they safely hold and protect fresh liquids from the process of fermentation. The author has seen these skin bottles numerous times while serving as a missionary in Africa.

(g) **New wine is better.** In using this term our Lord referred to His unique teachings as the Messiah of Israel as they related to His new kingdom. In Prov. 3:10, "new wine" was the *fresh* pressed blood of the grapes, which according to Isa. 65:8 is found in the cluster. It became potent *only* when men mixed additives or chemicals with it (Ps. 75:8 with Prov. 23:30). Most of the preaching and practices of Christ were so contrary to those of the scribes and Pharisees that the two were poles apart. His new doctrine was like "new wine," fresh, wholesome and designed to cheer the heart of man, and not make a half-drunken fool out of him. Refer to Section 27, John 2:9, footnote k, for further comments on the use of wine. In Sections 34 and 35, the Lord went among the Samaritans, and Section 50, to the feast at Matthew the cursed publican's house. These actions and many others caused great conflict between Him and the teaching of Jewish religionists. The only vessel that could hold Messiah's new teaching was the soul transformed by the miracle of saving grace. The Pharisees had tasted the "new wine" of Christ's teaching but fiercely rejected it, saying the "old wine" of their Mishna and oral traditions was better. See footnote h below. Ultimately, their theological "old wine" destroyed them and all who partook of it.

(h) Old wine will kill. Luke records another proverbial expression for Theophilus, the original recipient of his book. For other proverbs used by Jesus, see Section 38, Lk. 4:23, footnote i, and Section 96, Matt. 5:14. This maxim about "old wine" had direct reference to the false teachings of the scribes and Pharisees, who in their hatred of Christ rejected the "new wine" of His new kingdom. The Jews, full of the "old wine" (in this case) of their defective religion, with its thousands of rules and restrictions, were dulled into a fatal stupor and spiritual blindness. This proverb *perfectly* described the nation of Israel, especially its religious leaders, who were inebriated by Jewish traditionalism. They fiercely opposed Christ saying that "the [their] old [way] was better." Being reared in strict Hebrew asceticism of the oral law, they sternly rejected the "new wine" of Jesus' kingdom message. Most of what He taught flew in the face of these self-righteous, religious hypocrites and astounded His audiences as well. For example of this, see Section 47, Matt. 7:28-29, footnotes m and n.

2p-Christ opposed false traditions. Some of John's disciples, who came to challenge Christ on the subject of fasting and prayer, were bordering on the same fatal mistake as the Pharisees. See main heading in this Section along with footnote a above. Still drinking the "old wine" of Hebrew oral traditions, laws, and customs, the Jews argued with the Messiah that this was preferable to His teaching. Whenever the scribes and Pharisees taught the Law of Moses (or sat in his seat, Matt. 23:1-3), Christ admonished the people to obey Moses but not act like their teachers who did not obey his teachings. Read Section 119, John 7:19, footnote f, where Jesus charged them with not keeping the Torah Law of Moses. See footnote e above for more on the Jews and the law. They hated Jesus for opposing their legal system, especially their traditions or endless oral laws. These traditions and customs are explained in Section 52, footnote h; Section 89, footnote c; and Section 96, footnote d.

3p-Tradition's overwhelming power, be it religious, political, moral, or whatever is astounding. The author has seen this over the decades and wondered how much of it is demonic in origin and intent. Good and needed changes are often opposed and rejected based on some ancient tradition or custom no longer applicable or valid to the situation. For more on the dangers of this, see Section 12, footnote k and Section 45, the eleventh paragraph of footnote b. For a pungent but awful illustration of the power and grip of satanic false religious traditions, see Section 86, number 4 under footnote b. Because the supreme standard for saved Christians is the Word of God, this is often distorted, twisted, and perverted by evil men to suit their own purposes. History reflects this in the lives of such imposters as Joseph Smith, Brigham Young, Father Divine, Rev. Jim Jones, David Koresh, Herbert Armstrong, Rev. Jessie Jackson, John Ramirez, Cardinal Bernard Law, and thousands of others. Obedience to biblical teaching never frees believers from their duty of adhering to the laws of the land, be they local, state, or national. *True* Christians are faced with "time release legislation" designed to curb the witness of Jesus Christ in society. Millions in centuries past faced the same; however, they chose to be faithful to Christ rather than the *criminal* legislations of wicked persons who hate the Bible, things pure, upright, and honorable.

4p-Old wine of right and left wing politics and religion. For the origin of these terms, see Section 205, second paragraph of footnote e. America is blitzed by "talk-show hosts" and "right-wing stalwarts defending traditional values." *(Their religion is "conservative politics" not Jesus Christ.)* The truth they speak is bathed in cursing and offensive language. Jesus said that what is in the heart comes out of the mouth (Matt. 12:33-36). The usage of "damn," "hell," and sacrilegious statements about God and Christ denigrate moral and political truths. Know-it-all Keith Olbermann, ridicules "Jesus the Son of God," then tosses his script at the camera. He was recently fired from his position! Bill O'Reilly affirmed, "Jesus was a philosopher." Caught off camera he rages like a mad man with the popular four-letter dirt word pouring off his tongue. Arrogant Rush Limbaugh and blasphemous Bill Maher also fit into the verbal garbage can. Airwave trash is supposed to be controlled by the FCC (Federal Communications Commission), the watchdog for decency in broadcasting. It is another tax-funded government flop. Right-winger, Glen Beck, is not a *biblical Christian.* He calls on the government for moral and political responsibility (which is a joke), yet succinctly steps over the dark Mormon cult of which he is a defender. Would he give America a series on the history of his church? Never, because it reeks with polygamy, adulteries, occultism, mass murders, blasphemy, secret political intrigue, the sex abuse of women, children, and more. Beck's god is out yonder on a planet having babies with his spiritual wives! *No Bible obedient Christian can belong to the Mormon Church and be right with God.* Network executives fire men for racial and Islamic innuendos, and then allow the tsunami of electronic trash, sex perversions, nudity, adultery, sodomy, using God's Name in vain, profanity, cursing, and blasphemous insults to poison the airwaves. (Is this freedom of speech or freedom of verbal trash?) Meanwhile, the "talk-show hosts" crack their dirty jokes as the audiences laugh their way into hell. The Bible speaks of those "Whose mouth is full of cursing and bitterness" (Rom. 3:14). For more on the insane right and left wing scenarios in politics and religion, see Section 54, third paragraph of footnote h. *Today, either wing is just as rotten as the other!*

5p-The "lights out day" is coming for all men. God warns, "The lamp [light] of the wicked shall he put out" (Prov. 13:9). Old father time has long demonstrated that, "Fools make a mock at sin" (Prov. 14:9). Quoting Scripture to some people is like spitting on a fire to put it out. All you get is a short hiss. The old wine of rotten right and left wing radical politics, hypocritical religion, and dirt talk immorality continues. The objections of *true* Christians and *decent* non-Christian people alike will not change things as history reveals. However, we continue to object. At a time yet future, the judgment of God will beckon all of us in (Eccle. 12:14). *Who will laugh then?*

CHAPTER 10

PASSOVER NUMBER TWO IN JESUS' MINISTRY.* AGAIN, HE DEMONSTRATES HIS MESSIANIC AUTHORITY. VARIOUS EVENTS IN HIS LIFE UP TO THE THIRD PASSOVER A YEAR LATER. THE UPSETTING SYNAGOGUE DISCOURSE AT CAPERNAUM.

Time: The above events took one year.

Leaving Capernaum, He returns to Jerusalem. A cripple is healed on the Passover Sabbath. The Jews seek to kill Jesus. He defends Himself.

*For His first Passover, see footnote b below. During this second Passover, the Lord Jesus asserted again to be Israel's Messiah. This was before the Sanhedrin as seen in footnotes w, y, and z of this Section. The religious leaders sought to discredit Christ before the people who flocked to Him by the thousands.

Matt.	Mk.	Lk.	John 5:1-14—*Jerusalem and the temple*
			The unnamed feast
			1 After this[a] there was a feast[b] of the Jews; and Jesus went up to Jerusalem.[c] *(Assumedly, His second Passover as Messiah. See John 6:4 for the third, which He did not attend.)*
			Healing one out of hundreds
			2 Now there is at Jerusalem by the sheep *market* a pool, which is called in the Hebrew tongue "Bethesda," having five porches.[d]
			3 In these lay a great multitude of impotent folk, of blind, halt, withered, waiting for the moving of the water.
			4 For an angel went down at a certain season into the pool, and troubled the water: whosoever then first after the troubling of the water stepped in was made whole of whatsoever disease he had.[e]
			An infirmed man meets the Messiah
			5 And a certain man was there, which had an infirmity thirty and eight years.
			6 When Jesus saw him lie, and knew that he had been now a long time *in that case*, he saith unto him, "Wilt thou be made whole?"[f]
			7 The impotent man answered him, "Sir, I have no man, when the water is troubled, to put me into the pool: but while I am coming, another steppeth down before me."
			8 Jesus saith unto him, "Rise, take up thy bed, [pallet] and walk."[g]
			9 And immediately the man was made whole, and took up his bed, and walked: and on the same day was the sabbath.
			The Jews angered over the Sabbath day miracle
			10 The Jews therefore said unto him that was cured, "It is the sabbath day: it is not lawful for thee to carry *thy* bed."[h]
			11 He answered them, "He that made me whole, the same said unto me, 'Take up thy bed, [pallet] and walk.'"
			12 Then asked they him, "What man is that which said unto thee," 'Take up thy bed, [pallet] and walk?'"
			He did not know who it was that healed him
			13 And he that was healed wist [knew] not who it was:[i] for Jesus had conveyed himself away, a multitude being in *that* place.
			Later, Jesus finds the healed man: he is warned
			14 Afterward Jesus findeth[j] him in the temple, and said unto him,

Matt.	Mk.	Lk.	John 5:14-28—*Jerusalem and the temple*
			"Behold, thou art made whole: sin no more, lest a worse thing come unto thee."
			The man innocently reports to the Jews
			15 The man departed, and told the Jews that it was Jesus, which had made him whole.[(k)]
			They seek to kill Jesus
			16 And therefore did the Jews persecute Jesus, and sought to slay him, because he had done these things on the sabbath day.[(l)]
			HE CAN WORK ON THE SABBATH FOR HE IS EQUAL WITH GOD IN NINE DIFFERENT WAYS.
			1. In working like God
			17 But Jesus answered them,[(m)] "My Father worketh hitherto, and I work."
			18 Therefore the Jews sought the more to kill him, because he not only had broken the sabbath, but said also that God was his Father, making himself equal with God.
			2. In doing what the Father does for He loves and shows the Son all things
			19 Then answered Jesus and said unto them, "Verily, verily, I say unto you, The Son can do nothing of himself, but what he seeth[(n)] the Father do: for what things soever he doeth, these also doeth the Son likewise.
			20 "For the Father loveth the Son, and sheweth him all things that himself doeth: and he will shew him greater works than these, that ye may marvel.
			3. In having the quickening power of God
			21 "For as the Father raiseth up the dead, and quickeneth [gives life to] *them*;[(o)] even so the Son quickeneth whom he will.
			4. In having all judgment placed into His hands
			22 "For the Father judgeth no man, but hath committed all judgment unto the Son:[(p)]
			5. In being honored as the Father is honored
			23 "That all *men* should honour[(q)] the Son, even as they honour the Father. He that honoureth not the Son honoureth not the Father which hath sent him.
			6. In giving eternal life to the spiritually dead
			24 "Verily, verily, I say unto you, He that heareth my Word, and believeth on him that sent me, hath everlasting life, and shall not come into condemnation; but is passed from death unto life.[(r)]
			25 "Verily, verily, I say unto you, The hour is coming, and now is, when the dead shall hear the voice of the Son of God: and they that hear shall live.[(s)]
			7. In having God's life and authority to mete out judgment
			26 "For as the Father hath life in himself; so hath he given to the Son to have life in himself;[(t)]
			27 "And hath given him authority to execute judgment also, because he is the Son of Man.
			8. In calling the physical dead from their graves at His return
			28 "Marvel not at this: for the hour is coming, in the which all that are in the graves shall hear his voice,

Matt.	Mk.	Lk.	John 5:29-47—*Jerusalem and the temple*
			29 "**And shall come forth; they that have done good, unto the resurrection of life; and they that have done evil, unto the resurrection of damnation.**(u)
			9. In perfectly doing the Father's will
			30 "I can of mine own self do nothing:(v) as I hear, I judge: and my judgment is just; because I seek not mine own will, but the will of the Father which hath sent me.
			JESUS NAMES SIX WITNESSES THAT POINTED TO HIM
			1. The message of John the Baptist witnessed of Him
			31 "If I bear witness of myself, my witness(w) is not true.
			32 "There is another that beareth witness of me; and I know that the witness which he witnesseth of me is true.
			33 "Ye sent unto John, and he bare witness unto the truth.
			34 "But I receive not testimony from man: but these things I say, that ye might be saved.
			35 "He was a burning and a shining light: and ye were willing for a season to rejoice in his light.
			2. The works of the Father that He did witnessed of Him
			36 "But I have greater witness than *that* of John: for the works which the Father hath given me to finish, the same works that I do, bear witness of me, that the Father hath sent me.
			3. The Father whom the Jews did not know gave witness of Him
			37 "And the Father himself, which hath sent me, hath borne witness of me. Ye have neither heard his voice at any time, nor seen his shape.
			38 "And ye have not his word abiding in you: for whom he hath sent, him ye believe not.
			4. The Hebrew Old Testament Scriptures testified of Him
			39 "Search the Scriptures; for in them ye think ye have eternal life: and they are they which testify of me.
			40 "And ye will not come to me, that ye might have life.
			41 "I receive not honour from men.
			42 "But I know you, that ye have not the love of God in you.
			43 "I am come in my Father's name, and ye receive me not: if another(x) shall come in his own name, him ye will receive.
			5. Moses accuses the Jews to the Father for rejecting the Son
			44 "How can you believe, which receive honor one of another, and seek not the honour that *cometh* from God only?
			45 "Do not think that I will accuse you to the Father: there is *one* that accuseth you, *even* Moses, in whom ye trust.(y)
			6. Moses' wrote of Christ but the Jews refused to believe his record
			46 "For had ye believed Moses, ye would have believed me: for he wrote of me.
			47 "But if ye believe not his writings,(z) how shall ye believe my Words?" (Next chap. John 6:1 cont. in Section 93 .)

Footnotes-Commentary

(a) **"After this,"** speaks of His northward trip through Samaria, recorded in Sections 34 and 35. Refer to Section 37, footnote i for an explanation of the one-year silent period between the end of John 4 and the beginning of John 5:1. John rarely mentioned our Lord's ministry at Capernaum, in its synagogues, by the seaside, and numerous places across the land of Galilee. Nevertheless, Matthew, Mark, and Luke recorded most of His Galilean ministry as the Holy Spirit directed them to write.

(b) **"There was a feast."** Highlighted in gray for it is strategic in determining the length of Jesus' public ministry. The natural reading of John's book compels one to believe that this "feast of the Jews" was a Passover. This harmony commentary follows that line. For our reasoning in holding that verse 1 above speaks of a Passover, see all by the asterisk under main heading in Section 35. The *Harmony of the Four Gospels*, by Benjamin Davies, Appendix 36, contains a helpful discussion of this subject. This would be the second Passover attended by Jesus after His baptism. John alone recorded the accounts of Christ attending several Passovers during his public ministry as well as other annual celebrations of Israel at the temple. Alfred Edersheim does not hold that this was a Passover. See his reasons in, *Life and Times of Jesus the Messiah*, Appendix 15, part 3. Jesus attended the following celebrations:

1. His first Passover following baptism, see Section 29, John 2:13 and 23.
2. The second feast (assumed to be a Passover) attended during His ministry (John 5:1).
3. A third Passover, which apparently He did not attend, is mentioned in John 6:4.
4. A Feast of Tabernacles about six months before the cross mentioned in John 7. It is also called "feast" in John 7:2, 8, 10, 11, 14, and 37.
5. Feast of Dedication about four months before His death. See Section 123, John 10:22. This celebration is also called Hanukkah, Chanukak, and the Feast of Lights.
6. His fourth and final Passover mentioned numerous times in the gospel of John. Note, John 11:55; 12:1; 12, 20; and John 13:1, 29.

(c) For a colorful picture of this happy celebration at Jerusalem and among the Jewish people, see Section 29, John 2:13, second paragraph of footnote a. At this *second Passover* in His ministry, the Holy Spirit has given us only one miracle performed by our Lord. Next, we have His clash with the scribes, Pharisees, and leaders of the Jews. Not a single formality of the Passover supper is mentioned. However, Christ defends Himself before the Jews. He gives unique insight to His relationship and equality with God the Father, as in no other place of Scripture. Jesus continually asserted Himself to be the Messiah.

2p-"There is at Jerusalem." The gospel of John could not have been written *after* the destruction of Jerusalem and the temple in A.D. 70. The wording of John 5:2, "there is at Jerusalem," reveals that the city *was* standing when John wrote his book. (See *Appendix Seven* for more on this thought.) The very meaning of Bethesda (see footnote d below) is senseless if the angel did not appear and perform great wonders. It could not have been a "house of mercy."

(d) **"Five porches."** Located on the northern side of Jerusalem, this pool was near the entrance used for taking animals into the temple for sacrifice. Nehemiah also mentioned the sheep gate in Neh. 3:1, 32. The Pool of Bethesda ("house of mercy") was given this name because of the mighty acts of God's mercy, which miraculously took place there. The five porches were covered. To these shelters resorted the sick and suffering for protection from the sun's searing heat and the various elements of nature. These porches covered a vast area about 360 feet long and 130 feet wide into which thousands flocked for healing. No wonder John describes these porches by writing, "In these lay a great multitude . . ." (John 5:3). Sprawled over this vast area was a sea of hurting, suffering, humanity, all wanting to be healed; yet our Lord only healed one out of the multitude. This fact hits hard at the "God wills to heal everybody" teaching so popular today. Skeptics write on their websites that the location of this pool was originally a pagan temple to the god Asclepius; that Jesus used the magic of this (demonic) entity to perform His miracle! (No one knows what originally stood on any piece of earth anywhere!) According to these people, everyone who believes the Bible is sick except them! Their ridicule of Jesus, God, and the Scriptures will condemn them. Other pools in Jerusalem at this time were the Sparrow Pool, the Almond Pool, and the Pool of Siloam.

(e) It is futile to try to explain this clear statement away through the medium of "scholarly textual criticism." See asterisk under main heading, Section 120, for comments on the verses dropped out of the "better versions" of the *Bible*. It means what it says and is in accord with the belief that the ancient Jews attributed all favors from God to the ministry and work of angels. Which "season" it was when God's angel troubled the waters is not disclosed. John, in writing this place, "For an angel went down," may imply that at the time of his writing this miracle had ceased. Those who deny this miracle take a miserable step into the wretchedness of calling Holy Scripture into question. The late Dr. A. T. Robertson wrote in *Word Pictures in the New Testament*, vol. v, page 79, this shocker: "It is a relief to many to know that [this] verse is spurious." What kind of relief does Robertson mean? As helpful as some of Robertson's works are, it is a shame that he would pen such irresponsible statements as the above. His words only gender unbelief in Holy Scripture and assist the cause of Satan and his people. Thousands of sermons have been preached from this passage, resulting in the salvation of lost souls. God saving sinners through the preaching of a "spurious text" is ludicrous. He uses His Word blended with the work of the Holy Spirit in bringing men to eternal life. This is laid out in 1 Cor. 4:15; Eph. 6:17; Heb. 4:12; James 1:18; and 1 Peter 1:23. When men feel themselves qualified to remove from the *Bible* what they think is "spurious," then they are out of touch with Divine reality.

2p-Verse 5. This fellow had been infirmed for thirty-eight years. He was suffering from his terrible malady even before our Lord was born.

[(f)] In putting this strange question to the impotent man, Christ sought to arouse in his heart an expectation to receive something greater than the healing waters could give. In a curious sense, each time the saving gospel is preached Christ asks the same question to the unsaved. This man received a miracle of instant healing without having faith in Christ or even knowing who He was at that time. See footnote i below.

[(g)] **"Take up thy bed, and walk."** It was believed among the Jews that since Messiah would restore the nation of Israel, He *alone* had the right to heal on the Jewish Sabbath day. At Christ's pungent command, the crippled man was instantly healed, raised from the floor by the power of God, and walked and danced about with his pallet (bed) under his arm! Therefore, Christ must be Messiah. Some months prior at the house of Peter, in Galilee, the man let through the roof was given a similar command and responded in like fashion.

[(h)] **Fences about the law.** Immediately, some of the hypocritical religious leaders spotted the man walking past with his bedroll (pallet) under his arm or over his shoulder. As this miracle occurred on the Sabbath day, he was committing a horrendous sin according to the laws of the Mishna or tradition of the elders. The Jewish Talmud or Mishna consists of countless thousands of verbal commands and rules, put to memory by the Jews, which were *not* a part of the 613 written precepts of the Torah Law of Moses given at Sinai. The scribes called these endless commands "fences." They had been constructed in the dark hallways of rabbinical imagination and placed around the written Law of Moses with the belief that they would protect Israel from ever again breaking the original Torah Law. For example, there were some 2,000 of these fences built around the Sabbath day command alone! One of them was that no person could carry objects of any sort on this day: hence, the Jews' anger at the man carrying his bed. Christ sharply *condemned* these fabricated rules. The historian Josephus, wrote of the oral laws, "The Pharisees have delivered to the [Jewish] people many observances by succession from their forefathers, which are not written in the Law of Moses" See *Antiquities,* Book 13:10. 6, line 297. F. W. Farrar gives a brief but clear explanation of the Talmud in *Life of Christ,* pages 742-743.

[(i)] It is amazing to discover this man did *not* know that it was Jesus of Nazareth, the Messiah of Israel, who had healed him! Here is clear evidence of one healed by a miracle of God, who did *not* have faith or believe! See footnote f above. *He did not even know who Jesus was!* This miracle was a demonstration of the sovereignty of God in action, beyond the understanding of men. See a similar case in Section 121, footnote r, of the blind man healed at the temple gate. Though this is all true, God's rule today is that we have faith in and trust Him (Heb. 11:6). He may make exceptions as His infinite wisdom sees best.

[(j)] Later, Jesus found him in the temple. There is nothing more proper than, when men have been blessed and delivered from sickness and pain, that they should have recourse to the house of God to thank and praise Him for His sure mercies. In our Lord's words, "sin no more, lest a worst thing come upon thee," Christ was attempting to reveal to this happy man who He was! Surely, he was startled that the One before him knew of his secret past, revealed in His instructions "sin no more." The intimation is clear: his former sins had produced his miserable state. Messiah's stern warning must have shaken his soul when he heard, "lest a worse thing come upon thee." This pronouncement clearly reveals Christ's knowledge of the past and future. Those who have been saved and restored from the ravages of sin should with all diligence flee from every alluring evil. Men who profess salvation and later *permanently resume* their former sins are described as "dogs returning to their vomit" (Prov. 26:11 with 2 Peter 2:22).

[(k)] Men know when God has touched them. Totally unaware of the fierce war between Messiah and the religious leaders, this unnamed person reports to them in joyful innocence that it was Jesus, who cured him. Upon hearing this, they exploded with hostility. What did the healed man think of their reactions?

[(l)] **Sabbath fanaticism.** Raging with fury, the Jews determine to kill the Man, who had healed a helpless cripple on their beloved Passover Sabbath day. Worse, He had instructed him to carry his bed. Alas! How awful are the criminal aspirations of religious men who do not know the saving grace of God. They are the dearest friends the Devil ever had. The oral law or tradition of the elders was filled with thousands of infinitesimal rules regulating the most absurd things for the people of Israel. Such ridiculous rules forbid carrying a pen in clothing, putting out a lamp, and thousands of other absurdities. They had ruled in their religious fanaticism that nothing was to be carried on the Sabbath, and here comes this man carrying his bed! Note Section 38, Lk. 4:29-30, footnote l and m, for other occasions when they tried to kill the Lord Jesus for Sabbath violations. God finally *hated the Sabbaths* and predicted that He would abolish them (Isa. 1:13-17; Hosea 2:11; and Col. 2:14-17). The Lord of heaven hates any church, religion, creed, code, custom, ritual, day, or practice that is exalted above the Lord Jesus and draws attention from Him. Beware of those who talk much about "Sabbath keeping" and little about the blessed Savior! They think they are saved by grace but kept by keeping the Sabbath and selected portions of the Torah Law. It is written, "God is angry *with the wicked* every day" (Ps. 7:11).

(m) **"Them,"** meaning that Messiah was arraigned before the Jewish Sanhedrin for working on the Sabbath day. *Only they had authority to deal with such supposed offenders.* This verse reveals they "sought the more" to kill Him. Other attempts to destroy the Savior as recorded by John are found in John 7:1; 8:37, 40, 59; 10:39; and 11:53-54. The Sanhedrin alone could issue the death sentence; and at times, this was only by consent of the incumbent Roman governor. In this Section, we see Christ giving His defense against their false charges.

2p-My Father worketh hitherto, and I work." What a profound declaration. Jesus informed the angry rulers that as God His Father had worked on the Sabbath, doing His wonders across the whole of creation, so He also works on the Sabbath, doing His wonders: one of which was the healing of the impotent man at the pool.

3p-Verse 18. "Sought to kill him." Their basis of condemnation was that He had healed a crippled man on the Sabbath. See footnote g above. This was "work;" however, no sort of "work" would be tolerated during the length of their "Queen Sabbath" from sunset to sunrise. Had not Jehovah God clearly laid this down in the fourth commandment of Ex. 20:8-11? To their shock, Christ answered by calling God His Father! This was tantamount to blasphemy. Jesus informed them that since God had worked on the thousands of Sabbath days of the past, so He, as God's Son, could work, likewise. The idea here is clear: God rested (ceased) from all works of *creating* on that original Sabbath. However, He has never ceased to work (seven days a week) in sustaining, securing, governing, and keeping creation in orderly operation, and blessing mankind every second of life with His manifold goodness. Jesus informs the Sanhedrin that both, He and His Father work continually, every day, and this included their Passover Sabbath. He declared that the Father's work was the *same* as His, because He and His Father were One. The members of the court were utterly confounded at such astounding Words from Jesus. However, this was not their first clash with Him on a sacred Passover Sabbath. It all started a year earlier when He had purged the temple, demonstrating to be the Messiah, and had clashed with these men. For this, see Section 29, John 2:18. Their spies had dogged His footsteps every day since. See His works performed on the Sabbath listed in Section 54, footnote a.

(n) **Christ laid aside none of His equality with God.** No man can discover (or understand) the whole being and work of God except His Son. For it was the Son, who lay in the bosom of the Father in eternity past. Here, Christ states that He observed what God did and was both intimately and thoroughly acquainted with all of His purposes. All the Father's plans and counsels were ever before the Son. The Father had shown the Son *all things.* However, on earth in a body of flesh, He was still One with the Father in Heaven. It is seriously incorrect theology to teach that Christ laid aside certain levels of His equality with God. At no time did the Master do this, for if so, at this point, He would have ceased to be equal with the Father. Rather, He chose not to use some of His God attributes while still possessing every one of them. See more on this in footnote t below.

(o) To the amazement of the Sanhedrin, the carpenter from Nazareth *again* claims equality with God, in giving back life once it had been extinguished. Now, the "son of Joseph" standing before them declares that He has the exact power and authority of Jehovah Elohim, the true and living God. Again, in their hearing, He declared Himself the promised Messiah of their nation. Over the coming months, He raised many from the dead and restored them to new physical life. Every miracle of this nature must have greatly stirred the Sanhedrin. They saw that this man, who purported to be the Messiah, was actually doing the works that only God could do. At least, two members of this august court were in sympathy with Jesus, they were Nicodemus and Joseph, the rich man from Arimathaea.

(p) This confirmed what Christ had just said in verses 17 and 19 that the Father does not act independently of the Son or the Son of the Father. All their acts are shared and equal. Only they can judge the world, thus, these Words again show that Christ is divine and very God. He is the God-appointed Judge, and God the Judge.

(q) Equally, men must honor both God and Christ. To the utter consternation of the Sanhedrin, the Man standing before them claimed the right to be honored as God Himself was honored! Men today speak long and loud about God. Politicians clamoring for office are frequently heard talking to their constituents about God. Oddly enough, the Name of God's blessed Son, the Lord Jesus Christ, rarely, if ever, falls from their lips. Where is the political leader that will dare to mention the Name of the only begotten Son of the Living God? The President of the United States says many touching things about God, but he never mentions the precious Name of the Lord Jesus Christ. He shuns the National Day of Prayer but goes to a Mosque and bows before Allah. Those who refuse to honor Christ do *not* and can *never* honor God. The Savior said in John 5:23, "He that honoureth not the Son honoureth not the Father which hath sent him." The Almighty will not accept the adoration of any mortal, regardless of how sincere he is, who does not honor His beloved Son. Religion without Christ is a curse from Satan that millions have believed. The Jews of this time expected their Messiah to be a powerful human Prince, but they never thought of Him coming as a Man enrobed with *all the deity and attributes* of Jehovah God. Holy Scripture is explicit that "Whosoever denieth the Son, the same hath not the Father" (l John 2:23). The sincerity of the followers of the world's religions will not save them if they deny that Jesus Christ is the Son of God and the only Savior of mankind.

(r) Jesus Christ makes the absolute claim to be the *sole* Savior of men. In Him, all born again believers *have already* passed from death into His eternal life. From the consideration of God, it is a "done thing." John the Baptist had earlier spoken similar words in John 3:36. Note the exclusiveness of Jesus the Messiah in 1 John 5:12, and

Peter's words also spoken before the Sanhedrin a few years later (Acts 4:12). Christ, in His death for our sins bore the full condemnation of God's judgment on our sins. He literally took our place. In His resurrection, He was proclaimed Lord of all. *There is therefore, no sin for which the saved believer can be condemned.* Christ bore our full condemnation for us on the cross in His atonement. Our Savior's promise that those who believe "shall not come into condemnation," stands as sure and eternal as the throne of God in heaven (John 5:23-24).

2p-Deficit religions of the world! Every religion that has ever been or will be is in debt to their god or gods. The adherents must work their way into some kind of forgiveness, good favor, merit, or blessing. By their deeds and sacrifices of whatever sort, they hope to procure eternal life at the end. From the beginning, this has been the hallmark of spiritual darkness as seen in the offerings of Cain versus Able in Gen. 4:1-6. The true and living God offers eternal life and the forgiveness of all sins freely to all. These gifts cannot be obtained by works, rituals, or any pious actions. They are received by faith in the finished work of Christ in His death, burial, and resurrection.

(s) This is a general repetition of Christ's Words uttered in verse 21. Nevertheless, in this He adds that "the hour" *had* arrived and was taking place. The meaning is that sinners held in the death-grip of sin were now being saved through faith in the Words (or voice) of the Lord Jesus. Later, in His public ministry, many of those who were physically dead would hear His voice and resurrect to new life. There are only three examples with details of Jesus raising the dead. They are Lk. 7:14-15; Mk. 5:41-42; and John 11:43-44.

(t) Phil. 2:8. The Kenotic or kenosis emptying myth. The Son had *always* shared (or had) equal "life" and "authority to execute judgment" with the Father. However, He was *now* on earth, clothed in the natural limitations of human flesh, something different from the everlasting consistence He shared with God in a timeless eternity past. In verse 26 above, the Lord Jesus refers to the physical life the Father had placed in His frame at conception. Yet, in the eternal plan of the Trinity for the redemption of mankind, the Son, while on earth, still maintained the same powers as He possessed in Heaven. The theological wrangling about Jesus emptying Himself of His God attributes is more academic verbiage. It is another example of men prying into the mysteries of the Holy Trinity; something forbidden by the Almighty. The eternal God dwelling outside earth's time and space now entered human time and space by becoming incarnate in the Person of the Son. As explained above in footnote n, there was never a *time in the earthly life of Jesus the Messiah when He laid aside any of His God-attributes, of which He possessed all. However, at certain times during His ministry, He chose not to use some of them.* This is vastly different from emptying Himself of them. See again footnote n above, and then compare Mk. 13:32 where *He temporarily chose not to know the time of His return,* with John 2:24 where *He chose to know all men.* Note Peter's words *after* His resurrection in John 21:17: "Lord, thou knowest all things," meaning that His earthly work was finished, and that He had reverted to His omniscience. *After* our Lord's resurrection and glorification, there was no longer any need for him to *choose* not to use certain of His God equal attributes as He had during His earthly ministry. His work was completed (John 17:1). It is a serious theological error to teach that Christ "laid aside" particular attributes during His work on earth. If He did so, He ceased at that point to be equal with God. Such a scenario is impossible.

2p-The great Baptist educator, Augustus H. Strong (died 1921), in his work, *Systematic Theology,* pages 710-719, gives some nine pages in which he hopelessly struggles to explain how Christ could lay aside (empty) His divine attributes and still be perfectly equal with God. (Dr. Strong's thesis on this subject is like the fish who tried to prove water was wet.) Christ is God and God is Christ. This indissoluble union will never cease. Only meddling, immature minds will attempt to explain this glorious mystery. "Canst thou by searching find out God?" (Job 11:7).

(u) "Resurrection of damnation." An interpretive quotation based in part on Dan. 12:2, thus highlighted in gray. It is not a resurrection to annihilation or soul sleep. The Jews believed that only God and Messiah would raise all the dead and judge mankind. Hence, in this Jesus claims *again* to be Israel's promised Messiah. See footnote o.

(v) See footnote t above for comments and an explanation of this statement.

(w) His witnesses. In verses 31 through 47, the Lord Jesus lays before the Sanhedrin six infallible witnesses demonstrating that He was the Messiah. The Torah Law called for "two or three witnesses" to establish facts before a court (Deut. 19:15). Christ did better: He presented six witnesses before the Supreme Court of Israel.

1. John the Baptist bore witness that He was Israel's Messiah, in verses 31-35. The Baptist had been imprisoned some four months *prior* to the time Jesus said this.

2. His works demonstrated He was Israel's Messiah sent from God, in verse 36. See asterisk under main heading, Section 48, for an explanation of His exclusive Messianic miracles.

3. God's witness. However reputable the judgments of John the Baptist, nevertheless, Christ did not depend on his testimony *alone* to confirm His Messiahship. He had a greater witness than John, even the One whom the Jews acknowledged to be their God. Starting at His baptism, the Father had borne continual witness of Christ's works, in verses 37-38. He had just approved the command spoken by Jesus, which healed the man infirmed for thirty-eight years. Reports of His astounding miracles across Galilee had also reached the ears of these men of Israel's great court. In summary, our Lord told the Sanhedrin these Words, "Can't you see that God has attested Me as your Messiah?" (Acts 2:22). Truthful willingness was not in their hearts. If it had been, they would have recognized Him as

Messiah, Prince, and Savior. For a review of how long men remembered John the Baptist after his death, see Section 32, fourth paragraph of footnote b.

4. Next, the Lord Jesus told the Sanhedrin, "The Scriptures you purport to love, memorize and live by have never taken root in your souls. You have not entered into their sacred meaning." At this time, the rabbis taught that a man could help himself to obtain eternal life by diligently searching the Scriptures and thus be ready for the coming Messiah (verse 39-40). However, the very Scriptures they read so fervently pointed to Jesus of Nazareth, their Messiah, and they had rejected Him.

5. Lastly, the Jews taught that Moses wrote of the coming Messiah in the Torah Law. Hence, the Lord Jesus reminds them of their theological teaching. To the horror of the Sanhedrin, Moses, their great lawgiver was now His defender (45-47). Alas! There He stood before the Supreme Court of the nation, and they did not know Him! See footnote o above and y below. They purposely refused to "come to Him" and receive Him as their Messiah and Lord (verse 40). Those wretched Hebrews, void of the love of God, hated and sought to kill Him whom God had sent, while competing for human honor among themselves rather than seeking for honor, which comes from above (verse 44).

6. Moses wrote of Messiah. Refer to footnote z for explanation of this sixth witness of Christ.

2p-Verse 34. "That ye might be saved." Surely, the Lord from heaven knew if these men were numbered among the elect supposedly chosen before the foundation of the world, while all others were sentenced to hell. The reason for their doom is in verse 40. The Savior states that they "would not come to Him" for eternal life.

(x) Israel had a notorious history for being led away by claimants pretending gifts and great powers, many of whom announced themselves as "the Messiah." At the time Christ charged them with this sin, their nation was divided between two famed theological teachers who had separate schools: Hillel and Shammah. The Pharisees and Sadducees hated each other. They were famed for their fierce theological battles and physical fights (see Acts 23:1-10). The everyday people of Israel were fed up with strife, divisions, and corruption prevalent among their religious leaders. Dr. David Stern in his *Jewish New Testament Commentary*, writes on page xvii, "Of some 50 false Messiahs known to Jewish history, none of them has fulfilled more than a few" (of the Old Testament prophecies relating to the Messiah). For a look into the subject of Israel's false Messiahs, see *Bandits, Prophets, and Messiahs: Popular Movements at the Time of Jesus*, 1985 edition, by R. A. Horsley and J. S. Hanson.

2p-Verse 43. "Him ye will receive." Some see in this a prediction of the future Antichrist that would come over two thousand years later and the nation of Israel would "receive." It takes an unordinary imagination to read this extremism into the historical and theological context of this passage. Such bizarre interpretations hurt the *true doctrine* of premillennialism. They give our opponents occasion to ridicule our belief in this system of eschatology.

(y) "Moses in whom ye trust." It was a common saying among the Jews of this time that "none could accuse them but Moses," their revered lawgiver. See this in *Adam Clarke's Commentary,* vol. 5, page 555. Christ had just laid serious charges against them in His defense. He suddenly changed His approach by declaring that Moses himself was also accusing them before Jehovah in the Scripture that he had written. The Sanhedrin attempted to make Moses a prime witness against Christ in their attack. Our Lord reversed their argument and informed them that the great lawgiver of Israel had written of Him in their Torah and was thus defending Him before God (verse 45). The Torah was the *primary* portion of the Old Testament, which they habitually searched day and night, hoping to receive eternal life for their labors (verse 39). Yet, they were blind concerning the Person to whom it pointed.

2p-Verse 46. Moses wrote of Christ. This is in every sacrifice, offering, the priestly garments, the tabernacle with its beautiful ornate furniture, all rituals and scores of other ways. *Appendix Three* contains forty-two Old Testament predictions that pointed to the coming Messiah. For more on this, see Lk. 24:25-27, and 44-46 with Acts 10:43. Peter interpreted Moses' words in Deut. 18:15, 18-19, regarding a future Person "like" Moses as strictly applying to the Lord Jesus (Acts 3:22-26). Did not Moses discuss with Jesus His upcoming death when they met on the Mount of Transfiguration in Section 105? No writer across the Old Testament gave such an enormous witness to the coming Messiah, as did Moses in his voluminous books. The benighted Jews totally trusted his writings. Ironically, they shouted from every page, "Look! See here, there, and everywhere is your Messiah. He is our great theme." Thus, it is today. Many profess to believe the Bible but oddly lose this firm resolve when it exposes their sins. Then, like the Jewish religious leaders of old, their "precious Scriptures" suddenly become their enemy. An old work, *The Gospel in the Law*, by C. M. Taylor, 1869 edition, beautifully pictures Christ in the Law of Moses.

(z) His writings. Moses wrote the Pentateuch, Psalm 90, and perhaps the book of Job. This statement by Jesus was not a specific prophecy, yet highlighted in gray because Moses' writings spoke of the coming Messiah and Savior in many different ways. See second paragraph of footnote y above, for details on this. In essence, Christ concluded His defense before the Sanhedrin and responded to the charges against Him with something like this: "Since you refuse to believe what your hero Moses wrote, you therefore, cannot believe Me, for his chief message was about Me, your Messiah. Hence, you have rejected both Moses and Messiah." *Our Lord is saying that the key to believing Him is to believe first the inspired Scriptures that point to Him!* Again, He had silenced the religious leaders. One wonders if Nicodemus and Joseph of Arimathaea were present at this setting of the Sanhedrin?

The disciples pick and eat grain on the Sabbath day.* The Pharisees object.

After completing the Passover observance, with none of the formalities mentioned, He heals a crippled man, wages a verbal war with the Sanhedrin in Section 52, and returns north with His disciples to Galilee. The enraged Jews were seeking to kill Him, hence His urgent exodus from Jerusalem and Judaea. Along the way, the disciples became hungry and plucked heads of wheat or barley from the fields of grain Jesus led them through. The omnipresent Pharisees following Jesus back to Galilee, instantly attack the disciples for breaking one of their fabricated Mishna Sabbath rules.

Returning to Galilee from the Passover

Matt. 12:1-4	Mk. 2:23-26	Lk. 6:1-4	John
His disciples rebuked[a]	***His disciples rebuked***[a]	***His disciples rebuked***[a]	
1 At that time	**23** And it came to pass,	**1** And it came to pass on the second sabbath[b] after the first, that he went	
Jesus went on the sabbath day through the corn; and	that he went through the corn fields on the sabbath day; and	through the corn fields; and his disciples	
his disciples were an hungred, and began to pluck the ears of corn,[c] and to eat.	his disciples began, as they went, to pluck the ears of corn.[c]	plucked the ears of corn,[c] and did eat, rubbing *them* in *their* hands.	
2 But when the Pharisees saw *it*, they said unto him, "Behold, thy disciples do that which is not lawful[d] to do upon the sabbath day."	**24** And the Pharisees said unto him, "Behold, why do they on the sabbath day that which is not lawful?"[d]	**2** And certain of the Pharisees said unto them, "Why do ye that which is not lawful[d] to do on the sabbath days?"	
Jesus' response: they did not know their Scripture	***Jesus' response: they did not know their Scripture***	***Jesus' response: they did not know their Scripture***	
3 But he said unto them, "Have ye not read[e] what David did, when he was an hungred, and they that were with him;	**25** And he said unto them, "Have ye never read[e] what David did, when he had need, and was an hungred, he, and they that were with him?	**3** And Jesus answering them said, "Have ye not read[e] so much as this, what David did, when himself was an hungred, and they which were with him;	
4 "How he entered into the house of God, and did eat the shewbread,	**26** "How he went into the house of God in the days of Abiathar[f] the high priest, and did eat the shewbread,	**4** "How he went into the house of God, and did take and eat the shewbread, and gave also to them that were with him;	
which was not lawful for him to eat, neither for them which were with him, but only for the priests?"	which is not lawful to eat but for the priests, and gave also to them which were with him?"	which it is not lawful to eat but for the priests alone?"	

Matt. 12:5–8	Mk. 2:27–28	Lk. 6:5	John
5 "Or have ye not read in the law, how that[g] 'on the sabbath days the priests in the temple profane [or work on] the sabbath,' and are blameless? **6** "But I say unto you, That in this place is *one* greater than the temple.[h] **7** "But if ye had known what *this* meaneth,[i] 'I will have mercy, and not sacrifice,' ye would not have condemned the guiltless."			
	27 And he said unto them, "The sabbath was made for man, and not man for the sabbath:[j]	**5** And he said unto them,	
He is Lord of all	*He is Lord of all*	*He is Lord of all*	
8 "For the Son of man is Lord even of the sabbath day."[k] (Verse 9 cont. in Section 54.)	**28** "Therefore the Son of man is Lord also of the sabbath."[k] (Next chapter Mk. 3:1 cont. in Section 54.)	"That the Son of man is Lord also of the sabbath."[k] (Verse 6 cont. in Section 54.)	

Footnotes-Commentary

(a) **Attacked for breaking their traditions.** Refer to Section 52, John 5:10, footnote h; Section 89, footnote c; and Section 96, footnote d, for an explanation of these oral or Mishna Sabbath rules. Our Lord was accused of breaking these by the religious leaders of Israel. See footnote d below. Note Section 157, footnote a, for information about an odd sectarian group within the Pharisees that did not hold to these man made rules, called the tradition of the elders. They were known as the Karaite Jews.

(b) **"The second sabbath after the first."** With these words, Luke designates precisely which Sabbath this was. The expression "first" Sabbath had reference to the Passover Sabbath day that had just recently been celebrated by our Lord. This "second" Sabbath had to be *after* the actual "first" Passover Sabbath, for the law clearly forbade any Jew to eat "green ears" (or heads of grain) until *after* the great Passover was over (Lev. 23:14). The Messiah and His disciples had probably already reached Galilee when this Sabbath day "corn field clash" with the Pharisees occurred. Some think that since it was a Sabbath, the Lord Jesus was going with His disciples to a synagogue service. The rabbis ruled in their oral law that no person could eat until *after* the Sabbath morning synagogue meeting was over. Then they would gorge themselves! Clearly, we have here the legitimate hunger of the disciples' versus the anger of the self-righteous, hypocritical Pharisees.

2p-**"Went through the corn [grain] fields."** Across the areas of grain near public concourses were "field paths" purposely left for the convenience of travelers to pass over without treading down the stalks. Note Section 47, Matt. 7:13, footnote f, for more on Jewish roads and travel ways.

(c) **"Corn"** here does not have reference to American corn or maize, as it is called. This word in the New Testament is a generic term referring to wheat, barley, rye and other grains. Corn, as used by the aboriginal American Indians, was mostly unknown until the discovery of America. As the Passover was usually in April, and barley was in full ear during this month, this was probably the grain eaten by the disciples of Jesus. Nowhere does it say that Jesus Himself ate of the heads of grain. In their oral law, the Pharisees counted "rubbing" (the husks off) to be the same as threshing the grain. They considered it a heinous sin! See number 2 under footnote d below.

(d) On any ordinary day, this act of plucking and eating would have been lawful (Deut. 23:25). According to the oral law, called tradition of the elders, Talmud or Mishna, the disciples committed the three following horrific sins:

1. **Plucking of grain.** They had decreed this amounted to reaping and carrying on the Sabbath.
2. **Rubbing grains.** This removed the husks. This was counted as threshing on the Sabbath. Luke specifically mentioned the rubbing of the grain. Thus he was familiar with the particular Mishna regulation (Lk. 6:1).
3. **Eating grain.** This was compared to storing on the Sabbath. See Talmud tractate, Shabbath 70a and 142b for examples. The entire Shabbath tractate deals with numerous oral restrictions of the Sabbath day. See footnote a above for references regarding these oral commands over which the Jews were incensed at Christ's disciples. Jesus the Messiah kept all 613 precepts of the written Law of Moses but strongly condemned the countless oral traditions of the scribes, which had *replaced* the Word of God. See Mk. 7:5-13, where Christ justly condemned the Pharisees over their Mishna or (as they were later called) Talmudic traditions. See footnote g below for more on this problem.

(e) **"Have ye not read?"** *What a question!* Verses 4, 26 and 4 are highlighted in gray because of their origin in the Old Testament. Messiah aims this at the Pharisees, who prided themselves in knowing Scripture better than anyone in Israel. He makes a general reference to the events recorded in 1 Sam. 21:1-6. The Pharisees charged that the Master and His disciples had broken the law. He responds by asking them if they had never read what David did when he was hungry. Note the text states that our Lord's "disciples were an hungered" (Matt. 12:1). Christ points them to the Old Testament, with which they should have instantly been familiar. He cites the time when David and his men, fleeing from Saul, were hungry and weary. What did the illustrious person of David do with his men? All three writers affirm that they went into the house of God (in this case meaning the tabernacle, as the temple was not yet built), and the priest on duty gave them the sacred shewbread to relieve their hunger. The law commanded that twelve loaves of bread should be laid on the golden table in the holy place of the tabernacle. There they remained for a week and were eaten by the priests *only* (Lev. 24:5-9). However, David and his men ate the shewbread without infraction of Moses' code. Clearly, the need of David and his men was *superior* to the ceremonial precepts of Leviticus, and he bypassed them without incurring the wrath of God.

2p-Rabbi David Kimchi, born in France in 1160, relates in his commentary on 1 Samuel that the older *rabbis* actually justified David in eating the shewbread. The Pharisees who had attacked Christ and His disciples would surely have known this earlier rabbinical ruling mentioned by Kimchi. In drawing their attention to this fact in Hebrew history, the Lord Jesus shut their mouths. See details in *Commentary on the New Testament . . . ,* vol. 2, pages 198-199, by John Lightfoot. The ancient rabbis had decreed, "Danger to life drove the sabbath away." See also Edersheim's excellent comments in *Life and Times of Jesus the Messiah,* page 513.

(f) "House of God." This term was used of the tabernacle as well as the Temple of Solomon. At this time, the temple was not built, thus it was the tabernacle our Lord spoke of in these verses. Refer to 1 Sam. 1:3, 7 and 9.

2p-**"Abiathar."** Mark names him as the high priest. However, in 1 Sam. 21:1, we note that his father, Ahimelech was holding the office. The unbelieving critics rush about trying to understand this "discrepancy." The son of the high priest was automatically his successor and continually assisted him in his various duties of service. It was normal to designate him also as "high priest" during his father's life, since that was the title by which he would be later known. Thus, Mark called Abiathar high priest, as though he were in the office of his father Ahimelech. This was the standard priestly procedure known and understood by the people.

(g) Here, Jesus is alluding to Num. 28:9-10, where the law commanded the priest to work on the Sabbath by offering a certain gift on the altar. Our Lord attempted to point out to the Pharisees the wickedness of their oral laws, or Mishna as they were later called, and the impossibility of their rigid decree of "no work of any sort on the Sabbath." He reminded them that *every* Sabbath the priest serving in the temple at Jerusalem had to work! Hundreds of priests and Levites were continually offering up various sacrifices, flaying, cutting them into pieces, lifting the carcasses to the altar, cutting wood, kneading dough, baking bread, and dozens of other necessary services each Sabbath day. Should not they also condemn the priests for breaking the oral laws by their Sabbath labors? Yet, the priests were blameless before God. What absolved these priests of law breaking was the fact that they served in the temple. Simply, their service to the needs of men was superior to the Sabbath. The rabbis had ruled that what was forbidden on the Sabbath was allowed in the temple. The disciples served Christ, who was "greater than the temple." Therefore, they were exempt from all condemnations.

(h) "Greater than the temple." This claim must have shaken the Pharisees. The Talmud records the deep rabbinical veneration for the temple. It was purported to be "the light and eye of the world" in Baba Bathra 4a. They held that the very building of the temple "sanctified the gold plates that were attached to its stones," and that to swear by it was the greatest confirmation of an oath (Matt. 23:16-17). How dare a lowly carpenter from the ignorant state of Galilee, standing in a field, speak such blasphemous words! Our Lord's statement is simple yet profound. The priests were excused for working on the Sabbath in the temple to satisfy the needs of the people, how much more ought the disciples of One greater than the temple be excused for satisfying their hunger on a Sabbath.

2p-The Jews longed for the presence of Jehovah God to dwell in their beloved temple. They failed to see that in Christ the Messiah dwelt the very "fullness of the Godhead bodily," and that He was the "true Light" of the world (John 1:9). For earlier comments on Jesus the Light, note Section 1, Part 1, and John 1:4, footnote e. Our Lord clearly declared that works of necessity and mercy were acceptable on any Sabbath day. The prevailing hunger of the disciples was one of necessity. For a forgotten classic dealing with many aspects of the Sabbath question, see *Seventh-Day Adventism Renounced,* first published in 1899, by D. M. Canright. It may be located at a larger theological library or on an Internet site for religious book sales.

(i) A nonspecific, general quotation from 1 Sam. 15:22 blended with Hosea 6:6. Our Lord had previously quoted this passage to the religious leaders, as seen in Section 50, Matt. 9:13, footnote g. This is another example of Christ repeating Himself. See also the asterisk under main heading in Section 71. At the temple in Jerusalem, men offered sacrifices, seeking to obtain God's mercy. Jesus, the One greater than that earthly structure, offered free mercy to whosoever will. In this citation from the prophet Hosea, Messiah charges the Pharisees with ignorance of the Scripture, of which they boasted to know thoroughly. Yet with their (supposed) knowledge of God's Word, He exposed their gross inhumanity as they condemned innocent persons for plucking, rubbing, and eating ears of grain from the fields to meet honest needs. He was saying, "You quote the Scripture, but you do not know its meaning.

God, whom you pretend to worship, requires acts of love, compassion, and mercy, instead of your cold words, heartless ceremonies, and meaningless sacrifices." The Scripture-ignorant Pharisees had just condemned the guiltless disciples in this act. With this statement in mind, read the beautiful passage of Micah 6:8.

(j) Meaning, that the Jews should *correctly rule* the day and *not* the day rule the Jews. The law cults do the exact opposite. Christ had just shown His sovereignty as "Lord" of the Sabbath by allowing His disciples to eat from the grain field. In meeting their need, He showed them how to use correctly the Sabbath day.

(k) **Who is Lord of the Sabbath?** The Jews held that God, who created the Sabbath, was its "Lord" and could therefore, dispense with it at His choosing. Rabbi David Kimchi, in his ancient commentary on Joshua chapter 6 wrote the above statement over nine hundred years ago. He further stated that the fall of Jericho occurred on the Sabbath, and that God set it aside to allow for the destruction of this pagan city. This setting aside of the Sabbath for the purposes of God to be realized was well known to the Jews in Christ's day.

2p-Jesus Christ is the Lord of the Sabbath. To the utter dismay of the Pharisees, Jesus claimed to be God in stating that He was "Lord of the Sabbath." Therefore, as such, He could set its restrictions aside for His work to be done. Either their beloved Sabbath had two Lords, or God and Christ were the same. Christ not only claimed to be "Lord" of the Sabbath (because as the Creator, Eph. 3:9, He had instituted it in the beginning), but the lesson goes deeper. He was now standing in a Galilean grain field as the "Son of man" in human flesh; therefore, as such He was also one of those for whom the Sabbath was made. Since it was made for Him, He had used that Sabbath day honorably in approving the actions of His disciples who had a legitimate need because of physical hunger.

3p-Cults and Sabbath day abuse. Law cults hung up on Sabbath keeping should read and obey Paul's words in Col. 2:14-16 regarding judging others concerning this Jewish day or any other day, for that matter. It is the lie of certain Adventists, that those who worship on Sunday have or will receive the mark of the beast. One Adventist website goes so far into heresy as to write, that our salvation depends on knowing the mark of the beast. This gross untruth stands for correction. Our salvation depends on whether or not we know Jesus Christ as *personal* Lord and Savior by the miracle of the new birth. This heavenly birth is received through repentance and faith in the finished atonement of God's Son. It is not by works of any sort; not even knowing the mark of the beast! For more on the Adventist sect, see Section 45, twelfth paragraph of footnote b. Dale Ratzlaff's work, *The Cultic Doctrine of the Seventh Day Adventists . . .* , is a classic in exposing the untruths of this cult masquerading so well (like the Mormons) as a valid traditional Christen Church.

4p-Some Messianic Jews adamantly slap their sabbatical demands on all Gentile believers in Christ the Messiah. The word Sabbath is found some sixty times in the New Testament; and in *every case,* it has reference to the *weekly* Sabbath. This includes the one recorded in Col. 2:16. In Col. 2:14, Paul affirms that these ordinances, holy days, and new moons, have all been "blotted out" and "taken out of the way" by Jesus' death on the cross. It is amazing how groups possessed with cultic propensities seek to "un-blot" and "bring back" what God has swept away. Often, they demand that this is necessary for acceptable Christian living and in some cases for salvation. Refer to the next Section, Matt. 12:10, footnote d, for further details regarding the Jewish usage of the Sabbath day.

5p-Cults seek acceptance. The author counts the Seventh Day Adventist Church a false cult. While holding some major tenants of the Christian faith, they strongly deny and oppose others. Adventists are prisoners of the Jewish Sabbath, due to the earlier heresies of their founders, William Miller and Ellen G. White. Other comments on the successors of White are in Section 45, twelfth paragraph of footnote b, and Section 110, fifth and sixth paragraphs of footnote k. The theological poison of Ellen G. White (died 1915), Herbert W. Armstrong (died 1986), and their hundreds of law cult splinter groups continues to this day. The Jews in Christ's days taught that the pains of gehenna fire ceased on the holy, happy Sabbath day! All law cults are trapped in similar extremes. The originators of these groups used enough of Scripture to persuade the ignorant and uninformed that what they propose was divine truth. An example is Charles Taze Russell (died 1916), a prime founder of the Jehovah's Witnesses monstrosity. Growing up in the *early* Congregational Church and hearing about hell, he was terrified. Later, Russell established the Witness cult. Like the Adventists, both deny the eternal suffering of the damned and the reality of the human soul. The Church of Jesus Christ of Latter Day Saints (LDS) is also rotted with doctrinal heresies. They try hard to present themselves as a valid Christian church. In their TV ads and door visits, they never mention their sex insane founders and theological blasphemies, such as, that God was once a man and gradually rose to the status of a god. After "faithful Mormons" finally become gods, they go to a future sex heaven and will produce spiritual babies forever! (Shades of Islam with Muslim maniacs killing themselves and going to "heaven" to enjoy their virgins.) *The greatest blasphemy of the Mormons is their teaching that Jesus and Lucifer are spiritual brothers!* For more on this "church," see Section 27, all of footnote a. Some of these groups have extreme heresies, heterodoxies, and shocking immoral origins. Doctrinal distinctions are not wrong if based on rightly divided Scripture. The founders of all false religions originally injected various theological untruths into their belief systems, and they remain to this day. Cult representatives conceal these when trying to persuade prospective converts into their church. These poor people must be loved for they are God's creatures, lost in sin. Only in the saving gospel will they find rescue and salvation. We too were once lost without hope. *Dare we forget that someone in great love brought us to the Savior?*

Jesus works again on the Sabbath day. More trouble erupts from the ranks of the Jewish religious leaders.

The synagogue at Capernaum

Matt. 12:9-12	Mk. 3:1-4	Lk. 6:6-9	John
The Jews' trick question 9 And when he was departed thence, he went into their synagogue: 10 And, behold, there was a man which had *his* hand withered.(b) And they asked him, saying, "Is it lawful to heal on the sabbath days?"(d) that they might accuse him. *His response* 11 And he said unto them, "What man shall there be among you, that shall have one sheep, and if it fall into a pit on the sabbath day, will he not lay hold on it, and lift *it* out? 12 "How much then is a man better than a sheep? Wherefore it is lawful to do well on the sabbath days."	*The Jews' trick question* 1 And he entered again into the synagogue; and there was a man there which had a withered hand.(b) 2 And they watched(c) him, whether he would heal him on the sabbath day; that they might accuse him. *Jesus addresses the man and the Jews* 3 And he saith unto the man which had the withered hand, "Stand forth."(e) 4 And he saith unto them, "Is it lawful to do good on the sabbath days, or to do evil? To	*The Jews' trick question* 6 And it came to pass also on another sabbath,(a) that he entered into the synagogue and taught: and there was a man whose right hand was withered.(b) 7 And the scribes and Pharisees watched(c) him, whether he would heal on the sabbath day; that they might find an accusation against him. *Jesus addresses the man and the Jews* 8 But he knew their thoughts, and said to the man which had the withered hand, "Rise up, and stand forth(e) in the midst." And he arose and stood forth. 9 Then said Jesus unto them, "I will ask you one thing; Is it lawful on the sabbath days to do good, or to do evil? To	

Matt. 12:13-14	Mk. 3:4-6	Lk. 6:9-11	John
	save life, or to kill?" But they held their peace.	save life, or to destroy *it*?"	
	He is angry at sin	*He is angry at sin*	
	5 And when he had looked round about on them with anger, being grieved for the hardness of their hearts,	**10** And looking round about upon them all,	
The man is healed	*The man is healed*	*The man is healed*	
13 Then saith he to the man, "Stretch forth thine hand." And he stretched *it* forth; and it was restored whole, like as the other. [(f)]	he saith unto the man, "Stretch forth thine hand." And he stretched *it* out: and his hand was restored whole as the other. [(f)]	he said unto the man, "Stretch forth thy hand." And he did so: and his hand was restored whole as the other. [(f)]	
The religious leaders plot to kill Him	*The religious leaders plot to kill Him*	*The religious leaders plot to kill Him*	
14 Then the Pharisees went out, and held a council [(g)] against him, how they [(h)] might destroy him. (Verse 15 cont. in Section 55.)	**6** And the Pharisees went forth, and straightway took counsel [(g)] with the Herodians against him, how they [(h)] might destroy him. (Verse 7 cont. in Section 55.)	**11** And they were filled with madness; and communed [(g)] one with another what they [(h)] might do to Jesus. (Verse 12 cont. in Section 57.)	

Footnotes-Commentary

[(a)] **Jesus and the Sabbath.** Luke explained to Theophilus in verse 6, that this encounter of Christ with the religious leaders occurred on a Sabbath day in the synagogue. However, it was a different Sabbath from the one on which He had previously clashed with them. Nor was it the conflict He had with them in the fields of grain previously mentioned in Section 53. Neither Matthew nor Mark clarified this point. This shows inspiration. Below, the four gospel writers have recorded at *least* ten times when Messiah did miracles on the Sabbath day and made specific Messianic claims. On each occasion, the Jews were seriously angered. This surely happened hundreds of times, which are not recorded in Scripture. The fanatical Jews had turned the Sabbath into a day of idolatry. They worshiped it, not God. This is reflected in their calling it "Queen Sabbath," as seen in the Talmud tractate, Shabbath 119a. Below are recorded a number of places where the Lord did miracles on this day and the Jews' reaction.

1. In John 2:13 and 23 is the Passover Sabbath where Christ first presented Himself as Messiah in the temple. On this occasion, He also performed various miracles among the crowds.
2. In Mk. 1:21, 26, the healing of a demon-possessed man on the Sabbath.
3. Our Lord heals Peter's mother-in-law in her house immediately after the Sabbath synagogue service at Capernaum. See Lk. 4:38-39.
4. In Matt. 4:23-24, mention is made of many great miracles in the synagogues of Galilee. These obviously had to occur on the Sabbath, which was the main day for religious services to be conducted.
5. The healing at the Pool of Bethesda in John 5:8-9.
6. In Matt. 12:1-2, the conflict in the corn field on the Sabbath over the disciples plucking and eating grain.
7. In this Section in Matt. 12:9-10, 13, Messiah heals the man with the withered hand on the Sabbath.
8. In John 9:6, 7, 14, He heals a man born blind—a miracle that only Messiah could do. Note the heading at the beginning of Section 121 for more on this thought.
9. The story of the woman with a crooked back is recorded in Lk. 13:10-17.
10. Lastly, the man with dropsy in Lk. 14:1-6. See footnote d below, and Section 52, John 5:8-9, footnotes g and h, for more on the Jews and the Sabbath-breaking charges they lay against the Lord Jesus.

[(b)] **The withered hand.** As a trained physician, Dr. Luke informed Theophilus this fellow's "right hand" was withered or atrophied. The good doctor remembered this detail because the Holy Spirit of God brought it to his memory years later as he looked back and wrote about this miracle. With this in mind, there is an interesting story running through portions of ancient tradition/history regarding this man. It was reported that he was a plasterer and bricklayer by profession, with his *right hand* withered, he was unable to procure his daily bread. Refer to Matthew

251

Henry's *Commentary on the Whole Bible*, vol. 5, page 132, for a brief review of this ancient story.

(c) This whole scenario was a possible "setup," arranged by the rabbis seeking *again* to entrap our Lord. Refer to Section 64, Lk. 7:36, footnote a, for another possible trap at suppertime! Both Mark and Luke record the words "they watched him whether he would heal him on the Sabbath day; that they might accuse him" (Mk. 3:2 and Lk. 6:7). Surely, "*they*" cannot refer to the common people, who mostly had nothing but praise for the miracles of the Messiah. It can only direct us to the religious leaders who despised Jesus and had sought already on several occasions to kill Him. One can almost see them sitting in their prominent places of authority in the synagogue, whispering and leaning forward, so carefully watching the Lord as He taught. The fierce hatred and jealousy that filled their hearts was reflected in their dark, menacing faces as they scowled at the Prince of Life. Again, they sought for the opportunity to belittle Him before the people. It backfired in their faces! See footnote d below.

(d) **"That they might accuse him."** This proves ill intentions (Matt. 12:10). They knew that their ancient rabbis had prescribed various works that might be done on the Sabbath without incurring wrath for breaking the fourth commandment. According to both the Jerusalem and Babylonian *Talmuds*, certain "works" were allowable on the Sabbath for the humane good of Israel. However, some of the older sages and rabbis debated the validity of these permissible deeds on the Sabbath day. Such things as "swallowing oil and rubbing the teeth with spice" were allowable if it was not being used for treatment. Blood letting for infection and treating one bitten by a mad dog, of all things, was treated with a hog liver! In extreme danger of life, a fire may be kindled for heat or food preparation. In the most serious cases, "medicine might be prescribed by a physician." See examples in the Talmud tractate, Shabbath 14c and d. For more details, note *Gill's Commentary*, vol. 7, page 128. For a list of over fifty meticulous and ridiculous rules translated from the Talmud concerning Sabbath keeping, see *The Victor Bible Background Commentary*, page 54, by L. O. Richards.

(e) **"Rise up, and stand forth in the midst."** Knowing their covert purposes, Christ stopped teaching and suddenly addressed the infirmed man with this startling command. This action unduly alarmed the Pharisees and instantly threw them off guard! With the man standing amid the vast congregation of Jews, Christ had just put several questions to the congregation: "What man shall there be among you, that shall have one sheep, and if it falls into a pit on the sabbath day, will he not lay hold on it, and lift it out? How much is a man better than a sheep? Wherefore is it lawful to do good on the sabbath days?" At this point, only Mark and Luke add the remainder of Christ's Words, "To save life, or to kill?" (Mk. 3:4 and Lk. 6:9). Everyone present knew the answer to Messiah's questions. To do certain good on the Sabbath was freely admitted by all teachers of the law and the common folks as well. However, the prelates of Jewish religion fiercely resented Christ for the good He was doing on *their* Sabbaths. See footnote d above. He dared to break their revered traditions and oral law. The religious leaders who had set this trap must have felt sick at their stomachs upon hearing these questions. They also knew the answer and would not *publicly* deny its obvious truth. In great wisdom, our Lord draws His argument from their own code of oral laws and conduct. If a sheep fell into a pit upon the Sabbath day, any Jew would exercise the common office of human compassion and draw the helpless beast out.

2p-Many Hebrew men sitting in that congregation had done this very thing! In addition, among the Pharisees and religious leaders present were those who had rescued their domestic stock from the same or similar plights. The Talmud, written centuries later, contains carefully detailed instructions about what to do when a beast had fallen into a ditch or water and was helpless to extract itself. By a reference to their own laws and conduct, Jesus silenced them all. It must be noted that Mark adds these terse words: "And he looked round about on them with anger, being grieved for the hardness of their hearts" (Mk. 3:5). Their overt wickedness stirred holy indignation in His pure soul. His anger over their sin was the very anger of God (Ps. 7:11). See an earlier example of Christ's holy anger and what He did in Section 29, John 2:13-17, footnote d.

(f) A deathly awe fell over that synagogue scene as all sat dumbfounded; no one could respond to the questions of this great and fearless Man. His voice echoed like a rifle shot off the stonewalls and through the silent atmosphere as He commanded the man to stand in their midst where all could see. His directive was, "Stretch forth thine hand." How can a hand wrinkled and withered into helpless atrophy respond? It responded because God in human flesh commanded it so! He who measures the seas in the hollow of His hand now instructs a man's hand to be whole (Isa. 40:12). God will command us to duties, which we ourselves are unable to perform. They oft seem as impossible as was the command spoken to this fellow standing in the synagogue. Despite this, by the avenue of faith, contact is made with fresh physical life and divine grace. And the end of the command is realized.

2p-**"Whole as the other."** Who can imagine the profound impact this instant healing had on the hundreds sitting in the Jewish house of worship? The place was shaken! With their own eyes, they beheld a genuine Messianic miracle take place. *Both hands were now the same!* However, not all present were filled with praises to God for this marvelous wonder. Surely, the healing of this man was of higher grace than pulling a sheep from a pit. It was acceptable to God in heaven and must therefore, be accepted on their Sabbath day as well. However, the religious leaders of the place sank into resentment and revenge. This carpenter from Nazareth dared to break their rules and regulations in healing a suffering human. They went into a huddle and plotted to kill Him!

(g) Though the translators have rendered the Greek word as "council" in Matt. 12:14, and as "counsel" in Mk. 3:6, they are, nonetheless, correct. The religious leaders did *both* in their frustration to entrap the Savior. We could say, "The *council* held a *counsel* and *communed* with each other." They could take no more of this Man and His mighty works. Storming out of the synagogue, the scribes, and Pharisees again plotted His death.

2p-A thousand years before the birth of Christ, David predicted in Ps. 2:2 the time when the rulers of Israel would take "counsel against the anointed of God" or Messiah. This was fulfilled repeatedly during the ministry of Jesus, as seen in Mk. 3:6 above, with John 11:53; and 18:14. During the various trials of our Lord, both Roman and Jewish rulers played a part, as they unwittingly fulfilled the plan of God.

(h) **"Destroy him."** The self rancor of the Pharisees and their followers in false religion toward Christ was obvious. Mark 3:6 points out how they now united with their previous enemies, the Herodians, a religious–political sect. Their *common* passion was to kill the Son of God. Filled with "madness" at His unanswerable arguments against their hypocrisy, the Pharisees *again* plotted His death with the aid of this group. Some historians think the Herodians were strong adherents of Herod Antipas and opposed to the Pharisees. For a review on Antipas and the other sons of Herod the Great, see Section 21, Part 1, numbers 3 and 4, under footnote b. Whoever they were, they became friends of those who hated the Savior and sought His death as well. Normally, the two groups violently opposed each other. Soon, they would learn (in A.D. 70 at the destruction of Jerusalem and the Jewish state) that the sword of hatred hurts worse at the hilt than it does at the point. Another united effort between the Pharisees and Herodians to snare the Lord Jesus occurred two days before His death. See Section 155, footnote a.

2p-Universal hatred for Christ and the biggest lie of all. Malice for the Son of God, *true* Christianity, and the Bible, prevails worldwide. Satan and demons have worked through every channel imaginable to discredit, malign, and silence the witness of Jesus Christ. Even within the ranks of so-called Christian churches and organizations, the Devil has succeeded. This harmony commentary briefly documents the murders committed by pagan governments, the Crusaders, insane emperors, the Roman Catholic Church, and other religious tyrants killing all who disagreed with them. History reveals the barbarity of Bolshevism across Russia and parts of Europe from 1903 to 1917. Mao's communist China is the prime example of hatred for God, Jesus Christ, and Christianity. The *Guinness Book of World Records,* 1979 edition, page 397 says Mao committed "the greatest massacre [of people] in human history." Radical Islam wades through the blood of her murdered millions. In Africa, insane Muslims have killed thousand, burning churches and homes of Christians while the tax funded "International Community" sucks its thumb and looks the other way. Women have their hands hacked off, men their eyes punched out, and children chopped to death with machetes at the behest of this "peaceful religion." There are documented cases of where Muslims have killed their children, sisters, husbands, and wives for the "honor of Allah," for leaving Islam, converting to Christianity, or some other religion. Steel faced Muslims sit before millions on Fox Television and lie about their intentions. Shari'a law should be spelled "H-e-l-l." Meanwhile, American politicians let them build a "Mosque of friendship and reconciliation" near the site of the Twin Towers and 911, and Hollywood is called in to prove it is right. However, there is another hatred for the truth of God, far worse than the above. Like an unseen cancer, non-salvation liberalism, denying the Bible, slowly eats away at the souls of men. *Their educated denial of Jesus Christ is the most diabolical lie of all.* His deity, birth, ministry, miracles, and atoning death for our sins, and resurrection from the dead, are reduced to myths, word pictures, or accommodating theology. Sin is an epic Dark Age concept. In time, it will be cured by education, cooperation, sharing the wealth, dialog, and respecting what every man believes! (How would that have worked with Hitler or Joseph Stalin?) According to these Judas Iscariots, we are to believe that Jesus was a "nice guy who spoke some truth," but He is not the world's only Savior. We are now hearing that *true* Christians are religious nuts and far worse than the radical Muslims described above.

3p-Talk show garbage. It says, "Respect all political leaders, social customs, and the religions of the world." This is New Age darkness talking. Genuine Christians refuse to tickle Buddha's navel, put on their shoes according to Mohammed, burn incense to Hare Krishna, praise Harry Potter, laud adulterous presidents, lying members of Congress, and thieving politicians, kiss the Pope's hand, while priests molest thousands of children. We are not "one international family!" Their biggest lie is that if we extract Jesus Christ from the equation everyone will be happy for all religions are good except *true* Bible Christianity. Peddlers of this myth should assist the aboriginal witch doctors as they kill the weakest of twins by pouring sand down its throats. Even better, they could watch religious Africans throwing certain babies to the crocodiles. A "Sixty Minute" documentary about the tribes of New Guinea, slashing the faces of their children, and knocking the girl's front teeth out would be educational. Who can respect the hypocrites in the churches, *radical* Muslims killing themselves and thousands of others? Would our "network anchors," "talk-show hosts," "cultural anthropologists" or "liberal ecumenists" eat the flesh of a dead family member, three days rotted because in India, a religious cult requires this? For other comments on these things, see Section 95, the sixth and seventh paragraphs of footnote r. God explicitly commands believers, "To speak evil of no man" (Titus 3:2). *Sharing needed facts is not evil or judgmental; it is necessary to warn honest men.* Awareness of the truth may rescue some from the religious, political, and moral deceit being heralded over the land. Refer to Section 51, the fourth and fifth paragraphs of footnote h for more on "talk-show" ignorance and hypocrisy.

Aware of their death plot, the Savior withdraws from the synagogue and Capernaum to the shores of Galilee. Thousands, including many Gentiles, trusted in His name, fulfilling another Old Testament prophecy.

Capernaum and the Sea of Galilee

Matt. 12:15-21	Mk. 3:7-12	Lk.	John
He leaves: the crowds follow	*He leaves: the crowds follow*		
15 But when Jesus knew *it*,[a] he withdrew himself from thence: and great multitudes followed him,	**7** But Jesus withdrew himself with his disciples to the sea: and a great multitude from Galilee followed him, and from Judaea, **8** And from Jerusalem, and from Id-u-mae-a, and *from* beyond Jordan; and they about Tyre and Sidon, a great multitude,[b] when they had heard what great things he did, came unto him.		
	A boat is His pulpit		
	9 And he spake to his disciples, that a small ship[c] should wait on him because of the multitude, lest they should throng him.		
and he healed them all;	**10** For he had healed many; insomuch that they pressed upon him for to touch him, as many as had plagues.		
	Evil spirits recognized Him		
	11 And unclean spirits,[d] when they saw him, fell down before him, and cried, saying, **"Thou art the Son of God."**[e]		
His humility fulfilled prophecy			
16 And charged them that they should not make him known:[f]	**12** And He straitly charged them that they should not make him known.[f] (Verse 13 cont. in Section 57.)		

17 That it might be fulfilled which was spoken by E-sa-ias [Isaiah] the prophet, saying,[g]
18 "Behold my servant, whom I have chosen; my beloved, in whom my soul is well pleased: I will put my Spirit upon him, and he shall shew judgment to the Gentiles.
19 "He shall not strive, nor cry; neither shall any man hear his voice in the streets.[h]
20 "A bruised reed shall he not break, and smoking flax shall he not quench, till he send forth judgment unto victory.
21 "And in his name shall the Gentiles trust."[i] (Verse 22 cont. in Section 66.)

Footnotes-Commentary

(a) This text is explicit in stating that Jesus "knew it," meaning the plot of the Pharisee-Herodian murder teams as described in the previous Section 54, Matt. 12:14, footnotes g and h. However, as His hour for dying on the cross had not yet come, He thus moved into other places. By remaining near the synagogue or in the city of Capernaum, our Lord would have only further provoked these men of evil intentions. Acting under the dictates of inspired prudence, Mark informs us in verse 7 that He takes His disciples and withdraws to the shores of Galilee. Christian charity will work hard to avoid *unnecessary* conflict with friend or foe wherever possible. Great crowds of suffering humanity gathered to the Son of God as His fame again swept abroad. Reaching out in mercy, He received them.

(b) Verse 8. **"Beyond Jordan"** speaks of the near and far eastern cities of many pagan nations. The geography from which these countless thousands came is amazing. North, south, east and west, all meet here with the lowly Messiah. Several of these western places such as Tyre and Sidon were outside the boundaries of strict Jewry and Judaea. Thousands of Gentiles were among the throngs who pressed upon Christ, seeking His loving, sure mercies. They came "when they had heard the great things he did." His Name and deeds were on everyone's lips! See Section 71, Lk. 12:1, footnote a, where the pressing crowds actually trampled upon one another to reach the Savior.

2p–"Came to him." This means that among these were many who believed on Christ. Believing on the Lord Jesus does mean that a lost person must understand all theology, the doctrines of the Bible, have knowledge of history, economics, society, and so forth, then God will save him. We are not saved from sin and hell by education, reformation, confirmation, or anything else! When the Holy Spirit and God's Word convicts any person, regardless of who and where they are, that they are lost in sin, going to hell, and that Christ is the only Savior of mankind, he is close to salvation. The second he trusts, in simple faith, Jesus Christ as Lord and Savior, He is forgiven, pardoned, and saved forever! This is what it means, in a nutshell, to believe on the Lord Jesus Christ. *The greatest display of God's grace is Jesus dying on the cross for the sins of mankind.* The second greatest display is the millions saved by this grace. A religion that does not give the heart of man absolute assurance of forgiveness, peace with God, and a home in heaven is false. It should be denounced and forsaken. Loyalty and dedication to a lie is the height of deceit, and its end is eternally bitter. At the close of World War II, with the collapse of the Hitler regime, in Berlin alone, over three thousand Germans committed suicide. Too late, they saw the folly of putting their trust in a demon–possessed man who had promised them a world of white supremacy with no Jews or blacks, only blond haired and blue eyes Arians ruling in peace. Millions who embraced this lie are now in hell.

3p–Religiosu radicals. Jim Walker, in his elaborate website, presents Hitler as a Christian because he quoted Scripture. *So did the Devil Mr. Walker, (Matt. 4:5-7). Does he qualify?* Apparently, Jim does not know that insane tyrants use the Bible when it is to their advantage and curse it when it is otherwise. The mass murderer Joseph Stalin attended a seminary at Tiflis, Georgia, in Russia studying for the Orthodox Church. Only a fool would classify him as a "Christian." For more on this, see Section 194, second paragraph of footnote d.

(c) A small boat frequently became the pulpit of Christ. One can see the multitudes packing the shoreline, many sick, diseased and suffering, listening attentively to every word falling from His lips. Note Section 43, Lk. 5:3, footnote c, for an earlier sermon from a boat. We are staggered at Matthew's comment "and he healed them all" (Matt. 12:15). It is impossible to believe that *each* one of these teeming thousands *fully* understood (at that time) who Jesus was and His mission on earth. Like the man in John 5, that was healed without knowing who Christ was or believing in Him, so thousands of these received His mercy without preconditions or prior requirements. Now, God requires that men, upon hearing the gospel, in the conviction of the Holy Spirit, repent of their sins and believe on the Lord Jesus (Rom. 10:13-15; Acts 13:38-39, 16:31 with Heb. 11:6). What a glorious sight. The hated carpenter from Galilee, though despised and rejected by the custodians of Jewish religion, now embraces all of hurting humanity in love and compassion. Both Jews and Gentiles meet *in* Him. No scene could be more sublime than this.

(d) **"Unclean spirits."** Called "unclean" because of the unspeakable filth they often produce wherever they find access. Herein, we discover the answer for the shocking and outlandish deeds being committed by people across the land and around the world. Most modern medicine puts it down to different levels of insanity and various psychiatric delusions. God's Word is clear that in *some cases* these people are demon possessed! For more on this terrible thought, see Section 40, footnotes c, d and e. On the other hand, there are levels of demons that inspire uprightness and moral purity as long as this keeps them from trusting Christ as Lord and Savior. *Morality without Christ is sin looking good.* It is one of Satan's chief tactics to deceive men about preparing for eternity. God considers the "plowing of the wicked" as "sin" if they are without Christ (Prov. 21:4 with John 15:5). Satan will do what is necessary to damn the souls of men, whether by demonic possession or high moral contrivances. *This truth does not dismiss the fact of legitimate brain damage, diseases, and neurological maladies in which demons have no part. To confuse the two could be disastrous. Expert medical and theological counseling is needed.*

2p–No doctors and no medicine needed? Within the Christian community, there are radicals who put every ailment down to the work of Satan. In their distorted thinking, going to the doctor and taking medication is a sign of no faith. Such rashness has caused untold problems within society and the church. These charlatans should be warned to stop their nonsense or shown the door. The "faith healer," Peter Popoff, of Upland California is an example of this. He instructs, "Throw your medications on the stage and break free from the Devil." "Popping off Popoff," promises his listeners that their mortgages will be paid off if they support his ministry!

(e) Another ancient title for Israel's Messiah, was confessed by demons! See footnote f below. This verse proves that evil spirits may speak audibly through the mouths of their victims and be heard by others as well. This experience was repeated later on in the ministry of Christ. Refer to Section 88, Matt. 8:29, footnote c for details.

(f) **"Not make him known."** It is noted that demons knew who Jesus Christ was! See Acts 19:12-16 for a terrible confirmation of this fact! Wherever the Son of God went, they trembled and howled at His presence while bowing to His Majesty. Our Lord's charge to the wicked spirits to "not make him known," reveals that He refused even truthful recognition from Satan's kingdom. He had higher and purer witnesses than that of cringing evil spirits of darkness. See Section 52, footnote w, for His six unique witnesses. Several years later, during His last night on earth in the upper room, He declared triumphantly to His apostles "the prince of this world cometh, and hath nothing in me" in John 14:30. Note the *final* destiny of Lucifer and his demons in Section 88, Matt. 8:28-29, footnote c, with Section 166, Matt. 25:41 with Rev. 20:10.

(g) A general quotation from Isa. 42:1-4. The rabbis pointed to this prophecy as speaking of their Messiah being anointed with the Holy Spirit. Refer to Section 38, Lk. 4:17-19, footnote d, for another prophecy from Isaiah of Jesus being empowered by the Spirit. Now, Matthew presents this to his Jewish readers to show them that Jesus of Nazareth is their Messiah; and that in God's plan of the gospel, the door of salvation is open for *every* man. By the time Matthew wrote his book, some years after Christ's ascension, many Gentiles had trusted Israel's Messiah. Jews across the known world were provoked to wonder about the man Jesus of Nazareth, who received all without racial prejudice. This was different from the restricted religion of the scribes and Pharisees at Jerusalem.

2p-Verse 18. "Show judgment to the Gentiles." "Judgment" in this passage means that He made known the truth of God to the pagans. This He busily did as thousands were blessed and healed amid the crowds along the seashore. Because of this, *many* among the heathen believed in Him and carried the news of this great man back to their lands and homes. Matthew was inspired to quote these passages from Isaiah in order to convince his original Jewish readers that Jesus was Messiah, and He literally fulfilled these Old Testament verses in going to the Gentiles.

3p-Both the Jews and Christ's disciples had been taught that Messiah would appear as a mighty conqueror, shouting out His authority, and vindicate Israel in terrible wrath over all Gentile nations. When they saw Jesus, who continually claimed to be the Messiah, meek and lowly, refusing (at this point) to combat any of Israel's political enemies, especially the Romans, they were confused.

(h) Verse 19. No "Gentile-destroying Messiah" is presented here! Shouting, wailing, crying, and calling out loudly on various occasions and for different reasons were standard parts of Jewish and eastern culture. This is especially true in the streets and marketplaces where the people gather. Continually, a noise is made by vendors to attract public attention to their wares (Matt. 12:19). However, Messiah employed none of these traditional methods to call people to Him. His different tender approach to the needs of men is explained in the two paragraphs below.

2p-Verse 20. "Bruised reeds." Basket weavers cutting reeds along the Jordan River would take sharp knives and slash the bruised plants down then throw them aside; they were considered unfit for basket making. The Son of God, filled with the Holy Spirit and divine compassion, reached out to the bruised reeds of humanity along His way. He rescued them from sin to new life and a place of wonderful service in His kingdom. No work on earth is as blessed and rewarding as the gospel service of Jesus Christ to our fellow men. It is written, "The labour of the righteous *tendeth* to life" (Prov. 10:16). Again, we read, "He that goeth forth and weepeth, bearing precious seed, shall doubtless come again with rejoicing, bringing his sheaves *with him*" (Ps. 126:6). The great missionary of the early church wrote of his converts, "For what *is* our hope, or joy, or crown of rejoicing? *Are* not even ye in the presence of our Lord Jesus Christ at his coming?" (1 Thess. 2:19). The wisest man who ever lived said, "The fruit of the righteous *is* a tree of life; and he that winneth souls *is* wise" (Prov. 11:30). God delights in using broken things for His glory and our good. Only after he had carried the painful thorn in his flesh for many years did Paul understand that his sufferings brought the power of God to rest upon his ministry (2 Cor. 12: 5-10). Some day in the future, every real Christian will kiss the heavenly hand that wounded them.

3p-"Smoking flax." Lamp wicks were produced of flax. When a wick had burnt down, flickering its last vestiges, it would be "quenched" or pulled from the lamp and thrown aside. Never once in His perfect earthly ministry and to this present moment has the Master quenched the smoking flax of a burnt out, wasted sinful life that wanted help. A classical example is that of the woman taken in adultery in Section 120. In grace, He forgives and imparts to every repenting believer eternal life and new light . See Matt. 5:14-16 and Phil. 2:15.

(i) "Gentiles." Again, reference is made to the pagans trusting in the Messiah. Mark, in verses 7 and 8 lists several places from which these Gentiles came. See also footnote b above. Long after Matthew had written his book, thousands of Jews looked back and knew that the Gentiles had trusted in their Messiah. Over the centuries that followed, millions have joined the happy train of these early believers and trusted in His Name to be saved. For more on this truth, refer to Section 60, footnote h, and Section 127, second paragraph of footnote l.

2p-What does it mean to believe on the Lord Jesus Christ? When a person has received enough of God's Word to understand that they are lost in sin, and the Holy Spirit convinces them of this truth, they are ready to be saved. The moment, they turn from (repent) of their sins, trust Christ to save them, they become a child of God forever. All the numerous rituals, rites, baptisms, announcements, and public or private exercise of the church must follow salvation. It has been repeated that works will not save one from hell, but Jesus Christ can. And He is received into one's life by child-like trusting faith: there is no other way to heaven. Again, any church or churches that claim they are right and all others are wrong, by that very admission confess that they are cultish, ignorant of God's word, and living in bigoted error. *Trust Christ and nothing else. A good church has it place, too.*

Matthew and Mark alone mention His fourth Galilean tour.* Overwhelmed by the pitiful multitudes and their needs, Christ delivers a touching plea and calls prayer for workers to enter the harvest of lost mankind.

See Section 38 for His first tour without the disciples, Section 39 for the second trip, Section 42 for the third, and this Section 56 for the fourth. His fifth missionary effort across Galilee is in Section 65. No doubt, many trips were made that are not recorded in the brief record of His life as laid down in the four gospels.

Galilee

Matt. 9:35-38	Mk. 6:6b – cont. from Section 91	Lk.	John
The traveling preacher **35** And Jesus went about all the cities and villages, teaching(a) in their synagogues, and preaching the gospel of the kingdom, and healing every sickness and every disease among the people. *The pitiful plea: "pray workers into the harvest fields"►* **36** But when he saw the multitudes, he was moved with compassion(c) on them, because they fainted, and were scattered abroad, as sheep(d) having no shepherd. **37** Then saith he unto his disciples, "The harvest truly *is* plenteous, **but the labourers are few;**(e) **38** "Pray(f) ye therefore the Lord of the harvest, that he will send forth(g) labourers(h) into his harvest." (Next. chap. Matt. 10:1 cont. in Section 57.)	*The traveling preacher* **6b** And he went round about the villages,(b) teaching. (Verse 7 cont. in Section 59.) ◄*The heart of our Lord was troubled as He saw the people without Him as their Savior. Those who have limited this plea of Jesus for workers in the harvest fields to only doing philanthropic deeds for fellow men, helping, and aiding the needy are wrong. They have a defective vision of eternity and men dying without salvation. No sane Christian would decry helping those honestly in need in every way possible, but woe be those who spend their lives in charitable actions, ever assisting mankind, but die without being saved! See Matt. 7:21-23, and Rev. 20:15, with Prov. 16:25.*		

Footnotes-Commentary

(a) Matthew carefully explained to his Jewish readers the Messiah's ministry during the months of this particular Galilean tour. He divided the work of Jesus into three distinct categories.

1. **Teaching.** In New Testament Greek, this word carries several similar meanings: "To instruct, deliver a discourse, to impart knowledge, instill doctrine into another, and explain." The Savior was the greatest teacher in world history. Across Galilee, the people marveled at what He said, *not* at His bodily gymnastics, loudness of voice or movement of hands. Ministers today, who are powerless, substitute these antics for the power of God and kid themselves into believing this is the work of the Holy Spirit! All teaching should be done in an informal way, with respect to culture and customs of the audience, and under the anointing of the Holy Spirit. Questions should be permitted afterward until everything taught is clear to the audience.

2. **Preaching.** Here, the word means sounding forth. It was used of a "street crier or proclaimer." The Savior preached like a public herald with the intention of troubling their souls and convicting their consciences regarding both earthly and eternal matters. He did this through various means and methods, but always in the power of the Holy Spirit. Unlike many of the preachers of today, our Lord was not a screaming, ranting, raving public speaker. It pleases God to save all men who will repent and believe the gospel delivered unto them through "the foolishness of preaching" (1 Cor. 1:21). Wonderfully, more than men preach the message of hope. A tract, a gesture, a word in season, a billboard, a bumper sticker, the innocence of a little child, an accident or brush with death and more, God has used to snap men into a sober contemplation of eternity and their need for sins to be forgiven. There is a delicate balance between teaching and preaching. All teaching and the church will *dry up*; all preaching and it will *blow up*. A proper balance between the two and the church will *grow up*.

3. **Healing.** This carries a wide variety of meaning. He healed every kind of sickness and disease. The high intention of the thousands of extraordinary miracles performed by Christ were *first* to show the Jewish people that He was their Messiah. Note Section 119, John 7:31, footnote l, clearly reflect the Jews' miraculous expectations of their Messiah. See also the asterisk under main heading in Section 48 for other exclusive miracles attributed solely to the Messiah.

(b) In Section 42, footnote c, note the ancient comments regarding the number of cities and villages located in Galilee. This work of traveling over Galilee required tremendous effort on the part of our Lord and His disciples.

(c) **"Moved with compassion."** This signifies the human bowel and was used by the Jews and ancients to express the deep seat of man's emotions and feeling pain. The scribes and Pharisees, swelled by their arrogance over the Torah Law and tradition of the elders, had utterly rejected the common person, whom they classified as "cursed." This awful statement is recorded in John 7:49. Because of this, our Lord was moved and distressed at the misery and suffering of the ordinary people as the religious leaders of the nation scorned them. The sight of lost sinners caused pity to grip His great heart; He instantly opened His mouth and spoke the Words of verses 37 and 38. *It was a plea for help!* Rarely today does one hear a prayer being petitioned to God for workers to be "thrust out" into the harvest fields of lost souls. See footnote f below. Other methods have now supplanted the masterful work of prayer and the astounding results it brings in God's time and way. The past few decades have demonstrated that these new methods of "selling the church" to the ungodly world are proving to be miserable failures.

2p-**"Fainted."** Historians use the word here to picture men seriously wounded and falling in battle. It signified the exhaustion that goes with bringing men to Jesus as well as the condition of the lost.

(d) **"As sheep."** No metaphor employed by human imagination could better reflect the appalling condition of Adam's fallen race than pitiful, trembling sheep, lost and without a caring shepherd. This illustration of men without God was again used a while later by our Lord in Section 93, Matt. 14:14, footnote f. Everyone hearing His plea of deep pathos instantly related to what Jesus was teaching. The land was filled with shepherds and flocks. One can believe the hearts of His apostles were moved by the loving, caring pity in their Master's emotional plea bathed in compassion. In days past, we got down on our knees, wept, prayed, and pled with God for souls to be saved. Then we stood on our feet and preached the gospel with the Holy Ghost sent down from heaven. Men were born into the kingdom of God and Christ. The Son spoke of lost sinners in tones that stirred the hearts of every listener of good will. Rarely do we find those lonely prayer vigils in the night watches, when men who worked hard all day were moved to pray all night! Old-fashioned evangelism anointed of God broke people to weep over their sins. Today, we hear, "Is everybody happy?" or "Let's have a good time tonight." Hymns and choruses must have that rock and roll (subliminal) beat, or "we cannot reach the young people." It is vicious untruth that one must look like a tramp or Vietnam hippie in order to reach the youth for Jesus. Jokes, jokes, and more jokes "warm them up." Singing the same chorus twelve times in succession is a form of self-hypnosis, not the Spirit moving on the people. The blessed Holy Spirit will not work in a "Christian" frivolous atmosphere, for He is *holy*. Jesus was painfully serious as He begged workers to become "hell robbers" by reaping the vast harvest of lost souls (Jude 23).

2p-In 1973, near Cape Town, South Africa, I witnessed a *genuine* spiritual awaking, which resulted in a vast harvest of lost souls. Strongmen fell to their knees and cried aloud for mercy; a fearless police officer lay in a flowerbed for what seemed to be a full hour, transfixed in the spirit of prayer as he called on the Name of the Lord. A former "Olympic champion" was instantly saved as he walked through the side door. This went on for weeks. There was little singing, and not one "sermon" was preached for seven nights. As the people quietly assembled in the hall on a particular evening, I sat on the stage looking over the vast congregation, arrested at the fearful presence of God. A hush so wonderfully strange held every tongue. One man stood with a Bible in hand and moved toward the pulpit; suddenly, he broke the convicting silence. Trembling, sobbing, then weeping loudly, he fell on his knees and begged God for forgiveness of his sins. Dozens bowed at their pews. Others rushed forward kneeling everywhere. A holy noise gradually filled the place as hundreds of voices blended in prayer. This spontaneous, unorganized prayer meeting lasted for over two hours! That congregation experienced a rare visitation from God. Burdened for the souls of men, they had caught a glimpse of hell and sin's wages. So many were saved during the months that followed the pastor left off counting. His profound words were, "God is doing this: we must hurry and get out of His way." This explains what Jesus meant in Matt. 9:38 about sending out workers into the harvest.

3p-Few local assemblies today could understand such a move of the Spirit as briefly described above. Outbreaks of God's saving grace are so abnormal to the program that most Christians would draw back in horror.

(e) Highlighted in gray. Some see in this an allusion to different words found in several Old Testament passages, such as Prov. 10:5 with Joel 3:13. Christ's language here is reminiscent of His Words spoken almost two years prior to the disciples at the well in Sychar, Samaria. For details on this, see Section 35, John 4:35, footnotes e and f. Some expositors also see in these Words of Jesus an allusion to Jer. 8:20.

(f) **Verse 38. "Pray."** With thousands thronging, pushing, and reaching out to Him, the Son of God was moved with compassion, and admonished His followers to "pray" for workers to "be thrust" into the harvest. Christ saw the people burdened with the hypocritical religion and false doctrines of the Pharisees. They were harassed, importuned, and bewildered by those who taught them. They were hindered from entering the kingdom of God. In the previous Sermon on the Mount, He had unleashed a scathing denunciation of Israel's religious leaders and the news of this spread everywhere. Continually, the hoards of humanity gathered to Him and were hungry to hear more. Audible prayers to "the Lord of the harvest" for more reapers are rarely heard in today's modern prayer meetings. Refer to footnote c above. A gigantic harvest with few laborers equals irreparable loss of precious grain. The scarcity of *true* ministers, missionaries, and workers is because men have not prayed for them. How all this works, we cannot know, but we can know that prayer for laborers does produce results in God's time and grace.

(g) **What is going on in the church today?** A sober look into the normal church today and the compassionate, thinking Christian is in for a religious shock. Concern for soul harvesting has been mostly ditched or humbly explained away. Instead, there are the colorful and grand displays of humanity as believers busy themselves with "ministries" of the flesh and the methodologies of unsaved, "scholarly academicians." Basking in the applause of the congregation, the actors in this religious "Gone with the Wind" drama continue. It slithers forth Sunday after Sunday, month after month, and year after year. Music, singing, specials, presentations, and accolades for certain duties well performed are front and center stage. (God forbid that *heavenly anointed* music, singing, and correct recognition of fellow believers vanish from the house of God.) However, today one must have, "at least, a Bachelor's degree before God can use him." With the above kept in balance, we wonder, "Where is the Holy unction that exposes our 'little sins,' and 'brings to light the hidden things of darkness,'" snuggled down in the hearts of many Christians? Our announcements about "family camps," "in-depth Bible studies," "retreats," and "handling our problems scripturally," or "reading the new study guide," have added little *long term* worth to the church corporate body. A brother or sister, who is busy serving God in the local church today, may be in prison next year! There is a difference between professing a faith and possessing Christ who possesses us. God saved the author of this work in 1946. It is still valid today in 2011. He is not advocating a trouble-free, holier than heaven, and wiser than God assembly of Christians. Refer to Section 63, second and third paragraphs of footnote h for more on this.

2p-Countless books have been written about "Self Help," "Improving Relationships," "Loving them to Jesus," "How to Build a Mega Church," "Anger Control," and so on. They are, for the most part, a "flash in the pan." Soon old man time will sweep them into the long hallways of human forgetfulness. Every tool, device, power point presentation, scheme, plan, program, aid, cantata, help, and "God given idea," has been tried in an effort to bring divine life back into the church. Eventually, they too fall by the wayside. Men must return to the naked truth of the Holy Bible and the authority of the Holy Spirit if *eternal fruit* is to be produced. Holiness and inspired truth must always be front and center stage, not religious entertainment. When this is so, other things may follow. Most Christians resent or even hate a pastor, minister, Bible teacher, or missionary, who will correctly deal with their sin, and refuse to (knowingly) allow it to be brought into the fellowship of the saints. Million dollar "sanctuaries" loom with their (occult origin) steeples pointing upward; while under these massive roofs sit thousands of confused, bewildered, unhappy, defeated, weary, unsaved, and worried believers. Only in God's Word and the fellowship of the Holy Spirit in Christ, and the heavenly Father, will we find strength, help, and victory in a world gone mad. (This does not rule out the fellowship and loving support of fellow Christians as we pass through the unmitigated storms of human life.) However, it does put God, His Word, Jesus Christ, and the blessed Holy Spirit, *first.* All other worthy ideals, plans, programs, and whatever must follow behind the Holy Trinity and the Word of God.

3p-Million dollar buildings will not draw in the harvest of souls. This is a popular Baptist myth. While our Reformed and Presbyterian friends are waiting for God to "effectually call His elect," the Baptists are busy "adding to their membership rolls." Methodist and Episcopalians are ordaining homosexuals, and the *extreme* charismatics are "speaking in tongues," "having visions," and "performing signs and wonders." Meanwhile, thousands are dropping into hell. All the glib revival talk is a joke. Calling in a "famed evangelist who has won thousands to Christ" is sucker bait swallowed by believers who cannot pray or think a situation through. David lamented after his sin with Bathsheba, "The sacrifices of God *are* a broken spirit: a broken and a contrite heart, O God, thou wilt not despise" (Ps. 51:17). The Lord told us with whom He delights to abide, "For thus saith the high and lofty One that inhabiteth eternity, whose name *is* Holy; I dwell in the high and holy *place*, with him also *that is* of a contrite and humble spirit, to revive the spirit of the humble, and to revive the heart of the contrite ones" (Isa. 57:15). Brokenness today is because a truck ran over the house cat, or the mother-in-law moved in to spend a week!

(h) **"Labourers."** Ancient rabbis referred to their theological students as "reapers," or "labourers," warning them that "time is short and the harvest perishing." They were to bring Gentile proselytes into the Jewish religion. The disciples instantly understood this rabbinical symbolism so fittingly used by Jesus. The painful sight of lost mankind moved Jesus into the action of evangelism recorded in the following Section 57. He not only *said something,* but He *did something* to reach those great multitudes of lost humanity. Calling twelve men from among the thousands, He endued them with special power to go among the Jews of Galilee. Waving fields of golden grain calls for reapers and demands haste coupled with diligence. Across Galilee, the disciples heralded out in both words and works that the Messiah's new kingdom was being slowly established. On the Jewish materialistic misunderstanding of the kingdom, see Section 39, footnotes a and g for comments.

TWELVE APOSTLES ARE CHOSEN.

Jesus spends the night in prayer on a mountain. The next morning He selects twelve out of the masses to become special apostles.* They are endued with unique power and will be sent out as apostles into the harvest fields of Galilee.

*As explained by the asterisk under main heading in Section 44, Matthew gave the calling of the twelve after the Sermon on the Mount, as seen below. Luke placed their calling as occurring before the sermon. His shorter version of the same sermon as given later in Section 58, Lk. 6:20-49. Luke did not pen the exact message as Matthew. Mark was inspired to omit the Sermon on the Mount altogether but wrote about the calling of the twelve. This diversity demonstrates that these men wrote independent of each other by the authority of divine inspiration.

An unknown mountain in Galilee

Matt. 10:1-2	Mk. 3:13-18	Lk. 6:12-14	John
		The twelve are called 12 And it came to pass in those days,(a) that	
	The twelve are called 13 And he goeth up into a mountain,	he went out into a mountain to pray, and continued all night in prayer to God.	
The twelve are called 1 And when he had called unto *him* his twelve(b) disciples,	and calleth *unto him* whom he would: and they(b) came unto him. 14 And he ordained(c) twelve, that they should be with him,(d) and that he might send them forth(e) to preach,	13 And when it was day, he called *unto him* his disciples:(b) and of them he chose(c) twelve, whom also he named apostles;	
Given special powers he gave them power *against* unclean spirits, to cast them out, and to heal all manner of sickness and all manner of disease.	**Given special powers** 15 And to have power to heal sicknesses, and to cast out devils:		
Their names 2 Now the names of the twelve apostles(f) are these; The first, Simon, who is called(g) Peter, and Andrew his brother; James *the son* of Zebedee, and John his brother;	**Their names** 16 And Simon he surnamed(g) Peter; 17 And James the *son* of Zebedee, and John the brother of James; and he surnamed them Bo-a-ner-ges, which is, "The sons of thunder:" 18 And Andrew, and	**Their names** 14 Simon (whom he also named(g) Peter,) and Andrew his brother, James and John,	

Matt. 10:3–4	Mk. 3:18–19	Lk. 6:14–19	John
3 Philip, and Bartholomew; Thomas, and Matthew the publican; [tax collector] James *the son* of Alphaeus, and Lebbaeus, whose surname was Thaddaeus; **4** Simon the Canaanite,	Philip, and Bartholomew, and Matthew, and Thomas, and James the *son* of Alphaeus, and Thaddaeus, and Simon the Canaanite,	Philip, and Bartholomew, **15** Matthew and Thomas, James the *son* of Alphaeus, and Simon called Zelotes. **16** And Judas *the brother* of James,	
and Judas Iscariot, who also betrayed him. (Verse 5 cont. in Section 59.)	**19** And Judas Iscariot, which also betrayed him: and they went into an house. (Verse 20 cont. in Section 66.)	and Judas Iscariot, which also was the traitor. **17** And he came down with them, and stood in	
the plain, and the company of his disciples, and a great multitude^(h) of people out of all Judaea and Jerusalem, and from the sea coast of Tyre and Sidon, which came to hear him, and to be healed of their diseases; **18** And they that were vexed with unclean spirits:⁽ⁱ⁾ and they were healed. **19** And the whole multitude sought to touch him: for there went virtue^(j) out of him, and healed *them* all. ^{(k) – (l) – (m)} (Verse 20 cont. in Section 58.)			

Footnotes–Commentary

(a) **In those days and all night in prayer.** How many days there were, we cannot know. These were times of great burdens, for the waves of humanity were pressing to Him. The savage opposition by the Pharisees and their companions pressed hard upon His humanity. Some ask the question, "Why did the Son of God need to pray at all if He was divine?" We reply that He was also human. As such, He was subject to the same suffering, sorrows, and pains as all other men. As a man, He too sought blessing from God. Had He not just pled for His disciples to pray laborers into the perishing harvest fields? There is no more inconsistency in Jesus praying than there was in His eating or sleeping. The Jews had built places of prayer across the land where they could retire from the distresses of life and have private communion with Jehovah. These were found on riverbanks (Acts 16:13), hills, groves, valleys, and other locations. Perhaps it was to one of these that our Lord retreated. *We are amazed that Jesus took one minute to raise Lazarus but spent all night in prayer to God.* If He found it necessary to tarry with heaven that long how much more should we poor mortals of time and flesh? Citizens of this world spend nights in partying and reveling, and go about their affairs the next day despite the discomfort. Many saints unfamiliar with prayer cringe at the thought of spending time with God. For more on our Savior and His life of prayer, see Section 42, footnote a, and Section 48, footnote h.

(b) **"Twelve."** Much conjecture exists as to *why* our Lord selected the number twelve. The most reasonable answer seems to be that they were representative of the twelve tribes of the nation of Israel or the twelve sons of Jacob from which the tribes came. It is incorrect that one apostle was selected from each of the tribes. The holy angel identified eleven of them as "men of Galilee" (Acts 1:11). Judas the traitor was not from Galilee, but Judaea.

(c) **"Ordained."** This comes from the Greek word "poieo." Among several things, it means, "to make." In some cases, it is employed in a technical sense. In this text, it means that the Lord Jesus "selected" or "chose" them from the crowds "to make" them something out of them. See footnote d below. It has nothing to do with a churchy, pompous, religious ceremony, which is supposed to give men the "right" to preach God's truth. The word is translated over *seventy* different ways in the New Testament; all of them carry slightly similar meanings.

2p-Nevertheless, it is true that the numeric twelve signified a peculiar divine attachment among the ancient Jews. Twelve was almost "God's number." Wherever mentioned it suggests that He was mystically involved; this number signaled His sovereignty and purposes in the affairs of things, nations, and especially Israel. For example, we read of the five nations that served Chedorlaomer for twelve years (Gen. 14:4). Twelve princes came from

Ishmael (Gen. 25:16). Jacob had twelve sons (Gen. 35:22). From these came the twelve tribes of the nation of Israel (Gen. 49:28). There were twelve wells of water in the wilderness (Ex. 15:27). Twelve oxen were brought as a special offering to the Lord (Num. 7:3). Twelve men were chosen by Moses to spy out the land of Canaan (Deut. 1:23-25). There were twelve stones in the breastplate of the high priest (Ex. 28:21). How impressive that twelve memorial stones were taken out of Jordan and erected for the future generations in Israel to learn from (Josh. 4:1-7). Lastly, heaven's beautiful city has twelve foundation stones garnished with unspeakable luster, and twelve gates, each made from a single pearl (Rev. 21:19-21).

(d) He wanted these twelve to be especially *close* to Him. At His side, they would learn His teaching, watch His conduct, and observe His compassion and genuine love for lost mankind. No man can do the work of Christ, unless he is daily living close to Him. Such are the experiences and actions that make real disciples of Christ.

(e) **"Sent them forth."** Various writers have noted that the departure of Christ and His disciples from Capernaum marked a crisis in that city's history. See main heading of Section 55 for His leaving the city at this time. Jesus cursed Capernaum and two other cities with a most horrible injunction of doom. See main heading of Section 63. No longer would it be the prime center of His activity. Opposition from the Pharisees and the frown of Herod Antipas, who resided at nearby Tiberias, were casting a shadow over His work in that location. From this time forward, we behold our Lord as the man "Who had no place to lay His head." This *human* loneliness and pressing workload is reflected in that night of prayer before selecting His twelve apostles the following morning. The Holy Spirit did *not* give the names of the twelve exactly alike in the three lists. We should not attempt to build one. Several brothers are listed as apostles, Peter and Andrew, James and John, and Judas and James (of Alphaeus) Lk. 6:16. It is beautiful when brothers in the flesh are brothers in grace and together serve Christ. Judas was put last on each list. In death, he "went to his own place" (Acts 1:25).

(f) **"Apostles."** This word in Scripture conveys the idea of "One sent on behalf of and in the authority of another to execute a specific duty." The term was used in a *general* sense of a slave sent by his master to perform a certain task, or even of a child sent by his parents to the market. In this elastic usage of the word, we note that Barnabas was called an apostle (Acts 14:4, 14); Silas and Timothy were apostles (1 Thess. 1:1 with 2:6), and even a woman named Junia was designated as such (Rom. 16:7). They were all sent to do whatever was assigned as their work duties. However, in the case of Christ selecting these twelve men, it became an exclusive *one-time-only* designation. These twelve unique persons (with Matthias who replaced Judas) were God's gift to the *first* churches and are described as being its foundation (1 Cor. 12:28 with Eph. 2:20). Their offices were *not* hereditary or passed on to a future group of apostles. *The widely acclaimed notion of apostolic succession today is foreign to the New Testament doctrine.* The "apostolic age" ended with the death of the last apostles of Christ. One of the highest qualifications of an apostle was that he had seen the Savior after His resurrection (1 Cor. 9:1). The sending of the seventy in Section 113, Lk. 10, was a different event that took place much later in the ministry of Christ.

2p-**Paul.** When Paul was saved and called to be an apostle, even he was *not* ranked among the unique twelve (1 Cor. 15:9). In Rev. 21:14, *only* the names of "the twelve apostles of the Lamb" are upon the foundations of heaven's city. After the death of Judas, Matthias was approved of God and chosen to take the traitor's office, thus restoring the original number of twelve (Acts 1:15-26). All the twelve were from the "ignorant and backward" state of Galilee, except Judas. His name "Iscariot" referred to a town in Judaea where he was born. None of the twelve had been trained in theology. They were rustic, simple men of little social importance, in some cases, ignorant, obscure, and inferior. Each one was filled with typical Jewish prejudices, holding all Gentiles in contempt and possessed by the false teachings of the rabbis; yet the Son of God chose these men to be with Him. It does not take "great men" to be witnesses for Christ. Little men are needed in the service of God as well as the greater ones. The original twelve were all trained by the Son of God, the greatest of all apostles (Heb. 3:1).

(g) Below, under footnote l, are the four name lists of the twelve apostles: three in the gospels and one in Acts. In each listing, the order of the names varies, but with a remarkable agreement that they are *always* given in three groups. The first apostle in each group is the same (Peter, Philip, and James the son of Alphaeus), while the other three, though they vary in order within the group, are never given anywhere in different categories. Matthew identifies himself as "a publican" (verse 3). For earlier details regarding the followers of the Lord Jesus, see Section 26, footnotes b, c, and c.

2p-The question is frequently put, "Why are the names not identical in the lists?" This is because God seeks to teach us of the actions and glory of His grace. Our Lord's *true* servants may never clamor or claim permanent places of superiority in His work. There is no room for "name fame" or "popularity" among the ministers of Christ. One who has his name put at the top of the list today may, by the will of God, be put at the bottom tomorrow or he many vanish into obscurity. Does not the Lord of heaven put up one and set down another? Some remain; others vanish. So are the ways of God with His servants.

3p-**Verse 17. House or plain?** Mark in verse 19 wrote that after Jesus called them, they "went into a house." Luke, in verse 17 stated that they "stood in the plain." They did both, probably going into the house first, then out into the plain area where the suffering people met them.

(h) Countless thousands from every direction flocked to Messiah. A few months prior to the cross, Jesus purposely thinned out the crowds, seeking only those that would follow Him regardless of the cost. Note the main heading under Section 95 for His offensive sermon in the Capernaum synagogue where he deliberately purged out those who were insincere in their dedication.

(i) **"Evil spirits"** again! Wherever Christ went, He confronted demonic powers, even in the Jewish synagogues, where God was worshiped and His Word was read and taught.

2p-Demon-possessed girl. The author of this work went into a large Indian church in Chatsworth, near Durban, South Africa, in 1973. During the service, a teenage girl suddenly began hissing loudly and fell to the wooden floor with a resounding thud. She took on the horrible semblance of a snake and began sliding across the floor and over the pews! People fled, and children screamed as bedlam broke loose. The wise pastor (himself a convert from a pagan Indian religion that worshiped snakes) knew what was taking place. He instantly mastered the chaotic situation. Speaking with holy unction, he commanded the demon(s) to leave the girl in the authority of Jesus Christ the risen Lord. Instantly, she stopped hissing, sliding, and floundering over the floor. Sinking into a limp posture, she lay under a front pew. The devils had departed from her frail body. I cannot describe the explosion of joy that came forth from those dear Indian Christians, especially the mother. One can easily believe that over the course of His ministry, there must have been hundreds if not thousands of demonic encounters in the life of our Savior.

3p-For our Lord's first recorded confrontation with satanic spirits, see Section 40, especially footnotes b through e. For demonic recognition of the Son of God and pagan distortions of the truth regarding Satan and his evil minions, refer to Section 41, footnotes d and g.

(j) Later, we read of another case of virtue or healing power going out of Christ to cure a woman who dared touch His clothing. For this amazing event, see Lk. 8:46.

(k) **Apostolic healings. "Healed them all."** This means just what it says. Yet, it hardly gives grounds for the extreme faith healing movements, which proclaim that healing for everyone is the will of God. On this and other occasion, the Lord Jesus healed every person present, meaning countless thousands. Note Section 41, footnote f, for more on the healings performed by the Savior. For the healing of a man who *did not know* who Jesus was, see Section 121, John 9:36, footnote r. God chooses who shall be healed and who shall not; puny man cannot force His will into anything. "He *hath* his way in the whirlwind and in the storm, and the clouds *are* the dust of his feet" (Nahum 1:3). *Radical faith healings have brought death to the innocent and wrought havoc to the cause of Christ.*

2p-Regarding being healed by His stripes, refer to Section 41, Matt. 8:17, footnote g for details on this subject. Divine healers have become a curse to the cause of Christ in the western world with their glowing promises and ill handling of Holy Scripture. Even the media have infiltrated the healing movements and demonstrated the falsity of their flamboyant claims, the havoc, and despair left in the lives of thousands who "went forward for healing" and were not healed. Worse, most of their champions and "anointed leaders" live like billionaires in plush mansions, wallowing in millions of dollars while fawning to love the poor, homeless, and distraught members of society. This lifestyle has been noted by the clever but unsaved observant public and has turned people away from the Lord Jesus Christ. The Holy Bible and saving gospel are traduced by these scowling unbelievers as they point a justified finger at the "healthy wealthy" movements running amuck in the name of Christianity. This is not to decry praying for the sick and suffering, but it is to renounce the blood-sucking charlatans with a Bible in their hand preying on ignorant, untaught, and hurting people. Sincerity apart from the truth is a charming but deadly serpent. For further comments on this awful truth, see Section 95, sixth paragraph of footnote r.

(l)**Name lists of the twelve apostles as found in the New Testament**

	Matt. 10:2-4	Mk. 3:16-19	Lk. 6:14-16	Acts 1:13, 26
1	**PETER**	**PETER**	**PETER**	**PETER**
2	and Andrew his brother.	and Andrew his brother.	and Andrew his brother.	and Andrew his brother.
3	James and John his	James and John his	James and John his	James and John his
4	brother.	brother	brother	brother.
5	**PHILIP**	**PHILIP**	**PHILIP**	**PHILIP**
6	and Bartholomew[i]	and Bartholomew[i]	and Bartholomew[i]	and Thomas
7	Thomas	and Matthew	Matthew	Bartholomew[i]
8	and Matthew	and Thomas	and Thomas	and Matthew
9	**JAMES-SON OF ALPHAEUS**	**JAMES-SON OF ALPHAEUS**	**JAMES-SON OF ALPHAEUS**	**JAMES-SON OF ALPHAEUS**
10	and Lebbaeus[ii]	and Thaddaeus[ii]	and Simon[iii] (Zelotes)	and Simon[iii] (Zelotes)
11	Simon[iii] (Cana.)	and Simon[iii] (Cana.)	and Judas[ii] (of James)	and Judas[ii] (of James)
12	and Judas Iscariot.	and Judas Iscariot.	and Judas Iscariot.	Matthias replaced Judas.
				See next page by ●

i Bartholomew also called Nathanael. He is with Philip in John 1:44-46 and with Thomas in John 21:2.

ii Lebbaeus listed as number 10 in first column above was also called Thaddaeus, as well as Judas the brother of James, to distinguish him from the traitor Judas Iscariot. See number 10 below.

iii Simon also called the Canaanite or Cananean. He was *not* a Gentile. The title "Canaanite," as used here is an Aramaic word signifying the same as Zelotes, explained in number 11 below.

●Matthias filled Judas' place in the apostolic twelve. The twelve are mentioned some thirty times across the book of Acts by the word "apostles,'"if we include the plural possessive "apostles." Their final mention in the New Testament is in Rev. 21:14.

It is incorrect that Paul filled the vacancy left by Judas. He was the great apostle to the Gentiles but not of the class of the twelve, whose names are engraved in the foundation stones of heaven. For further details on the apostles and Paul, see footnote f above.

(m)Further detailed particulars regarding the twelve apostles

1. **Simon** (Matt. 10:2; Mk. 3:16; Lk. 6:14; and John 1:42). **"Peter"** (Acts 1:13), so surnamed (Matt. 10:2) by Christ (Mk. 3:16 and Lk. 6:14), who first called him **"Cephas"** (John 1:42). He was the son of Jona (John 1:42) and a native of Bethsaida (John 1:44). He was an apostle with three names. *See number 10 below.*

2. **Andrew** (Matt: 10:2; Mk. 3:18; Lk. 6:14; and Acts 1:13), from Bethsaida (John 1:44), and Peter's brother (Matt. 10:2; and Lk. 6:14).

3. **James** (Matt. 10:2; Mk. 3:17; Lk. 6:14; and Acts 1:13), the son of Zebedee (Matt. 10:2). Surnamed **"Boanerges"** ("sons of thunder") by Christ with his brother John (Mk. 3:17). *See number 4 below.*

4. **John** (Matt. 10:2; Mk. 3:17; Lk. 6:14; and Acts 1:13), the brother of James (Matt. 10:2). He was also given the epithet **"Boanerges"** ("sons of thunder") by Christ, with his brother James (Mk. 3:17). *See number 3 above.*

5. **Philip** (Matt. 10:3; Mk. 3:18; Lk. 6:14; and Acts 1:13) of Bethsaida (John 1:44).

6. **Bartholomew** (Matt. 10:3; Mk. 3:18; Lk. 6:14; and Acts 1:13). He is also called **"Nathanael"** (John 1:45).

7. **Thomas** (Matt. 10:3; Mk. 3:18; Lk. 6:15; and Acts 1:13), called **"Didymus"** (John 11:16; 20:24; and 21:2).

8. **Matthew** (Matt. 10:3; Mk 3:18; Lk. 6:15; and Acts 1:13), the publican (Matt. 10:3 and Lk. 5:27), also called **"Levi"** (Mk. 2:14 and Lk. 5:27), the son of Alphaeus (Mk. 2:14). This is not the Alphaeus at number 9 in the apostle's name list on the previous page under footnote l.

9. **James** (Matt. 10:3; Mk. 3:18; Lk. 6:15; and Acts 1:13), the son of Alphaeus (Matt. 10:3; Mk. 3:18; Lk. 6:15; and Acts 1:13).

10. **Lebbaeus** (Matt. 10:3), whose surname was **"Thaddaeus"** (Matt. 10:3 and Mk. 3:18); also called **"Judas"** brother of James (Lk. 6:16 and Acts 1:13), and "Judas not Iscariot" (John 14:22). He also was an apostle with three names. *See number 1 above.*

11. **Simon** (Matt. 10:4; Mk. 3:18; Lk. 6:15; and Acts 1:13), the Cannanite (Matt. 10:4 and Mk. 3:18), called **"Zelotes"** (Lk. 6:15 and Acts 1:13). The term "Zelotes" connects Simon with a Jewish revolutionary political party, fiercely opposed to foreign taxation. They were engaged in terrorist warfare against the Romans. Matthew had betrayed his Hebrew people and collected taxes for the Romans. Simon the Zelote hated all tax collectors. Together, they now walk with Jesus in divine service to God and men. O the glory of saving grace!

12. **Judas Iscariot** (Matt. 10:4; Mk. 3:19; and Lk. 6:16); Iscariot (Matt. 10:4; Mk. 3:19); the traitor (Lk. 6:16) who betrayed The Lord Jesus (Matt. 10:4; Mk. 3:19; John 6:71; 12:4; and 13:2); and the son of Simon (John 6:71; 12:4; and 13:2, 26). Satan entered his body (Lk. 22:3 and John 13:27). Judas betrayed Jesus, committed suicide and went to his own place in hell (Matt. 26:14-16; 27:3-10; with Acts. 1:25). See David's prophecy of Judas' life, wife, children, parents, cursing, and fate in Ps. 109:6-20, and how this was interpreted and applied by Simon Peter in Acts 1:16-20. Refer also to Section 95, footnote x, and Section 146, footnote h, for further comments on Judas. For a review of his life, see Section 172, footnote e. For the other Judas (not Iscariot), with three different names, see number 10 above.

Matthias. For the brief history of Matthias, chosen to fill the vacancy left by Judas, see Acts 1:15-26.

THE SERMON ON THE PLAIN*AS RECORDED BY LUKE.

The original edition* of this message was the Sermon on the Mount in Matthew 5-7. Below, Luke records a later version when Christ gave parts of the same discourse but in a shorter form. The lesson here was delivered to His disciples and a wide variety of people from across the land.

*See asterisks below main headings in Section 44 and Section 57 for more on this subject. Matthew describes Jesus' sermon in 111 verses. Luke uses 30 verses in his record. Out of these 30 passages, 23 have a parallel in Matthew's record, meaning that Luke recorded about six or seven statements of Christ not found in the record given by Matthew. All this was by the direction of the Holy Spirit and not because the authors borrowed from one another. Religious academicians who do not believe in the total inspiration of Holy Scripture invented the synoptic problem myth. For a brief review of the origin and spread of this fable, see the Author's Introduction. It is another lie fostered off on the credulous and gullible.

Matt.	Mk.	Lk. 6:20-36—Galilee	John
		The beatitudes as recorded by Luke	
		20 And he lifted up his eyes on his disciples, and said,**(a)** "Blessed**(b)** *be ye* poor: for yours is the kingdom of God.	
		21 "Blessed *are ye* that hunger now: for ye shall be filled. Blessed *are ye* that weep now: for ye shall laugh.	
		22 "Blessed are ye, when men shall hate you, and when they shall separate you *from their company*, and shall reproach *you*, and cast out your name as evil, for the Son of man's sake.	
		23 "Rejoice ye in that day, and leap for joy: for, behold, your reward *is* great in heaven: for in the like manner did their fathers unto the prophets.	
		24 "But woe unto you that are rich! for ye have received your consolation.	
		25 "Woe unto you that are full! for ye shall hunger. Woe unto you that laugh now! for ye shall mourn and weep.	
		26 "Woe unto you, when all men shall speak well of you! for so did their fathers to the false prophets.	
		His new kingdom commands: love, bless, accept wrong, give	
		27 "But I say unto you which hear, Love your enemies,**(c)** do good to them which hate you,	
		28 "Bless them that curse you, and pray for them which despitefully use you. **(d)**	
		29 "And unto him that smiteth thee on the *one* cheek**(e)** offer also the other; and him that taketh away thy cloak forbid not *to take thy* coat also.**(f)**	
		30 "Give to every man that asketh of thee; and of him that taketh away thy goods ask *them* not again.**(g)**	
		31 And as ye would that men should do to you, do ye also to them likewise. **(h)**	
		32 "For if ye love them which love you, what thank have ye? for sinners also love those that love them.**(i)**	
		33 "And if ye do good to them which do good to you, what thank have ye? for sinners also do even the same.**(j)**	
		34 "And if ye lend *to them* of whom ye hope to receive, what thank have ye? for sinners also lend to sinners, to receive as much again.**(k)**	
		35 "But love ye your enemies,**(l)** and do good, and lend, hoping for nothing again; and your reward shall be great, and ye shall be [like] the children of the Highest: for he is kind unto the unthankful and *to* the evil.	
		36 "Be ye therefore merciful, as your Father also is merciful.**(m)**	

265

Matt.	Mk.	Lk. 6:37-49—Galilee	John
		37 "Judge not, and ye shall not be judged: condemn not, and ye shall not be condemned: forgive, and ye shall be forgiven:(n)	

37 "Judge not, and ye shall not be judged: condemn not, and ye shall not be condemned: forgive, and ye shall be forgiven:(n)

38 "Give,(o) and it shall be given unto you; good measure, pressed down, and shaken together, and running over, shall men give into your bosom. For with the same measure that ye mete withal it shall be measured to you again."

Blind leading the blind similitude

39 And he spake a parable unto them, "Can the blind lead the blind? shall they not both fall into the ditch?(p)

Don't judge hastily

40 "The disciple is not above his master: but every one that is perfect [mature] shall be as his master.(q)

41 "And why beholdest thou the mote [speck] that is in thy brother's eye, but perceivest not the beam [plank] that is in thine own eye?(r)

42 "Either how canst thou say to thy brother, 'Brother, let me pull out the mote [speck] that is in thine eye,' when thou thyself beholdest not the beam [plank] that is in thine own eye? Thou hypocrite, cast out first the beam [plank] out of thine own eye, and then shalt thou see clearly to pull out the mote [speck] that is in thy brother's eye.

Tree and fruit similitude

43 "For a good tree(s) bringeth not forth corrupt fruit; neither doth a corrupt tree bring forth good fruit.

44 "For every tree is known by his own fruit. For of thorns men do not gather figs, nor of a bramble bush gather they grapes.

45 "A good man(t) out of the good treasure of his heart bringeth forth that which is good; and an evil man out of the evil treasure of his heart bringeth forth that which is evil: for of the abundance of the heart his mouth speaketh.

Words without deeds

46 "And why call ye me, 'Lord, Lord,'(u) and do not the things which I say?

Results of obedience compared to building on the rock foundation

47 "Whosoever cometh to me, and heareth my sayings, and doeth them, I will shew you to whom he is like:

48 "He is like a man which built an house, and digged deep, and laid the foundation on a rock: and when the flood arose, the stream beat vehemently upon that house, and could not shake it: for it was founded upon a rock.

Results of disobedience compared to building on no foundation

49 "But he that heareth,(v) and doeth not, is like a man that without a foundation built an house upon the earth; against which the stream did beat vehemently, and immediately it fell; and the ruin of that house was great."

(w) (Next chap. Lk. 7:1, in Section 60.)

Footnotes-Commentary

(a) Where was the Lord Jesus when He gave this *shorter* version of His original Sermon on the Mount? Lk. 6:17, states that He came down from the mountain after a night of prayer (verse 12) and "stood in the plain." (This hardly means that He stood up for the entire discourse, as the posture of a teacher was that of sitting.) This word signals a "level place," or we would call it a "plateau." These lessons were spoken somewhere in Galilee on a mountain tabletop accessible to the crowds and apparently not far from Capernaum.

(b) Verses 20-26. "Blessed." We note that on this occasion the Savior gave only *three* of the original nine beatitudes written earlier by Matthew. Unsaved critics and "scholars," who disdain any notion of a Bible that is trustworthy and fully inspired of God tell us that *later editors* took the manuscript of Matthew and injected into its text the words missing in Luke's work and vice versa. Hence, the differences in the two! For an outstanding example of this infidel approach to the Sermon on the Mount and other paralleled Scriptures, see *Extra Volume to Hastings Bible Dictionary*, 1906, pages 1-45. A healthy, well-balanced belief in the absolute inspiration of the Bible serves as a sure deterrent to "forced interpretations," "radical exegesis," and "preposterous preaching" so obviously void of the fear of God and sensitivity to the Holy Spirit. Below is a short comparison of part of the records as given by Matthew and Luke.

1. Lk. 6:20 contrasted with Matt. 5:3. Christ's usage of "poor in spirit" in Matthew reads in Luke as "Blessed be ye poor" with "spirit" left out (Lk. 6:20). See Section 44, fourth paragraph of footnote f for comments on "poor in spirit."

2. Lk. 6:21 contrasted with Matt. 5:6. Christ's usage of "hunger and thirst after righteousness" in Matthew reads in Luke as "Blessed are ye that hunger now." What Matthew wrote fully, Luke wrote briefly in his letter. See Section 44, footnote k, for details.

3. Lk. 6:22-23 with Matt. 5:11-12. Matthew recorded Jesus as saying, "when *men* shall revile you, and persecute *you*, and shall say all manner of evil against you falsely, for my sake." In Luke's version the Savior said, "When men shall hate you [and] shall separate you *from their company*, and shall reproach *you*, and cast out your name as evil, for the Son of man's sake." Seemingly, both were first directed at the apostles of Christ (and all true believers to follow) whose names were scandalized by being labeled as "Nazarenes" and "Christians." Both words were used as terms of ignominy and reproach. James 2:7 reads that they (the Christ-hating Jews and Gentiles) "blaspheme that worthy name by which ye are called." We read in the works of Governor Pliny the Younger, Epistle x. 97, where he inquired of the Roman Emperor if he "should punish the name Christian." The word "separate" has reference to being excommunicated from the exclusive fellowship of the Jews. Each of Jesus' disciples understood what He was saying. A shudder must have fallen over all of them. For details on the awfulness of excommunication from the synagogue and Jewish religion, see Section 121, third paragraph of footnote j.

4. Lk. 6:23 with Matt. 5:12. Matthew records Jesus as saying, "rejoice and be exceeding glad: for great *is* your reward in heaven." He writes that Jesus spoke about the persecution of the prophets who lived before His disciples. See 1 Kings 18:4 with Heb. 11:32-39 for many examples. Luke wrote that Jesus said they were to "leap for joy," for their reward would be "great." It was a social custom for Jews filled with joy to dance about and leap into the air, waving their hands in high ecstasy.

5. Lk. 6:24-26 are not in Matthew's record. The words "Woe unto you that are rich" may be an allusion to Amos 6:1. Hence, they are highlighted in gray. Probably, they were addressed to the Pharisees and their companions, who prided themselves in their wealth and haughty religion. See Section 44, fifth paragraph of footnote f, for the Pharisee's teaching on riches.

(c) Verses 27-28. Matthew's words as spoken by Jesus, "Love your enemies, bless them that curse you, do good to them that hate you," are more or less the same as those of Luke. Refer to Section 45, Matt. 5:44-45, footnotes n and o, for details. Now, the Savior speaks of one of the most glorious laws in His new kingdom, the law of self-abandon and bearing the reproaches of those who hate and accuse us out of spite. We are to forgive them. *See the shocking rabbinical law on forgiveness in Section 110, footnote h.* This was new teaching in the ears of the disciples and those listening. No such message was heard from the synagogue chair or lips of the rabbis. Jews were taught to love their neighbors who were strictly fellow Jews. Jesus' teaching in Luke 6:29 is similar to those He spoke in Matt. 5:39-40. They are not placed in the same order as Matthew has them. This message of Jesus as recorded by Luke was given at a different time and in a different order.

(d) Verse 28 has a short parallel in Matt. 5:44. Many years later Paul writes along *similar* lines in Rom. 12:14. Was the apostle quoting these sayings of Christ and thus demonstrating that the book of Matthew was written and in circulation? On the question of when the gospels were written, see *Appendix Seven*.

(e) Verse 29. Jews loved only Jews if they were strict adherents to the law and tradition of the elders. A slap on the right cheek was a most grievous insult in the east. It was an offence usually settled by war and bloodshed! The command of Jesus for the members of His new kingdom must have stunned every person who heard it. "Offer your offender the other cheek to smite." Never had the rabbis taught such things! It flew in the face of hundreds of years of rigid Jewish culture and practice. Jesus' teachings were astonishing to every law-abiding pious Jew, *especially* those chained to the oral teachings of the rabbis. Christ teaches patience and longsuffering in bearing injuries and affronts the poor unsaved often lay upon us. Often, they seem to be on all sides ready to contend and debate over the most unimportant things.

(f) "Thy cloak and coat." This has roots in eastern dress styles. The "cloak" speaks of the *outer* garment while

267

"coat" the *inner* or under garment. The Jews and others of that era usually wore such. Most people owned only *one* of each, and to take either was to leave one in a condition of semi-nakedness. Earlier John Baptist had required those who had *two* coats to give one to the poor. In the minds of the people, this was a high and great requirement, and only the person exercising true repentance would do such a thing. The Talmud in tractate, Baba Bathra 46b also speaks of "taking a coat in payment" for a debt. Matthew's parallel of Luke's text adds, "sue thee at law" in Matt. 5:40. Jesus requires that the members of His family must be willing to lose everything (stripped of all if necessary) in order to show the spirit of the true religion, reflecting His beautiful image and the love of God in dealing with those who hate and despise us. This law of the kingdom-church of God has been abandoned today. Men are quick to sue and clamor over the smallest of earthly trifles, having no regard for matters of eternal weight and consequence.

(g) **Matt. 5:42,** is similar to the passage in Luke 6:30. Jesus is not being "politically correct" in His statement. *At no place in Scripture does Christ defend laziness, loitering, borrowing with intent to steal or welfare theft.* This command had direct reference to the beggars and the poorer class of that day and time, who often sought help from others to alleviate their misery. The rabbis and Jewish society in general made a big noise about charity and giving to the poor. Here, the Lord Jesus confirms this rabbinical teaching as true, and that it was to be practiced by those who follow Him in the new kingdom. On Christ's approval of certain rabbinical teachings, portions of which were later recorded in the Talmud, see Section 45, ninth paragraph of footnote b.

(h) Verse 31 has its match in Matt. 7:12. See Section 47, second paragraph of footnote e.

(i) See Section 45, Matt. 5:46, for similar words.

(j) Verse 33 is paralleled in Matt. 5:47. Another proof that this message recorded by Luke was in parts different from that penned by Matthew. The Jews spoke of the heathen who loved their fellow heathens. Messiah is herewith telling the Jews (who loved only fellow Jews) that they are no different from the pagans who lived so close to the people of Israel. Unthankfulness is one of the greatest crimes of humanity. Paul lists it among the gross sins of men in 2 Tim. 3:2. The proverb, "Plenty makes picky but a hungry man does not argue with the cook" is applicable to America. Ralph Waldo Emerson, a worldly philosopher and defunct Unitarian minister (died 1882) wrote, 'If the stars only shined once a year the whole world would be waiting to see them." God often wrings the truth from the mouth of His enemies. Sadly, because they shine continually few note their beauty. A thing ever at hand is valued less than that which is rare or hardly seen by human eyes.

(k) See Section 45 Matt. 5:42, footnote m.

(l) See Section 45, Matt. 5:46, and Lk.6:27, footnote c above for a similar statement.

(m) See Section 45, Matt. 5:48, footnote a, for a slight parallel of part of Matthew's original verse. Matthew records Jesus as saying on that earlier occasion, "Be ye perfect" (or mature), and then He uses God in heaven as an example of dealing with men in the perfection of absolute divine maturity.

(n) No hasty, immature judgments, and generalized condemnation of men are allowed in the new kingdom-Church of Christ. Quick and carnal Christians, walking in the flesh and filled with pettiness, are daily guilty of this sin. It is a curse to every local assembly of believers and continually creates unrest and problems. See Section 47, Matt. 7:1-5, footnotes a, b and c, for the whole of Christ's original teaching on this subject.

(o) **Verse 38. "Give."** There is no parallel for the first part of this passage in Matthew's version of the Sermon on the Mount. Our Savior added this statement to the later edition of this same message. *This has nothing to do with prosperity or getting rich by giving to God. These words do not promise that if a man gives, God will give back more.* Rather Christ is again using familiar local color in His teachings. He was referring to the "tithing vessels" used among the Jews called "decimaries." When tithes of money were brought to the temple, they were poured into these consecrated containers. The giver would often shake and press down the contents of the decimarie, even to the running over stage, in order to give God more than the tenth! This was especially true of tithes of small grain, and the fine flour used in the meat offerings (Lev. 2:7). Thousands of good-hearted Jews did this before presenting their tithes and offerings to the officiating priests. The Talmud also mentions this custom among the Hebrews in tractate, Menachoth 87a, b, and 90a. The tithe of "fine flour" is mentioned in Yoma 73a. Pointing to this passage as proof of financial benefit through big giving misses the mark. *There is nothing here about mass wealth for those who give abundantly.*

2p-The author of this work has seen thousands of saints who had nothing to give. Once, in the wild "outback country," I participated in a communion service with Australian aboriginal Christians. They only had a tin cup of water and a "bush sweet potato" for the emblems! It was the sweetest communion service in which I have ever shared. The so-called Bible promises of sure wealth and "name-it-claim-it" so fervently preached by certain people, would never apply to those poverty-stricken, gracious people and thousands of other believers worldwide. These high-sounding claims of financial and physical prosperity are misrepresentations of Bible doctrine. They are profoundly contradicted by the past two thousand years of *true* church history. Paul's famed words in Phil. 4:19 is ripped from context by these cults. *God supplies what He sees we need!* From His sovereign understanding of our lives, He may see it right to supply us with cancer, severe loss, financial ruin, or other trials, which are designed for our final good and His glory! Paul, who penned Phil. 4:19, a few years later also wrote that he had suffered in weariness and painfulness, in watchings often, in hunger and thirst (2 Cor. 11:27). In 1 Cor. 4:11, Paul stated that he had been "hungry, thirsty and naked" in the service of God. This is hardly compatible with the "gospel of health and prosperity" ministers of today. Scripture declares that God has chosen the "poor of this world rich in faith" (James 2:5).

(p) **Verse 39.** This passage has no parallel in Matthew's record of the Sermon. It was a general proverb often employed to describe a hopeless situation. Christ used it earlier when describing the Jerusalem Pharisees and their blindness in exalting and obeying the oral or Mishna traditions in preference to the beautiful Torah Law of Moses. Jesus spoke this same proverb two days before His death and employed it to describe the religious leaders of Israel. They were spiritually blind (Matt. 23:17).

(q) This seems to have been a maxim known to the Jews. It has no roots in Matthew, but was used later by Christ, the night before His death (John 13:16 with 15:20). The idea is that every mature (perfect) believer will suffer similar things as his Master. Often what befalls the Master befalls His followers.

(r) **Verses 41–42.** These verses find their source in the original version of the Sermon on the Mount. See section 47, Matt. 7:3–5 with footnotes a, b, and c where this was first mentioned.

(s) **Verses 43–45.** This is a slightly revised version of the original words recorded in Matt. 7:16–19. The Holy Spirit supervised all such revisions.

(t) The first part of this passage has no parallel in the Sermon on the Mount. Christ did use it a short time later in Section 66, Matt. 12:35. The only way a man's heart had good treasure was by the Holy Spirit of God performing the miracle of the new birth, resulting in *total* justification by faith and *perfect* righteousness before the Almighty. Justification before God is received by faith in the finished work of Christ in His death, burial, and resurrection. It is not salvation but one of the major fruits of salvation in the life of the born again Christian. Genuine, acceptable, inward goodness is then possessed because "Christ dwells in our hearts by faith" (Eph. 3:17). Apart from this divine plan, all of our good deeds are as filthy rags before God (Isa. 64:6). On the utter wickedness of the human heart apart from the saving grace of God, see Section 96, Matt. 15:18, footnotes l and m.

(u) **Verses 46–48.** A condensed version of Matt. 7:21–22 with 24–25. See related footnotes in both places.

(v) This final statement of Christ is also a revised form of what He had said earlier in Matthew's version of the Sermon on the Mount. Note this in Section 47, Matt. 7: 26–27.

(w) **"Great ruin"** has reference to the eternal, conscious sufferings in the lake of fire for all eternity. Men may discover a glimpse of their destiny by the examination of their hearts, for in some unspeakable way, what is there strangely prognosticates our eternal state. How appalling is the fact that these troubling voices of doom are often silenced by the power of dominating sin, and obstinate unbelief. The design of such is to deceive and lastly damn the unsuspecting victim who is a prisoner of such.

2p-Another side to the awful drama. All men are endued with rational and immortal souls, and have understanding and wills capable of most excellent things. However, they are out of tune with the Lord of heaven and eternity by sin and wickedness. These vices have disfigured them beyond measure and turned them into aliens before God and the commonwealth of Israel. They pursue their lot and success in this earthly life, blind to what lies ahead! These facts ought the more to raise the height of love and compassion in our hearts, for as they are, so once were we! Seeing a fellow mortal chained in the fatal distempers of sin, rendered helpless by the curse of Adam, and doomed for hell, converts our false aversions into compassion and pity. By nature, it is hard to love the vile, dirty, foul smelling, and harmfully wicked. Nevertheless, we must be brave and exert every effort to reach them with the saving gospel of Jesus Christ. Alas! This is their only hope of rescue. What will our fame and proud reputation, great learning, higher academic degrees, massive libraries, and much experience be worth a hundred years from now? "Great ruin" waits for all souls that are outside God's saving grace found only in the Lord Jesus Christ. This alone can render them into new creatures, fit to be companions of angels and a spiritual stone in the temple of the Holy Ghost. Any dissimulation that takes us from this highest of duties is surely from Satan or his agents. O Christian reader, "work for the night is coming when no man can work." Sadly, most are dumb to these truths. When Napoleon saw the shattered and beaten remnant of his proud army, which had marched through the killing winter of Russian snow and ice, he broke down, fell to his knees, and sobbed. Now, the arrogant warlord who boasted that he "did not need God to conquer Europe," met his match! In this lament, we see demonstrated again that the Almighty reigns in heaven and earth. Alexander, miscalled "the great," wept when he could find no more empires to conquer! After one fierce battle, he sold 30,000 men into slavery! Nations, kings, and kingdoms were terrified of this haughty little Greek. Yet, "the great" died drunk in 323 B.C. with wine and pneumonia while in a tent with his pregnant mistress. Thomas Hobbs, that "eminent philosopher of philosophers" muttered as he died in 1679, "I am about to take a fearful leap into the dark." These and a million more over history demonstrate for thinking men that life without God and Christ is empty and vain. At the end of the road waits "great ruin." For other comments on dying atheists and skeptics, see Section 87, footnote j.

The twelve selected in Section 57 go out two by two on a limited commission to the house of Israel. They are endowed with unique Messianic power, and given instructions, and various warnings.* Christ leaves to teach and preach.

At this junction in the ministry of Jesus, it is impossible to trace an exact chronology. The twelve rejoined Him on a brief, temporary basis after beginning this restricted commission. This is because some months later, they will be with Him on the fifth Galilean tour as seen in the main heading of Section 65. Their work among fellow Jews in Galilee was interrupted by the news that Herod Antipas, the ruler of Galilee, had murdered John. This occurred while the disciples were busy in Galilee where Herod Antipas ruled. Hearing this they stopped their labors and went immediately to meet their Master at Capernaum. See asterisk under main heading of Section 93 for their return and meeting with the Savior. With this, the limited Galilean commission ended.

Galilee

Matt. 10:5-10 (Matt. 11:1)	Mk. 6:7-9 (Mk. 6:12-13)	Lk. 9:1-3 (Lk. 9:6)	John
Their first mission, message, and power	***Their first mission, message, and power***	***Their first mission, message, and power***	
5 These twelve Jesus sent forth,	7 And he called *unto him* the twelve, and began to send them forth by two and two; and gave them power over unclean spirits;	1 Then he called his twelve disciples together, and gave them power and authority over all devils, and to cure diseases.	
Limitations imposed and commanded them, saying, "Go not into the way of the Gentiles, and into *any* city of the Samaritans[(a)] enter ye not: 6 "But go rather to the lost sheep of the house of Israel.[(b)] 7 "And as ye go, preach, saying, The kingdom of heaven is at hand. 8 "Heal the sick, cleanse the lepers, raise the dead, cast out devils: freely ye have received, freely give.[(c)]	8 And commanded them that they should	2 And he sent them to preach the kingdom of God, and to heal the sick.	
Equipment 9 "Provide neither gold, nor silver, nor brass in your purses, 10 "Nor scrip[(d)] [bag] for *your* journey, *(Shoes and sandals were not the same among the ancients)*▶ neither two coats,[(e)] neither shoes, nor yet ▶staves: for the workman is worthy of his meat.	***Equipment*** take nothing for *their* journey, save a staff only; no scrip,[(d)] [bag] no bread, no money in *their* purse: 9 But *be* shod with ◀sandles; and not put on two coats.[(e)] *Luke puts staves in verse 3* ◀*above.*	***Equipment*** 3 And he said unto them, "Take nothing for *your* journey, neither staves, nor scrip,[(d)] [bag] neither bread, neither money; neither have two coats[(e)] apiece.	

Matt. 10:11–19 (Matt.11:1)	Mk. 6:10–11 (Mk. 6:12–13)	Lk. 9:4–5 (Lk. 9:6)	John

Conduct and reception
 11 "And into whatsoever city or town ye shall enter,(f) enquire who in it is worthy; and there abide till ye go thence.
 	
 12 "And when ye come into an house, salute it.(g)
 13 "And if the house be worthy, [sympathetic] let your peace come upon it: but if it be not worthy, let your peace return to you.
 Opposition coming from four different places
 14 "And whosoever shall not receive you, nor hear your words, when ye depart out of that house or city, shake off the dust of your feet.(h)
 	
 15 "Verily I say unto you, It shall be more tolerable for the land of Sodom and Gomorrha(i) in the day of judgment, than for that city.
 16 "Behold, I send you forth as sheep in the midst of wolves:(j) be ye therefore wise as serpents, and harmless as doves. (k)
    1. From Jewish religion
 17 "But beware of men: for they will deliver you up to the councils, [Sanhedrin] and they will scourge you in their synagogues;
    2. From Gentile rulers
 18 "And ye shall be brought before governors and kings for my sake, for a testimony against them and the Gentiles.
 19 "But when they deliver
	Conduct and reception
	 10 And he said unto them, "In what place soever ye enter(f) into an house, there abide till ye depart from that place.
	
	 Opposition coming
	 11 "And whosoever shall not receive you, nor hear you, when ye depart thence, shake off the dust under your feet(h) for a testimony against them. Verily I say unto you, It shall be more tolerable for Sodom and Gomorrha(i) in the day of judgment, than for that city.
	
	 ◄ *Several of the instructions given to the twelve in this Section concerning opposition they would meet across Galilee, are similar to those given later during our Lord's Olivet Discourse in Section 163. This reveals that satanic opposition to God's Word is often the same regardless of the time in which it occurs. Several of these similarities are seen by comparing Matthew 10:17 with Mark 13:9 and Matthew 10:18-21 with Mark 13:11-12. The Devil is the Devil, whether it was a thousand years ago or today. He hates God's Word, work, and people with unmitigated passion.*
		Conduct and reception
		 4 "And whatsoever house ye enter(f) into, there abide, and thence depart.
		
		 Opposition coming
		 5 "And whosoever will not receive you, when ye go out of that city, shake off the very dust from your feet(h) for a testimony against them.	

271

Matt. 10:19-37 (Matt.11:1) (Mk. 6:12-17) (Lk. 9:6)—*Galilee*	Mk.	Lk.	John
you up, take no thought how or what ye shall speak: for it shall be given you in that same hour what ye shall speak.			
20 "For it is not ye that speak, but the Spirit of your Father which speaketh in you.			
3. From relatives			
21 "And the brother shall deliver up the brother to death, and the father the child: and the children shall rise up against *their* parents, and cause them to be put to death.			
4. From the world			
22 "And ye shall be hated of all *men* for my name's sake: but he that endureth to the end shall be saved.			
23 "But when they persecute you in this city, flee ye into another: for verily I say unto you, Ye shall not have gone over the cities of Israel, till the Son of man be come.[(l)]			
Be like Christ in suffering			
24 "The disciple is not above *his* master, nor the servant above his lord.			
25 "It is enough for the disciple that he be as his master, and the servant as his lord. If they have called the master of the house Beelzebub,[(m)] how much more *shall they call* them of his household?			
Make truth known publicly			
26 "Fear them not therefore: for there is nothing covered, that shall not be revealed; and hid, that shall not be known.			
27 What I tell you in darkness, *that* speak ye in light: and what ye hear in the ear, *that* preach ye upon the housetops.[(n)]			
Beware of men: God is with you: confess Me before men			
28 "And fear not them which kill the body, but are not able to kill the soul: but rather fear him which is able to destroy both soul and body in hell.[(o)]			
29 Are not two sparrows[(p)] sold for a farthing? [one forth of a penny] and one of them shall not fall on the ground without your Father.			
30 But the very hairs of your head are all numbered.			
31 Fear ye not therefore, ye are of more value than many sparrows.			
32 "Whosoever[(q)] therefore shall confess me before men, him will I confess also before my Father which is in heaven.			
33 "But whosoever shall deny me before men, him will I also deny before my Father which is in heaven.			
Division coming: cross bearing, and losing life			
34 "Think not that I am come to send peace on earth: I came not to send peace, but a sword.			
35 "For I am come to ʻ**set a man at variance against his father, and the daughter against her mother, and the daughter in law against her mother in law.**ʼ			
The most painful of all opposition: choose to follow Jesus			
36 "**And a man's foes *shall be* they of his own household.**ʼ[(r)]			
37 "He that loveth father or mother more than me is not worthy of me: and he that loveth son or daughter more than me is not worthy of me.			

Matt. 10:38-42, Matt. 11:1, Mk. 6:12-13, Lk. 9:6—*Galilee*	Mk.	Lk.	John
38 "And he that taketh not his cross, and followeth after me, is not worthy of me. **39** "He that findeth his life shall lose it: and he that loseth his life for my sake shall find it. ***Receiving God's servants: smallest deeds will be rewarded*** **40** "He that receiveth you receiveth me, and he that receiveth me receiveth him that sent me. **41** "He that receiveth a prophet in the name of a prophet shall receive a prophet's reward; and he that receiveth a righteous man in the name of a righteous man shall receive a righteous man's reward.**(s)** **42** "And whosoever shall give to drink unto one of these little ones a cup of cold *water* only in the name of a disciple, verily I say unto you, he shall in no wise lose his reward." *(It is clear that the above instructions given by the Savior to the twelve are concluded in Matt. 11:1, below. Technically, Matt. 11:1 should read as Matt. 10:43. For more on this, see footnote t below.)*			

Matt. 11:1**(t)**—*Galilee*	Mk. 6:12-13—*Galilee*	Lk. 9: 6—*Galilee*
He departs for the cities **1** And it came to pass, when Jesus had made an end of commanding his twelve disciples, he departed thence to teach and to preach in their cities.**(u)** (Verse 2 cont. in Section 62.)	***Their obedience*** **12** And they went out, and preached that men should repent. **13** And they cast out many devils, and anointed**(v)** with oil many that were sick, and healed *them.* (Verse 14 cont. in Section 92.)	***Their obedience*** **6** And they departed, and went through the towns, preaching the gospel, and healing every where.**(w)** (Verse 7 cont. in Section 92.)

Footnotes-Commentary

(a) In Section 33, Jesus departed Judea for Galilee. It was noted in Section 34, John 4:4, footnote a, that He passed through Samaria on His return to Galilee. Section 65, Lk. 8:1, footnote d explains who accompanied our Lord on His fifth Galilean tour, which occurred some months *after* the limited commission as given above in this Section. For the hurried return of the twelve apostles from this Jewish only commission, following the murder of John the Baptist, see asterisk under main heading Section 93.

(b) **"Go only to Israel."** As seen in Sections 34 and 35, our Lord and a few of His earlier disciples had previously walked through Samaria and spent several days and nights preaching to the people at the city of Sychar. Now, He forbids His apostles to set foot in this land. Instead, they are to go to Jews, who resided within Galilee. It was to Galilean Jews, that He sent the twelve in this limited commission. The time was now ripe for Israel to become the object of *total* attention and have the opportunity to hear the message and see the miracles of their great Messiah. Paul wrote that the gospel is for the Jew first (Rom. 1:16). This declaration of Paul is valid to the present moment but not with the exclusion of the Gentiles. There can be no doubt that one reason for this missionary effort was a training exercise for the twelve. Gradually, they must learn to face the crowds without the Master's sheltering presence. These men could, at this point, only proclaim, "The kingdom of heaven is at hand" and (to their amazement) perform many miracles and wonders. As of yet, none of them understood the death, burial, and resurrection of their Messiah. This glorious mystery was still veiled. The amazing wonders and miracles they performed signaled to every informed Jew, that the Man in whose Name they were accomplished was *indeed* the Messiah of Israel. When their tour was completed, the entire province of Galilee was (again) shaken into the realization that Israel's Messiah had come; and that these crude men of menial occupations were His valid representatives. The leaders of religion fell into utter dismay as they witnessed innumerable masses following both the twelve and their Master. News of this great stir across Galilee went even into the palace of Herod Antipas who resided at Tiberias, which was part of Galilee.

(c) **"Freely give."** This was a well-known rabbinical expression. Teachers of the Torah Law were to share it as "freely" as God had given it to them. Jewish teachers strictly forbid accepting payment for teaching the Torah Law because it was "freely given" from God to Israel. Therefore, Christ required the same principle of His twelve as they went forth among the nation of Israel teaching the truth of His new kingdom and its new laws. His audience understood what He was saying, being very familiar with this rabbinical rule for teachers.

2p-Jesus' commission abused by radicals. "We can do the things Jesus did!" Certain prime-time TV evangelists preach this commission as given by Christ and assure their listeners, that "we must do as Christ commanded in these passages." Yet, we have never seen one of them "raise the dead," as the twelve were instructed to do. See Section 98, third paragraph of footnote f, for other comments on these imposters. Because a certain miracle or event is recorded in Scripture hardly means that this is our license to do the same. Various descriptions of human experiences are found in Scripture, not as models for imitation, but as illustrations of the doubts, struggles, and needs of the soul. It is sheer foolishness to hold that because Jesus, Paul, or Peter did certain miraculous things, we are thus commissioned to do the same! Here, is the *first* commission recorded in the New Testament that Messiah gave to His apostles, and it was *limited* strictly to the nation of Israel within the province of Galilee. While carrying out these instructions, upon hearing of the murder of John the Baptist, the apostles *suddenly* ended their work. They hurried off to meet Christ at Capernaum and report what had transpired in their work.

(d) **"Scrip."** This was a leather or cloth bag worn about the neck or waist. It carried dried fruits, bread, nuts, and small items. Travelers making long trips carried these food bags. G. M. Mackie records the details of this in the excellent little book *Bible Manners and Customs,* pages 30-31. It is probably similar to the "scrip," mentioned in 1 Sam. 17:40. Another lesson is that professional beggars and heathen priests making their rounds on behalf of various gods and goddesses also used the leather bag; thus, the Lord required his ministers to avoid all appearances of beggars and pagans before those to whom they preach His kingdom message. They were to look and act differently without pretense and obvious show. See footnote e below.

2p-"Staff." There is no contradiction in Mark's words about "taking a staff" (6:8), and Luke's version "take no staves" (Lk. 9:3), or Mark's statement about "taking sandals" (6:9), against Matthew, who wrote, "take no shoes" (Matt. 10:10). What Jesus said here has been translated correctly in order to preserve the clear-cut distinction *among the Jews* between shoes and sandals, staffs and staves. The temple officials were adamant, especially when it pertained to bringing various articles into their sacred house. They wrote, "No one might enter with a staff, shoes on (though he may wear sandals), a scrip, dust on his feet, use course or irreverent language, make worldly gestures, pray with his head uncovered, talk loudly, must worship with feet close together, eyes to the floor, hands upon his breast with the right one higher than the left." For more on these regulations, see the *Biblical, Theological, and Ecclesiastical Cyclopaedia,* vol. x, pages 264-266, by M'Clintock and Strong. Jewish veneration for the temple was astounding. Yet the leaders of religion broke their own rules and hated the Lord Jesus.

(e) **"Two coats."** A single coat reflected a humbler state of life, while two coats suggested over plenty. The orders of John the Baptist were, "He that hath two coats, let him impart to him that hath none" (Lk. 3:11). Christ forbids His preachers to be clothed with double (two) garments. Priests on duty in the vast temple wore only a single garment (which probably included a woolen undershirt) and went barefoot. Is our Lord drawing a lesson from the servants at the earthly temple in Jerusalem and applying it to the servants in His kingdom for the heavenly temple? Such dress would have caught the attention of every pious Jew and would have reflected the low estate of Christ's kingdom servants in comparison to that of the Pharisees dressed in splendor and costly finery. From this difference, the Jews would quickly frame the right judgment of their Messiah and His preachers. True ministers of Jesus Christ are not to reflect worldly pomp or make themselves overly fine. This has become a curse in present day society amid the clamor of healthy wealthy preachers and television evangelists. The lie of "seed faith" teaching has devastated many Christians, especially the poor and untaught. (For example, if you give God in faith a thousand dollars seed, He will give you ten thousand in return!) The lesson here is that the habit and guise of Jesus' men should reflect mild simplicity and genuine humility. Though working under many inconveniences (especially in the winter seasons), the disciples were a blessed lot, joyfully serving their Master and preaching His Word, while keeping their eyes on the angry religious leaders of Israel. Later, the apostles of our Lord fell into quarreling and bickering among themselves over position and power in the misunderstood kingdom of Christ. See this sad story in Section 109, footnote a, and the third paragraph of footnote n, with Section 159, footnote h. Note also all in italics under main heading of Section 169.

2p-"Shoes." These were more for endurance and longer lasting. Shoes were made of soft leather, fastened by a latchet, and sandals of the harder type leather. Some sandals were made with the sole of wood and the upper part of leather. Others were manufactured out of rushes or the bark of palm trees. There was an established difference between shoes and sandals among the Hebrew people, and a wide variety of both types of this footwear were used. Sandals are mentioned twice in Scripture, Mk. 6:9, and Acts 12:8. John Baptist spoke of fastening the latchet of Jesus' shoes in Mk. 1:7.

3p-Verses 9-14. These speak of Hebrew culture. The rabbis had decreed that *no one* must take shoes (not sandals), scrips (food and collection bags), money purses (girdles), and staves (not staffs) into the temple precincts. However, the temple police used staves as both a defensive and offensive weapon and carried these on their person. Every one of Christ's apostles clearly understood this injunction and as pious Jews, followed it to the letter when at the temple. Now, our Lord uses rabbinical language to convey a serious lesson to His twelve evangelists. They must feel as though they were entering into "the temple of their nation" as they went out to preach, heal, and bless. The instruction to preach their message "freely" was another common saying of the rabbis who taught they were freely given the Torah Law and were to share it equally so with all Israel. The twelve have been given the superior message of Christ's new kingdom, and they are to share it with all at no cost. See footnote c above.

(f) It was considered rude and insulting not to continue with the one who had invited you into his house until *he gave permission* for his guests to leave! The author of this work experienced this very custom while preaching in the Holy Land in 1966. We were an hour late for a scheduled meeting because our Arab Christian host would not give the *spoken* permission to leave his home. He was "enjoying the fellowship." Western minds have difficulty with these customs, yet they are to be respected and adhered to by all believers as long as one is not called upon to compromise with clear, known sin.

(g) Showing sincere hospitality by taking in travelers was one of the highest honors in eastern antiquity, especially among the Hebrews. Only the lowest of persons evaded this delightful duty. A rabbi entering a house would chant "Peace be upon this place." This was considered a salute. Christ transfers this *exclusive* rabbinical privilege into the hands of His preachers who carried the true message of peace. A Christian Jew visited our home in Africa on several occasions. Each time upon entering, he would raise a hand and say, "Peace be upon this house!"

(h) Deeply religious Jews when returning to the holy ground of Israel would shake off the dust of pagan soil clinging to their shoes or sandals. In this act, the Hebrews signified their belief in the purity of the soil, which God had given their nation. The Talmud tractate, Sanhedrin 64a speaks of the "dust of idolatry" clinging to a Jew. The obvious meaning was that he must shake it off.

(i) "Sodom and Gomorrha" are the apex of God's judgment on wickedness. The prophets selected these cities as being so evil that they deserved the worst judgment of God for their sin (Isa. 13:19; Jer. 50:40; and Zeph. 2:9). This same thought is found in the New Testament. See Gen. 13:13; Lk. 10:12; 2 Peter 2:6; and Jude 7. The astounding lesson here is that they who reject the messengers of Christ will receive a *harsher judgment* than the corrupt people of Sodom and Gomorrha, who rejected the angelic visitors. There is something frightfully terrible in this teaching of Jesus that lay such stress on the message of eternal life. This message, men often reject, scorn, or tread underfoot. See Section 63, Matt. 11:23-24, footnote c, where Jesus again uses these cities as illustrations.

(j) Only God would send sheep among wolves!

(k) "Serpents and doves." In Hebrew thinking, the serpent was the wisest of all creatures *before the fall* and the dove was the most harmless. This was a common term among the Jews, and everyone knew of what He was speaking. In addition, to them, the dove was the epitome of meekness. Hence, Jesus uses two popular illustrations to bring home His lesson. All the apostles understood Him to be saying, "You must be the *wisest* and *gentlest* of all men as you represent Me and My kingdom." Gentle wisdom and meekness powerfully reflect the likeness of Christ.

2p-Verse 20. "It is not ye that speak." The Holy Spirit would speak through them. He would get the work done! Starting with verse 16 through verse 42, our Lord's instructions to the twelve went further than the limited commission, He had just given in verses 5-15. The scope of verses 16 through 42 somehow in their *totality* reached beyond the personal ministry of the apostles on this occasion. Neither Mark nor Luke wrote Jesus' instructions as recorded by Matthew. The persecutions He warned of did not happen during their Galilean missionary work. Such things as the twelve appearing before "councils" (or the Sanhedrin), being beaten in the synagogues, and brought before (Roman) governors, rulers and so forth occurred at a later time. For explanation of the Sanhedrin, see Section 30, footnote b. There can be no doubt that from verses 16 through 42, Christ projects from the present into the future regarding the work of His apostles. Our Lord's Words are similar to warnings given later regarding conditions prior to A.D. 70. Refer to this in Section 163, at Mk. 13:11 with Lk. 21:14-15. Jesus said in Matt. 10:20 that the Holy Spirit would miraculously assist them in responding to their enemies during these times of future persecution. This did not mean that they were without the Spirit of God at that time (Rom. 8:9). At this point, in the ministry of Christ, John wrote that the Holy Spirit was "not yet given." He was stating that the Spirit had not come in fullness at the time of the events recorded in John 7:37-39. It is to be remembered that John wrote this looking back some years *after* the coming of the Spirit on Pentecost. See Section 10, Lk. 1:41, footnote b, for more on the Person and work of the Holy Spirit during this era.

3p-Jesus' Words in verses 17 through 42 were primarily a forecast of *later* apostolic activity. Verse 23, and the words "till the Son of man be come" are something of a parenthesis spoken in the middle of His message. See footnote l below for explanation of this. The wave of suffering for the apostles and early Christians started in the book of Acts, under the fists of the Jews and continued the rest of their lives. Later, various Roman emperors unleashed satanic fury upon believers in the true and living God, and His Son. We have no systematic record of when and where *all of these things* happened. However, they did occur for Christ forewarned of them in these passages. If God had given us books containing every event in the lives of the apostles and first Christians, we would have thousands to read! What we do have in Scripture is sufficient. It contains what God wants us to know that is trustworthy and reliable. Our incomplete knowledge of these things is God's will, for the time being. The wise man will be content with this and not pry into that which God has not given us. This is not to decry the art of study or researching Bible background, manners, and social customs, language, politics, and so on. Those super Christians, who dogmatically affirm that the Holy Spirit shows them *all truths,* and that they need no outside help, are like the rooster who was confident that he crowed the sun up every morning! Paul requested prayer that he might "be delivered from unreasonable men" (2 Thess. 3:2). God will do for no man what he can do for himself.

(l) **"Till the Son of man be come."** Our Lord *cannot* be referring to His second coming, which now, some two thousand years later, still has not occurred. Three possibilities have been offered to explain this difficult statement:

1. The Master was making reference of His coming to meet the apostles (at Capernaum) after they had finished their work assigned in this limited commission. The asterisk under main heading above explains this meeting. *This is the most sensible explanation of Jesus' teaching.*

2. Some believe that He was speaking of "an invisible coming" during the utter destruction of the temple and Jerusalem, which occurred some forty years later in A.D. 70. This is impossible; for at the time, none of the apostles understood the coming devastation of Jerusalem and their grand temple. At this point, none of them even understood His death on the cross, resurrection, and ascension. The destruction of Jerusalem in A.D. 70 is discussed more fully in Section 163.

3. Some interpret this as the "twelve apostles being resurrected" and somehow becoming the "144,000 Jewish representatives preaching to fellow Jews during a future great tribulation period." This is grievously misinterpreting Holy Scripture. Refer to Section 44, second paragraph of footnote u.

(m) **"Beelzebub."** Being the name of a god of the pagan Ekronites, this was a horrid statement of blasphemy (2 Kings 1:2). Jews were loathed to all idolatry and rightly so. They decreed it was lawful to belittle, ridicule, jeer, and mock all idols (Isa. 30:22). Among the numerous ignominious names bestowed upon the pagan idols, the most common one was "Zebul" meaning "dung or a dunghill." The word eventually came to mean "lord of filth or flies." (This probably had reference to the swarms of flies swarming about the repulsive blood splattered altars of this heathen deity.) The Jews applied the name to Satan as an expression of contempt and aversion. The scribes and Pharisees have now placed this highest verbal slander upon Messiah in their hatred for Him. See Section 66, Matt. 12:24, footnote c, where *again,* the scribes and Pharisee threw this awful accusation at the Savior. All this is compatible with the Talmudic slander that Jesus learned magic as a boy while in Egypt. Refer to Section 6 and second paragraph of footnote d for more on this dreadful thought. Christ is warning His apostles that (in time) they will fare no better than He has at the hands of the Jewish leaders of religion.

(n) **"What ye hear in the ear."** The Lord alludes to two well-known Jewish customs. First, He points to the scribe whispering specific teachings into the ear of the reader of Scripture during the synagogue services. This was the standard practice. Next, the "chazan" or minister of Jewish religion also served as the town crier. In this work, he made important public announcements from the flat top houses of the village or city. After blowing a loud trumpet to get the attention of the people he would then read the proclamation or (as Jesus said) "preach it from the housetops." This is explained in *Manners and Customs of Bible Lands,* by F. H. Wight, pages 32-34. Jesus, is thus referring to these familiar customs; and in so doing, He warns that men cannot hide their sins from God, though they whisper and connive. They will all be revealed in judgment for nothing shall be hidden in that terrible day!

(o) **"Soul and body in gehenna."** In verse 28, Christ speaks of *eternal* damnation and makes a clear distinction between the human body and the soul. He warned His congregation to "fear God" who alone has the power to *eternally* destroy the wicked. Woefully, the fear of God is vanishing from society. The word "destroy" in the verse speaks of "eternal destruction" as recorded by Paul in 2 Thess. 1:9. Never in human history has there been such a lack of the wholesome fear of God among mankind. "Hell" in this passage comes from the word "geenna." This had first reference to the "city dump" on the southern end of Jerusalem outside the walls. In former days, pagans used this site to offer their children to the god Moloch, as heathen priests beat on drums to drown out the screams of the burning infants. Geenna (or gehenna in the marginal reading) was a place of permanent fire, sickening smells, and unbearable stench. Christ used it to illustrate the everlasting *conscious* torment of the damned in the lake of fire (Rev. 20:10 and 15). No annihilation of either the body or the soul is taught in this sobering passage. It reveals the horrible consequences of sin in a place called the "second death." According to Dan. 12:2, the lake of fire is a place of "everlasting contempt." The "first death" is physical. Christ conquered this in His resurrection for those who know Him as personal Lord and Savior (Rev. 1:18). For more on geenna or gehenna, see Section 45, ninth paragraph of footnote f. Refer also to Section 131, footnote f, and Section 190, second paragraph of footnote i for what waits in the after life for the souls of men. Note twenty-one things the Bible says about hell–lake of fire in Section 103, number 8, under footnote g. The general philosophy of today is that hell is a convenient swear word or at the best a joke. After all, "A God of love would never create such a place." Men are quick to speak of love but slow to mention their sin and rebellion against the Lord of heaven. *If there is no eternal suffering of the damned, then Christ died to save us from annihilation! Such proposal is ridiculous.* In the afterlife, the soul is not deprived of thought and perception. It is forever capable of bliss or misery and continues in conscious sensation. How awful the nightmare of dying in sin without the atonement of Jesus Christ to prepare us for eternity.

2p-Heathen philosophies regarding hell. Refer to Section 104, footnote g for brief comments regarding Plato and other heathen Greeks, who spawned so many preposterous philosophies regarding the human soul, hell, and the afterlife. These were inspired by demons to deceive and damn all who embrace them.

(p) Messiah encourages His apostles not to fear by giving them two examples:

1. **Sparrows.** God takes care of the small sparrows. Not one falls without His attention. See Matt. 6:26 for an earlier mention of the fowls of heaven. The rabbis continually pointed to the creatures of nature as a public example of Jehovah's great care over creation. Now, heaven's greatest Rabbi and Teacher did the same and assures the people that when a sparrow falls to the ground "God is with him." What comfort this must have given His apostles, especially in the years to come as they went out and carried the gospel over the known world of that day. Most of them died as martyrs. A million and more sparrows fall every day. God attends the funeral of each one. When we fall in Christian service, no one understands and helps like Jesus. The watchful friend of sparrows is the sure friend of hurting mankind.

2. **Hair count.** In verses 30 and 31, He informs them that God in heaven has counted the number of hairs in each of their heads! What glorious sovereignty and infinite care! In the Talmud, the Jews speak over two hundred times about counting body hair. They understood the meaning of Jesus' teaching.

(q) Verses 32–33. The son of God again calls for unashamed dedication to His cause. Confession and self-denial played a major role in Jewish religion. Now, Christ transfers these truths over into serving in His kingdom. In verse 34, Christ sought to correct a wrong Jewish thought about Messiah. It was held that Messiah would bring peace to the world. He alarmed His apostles by informing them that He had not come to establish world peace. The Jews held that Messiah would bring lasting peace and worldwide tranquility when He came. Note Section 82, footnote d, for explanation of different Jewish time periods in which they believed their Messiah would work. The peace our Lord brings is *only* by the blood of His cross in the salvation of *individual* sinners. At this time, neither the Jews nor the twelve understood this truth. This message would later become their life's theme as they went for every creature. In verse 38, the allusion is to persons sentenced to be crucified. The idea of cross carrying was unthinkable to the Jewish mind. Any man who took a Roman cross over his back was nailed to it down at the end of the road. Like so many things Christ tried to teach His followers, only in time did the right meaning blossom into a reality and daily experience. Messiah's sayings in verse 39 have troubled some. He stated in the form of a maxim, that those who struggle and scheme to have the temporal pleasures of this world and "find" life in them will at death lose all. On the other hand, believers who are willing to forego the pleasures of sin and the wickedness of the world, shall upon death find their souls were fully possessed with eternal life and step into the presence of God their Father and into the everlasting pleasures of heaven (Ps. 116:15).

(r) "Foes in his own household." Our Lord gives this free and general quotation from Micah 7:6. This verse is similar to the quote found in Section 8, Lk. 1:17, which comes from Mal. 4:5-6. The Talmud in tractate, Sota 49b contains almost these exact words. Devout Jews listening to Christ knew what He was saying. However, He, the Messiah, not the Torah Law, was the catalyst. It is a fact of church history that when a man is saved by the blood of Christ, often the members of his household will rise in fierce hostility to oppose him. It is the wickedness of man's heart and *not* the saving gospel that causes the hostility. The sword that divides is the message of Jesus the Messiah. These truths were especially felt in the days of the apostles and early church.

2p-Over the centuries many Jews have, upon hearing the gospel and being saved, instantly become outcasts to their own families. The late Russian Jew and world-renowned evangelist Dr. Hyman Appleman is a classic example of this ugly fact. After being saved, his staunch Hebrew family actually buried a coffin and counted him as a dead man. In many cases, Orthodox Jewish hatred for the Messiah and His salvation is expressed to this day. Many other religions equally hate the claims of Christ. The author of this work knew a Muslim university professor who was saved in Durban, South Africa. The members of his Islamic community became so fierce in their efforts to kill this humble Indian gentleman that he was forced to flee South Africa and go into hiding. Even now Christians are suffering, imprisoned and in many cases being put to death in lands where the religion of radical Islam rules. This religion allows a place in their theology for Jesus Christ but relegates Him lower than Mohammed. They vehemently deny His deity, death on the cross for our sins and resurrection from the dead.

3p-Verse 40. "Receive you and receive Me." What a sweeping and profound warning. Those who do not receive God's *true* ministers, and preachers do not receive either Jesus Christ or God the Father!

(s) In concluding His instructions to the twelve, our Lord then set before them the promise of "reward" for faithful service. Rewards will be given based on the heart's motive of Christian service, and because men were saved and spent their life's little day in the service of God and men. The Jews made much of hospitality to strangers and would receive them with open arms. The rabbis taught that those who did so would be blessed or rewarded like the house of Obed-Edom, because he had taken in the ark of God (1 Chron. 13:14). Paul refers to the rewards for faithful service in Rom. 4:4, and losing them in 1 Cor. 3:11-15.

2p-Verse 42. So infinite is God's observation of our service that "a cup of cold water" given in Jesus' Name shall not be forgotten. The Lord Jesus counts what we do to His children as being done to Himself (Matt. 25:37-40). Riveted in my mind is a picture of "giving the cup of cold water" to one in need. In the mid 1970s, while working in South Africa as a missionary, I drove my wife into uptown Johannesburg to run an errand. It was a blistering hot day in the "concrete city." Parking at the front of the shop, I sat waiting for her with the windows all down, sweltering in the heat. I heard the sound of someone strumming on a guitar. Sitting there on the hot concrete by the entrance into the store was an African with both legs off, playing his tattered instrument—begging. He was also blind! My heart leaped forth in pity. At the same moment, a shining new Mercedes Benz parked in front of me and out stepped a well-dressed and obvious affluent woman in her mid 50s. As she walked by the beggar I thought, "He'll get nothing from her." I sat and watched the pitiful scene. Shortly, this same "rich lady" came out of the store with an umbrella and big ice cream cone in her hand. Leaning out of the window, I saw her kneel beside the beggar, give him the umbrella, and ice cream. She said in broken English, "I give you this in the Name of Jesus Christ my Lord and Savior!" Instantly, I was struck guilty at my wrong judgment of this unknown Christian woman. I had just witnessed the right meaning of Christ's teaching about giving a cup of water in His Name.

(t) This verse belongs to the end of chapter 10 and should not be separated from it. Clearly, Matt. 11:1 has no connection with Matt. 11:2. They speak of entirely different time periods. In 1557, William Whittingham was the first person to put *total* verse divisions in the New Testament. He was a brother-in-law to John Calvin. Others had tried in the past but with little success. The first Bible in English to have both chapter and verse divisions was the Geneva Bible in 1560. In several places, Whittingham, failed to number properly the Scriptures, inadvertently blending totally separate events. This has nothing to do with the trustworthiness or the verbal, plenary inspiration of God's Word. Those who object would do well to remember that in the ancient manuscripts, there are no punctuation marks or numerical characters for verse division. Paul's use of the term "the second Psalm" (Acts 13:33) does not mean that the existing Old Testament books had chapters and verse numbers in the days of David, a thousand years before Christ. The *Author's Introduction* deals with the subject of inspiration and the reliability of our *Authorized Version of the Bible.*

(u) Seemingly, Christ sent the twelve away and then went on an independent missionary endeavor preaching and teaching in the cities across Galilee.

(v) **"Anointed with oil."** The apostles were also engaged in casting out demon spirits. Refer to Section 106, where later they were unable to cast the demon out of a small child. In this Section, see particularly footnote k. The apostle's use of oil in these healings presents no alarm. Jews were familiar with the application of oil throughout their history, especially in the commissioning of their priests and kings. In sending out the twelve, Christ must have instructed them to use oil. This signified, in Jewish thinking, the *approval* of God, and His *blessing.* The crowds watching would have instantly understood this. The oil used here was not a "medicine to heal"; otherwise, there would have been no miracle in the cure. The Jews used various oils (often mixed with wine and herbs) for physical ailments, but here it was not the case. See Section 116, Lk. 10:33-34, footnote k, for an example of oil and wine used as disinfectant. Jewish writings reflect that cures or progressive healings were not always affected by such means. Anointing is mentioned over four hundred times in the Talmud.

2p-In the work of the apostles, those anointed and prayed for were instantly healed by the power of God. In these miracles, the Lord Jesus chose to enjoin the application of oil with divine healing, though the oil itself was powerless. *Usage of oil was a Hebrew custom and understood by all.* Many years later, Jewish believers among the twelve tribes scattered abroad continued to practice the use of anointing oil when praying for the sick (James 5:14-15). This text is explicit that it is "the prayer of faith" that saves (heals) the sick. The oil had nothing to do with healing. Though the Greek word used here also had reference to "rubbing" in the sense of applying medication, it is wrong to explain away these verses in James and Mark by faulty exegesis. *Whatever* happened in those early miracles of healing, everyone watching knew that God was doing wonderful things, *not* the oil.

(w) **"Every where."** This means what it says. The ministry of these men touched the entire country. The twelve being sent out two by two. Who went with Judas Iscariot the arch-traitor (Mk. 6:7)? Regarding Judas' ability to perform miracles, see Section 47, footnote j, with Section 95, footnote x. The absurdity of Judas being the future Antichrist is discussed in Section 178, John 17:14, footnote m. For other verses that mention Judas Iscariot, refer to Section 57, number 12 in the block of apostles' names near the end of the footnotes.

Returning to Capernaum, He heals the servant of a Roman army officer.* This man's faith in Christ foreshadowed millions of Gentiles, who would believe. Here, is the second recorded case of Christ healing without being present.**

*If by the word "faith" (Matt. 8:10), it is meant that this Roman soldier was saved, then here we have the first Scriptural record of a Gentile heathen being converted to the Messiah. This man was the earliest fulfillment of the prophecy quoted in Section 38, Matt. 4:15-16. He became the "first fruits" of what would follow when millions of Gentiles would trust Jesus Christ the Son of God as their personal Lord and Savior. Was he the first "wild branch" grafted into the "good olive tree of Israel" during the earthly ministry of Christ? Paul wrote about this grafting many years later in Rom. 11:17-24. The prophet Isaiah foretold of the conversion of Gentiles some seven hundred years prior in Isa. 11:1, 10. This is quoted in Section 55, Matthew 12:21, where other Gentiles were coming to Christ. However, no specific cases are so uniquely singled out like the Roman soldier above. Almost thirty years later, Paul cites this same Isaiah text in Rom. 15:12, and he applies it to the Gentile converts of his missionary ministry. **See footnotes i and j below for another example of the Savior healing without being physically present.

Capernaum

Matt. 8:5-9	Mk.	Lk. 7:1-8	John
Jesus hears of the sick servant **5** And when Jesus was entered into Capernaum, there came[(a)] unto him a centurion, beseeching him, **6** And saying, "Lord, my servant lieth at home sick of the palsy, [paralysis] grievously tormented."[(b)]		***Jesus hears of the sick servant*** **1** Now when he had ended all his sayings in the audience of the people, he entered into Capernaum. **2** And a certain centurion's servant, who was dear unto him, was sick, and ready to die.[(b)] **3** And when he[(c)] heard of Jesus, he sent unto him the elders[(d)] of the Jews, beseeching him that he would come and heal his servant. **4** And when they came to Jesus, they besought him instantly, saying, That he was worthy for whom he should do this: **5** "For he loveth our nation, [Israel] and he hath built us a synagogue."	
7 And Jesus saith unto him, "I will come and heal him."			
The Gentile soldier's humility **8** The centurion answered and said, "Lord, I am not worthy that thou shouldest come under my roof:[(e)] but speak the word only, and my servant shall be healed.[(f)] **9** "For I am a man under authority, having soldiers under me: and I say to this *man*, 'Go,' and he		***The Gentile soldier's humility*** **6** Then Jesus went with them. And when he was now not far from the house, the centurion sent friends to him, saying unto him, "Lord, trouble not thyself: for I am not worthy that thou shouldst enter under my roof:[(e)] **7** "Wherefore neither thought I myself worthy to come unto thee: but say in a word, and my servant shall be healed.[(f)] **8** "For I also am a man set under authority, having under me soldiers, and I say unto one, 'Go,' and he	

Matt. 8:9-13	Mk.	Lk. 7:8-10	John
goeth; and to another, 'Come,' and he cometh; and to my servant, 'Do this,' and he doeth *it*."		goeth; and to another, 'Come,' and he cometh; and to my servant, 'Do this,' and he doeth *it*."	
A faith greater than any Jew had **10** When Jesus heard *it*, he marveled, and said to them that followed,[g] "Verily I say unto you, I have not found so great faith,◄ no, not in Israel.[h]		***A faith greater than any Jew had*** **9** When Jesus heard these things, he marveled at him, and turned him about, and said unto the people that followed him,[g] "I say unto you, I have not found so great faith,◄ no, not in Israel."[h]	
Many Gentiles saved before Jews **11** "And I say unto you, [Jews] That many [Gentiles] shall come from the east and west, and shall sit down with Abraham, and Isaac, and Jacob, in the kingdom of heaven.			
Jews without Christ are doomed **12** "But the children of the kingdom [Jews] shall be cast out into outer darkness: there shall be weeping and gnashing of teeth."			
The officer believes **13** And Jesus said unto the[i] centurion, "Go thy way; and as thou hast believed, *so* be it done unto thee." And his servant was healed in the selfsame hour.[j] (Verse 14 cont. in Section 41.)		**10** And they that were sent, returning to the house, found the servant whole that had been[k] sick. (Verse 11 cont. in Section 61.)	

►**"So great faith in Israel."** The Savior takes occasion from the faith of the Roman soldier to inform His *Jewish audience* that this man's conversion will not be a solitary thing; many Gentiles would be saved and brought into His new kingdom, while the Jews to whom it first belonged would be cast out. This was because they had rejected Him. Above in Matt. 8:11-12, the blessings of heaven shared by saved Gentiles are described under the similitude of a great banquet, which was in eastern society their way of expressing joy and fellowship. See Lk. 14:7-11 and Lk. 22:30, for other examples. At these banquets, it was the highest honor to sit with distinguished men of renown. They were stunned to hear that Gentiles would be in His new kingdom and most Jews cast into hell. For more on this, see second and third paragraphs under footnote h below. A few days before His death, the Lord Jesus gave the Jews a solemn parable in which He spoke of the kingdom being taken from them and given to the Gentiles. Refer to this in Section 153, Matt. 21:33-46. See especially verse 45, footnote m where it reads that the Jews knew exactly what He was saying and became angered. To this very moment, God's kingdom is still in the hands of saved Gentile believers scattered over the face of the earth. Every Hebrew who has trusted Messiah-Christ as his Savior is also part of this spiritual kingdom. Within its blessed number are neither Jew nor Greek, bond or free. All are one in Jesus the Savior (Gal. 3:28). For extended comments on the Jewish rejection of their Messiah, and how this was predicted in their Old Testament, see Section 74.

Footnotes-Commentary

(a) **The centurion or the elders?** Matthew wrote that the centurion came to Jesus in person. However, Luke wrote that the elders of the Jews came to the Savior. This diversity is explained once we understand the custom of that day: what one did through the actions of another was counted as though he did it himself. In like manner, Jesus is said to baptize; though, in fact, He did not (John 4:1-2). Pilate is said to have scourged Jesus, though a soldier was assigned to do the whipping (John 19:1). Both Matthew and Luke wrote according to the social traditions of their day, and their original readers understood. They were inspired to present *both* sides of the custom. We note, according to Matt. 8:13, the centurion came to Christ. According to Lk. 7:3, a second party called "the elders" representing the soldier also approached the Savior, probably arriving just ahead of the distraught officer. Refer to footnote d below for more on these elders. From the flow of the story, one gathers that it was both who came to Jesus, one on the heels of the other due to the urgency of the slave's critical sickness.

2p-Both Matthew and Luke give the rank of this man as a "centurion." In the Roman military structure, he would (normally) be in command of one hundred men, hence our word "century." See footnote c below for more on this subject.

(b) Whatever type of palsy or stroke the servant had, he was at the point of death, suffering excruciating pain. It touches us deeply that such a bond of caring love existed between this high-ranking officer and one of his slaves. A centurion was the equivalent to the rank of captain by today's standards. What a lesson for the employer and employee relationships in today's cutthroat corporate world of big business, especially the "Christian business" sector.

(c) "He" has reference to a Roman military officer. He held the command of usually a hundred men. This could vary according to emergencies that arose. A centurion carried a staff made of vinewood as a badge of his office. There were at least three different levels of rank among these men. Because Judaea was a Roman province, many garrisons of men were stationed there as well as in other strategic locations over the land of Israel. They were something of a peacekeeping force. See *The Roman Soldier,* by G. R. Watson, and *Greece and Rome at War,* by Peter Connolly. These two works give intricate details of life in the Roman military from enlistment to retirement. Watson's book has twenty-six interesting illustrations so that the student may see much of what he is reading.

2p-This soldier was a Gentile stationed at Capernaum. Like every person across the city and country, he too had heard of Christ. Word of His miraculous works had spread everywhere. Even within the Roman military barracks, hard-bitten men spoke of the great and wonderful Person, who loved all people and helped them.

3p-Earlier John the Baptist had preached to the military present in his audience and warned them to repent of their sins and produce the fruits of *genuine* repentance before requesting baptism. See all of Section 21, Part 3, footnote l for details on John's requirements before he witnessed their baptism. Now, the Messiah of Israel reaches out to the hated Gentiles and gives an illustration declaring the conversion of millions of Gentiles to the damnation of the unbelieving Jews. The Pharisees saw to it that everyone knew that Jesus had spent several days in the unclean Samaritan village of Sychar. His visit there is found in Section 36, John 4:43-44, footnote a. Yet in this critical situation, the rulers of the synagogue approached Christ pleading for help. The Master lovingly receives their requests. See footnote d below. The prediction of Matt. 4:15-16 was being fulfilled as eternal light was now shining across Galilee into Gentile hearts. How marvelous that it found home so early in the soul of a Roman army officer.

(d) "The elders." Here is an amazing thing: a pagan had such amiable relations with the local Jews, that he sent some of their "elders" to Jesus to represent his cause. On the other hand, was he any longer a pagan? *Some believe he was a proselyte to the Hebrew religion, which would explain why the Jews were eager to help him.* Normally, only fierce hatred existed between the Hebrews and their Gentile oppressors. "Elders" has reference to either the local Jewish magistrates or leaders within a synagogue that often held the same office. Their grounds for presenting proof to Jesus that this centurion was worthy were that he "loved their nation" and "he hath built for us a synagogue." Whoever this soldier was, he had the money and joyfully laid it out for the high costs of such a noble project at his own expense. Years later, another centurion turned from the worship of pagan gods and sought the true Lord of heaven (Acts 10). According to Matt. 8:5, all this occurred at the entrance (gates) to the city of Capernaum. Our Lord had already clashed with the religious leaders of that city and its synagogue. See Section 40 for a terrible battle in this house of worship over the healing of a demon-possessed man during a Sabbath service. Now, on behalf of the soldier, the Jews come asking a favor of the man they hated so fiercely, and He graciously complied! Later, the meek and lowly Jesus placed a curse upon this vast city. Note this in Section 63, Matt. 11:23, footnote b, where He compared Capernaum with wicked Sodom. His conclusion: Capernaum was greater in wickedness than Sodom- that infamous Old Testament city that God destroyed by fire and brimstone (Gen. 19).

(e) Upon hearing that this marvelous Man would actually come into his house to heal the beloved servant, the Roman officer was overwhelmed by a deep sense of personal unworthiness. He had a rare case of genuine humility! Being a Gentile and knowing the feelings of the Jews toward his people, he may also have been afraid to ask the greatest of all Jews into his home. His plea of being a man with powerful authority over others was neither pride nor false humility. Every soldier knew how to exert authority or how to bow before others who wielded it from a higher rank. Roman soldiers were the most disciplined men of any known military of that era. See his rank in footnote b above.

(f) "But speak the word only, and my servant shall be healed." What a demonstration of childlike trust in the power of the spoken Words of Christ. However, how did he know this? Had he heard Christ speak Words of healing power on some prior occasion? Had he heard about Jesus healing the nobleman's son while He was visiting in Cana, even though the lad was miles away at Capernaum? He begs the Messiah to "speak the word only," and his beloved servant and friend will be healed. His confidence in the Word's of Christ was total and absolute. He was a genuine believer in the Son of God, while most of the Jews standing there had rejected Him in their wicked unbelief.

(g) **"He marveled."** Jesus revealed His moral joy because the military commander had believed in Him with all his heart, while His own people rejected Him. Though Christ knew the officer's faith before the foundation of the world, when it actually happened, His divine pleasure was reflected through His humanity. Heb. 12: 2 spoke of the "joy that was set before Christ" in bringing men to Himself by the cross. We read of the Savior marveling because of the unbelief of the Jews in His hometown of Nazareth. Refer to Section 91, footnote g for this event. On this occasion, He was humanly amazed at their wicked unbelief and rejection of their Messiah.

2p-Thousands followed the Messiah and many of them witnessed this encounter with the soldier. Luke is careful to write that upon hearing the centurion's sincere request, Jesus turned His attention from the officer and spoke to the Jews, who followed him. In the hearing of these people Christ said, He had "not found so great faith," not even among His own Hebrew people. What a profound statement in view of the thousands of Jews who had trusted Christ up to this point. *Now, a heathen Gentile had shown the greatest faith of all.* In addition, this Gentile was a cursed Roman soldier! Within military life today, one still finds those saved by God's grace who are faithful servants of Christ Jesus.

(h) Taking (as it were) His cue from the faith of the Gentile soldier, Christ used this to remind His Hebrew audience, that, unless they too, trust Him through simple faith, they will be shut out of His kingdom in its *final* consummation. (For a description of the Jewish understanding of various ages and time periods, see Section 82, footnote d.) Here, our Lord used well-known Jewish terminology when He spoke of a future banquet in God's kingdom. The rabbis taught that only all circumcised Hebrews, the children of Abraham, who kept the Torah and oral law, would enjoy the kingdom. Christ gives it new meaning by affirming that it is faith, as just demonstrated by the Roman soldier, that will bring men into His kingdom. In eastern gatherings, guests were seated at banquets according to rank. Table fellowship signified intimacy; thus, to be seated beside the great patriarchs of Israel, Abraham, Isaac, and Jacob, was counted the highest honor. However, Christ had just given a new twist to this belief, one that shocked them! They must believe in Him as the Messiah-Savior or be shut out of the kingdom of God.

2p-Verse 11. **"Sit down with Abraham."** Every deeply religious Jew firmly believed that it was a sin of the highest order to sit at the same table with a Gentile, and that the Jews alone were the rightful heirs to God's kingdom. Those unfamiliar with ancient rabbinical teachings have taken many extremes from the Words of Jesus in Matt. 8:11. Some hold it has reference to a literal, physical banquet of drink and food at the end of a particular age yet to come. Other expositors carry it over into a millennium of good times, sort of a "thousand years' party for God's children." Later, Christ made other comments about similar things in Lk. 13:28-29; and Section 139, Matt. 19:28, number 2 under footnote m. *Ultra* dispensationalists have attached many wild interpretations to these Words of Christ, claiming all sorts of fantastic things for themselves in the eternal and perfect rule of Christ on earth. Despite their sensational exegesis, one thing is sure: in the context of these passages, Jesus sternly informed *all Jews present* that, unless they trusted Him by faith (as the soldier had done), they would be shut out of God's bliss and cast into the fires of the damned. Messiah's statement, "the children of the kingdom shall be shut out," and the expression "weeping and gnashing of teeth" contextually had direct reference to the Jews, who, had rejected Him as their Messiah. Every circumcised, Torah abiding Jew referred to himself as "a child of the kingdom" who had been "born of water." This latter expression meant that he was a true Hebrew of pure descent in Israel. See Section 30, footnote f for an explanation of this term. For extended comments on "eating and drinking" in eternity, see Section 169, first and second paragraphs below footnote f.

3p-Verse 12. **"Outer darkness of hell's eternity"** is set in contrast to the "inner darkness" of earth's night. It is found in Matthew's book in the following places: Matt. 13:42, 50; 22:13; 25:30, 41. The people got the message, for their rabbis often spoke of the outer "darkness of gehenna." This is mentioned in the Talmud tractate, Chullin 133b. Gehenna fire was reserved for Gentiles and all non-Jews. Again, the carpenter from Galilee, claiming to be Israel's Messiah, shatters their false beliefs. For twenty-one things the Bible says about suffering in hell-lake of fire, see Section 103, number 8, under footnote g. Only cults could interpret these august words as having reference to the grave. For the *original* meaning of "outer darkness" see Section 165, footnote n. It did not always refer to the torments of the damned. This meaning gradually evolved in Hebrew eschatology.

4p-**"East and west."** This term was well known among the Jews as having reference to the Gentile nations of the world and faraway places. It is found in the Talmud some twenty-two times. Several examples are tractates, Eiruvin 38a with Sotah 34a. In using this expression, Jesus was referring to the millions of Gentiles, who would be saved over the coming millennia of church history and would share the eternal blessedness of God's presence forever. The staunch Jews in His audience were both amazed and angered at His teaching.

5p-To their utter confoundment, Christ informs them that at the end of the age, Gentiles from "east and west" will be the majority guests at that great celebration in heaven that is in comparison to a banquet. However, the rightful heirs, the Jews ("children of the kingdom") will be cast into hell. Later, Paul wrote that the (Jewish) branches are broken off, and the Gentiles are grafted into God's olive tree. It was because of "unbelief" that the Jews were broken off (Rom. 11:19-20). The rabbis spoke of the wicked in hell as gnashing teeth in agony and torment in the Talmud tractate, Sanhedrin 105a. It is also mentioned in Ps. 112:10. Ironically, Christ picks up these rabbinical expressions and transfers the fate of devils and evil men onto all those of Israel, who will not receive Him as the Gentile soldier had done. One can imagine the raging fury of the religious leaders in the crowds following Jesus as they heard Him speak these Words.

(i) **Distance healing.** Having now finished with His digression in addressing the Jews present (footnote h above), Christ turns His attention back to the waiting military commander. Jesus did not say that his request was answered according to this man's prayer, his righteousness or the intercession of the Jewish elders; but simply "as thou hast believed, so be it done unto thee." What rejoicing must have filled the house of that centurion when his dear servant rose from the bed of anguish "in the selfsame hour" and announced that he was whole. Here, we have a classic case of "long distance" healing without the bodily presence of the Lord Jesus being there. As with every miracle performed by the Messiah, the city of Capernaum was again shaken at such astounding news. Months before, thousands had flocked to Peter's house as the entire city had been moved over the ministry and miracles of Christ. Refer to Section 41, footnote d, for this great awaking in Capernaum.

2p-What did the fellow soldiers under the command of this officer think when he shared with them this amazing story? Both the centurion and his servant undoubtedly related this news to strangers, neighbors, friends, family members, and even their grandchildren in years to come: like the household of the nobleman (several weeks prior to this miracle), whose son was also healed from the point of death, joy reigned supreme. We wonder if every person within the Roman soldier's house came to believe in Christ as he had. Could we not say he was now a true Israelite, one whose circumcision was in the heart and not the flesh (Phil. 3:3)? The Jewish authorities from the synagogue sent their men to appeal before Christ for the healing of the servant. As they walked back to the soldier's house, somehow, in their hearts did they also know that the dying slave would be healed?

(j) **The second case of distance healing in the New Testament.** For the first recorded event of this nature (healing without Jesus being physically present), see Section 37, John 4:46 and 52, footnote f. There stood the previously ill servant watching for his master's return. No doubt, he ran to meet them waving his hands and shouting praises to God. Smiling, dancing, clapping, and rejoicing, as all slaves did when blessed with some good fortune! He was well from head to toe; the killing paralysis had vanished. Everyone in that band of Jews who went and appealed to Jesus had only praises for that good Man, who claimed to be their Messiah. How many of them immediately believed on Him? Surely, they had told the servant about Jesus before going out to seek Him. Perhaps he already knew. Talk of this miracle spread over the whole land, and it is easy to believe that the officer shared it with every man under his command.

2p-Capernaum rocked again with the stories of "Jesus of Nazareth, the carpenter's Son," who claimed to be Israel's Messiah. He had healed the slave of a Roman army officer and officials from a local synagogue helped make it possible. The wonder of it all (just like the nobleman's son who was healed, Section 37), was the absence of Jesus at the house when the sick man was cured. Distance does not hinder God or His Son, since they created it as part of this life and human experience. There is no distance or time in eternity! It is a togetherness that lasts forever, whether in heaven or hell, and is beyond the comprehension of mortal mind. All events, past, present, and future are known to Him because the extent of His knowledge is unlimited. He knows all things possible and all things actual, though He is not necessarily the author of all things. Because something happens does not always signify that God caused it. Man has a free will and can choose to do or not do. When the Word of God and the Holy Spirit have enlightened man's will, he may exercise it to do right or wrong. The Lord sees all things present but not as men do, and He remembers the past differently from the way human memory does. Because He is God, He chooses to blot from His infinite memory all the sins of those who trust Jesus Christ as Lord and Savior (Heb. 8:12 and 10:17-18). The newborn heresy floating about churches that "God cannot know something until it happens" is another doctrine of demons (1 Tim. 4:1). The rise of these new heresies is a call for believers to rise up, take their places, and stand against further "high sounding, philosophical lies" as they continually seek to invade the domain of God's people causing division and confusion. We have been warned to never "give place to the devil" (Eph. 4:27), and, "Be not carried about with divers and strange doctrines" (Heb. 13:9). Paul instructed Titus on the island of Crete continually to be "Holding fast the faithful word as he hath been taught, that he may be able by sound doctrine both to exhort and to convince the gainsayers" (1:9). If men in willful stubbornness refuse the rightly divided truth of Holy Scripture, they should be told to leave the local assembly and go elsewhere with their heretical prattle.

(k) **He left him sick and returned home to find him whole.** The Roman solider simply believed Jesus' statement of hope. The Son of God alone rescues men from the steel-like grip of all false religions, self-deceit, misplaced affections, arrogant ambitions, and the mad pursuits that drive them into wasted lives, and at last a home in hell. As with Israel of old God pled, "O Israel, thou hast destroyed thyself, but in me *is* thine help" (Hosea 13:9). Wisdom, personified as a loving mother calling out to humankind in the streets of life, "How long, ye simple ones, will ye love simplicity? and the scorners delight in their scorning, and fools hate knowledge?" (Prov. 1:22.). Mature, thinking Christians also enquire, *Yes, how long?*

The Lord Jesus stops a funeral procession. The former dead man is sent home! The people are shocked into holy fear. This is the first recorded case of Messiah raising someone from the dead.*

The similarity between Elijah raising the widow's son, some seven hundred years prior (1 Kings 17:17-24), and this event must not be overlooked. Zarephath, where Elijah's miracle took place, was about thirty miles northeast on the sea-coast between Tyre and Sidon. See footnote f below. Earlier, while preaching in His hometown synagogue at Nazareth, Christ mentioned this very miracle and His application of it infuriated the Jews so greatly that they attempted to kill Him (Section 38, second paragraph of footnote k). There are only three recorded cases in Scripture of Jesus raising the dead. Below is the first one. For the second, see the asterisk under main heading of Section 89. For the third, see Section 124, second paragraph of footnote w. This third miracle incurred the wrath of the Sanhedrin for it demonstrated again that He was the true Messiah of Israel, the Son of God.

Matt.	Mk.	Lk. 7:11-18—At Nain in Galilee near Mt. Tabor	John
		Jesus meets a massive funeral procession	
		11 And it came to pass the day after,[a] that he went into a city called Na-in; and many of his disciples went with him, and much people.	
		12 Now when he came nigh to the gate of the city, behold, there was a dead[b] man carried out, the only son of his mother, and she was a widow: and much people of the city was with her.	
		Moved with compassion He calls the dead back to life	
		13 And when the Lord saw her, he had compassion[c] on her, and said unto her, "Weep not."	
		14 And he came and touched the bier: [platform] and they that bare *him* stood still. And he said,[d] "Young man, I say unto thee, Arise."	
		15 And he that was dead sat up, and began to speak.[e] And he delivered him to his mother.	
		Word of this miracle shook the countryside	
		16 And there came a fear on all: and they glorified God, saying, "That a great prophet is risen up among us;" and, "That God hath visited his people."	
		17 And this rumour of him went forth throughout all Judaea, and through-out all the region round about.[f]	
		18 And the disciples of John shewed him of all these things.[g] (Verse 19 cont. in Section 62.)	

Footnotes-Commentary

[a] Yesterday, the Gentile centurion's servant was healed. Rising early the following morning, Christ, accompanied by even a larger group of people and disciples, walks some twelve miles down into the southeast portion of Galilee. At the entrance into the beautiful city of Nain, He meets a Jewish mother whose heart is weighted down with overmuch sorrow. Her *only* son, cut off in the flower of his life has died. Being a "widow," she had tasted from this bitter cup before. Just as (the supposed) rabbinical defilement of contact with a heathen soldier did not attach itself to the Messiah of Israel, nor could His intrusion into the realm of the dead. Just outside that city, the Lord of life will tear open the gates of death and command the captive's release. Those among the crowds who had precipitately attached themselves to follow Christ were in for the biggest shock of their lives! Here is the *first* Scriptural account of Christ raising the dead. See asterisk under main heading above for other resurrections performed by the Messiah. There were surely hundreds of cases that are not recorded in Scripture (John 20:30-31). *It should be remembered that the four gospels briefly record only about one-fourth of the life of Christ!* The glorious rest of the story has never been written.

[b] **When death came to town. Preparing the body.** With the well-known blast from a ram's horn at the hand of a rabbi, the citizens of any city or town in Israel were informed that someone had died behind their walls. At death, all Jews except the Sadducees believed the soul departed from the body. The family, kindred, and friends grieved for seven days. This was to emulate Joseph, who lamented the decease of his father for the same period (Gen. 37:34). At death, all water was thrown into the street to show that someone had died in that house. Some held that this act was in memory of the prophetess Miriam, of whom it is written that when she died, Israel had no more

water (Num. 20:1-2). The face of the deceased was covered. A thumb was bent inward and tied into the palm with threads from the prayer shawl. When thus folded, three of the fingers formed a schin-ש, the twenty-first letter of the Hebrew alphabet. This figure suggested the word "Shaddai" which was one of God's Names. Because the hands of the dead relax and open, the ancients believe this signaled that they could carry nothing out of the world. A baby is born with both fists clenched. This indicated that God had given him all good things to enjoy; they were held in his tiny hands! The corpse, with hair and nails cut, would be laid upon the ground, washed with warm water, wrapped in strips of cloth, and a white linen gown both depending upon the financial state of the family. The more pious of Israel wore these linen gowns on the Day of Atonement. The head of the deceased was covered with a mixture of eggs and wine, which served as a perfume. Then, the body was anointed with various burial spices. The mother would sit on the floor and not eat nor drink. When she did, it must always be with her back to the dead. A flute was provided for her to be blown in somber, mournful tones at the burial site. Neighbors came to offer words of condolence and consolation and do deeds of kindness. If money was available, professional mourners were hired to make dreadful noises with their voices and weird sounding instruments. Refer to Section 89, Mk. 5:38, footnote o for an explanation of this custom and how the Lord Jesus handled them.

2p-Jewish burial customs. When being removed from the house for burial, someone would throw in its direction an earthen vessel and shatter it. This meant that all sadness and sorrow would be removed from the house of the deceased. Bodies were carried on large open platforms made of various materials, especially wicker; face upward with hands folded over the chest. Friends and neighbors all sought to share in carrying out the body, swapping places, and frequently relieving each other along the way to the burial site. Each participant must walk barefooted as a sign of sorrow. People customarily stopped whatever they were doing and out of courtesy would join in the funeral procession. At each stop to change pallbearers, someone would speak a verbal eulogy on behalf of the dead. All such actions were looked upon by the Jews as merits unto eternal life. The Jews would not bury their dead within the walls of a city in Israel, but carried the corpse a specified distance away. This was to prevent defilement. The rabbis had ruled that since by a woman death came into the world, it was fitting that a woman should lead each funeral to the burial site. For more on the burdens carried by Jewish women through life and even to death, see Section 16, footnote b. Hence, this mother led the procession for her son. Before interment, the body was placed near the open grave, and family members would circle it seven times chanting long prayers. The closest friend would throw dirt upon the grave site. Returning home, all would pull pieces of grass throwing these backward to indicate they believed in the resurrection to come. A lamp burned from three to seven days in the home for the ancient Jews believed that the soul tried to re-enter the body for three days after its departure. See Section 124, second paragraph of footnote w for more on this curious belief. It was held that the Angel of Death came and sat on the grave seeking to claim the returning soul of the deceased. He was warded off by numerous rituals, incantations, and prayers. Oddly, the rabbis taught that Jews, who died in foreign lands, had to roll underground to reach the beloved land of Israel. Those who did not participate in the "rolling" could not be in the final resurrection of the dead. All of these were simply more rabbinical exaggerations and fables.

3p- So close, yet so far. Some years ago, I was flying from San Antonio, Texas, to Louisville, Kentucky. My seat placement was beside a Hebrew rabbi from New York. We fell into conversation about various topics. When he inquired of my occupation, the door was open for witness. I explained that I was a born again Christian and had spent my life serving as a foreign missionary. We talked about Josephus, the plights of the great Jewish people, and then his Old Testament or Tanakh. I asked him why Jews did not believe the New Testament, which confirms that Jesus is the Messiah of the Old. He looked at me and said, "O, surely you know that the New Testament documents are not reliable." I responded, "What would it mean for men like you if they are reliable." His wife Ruth was listening to our conversation. She answered, "That would mean that we are so close, yet so far from our Messiah." This is the sad plight of millions sitting in church buildings, synagogues, and places of worship, but lost in the deceitfulness of sin without the saving knowledge of Jesus Christ. Millions of religious people have been taught to trust rituals, ceremonies, deeds, good works, creeds, men, confessionals and more. However, the major thrust of the entire Bible is that we are saved from our sin, made children of God, by simple faith in what Jesus did on the cross and in His resurrection. Reader, in what do you trust? Flee all things and cling to the cross of Christ for only there all of your sins were atoned for to the satisfaction of God. Abandon the woeful company of those who are "so close, yet so far." It is written, "But now in Christ Jesus ye who sometimes were far off are made nigh [near] by the blood of Christ' (Eph. 2:13).

(c) **"Had compassion on her."** What a beautiful thing. Our wonderful Savior was touched by pity and sympathy over the sorrows of one whom He had never met. We saw Him earlier moved by compassion on the unsaved crowds in Section 56, Matt. 9:36, footnote c. Stepping close to the wicker carrier, the Messiah reached out and did the unthinkable. He touched it! The pallbearers stopped in their tracks. Everyone was horrified: that signaled He was now defiled by the work of death, which was considered the severest form of all ritual impurity in Israel. The Torah Law deemed all unclean who touched the realm of the dead (Num. 5:2-3). Christ raised His hand, the standard signal to the pallbearers that He desired to speak a word. To the absolute shock of all present, He turns and addresses the dead man! Never had a funeral like this been seen or heard of in the history of Israel. (Earlier He had placed his fingers upon an unclean leper in Section 48, Matt. 8:3, footnote c.)

(d) **"Young man, I say unto thee, Arise."** He touched the forbidden domain of death, and then spoke to the corpse! See footnote c above. Messiah's clear, pungent command rumbled like thunder over those standing about the scene. Everyone heard Him. "Now, He talks to the dead!" one must have muttered. Stunned, the crowds reeled under the shock of the whole scene. None of them knew, that veiled behind the flesh of that humble preacher from Galilee was the very God of heaven and earth. Death met its match, yielded its prey, and backed off at His beckoned command. See another case of Christ touching the dead in Section 89, Matt. 9:25, footnote r.

2p-Eternity and the real person. The deceit of this world exerts itself even to the grave! In the funerals of unsaved men, Satan works madly to conceal what sin is, and what its final consequences are. See the corpse looking so well dressed, the kindness of the funeral attendants, and the (fading) flowers with their pleasant aromas: what vain empty pomp one observes on these occasions. Sin clocks in for overtime to conceal the vanity and wretchedness of life's end for those without Christ. The costly adornments and bright colors, the artificial palls, scarves, cloaks, burning candles, kingly caskets, and the kind (but so often lying) words of the "good minister of religion" over one who has perished in sin are for naught. Alas! When sin and pride are the pallbearers to the sinner's grave, most bystanders and curious observers are hoodwinked as to what the deceased now feels, thinks, and experiences, forever! The real person is not terminated in the form of a rotting corpse; rather, he or she is a soul departed from its house and this world, now permanently fixed in eternity. See the true story of one who died damned and his plight in eternity as given by the Lord Jesus in Section 131. Other comments on these serious things are recorded in Section 65, the second paragraph of footnote h. According to the skeptics all this is "scare talk" designed to frighten people into religion. Someone remarked, "It is better to be scared into heaven than educated into hell." *Of course, both are ruinously wrong.*

(e) **The dead man is now alive!** Falling back in a terrified shudder, the people gripped in awe were stunned as they saw the dead man rising up from the bier. *He was no longer dead!* He is alive and begins to talk. *(What did he say?)* This was a great for mortal eyes. That broken, weeping widow, now twice tied to death's whipping post, reached out to her dear son as he stepped off the death cart. That wonderful Man, Jesus of Nazareth, had (again) turned the "shadow of death into light" (Amos 5:8). Surely at this point, the poor pallbearers were thoroughly confounded, as they no longer had a corpse to carry. Who could describe the explosion of joy mingled with fear that shook the bewildered crowds? Someone was deputized to run ahead to the burial site and inform the waiting attendants, "The funeral is off for the dead man is now alive!" Glorious confusion prevailed that day and for months that followed in the city of Nain. One can imagine the hundreds that tramped their way to the widow's door over the upcoming weeks, and after a soft but embarrassing knock, requested to "see" her son! What were public reactions when he, the former dead man walked *again* the familiar streets of his city? Without hesitation, we know the topic of all conversations for months was "Jesus of Nazareth had raised the widow's son. He must be the Messiah of Israel." The text is clear "all Judea" and the region round about heard this marvelous story. Meanwhile, the scribes and Pharisees smoldered in confused rage at the news.

2p-Satanic cults that deny the separation of the soul from the physical body at death are quick to put their infamous question, "Where was his soul while his body was on the cart?" The answer to their chicanery will always remain the same, "It was where God wanted it to be." The (*very*) late Joseph Smith, Brigham Young, Ellen G. White, and Charles Taze Russell could not handle that one. They and their false religious organizations blatantly deny the fact of body, soul, and spirit constituting the human man and all his posterity. They deny that there is a separation of the soul from the body at physical death. Unconsciousness of the *entire* man at death, soul sleep, and annihilation are lies with which the Devil has rocked millions into hell. See the second paragraph of footnote d above for more on this awful subject, along with Section 59, Matt. 10:28, footnote o. For Lazarus and the rich man refer to all of Section 131, especially footnote d.

(f) A reverential sense of divine Presence and holy awe swept over that scene and region. Some wept, some shouted, children cried out of confusion, and others burst out with unbridled praises to the God of heaven for such a miracle. Among the rejoicing multitudes were those who declared, "A great prophet has risen" among the Jewish people. No doubt, some of them remembered that Elijah, the greatest of the Old Testament prophets, had raised the widow's son hundreds of years before near this area. See comments by the asterisk under main heading above. In 1 Kings 17:23, it is written that Elijah "delivered the child unto his mother." Similarly, in Lk. 7:15, we read that Jesus "delivered him to his mother." A mighty tidal wave of praises to Jehovah swept over the nation even into the prison cell where John the Baptist waited for the executioner's sword. The story of John's death is given in Section 92. Some of John's disciples were present and others hearing of this mighty miracle rushed away to tell their depressed master this amazing news. For the *intricate* details regarding ancient Jewish burials, see the second paragraph of footnote b above, and the Talmud tractates, Moed Qatan; Shabbath; and Kethubbot.

(g) This verse reveals that there was communication between John and Jesus, although John was incarcerated waiting execution in Machaerus fortress some forty miles away. The next Section explains John's suffering and doubts about Jesus as he languished in Herod's prison and the Savior's public defense of His forerunner.

Suffering in prison,* John the Baptist is overwhelmed with tormenting doubts. He sends messengers to inquire if Jesus was the real Messiah or not.

*For John's imprisonment, see asterisk under main heading Section 21, Part 1. For details surrounding His death, see footnote a below, and Section 92, footnotes k, l, and m.

Machaerus prison on the eastern side of the Dead Sea

Matt. 11:2–8	Mk.	Lk. 7:19–25	John
(The Sermon on the Mount concludes in Matt. 11:1. See Section 59, Matt. 10:42 and 11:1, footnote t for explanation.)			
John's doubt expressed		*John's doubt expressed*	
2 Now when John had heard in the prison[a] the works of Christ, he sent two of his disciples,		19 And John calling *unto him* two of his disciples sent *them* to Jesus, saying, "Art thou he [the Messiah] that should come? or look we for another?"[b]	
3 And said unto him, "Art thou he [the Messiah] that should come, or do we look for another?"[b]		20 When the men were come unto him, they said, "John Baptist hath sent us unto thee, saying, 'Art thou he [the Messiah] that should come? or look we for another?'"	
		21 And in that same hour he cured many of *their* infirmities and plagues, and of evil spirits; and unto many *that were* blind he gave sight.	
His works and Words reveal that He is the Messiah		*His works and Words reveal that He is the Messiah*	
4 Jesus answered[c] and said unto them, "Go and shew John again those things which ye do hear and see:		22 Then Jesus answering[c] said unto them, "Go your way, and tell John what things ye have seen and heard;	
5 'The blind receive their sight, and the lame walk, the lepers are cleansed, and the deaf hear, the dead are raised up, and the poor have the gospel preached to them.'		'how that the blind see, the lame walk, the lepers are cleansed, the deaf hear, the dead are raised, to the poor the gospel is preached.'	
6 "And blessed is *he*, whosoever shall not be offended in me."[d]		23 "And blessed is *he*, whosoever shall not be offended in me."[d]	
He questions the people about John		*He questions the people about John*	
7 And as they departed, Jesus began to say unto the multitudes concerning John, "What went ye out into the wilderness to see?[e] A reed shaken with the wind?		24 And when the messengers of John were departed, he began to speak unto the people concerning John, "What went ye out into the wilderness for to see?[e] A reed shaken with the wind?	
8 "But what went ye out for to see? A man clothed in soft		25 "But what went ye out for to see? A man clothed in soft	

Matt. 11:8–14	Mk.	Lk. 7:25–30	John
raiment? ▶<u>b</u>ehold, they that wear soft *clothing* are in kings' houses. ▶ *The lowercase used above in the word "behold" (verse 8) in comparison to the upper- case in Luke 7:25 is an example of one of the changes needed in this version of the KJV Bible. This has nothing to do with inspiration. It is rather a proofreaders and typesetters oversight. Grammatically, both should be uppercase as they begin sentences. Both of these verses have caps in the original 1611 version. See verses 10 and 27 just below with 19 and 34 for examples of correct capitalization of the same word.* 9 "But what went ye out for to see? A prophet? yea, I say unto you, and more than a prophet.[(f)] 10 "For this is *he*, of whom it is written, 'Behold, I send my messenger before thy face, which shall prepare thy way before thee.'[(g)] ***Jesus highly extols John*** 11 "Verily I say unto you, Among them that are born of women there hath not risen a greater than John the Baptist: notwithstanding he that is least in the kingdom of heaven is greater than he." ***Battling hypocrisy to get into the kingdom*** 12 "And from the days of John the Baptist until now the kingdom of heaven suffereth violence, and the violent take it by force.[(h)] 13 "For all the prophets and the law prophesied until John.[(i)] ***John is the promised Elijah*** 14 "And if ye will receive *it*, this is E-li-as, [Elijah] which was for to come.[(j)]		raiment? ▶<u>B</u>ehold, they which are gorgeously apparelled, and live delicately, are in kings' courts. 26 "But what went ye out for to see? A prophet? Yea, I say unto you, and much more than a prophet.[(f)] 27 "This is *he*, of whom it is written, 'Behold, I send my messenger before thy face, which shall prepare thy way before thee.'[(g)] ***Jesus highly extols John*** 28 "For I say unto you, Among those that are born of women there is not a greater prophet than John the Baptist: but he that is least in the kingdom of God is greater than he." 29 And all the people that heard *him*, and the publicans, justified God, [demonstrated Christ was right] being baptized with the baptism of John. ***Rejecting John's message is tantamount to rejecting God*** 30 But the Pharisees and lawyers rejected the counsel of God against themselves, being not baptized of him.	

Matt. 11:15 -19	Mk.	Lk. 7:31-35	John
15 "He that hath ears to hear, let him hear.[k]			
The Jews act like pouting children[l]		*The Jews act like pouting children*[l]	
16 "But whereunto shall I liken this generation?[m]		31 And the Lord said, "Whereunto then shall I liken the men of this generation?[m] and to what are they like?	
It is like unto children[n] sitting in the markets, and calling unto their fellows,		32 "They are like unto children[n] sitting in the marketplace, and calling one to another,	
17 And saying, 'We have piped [played flutes] unto you, and ye have not danced; we have mourned [pretended sorrow] unto you, and ye have not lamented.'		and saying, 'We have piped [played flutes] unto you, and ye have not danced; we have mourned [pretended sorrow] to you, and ye have not wept.'	
The Jews falsely accuse Jesus just as they did John		*The Jews falsely accuse Jesus just as they did John*	
18 "For John came neither eating nor drinking, and they say, 'He hath a devil.'[o]		33 "For John the Baptist came neither eating bread nor drinking wine; and ye say, 'He hath a devil.'[o]	
19 "The Son of man came eating and drinking, and they say, 'Behold◄ a man gluttonous, and a winebibber,[p] a friend of publicans [tax collectors] and sinners.'		34 "The Son of man is come eating and drinking; and ye say, 'Behold◄ a gluttonous man, and a winebibber,[p] a friend of publicans [tax collectors] and sinners!'	
But wisdom is justified of her children."[q] (Verse 20 cont. in Section 63.)		35 "But wisdom is justified of all her children."[q] (Verse 36 cont. in Section 64.)	
► *See under Matt 11:8 above for explanation of this symbol.*		► *See under Matt 11:8 above for explanation of this symbol.*	

Footnotes–Commentary

(a) Herod Antipas knew the fame and national interest throughout his domain of both Jesus and John the Baptist. He had thrown John into prison because the Baptist had reproved him for his adulterous affair in stealing his half brother, Philip's wife. She was a granddaughter of the infamous baby killer, Herod the Great. Antipas was his son. See Section 8, footnote a, for other comments on Herod Antipas. Herodias married her uncle, Herod Philip, by whom she bore the birthday party dancer, Salome. Refer to Section 21, Part 1, number 4, under footnote b for information on Philip. Then she abandoned him and lived openly with his half-brother Herod Antipas, (her former brother-in-law) who had recently deserted his wife, the daughter of King Aretas (2 Cor. 11:32-33). Aretas waged a savage war on Herod for putting away his daughter, during which Herod's military was cut to pieces by the superior Arabian forces of King Aretas. Many of the Jews believed his defeat was an act of God because he had killed John the Baptist. For Herod's birthday party and the events that led to the death of John the Baptist, see Section 92 footnotes k and l.

2p-The wretched Herodias was the ruin of Antipas. She pressured her husband to travel to Rome in 39 A.D. There he requested kingship from the Emperor Caligula. This vanity trip resulted in disaster, for both were banished into foreign exile in France by the enraged emperor. As Antipas ruled over Galilee and Peraea, the ideal place of confinement for John was in his infamous Machaerus prison located at the southern end of Peraea. A city and strong fortress stood in that place. History has left tiny sketches of this city and mountain fortress standing in a threatening position overlooking the Dead Sea. The Jews said that on a clear day its imposing figure could be seen from Jerusalem! Scattered remains of the place are still visible. A series of upturned concrete slabs and stones reveal the road to Machaerus was built by Roman engineers. Fragments of large paving stones, broken cisterns, foundations of the walls, and the scanty ruins of a temple to the pagan sun god of Syria are there. This place covered nearly a square mile of both city and prison area. Two large shafts, sunk deep into the hot earth, reveal where prisoners were kept! Those familiar with the horror of eastern dungeons can well imagine the agonizing torture of such a dark and foreboding place. Chain holes chiseled into the stone may still be seen. In one of these deep pits, the ministry of John slowly ended! From here, he communicated with his disciples trying to keep abreast with the ministry of Christ. Josephus expressly states that John the Baptist was murdered in Machaerus prison in *Antiquities,* Book 18:5. 2, lines 116-119. See the old work, *Holy Places of the Gospel,* pages 141-142, by C. Koop, for the interesting details of this horrible place.

(b) "Art thou he that should come?" When great men doubt. Commentators have written puzzling things about this statement of John. Those who are unfamiliar with suffering *cannot* fathom the actions and words of those who do. Often, the pressure of unbearable captivity has crushed strong and dauntless spirits. Maddening solitude, with an iron fist of despair, will ultimately beat down and crush the strongest of wills and the most resolute heart. A life left to rot in hot darkness cannot be held accountable for what it sometimes says and does. From freedom in the wilderness of Judaea to Herod's horrifying Machaerus prison was the journey of John! It remains a terrible but glorious paradox that often in world history, God chooses for His greatest of servants to drink the dregs from the cup of seemingly miserable failure and endless suffering. Some saints by a lingering disease, terrible misfortunes, abandonment even by dearest of family, financial collapse, and a thousand other calamities, the Lord of heaven seems to have flung aside like broken instruments. However, it is never true according to His promise in Heb. 13:5. To have the image of Christ formed upon our souls is a costly process with so few willing to pay the wonderfully awful price. No duty in Christian love requires more delicacy than that of comforting the crushed and fallen. O to be a helping hand from God, reaching out to fellow men.

2p-Several of John's disciples obtained entrance into the maddening prison of Machaerus and reported to their depressed master. They told him of Jesus' miracles and wonders and no doubt the recent healing of the centurion's servant and the raising of the widow's son at Nain. The great forerunner was informed of Messiah's eating and drinking with publicans and sinners. Did they also tell John about the sectarian group from his followers that sided with the Pharisees against Christ? See Section 51, footnotes a, and e. John, bowed reluctantly under the shadow of Antipas' sword and wilting in prison, tried to make sense of the whole thing. Was this the cost of doing that, which was right? Earlier John was convinced that Jesus was the Messiah and publicly said so. God had vouchsafed this truth to him by divine methods. Had he not fearlessly heralded Him as "the Lamb of God" that would take away the sin of the world? Now, suffering had done something to this greatest of men. He questions if Jesus was the Messiah or not! Beckoning two trusted disciples, he sent them to inquire of Jesus "Art thou he that should come? or look we for another?" (Lk. 7:19). Many things about Jesus were strange and inexplicable. What troubling contrasts: John, dirty, broken, confused, and overwhelmingly depressed, while Messiah is mixing with sinners at a great banquet in the house of a former chief publican! This "greatest born of women" needed answers. Therefore, he sends two of his disciples to get them, for nothing made sense anymore.

(c) The response of Jesus to John's disciples was conclusive. Among the Jews, there were various signs by which their real Messiah could be identified. He would be singled out from all the prophets and great men of Israel by two marks, His Words, and works. This is explained by the asterisk under main heading Section 48. Our Lord did not directly answer their question, but rather He allowed the men to behold with their eyes His Messianic wonders! Luke 7:21 explains in "that same hour he cured many of *their* infirmities and plagues, and of evil spirits; and unto many *that* were blind he gave sight."

2p-Verses 5 and 22. Highlighted in gray being Messianic predictions. The prophecy He had read back in the Nazareth synagogue was being fulfilled (Lk. 4:19-20). The rabbis had pointed out numerous passages from their Old Testament that forecast the miraculous deeds of their coming Messiah. He would open the eyes of the blind, make the lame to walk, liberate captives from all diseases and demons (Isa. 61:1) and cause the deaf to hear (Isa. 29:18). John's inquirers *saw* these things happening before their very eyes! They were convinced that He was the Messiah of Israel! We have no record of their return to the Baptist, but can believe they surely carried to his heart renewed hope that Jesus of Nazareth was indeed the Messiah and Savior of the world. John had been right after all! The author of this work was acquainted with the late, Pastor Harlen Papov, who suffered unspeakable tortures in Bulgarian communist prisons for his faith. Once he shared with us how he was so beaten, tortured, and deprived of sleep and food that he signed a confession of crimes he had never committed! Such irrational acts are produced by a mind that has been broken and temporarily deranged through intense pain. *God understands and keeps the wounded victim in His loving grace.* It is written in Prov. 15:13, "by sorrow of the heart the spirit is broken." In view of this, we also note Prov. 18:14, "But a wounded spirit who can bear?" Such verses describe something of the changes reflected in the life of John the Baptist. No Christian knows how his life will end; it behooves us to pass the time of our sojourneying in fear and commit the keeping of our souls to God in well doing.

3p-Matt. 11:5 with its parallel of Lk. 7:22 are but a selection of words from various Old Testament verses speaking of the works and wonders of Messiah.

^(d) **"Offended at Christ."** Does this suggest that John had somehow become offended at Christ? The scribes, Pharisees, and Jews in general had also become offended and then infuriated at His claim to be Israel's Messiah. After all, had He not rejected their oral laws and gone among the foul Samaritans and cursed publicans at Matthew's house? Had He not called the religious leaders of the nation hypocrites and then opposed their hypocrisy? Their Messiah would never do such insulting things, so they thought! A sectarian group of John's disciples was also offended at Him over the issue of fasting and separation from "sinners." For more details, see main heading Section 51, footnotes a, and e.

2p-Happy is the Christian, who does not take offence as he follows Christ into poverty or riches, sickness or health, suffering, loss, misunderstanding, heartache, personal obscurity, public infamy, and even death. Men who embrace Christ by faith and abandon all to love and serve Him are peculiarly "happy" and "blessed." Our Lord seems to be sending the message back to John, that even though He is the Messiah, John will not be freed from prison. "John, do not be offended in Me because of this trial you are suffering; you shall die as a martyr for preaching the truth." The author serving as a foreign missionary for half his life, has seen fellow workers become "offended at Christ" due to some overbearing problem, great calamity or other inexplicable sorrow that fell into their lives. Not being able to "figure it out," they were "offended" and abandoned the Lord they had previously professed to love. This was the temptation of John as he languished in that dreadful prison called "Machaerus." See second paragraph of footnote a above for more on this ancient prototype of Alcatraz or Devil's Island prisons.

^(e) **"What went ye out to see?"** The nature of this question proves that these people had heard John preach. Thus, they quickly interpreted the Savior's illustrations of His forerunner. The crowds had listened to the conversation between Christ and John's two disciples. Upon their departure, Christ turned His attention to the curious bystanders and spoke of John's character and ministry. What Matthew had previously written of Messiah, "a bruised reed shall he not break," is now beautifully demonstrated in His treatment and defense of John, bruised unto death by the foulness of Herod's prison. The rabbis used the metaphor of the reed "shaken by the wind" to describe a trembling soul, terribly distraught, nevertheless, rooted deep under water, to picture great stability under adversity. John's image was not that of a soft person, delicate and timid to speak the truth. Both his dress and food betokened the opposite of pampering or overly caring for the body, as the people continually saw in the court officials of Herod Antipas. John had been strong, stable, and had served Messiah well. It is indeed touching that our Lord speaks not one word of condemnation or rebuke to the hurting, doubting preacher writhing in the filth and dark despair of Machaerus. He has only praise for His forerunner! For the story of John's death, see Section 92.

^(f) **"More than a prophet."** Peter preached to Captain Cornelius and his fellows that to Christ "gave all the prophets witness" (Acts 10:43). However, John did even greater things. Old Testament seers pointed in various ways to the coming Messiah, but John presented Him visibly to Israel. John was Malachi's Elijah, the last link *before* Messiah appeared amid the Jewish people. By fulfilling Mal. 3:1, John became more than just a herald, now he was the single and direct announcer of Messiah. In fulfilling Mal. 4:5-6, he literally became the Elijah, which was to come. As Messiah's forerunner, John pointed Him out to the people; he saw Him, talked to Him, baptized Him, and preached Him. God gave John a unique revelation on how to recognize the Messiah as explained in John 1:33. And this he did! The ministry of John introduced a new era in Israel's history – an abrupt ending, followed by a glorious beginning for "All the law and the prophets prophesied until John" (Matt. 11:13). The son of Zacharias and Elizabeth became "greater than all other prophets." Our Lord used the occasion to announce the infinitesimal value of humility in His kingdom. The smallest of His servants are greater than the greatest! Those who seek to serve God with a small opinion of themselves, but a big opinion of Christ and others are His best servants. *To be humble and not know it is a pearl of great price.*

^(g) Jesus suddenly quoted Mal. 3:1, a passage familiar to all devout Jews as forecasting the coming of Messiah's forerunner. Then He applied it to John. It is of interest that some thirty years prior, the angel Gabriel quoted, selected parts of Mal. 4:5-6 and also applied them directly to the son of Zacharias (Lk. 1:17). Even heaven's angels are familiar with God's Word and use it as the final authority! Thus, *both* citations found their completion in John the Baptist. See Section 24, footnotes a and b, for detailed explanation of this matter.

2p-Verse 29. "Justified God." A vast array and varied assortment of sinners sincerely believed John's flaming message about the Messiah, repented of their sins and trusted Him. Next, they were baptized to show their faith in Israel's Messiah. By these actions, they were publicly demonstrating that God was "justified" or "right" in sending the Messiah and John His grand herald. This is what Luke was telling his friend Theophilus in this passage.

^(h) **"And from the days of John the Baptist."** That is, from the time when John began to preach. It is unknown precisely how long this was.

2p-"Violence and force." Jesus is saying that there had been a "violent" rush of people pressing hard to hear John's message regarding the kingdom of God (Matt. 3:5 with Mk. 1:5). Most of these were tax collectors, common people, and even Gentile soldiers. Upon hearing the message of John, many of their hearts were fired to fresh hope of sins forgiven and peace with God. These "violent" masses were rejected and hated by the scribes, Pharisees, and religious masters of Israel. This is the meaning of Lk. 7:29 above. Christ said that the publicans and harlots (who were pressing through the crowds to hear John) would enter the kingdom *before* the religious leaders would. In our Lord's Words, there is an allusion to soldiers rushing to take a city and gather its spoils. Thus, great numbers of people thronged around both, Him and the Baptist to hear the kingdom message they preached. The idea here is that many of the common people fought hard against the religious bigotry and hatred of the scribes and Pharisees; being unstoppable, they surged forward seeking entrance into the wonderful new kingdom of Christ and God. Western believers have no idea of the cost some pay or the fierce struggles they press through in coming to salvation.

3p-**"Violence and force" in today's world.** The story of Saleema, a young Pakistani Muslim woman comes to mind. She was saved in August of 1999 through the witness of a friend in her village who had been secretly reading the New Testament. The friend was put to death. Saleema, imprisoned by her Muslim family, suffered rape, beatings, starvation, and torture for months. Both ankles were broken. Through international pressure on the Pakistani Embassy in Washington D.C., she was released. A covert courier found her as a bent-over cripple, with legs twisted, and face distorted. This was her violence for the kingdom of God. She vanished a few months later and has not been heard of since. Our Lord's usage of the terms "violence" and "force," well describe the pathway thousands have trodden to find the kingdom of Jesus Christ and eternal life.

4p-**Verse 30. "Lawyers."** His usage of this word had reference to "specialists" in the Jewish Torah Law of Moses, not the attorneys of our present day legal system. For more on Hebrew lawyers, note Section 116, Lk. 10:25, footnote a. However, many attorneys today are thieves and scoundrels just as the scribes and Pharisees were. In contrast to the crowds, the religious leaders of Israel had condemned themselves in *finally* rejecting John's message of the Messiah, thus refusing baptism as a public proclamation of their faith in Him. Their censure of the Baptist's message reflected their contempt for both him and Christ. Over a year later, and about two days before His death, the Lord Jesus *again* declared to the scribes and Pharisees very similar words when He said, "Verily I say unto you, that the publicans and the harlots go into the kingdom of God before you. For John came unto you in the way of righteousness, and ye believed him not: but the publicans and the harlots believed him: and ye, when ye have seen *it*, repented not afterward, that ye might believe him" (Matt. 21:31-32). According to John 5:35-36, Christ said the religious leadership of the Jews *originally* "rejoiced for a season" with the appearing of John. Witnessing the people flocking to him for baptism, and then to Christ was too much. This served to condemn their self-righteous ways. The Jews in anger turned away and rejected John's message of Christ. See footnote d above. They would not, after seeing all these things and having several years to evaluate Christ's ministry, reconsider, repent, and believe.

5p-**Were the religious leaders of Israel predestinated to reject the Messiah?** This will be briefly dealt with in Section 74, first and second paragraphs of footnote e. Men *post*-ordain themselves to hell by their unforgiven sins. Consigning millions to damnation before the foundation of the world is the heresy of Augustine-Calvin. Some of these people are so twisted in mind that they condemn inviting sinners to the Savior, even though He invited them to himself (Matt. 11:28). The late evangelist, W. E. Best, associated with the South Belt Assembly of Christ, in Houston, Texas, wrote in *Honoring the True God,* page 9, "The preacher who commands people to come forward to be regenerated assumes the prerogative of the Holy Spirit." Best's ignorance of church history is appalling. Millions came to Christ through the public invitational ministries of the Wesley brothers, General Booth, Billy Sunday, Dwight L. Moody, Gypsy Smith, W. P. Nichols, Charles G. Finney, Hyman Appleman, and hundreds of others. The great Dutch Reformed preacher and Calvinist, Andrew Murray of South Africa, continually gave public invitations and thousands were saved. *Common sense dictates that a gift has to be received!* Affirming that all evangelists who give invitations neglect the Holy Spirit and try to do His work is absurd. Like all red-hot Calvinists, Best was eventually snared by his own words. On page 30 of the above booklet, he wrote of his church, "The assembly is on a hunting expedition for Christ's sheep." Amazing! Since according to these people "irresistible grace" will bring in the elect *regardless*, why are they "on a hunting expedition" looking for them? Years ago, while in Pasadena, Texas, I put this objection to Dr. Peter Connelly, a famed Scottish five point Calvinist. He responded, "It is the sovereign will of God that we help Him do His work." I wondered, "What does God do when many of His elect will not help Him do His work? Who then will bring in those ordained to be saved before the foundation of the world? Could some of those Christians, who reject the T-U-L-l-P heterodoxy of Calvinism bring them in? For more on this, see Section 91, the first paragraph of footnote g.

[i] **Verse 13. "Prophets and law until John."** This statement of Christ must be interpreted in its context back to verse 11. They are reveal that the Baptist was greater than the sages and prophets who were before him. All of them declared that Messiah was coming; John heralded that He had come! The countless shadows, figures, similes, types and markers used by that army of holy men across the Old Testament, all met their terminus as John pointed toward, and shouted "Behold the Lamb of God" (John 1:29). John witnessed Messiah's baptism, introduced Him to men, and urged his disciples to abandon him and follow Jesus. It was firmly believed among the rabbis that the law and all prophets would prophesy *only* (or come to fulfillment) in the days of the Messiah. This is what our Lord affirmed in Matt. 11:9. With the appearing of John, the "days of the Messiah began." Christ agreed with the rabbinical saying in His statement, "For all the prophets and the law prophesied until John." See Section 82, footnote d for the ancient Jewish divisions of time within which the proposed Messiah would do His work.

(j) For the benefit of His audience, Christ reaffirmed that John the Baptist was the predicted Elijah of Malachi. His Jewish congregation understood. On the return of Elijah during the tribulation, see Section 58, footnote i.

(k) As if to check all opposition to this fact, the Lord Jesus adds a terse warning for men to "hear" what He had just said. Many years later, the glorified Christ issued the *same warning* in His messages for the seven churches in Asia (Rev. 2:7, 11, 17, 29, 3:6, 13, 22). It remains valid to this present moment. Refer to Section 73, Matt. 13:9 and all of footnote k, for more on this rabbinical expression used in the synagogue.

(l) No better illustration of the stubborn Jews, especially their religious leaders, could be given than that of self-willed, spoiled children who will not listen to their parents or peers when sound advice is given. As naughty children wrangle to have their way and disregard what is right, so did the Jews to their Messiah.

(m) **"This generation."** In using such a specific term our Lord was positively speaking of the Hebrew generation standing *immediately* before Him. No other interpretation makes sense. See Section 67, footnote b, and notes by the asterisk under main heading in Section 68, footnote g for more details. Christ addressed the Jews in general, but explicitly their religious leaders, and gave a most appropriate allegory of their wicked foolishness. Their fatal crime was to reject John and his message of Jesus their Messiah. In so doing, they were acting as spoiled children playing their games of imitating adults in weddings, funerals, and numerous other activities. Suddenly, one child is offended, and in peevish anger, refuses to join in with the others. Unwilling to cooperate, he or she will not dance to the play-music or chant back to the imitation of mourning. Such was the evil and perverse practices of those religious charlatans who pretended so hard to be holy and spiritual before the common people of Israel.

(n) **Maxim of quibbling children.** In playing games, arguing, and refusing to respond to their playmates, the Savior was saying to the scribes and Pharisees something like this, "You are the generation which did not respond to John, who came as a Nazarite neither eating nor drinking." (This does not mean that John did not eat at all, but he was noted for remarkable abstinence, eating and drinking only the *right* things.) "You went so far as to accuse him of having a demon because of his stern asceticism! Then I, your Messiah, came doing the opposite, eating and drinking, taking part in feasts, weddings, and other public events. Conversely, you call me gluttonous, a winebibber, a friend of publicans and sinners. You condemn me on one charge and John on something totally opposite. Stop acting like silly children who are divided into petty groups over who does what in their games and will not respond to each other." Jesus was saying, "Make up your minds, *both* John, and I cannot be wrong! Why do you not believe us for we have preached the same things? Will you continue to reject us both?"

2p-In these charges against our Lord, the Jews sought to discredit Him before the people. They were saying that the perfect Son of God partook of sinful pleasures. For "Christians" who plead that Jesus turned the water to intoxicating wine to justify their "disciplined drinking," see Section 27, footnote k. The crowds pressed forward to hear every Word Christ spoke to the Jewish clergy. He said they were erratic, inconsistent, and could not be trusted. Later, He called them the children of the Devil (John 8:44). Note more of His stern Words to them in Matt. 23:15.

(o) **"John had a devil."** The religious leaders accused the Baptist of having a devil or demon. This was a standard practice among the Jews. If they could not handle the arguments of their opponents, they would resort to declaring them as being "demon possessed." We note later, this same charge was laid upon the Lord Jesus again by these Jews (John 7:20 and John 8:48).

(p) **"Jesus a drunkard?"** Like the charge in John 10:20, "He hath a devil and is mad," this too was another malicious slander leveled at the sinless Son of God by the hate filled Jews. His friendship with sinners was of such divine nature and heavenly purpose that the religious leaders could not understand. They were so self righteous that they hated anyone not of their persuasion, and bitterly opposed all who dared reach out to bring sinners to hope and forgiveness. For example, see their rotten attitude towards those not of their hypocritical religious practices in Section 50, footnote c, and the "exceeding sinful women," in Section 64, Lk. 7:38, footnote g.

(q) This was another well-known saying or proverb among the people. Christ was telling His audience that the conduct of John, contrasted with that of Himself, were *both* the products of God's wisdom and were therefore, justified (right). John more aptly fit the role of an ascetic ancient prophet, while the Lord Jesus was vastly different in His ministry continually being a public figure. All believers with God's wisdom in their hearts will understand these diversities in disposition and deportment and see in them the unique will of God for each person involved. We need to remember that God does not will that we all be alike in everything. Believers must not be as the scribes and Pharisees, who were blind to the diverse wonders of the Almighty's grace in the lives of His children. *They demanded that all men be as they were!* Neither Christ nor John would fit into their religious box. God knew what He was doing in sending John as He did, and in sending His Son, who practiced an opposite behavior to that of the Baptist. Both brought glory and honor to the Lord of heaven. God's wisdom is exhibited and justified in the *upright* but often varying conduct of His children, regardless of what their circumstances and sufferings may be. The vain opinions of unsaved men and a Christ hating world change nothing regarding the facts of true Christianity. Those "Christians" who give a sickly nod to the Lord Jesus then return to their sins are described this way, "As a dog returneth to his vomit, *so* a fool returneth to his folly" (Prov. 26:11). They are God's enemies (James 4:4).

Judgment pronounced on three great cities in Israel. Jesus rejoiced over the apostles' unique privilege of sharing His ministry. True soul rest promised to all Jews weary with the empty synagogue rituals.

Matt. 11:20-30—*Capernaum?*	Mk.	Lk.	John
Chorazin and Bethsaida doomed			
20 Then began he to upbraid [censure] the cities[a] wherein most of his mighty works were done, because they repented not:			
21 "Woe unto thee, Chorazin! woe unto thee, Bethsaida! for if the mighty works, which were done in you, had been done in Tyre and Sidon, they would have repented long ago in sackcloth and ashes.			
22 "But I say unto you, It shall be more tolerable for Tyre and Sidon at the day of judgment, than for you.			
Capernaum doomed			
23 "And thou, Capernaum,[b] which art exalted unto heaven, shalt be brought down to hell: for if the mighty works, which have been done in thee, had been done in Sodom, it would have remained until this day.			
24 "But I say unto you, That it shall be more tolerable for the land of Sodom in the day of judgment, than for thee.[c]			
His prayer of praise			
25 At that time Jesus answered and said, "I thank thee,[d] O Father, Lord of heaven and earth, because thou hast hid these things from the wise and prudent,[e] and hast revealed them unto babes.			
26 "Even so, Father: for so it seemed good in thy sight.			
27 "All things are delivered unto me of my Father: and no man knoweth the Son, but the Father; neither knoweth any man the Father, save the Son, and *he* to whomsoever the Son will reveal *him*.[f]			
His invitation to the religious weary Jews			
28 "Come unto me, all *ye* that labour and are heavy laden, and I will give you rest.			
29 "Take my yoke[g] upon you and learn of me; for I am meek and lowly in heart: and ye shall find rest unto your souls.			
30 "For my yoke *is* easy, and my burden is light."[h] (Next chap. Matt. 12:1 cont. in Section 53.)			

Footnotes–Commentary

[a] "**Chorazin and Bethsaida.**" With the mention of these two cities, we have proof of our meager knowledge of the events in the life of Christ, and the countless things *not* related to us in the four gospels. Twice, our Lord pronounced this awful curse, here and in Lk. 10:13, which was given *later* in His ministry. Nothing is known for sure of Chorazin ("woody place"), save it is named twice in Scripture. Archaeologists and historians are still guessing its location. Seemingly, it was situated near Bethsaida ("house of game or hunting"), being mentioned in the same censure given by Jesus. See Section 93, footnote c for more on Bethsaida. Both cities had seen, heard and felt the impact of the "mighty works" of the Messiah and had blatantly rejected both. Bethsaida was no stranger to the Word of God either, for as bad as this city was, the grace of God had called out of it no less than three of Christ's apostles, Philip, Andrew and his brother Peter (John 1:44). Yet like Chorazin, Bethsaida also in its sinful madness rejected the works and Words of their Messiah. They refused to repent of their sins. How strange that these people, who according to Calvinism were of the "non elect," should have this written about them for it would make no difference anyhow. If this does not mean that they rejected their opportunity to salvation then words no longer make sense. Whoever heard of the "non elect" refusing salvation when they were never chosen to it in the first place?

2p-"**Wherein most of his mighty works were done.**" Here is another mark of inspiration. Regular authors would have written many pages about the cities that had witnessed Jesus' greatest works. Divine Scripture says very little of these places. Christ in announcing this curse compared these Jewish cities with two pagan Canaanite locations, Tyre and Sidon. Both were well known to His audience. Normally, this would have highly insulted a typical Jewish congregation, for He was telling the Hebrew inhabitants of Chorazin and Bethsaida that, the heathen Tyrians and Sidonians were better than they were! However, the austerity of our Lord must have struck a fearful and somber mood in their hearts. According to 1 Kings 17:9-24 (some seven hundred years prior), the Word of God had been delivered in these regions, and some had believed on the true God of heaven. The Messiah sternly informs them that, if these pagan cities had heard and seen what they had, both would have repented of their sins in deep sorrow. However, the Jews had hardened themselves to such a degree of madness and obstinacy against that it was too late! Many of the ancients wore rough sackcloth and adorned ashes to show their regret and dismay. Christ concluded His terrible anathema by declaring that the sinners of these idolatrous cities will suffer *less punishment* in God's judgment than they will. Their degree of damnation will be lighter than that of Israel; for to whom much is given, much is required. This is explained in Lk. 12:48. Later, our Lord returned to the vicinity of Bethsaida and healed a blind man by using strange methods. This event is described in Section 102, Mk. 8:22-25 footnote a.

(b) **"Capernaum."** Meaning "village of Nahum," it is mentioned sixteen times in the four gospels. The Hebrew expression "exalted into heaven" denoted being highly blessed of God. This was especially true because our Lord dwelt in Capernaum after departing from Nazareth. Note Section 19, footnote a, for more on this move. The Savior spent much time in Capernaum and surrounding districts performing His most fantastic miracles, and preaching and teaching hundreds of times in their synagogues. The truth of God had been poured into this city and surrounding area, but they chose to reject and abuse it. The term employed by Christ "remained unto this day," was standard rabbinical talk. The Talmud uses heathen cities as emblems of God's terrible judgment on the wicked, thus Christ's audience understood His illustrations. See this in Yoma 38b, Baba Metzia 48a and 49b with Sanhedrin 38b. Messiah tells His Jewish listeners that the worst of pagan cities were better than their highly prized Capernaum, which was now forever doomed. If His works had been performed behind the walls of ancient Sodom, it would have remained to that very moment. At God's judgment, the wicked men of Sodom (Gen. 13:13) would, like the people of Tyre and Sidon, fare better than the self-righteous Christ haters of this city. *There is something terrible in these Words of Christ.* Normal people consider sodomy the worst of sins; yet the Son of God affirmed that to reject Him is even more dreadful than the unspeakable filth and evil of sodomy. Here, as before, Christ revealed the horrid stiffness and impiousness of the Jews. They had one fate in eternity—hell! Yet, in an amazing demonstration of extended mercy, Christ returned to Capernaum numerous times after speaking this curse! Grace lingers long at the door.

(c) **Sodom better off than Capernaum.** Though the former citizens of Sodom and the cities of the plain had been dead some two thousand years, the Lord affirms they were *still* alive and would rise to stand in the last judgment! Some forty years later in the Roman wars of A.D. 70, these cities were destroyed. During these fierce battles, Jews were slaughtered by the millions and brought down to hell, as Messiah had warned (verse 23). In this, we see the stubbornness of the Jews, who are now cursed above their pagan neighbors whom they so fiercely hated.

(d) After announcing these ghastly judgments, the Savior suddenly breaks out in a prayer of praise to the Father in heaven (verses 25-26). Portions of Matt. 11:25-27 are later repeated by Christ in Lk. 10:21-24. Christ blesses God for allowing His apostles to hear and see the things they have up to that time. All the marvels of the former prophets, astounding works that eclipsed those of the great seers of the Old Testament, and words more sublime than the Psalms of David, Solomon and the rest; the lowly twelve were now witnessing and hearing. In this brief prayer, the Messiah is seeking to impress on the hearts of these fearful disciples the vast magnitude of their privilege in serving Him. Former generations of Israelites had witnessed wonderful things, but nothing to be compared with what the apostles of Christ were seeing and hearing as they followed the carpenter from Galilee—their Messiah.

(e) **"Wise and learned."** In this, the Lord Jesus refers to the scribes and Pharisees, who believed they knew more about God than any other people on earth. In reality, they did not know Him at all and had blatantly rejected His Son, their Messiah, and Savior. This sin sealed their doom. National judgment fell upon Israel in A.D. 70 with the destruction of Jerusalem, the temple, and Jewish state. This is recorded in Section 163. Their adamant rejection of Messiah resulted in God hiding great truths from them but making them known to the simplest of believers.

2p-**"Revealed them unto babes."** Adam Clarke well explains this curious statement of Christ, "This is a great truth, and the key of the science of salvation. The man Jesus Christ receives from the Father, and in consequence, of His union with the eternal Godhead becomes the Lord and sovereign dispenser of all things. All the springs of the divine favor are in the hands of Christ, as Priest of God, the atoning sacrifice for men; all good proceeds from Him, as Savior, Mediator, Head, Pattern, Pastor, and Perfect Judge of the whole world." *Clarke's Commentary*, vol. 5, page 132.

(f) **The Son reveals the Father.** What a profound statement! The Lord Jesus was the sole revealer of God the Father in absolute truth to mankind during His earthly ministry. Thus, when Christ is hated and rejected, men cannot come to know God. He reveals God by the work of the Holy Spirit through various channels, the primary one being the written Word of God. For a brief explanation of this truth, see Section 1, Part 4, footnote m. Regarding the possibility of Natural Theology revealing God and man's need for salvation, refer to Section 1, Part 4, fourth and fifth paragraphs of footnote g. Today, the Holy Spirit and God's Word are the *greatest* revealers of divine truth.

(g) **A synagogue chant.** Here, the Savior reconstructs a popular recitation spoken regularly in the synagogues and Jewish schools. The doctors of the law could be heard chanting with hands raised, "First accept upon you the yoke of the kingdom of heaven, then take upon yourself the yoke of the commandment." This is recorded in the Talmud tractates, Bereachoth 13a and Sanhedrin 55a. Every person of understanding knew the source of the Messiah's Words; it was a rabbinical plea for all Hebrews to become thorough Torah Law Israelites and thereby (they thought) find rest. The rabbis taught, "The law will give you rest." They continually spoke of "the yoke of the law," "the yoke of the precept," and "the yoke of the kingdom." It is noted that Rabbi Jesus has deliberately altered the wording of the great synagogue chant! His public invitation was different. He called on fellow Jews to come to *Him,* not the synagogue or Torah Law or precept (which pointed to Him): take upon them *His yoke* and learn of true rest. As the dove loosed from Noah's ark, no man will find rest until he returns to the Son of God. Christ, the greatest teacher, was meek and lowly in heart; this could hardly be said of the scribes and Pharisees. He had no rituals, dogmas, harsh overbearing traditions, or oral laws to strap upon the people and bring them into further bondage. They would find His yoke easy, His burden light, and above all else, rest for their weary souls (Jer. 6:16). To Christ, His cross and empty tomb, men must be directed.

2p-Several years ago, a police magazine carried the following story. "A little boy was lost in a suburb of the vast city of Chicago. He was found by a police officer who took him to headquarters. In vain, they tried to obtain his address, parent's name, or place of residence. Frightened, the little fellow could not remember these things. Suddenly, he leaped to his feet and with absolute confidence said, "Mr. Policeman, near my house is a church with a big cross on top; take me to the cross and I can find my way home." It has ever been the same. Only at the cross and in its glorious atonement for sin will men find their way to heaven's eternal home. This will never change.

3p-Men are *permanently* "yoked" to the Lord Jesus, by repentance of sin and faith in His atoning death and resurrection. Untold millions have taken upon themselves this glorious salvation yoke for freedom from the ravages of sin. In so doing, they learned that Jesus is meek and lowly of heart, full of tender mercies, ready to forgive and save *all* who come to Him. See Section 55, Matt. 12:18-20, footnote h for an Old Testament prophecy of Jesus' extraordinary meekness. In Zech. 9:9 it is predicted that Messiah would be a man of lowly posture, meek civic stature, and humility, riding on a donkey. Never had the Jews heard preaching like this. Again, they were amazed.

4p-**"Rest for your souls."** The psalmist cried to God that his soul was "disquieted within" him (Ps. 43:5). Clearly, he spoke of his soul as being a separate entity from his body but dwelling within it. No part of man needs "rest" as does his soul, lost in sin without hope. Refer to Section 59, Matt. 10:28, footnote o for more on this subject.

(h) "My burden is light." The burden of living life for the Lord Jesus is "light" in comparison to the burdens of a life spent in sin and rebellion to God. His "yoke" is unlike that of Satan; it is blessed! "The way of the transgressor is hard" (Prov. 13:15). Heaven's highway, though paved with blood, sweat, and tears, is made graceful by such promises as "For our light affliction, which is but for a moment, worketh for us a far more exceeding *and* eternal weight of glory' (2 Cor. 4:17). With Joseph, all faithful Christians can say, "For God hath caused me to be fruitful in the land of my affliction" (Gen. 41:52).

2p-**What kind of cross?** The cross is the foundation of the believer's faith and life. (Beyond it stands the empty tomb!) Christ's cross, a former emblem of pagan antiquity has two sides. It is our rudder through the storms of life bringing us pain and peace, hopelessness and help, crushing and cheer. From one side, it sheds glorious light while the other genders darkness. The cross of Christ brings us many tears before great triumph. This has greatly changed in American churches today. Flesh driven ministers, youth leaders, choirmasters, and others have gradually introduced an army of "harmless attractions" into the services of God. It is called "sanctified entertainment." Spiritually retarded saints think these new things are a move of the Holy Spirit for, "it brings the people in." They get a load of entertainment and laughs but only a pinch of Scripture and serious instruction. Salvation is a "joy kick" in which "the best life is now," and the road to heaven is paved with laughs, prosperity, and good times. *Thankfully, there are still churches where the real cross of Christ is the prime attraction and saints joyfully live in its shadow.*

3p-**Tail wagging the dog?** Could it be possible that some children and young people are being *sincerely* miss-instructed in our Sunday schools and VBS (Vacation Bible School) endeavors? Are they being conditioned to believe that the Christian life is a happy waltz to heaven? Before the shining crown, looms the old rugged cross. Before heaven, there is life that often leads to various hell-on-earth experiences. Most advertisements for neighborhood Vacation Bible Schools tell unsaved parents that it will be a "week's blowout of fun and games." After five days of videos, musical chairs, superheroes, basketball, Sponge Bob, laughing, shouting, and coloring books, text messaging, twitter, and plenty to eat, what is left of eternal value? (This is not intended to knock proper, well-controlled games and fun for children and youth or to make paranoid religious zombies out of them.) Nevertheless, could it be that we often have the tail wagging the dog? Who can imagine Titus or Timothy sharing a "fun gospel" with the kids at the Ephesus Church? It is written in Isa. 32:17, "And the work of righteousness shall be peace; and the effect of righteousness quietness and assurance for ever." Where is the divine "quietness" that God's righteousness brings? Why did Paul instruct the Thessalonian Christians, "study to be quiet" (1 Thess. 4:11)? Who among us has a degree in this holy discipline? Have we equated noise and crowds for God's blessing? *The great and first duty of all teachers is to point others to the Savior and to comfort the weak and wounded.* For continued comments on these subjects, see Section 73, footnote c, and Section 192, second and third paragraphs of footnote g.

His first recorded meal* in a Pharisee's house. During the supper, an exceedingly sinful woman slips in and anoints Jesus' feet. He gives a beautiful lesson on the depth and magnitude of instant divine forgiveness.

*See Section 70 for the Master's second meal with a Pharisee. Here, He was condemned for not adhering to the tradition of the elders. At the dinner given below, Christ was condemned for letting a sinful woman touch and anoint His feet. He responds to the allegations of the Pharisee with the Parable of the Creditor. This lesson demonstrated the amazing depths of His forgiveness, which He granted to the woman kneeling at His feet.

Matt.	Mk.	Lk. 7:36-49—Galilee	John
		An unwelcome stranger intrudes during supper	
		36 And one of the Pharisees[(a)] desired him that he would eat with him.[(b)] And he went into the Pharisee's house, and sat down to meat.	
		37 And, behold, a woman in the city,[(c)] which was a sinner,[(d)] when she knew[(e)] that *Jesus* sat at meat in the Pharisee's house, brought an alabaster box of ointment,[(f)] (a costly perfumed oil)	
		38 And stood at his feet behind *him* weeping, and began to wash his feet with tears, and did wipe *them* with the hairs of her head, and kissed his feet,[(g)] and anointed *them* with the ointment.	
		Simon the Pharisee is upset: Jesus responds	
		with a parable showing him the depth of God's forgiveness	
		39 Now when the Pharisee which had bidden him saw *it*, he spake within himself,[(h)] saying, "This man, if he were a prophet, would have known who and what manner of woman *this is* that toucheth him: for she is a sinner."	
		40 And Jesus answering[(i)] said unto him, "Simon, I have somewhat to say unto thee." And he saith, "Master, say on."	
		41 "There was a certain creditor which had two debtors: the one owed five hundred pence, [1 pence = 17 cents or about $85.00] and the other fifty [about $8.50].	
		42 "And when they had nothing to pay, he frankly forgave them both. Tell me therefore, which of them will love him most?"	
		Simon the Pharisee "supposes" about forgiveness	
		43 Simon answered and said, "I suppose that *he*, to whom he forgave most." And he [Jesus] said unto him, "Thou hast rightly judged."	
		A living example of God's grace to save and forgive	
		44 And he turned to the woman, and said unto Simon, "Seest thou this woman? I entered into thine house, thou gavest me no water for my feet: but she hath washed my feet with tears, and wiped *them* with the hairs of her head.	
		45 "Thou gavest me no kiss: but this woman since the time I came in hath not ceased to kiss my feet.	
		46 "My head with oil thou didst not anoint: but this woman hath anointed my feet with ointment. (a costly perfumed oil)	
		The intruder is forgiven her great sin debt	
		47 "Wherefore I say unto thee, Her sins, which are many, are forgiven; for she loved much: but to whom little is forgiven, *the same* loveth little."[(j)]	
		48 And he said unto her, "Thy sins are forgiven."	
		49 And they that sat at meat with him began to say within themselves,	

297

Matt.	Mk.	Lk. 7:49-50—Galilee	John
		"Who is this that forgiveth sins also?" **50** And he said to the woman, "Thy faith[(k)] hath saved thee; go in peace." <small>(Next chap. Lk. 8:1 cont. in Section 65.)</small>	

Footnotes-Commentary

[(a)] From among His bitterest foes, a Pharisee named Simon appeared on the scene and invited Jesus into his home for a meal. This same thing occurred again a short time later in Section 70, Lk. 11:37, footnote a. "Simon" was a popular name, with some nine persons bearing it, in the New Testament. Josephus mentions some twenty different Simons in his work. See Index page 923 for the listing of this name. Some believe that the strangeness of the circumstances attached to this occasion suggests it was another "set-up," designed to ensnare the Messiah. The general "feel" of the story suggests this opinion is incorrect. If it was a trap, the whole affair backfired in the face of those who planned it. See Section 54, Mk. 3:2, footnote c for an earlier "set-up" by the Pharisees in one of their synagogues. The reason for the invitation will remain uncertain, but one may be sure that the Pharisee Simon remembered what had happened at this meal the rest of his life!

[(b)] It was believed by the Jews that the prayers offered within that structure hallowed all carpets, mats, even the floors of their houses. Hence, all shoes and sandals were removed before entering to prevent bringing any pollution from the streets into the sanctified area. The Lord Jesus, complying with this custom removed His footwear like all courteous Jews entering another person's home.

[(c)] **"A woman in the city."** Thousands of women were this unnamed Galilean city. Luke wrote as though this event occurred on the same day as the miracle at Nain. Had this unnamed woman stood among the crowds and heard our Lord's tender invitation for the heavy laden to come to Him for rest? We can only wonder with awe. Had she witnessed the raising of the widow's son? Refer to Section 61, footnote f about the spread of His notoriety.

[(d)] See Section 50, footnote d for the meaning of the word "sinner," as used to identify this unnamed woman. Some commentators attempt to make this woman the Mary Magdalene of Lk. 8:1-2. This is totally unfounded. Whoever this "sinner" was, she had "many sins" to be forgiven (verse 47). They weighed an overbearing load on her heart. Somewhere and in some way, she had heard of this man Jesus, and she believed that He could help her.

[(e)] **"When she knew." Washing Jesus' feet with tears.** Having received prior intelligence that Jesus was supping at Simon's house, this fallen woman, a slave to sin, ventured there and somehow gained access amid the visitants. We inquire, "How did she gain entrance?" Simon, being a Pharisee, had servants. The duty of the more responsible servant was to attend the door and clear each visitor seeking entrance into the master's house. If she were a Gentile (as some tell us), she would have been detected instantly by her dress, sandals, hairstyle, speech, and even accent, and refused admission. Perhaps she slipped in unnoticed, secretly carrying on her person a valuable little bottle made of precious alabaster (mined in Egypt or Damascus). We note that Simon immediately recognized her knowing "what manner of woman she was" (verse 39). How did he do this? Some think she was dressed in "the attire of a harlot" (Prov. 7:10). This is surely incorrect, for admittance would not have been granted, unless it was a premeditated trap. However, was this a trap with the woman being used as a pawn? If so, the whole failed for she was smitten over her sin at the sight and presence of the Lord Jesus Christ. Perhaps she was known over the city or village where this took place. Did the doorkeeper whisper into his master's ear what had happened and point her out? Regardless of our assumptions and her covert motives, wonderful things were about to take place! Simon, the haughty Pharisee had not included these in his supper plans.

[(f)] **"Alabaster box."** Then as now, women were fond of perfume. Flasks containing the substance were hung about the necks of adult females. So common was its use that the rabbis had decreed it could be used and worn on the Sabbath. It was carried in bottles of glass, glazed clay, silver and even gold. The popular "rose perfume" was placed on the tongue to sweeten the breath and to give pleasantness to the person. Particular brands were very costly. The ancients considered alabaster as the most appropriate container for this precious substance. It was the highest of social courtesy to bring a gift to respected persons especially when seeking a favor. This woman had previously planned in her heart to bring the ointment to the Lord Jesus and (according to custom) lay it at His feet. Once in His divine presence her heart melted, her tears flowed. The flask of precious oil she intended to present to the Lord Jesus as a gift had suddenly become appropriated on this occasion. Along with the costly ointment, she first gave Him her heart! For another mention of alabaster, see Section 146, Matt. 26:7, footnote e.

[(g)] **She mysteriously appears.** Amid the clamor and noise of that occasion, suddenly, out of nowhere, there crouched at the feet of Jesus, a publicly notorious woman! Any healthy imagination can picture that electrifying scene. Eastern meals were not served as those in the West. Sitting upright in chairs at meals was unknown. The Hebrew eating posture was to lie in a reclining position, leaning on the elbow, with the other hand free to take up food and drink. (This reverse custom was probably adopted during the Babylonian captivity.) Consequently, the uncovered feet would hang over the end of the couch. Simon, at the head of the table, and all the guests present were jolted into silence; suddenly, they could hear someone weeping bitterly! There she was, a wretched, disheveled street woman! Tremblingly, she sank to her knees. Foot washing was the duty of the most common slaves. It was standard courtesy to remove the sandals, wash the feet of all guests, greet them with a kiss of welcome, and then place drops of oil upon their heads (verses 44-46 with footnote b above). Christ had received none of the above social graces from the Pharisee Simon, who was His host. Some expositors are prone to suspect Simon's motives in inviting the Messiah into his home. Not to offer the washing, kiss, and anointing was a high insult among even the poorest of the land. The irresistible appeal to pity that despairing and broken-hearted mourner did not move the calloused Pharisee. His religion had hardened his heart. One can imagine the frigid demeanor and contemptuous expression of countenance that flushed in the face of Simon. Over a year later and just before His death another woman wept at Jesus' feet, wiped them with her hair, and anointed Him. Because of this act of faith in His soon death, burial, and resurrection, Jesus said that she was to receive continual *international recognition* for this deed. Read this glorious declaration of Christ and its meaning in Section 146, Matt. 26:12-13, all of footnote l.

2p-Something wonderful was pending. As this "sinner" drew near to the feet of Christ, the dreadful panorama of her wickedness flooded her soul; her heart burst open as she knelt at the couch of the Redeemer from heaven! Deep sorrow and remorse crushed her spirit, as she, the vile one, touched the purest One. Her wretchedness had overwhelmed her soul. She was as Isa. 9:18 states, "For wickedness burneth as the fire; it shall devour the briers and thorns, and shall kindle in the thickets of the forest." As David in the depth of regret and repentance, she too could lament, "My sin *is* ever before me" (Ps. 51:3). Everyone present recoiled in horror as this fallen woman dared lay her hands on the Messiah. What Simon had failed to do for his honored Guest, she did. Tears flowing like rivers of small diamonds washed the dust of the roads from His feet. On her knees, hair unloosed flowing long and thick, she gathered it together as a towel and dried His wetted feet in tender love. The missionary William M. Thomson in his classic work, *The Land and the Book*, page 30, wrote, "A Jewish matron [woman] must on no account allow her own hair to be seen." Tenderly kissing those tear washed feet, (still today a form of deep respect in the East), breaking the seal of her little bottle, she anointed Him with the precious substance. (It is noted from Prov. 7:17, harlots in pursuing their deadly craft used that perfume.) Sick of her sin, she comes to the Messiah for help! Never had Simon the Pharisee and his guests witnessed such a scene. A deafening silence permeated the room! All were muted by the conduct of the shady figure as she touched Christ's feet. According to the Jews, He was now ceremonially unclean. He spoke no rebuke. Somehow, she knew He would receive her; that her deepest sinfulness moved His deepest sympathy. This bruised reed He did not break or smoking flax He did not quench. Not only did "sinners" and the "unclean" touch Christ, but He touched them. See Section 48, Matt. 8:3, footnote c where the Lord Jesus reached out, touched a rotting leper, and healed him.

(h) Being God omniscient, the Messiah knew the thoughts of *both* the woman and the Pharisee (verse 39). To Israel, God had declared, "for I know the things that come into your mind, *every one of* them" (Ezek. 11:5). *Christ heard them thinking!* An ancient proverb declares, "Guard well thy thoughts, for they are heard in heaven." After reading Simon's mind, Christ addressed the secret doubts of his heart with a parable.

(i) **Verses 40-43.** Jesus laid before Simon the Pharisee and all present, what has been named "the Parable of the Two Debtors." Obviously, Christ's lesson was intended to respond to the *present* situation that had suddenly developed during the meal. It is plain in this parable that God is the creditor, and the two debtors Christ spoke of, were the woman and Simon. One owed five hundred denarii or pence (about $85.00) and the other fifty (about $8.50). One denarii was a day's wages. Amazingly, out of the goodness of his heart, the creditor forgave *both* their debts, and they were free. Christ put the question to Simon "Tell me therefore, which of them will love him most?" Simon's *halted response* indicates he understood the parable but was reluctant to answer (verse 43). Covertly, Christ stealthily inquired something like this, "Which one of you loves me the most?" The answer was obvious. That fouled and soiled woman, so despised and hated by religion, bundled at Jesus' feet now loved Him supremely! The self-righteous Pharisee struggled to save his red face.

(j) **Love much or love little.** These words explain *why* some serve Christ with a burning fervency, while others reflect a half-hearted devotion. The great sinner, the woman who owed the five hundred pence, was forgiven. The terrible burden of her awful sin debt had vanished! No marvel she knelt weeping before her Savior. From an evil soul came clean tears. Simon the Pharisee, still numbered among the hateful enemies of Christ, had little to weep about in his self-righteous life. Alas! How much this reminds one of certain church members today. Rising from the couch, the Lord Jesus looks down at the broken woman; His voice rang pungent and clear as He spoke in tones that boomed like a thunderclap across the room.

2p-Verse 48. **"Thy sins are forgiven."** Never had sweeter words sounded in her ears. Nor was this the first time that Christ had made such a startling announcement. We heard this blessed pronouncement earlier to the man twisted by palsy. Note this in Section 49, Matt. 9:2, footnote i. While the Pharisees and scowling guests murmured, the beaming woman rejoiced. Woeful is the misery and terrible the burden of religion without Christ. It is like a deceitful distemper that ends in hell. Even worse is a false religion that teaches scraps of God's truth but does not point its communicates to Christ dying for their sins and the sure gift of eternal life.

(k) In direct opposition to the theology of the scribes and Pharisees, Christ sent away this *former* sinful woman with heaven's joy bells ringing in her heart, "Go in peace" (verse 50). In peace, she went, changed, new, totally forgiven and a product of saving grace. And she was not baptized! Appealing that this was a different dispensation when men were saved without baptism is sheer nonsense. Baptism always follows salvation by showing outwardly, what salvation has already done inwardly. God considers that the born again soul was washed in the blood of the Lamb on the inside, as the body is washed with water on the outside. The latter depicts the former. Like the woman of Samaria, she too vanished from the pages of Scripture. See Section 35, second paragraph of footnote k for the beautiful story of this woman.

2p-"Thy faith hath saved thee." Here, it is clear, that people were saved through faith *before* the death of Christ on the cross. The woman to whom Jesus spoke these words trusted Him for all she knew Him to be at that time. Like most others at this period in His ministry, few understood their Messiah would die on a cross for the sins of the human race. See Sections 104-105 and 107 for comments on the disciples not understanding Jesus' death. The four gospels reveal that many wonders were accomplished through the faith of individuals placed in Christ. Likewise, their faith in Him as the Messiah-Savior was a tiny blossom that culminated into beautiful fruit at His resurrection. *Christ announced that this woman was "saved" through "faith."* This was so, for He "calleth those things which be not as though they were" (Rom. 4:17). For a later example of a publican who was saved before Jesus' death, while setting in a tree, refer to Lk. 19:9-10! The thief on the cross also found forgiveness and the sure promise of paradise at death (Lk. 23:39-43). Concerning salvation during the Old Testament era, see Section 10, footnote b, and Section 30, footnote h. In Section 203, third paragraph of footnote d, salvation, and forgiveness without baptism is discussed.

3p-Baptism puts one into salvation? The world's greatest missionary wrote, "Christ sent me not to baptize, but to preach the gospel" (1 Cor. 1:17). Many objections are hurled at these words for they threaten the heresy of salvation by baptism. If baptism puts one into Christ, then how were the above persons saved without it? None of them had yet been baptized, but their sins were forgiven. Appealing that this was an older period in history and men were converted differently is absurd. *There exists only one plan or way of salvation, not many.* Over time, men who received forgiveness and the gift of eternal life did so by the grace of God, minus nothing plus nothing. The repentance and faith produced by the Holy Spirit and God's Word are prerequisite to salvation. They are not professional human actions performed with machine like precision. Nor are they a road or five-point plan leading men to God. The gifts to repent and believe may be received or rejected. This does not upset God or shame His grace. Like the woman in the story above, repentance and faith came softly and sincerely from the womb of divine regret over her sins as God worked in her heart. Some express their remorse of sin and need for the Savior by tears, others by silence, by words, reading the Bible, kneeling, praying, or clapping their hands and dancing about as the black Africans do. I once saw a Zulu youth, backstage of the Town Hall in Kokstad, South Africa, fall to his knees, and beat fiercely upon his chest as a way of expressing sorrow for his sin. When one receives Christ by faith then grace receives that *surrendered* soul, and it is instantly born again. John 1:12 states that we "receive him," while Rom. 15:7 affirm, "He receives us." This was a divine transaction; somehow heaven and earth kissed each other (Lk. 15:7, 10). *Sinners are made saints by the epic miracle of the new birth taking place in their souls and not by baptism.* The blessing of baptism takes place after salvation, not before. Baptism and communion before salvation are actually "unbeliever's baptism," and "unbeliever's communion." Scripture allows for no such thing.

4p-A dancing Jew. Almost sixty years ago, the author of this work watched as a little Jewish man, named Solomon, in his mid fifties, who had just received Christ the Messiah by faith. He literally danced over the stage, kissing a Bible, crying, singing, and loudly rejoicing. Repeatedly, he shouted, "I have found the Messiah, I have found the Messiah!" According to the theological skeptics, he was rejoicing over a Messiah, who had been dead for almost two thousand years, was a fake, or possibly did not exist. And according to those who require baptism for forgiveness, the poor man was not yet saved. Someone later said, "He was too emotional!" I replied, "No, Solomon found the Messiah of Israel and was saved. He should rejoice," Religious people, who are unsaved, be they ever so good and devout cannot understand these things because they have never been born from above. Paul wrote that upon salvation, men are delivered from the power of darkness and placed into the kingdom of God's dear Son (Col. 1:13). This transformation takes place inside and is often manifested on the outside as in the case of that little Hebrew, who, out of curiosity, wandered into a Sunday night church service.

5p-Joyful lady from Switzerland. In the early 1960s in Gladstone, Queensland, Australia, after a Sunday night service, a woman came to our little house on Off Lane in a pouring monsoon rain. She walked in, dripping wet, bowed on her knees at the couch, and said, "Mr. Pike, I want to pray!" I said, "Helen, do you mean you want to be saved?" She responded *loudly*, "Yes!" This dear Swiss woman served God until the night she was called to heaven in her sleep thirty years later. The joy of knowing Christ never left her face and actions. Not all men come alike to the Savior, but He redeems all of them the same way. The wonderful ways of saving grace in the heart of men and women are more beautiful than the patterns of snowflakes. O reader, do you know this Christ as personal Lord and Savior? If not receive Him now, then hurry to the waters of *believer's* baptism in a *sound* Bible believing and practicing church.

Messiah and His men supported by believing women as they tour* Galilee for the fifth recorded time. Masses followed Christ, wherever He went.

See asterisk under main heading Section 38, for the other Galilean tours Jesus made. There is no exact data regarding how many trips were undertaken. For more on this thought, see footnotes b and d below.

Matt.	Mk.	Lk. 8:1-3—*Across Galilee*	John
		Great women who supported the work of Christ **1** And it came to pass afterward,[a] that he went throughout every city and village,[b] preaching and shewing the glad tidings of the kingdom of God:[c] and the twelve[d] *were* with him, **2** And certain women,[e] which had been healed of evil spirits and infirmities, Mary called Magdalene, out of whom went seven devils, *One lived in the palace of Herod Antipas* **3** And Joanna[f] the wife of Chuza Herod's steward, [household manager] and Susanna,[g] and many others,[h] which ministered unto him of their substance. (Verse 4 cont. in Section 73.)	

Footnotes-Commentary

[a] **"And it came to pass afterward,"** meaning *after* Christ had healed the centurion's servant at Capernaum, raised the widow's son at Nain, comforted John in his prison sufferings and attended the meal at the Pharisee's house. *Then,* He went forward on this fifth evangelistic tour of Galilee, temporarily accompanied by the twelve who were still busy with the assignment given them in Section 59. Seemingly, they moved back and forth between different areas of service as they sought to obey their Lord's instructions. See asterisk under main heading above.

[b] **"Every city and village."** What a sweeping statement! The number of villages and cities across Galilee were in the hundreds according to Josephus. See Section 42, footnote c. Such an enormous task must have taken months, even if the evangelists were divided up into teams (which surely they were) to cover this area. In our Lord making numerous missionary tours across Galilee, we learn the abiding lesson over the history of Christian evangelism that men must hear the Word of God repeatedly. In our vastly populated world of today, there is no such thing, as "they all have heard it enough."

[c] For comments on the two aspects of the kingdom of God, see Section 39, footnotes a and g.

[d] Luke affirms in this verse that the twelve went with Christ on this fifth Galilean preaching tour. Seemingly, the apostles at this time were still engaged in their work as commissioned earlier by Christ. See asterisk under main heading of Section 59 for details of this limited commission. There was overlapping of their initial assignment to go to the nation of Israel with other missionary endeavors such as the one mentioned above. See footnote b above.

[e] **The first "Women's Missionary Society."** Here we meet two of its charter members, Mary and Joanna. This band of faithful women is last seen standing in sight of the cross as their Lord died (Mk. 15:40-41). They were also at His tomb early on resurrection morning as seen in Lk. 24:10. It must not be thought that these women traveled day and night with Christ and his band. Such an act would have been considered scandalous. Probably, it means they were among the thousands of other followers who continually flocked about the Messiah and were coming and going. At some previous time, these particular women had been healed of various physical infirmities and demonic problems. There are six Mary's in the New Testament. These are listed in Section 9, footnote c. Of Mary Magdalene, Luke informs us that she was dispossessed of seven devils. This is *not* figurative language. On the exorcism of foul spirits, see Section 55, footnote d. According to Mk. 16:9, it was a literal, physical deliverance from demon possession. (See a curious reversal of this demonic reality in Section 68, Matt. 12:45, footnote e.) In this text she is called "Magdalene" to distinguish her from other women bearing the name of Mary.

2p-For centuries the Papal Church as well as many liberal "Protestants" have preached, painted, and sculptured her as a prostitute. The Roman system even made her the patron of penitent prostitutes for which there is not one scrap of evidence for this allegation. After her deliverance from "seven demons," she became a woman of stability and candor, as evidenced by Joanna the wife of Chuza (from the royal court of Herod Antipas) associating with her. See footnote f below for more on Joanna. Yet to have been possessed with "seven devils," she had given place through some kind of heinous sins for these evil entities to have entered her human body (Eph. 4:27). What her past sins were will remain a matter of conjecture among men but forgotten by God! See asterisk under main heading Section 40 for more on this thought of demon possession. Mary *never* forgot what the Lord Jesus did for her. Later, in the life of Christ, we see her at His crucifixion (John 19:25), and burial (Mk. 15:47) and among those who prepared the materials to embalm His body (Lk. 23:55-56). It is deeply instructive that she was the *first* to whom our Lord appeared after His resurrection (Mk. 16:9). Mary's conversation with the risen Christ is one of the most sublime pieces of Christian literature found in Holy Scripture. It is recorded in John 20:11-18.

(f) **Joanna.** *What an intriguing and mysterious woman!* She found time to travel amid the followers of Christ and assist them materially. Her name means, "Jehovah has been gracious." She was the wife of Chuza, Herod's steward, a prominent court official. Her name confirms she was Jewish. See footnote e above. Our Savior had disciples even in the halls of wicked Antipas' great palace! No wonder he had heard so much about Jesus.

2p-Chuza was a *chief* servant of Antipas and promoted to the high office of attending to the domestic affairs of the palace. Only absolute fidelity and complete trustworthiness could earn this position of service. Such persons were frequently referred to as "noblemen." Apparently, he did not oppose his wife's material assistance to the Savior and His twelve. Oddly, his name means "little pitcher." He may have been a Jew though some doubt this assumption. Some have tried to trace Chuza's genealogy to the book of Esther, and the infamous wretch named Haman. See Lightfoot's *Commentary on the New Testament . . . ,* vol. 3, pages 85-86. Further, it seems unfeasible (but not impossible) that Chuza was the *same* court official ("nobleman") as the one mentioned in the main heading of Section 37, John 4:46, footnote b, whose son Jesus healed. Over a year later, his wife Joanna is mentioned on the resurrection morning of Christ as still being in the company of Mary Magdalene (Lk. 24:10). Apparently, these two women were close friends in the service of Christ: their hearts filled with devotion and love for the Lord Jesus. Regarding the old scoundrel, Herod Antipas; years later, the grace of God again invaded his dark domain and saved Manaen, his foster-brother, who was listed among the great men in the first missionary church (Acts 13:1).

(g) **Susanna.** Found only here in Scripture and meaning "lily." One cannot help but connect the *etymology* of her name with our Lord's words about flowers in Matt. 6:28-29.

(h) **"Many others."** These two words embrace scores of faithful *female* disciples. Within this periphery of unnamed saints standing about the Lord Jesus, we can feel the heartbeat of God's work over the course of church history. In 1973, while the author was ministering God's Word in the Newholme Township, east of Pietermaritzburg, South Africa, he slipped and fell across a concrete curbing seriously bruising his left arm. Long will he remember the elderly Indian saint, "Mother Thomas," (as she was called) who so carefully bathed his arm in warm salt water, praying and speaking of God's love and care for me through the whole process. Surely, this kind woman (now in heaven) mirrored the heart of those *first* female saints who loved and served Jesus and His twelve. (We wonder who served Judas the traitor!) Though not inscribed on the pages of earth's books, they are written in the "Lamb's Book of Life." These nameless millions are the unseen and unsung heroes of the Christian faith; they are the spiritual Florence Nightingales of the cross: those who *give and give and give!* Here, the old proverb whispers to us "Blessed is the one who can give without remembering and receive without forgetting." Of such high character were these good and noble women who assisted the Messiah in His work. Their unselfish service of love has been forever inscribed on the pages of Holy Writ. For a look at all the women mentioned in the gospels, see *Gospel Women: Studies of the Named Woman in the Gospels,* by Richard Buckham. Herbert Lockyer, in his classic, *All the Men of the Bible: All the Women of the Bible,* deals with every female mentioned in Scripture.

2p-Lying love! Whatever happened to sin? These women followed Jesus out of love and loyalty. God's love (despite what radical Calvinist say) embraces all men but none of their sin for His perfect justice demands that sin be punished. "Lopsided" ministers talk *only* of "God's love." At the funerals of the violent and wicked, we hear great swelling words that they are "resting in peace," because "God loves everyone." One rarely hears the rest of the story. Sin's awful retribution in hell is suppressed or explained away. Bible statements that "The wages of sin is death" (Rom. 6:23), and "The wicked shall be turned into hell" (Ps. 9:17) are missing. God's love does not negate His other eternal attributes. They remain. He is infinitely holy, and His holiness has been offended by our sins. Only Jesus' atoning death can appease this offence. Apart from this, men are doomed. Preaching people into heaven because "God is love," is a vicious untruth. John 3:16 with 1 John 4:9-10 teaches that the highest demonstration of God's love was in giving Christ to die for our sins on the cross. Those who decease in their sin without Christ as Savior are doomed (John 8:21). Some twelve years ago, the wife of a prominent attorney died. I was to speak at her funeral. She had attended a notoriously liberal Baptist Church, and her funeral was to be held there. It was another "Baptist social club" and gathering station for young people to rock and roll their problems away. The pastor's habitual message was "love," "love," and more "love." Sin and salvation were taboo for this élite wealthy congregation. Locking my leg braces, I stood at a pulpit on floor level, and gave a simple gospel message on "How to go to heaven." The congregation was stunned. Some became angry, several older people walked out, a few nodded their shy approval. At the conclusion, I appealed for all who were unsaved to receive Christ as personal Lord and Savior. As I was being seated, the pastor leaped into the pulpit and said, "A funeral is a place for comfort not for preaching." As the people exited the building, some refused my handshake, others were visibly angry, a few thanked me. One older woman literally turned her face away and walked by. For years, these people had been fed "lying love" by a Judas pastor, and it was sending them to hell. *The love of God that saves us from sin and eternal damnation is the love of the cross and empty tomb.* It does not wink at evil, tolerate unrepentant, wicked church members, or give hypocrites and the Devil's crowd a front seat in heaven. Refer to Section 61, the second paragraph of footnote d for more on these things.

Thousands pressed upon the Savior to see and hear Him. Family and friends oppose His work. A second unique miracle*demonstrated He was the Messiah. The furious Jews blaspheme the Holy Spirit. Christ announces a terrible judgment on them.

Luke's version below of the healing of the blind and dumb man, and the blasphemy of the Spirit by the religious leaders, is indisputably the same as that recorded by Matthew and Mark. His account of this miracle has been lifted from its much later placement by Luke in chapter 11, and transferred back into Matthew's period for harmonizing them. It should be left as originally given.

*For the first recorded public miracle affirming that He was Israel's Messiah, see asterisk under main heading of Section 48. Note all four listings of exclusive Messianic signs under this Section.

Galilee

Matt. 12:22–25	Mk. 3:20–23	Lk. 11:14–17	John
	Crowds and conflict 20 And the multitude cometh together again, so that they could not so much as eat bread. 21 And when his friends heard *of it*, they went out to lay hold on him: for they said, "He is beside himself."[(a)]		
A Messianic miracle 22 Then was brought unto him one possessed with a devil, blind, and dumb: and he healed him, insomuch that the blind and dumb both spake and saw. 23 And all the people were amazed, and said, "Is not this the son of David?"[(b)]		***A Messianic miracle*** 14 And he was casting out a devil, and it was dumb. And it came to pass, when the devil was gone out, the dumb spake; and the people wondered.	
The Jews blaspheme 24 But when the Pharisees heard *it*, they said, "This *fellow* doth not cast out devils, but by Beelzebub the prince of the devils."[(c)]	***The Jews blaspheme*** 22 And the scribes which came down from Jerusalem said, "He hath Beelzebub, and by the prince of the devils[(c)] casteth he out devils."	***The Jews blaspheme*** 15 But some of them said, "He casteth out devils through Beelzebub the chief of the devils."[(c)] 16 And others, tempting *him*, sought of him a sign from heaven.	
Jesus' response 25 And Jesus knew their thoughts,[(d)] and said unto them,	***Jesus' response*** 23 And he called them *unto him*, and said unto them in parables,	***Jesus' response*** 17 But he, knowing their thoughts,[(d)] said unto them,	

Matt. 12:25-30	Mk. 3:23-27	Lk. 11:17-23	John
"Every kingdom divided against itself is brought to desolation; and every city or house divided against itself shall not stand:(e) 26 "And if Satan cast out Satan, he is divided against himself; how shall then his kingdom stand?	"How can Satan cast out Satan? 24 "And if a kingdom be divided against itself, that kingdom cannot stand. 25 "And if a house be divided against itself, that house cannot stand.(e) 26 "And if Satan rise up against himself, and be divided, he cannot stand, but hath an end.	"Every kingdom divided against itself is brought to desolation; and a house divided against a house falleth.(e) 18 "If Satan also be divided against himself, how shall his kingdom stand? because ye say that I cast out devils through Beelzebub.	
27 "And if I by Beelzebub cast out devils, by whom do your children cast them out?(f) therefore they shall be your judges. 28 "But if I cast out devils by the Spirit of God,(g) then the kingdom of God is come unto you.▶		19 "And if I by Beelzebub cast out devils, by whom do your sons cast them out?(f) therefore shall they be your judges. 20 "But if I with the finger of God(g) cast out devils, no doubt the kingdom of God is come upon you.	
	◀This means just what it says. The kingdom was a present reality but with future events and blessings yet to come.		
		Bind the strong man 21 "When a strong man armed keepeth his palace, his goods are in peace:	
Bind the strong man 29 "Or else how can one enter into a strong man's house, and spoil his goods, except he first bind the strong man? and then he will spoil(h) his house.	**Bind the strong man** 27 "No man can enter into a strong man's house, and spoil his goods, except he will first bind the strong man; and then he will spoil(h) his house.		
		22 "But when a stronger than he shall come upon him, and overcome(h) him, he taketh from him all his armour wherein he trusted, and divideth his spoils.	
30 "He that is not with me is against me; and he that gathereth not with me scattereth abroad.(i)		23 "He that is not with me is against me: and he that gathereth not with me scattereth."(i) (Verse 24 cont. in Section 68.)	

304

Matt. 12:31-37	Mk. 3:28-30	Lk. 11	John
They had committed the unpardonable sin **31** "Wherefore I say unto you, All manner of sin and blasphemy shall be forgiven unto men: but the blasphemy[j] *against* the *Holy* Ghost shall not be forgiven unto men.	*They had committed the unpardonable sin* **28** "Verily I say unto you, All sins shall be forgiven unto the sons of men, and blasphemies wherewith soever they shall blaspheme: **29** "But he that shall blaspheme[j] against the Holy Ghost hath never forgiveness, but is in danger of eternal damnation: *He is falsely charged* **30** Because they said, "He [Jesus] hath an unclean spirit." (Verse 31 cont. in Section 69.)		

How this sin was committed

32 "And whosoever speaketh a word against the Son of man, it shall be forgiven him: but whosoever speaketh against the Holy Ghost, it shall not be forgiven him, neither in this world, neither in the *world* to come.
33 "Either make the tree good, and his fruit good; or else make the tree corrupt, and his fruit corrupt: for the tree is known by *his* fruit.[k]

The scribes and Pharisees were a generation of self-condemned vipers
34 "O generation of vipers,[l] how can ye, being evil, speak good things? for out of the abundance of the heart the mouth speaketh.
35 "A good man out of the good treasure of the heart[m] bringeth forth good things: and an evil man out of the evil treasure bringeth forth evil things.
36 "But I say unto you,[n] That every idle word that men shall speak, they shall give account thereof in the day of judgment.
37 "For by thy words thou shalt be justified, and by thy words thou shalt be condemned."[o]
(Verse 38 cont. in Section 67.)

Footnotes-Commentary

[a] **Splendid insanity. "He is beside himself."** Our Lord's discourse was halted at this point by a sudden interruption. News of His miraculous work and fierce conflict with the nation's religious leaders had reached home in Galilee and spread among His friends. They heard the news that Jesus had boldly repudiated the scribes and Pharisees with public rebuke and correction. Alarm gripped the family and friends of Christ, and they have now arrived amid thousands to take Him away. Even His relatives did not understand Him, His message, and work. However, this is good insanity! Would to God that more people were infected with this heavenly virus.

2p-At this point, the whole country was in great tumult over the carpenter from Nazareth. The question on all lips was, "Is He our Messiah or not?" See footnote i below. The "friends" mentioned here (Mk. 3:21) have reference to both His neighbors and family members. They decided that He had lost His mind and went to take Him home by force. A short time later in Mk. 3:31-32, it is made clear that both His mother and half-brothers were among the "friends" standing outside the house, where He was. They sent word for Him to come out saying, "He is beside himself." We also note the mocking ridicule of His half-brothers about six or seven months before the cross in Section 111, John 7:3-5, footnote d. These verses affirm that even at this late point in the ministry of the Savior neither family nor friends yet understood the real purpose of His work. Let a man find and receive the saving grace of God, have his life utterly transformed, withdraw from the wild and daring amusements or crooked business of this

305

life, begin to warn his friends and neighbors of eternity, and he will soon be put down as being deranged! However, the unsaved man can endanger his life in work, sports or some daring, plunge into the damning vortex of sin and earthly follies, and he is hailed as "hero," a "great adventurer," and "a model for the youth." Such is the caviling prattle of a world living in horrible spiritual darkness without Christ. *Few men realize that there was a time in the past when they were not, but there will never be a time in the present and future when they will not be!*

(b) **"Son of David"** was the highest Name for Israel's Messiah. It is used of Him in the Talmud tractates, Chagigah 16a; Eiruvin 43b; and Sukkah 52b. To the shock of the people, He instantly expelled the demon causing dumbness. See number 2 by the asterisk under main heading, Section 48, where this was strictly considered an exclusive Messianic miracle. Crowd reaction to this cure confirmed the people knew that *only* Messiah could perform such a marvelous work. The amazed onlookers instantly identified Jesus by their interrogatory question: "Is not this the Son of David?" or "the Messiah?" For details of Christ descending from King David's family line, see Chapter 3, Section 7, blocks number 4 and 5. Many times, they had heard the rabbis explain Isa. 35:5, for it predicted *one* of the unique Messianic miracles. "Then shall the eyes of the blind be opened, and the ears of the deaf shall be unstopped." Jesus had cured a deaf mute, but *only* Messiah could do such a wonder. The rabbis reasoned that in casting out demons, one must contact the evil spirit, and command it out by name to leave. However, with a deaf mute this was impossible for he could not hear. Consequently, this was a wonder that only Israel's true Messiah could do.

(c) **The prince of hell, a vicious slanderer.** Realizing to their horror that Jesus had *again* shown that He was Israel's Messiah, the purveyors of the Jewish religion resort to blasphemy to save their faces. The Messianic work just done must be accredited to another source, not to Jesus of Nazareth. In Matt. 12:24, they claimed that Jesus' source of power was "Beelzebub." See Section 59, footnote m for the meaning of the pagan term Beelzebub. The scribes and Pharisees were equating Christ's miracle as having its origin with the Devil! There prevailed a belief among the Jews, that only *one* Devil existed, who was head or god over all evil and foul spirits. He was referred to by such names as the "prince of hell," "the angel of death," and often by the name "Asmodeus." Later, in the fluxion of the Hebrew language amid pagans, he became known among the Jews as "Beelzebub." Every person in the audience understood the vicious slander their leaders had laid upon Christ. It was the highest of insults. For an excellent excursus on ancient Jewish beliefs concerning Satan, demons and angels, refer to Alfred Edersheim's *The Life and Times of Jesus the Messiah*, Appendix 13.

(d) See Section 64, footnote h for how Christ knew their thoughts. This is evidence that He was God in human flesh. Regarding the Jewish mania for Messiah to produce signs (verse 16), refer to Section 29, footnote e, and notes by the asterisk under main heading Section 48.

(e) Seemingly, this was a common saying among the Jews. Instantly, Messiah made their wicked accusation recoil upon their heads. The great Presbyterian minister, Dr. Albert Barnes, gives a clear explanation with these words, "It is your doctrine that Satan has helped me to undo what he had done. He has aided me [and] cast himself out, that is, to oppose and discomfit himself. If this is true how can there be any stability in his kingdom?" See *Barnes' Notes on the New Testament,* pages 130-131 where he demonstrated the gross absurdity of the Pharisee's charge that Satan could be his own enemy and cast out his own demons as the Jews affirmed in verse 24.

(f) **"By whom do your children cast out devils?** This reveals that some of the children of the religious leaders were involved in exorcism. Our Lord takes their blasphemous charge even deeper and points out that it should be laid upon their children. He was saying, "If your argument is right then your children are also in league with the Devil for they too cast out demons." We have a classic example of Jewish exorcism in Acts 19:13-17. Among the Jews of this time and for many years prior, were traveling exorcists. They did their work for a fee! Christ here refers to these as "children" or "disciples" of the Pharisees. They were infamous for the use of magical incantations, washings, red cloth, black strings, roots, and animal skins used to exorcise evil spirits. (Witch doctors in Africa use many of these exact methods today in attempting to "deliver" those who are demon possessed.)

2p-For other comments on the Jews and evil spirits, see Section 41, second paragraph of footnote g. A brief explanation of "Jewish demonology" as it existed in the days of Christ, is found in F. W. Farrar's *Life of Christ*, pages 745-746. Josephus wrote about expelling demons in *Wars of the Jews,* Book 7:6. 3, line 185. He also mentioned Solomon's use of exorcism in *Antiquities*, Book 8:2. 5, lines 47 through 49. It is to be noticed that the story about Solomon, smacks of typical rabbinical exaggeration. For King Saul's strange demonic experience, refer also to *Antiquities,* Book 6:8. 2, line 166.

(g) **"By the Spirit of God."** In this statement, Christ lays a terse claim to being the Messiah. With the conclusion of the book of Malachi, it was taught by the rabbis that the Holy Spirit had departed from Israel, and He would only return with the appearing of Messiah. His presence would be irrefutable proof that the kingdom of God had appeared for the nation of Israel, so they believed. Every informed Jew understood that the Lord Jesus was claiming again to be the Messiah. Our Lord's Words here, demonstrate that the (spiritual) kingdom was a *present reality* among them at that time (Matt 12:28). It was not a future entity thousands of years away. As stated in this work, this kingdom gradually became known as the church as we follow the progression through the book of Acts and Paul's letters. There will yet be some kind of kingdom in which saved Israel will play a leading role. It will be shared by Gentile believers and will last forever.

2p-"Finger of God." This was a Jewish expression for a particular action caused by God. The Jews explained the finger as being one of the five in the hand; it worked by the power of Elohim. When the Almighty was doing a particular work this was often described as the "hand of the Lord." The magicians of the pagan King of Egypt used these words to confess that Israel's God was the cause of the judgment falling upon their land (Ex. 8:19). It was the "finger of God" that inscribed the Torah Law into the tables of stone (Ex. 31:18). Jesus adamantly affirmed that He had cast out the demon and performed this exclusive Messianic miracle by "the Spirit of God" or "finger of God" (Lk. 11:20). With the finger of God, the Lord Jesus wrote in the dust of the temple floor a message that sent his enemies to flight (John 8:6). It is indeed interesting that the Savior used the expression here and applied it to the blessed Holy Spirit in His work against demonic powers.

(h) To refute the lie of the long-robed Pharisees, Christ draws another illustration; that of a house being broken into. He had previously employed a similar metaphor in the Sermon on the Mount in Section 46, Matt. 6:19-20. In Jesus' lesson, the "strong man" is the demon dwelling securely inside the human house or body. Only one superior to this emissary of Satan can enter the captive house and then overthrow, spoil, or drive out the "strong man." Before their very eyes, both the people and the Pharisees had witnessed this supernatural overthrow successfully accomplished by Jesus. He must be the Messiah for now a man formerly blind and dumb, sees, and hears! Christ's astounding miracle answered the people's question: "Yes, He is the son of David our promised Messiah."

2p-About thirty years later, the apostle Paul stood before King Agrippa, a man well acquainted with Jewish theology, and declared that Jesus of Nazareth was the "hope to come" for the nation of Israel (Acts 26:3, 7-10). As mentioned previously, all the "academic speculation" regarding whether or not Jesus was that Messianic Person is a brainy pursuit into vanity and unbelief of Holy Scripture.

(i) After an irrefutable demonstration that He was Messiah, our Lord issued this decisive and powerful charge. "If you are not for me, you are against me." There are no neutral grounds! Surely, this must have shaken those wavering between two opinions of Him. "Is He our Messiah or is He not?"

(j) "Blasphemy." In the most dreadful terms, the Son of God charges the religious leaders of Israel with blasphemy of (or speaking hurtfully against) the Holy Spirit. The Jews had a saying that "God pardons all sins except lasciviousness." Here, the Messiah publicly disagrees with another rabbinical maxim and informs them that they have just committed the *only* sin that God will *not* forgive! Controversy has raged over what this sin was. Contextually, Christ carefully explained it to His audience. Matt. 12:32 clearly says that it is "speaking against the Holy Ghost." On all sides today, we hear men with foul tongues employing the Names of both God and Jesus Christ in their verbal insanity. God is flippantly called upon to "damn" this or that. The Name Jesus Christ is articulated in ways that are both sacrilegious and vile. *However, never does one hear the Name of the Third Person of the Holy Trinity invoked in such reckless profanity.* The Pharisees, in assigning the work of the Holy Spirit to Satan and acclaiming that Jesus had produced this miracle by the aid of a demon, had stepped over the line into the dark realm of no forgiveness. Mark settles the meaning of Christ's terrible Words by writing, "in danger of eternal damnation" (Mk. 3:29). The term "danger" signals that it is pending; something yet to come. How many times one may blaspheme by evil words the blessed Spirit of God, before crossing the fatal line is not stated. However, we gather from the text that the scribes and Pharisees had gone too far. It is noted that a short time later in Section 68, Christ compared Israel to a man who was demonized seven times over and his last estate was worse than his former. This was a perfect description of the Jews in general and *most* of their religious leaders, in particular.

2p-There are some Messianic Jews and Christians who believe this was a sin *exclusive* to Israel's religious leaders at that time, that it is no longer possible for men of this present age to commit this dreaded offense. Contextually, strong merit exists for this interpretation. Regardless, the wise man will guard his heart and lips with all caution to refrain from using the Name of the Holy Spirit in a glib, vulgar, suggestive, joking sort of manner. Normal Christians may enjoy clean humor at the right time and place; however, every mention of Holy things should be left out of all acceptable and merry conversations. Jokes about Jesus, Paul, Saint Peter, and so on, are taking things too far, and have no place in the conversation of born again believers. There are too many other things to converse about without dragging God's Word into the story.

(k) Christ has spoken similar Words during the Sermon on the Mount. See Section 47, and Matt. 7:17-20, footnote i. This is another example of Jesus repeating Himself with only slight word changes to fit the occasion. The Lord Jesus was laying this expression upon the heads of the religious leaders of Israel. Their rejection of Him as Messiah led them into producing only bad fruit and thousands of believers knew this.

(l) "O generation of vipers." What a damning declaration! The meaning here is that the scribes, Pharisees and Israel's religionists were actually the offspring of vipers; their parents were of the same stock! The word means "brood of snakes." Later, in Matt. 23:29-33, He again spoke of their serpentine origin. The viper was a poisonous asp or adder. The most common ones are about four inches long, no thicker than a wire, lurking under stones, in cracks, in the sand, along footpaths even in houses, beds, and buildings. They look harmless and helpless. Children, reaching out for them, were often struck a deadly blow. They become fierce and aggressive when disturbed. John the Baptist called the religious leaders "vipers," in Matt. 3:7. It was a standard word, commonly used among the ancients, to describe the worst of dangerous men. Two days before His death, Christ used this term again in describing the religious leaders of Israel. See this in Section 159, Matt 23:33, footnote u.

2p-Is the face a window to the soul? Yes, but no! Some people wear on their faces what they are in their hearts. Others are too clever for this. What we really are has its origin inside not outside. The Savior's words, "from out of the abundance of the heart the mouth speaketh" (verse 34) remain true. Often, men and women who seem deeply pious, devoted to moral and religious ideals suddenly turn into verbal monsters. In these times, the most vile and violent language known to mortal ear pours from their tongues. These people have an inward problem, not outward. Many a black and bloody heart is hidden behind a white shirt or pretty blouse. The reason that filth and corruption pours from so many mouths is that it comes from the filth and corruption inside. Therefore, the inside of man must be miraculously changed; only God can do this. Our Savior declared in verse 37, "For by thy words thou shalt be justified, and by thy words thou shalt be condemned." In the context of Jesus' statement, the religious leaders of Israel had just accused Him of being in a league with Satan (verse 24). These awful words demonstrated the hatred of their hearts toward Messiah. Instantly, the Lord Jesus affirmed that a man's words would condemn or justify him. That is, the one who speaks right and truth reflects his correct standing or justification before God. The one who *habitually* utters lies and evil moves under God's awful condemnation. See footnote o below for more on this serious thought and the illustration in Section 203, fourth paragraph of footnote e.

(m) See Section 58, Lk. 6:45, footnote t, for the only way a wicked heart is made "good."

(n) With these august statements, Messiah concludes the address to His hostile hearers. He issued a final solemn warning: they were headed for the judgment of God! Contextually, all the evil things they had said about Him, their Messiah, even every "idle word" would be accounted for. At this point, the religious leaders had already laid enough blasphemous charges against the innocent Jesus to condemn themselves forever. Their heinous hatred and verbal traducing of our Lord sprang from their *intentional* and *deliberate* rejection of Him as the Messiah of God and Savior of men. Refer to Section 52, John 5:40 for an earlier encounter with the Sanhedrin, in which He bluntly told them "And ye will not come to me, that ye might have life" Void of all reverence toward the Son of God, these pious, fringed and pompous clerics willingly made their beds in hell (Ps. 139:8).

(o) The Son of God warns that the whole tenor of our conversation will give evidence of our relationship with God and the content of our hearts. The religious leaders had just uttered the most heinous statement against the Lord Jesus Christ. Their awful words are found in Matt. 12:24, footnote c. Did their words not exhibit solid proof that they were condemned and unjustified before Him, whose dear Son they had so wickedly scorned? See second paragraph of footnote l above for other comments on this, as well as the second paragraph below.

2p-*Gill's Commentary,* vol. 7, page 136 informs us that this was a common saying among the Jews. It was solemnly used in court proceedings to warn the accused of the consequences of their words. Christ takes this well-known expression and lays it upon the religious leaders. Men who act so deeply pious, but have *never ending* poison pouring from an unbridled tongue, are sure subjects for hell fire. Our Lord using this saying may have taken it from Job 15:6. Solomon wrote, "Death and life are in the power of the tongue" (Prov. 18:21). The Pharisees were their own judge and jury, and their dreadful blasphemous words firmly condemned them.

The scribes and Pharisees request a second sign* from Jesus to prove He was the real Messiah. He predicts that the men of Nineveh, and a queen will rise in judgment and condemn their generation. Being full of darkness and sin, Israel deliberately rejects Him as their Messiah and seals their fate.

*Originally, the Jews requested the first sign over a year ago at the Passover. Refer to asterisk under main heading, Section 29, John 2:18, footnotes e and g. On that occasion, He first publicly presented Himself as Israel's Messiah and told them to look for the sign of His resurrection. Their second sign request is below (verse 38). The third is in Section 100. On each occasion, He informed the religious leaders that there would be only one sign for Israel: His resurrection from the dead, which would prove that He was indeed God. Refer to Section 199 for the reaction of Israel's religious leaders when confronted with the fact of His resurrection.

Galilee

Matt. 12:38–42	Mk.	Lk. 11:29–32	John
		The Jews seek a sign: His response 29 And when the people were gathered thick together,	
The Jews want a sign: His response 38 Then certain of the scribes and of the Pharisees answered, saying, "Master, we would see a sign from thee."[a]			
Only evil men seek a sign 39 But he answered and said unto them, "An evil and adulterous generation[b] seeketh after a sign; and		*Only evil men seek a sign* he began to say, "This is an evil generation:[b] they seek a sign; and	
They shall be given one sign: *His resurrection from the dead* there shall no sign be given to it, but the sign of the prophet Jonas:[c]		*They shall be given one sign:* *His resurrection from the dead* there shall no sign be given it, but the sign of Jonas the prophet.[c] 30 For as Jonas was a sign unto the Ninevites, so shall also the Son of man be to this generation.	
40 "For as 'Jonas was three days and three nights in the whale's belly;'[d] so shall the Son of man be three days and three nights in the heart of the earth.			
Condemned by Gentiles 41 "The men of Nineveh[e] ◀ shall rise in judgment with this generation, and shall condemn it: because 'they repented at the preaching of Jonas;' and, behold, a greater than Jonas *is* here.		◀*Matthew places the men of Nineveh at verse 41 in his narrative, while Luke puts it in verse 32 below.*	
A Gentile queen was wiser than you 42 "The queen[f] of the south shall rise up in the judgment with this generation, and shall condemn it: for 'she came from the uttermost parts[g] of the earth to hear the wisdom of Solomon;' and, behold, a greater than Solomon *is* here." (Verse 43 cont. in Section 68.)		*A Gentile queen was wiser than you* 31 "The queen[f] of the south shall rise up in the judgment with the men of this generation, and condemn them: for 'she came from the utmost parts[g] of the earth to hear the wisdom of Solomon;' and, behold, a greater than Solomon *is* here.	
Luke places the men of Nineve[h] in verse 32 ▶		*Condemned by Gentiles* 32 "The men of Nineve[h] shall	

Section 67: Again, the religious leaders of Israel seek to trap Christ. He responds to their folly.

Matt.	Mk.	Lk. 11:32-36	John
of his record. Matthew puts it in verse 41 above. For more on how the gospels were written, see the explanation given just before Section 29. This style was the choice of divine inspiration. It has nothing to do with the critical myth of various writers compiling the four gospels or books of the New Testament over many decades of time.		rise up in the judgment with this generation, and shall condemn it: for they 'repented at the preaching of Jonas;' and, behold, a greater than Jonas *is* here.	

Let your light shine for Me

33 "No man, when he hath lighted a candle, putteth *it* in a secret place, neither under a bushel, [basket], but on a candlestick, [light holder], that they which come in may see the light.[(h)]

Beware of darkness in your soul: choose rather inward light

34 "The light of the body is the eye: therefore when thine eye is single, thy whole body also is full of light; but when *thine eye* is evil,[(i)] thy body also *is* full of darkness.

35 "Take heed therefore that the light which is in thee be not darkness.

36 "If thy whole body therefore *be* full of light, having no part dark, the whole shall be full of light, as when the bright shining of a candle doth give thee light."[(j)] (Verse 37 cont. in Section 70.)

Footnotes-Commentary

[(a)] **"Signs, signs, and more signs."** On the Jew's obsession with signs, see all of Section 29, footnote e, and the asterisk under main heading in Section 48. In requiring a sign from Jesus, the Jews were saying, "Perform a great miracle now, and we will believe you are the Messiah." Though Christ had performed hundreds of amazing wonders, He refused to produce a "miracle on demand" for these religious hypocrites. It is noteworthy that they wanted "a sign from heaven." However, the Messiah would give them one from the earth-His resurrection from the dead. A short time later, the religious leaders approached Jesus again and requested another "sign from heaven." See Section 100, Matt. 16:1, second paragraph of footnote a for more on this subject.

[(b)] **"Evil and adulterous generation."** This was an expression used by the Hebrews of the Gentiles. However, the Lord Jesus described this generation of Jews as being both "wicked and adulterous." For a review of every place Matthew used the word "generation" in relationship to the Jews, see Section 106, footnote c. Certain dispensationalists have distorted the word "generation" along with the even more extreme postmillennialists. All the talk about it meaning, "a race," or "a people," or "stock," or "family," or "it can be substituted for the nation Israel," is wrong. Alfred Plummer put it this way "Here, [in Matthew 12] as elsewhere in the gospels, this expression [generation] can hardly mean anything else than Christ's own contemporaries." To make it mean the "Jewish race or a race of believers or the whole race of mankind," is unacceptable. See Plummer's *The Gospel According to St. Mark*, page 305. His comment is especially applicable to the over worked "double usage" of this word that is employed by the various "authorities" when interpreting Matt. 23:33, 36. This is done to make the text fit a prior eschatological error. Five times in Matt. 12:34-45, Jesus used the term "generation." *It was His Jewish audience in front of Him that He was rebuking, not the Hebrew nation over two thousand years later.* The Jews standing there were that evil and adulterous generation who were looking for a Messianic sign. In Lk. 11:30, the Savior said He was a sign to "this generation," which meant *that* generation! Their only sign of Him would be His empty tomb illustrated in the story of Jonah. It must be remembered that *a single generation of Jews* actually witnessed the sign of Christ's death, burial, and resurrection. In addition, some of these were among the people listening to Him teaching on this occasion. He was speaking to them!

2p-One can safely embrace the obvious truths of balanced premillennialism without distorting Scripture. The large amount of religious literature promoting semantic hairsplitting, date picking and forcing the text into arbitrary interpretations of the word "generation" has done irreparable damage to the truth of our Lord's return. *Leave this word alone. It means just what it says!* Beware of the teaching that makes the word "generation" have reference to people living two thousand years later. These teachers seem to have forgotten that Israel again became a nation on May 14, 1948. They affirm that a "generation is about forty years." Thus, from 1948 forward, forty years, would be 1988, the year of Christ's return! Hal Lindsey used this time setting blunder in his best selling book, *The Late Great Planet Earth,* pages 53-54. For further comments on "generation" see asterisk under main heading Section 68, footnote g. For well over half a century the author of this work has heard men preach, teach and affirm, "Jesus is coming soon, even in our lifetime, for all signs point to this fact." Many of these men have been dead for decades and Christ has not come! Who was wrong? In 1919, the great Methodist preacher, Luther B. Bridgers, published the beautiful hymn, *He Keeps Me Singing*. The fourth verse reads, "Soon He's coming back to welcome me ..." Bridgers penned this hymn after losing his wife and children in a terrible fire. That was over ninety years ago.

Another "soon" for our Lord's return has proven wrong. The prudent minister will affirm, "Christ is coming for He said so, but we do not know when it will occur." He will leave the "soons" and "signs glitches" out of his message. For more on this popular but greatly abused subject, see *Appendix Eight.*

3p-"Seeketh a sign." The word "sign" is found in the Talmud five hundred and fifteen times. Many of these usages have reference to end-time and Messianic signs. See footnote a above for more on Jews and signs. Everyone understood what Jesus was saying. It was serious when Christ charged that those Jews were "evil and adulterous" sign seekers. Here, Jesus' Words should warn that vast army of "sign seekers" within the church today. They are forever looking here and there for a shred of evidence that will reveal (to them) the date of our Lord's return. Such speculative saints are hindrances to the cause of Christ; always talking about "the Jew," or "war in the Middle East," or "seeing prophecy fulfilled in newspaper headlines," and "world events." Almost two thousand years of church history *continually* proves them shamefully wrong. Swift to condemn the cults for setting dates, they habitually do the same thing. Such practices have brought great reproach upon the cause of Christ. Every *true* sign in Scripture is for warning the saints to be ready that He is coming. *None of them tell us when that time will be.* In the context of Matt. 12:39, the Messiah was directing His remarks to the scribes, Pharisees, their associates in religion, and the people in general. He was speaking to *that* "generation" of Jewish people sitting and standing *immediately* in front of Him, especially the religious leaders. *They* were the sinful "generation" of which He spoke. As explained in footnote a above, they asked Him for Messianic signs to prove that He was Messiah, not signs of His second coming. At this point, in His ministry, they did not understand His death on the cross, and resurrection, much less His return several thousand years later for the church. Their request for signs could not have included anything pertaining to the appearing of Christ for His church. This was only revealed later, mostly in Paul's letters.

4p-Jewish signs for the coming Messiah. Hebrew religion rotted to the core. The Jewish sages laid down numerous signs proving *when* their Messiah would come to save Israel and set up His political kingdom. None of these pointed to His second advent as we know it today; they had never heard of such a thing! In the Talmud, it states that in the day Messiah appears [to establish His earthly kingdom] sin would be rampant in Israel: corn and wine costly, government corrupt, disrespect of elders would prevail among children, and the synagogues would become brothels. See Talmud tractate, Sanhedrin 97a and 98a. When Christ called these Jews "wicked and adulterous," morals had dropped so low that the "bitter water test" given by God, through which those guilty of adultery could be detected, had been discontinued. See Num. 5:11-31 for the strange story of this test. This discontinuance was made official by the voice of Rabbi Jochanan ben Zacchai because Israel had been nicknamed "an adulterous race of people." Everyone listening knew what Jesus meant when He called them "an evil and adulterous generation." Josephus was lived contemporary with some of these people or at least their children. He wrote these scathing remarks about their moral and spiritual decadence, "For that time was fruitful among the Jews in all sorts of wickedness, so that they left no wicked deed undone; nor was there any new form of wickedness which anyone could invent if he wished to do so. Thus, they were all corrupt in both their public and private life relations, and they vied with each other over who should excel in impiety toward God and injustice to men. The more powerful oppressed the common people, and the common people eagerly sought to destroy the more powerful . . ." Quoted from, *Introduction to the Gospel Records,* by William Nast, page 145, printed in 1866. The pious talk heard today that "the temple was a place of learning the truth of God and to receive instructions from the noble rabbis and teachers of the law" is a joke. The above quotations, even from one of their own who lived among them during this era, belies this claim. God judged these religious hypocrites in the horrific destruction of A.D. 70 at the hands of the vicious pagan Roman armies. Also, read Christ's fierce denunciations of them in Section 159, Matt. 23.

(c) "The prophet Jonas." Devout Jews were familiar with the story of Jonah recorded in their Scriptures. Nevertheless, the rabbis taught some odd things about the running prophet. An example of this rabbinical extremism is noted in the Talmud tractate, Nedarim 38a, where a certain rabbi said that Jonah rented (hired) the entire ship on which he sailed for the sum of four thousand gold denarii! These were several years' wages! In this, the Messiah selected this prophet and his real experience as pointing to the only sign the Jews will get from Him. No other would be given. Christ did not mean that He would work no further miracles, for He did. Rather, He is informing the religious leaders that they will not get the sign they have requested. Up to this point in His ministry, our Lord had performed thousands of signs, miracles, and wonders, but these wicked religionists wanted something better. They could not deny that His works were real. They ask for an extraordinary performance on His part. One is struck by the audacity of these hypocrites who had just accused Jesus of performing miracles by a league with the Devil. Now, they ask Him for one! See Section 100, Matt. 16:4, footnote e for a later mention of Jonah.

(d) A general quotation from Jonah 1:17 confirms that Christ accepted the story as literal history. Couched in this statement, He makes another covert mention of His death on the cross and burial. Every Jew standing in that congregation knew the story of Jonah and his confinement within the sea creature for "three days and nights." *Assuming* that Jonah died, by a miracle of Jehovah he was resurrected back to life. Some eighteen months later, Jesus' body also rose from the tomb after "three days and nights" of confinement. How many Jews upon learning of His resurrection, recalled later the words spoken on that occasion and *then* understood their significance? He was informing the scribes and Pharisees of His upcoming death, burial, and resurrection, prefigured in the factual history of Jonah. They missed it again, yet what He said greatly troubled their minds. This is seen in their requesting soldiers to guard His tomb after burial and their terror at His resurrection. Refer to this in Sections 194 and 199.

2p-"In the heart of . . ." was a common Hebraism. For example, in Ex. 15:8, it is "the heart of the sea," in Ps. 10:6 a certain person "said in his heart." Nevertheless, here it is more than a Jewish by-word. *The "heart of the earth" was not Joseph's tomb!* That was on top of the earth. In using these terms, Christ referred to where His soul would be while His corpse lay in the grave. The real Person Jesus Christ moved out of His human body when it expired on the cross. A thousand years before, the Psalmist had predicted of Messiah, that at His death His "soul would not be left in hell, neither would His body see corruption or decay" (Ps. 16:10). The word "hell" in this text is "sheol," which is the exact equivalent to the Greek word "hades." On the day of Pentecost, Simon Peter quoted this very passage (Ps. 16:10) in Acts 2:31, and here the "sheol" of the Psalm is translated by "hades" in the Greek. These two words have reference to *one* place in the "heart of the earth" divided into two different compartments or sections. They are separated by a "great gulf" or impasse. One side was a region of horrible conscious suffering amid fiery torments; the other was that of conscious tranquility and rest amid divine bliss. Refer to Section 131, for further explanation of sheol-hades in the story of Lazarus and the rich man.

3p-Hell's house under the earth. The souls of all believers who died physically *before* the perfect and final atonement of Christ, and His resurrection went into the blissful side of sheol-hades to rest, waiting for Christ's eternal atonement and victory over death and the grave. Peter interprets Ps. 16:10 as saying that Jesus' soul left his physical body at death and went down into this place; but He did not stay, for the text reads, "his soul was not left" in hell or sheol-hades. Later, as an old man, Peter wrote that Jesus went there and preached (1 Peter 3:18-20) to the millions the grand news that the eternal redemption was accomplished, and death defeated. In 1 Peter 4:6 it expressly affirms that Christ "preached the gospel" to these saved, Old Testament believers waiting for God's final redemption to be historically accomplished. He told them that He had died and would rise victorious over death, hell and the grave. Then, the Lord Jesus led them from this holding station where they were waiting as captives of God: He took them and ascended far above all heavens. Eph. 4:8-11 is clear that He escorted these saints from the "lower parts of the earth" and into heaven. Regardless of how much pagan mythology has been mixed over the centuries with the Bible doctrine of hell and heaven, they remain solid facts of Holy Scripture. Hell is still hell and heaven is still heaven. *Most men will only be convinced of this after their arrival in one of the other.*

4p-Hell and heaven are not pagan myths. The fact of sheol-hades was known from the beginning. After the scattering of the human race from the Tower of Babel, millions of gods and goddesses were fashioned by heathen families, tribes, priests, clans, and nations around the world. Inspired by Satan and demons, they created countless perversions of God, Jesus Christ, and eternal truth. Every nation in antiquity of which there are extant records had their unique *perversions* of hell or sheol-hades. Egypt, Babylon, Persia, Assyria, Greece, Rome, the savage tribes of Europe, England, the isles of the sea, and the cruel Norseman of Scandinavia; all believed in an afterlife. The bloodthirsty Mayans of Central America offered human sacrifices to avoid going to a large cave-like house of fire and torment located under the earth after death! Others practiced similar rituals. One is aghast at the "professional theologians" appearing on national television who so eloquently explain away the fact of sin, hell, heaven, and the after life. *All* of them will someday be totally convinced upon arrival in the place they have denied. Their verdict is always the same: the biblical teaching of an afterlife, in a glorious heaven, or horrible hell was borrowed from the earlier pagan beliefs. Some of them affirm that Jesus "used pagan teachings" when He spoke of the afterlife. This is another academic lie designed to shunt men from Christ and eternal life. From the beginning, the Devil perverted God's truth about these things, then commenced and continued this through idolatry and religious heathenism. He continues it today in the "civilized world" through Antichrist theologians, institutions of learning, churches, religions, and the secular media. Nevertheless, God has always had a remnant that knew truth and held to it. For more on the above successful devices of the Devil, see Section 1, Part 2, second through fourth paragraphs of footnote f. Regarding the way to heaven, Christ warned, "Few there be that find it" (Matt. 7:14 with John 14:6).

(e) **"The men of Nineveh"** Though dead and gone for over seven hundred years, nevertheless, they were still alive somewhere and would rise in God's judgment with *that generation* of Jews and condemn them for rejecting Messiah. Luke wrote, that as Jonah in his resurrection from the whale was a "sign unto the Ninevites," so likewise Christ in His resurrection was a sign to Israel (Lk. 11:30). For more on this, see first paragraph footnote d above. In contrast, the preaching of Jonah brought the pagans of the vast city down into the dust of repentance, whereas the preaching of Christ infuriated the Jews so madly that they continually sought to destroy Him.

(f) **"The queen of the south."** This is another general quotation from either 1 Kings 10:1 or 2 Chron. 9:1. She woman is called the "Queen of Sheba" in 1 Kings 10:1. A man bearing the name Sheba was one of the sons of Joktan, a grandson of Arphaxad, who settled in the southern parts of Arabia (Gen. 10:28 with 1 Chron. 1:22). Tradition has given the Queen of Sheba many names such as "Zemargad, Maqueda, Balkis, Nicolaa, and Jaman." An ancient *legend* relates that Solomon married her and had a son named Menelek. (It is often difficult to distinguish between legend and truth.) From him supposedly came the Falasha or Black Jews of Ethiopia so prominent in later Hebrew history. Whoever she was, she had enough sense to turn from paganism and believe in the true and living God after hearing and seeing the evidence for His existence in the court of Solomon. This was better than the Jews did to Christ. After witnessing His Messianic miracles for some three years, they rejected Him.

2p-Modern day pagans. They resent hearing that Jesus is the only Savior. Nature is their religion but rarely talk about where nature came from. "Civilized" pagans no longer dance around blood sacrifice, or cut their bodies, and slaughter their enemies. *Any "Earth spiritual path" that replaces Christ leads to doom (Acts 4:12).*

(g) "Uttermost parts." This was an eastern euphemism for the extreme distances. Having traveled far to meet King Solomon, the Queen of Sheba *saw* and *heard* the wonders of his God and kingdom. She melted into humility and instantly believed Jehovah as the only true and living God (1 Kings 10:4-10). See footnote f above. On the other hand, the Jews had both *seen* and *heard* the works and Words of Christ, who had traveled from heaven to earth, but despised Him as Messiah and blasphemed His miracles. See footnote e above for comments about former dead men appearing in judgment to condemn these Christ rejecters. God's judgment upon sinners will have witnesses even from among the dead in His terrible day of reckoning. In this awful time, the Jews will have the cursed Gentiles stand in judgment and condemn them for their blatant rejection of Messiah. However, the Gentile pagans of Nineveh received the Hebrew prophet Jonah and obeyed his message. The expression, "the wisdom of Solomon" was a Jewish saying that lives to this day. It is also found in the Talmud tractate, Megilah 7a.

2p-"The wisdom of Solomon." Great stress is placed on human wisdom. Old works, such as *The Art of Worldly Wisdom,* written in 1647 by a Jesuit priest, attracts some with its pert comments about life. However, at the end of the road, the man who dies without Christ as personal Lord and Savior is the biggest of all fools, void of the wisdom of eternal value. For God's comments on worldly wisdom, see Jer. 9:23-24 with 1 Cor. 2:6.

3p-Verse 32. "Nineve." An older way of writing the name of Nineveh. See Section 6, second paragraph of footnote a for other differences in biblical spelling. This has nothing to do with inspiration of Scripture. It is rather a matter of the gradual and historical progress of word spelling changes.

4p-"They repented." Matt. 12:41 with Lk. 11:32. Highlighted in gray for it seems to be a summation of Nineveh's repentance from their sins as recorded in Jonah 3:4-10. For several million people to change their minds about their sins at the preaching of a strange Jew, who suddenly appeared in their streets, is a most extraordinary thing! What was the full content of his message, which so shook that wicked city and turned them from paganism to the true and living God? Had they heard of his experience in the fish's stomach and the fearful events that led up to it? Whatever it was, we rejoice to read that Christ is greater than Jonah. Over the past two thousand years, countless millions of Gentiles have turned to Him in saving faith. *He is greater!* The religious leaders of Israel firmly believed the story of Jonah, nevertheless, rejected the Man, who was greater than the fishy preacher!

5p-The turning of the heathens behind the walls of Nineveh to Almighty God also had a future side not so glorious. About one hundred and forty years *later* the prophet Nahum wrote, "The burden of Nineveh." The forty-seven verses of this book pronounce God's fierce judgment upon the same city! In the year B.C. 612, it fell to the cruel armies of Babylon, and thousands died. The book of Nahum reveals the sins into which the fifth generation of Ninevites had fallen and the judgment that came upon them. It is the sad commentary on nations that forsake God (Ps. 9:17). For a disturbing work on this awful subject, see *When a Nation Forgets God,* by Erwin W. Lutzer.

(h) With these words, the Savior repeated a teaching He had given during Sermon on the Mount. At that time, it was directed to His disciples (Matt. 5:14-15). Now, He lays it upon the religious leaders, warning them of their fatal mistake in snuffing out His great light. They had pushed it under the "bushel" of their oral law and traditions. For explanation of the oral law, see Section 52, footnote h; Section 89, footnote c; and Section 96, footnote d.

(i) "Evil eye." Jews taught in their schools that an "evil eye," or eye, which was not "single," signified wickedness. In the Orient and countries of the East to this day there is the "evil eye," the "bad eye" versus the "good eye" or the "enlightened single eye." Because both eyes see *together*, they become a "single eye" in beholding the same object. Thus, the rabbis spoke often of the "single" or "good" eye. This expression conveyed the idea of "oneness" or "singularity." It spoke of the acceptance of wholesome teaching and seeing clearly the truth. The "evil eye" was among other things, wickedness within one's life. Using everyday colloquialisms, Christ hit home with every listener. Those Jews who rejected Him had an "evil eye" and were full of darkness. Those who received Him as Messiah had a shining candle lit in their souls and were full of light. To His audience, the Son of God warned, "Take heed therefore that the light which is in thee be not darkness" (verses 35-36). To the scribes and Pharisees, He said, "If you had the 'single' and 'good eye' you would see that I am the Messiah."

(j) One of the rabbinical titles for the Messiah was "the light of the world." Refer to Section 1, Part 1 and all of footnote e for more on Messiah the light. The "lighted candle" in *this instance* was the saving knowledge of Jesus the Messiah, ignited within the hearts of men and shining so that all who "come in" (verse 33), may see. He had previously used this metaphor in His original Sermon on the Mount; however, at that earlier time, He applied it to testimony or witness of His disciples. This is noted in Section 44, Matt. 5:14, footnote r. In this relation, see 2 Cor. 4:6-7. The Messiah's reference to Himself as the Light was highly offensive to the rabbis. They continually spoke of themselves, the law, the temple, and Messiah as the light of the world.

Israel and its religious leaders are demonized seven times. They are worse than all previous generations.* The unspeakable blessing of hearing and keeping God's Word is the greatest prize for any believer.

*See main headings in Sections 67, 70, 71, and 72 for other judgments pronounced upon Israel. To understand Christ's illustrative response the context should be noted. The scribes and Pharisees had just requested another sign from Jesus that would decisively prove He was the Messiah. See Section 67, and all of footnote a, for explanation of this. Beyond all His astounding works, the impeccable sign would be His resurrection from the dead shadowed in the experience of Jonah. The use of the word "generation" must not be missed. John the Baptist had previously described the religious leaders as "a generation of vipers" (Matt. 3:7). Christ likened them to a "generation" of spoiled children in Section 62, Matt, 11:16, footnote m. No form of honest exegesis can take this biblical word "generation," lift it from the context, and then apply it to the nation of Israel over two thousand years later. Christ's Words in this Section were directed at the Jews, who for the greater part perished in the terrible judgment of Jerusalem and the temple in A.D. 70. They and their companions in evil were that wicked "generation" of which the Son of God spoke. For our Lord's vivid description of their destruction, and warnings for His followers to watch and be ready for this catastrophic event, see Sections 163 through 165.

Galilee

Matt. 12:43–45	Mk.	Lk. 11:24–28	John
A wandering displaced demon returns home **43** "When the unclean spirit is gone out of a man,[a] he walketh through dry places, seeking rest, and findeth none. **44** "Then he saith,[b] **'I will return into my house from whence I came out;'** and when he is come,[c] he findeth *it* empty, swept, and garnished.[d] *He returns to his former house and takes others with him* **45** "Then goeth he, and taketh with himself seven other spirits more wicked than himself,[e] and they enter in and dwell there: and the last *state* of that man is worse than the first.[f] Even so shall it be also unto this wicked generation."[g] (Verse 46 cont. in Section 69.)		*A wandering displaced demon returns home* **24** "When the unclean spirit is gone out of a man,[a] he walketh through dry places, seeking rest; and finding none, he saith,[b] **'I will return unto my house whence I came out.'** **25** "And when he cometh,[c] he findeth *it* swept and garnished.[d] *He returns to his former house and takes others with him* **26** "Then goeth he, and taketh *to him* seven other spirits more wicked than himself;[e] and they enter in, and dwell there: and the last *state* of that man is worse than the first."[f] *A woman breaks out in praise to Jesus' mother: He corrects her*	
27 And it came to pass, as he spake these things, a certain woman[h] of the company lifted up her voice, and said unto him, "Blessed *is* the womb that bare thee, and the paps [breasts] which thou hast sucked." (nursed) *The highest of life's blessings* **28** But he said, "Yea rather, blessed *are* they that hear the word of God, and keep it."[i] (Verse 29 cont. in Section 67.)			

Footnotes-Commentary

[a] If there had been no reality in demonical possession, our Lord would have scarcely appealed to a case of this nature to point out the condition of the Jewish people and the desolation, which was coming upon them in A.D. 70. His mention of demons was not borrowed from pagan mythology, but horrible reality. For a comprehensive survey of the numerous aspects of demonology, see *The Handbook for Spiritual Warfare* by Ed Murphy. The experiences recorded in his book will not necessarily be ours. Note the third paragraph of footnote e below for other dependable publications dealing with this subject. For the meaning of "unclean," see Section 55, footnote d.

2p-**Verse 43. "Dry places."** An expression having reference to places where there was not life. Departing from the unnamed man's body, this single demon walked through something called "dry places." Christ expressly said he was "seeking rest." It was the common belief among the Jews, that Satan and demons inhabited and haunted desolate places of the wilderness. See John A. Broadus' *Commentary on Matthew,* pages 279-280, for clear details on this thought. The Old Testament gives affirmation to this curious Jewish notion. Note Isa. 13:21 and 34:14 where "satyrs" dwelling in wild places are references to demonic entities. Evil spirits seek abandoned and dark places where they devise and later practice their unspeakable ills upon the children of Adam's fallen race. Was it not in the "wilderness" that Satan had preciously attacked the Son of God (Mk. 1:13)?

3p-Satanic forces cannot "rest" unless they are creating havoc, pain, and sorrow, injuring the physical bodies of men or damning their souls. In these calamities, they find their evil satisfaction! Their prime base of operations for all malignancy is the sinful, polluted human heart. If wandering demons find no place within human frames, they take second best: the fleshly bodies of lower beasts and creatures. We read of them pleading with Christ to be sent into thousands of swine (Matt. 8:31). Upon entrance, the evil spirits immediately drowned them in the sea! Herein may be found the explanation for *viciously* dangerous mad cats, dogs, horses, cows, wolves, and even people who brutally attack others, violently mutilating and killing in the most shocking manner. Joseph Stalin, Adolf Hitler, Charles Manson, and Saddam Hussein are classic examples, to name a few.

4p-History indisputably demonstrates that some buildings such as old prisons, hospitals, and even battlefields where tortures, rape, fierce and brutal killings occurred may be demonized. A "prohibited area" of former Alcatraz Prison and a "forbidden area" of the Gettysburg battlefield are present day examples of this. Hundreds of tourists have had horrible experiences at these sites. The author knows of an old pre-Civil War building in the state of Tennessee where slaves were ruthlessly killed, and helpless wounded soldiers were beaten and bayoneted to death on the floor. To this day demonic apparitions and loathsome manifestations appear within these decrepit remains.

5p-While on furlough in 1979, a local pastor asked me to accompany him in visiting a home on Augusta Road in Greenville, South Carolina. The resident family approached him for help after the Sunday morning service. A visitor spending the night went to the basement to sleep. Later, in the evening, she was awakened as something touched her body. Sitting up on the portable cot, she was slapped across the face by a powerful, unseen force and crashed onto the concrete floor badly injuring her arm. A strong smell of rank, sickening perfume filled the basement. We arrived at this place mid Sunday afternoon. Before going in the pastor, we visited several neighbors to inquire about the history of the old brick house. An elderly man informed us that years ago, several prostitutes were murdered in an upstairs room of the "haunted house." Their bodies were thrown over the back balcony to a concrete pad below. In this act, we discovered the grounds for the demonic activity that had terrified the woman visitor the previous night. They were miming the murder of the two women that had occurred years before. The concrete pad was just outside the double doors leading into the basement where the visiting mother-in-law had been assaulted. As it was in the days of Christ, so it is today. The emissaries of Satan still inhabit the places of sin, injury, violence, darkness, fear, and death. Only the Lord Jesus Christ has triumphed over them and their unspeakable evils. His resurrected power and authority over all the forces of darkness must be appropriated upon every such case as those mentioned above. Conversely, some men often pack on the shoulders of Satan many of the calumnies for which they alone are responsible. They act like father Adam of old who responded when caught in his sin, "The woman whom thou gavest to be with me, she gave me of the tree, and I did eat" (Gen. 3:11-12).

(b) Evil spirits can talk. All words spoken by Satan and demons are in a heavy font style for easy recognition. This demonstrates that evil spirits may talk not only among themselves but also through the mouths of their captives. See Section 40, Mk. 1:23, footnote c, and Section 41, Mk. 1:34, footnote g, for other examples of this. Now the Savior gives a lesson on demonic activity, especially what their intentions are after voluntary moving out of the human house they had previously occupied. Christ spoke on this subject with absolute authority. Here, is an area where abysmal ignorance prevails within most churches. It was noted in Section 66, Matt. 12:22-24, footnotes b and c that He had expelled a demon out of the blind mute, which was a miracle that only Messiah could perform. See asterisk under main heading Section 48, number 2 for exclusive meaning to the Jews of a deaf mute being healed. Messiah applied His lesson about the possessed man *strictly* to the nation of Israel, and especially its religious leaders. They were "empty, swept, and garnished" according to all the external requirements of their oral law. Upon this last *rejection* of the Messiah, the Jews had sealed their fate and were possessed with many demons instead of one. See this *final rejection* and terrible blasphemy of the Jewish religious leaders in Section 66, Mk. 3:28-30, footnote j. Their last condition (filled and controlled by demons) was far worse than their earlier condition. Jesus showed total insight into the nature and machinations of spiritual powers in this brief discourse.

(c) "My house." The foul entity claimed ownership of the man's physical body as his house. Another personal illustration may help to explain what is meant in this verse. Evil spirits operating today often may make this same claim from the mouths of their captives. In 1973, while praying for a prominent Jewish business woman in South Africa, she suddenly stiffened and threw her head back as a deep *male voice* growled through her mouth, "This is my house, I will not leave." Evil spirits claim various bodies as their own. The Savior said that after it was vacated, the man's body was described as "empty, swept and garnished." This meant that during the absence of the foul entity, the man seemed to be in his right mind again. For garnished, see footnote d below. The man was *temporarily* freed from the influences of the indwelling, controlling evil power, but not safe from the demon's ability to reenter and repossess his body for the second time. No believer is protected from satanic assaults, who dabbles in sin, lives in willful disobedience, and flippantly toys with the things of God. Though his soul is safe in Christ, his physical body and human life may be wrecked, ruined, and destroyed by the forces of darkness or an act of chastening from the hand of God (2 Sam. 7:14; Ps. 6:1; Heb. 12:5-13; 1 Cor. 5:1-5; 1 John 5:16-17; and Rev. 3:19).

2p-In the antitype, our Savior made reference to the nation of Israel but especially its religious leaders; clean outwardly by observation of the oral law and countless traditions, but inwardly they had become an abode for the Devil, their father, and many evil spirits (John 8:44). John the Baptist identified them as a "generation of vipers" (Matt. 3:7), and the Lord Jesus said they deserved "greater damnation" (Matt. 23:14). This was preeminently reflected in their hatred for the Messiah. However, a few exceptions to these awful indictments were Nicodemus and Joseph of Arimathaea (John 19:38-42). No doubt, there were others who are unnamed in Scripture (John 9:22).

(d) "Garnished." This speaks of something being put in neat and correct *external* order. Hence, the *outside condition* of this unnamed man. Returning, the demon found him cleaned up outwardly. He appeared normal and had enjoyed a reprieve during the absence of the spiritual entity that had tormented him. How long the evil spirit was out of his body, we are not told. However, the Devil will not leave his victims long to enjoy peace. The obvious meaning is that prior to this while the demon lived in his body, he was *not* empty, swept or garnished, but disorientated, keeping an unclean house or physical body. There is a dark affinity between demons, human filth, violent personal disorder, self-inflicted bodily injuries, and other wild abnormalities, especially in lewd, vulgar dress styles, orgies, violent language, ghastly nude emblems, signs, and satanic motifs tattooed on the skin. The original demon that lived in him is described as "unclean?" See footnote c above. The Jews, who had so adamantly abandoned and banished every form of idolatry, were now themselves captives of the evil spirits. For explanation of the origin and cause of idolatry, see Section 1, Part 4, third paragraph of footnote j and each of the cross-references.

(e) "Taketh with him seven other spirits." With this, the Lord Jesus opened the dark world of collaboration among devils for the destruction of men. Here, is a brief glimpse into the machinations of wickedness. This reveals that evil spirits converse among themselves as they plot and scheme to hurt men and that God hears their conniving. See Section 40, footnote d for more on demons speaking audibly. In Scripture, we read of them speaking through the mouths of their victims (Matt. 8:29; Lk. 8:30-31; with Acts 19:15). "Finding no rest" (or place from which he could produce further ill and hurt), the foul spirit returned to his former house. The lesson here is that evil powers only find peace or rest in creating sorrow, pain, confusion, and sin in human lives. See Section 106, Mk. 9:25, footnote f for another mention of demons returning to their former dwellings. This spirit had no trouble reentering his previous domain. In trekking through desolate places, the foul entity found no dwelling as suitable as that of his former prisoner for producing havoc and suffering. Taking "seven other spirits far more wicked than himself," he freely reenters this cleaned up human house. See where another seven demons were cast out of a woman in Section 65, Lk. 8:2, footnote e, footnote f below. We also note the various degrees of wickedness that exists among evil spirits. The first demon was called "unclean" but his seven companions exceeded him in their wickedness! This explains the high and low levels of violence that demonically enslaved people manifest time by time. *Not all physical maladies and reactions of violent nature should be accredited to evil powers.* Numerous legitimate body ailments frequently reflect themselves in actions or reactions similar to those by people who are demonically controlled. Patience, prayer, discernment with caution and in many cases medical consultation from an informed Christian physician is needed. The Roman proverb "Hurry slowly" is helpful in such situations.

2p-Demon-possessed people may become helpless, screaming, sprawled on the floor, vomiting, trembling violently, and whimpering like children. Others may charge across the room shouting, "I'll kill you, Christian!" In one case, a young woman at a hospital guest room was lifted from her chair, sailed through the air, slammed into the wall, and slid down the wall to the floor. She was delivered after a terrible battle when a demon using the name "Ricardo" spoke through her mouth and fled out of her frail body. Ricardo was the name of her brother in Chicago, who was involved in a satanic cult. He had put a curse on her for attending a Christian institution. She had entered this place to study. However, her life was full of sin and rebellion. *This is not propagating the destructive error that saved people can be demon possessed; but it does affirm that evil spirits may find grounds or a place in the depraved flesh and perform their wickedness from this base of operations.* See Rom. 7:18 and 24 with Eph. 4:27. These verses were written to saved people. The Holy Spirit lives within the redeemed soul of every believer (Eph. 3:16), *not the human flesh*. Until this distinction is made, pastors will continually find themselves in great frustration when counseling long-time troubled Christians, who may have this problem. The power of evil spirits over men is *not* independent of the human will. The devices and unspeakable evils of these things cannot be exorcised without the consent of the captive's volition being brought into play. In cases of demonic inheritance passed to family members and little children, someone in the family line gave place to Satan for this to occur. For an example of this, see Section 106, Mk. 9:21, and all under lengthy footnote d.

3p-How puzzling when "learned theologians" write wonderful things about God and Christ, yet when confronted with the kingdom of darkness they play down, or attempt to explain away these awful realities. Examples of this are seen in Augustus Strong's *Systematic Theology,* pages 458-459, and *The Christian Counselor's Manual,* pages 127-129, by Jay Adams. Professor Adams suggests that after conversion the Devil leaves town! These men exalt our Savior, then write the exact opposite regarding Satan. The two will not mix! For a shocker from the pen of Adams, see Section 1, Part 3, third paragraph of footnote i. Sound teaching on this difficult subject, void of sensationalism, is given by Neil T. Anderson, Mark Bubeck, and Kurt Kock. *Could this be the reason their works are attacked on the internet by certain "authorities" who have never had one demonic encounter?*

4p-Examples of "Christian" tyrants. Along with the Roman Catholic Church, another prime example of this in religious history is that of John Calvin and his Reformers in Geneva. For coverage of this bloody period of *enforced* purity and *mandated* righteousness, see Will Durant's, *The Story of Civilization*, vol. 6, pages 459-490. Believing they were the elect of God, nothing moved the Reformers from their course; they crushed and killed anything that stood in the way, with "God's approval" and blessing! Calvin adhered to the barbarities of the Catholic Church out of which he came. Those who disagreed with him were called "filth" and "villainy," "mad dogs who vomit their filth against the Majesty of God." Four men who fell out with Calvin over the Lord's Supper were beheaded, quartered, and their body parts hung in strategic locations in Geneva as a warning to others. The notoriously liberal historian Philip Schaff (died 1893) wrote of these things in, *History of the Christian Church,* vol. 8, pages 489-493. A mentally deranged break off group from the Anabaptist went to Münster, Germany (1533 to 1535). They killed and plundered to establish a "New Jerusalem" and picked a date for Jesus' return! Enthusiasm, like fire, must not only burn, but be controlled. This is only part of the horrific history of zealous religious people in action without the saving grace of God in their souls. Men who murder for their religion are animals (2 Peter 2:12). Those who justify their atrocities are worse. See Section 1, Part 3, second paragraph of footnote i, Section 12, twelfth paragraph of footnote k, and Section 14, third paragraph of footnote f for more on these awful truths.

5p-Later, two of Jesus' apostles connived with their mother in a special little plot. In Section 142, second paragraph of footnote b, they attempt to secure for themselves exalted (carnal) positions in Christ's literal kingdom. (They thought it was soon to appear.) Men have always wrangled for prominence in politics, religion, and even *true* Christianity. This gives them a (false) sense of spiritual superiority. They believe that their way is the only way. The message of the Holy Bible is clear: Jesus Christ the Son of the Living God is the sole way, the truth and the life. Beside Him, there is no other. When religious zealots use His Name and Word to achieve their unholy purposes, it is enough to make the angels weep! Worse, are those "Christians" who today vehemently deny the established facts of church history, as mentioned above, and work to cover up this cancer that so besmirches their church name.

(f) Degrees of satanic bondage. The first state of the poor man was bad; now with eight unclean demons dwelling in this frame he became worse: even a human battering ram for Satan. According to Scripture, various numbers of demons may dwell within physical bodies and can move in and out. Refer to Section 170, John 13:2, footnote c for the example of Judas with Satan moving in and out of his body. Sin is always the basis for such horrific realities. See Section 65, Lk. 8:2, footnote e for a reversal of this demonic situation in a woman who was delivered of seven devils and then followed Christ. See footnote e above for more on this thought. The wild man named Legion had thousands of demons living in his physical body; hence, his self-destructing insanity and savage, super-human tendencies. This awful story is given in Section 88. See especially footnotes b and f.

(g) "Wicked generation." Our Lord was speaking of *that present generation of Jews* and particularly their religious leaders. See asterisk under the main heading of this Section for comments on the word "generation" and the relevant parallel references.

(h) "A certain woman" amid the crowd, suddenly called out with this frequently heard form of female Jewish praise. She had seen the miracle on the blind mute, heard Messiah's terse answers to the scribes and Pharisees, and rejoiced in the prudent way He had cleared Himself of their charges against His Holy character. Whether she personally knew Mary, the mother of Jesus, is not known. She spoke well but womanly. Her little beatitude reminds us of Elisabeth's lofty words in Lk. 1:42. This unknown woman is to be saluted for shouting out this public commendation to Mary and her Son, in the presence of the hateful religious leaders of the nation. It is noteworthy that the expression "Blessed be" was common among the Jews. It is mentioned in the Talmud over one thousand times! Saints like this one have been fulfilling Rom. 10:11 for some two thousand years. According to Section 69, Matt. 12:46, footnote a, the family of Jesus was present at this occasion.

(i) Our Lord deliberately diverted the words of misplaced praise for His mother spoken by the unknown woman. He instructed His listeners regarding the source of true blessedness. Many are the distinctions and earthly honors bestowed by men upon men. Though Mary was blessed to mother the Savior and rear Him from childhood, and she should be honored for this, there is something more important. Life's foremost and venerable privilege is to read and hear the Word of God, to be saved by its gospel, live by its teachings, bring others to Christ, and lastly to arrive in heaven when life has ended. No duties of men are as holy and reverenced as these are. Earlier, at the conclusion of the Sermon on the Mount, Christ spoke of the security and blessing of hearing and keeping His Word. One is struck upon remembering that when Jesus said this, only the Old Testament portion of God's Word existed. See *Appendix Seven* dealing with the question of *"When were the four gospels written?"*

Christ's true relatives are publicly identified.* They are those who are saved, do the will of God in heaven, and obey His Word on earth.

See Section 66, Mk. 3:20-21, footnote a, for the first mention of our Lord's family and friends since He began His ministry and how they misunderstood His work, seeking to restrain Him. See also the previous Section 68, footnotes h and I, for further comments on this subject.

Galilee

Matt. 12:46-50	Mk. 3:31-35	Lk. 8:19-21	John
Mary and her sons seek Jesus 46 While he yet talked to the people, behold, *his* mother[a] and his brethren stood without, [outside] desiring to speak with him. 47 Then one said unto him, "Behold, thy mother and thy brethren[b] stand without, [outside] desiring to speak with thee." ***His true family*** 48 But he answered and said unto him that told him, "Who is my mother? and who are my brethren?" 49 And he stretched[c] forth his hand toward his disciples, and said, "Behold my mother and my brethren! ***"Do the will of God"*** 50 "For whosoever shall do the will[d] of my Father which is in heaven, the same is my brother, and sister, and mother."[e] (Next chap. Matt. 13:1 cont. in Section 73.)	***Mary and her sons seek Jesus*** 31 There came then his brethren and his mother,[a] and, standing without, [outside] sent unto him, calling him. 32 And the multitude sat about him, and they said unto him, "Behold, thy mother and thy brethren[b] without [outside] seek for thee." ***His true family*** 33 And he answered them, saying, "Who is my mother, or my brethren?" 34 And he looked[c] round about on them which sat about him, and said, "Behold my mother and my brethren! ***"Do the will of God"*** 35 "For whosoever shall do the will[d] of God, the same is my brother, and my sister, and mother."[e] (Next chap. Mk. 4:1 cont. in Section 73.)	***Mary and her sons seek Jesus*** 19 Then came to him *his* mother[a] and his brethren, and could not come at him for the press. (crowds) 20 And it was told him *by certain* which said, "Thy mother and thy brethren[b] stand without, [outside] desiring to see thee." ***His true family*** 21 And he answered and said unto them, "My mother and my brethren ***"Do the Word of God"*** are these which hear the word of God, and do it."[d] (Verse 22 cont. in Section 87.)	

Footnotes-Commentary

(a) Both Matthew and Mark placed the visit of the mother and brothers of Jesus *before* the Parable of the Sower. We note that Luke was inspired of God to place it *after* the parable. See Section 2, footnotes c and e regarding Luke's use of chronology in writing his book. The half-brothers and half sisters of Jesus were not at this time sympathetic with His ministry, especially since He had been rejected and almost killed in the uproar at their hometown synagogue at Nazareth. This event is recorded in Section 38, Lk. 4:28-29 and its supplement. We saw them earlier coming to lay hands on Him and take Him away in Section 66, Mk. 3:21, footnote a. This sincere family attempted to stop His preaching and work, but they failed. At this point, *none* of them understood His life, who He really was, and His work. This would all come later. Refer to Section 20, footnotes g and i, for more on Joseph, Mary, and Jesus as a boy. For the names of Jesus' half-brothers and mention of His half sisters (plural), refer to Section 91, Matt. 13:55-56, footnote d. Footnote b below also contains other details on this subject. On Joseph being called "the father of Jesus," see Section 38, footnote h.

(b) **"His mother and brothers."** This text means what it says. The obvious teaching here is that these were the children of Mary. It seems that the person who bore this message to Jesus may have been familiar with some of His family. See Section 12, footnote k, especially the second paragraph for more on the family of our Lord, with footnote a above. On the other side of this story, it was natural for Mary to be concerned for her beloved Son. Like any good mother, she wanted to take Him home for rest and freedom from the pressures that weighed so heavy on His great heart. For further comments on Mary and Joseph, see Section 6, footnotes d and e.

(c) Christ looked over the crowds, then stretched forth His hand in a dramatic wave toward His disciples and answered His own question. In this action, He literally pointed out His closest relations. Those who had anchored their faith in Him as the promised Messiah, and were learning of His new kingdom, were nearer to His great heart than flesh and blood kin. It is the same today. Godless family members who reject Christ and glory in their shameful sins are often like total strangers. With this thought, see footnote e below. In saying, "Behold my mother" one wonders if He pointed to that band of women who followed and ministered to Him and the twelve, out of their possessions. See this in main heading Section 65, Lk. 8:1-3, where several of their names are given.

(d) **"Doing the will of God."** The Savior explained exactly who qualified as members of His spiritual family or new kingdom. Matthew and Mark wrote part of it as "whosoever shall do the will of my Father [God] which is in heaven" (verse 50 and 35). Luke completed our Lord's Words with "these which hear the Word of God and do it" (verse 21). Men can only do the will of God as they hear the Word of God and obey it. God has various wills for different people; however, His preeminent will for all men everywhere is that they "believe on His Son" and be saved. This is made clear in Section 95, John 6:40. At this time only the Old Testament portion of Scripture had been written. It was considered the infallible message from God to Israel. Later, the Scriptures of the New Testament were written and counted on *equal* footing. Together *both* Testaments constitute the eternal written Word of God. It is the will of Jehovah that men hear and do (obey) His Word. Christ had previously and dramatically illustrated the results of doing or not doing His Word in the Sermon on the Mount in Section 47, Matt. 7:24-29.

(e) **A new and divine relationship.** The Son of God is not teaching that natural affections for filial family and dear friends may be discarded when one comes to know Him as personal Lord and Savior; or that we may be disrespectful to parents, kindred and associates because we are now saved. *God forbid!* Rather, He is saying that at this critical moment in His work, the lesser duties (of receiving family and friends), are to stand by and wait while the more serious and eternal things are attended to. Thus, He *politely* called upon His family members to wait until He had completed the work of God for that occasion. Faithfulness to Christ in this wonderful new relationship always takes preference to lesser matters. Yet, even these are to be diligently handled with honor and respect. *With such conduct and actions, God is well pleased.*

2p-The beautiful wonder of Christ-like meekness in God's family relationship. Over the decades, the author has witnessed the amazing change made in the lives of people converted to Christ. This new and divine relationship, mentioned above by the Savior, is first marked by the flower of humility and meekness as it blossoms out of their lives. Meekness is not popular in today's world. Unsaved men call it a "craven spirit that leads man to remain quiet, under insult, to endure a wrong without resentment, to be treated badly and give kindness in return. Such a disposition is considered "unmanly," it shows "weakness and cowardice," they tell us. (The author is not talking about modern day passivism.) It is by the grace of God that any person could become kindred to the Savior. Jesus Christ was the only perfect Person to walk on this earth. Out of His life flowed the sweet fragrance of genuine meekness; He was gentle in disposition, not easily provoked, patient under awful wrong, silent amid fierce reproach. When He suffered, He threatened not, when reviled He reviled not again. Never did Jesus lift a finger or raise His voice to avenge personal insult or injury. His response to the wrath of evil men was tender love and ready forgiveness. I once read a story of a woman who was stabbed by a robber. Dying, she said in tears, "I wish to have him with me in heaven." Her words reflect the very heart of real Christianity, which is the heart of God, to forgive all men and have others with us in paradise. Nailed to the cross and in pain unspeakable, Jesus first prayed for His tormentors to be forgiven. Meekness is not a craven spirit; it is heavenly to forgive those who have wronged us. Born from above, every *real* Christian is in this unique family of God, somehow counted as the Savior's mother, sister, or brother. What a humbling thought. True believers mirror the likeness of Jesus as they love those who hate them. Ours is to oppose all evil, yet loving those who commit it, seeking their salvation. *There is no higher or nobler way for men to live!* For God transforming the life of an army officer, to the amazement of his men, see Section 203, the fourth paragraph of footnote e. This heavenly transformation is called the "new covenant." It is briefly explained in Section 95, the second paragraph of footnote u. It starts when one is truly saved by God's grace.

The second recorded meal of Jesus with a religious leader.* Again, He denounced the Pharisees, lawyers, and scribes who were present. Fiercely enraged, they hurl many charges at the Savior seeking to trap Him into a contradiction of Words.

*See Section 64 for His first meal with a Pharisee named Simon. On that occasion, He was condemned for allowing a sinful woman to touch Him. At this second meal, He was attacked for not obeying the tradition of the elders or oral law in washing His hands a specific way for ritual cleansing. See footnote d below. The Savior tangled again with the religious leaders over this issue in Section 96, footnote b passim.

Matt.	Mk.	Lk. 11:37-52—Galilee	John
		A Pharisee is upset over Jesus neglecting the oral law washings	
		37 And as he spake, a certain Pharisee[a] besought him to dine[b] with him: and he went in, and sat down [reclined] to [eat] meat.[c]	
		38 And when the Pharisee saw *it*, he marvelled that he had not first washed[d] before dinner.	
		He speaks terrible judgments on the scribes, Pharisees, and lawyers	
		39 And the Lord said unto him, "Now do ye Pharisees make clean the outside of the cup and the platter; but your inward[e] part is full of ravening and wickedness.	
		40 "*Ye fools,*[f] did not he that made that which is without make that which is within also?	
		41 "But rather [dedicate your inward self and then] give alms of such things as ye have; and, behold, all things are clean unto you.	
		42 "But woe unto you, Pharisees! for ye tithe[g] mint and rue and all manner of herbs, and pass over judgment and the love of God: these ought ye to have done, and not to leave the other undone.	
		43 "Woe[h] unto you, Pharisees! for ye love the uppermost [front] seats in the synagogues, and greetings in the markets.	
		44 "Woe unto you, scribes and Pharisees, hypocrites! for ye are as [unmarked] graves which appear not, and the men that walk over *them* are not aware *of them.*"	
		An offended Torah lawyer objects to the Savior's Words:	
		Jesus responds with a scathing rebuke and promise of coming judgment	
		45 Then answered one of the lawyers, and said unto him, "Master, thus saying thou reproachest us also."	
		46 And he said, "Woe unto you also, *ye* lawyers! for ye lade men with burdens grievous to be borne, and ye yourselves touch not the burdens with one of your fingers.	
		47 "Woe unto you! for ye build the sepulchres [tombs] of the prophets, and your fathers killed them.	
		48 "Truly ye bear witness that ye allow the deeds of your fathers: for they indeed killed them, and ye build their sepulchres. (tombs)	
		49 "Therefore also said the wisdom of God, I will send them prophets and apostles, and *some* of them they shall slay and persecute:	
		50 "That the blood of all the prophets, which was shed from the foundation of the world, may be required of this generation; [of Jews]	
		51 "From the blood of Abel unto the blood of Zacharias, which perished between the altar and the temple: verily I say unto you, It shall be required of this generation. (in A.D. 70)	
		52 "Woe unto you, lawyers! for ye have taken away the key of	

Matt.	Mk.	Lk. 11:52-54—Galilee	John
		knowledge: ye entered not[i] in yourselves, and them that were entering in ye hindered." **_Seriously offended, the religious leaders fiercely attack Him_** **53** And as he said these things unto them, the scribes and the Pharisees began to urge *him* vehemently,[j] and to provoke him to speak of many things: **54** Laying wait for him, and seeking to catch something out of his mouth, that they might accuse him.[k] (Next chap. Lk. 12:1 cont. in Section 71.)	

Footnotes-Commentary

[a] **Dining with an enemy.** Probably, He gave this scathing discourse to the people in general but specifically to the Pharisees and their companions in hypocrisy. Surprisingly, a Pharisee present on this occasion steps forward and invites the Lord Jesus into his home for a meal. As already noted, Messiah had continually blasted the religious leaders for their double standards in living out the Torah Law. Now, one of these abashed religionists calls for the Master to dine with him. This was not our Lord's first invitation to dine with an enemy. It had occurred earlier in Section 64, Lk. 7:36, footnote a. See asterisk above under main heading for special observations of this occasion.

[b] According to *Thayer's Greek Lexicon*, page 73, the word, "ariston," (from "aristos") has reference to the *first* meal of the day, which was a combination of our breakfast and lunch. The word means the best! The Jews ate two primary meals over the course of a day; the first, shortly before the noon hour and the second at early evening. The unnamed Pharisee invited Christ to the first meal of the day. See Section 127, Lk. 14:12, where both meals are clearly distinguished "dinner and supper" or "ariston and deipnon."

[c] **"Sat down to meat."** Actually, He reclined at the table, which was the normal posture in dining. Refer to Section 64, Lk. 7:36, footnote b for other details of practices employed at this time in history.

[d] **"Unwashed hands."** The Pharisee's fierce resentment rose from the fact that Jesus flatly rejected rules and commandments laid down in the Mishna or oral law. He did not dip His hands deep into the water or scrub His arms the required number of times (according to their tradition) before eating the meal. This was a religious ritual and had nothing to do with personal hygiene. The exact problem erupted later in our Lord's ministry. Refer to Section 96, Matt. 15:3-20 for the response of Jesus. Following the verbal blessing, He lay across the couch and commenced to eat. Every eye was upon Him; they were horrified that He did not vigorously wash His hands before eating. The Jews believed there was a demon named Shibta, whom they feared could be picked up on their hands in the markets and brought home. Washing hands and elbows in water according to the oral law was the only way to remove him! Shibta is mentioned in the Talmud tractate, Yoma 77b. None of these ridiculous rules and extra laws can be found in the Old Testament. The rabbis twisted and perverted the Scriptures in an attempt to justify their wild extremes. See Alfred Edersheim's, *Life and Times of Jesus the Messiah*, pages 477-491, for a good exposition on the subject of the Mishna, tradition of the elders or oral law. The rulers of religion continually failed to entrap Christ in breaking the Law of Moses, which He kept perfectly. Countless charges were laid against Him for breaking their fabricated Mishna commandments. The Talmud tractate, Celim (vessels) is packed with rigid stipulations about what is clean or unclean, what to wash and so on. This was the basis of our Lord's Words, "and many other such like things ye do," when speaking of the tradition of the elders (Mk. 7:8). These thousands of extra Torah rules and stipulations were not fully collected into the Talmud until several hundred years after the ascension of Christ.

[e] **"Rotten inside."** Here, the Messiah lays His finger on the real problem of the Pharisees. Scrupulously, they labored day and night to be clean in body and appearance before men. He was saying, "You cleanse yourselves outwardly with various washings of your oral laws but your source of defilement comes from within." Later, Christ repeated this same charge against them in Section 159, Matt. 23:25, "Ye make clean the outside of the cup and platter, but within they are full of extortion and excess." Their hearts, the fountainhead of human conduct, were polluted and wicked. Like religionists in churches today, these men lacked a miraculous change wrought inside their hearts by the grace of God. Those who assume religious leadership and have never been saved are a curse to the cause of Christ and the genuine spiritual needs of men. They are intruders and enemies within the holy camp, even *modern day* scribes, and Pharisees. Sincerity in the service of Christ apart from biblical truth and the work of the Holy Spirit is among the worst of human errors (Prov. 14:12). Refer to Section 95, sixth paragraph under footnote r for more on the subject of sincerity in action void of divine truth.

[f] **"Ye fools."** Why did the meek and lowly Jesus speak out during this meal and call his host and many of the guests "fools." The lesson is that churchy men who have never been saved, and lead others into the torments of hell are the biggest "fools" on earth. Somehow, religious "fools" are deadlier than those mentioned in Ps. 14:1. Refer to Section 101 where He later warned His disciples about the false teaching of the Pharisees and their fellows.

2p-Verse 41. "Give . . . and behold all things are clean unto you." The meaning of this curious statement

321

is found in the previous verses 39 and 40. The Savior reprimanded the religious leaders for making the outside so scrupulously clean and well appearing to public eyes, yet their hearts were cesspools of gross wickedness. In verse 40, the Lord Jesus warns them that God made both the outside and inside of men. Thus, He alone can correct the inward heart's avarice, extortion, corruption, and sin. The Son of God informs them of the need to correct first the inner source or root of their vileness, and then they can give alms of all they have. With this inward cleansing of their hearts, all gifts will be received and counted clean before God. Sadly, verse 42 reveals they left this command of Messiah "undone." There are millions today, who believe that their contributions of charity will cleanse the inside of its darkness. Gentiles, Jews, Muslims, and church people by the millions hold to this awful untruth. It is written in Scripture that God *only* forgives men of their sins "for Christ's sake" (Eph. 4:32 with 1 John 2:12). "We also joy in God through our Lord Jesus Christ, by whom we have now received the atonement" (Rom. 5:11). The prophet Micah puts the serious question, "Will the LORD be pleased with thousands of rams, *or* with ten thousand rivers of oil? Shall I give my firstborn *for* my transgression, the fruit of my body *for* the sin of my soul: (Micah 6:7)? "Not by works of righteousness which we have done, but according to his mercy he saved us" (Titus 3:5).

(g) **The Jews and tithing.** They were highly sensitive in the performance of their religious duties but woefully neglectful of attending to the welfare of their souls, their relationship with others, and the practice of genuine godliness. They gave no thought to *correct* judgment and God's love toward others (Micah 6:8). Their giving tithes of the smallest of things were called "pot plant tithing." The Pharisees were hyper sensitive to give tithes of even the lesser garden produce (Lev. 27:30). **"Mint"** was a small plant, smelly, tasty, and used in cooking and decoration. **"Anise"** has reference to a form of "dill" and was used to give a good taste to cooking and perfuming the house or physical body. **"Cummin"** was also a seed but threshed out by a stick or rod. It was costly and employed in preparing meals or dropped about the house to leave a delightful fragrance. Professional confectionaries sought out all three of these herbs for business usage. Some of the Jews debated on the validity of tithing from herbs. However, the more pious and self-righteous ones practiced this faithfully, basing their reason on Deut. 14:22. Yet the Law of Moses said nothing specifically about tithing from herbal plants.

(h) **"Woe."** Starting with verse 42, the Lord pronounced a series of successive woes upon His audience. Though it is difficult to separate all of these dooms upon the Pharisees and lawyers, what they say is terribly clear.

1. **Verse 42. "Pharisees."** The arrogance of the Pharisees and scribes was condemned along with their love for prominence, and public praises of men. They enjoyed tithing publicly! See footnote g above for explanation of their tithing habits. Religion to them consisted *only* of the external. They made a great fuss about washing things outside but were blind to the need of divine cleansing within where abode all manner of malice, hatred, envy, and great wickedness.

2. **Verse 43. "Pharisees."** They struggled among themselves for the front row seats in the synagogues and loved to hear the praises of men in open market places. For explanation of these men and their religious hypocrisy, see Section 159, Matt. 23:6, footnote e.

3. **Verse 44. "Pharisees, hypocrites."** The Lord Jesus refers to a common Jewish saying "You are as grass grown over a grave, and it cannot be seen." Worshipers walking to the temple to perform religious duties would unknowingly step on these grass-covered tombs and thereby incur defilement. This would render them unfit to complete their service to God. The scribes and Pharisees, in their pretense of knowing God, had defiled the nation with their hypocrisies and damning untruths. However, the bold preaching of Christ had opened many eyes and produced a keen awareness regarding these vile men of false religion. Pious and honest Jews knew He spoke the truth.

4. **Verse 45. Lawyers in Israel.** Contextually, all Jesus said from verse 45 through verse 52 was addressed to these men. They were "specialists" in the Law of Moses. Christ responds to the complaint of one of the lawyers present at the meal (verse 45). He then charges them with three terrible sins and lays on them three separate woes. For a good explanation of Jewish Torah lawyers, and their operational system, see Lightfoot's *Commentary on the New Testament . . . ,* vol. 3, pages 100–103. Joachim Jeremias' work, *Jerusalem in the Time of Jesus,* pages 147-213 gives excellent coverage of this subject. For continued and needed comments on Jeremias and his writings, second paragraph under footnote l below.

5. **Verse 46.** They loaded down fellow Jews with the unbearable burdens of the oral law and its endless, traditions. Christ charged them with the following sins. Refusing to assist other Israelites, who were struggling with trying to keep the tradition of the elders. As enforcers of the oral law, they had burdened the common Israelite with their finicky, hair-splitting demands, which were not of God and impossible to keep. The lawyers present became seriously offended at the cutting remarks made by Christ. In verse 45 one of them vocally objected because he was deeply insulted by the truth Jesus had spoken.

6. **Verses 47-49.** The lawyers were builders and custodians of the burial sites of the Old Testament prophets, whom their fathers had murdered for preaching the truth. Ironically, they now hate and seek to kill the Messiah, who was doing the same thing. Jesus was saying, "One of you murders God's man and the others cover up for him." The Savior did not ridicule or abuse any of His angry audience. He spoke

Words of truth couched in love that cut into their wicked souls; hence, the hostile reaction. Their conscience told them they were guilty, thus in madness, they hated the Son of God for being fair and truthful with them. They were the co-murderers of God's prophets! Some historians think that there was at that time a book called *The Wisdom of God*, and Jesus referred to it. Regarding the wisdom of God, it is sure that He did not mix it with human ignorance. Others hold that He referred to Himself (1 Cor. 1:30 with Col. 2:9). There is a possibility that this was a paraphrase from 2 Chron. 36:15-16. Regardless of its source, the Savior quoted it as valid and applied it to the religious leaders of Israel. The warning that all the blood of innocent men of God, shed since the foundation of the world (starting with Abel) would be required of that "generation" was horrible. This was literally fulfilled in A.D. 70. See Section 163 for the story.

7. **Verse 50-51a. "From Abel."** What a terrible curse. The blood of all God's murdered preachers and prophets was to be required of *that* generation of Jews, especially the religious leaders. This payment for their horrendous, accumulative sins over the centuries finally occurred in A.D. 70. This resulted in the destruction of Jerusalem, the temple, the Hebrew state, and political body. See Section 163 for an explanation of this unprecedented calamity in the history of Israel. It is impossible to believe that the Jews did not understand what He was saying. Jesus selected words from Gen. 4:4-8, and 2 Chron. 24:20-21, then blended them into this inspired quote. (Dozens of quotations lifted from the Old Testament and found in the New Testament are of this nature.) Abel, the son of Adam, became the first martyr because of his belief in salvation by the blood of the Lamb (Gen. 4:4-8; 1 John 3:12; and Heb. 11:4). Christ placed Zacharias at the end of His martyr's list. Here, Zachariah, the son of Jehoiada, being empowered by the Holy Spirit, spoke a curse upon his killers, whereupon it was recorded, "And they conspired against him, and stoned him with stones at the commandment of the king in the court of the house of the LORD" (2 Chron. 24:20). Hundreds of years later, in another rebuke aimed *again* at the religionists, Christ said that Zachariah was the son of Barachias (Matt. 23:35) and not Jehoiada, as it is recorded in 2 Chronicles. This difference in names means nothing. Single persons often carried a variety of names. The Lord Jesus used the name designation they best understood at that time, and the company of religious hypocrites standing before Him got His message. Among the ancients, personal names were as different in size and flexibility as our present day rubber bands. See Section 5 left column, footnote b, and Section 6, footnote a, for the variety in usages of names in Scripture.

8. **Verse 51b. "To the blood of Zacharias."** An eerie legend rose among the Jews over the murder of Zacharius. It was reported that his blood did not dry up but bubbled out from the floor of the court pavement within the temple of God where he was murdered. It was said to have only ceased after the Babylonians destroyed the city in 586 B.C. With this, vengeance upon the Jews, who killed Zachariah, was apparently satisfied. See Talmud tractate, Sanhedrin 96b. The brutal killing of the prophet Zacharias stood prominent as a national crime across Jewish history. It is not to be confused with Josephus' record of a man with a similar name who was also killed within the temple precincts in A.D. 70. This is recorded in Josephus' *Wars of the Jews* Book 4:5. 4, line 343. There is something divine yet uncanny about this story given by the Lord Jesus to the Jews. The Hebrew Bible was arranged with Genesis as the first book and 2 Chronicles as the final one. Thus, Christ scans the entire Old Testament from the first to the last martyr. Also note as Abel's blood cried out from the ground for vengeance (Gen. 4:10), so Zacharias in dying called on God to avenge his innocent death (2 Chron. 24:22). This vengeance took force about four decades after Jesus spoke these Words.

9. **Verse 51c. "Required of this generation."** For explanation of this term, see asterisk under main heading in Section 68. This bloodguilt debt was required of the Jews, and they paid it forty years later with millions being killed, enslaved, banished, and slaughtered in the Roman gladiatorial arenas. With this the Lord Jesus was saying, "You admit that your fathers in former years murdered God's prophets. You are now showing by your hatred toward Me, that you are as evil as they were, and will in time murder both, Me and My apostles." They were the heirs of the guilt of their ancestors. These men maintained and garnished the tombs of the Old Testament prophets that their fathers and grandfathers had murdered. What hypocrisy! Refer to number 6 above.

10. **Verse 52. Lawyers and the stolen key of knowledge.** This final curse or woe was intended for every hypocrite in earshot, including the caviling lawyer who was offended back in verse 45. They had stolen from Israel the "key of knowledge." God alone, who can search the heart (Jer. 17:9-10) would, in time unmasked these pretentious hypocrites. And this the Lord Jesus Christ did! "The key of knowledge" (or Law of Moses) was a maxim among the scribes and teachers. When one was ordained a teacher of the law, he was given a metal or wooden key called the "key of knowledge." In a *symbolical* sense, he was thenceforth to use it in "opening the Scriptures" for the people of Israel. Little did they realize that Christ alone could do this (Lk. 24:45). Rabbinical decisions were looked upon as having power to "bind and loose" all Israelites. At death, this key was often buried with these famed teachers of religion. More

details on the Jewish usage of keys are found in Section 103, Matt. 16:19, footnote h; and Section 110, Matt. 18:18, footnote f. The Savior was correcting another Jewish myth that the rabbis alone had true knowledge of God and His law. Here, He denounced the lawyers for perpetrating it. Since they were specialists in the Torah Law, they should have gladly accepted Christ and rejoiced in His preaching and teaching. Failing to attend to their duties, they did not use the key of knowledge to open the Old Testament Scriptures that pointed to the Messiah. This is briefly discussed in Section 52, John 5:45-47, footnotes y and z. See *Appendix Three* for a list of some forty predictions found in the Old Testament that pointed to the coming Messiah.

(i) In rejecting Christ, they shut themselves out of the new kingdom of God or the church and hindered or prevented others from entering. Many that were saved during the ministry of our Lord came into His kingdom through great "violence" and suffering. This curious statement of Jesus in Matt. 11:12, is explained in Section 62, second and third paragraphs of footnote h. There is no better in-depth, documented, and concise review of the scribes and Pharisees in the English language than *Jerusalem in the Time of Jesus*, pages 233-267 by Joachim Jeremias (died 1979). He was a Lutheran theologian whose spiritual insights in theology and Christology are worthless. However, Jeremias' information is of great value in understanding Bible background and history. Any man who is blind to the inspiration of Holy Scripture and the deity of Christ is handicapped from the start. When he *rarely* writes about eternal matters and the salvation of Jesus Christ, he is always wrong. For more on Jeremias, see number 4 under footnote h above. Being a brilliant historian, linguists, philosopher, theologian or whatever, accomplishes nothing if a man ends his life in hell. As Jesus said of Judas, so it can be said of these people, "good were it for that man if he had never been born" (Mk. 14:21).

(j) **The furious Pharisees.** The majestic Messiah again exposed publicly the malignant Hebrew religionists. Infuriated, they flew into fits of rage attacking Him violently with dozens of accusations and contradictory questions. Greatly incensed, they poured out their envy hoping to ensnare Him in some minute detail of their oral law and countless traditions. The beautiful meal turned into a verbal battlefield. The psalmist had written a thousand years earlier in a Messianic eulogy, "all their thoughts are against me for evil" (Ps. 56:5). We would do well to "consider him who endured such contradiction of sinners against himself" (Heb. 12:3). Christ had felt the fury of these wicked men many times, starting in His hometown synagogue some two years earlier. Later, while hanging on the cross, He felt the fullness of their hatred and wrath, as well as that of all men. Nevertheless, He prayed the Father to forgive them (Lk. 23:34).

(k) **Accuse the sinless Son of God from heaven!** Alas, the devices of religious men who are unacquainted with the saving grace of God. When in positions of leadership and responsible for the care of men's souls, they are the most dangerous people on the face of this earth. See footnote e above for the source of their problem.

2p-**The light of hope and help still shines.** It has been continually repeated in this work that the most dangerous people on earth (from the eternal point of view) are deeply religious men and women who are void of the saving knowledge of Jesus Christ, and have substituted something else for Him. Thus, it was with these Jewish religionists in the Scriptures of this Section. They hated the Savior because He would not agree with their pious unbelief, secret sins, colorful but empty rituals, boisterous acclamations, void of God's true love and saving grace. It is not much different in today in a large part of America's religious circus. Many "Christian ministers and laypersons" would have us to believe that God may have sent His Son into the world but He did not leave humanity a trustworthy, infallible record of this. To these people the Bible is a fable of sorts, mixed with scrapes of philosophical truth and nice sayings. Therefore, the interpretation of these things is open to anyone's opinion! Such conjectures are impious idiocy of the lowest level. Unsaved religionists and do-gooders cannot stomach the thought of a divinely inspired and God-give Book; it chills their wicked souls, and spells their eternal damnation. The Savior described the religious Pharisees and lawyers that stood about Him, as "fools" (verse 40). The unique and exclusive claims of Jesus Christ as recorded in the Bible, are today scorned, lied about, twisted, distorted, ridiculed, perverted, despised, and burnt in hard line Islamic countries. Men want a milk-toast Jesus that is sick like they are, a Savior who winks at their wickedness, and smiles at their Jerry Springer barnyard morals, and animal behavior. For the most part, *true* Christianity is as unpopular as a pork chop in a synagogue or a pig in a mosque! This opposition will increase as creation and humanity move toward the consummation of all things. *When that will be no man knows, but all wise men know it will be!* God has not abandoned creation and human society. He has given and preserved His truths for Adam's broken race; they are in that old book, called The Holy Bible. The light of sure hope and help still shines amid the encroaching darkness of humanistic immorality, political vanity, and indescribable sin. It teaches and aspires men to a higher and nobler way of life. *This begins with the new birth which is a miracle that God alone performes in the soul of man. It occurs when one receives Christ as personal Lord and Savior.* Salvation shows them true love and compassion as they pass through this world, reaching out to help their fellow men and upward to praise their Father in heaven. The narrow and exclusive way is Jesus, the Son of the only true and living God. For continued comments on these things, refer to Section 47, fourth paragraph under footnote c, Section 101, fourth paragraph under footnote b, and Section 176, footnote s.

Multitudes stampede to see and hear the Savior. Again, He warns of the religious authorities in Israel. Jesus gives twelve unique lessons* to His disciples.

The obvious similarities contained in this discourse with those given in previous messages demonstrate again that the Son of God frequently repeated Himself. See footnotes d through g below for examples.

Matt.	Mk.	Lk. 12:1-15—Galilee	John
		1. About hypocrisy	
		1 In the mean time, when there were gathered together an innumerable multitude(a) of people, insomuch that they trode one upon another, he began to say unto his disciples first of all, "Beware ye of the leaven(b) of the Pharisees, which is hypocrisy.	
		2 "For(c) there is nothing covered, that shall not be revealed; neither hid, that shall not be known.	
		3 "Therefore whatsoever ye have spoken in darkness shall be heard in the light; and that which ye have spoken in the ear in closets shall be proclaimed upon the housetops.(d)	
		2. About fear of man	
		4 "And I say unto you(e) my friends, Be not afraid of them that kill the body, and after that have no more that they can do.	
		5 "But I will forewarn you whom ye shall fear: Fear him, which after he hath killed hath power to cast into hell; yea, I say unto you, Fear him.	
		6 "Are not five sparrows sold for two farthings, [smallest coins] and not one of them is forgotten before God?	
		7 "But even the very hairs of your head are all numbered. Fear not therefore: ye are of more value than many sparrows.	
		8 "Also I say unto you, Whosoever shall confess me before men, him shall the Son of man also confess before the angels of God:	
		9 "But he that denieth me before men shall be denied before the angels of God.	
		3. About blasphemy	
		10 "And whosoever shall speak a word against the Son of man, it shall be forgiven him: but unto him that blasphemeth against the Holy Ghost it shall not be forgiven.(f)	
		4. About opposition	
		11 "And when they bring you unto the synagogues, and *unto* magistrates, and powers, take ye no thought how or what thing ye shall answer, or what ye shall say:	
		12 "For the Holy Ghost shall teach you in the same hour what ye ought to say."(g)	
		5. Concerning covetousness: two brothers *ask Jesus to solve their problem about an inheritance*	
		13 And one of the company said unto him, "Master, speak to my brother, that he divide the inheritance with me."(h)	
		14 And he said unto him, "Man, who made me a judge or a divider over you?"	
		15 And he said unto them, "Take heed, and beware of covetousness: for a man's life consisteth not in the abundance of the things which he possesseth."	
		The Parable of the Rich fool	

Matt.	Mk.	Lk. 12:16-35—Galilee	John
		16 And he spake a parable unto them, saying, "The ground of a certain rich man brought forth plentifully:	

16 And he spake a parable unto them, saying, "The ground of a certain rich man brought forth plentifully:

17 "And he thought within himself, saying, 'What shall I do, because I have no room where to bestow my fruits?'

18 "And he said, 'This will I do: I will pull down my barns, and build greater; and there will I bestow all my fruits and my goods.

19 'And I will say to my soul, Soul, thou hast much goods laid up for many years; take thine ease, eat, drink, *and* be merry.'

20 "But God said unto him, '*Thou* fool, this night thy soul shall be required of thee: then whose shall those things be, which thou hast provided?'

21 "So *is* he that layeth up treasure for himself, and is not rich toward God."

6. About anxiety

22 And he said unto his disciples, "Therefore I say unto you, Take no thought for your life, what ye shall eat; neither for the body, what ye shall put on.[i]

23 "The life is more than meat, [food] and the body *is more* than raiment.

24 "Consider the ravens: for they neither sow nor reap; which neither have storehouse nor barn; and God feedeth them: how much more are ye better than the fowls?

25 "And which of you with taking thought can add to his stature one cubit? (18 inches)

26 "If ye then be not able to do that thing which is least, why take ye thought for the rest?

27 "Consider the lilies how they grow: they toil not, they spin not; and yet I say unto you, that Solomon in all his glory was not arrayed like one of these.

28 "If then God so clothe the grass, which is to day in the field, and to morrow is cast into the oven; how much more *will he clothe* you, O ye of little faith?

29 "And seek not ye what ye shall eat, or what ye shall drink, neither be ye of doubtful mind.

30 "For all these things do the nations of the world seek after: and your Father knoweth that ye have need of these things.

31 "But rather seek ye the kingdom of God; and all these things shall be added unto you.

32 "Fear not, little flock;[j] for it is your Father's good pleasure to give you the kingdom.[k]

7. About earth's possession for His followers at that time

33 "Sell that ye have,[l] and give alms; provide yourselves bags which wax not old, a treasure in the heavens that faileth not, where no thief approacheth, neither moth corrupteth.

34 "For where your treasure is, there will your heart be also.[m]

8. About readiness for His coming

35 "Let your loins be girded[n] about, and *your* lights burning;

Matt.	Mk.	Lk. 12:36-52—*Galilee*	John
		36 "And ye yourselves like unto men that wait for their lord, when he will return from the wedding;[o] that when he cometh and knocketh, they may open unto him immediately.	

37 "Blessed *are* those servants, whom the lord when he cometh shall find watching: verily I say unto you, that he shall gird himself, and make them to sit down to meat, and will come forth and serve them.

38 "And if he shall come in the second watch, [pre midnight] or come in the third watch, [post midnight] and find *them* so, blessed are those servants.

39 "And this know, that if the goodman[p] [lord-owner] of the house had known what hour the thief would come, he would have watched, and not have suffered [allowed] his house to be broken through.

40 "Be ye therefore ready also: for the Son of man cometh at an hour when ye think not.

9. About unfaithfulness

41 Then Peter said[q] unto him, "Lord, speakest thou this parable unto us, or even to all?"

42 And the Lord said, "Who then is that faithful and wise steward,[r] [slave] whom *his* lord shall make ruler over his household, to give *them their* portion of meat in due season?

43 "Blessed *is* that servant, whom his lord when he cometh shall find so doing.[s]

44 "Of a truth I say unto you, that he will make him ruler over all that he hath.

45 "But and if that servant say in his heart, 'My lord delayeth his coming;' and shall begin to beat the menservants and maidens, and to eat and drink, and to be drunken;[t]

46 "The lord of that servant will come in a day when he looketh not for *him*, and at an hour when he is not aware, and will cut him in sunder, and will appoint him his portion with the unbelievers.

47 "And that servant, which knew his lord's will, and prepared not *himself*, neither did according to his will, shall be beaten[u] with many *stripes*.

48 "But he that knew not, and did commit things worthy of stripes, shall be beaten with few[v] *stripes*. For unto whomsoever much is given, of him shall be much required: and to whom men have committed much, of him they will ask more.

49 "I am come to send fire on the earth; and what will I, if it be already kindled? [w]

10. About His soon coming death

50 "But I have a baptism to be baptized with; and how am I straitened [hindered] till it be accomplished!

11. About false peace, divisions, and signs

51 "Suppose ye that I am come to give peace on earth? I tell you, Nay; but rather division:

52 "For from henceforth there shall be five in one house divided, three against two, and two against three.

Matt.	Mk.	Lk. 12:53-59—Galilee	John
		53 "The father shall be divided against the son, and the son against the father; the mother against the daughter, and the daughter against the mother; the mother in law against her daughter in law, and the daughter in law against her mother in law." **54** And he said also to the people, "When ye see a cloud rise out of the west, straightway ye say, 'There cometh a shower;' and so it is.**(x)** **55** "And when *ye see* the south wind blow, ye say, 'There will be heat;' and it cometh to pass. **56** "*Ye* hypocrites, ye can discern the face of the sky and of the earth; but how is it that ye do not discern this time? **57** "Yea, and why even of yourselves judge ye not what is right?"**(y)** ***12. About failure to reconcile: a lesson on chastisement*** **58** "When thou goest with thine adversary to the magistrate, *as thou art* in the way, give diligence that thou mayest be delivered from him;**(z)** lest he hale [haul] thee to the judge, and the judge deliver thee to the officer, and the officer cast thee into prison. **59** "I tell thee, thou shalt not depart thence, till thou hast paid the very last mite." (one-fifth of a cent) (Next. chap. Lk. 13:1 cont. in Section 72.)	

Footnotes-Commentary

(a) "Innumerable multitude." The word here is "myriads" or "ten thousands," and is translated as such in Jude 14. It means that multiplied thousands swamped the Savior on this occasion. There were so many that they trampled upon each other. Most of these were not believers. People from all occupations gathered to see and hear this mystery Man. Again, news spread over the country of His compassion on the outcasts of Jewish religion, especially the lepers, sick, and deformed. Even Gentiles amassed to see and hear Him. Everyone knew of His pungent, fearless exposure of the scribes and Pharisees. Curious as it is, the consciousness of many men is on the side of him who is faithful to expose their wickedness: all, except religious hypocrites. Though *honest* sinners deeply feel the sting of their reproach, they secretly admire any man who speaks what they know is right. Among those that followed Jesus, many were of this mind.

(b) "Beware of the leaven." The meaning here is that Jesus sought to warn first His preachers about the spiritual decadence of the religious leaders of Israel. He repeated this warning later, in Section 101, Matt. 16:5-6, footnote b. If the ministers and missionaries of Christ do not know *who* their enemies are, then half the battle is lost! As seen in the previous Sections, the disciples had been present during His violent clashes with the religionists and heard His numerous warnings about the doctrine of the scribes, Pharisees, and lawyers. Now, it is given again under the symbolism of "leaven," a fermenting element that spreads throughout that in which it is found. See Section 80, Matt. 13:33, footnote b for other meanings of leaven. The Messiah attempted to engrain this warning into the very souls of His apostles-disciples. After His departure to the Father, the scribes and Pharisees became their chief enemies. The doctrine condemned by Christ was their oral law, traditions, and distorted interpretations of the Mosaic code. See Section 52, footnote h; Section 89, footnote c; and Section 96, footnote d for explanation of the Hebrew oral law. Their chief sin was pretending or playacting to be something they were not.

(c) The following discourse of Christ consisted of various admonitions, some of which He had mentioned on previous occasions and at different times. We observe from these verses how He often repeated Himself. Several of the repetitive statements may be traced in the following footnotes.

(d) Verses 2-3 were originally spoken in Section 59, Matt. 10:26-27. See footnote n.

(e) Verses 4-9 were first spoken in Section 59, Matt. 10:28-33. Here, note footnotes o and p.

(f) Verse 10 was first spoken in Section 66, Matt. 12:31-32. At this place, refer to footnote j.

(g) Verses 11-12. This was originally spoken in Section 59, Matt. 10:17-20. Also, note Jesus' Words in Section 163, Mk. 13:11 and Lk. 21:14-15. It is the anointing of the Holy Spirit that makes the difference in ministering God's Word; not academic degrees, loudness, bodily gymnastics, and theatrical antics. This statement does not decry the need for diligent study and correct understanding of Holy Scripture. Yet, even this at its best is a joke apart from the power of God. Read the admonitions about teaching-preaching in 1 Cor. 2:1-5 and 1 Peter 1:12.

(h) Verses 16-21. The Parable of the Rich Fool is found nowhere else in the New Testament. Someone in the audience felt that Christ could resolve a dispute with his brother over an inheritance. Among the Jews, it was customary that the elder brother received two shares and the remainder was equally divided among the others (Deut. 21:17). The response of Christ in verse 14 is enlightening. The Messiah affirmed that He had not come to get involved in financial controversies. His mission was to march to the cross and die for the sins of the world. The *priority* business of ministers is to attend to the souls of men by steady obedience to Acts 6:4. This is not to deny that God's men should assist and bless all in every possible way, but it is to state that our *first* calling is to rob hell of dying souls, "pulling them" as it were "out of the fire" with the gospel rope (Jude 22-23). It is also our sacred duty to strengthen the brethren. Christ responded to His inquirer with a parable that demonstrated the folly of pursuing earthly goods and leaving one's soul famished, without eternal life. There is a strong intimation in Christ's Words that His inquirer was unprepared to meet God, and his fate was shadowed in that of the rich fool. The wealthy of this world (with a few exceptions) will die damned without hope. They are paupers toward God and heaven. The farmer in our Lord's parable was the "perfect fool." Note the actions of his heart in the midst of great abundance. He was deceived by five different negative deeds.

1. **He left God out of his "thoughts"** (verse 17). Few men can acquire great plenty and maintain the proper mental and religious balance. With abundance, often there is disquieting care and great anxiety.

2. **He left God out of his "room"** (verse 17b). Hundreds of gigantic stone castles with thousands of rooms lavish Europe. They are cold, mute testimonies of the eternal calamity of leaving God out of one's dwelling.

3. **He left God out of his "building"** (verse 18). The warning, "Except the LORD build the house, they labour in vain that build it" (Ps. 127:1) was left unheeded by this busy fellow.

4. **He left God out of his "years"** (verse 19). This sorely manifested itself in his later days of life. Visit that old age home! Look hard at those wrinkled frames; catch that dreadful smell of slow death, trembling hands, dim eyes, deaf ears and cracking voices of hopelessness from those who never had time for Christ. How helpless and lost they are. Life lived without Christ is better to have never been lived.

5. **Finally, and *fatally*, God is left out of this man's "soul"** (verses. 19-20). Heaven announced, "Thy soul is required of thee." This divine proclamation for all men of all languages is inevitable. Not his body, not his barns, nor his wealth, but his soul was wanted! At death, it departed his human frame and stepped into eternity, but where? How could we ever forget another rich man who died? It was of him our Lord said, "And in hell he lift up his eyes, being in torments" (Lk. 16:23). He, who refuses God's entrance to his soul in this life, will find God leaves him out of the life to come (1 Tim. 6:6-12). *Thus, the "perfect fool."*

(i) **Verses 22-31.** This was originally spoken in Section 46, Matt. 6:25-34, during the Sermon on the Mount but in a different arrangement and with more specifics than given above in Luke's record. Here, Jesus warns His disciples about the killing fret of anxiety over earthly things that so often seize the minds of believers.

(j) **Verse 32. "Fear not little flock."** These words of comfort are found nowhere else in the four gospels. After the recent uproar with the Pharisees at a supper (Section 70), the apostles were shaken and fearful. Now, the Master seeks to comfort His trembling sheep. "Fear not" and its parallels are found 366 times in Scripture, one for each day of the year and the extra for leap year. We have a "fear not" for every day of life. No more beautiful expression could describe God's children than that of trembling sheep. First, they were used of the apostles and earliest followers of Christ, and then became applicable to believers of every age. *True* Christians have always been a "little flock" in comparison to the thousands of unconverted church members and the unsaved world at large. Many believers in Christ frighten themselves with an apprehension of some evil to come. How awful to torment one's mind and heart with evil fantasies. Woe be those who borrow sorrow from tomorrow and take out a loan on next year's troubles. *Have we forgotten that God is already there waiting for us?* Our blessed Lord has commanded "Fear Not." Reader, claim yours for today and (if there is one) for tomorrow. David's remedy for fear was, "What time I am afraid, I will trust in thee" (Ps. 56:3). The giant killer found fear hovering near long after his fight with Goliath.

2p-One can imagine the sheer horror of the twelve as they sat and listened to their Lord over and over expose the religious leaders of the nation as self-righteous "hypocrites" and "fools." No wonder they were afraid!

(k) To that miniature flock, God had "pleasure" in giving them His Son's kingdom. This beautiful Jewish expression speaks of the bestowment of all the blessings and benefits of knowing God. With the coming of Christ, it included the saving gospel and the comfort of the Holy Spirit in times of fear and uncertainty. All who believed in Him would later understand these mercies of God's great kingdom. The life to follow becomes theirs forever. They are ours today and will in the future be totally understood and fully enjoyed in sweet heaven to come.

(l) **"Sell that ye have." Christian socialism?** Over the ages, various cults have pointed to this text to justify their condemnation of private ownership of property. These poor people have never realized that free men are not equal and equal men are not free. Marxist infected liberal ministers, educators, and communal living sects have used this passage to propagate their "equal sharing" and so-called "Christian socialism." Winston Churchill once said, "Socialism is a philosophy of failure, the creed of ignorance, and the gospel of sharing misery." Here, Christ speaks in comparative terms as in Lk. 14:26 (hate parents and family), and Mk. 9:43, 45 and 47 (cutting off the hand, foot, and tearing out the eye). This is the same powerful language of imagery. The first church at Jerusalem in unconsidered haste attempted this "sell out policy" in Acts 2:44-45. It had such a disastrous effect on the believers that in years to come, they became a church of paupers. Their material and economic situation became so dire over the coming years that missionary Paul and others found it necessary to collect help for them (Rom. 15:25-26; 1 Cor. 16:2-3; 2 Cor. 8:4 and 9:1). Here, the Savior refers to *hoarding* earthly treasures, not ordinary dwelling houses and the necessities of mortal life. Scripture is clear that we are responsible to provide for our own and if possible assist those who are not able to provide for themselves. "Christian men" who do not take care of their families when they are physically able have "denied the faith, and are worse than an infidel" (1 Tim. 5:8 with 11 Thess. 3:10). The word "bags" in this text has its general equivalent in our modern day carrying purses.

(m) See Section 46, Matt. 6:19-21, footnote j, where He had earlier and briefly taught similar things during the Sermon on the Mount. Truer things were never spoken for both the sinner and the saint.

(n) **"Ready for His coming."** As frequently stated, none of the apostles understood the death, burial, and resurrection of Christ. This statement from the Savior must have puzzled them at that time. Christ made a second brief reference to His return a short time later in Section 135, and the seventh paragraph of footnote e. Refer to Section 163, eighth and ninth paragraphs below footnote c for an explanation of why His apostles could not understand this. For the apostle John's comments on their disbelief in Jesus' resurrection, written some years after it had occurred, see Section 196, notation by the symbols ▶ and ◻ at John 20:9.

2p-"Loins be girded." Here is another illustration peculiar to Luke. It was a term among both Jews and pagan Gentiles. It alluded to the style of eastern dress. A long robe served as the outer garment. When engaged in work, fast walking or swift labor, the robe was tied up with a sash about the waist or tucked beneath it. Hence, their labors were not impeded. Christ said, "Be actively unhindered, busily engaged in my service, and always prepared."

3p-"Burning lights" were a symbol of clear-sighted and bright readiness in view of expecting someone during the night hours. God's servants are to be always ready (Rom. 13:11-14 with 1 Peter 3:15).

(o) Every person in Jesus' audience understood this illustration. The lord or master of the house would return late at night from a wedding. No servant knew the exact hour. It could be during the "second watch" (9:00 to 12:00 p.m.), or even as late as the "third watch" (12:00 to 3:00 a.m.). At sundown, the master's servants would lock and bar all doors of the house to ensure security and protection. Upon arrival, the master would knock at the door of his own house and call out; waiting servants scrambled among themselves to be *first* to open and greet their master. He would honor with gifts those who loved him so much as to wait through the long night for his return. There were cases of the lord or master actually taking the place of a servant in bestowing his appreciation on those loyal to him and his household. This custom was practiced in early England for years, when out of joy the bridegroom would don common work clothes and serve his guests. Various pagans borrowed this habit from the Jews. At particular heathen celebrations, the slave owners would exchange places and clothes with the slaves and wait upon them. We see our Lord practicing a similar thing in total honor to the true and living God, in washing the feet of His apostles to their consternation in Section 170, John 13:1-7. However, Christ washed their feet *not* out of gratitude but to leave them lasting lessons on humility and servitude for others.

(p) **Verses 39-40.** This does not seem to speak of the coming of Christ in the air for His church. At this point, none of His disciples understood this truth or even His death on the cross. Exegetically, it has reference back to a lord of the house returning from the wedding unannounced and finding the servants careless and slothful (verses 36-38). See footnote o above. *The lesson here is to be always ready in God's service for unexpected things to happen!*

2p-"Goodman" has the meaning of "lord, head or owner" as reflected in verses 36-37. It was probably taken from Prov. 7:19, and is the same as "master of the house" in Matt. 10:25; Lk. 13:25; and 14:21. "Goodman" was later used in Matt. 20:11; 24: 43; Mk. 14:14; and Lk. 22:11. The astute and alert "goodman" cared for his property to keep it from being plundered. The conclusion of this parable is watchfulness; "be ready, for your master [lord or head] will come when you are least expecting him." He warns them against unreadiness. Some commentators think it speaks of Christ returning unexpectedly to this particular region of Galilee or to the village, city, or people to whom He had spoken these things. Some believe it may have reference to Christ coming at death to take His servants home. (This interpretation is farfetched.) However, Christ could have been speaking of His coming back for the church, realizing that His disciples would *later* understand the whole story, after being thoroughly illuminated by the Spirit on the day of Pentecost (John 14:26 and 16:13).

(q) **Peter's pertinent question.** He listened intently to the Word's of Jesus and understood both the parable and lesson His Master had just given. Now, he puts a thoughtful question to Jesus. He had pondered if it was the crowds, or the twelve that represented the waiting servants after the wedding, or the servants at home watching over the household during their master's absence. His interruption of Christ's preaching reflected his synagogue background. It was quite in order to put an inquiry to the teacher-rabbi when a certain point was not clearly understood. This demonstrated Peter's desire to be right and ready before the Messiah. He wanted to know if these parables were for the crowds or just for the disciples.

^(r) It is deeply instructive that in replying to Peter's inquiry, Christ gave another parable concerning wealthy householders and landowners who often had a slave known as a "steward." The steward was a business manager who took charge of things in the absence of his master or lord. He was not necessarily a slave. This person was looked upon as the "ruler" or "overseer" of his lord's total estate. He actually controlled the food, shelter, and raiment given to lower ranked servants.

^(s) Clearly, our Savior reveals that His estate (or work) in this world has two kinds of "stewards" working for Him during His absence. The sovereign Landowner of heaven and earth has been absent from His estate for some two thousand years. Many "stewards" (servants) have come and gone from the scene of service and duty to their Lord over this long period. Christ explained in verses 43-44, that the "steward" who had served faithfully during his lord's vacancy and had discharged his trust with prudence would be rewarded. His reward is to be "ruler over all that he had." This was an ancient adage used to denote that the beneficiary will enjoy all the blessings of his Master, and thereby "enter thou into the joy of thy Lord" (Matt. 25:23). It has nothing to do with believers ruling during the millennium: rather, these beautiful sayings picture the eternal bliss of God's good favor. Some slaves were paid so well for their long-time, exemplary service that the money was used to buy their freedom. May the grace of God so work in our lives that we may be counted within this happy number of "faithful and wise" stewards (happy slaves) who have been true to Christ, serving Him from a heart of love over the course of life's little while. Those who thus work will "enter into the joy of God forever."

^(t) **"When the cat's away the mouse will play!"** Verses 45-46 mention a regular occurrence within the circles of stewardship servitude in ancient times. Landowners were frequently absent from their properties, especially if they lived great distances. This provided many temptations for ruling stewards or servants to become negligent, cruel, and even physically abusive. The ruling servant often became a monster as control and power corrupted his sense of fairness and integrity. Beating fellow servants, wild, gluttonous behavior mixed with sordid eating and drinking soon ruled their lives. The term "menservants and maidservants" also carries the meaning of "boys and girls." This is indicative of how heartless and abusive this steward became with the master's workers during his absence. Our Lord speaks here of those within the *visible* and *corporate* ranks of various churches and religions, who claiming to serve Him, are, in fact, monsters of sin and lusts, having never been saved.

2p-Unconverted people trying to do God's work are a curse. Some of these are like coiled vipers waiting to strike. Encyclopedia like quantities of documentation has been written about the vast army of *human devils*, who flagging themselves as "Christians" or "servants of God and humanity" were in reality sons of Satan. Rape, murder, sodomy, child abuse, theft, lying, fraud, adultery, fornication, gossip, slander, heresy, divisions, and a thousand other sins could be laid at their feet. In these Scriptures, Jesus tells of their sins and fate. He explicitly said their portion is with unbelievers (verse 46). For example, the horrible revelations of thousands of priests guilty of child molestation are but the tip of the iceberg. All the television ads about "Come home to the Catholic Church" are like inviting the fly into the spider's den. Any church claiming *infallibility* and to be *God's only true voice on earth* that has such a record should apologize to God, and the world, and go out of business. See Section 104, the first paragraph of footnote e for more on the horrors of the Papal system among myriads of well meaning people trying to find forgiveness and peace.

3p-The Savior repeated this same illustration about gluttony and drunkenness, with several minor differences, a few days before His death (Matt. 24:45-51). He spoke of the unfaithful servant as being a hypocrite and going to a place where there is "weeping and gnashing of teeth" (verse 51). This was a common rabbinical term used to describe the torments of the damned. For twenty-one things the Bible says about suffering in hell-lake of fire, see Section 103, number 8, under footnote g. Our Lord approved this rabbinical expression because of its truthfulness. The wicked steward does *not* picture saved Christians, who backslide and are chastened for their sins. He is pictured later in the illustration of the tares mixed with the wheat. For details on this, see Section 82, Matt. 13:40, footnote e.

^(u) **Degrees of punishment.** With this, we are introduced to the standard Jewish custom of beating (punishing) offenders and law-breakers. Every person in His audience understood exactly what He was saying in light of their judicial customs. According to the Torah Law, an offender could not be beaten over forty stripes (Deut. 25:3). This was considered a high sum of severity to which a beating could extend. It was also right that in some cases, if a man had committed double crimes, his stripes in a public whipping could be doubled to twice thirty-nine!

2p-Verse 47. "Beaten with many stripes." Hence, our Lord's Words have root in the practice mentioned above. The servant, who knew his lord's will and did it not, who had received much light, and had knowledge of what would please his master, points to the one who knew the message of Christ but deliberately rejected it. Contextually, Christ can only be speaking (again) of the scribes, lawyers and Pharisees, who above all others in Israel had committed this heinous crime. We learn from these words that there are varying degrees of punishment in eternity. Just *how* this works, we are not told (Matt. 23:15). Christ warned the scribes and Pharisees of a twofold or double-hell punishment for their wickedness. In plain words, hell will be hotter for some people than it will for others. Read the story of a man in hell and what he said about his suffering. Refer to Section 131, Lk. 16:24.

^(v) **Verse 48. "Beaten with few stripes."** Here the Son of God informed not only His listeners but also all men,

that those who have had no light (or understanding of Him), shall have the lesser punishment in eternity. Some men cavil with God on this and quickly point to these verses to prove that ignorance of divine things will excuse men of their sins. No criminal is excused because he is ignorant of the law. Those who attempt to plead their ignorance of godly commands are sheltered in a refuge of lies that will collapse upon their heads. The most ignorant man on earth, *without Christ* and in sin is doomed (1 John 5:11-12). Only by the saving gospel of Jesus Christ (Rom. 1:1 and 16), are men redeemed and prepared for heaven. It is dreadful to contemplate the realities of men suffering in the fires of the damned for their unforgiven sins. See footnote u above for comments on degrees of punishment.

2p-It is obvious that some people have extraordinary talents and unusual mental abilities. Then, on the contrary, we note others who struggle hard but can never excel. They are good, sensible, clean living saints who seem to be always behind the cheering crowds. Little applause is afforded these dear ones: they are never found on the platform or in the public spotlight. These are those of whom our Lord said that they "knew not," and thus the weight of known responsibility does not lie so heavy on them. However, those believers who have greater capacities of mind, much knowledge and learning, possess deep acquaintance with Holy Scripture, but do not use these gifts will have more to answer for at the judgment seat of Christ than the ordinary Christian.

(w) Verses 49-50. Christ warns the Jews that most of them are kindling wood seasoned for hell. In verse 50, the Savior speaks of His future death on the cross for our sins. He called it a "baptism," and at this time earnestly desired that it be over. "Since the sufferings of Calvary must be endured for the salvation of men," He says, "I am anxious that it should soon be." The death of the pure and spotless Son of God was sad and terrible, yet so wonderfully glorious! It is impossible that we should look at it without trembling souls, bowed heads, and humble hearts. Later, Jesus used the same expression ("baptism") to refer to His upcoming death in Matt. 20:22.

2p-Verse 51. Christ is not the world peacemaker! The results of His death for our sins and resurrection have been curiously diverse. For some, redemption brings peace and love, for others division and hate. Families have been united in a bond of love because of the gospel, or they have split into fragments and terrible divisions. In lands where radical Islam dominates all, there are documented cases of parents putting their children to death for trusting Christ as their Lord and Savior! (If radical Islam vanished, terrorism would fall to an all-time low.) This reveals the age long hatred of false religions for the redemption found exclusively in Jesus Christ. Let it be noted that this is because wicked hearts reject Him in their blind folly and love for sin, their embracement of satanic beliefs or in defense of falsity and doctrinal error. It started in the very sunrise of antiquity when Cain murdered his brother over the question of salvation by the blood of the Lamb or one's good works (Gen. 4:1-11; Heb. 11:4; 1 John 3:12; and Jude 11). For more on religion's opposition to Christ's salvation, see Section 59, Matt. 10:36, footnote r.

(x) Messiah's prediction of ominous weather fell upon the hypocritical Jews with momentous consequences about forty years later in A.D. 70. It would be the most catastrophic destruction in Israel's long history. Several months later, He again tangled with the Jews and used their accurate meteorological abilities to point out their blindness regarding Him. Refer to this in Section 100, Matt. 16:1-4, footnote b. In Section 72, Lk. 13:3 and 5, footnote f, our Lord warned that, unless they repent, doom is certain: their fate was illustrated in the fig tree that would not produce fruit after several years of tedious care and attendance.

2p-Verse 56. "Ye do not discern this time?" This was a warning of the doom of A.D. 70. See Section 163 for the horrific story of the fall and destruction of Jerusalem.

(y) This cutting denunciation was directed at those amid the crowds who had sided with the religious leaders and hatefully rejected the Lord Jesus. These Jews, with expert precision, could predict the changes of weather, but were blind to who Christ was, and what He offered them. In verse 56, He says that they could not "discern" the time that was upon them. It was the time of the presence of their Messiah and the message of hope and salvation for Israel. Blinded by their father the Devil, these men despised their lowly Messiah (John 8:44). He predicts that a storm of terrible judgment is gathering for them and their nation.

(z) Verse 58. Reconcile quickly. Christ had spoken earlier in the Sermon on the Mount along these lines of the magistrate or judge and prison. Here, the Savior refers to a Roman Law. See Section 45, Matt. 5:25-26, footnote g. This was a form of incarceration known as "debt imprisonment" and is briefly mentioned in the Torah Law (Lev. 25:39-41). The congregation would have instantly understood what Jesus was saying. The lesson is, hurry and get right with God and settle your personal grudges. Sadly, the Jews never reconciled with their Messiah.

2p-A lesson on chastisement. Christ is showing guilty believers that there is great urgency to make reconciliation with their enemies while they can. If not, an awful price will be paid for this neglect. Eventually, it will bring the chastisement of God upon their lives. For a review of this commonly overlooked biblical teaching, see Section 46, eleventh paragraph under footnote g.

3p-Verse 59. This reveals that men could connive with friends and family and eventually pay their way out of ancient prisons. "Mite" or "lepton" was the smallest copper coin worth about one-fifth of a cent. Such tiny indebtedness could be paid in time, and the prisoner released. (The pagan myth of purgatory is not taught here.) In eternity, there is no parole or pardon. Over there it will be too late to settle these matters.

Factious Jews seek a confrontation with Jesus by telling Him about Pilate's murder of the Galileans in their temple. Messiah corrects their erroneous views. He again publicly forecasts Israel's coming judgment in A.D. 70* in the Parable of the Fig Tree. This lesson portrayed the nation's pending but certain doom.

*See Sections 67, 68, 70 and 71 for the previous condemnations spoken upon the Jews. The nearer Jesus drew to His death, the more frequently He warned the Jews of their sure judgment. In Section 163 is His final discourse in which He graphically describes the partial destruction of Israel, the Jewish state, Jerusalem, and the temple.

Matt.	Mk.	Lk. 13:1-9—Galilee	John
		Pilate's murderous deeds: Jesus responds **1** There were present at that season[a] some[b] that told him of the Galileans, whose blood Pilate[c] had mingled with their sacrifices. **2** And Jesus answering said unto them, "Suppose ye that these Galileans were sinners above all the Galileans, because they suffered such things?[d] **3** "I tell you, Nay: but, except ye repent, ye shall all likewise perish. **4** "Or those eighteen, upon whom the tower in Siloam fell,[e] and slew them, think ye that they were sinners above all men that dwelt in Jerusalem? **5** "I tell you, Nay: but, except ye repent, ye shall all likewise perish."[f] ***The Jews are warned by the Parable of the Fig Tree*** **6** He spake also this parable;[g] "A certain *man* had a fig tree planted in his vineyard; and he came and sought fruit thereon, and found none. **7** "Then said he unto the dresser [keeper] of his vineyard, 'Behold, these three years[h] I come seeking fruit on this fig tree, and find none: cut it down; why cumbereth [or deplete] it the ground?'[i] **8** "And he answering said unto him, 'Lord, let it alone this year also, till I shall dig about it, and dung [fertilize] *it*: **9** 'And if it bear fruit, *well*: and if not, *then* after that thou shalt cut it down.' "[j] (Verse 10 cont. in Section 125.)	

Footnotes-Commentary

(a) "That season." Because of this wording, some believe this could have reference to a particular Jewish feast or celebration. If so, we have no clue as to which one, it was. Regardless, innumerable multitudes had just heard the twelve lessons given by the Lord Jesus in the previous Section 71. In that discourse, He continued to utter dreadful warnings about the Pharisees and their companions, and concluded it with a prediction of their doom. Perhaps such strong statements incited them to attack the Savior with their groundless charges. In the nine verses above, Christ illustrated the impending judgment coming upon the nation of Israel and its religious leaders, by use of a barren fig tree. See footnote j below.

(b) "Some that told him." Whoever these people were, they appear to be among those *elite Jews,* who despised the Galileans and sought for an occasion to condemn them. The leadership of Jewish religion and many of the people believed that those who lived in Galilee were "ignorant" and "backward." They were commonly referred to as "Galilean fools." Refer to Section 9, footnote b for more on this. Certain historians have characterized the Galileans as "fanatics" and "disturbers of the peace." *A History of the New Testament Times,* page 12, by A. Hausrath, states that the Galileans incited tumults at the feasts in Jerusalem. *Jesus of Nazareth*, pages 143-144, by Joseph Klausner, carries the same line of thought regarding Galileans. Hence, Peter, the Galilean, his intemperance and eagerness to fight at the arrest of Jesus in the garden (John 18:10-11). However, such a conclusion of all dwelling in this place is unrealistic. It is grossly unfair to taint all the people of Galilee because some were of a hot headed and warlike nature. If one will study the trials of Jesus at the hands of the religious leadership of Israel, he will discover their fierce and unlawful actions far surpass anything recorded about the people of Galilee.

(c) Pilate. For more on this Roman politician, see Section 21, Part 1, number 2 under footnote b. For Pilate's actions during the trial of Jesus, peruse selected verses in Sections 181 through 187. The expression "mingled blood" was a common Jewish term used in their literature. It is also found in the Talmud seventeen times. Two examples are in tractates, Beitzah 8b and Menachoth 59b. Though these particular Galileans perished at the hands of Pilate, countless thousands more died at the fury of the mighty Roman legions some forty years later when Jerusalem fell in A.D. 70.

(d) Some believe this refers to the slaughter mentioned by Josephus in *Antiquities,* Book 18:4. 1, lines 85-87. Others think this murder of the Galileans occurred during a celebration at the temple. They point to a rebel fighter called "Judas of Galilee" and his army mentioned in Acts 5:37. The possibility lingers that the ongoing feud between Pilate and Herod may have incensed Pilate to slaughter some of Herod's subjects at some particular time (Lk. 23:12). Regardless of who it was, it is certain that because those murdered were Galileans, the Jewish talebearers who came to Christ (with their superior religion) rejoiced in this inhuman calamity. They saw this slaughter as firm evidence that Galileans were godless people. Like millions today, these Jews subscribed to the philosophy that "bad things *only* happen to bad people." The implication was obvious: since Christ had just forecasted a storm for the Jews in footnote a above, and He was also from Galilee, then He, like those murdered by Pilate would suffer some awful judgment, for this was the fate of wicked people. The Jews connected special sins with great punishments. Christ's unforgivable sin in the eyes of the Jewish religionists was His rejection of the tradition of the elders or oral law.

(e) **"The tower fell."** This calamity was a matter of current interest to the talebearers of Jerusalem. The Savior turned this piece of fact into a powerful lesson on sin and repentance. There is no extant record in history that explains this event. Though it is a mystery to us, it was hardly that to our Lord's congregation at this time. Knowing the thoughts of their evil hearts, Christ's answer devastated these conniving Jews. He flatly responded, "No, you are wrong in your thoughts." As these Hebrew hecklers pointed to the illustration of the Galileans dying on God's altar at the temple (because they were so wicked), Jesus instantly pointed them to the death of eighteen Jews, who were killed in their beloved Jerusalem, and of all places at Siloam! This word means "sent" and had reference to a place of joy, especially during the Feast of tabernacles. Refer to Section 121, John 9:7, footnote f for further explanation. Nothing else is recorded of this slaughter except it was a well-known fact of that time and brought joy to no one other than the hate-filled religious leaders of Israel.

2p-The Messiah profoundly argued that it was just as wrong to infer God's judgment had fallen on the Galileans because they were from Galilee, as it was to say the tower had killed the eighteen Jerusalemites because they were from Jerusalem or Judaea. He cautioned His hearers *not* to censure or condemn great sufferers, as if they were to be counted as great sinners. (Immature Christians, who are quick to draw the same conclusion of human tragedies, are as wrong as those quarrelsome Jews were.) Nor is it *always* true, that an unusual deliverance signals great righteousness. Christ's warning was something like this, "Do you who live at Jerusalem, near the temple and close to the law, count yourselves exempt from the sure judgment of God?" Ultimately, only few of them seemed to have escaped the bloody holocaust of A.D. 70, by the sword of Titus and the Roman legions. See footnote j below. Christ had pointed out on numerous occasions that the *whole* nation stood guilty before God, whether from Galilee, Judaea, or wherever. A terrible storm was brewing for the house of Jacob.

(f) **Verse 5. "Repent or perish!"** What a dreadful warning! Based on the two stories about people dying by such horrible means, the Lord Jesus established His call for repentance. He informed the Jews that they were, likewise, doomed, unless they realize their sin of rejecting Him, the Messiah, and repent of this crime. This was the cardinal sin, He required them to "change their minds" about Him immediately, repent of their sin of rejecting Him. It has been noted that the rabbinical understanding of repentance was far from what Jesus required. See further comments on repentance and the distorted Jewish teaching of this subject in Section 50, Matt. 9:13, footnote h.

2p-At the end of life, it is not *how* a man dies physically, but what follows his death that is infinitely serious. Whether the wicked suffer in this world or not and whether the righteous are delivered or not, is a moot issue. *What is reserved for them in eternity is the ultimate: heaven or hell!* The Greek word for repent is "metanoeo." It signifies to change one's mental attitude about sin, then, turn from it to Christ. This act of turning is called "metanoia." Man's ability to repent (change his mind about sin) then turn from it to the Savior, is given by the grace of God. This can happen *after* he has been touched with the gospel and awakened by the Holy Spirit of its truth. God's goodness in "giving" or "granting" man the ability to repent is stated in Acts 5:31; 11:18; and Rom. 2:4. This miserable blessedness is called "conviction" or "space to repent." It is the frightful dawning of a terrible awareness that one is lost in sin and damned without Christ. At this critical point, the convicted sinner may repent or change his mind and believe in Christ or refuse to believe. See Rev. 2:21 where Christ gave "space" (time) to a wicked woman to repent, and she refused His extended offer of God's goodness. Every mortal on earth of intelligible, responsible age, and rational mind has been commanded by Jehovah to repent (Acts 17:30). One of the major purposes of Christ coming to this world was "to call sinners to repentance" (Matt. 9:13). God hijacks no one to heaven nor does He actively force repentance down the throat of an unwilling man. It is base religious fiction to teach that men can only repent *after* they have been saved. Paul's orders for repentance, pungently expressed in Acts 20:21 do not fit with that of staunch Reformed doctrine. The stubborn Jews refused to repent (change their minds) then turn from their sins and believe in Jesus of Nazareth as their Messiah-Savior. When giving the Great commission the first time Jesus said, "that repentance and remission of sins should be preached in his name among all nations, beginning at Jerusalem" (Lk. 24:47). If men can only repent after salvation then the Son of God had it wrong! He should have said, "Preach that after salvation men can repent." However, the order laid down here is first to "repent and [then receive] remission of sin." For further comments on this theological caviling, see Section 201, second and third paragraphs below footnote n.

(g) **"Also this parable."** With this lesson, our Lord again reinforced the things He has just spoken. In great patience, He lays before His Jewish haters a parable that they would quickly understand. A standard custom was to plant fruit trees of various sorts within the confines of a vineyard. In this, the Lord Jesus uses a *single lesson* about a fig tree to illustrate the nation of Israel and its decisive fate at the hands of the Romans in A.D. 70. It is not true that the fig tree in Scripture always symbolizes Israel. See a detailed explanation of this in Section 163, Matt. 24:32-33, footnote s. According to Romans 11, the olive tree is the biblical figure for the nation of Israel. It is correct that God chose the vine as a long-standing emblem of the nation of Israel in her rebellious and sinful condition (Isa. 5:1-7). As the man in this parable had a "certain fig tree" and tenderly looked after it, so Israel was chosen by God and separated from other nations for His purposes. Now, she has rejected the Messiah. The owner (God) had visited the vineyard in the Person of Christ and inspected His tree for several years. He found it fruitless. See footnote h below.

(h) **"Three years."** Great surmising has risen from the owner's plea. Some interpret this as the length of Jesus' earthly ministry not counting the early months. It is correct that the dresser's intercession for the doomed tree points to the coming of Christ into the world, first, for "His own" Jewish people (John 1:11). Yet, reprieves for mercy have their limits. "One year" was granted. It is within this period that some place the remainder of Christ's ministry (after giving this parable) in which He was ultimately rejected as Messiah and crucified. Another view regarding the "three years," is that the nature of a certain fig tree is alluded to in this lesson. It does not bring its fruit to *perfect maturity* until after three years. Only then was its produce gathered. At the end of our Lord's ministry, Israel should have been bowing to the earth before its divine owner, laden with precious fruit. The rabbis interpreted Lev. 19:23 as commanding that fruit from newly planted trees was forbidden until after three year's growth. This later interpretation is unacceptable, as Israel had been considered a nation (for *almost* two thousand years) since the time of Abraham its federal head. Regardless of the various ideas, one thing is sure: the barren tree, which represented Israel, especially its religious leaders was doomed. The Jews were called upon to repent of their heinous sin of rejecting Jesus of Nazareth. They refused and were doomed. See footnote j below.

(i) The owner complained to the dresser (keeper) that for three years it was unproductive and suggested that it should be cut down. See footnote j below. The Talmud reads in tractate, Eiruvin 54a, "Whoso keepeth [or owns] the fig tree shall eat the fruit thereof." Conversely, the Talmud also refers to trees that do not produce fruit in tractate, Tamid 29b. According to the Torah Law, it was a serious thing to cut down a fruit tree of any variety (Deut. 20:19-20). Hence, the keeper's great concern for the barren tree. Only in extreme cases was cutting it down allowable. The barrenness of the fig tree pointed to the sin of Israel: they stood barren of fruit, even naked, and shameful before God their owner. Had they not rejected His Son? This was the worst sin in their national history. They were destined for the ax of holy wrath, and it fell upon them in A.D. 70.

(j) **"Cut it down"** was the verdict of *God the sovereign owner* of the stiff-necked, hard hearted, nation of Israel. Judgment would have been suspended if they had repented and believed their Messiah. In a few more decades, the legions of pagan Rome would encamp about Jerusalem. The blood of a few Galileans that poured out upon the temple altar was nothing in comparison with the blood of several million Jews that died in the destruction of their city. See second paragraph of footnote e above. The awesome verdict "Cut it down," signaled the final doom of *that* Christ hating "generation" of Jews. Refer to Section 163, which deals with the destruction of Jerusalem in A.D. 70. See asterisk under the main heading of Section 68, footnote g for more on the correct usage of the word "generation." There is no hermeneutical way that this word can be lifted from its context and syntax and have reference to the nation of Israel over two thousand years in the future during the millennium.

A TABLE OF CHRIST'S TEN KINGDOM PARABLES. THESE ARE IN SECTION 73 THROUGH SECTION 86. THEY ARE RECORDED IN MATTHEW, MARK, AND LUKE, AND PLACED IN ORDER ACCORDING TO EACH OF THE AUTHORS.

This table illustrates how the Holy Spirit inspired the gospel writers to relate the story of Christ preaching the Parables of His new kingdom. Matthew, the first of the four gospels written gives eight of our Lord's parables, while Mark and Luke repeat several of those recorded by Matthew. Both writers included the story of the *Candle* not given by Matthew. The Scriptures reveal that our Savior spoke ten parables on this occasion. Mark wrote that He also gave "many" others. However, none of these others were penned by the four evangelists (Mk. 4:33-34). The order employed by Mark and Luke in listing their parables differs somewhat from that used by Matthew. Luke recorded the parables of the *Mustard Tree* and *Leaven* in chapter 13 of his book. These two given by Luke were spoken over one year *after* those recorded in Matthew 13. This confirms again that the Master repeated Himself.

Below is a partial synopsis of these ten parables. Mark gives two not recorded by Matthew, the *Candle*, and *Growing Seed*. From the lists of Matthew, Mark, and Luke, we observe that Christ spoke the first six by the seaside, and the last four were probably given in Peter's house. These four begin in Matt. 13:44, and end with Matt. 13:53. Adding the *Candle* and *Growing Seed* parables to the eight given by Matthew as listed below give us a total of ten. In addition, they are all recorded only in the first three gospels. John was not inspired to write about any of these majestic, new kingdom or church lessons given by our Savior.

All of these are instructions for His church. They were given first to a Jewish audience but also carry lessons relating to the future conversion of Gentiles. Jesus spoke many other parables that are unrelated to these ten. The others are located across the four gospels. It remains a matter of individual opinion as to the exact number of parables that were given by Christ. *Smith's Bible Dictionary,* vol. III, 2327– 2331 carries an excellent article on this subject. Herbert Lockyer's, *All the Parables of the Bible,* is one of the best sources in the English language. The exact number of parables given in the four gospels is still being debated. The most reliable sources find approximately thirty. This count usually excludes Jesus' message about Lazarus and the Rich Man, which was not a parable.

Matthew's Order	Mark's Order	Luke's Order
[1]Sower—13:3-9	[1]Sower—4:3-9	[1]Sower—8:4-8
	[1]Candle—4:21-25	[1]Candle—8:16-18
[1]Tares & Wheat—13:24-30		
	[1]Growing Seed—4:26-29	
[1]Mustard Seed—13:31-32	[1]Mustard Seed—4:30-32	
[1]Leaven—13:33		
[2]Hidden Treasure—13:44		
[2]Pearl—13:45-46		
[2]Net—13:47-50		
[2]Householder—13:51-53		
		[3]Mustard Seed—13:18-19
		[3]Leaven—13:20-21

[1] Given by the Galilean seaside from a boat. See Matt. 13:1.

[2] Given in a house at Capernaum. See Matt. 13:36.

[3] Given in a revised form over a year later at Ephraim in north-eastern Judaea or possibly in Galilee. See John 11:54, where He went into a city called Ephraim for a time.

FIRST: THE PARABLE OF THE SOWER.

After His rejection*by the Jews, Christ gave ten parables relating to His new kingdom, which would replace their material one. Matthew, Mark, and Luke record eight of them while Mark and Luke give the remaining two.

*See the Jews blasphemous rejection under main headings in Sections 66, 67, and 68. In these ten parables, the Lord Jesus depicted events inside the sphere of professing Christendom from its beginning with His earthly ministry to the present hour. Within this periphery are both saved and lost. The first parable of the sower reveals how His kingdom is advanced by the continual propagation of the gospel with all the difficulties, set backs and victories it experiences. This parable is explained in Section 75. The gospel age will end with the final sweep of the dragnet as seen in Section 85, when God separates the saved from the lost at the removal of the true church. According to Mk. 4:33-34 in Section 81, many other parables were given on this occasion but these are not recorded in Scripture. It would take thousands of books to contain everything Jesus preached and taught during His earthly ministry (John 20:30-31). God has given in the four gospels what He wanted us to have and this is what we need.

By the Sea of Galilee

Matt. 13:1-5	Mk. 4:1-5	Lk. 8:4-6	John
He teaches in parables 1 The same day(a) went Jesus out of the house, and sat by the sea side.	*He teaches in parables* 1 And he began again to teach by the sea side:		
2 And great multitudes(b) were gathered together unto him,	and there was gathered unto him a great multitude,(b)	*He teaches in parables* 4 And when much(b) people were gathered together, and were come to him out of every city,	
so that he went into a ship, and sat;(c) and the whole multitude stood on the shore.	so that he entered into a ship, and sat(c) in the sea; and the whole multitude was by the sea on the land.		
3 And he spake many things unto them in parables,(d) saying,	2 And he taught them many things by parables,(d) and said unto them in his doctrine,	he spake by a parable:(d)	
The seed and the wayside "Behold, a sower went forth to sow;(e) 4 "And when he sowed, some *seeds* fell by the way side,(f) and	*The seed and the wayside* 3 "Hearken; Behold, there went out a sower to sow:(e) 4 "And it came to pass, as he sowed, some fell by the way side,(f) and	*The seed and the wayside* 5 "A sower went out to sow(e) his seed: and as he sowed, some fell by the way side;(f) and it was trodden down, and	
the fowls came and devoured them up:	the fowls of the air came and devoured it up.	the fowls of the air devoured it.	
The seed and the stones 5 "Some fell upon stony places,(g) where they had not much earth: and forthwith they sprung up, because they had no	*The seed and the stones* 5 "And some fell on stony ground,(g) where it had not much earth; and immediately it sprang up, because it had no	*The seed and the rock* 6 "And some fell upon a rock;(g) and as soon as it was sprung up,	

337

Matt. 13:5–9	Mk. 4:5–9	Lk. 8:6–8	John
deepness of earth: 6 "And when the sun was up, they were scorched; and because they had no root, they withered away.	depth of earth: 6 "But when the sun was up, it was scorched; and because it had no root, it withered away.	it withered away, because it lacked moisture.	
The seed and the thorns 7 "And some fell among thorns;[h] and the thorns sprung up, and choked them:	**The seed and the thorns** 7 "And some fell among thorns,[h] and the thorns grew up, and choked it, and it yielded no fruit.	**The seed and the thorns** 7 "And some fell among thorns;[h] and the thorns sprang up with it, and choked it.	
The seed on good ground 8 "But other fell into good ground,[i] and brought forth fruit, some an hundredfold, some sixty fold, some thirtyfold.[j]	**The seed on good ground** 8 "And other fell on good ground,[i] and did yield fruit that sprang up and increased; and brought forth, some thirty, and some sixty, and some an hundred.[j] 9 And he said unto them,	**The seed on good ground** 8 "And other fell on good ground,[i] and sprang up, and bare fruit an hundredfold."[j] And when he had said these things, he cried,	
A stern warning 9 "Who hath ears to hear, let him hear."[k] (Verse 10 cont. in Section 74.)	**A stern warning** "He that hath ears to hear, let him hear."[k] (Verse 10 cont. in Section 74.)	**A stern warning** "He that hath ears to hear, let him hear."[k] (Verse 9 cont. in Section 74.)	

False gospel tares: Refer ahead to our Lord's lesson in Section 77, and the main heading. Here, He reveals *another* enemy to the saving message of God's Word, which is not mentioned in the Section above. This opponent is the tares or false gospel that so closely resembles the truth of Christ, yet is a clever lie, disguised to entrap the untaught and ignorant. As sure as God is in heaven, the Devil is on earth, walking about as a roaring lion seeking whom he may devour. There is the true saving gospel that gives men eternal life, and satanic counterfeits designed to deceive and lastly damn their souls. "Greatly learned academicians" accuse us of using "fear mongering" or "scaring people" to faith in Christ. Their haughty secular intelligence and brainy but dark objections will serve to augment their own damnation when life is over. Seminaries, Bible schools, halls of divinity, churches, and pulpits across America are full of unsaved men and women who feign to teach others about the Bible, yet it is a book in which they do not believe. The true and living God of the Bible they do not know, nor Jesus Christ, whom they strip of His deity, and demote to the category of "thinkers" and "world philosophers." The Son of God described these people as "wolves in sheep's clothing" (Matt. 7:15). Peter wrote that their end is "swift destruction." They have reservations in "the blackness of darkness for ever" (2 Peter 2:1–2, 17). *Life is too short and eternity too long to play silly games with the Son of God.* Curiously, at times even the wicked blindly recognize this as flashes of truth slip unconsciously from their soiled lips. The godless Irish playwright, George Bernard Shaw, (died 1950), a fierce Fabian Socialist and Christ hater once said of himself, "I died at thirty and was buried at sixty!" Men who know the Son of God in truth have a higher hope that endures this life, survives by the grace of God, and lives into all of eternity.

Footnotes-Commentary

(a) **"The same day."** This specific statement establishes the chronology of this chapter as coming immediately after chapter 12. Matthew wrote that this group of parables were given on the "same day" as the blasphemous accusations of the Pharisees were spoken, and the visit of Jesus' mother and His half-brothers. Our Lord left the stuffy house where he had been teaching; and surrounded by the pressing thousands, made His way to the shores of Galilee. According to Matt. 8:14, this was the house of Simon Peter. Such openness on the shore would give unlimited room for His auditory to be heard by the multitudes. Here, it is suggested that Jesus appears rarely to take any rest for His weary frame. He was incessant in His labors for the souls of men. What a wonderful example for His successors in this gospel ministry. *True servants* of God rarely find a spare hour of the day in which to retire their exhausted bodies amid the demands and pleas of unsaved and suffering humanity clamoring for help.

(b) **"Multitudes."** This word is used in *both* the singular and plural over forty times in the four gospels. It has reference to the hoards of mankind that continually followed Christ. See Section 71, Lk. 12:1, footnote a where we read that the people actually stepped upon one another in their rush to see and hear the Savior.

(c) His pulpit was a borrowed ship. This was seen previously in Lk. 5:3. What a glorious spectacle; the Son of God from heaven, on the edge of a tranquil sea, sitting in a fishing boat. Thousands stand or sit motionless, giving rapt attention to the Galilean carpenter, as He explained to them, the great interests of eternity as found in His kingdom. In our present day, too much emphasis is being laid on "making men comfortable" or "relaxed" in the service of God. One church advertised, "Jesus wore sandals so you can!" (He also raised the dead!) Pastors and spiritual leaders knock themselves out trying to make Jesus attractive to a godless world! Just about every device known to men has been brought into the church in order "to win them." Jesus Christ has become something of a Six Flags over Georgia attraction; after all everyone needs some religion. However, a Man dying on a bloody Roman cross for the sins of others is the highest offense to the godless world. Pastors, ministers, missionaries, and Christian workers who try to get around the "offense of the cross," have crossed the river without getting into the boat. Meanwhile, sinners are dropping into hell amid the comforts of plush carpets, padded pews, and air-conditioned "sanctuaries." (There is nothing wrong with having these things if they do not have us.) Only when people are convicted by the Holy Spirit over the sinfulness of their sins, illuminated by the Word of God, and horrified at the prospect of eternal damnation will they be saved. One hardly "feels good about themselves," amid the *glorious* terror of Holy Spirit conviction that leads to the joy of personal peace and everlasting redemption. For further comments on these things, see Section 63, second and third paragraphs of footnote h, and Section 192, second and third paragraphs of footnote g.

(d) **"Parables."** Many opinions have been cast about the *final* meaning of parables. The etymology of the word signifies "to lay along side for comparison." Some parables in the Bible were *created* by the speaker as he sought to present spiritual and moral lessons. Often, the persons and events mentioned in these were fictitious: as the popular children's story, *Little Red Riding Hood*. However, other parables in Scripture were built from genuine life experiences. See Section 130, footnote a for further explanation. All ten of Jesus' parables given in the following Sections are built upon common everyday experiences with which the Jews were familiar. The grand intent of His parables, as given here, was to present *a brief sketch* of the workings of His new kingdom from beginning to end. There is *not* one myth, fable, half-truth or lie to be found in any of these lessons. Though correctly called parables, these things happened daily in Jewish life. In them are presented eternal truths applicable to this life and that which is to come. His audience compared themselves with His parables and fell shockingly short!

2p-For an older treatment of Bible parables, see *Notes on the Parables of our Lord*, by Richard C. Trench. Oddly, many commentaries tell us this was the *first* time Jesus employed this method of teaching. However, He had *previously* communicated in this form. See examples of this in Matt. 5:13-16; 6:26-30; 7:3-5, 13, 15, 17-20, 24-27; and Lk. 5:36. On this occasion, our Lord purposely introduced a straightforward systematic form of parabolic teaching. His design was to explain some of the functions of His new kingdom, then refute the Jews, who had so fiercely blasphemed the Holy Spirit and rejected Him as their Messiah in the previous chapter. Even though no figure of eastern rhetoric was more commonly understood than that of the parable with the Jewish rejection of Messiah and His ministry, He continued to use this accepted form of communication. With it, He amazed His audience as He described this wonderful new kingdom. Christ's kingdom was *totally different* from that of the scribes and Pharisees. In this discourse, a reverberation of divine justice is dreadfully sounded for those who had rejected and blasphemed His glorious works and Words of truth. Ancient books, especially the Talmud, contain some of the expressions and illustrations used by Christ in this seaside sermon.

(e) **The sower sowing.** This was a common springtime sight across the farmlands of old Galilee. In the order of human things, plowing comes before sowing. The ground must be broken up, worked, and prepared for the seed. With this in view, we recall how God sent the greatest of plowmen, John the Baptist, to break the fallow soil preparatory for the seed Messiah would sow. John had denounced their hypocrisy and exposed their vices, sparing none. His mighty preaching unmasked all pretenders. Thousands were broken and shaken to their souls by the ministry of the Baptist. Then Jesus appears as the greatest of all sowers. The Talmud tractate, Bereachoth 63a, speaks of those who disseminate seed. Christ used the sower illustration to launch His first parable on this occasion. It is noteworthy that Mark introduced the parable with "Hearken" and "Behold" (verse 3) informing his readers that it is a lesson of urgent importance. In Mk. 4:11, our Lord referred to His parables as mysteries. The noun "musterion" signifies a truth previously hidden *but now made known*. This word was well understood, for at that time countless pagan religions had their dark "mysteries" known only to a *few* initiates. However, Messiah was not preaching that God's kingdom was a mystery to be understood by a handful of "elected" super saints. Although this is exactly what the scribes and Pharisees so strongly believed, considering themselves the elite and exclusive insiders of God's truths. *They alone* among all Jews were specially blessed of Jehovah. What Christ had preached and affirmed up to that time (for the most part) was not compatible with the scribes' and Pharisees' false view of the kingdom of God. With His rejection by the Jews, the doors of God's kingdom would gradually be opened for all. Refer to the main heading in Section 67 for their rejection of the Messiah. However, men who were concerned about their soul's welfare would gradually understand its meaning and press into it. See Section 130, Lk. 16:16, footnote o. For an explanation of Christ's spiritual kingdom, see Section 39, footnotes a and g.

2p-Christ later explained these parables to His apostles. Their work was to carry the gospel over the known world of that era (Matt. 13:10-11). This they fully understood and began to do after Pentecost as explained in Section 163, footnote f, third paragraph under number 16. The earlier introduction of this new kingdom (later known, among other things, as the church), the Jewish religionists had not understood. Now, it was concealed to them due to their *deliberate* rejection and blasphemy of the Holy Spirit. To His disciples and apostles, Christ gradually revealed the meaning of these parables. By the end of this discourse, they were beginning to understand what He was teaching. In Matt. 13:51 the Savior inquired of them to this end.

3p-The kingdom of God or Christ *begins* with a man going out and sowing seed. In Section 75, Lk. 8:11, it is emphatically affirmed that the "seed is the Word of God." Every mortal enterprise that does not have its origin in the Word of God is doomed for failure. This has nothing to do with a "Jewish remnant" preaching the gospel during a tribulation period over two thousand years in the future! Such exegesis is absolute folly. The first sower going out is the precursor of the Great Commission that was given to the eleven several years later. See footnote f below. Chapter 19 of this work contains the record of our Lord giving the Great Commission five different times in five different places to his preachers and disciples. This was done in the forty days between His resurrection and ascension (Acts 1:3).

(f) "The wayside." Firstly, the seed sown by the unnamed laborer fell into four different places. Probably, the *original* sower of the kingdom message had been John the Baptist. Now, it is our Lord Himself (assisted by His disciples and apostles) as He disseminated God's Word among His own Hebrew people and their hostile religious leaders. Over the centuries, millions have followed in their train taking the saving gospel to their fellows. In Matt. 13:38, "the field is the world," while verse 19 is clear that each of the four places where the seed fell, represented the different conditions of the human heart within this field-world. The "way side" of verse 4, speaks of the "field paths" running through and along side, the areas of grain. All such waysides were untouched by the worker's plow. These traveling paths are discussed in the Talmud tractates, Nazir 8b and Chullin 52a. They were designed to keep travelers from treading upon the growing stalks and thus destroying the prospective grain. Otherwise, it would be beaten down by thousands of human feet, wagons, and riding animals. These avenues of concourse became hard as stone. Here, some of the seed first fell and was quickly stolen away by the fowls always present at freshly plowed fields. Luke gives Christ's interpretation of fowls or the seed-thief as being Satan. He and his demons unceasingly labor to steal God's Word from the hearts of men "lest they should believe and be saved." Note this in Section 75, Lk. 8:12. His chief work is to "steal, and to kill and to destroy" (John 10:10). All who impede or oppose the propagation of the saving gospel of Christ do a helpful service for the cause of evil. For a *different interpretation* of the fowls also used at this same time, see Section 79, footnote e.

(g) "Stony places" or rocky soil. The servant's plow had been pulled over these areas, but the loose stones had not been removed from the newly tilled earth before the sowing. The Talmud tractate, Mo'ed Katin 13a mentions the need for clearing the soil. Here, the seed sprang up; but unable to strike root (depth), the scorching sun killed the tender plants. Matthew and Luke record our Lord's interpretation of this part of the parable. It illustrates those who profess to be part of His kingdom but *without possession* of the new birth (root). In time, they succumb to temptations, afflictions, and persecutions, which came because of their earlier identification with the Word of God. The devious stones of sin lurking in hearts, well plowed but never purged by the grace that always accompanies genuine repentance, *will* deal the fatal blow (Rom. 6:23 with James 1:15). The concealed appendices of sin eventually demolish all who do not ruthlessly deal with them. According to Isa. 53:2 and Rev. 5:5, Christ is the "root" that gives life to men. These "stony place professors" of the kingdom had "no root" and perished.

(h) "Some fell among thorns" and were gradually choked to death. Even though the plow also tilled this part of the field, yet (like the stones mentioned above in footnote g), the brambles were not removed from the soil. Jewish history speaks in the Talmud tractate, Metzia 83b of removing all excess from freshly plowed fields. Again, one sees *why* so many within the sphere of Christian profession return to their former evil ways (2 Peter 2:21-22). Thorns, being a product of the Edenic curse, speak of sin in its poison and painful end (Gen. 3:17-18 with Heb. 6:8). Mark gives the Master's explanation as having reference to those who are "overcome by the cares of this world, the deceitfulness of riches and the lusts of other things" (Mk. 4:19). Luke adds the "pleasures of *this* life" in Lk. 8:14. Matthew's pungent comment (verse 22), that this counterfeit member of Christ's kingdom became "unfruitful," reminds one of the fig tree in the previous Section. This tree typified the nation of Israel. In *both* the stony and thorny persons, we see reflections of those who make hasty professions, without paying any heed to the serious duties and consequences that go with being a Christian. The church of today is burdened down with the people who have never been converted to Christ.

(i) **"Good ground."** This is the fourth and final place where the seed fell. "Good ground" is a term also mentioned in the Talmud tractate, Gittin 67a. All three of the gospel writers defined these converts to Christ's kingdom as a product of proper, faithful seed sowing in ground that had been correctly prepared. In Section 75, Matt. 13: 23 we read, "But he that received seed into the good ground is he that heareth the Word, and understandeth *it*." The converts are defined as those who "hear the Word, and receive *it*" (Mk. 4:20. It is noted that Lk. 8:15, in Section 75, aptly reads, "But that on the good ground are they, which in an honest and good heart, having heard the word, keep *it*." In this part of the field, the plowman did his work thoroughly. *Before* sowing, he removed all stones, thorns, brambles, and weeds from the tilled soil. This lesson forgotten today by easy-believe Christianity.

2p-As a rule, men do not come to Christ easily. Satan fiercely opposes the salvation of lost souls. Not only does he seek to steal the saving gospel seed from the hearts of men, but also he deceives them into believing they can be converted to Christ *along with* their sin. The Son of God never saves men *in* their sin: He redeems and delivers them *from* it. Whatever particular wickedness of the human race is illustrated in the stones, thorns and brambles, it is sure that *only* those who (under conviction of the Holy Spirit) repent and believe the gospel are soundly converted to Christ and freed from such. Never, had the scribes, Pharisees, and Jews heard such teaching. They were astonished at this first parable describing *how* men are brought into the new kingdom, and at the man claiming to be their Messiah, who spoke these things. In Jewish thinking, to be born into the family of Abraham (or born of water), keeping the Torah and oral laws were among the first steps into their earthly, political kingdom of God. For a thorough discussion of the Hebrew understanding of "born again," see Section 30, footnote e.

(j) Note how the three authors were inspired to describe the yields from the good-ground saints. Not all are alike in fruit bearing. Some who begin profusely do not end so. Nor do all who begin small conclude this way:

1. **Matthew: "some an hundredfold, some sixtyfold, some thirtyfold"** (verse 8). These Words of Jesus reflect a downward regression in the lives of *genuine* converts to Christ. This does not necessarily suggest sinfulness on the part of the fruit bearer of God. This pictures those believers who begin big, but end small in their work and service for Christ. Some Christians are more fruitful than others are. Quality pleases God first. Grace has various degrees of efficiency. One believer raises himself high in knowledge, experience, and fame; others remain obscure and unknown. Both love and serve the same Lord. Physical age produces weakness and inability to go and do in God's service. Sickness may ravage a hard working believer and reduce him to waste and nothing. However, the Father in heaven will bountifully reward all, who with clean heart and dedicated life, have labored for Christ. Christians who through loss and suffering are finally reduced to the "thirtyfold" category will be as blessed as those who have continued in the ideal "hundredfold." "Shall not the Judge of all the earth do right?" (Gen. 18:25). "*As for* God, his way *is* perfect" (Ps. 18:30).

2. **Mark: "brought forth thirty, some sixty, and some a hundred"** (verse 8). This suggests an upward advance in the lives of some believers starting at the lower figure and working to the highest. Here, we see those who being most humble, have "small beginnings" in their service for Christ but gradually over the course of life move upward into the greater things of God.

3. **Luke: "and bare fruit an hundredfold"** (verse 8). This is the highest ideal for every born again Christian. It should be remembered that each one has their place in the body of Christ. Though some members occupy a high place of honor and others a lowlier slot of service, the Lord of heaven equally loves all. Even a cup of cold water is not overlooked (Matt. 10:42). God has no favorites (Rom. 2:11).

(k) This common proverb was used by the rabbis. It has reference to the ears not only externally but much more internally! See Section 62, Matt. 11:15 footnote k for its previous usage. The Savior also employed it months later in Section 96, Mk. 7:16. The Talmud tractates, Avodah Zarah 5b, and Berachoth 31b have examples of this expression being used where it was based on Deut. 29:4. This verse tells us that God had given Israel "ears to hear." This rabbinical expression about having "ears to hear" was well known to the people; everyone understood what He was saying. Jesus also used it over forty years later in His messages to the seven churches of Asia. See Rev. 2:7, 11, 17, 29; 3:6, 13, 22, with a change from the plural to the singular.

2p-In concluding this first lesson of the sower, Christ gave a solemn warning for His audience to take heed to what He had just spoken. Christians must disseminate the Word of God by practical work and financial support over the whole of their lives. Duty is ours to do this and the consequences from our labors are in the hands of God. Not all of our efforts seem to result in good; nevertheless, the Lord of heaven attends to His Word. It is easy to believe that Christ first aimed this lesson at His original disciples and preachers, many of whom, in days ahead gave their lives sowing the precious seed. A thousand years before the birth of Christ, David predicted, "The Lord gave the word: great *was* the company of those that published *it*" (Ps. 68:11). For the gospel being carried across the known world of their era, see how the first church accomplished this amazing task. Refer to Section 163, third paragraph of number 16, footnote f.

Christ's parables were especially designed for the Jews. Their sin of rejecting Him turned them into reprobates; spiritually blind, deaf, and dumb to His Words.* The disciples who were blessed above all prophets and righteous men would later understand His kingdom parables and mysteries.

*See footnote e below for further details on the spiritual and moral condition of Israel's religious leaders.

By the Sea of Galilee

Matt. 13:10–14	Mk. 4:10–12	Lk. 8:9–10	John
The problem of parables 10 And the disciples came, and said unto him, "Why speakest thou unto them in parables?"(a)	**The problem of parables** 10 And when he was alone, they that were about him with the twelve asked of him the parable. (a)	**The problem of parables** 9 And his disciples asked him, saying, "What might this parable be?"(a)	
The Jews had crossed the deadline: it was too late 11 He answered and said unto them, "Because it is given unto you to know the mysteries of the kingdom of heaven, but to them [the Jews] it is not given.(b)	**The Jews had crossed the deadline: it was too late** 11 And he said unto them, "Unto you it is given to know the mystery of the kingdom of God: but unto them [the Jews] that are without,◄ all *these* things are done in parables: ► *This means "without" the Lord Jesus as savior and outside His family of saved believers.*	**The Jews had crossed the deadline: it was too late** 10 And he said, "Unto you it is given to know the mysteries of the kingdom of God: but to others [the Jews] in parables;	
12 "For whosoever hath, to him shall be given, and he shall have more abundance: but whosoever hath not, from him shall be taken away even that he hath(c)			
Israel blind and deaf 13 "Therefore speak I to them• in parables: because they• seeing see not; and hearing they• hear not, neither do they• understand.(d)	**Israel blind and deaf** 12 "That seeing they• may see, and not perceive; and hearing they• may hear, and not understand;(d) lest at any time they• should be converted, and *their•* sins should be forgiven them."• (Verse 13 cont. in Section 75.)	**Israel blind and deaf** that seeing they• might not see, and hearing they• might not understand."(d) (Verse 11 cont. in Section 75.) •*Some twelve times the plural pronoun is used in these verses to address only the Jews. See Matt. 13:15 below.*	
Jewish stubbornness had fulfilled prophecy 14 "And in them• is fulfilled the prophecy of			

Matt. 13:14–17	Mk.	Lk.	John
Esa–ias, [Isaiah] which saith, (e) 'By hearing ye shall hear, and shall not understand; and seeing ye shall see, and shall not perceive: **15** 'For this people's▶ heart is waxed gross, and *their* ears are dull of hearing, and their eyes they have closed; lest at any time they should see with *their* eyes, and hear with *their* ears, and should understand with *their* heart, and should be converted, and I should heal them.' *Unlike the Jews, the disciples believed and were blessed above all great men* **16** "But blessed(f) *are* your eyes, for they see: and your ears, for they hear. **17** "For verily I say unto you, That many prophets and righteous *men* have desired to see *those things* which ye see, and have not seen *them*; and to hear *those things* which ye hear(g) and have not heard *them*." (Verse 18 cont. in Section 75.)	◀*What people? Contextually and historically, Jesus was addressing the Jewish people. He demonstrated how they were fulfilling the prediction made by the prophet Isaiah centuries before. Note the comments by the marker ● at the end of Lk. 8:10 above. See also footnote e below for other details.*		

Footnotes–Commentary

(a) Not the twelve only, but others that were gathered about listening as He spoke. This is noted in Mk. 4:10. The disciples asked the question and everyone got the answer.

(b) This does not mean that Jesus adopted a special style of teaching for the select purpose of concealing the truth from the people that they might be damned. Even though speaking in parables was a most common mode of communication and understood by all, on this occasion the Messiah's efforts to define and elucidate the functions of His church were not understood by the religious leaders. One reason was that the people had never heard such things as He was teaching! The text is clear that not only did the Jewish elite fail to understand, but also the twelve missed the meaning. It all sounded strange, so un-Jewish, and un-rabbinical to them. Never had their trusted teachers spoken this way. Therefore, the twelve and the other disciples requested an explanation for themselves as well as the audience (Matt. 13:10 with Lk. 8:9). Neither the disciples nor the common Jews had ever heard God's kingdom explained as Christ had done.

2p-Believers and unbelievers alike were continually astounded at the teaching of Christ regarding His new kingdom and its commandments. Refer to main heading Section 45, for examples of this as our Lord gave it during the Sermon on the Mount. The parables given here only added to the mystery of His glorious teaching. Now, with

Messiah's interpretation of them, the apostles began to comprehend slowly the meaning of their Lord's teaching. In Matthew's version, it is noted that the plural pronouns "them," "their," and "they," are given some twelve times in verses 11 through 15. Clearly, He singled out a *specific group* of persons by use of these pronominal terms. Jesus' quotation from Isa. 6:9-10, unequivocally in the context pinpoints the nation of Israel, but specifically, its religious leadership. See footnote c and all of e below for the reasons why the Jews could not fathom His kingdom teachings.

(c) **"Taken from him who hath."** This odd saying falls hard on western understanding. Here, the Lord Jesus alludes to a common custom in eastern countries. It was used of one who possessed much or was rich, and gifts were continually bestowed. While the poor man with but little so often had his small amount violently taken away by the unscrupulous. Christ is warning the Jews, "He who does not add upon the truths heard from Me stands in danger of losing even that which they have received." This is precisely what Israel did! A man who seeks to advance what light and grace he has from the hand of God shall surely have them increased from the same good hand. The scribes, Pharisees, and their companions in hating the Messiah had many opportunities to learn the truth of God from His lips. Being overly materialistic, chained to their Mishna rules or oral traditions, and filled with hatred for the Galilean preacher, what little truth they possessed would be taken away as Satan stole the seed from their unrepentant hearts. For explanation of the Mishna laws of the Jews, see Section 52, footnote h; Section 89, footnote c; and Section 96, footnote d

(d) **"And not understand."** See comments under first paragraph of footnote b above, and e below.

2p-Verse 14. "Fulfilled in them." The Son of God states emphatically that Isaiah's Old Testament prediction was fulfilled in the Jews, who despised and rejected Him, their Messiah. See footnote e below for more on this thought.

(e) **Too Late!** Christ quotes the substance but not the entirety of Isaiah's prediction found in Isa. 6:9-10. In the context of the prophet's marvelous vision, he both saw and spoke of Israel's Messiah in His glory. What Isaiah wrote was literally fulfilled in his days by the stubborn Hebrews. About seven hundred years later in the time of Christ, the Jews had the *same twisted character* and emulated the example of their fathers of old in rejecting God's Messiah. This awful pronouncement fitted the Jews, especially their religious leaders, right across the ministry of the Lord Jesus, as well as that of Paul, and is valid to this present moment for both Jews and Gentiles. They had succumbed into a reprobate mind: the horrible blind deafness of eternal doom. See Section 100, footnote d for the moral wickedness of the Jews at this time.

2p-The ancient prophecy. Isaiah's words are partly repeated in the parallel verses of Mk. 4:12; Lk. 8:10. They are also mentioned in John 12:37-41; and Rom. 11:8. In Christ's quotation from the prophet, He expressly says, "they closed their eyes" (verse 15). *Israel was blind because they chose not to see!* About thirty years later, Paul used the same quotation from Isaiah and applied it to the stubborn Jews in Rome, Italy, who came to his rented house to hear what he had to say. This was about several years before the destruction of Jerusalem. In Rom. 11:8, we read that God had given the Jews the "spirit of slumber, eyes that they should not see, and ears that they should not hear." This is explained in Rom. 11:20. It reads that they were "broken off because of unbelief." Yet verse 23 declares that if they continue *not* in this unbelief, they "shall be grafted in, for God is able to graft them in." Can this mean that the fixed decrees of God, before the foundation of the world are changed *each time* a Jew repents and believes in Jesus the Messiah? John in quoting these same verses from Isaiah wrote that the Jews "believed not on him" (John 12:37). There is nothing here to suggest that God predestinated these people to this fate by His own "sovereign good pleasure." He decreed to stop their ears and blind their eyes in order to damn them *after* they had crossed the deadline in rejecting Messiah. They went to hell because they *chose* their sin, while hating and rejecting Christ as their Messiah. This resulted in their being, cut off, and dying without hope. For the doom of Jerusalem, the temple and the Jewish state, see Section 163 where the Lord Jesus, just two days before His death, predicted the horrific calamities of A.D. 70.

3p-The "Israel of God." Paul used this term in Gal. 6:16. It denotes that *both* believing Jews and Gentiles in Christ are without national distinctions. The New Testament is clear that the new Israel is considered different from the old Israel. They were the believers in Messiah among the "twelve tribes scattered abroad" (James 1:1). And "the strangers scattered" (1 Peter 1:1), were designated as "a chosen generation, a royal priesthood, an holy nation, a peculiar people" (1 Peter 2:9). Originally, the nucleus of this new Israel was Jewish (Rom. 11:18). Later, the Lord Jesus said that there were "other sheep" to be brought into His fold (John 10:16). This spoke of the millions of Gentiles yet to be saved and made part of the original new Israel of God. The Savior later warned the religious leaders of Israel that the kingdom would be taken from them and given to those (Gentiles) who would bring forth fruit. Note this profound statement in Section 153, Matt. 21:43, footnote k. Present day Israel "according to the flesh" is prevented from entrance into this great spiritual entity by their personal choice to reject Jesus of Nazareth as their Messiah, Lord, and Savior. This rejection of Israel's ancestral Jesus has blinded their eyes and hardened their hearts. Scripture declares that the veil of blindness will finally be removed (upon trusting Christ), and they will be re-established by faith into the true "Israel of God" (2 Cor. 3:16). In this, "all Israel" (who repent and believe on Jesus the Messiah-Savior) will be saved (Rom. 11:26).

(f) **"Blessed"** was a common rabbinical benediction used especially of God and to praise particular attainments of wise men and teachers of the Torah Law. See its meaning in Section 44, and Matt. 5:4, footnote h. It is found in the Talmud over fourteen hundred times. Because the apostles had trusted Jesus as the Messiah, He pronounced a blessing on their eyes and ears for they were true wise men! This was the opposite of other Jews, who had their eyes blinded and ears stopped through rejection of Christ. See footnote e above. Now, Christ gives unique insight as to what prophets and righteous men of the Old Testament era longed to see and hear over the course of their lives.

(g) **The privileged twelve.** On serious contemplation, one is staggered at what the twelve apostles' saw and heard as they followed Jesus, the traitor Judas included! This confirms that *miracles alone* cannot convert men to the saving knowledge of Christ, for Judas saw thousands of them. In reflection, we note that Adam and Eve viewed the wonders and beauty of that pristine creation. Noah saw the worldwide flood that destroyed every living creature under the whole heavens save those in the ark. Abraham foresaw Messiah's great day (John 8:56). The prophets "searched" diligently for the Messiah of whom, they wrote (1 Peter 1:10-11). Moses beheld the terrible plagues in Egypt, the parting of the Red Sea, and the miracles in the wilderness. Who could sufficiently describe the sights, scenes and sounds as experienced by David, Daniel, and Ezekiel to name a few? Yet, the little band of apostles who stood at the end of the line were the final benefactors of all that the sages had written and said. The shadowy images of the Old Testament became substance and reality in the New Testament. Their eyes and ears were blessed indeed!

2p-The apostles' experiences were greater than those of kings, sages, prophets, and wise men. They saw, heard, and handled the very Word of life, Jesus of Nazareth the promised Messiah! His miracles continually dazzled them! His grace, love, patience with sinners, and His truthfulness with the hypocrites of Jewish religion; His surrender to Pilate, the Jews, and Gentiles to die for all men they summarily witnessed. Then we have His glorious resurrection and many infallible proofs demonstrating that He had risen and was alive forever; this and *much* more they saw and heard. They were the privileged twelve, with Judas Iscariot being among the number. Who has the talent of a divine vocabulary to describe the glories that will be seen and heard by the child of God in heaven's never ending day (2 Cor. 4:17-18)? We finite beings (especially preachers) like to believe that we have special insights into things eternal. God dares not reveal very much about the glories of the after life. Our weak frames could not bear the wonder of such unspeakable realities. For other comments see Section 156, second paragraph of footnote g.

3p-**Hopeless religion or living the life that counts forever.** Meanwhile, the purveyors of Israel's religion were deaf, dumb, and blind to these things; this was by *their* choice. God still chooses the weak and most insignificant of His children to partake of His unique and glorious wonders. The great minds are those who know Jesus Christ as personal Lord and Savior, and live for Him. *Wise men and women have always taught more by deeds than by words.* This kind of Christian living does not end with the grave and the awful conscious darkness that awaits those who are unsaved. It continues forever in heaven's bright eternity. Christ later spoke similar things to His seventy as they returned from their first mission. It was another holy benediction that He placed upon their labors as wise men who were serving Him. This beautiful story is recorded in Section 115, Lk. 10:23-24, footnote d.

4p-**Super holy Christians?** Scripture warns us, "Be not righteous over much." (Eccle. 7:16). Long-time Christian workers know those "super saints" who always have the Devil by the throat and the world under their fist! Their lofty acclamations of personal success remind one of the Long Ranger galloping off into the sunset after winning the last gun battle. *Beware of the Christian, who is the hero of all his stories and everyone he meets is saved.* Truth can be twisted into an untruth. Because truth is truth, it has steel wall limits to finite men. To cross these boundaries is unwise. Even in times of correction, the extreme may take precedence over the correction. This is illustrated in the pastor who was given to terrible exaggerations. One elderly deacon approached him with a plan to correct the problem. He said, "Pastor when you go too far, I will softly whisper 'check.'" Next Sunday amid a red hot sermon on Noah's ark, the pastor shouted, "And Noah built the ark ten miles long." Instantly, he heard "check." Pulling himself back into reality he snorted, "And an inch wide!" Once I heard a boastful Baptist pastor say, "Nothing bothers me, for I keep myself right with God." Exaggerated honesty and over self-confidence can become a knockout punch. Some five years later that same trouble proof pastor quit the ministry, went into the secular world, when his only daughter became pregnant out of wedlock. In the 1930's "Big boy Blalock" was a famed boxer who knocked them all out with his famed "roundhouse punch." During a match, his opponent stepped in closely. Blalock's swing went around the man's neck; he knocked himself cold! *Thus, some super holy Christians!* Genuine uprightness before men has its origin on the inside first. It is there by the grace of God. Self righteousness with its charming public displays is foreign to heaven. Everyone wants to be like someone else instead of himself or herself. *Our highest mark is Jesus Christ; to be but a little like Him would be heaven on earth!* In time of crushing sorrow, we often discover that our personal invincibility was not as we had imagined. Let your righteousness be only the righteous of God in Christ, never your own; do not pretend. Here is a spiritual safety zone. To have Jesus pronounce upon us His blessing as He did those preachers in verses 16 and 17 above is worth living this life a dozen times. Amid that distinguished company of the "privileged twelve," there is a little place somewhere in the back where the servants of Christ may also stand, blessed, and approved of their Lord.

The Parable of the Sower* is interpreted by the Lord Jesus.

This parable was originally given by the Lord Jesus in Section 73. Below, He explains its meaning to the apostles. It reveals the four conditions of the human heart and their reaction to the Word of God and the Word's reaction toward these four conditions. This single lesson explains most of the trouble found in churches today.

By the Sea of Galilee

Matt. 13:18–21	Mk. 4:13–17	Lk. 8:11–13	John
	You need to know **13** And he said unto them, "Know ye not this parable? and how then will ye know all parables?		
The parable explained **18** "Hear ye therefore the parable of the sower.	***The parable is explained*** **14** "The sower soweth the word.	***The parable explained*** **11** "Now the parable is this: The seed is the word of God.	
Wayside ground **19** "When any one heareth the word of the kingdom, and understandeth *it* not,	***Wayside ground*** **15** And these are they by the way side, **(a)** ◄ where the word is sown; but when they have heard,	***Wayside ground*** **12** "Those by the way side **(a)** ◄ are they that hear;	
Satan hates the seed and works to take it away then cometh the wicked *one*, and catcheth away that which was sown in his heart.	***Satan hates the seed and works to take it away*** Satan cometh immediately, and taketh away the word that was sown in their hearts.	***Satan hates the seed and works to take it away*** then cometh the devil, and taketh away the word out of their hearts, lest they should believe and be saved.	
This is he which received seed by the way side. **(a)** ►	◄ *Matthew puts the "way side" verse here. Mark and Luke place them in verses 15 and 12 above.*		
Stony ground: suffering and persecution effect the seed **20** "But he that received the seed into stony**(b)** places, the same is he that heareth the word, and anon [immediately] with joy receiveth it;	***Stony ground: suffering and persecution effect the seed*** **16** "And these are they likewise which are sown on stony**(b)** ground; who, when they have heard the word, immediately receive it with gladness;	***Stony ground: suffering and persecution effect the seed*** **13** "They on the rock**(b)** *are they*, which, when they hear, receive the word with joy;	
21 "Yet hath he not root in himself, but dureth for a while: for when tribulation or persecution ariseth because of the word, by and by	**17** "And have no root in themselves, and so endure but for a time: afterward, when affliction or persecution ariseth for the word's sake, immediately	and these have no root, which for a while believe,	
		and in time of temptation	

Matt. 13:21-23	Mk. 4:17-20	Lk. 8:13-15	John
he is offended.	they are offended.	fall away.	
Thorny ground: greed and worldly cares choke the seed	*Thorny ground: greed and worldly cares choke the seed*	*Thorny ground: greed and worldly cares choke the seed*	
22 "He also that received seed among the thorns[c] is	**18** "And these are they which are sown among thorns;[c] such as	**14** "And that which fell among thorns[c] are they, which, when they have	
he that heareth the word; and the care of this world, and the deceitfulness of riches,	hear the word, **19** "And the cares of this world, and the deceitfulness of riches, and the lusts of other things entering in,	heard, go forth, and are	
choke[d] the word, and he	choke[d] the word, and it	choked[d] with cares and riches and pleasures of *this* life, and bring	
becometh unfruitful.◄	becometh unfruitful.◄	no fruit to perfection.◄	
Good ground: it loves the seed and produces fruit	*Good ground: it loves the seed and produces fruit.*	*Good ground: it loves the seed and produces fruit.*	
23 "But he that received seed into the good ground[e] is he that	**20** "And these are they which are sown on good ground;[e] such as	**15** "But that on the good ground[e] are they, which in an honest and good heart,	
heareth the word, and understandeth *it*; which also beareth fruit, and bringeth forth, some an hundredfold, some sixty, some thirty."[f] (Verse 24 cont. in Section 77.)	hear the word, and receive *it,* and bring forth fruit, some thirtyfold, some sixty, and some an hundred."[f] (Verse 21, cont. in Section 76.)	having heard the word, keep *it*, and bring forth fruit with patience."[f] (Verse 16 cont. in Section 76.)	

►It is curious what sin may do to God's Word, rendering it ineffective in the lives of some people. This is because the written Word unleashes its power to save, bless, and produce fruit in the atmosphere of simple honest faith. It will not accomplish divine purposes where men are filled with unbelief, sin, and worldliness, walking in the flesh and void of intimate fellowship with God. This is illustrated in Lk. 4:19, where it is "chocked." Like Israel in the wilderness, those who heard it (Heb. 4:2) did not mix the Word with faith. The Savior "marveled at the unbelief" of the people in His home town of Nazareth (Mk. 6:6). The statement that God's Word will "not return void" (Isa. 55:11) *in its context,* refers to various judgments that God had pronounced upon Israel. In time, they all happened just as He said. His Word was not void. Many look upon the inspired Scriptures, as though they contain magic. There is nothing magical about the Bible, but there is everything divine about it. It is God's infallible Word, breathed out by the Holy Spirit. It is living, effective, and totally reliable. Men can believe it and be blessed or reject it and be damned. For more on this subject, see Section 91, footnote g, and the *Author's Introduction.* God forces no one to believe or produce good fruit while living in sin and unbelief. Newborn Christians do not automatically do everything right and instantly produce every fruit of the Spirit in their lives (Gal. 5:22-26). God's plan is for His children to "grow in grace" (2 Peter 3:18). This is a life-long process. It does not keep us saved but does reflect that we have been saved. An apple tree is an apple tree even if it never produces fruit. The creative plan of God is for it to produce fruit in due season; some more and some less. The thief on the cross who trusted Christ had little time to bring forth fruit. His one great effort was to witness to his dying companion (Lk. 23:39-41).

Footnotes-Commentary

[a] **"The way side."** For our Lord's interpretation of this part of His first parable, see Section 73, footnote f. The enemy of men's souls and the stealer of the seed is described by Matthew as "the wicked one" (verse 19), by Mark as "Satan" (verse 15), and by Luke as "the devil" (verse 12). Since the Garden of Eden, the Devil has been the

archenemy of God's truth. His first recorded words spoken to the mother of us all were, "Yea, hath God said …" (Gen. 3:1). *Thus, we have the world's original "textual critic."* He succeeded by casting doubt on the command of Jehovah given to Adam and Eve. To this moment, Satan hates the Word of God presented in truth and power. Every conceivable attempt is being made to change, water down, retranslate, reinterpret, rework, and cast shadows of doubt on its veracity, reliability, and trustworthiness. We read of Lucifer actually quoting Scripture in his futile efforts to bring down the weakened humanity of the Son of God during the temptation (Matt. 4:5-6). From Eve to the end, the chief work of the wicked one is to steal the infallible Word of God from the hearts of men by every means possible. Mankind's *only hope* for sure instruction about salvation, forgiveness, and peace with God is contained within the pages of Holy Scripture; thus, Satan and his people hate this Book.

2p-Three names, same person. This is explained in footnote a above. Later, the Lord Jesus stated that everlasting fire was originally prepared for "the devil and his angels" (Matt. 25:41 with Rev. 20:10). Hell denying cults are quick to point out that this place was prepared for Satan not men! All who follow him will also move into his eternal hell fire lock-up some day. For further explanation of this evil spirit person, the archenemy of God and man, see Section 23, footnote c. Unsaved critics scoff at the above for in their "superior learning" they know more than the Lord of heaven.

(b) **"The stony ground."** In Section 73, footnote g the meaning of the stony ground or "rock" (as Luke puts it in verse 13) is given. The seed fell both on stony ground and on a rock. This hardened substance *first* pictures the coldness of the religious leaders of Israel to Christ their Messiah and His message to them. Next, it illustrates the hearts of all mankind.

(c) **"Among thorns."** Refer to Section 73, footnote h, for explanation of the seed among these noxious plants.

(d) **"Choke."** The idea here is that of an unnoticed, gradual take over of "creeping thorns" so common in the Holy Land. Sin in its various disguises, some powerfully beautiful and appealing, enters the life of an individual and will, in time bring decay and physical death, unless it is dealt with. Some expositors hold that this illustration portrays a saved individual who fails to grow in grace and thus becomes fruitless or has no fruit to perfection or maturity. Taking the parable as a whole, this seems to be the preferable interpretation. The teaching, that if one is saved, they will *automatically* become a full-blown Christians loaded down with spiritual fruit, is not found in Scripture. Rather, the lifetime process of growing in grace is the biblical teaching. Churches are filled with these "choked out" believers, who spend their lives weighing down others in their spiritual impotence or causing problems that cannot be solved. Whether we accept it or not, the local assembly will always have this conflicting mixture until death or Christ returns. The letters of Paul written back to churches and friends reflect this unpleasant truth repeatedly. Someone said, "Paul spent as much time encouraging and building up believers as he did winning the lost." The teaching that when a person is saved, he will always do right and continually live for Christ is seriously incorrect. Such dogma is a disgrace to the grace of God and leaves struggling believers in utter despair.

(e) **"Good ground."** The meaning of this is described in Section 73, footnote i. This person becomes a genuine convert to Christ because he hears God's Word and understands it. They receive in an honest and good heart, the message of salvation and keeps it. These people were not saved, then repented and believed the gospel as taught by perverted reformed doctrine. The Bible order is hearing, understanding, and then believing (Rom. 10:13-15). For a look at repentance and salvation, see Section 91, footnote g. There is much hearing today with little understanding of what is heard, while others know the truth and live in disobedience. This does not teach salvation by works. A soundly converted man keeps God's Word because he is saved, not to be saved. It is further true that some of God's children do fall away, but in time, they will return to the Christ, who saved them. The process may be both bitter and painful, but the end is glorious (Heb. 12:5-11). In this first parable, a host of opponents align themselves against God's Word. They include hardness, fowls, stones, thorns, sun and so on. Christ interprets these hindrances into such common things as "tribulation or persecution, cares of this world, deceitfulness of riches, lusts, and pleasures of this life." The original mastermind *behind* the various attacks on the spreading and success of the saving gospel has always been "Satan," "the devil" or the wicked one," regardless of the channel through which he works.

(f) See Section 73, footnote j for explanation of the varying amounts of fruit produced in the lives of believers and the different levels of its measurements listed in harmonization of verses 23, 20, and 15. This demonstrates that each has a place of service, some greater and some lesser. Regardless, all serve for the glory of God and the blessing of fellow men. Too much emphasis is put on the amount of service and too little on quality.

2p-Two trees made different by God. In 1966, I was spending time with a Christian Arab in Jericho. One morning he escorted me into his front garden full of fruit trees. Pointing out a bush loaded down with small yellow fruit he inquired, "What do you see?" I replied, "This tree has done a good job." Moving across the garden, he pointed out another bush and said, "And what do you see here?" Pushing the branches apart with my crutch, I counted only four pieces of fruit. My answer was, "This tree has not done a good job." Laughing loudly, he informed me that by nature, this small bush only produced a few pieces annually. The other was loaded with its produce. The lesson was, "Do what you can." Both plants did the work God made them to do. So it should be with Christians, each one doing what grace enables them to do. *Bigness does not always signify blessing.*

SECOND: THE PARABLE OF THE CANDLESTICK.*

Jesus admonishes the disciples that His teaching must not be hidden. Rather, it is to be shared like the light of a shining candle so that all may see.

Neither Mark nor Luke gave all eight of Matthew's parables. Mark alone records the story of the seed growing mysteriously, while both, he and Luke give the illustration of the candle. Jesus had previously used the candle parable in Section 67, Lk. 11:33. Matthew recorded the Parable of the Candle much earlier in the Sermon on the Mount in Section 44, Matt. 5:15-16. In this, we note again, we note our Lord repeats Himself at various occasions, often saying the same thing with different Words and illustrations. Luke recorded Jesus' condensed version of the mustard seed and leaven parables given much late inn Section 125, Lk. 13:18-21.

By the Sea of Galilee

Matt.	Mk. 4:21-25	Lk. 8:16-18	John
	A candle illuminates **21** And he said unto them, "Is a candle brought to be put under a bushel, [container] or under a bed? and not to be set on a candlestick?[a] (lightholder)	*A candle illuminates* **16** "No man, when he hath lighted a candle, covereth it with a vessel, or putteth *it* under a bed; but setteth *it* on a candlestick,[a] [lightholder] that they which enter in may see the light."	
	Everything will be revealed **22** "For there is nothing hid, which shall not be manifested; neither was any thing kept secret, but that it should come abroad.[b]	*Everything will be revealed* **17** "For nothing is secret, that shall not be made manifest; neither *any thing* hid, that shall not be known and come abroad.[b]	
	Careful "what" you hear **23** "If any man have ears to hear, let him hear."[c] **24** And he said unto them, "Take heed what ye hear:[d] with what measure ye mete, it shall be measured to you: and unto you that hear shall more be given. **25** "For he that hath, to him shall be given:[e] and he that hath not, from him shall be taken even that which he hath."[f] (Verse 26 cont. in Section 78.)	*Careful "how" you hear* **18** "Take heed therefore how ye hear:[d] for whosoever hath, to him shall be given;[e] and whosoever hath not, from him shall be taken even that which he seemeth to have."[f] (Verse 19 cont. in Section 69.)	

Footnotes-Commentary

(a) With this question, our Lord explains "why," He has been teaching in parables. His lessons, once understood by the disciples, would transform them into individual lights, shining like candles before all in their presence. None of the lessons within these parables were to be made secret or hidden away: they will give the light so greatly needed by the nation of Israel and others. In essence, Christ said, "As you apostles and disciples do not fire a candle in order to conceal it, neither must you understand these eternal truths only to hide them from others. Take my teaching and spread it wherever you are. Just as the little candle becomes a *public* object (by being put on a candlestick or holder), then it spreads its light wherever it is placed." The design in Christ's preaching was to enlighten men; and once enlightened, His followers were to share this glorious gospel. The absurdity of taking a candle, lighting it, only to conceal its cheery rays, was comparable with the disciples now hiding the amazing truths they have received from Messiah's great heart. Christ had earlier spoken of these things during the Sermon on the Mount in Section 44, Matt. 5:16. After Pentecost, these men became candles shining for Christ.

(b) Here, the Lord Jesus warns His disciples, the first servants in His new kingdom that even though they *could* hide the enlightenment and the profound teaching found in His parables, the time would come when every hidden thing (good or bad) would be manifested. Untold thousands of believers, enlightened by the grace of God, have put this marvelous enlightenment (as it were) under a bed, bushel, or vessel. Hiding the illumination of hope for lost mankind, they seldom witness to others. Every truly born again Christian who conceals the gospel light, when clearly, it should have been shared, will regret it on this terrible day of divine public exposure (2 Cor. 4:3-4).

(c) See Section 73, Matt. 13:9, footnote k for more on ears that hear. Jesus used this illustration several times in His preaching-teaching. For another example, see Section 82, Matt. 13:43, footnote i.

(d) **"Take heed [consider] what ye hear."** Luke pens these Words of Christ as being "how ye hear." *The Master said both.* In the term, "what," He was warning His disciples to beware of the "doctrine" of the religious leaders of Israel. This is noted in the main heading of Section 101. Here, Jesus instructs them to let into their ears *only* the truths that they have heard Him speak. Previously, these same men had been seriously corrupted by the foul teachings of the rabbis. "How" men hear is urgently important. Some hear the Word of God with bias, others filled with secret resentment, and many hear it with doubt and skepticism. Some by repentance throw open the doors of their weary hearts at its wonderful proclamation and hope (Rev. 3:20). The Savior calls for men to hear, understand, and receive His Word with a heart cleared of stones and thorns as explained in Section 73, footnote i. This is called "good ground." The disciples and apostles were repeatedly amazed at Messiah's profound and lofty teachings. They embraced all men everywhere and were mostly opposite to the synagogue message. As sure as the skies receive all the fowls that can fly, so the love of Christ welcomes all who repent and believe. Our Lord's stern opposition against much of the doctrine of the scribes and Pharisees startled everyone listening. It is most serious for those who hear the Word of God, to mark *what* they hear and to live it before others. "Measure" out to all who stop to consider the claims of Christ, a good amount of God's blessed Word, for someday it will return to you. The disciples of Christ's new kingdom are to shine as burning *public* candles that others might see the way to salvation.

(e) In these passages, Christ is saying, that those who "hear" and "have" my Word and unsparingly give themselves to its sowing shall receive a bountiful return (2 Cor. 9:6). This is not the healthy wealthy gospel.

(f) The Lord Jesus declares that believers who attend to His Words shall increase more and more in the knowledge of the truth. James explained it this way, "But be ye doers of the Word, and not hearers only, deceiving your own selves" (James 1:22). Conversely, he who does not render great diligence to the study of God's Word, but neglects it, will diminish in Christ's service and usefulness in His kingdom. This truth rings similar to the previous warning Jesus had given in concluding His Sermon on the Mount. Refer to Section 47, Matt. 7:24, footnote l. Our Lord told the Devil at the beginning of His ministry that man cannot live by bread alone. He must include every applicable thing God has written in His Word (Matt. 4:4). Satan seeks night and day to steal, take away, and draw the hearts of men from the infallible Word of God and a personal sensitive acquaintance with the Holy Spirit.

2p-Strange changes in churches. Many are gradually turning from the ministry of God's Word. We have "group discussions," "weight loss classes," "makeup face lifts," "self-help seminars," "anger management programs," "debt-free free counseling," "advice on purchasing insurance," "Tupperware demonstrations," and the lot. One "slick-chick sister," wrote a best seller named, *Slim for Him.* The "minister" sits on a bar stool or park bench, wears a grubby shirt, sips coffee with his sleeves unbuttoned, and grasps the hand mike while soothing his congregations with stories from *Time, Life,* or *Readers Digest.* We hear more about *"The Best Life Now"* than "the blessed life to come." Peek through the back door of the average church hall on a Wednesday evening and what do you see? Dozens of "overweight" men and women, huffing and puffing amid a frenzy of sweaty calisthenics. Note the altar for prayer in the dark auditorium! We wonder why the power of God to save sinners has departed from our presence. The *first* business of any Christ honoring local assembly be it ever so large or small is to "give themselves to prayer and the ministry of the Word" (Acts 6:4). If any time remains after this arduous task, churches may consider wholesome physical enterprises outside the royal commands of Scripture. Programs are to serve the people, not people the programs. For more on strange changes in churches, see Section 175, third paragraph of footnote e.

3p-Things have changed. A hundred years ago the *main line* churches, Methodist, Presbyterian, Baptist, Congregationalist and others were rescue stations for mankind. Today, this concept is voted out, ruled out, embarrassed out, and hated out. The average church building has become a hot house of human activities. No longer do sinners weep, or saints groan in prayer, or ministers preach in the power of God. How can we suffer our generation to perish in the slave labor camp of moral bondage, while Lucifer, with millions chained to his infernal chariot, gallops off into eternal damnation? Most denominations are paralyzed by "acceptable sins," "heretical teaching," "sick pulpits," and "prayer less pews," while riding a mad merry-go-round of religious sensuality. "Social justice" is the new theme not the salvation of lost souls. *Will there be underground churches in America?*

4p-Apostate hymnology. The hymn *Faith of our Fathers* was written by an Anglican turned Catholic priest, Frederick W. Faber (died 1863). It was a memorial prayer to Mary, fellow priests, and Catholics, who had been murdered in the sixteenth century during the reign of mad man, Henry VIII. Publishers, knowing that "Protestants" would not use this hymn, secretly dropped out a key verse from the original text. The aborted stanza reads, *"Faith of our fathers! Mary's prayers, Shall win our country back to thee; And through the truth that comes from God, England shall then indeed be free."* Faber made no secret of his longing for England to return to the Papal fold and expressed it in this hymn. "Protestants" sing this with gusto each Lord's Day, not realizing they are calling on Mary to save men for Popery! See *Singing With Understanding,* pages 105-107, by Kenneth W. Osbeck, and *The Gospel* *in Hymns,* pages 202-204, by Albert E. Bailey. Another example is the Catholic monk, Bernard of Clairvaux (died A.D. 1153) who penned, *Jesus the Very Thought of Thee.* He said that Mary visited his cell, exposed her breasts, and let three drops of milk fall onto his lips! Can demonic apparitions inspire one to write beautify worded hymns? On another occasion as he walked past a statue of Mary, it spoke, "Hail, Bernard." He wrote that Mary was the "aqueduct" between God and man. See *Alone of All Her Sex,* by Marina Warner page 198, and *Dictionary of Mary,* (passim), by Alphonse Bossard, translated by John Otto. Ill informed Christians often praise Saint Francis of Assisi, Italy, (died A.D. 1228). He was a "Roman Catholic patron saint," who spent much of his life talking and "preaching to animals and birds, and doing good deeds of charity." He supposedly "performed many miracles." Like Augustine, Francis is one of the esteemed doctors of the Papal Church. "The faithful saints to ward off evil" wear charms bearing the name "Francis." *The silence of these "saints" about personal salvation by faith in Christ is deafening.* See Section 33, third paragraph of footnote c for the difference between being good before men and righteous men before God. Apostate hymnology should be forbidden in the local church. A modern day example is much of contemporary music and signing. Traditional gospel filled hymnology has gradually been replaced. Much contemporary church singing (but not all) is void of *basic* Bible doctrines. The call for biblically separated living is often missing. It is about being "happy," "feeling good," and the next adrenalin rush!

5p-Leaving unchanged. Exiting "the house of God" after the Sunday morning sermon, most attendants mutter some form of approval to the Reverend, Doctor, Mr. Whoever's "nice sermon." After all, "He is an expert in Hebrew and Greek, and has five earned degrees!" No tears over sin but much tripe for nonsense. We have mastered the doctrines of Christianity, but they have never mastered us. Our prayers are like the little boy who rings the doorbell, but runs away before it is answered. Meanwhile, we continue to stumble forward in the service of Christ. *Sin is no longer the chief enemy of mankind; sadness is!* Pastors must find a way to keep the people "excited about God." The Bible has become a devotional guide written to make us feel good about self. We are "discovering our image," and then polishing our self-worth esteem. How happy God must be to have us on His side!

6p-Mega mania. A new wave slowly moved across America's "evangelical community" some thirty years ago. The religious press labeled it "Mega Church." Thousands were romanced by this "daring approach" to the gospel. Gradually, everything, we had been taught as basic Bible doctrine was replaced with a fresh dimension or approach to getting Christian work done. God was marketed, the Scriptures made pleasing to the vilest of men, while a smiling guru pastor and bouncing "praise leader" led thousands into the new experience. The enormity of the crowds instead of the needs of the heart determined the success, for if the crowds came "God was blessing." Bigger is better! Youth evangelists, who "specialize in leading the younger generation to Jesus," believe that they must look like tramps sleeping in a barn to win teenagers to Christ. For a shattering exposure of the failure of the mega mania nightmare, see *Taking Back your Faith from the American Dream,* by Pastor David Platt. It is a revelation, indeed!

7p-"Exciting churches." Professional engineers, strategists, and demographic experts are called in to blueprint the new auditorium, known as "the sanctuary." Sin, salvation, sanctification, hell, and heaven have been replaced by the Starbucks mentality. Satellite seminars were next, as thousands of ministers hung on every piece of advice as how to build a Mega Church. (There is nothing wrong with these seminars when folks can do no better.) Regretfully, flashy pastors forgot what the people needed and gave them what they wanted. Traditional church building fell by the wayside as they raised their new edifice on foundations of sand. Thousands of "Christians" travel hundreds of miles to hear the "prophecy expert," announce the near date of Christ's return. They will hock their souls to buy a new Mercedes but complain about giving extra for missions. American churches grow because people come from other churches. Men are only added to God's work by the new birth, resulting in a changed life.

8p-The glorious new Bibles. One can find a version that will teach just about anything they want to believe and a "church" that practices it. A debunked British Baptist minister, John Henson, produced the *Good as New Bible* in 2004. He promotes the "anything goes" church, and the "Playboy style Jesus." It mocks Christian core values, calls Peter "Rocky," Mary Magdalene "Maggie," and Aaron is now "Ron," while John the Baptist is "The dipper." The robed religious infidel, Archbishop of Canterbury, Dr. Rowan Williams, head of the Anglican Church, approved it. Staunchly conservative members of his church have called for his resignation for years. Williams goes to Zimbabwe and confronts the tyrant Robert Mugabe, but denies Jesus is virgin born son of God. He continually spouts his godless, secular humanistic philosophy, and apostate theology. *His approval affirms it is a rotten Bible!*

9p-When Scripture is rejected, sin covered up, "justice, dignity, and civil rights for all" are exalted, the cart is before the horse. Political ideals sprinkled with God are "easier to understand" for the religiously bent unsaved masses, than their need for the new birth. People march in the streets demanding freedom to do what they want. Meanwhile, we are sailing around in a whirlpool of "Christian pleasures," and Satan is captain of the doomed ship. Decades ago in Zululand, South Africa, an old black farmer said, "Bossie, we destroy ourselves and don't know the enemy is us!" *Honest,* hard-bitten sinners (secretly) want a religion that works, not one that entertains. As contradictory as it sounds, men often see better through sinful honesty than religious people do through their super pious churchanity! Does *true* Christianity work? Ask those thousands murdered by the bloody hands of communism, radical Islam, Papal inquisitions, paganism, and the millions of martyrs of church history. From heaven's glory, they all shout back "Yes!" Note God's view of the death of His children in Ps. 116:15.

THIRD: THE PARABLE OF THE TARES OR POISONOUS SEED.*

Be alert as my messengers. Fierce opposition waits for all who become active in the work of spreading God's Word. Evil men, undetected, are among those of you who labor for me. They will sow discord, doctrinal poison, and deadly untruth.

This lesson reveals that something else attacks God's Word besides the three things mentioned in the parable of Section 73. These three are the hard wayside, stones, and thorns. Here, our Lord informs us that when believers are engaged in sowing God's Word into human hearts, the Devil instantly becomes hostile. He not only seeks to steal the message of life and hope from men but his servants cleverly counterfeit the saving gospel. Satan has plans for the souls of men; to deceive and damn them into eternal hell. His false gospel is pictured in the poisonous tares. The Lord Jesus explains the meaning of this parable in Section 82.

Matt. 13:24-30 —By the Sea of Galilee	Mk.	Lk.	John
Good and bad seed sown			
24 Another parable put he forth unto them, saying, "The kingdom of heaven is likened unto a man which sowed good seed in his field:(a)			
25 "But while men slept,(b) his enemy came and sowed tares(c) among the wheat, and went his way.			
26 "But when the blade was sprung up, and brought forth fruit, then appeared the tares also.(d)			
The servants' report			
27 "So the servants of the householder(e) [land owner] came and said unto him, 'Sir, didst not thou sow good seed in thy field? from whence then hath it tares?'			
28 "He said unto them, 'An enemy hath done this.' The servants said unto him, 'Wilt thou then that we go and gather them up?'(f)			
29 "But he said, 'Nay; lest while ye gather up the tares, ye root up also the wheat with them.			
The solution: separate them at harvest			
30 'Let both grow together(g) until the harvest: and in the time of harvest I will say to the reapers, "Gather ye together first the tares, and bind them in bundles to burn them: but gather the wheat into my barn." ' " (h) (Verse 31 cont. in Section 79.)			

Footnotes-Commentary

(a) In the first parable of Section 73, the good seed of God's Word fell upon four different types of human hearts. In this lesson, the Lord Jesus reveals a unique situation that gradually develops among the general masses that make up His new kingdom. Later, in explaining this parable Christ said, He was the sower of the good seed and "the field is (or represents) the world." See this in Section 82, Matt. 13:37-38. With this in mind, note the following:

1. We see Messiah taking God's Word *first* to the Jews. They willingly harden their hearts, and the Devil, being their father (John 8:44), steals the seed and molds them into genuine hypocrites. They lived in blind obedience to their oral laws and tradition of the elders. See Section 52, footnote h; Section 89, footnote c; and Section 96, footnote d for a comprehensive explanation of the Hebrew oral law.

2. We observe another side of Messiah's new kingdom or the church, especially in centuries that were to come. It is indisputable that the righteous, and the wicked are mingled within the *visible local churches.* Every Christian congregation of any size, regardless of how pure it appears outwardly, has tares or "bastard wheat." See footnote c below. Even that first great church at Jerusalem had its Ananias and Sapphira (Acts 5:1-11). Satan waits patiently for the opportunity to sow *another* Potiphar's wife or Judas Iscariot within every vibrant, soul winning assembly of saints. This is intended to shame its testimony before the unbelieving, but watching world. Religious infidels in the pulpits and positions of leadership in local churches are wolves in sheep's clothing. Some three-thousand years ago, Solomon wrote that there is wickedness in the place of righteousness (Eccle. 3:16). While on furlough years ago, the author went to speak at a church in Florida. Arriving early, I sat on the front pew and asked the pastor if they would move the pulpit down to the floor level. As two men lifted the pulpit up, a deadly coral snake raised up and struck at them! *Many serpents still wait in the pulpit and strike at God's people.*

(b) **"While men slept."** Alas! It is the same today. In the time of Christ, these "men" were servant-watchmen appointed by their master to keep oversight of his well-sown field. This was a standard custom. It was a common practice in the land for an enemy to sow the bad seeds in the fields of those upon whom they sought vengeance. How disastrous, when God's pastors, church keepers sleep, and the enemy creeps in. Satanic cults such as the Mormons and Jehovah's Witnesses cunningly entice weaker, untaught Christians into their web of death. The consequences of indifferent or ignorant pastors in their indolence are horrifying. Never has there been a time when shepherds of the flock are so careless of their duties. Sin is glossed while the Christ hating world sits in the sanctuary, often directing the actions of the church. Shameful and blatant wickedness is winked at. The uncircumcised are in the camp of God. The Philistines have stolen the ark of power as the Devil's wheat (darnel) stealthily grows amid the *local* congregations. See footnotes c and d below. Many churches are crippled because Christians sleep in times of prayer, diligence, alertness to sin, satanic opposition and demonic invasion of their congregations. On the other side, true conservatives and fundamentalists Baptists "believe" they have done God a grand favor by preaching "such a wonderful message on Sunday morning," continually reminding their flock that *they* "will not compromise." This is true for their people compliment them at the door after the meeting is over.

(c) **"Sowed tares" or "bastard wheat."** Counterfeiting real Christianity has ever been a chief scheme of Satan and demons. At this point, in the history of Israel, Lucifer had riddled the Jew's religion with falsity and hypocrisy. Jesus continually confronted this lamentable situation. For a dreadful testimony of their sin, see Section 67, fourth paragraph of footnote b. Today, this points to the *local churches* so burdened with heretics, heresy, and hypocrites. However, there is another side to Satan's devices. The tares *also* depict the countless thousands of good, morally upright people, within local churches, who have never been saved. Geographically, the tares had reference to a "bastard wheat" common to the land of Israel. It was called "bearded darnel" or "bastard wheat." The Jews called it "kilayim," and classified it a toxic plant. In outward appearance, it was the *exact duplicate* of wheat and grew side by side with the true product. It was impossible to distinguish between tares and wheat until they reached a full head. The Talmud speaks of darnels or "kilayim" in tractate, Baba Bathra 37b. Being closely allied, with its roots intermingled with the original wheat plant, to pull the darnel from the ground *always* uprooted the nearest wheat stalk. To remove one is to destroy the other, for their roots were hopelessly tangled.

2p-Extracting the good from the bad *cannot* be speaking of church discipline being scripturally applied to believers within the local assembly. Paul wrote of this practice later in 1 Cor. 5:1-13. If so, then believers are destroyed in the process. Rather, it has reference to that body of unconverted people, who partly make up the "membership" of thousands of *local churches*. Outwardly, they appear as wheat, and have the visible markings of wheat. They stand beside the genuine wheat of the congregation, but their inward content is concealed until the end. Oddly, Solomon wrote that iniquity was found in the place of righteousness (Eccl. 3:16). The seed of counterfeit darnel is pitch black, barbed, and poisonous. It is only exposed by vigorously rubbing the head back and forth in one's hands; then, the toxic villain revealed. Those who consume it become ill, suffering from violent dizziness and vomiting. It would often affect or even kill fowls that ate it from the threshing floors. At judgment day, with each man giving an account of himself, the scrutiny of God will expose all persons for what they are (Rom. 2:16). The outward husks or showcase will be rubbed off, and then the inside will appear! For a very enlightening article on darnel, see Dr. W. M. Thompson's, *The Land and The Book*, vol. ii, pages 111-112. Thompson's classic published in 1858, remains among the best in the field of customs and manners in Bible lands.

(d) **The tares appeared.** It is notable that the "shoots of Satan" did not appear until *after* the tender, early blades of good wheat began to surface from the ground. There is a counterfeit sprout of sin for every appearing of grace. As sure as God's grace begins a new and blessed work with souls being saved, lives changed, and sin trampled down, here comes the "enemy" with deadly seeds. Wise ministers will listen for those early whisperings, and contrary rumblings; all are poison darnel, intent on discrediting the labors of real wheat (or children) of God.

(e) Upon hearing the announcement of the servants, the "householder" (land owner) instantly discerned the enemy had been operative within the confines of his property. Blessed is the minister of the gospel who can spot the works of Satan. The closer a lie is to the truth the more indistinguishable it becomes. Satan's schemes are introduced by covert strategies into God's work. Men and women of both good and foul intentions often do this ignorantly. The devilish aim is to dicredit publicly God's work before the unsaved world. Whoever this "householder" was, he was a prudent man. Men and women of such discernment are sorely needed in the Church of God today.

(f) The great zeal without knowledge of these servants reflects the lack of practical sense of many church workers. Those who tear into a difficult or problematic situation without consulting God in fervent prayer, and seeking counsel from His Word are great wreckers. Hasty men rush into God's presence with a mouth full of words and a heart empty, often without pause for serious contemplation, and consulting heaven in the realm of holy prayer.

(g) **"Let both grow together."** There are things within the *earthly local* church that cannot be rooted out or resolved by practical action or church discipline. There is a side of Christ's kingdom (as seen within the local churches) that remains untouchable to the best of ministers, pastors, or missionaries. Not all darnel will be expunged from the fellowship of saints on earth; as much as we wish, it would. Always, in the local church there will be those things that load us down in grief and sorrow. We seem helpless to resolve them. It is impossible for the best of saints to distinguish perfectly between every single seed of tare or wheat. Those who take on this task, without the blessing of God, in time will create more problems than originally existed. Nevertheless, it is sure that scandalously living church members are to be dealt with according to the teaching of the New Testament.

2p-**Balance is needed.** Too often, church authorities are nice to sin, even excusing it in the lives of openly disobedient Christians. On the other hand, there are spiritual leaders who are mean, harsh, and utterly void of compassion when handling such matters. Woe be the congregation whose minister is a dictatorial tyrant, always right, never wrong, and quick to exert his authority and crush any voice of honest questioning. Many entrapped by their sin and failures are only further bruised, shamed, and driven away by these men. Defeated Christians are as pieces of smoking flax and broken reeds. Great caution and wise moderation must be employed in counseling such, and applying the verdict of God's Word to their lives. If not, the struggling wheat may be trodden down or even plucked up! See an illustration of this in Section 137, the fifth footnote of footnote f. Then, there are those problematic individuals that "oppose themselves" and yet continue reaching out for help. They too must be received and instructed in meekness and patience by mature Christians (2 Tim. 2:24-26). As dogmatically stated above, no person must be comforted in his sin, but by the grace and patience of Jesus Christ, they must be rescued from it. Such work is not quickly accomplished by following a set of rules, or a little "prayer of rededication," especially, if the victim is in demonic bondage. Sin's mark has struck deep in the souls of millions. In Christian counseling, it is often difficult to distinguish if the problem is physical or caused by sin. There are physical maladies that cause some individuals to react as though he were under satanic bondage, when it is not true! Great discernment is necessary in dealing with fellow mortals that are badly wounded by their past actions and wrong decisions. Deliverance from spiritual evil is found only in Christ, God's Word, and the power of the Holy Spirit. Instructions to secure freedom should be given by a competent Christian counselor, preferably one with years of experience. *Medical aid should not be refused. Those "Christian counselors" who teach that proper medical attention is wrong are seriously mistaken.* See Section 50, footnote f for more on this. Woefully, there are those that enjoy "talking about their problems," to the wearing down of the counselors. These "time killers" should be told that prisoners in bondage must want deliverance more than life before they get it! It is so important that balance be used in dealing with wheat that is not yet in the God's barn. Refer to footnote h below for more on this.

3p-**In time it will all be clear.** It is a wicked lie that God has chosen to save some while rejecting and damning others. Those defending this foul teaching have their consciences seared by theological error. Worse, they propagate a one-sided gospel wherein all things are predetermined. What they think they are doing "for the glory of God" is something that will be done regardless of what they do! Concerning life's manifold calamities, the Lord Jesus teaches in this parable that it is not until *final harvest* that all the contents of men's hearts will be revealed and resolved. God predestinated no man to sin and to nurse evil in his heart. Judgment day will prove that. At this point, in giving the Parable of the Tares and Poison Seed, the Lord Jesus had not yet started teaching *categorically* concerning these serious matters. Here, He was speaking in a broad sense, using Jewish terminology that his Hebrew audience easily understood. Later, the Holy Spirit gave precise instructions with limited details about end-times and judgment that would finally come. These are recorded *especially* in the epistles of Paul. In Sections 163 and 164, the Savior gave the earthshaking discourse on the destruction of Jerusalem, the temple, the collapse and demise of the Jewish state, which occurred in A.D. 70. Most of this awful judgment must not be confused with the "time of harvest" in verse 34 above. In God's time, all things will be resolved and made clear.

(h) **"My barn."** The context of this verse "my barn" surely speaks of heaven, the home of the redeemed. Christ symbolically calls it "my barn." In the land of ancient Israel, the hypocritical darnel, or false wheat, both stalk and seed had one common use. *It was gathered as fuel for burning!* Conversely, precious wheat was carefully gathered into the underground stores or barns. Someday, every born again believer will be taken into the "house of the LORD forever" (Ps. 23:6). Everyone present instantly understood the inferences of the Messiah in using these terms.

2p-**What God's barn or heaven is not**. Over the centuries, Christians have surmised and speculated what heaven will be like. Many have tried to paint the total picture from the final chapters of the book of Revelation, but failed. The best of pure imaginations collapse miserably in an effort to explain the Home of God and His people! Likewise, no one can describe the prison house of the Devil and his own! Every cult has its demonic distortion of heaven. Groups such as the Church of Jesus Christ of Latter Day Saints have an eternal sex paradise begetting millions of spiritual children. Their heaven has three degrees of glory. The first is called "celestial' and reserved for good Mormons, who were able to cease from sinning in this life! The second is "terrestrial" which is for good people who did not comply with all the teachings of Mormonism. Lastly, is the "telestial" part of heaven, which is designed for all who lived unclean earthly lives? However, God's heaven as described in the Bible is not the sex perversions of the Mormon cult and its numerous offshoots.

3p-Regarding the question of eating and drinking in eternity, refer to Section 168, footnote h; Section 169 first and second paragraphs of footnote f; and Section 171, third paragraph of footnote b. For a provocative look into "God's barn," void of the extremes often found in writings dealing with this subject, see *Heaven*, by Randy Alcorn, published in 2004. It is a refreshing look into a subject of which we know so little in this life.

FOURTH: THE PARABLE OF THE SEED GROWING MYSTERIOUSLY.*

The puzzling yet amazing mystery of the effect and growth of God's kingdom as its members disseminate the saving gospel. This glorious message produces fruit in the lives of all who receive it in sincerity and truth. It will continue to do so until the end at harvest time.

*In all the parables recorded by Matthew, Mark, and Luke, the Lord Jesus first addressed the religious leadership of the Jews and their adherents. Secondly, His teaching then spanned the entire course of church history and is pertinent to this entire period. This parable reveals that God's work is finally accomplished, not by the physical labors of men (though that is necessary), but by the glory of His marvelous grace working quietly over the long periods of human history. This is beyond the understanding of men.

Matt.	Mk. 4:26-29—By the Sea of Galilee	Lk.	John
	The kingdom grows mysteriously until the end 26 And he said, "So is the kingdom of God,(a) as if a man should cast seed into the ground; 27 "And should sleep, and rise night and day, and the seed should spring and grow up, he knoweth not how.(b) 28 "For the earth bringeth forth fruit of herself; first the blade, then the ear, after that the full corn in the ear.(c) 29 "But when the fruit is brought forth, immediately he putteth in the sickle, because the harvest is come."(d) (Verse 30 cont. in Section 79.)		

Footnotes-Commentary

(a) See Section 39, the first paragraph of footnote a, for an explanation demonstrating that the kingdom of God and the kingdom of heaven mean the same thing in the four gospels. In the early days of Christ's ministry, they were both the church in its embryonic form. There were believers across the history of the Old Testament. Stephen referred to the nation of Israel as "the church in the wilderness" (Acts 7:38). The "church" as used by Stephen spoke of an assembly of people and did not carry the connotation that it did later across the book of Acts and other New Testament letters. For the benefit of those who disclaim that people were saved before Christ came, they should read Hebrews chapter 11. The teaching that no one was saved from sin and made a child of God until Christ died and rose is viciously false. By faith, they of earlier times looked forward to the coming of Christ, and trusted Him. We today, look back and anchor our faith in Him as well.

2p-The good seed clearly pictures the saving gospel of Christ. Any other seed that promises eternal life and the forgiveness of sins, apart from this, is false and fatal. The carrier of this good news often feels despair as he seems to see nothing promising in his life long labor. The eternal God of heaven, who sees each sparrow fall to the ground, will attend to the Word that is exalted about His name. The springing up of natural seed is a glorious mystery of nature. Men marvel as a drab field is gradually transformed into a blanket of fresh green. Without controversy great is the mystery of godliness, even in the power and effect of His eternal Word. See the second paragraph of footnote c below for the wonder working power of the gospel, twenty years after it was sown in the heart of a child. For the other side of this truth, see the Information Box at the end of the Scriptures in Section 75.

(b) **"Man knoweth not how" My kingdom appears and grows**. The Lord Jesus first addressed these parables, and "many such parables" that are not recorded in Scripture, to the Jewish people, especially the religious authorities of the nation (Mk. 4:33-44). Only when this is paramount in study will the above parable concerning the mysterious seed be understood. The Jews were looking for Messiah to come and establish a worldwide, earthly political rule. Then the nation of Israel would master the world under His authority. The pious Jews were forever chanting such slogans as, "Lo here! or, lo there! is the kingdom of God!" Note our Lord correcting this error in Section 134, Lk. 17:20-21. They believed that these loud, verbal chants would actually hasten its sudden appearing. Frequently, highly zealous Jews would stand in the temple and point eastward, chant and softly shout, "The kingdom cometh." This was based in Ezek. 43:2 from which the rabbis maintained that Messiah would finally come from the east and His kingdom would be instantly established. This would begin Messiah's physical, material, theocratic rule. It was these rabbinical extremes that Jesus also sought to correct in the above parable. A glaring example of these Jewish extremes is found in the Talmud tractate, Nidah 13b. It reads, "Proselytes and those who play with children postpone the coming of the Messiah."

2p-However, God's kingdom does not suddenly appear by noise or through clamor, show, and pomp. Jesus' parable of the secret, slow growing seed, that puzzled men, flew into the face of the loud-mouthed Jews trying to make the kingdom appear by incantations and noisy public show. The Messiah was telling them, "His kingdom was not like that of the rabbis. It had a small beginning with John's preaching, grew slowly, quietly, and is already here, even though in infant stages. When it has accomplished its purpose, the end will come, and no man knows how or when this will be. Not even the "end time barons."

(c) As sure as the earth mysteriously produces her fruits for the joy and good of men (and has done so since creation), so too the gospel of Messiah's new kingdom works in glorious mystery. Nature's secret processes do not fail to operate because we are ignorant of them. How a derelict, down-and-out human can be transformed into a beautiful saint of God is a wonder that amazes sinners and saints alike! We can no more fathom how a seed works beneath the soil than we can the gospel working in the heart of man. One hears the good news of Jesus and rejects it while another is smitten by the Holy Spirit and brought into eternal life. We marvel at the wonder of salvation by the grace of God and the streams of mercy that flow into our lives. However, all thinking heads bow and tongues confess, "We know not how."

2p-The following story illustrates the mystery of saving grace as depicted in this lesson. During World War II, a long time AWOL sailor sat on a bed in a rat-infested hotel located on the south side of Chicago. Placing a pistol, wrapped in a pillow, to his head, he reached over to turn the radio up to muffle the sound of gunfire. Suddenly, he noticed a shaft of light streaming under the door from the hallway into his dark room. Then into his mind flashed the passage from John 8:12, that a Sunday school teacher had drilled into his heart some twenty years prior, "Jesus said, I am the light of the world: he that followeth me shall not walk in darkness, but shall have the light of life." The Spirit of God took the sword of that passage and fiercely convicted the distraught sailor of his sins; the precious gospel unfolded afresh into his memory. Russell dropped the pistol to the bed, fell to his knees, received Christ by faith, and was gloriously saved. After the war, that same ex-sailor spent the remainder of his life on a foreign mission field preaching the gospel of Christ in Japan. He is now in heaven as I write this line.

3p-As we do not know "how the bones grow in the womb of her that is with child" (Eccles. 11:5), so we shall never comprehend the manifold ways of saving grace as it works through God's Word, especially the gospel. The kingdom-church of Jesus Christ spreads its mysterious and marvelous influences across the globe at all times, even while men sleep on one side of earth and work on the other. The sun of heaven never sets on the work of God. The scribes and Pharisees rejected the kingdom that was being preached by their Messiah, it was not like their carnal, materialistic, political kingdom.

(d) **"The harvest is come."** Christ's commission is, "preach the gospel to every creature" (Mk. 16:15). For explanation of how this commission was fulfilled by the *first churches*, see Section 163, third paragraph of number 16, footnote f. However, this has never been realized again since that time to the present. Therefore, each new generation needs the saving gospel of Christ. In the grand service of seed sowing the Scriptures, we rest in knowing that duty is ours but consequences are God's. The messengers of the gospel should be content to know that the Word of God will only grow in a divine manner. Those who engage themselves in "forcing results," are like foolish men who attempt to make seed grow without sowing it. They court loss and calamity. A motivating factor that compels men to sow the Word is the clarion call that "the harvest is coming" for every man, and that eternal hell is a ghastly reality. The harvest in the parable above was specified as occurring when the fruit was brought forth or had completed its growing cycle. This signifies that all earthly things will eventually run their course and must end. Here, in Christ's parable, we see physical death and the final judgment of God. Woe be those unsaved in that terrible day (Jer. 8:20).

2p-The message in the parable must have greatly alarmed the Jews, who were hostile to what our Lord was preaching concerning His new kingdom. See footnote b above for more on their kingdom. Some two thousand years have now passed since the original sowing of verse 26. The *future* "full corn in the ear" of verse 28 has not occurred yet! When verse 29 "putting in the sickle" will be realized, no man knows. Whenever that time comes, it will signal the end of sowing and reaping for the last generation of workers in Christ's kingdom-church. *Dear reader, are you ready?*

FIFTH: THE PARABLE OF THE MUSTARD SEED.*

The spiritual side of the kingdom, which is the church, as it was later called, will have a unique but small worldwide impact over the course of human history. It has done this, with highs and lows, for two thousand years and continues to the present hour.

*This parable reveals that Christ's kingdom began in dire insignificance, but its message has brought salvation, hope, and shelter from sin to millions. It is noteworthy that the Lord Jesus during the final six months of his ministry again gave a portion of this same parable in Section 125, Lk. 13:18-19. As expressed numerous times in this harmony commentary, here again is evidence that the Son of God frequently repeated Himself in preaching and teaching.

By the Sea of Galilee

Matt. 13:31-32	Mk. 4:30-32	Lk.	John
God's kingdom begins small	*God's kingdom begins small*		
31 Another parable put he forth unto them, saying, "The kingdom of heaven[a]	**30** And he said, "Whereunto shall we liken the kingdom of God?[a] or with what comparison shall we compare it?		
is like to a grain of mustard seed,[b] which a man took, and sowed n his field: **32** "Which indeed is the least of all seeds:	**31** "*It is* like a grain of mustard seed,[b] which, when it is sown in the earth, is less than all the seeds that be in the earth:		
It slowly becomes great, offering shelter and hope	*It slowly becomes great, offering shelter and hope*		
but when it is grown, it is the greatest among herbs,[c] and becometh a tree,[d] so that the birds of the air come and lodge in the branches thereof."[e] (Verse 33 cont. in Section 80.)	**32** "But when it is sown, it groweth up, and becometh greater than all herbs,[c] and shooteth out great branches;[d] so that the fowls of the air may lodge under the shadow of it."[e] (Verse 33 cont. in Section 81.)		

Footnotes-Commentary

[a] For a similar lesson on the mystery of how God's kingdom spreads, see Section 80. Section 39, footnotes a and g contain an explanation of this kingdom and its two different aspects. It is noted Matthew calls it the kingdom of heaven. Mark wrote that it was the kingdom of God. This is because they are the same. Hyper dispensationalists have distorted this fact in order to "prove" or prop up a previous erroneous eschatological teaching.

[b] The Savior now explains how small His kingdom or church (as it was later called) was at its beginning during His ministry. It was as small as a mustard seed! It did not step onto the stage of human history with phenomenal splendor visible to mortal eyes. Like the stone cut out of the mountain (Daniel 2:45), and the leaven in the next Section, His kingdom began without fanfare and sound of trumpets. Following His ascension, and on the day of Pentecost, with the coming of the Holy Spirit in fullness, the new kingdom of God and Christ received all those saved over the Old Testament starting with Adam. Through some two thousand years of blood, sweat, and tears, the church of our Lord has slowly moved forward to this present moment. Though often torn by division, heresies, strife, prisons, exiles, suffering, persecutions, and death, it lives and marches on to its final goal.

2p-A grain of mustard was a popular expression for the smallest of something. Even though the mustard seed was the smallest seed *known in that land,* it is not the smallest of earth's seeds. Our Lord was speaking within the context of the land of Israel. Jesus used this same seed illustration later. See Section 106, Matt. 17:20, footnote i, and Section 132, Lk. 17:6, footnote g for more on the subject of little faith and seed. Jews were familiar with the term. The Talmud in tractate, Nidah 5b also contains the expression when referring to a drop of blood. Although there were seeds smaller than the mustard, the Jews employed it to symbolize tiny things. Christ was not giving a lesson on the specifics of botany! He was using local color as He addressed the people. Mustard seeds were highly prized for cooking and giving food something of a sharp, tart taste. It has no resemblance to the western-style mustard seed converted into a yellowish paste, used for sandwiches, and cooking.

(c) In some cases, this plant would grow into an enormous size tree. Thus, it was considered among the greatest of herbal bearing plants. Smaller ones were said to reach the height of a horse and rider. See next footnote.

(d) It took years for the mustard plant to reach a large size and taller heights; then it became a shelter for the fowls of the air and shade for men and beasts alike. Christ is pointing out that the small mustard seed grew over a long period of time into something that blessed both man and the lower creatures. His new kingdom had a tiny beginning just as a single mustard seed did. It was little, unimportant and held in contempt by the makers and custodians of the Jewish religion. The early disciples were poor and despised by the scribes and Pharisees. In time, the kingdom-church of our Lord cast its bright light over the known world of that era. To this present moment, the "fullness of the Gentiles" is still being brought under its shadow of rest and shelter from sin. In contrast to this world and its evil systems, the kingdom of Christ is small and insignificant. In comparison to the countless thousands of false religions of this world, the kingdom-church is the greatest organism to appear amid human society.

(e) The Savior is not teaching any fashion of postmillennialism, which propagates the error that the gospel will spread and finally conquer most of human society. Then, when the majority of mankind are saved, Christ will return to a wonderfully good world! This curious doctrine is outlined in *The Millennium*, pages 58-62, by Loraine Boettner. To interpret the "fowls of the air" as *always* having reference to demons and evil powers is incorrect. However, in the earlier parable of the sower, the fowls stealing the precious seed were given this meaning as noted in Section 75, Matt. 13:19, footnote a. In other places, Christ used the birds or fowls as symbolic of good things that were watched over and cared for by the Father in heaven (Matt. 6:26). Fowls by the thousands, *especially doves,* would swarm over the mustard trees enjoying the seed as a delicate food. This is in sharp contrast to the poisonous darnel mentioned in Section 77, footnote c. Later, in Rev. 18:2, we read of Babylon, a "cage of every unclean and hateful bird." Nevertheless, the dove, as seen in Matt. 3:16, symbolizes the Holy Spirit. Christ may have drawn His allegory of the tree from Dan. 4:20-21, with which His Jewish audience would have been familiar.

2p-The scribes, Pharisees, and their adherents failed to understand this parable given by Messiah. It was taught by the rabbis that a tree spreading its branches, and affording lodgment for the feathered creatures of the air, was a common figure for the Hebrew kingdom of heaven (Ezek. 17:23), they (again) missed the Messiah's lesson. The Jews longed for a material kingdom in which they would rule the world. Some of the rabbis held that it would become a haven for millions over the ages: they believed that Gentiles from every nation on earth would come into it. Now, some two thousand years later, looking in retrospect over the course of church history, we see the meaning of this third parable in Matthew's order and fourth in Mark's. It prefigures the church or new kingdom of Christ, "slowly growing into maturity." At last, it will be triumphant and victorious over the world. It is the church, or spiritual kingdom, which has provided hope, forgiveness, and shelter through the saving gospel she has preached.

3p-The word "church" as used above is to be understood as those local assemblies or groups where the Son of God is honored and exalted above all others. It does not speak of a building! Within these various bodies, the Word of God is taught and lived by as far as possible. Within these assemblies are both saved and unsaved people. Apart from the churches of the western world, there are thousands of Christians trapped in pagan religions, radical Islam, and apostate versions of Christianity. Under these satanic systems, believers, for the most part, secretly worship God in clandestine manners. Others languish in prisons, slave labor camps, and exist under the most appalling conditions, yet their faith remains undaunted. They spread out their branches in the most amazing places and bring others, often their fierce enemies, to the saving knowledge of Christ. These ragged, dying, suffering saints are the church and Christ's kingdom in the truest sense. They are the modern day version of Hebrews chapter 11. For other comments along these same lines, see Section 177, third paragraph of footnote z.

4p-**Trouble and Jesus.** By nature, the birds of heaven seek shelter among the branches of trees. Last summer I sat in my wheelchair and watched a hawk, chase a small sparrow. The little fellow flew into the thick foliage of large Oak trees; the hawk could not follow. Many hawks of sorrow and suffering pursue the lives of God's people. On all sides, there are manifold temptations, while inside dark thoughts rise to harass. Trouble storming into a home has often sent the occupants hurrying to Jesus. We must discipline ourselves to remember that whatever assails us as God's children, there is a divine purpose. The trouble that touches us is the merciful hand of God with the design to form the image of Christ in our lives. Many people have knelt beside the deathbed of a dear child or loved one; there they found Christ as personal Lord and Savior. It was not until the prodigal son was in sore want, with every resource exhausted, nigh starvation, and without friends, that he turned his thoughts to the father and home. A man was traveling through a deep forest, having eaten nothing for three days he fell into great hunger. Suddenly, a violent storm broke upon the scene, compelling him to seek shelter. Fleeing under the high roots of a giant berry tree, he found both protection and food. The storm had brought down the sweet fruit, dropping many pieces into his hiding place. Those whom fierce troubles drive to Christ also find both shelter and food. Romans 8:28 makes sense by looking back on it instead of looking forward and trying to make it fit into our situations. Our lives are about something bigger than ourselves. Let God make things fit! In eternity, you will be thankful.

SIXTH: THE PARABLE OF THE LEAVEN.*

The secret effectiveness and self-propagating power of the gospel works as it is kneaded (disseminated) by the Holy Spirit into the hearts of men. Christian history reveals that this process alone saves the souls of men. God's grace does it's work despite militant communism, evolution, radical Islam, non-redemptive theological liberalism, paganism, and the rest. They all ultimately oppose the message of Jesus Christ and hate what the Bible really teaches.

*This lesson is similar to that of the mysterious growth of the seed in Section 78, and the mustard seed in the previous Section 79. The work of the leaven does not speak of the gospel converting the world to Christ before the end. As with the Parable of the Mustard Seed, our Lord also repeated this lesson later in Section 125, Lk. 13:20-21 where it was called the kingdom of God, demonstrating again that they are both the same. There is no postmillennial winning of the world to Christ to be found anywhere within this parable. It is wistful theology to believe that sinful humankind will mostly be converted to Christ before the Savior returns. Regarding the way to heaven, Christ said, "Few there be that find it" (Matt. 7:14).

Matt. 13:33—*By the Sea of Galilee*	Mk.	Lk.	John
How God's kingdom spreads **33** Another parable(a) spake he unto them; "The kingdom of heaven is like unto leaven,(b) which a woman took, and hid in three(c) measures of meal, till the whole was leavened."(d) (Verse 34 cont. in Section 81.)			

Footnotes-Commentary

(a) This parable is in harmony with the previous one of the mustard seed in Section 79. It also reveals that Christ's spiritual kingdom starts small and unimportant, but will increase in its worldwide influence. Such increase comes, as men believe the saving gospel of Christ. *This does not mean the entire world will gradually become better, and most men will be saved.* Rather, it portrays the silent and glorious way Christ's new kingdom or the church affects individual lives across the ages of human time. The mystery of God's Word, blended with the Holy Spirit working in the souls of men, is beyond explanation.

(b) **"Leaven" does not *always* represent evil or sin.** Popular fallacies such as these have been taken for granted only because some writer or preacher said it to be so a hundred years ago. Clarence Larkin, in *Dispensational Truth,* is a chief source for this error along with several footnotes in the *Scofield Reference Bible.* In 1 Cor. 5:7–8, Paul reveals his Jewishness in using leaven as a symbol of evil that was rampant in the Corinthian assembly. However, this was not true in every usage of the substance. This Paul would have known, being a former rabbi. His words reveal the emblematic moral influence in general, whether good or bad, of anything taken into our lives. In the parable above the Savior uses leaven to illustrate the mysterious growth of His kingdom through the preaching of the saving gospel. There were cases when leaven was used in the good sense in the Torah Law. It was forbidden during Passover, the week afterwards, and in all offerings given to the Lord by fire on the altar. Yet, the two wave loaves baked for usage on the day of Pentecost contained leaven by the command of God (Lev. 23:17). The temple bakers had to have leaven in the house of God in order to produce these loaves. Neither of the loaves used at Pentecost symbolized evil. They pointed to *both* Jews and Gentiles united in peace by the Spirit *through the gospel* and the empowering of the church or kingdom on the Day of Pentecost (Acts 2). The picture symbolized in the two loaves filled with leaven reveals the secretly penetrating and diffusive power of the gospel. This gospel, blended with the Holy Spirit, brings believing men to praise God for peace brought into their lives by Christ. "For he is our peace" (Eph. 2:14).

2p-The "peace offering" cakes used in the temple also contained leaven (Lev. 7:13). They were presented as a thanksgiving gift to God. Leaven is spoken of in a sarcastic manner in Amos 4:5. This verse affirms that the temple bakers used leaven to produce this type of bread. Several different examples of the *misusage* of leaven as only representing evil are as follows: "Oil always pictures the Holy Spirit." Yet according to Prov. 5:3 it also illustrates the appealing words of a harlot! "A lion always represents evil, as in the case of Satan" (1 Peter 5:8). Such exegesis collapses when we read of Christ "the lion of the tribe of Judah" (Rev. 5:5). Nor does the serpent *always* point to the Devil as in Rev. 12:9. It also represented the Son of God in His death for our sins by crucifixion. Refer to this in John 3:14-15. The serpent was counted the wisest of creatures before Adam sinned. Refer to Section 59, and Matt. 10:16, footnote k for the Jewish opinion of the serpent *before* the fall.

3p-In daily activities, the Jews used leaven in various ways other than in baking homemade bread. We read in the Talmud tractate, Gittim 19a, that it was mixed in boot maker's polish. Talmud tractate, Shabbath 18b, gives instructions on how a Jew can sell leaven to a Gentile. Obviously, the Jew would have it in his possession before he could sell it. The word "leaven" is found in the Talmud 765 times. Most of these have to do with Passover and the Feast of Unleavened Bread that followed. Beginning with the annual Passover, no leaven was allowed in Jewish homes for eight days (Lev. 23:6–8). (Some greatly sensitive Jews searched out all leaven several weeks before Passover commenced.) At the end of the Unleavened Bread celebration, the ban was lifted and things returned to normal. It has been noted above, that the wave loaves baked for the Feast of Pentecost contained leaven and were called "the firstfruits unto the LORD" (Lev. 23:17). Thousands of these were baked. They served as food for the ministering priests. However, they could not be eaten in the temple court. Leaven points to evil in many places; but in other places, it does not. As explained, the lion and serpent do not *always* denote Satan, and leaven does not always signify evil.

(c) **Three measures of meal"** was a common term among the Jewish women. It was equal to about a bushel. The number three seems to be of no special significance in this passage and apparently points to nothing of profound importance. The ancients often said, "Three women may be employed in one lump of dough; one to knead, one to make loaves, and one to bake it." Consequently, it was thus described as "three measures." Our Lord may have alluded to this popular saying. Nevertheless, three measures were the standard deal of flour kneaded by Hebrew women to provide bread for a large group of people. Others see in this a reference to the three-fold nature of man: his spirit, soul, and body, which are affected by the saving gospel (1 Thess. 5:23 with Heb. 4:12). Several older expositors think Jesus was referring to the world of that day which had been geographically divided into three parts by the rabbinical teachers. From the viewpoint of historical background, this may be the meaning used by our Lord. At least, he crowds would have understood the usage. Some, with very elastic imaginations see in this, the Trinity and others the "three wise men." Regardless, into this quantity of flour the women kneaded the leaven. This measure of flour could point to those of the human race who will be saved by the glorious work of the gospel, which is singularly pictured in the leaven. Even so, three measures of flour meal are but a drop in the bucket in comparison to the countless millions on earth who have never been kneaded by the Holy Spirit with the good news or those who have rejected the gospel and died without Christ.

(d) **"Till the whole was leavened,"** reveals a period of time involved in the process of God completing His kingdom. From this sixth parable, we learn that the gospel message of the kingdom of God or Christ, when received within a man's heart, works mysteriously and secretly like unseen leaven. In time, it would spread, assimilate, prevail, and then transform the whole person. (This is *not* salvation by a process but the process that brings salvation.) In this parable, the leaven works similar to the mustard seed as noted in the previous Section. The tiny seed slowly grew into a powerful entity for God over the earth in the form of the church. Thus, the small amount of leaven touches the lives of millions. Out of these groups some repent, believe, and are converted to the Savior. Others, like the religious leaders of Israel, reject and traduce the saving gospel of Christ.

2p-Perhaps the unnamed woman working so hard kneading the dough points to those faithful believers who have spent their lives disseminating the message of the Savior. To make the entire kingdom of heaven (or the new kingdom of Christ as mentioned in this parable) gradually become totally evil by the process of the leaven is a ridiculous interpretation. Those who object to the usage of leaven as *singularly* representing the gospel in this parable and acclaim that it always pictures evil are incorrect. For more on this error, see first paragraph of footnote b above. Concerning details on the our Lord's kingdom in its two different manifestations, the spiritual and material, see Section 39, footnotes a and g.

3p-**The end, then what?** A time is coming when the leavening process of the saving gospel, as mentioned above will end, and the God of heaven will have concluded His plan for the church or new kingdom of Christ among mankind. It has been some two thousand years since the Lord Jesus spoke these Words, meaning that it is two thousand years closer than before. The concluding date when God's will for the church has run its course, and it is taken out, no man knows. Thus, it behooves us to be ready at all times. We are all destined to leave this world and step into eternity! *Reader now is the time to prepare.* Read several testimonies of men who died lost without Jesus Christ as Lord and Savior. Refer to these in Section 115, third paragraph of footnote e. It is to be remembered that the Devil is far too clever to let all his children decease, screaming, "My feet are in the fire. Help, help!" Many unconverted people seemingly die quiet peaceful deaths. It is what happens on the other side of this life, after their souls leave their bodies that counts. See Section 131, for a true story the Savior gave of two men; their lives here and in eternity! And both of them are still there now over two thousand years later.

Matthew explains why Jesus used parables. This method of instruction fulfilled another Old Testament Messianic prediction.* Jews familiar with their Scripture would have discerned this in Christ's teaching as Matthew had.

See all of Section 3, demonstrating that Matthew wrote his book to fellow Jews, and how he was inspired to show all readers that Jesus of Nazareth was the true Messiah of Israel.

By the Sea of Galilee

Matt. 13:34–35	Mk. 4:33–34	Lk.	John
34 All these things spake Jesus unto the multitude in parables; and without a parable[(a)] spake he not unto them: **35** That it might be fulfilled which was spoken by the prophet, saying,[(b)] **"I will open my mouth in parables; I will utter things which have been kept secret from the foundation of the world."** (Verse 36 cont. in Section 82.)	**33** And with many such parables spake he the word unto them, as they were able to hear *it*. **34** But without a parable[(a)] spake he not unto them: and when they were alone, [away from the crowds] he expounded all things to his disciples.[(c)] (Verse 35 cont. in Section 87.)		

Footnotes-Commentary

[(a)] **Mk. 4:33. "Able to hear it."** Too much of God's Word can overwhelm young believers. Note Prov. 25:16. The meaning is that on this occasion, He spoke only in parables. At other times, He did not follow this method of teaching and preaching. See Section 73, footnote d for notes on the word parable.

[(b)] From Ps. 78:2. Here, *again*, Matthew, reaching out to fellow Jews, pens this quotation from an Old Testament person named Asaph. It is to be noted that Asaph was called a "seer" in 2 Chron. 29:30. This was the source of his Messianic predication. The family of Asaph was one of the three families given responsibility for the music and singing in the temple. It is noteworthy that Matthew calls Asaph "the prophet." Hence, his divine forecast pointing to Israel's coming Messiah. The rabbis predicting the way their Messiah would teach the nation of Israel often quoted this Psalm. In addition, this was exactly what He had been doing since their rejection of Him. Matthew cites this passage and informs his Hebrew readers that Christ fulfilled it; therefore, He *must* be their Messiah. See main heading under Section 74, footnote e for more on His rejection by the religious leaders. There is nothing in this quotation from Asaph pointing to a "remnant of Jews, who will be saved during the tribulation period."

[(c)] **"Expounded all things."** After Messiah had taken His little band of disciples away from the restless, milling crowds, He then explained to them the meaning of His various lessons. On the afternoon of the Resurrection Day, He gave two of His disciples a comprehensive survey of Himself as found in their Old Testament Scriptures. Refer to this in Section 200, Lk. 24:25-27. Later, on the day of Pentecost, the Holy Spirit came to dwell in their souls in absolute fullness as members of Christ's body. Then the same Spirit instructed them in all things, and brought to their remembrance, with perfect understanding everything Jesus had previously taught (John 14:26).

2p-Verse 34. "All these things" can only mean "all" up to that point. At this time in the lives of our Lord's disciples, they did not yet know or understand His death, burial, resurrection, and ascension. The last question the eleven apostles put to Jesus before His ascension was, "Lord, wilt thou at this time restore the kingdom again to Israel" (Acts 1:6). They were still looking for this even when Jesus ascended! For further details regarding this material, physical kingdom the apostles looked for, see Section 39, paragraphs three, four and nine, under footnote a.

3p-It was not until ten days after His ascension, with the coming Holy Spirit, that they then understood the literal, physical, political kingdom of Israel was now a spiritual entity, soon to be known as the church or assembly of called out ones. For explanation of this, see Section 9, Lk. 1:32, footnote g. This does not negate some unique place for *redeemed* Jews and Gentiles sharing in a glorified reign on a new earth. Whatever this is, it will not be a carnal, sin poisoned, earth-cursed event, or a priesthood of ungodly Jews, offering animal sacrifices in a rebuilt temple at Jerusalem. For an explanation of these things, see Section 134, all of footnote d. The teaching of a literal temple in the land of Israel functioning with animal sacrifices needs eschatological rehab. It shames the death of Christ!

The Parable of the Tares or Poison Seed interpreted by the Savior.*

See Section 77 where Christ first gave this third parable. Later, after leaving the seashore of Galilee, He was requested by His followers to explain what this strange lesson meant.

Matt. 13:36-43 —*In Peter's house at Capernaum*	Mk	Lk.	John
Their request **36** Then Jesus sent the multitude away, and went into the house:[(a)] and his disciples came unto him, saying, "Declare unto us the parable of the tares of the field." ***The Savior's explanation*** **37** He answered and said unto them, "He that soweth the good seed is the Son of man;[(b)] **38** "The field is the world; the good seed are the children of the kingdom;[(c)] but the tares are the children of the wicked *one*; **39** "The enemy that sowed them is the devil; the harvest is the end of the world;[(d)] and the reapers are the angels. **40** "As therefore the tares[(e)] are gathered and burned in the fire; so shall it be in the end of this world. ***The fate of the wicked*** **41** "The Son of man shall send forth his angels, and they shall gather out of his kingdom all things that offend, and them which do iniquity;[(f)] **42** "And shall cast them into a furnace[(g)] of fire: there shall be wailing and gnashing of teeth. ***The future of the righteous*** **43** "Then shall the righteous[(h)] shine forth as the sun in the kingdom of their Father. Who hath ears to hear, let him hear."[(i)] (Verse 44 cont. in Section 83.)			

Footnotes-Commentary

[(a)] **"The house."** This is the same house as mentioned in Section 73, Matt. 13:1-2, footnote a. Originally, Jesus left it and went to the boat pulpit to preach to the people these parables. He leaves the boat and returns to Peter's house in Capernaum. Once behind the shelter of this dwelling, the disciples felt comfortable to inquire of Messiah the meaning of tares or poison seed. They were now out of earshot of the religious leaders. There were great benefits to be gained by the apostles privately inquiring of His lessons away from the noisy, factious crowds. Men, who *only* attend to the public preaching and teaching of God's Word, are not so likely to understand more fully the secrets of eternal truth. Those who seek further to understand, to grow in grace, and to attain to some height of maturity (like the disciples) are those who continually enquire and ask many questions, spend much time in private prayer and study, seeking to satisfy the hunger of their souls. In such divine exercises, the Word of God sinks deeply into these broken souls. Later in their season, they will produce fruit to His glory.

[(b)] **"Son of man."** For more on this unique title, see Section 103, footnote b, and Section 161, footnote l. Now the Lord Jesus narrows down the meaning of this parable. From the ministry of John the Baptist, the Messiah entered the scene and worked among the nation of Israel. He "sowed" the best seed that the nation had heard in centuries, "Your Messiah has come!" (His ministry carried the seed of God's Word over the world of that era, through the apostles and early missionaries.) Christ diligently reached out to the stubborn Jews and sowed the good seed of His new kingdom. He came first to save and bless Israel; but for the most part, they rejected Him. This was originally mentioned in Section 1, Part 3, John 1:11-12, footnote g.

[(c)] **The meaning of the seed is now changed.** In the interpretation of this parable, the good seed changes character. In the first parable, it represented the Word of God. Now, it has strict reference to the original disciples and early apostles; then the thousands who later believed on Him and were saved. They were called the "children of the kingdom." Therefore, "seed" had a twofold meaning within this series of parables, just as we have seen that leaven does not always point to evil. In Section 80, footnote b, the two meanings of leaven are explained. Yet amid all these saved ones (good seed), stands wicked men, the tares or children of the Devil, planted within the *visible local* churches. They are always the channels of upheaval, hypocrisy, and division in His kingdom as seen in the various assemblies of God's people on earth. As Christ has begotten the children of God (good seed), so likewise

Satan fathers the children of wickedness or the poison tares (1 John 3:10). For a time, they are mingled among true believers, wherever they may be found. The great separation will come at the return of our Lord when He calls His church to meet Him in the air (1 Thess. 4:17).

(d) **"End of the world."** The Greek noun for "world" and several other similar terms in this verse is "aion." Here, it had strict reference to the end of a fixed time period. Across the New Testament "aion" has several kindred meanings with each one embracing elements of time. For example, it speaks of "a limited period of time," or "an age wherein certain events transpire," or "the final end of something, which has no more time." In this passage, as just stated, it speaks of "the end of a specific age." It does not speak of the end or consummation of the *whole* world, mankind, and *all* earthly activities. The term "end of the world" in Section 204, Matt. 28:20, footnote f, also means "the end of a specific but limited period of time." When this period has ended, another time or age will follow. It is noted that *after* "the end of the world" in Matt. 13:39, and the holy angels have completed their work of removing the tares and offensive things, God's plan for man continues throughout all eternity. It does *not* mean the end of all things finally and forever, but only of a limited age. This wonderful prospect is expressed in these words "Then shall the righteous shine forth as the sun in the kingdom of their Father" (verse 43). Long before the birth of Christ, the Jewish teachers of religion had divided their coming Messiah's life and reign into at least three divisions. Below, is a review of each Messianic period as established by the ancient rabbis. Christ's apostles would have been familiar with these rabbinical categorizations of time. It is seriously incorrect, that in Jewish eschatology there were only two ages of time. The *three ages* known to the ancients are reflected in many of the New Testament writings. They are as follows:

1. **The days of the Messiah.** This age or time period was to start with *the appearing* of Messiah. It was called "the end," "the end of the world or age," "the last days," "the latter times," "the last times," and "the last time." These Jewish terms surface numerous times in the letters of the New Testament. The reader must keep in mind how the ancients catalogued and named things. The rabbis, with their outrageous exaggerations, seemed to have picked whatever date they fancied, and then taught that it was the length of time that the Messiah would work in Israel to bring them back to God. Some believed it would be three generations, some forty years, one thousand years, seven thousand and one group ten thousand. Notably, the appearing of Messiah in Israel was spoken of as being "the end of all things," (1 Peter 4:7), meaning "things" occurring during that particular time would finally end. This included Messiah dealing with the sins of the Jews, the malfunction of the temple, and the corruption of Jewish youth. The verse above from 1 Peter cannot speak of the coming of our Lord for His church. There is no way that honest exegesis can turn Simon Peter's words "at hand" into some two thousand years later and Jesus has not returned! Similar comments may also apply to Paul's words in Rom. 13:12-14. For a general review of end-times, Antichrist, mark of the beast, and relative subjects, see *Appendix Eight*.

2. **The coming days or age.** The "days of the Messiah" (above), would end with complete victory for the nation of Israel and their Messiah ruling over the world. All strife, wars, and conflicts would end and the Messiah would usher in "the coming days or age" for the Hebrew nation. According to the rabbis, in this "coming age" Messiah would rule worldwide for a limited period. They have guessed this to range from one year up to seven thousand! A final resistance to Messiah's rule would end in a dreadful war called "the battle of Gog and Magog" led by the Antichrist called "Armilius," in which he would be defeated. (This ancient Antichrist has no resemblance to the several thousand different Antichrists that have been *invented* by over zealous Christians for the past two thousand years. In the Jewish Talmud, Sanhedrin 17a, Gog and Magog represented all hostile Gentile nations of earth or aggerated evil, instead of two individual nations of people.) After this battle, there would be a great judgment throne for all men, and two books would be opened at this terrible event. One can detect fragments of New Testament teachings in this exaggerated rabbinical scenario, especially in the book of Revelation. However, the differences as recorded in the Scripture far outweigh the likenesses in Hebrew myths.

3. **The world to come.** Many Jews believe that this is a span of time, not a place. It is *the final stage* in ancient Jewish eschatology. The first two periods mentioned above moved forward into this grand climax of time. Pious Jews called this "Olam Ha-Ba," the "World to Come," or the "Messianic Age." (*Today* this period is often referred to as "tikkun olam," meaning the final perfection of the world.) During this time, the dead will be raised and all souls brought back from their waiting place called the "world of souls." Refer to Section 104, paragraphs four through seven of footnote g for other details. During this time, there will only be the Jewish religion: murder, robbery, jealously, and all evil will vanish. It was more or less believed by pious Jews in the days of Christ that there would be both a New Jerusalem and new temple built by the Messiah. Sacrifices limited to the thanksgiving offering would recommence. There will be no expiatory offerings. The dimensions of this city and temple are a grand example of the wildest rabbinical extremes. It would reach some nine miles into the air and cover hundreds of square miles over the land of Israel. Jewish women would give a quick and easy birth to a child every day. Messiah would rule the world from this fantastic temple. With all this, Israel at last

would be safe and happy forever under the rule of their glorious, all conquering, human Messiah and King. Among some of the Jews during this era and today, there exists a belief in *two different* Messiahs. One would be killed and the other would be the ruling prince over Israel and live forever, after His earthly work was completed. Today, many Jews believe that this Messiah will rule as king and after many years will die. Then his son will reign; afterwards a grandson and so on. Jewish rabbis and scholars still debate just how long this scenario will continue. How sad and touching that the great Hebrew people are blind to the fact that Jesus of Nazareth was their promised Messiah, that His death on the cross and resurrection from the dead was for the sin's of all mankind. His saving gospel is still for the Jew first (Rom. 1:16).

2p-It is impossible to say exactly how many of these rabbinical extremes were believed in the earthly days of Christ. That they were in vogue and embraced in whatever form by pious Jews is indisputable. In the decades following the resurrection and ascension of Christ, Hebrew scribes added extra and often wild interpretations to their eschatology. There is no mention in the gospels or the New Testament of the rabbinical teaching of two Messiahs, which may signal that a minority of radical Jews held this error. For more on the two Messiahs, refer to Section 6, sixth paragraph of footnote d. Part of these ancient teachings (especially the coming of Elijah) were known by the apostles of Christ and His followers. This is mentioned in Section 105, Matt. 17:10-13, with footnotes j, k, and l. See *Appendix Four* for more on what the rabbis taught about their "coming Elijah."

3p-The Savior had to undo gradually every false teaching about Himself in the minds of His faithful followers, especially the apostles. With the coming of the Holy Spirit at Pentecost, the apostles and disciples *fully* understood God's plan, the entity of the church, its Great Commission, and work. Gradually, the term kingdom gave way to the more descriptive and appropriate word "church." Later, Paul was inspired to pen letters of instruction and explanation for this kingdom-church. These were accepted as the divinely given Magna Carta and compass for the Church of the Living God during her earthly journey. It remains so to this present hour. For an excellent guide to present day Jewish beliefs and traditions, see the source previously mentioned, *Living Judaism,* by Rabbi Wayne Dosick, a non-Christian Hebrew.

(e) Refer to Section 77, footnote c for the tares. Wicked men and women embedded within the assembly of the saints are represented as bastard wheat, even the seed of the serpent. They are satanically inspired and their destiny is everlasting damnation. See footnote g below.

(f) See Section 77, footnote g.

(g) The Jews used the metaphor of a burning furnace and gnashing teeth to illustrate earthly human suffering, and the punishments of the damned in gehenna-hell. See the Talmud tractates, Pesachim 118a; Sanhedrin 92b; Berachoth 54b; and Sotah 12b for examples of this. In Hebrew thinking, hell was reserved for all who did not keep the tradition of the elders (Mishna) and the Torah Law. For an explanation of the Mishna oral laws, see Section 52, footnote h; Section 89, footnote c; and Section 96 footnote d. In modern day Jewish theology, hell is not eternal but only a temporary place. This is a revision of the mythical Roman Catholic purgatory. It was from Gen. 15:17 that the rabbis first interpreted the furnace (or oven) as being symbolic of hell. In the verses above, Jesus was teaching the *conscious* suffering of the damned. Every Jew in His audience understood what He was saying, especially the scribes, Pharisees, and their disciples. Later, the spiritual side of the kingdom of Christ manifested itself within the *visible local* assembly, or church. The time is coming when all born again believers (the real body of Christ) will be separated from the unsaved hypocrites that burden the work of God. It will be a terrible day when Christ's true church is removed from the earthly scene. For twenty-one things about suffering in hell-lake of fire, see Section 103, number 8, under footnote g. *For the meaning of "outer darkness," see Section 165 footnote n.*

(h) The "righteous" do not *fully* "shine forth as the sun" until after the wicked have been judged and cast into their eternal abode. Whatever this difficult expression finally means, it is a free quotation or possibly a paraphrase taken from Dan. 12:3.

(i) **"Ears to hear."** For more on this popular expression, see Section 73, Matt. 13:9, footnote k. It was well known by the Jews and is mentioned in the Talmud tractates, Berachoth 31b and Avodah Zarah 5b. Job said of God, "I have heard of thee by the hearing of the ear" (Job 42:5). The rabbis made much fuss about this statement, affirming that the human ear was first designed to hear and learn the Torah Law of Jehovah the only true and living God. The implication from the Lord Jesus was that though men have ears, they do not use them to hear and heed things of eternal worth. Never has the world been as loud with so many noises and appeals to the ears of unsaved men, women, and youth. Like the sea nymphs in pagan Greek mythology, whose sweet singing lured sailors to their doom on the hidden rocks and deadly shoals, so these attractive sounds offer a deceitful satisfaction ending in the everlasting home of the damned. No wonder the Lord Jesus pled with men to use their ears right!

SEVENTH: THE PARABLE OF THE HIDDEN TREASURE.*

The Lord Jesus reveals that His kingdom or church and its glorious message must become the personal possession of men at all cost.

Stories about hidden treasure have always been common among men, especially the poorer classes of society. Here Messiah employed a hidden treasure story to illustrate again another aspect of His kingdom. The deeds of the man dispensing all that he had to secure this great treasure, were designed to show the Jews their need to repent, (change their minds) and turn from their self righteous, fatal fanaticism of empty traditions, and the oral law, to joyfully trust Him as their Messiah at all costs. This they refused to do while the Gentiles received Him gladly.

Matt. 13:44—*In Peter's house at Capernaum*	Mk.	Lk.	John
What the kingdom is compared to **44** "Again, the kingdom of heaven is like unto(a) treasure hid in a field; the which when a man hath found,(b) he hideth,(c) and for joy thereof goeth and selleth all that he hath, and buyeth that field.(d) (Verse 45 cont. in Section 84.)			

Footnotes-Commentary

(a) **"Is like unto."** In these words, Christ states that this treasure is in comparison to or like His new kingdom. See Section 39, footnotes a and g for more on the various aspects of the kingdom. This does not teach salvation by works but rather how salvation does work. The Master used terminology that the crowds understood. Here, He makes a comparative statement. His kingdom is compared to the precious treasure in a field and is like an ancient business transaction. The *original* owner of the field (the Holy Land) may point to the nation of Israel. The Jews, for the most part, flatly refused to believe that amid them stood Messiah, the Son of God, Savior of mankind, and the greatest of earth's treasures. They did not reject a "kingdom offer," rather they rejected Him as their Messiah and Savior. With this, He and His new kingdom were hidden from them, as so profoundly explained by the Lord Jesus (Matt. 13:13-15). After their final rejection, they became decidedly self-blind and deaf to their Messiah. For more in Israel's refusal of Jesus the Messiah, see fourth paragraph of footnote d below. Concerning the "field" and its several usages in the preaching of Christ, see footnote b below.

(b) **Correct but wrong!** Often, Christians are self-snared by the obsession to be *more* than right in expounding Scripture. It is orderly and astute for preachers and Bible teachers to seek accuracy in sharing God's Word. To do less is unacceptable. However, biblical "correctness" can be taken into the realm of absurdity. The same lesson prevails in politics as well. Born again believers and political leaders should work for truth and uprightness. Over the past twenty years, this has been taken into the realm of the ridiculous. An example is the so-called "political correctness" in the renaming America's black people, "African Americans." I have met hundreds of blacks who were not born in Africa. They were born in America. They are Americans. How can they be "African-Americans?" Black people of honor and dignity reject the pseudo semantics of racial politics that demeans their race and attempts to make them something God has never intended. They are proud to be "Black Americans" as I am to be a White American. Sick men unable to face the genetic facts of life invented these racists terms. In everyday life and limb, distinctions are often necessary. This is especially true in body identification, police work, and so forth. My paternal family lineage on one side comes from Ireland and Scotland. The maternal line is traceable to Ireland and the American Indians. According to the muck raking wing of the media and smooth talking ethnic politicians, I should be called "Irish-Scottish-Indian-American." These ill distinctions are made because honest reasoning is distorted by sin. Other examples are couples living together and unmarried. They were once described as "adulterers." Today, they are "in a relationship." The drunkard of yesterday is the "alcoholic" of today. The dope head of former years is now a "chemical dependent" or victim of "substance abuse." Years ago, in American society females were addressed as "she," and the males, as "he." To avoid discrimination they are now "persons." In Australia, I heard a former underground pastor from Bulgaria say, "We have learned there is only one good thing about sin and ignorance; Jesus died to save us from both. Otherwise, they will distort honesty, twist truth, and change us into something we are not." This is where we are in America. The covert language of unsaved men must be decoded to understand what is really being said.

2p-Extremism in the Christian faith is another disaster. The Bible is *concretely* dogmatic on eternal issues and allows for no secondary interpretation. On lesser matters, there are exceptions. The word "field" that Jesus used in the above parable reveals the flexibility that some terms may have in Scripture. In His interpretation of the Parable of the Tares or Poison Seed, Jesus said, "the field is the world." See Section 82, Matt. 13:38. Earlier in the Parable of the Sower, Christ interpreted the field (into which the seed fell) as representing the various conditions of the human heart. Thus, we have *two different meanings* given to the same word. It is not exegetically correct to always apply the same interpretation to a specific term. The "law of first meaning" is the rule of hermeneutics but it does not hold true throughout all Scripture. It was noticed in the Parable of the Tares that Christ interpreted the seed as being both good and bad men (Matt. 13:38). Yet in the first Parable of the Sower, seed had exclusive reference to "the word of God" (Lk. 8:11). In the parable given here by Jesus, we meet the frequently overlooked Bible rule of two opposite meanings for the same word.

3p-The above thought is continued in Section 80, footnote b, where it is noted that leaven does not *always* have reference to sin. As previously mentioned, this common error was popularized over a century ago by a footnote in the *Scofield Reference Bible*, page 1016, footnote 3. Thousands have accepted this without question. Similarly, neither does "oil" *always* represent the Holy Spirit in Scripture. See Scofield's footnote number 2 on page 1035. Later, the Baptist pastor, F. E. Marsh continued this in his popular book, *Emblems of the Holy Spirit* published in 1911. In Prov. 5:3, it reads that the words of a prostitute are "smoother than oil." Only the most credulous would attempt to lay that one on the Spirit of God. In using the word "field" in this seventh parable, our Lord changed the use of its earlier meaning into something entirely different. As stated in the 2p- above the field represented the human heart, where the seed fell (Matt. 13:19), as well as the whole world (Matt. 13:38). In the above lesson, the field points to a part of earth with something precious buried or concealed in it. This field may also represent the Holy Land with Christ-Messiah there, but rejected by the Hebrew people He came to saved. The unnamed man who later discovered the treasure could perhaps mirror the Gentiles, who gladly repented of their sins and accepted Him as their Savior. This is strictly the author's conjecture. See footnote c below.

(c) "He hideth" the treasure. Some commentators hold that the actions of this man were dishonest. This is not necessarily right. Rather, it was in strict accord with ancient business practices. In Jewish customs, if a treasure was found in unmarked public land, he could claim it for his own. If it were marked, he could purchase the land, and the treasure was, automatically his. This was not considered fraudulent business practice but an accepted custom. In this parable, the Lord Jesus was not vindicating the conduct of the purchaser. He was stating the way in which men worked in those days to secure wealth, and from that drew His lesson. Christ was informing His audience of the need for them to be willing to give up ("selleth all that he had") anything and everything to secure life's greatest treasure, the saving knowledge of Himself, which gave them entrance into His kingdom. This "giving up" has nothing to do with good works for salvation, but rather points to repentance or turning from sin.

(d) In buying the field, he secured the treasure. The field in this parable *cannot* mean the geological world, for no man has ever bought that with money. In footnote a it is suggested that this may have reference to a specific section of earth; perhaps the land of Israel into which God sent heaven's greatest treasure, His beloved Son. Christ became hidden to the nation of Israel because the Jews refused to believe on Him as their Messiah. As suggested in footnote a, above, this field may picture the place in which our Lord executed His public ministry among His own people, died for their sins and rose again. The unnamed man only purchased the field as a secondary item: his real interest was the great treasure, which became his. The whole emphasis of the parable is not the field but the treasure in it. See footnote b above, for comments and a warning regarding those Christians who are overly pedantic in every biblical interpretation. With the *major doctrines* of the faith, one must not budge an inch; with the minor doctrines of Holy Scripture and personal preferences about unclear nonessentials, there is room for courteous disagreement among God's people. This peace making truth of Christianity, many have never learned.

2p-With the Jewish rejection of Jesus as their Messiah, some worthy commentators hold that this unnamed buyer pointed to the Gentiles, who, upon learning of Christ, gladly gave up and expended whatever was necessary to have Him as personal Lord and Savior. No *man* has ever found Christ in forgiveness of sins without wanting others to know Him! He is compelled to cry, be it ever so feeble "Ho, every one that thirsteth, come ye to the waters, and he that hath no money; come ye, buy, and eat" (Isa. 55:1). The treasure of the knowledge of Jesus Christ in the earthen vessels of humanity is the greatest of all possessions. Only those truly saved and in fellowship with their Lord work long and hard to share Christ with others. This is illustrated in the life of Legion, immediately after his conversion and deliverance. See this beautiful story in Section 88, Mk. 5:18-20, footnotes j, k, and l.

3p-A *true* Christian wife does not pine that her husband loves Jesus more than he loves her. No Godly mother, however deep the pain of parting, fails to rejoice in that her only son tears himself from her kind arms and goes to plant the cross of Christ on distant heathen shores. This youthful son knows well that those dwelling in the darkness of sin need this treasure too and his heart burns to share it with them. The author of this harmony commentary and his wife understand the meaning of these words; they have *happened* to us many times! Salvation is all of grace and what it commands a man to do. Our Lord had earlier warned His little flock in the Parable of the Hidden Treasure, about the calamity of placing their lighted candles under a bushel. This is in Section 44, footnotes q, r, and s. Perhaps this single man portrays the millions of Gentiles, who have received the blessed Messiah, though spurned by His own people. (John 1:11-12)? This *conjectural* interpretation warms the heart and fills the soul with love and good cheer. It rekindles a renewed impetus to bring men to Jesus (Prov. 11:30).

4p-For Israel's earlier fatal and final rejection of their Messiah, see the main headings under Sections 66, 67 and 68. This does not signal that God is forever through with His ancient people. For more on Israel and her future, and the new covenant, see Section 9, Lk. 1:31-32, footnote g, and Section 95, second paragraph of footnote u.

EIGHTH: THE PARABLE OF THE PEARL OF GREAT PRICE.*

This discourse is strikingly similar to the previous one in Section 83. It also carries the lesson that life's most important event is to know Christ as Lord and Savior. Losing or giving up everything is worth having Him. Again, we repeat the word's of martyred missionary Jim Elliott "He is no fool who gives up that which he cannot keep to gain that which he cannot lose."

Matt. 13:45-46—*In Peter's house at Capernaum*	Mk.	Lk.	John
What the kingdom is compared to **45** "Again, the kingdom of heaven[a] is like unto a merchant man,[b] seeking goodly pearls:[c] **46** "Who, when he had found[d] one pearl of great price, went and sold all that he had, and bought[e] it." (Verse 47 cont. in Section 85.)			

Footnotes–Commentary

[a] **"Kingdom of heaven."** As in all these ten parables, the kingdom of heaven represented the presentation of Christ and His saving gospel for Jews and Gentiles alike. Later, this kingdom became known as the church. In the lesson given above, it does not mean a literal kingdom some two thousands years in the future. This *genuine* aspect or side of the kingdom is discussed in Section 39, footnotes a and g.

[b] **"A merchant man seeking."** Over the years, *dependable* commentators have found different as well as similar lessons in these various parables: yet most of them oddly convey portions of heavenly truth! We do well to remember that the Bible has many inspired paradoxes! Some things appear contradictory, such as fire and water: which are enemies, yet friends. The Lord Jesus is the creature and yet the Creator; the Son of man, yet the Son of God. Paul wrote that Christians are "unknown" yet "well known," "living, yet dying," "sorrowful, yet always rejoicing;" "poor, yet making many rich" (2 Cor. 6:9-10). How can robes washed in the blood of the Lamb become white as snow? All biblical opposites blend in the eyes of God from above, while they may confound man below. As leaven in Section 80 carries several different meanings so it is with the Parable of the Pearl. *The divine paradoxes of Scripture surely must smile at our frustrations as we struggle to rightly divide them.* The truth of paradoxical meanings in the New Testament must be kept within the bounds of doctrinal propriety. Cults continually use this to prove just about anything. See Section 83, footnote b, for an important comment on this thought.

2p-While we cannot doubt the identity of this dauntless merchant as a man only (footnote e below), he also must point to the Lord from heaven, even our Savior, who said He had "come to seek and save that which was lost" (Lk. 19:10). Did not the Son of God give up all that He had, and come to earth to buy lost man back to God? "Out of the ivory palaces" He came, whereby we have been made glad (Ps. 45:8). The awful, but wonderful atonement that appeased the wrath of God because of our sins was His precious blood (Acts 20:28). For our sakes, He became poor (2 Cor. 8:9). He is the True Shepherd out in the wilderness of a vicious world searching for the lost sheep (Lk. 15:4). Heaven's "merchant man" stepped onto the stage of earth at Bethlehem's manger, beginning His hunt for the souls of men who would believe in Him. The "great price" He willingly paid in His death on the cross "for the joy [of saving sinners] that was set before him" (Heb. 12:2).

3p-Public notice board! Our Lord's use of the term "finding that which was lost" and so forth, was well known to all Jews, dwelling at Jerusalem. Near the middle of the city, there was a location named "The stone of lost things." Here, notices were posted by any person who had lost some cherished object or thing. Thousands of people read these notices, which often resulted in the lost items being found by the original owner.

[c] **"Pearls."** The most famed jewel mentioned by ancient writers was a pearl, which belonged to that wanton, wicked woman, Queen Cleopatra of Egypt. Informed Jews knew her sordid story. Among the insane Roman emperors wishing to exhibit their power and extravagance, some would have beautiful expensive pearls placed in goblets of vinegar until they dissolved, and then drink them in wine! Holy Scripture uses the pearl in a variety of ways to project to the reader several different lessons. Not only are lost souls portrayed in the pearl of great price but God's eternal truths are as well. Had Jesus not previously warned during the Sermon on the Mount, to beware of how they dispensed sacred teaching and selected the pearl to illustrate His great doctrines? Refer to this in Section 47, Matt. 7:6. In other Scriptures, pearls denote things of extreme value in the hands of wicked people (Rev. 18:12), as well as part of heaven's eternal city (Rev. 21:21).

2p-Pearls are uniquely different from all of earth's precious gems, belonging solely to the depths of the ocean. They are imprisoned at her lowest level in awful darkness and great are the dangers incurred in bringing them up to the light. Pearl fishers risk life and limb to redeem these precious treasures from their sentence of lasting darkness on the ocean floors. What a picture of the Lamb of God seeking and saving the lost. This single pearl purchased at such great cost, becomes a fitting symbol of the redeemed that constitute the kingdom-church.

(d) The seeking merchant, at last, found that for which his soul had long sought, the "one pearl of great price." The wording of this parable reveals that the "kingdom of heaven," "the pearl" and "the redeemed," are all the same thing. Thus, collectively united they picture the children of God or the kingdom of Christ. The beauty of pearls is formed through the suffering of a particular variety of shellfish. Thus, the beauty of the saints is slowly sculptured upon their lives as they follow their Lord in the footsteps of His sufferings and sorrows. We *cannot* buy eternal life or entrance into the kingdom of Christ and God. Instead, we must be bought into this blessed estate by the grace of another. Only our Lord Jesus has this grace, and only He laid aside heaven and the presence of the Father, to come into this world to seek, find, and purchase helpless sinners. For such was the sole business of heaven's great merchant. In a similar but lesser sense, as Christ came to seek out the lost and provide perfect redemption for them, thus it behooves us to make the pursuit of sinners our chief aim in life. Would to God that the work of eternity had an over powering grip upon our poor distracted lives. The glorious quest to love and serve the Lord Jesus and win men to Him was beautifully expressed by Dr. Thomas Guthrie in 1840, when he penned these stirring words: "Were I on one bank of a river and saw Jesus on the other, and that river ran [with] burning fire, I would dash into the flames to reach Him." From his little book *Parables of Christ,* page 184.

2p-Those who make the pearl the nation of Israel, even a "Jewish remnant in the future tribulation period," have made this parable something the Son of God never intended. Not one person in His congregation would have understood such a curious interpretation or application.

(e) Some expositors hold that "selling all" referred to our Lord laying aside all the glory of heaven and coming into this world. Christ bought the church or His new kingdom with His own precious blood (Acts 20:28; 1 Cor. 6:20 with Eph. 1:7). It was His by the purchase price. Others believe this pictures an unsaved man, stirred by conviction and guilt, gladly turning from all sin and finding forgiveness and peace with God. Probably, both figures are seen in this "merchant man" illustration. As with some of the parabolic teachings of Scripture, and certain areas of eschatology, one must be cautious not to carry their interpretations into the realms of the extreme in order to prove a moot point. There are times when it is better to be silent and sure instead of vocal and uncertain. Our words are like bullets; when fired, we cannot bring them back.

2p-The *radical* dispensationalists relegate every mention to the kingdom of God or Christ into a "Jew only thing." They fail to distinguish between the present spiritual manifestation of the kingdom in the form of the church or body of Christ, and a glorified future kingdom yet to be when the world will rest in everlasting peace. Some things in Scripture are for the Jews only while others are not. Such verses must be rightly divided.

3p-Neutral society? According to Gal. 3:27-28, among the redeemed there is neither Jew nor Gentile, bond or free, male or female (Gal. 3:27-29). These verses intimate some kind of free, sexless condition known only in eternity where natural earthly differences no longer exist. They speak of saved people as God sees them from the viewpoint of heaven. However, in human life on earth, these verses do not abolish genders, places, nationalism, and the physical distinctions of anatomical geometry. The feminists call God "she," wanting a neutralized society. They have lost their way in life, often refusing divine help, and *true* spiritual enlightenment. Traditional and ethical guidelines, common sense morals are missing or changed. Brash and bawdy, vulgar and vile, many "liberated feminists" marry each other; adopt children that normal people have. Some of these become national icons. Their television audiences are filled with screaming, cheering, erotic maddened sympathizers. The "fairer sex" is not alone in its unnatural lesbian madness. Males calling themselves "gays," imagining that they are females, reflecting the mannerisms of women, travel the same broad way. *They reinterpret what God did to Sodom and Gomorrah.* The "pearl of great price" (Jesus Christ), mentioned in verse 46, is made to agree with their lifestyle. Toss out the Bible, and we can all live like hell and go there when we die! Amid this perverted madness, God still reaches out in love, ready to save, forgive, and restore all willing individuals to normal living. Mike Haley's book, *101 Frequently Asked Questions About Homosexuality,* has been a help to many who struggle with these tormenting sins.

4p-Silence truth. In some states, "hate crime laws" are in place to silence public objection of the wickedness of godless people. The ancient Torah Law of Israel demanded the death sentence for the sins mentioned above In Lev. 20:13 it reads, "If a man also lie with mankind, as he lieth with a woman, both of them have committed an abomination: they shall surely be put to death; their blood *shall be* upon them." Today, these crimes are legalized. Among certain heathen tribes in Africa, those practicing these abominations are put to death. See Section 155, the third paragraph of footnote f. About two thousand years ago, the apostle Paul wrote a damning diatribe about unnatural conduct (Rom. 1:24-32). In time, this very chapter from the Holy Bible may be banned! "Gay and lesbian pastors" have reinterpreted Paul's words to accommodate their "life styles." It is the work of Christians, as far as possible, to demonstrate genuine love and offer help to those caught in this eventual death. *However, most scorn any offer of the gospel or distort it to suit their wickedness.* Nevertheless, some caught in these perversions long for deliverance but are terrified not knowing where to turn. In another letter, Paul wrote of those who had been saved from these abominations during his ministry in the vile Greek city of Corinth (1 Cor. 6:9-11). Men and women who are saved from their sins, by the grace of God are the goodly pearls of our Lord's parable given above. The worst of sinners, wallowing in the lowest of sin, may find forgiveness and new life in the Lord Jesus Christ. *This beacon of divine hope shines for all! Prison, legislation, persecution, banishment, or death cannot extinguish it.*

NINTH: THE PARABLE OF THE DRAGNET.*

This lesson is kindred to the Parable of the Tares or Poison Seed in Section 77. The Savior teaches a final separation of the wicked from the righteous.

The Messiah affirms that His kingdom on earth will conclude with the lost being severed from the saved and confined to the regions of the damned. Refer to the Introductions of Section 166 and their relative footnotes for the Parable of the King Coming to Judge all Nations.

Matt. 13:47-51—*In Peter's house at Capernaum*	Mk.	Lk.	John
Kingdom work is finished: a terrible separation follows **47** "Again, the kingdom of heaven is like unto a net,(a) that was cast into the sea, and gathered of every kind:(b) **48** "Which, when it was full, they drew to shore,(c) and sat down, and gathered the good into vessels, but cast the bad away.(d) **49** "So shall it be at the end of the world:(e) the angels shall come forth, and sever the wicked from among the just, **50** "And shall cast them into the furnace of fire: there shall be wailing and gnashing of teeth."(f) **51** Jesus saith unto them, "Have ye understood all these things?" They say unto him, "Yea, Lord."(g) (Verse 52 cont. in Section 86.)			

Footnotes-Commentary

(a) This was the common dragnet used while fishing selected waters that were not so deep. Here, is the only place it is mentioned in the New Testament. This was similar to our seine, but much larger floats were attached to the top and weights to the bottom. It was carried to the seabed by these weights. After being dragged over a distance through the water, it was drawn together on both ends and pulled to the shore. See the only mention of hook fishing in Section 108, Matt. 17:27, where Peter went fishing to pay temple taxes.

2p-**The kingdom of heaven.** Incorrect views respecting the nature of Christ's present kingdom have produced much harm to the cause of our Lord. A visible ecclesiastical organization, distinguished by the observance of external rituals, swimming with pomp and colorful pageantry, has claimed to be the kingdom. The ecumenical movement, struggling to "build bridges to those of other faiths" and bring about a world religious unity, is an apostate organization. The exalted Son of God, seated even now at the Father's right hand, exercises a mediatorial rule and reign in His own unique and curious way. He does break the potter's vessel (Ps. 2:9), as He deems it right. The visible side of His kingdom has good and bad mixed together. However, on the other side, only those who are saved by the grace of God constitute the authentic kingdom. It is often difficult to distinguish the tares from the wheat. At the appointed time, God will separate the two when Christ returns for His own. One is appointed to eternal bliss, the other eternal damnation. The born again children of God have been translated by divine power into the kingdom of His dear Son (Col. 1:13). This miracle is considered eternally valid from the viewpoint of the Almighty, regardless of varying theological opinions. It should be singularly understood that this part of the spiritual kingdom of Christ or His church is distinct from a great visible organization, consisting of saved and lost, good and bad, all united together by some ecclesiastical doctrine or ecumenical bond. Sheep are not goats and goats are not sheep! For more on the two aspects of the kingdom, see Section 39, footnotes a and g.

3p-**Religious and ecumenical pluralism.** Men without the saving knowledge of Jesus Christ, and a *true* understanding of biblical soteriology, developed various philosophies regarding the origin and existence of things, mankind, solutions, and salvation. Creeping into churches, they gradually became compatible with the kingdom of God. The "worldview" of pluralism affirms that there is no exclusive faith that contains the absolute truth that God wants men to know. It says that religious truth is blended more or less into all religions. This is Antichrist ecumenism in action through "interfaith dialogue." Politically, freedom of religion encompasses all religions within the framework of constituted law. Under this umbrella, *honorable men* do not attempt to take this freedom from any fellow. However, they may exercise their disagreement with and expose the errors, falsity, and deceit (as they see it) of any religious person or organization. Over the past decades, the national media and secular institutions of lower and higher education have traduced the Christian faith, Holy Bible, and the Person and work of Jesus Christ. A concerted effort, sponsored by Satan and made operative by demon spirits, has set itself to denigrate anything that smacks of rock solid, conservative Christianity. For the unmasking of this lie, see *The Gagging of God; Christianity Confronting Pluralism*, by Dr. Donald A Carson. This work reveals how pagan pluralism is presented as relative to all things, including all religions. Its influence on western culture has given birth to a confused and corrupted society who believes there are no absolutes and concrete moral guidelines. Adultery is renamed "relationship." A drunkard is an "alcoholic." The jailbird is an "incarcerate." The dope head is a "chemical dependent." Abortion is now respectable, for "women have their rights." President Obama signs into law a bill that frees taxpayer's money to pay for the murder of millions of babies. "Jesus Christ" has become a national swear word, while Hollywood and the media present Him as a ignorant Jew wandering about Israel. Religious pluralism makes salvation a potluck supper. Take a shot and hope you get what you want! The biggest lie is, "Any religion will do for they all contain elements of truth." These apostate dreamers reject the Son of God and His exclusive atonement on the cross as humankind's only answer. Divine provision has been made for our dilemma. It is found in Jesus Christ. Because this is true, we understand why He is the world's most hated Man. Ecumenism, idealism, and inclusivism degrades God, Christ, the Holy Spirit, and the Bible in the name of unity and fellowship. For the sheer fallacy of the "any religion will do" myth, see Section 95, sixth paragraph of footnote r.

4p-The Emerging Church. This appeared in the late 20th and early 21st centuries. Its origin and roots seem to be in Australia and Britain. It is a conglomeration of Protestants, post evangelicals, Roman Catholics, Seventh Day Adventists, Anabaptists, amoral moralists, and a wide assortment of just about anything that smells religious. A neo-liberal, apostate cult, with a profusion of "who's who" in the heresy hall of fame, they crossed established fundamental theological boundaries and disdain traditional Bible doctrines. Their agenda of pro homosexuality among young people, a false view of biblical inspiration, and human depravity provides Satan with an open door. With a "transcendent" view of the virgin birth, Christ's miracles, blood atonement, and resurrection, the Emerging Church is a synagogue of Satan, another off-ramp to hell. In this relevant, sin denying cult, "transforming secular society," one sees another demonic inspired ecumenical blunder seeking to blend all faiths. The Emerging Church is a fake and will shunt men from the salvation of Jesus Christ into the pits of hell. *The "good people" who are in it are their because of their ignorance of Scripture, dumb disobedience, or they have never been saved.*

(b) A variety of things were scooped up in dragging along the shallow floor of this part of the Sea of Galilee.

(c) Towing and pulling a full net to the shore was no little task. With hundreds of struggling, flopping fish, and various items lifted from the bottom, up to six strong men could be called in to bring the mixed catch to shore.

(d) Once the net was hauled to the shoreline, the laborious work of clearing its contents commenced. Only those with an eye to discern the good sea creatures from the bad were assigned this task. This could take many hours.

(e) **"End of the world."** For the meaning of this term in Jewish thinking and eschatology, see Section 82, Matt 13:39, footnote d. Immediately after speaking this parable our Lord commenced to give its meaning, beginning at verse 49. The preaching of the gospel of Christ's kingdom is likened unto casting a great net over the earth. Found in this net are good and bad, genuine and counterfeit, treasure, and trash. The *visible local* church has in it everything from the great saints of God to the servants of sin. This has been examined in Section 77, footnote g, and the Parable of the Tares or Poison Wheat. By no means is the *visible local* church to be confused with the true body of Christ. The former is a mixture of good and bad, while the latter consists *only* of those who have been born of the Spirit of God and added into the body of Christ, which is His church or spiritual kingdom. This inclusion of a converted soul into the body of Christ is the sovereign work of the Holy Spirit as seen in 1 Cor. 12:13. In this present dispensation or time period (commonly called the church age), saved Christians are normally found within the thousands of local assemblies scattered over the world. All too often, side by side with believers are the Devil's tares, tangles, trash, and bad fish. At the end of this age (or period), the saved saints of God will be separated or severed from the godless by the removal of the church. Regarding this separation and the "severing of the wicked from among the just," refer to Section 77, Matt. 13:30. Each field of eschatology seems to have a more or less different idea regarding this "severing." For a general coverage of these various beliefs, and often bizarre opinions on this subject, see the Introduction, just before Section 166 and all of *Appendix Eight.*

(f) **"Wailing and gnashing of teeth."** Where is annihilation or soul sleep found in these awful words? If this does not describe a *real* suffering in the fires of torment, then words are not vehicles to transport meanings anymore. These wicked are said to be severed from among the just, exactly as the tares were gathered out from the wheat and thrown into the fire. "Gnashing of teeth" has been a universal symbol used to express the worst of human pain. Soul sleep in the grave is not found here. For twenty-one things the Bible says about suffering in hell-lake of fire, see Section 103, number 8, under footnote g.

(g) With the conclusion of this parable, so passionate and expressive of the fate of the damned, the disciples *now* understood their Lord's teaching. The "them" and "they" of this passage are the disciples whom He had previously taken into the house. Despite their sluggishness in comprehending the earlier lessons, *now* with the horrible story of the dragnet, they are shaken into a fearful reality of what their Messiah has been teaching. Never had the rabbis taught such straightforward, soul-searching truths. And never had a kingdom like His been proclaimed to the people of Israel. Indeed, even His enemies testified, "Never man spake like this" (John 7:46). See the main heading Section 81, Mk. 4:33-34, where the Lord Jesus privately explained many of these parables, and they *slowly* began to comprehend. With this ninth parable, their understanding is jolted again. It was all beginning to make a little more sense. However, with the coming of the Spirit in His fullness on the day of Pentecost, everything, He taught came into focus. Then they clearly understood everything Jesus had said.

TENTH: THE PARABLE OF THE HOUSEHOLDER.

In the final parable of this series, the Messiah singularly addressed His disciples and apostles.* They are to become true experts in handling the treasure of God's Word.

*To their amazement, He bestows upon them a new and highly respected title with its awesome responsibilities. Now, they are becoming true "scribes" instructed in the kingdom of heaven. Having just given a brief parabolic survey of His new kingdom or church from beginning to end, they are to act as God's true scribes ministering and serving in this kingdom. Their work was to bring forth its truths: both the new teachings as He had spoken and the old ones already known, win men to Him and shine as lights in their dark world. A survey of the book of Acts, which commences immediately after His ascension, reflects that after the day of Pentecost, they did exactly as their Lord had commanded them.

Matt. 13:52-53—*In Peter's house at Capernaum*	Mk.	Lk.	John
Those who understand are well equipped to serve **52** Then said he unto them,[a] "Therefore every scribe *which is* instructed unto the kingdom of heaven is like unto a man *that is* an householder, which bringeth forth out of his treasure *things* new and old."[b] **53** And it came to pass, *that* when Jesus had finished these parables, he departed thence.[c] (Verse 54 cont. in Section 91.)			

Footnotes-Commentary

[a] **"Them."** This plural pronoun has reference to His disciples now back in the house. See Section 82, Matt. 13:36, footnote a where it states that Jesus "went into the house." The inference is clear: Christ's apostles were now the true scribes, while those religious scribes of Israel were uninstructed regarding the real kingdom of heaven and its treasures.

2p-"Instructed in the kingdom." The religious leaders of Israel were thoroughly "instructed" in the kingdom of their material and political dreams. However, they did not understand the kingdom or Church of Christ at this time. With their scrambled eschatology, they looked for a superman Messiah of dynamic abilities who would destroy or subdue all of Israel's Gentile enemies and lead them into ruling the world. For an explanation of how the ancient Jews had established various time periods within their system of eschatology, see Section 95, footnote k.

[b] This closing remark was a grand benediction upon the nine parables He had just given. With this conclusion, our Lord conferred a *new* and high title upon His disciples-apostles. The Lord Jesus addressed three important things to these men, who were slowly becoming the *original* foundational layers of His kingdom-church:

1. **A promotion.** He promoted them to the status of "scribes" in the service of His kingdom. In Israel, "scribes" were greatly revered for their learning. They are mentioned many times in the Talmud with passages that affirm their power and dreaded control over the people. See Talmud tractates, Yevamoth 20a, 85b, and Rosh Ha Shana 19a for two examples. Messiah's disciples were beginning to learn from the Chief of rabbis, the Son of God. Soon, they would be inducted into the true school of Scribes; as men who were equipped to teach others about the Savior of the world! Their work was to instruct all willing hearts in the things of God, but first they must know themselves of what they speak. How painfully pitiful to hear a "minister of God" address a subject of which (it is obvious), he is greatly ignorant? Such was the continual prattle of the scribes and Pharisees regarding their promised Messiah. Christ trained His men to be and do otherwise. See examples of their future preaching in Acts 4:33, 6:10, and 7:51-60.

2. **A comparison.** He compared them to a householder (wealthy estate owner), who brings "things new and old" out of his treasures or vast storehouse. Later, Paul instructs us that the man of God is to be "throughly furnished" (2 Tim. 3:16-17). This is because we have a boundless storehouse in God's infallible Word. The Lord Jesus tells His men that the small amount of knowledge they have *now* attained, unless taken further, is not sufficient for the work of His great kingdom. A preacher of God's Word must have for his supreme treasure the Holy Scriptures. By continually drawing from these, he understands better the problems of life and can answer sensibly those who inquire. He is not so much to be furnished with a great amount of worldly learning or wisdom. Rather, *first* he must be instructed and grounded in the *major doctrines* of Christ's kingdom: laboring in continual prayer, the art of soul winning, supporting the weak, upholding truth, and blessing mankind, saved and lost alike in general. It is not enough for a man to possess these advantages, but he *must*, in the power of the Holy Spirit, share them with all who would stop to give attention along life's highway. The man of God must guard his heart and keep it always before the cross. One is constantly astounded at the flippant, careless attitude of

371

believers and ministers who show little or no interest in the salvation of work mates, strangers, and passers by, neighbors, friends, hateful enemies, and even beloved family members.

3. **A duty.** They were admonished to "bring forth" or share the truth they had learned from His parables and sow it in the hearts of others. Had they not watched Him do this hundreds of times? Some see in Jesus' usage of the terms "old and new" a reference to both divisions of God's Word, as found in the Old and New Testaments. The able ministers of Christ can joyfully present the gospel equally well from either part of the inspired Canon. He who preaches the same sermon week after week is reflecting his weakness in understanding truth from both covenants. How empty is the pastor or minister who knows not the thrill of fresh explorations and discoveries from Holy Scripture. Ezra prepared his heart to teach in Israel (Ezra 7:10). Those who have the duty to instruct others in the things of God and Christ should first be instructed and prepared themselves. It was the duty of the priests to keep knowledge in their heads and hearts and distribute it with their lips (Mal. 2:7). A man may be a great philosopher, politician, scientist, or an authority in the peculiar matters of life; yet if he does not possess the saving knowledge of Jesus Christ, he is of all men most miserable. The Master described His little flock of preachers as men who dispense eternal truth, and as "scribes instructed unto the kingdom of heaven." No more honorable titles could have been given His preachers. Here, was another rebuke for the scowling scribes and proud Pharisees, who made public claims to have the correct knowledge of God; yet, they continually opposed and contradicted their Messiah. It is not much different today. As explained, those churches and individuals, who claim to *alone* have the truth and all others are wrong; that men must become one of their number to find God's grace and salvation, are imposters. They speak falsehood and deceive many. The issue is not a particular religion, church, clan, or organization, but rather the Man, who died on the cross, rose from the dead and lives forever! It is Him with whom we shall all have to do (John 5:22-24). Many preach Christ, make a grand noise about Him and His death for sinners, and then require their adherents to do all sorts of things in order to be saved. With some, there is the mass, confessional, stations of the cross; others demand baptism by various means, and good works. The law cults require their members to keep the Ten Commandments, observe the Sabbath day, eat certain foods, wear particular clothing, and head coverings. For years, we have had the distortion that God's salvation is found in five points called T-U-L-I-P, or the other extreme that the exercise of the free will brings eternal life. The TV charlatans, promising to make men rich, heal every disease, words of knowledge claims and so forth, offend believers who know God's Word. *Let the reader please note, this does not decry order, decency, doctrinal accuracy, and proper Scriptural authority among Christians.* It is our duty to bring forth truth and strike a hopeful deathblow at legalism, sectarianism, and the clever heresies that are storming through true churches. The final design of all this is to destroy weak Christians and deceive the lost about the saving grace of God.

4. **The gutter sweeper from Denmark.** Those trapped in false religions oppose the saving gospel and its simplicity. They eloquently debate against divine truth, arguing for their own damnation, clinging to the most absurd things that blind them to faith in Jesus Christ. The following story illustrates this. When working in Australia in the early 1960s, in a small village, I made friends with the town "gutter sweeper." He had immigrated to Australia from Denmark as a young man some fifty years prior. Frank and his family often attended services and appeared to have no opposition to the gospel of Christ. While driving to the hospital early one Monday morning, I saw him sweeping a gutter and stopped to chat. During our conversation, I inquired, "Frank, when are you going to receive the Lord Jesus Christ as your personal Savior?" Suddenly, he dropped the broom, reached into his shirt and ripped out a curious object attached to a chain about his neck. Instantly, I discerned that it was an occult charm! Trembling and shaking, he loudly shouted, "Mr. Pike, my faith is in this medal my mother gave me when I left Denmark years ago. It is a family tradition and my salvation. I will never give it up." He was red-faced and loudly adamant. Dismissing myself, I drove to the hospital. Late, that afternoon, I learned that Frank dropped dead in one of the gutters he was sweeping! The Devil has shaded the minds of those who do not believe in the Savior. He and demons work to keep them in darkness until death slams their souls into eternity. Even an occult charm from the hand of a sincere mother will do the job! False traditions that turn men from Christ are among the most successful tools employed by the forces of darkness to damn lost souls. Anything that prevents us from receiving Jesus Christ as personal Lord and Savior is a lie. Men who trust something or someone other than Christ are among the biggest fools who ever lived. Though they curse us now for speaking these words of truth, in time, they will come to know, but often it is too late!

(c) This lengthy teaching session of our Lord must have taken several hours. Having finished His discourse on the parables, the Savior departed from Peter's house and returned to the shores of Lake Galilee. He prepares to cross over to the eastern side. Great multitudes continue to follow Him. See Section 87, Matt. 8:18 for mention of the thousands that pursued the Lord Jesus, wherever He went over land or sea. See Section 42, Matt. 4:23-25 for an earlier mention of the thousands, from all directions coming to the Savior.

While directing His apostles to cross the sea, Jesus stopped to give His requirements for discipleship to several inquirers. A fearful storm on Lake Galilee* is stilled.

This miracle is not to be confused with Christ walking on the water, which occurred some days later. See Section 94 for explanation of this second wonder that also took place on the turbulent waters of the Sea or Lake of Galilee.

The Sea of Galilee

Matt. 8:18–25	Mk. 4:35–38	Lk. 8:22–24	John
18 Now when Jesus saw great multitudes about him, he gave commandment to depart [a] unto the other side.	**35** And the same day, when the even was come, he saith unto them, "Let us pass[a] over unto the other side."	**22** Now it came to pass on a certain day, that he went into a ship with his disciples: and he said unto them, "Let us go[a] over unto the other side of the lake."	
Two proposals to follow Christ: His response 1. A Jewish scribe **19** And a certain scribe[b] came, and said unto him, "Master, I will follow thee whithersoever thou goest." **20** And Jesus saith unto him, "The foxes have holes, and the birds of the air *have* nests;[c] but the Son of man hath not where to lay *his* head." 2. A wistful disciple **21** And another of his disciples said unto him, "Lord, suffer [let] me first to go and bury my father." **22** But Jesus said unto him, "Follow me; and let the dead bury their dead."[d]			
23 And when he was entered into a ship, his disciples followed him.	**36** And when they had sent away the multitude, they took him even as he was in the ship. And there were also with him other little ships.[e]		
		And they launched forth. *A terrible storm hits* **23** But as they sailed he fell asleep:[f] ▼ and there came down a storm of wind on the lake; and they were filled *with water*, and were in jeopardy.	
A terrible storm hits **24** And, behold, there arose a great tempest in the sea, insomuch that the ship was covered with the waves: but he was asleep.[f] ▶	*A terrible storm hits* **37** And there arose a great storm of wind, and the waves beat into the ship, so that it was now full. **38** And he was in the hinder part of the ship, asleep[f] ▶ on a pillow:	◀ *Matthew and Mark first record the storm, then Jesus asleep. Luke reverses the order in verse 23 above.*	
Fear's foolish question **25** And his disciples came to *him,* and awoke him, saying, "Lord, save us:	*Fear's foolish question* and they awake him, and say unto him, "Master, carest thou not	*Fear's foolish question* **24** And they came to him, and awoke him, saying, "Master, master,	

Matt. 8: 25-27	Mk. 4:38-41	Lk. 8:24-25	John
we perish."[g]	that we perish?"[g]	we perish."[g]	
	He commands the wind and sea; they obey!	*He commands the wind and sea; they obey!*	
	39 And he arose,[h] and rebuked◄ the wind, and said unto the sea, "Peace, be still." And the wind ceased, and there was a great calm.	Then he arose,[h] and rebuked◄ the wind and the raging of the water: and they ceased, and there was a calm.	
►*Matthew places this act of the Savior in verse 26 below. These differences are marks of divine inspiration.*			
26 And he saith unto them, "Why are ye fearful, O ye of little faith?"[i]	**40** And he said unto them, "Why are ye so fearful? how is it that ye have no faith?"[i]	**25** And he said unto them, "Where is your faith?"[i]	
He commands the winds and sea; they obey!			
Then he arose, and rebuked► the winds and the sea; and there was a great calm.	◄*Matthew pens Jesus rebuking the elements here. Mark puts it in verse 39 and Luke in verse 24 above.*		
The amazing Messiah	*The amazing Messiah*	*The amazing Messiah*	
27 But the men marvelled, saying, "What manner of man[j] is this, that even the winds and the sea obey him!"[k] (Verse 28 cont. in Section 88)	**41** And they feared exceedingly, and said one to another, "What manner of man[j] is this, that even the wind and the sea obey him?"[k] (Next chap., Mk. 5:1, in Section 88.)	And they being afraid wondered, saying one to another, "What manner of man[j] is this! for he commandeth even the winds and water, and they obey him."[k] (Verse 26 cont. in Section 88.)	

Footnotes-Commentary

[a] **"Depart,"** or **"let us pass over."** The Savior had been in Capernaum, a city on the north-west corner of the Sea of Galilee. Leaving here, He makes His way to the sea, which was also known as Gennesaret and Tiberias. In verse 22, Luke refers to it as a lake. It was some fourteen miles long from north to south, nine miles wide from east to west, and lay "680 feet below the level of the Mediterranean Sea." This low geological feature formed a natural vortex for the powerful winds, which swooped down from Mount. Hermon's summit and then fell into the sea like an explosion. The place Jesus purposed to go was located on the upper eastern shore of this sea or lake. Refer to footnote g below, for more regarding the curious weather patterns that prevail over this vast body of water.

[b] **The first inquirer**. This fellow was a scribe (one of the most hostile enemies to the Messiah) and with this large following in Galilee. He openly confessed a desire to follow the Lord Jesus. Apparently, his motives were not sincere, as one may see in the answer given to him by Christ. See footnote c below, for explanation. Even though some of Jesus' Words spoken at this time were similar to those used several months later when a "certain man," proposed to follow Him, this was a different event. For another lesson on discipleship, note Section 128 and the three parables given by the Lord Jesus on the cost required of those who follow Him.

[c] How strange and unfair it seems, that the creatures of sky and earth have places to rest, but their Creator did not! What a startling manifestation of heavenly love for sinful men. "For ye know the grace of our Lord Jesus Christ, that though he was rich, yet for your sakes he became poor, that ye through his poverty might be rich" (2 Cor. 8:9). The rabbis often spoke of the birds and their nests. See the Talmud tractates, Beitzah 10b and Chullin 138b. Now, Rabbi Jesus uses similar terminology but with a vastly different application!

2p-**"Son of man."** Christ's usage of this title for Himself, as expressed here for the *first* time, has puzzled some. Being used of common ordinary men across Jewish history, it seems strange that Christ would call Himself as such. Because the title "son of man" is employed in different significations means nothing in relation to Christ's application of it. Ezekiel used it some ninety times of himself. Hundreds of like words are similarly used. The Savior took the "Son of man" designation because He was indeed that in His frame of humanity, yet, He was that exclusive Person, God in mortal flesh. "Son of man" was also another Old Testament title for Israel's coming Messiah (Dan. 7:13-14; Matt. 16:28; and Rev. 1:13). During His earthly humanity, our Lord applied this Messianic term to Himself and fulfilled its predictions. It denoted that He was the divine Messiah, and at the same time, He had a peculiar human connection with mankind. "Son of man" reflected His coming among us, partly as a Man to provide salvation for Adam's fallen race, sharing in their woes and infirmities; yet, Himself as true God, always without sin. Jesus Christ is the Son of man, as He proclaimed Himself to be. Thus, as such, He is the true and highest representative of all earthly mortals. In Him, all the lines of our common humanity converge; yet, He was the perfect Human without sin. What He became in His bodily resurrection, we shall be someday (Rom. 6:5 and 9). For our Lord as a human in boyhood days, see Section 20, first paragraph of footnote j. For more on the title "Son of man," refer to Section 103, footnote b.

(d) **Verse 21. The second inquirer**. He was a disciple of Christ and not the scribe mentioned in verse 19 and footnote b above.

2p-Verse 22. "The dead bury their dead." Here, we meet another of those curious statements that prove so difficult for western Christians. It has drawn deep from the well of human imagination. Looking at it *strictly from the Hebrew culture* of that era and the understanding of the people who heard Jesus speak, we discover its meaning. Note the following three things:

1. Pious Jews considered all who did not obey the Law of Moses or did not know it, as being "dead men." It seems impossible that the inquiring disciple was using this well-known expression in such a manner on this occasion.

2. To bury the dead was counted one of the most honorable deeds a Hebrew could perform; it was to be executed as quickly as possible. Jews would *not* leave their houses for work or any venture until *after* the dead had been buried. Hence, this second option seems incorrect, for this man was with Christ on the shores of Galilee, *not* at home with his dead. It is sure that he was not traveling with Jesus while his father's corpse lay in the house decaying. The truth is that his father was *not* dead. Apparently, he wanted to return home, and live in its comforts until the decease of his father. Often pious Jews would not venture out into life until the decease of the father. After the normal ritual of burying him was over, he would *then* follow the Messiah unimpeded.

3. There was a *second* burial meticulously observed by the ancient Jews. Approximately, *one year* after the burial of the corpse when the flesh had totally decomposed, the bones were exhumed, and then the eldest son would place the remains into a special box and give them sacred interment in the walls of the family tomb. Hundreds of these have been discovered over Israel. The *Biblical Archaeology Review,* Nov.-Dec. 2002, pages 24-33, carried a brilliant article about an ossuary recently discovered. It had the inscription in Aramaic letters "James, the son of Joseph, brother of Jesus." Apparently, it was the exhumed type of a second burial that this disciple appealed before Messiah to be completed. According to Jewish custom, it was the duty of the first son to perform this honorable deed. The Savior says emphatically that His service and divine call are above the most delicate and sensitive issues of human life. Someone else at the home of this man could perform the *second* burial. (This was allowable should the oldest son not be available.) Nothing rude or disrespectful is found here. However, odd Christ's response may sound to the western ear, this man and all those standing nearby instantly understood it. For an explanation of various Hebrew customs when dealing with their dead, see Section 61 first and second paragraphs of footnote b.

3p-In this proverb, "Let the dead bury their dead," the Master informed this disciple that there are always plenty of spiritually dead people who can attend to the business of burying the physically dead. Based on the man's plea, "I will follow thee whithersoever thou goest," the Savior, demanded from him absolute devotion and undivided loyalty to His kingdom and cause. His excuse of requesting to return home first, wait until his father had deceased, then follow the Messiah was unacceptable. At this later period, we notice that the Lord Jesus called for unqualified love and absolute devotion above all things in human life. Preachers who make a big deal out of our Lord's words have sorely missed the mark. The matchless and precious Son of God simply says, *"Put Me first or not at all."* Who needs a one hour sermon, Sunday school lesson, or weekend seminar to understand what this means?

4p-There are those high and curious hours in the lives of God's servants when they are called upon to set side, temporarily, natural feelings, pressing moral obligations, and other wholesome aspirations to attend the most sacred of all duties: the urgent work of Christ. In summary, this was what our Lord told this would-be disciple.

(e) **"Other little ships."** Only Mark writes of these sailing close to the Lord Jesus' boat. One wonders who was aboard these small vessels and what became of them when the terrible storm fell upon the sea (Mk. 4:37).

(f) **"Asleep on a pillow."** Here is the only mention of Christ sleeping in Scripture. Mark tells us he was in the "hinder part" of the craft. This was the stern, which had a higher platform built into the end of the ship above the floor level. It was here that Jesus slept as the raging waters poured in, covered the floor of the vessel, and began to rise slowly. See verse 37 below. Worn and fatigued from travels, crowds, continual teaching and preaching, He laid His head "on a pillow," in a deep and restful sleep. We have often wondered who gave our Lord that pillow on which to rest His head? *Men do not give pillows to one another!* This loving act, was beyond doubt, from the foresight of a prudent female disciple. Was this comfort from the hand of one of the Galilean women that assisted His great ministry? Regardless, such conjecture is dear to one's heart and moves us to offer our pillows to those servants of Christ, who may come our way. This marvelous picture of the "sleeping Savior" reflects His humanity and sharing in our physical needs and weaknesses.

2p-**Verse 37**. Here, is a miracle of the New Testament unmentioned by the commentators. Mark explicitly wrote that the boat was "now full" of water. For Jesus sleeping in this situation, see paragraph just above. Every sensible man knows that a boat full of water sinks! *This one did not.* This is one of those "overlooked miracles" that occurred in the life of Christ.

(g) Dr. W. M. Thomson in *The Land and the Book*, vol. ii, page 59, gives a vivid description of the danger that could suddenly fall upon this body of water. The lake will be placid as a molten mirror; when without warning, it will quiver, leap up, and boil as though it were going to explode. Fierce, howling winds of terrible speed churn the waters into foaming wet mountains of destruction to all in their path. Worse, it was at night and the feeble lights carried aboard would be soon extinguished by the tempest. Though totally familiar with this body of water, these men were terrified as this "storm of storms" came down and fiercely threatened their doom. (Refer to footnote a above for more on the turbulence of this vast sea.)

2p-Falling, slipping, feeling about in the darkness and rain, the terrified apostles hurried to awake their sleeping Messiah. Holding high their flickering lanterns, they frantically pled to be saved from this typhoon of death. The best of men are prone to ask foolish questions amid times of great fear and pending doom. These apostles acted as most of us would have, shouting loudly, "Master, carest thou not that we perish?" What a ridiculous question! Yet, are not all of us guilty of hasty and rash conclusions to emergencies that so often fall like this fearful storm upon our lives? *Would any of us have done any better?* The dominance of inordinate fears reflects our lack of faith in the blessed Son of God to assist us in those terrible times of dark and dreadful storms. See footnote i below, for the response of the Savior to His terrified preachers.

3p-There is a story of a Christian army officer of many years ago. He was at sea with his wife and little children when suddenly a terrible storm befell the ship. Great terror came over all the passengers, and they screamed and shouted in fear. Oddly, the officer was calm amid the chaos! His wife in her dilemma chided him and cried out "Why are you not concerned for me and your children? We are all going to perish!" To her shock, he unsheathed his glittering sword and placed its point at her throat. She was not in the least alarmed at this action but looked up into his face with a smile. "What!" said he, "are you not terrified with a drawn sword at your throat?" "No," she replied, "not when I know it is in the hand of the one who loves me." "And would you have me" he asked, "to fear this tempest when I know it is in the hand of my heavenly Father, who loves me?"

(h) **The authority of Jesus' Words.** Rising from human sleep, He stood tall in the tossing ship and verbally commanded the elements of nature! All three gospel writers state that Jesus "rebuked" the winds and raging sea. On a previous occasion, we have noted our Lord "rebuking" demons or devils and their obedience to Him (Mk. 1:25). Those who propose that Satan was the origin of this particular dreadful storm, designed to kill the apostle's of Christ, may not be wrong. Was Messiah's rebuke aimed at the lord of terror, death, and darkness? Was the Devil in this mighty blast as he had been in the killer whirlwind of Job some two thousand years previously (Job 1:19)? Whoever or whatever it was, the Master's orders were immediately obeyed. The atoms of meteorology instantly bowed at His feet in reverence. A great peace fell and wonderfully tamed the raging sea. Normally, after a storm over a large body of water, there is a gradual fretting of the waves, a time in which it settles down becoming placid again. Not so here, for *suddenly* there fell a great calm. Of old, the prophet had written, "At his rebuke, the waters fled" (Ps. 104:7). See footnote j below for more on this wonder.

(i) **Lk. 8:25. "Where is your faith?"** This admonition would later strike root in their lives. He was gently asking them, "Don't you believe I am able to handle this raging torrent?" Now, however, only one thing mattered: this hair-raising experience overwhelmed them. In a shock, the apostles are confronted again with the fact that Jesus of Nazareth, their Teacher and Messiah, is more than a mere man. Only God could do what He just did. With a frightening alarm and swift suddenness, the howling storm subsided; the ship again glided smoothly along; danger fled; and death's chilling fear vanished! The apostles, trembling over their near destruction, are confounded at this strange but wonderful Person. They were struck again with awe and glorious terror, no longer at the winds and waves, but at that marvelous Man standing before them in the shimmering darkness, as a loving shepherd gently caring for His trembling little flock.

(j) **"What manner of man is this?"** He was God dwelling in human flesh, yet manifested to all observers in the Person of Jesus Christ of Nazareth. Note Section 1, Part 1, footnotes a and b, for details on this gloriously overwhelming subject. The entire foundation of Bible Christianity is that Jesus was God in a human frame. If that truth is altered, adjusted, reinterpreted, or even *slightly changed,* then the whole superstructure of the Christian faith crashes to the ground. We are left to assume that Christ was a shameless impostor, or that He was a lunatic, suffering from religious delusions. With either, He would be disqualified from being mankind's only Savior. If this were so, then the most astounding phenomenon in history is left without explanation. Though denominations and abominations alike rattle their little sabers against the deity of Christ, at the end of life's human highway, the rest of the story often slips out. Joseph E. Renan (died 1892), the famed French infidel, whose poisoned words rule millions from hell to this day, near the end of life wrote of Christ this final sentence. "Thy divinity is established. Between Thee and God there will no longer be distinction. Jesus will never be surpassed." Such a profound confession from the pen of a dying infidel, so near hell's opened gates is the testimony of brutal history. It signals a warning for all who would "toy" with their souls. On the other hand, unsaved men in their dark derisions often utter vain and futile words against God and His Son. For more on the deathbed confessions of the ungodly, see Section 58, second paragraph of footnote w, Section 115, the third paragraph of footnote e, and the *Dying Testimonies, of Saved & Unsaved,* by A. B. Shaw. *To Hell and Back*, by Dr. Maurice S. Rawlings, a former skeptic, wine maker, and renowned cardiologist, is electrifying in its contents. It answers the scorners rebuttal that only "country bumpkins and uneducated ignoramuses believe in God, Jesus Christ, and life after death." There are no unbelievers in eternity.

(k) Soon, these terrified preachers would learn that all of creation rushed to heed His beck and command. Did those few disciples, who had been present at the Cana wedding, suddenly remember that He had turned water into new wine? As He had commanded water on that earlier occasion, and it obeyed Him, so He does it again. Refer to Section 27 for the story of Jesus' first miracle performed at Cana. He had spoken to the raging Sea of Galilee, and it instantly obeyed Him! And this was not the end of it. In a short while, He will walk on the waters of this same sea, while in the midst of another fearful stormy night. See Section 94 for this later, but equally amazing, water adventure with the Son of God. Again, it will be to the shock of these men. He had commanded fish to swim into nets and one with a large coin in its mouth to bite Peter's hook! Only God could do this. One can believe that these men had some interesting stories to tell their grandchildren!

2p-**Which is right?** The careful eye will note the punctuation differences in these three passages found in the *Authorized* or *King James Version*. The translators have written Matthew's verse as an exclamation spoken by the disciples. Mark's passage has been punctuated as an interrogative or question. Luke's record is punctuated as also being an exclamation, but the exclamation mark has been placed after the sentence, "What manner of man is this!" In view of the trauma of that experience, all three forms of grammar are surely correct, for they express the varying intensity of that terrifying event. Regardless, the best grammarian on earth would have a problem deciding this one.

3p-**Your next storm.** As sure as the Savior sent His preachers into the dreadful storm of Galilee, so today, He continues to direct His servants into difficult adventures. Often, God's commands seem absurd. In Zech. 11:1, it is written, "Open thy doors, O Lebanon, that the fire may devour, thy cedars." This is quite a command. When you see fire coming, open your doors that it may devour all you have! Who among sane men would fling back the doors of their homes and welcome the devouring flames. The unsaved world cannot understand divine things. They look upon *true* Christians with pity and resentment. The author heard the late Harlan Popov tell of fellow prisoners who danced with shinning faces amid their sufferings in cold, filthy Bulgarian communist prisons. Christian joy is mingled with tears. Once there was a fiddler who played so beautifully that everyone in the village danced. A deaf man sat nearby. Not being able to hear the music he thought they had all gone mad. Believers, who walk with Christ through the piercing sorrows of life, also dance to heavenly music. They are unconcerned what the Christ hating world thinks. God does things differently from men. Conquering kings upon entering a vanquished city would ride in with pomp and great splendor mounted on the back of a strong prancing stallion. Jesus' disciples and friends were greatly disturbed that He rode into Jerusalem on the back of a poor donkey, the slowest of riding animals. He chose the pace. Dashing about, they placed coats, garments, and many branches before their Lord, trying to make their King look kingly. These were trampled beneath the hoofs of the lowly animal. To them, He did not appear much of a king. Thus, the ways of God. All true believers have their seas to cross, storms to wither, and donkeys to ride. Fellow Christian, ride well your donkey for King Jesus; He rode well for you!

4p-**God's strange way of doing things.** Years ago, Sabina Wurmbrand told the author of this work something she had witnessed in 1952 while a prisoner in a communist slave labor camp on the banks of the Danube River. As the female prisoners marched each morning to their work, an elderly woman would spontaneously break out into singing Christian hymns. She danced and skipped about with great joy waving one hand upward in the sky. The guards would beat her without mercy, but every day it was the same. Running parallel with the roadside was a long fenced-in ditch, with savage guard dogs, to prevent escape. The old woman was warned that another singing and she would be thrown to the dogs. Sure enough, the next morning, Lola broke out in loud praises to her Savior. Instantly, two guards fell upon her, dragged the old woman to a gate, and threw her into the muddy ditch. Everyone rushed forward to watch. The dogs, with tails between their legs, gathered in a pack about the old woman and bowed before her. Slowly, they rose and walked away standing subdued and quiet at a distance. Stunned, the guards opened the gate and pulled her up. For the next year, she sang every morning marching to work; no one dared to touch her! Later, Lola died of pneumonia in a common cell praising Jesus as her Savior amid dozens of amazed prisoners. She was ninety-two years old. Her testimony lives to this day as an example of the strange way God does things.

Arriving on the eastern shore of Lake Galilee, Jesus and His apostles meet two demon-possessed mad men with super-human strength.*

*Matthew wrote about two wild men, while Mark and Luke were inspired to give the story of the fiercer of the two. See footnote b below. This is literal history. It should not be dismissed as fable or interpreted symbolically.

The south – east coast of Galilee

Matt. 8:28-29	Mk. 5:1-7	Lk. 8:26-28	John
Meeting two wild men **28** And when he was come to the other side into the country of the Gergesenes,[a] ***Demonic psychopaths*** there met him two[b] [men] possessed with devils, coming out of the tombs, ◄ exceeding fierce, so that no man might pass by that way.	***Meeting one wild man*** **1** And they came over unto the other side of the sea, into the country of the Gadarenes.[a] ***Demonic psychopath*** **2** And when he was come out of the ship, immediately there met him out of the tombs◄ a man[b] with an unclean spirit, ►*They were in both the tombs and the city terrifying everyone.* ***Living among the dead*** **3** Who had *his* dwelling among the tombs; and no man could bind him, no, not with chains: **4** Because that he had been often bound with fetters and chains, and the chains had been plucked asunder by him, and the fetters broken in pieces: neither could any *man* tame him. **5** And always, night and day, he was in the mountains, and in the tombs, crying, and cutting himself with stones. **6** But when he saw Jesus afar off, he ran and worshipped him,	***Meeting one wild man*** **26** And they arrived at the country of the adarenes,[a] which is over against Galilee. ***Demonic psychopath*** **27** And when he went forth to land, there met him out of the city◄ a certain man,[b] which had devils long time, and ware no clothes, neither abode in *any* house, ***Living among the dead*** but in the tombs. ◄*This reveals the super-human strength of certain demonic entities.* **28** When he saw Jesus, he cried out, and fell down before him,	
Demons recognize Jesus: ***He commands them out*** **29** And, behold, they cried out, saying, **"What have we to do with thee, Jesus, thou Son of God?**[c] **art thou come**	***Demons recognize Jesus:*** ***He commands them out*** **7** And cried with a loud voice, and said, **"What have I to do with thee, Jesus, *thou* Son of the most high God?**[c]	***Demons recognize Jesus:*** ***He commands them out*** and with a loud voice said, **"What have I to do with thee, Jesus, *thou* Son of God most high?**[c]	

Matt. 8:29–33	Mk. 5:7–14	Lk. 8:28–34	John
hither to torment us before the time?"	I adjure thee by God, that thou torment me not."	I beseech thee, torment me not."	
	8 For he said unto him, "Come out[(d)] of the man, *thou* unclean spirit."	**29** (For he had commanded the unclean spirit to come out[(d)] of the man. For oftentimes it had caught him: and he was kept bound with chains and in fetters; and he brake the bands, and was driven of the devil into the wilderness.)	
	9 And he asked him, "What *is* thy name?" And he answered, saying, **"My name *is* Legion:[(e)] for we are many."**	**30** And Jesus asked him, saying, "What is thy name?" And he said, **"Legion:"[(e)]** because many devils were entered into him.	
	10 And he besought him much that he would not send them away out of the country.	**31** And they besought him that he would not command them to go out into the deep.	
Violent reaction	*Violent reaction*	*Violent reaction*	
30 And there was a good way off from them an herd of many swine feeding.	**11** Now there was there nigh unto the mountains a great herd of swine feeding.	**32** And there was there an herd of many swine feeding on the mountain:	
31 So the devils besought him, saying, **"If thou cast us out, suffer [let] us to go away into[(f)] the herd of swine."**	**12** And all the devils besought him, saying, **"Send us into the swine, that we may enter into[(f)] them."**	and they besought him that he would suffer [let] them to enter into[(f)] them.	
32 And he said unto them, "Go." And when they were come out, they went into the herd of swine: and, behold, the whole herd of swine ran violently down a steep place into the sea,	**13** And forthwith Jesus gave them leave. And the unclean spirits went out, and entered into the swine: and the herd ran violently down a steep place into the sea, (they were about two thousand;) and were choked in the sea.	And he suffered [let] them. **33** Then went the devils out of the man, and entered into the swine: and the herd ran violently down a steep place into the lake,	
and perished in the waters.		and were choked.	
Terrified, the keepers flee	*Terrified, the keepers flee*	*Terrified, the keepers flee*	
33 And they that kept	**14** And they that fed	**34** When they that fed *them* saw what was done,	

Matt. 8:33–34	Mk. 5:14–19	Lk. 8:34–39	John
them fled,(g) and went their ways into the city, and told every thing, and what was befallen to the possessed of the devils.	the swine fled,(g) and told *it* in the city, and in the country.	they fled,(g) and went and told *it* in the city and in the country.	
	And they(h) went out to see what it was that was done. **15** And they come to Jesus, and see him that was possessed with the devil, and had the legion, sitting, and clothed, and in his right mind: and they were afraid.	**35** Then they(h) went out to see what was done; and came to Jesus, and found the man, out of whom the devils were departed, sitting at the feet of Jesus, clothed, and in his right mind: and they were afraid.	
▶ *Both singular and plural were true.*	**16** And they that saw *it* told them how it befell to him that was possessed with the devil,◀ and *also* concerning the swine.	**36** They also which saw *it* told them by what means he that was possessed of the devils◀ was healed.	
34 And, behold, the whole city came out to meet Jesus: and when they saw him,		**37** Then the whole multitude of the country of the Gadarenes round about	
"Get out of our country" they besought *him* that he would depart(i) out of their coasts. (borders) (Next chap., Matt. 9:1 in Section 49.)	*"Get out of our country"* **17** And they began to pray [request of] him to depart(i) out of their coasts. (borders)	*"Get out of our country"* besought him to depart(i) from them; for they were taken with great fear:	
	"Let me go with Jesus" **18** And when he was come into the ship,	*"Let me go with Jesus"* and he went up into the ship, and returned back again.	
	he that had been possessed with the devil	**38** Now the man out of whom the devils were departed	
	prayed [asked] him that he might be with him.(j) **19** Howbeit Jesus suffered [allowed] him not, but saith unto him,	besought him that he might be with him:(j) but Jesus sent him away, saying,	
	"Witness at home first" "Go home to thy friends, and tell them how great things the Lord hath done for thee, (k) and hath	*"Witness at home first"* **39** "Return to thine own house, and shew how great things God hath done unto thee."(k)	

380

Matt.	Mk: 5:19-20	Lk: 8:39-40	John
► *Verse 20 compared with verse 39 seems to distinguish between the various ten cities of Decapolis and the city in which was the man's home.*	had compassion on thee." 20 And he departed, and began to publish ►in Decapolis [ten cities] how great things Jesus had done for him:[l] and all *men* did marvel. (Verse 21 cont. in Section 89.)	And he went his way, and published throughout the whole city how great things Jesus had done unto him.[l] ***Jesus returns later: The converted man's work was rewarded*** 40 And it came to pass, that, when Jesus was returned,[m] the people *gladly* received him: for they were all waiting for him. (Verse 41 cont. in Section 89.)	

Footnotes–Commentary

(a) The academic harangue about the different spellings for this place and its inhabitants are another exercise in vanity. Over the progress of recorded history, thousands of names have been spelled, pronounced, and written differently. For more on this, see Section 5, footnote b, and Section 6, footnote a. Both Mark and Luke wrote it as the "country of the Gadarenes." Gadara was a city not far from the Sea of Galilee, and one of the ten cities in a vast region called Decapolis, which was mostly inhabited by Gentiles. Matthew wrote of the Gergesenes, which were people from Gergesa located about twelve miles southeast of Gadara. Messiah came into the region of *both* places and encountered a mixture of folks from the entire area. One gospel writer mentioned the people while the others named a place. This alone affirms that the writers had not agreed to impose upon their readers a prefabricated story, and that they were familiar with the country and people of which they wrote.

(b) **Two or one?** Matthew is inspired to write about two demoniacs, while Mark and Luke deal with a specific one. Luke tells us that they had originally lived in the city, while Matthew and Mark state, they were now tomb dwellers. It is incorrect that one of them ran off, and Christ healed the other. Both were saved and delivered. However, only one featured in the inspired record. This is seen in Luke's definitive words "a certain man" (verse 27). No better explanation of this so-called "contradiction" of how many men there were can be found than that in *Davies Harmony of the Gospels*, footnote page 51. It reads thus, "Mark and Luke speak of only one demoniac; Matthew of two. Something peculiar in the circumstances or character of one of these men rendered him more prominent, and led the two former evangelists to speak of him, particularly. However, their language does not exclude another." No sooner had our Lord disembarked and set foot on the shore, than these naked homicidal men burst upon the scene, galloping about, ranting and raving. What did the apostles think? Due to the seriousness of this dramatic event, the following points have been listed for consideration:

1. This was *real* history. Certain doctors of theology, science, and "greatly learned psychiatrists" tell us that the superstitious Jews described these two "deranged madmen" as being demon possessed. Theological skeptics say they were mentally ill. It is sure that he who denies divine inspiration also denies the reality of Satan and demon spirits, hence the origin of their problem. Those who relegate *all* such happenings to folklore are wrong. A good example of this is found in William Barclay's *The Gospel of Mark*, page 119, where he wrote that it is not important if we believe in demon possession or not, and then wrote about Legion having a disordered mind. Despite Barclay's terrible unbelief in this truth, Legion's mind *was* clearly disordered by the power of indwelling evil spirits who tormented him into fits of wild madness and immoral insanity, accompanied by super-human strength. *It makes a tremendous difference, whether we believe this or not.* For other comments on the famed Scottish writer, William Barclay, see Section 16, fourth paragraph of footnote h.

2. These men were *literally* demon possessed. Evil spirits lived *inside* their human bodies. The one on whom Mark and Luke dwell is given special attention, being the fiercest. He lived among the tombs of the dead. He had superhuman strength, snapping chains and fetters, was untamable, wild and naked. For more on this, see Section 40, footnote c. The indwelling spirits endued him with extraordinary satanic power. Night and day, wild, running about the hills, crying, and screaming, his voice terrified all who heard it. Reflecting their desire to bring hurt to those who carry the image of God, the demons inflicted

his physical body with unspeakable pain and suffering. Public exposure of human nakedness has always been a tactic of demons, to demoralize and shame the temple of God. Travelers dared not pass near this wild man; both life and limb were endangered. For miles in every direction, all knew of this human monster. This is not some isolated case. The mental institutions of the world are filled with thousands in similar conditions. However, time and experience show God's servants that not all cases of demon possession are this vicious. Also, there exists legitimate mental illness having its origin in genuine human maladies, blunt trauma, and so on. To distinguish between the demonic and the physical is the most serious duty of any who are involved in these things. To confuse the two has often resulted in disaster for the victim seeking help.

3. Note both *singular* and *plural* among these demonic entities. Among the fiercest types of evil spirit possession, there is a chief demon in command of others dwelling within the physical body of the victim. In this case, the superior demon gave his name as "Legion" (Mk. 5:9). In so doing, he drops from singular "my name," to the plural, "we are many." A legion was a division in the Roman army. At the time of Christ, it consisted of about six thousand men. In time, the word came to signify a large number without exact numeric determination. Legion stated that he and the others constituted thousands of evil spirits, which dwelt *inside* this man's physical body. He was their chief spokesman. Thus, we discover the *source* of the poor man's titanic strength, immoral nakedness, infliction of pain, dwelling in habitats with the dead, screaming, and wild; no man could tame him. The root of his problems was singularly spiritual, not physical. His wild anatomical antics and super strength were caused by the satanic entities. For an earlier case of this move from singular to plural, see Section 40, second paragraph of footnote d.

4. The Savior only talked with the demon named "Legion." In some cases, indwelling demons will audibly speak through the mouth of their captives. They sometime give their names, which range from weird to the wonderful. Months before this encounter, Christ had informed the people, "The strong man of the house must be bound" before his house can be spoiled or cleaned out (Matt. 12:28-29). Now, Messiah had commanded Legion, the source of all suffering in the body of this man to come out of him (Mk. 5:8). He was binding the strong spirit in command of this battered human house! With this command from the Savior, all others had to surrender their grounds and flee their dwelling.

5. The demons moved *from* the man into the swine at the command of Jesus. Mk. 5:13, reads that there were some two thousand hogs present. Luke 8:32 tells that they were feeding on the mountain. It is known among pig farmers that hogs *cannot* run down a hill. All scoffers of these terrible events will have to reckon with the hogs and God! One cannot charm or entice swine to run down hill, leap over a precipice, and kill themselves. Matt. 8:32 records that they ran "violently down a steep place into the sea." Here, we see a demonic transference explained in the words "Then went the devils out of the man and entered into the swine" (Lk. 8:33). Evil spirits can shift from one dwelling into another and increase their number in the process (Matt. 12:43-45). Regardless of the move, their final intent is to inflict pain and death. For a well-balanced and helpful work on the subject of demonology and believers, see *Demon Possession and the Christian,* by C. F. Dickason. For an excellent summary of this subject, see *Scofield Reference Bible,* page 1004, footnote 1.

(c) **Mk. 5:7. "Son of the most high God."** All three gospel writers record that the evil spirits *knew* who Jesus Christ was. They had confessed Him as the Son of God from the early days of His ministry. This is stated in Section 40, footnote d, yet the custodians of the Jewish religion rejected Him! "The Son of God" or "Son of the most high" was among the supreme titles given by the Jews for their Messiah. Later, we hear it in the form of a question from the lips of the high priest during the trial of Christ (Matt. 26:63). The scorning Jews repeated this again during His crucifixion (Matt. 27:39-40).

2p-"Adjure thee." Note these same words coming from the mouth of the high priest during the trial of Jesus! See Section 181, Matt. 26:63, footnote g. Is there a link between the two?

3p-"Torment me not before the time." These verses reveal that demons know a day of judgment is coming, and they will be confined to the flames of eternal suffering forever. Every hell-denying cult shadowed under the umbrella of Christianity, had better listen to these demons regarding the duration of torment. At the climax of human history, Satan and all his workers will be cast into the lake of fire to suffer forever (Matt. 25:41 with Rev. 20:10). These demons were alarmed at the presence of the Son of God and feared that the dreadful day of doom was coming upon them. All malignant, dark spirits of evil believe in hell and know ultimately they will be confined there. It is of interest that the term, "What have we to do with thee" was a typical Jewish expression. It signified an abrupt refusal of some request and was employed by the rabbis in rejecting the arguments of their opponents. Now, the demons speak the language of the Christ hating rabbis but this time they confess to the truth. For a review of twenty-one things that men will experience in hell, refer to Section 103, number 8, fourth paragraph, under footnote g.

(d) Obviously, the evil spirits had to be *in* the man before they could come out. The words "oftentimes it had caught him," speak of the sudden and unexpected attacks of demons upon their helpless captives. In some cases, they have liberty to come and go upon or within their victims causing unspeakable suffering and pain. There are cases where indwelling demons give their captives a time of reprieve, seemingly, the prisoner is free; and then suddenly he is again writhing under the horrible agony of satanic attacks. Such "cat and mouse" tactics reveal the hatred of evil spirits and Satan toward humans and their desire to inflict every pain and suffering possible. Christ said, "The thief cometh not, but for to steal, and to kill, and to destroy" (John 10:10).

2p-The great mistake. How awful when a Christian counselor, minister, or missionary credits *all* visible physical maladies to the work of Satan and makes no allowance for legitimate body illness. This ill-informed diagnosis has left a wake of suffering, frustration, and sorrow among thousands who reach out for help. There are times when genuine physical symptoms may be identical with those produced by indwelling evil entities. In such cases, the highest form of caution must be exercised without a quick diagnosis from the counselor assisting the victim. No person should ever be told, "You have demons," unless there is *incontrovertible evidence* to substantiate such an awful affirmation. Refer to our Lord's first recorded encounter with demons in Section 40.

(e) **"My name is Legion for we are many."** This man's real name had been absorbed into a hideous tyranny of foul spirits under whose influence his own personality was subdued. It is a fact of history that demons use thousands of names and titles: sometimes they signify the work(s) they perform through and in the bodies of their victims. The author, over the years, has heard the following names from the mouths of those who were possessed by demons. They include "Hatred, death, tiger, fox, fish, prayer, headache, liar, jealously, and smoke. Others were, cat, King Fisal, Satan, Devil, sodomy, cry, reading, church, pornography, witchcraft, neck, back, kill, twin, big chief blue beast, Ricardo, hand, throat, communism, socialism" and even "Jesus." There are thousands of others. At times, chilling and dramatic voice changes may be heard coming from the mouths of those who are possessed. (Could this be the reason that many male homosexuals have such obvious feminine tones in their voices?) These range from soft female whisperings, from men who are often associated with homosexuality, whining, growling, hissing, and violent sobbing, to ear-bursting screams and roars like the African lion. A young mother at a church just outside Pretoria, South Africa slipped into something like a coma and actually had a loud fish tank bubbling sound in her throat. This demon entity inside her body spoke audibly through her mouth and said his name was "fish." The evil spirits spoke in four different languages through the voice of this woman. She had learned none of these languages. She had purchased a divider curtain from a Hindu priest who had dedicated it to the spirits. It was hung in her house!

2p-Satanists infiltrating churches. A real Christian psychologist, Dr. James G. Friesen in his groundbreaking work, *Uncovering the Mystery of MPD*, pages 279-280, tells of satanic cult groups that train selected persons to infiltrate effective churches, and then work their way into positions of recognition and leadership. At the right time, they will commit suicide in the church office or amid the services if possible! Such a disaster would discredit the church, empty the building, and bring legal challenges upon the leadership of the congregation. Friesen clearly demonstrates that the *final* answer to this shocking plot is the Lord Jesus Christ! Such ghastly actions reveal again the power of Satan, his cults and demons, and their fierce hatred for true churches that are doing the work of Christ. The story recorded of Legion is but one of the untold millions that have literally occurred over the course of history. Most are not reported. And they are here to this present hour. For more on these awful things, see Section 27, fourth paragraph of foot note k.

(f) **"Go,"** was the Savior's command (Matt. 8:32). The devils obeyed His command. See number 5, under footnote b above. This calls to mind the command of God to Satan in Job 1:12 and 2:6 where he went forth to torment Job. Eventually, this became Satan's defeat. Though mighty in power, his strength is *not equal* to his wrath and hatred for God and mankind. Later, Christ spoiled (defeated and conquered) Satan in His death, burial, and resurrection (Col. 2:14-15 with Rev. 1:17-18).

(g) Matthew wrote that the evil spirits went *out* of the men into the swine (verse 32). These invisible entities exited the human body and sped through the air into the bodies of the unaware beasts, though they were a good way off. Suddenly, the several thousand hogs broke out into squealing, bolting, snorting, and madly stampeded down hill and over the precipice into the ocean below. Satan bears fierce malice towards *all* of God's creation, both animate and inanimate. However, Adam's race is his chief interest.

2p-The swine keepers fled in terror! There has been great debate over who were the owners of these animals. Some argue that the Jews would never traffic in unclean creatures based on Lev. 11. However, as had been pointed out at this era in Hebrew history, the Jews were corrupt politically, decadent morally and apostate religiously. The Talmud states in tractate, Baba Kama 82b, "Cursed be the man who would breed swine." Yet, *Gill's Commentary*, vol. 7, page 86, mentions Jews, who were allowed to purchase items such as fat or lard made from hogs, but not the actual flesh itself. Talmud tractate, Sabbath 90b, speaks of the Jews using "stiff bristles of swine." Others believe that these animals were sold to the Romans, who relished pork and paid great prices to obtain it. Regardless, whoever these swine breeders were, apostate Jews or pork loving Gentiles, they were terrified at the power and authority of Christ over the devils that had controlled these poor men. Instead of fleeing from the insane demoniac, they now fled from the presence of Christ, who had delivered and saved him (Lk. 8:34). *Some men make the stick with which God beats them.*

(h) Several hours after the ordeal, thousands of people, curious, and cautious return to the scene. Lk. 8:37 reads, "the whole multitude of the country" came out. The report of this miracle spread everywhere. Stunned and amazed, the people see the *former* maniac, properly clothed and in his right mind. Surely, he had bathed his bloody, filthy body. Upon receiving clothing from one of the disciples, Legion dressed himself and sat before his newfound Lord. The wisdom and teaching of this wonderful Man blessed his soul with joy. Face shining, eyes clear, and countenance radiant, he gazed upon the One who had delivered him from Satan's fierce power. *The carpenter from Galilee had tamed the demoniac.* What a triumph for the grace of God!

(i) **"They besought him to depart."** This is one of the saddest statements in the gospels. Incredible as it seems the thousands of people gathered on the scene and pled for Christ to leave their country! See footnote l below. Lk. 8:37 reveals they were greatly terrified. Amazing indeed: they were more afraid of the blessed Son of God than the devils that dwelt in that place. How twisted and warped are the values of men without Christ, God's Word, and the indwelling Holy Spirit. Did some of the demons left the swine and enter the people? Instead of inviting Messiah into their cities as the Samaritans had done months prior, they wanted Him out of their country. Angered but fearful, they cared more for the swine and financial profit than their souls. This crazy mob of pig lovers mirrors the unsaved today. It is no uncommon thing for men to desire for Christ to depart from them. His holy presence and inspired Word greatly disturbs the wicked in their pursuit for the gains and pleasures of sin. False religions, base morals, and sinister politics may give the Son of God a nod or faint smile, but they hate His demands for a changed life, reflected in conduct, speech, private, and public life.

(j) How beautiful beyond words! His heart bursting with thankfulness, this new man sought to go with Jesus across Galilee. Men and women who have been saved from notorious and highly vicious sins relate well to the aspirations of this *former* possessed lunatic. "O blessed Jesus, we give our lives to thee," has been the prayer of millions delivered from the terrible bondage of sin and Satan.

(k) **Every man is saved to serve be it short or long term**. Now, this man's assignment was to return to his city, family, kindred, and friends to tell them of Jesus. The Samaritan woman did this and seemingly brought her city to Christ. The Church of God suffers greatly from the appalling lack of those who witness of the great things Christ has done in their lives. See footnote m below for two examples of converts witnessing for the Savior.

(l) Whoever this fellow was, he immediately went to work and fulfilled the commission given by his newfound Lord. Luke writes that Christ instructed him to return to his "own house" (Lk. 8:39). Did he have a wife and children, brothers, sisters or what? Imagination can run riot at the thoughts of this fellow as he returns "home *again*" saved, delivered and a new creation in Christ. The neighborhood was shaken. Everyone heard "Legion has returned!" "Decapolis" had reference to ten cities over a vast area, and these became his mission field. For details on this large region, refer to Section 42, second paragraph of footnote h, and footnote a above. Like all who are seriously demonized, during his bondage to the savage spirits, he was intermittently aware of his condition but helpless to free himself. He had been unchained from the power of Satan and declares the most amazing story ever heard across Decapolis! Vast crowds stopped to listen, being filled with the fear of God. One can easily believe that thousands gathered to hear him speak; many of them having seen and heard him in the wild animal–like state of his former life. Mark wrote so aptly "and all *men* did marvel" (verse 20). Oh, the amazing grace of God!

2p-Lk. 8: 39. God hath done and Jesus hath done. In this statement, the Savior claims equality with God, for He as God performed this amazing miracle.

(m) His work of witnessing was not in vain! Months later, when Christ *returned* to this district, we read of how "multitudes" upon hearing this news flocked out to meet Him. Luke wrote that the people were "all waiting for him" (verse 40). Prior, they had begged Him to leave their country as seen in footnote i above. Now, everyone wanted to see that wonderful Person, who had so gloriously changed Legion.

2p-Tomba the martyr. In 1975, while preaching (through three different interpreters) under a tent outside Salisbury, Rhodesia (now Harare, Zimbabwe), an African in his early twenties was saved out of a terrible pagan background. This young man overflowed with the joy of sins forgiven! The next day he left Salisbury and walked eastward for seven days into the neighboring country of Mozambique, which was under the rule of a Marxist, anti-God government. Tomba made this hazardous journey to find his brother and share what Christ had done in his life. After several weeks, he was found. He received the Savior that had so radically changed his brother. Word spread of this among the natives; he was arrested and vanished in one of their infamous prisons. Tomba was never heard from again. As it was with Legion some two thousand years ago, and that African youth, it remains the same today. Nothing has changed except men who have *not* been changed by the power of the new birth.

3p-Where are the men and women so wonderfully transformed by God's grace? They are the Christians, who do not *overly* care for life or limb, but only that others may also know their Lord. We of the western world are suffering because the "Legions," and "Tombas," are disappearing from the local church scene and amid an unsaved society. In the lands where extreme Islam rules or Antichrist paganism, Christians, who have nothing, can do just about anything as they bring others to Christ. The great missionary of the early church wrote, "As sorrowful, yet always rejoicing; as poor, yet making many rich; as having nothing, and *yet* possessing all things" (2 Cor. 6:10).

The two twelve's. Christ raises a twelve-year-old girl* from the dead. A woman touches the hem of His garment and is healed of a twelve-year-old ailment.

Though the Messiah raised hundreds from the dead (John 21:25), yet Scripture only mentions three of these miracles. Below is the second one. For more on this unique subject, see asterisk under main heading, Section 61.

Capernaum

Matt. 9:18–20	Mk. 5:21–26	Lk. 8:41–43	John
A little girl dies **18** While he spake these things[a] unto them,			
	21 And when Jesus was passed over[b] again by ship unto the other side, much people gathered unto him: and he was nigh unto the sea.		
	A little girl dies	*A little girl dies*	
behold, there came a certain ruler,[c]	**22** And, behold, there cometh one of the rulers[c] of the synagogue, Jairus by name; and when he saw him, he fell at his feet,[d]	**41** And, behold, there came a man named Jairus, and he was a ruler[c] of the synagogue: and he fell down at Jesus' feet,[d]	
and worshipped him,[d] saying, "My daughter is even now dead:• but come and lay thy hand upon her, and she shall live."[e]	**23** And besought him greatly, saying, "My little daughter lieth at the point of death:• *I pray thee, come and lay thy hands on her, that she may be healed;* and she shall live;"[e]	and besought him that he would come into his house: •*Verses 18 and 23. No doubt the distraught father said both things to Jesus.*	
		42 For he had one only daughter, about twelve years of age, and she lay a dying.	
19 And Jesus arose, And followed him, and *so did* his disciples. (Cont. at ▶ in verse 23 below)	**24** And *Jesus* went with him; and much people followed him, and thronged[f] him. (Cont. at ▶ in verse 35 below)	But as he went the people thronged[f] him. (Cont. at ▶ in verse 49 below)	
A woman healed **20** And, behold, a woman, which was diseased with an issue of blood twelve years,	*A woman healed* **25** And a certain woman, which had an issue of blood twelve years, **26** And had suffered many things of many physicians, and had spent all that she had, and was nothing bettered, but rather grew worse,	*A woman healed* **43** And a woman having an issue of blood twelve years, which had spent all her living upon physicians, neither could be healed of any,	

Matt. 9:20–21	Mk. 5:27–33	Lk. 8:44–47	John
came behind *him,* and touched the hem of his garment:(g) **21** For she said within(h) herself, "If I may but touch his garment, I shall be whole."	**27** When she heard of Jesus, came in the press behind, and touched his garment.(g) **28** For she said,(h) "If I may touch but his clothes, I shall be whole." **29** And straightway the fountain of her blood was dried up;(i) and she felt in *her* body that she was healed of that plague. ***The strange question*** **30** And Jesus, im- mediately knowing in himself that virtue had gone out of him, turned him about in the press, [crowds] and said, "Who touched my clothes?"(j) **31** And his disciples said unto him, "Thou seest the multitude thronging(k) thee, and sayest thou, 'Who touched me?'" **32** And he looked round about to see her that had done this thing. **33** But the woman fearing and trembling,(l) ***Her unashamed public confession*** knowing what was done in her, came and fell down before him, and told him all the truth.	**44** Came behind *him,* and touched the border of his garment:(g) and immediately her issue of blood stanched. (i) (stopped). ***The strange question*** **45** And Jesus said, "Who touched me?"(j) When all denied, Peter and they that were with him said, "Master, the multitude throng(k) thee and press *thee,* and sayest thou, 'Who touched me?'" **46** And Jesus said, "Somebody hath touched me: for I perceive that virtue is gone out of me." **47** And when the woman saw that she was not hid, she came trembling,(l) ***Her unashamed public confession*** and falling down before him, she declared unto him before all the people for what cause she had touched him, and how she was healed immediately.	

Matt. 9:22–24	Mk. 5:34–40	Lk. 8:48–53	John
The wonderful news **22** But Jesus turned him about, and when he saw her, he said, "Daughter, be of good comfort; thy faith hath made thee whole."[(m)] And the woman was made whole from that hour.	***The wonderful news*** **34** And he said unto her, "Daughter, thy faith hath made thee whole;[(m)] go in peace, and be whole of thy plague."	***The wonderful news*** **48** And he said unto her, "Daughter, be of good comfort: thy faith hath made thee whole;[(m)] go in peace."_	
	►**35** While he yet spake, there came from the ruler of the synagogue's *house certain* which said, "Thy daughter is dead: why troublest thou the Master any further?" **36** As soon as Jesus heard the word that was spoken, he saith unto the ruler of the synagogue, "Be not afraid, only believe."[(n)]	►**49** While he yet spake, there cometh one from the ruler of the synagogue's *house*, saying to him, "Thy daughter is dead; trouble not the Master." **50** But when Jesus heard *it,* he answered him, saying, "Fear not: believe[(n)] only, and she shall be made whole."	
	Jesus picks His company **37** And he suffered [let] no man to follow him, save Peter, and James, and John the brother of James.	***Jesus picks His company*** **51** And when he came into the house, he suffered [let] no man to go in, save Peter, and James, and John, and the father and the mother of the maiden.	
Musical scorners[(o)] ►**23** And when Jesus came into the ruler's house, and saw the minstrels [pipers] and the people making a noise, **24** He said unto them, "Give place: for the maid is not dead, but sleepeth."[(p)]	***Musical scorners***[(o)] **38** And he cometh to the house of the ruler of the synagogue, and seeth the tumult, and them that wept and wailed greatly. **39** And when he was come in, he saith unto them, "Why make ye this ado, and weep? The damsel is not dead, but sleepeth."[(p)]	***Musical scorners***[(o)] **52** And all wept, and bewailed her: but he said, "Weep not; she is not dead, but sleepeth."[(p)]	
The scorners expelled And they laughed him to scorn.[(q)]	***The scorners expelled*** **40** And they laughed him to scorn.[(q)]	***The scorners expelled*** **53** And they laughed him to scorn,[(q)] knowing that she was dead.	

Matt. 9:25-26	Mk. 5:40-43	Lk. 8:54-56	John
25 But when the people were put forth, he went in,	But when he had put them all out, he taketh the father and the mother of the damsel, and them that were with him, and entereth in where the damsel was lying.	54 And he put them all out,	
The child is raised and took her by the hand,(r) and the maid arose.(s)	***The child is raised*** 41 And he took the damsel by the hand,(r) and said unto her, "Tal-i-tha cu-mi;" which is, being interpreted, "Damsel, I say unto thee, arise." 42 And straightway the damsel arose,(s) and walked;(t) for she was *of the age* of twelve years.	***The child is raised*** and took her by the hand,(r) and called, saying, "Maid, arise." 55 And her spirit came again, and she arose(s) straightway: and he commanded to give her meat.(t) (food). ◄	
	Overwhelmed and amazed And they were astonished with a great astonishment. 43 And he charged them straitly that no man should know it;(u) and commanded that something should be given her to eat. ► (Next chap., Mk. 6:1 cont. in Section 91.)	***Overwhelmed and amazed*** 56 And her parents were astonished: but he charged them that they should tell no man what was done.(u) (Next. chap., Lk. 9:1 cont. in Section 59.) ► *Luke gives Jesus' command about feeding the child in verse 55 above. Mark records it just afterwards in verse 43. Matthew does not mention it. This difference is another mark of divine inspiration.*	
Everyone hears of Jesus 26 And the fame hereof went abroad into all that land.(v) (Verse 27 cont. in Section 90.)			

Footnotes-Commentary

(a) This passage reads that Jairus came to Jesus while He was giving His discourse on the wine skins during Matthew's great banquet supper. However, according to Mark and Luke, Jairus did not appear, begging help for his child until immediately *after* Jesus' return some time later from the eastern side of Lake Galilee. Lk. 5:33 reads "And they said unto him." The pronoun "they" apparently has an antecedent back to the speakers in verse 30, which were the scribes and Pharisees. In verse 30, the question was asked about Christ's disciples "eating and drinking." Further on in the context (verse 33), this same question was put again. This time the disciples of John are included in the "eating and drinking" controversy. Therefore, the same event is being given right through Lk. 5:29-39. Hence, all these things seemingly occurred at the same time. The harmonization that places Jairus coming to Jesus amid His message on the wine skins has merit. Yet it seems more natural, that the freshly converted ex publican would *immediately* give the great feast in honor of his newly found Messiah. It was during *this feast* that the scribes and Pharisees attacked the disciples of Christ over the issue of mixing with sinners. The syntax of Luke as *conjectured* above seems to demonstrate this is the better chronology for these events.

(b) As stated in footnote a above, this "passing over" has reference to Christ departing from the shores of eastern Galilee after His encounter with Legion, and *returning* to the western side and the city of Capernaum. Mark reveals in this verse that many people lined the shore waiting and watching for Messiah's return. No doubt, the word about Legion had already reached their ears. The curious crowds watched as the Lord Jesus and His little band of twelve stepped ashore again at Capernaum. See footnote f below for more on this thought.

(c) The synagogue. "Have any of the rulers . . . believed on him?" This was the chief question of the Sanhedrin (John 7:48). The answer was "yes!" Moreover, here is the prime example. Capernaum, being a large city had more than one synagogue. Matthew used the term "archon" (ruler) to describe Jairus' position in the Jewish religious community (verses 18, 23). Yet, Mark in verses 22 and 38 employed the word "archisynagogue" (denoting a wide variety of duties, even to the handling of finance). Hostile critics jump on these different terms to point out "another contradiction in Scripture." More learned assumptions! Jairus served in both capacities in his local synagogue. The origin of the synagogue may be traced (at least) back to the inter-testament period, but surely further. Some four hundred years before Christ, Ezra and Nehemiah left a settled form of government in the land. Ten men of "learning and leisure" were sufficient to start a synagogue. The number ten was taken from the spies sent out by Moses, but killed by God for their unbelief (Num. 14:36-38). Because only two of those sent out by Moses believed God (Joshua and Caleb), and ten doubted, the rabbis supposedly selected the number ten as a replacement of the unfaithful in Israel. These ten Jews chosen for the synagogue became leaders in the Jewish community. The term "ruler" as applied to Jairus had reference to one of the ten who had charge of organizational affairs in the synagogue. Jairus would be known as "chazan," "bishop," "overseer" or "angel" of the congregation. (We see how these titles were carried over into the leadership of the New Testament churches in Phil. 1:1; Rev. 2:1, 8, 12, 18; and 3:1, 7, 14.) He would appoint specific duties, such as reading Scripture, reciting the phylacteries, passing the ark of the Torah among the people. Jairus was honored and respected within the Jewish community at Capernaum and held a position of prominence. See footnote d below. He had believed on the Lord Jesus as his Messiah and Savior. For a comprehensive and enlightening study of the synagogue, see *The Ancient Synagogue, Second Edition. The First Thousand Years*, by Lee I. Levine. This classic work covers any angle of this subject.

2p-The leadership of Israel consisted of a council, elders, and priests who formed something of an ecclesiastical and civic court later called the Sanhedrin. Among other things, their main duty was to interpret and enforce the Law of Moses. Later, their consuming duty was to assure the strict practice of the oral law or traditions. In the early stages, they were known as the Great Synagogue. It supposedly consisted of 120 members. From this body ultimately came the Sanhedrin and scribes ("sopherim") who propagated the grand myth that the law of God for Israel had been given in two forms. *God's Word to Israel was contained only in their Old Testament.* Below is a brief description of the present day major Jewish religious literature:

1. **The written Torah Law.** "Torah" means "teaching." Originally, it consisted of Genesis, Exodus, Leviticus, Numbers, and Deuteronomy. It was codified into 613 commandments. This was by physical count of every law within the Torah. They are called "Taryag motzvos." These 613 precepts were then divided into 248 positive commandments, representing the numerous and diverse parts of the human body, and 365 prohibitions representing the days of the year. The famed Rabbi Maimonides (died A.D 1204) seems to be credited with this codification of Torah. However, some Jews argue that it was used before the Christian era and some think they find this in the Talmud. Thus, 613 laws are laid down in the code of Moses. This count is valid today among Orthodox Hebrews, yet nothing whatsoever is written of this in their Scriptures. It is another rabbinical conjecture. To this moment, Jews adamantly defend this myth as though it were established truth. To Jews, there is no "Old Testament" as Christians use the term. The New Testament is not a part of their canon of Scripture called Tanakh. In most services, Jews still use parchment scrolls with Scripture written thereon. These scrolls were not to be touched. The text is read using a pointer called a "yad," meaning "hand." This instrument is shaped like the hand with the index finger pointing. By the time of Jesus on earth, the term "law" embraced not only the Torah, but also the entire Old Testament cannon. Note this also in Section 176, footnote t. He endorsed the entire Hebrew Scriptures in Matt. 23:36; from Abel in their first book to the last book in 2 Chron. 24:20-21.

2. **The oral law** became known as the "tradition of the elders" or "Mishna." The word probably means "second instruction." This had reference to a second part of the Law of Moses. In Jewish tradition, these were said to have been *verbally* given to Moses on Mt. Sinai. They were (supposedly) passed down orally to all future generations of Jews for the next fifteen hundred years! The Talmud, which contains the oral law, is divided into two major parts, Mishna meaning the text, and Gemara, which is the rabbinical exposition of the Mishna text. These two divisions are subdivided into six parts, voluminous in content. These contain sixty-three tractates, or chapters. Both parts together (Mishna-Gemara) are usually called the Talmud. The Mishna is divided into six sections called "sedarim" or "orders" in English. These are oral laws and contain *thousands* of copious details not found written in the Torah. By the time of Christ, these were made superior to the great Torah Law by the scribes, who had control over the people. See all of Section 96, where the Lord Jesus clashed with the scribes and Pharisees over their traditions or oral laws, and what He said about them.

3. **The distorted *Talmud*.** Despite the exaggerated and preposterous claims in the Talmud, it has value. If one wanted to study all the Torah said about the Sabbath, he would need to read Exodus, Leviticus, Numbers, Deuteronomy, plus all the prophets. However, in the Talmud, everything the Old Testament states about Sabbath is found under the tractate, "Shabbat," which is Hebrew for Sabbath. It is stressed that the rabbis added thousands of silly rules and commandments (oral laws) to the Sabbath not found in the Torah of Moses or the prophets. For examples of the sheer blasphemy of parts of the Talmud, refer to Section 6, third paragraph of footnote d. Oddly, the Sadducees fiercely rejected the oral law as seen in selected portions of the Talmud such as tractates Nedarim 25a and Rosh HaShana 22a. The Pharisees defended it. On the argument that "Jesus upheld the oral law, and taught that His disciples and all Christians were to live by parts of the Torah Law," refer to Section 45, footnote b.

3p-**Two *Talmuds*.** The word in singular form means, "To teach or instruct." Historically, there are two *Talmuds,* the *Babylonian,* and *Jerusalem*. The former is the larger of the two and counted as authoritative. It is filled with abstruse, difficult, hair-splitting details regarding Jewish customs, laws, and thousands of fine points. Opposite to this, the *Jerusalem* Talmud is a vast work, but simpler, brief, to the point, and overflows with information about archaeology, geography, and history. The total Talmud is something of a mini library and was printed in the earlier versions in some four hundred volumes! The laws written in the Talmud were called "fences" and were built around each of the 613 written laws of the Torah Law. The contents of the Talmud began to be collected and slowly put into print in approximately 220 A.D. at Tiberius. This was long after the destruction of Jerusalem and the temple in A.D. 70. Prior to the fall of Jerusalem, the Jews boasted that the contents of their Talmud were strictly committed to the minds of the scribes and spoken verbally to the people. However, this typical rabbinical exaggeration is far fetched. The purpose of these fabricated traditions was to prevent future generations of Jews from getting to the actual written Torah Laws and breaking them. For example, there were some three thousand "fences" or oral laws built around the fourth commandment, "Remember the Sabbath day, to keep it holy" (Ex. 20:8 with Deut. 5:12). Rabbis believed that no Jew could possibly get through this many "fences" to the *actual commandments* of Moses and then break them.

4p-**Midrash.** Thought to be compiled between A.D. 400 and 1200, this work is second to the Talmud. Midrash means, "Search or explain." It is a commentary on the Hebrew Old Testament. It reeks with impossible and silly exaggerations. One explains why Moses was not a successful public speaker and needed Aaron to help him. It teaches that he put coals in his mouth as a child; this demonstrated that he was not covetous. The Midrash is divided into two parts, the Halakah meaning comments on the Torah Law, and Haggada with comments on entire Old Testament, including parables, proverbs, and Jewish folklore.

5p-**Tosefta.** Compiled in approximately A.D. 200 and meaning, "supplement." It is something of a commentary on the Talmud and filled with Jewish traditions similar to those in the Talmud. The Tosefta towers over all Hebrew religious literature. It is counted higher than their written Scriptures or Tanakh. To this day, pious Jews put supreme affection on their Talmud, even above their Old Testament.

6p-The imposition of these endless oral inventions upon the Torah Law or Word of God began several centuries before Christ was born. *The religious leaders hated Christ because He rejected and publicly condemned their oral laws; these had replaced the great Torah.* This vast collection remains an invaluable tool in Bible exegesis, but must be read with the greatest of caution due to some of its ungodly contents. Some parts of it in the older unexpunged versions are nothing less than shocking blasphemy. As mentioned in number 3 above, see Section 6, third paragraph of footnote d for details on this point. Its pages offer to us insight into Jewish history, philosophy, traditions, religion, and many other subjects. They speak of the extravagant luxury and excess of the final days of the Hebrew state before her destruction at the hands of pagan Rome. It mentions such delicacies as "Spanish fish, Cretan apples, Bithynian cheese, Egyptian lentils and beans, Greek pumpkins, Italian wine, Median beer, garments from India, shirts from Cilicia and veils from Arabia." For a brief and easy to understand explanation of the Talmud, void of the standard academic claptrap, see *The Trial of Jesus from a Lawyer's Standpoint*, pages 73-90. 1957 edition, by attorney Walter M. Chandler. This classic volume was first published in 1925, after the *conversion* of its author, a member of the New York Bar Association.

(d) **"Fell at his feet and worshipped him."** An extraordinary statement! Now, a prominent Hebrew, ruler in his local synagogue, bows down and worships the carpenter from Nazareth! No pious Jew would dare worship a man. What was behind Jairus' respect to the Lord Jesus? This was far more than an act of respect normally paid to a great teacher. Jairus and his family were *already* believers in the Messiah, hence the reason for his worship of the Lord Jesus. Refer to first paragraph of footnote c above for more on this great Jewish personality.

(e) How did Jairus know Jesus could heal the sick? See footnote g below. Again, here is confirmation that news of Messiah's mighty works had spread over the entire nation and further abroad. Christ had previously healed a man's withered hand in a Capernaum synagogue as seen in Section 54. Earlier, He had physically been forced out of the synagogue at Nazareth. News of these things had spread over the country. Jairus had heard of these things and (no doubt) much more about Christ. Luke is specific to inform Theophilus, the person to whom he sent this letter, that the little girl was twelve years of age. It is a curious note that the woman with the issue of blood had been in that condition twelve years (Matt. 9:20), and the child who had died was about twelve (Mk. 5:42). Swift flies the sands of life except in the hours of suffering and pain. Trouble and sorrows come to both young and old; the ravage of sin spares no one. Jesus was the answer in both cases, a truism that remains valid to this day.

(f) Not only the disciples, but also innumerable crowds flocked to Christ. We have continually noted this in the four gospels. Refer to Section 41, footnote d, and Section 73, footnote b, along with footnote b above for more on Jesus and the crowds that followed Him.

(g) As with Jairus, this woman also had heard of the Messiah and His power to heal. See footnote e above. She had suffered from continual menstrual flooding. It was regarded as incurable. All her life's savings had been spent on the physicians, but to no avail. This is not a condemnation of medical practitioners as various "divine healers" assert. According to the Torah Law, she was thus rendered unclean; and if she touched anyone or anything, it instantly became unclean for the remainder of that day. Her being in public was strictly forbidden. See Lev. 15:19-33 for the details.

2p-Verse 20. "Touched the hem of his garment." Jewish males in the time of Christ and some today, especially in Israel, still wear tassels or fringes hanging from the four corners of their prayer shawls. The four corners reminded pious Jews of the divisions of earth (north, south, east, west) and in whatever direction he turned, Jehovah was there. This garment article or tallit was something like a blanket or mantle thrown over the shoulders and left hanging down about the body. It was made of wool or linen and was a hand's breadth shorter in length than the under garment. They were worn in obedience to Num. 15:37-41 and Deut. 22:12. The tassels were made of blue and white cords woven together. Each tassel was called a "tzitzit" or fringe. Tying the tzitzit is a delicate practice involving all sorts of meanings and using the numbers 7, 8, 11, and 13. The fine arrangements of each thread and knot were woven to symbolize the 613 commandments of the Torah Law. See numbers 1 and 2 under footnote c above for details on this subject.

3p-In modern day synagogues where the tallit is worn, there is a rack carrying them for visitors. Before wrapping themselves in the tallit, a Jew will recite an ancient prayer for blessing. This is seen on the collar band as it is opened. The embroidered words read in part, "Blessed are you, Lord our God, Ruler of the universe, who makes us holy with commandments . . ." The purpose of this is to remind Israelis of the commandments of God. A. T. Robertson wrote, "The Jews actually counted the two words *Jehovah One*, from the number of twisted white cords or threads" in each tassel. See Robertson's, *Word Pictures in the New Testament*, vol. 1, page 74. Today, the prayer shawl is the most sacred piece of clothing for pious Hebrews. It is presented to the child when he is circumcised and carried through life. Later, in Section 159, Matt. 23:5, footnote e, the Lord Jesus *severely* reprimanded the scribes and Pharisees, because they greatly enlarged the tassels on their garments in their outward show of hypocrisy.

4p-It was one of these "holy tassels" hanging from our Lord's garment that this woman dared touch! They were considered the most sacred part of Hebrew clothing. Her physical disorder was of such a delicate nature that she could not make a public announcement of it to the Lord Jesus. As mentioned in footnote e above, how did she know Christ could heal her? She had heard the thousands of stories about this great Man and believed He could cure her illness. News spread about her healing through the touch of a tassel on Messiah's garment. See Section 94, Matt. 14:35-36, footnote o, where weeks later, hundreds were cured the same way by touching these tassels. The tassels themselves had *no* healing power; they represented the holy Law of Moses and were an outward sign of one's dedication and loyalty. No better touch of the Messiah could be found, for the entire thrust of the Torah Law was to point men to Him. *Only* Jews would approach the Lord Jesus in this manner, for they alone understood the symbolic meaning of these objects and therefore, sought to touch them. To touch such forbidden objects as the tassels signaled one's total faith in the person wearing them.

5p-Too many corrections. In 1983, David Bivin and Roy Blizzard, Jr. published a work, *Understanding the Difficult Words of Jesus*. Like most enthusiasts, they went overboard in their efforts to help us understand the background of different Greek and Hebrew terms in Scripture. Chapter Six begins with the shocker, "The Gospels are rife with mistranslations." It then follows some thirteen pages explaining why various Scriptures are wrong and thus cannot be trusted. Chapter six ends with these amazing words "With the tools now available, no effort should be spared in correcting every mistranslation and in clarifying every misinterpretation of the inspired text." The Scriptures are "inspired" so they write, but rife with "mistranslations." What a "scholarly" blunder! Inspired in "the original," yet partly wrong in the translation. One is amazed that a Bible, so replete with errors, could be used of the Holy Spirit to bring millions to a saving knowledge of Christ in centuries gone by. Histories greatest evangelists, missionaries, teachers, and soul winners of centuries past brought multitudes to Jesus, and they used the wrong Bible. Nor did they have "tools to understand," the latest "archaeological discoveries," and "the textual studies of the past 35 years . . .?" With scholars like Bivin and Blizzard Jr., to help, perhaps in another forty years or so, we will have the right kind of Bible and can get the job done for God and unsaved mankind. Men who write such things about God's Word are not aggressive soul winners. Many of them are so ecumenically minded that they would never inquire as to the spiritual welfare of a lost stranger or neighbor. Years ago, after lecturing at a South African university, I asked a professor of theology, who busied himself demonstrating the errors of Scripture, if he had won a lost soul to Christ over the past five years. The poor man flew into a red-faced shouting rage! Finally, he blurted out, "That's a job for common Christians not for academicians." God grant us more "common Christians" and less "academicians." *An academician who does not hold to the full inspiration of Scripture is a curse to God's work.*

6p-Hebrew and Greek will not totally explain Scripture. Men who set themselves to correct the "wrong translations" of Scripture trouble the church and promote unbelief in the trustworthiness of God's Word.. Their dreams of finding the *total* meaning of all God has written in His Word via the "original languages" are illusions grandeur. One cannot dip the ocean of written divine truth dry with a Hebrew and Greek teacup! What is recorded on the pages of the Bible is sufficient and efficient to be saved, miss hell, correctly live the Christian life, bring others to Jesus, then die, and go to heaven. *No sensible person could object to explaining associated and similar meanings to any biblical word.* The problem begins when the "experts" announce, "This verse is wrong, let me give you the correct translation." After almost sixty years of the ministry among thousands of people, in different lands, the author has never won a lost soul by explaining, "the original meaning" of a word in the Hebrew or Greek. Nor has he ever known of one person who was restored in the faith by this approach. Those, who were, are the rare exceptions to the proven rule. The term so often heard from the pulpit, "The literal meaning is . . .", implies that we do not have the meaning. For more on this subject, see Section 188, the first paragraph of footnote e. Referring to the original biblical languages is acceptable if it enlarges the meaning but does not change it.

(h) "She said within herself." Only by the illumination of the Holy Spirit could Matthew have known what this woman thought in her heart. Such statements as this give the unsaved critics fits, for they have no knowledge of divine inspiration working in the hearts of the four evangelists as they wrote their individual stories of Christ's life. Why did she believe that touching Jesus' garments could bring healing? Where did she learn about the miraculous power and deeds of the wonderful Man? She, like every person in the land, knew very well the stories that had blazed over the country about Jesus. See footnote g above. The idea here is that she must make contact with Christ, and the most appropriate and nearest place was His long flowing garment. It was through her simple yet daring faith that healing came, not touching a tassel.

(i) Instant healing. This miracle explains the words Jesus later prayed to the Father that awful night before the morning of the cross, "thou hast given me power over all flesh" (John 17:2). Messiah's power over *all flesh* was demonstrated in healing this untouchable woman. What a story she had to tell!

2p-Struggling through that dense throng of pushing, shoving people, finally she was close enough to touch Him. Lunging forward in desperation, she clasped one of the tassels dangling from His garment. However, her desperate faith went further, even into His great heart. Luke wrote that Messiah responded to her healing with these strange words, "virtue is gone out of me" (Lk. 8:46). This power did not flow from Christ as fragrance did from flowers, for if so, all healed by Him would have partaken of it. We know they did not. Moreover, why was it peculiarly so with her? Here is a manifestation of God's marvelous grace. This poor woman, dejected, rejected, a social outcast, refused to allow laws, crowds, rabbis, rules, and regulations to prevent her from reaching Messiah. Her determined faith was uniquely honored as the power of true deity flowed from Christ into her tormented body. An infinitesimal flash of healing filled her ailing frame, and she was made well. Only God could do such a work as this! Infidel critics have tried every trick in the Devil's book to explain this historical and biblical fact away.

(j) Verse 30. "Who touched my clothes?" Christ never asked a question because He did not know the answer. Instead, He wanted us to know! The Savior put this inquiry to His apostles in an effort to draw them into the wonder of this supernatural miracle.

(k) Thousands packed these streets to see, touch, or hear this Man. See footnote f above.

(l) "Fearing and trembling." Poor soul! Indeed, she was "poor," for all her livelihood had been spent on the physicians. Terrified at being discovered in public, yet knowing assuredly, this Man could help, she defied every social barrier in order to reach the Great Physician. Luke wrote that she came "trembling, falling down before him" (verse 47). Mark wrote that she came with "fearing and trembling" . . . "and fell down before him, and told him all the truth" (verse 33). She was, firstly, ashamed in her feminine modesty to reveal publicly the malady from which she was suffering. In the presence of Messiah, she is free to tell Him all, and those standing nearby heard the whole story. If the bystanders understood her confession, they were horrified that such a woman as this would be loose in the general public. What did the apostles think of this? The response of Christ was sweet music in her ears and weary heart.

(m) "Thy faith hath made thee whole." *Faith was the channel through which healing came from Christ, not the source. Faith itself has never saved or healed anyone.* She was a mystery woman, of whom we know mostly nothing, yet she knew who Christ was and put simple child-like faith in Him. She had prior knowledge of the Lord Jesus before seeking Him. Knowing her fears, the Savior spoke words of love and comfort to this distraught, pitiful woman. To bring peace to her troubled mind, He says to her in essence, "My child thou art saved from thy infirmity and all its consequences." To hold that *only* her body was healed, and not her soul saved is wrong. Christ addressed no other woman in Scripture by the title "daughter." For comments on the expression "fear not" as found in New Testament Scripture and its special meaning for God's children, see Section 71, Lk. 12:32, footnote j. See Section 144, footnote i for how people were saved before Jesus died on the cross. For a brief review of several people who were saved during the life of Christ, see Section 64, footnote k.

(n) "Be not afraid, only believe." These words of loving care were spoken to the distraught father in an effort to dispel his terrible fears. We cannot but marvel at the infinite concern of Jesus for mortal man. Messiah permitted only Peter, James, and John to enter the house where the little corpse lay. In a few years, these men would be pillars of His church. This was part of their exclusive training.

(o) Instantly, the professional mourners were present! This reveals they knew her death was imminent and were "waiting in the wings" to begin their doleful and costly work! Here, we meet a curious custom. In every village and community of Israel, there were hired mourners, mostly women, who were greatly skilled in this dreadful art. They were found among the Jews as seen in Jer. 9:17-19, with Amos 5:16 and the pagan Romans. At death, these women would sing mournful songs, make the most hideous noises, scratching, growling, hissing, and screaming in wild frenzy. Prominent among these were the flute players making their eerie sounds. In some cases, they would pluck hair from their heads, beat their chests, claw their faces, jump, dance, and even roll over the floor in dust or ashes. Mk. 5:40 states that Jesus put all of them out of the house. For more on this custom of mourning, see Section 61, Lk. 7:12, footnote b. Their demeaning antics were not welcomed or needed in His awesome presence. Their services were superfluous, for He, the resurrection and the life, was now present to transform that death into a sweet nap, from which His voice would arouse her. Their turbulence and scornfulness were discordant with the astounding work He was about to do. Jews were commanded to rend their garments when death entered their homes. In the Talmud, there are some thirty-nine different rules on how to rend or tear their clothing during these times. Parents were to rend the section just over the heart, so (for the male) the skin could be seen. The tear was to be large enough so that the fist could be thrust through the opening. These antics, with specific variations for women, went on for over thirty days among sorrowing Jews. Refer to the Talmud tractates, Mo'ed Katan 15a, 20b, 22b, 24a, 25a and 26b for some of the meticulous rabbinical details. If Jairus and his wife had already torn their clothing (as the sign of mourning), they must have hurriedly found a needle and thread after Jesus left their home! At this time in history, the Jews practiced *two types* of mourning for the dead:

1. **Aninuth.** This began at death and continued until the corpse was carried out of the house. Both hired and voluntary individuals partook in this service. It was considered the highest form of respect to share in the sorrow of families, friends, and neighbors whose loved ones had died. The Talmud has several hundred references to burying the dead. See tractates, Berachoth 16b and Kethubth 53a for details. *Afterwards, the family gave free food and drinks for all who were present!*

2. **Ebluth**. This was the correct way of mourning. Once the body was taken *from* the house, this began and continued for thirty days after burial. Wretched sounding musical instruments accompanied both types of Jewish lamentation. These dreadful dirges added even greater sorrow to the bereaved. The Jews considered this a solemn and necessary way of expressing grief. It is still employed in some eastern countries today. The author has seen and heard this in awful practice among the pagans of Africa. It echoes with a doleful beat of hopelessness. For continued details on the various customs of the Jews in burying their dead, see Section 61, all of footnote b.

(p) Our Lord's Words constituted something of a double negative in the mind of the vast crowds that stood in the courtyard and house of Jairus. The Jews said of a dead person, "He sleeps." Messiah contradicts this saying. He clearly distinguished between death and sleep! Death is not sleeping and sleeping is not death. Before the people at Jairus' house, the Lord Jesus affirmed that those who have believed in Him could not really die! Here is evidence that the household of Jairus had previously believed in Christ as the Messiah. See footnote d above. The expiration of the believer's physical body is but temporary, for it lapses into restful sleep from the toils of life. This sleep will be broken at the return of Christ, and every atom that constituted the human frame will be restored into its original likeness, only new and eternally perfect.

2p-When Stephen was stoned (killed) it was written, "He [his human body] fell asleep" (Acts 7:60). The Lord Jesus stood in heaven waiting to receive his soul, which was sometimes referred to as the spirit (Acts 7:59). A short time before His cross while at another funeral, Christ spoke these profound words, "And whosoever liveth and believeth in me shall never die" (John 11:26). The hornet of death lost its stinger when it assaulted Christ as He expired on the cross (1 Cor. 15:55). At His resurrection, Jesus had the keys of hell and death in His mighty hand (Rev. 1:18). Now, we realize the meaning of the verse, "Precious in the sight of the LORD is the death of his saints" (Ps. 116:15). What happened to transform death from its horror to being precious? Christ rose victorious and Lord over all things both natural and supernatural. Death becomes the channel through which all the redeemed may enter God's presence at the end of their earthly days; it is the doorway into heaven and home. Paul wrote that he desired "to depart [die] and be with Christ; which is far better [than anything on earth]" (Phil 1:23). Lastly, he stated in 2 Cor. 5:8 that physical death was to be "absent from the body, and present with the Lord." One of the hallmarks of false cults, feigning to be Christians, is their blatant denial of the departure of the soul from the body at death. They may claim to believe and support some of the other doctrines of the faith, but what happens to us at death is the great divider for these people. For a wider discussion of this subject, see Section 104, footnote g.

(q) Hearing but not understanding Messiah's words, the Jews scorned Him to *human* shame before the three apostles, Jairus, and his wife. Such vicious ridicule mirrored the contempt they held for the Son of God. Here, we see the true colors of the fickle mourners toward the Messiah. Christ expelled them from the room, for they were unworthy to behold such a miracle (verse 54). What did those cynics think when the child walked into their presence a few minutes later? Were they paid for their professional services, since she was no longer dead?

(r) **Again, He speaks to the dead, and they obey.** Ah! The touch of the Master's hand is the touch of life. With the sound of His voice creation snaps to attention. Three of the four evangelists mention this act. In touching the dead, one was considered ritually unclean by Jewish law. See a previous similar case of Christ touching death in Section 61, Lk. 7:14, footnote d. Leading the parents and three apostles, He steps into the inner chamber where the body lay. He speaks to a corpse, and it hears! Mark interprets the Aramaic Words of Jesus "Tal'i-tha cu' mi" into Greek for the benefit of his original readers, "Damsel, I say unto thee arise." Does this mean the little girl spoke and understood the Aramaic language? It must, for Jesus spoke it to her! Mark used the diminutive form of the word "korasion" meaning a *little* girl. The idea is that she was unusually small in body and stature. Old man death heard the command of God's Son and instantly turned the child loose! The Messiah had spoken and demonstrated His supreme authority over death. This was for His apostles to hear and see. About two years later, Peter used a similar verbal formula; and put the crowds out, when he raised Tabitha from the dead (Acts 9:39-42).

2p-All the scholarly writings about "Jesus speaking *only* Aramaic" are in error. Christ did speak Greek and Aramaic, but the language of that day for the Jews was Hebrew, regardless of what "corrupted form" it might have been both spoken and written. This was the language of our Lord. Years later, Paul spoke His native Hebrew in Acts. 21:40 to the thousands of Jews gathered at the temple. For a study about languages in the time of Christ written by an unsaved Hebrew, see *Jewish Sources in Early Christianity*, by Dr. David Flusser. For an examination of the Hebrew language, its history and related subjects, see *Hebrew: The Eternal Language*, by William Chomsky.

(s) The weakest imagination can touch this wonderful scene. Who can describe the awe and suspense of that breath-taking miracle? Suddenly, the child opened her eyes, looked up at Jesus and responded. Luke expressly records the words "And her spirit came again" (verse 55). See a similar case of a little boy in 1 Kings 17:17-22. Both events show that the inward person (soul) leaves the body at physical death. The little human frame, smiling and well, clasped the Master's hand as He escorted her back into the life of her home and world. No wonder "they were astonished with a great astonishment." Jubilant parents, shouting praises to God, embraced, with hearts full of joy and thankfulness, their *only* child. Amazed apostles, wide-eyed and stunned, watched aghast in silent but awesome wonder. The former death room now rings with anthems of glory to God and the joy of new life. A house filled with sorrow is suddenly filled with gladness. The scoffing professional mourners gathered up their instruments of sad music and fled. For an earlier miracle that produced joyful praises to God, see Section 49, footnote n.

(t) **"Walked."** Slipping from her bed, Mark records that she did this. Why? It must have been about the room (verse 42). Could her former malady have caused some sort of infantile paralysis? Did this precious child suffer from ambulatory impairment? Did she walk to demonstrate that she was wholly cured from such a disability?

2p-**Give her something to eat.** Not only was she now alive, walking, and in perfect health, but the Master of the universe commands that something be given her to eat. Her healing was thorough. *What normal twelve-year-old child is not hungry?* Though cured by extraordinary power, she now is to continue sustaining human life by the regular means of food and drink. Great rejoicing echoed through the house of Jairus, as family, friends, and neighbors shared in this overpowering wave of supernatural, heavenly bliss. No one slept much that night, and we can easily believe the little girl was allowed to stay up late!

(u) On other occasions, Christ had issued similar instructions as seen in Section 48, footnote d. The purpose was to keep down as much disturbance about His work as possible, for the hostility of the religions leaders increased with every report of His miracles and messages. However, such a command was simply impossible. News spread everywhere that He had healed the daughter of Jairus. Thousands spoke of this astounding miracle, and again, the entire country was moved to wonderment about Jesus of Nazareth. Matthew wrote that His fame went over the land (verse 26). Many of the Jews reading his letter would have called to remembrance this miracle as they reflected on the life of Jesus of Nazareth. They knew what Matthew had written to them was true.

(v) All attempts to suppress the good news of Jesus are tantamount to covering the face of the sun so that it cannot shine. Tyrants, despots, and maniacs have tried it for centuries, yet the light of Jesus Christ, the Son of God continues to beam forgiveness and hope into the lives of all who will believe. In this present century, radical world Islam, like a maddened animal, opposes and hates the gospel of the Savior. It has murdered untold thousands of Christians, especially in Africa and across Asia. Yet, the light of Jesus Christ shines on forever!

2p-Our Savior said that He was the light of the world. Refer to Section 120, John 8:12, footnote j for this claim. Note the person to whom this was spoken and the context in which it was stated.

Leaving Jairus' house, Jesus meets two blind men and a demoniac. Both confess Him as the Messiah and beg for mercy. They are healed. In curing the man with satanic dumbness, the Savior again demonstrated that He was Israel's true Messiah.* The crowds are struck with amazement. The Pharisees blaspheme.

*See asterisk under main heading Section 48 for the four miracles that would prove Jesus was the true Messiah among the Jewish people of that time.

Matt. 9:27-34—*Capernaum*	Mk.	Lk.	John
The two blind men are healed			
27 And when Jesus departed[a] thence, two blind men followed him, crying, and saying, "*Thou* son of David,[b] have mercy on us."			
28 And when he was come into the house, the blind men came to him: and Jesus saith unto them, "Believe ye that I am able to do this?"[c] They said unto him, "Yea, Lord."			
29 Then touched he their eyes, saying, "According to your faith be it unto you."			
30 And their eyes were opened; and Jesus straitly charged them, saying, "See *that* no man know *it*."[d]			
31 But they, when they were departed, spread abroad his fame in all that country.			
A man possessed with a demon of ***dumbness is healed: this was another exclusive Messianic miracle***			
32 As they went out, behold, they brought to him a dumb man possessed with a devil.			
33 And when the devil was cast out, the dumb spake: and the multitudes marvelled, saying, "It was never so seen in Israel."[e]			
34 But the Pharisees said, "He casteth out devils through the prince of devils."[f] (Verse 35 cont. in Section 56.)			

Footnotes-Commentary

(a) As Jesus was departing Jairus' house and Capernaum, two blind men had learned that He was in the city and found Him. As He exited Jairus' house they stumbled along behind the Light of the world! Shortly, they would see *both* the sunlight of the world and the glorious light of eternal life. They addressed Jesus by the term "Son of David" which was the pre-eminent Jewish title for Israel's Messiah. Refer to footnote b below for more on this thought. Note Section 66, Matt. 12:22-23, footnote b, where a crowd of onlookers had used it earlier, and Section 143, Matt. 20:30, footnote d where two blind men at Jericho employed it later. Both men knew exactly what this masterful title signified and because of this, they called to Him for mercy. The rabbis had taught for centuries that when Messiah came, he would "open the eyes of the blind." Now, that He did this, they angrily refused to receive Him as their Messiah.

(b) "*Thou* son of David." These two men plead with great importunity and the irresistible fervor of simple faith. The preclusion of this common Messianic title as applied to the Lord Jesus is most enlightening. Where had the two men who used it acquired this knowledge of their Messiah? It was obtained by attendance at the synagogues (and general public talk) because Israel's coming Messiah was a subject of discussion and debate among the Jews. Through the channels of national gossip, they had heard many things about Jesus of Nazareth and had come to believe that He was Messiah "the Son of David." As such, they knew He could perform great signs, wonders, miracles, and even open blind eyes to see. One of the frequently cited verses from the Old Testament about Messiah's miracles was Isa. 29:18, which prophesied, "The eyes of the blind shall see." Again, Isa. 42:7 (mentioned in footnote a, above) predicted that He would "open the blind eyes." They had this truth proclaimed many times by the rabbis. We have noted that this Messianic title "Son of David," was used earlier of the Lord Jesus in footnote a above. Refer to Section 97, Matt. 15:22, footnote c where a Gentile woman also called our Lord by the same Messianic description. For several diagrams that display Jesus' physical descent from Abraham down through King David's family line, see Section 7.

(c) Jesus exited the house and made His way across the city to the location where He was temporarily staying. These blind men followed Him in their darkness every step of the way! Though they cried with great intensity, He apparently paid no attention. Led by others, they entered the house where Jesus was.

2p-Verse 29. This passage reflects the loving kindness of our Lord. Touching their eyes was a sign of favor and kindness to them. He had just inquired if they believed He could do this wonder. Now, with His touch on the eyes that were in darkness, He states that through their faith, it will be done. He knew these men accepted Him as that marvelous Messianic Person, for had not their appeal been addressed in His supreme and highest title? That is precisely what they did and both were instantly healed. There were hundreds of dramatic events such as this in the ministry of Christ (John 20:30-31).

(d) This gag order was applied by Jesus on other occasions. Refer to this in Section 48, Mk. 1:44, footnote d, and Section 89, footnote u. With the former demoniac, the Master ordered him to spread the good news of his deliverance over the countryside. Probably, this was because it was predominately a Gentile region embracing ten cities and thousands of pagans.

2p-Verse 32. "They brought." The plural pronoun "they" has reference to the two freshly healed former blind men. Instantly, they brought to Jesus, another afflicted man struck dumb by a demon. It has always been true that God has those unnamed heroes of the faith who work day and night to bring others to Jesus. Someday yonder in the eternal joy and bliss of heaven, they will be revealed to the glory of the Holy Trinity and praises of all the redeemed. In 1960, (just before departing for the mission field of Australia) the author of this work met an elderly man in Houston, Texas. He was wrinkled and stooped. Quietly, with a sense of modesty, and blushing, Jim Doss shared with me how he had spent his life. Never marrying, without earthly obligations and no living relatives, he was known as "The traveling tract man" or "The hitchhiker for Jesus." As such, he had traversed America over a hundred times, witnessing, and passing out tracts or testaments to those who gave him a ride and responded to his testimony. Old, white-headed Jim was a noble figure. Praise God for the unnamed company, who still today are busy sowing eternal seed and bringing men to the Savior. Jim Doss went home to be with Christ some ten months after our unforgettable meeting at a Houston rescue mission. I can still see his clean, beaming face and snow white hair. His blue eyes were milky and dim. As a young missionary, I was *permanently* inspired to distribute gospel tracts because of the testimony of that aged saint and have done so for over half a century. Surely, "the memory of the just is blessed" (Prov. 10:7). Note the Savior's lesson on the man sowing seed, in Section 73 and 75.

3p-The dying witness for Jesus. Alas! How many professors of the Savior have their candles blown out by the first trial that falls upon them? In some cases, it will never be lighted again. Even amid the congregations of "Bible preaching churches," there are those that openly oppose speaking to others about their eternal destiny. Men run their souls out of breath and work over time to secure a piece of this world's vanity. Life's brevity is not a part of their faith in God. Most people act as though they are living on earth forever. In a strange blindness, they spin out their own heaven here, one constructed of sin, sorrow, poverty, fear, money, crosses, and curses. They cannot smell the sweet, afar fragrance of the city of God. Sharing the gospel of redemption from sin, divine escort through this wicked world and home secured at last, is not at all in their thoughts. Their fellows drop off into hell and most seem not to care. The noise of dark Christian silence has muffled the sound of the glorious gospel to many ears.

(e) **"It was never so seen in Israel."** This heated exclamation of the crowds was incorrect. Earlier in His ministry, the Savior had healed a dumb man who was demon possessed. Refer to this in Section 66, Matt. 12:22-23. The reaction of the multitudes at that time was earthshaking because their rabbis had taught them that *only* Israel's Messiah could heal one with a dumb demon. Another dumb demon was expelled in Mk. 9:17 and 25. The same miracle is mentioned in Matt. 15:30. *Again,* the religious leaders accused Messiah of being in a league with the Devil as seen in footnote f below. Jesus of Nazareth performed this Messianic miracle before their eyes! Cross-reference back to Section 48, and see number 2, by the asterisk under main heading for more on this unique Messianic wonder. Later, when Jesus healed a man at the temple gate, who had been born blind, the benefactor of this miracle said that such a thing was unheard of from the beginning of the world (John 9:32). When the people exclaimed, "It was never so seen in Israel," they were speaking of the supernatural, exclusive work, which *only* their Messiah could do.

2p-Another point of interest regarding persons in this physical condition, is that the rabbis believed that one born blind and dumb could not rejoice or offer sacrifices at the temple. See this in the Talmud tractate, Chagigah 2b where the normal meticulous rabbinical details are given. Christ gave no orders of silence to this poor man as He had just done to those healed from blindness. See footnote d above. Now, he had something to rejoice about, and the blessed Lord Jesus turned him loose to do it!

(f) Outraged at this miracle, which proved He was Israel's Messiah, the religious leaders resorted to blasphemy. How shocking the venom of these Jews without Christ. Months prior, they had laid this same vicious charge upon the Son of God. See Section 66, Matt. 12:22-24, footnote c, for this first defamatory calumny used by the Pharisees, when another demon-possessed dumb man was healed earlier in the ministry of Jesus. "The way of the wicked *is* as darkness: they know not at what they stumble" (Prov. 4:19).

Returning to the Nazareth synagogue for a second time,* He speaks and the people are again seriously offended. They reject Him anew. The Savior can perform only a few miracles because of their stubborn unbelief.

For His first visit to Nazareth shortly after beginning His ministry, and the Jews attempt to kill Him, refer to Section 38 with its supplement. On this return trip, He was again subjected to scorn and contempt after addressing the congregation. Few believed what He had to say. The Jews seeking to destroy Him earlier and now letting Him speak again reveals the deadly eastern temperament. Still today, they will greet one with great enthusiasm, and then two hours later seek to kill him in fierce anger and mob violence.

Nazareth

Matt. 13:54–58	Mk. 6:1–6a	Lk.	John
Back in Nazareth: *again, He is rejected as Messiah*	*Back in Nazareth:* *again, He is rejected as Messiah*		
54 And when he was come into his own country,(a)	1 And he went out from thence, and came into his own country;(a) and his disciples follow him.		
he taught them in their synagogue,(b) insomuch that they were astonished, and said, "Whence hath this *man* this wisdom,	2 And when the sabbath day was come, he began to teach in the synagogue:(b) and many hearing *him* were astonished, saying, "From whence hath this *man* these things? and what wisdom *is* this which is given unto him, that even such		
and *these* mighty works?"(c)	mighty works(c) are wrought by his hands?		
Names of His family members	*Names of His family members*		
55 "Is not this the carpenter's son?(d) is not his mother called Mary? and his brethren, James, and Joses, and Simon, and Judas?	3 "Is not this the carpenter,(d) the son of Mary, the brother of James, and Joses, and of Juda, and Simon?		
56 "And his sisters, are they not all with us? Whence then hath this *man* all these things?"	and are not his sisters here with us?"		
57 And they were offended(e) in him. But Jesus said unto them, "A prophet is not without honour, save in his own country, and in his own house."(f)	And they were offended(e) at him. 4 But Jesus said unto them, "A prophet is not without honour, but in his own country, and among his own kin, and in his own house."(f)		
The results of unbelief	*The results of unbelief*		
58 And he did not many mighty works there	5 And he could there do no mighty work, save that he laid his hands upon a few sick folk, and healed *them*.		
because of their unbelief.(g) (Next chap., Matt. 14:1 cont. in Section 92.)	6a And he marvelled because of their unbelief.(g) (Verse 6b cont. in Section 56.)		

Footnotes–Commentary

(a) **"His own country."** Refer to asterisk under main heading of Section 28 for important comments on this statement. Jesus returned to His home at Nazareth, where He had grown up with His mother, foster-father, half-brothers, and sisters. See footnote d below. Our Savior did not take His rejecters at their first word, but returns repeatedly with offers of saving and forgiving grace! One can assume that He had made numerous trips home, but

Scripture is silent on this point. See asterisk under main heading above, and under Section 111, for a later occasion when Jesus returned to Nazareth. Then it was amid ridicule and contempt from His half-brothers.

(b) Mark informs us that this teaching effort occurred on the Sabbath day (Mk. 6:2). The Lord Jesus was in and out of the synagogues of Galilee hundreds of times. It was a custom that any Jew had the right to address the congregation if called upon by the minister. It had been about two years since the tumultuous events described by Luke in Section 38, when our Lord spoke in this place. Every person in Nazareth had heard of His fame and fierce confrontations with Israel's religious leaders. Now, Nazareth had made its mind up: "He was a Messianic imposter!"

(c) **"Wisdom and works."** Did not their Scriptures predict this of Messiah? Wicked men often judge God's people by their level of education. If Christians are not pertly academic, they cannot know the truth. If they are not "greatly learned," they cannot comprehend the things of God. There is a curious paradox that offends the unsaved religious world. It is that men are *finally* converted to Christ not by super minds and academic excellence, but rather by the mysterious work of the Holy Spirit, blended with the Word of God, ministering in their hearts. And all of this is by grace. *However, this being so, we do not believe that God puts a blue ribbon on blatant ignorance as the chief qualification for divine service.* Academic excellence coupled with the power of the Holy Spirit is a rarity in these days; yet, it does exist in all its wonderful beauty. The citizens of Nazareth sat stunned as Christ preached from the synagogue chair. No doubt, many of them had heard Him speak elsewhere over the countryside. Never had they heard such doctrines taught in such a loving, powerful, and graceful manner. Every Jew present knew that this Man had grown up in their hometown, and He had no formal theological training from the schools at Jerusalem. Later, this was thrown into His face in John 7:15. They were confounded and inquired of His wisdom and the origin of His mighty works. At one time or another, all of them had heard of His miracles and wonders as news of these things had spread throughout Israel and into lands far away. In Section 92, Matt. 14:1, Herod Antipas in his palace on the western shores of Lake Galilee had received intelligence about Christ. We read, "Herod heard of the fame of Jesus."

(d) **"Is not this the carpenter's son?"** This affirms that Joseph was still alive, or they would have said, "Is not this the son of the carpenter who is deceased?" It seems also to suggest that they upbraided Jesus *along with* His foster-father. The reason for this we do not know, unless it was because the Jewish elite looked down upon the occupation of a carpenter. Much has been written trying to prove that the family persons mentioned in these texts were actually cousins and other indirect family members. There is no warrant whatsoever for departing from the syntax and obvious meaning of the verses. Note Section 6, Lk. 3:23, footnote e; Section 66, footnote a; and Section 69, footnote a, for details regarding our Lord's human family. It is of interest that Mark records the comments of the people when they described Christ as "the carpenter" (Mk. 6:3). This is not a statement expressing mean sarcasms or ridicule as some writers suggest. It was incumbent upon every Jewish father to circumcise his son, see that he was taught the Torah Law, and a trade: Joseph did this for Jesus. Little did he know that this youthful, tender lad, learning to be a "carpenter," had engineered and created all things! Refer to Section 1, Part l, footnote a, for Christ's work in creation. One is puzzled at the "scholars" who question Jesus being a carpenter. The Greek word translated "carpenter" is "tekton." It has reference to various crafts or trades, including woodcutters, builders, and a variety of vocations. Are we to believe that Joseph, though a carpenter, taught his stepson to be a stone mason, or tanner, and not a carpenter? Men who call into question the statements of the Bible are not the friends of God. Beware of men who only accept Scripture when they dig up a skeleton, an earthen pot of old manuscripts, or the bones of a "prehistoric" horse. After all, proof is necessary before an "educated person" will believe in anything that he cannot see. (Does this include electricity and the wind?) To believe only when it is academically proven is the pastime of fools. Hell is full of millions who lived and died in this falsehood. For more on the infidel "scholarly approach to Holy Scripture," see Section 18, first paragraph of footnote d, and Section 137, footnote d.

2p-Moses, of the Old Testament has been recognized by both friends and foes as one of histories greatest leaders. How did he acquire this honorable accolade? Not one academic today has the formal training of Moses in *all* the wisdom of the Egyptians, mighty in words and in deeds (Acts 7:22). These ancient people built things that confound the best of engineering, mathematical, and astronomical minds of today. Moses knew all the Egyptian arts, crafts, and skills, yet had enough sense to believe in one Almighty God, amid the millions of god and goddess of ancient Egypt. It is written that, "he endured, as seeing him [God] who is invisible" (Heb. 11:27). How appropriate is the statement of our Savior, "blessed *are* they that have not seen, and *yet* have believed" (John 20:29). Both Abraham and Paul had no problem of believing in the invisible things of eternity (Heb. 11:10, 14–16 and 2 Cor. 4:18). As stated later in this work, there are two places where *everyone* believes everything in the Bible, heaven, and hell. It is atheistic propaganda that most scientists do not believe in God, Jesus Christ, or the Bible. See Henry Morris' works, *21 Scientist who Believe in Creation* and *The Bible Basis for Modern Science.* It takes a far greater faith to be an atheist than it does a Christian. One ponders how these poor people ever make it, or do they?

3p-**War between faith and science.** This is a verbal red herring. The Bible is not a text book on science, yet when it touches upon any of them, it is accurate. In past history, as God allowed men to discover some of the wonders of *genuine* science, the Catholic Church censured, tortured, and killed thousands who would not bow to their demonic superstitions and ignorance of Holy Scripture. Galileo (died 1642) is a classic example of Papal torture and intimidation. Were it not for right thinking men in centuries past, who dared challenge the murderous religious quo, many would still think the earth was flat!

(e) **"And they were offended" or "scandalized."** Contextually these statements first had reference to our Lord's physical family. They were too proud to be taught by one of their own, a hometown carpenter whom they considered to be their equal or lower. These words reflect that at this late period in His ministry, Jesus' family, just as His disciples, did not yet understand His true mission. They too had been brainwashed by the rabbis about their literal, physical kingdom on earth, which had no place for a crucified Messiah dying for the sins of the world.

(f) As stated above in footnote e, it is pointedly clear that the members of Christ's own physical family rose up in opposition to His preaching and work. This was a proverb commonly used stating that a prophet had no honor in his country or hometown. Even though this was true in the case of Jesus' house disregarding Him, it is not a hard-fast rule. At times, a man of God is despised by his people and received more readily by strangers. However, there are occasions when he is loved and applauded by family and friends at home. As mentioned in footnote e above, this statement points us to Jesus' family members who *first refused* to honor His work. Their opposition continued to His death. For the wonderful climax to this "half-brothers' problem," note Section 207, footnote g.

(g) **"He marveled because of their unbelief."** Later it was written, "But without faith *it is* impossible to please *him*: for he that cometh to God must believe that he is, and *that* he is a rewarder of them that diligently seek him" (Heb. 11:6). On the Lord Jesus marveling over the actions of men, see Section 60, footnote g. This terse passage demonstrates that the Sovereign God of heaven will not necessarily overrule the wicked unbelief of men in order to perform His wonders. He forces no one to believe *in* their personal sins and deliberate rejection of truth. Scripture teaches that all men must repent of sin. Repentance, engendered by God's word and prompted by the Holy Spirit, is the prerequisite to genuine saving faith. It is vicious heresy to teach that men cannot repent and believe until *after* they are saved. For more on repentance, see Section 50, Matt. 9:13, footnote h. For a lucid examination of this teaching often referred to as "post salvation repentance," see *What Love Is This? Calvinism's Misrepresentation of God*, by Dave Hunt, and *The Other Side of Calvinism,* by L. M. Vance. These two works present a fair and comprehensive coverage of the false doctrine of Calvinism. For an examination of the equally erroneous teaching of Arminianism, see *Why I am Not an Arminian,* by M. D. Williams. Both beliefs are fragments of religious philosophies, mixed with scraps of biblical doctrine. Calvinism sparkles with the attraction of superior learning but so often genders deceiving arrogance resulting in awful division. It contradicts the Great Commission and biblical soul winning. Arminianism wears the rags of simplistic ignorance, infecting its adherents with the awful fear of being lost again, while they struggle to do enough good works to keep themselves saved. Each appeals to its own and grips the human mind with a steel-like vice, which in most cases is impenetrable. For more on the teaching of both Calvinism and Arminianism, see Section 1, Part 3, footnote h, with Section 50, fourth and fifth paragraphs under footnote h, and Section 135, footnote e. In 2010, James G. McCarthy released *John Calvin Goes to Berkeley.* This book presents a disjointed novel dialogue between students and others over the validity of Calvinism or Arminianism. It takes place, more or less within the confines of the University Christian Fellowship (UCF) at Berkeley. Amid an ocean of quotations from scores of people, it concludes with nothing positively helpful for a lost person seeking to be saved. Those who refuse to rise up and announce that *both* Calvinism and Arminianism are distortions of fundamental biblical truth, and try to walk a loving path between the two are "peacekeepers" of nothing. The suggestion that both sides are right, and they can reach a synthesis is more doctrinal nonsense. This is a revision of religious pluralism designed to please everyone and offend none. No honest Christian goes about looking for a theological fight. However, those who will not take an unflinching stand on *biblical truth proven by experience* will find themselves running with the hares and the hounds. In this scenario, no one catches anything!

2p-Repentance, the handmaid of faith. Believing on Christ involves repentance from sin, though this is not explicitly stated in verse 58 above. The ability to repent is given by God as His grace releases man's bondage of the will and offers him eternal life. He pushes no man over the edge or holds him back. Men may repent, believe, and be saved, or refuse this act of mercy. *Either way, saving grace is vindicated and God is glorified.* No one is hijacked into salvation, and God is not embarrassed because His gift of everlasting life is rejected. For other comments on the bondage of the will as propounded by Martin Luther, see Section 201, third paragraph of footnote n. In every verse where repentance is mentioned, faith may not be and vice versa. Doctrinal truths are not always expressed in a systematic order in Scripture. This is because different men, at different places, and at different times, wrote the books. One was inspired to emphasize a certain point while the other was not. Details on repentance are found in Section 50, Matt. 9:13, all of footnote h. During Jesus' return visit to Nazareth, only a *few* sick people believed in Him as the Messiah and were healed. Apparently, the majority of infirmed people living at Nazareth and those who traveled there to hear Him, refused to believe that He was Israel's Messiah, who could heal their maladies. This reflects the enormous depth of unbelief and resentment that had been built up against Him since His last visit to the Nazareth synagogue. So great was their scorn and rejection, that He walked out of His boyhood village and "marveled" at their lack of faith. What an amazing declaration in verse 6a that the Lord from heaven "marveled" at poor mortals who refused to believe in Him!

Herod Antipas is smitten by a guilty conscience. A brief recount of the imprisonment and murder of John the Baptist.* His burial by loyal disciples.

For other relevant events and John's imprisonment, see asterisk under main heading in Section 21, Part 1.

Southern end of Peraea at the stronghold of Machaerus in Edom

Matt. 14:1–5	Mk. 6:14–19	Lk. 9:7–9	John
Terrible memories	*Terrible memories*	*Terrible memories*	
1 At that time Herod[(a)] the tetrarch [ruler of a fourth part] heard of the fame[(b)] of Jesus,	**14** And king Herod[(a)] heard *of him*; (for his name was spread[(b)] abroad:) and he said,	**7** Now Herod the tetrarch[(a)] [ruler of a fourth part] heard of all that was done by him:[(b)] and he was perplexed, because that it was said of some,	
2 And said unto his servants, "This is John the Baptist; he is risen from the dead; and therefore mighty works[(c)] do shew forth themselves in him."	That "John the Baptist was risen from the dead, and therefore mighty works[(c)] do shew forth themselves in him.	that "John was risen from the dead;"	
	15 Others said, That "it is Elias." [Elijah] And others said, That "it is a prophet, or as one of the prophets."[(d)]	**8** And of some, that "Elias [Elijah] had appeared;" and of others, that "one of the old prophets[(d)] was risen again."	
It is reasonable to believe that ▶ *Herod said both things, as recorded in verses 16 and 9, amid his fear and frustration.*	**16** But when Herod heard *thereof*, he said, "It is John, whom I beheaded: he is risen from the dead."	**9** And Herod said, "John have I beheaded: but who is this, of whom I hear such things?" And he desired to see him.[(e)] (Verse 10 cont. in Section 93.)	
A review of John's death	*A review of John's death*		
3 For Herod had laid hold on John, and bound him, and put *him* in prison for Herodias'[(f)] sake, his brother Philip's wife.	**17** For Herod himself had sent forth and laid hold upon John, and bound him in prison for Herodias'[(f)] sake, his brother Philip's wife: for he had married her.		
4 For John said unto him, "It is not lawful for thee to have her."	**18** For John had said unto Herod, "It is not lawful for thee to have thy brother's wife."		
	19 Therefore Herodias had a quarrel[(g)] against him, and would have killed him; but she could not:		
5 And when he would have			

Matt. 14:5-9	Mk. 6:20-26	Lk.	John
put him to death, he feared the multitude, because they counted him as a prophet.[h]	**20** For Herod feared John, knowing that he was a just man and an holy,[h] and observed him; and when he heard him, he did many things, and heard him gladly.		
	A fatal birthday party		
	21 And when a convenient day was come, that Herod on his birthday made a s upper to his lords, high captains, and chief *estates* [rulers] of Galilee;		
A fatal birthday party **6** But when Herod's birthday was kept,	**22** And when the daughter of the said Herodias came in, and danced,[i] and pleased Herod and them that sat with him, the king said unto the damsel, "Ask of me whatsoever thou wilt, and I will give *it* thee."		
the daughter of Herodias danced[i] before them, and pleased Herod.			
7 Whereupon he promised with an oath[j] to give her whatsoever she would ask.	**23** And he sware[j] unto her, "Whatsoever thou shalt ask of me, I will give *it* thee, unto the half of my kingdom."		
The horrible request **8** And she, being before instructed of her mother, said, "Give me here John Baptist's head in a charger." (platter)	*The horrible request* **24** And she went forth, and said unto her mother, "What shall I ask?" And she said, "The head of John the Baptist."		
	25 And she came in straightway with haste unto the king, and asked, saying, "I will that thou give me by and by in a charger [platter] the head of John the Baptist."		
9 And the king was sorry:[k] nevertheless for the oath's sake, and them which sat with him at meat, he commanded *it* to be given *her.*	**26** And the king was exceeding sorry;[k] *yet* for his oath's sake, and for their sakes which sat with him, he would not reject her.		

401

Matt. 14:10-12	Mk. 6:27-29	Lk.	John
10 And he sent, and beheaded John in the prison. **11** And his head was brought in a charger, [platter] and given to the damsel: and she brought *it* to her mother. [(l)] *Love's last deed* **12** And his disciples came, and took up the body, and buried [(m)] it, and went and told Jesus. [(n)] (Verse 13 cont. in Section 93.)	**27** And immediately the king sent an executioner, and commanded his head to be brought: and he went and beheaded him in the prison, **28** And brought his head in a charger, [platter] and gave it to the damsel: and the damsel gave it to her mother. [(l)] *Love's last deed* **29** And when his disciples heard *of it*, they came and took up his corpse, and laid [(m)] it in a tomb. (Verse 30 cont. in Section 93.)		

Footnotes-Commentary

[(a)] **"King Herod."** This title applied to Antipas has caused some to point a finger of fault at Scripture. Technically, Herod Antipas was *never* crowned king of anything by the Roman government. Mark, chapter 6, referred to him five times by this title in verses 14, 22, 25, 26, and 27. Matthew, chapter 14, uses it in verse 9 of his gospel. The usage reflected a local custom of calling rulers by a courtesy title, even though officially it was not correct. It is noted that Matthew called Herod both tetrarch and king at the same time in verses 1 and 9. It is the same as Luke describing *both* Annas and Caiaphas being high priests that year. See this mentioned in Section 21, Part 1, Lk. 3:2. Technically, there could only be one high priest at a time in office. Regarding these men, Alfred Edersheim in *The Life and Times of Jesus the Messiah,* page 972 gives a complete list of all high priests from the accession of King Herod the Great to the destruction of Jerusalem in A.D. 70.

2p-**"Tetrarch."** A word that refers to ruling over the fourth part of a designated area. For Herod Antipas see Section 21, Part 1, number 3 under footnote b. This term became synonymous with governor or ruler over whatever country, after Rome's political sanction. Antipas' father, Herod the Great, was the baby killer who died shortly after the birth of the Lord Jesus. Refer to Section 18, footnote d for his murder of the infants. Antipas' mother was a Samaritan woman named Malthace, according to *The New Unger's Bible Dictionary*, page 83. Herod the Great left His kingdom to the rule of three sons, with the approval of the Roman Senate. One was Herod Antipas who ruled over Galilee, Jesus' home province, and Peraea a large area on the eastern side of the Sea of Galilee and the Jordan River. He is mentioned more often than any other Herod in the New Testament. See the fascinating little work *Ludwig's Handbook of New Testament Rulers & Cities*, by Charles Ludwig, for intriguing details about the Herodians and their legacy of intrigue, murder, adulteries, and horrible deaths.

[(b)] **"The fame of Jesus."** These verses reveal again that the notoriety of Jesus was known everywhere, even in the palace of Herod Antipas. Was not Joanna, the wife of Herod's steward, also a devout follower of the Lord Jesus? No doubt, Herod gathered intelligence about the Savior from this woman through her husband, whose name was Chuza, a prominent figure in his court. For more on Joanna and Chuza, note Section 65, Lk. 8:3, footnote f. Later, Antipas saw Jesus a few hours before His crucifixion, and his military fiercely mocked the Savior. See footnote e below for details.

[(c)] It was commonly believed that persons who were murdered in innocence would rise from the dead to haunt those who put them to death. See footnote d below. It was also believed that they would do great miracles to assert their power and mission. National gossip had accredited the mighty works of Jesus to John, who had returned from the shades of the after life to prove his innocence and to avenge himself. Troubled, Herod Antipas was pressed hard by this tormenting thought. One guilty conscience performs the work of a thousand accusers.

[(d)] Superstition was part of everyday life of the ancients. Here, it rears its ugly head in the belief that someone from the dead was appearing. Lk. 9:8 show us that the belief in the return of Elijah was still a paramount thought among the Jewish people at this time, and that many of them saw John the Baptist as the Messiah's forerunner. This statement of Luke also reflects the confusion that prevailed among the rabbis on this subject. Lightfoot's *Commentary on the New Testament* . . . . , vol. 3, pages 91–92 tells us that a fiction existed among the Jews at this time that Moses would rise from the dead and appear with Elijah. Hence, we read the words that "one of the old prophets was risen again." For more on this, see Section 103, Matt. 16:14, footnote c.

(e) **He desired to see Jesus.** What is said here of Herod Antipas, beyond doubt, could have been said of every informed person across the land and known world of that era in history. *All men wanted to see this Jesus.* Many months later, Herod did "see" the Lord Jesus, during His death trials at Jerusalem. It turned out a disaster for Herod Antipas, who flew into a rage and along with his soldiery mocked the Son of God. Those writers who attempt to portray Jesus as an insignificant figure of that day, with Rome paying Him but little attention, have seriously missed the obvious tenor of the four gospels.

(f) **"Herodias."** One of the most infamous females in Bible history, the wife of Philip, son of Herod the Great, by whom she bore a daughter named Salome. She abandoned Philip and eloped with Herod Antipas, another son of Herod the Great, who in turn had deserted his wife, the daughter of Aretas the king of Arabia. (Philip and Antipas were half–brothers.) Dreadful wars broke out between Aretas and Antipas. These ended with the crushing of Herod Antipas' vast armies according to Josephus' *Antiquities,* Book 18:5. 1, lines 109–115. Jewish gossip accredited his defeat and suffering to the judgment of God for his sins. Herodias and her depraved daughter proved to be the complete ruin of Herod Antipas.

2p-An old *legend* has it that this wicked female fell through ice on a lake, and a razor–sharp edge sliced her head from her body! It is ironic that some fables of ancient history oddly mirror truths that continually demonstrate God's providence in dealing with incorrigible sinners. Fable lovers should look at the other side of the picture and remember that eternal hell is far worse than being decapitated by a piece of ice! *The sinful daring and shamelessness of a godless woman makes even hell to weep.*

(g) This suggests that John had previously clashed with this pernicious woman. See footnote f above for a brief review of Herodias. Hating God's preacher who rebuked her sins, she seethed in anger waiting for the opportune moment to have him killed and silence his message of truth. History has been replete with these people. Hell is full of them with room to spare for all the others.

(h) It seems odd that Herod feared the people. This was because of the great influence the Baptist had over them. Instant uprising over the smallest trifles was common at this time in Jewish history; possibly Herod feared something of this nature. The Jews held that to touch one considered a true prophet was serious business (1 Chron. 16:22). It could cause great unrest in his domain. John, having learned of the incestuous marriage, apparently went to Herod and reproved him face–to–face. Luke 3:19 adds these words "and for all the evils which Herod had done." Here, we see a reflection of the "spirit of Elijah" flashing from the Baptist as he boldly confronts the ruler over his sins (1 Kings 18:17-18). Herod Antipas was shaken by the fearless presence of this man of God and stung to the core by his daring rebuke. Then the Holy Spirit gives us a brief profile of the real Antipas: "He feared the multitude," meaning the thousands that were part of John's ministry and had followed the Baptist, and others who were sympathetic with his message and ministry. We read in Mk. 6:20 that "he feared John, knowing that he was a just man and an holy, and observed him." Upon hearing the Baptist preach, Antipas was greatly moved. We note the curious words, "he did many things, and heard him gladly." What the "many things" were and *why* he did them, we will never know. However, all works of reformation from an unregenerate heart avail nothing. Compromise with a guilty conscience leaves the victim sinking deeper in doleful despair. John's requirements *before* he witnessed baptism in Section 21, Part 2, footnote i, reveal his feelings about sin. Antipas is the portrait of a royal weakling, who struggled to rise above his horrendous sins of adultery and incest, and the trauma they wrought in his mind; yet at the same time he was dominated by a ruthless woman, madly pursuing her ghastly ambitions. Alas! Who could begin to relate the manifold devious machinations of sin and its dreadful results in the lives of men?

2p-Verse 6. "Herod's birthday was kept." The Jewish schools and their teachers were loath to esteem birthday celebrations. They were counted as heinous pagan customs. Nevertheless, the Jews would assign a "birthday text" to each child when it was born. The child was to quote the passage each day in prayer. These were referred to as "guardian words." The verse had to begin and end with the same letters of the child's Hebrew name. The only other mention of a birthday in Scripture is that of Pharaoh in Gen. 40:20. Many of our present day birthday celebrations are loaded with pagan customs and antics. Even the cake with candles has its origin in the heathen Greeks as they worshiped a female goddess. However, the ancient birthday parties and antics of godless men in the past are not part of our celebrations of today. There is no sin in the joy of remembering the birth of a loved one. The problems start when these happy occasions are drinking bouts; sensuous acts of dancing, removing clothing, crawling over the floor in a drunken state and so forth. When strong drink enters the human system, the brain slips out of gear, and things become hilariously evil. Thus, it was with Herod's happy birthday party. For more on these things and associated matters, see Section 98, paragraphs three through five of footnote c.

3p-History of birthday celebrations. Historically, the earliest birthday celebrations have been traced back to Egypt as a practice for the Pharaohs. Two ancient female birthdays are documented. From Plutarch, the first century

Greek biographer, we learn that Cleopatra, threw a great birthday celebration for her companion in adultery, Mark Antony. They were lavished with rich gifts on the occasion. An earlier Egyptian queen, Cleopatra II, who had incestuously married her brother Ptolemy, had a son by him. She received from her insane husband one of the most macabre birth presents in all history: the dismembered body of their son! Regarding such heinous deeds, see footnotes f above and l below for the head of John the Baptist being presented to another debauched woman.

4p-Paganism and birthdays. Among the heathen, there were birthday gods and goddesses. These idols were often worshiped with a lighted birthday cake being presented to the appropriate deity. Both pagan Greeks and Romans took up the custom, and it has (with various alterations) been handed down to us today. The first and earliest Christians, who were persecuted by both Jews and pagans, disdained to celebrate birthdays for the above reasons. Instead, early believers in Christ quietly observed what they called "death days." They held that death liberated the suffering ones from their enemies and transported them into the eternal presence of their Lord. By the fourth century A. D., the apostate church began to make a noise about the birth of Christ. This resulted in the tradition of celebrating Christmas and Jesus' birth. It was with the celebration of Christ's nativity that the western world gradually went back into the original pagan custom. By the twelfth century, parish churches in Europe made records of birth dates of women and children; families got busy observing the dates with annual celebrations. It was during this time that the candled decked birthday cake reemerged. For details, see *Extraordinary Origins of Everyday Things,* pages 31-35, written by the skeptic infidel Charles Panati. The largest birthday celebration in relevant history was that of Hitler at fifty years of age. It was observed by millions of duped German people, worshiping a human Devil. His insanity is seen in *Mein Kamph* where he wrote that he was doing God's work in killing Jews!

(i) **Danced before them in Herod's castle at Machaerus.** Still today, there are traces of an old Roman paved road leading up the mountain side to the ancient town and prison tower of Machaerus. Ruins of large broken stones and traces of a temple to the Syrian Sun god, cisterns, and desolation are on every hand. The entire complex was built in a sprawling gorge on a ridge 3,860 feet above the Dead Sea, which can be seen some six miles westward. The infamous prison was located to the east of the town. The name "Machaerus" means "the Black Fortress." At this strategic location, Herod Antipas had built a royal palace complete with kitchens, dining halls, baths, sun parlors, and many rooms. Amid riches, power, and too much of everything, the Devil is quick to provide every occasion for men to sin and realize the gratification of their most wicked thoughts. Matt. 14:6 with Mk. 6:21 reveals that, in time, a government birthday party was thrown in honor of Antipas. In Mk. 6:21 it is clear that hundreds, if not thousands, were present on this occasion of revelry and wild partying. Pious Jews looked upon the celebration of birthdays as a heathen custom, during which demons were worshiped and sin's follies were enjoyed. Wild music, loudness, frolicking, limitless drinking, and the exhibiting of vivacious females in passionate and seductive dances were the highlight of these occasions. (Those commentators who write that there is no evidence that this was a drunken orgy need an introduction to reality.) Salome, the daughter of Herodias, (who was apparently not present) was called upon to come forward and perform her special act. She out danced every girl on the floor! The inspired text declares explicitly that she "came in, and danced" (Mk. 6:22). One can imagine the vast hall packed with political dignitaries; hundreds of lamps burning; sweaty, busy servants rushing back and forth; the coarse joking, loudness, eating, drinking, cheering, and sinful frivolity that accompanies such events. Both Herod Antipas and "those that sat with him" roared their approval as Salome swung and whirled across the marble floor of the banqueting hall in a most provocative and sensuous manner. See Esther chapter 1, for a *reverse* example of this, when a *modest pagan* woman refused to exhibit her body before wine filled fools at a Persian feast. "Bible scholars" who attempt to explain this away or state that it never happened should change occupations and do something honest for a living.

2p-Dancing on festive occasions was common among both Jews and pagan Gentiles. Youths and virgins, singly or separated into bands would dance, but *never* did the sexes intermingle and dance, body pressed against body. Pagans would dance to a god, goddess, or a hero, during times of joy and solemnity. In the Old Testament, Miriam danced (Ex. 15:20), the daughter of Jephthah danced (Judges 11:34), and even David (2 Sam. 6:14). The famous dance of lights during the Jewish Feast of Tabernacles is well known in Hebrew history. For explanation of Tabernacles, note Section 119, third paragraph of footnote a, especially paragraph six, for a detailed description of this fantastic religious expression. However, male and female dancing in pairs was unknown in the East. It came about due to the elevation of women from their lower status in society. The consequences of body–to–body dancing and the final fruits of the dance floor are horrific.

(j) **The oath.** Herod's words are often misunderstood by the western mind. This was *only* a way of speaking employed by rulers, princes, and kings to express their appreciation to the highest degree for some act performed. "Half of my kingdom" meant that regardless of the costs, the request would be granted. It did not signify that the ruler would literally relinquish half of his domain. Antipas could have never done this without Emperor Caesar Augustus and the entire Roman Senate rising up against him. See Esther 5:3, 6 for another ancient example of this statement. Historically, it is true that Herod had no kingdom to give anybody! He was a vassal of Rome, and what he had belonged to Caesar and the senate. Critics have denied just about every detail of this event. Harold W. Hoehner in his classic work *Herod Antipas a Contemporary of Jesus Christ* deals with every one of their objections. Those who think Herod was sober and had drunk in strict moderation are seriously unrealistic! His wild rashness spelled his doom! It reminds one of the hasty vows of Jephthah in Judges 11:31. Salome, the benefactor of his offer, requested time to consider; then she would make her request. Hurrying to her mother (who would also have been present somewhere at the wild party), Salome enquired of her maternal advice! For weeks, this evil female had sought to avenge herself on the man who publicly denounced her sins. The shocking instructions given from mother to daughter reveal the hideous evil of both. How sweet was her revenge on the preacher who had publicly condemned her shameful sin. Herodias would silence the man who had disturbed her evil life. Her chilling instructions were, "Salome, ask of your step-father the head of John on a meat platter!" See second paragraph of footnote f above for comments on Herodias' alleged death. In conclusion, to this sordid act, we must remember that no oath is binding that requires one to sin by taking another man's life! That is not his to give or take.

 (k) Too rash and too late. Upon hearing the request from Salome, Herod realized he was trapped by his own rashness and probably half-drunken vow. No ruler would dare to recant such an oath as the one he had made in the presence of hundreds of dignitaries. One can be sure that he knew the source of such an appalling request. Immediately, the orders were given and relayed to the prison executioner on the other end of Machaerus. Refer to Section 62, footnote a, for several precise details on this infamous prison in which John was languishing. Hurriedly, an executioner was dispatched to decapitate the mighty forerunner of Israel's Messiah. Josephus wrote in *Antiquities,* Book 18:5. 2, lines 116 and 119, that John was executed in this prison. The gory head was placed on a charger or platter and rushed to Salome the youthful dancer. The expedition or swift fulfillment of her request is understood because the dancing party was held at Herod's magnificent palace, which stood on a mountainside adjacent the fortress of Machaerus where John was held. For brief details of this palace, see Josephus' *Wars of the Jews,* Book 7, and all of chapter 6. Herod Antipas also had a palace-residence built at Tiberias on the lower western shore of Lake Galilee, which was his place of regular abode. For the unholy and cursed ground on which Antipas built his Tiberias mansion, see Section 95, footnote b.

 (l) "Gave it to her mother." We are stunned at what this verse says! Salome received the bloody platter, lifted the cover, and there lay the grizzly head of her mother's tormenter. She in turn presented this gift to her demon-possessed mother. An old tradition relates, "Herodias took a needle and continually pricked the tongue of John's head." Her hatred for that member of the Baptist's body that had spoken the truth of God about her awful sins is reflected in this ancient legend. The triumph of this vicious woman and her weakling husband were short lived. Soon, the Roman Emperor Caligula in about A.D. 39, would banish both. Following their exile in (Gaul) France and later in Spain, both died. See second paragraph of footnote f above for other comments on the death of Herodias.

 (m) Bodies of executed persons were thrown out to rot and as food for the beasts and fouls. This story of horror has a beautiful ending. Upon hearing of their master's death, the disciples of John retrieved the corpse and buried it. This was their last office of love for the great preacher who had pointed them to the Messiah. Wonderfully, we read later in Scripture of the souls of those that were beheaded for the witness of Jesus before the throne of God (Rev. 20:4). This passage confirms that souls depart bodies at death and move into eternity. All false cults and sects *fiercely* deny this blessed and comforting truth. For needed comments on sincerity without the truth, see Section 95, sixth paragraph of footnote r, and Section 33, third paragraph of footnote c.

 (n) "And went and told Jesus" (Matt. 14:12). How precious are these words of solace in this time of overwhelming sorrow. What a glorious comfort, that in the worst of life's physical calamities, we can tell Jesus. At the end of each day, we should report in and tell Him everything. It would be terrible to think that there was something in our lives that we could not share with the Savior before a night's rest! How comforting to know that He understands us in mercy and love. *O children of God, and weary sinners, hurry to Jesus and tell Him all!* In England of old, the flag flew over the king's palace to signal to the people that their sovereign was at home. Day and night God flies His flags of sun, moon, stars, and all the emblems of nature to remind us that He is always on duty, caring for us. Even amid the worst of natural disasters, He remains eternally vigilant and watchful. Those poor souls that demand a God that prevents all world calamities and suffering, then they will believe on Him, are unrealistic with life and live in a cocoon of self deception. Honest men will eventually face the fact that something is drastically wrong with the human race. Sin and its perpetual consequences shout at us from all sides. Worse, are those who have never gone to Jesus, received Him as personal Lord and Savior, thus knowing peace of mind and heart amid a world gone mad. Look up, reader the King is at home! Eternity's great sovereign welcomes all of honest motives into His throne room. He desires to hear everything we have to say. David wrote, "Pour out your hearts before him:" (Ps. 62:8). "Cast thy burden upon the LORD, and he shall sustain thee: he shall never suffer the righteous to be moved" (Ps. 55:22). Jesus Christ our Lord and Savior is touched with the feelings of our infirmities (Heb. 4:14).

 2p-After the disciples of John had shared their grief with Jesus, something beautiful takes place. In the main heading of the next Section 93, the Savior took them under His love and carried them in a boat across Lake Galilee for an *attempted* time of rest. It is wonderful to read that the Son of God from heaven cares that we have seasons of rest for these weary houses in which our redeemed souls temporarily dwell. In Ps. 139:17-18 we read of the countless thoughts God has toward His children. They are as the sand in number and new each morning!

CHAPTER 11

THE THIRD PASSOVER IS APPROACHING AT JERUSALEM.*

Hearing that Herod Antipas had murdered John the Baptist, the apostles discontinue their work across Galilee, and hurry off to meet Jesus at Capernaum. ** They all depart for the eastern shores of Lake Galilee to rest. The ever-pressing multitudes find them. Jesus teaches the people of His Kingdom, heals, and miraculously feeds more than five thousand.*

*It is assumed that the Savior did not attend this Passover. See details in footnote e below. **Months prior, Christ had given supernatural power and a limited commission to the twelve apostles, who went only to the lost sheep of Israel in Galilee. See Section 59 for this commission. With the country shaken over the death of John, and the uncertainty of Herod Antipas' next move, the apostles stop their work and go to meet Jesus. He takes them to Bethsaida, for a time of rest. This place was outside Antipas' jurisdiction. ***See Section 99 for the feeding of another group of people with seven loaves and two fish several weeks later.

Capernaum and northeast shore of Lake Galilee

Matt. 14:13	Mk. 6:30-33	Lk. 9:10-11	John 6:1-3
	They return and report	***They return and report***	
	30 And the apostles gathered themselves together unto Jesus, and told him all things, both what they had done,(a) and what they had taught.	**10** And the apostles, when they were returned, told him all that they had done.(a)	
	31 And he said unto them, "Come ye yourselves apart into a desert place, and rest a while:" for there were many coming and going, and they had no leisure so much as to eat.(b)		
They retire to rest: but the masses follow	***They retire to rest: but the masses follow***	***They retire to rest: but the masses follow***	***They retire to rest: but the masses follow***
13 When Jesus heard of it, he departed thence by ship into a desert place apart:	**32** And they departed into a desert place by ship privately.	And he took them, and went aside privately into a desert place belonging to the city called Bethsaida.(c)	**1** After these things Jesus went over the sea of Galilee, which is *the sea of* Tiberias.
and when the people had heard *thereof*, they followed(d) him on foot out of the cities.	**33** And the people saw them departing, and many knew him, and ran(d) afoot thither out of all cities, and outwent them, and came together unto him.	**11** And the people, when they knew *it*, followed(d) him:	**2** And a great multitude followed(d) him, because they saw his miracles which he did on them that were diseased.
			To a mountain
			3 And Jesus went up

Matt. 14:14–15	Mk. 6:34–36	Lk. 9:11–12	John 6:3–7
			into a mountain, and there he sat with his disciples.
		► *For His first Passover as Messiah, see Section 29, John 2:13, footnote a. For the second, see Section 52, John 5:1. This present Section in verse 4 is the third. The fourth and final Passover shared with the apostles is in Section 171.*	◄ ***The third Passover*** **4 And the passover, a feast of the Jews, was nigh.** [(e)]
14 And Jesus went forth, and saw a great multitude, and was moved with compassion [(f)] toward them,	**34** And Jesus, when he came out, saw much people, and was moved with compassion [(f)] toward them, because they were as sheep not having a shepherd: and		**5** When Jesus then lifted up *his* eyes, and saw a great company come unto him,
and he healed their sick.	he began to teach them many things.	and he received them, and spake unto them of the kingdom of God, and healed them that had need of healing.	
			Philip tested he saith unto Philip, "Whence shall we buy bread, that these may eat?" [(g)]
			John understood later **6** And this he said to prove [(h)] him: for he himself knew what he would do. **7** Philip answered him, "Two hundred pennyworth [$40.00] of bread is not sufficient for them, that every one of them may take a little."
"Feed the hungry:" ***the disciples are tested*** **15** And when it was evening, his disciples came to him, saying, "This is a desert place, and the time is now past; send [(i)] the multitude away, that they may go into the	***"Feed the hungry:"*** ***the disciples are tested*** **35** And when the day was now far spent, his disciples came unto him, and said, "This is a desert place, and now the time *is* far passed: **36** "Send [(i)] them away, that they may go into the	***"Feed the hungry:"*** ***the disciples are tested*** **12** And when the day began to wear away, then came the twelve, and said unto him, "Send [(i)] the multitude away, that they may go into the towns and	

Matt. 14:15-19	Mk. 6:36-40	Lk. 9:12-15	John 6:8-10
villages, and buy themselves victuals."	country round about, and into the villages, and buy themselves bread: for they have nothing to eat."	country round about, and lodge, and get victuals: for we are here in a desert place."	
16 But Jesus said unto them, "They need not depart; give ye them to eat."*(j)*	**37** He answered and said unto them, "Give ye them to eat."*(j)* And they say unto him, "Shall we go and buy two hundred pennyworth [$40.00] of bread, and give them to eat?" **38** He saith unto them, "How many loaves have ye? go and see."	**13** But he said unto them, "Give ye them to eat."*(j)*	*A lad is found with barely bread and fish* **8** One of his disciples, Andrew, Simon Peter's brother, saith unto him.
Five loaves and two fish **17** And they say unto him, "We have here but five loaves, and two fishes."	*Five loaves and two fish* And when they knew, they say, "Five, [loaves] and two fishes."	*Five loaves and two fish* And they said, "We have no more but five loaves and two fishes; except we should go and buy meat for all this people."	**9** "There is a lad*(k)* here, which hath five barley loaves, and two small fishes: but what are they among so many?"
		14 For they were about five thousand men.	◄*Matthew and Mark give the number in verses 21 and 44. John inserts the same number in verse 10 below.*
18 He said, "Bring them hither to me."			
The orderly Savior **19** And he commanded the multitude to sit down*(l)* on the grass,	*The orderly Savior* **39** And he commanded them to make all sit down*(l)* by companies upon the green grass.	*The orderly Savior* And he said to his disciples, "Make them sit down*(l)* by fifties in a company."	*The orderly Savior* **10** And Jesus said, "Make the men sit down."*(l)* Now there was much grass in the place.
	The hungry masses are quick to obey **40** And they sat down in ranks,	*The hungry masses are quick to obey* **15** And they did so, and made them all sit down.	*The hungry masses are quick to obey* So the men sat down, in

Matt. 14:19–21	Mk. 6:40–44	Lk. 9:16–17	John 6:10–13
	by hundreds, and by fifties.		number about five thousand.
First prayer, then distribution	*First prayer, then distribution*	*First prayer, then distribution*	*First prayer, then distribution*
and took the five loaves, and the two fishes, and looking up to heaven, he blessed,[m] and brake, and gave the loaves to *his* disciples, and the disciples to the multitude.	41 And when he had taken the five loaves and the two fishes, he looked up to heaven, and blessed,[m] and brake the loaves, and gave *them* to his disciples to set before them; and the two fishes divided he among them all.	16 Then he took the five loaves and the two fishes, and looking up to heaven, he blessed[m] them, and brake, and gave to the disciples to set before the multitude.	11 And Jesus took the loaves; and when he had given thanks,[m] he distributed to the disciples, and the disciples to them that were set down; and likewise of the fishes as much as they would.
Everyone had enough 20 And they did all eat, and were filled:	*Everyone had enough* 42 And they did all eat, and were filled.	*Everyone had enough* 17 And they did eat, and were all filled:	*Everyone had enough* 12 When they were filled, he said unto his disciples,
			Jesus was no waster ▼ "Gather up the fragments that remain, that nothing be lost."
Jesus was no waster and they took up of the fragments that remained twelve baskets[n] full.	*Jesus was no waster* 43 And they took up twelve baskets[n] full of the fragments, and of the fishes.	*Jesus was no waster* and there was taken up of fragments that remained to them twelve baskets.[n] (Verse 18 cont. in Section 103.)	13 Therefore they gathered *them* together, and filled twelve baskets[n] with the fragments of the five barley loaves, which remained over and above unto them that had eaten. (Verse 14 cont. in Section 94.)
			▲ *Only John is inspired to write in verse 12 that Jesus instructed to save all the remnants from this miracle meal.*
Thousands were fed 21 And they that had eaten[o] were about five thousand[p] men, beside women and children. (Verse 22 cont. in Section 94.)	*Thousands were fed* 44 And they that did eat[o] of the loaves were about five thousand[p] men. (Verse 45 cont. in Section 94.)		

Footnotes-Commentary

[a] They told Him all things. This is deeply instructive. The twelve share with Jesus all their adventures, experiences, and what they had taught during the long preaching tour across Galilee. Beyond doubt, they spoke of the murder of John at the hands of Herod Antipas. Our Lord, upon hearing of the death of John and the madness of

Antipas, immediately took His little flock of preachers and departed to a safer region across the sea. See footnote c below. Here, we note the lesson that it is lawful and correct for God's people to avoid dangers whenever possible. Such moves never demonstrate a lack of faith, but rather an abundance of wisdom. See Section 36, footnote a, and Section 38, footnote m for earlier examples of Jesus escaping the angry mobs and the fury of the religious leaders. "A prudent man foreseeth evil, and hideth himself: but the simple pass on, and are punished" (Prov. 22:3).

(b) This brief statement reveals the tremendous demands that the crowds laid upon Christ and His apostles. Note it was two-way traffic, described as "coming and going." We are overwhelmed when we remember there were countless thousands of people, continually pressing day and night, to see and hear the Lord Jesus. The words of the prophet deeply touch us when we read, "Surely he hath borne our griefs, and carried our sorrows" (Isa. 53:4). One Man, the sinless Son of God from heaven, carries the weight of the world on His heart. See footnote d below.

2p-**Verse 13. "Desert place."** This expression does not signify a howling desert of blistering heat and sand as known in the western mind. It spoke of a place without human inhabitants, villages, or cities in that proximity. Regardless of its emptiness, it was somewhat amiable, for Christ commanded all the people to be seated "upon the green grass" (Mk. 6:39).

(c) **"Bethsaida,"** meaning "the house of fishers" was out of the jurisdiction of Herod Antipas and under that of the Tetrarch Philip, his mild half-brother. See footnote d below for more on Bethsaida. The apostles would have felt safer here due to Herod's distraught mental state over the murder of John the Baptist. Jesus and His preachers had crossed over the Sea of Galilee and were out of his territory. The Lord Jesus later revisited Bethsaida. This is recorded in Section 102, Mk. 8:22, footnote a. Earlier in His ministry, Christ had pronounced a curse upon this city; but like Capernaum, He returns to the vicinity to offer them a final call of God's mercy and forgiveness. Note this event is recorded in Section 63, Matt. 11:21-22, footnote a. John is the *only* gospel writer to call Lake Galilee by the name Tiberias. *The King James Study Bible* carries this footnote on page 1618, "Following the destruction of Jerusalem (A.D. 70), the Sea of Galilee was renamed Tiberias after (Emperor) Tiberius Caesar." (The differences in name spellings are correct.) If this is right, some assume that John wrote this book *after* A.D. 70. The author holds that all four gospels were written before the city, and temple fell. This is discussed in *Appendix Seven*. The Roman Senate often named and renamed things years in advance.

(d) Continually, the people rushed to follow Jesus. Bethsaida was located in the upper eastern side of Lake Galilee or Tiberias. See footnote b above. Christ led His preachers to some secluded area seemingly outside the hustle of the city that they might find rest. However, rest they did not find because of the surging crowds ever looking for the Lord Jesus. Bethsaida was the home of three of the apostles, Peter, his brother Andrew, and Philip (John 1:44).

(e) **Highlighted in gray** because of its importance in determining the length of Christ's public ministry. Did the Lord Jesus attend this Passover? If so, no details of any fashion are given. Regardless, it was seemingly the third one since His baptism. See asterisk under the main heading of Section 96 for explanation. Some think that the wording of John 7:1 suggests, He had reentered to Judaea (after the Capernaum synagogue sermon in Section 95), then quickly returned to Galilee because the Jews laid in wait there to kill Him. (Being God, He by passed the Torah command to keep Passover as recorded in Deut. 16:6. It should be remembered that His family or part of them would have been present on this occasion.) We note that during the previous Passover, the year before, it was explicitly stated that they sought to kill Him (John 5:18). Even more relevant was the upsetting sermon at Capernaum on "eat my flesh and drink my blood" which only enraged them further. *If indeed, the Lord Jesus attended this third Passover, then total silence falls over the whole event.* The bitter hatred of the religious leaders at Jerusalem and in Judaea was so fierce that Christ deliberately avoided another confrontation with them on this great national occasion. Six months later, we read that the Feast of Tabernacles celebration was at hand and Jesus was going to Jerusalem for that occasion. However, he went in secret and only revealed Himself on the last day of this feast. This was done for prophetic reasons in which He again presented Himself as Israel's Messiah at this annual celebration. For details on this, refer to Section 111, John 7:2 and relative footnotes.

2p-In Mk. 6:33, we note that thousands of people actually ran around the upper northern end of Lake Galilee in pursuit of Messiah. The distance by foot was shorter than the trip by boat, which took several hours. The Lord Jesus chose this method of travel trying to avoid public attention. However, the crowds were standing on the shores of Bethsaida, waiting for Him to arrive, straining hard for a sight of His boat. This was familiar territory for the apostolic band. Just a few miles south, the healing of the demoniacs had recently taken place as described in Section 88. John is precise and writes that most of the people were curious sightseers who wanted to watch another miracle (John 6:2). Despite the overbearing pressure of the mobs, Lk. 9:11 wonderfully reads that "he received them" and He spoke to them of "the kingdom of God, and healed them that had need of healing." One cannot comprehend what these words are really saying. We can imagine the thousands, healed of every malady and disease known, returning to their homes and places of life, telling all who would listen, the praises of this great and good Man, Jesus of Nazareth. Again, the countryside blazed with the story of Christ, the Messiah of Israel.

3p-In John 6:4, we learn that these hoards of humanity were going to Jerusalem. It was almost Passover time down south at the temple. Pilgrims by the thousands, traveling from the known world of that era, were making their way to the city to keep this great celebration of Israel. They had heard of Jesus of Nazareth, who claimed to be the Messiah of Israel, and natural curiosity drove them to seek out this Person to see and hear Him. All roads, traveling lanes, and footpaths, were packed as Jews turned their hearts again to the temple of God and remembered their deliverance from Egypt. Refer to Section 29, all of footnote a, for an explanation of Passover. For John to describe this as "a feast of the Jews," suggests that he wrote to people who lived far away from the land of Israel, and were unacquainted with Jewish national customs. Also, see Section 1, Part 1, all of footnote b for evidence that John first wrote to Hebrews, some of whom were familiar with synagogue liturgies, customs, and so forth. Secondly, he wrote to a vast body of uninformed readers and thus gave detailed explanations for their benefit. Millions, for almost two thousand years have read this beautiful book!

(f) **"Moved with compassion."** Again, we read this statement concerning our Lord. He had taken the twelve into a secluded location for a time of renewal and rest. However, it was short lived. The possibility of physical rest fled as lost souls surged forward to hear the Savior. Every representation of Adam's fallen race moved within that vast ocean of sinful, hurting humanity to reach the Savior. In Mk. 6:34 we read that when Jesus "came out," He saw the people like shepherdless sheep and was moved with tender compassion. These pitiful crowds reminded Him of defenseless sheep harassed by their enemies, thirsty, starving, and neglected, without a shepherd. See Section 56, Matt. 9:36, footnote d for a previous usage of the metaphor of lost and wandering sheep. Later, our Lord employed this illustration a third time in Lk. 15:3-7. Leaving the house or shelter where they were staying, He sat down and began to teach them of His kingdom. He wanted to be their Shepherd. How touching are the words in Matt. 11:5, where we read that the "poor have the gospel preached unto them." These preaching-teaching classes continued all day, until sunset.

(g) Note Philip's request to Christ over a year later, the night before the morning of the cross in the upper room at Jerusalem in Section 175, John 14:8.

(h) **"To prove him."** How many times have we been sent into those impossible situations so that God may prove us? This proving is for our betterment and good. Jesus' Words stunned them. They have been ordered to give bread to some five thousand men not counting the women and children. Suddenly, Andrew speaks out and informs Christ that a lad has been found who has five loaves and two fishes, but even that is not enough. John 6:9 reads that Andrew described the loaves as made of barley and the fish were small. He cannot figure out his Master's reasoning, for this will never feed so many people! The area about Lake Galilee was a land of wheat and barely, according to Deut. 8:8. Barley was harvested just as the Passover occurred, normally in April. On the second day after Passover, the first fruit sheaf was waved before the Lord (that symbolized the resurrection of Christ, 1 Cor. 15:20). This sheaf consisted of fresh barley stalks heavily laden with grain. For a clear explanation of the ancient Jewish calendar, with seasons, festive occasions, rainfall, sowing, reaping, and harvests all mention, see *The Illustrated Bible Dictionary*, Part 1, page 223.

(i) **"Send them away."** The apostles believed that this was the solution to their problem and quickly suggested it as the answer. It reflects their despair. Only John mentions Andrew, Philip and the lad. With the people lingering before Him, and the sun setting, the Lord Jesus looked at Philip and inquired where they may purchase bread to feed the people. Philip being from Bethsaida, (John 1:44), it was natural for Christ to inquire of him. In our speech today, Christ would be asking, "Where in your hometown is a baker from whom we may purchase bread to feed these people?" It strikes us that Jesus was putting the question in order to "prove" Philip. Being God, the Master knew what He would do. However, in grace He attempts to *draw out* not only Philip, but also all the twelve into the needed understanding that with Him present, every situation was under control. At this point, both Philip and the others missed the secret appeal of Christ. He wanted them to respond thus "Master, with thee all things are possible: You know what to do, we don't." Philip's evaluation of the finance needed to purchase bread at a Bethsaida shop, was that "two hundred pennyworth" would only barely feed them (John 6:7). This amounted to some two hundred days' wages. Some commentators believe that Philip was saying the apostles' treasury (attended to by Judas the traitor) did not contain that much (John 12:6). At this time, a penny or denarius (which was a day's wages) with the Jews, would purchase enough bread to feed some ten men. The two hundred pennies (denarii) amount to some $40.00. Philip could have solved the supper problem for a few but the Son of God solved it for everyone present! Now, Christ waited for the verbal response from the remainder of His preachers. All of them surely heard the discussion between Messiah and Philip.

2p-**Desert place.** Not a sand desert of heat and barrenness as considered in the western world. Luke writes of an area without villages, cities, accommodations, and food.

(j) **"Give ye them to eat."** This command for the people to sit upon the grass in orderly fashion, and for the twelve to feed them must have floored the apostles. The sun was setting, and they were growing more anxious every moment. They knew that it was humanly impossible for them to feed this army of people. In their apostolic collection bag, carried by Judas, could not be found two hundred pennies for purchasing bread. They had just suggested to Jesus "Send them away to the towns and villages to buy for themselves." Now, Jesus tells the apostles to feed them!

2p-Richard Wurmbrand, made a statement in his book, *Christ on the Jewish Road*, page 76. He wrote, "Jesus had compassion on men and women because they were hungry, and not only because they were not saved." This truth overshadows the whole miracle performed on this occasion. In parts of Africa and Asia, true missionaries soon learn that a *starving* man first needs food for his stomach before he will receive the gospel for his soul.

(k) **"There is a lad here."** They were called "small fish." Young boys with baskets of bread were common sights across Israel. They were called "baker boys" and sold their wares to the general public. During Passover, with hundreds of thousands of Jewish pilgrims traveling to Jerusalem, "baker boys" were seen everywhere with their baskets filled with black barley loaves and dried or pickled fish. Whether the apostles paid the lad for his basket, or if he gave it, we are not told. What did the stunned apostles think as Christ took the small basket and stepped forward before the hungry masses? We can almost hear Peter muse, "What on earth will He do now?"

(l) The weary Savior commanded proper organization for the large feeding effort. Instantly, the apostles, probably assisted by other believers, were ordered to instruct the hordes of people to sit on the grass in groups of hundreds and fifties (Mk. 6:40). This was for easier feeding and perhaps for a count of precisely how many men were there. It was normal for the Jews to count men but ignore the women and children. The reason for this was that Jewish men provided for the latter. With this, we may learn from our Master the need for things to be done orderly. This action serves as an example of how spiritual work should be enacted. The kingdom of Christ suffers beyond words because of the impropriety of ministers, pastors, and various church leaders.

2p-The execution of divine business has sunk to a shameful level of decadence. This is because of half-hearted planning, incompetent labor, and laziness. It is difficult to find one who will keep his word, answer his mail, and return his phone calls. Religious deadbeats in positions of authority and leadership in the local assemblies should be replaced with persons of sterling character, vision, and the fear of God. These traits are reflected in outward life and conduct. Christ still commands His people to "sit in companies" that are businesslike, aware, composed, well managed, sensitive to His leadership, and instantly dispatch His work. Nothing less is acceptable. Woe be the congregation where the pastor preaches well but lives badly in the exercise of practical everyday Christian service.

(m) **"Looking up to heaven."** Matthew, Mark, and Luke record the beautiful picture of Christ, standing before the thousands, with His face raised upward to heaven, and thanking God, His Father for the basket of bread and fish. (See Acts 27:35 for a parallel of this prayer spoken by Paul from the deck of a storm-driven ship.) For the standard Hebrew prayer at mealtime, see second paragraph below. To this day, many Jews pray with their eyes open, whereas Christians do the opposite. The author of this harmony commentary was personally acquainted with the Romanian Jewish Christian, Richard Wurmbrand, mentioned in footnote j above. Having spent hundreds of hours with Richard, I noticed that he never prayed with his eyes shut! On one occasion while driving from Johannesburg to Pretoria, South Africa, I enquired why he did this. He responded with a smile over his worn face, "Brother Pike, the Savior told us to 'watch and pray;' we cannot watch with our eyes closed!" There are several places in the gospels where Jesus prays looking up to heaven with His eyes open (Mk. 7:34; John 11:41; and John 17:1). It was normal for Jews to pray looking upward. For years to come, hundreds of the people carried in their memory that glorious silhouette against the early night skies, of Christ the Messiah praying over the basket of that little baker boy.

2p-"And brake." Pious Jews would not cut bread with a knife as it was considered the "staff of life." To do so would be highly insulting. The standard Jewish prayer blessing offered for over two thousand years *before* receiving food was "Blessed [or praise be] art thou, our God, King of the universe, who bringest bread out of the earth!" Though there is no record in this event of the "after food prayer," the Jews would utter the following words upon completing a meal, "Blessed [or praise] be our God, the King of the universe, the Creator of the fruit of the vine!" *Clarke's Commentary* explains these prayers in vol. 5, pages 158-159.

(n) **"Twelve baskets full."** It should be noted that the baskets were "full." Everyone had their needs for nourishment met through obedience to the commands of Christ. At least a ton of food would be required to feed these hungry people. John wrote that the Savior ordered all fragments be gathered up, and nothing wasted. *The amount taken up after the miracle was more than they started with!* Apparently, each apostle filled his own basket. We have wondered, what became of these twelve baskets full after the people were fed? There can be no doubt that many of these were pilgrims moving toward Jerusalem for Passover, of which John wrote that it was "nigh" (verse 4). See third paragraph of footnote e. Adam Clarke informs us that during the Feast of Passover, the Jews would often carry baskets filled with straw to remind them of their ancestor's bondage in Egypt. Note *Clarke's Commentary*, vol. 5, page 159 for the interesting details. The pilgrims, upon their arrival at Jerusalem could purchase these baskets. In addition, these crowds had not yet reached the city, which was some ninety miles south.

2p-Never has there been so much waste among believers as today. While much of the world starves to death, many western Christians are criminal wasters with the goods and necessities of mortal life. In few homes today are the "fragments gathered" and eaten later. Here, Jesus teaches a good lesson on saving leftovers for tomorrow.

(o) By the time this feeding effort had ended, it was dark. Small and large fires burned everywhere for light. Hundreds of flaming hand torches could be seen dotting the night skies. Messiah had fed and satisfied all of them. The Jews counted it an ill omen, if after a meal, anyone was still hungry and nothing was left over. We are amazed with joy to read that twelve baskets full were gathered and that nothing was lost or wasted. Does this mean that among the crowds were eleven other "baker boys" who had sold all, and their empty baskets were now refilled? See footnote k above for explanation of the "baker boys." Can this be the source for the other baskets? It is noted that all four evangelists use the same Greek word "kophinos," or "wicker-basket."

2p-As part of Passover celebration, many Jews would carry to the temple small baskets filled with straw to remind them of their nations suffering in Egypt (Ex. 5:10-12). From somewhere amid the crowd, twelve empty baskets were retrieved and filled with delicious, *freshly created* barley bread and fish! Everyone saw Christ as He stood continually producing both bread baked and fish already dried. They strained their eyes in the early night shadows, staring as He placed it into the hands of His preachers. They in turn gave it to the people. The entire operation must have taken several hours at the least. This miracle reminds us of Elisha, who, some seven hundred years prior, fed one hundred people with twenty barley loaves and also had left some left over (2 Kings 4:42-44).

(p) **"Five thousand men beside women and children." National Geographic attacks Christ.** Matthew wrote that this number was "beside [apart from] women and children." Unexaggerated estimates put this crowd at some ten thousand people! This shames the clamor of the "learned academics" who belie the fact that Jesus had massive followings. National Geographic channel presents Him as a teacher trying to get attention and ultimately dying on a Roman cross for his political activities. The "theologians" and "historians" who make these programs are unsaved people who talk so eloquently about something of which they know nothing by experience. Their arrogance emerges as they speak "sincere" trash about the Son of God and Holy Scripture. Poor unsaved religious academics struggle to explain away the supernatural; it terrifies them! They must do this to keep their credentials valid. This miracle of feeding the masses is one of their favorite objects of smiling scorn and wicked unbelief. Like Jesus' substitutionary death on the cross and resurrection from the dead, it offends their spiritually unenlightened intellect. The miraculous feeding required carful order and control of such a vast number, especially so many children. And this had to be done before sunset. The apostles, who were perturbed about how to feed this massive crowd, were instructed to delivered the never-ending supply of food to them. Amazingly, at the end, they stand, each one, with a full basket of fresh bread in hand! Surely, they were astounded. *What a Messianic act! It is the only miracle performed by Christ that is recorded by all four evangelists.* Some two and a half years earlier, Satan had dared the Son of God to turn stones to bread. See Section 23, for the story. Now, He created and distributed a miraculous supply of bread and fish, revealing that He is the Lord of nature and the Son of the living God.

2p-**Make Him King.** Among the milling crowds, whisperings continued throughout the night. This group of Jewish men had reached the conclusion that Jesus of Nazareth was their Messiah. Therefore, He must be crowned King of Israel immediately. We note in the next Section that some five thousand men actually attempted this forced kingship on Him. See this dramatic event recorded in John 6:14-15. Matthew wrote that Christ instructed (meaning "constrained with strong words") His disciples to get into a boat and cross over the sea, as He attempted to dismiss the people and send them away to the nearby villages to find shelter for the night. Afterward, He went to a lonely mountain to pray! How touching that our Lord again resorted to the holy art of prayer in pressing situations that rose in His life. God draws a curtain of silence over this scene. It is too much for mortal man to behold and hear.

3p-**"A good report [testimony] through faith," (Heb. 11:39).** The crowds, wild with enthusiasm were ready to crown Him as their Messiah-King, while His disciples and apostles did not yet understand His true mission. Deliberately pushing the twelve into the ship at night, He beckoned them to go. Little did they know that He was sending them into another terrifying storm in the midst of the Sea of Galilee! Refer to Section 87, Mk. 4:38 for the first storm in which He slept on a pillow in the boat. *True* Christians must remember that wherever the Savior sends them, it is the safest place this side of heaven. Whether a Joseph in Egypt, a Daniel in Babylon, or a Paul in prison, it does not extract God from the situation. History has powerfully demonstrated this many times. Queen Ranavalona ruled the island of Madagascar until her death in 1861. She hated Christians because they opposed slavery, and their converts abandoned the darkness of demonic paganism. All missionaries were ordered out of the country, and Bibles burned. Nationals who were Christians had all goods confiscated and were killed or sold as slaves. Hundreds of thousands died under her bloody reign only equaled in history by the Papal inquisitions and radical Islam. Believers were boiled in tar and water, dismembered, impaled, and burned alive, thrown from cliffs, disemboweled, beaten to pulp, crucified, and decapitated. Many fled into hiding. Rasalama, a firm believer, was sentenced to death by burning. She sang hymns of praise to Jesus as they threw her into the devouring flames. These awful things did not dismiss God's amazing peace and presence from among those martyrs. *He was more real in death than in life.* For a chilling history of the murder of Christians by heathen tyrants, on this island off the southeast coast of Africa, see the *Female Caligula: Ranavalona the Mad Queen of Madagascar,* by archaeologist Keith Laidler for the story. The illustrated cover of this book alone is a horror! Laidler's work shocks the decency of sinners and saints alike. It is another revelation of the depravity of man without the *true* saving knowledge of Jesus Christ.

Excited Jews attempt to crown Him King of Israel.* The twelve are sent across Lake Galilee at 3:00 a.m. Retreating to the mountain, He prays. Afterwards, the Lord Jesus walks on the sea to join the apostles. Simon Peter attempts a water-walk but fails the test. Jesus rescues him.

*This event alone proves that Christ did not come to first offer Himself as the King of the Jews and to establish some sort of literal kingdom for the nation of Israel. Refer to Section 39, footnotes a and g for an explanation of His kingdom. In Section 87, the Lord Jesus had earlier stilled another storm on the waters of Galilee.

Near Bethsaida and along the north east shores of Lake Galilee

Matt. 14:22–24	Mk. 6:45–48	Lk.	John 6:14–19
			A forced kingship **14** Then those men, when they had seen the miracle [of the loaves] that Jesus did, said, "This is of a truth **'that prophet that should come into the world.'** **15** When Jesus therefore perceived that they would come and take him by force, to make him a king,(a) he departed again into a mountain himself alone.
Leaving the masses **22** And straightway Jesus constrained his disciples	*Leaving the masses* **45** And straightway he constrained his disciples		*Leaving the masses* **16** And when even was *now* come, his disciples went down unto the sea,
to get into a ship, and to go before him unto the other side,(b) while he sent the multitudes away. **23** And when he had sent the multitudes away, he went up into a mountain apart to pray:(d) and when the evening was come, he was there alone.	to get into the ship, and to go to the other side(b) before unto Bethsaida,(c) while he sent away the people. **46** And when he had sent them away, he departed into a mountain to pray.(d) **47** And when even was come,		**17** And entered into a ship, and went over(b) the sea toward Capernaum.(c) And it was now dark, and Jesus was not come to them. (yet)
A storm hits **24** But the ship was now in the midst of the sea, tossed with waves: for the wind was contrary.(e)	*A storm hits* the ship was in the midst of the sea, and he alone on the land. **48** And he saw them toiling in rowing; for the wind was contrary(e) unto them:		*A storm hits* **18** And the sea arose by reason of a great wind that blew. **19** So when they had rowed about five and

414

Matt. 14:25–32	Mk. 6:48–51	Lk.	John 6:19–21
Jesus walks on the sea: the disciples are terrified	*Jesus walks on the sea: the disciples are terrified*		twenty or thirty furlongs, (four miles)
25 And in the fourth watch of the night [between 3:00 and 6:00 a.m.] Jesus went unto them, walking on the sea.	and about the fourth watch of the night [between 3:00 and 6:00 a.m.] he cometh unto them, walking upon the sea, and would have passed by them.		
			Jesus walks on the sea: the disciples are terrified
26 And when the disciples saw him walking on the sea,	**49** But when they saw him walking upon the sea,		they see Jesus walking on the sea, and drawing nigh unto the ship: and they were afraid.(f)
they were troubled,(f) saying, "It is a spirit;" and they cried out for fear.	they supposed(f) it had been a spirit, and cried out: **50** For they all saw him, and were troubled.		
27 But straightway Jesus spake unto them, saying, "Be of good cheer; it is I; be not afraid."(g)	And immediately he talked with them, and saith unto them, "Be of good cheer: it is I; be not afraid."(g)		**20** But he saith unto them, "It is I; be not afraid."(g)
Peter attempts a water–walk and sinks **28** And Peter answered him and said, "Lord, if it be thou, bid me come unto thee on the water." **29** And he said, "Come." And when Peter was come down out of the ship, he walked on the water, to go to Jesus.(h) **30** But when he saw the wind boisterous, he was afraid; and beginning to sink, he cried, saying, "Lord, save me." **31** And immediately Jesus stretched forth *his* hand, and caught(i) him, and said unto him, "O thou of little faith, wherefore didst thou doubt?" **32** And when they were come into the ship, the wind ceased.			
	51 And he went up unto them into the ship; and the wind ceased:		
			21 Then they willingly received him into the ship:

415

Matt. 14:33–36	Mk. 6:51–56	Lk.	John 6:21
	and they were sore amazed in themselves beyond measure, and wondered. **52** For they considered not *the miracle* of the loaves: for their heart was hardened. (j)		
The amazing Messiah **33** Then they that were in the ship came and worshipped him, saying, (k) "Of a truth thou art the Son of God."			
An overlooked miracle **34** And when they were gone over, they came into the land of Gennesaret. (l)	*An overlooked miracle* **53** And when they had passed over, they came into the land of Gennesaret (l) and drew to the shore.		*An overlooked miracle* and immediately the ship was at the land whither they went. (l) (Verse 22 cont. in Section 95.)
Humanity gathers to Jesus **35** And when the men of that place had knowledge (m) of him, they sent out into all that country round about, and brought unto him all that were diseased; (n)	*Humanity gathers to Jesus* **54** And when they were come out of the ship, straightway they [the people] knew (m) him, **55** And ran through that whole region round about, and began to carry about in beds those that were sick, (n) where they heard he was. **56** And whithersoever he entered, into villages, or cities, or country, they laid the sick in the streets,		
The touch of faith **36** And besought him that they might only touch the hem of his garment: (o) and as many as touched were made perfectly (p) whole. (Next chap., Matt. 15:1 cont. in Section 96.)	*The touch of faith* And besought him that they might touch if it were but the border of his garment: (o) and as many as touched him were made whole. (p) (Next chap., Mk. 7:1 cont. in Section 96.)		

Footnotes-Commentary

(a) **Verse 14.** "Those men," meaning the five thousand, He had just fed as recorded in Section 93, Matt. 14:21.

2p-"That prophet." Highlighted in gray. These are the words of someone in the crowd who gave a general quote from Deut. 18:15. Here, Moses predicted the coming of Messiah about fifteen hundred years in advance. This vast multitude of Jewish men, upon witnessing the miracle of the loaves and fishes, reached the conclusion that Jesus was Messiah based on this specific miracle. Instantly, they connected it to Moses' prophecy. Lightfoot's

Commentary on the New Testament . . . , is helpful at this point. In volume 3, page 305, he wrote about an ancient Jewish belief that when their Messiah came, He would "lead Israel into the wilderness … and make manna descend from heaven." Was this old story along with Moses' prediction the reason for the crowd's mad rush to suddenly make Jesus their king? They called Him "that prophet," revealing they understood Moses' words in Deut. 18:15-19 as pointing to Messiah. They related Moses feeding Israel with manna from heaven to the miracle just performed by Christ. George Sasson's book, edited by Rodney Dale, entitled *The Kabbalah Decoded. A new translation of the 'Ancient of days' texts of the Zohar,* states on page 19, that there were "traditions [among the ancient Jews] that manna supplies will be restored at the coming of the Messiah." The ancient Hebrew writing, *Midrash Ecclesiastes* 1, by Rabbah Nosso, spoke of Messiah riding on an ass (Section 148, Palm Sunday), and bringing manna (bread) down from heaven. Did such beliefs move the crowd into action? Plans were made to kidnap Christ and crown Him the King of Israel. Again, we see the folly of the teaching that Christ offered Himself as the political King of Israel only, and *they* rejected the offer. With hundreds of thousands following the Savior from all over the country, He could have at any time presented Himself for the royal position, and they would have responded. See Section 21, Part 4, footnote q, regarding the message of John the Baptist. Continually, we see Him trying to escape the mobs and ever pressing forward to do the will of God. Now, He seems to be trapped somewhere near Bethsaidia by the pressing crowds, who will force on Him the kingship of Israel. The inspired text informs us that He "perceived" their intentions and went into the mountains alone. Refer to Section 93, second paragraph of footnote p, for the aborted attempt to crown Jesus as King of the Jews.

3p-A forced kingship of Christ. If this had been attempted in either the territory of Herod Antipas, Herod Philip, or Pilate it would have been counted as treason against Rome. See footnote d below. Dr. Charles Ryrie in the *Ryrie Study Bible,* page 1610 makes this strange comment, "Jesus had to escape from the enthusiasm of the crowd, which would have forced Him to lead them in revolt against the Roman government. Jesus refused to become a political revolutionist." *Nothing* could have "forced" the Son of God into a revolt against Rome! This is appallingly incorrect. If the Son of God had ever offered the Jews a literal, political kingdom, then why on this occasion did He flee from what He was supposed to have offered them? *Being in Galilee had nothing to do with it.* Not one time across the whole of His ministry did Jesus offer the Jews a physical or material kingdom. Dwight Pentecost in *The Words & Works of Jesus Christ,* page 234, wrote, "Christ had offered Himself as a King." This is another example of reckless dispensationalism that continually backs itself into an eschatological corner. Instead, He offered the Jews Himself as their Messiah, His soon atonement on the cross and entrance into the spiritual new kingdom or church He was building. (This does not negate the fact that there will be some kind of rule of Christ in a glorified state among saved Jews.) For the "kingdom offer" myth, see Hal Lindsey, *The Late, Great Planet Earth*, pages 20-21; and *Premillennialism or Amillennialism*, pages 199-200, by C.L. Fienberg. Note Section 39, footnotes a and g, and Section 134, footnotes c and d, for an explanation of both manifestations of the kingdom.

(b) Our Lord, sensing the scheme of the frivolous, stomach-filled crowds instantly sent the twelve across the lake. Was this because they too might have become embroiled in the kingly plot of the masses? With the crowds pressing upon Him, He quickly retreated through the dark night to a nearby mountain for a time of prayer with the Father. How oft have we failed to hurry to our Lord amid the early signs of terrible conflict and pending trouble?

(c) Mark records that the apostles were to sail ahead to Bethsaida (verse 45), while John wrote that, they went toward Capernaum (verse 17). This means they went over the sea toward Capernaum and steered their course *from* Bethsaida, for it was here their journey began. These two places were about four miles apart and located at the northern side of Galilee, in a district called Gennesaret. Bethsaida was on the east and Capernaum on the west upper end of the conclave of the sea. Sailing around this curve, they would pass Bethsaida and then reach their *ultimate* destination of Capernaum in the Gennesaret area.

(d) **"Up into a mountain to pray."** While the excited crowds were planning their coronation of Christ as the King of the Jews, He was hiding in the mountain engaged in prayer. Meanwhile, the apostles were riding their little boat into the moonlit, tumultuous Galilee waters. We cannot help but wonder in deep reverence *for whom* and *for what* Jesus prayed that troubled night. Was it for His little flock of preachers soon to crash into another violent storm? Was it for the people who failed to understand that He would not be their King at that time? Could He have been in prayer over the upcoming cross, ever drawing near. Alternatively, was it perhaps for us, for you and me? Silence falls over this sacred scene. Divine things are too high for our low understanding. Angels viewed that sight with awe. Creation's stars and old Mr. Moon shined their lights upon that glorious but awesome spectacle.

(e) **"The wind was contrary."** So reads Mk. 6:48. The meaning is that the men were rowing their boat contrary to the fierce winds sweeping over the lake. The sea swelled, was tumultuous and raging. See footnote l below for their miraculous trip after the storm had ceased. For our Lord's final trip through this city, refer to Section 100, footnote f. Among the twelve were (at least) four professional fishermen who knew these waters by night and day. Fishing at night was common work. Both Matt. 14:25 and Mk. 6:48 inform us that it was "about" the fourth watch when the storm struck. See footnote f below for explanation of this time. They were toiling at the oars, meant this was a smaller vessel and not one with sails offering more safety amid storms and turbulent waters.

2p-Matt. 14:25. He walks on the sea! Religious infidels over the ages have attacked this miracle as well as the others recorded in the Bible. A "learned professor," in a northern theological seminary, invented the "brilliant" conclusion that due to a dramatic change in the weather, the top of the sea froze over and Christ walked on ice! These are normal responses from men who have never been saved and changed by the grace of God. It is not that alarming, as we can sadly expect nothing better from these poor souls without the Lord Jesus Christ.

3p-From a battlefield of the Civil War history we see the wonder of God bringing salvation to men. Daniel Webster Whitter (died 1901) was an officer in the Union Army, holding the rank of major. He was unsaved but deeply concerned in his soul's welfare. Being severely wounded with an arm blown off, he was taken prisoner in the southern United States. While in a makeshift Confederate hospital, an orderly noticed Whitter reading a Bible. Thinking he was a Christian, he requested the major to go and pray with a young soldier that was dying. Confounded as to what he should do, he knelt beside the cot of the dying youth, took his hand, and inquired, "Are you prepared to meet God?" His question pierced his own heart! The soldier said nothing, but tightly gripped the major's hand. The officer reposed his weary head over the young man, mumbled, "Trust Jesus Christ", and then prayed. The dying man nodded in the affirmative, smiled, and passed into eternity. Daniel Whitter, later testified that God saved him as he prayed for the other man to be saved. Both came to Christ in this way of grace and mercy and have now been together in heaven for over a hundred years! "His [God's] ways are past finding out" (Rom. 11:33).

(f) "They were troubled or afraid." It was commonly believed by mariners and superstitious Jews frequenting Galilee, that the spirit or apparition of drowned persons would walk during fierce storms amid full moonlight. John informs us that the boat was "five and twenty or thirty furlongs" (or four miles) into the sea (verse 19). This would put them mid way in their journey to Capernaum, as this body of water was nine miles across. "About the fourth watch of the night" was between 3:00 and 6:00 a.m. Earlier when the Master had commanded them to depart across Galilee it was nearing sundown (John 6:16). Now, it is close to sunrise, signifying, they had been battling the raging waters many long hours. Paralyzing terror fell upon the apostles. They believed that their Master had drowned and His spirit walked in their sight to warn them of danger and a possible similar fate. It was also believed that such nocturnal phantoms would *never* enter a ship. Hence, Mark writes that Jesus walked as though He "would have passed them by" (verse 48). Mark is explicit to write, "They all saw him" (verse 50). The question of how Christ moved so swiftly from the mountain where he prayed into the middle of stormy Galilee is not answered. God saw no need to minister to human curiosity by answering this childish inquiry. Eleven of these apostles had a similar experience (with an assumed "spirit") on the night after the resurrection of Christ.

(g) "It is I; be not afraid." Knowing the terror of their superstitions, the Lord Jesus deliberately spoke words of good cheer seeking to assure them that He was present and all would be well. There was a sudden and almost frightening lull of crashing waves and howling winds; the next sound was that of their Master's voice, clear, kind, and filled with assurance and comfort. The silver shimmering of moonbeams illuminated the scene as the horrified apostles, wide-eyed, gazed upon their Lord. Now, He walks upon water, and it holds Him up! No wonder they were terrified. The question of Ps. 114:5 is most appropriate "What *ailed* thee, O thou sea that thou fleddest?" Again, we read, "Thy way, O God, *is* in the sea and thy path in the great waters" (Ps. 77:19). If He could turn water into fresh wine, then He could walk on it as well!

(h) Only Matthew tells of Peter attempting his walk on the water. Amid the uncanny stillness of that moment, the voice of Peter booms loudly! The storm of terror that raged in their hearts, now, like that on the sea was silenced by His presence. Naturally, Peter must say something or burst! "Lord, if it be thou …" Amazing words indeed! Had He not just identified Himself to them? Regardless, daring Peter questions His Lord. Upon hearing spoken permission from Christ, he swings over the side of the boat, and his feet hit *solid water!* For whatever task the Lord Jesus commands, He will give the sufficient grace to accomplish it. Suddenly in the middle of his water walk, the wind and waves again come unleashed and drop upon the scene with renewed fury. The moonlit scenario before Peter instantly became a fisherman's nightmare. Tall waves slam boisterously about him and his solid water footing begins to roll and weave beneath his feet. Early glimmers of good faith, when all was quickly made peaceful, vanished as Peter feels the wetness of Galilee's cold water moving over his ankles up his legs. The word means he was sinking slowly into the sea. Although being a good swimmer as a Jewish fisherman, this ability could not save him now. He is sinking and will die! It was a dramatic moment that wrung from Peter's soul the cry "Lord save me," as his body sank! When pig headed men sincerely call upon the Lord for mercy, they will find it.

(i) In loving care, the Lord of creation reaches out to rescue His impetuous preacher while at the same time whispering in his ear the needed rebuke, "O thou of little faith, wherefore didst thou doubt?" Peter had more ardor than his faith would justify, and more forwardness than humility could endure. He was afraid when in danger but brash when not. Such saints as these the Lord of glory will permit to learn their lessons by costly experiences. Have we not all attempted our own walk on Galilee? In verse 32, Matthew informs us that *both* Peter and Jesus walked to the boat, revealing that Jesus' rebuke restored the fisherman's faith once again! About three decades later, Peter wrote about faith tried by fire (1 Peter 1:7) or in this case water! The eternal God who caused the iron to float on water (2 Kings 6:6), now caused His hasty preacher to walk on water. Job said of God, "He treadeth upon the waves of the sea" (Job 9:8).

2p-The whole drama of Peter's water-walk was both seen and heard by the remainder of the apostles watching from the boat that moonlit morning. John wrote, "They willingly received him into the ship" (John 6:21). Terrified they "all" quickly assisted both Peter and the Lord Jesus aboard.

(j) **"Hard hearts."** The meaning is clear. These men had forgotten the miracle of feeding the crowds only the day before. The terror of the storm had hardened their poor hearts. They were not quick to learn from the wonderful Man they had just confessed was their Messiah. We today are not much better! Almost every day brought another "shock experience" into their lives! His teachings continually amazed them, His miracles staggered their imagination, and several of His commands left the apostles stunned, confused, and even fearful. One may believe that later when they recalled these experiences; surely, their hearts were cheered and spirits warmed anew upon remembering such events as these shared with their glorious Master and Messiah.

(k) A pious title for Israel's Messiah, spoken as the apostles worshiped Him from the wet floor of their boat. They knew Messiah was called the Son of God. (What did Judas think of all this?) Matthew reported that as this worship service commenced "the wind ceased" (verse 32). The atoms of nature's structure instantly recognized Him as their creator and supreme Lord of the universe. For an extended explanation of this glorious Messianic title of the Savior, see Matt. 16:16. Also, see Matt. 26:63 for the high priest's question to Jesus during His trial. Note, the Devil's usage of this title, in Section 23, Matt. 4:3, third paragraph of footnote c.

(l) The four-mile journey to this district and the city of Capernaum was traversed in a split second. See footnote f above for the distance they had traveled when Christ came to them. *Here, is one of those overlooked miracles of Christ.* Only John reported this supersonic trip across half of Lake Galilee. In the Old Testament, the Spirit of God transported men instantly from one place to the other (1 Kings 18:12; Ezek. 8:3; with 11:1).

2p-"Gennesaret." Meaning "garden of riches," was the name of a geographical district located on the western side of Lake Galilee, in which stood the cities of Capernaum and Tiberius. It was also applied to the Sea of Galilee (Lk. 5:1), as well as a specific town in the Old Testament (Josh. 19:35). The district is still today a rich plain some four miles long and two broad. Jesus had earlier pronounced a curse upon Capernaum, but continued to return offering them the last measure of mercy. The earlier curse upon this city is given in Section 63.

(m) It was now full sunrise. The people standing along the shoreline where the boat docked instantly recognized the Master and His little band of preachers. They went in every direction alerting the people of this area that Israel's Messiah had arrived on their shores. See footnote n below.

(n) Word spread across the district and into every city, village, hamlet, and home that Jesus of Nazareth was present. Mayhem broke loose as thousands of people, running in every direction, brought a tidal wave of sick, and suffering humanity to the Savior. Untold hundreds were blessed, healed, and believed in this wonderful Man. In Mk. 6:56 we discover a new dimension to the ministry of Christ in the region of Gennesaret. We read that whole "cities and villages" in the district were aroused and rushed out to see and hear Him. This meant thousands of people. The whole country was aflame with word of Him. He was not an obscure Jew, mostly unknown. See footnote m above.

(o) News of the woman who had touched the hem of His garment months before and was instantly healed had spread over this part of the land. See her healing in the main heading of Section 89. Now, hundreds scramble to make the touch. Never in the history of Israel had such wonderful things happened. Contemplation of all this leaves one in a sense of awe, transfixed by a deep reverential fear of God and unspeakable love for Christ, *always* reaching out to hurting humanity, whether they love and honor Him or not. The Savior's *last miracle* before His death was to heal the ear of one of His enemies during the night skirmish in the garden of Gethsemane. Refer to Section 181, John 18:26, footnote o for this amazing manifestation of love and compassion.

2p-Big time religious phonies. This wonder accomplished by touching His hem hardly gives grounds for the absurd practices abounding today by the popular TV preachers and religious personalities. These people are mailing out "prayer cloths," "bottles of water," even "grass and soil from the Holy Land," so that the sick may be healed, the possessed delivered, and prosperity come. Such ill practices reflect abysmal ignorance of God's Word, take on an authority that has never been delegated, and show deep irreverence in handling divine things with shameless frivolity. Worse, they play on the gullible. leaving them in despair and often using them for financial gain. For a classic example of this today, see Section 55, second paragraph of footnote d.

(p) **"Perfectly whole."** Almighty God alone could perform such miracles as these. This is another affirmation that Jesus is everything God is and is therefore, God. The shameful examples of "faith healing" as seen on national television, performed by "anointed men and women of God," are mockeries when laid beside these miracles of the Lord Jesus. For further thoughts on this and related subjects, see Section 207 second and third paragraphs, footnote i. For the *original* and divine reasons of Jesus' thousand of miracles and supernatural wonders, see Section 48, all in italics under the main heading.

THE UPSETTING SYNAGOGUE DISCOURSE.*

Messiah intentionally gives a disturbing message. The Jews are greatly angered. Many disciples leave. The twelve threaten to abandon Him. Simon Peter saves the day. The Lord Jesus continued to stay in Galilee because the Jews in Judaea sought to kill Him.

*At this place in the life of Christ, we are introduced to His memorable discourse, which gave so great offence to both friends and foes alike. With the shadow of the cross hovering so near, Jesus deliberately began to sift the false disciples from His true ones. This difficult message began the great separation among His followers. He deliberately couched it in terms that offended the non spiritual and think less people who pretended to follow Him. To this present day this great lesson given by our Lord has been distorted and perverted from its high spiritual faith meaning into a cannibalistic form of literalism that has become a blasphemous lie deceiving millions.

Matt.	Mk.	Lk.	John 6:22-35 (John 7:1)—*In a Capernaum synagogue*
			He cannot be found the next day: the masses go to Capernaum
			22 The day following,[a] when the people which stood on the other side of the sea saw that there was none other boat there, save that one whereinto his disciples were entered, and that Jesus went not with his disciples into the boat, but *that* his disciples were gone away alone;
			23 (Howbeit there came other boats from Tiberias nigh unto the place where they did eat bread, after that the Lord had given thanks:)[b]
			24 When the people[c] therefore saw that Jesus was not there, neither his disciples, they also took shipping, and came to Capernaum, seeking for Jesus.
			25 And when they had found him on the other side of the sea, they said unto him, "Rabbi, when camest thou hither?"
			Christ rebukes the multitude's insincerity
			26 Jesus answered them and said, "Verily, verily, I say unto you, Ye seek me, not because ye saw the miracles, but because ye did eat of the loaves, and were filled.
			What to work for
			27 "Labour not for the meat [food] which perisheth, but for that meat which endureth unto everlasting life, which the Son of man shall give unto you: for him hath God the Father sealed."[d]
			28 Then said they unto him, "What shall we do, that we might work the works of God?"[e]
			To believe on Jesus is to do the greatest work of God
			29 Jesus answered and said unto them, "This is the work of God, that ye believe on him whom he hath sent."[f]
			30 They said therefore unto him, "What [Messianic] sign[g] shewest thou then, that we may see, and believe thee? what dost thou work?
			31 "Our fathers did eat manna in the desert; [wilderness] as it is written,[h] **'He gave them bread from heaven to eat.'"**
			God gives the true eternal bread not Moses
			32 Then Jesus said unto them, "Verily, verily, I say unto you, Moses gave you not that bread from heaven; but my Father giveth you the true bread from heaven.
			Christ sent from heaven is the true bread
			33 "For the bread of God is he [Jesus Christ] which cometh down from heaven, and giveth life unto the world."
			34 Then said they unto him, "Lord, evermore give us this bread."
			35 And Jesus said unto them, "I am[i] the bread of life: he that cometh to me shall never hunger; and he that believeth on me shall never

Matt.	Mk.	Lk.	John 6:35–54 (John 7:1)—*In a Capernaum synagogue*
			thirst.
			36 "But I said unto you, That ye also have seen me, and believe not.
			God given men will come to Jesus
			37 "All that the Father giveth me shall come to me; and him that cometh to me I will in no wise cast out.**(j)**
			38 "For I came down from heaven, not to do mine own will, but the will of him that sent me.
			39 "And this is the Father's will which hath sent me, that of all which he hath given me I should lose nothing, but should raise it up again at the last day.**(k)**
			40 "And this is the will of him that sent me, that every one which seeth the Son, [by faith] and believeth on him, may have everlasting life: and I will raise him up at the last day."
			He addresses the Jews and explains the bread
			41 The Jews then murmured at him, because he said, "I am the bread which came down from heaven."
			42 And they said, "Is not this Jesus, the son of Joseph, whose father and mother we know?**(l)** how is it then that he saith, 'I came down from heaven'?"
			43 Jesus therefore answered and said unto them, "Murmur not**(m)** among yourselves.
			44 "No man can come to me, except the Father which hath sent me draw him: and I will raise him up at the last day.**(n)**
			45 "It is written in the prophets,**(o)** 'And they shall be all taught of God.' Every man therefore that hath heard, and hath learned of the Father, cometh unto me.
			46 "Not that any man hath seen the Father, save he which is of God, he hath seen the Father.**(p)**
			47 "Verily, verily, I say unto you, He that believeth on me hath everlasting life.
			48 "I am that bread of life.
			49 "Your fathers did [physically] eat manna in the wilderness, and are dead.
			50 "This is the bread which cometh down from heaven, that a man may eat [by faith] thereof, and not die.
			51 "I am the living bread which came down from heaven: if any man eat of this bread, [by faith] he shall live for ever: and the bread that I will give is my flesh, which I will give [on the cross] for the life of the world."**(q)**
			The confused and factious Jews argue
			52 The Jews therefore strove among themselves, saying, "How can this man give us *his* flesh to eat?"**(r)**
			A final warning given to the masses: "eat and drink or die"
			53 Then Jesus said unto them, "Verily, verily, I say unto you, Except ye eat the flesh of the Son of man, and drink his blood, [by faith] ye have no life in you.
			54 "Whoso eateth my flesh, and drinketh my blood, [by faith] hath eternal life; and I will raise him up at the last day.

Matt.	Mk.	Lk.	John 6:55-7—John 7:1—*In a Capernaum synagogue*
			55 For my flesh is [spiritual] meat indeed, and my blood is [spiritual] drink indeed.

56 "He that eateth my flesh, and drinketh my blood, [by faith] dwelleth in me, and I in him.

57 "As the living Father hath sent me, and I live by the Father: so he that eateth me, [by faith] even he shall live by me.

58 "This is that bread which came down from heaven: not as your fathers did eat manna, and are dead: he that eateth [by faith] of this bread [the Messiah] shall live for ever."

The disciples also complain

59 These things said he in the synagogue, as he taught in Capernaum.

60 Many therefore of his disciples, when they had heard *this*, said, "This is an hard[(s)] saying; who can hear it?"

61 When Jesus knew in himself that his disciples murmured at it, he said unto them, "Doth this offend you?

62 "*What* and if ye shall see the Son of man ascend up where he was before?[(t)]

He explains that He was using spiritual language; they should not be offended but believe

63 "It is the Spirit that quickeneth; [gives life] the flesh profiteth nothing: the Words that I speak unto you, [about eating my flesh and drinking my blood] *they* are spirit, [symbolic] and *they* are life.[(u)]

64 "But there are some of you that believe not." For Jesus knew from the beginning who they were that believed not, and who should betray him.

65 And he said, "Therefore said I unto you, that no man can come unto me, except it were given unto him of my Father."

He is forsaken by many: the twelve also consider leaving

66 From that *time* many of his disciples went back, and walked no more with him.[(v)]

67 Then said Jesus unto the twelve, "Will ye also go away?"

Peter confesses again: Jesus is declared to have the words of life and to be the Messiah of Israel

68 Then Simon Peter answered him, "Lord, to whom shall we go? thou hast the words of eternal life.

69 "And we believe and are sure that thou art that Christ, [Messiah] the Son of the living God."[(w)]

The dreadful warning: "there is a devil among you"

70 Jesus answered them, "Have not I chosen you twelve, and one of you is a devil?"

Looking back later, John understands and explains to his readers

71 He spake of Judas Iscariot *the son* of Simon: for he it was that should betray him, being one of the twelve.[(x)] (Next chap., John 7:1 cont. below.)

Matt.	Mk.	Lk.	John 7:1—*He remains in Galilee*

Knowing of the Jewish death plot He disdains to go into Judaea

1 After these things[(y)] Jesus walked in Galilee: for he would not walk in Jewry, [Judaea] because the Jews [there] sought to kill him.[(z)] (Verse 2 cont. in Section 111.)

Footnotes-Commentary

(a) It is now the morning *after* the miracle of loaves and fishes and the apostles' terrifying voyage across the sea, as given in Section 94. Hundreds gathered along the shoreline looking for Jesus, who had spent the night away from them in the mountains praying. Noticing the boat in which the apostles traveled was missing and knowing that Jesus did not go with them, they concluded that He was still on their side of the sea. They did not know that the Lord Jesus had water-walked through the night to the apostle's boat and climbed aboard.

(b) This fact, though mentioned in John 6:11, is added to show again that the miracle of the loaves and fishes took place through prayer and the power of God resting on Jesus the Messiah. Tiberias was reputed as a center of learning for Jewish doctors and wise men. Herod Antipas built this vast city in honor of the Emperor Tiberius. For details on Herod, refer to Section 21, Part 1, number 3 under footnote b. A famed university was there, and behind its walls, a newly organized Sanhedrin, led by Rabbi Yochanan ben Zakki, sat for a time after the destruction of Jerusalem in A.D. 70. All this is extraordinary, given that Antipas built the city on the site of an ancient graveyard, which would make it repugnant to all pious Jews. Both the *Jerusalem* and *Babylonian Talmuds* were supposedly compiled at Tiberias.

(c) The fickle crowds crossed the sea and went to Capernaum. Some took boats, but most walked, being a vast multitude of some five thousand people. It was seemingly the Sabbath day, and they hastened to the synagogue where they found the Lord Jesus teaching (verse 59). Purposely diverting from their question in verse 25, the Messiah exposed their true reason for seeking Him out. They were hungry again and sought another miracle meal from Him (verse 26). This was the very crowd who attempted, only yesterday, to force kingship upon Him! Knowing their selfishness, He lays before them their real need, which was something greater than physical bread. He presented Himself as God's *only* source from which men may receive the "meat [food] of everlasting life." Just the day before, they had received from Him the fishes and loaves to sustain human life.

(d) **"Sealed."** Our Lord warns us to attend first to spiritual things. In so doing, we find unspeakable comfort in the truth that Jesus Christ has been "sealed" or "approved" as being truth incarnate. The congregation instantly understood the meaning of Christ's Words for they were a well-known Jewish expression. No sacrifice was offered at the temple, no priestly garments worn, no wood burned on the altar, no cakes accepted for showbread, no oil for the candlesticks, yea, hardly anything was offered to Jehovah, unless first it had been "sealed" or declared acceptable, clean, or truth by the priests. Christ claims for Himself the very approval and seal of Israel's God! *This was something that only Messiah could do.*

2p-The rabbis dictated that the word "truth" was composed of three digits from the Hebrew alphabet. *"Aleph"* being the first letter, *"mem"* the middle, and *"tau"* the last. Together they make the word "emeth" or "truth." This is stated in the Talmud tractate, Shabbath 104a. The sages reasoned that God is א *"Aleph,"* the first with none before Him. He is מ *"mem"* or the absolute middle and none dare to mingle with Him. Finally, He is ת*"tau"* the last. There are none after Him. In Rev. 1:11, Jesus makes the exact claim for Himself. The obvious conclusion is that they are both the same Person. For more on "sealing," note Section 32, John 3:33, footnote c.

3p-Verses 26-27. He rebukes the excited crowds who labored hard to find Him but for wrong purposes. The message Christ gave was for them to find the food that would endure forever: to do this, they *must* come to Him. He alone is truth or "emeth" from God. He was exclusively "sealed" by the Father. If they are only seeking another breakfast, He cannot help. Later, He claimed again to be "the truth" that makes God known to men (John 14:6).

(e) Seemingly an earnest inquiry. These people also wanted to do works for God. Being loyal Jews, they only understood that the "works of God" consisted of hundreds of rules, regulations, traditions, oral laws, and many other things. Therefore, the response "What shall we do?" However, none expected the answer that came from the Savior.

(f) **The greatest work to be done for God.** The profound simplicity of this is striking. Christ responds to their query by telling them of the Father's most important work that they can do. It is that they believe on Him as their Messiah, sent to them and sealed by God! *Saving faith in the Son of God is the greatest of life's works!* However, it is not a human work, but one instilled by grace and responded to by the willing heart. Sadly, it can be rejected as well. God arranged it this way, not man! Here, the Lord Jesus presents Himself and His work on the cross and in resurrection as being spiritual bread that they must eat. Puzzled, they mused, "How can we eat bread we cannot touch, hold, or see?" It is received into our souls the moment we repent of our sins and trust Christ as Lord and Savior. This is done by simple faith. *God considers this as doing His greatest work and as eating of the eternal bread from heaven!* Men who have done this have accomplished the highest work of God. The Father is satisfied and saves his soul from sin's awful wages. Herein, we feed on Christ the living bread from heaven. In 1 Thess. 1:3, Paul described this as "the work of faith." Refer to footnote j below for more on this thought. Nevertheless, the religious leaders of Israel, along with many of the Hebrew people refused to do this. See main headings in Sections 67 and 68 for their rejection of Jesus as the Messiah.

(g) **Signs again!** Had they not just the day before witnessed the feeding of thousands probably from a baker boy's basket? Did that miracle not stir them to attempt a forced crowning of Him as the King of Israel? There prevailed a belief among the more pious Jews that Messiah would feed Israel with "everlasting" manna from heaven when He came. How could they forget so soon? Now, they demand *another* sign, for that of yesterday had passed from heart and memory. See Section 29, second paragraph of footnote e for a list of the times they wanted Jesus to give them great signs proving He was the Messiah. Refer also to note by the asterisk under main heading Section 48, for the four unique signs that only Israel's genuine Messiah could perform.

(h) In verse 31, someone in the crowd gave a general quotation by selecting several words from various Old Testament verses (Ex. 16:4, 15; Num. 11:8; Ps. 78:24; and 105:40). Hence, it is shaded in gray. It is interesting that whoever spoke these words had their exegesis seriously out of order. The words "He gave…" (verse 31) had reference to God *not* Moses. Christ corrects their interpretation in verse 32, by explaining that it was "Moses who gave you not that bread but my Father." Whoever gave this quote, their argument went like this: "You fed more than five thousand in the wilderness yesterday with the loaves and fishes, but what is that in comparison to Moses, who for forty years fed millions of Jews in the wilderness with manna from heaven? Show us a sign miracle like this and we will believe you are the Messiah." Here, again we see the signs mania that infected every religious Jew. In the latter portion of verse 32, Christ declared that God His Father alone gives the true bread from heaven. In verse 33, Messiah emphatically declared that He was that special bread from God, who had come down from heaven to give life to the world. He *reemphasized* this singularly exclusive truth again in verses 35, 38, 41, 50, 51, 57, and 58.

(i) **"I am."** John records at least thirteen times where the Savior applied this ancient Name of Jehovah God to Himself. It was first mentioned in Ex. 3:13-14. Here, it was the Sacred Name whereby God introduced Himself to Moses from the burning bush. Jesus applied it to Himself in the following places during His ministry, thus telling the Jews that He was the God of Moses, who had appeared in the desert bush some fifteen hundred years prior. See Section 120, footnote y, and Section 122, footnote g, for more on the Name "I am." Several of the verses where this term is used in John's gospel are as follows. Some are doublets:

1. Section 34, John 4:26—"I am *he*" (Messiah).
2. Section 95, John 6:35—"I am the bread of life." See footnote h above.
3. Section 95, John 6:41—"I am the bread which came down from heaven."
4. Section 95, John 6:48—"I am that bread of life."
5. Section 95, John 6:51—"I am the living bread which came down from heaven."
6. Section 120, John 8:12—"I am the light of the world."
7. Section 120, John 8:23—"I am from above."
8. Section 120, John 8:23—"I am not of this world."
9. Section 120, John 8:28—"Ye shall know that I am *he*."
10. Section 121, John 9:5—"I am the light of the world."
11. Section 122, John 10:7—"I am the door."
12. Section 122, John 10:9—"I am the door."
13. Section 122, John 10:11—"I am the good shepherd."
14. Section 122, John 10:14—"I am the good shepherd."
15. Section 124, John 11:25—"I am the resurrection and the life."
16. Section 175, John 14:6—"I am the way, the truth, and the life."
17. Section 176, John 15:1—"I am the true vine."
18. Section 176, John 15:5—"I am the vine."
19. Section 180, John 18:5—"I am *he*."
20. Section 180, John 18:8—"I am *he*."

2p-John 6:35 is another plea from the Lord Jesus affirming that He was the Messiah of Israel. Rabbis taught that the manna in the wilderness pointed to their Messiah. Jesus invites the Jews to "come to Him" (or trust Him) for He is God's genuine manna or Messiah sent down from heaven. Those who believe on Him in trusting faith will *never again* thirst or hunger to be saved. After the new birth, we long for numerous things in life, but no truly saved man has ever longed to be saved the second time. Such a thing is impossible and decries the false teaching of Arminianism. For one to be saved the second time would require the Lord Jesus to die *again* for their sins! Hebrews 10:12 is emphatic that Christ "offered one sacrifice for sins for ever." His one sacrifice saves individuals one time forever, not many times. See how this is illustrated in Section 50, fifth paragraph of footnote h.

(j) **"I will in no wise cast out."** This is one of the most comforting promises in the New Testament. We inquire, "Who does the Father give to the Son?" The answer, "All who do the 'work' of believing on Him as previously expressed in verse 29. It was seen in footnote f above that believing in Christ is spoken of as "work." Indeed it is a "work of grace" created in our hearts to which the convicted sinner may respond or choose not to respond. His rejection hardly negates sovereign grace. How do men believe or have faith in Christ? "So then faith cometh by hearing, and hearing by the Word of God" (Rom. 10:17). Shortly after His statement about not casting men out, the Lord Jesus said, "No man can come to me, except the Father which hath sent me draw him" (verse 44). Lost sinners are awakened over their plight, and drawn by the combined work of the Holy Spirit and God's Word illuminating their hearts. Prior to this, God may use numerous things to arouse concern in the thoughts of man toward Himself and eternity. Great sorrows, loss, death, unmitigated suffering, and a thousand other calamities have stopped men in their tracks and turned their thoughts to the Almighty. Yet, *only* the Holy Spirit and the Word of God can produce the new birth in the souls of men. In this sense, it is a pure work of grace. Refer to footnote f above for more on this.

2p-One of the deeds of Christ, now exalted at Gods' right hand, is to "give repentance and forgiveness of sins" to Israel and all others who hear the saving gospel and believe it (Acts 5:31). However, the "space" (or time) Christ grants men the ability to repent can be trifled away as seen in Rev. 2:21. It is written that the "Corinthians hearing, believed and were baptized" (Acts 18:8). Men who come to the Savior, smitten over their lostness and sin will be instantly forgiven, saved, and received into God's family the moment they believe from a heart of true repentance. The Lord of heaven has never turned away such supplicants of heavenly grace.

3p-The ditch on both sides of the road. As stated above, on the other hand, men can refuse to come to Christ with the work of grace seeking to bloom in their hearts. This is discussed in Section 52, John 5:40, where Jesus told the Jews "ye would not come to me, that ye might have life." He did not say, "Ye *could* not," but "ye *would* not." Jude wrote of certain people who "turn the grace of God into lasciviousness" (Jude 4). Peter said that they "deny the Lord that *bought* them" (2 Peter 2:1). "Bought" is from the Greek word "agorazo," meaning to purchase by paying the price. How amazing that those "bought" by the blood of Christ, deny Him to their damnation. Could we say, these elected bought ones suddenly got unelected? It remains right that one cannot blend Calvinism with Arminianism, for both are opposite departures from fundamental basic truths of Scripture. *Each doctrine becomes wildly heretical when taken into arrogant extremes.* They are as toxic ditches on either side of the gospel road. For a balance in this conflict, note Section 203, paragraph five, under footnote d.

(k) "The last day" is used by our Lord in this passage as well as verses 39, 40, 44 and 54. Later, in John 11:24, Martha also employed the same Jewish terminology. The rabbis taught that when Messiah came, He would raise the dead, which meant the "last day" for them to sleep in their graves but not the end of the world as such. Messiah appearing in His earthly ministry did *not* signify the "last day" or the *final* "end of all things" as some teach. In rabbinical eschatology, there were not only days, but also years of time during which many things would transpire before the *end* and absolute consummation of earth's affairs. This end the Jewish doctors called "Olam Hab-Ba" or the "World to come." There would be a long drawn out scenario, taking in many years *after* Messiah appeared in Israel and before the grand day of "Olam Ha-Ba" finally came. The Lord Jesus had to undo gradually the numerous myths taught by the rabbis and believed by the Jews as well as the twelve. Later, the apostle Paul was inspired to write his letters in which the *true outline* of end-time things was laid down once for all. For the Jewish understanding of the various events that would lead to great "Olam Ha-Ba" or last day, note Section 82, footnote d. Our Savior was *not* teaching a general resurrection and judgment in His usage of the common Hebrew term "last day." Rather, He was speaking in their language and using their eschatological terms. As stated above, Paul's letters written later clarified some of these things. They give us a brief understanding of Christian eschatology. Nowhere in Scripture has God penned the *whole story* of Christian eschatology. It is only given in parts.

(l) "Whose father and mother we know." On Joseph being called Jesus' father, see Section 38, footnote h. In that vast audience of thousands were hard-line Jews, without one grain of real spiritual discernment. They attempted to figure out the Lord Jesus by human reasoning. Some of them knew the mother and foster-father of Christ and said so in this verse. This demonstrates that Joseph was still alive at this time, which was about one year before the cross. Christ's claims to have come down from heaven, to be God's bread of eternal life, were ridiculous in the carnal thinking of these Jews. For more on Jesus' human family, see Section 66, footnote a, and Section 190, John 19:25-27, footnotes k through m.

(m) Knowing the thoughts of their evil hearts, Christ rebuked their surmising, whisperings, and murmurings against His message. No man in the colorful history of Israel had caused such a stir among the nation, as did Jesus of Nazareth. He remains a problem to all thinking and informed Jews today. They have invented a thousand stratagems and philosophical devices to re-explain or have rejected Him all together. *Nevertheless, He remains!*

(n) See footnote k above for the expression "last day." In addition, who does the Father draw or bring to Christ? See first and second paragraphs of footnote j above and footnote o below for the answer to this question.

(o) "And they shall all be taught of God." Christ built this quotation by selecting various words from Isa. 54:13 with Jer. 31:34, and perhaps Micah 4:2. The rabbis applied these several Old Testament passages as being fulfilled in the days of Messiah. They believed it had reference to the Gentiles, who would be converted or proselyted to their faith in the days of Messiah among them. The Savior constructs from these verses His own unique passage and informs His hearers that every man, whom God has taught about the Messiah, will come to the Messiah. However, many who come to Christ then reject Him, as seen in the rich young ruler in Section 139. Others receive Him as personal Lord and Savior. The inference is clear: God, in their Torah Law, had taught all the Jews sitting before Him that Messiah was coming to save them. The rabbis had so foiled this message of hope with their materialistic ambitions and dreams of a physical world-rule, that they rejected Jesus of Nazareth as their Messiah-Savior. Though He had revealed His Messiahship in countless ways, they refused to come to Him (verse 47). In short, they would not "eat of his flesh or drink of his blood," meaning they refused to receive Him by faith as Lord and Messiah. See footnote r below for explanation of eating His flesh and drinking His blood.

(p) **"Not that any man hath seen the Father."** God does not come down in person and visibly appear before men as He teaches them. The Lord Jesus informs the Jews that He had seen and had been taught (instructed) by God. Indeed, He was totally equal with God! Refer to Section 1, Part 4, John 1:18, footnote m, for Christ being with God and equal with God before the foundation of the world. Refer to Section 19, footnote c for the way the Father taught Jesus from childhood. Christ continually claimed that His teaching and preaching was what the Father had taught and commanded Him. See this mentioned in such places as John 8:26; 12:49-50; 14:10, 24; 15:15; 17:8; and 14. Men who reject and ridicule the teachings of Jesus Christ are, in fact, scorning God Almighty!

(q) **"Give my flesh."** This is another veiled mention of His death on the cross as seen in verses 33, 53-58. He informed the Jews that He would give His physical body (flesh in death on the cross) for the life of the world so that the world may have life through this act. This is a direct reference to His upcoming atonement for the sins of mankind. He plainly affirms that His death would be a vicarious sacrifice in which atonement would be established once and forever. When Messiah invited the Jews to eat of His flesh and drink His blood, it was not a new thing for the *older* people. They had heard something similar on numerous occasions. Hundreds of years before Jesus came, the rabbis spoke of "eating Messiah," an expression meaning to be filled with His glory. This saying is recorded in the Talmud tractate, Sanhedrin 98b. A thousand years before Christ, the psalmist wrote, "O taste and see that the LORD [Messiah] is good" (Ps. 34:8). This spoke of their coming Messiah. Over thirty years *after* the ascension of Christ, Peter still used this Hebrew terminology. He wrote, "If so be ye have tasted that the Lord is gracious' (1 Peter 2:3). Thus, our Lord's appeal should not have fallen so hard on their ears! Yet, it did. They immediately fell into quarreling with each other over what Jesus meant. "Eating and drinking" were common expressions in the Jewish schools as well as daily life and were continually used in a metaphorical sense. It is found in the Talmud well over two thousand times! It was used in reference to great social and spiritual benefits as well as the material blessings of God on Israel. Messiah shortly told them that He is speaking in spiritual language, not literal (verse 63). Their earlier enthusiasm, in verses 24-25, was beginning to fade slowly away.

2p-Verse 53. "Eat and drink." In Hebrew schools, this was a thoroughly known metaphor and continually used by the rabbis in teaching and everyday conversation. The book of Ecclesiastes uses this term numerous times. Often students would hear "eat and drink of the Torah," or "eat and drink of the things of God." All who heard these expressions automatically understood their teachers were using them in a figurative sense. Now, their Messiah uses their very method of teaching, and they fly into a rage of anger! The old maxim "There are none as blind as those who choose not to see," is fitting of the Jews on this occasion. Some of the ancient rabbis taught that Israel would "eat Messiah" when He came, meaning they would totally receive Him without hesitation. Was the Lord Jesus alluding to this teaching? John Lightfoot documented this in his *Commentary . . . ,* vol. 3, pages 307-308.

(r) **Jesus used symbolic language.** Everything said by our Savior in verses 50 through 58 are repetitious warnings for the benefit of the unsaved Jews. The Words of Christ in verse 53, "Except ye eat the flesh of the Son of man" are comparable to His previous warnings "Except ye repent, ye shall all likewise perish" (Section 72, Lk. 13:3, 5), and "Except a man be born again he cannot see the kingdom of God" (Section 30, John 3:3). Repeatedly, He appeals with the Jews to believe on Him. Some six times in this single chapter, Christ pleads for this in the words "eat my flesh" and/or "drink my blood." Our Savior was saying, "Believe on me; trust me as your Messiah and Savior." He was speaking of a spiritual act not something literal or physical. *The words eat and drink referred to receiving Christ into one's life by faith.* See footnote q above. Throughout this synagogue discourse, eating, drinking, and believing were used interchangeably as exact equivalents. When the Savior claimed to be the "light of the world," (John 8:12), and "the door," (John 10:9), He did not mean that He was a literal door swinging on hinges or a metal fixture light attached to a wall. In this message on eating His flesh and drinking His blood, our Lord was using the same kind of symbolic language. See footnote u below for more on this same thought.

2p-The error of Mass and Mithraism. Here, is the foundational error of the Roman Catholic Church. It teaches that the officiating priests have the power to turn the wafer into the literal flesh of Christ, and the contents of the cup into His literal blood. Worse, partaking of these brings salvation to the consumer. What could be more blasphemous than to teach that man is saved from sin and hell by taking Christ into his mouth, and swallowing Him into the digestive tract? Why don't they finish the journey and explain that whatever goes this route finally reaches the colon and then is excreted as waste! *No one "eats" or "drinks" his way to heaven.* The notion of "eating *real* flesh and drinking *real* blood" before a deity, finds its historical origin in a pagan religion called Mithraism and not in Holy Scripture. The earliest known origins of this cult are traced to India in 1400 B.C. Its beginnings are buried in a mountain of fables, myths, mysticism, and satanic distortions. In time, it became one of the major religions of the Roman Empire, especially among the military. Hostile infidel critics maintain Christianity borrowed communion concepts from this religion. Men and women who despise the Bible often point to the heathen labyrinth of dark rituals. We are told that Christianity took its doctrine of communion from pagan Mithraism! They see the following similarities: Mithra (according to heathenism) was born of a virgin in a cave with stars in the ceiling; another source depicts him coming from an egg. He was called a son of God; had disciples, was crucified, rose from the dead, and returned to heaven. Ancient Mithric rituals celebrated eating the flesh and drinking the blood of the gods. See the fourth paragraph below for more on this. *Oh, mortal man, is there anything you cannot be persuaded to believe?*

3p-Evil in its origin. The above perversion of the *true* Lord's Supper was invented by demons thousands of years before the birth of Christ. Later, it was practiced in a "Christianized version" by the heretical church fathers. Gradually, this heathen philosophy came into the state church of Emperor Constantine, by thousands of pagans being forced into its ranks under threat of baptism or death. In time, this religious monster became the Roman Catholic Church. It became their "unbloody mass." Later, it raised its ugly head in the worldwide so-called "Christian churches." For a brief review of the pagan Mithra religion, see *He Walked Among Us*, pages 190-192 and relevant references, by Joshua McDowell and Bill Wilson. Dr. Lee I. Levine, in, *The Ancients synagogue. The First Thousand Years,* pages 142, 143 wrote about the pagan cults and their observing various meals and feasts in honor of gods and goddesses. In footnote 38 on page 142, Levine lists sources translated from French that deal exhaustively with the heathen Mithraic cult and its practices.

4p-Can blood make someone drunk? The Papal Church teaches that the wine in the mass becomes the *literal* blood of Christ though in an "unbloody" form. Next, the wafer becomes His *actual* flesh or body. If this is correct, then why have so many priests, who are habitual wine drinkers, and consume what is left in the chalice, become drunkards and are sent to institutions to "dry out." They become unfit to perform their duties. Blood makes no one become a drunkard, but *real wine* does. Drinking blood, from the Jewish view was condemned in their Torah Law (Lev. 17:12-14 with Ps. 16:4), and by the leadership of the first and earliest churches (Acts 15:29). For more on the shocking errors of the Roman Catholic system regarding the forgiveness of sins and salvation, refer to Section 45, footnote g. Refer to the sixth and eighth paragraphs below, for more on blood baths and drinking.

5p-Stoddardism in early America. Solomon Stoddard (died 1729) was the grandfather of Jonathan Edwards. He was a noted figure in early New England Congregational churches and invented a thing called the "Half Way Covenant." "Pope Stoddard," as his enemies called him, taught that all who lived outwardly decent lives should partake of communion, even though they were not saved. By doing this, the participants would learn their need for Christ as personal Savior and be redeemed! Many of the early Congregational Churches rejected his heresy. Stoddarism, was nothing more than a revised version of the Catholic dogma of mass. Stains of Stoddarism still exist in the more liberal Congregational Churches. Since 1957, some Congregational Churches have been absorbed into the United Church of Christ. This is a left wing polarized group preaching a social gospel laced with Marxism, bantering to political revisionism, defending sodomy, gays, lesbians, same-sex marriages, and other issues that have been abominations from the sunrise of antiquity. Behind this stands Satan to grind America down by dismantling her *true* spiritual life, ballyhooing the Bible, discrediting genuine moral values, and strangling patriotism.

6p-Sincerity in religion is not enough. A heathen tribe in South Africa hangs up a black bullock by its back legs and cuts its throat. As the animal dies, all women and girls of that tribe dance wildly beneath the beast drinking and bathing in the hot blood as it pours from the wound. Dozens of them fall into demonic fits and convulsions; kicking, screaming, dancing, shouting, madly snapping their heads up and down, waving sticks and knives amid the frenzy. The witch doctor assures them that this will purge their souls of evil. The South African Press Association reported on May 26, 2010 that an ox was slaughtered at Soccer City, Soweto, near Johannesburg. This was to "invoke the spirits of . . . African ancestors to usher-in their wisdom and energy . . ." Some three hundred witchdoctors, both black and white, took part in this act of Devil worship as the animal was speared in the back of its neck by a Xhosa warrior. In the nomadic regions of Australia, to this day, the Aboriginal witchdoctor sifts sand down the throat of the weakest of twins, for this infant is a bad omen; it must be destroyed. In Tanzania, Africa, witch doctors kill albinos and use their body parts to make magic potions. South Africa is rife with its "Isangomas" or religious witch doctors, busy making their "muti" (medicine) from body parts. Though "outlawed" (on paper but not in practice) in other African states, this practice of deadly false religions continues. A South American pagan tribe, obeying its religious beliefs, eats the flesh of their dead after they have rotted for three days. Some become violently ill and die. Across India, the Hindu Agori sect feasts on dead human flesh, and worships snakes, rats, monkeys, birds, bugs, and whatever the Devil puts before them. *These facts indisputably demonstrate that divine truth is the prerequisite before sincerity in religion.* This truth is found only in the rightly divided Holy Scripture. Hell will be full of people who were sincerely wrong because their religion steered them from Jesus Christ.

7p-Crusader insanity. Among the mentally deranged "crusaders," a group called "Tafurs" ate the flesh of their Muslim enemies. These religionists are examples of what men do without the personal saving knowledge of Christ. Only the precious blood of Jesus, appropriated by faith, not the digestive tract, cleanses from all sin. Nothing else is acceptable in God's viewpoint (Lev. 17:11; Heb. 9:14; 1 Peter 1:17-20; 1 John 1:7; with Rev. 1:5). The ecumenical prattle about "sincerity in religion is all that counts" is spiritual poison. It must be opposed and exposed, for it is a lie! Those angered at these words should also try *"sincerely"* eating the hand of a dead family member as mentioned in the 6p above. For the crusaders, see Section 14, number 7, under third paragraph of footnote f.

8p-One sacrifice forever. Regarding the Catholic Mass, see the first two paragraphs under footnote r above. It is dogmatically reasserted that the sacrifice of Christ on the cross was a once for all, settled, and a finished forever accomplishment. Scripture declares of our Savior, "But this man, after he had offered one sacrifice for sins forever, sat down on the right hand of God" (Heb. 10:12). One sacrifice forever, is forever! It cannot be continued on the altars of the Papal Church or any other church. "Christians" attending this altar, pit themselves against the fundamental teaching of the New Testament. Worse, they reveal their ignorance of the *finished work* of Christ on the cross (Heb. 9:24-28). Men without the saving knowledge of God's Son are the highest form of wickedness when they create a substitute for His eternal atonement. It is sincere blasphemy of the darkest proportions.

9p-Verse 58. The Master warned the Jews that Moses' manna sustained Israel for only forty years and then that generation of people died. He the true bread from God and heaven and He will give them everlasting life. To "eat" of Him by faith, they will never [eternally] die! There is not the slightest hint of communion or the Lord's Supper found in these passages. Those upholding and practicing the pagan infected doctrines of "transubstantiation" or "consubstantiation" have grievously misinterpreted Scripture. Christ did not institute the Lord's Supper until about a year later, at His fourth and final Passover. He did this on the night before the morning of the cross. When Christ spoke these things, none of the apostles understood that their Messiah would end His physical life by death on a Roman cross. The apostles' understanding of His death and resurrection came later on the day of Pentecost. For Martin Luther's explanation of communion and baptism, refer to Section 203, the eighth paragraph of footnote d.

10-Rome and the redeemed. Ecumenically blinded "evangelicals" and "conservatives" are bending over backwards to accommodate the Papal system. The plan of salvation as laid down in the New Testament is not that of the Roman Catholic Church. Nor is this church "God's appointed place for Christian Communion." Men are instantly, once and for ever saved through faith, from sin and hell, by the finished work of Christ in His death and resurrection. The officiating priest at the altar does not offer a fresh sacrifice of Christ's body and blood. That is high blasphemy. *The Son of God does not become liquid in a cup or a round wafer!* See footnote q above. Those who die trusting this abomination die damned; those who die trusting Christ and Him *alone* are forever saved.

11p-Eyes are opened. Having seen many Roman Catholics saved over the past half century (including a priest and several altar boys) an amazing change takes place. Their spiritual eyes are *instantly* opened to see what Christ has saved them from. The joy of the new birth fills their souls. Acts 26:18 beautifully describes what occurs when religious people are redeemed by the grace of God! They understand the religious errors out of which God delivered them. Wonderfully, with salvation comes a burden for fellow Catholics to be saved and share this joy of Christ. I have seen this amazing wonder many times. Papal apologists have fits trying to re-explain the miracle of personal, know-so salvation through faith in Christ. They deny, change, mitigate, re-interpret, and oppose the biblical plan of salvation. They go to any length trying to circumvent the teaching of Scripture (even in their Bible with doctored footnotes) on the most important of all subjects. *It is not true that the Roman Church denies salvation, eternal life, and forgiveness of sin. Never! Rather, it teaches men the wrong way to partake of these gifts.* Salvation of the soul is not in the "unbloody mass" of a Papal altar, its rituals, baptisms, and so forth. It is not secured by confessionals, wearing a scapular, the rosary, Stations of the Cross, prayers to Mary, the saints and so forth. No denomination has a copyright on eternal life! Jesus Christ does! When one receives Him by repentance from their sins and faith in His atonement, they are forever saved. *This is the only way to heaven.*

12p-The "requiem mass" for the dead has its origin in the pagan ritual called "manes," in which blood offerings were given for the souls of the deceased. Purgatory is one of the biggest religious frauds and moneymaking rackets ever saddled on innocent people. For a further look into the pagan myth called "purgatory," believed and practiced in the Papal Church, refer to Section 45, second paragraph of footnote g.

13p-Nuns, priests, and vows of celibacy. Nunnery originated in the "vestal virgins" of ancient heathen temples who "married various gods" and sexually served them. Regarding Peter being the "rock" on which Christ would build His church, see Section 103, number 2 under footnote g. The "sacred celibacy" of Catholic Priests also has its origin in the early pagan worship of a goddess mother, Queen of heaven, called Cybele. She was the "Magna Mater" (great protector) of the hills of Rome. Priests serving this demonic idol were eunuchs by castration. It is of interest that the goddess Cybele had a *eunuch* son, named Attis. Heathen priests believed that by castration, they eliminated the distraction of sexual urges and would gain access into mysteries unknown to others. Men and women locked in monasteries and convents waste their lives in ignorant isolation and may die without salvation.

(s) Verse 60. "Hard saying." His message was too much for the stubborn Jews. Discontent also broke out among His own ranks at what He preached. It was the normal practice during synagogue preaching for persons to interrupt and call the speaker into question on points they did not understand. One can be sure the "fur was flying" at this point in Jesus' message. Among the hundreds present on the Sabbath day were many who had followed Him as their Messiah. Thousands across the land of Israel were His ardent supporters. However, with this puzzling message, a decisive point was reached! A demonic spirit of faction, grumbling and unrest settled over the congregation as they fell into murmuring. With this, Jesus pointedly addressed His disciples, who were grumbling and calling into question what He had preached. Just as carnal and earthly minded as the literalistic Jews, who only looked for a material kingdom and Messiah, the disciples too were dumbfounded at His Words "eat my flesh and drink my blood." They understood so little of a spiritual kingdom, of imputed righteousness, and a living personal relationship with the God of heaven. These things being greatly unknown by the sincerest of them, they stood aghast at Jesus'

Words. He was not the Man they had taken Him for; He was not going to set up their political kingdom. It was clear; He had no plans to overthrow the Romans. Had He not only yesterday fled the Jew's intentions of making Him king in Section 94, footnote a? This kind of Messiah they did not want! How revolting He was! His thousands of miracles and wonders vanish from their memory because He would not take the sword in hand and lead the fight against cursed Edom, the popular euphemism for Gentile pagan Rome. For how people were saved during this time, not understanding the full purpose in Jesus' coming into the world, see Section 144, footnote i for explanation.

(t) This was a profound response from our Lord to their faithlessness when they thought that He was commanding them to eat *literally* His flesh and drink His blood. In essence, He said, "I am going to ascend back to my Father in heaven. How can you literally eat my flesh and drink my blood if I am not here? Can you come up into heaven and there eat of me? Don't you understand I am speaking to you in spiritual language not literal?" See all of lengthy footnote r above for more on this thought. Interestingly, these very men, all except Judas, watched Christ ascend up into heaven about one year later. Note this in Section 207, Acts 1:9-11 with footnotes a, and b.

(u) **"I am speaking in symbolic or spiritual terms."** It could not be any clearer. The Jews and His disciples were thinking of eating physical flesh. Christ was speaking of nonliteral, spiritual things. Refer to second paragraph of footnote q above, for further explanation. Exactly, the same problem exists today in the church: many cannot discern between the two. Analyzed, Christ said that all who ate His flesh (or believed on Him) will "not die" (verse 50), "shall live for ever" (verse 51), "hath eternal life" (verse 54), "dwelleth in me and I in him" (verse 56), "shall live" (verse 57), "shall live for ever" (verse 58). For more on this, see first paragraph of footnote r above. Jesus attempted to correct the misunderstanding when He said, "It is the Spirit that quickeneth [gives life] the flesh profiteth nothing" (John 6:63). Roman Catholics and others take Christ's Words literally when He said, "this is my body" (Matt. 26:26). Why do they stop here? The Savior also said that the cup was the new covenant or testament (Matt. 26:27-28). Did He mean that the metallic Passover cup he held contained the twenty-seven books of the New Testament, and they were to drink them? For explanation of this new covenant, see the next paragraph.

2p-**What is the new covenant?** Some five hundred years before the birth of Christ, God promised the house of Israel and the house of Judah that He would make a covenant with them (Jer. 31:31). Centuries later, the writer of Hebrews makes it clear that this "new covenant" replaced the old one (Torah Law). He wrote that Christ had established this new entity by His death and resurrection (Heb. 8:13; 9:1-28). His atoning death was declared to be "the blood of the everlasting covenant" (Heb. 13:20). This new covenant would first change the hearts of men on the inside, then their conduct on the outside (Jer. 31:33-34 with Ezek. 36:26-27). *That the prophecies pointing to the future new covenant nullify salvation before the cross is absurd.* The new covenant announced by God through Jeremiah had been effective from Adam down. Jeremiah simply reaffirmed this fact and was inspired to write about this. Its prior existence is beautifully portrayed in Hebrews chapter 11. This entire chapter speaks of hundreds who were saved in the centuries before Jeremiah wrote. For salvation during the Old Testament era, see Section 30, footnote h. On the Holy Spirit indwelling men in the Old Testament, see Section 10, the second paragraph of footnote b. Every mention of Christ about the future coming of the Spirit had reference to day of Pentecost and the church. Dwight Pentecost, in *Thy Kingdom Come*, page 172 wrote, "Israel has not yet entered into the benefits that flow from the New Covenant, [spoken by Jeremiah] its ultimate fulfillment must still be viewed as yet future." This is radical dispensationalism and a denial of salvation by the grace of God across Old Testament history. It was *invented* and popularized by C. I. Scofield in his *Reference Bible,* page 1044, footnote 1, and page 1115, footnote 2. The *first* Hebrew (Gen. 14:13), Abraham, was saved and made righteous by faith in the coming Messiah according to Paul (Rom. 4:1-5 with John 8:56). Abraham lived "four hundred and thirty years" before Moses, and the Torah Law existed (Gal. 3:17), and before Jeremiah was born. Through Jeremiah, the Spirit reaffirmed the everlasting atonement of Christ on the cross. It is not a future exclusive blessing for Israel only; rather, it had been and still was a promise for all men, of all times, and all places. Further, it had been operative from the beginning (Lk. 1:70 with Acts 10:43). Peter said that *both* Old and New Testament people are saved by grace (Acts 15:11).

3p-**Wounds in Jesus' hands.** This is another invention of radical dispensationalism. It teaches the *Jewish nation* or a *tribulation remnant* will all be saved when Christ returns, as they look at the wounds in His hands (Zech. 12:10; 13:6; with Rom. 11:26). Jews, like all other men can only be saved by trusting Jesus the Messiah as personal Lord and Savior. No one is converted from sin and hell by looking at scars. Men are saved by repentance and faith in the finished work of Christ, be they Jew or Gentile (Acts 15:11 with Eph. 2:8). This miracle occurs in the heart and not by seeing with the eyes. Jesus said, "blessed *are* they that have not seen, and *yet* have believed" (John 20:29). Read *when* John said this wounding of Jesus took place, in Section 193, number 2, under footnote d.

(v) **The great departure.** Vast hoards of people, many of them previously announcing loyalty to Jesus Christ, suddenly stormed out of the synagogue (verse 66). The word "many" has reference to people following the Savior after feeding the five thousand, but now they desert Him. His message was too much for them! This reveals their abysmal lack of spiritual insight into His teaching and the things of God. It is not much different today.

(w) **"We believe and are sure."** In a flash of brilliance, Peter the recent water-walker and spokesman for the apostles responded to Jesus' troubling question, "Will ye also go away" (verse 67)? Here, we catch a glimpse of the *true* Simon Peter. Poor, boisterous, and rude, he will yet become a stone! Though obtusely loud, talking ever so much, making his preposterous claims, now, we see the heart of the real man. Speaking again for the eleven, he used the pronoun "we" in his confession to Christ. Peter imperceptibly knew this strange Man, this Person he had abandoned all to follow, spoke "the words of eternal life." In contrast to the Jews, bickering and complaining as they exited the synagogue at Capernaum, Peter reveals that even though they do not understand what Jesus had preached, He was "The Christ (or Messiah) the Son of the living God." And he was staying with Him! Earlier, both Satan and his demons had shrieked out a similar confession regarding who Jesus was. Refer to this confession in Section 23, footnote c, and Section 41, footnote g. Simon Peter saved the day! Both exclamations about Jesus were standard rabbinical verbalizations of their Messiah. Later, Peter confessed the same in Section 103 Matt. 16:15-16, footnote f.

(x) **More on Judas.** Looking back on history, John, now understood the whole story and is inspired to pen this editorial comment. *At the time Jesus said this in the Capernaum synagogue, John had no idea who Judas really was or his evil intentions.* Contextually, verses 70 and 71 must be tied back to verse 64. Christ responded to Peter's confession in deep melancholy with words meaning something like this, "I have good reasons for asking if you twelve would also desert me; for there stands one among you who pretends to love me, and he is a devil." Here, the word for "Devil" is "diabolos," which is not the word for demons. It means "accuser," and "slanderer." How awful that Jesus called Judas "the devil." It is right that people who are in such league with Lucifer, should be addressed by his name. *There was far more to the evil life of Judas than Scripture reveals.* At this point, none of the eleven knew of whom Jesus spoke. Many in the church who seem to be saints are serpents in disguise. It is alarming to read that Judas was given power to "cast out devils" (Matt. 10:1), yet he was identified as the wicked one himself! Perhaps this is a classical example of evil conniving with evil to deceive and secure his final damnation. For the opportunities of Judas being with Jesus, see Section 74, footnote g.

2p-**A last appeal?** Were Christ's Words in verse 70 a sharp appeal to Judas the traitor, even his *final opportunity* to forsake his devious plan of betrayal? Had not hundreds of half-sincere and false disciples just walked out on Him (verse 60 with 66)? If this was his "way out," the Messiah's personal plea was rejected and the man from Kerioth plunged himself deeper into the abyss of secret sin. Refer to Section 107, footnote c for Jesus' second mention of the traitor. Because Judas was among the unique eleven does not ill repair their name and labors. Within the local assembly of true believers, there is an exclusive society of born again saints, into which modern day Judas's still infiltrate and play havoc within the church. It will be this way until the end.

(y) **John 7:1. "After these things"** can only have reference to the message He had just given and the uproar that occurred in the Capernaum synagogue. *There is apparently a time span between verse 1 and 2 in this seventh chapter of John.* Luke filled in *some* of this gap in chapter 9:51 through chapter 18 of his book. The rest is left to imagination and hopeful conjecture. Because of these divinely inspired gaps, one cannot build a straightforward, unbroken chronology of the life of Christ. God had the four gospels written this way. Refer to Section 6, footnote a for more on this subject. His purpose was to give mankind a condensed but reliable version of the earthly life of His Son. If every act of Christ had been written, we would have thousands of books to work through. For more on this thought, refer to Section 202, John 20:31, footnote j. However, God in His mercy has given us four dependable and trustworthy gospels. As already said, if they were all *exactly* the same, we could dispense of three and use only one.

(z) **They "sought to kill him."** Refer to Section 123, footnote f, for other plots devised by the religious leaders of Israel to destroy the Lord Jesus. The Jews went wild about His message, "eat my flesh and drink my blood." The text of John 7:1 suggests that some kind of enticement was made to allure Him south into Judaea. However, He refused, knowing the Jews waited there to kill Him. Again, we see the wise actions of our Lord when pending danger lurked ahead. Christians should exercise the same kind of practical sense in their service for Christ. There are times for believers to flee, hide, and preserve life and limb for future Christian service (Matt. 2:3, 10:23; Acts 17:13-14 and 2 Cor. 32, 33). Then, there are times when we must "stand" regardless of the cost (Eph. 6:11-18).

2p-**We are commanded to keep ourselves**. 1 John 5:18 reads, "but he that is begotten [born] of God keepeth [guards] himself, and that wicked one [Satan] toucheth him not." The doctrine of keeping ourselves in a guarded state of mind concerning sin and Satan is rarely heard. *This personal, self-practiced discipline has nothing to do with gaining or keeping salvation.* Nor is it a rule for legalist standards. It is a practical way that the benefits of salvation work when exercised in the Christian life. It is obeying the word, "Put on the whole armour of God, that ye may be able to stand against the wiles of the devil" (Eph. 6:11). Jude 21 commands, "Keep yourselves in the love of God." A thousand years prior David wrote, "I kept myself from mine iniquity" (Ps. 18:23). Paul exhorted Timothy to "flee youthful lusts" (2 Tim. 2:22). What happens to a Christian's testimony if they do not "keep themselves," or "put on the whole armour," "shun iniquity," and "flee lusts?" The answer is in I Cor. 3:16-17. The salvation of the soul is a one-time event forever. The saving of *our earthly lives* for God's glory is an entirely different story! This requires self-discipline, dedication, and obedience to the Word of God, activated by grace in daily living. Christ came not only to save our souls from sin and hell, but also to save our years on earth for His glory and man's good (Lk. 9:56 with 3 John 4). Many "Christians" bleat with the sheep and howl with the wolves, then try to convince others that they "are right with God." He inquires, "Can two walk together, except they be agreed?" (Amos 3:3).

APRIL, AND THE THIRD PASSOVER* HAS ENDED. APPARENTLY, JESUS DID NOT ATTEND. EVENTS IN HIS LIFE UNTIL HIS DEPARTURE FOR THE FEAST OF TABERNACLES SOME SIX MONTHS LATER IN OCTOBER.

Fierce conflict erupts over the oral law or Jewish traditions and unwashed hands. Christ charges the religious leaders with subverting God's Word in the Torah Law, spiritual blindness, and having evil hearts poisoned by many heinous sins.

Time: The above happenings took about six months
This third Passover is mentioned in Section 93, John 6:4, with comments at footnote e. If our Lord attended this cel- ebration, the details are shrouded in silence. The weight of evidence indicates that He did not, due to the fierce hostility of the Jews at Jerusalem. This was especially so since the news of His disturbing synagogue sermon given at Capernaum (Section 95, footnote y), had quickly traveled south to Jerusalem and the Sanhedrin. In harmonizing this period in the life of Christ, this present Section takes up the narrative by assuming that this silent Passover was completed after the end of Section 95, John 6:71. After this, John condensed the next months of His life down to the Feast of Tabernacles as seen at the end of Section 95, John 7:1, footnote y. Nevertheless, the other three gospel writers have provided informa- tion about these months. From their records, the following Sections 96 through 118 of this harmony have been built. At best, most of these twenty-three placements are a matter of personal conjecture. They are not presented here as established biblical chronology.

Capernaum

Matt. 15:1–3	Mk. 7:1–6	Lk.	John
The oral law conflict between Jesus and the Jews **1** Then came to Jesus scribes and Pharisees, which were of Jerusalem,(a)	***The oral law conflict between Jesus and the Jews*** **1** Then came together unto him the Pharisees, and certain of the scribes, which came from Jerusalem.(a) **2** And when they saw some of his disciples eat bread with defiled, that is to say, with unwashen, hands, they found fault. ***Mark gave his readers a brief description of the oral law*** **3** For the Pharisees, and all the Jews, except they wash *their* hands oft, eat not, holding the tradition of the elders. **4** And *when they come* from the market, except they wash, they eat not. And many other things there be, which they have received to hold, *as* the washing of cups, and pots, brasen vessels, and of tables.		
The Jews ask Jesus the wrong question saying, **2** "Why do thy disciples transgress the tradition of the elders?(b) for they wash not their hands when they eat bread."	***The Jews ask Jesus the wrong question*** **5** Then the Pharisees and scribes asked him, "Why walk not thy disciples according to the tradition of the elders,(b) but eat bread with unwashen hands?"		
He exposes their wickedness **3** But he answered and said unto them,	***He exposes their wickedness*** **6** He answered and said unto them,		

431

Matt. 15:3–10	Mk. 7:6–14	Lk.	John
▶ *Matthew was inspired to place Mark's partial quotation of Jesus in verse 8 below.*	"Well hath Esaias [Isaiah] prophesied of you hypocrites, as it ▶is written,[(c)] **'This people honoureth me with their lips, but their heart is far from me. 7 Howbeit in vain do they worship me, teaching for doctrines the commandments of men.'** 8 "For laying aside the commandment of God, ye hold the tradition of men, *as the washing of pots and cups: and many other such like things ye do.*" 9 And he said unto them, "Full well ye reject the commandment of God, that ye may keep your own tradition.[(d)]		
"Why do ye also transgress the commandment of God by your tradition?[(d)] 4 "For God commanded, saying,[(e)] **'Honour thy father and mother:' and, 'He that curseth father or mother, let him die the death.'** 5 "But ye say, 'Whosoever shall say to *his* father or *his* mother, "It is a gift," [or Corban] by whatsoever thou mightest be profited by me;[(f)] 6 'And honour not his father or his mother, *he shall be free.'* (from helping his parents according to your rules)	10 "For Moses said,[(e)] **'Honour thy father and thy mother;' and, 'Whoso curseth father or mother, let him die the death:'** 11 "But ye say, 'If a man shall say to his father or mother, "It is Corban," that is to say, a gift, [from God] by whatsoever thou mightest be profited by me;[(f)] *he shall be free.'* (from helping his parents according to your rules) 12 "And ye suffer [let] him no more to do ought for his father or his mother; 13 "Making the Word of God of none effect through your tradition, which ye have delivered: and many such like things do ye."		
"Thus have ye made the commandment of God of none effect by your tradition." ***The prophet also spoke of them*** 7 "*Ye* hypocrites, well did Esaias [Isaiah] prophesy of you, saying,[(g)] 8 ▶**'This people draweth nigh unto me with their mouth, and honoureth me with their lips; but their heart is far from me.** 9 But in vain they do worship me, teaching *for* doctrines the commandments of men.'"[(h)] 10 And he called the multitude, and said unto them,	◀*Mark was directed by the Holy Spirit to place Matthew's quote of the Savior in verse 6 above. Again, this demonstrates there was no copying of one evangelist from the other. Each wrote independently as the Holy Spirit led them.* 14 And when he had called all		

Matt. 15:10–19	Mk. 7:14–21	Lk.	John
"Hear, and understand:[i]	the people *unto him*, he said unto them, "Hearken unto me every one *of you*, and understand:[i]		
Sin defiles the inside first	***Sin defiles the inside first***		
11 "Not that which goeth into the mouth defileth a man; but that which cometh out of the mouth, this [sinfully] defileth a man."	**15** "There is nothing from without a man, that entering into him can defile him: but the things which come out of him, those are they that [sinfully] defile the man. **16** "If any man have ears to hear, let him hear."		
The Pharisees offended at truth: they were doomed blind men	***The Pharisees offended at truth: they were doomed blind men***		
12 Then came his disciples, and said unto him, "Knowest thou that the Pharisees were offended, after they heard this saying?" [j] **13** But he answered and said, "Every plant, which my heavenly Father hath not planted, shall be rooted up. **14** 'Let them alone: they be blind leaders of the blind.' And if the blind lead the blind, both shall fall into the ditch." **15** Then answered Peter and said unto him, "Declare [explain] unto us this parable."	**17** And when he was entered into the house from the people, his disciples asked him concerning the parable.		
The disciples do not yet understand this teaching of Jesus	***The disciples do not yet understand this teaching of Jesus***		
16 And Jesus said, "Are ye also yet without understanding?[k] **17** "Do not ye yet understand, that whatsoever entereth in at the mouth goeth into the belly, and is cast out into the draught?	**18** And he saith unto them, "Are ye so without understanding[k] also? Do ye not perceive, that whatsoever thing from without entereth into the man, *it* cannot defile him; **19** "Because it entereth not into his heart, but into the belly, and goeth out into the draught, purging all meats?"		
Mankinds' depravity has its origin within	***Mankinds' depravity has its origin within***		
18 "But those things which proceed out of the mouth come forth from the heart;[l] and they [sinfully] defile the man. **19** "For out of the heart proceed[m] evil	**20** And he said, "That which cometh out of the man, that [sinfully] defileth the man. **21** "For from within, out of the heart of men, proceed[m] evil		

433

Matt. 15:19-20	Mk. 7:21-23	Lk.	John
thoughts, murders, adulteries, fornications, thefts, false witness, blasphemies: **20** "These are *the things* which [sinfully] defile[n] a man: but to eat with unwashen hands defileth not a man." (Verse 21 cont. in Section 97.)	thoughts, adulteries, fornications, murders, **22** "Thefts, covetousness, wickedness, deceit, lasciviousness, an evil eye, blasphemy, pride, foolishness: **23** "All these evil things come from within, and [sinfully] defile[n] the man." (Verse 24 cont. in Section 97.)		

Footnotes–Commentary

(a) **"Which were of Jerusalem."** The distance from Jerusalem to Capernaum, Galilee, was some ninety miles one way. The religious leaders of Israel had walked this three day's journey from Jerusalem to Capernaum for the purpose of attacking Christ and His disciples over their oral law.

(b) **"Tradition of the elders."** For explanation of these traditions, also called the oral or Mishna law, see Section 52, footnote h; Section 89, footnote c, and footnote d below. The religious leaders had attacked Him earlier on the same issue, for they placed more value on these than the Word of God in their Tanakh or Old Testament. Lightfoot, in his *Commentary . . .* , vol. 2, page 222, cites some shocking quotations from ancient Jewish writers where they actually state that their traditions were higher than the law and prophets! Refer to Section 70, Lk. 11:38, footnote d for more details on these fabricated rules of the Jews. Among these traditions, hundreds of various washings of furniture, doorways, windows, arms, elbows, hands, tools, and dishes were required for ceremonial purity. The many water pots at the Cana wedding were used for the traditional washings staunchly practiced by the Jews. See Section 27, John 2:6, footnote h for notes on these massive water containers.

(c) A general quotation by our Lord built from word selections found in Isaiah 29:13. Mark placed this quotation *before* the Words of Jesus about the Jews breaking the Torah Laws in verses 8-11. Matthew was inspired to place the same quotation from Isaiah after his mention of the Torah Laws being broken by the religious leaders, in verses 3-6. This different placement well illustrates that the two evangelists wrote as the Holy Spirit moved them, and that Matthew did not copy from Mark. Refer to footnote g below, for more on this.

(d) **"Your tradition."** We *are not to understand by this that all Jewish traditions were bad.* Even the New Testament speaks favorably of traditions or ordinances when they soundly relate to the new covenant (1 Cor. 11:2 with 2 Thess. 2:15). For the meaning of this new covenant, see Section 95, second paragraph of footnote u. These New Testament traditions had reference to certain instructions Paul had previously given believers. They had nothing to do with thousands of ridiculous claims recorded in the Talmud. Any tradition, which supplants, overrules or changes God's Word (as contained in the closed canons of both Testaments) is wicked and must be sternly rejected. We have a tradition to salute the flag, solemnly bow our heads in times of prayer, and heartily shake hands with our friends and so on. These things are honorable. Among the Jews, the term tradition signified what was called the "tradition of the elders" (meaning the older generations of scribes) or oral law, and sometimes called the *oral* Torah. Specifically, this *oral* Torah is the Mishna (text) with the Gemara (interpretation of the text). These two constitute the Talmud and are contained in numerous volumes larger than the entire *Britannica Encyclopedia*. See footnote b above. The origin of the Hebrew Talmud is explained below. For other helpful details, see also Section 45, second paragraph of footnote b regarding the division of the Torah Law into 613 parts or percepts.

2p-According to traditional Judaism, the written books of the Tanakh (Hebrew Bible) were transmitted along with the oral traditions down to each generation. Moses received both the written Torah Law and the oral (unwritten) laws on Mount Sinai. The latter was supposed to interpret correctly the former. Thousands of extra commandments were compiled to make up this conglomeration of rules and regulations. For example, amid the labyrinth of foolishness, the Jews invented the story of "Shibta," a demon present at night and in the fruit markets. Some writers described this spirit as an odor! This loathsome entity would sit on food, water, and fruit. Unless one meticulously washed (dipped and scrubbed) his hands, Shibta might leap down his throat or leave a deadly substance where he sat! See the Talmud tractate, Yoma 77b for the mention of Shibta. These rules of extreme washing had nothing to do with physical cleanliness. Rather, they were an effort to make one ceremonially acceptable to God. See footnote b above for other references. Staunch Jews tenaciously cling to their oral law and claim that all Hebrews must adhere to it. For the Gentile world, they invented the "Seven Laws of Noah" from the book of Genesis. These include no idolatry, blaspheming the Name of God, murder, and stealing, sexual immorality, eating the limb of a living animal or blood, and establishing courts of justice.

3p-Unsaved Orthodox Jews and *many* Messianic (saved) Jews are still chained in conscience to parts of the Mishna traditions. George Foot-Moore, wrote in his work *Judaism,* vol. I, page 271, that "the unwritten law will remain beside the written, and there must of course be schools for the study of both." This is the sentiment of thousands of Hebrews today. Some Messianic Jews point to the Word's of Christ in John 7:37, spoken at the Feast of Tabernacles, and tell us that Christ was observing part of the oral law. This particular act was the water drawing ceremony (mentioned in this text) and is not found in the Old Testament, but in the Mishna. However, this is a very ambiguous handling of the text recorded by John. Rather, could it not be that many of the *acceptable* Jewish customs that were practiced in the days of Christ and long before were later taken by the rabbis and included in their Talmud? The problem is that the thousands of religious customs that existed in Jesus' days were given a status *above* the Torah Law of God. This naturally resulted in a blind obedience that neither Christ, God, the apostles, nor the early church accepted. *Christ only observed those parts of the oral law that clearly pointed to Him or some aspect of His work as the Savior and redeemer of mankind.* Otherwise, He fiercely opposed them. There is nothing in New Testament Scripture about Christians living under the oral traditions of the Jews. If every Messianic Jew on earth wishes to return to the chains of the Mishna or oral law, let them go. However, they must not lay this unbearable yoke upon the necks of their saved Gentile brethren. For a good example of the apostles before Pentecost, not yet delivered from the tradition of their fathers, see Section 207, Acts 1:12, footnote d. This reference deals with the problem of walking a limited number of steps on the Sabbath day as regulated in the oral law.

4p-Both the *Babylonian* and *Jerusalem* Talmud were extant by about A.D. 500. (The Babylonian work is considered the superior of the two.) In these were written the entirety of the oral laws. Many Orthodox Jews hold these rules of more importance than the glorious Torah Law of Moses, or the words of the prophets. See Section 6, footnotes d for more regarding the Jewish Talmud. Many Hebrew writers try hard to play down our Lord's fierce condemnation of their traditions in the above verses of this Section. Some Christian Jews tell us that this was only something of a "Jewish family argument" between our Lord and the religious leaders! Was Messiah's scathing reply in Section 159, to the Jews, also a little family disagreement? If it was one could not bear to read what He would have said in a genuine feud. Were the awful judgments uttered by Jesus in Section 163 real or not?

(e) The Master cites this from Ex. 20:12 with 21:17. What a rebuke to these legal hypocrites who prided themselves in meticulously keeping every precept of Moses' Law. Two days before His death, our Lord again charged the Pharisee with thievery. Refer to Section 159, Lk. 20:47, footnote j. The Messiah now quotes their law back to them. He charged them with breaking the commandments of God that they demanded others to keep. Then He proceeded to give several illustrations of their heinous trespasses. These are mentioned in footnote f below.

(f) Matt. 15:4-9 with Mk. 7:9-13. In these verses, Jesus sorely rebukes the scribes and Pharisees. They had committed one of the worse transgressions forbidden by the Law of Moses. The ancient Jews originally looked upon the commandment to honor one's father and mother as among the highest of God's precepts. By the time of Christ on earth, the nation of Israel, especially its religious leaders, had fallen into apostasy and moral decadence. In *earlier Hebrew* tradition, it was taught that, "A son was bound to provide his father (or parents in old age) meat, and drink, to cloth him, to cover him, to lead him in and out, to wash his face, hands, feet, buckle his shoes and even beg for him." Quoting from their Torah Law, (see footnote e above), the Lord Jesus fiercely condemns the Jews for exalting their traditions *above* the written commandments of God. Messiah then gives an outstanding example of their violation of truth, which Hebrew traditions had made null and void. It was the fifth commandment of the great Decalogue.

2p-"Corban." Mark, in verse 11 of his account, uses this word. It meant something "dedicated" to God and/or the temple. Over time, this term had evolved into something of a financial incantation among the Jews. Any Hebrew so minded could take his money, stand in the temple compound, and vow it exclusively to God by speaking aloud the word "corban." *With this, he was freed from all obligations to assist his infirmed or aged parents.* The whole plot was that the scribes and Pharisees pretended to use the money for God. When any man had made such an impious vow, it stood firm and could not be altered. He no longer was under duress to support his parents or other who were in need. No wonder the Lord Jesus charged these hypocrites, that they had made the commandment God useless by their traditions. Men often make loud and long speeches about spiritual matters, but when it touches their money things can change quickly!

3p-It is of interest that among the Jews of this period were two types of vows. Briefly, they are as follows: first, the vow of consecration; and second, a vow of obligation-prohibition. The first embraced anything that was devoted to holy uses, such as to the temple altar or the temple itself. The second, had reference to anything that a man was bound to give to himself. If a Hebrew wanted something for himself, he would invoke the latter and thereby secure it as his own. The Talmud tractates, Nedarim and Nazir are filled with instructions for Jews regarding vows, but much of this material is conflicting and confusing.

(g) See footnote c above for explanation of the different placements of this quotation by Matthew and Mark. The religious leaders purported to know all their Torah Law Scriptures. To their shock, the Son of God cites this statement from the prophet Isaiah, and announces that it spoke directly of them and their sins centuries in advance. The prophet had written these words some seven hundred year prior!

(h) The worship of these religious prelates was in vain, for they had nullified God's Torah Law and replaced it with their fabricated oral traditions. What a cutting rebuke. All their prayers, readings, customs, service, temple and synagogue rituals were empty and rejected by God. Why? Because they had substituted the infallible Word of God for the "doctrines and commandments of men," which was another name for their oral law. When the doctrines of Holy Scripture are neglected or subverted by other things, then duty to God becomes an exercise in vanity and will be cursed at the end of the day. The Jews had abandoned God's Word as laid down in the Torah for the impossible thousands of external rules contained in their infamous tradition of the elders. They meticulously and with great scruples cleaned up the outside, but left their souls to be ravaged by Satan and ten thousand sins. Two days before the cross, He again laid this terrible charge against the scribes and Pharisees (Matt. 23:25-26).

(i) His call to the "multitude" or "all the people." This makes it clear that hundreds heard this debate between Christ and the religious leaders. These men threw off all convictions of their sins; they were obstinate about the Messiah and His message. Now, He warns His audience to draw near to Him, to *both* hear and understand what He had preached and taught (Mk. 7:16). Gathering the people in close, He gave this enlightening discourse on the source of man's wickedness. See footnote l below. It behooves every honest man to pay the most serious attention to that on which he has hung his hope for the forgiveness of sins and life everlasting. Refer to Section 73, Matt. 13:9, footnote k for details on having "ears to hear." For a later mention of this common Jewish expression used often by the Lord Jesus, refer to Section 128, Lk. 14:34-35, second paragraph of footnote j.

2p-Verse 11. What defiles a man? No food we eat touches the soul. A coal miner may be black and grimy due to his common labor beneath the earth and yet have a soul whiter than snow! What comes out of men and woman signals what is on the inside. A foul mouth, cursing, swearing, and blaspheming are proof of corruption within. Beware of those church people who spend their time in idle gossip, slander, criticism, maligning, and degrading others with tongues that drip of poison; their hearts are not right with God or man. This charge our Lord laid against the religious leaders of Israel! See footnote l below for more on this statement.

(j) "The Pharisees were offended." This reflects the fear of the scribes and Pharisees that had hold on the disciples. To their amazement, the Messiah informs them that the religious leaders of Israel are not the work of God's care. It was common for the rabbis to speak of God planting and rooting up things with which He was displeased. The disciples had heard this many times from the synagogue chair.

2p-Verse 14. "Let them alone." Rightfully offending. Highlighted in gray because our Lord builds this citation by selected words taken from Hosea. 4:17 and Isa. 42:18-19. It was a long-time rabbinical teaching that there would be "blind teachers within Israel" in the days of Messiah on earth. This was based on Isa. 42:19. In these terse words, the Lord Jesus again uses their own maxims to condemn them. The blind leading the blind and both falling into a ditch was also a well-known proverb. Everyone standing in that vast crowd clearly understood what Messiah was saying about the religious leaders in the usage of these familiar terms. They were spiritually blind and those who followed them would crash into the ditch of eternal hell. See a later mention of "offending" in Section 132, footnote a and b. The Talmud carries a pertinent tractate (previously mentioned) that spoke of the wickedness of the Jews in the days of their Messiah in Sanhedrin 97a. It reads, "In the generation of Messiah coming impudence will increase, esteem be perverted, the vine yield her fruit, yet shall wine be dear, and the kingdom converted to heresy." (The word "heresy" seems to refer to the Gentiles taking the kingdom.)

(k) Despite what is said in footnote i above, this question introduces us to a prevailing calamity present within the church for some two thousand years. In this, we see Peter and the other disciples inquiring about the meaning of their Lord's words. As the Master responded then, so He must today, "Are ye also yet without understanding?" The absence of the true knowledge of the *spirit and power* of the gospel and God's Word in general is still a paralyzing monster within the Church of God on earth. Even among many of those hailed as "scholarly academicians," there exists a shocking ignorance of the most simple and elementary truths of Holy Scripture. *The major crime is that no longer do many believe that we have a dependable, trustworthy, and inspired copy of the Holy Scriptures.* They preach and teach from a Bible that is "not inspired," or "partly inspired," or "it *contains* the Word of God." We wonder who among their celebrated company is wise enough to locate the verses that are inspired and those that are not! I once challenged a South African Anglican priest if he could show me what part of Scripture was inspired and what was not. In clear honesty he confessed, "I cannot do that." One will read the Preface or *Author's Introduction* to most of the "best sellers" or an "easier to understand translation" and will not find one word of praise to God for saving the soul of the authors, editors, or translators. *It is never there!* Why?

2p-Too many seminary graduates now spend their time telling us what is wrong with the Bible instead of preaching what it says. The author recently heard a twenty-seven-year old year-old Ph. D. theological graduate, labor confidently on Sunday morning to correct a single passage in the *Authorized Version Bible* by means of his "expertise" in the Greek grammar and language. He assured his congregation it was translated wrong, and that he had corrected the error! (Is some of the grammar used to make these corrections wrong?) Something is seriously amiss in the church when these things are allowed. We may rest assured that in most cases, it will not be corrected. The author has proven the *Authorized Version (KJV)* for over fifty-five years of Christian ministry. This does not mean that it is without problems and difficulties. However, problems and difficulties do not constitute contradictions! They all have their origin in the mind of the reader, not the inspired Scriptures. Men who preach and teach from a Bible that is not trustworthy in *every line* are deceiving the people. They are proclaiming something that God has never said. Only with the emergence of the hundreds of "easier to understand translations" was war declared on the *Authorized Version* of Holy Scripture. (The author is not part of the King James Bible cult, which is destroying churches, confusing untaught Christians, and spreading havoc in the name of "defending God's Word.")

(l) **"From out of the heart" or total depravity.** Here, we discover what is wrong with the human race. "Heart," has reference to the real person inside, the fountain head from which we flow. It is ravaged by sin. The fruits of this are manifested through the words and deeds of the physical body. In Matt. 15:18, the Savior served notice on the scribes and Pharisees that their traditions and oral laws, obeyed with such pedant scruples, could not cure their *inward problem* of sin. Worldly-wise philosophers scorn the fact of sin. Hitler's death camps, Mao and Stalin's genocides, Asia's barbaric child prostitution, millions of starving children in Africa, and a billion untold evils are not due to a "lack of education" or "sharing the wealth." Man's inhumanity to man, flows from the fact of universal sin. While American society slowly rots from within, secular educators pump humanism into the heads of each new generation of students. This is nothing new. In decades past, the infamous pediatrician, Dr. Benjamin Spock, decried the fact of sin. He warned millions of parents not to spank their children; "It would warp their personality." (Spock's son committed suicide.) The masses embraced his "non-violent" method of rearing their kids. Today, we are reaping the curse of Spock's idiocy with an army of "unwarped personalities" defying law and order, decency, parental authority, needful boundaries, and time proven traditional values. They burn down a city block when their ball team wins or loses the game! If the police "interfere" in their "civil rights," they are sued for excessive force. *(And brutality should be dealt with!)* "Freedom" in twisted minds is to do whatever one chooses, without respect, proper constraint, or consideration of life, limb, and the property of others.

2p-**Sin's curse in action is satanically inspired.** Wise men affirm that something is wrong with mankind. We detect evil in the life of another while it often lurks in our bosom. All extant history witnesses to the universality of sin. It has cursed and poisoned all creation. Sin is not merely a negative thing, or an absence of love, it is a disease, a dreaded distemper that kills and damns; a brute inheritance that every man carries within him. It affects mental decisions made by world leaders. We behold fool politicians legislating to support the adulteries of unmarried women having babies and living off tax dollars. They give billions to our enemies who cut off the hands of nursing mothers, murder children, burn church buildings and Bibles, and slash the throats of their prisoners in parts of Africa and Asia amid dancing and shouting, "God is great." The Koran calls for cutting off the feet and hands on alternate sides of non Muslims, especially "Jews" and "People of the Book"(Christians) in Shurah, Al-Ma'idah line 34. In Quran 48:29 Mohammad states, "Be ruthless to unbelievers" (non muslims). Radical Muslims lie and say, "These verses are to be interpreted spiritually, not literally." Would Daniel Pearl's wife believe that? During February 2002, in Pakistan, Al Qaeda Muslims cut his head off, hacked his body into ten pieces, and videoed it for the world to see! *And this is spiritual?* Radical "fundamentalist Muslims" murder their friends, children, and family members "in the name of Allah" their god. The Islamic husband, wife, and son who recently murdered four family members in Canada illustrate this. They responded that it was an "honor" to kill them being loyal Koran obedient Muslims! This illustrates the satanic insanity that grips some of these people. In view of all this, how dark it is when ignorant men are inducted into the Shriners. They must *swear on the Bible and the Koran,* in the name of Mohammed! The oath reads in part, "I do hereby, upon this Bible, and on the mysterious legend of the Koran, and its dedication to the Mohammedan faith promise and swear and vow . . ." This oath calls for having the eyeballs split, feet flayed and so forth. (The Masons swear to cut their throats from ear to ear and to be disemboweled if they betray Lodge secrets!) The potential of spiritual bondage by taking such oaths is horrifying. However, mentally deranged Muslims are not the only religious killers. Men calling themselves "Christians," have also been vicious savages. Some of their crimes are mentioned in Section 12, tenth paragraph of footnote k, and Section 203, the sixth and seventh paragraphs of footnote d. Humanistic academics, corrupt antichrist politicians, immoral moralists, killer Muslims, and unsaved "Christian" religionists do not have the answer to man's spiritual need. In America, with each new administration, political fools ruling in the Senate and Congress vote society deeper into darkness and shameful shamelessness. God warns, "I will punish the world for *their* evil, and the wicked for their iniquity . . ." (Isa. 12:11). If we did not have the sweet consolation of Christ, abiding in our hearts, we could wail with John Morrison as the Hindenburg exploded in 1937, "O humanity! O humanity!" Only Jesus Christ forgives and restores to new life amid human society going mad. Happily, we are not past redemption. Jehovah's plea to Israel in her darkest hour remains valid for all, "O Israel, thou has destroyed thyself; but in me *is* thine help." (Hosea 13:9).

3p-**Verse 18. Change must occur inwardly.** Jesus was saying that external washings, baths, and reformations could not change the dark and godless hearts of the scribes and Pharisees. Their scrupulous *outward* dedication to the oral law would not save their souls from hell. Today, as then, millions cling to and trust in good works, church membership, water baptism, christening, sprinkling, confirmation, turning over a new leaf, and hundreds of other deeds for the salvation of their souls. The sinfulness of the human heart is beyond self-correction. Only He, the Messiah of Israel, the Son of God, can change one's heart, pardon, forgive, and save. *He freely welcomes into His love and forgiveness all who repent of their sins and trust Him as personal Lord and Savior* (Acts 4:12, 1 John 5:12, and Rev. 3:20). Apart from the saving grace of God found in Jesus, poor humanity can only repeat the words of Prov. 20:9. "Who can say, I have made my heart clean, I am pure from my sin?" In Christ, man's heart can become a dwelling place for God. It is written in 1 Peter 3:15, "But sanctify the Lord God in your hearts." Reverse this truth and read that man's heart after conversion is also a dwelling place for Christ (Eph. 3:17). Lastly, according to Gal. 4:6, the Holy Spirit is in our hearts "crying, Abba, Father." Thus, the redeemed soul or heart is home for the Holy Trinity! "Conversion" apart from Christ is like a nightingale that cannot sing or a fish that cannot swim. It does not work! Further comments on the heart of man are found in Section 44, footnote m. The Holy Spirit revealing Jesus through the gospel and wakening the human will to respond by repentance and faith is a divine miracle. For more on these things, see Section 201, third paragraph of footnote n.

(m) Evil in the human heart. Matthew lists various deadly sins that originate in mankind (verse 19), while Mark enumerates (with several parallels) even more (Mk. 7:21-22). For definition of the "heart," see footnote l above. These sins lurk in man's bosom, coiled as a deadly viper ready to strike at the opportune moment:

1. **Evil thoughts**. Translated a variety of ways but having reference *first* to all mental and intellectual reasoning that pits itself against God and His Word.
2. **Murders.** Intentionally taking the life of another without warrant from God's Word or constituted law.
3. **Adultery**. Illicit sexual relations between married persons and not one's wedded mate.
4. **Fornications**. Sexual relations between unmarried persons. The word includes all manners of unlawful intimate actions, perversions, and anatomical debasements.
5. **Thefts**. Stealing or taking away the property of another by whatever means.
6. **False Witness**. Untrue testimony spoken against any person including statements given under oath in deposition or law court.
7. **Blasphemies**. To speak evil of, rail against, revile, defame, slander, or insult.
8. **Covetousness**. A progressive, passionate, burning greed for that which is not one's own.
9. **Wickedness**. Every sort of base, vile conniving that rises within the human heart.
10. **Deceit**. Cunning with evil intent and plans.
11. **Lasciviousness**. Vicious wanton desires, licentiousness, lustfulness, and shameful lewdness.
12. **Evil eye**. An undisciplined eye that wanders from sin to sin, thus inflaming the heart and imaginations into dark and base surmising. Refer to Section 46, footnote k for Christ's first mention of this "evil."
13. **Pride**. An arrogant and superior opinion of one's self and a low opinion of all others.
14. **Foolishness**. Ungoverned and intemperate folly that leads to senseless, reckless words, and wild actions often accompanied by obscene antics and scandalous behavior.

2p-The Lord first laid these sins to the charge of the scribes, Pharisees, and their associates in religious hypocrisy. Next, He reveals a dreadful array of festers in the hearts of *all* mankind. Galatians 5:19-21 lists another mountain of sins in which it is revealed that the "flesh" is the channel through which Satan and demons operate to promote these atrocities against God and man. The *fact* of man's utter sinfulness and depravity is fiercely hated by sham religions and the secular educational systems. Until men are changed by a miracle of God's saving grace they will continue as self-loving sub humans denying the Creator while worshiping their egos. In 1 Cor. 6:9-11 we read of the forgiveness of the most heinous sins, restoration to normality and true life, all made possible by Jesus Christ.

(n) Sinfully defiled, not physically. Jesus was not referring to the standard modes of personal hygiene. He spoke rather of the hundreds of Jewish religious ritual washings, which according to their traditions, made them better than all other men. See footnotes in b and d above for more on this subject.

2p-**Heretical Jewish religion.** At this time in history, the religion of the Jews consisted of traditions and human inventions. It was almost bewitchery. Thousands of endless traditions and oral laws had seduced them. These, along with perverted interpretations of their Scriptures, had falsely taught that Messiah would administer an earthly, carnal kingdom in all human pomp and glory. He would wonderfully promote Judaism or their religion. Messiah would redeem Israel from the yoke of heathenism, especially the Romans. They believed that by amazing miracles and glorious words, He would assert Himself as King of the Jews. However, Jesus did the opposite!

3p-**The Messiah was different.** Though Jesus of Nazareth met their Messianic criteria, He was different from their materialistic expectations. He advised to pay tribute to Caesar, touched lepers, went among publicans and sinners, reached out to the poor, conversed with women of ill repute, and taught much that was contrary to the doctrine of the scribes and Pharisees. Several years later, Peter made it clear that the Jews had rejected Jesus (Acts 3:13-15). This was their *willful and deliberate* choice (John 5:40). Like the millions of pagan Gentiles, who so fiercely hated the Jews, they too will someday stand before God without excuse. When that time occurs no man knows, but it is as sure as the throne of God in heaven. Again, wise men prepare, while fools march on unabated. We cannot get out of this world alive! Two things never change, taxes and death, and we are all faced with both.

The little daughter of a Gentile woman is delivered from an evil spirit. This is the first recorded case in Scripture of long distance exorcism without the Lord Jesus being physically present to perform the work.*

*See Section 106 for a little boy being healed of demons with the Savior present. *In Section 37, He had previously healed a nobleman's son and was not present. Distance did not hinder Christ's work.*

Somewhere in the region of Tyre and Sidon

Matt. 15:21-28	Mk. 7:24-29	Lk.	John
A woman approaches Christ **21** Then Jesus went thence, and departed into the coasts [borders] of Tyre and Sidon.(a)	*A woman approaches Christ* **24** And from thence he arose, and went into the borders of Tyre and Sidon,(a) and entered into an house, and would have no man know *it*: but he could not be hid.		
She uses the great Messianic title in pleading for her child **22** And, behold, a woman	**25** For a *certain* woman, whose young(b) daughter had an unclean spirit, heard of him, and came and fell at his feet:		
of Canaan came out of the same coasts, [borders] and cried unto him, saying, "Have mercy on me, O Lord, *thou* son of David;(c) my daughter is grievously vexed with a devil."	**26** The woman was a Greek, a Syrophenician by nation; and she besought him that he would cast forth(d) the devil out of her daughter.		
The misunderstood method of God: silence draws out her faith **23** But he answered her not a word.(e) And his disciples came and besought him, saying, "Send her away; for she crieth after us." **24** But he answered and said, "I am not sent but unto the lost sheep of the house of Israel." **25** Then came she and worshipped him, saying, "Lord, help me."(f)			
Her unworthiness confessed **26** But he answered and said, "It is not meet to take the children's bread, and to cast *it* to dogs."(g) **27** And she said, "Truth, Lord: yet the dogs eat of the crumbs which fall from their masters' table."(h)	*Her unworthiness confessed* **27** But Jesus said unto her, "Let the children first be filled: for it is not meet to take the children's bread, and to cast *it* unto the dogs."(g) **28** And she answered and said unto him, "Yes, Lord: yet the dogs under the table eat of the children's crumbs."(h)		
Faith always pleases Christ **28** Then Jesus answered and said unto her, "O woman, great *is* thy faith:(i) be it unto thee even as thou wilt."	*Faith always pleases Christ* **29** And he said unto her, "For this saying go thy way; the devil is gone out of thy daughter."		

Matt. 15:28	Mk. 7:30	Lk.	John
The long distance miracle is done And her daughter was made whole[j] from that very hour. (Verse 29 cont. in Section 98.)	*The joyful return home* **30** And when she was come to her house, she found the devil gone out, and her daughter laid upon the bed.[k] (Verse 31 cont. in Section 98.)		

Footnotes-Commentary

[a] Meaning the Savior departed from the presence of the wrangling, factious scribes and Pharisees, whom He had so powerfully silenced. Moving from the shores of Lake Galilee, He traveled some twelve miles in a northwestward course to the "coasts" (borders) of Tyre and Sidon. They were two large seacoast cities located in heathen Phoenicia. It is not clear that our Lord ever departed from the land of Israel, nor does this text say so. Some believe that in Jesus' time, it was necessary to pass through the territory of Syrophenicia in order to move from Galilee into Caesarea Philippi. According to older maps, this may have been the case. However, the contextual thought is that He went to some particular border location, attempting again to hide from the crowds that dogged His every step. In typical Bible language, these two cities are spoken of as being together, though they were several miles apart. This unnamed person is called a "woman of Canaan," a "Greek," and a "Syro-Phoenician by nation." Seemingly, she was born in Syria, but now dwelt in Phoenicia. All of these statements were true! In ancient times the entire land, including both Tyre and Sidon, belonged to the Canaanites and was called Canaan. Over the progress of history, the Phoenicians descended from the Canaanites; while hundreds of years later they all fell to the Greeks under Alexander the Great. Because of his conquest, the Gentiles in both cities and the entire country became hellenized or Greek orientated in life and culture. All their religions were grossly pagan. There can be no doubt that this woman spoke Greek being a product of that environment. Despite her dark heathen background, she proved to be an amazing person! See all of footnote c below.

2p-Mk. 7:24. "He could not be hid." The fame of Christ had gone out too widely over the whole land for Him to travel anywhere without being recognized. He wore no white linen gown and had no pagan halo; He was not blue-eyed and blonde-haired as depicted by the early church fathers and critics of today. We cannot believe that He was always dressed in spotless white robes. About seven hundred years before His birth, the prophet had predicated of Jesus the Man, that "He hath no form nor comeliness: and when we shall see him, *there is* no beauty that we should desire him" (Isa. 53:2). This means that He appeared as another ordinary man. The difference of Christ our Lord was in the words He spoke and the deeds He did! If outward appearance *alone* determines the true worth of a man, it is sure that most of us will never see the lights of heaven's holy city! However, in a unique sense, the Son of God cannot be hidden. One may conceal the sweet flowers so that they cannot be seen, but their fragrance will disclose their presence and hiding place. The glory of Jesus' forgiveness entering into a man's heart cannot be hidden. As a missionary serving in Australia and Africa, the author has repeatedly seen the amazing change God's Son makes in the lives and conduct of those He saves from sin.

[b] **"Young daughter."** The word means a small child. She was demon possessed and vexed or tormented by the wicked entity. The mother with genuine spiritual discernment had correctly diagnosed the problem: also, she knew who could help! It strikes us that a small child (not adult) *had a demon living inside her physical body* (Mk. 7:30). Later, we meet a little boy who was demon possessed as a tiny infant. Both cases are historical facts and fly into the face of popular theology being bounced around in many seminary classes. *This story teaches that children may have demons!* The causes are not given in these stories, but the results are. The Devil and his associates can only operate where sin is rampant and self-control is has vanished. For a discussion of this terrible subject, refer to Section 106, Mk. 9:21, footnote d. Regardless of the severity of these cases, and their shocking reality, Satan and all demons knew who Jesus Christ was and bowed to His supreme authority. The same inviolable rule exists to this moment. Jesus Christ is "Lord of all." See the second paragraph of footnote c below for more on this.

2p-Mk. 7:25. "Heard of him." His notoriety had spread over into pagan regions and countries near the land of Israel. Someone there had told her the wonderful news of Jesus of Nazareth, the man claiming to be the Messiah of Israel. See footnote below for more on this intriguing thought.

[c] **"Thou Son of David."** We are struck with amazement that this Gentile pagan called upon Jesus by His most popular Hebrew Messianic title; and she prefaced her plea with "Have mercy on me." Where did she gain this insight into the Old Testament passages that spoke of the Jewish Messiah by this designation? Was it from Dan. 9:25-26? Thousands of Jews lived across Phoenicia and retained their Hebrew faith and religion amid a demoralized heathen society, and they knew about Jesus of Nazareth, the proclaimed Messiah of Israel. Many of these Jews had spoken of Him to their more amiable heathen neighbors. Note Section 90, Matt. 9:27, footnote b, where later two blind men also used the same title when referring to the Lord Jesus. In the earlier days of Christ's ministry, we read

that many had heard of Him in distant Syria and brought their sick and suffering for healing. Thousands returned to Syria and other regions with news that Israel's Messiah had come. Months prior to this event, great multitudes from Tyre and Sidon flocked to hear and see Christ. Note this in Mk. 3:8. How easy to believe that this distraught women had learned of this wonderful Man through these fellow citizens. She had heard many stories of His miracles and wonders.

2p-The word here is "daimonizomai." It means to be "controlled by a demon." See footnote b above. Regardless of her former heathen background, now she confessed Jesus openly and publicly as the Messiah. In this heathen, we have another example of Gentiles entering into the kingdom of Christ.

(d) This distraught mother knew well that Christ could expel the demon from her child. Her daughter's sorrow and suffering became her own. She had acquired the knowledge that Christ could help her child. Being so convinced of this truth, she stubbornly refused to be turned away. Refer to footnote c above for more on this thought.

(e) "He answered her not a word." There is something indeed remarkable in the silences of Christ. Usually, He was quick to respond to all who called upon Him. Now, He stands and hears this pitiful plea but remains in terrible silence! Why? It was not that He was engrossed in His own approaching sorrows as the cross hung so near. Even in His most terrible sufferings, He reached out to aid the hurting. He wants from her an end of self, to an absolute trust in Him. So often in our lives, similar situations arise. God seems to have forgotten or is no longer concerned in our sorrows. Again, holy silence will eventually end with His glorious will being realized in the lives of all broken suppliants. This is another of the strange ways of God in dealing with His children and answering their prayers for mercy and help.

2p-With all the clamor amid this crowd, the poor disciples were deeply embarrassed, disliking this form of public attention, especially from a pagan female. Trying to hide from the crowds, they are more highlighted than ever. This strange woman wailing and screaming now cries after them, pleading for help. Her dress revealed she was a Gentile; and they, being stern Jews, were deeply shamed by her continual pleadings. See Section 35, John 4:40, footnote j for earlier embarrassments experienced by several of the disciples due to Christ's association with another wrong kind of woman; this one was a "cursed" Samaritan.

(f) Falling before Christ, she begs her case in a worshipful posture. Did this ex-pagan remember, in the history of Sidon, the story of a woman who had gone to Elijah the Hebrew prophet begging for help (1 Kings 17:18-19)? Did she know the history of the Shunammite woman and Elisha that had also occurred in her country (2 Kings 4:12-16)? Both women refused to take no for an answer; both pleaded with God's man until their petitions were granted. One can believe, somehow, she was almost emulating these examples now centuries later. We can easily believe that these *literal* case histories lived in the memories and folklore of these Gentile pagans. Beyond doubt, they were just as well known to all pious Jews residing in these areas.

(g) "To the dogs." This was the popular title employed by the Hebrews in their spite and contempt for all Gentiles. It is used this way in the Talmud tractates, Beitzah, 21b, and Megilah 7b. The Jews, since the call of Abraham (Gen. 12:1-3 with Acts 7:2-4), had considered themselves the peculiar children of God. For all other nations, they only had contempt. Messiah's answer employed standard everyday Jewish terminology. Every Gentile knew that the Hebrews referred to them as "dogs," and the Gentile epitaphs for the Jews were no less harsh. In His reply to the woman, Christ, (as it were) makes a test case of her professed faith in Him as the "Son of David." He draws out of her the glory of a simple, yielding, child-like trust.

2p-"Children's bread" speaks exclusively of the doctrines and things of God and even of Christ. He was the bread, which came down from heaven. Christ offered Himself and the doctrines of God, *first* to the Jewish people and especially their religious leaders. As previously affirmed, the Jews had (for the most part) rejected Christ and all He offered them. Our Lord is saying to this Gentile woman that He must make every effort to turn Israel to Himself, the bread of life, to convert them and bring them to know the true and living God. The chief benefits of the kingdom of God were for the Jews first, but they had rejected and scorned them all. With this, the Messiah turned to the Gentiles. A few days before His cross, the Savior gave the religious leaders three successive parables in which the demise and doom of the Jews were depicted, and the kingdom was being taken from them and given to the Gentiles, who would produce fruit pleasing to God. See Section 152 through 154 for these warnings. Note, especially Section 153, the Parable of the Vineyard Workers and its meaning.

(h) "The dogs eat the crumbs." Her reply is astounding! It sounds as though she knew Israel had crossed the line, that the Jew's cup of iniquity, in rejecting their Messiah, had almost reached its fullness. Yet, she took no offence in being referred to as a dog. With something of a quick wit, she took the Master's words and turned them into her own advantage! In essence, she replied, "Dogs eat the crumbs under their masters' tables, even the crumbs of the children." This benighted woman used the diminutive Greek word "kunarion," which has reference to "puppies," or "little dogs" licking up crumbs. Her keen rejoinder and undaunted faith stole the Master's heart! The seeming denial of her request was transformed into an exhibition of importunate, unswerving faith. With a holy earnestness of desire, she prosecutes her pitiful petition in the courtroom of Christ's great heart and wins the case! She acknowledged her position as undeserving and without the legal covenant rights of Israel. O, the wonder of amazing grace! She, a Gentile, who could never eat the children's (Jew's) bread, not being a member of the Hebrew nation, is suddenly granted honorary citizenship into the commonwealth of Israel! Instantly, and by faith divine adoption "pertaineth to her" (Rom. 9:4). *Now,* she is a true child of Abraham, which is one inwardly (Rom. 2:29 with Gal. 3:29). Are not the smallest crumbs of His grace better than the riches of this world?

(i) **"Great *is* thy faith."** Note that the Lord Jesus had words of praise regarding this woman, for one thing, she had great faith. Her faith in Christ reflected great confidence in His power to heal. In all the graces of God, the Savior honors faith most of all. As he had previously commended the faith of the Roman centurion, also a Gentile, now he blesses the faith of another Gentile, a former heathen from Phoenicia. For the story of the centurion, and his simple faith in Christ, see Section 60, Matt. 8:10, footnote h. The greatness of faith is given strength and motivation by the iron will of personal discipline, by *refusing* to yield any known place to Satan, and by clinging to Him, who at *the right time* will rise and give the needed bread. This was the "kingdom of God at hand." Apparently, the instant this woman believed, the evil spirit fled from out of the body of her child who was miles away. See footnote j below.

(j) **"Her daughter was made whole."** The reply of Jesus recorded in Mk. 7:29, "the devil is gone out of thy daughter" is conclusive. *For the demon or devils to go out of her, it had to be in her body.* He, whom all devils recognize and in whose presence they screech and howl, had spoken. For demons recognizing the Lord Jesus and their wild reaction, see Section 88, Mk. 5:7, footnote c, and its related references. "From that hour" was an expression meaning it happened instantly.

(k) **Verse 30.** Again, how could the demon have come out had he never been in? Wicked men ridicule the truth of these things but will be eternal believers upon their arrival in hell. Read of such a person in Section 3. Hurrying home after a five-hour walk, this hopeful mother raced into the house and found her child "whole from that very hour" and "laid upon the bed." The expression in Mk. 7:30 reveal that the child's struggling, convulsions, fits, and ravings were produced by the indwelling demons. Now, her little body, so torn and tossed by this foul spirit, rested; composed in the peace of God. The child was thoroughly exhausted after being delivered from the grip of demon spirits. It is an established fact that some people who have been freed out of fierce bondage are totally worn out following exorcism. Some are unable to walk until normal strength has returned to their bodies. The words "that very hour" have reference to the moment that Christ's promise was spoken to the distraught mother in Mk. 7:29. This mother had deep discernment and instantly recognized the evil spirit had left the body of her child. A reunion of unspeakable joy exploded in that house, and throughout the neighborhood as everyone knew Jesus of Nazareth had been at work. Again, this Man from Nazareth shook the borders of Tyre and Sidon.

2p-The unspeakable joy of knowing Christ. In a moment of contemplation, we can imagine how this saved mother shared the news of this good man, Jesus the Messiah, though physically far from her little daughter had wrought a miraculous deliverance from Satan. We can easily believe that both mother and child became fervent witnesses for their wonderful Lord throughout the pagan cursed land in which they lived. It remains a glorious fact of *true* Christianity that when one is saved or blessed in an extraordinary manner, he will spontaneously and wonderfully share the news with anyone who gives a listening ear. The express joy of sins pardoned, and the sure knowledge of genuine forgiveness is something no religion on earth gives its communicates, except Bible Christianity. This is because our Savior defeated sin on the cross, and the Devil and death in His resurrection. The wonder, simplicity, and charm of new converts to Christ, witnessing for their Lord is a sight that must capture the attention of heaven's angels. For two marvelous illustrations of the joy of salvation, a dancing Jew, and a women from Switzerland, see Section 64, fourth and fifth paragraphs of footnote k.

Crossing the Sea of Galilee, Jesus returns to Decapolis.* He is met by great multitudes of people. Amid hundreds of miracles, a deaf and dumb man is cured in a most extraordinary manner.** The maimed are made whole!

The "maimed" are healed (Matt. 15:30). This is one of the most remarkable statements ever written about the miracles of Christ. It furnishes incontrovertible proof that He is God the Creator. Only God Almighty could create new limbs on a human body!***

*See Section 42, Matt. 4:25, second paragraph of footnote h, for more on Decapolis located on the eastern side of Lake Galilee. It was here that Christ had recently delivered Legion from evil spirits and then sent him home to witness of his miraculous experience. See Section 88, footnotes j and k for the glorious history. Upon news of Christ's return to this district, countless thousands flocked out to see and hear Him. Legion, the former wild man had done his work of evangelizing exceedingly well. **See Section 102 for a second peculiar method used by Jesus a few days later in healing a blind man at Bethsaida. There was a third healing at the temple in Section 121, John 9:6. This involved making clay from His spittle. ***For more on this miraculous phenomenon, see footnote f below.*

Decapolis

Matt. 15:29–31	Mk. 7:31–36	Lk.	John
On a mountain top He heals hundreds 29 And Jesus departed from thence, and came nigh unto the sea of Galilee; and went up into a mountain, and sat down there.(a)	***On a mountain top He heals hundreds*** 31 And again, departing from the coasts [borders] of Tyre and Sidon, he came unto the sea of Galilee, through the midst of the coasts [borders] of Decapolis. ***A deaf and dumb man healed*** 32 And they(b) bring unto him one that was deaf, and had an impediment in his speech; and they beseech him to put his hand upon him. 33 And he took him aside from the multitude, and put his fingers into his ears, and he spit,(c) and touched his tongue; 34 And looking up to heaven, he sighed, and saith unto him, "Eph-pha-tha," that is, "Be opened."(d) 35 And straightway his ears were opened, and the string of his tongue was loosed, and he spake plain. 36 And he charged them that they should tell no man: but the more he charged them, so much the more a great deal they published *it*;(e)		
The dumb, maimed, crippled, and blind are healed: the people are astonished 30 And great multitudes came unto him, having with them *those that were* lame, blind, dumb, maimed,(f) and many others, and cast them down at Jesus' feet; and he healed them: 31 Insomuch that the multitude wondered, when they saw the dumb to			

443

Matt. 15:31	Mk. 7:37	Lk.	John
speak, the maimed to be whole, the lame to walk, and the blind to see: and they glorified the God of Israel. (Verse 32 cont. in Section 99.)	***Again, the masses are amazed*** 37 And were beyond measure astonished, saying, "He hath done all things well: he maketh both the deaf to hear, and the dumb to speak."(g) (Next chap., Mk. 8:1 cont. in Section 99.)		

Footnotes–Commentary

(a) **On a mountain.** Finding no place to rest, the Lord Jesus leaves the border region of Tyre and Sidon and moves eastward into the lower area of Lake Galilee. Unless He had various stops along the way, this walk took at least one full day. Arriving at the Jordan River, He crosses over and travels in a general southerly direction through portions of Decapolis, doing many great works while in transit. The wording of Matt. 15:29 ("a mountain") seems to suggest our Lord was accustomed to visiting this particular mountain site, wherever it was. Making a temporary camp at this place, the Savior received the great crowds that followed Him. One wonders what mountain this was, as Matthew mentions it in several passages of his work. See Matt. 14:23 with 28:16. When news spread across Decapolis of His return to the area, the populace of the entire region rushed to His campsite.

(b) **"They."** This single word reveals that friends brought this fellow to the Master upon hearing of His return to their region. Mark was inspired to single out this particular miracle performed on that occasion. For more on these called "they" in the service of God, see Section 90, second paragraph of footnote d. Apparently, he was not totally dumb, but spoke with some impediment or extreme difficulty, probably caused by the dumbness. The afflicted man's helpers requested Messiah "to put his hand upon him." Had they seen these hands in prior action? Had they heard the marvelous stories about this great person and the power of His touch? Surely so, or they would not have been there with their afflicted companion. *To those who brought us to Christ, we are eternally indebted.* Refer to Section 41, footnote b where Christ had previously "touched" another person who was ill with a raging fever.

(c) **"Into his ears and spit." A heathen custom?** The strange method Christ employed in healing this man is difficult to understand. He could have been healed through the channel of silence, but Messiah chose another means. Some spiritualize this by pointing to all sorts of emblems, types, and shadows. With none of these, have I been satisfied. There is something here more wonderful and glorious. It was *His* finger, spittle, look into heaven, and *His* "sigh" that were featured. Can this signify that every sovereign act of the Savior, put upon men, be it ever so strange, works for their good and His glory? Did not the painful "thorn in the flesh" help produce the world's greatest missionary (2 Cor. 12:7-10)? Was this not the same divine Person, who some fifteen hundred years prior spoke thus to Moses at the burning bush? "Who hath made man's mouth? or who maketh the dumb, or deaf, or the seeing, or the blind? have not I the LORD?" (Ex. 4:11). Could we say, that He now *unmakes* these physical disabilities and acts to bring new life instead and glorify His great Person? There was a tradition among the Jews of this era that the "spittle of the firstborn heals." See Talmud tractate, Baba Bathra 126b. With the Jewish "healers," it did not work. Could this have something to do with Christ, the *firstborn* of Mary, the great healer using His spittle? Regardless, His miracles *always* worked with or without spittle.

2p-The fact that ancient heathen physicians often employed similar means to produce "cures" as Christ did in this event means nothing. They also ate food and drank water! *Our Lord's work was thoroughly divine and strictly miraculous, thus setting it apart from all others.* The ancient "healers" would push their fingers into the ears, speak curious incantations, and in some cases, spit upon or near the afflicted one. The Jewish physicians would, at times, rub spittle upon eyes (except on the Sabbath) and counted it a healing application. The Talmud in tractate, Shabbath 108b speaks of spitting on the tongue as a method of healing. Contrary wise, spitting in the face was the grossest insult (Num. 12:14). Moreover, saliva emissions were forbidden in the temple precincts. One would never spit in the presence of dignitaries. If one had to spit, he must use his garment to catch the substance. The Talmud has over one hundred entries about spittle, many of which are ridiculous. In His actions, our Lord countered and exposed the folly of these quack medical practitioners. He *instantly* affected supernatural cures upon human bodies in the most amazing fashion, something no Jewish physician or ancient healer ever did after performing their silly antics. See Section 102, Mk. 8:23, footnote b for similar case. Messiah was superior to the doctors of medicine, healers, and health wizards of that day. Those watching instantly saw the difference and were stunned at the works of this Jesus.

3p-**The Papal Church** has incorporated this event from the life of Christ into one of their rituals. In their baptisms, the priest cites a pagan chant of exorcism, rubs spittle near the eyes and nostrils of the one being baptized (sprinkled) and then speaks the exact Words of Christ as recorded in Mk. 7:34. He then utters a curious incantation in which he proposes to put Satan to flight from the life of the child. All such rituals are residues from ancient heathenism, and they constitute a large part of the liturgy of the Roman Catholic and Orthodox Churches. Within so-called "Protestant churches," there are celebrations, holidays, and other rituals that had their origin in evil. "Astarte" or "Easter" is one of the famed names in heathen mythology, history, and demonology. *Pagan Easter, with its sex goddesses Astarte, has nothing whatsoever to do with the resurrection of Jesus Christ.* Because He rose from the dead when heathens worshiped Astarte, means He is right, and they are wrong. While her image stands in museums. Christ lives forever in heaven. For more on Easter, see Section 195, third paragraph of footnote a.

4p-Part of Christmas ritual also reaches back several thousand years *before* the birth of Jesus. The Romans revived this custom with the introduction of a holiday called Saturnalia, which overlapped December 25. Unsaved pagans in churches blended various heathen religious concepts into their liturgy and services, including the Roman Saturnalia. The *Britannica Encyclopedia,* not sympathetic to Christianity, carries helpful articles on the subjects of Easter and Christmas. The Puritans in early America banned Christmas then murdered those accused of witchcraft! The popular kitchen cleaning powder, Ajax, was named from a Roman god. Certain automobiles imported from Japan have heathen names. "Mazda" is the Persian god of life! However, these things long ago lost their pagan connotations. Even the business world makes a "fast buck" from the dead residues of heathenism. Zealous Christians have sought to purge all vestiges of paganism from the church and society, but have failed. The name of every month and weekday came from heathenism. To extract all of this from society would throw civilization into chaos, especially renaming the months and days. It is our duty to handle these things wisely while not falling victim to the Devils devices (2 Cor. 2:11).

5p-The steeple and paganism. The church steeple originated in heathen sex worship. For documentation, see *Ancient Pagan & Modern Christian Symbolism Exposed & Explained*, pages 368–370, by Thomas Inman, published in 1922. The late atheist Clifford Howard in *Sex Worship: and Exposition of the Phallic Origin of Religion,* published in 1909, wrote on page 96 the following (revised) words, "A church building is considered incomplete without a steeple or tower. This distinguishing feature in much of church architecture is a relic of the primitive symbol of the [pagan] idea of a creator. Its function was to hallow the place in which the deity of procreation was worshiped." Many of Howard's conclusions are right, but his blindness to the reality of the Devil and sin that originally inspired these perverted objects is obvious. Originally the church bell was installed to drive demons from the building! For more on heathen practices that crept into the early churches, see Section 1, Part 4, and third paragraph of footnote j. Today, these pagan gods are extinct and wise men remind us that the dark celebrations associated then, have, over the centuries lost their evil connotations. No doubt this is true. Yet, it is written in Eccle. 3:15, "God requireth that which is past," meaning, unless it has been forgiven. Two icons of pagan origin, still functioning around the world are "transubstantiation" and "consubstantiation." These distorted corruptions of the beautiful Lord's Supper are practiced by many churches serving under a so called Episcopacy. See Section 95, paragraphs 1 through 4 of footnote r for explanation.

6p-Overall, the mechanics employed by the Son of God in affecting the healing on this occasion are best left as they are. If Christ decides to spit near me, touch my tongue or put His finger into my ear, it will be only good for my disorders, and honoring for His glory! Could this mean that little man will not discover most of God's wonders?

7p-"He touched his tongue." It is a glorious thought that our Lord "touches" men in the worst of life's calamities and the physical member that is "full of deadly poison" (James 3:8). Friends stand over us in our sufferings and heave a sigh of sympathy then pass on to the duties of earthly life. Often, this is all they can do. Human sympathy amid suffering is wonderful, but it soon fades. It is not so with the Lord from heaven (Heb. 13:5). His presence does not guarantee freedom from pain and trouble but assures us we can bear it with Him close by. One can rejoice even when God finds us deaf to all the sweet voices of His love and grace; because He is ready to unstop our ears to hear the sweetest melodies of sins forgiven and life eternal. Upon repentance from sin and faith in Christ, the ears of our souls are fitted to hear the voice of God and the harmonies of heavenly music. Once dead to divine truth, now we hear sounds of joy and eternal hope. There are men among us who are eloquent when they speak of business, the sciences, arts, farming, music, machinery, and so forth, but the moment the subject of Christ is introduced their eloquence vanishes! Their tongues can be loosed by the saving grace of God.

[(d)] **"Looking up to heaven he sighed."** O, how we earthly mortals relate to this look and sound! Who among us has not done the same? Here, the pure humanity of the Son of God beams forth and touches all who daily sigh their way through the hardships and sorrows of life. The great heart of the Lord Jesus was saddened as He walked through the sorrows and sufferings of mankind. There is a story of a famed sculptor who wept continually as he saw at his feet the fragments of his work, shattered by one slip of his tool. Our Lord walked with a heavy heart through the shambles and ruins of Adam's race, the noblest work of His creative hands. We will hear Him a short time later sigh, again, over the religious leaders and their devices to entrap Him. See Section 100, Mk. 8:12, footnote c.

2p-"Ephphatha" is Syrian in origin. Could this infer that both the poor man and Christ understood that language? By interpretation, it means, "be opened." Mark translates it for his original readers. This expression was common among the Jews and used in reference to many things. We are deeply stirred as we read, "he sighed," being moved with compassion on the sufferings of fallen humanity. The Word's of Jesus, "be opened" are significant: a divorced person, a fool who had found his senses, a sick man now healed, a Gentile, who became a proselyte, all were said to "be opened" or "freed." A person who had various impediments in speech and hearing, once cured, was also described as "being opened." Verse 35 states that "he [now] spake plain." Here, we note that Christ frequently used the speech and colloquialisms of that day. Those standing by understood what He was saying.

(e) **"He hath done all things well."** This exquisite eulogy has been and will be from everlasting to everlasting the crown of Christ. In creation, revelation, and salvation, He has done all things well. Wise men concur that looking over the whole of all things, it would be impossible to improve on them. Everything has been made right, in substance, weight, measure, and time. One is overwhelmed as he surveys the handiwork of the Holy Trinity. However, deaf ears hearing, lame legs walking and blind eyes seeing are but a trifle in comparison to His glorious work of redemption and eternal life for the individual. Salvation is heaven's glorious jewel for mankind.

2p-Apart from God's perfection in the creation, we note the results of sin. See the horrific devastation of human wickedness and its effects on fellow mortals and natural creation. However, many turn blind eyes upon these things. "Sin cannot be the original cause of our misery," so argued an Australian geologist. Cleverly, looking over *their personal evil,* men blaspheme, curse, hate, lie, cheat, steal, spit on the Bible, shake a fist at God, the church, and ridicule *true* Christians. (Oddly, God does not exist, but He is blamed!) Others, not so intemperate step over these facts without comment. Mortal life trembles with innumerable sorrows and sufferings. As this line is typed, millions around the world writhe, plead, pray, beg, and hurt, with no relief. Starvation, depravation, distorted physical bodies, twisted children, religious hatred, political corruption, greed, unspeakable forms of vile immorality, with famines and wars are omnipresent. The author has seen the bodies of African children axed to pieces, and men and women with lips and ears cut off by the terrorist's bayonets. On one occasion in the bush of Rhodesia, at an isolated mission station, there lay the corpse of an emaciated Salvation Army girl. She had been raped and murdered by African "freedom fighters." (American tax dollars and the World Council of Churches supported these butchers!)

3p-There have always been ill set humans who blame God for life's calamities. A distraught father, struggling in despair, cursed God because his twenty-year old daughter lay twisted and helpless in her bed. She was born that way. Most of life's disasters have no answers, and only a fool would invent one. *A bigger fool will blame God.* Today, most men cannot bear or control their compelling vices and hate their divine remedies. Society is in a revolting and melancholy state. How dreadful to live a little while, die, and face God, who was blamed for our confederate wickedness. Millions today discard and disrespect all that is both good and righteous. No longer do they conceal their sin, but shamelessly exhibit their depravity like puppets dancing on the precipice of hell. Religious hypocrisy, moral decadence, political wickedness, and every vice, though joined hand in hand will be punished. No man, however wise, can *fully* explain the age long fact of suffering, even though sin is the original mother of it all. Jesus Christ is our only Savior and final refuge from sin and its eternal results. The God of all grace reaches out to opposing souls; He offers His Son as their cure. Even to those who blame Him for their ills and misfortunes, He seeks in love. As in the text above, some day every tongue will confess, "He hath done all things well."

(f) **"Maimed."** This word introduces us to the most extraordinary miracles performed by Christ. The Greek word here is "kullos." It conclusively shows that Matthew is writing of those who had literally lost feet, legs, hands, or arms and were healed. The *New Strong's Dictionary of Hebrew and Greek Words*, under article number 2948, gives the definition as, "rocking about i.e. crippled, maimed in feet and hands." The Greeks used it in referring to dismembered body parts. It does *not* mean crippled only, as the marginal notation incorrectly reads. *Thayer's Greek-English Lexicon*, page 864, under number 2, renders "kullos" as meaning, "maimed, mutilated …" Thayer cross referenced this word to Matt. 18:8 and Mk. 9:43, where the Lord Jesus spoke of "cutting off a hand or foot."

2p-With a mere word or touch, human limbs were instantly and newly created: hands, feet, legs, arms, and fingers! Here are further supernatural acts of creation streaming from the Memra-Logos described in Section 1, Part 1, second paragraph of footnote b. He had previously created fresh bread and fish to feed the hungry people on two difference occasions. Now, He shines as Creator-God calling human limbs into existence, correctly attached to the anatomy, perfectly functioning. Only the omnipotent God could do such. This *is unarguable proof that Jesus of Nazareth was God in human flesh.* Creation, which is causing something to be that had no prior existence, can only belong to the Almighty. This is the impregnable proof of the Divinity and Deity of Jesus of Nazareth.

3p-Let the omnipresent "faith healers" who boast of "God's healings, wonders, signs, and miracles" take acute notice! *Dare but one of them to duplicate such epic miracles of Christ.* Let the gullible people supporting these charlatans look ever so hard to see new limbs, arms, feet and fingers suddenly appear on the maimed physical trunks of the infirmed. Has this occurred? These "miracle workers" teach and preach, "They do the works of Christ and even more" on their TV programs. For further comments on these fakes, see Section 58, footnote o and Section 59, second paragraph of footnote c. The Greek word "kullos" in the first paragraph of footnote f above, and as used in Matt. 15:30, stands like a steel impasse, and identifies these smiling, slick dressed, and well spoken imposters as clouds without water and trees whose fruit withereth (Jude 12). They are sentenced in Matt. 7:21-23.

(g) See asterisk under main heading Section 48 for other comments on the *exclusive* meaning of Messiah healing those who were dumb.

Miracle of seven loaves and a few fish. Over four thousand are miraculously fed. Earlier the Lord Jesus had fed more than five thousand from five loaves and two fish.* Below is the record of the second miracle of this nature.

*See Section 93 for details of the previous food miracle of fish and bread performed a few days prior.

From Decapolis to Magdala–Dalmanutha

Matt. 15:32–39	Mk. 8:1–9	Lk.	John
	He feels for the hungry masses **1** In those days the multitude being very great, and having nothing to eat, Jesus called his disciples *unto him*, and saith unto them,		
He feels for the hungry masses **32** Then Jesus called his disciples *unto him*, and said, "I have compassion on the multitude,(a) because they continue with me now three days, and have nothing to eat: and I will not send them away fasting, lest they faint in the way."	**2** "I have compassion on the multitude,(a) because they have now been with me three days, and have nothing to eat: **3** "And if I send them away fasting to their own houses, they will faint by the way: for divers [various ones] of them came from far."		
The disciple's question **33** And his disciples say unto him, "Whence should we have so much bread in the wilderness,(b) as to fill so great a multitude?" **34** And Jesus saith unto them, "How many loaves have ye?" And they said, "Seven,(c) and a few little fishes."	*The disciple's question* **4** And his disciples answered him, "From whence can a man satisfy these *men* with bread here in the wilderness?"(b) **5** And he asked them, "How many loaves have ye?" And they said, "Seven."(c)		
Be still and believe: the masses fed **35** And he commanded the multitude to sit down on the ground.(d) **36** And he took the seven loaves and the fishes, and gave thanks,(e) and brake *them*, and gave to his disciples, and the disciples to the multitude.	*Be still and believe: the masses fed* **6** And he commanded the people to sit down on the ground:(d) and he took the seven loaves, and gave thanks,(e) and brake, and gave to his disciples to set before *them*; and they did set *them* before the people. **7** And they had a few small fishes: and he blessed, and commanded to set them also before *them*.		
Again, Jesus saves the scraps **37** And they did all eat, and were filled: and they took up of the broken *meat* that was left seven baskets full.(f) **38** And they that did eat were four thousand men, beside women and children.	*Again, Jesus saves the scraps* **8** So they did eat, and were filled: and they took up of the broken *meat* that was left seven baskets.(f) **9** And they that had eaten were about four thousand:		
Sending them away, He departs for Galilee's western shore. **39** And he sent away(g) the multitude,	*Sending them away, He departs for Galilee's western shore.* and he sent them away.(g)		

Matt. 15:39	Mk. 8:10	Lk.	John
and took ship, and came into the coasts [borders] of Magdala. [h] (Next chap., Matt. 16:1, cont. in Section 100.)	**10** And straightway he entered into a ship with his disciples, and came into the parts of Dalmanutha. [h] (Verse 11 cont. in Section 100.)		

Footnotes-Commentary

[a] **Multitudes, multitudes, multitudes!** They were always about the Lord Jesus. He had previously fed a crowd of more than five thousand at the northeastern end of the Sea of Galilee. Repeatedly, we have noted in this harmony commentary how the milling multitudes continually followed Christ, wherever He went. Note the comments in Section 41, footnote d for more on this.

2p-**"I have compassion on the multitude."** What a lesson for present day believers, especially those who dote on themselves as "non-compromising, militant fundamentalists," who will have no associations with anyone save their own. Their common notion that we love those who agree with us and lend assistance to them *only* is viciously spurious. The Pharisees practiced the same thing. No one can honestly think that every person in that large crowd believed on the Lord Jesus and were dedicated followers. Regardless, the Messiah felt compassion for all and fed them without distinction. Herein, we should learn one of the noblest features of God's great love. It embraces all! It is written, "Christ died for the ungodly" (Rom. 5:6). The Lord Jesus did not gather aside those few who trusted him as Lord and Messiah; He fed every person without religious distinction or selection. We do not advocate *the support* of those who "hate the Lord" as recorded in 2 Chron. 19:1-2, nor the infraction of such commandments as those found in Rom. 16:17; 2 Thess. 3:6-7; Titus 3:10-11; and 2 John 9-11. However, the Bible doctrine of separation, with many, has become the doctrine of insulation. It is our duty to go to all men, everywhere possible, and reach out a sincere hand of love and compassion like that of Jesus.

3p-The late Dr. James Crumpton, of Natchez, Mississippi, often visited the pubs in his city, going from stool to stool, and table to table speaking to all, witnessing of Christ and passing out gospel literature. The owners of these drinking establishments welcomed this gesture with amazement. Meanwhile, a fellow Baptist pastor blasted this elderly good man as "compromising the doctrine of separation." For the Savior *deliberately* mixing among notorious sinners in an effort to win them to Himself, see Section 50, Matt. 9:10-11. We should carefully give attention to the reaction of the leaders of religion to these offensive actions of our Lord. It is still the same today. *If a man's religion prevents him from going into the gutters and among the foul smelling, filthy derelicts of human society, and from witnessing to the cults and sects that plague the cause of Christ, then he has the wrong religion.* Refer to Section 33, third paragraph of footnote c for more on this thought. When biblical separation is confused with social isolation nothing, but a self righteous disaster can follow. For an example of mixing with the ungodly and debating for the truth, see Section 50, forth paragraph of footnote g. The author while serving as the principal of a small Bible school in Queensland, Australia was invited by a local farmer to visit and speak to him about Christ. Upon arrival at Trevor's house, five Seventh Day Adventists preachers confronted me! It was a trap! Refusing to give the Devil an inch I verbally fought it out with these law cult Sabbath day deceivers. I did not change, and they did not change. Some months later, I hired this same farmer to dig some postholes for me. In a sheepish manner, the poor fellow tried to explain why the cult representatives were at his house that night. I prayed with Trevor, paid him for the work, and thanked him for a job well done. Over the next few years, we would occasionally meet. He was warm, friendly, and eager to take tracts from me. Later, I visited his home again when his son was born and prayed for that little baby to be saved and live for Jesus. What came out of this I do not know. We serve God and leave the results in His hands and time. *If surprises occur in heaven, we all may be astounded as to who will be there and who will not!*

[b] **"Seven and a few."** Earlier, it was **"five and two"** (Matt. 14:17). Though these disciples had witnessed the former miraculous feeding, they lacked simple trust that their Lord could again do such wonders. Human foresight even among the closest of Christ's disciples is somewhat short at the best of times. Oddly, the graces of yesterday are not so clearly remembered by most of us today.

[c] There seems to be no special significance in the number seven in this miracle, although some have built an entire theological system from it. The Savior inquired, "How many loaves have ye?" Apparently, this small amount of food was found among the personal supplies of His disciples.

[d] Christ required exact order for the distribution of the food to be done quickly and efficiently. With the thousands sitting quietly on the ground, confusion was eliminated. No doubt, families sat together, and children were kept orderly by their parents as the disciples distributed the food. The entire process of feeding over four thousand people must have taken several hours.

[e] **Jesus giving thanks.** What a marvelous sight, the Son of God, with face uplifted thanking the Father for His food. See this same posture earlier in Section 93, footnote m. The Jews had unique rules for giving thanks for food. When three ate together, they must give thanks: meaning that one offers thanks for them all. When hundreds or

thousands were present, then one would stand and offer thanks for the multitude, at the end of which all would say "amen" or recite some word of blessing. See the Talmud tractate, Berachoth 54b for an illustration of how thanks were given when many ate together. It is clear in this miracle that our Lord prayed over the food for all the thousands present. See comments in Section 93, second paragraph, footnote m on how the ancients prayed.

(f) The word here is "spuris." It signifies a large reed basket, plaited like a big hamper. It seems the amount left over was also something of a miracle. Section 93, Matt. 14:20, footnote n on how many baskets were gathered after the first miracle of this nature. It is noted that the baskets used to receive the left-overs from the previous miracle were not of this nature. The word here is "kophinos" meaning a hand basket. See this in Matt. 14:20 with 16:9.

(g) **"Sent them away"** only after He had supplied the need for their hungry bodies and offered them the bread of eternal life for their dying souls.

(h) Sailing westward from the eastern shore of Galilee, Jesus and His disciples arrive at the border of a place called Magdala ("tower") by Matthew, but Dalmanutha by Mark. Today, a ragged Arab village stands on the supposed site of Dalmanutha. The inhabitants call it "cold fountain." Over history, many ancient cities, regions, and people have passed through multiple name changes. This was also discussed in Section 88, footnote a. In these verses, one writer speaks of the city and the other of the district. However, we do not know which is which: or is there any reason that we should know. The original recipients of these two letters understood the distinction given by the writers, and that was sufficient. Because we do not understand this today hardly means that, it is incorrect. Both places seemed to have been situated on the mid-western shore of Lake Galilee. Some writers hold that these were two different names for the same place.

2p-God's Word, archaeology, and history. In considering the historical reliability of the gospels regarding their usage of names and places such as these given above, Dr. Joseph P. Free in his *Archaeology and Bible History*, page 1 says, "Numerous passages of the Bible which long puzzled commentators have yielded up their meaning when new light from archaeological discoveries has been focused on them." Though these things are helpful; nevertheless, saved Christians, who know God's Word need no "outside confirmation," and know that the Scriptures are valid. Proof of the validity of biblical statements is a requirement of "religious skeptics," and "academic infidels," most of whom do not intend to seek the salvation of their souls. In fact, they scorn the very idea. *Scripture is true whether archaeology ever confirms anything.*

3p-Believe God regardless. To embrace the truths of God's Word, only when they have been proven by some extra-biblical discovery is absurd. (Why don't these "experts" apply this method of judgment to all historical documents and see how far they get?) However, we may use established history in the art of biblical interpretation when it agrees with or throws illumination on Scripture. This use of history is well demonstrated in Daniel chapter 8, in the death of Alexander the Great, and his kingdom divided among his four generals: Cassander, Lysimacus, Seleucus, and Ptolomey. History is the backdrop of every event in the Bible; if one is familiar with it, then he knows better the Word of God. Biblical archaeology attempts to prove the Bible right, while reliable history may clarify portions of the Bible. For example, the historical works of Josephus explain the meaning of some of our Lord's sayings during The Olivet Discourse. This is illustrated in the large commentary of Section 163, dealing with the fall of Jerusalem in A.D. 70 and associated events. Many classic examples of trying to prove the Bible right by secular evidence is found in Dr. A. T Robertson's old work, *Luke the Historian,* published in 1910. As interesting as this work is, it falls on its face, trying so hard to demonstrate that the historical data of Holy Scripture is true after all. God's Word is correct whether ancient history agrees with it or not. For an earlier comment on the opinions of unsaved "scholars" who busy themselves distorting God's Word, see Section 18, footnote d.

4p-How and when men are saved. When the saving gospel happens to a man, and he is born again, he becomes a convinced believer in everything the Bible declares, whether he understands it all or not. This is a miracle of saving grace. Salvation is not against *true intellect*, but above it. Therefore, only through the channel of divine faith will one grasp the blessed reality of sins forgiven and the unspeakable joy of the new birth, which brings life eternal in Christ. On the other hand, we do not expect the unconverted to believe God's Word. They live in a state of spiritual blindness produced by Satan in their minds (Acts 26:17-18 with 2 Cor. 4:4). The awful sin of rejecting the saving gospel of Christ is the first step into solidifying the darkness that already rules the hearts of those without God's Son. If continued, it will result in their eternal damnation because of their sins not atoned for by receiving Christ as Lord and Savior. For more on the question of *how* and *when* men may believe on Christ and be saved, see Section 1, Part 1, number 2, under the fifth paragraph of footnote h, and Section 95, footnote f. One of the biggest frauds in all theology is that of "baby faith." The nefarious teaching that God has planted a "seed of faith" in the soul of all elect infants, and that this will spring up into salvation later in life is another doctrine of demons. For other references on this monster soteriology, see under *Baby faith,* in the *General Subject Index.*

5p-The awful statement of our Lord, in John 8:21, hangs like a death sword over the heads of all men without Him as personal Lord and Savior. Those who die in their sins, die damned. Satan has invented a million contrivances to divert the world from God's gift of forgiveness and salvation through His Son. For the answer to the biggest question, "Which religion is right?" see Section 175, sixth paragraph of footnote e. *You may be surprised!*

Again, the Jewish religious leaders seek to trap the Savior.*
They required Him to produce a supernatural sign from
heaven to prove He was the genuine Messiah of Israel.

See asterisk under main heading Section 48, for explanation of the Jewish demand for Jesus to perform a grandiose wonder upon instant request. For a list of the six different times, Christ was requested to perform unique signs to demonstrate that He was the genuine Messiah of Israel, see Section 29, second paragraph of footnote e. Though He had previously given them indisputable Messianic signs, His opponents rejected their validity. Refer to Section 66, Matt. 12:22-24, where they charged Him with being in a league with the Devil. They claimed this was the source of His miracles.

Magdala or Magadan on the western shore of Lake Galilee

Matt. 16:1-4	Mk. 8:11-13	Lk.	John
Again, they tempt Him for a sign **1** The Pharisees[a] also with the Sadducees came, and tempting desired him that he would shew them a sign from heaven.	*Again, they tempt Him for a sign* **11** And the Pharisees[a] came forth, and began to question with him, seeking of him a sign from heaven, tempting him.		
2 He answered and said unto them, "When it is evening, ye say, *It will be* fair weather: for the sky is red. **3** "And in the morning, *It will be* foul weather to day: for the sky is red and lowring.[threatening] O *ye* hypocrites, ye can discern the face of the sky; but can ye not *discern* the signs of the times?[b]			
Being evil men: He would give them only one sign. **4** "A wicked and adulterous generation[d] seeketh after a sign; and there shall no sign [except one] be given unto it, but the sign of the prophet▶ Jonas."[e]	*Being evil men: He would give them only one sign.* **12** And he sighed[c] deeply in his spirit, and saith, "Why doth this generation[d] seek after a sign? verily I say unto you, There shall no sign [except one] be given unto this generation. ◀*Mark was not inspired to write the statement about Jonas.*		
And he left them, and departed.[f] (Verse 5 cont. in Section 101.)	**13** And he left them, and entering into the ship again departed to the other side.[f] (Verse 14 cont. in Section 101.)		

Footnotes-Commentary

(a) Verse 1. "The Pharisees also with the Sadducees." For more information on the Pharisees, refer to Section 30, first paragraph of footnote a. Historically, these two religious groups were bitter enemies, fiercely despising each other. Now, we see them united in their common opposition to the Lord Jesus Christ. *Hatred makes strange bedfellows.* They despised Jesus more than each other. He had sharply rebuked both groups pointing out their doctrinal errors, hypocrisies, and heresies. Later, he informed the Pharisees they were doomed for hell (Matt. 23:14-15).

2p-The Sadducees had their origin and name from one Zadok, a Jewish teacher who had lived about two hundred and sixty years before the birth of Christ. He taught there were neither punishments nor rewards for serving God. Thus, there would be no resurrection of the dead! Zadok (also spelled Sadoc) and his disciples embraced the doctrine that there was no afterlife, soul, spirit, or angels in the unseen world. Men were rewarded or punished in this life for their good or evil. Scripturally, they accepted only the Five Books of Moses. They were the "theological liberals" of that day. Their doctrine was riddled with cult heresy, including Greek annihilation philosophy and blasphemy. For more on both the Pharisees and Sadducees, refer to Section 101, numbers 1 and 2 under footnote b. For an exhaustive article on this sect in Judaism, see the *Biblical, Theological, and Ecclesiastical Cyclopaedia,* vol. ix, pages 234-241, by M'Clintock & Strong. It is of great interest that the Sadducees rejected the oral law or tradition of the elders, while the Pharisees placed it higher than the Torah Law of Israel! See the details on this conflict in Section 96. Belief differences are manifested throughout religious history. One group holds to one doctrine while another denies it. Regardless, men can be absolutely sure about how their sins are forgiven, their souls saved, and heaven will be their home when life is over. Thankfully, we have the answer. He is Jesus Christ, the Son of God, redeemer, and only Savior of mankind.

3p-"Shew them a sign from heaven." *At this time in history, the Jews were signs mad!* On the last day of the Feast of Tabernacles, they carefully studied the smoke rising from the great temple altar. If it moved northward, the poor rejoiced and the rich were troubled. This meant there would be too much rain the coming year, and their crops would rot. If it went southward, the poor grieved and the wealthy Jews rejoiced, for this signified less rain that year. Again, their madness for seeing signs surfaces. Both Matthew and Mark wrote that their request was for the purpose of "tempting him," meaning they hoped He could not do this, thus, He would not be Messiah. *We note the first person to tempt the Lord Jesus was Satan, and the second temptation came from the religious leaders of Israel.* In this, they were acting like their "father, the devil" (John 8:44). They had read many times the warning, "Ye shall not tempt the LORD your God" (Deut. 6:16), but failed to apply it to Christ. Their call for a "sign from heaven" was pure Messianic language. Hebrews believed and taught (especially the Pharisees) that their true Messiah would produce the most extraordinary and amazing signs for them to behold. In an ancient Jewish writing called *Zohar* 52:2, there is a line stating, "The appearing of the rainbow in a strange way is a sign of Messiah's coming." Joseph Klausner in *The Messianic Idea in Israel,* pages 178-183, 278-280, 442-449, and 503-517, gives many pages dealing with the ridiculous signs the Jews believed their Messiah would perform when He appeared in Israel. Though Jesus had done hundreds of genuine signs and wonders that amazed His observers; nevertheless, these men demanded, "Signs on request." This could include hundreds of things, such as calling down fire, creating a rainbow in heaven, producing manna, staying the light of the sun, and other phenomena. These amazing deeds would have vindicated His Messiahship. *This they will not get!* Every sign, miracle, and wonder He did was for God's glory and not man's curiosity. He refused to perform any deed of extraordinary consequences for the benefit of silly spectators or tricksters, such as the Jewish religionists. Yet, there was one sign He would show not many months hence; this would come from out of the earth not down from heaven. It was His resurrection from among the dead! See footnote e for this final sign by which all men will be saved or damned. When our Lord died, nature yielded alarming proofs for the Jews to see as "darkness covered the earth" (Matt. 27:45). The most terrifying sign was when the temple veil was rent at the death of Christ, from top to bottom, exposing the forbidden holy of holies (Matt. 27:51).

4p-Signs madness. Religious Jews were obsessed with a passion for Messianic signs and slavishly chained to vain traditions. They had rejected the thousands of wonders and miracles He had performed. See Section 29, second paragraph of footnote e for a listing of the times they requested signs from the Lord Jesus. They had previously asked for "a sign from heaven" by the Messiah in Section 67, Matt. 12:38, footnote a. Again, they are feigning to see evidence proving He was the Messiah. In reading through the Talmud, one is struck by the deep superstition of the ancient Hebrews about signs regarding the weather, winds, smoke, fire, and so on. We read, "Cloudy weather at Pentecost was a sign of a good harvest," according to Baba Bathra 147a. "Vinegar was considered helpful in hot weather," so affirmed a rabbi in Shabbath 43b; "smoke rising from wood on the altar had five different signs," according to Yoma 21b; "One can pour hot water into cold, but not cold into hot," Shabbath 42a. The Sadducees said in Chagigah 23a, "Sunset was only for those who were [ritually] unclean." Lightfoot's *Commentary on the New Testament . . . ,* vol. 2, page 232, states that the rabbis lamented the terrible things that would befall Israel just before their Messiah came. "Can ye not distinguish that the times of the Messias [sic] are come, by those signs which ye plainly declare it? Do ye not observe Daniel's weeks now expiring? Are ye not under a yoke, the shaking off of which ye have neither any hope at all or expectations to do? Do ye not see how the nation drowns into all manner of wickedness? Are not miracles done by me [Messiah], such as were neither seen nor heard before?" These are but a few quotes from Jewish literature that speak of the signs within Israel when Messiah will appear. To understand more of the Hebrew obsession with signs regarding Christ, see all references by the asterisk under the main heading above. Edersheim in *Life and Times of Jesus the Messiah,* pages 519-521, lists an amazing array of signs the Jews claimed to have been wrought by their power! They range from a rabbi moving a locust tree hundreds of cubits backwards, water flowing backwards, walls leaning over, and turning water to blood! All of these were typical Jewish exaggerations demonstrating their madness to see signs. Those recorded above by Lightfoot occurred before and during the earthly days of Jesus, the real Messiah.

5p-Guesses, guesses, and more guesses. *Appendix Eight* carries coverage of some of the prognostications and assumptions about the appearing of both Christ and the Antichrist. However, this was not strictly a Jewish thing. In 1924, at Balmoral, near Sydney, Australia, a group of second coming fanatics built a large amphitheater facing the sea. Tickets were sold, and every seat was booked. They would be able to see the Lord Jesus returning on the waters of the sea at a place called Sydney Heads! Christ did not appear, and thousands of disillusioned people went their ways. The story of this end-time fluke is found in the *Australian Post*, December 13, 1984. America also has its share of second coming prophets. The *New York Times*, April 25, 1982, carried an article written by another group of religious fanatics. It stated that Christ is now present and would "speak to the world in two months by telepathic" communication! That was over twenty-seven years ago, and He has not yet spoken. What Christ wants us to know is recorded in the Bible. End time guessing nonsense continues to this present moment.

(b) **"Can ye not *discern*?"** Our Lord's Words to the Pharisees and Sadducees have *nothing* whatsoever to do with His return or second coming. Contextually, they have reference to the signs that pointed to the first coming of Israel's Messiah, His rejection and the nation's demise as described in footnote d below. At this place in history, no one had ever heard of the "rapture of the church," "the tribulation period," and the "beast out of the sea" as revealed in the later books of the New Testament. (None of them even understood His death, burial, and resurrection at this time!) Among rabbinical interpreters, the emblems in the book of Daniel were still a matter of dispute, and most of their meanings were unsettled. Ancient rabbis agreed that Dan. 9:26-27 spoke of their coming Messiah, yet its finer details were fiercely debated. The signs mentioned here by our Lord have to do *exclusively* with Israel's rejection of Him, and the later doom of their city and temple in A.D. 70. One is amazed to hear Bible teachers, pastors, theologians, and missionaries read this passage, build their signs scenario, and then assure their congregations that this proves the coming of Christ is very near! For decades, we have heard about such things as the "radio, telephone, TV, radar, sonar, airplane, automobile, atomic bomb, world wars, various world dictators, oil, the mark of the beast, 666, computer chip implants, communism, the KGB, the Pope's hat, world trade center, and the Great Pyramid being signs of the end. They were dogmatically heralded to be proofs that the end was near. It is striking how every (would be) world tyrant to rise up is pointed to as being "the Antichrist." Books are written, "proving" this myth and several million copies sold. Suddenly, the prospective Antichrist dies, is assassinated, retires, or vanishes. Henry Kissinger, was a popular candidate for Antichrist decades ago. Later, he retired from politics. At this writing, Kissinger, "the Antichrist" is now a feeble old man hardly able to walk.

2p-The passing years of world history have continually proven these "end-time experts" wrong. Worse, they are misinforming thousands of weaker Christians, who thrive on speculation. This is nothing new, for the ancient rabbis also had their *distorted* notions of Antichrist, Messianic rule, the kingdom, and judgment. They were eschatological nightmares designed to glorify carnal Israel and were foreign to the teaching of Jesus and the record of the New Testament. Rabbinical distortions are missing from Paul's (later) revelations and inspired writings. The various terms we use today to categorize eschatology came much later in church history. *They were unheard of in the days of Jesus and only developed centuries later from the writings of Paul, Peter, and John.* In time, future debates about the finer points of eschatology gave rise to more descriptive terms.

3p-**Expertise in the wrong field.** The Pharisees and Sadducees were good meteorologists but dreadfully wet and cold theologians, especially in the field of eschatology. See first paragraph of footnote a above, for more on this. With great skill, they would scan the heavens, cloud formations, wind movements, hot and cold temperatures, and sun reflections. Their predictions of fair or foul weather were amazingly dependable. However, they were stone blind to the spiritual signs of decay and death within their own souls, nation, and religion. Sadly, they were oblivious to the infallible signs revealing that Messiah had come to earth and was standing in their presence, irrefutably proving that He was the promised One of Israel. Genuine Messianic signs were being seen over the land of Israel daily through the words and works of Jesus of Nazareth. The sceptre had departed from Judea, and Daniel's weeks were swiftly running their course. Shiloh had come, and they had rejected Him! Experts in weather forecasting, but blinded by their religion, the Jews failed to see the dark clouds of awful judgment gathering over their nation and city. Christ put the pressing question to these men, "Can ye not discern the signs of the times?" "Look," He says, "Can't you see that your Messianic signs point to Me and the storm of God's judgment will soon fall upon Israel?" They did not see. Jesus had earlier used an illustration of weather in Section 71, Lk. 12:56-57.

(c) **"Sigh."** We heard this from the Savior on another occasion in Section 98, Mk. 7:34, footnote d. What a powerful flash of His humanity! Jesus' great heart was sorely touched by the hypocrisy and wickedness of these men, who were Israel's religious leaders. "Sigh," means that He drew deep groans from His breast. Their obstinacy and hardness of heart deeply touched the sinless humanity of Jesus. How He loved those who hated Him so much!

(d) **"Wicked and adulterous generation."** This was Christ's description of the Jews! These were cold facts not allegories or symbolic language. Josephus, a former Pharisee among some of these Jews wrote the following remarks about their ungodliness during this period. "For that time was fruitful among the Jews in all sorts of wickedness, so that they left no evil deed undone: nor was there any new form of wickedness which anyone could invent if he wished to do so. Thus, they were all corrupt in both their public and their private relations; and they vied with each other, which should excel in impiety toward God and injustice to men. The more powerful oppressed the common people, and the common people eagerly sought to destroy the more powerful, for the former class was governed by the love of power and the latter by the desire to seize and plunder the possessions of the wealthy." The above quote is from the 1886 work by Dr. William Nast, *Introduction to the Gospel Records*, page 145. While studying at the notorious University of Tubingen in Germany, Nast, though unsaved, became disgusted with their liberalism and came to America. After a "life changing" conversion to Christ in January 1835, he served as a Methodist missionary among the German speaking population in Ohio. Despite great physical difficulties, thousands came to a saving knowledge of Christ in his ministry. He died in 1899. Nast's work, cited above is an outstanding early apologetic for the defense of God's Word. The Anglican writer, Dr. John Lightfoot, also wrote of the wickedness of the Jews at this time. In *Commentary on the New Testament . . .* , vol. 2, pages 315-316, he stated, "There were hardly any people in the whole world that more used, or were more fond of, amulets, charms, exorcisms, and all kinds of enchantments."

2p-For more on Jewish wickedness in the days before, during and after the earthly life of Christ, see *The Messianic Idea In Israel*, Chapter V, by the late Joseph Klausner, an unsaved Hebrew. As a Christ rejecter, in the Appendix of his book, he reduces Jesus to a hero figure in conflict with the writings of Paul about Israel's Messiah.

3p-In their madness the Jews had deliberately rejected Christ. Even though He had done many signs and would yet do more, they would not get their "sign from heaven." By thousands of astounding deeds, He had soundly demonstrated His Messianic mission and deity. He said that responding to their request would be casting pearls before swine and giving the holy unto dogs. The Talmud, in tractate, Sotah 49a carries a long lamentation regarding the sins of Israel and her leaders before the temple was destroyed in A.D. 70. Then Sotah 49b reads, "The meeting place [of scholars] will be used for immorality." This has reference to the temple, synagogues, and possibly the "hall of hewn stones," where the Sanhedrin met. Within this post funeral dirge for the nation (written after A.D. 70), one reads the terrible line that the "fear of sin ceased" among the Jews prior to their doom. Christ classified those ancient Jewish "sign seekers" as "wicked and adulterous." Could this be a warning signal for "date setters" who have plagued the Church of God with their (false) predictions regarding the time of Christ's return?

4p-"Generation," Concerning this word, refer to the comments and cross-references by the asterisk under main heading of Section 68. In using this term, Jesus was speaking of *that present generation, (then and there)*, not some distant generation of Jews, thousands of years in the future. For an explanation of how the ancient Jews reckoned time before, during, and after the life of Christ, see Section 82, footnote d, and *Appendix One*.

(e) "The sign of Jonah" was the sign of resurrection. Here, the Savior speaks again of His death, followed by resurrection. Jonah's experience in the whale's stomach for three days and nights mirrored the resurrection of Christ. His preaching to pagan Nineveh reflected the message of Christ taken to the Gentiles. Refer to Section 67, footnotes c and d for an earlier mention of Jonah. Christ's resurrection has sounded the death-knell on *all* the world's religions. None of them has a savior, founder, teacher, mantra, guru, or whatever, who conquered death, rose from the grave and lives forever. Jesus, the Son of God, is singularly above all others and exalted at God's right hand as the only Savior of lost men (Acts 4:12). By simple faith, millions of Gentiles have found Him "greater than Jonah" and more precious than life itself. The great Puritan, Samuel Rutherford wrote, "To be in heaven without Jesus would be hell. To be in hell with Jesus would be heaven. He is all heaven to me regardless of where I am!" Like all others, the Puritans also had their share of baptismal heretics and tyrants. Believer's baptism reflects their prior faith in Christ's death, burial, and resurrection typified in Jonah. This simple ordinance became so perverted that early believers were taught they must be baptized naked; they should "take nothing into the water except their bodies." Thus, they were guaranteed that all their sins were washed away! The murderous Emperor Constantine was baptized this way shortly before he died in A.D. 337. Kenneth S. LaTourette, in *A History of Christianity*, vol. 1, page 194, wrote of this odd practice. It reveals how far some early believers had drifted from the original New Testament doctrine of baptism for believers. For more on this slow departure from Bible truth, see Section 12, seventh paragraph of footnote k. After the death of the apostles, the doctrine of baptism was corrupted by the so-called church fathers, and then taken into the Catholic Church. The Reformers and Puritans were contaminated by this when they came out of the Papal system and passed it to their successors, where it continues with *some* (but not all) of them to this present day. For the unspeakable barbaric deeds of some of America's early Puritans, see Section 155, the sixth paragraph of footnote g, and Section 203, the sixth paragraph of footnote d. Oddly, devils seem to have wings as well as angels.

2p-For an exhaustive coverage of many of the cults, sects, and secret societies in America, and their false teachings, see *AMG's Encyclopedia of World Religions, Cults and the Occult*, by Mark Water.

(f) We learn from Section 102, Mk. 8:22, footnote a, that upon departing this area of Magdala, Jesus traveled across the sea back to Bethsaida, located at the northeastern side of Lake Galilee. Over a year before, He had pronounced doom upon this city as noted in Section 63, Matt 11:20-22, footnote a. Later, He went into the Bethsaida district again with His weary apostles for a time of rest but was swamped by the people. See Section 94, Mk. 6:45, footnote for this event. Now, He passes through Bethsaida for the *final time* and heals a single blind man, but only after leading him out of that cursed place. Later, while sending out the seventy, the Lord Jesus spoke a final curse upon Bethsaida. This was about six months before His death.

A warning about the Pharisees, Sadducees, and Herod Antipas.

North-east coast of the Sea of Galilee

Matt. 16:5–12	Mk. 8:14–21	Lk.	John
The best of men often forget **5** And when his disciples were come to the other side, [of the sea] they had forgotten to take bread.[a]	**The best of men often forget** **14** Now *the disciples* had forgotten to take bread,[a] neither had they in the ship with them more than one loaf.		
The poison of false religion **6** Then Jesus said unto them, "Take heed and beware of the leaven [teaching] of the Pharisees and of the Sadducees."[b] **7** And they reasoned among themselves, saying, "*It is* because we have taken no bread."	**The poison of false religion** **15** And he charged them, saying, "Take heed, beware of the leaven [teaching] of the Pharisees, and *of* the leaven [politics] of Herod."[b] **16** And they reasoned among themselves, saying, "*It is* because we have no bread."		
The turmoil of faithlessness **8** *Which* when Jesus perceived, he said unto them, "O ye of little faith, why reason ye among yourselves, because ye have brought no bread? **9** "Do ye not yet understand, neither remember [c] the five loaves of the five thousand, and how many baskets ye took up? **10** "Neither the seven loaves of the four thousand, and how many baskets ye took up? **11** "How is it that ye do not understand[d] that I spake *it* not to you concerning bread, that ye should beware of the leaven of the Pharisees and of the Sadducees?" **12** Then understood they how that he bade *them* not beware of the leaven of bread,[e] but of the doctrine [teaching] of the Pharisees and of the Sadducees. (Verse 13 cont. in Section 103.)	**The turmoil of faithlessness** **17** And when Jesus knew *it,* he saith unto them, "Why reason ye, because ye have no bread? perceive ye not yet, neither understand? have ye your heart yet hardened? **18** "Having eyes, see ye not? and having ears, hear ye not? and do ye not remember?[c] **19** "When I brake the five loaves among five thousand, how many baskets full of fragments took ye up?" They say unto him, "Twelve." **20** "And when the seven among four thousand, how many baskets full of fragments took ye up?" And they said, "Seven." **21** And he said unto them, "How is it that ye do not understand?"[d] (Verse 22 cont. in Section 102.)		

Footnotes-Commentary

(a) **"Forgotten to take bread."** In the previous Section, Jesus clashed with the Jews over signs. This confrontation took place somewhere near Magdala or Magadan on the Midwestern shore of Lake Galilee. Then, they crossed the sea again to the eastern side. Disembarking from the ship, they walked the road in the northerly region where the city of Caesarea Philippi stood. *Here, we learn an all-important lesson, that even the best of men can forget important things.* The chief butler forgot Joseph's kindness centuries before (Gen. 40:23). Amid the distress of forgetting, Christians must learn that good humor often helps. The Jewish people have a popular joke they tell. A rabbi named Rubenstein boarded a train and was seated. Suddenly, outside on the station platform a woman shouted loudly, "Rubenstein, Rubenstein, where are you? Show me your face, you rascal!" The rabbi stuck his head out of the window to see what was going on. Suddenly, a woman ran up and slapped him so hard that his skullcap flew across the coach! Everyone in the compartment roared with laughter. To their amazement, he laughed harder than everyone did. An elderly man inquired, "And why do you laugh rabbi, you were the one who got the slap?" Shaking all over with hearty laughter he responded, "I'm not Rubenstein!"

2p-Mark comments that there was but one loaf of bread in the ship. Did the continual conflict with the leaders of Jewish religion, keep the disciples so troubled that they simply forgot to take food for their journey? Men do not easily forget their food, unless the circumstances are radically extreme! Some commentators have hypothesized that the disciples purposely left off taking bread so that they could see Jesus perform another miracle. However, the word "forgotten" seems to nullify this conjecture. It seems best to believe that the disciples purchased food and supplies at places most proper and carried these along as they journeyed over the land with their Lord. In Section 172, John 13:29, footnote j we note that the traitor Judas was in charge of spending money from their treasury for what was needed on various occasions.

(b) **Warning about false teaching.** Having just clashed with the Pharisees and Sadducees over the signs question (Section 100), the Savior sought to *reconfirm* in the minds of His preachers just how evil the teachings of these men were. He used leaven as a symbol of the slow, deadly effects of their false doctrine. See Section 80, Matt. 13:33, footnote b for explanation of the various usages of leaven. Jesus had given an earlier warning about the false teaching of the religious leaders and used the same symbol in Section 71, Lk. 12:1, footnote b. It is amazing that at this point, the disciples did not yet comprehend that the religious teachings of the Jews were (mostly) poison! Had He not just *again* clashed with them over serious doctrinal points and proven them wrong? Did the apostles not witness the whole conflict a few hours before at Magdala, as recorded in the previous Section? It is puzzling that often those who seem to follow so close to Christ are in a lamentable state of blindness when it comes to the major doctrines of God's Word, especially when confronted with the sophisticated forms of heresy and error. Thus, we see the spiritual condition of our Lord's chosen apostles! This terrible drama was precipitated by lack of faith in what they had been hearing from their Lord; hence, the Savior's cry, "O ye of little faith." Even though the apostles shared in this clash of beliefs, they did not yet comprehend the meaning. Realizing His band of preachers and missionaries did not yet understand the false teachings of the Pharisees and Sadducees (Mark adds Herod Antipas to the list), the Son of God attempts to instruct them as they sail to the eastern side of Lake Galilee. One can check the Index in the *Works of Josephus* for extended information about these three groups operating in the days of Christ. The following is a short review of what they taught and believed:

1. **The Pharisees**. They taught the Law of Moses; but in practice, they canceled it by putting the greater emphasis on the tradition of the elders or oral law. See Section 52, footnote h; Section 89, footnote c; and Section 96, footnote d, for explanation of the oral law of Israel. For a brief and amazing description of the seven different kinds of Pharisees in Jesus' time, see Section 30, third paragraph, footnote a.

2. **The Sadducees**. They were the theological liberals denying the very foundational truths of God's Word as laid down in the Old Testament. *They did not hold to the oral law or traditions as did their enemies the Pharisees, and denied the resurrection of the dead.* A few days before His death, the Sadducees attempted to trap the Lord Jesus by questioning Him regarding the resurrection. See this in the main heading of Section 156 and relative footnotes.

3. **Herod and his Herodians**. They were men of corrupt morals, interested in political advantage and gain. Some commentators write that many of the Sadducees were sympathetic with Herod Antipas and served in his government. Basking in the sunlight of Herod's political tyranny, they served him for their own good and profit. Men, who reject God's Son and His Word, gradually become destitute of genuine hope. To fill this dark void, they often vent their half-truths and whole lies via *corrupt* moral, civic, legal, and political systems and make laws to protect their sins. For more on the corrupt Herodians, see Section 54, Mk. 3:6, footnote h. For a review of Herod Antipas, note Section 21, Part 1, number 3 under footnote b.

2p-It is interesting that the Lord Jesus on this occasion "got involved in politics," when He exposed the wretched doctrine of Herod Antipas. We have often wondered what religious "doctrine" this scoundrel advocated. Years ago the unsaved Jew, Joseph Klausner, in his work *The Messianic Idea in Israel*, pages 374-375 may have given us the long sought for clue. He wrote, "We have evidence that Herod regarded himself as Messiah." In a footnote on page 374, Klausner cites several ancient sources for this claim. If indeed, Antipas presented himself as a Messiah, then we instantly understand why the Lord Jesus condemned his doctrine. Even worse, F. W. Farrar, in his *Life of Christ*, footnote 1, page 556, informs us that the Herodians had earlier attempted to represent Herod the Great (the infamous baby killer) as the Messiah! This plot was foiled by the Sanhedrin, who appealed to Deut. 15:17, and affirmed that Herod's ear was not marked, thus he was not Israel's servant as Messiah would be. Apart from these yarns about the politicized Herodians, all of this informs us that knowledge of the coming Messiah was common among the various religious and political bodies in the land during these years.

3p-The Savior described the teachings of all three groups as "leaven." His admonition "Take heed and beware" is applicable to our present situations. Christians must be continually warned concerning evil persons, false religions, and corrupt political organizations. Unsaved lawmakers, who have no solid moral or spiritual foundation, and no infallible guide to decision making, legislate out of their blindness. Among their shocking legal injunctions are the approval of abortion or murder of the unborn, the abomination of same sex marriages, protection of sodomy and lesbianism. In some states, it is becoming a crime to speak out for Christ, the Bible, divine, and moral truth. Things are in the lowest decadent condition when laws are made to protect the guilty in their abominations and condemn the innocent who are brave enough to speak out against such deeds. *Even the amoral animal world does not behave like some men and women.* Among the religious protectors of these sins is a poison called "Revisionist theology." See Section 191, fifth paragraph of footnote i for more on this. The warning to ancient Israel is valid today. God "will remember their iniquity" (Hosea 9:9). Wicked men rage at such statements for it troubles them in their sins. Meanwhile, the Christ they hate waits patiently to forgive and pardon.

4p-Christianity is hated. In American society, one can speak openly of Buddha, Mohammed, murderous *militant* Islam, Abraham, Moses, Judaism, Hare Krishna and any other religion, person, cult or sect; but he dares not freely and *openly* speak of Jesus Christ as the *only* Savior of mankind. To invoke His Name in public prayer often infuriates certain religious leaders, politicians, lawmakers, school principals, teachers and others. Evolution is rigorously taught at every level of education but rarely is the biblical account of creation considered. In some schools, it is declared as unacceptable to children and young people. American Christians are gradually muzzled by the higher legal and secular educational systems. These predominately legislate and write in favor of sin and wickedness, against God, Christ, and right. The most heinous sins in human history are now respectable under the guise of "human rights" and "political correctness." One atheist wrote in his local newspaper that he resented Christians sharing their "brainwashed superstitions." (He is an evolutionist!!) *True Christians are not what these people resent; rather, it is what God has written in the Bible about their sins.* They hate that! If one wishes to behold some of these haters, let him spend several hours in the "Teacher's Lounge" of the average secular institution of learning. He will discover everything from "doctrinaire monkeys to educated screwdrivers." These are the "academics" and "professionals" training minds for tomorrow! (Thank God, there are some exceptions to this rule.)

5p-Majority vote failure. Editor David Kupelian produced a devastating exposure of the attacks on America, and Christianity in his book, *The Marketing of Evil: how Radicals, Elitists, and Pseudo-Experts Sell us Corruption Disguised as Freedom.* In this masterpiece, Kuperlian reveals how intellectual numbskulls, and money mad, morally rotted out policy makers are conning millions into accepting beliefs and behaviors that would have horrified all previous generations of Americans. The agenda of secular intellectuals, political pawns, and "Hollywood celebrities" is to vomit out their hatred for Bible directives, conservatism, family values, and *responsible* politics. They tell us that promiscuity is a choice, abortion as a right, flag burning a privilege, and selling evil, sin, and immorality of any kind as socially acceptable. These monsters dominate our society via the educational, judicial, and entertainment systems, halls of Congress, and media, while finding legal protection in the (some time) corrupt court systems entrenched like festered sores across America. For example, the citizens of California voted against same sex marriage. Regardless, a federal judge threw out their votes and ruled in favor of the highest of human abominations. *It is high time these kind of judges were thrown out.* Godless persons positioned in critical places have packaged and perfumed evil to make it look good and acceptable. Millions with no Bible knowledge of what is right or wrong, rush forward to buy this new moral, educational, social, and political garbage: it is then publicly and privately practiced. Past generations of older Americans would have been horrified at what is being said and done openly today. And it is all in the name of "Civil rights." The hard fought for glory of "majority vote" is gradually strangling the country to death. *When there is a majority of devils and a minority of good people, the devils always win the vote.* This is where the voting system stands today. It is a guaranteed loser for family, country, honor, righteousness, and genuine dignity. The poisoned leaven of the religious leaders in the time of Christ on earth has spilt over into every strata of American life, even in many churches. Men once looked up to and held in high esteem for their positions, and office are continually being exposed as thieves, crooks, immoral animals, adulterers, liars, child molesters, hypocrites, and the rest. This is especially true in American professional sports, politics, and certain places of religion. After being exposed, their superiors often let them continue in their professions after a soft reprimand or two weeks dismissal with full pay! The warning of our Lord in verse 6 above, "Take heed and beware of . . ." has been forgotten. And we are now paying for it. As America slowly dies, communist China, *radical* Islam," and the worst of immoral rottenness rises like demonic apparitions from the pits of hell. Unless, America's mass media, educational, judicial, *true* religious and political systems are changed by the grace of God, we are eventually doomed. Sinister skeptics scorn these words; one minute in hell will change their minds.

6p-In far off Sweden, a faithful Lutheran pastor was jailed for preaching against the sin of sodomy. Since when is it "discrimination" to oppose the deeds of people who live lower than animals. The final aim of this trash bag scenario is to turn society into a happy animal farm, where no such thing as wrong exists and everyone does their own thing. Thousands, even in churches, scorn the fact of original sin and ridicule the Bible's message for moral uprightness and purity of life. Their answer to the crisis is education, jobs, money, abolish racism, and equalize humanity by some form of Marxist socialism. Apart from Marxist socialism, no sane person would disagree with the above goals. Liberal pastors now practice what they call a "centrist ministry." *Their* gospel receives men without the new birth, sinners without the Savior, and takes them to a heaven because there never was a hell. Falsely professing to believe the basics of Christianity, they dare not preach about morals, biblical standards, and divine inspiration of Scripture. Their nice talk about "sexual orientation" and "gender identity" is a satanic lie. Opposing the popular sins of today is now "discrimination." *What Scripture says about these things is rejected or changed to approve their evil.* Clergymen who are more concerned in getting a man out of the dumps than getting the dumps out of a man should get another job. For a shocking illustration of the "inside dumps," see the story of the Oxford trained African politician in Section 177, the second paragraph of footnote z. In time, after human madness has expired (whenever that may be) the Lord of heaven will triumph in universal judgment. Meanwhile, millions of *true,* non-fanatical Christians have gone to prison and death for Christ and right over the past two thousand years. The waiting list is just as long today.

7p-Informed, *dedicated* Christians know that here they have no continuing city; that crowns roll in the dust, and eventually every earthly kingdom will flounder and collapse. Believers, who know Christ as personal Lord and Savior, acknowledge a King, who men did not crown and therefore, cannot dethrone, because they are citizens of the city of God, which men did not build and cannot destroy. The Christ hating systems of this world are like an endless soap opera going on from century to century. Their shameless, erotically poisoned old props and mannequins litter the earth, as each new generation is only deeper charmed by their beautiful deceit. Sodomites and homosexuals in Paris and London often set the dress fashions, and the western world follows. This is also true of many spiritually sick "Christians," regardless of how provocative, sensuous, wrong, and vulgar these fashions may be.

8p-Nevertheless, while the human wolves howl, Jesus Christ remains the pivot of world history. Through Him only, God reaches down to man and man reaches up to God for perfect and eternal reconciliation. In our Lord, time looks into eternity and eternity into time, thus making now always, and always now. The rich and poor alike rot in the grave while endless eternity reckons with their souls. Though the cause of Christ is often reduced to ashes, yet, out of these smoldering heaps, it has always risen like the legendary Phoenix bird. And it has lovingly stretched out the hand of love and forgiveness to its hateful enemies, inviting them to join their blessed company. Our Savior has conquered sin, Satan, death, and the grave for all who trust Him. *We are not going to win; we have already won and are now waiting for the final act on the stage of human history!* Whether that last curtain call is soon or a thousand years away, it is coming. Prudent men prepare while fools march on into everlasting doom.

(c) **"Do ye not remember?"** In an effort to help the apostles understand, the Messiah reminds them that He had supplied bread on two other recent occasions, and they had much left over. See the main heading, Section 93. Therefore, the lack of bread is not the issue in the above statement of our Lord. He jogs their memory as to exactly how many baskets were taken up after the gigantic feeding efforts. Moreover, they knew the answer! How amazing that Christ previously had sent these same "spiritually handicapped" men out to represent Him and had endued them with supernatural powers for the job. Regarding insight into spiritual language, they were unable at this point to find meaning in the strange words of their Master. In time, this problem vanished. See last paragraph below.

(d) Both Matthew and Mark record that the disciples did not, at this point understand the lesson Christ was presenting to them. We are amazed at their senselessness in failing to realize that Jesus was not speaking of a literal leaven. However, their understanding of this would come later.

(e) Matthew concludes the story where Mark leaves off. He wrote that suddenly, by divine revelation, the disciples now understood what Jesus was saying. For a pious Jew to deny or reject the teachings of their rabbis was a sin of the highest caliber. This is reflected in the Talmud tractates, Baba Mezia 59b and 86a, where we read that several rabbis disputed with God over the Torah Law, and in one case actually defeated Him in the debate! One shocker is in tractate, Erubin 21b, where it infers that the commands of the rabbis are more important than the commands of God! Now, they hear Jesus say that the rabbinical teachings were poisonous. This statement had reference to *specific* doctrines, because not everything they taught was wrong. Their cardinal sin was the rejection of Jesus as Messiah, clinging to their man made oral laws and traditions for salvation.

2p-Christ's Words must have shaken these future servants of His new kingdom or church and preachers of the saving gospel. In time, they would understand with the coming of the Holy Spirit at Pentecost. Then, they were endowed with supernatural powers to perfectly comprehend all that He had previously taught them. Concerning how people were saved during the ministry of Christ and before His death, note Section 144, footnote i.

A blind man is healed. For the second time, the Savior uses strange methods in performing another miracle of divine healing.*

*See main heading of Section 98, for a former healing in which the Lord Jesus employed odd but similar methods in curing a deaf man. See also Section 121, John 9:6, footnote e for another example of the curious methods employed by the Savior in healing another blind man.

Matt.	Mk. 8:22-26—Bethsaida	Lk.	John
	Men looked like walking trees		
	22 And he cometh to Bethsaida;[a] and they bring a blind man unto him, and besought him to touch him. **23** And he took the blind man by the hand,[b] and led him out of the town; and when he had spit on his eyes,[c] and put his hands upon him, he asked him if he saw ought. **24** And he looked up, and said, "I see men as trees, walking."[d] **25** After that he put *his* hands again upon his eyes, and made him look up:[e] and he was restored, and saw every man clearly. **26** And he sent him away to his house, saying, "Neither go into the town, nor tell *it* to any in the town."[f] (Verse 27 cont. in Section 103.)		

Footnotes-Commentary

(a) **"Bethsaida."** Refer to Section 63, footnote a, and Section 93, footnote c, for comments on this city. It was later named Julias after the daughter of Emperor Augustus, and was located on the northeastern side of Lake Galilee, not far from where Jesus had just fed more than five thousand. For more on Bethsaida, see the second paragraph of footnote f below. Christ had visited here previously, hence the excitement of the crowds upon hearing of His return.

(b) **Jesus took his hand and led him out.** The Lord Jesus had already pronounced a terrible curse upon this city and refused to do another miracle here. See the second paragraph of footnote f below, for more on this thought. What a touching statement and sight. This custom is still practiced today in many eastern lands by men. One also sees this frequently in South Africa among black males. It shows absolute trust between the two parties. It does not carry the evil connotation so well known in the West. The Son of God from heaven takes the hand of the blind man and leads him out of the city. Not in all his life had this poor fellow ever been led like this! Job of old once said that he had been "eyes to the blind" (Job 29:15). Now, Messiah will give blinded eyes the power with which to see. The words in Isa. 61:1-2 were used by the rabbis to point to Messiah. In the early days of His ministry, the Lord Jesus read these passages in His hometown synagogue on a Sabbath and claimed that He would fulfill them. Among the miracles predicted by Isaiah, was that Messiah would cause the, "recovering of sight to the blind." Refer to Section 38, Lk. 4:16-30, for this dramatic event and the uproar that followed. As far as the biblical record is concerned, this was the first physical attempt on His life from the angry Jews.

(c) **"Spit on his eyes."** Note Section 98, second paragraph under footnote c for the attitudes of many ancients toward human spittle used in healing practices.

(d) **"He looked up."** Meaning that he opened his eyes and lifted his head upward to see if he could really see. This is not the same look as in footnote e below.

2p-**"Men as trees walking."** A mountain of opinions has been raised regarding this man's curious answer given in response to Jesus' question. His eyeballs were covered with spittle from the mouth of Christ. Apparently, the miracle of healing did not remove the spittle. Though the actual eyes themselves were healed, the man could only see through as thick film. His response is greatly revealing. He had previously been able to see for he knew what trees and fellow men looked like. He even knew how men walked. Second, his odd statement, "I see men as trees, walking" will be understood by anyone who has ever spent time in the Middle East, especially their remote villages.

3p-The author of this harmony commentary has seen the exact thing as mentioned here by the former blind man. Arabs and pack animals walking the roads or through their villages often carry giant piles of straw, wood, and small limbs covering their heads, shoulders, sides, and back parts. While traveling a few miles north of Jerusalem in 1966, I saw a man so loaded with straw it appeared that the entire stack was actually walking! My Arab Christian friend said to me "Look, see men walking as trees!" Also traveling the same dusty road, there was a donkey covered with hay. The shuffling hoofs of the beast were not visible: a haystack appeared to be bouncing along the ground! Probably, this is what the newly seeing man beheld as he peered through the film over his eyes. See *Strange Scriptures that Perplex the Western Mind*, by Barbara M. Bowen, page 68, for more on this intriguing subject. Most of the super spiritualizing applied to this event usually makes things just about as blurred as they were to the poor fellow looking through the spittle in his eyes. In cases like these, we best let the traditions and culture of these ancient people speak for us instead of human imagination.

(e) **"Made him look up."** Upon hearing the blind man's response, Christ touched his eyes a second time and guided his head in an upward direction. Suddenly, he clearly saw the blue skies above, the excited crowds standing about, and above all, the wonderful Man standing before him. There is nothing here about a "gradual healing process" as often heard. It was just the way Jesus did things in this particular case. Some seventy-four years ago, the author heard an old white headed, Tennessee, Methodist preacher make a terse comment on this text. Pastor Cotton declared, "No man will ever see things clearly until he first looks up to Jesus!" Even though the Savior led him "out of town," the curious crowds followed, always anxious to see another miracle.

(f) **"Sent him to his house."** How beautiful that he was sent home apparently to one of the neighboring villages where he lived. *First,* his own household must hear of his healing and the Man Jesus of Nazareth, Israel's Messiah. See Section 88, Mk. 5:19, footnote k, where the Master sent Legion home to testify of his deliverance from the bondage of Satan. See also Section 89, Lk. 8:56, footnote u; Section 98, Mk. 7:36, footnote e; and Section 103, Matt. 16:20, footnote j for other occasions where Christ forbade most of those He healed to testify of His miracles. This was an attempt to calm the mass hysteria that had swept over the country regarding His ministry. However, the hatred and opposition of the religious leaders of Israel only increased.

2p-"Stay out of Bethsaida." *What a dreadful restriction!* The Savior forbids the man to return into the city of Bethsaida out of which He had just led him. For more on Bethsaida, see footnote a above. In Section 63, Matt. 11:20-22, footnote a, we noted that the Master had spoken a curse upon two cites, Chorazin and Bethsaida. Both had refused to repent of their sins and believe in Him. This is apparently the reason for the Lord Jesus forbidding the former blind man to re-enter Bethsaida, the great city that had slighted His miracles and message. If His wonderful works, miracles, and preaching seen and heard in these two cities had been heard and seen in the pagan cities of Tyre and Sidon, they would have repented long ago. Sadly, it was not so with Bethsaida. She had sealed her doom from the cruel hands of the Romans, as they swept through Galilee, in their southward march to Jerusalem. The awful truth is that the most infamous heathen cities would have received the Messiah quicker than the famed religious cities of the Jews. Jerusalem stands as the supreme example of this. By continually blaspheming and contradicting their Messiah, in time, they made themselves unworthy of the message of forgiveness and eternal life.

3p-The stiffnecked Jews. This was not the first time that Israel as a nation had gone too far in rebellion against God. Shortly before the invasion of Judaea and the final destruction of Jerusalem and its temple at the hands of Nebuchadnezzar in 586 B.C., something unspeakable happened. Their wickedness had gone so far that God commanded no further prayers should be offered for the nation of Israel. They had crossed the deadline and exhausted divine patience. See Jer. 7:16 and 11:14 for one of the chilling statements of awful finality when wicked men had pushed God's patience too far. In Section 100, first and second paragraphs of footnote d, there is a description of the decadence into which the nation of Israel had fallen. Near the end of His ministry, the Lord Jesus pronounced awful judgments upon the men of Israel, who were responsible for the spiritual welfare of their fellows. This terrible anathema is found in Section 159.

4p-Stubbornness and plowing into hell. The above statement regarding Israel's rebellion against God's warnings may be graphically illustrated by the following story. The author of this work grew up in the farming area of middle Tennessee. An old man in the community had notoriety for cursing, beating his wife, and terrifying his children, and neighbors. Even his dog was afraid of him! Late, one afternoon while plowing, a fierce lightening storm fell over the entire area. Fearful for his life, the old man's wife ran to the edge of the field and plead with him to "take the animals and go to the barn for shelter." Flying into a rage he shouted, "Go away woman, I going to make one more round or drive this thing into hell!" Turning the team of mules back into the furrow, he set out to make one more round. Reaching the end of the furrow, a bolt of lightening hit him, his metal plow, and team of two mules. They were blown into thousands of pieces. *This old fool did plow into hell!* The Bible warns, "He, that being often reproved hardeneth *his* neck, shall suddenly be destroyed, and that without remedy" (Prov. 29:1). Further, we read that stubborn people have a heart that is not right with God (1 Sam. 12"8). Worse, Scripture declares that rebellion is as witchcraft, and stubbornness are compared to idolatry (1 Sam. 15:23). Most stubborn people are fools at heart. Pig headed "Christians" who demand their way in every church business meeting, and enjoy expressing themselves with a boisterous authoritative voice, are a curse to God's work, and the testimony of Jesus Christ. One can imagine how these people act at home! Walking softly in genuine humility is the way of real Christianity. *When sternness and sharp rebuke are necessary, the child of God can perform this duty with the same spirit of humility.* The Savior was the meekest man every to appear amid human society. Not once did He hesitate in uncertainty when dealing with things and people. Jesus was never unsure. He never questioned whether He was too severe or too soft. He came to each new duty untainted by accusing memories. He was perfect in all things. It is from Him that we learn the art of true humility, real love, respect, and dignity. Stubbornness is the first step into a life of hurt, sorrow, and regret. For millions, it is their last step into hell.

Peter makes the great confession. Jesus of Nazareth is the promised Messiah of Israel, the Son of the living God.

Region of Caesarea Philippi

Matt. 16:13-17	Mk. 8:27-29	Lk. 9:18-20	John
		The greatest question 18 And it came to pass, as he was alone praying, his disciples were with him:	
The greatest question 13 When Jesus came into the coasts [borders] of Caesarea Philippi,(a) he asked his disciples, saying, "Whom do men say that I the Son of man am?"(b) 14 And they said, "Some *say that thou art* John the Baptist: some, Elias; [Elijah] and others, Jeremias, [Jeremiah] or one◄ of the prophets."(c)	*The greatest question* 27 And Jesus went out, and his disciples, into the towns of Caesarea Philippi:(a) and by the way he asked his disciples, saying unto them, "Whom do men say that I am?"(b) 28 And they answered, "John the Baptist: but some s ay, Elias; [Elijah] and others, ►One of the prophets."(c) ▲ *The above verse 28 is an example of a grammatical correction needed in the present day KVJ text. "One" should be with lowercase "o" as seen in Matthew and Luke, not upper-case. This has nothing to do with the inspiration of Scripture, but rather a single letter oversight by proofreaders or typesetters. The lowercase is in the first printed, original edition of the 1611 Bible at verse 28 above.*	and he asked them, saying, "Whom say the people that I am?"(b) 19 They answering said, "John the Baptist; but some *say*, Elias; [Elijah] and others *say*, that ►one of the old prophets(c) is risen again."	
15 He saith unto them, "But whom say ye that I am?"(d) *The greatest answer* 16 And Simon Peter(e) answered and said,(f) "Thou art the Christ, [Messiah] the Son of the living God." *Peter's unique blessing* 17 And Jesus answered and said unto him, "Blessed art thou, Simon Barjona: for flesh and blood hath not revealed *it* unto thee, but my Father which is in	29 And he saith unto them, "But whom say ye that I am?"(d) *The greatest answer* And Peter(e) answereth and saith(f) unto him, "Thou art the Christ." [Messiah]	20 He said unto them, "But whom say ye that I am?"(d) *The greatest answer* Peter(e) answering said, (f) "The Christ [Messiah] of God."	

Matt. 16:17–20	Mk. 8:30	Lk. 9:21	John
heaven.			
The greatest foundation			
18 "And I say also unto thee, That thou art Peter, and upon this rock[(g)] I will build my church; and the gates of hell shall not prevail against it.			
The greatest privilege			
19 "And I will give unto thee the keys[(h)] of the kingdom of heaven: and whatsoever thou shalt bind[(i)] on earth shall be bound in heaven: and whatsoever thou shalt loose on earth shall be loosed in heaven."			
The great temporary secret	***The great temporary secret***	***The great temporary secret***	
20 Then charged he his disciples that they should tell no man that he was Jesus the Christ.[(j)] (Messiah) (Verse 21 cont. in Section 104.)	**30** And he charged them that they should tell no man of him.[(j)] (Verse 31 cont. in Section 104.)	**21** And he straitly charged them, and commanded *them* to tell no man that thing;[(j)] (Verse 22 cont. in Section 104.)	

Footnotes-Commentary

[(a)] This means they had departed from the city of Bethsaida and Galilee and moved into Caesarea Philippi, which was in a northerly direction. To get there, it would require walking some five hours over twenty miles of rough, hilly, terrain. Now, they were in the jurisdiction of Philip, half-brother of Herod Antipas. Philip was the ruler of Iturea and Trachonitis. Two cities bore the name of Caesarea; one being located on the coasts of the Mediterranean Sea (Acts 8:40) and the other is mentioned here. Greeks colonized this entire area after the conquest of Alexander the Great some three hundred years before Christ. They changed the name of this specific site to Paneas or Panias in honor of a cave at the base of one of the mountains. Pagan mythology taught that a grotto was there in which was born and lived the (demonic) god, Pan. The original city built here was later greatly enlarged and enhanced by Philip the tetrarch. For information on Philip, refer to Section 21, Part 1, number 4 under footnote b. He was the son of King Herod, the baby killer, mentioned in Section 8, footnote a. Philip renamed the city in honor of Emperor Tiberius who ruled from A.D. 14 to 37. Later, it was called Caesarea Philippi or Caesarea of Philippi.

2p-Praised for its beauty, the city was situated in the boundaries of Naphtali at the foot of the snow-capped peaks of Mount Hermon mentioned in Ps. 42:6. These peaks stand some nine thousand feet above sea level. The melting snows, glaciers, and a lively river flowing from their base provide the major source of water for the Jordan River. It is noted for heavy dews in the summer months, hence we can understand the words recorded in Ps. 133:3. The snow dressed caps of Hermon can be seen from the Dead Sea about one hundred and twenty-five miles to the south! Presently, the thriving tourist city of Banias (a form of Panias) is situated at Hermon's sprawling base. Continuing their journey, Mark pens that as Christ traveled through the towns of the area, He put a serious question to the twelve along the way (Mk. 8:27). Arriving at the site, the Lord Jesus enters into a season of lone prayer (Lk. 9:18). Matthew takes up the narrative by explaining that when they arrived in the "coasts" (or district) of Caesarea Philippi the Lord pursued a full discussion of His previous question.

[(b)] **"Who do men say that I the Son of man am?"** No greater inquiry could ever be put to mortal man. The Savior did not ask because He was ignorant of the answer. This was intended to draw from the twelve an absolute declaration regarding who He was. Our answer and response to this will determine our destiny in heaven or hell.

2p-"Son of man" was the favorite title used by the Lord Jesus for Himself. It is recorded some eighty-two times in the four gospels. Every time, except two, this title is found on the lips of Christ. The two exceptions are Lk. 24:7, and John 12:34. It was an Old Testament designation used of men in general, but singularly a prophetic title for Messiah (Dan. 7:13). The term is used some ninety-two times of Ezekiel, thus reflecting his human experiences

461

and sorrows as a prophet of God among the captive Jews in Babylon and those remaining at Jerusalem. It is also found in various Jewish writings such as, the Book of Enoch, 2 Esdras, and the Sibylline Oracles. When applied to our Lord, it is an exclusive and *combined* designation for both His deity and humanity. It denotes His unique deity. As "the Son of man," He has the authority to forgive sins (Matt. 9:6), to interpret the Sabbath law (Matt. 12:8), to execute judgment (John 5:27), to give His life a ransom for many (Matt. 20:28), and to send His angels to gather out the tares (Matt. 13:41). Then He will sit on His throne in judgment (Matt. 25:31). His deity is silent in such places as Matt. 8:20, where He had no place to lay His head; in Matt. 11:19, where He ate and drank; and in Lk. 9:44, where He was delivered into the hands of men. Thus, the title signals both the deity and humanity of our Savior. Sigmund Mowinckel, in his work *He that cometh. The Messiah Concept in the Old Testament & Later Judaism,* pages 370-379 gives a historical coverage of this subject (the Son of Man). This work is flawed by his failure to believe in the total inspiration of the four gospels and his critical late dating of the book of Daniel.

3p-Pagan gods and their sons. Because this title ("son of god") was used continually among heathen priests, infidel theologians have assumed that Christ borrowed it from them in an effort to deify Himself. Concerning the history-long pagan imitations of Christ, note Section 12, footnote b. In 1676, Theophilus Gale produced one of the most exhaustive and definitive works ever compiled on this subject. It is entitled *The Court of the Gentiles* and is a comprehensive coverage of this historical truth. Infidel critics have scorned this old classic for centuries because it reveals the origin of their unbelief and hatred for an inspired and trustworthy Bible. For earlier comments on Gale's work, see Section 1, Part 1, fourth paragraph of footnote b. Jesus of Nazareth used "Son of man" to stress His common humanity with all mankind; showing that He took upon Himself the form of a servant (Phil 2:7). In this unique sense, He was the "Son of man" who was linked physically and humanly with the feelings and sorrows of all Adam's posterity. For Jesus, *the human* Son of man carrying our sickness and sins, see Section 41, footnote h. For other comments on the title the "Son of man," see Section 161, footnote l.

4p-Augustus Neander, in his work *The Life of Christ,* written in 1853, penned these pertinent words on page 100 about our Lord's usage of the titles "Son of God" and "Son of man." He said, "These two titles . . . therefore bear evidently a reciprocal relation to each other. And we conclude that as Christ used the one to designate his human personality; so he employed the other to point out his divinity."

(c) At this point in the ministry of Christ, His fame had created an avalanche of stories, myths, fables, gossip, and rumors of every imaginable sort. His name was on the lips of kings flourishing in their palaces, prisoners languishing in their dungeons, and soldiers in their barracks. Among the public, guesses regarding who Jesus was, were John the Baptist, who was now supposed to be raised from the dead, Elias [Elijah] , Jeremias (Jeremiah), or one of the famed prophets of Israel. Ancient Jews held the prophets in high veneration, and for the public to consider Christ being one of them, suggests that many still held Him in great esteem and honor. The rumor that Christ was John the Baptist raised from the dead seemingly originated in Herod's court. Was it another echo from his guilty conscience?

(d) **"Whom say ye that I am?"** It is more important what we think about Christ than what the world thinks about Him. One can quote the creeds of Christendom, give, faithfully attend church, and read the Bible without knowing Him as personal Lord and Savior. If Jesus was only a good man and not divine than all His promises, love, and support ends at the grave. However, the cross and empty tomb declare that He is God our only hope! At this place, the Savior deliberately laid this serious question upon the twelve. In verse 13, it was what "men" thought of Him. He inquires what do "you" think? It was critical that they understood who He was; even the promised Messiah of Israel and Savior of men. Yet, His actions and words were so contrary to what they had been taught about Messiah. His death on the cross was, at this point, the catalyst that divided them from Him. They had no idea their Messiah would die on a Roman cross for the sins of the world. See Section 26, footnote i; Section 27, footnote n; and Section 29, footnote j for details on this subject. Even at this late hour, the apostles did not yet understand about His atonement on the cross. This would come later. Read of this in Sections 104, 105, 107, and 141.

2p-Jewish beliefs about Israel's coming Messiah at this period were fragmented, violent, nationalistic, ignorant, destructive, and vengeful. Their warlike Messiah would destroy all who opposed Him and then rule the world. Old non-biblical literature, written mostly during the inter testament period, contains many lines about the awful doom and victory Messiah would bring. The ancient writings called the Sibylline *Oracles,* chapter 3:363-372 paints a gruesome picture of this time. "The kings of the nations shall throw themselves against this land [Israel] and bring retribution on themselves." In the non-canonical book of 4 Ezra 13:33-35, we read the following of the nations that gather to fight the Messiah, "It shall be that when all nations hear his [Messiah's] voice. Everyone shall leave his own land and be gathered together, desiring to fight against him." This final conflict of the Gentile nations of earth against the Jewish King would conclude according to these words in Enoch 52:9, "And all things shall be destroyed from the surface of the earth." Further, we note that 4 Ezra 9:3 mentions the "earth quakes in [various] places, tumult of peoples, scheming of nations, confusion of leaders, disquietude of princes." *(All these things were to happen at the first coming of Messiah.)* It is true that this universal gore and bloodshed would end in the perfect reign and eternal peace of Messiah. He would build a New Jerusalem (some sources say refurbish it) and a new temple; the dispersed of Israel, He would gather back home again to the holy city. All nations would then acknowledge Messiah and come to the temple to worship him, according to the *Sibylline Oracles* 3: 690. However, before this, He would be the most thorough and total conqueror in all human history. For an excellent review of the wild rabbinical opinions of their coming Messiah, see John Lightfoot's *Commentary on the New Testament . . .* , vol. 2, pages 232-234.

3p-In view of these grandiose rabbinical dreams about the Hebrew Messiah, it is no wonder that the little band of apostles *could not* reconcile (at this time) the meek and lowly Jesus of Nazareth with this kind of Jewish superman! Refer to the main heading of Sections 104, footnote a, and Section 141, for their fearful reaction to Jesus' mention of dying and rising from the dead. The rabbis had never taught such things about their coming Messiah. The apostles were simply dumbfounded every time Jesus mentioned dying on the cross.

(e) "And Peter answered." The voice often heard *first* from within the apostolic band was that of Simon Peter. This time, however, he speaks inspired words of great spiritual discernment. "Christ" and "Son of the living God" were direct terms used to signify the Messiah of Israel. *No Jew on the face of the earth could have said it better!* Peter's acclamation embraced the sum total of what Messiah was. In addition, the impetuous fisherman speaks them! The apostles had previously confessed Him as such, along with others as seen in John 1:41, 4:25-29, and Matt. 14:33. As it was on previous occasions, they confessed Him as Messiah, but it was based upon their prior knowledge gained from the rabbis. It is noteworthy that Mark wrote, "Thou art the Christ" (or Messiah) in verse 29, while Luke put it down as "the Christ (Messiah) of God" in verse 20. On His Messiahship, see Section 5, footnote a; Section 14, footnote d; Section 24, footnote a; and Section 29, footnotes e, j, and k.

(f) "Christ the Messiah." What memorable words! This man was "Yeshua ha'Mashiach" or "Jesus the Messiah." Highlighted in gray, because contained in this confession are segments of numerous Old Testament predictions that pointed to Israel's Messiah, who was Jesus of Nazareth. He was predicted in such verses as Ps. 2:2, 7; Prov. 30:4; Isa. 9:6; Dan. 8:25; and 9:25-26. *Appendix Three* contains a list of many Old Testament verses that spoke of Israel's coming Messiah. It must be noted that Jesus did not charge Peter with a preposterous or hasty conclusion. Rather, He approved the apostle's words. (Several years earlier Nathanael had made a similar confession. See Section 26, John 1:49, footnote i.) Simon had the right title for Jesus*, but at this point,* the wrong concept of His work yet to be done on the cross. For more on, "the Son of the living God" and its meaning to Jews, see Section 181, footnotes g and h. Conjectures regarding Peter's confession and Jesus' response are as follows:

1. Peter is pronounced, "Blessed" because he knows Jesus is the Messiah. The same glorious coronation word crowns the hearts of all who come to know Christ as personal Lord and Savior, the promised Messiah of Israel.

2. "Simon Barjona" means most likely "son of a dove [peace] or graciousness." Here, Jesus reminds him of his parentage. Though it may have been ever so peaceful and gracious, yet no genealogical descent or noble family line could bring upon him the blessedness of God that his Lord had just announced. This had been received by his faith in the Messiah, man's only source of *eternal* peace and graciousness.

3. The boisterous fisherman had been in touch with God Almighty! Amid the national furor regarding this man Jesus Christ, and beyond all the variations of human opinion, Peter had the truth, and it came straight from his heavenly Father. "Flesh and blood" is a common term found profusely in Jewish writings. It is used to distinguish man from God. See examples in Talmud tractates, Shabbath 30a and Megilah 14a. Paul, the Jew, used it in Gal. 1:16 and Eph. 6:12.

4. Peter knew that the man Jesus of Nazareth was the Messiah, the "Son of the living God." He uses a pre-eminent Jewish description for their King. Even demons confessed this truth as noted in Section 41, footnote g. He had secured this intelligence by divine revelation from God in prayer and meditation. The objection often heard that ancient Jews did not believe God had a Son, collapses in view of Peter's confession. Caiaphas, the high priest of Israel, asked Christ during His first trial if He was "the Christ [Messiah] the Son of God," in Matt. 26:63. God everlastingly had a Son, and the ancients confessed it in Scripture. The humanity of Jesus was conceived and developed in the womb of the virgin Mary. For a review of the original and early Jewish opinions of Jesus Christ, see Section 14, footnote f.

5. He was that uniquely divine Person spoken of so often by the rabbis and written about in their literature and Scripture. Finally, Peter and the eleven had come to realize what the demons and Satan already knew, that this man was God in human flesh.

(g) "Thou art Peter." *They all knew his name was this!* The western mind struggles with these words. This was an ancient way of stressing a profound truth someone had just stated. The Greek for Peter is "Petros" a moveable stone. It is the same word translated "Cephas" in John 1:42, where Christ bestowed it upon him at their first meeting over three years ago. Thus, not the giving of the name but rather its meaning is the prime lesson. Vincent informs us that in classical Greek, "petros" meant a "piece of a stone," and lists several illustrations from the ancient literature of that age. The second usage of the word in verse 18, "upon this rock I will build my church," is the feminine form "petra." This had reference to "a massive rock" or "stone" that was immovable and *not* a piece broken off. See

Vincent's Word Studies of the New Testament, vol. 1, pages 90-91. As with every *major* text in Scripture, this one also has been subjected to various attacks and interpretations. Several are as follows:

1. **The Papal Church** teaches that Peter was the rock and that from him has succeeded an unbroken line of Popes to rule the church on earth. See Section 41, Matt. 8:14, third paragraph of footnote a for more on the myth of "Pope Peter." Romanism claims a transmitted infallibility, from one Pope to the next. Men who think they hold God in their custody and then distribute Him to whomsoever they will are either mentally deranged or demonized. God has never appointed a Vicar or mouthpiece for the Holy Spirit on earth. *True* believers have one rallying point: the closed canon of infallible Holy Scripture and the indwelling Spirit of God. Christians, who put unity before Bible truths, are soon contaminated by the schemes of the ecumenical movement. Mixed into this religious Trojan horse today are the Christ denying "Protestants," the Papists, and fragmented philosophies from various pagan religions of the world. Now, the Roman Catholic Church is selling "Original Pope Water" on the internet for about $20.00 per bottle. The ads say that it was "blessed by the Pontiff." This is another heathen superstition that permeates this system. Pagans and Wiccan witches also use "holy water" in their rituals. In ancient Egypt and Greece, the idolatrous priests employed salt ("holy") water to ward off evil and heal. (The use of "holy oil" in the Hebrew Levitical priesthood (Ex. 30:35), was stolen by the pagans from the Jews and used in their heathen practices.) As previously stated in this work, heathen religions gradually corrupted many Christian doctrines thousands of years *before* the Savior came. Later, with the bewildered church fathers and Constantine's compulsory state church, these doctrinal corruptions found their home. For information given previously in this work on the original schemes of the Devil in distorting what would become Christian doctrine, see Section 1, Part 4, third paragraph of footnote j. Nevertheless, thousands of true believers fled Constantine's first version of the apostate World Council of Churches, refusing to compromise the core truths of Scripture. God has had His people "since the world began" and always will (Lk. 1:70).

2. **Peter the rock**. It is taught by some that the rock-stone was Peter, but only in the sense of his soundness and stability as a believer in the truth of God. How one gathers these things from Scripture is a mystery. Our Lord did not say, "upon thee" but "upon this rock," clearly referring to something distinctly apart from the apostle. As a rule, Peter was an ineffective believer from the start, yet rare flashes of good sense, choice, and intimacy with God mitigated his bad temperament. Some nine years after his triumph at Pentecost, he was so hung up in the Mosaic law that he argued with God over what he would or would not eat (Acts 10:9-14). Then about ten years later during Paul's first missionary journey, Peter visited the Antioch Church and played a part in creating a faction among the believers. Again, it was over certain Jewish traditions and the oral law. Upon Paul's return to the home church at Antioch, he found that assembly of believers torn to pieces by the legal questions of the law. Who was a ringleader in the faction? Peter was the culprit! It came to a showdown where Paul "withstood him [Peter] to the face" for his part in the trouble (Gal. 2:8-14). Peter's preeminence was the honor of being the one to open first the gospel door on the day of Pentecost to the nation of Israel. Then a few years later, he went to the Gentiles at the house of Cornelius (Acts 10). A survey of the life of Peter gives enlightenment as to why he steps from the Bible with the profound words and warning of 2 Peter 3:18.

   The Pope's attire is the epitome of blasphemy! His crown-like mitre (headgear) bears the Latin words "Vicarius Filee Dei," the "Vicar of the Son of God." "Vicar" means, "substitute." It is the highest of insults for a mortal man to claim that he is the substitute for Christ on earth. Catholic apologists dodge this by writing that this claim is no more than a Christian minister claiming to speak for Christ! *The Catholic Church claims to be the only means of salvation, while soaked in the blood of the millions she has murdered!* The horrific slaughter of thousands in France on Saint Bartholomew's Day in 1572 infallably demonstrate this fact. God will avenge these crimes that were approved by the Pope. Recent pictures show the Pope kissing the Koran, a book that denies the deity of Christ and His death on the cross. This Islamic blasphemy is found in Shurah 4:157. Jesus is the only way to eternal life. Men who believe God has exclusively deposited salvation within the Papal Church are deceived. It is found in the storehouse of grace called "whosoever will." It is not the great treasure of any church, denomination, movement, society, group, club, person, or organization. *Those who teach that they alone have the total truth and that all others are wrong, by that very admission, are false claimants of God and Christ.* The Roman Catholic Church and many others make this boast. Even Peter was a married man and according to rules was disqualified from being the Pope. See this in Section 41, the third paragraph of footnote a.

3. **The twelve.** Some hold that Christ referred to all twelve of His apostles as being the rock on which He would build His future church. Several passages do speak of persons as being rocks on which others may build. This was said of the apostles and prophets in Eph. 2:20.

4. **Peter's confession of Christ.** The most sensible and contextual meaning is that Jesus Christ referred to Peter's profound confession in answering the question, "who" Jesus was. Because Peter's words were true, men have the guarantee of present salvation, the solid assurance of sins forgiven, and God's

infallible promise of heaven when this life is over. If Peter's words were false, then we are of all men most miserable. His confession at this time was not the utterance of a rude fisherman but of the God of heaven speaking through his mouth, the most irrefutable and profound truth of all times. Clearly, the rock was the confession of Peter; not Peter himself, as the Papal Church teaches. Years later, the apostle Paul wrote, "For other foundation can no man lay than that [which] is laid, which is Jesus Christ" (1 Cor. 3:11). Peter confessed that the stone or rock is the Son of God. It was not, nor ever has been Peter! (1 Peter 2:6-7). For a brief discussion of the Roman Catholic Church and its major heresies, see Section 95 and all of footnote r.

5. **Matt. 16:18.** Some believe that Jesus selected part of these words (with a few additions) from Isa. 28:16. Regardless, the rabbis pointed to this verse as a prediction of their coming Messiah. Its interpretation and application should strictly be applied only in the Messianic context.

6. **"My church."** Here is the first of the three usages of the word "church" in the four gospels. Refer to Section 110, Matthew 18:17 footnote e. The Greek word "ekklesia" means a "called out" assembly of people. It never speaks of a building. It was used among the Greeks hundreds of years before Christ in reference to a body of citizens called out for whatever reason. See Acts 19:39, where it was translated as such. In Acts 7:38, it is translated "church" but speaks only of the nation of Israel in the wilderness as an assembly of people. There is nothing here about God having a church in the Old Testament. It referred strictly to a group of Jews that He had "called out" of Egypt. In the present text, Jesus applied it to those who have trusted Him, who, within the nation of Israel, were a distinct and minority assembly of people. Later, in New Testament writings, the word had exclusive reference to all the redeemed who are called by God through the Spirit and gospel to a saving knowledge of Christ. At this point, in the ministry of Christ, the church did not exist as it would later in New Testament history, especially in Acts and in the letters of Paul. During the ministry of Christ, it was known mostly as the kingdom.

7. **"Gates of hell."** A Hebrew expression pointing to a dark spiritual world in eternity. This was a Jewish way of saying that no device of Satan will prevail over (Israel) God's people. The rabbis had created many odd superstitions about life after death. One was that there were three different gates to hell: one in the sea, one the wilderness, and the other at Jerusalem. They had invented a special after-life angel named "Dumah," who was powerful, illusive, and totally in command of the souls of the departed. See Talmud tractates, Eiruvin 19a and Sanhedrin 94a for more on these ridiculous Jewish myths. Perhaps the Lord Jesus was trying to undo some of these fables invented by the rabbis. What He said about the afterlife was absolute, final, and void of all rabbinical myths. Early in heathenism, the word "Hades" had reference to a pagan god also known as Pluto, who presided over the nether realm of the dead. He ruled this dreaded place with Persephone, his kidnapped wife. Briefly, entrance into this pagan mythological hell was through groves named after Persephone. A wild dog, who admitted all, guarded the large gates; but once in. he would not allow any to leave. There were several rivers to cross before arrival, after paying a ferryman a small fee. Pagan eschatology divided hell into different parts: one was a place of peace and rest called the Elysian Fields. This was the counterfeit of the rest side of Sheol-Hades.

8. **Satan's imitations. Hell is not the grave.** These thousands of pagan corruptions, given above, were satanic efforts to divert thinking men from the truth about the reality of hell. With the passing of time, Hades gradually evolved into several similar meanings. The Hebrew word used for "hades" was "sheol." Christ went into Sheol-Hades at His death on the cross Acts 2:27, 31. This shows that it was a real place. In the history of Lazarus and the rich man, the Savior reveals Sheol-Hades to be a place divided into two different compartments, separated by a great gulf. See Section 131, Lk. 16:19-31. His congregation understood Christ's explanation of the two men in Luke 16. In one side, the occupants with full memory of their past lives suffer the torments of the damned, while in the other, they knew the joys of the happy after-life for the redeemed. It was into this latter compartment that our Lord descended after the death of His body on the cross (Eph. 4:8-11). According to Arndt and Gingrich's *A Greek-English Lexicon of the New Testament*, page 16, hell is defined as "the underworld ... the place of the dead." A.A. Hodge wrote in his *Evangelical Theology*, pages 372-373, "Never on a single occasion in the Bible [does Sheol and Hades] mean the grave." Satanic cults, skeptic theologians, and religious infidels in general, fiercely oppose this truth and go to no limits to undo, alter, reinterpret, and change the meaning of this horrible place that waits in the after-life for all who die without the forgiven of their sins.

Both Jews and pagans used the words Sheol-Hades in reference to destruction and death wrought by sin and Satan. As stated above, it was also considered a place of felt sufferings located in eternity. Because the meaning of Sheol-Hades over the course of linguistic history was obscured by paganism, one discovers in this obscurity the trail of the serpent deceiving the souls of men. In the gutter language of men today, the two words most used, abused, made glib, and humorous are the words "hell" and "damn." National television and radio have so popularized and then bled these dreadful terms of their horror that they have become void of true original meaning among men. Everyone seems to be damning someone else. Hell is no longer that dreaded word of yesteryear rarely heard in daily circles. Now it is accepted secular vanity, vulgarized into another minced oath.

Regardless of the above facts, the arm of Omnipotence will prevail. Whatever interpretation people assume from these terms, Christ here declares, "The Church of God would be hell-proof." This cannot mean the grave, for millions of Christians have died over the centuries, and their bodies buried. If hell in this verse means the grave, then the gates of the grave overcame all the saints of yesteryear.

The eternality and permanence of hell mixed with lasting fire, unspeakable suffering, and darkness are soundly established in the following twenty-one New Testament subheadings. To hold that all of this has reference to an unconscious state of men after physical death is abysmal ignorance:

a. "Unquenchable"–Matt. 3:12.
b. "Hell fire"–Matt. 5:22, 18:9 with Mk. 9:47.
c. "Fire"–Matt. 7:19, 13:40.
d. "Weeping and gnashing of teeth"–Matt. 8:12, 22:13, 24:51, 25:30 with Lk. 13:28.
e. "Damnation of hell"–Matt. 23:33.
f. "Everlasting punishment"–Matt. 25:46.
g. "Eternal damnation"–Mk. 3:29.
h. "The fire is not quenched"–Mk. 9:44, 46, 48.
i. "Fire unquenchable"–Lk. 3:17.
j. "Torments"–Lk. 16:23.
k. "Tormented in this flame"–Lk. 16:24.
l. "Place of torment"–Lk. 16:28.
m. "Resurrection of damnation"–John 5:29.
n. "Everlasting destruction"–2 Thess. 1:9.
o. "Eternal judgment"–Heb. 6:2.
p. "Darkness . . . reserved for ever"–2 Peter 2:17.
q. "Everlasting chains"– Jude 6.
r. "Blackness of darkness for ever"–Jude 13.
s. "The smoke of their torment ascendeth up for ever and ever"–Rev. 14:11.
t. "Shall be tormented day and night for ever and ever"–Rev. 20:10.
a. "And death and hell were cast into the lake of fire"–Rev. 20:14.

With these twenty-one different descriptions of hell and the lake of fire in Scripture, the Devil still persuades men that they speak of the grave, and not a place of eternal suffering. If these terms point to the unconscious ashes of the unsaved, then linguistic sanity has died by the wayside. The teaching that this was more rabbinical story telling, and not to be understood as literally happening, is a wrong. Christ's source for this was not the Talmud (it did not exist at this time), but eternal reality.

Godless men instinctively labor to explain hell away, or dilute its awfulness with wordy force or colorful vocabulary. One cannot judge the truthfulness of Bible doctrine by the intuitive sense of right and wrong, for these have been fouled by sin. The holiness of God, ever offended by sin not atoned for, and dreadful retribution, fiercely insults the unenlightened mind of unsaved men. The fact of heaven and hell is beyond human logic. Some express opposition outwardly in bitter rage; others subdue their hateful passions of "God resentment" in smoldering silence. Cults such as the Seventh Day Adventist and Jehovah's Witnesses tell us that the word "hell" means the grave. In their heresy, no intermediate state after death exists. Scripture teaches there are five locations for departed souls or spirits. These are **(1) Tartarus**, a prison for fallen angels, (1 Peter 3:19, 2 Peter 2:4 and Jude 6-7). **(2) Paradise,** or the rest side of Abraham's bosom where the saved went until the resurrection of Jesus (Lk. 16:19-31 with Lk. 23:43 with Eph. 4:8-12). **(3) Hell**, which is the torment side of Abraham's bosom where all the unsaved go at death, waiting for final judgment, (Matt. 16:18 and Lk. 16:19-31). **(4) The abyss or bottomless pit.** This is the awful abode of demons and probably some evil angelic beings (Lk. 8:31. Rev. 9:1-3, 11:7, 17:8, and 20:1-10). **(5), The lake of fire or gehenna.** Here, is the eternal hell and perdition of unsaved men, fallen angels, Satan and demons, (Rev. 20:6, 11-15, 21:8, 22:15, Matt. 25:41, 46). The ancients looked upon death, a corpse, an open grave, burial conclave, or cave tomb, as doorways that led into eternity. For the soul leaving the body at physical death, see Section 104, second paragraph of footnote g.

9. **"I will build my church."** Verse 18. As stated above, here is the first mention of "church" in the New Testament. Mostly, our Lord referred to His work or those who had trusted Him as the kingdom, often written in this harmony commentary as the new kingdom of Christ. For explanation of the church, see number 6 above. With the advancement of the gospel, the word "kingdom" gradually faded out, and "church" became the predominant term for God's people. In employing the word "church" in this passage, the Lord Jesus spoke exclusively of all those who are born again and thus saved by His atoning

death and resurrection. This is not the physical, local assembly, but those who are saved within all local assemblies, or wherever they may be, across the face of planet earth.

(h) Peter and the keys. Keys lock or unlock. They have no other purpose. Here, they point to those who have the God-given authority to admit others into Christ's kingdom or to refuse admittance. And who are these? *Every saved Christian, by use of the gospel of salvation, exercises this unique authority.* Entrance stands upon salvation from sin, which comes by believing Peter's grand confession that Jesus of Nazareth is "the Christ the Son of the living God." With awful solemnity, the Savior directed His Words at Peter and the other apostles. For more on sins being remitted, see Section 201, footnote t.

2p-In the interpretation of this verse, we meet another Roman Catholic distortion of Bible truths. This was not a "Peter only" command. Christ intended it for all the apostles. This is profoundly clear, for a short while later, *all* the apostles were endowed with this same authority (Section 110, Matt. 18:18). It is historically true that Peter took the gospel keys and *first* opened the door of faith for the Jews at Pentecost (Acts 2:14), then some nine years later to the Gentiles in the house of Cornelius (Acts 10). Peter confirmed that he did this when he later spoke to the church council. His Words were "A good while ago God made choice among us, that the Gentiles by my mouth should hear the word of the gospel, and believe" (Acts 15:7). Surely, he referred here to words Christ had spoken to him as recorded in Matt. 16:17-19. It is further true that all the eleven apostles took the gospel keys of the new kingdom of Christ (the church) and opened countless doors to myriads of souls over the ensuing years of early church history. The author of this harmony commentary, and his wife spent over half of their lives opening doors of everlasting life to thousands on the foreign mission field. Many stepped through, and many did not! Every born again believer has a set of the gospel keys. Reader, are you using yours? For several details on the use and meaning of keys by the ancient Jews, see Section 70, Lk. 11:52, number 10 under footnote h.

(i) "Binding and loosing" were common terms understood by the Jewish people. Hebrew writings are replete with this expression. For examples of the Jewish usage of these words, see the Talmud tractates, Berachoth 14b, 20b, 58b; and Shabbath 104a. The rabbis and doctors of law were continually "binding and loosing" such things as doors, looking glasses, letters, women, animals, trips to the toilet, leaven, and dozens of items. From the oral law Jewish scribes believed, they had special judicial and legislative powers to bind or set free whatever they choose.

2p-Some Hebrews postulated the myth that there was a *heavenly* Sanhedrin Court, which would bind what the *earthly* Sanhedrin Court had bound on earth, and loose whatever they had freed. A. T. Robertson in *Word Pictures in the New Testament*, vol. 1, page 134, wrote that the two Jewish theological schools in the days of Christ (Hillel and Shammai) busied themselves with "loosing" and "binding" what the other school had bound or loosed. For more on these schools and their opinions of marriage and divorce, see Section 137, footnote c.

3p-In *Wars of the Jews*, Book 1:5, lines 107-119, Josephus informs us that the Pharisees, under Queen Alexandra (75–67 B.C.) became administrators of all public affairs [of the Jews] so as to be empowered to banish and readmit whom she would, as well as to loose and bind. Furthermore, that "the different Jewish schools had the power to bind and loose, to forbid and to permit" as they saw fit. This (imaginary) authority was passed onto succeeding rabbinical groups of each age. They even received some kind of official sanction from a court of justice! The common everyday Jews were terrified at this rabbinical claim lest it be placed upon them. Christ denounced the Jews for "binding heavy burdens on men" which sprang from this pseudo authority. His sharp denunciation is found in Section 159, Matt. 23:2-4.

4p-On the other side of this dilemma are those who advertise their "specialized ministry of binding and loosing." They have lifted these passages out of their historical context and taken from them something never intended. The so-called "ministry of binding and loosing," much acclaimed on national television, was unheard of over the course of church history. It was only within the last century that this monster gradually appeared on the church stage and has claimed many victims. The psychotic and psychological wounds left behind by these religious charlatans should warn serious Christians to "Prove all things; hold fast that which is good" (1 Thess. 5:21).

5p-The above statement does not deny that in some cases, believers may face the reality of demonic presence or activity and must deal with them according to Holy Scripture. Those who affirm that such things were only an apostolic experience have not advanced in the Word and work of God. Necessary times of demonic confrontation are altogether different from the phony professional exorcists so prevalent today, especially on national television.

6p-The correct meaning of binding and losing. Messiah takes this rabbinical tradition and gives it correct meaning. Later, the keys of the saving gospel were issued to them on the day of Pentecost. Afterward, they and their successors were sent forth across the world of that era. All who believed their message were declared, "loosed" from the bondage of sin by the authority of God in heaven. Those who *finally* rejected were eternally "bound" by their sin and doomed for endless perdition. Jesus told the eleven the same thing on the evening of His resurrection in Section 201, John 20:23. The Papal Church with its popes, bishops, and priests, calming the power to absolve sin is a perversion of what Jesus Christ taught in these passages. See footnote h above.

7p-Church fathers' heresy. In early church history, religious heretics before, during, and after Tertullian (died A.D. 220), claimed for themselves the exclusive power to forgive or remit sins. Tertullian stated that baptism brought "the remission of sins, deliverance from death, regeneration, and the bestowal of the Holy Spirit." See more on the ex-lawyer from North Africa and his teachings in *The Christian Tradition: A History of the Development of Doctrine*, vol. 1, pages 162-165, by Jaroslav Pelikan. Professor Pelikan, a Lutheran writer, also mentions the baptismal beliefs of the church fathers in *History of the Christian Church*, vol. 2, page 253, and vol. 3, page 481 passim. It is an unarguable fact that *every* church father held to salvation and the forgiveness of sins through the Lord's Supper and baptism, mostly by sprinkling. *Though some of them wrote excellent books defending the doctrines of the Christian faith, they missed the mark on "how one is saved."* They had drifted miles from the original apostolic doctrine (Acts 2:42). The famed Cyril of Jerusalem (died A.D. 386) stated that in baptism, "We are reshaped into the divine image of Christ." See Pelikan's second work, listed above, vol. 1, page 237. Adding to this untruth, Cyril also said that we should worship Mary as the mother of God! The fathers would defend the deity of Christ, His death and resurrection, and then declare that communion and baptism saves men from sin and hell! It was a miracle that God's written truth was preserved and handed down over the centuries in view of the sweeping apostasy, heresies, unbelief, perversions, and religious sword of the state that appeared in this era. Thousands of Christians rejected the doctrinal perversions of the church fathers and their numerous split off factions. For other details regarding their apostasy, see Section 12, sixth and seventh paragraphs of footnote k. Thousands of history books, both secular and religious, that carry the story of the fathers. Oddly, many authors, historians, and writers exonerate these men of their doctrinal perversions regarding *how* one receives the gift of eternal life in Christ.

8p-Paul's seven ones. In his letter to a church, he had previously started, the apostle Paul wrote in Eph. 4:4-6 about a series of seven ones. They are as follows:

1. **"One body."** This is Christ's Church or spiritual kingdom. Though thousands of divided pagan religions existed, there was *only one* true community of born again believers known and owned by God. Entrance into this exclusive body was open to all by repentance and faith in the finished work of Christ.
2. **"One Spirit."** This is the Holy Spirit. Demon entities abounded then as now and are but deceivers and liars to all who lend them an ear. Only one Spirit is eternal and divine: the Holy Spirit of the Trinity. It is He Who quickens, and actuates believers. He convicts of sin, enlightens, and regenerates lost men and then dwells forever in the soul of every saved believer seeking to produce the fruits of righteousness.
3. **"One hope."** This is the sure anticipation of God fulfilling every promise to His children of the things laid up in heaven for them. The sorrows of human life will fade as heaven and home draw closer each passing day. Every hope of this world and those of false religions are as sparkling bubbles, soon to burst in bitter disappointment. Our hope in Christ is as sure as the throne of God!
4. **"One Lord."** Here, the reference is to the Lord Jesus Christ. He, by creation of the world, is Lord of all, and by redemption is the Savior of all who believe. He conquered sin, death, hell, and the grave and is "Lord of all." At an appointed time, all men will bow and confess this truth (Phil 2:9-11).
5. **"One faith."** This speaks of saving faith in Christ that brings forgiveness and eternal life. It is produced in the heart of unbelievers by "hearing the Word of God" (Rom. 10:17), and may be responded to or rejected. For the Reformed error of "baby faith," see Section 150, second paragraph of footnote f.
6. **"One baptism."** He did not say "one mode" of baptism, for water baptism is *not* the subject under consideration here. Many were the baptisms or washings under the Torah Law, but only one under grace that secured eternal life. This is the baptism of the Holy Spirit, the third Person of the divine Godhead, who mystically and wonderfully places each saved soul into the body or *true* church (1 Cor. 12:13; Gal. 3:27; Col. 2:12; and Rom. 6:3-7). This exclusive work of the Spirit guarantees that no unsaved person is among God's children. He immerses into Christ and His body, only those that have been born again. This is the "one baptism." The Holy Spirit *sprinkles or circumcises* no one into eternal life. For a continued discussion on these things, see Section 206, second and third paragraphs of footnote e.
7. **"One God."** Amid millions of idols, gods, and goddesses, the apostle lays down the great eternal truth. There is only one God: this is the voice of both nature and revelation combined. The silly and fictitious deities of the pagan nations were but channels of demonology and bondage to their worshippers. The Thessalonian Christians, upon conversion to Christ, "turned to God from idols to serve the living and true God" (1 Thess. 1:9). *All* idolatry is finally the worship of Satan through the medium of evil spirits (1 Cor. 10:19-21). Hence, it is cursed throughout all of Holy Scripture. It is worthy of note that all three Persons of the Holy Trinity are listed in Eph. 4:4-6.

(j) **"Tell no man."** Repeatedly, we read of Christ imposing this "no talk" command on His apostles and converts. His orders were not to divulge that He was the "Christ" or "Messiah" of Israel. This was an effort to quite the national uproar about His Messianic claims, which had spread over the land and infuriated the religious leaders. Even the demons knew this truth and openly confessed it, but He muzzled them as well. See the main heading of Section 40, footnote d, and the main heading of Section 41 for more on this thought. Though our Savior mostly forbade men to speak of His Messiahship, He, nevertheless, continually demonstrated it before all who watched and heard Him. He chose to show onlookers that He was Messiah above the testimonies of those delivered and healed, as well as the gossip and hearsay of excited men (John 5:41).

Jesus speaks of His soon death and resurrection. Peter fiercely objects and is rebuked. Cross bearing, suffering, and death are theirs in His service.*

See asterisk and all under the main heading of Section 107, for further details on His crucifixion.

Caesarea Philippi

Matt. 16:21-25	Mk. 8:31-35 (Mk. 9-1)	Lk. 9:22-24	John
The glorious awful truth that Jesus will die 21 From that time forth began Jesus to shew unto his disciples, how that he must go unto Jerusalem, and suffer many things of the elders and chief priests and scribes, and be killed, and be raised(a) again the third day. (For third day, see Appendix One.)	*The glorious awful truth that Jesus will die* 31 And he began to teach them, that the Son of man must suffer many things, and be rejected of the elders, and of the chief priests, and scribes, and be killed, and after three days rise(a) again.	*The glorious awful truth that Jesus will die* 22 Saying, "The Son of man must suffer many things, and be rejected of the elders and chief priests and scribes, and be slain, and be raised(a) the third day."	
Peter's sincere ignorance 22 Then Peter(b) took him, and began to rebuke him,(c) saying, "Be it far from thee, Lord: this shall not be unto thee."	*Peter's sincere ignorance* 32 And he spake that saying openly. And Peter(b) took him, and began to rebuke him.(c)	◄Peter not understanding the death, burial, and resurrection of Jesus flew into a rage of opposition at His Lord's hard statement. For the failure of all the apostles and disciples to understand this, refer to Section 195, Lk. 24:7, with comments by the ◄ symbol. In the next Section 105, at Lk. 9:31, we see Moses and Elijah discussing with Jesus His soon coming death on the cross. Read all of Section 107 for the fear that came on the apostles at the mention of this subject.	
From blessed to Satan 23 But he turned, and said unto Peter, "Get thee behind me, Satan:(d) thou art an offence unto me: for thou savourest [mindest] not the things that be of God, but those that be of men."	*From blessed to Satan* 33 But when he had turned about and looked on his disciples, he rebuked Peter, saying, "Get thee behind me, Satan:(d)◄ for thou savourest [mindest] not the things that be of God, but the things that be of men."	◄How strange that Peter spoke so great of Christ earlier in the previous Section, in Matt. 16:16. Now, a few moments later he speaks for the Devil in opposing the death of His Lord. See italicized comments above and footnote d below.	
Love Christ above all else: take up His cross 24 Then said Jesus unto his disciples, "If any *man* will come after me, let him deny himself, and take up his cross,(e) and follow me. 25 "For whosoever will	*Love Christ above all else: take up His cross* 34 And when he had called the people *unto him* with his disciples also, he said unto them, "Whosoever will come after me, let him deny himself, and take up his cross,(e) and follow me. 35 "For whosoever will	*Love Christ above all else: take up His cross* 23 And he said to *them* all, "If any *man* will come after me, let him deny himself, and take up his cross daily,(e) and follow me. 24 "For whosoever will	

Matt. 16:25–28	Mk. 8:35–38 – Mk. 9:1	Lk. 9:24–27	John
save his life shall lose it: and whosoever will lose his life for my sake shall find it.[f]	save his life shall lose it; but whosoever shall lose his life for my sake and the gospel's, the same shall save it.[f]	save his life shall lose it: but whosoever will lose his life for my sake, the same shall save it.[f]	
Man's greatest loss 26 "For what is a man profited, if he shall gain the whole world, and lose his own soul?[g]	*Man's greatest loss* 36 "For what shall it profit a man, if he shall gain the whole world, and lose his own soul?[g]	*Man's greatest loss* 25 "For what is a man advantaged, if he gain the whole world, and lose himself,[g] or be cast away?	
or what shall a man give in exchange for his soul?"	37 "Or what shall a man give in exchange for his soul?		
	Shame is one of Satan's most effective weapons. 38 "Whosoever therefore shall be ashamed[h] of me and of my words in this adulterous and sinful generation; of him also shall the Son of man be ashamed, when he cometh in the glory of his Father with the holy angels." (chap. 9, verse 1 below.)	*Shame is one of Satan's most effective weapons.* 26 "For whosoever shall be ashamed[h] of me and of my words, of him shall the Son of man be ashamed, when he shall come in his own glory, and *in his* Father's, and of the holy angels.	
27 "For the Son of man shall come in the glory of his Father with his angels; and then he shall reward every man according to his works.		◀ *See Information Box below for more on this placement.*	
	The correct placement Mk. 9:1		
A difficult text 28 "Verily I say unto you, There be some standing here, which shall not taste of death, till they see[i] the Son of man coming in his kingdom."[j] (Next chap., Matt. 17:1 cont. in Section 105.)	*A difficult text* 1 And he said unto them, "Verily I say unto you, That there be some of them that stand here, which shall not taste of death, till they have seen[i] the kingdom of God[i] come with power." (Next verse 2, cont. in Section 105.)	*A difficult text* 27 "But I tell you of a truth, there be some standing here, which shall not taste of death, till they see[i] the kingdom of God."[j] (Next verse 28 cont. in Section 105.)	

▶**The correct placement.** It is clear by reading Matthew and Luke's parallels that Mk. 9:1 is the end of Mark chapter 8 and numerically should be Mk. 8:39. *Total* chapter and verse division did not appear in the Scripture until the year A.D. 1560 with the Geneva Bible. William Whittingham produced the first New Testament with verse division in 1557. This had nothing to do with verbal and plenary inspiration of Scripture. God had *forever* inspired His Word hundreds of centuries before Whittingham was born. Divine inspiration did not run out, wear out, fade out, play out, or somehow partially vanish over the ensuing years. "For ever, O LORD, thy Word is settled in heaven" (Ps. 119:89). The Holy Scriptures are just as reliable now as when the original writers penned them. See the *Author's Introduction* along with Section 3, footnote a, and Section 59, footnote t for more details on this. Not understanding certain things in the Bible is our problem, not God's. He has provided what we need to wield in confidence, "the sword of the Spirit" (Eph. 6:17).

Footnotes-Commentary

(a) **"From this time forth."** Shaded in gray as this speaks of His soon death, burial, and resurrection. With these words, Matthew is explicit in telling his readers that Christ made a deliberate effort to explain to the apostles His upcoming death at Jerusalem. These grave communications were unwelcome by His preachers, especially the terrifying words that He would be "killed," or "slain." The Savior's usage of "elders, chief priests, and scribes" must have struck great fear into their hearts, for they signified the Sanhedrin Council or Supreme Court of the nation of Israel. The apostles had witnessed their Master tangling with them many times, and they knew that these religious men raged with anger and had attempted to kill Him on numerous occasions. Regarding their efforts to destroy the Messiah, see Section 52, footnote l, and Section 55, footnote a. For details on the apostles *not* understanding Christ's death and resurrection, refer to Sections 104, 105, 107, and 141.

(b) **Belligerent Peter.** At this time, the *twelve* had been with Christ over two years. (He preached for about one year before selecting the twelve out of the crowds.) One is amazed that the leading apostle, Simon Peter, did not yet understand about the cross and his Lord's atoning death for sin. Even His resurrection was not understood! Jesus had gone to great lengths to convince them that He was the Messiah. Peter's confession reflects that he understood Jesus in a literalistic Jewish sense. See Section 103, Matt. 16:16, footnotes d, e, and f. Our Lord had spoken previously of His death or attempted to portray it to the disciples. It had been presented in softer terms mostly couched in symbolism. For example, in His baptism by John, one sees that His future death and resurrection were prefigured as explained in Section 22, first and second paragraphs of footnote c. At the Cana wedding He said, "mine hour is not yet come," in Section 27, footnote f. Before Nicodemus, He spoke of the "brazen serpent" in Section 30, footnote j.

2p-Knowing they could not bear the entire story, Jesus had slowly worked up to this time. The eschatology of the rabbis gripped the apostles with steel fingers. Like all Orthodox Jews, they held that their Messiah would be a man of extraordinary power, crushing the Romans and ruling the world for Israel. It allowed no place for their glorious Messiah to be nailed on a Roman cross and die in such shame and infamy. *Now,* He bluntly speaks to them about going to Jerusalem and the leaders of their religion putting Him to death. *By physical count, it has been determined that over the course of His ministry, the Lord Jesus mentioned His death at least fifty-four times in various ways.* The length of His public ministry was about three and a half to four years. Despite all this, His disciples–apostles still did not understand His atoning death. They never dreamed that the cross was His destiny. On Pentecost, this truth was clearly understood. For salvation before the cross, see Section 144, footnote i.

(c) **"Rebuked him."** It was unheard of for a pupil to *correct* his teacher. Such would be considered a shameful deed. This was not the same thing as asking questions, which was the normal procedure amid teaching and preaching. Peter's fierce reactions reveal again that neither he, nor his apostolic companions comprehended the atoning death of Christ on the cross. He publicly contradicts the Savior with his brash personality. Yet, we need to understand that Peter was strongly attached to Jesus and dearly loved Him, greatly believing that He would soon establish Israel's literal kingdom on earth. This being so, there was no place for the King of the Jews to die on a pagan Roman cross. It is amusing that the fisherman from Galilee "rebuked" the Lord from heaven!

(d) **"Get behind me Satan."** Christ's response enlightens us concerning the forbidden world of Satan and occult powers. It seems that in this verse, Messiah spoke to both Peter and the Devil. This strange compound of good and evil, detected here in Simon, may be seen in all of us at times. A brief, but real collaboration between the two became a horrendous moment and must not be explained away by nice academic words. Mark. 8:33 records that Jesus now reversed the attack and He "rebuked" Peter. What a lesson to be learned from this event. The bravest and the most forward Christian, who does not walk with God, is liable to become a mouthpiece for the Kingdom of darkness. In a sense, it can be said that Peter was *momentarily* devilized. Any man, institution, or religion that opposes the death and resurrection of Christ for our sins, or adds to it, does a masterful work for Satan. All such are an "offence" or "stumbling block" to the cause of Christ. There can be no doubt, that at this point, the Devil had taken advantage of Peter's weakness, arrogance, and most notably his ignorance concerning the death of Jesus. Now, under satanic influences, Simon Peter attempts to dissuade the Lord Jesus from Calvary where the atonement for our sins will take place. The old adage, "Give the Devil an inch, and he will become your ruler" is not wanting in this story. He whose confession was called "the rock" moments ago is *now* called "Satan." Strange and mystic are the changes of human mood and message when one falls into the hands of the wicked one. In the rebuke spoken by the Lord Jesus "thou savourest [mindest] not the things that be of God," our Lord was saying, "Peter, you are not thinking about right things." Those who tell us there is no Devil, but only evil influences, speak untruth and do a service for Satan. They are neither thinking nor minding right things. Later, Simon had another bout with Satan the night before the morning of the cross (Lk. 22:31-34 with 1 Peter 5:8-9).

(e) **On a street in Madrid. False redemptive suffering and vain self-denial of the Catholic Church.** At no place do people reflect their sincere ignorance more than in their efforts at religious self-denial. One person will eat no meat on Friday. Another gives up drinking or a social habit for forty days during a ritual called Lent. Still others lock themselves away in a monastery or convent under the pretense of "serving the Lord." In certain foreign lands where the Papal Church rules through ignorance and poverty, many have their hands nailed to a cross; others are whipped and beaten publicly to show their denial of sin. During the Easter season in the Philippines, thousands of Roman Catholics do these things. Blind to biblical teaching, they demonstrate their utter bondage to the Papal system and Satan. In San Fernando City, the Philippines, flagellants dressed in dark robes beat hundreds of fellow Catholics unmercifully during religious rituals. Many have spikes driven into their hands, and others are literally nailed to crosses. This is to emulate Christ's death and secure forgiveness of their sins! This is called "redemptive suffering" and is a gross untruth. In 1966, I stood on a street in Madrid, Spain, during Easter, and watched with horror as thousands paraded by. Old women carrying giant crosses, others dragging heavy chains, some with bleeding feet, and large crucifixes over their shoulders. This was done to secure forgiveness. It is a monstrous lie, a counterfeit of divine truth, and a masterpiece of religious deceit. These poor people are trying to punish their way into heaven! They do not know that Christ died on the cross for *all* their sins; He did *all* the suffering for them, and they can be saved and instantly forgiven. These antics depict the hopelessness of millions of Roman Catholics. For more on this, see Section 95, and all thirteen subheadings under footnote r.

2p-"If any man will." Following Christ *not for salvation* but in Christian service, first involves an act of the individual's will. A man can "will" to follow Jesus or "will" not to follow. No Calvinism here! Biblical self-denial is the glad offering of any sacrifice that love and loyalty to our Savior requires: even to one's own life. It is a *daily disciplined* work of surrendering everything to Christ, and is continued over a lifetime. Whipping one's self across the back or chest, as practiced by the Papal Church, and mentioned above, is not biblical self-denial; rather, it is a demonic act designed to produce pain and deceive the actor. As previously stated, all the suffering for humankind's sins, Christ has borne in His atoning death. Those who inflict self-torture to pay for their trespasses and sins, toy with blasphemy. They are denying the *finished atonement* of Christ on the cross and attempting to add their sufferings to what He has completed. God will never accept such high insults to the death of His Son for our sins.

3p-"Take up his cross." Again, this speaks of service not salvation. In verse 23, Luke adds the word "daily." Matthew's record of what follows in verses 24-28, continues the previous instructions just given by Messiah. There is no break in the continuity of thought and lesson. After quelling the vociferous Peter, Jesus explained to the apostles and people (Mk. 8:34) that they too, have crosses! One hard announcement comes after the other. First, He is going to be put to death; and now, they must deny themselves and carry crosses if they will follow Him. *And each one has a cross to carry.* At this place in history, the cross was the most abominable emblem for pain and suffering known. When a man took up a cross, he was always nailed on it at the end of the road! No man spoke of cross bearing except the condemned who were to be nailed to its terrible wood. Sadly, the cross in this day of "evangelical Christianity" is not the cross of those infant churches. It is a worldly-wise philosophical ornament, one that entertains, excites, charms, hangs from the neck, waists, wrists, ankles, or over a baptistery. It is adorned by the shameless citizens of a vulgar unsaved society. It is displayed amid cursing, swearing, drunkenness, adultery, profanity, and verbal filth of the basest sort. Sin's human animals have their crosses too! However, it is not the cross of Holy Scripture. The true cross of Christ *in its message and impact* weighted men to their knees, rent their hearts, and drove them into the chambers of secret prayer. It has sent millions of saints into agony and weeping, as they wrestled with God for lost souls and wrecked lives. Gloriously, its stigma and death brought new life and hope for all who trusted the Christ of that tree. Its darkness gave great light, its pain delivered comfort, and its raging tumults rendered eternal peace! This is the kind cross that Jesus ordered His followers to "take up daily."

4p-"Follow me." Jesus had just informed the twelve of His death at the hands of the Sanhedrin and religious leaders. Now, He informs them that their call to service will not fare much better. Here, the Son of God established the rule for discipleship, which is "cross bearing" and "following Him." This law is not just for the twelve apostles or the people of that time, but also for believers of all ages. The King of the Kingdom laid down this universal truth, and it is binding upon His subjects. "Every one who follows me carries his or her cross." Here, the cross does not point to the external and physical death it brought: rather, it signifies all trials and sufferings that come to those who sincerely, endeavor to live for Christ. It reveals the sure consequences of following the Lamb wheresoever He leadeth. It is drinking of His cup and filling "up that which is behind of His afflictions" (Col. 1:24). These things are not to complete some unfinished part of His atonement but to glorify it. "We must through much tribulation enter the kingdom of God" (Acts 14:22). There is no "cheap grace." We are called to "die daily" as we follow our Lord. For a later mention of "cross carrying," see Christ's Words in Section 128, Lk. 14:27, footnote d. For a soundly documented investigation into the history of death by the cross, see *Crucifixion* by Martin Hengel. More may be learned about execution by ancient crucifixion from this little book than most sources. Sadly, Hengel is totally off on the reason for Christ's death. This error marks all *unsaved* scholarship that rejects an inspired and trustworthy Bible.

(f) Losing one's life in the service of God. What mysterious words for millions of Christians. The great ambition of many people outside the church and many within is to live like happy animals. "Give us pleasure, excitement, money, power, influence, and a tad of religion," they brazenly affirm. A "new church" was recently started near to where the author of this work lives. Their colorful advertisement read, "Life is made to be enjoyed. You should be having a good time." There was no word regarding eternity, the devises of sin, death, salvation, and the service of God. Most will not *voluntarily* endure hardships for the glory of God and the salvation of lost souls. However, they will run themselves sick in a cross-country marathon. Everything must be easy. All menial work done in the church building must be paid for. The prime duty of the "new church of today" is to make men feel good about themselves, enjoy life, offer the latest "self-help" program, "how to do it seminar" or "anger management" sessions, and be comfortable. Inside many church halls, men and women are knocking themselves out trying to slim up or trim down. Try calling these "shapely, slim for Him," and "trimmed out curvaceous saints" to a night or half night of prayer! One dare not mention sin or warn the people about things that damn souls, wreck lives, and destroy homes. Cross bearing, self-denial, and following Christ were relics of those who lived and died in the Roman catacombs, the shadow of Marxist-Leninist communism, or the bloody crescent and star of radical Antichrist Islam.

2p-Winds of change. Contemporary Christianity. Amid the chaos described above, we note "*radical* contemporary Christianity" with its casual everything. *(Not all contemporary churches are of the nature described below.)* We have seen their carnal appeal to undisciplined youth, rocking in the sanctuary amid the beat of jungle music. Some (always "in moderation") drink their table wine, alcohol, and puff at their cigarettes, betting on the horses at the Kentucky Derby or the Florida greyhounds, while "growing in grace." This does not necessarily make them bad, but it does make them disgraceful "witnesses for Christ." Now we are hearing from a popular *radical* counterparty outfit that "even Abraham had trouble with pornography! And all this is accomplished through a single "praise service" on Sunday morning. "The Old Rugged Cross" of yesteryear has been exchanged for the new cross of today. "Great spiritual leaders," with their latest, easy-to-understand modern translation of the Bible, and new hymnology bathed in the subliminal beat of Pavlov's dogs, have erected a new cross. It glorifies the flesh amid a Jesus revolution type "worship service." Grubby looking men, women, and youth, often three quarters-naked, leg kicking, head snapping, "light the fire." A veteran identity expert with the F.B.I. could not distinguish many of these antics from those of a Vietnam War protest, rock and roll convention, or a pot-smoking Willie Nelson sing-out at Woodstock, New York. *The subject never mentioned in any of these events is the thing called "sin."* One might very well lose his life amid these circus performances, but it would hardly be for the glory of God and the salvation of lost souls. If people want to express their joy by clapping and waving their hands, it is not necessarily wrong. (Those who object should attend the meetings of most Hebrew, African, and Asian Christians!) The musical program of many Baptist churches is more professional than powerful; both are needed. It is not necessary to wear a suit and tie, but *decent clean dress* has priority everywhere except in the shower! (Several men in our church in Australia had never had on a tie in their lives!) Winds of cultural change have blown over many believers. Bible convictions about sin, hell, heaven, and eternity are vanishing. Life is built on "things" and not Jesus Christ. Role models for many Christians are in the Christ hating world, Hollywood trash, sports stars, or rock and roll artists glorying in their shame (Phil. 3:18-19). Historically, contemporary worship came out of the Jesus Movement in the 1960s, and the "Charismatic Renewal Movement." Some of their basic theology reads good on paper but was often non practiced truth. For demonic manifestations in *some* of the more radical groups, see Section 175, third paragraph of footnote e.

3p-Baptist bloopers. On the other extreme side of this amoral-religious circus, we have the "militant, Bible believing, separated, missionary minded, fundamentalist Baptists." *Within this camp, there are some of the finest Christians on earth.* One also encounters ruthless dictators, playing church politics and crushing those who *slightly* disagree on the smallest theological point. Arrogantly smug, they do everything right. Among these "non compromising Baptists," one will find some of the biggest gossipers on the face of the earth. They glory in their sins forgiven but will not allow the same for certain others. For a devastating look into these things, see *Churches that Abuse,* by Professor Ronald M. Enroth. Baptists have "famous speakers" but no famous kneelers; experts in prophecy, but none in prayer; family retreats on "How to have a happy home," but nothing on what to do when it did not work like the "famed speaker" promised! The rasp of anointed Scripture cuts cleaner than the silk sandpaper of smooth sermonizing from a contemporary church bar stool or the "jealously guarded fundamentalist pulpit." If every Baptist of whatever stripe, who reads these lines had only one more day to live, how would he spend the last day? We can be sure that *radical* changes would instantly occur within their homes, at the workplace, and amid the church fellowship. Loving God and our fellow men, regardless, while hating and opposing sin at the same time requires a delicate balance. Jesus did this. He was the "friend of sinners" (Matt. 11:19), yet "separate from sinners" (Heb. 7:26). This is the standard. Whether it is the mean fundamentalist religious right, who think they keep God's work afloat, or the radical left who will sleep with the devil, both camps need cleaning up. *Fellow Christians, avoid extremes. If you cannot be the best, be the second best for Jesus and others.*

4p-Overlooked harvest fields. It is ever true that the tears of God's people are the diamonds that make heaven shine. The groans and sorrows of history's Christian Martyrs are transformed into beautiful music before the throne of God. Having reinterpreted or despised Bible truth and the way of practical righteousness, our chickens are now coming home to roost. American churches send missionaries everywhere, except to Hollywood, the halls of congress, the judicial systems, and the national media networks. These overlooked fields, long white unto harvest, have now become a progressive tidal wave of poison and immorality flooding this land. Across America, the present generation of children and grandchildren are paying an unspeakable price for our incorrigible failure. *Outside, A*ntichrist, God and Bible hating secular educational institutions, and higher court decisions that cannot be overturned, destine us for destruction. *Within,* our own failures hiss like a serpent while we are too polite to deal with sin, and the cancer of vain pleasures eats away the higher purposes of life, leaving future generations without hope. The great meaning and value of human existence are lost in these satanic vortexes of disguised violence and death. Someone said, "The two greatest discoveries in my life were when I realized I was born, and why!"

(g) "Lose his own soul" or "lose himself." What fearful words! The soul is counted the same as one's self or the real person living inside the physical body. Whatever one may wish to say about this, Christ informs us that he who loses his soul has played the fool. A man can have a saved soul, know it, and be a right-minded Christian at the same time. Those who gain a scrap of this world at the cost of their inward person have eternally lost. The Devil puts no market price on the human soul, but most men never learn that. *Anything that works to deceive and damn is his terrible bid.* Alas! Who can describe a soul lost forever; what would the loser give to retain it again? The redemption of the soul is precious and Christ alone has provided that redemption. And it is for whosoever will.

2p-Judaism and the soul. The word "soul" is translated in a fluid manner across the Bible. This is because there is no single term that can fully describe this mysterious, eternal being in man. Divine inspiration employs a variety of words to inform us of his most valuable possession. Yet, these do not *fully* explain the soul of man. Whether it is, life, wind, spirit, self, will, persons visible or invisible, or whatever, they are indescribably related. The human soul (sometimes called spirit) leaves the physical body at death (see Gen. 35:16–18; 1 Kings 17:17–24; Job 27:8; Lk. 12:20; and James 2:26). And where does it go after physical death? The answer is heaven or hell! Cults fiercely deny this truth, telling us that the soul is only the human body with life force or breath in it. Who can imagine the Son of God warning, "What is a man profited if he gain the whole world and lose his human body or life force?" Does our Lord not speak of the physical life in Matt. 16:25, and then dramatically changes to the soul in verse 26? Ezekiel's warning in 18:4, "the soul that sinneth, it shall die," has reference to the everlasting or eternal, never ending, *conscious* death of a man's soul, not pagan annihilation. Peter's terse warning in 1 Peter 2:11, "Abstain from fleshly lusts, which war against the soul," shows the clear distinction between the human frame and the soul abiding therein, as well as the conflict between the two. Refer to Section 59, footnote o for more on the soul of man. See various footnotes in Section 131 for the souls of two men speaking to us from the after-life world. Note the fourth paragraph below for animals and souls. See the following paragraphs for more on this subject.

3p-Souls can be seen in eternity. Years ago, after speaking at a Christian school graduation in Australia, a skeptic surgeon approached me with a question. "I have looked inside thousands of human bodies on the operating table but have never seen a soul; can you tell me what it looks like?" I replied that he had never seen the wind or electricity either. Thus, based on his words, they cannot exist. Every cult, atheist, "greatly learned academic," or infidel struggling to deny the reality of man's soul and its place in eternity uses these and other objections. The spiritual world cannot be seen by human eyes. It is written, "But the things which are not seen are eternal" (2 Cor. 4:18). Moses endured the hardships of Egypt and the wilderness because he saw Him (God) "who is invisible" (Heb. 11:27). He did this by faith. There are things natural and things spiritual (1 Cor. 15:44). In timeless eternity, the apostle John was divinely transported into that realm called heaven. He then wrote, "I *saw* the souls of them . . . [whose bodies] were beheaded [on earth] for the witness of Jesus, and for the Word of God" (Rev. 20:4). Clearly, their souls departed from their bodies at the time of execution. John could see these souls in eternity! Refer to Section 131 for the story of Lazarus and the rich man. In this history given by the Savior, we note again two souls had departed from their physical houses at death. In that other world, they were very much alive, talking, hearing, seeing, and feeling. *(If all these things happened in the grave, it is sure that they were both buried alive!)* One of them was begging for help amid his torment. He pleads for someone to return to earth and warn his five brothers regarding the home of the damned. He was told that their only hope was in believing God's Word. These things and much more transpired in a real eternity. The two illustrations given by Jesus in Lk. 16 represents billions that are there now. Human eyes cannot see into that "world which is to come" (Heb. 6:5). Paul wrote of "the life which now is, and of that which is to come" (1 Tim. 4:8).

4p-Do animals have souls? A common myth among Bible believing Christians is, "Only humans have souls, animals do not." This is incorrect. In Num. 31:28, we read where God speaks of the "souls of the beeves, [oxen] and of the asses, and of the sheep." No amount of running to "the original Hebrew" will change this statement. These animals had souls. However, whatever the souls of the lower creatures are, they cannot be the same as that of man who bears the image of God (Gen. 1:27 with Mat. 16:26). The word "souls," when used of lower creatures, refers to life within their bodies. A similar objection that lower creatures do not have spirits is also error. The unique passage in Eccles. 3:21 speaking of death reads, "The spirit of man that goeth upward, and the spirit of the beast, that goeth downward in the earth." Again, a distinction is made between the two, one going up to God and the other down into earth's dust. Man alone was made in the image of God, and this likeness carries eternal being, especially with his soul and spirit. The destruction of the soul in Matt. 10:28 lasts forever according to Matt. 25:41 and 2 Thess. 1:9.

5p-Plato and the soul. Theological liberals and secular philosophers make a great noise regarding "Plato's theories of the human soul." Whatever mainstream fifth century Greek culture and its satanic philosophers' wrote concerning this subject, one thing is sure: all of them plagiarized bits and pieces of truth from the Hebrew Old Testament or by contact with the Jewish people, and perverted these truths by mixing them with paganism. The absurdity that the inspired writers dipped their pens into the heathen pot of demonism, and then developed their understanding of man's soul, shows that unsaved men are blind to the truth regarding spiritual matters.

6p-Judaism and the soul. Much of Orthodox Judaism *today* (like the cults within Christianity) rejects the *biblical teaching* that man has a distinct, separate entity within his human frame, known as the soul. They affirm that the soul "is not a one-piece item." This error springs from the belief that "there is no eternal hell." To them, the soul is something of a conglomerate of various mystic elements including physical life, which is in the blood, and a desire to reach out to spiritual things. A part of Judaism teaches that when a person dies, not all of his spiritual person departs the dead body! Some portions remain for up to seven days or even in the house where he formerly lived. In some Hebrew communities, mourners walk around the block for seven days after their original seven-day period of mourning. This walk is supposed to "symbolically escort" the departed away from his house! This "seven day walk" seems to be a revision of an ancient belief that the soul of the dead hovered over the body after physical death. This is discussed later at the resurrection of Lazarus in Section 124, second paragraph of footnote w.

7p-Rabbinical mythology. They invented a future, but dormant "World of souls" out yonder somewhere! In this mystic place, men who recall the Torah Law that they have studied in this life will gradually absorb holiness! Worse, these people hold that men who study in this life can provide merits for the dead. This will be counted as if the dead studied the Torah. (This is something of a Jewish Roman Catholic purgatory.) After a thousand years of waiting in this lifeless limbo, they will return to earth for resurrection. Mixed into this muddy eschatology is a system of good works, holiness, guiding angels, and numerous other things. It is another of the millions of "salvation by good works" beliefs that permeate human society. *Any religion without a Savior who did not beat sin, death, and the grave is a false religion.* Those who reject this foundational fact of history resort to their vain imaginations. They invent answers to the question "Where do I go at death?" Only in Christ has this been resolved.

8p-Refer to Section 103, number 8 under footnote g for a list of twenty-one things the Bible says about the place known as hell-lake of fire.

(h) "Ashamed." Realizing that many who heard His stern words would be struck with a mixture of shame and fear, the Lord Jesus admonished them to put aside timidity concerning His instructions. He warns that there looms the danger of Him being ashamed of them in that great day of His coming, when His own shall be rewarded. The word reward here means, "recompense." Mark adds in his record these Words of Jesus, "be ashamed of me and my words in this adulterous and sinful generation" (verse 38). Again, we meet the expression "this generation." As mentioned before, our Lord cannot be speaking of a generation that would live two thousands years in the future. He was speaking of the people who were standing there. Probably, He meant that their wicked generation would feel the sting of being ashamed of Him at some judgment yet to come. Peter exemplifies this, yet he found forgiveness and served His Lord even unto death.

2p-"The son of man shall come." Matt. 16:27 and its parallels are all highlighted in gray as this is a free quotation probably taken from Dan. 7:13. The latter portion of verse 27 may be a quotation from Ps. 62:12.

(i) "Till they see." In Matt. 16:28 with Mark and Luke's parallel verses, we find one of the most difficult statements in the four gospels. In its immediate context of Matt. 16:27, Jesus introduced His coming to "reward every man according to his works." Then in the following passage (verse 28), He speaks of the kingdom of God coming with power, and of Himself coming in that kingdom. This was also a quote from Dan. 7:13 as mentioned just above. To our amazement, the Lord then informs His audience that "some standing here" would not die or "taste of death" until they had seen the "the Son of man coming in his kingdom" (verse 28). Further, He said that they would "see the kingdom" itself come with power (Mk. 9:1). In other words, He told the Jews standing in front of Him, "Some of you will be living when my kingdom comes." (Honesty forbids taking these words of our Lord and projecting them over two thousand years into the future to some Jewish remnant.) *Christ Jesus clearly stated that some of that contemporary generation would see His kingdom come.* Contextually, one must connect this kingdom to His literal coming with angels, just previously mentioned in Matt. 16:27; Mk. 8:38; and Lk. 9:26. Presently, we are two thousand years *after* Christ spoke these things, and His kingdom has not yet come in the glory of His Father, attended by angels. None of those standing in His congregation at that time are alive today; hence, the dilemma. Opinions vary as to what these words mean. Among many saved Jews, one notices a frantic struggle to make this have reference to their literal, political kingdom on earth. Some go so far as to have King Messiah ruling, while down the street in a rebuilt Hebrew temple, the restored priesthood are busy offering blood sacrifices as "memorials" to His death, burial, and resurrection, while the world lives under the Torah Law. Whatever this kingdom will be, it will not be of this nature, even with all the verses taken out of context to prove this nightmare of foul, stinking, burning animal flesh and hair. The most common interpretations of Jesus' Words are as follows:

1. **Transfiguration.** Our Lord was referring to His glorious transfiguration that occurred a few days later. Some believe that the transfiguration was a brilliant but miniature "introductory anticipation" of His return for His own. It was in this transfiguration experience that some of those "standing there" did see a prefigure of the kingdom that was to come with might and wonder. The fact that Christ took Peter, James, and John with Him to behold this wonder, means they were the ones who saw this preview of the future kingdom in its glorified fullness. This happened before their deaths occurred ("taste of death"

verse. 28). Many conservative believers hold this interpretation. On the mount, we read nothing of angels being present, though they could have been there, but the inspired writers did not record it.

2. **Entry into Jerusalem.** He was speaking of His triumphal entry into Jerusalem shortly before His death, which occurred about six months later. At this event, the crowds gathered at the Eastern Gate of the city and shouted various slogans and quoted kingdom Messianic Scriptures to welcome Him (John 12:12-16). Therefore, the kingdom made its *initial and spiritual,* but not eternal appearing as He rode into the city. As in the transfiguration mentioned above, we find no place, where angels shared in this event. Some expositors seeking to avoid this difficulty, appeal to the invisibility of holy angels to resolve the problem.

3. **Pentecost.** This is a popular interpretation of these Word's of Jesus. On this day, the Holy Spirit joined together the New Testament believers with *all* the Old Testament saints. This constituted the *first and totally united* manifestation of the church or new kingdom of Christ to appear on earth. At Pentecost, in Acts 2, the kingdom-church was empowered and given unique gifts of the Spirit for service in taking the gospel to the world at that time, and every succeeding generation. The appearing of His kingdom at that time, in its spiritual form, does not negate His kingdom on earth yet future. We must distinguish between the spiritual and literal aspects of the kingdom. Some hearing Him speak these things were at Pentecost.

4. **The year of A.D. 70.** Some hold that Christ, angels, and His kingdom all came (invisibly) at the destruction of Jerusalem and the Jewish state in A.D. 70. That this calamity was *seen* by the eye of faith along with all ensuing events of that terrible time. *We do not doubt that the Son of God was involved in this judgment, but that was not His real coming as taught in Scripture.* Various reliable commentators believe several of the New Testament verses that have been popularly attached to the real return of Jesus Christ should rather be applied to A.D. 70. Several of these are Acts 2:20; 2 Thess. 2:11; Heb. 10:37; James 5:9; 1 Peter 4:7. In Rev. 1:1 "shortly come to pass," may also speak of this time. The "day of the Lord" was the destruction of Jerusalem and the Jewish state, not the tribulation period millenniums later. Refer to Section 134, fourth paragraph of footnote k for more on this "day." Among the congregation of Christ, as He spoke, *some* of His apostles and others lived to hear or see Jerusalem's demise and the destruction of their beloved city and temple. For example, the apostle John lived until A.D. 100. Some think that the words the Savior spoke to him at Lake Galilee, suggesting that he would not die until he had seen Jesus' return, may have reference to A.D. 70 and Jerusalem doom (John 21:18-22). This is supposed to mean that John saw Jesus return in this judgment in a concealed manner! Amid all the horrible things that occurred at this time, Christ did not *literally return* with angels, either for, or with His kingdom to reward anyone. He came to punish! His spiritual kingdom had already been here for some forty years. It was generally called "the church" by the time Jerusalem fell. This horrific destruction may have reflected the last judgment of this world, but it was not that final all-inclusive event.

5. **Martyrdom.** A peculiar interpretation is that some of the apostles suffered martyrdom, in this, they saw the kingdom of God, and angels come to receive them into heaven. This is unworthy of consideration.

6. **John saw it all on Patmos.** Some understand the Savior was speaking of a unique kingdom manifestation that would occur in the future. They believe that this came to pass when John, in a vision, saw the glories of the kingdom as he penned the final chapters of the book of Revelation.

2p-The problem is to determine which of the above is correct. Even greater is the question yet to be answered, "In what way did the Lord Jesus come in His kingdom to reward His servants during any of these above eschatological assumptions?" Was this fulfilled by some unmentioned, invisible return of Christ in fierce judgment upon Jerusalem and Israel? John Bray postulates this view in, *Matthew 24 Fulfilled.* Many think that number 3 makes more sense in that the apostles lived to see the day of Pentecost occur and its relative events for years ahead. For many of the interpretations given to these verses, see *Jesus and the Kingdom of God,* by G.R. Beasley-Murry. His trust in the opinions of theological infidels and unbelief in the total inspiration of all Scripture makes his thesis unreliable. For a review of the kingdom question and its two manifestations, see Section 39, and all of footnote a.

3p-Religious skeptics such as the late Professor T. W. Mason, gave a startling answer to this problem. He wrote of our Lord, "And it is quite possible Jesus could have been mistaken." See Mason's, *Teachings of Jesus,* 1935 edition, page 283. A mistaken Savior is the best infidel scholarship can produce.

4p-**A rabbinical belief about Messiah and clouds.** There was a belief that Messiah would be *revealed* in the clouds of heaven. The name "Anani" recorded in the fifth and final generation after Zerubbabel, in the family line of David, was interpreted as meaning "cloud man," and thus pointed to their Messiah (1 Chron. 3:24 with Isa. 60:8). Hence, His identification with clouds in Jewish eschatology. This may explain the verses that connect Christ with clouds in Acts 1:9-11, 1 Thess. 4:16 with Rev. 1:7. Was He alluding to this ancient rabbinical belief?

(j) Highlighted in gray, as this is a repeat of Dan. 7:13. These three parallel verses again show us that the "Son of man's kingdom" and the "kingdom of God" are identical. Clearly, Matt. 16:27 and its parallels must be connected with the words in verse 28 about the Son of Man coming again. In verse 28, Jesus quoted this Old Testament passage from Daniel, several times during His ministry, especially during the latter days. An example of this is found in Section 181, Matt. 26:64, footnote i.

The Mount of Transfiguration miracle occurs at night. Moses and Elijah appear and talk to Jesus about His soon death at Jerusalem. Peter, James, and John hear the audible voice of God speaking from heaven. Terrified, they do not understand.*

*It has been continually pointed out that the apostles did not know about Jesus' death, burial, and resurrection. They were shocked at every mention of this. Later, they understood. See asterisk under main heading of Section 107.

On a mountain near Caesarea Philippi

Matt. 17:1-4	Mk. 9:2-5	Lk. 9:28-33	John
Glory on the mountain **1** And after six days[a] Jesus taketh Peter, James, and John his brother, and bringeth them up into an high mountain[b] apart, **2** And was transfigured[c] before them: and his face did shine as the sun, and his raiment was white as the light.	*Glory on the mountain* **2** And after six days[a] Jesus taketh *with him* Peter, and James, and John, and leadeth them up into an high mountain[b] apart by themselves: and he was transfigured[c] before them. **3** And his raiment became shining, exceeding white as snow; so as no fuller on earth can white them.	*Glory on the mountain* **28** And it came to pass about an eight days[a] after these sayings, he took Peter and John and James, and went up into a mountain[b] to pray. **29** And as he prayed, the fashion of his countenance was altered,[c] and his raiment *was* white *and* glistering. (dazzling white)	
Representatives of the law and prophets **3** And, behold, there appeared unto them Moses and Elias [Elijah] <mark>talking[d] with him.</mark>	*Representatives of the law and prophets* **4** And there appeared unto them Elias [Elijah] with Moses: ◄ and they <mark>were talking[d] with Jesus.</mark> ► *Mark is inspired to reverse name-order and list Elijah first and Moses last. Another proof they wrote independent of each other. Luke puts Moses first. In verse 30.*	*Representatives of the law and prophets* **30** And, behold, there talked with him two men, which were Moses and Elias: [Elijah] **31** Who appeared in glory, <mark>and spake[d] of his decease [death] which he should accomplish at Jerusalem.</mark> **32** But Peter and they that were with him were heavy with sleep:[e] and when they were awake, they saw his glory, and the two men that stood with him.	
Peter's building program **4** Then answered Peter, and said unto Jesus, "Lord, it is good for us to be here: if thou wilt, let us make here three tabernacles; [booths] one for thee, and	*Peter's building program* **5** And Peter answered and said to Jesus, "Master, it is good for us to be here: and let us make three tabernacles; [booths] one for thee, and	*Peter's building program* **33** And it came to pass, as they departed from him, Peter said unto Jesus, "Master, it is good for us to be here: and let us make three tabernacles; [booths] one for thee, and	

Matt. 17:4–9	Mk. 9:5–10	Lk. 9:33–36	John
one for Moses, and one for Elias."(f) (Elijah)	one for Moses, and one for Elias."(f) (Elijah) **6** For he wist not what to say; for they were sore afraid.	one for Moses, and one for Elias:"(f) [Elijah] not knowing what he said.	
God's audible voice **5** While he yet spake, behold, a bright cloud overshadowed them: and behold a voice out of the cloud, which said,(g) *"This is my beloved Son, in whom I am well pleased; hear ye him."* **6** And when the disciples heard *it*, they fell on their face, and were sore afraid.(h) **7** And Jesus came and touched them, and said, "Arise, and be not afraid."	*God's audible voice* **7** And there was a cloud that overshadowed them: and a voice came out of the cloud, saying,(g) *"This is my beloved Son: hear him."*	*God's audible voice* **34** While he thus spake, there came a cloud, and overshadowed them: and they feared as they entered into the cloud. **35** And there came a voice out of the cloud, saying,(g) *"This is my beloved Son: hear him."*	
8 And when they had lifted up their eyes, they saw no man, save Jesus only.	**8** And suddenly, when they had looked round about, they saw no man any more, save Jesus only with themselves.	**36** And when the voice was past, Jesus was found alone. And they kept *it* close, and told no man in those days any of those things which they had seen. (Verse 37 cont. in Section 106.)	
"Keep it secret until I have have risen" **9** And as they came down from the mountain, Jesus charged them, saying, "Tell the vision to no man, until(i) *the Son of man be risen again from the dead."*	*"Keep it secret until I have have risen"* **9** And as they came down from the mountain, he charged them that they should "tell no man what things they had seen, till(i) *the Son of man were risen from the dead."* **10** And they kept that saying with themselves, questioning one with another what the rising from the dead should		

Matt. 17:10–13	Mk. 9:10–13	Lk.	John
10 And his disciples asked him, saying, "Why then say the scribes[j] that 'Elias [Elijah] must first come?'" **11** And Jesus answered and said unto them, "Elias [Elijah] truly shall first come, and restore all things.	mean.▶ **11** And they asked him, saying, "Why say the scribes[j] that 'Elias [Elijah] must first come?'" **12** And he answered and told them, "Elias [Elijah] verily cometh first, and restoreth all things; and how it is written of the Son of man, that he must suffer many things, and be set at nought.	For other references on the disciple's not understanding the death of Christ, see Section 104, Mk. 8:32, side note attached by the ◄ symbol. Note all of Section 107, and Section 196, John 20:9, with relative notes for more on this amazing subject.	
John Baptist is Elijah **12** "But I say unto you, That Elias [Elijah] is come[k] already, and they knew him not, but have done unto him whatsoever they listed. (desired) Likewise shall also the Son of man suffer of them."	*John Baptist is Elijah* **13** But I say unto you, That Elias [Elijah] is indeed come,[k] and they have done unto him whatsoever they listed, [desired] as it is written[l] of him." (Verse 14 cont. in Section 106.)		
Now, they understand **13** Then the disciples understood[m] that he spake unto them of John the Baptist. (Verse 14 cont. in Section 106.)	◄*They understood only about John and no more. However, this must have further confused these disciples. Their rabbis had (wrongly) taught them that the real Elijah of their Old Testament would reappear before Messiah came. At this point, they did not yet realize that John the Baptist was the symbolic representation of the Old Testament prophet. In time, they would come to understand the whole story. On the apostles early failing to comprehend the death and resurrection of Christ, see Sections 104, 105, 107, 141, and related footnotes.*		

Footnotes–Commentary

(a) **Six days or eight days?** Both Matthew and Mark wrote that it was "six days" *after* Peter's confession and rebuke of Christ that this marvelous event took place. Meaning six days from their conversation recorded in the previous chapter of Section 104. Yet, Luke speaks of it as "about an eight days" (verse 28). Liberal critics smile at such statements thinking they see another contradiction in Scripture. Matthew and Mark wrote of the "six days" that had passed *after* Peter's opposition of Christ's words and *before* the transfiguration. Luke included both the conversation day of Peter, and the transfiguration in his calculation, making a total of "about eight days." Matthew, in writing to fellow Jews, may be alluding back to the time when God spoke to Moses from a cloud on Mount Sinai (Ex. 19:1, 9), and later when his face was transfigured with glory and the Israelites were struck with glorious fear (Ex. 34:29-30). Every pious Jew reading Matthew's report could relate to this history of their nation.

2p-"Jesus taken Pater, James, and John." These three men belonged to the inner circle of our Lord's disciples. Jesus often selected these three apostles for special private training. Though Peter had been curt and offensive toward his Lord, yet we see the kind patience of Christ in selecting him for this grand experience. How marvelous that a brash man like Peter, so full of blunders and loud boastful talk, and lastly denying his Savior with foul language was admitted into this divine and heavenly experience. What a demonstration of grace in action! In so much of today's church "fellowship circles," everyone must be exactly as we are. If they do not measure up to our standards, then they are counted as second or third class Christians. This is not to deny that God's Word has sure standards for Christian living, rather it is to point out the hypocritical bigotry often exists among Christians. There is a vast difference between the imputed righteousness of Jesus Christ and its impact on others, and polished up self-righteousness of so many people today. God's righteousness works through love; man's righteousness works through personal selection or choice and disregards the teachings of Holy Scripture. It is blind to things of eternal value (2 Cor. 4:18). Alas! There is such a difference between being good and being Godly! A Godly man is not like himself; *somehow*, he is like God. What a demonstration of grace this is for all who watch and listen. I have often wondered how we would fair, if Simon Peter should be a close neighbor, member of the Bible class, boss, or foreman on our job.

(b) A high mountain in Galilee. Some believe it was Mount Hermon, since He was in that area, according to Section 103, footnote a. History reveals that Mount Tabor at this time had a city built on its top, thus making it unsuitable for this grand event. Luke is careful to inform his friend Theophilus that Christ went there to pray. There is something in the lonely solitude and stillness of such places that is favorable to devotion and communication with God. Often, we note our Lord slipped away into the retreat of prayer to refresh His weary and saddened human frame. See this mentioned in Section 48, footnote h; and Section 57, footnote a. Did He not take these same three apostles into the terrible shadows of the garden that lonely night before the cross? We are struck to note the conversation that followed on that occasion was also His death on the cross! See footnote d below.

(c) "Transfigured." Textbook definitions of this word slightly vary. Whatever it finally means, at this time it is saying that the inward fullness of the Godhead *momentarily* flashed through Jesus' human frame. *It must be remembered that this event occurred at night.* Note Section 106, footnote a for more on this. The overwhelming impact upon the three apostles was more than just the shining of their Lord's face as a sun at midnight or the dazzling glister of His garments. To be sure, that alone must have raised the hair on their heads, but something more daring, bold, and divinely fearful occurred. There was a presence and *power* in that scene of brilliance, with the two men from eternity, which history could not convey. The *full* sight and unspeakable revelation of deity breaking forth from the strange but wonderful carpenter from Galilee, stunned these men. The spot where our Lord knelt was illuminated as though a million mega watts of sun power had focused upon that human, but so divine, scene. The superior light of the Son showed itself on that night. There is no evidence in this story to justify the teaching that His anatomy changed and was glorified. His human frame remained the same, but was gloriously immersed for a short time in the brilliance of pure divinity coming from God dwelling within.

2p-Whatever our Lord prayed about that moonlit night, it is right to believe that the glorious event that followed was the answer to that prayer. Yea, even while solemnly engaged in prayer, our blessed Savior was changed as the fullness of God beamed forth from within His physical body. Because the entire transfiguration, firstly, had to do with His upcoming death, burial, and resurrection, we inquire, "Was this the burden of His lonely supplications to the Father in heaven?" A most notable thing about this breathtaking event was that it occurred at night! Alfred Edersheim described it so eloquently in his *Life and Times of Jesus the Messiah*, pages 537-544. We are overwhelmed to ponder this holy event. Yonder in bowed loneliness on a cold mountain peak one can envisage the Son of God, laboring in prayer, while fresh beams of a full moon joyfully dance about to illuminate their weary creator. Such a divine thing had never in human history been vouchsafed to mortal man, and (to our amazement) the cantankerous Peter was one of them. What was about to transpire was no "vision" or product of "hallucination." It was a visible, audible reality coming to three apostles and us from that pure world above.

(d) Moses and Elias [Elijah] talking with Him. Highlighted because they were speaking of His soon death on the cross. See *Appendix Three* for dozens of Old Testament predictions pointing to the birth, life, death, and resurrection of Christ. It was proper that both figures should come to Christ, for in about six months, He would fulfill their highest predictions by dying for the sins of mankind. All saints who had died under the Old Testament system had a special interest in the death of Christ, for they had put faith in that event that was yet to come. Now, their faith would give way to sight and their hope of eternal redemption would become a firm reality. For the Holy Spirit in the Old Testament, see Section 10, second paragraph of footnote b. For how people were saved before Jesus died on the cross, see Section 144, footnote i. A number of things capture our attention in this drama on a Galilean mountaintop:

1. This event reveals the reality of life after death and that there is another realm, a real spirit world in which the souls of men live after departing from this world. Moses' physical body did not resurrect from its corruption after burial fifteen hundreds years prior (Deut. 34:6 with Jude 9). This was the *real* Moses, who had lived in a human frame for one hundred and twenty years before death (Deut. 34:7).

2. These two men did not lose their personal identities after death. Moses and Elijah still looked like Moses and Elijah. *The three apostles knew them!* How? Moses had been dead some fifteen hundred years (Deut. 34:5-8) and Elijah had been translated to heaven about 900 years prior (2 Kings 2:11). Amazingly, the apostles recognized them. This affirms that in eternity, we shall know as we are known, and that earth's "glass darkly" will be removed forever (1 Cor. 13:12). They appeared in glorified forms (verse 31). Was this a pledge for the resurrection of the saints yet to come and the sudden translation of the living at the return of Christ (1 Thess. 4:17-18)? All the fuss about "poor Moses being shut out of the Promise Land," now vanishes! In these verses, he *is there!* Even better, he is there with the Messiah, of whom he wrote so much. For Moses writing about Jesus, see Section 52, John 5:46-47, footnote z.

3. Their conversation: Moses and Elijah had one mission, which was to discuss with Jesus, the Messiah, His decease, soon to occur at Jerusalem. Matthew could have not written anything more un-Jewish than Israel's Messiah dying on a Roman cross! However, he writes thus, for this Messiah had saved his soul and changed his life. Moses was the greatest leader in human history and the chosen Legislator of God's Torah Law to Israel. Now, his honor and fame disappear in the light of history's most profound drama, the death of Christ for the sins of the world. Had he not painted many portraits across the entire Torah, perhaps a thousand pictures or so that pointed ahead to some aspect of the life and work of Messiah. Back in the Old Testament God had informed Moses that this coming Messiah would be "like unto" him (Deut. 18:18). The Law of Moses, each of its 613 precepts, run to this brilliant scene and bow before the One who has fulfilled and filled full their every requirement. He alone met their *every* strenuous demand, and they knew this very well. *The law hands its sharp sword to Christ; He accepts the surrender.* Descending the sides of old Sinai, Moses' face shone bright and had to be veiled (Ex. 34:29-33). Some fifteen hundred years later, Jesus had fulfilled every jot and tittle of Moses' code. Then He brought salvation by grace with an unveiled countenance that shines brighter than the sun and His clothing became white as light. Glorious is the superiority of grace over the glory of Moses' Law and all the prophets (2 Cor. 3:6-18). This is not antinomianism as the law cults charge; rather, it is true sovereign grace in action (John 1:17).

2p-Why the presence of Elijah at this time? Being called by the Jews the "chief of the prophets," he is the appropriate prophetic representative. In *both men,* we see the law and the prophets giving total acquiescence as they bear full testimony to the dying of the Messiah. In His life and death, He had met their every criterion. Peter, some nine years after this scene, preached to the Roman officer and his men stationed at Caesarea, that "To him give all the prophets witness, that through his name whosoever believeth in him shall receive remission of sins" (Acts 10:43). It is of interest that Jewish writings spoke of Moses and Elijah being together in various undertakings. See Talmud tractates, Pesachim 54a; Sukkah 5a; and Megilah 19b, for examples of this. As previously mentioned, the Jews held that Elijah would prepare the way for Messiah to appear. Refer to this in Section 8, footnote h, and Section 24, footnote b. John the Baptist fulfilled this prediction in a spiritual sense, but here on the mountaintop the real Elijah of the Old Testament appeared.

3p-Looking too late. How sad that the great people of Israel continue to look for Elijah to appear at every Passover during the seder meal. They set a place for him at the table, prepare a chair, and open the door to welcome him, should he appear. O that they only knew John the Baptist came to their nation some two thousand years ago; that he was the Elijah of their Scriptures, and prepared the way for their beloved Messiah or Mashiach, who was Jesus of Nazareth. Christ had previously explained to His apostles that John was Elijah, and had already appeared and fulfilled his ministry. It took them several years to understand what Jesus was teaching. Finally, it all came together on the day of Pentecost.

(e) Heavy with sleep." This event occurred in the night at the top of the mountain. The apostles must have been frightened out of their wits. See footnote h below. For confirmation that this event happened at night, see Section 106, Lk. 9:37, footnote a.

2p-"Make three booths." Being late at night, surely there was some type of campfire burning nearby and a shelter (tabernacle) of some sort. See footnote f below for more on the brush shelter or tabernacle. What a rude but wonderful awaking! Rubbing their eyes and gasping in fear and wonder, they see all three marvelous persons standing nearby shrouded in the most dazzling light. The three disciples not only heard their conversation but also understood it as they discussed Jesus' death on the cross. See footnote note i below. What language did these visitors from eternity speak? Whatever it was, it was understood by the three apostles.

(f) It is noted that Peter blurted out this statement. Even though he did not know what to say, he still had to say something! Mightily astonished at the wonderful terror of God's glory, he said the wrong thing (again). In the ecstasy of that marvelous moment, the Galilee fisherman wishes that this glorious trio would stay for a while. Haltingly, he offered on behalf of fellow apostles to "build three tabernacles" (makeshift tents or booths from tree limbs) as he saw Moses and Elijah beginning to move away (Lk. 9:33). Mark wrote, "For he wist not what to say; for they were sore afraid" (verse 6). Some wrongfully hold that Peter wanted to observe the Feast of Tabernacles with these heavenly visitors. This is in error, as *all the* annual Jewish feasts could only be correctly enacted at the temple in Jerusalem (Deut. 12:5-7).

2p-Various interpretations have been given to this event. Some note in it a picture of the future millennial reign and base this on Zech. 14:16. Some find here the church in its infant stages! Others see it as a precursor to the Feast of Tabernacle a few weeks ahead, during which devout Jews built booths for the occasion. Probably, Peter meant no more than some act of blundering, frightened courtesy, wanting to provide a temporary shelter from the harsh conditions of the mountaintop. Further, we cannot doubt that he wished to have had more time to converse with these two famed personages of Jewish history. This, God would not allow. At this time, the law and the prophets, wherever they spoke of the Savior, had just about run their course. The arresting voice from the cloud commanded that the Son was to be heard. Perhaps a prevailing lesson was that those men, now in divine glory, would not come down to the level of earthlings anymore; Peter must come up to them. And this he did about thirty- four years later (2 Peter 1:14).

(g) **Highlighted in red, for it is the voice of God speaking audibly.** For the third and final time that God spoke in the four gospels, see Section 161, John 12:28. Refer to Section 22, footnotes f and g for the first time He spoke audibly in New Testament history. A *bright* cloud suddenly eclipsed the scene. Such a cloud was the symbol of divine presence as God went before Israel in a cloudy pillar by day and night (Ex. 14:19 and 24). Fear gripped the apostles as it engulfed them. Suddenly, the voice of God spoke from that cloud. In Section 104, footnote c, we noted that Peter had challenged Christ upon hearing of His death at Jerusalem at the hands of the religious leaders. Now, some six days later, God challenges Peter. His message to the tough but tender fisherman was clear: "Peter, six days ago you argued with my Son about His death at Jerusalem. Now, you have heard Moses and Elijah speak of it." In this command, God referred to Christ's recent declaration of His upcoming death, which had been so hotly debated by Peter. On this mount, Jehovah renewed the truth of this eternal fact, especially to Peter, who had listened more to his own voice than that of his Lord. The thrust of this scene is that the death of Christ for man's sin would soon be an accomplished fact of divine history, and the apostles had better get that straight.

(h) **Matt. 17:6. "Sore afraid."** And who would not be? Terrified, they dropped to the ground, faces hidden and minds awed at the presence and voice of God. The scene is reminiscent of Israel in the wilderness, the pillar of cloud by day and fire by night in which God abode over His people and often spoke to them (Num. 9:17). It reminds us of Daniel, who was physically ill after the glory of God appeared to him (Dan. 10:2-8), and is similar to John on Patmos, when his mortal flesh was overwhelmed by divine glory (Rev. 1:17). The reassuring voice of their Master gave comfort and soothed their fears. Rising up they "saw no man save Jesus only." Moses and the law, and Elijah of the prophets had vanished; the Son stands alone. Pavilioned in splendor, the Son of God had left them breathless! All things must finally give way to Jesus the Christ (Phil. 2:9-11). *He is forever centrally pre-eminent.*

(i) This is a general gathering from numerous Old Testament verses that predicted the death, burial, and resurrection of Christ. *The New Open Bible,* pages 1489-1495, has a list of some forty-four different Old Testament prophecies pointing forward to various aspects of the life, ministry, death, resurrection, and ascension of the Lord Jesus. Several decades ago, Kregel Publications reprinted the classic volume *Christology of the Old Testament,* by E. W. Hengstenberg. This has been described as one of the greatest works ever written on the Messianic prophecies of Christ. Alfred Edersheim, in his work *The Life and Time of Jesus the Messiah,* lists in Appendix 9, many Old Testament passages the rabbis said pointed to the coming Messiah. The prolific British writer, Herbert Lockyer, produced the outstanding book, *All the Messianic Prophecies of the Bible.* This is a straightforward effort, easy to understand and packed with helpful information on this subject.

2p-Again, the Lord Jesus forbids any mention of this fantastic event. The three apostles were not allowed to mention this experience even to their fellow apostles at that time. Perhaps this was because it would have been spread across the land and further angered the religious leaders. Only after His resurrection could they tell this unusual story. Many years later, Peter wrote about it in 2 Peter 1:15-18. Mark records something of a private discussion the three men had among themselves. They were "questioning one another what the rising from the dead should mean" (verse 10). It is noteworthy that there is no recorded mention of Christ's resurrection being spoken of anywhere within the verses describing the transfiguration event. So where did they hear this? It could have only been from the conversation between Moses, Elijah, and Jesus. No doubt much more was spoken of at that time. We have only a brief record of that glorious event. It is clear that the disciples were totally oblivious to the resurrection of the Messiah as well as His death on the cross. They would, however, understand it later.

(j) **Elijah comes first.** Set in a gray background. Not a direct Old Testament quotation as such, but a truth gathered from certain words in Mal. 3:1-3 with 4:5-6. Making their way down the mountain, the three apostles were confused. Jewish rabbis and teachers had pounded into them that Elijah will come to Israel *before* Messiah's appearing. This belief is renewed at every Passover in the seder meal. Had Peter and his companions not just seen Elijah? However, something is wrong, for Jesus the Messiah had come on the scene *before* the real Elijah did! Things were backwards and not working according to the theology of the rabbis. In verse 11, the Lord makes it clear that "Elias [Elijah] truly shall first come, and restore all things." He did not mean that Elijah was *yet* to appear at a future date, for He then told them in the same breath, "That Elias [Elijah] is come already" (verse 12b). See footnotes k and m below. John Lightfoot, in *Commentary on the New Testament . . .* , vol. 2, pages 246-247, partly explains the meaning of "restoring all things." He wrote that Elijah would "purify the bastards, and restore them to the congregation" [of Israel]. He would bring back "the pot of manna, the vial of holy oil, the vial of water, and the rod of Aaron." For other details of Elijah's alleged works, see *Appendix Four*, the second sub heading under title, What Elijah would do when he appeared in Israel. John the Baptist did none of these things, demonstrating again the vanity of Hebrew mythology and a misunderstanding of their Scriptures regarding Messiah and His forerunner.

2p-In the above words, our Lord did not refer to the appearing of the real Elijah, whom they had just seen. Rather, He spoke of the appearing of John the Baptist several years previous, who had come in the spirit and power of the original Elijah; he was His forerunner and prepared (or restored) a people out of Israel for Him. It is noted that Christ said of John, "they [the religious leaders of Israel] knew him not" (verse 12). Meaning they did not understand that John was the fulfillment of their Old Testament predictions of Elijah coming again. The scribes, Pharisees, and leaders of the nation were looking for the physical Elijah to return. (Exactly the same problem exists today among the vast army of "end-time experts.") When John the Baptist fulfilled his role of getting things ready for Jesus, the Jews *totally* missed the meaning of their own Scripture.

3p-Verse 12. "He must suffer many things." Mk. 9:12 is highlighted in gray. This was another general reference to the various predictions recorded in the Old Testament that spoke of Christ's death for the sins of mankind. He knew these verses spoke of Him. Refer to first paragraph of footnote i above for other details regarding these prophecies that pointed ahead to the Lord Jesus. For many predictions concerning the birth, life, death, burial, and resurrection of Christ, see *Appendix Three*.

(k) Elijah has already come. There is no intelligible way these words can mean that Elijah *had not come*, but that he would appear over two thousand years later and preach during the tribulation period. It takes a wild imagination to read this proposal into these Word's of our Lord. Note the bewildering explanation given of this in the *Scofield Reference Bible*, page 1023, footnote 1.

(l) Meaning that everything written about the Baptist in the Old Testament Scriptures was fulfilled according to the will of God for his life and ministry. He was clearly predicted in Isa. 40:3 with Matt. 3:3, and in Mal. 3:1 with Mk. 1:2. Even his being a Nazarite, which was a group that had its roots back in Num. 6:1-21 was another fulfillment of Scripture. For more on the Nazarites, see Section 8, Lk. 1:15, footnote g. In 1954, F. B. Meyer wrote an excellent book entitled *John the Baptist*. A few years later, M. L. Sloan produced *John the Baptist as Witness and Martyr*. These two works fairly cover the life and ministry of Jesus' forerunner. For likenesses between John the Baptist and Elijah, note Section 21, Part 1, footnote f.

(m) "Understood that he spake of John the Baptist." The apostles [then] understood Jesus' Words, but still could not put the puzzle together. They now knew that John the Baptist was the fulfillment of the coming of Elijah as proclaimed by the rabbis. There are thousands who take these passages and see in them a "second coming of Elijah" to earth at a future date, who will preach to Jews during the tribulation period. The associated verses used to prove this theory are in Rev. 11:3-12, which speaks of two witnesses. These passages are anything but conclusive. They must be forced to speak of Moses and Elijah by association, not facts. Hippolytus (died A.D. 236), said they represent Christians, who died for their faith! Over the past century, these two *unnamed* persons have been identified as Moses, Elijah, Adam, Enoch, Abraham, Daniel, Joel, and Elisha, to list a few. Putting names on persons when God has not is sorry exegesis of Holy Scripture. On this problem, see all of Section 8, Lk. 1:17, footnote i, for the Archangel Gabriel's interpretation of who Elijah would be. Surely, Gabriel knew what he was saying!

2p-In Mk. 9:13, the Master settles the question by explaining that it was all done according to Scripture, and that "they" (meaning the Jews and Herod Antipas who killed John) had fulfilled these prophetic forecasts. Thus, if they have been fulfilled, how will they be fulfilled again? The only answer to this is the same answer that various "specialists" appeal to in order to be saved from further eschatological contradictions. This is the "double fulfillment" exegesis, which over the decades has been used to prove just about anything. For other comments on the double fulfillment hermeneutic, see Section 8, footnote i. Nevertheless, it is interesting that some believe there is a prophetic forecast of John's ministry, message, and death in Isa. 40:8, when this verse is coupled with John's testimony of his work in John 3:30. For other comments on the appearing of Elijah, see number 3, of footnote d above, along with footnote j.

Descending from the mount, He delivers a child from demonic torment* and suffering. The apostles learn why they were unable to help the little boy.**

*See main heading Section 48, for four unique Messianic miracles that only Jesus produced. **See Section 97 for a little girl who was healed of demon possession and further comments on this subject.

At the foot of the Mount of Transfiguration near Caesarea Philippi

Matt. 17:14–17	Mk. 9:14–19	Lk. 9:37–41	John
The morning after the transfiguration	***The morning after the transfiguration***	***The morning after the transfiguration***	
14 And when they were come to the multitude,[a]	14 And when he came to *his* disciples, he saw a great multitude[a] about them, and the scribes questioning with them. 15 And straightway all the people, when they beheld him, were greatly amazed, and running to *him* saluted him. 16 And he asked the scribes, "What question ye with them?"	37 And it came to pass, that on the next day,[a] when they were come down from the hill, [the Mount of Transfiguration] much people met him.	
The distraught father	***The distraught father***	***The distraught father***	
there came to him a *certain* man,[b] kneeling down to him, and saying, 15 "Lord, have mercy on my son: for he is lunatick, and sore vexed: for ofttimes he falleth into the fire, and oft into the water.	17 And one[b] of the multitude answered and said, "Master, I have brought unto thee my son, which hath a dumb spirit; 18 "And wheresoever he taketh him, he teareth him: and he foameth, and gnasheth with his teeth, and pineth away: and I spake to	38 And, behold, a man[b] of the company cried out, saying, "Master, I beseech thee, look upon my son: for he is mine only child. 39 "And, lo, a spirit taketh him, and he suddenly crieth out; and it teareth him that he foameth again, and bruising him hardly departeth from him.	
16 "And I brought him to thy disciples, and they could not cure him."	thy disciples that they should cast him out; and they could not."	40 "And I besought thy disciples to cast him out; and they could not."	
The patient Savior	***The patient Savior***	***The patient Savior***	
17 Then Jesus answered and said, "O faithless and perverse generation,[c] how long shall I be with you? how long shall I suffer [bear with] you? bring	19 He answereth him, and saith, "O faithless generation,[c] how long shall I be with you? how long shall I suffer [bear with] you? bring	41 And Jesus answering said, "O faithless and perverse generation,[c] how long shall I be with you, and suffer [bear with] you? Bring	

Matt. 17:17–18	Mk. 9:19-27	Lk. 9:41–43a	John
him hither to me.”	him unto me.”	thy son hither.”	
	20 And they brought him unto him: and when he saw him, [Jesus] straightway the spirit tare him; and he fell on the ground, and wallowed foaming.	**42** And as he was yet a coming, the devil threw him down, and tare *him.*	
	Since a small baby **21** And he asked his father, “How long is it ago since this came unto him?”**(d)** And he said, “Of a child. ▶		
	22 “And ofttimes it hath cast him into the fire, and into the waters, to destroy him: but if thou canst do any thing, have compassion on us, and help us.”	◀*What a disturbing answer from this distraught father! See all of footnote d for comments on this awful thought.*	
	23 Jesus said unto him, “If thou canst believe, all things *are* possible to him that believeth.”		
	24 And straightway the father of the child cried out, and said with tears, “Lord, I believe; help thou mine unbelief.”**(e)**		
18 And Jesus rebuked**(f)** the devil;	**25** When Jesus saw that the people came running together, he rebuked**(f)** the foul spirit, saying unto him, “*Thou* dumb and deaf spirit, I charge thee, come out of him, and enter no more into him.”	And Jesus rebuked**(f)** the unclean spirit,	
and he departed out of him:	***The demon's final bid*** **26** And *the spirit* cried, and rent him sore, and came out of him: and he was as one dead; insomuch that many said, “He is dead.”		
and the child was cured from that very hour.	**27** But Jesus took him by the hand, and lifted him up; and he arose.	and healed the child, and delivered him again to his father.**(g)** **43a** And they were all	

485

Matt. 17:19-21	Mk. 9:28-29	Lk. 9:43a	John
		amazed at the mighty power of God. (Verse 43b cont. in Section 107.)	
The apostles' question **19** Then came the disciples to Jesus⁽ʰ⁾ apart, [alone] and said, "Why could not we cast him out?" ***Their question answered*** **20** And Jesus said unto them, "Because of your unbelief: for verily I say unto you, If ye have faith as a grain of mustard seed,⁽ⁱ⁾ ye shall say unto this mountain,⁽ʲ⁾ 'Remove hence to yonder place;' and it shall remove; and nothing shall be impossible unto you.	***The apostles' question*** **28** And when he was come into the house,⁽ʰ⁾ his disciples asked him privately, "Why could not we cast him out?"		
Their question answered **21** "Howbeit this kind⁽ᵏ⁾ goeth not out but by prayer and fasting." (Verse 22 cont. in Section 107.)	***Their question answered*** **29** And he said unto them, "This kind⁽ᵏ⁾ can come forth by nothing, but by prayer and fasting." (Verse 30 cont. in Section 107.)		

Footnotes–Commentary

⁽ᵃ⁾ **Multitudes and the next day.** It is the morning, *after* the night of the transfiguration. Luke affirms this in the words, "on the next day" (verse 37). Note Section 105, footnote e for more on this. Christ and three apostles make their way down the mountainside where the other nine apostles and a "great multitude" had been waiting for their return. Someone in the crowd sees Jesus and announces His return. Upon hearing this, the people surged forward to meet the Lord Jesus. During the absence of Christ, a certain unnamed man had appealed to the nine apostles on behalf of his only child, a small boy who was seriously demon possessed. Though Christ had previously given them authority over evil spirits to cast them out, this case was beyond their ability. Apparently, the vast multitude and even the scribes who were present had become involved in the despair of the father and condition of his son. Hence, they questioned the apostles as to why they could not out drive the spirit (Matt. 17:16 with Mk. 9:14). At the sight of Jesus, hopes rose high with great anticipation. Seeing Him, from within the body of the child, the demons flew into fits of rage, and made their last efforts to inflict pain and injure him before being driven out.

⁽ᵇ⁾ **The distraught father.** Falling before Jesus, he begs for mercy. In Matt. 17:15 he described his son to the Savior as "lunatick." Refer to Section 42, Matt. 4:24, footnote g for comments on what the word meant to the ancients. This little boy was in a dreadful condition. The evil spirit had attempted on numerous occasions to kill him by fire or water. Torn by the indwelling demons into fits and convulsions, and grinding his teeth, they slammed his frail body to the ground. He is described as wasting away. There are millions of cases like this around the world. *See the second paragraph of footnote d below, for a warning about prejudging these things.*

2p-**"Dumb spirit."** Mark wrote that the father reported to Jesus that the little one had "a dumb spirit" or demon (verse 17). In Mk. 9:25, Jesus said the demon was both a "dumb and deaf" spirit. Matthew describes the demon as a "devil" (verse 18), Mark as a "foul spirit" (verse 25), and Luke as an "unclean spirit" (verse 42). *The Jews believed that only their Messiah could heal one struck with dumbness by demonic possession. Christ's healing of this child demonstrated, without argument, that He was Messiah.* See Section 66, footnote b for a brief explanation of this belief and main heading of Section 90.

⁽ᶜ⁾ **"Generation"** Again, we hear this word from the lips of Christ. It was addressed *exclusively* to the unbelieving Jews of that time. Matthew uses the word "generation" thirteen times in his book. They are as follows, Matt. 1:1; 3:7; 11:16; 12:34, 39, 41, 42, 45; l6:4; 17:17; 23:33, 36; and 24:34. In every case except the first reference, it is used as a warning to the Jews, especially the scribes and Pharisees. For more discussion on the word "generation," see main heading Section 68 along with footnote g. Contextually, and historically, it cannot speak of a time thousands of years in the future and Israel in the tribulation period.

2p-As on previous occasions, again our Lord laments the unbelief of the Jews, including this distraught father. "O faithless and perverse generation" was uttered after reading their hearts, which had no trust in Him. Messiah issues the command, "Bring thy son hither" (verse 41). The violent reaction of the evil spirit when he saw Christ standing before him reveals their terror of God's Son. This was also seen earlier in Section 88, Matt. 8:29.

(d) "When did this happen to your son?" This inquiry of Jesus constitutes one of the most important questions regarding the subject of demonic possession. Mark only records the question Jesus put to the father before effecting deliverance for the child. "How long is it ago since this came unto him" (verse 21)? Such inquiry was for apostolic instruction and to inform believers throughout all ages of Christian history. It was not because the Master suffered from lack of information. This single event remains one of the most critical examples in *all Scripture* of dealing with children who are genuinely demon possessed. Note the following:

1. **"Of a child."** Here was the father's response to the Master's question. The Greek word for child is "paidion." It is used of both newly born infants and older small children. In this case, it can *only* mean a small child, for the tenor of this whole narrative reveals this fact. The father affirmed that the terrible malady had befallen him at an *earlier time,* even as a baby. This child was afflicted from the cradle. We are amazed! One is struck at the discernment of the wise father in detecting what was wrong with his son. A work on the subject of demonic activity with children is *The Seduction of Our Children,* by Neil T. Anderson. It has helpful insights to this dreadful subject. Woe be those who scorn such things, or relegate them to the realm of myth or heathen superstition. Even among many "conservatives" and "fundamentalists," this is played down or flatly denied. Such evasive theology pleases Satan and furthers his awful work among the children of men. The Jews believed in a demon named "Shibta." They held that he would take hold of children on their necks, then dry up, and contract their nerves. He could produce all sorts of diseases and physical contortions. Could this *Hebrew myth* have been a distorted corruption of some original truth? For more on "Shibta" and his alleged habitation of market places and fruit, see Section 70, footnote d, and Section 96, second paragraph of footnote d.

2. **How can evil spirits enter the bodies of helpless children?** Here is the central question of this whole event. One thing is sure: the child was not suffering demonic trauma for sins he had committed, thereby giving grounds for this thing to enter his body (Rom. 9:11). Yet, the fact remains that an unclean, foul, or demon spirit had tormented him since infancy. *Sin has always been the basis or grounds for demonic activity of every sort.* Since the child *could not* sin, what opened the gate for this awful invasion into his little body? Scripture teaches that the sins of wicked or incorrigible parents, who *"hate God,"* may be transmitted to their children (Ex. 20:5; Lam 5:7; with Ezek. 18:2). Others believe this type of possession, like sin, is hereditary, being passed on, *somehow,* perhaps genetically (Neh. 9:2; Ezek. 16:44; Dan. 9:16; with Rom. 5:12). There are cases where satanic parents have dedicated their unborn children to Lucifer. Often, these children are born possessed. Little investigation has been put into searching for the cause, and finding the cure. The *grounds* for demonic activity in children will never be fully known, but apparently may be traced back into the family line. Regardless, this awful reality had better be believed and not explained away! It is sure that God has given us the cure: His Son, the Lord Jesus Christ. He came to "destroy the works of the devil," regardless of where they are (Acts 2:39; 10:38; Col. 2:15; with 1 John 3:8). For more on this, see *What Demons Can Do to Saints*, by Merrill F. Unger. For an examination by a professional psychologist into the Satanic Ritual Abuse (SRA) of children, and multiple personality disorders, see *Uncovering the Mystery of MPD*, by Dr. James G. Friesen.

3. **All devils know Christ.** The entire kingdom of darkness knows who Jesus Christ is. They are terrified at His divine Person and power. A solemn hush fell over the milling, restless crowds, as the broken father with his only child in arms approached Messiah! Suddenly, the demon beheld the glory of that majestic Man standing before him. Things exploded! The lurking spirit knew Him. His associates in evil had felt the sting of defeat from Him hundreds of times. Madly, the foul spirit makes his final attempt to inflict pain and injury upon the innocent child. On other occasions, their wicked counterparts had confessed Jesus Christ in terror. See Section 40, footnote d, and Section 41, footnote g. Christ had bound the strongest of their number and spoiled their captive houses throughout His ministry. This case was no different. In a fierce final strike, the demon slammed the child out of his father's arms to the earth; he was thrown into kicking, screaming, frothing, and wallowing like a wounded animal. Typical of Satan we read, "The thief cometh not, but for to steal, and to kill, and to destroy" (John 10:10). For the deliverance of this child from the clutches of Satan, see footnotes f and g below.

2p-What demons did to this child. Matt. 17:15, with its parallels in Mk. 9:18 and Lk. 9:39 lists an array of sufferings the evil spirits put this boy through. These included "falling into fire and water," "tearing him," "gnashing" or "grinding his teeth," "pining away," "foaming at the mouth," and "bruising him." Not everyone who may reflect these symptoms is troubled by demons. Genuine physical maladies of many sorts may also cause similar bodily manifestations. *It is dangerously harmful to assert that all such reactions are the work of demons.*

(e) **"Help."** All believers, at one time or another, have prayed as this poor father. Our best of faith is often tempered with unbelief. In the human heart, a nagging voice whispers dark things to our soul. It is this lurking element of unbelief that needs the "help" of God in heaven. And this help is readily available.

(f) **"Jesus rebuked the devil."** After speaking the word of command, obedience to the Son of God must follow. Our Savior's orders, "enter no more into him," make it clear that demons can return to their former dwellings. See Section 68, Matt. 12:44, footnotes b and c, for an earlier mention of this happening. Throughout His ministry wonderful things happened: Galilee's howling storms harkened to His charge, blind eyes, deaf ears, and dumb tongues, obeyed His Word; even body stumps once maimed by war or accident suddenly grew new members. "But how can this be?" inquires the scoffing infidel. It is because He is Very God dwelling among mortal man. Commanding the evil entity to depart and *never enter again,* the howling imp fled in terror. As the demon departed, the child's distorted little body collapsed. Amazed spectators cast their startled opinions, "He is dead" (Mk. 9:26). Who could imagine the mixed reactions of those hundreds of spectators? Stunned, the crowds fell back in horror. The apostles were shocked, amazed, and confounded, as they stood aghast before the whole spectacle.

(g) **A glorious delivery!** Who has words to describe the joy of this once distraught father? Now, his only child has been delivered from devils and healed of the horrible effects of their malignant activities. The unceasing agony of caring for such an afflicted little one was over. See number 1 under footnote d. The sunrise of everlasting hope had risen in the shattered life of that worn, weary father. What unspeakable and marvelous changes the Lord Jesus makes in our lives. He is precious indeed! No marvel it is written, "His name shall be called wonderful" (Isa. 9:6).

(h) **The troubled disciples.** Entering into a "house" (Mk. 9:28), the apostles question their Lord as to why they could not cast out the spirit. (Who among us has not been troubled by our seeming inability to do successfully the work of God?) Christ informs them that unbelief brought about their failure. Prior, to this, they had success in exorcism, healing the sick, and raising the dead. See this in Section 59, Matt. 10:8. Something happened! It is possible for men of God to become so preoccupied in their work, even in the art of study, that they lose power with the Father in heaven. The apostles had seen more than any mortal! They were followers of the Messiah and were His special chosen ones. However, in prayer, they had failed. Prayerlessness breeds faithlessness. Matthew wrote that Jesus rebuked them for faithlessness by using the example of the mustard grain. Jews frequently used the mustard seed as illustrative of small things. The apostles understood their Lord's rebuke. With the smallest measure of true faith, they could (in God's time) pass through the most difficult circumstances. These men of public notoriety in their Messiah's service are suddenly unable to help a child writhing under the afflictions of Satan. Christ's Words "nothing shall be impossible unto you" are to be understood as meaning nothing impossible that is in the will of God for one's life (1 John 5:14). It is not, nor has faith ever been a blank check, for *whatever* one desires to have. Those who teach this propagate demeaning error and do serious harm to weaker Christians.

2p-More to the story. As odd as it sounds, the genuine Christian life has mysteriously built into it a certain expectation of failure. There is a nagging little voice down inside every believer that infrequently and cunningly whispers, "You are a failure." The high-sounding claims that we must *always* be spiritual, winners, victors, and never lose heart in any battle does not correspond with genuine Christian experience. *No believer exists who does not have terrible difficulties in this world.* Only Christians who have died have that kind of peace! The apostles struggled with their inability to help this child. The rebuke of Jesus regarding their faithlessness may fit this embarrassing situation. And it fits into ours as well! Few people have courage enough to appear as good as they really are. For many Christians it would prove most embarrassing!

(i) **"Mustard seed."** Here again, the Lord Jesus repeats Himself in the use of this term. See Section 79, Matt. 13:31-32, footnotes b, c, and d, where earlier He employed this to illustrate His kingdom and its mysterious growth in the world. See Section 132, Lk. 17:5-6 for a much later usage of the mustard seed.

(j) Among the ancients, especially the Jews, mountains were looked upon as being the supreme example of stable things on earth (Ps. 46:2 with Isa. 54:10). "Removing mountains" was a term used to express the most difficult of tasks or superior learning. The Jews were fond of the words, "remover of mountains," and applied them to their most knowledgeable rabbis to flatter their great wisdom. Now, Messiah employs this to glorify the power of a speck of faith, and what it can accomplish when exercised within the will of God. Everyone listening understood what Jesus was saying. For more information on the Jewish "rooter up of mountains," see John Lightfoot's *Commentary on the New Testament . . .* vol. 3, pages 283. There are no grounds here for the "healthy, wealthy, faith healers" who get everything they want from God regardless of His will for their lives.

2p-The words "this mountain," had reference to the Mount of Transfiguration from which He had just descended. One can believe that He pointed to it as He spoke. Christ was *not* teaching the disciples that they were to shift land terrain, restructure earth's geology, or moving literal mountains. Such an interpretation is sheer nonsense. Rather, He taught them (and us) that our faith is to increase gradually and grow (like the mustard seed), as we labor in His service. Through faith, the most difficult things, that are within the periphery of His sovereign will for our lives, may be accomplished. Later, we hear our Lord again using similar language when He speaks of a "mountain being cast into the sea" in Matt. 21:21-22 with Mk. 11:23. The apostle Paul used similar words some twenty years afterwards in 1 Cor. 13:1-2. Was he quoting a common expression or was this from the book of Matthew, the first of the four gospels to be written? If so, this demonstrates that Matthew's work was in circulation by A.D. 54, the time Paul wrote his first letter to the Corinth church. Refer to Section 113, footnote g, for more on this thought.

(k) **"This kind."** There are at least three lessons here that should be noted:

1. **Different kinds.** In using the words "this kind," Jesus referred to *specific* types of demons that cause dumbness in the human anatomy. This child's dumbness was caused by a demon and not genuine physical maladies. It is psychology devastating for those suffering these things to be told they have demons, when they may not. Counselor(s) must make a careful diagnosis before anything is said or done. Jesus told the apostles, that *such cases* as this are only cured by earnest prayer, faith, and fasting.

2. **The only basis for exorcism.** There are degrees of spiritual, physical, and moral evil deep and fierce, so obstinate and intense, that only fasting and prayer to God for mercy can destroy them. The work of deliverance should be motivated first by simple faith, without which, the petitioners cannot please God (Heb. 11:6) Genuine exorcism must be totally based upon the atoning work of Christ in His death, burial, and resurrection. He alone has the power to break demonic bondage. Those assisting the ones held in a satanic grip must verbally appropriate the authority of Christ against the evil powers. The author has audibly heard demons screeching out in fear at the reading of Scripture and at the application of the authority of Jesus Christ against them.

3. **Not for apostles only.** Expulsion of evil spirits in the New Testament was a work the apostles exercised, but not exclusively. The belief that this was strictly an apostolic thing, and it cannot be exercised today, is an error. Many well meaning pastors have fell for this untruth and find themselves paralyzed to help those in this awful bondage. *However, it is also true that certain gifts and abilities were strictly apostolic and never intended for Christians in general.* A short time later, Christ sharply reprimanded the twelve for the mistake of thinking that, they alone, were the only ones to aid those in satanic bondage. Refer to this in Section 109, Mk. 9: 38-41, footnotes h and i for the story. Over the course of church history, many Christians have suddenly been faced with dark entities and soon learned that exorcism was not limited to the twelve! Below are examples of demonic possessions different from those in the little boy that was brought to Jesus.

3p-**Demon-possessed nurse.** The author was praying for a nurse in a Johannesburg high-rise office building in early 1973. Suddenly, a powerful burst of wind gushed from her mouth as she was lifted into the air and fell behind the chair in which she had been sitting. (Shock experiences such as these will test the best of one's faith.) An elderly Christian man who was present took charge of this situation. The young nurse was instantly delivered. *When confronted with devils, one cannot go looking for the rulebook or check it out with his college professor.* It must be established in our hearts that only in the risen Christ is deliverance received for those in bondage. This is accomplished through the power of the Holy Spirit, by faith in the finished work of the cross. Some cases may require persevering-enduring faith and pastoral care for extended periods of time. Exorcism is a grace that thousands of saints have employed when the situation so demanded it. *Arrogant curiosity in these things can prove a calamity for the flippant Christian.* See the horrific illustration of this in Acts 19:14-16.

3p-**The pastor.** A minister in Durban, South Africa, related the following experience. It illustrates the need for constant vigilance in God's service. While visiting in a home one evening he spoke of the salvation of Christ being available for the man of the house. Suddenly, the husband leaped from the couch, smashed the end off a coke bottle, and charged the pastor, screaming, "I will kill you, Christian!" The stunned pastor shouted loudly, "Jesus, thou Son of God, save me!" Suddenly, there was a loud thump. The enraged husband sailed across the room and crashed into a corner, unconscious! At the behest of the terrified wife, the pastor fled. Later, he learned that her husband was a priest in the satanic worship circles in the Durban area. He fiercely opposed the gospel of Christ.

4p-**Walking prudently amid mass deceit.** Satan has counterfeited Biblical exorcism among certain evangelists and popular ministers. Men who publicly advertise their "gifts" are to be shunned. Beware of the so-called "deliverance ministries" that abound across America today. Much of it is a sham and flashes with danger signals when many of these "anointed ministries" finish in disaster, financial, and moral scandals, total shipwreck of faith, and in some cases, suicide. "Evangelists" who flippantly "take on the Devil" may find that "they have been taken on." Michael, God's holy angel, would not bring "railing accusations" against Satan (Jude 9). Christ spoke of the Devil's exorcists in Section 47, Matt. 7:21-23, and warned of the terrible consequences in judgment. Though saved, and saved forever, our shelter and safety in practical everyday life is found in wearing the whole armor of God (Eph. 6:10-18), watching in prayerfulness (Lk. 18:1), living in Scripture (Matt. 4:4), and old-fashioned self-discipline (Ps. 18:23 with 1 John 5:18b). According to Prov. 18:10, "safety" is also found in our Lord. James 4:8 is valid to this present moment. *Helping those in need is not salvation by works, but how salvation does work.* Regarding Jesus' doing good and helping others, see the beautiful statement recorded in Acts 10:38.

5p-**Little children preaching?** The weird phenomena among *wild* Pentecostals and others of small children preaching amid screaming and yelling is not of the Holy Spirit. *It is a clever and successful invasion of Satan.*

Traveling back to Capernaum, again the Savior mentions His death.
The apostles, filled with sorrow are afraid to inquire for the meaning
of His somber and terrifying Words about death* and resurrection.

Over the past few days, Messiah had spoken several times of His death to the apostles. See main headings of Sections 104-105. Each time they failed to grasp what their Lord was saying. For more on this, refer also to Section 26, footnote e; Section 27, footnote n; and Section 29, footnote j. They could not believe the Messiah of Israel would die and thus fail to bring about their long looked-for physical, political kingdom on earth.

Galilee

Matt. 17:22-23	Mk. 9:30-32	Lk. 9:43-45	John
		Aftermath of the miracle 43 And they were all amazed at the mighty power of God. But while they wondered every one at all things which Jesus did,	
He speaks of His death: the disciples are confused and fearful 22 And while they abode in Galilee, Jesus said unto them,	*He speaks of His death: the disciples are confused and fearful* 30 And they departed[a] thence, and passed through Galilee; and he would not that any man should know *it*. 31 For he taught his disciples,[b] and said unto them,	*He speaks of His death: the disciples are confused and fearful* he said unto his disciples,[b]	
"The Son of man shall be betrayed into the hands of men:[c] 23 "And they shall kill him, and the third day he shall be raised again." ▲ *For other references on the disciple's not understanding the death of Christ, see Section 104, Mk. 8:32 with side note, and Section 196, John 20:9, and relative notes.*	"The Son of man is delivered into the hands of men,[c] and they shall kill him; and after that he is killed, he shall rise the third day." *(For third day, see Appendix One.)*	44 "Let these sayings sink down into your ears: for the Son of man shall be delivered into the hands of men."[c]	
They do not yet understand His death on the cross And they were exceeding sorry.[e] (Verse 24 cont. in Section 108.)	*They do not yet understand His death on the cross* 32 But they understood not that saying, and were afraid[d] to ask him. (Verse 33 cont. in Section 109.)	*They do not yet understand His death on the cross* 45 But they understood not this saying, and it was hid from them, that they perceived it not: and they feared[d] to ask him of that saying. (Verse 46 cont. in Section 109.)	

Footnotes-Commentary

(a) **"They departed."** Leaving the area of the Mount of Transfiguration and the scene of the healing of the demoniac child, the Master and His little flock of twelve moves in a southerly direction back to Capernaum. They left behind a crowd of amazed people and a father who shouted praises to God all the way home. From verse 30, we learn that our Lord attempted to remove Himself from the flocking, curious crowds. Seemingly, He wanted a private

490

time with His preachers in order to teach them those invaluable lessons they so greatly needed, especially the facts of His upcoming death at Jerusalem, resurrection, and ascension to heaven.

(b) **"He taught his disciples."** It has been over a week since the fierce opposition of Peter against Jesus' announcement of His approaching death at Jerusalem. This event is recorded in Section 104, Matt. 16:22. Shortly afterward, Christ takes Peter along with James and John up to the mount, and there amid the glory of God, they actually hear Moses and Elijah speaking with their Lord about His death. Refer to Section 105, Lk. 9:31, footnote d for more on this. Now, while walking back to Galilee and Capernaum, the Lord Jesus again brings up the troubling subject to the twelve and pleads with them that what He says must "sink down into their ears" (verse 44). Unless the truth of Christ's death, burial, and resurrection is fixed in our hearts, we will be unbalanced, defective believers all of our lives.

(c) Though not a prophecy within itself, yet highlighted in gray, for here is another hint about the dastardly deed of Judas Iscariot, one of the twelve. He was a noted subject of various Old Testament predictions (Ps. 69:25, 109:6–20). Jesus' *first recorded public* mention of the traitor is in Section 95, John 6:70-71, footnote x. This original mention of Judas occurred shortly after the uproar over His message in the Capernaum synagogue. At this time, none of the eleven knew that a traitor walked with them along the roads of Israel. Our Lord also speaks of His death, burial, and resurrection at Jerusalem. See footnotes d and e below for the reaction of the apostles concerning the decease of Jesus their Lord.

(d) **"Afraid and feared."** The most eloquent vocabulary could not describe the storm that howled in their hearts. Everything they had been taught by the rabbis about Israel's all conquering Messiah was gradually fading before their eyes. Here, they hear from His mouth that He will be killed! *This was impossible.* They had been taught that Messiah Son of David would establish a literal kingdom for Israel, and that He would rule the world. For more on this, see Section 9, Lk. 1:32, footnote g. Later, the whole story would be fully understood: but for now, it was a mystery and a terrible burden of confusion that weighed heavily on their minds. No wonder they were described as being "afraid."

(e) **"Exceeding sorry."** Jesus employed straightforward, clear speech. One would think that His Words "kill" and "rise the third day" would be plain enough. However, it was not so. The apostles did not, indeed could not, at this point, relate to what their Lord was saying. Refer to main heading Section 104, footnote a, for more on this subject. Luke informs us "it was hid from them" (verse 45). The meaning is that they were unable to comprehend what Christ said because they were the victims of rabbinical teaching about a political Messiah, who would lead Israel to conquer and rule the world. The thought of their Messiah being crucified on a Roman cross was a scandal and a blatant contradiction to all they had ever been taught about Israel's glorious King. Even Peter, with his amazing confession of "who" Christ was, did not include anything about His death on the cross. Both Mark and Luke wrote that the apostles were "afraid to ask him." They knew He was their Messiah, but He was *doing and saying* things that continually shocked all of them: things that did not correspond with the Messiah, as preached by the religious leaders of Israel.

2p-For the most profound and surprising admission of the two major apostles not knowing of their Lord's death and resurrection, see the symbols ◄ and ▫ by John 20:9 in Section 196.

The Lord Jesus sends Peter hook fishing to pay their temple taxes.* Catching one, He miraculously finds sufficient money in its mouth. In Israel, these taxes were levied annually to pay for maintenance of the temple** at Jerusalem.

*See main heading under Section 43 where an earlier miracle was performed in a great catch of fish after which the disciples forsook all to follow Jesus. Staying somewhere near the sea, Peter is sent fishing. **Two days before His death the Lord Jesus tangled again with the Jews, this time over paying taxes to the pagan Roman government. Refer to Section 155 and relevant footnotes, especially g.*

Matt. 17:24-27—*Capernaum and Sea of Galilee*	Mk.	Lk.	John
Jewish tax collectors visit Peter			
24 And when they were come to Capernaum,[a] they[b] that received tribute *money* came to Peter,[c] and said, "Doth not your master pay tribute?" (Annual temple tax. About two days wages or thirty-two cents.) **25** He saith, "Yes." And when he was come into the house, Jesus prevented [spoke first to] him, saying,[d] "What thinkest thou, Simon? of whom do the kings of the earth take custom or tribute? of their own children, or of strangers?" **26** Peter saith unto him, "Of strangers." Jesus saith unto him, "Then are the children free.			
Avoid unnecessary offences: go pay our taxes			
27 "Notwithstanding, lest we should offend them,[e] go thou to the sea, and cast an hook,[f] and take up the fish that first cometh up; and when thou hast opened his mouth, thou shalt find a piece[g] of money: that take, and give unto them[h] for me and thee." (Next chap., Matt. 18:1 cont. in Section 109.)			

Footnotes-Commentary

(a) Their journey from the Mount of Transfiguration, located at the uttermost northern limits of the Holy Land, now ended back at Capernaum. After their arrival, Peter was visited (probably at his house) by Jewish tax collectors from the temple at Jerusalem. There was also a tax, which was collected from the Jews strictly for the Roman Emperor. It is mentioned in Matt. 22:17 and Lk. 23:2 and was totally different from the Hebrew temple tax mentioned in this story.

(b) The Hebrew tax officer inquired whether Christ paid tribute. This payment was commanded in the Torah Law (Ex. 30:11-16) and was collected for use in the services of the temple. It was described in the law as "a ransom for a soul," in which each man, rich or poor, paid the same. A lesson here reveals that all souls are precious before God. The amount collected annually paid for "public sacrifices," meaning those offered on behalf of the entire nation of Israel. It was also used for incense, showbread, pay of the rabbis, copyists, temple bakers, judges, the dozens of women, who wove or washed the temple linen, and other items used in temple service. Every male twenty years of age and older, including all proselytes, were expected to pay this annual sum, which was collected in the month of Adar (February and March), just before the Passover in April. Jews who resided outside the land of Israel might bring their payments while attending the Passover celebration. See more about this in the Talmud tractate, Kiddushin 54a. This method of collecting funds began only after the Babylonian captivity of Israel had ended in 536 B.C.

2p-Strict records were kept of who paid and who did not. The collecting officers sometimes conducted a canvass from village to village and city to city. On the first day of the month (see paragraph just above), before the Passover Feast, messengers went over the land to inform the people that it was "temple tax time again." Fifteen days later, stalls were erected in a central location accessible for the populace of the cities and villages; just inside each of these stalls were two large chests. The tax officers were present, watching the proceedings. Into these chests, the Jews dropped their money. The deadline for this payment came on the twenty-fifth of the month. After this date, all payments had to be made at the temple in Jerusalem. Payment amounted to about twenty-five cents annually, and could be paid only in the ancient money of Israel, which was the regular half shekel. Money changers appeared en masse on the scene during these days of tribute collection. See Section 29, footnote b for more on money changers and business in the temple. They shouted and clamored to the passing crowds, seeking their business. All foreign coins (bearing the images of gods and pagan rulers) had to be changed into the proper Hebrew currency. The exchange rate, which was fixed by law, was between four and five cents on each half shekel. The annual revenue collected from this was estimated at about forty-thousand dollars, which was a large fortune. *Every Jew who loved his nation and religion gladly paid this tribute.* It is painfully ironic for Israel, that after the destruction of Jerusalem and the temple, Emperor Vespasian ordered that this tribute money should continue to be collected from the conquered Jews. However, it was then used for the building of a temple for the heathen god, Jupiter!

(c) Apparently, the receivers of the tribute went to Peter, preferring not to approach Christ over the matter.

2p-**"Tribute."** The word here is "didrachmon," and is equivalent to about 32 cents in present day (2011) currency exchange. As mentioned in footnote b above, this money was collected annually and used in the various services of the temple. It is noted that when Peter hoisted his prize catch from the water the "piece of money" in its mouth was a "stater," which amounted to about .64 cents (verse 27). Amazingly, this was enough to pay taxes for both Peter and the Savior! For more on this miracle, see all under footnote f below.

(d) Christ spoke to Peter a question concerning "from whom do the kings and rulers of earth collect taxes" (verse 25). Then the Master adds, "of their children or strangers?" The lesson means that the kings of earth do not collect payments from their family and children to sustain financially their kingdom. Only their subjects pay what is required. In this, our Lord said that He was the King of all, including the temple. Thus, His children (in this case the apostles) were not required to pay any taxes. They were technically "free" from this obligation because of the authority of Jesus, who was Lord of all. See next footnote e for more on this thought.

(e) **Avoid all unnecessary offence.** Various persons have risen on the stage of church history and seized upon this statement as proof that they are exempt from paying taxes. *This is political heresy.* Our Lord's response was not an argument against tax paying, but rather an explanation of why He paid it. The children of God are subject to civil laws wherever they live, and should pay the taxes levied on them by public, state, and national authorities. Even though much of this will be used in the most unjust and hideous ways. Christians must let retribution for such crimes come from the hand of God. "Vengeance belongeth unto me, 'I will recompense,' saith the Lord" (Heb. 10:30). The Lord Jesus paid His temple tax even though the functions of the religious system were in the hands of evil men. Later, during His trial, the Jews distorted His reply and used it as an accusation against Him before Governor Pilate. This proves that some of them were present and heard our Lord's reply to Peter about paying taxes. The twisted inference was that He had refused to pay the tax levied by the Roman Government, but the verses say nothing of the kind. Note Section 155, footnote g, where Christ affirmed the correctness of paying taxes to civil rulers. In the Talmud, Tractate Sukkah 30a, there is found a curious story of a king who paid the toll at a common crossing like all other men! His shocked attendants inquired of him why he did such a thing, being the king. He replied, "All travelers would learn from me not to evade their payments of taxes."

2p-**Our Savior was careful to avoid unnecessary offence.** This needed lesson is unknown to many of us present day Christians. Much rudeness, careless words, and quick judgments fly about in the company of believers. Our words are like bullets, once fired, they will not come back for a second shot. Observe how carefully the Savior answered Peter's question. He did not leave the impression that He and His followers despised the temple and its great system of worship. On two different occasions, He had used small whips and purged it of evil merchandising. Even though He and His apostles were divinely exempt from paying the temple tribute, to prevent further bitterness among the leaders of religion, it would be paid. Years later, Peter wrote these beautiful words, "For *it is* better, if the will of God be so, that ye suffer for well doing, than for evil doing" (1 Peter 3:17). The Savior instructed him to go to the sea and cast in a line with a hook. Whoever heard of paying taxes from a fish's mouth? Pulling up the first catch, Peter haltingly pulled open its mouth and there lay the large coin ("stater") good for *two* full payments! This falls out to about 64 cents in today's economy. As the ravens had fed Elijah (1 Kings 17:2-6), now the fish pays taxes for Peter and Jesus. The omniscience and omnipotence of Christ are seen in this miracle. Whether our Lord created the coin in the fish's mouth, or whether He ordered the fish to scoop it from the bottom of the lake, and then directed the creature to Peter's baited hook are interesting points. In this very miracle, He proved Himself exempt and far above all kings and rulers of earth: the One to whom they should bring tribute. Why the money was not enough to pay for the other eleven apostles we do not know. Perhaps they had previously submitted their payments to the collection officers. Teddy Roosevelt once said, "Income taxes had made more men liars than fishing." Nevertheless, now Peter had one fish story to tell that nobody would believe, not even the Hebrew Internal Revenue Service!

3p-It is of interest that this very tribute money was referred to as "ransom for a soul" (Ex. 30:12) and the Lord Jesus paid it in full. Read the first paragraph of footnote b above where this was previously mentioned. Later, nailed to the cross, He paid the absolute and total ransom for the souls of all mankind. Moreover, those who become recipients of this ransom are those who repent of their sins and believe the gospel message of His salvation.

(f) **"Go fishing, Peter!"** Here is the only mention of hook fishing in the New Testament. For the singular mention of *dragnet fishing* in the New Testament, see Section 85, footnote a. In Lk. 5:1-3 they were washing nets. In John 21:6 they were using casting nets. The fishing in Shame on those rationalist infidels who teach that the instructions of Jesus to Peter were just an expression; that He was actually instructing him to go and sell fish and acquire the needed tax money! If the coin was in the mouth of the fish when Peter caught it, we are amazed at the wisdom of Christ, who knew it. If the fish picked up the coin just before Peter caught it, we are still amazed at His power to put it there. Further, if the coin was not already in the sea, then Christ created it for that particular fish to swallow. Next, He compelled the creature to bite Peter's hook. Regardless of how we look at it, only God could have arranged such a miracle.

2p-For a comprehensive article describing the art of fishing and fish in the Middle East, see the *Biblical, Theological, and Ecclesiastical Cyclopaedia,* vol. III, pages 574-580, by M'Clintock & Strong. All the prattle about there being no fish large enough in the waters of Lake Galilee to hold this coin is wrong. There is even now in the waters of Galilee a fish, not of particularly enormous size, with a flexible pouch inside its mouth. In this pouch, articles the size of a golf ball have been found. Regardless of what kind of fish it was, it did the work God commanded! If God made a fish large enough to swallow Jonah, surely He had no problem creating one large enough to hold a tax coin, which was a bit larger than the American half dollar piece. The author of this work saw one of these ancient coins (half shekel) years ago in Durban, South Africa. It was the property of an elderly Christian gentleman, who, at that time had the world's only complete collection of biblical coins. Later, he sold this invaluable prize and gave the money to build a Bible school. He died shortly afterwards. What an example of laying up treasure in heaven.

(g) A Hebrew legend. In Jewish folklore, an interesting legend was built from this factual event in the life of Christ. It is recorded in the Talmud tractate, Shabbath 119a. Among the Christians in Rome, the story was related that a poor tailor went to market to purchase a fish for a special Sabbath meal. He had previously sold his property and bought a precious stone of great price. While crossing a bridge the wind blew the stone from his turban into the water, and a fish swallowed it. The same fish was later caught and taken to the fish market where the poor man went to purchase his food for the meal. The fishmonger cut open the selected fish and there was the jewel, which had blown off his turban! The prudent reader can scarcely fail to note the sharp difference between the Bible records of truth against the fable that rose later in human history. It is beyond doubt that the rabbis invented many of these Jewish legends. This was an effort to discount or counter the historical facts recorded in the pages of the New Testament regarding the life and works of Jesus the Messiah.

(h) Knowing whom the temple tax collectors were and where to find them in the vast city of Capernaum, Peter took the money and made the necessary payment. One wonders if he told them *how* he had gotten the coin. Knowing Peter, he probably did! Could this have been the origin of the Hebrew legend mention in the paragraph just above?

The apostles bicker about their individual greatness. Taking a little boy as His text, Christ teaches them a lesson on pride and vanity. John seems to have changed the subject as Jesus responds to his question with a lesson on brotherly love. Jesus gives a warning about offending one of God's children who was not in their group.

Capernaum

Matt. 18:1–5	Mk. 9:33–37	Lk. 9:46–48	John
Struggle for prominence **1** At the same time came the disciples unto Jesus, saying, "Who is the greatest[a] in the kingdom of heaven?"		*Struggle for prominence* **46** Then there arose a reasoning among them, which of them should be greatest.[a]	
	Christ's question **33** And he came to Capernaum: and being in the house he asked them, "What was it that ye disputed among yourselves by the way?"[a] **34** But they held their peace: for by the way they had disputed among themselves, who *should be* the greatest.		
		47 And Jesus, perceiving the thought of their heart,	
	Christ's answer **35** And he sat down,[b] and called the twelve, and saith unto them, "If any man desire to be first, *the same* shall be last of all, and servant of all."		
Christ's supreme example **2** And Jesus called a little child[c] unto him, and set him in the midst of them,[d]	*Christ's supreme example* **36** And he took a child,[c] and set him in the midst of them:[d] and when he had taken him in his arms, he said unto them,	*Christ's supreme example* took a child,[c] and set him by him,[d]	
		48 And said unto them,	
3 And said, "Verily I say unto you, Except ye be converted,[e] and become as little children, ye shall not enter into the kingdom of heaven. **4** "Whosoever therefore shall humble himself as this little child, the same is greatest in the kingdom of heaven.[f] **5** "And whoso shall receive one such little child in my name receiveth	**37** "Whosoever shall receive one of such children in my name, receiveth	"Whosoever shall receive this child in my name receiveth	

495

Matt. 18:6–8	Mk. 9:37–43	Lk. 9:48–50	John
me.[g]	me:[g] and whosoever shall receive me, receiveth not me, but him that sent me."	me:[g] and whosoever shall receive me receiveth him that sent me: for he that is least among you all, the same shall be great."	

	Sectarianism rebuked	**Sectarianism rebuked**	
	38 And John[h] answered him, saying, "Master, we saw one casting out devils in thy name, and he followeth not us: and we forbad him, because he followeth not us." **39** But Jesus said, "Forbid him not: for there is no man which shall do a miracle in my name, that can lightly speak evil of me. **40** "For he that is not against us is on our part. **41** "For whosoever shall give you a cup of water to drink in my name, because ye belong to Christ, verily I say unto you, he shall not lose his reward.[i]	**49** And John[h] answered and said, "Master, we saw one casting out devils in thy name; and we forbad him, because he followeth not with us." **50** And Jesus said unto him, "Forbid *him* not: for he that is not against us is for us." (Verse 51 cont. in Section 112.)	

Punishment of offenders	**Punishment of offenders**		
6 "But whoso shall offend one of these little ones which believe in me, it were better for him that a millstone[j] were hanged about his neck, and *that* he were drowned in the depth of the sea. **7** "Woe unto the world because of offences! for it must needs be that offences come; but woe to that man by whom the offence cometh!	**42** "And whosoever shall offend one of *these* little ones that believe in me, it is better for him that a millstone[j] were hanged about his neck, and he were cast into the sea.		

Deal with your sin before it deals with you	**Deal with your sin before it deals with you**		
8 "Wherefore if thy hand or thy foot offend thee, cut them[k] off, and cast *them* from thee: it is better for thee to enter into life halt or	**43** "And if thy hand offend thee, cut it[k] off: it is better for thee		

496

Matt. 18:8–10	Mk. 9:43–50	Lk.	John
maimed, rather than having two hands or two feet to be cast into everlasting fire.	to enter into life maimed, than having two hands to go into hell, into the fire that never shall be quenched: ***Damnation is eternal*** **44 "Where their worm dieth not, and the fire is not quenched.** [(l)] **45** "And if thy foot offend thee, cut it off: it is better for thee to enter halt into life, than having two feet to be cast into hell, into the fire that never shall be quenched: ***Damnation is eternal*** **46** "Where their worm dieth not, and the fire is not quenched. [(l)]		
		◄ *Mark places Jesus' Words about the foot in this verse. Matthew recorded them earlier in Matt. 18:8 and combined hand and foot together. Mark's statement about the hand is in verse 43 above. This is another one of the peculiar marks of inspiration of Scripture.*	
9 "And if thine eye offend thee, pluck it out, and cast *it* from thee: it is better for thee to enter into life with one eye, rather than having two eyes to be cast into hell fire."	**47** "And if thine eye offend thee, pluck it out: it is better for thee to enter into the kingdom of God with one eye, than having two eyes to be cast into hell fire:	◄ *"Life" and the "kingdom of God" are the same.*	
	Damnation is eternal **48** "Where their worm dieth not, and the fire is not quenched. [(l)] **49** "For every one shall be salted with fire, and every sacrifice shall be salted with salt. [(m)] **50** "Salt *is* good: but if the salt have lost his saltness, wherewith will ye season it? Have salt in yourselves, [(n)] and have peace one with another." (Next chap., Mk. 10:1 cont. in Section 137.)		
Warning: angels are watching! **10** "Take heed that ye despise not one of these little ones; [(o)] for I say unto you, That in heaven their angels do always behold the face of my Father which is in heaven. (Verse 11 cont. in Section 110.)		◄ *What a lesson! Continual strife among the apostles would affect their witness for Christ. Ministers and missionaries of God today are saltless due to this very sin. Peace must reign among the children of God. Great sermons and Bible oratory are often given, but miserably void of the anointing of the Holy Spirit due to bickering among God's servants. Note Zech. 4:6; Micah 3:8; Eph 4:30; and I Cor. 2:4 with 1 Peter 1:12.*	

Footnotes-Commentary

(a) **"Ye disputed among yourselves."** The apostles fall into an argument as to which of them was the greatest! After healing the demonic child and departing from the crowds at the base of the Mount of Transfiguration, during their walk back to Capernaum, a spirit of rivalry erupted among the twelve. Arriving at the house, Jesus asked them about their dispute along the way (Mk. 9:33-34). Three had been selected out of the number to ascend and behold the transfiguration. Peter had made the great confession of Messiah, and the tax collector went to him as a representative of the apostolic body. Now, wrangling and debate emerge as they follow along behind their Lord. Apparently, they did not know He was listening to their ministerial quibbling. One is amazed at the apostles' bickering among themselves over position and authority in their long-looked-for material kingdom on earth. This was not the kingdom of Jesus at this time.

2p-The kingdom of heaven. Their very argument proves that they viewed the kingdom of heaven or God as only a temporal thing. For explanation of Christ's new kingdom, see Section 39, footnotes a and g. Perhaps they wished to know which one of them would be made the Prime Minister of Israel's would-be literal kingdom. Note the main heading, Section 142, for the *continuation* of this argument many weeks later. On this occasion, we note that James and John, aided by their mother, sought by craft to secure a chief place for themselves in their imaginary Jewish material kingdom. This conflict surfaced again the night before the morning of His death, as they sat at the Passover table.

(b) Mark wrote that Jesus "sat down" (reclined) and called the twelve to gather about Him. The words about being last and first were strange to the Hebrew ear. This was based on Jesus' statement in Mk. 9:35 about who will be first and last. Jews believed that in the literal kingdom on earth, with their all-conquering political Messiah ruling, various positions of authority would be given to the faithful in Israel. Only the most pious would be first and all others last. There can be no doubt the apostles believed these things and were debating their positions in this future era.

(c) **The grand example.** To illustrate His response to their argument, the Master takes a child and lifts the little one into His arms before the twelve. If this occurred in Peter's house, it was probably one of his children. Several weeks later, our Lord gave *another* lesson on humility to His apostles, using tiny children as His illustration.

(d) Taking the little one into His arms, and then placing him on the floor in front of them, He begins to speak. As these men looked upon the lad, they must have held their breath waiting for their Master's Words. Luke is terse to write, that He "Perceived the thought of their heart" (verse 47). With this, note Ezek. 11:5! Jesus said that unless they were "converted" or "turned from" their arrogance, and became as that child, they would have no place for service in His new kingdom. The lesson here is not that this child humbled himself, but that he was humble from the nature of his relation to older persons. Self-humbling is the most difficult thing in the world for *both* saint and sinner. There sat the Lord of heaven pointing to a little child; this was His powerful text for the disputing preachers.

(e) **"Converted."** This is an action word meaning to "turn from something." Our Lord affirmed to His band of apostles that, *unless* they "turn from" struggling for power, and position in their (allusive) political kingdom, and realize that for the present, God's kingdom is not of this world, they would be worthless in His service. Greatness in the kingdom of God finds its beginning in littleness. The way up is down, and the way down is up. The right road to a high place in the kingdom of Christ is the low road of serving Christ and others. These men were shaken by His forthright words, as they flew into the face of their traditional Jewishness and bigoted national prejudices.

(f) **"Greatest in the kingdom."** Here, the Messiah makes known the results of abandoning all self-interest and personal ambitions to seek genuine greatness. The disparity between the kingdom of Christ and the kingdom of this world is so great that the only way to rise to honor, and blessing in the former is to be as a little child: clean, humble, and totally trusting. In this, the Lord Jesus shows them that they are all equal; no one is superior to the other. They all need each other as they serve Christ. A king's child will happily play with the son of a beggar all day long and never know the difference. Fame and prestige mean nothing to either. Their innocent hearts are cheerful in play, inviting friendship. Christ wills for His servants to "humble themselves" even to the level of simple, loving children. What a lesson for all of us today! See an illustration of this in the second paragraph of footnote g below.

(g) Nestling the child in His arms, then watching him move about the floor, the Son of God issued another warning to the twelve. Now, the Master instructs them about receiving little ones. Jesus speaks first, of children in the literal sense and second, of receiving all the things that portray real goodness and innocence as reflected in the child before them. Beware of those in the service of God, who have no time for, or even despise children. The author of this work has seen many of these dangerous people. Abuse, rape, and molestation of little ones are commonplace occurrences. Harshness and a bent to dictatorship mark all the servants of Christ, who have given themselves to high and lofty ambitions of carnal fame, and will not reach down to the small and lowly. They dig the pit into which they shall finally fall. In some strange manner, little children, with almost a sixth sense, can sometime detect the insincerity and falsity dwelling in the bosom of the Judases of the church. True born again saints, who walk with their Lord are quick to receive their Master's fellow servants who reflect these "child-like" characteristics.

498

2p-In November of 1971, while preaching in Cape Town, South Africa, the author of this work met an old man who "carried" the famed Dr. Andrew Murray (died 1917) to his last meeting. I inquired of the elderly Mr. Rowland (who was one hundred years old), "What touched you most about Murray?" He replied *"His humility! He was so gentle and easy to love and I knew he loved me!"* This is what Christ said to His quarreling preachers.

(h) **"And John."** Suddenly, the Savior's lesson is cut short! John's abrupt interruption had nothing to do with the Master's rebuke of their petty quarreling. Rather, it was an embarrassing effort to "get off" the painful subject of accepting others, who were also doing God's work but would not follow the apostles. This was embarrassing for John, the apostle of love. In a previous preaching tour, they had observed a man *not of their company* who successfully cast out demons. Luke informs us that the apostles "rebuked him" because he would not join with them (verse 49). In an effort to correct their misunderstanding of His work, our Lord gently rebukes them and defends this unnamed servant in His new kingdom! The apostles felt they alone were the true servants of their Messiah; that all others must be cleared for service by their superior knowledge and experience. Such arrogant deception is rampant today among the people of God. It is crucial for saints to know and understand the difference between loyalty to Christ and His Word, and drowning themselves in the debates over nothing. Previously, our Lord had said, "He that is not with me is against me," (Matt. 12:30). Apparently, the twelve had forgotten this admonition, for (to their shock) there was someone else serving Christ besides them. Worse, this person flatly refused to join in with the apostles. This, they could not understand.

(i) **"Reward"** for faithful service in the least of things that had been mentioned earlier. There have been multiple cases across church history where the people of God have been reduced to a cup of water. We know not what the morrow holds. If we bless our fellows today, God may see it good to bless us on the next. A cup of cool water in the Middle East is no small thing. It is considered an act of high charity even for one's enemies. Jesus had mentioned this earlier in Section 59, Matt. 10:41-42, footnote s.

(j) **Verse 6 and parallel in 42. "Millstone."** The Jews used two millstones: one turned by hand and the other by an ass, (donkey) known as the "ass millstone." It is the latter to which Christ refers. History reveals that on one occasion, the Romans inflicted this punishment on those who led an insurrection against their rule in Galilee. The guilty were drowned in the lake this way. Jewish literature, especially the Talmud speaks often of the millstone and its usage. One curious tractate, Kiddushin 54a speaks of studying the Torah with a millstone about the neck. In the context, it speaks of a man who married a wife and then attempted to learn the law. The marriage added an extra burden to his life, is the supposed lesson. However, Messiah's audience needed no explanation. Here, the Lord stated that whoso receives, helps, and loves one with a spirit (like the little boy He embraced), and is without guile, meek, and trusting, will be counted the "greatest in His kingdom." To receive or welcome such is tantamount to welcoming the Savior Himself. Our estimations and judgments of who is or who is not a true believer are often far removed from the teachings of Christ as laid down in this story. To "offend" a true child of God carries such awful consequences that one loathes speaking of these things. The terror of drowning in the sea, choking to death by water and weight, is heaven compared to the doom that waits in hell. The warning of verse 7 "Woe to the world" trembles with horror for those without Christ.

(k) **Verses 8-9 with parallels in Mk. 9:43, 45, and 47. "Hand, foot, eye."** Over a year ago, our Lord had used this expression during the Sermon on the Mount. Here, it is generally repeated again. As seen numerous times in this harmony commentary, there is plenty of evidence that Christ repeated Himself. Refer to Section 45, Matt. 5:29-30, the last paragraph of footnote h for an explanation of what our Lord conveyed using such harsh illustrations.

(l) **"Not quenched."** A quotation from Isa. 66:24. Mark pens these words three times in verses 44, 46, and 48. It is a repetitive emphasis given by Christ on the *eternal hopelessness* of souls languishing in hell-lake of fire. He did this to impress upon His audience the awfulness of that place. The ancients, in their superstitions, believed that a worm gnawed upon the conscience of each damned soul in eternity. Whatever our Lord intended to depict, He attached to the horrible thought of eternity without Him, the similes of the gnawing worm and the burning fire. Annihilation, soul sleep, and pointing to Jerusalem's city dump called gehenna, where pagans had once offered human sacrifices, do not mitigate Christ's Words. The Old Testament was replete with warnings against human sacrifices in fire offered by pagans. *This is not our Savior's lesson here.* Heathen sacrifices offered to gods and goddesses were, in reality, offerings to Satan via demon spirits. This is explained in Section 1, Part 2, the fourth paragraph of footnote f. The Savior was not talking about sacrifices in the above verses, but the eternal death of the soul. For more on this, see Section 59, footnote o, and Section 131, footnotes d and e. For twenty-one things the Bible says about hell-lake of fire, see Section 103, number 8, under footnote g. No-hell cults work hard to reinterpret these Bible facts and make them fit their annihilation heresies. *Christ did not die to save us from annihilation!*

2p-Hell is no joke. Apart from Christ's deity, His resurrection, and the doctrine of man's utter depravity in sin, no fact of Scripture is so hated as the truth of eternal conscious suffering in hell. The powerful, Christian Jewish evangelist, the late Hyman Appleman, often quipped, "It will take hell to make some people believe in hell." A scoffer once harangued me with the question, "How can you believe in hell, you have never seen it?" I replied, "I have never seen the wind, either." The most frequently used curse words in American society today, heard on every hand are, "hell" and "damn." After all, it's a big joke believed only by country bumpkins, fanatics, and religious cranks. *In time, all men everywhere will learn that hell is no joke!*

(m) Every sacrifice salted. At the temple altar, every sacrifice was salted by the officiating priests (Lev. 2:13). Seemingly, the Messiah had this in mind. As the sacrifices at the temple were covered in salt and then placed upon the fire, likewise, shall the wicked in hell be eternally *preserved* to suffer their everlasting fate (2 Thess. 1:9). For an earlier mention of salt by the Lord Jesus, refer to Section 44, Matt. 5:13, and for a later mention, see Section 128, Lk. 14:34–35, footnote h. Again, we see in this statement the Lord repeating Himself as He taught.

(n) Mk. 9:50. "Have salt in yourselves." The idea here is that the apostles were admonished to have in their lives those things that salt represented: such traits as soundness of doctrine, holiness of life, wisdom, perseverance in trial, and the spirit of endurance. Without these, they would be as savorless salt, fit only to be cast out. For explanation of the interesting Jewish view of salt, note Section 44, footnote q.

2p-"Have peace one with another." What a sorely needed admonition for then as well as today. Strife and faction among believers are at epidemic proportions, as carnal men and women attempt to lead the Church of God. Christ began this private discourse aimed at His twelve in an effort to resolve their silly arguments about personal greatness. He pointed out that genuine child-like humility was a prerequisite for His kingdom service. Deliberately offending one of His children was serious indeed! The source of offences was to be dealt with even if it seemed as painful as cutting off a body member! He concluded this lesson by declaring that some who fain His service are offenders, and will be banished into the flames that shall never be requited. Previously, He warned that when salt loses its saltiness, it is cast out as pavement for the streets on which men tread.

3p-"No more arguing." In conclusion, He admonished His preachers to stop their bickering about prestige and fame. Instead, they were instructed to be as innocent children and work for peace among themselves and others of like faith, who (for whatever reasons) will not join their group (Mk. 9:38). There are no grounds for ecumenical church relations in these words. The "inter-faith" groups that throw out the fundamental doctrines of the Bible in order to have fellowship with, and build bridges to all religions, are nothing but a conglomeration of Bible ignorant religionists. They blatantly disobey the teachings of the New Testament on Christian separation from major doctrinal error (Rom. 16:17-18). In 2 John 8-11, it is clear regarding the correct and God-honoring attitude that saved believers should demonstrate toward the ecumenists. In these passages, there is nothing unkind or without charity; rather, they are divine instructions for God's people who confront these things. The genuine love of God in a man's heart will compel him to stand when it is *the right time,* and oppose anything that denies His Savior and the *clear* teachings of God's Word. This is real love in action, and if needs be, it can be tough love as well.

(o) "Little ones." Jesus refers to the child He had taken into His arms (Mk. 9:36). The subject of children raised by the Lord, firstly, had antecedent back to John's interruptive question at Mark 9:38-39, and secondly to the apostles continual debating among themselves. Whoever that genuine exorcist was that John mentioned, he was counted by Christ as a true servant in His new kingdom. When he refused to abandon his work and follow the apostles, they accrued a sense of "indignation" and "rejection" toward this unnamed follower of Christ. *"How could he not go with the great twelve apostles?"* Now, the Son of God deals with this arrogant attitude. Christ described him as "one of these little ones," a heavenly title not yet (at this time) understood by the "famed" apostles. First, the "little child" here points to all of God's "children of faith," and is illustrated in the nameless man who refused to join the apostolic band. A second meaning seems to be embedded in this text. Was Jesus warning the apostles against physically turning little children away from His kingdom? *It was a firm custom among the Jews that children were not to be seen in public places; parents were to keep them out of sight.* Though the Jews fiercely loved their children, they were not to intermix in gatherings such as those that flocked around Christ and His disciples. This is a difficult text, but it seems that (along with the contextual thoughts just mentioned) the Savior is correcting a traditional social error about children. It was also a mind-set among His apostles. Later, in Section 138, Matt. 19:13-14, we note the apostles missed this lesson. Here, again, they try to prevent children from coming to their Master!

2p-Angels watching. The Jews believed that each person had a guardian angel, based on Ps. 34:7. This is also suggested in Heb. 1:14. Our Lord may have had this in mind when He spoke of angels beholding God's face. There was a Hebrew belief that pure and unique happiness was to behold the face of God! The Lord Jesus was saying something like this, "Don't you know that each little one has an angel standing before the Father in heaven? You must understand that angels are concerned in them. See me, the Son of God, sitting here with this lad in my arms. Behold, I came down from heaven to save also children from their sins; therefore, forbid them not to be brought to Me." What a lesson on child evangelism! Those who see in this grand event, Jesus sprinkling water on little ones to remit their sins, are having hallucinations. The belief that infants enter the kingdom of Christ or His church by dropping water on their heads in "baptism" is wrong. The absurdity of Reformed "baby faith" is discussed in Section 150, the second paragraph of footnote f. For extended comments on salvation by baptism or communion, and some of the "great men" who believe this untruth, see Section 203, Mk. 16:16, and all eleven paragraphs of footnote d.

Why the Savior came. The apostles are instructed concerning prayer in the new kingdom. Later, at Pentecost, the Holy Spirit endued the twelve* with unique authority, perfect doctrinal knowledge, wisdom to censure the incorrigible, and extraordinary privileges in prayer. Several of these gifts pertained exclusively to them and were never intended for believers of all ages. Many ill-taught Christians have been wounded in their faith, expecting to perform apostolic works and miracles, only to discover they could not.

*Judas Iscariot was replaced by Matthias. The story of his being chosen is recorded in Acts 1:23-26.

Matt. 18:11-25—*Capernaum*	Mk.	Lk.	John
The ultimate purpose of Christ coming into the world(a)			
11 "For the Son of man is come to save that which was lost.(b)			
12 "How think ye? if a man have an hundred sheep, and one of them be gone astray, doth he not leave the ninety and nine, and goeth into the mountains, and seeketh that which is gone astray?			
13 "And if so be that he find it, verily I say unto you, he rejoiceth more of that *sheep*, than of the ninety and nine which went not astray.			
14 "Even so it is not the will of your Father which is in heaven, that one of these little ones should perish.			
Handling offenses correctly			
15 "Moreover if thy brother shall trespass against thee,(c) 'go and tell him his fault between thee' and him alone: if he shall hear thee, thou hast gained thy brother.			
16 "But if he will not hear *thee*, *then* take with thee one or two more, that(d) 'in the mouth of two or three witnesses every word may be established.'			
17 "And if he shall neglect to hear them, tell *it* unto the church:(e) but if he neglect to hear the church, let him be unto thee as an heathen man [Gentile] and a publican. (tax collector)			
18 "Verily I say unto you, Whatsoever ye shall bind(f) on earth shall be bound in heaven: and whatsoever ye shall loose on earth shall be loosed in heaven.			
19 "Again I say unto you, That if two of you shall agree on earth as touching any thing that they shall ask, it shall be done for them of my Father which is in heaven.(g)			
20 "For where two or three are gathered together in my name, there am I in the midst of them."			
Peter's question: its answer			
21 Then came Peter to him, and said, "Lord, how oft shall my brother sin against me, and I forgive him? till seven times?"(h)			
22 Jesus saith unto him, "I say not unto thee, Until seven times: but, Until seventy times seven.(i)			
Answer illustrated by the Parable of the Unmerciful Servant			
23 "Therefore is the kingdom of heaven likened unto a certain king, which would take account of his servants.(j)			
24 "And when he had begun to reckon, one was brought unto him, which owed him ten thousand talents. [if silver about 30 million dollars: if gold about 200 million]			
25 "But forasmuch as he had not to pay, his lord commanded him to			

Matt. 18:25-35—*Capernaum*	Mk.	Lk.	John
be sold, and his wife, and children, and all that he had, and payment to be made.			
26 "The servant therefore fell down, and worshipped him, saying, 'Lord, have patience with me, and I will pay thee all.'			
27 "Then the lord of that servant was moved with compassion, and loosed him, and forgave him the debt.			
28 "But the same servant went out, and found one of his fellowservants, which owed him an hundred pence [about $20.00]: and he laid hands on him, and took *him* by the throat, saying, 'Pay me that thou owest.'			
29 "And his fellowservant fell down at his feet, and besought him, saying, 'Have patience with me, and I will pay thee all.'			
The sin of unforgiveness			
30 "And he would not: but went and cast him into prison, till he should pay the debt.			
31 "So when his fellowservants saw what was done, they were very sorry, and came and told unto their lord all that was done.			
32 "Then his lord, after that he had called him, said unto him, 'O thou wicked servant, I forgave thee all that debt, because thou desiredst [asked] me:			
33 'Shouldest not thou also have had compassion on thy fellowservant, even as I had pity on thee?'			
34 "And his lord was wroth, and delivered him to the tormentors, till he should pay all that was due unto him.			
The conclusion of the matter:			
beware of not truly forgiving those who offend you			
35 "So likewise shall my heavenly Father do also unto you, if ye from your hearts forgive not every one his brother their trespasses."(k) (Next chap., Matt. 19:1 cont. in Section 137.)			

Footnotes–Commentary

(a) In view of the horrific warnings given by the Lord Jesus in Mk. 9:44, 46, and 48 regarding the eternal suffering of the damned, He suddenly declares His chief reason for coming to earth and dwelling among men. In verses 12-14, He illustrates this by the example of the lost sheep being sought, found, and saved.

(b) **Verse 11. "Save the lost."** Contextually, this has first reference to unsaved children who are old enough to understand the gospel. Declaring again, His chief purpose for coming to earth, our Lord in this passage ties His great mission to the salvation of children, as previously mentioned in Section 109, Matt. 18:10. He then proceeds to illustrate this in verse 12-14 by the common example of a lost sheep. Note Section 129, Lk. 15:3-7 for a later use of this same parable. Verse 14 above is conclusive that His lesson was to reveal that God in heaven does not want one of these children to perish. Near the end of His work, Jesus beautifully demonstrated that He was seeking the lost when He found the publican, Zacchaeus, up in a tree near Jericho. See this in Section 144, Lk. 19:10. His claim of searching for the lost had been thoroughly exhibited over the course of His ministry. The child He embraced at that moment was like the sheep, helpless, without understanding, and depending upon someone else for rescue or salvation. He instructed the apostles to go "into the mountains" (the unknown and dangerous places) to seek the straying ones for God. This means all, including little children, for they must be instructed in the gospel preparatory to their personal salvation through faith in Christ (2 Tim. 3:14-15).

2p-**Verse 14. "Little ones should perish."** Again, the Savior is speaking by illustration of the little one in His arms (Mk. 9:36. Those who teach that children are saved by infant baptism speak a vicious untruth. The "baptizing of infants" for remission of sins, and praying for "elect children to be born into Christian families" is as pagan as the heathen priests bowing before the altars of Baal and Ashtaroth. For comments on Israel being the church and circumcision pointing to baptism, see Section 138, and all under footnote a. On the Reformed myth of "baby faith," see Section 150, second paragraph of footnote f.

(c) A free quotation apparently taken from Lev. 19:17, where the Law of Moses commanded the people of Israel to seek quick reconciliation in every conflict situation. Contextually, our Lord makes direct reference *back* to the argument that had again exploded among the twelve, as explained in Section 109, Mk. 9:33, footnote a. His remarks at this place were spoken first to the apostles, because of their hostile attitudes against each other. Most problems among Christians, who are of reasonable and honest disposition, would be resolved quickly if this Word from Christ was heeded. The command *"between thee and him alone"* (a private discussion) would cut the tongue out of old man gossip.

(d) Cited generally from Deut. 19:15. Being thorough Jews, the Lord quoted to the twelve the demands of Moses' Law as an example of how to resolve personal conflicts. This is an excellent example of a spiritual lesson being taken from the Torah. The rabbis wisely stressed that individuals meet and end their difference to avoid public scandal and courts of law. If this failed, then several witnesses were called to hear the dispute. Christ takes certain lessons from the Jewish teachers and the Torah Law, and lays them before the apostles as guidelines in handling their disagreements. The apostles will be the unique future leaders of His new kingdom, especially when it later became popularly known as the church, as seen in the history of Acts. They must get these things straight, in view of the serious work ahead. In all such instances as this one, the citation from the law was *again* a very good schoolmaster. For Christian usage of parts of the Torah Law during this present age and various spiritual meanings found in the law, see Section 45, number 5, the third paragraph under footnote h.

(e) **Verse 17. "Tell *it* unto the church."** *At this time in the ministry of Christ, "the church" did not exist, as it was known later, especially in the book of Acts and the epistles.* However, it did exist in embryo form in the presence of His new kingdom, but this was not yet understood. It has been continually pointed out in this harmony commentary, the apostles, disciples and all religious Jews were looking for a literal, material kingdom to be established, with Israel ruling the world. They were fed this rabbinical teaching, as they had been their mother's milk! In view of this fact, the concept of the New Testament church was foreign to their thinking at this time. The Savior can only be speaking of a *future* function that would be practiced in the local assemblies yet to be established. In addition, it would be the unique responsibility of the apostles to execute their Lord's commands in these assemblies during the early decades. In time, Paul's letters containing directions for church polity became the *permanent* guide sources for the correct functioning of the Christian assembly.

2p-Later, the apostles remembered these things, *after* the coming of the Spirit at Pentecost. Note the promise of Section 175, John 14:26, footnote n, which was given exclusively to these men. Christ pre-instructs them about specific problems that will rise within the local churches. Here, we meet those incorrigible persons, who by design and wickedness, refuse to be reconciled with God or man. Many of them audibly say so. The apostles were told to count such as "heathens and publicans," after they have rejected every appeal to return to God. The Jewish apostles instantly understood their Lord's use of these two descriptive terms. (What church today would count someone as a heathen-Gentile or publican?)

3p-Christ warns that there will be men in the future churches who will not get right with God and their fellows; they were to be removed by special apostolic authority from the assembly of believers, just as heathens and publicans were shut out of the inner court of the temple and synagogues. When the apostles could not be present to handle such affairs, it was committed into the hands of the leaders of the local church. See 1 Cor. 5:1-8 for a clear example, and Section 47, Matt. 7:6, third and fourth paragraphs under footnote c, for more on incorrigible persons in the local church. Prov. 22:10 gives the exact instruction on how to handle this kind of people.

(f) **"Binding and loosing."** For comments on this strange subject, see Section 103, Matt. 16:19, footnote i.

(g) **"Two or three agree."** This is a positive promise that whatever the issue, God will grant the answer in prayer. It was a prerogative guaranteed *only* for the twelve and exercised by them in the first and early churches. See main heading above in this Section, for further explanation. The numeric used here had reference back to the "two or three" called in to settle disputes as commanded in the Law of Moses (verse 16). See footnote d above. What the law did well, grace did better. Keeping the *historical interpretation* of this text in view, the Lord Jesus was *not* establishing a fixed quorum for an approved prayer meeting, in which prayer was infallibly guaranteed to be answered.

2p-In the Jewish communities of this time, "two or three" men would come together to decide certain issues and resolve various problems among the Hebrew people. See footnote h below, for more on this subject. The rabbis based this on Eccles. 4:9-12. In the synagogues, ten men would resolve the questions at hand. It was from these well-known and long practiced Jewish customs, that our Lord took His lesson and laid down directions for His twelve, as they would lead His spiritual kingdom or church in the years ahead. It should be remembered that Matthias replaced Judas (Acts 1:26). The author of this work is not saying that "two or three" must never assemble for special times of prayer, especially in emergencies. However, he is saying that a guaranteed answer to their requests, as laid down by Christ in verse 19, *was first* vouchsafed for the apostles, who were the supreme leaders of the original and earliest churches. Because this is not understood among many Christians, it has resulted in bitter disillusionments, because various things have been "claimed" from God (in prayer groups) that did not happen.

3p-The following illustrates the above lesson: years ago, the author was lecturing at a Dutch Reformed Church in the Eastern Cape Province of South Africa. During these meetings, a farmer's wife drove some two hundred miles in order to inform me, "God's Word was not true about two or three agreeing in prayer." Upon asking, "why" she replied in tears, "My mother-in-law was dying with cancer. We gathered about her bed and claimed these passages from Matt. 18:19-20. She was not healed and died a week later." I tried to explain to her the background and history of these passages. However, to no avail! This woman left the meeting, and drove the two hundred miles home, thoroughly disillusioned because her prayers were not answered for the greatly loved mother-in-law. *The many grievous ills that result from a misinterpretation and then misapplication of Scripture are as high as the mountains.* This is not the fault of God's Word, but finite man, who has failed to study and understand what a particular text may be teaching from its historical and cultural background.

(h) Verse 21. "Till seven times?" For the meaning of "two or three," see the second paragraph of footnote g above. At this period in Hebrew history, there existed a firm practice among the Jews that one should forgive his fellow *only three times* and no more! See the Talmud tractate, Yoma 86b for an illustration. They based this on another perverted rabbinical interpretation of Scripture, this time from Amos 1:3 and 2:6. For a later discussion of the subject of forgiveness, see Section 132, footnotes e and f. In view of what his Lord had just said to them about forgiveness, the apostle Peter was dumbfounded. Again, the false rabbinical teachings clashed with the commands of the Messiah. Peter, inquiring about this theological teaching, selected a number ("seven times") one more than doubled that required by the Torah teachers for forgiveness.

(i) First, read all of footnote h above. In response, the Lord Jesus quotes another rabbinical maxim to Simon Peter, the bewildered former fisherman. The Jewish teachers affirmed that the numbers "seventy times seven" signified infinity. This was based on Gen. 4:24. Thus, our Lord informs His troubled apostle that forgiveness of others is without bounds or limits; it lies within the endlessness of infinity! It must have amazed Peter to hear that a man can be forgiven and should forgive thousands of times (unlimited) over the course of his life. He had never heard any rabbi teach such amazing things!

(j) The Savior responds to Peter with the Parable of the Unmerciful Servant. Realizing that he was again dumbfounded at His teachings, the Lord commenced to illustrate what He had just said. He introduced the lesson as applicable to His kingdom. According to verse 35, (where Jesus explains the meaning of His lesson) this parable in no way depicts the conversion of the unsaved. It deals with forgiveness. The meaning is, "We had better forgive from our hearts every person who sins against us." It is clear from Section 109, Mk. 9:33-34, footnote a, and the main heading of Section 142, that there was a power struggle among the apostles. They harbored grudges, and held ill feelings against their fellows; hence, our Lord's strong Words on this subject. Note the second paragraph of footnote k below for more on this. In this parable, we note the following:

1. Two men were in debt; one to his king, the other to his fellow. One owed ten thousand talents, or loosely thirty million dollars, if silver was the coinage meant. The second owed a hundred pence, or approximately twenty dollars (verses 23-24 with 28).
2. Being summoned before his king to whom the money was owed, the first man fell before his majesty and begged mercy, lest his family be sold to reduce his enormous debt. To his amazement, the king, moved by compassion, frankly forgave him of all. He secured absolute forgiveness because his lord was a man of compassion and mercy (verses 24-27).
3. The forgiven servant found a fellow who was indebted to him for the sum of a hundred pence. In wild fury, he choked his fellow servant and had him thrown into prison until the debt was paid. He refused to show mercy with the servant who had begged for pity (verses 28-30).
4. Word of the ruthlessness of the first servant traveled to the king (verse 31).
5. Raging with indignation, the king reprimanded the servant. He had received a free pardon but refused to show the same mercy to a fellow servant (verses 32-33).
6. The cruel servant was thrown into the torture chamber of the prison. He was sentenced to suffer until he had repaid his debt, which was laid again to his charge (verse 34). Friends and family members would often raise the needed money to pay the amount owed, and thus secure his release.

(k) Verse 35. It is impossible to portray free salvation and the forgiveness of sins in this parable. In no way can the king picture God. Though he forgave the first servant, he later reinstated his forgiven debt, threw the man into prison and left him there until all was paid (which according to verse 24 was an impossible amount). At this period in history, no servant could have repaid thirty million dollars to anybody, not even his king. God does not change His mind about our sins after they are forgiven. See number 6 above. The prison cannot picture hell. Men are *not* promised deliverance from torment if they repay what they owe. One believer cannot cast another believer into hell.

2p-"Likewise shall my heavenly Father." These Words of Christ mean that God will act similarly (but not altogether) as the king did in Jesus' lesson. He will deal with men in whatever way He sees fit, to those who do not forgive "from their hearts" the trespasses committed against them. *This speaks of fellowship forgiveness, not salvation forgiveness.* Fellowship forgiveness is horizontal and runs across the earth from man to man; salvation forgiveness is vertical and runs from God down to man. The chief purpose of this lesson was for His apostles, who were entangled in wrangling with one another. The Master sought to ward off the dark shadow of petty feelings, struggles for fame, carrying, personal supremacy, and the awful blight of continual jealously among His preachers.

3p-Again, see Section 109, Mk. 9:33-34, footnote a, for more about their bickering along with the first paragraph of footnote j above. *To these fussy, antagonistic preachers, this parable was first spoken.* Later, the meaning struck deep in their hearts and manifested itself in their lives and ministry.

4p-The closed canon of Holy Scripture. The lesson given here was applicable to His kingdom or church, especially in the years ahead. He was training them well. Regardless of how enormous the trespasses are against us, they are to be forgiven as the king forgave his debtor in verses 26-27. Later, the Holy Spirit would bring the total of Christ's teachings to their memory with perfect understanding of everything He had taught them. Endued with this, they became the able leaders of the first churches in the New Testament. As these uniquely endowed apostles died out, God gave His people the closed and complete New Testament. It was joined to the Old as His full and final revelation to mankind. God's progressive revelation finally culminated in the twenty-seven books of the New Testament. Numerous interpretations often abound regarding various biblical doctrines. It is further true, that on the basic, fundamental teachings of the Christian faith, such as the virgin birth, blood atonement of Christ, His bodily resurrection, and ascension, and salvation through repentance and faith, there is no room for disagreement. Men either believe the basics and are saved, or they die damned. *Seasoned soldiers of the faith refuse to budge one inch on any of these essential doctrines of eternal truth!*

5p-Cults covering up their record. Persons operating under the guise of Christianity often add the "writings of their founders" to the closed canon of Holy Scripture. This is demonstrated in the Church of Jesus Christ of Latter Day Saints, the Seventh Day Adventist and others. They continually refer to their Book of Mormon and the writings of Ellen G. White and place these on equal footing with the Bible. Of course, the advocates of these cults strongly deny this, but one reading of their literature reveals otherwise. This does not decry the use of helps in the study of God's Word, but it does oppose any writing that places itself on par with or above the closed canon of inspired Holy Scriptures. If extra biblical literature agrees with the Bible, it is right. If it disagrees with the Bible, it is wrong. This is the litmus test for the children of God. Doctrinal integrity is one of the most urgent issues for any local church. The Adventists defend the inspiration of Scripture, the fact of creation, the deity of Christ, and other critical doctrines of the Bible. However, they openly deny the reality of hell, the fact of the human soul being a separate entity from the physical body, and other teachings. Their defense of *some* of the traditional truths of Holy Scripture is the bait on a sucker's hook, taken by the gullible. They deny that they rely upon Sabbath keeping (and other things) as a means of salvation. We are not saved by grace and then kept saved by keeping parts of the law.

6p-Sheep that are wolves. The author of this work served as principal of a small Bible School on the central coast of Queensland, Australia. Nearby was an Adventist training center and stronghold. He had many encounters with these people. On one occasion, a farmer invited him to his home to "discuss the Bible." Entering Ian's house, there sat four Adventist preachers ready to fight! After two hours of verbal discussion, not one of these men could give a clear-cut testimony of their conversion to Christ. Continually, they pressured me about worshiping on the Sabbath; man does not have a soul which is a separate entity from the human body; there is no eternal conscious suffering of the damned, and that their church had God's truth for the world. Any church or individual that denies the reality of hell, personal know-so salvation, and seeks to live under any of the 613 parts of the Hebrew Torah Law is wrong. In *The Kingdom of the Cults*, by Walter Martin (a "cult expert") and general editor Ravi Zacharias, one is stunned, that in Appendix B, are over a hundred pages that present this cult as Christian, while calling some of their teachings "heterodox concepts." The late Dr. Walter Martin practically stood on his head to clear Ellen G. White, William Miller, and other Adventists of their demonic doctrines. Someone described it as "whitewashing the Devil." In the early 1955 edition of *The Kingdom of the Cults,* Martin classified the Adventist Church as a cult but later changed his mind. In *Christianity Today,* Dec. 19, 1960, page 15 he wrote, "Adventists should be recognized as Christians and that fellowship should be extended to them we do not deny." Thousands saved out of this false religion would disagree with him. Any church that claims to be right and all others wrong, by this admission classify themselves as a cult. In the *Seventh Day Adventist Church Manual,* revised edition 1995, pages 30-31, we read one of the requirements before administering baptism to a prospective church member. They are asked, "Do you accept and believe that the Seventh-day Adventist Church is the remnant church of Bible prophecy . . . ?" Regardless of the Ellen's White heresy, Jesus is not Michael, the archangel. He is God and always has been. There is a burning, conscious hell, and men do have souls that leave the physical body at death. The mark of the beast is not going to church on Sunday. Christians do not live under the Ten Commandments and Sabbath keeping vanished at the cross. Miller and White's "Investigative judgment" is blasphemy. Why does the "Seventh Day Adventist remnant church" sneak about and conceal their identity behind health foods, archaeological seminars, radio and television broadcasts, slick colored children's books, magazines, and so forth? The author of this work left a church Sunday service early due to prior commitments. Setting at the door was a box filled with Adventist books about Sabbath keeping. Two women were running across the parking lot and would not stop when we called to them! The older woman was identified as a member of the Adventist cult.

Jesus returns to Nazareth.* He is ridiculed by His half-brothers because of His national fame. They challenge Him to attend the Feast of Tabernacles and publicly demonstrate His Messiahship.** After His family departs, Christ starts for Jerusalem but travels covertly through Samaria. ***

*It is being assumed that our Lord's family still lived at Nazareth. See Section 91, footnote a, for His previously recorded visit to this small town in which He grew up and the surprising aftermath of that visit. According to the syntax of verse 3 below, He was with family members, apparently at Nazareth. **This is precisely what He did midway during this great celebration. For details, see Section 119. ***For His secret trip through Samaria to Jerusalem, see verse 10 below, with the main heading of Section 112, Lk. 9:51-52, footnote b. One can only build a fragmented chronology for Christ's life during this time. God inspired it to be written this way.*

Matt.	Mk.	Lk.	John 7:2-10—Galilee and Jerusalem
			His half-brothers reveal their contempt
			2 Now the Jews' feast of tabernacles(a) was at hand.
			3 His brethren(b) therefore said unto him, "Depart hence, and go into Judaea, that thy disciples [there] also may see the works that thou doest.
			4 "For *there is* no man *that* doeth any thing in secret, and he himself seeketh to be known openly. If thou do these things, shew thyself to the world."(c)
			5 For neither did his brethren believe in him.(d)
			His response and secret departure for Jerusalem
			6 Then Jesus said unto them, "My time(e) [to go to the feast] is not yet come: but your time [to go] is alway ready. (whenever you choose)
			7 "The world cannot hate you; but me it hateth, because I testify of it, that the works thereof are evil.(f)
			8 "Go ye up unto this feast: I go not up yet unto this feast; for my time [to go] is not yet full come." (or ready)
			9 When he had said these words unto them, he abode *still* [a short while] in Galilee.(g)
			10 But when his brethren were gone up, then went he also up unto the feast, not openly, but as it were in secret.(h) (Verse 11 cont. in Section 119.)

Footnotes-Commentary

(a) **Feast of Tabernacles.** This celebration of joy at harvest usually occurred in October. An explanation of this grand event in Israel is given in Section 119, footnote a. From the April Passover in John 6:4, to this Feast of Tabernacles in John 7:1-2, was a period of about six months. *Assuming* that the Passover in John 6:4 occurred *after* the feeding of the five thousand and the uproar in the Capernaum synagogue, John tells us *nothing* of what transpired over this six-months, period of time. (It is *conjectured* that Christ fed the five thousand *before* this particular Passover, otherwise the crowds of people would have been at the temple preparing for the feast instead of up north in Galilee following Jesus.) This harmony commentary considers Sections 112 (when He departed for Bethany), through Section 117 (when He arrived at Bethany), as occurring over these six months ending with the Feast of Tabernacles. Only Luke was inspired to record the events in Sections 112 through 118.

(b) **Jesus' half-brothers.** Oddly, various commentaries attempt to reinterpret these words. They mean exactly what they say: His four half-brothers did not believe at this point that He was the Messiah and were hostile to His ministry and public fame. It appears, they deliberately tried to entice Him into Judaea (verse 3) where death was waiting at the hands of the Sanhedrin. Whether they were aware of this or not is unknown. See Section 91, Matt. 13:55-56, footnote d for more on Jesus' family and the names of His four half-brothers.

(c) **"Shew thyself to the world."** This sarcasm was addressed to the Lord Jesus by His half-brothers. It reeks with animosity. They were saying, in effect, "Let everyone see your great works as the Messiah of Israel and go to Jerusalem that all may see." Apparently, they had forgotten that He did this at the outset of His ministry, about three years prior, when He exhibited His Messiahship before the Passover crowds. See Section 29 for the story.

(d) Meaning that they did not believe on Him as the Messiah. The household of Christ was disturbed and fearful about His disfavor with the leaders of religion, and the serious divisions among the Jewish people over His ministry and claims. The Master could have fallen into a debate with His family over this issue, but He did not. *Arguing among family members over the things of God is a sign of serious trouble; it should never be allowed.* Later, their unbelief was corrected. Lastly, we find His family in the upper room just before Pentecost, waiting for the coming of the Holy Spirit in unprecedented power. Note this in Section 207, Acts 1:14. After Pentecost, Jesus' family vanishes from the inspired pages of Scripture. Early tradition assigns the books of James and Jude to His half-brothers.

(e) **"My time."** As explained above in the text brackets of verses 6, 8, and 9, referred to the time when Jesus would walk down to Jerusalem from Nazareth of Galilee and observe the feast. It is to be noted that He did not appear at the temple until the middle of its eight days, as seen in John 7:14. Hence, the words to the half-brothers that, "His time had not come to go down to the feast." Contextually, these are not words that spoke of His time to die on the cross, but rather to depart from Nazareth for Jerusalem. For the usage of the terms "my hour," and "my time," when referring to His crucifixion, note Section 27, John 2:4, footnote f.

(f) **The world is evil.** This is the final analysis of the *unsaved world's* attitude regarding the higher things of God and Christ. The believer, who *correctly* speaks out against the sin and folly of this world, will eventually find himself the object of scorn and hatred. It was so with our Lord, and it will ultimately be no different with Christians of every generation. *This world system is not the friend of God, His dear Son, or His people.* In this verse, the Son of God has well described the entire world system which is under the control of Satan (2 Cor. 4:4 with Rev. 12:9 and 1 John 5:19). He spoke a similar thing the night before the morning of the cross in Section 176, John 15:18, footnote o. This does not mean that Christians are to withdraw from society and live as hermits or in recluse places. Rather, the people of God are to be the best citizens, law abiding, always seeking to conduct themselves in a noble and honorable fashion toward all men. Where radical Islam, raw paganism, and godless communism, or other Antichrist systems of government rule, Christians are often forced to withdraw from society, live, and worship God in a covert manner. James 4:4, "whosoever therefore will be a friend of the world is the enemy of God" has reference to believers supporting obvious wicked things and the devices of darkness. 1 John 2:15, carries a similar message for God's people. Jude warned believers to keep themselves "unspotted by the flesh" (Jude 23). The unsaved world systems of today often give some sickly nod to the Bible, God, and Jesus Christ. However, at the end of the day, they are the enemies of genuine righteousness and faith in Christ. "The world by [it's] wisdom knew not God" (1 Cor. 1:21).

(g) Meaning He deliberately waited until His mocking brothers had departed for Jerusalem. See footnote h below. Several months earlier, He had previously *avoided* re-entering Judaea ("would not walk in Jewry"), because the Jews in Jerusalem wanted to kill him. See Section 95, John 7:1, footnote y, located at the end of Scripture verses in that Section. At this time, Galilee and Judaea were each under separate jurisdictions. Herod Antipas ruled over Galilee, while Pilate served as procurator over Judaea. These two rulers hated each other and frequently, someone in trouble in one jurisdiction would flee to the other for protection. For the quarrel between Pilate and Herod, and how Christ resolved it, see Section 184, Lk. 23:12, footnote f.

(h) **Jesus travels in stealth.** It is noteworthy that Christ made His way south to the temple and the Feast of Tabernacles celebration *after* the departure of His half-brothers. Only then was He free to begin the trip of about three days' journey. Yet, He went by stealth under some method of secrecy or disguise and took the forbidden route through Samaria. Some Jews would take this road when walking to Jerusalem, as it was by far the shortest route. However, it could be dangerous, for occasionally, hostile Samaritans attacked Jews traveling their roads, and killed many of them.

2p-Normally, the Samaritans only objected to Jews traveling southward through their land to Jerusalem during their seven annual celebrations at the temple. These events are explained in Lev. 23. Travelers moving from Judaea through Samaria in the northerly direction usually met no opposition from the Samaritan people. Regardless, it was true that most Jews would not travel this route out of sheer contempt for the Samaritan people. We have previously noted the Lord Jesus traveling through Samaria moving northward for Galilee and the great spiritual awakening that occurred when He met the Samaritan woman at the well. This wonderful story is recorded in Sections 34 and 35. At best, it was risky business to travel this road to Jerusalem during the annual Jewish Feasts. Pilgrims going to these various celebrations usually traveled together as families. Often, entire villages traveled as a large company if they were passing via Samaria. This promoted a sense of security among the pilgrims.

3p-The Lord Jesus deliberately avoided public attention from the crowds making their way down the eastern side of the Jordan River to the temple for the celebration of Tabernacles. Being "wise as a serpent," He walked the lesser traveled road that led through Samaria. Note Section 59, Matt. 10:16 footnote k, for the meaning of "wise as a serpent." He knew the religious leaders and thousands of curious Jews would be watching for Him along the main roads that led to Jerusalem. Thus, He avoided them. His fame had spread across Samaria as well, and thousands of these people knew Him. They had heard Him preach and witnessed His mighty works. His previous visit to Sychar in Samaria (now well over two years ago), and the hundreds that believed on Him in that village demonstrate this fact.

Jesus leaves Nazareth for Bethany and Jerusalem. Selected messengers are sent ahead to prepare for His arrival along the way.* Upon His rejection by a Samaritan village, James and John react inappropriately. He sharply rebuked them.

*See Section 21, Part 1, footnote a, for comments on the origin and work of a forerunner who was to prepare the way for persons of great notoriety soon to appear. Following this rejection, Jesus sent seventy other evangelists ahead to prepare for His arrival as He passed through the land. This event is recorded in Section 113, Lk. 10:1. For the Samaritans receiving the Son of God, refer to footnote b below.

Matt.	Mk.	Lk. 9:51-62—Galilee - Samaria	John
		Making ready His trip through	
		Samaria He sends messengers or forerunners ahead	
		51 And it came to pass, when the time was come that he should be received up,(a) he stedfastly set his face to go to Jerusalem,(b)	
		52 And sent messengers before his face: and they went, and entered into a village(c) of the Samaritans, to make ready for him.	
		A certain village refuses to receive Him: the reaction of	
		two apostles and Jesus' strong rebuke	
		53 And they did not receive him, because his face [turned south] was as though he would go to Jerusalem.	
		54 And when his disciples James and John saw *this*, they said, "Lord, wilt thou that we command fire to come down from heaven, and consume them, even as Elias [Elijah] did?"(d)	
		55 But he turned, and rebuked them, and said, "Ye know not what manner of spirit ye are of.(e)	
		56 "For the Son of man is not come to destroy men's lives, but to save *them*." And they went to another village.(f)	
		Jesus deals with two half-hearted followers	
		1. "I will follow thee regardless"	
		57 And it came to pass, that, as they went in the way,(g) a certain *man* said unto him, "Lord, I will follow thee whithersoever thou goest."	
		58 And Jesus said unto him, "Foxes have holes,(h) and birds of the air *have* nests; but the Son of man hath not where to lay *his* head."	
		2. "I will follow thee but first"	
		59 And he said unto another, "Follow me." But he said, Lord, suffer [let] me first to go and bury my father.	
		60 Jesus said unto him, "Let the dead bury their dead:(i) but go thou and preach the kingdom of God."	
		61 And another also said, "Lord, I will follow thee; but let me first go bid them farewell, which are at home at my house."(j)	
		No looking back in God's work: press ahead	
		62 And Jesus said unto him, "No man, having put his hand to the plough, and looking back, is fit [for service] for the kingdom of God."(k)	
		(Next chap., Lk. 10:1 cont. in Section 113.)	

Footnotes-Commentary

(a) **"Received up."** This refers to His hour of death, which was at this time some six months away; here, the Lord Jesus departed His family home at Capernaum heading for Jerusalem. He began making His way southward toward Judaea for the observance of the Feast of Tabernacles celebration. His apostles and others accompanied Him. This trip must have taken several weeks.

(b) **"Set his face to go to Jerusalem."** We cannot know what lies before us in life. Some awful sorrow may be waiting on the morrow, but it casts no gloom over our spirits today. This is God's merciful provision. If we knew all that we must pass through in the future, it would make us prisoners of fear. It is good that we cannot know until God leads us to the edge of the experience. However, there was no such kind veiling of the future from the eyes of Jesus.

He foresaw every step of the sorrowful way to the close of His human life. This makes it all the more glorious. Knowing it all, see how eagerly He presses to the cross. Setting His face to Jerusalem, Gethsemane, Gabbatha, and finally Golgotha, each step was taken with intense haste. Here, before us is the greatest example of heroism in all the pages of history. The accomplishment of His mission would bring forgiveness and eternal life for all who trust Him as personal Lord and Savior. Shame should blush our faces and hearts with red as we behold our slackness and procrastination to give all to Him and His grand service.

2p-"Setting one's face" was an eastern expression meaning to do something with strong determination. Taking the more direct, but often forbidden road that led through Samaria, He sent several disciples ahead to secure lodging and ask permission to preach and teach in certain villages on His route. Seemingly, the Lord Jesus was mostly received by the Samaritans as He passed through their land. This is strange indeed, in view of the fierce hatred that existed between these two nations. During the times of Israel's annual celebrations, few Jews would walk the shorter distance to Jerusalem via Samaria. There were times when the Samaritans would ambush and kill them in great companies. Perhaps the good name of Jesus, His works and love for all men, had spread over Samaria and these people saw in Him a different kind of Hebrew. Beyond doubt, His visit to the village of Sychar, almost two years earlier and what came out of that had spread over the land. Refer to this in Sections 34 and 35. Whatever the reason, many of the outcast Samaritan people held sympathy with Christ while the religious Jews hated Him.

(c) Verse 52. Messengers. These men are different from the seventy preachers sent out shortly afterwards, as seen in Lk. 10:1. Somewhere along the way, a particular Samaritan village had flatly refused to prepare accommodation for the coming Savior. To do so was a high insult in that culture. The reason is given, "his face was towards Jerusalem." This expression meant that the Samaritans knew that Jesus, and His followers were going south to keep the Feast of Tabernacles to be celebrated at Jerusalem. Note Section 119. footnote a for explanation of this.

2p-As previously mentioned, there were times when the Samaritans killed Jews traveling toward the temple to keep their annual religious celebrations. For more on the Hebrew-Samaritan conflict and hatred, see Section 116, footnote j. For some unknown reason, this particular village was hostile to Christ and refused Him entrance. For more on the hatred that prevailed between the Samaritans and Israel, refer to Section 34, all of footnote a.

(d) Over zealous preachers. Apparently, James and John were the two messengers sent ahead to prepare the way for Christ. They were offended at this blunt refusal of hospitality! It was considered one of the highest insults among the people of this land. Such an act only ignited the flame of vengeance in the hearts of the "sons of thunder." Their remedy boomed out, "Let's kill them like Elijah did." (Apparently, they remembered the fierce hatred the rabbis preached that the Jews should have for *all* Samaritans.) Recalling that Elijah had brought fire down twice on God's enemies, therefore, why not do the same to these men who had refused to welcome the Messiah into their village (1 Kings 18:38 with 2 Kings 1:10, 12)? This action of the two apostles reveals that men can pluck a verse here and there from Holy Writ and "prove" anything they choose. On this occasion, James and John stand as a classical example of forcing God's Word to accommodate their attitude be it good or bad. When wild zealotry seizes a man's mind, he instantly believes that the Almighty approves whatever his religious passions dictate. He can burn, imprison, ban, torture, and kill, all in the Name of God! Worse, he believes the Lord of heaven blesses his madness and cites verses from the Bible to prove it!

2p-**Examples of "Christian" tyrants.** These religious monsters included the Roman Catholic system, Anglican, Presbyterian, radical Anabaptists, various separatist's bodies, secular governments, and others. John Calvin's control over Geneva through the sword of the magisterial reformers, demonstrated this. For a brief coverage of these things, see Will Durant's, *The Story of Civilization*, vol. 6. pages 459-490. Believing they were the elect of God, nothing moved the Reformers from their mad course. They banished, crushed, and killed anything that stood in their way, but always with "God's approval." John Calvin adhered to the barbarity of the Catholic Church out of which he came. Those who disagreed with him were called "filth," "villainy," and "mad dogs who vomit their filth against the Majesty of God." The Papal Church has struggled to clear herself from horrific sex scandals, infamy, perversion, murder, and the awful bloodguilt of her history. Her claims of infallibility are trampled into the dirt by her wicked deeds. Likewise, many Anglicans, Reformed, and Presbyterian "Christians" refuse to accept the barbaric deeds of their religious ancestors. Equally hypocritical are those Baptists, who attempt to exonerate the ruthless Anabaptist of Münster, Germany (1533-1535) who murdered and butchered to establish the "New Jerusalem," and wait for "Jesus to return." Others could be added to this religious black list. Scripture calls religious men who commit such deeds, "natural brute beasts" (2 Peter 2:12). Read about the first religious murderer in history in 1 John 3:11-12. On the other side are the ecumenical religionists who throw out the foundational Bible doctrines in the name of "reconciliation and unity." The words of the humanistic, Anglican philosopher, Sir Francis Beacon (died 1626) fits this scenario, "We prefer to believe what we prefer to be true." Nevertheless, how refreshing to find those Christians, who will not "dance to the piper's music" in the work of God. Like Nehemiah of old, they hurry to confess their sins and the sins of their fathers (Neh. 1:4-11). In much of today's ecclesiology, the ugly facts just mentioned above have become "philosophical assumptions," open to anyone's interpretation. In the days of Malachi, the priests were the teachers of God's truth. To them, Jehovah said, "For the priest's lips should keep knowledge . . ."

(Mal. 2:7). "Learned theologians" often "shuffle history" to justify their denominational line or personal agendas. A long-time professor of church history in a "fundamentalist institution" said that the barbaric deeds of certain Christian men of centuries past are "relics of yesteryear." Scripture disagrees with this venerable old gentleman. It reads, "For God shall bring every work into judgment, with every secret thing, whether *it be* good, or whether *it be* evil" (Eccles. 12:14). Those "church history experts" who cover up the wickedness of Christian tyrants of the past and present, live in a dark corner. What they fain not to know, the Lord of heaven knows! Nahum 1:3, states that God will "not acquit" the wicked. The Bible is emphatic "that no murderer hath eternal life abiding in him" (1 John 3:15). "Christian" tyrants are no different from non-Christian tyrants. Unless saved and forgiven, *both* have reservations in hell.

3p-The conniving of James, John, and their mother. Regarding the ill-founded actions of James and John, mentioned in footnote d above, we note that later they invented a special plot! In Section 142, second paragraph of footnote b, the two brothers attempted to secure for themselves exalted but carnal positions in Christ's literal kingdom. (They wrongly thought it was soon to appear.) Their mother assisted them in this scheme. From the beginning, men have wrangled for prominence in politics, religion, and even Christianity. This would give them a sense of spiritual superiority. They believe that their way is the right way. The pages of the Holy Bible are clear: only Jesus Christ, the Son of the Living God, is the way, the truth, and the life. *Besides Him, there is none other.* When radical religious zealots use His Name and Word to achieve their unholy purposes, it is enough to make the angels weep! There have been millions of these spiritually deranged people over the course of church history.

(e) Turning about, Jesus looked with stern countenance upon the two brothers and set forth to rebuke their uncontrolled zeal. After following the Lamb of God for over two years, these men did not yet understand what it meant to be His disciple-apostle. Had they not by personal observation seen that He was the friend of sinners? His response touches us deeply. How comforting to hear our Lord say that He came "to save men's lives." He not only delivers our souls from eternal perdition, but also saves our lives from the ravages and depredations of sin and Satan in this world. What a wonderful Savior we have, whose infinite care for His own covers our every step in this perilous world, and will continue with us throughout all eternity (Heb. 13:5).

(f) **Jesus passed them by.** What a pitiful epithet to be inscribed on the tombstone of that unnamed Samarian village. Standing at their gates had been the Son of God from heaven, the Savior of the world. *They refused Him entrance!* Men in today's world commit the same crime. This does not mean that every village in Samaria rejected Christ. Turning on His heel, the Shepherd of the flock led them "to another village." A stark contrast to this eternal mistake made by these people had occurred almost three years prior, when the village of Sychar invited the Lord Jesus to come home with them. See the beautiful story in Section 35, footnotes j and k.

(g) "Went in the way," meaning "on the road," as they travelled through Samaria for Bethany and Jerusalem.

(h) For explanation of these words, see Section 87, Matt. 8:20, footnote c.

(i) Here is another odd term in Scripture. It is explained in Section 87, Matt. 8:22, footnote d.

(j) Apparently, our Lord had drawn to Himself an enthusiastic band of "would be" evangelists who wanted to follow Him at their convenience! Christ is not mitigating the blessing of showing family and filial respect. Rather, He is saying, "You must hold Me first above any duty, regardless of how honorable and noble it may be." To love and honor the Son of God above all things in this life is to love all things in this life correctly (Phil 2:9-11).

(k) **Looking back while plowing.** This ancient expression has been used for thousands of years. Our Lord employed this metaphor to illustrate a wholehearted dedication in serving Him. To "put one's hand to the plough" [plow] was a proverb that signified the undertaking of whatever business or duty that was at hand. The plowman must remain intent on his work, never looking back. *Those who continually look back to this world as they serve God, leave behind rows that are crooked or snaked.* The twisted rows left by those who did not seriously consider what they were doing in "Christian service" must number in the millions. The testimony of Christ has been deeply scarred over the past two thousand years by these incompetent laborers. Wherever men plow, it is a great pride for them to make perfectly straight furrows into which seed will be sown. In the Talmud tractate, Makkoth, precise instructions are given for Hebrew plowmen. Every mature person in His audience understood this lesson.

2p-Contextually, Christ is telling this pretended evangelist (verses 61-62) that he should return home and stay; for having a double mind, he could only produce "snaked rows." This rebuke has nothing to do with salvation; men are not saved from sin and hell because they work ("plough") in the kingdom of God. It speaks of service. No man dares to enter divine labor with a divided mind, heart, or house. Plowing is done in view of sowing. If it is not done right, the sowing will be wrong. Men and women, who attempt service for Christ with divided loyalties, are in for big trouble. *Christ is everything or nothing. It is wholehearted or no hearted.* A true missionary has eternity in his soul. He cannot beg a day off in the work of God, unless God in His wisdom should grant it so. This would-be follower of Messiah was guilty of speaking before he had thoughtfully considered the prospect before him. This is called an "inconsiderate, hasty impulse." All of us have fallen victim to this sin time-by-time. In verses 61 and 62, there seems to be a reference back to the call of Elisha working in the field, and his response (1 Kings 19:19-21).

LUKE'S EXCLUSIVE CHAPTERS 10 THROUGH 18 CANNOT BE HARMONIZED WITH JOHN'S GOSPEL, IN CHAPTERS 8 THROUGH 11. THE DOCTOR'S STYLE OF PLACING EVENTS IN A DIFFERENT ORDER IS A MARK OF DIVINE INSPIRATION AND NOT OF HUMAN CHOICE.

About six months stood between the celebration of the Tabernacles Feast (John 7: 2, 10) and Christ's arrival at Bethany "six days before the Passover," when His death occurred (John 12:1). Luke alone wrote of certain events that occurred during this time in the life of Christ. These are found in chapters 10:1 through 13:22 into 17:11 ("as he went to Jerusalem"), and ending at 18:31. Here, Jesus said to the twelve, "Behold we go up to Jerusalem." Luke was not inspired to put these particular experiences of His Savior into a successive chronology. Dr. Benjamin Davies, in his *Harmony of the Gospels*, page 84, comments, "For this portion of his (Luke's) Gospel presents very much the appearance of a collection of distinct discourses and transactions in themselves disconnected" (from the other three writers). Because of this, the question is often raised, "Did Luke copy these special events from an existing document, previously written by someone who had no interest in their chronological order?" In the beginning of his letter, he informed Theophilus that some of his narrative had been "delivered to him" by others who had been "eyewitnesses and ministers of the Word" (Section 2, Lk. 1:2, footnotes c and d). This method of copying from older documents or acquiring truth about Christ from others was under the absolute superintendence of the Holy Spirit. Nothing was by guesswork. If Luke copied, he was motivated of God to do so. The difficulty is to take Luke's nine chapters of historical *facts* about Christ, and correctly place them within the record of John in chapters 8 through 11:54. As seen in the Table of Contents of this work, various chapters are taken out of their regular numerical sequence in an attempt to harmonize. For example, the events in Lk. 11:1-13 are placed in Section 118. Those that follow in Lk. 11:14-23 are in Section 66. Note that Lk. 11:24-28 is placed in Section 68, with Lk. 11:29-36 being placed in Section 67. After this, Lk. 11:37-54 concludes in Section 70. The events of Lk. 12:1-59 are in Section 71 with the first part of the next chapter, Lk. 13:1-9 in Section 72. This reveals that the writer was not directed to follow an unbroken, chronological line as he penned these events in the life of Christ. In such cases, the events were more important than the order in which they happened. In other places, the time was of more interest than the transactions. Regardless, it is firmly held that the Holy Spirit directed the whole enterprise.

A cursory glance at the above examples from Luke's gospel reveals that any attempt to harmonize perfectly this part of sacred history is something God will not allow! This also shows that some of these events occurred before Christ went down to Jerusalem for the Feast of Tabernacles celebration in John 7:2, 10. As reflected in the paragraph above, everything from Lk. 11:1 through 13:1-9 has been harmonized. The author of this work has made some of these placements with reluctance, not feeling comfortable with them, even though he has stated that they are personal *conjectures*. In attempting to harmonize the exclusive stories as recorded by Dr. Luke, I have loosely followed the pattern laid down in the old *Davies' Harmony of the Gospels*. Others take a different view, such as Alfred Edersheim in his classic *Life and Times of Jesus the Messiah*. After any attempted harmonization of these events, the Scriptures that are used should be arranged as they were originally written in the New Testament. Luke's curious order reflects heavenly inspiration. The four evangelists wrote and arranged their accounts as God directed them. Unbelieving skeptics struggle with this fact and work hard to disprove the gospels were given from God to mankind.

A scrutiny of John's account in chapters 8:1 through 10:21 reveals that Christ remained in Jerusalem *after* the Tabernacles for a short time. The contextual flow between the last verse of John 8:59 with the beginning of John 9:1 is obvious. In the former verse, our Lord exited the temple and "so passed by," while the later reads "And as Jesus passed by." Therefore, the end of John 8 is continued at the beginning of John 9:1. There is no chronological break between these two chapters, as well as the next discourse given in chapter 10. His parable of the sheep in chapter 10 is clearly a continuation from the last verse of chapter 9. This discourse ends in a verbal brawl with the Jews, who are divided again among themselves about the Messianic claims of Jesus (John 10:19-21).This *Selah! Harmony Commentary of the Four Gospels* follows the speculation that our Lord departed from Jerusalem immediately after this fierce conflict and returned to Galilee. The bitter hatred of the Jewish religious leaders does not warrant His staying in the city to wait for the Feast of Dedication, which did not take place until about three months later, in December. *Conjecturing* that Christ departed from Jerusalem at the end of John 10:21, and returned to a lesser hostile environment in His home state, the author has inserted the infidel critics' infamous "Interpolations of Luke" as all occurring *after* this return to Galilee. This includes the event of Luke 10:1, where He sent out the seventy in lieu of His upcoming trip across parts of Samaria, as seen in Luke 13:22 and 17:11, ending with 18:31. These verses seem to record *another* journey to Jerusalem via Samaria, Galilee, and into Peraea. (The context is firm that He was traveling through Galilee, which was the domain of Herod Antipas, as written in Lk. 13:31.) In so doing, He "went through the cities and villages, teaching and journeying toward Jerusalem" according to Lk. 13:22. He had to be in Galilee in order to make this trip out of Galilee. Our Lord's departure here cannot be the same one mentioned back in Lk. 9:51, which was His journey to the Tabernacles Feast. Thus, it *seems* correct to hold that Christ returned to Galilee following the celebration of Tabernacles, and later made this next trip. This proposed arrangement does not crowd too many events into the Savior's travels.

The difficulty is locating the time when His departure from Jerusalem for reentry into Galilee occurred. As stated above, I have placed this reentry between John 10:21 and 22, for in verse 23, He was in the temple. Between these two verses is a period of about three months, being the time between the end of Tabernacles in October and the Dedication in December. This would allow the time needed for Messiah to perform the numerous works listed in Lk. 10:1 through 17:11. John's three-month silence between verses 21 and 22 is another fingerprint of inspiration. This curious prerogative is frequently seen in the Word of God and marks it as not being the product of man's genius.

Because neither Matthew, Mark, nor Luke recorded the Savior attending the Feast of Tabernacles (John 7), we seek to harmonize this part of His life without their aid. However, Luke wrote of at least three trips Christ made from Galilee to Jerusalem. The first was apparently His attendance of the Tabernacles (Lk. 9:51). The second was when He went back to the Dedication Feast in December, with Lk. 13:22 through 17:11 seemingly speaking of the same trip. Lastly, Christ attended *the final Passover* at which time, He died (Luke 18:31-35 through 19:1, 11, 28 and John 12:1). This was His third trip to the city as recorded by Luke in the passages above.

When Jesus returned to Jerusalem for the Feast of Dedication in the winter month of December (Section 123, John 10:22-23), He fell afresh into conflict with the Jews. Again, they sought to kill Him. Escaping their hands, He went to Bethabara, some twenty miles east of Jerusalem (John 10:31-41 with John 1:28). Matthew's words in 19:1, that He "came into the coasts (borders) of Judaea beyond Jordan," seem to describe this escape to Bethabara. Again, the Savior taught the thousands flocking to Him and responded to the questions of the Pharisees, who continually hounded His footsteps. It was from Bethabara that He received the call to hurry to Bethany, where His beloved friend Lazarus was dying. After the exclusive Messianic miracle of raising Lazarus from the dead, He was again threatened by the Sanhedrin and moved this time to a new location called Ephraim, situated about twenty miles north-east of Jerusalem near the Samaritan border. See Section 124, John 11:48-54 for the details.

According to John's record, with the final Passover approaching, Christ began His *last* journey from the north, to Jerusalem by departing from Ephraim. It is *conjectured* that He walked northward less than a mile, and crossed into Samaria where He did many works. Next, He moved over parts of Galilee for the final time, crossed Jordan to the eastern side, then, gradually worked His way southerly through a portion of Peraea. Finishing His work in Peraea, the Savior picked up the main road leading to Jerusalem, located on the east side of the Jordan River. Hundreds of thousands of pilgrims would have been traveling this route, heading for Jerusalem to observe the Passover. Crossing the fords at the extreme southern end of the Jordan River with the crowd of pilgrims, the Lord Jesus moved westward and entered Jericho, where He healed two blind men. Preaching, teaching, and healing along the way, He finally arrived at Bethany and entered the house of the resurrected Lazarus (John 12:1). During supper, Mary revealed her unique insight of His upcoming death, burial, and resurrection by anointing His body (Section 146, John 12:2-8). This was about six days before His *final* Passover and death on the cross.

There is an excellent discussion on this subject containing sensible but different views from the one postulated by the author, see *Davis Harmony of the Gospels*, pages 82-85, and the amazing work *Historical Chart Of The Life And Ministry Of Christ, With An Outline Harmony Of The Gospels*, by George E. Croscup, printed in 1912.

For an exhaustive treatment of the various harmonies written over the course of Christian history, up to 1872, see the article "Harmony" in the *Biblical, Theological, and Ecclesiastical Cyclopaedia*, vol. iv, pages 76-82, by M'Clintock & Strong. The first paragraph under the heading *HOW TO USE THIS HARMONY COMMENTARY* contains brief information on the most ancient commentary known.

Seventy missionary forerunners* are sent after the messengers to spread the glad tidings of Jesus. They are endued with power to preach, perform miracles of healing, and exorcisms along the way. Traveling first the southerly roads through Samaria, their mission must have taken several weeks. It is conjectured that these seventy met Jesus later at Bethany. ****

*The seventy are not to be confused with the "messengers" Jesus had sent out earlier to shelter and lodging for Him during the long trip to Jerusalem. Refer to Section 112, Lk. 9:51-52 for this and the reaction of two of them to a certain village that refused the Lord Jesus customary accommodation. **See the arrival of Christ at Bethany in Section 117, Lk. 10:38 after the seventy missionaries had prepared the way ahead of Him. On the Samaritans receiving the Savior and His men, refer to Section 112, second paragraph of footnote b.

Matt.	Mk.	Lk. 10:1-15—*Galilee, Samaria, and Judaea*	John
		The seventy are selected **1** After these things the Lord appointed other seventy also, and sent them two and two before his face into every city and place, whither he himself would come.**(a)** ***The seventy are instructed*** **2** Therefore said he unto them,**(b)** "The harvest truly *is* great, but the labourers *are* few: pray ye therefore the Lord of the harvest, that he would send forth labourers into his harvest.**(c)** **3** "Go your ways: behold, I send you forth as lambs among wolves.**(d)** **4** "Carry neither purse, nor scrip, [food bag] nor [extra] shoes: and salute no man by the way.**(e)** **5** "And into whatsoever house ye enter, first say, Peace *be* to this house.'**(f)** **6** "And if the son of peace [a believer] be there, your peace shall rest upon it: if not, it shall turn to you again. (to seek another place of lodging) **7** "And in the same house remain, eating and drinking such things as they give: for the labourer is worthy of his hire.**(g)** Go not from house to house. **8** "And into whatsoever city ye enter,**(h)** and they receive you, eat such things as are set before you: **9** "And heal the sick**(i)** that are therein, and say unto them, 'The kingdom of God is come nigh unto you.' ***Fate of all who rejected the seventy*** **10** "But into whatsoever city ye enter, and they receive you not,**(j)** go your ways out into the streets of the same, and say, **11** 'Even the very dust**(k)** of your city, which cleaveth on us, we do wipe off against you: notwithstanding be ye sure of this, that the kingdom of God is come nigh unto you.' **12** "But I say unto you, that it shall be more tolerable in that day for Sodom,**(l)** than for that city. **13** "Woe unto thee, Chorazin! woe unto thee, Bethsaida! for if the mighty works had been done in Tyre and Sidon,**(m)** which have been done in you, they had a great while ago repented, sitting in sackcloth and ashes. **14** "But it shall be more tolerable for Tyre and Sidon**(n)** at the judgment, than for you. **15** "And thou, Capernaum,**(o)** which art exalted to heaven, shalt be	

Matt.	Mk.	Lk. 10:15-16—*Galilee, Samaria,, and Judaea*	John
		thrust down to hell.	
		A warning for all men of all times: listen to the right person	
		16 "He that heareth you heareth me;[p] and he that despiseth you despiseth me; and he that despiseth me [Jesus Christ] despiseth him [God] that sent me."[q] (Verse 17 cont. in Section 114.)	

Footnotes-Commentary

[a] **Preparing the way for Jesus.** In Matt 10:5, the Lord Jesus sent out previously the twelve apostles on a special, but restricted missionary effort across Galilee to reach the "lost sheep of the house of Israel." For this work, they had been endued with supernatural power. That had been almost two years ago. Now, as He journeyed to Jerusalem to observe the Feast of Tabernacles, along the way He was rejected by an unknown Samaritan village, as recorded in the main heading of Section 112. Immediately, after this rejection, He commissioned seventy other missionaries and thrust them out into unnamed Samaritan "cities" (verses 8, 10-11). These seventy men were not only busy speaking of their Messiah, and doing great miracles in His name, but they were also preparing accommodations for Him and the twelve, as they were soon to pass that way going to Jerusalem. Matthew Henry, in his *Commentary,* vol. 5, page 548, sees in these numbers a picture of the twelve wells of water and the seventy palms at Elim (Ex. 15:27). Their chief announcement was something like this, "Messiah will soon arrive at your village: prepare for Him!"

2p-Different from the messengers. As stated above, these seventy men are not to be confused with the "messengers" of Section 112, Lk. 9:51-52, footnote c. In verse 1 above, the word "also" means in "addition to." Seemingly, the messengers were sent first to arrange accommodations for Christ and the seventy who followed.

3p-Why were there seventy? Some think this selection of Christ was patterned after the seventy elders of Israel that assisted Moses (Num. 11:24-25), for it was written that Christ would be like Moses (Deut. 18:18). There existed the rabbinical belief that the Gentile nations of the world were seventy in number. This is based on a tradition that when God divided the nations of earth (Deut 32:8), He appointed an angel named "Samael" to be in charge of this division. "Samael" was another name for Satan. Hence, the origin of his title, "the prince of this world," as he ruled over them from the heavens. For our Lord's use of this title, refer to Section 161, footnote j. Other intimations of the number seventy appear in Jewish literature. During the Feast of Tabernacles, seventy bulls were offered as commanded in Num. 29:12-34. According to the Talmud tractate, Sukkah 55b, these seventy sacrifices were to make atonement for the Gentile nations, which they reckoned to be seventy. Rabbis held that this large sacrifice of seventy animals pointed to the Jewish belief that Messiah would gather in many Gentile nations when He came! Some see in this our Savior trying to reach the many Gentiles living in Samaria and along His road to Jerusalem. He was harvesting from the seventy nations. They were to be evangelized by His thirty-five pairs of forerunner preachers, soon to pass their way.

[b] In verses 2 through 16 of the above Section, some of the instructions given in this commissioning of the seventy are identical with those previously given to the twelve in Section 59. Several of our Lord's comments were also given elsewhere in a setting totally apart from the sending out of the twelve and seventy. Throughout this work, we have noted that the Son of God *repeated* truth over and over. See footnote a above. Not being able to determine their time of return to Christ, it has been placed in the next Section. How long was required to fulfill their commission is unknown. See main heading under Section 114 for the *assumed* end of this particular commission of the seventy to these Gentiles and their Samaritan neighbors. Oddly, Edersheim holds that the seventy did not pass through Samaria, but rather into Peraea and then Judaea. For his comments, see *Life and Times of Jesus the Messiah,* page 568. However, it seems they went into Samaria first, then over into Peraea and down into Judaea.

2p-In this harmony commentary, we have conjoined the verses in the previous Section 112, Lk. 9:51-52, where our Lord was moving to Jerusalem and sent James and John to announce His soon arrival at an unnamed Samaritan village. *This confirms that He was passing through Samaria.* After the events that occurred "as they went in the way" (Lk. 9:57), He then appointed "other seventy" to proceed ahead of Him, do their evangelization, preach, and prepare for His arrival, as seen in Lk. 10:1 above. The fact that this verse is a chapter break means nothing, and the words "After these things," can only have been antecedent back to the events at the conclusion of the previous chapter. It is a mistake to think that between *every* chapter division in the Bible, no time periods elapse. This does not hold true. For more on chapter and verse divisions in the Bible, see Section 59, footnote t.

[c] **Lk. 10:2.** Jesus had spoken this prior to calling and sending out the twelve. See Section 56, Matt. 9:37-38 for very similar Words used earlier by our Lord.

[d] See Section 59, Matt. 10:16. Here, it is changed from lambs to sheep, obviously meaning both.

[e] **Don't waste time.** This statement has perplexed some. Nothing discourteous is conveyed in these Words. Jews believed that one in the service of Jehovah must move swiftly when attending to divine business. Jesus tells His preachers to never waste time with trifles and small talk along the way, but *"Get at the work you have been sent*

to do." Here is a lesson badly needed by many pastors, missionaries, teachers, and leaders in God's service. The church is hindered by people who spend half a week talking about a needed project and the other half *not* getting it done. It was accepted among the Jews, that seriously urgent events required a man not to salute his fellow along the way. When mourning for the dead and during times of prolonged fasts for rain, Jews were not to greet or salute each other along the way. All the seventy ministers understood their Master's instructions on this point.

(f) See Section 59, Matt. 10:13 and notice the difference in the wording here.

(g) **Lk. 10:7.** This verse in a modified form was previously used by the Savior in Section 59, Matt. 10:11. It is of interest that Paul quoted a part of Luke's words "the laborer is worthy of his hire," in 1 Tim. 5:18. Paul wrote this to Timothy some thirty years after the resurrection and ascension of Christ. Does this mean that he had a copy of Luke's letter to Theophilus and cited this verse knowing that it was inspired of God and on equal footing with the Old Testament? Refer to Section 106, second paragraph of footnote j for more on this fascinating possibility. *Appendix Seven* treats this subject.

(h) **Lk. 10:8.** These words are partially mentioned in Section 59, Matt. 10:11. They suggest that many villages were contacted by the seventy about the Messiah, who was to pass their way.

(i) **Lk. 10:9. "Heal the sick."** This was briefly mentioned in Section 59, Matt. 10:8. Note that Matthew's instructions were broader. The seventy were to inform their hearers that with the coming of Jesus to their village, "The kingdom of God" would be very close to them. There is no way that this can have reference to a literal kingdom, over two thousand years in the future. He was speaking of the spiritual manifestation of His new kingdom, which was being slowly formed and would come into full birth on the day of Pentecost. Note Section 134, footnotes c and d, with various cross-references for details.

(j) **Lk. 10:10–11.** These verses were also used in Section 59, Matt. 10:14. For comments on the village that had earlier refused the Lord Jesus entrance, see Section 112, footnote f.

(k) The Jews held that even the dust from Gentile lands was defiled and, therefore, must be shaken from the feet of every true Israelite. The apostles later continued this Jewish practice as seen in Acts 13:51. Paul, in Acts 18:6, used the custom of shaking one's raiment as a sign of abandonment. By this time, both practices had acquired very different meanings. Now, the smallest vestige of unbelief and rejection of Christ was to be detached from the lives of God's traveling witnesses. *The same standard applies to this day.* It is noted that the most aggressive cults working as "Christians" still practice the ancient custom of shaking the dust off their shoes against all who will not subscribe to their heresies and blasphemies. Notable among these groups are the Jehovah's Witness and the Church of Jesus Christ of the Latter Day Saints (Mormons). For insight into the horrific doctrinal perversions of the Mormon cult, see Section 27, footnote a. See Section 33, third paragraph of footnote c for the reason why Christians must expose false religions and sects operating as Bible Christians. Note also, Section 95, sixth paragraph of footnote r for explanation of the deceiving "sincerity in religion" objection.

(l) **"Sodom."** Lk. 10:12 is the same as Section 59, Matt. 10:15, and Section 63, Matt. 11:24. This wicked city, along with several others previously doomed by the Savior, had now become the epitome of evil and God's fierce judgment, sure to fall on all who despised and rejected His Son. Included in these were Tyre and Sidon.

(m) **"Chorazin and Bethsadia."** Lk. 10:13 is a general repeat of the same curse as was pronounced by the Lord Jesus back in Section 63, Matt. 11:21. See comments in footnote l above.

(n) **"Tyre and Sidon."** Lk. 10:14 had been spoken earlier in Section 63, Matt. 11:22. See comments in footnote l above.

(o) **"Capernaum."** Lk. 10:15 was repeated in Section 63, Matt. 11:23. See comments in footnote l above. How absurd to teach that this means "cast down to the grave." All men will finally go into the grave. This means the real place called hell, not some local cemetery.

2p-Verse 15. "Down to hell." For twenty-one things the Bible says about hell-lake of fire, see Section 103, number 8, under footnote g.

(p) **Lk. 10:16.** This was later rephrased in John 8:47 and John 13:20. The meaning is clear: if men hear God's preachers, they hear God; if they refuse to hear His men, then they have refused to hear God.

(q) There is nothing in the other three gospels exactly like this statement recorded by Luke. However, on the night before the morning of the cross, Jesus said something close to this in John 13:20. A fearful warning is couched in these words. Those who hate the Son of God, legislate against His Bible, ban His Name from public, and forbid it to be uttered in open prayer are, in fact, expressing their hatred for Almighty God. They do not believe that He keeps good records and will not forget. Legislation against God is described in Isa. 10:1-4. It is written, "God is angry *with the wicked* every day" (Ps. 7:11). "*Though* hand *join* in hand, the wicked shall not be unpunished" (Prov. 11:21). We read a terrible warning in Ps. 50:22, "Now consider this, ye that forget God, lest I tear *you* in pieces, and *there be* none to deliver." A day of divine tearing is coming for America and those who hate God and His dear Son. *Unsaved men fiercely resent being told that God is angry over their sin and that it requires judgment or forgiveness.*

Luke's placement of the return of the seventy is immediately after their departure without any details of their adventures. Later, he mentioned only one event that occurred during these several weeks' journey.* When their work was completed, it is *conjectured* that the seventy then met Jesus** at Bethany. The Savior gives them a sound lesson on misplaced joy in God's service.

*This event was the story of the Jewish lawyer who attempted to trap the Savior with a trick question. See Section 116 for details and Christ's response to him in the Parable of the Good Samaritan. **We have no idea of the exact place and time when the seventy returned to the Lord Jesus and reported their work. It has been assumed as occurring after the Savior arrived at Bethany (Section 117) since they were sent ahead to prepare His way to this village. He could not have met with them until after His trip was over. Placing their meeting with Jesus herein, this Section keeps us in harmony with Luke's reporting of these events in the life of Christ.

Matt.	Mk.	Lk. 10:17–20—*On the way to Bethany*	John
		The seventy return and report **17** And the seventy returned[(a)] again with joy, saying, "Lord, even the devils are subject unto us through thy name."[(b)] ***Rejoice in the most important thing*** **18** And he said unto them,[(c)] "I beheld Satan as lightning fall from heaven. **19** "Behold, I give unto you power to tread on serpents and scorpions, and over all the power of the enemy: and nothing shall by any means hurt you.[(d)] **20** "Notwithstanding in this rejoice not, that the spirits are subject unto you; but rather rejoice, because your names are written[(e)] in heaven." (Verse 21 cont. in Section 115.)	

Footnotes–Commentary

(a) Where the returning seventy heralds meet their Master is not stated, as mentioned above. It could have been upon Jesus' arrival at the gate of Bethany (city gates being a common meeting place) or somewhere along the road prior to entering the village. Perhaps it was at His reception in Martha's house. It seems correct that they did return to their Master before the Feast of Tabernacles commenced, as they would have also attended. This was one of the three compulsory celebrations for the males of Israel. For more on these three feasts, see Section 119, the third paragraph of footnote a.

(b) Divine power. The seventy missionaries discovered that the power bestowed on them by Messiah was greater than they had realized. (We note that within the record of their original commission in Section 113, there is no mention of exorcism.) While occupied in healing the sick, someone in the group discovered that they also had power to cast out demon spirits. It is obvious that upon their return to Christ, they had become enamored with this extraordinary endowment. It was paramount in their minds. Yet they knew that all their miracles were accomplished only by the name of Christ. Here, we note that Messiah had *already* spoken of the authority of His Name and how His preachers could use it. These things took place about one year *before* our Lord's fantastic promise about using His Name. He gave this truth the night before the morning of His cross. Refer to Section 175, John 14:13. Phony Jewish exorcists employed all sorts of herbs, roots, powders, and colored cloth, while voicing strange noises and sounds, commanding demons to depart from their victims. The seventy drove them out "in the name of Jesus Christ the Son of God." Crowds gathering to watch were struck with the stark contrast. For a timely warning regarding would-be exorcists, who take upon themselves something God has not given them, see Section 106, the fourth paragraph of footnote k. The many doing this today, are playing with a dangerous power that is not divine.

(c) Detecting their joy, which was misplaced on exorcisms, the Lord Jesus startlingly informed the seventy that He saw Satan, the lord of all demons, expelled from heaven. They were stunned! He was saying, "While you cast out the Devil's servants, I saw the prince, himself, cast out!" For Christ to speak of Satan falling from heaven means that he actually fell from heaven. The seventy understood, for no further explanation ensued in their conversation. It has been observed that the more "scholarly" and "academic" some theologians become, the more they deny the reality of the Devil and his awful kingdom. He has been (sort of) educated out of existence.

2p-Messiah's Words "fall from heaven" may have reference to Isa. 14:4-17 and Ezek. 28:1-19, where contextually, pagan kings thought they were gods and ruled the world of their day. Isaiah and Ezekiel seem to have pointed to their pride, ruthlessness, and fate as appropriate symbols of Lucifer. As he had fallen, so would these kings also fall. It was from this truth that Paul based his warning for young ministers, not to be novices in God's work. They too could be "lifted up with pride" and "fall into the condemnation of the devil" (1 Tim. 3:6). If Satan did not fall from heaven, then Paul was misinforming Timothy. To palm this off as a Jewish tradition borrowed by Paul from ancient folklore is theological ignorance. One is regularly amazed and even confounded how the "authorities" so eloquently explain away the fact of a dark spiritual kingdom ruled by the Devil and engineered by billions of demon spirits. Among "conservative believers," the author often hears words of courteous sneering and objections of high theological nature couched in many biblical verses! American television reeks with documentaries of ignorant persons who are "investigating the supernatural." With their sensitive electronic meters, sophisticated cameras, and sound instruments, they are trying to prove the paranormal. Infrequently, in these divinely forbidden experiments, a demon will slap a face, pull hair, shove someone down the stairs, or toss them through the air, and so forth. Some have been clawed across the face or down their backs by an "invisible force." The unsaved, and biblically ignorant "ghost seekers," continue to pursue their madness in a realm forbidden by God. In time, if this madness continues someone (usually younger women) will be brutally killed by these invisible entities of darkness. God's Word has warned in Prov. 6:27, "Can a man take fire in his bosom and his clothes not be burned?" Scripture warns, "whoso breaketh an hedge, a serpent shall bite him" (Eccles. 10:8).

3p-The Adam Clarke surprise. The text from Isa. 14:12, cited above, is rejected by the great Adam Clarke as having any reference to the original fall of Satan or Lucifer! See his *Commentary,* vol. iv, page 82. He comments that "Lucifer" could be an incorrect translation in this verse, that the word translated Lucifer means "Howl, yell, shriek." Apparently, he failed to remember that Satan and all his associates will conclude their dirty work in a place where there is "weeping and wailing and gnashing of teeth," forever! It is to be noted, that Clarke in his comments on Lk. 10:18 and 1 Tim. 3:6 does not refer to the text of Isa. 14:12. Even demons know they are bound for "torment," according to their confession in Matt. 8:29. Such passages as, Matt. 25:41 with Rev. 20:10 are verses those who reject the biblical doctrines of hell, and a real invisible spirit person called the Devil, they struggle to explain away. For twenty-one things the Bible says about conscious suffering in hell-lake of fire, see Section 103, number 8, under footnote g. For Christ telling the true story of two men who died and what became of them in eternity, see Section 131.

(d) "Nothing shall hurt you." Our Lord reiterates to the seventy regarding the unique power and extraordinary protection He had given them during their missionary activities. The very sovereignty of God delivered them from "hurt" of any form. Scorpions and serpents are to be understood in both literal and spiritual forms; as creatures, not metaphors, yet as metaphors, not creatures. This reflects the infinite care of God over these men in both spiritual and physical realms of human activity and divine service. To read into the words "not hurt you," as meaning that God's servants will never suffer pain in the Master's work is incorrect. There have been millions of martyrs for the cause of Christ over the centuries. Even now, Christians are suffering and dying for their faith in the Sudan and other countries as bloody Islam pursues her demonic religious jihad. Apparently, the promise of Christ in this text was an *exclusive thing* for these seventy evangelists sent out for this specific mission. On suffering in the work of Christ, read missionary Paul's incredible list of sufferings in 2 Cor. 4:8-12 and 11:23-30.

(e) Life's greatest joy. Among the Jews of this time, and even today, the idea of one's name being written in heaven was strongly believed. During Rosh-HaShanah (the Jewish New Year) as well as Yom Kippur (Day of Atonement), a prayer is offered requesting that the names of the faithful be recorded and sealed in the "book of life." A prominent interpretation of this book was that it had reference only to "this present [physical] life," and not that, which is to come. In Mal. 3:16 with Dan. 12:1, it was called "a book of remembrance." On Yom Kippur, it was believed that God opened the heavenly books and judged all Jews according to their works up to that time. He decided who would live and who would die in the coming New Year. Then He sealed the book. The Lord Jesus was correcting these Hebrew distortions of truth when He spoke of the seventy as *already* having their names in heaven's book of life. Beyond doubt, all of them were thinking of the rabbinical "book of remembrance," known to all pious Jews, while Jesus had in mind the book of eternal life or salvation.

2p-While entering into their joy, Christ quickly checked their dangerous enthusiasm about demons and traditional Jewish misunderstanding about the book of life. There was another subject deeper, yet higher, more wonderful, and personal than "casting out devils." Moreover, there was a book greater than the one the rabbis prayed about so much on Yom Kipper. The Lord Jesus was saying to the seventy, "Remember, above all the success of divine service, that your names are written in heaven; in the very place from which Satan was expelled." He speaks here of the book of eternal life in which are inscribed the names of the redeemed of all ages, not another rabbinical myth mixed with scraps of truth. Scripture teaches there is a book of physical life and another of eternal life. When one dies *physically,* his name is blotted out of the book of human life (Ex. 32:32-33; Ps. 69:28; with Isa. 4:3). Upon conversion to Christ, one's name is recorded in the book of eternal life, which act was foreknown by God before the foundation of the world. This holy foreknowledge is reflected in Rev. 17:8. Donald Guthrie, in his work, *Jesus the Messiah; an illustrated life of Christ*, page 194, well summarizes the whole matter by writing, "They [the seventy] should have been rejoicing that their names were written in heaven. This was a spiritual triumph of greater proportions than exorcism."

3p-In Rev. 3:5; 13:8; 17:8; 20:12, 15; and 21:27, we find other books are mentioned. All of these verses speak of eternal life except the passage in Rev. 3:5. This verse has reference to a custom of the high priest. When one met the criteria for admission into the priesthood, his name was inscribed in a book. Oddly, this priestly list of names was called "the book of life." It was a public register listing the names of those participating in temple service. The idea for this listing came from a registration scroll used in the days of Zerubbabel (536 B.C.). It was a name list of Jews, who returned from Babylonian captivity (Ezra 2:62). If a priest was dismissed for whatever reason, his name (written in black soot ink) was removed or wiped out with a wet cloth from the velum register. This had nothing to do with eternal life or salvation, but rather a Jewish priest being "fired" or "released" from his duties in the house of God. Those who think they find the shameful doctrine of "falling from grace" (Armininism) in Rev. 3:5, have sorely misinterpreted another passage in the Bible by overlooking its historical background meaning. Edersheim briefly mentions this in his work, *The Temple,* pages 95-96, of the 1959 edition. This passage speaks of those who through sin disqualified themselves from God's work in the temple. This fact strongly suggests that John wrote the Revelation to people who thoroughly understood Jewish customs and were familiar with the labors of the Hebrew priesthood. Salvation is not the subject in Rev. 3:5, rather, it is reward for divine service. And it comes from a religious custom of the Jewish priesthood that ended with the destruction of the temple in A.D. 70.

4p-How sober are these words as the Lord from heaven warns of misplaced joy due to a prior misunderstanding of Scripture and false teaching. Are we not the same today? On what, dear reader, is your heart centered? The most comforting hope of human life is to *know* one's name is written in the Lamb's book of (eternal) life. Jesus called upon His seventy preachers to keep this foremost in heart and mind: they belonged to God and were His servants. In short, He said, "Let this be the highest joy and chief subject of discussion among you." A thousand years prior, the Psalmist wrote, "Let the redeemed of the LORD say so, whom he hath redeemed from the hand of the enemy" (Ps. 107:2). Note Phil. 4:3 compared with Rev. 20:15. We read there is rejoicing in heaven over those who repent of their sins and are brought to Christ. See this in Section 129, Lk. 15:7, second paragraph of footnote d.

5p-Is the above not the same today? In some way not explained in Holy Scripture, the halls of heaven reverberate with unspeakable joy over every lost soul saved by the grace of God. Does this not lay hold on our hearts and sternly reminds us that bringing lost men to Christ is the most serious work in all human life? A hundred years henceforth, our bank account, house, car, weight, education, social status, and public prestige will be of no importance. Only what we have done for Jesus, in winning the unsaved to Him and blessing others for His glory will be of eternal importance. "*This is* a faithful saying, and these things I will that thou affirm constantly, that they which have believed in God might be careful to maintain good works. These things are good and profitable unto men" (Titus 3:8). The Lord Jesus said, "Herein is my Father glorified, that ye bear much fruit; so shall you be my disciples" (John 15:8).

6p-Amazing grace and Tom Fox from London. Who can explain the wonders of grace in the salvation of men? During overseas missionary endeavors, after we had completed our work on the east coast of central Queensland, I flew to Alice Springs, in the heart of Australia, to spy out the land. Arriving at the Alice airport late at night I went to a small restaurant to eat. After waiting for over an hour, with no server in sight, a stranger walked in and sat at my table. He was Tom Fox; about sixty years old, a builder from London, England. I told him we would get no food there. Tom invited me to ride with him to a small restaurant on the banks of the (dry) Todd River. We arrived there in the early morning hours, gave our orders, chatted, and waited. When the waiter sat the plates of food before us, without any thought, I bowed my head and gave thanks to God. Looking up, Tom glared at me across the table and inquired, "What did you do?" I replied, "I offered thanks for my food." Gasping, he said, "Do you know God? For years, I have wanted someone to help me know God. Can you?" Taking out my pocket New Testament, I spent the next hour explaining to him why Christ came into the world, and God's plan for the salvation of men. He asked many questions. Lastly, we ate the cold food and returned to the motel. I discovered that his room was near mine. Walking me to the door, I said, "Tom, if you are serious about wanting to know God, and want to be saved, knock on my door at seven in the morning." After a few hours of sleep, I rose well before seven, sat, prayed, and waited. Sure enough on the hour, Tom Fox appeared at the door. Within five minutes, he was led to a saving knowledge of Jesus Christ. Tom had to leave for the city of Darwin early. I took his mailing address, bade him God's speed, and have never seen him since. Upon arriving back in Gladstone, Queensland, I mailed him a Bible with a letter of good cheer and encouragement to follow Christ. A missionary from America, met a man from London, at a restaurant in the middle of Australia; this man had been looking for God all of his life! Poor Tom, over the course of life had been like the fellow who searched for a rose but had overlooked the beautiful orchid. God met his eternal need in a little motel room in 1965, amid the dust and sand storms of Alice Springs, Northern Territory, Australia. With his conversion to Christ, another name was found to be written in heaven. This adventure was all the work of heaven, not man. How sweet the thought that divine saving grace (in time) appears in some way to all men (Titus 2:11). For more on this mysterious but blissful truth, see Section 1, Part 2, the second paragraph of footnote f.

The seventy end their reporting to Jesus. He then thanked the Father for the simplicity of truth revealed to His preachers. The Lord pronounces a special blessing on the seventy for the service they have so faithfully performed.

Matt.	Mk.	Lk. 10:21-24—*On the way to or at Bethany*	John
		Great joy moves Him to pray to the Father **21** In that hour[a] Jesus rejoiced in Spirit, [the Holy Spirit] and said, "I thank thee, O Father,[b] Lord of heaven and earth, that thou hast hid these things from the wise and prudent, and hast revealed them unto babes: even so, Father; for so it seemed good in thy sight. **22** "All things[c] are delivered to me of my Father: and no man knoweth who the Son is, but the Father; and who the Father is, but the Son, and *he* to whom the Son will reveal *him*." *He blesses the seventy who have heard and seen unique things* **23** And he turned him unto *his* disciples,[d] and said privately, "Blessed *are* the eyes which see the things that ye see: **24** "For I tell you, that many prophets and kings have desired to see those things which ye see, and have not seen *them*; and to hear those things which ye hear, and have not heard *them*."[e] (Verse 25 cont. in Section 116.)	

Footnotes–Commentary

[a] **An hour of rejoicing.** The man of sorrows rejoices at last! Here is the only occasion in the *earthly life* of our Lord where Scripture speaks of His rejoicing. (See Heb. 12:2 for His joy in bringing souls to Himself after the ascension back to heaven.) It seems that in these words, the Lord Jesus praises the Father for answered prayer made on behalf of His seventy missionaries. The unknown hour and place when they returned to Him is hidden in history, yet their report filled His great heart with joy, and His mouth spontaneously opened in a prayer of thanks to God. Nothing so thrills the heart of Jesus than to know of the progress of His Word and saving gospel. See the previous Section 114, Lk. 10:17, footnote a. The word "spirit" has reference to the Holy Spirit, who had filled Jesus at His baptism over three years prior. Note this recorded in Section 22, Lk. 3:22, footnotes d and e.

2p-The Jews had very stern rules, which they observed in times of prayer. The Talmud informs us that prayer was not to be interrupted to salute a king, or even to uncoil a serpent that had wound about the foot, as recorded in tractate, Berachoth 33a. These high-sounding rules practiced by the scribes and Pharisees were only further proofs of their evil hypocrisy. As with most everything else, the rabbis were wild in their extremes, even regarding prayer. The Talmud tractate, Kiddushin 29b, relates the myth concerning a haunted schoolhouse. A rabbi spent the night there in prayer, and a seven-headed demon appeared before him. Each time he prayed a head fell off, until the spirit was destroyed! Earlier in His Sermon on the Mount, the Lord blasted them for being hypocrites in prayer. Refer to Section 46, Matt. 6:5, footnote d for this stern rebuke. Prayer is not following a set of rules; it is the heart speaking to God in words that the Holy Spirit alone interprets (Rom. 8:26-27). The mouth may articulate words, or it may not. *They are first heart-words.* In times of prayer, we may rejoice, as did our Lord; in others, we may also drop bloody sweat amid the frequent Gethsemanes of human life and experience. It remains curiously true, that as He was in the world, as a Man, so are we.

[b] **"Father."** The Lord Jesus used this word at least one hundred and seventy-six times when referring to or addressing God in prayer. It is found a hundred and twelve times alone in the Gospel of John. Immediately, after informing the seventy that their names were written in heaven, the Son of God broke forth into a brief, but beautiful prayer of praise. God the Father was thanked for the victories reported by the seventy missionaries; for every infirmed body healed; for every demon driven into the pit; and for every soul who believed their preaching about His spiritual kingdom. The Father was extolled for revealing to His preachers that their names were written in heaven. This was a prayer of supreme fellowship between Father and Son; a brief glimpse is given into the glorious relationship of the Triune God. All Three are seen in verse 21. As it was the "glory of God to conceal a thing" (Prov. 25:2), now it was "good in His sight" and for His glory to reveal eternal secrets to the humble seventy, described here as "babes." See Section 63, Matt. 11:25-26, footnote d for another earlier usage of these magnificent words where Christ had said similar things. The question in Job stands before us at this place. "Canst thou by searching find out God" (Job 11:7)? Yes! "Babes" now have limited insight into the mind of Jehovah. They have seen His power at work through their lives. They are experimentally being elevated to positions higher than earth's kings and Israel's sages and prophets of old. See cross-reference in footnote e below for more on this enthralling thought. For

later thoughts on the Father, note Section 178, footnote t where the Lord Jesus prayed His high priestly prayer on the night before the morning of the cross.

(c) See Section 63, Matt. 11:27 footnote f where the Lord Jesus had said the identical Words earlier in His ministry. These are further examples of Christ repeating eternal truths about God and Himself.

(d) **Verses 23-24.** As with the above, this was also spoken earlier when Christ was giving the Ten Parables. Refer to Section 74, Matt. 13:16-17 footnotes f and g for detailed explanation of these words of praise and their profound meaning. Israel's greatest rabbis or the Gentile kings and philosophers of the world had not been blessed to hear and see what the lowly twelve, and the seventy had witnessed. This glorious exaltation was because of their faith in and fellowship with the Lord Jesus Christ. Men who are unsaved and do not walk through life with Christ are the most spiritually ignorant beings in the whole of creation (John 15:5). See footnote e below. Sadly, they only discover this in irreversible haunts of eternity.

(e) **"You are privileged men."** Earlier, the Savior said similar things regarding the blessedness of hearing Him teach parables. Numerous similarities and expressions spoken by our Lord are mentioned repeatedly in this harmony commentary. These demonstrate that He frequently used repetition. They have nothing to do with the critical myth of "later additions or interpolations to the text of the four gospels." For further details, regarding this "academic" fable postured by the "experts," see *Author's Introduction*.

2p-Having spoken to the Holy Father, the Savior now addresses His preachers. He informs them that what their eyes had seen, and ears heard, elevated them a step above those thousands who went before them. The greatest kings and prophets of the Old Testament history did not share their honor. Matthew Henry put it in this succinct language, "The honour and joy of the New Testament saints far exceed those of the prophets and kings of the Old Testament. The general ideas which the Old Testament saints had, according to the intimations given them, of graces and glories of Messiah's kingdom, made them wish a thousand times that their lot had been reserved for those blessed days, and that they might see the substance of those things of which they had "faint shadows. . . ." See *Matthew Henry's Commentary,* vol. 5, page 552. We, of this era in history, no longer hear the amazing teaching from the mouth of our Savior, as did those of old. However, His audible truths remain before us in the form of Holy Scripture. The dim but wonderful light of the Old Testament is now bright and glorious as we trace it into the pages of the New. To share this eternal word with a fellow human along the brief road of life is the highest honor bestowed on any mortal saved by the grace of God. Few stop to consider its claims while others tread it under foot. Groups such as the Freedom From Religion Foundation (FFRF), and other atheists fiercely hate the Bible because it condemns their godless lifestyles, and speaks too much about judgment and hell for their comfort..

3p-**Testimonies of the damned.** In what do men find support as eternity beckons them away? Does evolution, atheism, skepticism, money, power, fame, socialism, communism, capitalism, Marxism, or "superior learning" give the support to move through death's door into the other world? Millions proudly boast of their infidelity, while pointing out the foolishness of Bible Christianity. They tell us that the church is a fraud for moneymaking, its adherents are *all* hypocrites, and their preaching of hell is based on intimidation and fear. (Surely, this is true for many but hardly all!) The famed atheistic skeptic, Sir Francis Newport (died 1708) articulated his blasphemies against heaven and earth, until death knocked on his door. Rolling, tossing, and clawing the mattress he wailed, "Oh that I could lie for a thousand years upon the fire that is never quenched, to purchase the favor of God and be united to him again. Millions and millions of years will bring me no nearer to the end of my torments than one poor hour. Oh, eternity, eternity forever and forever!" The celebrated Thomas Paine (died 1809) who sought God in nature apart from Holy Scripture, at last became a blasphemous skeptic. From his deathbed, he begged, "Stay with me, for God's sake; I cannot bear to be left alone . . . O Lord, help me! O God, what have I done to suffer so much? What will become of me hereafter?" Paine held to the myth of Natural Theology, or finding God in the glory of nature. Men only find God in truth in the pages of Scripture and the Lord Jesus Christ. For explanation of this, see Section 1, Part, 4, fourth paragraph of footnote m. The infamous Voltaire (died 1778) screeched as he perished, "I am abandoned by God and man . . . I shall die and go to hell." Thomas Hobbes was a philosopher who had all the answers but did not know the questions. As he succumbed in 1679, he wailed, "I am about to take a leap into the dark." For more on famous and infamous sayings of dying men, see *The Speaker's Quote Book,* by Roy. B. Zuck. Serious readers may Google the "testimonies of dying men" and learn more of this subject. Near the end of his life, the famed British infidel, critic, and author, H. G. Wells (died 1946) stunned everyone with his honesty. See Section 122, second paragraph of footnote j for his admission. The jovial and greatly loved British Prime Minister, Winston Churchill, mumbled just before death in 1965, "I'm bored with it all, what a fool I have been." Reader, have you contemplated what your last words might be? Ludwig van Beethoven (died 1872) said, "Friends applaud the comedy is finished." (No Ludwig, it had just begun.) And what awaits blasphemers and skeptics? A granite urn, a hole in the ground, maggots, decay, and Rev. 20:15! God's wisdom issues a warning in Prov. 1:24-33. It has a glorious response in Rev. 3:20. *Everyone is a total believer in the Bible, and the Savior, after death!* For most of them it is too late. Read the self-eulogy of the world's greatest missionary, chained in a Roman prison waiting execution (2 Tim. 4:6-8). For other comments along these lines, see Section 78, footnote d.

Traveling to Bethany and Jerusalem a Jewish Torah lawyer attempts to trick Jesus with a devious question. He answers with the Parable of the Good Samaritan.* Surprisingly, the lawyer agrees with the Savior's answer.

This lesson was probably given somewhere in Samaria or amid a group of Samaritans. At its conclusion, the Lord Jesus had said, "Lawyer, the Samaritan in my parable was a better person than either you, or your Jewish priests and Levites, for he was the true neighbor who had compassion on the wounded, helpless man."

Matt.	Mk.	Lk. 10:25-37—*Traveling to Bethany via Samaria?*	John
		A lawyer's question	
		25 And, behold, a certain lawyer stood up, and tempted him, saying, "Master, what shall I do to inherit eternal life?"[a]	
		26 He said unto him, "What is written in the law? how readest thou?"[b]	
		27 And he answering said,[c] "Thou shalt love the Lord thy God with all thy heart, and with all thy soul, and with all thy strength, and with all thy mind; and thy neighbour as thyself."	
		28 And he said unto him, "Thou hast answered right:[d] this do, and thou shalt live."[e]	
		29 But he, willing to justify[f] himself, said unto Jesus, "And who is my neighbour?"	
		Christ responds with a parable	
		30 And Jesus answering said, "A certain *man* went down from Jerusalem to Jericho,[g] and fell among thieves, which stripped him of his raiment, and wounded *him*, and departed, leaving *him* half dead.[h]	
		31 "And by chance there came down a certain priest that way: and when he saw him, he passed by on the other side.[i]	
		32 "And likewise a Levite, when he was at the place, came and looked *on him*, and passed by on the other side.	
		33 "But a certain Samaritan,[j] as he journeyed, came where he was: and when he saw him, he had compassion *on him*,	
		34 "And went to *him*, and bound up his wounds, pouring in oil and wine,[k] and set him on his own beast, and brought him to an inn, and took care of him.	
		35 "And on the morrow when he departed, he took out two[l] pence, [a Roman coin for two day's wages at about .20 cents each] and gave *them* to the host, and said unto him, 'Take care of him; and whatsoever thou spendest more, when I come again, I will repay thee.'	
		Christ's question; the lawyer's response: Christ's command	
		36 "Which now of these three, thinkest thou, was neighbour unto him that fell among the thieves?"	
		37 And he said, "He that shewed mercy on him." Then said Jesus unto him, "Go, and do thou likewise."[m] (Verse 38 cont. in Section 117.)	

Footnotes-Commentary

[a] **"Stood up."** This parable came out of a question that a lawyer proposed to the Lord Jesus. Public debate began when the questioner stood up and addressed the speaker. For the meaning of lawyers, see Section 70, number 4 under footnote h. This fellow was a doctor in the Torah Law, and a scribe. At this time, Christ was passing through Samaria going to Bethany, and then to Jerusalem for the Feast of Tabernacles. Among the crowds, ever following Him, was a lawyer probably planning to keep the Feast himself. An examination of this event reveals that the lawyer *first* questioned Jesus with malicious intentions. The occasion seems to have been a public gathering, for the verse reads that he "stood up," which was the accepted posture in putting questions to or debating a public speaker. However, by the time this discussion was over it appears that he was in agreement with the Master (verse 36-37). In

other cases, the religious leaders purposely laid snares to trap Him in His Words and deeds. See Section 54, Mk. 3:2, footnote c. This Hebrew scribe presented to Christ mankind's most serious question. It should be noted that two days before His death on the cross, another specialist in the Jewish Law came to Christ with a similar question. See Section 157, Matt. 22:35-39, footnotes c and d for details of this event.

(b) "How readest thou?" Christ's Words were the standard rabbinical response to questions in discussing Scripture with inquirers. Jesus turned this man over to the very law in which he was supposed to be an authority. In other words, Christ was saying, "Can't you find the answer to your question in the law of which you are a specialist?" As a scribe, it was his business to know the facts of the Torah Law and the correct interpretation of each of them. Because he was an "expert" in this field, the Lord Jesus responded to his question with a question and asked him to explain what the law said on this subject.

(c) Highlighted for He answered from the Shema prayer of Deut. 6:4-9. Several verses from this part of the Old Testament were handwritten on kosher skin or parchment and placed in phylacteries (small boxes worn on the forehead and forearm). They were regularly cited in the synagogues and inscribed on right side doorposts of all observant Jewish homes. Later, these verses were placed inside little cylinder-like boxes with the Hebrew Name for God "Shaddai" showing through a small opening. These religious fixtures are called "mezuzah." The plural form of the word "mezuaot" means "doorposts." The mezuzah served to identify the home as Jewish wherein the mitzvoth or commandments of God, are loved and obeyed. In the staunchly pious Hebrew homes, the mezuzah is placed on every door except the bathroom. The Shema is considered the holiest prayer within Judaism and is recited daily. The lawyer's second quotation from the Old Testament "thy neighbor as thyself" was taken from Lev. 19:18. He appended this passage to the Shema prayer, but it was *not* originally a part of it. These citations from the Old Testament reveal that this man knew the law well, and that he wanted to obey its injunctions, yet his heart was void of the peace of eternal life that only came by believing in Jesus as the Messiah and Savior.

2p-As mentioned above, a few days before His death, while standing in the temple, Jesus explained the "great commandment" of the Torah Law. This came in response to a question from another Jewish lawyer and was "loaded" with the intent to trap Him (Matt. 22:34-40). On this occasion, our Lord quoted the Shema prayer and made the same Lev. 19:18 addition to it as did the lawyer in the above Section. The essence of this commandment was that all of man's four powers (heart, soul, strength, and mind) are to love God supremely, and then his neighbor as himself. The Shema was an expression of God's highest purpose for Israel, toward Himself, and toward all fellow men. (It should be remembered that Jews hated both Samaritans and Gentiles). No Hebrew had ever fulfilled these requirements, save the Son of God. Here, we see the holiness of the law slays every Jew for failing to render *total obedience* to its just and high demands. The lesson is that someone must come and rescue the Jews from trying to be saved by law keeping. Later, Christ affirmed that none of them kept the Torah Law (Section 119, John 7:19). Thus, being broken, it pointed a finger of condemnation at Israel, but especially the spiritual leaders who were obligated first to keep the commandment. Whoever this scribe-lawyer was, he was beginning to see his need for help from the entrapment he fell into by trying tempting the Savior.

(d) "This do, and thou shalt live." What does this mean? Christ commended the lawyer, for he had correctly responded to His question. Is He saying that eternal life is acquired by adherence to the Mosaic Law, and in this particular case the Shema with the Lev. 19:18 addition? See the first paragraph of footnote c above for explanation of this Jewish term. Years later, Rabbi Paul, the great expositor of the Torah, wrote that the law was a schoolmaster that led or *pointed* the Jews to Christ. He did not say, "The sacrificial law only is the schoolmaster because you are to live by the rest of it." After coming to Christ for eternal life (through repentance and faith), the schoolmaster was no longer needed (Gal. 3:24-25). They believed that if any Jew perfectly kept all 613 precepts of the Torah Law, he would be accounted acceptably righteous before God. Devout Hebrews on earth in the days of Christ sought to attain to righteousness (or eternal life) by law-keeping (Rom. 9:31-32), for this was the message of the synagogues and rabbis without exception. Yet, they were ignorant of God's true righteousness (Rom. 10:3), which was found *only* in the Lord Jesus their Messiah (Rom. 5:17, 21). Jewish thinking was seasoned to believe that they had to do *many things* to appear righteous before God. (Every false religion on earth today teaches the same thing.) See Section 52, footnote h, Section 89, footnote c, and Section 96, footnote d for explanation of the oral law. In the Sermon on the Mount, the Savior sternly warned the common people that they must have righteousness greater than that of their religious leaders, or they would not be part of His kingdom. Note this in Section 45, Matt. 5:20, footnote e.

2p-The written Torah Law was considered a *complete entity,* perfect in its entirety. Nowhere in Scripture is it divided into three parts as the law cults teach. To keep 612 of the 613 precepts of Moses' Law and break only one, brought full condemnation upon the offender, for in breaking one, he had broken all (James 2:10). One of the chief purposes of the code of Moses was to convict Israelites, that they were unable to procure eternal life by works of righteousness. Nevertheless, men living under the law were saved despite the law's inability to save them. For how people were saved under the law and before Christ's death on the cross, see Section 10, footnote b. The Torah condemned without impunity every offender by various and sundry penalties. For explanation of this, see Section 45, footnotes c and d. Our Lord told this lawyer that he was living proof that the law could not save, even though he was one of its esteemed doctors, and an expert in its teachings. (Later, the rich young ruler in Section 139, Matt. 19:20 footnote f, also confessed the law could not save.) This expert knew the Torah perfectly and had directed his every step accordingly, yet he did *not* have eternal life and admitted to this in his initial question to the Savior. See footnote a above. Dedication and a rigid blind obedience to the law throughout his life had failed to bring to his heart the sure hope of salvation. He had woefully missed the supreme lesson of the great Torah Law and the prophets: they all pointed men to Christ, the Messiah, for salvation and forgiveness of sins (Lk. 24:27, John 5:45-47 and Acts 10:43).

3p-The code of Moses revealed the Savior to Israel in many ways. However, most Jews looked to the *letter* of the Torah, instead of its greatest single lesson which was Messiah-Christ, the One to whom its letters pointed. The clamor being made about "Torah based faith plus nothing equals salvation" is deathly sick. The correct motto should be "Torah based faith, which is based solely on the Messiah, who was to come, is saving faith." Later, the books of the New Testament were added to give specific instructions about living the Christian life. All Jews who put faith in this coming Messiah (pictured hundreds of times in their law) received salvation. Those who did not trust Him but put faith in their obedience to the Torah, were damned. Jews who hope *only* in the great Torah Law have no hope. All Jews, therefore, who trust the Christ *pictured in the Torah Law* are saved Jews, who now possess eternal life. Messianic Jews who write, "Keeping the Torah Law is part of the faith that gets you to heaven" have written heresy and by their own words are guilty of *mixing* works with grace. See last paragraph of footnote m below. According to Rabbi Paul, the two will not mix (Rom. 11:6). Beware of those who seize upon *every* mention of the word "command" or "commandments" in the New Testament and automatically force all of them to mean "the Ten Commandments" or "the commandments of the Torah." This is a standard cult approach for distorting God's Word. The chief response of the *radical* "Torah keeping Jews" is to slander those who will not be brought under legal bondage by calling them "anti Semitic." These people are always correcting the Bible and pointing out why *their* Greek and Hebrew translations are superior, and all others are wrong. *It should be carefully noted that not all saved Jews are of this dark and thunderous Mount Sinai nature.*

(e) First, Christ attempted to show this lawyer that Shema keeping would not save his soul. No part of the Mosaic commandments had the power to save one's soul from hell "for if righteousness come by the law, then Christ is dead in vain" (Gal. 2:21). Paul did not say, "by the ceremonial law." In essence, our Lord said, "You have kept the Shema faithfully, so has this given you eternal life?" The lawyer was saying, "I have kept the Shema and still do not have everlasting life." The conclusion of the matter was, "Can't you now understand that eternal life does not come by any of your Torah commandments or reciting the Shema? You have kept these commands of Moses, yet you do not have the hope your heart longs for." Like most Jews of that era, this lawyer failed to see Christ shadowed, prefigured, and presented throughout his beloved Torah. For the Savior pictured in the law, note Section 52, John 5:45-47, footnotes y and z. The Torah, *emptied* of Christ the Messiah and His work in redemption, was like a sun that cannot shine. This was how the religious leaders and most Jews in the days of Christ on earth viewed their law. They were intoxicated by their man-made tradition of the elders (oral law), and blinded by their passion for a material, political kingdom. Further, they hated with fierce intentions Jesus of Nazareth because He would not fall in line with their religion of works, outward noise, show, pomp, and rejection of what the Torah Law correctly taught. The Savior fearlessly and publicly condemned their sin repeatedly.

(f) Verse 29. "Justify himself." Greatly embarrassed by the response of Christ, he put the question about who his neighbor was. Being an Orthodox Jew and scribe of the law, he would automatically *exclude all Gentiles* from the neighbor category. Here, we must understand a peculiar thing that the Jews believed at this time. It was a common notion among the Jews, that one must "justify himself" before God while living on earth. This was accomplished by obedience to the Torah as well as the thousands of oral laws of Israel. Any devout Hebrew who worked faithfully at this, would, at the end of life, be counted one of those who had "justified himself" *before God*. The idea here is not that the lawyer fell into a hot debate with Christ and struggled to prove his viewpoint. He inquired of Jesus, who his neighbor was, because he sincerely wanted to "justify himself" before God by loving his neighbor as himself. In quoting the Shema to Christ, he *added to it* the passage of Lev. 19:18 as previously mentioned in the first paragraph of footnote c above. This passage commands love towards one's neighbor. *Now,* the Lord Jesus will show him how he has failed to keep his addition to the Shema quotation. He does this by giving the Parable of the Good Samaritan.

2p-The rabbis and doctors of the law had propounded for years that a Jew's neighbor was strictly a fellow Jew. No Gentile, especially a cursed Samaritan, would ever be classified as a neighbor by any pious Jew. In giving this parable, the Lord proved to the lawyer that he had broken the command of Lev. 19:18, which he has just quoted. In so doing, he had not "justified himself" on earth and was therefore, not "justified before God" in heaven. Even worse, as already explained, in breaking this one commandment, he was guilty of breaking the entire Torah Law. See second paragraph of footnote d above.

(g) "From Jerusalem to Jericho." This was a common expression denoting serious danger. For more on Jericho, see footnote h below and Section 143, footnote a. Most parables had one specific thrust-point designed to answer a particular question or present a specific lesson. By giving this parable, the Lord Jesus' main purpose was to show the lawyer (and all present) that one's neighbor was not just a fellow Jew, but also *any man* who showed mercy to those in need regardless of their national origin, race, creed, or color. In western culture, a neighbor is the person across the street or next door. Not so in the language of the scribes and Pharisees of this era in Hebrew history. In this parable, Christ portrayed the callousness of the Jewish religious leaders (a priest and Levite) towards *all men* who were not like them. Then He told of the "cursed" Samaritan, who manifested genuine neighborly mercy and love to a helpless man on the roadside. The entire parable was a slap in the face of the self-righteous Jewish religious leaders, and a sharp lesson to the lawyer by showing him who a true neighbor really was. Christ's reply was not what the lawyer had been taught in the synagogue, or schools of the Jews, nor what he had taught others.

(h) The ancient road from Jerusalem to Jericho was a steep descent every mile of the way in a northeasterly direction. It was the most traveled road in the land. Jericho was about sixteen miles east of Jerusalem and six miles west of the Jordan River. History calls it "the red" or "blood way," because it was infected with robbers and murderers who spilt much human blood. Jericho itself was known as the "city of palm trees" (Deut. 34:3). This was the most traveled road because it led over Jordan into Peraea and intersected with the road that led north into Galilee. Jews traveling this route avoided passing through Samaria. See footnote j below. The place derived its hostile character from a howling wilderness through which the road passed. Ravines, cliffs, caves, and such afforded a lurking place for thieves, murderers, and bandits. It was in this terrible region that the Lord Jesus was tempted by the Devil at the beginning of His ministry. Thousands of priests and Levites resided at Jericho and traveled back and forth to their work at the temple in Jerusalem. See Talmud tractate, Tamid 30b for mention of Levites (who were in command of temple music) singing in the city of Jericho. This "city of palms" was divided into two close but separate sections, one being the old city and the other a newer division built by the Romans. Herod the Great had built himself a palace in this city, in which he later died. See Section 17, footnote b for more on Herod's death date.

(i) **Verses 31–32. "The other side of the road."** This reveals the attitude of Jerusalem's religious functionaries towards a dying man who was not a fellow Jew. The priests served in the sacrificial system attending to all offerings brought into the temple. The Levites did the never-ending manual work and supervised all music and singing. These two men somehow represent the Law of Moses and its inability to save from sin and restore to new life. Returning home ("went down") from their work tenure, neither of these men dared to touch the victim of the robbers. Perhaps they feared defilement that would render them unclean for seven days (Num. 19:16), or was it typical racial hatred and bigotry? Christ selected these two members of the Jewish religion and their compassionless, hardhearted attitudes to make the lawyer understand that the true neighbor was the one who showed mercy. Both were professional religionists and worked in God's temple, yet both were void of a heart of pity and concern for the wounded stranger. Woe be to the church that has spiritual leaders who are void of genuine compassion and sincere love for those whom they can reach. Too many believers in the local church take the "other side of the road" to avoid reaching out to sinful, hurting humankind. In that lane, there is no giving, sharing, helping, praying, tithing, working, hurting, suffering, sacrificing, and above all else, bringing lost men to Jesus.

(j) **A "certain Samaritan."** Whoever this fellow was, his deeds of compassion and unselfishness have inspired millions over the ensuing ages. Mission boards, churches, charitable organizations, and countless others have taken up the title "the good Samaritan," and proudly wear it to demonstrate their attitude towards those who are in need. Though his name is not given, his deeds of genuine love and concern have lived for over two thousand years of history! Even among the godless of today, this story lives on.

2p-If we remember, the Lord Jesus was passing through Samaria when He gave this parable, and that the lesson was given in response to a Jewish lawyer, made it more acute. Jews hated Samaritans and vice versa. Josephus records that Samaritans on one occasion threw dead bodies into the temple precincts to pollute the place and had killed Jews traveling through their land, to attend one of the annual feasts at the temple in Jerusalem. See *Antiquities*, Book 18:2. 2, lines 29-30 for some of this story. Rivalry was fiercely vicious between the two groups. The Jews looked upon the Samaritans as a mongrel race, sprung from the heathen Assyrians. Yet, Christ deliberately gave His parable and in it, He revealed the meaning of "neighbor" in response to the lawyer's question. The "evil Samaritan" was moved with compassion and rescued the half-dead man, while the figures of Hebrew religion contemptuously passed him by. The conclusion was that the cursed Samaritan was the true neighbor, not the Jewish religionists. Jesus our Lord, as meek as He was, had a bundle of terrible thunderbolts reserved for the hypocrites and self-righteous monsters of Israel. *Was this wounded man was a Jew?*

(k) **"Oil and wine."** The Jews used this combination for all sorts of wounds and deep cuts. It served as an antiseptic and disinfectant. They strongly believed that this mixture would quickly heal the wound caused by circumcision. After being administered medical attention, the disabled man was then taken to the shelter of an inn that was surely nearby and out of the danger zone of robbers and bandits. The Samaritan cared for the injured, helpless man and paid all costs necessary for his recovery. There can be no doubt, that in this story one may see a type or allegory of Christ coming to save the lost, after the law (represented in the priest and Levite) proved unable to do so. However, the *main thrust-point* of the entire parable was to answer the lawyer's sincere question, "who is my neighbor?" See footnote g above. Moreover, was it ever answered? Now, he understood from Messiah, who his neighbor was in a sense never found in his Torah Law. The law showed no mercy; it was to be kept or else! Jesus was the opposite. He showed great mercy to sinners. The lawyer's thinking was now freed from the bondage of the rabbis and the exclusiveness of their hatred for all who were not Jews. This expert in the commandments of Moses had received light never seen before and had answered his own question. *The one who shows mercy is the real neighbor* (verses 36–37). Smitten by his conscience and knowing that he had shown mercy *only* upon fellow Jews, he understood the meaning of Jesus' parable.

(l) **"Two."** Some hyper enthusiasts over the past fifty years have seen in this word a sure prophetic sign that Jesus would return by the year A.D. 2000. It is now A.D. 2011. They missed again! Others have found in the coins a picture of both Old and New Testaments, some of the ordinances of the church, baptism and the Lord's Supper. One fanatical group holds that these pieces of money point to the gifts the Holy Spirit gives to the body of Christ. One can easily believe (that in time) some "anointed interpreter of the word," with "great insight into prophecy" may see in these two coins peanut butter mixed with jelly! Good sense dictates that we leave the coins to mean "two pence" just like the Lord Jesus said.

(m) **What a command!** "You now know who your neighbor is: go and act accordingly." He had never found anything like this written in the Torah Law. Surely, conviction fastened upon his soul with these final words spoken by the Lord Jesus. Did he obey Messiah? Being a thorough Hebrew and highly polished in the Torah Law, things backfired in his face. The Savior pointed him to (of all people) a Samaritan to learn his real duties before God and all men! Nothing could have been more humiliating than this. Often in this life, we must be brought low in our shame before we learn those special lessons from God.

2p-Genuine faith is seen in good works. There is an overriding lesson in this parable: it shadows for us a picture of the good we are to do in this life as saved Christians. Doing good and seeking to bring blessing to others (regardless of who, or what they are) are the natural results of saving faith. So much has been preached in Baptist Churches about "good works do not save," that many believers have swung in the opposite direction. *True* faith produces authentic works. Titus 3:8 makes this clear. Without this evidence or fruits, one is suspect of the salvation of some in the local church. Our Lord "went about doing good," (Acts 10:38). A thousand years before Christ came to earth, David wrote, "Trust in the LORD, and do good," (Ps. 37:3). The words of Gal. 6:10 hang as a beautiful rainbow over the earthly life of every Christian: "As we have therefore, opportunity, let us do good to all men, especially to them who are of the household of faith." This verse could be a grand conclusion of the Parable of the Good Samaritan: one that we should not so quickly forget. The popular and common notion that we can somehow get good enough to enter heaven is like putting lipstick on a pig, it does not work. One of the chief hallmarks of all false religions is their struggle to be forgiven and saved by what they do, instead of what Christ has already done in His death, burial, and resurrection. *We are saved, not by works, but to go to work for God and man.*

3p-Primitive or early Christianity in action. Once while preaching in Germany, a Christian Jew told the author of a peculiar custom practiced among inmates languishing in a Romanian communist prison. Someone had procured a small lump of sugar. This was highly prized. Among the dozens of men in the common cell were atheists, robbers, murderers, political fighters, and a small group of Christians. They had agreed among themselves that sugar would be given to the weakest and sickest prisoner. A Presbyterian pastor lay dying on a rotted blanket. Refusing the sugar, he requested that it be given to a raging atheist who had severely beaten him across the face. Holding the tiny morsel of sugar toward his persecutor, with trembling hand, the man of God smiled and slipped into eternity. This was primitive Christianity in action! Only Jesus Christ could inspire men to such unselfish love and behavior that expresses the glorious image of His person (Heb. 1:3). In these actions, we understand the verse that reads, "faith that worketh by love" (Gal. 5:6).

4p-Some observation on faith. Like light and illumination, faith and belief are synonymous. True saving "faith comes by hearing the word of God" (Rom. 10:8 and 17). After the new birth, abiding faith that produces fruit to the glory of God comes by genuine fellowship with the Father and the Son (1 John 1:3). There are thousands of false faiths in this world, but only one faith that is acceptable and honored by God (Eph. 4:5). This divine faith is seen or revealed from one believer to the other, in their lives and conduct (Rom. 1:17). The greatest of faith without God's love is useless (1 Cor. 13:2). When a professor in Christ departs from the faith, this is his choice not one of real faith (1 Tim. 4:1). Faith placed in the *wrong* things is inactive (1 Cor. 15:14). In Scripture, faith is called a work (John 6:29). It is a work God requires, yet He enables man to perform. Upon hearing divine truth one may choose or refuse to respond (Acts 17:32). Because it is a gift of God and an offering of mercy, it is clearly excluded from the category of works upon the basis of which man may claim salvation. Thus, faith is not the procuring cause of salvation, but it is only the instrumental cause. The blessed procuring cause is the Son of God Jesus Christ, whom ready faith embraces. How sad when *radical* Reformed believers put doctrine before Christ, and *timorous* Arminians put human will before God's grace. Both aim at nothing and hit it.

He arrives at Bethany* before the Feast of Tabernacles. It is *assumed* that Mary and Martha were previously informed of His upcoming arrival by a team from the seventy** forerunners. Thus, they had prepared lodging and a meal*** for Christ and His disciples. The two sisters contrasted.

*According to Section 124, John 11:1 the two sisters lived at this village. See footnote a below for other details.** See all by the two asterisks under main heading of Section 114 for more on the seventy meeting Jesus.***This is not the special supper given for Jesus and Lazarus in Section 146, John 12:1, six days before the final Passover.

Matt.	Mk.	Lk. 10:38-42—Bethany	John
		38 Now it came to pass, as they went, that he entered into a certain village:(a) and a certain woman named Martha received him into her house. **39** And she had a sister called Mary, which also sat at Jesus' feet, and heard his word.(b) **40** But Martha was cumbered [distracted and troubled] about much serving,(c) and came to him, and said, "Lord, dost thou not care that my sister hath left me to serve alone? bid her therefore that she help me." **41** And Jesus answered and said unto her, "Martha, Martha, thou art careful and troubled about many things:(d) **42** "But one thing is needful: and Mary hath chosen that good part, which shall not be taken away from her."(e) (Next chap., Lk. 11:1 cont. in Section 118.)	

Footnotes-Commentary

(a) **"Certain village."** We learn from Section 124, John 11:18 and Section 146, John 12:1-2, that this Bethany was located about two miles east of Jerusalem. It was situated on the main road that led down to Jericho and into Peraea on Jordan's eastern side. *Assuming* that the Lord Jesus had arrived here just before the Feast, the women of the house were ready for His visit. Among the seventy messengers sent ahead, the Savior surely instructed two of them to this humble home to announce a fixed day for His soon arrival. It was an honored occasion for householders to receive into their homes famed rabbis and great teachers of the law. We note the absence of the brother Lazarus, in Luke's narrative of this history. Section 119 and John 7:14 inform us that Jesus did not go up to the temple until the "middle of the feast," which was eight days long. Did our Lord arrive at the home of Martha *after* her brother had already gone up to the Feast? Apparently, this explains his absence from the house. It was not required that women attend this particular observance, though some did.

2p-During the eight days of the Feast of Tabernacles or Shavuot, the Jews built pens and leafy booths outside their houses. Those dwelling in, or near Jerusalem built thousands of booths, which dotted the landscape about the great temple and the area behind the walls of the city. These served as makeshift or temporary apartments during the celebration and were somewhat open yet still shady. Men, women, and children dwelled in separate booths. According to Jewish tradition, it was the duty of all Hebrews to eat, sleep, pray, and *study* God's Word during this grand event. These days concluded with a spectacular dance called the "dance of lights." This is discussed in Section 119, the eighth paragraph of footnote a. At the home of Mary and Martha, a number of individual booths had been erected in the courtyard adjacent to the house, during the feast period. These were considered as secondary dwellings for family, guests, and friends attending the Feast of Tabernacles. It was here the Lord tarried as the first few days of the official celebration passed. He was waiting for the right moment to appear suddenly at the temple and make a most profound and shocking announcement to the thousands of pilgrims present.

(b) **"Heard his Word."** Studying the Scriptures during the Feast of Tabernacles was a joyous event shared by thousands of Jewish pilgrims. During this particular celebration, emphasis was put upon reading the book of Ruth. This was done while sitting in or near their booths. This again expels the myth that few copies of Scripture were available for the ordinary people. There were countless thousands of copies of the Ruth scrolls belonging to the families in Israel as well as the other books of their Tanakh (Old Testament). The Lord Jesus was looked upon as a rabbi and gave His teaching sessions from the doorway of the "great booth," which was situated in a central location near the house of Lazarus and his sisters. It was used in the daytime for fellowship, study, and communication. No doubt, many sat nearby listening to the gracious Words that came from His mouth. "Sitting at the feet" was the posture of students listening to the rabbis teach. See Acts 22:3, where Paul was brought up at the feet of Gamaliel. So intrigued was Mary with her Lord's instructions, that she forgot to assist her sister in serving the large number that was present. Joining the guests, she slipped to her knees before the Lord of glory to hear the Word of God that poured graciously from His lips. Earthly food must wait, for her soul was longing for manna from heaven.

(c) **"Much serving."** There was no small crowd of people at Mary's house on this occasion. Poor Martha was busy rushing about serving the appointed meals to those listening to the teaching of Jesus. She was left out of this blessing and quickly became perturbed with her sister for not helping. One is surprised at the bluntness of Martha as she registers her complaint with the Master. "Tell her to come and help me," were her angry words of frustration. This outburst sounds like something of a *female* Simon Peter!

(d) **Verses 41 and 42.** These verses are a revelation into an area of human life, missed by many of us. The character of these two sisters shows itself vividly in this story. We cannot doubt that Martha shared the piety and love for Jesus as did her sister; seemingly, she fails at first to rise to the high and lofty conception of this wonderful Person. Being the host for Messiah, His disciples and others required much work. It was unfair to deride Martha for her anxiousness; her labor surely represented the best display of love and devotion toward the Savior. *On the other hand, Mary's posture at the feet of Jesus was unheard of for a female!* This was the position for boys and men learning from their teacher-rabbi, not for a woman! Could it be that Martha was embarrassed by her sister's unusual conduct? The traditional role was to be doing what Martha was engaged in, attending to the guests. Not over looking the role to serve and bless all visitors who may perchance enter our homes, (but beyond this necessary courtesy) the Word of God must always take first place. Job put it this way, "I have esteemed the Words of his [God's] mouth more than my necessary food" (Job 23:12).

2p-Somehow, this scurrying, busy scene portrays many of today's believers. Let sister so-and-so miss that special sale at the local department store, and she is sick for a week. Let brother so-and-so lose his pocketknife, or miss that fishing trip to Canada, and he is ill tempered for weeks. However, the same persons may have a son, daughter, workmate, or parent lost and without Christ, and they rarely spend time in prayer or a few minutes witnessing to these poor unsaved creatures. Call upon the saints to attend a time of Bible study, extended prayer, and soul searching before God, and see what you get! A thousand like Martha are heard and seen dashing about the church today, ever grumbling because they are "over careful and distracted about many things" of this world.

3p-**All things in life must pass away.** It is disturbing to behold many believers in Christ, planning and living, as though they will be here forever. We mortals in the western world spend the first twenty years or so of life making a mess of things. The next forty are employed trying to correct the disasters of the first twenty. Just as we think it is all in order, we peek out the window, and there stands old man death beside his hearse. He beckoning us to come with him; life is over. The stage of life has many entrances and many exits. We all pass this way, play our little parts, say our words, and exit into eternity. The end of life begins when we are born; it arrives when we die. *What then?* It behooves all of God's true children to follow Christ with all their hearts. The heartaches and sorrows that befall Christians must never deceive us into losing faith's sweet consolation. Keep faith in God; He is too good to do bad. Look afresh at the cross and see the greatest demonstration of love and mercy ever manifested to Adam's fallen race. *Remember again, it was for you that Jesus died despite the horrendous lies of Calvinism and the hopelessness of Arminianism.* The Son of God died to make possible the salvation of all men and to make certain the salvation of those who repent and believe in Him. It is childish play on words to affirm that the death of Christ was *sufficient* for all but *efficient* only for those wholly believe it. Calvinists invent words to justify every deviation from the truth they invent. All the smart talk about "Christ died for all without *distinction* but nor for all without *exception*" is a classical example of their theological jargon. See another example of inventing names for doctrinal perversions in Section 9, the fourth paragraph of footnote g.

(e) **"Hath chosen that good part."** The gentle calmness of Jesus, grateful to both for their service, had only a tender reply. He justified Mary's conduct, but with such wisdom and candor that we could almost weep. If we are faced with the decision of choosing to sit near our Lord to hear His teaching, or to attend the good and needful work of serving others earthly manna, our first duty is to choose Christ. This does not signify that wives and daughters neglect their household duties, or let things degrade and decline to a dirty and sinful condition. Rather, it signals that during the *once-in-a-lifetime* opportunities, we give full attendance to Christ while lesser things must wait. Never would this event be repeated at this wonderful Bethany home. Mary was willing to jeopardize her reputation as a good housekeeper *for this one time*, while Martha seemingly did not consider the supremacy of that moment as did her wise sister. What we receive into our souls by diligent attendance to God's Word, and prayer will never be taken away! Putting all things in their correct perspective, it remains forever valid that to attend to the salvation of one's soul, and then to live life for Christ are the most important issues in a passing world. This is the one needful thing, and when done right it shall never be taken from us.

2p-Even though the above is so, we must remember that both types of service as performed by these good sisters is sorely needed today in the work of our Lord. Each one to be done at the proper time and place. Those overheated preachers who slam Martha and praise Mary seemed to have missed the mark in this great story. The Savior was reminding us not to be consumed with lesser duties at the expense of eternal affairs. Stay balanced fellow saints as you serve God and men. Both endeavours will be rewarded some day.

Prior to leaving Bethany for Jerusalem, He seeks God in prayer. An unnamed disciple is greatly moved as he beholds Jesus praying. He beseeches the Master to teach them this divine art. The Lord Jesus revises a prayer given earlier during The Sermon on the Mount and uses it as a teaching model for His disciples to follow.*

The original version of this prayer is found in Section 46, starting with Matt. 6:9.

Matt.	Mk.	Lk. 11:1-13—Bethany	John
		Messiah prays: an observer's request	
		1 And it came to pass, that, as he was praying[(a)] in a certain place, when he ceased, one of his disciples said unto him, "Lord, teach us to pray, as John also taught his disciples."	
		The Lord's response: a model prayer	
		2 And he said unto them, "When ye pray, say,[(b)] Our Father which art in heaven, Hallowed be thy name. Thy kingdom come. Thy will be done, as in heaven, so in earth.	
		3 "Give us day by day our daily bread.	
		4 "And forgive us our sins; for we also forgive every one that is indebted to us. And lead us not into temptation; but deliver us from evil."	
		The key: be persistent in prayer: never give up	
		5 And he said unto them,[(c)] "Which of you shall have a friend, and shall go unto him at midnight, and say unto him, 'Friend, lend me three loaves;	
		6 'For a friend of mine in his journey is come to me, and I have nothing to set before him?'	
		7 "And he from within shall answer and say, 'Trouble me not: the door is now shut, and my children are with me in bed; I cannot rise and give thee.'	
		8 "I say unto you, Though he will not rise and give him, because he is his friend, yet because of his importunity [persistence] he will rise and give him as many as he needeth.	
		9 "And I say unto you, Ask,[(d)] and it shall be given you; seek, and ye shall find; knock, and it shall be opened unto you.	
		10 "For every one that asketh receiveth; and he that seeketh findeth; and to him that knocketh it shall be opened.	
		God gives good things: the Spirit is His best gift	
		11 "If a son shall ask bread of any of you that is a father, will he give him a stone?[(e)] or if *he ask* a fish, will he for a fish give him a serpent?[(f)]	
		12 "Or if he shall ask an egg, will he offer him a scorpion?[(g)]	
		13 "If ye then, being evil, know how to give good gifts unto your children: how much more shall *your* heavenly Father give the Holy Spirit to them that ask him?"[(h)] (Verse 14 cont. in Section 66.)	

Footnotes-Commentary

[(a)] **"He was praying."** Here, our Lord went into a season of prayer before departing Bethany for Jerusalem and the Feast of Tabernacles. The rabbis encouraged times of prayer for all pilgrims *before* their actual attendance at the temple. Apparently, this was what Christ did. It was common for disciples to inquire of their master about praying, different kinds of prayers, when to pray, and so on. Most Jewish prayers of this era consisted of dry benedictions and doxologies. The Talmud tractate, Bereachoth, deals with many of these. However, watching and hearing the Son of God in prayer greatly moved the apostles on this occasion. Beyond the dry Jewish prayer, they longed to pray like

Jesus. They knew that John the Baptist had taught his followers the divine art of prayer, for some of them had been among his early disciples. Now, they were so touched by the praying Christ that their hearts burned to know more. Who was this disciple that expressed desire for a better prayer life, similar to that of his Master? Listening to the Son of God pray was the nearest thing to heaven on earth! For earlier comments on prayer made by the Lord Jesus, see Section 47, Matt. 7:7, footnote d. Apparently the unknown disciple who put this question to Jesus was not present at the Sermon on the Mount, in which Jesus gave a model for praying.

(b) "After this manner therefore pray ye." In Section 46, beginning at Matt. 6:9, we were introduced to the first recorded model or form prayer of Christ, which was given during the Sermon on the Mount. Now about two years later, we hear our Lord repeating portions of this same prayer in response to the request of His disciples about "how" to pray. It is of interest that Christ used the same model prayer in answering the question. Why? What is to be found in this example of praying that is so high and worthy, that it was mostly repeated some two years later? Does this teach us that even a form prayer, if Scriptural and from the heart, is heard by God as well as those from veteran believers? The author has seen many converts come to Christ, who had to be taught how to pray! Note the following remarks regarding this prayer. They reveal that Jesus repeated Himself, taking words from the same type of prayer as used earlier during the Sermon on the Mount:

1. For Lk. 11:2, see the Sermon on the Mount, in Section 46, Matt. 6:9, footnote g.
2. For Lk. 11:2b, see the Sermon on the Mount, in Section 46, Matt. 6:10, third paragraph under footnote g.
3. For Lk. 11:3, see the Sermon on the Mount, in Section 46, Matt. 6:11, which is slightly different.

(c) In verses 5-13, the Master gave several illustrations regarding urgent things that pertain to prayer. All prayer must be under the banner of "God's will be done" (1 John 5:4).

1. In verse 5, He introduces to His apostles one of the most important features of prayer, which is persistence. Jesus gave the illustration of a man whose friend visits at midnight, and he had no food to set before him. In oriental culture, this was a serious calamity or even, insult. Hospitality was a sacred obligation; the host *must* feed all visitors and travelers who might spend the night. In verses 6 and 7, the breadless man goes to a neighbor, knocks on his door in the wee hours of the morning, and asks for bread to feed his visitor. The neighbor's reply is not out of rudeness but one of simple facts.
2. The children would all sleep on straw mats on the floor of the one-roomed house. Father would sleep at one end of the wide mat and the mother at the other end. His response "my children are in bed with me" is correct. To get up, step over the sleeping family, light a lamp and unbolt the door would awaken the household! His objections were valid, and the man at the door outside, knew this. What Jesus said in verse 8 are the thrust line of His lesson on prayer. The man without food for his visitor was in a more critical situation than his neighbor in bed with all the family. Both knew this. Consequently, the man outside did not cease knocking on the door. If he continued, the children would be awakened. Christ said this man was finally given the bread he needed because of "his importunity" in refusing to take no for an answer. The word "importunity" carries the meaning that he was "shameless" in his persistent hammering on the door. His cause being right and just, he would not stop until the answer came. In the culture of this time, the entire village would have been shamed and humiliated had word spread that the needy man was refused bread by his neighbor. The lesson Christ gave His preachers was that when their cause is honorable and crucial, they must stay before God, refusing to relent or give up their honest cause, prayers, and supplications. As the sleeping man rose and gave his friend as much as he needed, thus God will rise at the right time to meet our just, and righteous pleas, according to His will.

(d) Again, our Lord repeats a similar statement given previously in His Sermon on the Mount. See Section 47, Matt. 7:7-8, footnote d.

(e) See Section 23, Matt. 4:3, fourth paragraph of footnote c for stones in the land that resemble loaves of bread.

(f) Numerous sea creatures are serpentine in form, such as the sea snake. We have no idea exactly what type of creature is referred to in this statement. However, both Christ and His disciples understood.

(g) Jesus' Words here, that liken a scorpion to an egg, are not as difficult as some make them. There is a white or very light colored scorpion found in this land. Rolled up in the sand, it resembled a small egg and was sometimes mistaken as such by unwary travelers. Those who touched it were stung and suffered excruciating pain or death. Christ's preachers knew what He was saying in this comparative lesson. See Dr. E. H. Thompson's classic work, *The Land and the Book*, vol. i page 379, for comments on the white scorpion.

(h) In Section 47, Matt. 7:11 during the original Sermon on the Mount, the Lord Jesus had used a similar expression in speaking of prayer. However, it is noted that in the earlier usage recorded by Matthew, He did not mention the Holy Spirit, but rather God, giving "good things to them that ask him." We do well to understand that the Holy Spirit is the greatest of "good things (gifts)" that the Father gives His children after salvation. (See next paragraph below.) It would be as wicked and improper for a loving father to give his children deadly and harmful things to injure them, as it would for God to do so in response to the prayers of His children. Our estimation of "good things" is usually *not* the same as that of the Lord in heaven. God "supplying all our needs according to His riches in glory by Christ Jesus" (Phil. 4:19) does not always mean a "box of chocolates with a red ribbon." Our Lord may see that we need to be broken, wounded, emptied, and torn away from those things that rob us of intimate fellowship with Him and steal His power from our lives. It took years for Paul to understand that his thorn in the flesh was a good thing, designed to mold him into a powerful instrument for God's service (2 Cor. 12:7-10).

2p-Verse 13. "Give the Holy Spirit to them that ask him." Luke wrote that Jesus said the Father would do this. Here, is the highest gift for believers, the source and power of all *true* prayer (Rom. 8:26-27 with Eph. 6:18). This is not speaking of an unsaved man praying for the Spirit of God. Scripture is clear: men who do not have the Holy Spirit are men who do not know Christ (Rom. 8:9). With believers, He lives in the "inner man" or the "souls" of those who are redeemed (Eph. 3:16). God giving the Spirit to "them that ask Him" has reference to several things:

1. **Support in prayer.** Contextually, these verses *first* speak of the Holy Spirit giving us assistance and power in prayer. In truth, men cannot pray without the aid of the Spirit. Paul laid this down clearly in Rom. 8:26-28. Prayer is not saying words into the air! In prayer, we kiss the face of God and touch His great heart. Without the work of the Spirit, no man could attain to such things. Christ promised us the gift of the Spirit's *assistance* in our prayer lives. It is right that men should pray, "Father, give me the intercession of the indwelling Holy Spirit as I seek your face." Jude 20 speaks of "praying in the Holy Ghost." This has reference to the Holy Spirit's *support* as we talk to our Father in heaven.

2. **Filling the saints.** Right service and leadership are promised for those who ask. This is for believers in whom He dwells. See the apostles praying for a *fresh filling* of the Holy Spirit some few days *after* Pentecost (Acts 4:23-31). As stated above, He lives within the saved soul of every real believer. Spirit filling is an *extrusion* of divine power moving from the inside to the outside. It is not an intrusion coming from the outside in! For the apostles' unique filling with the Spirit, and the *exclusive* authority, this gave them as leaders of the early churches, see Section 177, John 16:13, footnote i. There is no such thing today as apostolic succession. In the first church, Matthias was selected to take Judas' place (Acts 1:22-26). Later, at the death of James, no one was chosen to fill his vacancy (Acts 12:1-2). The teaching of the apostles continued, but their order, succession, and unique authority did not.

3p-There are about two years between these two statements of Christ regarding the Spirit. The first was spoken during the Sermon on the Mount in Section 47, Matt. 7:11. The second is given above. Both are correct. If these were spoken exclusively to the twelve on this latter occasion, then we learn from this that some of them were married with children. It is clear from 1 Cor. 9:5 that Peter was a married man. Refer to Section 41, third paragraph of footnote a, for comments on Peter, the Pope with a wife. The 1959 edition of the classic *Halley's Bible Handbook,* pages 771-784, (and all succeeding editions) has a review of the history of the Roman Catholic Church, especially the hideous crimes of certain Popes with their wives and mistresses. Billy Graham's organization reprinted a *Crusade Edition of Halley's Handbook* in 1962, and dropped out the pages about the Papal church. For Graham's shocking sympathies with this evil system, see Section 4, the third paragraph of footnote d, and Section 30, forth paragraph of footnote f. Paul's' words in Gal. 1:8-10 describe those who go to or defend a false gospel.

4p-"Confirmation" and the Holy Spirit? This word is found three times in the New Testament (Mk. 16:20, Acts 14:22 with 15:41). Its root meaning is to "lean upon and support." The Papal Church has perverted "confirmation" into a false doctrine. Nowhere in the Bible is "confirmation" called a "ritual," "sacrament," or an act whereby one receives the Holy Spirit. Nowhere in the Bible is a Catholic bishop or priest said to minister this. (The Roman and Orthodox Churches did not exist during the New Testament era. They came into being out of the state church of Emperor Constantine, hundreds of years later.) When Paul retraced his missionary steps to former converts and churches, he "confirmed" or gave them something to "lean upon." This leaning post for believers is the Word of God (Matt. 4:4 with 2 Tim. 3:16). There was no pageantry with gowns, ornate crosses, colorful vests, collars, and religious accolades. No bishop, priest, minister, missionary, pastor, or anyone else imparts the Holy Spirit. Nor is this the meaning of Acts 8:14-17 and 19:1-6, that describes an *exclusive* apostolic act that is no longer valid. When a person is saved by the grace of God, he *instantly* receives the Spirit as the new birth is imparted to his soul (Eph. 3:16 and Rom. 8:9b). In prayer, as saved Christians, we should ask for renewed fillings of the Holy Spirit (Eph. 5:18). Apart from the Holy Spirit, we accomplish nothing of eternal value in God's work. This is the essence of what Christ taught His preachers in verses 11-13 above.

5p-Confirmation as practiced by Paul. This was to encourage Christians, giving them solid hope during times of trouble and suffering. God's Word provided the eternal truth to lean upon in daily living. "Confirmation has nothing to do with pretty dresses for little girls, or suits for boys, and a pompous religious show for the benefit of proud parents. There should be no objection to having biblical confirmation studies, if the participants are saved Christians. In the churches mentioned above, these dear people do not believe in *personal,* know-so salvation, obtained by faith in the finished work of Christ's death, burial, and resurrection. In Catholic and Orthodox Churches mentioned above, salvation is hopefully obtained after a life of self-works, ordinances, rites, rituals, baptisms, confessions, indulgences, abstinences, and other human deeds. All the religious chicanery about good works for salvation explains the warning verse, "Satan deceiveth the whole world" (Rev. 12:9).

CHAPTER 12

MIDWAY IN THE FEAST OF TABERNACLES.

AGAIN, JESUS PUBLICLY CLAIMS TO BE THE MESSIAH AND FALLS INTO FURTHER CONFLICT WITH THE JEWS. EVENTS OF THE NEXT SIX MONTHS UNTIL HE RETURNS TO BETHANY AND RAISES LAZARUS FROM THE DEAD. THE SAVIOR AND HIS MEN WITHDRAW TO EPHRAIM UNTIL THE FOURTH PASSOVER.

Time: The above events took at least six months.

Passover pilgrims fearful of the Sanhedrin secretly discuss the Messiah. His public proclamation on the last day of the feast. The people are divided and the Sanhedrin confused as Nicodemus softly attempts to defend Christ.

Matt.	Mk.	Lk.	John 7:11-25—*In the temple at Jerusalem*
			Division and fear
			11 Then the Jews sought him at the feast,[(a)] and said, "Where is he?"
			12 And there was much murmuring among the people concerning him: for some said, "He is a good man:" others said, "Nay; but he deceiveth the people."
			13 Howbeit no man spake openly of him for fear of the Jews.[(b)]
			He teaches openly: the Jews are amazed
			14 Now about the midst of the feast Jesus went up into the temple, and taught.
			15 And the Jews marvelled, saying, "How knoweth this man letters, having never learned?"[(c)]
			The source of His doctrine: the law
			breaking Jews are sternly rebuked and their intentions exposed
			16 Jesus answered them, and said, "My doctrine is not mine, but his that sent me.[(d)]
			17 "If any man will do his will, he shall know of the doctrine, whether it be of God, or *whether* I speak of myself.[(e)]
			18 "He that speaketh of himself seeketh his own glory: but he that seeketh his glory that sent him, the same is true, and no unrighteousness is in him.
			19 "Did not Moses give you the law, and *yet* none of you keepeth the law? Why go ye about to kill me?"[(f)]
			20 The people[(g)] answered and said, "Thou hast a devil: [demon] who goeth about to kill thee?"
			21 Jesus answered and said unto them, "I have done one work, and ye all marvel.
			22 "Moses therefore gave unto you circumcision; (not because it is of Moses, but of the fathers;) and ye on the sabbath day circumcise a man.
			23 "If a man on the sabbath day receive circumcision, that the law of Moses should not be broken; are ye angry at me, because I have made a man every whit whole on the sabbath day?
			24 "Judge not according to the appearance, but judge righteous judgment."[(h)]
			"Is He the Messiah?" The greatest of all questions
			25 Then said some of them of Jerusalem, "Is not this he, whom they seek to kill?

Matt.	Mk.	Lk.	John 7:26-45—*In the temple at Jerusalem*
			26 "But, lo, he speaketh boldly, and they say nothing unto him. Do the rulers know indeed that this is the very Christ?[(i)] (Messiah) **27** "Howbeit we know this man whence he is: but when Christ [Messiah] cometh, no man knoweth whence he is."

His response: some believe

Matt.	Mk.	Lk.	
			28 Then cried Jesus in the temple as he taught, saying, "Ye both know me,[(j)] and ye know whence I am: and I am not come of myself, but he that sent me is true, whom ye know not. **29** "But I know him: for I am from him, and he hath sent me." **30** Then they sought to take him: but no man laid hands on him, because his hour was not yet come.[(k)] **31** And many of the people believed on him, and said, "When Christ cometh, will he do more miracles than these which this *man* hath done?"[(l)]

Temple police: Jews confused

32 The Pharisees heard that the people murmured such things concerning him; and the Pharisees and the chief priests sent officers[(m)] [temple police] to take him.

33 Then said Jesus unto them, "Yet a little while am I with you, and *then* I go unto him that sent me.[(n)]

34 "Ye shall seek me, and shall not find *me*: and where I am, *thither* ye cannot come."

35 Then said the Jews among themselves, "Whither will he go, that we shall not find him? will he go unto the dispersed [Jews] among the Gentiles, and teach the Gentiles?

36 "What *manner of* saying is this that he said, 'Ye shall seek me, and shall not find *me*: and where I am, *thither* ye cannot come?'"[(o)]

Source of salvation and the Holy Spirit: believe on Him

37 In the last day, that great *day* of the feast, Jesus stood and cried, saying, "If any man thirst, let him come unto me, and drink.[(p)]

38 "He that believeth on me, as the scripture hath said,[(q)] 'out of his belly shall flow rivers of living water.' "

39 (But this spake he of the Spirit, which they that believe on him should receive: for the Holy Ghost was not yet *given*; [at Pentecost] because that Jesus was not yet glorified.)[(r)]

Again the people are divided

40 Many of the people therefore, when they heard this saying, said,[(s)] "Of a truth this is **the Prophet.'"**

41 Others said, "This is the Christ." [or Messiah] But some said, "Shall Christ come out of Galilee?

42 "Hath not the scripture said,[(t)] **'That Christ cometh of the seed of David,' and 'out of the town of Bethlehem, where David was?'"**

43 So there was a division among the people because of him.

44 And some of them would have taken him; but no man laid hands on him.

The temple police return dismayed

45 Then came the officers [temple police] to the chief priests and Pharisees; and they said unto them, "Why have ye not brought him?"

Matt.	Mk.	Lk.	John 7:46-53—*In the temple at Jerusalem*
			46 The officers [temple police] answered, "Never man spake like this man."[u] **47** Then answered them the Pharisees, "Are ye also deceived? **48** "Have any of the rulers or of the Pharisees believed on him? **49** "But this people who knoweth not the law are cursed." *Nicodemus defends Jesus: the Sanhedrin returns home* **50** Nicodemus saith unto them, (he that came to Jesus by night, being one of them,) **51** "Doth our law judge *any* man, before it hear him, and know what he doeth?"[v] **52** They answered and said unto him, "Art thou also of Galilee? Search, and look: for out of Galilee ariseth no prophet."[w] **53** And every man went unto his own house.[x] (Next chap., John 8:1 cont. in Section 120.)

Footnotes–Commentary

[a] **"The Jews."** John uses this term at least sixty-three times in his book. Obviously, the Holy Spirit was seeking to single out this people across John's work. In these first three verses, John gives something of the history of that occasion that he now looks back upon as an old man. He remembered it well, for he was there with Jesus!

2p-"Sought him at the feast." We read of similar things some six months later at the next Passover. This statement reveals that this Man, Jesus of Nazareth, had intrigued all Israel. At the next Passover, a year later, we note that Greeks sought to see Him. This affirms that His fame had reached into distant lands. Refer to Section 146, John 11:56, footnote b, and Section 161, John 12:20-21, footnote a, where the Passover crowds were curious about the Son of God and His presence on that occasion.

3p-Tabernacles celebration was one of the popular names of the seventh and final annual feast commanded in Lev. 23:33-43. Rabbis commenced giving lectures several weeks before the commencement of all the annual celebrations. The crowds were instructed the correct way to observe the feasts and were refreshed in the teachings of the Torah Law. The Tabernacles celebration was, likewise, known as "Sukkoth," a Hebrew word having reference to "booths" or "huts." During the feast, all Jews were required to dwell in "booths" to remind them of God's provisions for Israel during the forty years of wilderness trek. It was also known as "Feast of Ingathering," for it occurred *after* all crops had been harvested (Ex. 23:16 and 34:22). Like Passover, Unleavened Bread, and Pentecost, this was one of the three compulsory feasts. During these events, all Jewish males (or a representative from each household) were required to travel to Jerusalem (Ex. 23:17 and 34:22-23). It began on the fifteenth of Tishri, which was the seventh month, according to the Jewish religious calendar, and lasted for eight days. This rarely fell in late September but mostly in early October. Among the highlights of this occasion, the people were required to bring their tithes and offerings to the temple, for it was commanded in the Torah Law that they were not to "appear before the LORD empty [handed]" (Deut. 16:16). This Feast was primarily agricultural in nature but also spoke of the need for rain to fall upon the land, as well as being commemorative of the nation wandering in the wilderness. No annual and national celebration was as joyful as this one, not even the great Passover. The rabbis said, "He who had not seen Jerusalem during the Feast of the Tabernacles does not know what rejoicing means." See *The Gospel in the Feasts of Israel*, page 38, by Victor Buksbazen.

4p-Booth building. Jewish pilgrims flocked into Jerusalem by hundreds of thousands, having traveled from over the known world. They dressed in all sorts of bright clothing, and often the colors reflected their country of origin. It is known that Jews from distant Babylon dressed in white linen, while those from Asia chose blue, red, and even bright orange colors. Upon arrival, they immediately set themselves to erecting booths across Jerusalem, in lanes, roads, streets, courtyards, on housetops, and in all surrounding fields within a "Sabbath day's journey" of the temple. The "Sabbath journey" was a little less than one mile, being strictly part of the oral law or tradition of the elders. Note Section 52, footnote h, Section 89, footnote c, number 2 under second paragraph, and Section 96, footnote d for explanation of this law. These three Sections briefly define the traditions and oral laws of the Jews. The Talmud tractate, Sukkah is packed with intricate details regarding the correct way to erect these booths. Builders were excused if it rained but had to complete their booths after the rain ceased. At sundown, a sharp blast of the shofar or ram's horn sounding from the temple tower signaled over the land that the time of the great Feast of Tabernacles had arrived.

5p-This celebration was also associated with the weather. It occurred just *before* the winter rainy season began. These seasonal rains were critically necessary to prepare the soil for next year's crops. Without them, great famine and loss would follow. At daybreak each morning, thousands of people came out of their booths and tents pitched about the city, banded together like a vast army, and marched towards the temple. Upon arrival, they divided into two companies. Part of them followed the high priest and slowly walked to the Pool of Siloam, located *within* the walls at the southeastern end of the city. The pool drew water from Gihon spring, which was situated outside Jerusalem itself. After the priest had filled a golden bowl or pitcher (about one quart in size) with water from Siloam, the happy band returned to *the temple*. Meanwhile the other company of Jews went to a place known as Motza, located on the *outside* of the south wall of the city. Here, willows grew in great abundance. After gathering bundles of long thin willow branches, they too returned to the temple. These limbs were placed about the forty-foot square stone altar, forming something of a leafy wall. Every Jew entered the temple holding a "lulav" or branches of palms and an "ethrog" or citrus fruit in hand. These ceremonies were supposedly added to the Tabernacles celebrations because of a controversy that erupted between the Pharisees and Sadducees several hundred years previously. They are not commanded in the Law of Moses. Christ being present on this occasion hardly demonstrates that He approved of their oral law and thousands of overbearing traditions. He approved and fulfilled the Torah Law of Israel. John 7:37 reads that our Lord did not appear until the last day of the celebration.

6p-When the high priest and his vast entourage reached the temple Water Gate (named from this ceremony), there three powerful blasts from the silver trumpets of the temple musicians were sounded. At this point, all priests on duty shouted in unison the text of Isa. 12:3, "Therefore with joy shall ye draw water out of the wells of salvation." This was a united prayer for the return of the Holy Spirit to the nation of Israel and rains for next year's crops. The rabbis taught that the Spirit would return when Messiah appeared, and many Gentiles would be gathered to Him. Ascending the altar, the priest moved towards one of the silver funnels inset at the corners of the altar and lifted high the golden pitcher of water. At this signal, the people loudly shouted, "Raise your hand!" He then raised it so all might see. As he poured the water into one of the funnels, an assisting priest poured a libation of drink offering (wine) into the other. These funnels led to a sophisticated drainage system connected at the bottom of the altar and then ran underground to the Brook Kedron in the valley on the lower eastern side of the city. Here, blood from the thousands of sacrifices drained and when dried was sold as fertilizer to Jewish farmers. The ritual of water pouring occurred six nights in a row and concluded on the final day by the priests marching around the altar seven times. During these laps, all present were chanting in loud unison to God, "Favor us."

7p-Each day, for seven days, many offerings were given. On day one, thirteen bullocks were slain; day two, twelve; day three, eleven; day four, ten; day five, nine; day six, eight; day seven, seven were offered: thus seventy offerings. In rabbinical thinking, it pointed to "atonement for the seventy Gentile nations of their world." See Talmud tractate, Sukkah 55b. Fourteen lambs were offered each day for seven days. However, on the eighth or final day of Tabernacles only one lamb was offered. Throughout these eight days, seventy bulls, fifteen rams, one hundred and five lambs, and eight kids or goats, along with numerous drink offerings were presented to God. Num. 29:12–40 gives the details.

8p-The dance of lights. A *breathtaking* ceremony unfolded in the Court of Women or Temple Treasury on the final night after the day's activities. In the court center stood four giant golden candelabra (menorah), nearly eighty feet high. Each had four long branches leading up to reflecting lamps fueled by olive oil. Jewish writers claim the lights from these flooded across the entire temple area and over many parts of Jerusalem. Wicks were manufactured from the worn out linen garments of the priests. Long ladders, attached to the sides and attended by the sons of the priests, reached the massive brass lamps. Through the night, the elders of Israel and others performed amazing torch dances on a raised platform amid the light of the giant lamp stands. The dancers were called "chasidim" or "men of deeds." Thousands of spectators, each one carrying a burning torch or lamp, gathered to watch these events. A waist high barrier was raised to separate the men from the women, as the men stood on a makeshift platform. The court shined like the sun in its strength! All this amid the harmonious sounds of flutes, trumpets, harps and numerous other stringed instruments were heard. At the far western end of the Court of Women were fifteen semicircle steps leading up to the Nicanor Gate, which gave entrance to the sacrificial area. (Oddly, this gate was allegedly named after a Greek general, who fiercely hated Jerusalem and was slain by the Maccabeus. His thumbs and big toes were hung in the massive gate bearing his name. See the Talmud tractate, Tannith 18b.) Starting at the top step, the temple choir sung loudly the fifteen Psalms of Degrees (Ps. 120-134). With each new Psalm, they descended to the next step, reaching the bottom one and singing the final hymn of Ps. 134. This impressive event was repeated each night from the second until the final evening of Tabernacles. It was into this joyous ceremony at the house of God in Jerusalem that our Lord Jesus went. *He had something to say to Israel for the last time!* For a beautiful description of the Feast of Tabernacles, see *The Temple*, chapter XIV, by Alfred Edersheim.

9p-The question of verse 11 shows again that Jesus of Nazareth had stirred the nation of Israel when He claimed to be their Messiah. His Name was on the lips of the thousands of Jews present for the celebration of the Tabernacles. In verse 12 it is clear that there was a sharp division among the Hebrews concerning Him. It is the same today. The Son of God's claim to be the only hope of salvation for a lost and dying world is fiercely hated by some but loved by all who know Him as personal Lord and Savior.

(b) "Jews" here has reference to the powerful Sanhedrin and their companions who habitually clashed with Christ, and were continually silenced by His Words of wisdom and power. Most of them hated Him fiercely.

2p-Verse 14. "The midst of the feast." The entire celebration lasted about eight days. This means that Jesus purposely waited before making a personal appearance among the people. Apparently, He had dismissed His disciples to go ahead for all eight days while He tarried behind. The Jews forbade traveling long distances on the first two festive days; but this was another of their oral laws and traditions. Hence, Christ would have walked the two miles from Bethany and entered the temple in the middle of the grand event. One can imagine the tidal wave of anxiousness that fell over the people when He was spotted among the crowds! Word of His presence swept across the temple and city: "Jesus of Nazareth is here!"

(c) **"Never learned."** Jesus knew their Scriptures, traditions, history, and future better than all of them put together. Yet the sarcastic implication here is that Jesus was a "theological hick," having never studied the laws and traditions of Israel in the celebrated schools or at the feet of the "learned rabbis of the nation." The Sanhedrin hurled this same slander into the faces of Peter and John months after this (Acts 4:13). Later, Jewish antagonists of Christ accredited His superior learning to black magic. This is discussed in Section 20, footnote j, second paragraph. His understanding and insight amazed both the religious leaders and the common people. Note Section 19, footnote c for God teaching Jesus morning by morning. Refer also to Section 45, second paragraph of footnote i, and Section 52, footnote x for the two famed theological schools at Jerusalem. They are mentioned again in Section 137, footnote c.

2p-It is notable that a tradition recorded in the Talmud tractates, Sanhedrin 107b and Sotah 47a, reads that a most famed rabbi named Y'hoshua ben-Perachyah taught Jesus. This claim is wrong, since the rabbi bearing this name lived a hundred years *before* Christ was born. However, this Jesus fable in the Talmud proves that the early Jews did not really consider the Lord Jesus ignorant or unlearned! See footnote e below. The Sanhedrin provided many opportunities for Hebrews to learn. For example, according to the Talmud tractate, Shabbath 19a the rabbis held lectures, which were open to all for thirty days before each of the seven annual feasts of Israel began. If interest was high, they continued several days after the festive celebrations had ceased. Thousands of Jews and proselytes attended these events. Some think that it was at one of the post-festive lectures that the Lord Jesus tarried as a boy twelve years of age (Lk. 2:43).

(d) At least seven times, the Savior claimed to speak only God's Word and at His direction. See this in John 7:16; 8:28, 46-47; 12:49; 14:10, 24; and 17:8. Note also footnote c above. On how God communicated with His Son, refer to Section 19, footnote c.

(e) **A profound statement.** The religious leaders were highly offended because Christ undertook to teach though He had never attended their institutions of theological learning. His power in preaching and teaching made their academic credentials blush with shame. Refer to footnote c above for more on this. Further, He affirmed that His doctrine was of divine origin, from God Himself, that God had sent Him to teach and there was no unrighteousness in Him (verse 18)! See footnote d above. With this, our Lord declares that the person who is doing the will of God in heaven will know that Christ taught nothing but the eternal truth. Both the doctrines and doings of the Son of God are infallible proof that He is the Lord from heaven and the only Savior of mankind. *Therefore, it is concluded that all who deny, change, dispute, mitigate or argue against what Jesus taught, do not know the true and living God of heaven.*

(f) **"Why go ye about to kill me?"** **"None of you keepeth the law."** What a devastating rebuke! With hundreds standing about listening to the debate, our Lord lays upon the religious leaders and their partners in spiritual crime this dreadful charge. They were violating the Torah Law they professed to respect and obey. If they were Torah keepers they would have welcomed Jesus, for much of what Moses wrote pointed to Him. Nothing could have so pierced the heart of these wicked men as these Words of Jesus. Next, He accused them of plotting His murder! Their fiendish plans to destroy the Lord Jesus are mentioned numerous times throughout the four gospels. Messianic Jews, who demand that believers live under part of the Torah Law, should read these Words of Christ. The chiefs of Israel's religion were all master lawbreakers! "None" of them kept the commands of God.

(g) **"The people"** can only have reference to the religious leaders and their partners in hating Christ, *not* the visiting pilgrims attending the feast. Verse 21 reveals that these religionists were familiar with His work of healing the man on the Sabbath day at the Pool of Bethesda a year and a half previously (verse 23). Someone from the crowd retorted to His stinging charge "Thou hast a devil," and in the same sentence lied about their murderous intentions. This was the standard response used by the Jews against their opponents. It was thrown at Him a short time later in Section 120, John 8:48 and 52.

(h) The Lord Jesus was not detracted by their slander, but taking no notice of their blasphemy, He proceeded to refute their awful charge that He had a demon. They accused Him of a serious breach of the Sabbath when He had healed the thirty-eight-year-old paralytic lying by the Pool of Bethesda. The Jews continually harangued Him for doing the works of God on their Sabbath. In response, He has in view their *many* and *continual* violations of the Sabbath and then names one of which they were guilty: the circumcising of their children on this day. The Torah Law commanded no work to be done on the Sabbath day (Ex. 20:8-10). The same law commanded all male children to be circumcised on the eighth day after their birth (Lev. 12:3). Obviously, over the course of Jewish history millions of male children reached their eighth day on a Sabbath! Therefore, the strict law of Sabbath keeping had its exceptions. Christ points this out to the religious hypocrites standing about Him. See some of these in Section 54, footnote d, and Section 119. footnote h.

2p-As they circumcise their children to keep the law of Lev. 12:3, they at the same time are bypassing the law of Ex. 20:8-9. If they wounded a child in circumcising him on the Sabbath, was it sin for Him to heal a man (make him fully whole) on the same day? It is to be noticed that Christ made this man "every whit whole" suggesting that *every* ill and ailment was cured! They were blinded by hatred for Him and were incapable of rational judgments.

(i) "Is this the very Christ?" Jesus had demonstrated that He was the Christ or Messiah of Israel. It is ironic that these common Jews would say this to their rulers or the great Sanhedrin Court! For several references documenting that He was that unique Messianic Person, see Section 5, footnote a; Section 18, footnote h; and Section 21, Part 4, footnote m.

2p-Verse 27. This refers to a belief that was popular among the Jews at this period in history. They held that Messiah would give the first manifestation of Himself at Bethlehem, and then would vanish and hide from the world. Some rabbis said that after forty days, He would reappear, but from what place no one would know. This second appearing would fulfill the expectations of the Hebrew nation. This curious interpretation of their Messiah was based on Song of Sol. 2:8-9. The rabbis taught that the roe or young deer could easily appear and then disappear from human vision due to its marvelous camouflage. They held that during this second stage appearing of Messiah, He would make manna appear and feed great hoards of people! See main heading under Section 93 for Christ feeding the multitudes. Hence, the Jew's words, "but when Christ (Messiah) cometh [meaning *after* the Bethlehem appearing] no man knoweth whence [or where] he is" seem to have their origin in this ancient belief. Lightfoot's *Commentary on the New Testament . . . ,* vol. 3, pages 316–317 cites various old sources to confirm the Jewish belief that after Messiah had been born at Bethlehem, He would suddenly be "snatched away, they knew not whither." Afterward, He would come again but from a place totally unknown to them. With this, we can understand the proper meaning of the curious words of the Jews in verse 27.

3p-For a comprehensive article covering the various Hebrew ideas about their Messiah, see *A History of the Jewish People in the Time of Jesus Christ,* vol. II, pages 126-187, by Emil Schurer. It is noted that Schurer is miserably off in his dating of the book of Daniel, on page 137. Some of his comments about the "popular consciousness" of the Jews regarding their coming Messiah in the time of Christ are typical liberal unbelief.

(j) Standing in the temple, our Lord loudly spoke these Words after hearing the reasoning of the people in verses 26 and 27. He was informing the Jews "You know that I am the Messiah sent from God. The evidence of this is irrefutable in my Word and works. It is right and honorable that you believe this." He affirmed that He did not come of Himself into the world, that it was God, who sent Him on this mission of redemption for Israel and mankind.

(k) "They sought to take him." This has reference to the members of the Sanhedrin and their accomplices in hating the Messiah. For comments on His "hour," refer to Section 27, John 2:4, footnote f.

(l) "Will he do more miracles?" Here again is public confirmation that the Jews were looking for a Messiah, who would do countless miracles and wonders before the nation. See main heading under Section 48. Apparently, some of these Jews listening to the conversation were deeply stirred to have faith in Him as their Messiah because He had met the criteria by His Words and marvelous works performed among the people.

(m) "Sent officers" or temple police. With these words, we are introduced to the temple police. They are later mentioned in verse 45. This corps of trained men was commanded by one known as "the captain of the mount of the temple." Both night and day, the Levites kept perpetual watch at all the temple gates for the sight of any unclean thing. They also acted as a police security force. The "captain of the temple" is mentioned later in Acts 5:26. During the night hours, ten guards were placed in each of twenty-four stations about the gates and all the courts. A total of two hundred and forty Levites and thirty priests were on duty every night. Twenty-four priests watched over the temple and changed shifts every week. Nightly, the "captain of the temple" would secretly make his rounds, inspecting each station to determine if the guards were "alert, ready and in a watchful posture." The Jews divided "watches" into three parts, whereas the Romans used four. Hence, our Savior's Words take local meaning when He said, "Blessed are those servants whom the lord when he cometh shall find watching in the second and third watch." At the approach of the captain, the guard rose and passed on a salute. Any guard found sleeping on duty was beaten or his clothes set on fire. This is mentioned in the Talmud tractate, Tamid 27b. Now, we may better understand the admonition "Blessed is he that watcheth, and keepeth his garments" (Rev. 16:15).

(n) These remarks were addressed to the arresting officers who were sent to take Him. The "little while" spoke of His death in about six months at the next Passover. Here, standing amid vicious enemies who were filled with anger and hatred, the blessed Son of God speaks in love and tenderness! The warning is that they should seek Him then, because time will harden their hearts and their interest in Him will fade. The fierceness of this mob did not prevent the Lord Jesus from reaching out to them in compassion. He was returning to the Father, and if they failed to believe in Him, they could not go where He would be. How dreadful is this statement. What pathos of horror these words carry for sinners who procrastinate the salvation of their souls. Messiah's Words "Ye shall seek me, and shall not find me" (verse 34), may point to the destruction of Jerusalem in A.D. 70 (about forty years later). During those six months of death and destruction, they would find no comfort from their Messiah. It would be too late!

2p-Verse 35. Jews scattered among the Gentiles. Because of the Babylonian captivity, some five hundred years prior, the people of Israel had been scattered over the known world of that era. Jewish religious quacks would often leave the land of Israel, go among these dispersed of Israel, seeking to establish their apostate theology. The crowds were saying that Jesus was a failure among fellow Jews so perhaps the pagan Gentiles will hear Him! This is what the obstinate and angry crowds were suggesting about the Messiah.

(o) **"Ye cannot come."** Calloused by their sin and *deliberate rejection* of Jesus, they could not comprehend what He was saying. Thousands of Jews prayed for both God and His Messiah to save them from the sword and fire of the Romans in A.D. 70 during the national calamity of Israel. Their prayers were unanswered. Note Section 188, Lk. 23:28-31 where Christ warned of this as He walked to His death on the cross.

(p) **"Come unto me and drink."** Why did the Lord Jesus cry aloud such words at this moment? Read the following: The Jews did not reckon this last day (the eighth) as part of the actual feast. It was something of an appendage to the seven previous days. Nor did they sit in their booths or tents during this time. The final day with its various traditions and activities is described below.

2p-Leaving their booths at daybreak, the pilgrims made their way into the gigantic temple to participate in this final event of the Feast of Tabernacles. Thousands of Jews packed into the altar area preparing for the ceremony to follow; among them stood the lowly carpenter from Nazareth. Thousands of eyes fell upon Him: some in love and adoration, others with suspicion and hate. The priests, leading hundreds of marchers, made seven circuits about the giant altar instead of the usual one circuit. (Seven was reminiscent of Joshua marching around the walls of Jericho.) With this, three sets of seven blasts from silver trumpets were sounded. As the priest and people marched, they sang loudly Ps. 118:25, "the Hosanna verse." All Jews believed that it spoke of their Messiah and King, and they frantically waved their palm branches while encircling the altar. It was thought that Messiah would appear at the Eastern Gate of Jerusalem and that the people singing this Psalm and waving palm branches would be the first to meet him! A perusal of Christ's arrival at this gate about six months later and the Jews chanting this very Psalm reveals that they knew He was their Messiah. This is discussed in Section 148.

3p-With the completion of the parade, a priest stood on the ramp that encircled the vast stone altar. As he raised his hand holding a bowl of water taken from the Pool of Siloam, the temple resounded to the melody of the Hebrew musicians playing their instruments. In the background, a Levitical choir sang the Hallel of Ps. 113-118. The officiating priest emptied the bowl into a funnel at the eastern corner of the altar. *At the conclusion of this colorful ritual, a moment of silence fell over the amazing scene.* During the eerie quietness of that time, a piercing voice rang out over the temple precincts. It was that Man again, "that imposter," claiming to be the Messiah! In Jewish thinking, the ceremony of pouring out water signified a prayer to God for the return of the Holy Spirit to Israel and for rain from heaven to prepare the land for next year's crops.

4p-The Jews said that God had promised to send rains upon the land of Israel immediately after the great celebration. Hence, the pouring out of water symbolized this hope. The ceremony was not commanded in the Jewish Old Testament (Tanakh) but was added by the Jews. Later, it was recorded in the Talmud or oral tradition. *Our Lord followed these traditions only when they pointed to Him as the Messiah and Savior of Israel; all others, He condemned.*

5p-Verse 37. The Lord Jesus cried out for every Jew present to believe on Him, by saying, "come unto me and drink." He was trying to turn their hearts from the colorful traditions of that moment to Himself, their Messiah! He was shouting something like this: "You have rejoiced in the drawing and pouring of water from Siloam. However, he that believes in Me shall have 'rivers of living water pouring from his soul.'" Associated with the water outpouring on the vast altar was the belief that with the coming of Messiah, the Holy Spirit would return to the nation of Israel. This is exactly what Jesus was saying to the Jews in verse 38. At the baptism of Christ in the beginning of His ministry, the Holy Spirit went to work through Him amid the nation of Israel. He did indeed bring the Spirit back to Israel, but they rejected both their Messiah and the Holy Spirit.

(q) **"Out of his belly."** This citation was built by selecting certain words from different Old Testament passages and blending them together to make a single quote. Christ's quotation here came from Isa. 12:3; 43:20; 44:3; 55:1; Zech. 13:1; 14:8; Ezek. 47:1; and Joel 3:18. The Greek word for belly "koilia," used in verse 38, stands metaphorically for the inner most being of man, the saved soul, which is the dwelling place for the Holy Spirit (Eph. 3:16). See *Thayer's Greek-English Lexicon* of the New Testament, 1889 edition page 351, and definition number 5. From this redeemed citadel of man's soul, living waters of eternal life flow out to all who will drink. Over two years before, Christ had used similar language with the woman at the well (John 4:14). See further comments on this in next paragraph below.

2p-The ancient Israelites often compared the work of the Holy Spirit to water, rain, dew, wells, fountains, and rivers. See Ps. 36:8, 9; 133:2, 3; Isa. 44:3, 4; and Hosea 10:12. At the final day of Tabernacles, the Messiah said to Israel something like this, "You have only temporary joy over a little water being poured out upon the altar: but he that believes in Me shall have rivers of living waters streaming from his redeemed soul." The Jews believed that when Messiah came, He would procure water for them as Moses had for Israel in the wilderness (Ex. 15:22-27). Here, the offer of everlasting water is given, but they are deaf to the meaning of His Words. It should be noted that the cursed Samaritan woman asked Christ for this living water, while the leaders of Jewish religion at Jerusalem rejected it. Read her request in Section 34, John 4:15, footnote h.

3p-**Verse 38. Filled with the Holy Spirit.** There are many fillings of the Spirit in the life of the Christian, but one baptism. The one baptism of Eph. 4:5 puts the redeemed soul into the body of Christ (1 Cor. 12:13). *Being filled with the Spirit commences inwardly and flows outwardly.* All the noise about "come Holy Spirit," or "waiting for the Spirit," or "praying the Spirit down," are error. The sacred Third Person of the Trinity dwells within the soul of every born again believer (John 14:17; 1 Cor. 3:16; and Eph. 3:16). From the inside, He fills the believer with power to perform whatever service for God. The proof or fruit of being Spirit filled is not speaking in tongues. The nine marks of being Spirit filled and thus fruit bearing are listed in Gal. 5:22-26. The twelve apostles and others, waiting in the upper room for Pentecost, were all filled with the Spirit (Acts 2:4) and empowered to share the gospel with the crowds at the temple. They were instantly gifted to speak the gospel in languages they did not know. A few days later, the same group, after being threatened by the religious leaders of Israel, went to prayer and sought God for power to continue in His work. We read in Acts 4:31 that they were *again* "filled with the Holy Ghost." The book of Acts speaks freely of persons being Spirit filled and the attending results. Not one of them fell backwards or performed vulgar antics. These common features of many "evangelical mass meetings" today, but they were absent in the early and first churches. Meanwhile, a man named Montanus, with two "women preachers," Priscilla and Maximilla (who left their husbands), traveled to France and North Africa and started a false cult. Their converts began a "new prophetic movement" exercising "spiritual gifts," speaking in tongues and healing. They claimed, "revelations from God," swooned into "ecstatic unconscious states," and said the coming of Christ was near. This was a precursor for the wild modern day "slain in the spirit," "falling out," "healthy wealthy" *radical* movements. The prolific writer, heretic, and church father, Tertullian (died circa. A.D. 220), who believed in purgatory and baptismal salvation, was converted to the Montanus sect. For more on Tertullian, see Section 103, seventh paragraph of footnote i, and Section 138, seventh paragraph of footnote a. Typical of false cults, majoring on the Holy Spirit, the Montanists believed that the coming of Christ would be in their time. The date setting mania of these people has reappeared many times in church history. At this writing, it is again running rampant! See *Appendix Eight* for a historical review of two-thousand years of predictive failures of date setting Jesus' return.

(r) **"Jesus was not yet glorified."** John wrote his book *looking back* on the story. He said that at that time (when Jesus was standing there speaking in the temple) His death and resurrection were yet to be, and the Spirit had not yet come in fullness of power, as He did at Pentecost in Acts 2. We should remember that John was present at that grand event. Certain works and gifts of the Spirit have been vouchsafed from the beginning of the world to men, but the *unlimited* effusion of His graces were not granted until after the ascension of Christ to the Father's right hand. This would only occur as a consequence of the perfect atonement of Christ, which obviously did not happen until His death and resurrection. When Christ was glorified in His death, resurrection, and ascension to the Father, atonement became a *present* reality. Thus, the accomplishment of salvation foreshadowed and experienced in the Old Testament became a historical fact. It was for all mankind, especially the Gentile nations of the world. At Pentecost, the Spirit came in *unlimited* power to do His first *work* of revealing Christ to men through the gospel.

2p-The rabbis taught that the Spirit had departed from Israel with the conclusion of the books of Zechariah and Malachi. He would not return until Messiah came! This belief explains that curious band of disciples at Ephesus over twenty years after Christ, who bluntly exclaimed, "We have not so much as heard whether there be any Holy Ghost." They said this because they believed what the rabbis had taught (Acts 19:2). In historical meaning they were saying, "We have heard for years of the Spirit's departure from our nation centuries ago at the deaths of Zechariah and Malachi, but of His return to Israel, we have not heard." These men were staunch Jews and simply speaking what they had been taught and believed for years. Apparently, they were unaware of what had happened on the day of Pentecost (Acts 2). For the Holy Spirit in the history of the Old Testament, see Section 10, footnote b.

(s) **What Prophet?** This partial quotation was taken from Deut. 18:18. It reveals that the Jews were expecting a "prophet" to appear within Israel, as Moses had predicted some fifteen hundred years prior. Jewish writings called Moses "the savior of Israel," in the Talmud tractates, Sotah 12b and Sanhedrin 101b. See more on this in Section 7, inside block number 2, and Section 24, footnote c. We note that verses 41-42 above reveal that many knew Jesus was the Messiah but were puzzled that He was a citizen of Galilee. Further, they were also familiar with the Old Testament predictions that Israel's Messiah would come from the family line of David and appear at Bethlehem. His Davidic lineage is charted in Section 5, footnote c and d, and in Section 7.

(t) The first part of this quote is a general citation gathered from several different Old Testament verses such as Ps. 89:3-4, and 132:11. Whoever made this remark knew the Scripture on this point. It reveals that some of the Jews at the time of Jesus were concerned with the fact that Messiah, in order to be genuine, should have Davidic credibility. The second portion was predicted in Micah 5:2. Here, it was predicted that He would come out of the town of Bethlehem. The religious leaders correctly identified the time when our Lord was born and His birthplace. Note Section 17, Matt. 2:3-6, footnote h. It shows they had earlier pointed to Bethlehem as Messiah's birthplace.

(u) "Never man spake like this." This was the verdict of the temple police officers who were sent to arrest the Lord Jesus. Hearing the Words of grace and glory that came from His mouth convinced them, He was a righteous man speaking the truth of God. Amazed at His teaching, they returned to their lords without the prisoner. He had captured them! No marvel, for it had been predicted of Messiah, "grace is poured into thy lips" (Ps. 45:2), and "His mouth *is* most sweet: yea, he *is* altogether lovely" (Song of Sol. 5:16). Over three years prior, He had amazed the thousands in the Sermon on the Mount as seen in Section 47, footnotes m and n. Upon returning to His hometown synagogue, the crowds were stunned at His teaching. It is written of them, "And all bare witness, and wondered at the gracious words which proceeded out of his mouth." See this in Section 38, Lk. 4:22, footnote g. The Sanhedrin's response to the temple police was one of scorn, "Are ye also deceived?" Their verbal condemnation, "this people who know not the law" (meaning the common people) reveals the abysmal blindness of these religious leaders. They had rejected and blasphemed Him of whom Moses and the prophets spoke. Consequently, they were the Hebrews abiding under a fearful curse from God (verse 49).

2p-Verse 48. "Have any rulers believed on him?" This question was answered a few days later by John in Section 162, John 12:42, footnote e. Here, we note that "many" of Israel's rulers had secretly believed on the Lord Jesus as Messiah, but were terrified at the threat of being put out of the synagogue by the Sanhedrin.

3p-Verse 49. "These people are cursed." Again, we read the babbling of religious hypocrites! The scribes and Pharisees announced as "cursed" everyone except themselves. They considered their elite group of religionists as being the perfect law keepers, and all others were doomed. A few moments prior, the Jesus declared that they had not kept the Law of Moses (verse 19). This means that the curse of breaking the law now fell upon their heads.

(v) It is touching that Nicodemus asked justice for Jesus, and pleaded that He should not be condemned without a fair trial. This was a faint attempt to defend the Savior. See his first encounter with Christ recorded in Section 30. His statement here was a reflection of the fairness of Hebrew law at this period in their history. Later, at the trial of Jesus, this fairness vanished. Each person had the right to a fair trial as seen in Ex. 23:1,2; Lev. 19:15,18; and Deut. 19:15-18. It was held among very religious Jews that the law forbade any man to be put to death, though he was wicked, unless he was first condemned to die by the Sanhedrin Court. Their fierce condemnation of Jesus was a violation of the same Torah Law. Oddly, they had just cursed the common people for not knowing it (verse 49)! Hatred turns men into monsters of shameless deeds, often blinding them to every rule of fairness and justice.

(w) "Search and look." A popular Hebrew term having reference to the Jews looking into the Scriptures and national archives where births were recorded. Again, their *ignorance* of Israel's history on this point is demonstrated. Several famous Jewish prophets had come from Galilee. They should have known that Jonah, Hosea, Elijah, and Elisha were all from the northern kingdom. Some commentators hold that Malachi also came from Galilee. See more on this in *Dake's Annotated Bible*, New Testament, page 103, left vertical column, footnote p. It is noted in the Talmud tractate, Sukka 27b, that one rabbi said, "There was not a tribe in Israel, which failed to produce prophets." This affirmation hardly squares with the statement made by members of the Sanhedrin on this occasion. On the other hand, did they make this preposterous claim in their madness to discredit the Lord Jesus?

2p-It has been noted that these men of Hebrew religion hated, with fierce passion, Jesus the teacher from Galilee. They trailed Him across the land of Israel hundreds of times trying to entrap Him in some plot or scheme to discredit him before the people. As He was lifted up on the cross to die for their sins, they continually blasphemed Him. Some forty years later, in A.D. 70, the state of Israel, Jerusalem, and the temple were destroyed.

(x) On the validity of verse 53, see comments by the asterisk under main heading of the next Section 120. Was the challenge of Nicodemus to the Sanhedrin "Doth our law judge *any* man, before it hear him, an know what he doest?" taken to heart (John 7:51)? Apparently, their meeting ended with these words and each one returned home. Yet, there seems to be a note of disharmony among these seventy-one members of the Supreme Court of Israel. Were these men divided among themselves? Was this a case of God making the wrath of man to praise Him (Ps. 76:10)? Regardless, now, one of their own spoke as though he wondered about this carpenter from Nazareth, who was presenting himself as the Messiah of Israel.

2p-"To his own house." According to Section 120, John 8:1, the Lord Jesus went to the Mount of Olives, on the eastern side of Jerusalem. The seventy-one members of the Sanhedrin went to their respective homes. While foxes slept in their dens and birds in their nests, the Messiah had no earthly house at Jerusalem in which to spend that night. However, there was also a rule that the Sanhedrin *must* end all business and return to their respective homes before the evening sacrifice was offered. This occurred at or near sundown. It was counted evil for a Jewish court official to be out of his house during night hours. This is explained in Section 30, footnote c. The leaders of Israel had again "refused the waters of Shiloh" (Messiah) and fulfilled Isa. 8:6. We wonder what two prominent members of the Sanhedrin, Nicodemus, and Joseph of Arimathaea, did when they arrived home that night? For more on these two noble men, and how the death of Jesus totally changed their lives, see Section 181, second paragraph of footnote c.

Returning early to the temple, He resumes teaching. The religious leaders bring to Him a woman caught in adultery.* Christ pardons her and confounds them in a debate over the law. They attempt to stone Him. He escapes.

The controversy over the validity of John 7:53-8:1-11 is rejected by this harmony commentary. Many modern versions delete these twelve verses and insert the footnote "Most ancient authorities omit these verses." For over half a century the question has been, "Who are these ancient authorities?" In every case of expunging these passages and many others from the Authorized Version, "scholars" point to the Codex Sinaitic, Vatican, Alexandrian, and lesser sources. Yet, various smaller manuscripts written before the Sinaitic, Alexandrian, and Vatican carried these disputed passages. Yet, they say we are to believe they are not reliable. The fierce debate over the trustworthiness of God's Word as found in the King James Version was unknown until the "new and easier to understand versions" appeared. Why did it surface then? If the Authorized Version was so "full of mistakes," why were they mostly unnoticed by the "world's greatest scholars" for over three centuries? It only became an issue when the "corrected and better translations" appeared on the Christian book market. For more on this, see italics under the main heading of Section 197, and the Author's Introduction.

Matt.	Mk.	Lk.	John 8:1-14— *Temple treasury or the Women's Court*
			A woman brought to Jesus
			1 Jesus went unto the mount of Olives. [a]
			2 And early in the morning [b] he came again into the temple, and all the people came unto him; and he sat down, and taught them.
			3 And the scribes and Pharisees brought unto him a woman taken in adultery; [c] and when they had set her in the midst,
			4 They say unto him, "Master, this woman was taken in adultery, in the very act. [d]
			The Pharisees' devious question
			5 "Now Moses in the law commanded us, that such 'should be stoned:' [e] but what sayest thou?"
			6 This they said, tempting him, that they might have to accuse [f] him. But Jesus stooped down, and with *his* finger wrote on the ground, *as though he heard them not.*
			7 So when they continued asking him, he lifted up himself, and said unto them, "He that is without sin among you, let him first cast a stone at her." [g]
			8 And again he stooped down, and wrote on the ground. [h]
			9 And they which heard *it*, being convicted by *their own* conscience, went out one by one, beginning at the eldest, *even* unto the last: and Jesus was left alone, and the woman standing in the midst.
			He forgives her sin
			10 When Jesus had lifted up himself, and saw none but the woman, he said unto her, "Woman, where are those thine accusers? hath no man condemned thee?"
			11 She said, "No man, Lord." And Jesus said unto her, "Neither do I condemn thee: go, and sin no more." [i]
			He resumes teaching: the Pharisees object and He responds
			12 Then spake Jesus again unto them, [the woman and the people] saying, "I am the light of the world: he that followeth me shall not walk in darkness, but shall have the light of life." [j]
			13 The Pharisees therefore said unto him, "Thou bearest record of thyself; thy record is not true."
			14 Jesus answered and said unto them, "Though I bear record of myself, *yet* my record is true: for I know whence I came, and whither I

Matt.	Mk.	Lk.	John 8:14–35—*Temple treasury or women's court*
			go; but ye cannot tell whence I come, and whither I go.

go; but ye cannot tell whence I come, and whither I go.

15 "Ye judge after the flesh; I judge no man. (after the flesh)

Equal with God

16 "And yet if I judge, my judgment is true: for I am not alone, but I and the Father that sent me.

17 "It is also written in your law,[(k)] 'that the testimony of two men is true.'

18 "I am one that bear witness of myself, and the Father that sent me beareth witness of me."

19 Then said they unto him, "Where is thy Father?"[(l)] Jesus answered, "Ye neither know me, nor my Father: if ye had known me, ye should have known my Father also."

Where He taught

20 These words spake Jesus in the treasury, as he taught in the temple: and no man laid hands on him; for his hour was not yet come.

He resumes teaching again: the Jews are confused

21 Then said Jesus again unto them, "I go my way, and ye shall seek me, and shall die in your sins: whither I go, ye cannot come."

22 Then said the Jews,[(m)] "Will he kill himself? because he saith, Whither I go, ye cannot come."

23 And he said unto them, "Ye are from beneath; I am from above: ye are of this world; I am not of this world.

24 "I said therefore unto you, that ye shall die in your sins: for if ye believe not that I am *he,* ye shall die in your sins."

The greatest question

25 Then said they unto him, "Who art thou?"[(n)] And Jesus saith unto them, "Even *the same* that I said unto you from the beginning.

26 "I have many things to say and to judge of you: but he that sent me is true; and I speak to the world those things which I have heard of him."

27 They understood not that he spake to them of the Father.

28 Then said Jesus unto them, "When ye have lifted up the Son of man, then shall ye know that I am *he,*[(o)] and *that* I do nothing of myself; but as my Father hath taught me, I speak these things.

29 "And he that sent me is with me: the Father hath not left me alone; for I do always those things that please him."

Many believe: He admonishes them to continue in His Word

30 As he spake these words, many believed on him.[(p)]

31 Then said Jesus to those Jews which believed on him, "If ye continue in my word, *then* are ye my disciples indeed;

32 "And ye shall know the truth, and the truth shall make you free."[(q)]

Though believers, they are still greatly confused

33 They answered him, "We be Abraham's seed, and were never in bondage to any man: how sayest thou, 'Ye shall be made free?'"

34 Jesus answered them, "Verily, verily, I say unto you, Whosoever committeth sin is the servant of sin.

35 "And the servant abideth not in the house for ever:[(r)] *but* the Son abideth ever.

Matt.	Mk.	Lk.	John 8:36-55—*Temple treasury or women's court*
			36 "If the Son therefore shall make you free, ye shall be free indeed.
			37 "I know that ye are Abraham's seed; but ye seek to kill me, because my word hath no place in you.
			38 "I speak that which I have seen with my Father: and ye do that which ye have seen with your father."
			39 They answered and said unto him, "Abraham is our father." Jesus saith unto them, "If ye were Abraham's children, ye would do the works of Abraham.
			40 "But now ye seek to kill me, a man that hath told you the truth, which I have heard of God: this did not Abraham.(s)
			The big lie lives on
			41 "Ye do the deeds of your father." Then said they to him, "We be not born of fornication;(t) we have one Father, *even* God."
			42 Jesus said unto them, "If God were your Father, ye would love me: for I proceeded forth and came from God; neither came I of myself, but he sent me.
			43 "Why do ye not understand my speech? *even* because ye cannot hear my word.
			The Jew's spiritual father
			44 "Ye are of *your* father the devil,(u) and the lusts of your father ye will do. He was a murderer from the beginning, and abode not in the truth, because there is no truth in him. When he speaketh a lie, he speaketh of his own: for he is a liar, and the father of it.
			45 "And because I tell *you* the truth, ye believe me not.
			46 "Which of you convinceth [convicts] me of sin? And if I say the truth, why do ye not believe me?
			47 "He that is of God heareth God's words: ye therefore hear *them* not, because ye are not of God."
			The highest insult
			48 Then answered the Jews, and said unto him, "Say we not well that thou art a Samaritan, and hast a devil?"(v) (demon)
			49 Jesus answered, "I have not a devil; but I honour my Father, and ye do dishonour me.
			50 "And I seek not mine own glory: there is one that seeketh and judgeth.
			51 "Verily, verily, I say unto you, If a man keep my saying, he shall never see death."
			52 Then said the Jews unto him, "Now we know that thou hast a devil. Abraham is dead, and the prophets; and thou sayest, 'If a man keep my saying, he shall never taste of death.'
			53 "Art thou greater than our father Abraham,(w) which is dead? and the prophets are dead: whom makest thou thyself?"
			God's honor on Christ
			54 Jesus answered, "If I honour myself, my honour is nothing: it is my Father that honoureth me; of whom ye say, that he is your God:
			55 "Yet ye have not known him; but I know him: and if I should say, I know him not, I shall be a liar like unto you: but I know him, and keep his saying.

Matt.	Mk.	Lk.	John 8:56-59— *Temple treasury or women's court*
			56 "Your father Abraham rejoiced to see my day: and he saw *it,* and was glad."(x) **57** Then said the Jews unto him, "Thou art not yet fifty years old, and hast thou seen Abraham?" *He was before Abraham* **58** Jesus said unto them, "Verily, verily, I say unto you, Before Abraham was, I am."(y) *Again, they seek to kill Him: He escapes by hiding* **59** Then took they up stones(z) to cast at him: but Jesus hid himself, and went out of the temple, going through the midst of them, and so passed by. (Next chap., John 9:1 cont. in Section 121.)

Footnotes-Commentary

(a) **"To the mount of Olives."** See Section 119, second paragraph of footnote x for comments on this strange and lonely statement. Refer to Section 163, footnote d for other details regarding this favorite resort of the Lord Jesus and His preachers.

(b) **"Sunrise."** The word has reference to the time when the massive Shushan Gate, facing the east, was opened and the people flooded into the temple. This occurred at daybreak. Among the crowds were the hypocritical religious leaders with their prize catch of a woman caught in sin. They went straight to the Lord Jesus hoping to trap and discredit Him before the masses quickly gathering to hear Him teach. See footnote d below.

(c) **Adultery. "The scribes and Pharisees brought her."** This and numerous other sins were rampant among the Jews in this era and only grew worse until the destruction of the Hebrew state, the temple, and Jerusalem in A.D. 70. Josephus, who was a contemporary with many of these Jews, wrote of their extreme wickedness during this period. Refer to his words in Section 67, fourth paragraphs of footnote b. In Section 159, Mk. 12:40, footnote j, the Savior charged them with stealing from the widows of Israel. For more on the decadent condition of the religious authorities of Israel and the nation in general at this time in history, see Section 100, footnote d.

(d) **"In the very act."** Where was the man? Both culprits should have been arraigned before the Savior. This leaves one feeling highly suspicious of the real intentions of the Jews in bringing this woman to Christ for judgment. It was customary to bring such cases to a respected rabbi for his verdict; hence, she was taken to Jesus, but with ulterior motives. Leading their trembling prisoner, unveiled, and exposed before a crowd of men (the bitterest degradation to an eastern woman), they pushed her before Jesus. In the familiar tone of religious hypocrisy, one of them says, "Moses in the law said to stone such an one; but what is your opinion?" *Now, the trap had been set!*

(e) **"Stoned."** *The Law of Moses, given from God legislated morality!* New Testament Scripture does the same. All the talk about, "You cannot legislate morality" falls on it face. God did and has! Those guilty of adultery were put to death (Lev. 20:10, Deut. 22:22-24). Under pagan Roman occupation at this time, Jewish courts (apparently) could not enforce the death sentence without permission of the ruling governor; however, this rule was not strictly followed, as in the case of Stephen (Acts 7:58-59). The Torah Law laid down specific guidelines for a woman suspected of infidelity as seen in Num. 5:11-31. The husband took his wife to the priest officiating at the tabernacle or temple. She was "set before the Lord" as the priest gathered dust from off the floor, mixed it with holy water, and gave her to drink a portion of it. After putting her under a verbal oath, she drank the bitter mixture. He pronounced various curses upon her; such as, her body would swell and flesh rot if she lied. Next, he wrote these curses in a book in her view, and then washed them off with the remainder of the bitter water. This was to signify her innocence if proven not guilty. If the suspected wife was not stricken with these ailments after a period of observation, she was declared innocent by the priest and sent home with his blessing. The Talmud contains much information about the water test. It states that if a woman refused to drink the substance, her mouth was pried opened with pieces of iron! On the more pleasant side, if she were innocent, then "she would have a son like Abraham," so reads the Talmud in tractate, Sotah 20a. Edersheim, in his *The Temple its Ministry and Services,* pages 361-365 gives a coverage of the ordeal Jewish women endured when suspected of adultery. It is the duty of legally constituted governments to make proper and wholesome laws, and then enforce them. Present society has whitewashed just about every sin the in book as special-interest groups, lobbyists, human rights advocates, political activists and so on have legitimized the Devil, and evil. *Men do things today with public approval that they would have been hanged for fifty years ago.*

2p-As mentioned above in footnote c, adultery was so common at this time among the Jews, that the "bitter water test" had been abandoned. In Lightfoot's *Commentary on the New Testament . . . ,* vol. 3, page 426, we read, "Since the time that adultery so openly advanced under the second Temple, they left off trying the adulteress by the bitter water." It is noteworthy that Jesus "stooped down and wrote in the dust." What did our Lord write on this

543

occasion? Was He imitating the priest, who wrote the curses of God for the sin of adultery, with the dust water on his slate-book? Alternatively, did He write the sins of the Pharisees (who brought the woman to Him) on the floor for all to see? An interesting verse is Jer. 17:13, where God says, "They that depart from me shall be written in the earth." Did Jesus write their individual names? Surely, whatever He wrote in the dust on the marble floor of the temple, they saw and read; and whatever it was shook them!

3p-*There was a suppressed belief among the Jews at this time that if the water of jealously did not affect the wife, it would strike down the man who was guilty of the sin! Another group held that if the husband was an adulterer, the dust-water would not work on his wife.* Could this be the reason why the Pharisees fled the scene? Were all of them conscience stricken and dared not linger in view of this belief? Upon seeing Jesus writing in the dust, did they think that He was going to call for the administering of the dust-water test for each of them? Alas! What would have been their fate? See footnote h below for other comments on these men. Our Lord had previously described them as "an adulterous generation" in Section 100, Matt. 16:4, footnote d. John Gill in his *Commentary*, vol. 7, pages 840-841 has a lengthy discussion dealing with the cessation of the test for adultery, various punishments for crime, Jewish wickedness of this time and more. Dr. George Foot-Moore wrote that the dust-test law was not done away with until the year A.D. 66, (some thirty years after Christ). This is incorrect. He failed to explain to his readers "why" it had been canceled earlier. It was because adultery was one of the most prominent sins among the Jews! See Foot-Moore's work, *Judaism*, vol. 1, page 260. Regardless, it was not used in the case of the woman caught in adultery, and we know the reason why! (For those who are distressed over where the dust came from in the Women's Court, countless thousands of feet moving over the marble floors would have furnished enough dust for Jesus to write.)

4p-Jewish remiss in the execution of their Torah Law commandments at this period is appalling. Because of the loosening of judgment, violence, murder, thievery, and all kinds of shameful wickedness prevailed in Israel. The law was helpless, as evil was at its height and ran rampant, while punitive justice was slumbering. The religious leaders were to blame for His curse. In Section 163, we read the condemnation and judgment pronounced by Christ upon these people, their city, temple, and sins. It all happened some forty years later in A.D. 70.

(f) The religious leaders continually worked to ensnare the Savior into some contradiction with the Torah Law or the rules of their oral traditions. Note Section 54, footnote d, and main heading under Section 70 for other examples. Also, refer to the main heading of Section 137 for a classic illustration of the evil devices of the Jews to discredit the Savior before the people and throw Him into conflict with the two theological schools at Jerusalem.

(g) **"Cast the first stone."** Our Lord's Words in verse 7 were the final stroke. They knew their sin. These hypocrites of the Jewish religion were ready to take the speck from the eye of others, while blinded by planks and logs in their own eyes. The Lord Jesus was making direct reference to the sin of adultery and asked which of them was free from this scarlet stain. (Their subsequent actions revealed they were guilty.) This question of Christ was never intended as a blanket-cover for failure to deal with sin, by appealing to the old worn out cliché, "If you have no sin in your life then you can judge those who do." What Jesus said, in essence, was, "You that have not committed adultery, cast the first stone at this woman." Later, the apostle Paul gave plain instructions for dealing with *unrepentant* sinners in the local church (1 Cor. 5:1–8).

(h) **"Jesus wrote."** In verses 6 and 8, we find the several mentions of our Lord writing. What convicted these wicked adulterers? Why did the Lord Jesus kneel and write *again* in the dust? Moreover, they read every word! With each dusty inscription, conviction grew deeper and more terrifying in the hearts of these surreptitious men. God wrote with His finger on the tables of stone (Ex. 31:18). Later, He inscribed a message on the wall of Belshazzar's banquet hall (Dan. 5:5-6). Now, God in human flesh stoops to write in the dust of the temple floor a message that struck terror in the hearts of the religious leaders. Their insolent expressions, full of guile and malice, melted into shame and fear. Realizing the crowds were listening to the confrontation, (and some of them also reading the Master's Words) these embarrassed prelates of the Jewish religion, turned on their heels and from the oldest to the youngest fled the scene. Sin respects no age or person; it deceives and destroys old men as well as young. Every mortal in all stages of human growth is its victim. It always works its way from the oldest down to the youngest. It is written, "The fathers have eaten sour grapes, and the children's teeth are set on edge" (Ezek. 18:2).

2p-Verse 9. **Convicted by their conscience.** Conscience means knowledge. *Their own bosoms became their judges.* They were smitten by the burning knowledge of their pressing sins and the fierce voices of personal condemnation. Such things always cause unsaved religious men of evil to hurry away. What a glorious conclusion! The shame-filled woman now stands before Jesus of Nazareth, the Messiah of Israel. Shortly, righteousness and peace will kiss each other as the Savior announces her total forgiveness (Ps. 85:10).

(i) **"Neither do I condemn thee."** This poor woman was a human battering ram for the Devil. She was devastated in both body and soul. Her was like the words of David when he wrote, "For innumerable evils have compassed me about: mine iniquities have taken hold upon me, so that I am not able to look up; they are more than the hairs of mine head: therefore my heart faileth me. Be pleased, O LORD, to deliver me: O LORD, make hast to help me" (Ps. 40: 12-13). In verses 10 and 11, we see a marvelous display of grace and forgiveness for the worst of humanity. Surely, she knew who Jesus was, for His fame had spread across the camps of all sinners and saints throughout the land. In His presence, she was smitten over her sin and quietly repented in shameful sorrow. She wanted forgiveness. The Son of God, knowing her heart, spoke accordingly. Her misery and guilty conscience were instantly swallowed up in God's mercy. Again, our Lord reveals that His grace is superior to the Law of Moses. Knowing her heart, the Savior announced full pardon and sends her away a new woman. She left the temple with the light of another world shining in her heart and face. This immediate forgiveness is still available for all who are trapped in their shameful sins. Earlier, we heard the Lord Jesus say to the paralytic being lowered through the roof that his sins were forgiven. Refer to Section 49, Matt. 9:2, footnote i for details. God pardons our sin as He looks into our hearts and reads their deepest intentions and motives. *Every person truly longing for forgiveness, sick of their sin, who trusts Christ as Lord and Savior, is received into God's family with open arms and eternal love. Forgiveness is an instant transaction considered forever done in the mind of God.*

2p"**Go and sin no more**" In these words, the Lord Jesus was speaking of the specific sin in which she was formerly entrapped. He had instantly forgiven her. The imprudence of sinless perfection is not found in this benediction of Christ. A similar pronouncement was made upon the man healed at the Pool of Bethesda (John 5:14). On how people were saved *before* the cross, refer to Section 144, footnote i. Her former life of shame eternally vanished in the following promises, "Behold the Lamb of God, which taketh away the sin of the world" (John 1:29). "Come now, and let us reason together, saith the Lord: though your sins be as scarlet, they shall be as white as snow; though they be red like crimson, they shall be as wool" (Isa. 1:18). "And I will remember their sin no more" (Jer. 31:34). "Who *is* a God like unto thee, that pardoneth iniquity?" (Micah 7:18). Righteousness and peace have kissed *each other*" (Ps. 85:10).

(j) "**I am.**" Refer to Section 95, footnote i, footnote y below for more on this divine term. Jehovah had introduced Himself to Israel while in Egypt by this phrase. It affirmed a continuous existence from the beginning; even the One who claimed to be the uncreated Eternal Creator! Standing in the Court of Women, with its four gigantic oil lamps fading at the rising of the sun, and the light of early dawn shedding its fresh beams over that troubled scene in dazzling splendor, the lowly Jesus speaks. He openly claims to be "the light of the world." We can believe that all who heard this were stunned! The rabbis had taught them for years that the temple, the Torah Law, and Messiah were the lights of the world. They had also interpreted Gen. 1:3 as pointing to their Messiah "and God said, "Let there be light," meaning that God saw the light of His Son before the foundation of the world: that it would shine out to all men. Now, the man from cursed Galilee, the "carpenter's son," dares stand in their temple and acclaim Himself as their Messiah, the light of the world. For Jesus Christ the light of the world, refer to Section 1, Part 1, and John 1:4, footnote e.

2p-"**The light of life.**" Jesus used the word "light" because He was in the Women's Court of the temple where four massive lamps or menorahs stood, each almost eighty feet high. Powerful brass reflectors attached to the lamps shot beams over the temple area and into parts of Jerusalem. The rabbis referred to these in symbolic language as picturing, "the light of the world," that Messiah would bring to mankind. See the fascinating details of these giant luminaries in Section 119, eight paragraph of footnote a. In the synagogue, something called "the eternal light" was suspended just above the cabinet that housed the sacred Torah Law and other Hebrew Scriptures. This lamp was kept burning from morning to evening. Its earliest mention is traced back to the days of the tabernacle and little Samuel. When it burned out at evening that signaled, it was time for rest and prayers for Messiah to come. In 1 Sam. 3:3 it is written, "And ere the lamp of God went out in the temple [or tabernacle] of the LORD, where the ark of God *was*, and Samuel was laid down *to sleep*." The woman in this story, wrecked by sin, needed spiritual enlightenment. After her encounter with Jesus, she walked out of the Women's Court clean on the inside. His admonition for her to be done with her terrible past, flashed like a red beacon. See second paragraph of footnote i above. Without the Son of God, only darkness, misery, and eternal death wait for us at the end. Most people never realize this until it is too late. Jesus' kind Words of forgiveness settled permanently into her troubled heart. His love and compassion had brought her new life and eternal hope. One cannot but wonder where she went and to whom she testified of the Messiah, who had forgiven her sins and exchanged her awful darkness for light, never before known.

(k) **Verse 17. "It is also written in your law."** According to verse 13, these remarks are now addressed to the Pharisees, who were present. The Pharisees who brought the woman to Christ (verse 3) had fled (verse 9). Others had taken their place to continue the argument with our Lord. He suddenly gives something of a paraphrase from Deut. 17:6 and 19:15. Messiah said this because of the charge against Him in verse 13, which said that He was alone in His judgment; no one else agreed with Him. He responds by stating that their law affirms that the testimony or witness of two persons settles a case in Jewish court; His Words and deeds were the same as those of God in heaven. He was saying, "Therefore, you should heed your own law and let it show you that God and I are one and our testimonies agree" (verse 18). Again, Christ repeats Himself, as He has previously quoted this same Old Testament verse earlier in His ministry in Matt. 18:16.

(l) **Verse 19. "Where is thy father?" Born of fornication?** Their attempt to trap Him in condemning the woman had miserably failed. With this, they resort to an old slander and drag up His mother's past: the question of the virgin birth, and the vicious public gossip that had been attached to the whole affair. Their defamatory implication was "we are not illegitimate children like you are." Several centuries after the ascension of Christ, certain Jews resurrected the old lie that Mary, His mother, "was a hair dresser," which was a scandalous term for any woman in that culture. This is found in the Talmud tractate, Shabbath 105b where "Miriam" (Mary) was accused of being unfaithful to her husband. *Jesus in the Jewish Tradition,* pages 118–119, by Morris Goldstein also speaks of these things. A few moments later, these factious Jews brought up this awful subject again but in harsher language. See this in footnote t below. It is striking that the Jews inquire of Jesus about His Father. Later, in verse 44, He bluntly told them *who* their father was! See this in footnote u below.

2p-Verse 20. "His hour was not yet come." For explanation of this, see Section 27, John 2:4, footnote f.

(m) Verses 21–24. Again, the Jews reveal their abysmal ignorance of Messiah, His mission and work. "You shall die in your sins." Men who die in their sins cannot enter heaven. Christ pinpoints the spiritual origin of their sin as being "from beneath." This Jewish expression had reference to the dark regions of hell. The fearful warning that they will die in their sins, unless they believe in Him, remains valid for every member of Adam's race. It is a fact of history that many of the Jews committed suicide during the long siege and fall of Jerusalem in A.D. 70, thus dying in their sins. This calamitous and destructive end of the city and its people is thoroughly discussed later in Section 163. Millions of Jews died in their sins and went to hell during this horrible event of divine judgment.

(n) Verse 25. "Who art thou?" Here, the Jews were saying, "Who are you to deal out such threats to us?" Head strong and obstinate, they failed to understand what He was trying to tell them. In response to their fury, Christ announces that He has assumed no new character, and made no change in profession, preaching, teaching, and purpose. *He was still their Messiah, the Son of the Living God, and they were still rejecting Him.* At the beginning of His public ministry, He demonstrated at the Passover that He was the Messiah of Israel. Note this in Section 29.

2p-Verse 27. "They understood not." This was another editorial comment by John, as he looked back on that time, now long past. The *willful* rejection of Christ had blinded their minds to understanding who this Man was.

(o) "Lifted up . . . then shall ye know that I am *he*." *What a profound statement!* Can this mean that the Pharisees and their accomplices in hating Jesus would know for sure that He was Messiah when He died on the cross? Apparently, it does; this is reflected in the Sanhedrin paying the Roman guards to lie about His resurrection as seen in Section 199. This dreadful expression "lifted up" was understood as having *reference* to death by crucifixion. Note Section 30, John 3:14, footnote j for more on these words. This is mentioned a final time in John 12:32, a few hours before Jesus' death on the cross. The Messiah is telling His detractors that after they have crucified Him, He will rise and ascend back to heaven. This will prove that He was the true Messiah of Israel.

2p-Verse 29. "I always please God." No man who ever lived could make this profound claim, except Jesus of Nazareth, the Son of God.

(p) Scripture declares, that "faith comes by hearing the Word of God" (Rom. 10:17). Even as Christ debated and wrangled with the factious Jews, some among the vast crowds were convinced that He was the Messiah. *However, they had a wavering and unsure belief.* Knowing this in His great heart, He put their newly made confession to the test. Now, they hear that faithfulness and obedience were prerequisites for blessed service in His new spiritual kingdom. He admonished these professors to follow on and become disciplined workers in His service. At this time, they did not understand what it was to "continue in his Word." They were liars, potential murderers, the slaves of sin and children of Satan. Their faith in Messiah was fragmentary, then false, and ultimately fatal.

(q) Verse 32. "The truth shall make you free." In straightforward language, our Savior was saying to these half-hearted, wavering professors of faith, "You Jews have need of help, and I alone can help you, as long as you desire to be saved from the hypocrisy of the scribes and Pharisees and the tradition of the elders. As Israelites, you are in the great household of God but are not His sons or children; you are chained slaves of sin and Satan your father; you will continue to stumble in spiritual darkness. I know that you descended from Abraham, but it is only in a physical or bodily sense. You are not His spiritual seed and do not believe in Me like he did. I have told you what I have heard and seen of my Father: you have done to Me what your father has told you." *What Jesus said, the Jews put a material meaning onto it and thus failed to understand their Messiah had referred to their enslavement in sin.*

2p-Verse 33. "Never in bondage." What lying words! Taking offence, the Jews flew at Christ and shouted out another false statement regarding their past. History reveals the nation of Israel had suffered under the bondage of Egypt, Assyria, Babylon, Medo-Persia, Greece, and was, even at this very time, under the boot of the pagan Roman Empire. As the Jews wrangled with Jesus, Roman soldiers stationed along the walls of the Castle of Antonio were looking down upon this whole scene! They were in bondage, even as these words of untruth fell from their mouths. *Refer to the first part of footnote q above for the kind of bondage they were in, though blind to it.*

3p-Verse 34. Here, was the root problem of these men; it remains the same today. Those who are *slaves* to sin will commit or practice sin as easily as they breathe. It is that natural! Committing sin has its origin in all of our hearts. It is here that the poison fountain must be dealt with and changed. This miraculous change is only effected by the atonement of Christ and the work of the Holy Spirit in the evil heart. This change was unknown by the Pharisees, for they had rejected God's remedy, which was Jesus Christ their Messiah.

[r] **"The servant abideth not . . . for ever."** In this saying, Christ warns the Jews that they are sin's slaves (servants). Moreover, as such they will continually practice sin, unless He makes them free. Further, the servants (slaves) of sin will not live in God's house in heaven. Those who trust Him as Lord and Savior will be freed from this bondage. These alone "will dwell in the house of the Lord forever" (Ps. 23:6).

2p-"The Son abideth ever" Again, the eternal Sonship of Jesus Christ is affirmed. For the earliest mention of this truth in the four gospels, see Section 1, Part 1, footnote a. The Jews were surely astounded as they heard these words from the mouth of Jesus. Even though some of the rabbis proclaimed that Messiah would live forever, they could not comprehend a carpenter from Nazareth of Galilee, (of all places) claiming to be that divine Person.

3p-Verse 36. "Free indeed." In this bold declaration, the Messiah presented Himself as their only hope of being freed from their sin. Being born the physical children of Abraham, the Jews considered themselves free from the evils of the Gentile world. They were never an enslaved nation! Christ informs them that their father is neither Abraham nor God, for they fail to imitate either in their words and deeds (verse 37-38). *Now,* their Messiah puts the story straight! Without Him, they are in sin's bondage and will die doomed. See footnote u below for the father of the Jews. For more on the meaning of freedom, see footnote q above. This passage is quoted continually by ministers and Bible teachers, but *rarely* is the context explained and its original meaning as given by our Lord. The freedom Christ gives not only begins at personal salvation, with absolute and total forgiveness of sins, but also is a process that gradually continues over the course of life, as the child of God grows in grace and knowledge of his Lord. This will be so until we reach "the measure of the stature of the fulness of Christ" (Eph. 4:13), which will be when we are home in heaven.

4p-Verse 38. Two fathers are mentioned here. One is God Almighty, and the other is the Devil from whom these Jews had taken a lesson on how to hate the Son of God. For more on this, see footnote u.

[s] **"This did not Abraham."** What a word of revelation and enlightenment! Christ had appeared to Abraham under the title, "the Word of the LORD" and made known to him the truth about salvation some two thousand years prior (Gen. 15:1-4). The federal head of the nation did not rebel against the Messiah or His message, as did the religious leaders who had boasted that he was their Father. Abraham believed Christ's Words and was saved (Rom. 4:1-3 with Gal. 3:6-9). The scribes and Pharisees standing before Jesus could have done the same, but they refused. For continued comments on this beautiful story, see second paragraph of footnote x below.

[t] **"Not born of fornication."** See footnote l above where they attempted to lay upon Him the charge that He was conceived out of wedlock. His terse response is found in verse 46 where He challenges them to point out a single sin in His life! This carpenter from Galilee was heaven's pure model; He was piety at its highest, above that of all mortal men. No other human could hold such a religious attitude, unless He is distinguished above all others. His sinlessness was without one dash of repentance; one confession of wrong; one tear over personal failure; or one act of excessiveness. *How different from we humans.* No sooner does any one of us begin to be self righteous, and we slip into those outward sins that shame our very false conceit. The Son of God, over the course of all His human life, brought no stain on His conduct. Today, after some two thousand years of church history, He still affirms, "Which of you convinceth me of sin?" The world continues to hate Him. Refer to footnote l for more on this charge.

[u] **Verse 44. "Your father is the devil."** What a slam on the leaders of religion. The Jews boasted of Abraham as their father in the flesh. Messiah puts His finger on their real problem: they were the children of the Devil and reflect this dark relationship in their ongoing efforts to kill Him. This they actually attempted again a few moments later in verse 59. Woe be unto those who seek to tone down this terrible truth by claiming that the "Jews used this expression in their discussions and disagreements with each other. It was considered a friendly form of debate." The entire context of this chapter reveals there was no courteous disagreement here. It was a conflict between darkness and light, good and bad, heaven, and hell. *Christ used it because the religious leaders were children of the Devil.* As Satan inspired the first murder of Abel in the beginning (1 John 3:12), so they too, driven by the same Satan, seek to destroy the Son of God. Like Cain, they refused to hear Him because they were not of God but of the wicked one. Refer to the main heading under Section 159 where the Lord Jesus pronounced eight terrible woes on these same religious Jews. This was two days before His death on the cross. For a review of Satan and his human agents of evil, see Section 20, footnote l, and Section 23, footnote c.

[v] **"Thou hast a devil."** This was the greatest slander that a Jew could hurl at another Jew. All Samaritans were considered foul, unclean, and demon possessed. The scribes and Pharisees had never forgotten His visit among the "cursed Samaritans" about three years earlier. Note Section 34, footnote a for details on His time with these people. The accusation of demon possession was an old one, which they had previously used against the Savior in Section 66, Matt. 12:24, footnote c. A short while later, it was hurled at Him a third time in Section 122, John 10:19-20, footnote p. Those Messianic Jews, who tell us that this was no more than a harsh but friendly discussion and that Israelites always used this strong language in a debate among themselves, have confused their culture with Bible truth. These men hated the carpenter from Nazareth with implacable anger, and emptied their vengeance upon Him.

2p-Verse 51. "Shall never see death" was a pure Hebraism or Jewish expression. It is found in Ps. 89:48; Lk. 2:26; and Heb. 11:5. The rabbis had several spectacular interpretations of the term. In verse 52 it is "shall never taste of death" which is the same as the expression above. In the word "death," Jesus was referring to spiritual death, which is eternal conscious suffering of the damned in the lake of fire.

(w) **"Who are you?"** They sensed that Jesus claimed to be *greater* than father Abraham and the prophets. They were right! He tells them that God honored Him by supporting His every claim. He was really asking them "If He were your God, then why do you not support me as He does?" They were found to be liars like their father the Devil. See footnote u above for comments on this expression of the Jews. How terrible that demon spirits knew Him, and said so, while the leaders of religion despised and rejected Jesus as their promised Messiah. In Section 41, Lk. 4:41, the first paragraph of footnote g, we read their public confession to this end.

(x) **"Abraham saw my day and was glad."** He lived some two thousand years before the birth of Christ, yet he saw the day of Christ and rejoiced in it! The noun "day" embraces the life and ministry of Christ on earth, which culminated in His death and resurrection. Abraham was saved by faith in the gospel and counted righteous before God (Rom. 4:1-3). Looking ahead by the eye of faith, he saw Christ's life, death, burial, resurrection, and rejoiced. The Jews, who claimed to be Abraham's children, hated everything Jesus did or said. Abraham, whom they boasted to be their father, never did this! In footnote u above the Messiah told them who their spiritual father really was.

2p-Other things Abraham saw. In Section 131, Lk. 16:22-31, we read of Abraham talking from the rest side of sheol-hades in timeless eternity. Our Lord was warning men in this life and world that they had better heed the teachings of God's Word to miss hell.

3p-Those who tell us that Old Testament people could not be saved have seriously erred! The father of the great Hebrew nation foresaw the death, burial, and resurrection of the future Christ *pictured* in the offering of Isaac on the mount (Gen. 22:1-18 with Heb. 11:17-19). God preached the gospel to Abraham, and he believed it (Gal. 3:6-8). He knew that his greatest "seed" was the Son of God, born two thousand years after his death (Gal. 3:16). On how people were saved during the ministry of Christ, read Section 144, footnote i.

(y) **"I am."** He had just used this term "I am," to the woman taken in sin (verse 12). Now, it comes from His lips again. "I am" was one of the eternal names for Almighty God. See Section 95, footnote i for explanation, and footnote j above, for more on this term. The Jews knew exactly what He claimed by applying these sacred words to Himself, thus declaring His deity. It was the great "I am" who spoke to Moses from the burning bush fifteen hundred years earlier (Ex. 3:1-6, 13-14). The man from cursed Nazareth claims to be this very Person! His startling announcement to the scribes, Pharisees, and Jews was something like this, "I am from all eternity and have existed before all ages. You Jews look upon me as yourselves, persons in time. However, within this human frame, which you see and know, is another Person, the real Me dwelling inside this body: is the eternal God and great 'I am.' Both sides are united and subsist together co-equally. Abraham could distinguish them. He loved and worshiped Me as the true and very God. He foresaw Me in My future; he even predicted My coming into this world. This Abraham is not your father, the Devil is!" See footnote u above. To the horror of the Jews, the Lord Jesus had pronounced the Sacred Name of God in His usage of the words "I am." According to their interpretation of the Torah Law, He should be put to death (Lev. 24:15-16). This troublemaker from Galilee, affirming to be their Messiah, now dared to claim that He was the God of the burning bush. They were stunned and infuriated!

(z) **"They took up stones."** Another attempt to kill Jesus by the incensed Jews. With the temple in a continual state of building, stones were easily obtainable. Prudence demanded that Jesus should immediately withdraw from the temple compound after this outbreak of murderous fanaticism. They were livid about His claim to be equal with God, and that He is very God Himself. *The hallmark of every false cult on the face of this earth today is exactly the same denial.* They fiercely hate Christ's claim of equality with God and His death on the cross for mankind. Any religion, be it ever so amiable, that opposes, rejects, or reinterprets the deity of Christ should not be supported in their blasphemy. Islam is an example of this. Muslims adamantly deny the divinity and death of Christ for mankind. Converts to Christianity in some Muslim countries are often killed for holding these beliefs. In Sydney, Australia, the newspaper *The Telegraph,* May 31, 2011, carried an article of how Muslims are erecting billboards reading "Jesus a prophet of Islam." The sheer stupidity of this is seen when we know that Mohammed, the founder of Islam, was not born until some five hundred years *after* the birth of Jesus Christ. These people should be honest and put on their billboards that "Muslims deny the deity of Christ and His death for our sins." These eternal truths they fiercely hate. For a shocking look at the founder of Islam, see *The Truth about Muhammad,* by Robert Spencer.

2p-For other attempts made by the Jews to kill the Lord Jesus, see Section 52, John 5:16, footnote l; Section 55, footnote a; and Section 123, footnote j. Christ "hid himself," then slipped out of the temple to avoid their fury. Later, the Pharisees tried on several occasions to destroy Him again, but He escaped their hands each time. Some of these are discussed in Section 123, John 10:39, footnote j, and Section 124, footnote w. The word "kill" is found in John's book nine times and all of them, except John 10:10, refer to the Jews seeking to kill Jesus.

3p-"He hid himself." The Lord Jesus not only taught men the ways of God and salvation, He also demonstrated great practical foresight. John wrote that the Savior "hid himself" from the religious Jews. In this, He gives us the invaluable lessons on *prudence, planning, and common sense.* Here, we note Him using necessary and acceptable stealth to bypass danger as a human, when He could have smitten them dead.

Leaving the temple, Christ heals a blind beggar sitting at the gate. The disciples' strange question. Christ cures* the unnamed man and thus demonstrates again that He is Israel's Messiah. Another confrontation with the Pharisees.

The events recorded in John chapter 8 through 10:21 seemingly took place on the Sabbath day immediately after the Feast of Tabernacles and are harmonized according to this chronology.

*See asterisk under main heading Section 48, for explanation of the four miracles that were exclusive to Israel's Messiah. These attestations of Christ the Messiah appear repeatedly throughout the four gospels.

Matt.	Mk.	Lk.	John 9:1-17—At the temple gate used by beggars
			A blind man: the disciples' question
			1 And as *Jesus* passed by,[a] he saw a man which was blind from *his* birth.
			2 And his disciples asked him, saying, "Master, who did sin, this man, or his parents, that he was born blind?"[b]
			3 Jesus answered, "Neither hath this man sinned, nor his parents: but that the works of God should be made manifest in him.[c]
			4 "I must work the works of him that sent me, while it is day: the night [d]cometh, when no man can work.
			5 "As long as I am in the world, I am the light of the world."
			Curious methods
			6 When he had thus spoken, he spat on the ground, and made clay of the spittle, and he anointed the eyes of the blind man with the clay,[e]
			7 And said unto him, "Go, wash in the pool of Siloam," (which is by interpretation, 'Sent.') He went his way therefore, and washed, and came seeing.[f]
			The neighbors and the man
			8 The neighbours therefore, and they which before had seen him that he was blind, said, "Is not this he that sat and begged?"[g]
			9 Some said, "This is he:" others *said,* "He is like him:" *but* he said, "I am *he.*"
			10 Therefore said they unto him, "How were thine eyes opened?"
			11 He answered and said, "A man that is called Jesus made clay, and anointed mine eyes, and said unto me, 'Go to the pool of Siloam, and wash:' and I went and washed, and I received sight."
			12 Then said they unto him, "Where is he?" He said, "I know not."
			The Pharisees and the man
			13 They brought to the Pharisees him that aforetime was blind.
			14 And it was the sabbath day when Jesus made the clay, and opened his eyes.
			15 Then again the Pharisees also asked him how he had received his sight. He said unto them, "He put clay upon mine eyes, and I washed, and do see."
			Another division
			16 Therefore said some of the Pharisees, "This man is not of God, because he keepeth not the sabbath day."[h] Others said, "How can a man that is a sinner do such miracles?" And there was a division among them.
			17 They say unto the blind man again, "What sayest thou of him, that he hath opened thine eyes?" He said, "He is a prophet."

Matt.	Mk.	Lk.	John 9:18-38—*At the temple gate used by beggars*
			The parents and the Jews
			18 But the Jews[i] did not believe concerning him, that he had been blind, and received his sight, until they called the parents of him that had received his sight.
			19 And they asked them, saying, "Is this your son, who ye say was born blind? how then doth he now see?"
			20 His parents answered them and said, "We know that this is our son, and that he was born blind:
			21 "But by what means he now seeth, we know not; or who hath opened his eyes, we know not: he is of age; ask him: he shall speak for himself."
			22 These *words* spake his parents, because they feared the Jews: for the Jews had agreed already, that if any man did confess that he was Christ, [or Messiah] he should be put out of the synagogue.[j]
			23 Therefore said his parents, "He is of age; ask him."
			The Pharisees and the man
			24 Then again called they the man that was blind, and said unto him, "Give God the praise: we know that this man is a sinner."[k]
			25 He answered and said, "Whether he be a sinner *or no,* I know not: one thing I know, that, whereas I was blind, now I see."[l]
			26 Then said they to him again, "What did he to thee? how opened he thine eyes?"
			27 He answered them, "I have told you already, and ye did not hear: wherefore would ye hear *it* again? will ye also be his disciples?"
			28 Then they reviled him, and said, "Thou art his disciple; but we are Moses' disciples.[m]
			29 "We know that God spake unto Moses: *as for* this *fellow*, we know not from whence he is."
			The man's response
			30 The man answered and said unto them, "Why herein is a marvelous thing, that ye know not from whence he is, and *yet* he hath opened mine eyes.
			31 "Now we know that God heareth not sinners:[n] but if any man be a worshipper of God, and doeth his will, him he heareth.
			32 "Since the world began was it not heard that any man opened the eyes of one that was born blind.[o]
			33 "If this man were not of God, he could do nothing."
			34 They answered and said unto him, "Thou wast altogether born in sins, and dost thou teach us?" And they cast him out.[p]
			Jesus finds the man and asks him a question
			35 Jesus heard that they had cast him out;[q] and when he had found him, he said unto him, "Dost thou believe on the Son of God?"
			The man is willing to believe
			36 He answered and said, "Who[r] is he, Lord, that I might believe on him?"
			37 And Jesus said unto him, "Thou hast both seen him, and it is he that talketh with thee."
			38 And he said, "Lord, I believe."[s] And he worshipped him.

Matt.	Mk.	Lk.	John 9:39-41—*At the temple gate used by beggars*
			Blindness reversed **39** And Jesus said,[t] "For judgment I am come into this world, that they which see not [are blind by sin] might see; [if they believe] and that they [the Pharisees] which [think they] see might [unless they are saved shall] be made blind." (by rejecting me) ***The Pharisee's question about blindness is answered*** **40** And *some* of the Pharisees which with him heard these words, and said unto him, "Are we blind also?"[u] **41** Jesus said unto them, "If ye were blind, [or confessed you are in darkness] ye should have no sin: [for you would be forgiven] but now ye say, 'We see;' [and are not in darkness] therefore your sin remaineth."[v] (Next chap., John 10:1 cont. in Section 122.)

Footnotes-Commentary

[a] **"Passed by."** In Section 120, John 8:59, Christ escaped the presence of the murderous Pharisees. In so doing, He exited out of the Women's Court or treasury through the Beautiful Gate and "passed by" the location designated for beggars (Acts 3:1-2). Clearly, these words, "passed by," connect with the last words of the previous chapter. The blind and other disabled or handicapped persons lived from begging and public charity. It should be noticed that all the events that occurred here took place on the Jewish Sabbath, according to the complaint of the Pharisees in John 9:16. The hypocrites of the Hebrew religion took up stones to kill Christ on the Sabbath after He claimed equality with God. *Yet their law forbids killing on the Sabbath!* Now, they seek to execute Jesus for healing a blind man on their beloved day. We learn from this, that His encounter with the woman taken in sin also happened on this Sabbath, early in the morning. In both cases, our Lord was attempting to show the Jews that *their* interpretation of the Sabbath law was contrary to God's original intended purpose, and that neither He, nor His disciples were bound by their perversion of Torah truth.

2p-Making their way through the sea of beggars sitting about, the disciples drew our Lord's attention to one special person: a man born blind, sitting among the hundreds about the gate. How they knew he had been born blind is not stated. This fact was the basis of their inquiry.

[b] **"He was born blind."** The Jews held to various absurd myths regarding unborn children. Several of these are given in Lightfoot's, *Commentary on the New Testament . . . ,* vol. 3, pages 337 - 342. They believed God would punish a child in its mother's womb if it did undue kicking, twisting, or moving; further, that this man being born blind could be the results of various prenatal sins. Some Jews held that pious souls were reincarnated as a reward while the souls of the wicked were shut into a nether prison to suffer eternally. See Josephus *Antiquities,* Book 18:1. 3, lines 12-15 where he explains what the Pharisees believed regarding this oddity. The apostles' inquiry reveals that fragments of rabbinical teaching had corrupted them; hence their question to Jesus regarding this matter.

2p-Apart from rabbinical fables, modern science has demonstrated that the unborn child hears sounds, recognizes specific noises, and often responds accordingly by jumping, dancing, and kicking while in the mother's womb! For a previous mention of this, see Section 10, footnote a. Here, see Lk. 1:41 for an unborn baby hearing voices in its mother's womb. The amazing story of *nursing infants* and *little children* recognizing the Messiah standing in the temple a few days before His death, is found in Section 150, Matt. 21:16, footnote f.

[c] **Verse 3.** Christ hastens to correct their erroneous rabbinical theology. He informs them that this man is not the product of his own or of his parent's sin. This happened in the providence of God and will become a channel for the salvation of the blind man's soul and the recovery of his sight. In these Words, Jesus reveals His knowledge of the secret counsels of God and all things that were foreordained for His eternal glory and man's good.

[d] **"Night when no man can work."** Our Lord may have also had reference to the destruction of Jerusalem, its temple, and several million Jews in A.D. 70. This event was the darkest night in the history of ancient Israel. With it, the work of the Hebrew temple ended forever, being replaced by the temple of the church or the new kingdom. For explanation of this beautiful truth, see Section 153, footnote k. The hand of death will sweep every child of God from the stage of Christian service. This *physical* cessation of all divine labor is described thus, "Whatsoever thy hand findeth to do, do *it* with they might; for *there is* no work, nor device, nor knowledge, nor wisdom, in the grave whither thou goest" (Eccle. 9:10). What a warning about the end of human life and labor. This verse has nothing to do with the soul of man which departs the body at death; rather it speaks strictly of the end of all our earthly labors.

2p-Verse 5. **"I am."** for more on this sacred designation, see Section 95 footnote i. Similar words were spoken to the guilty woman in Section 120, John 8:12, footnote j. Our Lord is saying to His band of preachers and in the hearing of the blind man, "Like the sun in yonder heavens dispenses its rays of light, warmth, and hope wherever it shines, I too must neglect no opportunity to reach men, regardless of the darkness in which they sit." As the "Light of the world" had just shone into the awful darkness of the woman's adultery, now it will shine into the eyes and soul of one who had never seen. He made this appropriate statement in view of the miracle He was about to perform. Shortly, the blind man will see *both* the sun and the Son! For more on "Jesus the light," see Section 1, Part 1, footnote e. Christ's Words "while it is day" have reference to His ministry, which would finish in about six months.

(e) **Mixing clay and spittle. "He spat on the ground and made clay."** We wonder what the apostles and crowds thought as they saw Jesus spit in the dust, with His finger make thin clay, and rub it into the man's eye sockets! No doubt, they were astounded at His curious actions. For other occasions where Christ used spittle, see Section 98, Mk. 7:32-34, footnote c, and Section 102, Mk. 8:22-23, footnote c. Could there be some connection with Adam being created out of the dust of the earth (Gen. 2:7) and Christ creating from dust new optic nerves through which the man's sight was restored? Does this miracle somehow reflect back to the original creation? Could it be a lesser repeat of that supernatural event? It reveals that Jesus is the Creator of man and that "God created all things by Jesus Christ" (Eph. 3:9).

2p-As with unborn children (footnote b above), the ancient Jews also held to many bewildering fables, myths, partly pagan allegories, and folk lore regarding the medical value of human spittle. This subject is mentioned in the Talmud a hundred and forty-one times.

3p-**"By interpretation."** John is inspired to give the meaning of the word "Siloam" for readers who did not know. Every true missionary working among people of other languages understands this need. See method of writing used to explain words in Section 26, John 1:41-42, second paragraph of footnote f.

(f) **"Go wash."** This pool was located within Jerusalem itself, but its source, the spring of Gihon, was southwest of Jerusalem outside the city walls. It had been built by King Hezekiah some five hundred years prior (2 Kings 20:20). It is of note that John interprets for his original readers, the Hebrew word "Siloam" as meaning, "sent." The Jews considered this pool of clear water as being "sent from God." It was a distance of about two miles round trip from the temple. It would be no small task for this blind man to *feel* and *find* his way to this site, especially when we remember the vast crowds that packed the city for the Feast of Tabernacles! Even if led by another, it was hard work to arrive at the pool. This was a miracle where Christ did not speak the command to be healed instantly, but rather sent the patient off to be healed. He let Christ do what He pleased and did what He said. There can be no doubt that the blind man undertook this difficult task to the pool as a test of obedience to the Master's orders. The walk to the pool was vastly different from his walk back! *He went blind and returned seeing!* The whole process must have taken at least an hour or more. The Lord often sends His servants into the most arduous of journeys to test their obedience.

(g) **"Is not this he?"** According to these words, the blind man was well known at the temple gate and by others who frequented this location. Who could describe the commotion, wonderment, and excitement that filled the place upon his return, as he raced back to the gate, leaping, waving his hands, and praising God. For the first time, he can see. Quickly, someone explains, "*Look* those things are people, land, trees, houses, children, animals, flowers, birds, a gate, walls, sky, sun, and beasts." He sees his former companions in poverty and sufferings, who sat about the gate begging with him. Voices once heard now become visible forms and persons. Suddenly, he is the talk of the town! The people were held in amazement at this wonder. No doubt, many of them made him repeat the astounding story of his cure. The happy confusion was so profound that some were unsure if it was the same person or not. Others vowed it was the one who sat at the gate. The great question of that scene was "How did you get your sight?" He knew Jesus by Name and said so, but being blind had not seen Him. He re-explains the instructions Jesus had given him. He obeyed these and was healed! In all the confusion, the Savior conveyed Himself away and vanished among the vast crowds that were always at the temple. He could not be found at this time for comment.

(h) Among the crowds were many sympathizers of the scribes and Pharisees. The more they heard, the more incensed they became, for this miracle was done on *their* Sabbath day. They escorted the seeing man to the Jewish authorities, the Sanhedrin court officials. Now, they find new grounds to condemn a law-breaking healer, who claimed to be Israel's Messiah. The response of the Pharisees was amazing! They concluded that He was not of God because He had broken their holy day (verse 16). *However, the Sabbath of the hypocritical rabbis was not the Sabbath of God.* See footnote a above. Other religious bigots standing by said that Jesus was a sinner; but others, more thoughtful, yet puzzled over the whole miracle, mused, "How can a man that is a sinner do such a miracle?" Repeatedly the works and Words of the Lord Jesus threw the people into various divisions among themselves. It is no different today.

(i) **"They called the parents."** The Jews fiercely rejected this miracle of healing one born blind, for they taught that this was a work that only the true Messiah of Israel could perform. See footnote o below. Therefore, if this man was born blind and Jesus did heal him, then, He is Messiah! Such a thought was impossible, and they scrambled to prove it wrong. They called in his parents to settle the controversy. The Jews unfamiliarity with the man who was healed means nothing. Hundreds of beggars in all sorts of physical conditions haunted Jerusalem and sat at the temple gate. This poor fellow was just another one of the massive crowds.

(j) **Verse 22. "Confess that he was Christ."** *Here was the crux of the whole issue.* They despised Him for claiming to be their Messiah and refusing to follow the thousands of oral or traditional laws. As Messiah, He was Torah familiar and faithful to the words of Moses and the prophets, but opposed to the Jew's fabricated rules for salvation and their hypocritical wickedness. These religionists brought in the man's parents to confirm whether he had been born blind. The thought of Jesus being their Messiah was unbearable. They presented three questions to the terrified parents of this formerly blind man (verses 19-21). They went something like the following:

1. "Is he your son?"
2. "Was he born blind?"
3. "Do you know how he received his sight?"

2p-To the first two questions, the parents answered in the affirmative. To the third inquiry, they could not answer, apparently, because they were not present to see how their son was healed. The response that he was of age is noteworthy. A Hebrew male was counted of age at thirteen years. See sixth paragraph below for more on this.

3p-**Verse 22. "Put out of the synagogue!"** This means he would be excommunicated or "de-synagogued." These terrifying words shook the parents. Nothing sounded more dreadful in the ear of any religious Jew. This was the penalty for confessing Jesus as the Messiah. At this time in history, there were three forms of excommunication practiced within the synagogue communities. "Cutting off from the congregation," or "shammata," was the punishment for anyone who confessed Jesus as the Messiah! The Talmud describes several forms of this specific punishment. There was "Neziphah" (correction) which consisted of a light rebuke of the guilty person and lasted from seven to thirty days. This action was valid only in *one* synagogue and not compulsory for all others to follow. The *formal* judicial punishments were as follows. In the written sources, there is a little overlapping of these:

1. **Niddui** ("to thrust out"). Its duration was for a minimum of thirty days. At the conclusion of this period, another warning was given, it too, lasted thirty days. If the culprit was still without repentance after ninety days, then the final form of expulsion was enforced.
2. **Cherem** ("to ban") was a harder punishment. The duration of this was up to ninety days.
3. **Shammatha** ("to cut off"). This was the final excommunication from the Jewish community.

4p-If the first two failed, the third was enacted. It was also called "the greater excommunication" and was a terrible experience. During the ceremony performed within a particular synagogue, curses were read aloud and cast upon the guilty one; candles were often lit and then blown out to signify the person's light was extinguished in Israel. To be expelled from most public life and all social events, with loss of work, family, and friends, was a terrible blow. *The victim became something of a living dead person.* To walk on a public road was forbidden. He could buy the necessities of life, but only from a Gentile, and everyone was forbidden to eat with him. Even at his funeral, stones were cast to show contempt. The rabbi's listed twenty-four reasons for excommunication; one of these was working on the Sabbath. Yet, expelled persons were allowed limited access into the temple through a special door, all in hope of God's mercy upon them. The authority for expulsion from the synagogue was in the hands of the Sanhedrin. For a good review of Jewish excommunication, see *Gill's Commentary,* vol. 8, pages 4-7, and Talmud tractates, Pesachim 52a; and Mo'ed Katan 16a-17a.

5p-In view of the above, we can understand why the parents of the former blind man were horrified at such a prospect. No wonder they spoke the cold words of verse 23. The night before the morning of the cross, Christ warned His eleven apostles that they too would be expelled from the synagogue. This forecast is in Section 177, John 16:2, footnote b. There is an old *legend* recorded in the Talmud tractate, Sanhedrin 107b, which says that Christ was, "Excommunicated from the synagogue with the blast of four hundred trumpets." Whether or not this legend is true, we may rest assured that somewhere along the way, probably near the end of His ministry, Jesus was excommunicated from His hometown synagogue at Nazareth.

6p-**"He is of age."** A person was counted of age at thirteen years if he could produce the physical signs of puberty. If so, he was considered a responsible individual and allowed to give an independent witness in court during judicial proceedings. This seems to be what his parents were referring to in their strange statement.

(k) **"This man is a sinner."** The chief of sinners, in Jewish thinking, was one who did not keep the oral law or tradition of the elders. The terrible dark evils of sin-twisted minds echo from verse 24. They order the man to voice his praises and thanks to God, but not to the One, who had healed him! They continued by saying that Jesus the Messiah was a sinner. Alas! How hate poisons and distorts the minds of men. In verses 27, the innocent man asked a question that threw the Jews into fits of rage. They now attack him! He gives thanks to God for his healing. In verse 32, he actually cites the formal belief of many Jews: that only Messiah could open the eyes of one born blind; then, he dares to give the Lord Jesus credit in their presence. Infuriated by Satan and filled with malice, the religious leaders "cast out" the man who was healed, describing him as "born in sins" (verse 34). This derogatory term also referred to one who was born a bastard.

(l) **"Out of the mouth of babes and sucklings thou hast ordained strength because of thine enemies"** (Ps. 8:2). How interesting that the rabbis had taught for centuries that this verse spoke of their coming Messiah! A newly converted person may not be able to meet the cavils of the enemy; he may fail in responding to their polished theological objection, but he can say with confidence, "Once I was blind, but now I see!" This poor man, being harassed and reviled by the leaders of religion, tells them in so many words, "Say what you will, I know what happened to me. I can see!" They were unable to explain away that miracle. For a later example of this before the same Jewish religious leaders, see Acts 4:14.

(m) "We are Moses' disciples." Clinging tenaciously to the oral traditions and Torah Law for their salvation, these Jews, being satanically inspired, ridiculed the beaming, rejoicing man who stood before them. Their abuse and misuse of the law had filled them with renewed hatred and bitterness. Now, they can only find refuge in scorn, which is hurled in the face of the man who can now see. According to the Talmud tractate, Yoma 4a, the Pharisees claimed *exclusively* to be Moses' disciples, yet they were ignorant to the truth that Moses had written about Christ their Messiah hundreds of times in their law. Moses' record of our Savior is mentioned in Section 52, John 5:45-47, footnotes y and z. According to the Pharisees, the Lord Jesus had seriously desecrated their Sabbath in performing this miracle, and they believed that Moses was offended as well!

2p-Law cults. As it was in the days of the apostles and early church, so it is today. Splinter groups, sects, cults, and breakaway movements, entangled in the Torah Law of Moses, abound. Even among some of the major denominations of Christianity, one finds millions trapped in selected portions of the code of Moses. In many of the Reformed Churches, there is a continual doctrinal mixture of God's grace with the weak and beggarly elements of the law. For more on the law cults, see Section 53, third paragraph of footnote k. The biggest hoax is the appeal to sincerity. We hear, "If people are sincere in their religion, they are acceptable to God." For the objection that all religions are right and none should be exposed and condemned, see Section 33, third paragraph of footnote c. On this great deceiving error that is so contrary to God's word, see especially Section 95, sixth paragraph of footnote r. *God only accepts those into heaven who know Jesus Christ as Lord and Savior.*

(n) "Heareth not sinners." He is simply parroting rabbinical theology, which stated that sinners were Gentiles and those who did not keep the Torah Law and the traditions of Israel. The former blind man is saying that the Person, Who healed his eyes, cannot be a bad man or a sinner to have worked such a miracle, even according to the standards of the Pharisees. If Jesus were an imposter, as they claimed, God would have never heard Him, and He could not have performed this fantastic wonder! According to the man's words recorded in verse 31, Christ had prayed for him to be healed, and then sent him off to the pool to wash, though there is no record of His actual prayer.

(o) "Since the world began." Whoever this fellow was, he was familiar with the Jewish belief that only Messiah could open the eyes of one born blind. This is what he was expressing in these words. Note all by the asterisk, at number 3, under main heading of Section 48 for more on this Messianic belief. For previous Messianic wonders, such as the deliverance of those possessed with dumb demons, see Section 66, Matt. 12:22, footnote b and Section 90, footnote e.

2p-Verse 33. He dogmatically affirms that who ever healed his blind eyes is "of God." This must have grated the Jews!

(p) "Cast him out." These words are a condensed version of the fact that he was (later) expelled from the synagogue for defending the Lord Jesus, whom he did not really know at that point. See footnote r below. On the terrible consequences of being excommunicated from Jewish worship, see footnote j above. Being convicted in their wicked hearts by the simplicity and openness of the man they were interrogating, the Sanhedrin was shamed into anger and threw him out of his synagogue. John wrote his book years later, and looking back on the entire story, was thus inspired to fill in various other details.

(q) The greatest question. *Word spread across Jerusalem of this event.* The Lord Jesus learning of the man's fate in the hands of the Jews sought him out in loving concern. Verse 35 states, "and when he [Jesus] had found him." The Master put one question to His new friend, "Doest thou believe on the Son of God?" It should be noted that this fellow did not inquire, "What are you talking about? I don't know what you mean by the Son of God?" Though he was both blind and a beggar, like all informed Jews, he knew this exclusive title signified the Messiah of Israel. See Section 103, Matt. 16:16, numbers 4 and 5, under footnote f for more on the title "Son of God."

2p-"The Son of God." This divine title is known on earth, in heaven, and hell. Several months ago, two friends of the author entered a jail in a large Alabama city. Their weekly visit was to share the gospel with the inmates. The older of the two said to his companion, "I am going to try an experiment; watch and see the reaction." Approaching the cell and being unknown to this new batch of prisoners, he called out, "How many of you believe that Jesus Christ is the Son of God?" Spontaneously, they began shouting and cursing, "We don't believe that!" Some beat on the bars to express their objection. An elderly man, under a blanket, lifted his head and said, "I believe that!" Everyone railed upon him! This reveals that devils and wicked men alike hate this highest accolade for the Savior. As Israel's religious men despised it over two thousands years ago, it is still slandered today. Popular TV figures, such as Stephen Colbert (a real dirt mouthed blasphemer), Bill O'Reilly, Keith Olbermann and others also ridicule divine truth. Worse, the *WORLD* magazine for Oct. 8, 2011, pages 44-47 reported how the famed Wycliffe Bible Translators are trying to produce a Bible that will please the Muslims! Toying with the terms "Son of God," and "God the Father," they are looking for a less offensive rendering for Islamic readers. (This is because the religion of Islam viciously hates the deity of Christ and His death on the cross.) Wycliffe should defend the Word of God, or get out of the business of translating, apologize to their supporters, and return their money.

3p-The church sign that spoke to a man's heart. While serving as a missionary in Australia in 1963, we had a large church sign erected at a curve in the road in front of the local train station. It read across the top in large red letters, "Where will you spend eternity? Heaven or hell?" A native from Thursday Islands, who was employed at the local meat works, passed that sign every day for five days; its words pierced his heart. The following Saturday he came to my house; head down in utter humility and haltingly asked, "Mr. Pike, I read your sign; can you help me prepare for eternity?" Noel was saved that day at our kitchen table, served God for the next thirty years, and then went home to heaven. If ever a humble, poor, seeking man discovered who the Son of God was, Noel Johnson did! And it all started when he read a church sign on the side of the road (Heb. 4:12).

4p-While home on furlough in 1966 and showing slides of this very sign at a church outside Chicago, a businessman attacked me stating it was wrong to do such things. He vehemently demanded a verse to justify my actions. Suddenly, Ruth 4:4 flashed over my mind. It reads, "I thought to advertise thee." I quoted this passage to the whole church and *to my surprise, they broke out in loud applause!* The elderly pastor smiled. Before the series of meetings were over this objector became my friend. God's Word still works wonders in seeking hearts, whether it is on a road sign or a verbal Scripture quotation to an angry Chicago electrician. With this, see 1 Thess. 2:13.

(r) "Who is the Son of God, Lord?" We are amazed at this question. Even at this late hour, he did not know the Person with whom he held a conversation was the Messiah, the One who had cured his eyes back at the gate. This is another miracle of healing *without* the benefactor knowing who had healed him. Earlier, the man at the Pool of Bethesda had been healed without knowing His healer. Refer to Section 52, John 5:13, footnote i. Both cases are examples of the truth that "God will use whom He chooses to accomplish what He pleases." Responding to the man's inquiry, the Lord graciously reveals Himself as that very Person on whom he must believe. The former blind man's reaction (recorded below) to this profound revelation was spontaneous.

(s) Verse 37. "Lord, I believe." The Lord Jesus presented Himself as the Messiah of Israel. In the simplicity of faith, the man spoke this verbal confession. The beauty and wonderment of genuine conversion beams from his humble words, "Lord, I believe." The words of David written over a thousand years earlier had great meaning in this man's life: "When my father and my mother forsake me, the LORD will take me up" (Ps. 27:10). He confessed Jesus of Nazareth as his Messiah. Falling before the Lord of heaven, he "worshipped Him." Faith and works kissed each other. Bowing in worship is an eastern expression of respect. It must be noticed that Christ did not refuse worship. It is written, "Thou shalt worship the Lord thy God, and him only shalt thou serve" (Matt. 4:10 with Deut 10:20). *This either makes Christ equal with God or an imposter who broke the law of Israel.*

(t) Having spoken comfort to the poor man, Christ swiftly turns his attention to those Pharisees, who persecuted him. He now explains a truth to the Jews by borrowing a lesson from the healing of the former blind man. "They which see not might see." The example stood before them. Like this fellow, the Pharisees were spiritually blind. However, it they knew it and would ask for His forgiveness their spiritual eyes would open. Conversely, those religious leaders and their supporters who think they see, but rejected Jesus as Lord, Savior, and Messiah, had willfully made themselves blind. The hostile Jews standing about got His message. Note their instant reaction and obvious question in footnote u below. Our Lord had spoken earlier about the self-willed blindness of the religious leaders of Israel, predicted by the prophet Isaiah some seven hundred years prior. Refer to Section 74, Matt. 13:14, second paragraph of footnote e.

(u) "Are we also blind?" The Pharisees and Sanhedrin Court smarted sharply under the authority of Messiah's plain but powerful words. They retort in sarcasm, but their question signified, they understood the Master's allegory was intended for them. To these professional hypocrites, He replied, "If you accepted the truth that you are spiritually blind and walk in darkness because of your rejection of Me, then you could be saved, forgiven and enlightened to see: your sin would be removed, and you would have it no more. However, this you refuse to do: you pretend to see and to have light; therefore, you continue on to hell in your blindness." He had previously warned them of blaspheming the Holy Spirit and the consequences of this dreadful sin. Note this in Section 66, Matt. 12:31, footnote j. Their response is recorded in footnote v below.

(v) "Your sin remaineth." Another devastating statement from Jesus! And w*hat was their great sin?* That of rejecting Him as Savior and Messiah. In reply to numerous warnings from Christ, they roared back, "No! We are not blind. We will continue in our traditions and oral law. We will work for our righteousness. We want a Messiah, who will destroy the Gentile oppressors and set up a material and political kingdom where Israel will rule the world. You are an imposter. We will have none of you!" No marvel our Savior quipped back with these dreadful words. Sin remains unremitted for all who do not know or reject Jesus Christ as personal Lord and Savior. This was the damning evil for most of Israel's religious leadership; their awful physical judgment fell in A.D. 70 at the hands of the pagan Romans. Only a short time prior, Christ had warned them that they "would die in their sins" (John 8:21).

2p-For continued information on the "remaining" or "remitting of sins," see Section 201, John 20:23, footnotes t and u, and Section 203, second paragraph of footnote d.

After giving the Parable of the Good Shepherd, He departs Jerusalem. Upon hearing His lesson, the Pharisees learn that they are not part of His flock. Jesus speaks again of His death and resurrection. The Jews are divided over His Words. Many of them slander their Messiah claiming He was demon possessed.

Matt.	Mk.	Lk.	John 10:1-18—*At the temple sheep gate?*
			***The parable given*(a)**
			1 "Verily, verily, I say unto you, He that entereth not by the door into the sheepfold,(b) but climbeth up some other way, the same is a thief and a robber.
			2 "But he that entereth in by the door is the shepherd of the sheep.
			3 "To him the porter(c) [keeper] openeth; and the sheep hear his [the shepherd's] voice: and he(d) calleth his own sheep by name, and leadeth them out.
			4 "And when he putteth forth his own sheep, he goeth before them, and the sheep follow him: for they know his voice.
			5 "And a stranger will they not follow, but will flee from him: for they know not the voice of strangers."
			Parable explained
			6 This parable(e) spake Jesus unto them: but they understood not what things they were which he spake unto them.
			7 Then said Jesus unto them again,(f) "Verily, verily, I say unto you, I am the door(g) of the sheep.
			8 "All that ever came before me [claiming to be the door] are thieves and robbers: but the sheep did not hear them.
			9 "I am the door:(h) by me(i) if any man enter in, he shall be saved, and shall go in and out, and find pasture.
			10 "The thief cometh not, but for to steal, and to kill, and to destroy: I am come that they might have life, and that they might have *it* more abundantly.(j)
			11 "I am the good shepherd:(k) the good shepherd giveth his life for the sheep.
			12 "But he that is an hireling,(l) and not the shepherd, whose own the sheep are not, seeth the wolf coming, and leaveth the sheep, and fleeth: and the wolf catcheth them, and scattereth the sheep.
			13 "The hireling fleeth, because he is an hireling, and careth not for the sheep.
			14 "I am the good shepherd, and know my *sheep*, and am known of mine.
			A hint of His death on the cross
			15 "As the Father knoweth me, even so know I the Father: and I lay down my life for the sheep.
			16 "And other sheep I have, [Gentiles] which are not of this fold: them also I must bring, and they shall hear my voice; *and* there shall be(m) 'one fold, and one shepherd.'
			17 "Therefore doth my Father love me, because I lay down my life, that I might take it again.(n)
			18 "No man taketh it from me, but I lay it down of myself. I have power to lay it down, and I have power to take it again. This

Matt.	Mk.	Lk.	John 10:18-21—*At the temple sheep gate?*
			commandment have I received of my Father."
			Jews divided again: He is falsely accused
			19 There was a division(o) therefore again among the Jews for these sayings.
			20 And many of them said, "He hath a devil,(p) [demon] and is mad; why hear ye him?"
			Some of the Jews were sympathetic but unsure
			21 Others said, "These are not the words of him that hath a devil. Can a devil open the eyes of the blind?"(q) (Verse 22 cont. in Section 123.) *See the italicized sub heading in Section 123, footnote a, for the time gap occurring between verses 21 and 22 in this part of John's gospel.*

Footnotes-Commentary

(a) It is noted that the parable in this chapter is a continuation from the previous Section 121, John 9:41. This is clear from several observations. The usage of the word "Pharisees," in John 9:40 tied to the plural pronoun "them," in verse 41, and to "you," in John 10:1 give evidence that these are the same persons being addressed by our Lord. The Pharisees professed themselves to be the only true spiritual shepherds for the Jewish people, and that Israel alone was God's flock (Ps. 79:13). At the conclusion of the previous chapter, the Savior called them blind or unfit leaders for Israel. Every person listening, instantly understood the symbolic language used by the Master. The work of sheep herding was found everywhere across Judaea and known to all in His audience. Elite Jews had a low opinion of sheepherders. This is discussed in Section 14, footnote b. The Lord Jesus begins His lesson by stating emphatically that anyone who does not come into the fold of God by the door is an imposter. Later, in verses 7 and 9, He claimed to be that door. His message was clear: the religious leaders and all who joined hands with them, against Him, by refusing to enter His kingdom, were "thieves and robbers" amid the flock of Israel.

2p-Zechariah's Shepherd-Messiah. The ancient rabbis interpreted all of Zech. 11 as having reference to their coming Messiah and His functions as a pastor-herdsman among the children of Israel. Zechariah wrote his prophecy in about 515 B.C. In the Talmud tractate, Joma 39b, there is the story of a rabbi named Johanan ben Zakkai, who lived before the destruction of Jerusalem. On one occasion, he witnessed the gates of the temple suddenly swing open of themselves! He shouted out "O temple, temple, why doest thou terrify thyself? I know thy end will be destruction; for so Zechariah the son of Iddo, hath prophesied concerning thee." This prediction had reference to the fall of Jerusalem and was spoken by Rabbi ben Zakki forty years before A.D. 70. Lightfoot does an excellent work in explaining this from the Hebrew perspective in his *Commentary on the New Testament . . .*, vol. 3, pages 347–350. Zechariah begins his prophecy with a call for the doors of the temple to open so fire may devour the massive cedar, fir, and oak construction, imported from Lebanon, that was such a gorgeous part of this building (Zech. 11:1). Just before this calamity, Messiah manifested Himself among the Jews just as the nation was on the brink of utter destruction. He is instructed by God to "Feed the flock" or Israel (Zech. 11:4). Zechariah had forecasted their doom (which came in A.D. 70) and then brought in Messiah the Good Shepherd to save and care for them. All divine pity has been withdrawn from these stubborn people (Zech. 11:6). Messiah will feed them to slaughter and death but take the "poor" unto Himself (Zech. 11:7 with 11). Three of Israel's (false) shepherds will be destroyed (Zech. 11:8); these shepherds being later interpreted as the Pharisees, Sadducees and Essences. Because of Israel's incorrigible wickedness, Jesus the Messiah breaks His covenant with them and promises their destruction (Zech. 11:10 with 14). The true Shepherd, Christ the Messiah, is sold for thirty pieces of silver (Zech. 11:12-13) with the religious leaders of Israel paying the price to Judas the traitor. God will send an evil shepherd into the land of Israel; he will be merciless and fierce. In awful violence, he will destroy the wicked Jews (Zech. 11:16). This was General Titus with his Roman legions.

3p-In Zech. 11:17 we read of a sword upon the "right eye" of the evil shepherd that deserted the flock of Israel. After A.D. 70, this was interpreted to have reference to the religious authorities in Israel, especially the Sanhedrin. *The expressions "his arm shall be clean dried up," and "his right eye shall be utterly darkened," do not point to a future "one-eyed eyed Antichrist that would appear in the last days!"* Rather, these were common maxims employed by the rabbis to describe the utter destruction of a person or nation. The "last day experts" went ballistic when the one-eyed Jewish General, Moshe Dyan, appeared on the scene performing all sorts of military wonders for Israel. Instantly, they had their Antichrist! However, their "man of sin" or "Antichrist" died in 1981. For a review of the Antichrist, see *Appendix Eight.*

4p-Hundreds of the Jews listening to Christ give His discourse on the Parable of the Good Shepherd knew exactly what He was talking about. His interpretation of Zech. 11, however, was vastly different from that given by the rabbis who hated Him. Apparently, the Jews did not comprehend the meaning of this parable at first, though the common folk did. At its conclusion, the religious Jews were raging with fury over Jesus' Words and described Him as demon possessed (19 and 20).

(b) **"The sheepfold."** This was a rough enclosure, usually constructed of various things (sticks, poles, thorns, limbs, hewn planks, vines, and dried skins) in which the sheep were gathered at night for protection from foul weather, thieves, and beasts. The door was the means of access into the presence of the flock. The rabbis declared that only Israel was the exclusive flock of God; and that their Messiah would someday be the shepherd of their nation and the world. It was fervently taught that the Messiah was to be this shepherd (Ezek. 34:11-12, 23, 31, and Zech. 13:7). In verse 11, Christ declares emphatically that *He is the Messiah Shepherd*; He alone has the right to enter Israel as their only Savior and Shepherd. He came into the nation by the door of the virgin birth as the Person to whom all the Messianic predictions pointed. The Pharisees knew exactly that He was claiming, again, to be that promised Person of their Scriptures. They also knew He pinpointed them as the "thieves and robbers" of Israel, who refused to enter by Him, the only door.

2p-Two doors. A point commonly overlooked is that there were *two* doors to the standard Jewish style sheepfold. Not only the larger one by which the shepherd and his sheep entered at night, but also a smaller one constructed during the lambing season. Through this little entrance, the shepherds calculated their tithes of the lambs. This was done by putting all lambs inside the fold with the mothers outside. Then the small door was opened. Only two lambs at a time could exit. The shepherd, kneeling by the door, counted them as they scurried out. Every tenth one was marked with red as a tithe, holy unto the Lord. The bleating of the mothers without made the lambs hurry through their little door.

(c) **"The porter."** Our Savior probably gave this parable somewhere near the sheep market that served worshippers offering sacrifices in the temple. Here, hundreds of temporary folds were erected by the merchants for keeping their sheep penned up waiting for buyers. During the absence of the owners, a person called "the porter" cared for the flock. This "porter" would *only* open the door of the fold to the true owner and shepherd. See footnote d below for more on the porter. Standing amid this scene, the Messiah gave His great Parable of the Good Shepherd. *Every* porter knew the shepherd's voice, even amid the darkest and the most severe night. To him *only*, entrance was granted by the porter. Various emblems are given to this unnamed porter. Some have pictured here the great Holy Spirit, who alone can open the door for entrance to the Son of God. Others, see that body of faithful ministers of Scripture, who refuse to grant entrance into the local church to heretics, apostates, false prophets, and doctrines. They are known as "under-shepherds." However, he could not be the shepherd for he opens the door for "him."

(d) Several features seemingly distinguish the "porter" as being someone known and trusted by the shepherd. As just said above, possibly, here is the emblem of an *extraordinary* man of God, who with deep consciousness attends to God's flock under the shepherd's care. See verses 3-5. Note several things about the porter:

1. He alone has the authority to open the door that grants access to the sheep.
2. The sheep hear and know his voice.
3. He knows the name of *every* sheep in his flock.
4. He goes before, leading the flock, and they follow him in the absence of the shepherd.
5. The sheep know the porter's voice. They will not follow strangers who may imitate him ever so well. In 1966, we were returning to America on furlough. We stopped off in Iraq to visit the archaeological diggings of ancient Babylon, located about one hundred miles from Baghdad. Something happened that explained the meaning of Jesus' statement, "the porter's voice." As we arrived at the airport to depart Iraq, I looked onto the nearby street and saw a shepherd leading his flock through the bustling city! The English-speaking driver explained that he was taking them to new pastures. The sheep were terrified at the asphalt pavement, noise of traffic, and the normal racket of a large city. The poor animals were literally climbing upon one another's backs trembling and struggling to get near their shepherd. He was walking slowly backwards, facing the flock and making a cooing sound. The taxi driver explained that the terrified sheep wanted to "see the shepherd's face and hear his voice." This alone would calm them. Instantly, John 10:4 came to mind.

(e) The first five verses contain the parable. The people described as being those that "understood not" are explained in footnote a above. They were the religious leaders of Israel and by the end of His message, they understood what He had said. In verses 19 and 20, they hated Christ for giving this message and again charged Him with being demon possessed! Refer to the second paragraph under footnote g below.

(f) **"Again."** With this, the Lord Jesus commences to give a clear explanation of the parable He had just spoken. It is to be noted that He is both the door and good shepherd in this single parable. See footnotes h and k.

(g) **"I am"** For details on the Sacred Name and title, see Section 95, footnote i. See footnote h, below, for more on these two words. The rabbis, scribes, Pharisees, and Jewish teachers claimed to be the door to God's sheep as well as the nation's only spiritual guides. Nevertheless, here Jesus contradicts this pretense and clearly presents Himself as the door, the exclusive *door*, into God's fold. For centuries, the rabbis and religious leaders had claimed that their teaching of the law and obedience to the oral tradition would bring one to the knowledge of God. In a unique but single sense, this was true of the Torah Law, but *only* if one found in it the Savior to whom its 613 precepts pointed in one way or another.

2p-Verse 8. All are thieves and robbers. This is absolute Jewish language. The Talmud speaks of thieves and robbers hundreds of times. Two examples are the tractates, Nedarim 27b and Baba Kama 67a. It is beyond question that the Lord Jesus, in this narrow, sharp wording refers (again) to the religious leadership of Israel. See footnote a above for the false attitude of the scribes and Pharisees concerning the way to God. Refer to the first paragraph of footnote b above for more on the religious "thieves and robbers" in Israel at this time. Later, in Section 159, Mk. 12:40, footnote j, the Lord Jesus actually charged the scribes and Pharisees with *stealing* from the widows of Israel.

(h) **"I am the door."** This is Christ's second time in the parable to use the term. See footnote g above and verse 9 for its first usage. Over the course of world religion, every man who has stood and claimed to speak for God, but did not properly and honestly represent Jesus Christ as the *only* Savior and salvation for lost humanity, has lied to and deceived those who gave him ear. They are described as thieves and robbers: thieves, in that they steal from men the sure hope of heaven, and robbers, in that they openly and publicly do so, with no blush of shame. What a horrible description of Israel's religious leaders some two thousand years ago. It is the same of certain "Christian personalities" today!

(i) The Jews of this era held that pure Judaism was "the fold," and "the door." Such statements are rabbinical language. It was staunchly held that if anyone was of the seed of Israel and the stock of Abraham, it was enough for him to be a sheep of God in the flock, and could be fed and nourished into eternal life by the scribes and rabbis.

2p-"By me." Here, the Lord Jesus explodes another rabbinical myth! This was an affirmation of absolute narrowness. Christ is totally exclusive. He presents Himself as the *sole source for salvation* of humanity, and the only One to be followed in the work of God. If this is not true, then Jesus of Nazareth is the biggest religious liar in human history! *However, it is true!* None but those who follow this Good Shepherd will ever find pastures that will satisfy the high aspirations and longings of the human soul. How this affirmation must have slapped the religious leaders in the face! It was diametrically opposed to their entire doctrine of eternal life. In today's talk, we would say, "It is Christ or hell" for all mankind. See the second paragraph of footnote m below for more on this fact. This restrictive claim of Jesus is bitterly hated by the world and its Christless religions. Nothing so infuriates men as this *absolute opposition* of the Son of God to the ecumenicity of the false religious systems abounding on all sides. Jesus mentioned His unique exclusiveness later in Section 128, Lk. 14:27, footnote e, with its relative references, and Section 175, John 14:6, footnote e.

(j) **"Steal, kill, and destroy."** No better description is given of Satan and his minions of evil as they seek to work havoc among the little flock of God. Section 23, first and second paragraphs of footnote c, carries an explanation of Satan, his helpers and their intentions for mankind. For his final and everlasting end, and those who serve him, refer to Section 166, Matt. 25:41.

2p-"More abundant life." This is not the life that is preached by many American, prime time TV evangelists. It is not the counterfeit "healthy wealthy," "the good life now" preaching that has deceived millions. The greatest of Christians over the course of life have, in time, become disenchanted and fed up with this world, even the cleanest and best things it has to offer. *Fullness* of joy will never be totally realized in this pilgrim journey. Weeping has endured most of our nights, and we sigh for that land where there is no pain, sorrow, and suffering. Old age, feebleness, and trembling steps carry no abundance for the lives of millions of saved Christians. The world talks about the wonderful "golden years." Yet, for untold thousands of saints, they are nothing but a gradual surrender of health, work, mobility, strength, mind, and finally life. This is God's way of preparing many of us for eternity. Just ahead is something better, greater, and more enduring. Interestingly, the atheist author, H. G. Wells (died 1946) once said, "If this life is all there is to it then it is a very bad joke!" We reply, "There is more Mr. Wells, there is more!" The endless abundance of eternal life, found only in Christ, will finally and forever be enjoyed in heaven's sweet home, sharing eternity with Him who has loved us so. "In thy presence *is* fulness of joy; at thy right hand *there are* pleasures for evermore" (Ps. 16:11). "I shall be satisfied, when I awake, with thy likeness" (Ps. 17:15). Some day, prayer will give way to praise, and hope to sight, when we finally arrive home.

(k) **"I am the good shepherd."** On this Name-title, see footnotes g and h above. This term is repeated in verse 14. Christ *alone* is the Shepherd of God's flock. As the great, "I am," He is always in the continuous present tense. Woe be those who have trusted the salvation of their souls into the hands of Buddha, Hare Krishna, Mohammed, Brigham Young, Joseph Smith, Ellen G. White, Ron Hubbard, yoga, transcendental meditation, the Pope, and others. Only Christ died for the sins of all mankind, and only Christ rose from the bonds of death and the grave to live forever more! No other person in the ragged, messy history of earth's religions has His unique and infallible qualifications. In the New Testament, He is called "The good shepherd" (verse 11 above), "that great shepherd" (Heb. 13:20), "the Shepherd and Bishop of our souls" (1 Peter 2:25), and the "chief shepherd" (1 Peter 5:4).

2p-Verse 11. "Giving His life for the sheep" has reference to His soon death on the cross. He repeats this fact again, in verse 15 in the words, "I lay down my life for the sheep." As mentioned in verse 15 under footnote l below, there was a tradition among the Jews, that Hur was martyred when he opposed the Israelites for their worship of the golden calf. The rabbis would say of Hur, "He gave his life for the sheep" or Israel. Our Lord takes this phrase and gives it the correct meaning; He died for the sheep of God's flock. Dying for "the sheep" has nothing to do with the radical doctrine of Augustine-Calvinistic predestination. In Rom. 5:8 we read, "Christ died for sinners." Are we thus to conclude that only Calvinists and their elect are sinners? One radical Calvinist pastor in Louisiana went so far as to teach that all men are sinners, but all men are not lost!

(l) **"The hireling."** In verses 12 and 13 he is distinguished from the "porter." See footnotes c and d above. Several Talmud tractates mention the hireling, for example, Chagigah 5a and Kiddushin 14b. The word speaks of persons paid (hired) to attend the flock in the necessary absence of the owner. It seems that Christ used this derogatory term to describe the priests who served at the temple with outstanding wages and benefits, yet they cared nothing for the flock of God. For a brilliant explanation of this subject see, *Jerusalem in the Time of Jesus,* updated edition, pages 105-108 by Joachim Jeremias. A future meaning of "hirelings" may prophetically point to the thousands of false, wretched pastors who over the centuries have used God's flock for their greed and gain. Any minister who attends to his personal cares and safety and then neglects those of God's flock over which he has charge, is not to be trusted. Balanced attention should be given both. "Hirelings" fancy that the sheep may take care of themselves and often neglect or forsake them. Sheep by their very nature are dependent on the shepherd. They are defenseless, and will not bleat for help as they are being slaughtered.

2p-Years ago, the author was traveling at daybreak through a mountain chain in the Zululand region of South Africa. Rounding a curve in the fog, I saw ahead a most pitiful and heart touching sight. A trailer truck had just driven through a large flock of sheep standing in the road. Dozens had been killed, crushed, mutilated, and crippled. Some, still alive were hanging from beneath the truck's fenders and undercarriage. Stopping to survey the sight, I was struck by the eerie calm. Not one sound was heard from the wounded and dying animals or those standing in the road literally trembling in fear. Only the shouts of the excited Africans dashing about broke the eerie silence of that terrible scene. Slowly driving through the carnage, I remembered this chapter in the Gospel of John, and Christ's Words that sheep must have their shepherd to care for them. Speaking to the driver of the truck I learned that the sheep belonged to someone else, and that the "care boy" (hireling) had fled the scene when he saw the truck speeding around the corner towards the flock. This is the meaning of our Lord's Words.

3p-Verse 14. **Mutual knowledge.** What a wonderful statement! *The Savior affirms that He knows His sheep, and they know Him.* No better assurance of salvation could be found than these Words from the mouth of Jesus. Moreover, the most miserable religious persons on earth are those who flounder and wallow in the mire of doubt regarding the assurance of eternal life in Christ.

4p-Verse 15. **"I lay down my life for the sheep."** Some seven hundred years before Christ, the prophet Isaiah described the unsaved as "sheep gone astray" (Isa. 53:6). This is the meaning of Jesus' Words. The Savior makes direct reference to His upcoming death on the cross. As mentioned in the second paragraph of footnote k above, there was a tradition among the Jews, that Hur died as a martyr because he opposed the golden calf worship and its associated orgies of ancient Israel at Mount Sinai (Ex. 32). They said of Hur, "He laid down his life for the sheep." Now, the Lord Jesus gives the meaning of this traditional saying, for He alone died to save the sheep.

(m) **"One fold and one shepherd"** This is a selection of various words probably taken from Ezek. 34: 22-23. Here, it has direct reference to the millions of Gentiles, who would be brought into His original Jewish flock. The Great Shepherd, when He came, found that there was a flock to be gathered. As Rom. 11:5 states, it was "a remnant according to the election of grace." It means that all who repent and believe in Christ are God's flock, saved by grace. This began with the church after His rejection by Israel. For details, see information by the asterisk under main heading, Section 60. In God's time, all the saved of all ages would be *one* in Christ. It should be noted that Zech. 14:9 is a rabbinical prayer employed in specific synagogue rituals. It calls for the day when God (Jehovah) will be One over all the earth and His Name one. Our Lord may have also had this text from Zechariah in mind when He spoke these words. There is some similarity to the synagogue recital of Deut. 6:4, called "Shema."

2p-**A counterfeit unity.** The oneness spoken of here has nothing to do with a worldwide religion, blending all faiths together into a universal ecumenical conglomeration. Rather, it speaks of the gathering out of all nations those who will be saved into the final and perfect harmony at the end of time. This is not the infamous World Council of Churches or most national church councils, which consist of a mixture of infidels, unsaved religionists, cults, apostates, and pagans. The lost world hates the Lord Jesus because of His claim to be the *only* Savior of men. His declaration to be the sole way to heaven is opposed by governments, religions, false churches, most educational systems, sporting organizations, Hollywood, and the media in general. Marching in this satanic army are numerous social and civic groups, along with all pagan and Antichrist religions. Infrequently, these various groups may "tip their hat" to Jesus, the Son of God, but they reject His exclusive and singular claims and viciously oppose the slightest suggestion that they are lost in sin and need Him as their Savior. *Their hatred stands as impeccable evidence that Christ's Words and the Holy Scriptures are true, and they are wrong.*

3p-Is there a separate Gentile flock that will help Jews during the tribulation? For a response to this erroneous teaching that is not yet three hundred years old, refer to Section 166, footnote g.

(n) Another profound statement! A John 3:16 in minuscule form! See second paragraph under footnote k for an earlier mention of His decease on the cross. The death of Christ for the sins of the world was not by compulsion, coercion, force, or accident. It was planned before the foundation of the world. God in love gave His Son, and the Son in love willingly laid down His physical life and bore the death penalty for our sins. Though human instruments did the killing, divine sovereignty had arranged it in eternity past, and executed the plan in earth's time.

2p-Islamic theology considers it "repugnant and shameful" that God would give His Son to die for the sins of mankind. This reflects their abysmal ignorance of sin, its wages, and the holiness of God Almighty. Millions of religious people do not understand that personal salvation is only by God's grace. *The "Allah" of Islam is not the God of the Bible, for he denies and opposes the atoning death of Jesus for sins and His resurrection.* The prudent soul will carefully mark all other religions that boast this same lie and shamelessly decry the living Christ. In John 10:18, Christ's resurrection from death is mirrored in His Words, "I have power to take it [my life] again." He laid down His life in view of taking it up. Only God can raise the dead; thus as the Lord Jesus raised His body by the power of the Holy Spirit, this proved He was God (Rom. 8:11). A dead man can do nothing. Nevertheless, even in the throes of death at its worst, Messiah rose by the Holy Spirit, never to die again (Rom. 6:9). All who trust Him as Lord and Savior partake of this deathless life; it equally becomes theirs. This same thing was said in another way a short time later in Section 124, John 11:25–26, footnote k.

(o) A division among the Jews. Upon hearing the piercing Word's of Christ, the Jews flew into quarreling among themselves over His teaching. John uses the word "division" three times in his book, each one referring to the Jews at odds with each other over the messages of Jesus (John 7:43; 9:16; and 10:19). It is *not* the gospel that divides, but the wicked unbelief and sins of those who reject Christ as Lord and Savior. See Section 59, Matt: 10:36, and second paragraph of footnote r for other comments on this thought of the gospel dividing. This division among the Jews concerned whether or not Jesus was the Christ or Messiah of Israel. With this, see especially footnote o above. Refer to Section 119, John 7:43 for earlier divisions among the people. Other by-standers listening to the debate, who were more sober in their reasoning, objected because they had seen the miracle He had performed a few hours previously. The one born blind could now see. Only Messiah could heal one in this condition.

(p) Tazazith, "He hath a devil" (demon). Any person who opposed the theology of the religious leaders of Israel would be eventually dismissed with these words. The Jews had a demon for everything, even one that caused madness, hence their accusation "and is mad." During His debate with the Pharisees over the healing of the man born blind, the people were also divided. In verse 20, we meet a typical occult expression used by the Jews. They believed that madness was caused by a demon called "Tazazith," which was a foul spirit that stole one's sanity. These Christ haters had thrown this accusation into His face a short time earlier (John 8:48). Note also John 7:20, where "the people" had previously laid this same charge of demon possession on the Lord Jesus. Those who assure us that this accusation was nothing more than a Hebrew social rebuke, had better recheck their history. These men hated the Son of God with satanic fierceness, and their slander of Him had its origin in their spiritual father. Anyone who has spent time in the Middle East knows that both Jews and Arabs will argue, shout, and yell at one another *within their respective* national circles, then sit down, and drink tea as though nothing has happened. This is not what the religious authorities were doing with the Lord Jesus. *They wanted this Man killed!*

(q) This has reference to Section 121, where the man blind from birth was healed. As previously stated, an extraordinary feat such as this was considered a miracle exclusive for Israel's Messiah to perform. See asterisk under main heading of Section 48 for an explanation of the four unique Messianic wonders the Jews believed that only their Messiah could do. The devils (demons) could not open blind eyes, but they had caused blindness in eyes that could previously see. Read in Section 66, Matt. 12:22, where Christ had earlier healed such a person and reversed the works of Satan. It is indeed strange that evil spirit beings can subdue, control, and use certain organs of the human body causing chaos and suffering. This reveals that the spiritual world is neither hindered nor restricted by the material one. There are many examples of this in the life of Christ when He was dealing with those in demonic bondage. A classic example is the "crooked back woman" of Section 125, Lk. 13:16. Also at this verse, see the Section 125, first paragraph of footnote g for a mitigating word on the foolish teaching that all physical suffering and deformities are from evil spirits.

2p-Similarities and the eternal difference. It is written in Eccles. 9:2, "All *things come* alike to all: *there is* one event to the righteous, and to the wicked; to the good and to the clean, and to the unclean; to him that sacrificeth, and to him that sacrificeth not: as *is* the good, so *is* the sinner; *and* he that sweareth, as *he* that feareth an oath." Human life of both sinner and saint is fraught with calamities and suffering. Both good and bad, saved and lost, feel the sorrows and infirmities of this world. However, there is a difference. He who leaves God's Son, the Lord Jesus Christ, out in this life, God leaves him out of the wonderful life to come. At the end of it all the unsaved are assigned to the everlasting home of the Devil (Matt. 25:41). Those redeemed by the blood of Christ are ". . . present with the Lord" (2 Cor. 5:8). What a difference that makes, and it continues forever!

561

Cold December in Jerusalem. Christ returns to the temple for the Feast of Dedication or Hanukkah. The Jews quickly gathered about demanding to know if He was the Messiah. Enraged over His fearless Words they seek to take Him. He escapes again and goes to Bethabara east of the Jordan River.*

We have conjectured and harmonized Jesus leaving Jerusalem between John 10:21 and 22, due to the hostility of the Jews. From the end of Tabernacles in October to the Feast of Dedication in December was about three months, which must be fitted between these two verses. His whereabouts during this period is a matter of opinion. Some commentators think He went to Peraea on the eastern side of Jordan. The author conjectures that He returned to Galilee after the Feast of Tabernacles and ministered there. A few months later it would have been winter, and He went back to Jerusalem for the Dedication Feast as described in footnote a below.

Matt.	Mk.	Lk.	John 10: 22-39—Solomon's porch in the temple
			Feast of Dedication. "Are you the Messiah?"
			22 And it was at Jerusalem the feast of the dedication,(a) and it was winter. (b)
			23 And Jesus walked in the temple in Solomon's porch.
			24 Then came the Jews round about him, and said unto him, "How long dost thou make us to doubt? If thou be the Christ,(c) [or Messiah] tell us plainly."
			The Savior's answer
			25 Jesus answered them, "I told you, and ye believed not: the works that I do in my Father's name, they bear witness of me.(as Messiah)
			26 "But ye believe not, because ye are not of my sheep, as I said unto you.(d)
			27 "My sheep hear my voice, and I know them, and they follow me:
			28 "And I give unto them eternal life; and they shall never perish, neither shall any *man* pluck them out of my hand.(e)
			29 "My Father, which gave *them* me, is greater than all; and no *man* is able to pluck *them* out of my Father's hand.
			They seek to kill Him for claiming to be God
			30 "I and *my* Father are one."
			31 Then the Jews took up stones again to stone(f) him.
			32 Jesus answered them, "Many good works have I shewed you from my Father; for which of those works do ye stone me?"
			33 The Jews answered him, saying, "For a good work we stone thee not;(g) but for blasphemy; and because that thou, being a man, makest thyself God."
			Proof of His deity from the Torah Law
			34 Jesus answered them,(h) "Is it not written in your law, 'I said, Ye are gods?'
			35 "If he called them gods, unto whom the word of God came, and the scripture cannot be broken;(i)
			36 "Say ye of him, whom the Father hath sanctified, and sent into the world, 'Thou blasphemest; because I said, I am the Son of God?'
			37 "If I do not the works of my Father, believe me not.
			38 "But if I do, though ye believe not me, believe the works: that ye may know, and believe, that the Father *is* in me, and I in him."
			Again, they seek to kill Him: He escapes to Bethabara
			39 Therefore they sought again to take him: but he escaped out of their hand,(j)

Matt.	Mk.	Lk.	John 10: 40-42—*From Temple to Bethabara beyond Jordan*
			40 And went away again beyond Jordan[k] into the place [Bethabara] where John at first baptized; and there he abode. **41** And many resorted unto him, and said, John did no miracle:[l] but all things that John spake of this man were true. *Numerous converts from among the multitudes* **42** And many believed on him there.[m] (Next chap., John 11:1 cont. in Section 124.)

Footnotes-Commentary

[a] **"Feast of Dedication."** John informs his readers that his history of Jesus *now* reverts to Jerusalem. We find that it is another annual Jewish religious celebration. As explained in the main heading above, it appears that Jesus left the city after the conflict with the leaders; then several months later, He returned to Jerusalem for Dedication or Hanukkah. Judas Maccabaeus instituted this particular Jewish feast in the year 164 B.C. It was not a part of the seven annual celebrations commanded in Lev. 23, and is not mentioned in the law or any Old Testament Scriptures. Like many other things in the Jewish religion of this era, it was a good tradition with valuable historical meaning. However, over time, the Dedication was placed on equal footing with the Torah Law, and other Old Testament commands. This became another *fatal* error in the religion of Judaism.

2p-Frequently, certain Messianic Jews point to Christ being present at this celebration in their struggle to prove that He observed the oral law or tradition of the elders. See all of Section 96 for our Lord's earlier battle with the scribes and Pharisees over their oral traditions and what He told them! Messiah kept Hanukkah because it pointed to Him and His redeeming work for mankind, as explained in number two, in the paragraph just below. His observance had nothing to do with Him living by the oral law. Regarding the history of Hanukkah, an insane Greek ruler, Antiochus Epiphanes IV, king of Syria, had captured the temple and Jerusalem in 167 B.C. He had slain some forty thousand Jews and sold thousands more into slavery! The carnage was so vast that it took days to remove the dead from the temple and city and bury them. In hatred for the Hebrew people, Epiphanes erected a platform over the temple altar and sacrificed a sow on the sacred altar to the pagan god Zeus, made a broth from the carcass and sprinkled it over the temple site and the Torah scrolls. He forbade circumcision, observance of the Sabbath, and ordered that only pigs be offered in the temple. Josephus in *Antiquities,* Book 12:5. 4, lines 248 through 256 tells the awful story.

3p-Later, a pious Jew named Judas Maccabaeus led a revolt, overthrew the Syrians, liberated Jerusalem, and the temple. On the 25th of Kislev or Chislev (December), they rededicated the entire building and a new altar to God. The temple menorah light was relit, but the barrel of oil contained only enough to last one day. It would take the Jews at least one week to prepare more sacred olive oil for fuel. After prayer and seeking God for help, by a miracle, the barrel of oil had enough to last until a fresh supply could be produced by the Levites. During this time, the Jews renewed the temple area, decking it with gold and colored cloth and various ornaments. Many brilliant lights illuminated the scene. It was a time of great joy and public rejoicing among the wonderful Hebrew people and became an annual observance to this very day. This celebration has several names, which reveal different aspects of the event. They are as follows:

1. **"Feast of Dedication."** It was the dedication of the temple after its defilement by the pagan king.
2. **"Hanukkah. The "Feast of Dance or Lights.** This title points to the miracle of oil that provided light for eight days. The occasion is still a popular time among modern day Orthodox Jews. During every Hanukkah, candles are lit and a menorah (candelabra with nine branches) is set in the window for all to see. One candle is lit each evening in order from right to left. The center candle is called the "shammash" or "servant." All the other candles were lit from its strong flame. The unique *central candle* points to the Lord Jesus. It speaks of Him as the Light of the world and the only source of all mankind's valid spiritual and moral enlightenment. *Here, we find the reason why our Lord observed this event.* For brief historical details about the restoration of the beautiful celebration of Hanukkah, see Josephus' work, *Antiquities,* Book 12:7. 7, lines 323-326, and the apocryphal book of 1 Maccabees 4: 36-59.

[b] **"And it was winter." Here, is the only mention of Jesus and the weather or seasons.** It was the month of Khislev, equivalent to part of our November and December. During this time, fierce rains poured upon Jerusalem and Judaea. Christ spoke of these rains in Matt. 7:24-27. At night, there could be heavy frost. As one peruses the entire life of Christ as laid down in the four gospels, we mark that almost nothing is said of His life and ministry amid the changing weather and seasons of the land of Israel. Where was our Lord during the torrential rainy seasons, the bitter cold of Israel's harsh winters, mixed frosts, and deep frozen nights often accompanied by snows? (The storms on Lake Galilee were not seasonal.) Foxes had their holes and the birds their nests, while the Savior had only that which men gave Him. God draws a curtain of strange silence over the topics that occupy so much of men's thoughts in today's modern world. There are two other mentions of "winter" in the four gospels; one is Matt. 24:20,

which foretold of the Jews fleeing the destruction of Jerusalem in A.D. 70. The other is John 18:18 where Peter warmed himself at the fire during the cold night of Jesus' trial. This was during Passover, which occurred in late March or early April. Thus, even at this time of the year it was cold enough to have a fire built for personal warming. For an explanation of the ancient Hebrew calendar, seasons, crops, and harvest times, see *The Illustrated Bible Dictionary,* Part 1, p. 223.

2p-Solomon's porch. This was a large covered colonnade or portico in which thousands could maneuver about, despite bad weather. Seemingly, this part of the temple was untouched by the Babylonians in their final destruction of the city and temple in 586 B.C. This lone passage recorded by John takes us into the cold of winter when the Lord Jesus reappeared at the temple compound. Many charcoal fires were burning under the covers along the edges of Solomon's porch. It was something like a giant arcade located on the east and southern sides of the gigantic structure. Pans of hot coals were placed within these sheltered areas for the benefit of the thousands of Jews attending this celebration. Here, Jesus walked among the people and warmed Himself. His presence caused a great stir among the people and religious leaders. After a short absence, He was back in their temple again. They swooped down upon Him in the spirit of hate and confrontation.

(c) **"Are you the Messiah?"** Again, the troubling question that kept the nation of Israel in a constant uproar, "Is Jesus our Messiah?" This was the prevailing topic during His ministry; everything stood or fell upon the correct answer. The Savior responded to their inquiry in verse 25 with the Words "I have told you, and ye believed not." Then He pointed to His thousands of Messianic works as proof that He was Israel's promised One. The Jews would not believe this because they were unsaved and not of His sheep. Over twenty-five years later, Paul made it clear that the Jews were "broken off," because of their rejection of Jesus, in unbelief (Rom. 11:20). He also made it clear that if they abode not in this unbelief, they would be brought into the salvation of Messiah (Rom. 11:23).

2p-Messiah in Daniel. In the century following the ascension of Christ, the rabbis faced a terrible dilemma trying to explain the prophecy of Dan. 9:25. (Today some rabbis forbid the reading of Daniel's scroll!) Ancient Jews agreed that it spoke of Messiah. Verse 25 tells of His appearing in sixty-nine "weeks" (meaning sixty-nine sevens or a total of four hundred and eighty-three years), "after the commandment to restore and rebuild Jerusalem." As explained below, though the prophecy experts have miscalculated this date, the Messiah still came. Daniel's prediction unmistakably points to the beginning of the ministry of the Lord Jesus. Wise Jews knew this and struggled to explain it away. Christians witnessing for their Savior laid this passage from Daniel upon their Jewish friends. So what did these hard pressed Hebrews do with this problem? Years after Jesus' ascension, the rabbis said that the prophecy of Daniel 9:25 did not speak of Christ, but of a self-acclaimed Jewish Messiah, named Bar Kokba (or Cocheba) who was killed by the Romans in A.D. 135. This was another effort to dismiss Jesus of Nazareth as Israel's Messiah. See *Encyclopedia Judaica,* vol. 2, page 489 under heading "Akiva." Missionary Jack Moorman also discusses some of these things in his excellent work *Bible Chronology: The Two Great Divides.*

3p-The seventy weeks problem. Gabriel told Daniel, "Seventy weeks are determined upon thy people [Israel] and upon thy holy city, [Jerusalem] to finish the transgression, and to make an end of sins, and to make reconciliation for iniquity, and to bring in everlasting righteousness . . ." (Dan. 9:24). These seventy weeks are weeks of years not days. They have been calculated to mean 400, 434, 450, 470, and 490 years. The last figure is the most popular one. Some believe the first sixty-nine weeks ended with the birth Christ. Others, that week sixty-nine ended with the triumphal entry of Jesus into Jerusalem, just before His death. John Darby, born in London in 1800 invented a "gap" or "parentheses" between week sixty-nine and seventy. Prior to him, this was unknown in extant church history! Darbyite dispensationalists believe that the church age was a hidden thing; it was in the parentheses between the end of week sixty-nine and the beginning of week seventy. There is not one scrap of evidence for this anywhere in Scripture, not even Eph. 3:1-8. We are told that at the "end of week sixty-nine, the church will be raptured out." With this, week seventy (being seven years long) will begin with "the appearing of the Antichrist and start of the tribulation." Sir Robert Anderson's book, *The Coming Prince: the Marvelous Prophecy of Daniel's Seventy Weeks Concerning the Antichrist,* published in 1895, remains the major source for the 490 years dating of the seventy weeks of years. Anderson's chronology of exactly 490 years or sixty-nine weeks has calculation errors. Professor Harold Hoehner, a staunch dispensationalist, in *Chronological Aspects of the Life of Christ,* pages 136-138 impeccably demonstrates that Anderson picked the wrong starting time, the wrong ending, and missed various leap years. Reading into Dan. 9:24-27 a peace treaty between the Antichrist and the Jews, a rebuilt temple at Jerusalem, with the resumption of animal sacrifices is "imaginary" exegesis at its wildest. Nowhere do we read that Jesus the Messiah (verse 27) during His ministry "confirmed the covenant with many for one week." *However, it is sure that the cessation of sacrifice and the oblation (offering) occurred with His death on the cross.* We cannot find John Darby's gap. A search into fifteen major commentaries, from 1750 through 1800 reveals the gap or parenthesis between week sixty-nine and week seventy is missing. Darby invented it, then such good men as Harry Rimmer, C. I. Scofield, Clarence Larkin, Harry Ironsides, and others popularized it as established eschatology.

4p-Too much guessing. Parts of Daniel's prophecy are clear, while other parts are not. Setting *exact* dates, finding events and persons, and then making them fit specific prophecies is wrong. A teaching that was unheard of the first eighteen hundreds years of church history is false. Every *new* hermeneutic added to traditional biblical eschatology by the "end time specialists" is also wrong and should be rejected.

(d) "Not of my sheep." In these words, we have evidence that the Jews, who attacked Him upon His return to the temple for this December celebration, were the same ones that battled with Him prior to His departure months before. See Section 122 where He gave them the Parable of the Good Shepherd and to which He refers in this passage, by the words "as I said unto you." Verse 27 states a fact. The religious prelates did not "hear his voice." This was proof they were not of His sheep and did not have eternal life.

2p-Verse 27. "My sheep know and hear." In Section 122, John 10:4-5, footnote d, the Lord Jesus had made a similar statement. Years ago, while conducting gospel meetings, I was traveling through a part of Zululand, in South Africa. I stopped for a rest at a small bush store located on the backside of nowhere! There were hundreds of sheep milling around in the scanty grass about the tiny shop. I noticed a young Africa boy exit the store and make his way across the plains. As he went, he started making a curious humming sound. Suddenly, several dozens of the sheep popped their heads up, looked, and watched him intently. With machine like precision, they all fell into line, following their shepherd. The sheep knew him and his voice; they would not follow a stranger.

(e) Cannot be taken out of God's hand. This is the chief passage used by conservatives to confirm the teaching of the eternal security of the believer in Christ. However, security in Christ is based upon His atonement in which He died for all of our sins past, present, and future. This being so, there is no sin for which the saved believer can ever be condemned or suffer eternal death. Christ died and paid the sin debt for *all* the sins of *all* mankind. Those who trust Him as personal Lord and Savior are placed into the everlasting forgiveness and security of His atonement. In this, all of their sins are pardoned and everlastingly paid for and washed away in the blood of Christ. *The security of the believer is grounded in this and this alone, and it is because of this that no man can take us out of God's omnipotent hand.* As sure as no good work can save us, so no bad work can cancel eternal life in Christ. In other words, works, good and bad, have nothing to do with the new birth. To hold that good works keep us saved and bad works take away salvation is wrong. If good works keep one saved, we wonder how many of them, it takes. If bad works cause us to lose our redemption, we wonder how many it takes? This does not justify those so-called "Christians" who spend their lives living like the Devil, then argue that they have been converted to Christ.

2p-Verse 30. Equal with God. In these profound Words, Jesus, the carpenter of Nazareth, openly claims equality with Jehovah God. Every Jew was infuriated upon hearing these Words.

(f) Verses 31-33. "Stone him" and "stone me." We meet solid evidence again that Jesus was equal with God and therefore, God! Verse 31 reveals the Jews were incensed at His claim. With hands full of stones, they lifted them to kill Him because they understood exactly what He had said. Jesus did not deny or beg to correct His claims before these fierce men or the threat of death by stoning. If Jesus Christ were not God, He could never have spoken such words without blaspheming. The charge for this is explained in footnote g below. John wrote that the "Jews took up stones again." This was but another attempt to destroy the Messiah. On numerous other occasions, they had plotted to destroy Him. See Section 95, John 7:1 with Section 120, John 8:37, 40, 59, footnote z. Note how many times the word "kill" is used about the Lord Jesus in these verses. Refer also to Section 124, John 11:53, footnote w and the words "put him to death." Commentators who write about all the Pharisees being good men have seriously erred from the Scripture.

(g) Charged with blasphemy! Highlighted, for this is a general quotation from the Torah Law in Lev. 24:16. It called for death upon all who blasphemed the Name of God. Claiming to be His equal was considered just that. The Jews based their desire to kill Jesus on this passage from their law. Months earlier, He had charged them with not keeping their own Torah commandments, in Section 119, John 7:19, footnote f. Now, they prepare to kill Him for "breaking" one of the very laws that they did not keep! Later, in Section 181, Matt. 26:65, during Jesus' appearing before the Sanhedrin, the night before His death, the Jews again accused Him of blasphemy.

(h) The Lord Jesus described this citation from Psalms as being taken from the law. By the time of Christ on earth, the *entire* Hebrew Old Testament (Tanakh) was called "the law" even though it had been divided into three parts (Lk. 24:44). Taking up stones to kill Him, He responds to their charge in verse 33, by quoting from Ps. 82:6.

2p-"Ye are gods." In this verse, God, through the Psalmist Asaph, tells Israel that their "judges" or magistrates were like unto gods. This title was applied to them because of the honor and dignity that accompanied such a high office in the nation. Further, this passage reveals that the noun "god," (with lowercase "g") was applied to certain men, without any irreverence being intended or association with pagan idolatry. However, this use of the word is indeed rare in the Old Testament. See Ex. 4:16 and 7:1 for two examples. What our Lord affirmed before the Jews was simply, "If the Hebrew magistrates who spoke the truth and administered justice were called 'gods' (or greatly respected) by the people, then what is wrong with Me, the Messiah, who is greater than all, being called by the title and receiving the same respectful honor?" The furious Jews instantly understood what He was saying but would not bestow upon Him this deserved esteem.

(i) Verse 35. "Scripture cannot be broken." The meaning is that it cannot be "unfulfilled." This again proves the absolute confidence of Jesus in the Old Testament writings. As stated above, this is a direct citation from Ps.

82:6, which described the judges or magistrates of Israel. Christ was saying to the Jews, "If Asaph, the author of this statement was inspired to describe Israel's judges as 'gods' (Elohim in Hebrew), and these judges ministered the Word of God, then Scripture cannot be broken (misused) by Me, the Son of God employing the same description. I not only present myself as God in the supreme capacity as judge, but also was sent into the world as your Messiah. Further, I do the works you have said He would do. If I have not done His works, then reject me; if so, believe Me. Therefore, because this is true you should hear my Words as your Messiah; and judge, for I am fulfilling the Scriptures." Every Jew present knew that this term was used to describe Israel's magistrates, appointed by God, and no one would dare to accuse them of blasphemy. Why do they now lay this charge upon Him the One who is equal with God and has proven repeatedly that He was their Messiah? In James 5:9, Christ is the "judge" of all men poised at the door. Earlier, Jesus informed the Jews that God had put all judgment into His hands (John 5:22).

2p-Scripture's divine authority. The birth, life, death, resurrection, and ascension of Jesus Christ were predicted hundreds and thousands of years in advance across the Old Testament. This is illustrated in *Appendix Three*. Among the *chief works* of Satan and his demons is to undermine or cast doubts on the absolute inspiration of Holy Scripture. Once this is accepted in the minds of men, they find themselves without any trustworthy and infallible guide regarding the torments of sin, the struggles of life, death, and what awaits them in eternity. The creators and purveyors of this poison have been and are the *unsaved* religionists. They and their clones have, by choice, become channels of evil to undermine and destroy the faith of weak and untaught believers, and repel those without Christ, who seek help. The *Author's Introduction* carries a brief historical survey of the lives and theological perversions of many of these men. Heads packed with "great learning" and hearts locked in Christless darkness, they counsel, instruct, teach, lecture, pastor, minister, and advise the lost in spiritual matters. They have cooperated with Satan to damn millions of souls. The Savior said to the religious authorities of His day (who hated and rejected Him), "ye shall receive the greater damnation" (Matt. 23:14). That awful sentence remains valid to this moment. Almost two thousand years ago, a great missionary faced men of this same disposition. To them, he said, "Behold, ye despisers, and wonder, and perish: for I [God] work a work in your days, [the forgiveness found in Christ] a work which ye shall in no wise believe, though a man declare it unto you" (Acts 13:41). The apostle Peter wrote of such men and women, "their damnation slumbereth not" (2 Peter 2:3).

(j) Another attempt to capture the Savior is thwarted. See footnote f above for other assaults on His life. How He escaped, the evangelist is not inspired to tell us. See an earlier mysterious escape of Jesus two years previous in His hometown synagogue at Nazareth. Refer to Section 38, Lk. 4:28-30, footnotes l and m.

(k) **Verse 40. "Beyond Jordan."** Meaning He went across the river to Bethabara. Two locations have been given for this place. The author has selected the older one in preference to the newer, which is the opinion of infidel critics. *Smith's Dictionary of the Bible*, vol. I, page 284 has an article on the location of Bethabara. To reach this place, the Lord Jesus went eastward over the Jordan River into Peraea, which was under the rule of Herod Antipas. This was outside the political jurisdiction of those at Jerusalem seeking to kill Him. See Section 93, footnote c for an earlier example of Christ seeking to avoid Antipas' jurisdiction and moving into his half-brother, Philip's domain for protection, especially of His preachers and disciples from this mad tyrant.

2p-Verse 40. This passage is of importance in tracing the *final months* of the life of Christ. Following His conflict with the Jews at the Dedication Feast in December, and another attempt to kill Him, He immediately left Jerusalem and went eastward, across the Jordan River into the place where John first baptized (John 3:23). We learn from Section 24, John 1:28, footnote g, that the place where John *first* baptized was called Bethabara. The text is clear that He abode here. This harmony commentary leaves Christ and His preachers continuing at Bethabara until they received word of Lazarus' death. Mary and Martha knew the whereabouts of Jesus during this secret period, and sent for him when their brother fell severely ill. They knew His location through covert communications.

(l) **"John did no miracle."** A marvelous statement indeed! John the greatest man born of women, lived his life, preached God's Word, pointed men to the coming Savior, then died a martyr but did no miracle. What a slam on today's "healers and miracle workers" who boast of "raising the dead, opening blind eyes, healing the sick," "lengthening short legs," and "filling hollow teeth." This is "proof of God's hand on their ministry." *John's credentials were simple yet profound: everything he said about Jesus was true!* There was no exaggeration, over statement, or under statement. For a partial list of what this great man preached, said, and did, see Section 21, Part 4, and all of footnote q. John's suffering in prison and his strange question regarding the Messiah are in Section 62.

(m) **"Many believed."** Even while He was in hiding in self-imposed exile, great crowds sought out and found our Lord in this safer location. Upon hearing Him teach, "many believed" that He was the Messiah. We have harmonized Jesus leaving Jerusalem between John 10:21 and 22 due to the hostility of the Jews. From the end of Feast of Tabernacles in October to the Feast of Dedication in December was about three months, which must be fitted between these two verses. His whereabouts during this period is a matter of opinion. Some think. He went to Peraea on the eastern side of the Jordan River. This harmony commentary *conjectures* that He returned to Galilee after the Tabernacles celebration and ministered in that area. Later, He went back to Jerusalem in winter weather of December for the Dedication Feast as mentioned in the main heading of this Section.

Threatened by the Jews, He leaves* Jerusalem and walks twenty miles to Bethabara, east of the Jordan River. From here, the Savior is called back to Bethany where He raises Lazarus by another exclusive Messianic miracle. More debate erupts. The Sanhedrin laid plans to kill Jesus. He goes to Ephraim** and waits there with His disciples for the upcoming Passover Feast.

*See Section 123, footnotes j and k for the escape of the Lord Jesus from the angry Jews at Jerusalem to Bethabara. **A veil of silence falls over this sojourn in Ephraim. We can believe that Christ continued His work until it was time to begin the journey to Jerusalem and His final Passover. This is continued in the next Section.

Matt.	Mk.	Lk.	John 11:1-19—Bethabara to Bethany
			Lazarus sick: Jesus sent for
			1 Now a certain *man* was sick, *named* Lazarus, of Bethany, the town of Mary and her sister Martha.[(a)]
			2 (It was *that* Mary[(b)] which anointed the Lord with ointment, and wiped his feet with her hair, whose brother Lazarus was sick.)[(c)]
			3 Therefore his sisters sent unto him, saying, "Lord, behold, he whom thou lovest is sick."
			4 When Jesus heard *that*, he said,[(d)] "This sickness is not unto death, but for the glory of God, that the Son of God might be glorified thereby."
			5 Now Jesus loved Martha, and her sister, and Lazarus.[(e)]
			6 When he had heard therefore that he was sick, he abode two days still in the same place where he was.[(f)]
			Journey back to Judaea
			7 Then after that saith he to *his* disciples, "Let us go into Judaea again."
			8 *His* disciples[(g)] say unto him, "Master, the Jews of late sought to stone thee; and goest thou thither again?"
			9 Jesus answered, "Are there not twelve hours in the day? If any man walk in the day, he stumbleth not, because he seeth the light of this world.
			10 "But if a man walk in the night, he stumbleth, because there is no light in him."
			11 These things said he: and after that he saith unto them, "Our friend Lazarus sleepeth; but I go, that I may awake him out of sleep."
			12 Then said his disciples, "Lord, if he sleep, he shall do well."
			13 Howbeit Jesus spake of his death: but they thought that he had spoken of taking of rest in sleep.
			The shock announcement
			14 Then said Jesus unto them plainly, "Lazarus is dead.
			15 "And I am glad for your sakes that I was not there, to the intent ye may believe; nevertheless let us go unto him."
			16 Then said Thomas, which is called Didymus, [twin] unto his fellow-disciples, "Let us also go, that we may die with him."
			Arrival At Bethany
			17 Then when Jesus came,[(h)] he found that he had *lain* in the grave four days already.
			18 Now Bethany was nigh unto Jerusalem, about fifteen furlongs [two miles] off:
			Great crowds at the house of Martha and Mary
			19 And many of the Jews came to Martha and Mary, to comfort them

Matt.	Mk.	Lk.	John 11:19–40—*Bethany*
			concerning their brother.

Jesus and Martha

20 Then Martha, as soon as she heard that Jesus was coming, went and met him: but Mary sat *still* in the house.

21 Then said Martha unto Jesus, "Lord, if thou hadst been here, my brother had not died.

22 "But I know, that even now, whatsoever thou wilt ask of God, God will give *it* thee."**(i)**

23 Jesus saith unto her, "Thy brother shall rise again."

24 Martha saith unto him, "I know that he shall rise again in **the resurrection at the last day.**"**(j)**

25 Jesus said unto her, "I am the resurrection, and the life: he that believeth in me, though he were dead, yet shall he live:**(k)**

26 "And whosoever liveth and believeth in me shall never die. Believest thou this?"

27 She saith unto him, "Yea, Lord: I believe that thou art the Christ, the Son of God, which should come into the world."**(l)**

Jesus and Mary

28 And when she had so said, she went her way, and called Mary her sister secretly, saying, "The Master is come, and calleth for thee."

29 As soon as she heard *that*, she arose quickly, and came unto him.

30 Now Jesus was not yet come into the town, but was in that place where Martha met him.

31 The Jews then which were with her in the house, and comforted her, when they saw Mary, that she rose up hastily and went out, followed her, saying, "She goeth unto the grave to weep there."

32 Then when Mary was come where Jesus was, and saw him, she fell down at his feet, saying unto him, "Lord, if thou hadst been here, my brother had not died."**(m)**

His great compassion

33 When Jesus therefore saw her weeping, and the Jews also weeping which came with her, he groaned in the spirit, and was troubled,**(n)**

34 And said, "Where have ye laid him?" They said unto him, "Lord, come and see."

35 Jesus wept.**(o)**

36 Then said the Jews, "Behold how he loved him!"

Journey to the tomb

37 And some of them said, "Could not this man, which opened the eyes of the blind, have caused that even this man should not have died?"

38 Jesus therefore again groaning in himself cometh to the grave. It was a cave, and a stone lay upon it.

Unbelief and reasoning of Martha

39 Jesus said, "Take ye away the stone." Martha, the sister of him that was dead, saith unto him, "Lord, by this time he stinketh: [is decaying] for he hath been *dead* four days."**(p)**

Jesus admonishes her: "only believe"

40 Jesus saith unto her, "Said I not unto thee, that, if thou wouldest believe, thou shouldest see the glory of God?"

Matt.	Mk.	Lk.	John 11:41-54—*Bethany to Ephraim*
			The Savior's prayer **41** Then they took away the stone *from the place* where the dead was laid. And Jesus lifted up *his* eyes, and said, "Father,[q] I thank thee that thou hast heard me. **42** "And I knew that thou hearest me always: but because of the people which stand by I said *it,* that they may believe that thou hast sent me." ***Lazarus is raised*** **43** And when he thus had spoken, he cried with a loud voice, "Lazarus, come forth."[r] **44** And he that was dead came forth, bound hand and foot with graveclothes: and his face was bound about with a napkin. Jesus saith unto them, "Loose him, and let him go." ***Results of the miracle*** **45** Then many of the Jews which came to Mary, and had seen the things which Jesus did, believed[s] on him. **46** But some of them went their ways to the Pharisees, and told them what things Jesus had done. **47** Then gathered the chief priests and the Pharisees a council,[t] [Sanhedrin] and said, "What do we? for this man doeth many miracles. ***He will bring our destruction*** **48** "If we let him thus alone, all *men* will believe on him: and the Romans shall come and take away both our place [temple] and nation."[u] ***The unintentional prophecy of Caiaphas*** **49** And one of them, *named* Caiaphas,[v] being the high priest that same year, said unto them, "Ye know nothing at all, **50** "Nor consider that it is expedient for us, that one man should die for the people, and that the whole nation [Israel] perish not." **51** And this spake he not of himself: but being high priest that year, he prophesied that Jesus should die for that nation; (Israel) **52** And not for that nation only, but that also he should gather together in one the children of God that were scattered abroad. ***Planning again to kill Him*** **53** Then from that day forth they [the Sanhedrin] took counsel [a meeting] together [and planned] for to put him to death.[w] ***Jesus moves into hiding*** **54** Jesus therefore walked no more openly among the Jews; but went thence unto a country near to the wilderness, into a city called Ephraim,[x] and there continued with his disciples. (Verse 55 cont. in Section 146.)

Footnotes–Commentary

[a] All the noise about why John alone wrote of this extraordinary miracle is unnecessary. Have Christians forgotten that *each* of the four evangelists wrote as the Holy Spirit inspired them? They penned what He directed, no more and no less. This is why Matthew, Mark, and Luke did not record this Messianic miracle. Lazarus means "Eleazar," and was a common Hebrew name denoting, "God helps." Mary is the Hebrew form of the name "Miriam," meaning "bitterness," while Martha carries the connotation of "lady." For the six different Mary's in the New Testament, refer to Section 9, footnote c. This was not the beggar Lazarus of Section 131, Lk. 16:19-31. Regarding Bethany and the two sisters, see Section 117, footnotes a through e for details. What the deadly sickness was Lazarus had contracted, we do not know. For further comments on healing, see Section 41, footnote h.

(b) John wrote looking back on history and for people living outside of the land of Israel. He was inspired to explain to the recipients of his book that this is the Mary that anointed Jesus' feet and wiped them with her hair, apparently, to distinguish her from someone else bearing the same name with which his original readers were familiar.

(c) **Love's appeal.** This confirms that the sisters knew Jesus' whereabouts and quickly sent a messenger to Bethabara asking Him to come. The appeal of the distraught sisters "He whom thou lovest" is filled with simplicity, modesty, and assurance. On many occasions, they had seen the love of Jesus expressed toward their now dying brother, and they had heard of and discussed many times His great miracles. See footnote l below where Martha confessed that He was the "Christ" or "Messiah" that was to come into the world. All Jews believed their Messiah would perform extraordinary signs and wonders when He came.

(d) **"That the Son of God might be glorified."** Could this be the very message that Jesus had sent back to the anxious sisters? In relation to this, see the Words He spoke while later standing in front of Lazarus' tomb in John 11:40. God let him die so that the miracle of his resurrection might *again* demonstrate that Jesus of Nazareth was the Messiah of Israel. The sufferings of the saints carry a peculiar design: that the Lord of heaven may be glorified thereby. This fact should raise a high tide of peace in our hearts when we walk through the dark days designed by the workings of divine providence. As with the man born blind in Section 121, footnote c, so the untimely death of Lazarus will redound to the glory and Majesty of God.

(e) **Jesus loved them.** John, the author of these words had spent many hours with His Lord in the home of this family. These were intimate friends and familiar acquaintances of Christ, whom He visited often. John, the human author of this book, had seen and heard on numerous occasions the love Christ expressed toward Mary, Martha, and Lazarus. Years later, this lingered still as sweet melancholy in his old heart. What memories and impressions are we leaving upon those we touch and those who silently watch us? What will our unknown observers say of us years after we have stepped from earth's scenes?

(f) **"He abode two days still."** We think that Jesus should have made all haste to arrive at the Bethany home. What better way to show His love for this dear friend? Should not our Lord have hurried to the bed of Lazarus and instantly healed his ailment? That would have been no more than He had done for thousands. To our amazement, He tarried yet two more days at Bethabara. It was in this time span that Lazarus died, possibly even as the messengers returned to Bethany. This delay of Jesus reveals that His intentions were to raise him. The delays of Christ to respond to our prayers or needs are heavenly appointments arranged by the grace of God. A friend of the author had booked a plane to fly to Port Elizabeth, South Africa, from Johannesburg for urgent business. Driving to the airport, his car broke down, and consequently, he missed the flight. Distraught and frustrated, he learned several hours later that his plane had crashed into the Indian Ocean, with everyone aboard being killed! The starts, steps, and stops of a good man are still ordered by the Lord (Ps. 139).

(g) **"His disciples."** These men heard what the messengers said and Jesus' response to them. Two days later, He announced His plan to return to Bethany and Judaea. Horrified, the apostles reminded Him of the Jew's plan to kill Him. In verse 9, Christ is saying that His day or time of ministry has not yet ended. Though it is near to the cross, He still had several weeks left to bless and serve before His death. Therefore, the disciples must walk in the day of His presence and follow Him back into dangerous Judaea. In doing so, they will not stumble or fall because they are in the Light.

2p-Verses 11-15. Christ announced to His disciples that Lazarus was sleeping. This reveals His understanding of death for the believer. Sleep carries the idea of restful repose and peace after a life of toil in this world. The great awakening of the *sleeping physical body* of all believers will occur when Jesus calls forth all the saved at His return and the removal of the church.

3p-Verses 12-14. How odd that His apostles did not yet understand! Looking back on this event, John now understood the Master's Words, but when this happened, he, like the others, did not comprehend what the Lord Jesus meant. He shocked them into the meaning of His metaphor with the Words "Lazarus is dead."

4p-Verses 15-16. Now, the Lord Jesus again reveals His plan: the raising of a man long dead will lift the faith of the disciples to a new level. Poor Thomas still did not understand, yet, in loyalty to Christ, he invited his fellow believers to return also to Judaea and die with Jesus at the hands of the religious leaders. They had just fled the wrath of these men as seen in Section 123, John 10:39, footnote j.

(h) **He arrives at Bethany.** The four days since his death had been sad ones in this household at Bethany. It was a day's walk from Bethabara, across Jordan, then westward to Bethany village. Christ arrived at the town near sunset and apparently spent the night somewhere outside the village. All gates were closed at sundown and not opened until sunrise the next morning. For more on this, see footnote m below. Things had drastically changed in this beautiful home. The joy of former days had vanished because death had broken up that lovely family. The coming of the Lord Jesus was never so welcomed as at this sorrowful time.

2p-Many who resent the Christian minister amid their times of plenty and good health, welcome him with tears when death or sorrow strikes their awful blows. Need, was the open door for the Savior to manifest His preciousness. The only true preparation for life's devastating trials is a personal and daily fellowship with the Son of God: to know Him, love Him and trust Him. Someone once said, "If we would have Christ's sweet comfort when sorrow comes, we must welcome Him in days of gladness."

3p-**Verse 18.** It is interesting that John gives the distance from Bethany to Jerusalem, which again reveals that many of his *original* readers were unfamiliar with these places and the walking distance between them.

(i) Martha received word the next morning that Jesus was entering Bethany and rushed out to meet Him. Mary sat in the house. This was the posture of Jewish women in deep mourning. There are examples in ancient history of those who sat for hours on end, transfixed by the shock of sudden death or calamity falling upon a loved one (Job 2:13). Thus did Mary. *Martha's first words reveal she was familiar with the prayer life of her Lord!* They also may intimate that she hoped He would raise her brother back to life.

(j) **What did "last day" mean?** How did she know this doctrine of Hebrew eschatology? From rabbinical teaching heard in the synagogues. It was based in the Old Testament (Tanakh) in such places as Dan. 12:2 and Isa. 26:19. Jesus replied in the affirmative that her brother would rise again. Martha understood Him to be saying that Lazarus would be in the general resurrection in which pious Jews believed. For the Jewish understanding of "the last day," see Section 95, all of footnote k. For Hebrew beliefs at this time regarding "days," and "last days," see Section 82, footnote d. The term "last day," as understood by Mary, had first reference to the "last day" for the bodies of the righteous Jews to sleep in their graves; Gentiles were all cursed of God. The religious party, the Sadducees, denied the resurrection of the body and the fact of the human soul. Shortly before His death, our Lord fell into conflict with the Sadducees over the resurrection when they asked Him a trick question. Refer to Section 156 for this event.

(k) **"I am."** Our Lord had earlier used this title of Himself in John 6:35. Christ's Words *here* are one of the most profound statements ever made! He was pointing out to Mary that in Him alone was their resurrection to new life and eternal hope. Only God could say this. Jesus is telling the troubled sister that He is the very author of all resurrections from the dead. The doctrine of the resurrection finds validity in Him and comes from Him. He alone has the power to transmit this truth to others. Further, in verse 26, the Lord Jesus is clear that those who believe in Him will never die that awful eternal death. Living believers in Christ cannot die *the everlasting* spiritual death in the pangs of hell. They are saved forever from all condemnation (John 5:24).

2p-It was not easy, for a troubled spirit like Martha's, to distinguish between the deep thoughts and mystery of physical and spiritual death of which her Lord spoke. She was unable (as are we) to fathom it out into practical understanding. Being undisturbed by the profound answer of Christ she replied in tearful simplicity bathed in pure love, "Yea, Lord, I believe." Having spoken that blessed affirmation, she sent at once for her sister, about whom the Lord Jesus had already inquired.

(l) **"Thou art the Christ, the Son of God, which should come into the world."** This confession is similar to those spoken by others regarding who Jesus Christ was. Martha knew He was Israel's Messiah, the Savior, and that very Person the Hebrew Scriptures predicted would come into the world. See Section 5, footnotes a, c and d, in left vertical column for explanation of the word "Messiah." Yet she, like all the others, at this point did not understand His death on the cross and resurrection from the dead. Our Lord spoke of this later and so clearly in Section 141, yet according to Lk. 18:34 none of His apostles understood. *At the time, Jesus said this, it was about one week before His death on the cross.* One could almost believe that Martha had been talking to Simon Peter! Over two years prior, he had uttered a very similar confession regarding the Person of Jesus and used some of the same words employed by Martha. Peter's great confession is recorded in Section 103, Matt. 16:16, footnote f. Refer to Section 119, John 7:26, footnote i, where others had earlier spoken of Jesus as the Christ or Messiah. All this, and the "theological experts" still tell us that Jesus did not know He was the Messiah of Israel! These words conclusively demonstrate that the Messiah was also known among the Jews as "the Son of God." This same confession came from the mouth of the high priest during the trial of our Savior in Section 181, Matt. 26:63, footnote g. Refer to Section 14, first and second paragraphs under footnote f, for the Jewish opinion of Christ during the days of His earthly ministry, in the first century, and that of today.

2p-**Verse 31. "The Jews with her."** This family was well known across the country. Upon the death of Lazarus, a large concourse of friends, neighbors, and distinguished Jews were drawn to the home to console and mourn with the two sisters. Beyond doubt, there were hundreds of Jews present when the Lord Jesus arrived upon the scene and this crowd followed them to the burying plot.

(m) **"Had not died."** This sounds like she is blaming Jesus for his death! Her sister said the same thing in verse 21! Apparently, Lazarus died on the very day that Jesus received the message of his illness. Two more days elapsed while He lingered in Bethabara, beyond Jordan, with a third day spent in His return walk back to Bethany. Then, He spent the night outside the city walls and entered the next morning. See first paragraph of footnote h above. Turning quickly, Martha left the Master and hurried back to the house and whispers to her sister that Jesus had arrived. Running from the house, she found Him just outside the village, falls at His feet and repeats the very words her sister had spoken a few moments prior (verse 21). Seemingly, the two women had discussed this point during the long delay before Jesus came to help.

(n) **"He groaned and was troubled."** Here, we see a flash of His great humanity. Feeling the sorrows and pains of humankind, the blessed Son of God groaned in His spirit. Our Lord was the perfect human.

(o) **"Jesus wept."** *Love is an action not a feeling!* The shortest passage in all Holy Scriptures, yet one of the longest; it is filled with meaning and hope for all mankind. Walking to the gravesite, the human Christ meditated upon the scene as silent tears streamed down His cheeks. So often in this life, all we can do is to shed tears of grief too deep for mortal words. Death had struck His beloved friend Lazarus. Many weeping Jews, wailing loudly, followed in the sorrowful procession. In the distress of the hour, the burden of the Jews who hatefully rejected Him as Messiah and Savior pressed harder than all else on His pure soul. When they died, it would be death, final and eternal hell forever! Spontaneously, the Lord Jesus broke into open sobbing (not wailing as the professional mourners) because of it all.

2p-*However, wait!* Who ever heard of God weeping? Tears are the common lot of humanity, not divinity. How can such a thing be? It is the human nature, the house of Adam, mortal man reflecting one of its highest attributes— weeping. Here, the Man-side of God incarnate sobs in sorrow and catches the attention of the watching Jews. A few moments later, the God-side of this same Man, Jesus of Nazareth, will call the dead back to life. Perfect God and Perfect Man, and each is revealed at this marvelous scene.

3p-**Verse 36. "Behold how he loved him!"** The Jews looked only upon the human side, which resembles the fading flowers of earth's little while. They held a carnal, but humanly candid interpretation of Jesus weeping: a human opinion replete with emotion, yet pitifully void of eternal meaning. A few weeks hence, He would be lamenting again over them again, their city, and temple. Note this in Section 126, footnote k. Everyone present was in for the shock of their lives. The friend over whom they greatly wept would shortly require no tears; he would be restored back to the life he had so suddenly departed!

4p-**Verse 38. "Jesus cometh to the grave."** Cunningham Geikie, in his work *The Life and Words of Christ*, pages 614-615 gives us further information about death among the ancient Jews. He states that upon the death of Lazarus, "A lamp burned by his corpse from the moment of death as a symbol of the immortality of the soul; and an egg had been broken as a symbol of mortality. The funeral procession had been sad enough with its dirge flutes and wailing hired women. At the grave's mouth, the men had chanted the sublime ninetieth Psalm in a slow circuit seven times around the bier, on which laid the dead body wrapped in linen." Veiled women led all such processions. To the cave where the empty body of Lazarus lay, came the Son of God! Something awesome was going to happen! For various other fascinating details regarding ancient Jewish burials, see Section 61, all of footnote b.

(p) **"Move the stone."** Only the rich could afford a burial site such as this one, which was either a natural concave-cavity or man-made recess cut out of the rock. Upon arrival at the burial cave, Christ spoke His first command in verse 39. Stunned, Martha attempts to reject her Lord's orders. She knew that his body was already in the state of decay and corruption. Did she smell the terrible odor as some of the men rolled back the stone? If so, it would shortly become a sweet fragrance, she would never forget.

(q) **"Father."** For more on the Hebrew usage of this Name, see Section 46, second paragraph of footnote g. Over the ages, Jews have prayed with their eyes open and do the same today. According to these Words, Christ had already sought the face of the Father in prayer regarding Lazarus. It was God's will that he be raised. Did the Savior spend those two days' delay in prayer? Regardless, we may be sure that in the quietness of His own heart, He had also communed with the Father over this matter. He "lifted up his eyes" as He had done in a prayer of thanksgiving before feeding the five thousand. Refer to this in Section 93, Matt. 14:19, footnote m. Note Section 178, John 17:1, where later He "lifted up his eyes" the night before the morning of the cross.

2p-**Verse 42. "Thou hearest me always."** More glorious words from the lips of our Lord. We are touched by the absolute assurance of Jesus in prayer to the Father. No other can attain to such blessedness as our Lord did. He spoke as though the answer had already arrived! He makes known His reason for a public prayer. It was that those standing about might know that God had sent Him. The wicked Pharisees had accused him of using the power of the wicked one to perform miracles; being present, they observed that He employed the divine art of prayer alone in causing miracles among the people. There were no tricks, incantations, and mutterings in deep tones, only a short, simple, heart prayer to the Father! Such overwhelming simplicity and faith would corroborate His Word and openly show the power of God in startling and fearful action. His sole motive was first that they might believe in Him.

(r) **Verse 43. "Lazarus come forth."** Standing before the mouth of the dark cave, the Lord Jesus shouted loudly these Words of sovereign command into that black hole of death! Every soul present was terrified at the authority of that wonderful Man. Every eye was riveted on the dark opening. The great intensity and high emotion of that moment, no man can explain. It has been said that Jesus called Lazarus by name, or else all the dead of all ages would come out from the nether world! The people staring at the cave's mouth saw a shadowy figure, clad in white, suddenly appear at the opening!

2p-Verse 44. "He that was dead came forth." This passage bristles with mystery and glorious, but frightful meaning. Who could describe the suspense that froze the hearts of everyone present? Stepping back with a shudder, women screamed, children clutched their mother's skirts, and strong men were terrified, gasping at the sight before their eyes. Hands and feet bound, he could not walk; head covered with the burial napkin, he could not see! (Jews tied the napkin about the head to uphold the jaw that had dropped or sagged in death.) There he was; Lazarus, the man now dead some four days, was alive! *However, how did he emerge from that dark tomb?* Jesus of Nazareth, the Messiah of Israel, and Son of God had thus commanded death, and it turned him loose.

3p-Does this amazing event picture that man is saved by grace? Can it teach us that our deliverance from the terrible death of sin is by the command of Christ alone? Once Lazarus had *floated out,* Jesus charged those standing by to "loose him, and let him go." Another lesson may be seen here: though many have been saved, yet often some weaker saints need brotherly assistance to be "untied" or "loosed" from the lesser things of this world. Paul called it "comforting the feeble minded" or the "small souled" (1 Thess. 5:14). Peter described it as "growing in grace" (2 Peter 3:18). There is an ancient *tradition* that Lazarus, who had been a professional soldier, lived another thirty years after his resurrection. This seems impossible, as under Roman occupation, Israel had no army. *Regardless of how long he lived afterwards, we wonder what was said at his second funeral!*

(s) Miracles may sometimes bring people to the saving knowledge of Christ, but not always. See more on this in Section 146, first paragraph of footnote n. With the shocking resurrection of Lazarus from the dead, some of the Jews still refused to believe on Christ. Verse 46, informs us that even though many of them witnessed this profound miracle they went away and reported to the Pharisees in their passion to destroy Him. Earlier in His ministry, when our Lord returned to His home town of Nazareth, He could perform only a few miracles because of their unbelief. See this story in Section 91, Mk. 6:6a, footnote g.

(t) **"Council."** As explained in other places the word means a meeting was called of the Sanhedrin, the supreme court of Israel. For various details on the Hebrew council or Sanhedrin, see Section 30, footnote b. For a comprehensive article on the Sanhedrin, see *A History of the Jewish People in the time of Jesus Christ,* vol. 1. pages 163-195, by Emil Schurer. On this occasion, they met in the spirit of hatred and perplexity, not knowing what to do about the resurrection of Lazarus from the dead. It was irrefutable proof that Jesus of Nazareth was the Messiah of Israel. This they could no longer bear; something must be done.

(u) The idea is that because Jesus had created a continuous national stir and turmoil among the Jews, they feared the intervention of the mighty Roman armies. This intimates that Rome had become concerned in the life and deeds of Jesus. Their greatest fear was that someone would make Him a king of the Jews. See Section 94, John 6:15, footnote a, for an earlier attempt to crown Him king in the province of Galilee from which He fled. Such an act would be interpreted as rebellion against Caesar and bring the wrath of Rome upon the entire nation of Israel.

2p-"Our place" had reference to the temple at Jerusalem, which Rome did later destroy in A.D. 70, and the Hebrew nation was dispersed over the known world.

3p-Verse 49. We are told that Caiaphas was the high priest "that same year." John wrote looking back on history. The Jewish priesthood was hereditary and therefore, held for life; thus, Luke's words seem to conflict with the facts. However, at this time in history, the Romans appointed whom they would as priests, hence the wording "that year" is historically accurate. For further explanation of this curious contradiction in the Jewish priesthood, see Section 21, Part 1, numbers 6 and 7, under footnote b.

(v) **Verses 49–50. Caiaphas' prediction.** This was an *unconscious or unwilled* prediction from the mouth of Caiaphas, the wicked high priest, not premeditated or self enunciated. As a man, Caiaphas contrived for the death of Christ; as a prophet, God used him to spoke things, which he did not will or understand. Surprisingly, he informs the Sanhedrin that all their proposals were mere ignorance; that the only solution for this problem was to kill one person, whether he was innocent or guilty. That Person was Jesus of Nazareth, the national troublemaker. He stated that it was in the interest of Israel that Christ should be put to death. His growing influence and vast popularity, coupled with the raising of Lazarus, might incite the people to force Him into the kingship of Israel. This would bring Roman intervention, and they would destroy the Jewish state, city, and temple. Hence, Caiaphas reasoned it was better to kill Christ now and save their nation! Men do not know that history has no conscience and will destroy those who misuse it. The death of the innocent Jesus did not save the nation of Israel in A.D. 70. It precipitated into the doom of Jerusalem, Israel, and the temple they sought to save! See Section 163. Later, we note that the rules of the Sanhedrin for issuing the death sentence were totally bypassed by Caiaphas on the night of Jesus' trial. A period of four days was required to elapse for a witness to come forward and speak on behalf of the accused, *before* his sentence was passed. The late, hell denying Anglican, Dr. F. W. Farrar explains this in *The Life of Christ,* page 515.

2p-Verses 51–52. Years later, John looking back on this event, fully understood and thus wrote the true meaning of what Caiaphas had *unknowingly* said. God took the tongue of this evil man and compelled him to predict the soon death of His beloved Son. Caiaphas' words carried a deeper meaning than what he thought. His mention of Christ dying for the nation had nothing to do with atonement on the cross, but simply of getting rid of a troublemaker. Some fifteen hundred years prior, the Lord of heaven compelled the apostate prophet, Balaam to speak the truth, though he knew it not (Num. 22:38). These are examples of the wrath of man praising God. See more on this thought in Section 125, second paragraph, footnote b. John wrote of these events long after they had happened; now understanding the whole story he informs his readers that Christ died for *both* Jews and Gentiles, wherever they are found (verse 52). This is the "one fold and one shepherd" or new kingdom Jesus had spoken of earlier. Refer to the main heading of Section 60 and the explanation by the asterisk. Note also Section 122, John 10:16, footnote m, for details on the Gentiles coming to Christ.

(w) John 12:10. "Put Lazarus also to death." What satanic hatred! A dead man, four days deceased, now stands before them alive, and well! And they scheme to destroy him! In addition, the text declares that "from that day forward" (the day, he rose) the Jews began to lay new plans to kill Jesus and the one He raised. This affirms the truth, that it takes more than a profound miracle to bring one to the saving knowledge of Christ. First, it takes the Word of God as stated in Section 131, Lk. 16:31, footnote g. In this verse, a man (Abraham) had died some two thousand years prior to this event. Yet, he commanded from eternity for men to believe God's Word in order to escape hell. When the Sanhedrin met to vote on the death of Jesus and Lazarus, we know that two members cast their lots in the negative. Neither Nicodemus or Joseph of Arimathaea had part in this devious plan, as we later learn. Note this in Section 193, Lk. 23:50-53 and John 19:38-42. For the operations of the Sanhedrin Court of Israel, their structure, voting system, and so forth, see *Appendix Five.*

2p-Why were the Sanhedrin upset with the resurrection of Lazarus? Christ had raised hundreds; what made this one so different? The Jews believed that only Messiah could raise one from the dead three days after expiring. They held that the soul of the deceased hovered over the body, (some believed it went into the grave and waited) desperately seeking to re-enter. This continued for a period of three days. *After* this time, the countenance of the dead body so changed through decay that the soul could not re-enter. Lightfoot's *Commentary on the New Testament . . . ,* vol. 3, page 367 contains further information regarding the Jewish belief of the spirit attempting to re-enter the body after physical death. It was believed that only Israel's Messiah could bring back the soul, infuse it into the corpse, and raise it to life again after three days had lapsed! See *Gill's Commentary*, vol. 8, page 30 for sketchy details on this. The Jews were wont to say, "The soul is the preserver of the body." Hence, the *supposed* struggle for three days to re-enter the corpse and save it from decay. Thus, the resurrection of Lazarus was demonstratively a supernatural Messianic miracle. F. W. Farrar in his work, *The Life of Christ,* wrote briefly of this Jewish belief in footnote 1, page 510. The miracle of raising Lazarus *after three days* was undeniable proof that Jesus was the Messiah of Israel: the Sanhedrin knew this all too well. Hence, their fierce anger at this astounding miracle and they sought to kill Him. See asterisk under main heading Section 48, for the four unique miracles *only* Messiah could perform.

(x) Withdrawal to Ephraim. Only a few weeks remained of our Savior's human life. These He spent as a fugitive, continually seeking to avoid the enraged religious leaders. Knowing the fury of the Jews, He and His disciples leave Bethany and move some eighteen miles north-east of Jerusalem into a remote village called Ephraim, located near the south eastern border of Samaria. How long this much-imperiled retirement lasted, we are not told. Although the hour of His death was fixed in the determinations of God, yet the Lord Jesus never unnecessarily exposed His life to the bloodthirsty Jews. We should learn from this special example to exercise prudence in every threatening or dangerous situation of life.

2p-This harmony commentary follows the words written here (verse 54), that Christ went from Bethany to Ephraim. It is *conjectured* that later, He departed from Ephraim, worked His way northward into Samaria, and then eastward across Galilee, over the Jordan River into Peraea. Completing His work in Peraea, He moved southward, and later crossed over to the eastern bank of the Jordan River into Judaea and walked to Jericho. From here, He traveled to Bethany and lastly into Jerusalem to die. Here, He would become the final Passover Lamb and die for the sins of mankind. There is no chronological connection between verse 54 and 55. The events introduced in verse 55 could only have occurred months *later* (after verse 54) when the Lord Jesus finally arrived at Jerusalem for the last time, just before His death. Verse 55 is taken and placed in Section 146, where Jesus is at the house of Simon the leper. Now, Mary anointed Him six days before His death. None of the inspired writers of the four gospels penned their histories in a straight forward, unbroken chronological order. This is another mark that demonstrates these men wrote under divine inspiration, not personal choice. No normal author would have written his narrative in this curious order; God did! He wrote His book different, perhaps to reveal our trust or lack of trust in its message. Learned, *unbelieving* academics have always struggled with this fact; some to the doom of their souls! In Lk. 16:29-31 a voice comes from eternity that warns men they had better believe God's Word, even above someone returning from the dead! No book is so despised and maligned as the Holy Bible. Why? *Is this because it is not true?*

3p-Following verse 54, and His withdrawal to Ephraim, there is a period in the life of Christ not covered by John, until our Savior suddenly appears at the supper in John 12:1. It seems a sensible *conjecture* to place here, the exclusive portions of Luke chapters 10 through 18 during our Lord's time at Ephraim. It would be ill guessing to preclude the possibility that Jesus made various excursions and circuitous trips in and out of Ephraim. However, these did not include a return to Jerusalem where the Jews were thirsting for His destruction.

CHAPTER 13

Departing Ephraim for Jerusalem and the Passover, He travels through Samaria, Galilee, and moves eastward over the Jordan River into Peraea. Completing His work here, Jesus walks south, crosses the fords of Jordan, moves westward through Jericho, finally arriving at Bethany. A supper in His honor is held at the house of Simon the [former] leper. Mary, Martha, and Lazarus are present. Six days before Passover, Mary foreseeing His death, anoints His body. Luke only reports these events. Judas goes to Jerusalem and bargains to betray the Son of God.

Time: The above events took several months at the least.

A woman is delivered from Satan's bondage on the Sabbath. The synagogue ruler objects and is put to shame. Jesus repeats two parables previously given.

Matt.	Mk.	Lk. 13:10-21—*Ephraim-Samaria-Galilee-Peraea-Jordan-Jericho-Bethany*	John
		A crooked back woman is set free	
		10 And he was teaching in one of the synagogues on the sabbath.[a]	
		11 And, behold, there was a woman which had a spirit [demon] of infirmity eighteen years, and was bowed together, and could in no wise lift up *herself*.[b]	
		12 And when Jesus saw her, he called *her to him*, and said unto her, "Woman, thou art loosed from thine infirmity."	
		13 And he laid *his* hands on her: and immediately she was made straight, and glorified God.[c]	
		Reaction of an angry religious hypocrite: Jesus' response	
		14 And the ruler[d] of the synagogue answered with indignation, because that Jesus had healed on the sabbath day, and said unto the people, "There are six days in which men ought to work: in them therefore come and be healed, and not on the sabbath day."[e]	
		15 The Lord then answered him, and said, "*Thou* hypocrite, doth not each one of you on the sabbath loose his ox or *his* ass from the stall, and lead *him* away to watering?[f]	
		16 "And ought not this woman, being a daughter of Abraham, [Jewish] whom Satan hath bound, lo, these eighteen years, be loosed from this bond on the sabbath day?"	
		17 And when he had said these things, all his adversaries were ashamed:[g] and all the people rejoiced for all the glorious things that were done by him.	
		Parables of the Mustard Seed and Leaven briefly repeated	
		18 Then said[h] he, "Unto what is the kingdom of God like? And whereunto shall I resemble it?	
		19 "It is like a grain of mustard seed,[i] which a man took, and cast into his garden; and it grew, and waxed a great tree; and the fowls of the air lodged in the branches of it."	
		20 And again he said, "Whereunto shall I liken the kingdom of God?	
		21 "It is like leaven,[j] which a woman took and hid in three measures of meal, till the whole was leavened." (Verse 22 cont. in Section 126.)	

Footnotes-Commentary

[a] For the miracles of Jesus performed on the Sabbath, see Section 54, footnote a. It is worthy of note that the Son of God spent His Sabbaths in the synagogues preaching and teaching the Word of God and performing wonderful deeds of healing and help to those in need. It was the accepted custom to allow guest speakers time to

address the congregations of the synagogues after the standard rituals were over. The religious leaders continually opposed Him, wherever He went.

(b) "Could not lift herself up." We are touched by the dedication of this poor woman living in such terrible physical contortion. Nevertheless, she was present at the synagogue where Jesus was teaching and refused to let her ailment hinder her from attendance. The words "bowed together" meant her posture was bent face downward toward the earth, a condition being equally painful and humiliating. We learn that she had suffered in this state for eighteen years, *and that Satan was the cause of her crooked back* (verse 16). This was a long time for anyone to labor under the control and misery of the Devil. We read in Rev. 12:9, that he "deceives the whole world."

2p-One is aghast at the commentators who write about God *"allowing, letting,"* or *"permitting"* certain sins to be committed. Some years ago, I heard a pastor say, "God allowed David to commit adultery with Bathsheba, but He did not let David do this." This good man was trying to explain something beyond the realm of human understanding and stuck his foot in his mouth during the process. It is sure that God knows all things that have happened or will happen, but it is further sure that He is not always the *cause or author* of all these things. Man does have a free will and power to choose, and he is responsible for his choices, be they right or wrong. This obvious fact of human life hardly snatches sovereignty from God's hands or suggests He is not in control. *We do not credit the works of the Devil to the Almighty.* David committed murder and adultery and God had nothing to do with it! These sins were the choice of King David, not God. It is further true, that God could force every person on earth to do only, that which is honorable and upright. However, He does not operate a robot show! What the Almighty "allows" or "lets," for the most part, is beyond human comprehension. The wise man will not meddle into these secret matters. The high-sounding theological jargon about the "efficacious and permissive decrees of God" falls on its face when we remember that He overrules all things for His glory. For a brief discussion of these matters, see *Lecture in Systematic Theology,* chapter 10, by Henry C. Thiessen. Those "experts" who continually pry and meddle, often speak and write the most outlandish things about God's sovereignty. Over the course of church history, much of this has been used by the Devil to engineer disastrous calamities in the minds and bodies of people. For a shocking example of this, see Section 1, Part 3, first and second paragraphs, footnote i.

3p-In God's time, the Lord Jesus came on the scene to destroy Satan's works, then bring new life and hope to the former prisoners of sin (1 John 3:8). *In every such case, Christ was the cure for the maladies and ills, not the cause of them.* The curious story of God sending (forcing) an evil (demon) spirit to agitate King Saul is a classic example of the Lord making the powers of darkness do His will for a specific purpose to be accomplished. See this in 1 Sam. 16:14-23, 18:10, and 19:9. For a New Testament example of God compelling an evil man to speak the truth, see the prediction of the wicked high priest, Caiaphas, in previous Section 124, John 11:49-52, second paragraph of footnote v. For other comments on this difficult subject, see Section 137, fourth paragraph of footnote d. God is too good to do bad to anyone, whether we can figure it out or not (Nahum 1:7).

(c) The process Jesus employed in the public healing of this woman is noteworthy. In verse 12, "He called her" to Himself. We can easily picture the poor woman, struggling, holding on, no doubt assisted by friends as she dragged her crooked body to Jesus. With the command of His voice, shock waves reverberated across the hundreds present in that synagogue. Every eye fell on Him! First, He commanded her release from Satan's power and then laid His hands on her (verse 13). Instantly, she rose up straight; her back was healed. Never, had that synagogue congregation seen such a sight. She shouted, danced about, and waved her hands in ecstasy. We cannot doubt that dozens of friends wept and praised God loudly for this manifestation of power, while others sat stunned. The place was electrified with joy and the fear of God combined, except for one group present. They are described in the following footnote.

(d) "Ruler." The head of this synagogue was a hypocritical, cold hearted, ruthless pedant. Again, we are amazed at the calloused attitude of the religious leaders: in this case, the "ruler," or "chazan" of that particular synagogue and his companions in hypocrisy. He was a professional rabbi entrapped by the tradition of the elders. How dare this carpenter from Nazareth heal a member of *his* congregation! One could believe the demon exited the woman and entered his heart due to his vicious behavior. Repeatedly, the Jewish prelates were filled with rage and madness at the works of Messiah; while the common folks, beholding the effects of His power, publicly and unashamed voiced loud praises to God. Wherever the Master went, He was doing good and healing all that were oppressed of Satan. He was met by the taunts, depreciating remarks, and opposition of the Pharisees and those who resembled them in their false religion.

(e) "Not on the Sabbath day." The appalling spiritual condition of the Jewish authorities is reflected in the words of this ruler. Who could find such blinded bigotry, such corruption of religion, such sheer wickedness as emanated from this hypocrite? For a discussion of Hebrew rules regarding work on the Sabbath, see *The Jewish New Testament Commentary,* pages 117-118, by David Stern, and *The Victor Bible Background Commentary,* pages 53-56, by Lawrence O. Richards. They had invented thousands of extra rules and commands regarding the Sabbath. These were called the tradition of the elders or oral law. They were added to the Torah several hundred years before the birth of Christ. For the Sabbath day, the Hebrew scribes had invented over two thousand extra commands that had nothing to do with the Torah Law of Moses! In the Talmud tractate, Avodah Zarah 27b, these endless rules and restrictions are called "fences." This word describes the purpose of the thousands of extra rules and regulations. Like fences, they were raised about the original 613 precepts of the Torah Law with the intent of keeping the younger generations of Jews from breaking the commandments given at Mount Sinai to Moses for the nation of Israel.

^(f) **"Thou hypocrite."** This word in plural form is used fourteen times in Matthew alone. Each time it refers to the religious Jews. Fearless, the Son of God called the synagogue ruler for what he was. See Jesus' earlier rebuke of these evil men in Section 45, Matt. 5:20, footnote e, and Section 46, Matt. 6:5, footnote a. Dozens of Hebrew men sitting in that congregation had led their livestock to watering that very Sabbath morning. At this period in history, the Jews allowed a camel to be led to water with a halter on and a horse with a collar. However, if the horse should dip his collar in the water, then it all becomes unclean! Further, they permitted a man to draw water for his beasts and pour it into troughs, provided, he does carry the water. See Talmud tractate, Eiruvin 20b for a sample of the fine details and utter tripe of the Jews about attending to their livestock on the Sabbath day. They showed mercy on dumb beasts, but hated Christ for healing the bent over woman. The Messiah proved them wrong by their own practice in the use of this analogy. They were shamed before the people. The *distorted* values of unsaved men in positions of religious leadership have wrecked the lives and damned the souls of millions.

^(g) **Verse 16. "Whom Satan hath bound."** These words mean what they say! The Devil had literally bent her spine over and kept her in this posture for eighteen years. *This does not teach that all physical maladies have their origin in Satan.* What brought this into here life we are not told. Regarding the power of wicked spiritual beings to inflict torments, and suffering on human bodies, see Section 106, footnote d. Men, who know Christ as personal Lord and Savior and walk in disciplined fellowship with Him are protected from these evil entities (Eph. 6:10-18).

2p-"A daughter of Abraham." Christ reminded the ruler and his associates that the healed woman was a descendant of Abraham's seed. Moreover, since the Hebrews regarded all fellow Jews as the only benefactors in the world of God's mercies, then they too should rejoice that she was made whole. However, the Word's of the Lord Jesus go deeper than national ties. Our Savior informs the entire synagogue audience that this woman is now saved: she has followed in the steps of Abraham, who also trusted Christ by faith and was made righteous or saved. See Section 30, second and third paragraphs of footnote h for details on Abraham's salvation. The Master's words of unanswerable truth cut deep into the hearts of these angry men. The congregation roared their approval over the healed woman while their leaders, filled with hatred, were thoroughly embarrassed.

^(h) **Verses 18-19.** Our Lord added these two parables into the conversation in order to show the Jews, who were debating with Him, how vastly different His spiritual kingdom was from theirs in its attraction, growth, and mysterious effect.

⁽ⁱ⁾ **The Parable of the Mustard Seed.** It is to be noted that He had used this same parable almost a year earlier while preaching from a boat anchored off the shore of Lake Galilee. The Parable of the Mustard Seed was given earlier in Section 79, Matt. 13:31-31. Here, again, we note that our Lord repeated Himself.

^(j) **The Parable of the Leaven.** The Lord Jesus had given this earlier on the same occasion as mentioned in footnote i above. Here, see Matthew's statement that Christ called it "the kingdom of heaven;" while in Luke, the same parable is referred to as "the kingdom of God." *This reveals again that they both mean the same.* The same double identification is used in the Parable of the Leaven. For an explanation of the kingdom in its different phases, see Section 39, footnotes a and g.

2p-It is noticed the *second time* that the Lord Jesus gave this parable He spoke of "a woman" putting the leaven in the meal or flour; and here, He had just healed "a woman" of her infirmity. One cannot but wonder where she went telling the marvelous news of the Savior and her miraculous healing. We may be sure she spent the rest of her days "putting grand news" into every listening ear and heart. For an explanation of various usages of leaven in Scripture, see Section 80, and all of footnote b.

Christ continues en route to Jerusalem for Passover. The Pharisees warn Him to leave Galilee for its ruler, Herod Antipas would kill Him. He calls Herod "that fox." Jesus gives His first recorded eulogy of doom over Jerusalem and the temple.

Matt.	Mk.	Lk. 13:22-35—Galilee	John
		The traveling preacher-teacher 22 And he went through the cities and villages, teaching, and journeying toward Jerusalem.[a] 23 Then said one unto him, "Lord, are there few that be saved?"[b] And he said unto them, 24 "Strive to enter in at the strait gate: for many, I say unto you, will seek to enter in, and shall not be able.[c] *Parable of the Shut Door*[d] 25 "When once the master of the house is risen up, and hath shut to the door, and ye begin to stand without, and to knock at the door, saying, 'Lord, Lord, open unto us;' and he shall answer and say unto you, 'I know you not whence ye are:' 26 "Then shall ye begin to say, 'We have eaten and drunk in thy presence, and thou hast taught in our streets.'[e] 27 "But he shall say, I tell you, 'I know you not whence ye are; depart from me, all *ye* workers of iniquity.' 28 "There shall be weeping and gnashing of teeth,[f] when ye shall see Abraham, and Isaac, and Jacob, and all the prophets, in the kingdom of God, and you *yourselves* thrust out. 29 "And they shall come from the east, and *from* the west, and from the north, and *from* the south, and shall sit down[g] in the kingdom of God. 30 "And, behold, there are last which shall be first, and there are first which shall be last.[h] *Threats from Herod Antipas, the ruler of Galilee* 31 The same day there came certain of the Pharisees, saying unto him, "Get thee out, [of his territory] and depart hence: for Herod will kill thee."[i] 32 And he said unto them, "Go ye, and tell that fox,[j] 'Behold, I cast out devils, and I do cures to day and to morrow, and the third *day* I shall be perfected.' (will have completed my work here in Galilee) 33 "Nevertheless I must walk [in Galilee] to day, and to morrow, and the *day* following: [three more days before leaving] for it cannot be that a prophet perish [be killed] out [away from] of Jerusalem. *He bewails the fate* *of Jerusalem and the Jew's great temple in A.D. 70* 34 "O Jerusalem, Jerusalem,[k] which killest the prophets, and stonest them that are sent unto thee; how often would I have gathered thy children together, as a hen *doth gather* her brood under *her* wings, and ye would not! *The wonder of the world, the glorious temple would be "desolate"* 35 "Behold, your house [temple] is left unto you desolate: and verily I say unto you, Ye shall not see me, until *the time* come when ye shall say, 'Blessed *is* he that cometh in the name of the Lord.'"[l] (Next chap., Lk. 14:1 cont. in Section 127.)	

Footnotes-Commentary

[(a)] We discover from this verse that the Lord Jesus had left His hiding place at Ephraim. He was on a long trek that would finally end at the home of Simon the leper, Lazarus, and his two sisters. See this arrival in Section 146. A few days later, He would enter Jerusalem, and after a series of events become the Passover sacrifice for our sins in His death on the cross.

[(b)] **"Are only few saved?"** Again, it is stressed that what most of the Jews meant (at this time) by being saved was different from what our Lord taught. It was commonly known and accepted among the Hebrew people that "all pious Jews would share (or be saved for) the world to come" which was called "Olam Ha-Ba." This meant only those Jews, who obeyed the Torah, but especially their oral traditions. Whoever asked this question was apparently not speaking of *personal salvation* of one's soul from sin and its consequences. Rather, he was thinking of being saved to share in Israel's earthly kingdom. Salvation from personal sin was mostly unknown to the Jews: they looked for a physical kingdom only. See Section 145, Lk. 19:11, footnotes a, b, and c for the political kingdom the Jews thought would suddenly appear. In their thinking, salvation, redemption, and like terms carried the meaning of a physical, material salvation for the faithful Jews from the domination of Gentile powers, especially, the Romans at this time. The Hebrew political utopia embraced their physical Messiah sitting on David's throne ruling the world. For more on this thought, see Section 9, Lk. 1:32, footnote g.

2p-Had this person heard Christ say earlier in His Sermon on the Mount that only "few" would find His new kingdom (Matt. 7:13-14)? Repentance from sin and faith in Him as the Savior-Messiah were prerequisites for admission. Perhaps this unnamed man had heard that John the Baptist preached similar things. Having been taught by the rabbis "all Torah abiding Jews would share in the world to come," apparently he could not reconcile the two opposite messages. Hence, his puzzling question, "are there few that be saved?" Could it be that he was saying as a pious Hebrew, "Master, who will share in Israel's great earthly kingdom?" For details on both sides of the kingdom, see Section 134, footnotes a through c.

[(c)] **Verses 24-25.** Jesus had taught a slightly similar thing during His Sermon on the Mount, given many months before. See Section 47, Matt. 7:13 footnote f. This is another example of Christ repeating Himself. In this text, He uses the word "strive" in verse 24, while in the Matt. 7:13 it is the term "enter." The Master's answer was perfect for the scribes, Pharisees, and all devout Jews. Thousands of them were striving to enter their imagined literal kingdom, but it was by works of the law and Talmud or Mishna rules. These oral traditions are explained in Section 52, footnote h; Section 89, footnote c. Note Section 96, first paragraph of footnote d, for the Mishna. They had sternly rejected Jesus as their Messiah. Because of this, they would never be able to enter His spiritual kingdom. Here, the Master requires their great religious diligence to be re-employed in striving to obey His message. They needed to believe in Him so that they would have entrance into the true kingdom of God. The "striving" had reference to the awful battle that every pious Jew had to face, in shedding the impossible demands of the scribes and Pharisees and the thousands of oral traditions that had so bound their lives. This struggle and its explanation are discussed later under the term "presseth into the kingdom," in Section 130, Lk. 16:16, footnote o.

[(d)] **The Parable of the Shut Door.** Jesus warns the Jews that the master (Himself) of the house will wait with His door open for a limited time. Soon, it would be shut through their continued rejection of Him as the Messiah. Thus during the dark night that was coming upon their nation, it would be vain to seek entrance, for the door would be closed and locked. They would be shut out, and the door would be opened for the admission of all believing Gentiles to come in. There is a right time to seek and find admission into the Lord's kingdom and His house of eternal life. Beyond doubt, the Messiah *first* had in mind the destruction of Jerusalem and the temple in A.D. 70, then the scattering of the Hebrew nation to the four winds of the earth.

[(e)] **Verse 26.** Clearly, Christ addressed His Words of judgment upon those who were *there with Him.* The condemned would plead that they had heard Christ teach in their streets and had dined with Him, confirms to whom the Lord addressed these terrible Words. Verse 27 is a repeat of a former condemnation He had spoken to the Jews and religious leaders earlier during the Sermon on the Mount. See this in Section 47, Matt. 7:21, 23.

[(f)] Another repeat in the teaching of Christ. See Section 82, Matt. 13:42. footnote g for the definition of the term "weeping and gnashing of teeth" among the Jews. The Savior had mentioned this earlier in Matt. 8:12. For twenty-one things the Bible says about suffering in hell-lake of fire, see Section 103, number 8, under footnote g.

[(g)] **"Sit down."** This expression had also been employed by the Lord Jesus earlier in His preaching to the Jews as seen in Section 60, Matt. 8:11, footnote h. Verse 8, in Section 60, is solid proof that Abraham, Isaac, and Jacob were saved men, for they were sitting in the kingdom of God. The Lord Jesus made it clear that only those born of God will see His kingdom. Refer to this profound statement spoken to a member of the Sanhedrin, in Section 30, John 3:3.

[(h)] **"Last first and first last."** A proverbial saying popular among the Jews. It is found in the Talmud tractate, Rosh HaShana 18b. For comments on this old expression, see Section 139, Matt. 19:30, footnote p, and Section 140, Matt. 20:16, footnote j. It spoke of God choosing one group in preference to another based on their reaction to Him.

Here, our Lord is saying, the Gentiles, who in Jewish opinion were the lowest of all and were last in everything, would now become first with God. In accepting Christ as Messiah and Savior, they would share in the blessing of sitting down with the saved Hebrew patriarchs and prophets in the joy of heaven. The Jews, who were first before God, to whom His oracles were given, and to whom His prophets and the Messiah were sent, would be rejected. Surely, the men of religion understood what their Messiah meant by these awesome Words. Later, He gave another parable with a similar meaning, and the religious leaders became angry because they knew He spoke of them. Refer to this in Section 153, Lk. 20:19, footnote m.

(i) **"Get out or Herod will kill you."** This passage confirms that Christ was in Herod's territory of Galilee at this time; otherwise, the words of the Pharisees would have been meaningless. Galilee was a small area where it would be difficult to be unnoticed. Thus, the people soon detected His presence. Word of His presence spread everywhere. The entire place was only about fifty miles from north to south and twenty-five miles from east to west. For details on Herod Antipas, the ruler of Galilee, see Section 21, Part 1, number 3 under footnote b. Some commentators believe this was a scheme of the Pharisees (pretending friendship) to lure Christ out of Galilee into Judaea, where they planned to kill Him. To kill Him in the territory of Herod Antipas and not Judaea where Pilate ruled, could very well have caused further uproar between the two rulers. The reason for their on-going political feud is explained in Section 184, Lk. 23:12, footnote f. Christ's answer sent back to Herod reveals that this was indeed a real threat from the old fox. Whether Herod had entertained some plot to see Jesus put to death in his territory as he had murdered the Baptist is impossible to say. Refer to Section 92 for the death of John at the behest of Herod Antipas.

(j) **"Go tell that fox."** To their surprise, Christ sends to Herod Antipas a message via their lines of communication right into his palace. In verses 32-33, the Master said in so many Words, "Go tell that cunning killer that I have only a brief time to spend in his territory. I will continue to perform cures and miracles for several more days across Galilee but on the third day I will be perfected, or will have completed my business in his domain." In verse 33, Christ said, in essence, "I will walk across Herod's land but will not die here. My decease is fixed at Jerusalem, for only there can the Sanhedrin give judgment for my death. Herod shall not kill me, for my sentence cannot come from Galilee. I must die at Jerusalem, the city of the Great King." This answer from the Lord must have shaken the Pharisees. They surely mused among themselves, "What does He mean by this?" It is worthy of note that this is the only place in our Lord's ministry where He uses Words of contempt for a political enemy. The nearest thing to this was His denunciation of the leaders of religion in Section 159, Matt. 23, footnote p. Like anger at sin, the fury of true moral indignation against evil has its place as a righteous function in the heart of God's people. However, such things are rarely heard from today's plush pulpits and professorial chairs of theological education. Men have become so weak in God's Word, so blinded to the consequences of sin, that they almost apologize to the Devil for interfering with his business.

2p-If there was ever a ruler over Israel (during this time) that brought upon himself such apt and justified words, "that fox," Herod Antipas was the man. He was a perjured princeling, false to his religion (a Jewish proselyte), false to his nation, false to his friends, false to his soldiery, and false to his wife—a "fox" in the animal sense of the word. Whether this "fox" ever heard of the way Jesus had characterized him and his dominion, we do not know. One can believe that the Pharisees delivered Christ's message to this old devil. The late, non-Christian, Jewish writer, Joseph Klaustner, in *The Messianic Idea In Israel* states on page 126, that Herod had one time acclaimed himself to be a Messiah! We can easily believe that such a self-assumed title was normal for this political mad man, and that he could claim Messiahship to curry favor with the Jews, who bitterly hated him. His idiosyncrasies are reflected in a Talmud tractate, Beitzah 24a, which informs us that he bred domesticated house doves. Some mad men need a pastime hobby to sooth their guilt-ridden feelings. Adolf Hitler raised canaries, petted dogs, and fondled little children!

(k) **Verses 34. "O Jerusalem, Jerusalem."** What a cry of moving pathos! It revealed both divine and human emotions blended in one as the heart of Jesus burst open in love and pity for the city (or people) of Jerusalem where He would soon die. We have noted the Lord Jesus, earlier, weeping over Lazarus and his sisters in Section 124, John 11:35, footnote o. The rabbis taught that Israel was under the wings of God: when a Gentile converted to Judaism, he was also said to be under this divine protection. The Old Testament compares God to an eagle hovering over its little ones (Ex. 19:4 with Deut. 32:11) and protecting Israel under His wings (Ps. 17:8; 36:7; 57:1; and 91:4). The rabbis taught that God gathered Israel under His care as a mother hen would her chicks. No baby chick ever refused the shelter, warmth, and care of its mother's wings. Yet, Israel did this very thing to their Messiah, Jesus of Nazareth. The Talmud uses similar language in tractates, Shabbat 31a and Sota 13b.

2p-**Verse 35. "Your temple desolate."** This is another prediction of the judgment that fell upon the city and the temple ("your house") about forty years later in A.D. 70. This first lament is different from that recorded in Section 159, Matt. 23:37-39, which He said two days before His death. The latter one was spoken in or near the temple at Jerusalem, while the former was given somewhere in Galilee in the presence of the conniving Pharisees, as stated in footnote i above.

(l) Jesus quoted the latter portion of verse 35 from Ps. 118:26. Levitical choirs always sang this "hallel" (praise) during the Passover celebration. The rabbis taught that when Messiah arrived at the Eastern Gate of Jerusalem, He must be welcomed by the singing of *this* hallel. Christ informs the Pharisees, who had warned Him to depart from Galilee, that they would not see Him again until the Passover at Jerusalem, and that this hymn of praise would be sung when He entered the temple to teach for the final time before His death. A few weeks later when our Lord rode into Jerusalem, the people gathered about the Eastern Gate singing this welcome Messianic hallel. Note Section 148, Matt. 21:9-10, for the story. It was on this occasion that they literally fulfilled the prediction of Christ spoken in verse 35. Again, this demonstrates that they were oblivious of the atonement that He would accomplish on the cross a few days later. Their aspirations were *only* for a human, earthly monarch to rule them in physical power and worldwide control.

2p-Shortly after His entrance into Jerusalem, these same people, along with their religions leaders, screamed for His death. This was because they looked for an earthly king who would fight and destroy Israel's enemies, obey their oral law, destroy the Romans, and establish a material political kingdom. *This He did not do upon entrance into their beloved city.* The Psalm quoted by Christ has nothing to do with His return over two thousand years later and the establishment of a glorified reign on earth. Some commentators lift this out of its historical context and then incorrectly apply it to the church. For a brief discussion of God's promises to Israel being given to the church, see Section 9, third and fourth paragraphs of footnote g. Regarding the millennium period, see Section 171, third, fourth and fifth paragraphs of footnote b for explanatory comments on what this time will *not* be. The frequently heard, wild speculations of various "end time specialists" regarding the reign of Christ are enough to turn off any serious minded Christian. Unless one forces certain Old Testament verses to say what they do not say, we know only a little about this wonderful time yet to come. Every effort of men to measure this by the best of earth's standards and blessings is a miserable flop and should be rejected by sober Christians. The wise saint will refrain from filling in the eschatological gaps that inspiration has placed into Holy Scripture. For further comments on the reign of Christ in eternal perfectedness and joy, see Section 171, third, fourth, and fifth paragraphs under footnote b.

3p-Some extremists teach that Christ was speaking of His return at the end of the age, and that these very Pharisees would then sing this Messianic hallel of praises from the regions of hell! This sort of exegesis deserves a Nobel Prize for ignorance. People do not sing in hell; instead, they scream amid their unspeakable agony and torment. See Section 131, for the horrible story of a man in hell and what he said and did. *We find no singing in this terrible place.*

Jesus has His third recorded meal with a Pharisee. The Jews criticized Him for healing on the Sabbath. He gives two parables that portray their arrogance and rejection of Him as the Messiah.

Matt.	Mk.	Lk. 14:1-18—*Galilee*	John
		A meal time trap	
		1 And it came to pass, as he went into the house of one of the chief Pharisees[(a)] to eat bread on the sabbath day, that they watched him.	
		2 And, behold, there was a certain man before him which had the dropsy. [(b)] (swelling)	
		3 And Jesus answering spake unto the lawyers and Pharisees, saying, "Is it lawful to heal on the sabbath day?"[(c)]	
		4 And they held their peace. And he took *him*, and healed him, and let him go;[(d)]	
		5 And answered them, saying, "Which of you shall have an ass or an ox fallen into a pit, and will not straightway pull him out on the sabbath day?"[(e)]	
		6 And they could not answer him again to these things.	
		Parable of the Ambitious Guest	
		7 And he put forth a parable[(f)] to those which were bidden, when he marked how they chose out the chief rooms; [places] saying unto them,	
		8 "When thou art bidden of any *man* to a wedding, sit not down in the highest room;[(g)] [place] lest a more honourable man than thou be bidden of him;	
		9 "And he that bade thee and him come and say to thee, Give this man place; and thou begin with shame to take the lowest room.[(h)] (place)	
		10 "But when thou art bidden, go and sit down in the lowest room; [place] that when he that bade thee cometh, he may say unto thee, 'Friend, go up [to a] higher:' [place] then shalt thou have worship [respect] in the presence of them that sit at meat [the meal] with thee.'	
		11 "For whosoever exalteth himself shall be abased; and he that humbleth himself shall be exalted."	
		12 Then said he also to him that bade him, "When thou makest a dinner or a supper, call not thy friends, nor thy brethren, neither thy kinsmen, nor *thy* rich neighbours; lest they also bid thee again, and a recompence be made thee.[(i)]	
		13 "But when thou makest a feast, call the poor, the maimed, the lame, the blind:	
		14 "And thou shalt be blessed; for they cannot recompense thee: for thou shalt be recompensed at the **resurrection of the just."**	
		Parable of the Great Supper and its rejection by three excuses	
		15 And when one of them that sat at meat with him heard these things, he said unto him, "Blessed *is* he that shall eat bread in the kingdom of God."[(j)]	
		16 Then said he unto him, "A certain man made a great supper,[(k)] and bade many:	
		17 "And sent his servant at supper time to say to them that were bidden, 'Come; for all things are now ready.'	
		18 "And they all with one *consent* began to make excuse. The first	

Matt.	Mk.	Lk. 14:18-24—*Galilee*	John
		said unto him, 'I have bought a piece of ground, and I must needs go and see it: I pray thee have me excused.' **19** "And another said, 'I have bought five yoke [ten] of oxen, and I go to prove them: I pray thee have me excused.' **20** "And another said, 'I have married a wife, and therefore I cannot come.' ***The lord of the wedding sends servants across the city*** **21** "So that servant came, and shewed his lord these things. Then the master of the house being angry said to his servant, 'Go out quickly into the streets and lanes of the city, and bring in hither the poor, and the maimed, and the halt, and the blind.' **22** "And the servant said, 'Lord, it is done as thou hast commanded, and yet there is room.' ***The lord of the wedding invites whosoever will to come*** **23** "And the lord said unto the servant, 'Go out into the highways and hedges, and compel *them* to come in, that my house may be filled.' ***The original Jewish guests forbidden*** [l] **24** "For I say unto you, That none of those men which were bidden shall taste of my supper." (Verse 25 cont. in Section 128.)	

Footnotes-Commentary

[a] **"To eat bread on the Sabbath day."** In Section 129, Lk. 15:2, the religious Jews scorned Christ for eating with the ungodly. Here, we see Christ eating with a chief Pharisee and his companions in hypocrisy. How touching that our Lord sought to win all men to Himself; He made no distinction. The Jews counted eating bread together as a time of deep and intimate fellowship. To do so at a Sabbath meal only heightened the pious feelings. They turned the Sabbath into a day of great, extravagant feasting. This was done to honor the day! Hundreds of people were invited to these meals. "Chief Pharisee" probably meant that this fellow was a member of the Sanhedrin and according to verse 12, he had "invited" (or "bade") Jesus into his home. As on a previous occasion, this was another "set up," for the text reads "they watched him," or with evil intentions looked for something with which they could accuse the Lord of glory. For an earlier occasion when the Jews sought to entrap the Savior by inviting Him to a meal, see main heading of Section 70. Other attempted confrontations are mentioned in Section 54, Matt. 12:10, footnotes a through d, and the main heading of Section 72.

[b] **"Dropsy."** This was an ailment caused by large accumulations of water in various parts of the human anatomy, resulting in terrible swelling. It was unbearably painful, and during this era of history, was incurable. Many of its victims hurt themselves to death!

[c] **"Is it lawful to heal on the Sabbath day?"** Jesus put this question to the religious leaders. It reveals the wicked intentions of the "chief Pharisee" who invited Christ to his home and that of his colleagues in evil. As on numerous other occasions, they sought to throw Him into conflict with *their* Sabbath laws. See a similar Sabbath day situation in Section 125, Lk. 13:10, with an infirmed woman badly bent over.

[d] Jesus answered their question by healing him, and letting him go.

[e] This was the standard response given by Messiah to the wrangling Jews. It was something all of them had done. *Note verse 6 for their reply!*

[f] **He observed their hypocrisy.** The meal was a large gathering of many people. See footnote a above. The Savior noted how they scrambled for higher seats and exalted positions. Quest for glorified social status was rife among the Jews and made obvious by special seating places at public banquets. James 2:1-6 speaks of this very practice in the synagogues. The scribes, lawyers, and other religious leaders vied for these top positions. For more details, see footnote g below. Largely, the same thing is practiced today among the rich and famous. Taking advantage of this scene and the blinded arrogance of the Jews, He gave them the lesson of the ambitious guest who sought only for recognition and prominence in verses 7-14.

[g] **Verse 8. "Room."** This has reference to a higher seating or reclining place at the host's table. Important persons were always placed near the chief couch where the master of the house reclined. This position (room) reflected honor and esteem from everyone present. Note, further comments on this in footnote h below.

(h) **Verses 9-11.** These verses teach the lesson of humility and the danger of self-exaltation. Clearly, the Savior reproved the master of the feast ("Chief Pharisee") for inviting the rich and powerful and neglecting the poor and needy. The Lord Jesus continually faced the pride and arrogance of the Jews, including His own apostles. It is noteworthy that the rabbis would teach their students to "always take the lower seat, and you may be advanced higher." Jesus quotes almost their very words, for here amid this great feast and dining occasion, they did not practice what they preached. See Adam Clarke's *Commentary*, vol. 5, page 452 for details.

2p-Verse 10. Highlighted in gray; seemingly, the Lord Jesus took these words from Prov. 25:6-7.

(i) **Verses 12-13.** This is one of the greatest lessons ever uttered to believers who have an abundance of this world's goods. Giving to those who have nothing and cannot give back has always been God's way. He shows His favor to the poor and needy via these channels! *Where are the Christians today who practice this advice of the Savior?* He is not saying that it is wrong to invite friends, family, and associates to share our blessings. Rather, that we do a dreadful injustice by *not* calling in those who are in need and never sharing our substance with them. *Yet in today's vicious society one dare not invite every stranger into their home for fear of murder and robbery.*

2p-Verse 14. "At the resurrection of the just." In gray because it was seemingly quoted from Dan. 12:2. Our Lord has promised that those who share and give to those who have not, will be specially blessed and rewarded. In these words, Jesus clearly distinguished the "resurrection of the just," *from* those who are "unjust." The Old Testament does the same in Dan. 12:2. Refer to Section 124, footnote j, for more on the Hebrew idea of resurrection.

3p-Christ is not instructing His people to support "dead beats," and "drop outs," or persons who refuse to work (when they are physically able), living off the grace of others and tax dollars from the government. The rule is "if any man would not work, [when he is able] neither should he eat" (2 Thess. 3:10).

(j) **A great Messianic banquet.** This was another common saying among the Jews and often heard at feasts such as this one. It embraced more than a piece of bread! Who was this unnamed speaker? He was a fellow Pharisee or lawyer of some distinguished rank, in order to speak out and interrupt the conversation of others. Apparently, he had listened to the rebukes and instructions of Messiah, and he was stirred to speak out this popular expression. It should be noted that at this time in Jewish theology there existed some of the most *absurd and gross notions* about banqueting in the Jew's literal kingdom of God. Many of them believed that God would throw a unique Messianic banquet as never seen or heard of in all human history! The Hebrews would eat "the bread of the kingdom," with a vast variety of flesh, such as fish and fowl, and drink wine kept from the creation of the world. There would be a variety of delicious fruits, a cooked ox, which was the Behemoth of Job, a Leviathan or gigantic bird called Ziz, and other perversions invented by the rabbis. Ziz is mentioned in the Talmud tractate, Baba Bathra 73b. This interjector may have been speaking of this ridiculous myth, popularly believed among some of the Jews at that time.

(k) **"The Parable of the Great Supper."** The Savior takes advantage of the occasion to give a lesson regarding *another* feast, the meaning of which was understood by every pious Jew present. He told them that *they* would be left out of God's true kingdom! Later, at Jerusalem, Jesus gave a similar lesson. See Section 154, Matt. 22:1-14. Note the following about this parable:

1. **Verse 16.** It is God, who makes this great supper.

2. **Verse 17.** His servant is the Lord Jesus, who has just spent over three years of ministry among the Jewish people and was rejected by them. With the death, burial, and resurrection of Christ, "all things were ready" for the forgiveness of sins and eternal life. All Old Testament verses that pointed to the work of the coming Messiah met their fulfillment in Him. The untold thousands that had lived and died *prior* to the cross and resurrection, now had their faith confirmed, realized, and justified.

3. **Verses 18-20.** All those invited made excuses not to attend the great supper given in their honor. Their excuses were all in vain. One had purchased a parcel of earth, another five yoke (or ten) of oxen, and the third was newly married. These excuse makers represent the Jews, especially the religious leaders, who had spurned the invitation of their Messiah countless times and refused the plea to enter His kingdom. To reject the supper invitation would have been the highest of social insults. The Master of the house said, "Come; for all things are now ready" (verse 17), and they excused themselves. It is not much different today as men still give their "genuine reasons" for rejecting Jesus Christ.

4. **Verses 21-23.** The servant explained to his master the excuses given by all those who had been invited. The master grew angry at the indolence of those for whom he had prepared. They had insulted him and his gracious goodness, offered so freely. He immediately instructed his servant to go out "quickly" everywhere and invite *whosoever will* to come and enjoy his bounty.

5. **Verse 24.** What a terrible benediction! "None of those men which were bidden shall taste of my supper." The Jews, in their wicked rejection of Messiah, found themselves under the judgment of Jehovah and cast away, while Gentiles and strangers accepted His invitation. See footnote l below for more on the Jewish rejection of Messiah. For earlier predictions of the Gentiles coming to Christ and trusting Him as Messiah, Lord, and Savior, refer to Section 55, Matt. 12:18-21, footnotes h and i, and all of Section 74. There is no way this could have been a physical, material kingdom of real bricks, blocks, and stones

taken from Israel and given to Gentile believers in Christ. A further explanation of this is found in Section 153, footnote k. *This* kingdom had to be a spiritual one. However, this fact does not negate the truth of a future, perfect, and glorified rule of Jesus as King over the earth and all mankind, which includes redeemed Israel. For earlier thoughts on this, refer to Section 9, Lk. 1:32-33, footnote g. On the present spiritual kingdom of Christ, see Section 38, second and third paragraphs of footnote o.

(l) *Every* Jew and Pharisee present understood the awful meaning of His parabolic lesson. John the Baptist, Christ, and His preachers had given the invitation to them hundreds of times. They were doomed for rejecting God's Messiah, who was their only hope of salvation. None of them would partake of the supper of eternal life continually offered them by the Savior, for they had excused, blasphemed, and lied themselves out of it. In Prov. 24:20 we are told, "The candle of the wicked shall be put out." In A.D. 70, God put out the candle of the Jewish state and snuffed out the lives of several million Hebrews by the sword of the Roman armies. The most calamitous event in the history of Israel is described in Section 163. The wages of sin will always be eternal death, unless pardoned by the grace of God. The master grew angry at the indolence of those for whom he had prepared the supper of eternal life. They had insulted him and his gracious goodness, offered so freely. He immediately instructed his servant to go out "quickly" everywhere and invite whosoever will to come and enjoy his bounty. This depicts God turning from the lying, stubborn Jews, especially the leaders of religion, who for over three years have trampled the ministry and message of His Son, their Messiah. He now turns to the Gentiles.

2p-Verse 24. Out go the Jews, in come the Gentiles. What a terrible benediction! "None of those men who were bidden shall taste of my supper." In rejecting Messiah, the Jews found themselves under the judgment of Jehovah and cast away, while the hated Gentiles gladly accepted Jesus. Today, almost two-thousand years later, we disfavored Gentiles, whose ancestors dwelt in the darkest dungeons of sin, lift our hearts to God in thanks (Heb. 13:15). We have been accepted in the beloved and redeemed (Col. 1:13-14 and Eph. 1:6). The reaching out of God in Christ, so scorned by most of the religious leaders of Israel, finally turned its appeal of love and offer of forgiveness, to us! Once classified as "strangers, foreigners, aliens, dogs, unclean, and afar off," now, we are heirs of God and joint heirs with Christ (Rom. 8:17). This miracle is because of divine grace that saved us, mercy that spared us, and peace that comforts us in the bliss of eternal life (Titus 1:4). This wonder of total forgiveness calls to mind the ancient story of the man who had committed a capital crime. He was a friend of the king, one of his favorites. During the trial, everything pointed a finger of condemnation in his face. Helpless before such fierce evidence, there was no way to escape death by hanging. Oddly, he stood calm and reposed amid the trial. Friends and foes alike were amazed at his shining demeanor showing no signs of alarm. Did he know something they did not know? As the court official stood to announce the verdict of death, the accused drew a paper from his bosom and handed it to the judge. *It was the king's full pardon!* With that in possession, he had no cause to fear. We too were guilty Gentiles, aliens, and cut off from God. We possess in our hearts the charter of divine pardon. Forgiven, cleansed, and justified forever, we bask in the favor of the King of Kings and Lord of Lords. Our partaking of God's supper of eternal life came through repentance and faith in the gospel of Christ. This brought us forever into the kindness of heaven. Eternal pardon is ours! Once cursed Gentiles, we now have the unspeakable wonder of so great salvation, in which "There is neither Jew nor Greek, there is neither bond nor free, there is neither male nor female: for ye are all one in Christ Jesus" (Gal. 3:28). Contemplating this miracle, we understand the words, "Who shall lay anything to the charge of God's elect? *It is* God that justifieth" (us). (Rom 8:33). Men *truly* in Christ are as secure as God's throne! This great salvation is for both Jews and Gentiles alike, regardless of where they are! *Reader, have you received it?*

3p-For our Lord's *most pungent* statement regarding Gentiles coming into the kingdom of God, taking its leadership, and filling its ranks, to the demise of the unbelieving Jews, see Section 153, Matt. 21:42-45, footnotes m and n. On this occasion, the religious leaders of Israel clearly understood what Jesus was saying and became angry. Section 60 carries the beautiful story of a Gentile army officer who came to Christ as a believer. In this Section, see all in italics under the main heading and the Information Box at the end of the vertical Scripture columns. Was this officer the first Gentile saved in the ministry of our Lord; at least as far as the Scripture record is concerned? To this day, millions of born again Gentiles have swelled the ranks of the church, which is presently the spiritual kingdom of God in Christ. It is written of all Gentile believers, "But now in Christ Jesus ye [Gentiles] who sometimes were far off are made nigh by the blood of Christ" (Eph. 2:13). Earlier in His ministry, the Son of God warned the stubborn Jews, "And I say unto you, That many shall come from the east and west, and shall sit down with Abraham, and Isaac, and Jacob, in the kingdom of heaven. But the children of the kingdom [Jews] shall be cast out into outer darkness: there shall be weeping and gnashing of teeth" (Matt 8:11-12). Some four hundreds year prior, the prophet Malachi foretold of the mass of Gentiles coming to the saving knowledge of Jesus Christ. He wrote of their supreme love for the Name of God, and their great joy in offering special gifts to the Savior. This beautiful passage in Mal. 1:11 has been in the process of fulfillment for two thousand years. Refer to the 2p- above for more on this blessed subject. Every saved Gentile can rejoice that the plan of God for mankind has embraced all of humanity and ultimately all of creation. However, only those who know Jesus Christ as personal Lord and Savior will share in this everlasting bliss. False religions and unsaved men bitterly hate this exclusive truth of Scripture.

Great masses follow the Savior. His terms for discipleship are made clear. Now, all would understand. Three warning parables are given to the multitude of enthusiastic would-be followers of Jesus.

Matt.	Mk.	Lk. 14:25-35—*Galilee*	John
		Discipleship's priority: Christ above all others(a)	
		25 And there went great multitudes(b) with him: and he turned, and said unto them,(c)	
		26 "If any *man* come to me, and hate not his father, and mother, and wife, and children, and brethren, and sisters, yea, and his own life also, he cannot be my disciple.	
		27 "And whosoever doth not bear his cross,(d) and come after me, cannot be my disciple.(e)	
		DISCIPLESHIP EXPLAINED BY THREE LESSONS	
		1. Illustration of the Tower(f)	
		<u>Count the cost</u>	
		28 "For which of you, intending to build a tower, sitteth not down first, and counteth the cost, whether he have *sufficient* to finish *it*?	
		29 "Lest haply, after he hath laid the foundation, and is not able to finish *it*, all that behold *it* begin to mock him,	
		30 "Saying, 'This man began to build, and was not able to finish.'	
		2. Illustration of Going to War(g)	
		<u>Consider the enemy</u>	
		31 "Or what king, going to make war against another king, sitteth not down first, and consulteth whether he be able with ten thousand to meet him that cometh against him with twenty thousand?	
		32 "Or else, while the other is yet a great way off, he sendeth an ambassage, [envoy] and desireth conditions of peace.	
		33 "So likewise, whosoever he be of you that forsaketh not all that he hath, he cannot be my disciple.	
		3. Illustration of Bad Salt(h)	
		<u>Calamity of quitting</u>	
		34 "Salt *is* good: but if the salt have lost his savour, wherewith shall it be seasoned?(i)	
		35 "It is neither fit for the land, nor yet for the dunghill; *but* men cast it out. He that hath ears to hear, let him hear."(j) (Next chap., Lk. 15:1 cont. in Section 129.)	

Footnotes-Commentary

(a) The lessons given by the Lord Jesus in this Section do not speak of *salvation*. Rather, they inform us of *service*, *which* follows the new birth. Those who forsake, build, battle, and sacrifice in hope of eternal life will never find it in human merit, self-discipline, and charitable works. Men are saved from sin and hell through repentance and faith in the atonement of Christ. *Then*, they should request believer's baptism. Afterwards, they stand ready for entrance into God's service if they will accept and heed the terms as laid down in these verses. It must be remembered that when our Lord spoke these words, the church, as it was later and today did not exist.

(b) **The excited crowds.** Thousands followed Christ at this time and for many reasons; most were triflers, not sincerely interested in absolute dedication to the Messiah. (It is not much different today.) How zealous were these masses. It was a mixed multitude, like that gang who followed Moses out of Egypt (Ex. 12:38). As the Lord Jesus drew near to the hour of death, He purposely thinned out these religious loiterers. Here, He exerts another effort to disperse them from His ranks. Only genuine believers could handle and endure what was soon to fall upon Him and them. At this time in our Lord's ministry, He undertakes to warn the multitudes, that in following Him, they must count upon the worst and prepare to fight all the way. For an earlier attempt to drive off the light-hearted crowds some six months prior, see all under main heading of Section 95.

(c) **"Said unto them." "If any *man* come to me."** Again, the Savior calls human responsibility into action. Believers are often commanded to act physically and practically in God's service. Paul told the Corinthians to "quit you like men" (1 Cor. 16:13). There are some things that we are to "quit." This is accomplished by old fashion self discipline. See Section 95, second paragraph of footnote z for more on the believer's practical and moral duties. Turning to the people, Jesus laid down His awesome requirements for *genuine* discipleship. The high theme of this instruction is not deliberate alienation from one's family and friends, but rather what it will cost some to be disciples. They must be willing to wean themselves from the most affectionate of earthly ties, if necessary. The lesson is that nothing; not love for father, mother, wife, and children are to be greater than love and loyalty to Him and His cause. Not even love for one's own life can take precedence above Him. Jesus is preferred above life itself! Christ teaches that to be His disciple, one must (as it were) comparatively hate all else and must love them less than they do Him. This does not teach that the believer is to abandon His earthly *duties* or neglect his filial obligations. Family and friends may hate and forsake him, but he is to love and show sincere care for them, while cherishing the Son of God *supremely* above everything else in life. See first paragraph of footnote f below for more on this.

(d) **"Bear his cross."** The cross was the most infamous object in human thinking and had been for thousands of years. The Romans used it, among other things, to punish "murderers," "robbers," "political rebels," and "state criminals." From time immemorial, death by crucifixion was known. *Tradition* has it that the wife of Nimrod (Noah's great-grandson) invented this fate. The Egyptians, Babylonians, Assyrians, Greeks, and Romans alike employed it. It is woven in the myths and stories of pagan nations, which reflects a deep aversion to this cruelest of all penalties. In the days of Christ, when a man had the horizontal bar (crux or patibulum) of the cross laid over his shoulders, he was nailed to it at the end of the road. For the Savior to employ such a dastardly emblem and associate it with being His disciple, the crowds must have fallen back horror-stricken. A cross was the motif of suffering, pain, dejection, and rejection in the minds of the unconverted world who watched its pitiful victims. In symbolic language, Jesus was telling His thousands of followers: "Those who follow me, this will be your fate as it soon will be mine." This does not mean that every disciple of Christ was *literally crucified,* but it does inform us that all of them followed in the train and trial of their Lord's sorrow and suffering. Terror filled the hearts and faces of the crowds at the mention of the cross. They were thunderstruck at what He said! Had He not made an earlier mention of "cross carrying" in Mk. 8:34? For a mini classic on the cross and its terrible death, see *Crucifixion*, by Martin Hengel. This little book, is packed with rare and ancient documentation, was translated from German in 1977. Sadly, Hengel's book, though filled with invaluable historical information, is totally off on the reason for Jesus' death. This is the fatal hallmark of *unsaved* academic biblical scholarship.

(e) **"Cannot be my disciple."** At this time in Jewish history, there were thousands of teachers with their disciples. Cults, sects, factions, and schisms of religious thinking were in abundance over the land of Israel and pagan nations as well. With a total exclusiveness and absolute self-claim, the Lord Jesus affirms, that unless His conditions are met, not one person can be His disciple! There is no "bridge building" to discuss the differences with His enemies, no ecumenical jargon with the Devil and his imps, and no supporting the lies of the unfruitful workers of darkness. *Do it this way or you cannot be my disciple" proclaims the Savior.* How different from the religious jargon of today, where men throw out the basic and fundamental doctrines of the Christian faith in order to "fellowship" with the enemies of God and Christ. Unlike Satan, who shows the best now but hides the worst from his followers, the Messiah does the opposite. He is "up front" with all who were previously saved and now inquire of admission into His kingdom service. Many did not like what they heard! For the narrowness of Christ's teachings, see Section 175, John 14:6, footnote e, and Section 176, John 15:5, second paragraph of footnote f.

(f) **Verses 28-30. The illustration of the tower**. The Savior warns the danger of striking out in His footsteps without considering the consequences. Millions over the centuries, failing to do this, collapsed by the wayside. Others have continued despite all trials. The famed *Foxes Book of Martyrs* reveals the price thousands have paid in their service of the Lord Jesus. John Foxe (died 1587), being a staunch companion of Calvin, was purposely one sided in his great work. Writing prolifically about the murders committed by the Catholic Church, he failed to mention the barbaric deeds enacted by Calvin and his Reformers at Geneva. This was selective indignation. Historian Douglas F. Kelly also exonerated Calvin and his men of their atrocities. His book, *The Emergence of Liberty in the Modern World,* succinctly covers up their barbaric deeds, murders, and heinous acts. Kelly appeals to the customs and laws of that era as justification for their actions. One muses why these men do not appeal to Scripture and what it says about Christian conduct and the treatment of one's enemies. Innocent blood would not have flowed in Geneva (even a child's head cut off) if they had obeyed God's Word. Since most Calvinists are stuck in the Torah Law, why did those glorious Reformers not obey the plain truth of Ex. 20:13? Did the men who made Geneva "the purist city on earth," ever read Matt. 5:43-48 or Rom. 12:9-21? We read that Calvin was "the greatest exegete" in Christian history. Many of the people killed were martyrs for Christ. Who can number the millions that suffered and died under communism, fascism, paganism, radical Islam, and "Christless religions," not to mention the bloody inquisitions of the Papal Church? These martyrs counted the costs and paid it in full! First, the Lord Jesus warned the crowds of would-be disciples that the price is high and the path difficult if they follow Him. Hebrews

11:1-40 reveals the suffering of thousands for dedication to God. This has been true from the beginning and will continue to the end. See footnote c above. Building a tower of sterling testimony for Jesus requires dedicated, sacrificial labor, and great cost; in some cases, one's life. *It does not include killing your theological opponents as practiced by the Reformers at Genève and the savage Anabaptist at Münster, Germany.*

2p-Oriental teachers laid down rules for their followers and what it would cost those who were admitted. Jesus does the same, but never had such terms as these been heard. To make it clear, the Master illustrated what He had said by three illustrations. Now, the message is that prospective servants in the work of Christ had better decide if they are willing to pay the price of spending their lives in the work of God. The unfinished tower became an emblem of public scorn. In the ancient world, it spoke of a "watchtower" erected amid crops, at the grazing sites of livestock and near cities for security purposes. The welfare of thousands depended on the watchtowers functioning properly. The thing needed most in any community was the thing left unfinished by the thoughtless builder. This part of the gospel is missing in the average church. *Cost counting is unheard of today.* Instead, we hear about "how to be successful," "building a bigger church," "anger management," "weight reduction programs," "marketing the gospel," "God wants you to prosper, be happy," and "enjoy the best life now." This is not the message of the New Testament and the early church. Refer to footnote d above, for more on this thought.

(g) Verses 31–33. The illustration of going to war. Religious phonies. Prov. 20:18 declares, "With good advice make war." Here, the Lord Jesus admonished all who would follow Him to consider seriously the enemy. Every real believer in Christ is, upon conversion, born into a state of war. We are as men and women going into deadly battle and are warned to contemplate seriously the hazards, beforehand. In Eph. 6:10-18 it is explicit as to what we battle against in this life. When saved, the child of God draws his spiritual sword, he must throw the scabbard away! The evils of hell and darkness fall upon us with ten thousand devices while others come with twenty thousand. The ambassage (envoy) of peace that we send is the good gospel news of sins forgiven, redemption through the blood of Calvary's cross, and the empty tomb. No host of evil, regardless of how formidable and fierce they seem, can handle the word truth. Over the past thirty years, a new preaching has risen across America and parts of the world. We are bombarded with the perversion that Christianity is "pie in the sky." Big time TV evangelists live like kings, basking in their millions and bleeding their adherents of every penny possible, keep assuring the suckers that God will make them both healthy and wealthy if they follow Him. *This is not biblical or historical Christianity; it is a lie of the Devil.* Nor does this mean that God's people are to dress like tramps, sleep in shantytown, and eat from the trash can in order to demonstrate their faith in Jesus Christ. A life style of humility and meekness lived in honor is the way of the cross as believers pass through the wars of life. For more on this, see Section 55, second paragraph of footnote d, and Section 58, second paragraph of footnote o for more on these things.

(h) Verses 34–35. The illustration of powerless salt. Jesus warns the fickle crowd of would-be disciples, about becoming apostate from the faith; aliens by the demons of doubt to the great doctrines of God and Scripture. Previously, He affirmed that the members of His kingdom were the "salt of the earth." Men professing to serve God and His people, who gradually come to doubt, slowly change, then outright deny the basic dogmas of the Bible are many. They are in comparison to "salt that has lost its savour." Christ said it is fit to be cast out. He can only be speaking of the removal from the local church body of such scandalous ministers, missionaries, teachers, and false professors of the faith. Leaving men in positions of leadership, who flaunt their heresies and apostasy, will infect others, creating doubt in the inspired Scriptures. Such persons are not fit for the dunghill and will finally be cast out by the supreme Judge Himself. Alas! The calamity of losing confidence in the Scripture, then deserting God's work is unspeakably sad. How miserable are those who abandon Christ for the fading things of this life. Savour gone and hope diminished, they walk in the darkness of a hostile world and sin, rather than the sure light of God's Bible.

(i) The Jews and salt. The Jews spoke and wrote much about salt and its various meanings. It is mentioned in the Talmud four hundred and sixty eight times. "If salt has lost its savour" was a typical Hebrew saying. To the rabbis, salt was a symbol of the incorruptible and higher; they compared it to the human soul and Scripture; it sharpened the intellect and was a symbol of the covenant relationship between God and Israel. See Talmud tractates, Menachoth 20a and Kiddushin 62a, for examples. They affirmed that the world could not exist without salt, and that a disciple of the Torah Law could "lose his savour" if he ever abandoned Scripture. Jesus used various true synagogue sayings in His teaching. Refer to Section 44, Matt. 5:13, footnote q, for details on salt. In this reference, we see another example of the Master repeating the same lessons. He spoke of those who lose power with God and men while in His service. See footnote h above, for explanation on this calamity among believers.

(j) "Salt for the dunghill." The ancients used salt that had "lost its savour" as a deodorant and disinfectant in dunghills. Frequently, it was thrown onto the roads and served as a form of temporary paving. Christ had spoken of salt being cast out, earlier in His Sermon on the Mount (Matt. 5:13). This standard expression was well known to everyone listening to Him speak.

2p-"He that hath ears to hear" was a common saying used by our Lord on various occasions. It was a warning that what had just been spoken had better be heeded. See an earlier mention of this ancient maxim used by the Son of God in Section 74, Matt. 13:17, footnote g.

The Pharisees and scribes complain about Christ's social contacts with sinners. He responds to their murmurings with four parables. These depict the condition of all unsaved men including the religious Jews.

Matt.	Mk.	Lk. 15:1-17—*Galilee*	John
		His audience: sinners and hypocrites	
		1 Then drew near unto him all the publicans and sinners for to hear him. (a)	
		2 And the Pharisees and scribes murmured, saying, "This man receiveth sinners, and eateth with them."(b)	
		ONE PARABLE WITH FOUR PARTS	
		1. A Lost Sheep(c)	
		Insensible sinners	
		3 And he spake this parable unto them, saying,	
		4 "What man of you, having an hundred sheep, if he lose one of them,(d) doth not leave the ninety and nine in the wilderness, and go after that which is lost, until he find it?	
		5 "And when he hath found *it*, he layeth *it* on his shoulders, rejoicing.	
		6 "And when he cometh home, he calleth together *his* friends and neighbours, saying unto them, 'Rejoice with me; for I have found my sheep which was lost.'	
		7 "I say unto you, that likewise joy shall be in heaven over one sinner that repenteth, more than over ninety and nine just persons, which need no repentance."	
		2. A Lost Coin(e)	
		Senseless sinners	
		8 "Either what woman having ten pieces of silver, [Greek coin or ten day's wages at .16 cents each] if she lose one piece, doth not light a candle, and sweep the house, and seek diligently till she find *it*?	
		9 "And when she hath found *it*, she calleth *her* friends and *her* neighbours together, saying, 'Rejoice with me; for I have found the piece which I had lost.'	
		10 "Likewise, I say unto you, there is joy in the presence of the angels of God over one sinner that repenteth."	
		3. A Lost Younger Son(f)	
		Sensible sinners	
		11 And he said, "A certain man had two sons:	
		12 "And the younger of them said to *his* father, 'Father, give me the portion of goods that falleth *to me*. And he divided unto them *his* living.'	
		13 "And not many days after the younger son gathered all together, and took his journey into a far country, and there wasted his substance with riotous living.	
		14 "And when he had spent all, there arose a mighty famine in that land; and he began to be in want.	
		15 "And he went and joined himself to a citizen of that country; and he sent him into his fields to feed swine.	
		16 "And he would fain have filled his belly with the husks that the swine did eat: and no man gave unto him.	
		17 "And when he came to himself, he said, 'How many hired servants	

Matt.	Mk.	Lk. 15:17-32—*Galilee*	John
		of my father's have bread enough and to spare, and I perish with hunger! **18** 'I will arise and go to my father, and will say unto him, "Father, I have sinned against heaven, and before thee, **19** And am no more worthy to be called thy son: make me as one of thy hired servants."' **20** "And he arose, and came to his father. But when he was yet a great way off, his father saw him, and had compassion, and ran, and fell on his neck, and kissed him. **21** "And the son said unto him, 'Father, I have sinned against heaven, and in thy sight, and am no more worthy to be called thy son.' **22** "But the father said to his servants, 'Bring forth the best robe, and put *it* on him; and put a ring on his hand, and shoes on *his* feet: **23** 'And bring hither the fatted calf, and kill *it*; and let us eat, and be merry: **24** 'For this my son was dead, and is alive again; he was lost, and is found.' And they began to be merry. ***4. A Lost Elder Son***[g] <u>Sanctimonious sinners</u> **25** "Now his elder son was in the field: and as he came and drew nigh to the house, he heard musick and dancing. **26** "And he called one of the servants, and asked what these things meant. **27** "And he said unto him, 'Thy brother is come; and thy father hath killed the fatted calf, because he hath received him safe and sound.' **28** "And he was angry, and would not go in: therefore came his father out, and intreated him. **29** "And he answering said to *his* father, 'Lo, these many years do I serve thee, neither transgressed I at any time thy commandment: and yet thou never gavest me a kid, that I might make merry with my friends: **30** 'But as soon as this thy son was come, which hath devoured thy living with harlots, thou hast killed for him the fatted calf.' ***The father's response*** **31** "And he said unto him, 'Son, thou art ever with me, and all that I have is thine. **32** 'It was meet that we should make merry, and be glad: for this thy brother was dead, and is alive again; and was lost, and is found.'"[h] (Next chap., Lk. 16:1 cont. in Section 130.)	

Footnotes-Commentary

[a] **Jesus "receiveth sinners."** Another glorious statement, yet so contrary to the religion of the Jews. He who came to call sinners to repentance now has them flocking to Him. For an explanation of publicans and sinners, see Section 50, Matt. 9:10, and all of footnote d. The word "sinners" as used here and in Matt 9:10, denotes the *worst* of human society: criminals, prostitutes, thieves, and those considered of the lowest moral and social reputation. See footnote b below, for the wicked attitude of the Jewish religionists towards these people.

[b] Anyone not of the Jewish religion was considered a social and moral outcast. No dignified scribe, Pharisee, or pious Jew would have been caught dead in the company of such people. *Nevertheless, how different was their Messiah.* We have seen the Lord Jesus reaching out to the publican Matthew, and associating, during a great supper, with hundreds of derelict sinners in Section 50, Matt. 9:9-10. In Section 64, Lk. 7:37-39, He receives and forgives a notoriously evil woman. Later, in Section 144, Lk. 19:5, He entered the house of Zacchaeus, the chief publican at

Jericho, and brought salvation to all dwelling there. Why did the sinless, perfect Son of God continually mingle with the scum of society and befriend them? See Luke 19:10 for the wonderful answer. Where, in the church today, are Christians who would dare to emulate this example? They would be "called on the carpet," reprimanded and even threatened with dis-fellowship for "compromising with the world and sin." O how far we have drifted from the example of our Lord! How close we are to becoming a new generation of scribes, Pharisees, and hypocrites, while continually reassuring ourselves that we are the greatest defenders on earth of the Bible and truth! How urgent is the need for a return to the example set by the Savior in seeking those who are lost.

2p-On the other hand, behind the walls of "the church" and occupying professorial chairs in religious institutions of learning, we have discovered the awful presence of another band of Philistines. The January 10, 1994, issue of *Time* carried a shocking article about the Jesus Seminar, where a hundred "authorities" spent six years of study to identify the sayings of Christ in the four gospels that were authentic! The results? These "learned" infidels decided that only 18% of the more than seven hundreds sayings of Jesus were authentic. John's gospel faired the worst; they rejected all of it except one passage, John 4:4. What a contrasting contradiction! The "fighting fundies," who keep God's work afloat, sit at one end of the church stage loudly tooting their horns. While on the other side are the unsaved, liberal, Christ denying critics, who continually busy themselves subverting the very foundation of the Christian faith. There is the ancient story of a man lost in the blistering howling desert. Suddenly, he looked up, and there stood an old man before him. He cried, "Please, help me; where is the path?" Solemnly, the aged man replied, "I am the path, if you will, follow me to safety and home." It is the same today. Jesus remains the "path." Those who follow Him conclude their journey in heaven.

(c) Verses 3-32. Christ responds to the *true* charge the Pharisees and scribes had just laid upon Him. He gives one parable with four parts. Each one revealed the various conditions of lost sinners and the means whereby He was reaching them for Himself. *He was the friend of sinners, and amazingly, they knew it!* The Pharisees are included under the fourth part called "the sanctimonious sinners" (verse 25). The relative value of the lost items increases in each parable: one out of one hundred, one out of ten, and lastly, one out of two. *Jesus Christ is infinitely concerned in the ones, more so than the masses.* A brief explanation of the four parts of this parable is given below. Christ affirmed that the sheep and coin *both* represented lost sinners who had been found (verses 7 and 10). We proceed from that premise and note several lessons in each of His four parabolic illustrations. No attempt has been made to super spiritualize any of them.

(d) Verses 4-7. First: The Parable of the Lost Sheep or the **"Insensible sinner."** The Jews were fond of the numeric ninety and nine and used it to contrast gain and loss of various things. A rabbi would say, "Ninety and nine died in battle but one was saved." The Talmud carries this numerical expression in Pesachim 25a, and Baba Metzia 107b. It also speaks of "a lost sheep" as one who is not in the fold of Israel. This is recorded in tractates, Sanhedrin 109b and Makkoth 24d. Christ was using their language to reach them, and He pictured the Jews, who rejected Him, as lost sheep not in His fold. We also learn from this lesson that sheep do not *always* represent those who are saved, as seen in Isa. 53:6. He had spoken earlier about sheep in the Parable of the Good Shepherd in Section 122. Mark had compared the people to helpless sheep in Section 93, Mk. 6:34, footnote f. This lost sheep points to the "insensible sinner." "Insensible" speaks of a situation into which one is plunged, but does not know how to get out. This sheep was lost, knew it was lost, but did not know how to be found. The sheep was "insensible" (did not know) how to be saved from its perilous plight. Churches are filled with this type of people, especially the liberal assemblies where God's Word is toned to please the crowds. Thousands in attendance at these death-pits have heard just enough of the gospel to understand their lost condition. However, they are "insensible" over it (or like the sheep), do not know *how* to be found or saved! *This is the sheep sinner.* He depended on the faithfulness of the shepherd to seek his whereabouts and rescue him from sure death.

2p-Rejoicing. What a marvelous statement! Can it possibly be true that the Lord Jesus is saddened by those who wander astray and rejoices over those who return? This thought overwhelms us upon serious contemplation. We can understand a shepherd filled with joy that his lost animal has been found, or an anxious mother when her lost child is brought to the door. However, that the heart of Christ swelled with joy when He found us and bore us home, seems too amazing to be true! The prophet of old wrote, "The LORD thy God in the midst of thee *is* mighty; he will save, he will rejoice over thee with joy; he will rest in his love, he will joy over thee with singing" (Zeph. 3:17). O, how precious we are to Jesus! Would to God that He was so precious to us! As the saved animal was laid on the shepherd's shoulders and taken into the security of the fold, so the saved of all ages are thus secured. Christ was here presenting Himself (and those who serve in His kingdom) as seekers of helpless, insensible souls. In our Lord's first parable, His appeal was to those amid His congregations, who were lost and knew it, but did not know what to do about it.

3p-Verse 7. "Need no repentance" was also a common Jewish term. It referred to a believing Hebrew, who was pious in the Law of Moses and working ever so diligent to keep the tradition of the elders. Messiah selected this common rabbinical term to picture all those who had already believed in Him as Messiah. Regarding salvation before He had yet died on the cross, see Section 144, footnote i. Those who teach that *God given repentance* (which must be exercised) is not necessary for salvation are in serious error. *Repentance from sin and faith in the Lord Jesus Christ brings eternal life, and it is a one-time event.* In a short time, Messiah would give the message of Lazarus and the rich man. It was not by accident that the rich man, screaming in the pits of the damned pled for someone to warn his five brothers that they must repent of their sins or land in hell with him. Refer to Section 131, Lk. 16:30-31, and number 7 under footnote f for this terrible story.

4p-Verse 10 is a revelation of unique insight into the other world. Our Lord said that there is rejoicing *in heaven* over each lost person who repents and trusts Him. This reveals some sort of divine and mystic contact between those now with Christ and those who remain on earth! From heaven's side, they somehow share in our experiences of Christian service, but as it were through the eyes of God (1 Cor. 4:9 with Heb. 12:1).

5p-"Joy in the presence of angels." The youth of today consider it odd that elderly saints should publicly rejoice over lost souls being saved. How strange and even frightening to most in the church when someone lifts their voice in praises to God because a soul has been rescued from eternal hell! The same church members scream their lungs sore at the ball game on Friday night, but to bless the Lord of heaven for saving a loved one from eternal damnation is often frowned upon. Christ did not agree with these people. Two thousand years ago another missionary named Paul wrote, "Rejoice in the Lord always: and again I say, Rejoice" (Phil. 4:4). Refer to Section 114, Lk. 10:20, footnote e, for joy over believers' names written in the book of life. Most Christians rejoice more over the cat coming home than their neighbor being saved. The *inward* joy of knowing Christ as personal Lord and Savior is the second fruit of the Holy Spirit produced in the life of a believer (Gal. 5:22). So many churches today have grumpy Christians, who have been slowly soured over the years. Their pursuit for the fleeting things of this life have left them in old age, frustrated, miserable, and mean. Deceived by respectable little sins, they dread life and fear death. I once heard an old black preacher say, "All dim sour pusses will have a hard time in heaven."

(e) Verses 8-10. Second: The Parable of the Lost Coin or the **"Senseless sinner."** The ten silver pieces were probably the woman's dowry, usually worn across the forehead. Each coin or piece of silver was considered a day's wage. It pictured something like the engagement ring of today and was paid to the girl's father by her suitor. To lose one of these coins was a major calamity of which the loser bore the guilt. In this coin, a second kind of unsaved person is reflected. The lost coin was round in shape, bore the image of a man, and was dropped into helpless oblivion due to the blunder of a woman. *It became lost through a fall.* We may see in this fall the results of Mother Eve's willful transgression. Here, we meet the "senseless sinner." Being unable to think or reason, this coin would have remained lost, ultimately perish and its usefulness gone forever. What a picture of the pagan world, walking in darkness, minds blinded by the Devil, advancing into everlasting damnation without Christ the Savior. However, another side of the woman is introduced into this calamitous scene; she becomes burdened for that which is lost, lights a lamp, procures a broom, and turns the house upside down until her coin is found. Nothing can stop her pursuit for the lost! Could we see here a reflection of the *true* local church, born from Christ, the ultimate seed of Eve, with her *faithful* members daily on the hunt for lost souls? Her missionaries, worldwide, relentlessly pursue unsaved men until they are found. For her rejoicing, see the fourth paragraph of footnote d above.

2p-The "Theater of Absurdity." The curtain is raised; two men stand center stage. With this, the Theatre of Absurdity is open. One actor is a Calvinistic imbued missionary, going to distant foreign lands to "help God bring in His elect!" The other, poisoned by the dogma of Arminianism, preaches a redemption that depends on human works, an *unenlightened* human-will, and a human personal decision. Both sincerely play their parts. One diligently searches for the elect that will be saved regardless. The other offers his converts a gospel on crutches. It redeems men but cannot keep them redeemed. They must work hard to keep their salvation valid. Neither of these reflects the woman in footnote e above. She shines the gospel light of hope and deliverance into every dark place, seeking for the lost coin. When found, it is secured and greatly treasured. Those who understood the value of the lost coin shared in the wonderful experience. Great joy erupted in heaven over the rescue of that silver piece. Few today know the blessedness of bringing men to Christ. However, not all missionaries and Christian workers are performing in the "Theater of Absurdity." Millions are not. For other comments, see Section 1, Part 3, third paragraph of footnote i.

(f) Verses 11-24. Third: The Parable of the Lost Younger Son or the **"Sensible sinner."** It falls strange on the western mind to read of the youngest son requesting his inheritance before the father's death. However, it has been an immemorial custom in the East for sons to demand and receive their portion of the inheritance during their father's lifetime. According to the Torah Law, a Jewish father was not free to leave his property and goods as he liked. The elder son must get two-thirds and the younger one-third (Deut. 21:17). With secret motives, the youth takes his fortune and leaves the care of home. His destination was "a far country." Who could count the millions that have trodden the highway to this distant land? Many, upon achieving great academic status, fame, wealth, and notoriety, believe they no longer need God or His dear Son. "Things" become their security and confidence, even "superior learning" has sent millions to the "far country" from where they never return.

2p-Verses 15–16. "To feed swine." A Jew reduced to feeding swine! The oral law called a curse upon those who bred swine, according to Baba Kama 82b. Shame, contempt, and death are wedded to sin. The degradation it brings upon men is unspeakable. This silly youth had been demoralized and debauched by his willful and stubborn choice of wickedness and sin's sweet pleasures.

3p-"Husks" has reference to a bean pod called "carob" which grew in abundance in the Middle East. It was eaten by people and used for stock food during times of great famine and dire shortage. William M. Thomson, in his timeless work, *The Land and The Book*, pages 21-22, wrote of this food the following; "The husks . . . are fleshy pods somewhat like those of the locust tree, from six to ten inches long and one inch broad, lined inside with gelatinous substance, not wholly unpleasant to the taste when thoroughly ripe." He continues by writing that in neighboring countries "The pods are ground up, and a species of molasses expressed, which is much used in making certain kinds of sweet food." Thomson concludes that "Today [the mid 1800s] in the land of Israel it is often called 'John the Baptist food' from the tradition that he ate it." The "citizens" of sin's "far country" are varied and numerous. They entice all to join their dark ranks. Having deserted the best in his father's house, he is now reduced to starvation by the wretchedness of his wrong choice. Swine are his companions for "no man" would give him relief. The old adage "Out of money out of friends," is seen here. Satan is *finally* a ruthless taskmaster over those foolish enough to follow him.

4p-Verses 17–19. "Came to himself." The ancients used this term for a man who was deranged but suddenly regained his right mind. The suggestion is that during his folly of sin he was under a form of madness, mentally ill, even like a wild man. See *Vincent's Word Studies of the New Testament*, vol. 1, pages 387-388, for this fitting explanation. Here, we see the work of repentance, bringing one back into their right frame of mind. God, in mercy, sends into our lives many storms in an attempt to bring us "to ourselves," to repent of sin, to bring us out of our spiritual insanity. As the prodigal son rethinks life, he slowly changes his mind. Now, he is becoming sensible. Remembering the bounty of his father, the happy state even of the lowly servants back home, he is saddened. In his heart, he prepares a beautiful confession of sin. The words are ready in his mouth as he turns his feet homeward. It remains ever true that "Godly sorrow worketh repentance to salvation" (2 Cor. 7:10). For the Pharisees' false and perverted understanding of repentance, see Section 50, Matt. 9:13, footnote h; and Section 72, Lk. 13:5, footnote f.

5p-Verses 20–24. "A great way off." Did not God see us lost in sin, even before the foundation of the world? Did He not come down in the Person of Christ to this earth, wrapped in human flesh, to meet weary sinners in the highway of their failure and ruin? He embraces and receives in love and forgiveness all who come to Him in repentance and faith. Receiving the boy with kisses of love, upon hearing his confession, the father ordered a robe to cover his nakedness, a ring to signify his restoration into the family, and shoes to separate him from the world.

6p-Verse 21. His confession. This is worthy of special attention, and his confession must be noted. A genuine penitent feels and knows that his sins were committed *first* against God and *second* against his fellow men. (See David's confession in Ps. 51:4.) Jews were wont to refer continually to "heaven" as though it were God, which is noted in his self-confession of verse 18. *Not once in the entire text did the father bring up the son's sins, for when God forgives, He remembers no more* (Heb. 8:12). All blessings and new honors bestowed upon the weary lad were made efficacious by the shedding of blood of the fatted calf (verse 27), which was sacrificed at the father's command. Atonement was provided by the grace of the father, and the wayward son instantly came into its beneficence. Formerly, the young fellow had been a dead living man, now he was changed into a living dead man: dead to his sins by the pardon of the loving father. The old farmhouse rocked with joy as praises rang out to God that the son was saved, safe, and sure. He, despite a long voyage into that dark, far country, finally became a "sensible sinner." *The person, who considers his ill situation, turns from his sinful folly, and goes to the Father is the sensible one. God be forever praised that many of us have gone this way!* I once read the comments of Abraham Lincoln regarding how he would treat the southerners who had caused the terrible Civil War, resulting in the death of hundreds of thousands. He quipped, "I will treat them as if they had never been away." Similarly, this was the attitude of the father toward his son. Saving grace treats repenting, trusting sinners, as if they had never been away.

(g) Verses 25–32. Fourth: The Parable of the Lost Older Son or the **"Sanctimonious sinner."** Here, we behold the rotten attitude and conduct of the scribes and Pharisees. Yonder in the field, completing his duties, the elder son was walking to the house. Suddenly, a joyful commotion of music and dancing erupts from the home place (verses 25-26). Men dancing with men and women with women were common among the Jews (Ex. 15:20; Judges 11:34; 2 Sam. 6:14; and Ps. 30:11). See Section 92, second paragraph of footnote i, for more on ancient dancing. It had no resemblance to the sex-crazed dancing orgies of today, where many of the participants become inflamed, commit deeds, and say words that should not be put on paper. Upon news that the younger son had returned, the real character of the older son was exposed. If "good men" become angry over sinners being converted, they are "good-for-nothing men." There was something evil and satanic in his attitude. When "Christians" *angrily* refuse to share in the glory of others being saved, and even oppose it, they may well be aliens to the new birth themselves.

2p-The joy we first know when we come to Christ is normally greater than what we experience afterwards, but the *cause* of the joy remains the same. In times of great revival and spiritual awakening, it is sure that our hopes and expectations are higher for God and men than in the ordinary seasons. These fluctuations of feeling do not signal weakness, but normality. We must never allow the foul spirit of envy to sow in our hearts the seeds of jealously over the bounties that God has bestowed upon others; even sinners who have come home and who shine with such fresh joy and hope. Surely, He has given us more than we deserve. If it were not for His grace, our place in hell would be greatly enlarged. Over fifty years ago, the author remembers an "old deacon" who became publicly angry when a bone-weary, aged mother wept aloud at the conversion of her rebel son in a Sunday night meeting. Later, this same "deacon" (who had continually created *serious* problems in that church for many decades) fell, face down into a deep puddle of muddy water: unable to get up, he choked to death. Whether these verses applied to this situation or not I do not know. It is true that chickens do come home to roost (Num. 32:23), and we do reap what we have sown (Gal. 6:7). Therefore, *now* is the time to nest the right eggs and sow the good seed.

3p-Verse 28. The father, hearing of his elder son's anger, goes out and pleads with him to come in and rejoice over his brother, who has returned home. Filled with madness, he refused; yet at the same time he pled his good deeds and self-righteousness (verse 29). A jealous spirit is embedded in his sinister words, "thou never gavest me a kid, that I might make merry with my friends." Had he not also received his part of the inheritance along with his brother (verse 12)? How did he know his brother had associated with harlots (verse 30)? Good men of high morals flee interests in such base things. Pointing out his obedience as a sure mark of personal goodness, he disobeyed his father's invitation to enter the house and share in the return of his brother. *What a portrait of all religious hypocrites, and how descriptive of the scribes and Pharisees is this parable of the sanctimonious sinner.*

4p-Verses 31-32. The father's pleading to his hypocritical older son concludes this Section. How appropriate that our Lord would remind us of this: may the life of each believer who reads this line end like that of the old father. He stepped from the pages of sacred history begging for the lost to be found and the dead to be made alive again. If men could but understand that one sinner saved, especially that dear family member, does make it "meet" that God's Name be praised for the grace of everlasting life and forgiveness bestowed. The final book of the Bible reveals that the eternal hymn of heaven's saints will be praises to the Lamb for redemption through His precious blood (Rev. 5:9-14). Surely, rehearsal in this life would enhance the blessedness of that life which is to come.

(h) "Was lost, and is found." What sweet sentiments of hope our Lord used to conclude His message given first to the religious leaders of Israel. Undoubtedly, this word struck a dart of conviction into the hearts of the Pharisees and scribes who had criticized His association with sinners (verses 1-2). In this lesson, He revealed *their* spiritual condition before God, "lost." See footnotes b, and c above, for more on the "holier than thou" attitude of these men who were the religious masters for the Hebrew people. Only lost things can be found and found things are not lost. The Holy Spirit, blended with the Word of God, enlighten a man's mind into understanding his doom and need for Jesus Christ. This is not accomplished by great oratory or the contrivances of men, but by grace as it finds the lost and brings them to the Savior. God's people are normally the channels through which this works,

2p-Early America, lost and then found. By the mid 1700s, Colonial America was sinking into deep sin. The small witness of *true* Christianity was diminishing. Students at Yale and Harvard were busy with their worldly-wise philosophy and experimenting with self-moral religion. "Sin" was becoming a sinful word! Only the rude and rustic spoke of such things, and that was done in a quiet corner. Meanwhile, the murderous deeds of the Puritan leaders in Salem Village had sent a chill across Colonial America and frightened many who were looking to religion for answers. Refer to their horrific acts and the dark condition of early America in Section 155, fifth, sixth, and seventh paragraphs of footnote g, and Section 203, sixth paragraph of footnote d. Into this vacuum, God sent men anointed of the Holy Spirit to name sin, describe its calamities, wages, and cure. Jonathan Edwards (died 1758) was a Congregational minister of Calvinistic persuasions. He roared forth with powerful preaching, and thousands were saved. Edwards demanded a personal conversion to Jesus Christ that radically changed a man's life. Contrary to traditional Calvinism, He did not linger for the elect to appear; he went after them! His sermon, *Sinners in the Hands of an Angry God,* smote men to the floor, clinging to support posts, and crying to God for mercy. George Whitefield (died 1770), a Methodist clergyman, shared in the early awakening. His Calvinism was less cold and orthodox. He gladly worked with the Arminians, John, and Charles Wesley in England, where many were saved. Whitefield's powerful preaching, like that of Edwards, was also prominent in the early American awakening. The organized clergy and the "learned academics" fiercely opposed these acts of God. Their objection, "it was too emotional" continues to this day. As common folk came to Christ by the thousands over the colonies, the *radical wing* of the Puritans found themselves losing control of the ordinary people. As normal, Satan appeared amid the revival. James Davenport, a Congregational minister and self-appointed inquisitor, traveled across the colonies examining the gospel ministers. If they did not meet his radical standards or refused his request for an interview, they were renounced as being "unconverted." During a book burning, he pulled off his trousers, threw them into the fire and demanded believers destroy their worldly goods! He died suddenly in 1757. Out of these revivals, Colonial America slowly grew into the greatest nation in human history. Now, two hundred years later, she languishes again for spiritual awakening. Only by returning to God's Word and repentance from sin will this occur. Though absolutely necessary for organized, lawful society, politics, and human government cannot help. Only a few find the straight gate and narrow way that leads to heaven (Matt. 7:13-14). This is because men love darkness rather than light (John 3:19-21). For more on these things, see Section 155, fifth paragraph of footnote g.

Jesus gives a lesson on financial responsibility* in His new kingdom. The Parable of the Unjust Steward. The Pharisees hearing it are offended and mock Him because they were thieves. He responds to their ridicule and rebukes their sins of self-righteousness, and seeking the praise of men, rather than that of God. He also warns them regarding the sin of adultery.

*For a later lesson on the same subject relative to the new spiritual kingdom of Christ and His coming again, see Section 145, number 1, under footnote d. In the final months of His ministry, the Lord Jesus spoke often to His disciples on being financially responsible. He was preparing them for correct future service.

Matt.	Mk.	Lk. 16:1-11—Galilee	John
		Parable: the accused steward must give account	
		1 And he said also unto his disciples,[a] "There was a certain rich man, which had a steward;[b] [administrator] and the same was accused unto him that he had wasted his [master's] goods.	
		2 "And he called him, and said unto him, 'How is it that I hear this of thee? give an account of thy stewardship; for thou mayest be no longer steward.'[c] (administrator)	
		The steward's cunning plan	
		3 "Then the steward [administrator] said within himself, 'What shall I do? for my lord taketh away from me the stewardship: I cannot dig; [physically unable?] to beg I am ashamed.[d]	
		4 'I am resolved what to do,[e] that, when I am put out of the stewardship, [that] they [my master's debtors] may receive me into their houses.'	
		5 "So he called every one of his lord's debtors *unto him*, and said unto the first, 'How much owest thou unto my lord?'	
		6 "And he said, 'An hundred measures of oil.' [About nine hundred gallons.] And he said unto him, 'Take thy bill, [statement of debt] and sit down quickly, and write fifty.' (About five hundred and fifty gallons.)	
		7 "Then said he to another, 'And how much owest thou?' And he said, An hundred measures of wheat.' [About nine hundred bushels] And he said unto him, 'Take thy bill, [statement of debt] and write fourscore.' (About eight hundred bushels.)	
		The steward commended: sinners financially wiser than saints	
		8 [Jesus said] "And the lord [or rich man of verse 1] commended[f] the unjust steward, [administrator] because he had done wisely: for the children of this world are in their generation wiser than the children of light.[g]	
		Be true to others and responsible in all financial dealings	
		9 "And I [Jesus] say unto you, Make to yourselves friends of [those believers who have] the mammon [money] of unrighteousness;[h] that, when ye fail, [or have financial ruin] they [your friends] may receive you into everlasting habitations. (or will give you lifelong shelter like the steward in verse 4)	
		10 "He that is faithful in that which is least is faithful also in much: and he that is unjust in the least is unjust also in much.[i]	
		11 "If therefore ye have not been faithful in the unrighteous mammon, [handling money, possessions and wealth] who will commit to your trust the true *riches?* (Which are more than and all earthly gain.)	

595

Matt.	Mk.	Lk. 16:12-18—Galilee	John
		The warning question: divided loyalties unacceptable	
		12 "And if ye have not been faithful in that which is another man's, [handling his goods and money] who shall give you that which is your own?[j] (the true riches of life)	
		13 "No servant can serve two masters: for either he will hate the one, and love the other; or else he will hold to the one, and despise the other. Ye cannot serve God and mammon."[k] (money or anything on which you trust or rely apart from God)	
		The Pharisees ridicule Jesus: His response	
		14 And the Pharisees also, who were covetous, heard all these things: and they derided him.[l]	
		15 And he said unto them, [Pharisees] "Ye are they which justify yourselves before men; but[m] God knoweth your hearts: for that which is highly esteemed among men is abomination in the sight of God.	
		16 "The law and the prophets *were* until John:[n] since that time the kingdom of God is preached, and every man [who believes in Me] presseth[o] [fights his way out of the Jewish religious traditions] into it. (the kingdom)	
		17 "And it is easier for heaven and earth to pass, than one tittle of the law to fail.[p]	
		He rebukes the Pharisees for adulterous remarriages	
		18 "Whosoever putteth away his wife, and marrieth another, committeth adultery: and whosoever marrieth her that is put away from *her* husband committeth adultery."[q] (Verse 19 cont. in Section 131.)	

Footnotes-Commentary

[a] **"There was."** Here is a positive statement of historical fact. Refer to Section 131, footnote a, for the same words being used again by the Savior. Though called a parable, it was built upon people and real life experiences. Here, the Lord Jesus was teaching His disciples from literal illustrations the invaluable lesson that faithfulness to men in earthly affairs would prove them worthy of trust by God and honest fellow men. He then shifts His teaching from the four parables in previous Section 129, to this instruction dealing with financial matters among His children and the unsaved of this world. Not only was this parable directed to His followers but also, as seen in verse 14, to the Pharisees, who were money lovers and economic swindlers of notoriety. They "heard" the entire lesson and were instantly offended because they were guilty. The sort of parabolic reasoning Jesus used here was common to the Jews and well understood. The western mind, being grossly unfamiliar with eastern social customs and manners, struggles greatly with these things and often creates bizarre interpretations, which result in even worse applications.

[b] **"Steward"** in this verse was normally not a slave, but one employed for the administration of the rich man's business affairs and superintended all of his domestic and business concerns. He was the highest authority and comparable in his work to Eliezer, over the house of Abraham (Gen. 24:2) and to Joseph, who was over the house of Potiphar (Gen. 39:4). However, as reflected in Lk. 16:2 above, his lord who hired him could at any time dismiss him.

[c] Someone had accused the administrator-steward of squandering his master's goods. Thus, he was called before his lord and commanded to give an account. Then, he was ordered to reappear before his master later with a financial report showing the condition of the estate over which he had exercised authority. At this second meeting, he was given the opportunity to prove his innocence of the charges laid against him. Through clever conniving and manipulating, he exonerated himself of all charges, as seen in footnotes e and f below.

[d] **Verses 3-4. "He said within himself."** Some men trapped in their sins reason in dark secrecy for a way to escape the inevitable consequences. Note with this that an old proverb comes to fore, "What evil webs our minds conceive, when once we began to deceive." This steward began to scheme and connive in his heart as to how he might be saved from losing his job, income, home, and earthly securities. His fate was to become a digger in the soil, a tramp, or street beggar after dismissal from his work. He cringed at the thought of such degradation and shame for one who had held such power and position in his lord's estate. His "soft and easy" life had rendered him unfit for manual labor!

(e) Deciding that he will not dig in the fields or beg in the streets, he conceives a plan. Through this, he will have provisions and shelter against the time of destitution that seems inevitable, due to his pending job loss. His plan was clearly dishonest but promptly undertaken. His dishonesty is not applauded by our Savior, but rather his ability to "think, plan, and work" his way out of pending financial disaster. Hundreds of tenants worked for his lord. Each one had signed notes stating how much they were indebted to their master, and these written notes were in the keeping of the troubled steward. (Edersheim discusses the various forms of writing materials, inks, and contracts in *Life and Times of Jesus the Messiah*, pages 662-664.) The unjust steward takes these contracts and visits each of his lord's tenants. He said, "take thy bill," (verse 6) and then he instructs each of them to alter or change the wording and thereby state that they have received much smaller amounts from harvest than was actually the case! Because of this fraudulent maneuver, each tenant would be much *less* in the rich man's debt than they actually were. Because of this reduction in his or her original credit, each tenant felt a strong sense of loyalty to the wily steward. He believed that because of this plan, they would later help him if he were dismissed from his lord's service. From them, he would receive food, shelter, and the necessities of life. This is the meaning, of "they [the tenants] may receive me into their houses" in verse 4.

2p-Verses 5-6. The first worker owed a hundred measures of oil (about nine hundred gallons) and altered his contract to read fifty (about five hundred and fifty gallons). He paid it on the spot.

3p-Verse 7. The second, had contracted to provide a hundred measures of wheat, (about nine hundred bushels) and likewise, altered his note. Now, he owed only fourscore (about eight hundred bushels). He too paid it instantly to the steward. Going over the entire estate, he collected tons of goods and put them into the proper storehouses. Such visible bounty would prove he was not a "waster" of his lord's goods; however, it was crooked from the start. It should be noticed that the cunning head steward told the first tenant whom he approached to "sit down quickly and write fifty" as though he were fearful of detection (verse 6). The whole affair was a clandestine operation. Both the head steward and all tenants were collaborators together in swindling their master. He was ignorant of the plot, and it worked beautifully!

(f) Verse 8. The unjust man commended. When the accused steward stood to give an account, he requested his master to check the storehouses, grain bins, wine cellars, and every facility for containing the fruits of the earth. The lord was stunned at the report! Amazed, he commended the steward for "doing wisely." The abundance in the lord's stores disproved charges previously laid against him. The "doing wisely" has reference to his years of service as the head steward over the master's goods, and not the secret plot connived between him and the tenants. He was reinstated and had thus secured both his work and home. *Jesus is not commending the unjust steward for dishonest business practice. Rather, He carefully disentangles the steward's dishonesty from his foresight and ability to think ahead. Then, He informs His disciples that in the unsaved world, men usually exercise more prudence and planning, especially in financial matters, than do the children of God!* Footnote g below bears this out.

(g) Financial responsibility and Christian duties. The "children of this world" (who are unsaved) have more monetary wisdom and foresight, and can better manage money than the average Christian! The meaning of Christ's discourse here was to teach us regarding the correct "use of [the things of] this world," not the "abuse" or "misuse" of them. In this case, it was money. We are to manage earthly possessions in this life with exactness and long-range discretion. Our wisdom in such matters is to exceed that of the unjust steward mentioned in this parable and that of the best financial wizards of the unsaved world. See footnote i below. *Sadly, this is not being done very well in many churches and religious institutions.* Numerous congregations across America have appointed "superintendents," to see that things are done right. These men and women are usually exact and pedant in attending to church affairs. However, this is not the pressing issue in most true local assemblies. Far better, the need for Spirit filled leadership, where godly men and women see to it that first, the right things are done. Then, other affairs may be properly attended to. Right things are done in churches by obeying God's Word and divine common sense. Christian assemblies seem to have too many chiefs and not enough Indians. Years ago, in Toowoomba, Queensland, Australia, the author attended a series of meetings. At the conclusion of the Sunday night service, an appeal was given for those in need to come forward for prayer and counseling. How disturbing to see a young girl about sixteen years old, "counseling" an old white-headed man, bent over by time and work. Later, I asked the pastor about this. He responded that they had no men to do counseling, and that this young girl had been to Bible school! Fleas cannot tell lions what to do! A curious but relevant verse warns, "Let not him that girdeth on *his harness* boast himself as he that putteth it off" (1 Kings 20:11). Youth is not to be despised (1 Tim. 4:12), but the divine order is for the older to teach the younger (Titus 2:4). Are too many of us looking in the wrong as Moses did? It is written, "And he looked this way and that way, and when he saw that *there was* no man, he slew the Egyptian, and hid him in the sand" (Ex. 2:12). This occurred before his forty years in the wilderness tending his father-in-law's sheep. In hastiness, so many of us have committed those awful deeds because we did not first look up! *Christian responsibility is sorely missing!*

(h) "The mammon [riches] of unrighteousness." This was an ancient description for the goods of this world. For Jesus' earlier comments on "mammon" during the Sermon on the Mount, see Section 46, Matt. 6:24, footnote l. Material goods will never bring peace of mind, but they may be employed to bring comfort to weary bodies and blessing to those in need about us. Thus, we should make ourselves "friends of the mammon [money] of unrighteousness" by using it for the glory of God and the salvation of lost souls. In addition, like the unjust steward was received back into his master's care, and given life-long shelter, so believers at the end of their earthly tenure will be received into the *everlasting habitation* of God's wonderful heaven. This will not be because of our wise deeds, but by His grace. Our astuteness in handling money is a bonus that reflects our love and devotion to the Lord, who saved and called us into His service.

(i) What beautiful truth from the heart of our Lord. Christians, who have genuine principles of fidelity and upright character, make it a diligent work to attend carefully to the smallest things in life and Christian service. They keep their word, fulfill their commitments, answer their mail, return their phone calls, refrain from slander and gossip, love their enemies, pay their bills, and consciously look upon the small things as worthy of the same attention as the greater ones. See footnote g above.

(j) **Verses 11-12** are a summary of the parable just given. In conclusion, Christ said to His disciples and us today "If you are not faithful in life's little things, if you do not employ your earthly goods to bless men and glorify God, do not think that He will commit to you the true riches of life and service." Even the things which are "your own" (that can be used in His service) God will not give to you. How apt the words "Confidence in an unfaithful man in the time of trouble *is like* a broken tooth, and a foot out of joint" (Prov. 25:19). See Prov. 22:4 for divine instructions regarding true riches.

(k) Christ said this exact thing to His disciples almost three years prior during His Sermon on the Mount. See Section 46, Matt. 6:24. It is explained in this footnote that mammon was also an idol god of wealth worshiped by pagan Gentiles. This is another example of Jesus using repetition for the perpetuation of sorely needed truth. Again, our Lord admonished His disciples-apostles to make money their servant, and never let it become their master. The first major problem to rise in the early church had to do with Satan's lie about money to a husband and wife, and the apostles who handled it were the ones who had heard Christ bring these warning messages several years prior (Acts 5:1-11).

(l) **"The Pharisees also . . . heard all these things."** This is not a "disconnected remark" placed into Luke's text long after it was written by some "unknown Christian writer." Rather, it is a natural part of the conversation flow in progress. Luke wrote that the Pharisees also listened to the parable just given. Christ's message on financial honesty struck their hearts like a dart from heaven! They saw themselves and their covetousness mirrored in the chicanery of the unjust steward. Conviction smote them; their only resort was to "deride" or "turn up their noses" at the Son of God. The teaching He had just given showed their greed and love for money; they were furious at such public exposure. Refer to Section 159, Mk. 12:40, footnotes j and k, for the Pharisees *stealing* from the poor widows of Israel! Note the second paragraph of footnote q below. for more on this thought about the Pharisees listening to His message.

(m) **God knows the heart.** Highlighted because here, He seemingly paraphrased a favorite rabbinical passage from their Old Testament (1 Sam. 16:7) which spoke of God looking at man's heart. See also Jer. 17:9. Christ had earlier described the heart condition of the religious leaders of Israel in Section 96, Matt. 15:7-11. In response to their scorn, the Messiah replied by explaining their inward corruption and wickedness. The scribes, Pharisees, and their companions worked day and night to appear righteous before men. Their daily lives proved they had tried to reconcile mammon with God or money with the Master. As mentioned above in footnote l, later, the Savior charged them with stealing from Hebrew widows. These hypocrites sought justification *before men* by giving long prayers, wearing special robes, gowns, and receiving praises in the streets and markets. True justification, however, was found only in the Man they had just derided and scorned, Jesus of Nazareth, the Messiah. Their *outward* antics of piety, which men lauded and praised, were looked upon by God as an abomination. The word used here for abomination is the one used in the Old Testament to describe the worship of idols and devils by the Jews. Again, the Pharisees were horrified at the boldness of Jesus. They had a taproot heart problem caused by sin. Knowing the rottenness of their own hearts, they were shaken at Messiah's Words.

(n) **"The law and the prophets *were* until John."** Here, the Lord Jesus speaks of the end of something (the law and the prophets), and the beginning of something else (the new kingdom of God or the church). Knowing that the Pharisees (who were deriding Him) took refuge in their Torah Law, oral traditions, and prophets, and boasted of knowing them better than anyone in Israel, Jesus makes an abrupt announcement. Those parts of Moses' Law and the predictions of the prophets that pointed to Christ and His new kingdom, He was fulfilling.

2p-With the appearing of John the Baptist, a new spiritual kingdom of God was presented to the nation of Israel with Jesus as their Savior-Messiah. This was the supreme distinction and glorious difference. A new dispensation had dawned upon Adam's fallen race and it would embrace all men of all times. Soon, a new covenant would be established that did not evaluate men on how well they kept the oral law, the commands of Moses, the Hagiographa, or other Jewish holy writings. This new covenant is explained in Section 95, second paragraph of footnote u. Since John appeared on the banks of Jordan, better things were preached. Israel's old material kingdom, of sticks and stones, with a carnal human Messiah ruling the world was a bad dream that should be given up. See

Section 39 footnotes a and g for details on the kingdom. When John appeared, preaching the new kingdom and its true Messiah, things gradually started changing for Israel. Jesus was not saying that the Torah and prophets would be a part, of or an addition to His kingdom or church, and that the saved would live under these. Rather, He declared that they were valid "until" John began his ministry of presenting the Messiah. It took the Jewish converts of the first century some seven decades to understand this truth. Some Messianic Jews today still do not comprehend what their Messiah was affirming in this passage and work at living under the Torah and even (selected) portions of the oral law of their ancient fathers. See Section 45, footnote b for a discussion of this issue.

(o) **"Every man"** was an expression for "many men" in a specific predicament. It was in common use among the Jews. The people understood what Jesus was saying in using this term.

2p-**"Presseth."** The Words of our Lord "every man presseth into it," meant every Jewish person who repented of his sins, false religious traditions, and trusted Him as the Messiah, had become a part of His new kingdom. However, for every Hebrew, this was done at serious risk as it threw them into direct opposition to the leaders of Israel's religion. The word "presseth" means to "force entrance by great difficulty." The lesson is that any Jew, turning from the religion of the scribes and Pharisees, forsaking the oral law with its thousands of impossible demands, had to fight his way out of these burdensome requirements that strangled the conscience and blinded reasoning. Those who did so were saved by the grace of God. This *same struggle* was mentioned earlier in Section 126, Lk. 13:24, footnote c, under the word "strive." Their struggle to be free from the law and the thousands of killing oral traditions did not save them, but was the prerequisite (like repentance) to their salvation. It is about the same today, especially for an Orthodox Jew, to accept Jesus of Nazareth as Messiah and Savior. They pay a great price to be saved and often become the object of fierce persecution by members of the unsaved Jewish community. For a documentary on the history of various Hebrews who have been saved and the persecution they suffered from their fellow Jews, refer to Section 146, footnote o.

(p) As if to clinch His Words spoken in verse 16, the Lord Jesus says here, "The possibility of the law's predictions pointing to Me not be fulfilled is the same as the ability of heaven and earth to vanish from their places in the creation. You Pharisees, rest assured that *what* your law and the prophets have said of me, and my kingdom is slowly coming to pass before your eyes and ears, and you have rejected it." For a similar statement given earlier by Christ during the Sermon on the Mount, see Section 45, Matt. 5:18. These men made an everlasting fuss over keeping the Torah Law, yet they were blind to its grand and major theme, Jesus of Nazareth, the Savior and Messiah of Israel and all who will believe. Jews who receive Jesus of Nazareth as Messiah and Savior often pay a great price and become the object of fierce persecution by members of the unsaved Hebrew community. For a documentary on the history of various Hebrews who have been saved and the persecution they suffered from their fellow Jews, refer to Section 146, footnote o.

(q) **"Whosoever"** in the context had *first* reference to the all of the Pharisees, as seen in verse 14, and then a *second* reference to everyone. This is not an isolated saying or "interpolation," added later to Luke's work by some unknown editor as infidel theologians teach. See footnote l above, for more on this thought. Divorce and remarriage for just about any reason imaginable was rife among the Jews at this time, and the religious leaders of the School of Hillel were ringleaders. Most Pharisees subscribed to this school. For Jewish policy on this subject and other information, see Section 12, footnote a. Christ added these words to warn the Jews, and especially the religious leadership, that in His spiritual Kingdom, their sexual sins, and financial thievery would have no part.

2p-Israel was an adultery-ridden nation at this time in history. See Section 21, Part 1, second paragraph of footnote b, and Section 67, first paragraph under footnote b, for an explanation of their horrific sins. In this verbal effort to warn them of the consequence of their adulteries, Christ immediately commenced to give to them the story of a wealthy Hebrew, who died and went to hell. (What an appropriate discourse for the lying, thieving, adulterous Pharisees.) The obvious message was that they, like the rich man, were living life as he did and were traveling to the same destination that led to eternal damnation. One questions if this man of wealth had also been a Pharisee and a serial adulterer as many of them were. See Section 131 for Christ's stinging message on a rich man and a beggar: both of whom died and woke up in eternity. In Lk. 16:14, it is clear that the Pharisees heard His message. In relation to this, see footnote l above.

Lazarus and the rich man. This message has its basis in the previous Section 130 where he gave the Parable of the Unjust Steward. The Pharisees instantly derided the Savior being stung by conviction over their sins. He declares that their affluence and wealth will not rescue their souls from hell's eternal damnation, as it did not save the rich man. Further, that beggars whom they despised so greatly would be in heaven before them. All humanity is instructed in the lives of the two persons in this discourse. Lastly, Abraham warns men to hear God's Word above all things.

Matt.	Mk.	Lk. 16:19-31—Galilee	John
		Two men who represented all men	
		19 "There was[a] a certain rich man, which was clothed in purple and fine linen, and fared sumptuously every day:	
		20 "And there was a certain beggar named Lazarus, which was laid at his gate, full of sores,[b]	
		21 "And desiring to be fed with the crumbs which fell from the rich man's table: moreover the dogs came and licked his sores.	
		Death called both of them into eternity	
		22 "And it came to pass, that the beggar died,[c] and was carried by the angels into Abraham's bosom: the rich man also died, and was buried;	
		23 "And in hell[d] he lift up his eyes, being in torments, and seeth Abraham afar off, and Lazarus in his bosom.[e]	
		24 "And he cried and said, 'Father Abraham, have mercy on me, and send Lazarus, that he may dip the tip of his finger in water, and cool my tongue; for I am tormented in this flame.'	
		25 "But Abraham said,[f] 'Son, remember that thou in thy lifetime receivedst thy good things, and likewise Lazarus evil things: but now he is comforted, and thou art tormented.	
		The witness from hell: "Don't come to this place"	
		26 'And beside all this, between us and you there is a great gulf fixed: so that they which would pass from hence to you cannot; neither can they pass to us, that *would come* from thence.'	
		27 "Then he said, 'I pray thee therefore, father, that thou wouldest send him to my father's house:	
		28 'For I have five brethren; that he may testify unto them, lest they also come into this place of torment.'	
		The witness from Scripture: "Repent and believe God's Word"	
		29 "Abraham saith unto him, 'They have Moses and the prophets; let them hear them.'	
		30 "And he said, 'Nay, father Abraham: but if one went unto them from the dead, they will repent.'	
		31 "And he said unto him, 'If they hear not Moses and the prophets,[g] neither will they be persuaded, though one rose from the dead.' " (Next chap., Lk. 17:1 cont. in Section 132.)	

Footnotes-Commentary

(a) **Fact or fable?** Over the ages, men have wrangled about the historical validity of the discourse recorded here. This harmony commentary accepts it as literal history. Jesus began with the affirmative words, "There was," which is a statement of fact. These are the same words He used in Section 130, Lk. 16:1. Cults, disavowing the reality of a conscious hell where men suffer for unforgiven sins, have tried every trick in the catalogue of exegetical perversion to circumvent these words. Nor is this another example of the critics so-called "detached sayings of Christ." The characters in this lesson really lived just as those did in His previous message. In this story, the Lord

Jesus tells the Pharisees of real human events on earth, then lifts the curtain and offers them a quick glimpse into eternity. This is *not* given as a myth, fable or word pictures from which His audience was supposed to find bits and pieces of truth. The lesson previously given regarding the unjust steward was put into a parabolic format but came from real human events. In Scripture, some parables were stories *created* by the speaker to carry spiritual, moral, or practical meanings. Other parables were built from *real happenings* that had literally occurred in history. See Section 73 and all of footnote d for more information on parables

2p-The lesson given here of two men who lived and died is from a real life experience. All the prattle about the Lord Jesus borrowing this message from rabbinical parables means nothing. The fact remains that what He taught in this story was historical reality. It is true that the rabbis had all sorts of fables, and myths about sheol and the afterlife, but the Savior was not citing a fairy tale from rabbinical mythology. He spoke a terrible truth in this message. The Jews went so far that they even debated about how many angels it took to carry the righteous to Abraham's bosom! Edersheim wrote of these extremities in *Life and Times of Jesus the Messiah*, vol. ii, pages 279-281, then 1962 edition. First, the Savior's message was designed for the religious hypocrites and pretenders of Israel's religion. It was a dreaded warning about their fate for rejecting the Messiah and for not believing what their Scriptures said of Him. For confirmation that the Jewish Old Testament spoke of Christ, see Section 52, John 5:45-47, footnotes y and z. Secondly, this message briefly warns all men about life after death and eternity without Christ.

(b) "Lazarus." Personal names were never used in the parables that were invented by the speakers. In this message, the Savior gives two names (Lazarus in verse 20, and Abraham in verse 22), affirming that these events were genuine history. Note the following:

1. **Verse 19.** This introduces us to a wealthy, powerful Jewish man who had actually lived. His quality of dress and excellence of food were standard facts used by the Hebrews to single out and describe men of wealth and fame. Purple robes were expensive, and usually worn only by kings, nobles and princes or men of the highest position. The costly dye was obtained from the murex shell netted with great pains off the coasts of Greece Tyre, and surrounding areas (Acts 16:14). Fine linen was produced from flax grown mostly in Egypt. Slaves referred to it as "woven air." It was light, soft, and gorgeous to the eye. "Feasting every day" with friends and acquaintances was a standard procedure for the rich and famous. This was the life-style sought after by most of the religious leaders of the nation.

2. **Verse 20.** With this, the Savior gave a startling opposite! The religious elite of Israel despised beggars, who gathered at Jerusalem, especially about the temple, yet oddly, they counted it great merit to contribute to them. This curious paradox of despising yet supporting was based on a Talmud line, which speaks of Messiah sitting and binding up His wounds amid the poor and sick at the gate of Rome. See Sanhedrin tractate 98b. The Jewish merit of acquiring God's "divine presence" is promised to those who give to beggars in tractate, Baba Bathra 10a. Lazarus the beggar was crippled, full of loathsome sores, and helpless. Others "laid" ("carelessly dropped") him at the rich man's gate where he pleaded for sustenance. The picture of "dogs licking sores" is sickening to the western mind, yet this is still practiced among some of the primitive people of pagan lands. Their reasoning is that the "saliva of the dog has great healing properties" and should be procured if possible.

(c) They both died. All life must "come to pass" for at each day's end, death is another day closer. The arrest of the grim reaper is final, without bail, parole, or intermediacy. No suffering, be it ever so great, lasts forever, except in hell, and finally the lake of fire.

2p-At the decease of Lazarus' human frame, the real man inside moved out. See footnote e below for the place where his soul went. It was called Abraham's bosom. Chaperoned by holy angels, his soul (the real person) was escorted from earth's misery into a peaceful eternity. *They did not carry his dead body!* On earth, his body was borne by the unfriendly to a grave; in death, holy angels took his soul. The ancient Hebrews held that angels carried the souls of the righteous into God's company. See many lines on this in *Gill's Commentary*, vol. 7, pages 661-663, and the second paragraph of footnote a above. Our Savior affirmed this as truth in these words. Regarding the soul (sometimes called spirit) departing from the human frame at death, see the irrefutable evidence in Gen. 35:17-18; Job 27:8; 1 Kings 17:17-22; Lk. 12:20; and James 2:26.

(d) "And in hell." Many unsaved men (especially the cults) hate these truths and work day and night to explain them away. For explanation of hell, see Section 103, number 8, under footnote g. Jesus meant just what He said in this dreadful comment. The rich man's burial was mentioned due to the pomp attached to the funerals of the wealthy and famous. The Pharisees understood this perfectly as they considered prosperity as one of the marks of a good man worthy of paradise after death. Hence, no word of the beggar's Last Rites because he had none. Genuine religion teaches the doctrine of future retribution. Savages in far-flung places of earth have a conscience, which warns them, something terrible lies ahead; prepare! Demons pleaded not to be sent to this place in Section 88, Mk. 5:7, footnote c. God is to be properly feared, for beyond the destruction of the human frame, He can *eternally* destroy the spiritual soul. Vain are the dreams of the men of this world who hold that the only punishment for their sins falls upon them in this life. The fierceness of divine anger over sin not appeased and forgiven, finite intelligence cannot conceive. Those billions who have died unsaved and joined the infernal society of the damned, know the full wrath of God upon sin not atoned for by the blood of Christ. Heretics, like Rob Bell, pastor of the Mars Hill Bible Church, Grand Rapids, Michigan, write their books "proving there is no hell." False cults, antichrist sects, and demonic worldly philosophy fiercely oppose Bible truth. They work hard to explain away the Scripture teaching of hell's torments and heaven's joy.

2p-Heathen mythology and "Christian pagans." Cults write about annihilation and the unconscious state of soul sleep. Pagan mythology reeks with thousands of distortions of hell. Heathen literature with its re-coloring of hell and fabrications of gods and goddesses is embedded in the secular and religious conscience of western society. The dark teachings of heathenism, the glib usage of the words "hell" and "damn," becoming an accepted part of English vernacular change nothing. Amid all this, Hollywood continually pours its poison into the pot. Mentally deranged "clergymen," like the "Very Reverend" Jeffrey John, of St Albans in England, said on BBC radio, "The crucifixion of Christ makes God look like a psychopath," only affirm the reality of this hell and their front seat reservations. "Intellectual Christians," such as the late C. S. Lewis, who defended evolution, denied the resurrection, called Genesis a myth, rejected the depravity of man, believed in purgatory, confessed his sins to a priest, and prayed for the dead, demonstrate the deceitfulness of sin. The famed, Dr. Martin Lloyde-Jones wrote in *Christianity Today,* December 20, 1963, page 27 these words, "Because C. S. Lewis was essentially a philosopher, his view of salvation was defective in two key respects: (1) Lewis believed and taught that one could reason oneself into Christianity, and (2) he was an opponent of the substitutionary and penal theory of the atonement." The notoriously liberal Baptist, Dr. W. W. Shrader wrote in *Christianity Today*, February 28, 1964, pages 34-35, "C. S. Lewis would never embrace the Fundamentalist (literal-infallible) view of the Bible. He would not accept the theory of 'total depravity of man.' He rejected the 'substitutionary theory' of the Atonement." Years later, *Christianity Today*, December 2005, page 28 carried an article written by Bob Sietana, regarding Lewis' unbelief and dabbling with the occult. Lewis was the religious Elvis Presley of ecumenical evangelicals. These people despise *true* biblical and ecclesiastical separation. They detest one who is saved, knows it, and dares to believe and defend the authority of Holy Scripture. In their thinking, they are "wild fundamentalists." Professor Robert Millet, of Brigham Young University, headquarters of the Mormon cult, highly recommended Lewis' writings because of his "inclusive" approach to faith. In Lewis' book, *Mere Christianity,* pages 62-63, he stated that baptism and the sacraments were a means of finding "the Christ life." This is vicious untruth. Men only find real life by faith in the finished work of God's Son on the cross, and in His resurrection. Martin Luther's opinion of baptism and the sacraments was as foul as that of C. S. Lewis. It is discussed in Section 203, paragraphs three, eight, and nine of footnote d.

3p-Anti-hell advocates parrot the lie that the concept of men going to a place of torment first appeared in Jewish apocrypha literature in the years just before the birth of Christ. Cult adherents and fools in general bombard the internet with their blasphemies about Bible translations that do not teach eternal torment, and then attack the *Authorized Version* because it teaches the doctrine of eternal retribution. Of these people it is written, "the way of the wicked *is* as darkness: they know not at what they stumble" (Prov. 4:19).

4p-Cults and false religions propagate the untruth of annihilation. Because the Italian, Alighieri Dante (died 1321) partly misrepresented Bible truths about hell in his *Divine Comedy*, hardly means the place does not exist! Because the Roman Catholic Church was given the myth of purgatory by Saint Augustine, does not negate the Scriptural doctrine of hell. Because the Greek god Hades, or the Roman god Pluto were invented by darkened heathen minds does not invalidate hell's reality, it rather confirms it. *Paul did not blend mythology into his letters.* There are hundreds of heathen gods that mirror their creator the Devil, who is represented as the custodian of hell and "lord of the underworld." In pagan art, the god Hades is pictured carrying a two-prong fork with which he torments the damned. Hence, the source in comics and advertising that depict him carrying a pitchfork. A classic distortion of hell is also found in Norse mythology where a goddess named "Hel" rules over the dead, not in tormenting flames, but in awful unbearable cold. Ancient pagans mimed even the biblical heaven as they wrote of their "peaceful Elysian fields" over a river into which some would enter after physical death. The Hebrew word "sheol," in Ps. 16:10, and the Greek "hades" in Acts 2:27 are both translated by the world hell. This is a correct translation for both speak of the same infernal place. For explanation of the *two-fold division* of sheol-hades, see Section 103, number 8, under footnote g.

5p-Those who postulate that Christ died to save men from annihilation or everlasting unconsciousness accuse Him of robbing humanity of one of its greatest obligations: *nothing for which to answer for when life is over.* Jesus shed His blood to redeem men from sin and its eternal wages of conscious endless death in the lake of fire (Rom. 6:23; Matt. 25:41; Rev. 20:10; and 20:15). Into a real hell, the soul of the *former* rich Jew stepped as he entered eternity and the abode of the damned. To no purpose can it be called "everlasting destruction" (2 Thess. 1:9) if the subjects cease to consciously exist. The objection that literal fire totally burns things up, therefore, no one could survive hell, is refuted by the burning bush (Ex. 3:1-3), and Shadrach, Meshach and Abednego (Dan. 3:19-26). Neither the bush nor the three Hebrew children were *consumed* in flames. As sure as the bliss of heaven is eternal, so are the torments of the damned. Otherwise, we have an eschatological off balance; a one-sided eternity with saints blessed forever while sinners have vanished into nothingness. The duration of the damned is endless. It is not ash piles or dust heaps, but unspeakable reality such as were never known or experienced during life's short journey. The Son of God said, "These shall go away into everlasting punishment: but the righteous into life eternal" (Matt. 25:46). The rich man who screamed from hell over two thousands years ago screams from the same hell now. For a powerful exposition on this awful subject, see *Manual of Theology and Church Order*, pages 363-375, by J. L. Dagg, printed in 1857. Concerning the subject of salvation under the Old Testament, see Section 10, footnote b, with Section 144, footnote i.

(e) **"Abraham's bosom"** was an expression among the Jews and pointed to eternal rest found only in the presence of Jehovah. The idea was derived from the practice of reclining near a loved one during mealtime. Note this is illustrated in Section 172, John 13:23, with Section 205, John 21:20. In the verses above, it was used by the Savior to represent or depict the happiness of heaven under the figure of a great feast at which the guests recline on couches so that the head of the second person lay on the bosom (shoulder) of the first. This posture was the *highest* emblem of intimate fellowship among the ancients. The rabbis taught that Abraham was in God's paradise; and therefore, all who died in good grace with the law and tradition of the elders would go to rest in His bosom. Later, in Hebrew eschatology, Jewish teachers distorted the doctrine of hell into impossible myths, and esoteric experiences.

2p-Regarding the angels in this story, Scripture teaches that angels are sent to minister to the "heirs of salvation" (Heb. 1:14). They minister to us through life (Ps. 34:7), death (Lk. 16:22 with Jude 9), and share with us in eternity (Rev. 5:11).

3p-**Verse 24. His plea for mercy.** Is there water in eternity or was this a desperate plea? Being a thorough Jew, he addressed Abraham by the common Hebrew term "Father." The rich man was in hell and said so (verse 23). Who but the king of simpletons would cavil with such fearful words? How could any man today know more about hell than one who is there? No retreat to "the original languages," the multiple distortions of pagan teachings, or any form of "hermeneutics" can undo these words. His soul freed from bodily limitations at death, now in eternity realized, and felt its endless loss. Reposed in Abraham's bosom was the beggar that once lay at the rich man's gate back on earth. It is noted that Jesus said nothing about the rich man mistreating the beggar. According to number 2, under footnote b above, he had probably responded to Lazarus' pleas for crumbs from his table while back on earth. Nor was he in hell because of great riches. Rather, he was there for neglecting or rejecting the message of Christ contained in the writings of Moses and the prophets. Note Section 10, footnote b for how people were saved during Old Testament times. With a horrific introduction to hell, this former rich Jew now faced endless eternity in that horrible place. The wicked Pharisees and scribes must have shuttered at these words from Jesus; for at this time, they had perverted their teaching on this subject.

4p-**"I am tormented in this flame." Is this the grave?** What a wail of horror! Woe be those who wrest from this lament of a damned soul, its awful export, and change it into parables or word pictures. "O this speaks of the grave," cultists assure their prospective converts, or "Christ was making reference to the coming destruction of Jerusalem, and the subsequent sufferings of the Jews. Another unbeliever parrots the old lie that, "Jesus spoke here of the hardships of the former life coming to haunt the guilty." Still, another, "It means the pains of a guilt-ridden conscience in this life." Alas! What perverted prattle. This man was in hell, and he said so! Now, he begs for less than a crumb; he screeches for a moistened finger to touch his parched tongue. It strikes one curious that he first complained about the torment of his tongue. Infidels object by inquiring, "Are there fire and water in eternity?" and "Can a soul thirst?" Demonic cults ridicule the dialogue between Abraham and the rich man. They fail to understand that the human soul is more of a reality than the physical body in which it temporarily lives. The soul has eyes, tongue, mind, and feelings. Fire and water in eternity present no problem for God Almighty. Fools who taunt these things will know the truth immediately after death. Regardless of how confused the ancient Jews were on the subject, the Lord Jesus laid it down in plain words on this occasion. For twenty-one things the Bible says about suffering in hell–lake of fire, see Section 103, number 8, under footnote g.

(f) **"Remember thy lifetime." The torment of memory.** Here, the Son of God permits both the Pharisees and all living mankind to hear voices from eternity! Christ, in using the word "hell" speaks of one place separated by a fixed divide or gulf, with a compartment or vast area on each side. Some believe it is located in the heart of the earth according to Section 67, Matt. 12:40 footnote d. In the "rest side" of paradise where the saved of all ages were *until* the resurrection and ascension of Christ. During the three days and nights that Christ's body slept in Joseph's borrowed tomb, the real Person, Jesus Christ descended into the rest side of this abode of disembodied souls of the dead. He announced that perfect atonement had been accomplished. Further, that the saving gospel was now an established reality, that He would gather to Himself the millions of believers in that place and escort them to heaven. See more on this in Acts 2:31-35; Eph. 3:15; 4:7-11; Heb. 12:22-24; and 1 Peter 4:6. The damned of all ages up to that time were confined to the "torment side" where they await the great day Judgment. It was from his place in the "torment side" of sheol-hades that the rich Jew lifted up his eyes. Note several things about the senses and faculties of human souls in hell:

1. **Verse 23.** They know their former acquaintances of earth and persons who lived and died centuries before them. He could "see" Abraham afar off. Though the founder of the Hebrew nation had been dead

some two thousand years, the rich man instantly knew who he was. Everyone will know everybody in eternity. There will be no introductions and hand shakes in heaven or hell!

2. **Verse 24.** They sense, feel, recognize (number 1 above), and have need of comfort. They know what fire is and experience its pain. They remember what water is and how it soothed and satisfied. We learn here that the soul is more real than the human body in which it lived for a while.

3. **Verse 25.** They fully remember their former life on earth with all of its deeds and experiences.

4. **Verse 26.** They want to escape their sufferings but cannot "pass" out of the regions of the damned.

5. **Verses 27-28.** They have clear knowledge of earth's present affairs, know addresses or locations where people are. They beg someone to warn them not to come to their place and share their lasting fate.

6. **Verse 29.** Abraham died about four hundred and thirty years before Moses was born (Gal. 3:17). He also lived long before Israel's most famous prophets. However, in this verse, he knows that Moses, who gave the law, and the prophets all wrote about the coming of Christ the Savior. He knew that men were saved from hell by heeding the message of the Old Testament, which pointed them to the coming Messiah.

7. **Verse 30.** Every soul in hell believes and understands repentance, but too late. This former rich man now knew what his five brothers needed to do, but what he failed to do. He wanted someone to warn them of his dreadful suffering and sin's consequences. Those who scorn the command to repent, play it down, or describe it as "works" have embraced a corrupt theology. All such would do well to heed the plea of a man in hell who knows what it is to be there, and begged that others repent of their sins to avoid it. Regarding Jesus' command for men to repent of their sins, see Section 50, Matt. 9:13, footnote h.

(g) **"Moses and the prophets."** These words come to us from a man on the other side of eternity! It has been shaded in gray because it embraces the Hebrew canon of Holy Scripture. And what was the value of these writings? The Old Testament pointed with hundreds of fingers to the coming Messiah and Savior, Jesus of Nazareth. It foretold His birth, life death, burial, resurrection, and ascension. The entire Torah Law of Israel and the united witness of the prophets, all spoke of Christ the Savior to come. If a man studies the Old Testament and cannot see the shadow of Jesus moving to fulfillment in the New Testament, he has read with his eyes closed. Moses wrote of Jesus and the prophets also gave witness to Him (John 5:46-47 with Acts 10:43). The subject discussed during the transfiguration was "his decease which he should accomplish at Jerusalem (Lk. 9:31). As stated in the paragraph below, in eternity men realize the only hope for salvation is recorded in Scripture because these point to Jesus Christ. *Appendix Three* has dozens of predictions from the Old Testament that came to pass in the life of Christ.

2p-How did Abraham know about Moses and the prophets? Paul tells us in Gal. 3:17 that Moses lived some four hundred and thirty years after Abraham! Yet, here is Abraham speaking, as if he were familiar with the great lawgiver of Israel. He also spoke of the prophets who mostly lived centuries after his death. This reveals that in eternity, men will know all things; past, present and future, but for many it will be too late. Not even the glorious Torah Law existed when Abraham lived. Paul said that it came hundreds of years later. Nevertheless, Abraham knew that one could find salvation in what it taught. And how did he know this? Because in eternity men know all things! For Moses and the prophets writing about Christ, refer to Section 201, Lk. 24:44, footnote l.

3p-Abraham's response to hell's newest beggar is amazing. He dogmatically affirmed that the sacred Scriptures are the *first, foremost, and final* source through which men are saved from eternal damnation. If they will not hear God's Word and believe in salvation's truth it proclaims, then nothing will save them. Not even one released from the city of the damned and allowed to walk again among men would convince the lost. (Only the Old Testament existed at this time, yet its message was sufficient to save men from hell.) No messenger from the dead could ever say what Scripture says. This testimony of Israel's greatest patriarch reveals the absolute sufficiency and perfection of Scripture. Within its inspired writ is contained all that is necessary for life, death, and preparation for eternity. It is both presumptuous and wicked for man to determine divine things any other way. Those who seek after mediums, spirits, signs, birthmarks, necromancy, and so called "Spirit filled preachers," in order to know God's will are peeping into the forbidden realms of darkness. Some of them become burdened from this the rest of their lives! *The closed canon of the Holy Bible is the only divine medium for making God's will known.* Dreams, visions, revelations, word of knowledge, feelings, laying on of hands, and unknown tongues cannot be trusted.

4p-Only a few weeks prior, this statement made by Abraham had proven true. Though Christ raised another man named Lazarus from four days of death, it did not persuade the religious leaders to change their attitude toward Him. The Messiah rejecting scribes, Pharisees, and their friends who witnessed the resurrection of Lazarus went back to Jerusalem and began to plot his death as well as that of Christ. Read the terrible story in Section 146, John 12:10-11. This Messianic miracle of bringing Lazarus back to life further enraged them. At the conclusion of this startling miracle, the same Jews walked off with their hearts hardened into deeper hatred for the Messiah, who came to save them from the hell He had just so fearfully portrayed. Seemingly, our Lord also pointed ahead to the infidelity of the Jews, who refused to believe in His resurrection. Section 132 begins with a shift in the tenor of Messiah's teaching. The Savior suddenly changes His message from the horrors of hell to the need for humility and forgiveness among His followers. Was the story of Lazarus and the rich man another one of those *final warnings* to the religious leaders of Israel regarding their fate, which came in A.D. 70?

Another lesson on offences. The apostles are dumbfounded at what the Savior says about forgiveness. They ask for more faith to understand His teaching. He replies with the Parable of the Faithful Servant.

Matt.	Mk.	Lk. 17:1-10—*Galilee and into Samaria*	John
		A stern warning to the disciples **1** Then said he unto the disciples,[a] "It is impossible but that offences will come: but woe *unto him*, through whom they come![b] **2** "It were better for him that a millstone were hanged about his neck,[c] and he cast into the sea, than that he should offend one of these little ones. *Watch yourselves and be swift to forgive many times* **3** "Take heed to yourselves:[d] **If thy brother trespass against thee, rebuke him; and if he repent, forgive him.** **4** "And if he trespass against thee seven times in a day, and seven times in a day turn again to thee, saying, 'I repent;' thou shalt forgive him."[e] **5** And the apostles said unto the Lord, "Increase our faith."[f] **6** And the Lord said, "If ye had faith as a grain of mustard seed,[g] ye might say unto this sycamine tree,[h] 'Be thou plucked up by the root, and be thou planted in the sea;' and it should obey you. *Parable of the Faithful Servant*[i] **7** "But which of you, having a servant plowing or feeding cattle, will say unto him by and by, when he is come from the field, 'Go and sit down to meat'? **8** "And will not rather say unto him, 'Make ready wherewith I may sup, and gird thyself, and serve me, till I have eaten and drunken; and afterward thou shalt eat and drink?' **9** "Doth he thank that servant because he did the things that were commanded him? I trow [think] not. *After we have done all we can, grace gets the glory* **10** "So likewise ye,[j] when ye shall have done all those things which are commanded you, say, 'We are unprofitable servants: we have done that which was our duty to do.'"[k] (Verse 11 cont. in Section 133.)	

Footnotes-Commentary

[a] Here, we note a change in emphasis as we enter this Section. Jesus is no longer dealing with the hypocrites of Israel. Turning to His "little flock" of disciples, He warns against *wrongly* offending others, be ready to forgive all injuries suffered, and continue in faithfulness to love and serve their Lord. See *rightfully* offending in Section 96, Matt. 15:12, footnote j. A true man of God may find it necessary to give a scathing message to the congregation as Christ had just given the Pharisees in Section 131, and then instantly switch themes to one of love and forgiveness. The two letters of Paul to the Corinthian believers are filled with this approach.

[b] **"It is impossible."** This means that these things will not fail to happen time by time in this life. This dreadful "woe" falls on the guilty offender. We all offend unknowingly and unintentionally. This is not the subject of our Lord in these lines. Christ had earlier used similar language in Section 109, Matt. 18:6. Here, the Savior addresses children, who believed in Him, and the doom coming upon those who "offend" them. In verse 1 above, He did not use the term "little children" but in verse 2 refers to them as "little ones." This seems to signify that He was now addressing these words to His disciples, in particular. The words in Matt. 18:6 were spoken much earlier than those recorded here by Luke. Contextually, "trespass" in verse 3, must be the same as the "offence" in verse 2. He, therefore, was addressing adults under these terms and not innocent children. Obviously He used a different application.

[c] For an explanation of the millstone, refer to Section 109, Matt. 18:6, footnote j.

(d) Highlighted as this is something of a general reference to Lev. 19:17 but, is not framed into an actual Scripture quotation. Still, its roots are in the Old Testament. Rarely are these instructions of Christ followed by any local church. The innocent party is to "rebuke" the guilty. In the average church, this would cause a civil war! Yet, it is God's way for us to release our resentments and not smother them until they smother us. Grace has a better way than the Torah Law. See Paul's instructions for the church regarding such matters in Rom. 12:3-21 with 13:10. Again, Jesus had previously spoken similar things to his disciples.

(e) The Lord of heaven commands instant forgiveness when the offender shows genuine evidence of remorse and repentance. This is seen in the form of verbal apology, sorrow expressed, and often many tears of honest regret. In *some* cases, restoration is necessary as an outward fruit of the inward change (Matt. 18:21-22). For a classical example of true sorrow for many sins and a quick desire to make restitution to those done wrong, see Section 144, Lk. 19:8, footnote h. Every Christian needs a big graveyard where he can bury the faults of himself and those of others with whom he is associated. This does not mean that we wink at sin and think it will be alright.

(f) "Help Lord, that's hard to believe!" The magnitude of Christ's command amazed them all! Being staunch Jews, born and bred under the iron fists of the rabbis and captives to the oral law and traditions of the fathers, the twelve found it extremely difficult to comprehend their Master's Words about "forgiving seven times a day." Never had they heard anything like this. *To understand the depth of their frustration, see Section 110, footnote h, for the shocking rabbinical rule on forgiving offenders.* In view of this rule, which they had been taught and believed, the disciples-apostles spontaneously replied, "Lord, Increase our faith," or they were saying in so many words, "Help Lord, that's hard to believe. We need more faith to understand this, for it is contrary to everything we have been taught about forgiveness."

(g) In response to their request for increased faith (verse 5, footnote f above), the Lord Jesus used a common illustration. He had previously employed the mustard tree and its seed on several different occasions while teaching. The expression "as a grain of mustard seed" was commonly used over the Middle East. The Talmud also speaks of a man sowing mustard seed. This is recorded in tractate, Nazir 56b. See Section 79, Matt. 13:31, footnotes b and d where Christ had first used the expression earlier in His teaching. Afterward, He gave the same illustration again in Section 106, Matt. 17:20 footnote i. He gave it for a third time in Section 125, Lk. 13:18-19. Above in Lk. 17:6 is the last recorded mention of the term as employed by our Savior. In this illustration, the Lord Jesus is responding to the request of the disciples. The design of His teaching was to show his preachers what marvelous things might be done by genuine faith when it is the will of God. He was not instructing them to go into the business of transplanting trees from earth to sea! It is to be remembered that performing miracles was nothing new to any of these men. They had done this many times by the power that Messiah had given them. *The whole lesson is that they needed a super-super natural faith to be able to forgive those who trespass against them "seven times in a single day!"* This kind of forgiveness was unheard of in Israel and it astounded the apostles. See this explained in footnote f above with its relevant references.

(h) "Sycamine." This is not the same as the sycamore tree in Section 144, Lk. 19:4, the second paragraph of footnote d. One could imagine that the Master was actually standing by a sycamine tree when He spoke this. Dr. E. H. Thompson in *The Land and the Book* vol. i, pages 22-24 wrote that this tree was "planted by the wayside, in open spaces and where different paths met." It was as common as sand under one's feet. This marvelous tree bears several crops of small figs each year, and the figs grow on stems shooting from the trunk instead of the branches or twigs. The roots grow so deep that the ancients often said, "Only a miracle can pluck its roots from mother earth." Those who interpret our Lord's injunction (speaking to the tree, and it being transplanted into the sea) as being *literally possible,* and that all believers should exercise this type of faith, have missed the point. It was custom for ancient public speakers to employ an extreme or severe illustration to explain some simple point. This is exactly what Jesus does. Another place where our Lord had employed this form of public oratory is seen in Section 45, Matt. 5:29-30. This type of speaking is illustrated in Section 47, Matt. 7:3-5, footnotes b and c where He spoke of removing the "beam" (plank) and "mote" (speck) from your eye. (No one can have a plank in his or her eye!) All of His disciples-apostles understood the terminology used.

2p-Being grossly unfamiliar with the customs of the ancients, many modern day Christians "try hard" to get faith the size of a tiny mustard seed, so they can uproot the problems in their lives and move them elsewhere. Such endeavors are completely outside the scope of what our Lord said in this statement. This is not a blank check for a Christian to get whatever he wants! Jesus was telling the disciples and the twelve to be faithful *with* the small faith they had at that time. Then, it will, like the mustard plant, which begins ever so tiny, over the years become strong and productive. God may choose to uproot various problems, or He may not. *If not, then believers will need to exercise their faith!* Regardless, the main lesson is to be faithful with your little faith, and it too will grow. For helpful reading on the subject of the use of extreme illustrations and expressions by the ancients, see *Difficult Sayings in the Gospels,* by R. H. Stein, *Exegetical Fallacies,* by D. A, Carson, and *Has the Church Misread the Bible?* by Moises Silva.

(i) **Verses 7-10.** In order that the missionaries of Christ might remain humble amid such wonderful accomplishments and miracles that a small grain of faith might produce, Jesus gave them this parable. It was taken from a real life experience familiar to the Savior. Now, He uses it to teach His apostles that it is one thing to have faith but another to be humbly faithful. Here, the Lord affirms that what we do as believers in His service is normal duty. We cannot make the claim that because we have worked hard and served long, God is thereby committed to show us special favor, and we will be exalted above others. Never! Whatever blessing or reward the saints may receive for their service at the hand of God, still it is reckoned of grace and not of debt (Rom. 4:4).

2p-In this parable, the servant has been plowing all day in the field or feeding his lord's cattle. Upon return to the house, more duties are his; he must wait on his master's table. The lesson: It is proper that Christ our blessed Lord should be served before us! First, He must be given the glory and honor. It is not right that our Lord "thanks us," but rather that we praise Him throughout the ages of eternity. It is impossible that God gets a gain, or He will be benefited by our services; nothing we may do, be it ever so wonderful, will add to His divine excellence and glory. He saved us by grace, and we are his debtors all of life's day, even until the throes of death removes us from this frequently unpleasant scene.

(j) **"So likewise ye."** The Lord Jesus gave this parable to show His disciples that the great motive in kingdom service is not to be first, but is to serve with glad humility because of love and devotion to the Master. The greatest of all rewards is that of loyalty to Jesus. See footnote a above. We are to be tireless servants wanting only the best for our Master and others. For weeks, the twelve apostles had a power struggle among themselves with each one seeking an exalted place in their Lord's kingdom. The parable was designed to show them the right way to serve Him, especially in the hard days that were ahead as leaders in His church. In heaven at last, standing before the ineffable Majesty of the Holy Trinity, all knees will bow and all tongues joyfully confess, "We are unprofitable servants: we have done that which was our duty to do." We learn from these words that doing our total duty gains no credit with God's grace. We are "unprofitable," not in the sense of salvation, justification, adoption, sanctification, and calling, but rather in the sense that in His plan for the ages, He saw fit for us to share in His cause. When we are in His presence, *then* we will understand the depths of His love that sought us, the cost of His blood that bought us, and the patience of His longsuffering that brought us at last, into that glorious place called heaven and home.

(k) After we have fulfilled our duties in the cause of Christ, we are still as "unprofitable servants," for it was His grace that saved, called, and kept us all along the way. Therefore, no human work, deed, or merit will ever make us worthy; this will be the *glad confession* of all believers when standing before God.

Before entering Peraea, Jesus passes through parts of Samaria and Galilee. Nearing a certain village, He meets ten lepers and heals them. A hated Samaritan returns to give thanks to the Savior for his healing.*

The healing of leprosy was strictly a Messianic miracle. See asterisk under main heading of Section 48, for explanation of this truth.

Matt.	Mk.	Lk. 17:11-19—*Samaria and Galilee*	John
		Ten lepers along the road: their instructions 11 And it came to pass, as he went to Jerusalem, that he passed through the midst of Samaria and Galilee.(a) 12 And as he entered into a certain village, there met him ten men that were lepers, which stood afar off:(b) 13 And they lifted up *their* voices, and said, "Jesus, Master, have mercy on us."(c) 14 And when he saw *them*, he said unto them, "Go shew yourselves unto the priests."(d) And it came to pass, that, as they went, they were cleansed. ***The Samaritan banned from*** ***the temple at Jerusalem returns to give thanks*** 15 And one of them, when he saw that he was healed, turned back, and with a loud voice glorified God, 16 And fell down on *his* face at his feet, giving him thanks: and he was a Samaritan.(e) 17 And Jesus answering said, "Were there not ten cleansed? but where *are* the nine? 18 "There are not found that returned to give glory to God, save this stranger."(f) ***The results of faith in the will of God*** 19 And he said unto him, "Arise, go thy way: thy faith hath made thee whole."(g) (Verse 20 cont. in Section 134.)	

Footnotes-Commentary

(a) On His way to Jerusalem to die on the cross, the Savior passed through "the midst" (middle) of these places. We have only the briefest record of all the wonderful things that occurred during this trip.

(b) When lepers entered the temple to report to the priests, they could only stand before the Nicanor gate at the western end of the Women's Court but could go no further. Even then, all present would quickly move a great way from the infected person, lest they become unclean. Before the victim walked into the temple area a crier would call out, "A leper is entering to stand before the priest." As they did with the synagogue, wherever a leper set foot within the limited area of God's house, it was purged and made clean by one of the officiating priests. For details on this terrible disease, see Section 48, number 1 at asterisk under main heading, and comments in footnote a.

(c) **"Jesus, Master, have mercy on us."** Amazingly, they knew Him at sight! News had spread over the land and into every leper camp about Jesus of Nazareth purporting to be the Messiah and His healing of lepers. Lifting their voices and pleading in pitiful tones, they cried out to Him for "mercy." Here was sure hope of being healed from this debilitating, killing malady. See footnote f below.

(d) Christ did not call on them to believe in Him for healing as on previous occasions, but instructed them to go to the priests and show their infected bodies. (This demonstrates they were Jews, all except one.) He knew faith was swelling in their hearts, for they were later blessed for this in verse 19. On an earlier occasion, we noted that our Lord actually touched the rotting flesh of another leper; a thing strictly forbidden by the Jews. See this amazing event in Section 48, Matt. 8:3, footnote c. When he "touched" the leper in Matt. 8:3, he was "immediately" healed. Healing a leper was an exclusive miracle that only Israel's Messiah could perform. It must be noted that He did *not* touch these ten men. Instead, He spoke a note of instruction, which sounded as sweet music in their ears, "Go shew yourselves to the priests" (verse 14). Normally, it would have been thoroughly ridiculous for a rotting leper to do such a thing. The temple was many miles away, the road was long, these men were deathly ill, and they would not have gotten into the temple anyhow. The gates were carefully guarded for the possibility of something or someone unclean entering the holy site and thus defiling it. See Section 119, John 7:32, footnote m, for details on the temple police. However, despite all the seeming difficulties of Jesus' Words, they believed and obeyed Him instantly.

(e) "He was a Samaritan." We note here that the nine Jewish lepers were no longer ashamed to associate with a cursed Samaritan. Fatal disease and pending death often erase all social or racial distinctions and make the victims seek mutual comfort wherever it can be found, even among former enemies. The healing of these ten men occurred instantly, in the twinkling of an eye! Looking down at their fresh skin, seeing no ulcerated sores, and oozing wounds, they are astounded. Quickly turning on heel, they head south for Jerusalem and the temple. The people standing about observing this must have been astounded. However, one of the lepers was a Samaritan! In John 4:9, the Samaritan woman told Jesus that, "the Jews have no dealings with the Samaritans." Acts 10:28 is explicit that it was "unlawful for Jews" to keep company or come unto one of another nation." He remembered that Samaritans (unless proselytes) were not permitted entrance into the Jewish temple. (See footnote b above for lepers being allowed into the synagogue.) The nine Jews went to the temple of the Lord, while the Samaritan returned and thanked the Lord of the temple. Falling on his knees, bowing many times, and with quivering lips, he praised Jesus that his body was healed of the dreaded disease. See footnote g below.

2p-Lepers healed in Israel and the Torah Law. For further details into this subject, and Jesus' healing of lepers, refer to Section 48, footnote e. It was commonly believed that only the true Messiah of Israel could touch and heal lepers. Jewish Law forbids any Hebrew to have dealings with these people. See footnote b above for leper's being allowed into the synagogues to share in the services.

(f) "Thy faith hath made thee whole." Christ called him a "stranger," meaning He was not a Hebrew or member of the nation of Israel but a Samaritan. Faith itself did not procure his healing, but rather it was the channel through which Messiah performed this fantastic miracle. The Lord Jesus had earlier used this same word about faith. In Section 121, John 9:35-37 we note the Savior healing without faith being required. This was the exception not the rule (Heb. 11:6). The other nine ex-lepers were Jews. Not one of them came to bless *their* Messiah for healing; instead, it was a "stranger" or foreigner, one not of Israel. See footnote e above. It is ironic that this curious paradox happens in the work of God. The nine healed Jews should have been first to thank Christ their Messiah, for He had just saved them from so dreadful a death. Those from whom we expect much are frequently the ones who let us down the hardest.

2p-Repeatedly, we are amazed that the insignificant ones in the Christian community, the least, and the stranger, are continually the ones who get things done for God. Those who have so little are those who often accomplish so much! Where are the learned and mighty men of the church? Where are the esteemed professors with heads whitened by time, whose minds are storehouses of vast learning? Where are those Christians with enormous incomes, who bathe in luxury, who live in palaces of stone? It has always been the little and unimportant saints, filled with pure piety and honest devotion, that get the job done for Jesus. They have no drum to beat, flag to wave or horn to toot. As it was in this parable, so it is today. A half breed Samaritan (hated by the Jews) returns to give thanks and the Jews do not. *Gratitude was a rare entity then as it is now.* God, help us to be thankful Samaritans. We read in Heb. 13:15-16 that thanks and praise are part of the sacrifices to be offered by believers who please the heart of God.

(g) What a benediction and commission the Lord of heaven pronounced upon this stranger now cleansed in the body and saved in soul. The Words of Jesus "thy faith," signal that this man who had stood trembling among his fellow lepers as they called out for healing, was the one who had a faith that was grateful for every blessing. Real faith is adorned in the garment of thankfulness. He had secured total healing through believing in the Son of God. He knew this man was Israel's promised Messiah and Savior and rested his case upon this fact. See Section 144, footnote i, on how people were saved before they understood Christ's death on the cross. The man's wholeness was complete; for both body and soul were well. One cannot but wonder where he went and to whom he told his amazing story.

WHEN WILL THE KINGDOM OF GOD APPEAR?

Christ answers the Pharisees by explaining the spiritual nature of His new kingdom. The signs* that will signal the coming judgment appearing in A.D. 70 at the destruction of Jerusalem. He briefly describes what will soon befall their nation, city, temple, and those Jews, who have rejected Him as Messiah and Savior.

*This discourse is not the same as that in Section 163. There are numerous similarities and differences in the two.

Matt.	Mk.	Lk. 17:20-37—*Samaria and Galilee*	John
		Spiritual location of the kingdom	
		20 And when he was demanded of the Pharisees, when the kingdom of God[a] should come, he answered them and said, "The [true] kingdom of God cometh not with observation:[b]	
		21 " Neither shall they say, 'Lo here!' or, 'Lo there!'[c] for, behold, the kingdom of God is within you."[d]	
		Destruction of Jerusalem in A.D. 70: related signs and events	
		22 And he said unto the disciples, "The days will come, when ye shall desire to see one of the days of the Son of man, and ye shall not see *it*.[e]	
		23 "And they[f] shall say to you, 'See here;' or, 'See there:' go not after *them*, nor follow *them*.	
		24 "For as the lightning, that lighteneth out of the one *part* under heaven, shineth unto the other *part* under heaven; so shall also the Son of man be in his day.[g]	
		25 "But first must he suffer many things, and be rejected of this generation.[h]	
		26 "And as it was in the days of Noe, [Noah] so shall it be also in the days of the Son of man.	
		27 "They did eat, they drank, they married wives, they were given in marriage, until the day that Noe entered into the ark, and the flood came, and destroyed them all.	
		28 "Likewise also as it was in the days of Lot; they did eat, they drank, they bought, they sold, they planted, they builded;	
		29 "But the same day that Lot went out of Sodom it rained fire and brimstone from heaven, and destroyed *them* all.[i]	
		30 "Even thus shall it be in the day when the Son of man is revealed.[j]	
		Great personal calamities will fall	
		31 "In that day, he which shall be upon the housetop, and his stuff in the house, let him not come down to take it away: and he that is in the field, let him likewise not return back.[k]	
		32 "Remember Lot's wife.[l]	
		33 "Whosoever shall seek to save his life shall lose it; and whosoever shall lose his life shall preserve it.[m]	
		34 "I tell you, in that night[n] there shall be two *men* in one bed; the one shall be taken, and the other shall be left.	
		35 "Two *women* shall be grinding together; the one shall be taken, and the other left.	
		36 "Two *men* shall be in the field; the one shall be taken, and the other left."	
		The disciples big question and Jesus' answer	

Matt.	Mk.	Lk. 17: 37—*Samaria and Galilee*	John
		37 And they answered and said unto him, "Where, Lord?"[(o)] And he said unto them, "**Wheresoever the body** *is*, **thither will the eagles**[(p)] **be gathered together.**"[(q)] (Next chap., Lk. 18:1 cont. in Section 135.)	

Footnotes–Commentary

[(a)] Nothing was as dear to the heart of the Pharisees and their followers as the oral law and their long–looked–for kingdom of God that would be established first at Jerusalem. It would be a physical, political reign with great parade and pomp supervised by their glorious Messiah. Therefore, it is easy to see in what sense, they put this question to Messiah; they wanted their human earthly kingdom immediately. It is of interest that they "demanded" an answer. If He was the Messiah, then He could name the exact time when Israel's kingdom would appear and produce miraculous signs to confirm His prediction: hence, their question. It must be remembered that the kingdom Jesus came to establish *at this time*, was not a literal, earthly monarchy. (That would be later.) His kingdom then and now was to be rooted in the souls of born again men all over the world, and across every generation of mankind. It was an inward thing as explained in footnote d below. The teaching that Christ offered Israel their material kingdom, and they rejected it is more eschatological error. They did not hate and reject any kingdom, rather, it was Jesus of Nazareth that they despised. He did not perform, as they believed their coming Messiah would; He had not overthrown the Romans; nor was He was establishing an earthly rule. The leaders of Israel did not understand what He was doing. They were ignorant of the kind of kingdom He was now building.

[(b)] **"Cometh now with observation."** This is an astronomical term, used nowhere else in the New Testament. It means to look physically for something to appear. The Savior in these curious words seeks to correct a tradition believed among the Jews in that day. They held that the more spiritual Hebrews could literally see by careful observation their grand kingdom coming down from the eastern skies. Refer to footnote c below for more on some of their absurd tradition and practices. Dr. Lightfoot in his *Commentary on the New Testament . . .* , vol. 3, page 181 states that there are two senses in which the phrase "kingdom of heaven cometh" is to be understood apart from the carnal political notions of the Pharisees. "In some places it signifies the propagation of the gospels by the Messias [sic] and his followers . . . especially among the Gentiles: in other places, it denotes the Messiah's victory and vengeance upon the Jews, the enemies of the gospel." Jesus was saying that His kingdom was already present and in the very midst of the nation of Israel. Further, it would not be a world reality through the schemes of people like the Pharisees and their traditions, oral laws, chants, and devices. See footnote c below for explanation. Lightfoot wrote that the spiritual side of Christ's kingdom would ultimately be victorious by the following two things:

1. "The promulgation and establishment of the Christian religion." This began with the preaching of John, the appearing of the Lord Jesus and the establishing of His church. For salvation in the Old Testament and during the ministry of Christ before His death on the cross, see Section 144, footnote i. If Lightfoot meant by these words that the gospel would eventually conquer the world, he was wrong!

2. "The total overthrow of the Jewish polity." This has reference to the destruction of the temple and Jerusalem, the abolishing of the Hebrew state and scattering of the Hebrew nation over the face of the earth. It began in A.D. 70 under the Roman General Titus when he destroyed Jerusalem. After this calamity, the saving gospel of Christ leaped forward and has raced around the world many times, bringing salvation and sure forgiveness to all who repent and believe it. It was *after* the destruction of the temple that the new kingdom of God gradually broke from its Jewish, legalistic, and traditional chains.

[(c)] **"Lo here! lo there!"** With these statement, the Messiah responded to their demand by attempting to correct a ritual commonly practiced by the scribes and Pharisees. Pious Jews longing for their literal kingdom to appear would loudly shout, "Lo, here is the kingdom," or "lo, there is the kingdom," and then point at a designated place in the East. It was believed among the rabbis that Messiah would come from this direction, and it was based on Ezek. 43:2. The practice of chanting these incantations in a repetitive manner was employed only at the temple, as the caller would face the east and pray for Israel's kingdom to manifest itself. Our Lord informs the Pharisees that God's kingdom will not suddenly arrive by such auditory antics. In other words, He was saying, "This ritual you are performing is useless. It will not hasten the establishment of God's kingdom." His statement must have (again) rattled these hypocrites, for He sweeps away another of their vain religious ceremonies and pious public efforts to bring a Jewish rule over the world. Their kingdom and His were totally different. A short time later the Savior told the Jews the kingdom had been taken from them and given to the Gentiles. See this in Section 153, footnote k.

[(d)] **"The kingdom is in you."** Christ's affirmation that the "kingdom of God" was *within* men confounded the Pharisees to no end. The only kingdom *in them* was that of the Devil as Christ had previously said in John 8:44. What did Messiah mean by "within" you? The word "entos" in this passage is correctly translated in the *King James Version* as "within." Liddell and Scott's, *A Greek-English Lexicon,* Oxford edition 1940, page 577 render "entos" as meaning "in your hearts." Christ was speaking of a *spiritual kingdom* and its glory dwelling inside all born again believers. Some have *forced* "ethnos" to mean only something material and visible to accommodate a previous eschatological error. *Scofield Reference Bible*, page 1100 states that it was present in "the persons of Christ and His disciples." Neither Jesus nor His disciples *were* the kingdom. He was its King and the disciples its first preachers and representatives. The Jews had rejected all Christ taught on this subject. On every side stood the Romans enforcing their pagan authority, thus demonstrating they were ruling the land. And the Jews were their servants.

2p-The rebuilt temple myth. Dwight Pentecost in his book *The Words & Works of Jesus Christ,* page 349 wrote, "The kingdom "within you" literally means "in your midst," or "among." Then, he informs his readers that Jesus was telling the Jews that their "kingdom was possible and was being offered because the King [Jesus} was present." (What would have happened to the cross, and atonement had the Jews suddenly accepted this so-called kingdom offer?) Jesus was actually saying, "The kingdom of God, which is My kingdom or church, is already here; you cannot see it with the mortal eye for it is spiritual and establishes itself within the human heart (or soul) of all who believe in Me." Our Lord's kingdom is not the myth as propounded by postmillennial and amillennial eschatology, nor is it the carnal and ridiculous reign as portrayed by various overheated Baptists. Their fables about the ancient Jewish priesthood being reinstated in a rebuilt temple at Jerusalem during the millennium, offering blood sacrifices as a "memorial" to God are preposterous. *In view of Christ's finished work on the cross, such teaching borders on blasphemy!* The only memorials from God are believers' baptism by immersion and the Lord's Supper. They point back to the death and resurrection of our Savior. The Lord's Supper goes further and "shows his death till he comes" (1 Cor. 11:26). Neither of these ordinances will be needed in eternity. For comments on eating and drinking in the world to come, see Section 171, third and fourth paragraphs of footnote b.

3p-Sacrifice and offerings are forever over. The book of Hebrews is dogmatic that all sacrifices and offerings were fulfilled in the death of Christ. As said in the 2p- above, the only memorials during this present age in which the saved share are baptism and the Lord's Supper. At the end of His final Passover meal with the apostles, the Savior instituted communion. He said that He would not eat of it again until it was "new" in His Father's kingdom (Matt. 26:29). For explanation of this, see Section 171, footnote b, and Section 174, footnote d. This is not to deny that the Jews may attempt to rebuild their temple and restore the Aaronic priesthood. These industrious people are capable of trying just about anything! *However, there will never be another animal sacrifice or offering acceptable to God.* If Israel does reconstitute their old sacrificial system, Jehovah will have nothing to do with it. The temple is *now* His church (Eph. 2:17-22 with 1 Cor. 6:19-20). Every believer is a priest (1 Peter 2:9) offering unceasing thanks and praises to God (Heb. 13:15). An English architect, Henry Sully (died 1940) introduced the error of blood sacrifices in a rebuilt temple during the millennium. His book, *Temple of Ezekiel* printed in 1887 help launch this heterodoxy in book form. Sully was a Christiadelphian. This cult rejects the deity of Christ and teaches salvation by baptism. A false theological source is not the place to build sound doctrine. Where Sully based his beliefs about sacrifices being offered in a rebuilt Hebrew temple, we do not know. We do know, however, that early in the piece, the erratic church father Hippolytus (died A.D. 236), produced a treatise *On Antichrist.* In it, he propagated that Antichrist would build a temple and blood sacrifices would be reinstituted. With the appearing of Sully's new doctrine, among those who embraced it were John Darby, William E. Blackstone, Clarence Larkin, and C I. Scofield. This is how it found acceptance into *radical* dispensationalism. A poor insight into the totality of Jesus' death is the mother of the erroneous teaching of a rebuilt Hebrew temple and blood sacrifices again being offered to God. *The final, total, complete, and absolute sacrifice for sin was Christ on the cross.* No other solution for sin, regardless, in any period of history, and at any place is acceptable to God. That a reinstitution of sacrifices is to "remind us of man's depravity and need for forgiveness" is the height of ignorance. Who wants to live a thousand years being reminded of their past sins that are forever gone? That all sacrifices did not necessarily point to Christ's death for our sins is more nonsense. They all pointed to some kind of sin that needed pardon, regardless. During Christ's reign of eternal peace, there will be no lambs with their throats cut, cattle bolting at the smell of blood, sheep bleating, or the stench of burning carcasses and hair on a temple altar at Jerusalem.

4p-Writings on a rebuilt Jewish temple. For a comprehensive look into the alleged rebuilding of the Hebrew temple at Jerusalem, see *The Coming Last Days Temple,* by Randall Price. This is an intriguing work heavily documented and filled with interesting information. Like others, Price built many of his proposals on silence and filling in the spaces God has left blank. Dwight Pentecost in his *Things to Come,* pages 512-531, wrote many pages trying to describe a system in which sacrifices will be offered to God in a rebuilt temple during the millennium. Charles Ryrie did likewise, in his *Ryrie Study Bible* pages 1200-1216. This mythology is based primarily on the final eight chapters of Ezekiel. The prophet stated that the sacrifices to be offered in the temple that he wrote of were intended to make atonement or "reconciliation" for the sins of Israel (Ezek. 45:15). Does Israel revert to animal sacrifice for the atonement of sin? Do we now have two methods of forgiveness? *Even worse, for this interpretation of Scripture, "the prince" of this temple (who is supposed to be Messiah or Christ) will offer a sin offering for himself (Ezek. 45:22)!* The "authorities" avoid this by saying, "This prince was a human representative of Messiah." This same prince will have "sons" to whom he gives gifts (Ezek. 46:16)! Whatever all this finally means, it cannot point to the Lord Jesus, Israel's true Messiah offering sacrifices for His sins, or giving gifts to His sons during a thousand-year period. Such teachings are sacrilegious. The response that these animal sacrifices are only "memorials" pointing back to the cross is an insult to God. The word "memorial" is found thirty-two times in

612

the *Authorized Version*. Not one of these verses slightly intimates this bizarre teaching. *The correct view of Calvary and the empty tomb forever abolishes the question of a rebuilt Jewish temple and the old Levitical institutions being restored.* Some claim that the entire Levitical system will be operative during the millennial! If so, it would be a reversal of all it pointed too. Presently, in Israel, a group of Christ rejecting Jews are working to this end. They can work until doom's day but it will never be! The masterful book of Hebrews, especially chapters 8 through 10 settled this question forever. *Paul gloried only in the cross of Christ, the final and supreme sacrifice for the sins of mankind (Gal 6:14).* Anything else is disorderly, wrong, and an insult to the perfect atonement of Christ.

5p-Ezekiel's ideal city and temple never realized. Ezekiel was carried into Babylonian captivity in 597 B.C. While there, he was inspired to write a blueprint for a rebuilt Jerusalem and temple for fellow Jews in chapters 40-48. It portrayed the ideal place for sacrifice and worship of Jehovah when they returned to Jerusalem in 536 B.C. Nevertheless, this *model temple* was never realized due to the inadvertency and sin of the returned exiles as reflected in the books of Haggia, Zechariah, and Malachi. A scrutiny of the last nine chapters of Ezekiel reveals that only the first four of those chapters speak of a temple and it furnishings. The remaining five chapters deal with priestly duties, land areas, offerings, a river, boundaries, more land divisions, a city, and its gates. However, it would hardly have been a beautiful piece of real estate with sickening odors filling the air for miles about this "rebuilt Hebrew temple." Hundreds of dead beasts burning on its hot altar would be unbearable. The stench of burning flesh, blood, and animal hair alone would bring millions of flies, pests, and fowls. Will all of this occur during the great thousand years of peace on earth? Hygiene and sanitary conditions were one of the greatest problems with the temple in the days of Christ. There was a large underground drainage line starting at the altar and running down into the Kedron Valley. How ironic that Ezekiel closes with the words "and the name of the city [not Jewish temple] from *that* day *shall be,* The LORD is there" (Ezek. 48:35). The main thrust of these chapters has more to do with the rebuilding of a glorious Jerusalem and not so much the temple. Israel never realized Ezekiel's plan of a grand temple and peace in a glittering New Jerusalem. The exciting sermons about "the Jewish temple soon to be rebuilt," are the fruits of *radical* dispensationalism, not Bible dispensationalism. Several reasons for this are as follows:

1. To enter the temple ritually unclean incurred death. Those entering could only be made clean by the ashes of the red heifer or cow (Num. 19:1-22). For decades, Christian apologists have looked for the spotless red heifer to be born. On a ranch in Texas, strenuous efforts were made to breed this animal. It miserably failed. "Prophecy experts," tell us if found, this animal would be another "sign" of Christ's soon return! The excited Christian Gentiles and obstinate Christ rejecting Jews fail to realize that this animal pointed to Christ, who by his atonement, death, resurrection, and ascension can alone make men forgiven, clean, and qualified to enter the spiritual temple, which is His church (Eph. 2:16-21 with 1 Peter 2:4-6). If the people of Israel built a dozen temples and collect the ashes of a dozen red heifers, it will avail nothing. Jesus Christ is their only Messiah-Savior, and His blood alone takes away all sin.

2. Location of the altar. It must be at the exact spot of the original altar. Only a reliable witness can find this place. Many modern day Jews think this witness may be Elijah. Without the holy altar, all sacrifices are forbidden. By various electronic means, a group of Israelis thinks they have located the place. It is outside the Muslim Mosque. This speculation is fresh cannon fodder for the "end-time specialists."

3. A High Priest must be appointed for Israel. Only the Sanhedrin could do this after searching the temple genealogical records. These were all destroyed in A.D. 70. The Sanhedrin must consist of rabbis ordained with Mosaic ordination. This was transmitted from rabbi to rabbi since the days of Moses. The Mosaic ordination *ceased* when the mad Emperor Constantinius unleashed a bloody pogrom against pagans and Jews. By A.D. 358 all Mosaic ordinations ended for Israel. Details for this ceremony were long ago swallowed by the calamities of Jewish history. A skeleton Sanhedrin was formed in 2004 in Tiberius, Israel. This is a token of desperate Jews longing to relive their history but fail to realize their Messiah has already come. He was Jesus of Nazareth, the Son of the living God.

4. The sacerdotal garment of the High Priest must be of exact measure as in the days of Aaron. These measurements have been lost for over two thousand years.

5. An Islamic mosque built in A.D. 691 occupies the site for the construction of the rebuilt temple. To demolish this structure and build in its place a Jewish temple would create world chaos.

6. Staunch Orthodox Jews hold that their Messiah will rebuild the temple when He comes. A minority disagrees; they believe that human hands will erect it. This splinter group rejects plans for a third temple to be constructed. The primary teaching in the days of Christ was that Messiah would miraculously construct this edifice. Pious Hebrews believed that Messiah would come, their old temple would be destroyed, and He *alone* would build one more glorious than the former. See Section 163, eighth paragraph under footnote c for the apostle's understanding of a rebuilt temple. Refer to Section 39, footnotes a and g for details on *both* the spiritual and literal manifestations of the kingdom as presented in the New Testament. There exists in Israel a small group known as the Temple Institute. They focus on rebuilding a Hebrew temple in Jerusalem. The rabbis leading this movement have prepared numerous

ritual instruments to be used in their future house of God. Disagreement among these people is vicious with many and varying opinions as to exactly how and when this will be done.

7. The silence of the Talmud. Nowhere in the Talmud is there expressed a belief in a Messiah as contained in Christian doctrine. However, the story of Messiah is profoundly recorded in the Jewish Old Testament, and later fulfilled in the Scriptures of the New, especially the four gospels. Refer to *Appendix Three* for a sweeping illustration of this. The Talmud does speak of a supernatural era or time yet to come in human history during which their Messiah will rebuild the temple and guide the world into peace. Most Orthodox Jews embrace this teaching. These are the conjectures of rabbis who over the centuries have rejected the Lord Jesus Christ as their Messiah and personal Savior. No system of Jewish theology, regardless of what synagogue it comes from, allows for Christ's death on the cross for the sins of mankind and His resurrection. They all strongly reject these facts of Scripture.

8. No temple in the new world. The book of Revelation teaches that the present heavens and earth will pass away. They will be replaced by a new heaven and earth. In this glorious system, there will be no sea (Rev. 21:1). When this occurs, a temple will not exist. John looked upon this new world and wrote, "And I saw no temple therein: for the Lord God Almighty and the Lamb are the temple of it" (Rev. 21:22). The preaching about the "everlasting millennial temple" dies with this passage.

6p-Jesus' new kingdom message brought the blessing of absolute forgiveness of all sins and assurance of peace with God. Later, (after His death, burial, and resurrection) the basic kingdom message was then mostly known as the "gospel of Christ" (1 Cor. 15:1-3 with Rom. 1:16). In addition, this glorious herald continues to save from sin and hell, all who will repent and believe it. The inward spiritual kingdom of Christ is not a human system of brick, stones, mortar, men, roads, machinery, electricity, toil and sweat or earthly days and nights. The Pharisees not only did not understand this, but also rejected any suggestion of such a thing. The new kingdom message of Christ slowly found root within the hearts of those who trusted Him. Like the king's daughter, they were now "all glorious within" (Ps. 45:13), because His *spiritual* kingdom had arrived into their hearts. They simply trusted Jesus for all they knew Him to be at that time, both Messiah and Savior, even though the people did not yet comprehend His death on the cross, for sins. On His death not being understood, note Sections 104-105, 107, and 141. Refer to Section 144, footnote i, with Section 10, footnote b for the salvation of those under the Old Testament era.

(e) Continuing the thought just spoken in verse 21, of "His kingdom in the heart," Jesus turns to His disciples and seeks to comfort them regarding the destruction of their beloved Jerusalem and temple. They, like the Pharisees, were also expecting an earthly kingdom with all its external honors, positions, riches, and power. Jesus informed them that in the years ahead His disciples would wish to return to their Lord's side, walk with Him, sit and hear His profound lessons and be blessed from His corporeal presence among them. These things they enjoyed in the "days of the Messiah. This good rabbinical term spoke of Messiah's ministry. However, this will not be, for He must leave them and return to the Father's house. Now, they must know that after His departure, things will only get worse and days darker as time pushes them and their nation toward the horrendous disaster of A.D. 70. (See footnote m below for the escape of all Christians from the city before Jerusalem fell.) In a few dozen years, the vengeance of God was progressively poured out on both the land of Israel and its people culminating in the cataclysmic doom of A.D. 70. With this terrible event, the infant kingdom of Christ began to spread its mighty wings to take the gospel to every creature. See number 2 under b above.

2p-In verse 22, our Lord gives His apostles and disciples a *brief sketch* of what the days ahead hold for them. They will long to be with Him in a physical presence. Yet, He will not be there. In their future lives and work, they will not literally and physically see their Lord again. The blessed days, they were now sharing with Jesus would soon end. However, He would not leave His servants without comfort. The Holy Spirit would take His place with them (John 14:16-20). See footnote o below.

(f) Who are the "they" of verse 23 that would actually speak these things to the disciples ("you") of Jesus and other believers after His departure to heaven? The historian Josephus reported that the last few years before the fall of Jerusalem, many false prophets and Messiahs appeared in Israel. They sought to lead the Jews into various political causes. In *Wars of the Jews,* Book 6:5. 2, line 285, he referred to one such deceiver who "made a public proclamation in the city [Jerusalem] that God commanded them to get upon the temple, and that there they should receive miraculous signs of their deliverance [from the Romans]." He wrote that some six thousand people responded to the plea of this false prophet and gathered themselves into an empty storage room. The Romans learning of this, sealed off the entire area then torched it with fire. Consequently, the false Messiah and his several thousand disciples burned to death! S. W. Paher in his book *If Thou Hadst Known,* pages 66, quotes Josephus as writing that "the land [of Israel] was overran with magicians, seducers, and imposters, who drew the people after them into solitudes and deserts to see the signs and miracles which they promised to show them by the power of God." This has nothing to do with the Antichrist in a future tribulation period over two thousand years later, doing wonders, and seducing the people. It had strict historical and contextual reference to the disciples-apostles ("they" and "you") who were there and heard Christ speak. He was warning them, not Jews thousands of years in the future.

(g) Lightning flashing and the Son of man in his day. This symbolism seems to speak of Christ coming in powerful swift judgment upon Israel, Jerusalem, and the temple, not His return for the church. Paul wrote of His coming for the church years later in 1 Thess. 4:13-18. The context here speaks of the Jews asking about their literal kingdom suddenly appearing (Lk. 17:20-21.) As repeated in this work, at this time in history, the disciples had never heard of the removal of the church and so on. All this came later. The instrument through which the Savior "came" and accomplished this destructive lightning strike was the fierce legions of Rome. Christ used a simple illustration to counter the claims of the soon coming religious imposters who would swamp Jerusalem and further mislead the people. Dozens appeared on the scene prior to the fall of the city. They spoke swelling words, made fantastic promises, and assured victory for the people against all odds. Christ informs them that His judgment would be sudden and decisive. It was "His day." *Israel had crossed the deadline!*

2p-Contrary to the pretension of the false prophets moving over the land, Christ's wrath would fall, and then He would be gone. H. C. Heffren put it in these terse words, "There was nothing to indicate the exact time of judgment until the blow fell with an irretrievably disastrous and exterminating effect." See Heffren's work *The Mission of the Messiah,* page 51. Instead of a public announcement being made, the Son of God's wrath would appear as a flash of lightning and just as quickly vanish. That would be "His day," and the day of doom for Israel, Jerusalem and the temple. When the Jewish religious prophets ("they" in verse 23-24) approached the disciples, they were deterred upon hearing what the Savior had said about them. A few weeks later,

3p-Verse 25. "This generation" is paramount in understanding our Lord's Words. "But first," that is before any of the judgments that I have just said occur, I must be rejected of *this* generation. Among His sufferings were cruel mocking, spitting, buffeting, scourging, and finally death by Roman crucifixion. We must not sport with His statement about a certain generation. *"This generation" must and can only refer to that "generation" living then and there when He spoke these words.* A few hours later, the Master spoke a similar warning to the scribes and Pharisees. Note this in Section 159 Matt. 23:33, 36. To take the word "generation" and push it forward over two thousand years later, and force it to fit a future generation of Jews is absolute tomfoolery. For Jesus' usage of the word generation, see asterisk under Section 67, footnote b. After speaking these things, He then listed systematically what the signs would be, which would clearly distinguish this *unique generation* from others.

(h) Verses 26-29. These are shaded or highlighted in gray to show they are general ideas taken from the Old Testament. With this, the Lord Jesus drew numerous references from Genesis chapters 6, 7, and 19. This demonstrates that He accepted these writings as inspired, reliable history, and used them to buttress His teaching.

(i) These four verses that reveal the unspeakable wickedness that prevailed among the Jews in the days of Christ. Their horrendous evils led up to the fall of Jerusalem when terrible judgment was poured out upon Israel, their city and temple. Israel's sin was pictured by the wickedness in the days of Noah, Lot, and Sodom. For details on the corrupted condition of the Jews at the time, Jesus said this, see Section 67, third and fourth paragraphs under footnote b, and Section 100, footnote d. A short time later, Jesus again vividly predicted this destruction of the Jews on his way to death. Note this in Section 188, Lk. 23:27-31. It is incorrect to relegate these evils *strictly* to the times just before the Lord Jesus returns for His church. *Conditions then will be far worse than they were in the times of Noah, Lot, and Sodom.*

2p-A future picture is shadowed here. As it was in Noah and Lot's times, so shall it be at some distant date when our Lord shall come again (not in power of judgment) but in Person. The wickedness that prevailed at the coming of Christ to obliterate the wicked Jews in A.D. 70 bears a terrible resemblance to conditions that will dominate society when He returns personally to take away His kingdom or church. That *mysterious coming* of Christ's judgment upon the Jews in A.D. 70 has long been over. We look ahead with anticipation and hope for the wonderful triumphant next coming of our blessed Lord when we shall meet Him in the air. It may occur in our lifetime, and it may not: *no one knows the day or the hour.* The abominations that existed in Israel during the days of Messiah on earth will, likewise, prevail in a greater capacity in the later times. Jesus warned about the unbridled evils, the tidal waves of moral and spiritual corruption that swept the world of Noah's day; the booming economy and over-plenty in Lot's time; and that sickest of all sins practiced by the men of Sodom. All *of it* ended in terrible judgment. Noah's evil contemporaries drowned in the worldwide deluge. The citizens of Lot's time burned and choked to death in fire and brimstone behind the walls of their cities. Some forty years after Jesus spoke this warning, the Jews found themselves sealed behind the walls of Jerusalem and millions perished by the most horrible deaths imaginable. These old examples of fearful judgments of the past, pictured similarly the judgment of God upon His ancient chosen people, land and city: this happened in A.D. 70. The judgment of the Jews and their temple was the "day when the Son of man" was revealed in fierce wrath upon His worst enemies. Many of those who heard Jesus speak these dreadful things were, years later, trapped behind the walls of Jerusalem. Did they call to remembrance what He said, but too late! In these things are reflections of world conditions prior to His real return.

(j) Verse 30. Left Behind Series. This passage has nothing to do with judgment upon Israel some two thousand years in the "latter half of the great tribulation period." In Christ's Words "thus [or also] shall it be," He informed His disciples that as sure as destruction came in upon the wicked in olden times, so will destruction fall upon the

Jews, their city, temple and the land. First, the doom that fell upon the busy people of Noah and Lot's days mirrored the doom that fell upon the Jews in A.D. 70. It is sure that Christ was revealed as the judge or source of this horror. *This was not His return for the church.* Read the prediction of Messiah about the agony of Israel during the fall of Jerusalem. It was spoken in Section 188, Lk. 23:27-31, as Jesus made His way to the crucifixion site; these were fulfilled about forty years later. Firstly, the judgment of the Jews and their temple was the "day when the Son of man" was revealed in wrath to Israel. Secondly, our Lord's warning also pointed to future calamities that will befall the world, prior to His real return for the church. In 2004, Barbara R. Rossing, a professor of theology at a Lutheran School in Chicago, published *The Rapture Exposed. The Message of Hope in the Book of Revelation.* She demonstrates the error of the "secret rapture" myth and the *extremes* of the "Left Behind Series." Then suddenly, her bleeding heart liberalism shows its smiling face. This world is such a nice place that we are to save it. Jesus would never judge anyone for He is a lamb in Revelation! (Apparently, she missed Rev. 6:16-17, 19:11-21.) The church being "caught up" scares children, plays on fear, and is dangerous for the earth. Oddly, she overlooks salvation by the blood of the Lamb! Christ's death for mankind has a new slant. Whatever happened to sin, heaven, and hell with these people? Rossing's soteriology does not reflect that of the *early* speakers of the famed Lutheran Hour radio broadcasts. Those old men preached Christ with power and passion, pleading for lost souls to receive Him as personal Lord and Savior. Another sign of theological decay and rot in the Luthern Church.

(k) Verse 31. No "secret rapture." The wording of this verse precludes any reference to the removal of the church. When Christ returns no one will have time to hurry home and gather up his earthly goods. This describes social customs at the time Christ spoke the warning. Flattop houses were plenteous in Jerusalem and surrounding Judaea: people slept here at night and lounged there during the cool of the evening. Christ instructs those that would be living forty years later in A.D. 70, that when they see the Roman armies do not make an effort to save any possessions. He was telling them "Do not [if in the field] return to your houses in the city for anything; leave all and quickly flee Jerusalem and Judaea." Our Lord used similar terminology two days before His death in Section 163, Matt. 24:17, the eight paragraph of footnote w. In the same Section 163, in Matt. 24:41, He again spoke of the women grinding at the mill. Later, Christians in Jerusalem and vicinity fled when they saw the pending calamities especially the marching Roman armies. They "ran for their lives." See footnote m below for more on this.

2p-This cannot be speaking of the "rapture of the church," for that will be an instantaneous miracle occurring in the twinkling of an eye. At the taking out of the church, no one will return to his house and collect his earthly goods or leave the field to go home. Only by the wildest stretch of the imagination can the *sudden taking out* of the church be read into verse 31. The Savior could not have been making reference of this glorious event yet to happen. It spoke rather of pending judgment that loomed on the horizon in the form of the Roman armies, and these warnings were given to people who lived during this time. They were warned by the Messiah not to attempt any salvaging of their personal goods when these things begin to happen. It would then be too late. This warning was given a second time by the Lord Jesus in Matt. 24:17-18 and parallels. See the second paragraph under footnote h. The danger in "turning back" was illustrated in Lot's wife (verse 32). These speak of the rapture of the church, if so it will be a long, drawn out rapture, taking several hours at the least to be realized around the whole earth.

3p-Basis for the pseudo "secret rapture." In 2 Peter 3:10, it is written, "the day of the Lord will come as a thief in the night." It is "the day" that comes as a thief, *not* the Savior. The "secret rapture" is a relatively modern concept. In 1864, the famed Dr. S.P. Tregelles wrote in, *The Hope of Christ's Second Coming,* page 35, "I am not aware that there was any definite teaching that there should be a Secret Rapture of the church." The idea that millions of dead bodies will resurrect in total silence and millions of living Christians will disappear without it being seen, known, or felt is impossible. The Bible does not teach that the church will leave this world in universal silence and secrecy. The removal of the church will shake our planet like nothing since the flood of Noah. It will be a covert event. The secrecy will be the split second of His appearing, not the worldwide ramifications and aftermath when humanity will be turned upside down in shock and horror. It is sheer folly to teach that the "strong delusion" of 2 Thess. 2:11 will pacify the *terrified billions* left on earth after Jesus removes His church. This sensational eschatology is missing in Scripture. George Müller, Oswald J. Smith, and G. Campbell Morgan opposed "a *secret* rapture" but not "the taking out of the church." The words in Rev. 22:20, speak of *how* Jesus will return, "quickly," not the time. Two thousand years can hardly be described as "quickly."

4p-"The day of the Lord." Scofield assures us that "the day of God" or "the Lord," will begin "after the rapture," and will lead into the tribulation. *This was previously unheard of in extant traditional eschatology!* Originally, the Old Testament term, "the day of the Lord" included a wide variety of applications, relating to such things as judgment on lands, nations, persons, and various acts of God. Among other things, ancient Jews held that it spoke of the coming of Messiah. Narrowing it down to *strictly* "beginning after the rapture" is wrong. In the New Testament, it also embraces numerous things. The distinction between the "day of Christ" and the "day of the Lord [God]" is another myth. How odd that Christians were admonished to be "Looking for and hasting unto the coming of the day of God" (2 Peter 3:12-14). This means that believers are living on earth when this "day" occurs. The publication *Midnight Call,* page 21 of June 2000, carried a list of some thirteen differences between the "day of Christ," and the "day of the Lord." Only by adding to, and *forcibly* filling in the blanks that God has inspired in

Scripture is this list possible. "Blank filling" is the mother of the eschatological confusion that prevails today. At Pentecost, Peter preached that "the day of the LORD" in Joel 2:28-32, had its beginning *then* with the coming of the fullness of the Holy Spirit (Acts 2:16-21). His words, "This is that" (verse 16) stands despite every effort to reinterpret it. Dragging out the old "double" or "triple interpretation" of Joel's verses only takes one further from the truth. The above comments do not deny a time of unspeakable horror that is coming upon this world. If one wants to call this "the day of the Lord," or "the day of God," or "the day of hell," so be it! It is an elastic term in Scripture.

(l) **Verse 32. "Remember Lot's wife."** Christ refers to Gen. 19:26, but does not form this into an actual Old Testament quotation. He selected a few words from that event and turned them into a factual statement of His own. Every Jew in our Lord's audience knew about Mrs. Lot. Israel's rabbis and teachers often used her as a symbol of God's judgment. She is mentioned as such in the Talmud tractates, Berachoth 54 a, and b. The Savior selected her as the prime example of what happens when one is warned (even by angels) not to look back on earthly treasure when heavenly judgment is pending; but chooses to disobey (Gen. 19:17). She glanced behind sorrowing over the loss of her possessions left at Sodom. Jesus' audience understood Him to be saying, "If you look back and return to your houses and belongings, you too will perish; for only an angel warned Lot and his family, but I the Son of God your Messiah have forewarned you." See footnote note k above for more on this thought.

2p-All true believers heeded their Master's Words and none of them perished in the destruction of Jerusalem. Footnote m below carries more details on this subject. As with many things, the Jews have countless myths and fables. Some say that Mrs. Lot's name was Adith, others Erith, and that her bones were charred with brimstone and preserved in a hardened pillar of salt. They base this on Deut. 29:23. Josephus wrote that he actually saw this pillar during his lifetime (A.D. 37–100) in *Antiquities,* Book 1:11. 4, line 203, footnote c.

(m) **Verse 33.** This is the natural conclusion of Jesus' warning. As Lot's wife wanted to return to her house and save her possessions, so she lost all; those who lose all in obedience to Christ, save everything of genuine value. Our Lord affirms that those who remain in Jerusalem and Judaea, hoping to rescue their worldly belongings (during her time of judgment) will lose all. It is an unarguable fact of history that just *before* the Romans sealed off the city in April A.D. 70 that *all Christians* fled to a Gentile village across the Jordan River called Pella and saved their lives. W. R. Kimball gives the story in his work *What The Bible Says About The Great Tribulation*, pages 78-79. Eusebius of Caesarea was the ecumenical historian under Emperor Constantine, and also wrote of the believers' escape in *Ecclesiastical History,* III, 5. He said, "The whole body of the church at Jerusalem, having been commanded by a divine revelation, given to men of approved piety there before the war, removed from the city, and dwelt at a certain town beyond the Jordan, called Pella."

2p-In 1899, the English publishing firm, Paternoster Press, reprinted a book entitled *Renan's Antichrist.* Joseph E. Renan was a famed French infidel and theological skeptic. On pages 150-152, he gives a vivid account of the miraculous escape of believers from Jerusalem in A.D. 70. As a ridiculing infidel, he makes this remark, "It is probable that all [Christians] responded to the chief's [Christ] appeal. And that none of the brethren remained in the city, which, a very just instinct told them, was doomed to extermination." Renan continues with, "The place selected by the heads of the community [body of believers] to serve as the principle asylum [or protection] for the fugitive church was Pella, one of the towns of Decapolis. No wiser choice could have been made. Judaea, Idumaea, Peraea, and Galilee were in insurrection." In 1927, two unsaved Jews, M. L. Margolis and Alex Marx wrote in their book *A History of the Jewish People*, on pages 199-200 these words, "The Nazarenes, or those who accepted Jesus of Nazareth as the Messiah, indifferent towards the Hebrew national cause, sought safety in flight from Jerusalem; they settled in Pella beyond Jordan." Skeptics and non–Christian Jews confirm this escape of believers from Jerusalem.

3p-By way of summary note the following. Can these passages (verses 34-36) be speaking of the rapture of the church? *Only if they are extracted from their historical context can they be forced to carry this interpretation.* When left in their syntax and contextual background, exegetically they are speaking of some kind of final separation that fell upon various persons living at Jerusalem when it was attacked. "One taken" has reference to one being put to death; the "one left," points to those who remained to die in the terrible war that lasted some five to six months. (The numeric of "one" actually speaks of thousands.) Christ warned them far in advance that it was more urgent to flee than to prepare food! Those believers who took Jesus' Words seriously remembered them years later as the Roman legions entrenched about the city and fled. A. T. Pierson, in his *Many Infallible Proofs*, pages 62-78 has helpful information on this topic. Footnote l above carries the suggestion that Christ warned them not to even "look back" (as did Lot's wife) while they were fleeing the doomed city of Jerusalem.

(n) **Verse 34. "That night."** The Lord Jesus refers to the *darkest night* in the history of Israel, the destruction of their city, temple, statehood, and scattering over the earth. The massacres of Hitler, the pogroms of the Russian Czar could match the doom of A.D. 70. "Night" here does not speak of a literal twelve-hours. Rather, of many months before the city fell. By using the words "one taken and one left," Christ was telling his audience some would be spared and others not. There would be a ghostly cessation of all human activities during this time of retribution.

2p-As mentioned, we do *not* see the rapture of the church pictured in verses 34-36. However, it cannot be sensibly disputed that mirrored here is a shadow of that wonderful day when Christ returns for His own, couched in the events that fell upon Israel and Jerusalem. There is no catching out of the church in the words "taken" and "left" as used in this place by our Lord. Such an interpretation cannot fit the background discussion and the contextual flow of these passages. As stated in the final paragraph of footnote m above, the word "one" cannot mean just "one" single person only! It is a common euphemism for thousands. The siege ended after almost six months. The Romans sold some 93,000 Jews less than seventeen years old in slave markets. Thousands died from the internal faction fighting before the city fell, many committed suicide, while others starved to death.

3p-Many books describe the history of mayhem and judgment on Israel that spurned, hated, and rejected their Messiah. The Words of Christ were literally fulfilled in A.D. 70. When Jesus spoke of "one taken and one left," the twelve apostles had never heard the term "rapture of the church" or "tribulation period." At this late hour in Jesus' life, they did not understand His death, burial, and resurrection, much less His return for the church several thousand years later. For more on this see Section 26, footnote f with relative footnotes, along with Sections 104-105, 107, and Section 141. Paul described the real removal of the saints some twenty years later in 1 Thess. 4:13-18 and 1 Cor. 15:51-58. Objecting that the word "rapture" is not found in Scripture is nonsense. Neither is the word "depravity." For a response to this cat-chasing-his-tail eschatology, see Section 30, second paragraph of footnote k.

(o) "Where, Lord?" Those listening to Jesus were astonished at what they had just heard. He had explained that the kingdom of the Jews (they had just demanded to know when it would appear, verse 20) would not be established at Jerusalem, for the city would be destroyed: terrible days were ahead for Israel. These would be so bad that even the closest apostles would long again to have Jesus' comforting presence near. See second paragraph of footnote e above. He informed them that their city, temple, and national polity would be destroyed by divine judgment in the form of pagan armies. The wickedness of the Jews in general had reached its fullness. Some of them inquired of the *place* where these events would strike: hence, the question, "Where, Lord?"

(p) "Eagles." Jesus answered their inquiry with an ancient proverb, "Eagles gather where they find prey to kill and flesh to devour." His reply meant that wherever there would be Christ rejecting Jews within the confines of Jerusalem or over the land of Israel, the Roman soldiers would fall upon them to kill or enslave. The military ensign of the Roman legions was the eagle. These dreaded insignias were raised over every place of camping, combat, and conquering. Thousands of buildings in Rome carried these motifs. In time, the land of Judaea and Jerusalem would be covered with the pagan standards bearing this emblem. Tertullian (died A.D. 220), wrote in his book *Apologetic* 16. 162, "The entire religion of the Roman camp almost consisted in worshiping the ensigns, in swearing by the ensigns, and in preferring the ensigns before all the other gods." Their main insignia was the eagle. Every informed Jew knew this. Christ's usage of the eagles gathering was most befitting that dreadful occasion.

2p-Regarding Jesus' eagle parable, seemingly, He made a paraphrased quotation from Job. 39:27 and 30, in this warning, and then applied it to the Roman legions. For another mention of eagles by the Lord Jesus, where He again referred to the forces of Rome, note Section 163, Matt. 24:28, footnote m. This footnote carries a detailed explanation of this horrid creature that lived from the carcasses and corpses of the dead.

(q) Many things our Lord said on this occasion, He repeated a short time later to four of His apostles while sitting on the Mount of Olives looking over the city of Jerusalem and its temple. A comparison of the following verses taken from the two accounts reveal that Christ *again* repeated Himself. The discourse in this present Section of Luke 17 was given somewhere in Samaria or Galilee weeks earlier, while the one recorded in Matthew, Mark, and Luke were spoken two days *before* His death. See Section 163, Matt. 24:1-51; Lk. 21:5-36; with Mk. 13:1-37. John was not inspired to write this discourse. Only Matthew, Mark, and Luke recorded them. A few of the repetitions Jesus used in these two warnings given at two different times in the first three gospels are listed below:

1. Lk. 17:23 with Section 163, Matt. 24:4-5, 23 with Mk. 13:5-6, 21-22. He warns His own about going after or following false Christ's and prophets. See footnote f above for more on this subject.
2. Lk. 17:24 with Section 163, Matt. 24:27. His coming in judgment is compared to a flash of powerful lightning. See footnote g above.
3. Lk. 17:26-27 with Section 163, Matt. 24:37-39. The extravagances of the days of Noah ended in death. With this, also note the second paragraph of footnote i above.
4. Lk. 17:31 with Section 163, Mk. 13:15-16. On housetops and in the fields. Only paralleled in Mark. Not recorded by Matthew. See footnote k above.
5. Lk. 17:35 with Section 163, Matt. 24:40-41. These verses speak of being outside the home working in a field. Refer to second paragraph of footnote n above.
6. Lk. 17:37 with Section 163, Matt. 24:28. Coming of the eagles. Note footnote p above. For more on the eagles and their meaning, read the comments at Section 163, Matt. 24:28, footnote m.

2p-In these six comparisons Jesus tried to convince the Jews that their earthly kingdom of unregenerate hearts would never be realized. See footnote a above. His new kingdom or church, which brought salvation and the reign of the Holy Spirit within the lives of His children, was replacing the Jewish one. *This is not to deny a glorified rule of Christ on earth someday in total peace and everlasting harmony.* For more on this, glorious event, see Section 171, first through fifth paragraphs of footnote b.

The Parable of The Persistent Woman and Evil Judge. A lesson on prevailing prayer. In concluding this message, the Lord Jesus gave a unique but greatly overlooked sign which points to His return at a time unknown to any man.

Matt.	Mk.	Lk 18:1-8— *Samaria and Galilee*	John
		The parable given 1 And he spake a parable[a] unto them *to this end*, that men ought always to pray, and not to faint; 2 Saying, "There was in a city a judge, which feared not God, neither regarded man: 3 "And there was a widow in that city; and she came unto him, saying, 'Avenge me of mine adversary.'[b] 4 "And he would not for a while: but afterward he said within himself, 'Though I fear not God, nor regard man; 5 'Yet because this widow troubleth me, I will avenge her, lest by her continual coming she weary me.'"[c] *The parable interpreted* 6 And the Lord said, "Hear what the unjust judge saith.[d] 7 "And shall not God avenge his own elect,[e] which cry day and night unto him, though he bear long with them? *The overlooked sign: faith in persistent prayer* 8 "I tell you that he will avenge them speedily. Nevertheless when the Son of man cometh, shall he find[f] faith on the earth?"[g] (Verse 9 cont. in Section 136.)	

Footnotes-Commentary

(a) Never, stop praying! This parable encouraging the disciples to persevere in prayer, regardless of how bleak things may seem, was a fitting way to conclude the awful message of the previous Section 134. Jesus had just given them a fearful discourse about terrible days of judgment and suffering that were coming upon Jerusalem and the nation of Israel. He hangs before them the key that will unlock the door; He leads them to the solace of prayer as a sure source of strength and comfort in view of what was coming. Prayer is the soul after God, the salt for everything, the breath of the spiritual man. The urgency is shown in that Christ gave the meaning of the parable *before* giving it to His followers. The thrust of the lesson is to "Pray, pray, pray. Never give up or grow faint." See under number 3, under footnote f below for more on this serious thought.

(b) The mean city judge. We cannot know in which city this judge practiced law. He was under the authority of no one and the law unto himself. The magistrate who has no regard for God cannot be expected to have any regard for man. How appalling to see the men of the judiciary who are atheists attempting to pronounce sentences and judgments upon their fellows. This judge had neither character nor honor, either vertical or horizontal. One can see awful reflections of the Supreme Court of the United States in this godless magistrate. His conscience could only be touched when mental fatigue had beaten him down. The undaunted widow justly inflicted this upon him.

(c) Judges in ancient Eastern cities sat in the gates and heard their complainants one at a time. The rulers of the villages and cities in which they lived normally paid these judges. Bribery was rife and unless one had money, there was little possibility of getting his case heard and satisfactorily settled. Hence, the reason he slighted the widow which was a neglect of his duties. She appeared before him on many occasions until he became overly familiar with her problem. The widow's persistence and continual coming before his presence struck trouble in his wicked heart. "Least she weary me" were the inward thoughts of this wretched city judge. He knew she meant business, and that he did not! The only way to rid his conscience of this problem was to grant judgment on her adversary. This he did. We do not know her grievance, but she found the answer.

(d) After giving the parable, the Lord Jesus inquired of His audience "Did you hear what that unjust judge said?" Adam Clarke best explains our Lord's question. "If a person of such an infamous character as this judge was, could yield to the pressing and continual solicitations of a poor widow, for whom he felt nothing but contempt, how much more ready must God be, who is infinitely good and merciful, and who loves his creatures in the tenderest [sic] manner to answer our prayers in his chosen time." See Clarke's *Commentary,* vol. 5, page 471. There is no way this unscrupulous judge can picture the Lord. We are to learn from his conduct but not make him symbolize God.

(e) **"His own Elect"** was a term used among the Jews in speaking of fellow Jews. The word "elect" is found in the Talmud tractates, Megilah 92 and Sanhedrin 52b. In the verse before us, Christ was speaking to his disciples of coming calamities that He had just warned of in the previous Section 134. He assures them that God will avenge them of their adversaries, as the evil judge finally did the widow. The Hebrew usage of "elect" was brought over into the Christian faith and became one of the numerous names for all the saved of earth. Before the foundation of the world, God in His glorious sovereignty chose to save *all* who would repent and believe on His dear Son. *These and these alone, comprise the elect of God.* The condition of repentance and faith as per requisite to salvation has nothing to do with works. This was decided by wisdom of God. For more on repentance, see Section 50, footnote h.

2p-**Election's blessings start at salvation.** Men only become participants of divine election when they receive Jesus Christ as personal Lord and Savior. No mortal is forced, hijacked, or kidnapped into this. No man is born again, and then wakes up the next morning with the ability to repent of his sins now that he is saved! This fable was invented by men who tried to rescue the grace of God from being embarrassed by mixing it with the works of the human will. In their scramble, they turned grace "into lasciviousness" (Jude 4). Embraced in the election of God, for all who will believe on the Savior, is every blessing the Almighty bestows. For other comments on this subject, see Section 1, Part 3, footnote h. The Baptist Calvinist J. L. Dagg, wrote in 1824, that God's grace discriminates; that it is not bestowed on the grounds of previously existing faith. Then he wrote, ". . . a reason for this is known only to God." Dagg should have rechecked his words against John 3:16; Acts 16:31, Acts 18:8; Rom. 3:28; and Rom. 10:9-13. When did the persons in these verses believe, before or after salvation? See Daggs' *Manual of Theology and Church Order,* page 312, for his distorted soteriological views. How does the saying that, "God only requires what He gives," fit in with His rain and sun being shed on the just and unjust (Matt. 5:45)? The ultra Calvinist, Author Pink held that the non–elect are unable to believe because they are totally dead in sin; a dead man can do nothing. Then, he explains what the dead in sin elect *must do* to be saved! "Cry unto God for enabling power . . . to ask God for mercy to overcome his enmity and draw him to Christ; to bestow upon him the gifts of repentance and faith." See Pinks, *The Sovereignty of God,* 1930 edition, 198, 199. Quiet a feat for a spiritual corpse!

3p-The theological dogma about the sinner's "foreseen faith," and God saving him before the foundation of the world because of that faith is a heinous error. If God foresaw their faith, then they had it before salvation. This would negate their teaching that men cannot believe until after they are saved. These people do not understand that "faith comes by hearing the Word of God," and that this faith can be exercised by the recipient or not exercised (Acts 17:32-34). This is hardly "an exercise of human virtue or man's works." It is this way because God Almighty made these arrangements. There has never been such a thing as the Lord of heaven electing out of the human race so many for eternal life, and then reprobating all the others to hell, regardless. The text in Rom. 9:18, is not speaking of salvation but events in human history as God moves men and things to accomplish His sovereign will.

4p-Saint Augustine (died A.D. 430) the "brilliant intellectual" reflected his spiritual blindness in these words, "When an infant is brought to baptism . . . the infant so presented is reborn." See his *Letters* 98:2. He also stated, "God does not forgive sins except to be baptized." See William Jurgen, *The Faith of the Early Fathers, vol. 3:156.* Augustine is the church father who taught that baptized infants suffer less in hell than those unbaptized. He rejected the historical reality of Genesis. We hear eloquent preaching about the marvelous conversion of Augustine and Monica his "praying mother." (One wishes she had prayed him out of his distortions and perversions of Holy Scripture.) An examination of his doctrine years after conversion causes men to ponder, "Was he saved after all?" Like Martin Luther, much is written about their conversions to Christ, but so little about their doctrinal heresy and apostasy afterwards. One cannot look to such men for correct understanding of Christian doctrine. All the church fathers were infected more or less by the virus that baptism and communion saves and takes sins away. Cyril of Jerusalem (died A.D. 386.), who so vigorously defended the deity of Christ wrote this alarming statement, "If any man does not receive baptism he does not receive salvation." Refer again to Jurgens, *The Faith of the Early Fathers*, vol. 1, 8:11. Appealing to these "fathers" and men who murdered their opponents is an appeal to the Devil. No form of baptism saves and puts one *into* salvation. For further explanation of this, see Section 203, footnote d.

5p-**Spurgeon: preacher, Calvinist, moderate drinker, and cigar smoker.** An example of the above was the British Baptist preacher Charles H. Spurgeon. He once said, "The old truth that Calvin preached, that Augustine preached, that Paul preached, is the truth that I must preach today." In this statement, the eloquent Spurgeon was trying to reach over history and gather credence for the heresy of Calvinism that infected him. He did not preach like Calvin that baptism put one into the church. See Samuel Fisk's work, *Calvinistic Paths Retraced*, pages 151-152. Nor as Augustine, who said that infant baptism saved children from burning in hell. Spurgeon preached none of the doctrines of the Papal Church, some of which were originally laid down by Augustine, the ex-lawyer from Hippo, Africa. Further, Spurgeon did not practice killing his theological opponents, as did Augustine, Calvin, William Farel, and their kind. Calvinism did "thunder through" Scotland, Holland, Switzerland, South Africa, and into Colonial America. The appalling social, moral, spiritual, and political mess these countries are in today somehow reflects the aftermath of this "thunder." Many of us enjoy quoting the eloquent Spurgeon. His pithy sayings have blessed us for over a hundred years. So . true the words, "No one could say it like Spurgeon." However, what would be the reactions of the "non-compromising Baptists," if Spurgeon blew the smoke from his cigar in their faces or burped from a glass of wine? His claim that he smoked "to the glory of God" borders on stupidity. *Spurgeon later renounced his cigars and drinking and gave up both.* Could it be that oratory and charming words have blinded us to sin and paralyze us from opposing it? Do "little foxes" still spoil the vines? Regarding Calvinism, Spurgeon said, "God called me to preach. If I knew that all the elect had a yellow stripe painted down their backs, then I would give up preaching and go and lift up shirt tails." Lifting shirt tails of men when "they will be saved regardless of what we do" is more Reformed nonsense. Oddly, Spurgeon he gave public invitations and hundreds were saved! *Great men repent of their sins when they see them; weak men will not but struggle to justify them. Spurgeon was a great man!*

6p-God waited forty years to answer. The Lord answers the prayers of His children, but only in His time and according to the manner wherein He is glorified, and they are blessed. He surely "bears long" and seems at times disinterested. Often, we wait for years and are seemingly left to question in a hard silence. The popular notion that "If you have enough faith you can get what you want" is a form of mental telepathy and/or occult mind-control reasoning. Dr. John R. Rice once said, "God answers prayer three ways, yes, no, or wait." We would do well to remember that our Lord is never so near as when he seems so painfully absent. The author of this book worked with a farmer named Bill Clemons for some forty years, pleading with him to repent and believe on the Lord Jesus Christ. During every furlough over a period of some thirty-five years, from the foreign mission field, he went to Bill and his wife Jean in Lebanon, Tennessee. Each time he said, "No, I am not ready." A Calvinist who had spoken to him said, "He is not one of the elect!" Finally, in November of 1997, he was saved. Twelve months later, Bill was in heaven. How amazing that one of the "non-elect" was finally elected after decades of witnessing, praying, and waiting! For another example of God waiting forty years, see Section 139, third paragraph of footnote p.

7p-Verse 8. "When the Son of man cometh." At this point, none of His apostles-disciples knew of His death and resurrection. They did not now understand this statement as having reference to His return from heaven. For an earlier mention of His return, see Section 71, footnote n, where the same situation existed.

(f) There are three major views about Christ finding faith on earth when He comes again. They are as follows:

1. Some hold that the coming of Christ mentioned in this text refers to His invisible coming to bring judgment on the Jews, the temple and Jerusalem in A.D. 70. This may be so in a mystical sense, but it does not seem to be contextually or hermeneutically applicable in this verse.

2. It could have reference to a popular saying that existed among the Jews prior to the coming of Messiah. *Gill's Commentary*, vol. 7, page 677 mentions a common expression used by the Jews. He wrote that the ancient sages taught, "no faith found in Israel" when Messiah appeared. Another rabbi said, "There would be no faith among them [Jews]." Could it be in this statement that the Savior takes this well known expression and calls on the people to believe in Him; telling them that He has come and alone is worthy of their faith in Him as Messiah? This gives credence to the Jewish usage of this saying and better fits the text than number 1 above. Can we then blend number 3 below into this meaning?

3. There is a third approach to this verse. It speaks of that hour when He will come in the clouds of heaven for His own. Will He find prayer faith on the earth when His church is gathered out? The question of verse 8 has nothing to do with saving faith. Christ is not saying that only a few will be saved when He returns. He refers *back* to the persistent faith of the widow who would not give up. He asks, "Will there be anyone on earth, who like the widow will be persevering in prayer when I return?" Here, is a remarkable "sign of the times" that has been missed. It is rare to find Christians laboring long hours in prayer. *Whenever Jesus returns, there will be an absence of persistent prayer among His people.*

4. When Jesus spoke verse 8 above, none of them understood this to mean His return for the church, which they did not understand at this time. However, this understanding did come later.

(g) **Powerless prayer, a sign of Jesus' return.** There is more praying today than at any time in church history, yet less is happening in response. *What is wrong?* Will the commas in our lives never end? There was a time when prayer meeting was humble, modest, and saints in serious moods did business with God, and one another. Today, we cannot get the coffee cup out of their hand long enough to get them on their knees. *No man or woman is greater than their prayer life.* The beautiful sermons we hear have superimposed themselves over the prayer room. The average pulpit is a shop window for displaying human talents: everyone must hear "Dr. so and so," for he is a "great pulpiteer!" Conversely, the old prayer closet allows no showing off: there, only God sees and hears. Prayer is the fair maiden of the church; but she remains, shy, blushing, and unwooed. Not attired in the pearls of intellectualism or the glamorous silk of philosophy, she is therefore, unnoticed and unsought. The pure maiden of importune prayer wears the common cloth of homespun sincerity and meekness; her dress is rough, but clean; she is not afraid to kneel, weep, hurt, and wait. She, like the widow in this parable, is always present, pleading that we keep on asking, asking, and asking. This is the message of our Master in these powerful verses.

2p-When Christ returns, will He find any "undaunted prayer widows," choosing rather to die in their prayers and supplications to God than quit? They know that regardless of the outcome the "judge of all the earth will do right" (Gen. 18:25). Playing "prayer games," seems to have become something of a ritual among many Christians.

The Parable of the Pharisee and Publican Praying given to the religious leaders of Israel. In this, Christ reveals their self-righteous, haughty, arrogance, seen and heard even in their prayers at the temple.

Matt.	Mk.	Lk. 18:9-14—*Samaria and Galilee*	John
		The purpose of the parable **9** And he spake this parable unto certain which trusted in themselves that they were righteous,[(a)] and despised others: **10** "Two men went up into the temple to pray; the one a Pharisee, and the other a publican.[(b)] (tax collector) *The Pharisee's prayer* **11** "The Pharisee stood[(c)] and prayed thus with [to] himself, 'God, I thank thee, that I am not as other men *are*, extortioners, unjust, adulterers, or even as this publican. **12** 'I fast twice in the week, I give tithes of all that I possess.' *The publican's prayer* **13** "And the publican, standing afar off, would not lift up so much as *his* eyes unto heaven, but smote upon his breast, saying, 'God be merciful to me a sinner.'[(d)] *The interpretation of Jesus* **14** "I tell you, this man went down to his house justified[(e)] *rather* than the other: for every one that exalteth himself shall be abased; and he that humbleth himself shall be exalted."[(f)] (Verse 15 cont. in Section 138.)	

Footnotes-Commentary

[(a)] Here is another parable built upon a true human event that had previously taken place in the temple at Jerusalem. There can be no guessing as to whom our Lord directed these remarks. Observe here, the prevailing hypocritical character of the scribes and Pharisees woven into His strong Words. They are mentioned by act and name in verses 9-10. The Talmud firmly renounces hypocrisy and consigns all hypocrites to be shut out of heaven or God's presence, yet many of the rabbis who wrote these words were among the biggest hypocrites in ancient history. Refer to tractates, Sotah 42d and Sanhedrin 103a, for these Talmudic statements. Early in His ministry, the Lord Jesus warned the common people that if they did not have true righteousness from God, (not that of the scribes and Pharisees), they would *never* be part of His new kingdom.

2p-Jewish prayer. Steve Herzig in his book *Jewish Culture & Customs*, pages 86–89 relates some interesting information about Jews and prayers. He wrote, "After Herod's Temple was destroyed; prayer was regarded as a substitute for the sacrifices. Later, it came to be considered as a means to forgive sin." Then Nerzig adds, "The Hebrew word *L'hitpalel* [pray] . . . means to judge. When people pray they are in a real sense judging themselves." We see in the above lesson given by the Lord Jesus that nothing so reveals the heart of man as the words he speaks while in prayer. Both men speak out in prayer to God their opinion of themselves! In some inexplicable way, unsaved men cannot really pray. Years ago the author of this harmony commentary worked with several persons who had contact with the secret underground churches, struggling under communism in the former Soviet Union. One chief method these humble saints often employed to detect a suspected traitor within their midst: they would ask him to pray. *Without fail, traitors did not know how to call on the Lord!* The author actually tried this on an Anglican priest (suspected of communist ties) while staying in a hotel room at the Black Forest of Germany in 1971. As he was leaving, I asked him to kneel with me beside a chair and to "lead us in parting prayer." This popular British clergyman fell into obvious alarm, could not pray one word, jumped up, excused himself, and hurried out of the room! The only place when confirmed hypocrites will sincerely pray is from the torments of hell, but then it is too late. For an example of one praying from the home of the damned for mercy, refer to Section 131, Lk. 16:27.

3p-On the other side of this story, there are those who have attended church and religious services for decades. They smoothly parrot off the most beautiful words in prayer, yet their lives betray their speech. Praying well, while living bad is the high mark of a religious hypocrite. Most of us would do good to emulate Hannah of old. It is written of this broken little woman, "Now Hannah, she spake in her heart: only her lips moved, but her voice was not heard" (1 Sam. 1:13). Prayer that reaches the bosom of God begins first in the heart not the mouth. The Holy Spirit escorts it to the throne of heaven (Rom. 8:26-27). And there are those strange but unique times when we may learn more by listening to men pray, instead of praying. See what this Pharisee and religious imposter prayed under footnote c below.

(b) For a review of the Pharisees, see Section 30, first paragraph of footnote a. For publicans, see Section 50, footnote d. According to Section 150, Matt. 21:13 with Isa. 56:7, the temple should first have been called the "house of prayer for all nations." Because of this, even Gentiles and publicans were granted *limited access* into its precincts. Publicans, though hated to the core by every devout Jew, could still return to the temple and pray. It was believed that if one did this, he was possibly contemplating a return to the Torah Law of God and the nation of Israel.

(c) **The Pharisee's prayer:**

1. He judged himself "not as other men" but superior. He enumerated the sins of which he was not guilty. Looking at the publican a great way off, he thanked God that he was a better person. He fasted twice a week, even though the Torah Law required only one fast a year (Lev. 23:27-32). See Section 23, footnote b, and Section 46, footnote i, for more on Jewish fasts. Some five hundred years before this Pharisee, in the days of Zechariah the prophet, the Jews had invented four more fasts (Zech. 8:19). They were called the fast of the fourth, fifth, seventh, and tenth months. Each one of these called to remembrance a different calamity in the history of Israel. By the time of Christ, they had a hundred and four others added to the list! See *Dake's Annotated New Testament*, page 82, right vertical column. How relevant are our Lord's Words when he says that he "prayed with [to] himself." It was only a soliloquy within his ears; a recital of his own virtues, which satisfied his mind alone, not his soul. How this greatly mirrors the prayers of millions today. People who are praying into their own ears, enjoying what they hear are not talking to the listening heart of God.

2. He tithed faithfully and told God so! The Jews based their tithing on Lev. 27:30-33 and Num. 18:21-26. Jewish tithing is explained in the Talmud tractate, Maaseroth. However, he prayed not one word about his sins but many about his deeds of (self) righteousness. This is the model prayer of a genuine hypocrite. The Talmud in tractate, Berachoth 28b records the supplication of an ancient rabbi containing words strikingly similar to these. In this parable, Christ painted the precise picture of a self-righteous Jew as he prayed and held his deeds before the Lord of heaven. What a strange perversion of the human mind when men seek to make God their debtor because they see the blessings His mercy bestows upon them and think it was their goodness that made it so. George Foot-Moore in his work Judaism, vols. II-III, pages 212-238 wrote voluminously about the various aspects of Hebrew prayer life. He says nothing about the Jewish hypocrites whom the Lord Jesus continually rebuked for their false, self-righteous prayers, and two-faced practice of these men of religion.

(d) **The publican's prayer:**

1. Ashamed of his sin he "stood afar off" from the people gathered at that particular hour of prayer. Though the Pharisee and the publican are put together in this lesson, in fact, they are miles apart. The Pharisees feared contamination by being in the presence of these traitors to the Gentile Romans. Abashed, the publican would not lift his face to God, which was the standard posture in temple prayers. Beating on his breast (a sign of deep regret and grief), he outwardly demonstrated his inward broken condition. Jews would thrash their chests during the Day of Atonement to signify their sorrow over sin. See Section 192, Lk. 23:48 for Jewish reaction at the death of Jesus.

2. Seven words came from his contrite heart. "God be merciful to me a sinner." Who ever this unnamed man was, he was fed up with his sin and wanted peace for his troubled heart. He looked to God for justification and found it. The Pharisee appealed to himself for justification and missed it.

(e) **"Justified!"** See Rom. 5:1 for justification's channel and its results in the hearts of men. The hypocritical Pharisees continually sought justification through their deeds of many sorts but did not find it in the eyes of the Messiah. He walked out of the House of God (temple at Jerusalem) as evil and corrupted as he had entered. He had exalted himself in prayer, being blind to his sins. *No man who despises others in his heart can pray. This was a common curse of the hypocritical, ultra self-pious Jews of this era.*

(f) The "cursed publican" was a changed man! The weight of his sins had humbled his heart. By faith in God, broken sorrowfulness, and true repentance over sin, he went home a new man. See Section 144, footnote i for people being saved before the death of Christ. The unwritten benediction to this parable given first to the religious leaders (as well as all men) remains valid to this moment: "Pride goeth before destruction, and a haughty spirit before a fall" (Prov. 16:18). The Pharisees and all those present, who trusted in their self righteous works of the written and oral law, were highly offended by this lesson, for the text reads that Jesus directed it to them (verse 9).

2p-Promises to dead men and prayers? Several years ago, the author was in a dentist chair and witnessing to the attending nurse. She was a young woman from another country. Upon asking her about salvation she responded, "O yes, I am a Christian. When I was a child, I had a serious disease and my mother, a devout Catholic, made a promise to Saint Thomas in heaven, that if he would heal me, she would give me to God. He answered that prayer." This is a dark religious deceit. The Bible says nothing about praying to Paul, John, Thomas, Mary or any other saint. The greatest saint in heaven cannot give us eternal life and assistance. Scripture says, "The Lord *is* my helper" (Heb. 13:6). Those masses making promise to dead men aim at nothing and hitting it every time.

The Pharisees' trick question concerning marriage and divorce. They attempt to ensnare the Lord Jesus into a conflict of opinions between the two theological schools at Jerusalem. Their purpose was to discredit Him before the people.

Departing Galilee, He enters Peraea, and later eastward over Jordan, into Jericho, and Bethany

Matt. 19:1–8	Mk. 10:1–10	Lk.	John
Their devious question **1** And it came to pass, *that* when Jesus had finished these sayings, he departed from Galilee, and came into the coasts [borders] of Judaea beyond Jordan;[a] **2** And great multitudes[b] followed him; and he healed them there. **3** The Pharisees also came unto him, tempting him, and saying unto him, "Is it lawful for a man to put away his wife for every cause?"[c] *Mark places this act of Moses in verse 4.* ▶ *Matthew puts it in verse 8 below.* ***Jesus' response*** **4** And he answered and said unto them, "Have ye not read, that he which made *them* at the beginning 'made them male and female,'[d] **5** "And said, 'For this cause shall a man leave father and mother, and shall cleave to his wife and they twain shall be one flesh?' **6** "Wherefore they are no more twain, but one flesh. [e] What therefore God hath joined together, let not man put asunder."[f] **7** They say unto him, "Why did Moses then command to give a writing of divorcement, and to put her away?" **8** He saith unto them, "Moses because of the hardness of your hearts	***Their devious question*** **1** And he arose from thence, and cometh into the coasts [borders] of Judaea by the farther side of Jordan:[a] and the people[b] resort unto him again; and, as he was wont, [or did] he taught them again. **2** And the Pharisees came to him, and asked him, "Is it lawful for a man to put away *his* wife?" tempting him.[c] ***Jesus' response*** **3** And he answered and said unto them, "What did Moses command you?" **4** And they said, ◄ "Moses suffered [allowed] to write a bill of divorcement, and to put *her* away." **5** And Jesus answered and said unto them, "For the hardness of your heart he wrote you this precept. **6** "But from the beginning of the creation 'God made them male and female.'[d] **7** 'For this cause shall a man leave his father and mother, and cleave to his wife; **8** 'And they twain shall be one flesh:' so then they are no more twain, but one flesh. [e] **9** What therefore God hath joined together, let not man put asunder."[f] **10** And in the house his disciples asked him again of the same *matter*. ◄ *Matthew places this act of Moses here in verse 8. Mark puts it in verse 4 above.*		

Matt. 19:8–12	Mk. 10:11–12	Lk.	John
suffered [allowed] you to put away your wives: but from the beginning it was not so."			
His final answer on the matter	***His final answer on the matter***		
9 "And I say unto you, [Pharisees][g] Whosoever shall put away his wife, except *it be* for fornication, and shall marry another, committeth adultery: and whoso marrieth her which is put away [for fornication] doth commit adultery."	11 And he saith unto them,[g] "Whosoever shall put away his wife, and marry another, committeth adultery against her.		
	12 "And if a woman shall put away her husband, [unless for adultery] and be married to another, she committeth adultery." (Verse 13 cont. in Section 138.)		
The disciples are confused			
10 His disciples say unto him, "If the case of the man be so with *his* wife, it is not good to marry."[h]			
11 But he said unto them, "All *men* cannot receive this saying, save *they* to whom it is given.[i]			
Life's situations greatly vary: many people cannot accept what happens			
12 "For there are some eunuchs,[j] which were so born from *their* mother's womb: and there are some eunuchs, which were made eunuchs of men: and there be eunuchs, which have made themselves eunuchs for the kingdom of heaven's sake. He that is able to receive *it*, let him receive *it*."[k] (Verse 13 cont. in Section 138.)			

Footnotes–Commentary

[a] **"Beyond Jordan."** Apparently, this has reference to Judaea. Previously, He had been falsely warned by the Pharisees to leave Galilee, in Section 126, Lk. 13:31–32, footnotes i, and j. Some days later, He departs from His home province for the final time and after passing through part of it will minister in Galilee no more. Most of His sermons, lessons, miracles, and wonders had been performed across Galilee, but now having completed His work, He did not return until after His resurrection. This was a prearranged meeting on a mountain in Galilee with His disciples. It is recorded in Section 204. In Mk. 10:1, it is clarified where Jesus went at this time by the words "into the coasts [borders] of Judaea by the farther side of Jordan." Some believe this signals that Christ walked down the western banks of Jordan River, slowly moving south. However, the text of Mark informs us that He crossed eastward over the river and thus entered into Peraea (called "the farther side of Jordan") in His journey to Jerusalem and His final Passover. Regardless, the Lord Jesus began to work His way south toward the ford or crossing that led over the Jordan River into Judaea, and then He moved over the westward road to Jericho a few miles away.

[b] This was normal. The mixed multitude following the Savior consisted of everything human! There were thousands of them. Some believed on Him, some curious were only wanting to see miracles, some seeking healing of infirmed bodies, while others attempting to trap Him in some word or act.

[c] **"Put away his wife for every [any] cause?"** The Pharisees, whom He had publicly exposed for their hypocrisy, attempt to trick Him again. They asked Jesus if He held to the interpretation of divorce and remarriage as taught by the Jewish school of Hillel (which allowed divorce for almost any reason), or did He subscribe to the

teaching of Shammai (which granted divorce only for adultery). The Pharisees were hoping Christ would oppose free divorce for any reason, (which He did) and thus alienate Himself from the people. For a brief review on divorce and remarriage at this time as practiced by the ancient Jews, see Section 12, footnote a, with Section 45, first paragraph of footnote h and i. The Talmud tractates, Yevamoth, Kethuboth, and Gittin mention divorce over a thousand times! An example of the sinfulness in the school of Hillel concerning divorce and remarriage is found in the tractate, Gittim 90a and b which allowed divorce for the wife "spoiling the food," or should the husband "find a woman more beautiful" than his present wife! A Pharisee rule in their oral law stated this shocking concession, "A man must not marry a woman with the intention of divorcing her; but if he previously informs her that he is going to marry her for a season, it is lawful." For more on this, see *The Life of Christ*, pages 748-750, by Dr. F. W. Farrar.

2p-Dwight Pentecost, in *The Words & Works of Jesus Christ,* page 354, wrote that rabbis from the school of Hillel, when visiting a town would advertise for a woman to serve as their wife during this time! This reflects the abysmal moral decadence that existed during this time among the Hebrew rabbis. One is overwhelmed trying to wade through the hundreds of lines in the Talmud tractates to understand the Jewish mind on this subject during the days of Christ on earth. It must be remembered that our Lord was dealing with the feigned questions, wicked reasoning, and carnal subterfuges of the Jews, especially the Pharisees, in this encounter over divorce and remarriage. The lessons in this Section can only be understood when viewed in their historical and religious context.

1. In Matt. 19:4-6 and Mk. 10:6-8, Christ refers His opponents back to Genesis chapters 2 and 5.
2. In Matt. 19:8 and Mk. 10:4-5, He refers to Deut. 24:1-4.
3. In the above verses of Matt. 19:4-5, the Lord Jesus gives two general quotations by selecting various words from Gen. 1:27, 2:24, and 5:2. Again, this confirms that the Savior looked upon the Jewish Scriptures as God's *authority* in this question. At this time, the New Testament with its added commands on this subject had not been written. (The statement of Christ recorded in Mk. 10:6, reveals that He believed in the creation as recorded in Genesis.)

(d) **"Made them."** Here, Jesus affirmed that God created or "made" the first humans. He used the word "creation" in Mk. 10:6 above and later in Mk. 13:19. In secular academic circles, men of atheistic persuasions have poisoned the minds of millions over the centuries with their anti-God or no-God philosophies. They control and push their agendas against divine things. Dare a professional secular educator suggest that God created all things in the beginning, and they will be mocked, ridiculed, scorned, and fired for this "intellectual crime." America's secular institutions call for "intellectual freedom" and then deny it for their own. For a devastating exposure of this academic two-timing that rules in America's leading universities, see the work *Expelled. No Intelligence Allowed,* by the non-Christian Jew, Benjamin Jeremy Stein. This documentary shows the hatred of these "greatly learned" educators for God, Jesus Christ, biblical creation, and *true* Christianity. God's opinion of these people is interesting. See this recorded in Ps. 14:1 with Rom. 1:21-32. Their intellectual darkness has its origin in 2 Cor. 4:4. For more light on this awful condition, see *The Case for a Creator*, by Lee Strobel, the former atheist/lawyer/investigative reporter. He was saved and his writings have shaken atheists, skeptics, and freethinkers across America. The attacks on his defense of the Bible are touched upon in Section 42, the third paragraph of footnote i. Human society has always had atheists denying the fact of God. A thousand years before Christ was born, David wrote of them in Ps. 14:1, and called them "fools." During the second century, another fool named Celsus penned a thing called *On the True Doctrine: A discourse Against Christians*. He denied the deity of Christ, said that Jesus was the bastard son of Mary by a Roman soldier, named Panthera. Later, other Christ haters have used this ploy. See Section 137, first paragraph of footnote d, and Section 21, Part 2, fifth paragraph of footnote i for more on this awful subject.

2p-"But from the beginning." Quoted from Gen. 1:27. With this, the Lord Jesus takes them back to "the beginning." He affirms that divorce and remarriage were not the *original plan* of God at the creation of man and woman. However, with the entrance of sin and its attending curse, the entire human race and all of creation fell into indescribable chaos and darkness. When sin mastered creation and humankind, divorce became a sometime necessary option. Because of sin's calamitous, creation-wide effects, everything changed; nothing could or would be as it was originally created in that glorious beginning. The devastation of universal evil was so thorough that Paul later wrote, "That the whole creation groaneth and travaileth in pain together until now" (Rom. 8:22). Satan and sin ravished and raped what God did at the beginning. Everything changed, including marriage. The Words of Jesus in Mk. 10:9 are not the divine standard for today. God has never required men to live by the sinless and glorious conditions of the primeval Garden of Eden (and the perfect Adam and Eve). Sin decimated it all.

3p-Polygamy. Another point overlooked within the boundaries of this discussion is that multiple wives were popular among the Jews before, during, and after the days of Christ. Some of Israel's greatest leaders were polygamists and even had interfamily marriages. Abraham married Sarah, his half sister (Gen. 20:12), and had a concubine by whom he bore six sons (1 Chron. 1:32-34). Others with multiple wives were Gideon, Judges 8:30; Elkanah, 1 Sam. 1:2; Saul, 2 Sam. 12:8; and David, 2 Sam. 5:13. Polygamy had been practiced under the Jewish Law for almost fifteen hundred years and even prior to that as seen by the warning given in Deut. 17:17. This curse was in vogue before the worldwide flood of Noah's time (Gen. 4:19 and 6:2). The infamous King Herod had ten wives; several of which he murdered. In 1958, a group of "clergymen" in London produced a paperback on the subject *The Bible and Polygamy*. It was edited by E. G. Parrinder. It was a hopeless attempt by the Church of England to explain the *unexplainable*: why polygamy was permitted in the first place. *Smith's Bible Dictionary*, vol. 111, pages 1793-1806, has a comprehensive article covering about every aspect of ancient marriages. Smith gives reasons for polygamy, as the ancients understood the practice. The reasons given in present day writings are pitiful. Regardless of who had a plurality of wives in the Old Testament, it was a practice that resulted in turmoil and conflict. Dr. Craig S. Keener gives an excellent coverage of these matters in his work . . . *And Marries Another*. Many have looked upon this practice with outward disgust but secret envy. This is another signal of the utter depravity of man (Isa. 1:6) and his inability to determine the true purposes of life and their consequences.

4p-"Let or allow." Modern commentators, for the most part, hinge their thinking on the mythical expressions "what God allows," and "what God lets" happen. *When will Christians realize that they both mean the same thing?* If God "lets or permits it to happen," then He "allows it to happen." If God "allowed it to happen," then He "let or permitted it to happen." (If I *allow* a man to enter my home and murder my family, then I have *let* or permitted him to murder them and must be held responsible. These terms are synonymous.) Along with this reasoning comes the theological paradox of "God's permissive will," and "God's positive will," which at the end of the road means the same thing. As great as these terms sound, it does not help. It is man's feeble effort as he tries to exonerate God of doing evil, which is witless to say the least. It is like striking a match to see if the sun is shining. The above expressions "allow," let," and "permit," fail to satisfactorily address the problem of polygamy (and many other issues as well), nor do they even begin to explain the mind of God regarding these matters.

5p-God did not "let" or "allow" the unspeakable crimes and sins that were committed last year across the earth happen. *Men and women have a free will and exercise it accordingly.* The origin of all man's wickedness is found within His own heart, not in God "permitting" it to occur. If God "permitted," "allowed," or "let," that man in Florida abduct, molest, strangle, and bury alive the little eight year old girl, then He is the culprit! Further, if God "let" or "allowed" it to happen, how could the police pursue, arrest, and then the courts try the killer, since God "permitted" him to do his dastardly deed in the first place. Correctly, God should be charged with the crime! *Such reasoning borders on religious insanity.* The child murderer, of his own volition or choice, schemed, planned in his heart, then committed the heinous crime and should pay the ultimate price. God had nothing to do with it. Christ clearly explained the origin of man's wickedness in Section 96, Matt. 15:19-20, footnote m. We may be sure the guilty person was assisted by Satan or demons in his actions. A few things are mentioned in the Bible about these problems, yet God has chosen not to give us an exhaustive explanation or intricate details on any of them. They should be left as they are regardless of how much they trouble our conscience or disturb our "doctrinal beliefs."

6p-Polygyny and pagans. Missionaries continually meet this problem in heathen lands. The preach God's Word among natives who often have many wives. Some of these men were saved. Later, they requested of their missionaries or pastors, baptism, and admission into the local assembly. It was interesting how the "theological experts" back in America fell all over themselves trying to answer this one (and never did). The ramifications of ordering the new convert to "dismiss all of his wives except one" are devastating both socially and morally. This multiplies the problems, especially as many children were involved. Whatever one may *think* they scripturally understand on this subject of marriage, divorce, remarriage, and polygamy, one fact remains abundantly clear; things are different since the fall of man and creation's curse by sin. The ideal situation of Adam and Eve *before* the entrance of sin and disobedience does not exist today and has never existed since Mother Eve and Father Adam ate the forbidden fruit. It is therefore, impossible, wrong, and unscriptural to require any person to live according to the order of that long ago vanished perfect paradise. *Sin and Satan demolished it!* Even in the perfect redemption of Christ presently shared by every truly born again person on earth, the whole creation about us *still* "groans and travails in pain together until now" (Rom. 8:22). Not until we reach that perfect heaven and earth will all things be new forever (Rev. 21:1-5). Those who respond that the New Testament is clear on this issue are unread, inexperienced, or plain dumb. Like eschatology, there are so many varying opinions, that one is left bedraggled dealing with this issue. Nevertheless, we must have some established biblical guidelines when facing things of such sensitive nature and stay with these, unless time or God shows us differently. Not all things are of this difficult nature. In major issues, God has spoken clearly and with condensed absoluteness. *With all such, it is not a matter of interpretation but of acceptation and obedience.* Unsaved men, in the dark on eternal matters, call this "opinionated judgment." If the doctor says an arm must be amputated or a policemen gives a ticket, they are "opinionated," so we simply shrug them off and go on our way!

(e) "One flesh." Highlighted for it is a quotation from Gen. 2:24. This expression speaks of the legitimate sexual union of husband and wife in which they become united as one flesh. The resulting fruit of this union is (in normal physical circumstance) a child which is literally the flesh of both, now seen as "one" in the newly born infant. See with this thought 1 Cor. 6:16 with Eph. 5:31. The highest insult to this *divine* one-flesh intimacy, exclusive to marriage, are the sins of adultery, fornication, sodomy, lesbianism, molestation, incest, bestiality and same sex marriage (Prov. 6:32 with Heb. 13:4). Note, the ruling of the Hebrew Torah Law concerning several of these sins, in Lev. 20:13. It was based on these heinous sexual perversions that acceptable grounds for divorce and remarriage are a divine option after all honest efforts of reconciliation, and restoration have failed. See footnote g below for other comments.

(f) "What therefore God hath joined together, let no man put asunder," In His reply, Christ disagreed with the *free* divorce rule of the liberal School of Hillel. See footnote c above. The western world generally believes marriages are performed through the mutual exchange of vows with each one saying, "I do," while the eastern world knows nothing of such vows in the marriage ceremony. The great question of "how" God unites a man and woman together in matrimony as husband and wife is not answered in Scripture. Thousands of answers have been submitted; each one assuring us they are right! How a man and wife are *physically* joined together after marriage as "one flesh" in sexual intimacy is discussed in footnote e above. Husband and wife should hold this union as both sacred and secret. The proposals put forward in all of footnote e do not correspond to "God putting a couple together" in marriage. In the Old Testament, there is no record of a formal exchange of vows mentioned. Across the history of nations, marriage ceremonies are as varied as the patterns in the snowflakes. This is true for both Christians and pagans. The Roman Catholic Church at the Council of Trent in 1545 decreed that marriages could only be performed under *their* authority. All marriage unions performed outside this religion were considered invalid before God! With the Reformation in 1517, there was introduced the act of recording marriages and setting rules for the union. This was the function of the State and enforced by her sword. Like the Papal Church, John Calvin and his colleagues enacted a thing called the "Marriage Ordinance of Geneva." This edict required all weddings to be performed under the authority of Calvin's Reformed Churches. If not, they (like the Catholic Church) were "illegal before God." Later, in Colonial America Calvin's legal peers, respective churches, and spiritual leaders enforced many of these "old country customs" upon the people. (Civil marriages are performed by the civil authorities apart from any religious body or church.) The nice little expression, "all marriages are made in heaven," is a pious fable. Some are "made in hell." Marriage is a divine institution of the Creator, but He forces no one to "marry the right mate." In this, we see again the choice of human free will.

2p-Among the Jews in the days of Christ, a legal contract, called 'betrothal," valid for about a year, was drawn up between the proposed couple. This stood as proof of the written agreed union of a man and woman. In the case of proven adultery during this time, divorce was granted, which meant the cancellation of this contract. This was Joseph's decision about his contract with Mary when he discovered she was pregnant (Matt. 1:19). The guilty party was to be stoned, but in the days of Christ, the Jews turned their heads to this command in their Torah Law (Lev. 20:10 with Deut. 22:22). After the actual marriage had taken place, divorce for proven adultery was permitted. These Words from our Lord reveal that "man" may, through his evil devices, actually, disunion ("put asunder") what God has united! Here, the Lord Jesus opposes divorce easy and free as practiced by the Jews of the school of Hillel. Further, He added dimensions that the Jews, who supported the school of Shammai, had never heard. *His Words remain valid to this moment.* Expositors that claim this was strictly a Jewish thing and has no bearing on society today are seriously wrong. They have caused great frustration and heartache among believers. Biblical typology, such as the husband–wife union in Eph. 5:23–24, is not established doctrine and should not be used as proof for anyone's beliefs or convictions. Many heresies have been built on typology.

3p-The Jews who subscribed to the teaching of the theological School of Hillel (and they were the majority) divorced and remarried at a rate that would cause Hollywood to blush! Refer to Section 45, first paragraph under footnote i for details on how the Jews divorced their wives. The liberal theologian, William Barclay in his work *The Gospel of Matthew*, page 199, wrote that if after ten years of marriage a couple did not have offspring, then divorce was compulsory for them. The Old Testament Torah Law has no such ruling whatsoever. This was another rabbinical tradition from their oral traditions and imposed upon their Scriptures. It has nothing to do with God joining a man and woman together. The divine joining or putting together of a man and woman in marriage is also called "wedlock" in Scripture. It is first mentioned in Ezek. 16:38, which says that adultery, breaks this lock. For more on this, see footnote g below. The ancient Talmud mentions "wedlock" in Berachoth 16a; Mo'ed Katan 18b; Gitten 26b; and Kiddushin 64a. It is not by accident that the words "break wedlock" in Ezek. 16:38 come from the Hebrew word "adultery." Any standard lexicon or concordance confirms this. The Talmud tractates, Sotah and Gittin have seven hundreds pages dealing with adultery and divorce according to the ancient Hebrews.

4p-Matt. 19:7–8. "Moses suffered [allowed] you to put away your wives." Based on Deut. 24:1-4, thus highlighted in gray. This passage has given rise to fierce controversy. Did Moses sin against God in allowing some of the Jews to put away their wives? Did he contravene the intention of the Lord for marriage to be permanent, which was ordained from the beginning? If He did, then the Creator failed to tell us about it! God approved what Moses allowed, but He did not make Moses' words a *compulsory* commandment. In response to the question of the Pharisees in verse 3, Christ informs them that God granted permission to divorce, but did *not* command divorce for the innocent party in their Torah Law. *It was strictly optional and not a compulsory injunction that had to be obeyed.* (The only text in the entire 613 parts of the Torah Law dealing with divorce is Deut. 24:1-4 as cited above.) To argue that remarriage was forbidden after *valid* divorce is to argue that water is not wet, but dry. Jesus does not infringe or revoke the original grant, or permission of divorce given by Moses. However, He frees it from the false interpretations laid upon it by the wicked Jews. Jesus restored its ancient sense and meaning, which says that divorce, was allowed only for the cause of fornication. This word translated "fornication" in Matt. 19:9, among the Jews embraced a variety of sexual sins and perversions, which included such acts as adultery, incest, bestiality, sodomy and various unlawful copulations. Little or mostly no regard is held today for what God has said in the Bible about anything. The teachings of Scripture are scorned while people run insanely rampant to marry, divorce, and remarry. On the other side, thousands live together, unashamedly in open adultery-fornication without any guilt, or personal responsibility. This problem will only get continually worse in the western society.

5p-Innocent victims. Another side to this dilemma are the millions of single parents who are innocent victims of brutal physical abuse, desertion, and unwanted divorce; these people need love and support wherever possible. The church should rally to receive them with all haste instead of putting them into a religious "penalty box." A single parent mother whose husband had abandoned her for his secretary told me in Houston, Texas, years ago, that she was terrified to go back to a certain "Bible believing church" after hearing the pastor speak on the evils of divorce! Her tearful words were, "He made me feel like a piece of dirt." While on furlough in America, we lived near a lovely family. The wife had a previous marriage in which her husband had forced her into adultery with other men and often beat her into unconsciousness. Her only escape was divorce. This family began attending a "Bible believing, non-compromising church." The pastor upon learning of the woman's past refused to let her take any part in church activities. (However, she was allowed to tithe, attend all the services, work in the nursery, and help clean the building!) Sadly, some ten years later, this pastor's only daughter was snared into the same situation. Amazingly, he suddenly changed his mind about the staunch rules and regulations that he enforced. And guess who was permitted to play the piano? Why of course, his daughter, who had been the unwilling victim of marital chaos. Blood is still thicker than water! *Conversely, it is the duty of God's men to cry out against the evils of sexual sins and unjustified divorce. This must be done in Christian candor and under the anointing of the Holy Spirit.* There was an oral ruling that divorced women must have their former husband's permission to remarry.

(g) "I say unto you." Who are the "you" our Lord addresses? Contextually, Matt. 19:9 has first and direct reference to the Pharisees, who came seeking to trap Him with a loaded question in verse 3. "No" says the Lord, "it [divorce] is not lawful for every cause as taught by the School of Hillel." *Irreconcilable* fornication-adultery is the only valid grounds, affirms the Savior. God stated the same thing hundreds of years prior in Ezek. 16:38. For comments on this passage, see Section 12, third paragraph of footnote a. In Jesus' usage of the words "put away," He did not mean separation. In verses 3-9 the legal term "put away" is used some four times in this discussion, twice by the Pharisees and twice by Jesus. It is impossible that the Pharisees meant "divorce," while Christ meant "separation" only, or vice versa. The context is clear that both sides in the debate were discussing marriage as ended by divorce and not dissolved by death or broken by separation. The reference source by Dana & Mantey, *A Manual Grammar of the Greek New Testament*, 25th edition, page 259 says, that those who force Christ's Words to mean separation and not divorce, "ignore and defy the context, and bring in a strange and foreign thought." Dana and Mantey then conclude that interpreters who do this are like people "trying to open a lock with the wrong key." Guy Duty in his book *Divorce and Remarriage*, pages 39-44 gives a list of some fourteen lexicographical wise men who testify to the same thing. This was the Savior's final Word about the controversy contained in the Pharisees trick question. They stand! See footnote e above for further comments.

2p-A Jewish thing under the Torah Law? There are some things in Scripture that are only for the Hebrew people, but not everything. An example is in Section 74, which is strictly a Jewish thing. Our Lord was not exclusively addressing His answer here to Jews. This "Jew only" twist has become popular among ministers and Christians, who feel they are (somehow) doing God a favor by "defending the Bible." The word "whosoever" in verse 9 surely means just what it says. To force it to read "whosoever of the Jews" is piteous. Jesus' words in verse 11, "all men" can hardly mean "all Jewish men." Refer to footnote f above the fourth paragraph for Moses' law on this subject. Another extreme is the teaching that Matt. 19:9 allows for divorce but not remarriage. If this is true then we note that the inspired writer, Matthew, failed to make this point clear earlier in Matt. 5:32, where he again used the word "whosoever." The entire Sermon on the Mount in Section 44 through 47 was a charter given by the Savior for the people of His new kingdom, or as it was later called, the church. Afterwards, the letters of Paul were written and his instructions regarding permissible remarriage and other things were handed to the church.

3p-Paul's words on this subject. About twenty-five years later, Paul in 1 Cor. 7 was inspired of God to add a second reason for valid divorce, which was not mentioned in the Old Testament Scriptures or by the Savior. Refer to Section 45, fifth paragraph of footnote i, for explanation of this addition, and the last paragraph of this same footnote for a warning on this subject. Those who make a big noise about the *difference* between adultery (between married persons), and fornication (between the unmarried) have a tough time explaining what it is called when one party is married, and the other is not. To believe that one is committing adultery and the other fornication is giving different names to the same sin. In Matt. 19:9, Christ said a married wife could commit fornication. The sacred sexual act when committed across the limits God has drawn is horrendous regardless of the matrimonial or non-matrimonial state of the persons involved. Fornication destroys the preciousness of future marriage consummation, while adultery tears the already existing marriage union apart. These two crimes are demonic and are the number one sin of the world today. Attempting to compartmentalize these two sins and make them different misses the mark. The difference between adultery and fornication is the same as the difference between hell and hell.

4p-Mental abuse. Some well meaning pastors declare, "No divorce for any reason; all married couples must stay together." Many Christians are not acquainted with reality of sin in human life. The author of this work has known cases where wives (and even daughters) have been severally beaten, forced into prostitution-adultery for financial gain, and even murdered by "staying in it." While door-to-door visiting in Alice Springs, Australia in 1966, I met a distraught young woman, beaten black, and blue. Her husband picked up Aboriginal men on Todd Street at night and forced her into prostitution. (She professed to be a saved person.) This had been going on for two years. She asked me what to do. *I did not say, "Pray, be faithful to your husband, and in time God will work it out for you!"* I advised her to go to the local police station, file a complaint, and ask for protection. Later, it was learned that they offered her no help. She fled to Adelaide, nearly a thousand miles south as her enraged husband threatened to kill her. Counselors should not advise women to stay in such perilous situations. Thousands of wives have been forced to divorce ruthless husbands to protect life and limb. *To do so is not a sin.*

5p-In another case at a small town on the central Queensland coasts of Australia, a woman (to whom I had witnessed many times) was beaten to death by her husband with a metal lamp! This was literally "until murder do you part." Her minister advised her to stay in the marriage. There are millions of such cases across the world today. God does not force the will of any man to do right, nor does He force men to commit sin. No one is coerced into righteousness regardless of how much we believe and pray for them. The standard has always been "Whosoever will, may come," or "Whosoever won't, won't come." This does not negate the grace of God in personal salvation. In the case of the murder mentioned above, or life threatening physical and mental abuse, has God given any instructions? What does the warning "do thyself no harm" (Acts 16:28), or "doth not even nature itself teach you" (1 Cor. 11:14) mean? Does the Bible teach them to "stay in it, pray hard," and finally have your brains beaten out? (Some people need to read and obey Prov. 21:9 and 25:24 when they find themselves in dangerous situations.) The author once met a Christian nurse at the Royal Brisbane Hospital in Australia, whose husband deliberately gouged her eyeball out with a spoon. She said that she did not try to protect herself. Proverbs 22:3 reads, "A prudent *man* foreseeth the evil, and hideth himself: but the simple pass on, and are punished?" Did the great missionary Paul demonstrate prudence when he slipped away from danger and death by going over the wall at night in a basket (2 Cor. 11:32-33)? When he and Silas sneaked out of Thessalonica under cover of the night and fled to Berea, was this a lack of faith on their part (Acts 17:10)? *Better, true faith produces common sense in the lives of genuine believers!* Even the Son of God used practical wisdom and went to Jerusalem "in secret" to avoid unnecessary confrontation with the Jews as seen in Section 111, John 7:8-10, footnote h. It has been noted in Section 120, John 8:59, how the Lord Jesus "hid himself" when the religious leaders took up stones to kill Him.

6p-Unfortunately, the ancient dictum that worked wonders in older times on people's attitudes and conduct, "A whip for the horse, a bridle for the ass, and a rod for the fool's back" (Prov. 26:3) is now outlawed by "civilized" governments. Missing today are the brave, young knights of early manhood and the shy, little flowers of fresh and beautiful, blushing womanhood. Male and female psychopaths roam the land; they dominate the stage, screen, television, and in some places even the "churches." The bad side of the media, along with Hollywood and secular education presents them as heroes, good people who really mean well! These human animals are pointed to as role models for our struggling adolescents. The ugly truth is that many of them are sex crazed; self inflamed monsters, which have no respect for God or man. The popular con today is to marry then divorce; remarry; divorce; then remarry and divorce again. The Hollywood philosophy on marriage is another off-ramp to hell. *These horror stories can have a beautiful side. It is found in the absolute forgiveness of God, with a new life in Christ.*

7p-The Lord Jesus did not introduce into this debate with the Pharisees over marriage and remarriage, the Torah Law bitter water test used to identify those guilty of adultery within Israel. The command for this curious act is recorded in Num. 5:11-31. The rabbis had thrown out this law due to the rise of immorality and especially adultery in the nation. Read Section 120 footnotes c and e in conjunction with this paragraph. For a list of the hypocrisies of the Jews, given by Christ, especially the religious leaders, refer to Section 159, and all of footnote e.

8p-It is clear in Mk. 10:12 that the wife could also put away her husband but only under the most peculiar of circumstances. If the husband was a "dung-collector, tanner, or copper smelter," she could seek divorce. See *Jerusalem in the Time of Jesus,* pages 301-310, by Joachim Jeremias, for the ridiculous rabbinical details on this subject. All such divorces had nothing to do with God's Word. They reflected ignorance of the Genesis record.

(h) "Is it not good to marry?" The disciples who had heard the question of the Pharisees and their Lord's response were dumbfounded! *His teaching on this subject separated Him from both theological schools.* In Jewish thinking of that time, there were no other places to go for answers! He was even stricter than the school of Shammai, for He added things they had never taught. It was too high for the twelve and other disciples present to grasp. Their words revealed their consternation over His reply. They blurted out something like this, "Lord, then it must be best for a man never to marry in view of what you have just said." They were shocked for what Jesus had just stated was mostly contrary to everything they had heard or had been taught by the rabbis. Even the Talmud said that a man who is not married is not a full man. See tractate, Yevamot 62b, 63a. Divorce is not an easy thing in His new kingdom. The Savior' commands were superior to *both* theological schools on this subject.

(i) Knowing their hearts, the Messiah answered in concern to His preachers. He said, in essence, "You cannot receive my teaching on this subject now, but later you will; it will be given to you in full understanding." He was speaking of the coming of the Holy Spirit at Pentecost, Who would "teach them all things" and "guide them into all truth" (John 14:26 with 16:13). To this very day, controversy still rages over our Lord's Words about marriage, divorce, and remarriage. Each *true* minister of the gospel feels he is right and stands by that. It is obvious that such wide and often wild diversity on these matters is seriously incorrect and has caused terrible division among believers and within the local church. As with the *finer points* on eschatology, someone is wrong, but few admit to this. Our arrogant human hearts struggle to be always right, but secretly we know they cannot be.

2p-Looming over this subject are the mysterious Words of Christ, "All *men* cannot receive this saying." The differences of opinion from good men and women in understanding these issues may reveal that this mystery continues to the present time. Exegetically, one cannot limit this statement of Jesus to the apostles. Our Lord said, "All *men*." Why and how this is so, we make no pretense to understand. In present times, marriage and its responsibilities are debunked by the liberal media, Hollywood, secular educational systems, liberal religions and various churches. Fornication, sodomy, and adultery are presented as normal; while purity, devotion, and abstinence are hated and opposed. However, God's Word continues to speak on these subjects in such places as Prov. 2:16-19; 5:3-23; 6:20-35; 7:4-27; and 9:13-18. Let all who scorn these words dare to read Heb. 13:4 with Rev. 21:8. God has hung out a bright rainbow of hope and forgiveness for all who are entrapped in the awful mire of sexual perversions and sin. It reads in 1 John 1:7, "The blood of Jesus Christ, God's Son cleanseth us from all sin."

(j) **"Eunuch."** This word speaks of an emasculated male. Christ uses the term here in a wider sense to explain that a variety of persons will make up His spiritual kingdom. They are not all of the same physical propensities, drives, temperate in will, and purpose in life. The following are mentioned:

1. **Physically born eunuchs.** This speaks of those who are born without the normal sexual organs or functions of the male anatomy. They cannot perform the duties of the marriage state. Millions over the course of time have been born without hands, feet, fingers, normal sex organs and so forth. This is not a sin nor is it a sign of judgment on the individual. The various reasons for most of these and a thousand other physical malformations will *never* be really known or *fully* understood. It is to be noted that the rabbis also recognized different categories of eunuchs. The Talmud speaks of Jews, who were sterilized in Babylon (tractate, Sanhedrin 93b), and men being born impotent (tractate, Yevamoth 75b). Our Lord seems to be employing several rabbinical terms in His answer to the Pharisees. The Jews were very acute about this subject, when referring to males. Their Torah Law forbids someone who had by surgery become a eunuch (while involved in pagan worship) to enter the congregation of Israel (Deut. 23:1).

    2p-The Old Testament foresaw a time when this restriction in the law would be invalid. In Isa. 56:4-5, the prophet spoke of a period yet future when eunuchs would be engaged in the worship and service of God. According to the context, this occurred in the history of Israel during the return of the nation from Babylonian captivity in 536 B.C. (Isa. 56:8). Those who seize these passages to prove "Sabbath worship for the church" have missed it by about two thousand five hundred years!

2. **Made eunuchs of men.** Ancient kings and rulers would literally emasculate their slaves. These eunuchs were assigned the duties of attending to the females in their vast harems.

3. **Self made eunuchs.** Here, Jesus refers to those over the course of Christian history, who have *purposely* chosen to abstain from marriage in order to serve Him without the distractions of matrimony. This is a voluntary renunciation of marriage and family. Christ is not referring to the inhumane system of the Papal Church with its celibates, monks, priests, and nuns. He concludes by informing His disciples that there are *some,* who will, without mutilating their bodies or partaking of unnatural lusts, by sheer *discipline* live chastely without the use of women, for the sake of His kingdom. The author of this book knew the famed surgeon, Dr. J. E. Shelly, physician-aide to General Allenby of the British Army. He spent seventy years as a "eunuch by choice" in God's work. His fortune spread the gospel around the world. Church tells of Origen (died in A.D. 254) who took Christ's statement literally and had himself emasculated. This should warn all Christians against false interpretations of Christ's teachings on this subject. Later, Constantine's state church became the Roman Catholic system. It introduced and enforced a compulsory celibacy upon its erroneous nuns and false priesthood. The sufferings caused by this are unspeakable. For the origin of the "first Pope," see Section 13, third paragraph of footnote f.

(k) Realizing His disciples did not comprehend His strange Words, Jesus again informs them that for the present they cannot "receive" what He had said. In time this difficulty would be resolved with the arrival of the Holy Spirit in *fullness* on the day of Pentecost (Acts 2). Then, they would understand all things He had taught them. These men became the foundation builders of the first church; Jesus was its chief corner stone (Eph. 2:20). For more on the unique and exclusive authority of the apostles, see the main heading of Section 110, and Section 177, footnote i.

631

Infants and small children publicly brought to Jesus for prayer. The disciples object. Using the little ones as an example, He teaches them on humility and trust.*

See Section 109 for a previous lesson He had given on humility. This was because of the continual wrangling that prevailed among the twelve apostles, near the end of His earthly ministry.

Peraea

Matt. 19:13-15	Mk. 10:13-16	Lk. 18:15-17	John
Jesus and the children: the disciples are upset	***Jesus and the children: the disciples are upset***	***Jesus and the children: the disciples are upset***	
13 Then were there brought unto him little children, that he should put *his* hands on them, and pray: and the disciples rebuked them.**(a)**	**13** And they brought young children to him, that he should touch them: and *his* disciples rebuked those that brought *them*.**(a)**	**15** And they brought unto him also infants, that he would touch them: but when *his* disciples saw *it,* they rebuked them.**(a)**	
He rebukes them	***He rebukes them***	***He rebukes them***	
14 But Jesus said, "Suffer [let] little children, and forbid [hinder] them not, to come unto me: for of such is the kingdom of heaven."**(b)**	**14** But when Jesus saw *it,* he was much displeased, and said unto them, "Suffer [let] the little children to come unto me, and forbid [hinder] them not: for of such is the kingdom of God.**(b)**	**16** But Jesus called them *unto him,* and said, "Suffer [let] little children to come unto me, and forbid [hinder] them not: for of such is the kingdom of God.**(b)**	
	Humility is first	***Humility is first***	
	15 "Verily I say unto you, Whosoever shall not receive the kingdom of God as a little child, he shall not enter therein."**(c)**	**17** "Verily I say unto you, Whosoever shall not receive the kingdom of God as a little child shall in no wise enter therein."**(c)** (Verse 18 cont. in Section 139.)	
Never to be forgotten event	***Never to be forgotten event***		
15 And he laid *his* hands**(d)** on them, and departed**(e)** thence. (Verse 16 cont. in Section 139.)	**16** And he took them up in his arms,**(d)** put *his* hands upon them, and blessed them. (Verse 17 cont. in Section 139.)		

Footnotes-Commentary

(a) Jesus and little children. He had given a prior lesson on humility several months before. See Section 109, Matt. 18:1-10. At that time, He used a little boy to illustrate His message. It is noteworthy that immediately after Jesus' discourse on divorce and remarriage a host of parents brought their children to Jesus for prayer and blessing. *Smith's Dictionary of the Bible,* vol. 4, page 135, footnote c, informs us that parents would bring their "one-year-old" children to the rabbis in the synagogues on special occasions to be blessed. No doubt, many of these couples had just heard the Master's lesson on marriage in the previous Section 137, and hurried to place their children into the arms of Him who spoke such wonderful truths. They requested that He place His hands on their little ones and pray for them as their rabbis did. Here, they are received and blessed by heaven's greatest Rabbi. Surely some of these children in after days reflected on this occasion and thought, "Jesus, that good man from heaven blessed me as a child." The touch of a loving hand on one's head may linger all through life. Often, it is like a divine benediction.

2p-On the occasion mentioned in the verses above, the disciples attempted to chase the crowds away by rebuking them (Mk. 10:13). It was a social shame for small children to be visibly present when adults were in conversation or serious discourse over religious issues with important persons. Christ disagreed with this strict Jewish custom. No appointment was necessary for Rabbi Jesus to receive parents or their little ones into His arms and bless them in prayer. Again, the disciples must have been shocked at their Master's anti-social conduct. The omnipresent Jewish religious leaders were ready to explode! It is a tragedy to make children feel unwanted or in the way at home or church.

3p-Did Jesus baptize these little ones? Some teach that our Lord baptized these children! At this point, in history, the baptism Christ commanded His church had not yet been instituted. Jesus gave missionary and baptismal instructions to the church only *after* His resurrection. See just beneath the main headings of Sections 201, 203-206. Jews sought the imposition of hands or a touch from pious men and rabbis as a token of approval and God's future blessings. Jacob placed his hands upon the sons of Joseph when he spoke a blessing from God (Gen. 48:14 and Num. 22:6). To read baptism of infants, adults, or anyone else into this is adding to Holy Scripture.

4p-"Children made holy." 1 Cor. 7:14. The teaching that infants of believers become part of the household of faith at baptism is a grievous error. It is traced back to the Roman Church. Before this, to the so-called church fathers, then its origin is found in pagan religions. Certain pedobaptist (baby baptizers) affirm that infants are entitled to baptism on the faith of one or both of their parents. However, the word baptism is found nowhere in 1 Corinthians chapter 7. It is read into the text and then conjectured that infants are "made holy" by sprinkling water on their heads, because their parents were believers. Alexander Hislop in his *Two Babylons,* page 131, tells us that this is not salvation holiness but another kind! He further states, "God may, or may not, as he sees fit, give a new heart, before or at, or after salvation." The error of possible salvation for helpless, incognizant, infants who cannot mentally comprehend the gospel of Christ is wicked. It is a mystic form of "time released salvation," which is more religious nonsense. Paul affirmed that the "unbelieving wife is sanctified by the husband and the husband by the wife." That is, one may, or has already brought the other to Christ. The design of this is that the children of saved parents, when able to understand the saving gospel as taught by their parents, then have the opportunity to be saved. For extended comments on the subject of infants, their conversion, and baptism, see Section 203, fifth and tenth paragraph under footnote d. One is confounded at Hislop's words when he strongly opposed Papal baptism, yet leaves open the possibility of infant salvation, or "a new heart," by sprinkling. As repeatedly stated in this book, the early reformers brought this heresy out lf the Papal Church, and it lives to this day.

5p-Infant baptism has condemned millions of souls. While working in South Africa, the author met hundreds of people in the different branches of the Reformed Church. He preached and lectured in their services, synods, and ministered to thousands. Often, I would inquire of my hosts, "When were you saved?" The answer in countless cases was something like this, "O Reverend Pike, I was chosen by God before the foundation of the world and then baptized as a baby by Christian parents into the church." *None of those who made this confession could affirm that they were saved and knew it!* Persons holding to this have believed a lie. They will die damned, unless they come to personal saving faith in Christ. (It should be remembered that not all Reformed Christians believe this foolishness!) Augustus Strong in *Systematic Theology,* page 957, quotes the famed Presbyterian theologian, Dr. W. G. T. Shedd, (died 1894) as saying that infants of believers are "born into the church as the infant of a citizen is born into the state" by baptism. He postulated false doctrine in this statement. Souls are "born into the true church" or the body of Christ by the grace of God, through repentance and faith in the finished work of God's Son on the cross. There is no other way. Shedd's words reflect the toxic canker of Romanist doctrine still alive among many Reformed and Presbyterian people. His thesis on *Double Predestination to Holiness and Sin* is a classic example of a brilliant mind invading the inscrutable councils of God, attempting to explain them by philosophy mixed with Scripture. The conclusion of this is always a whirlwind of wordy, high-sounding, philosophical, religious nothing.

6p-Heidelberg Catechism. Some Presbyterian and Reformed Christians contend that infant baptism is not just a symbol, but it conveys grace, however, not justifying grace. (Another kind of grace!) Others teach that infant baptism saves, justifies, and puts one into Christ's body or church. Some teach that, as circumcision was the outward sign in the flesh of the covenant God made with Abraham, so infant baptism is the New Testament counterpart. Nowhere does the Bible say that baptism has replaced circumcision. Perhaps the main verse used for this is Col 2:11-12. To hold that this text, "The circumcision of Christ made without hands," means the same as Old Testament circumcision made with hands is ridiculous. Paul told the Colossians that when they were saved, the Son of God did a glorious *spiritual work* in their hearts or inward being. By faith in Christ, the cutting away (or removal) of sin was performed. With this, they became (as it were) Jews inwardly (Rom. 2:28-29). Moses pled the same thing for a rebellious and stiffnecked Israel when he called for them to "circumcise the foreskins of their hearts" (Deut. 10:16). Only men can undergo physical circumcision. The response that "sin came through the bloodline of males" is theological naivety. *Sin devastated male and female alike as well as all of creation.* The massive church meeting in Acts 15 was to settle the issue of whether or not Gentile believers should be circumcised and keep the Law of Moses. Surely, if baptism is the New Testament counterpart of circumcision, the whole matter could have been resolved by stating that Gentile believers had been baptized. The word baptism is not found in this chapter. Those who continually refer to the Westminster or Heidelberg Catechism to prove their point would do better to use the Word of God. See Section 203, the tenth and eleventh paragraphs of footnote d for more on infant baptism.

7p-Pointing to the church fathers for proof of infant baptism is like pointing to water because it is wet. They all embraced the error of infant baptism for salvation, except the erratic, Tertullian (died A.D. 220). *He did worse.* This former African lawyer (shades of Augustine) abandoned sprinkling and taught that immersion saved men from their sin. Later, he became part of the Montanist sect led by two women preachers, Prisca and Maximilla. This ascetic recluse group went into eschatological extremes and proclaimed that the New Jerusalem would soon appear! Their counterparts exist today in those who are busy discovering the date for our Lord's return. For more on the theology of the church fathers, some of whom died terrible deaths for their heresies, see Section 1, Part 1, footnote c, with Section 12, the sixth paragraph of footnote k.

8p-Abraham waited after he was saved fifteen years before circumcision. Scripture is clear *when* Abraham was justified or made righteous. In Gen. 15:6, he was saved by faith in the gospel (Gal. 3:6-8). *However, he was not circumcised until some fifteen years later!* The chronology is thus: Gen. 16:3 reads, "Abraham had dwelt ten years in the land of Canaan." Abraham was seventy-five when he entered the land (Gen. 12:4), to this add ten and arrive at eighty-five years of age. How interesting is Gen. 17:1, which reads that he was now, "ninety years old and nine." God established His covenant with him in verse 7, and he was circumcised at this age (Gen. 17:24). Does this teach that all persons in line for baptismal sprinkling should wait for fifteen years after their conversion to Christ before having water sprinkled on their heads? Is there a waiting period of many years today between actual salvation and baptism [circumcision?] as it was with Abraham? Worse, how can infants fit into this scenario?

9p-Israel, the church in the Old Testament? Jewish circumcision was a private thing that all males bore in their flesh. It was seen and known to them. If so, why make infant baptism such a public exhibition? If Abraham was justified by faith fifteen years *before* circumcision (which "represents infant baptism," so we hear), does this teach that men *must* be saved for fifteen years before they pass through the ordinance of baptism by sprinkling or any other mode? Again, how can this apply to infants? Abraham was saved years *before* his circumcision. All the original Israelite males who came out of Egypt had been cut or circumcised in the flesh but not their hearts (Josh. 5:5). This was the root cause of their problem. The children brought out of Egypt grew up during the forty years wandering, and were uncircumcised due to parental neglect (Deut. 1:39). Before crossing Jordan to enter the land, God commanded all the children, now adults, to be cut in the flesh (Josh. 5:2-4). The circumcised parents could not enter the Promised Land, for they refused to believe the gospel that "God preached to them" (Heb. 4:1-3). The original company of Jews coming out of Egypt consisted of stubborn sinners. God let *all* of them die in the wilderness, except Joshua and Caleb (Deut. 1:35-38 with Joshua 5:6). The prophet Isaiah, looking back wrote that they, "Rebelled, and vexed his Holy Spirit: therefore, he [God] was turned to be their enemy, and he fought against them" (Isa. 63:10). Here, we have the Spirit of God doing His work of conviction, yet men shun him. Israel's rejection of the gospel is stated again in Heb. 3:17-19. It reads, they "could not enter in because of unbelief." The gospel was given to a *circumcised Israel* en masse, but they refused to put faith in this message of salvation.

10p-Israel rejected the gospel forty years. If this motley army of pig-headed Israelis was "God's Jewish Church in the Old Testament," then there is no hope for the Church of Christ in the New Testament. These several million Hebrew males all bore the covenant mark of physical circumcision, but it was only in their flesh. They had the mark but rejected the gospel and resisted the Holy Spirit according to the author of Hebrews as mentioned in the 9p- above. This scenario continued in the wilderness for forty years. Hence, the reason Jehovah pled with them to be circumcised in their hearts (Deut 10:16), which was an operation that only He could perform (Deut. 30:6). Paul wrote centuries later, "For in Christ Jesus neither circumcision availeth any thing, nor uncircumcision, but a new creature" (Gal. 6:15). The only thing that counts with God is being a "new creature" in Christ Jesus (2 Cor. 5:17). The new birth comes with the grace of God in the saving gospel for all who repent and believe. As these circumcised Jews were unsaved, so a baptized baby is unsaved. Covenant theology that transforms the surgical procedure of circumcision into infant baptism for the children of saved parents, is like taking a bath without water.

11p-Baptist baby dedication. The practice of public dedication of infants with its tenderness and pomp did not begin in Baptist churches until the early 1800's in Key West, Florida. Due to the powerful inroads of the Roman Catholic Church in the city at that time, Baptist parents ignorant of Scripture began *secretly* to take their children to the local Methodist minister to have them sprinkled. Over time, this developed into the so-called "public dedication" of infants with sprinkling subtracted from the dedication ritual. Gradually, it became an established practice among Baptist churches. For the story of this tradition that crept into Baptist assemblies in America, see Augustus Strong's *Systematic Theology,* page 957. This is not to decry the need to pray for our little ones and bring them up in the nurture and admonition of the Lord, so that they may come to personal saving faith in Christ. However, we strive to make it clear that neither infant baptism, nor infant dedication saves children from sin and its wages of eternal death. *Baptist churches should have a "parent's dedication" first!* For the fallacy of "baby faith," see Section 150, the second paragraph of footnote f.

(b) "Suffer little children." Those who come to God basking in their arrogance will not be saved! Sinners convicted of their need for salvation must receive the Lord Jesus with a humble, docile, and broken heart. Christ does not say that little infants must come to Him like this, but only those whose humility and willingness resemble that of children. See number 4 below, footnote c for more on this serious thought.

2p-Of such is the kingdom." The citizens of His new kingdom must become like children by a change of heart, which is the first result of the new birth. *Humility is a tiny opinion of one's self and a big opinion of God and others.* Reading all three passages from left to right as harmonized here, clearly the kingdom of heaven and the kingdom of God are the same. See number 3 below for more on this subject. The Savior corrected a mistake His disciples had just made and in so doing, went against the social standard of that day! Mk. 10:13 reads that his preachers tried to prevent the children from being brought to Jesus! See the second paragraph of footnote a above for more on this. We also note that Mk. 10:16, reads that some of these children were so small that He took them up into His arms, praying over each one. This must have taken hours. Note several things about this marvelous event:

1. Our Lord is not teaching that "little children" are saved because of the merits of believing parents. *No one is saved from sin by the faith of another, be it mother, father, Godparents, or whoever.* Everyone is commanded to repent and believe on the Lord Jesus Christ to be saved (Acts 16:31 with Acts 17:30). Salvation is a personal thing for every mortal of responsible age and mind.

2. Scripture teaches that infants and small children are "safe" in Christ but not saved as older responsible persons are. The atonement provides eternal shelter for all little ones who died innocent of *knowingly* committing sin (Deut. 1:39, Rom. 9:11, Jonah 4:11). In 1 Cor. 7:14 it reads that when both parents are believers, their children may be brought to Christ by them and thus be made holy before God. Calvinists who propagate the damnation of "non-elect babies" teach a hideous lie that should be opposed wherever possible. Only when children are awakened by the Spirit and the Word of God over their sinful condition and believe on Christ, are they saved and become children of God. Sprinkling or pouring water on their heads or even immersing them (as the Greek Orthodox Church does) will not save the soul of any child. The promise of remission of sins is to children (who are big enough to comprehend) and to all that are afar off (Acts 2:38-39). For myth of "baby faith," see Section 150, second paragraph of footnote f.

3. What Matthew called "the kingdom of heaven," *both* Mark and Luke called "the kingdom of God," confirming again that they are the same. Note Section 39, footnotes a and g, and the diagram at the end of this particular Section for more on the kingdom question. In the verses above written by Matthew, Mark, and Luke, all three were speaking of the new kingdom of Christ, later called the church.

4. In His Words "of such [or like such] is the kingdom of heaven," the Lord attempted to show His disciples that those who are without humility, and are aggressive, mean, hateful, filled with self and pride are not true kingdom members. "Of such," has reference to those with child-like traits and dispositions. They reflect the *true church* or kingdom. He was speaking of persons who resemble these children in humility and like temper. The little ones who cuddled in His great arms and gathered about His feet were high emblems of what His own followers were to be. He had previously given a similar lesson in Section 109, Matt. 18:2-4, where He used a little boy as the example for all believers. His own disciples continually missed what He was trying to teach them as they bickered and debated among themselves.

(c) Herein may lay the answer to the tormenting question as to why so many make professions of faith, but in time demonstrate that they were never saved. Is it because they did not come to Christ empty, little, needy, trusting Him with the simplicity of a child? These Word's of Christ are as valid today as when He spoke them over two thousand years ago. *They mean what they say!* Pompous, haughty attitudes have no place in the *genuine service* of the kingdom or church of our Savior. We noted in the Parable of the Sower, given by the Savior almost two years previous, that the seed represented God's Word falling into four different places. However, only one out of four was genuine and fruitful. This is further discussed in Section 75.

(d) **"He laid *his* hands on them."** What a scene! The meek and lowly Jesus, the despised carpenter from cursed Galilee, with hundreds gathered about touches the children. Behold the anxious parents; mothers weeping for joy, fathers stand aghast as Christ takes *their* sons into His strong arms and lays hands on them. And of course, see the aged grandparents! Ah, the crown of their white heads cuddled in the bosom of Israel's mighty Messiah. How their weary aged hearts swelled with praise and joy! See the Son of God, revealing He is also the understanding Son of Man as He receives the little ones in loving compassion. Hear Him whispering sweet things in their ears. Watch Him hugging them to His pure heart, stroking their hair, holding their tiny hands as they mystically sensed, "This man loves me, and I love Him." One could wish we had a record of the verbal blessing He pronounced upon these little ones. Yet in all the wonder and glory of this heavenly scene, tender silence speaks louder than many words.

2p-Mark's statement that Jesus placed "his hands upon them, and blessed them" is touching (verse 16). This had reference to the standard rabbinical custom of blessing children. Our Lord approved this and practiced the same custom without the guile and hypocrisy of the scribes and Pharisees. It consisted of laying on of hands, prayer, and prayer for God's mercy upon the recipient. The Jews based this upon the custom of their ancient patriarchs blessing various persons as illustrated in Gen. 48:14. See first paragraph of footnote a above for more on this custom.

(e) Upon departing from this grand occasion, with parents and children waving a loving farewell to the Lord Jesus, suddenly a rich young ruler races to the Savior and kneels before Him. See Section 139 for this intriguing but sad story.

A rich young man runs to question the Savior but leaves deeply sorrowful.*
The dangers of wealth. Peter's question about the apostles who had forsaken
all to follow Jesus. The Lord explains their lowly place in His new kingdom.

*For more information about men forsaking all and coming to Jesus, see Section 39, all of footnote g.

Peraea

Matt. 19:16–21	Mk. 10:17–21	Lk. 18:18–22	John
The ruler's question	*The ruler's question*	*The ruler's question*	
16 And, behold, one[a] came and said unto him, "Good Master,[b] what good thing shall I do, that I may have eternal life?"[c]	17 And when he was gone forth into the way, there came one[a] running, and kneeled to him, and asked him, "Good Master,[b] what shall I do that I may inherit eternal life?"[c]	18 And a certain ruler[a] asked him, saying, "Good Master,[b] what shall I do to inherit eternal life?"[c]	
The Master's response	*The Master's response*	*The Master's response*	
17 And he said unto him, "Why callest thou me good? *there is* none good but one, *that is,* God:[d] but if thou wilt enter into life, keep the commandments."	18 And Jesus said unto him, "Why callest thou me good? *There is* none good but one, *that is,* God.[d]	19 And Jesus said unto him, "Why callest thou me good? None *is* good, save one, *that is,* God.[d]	
	19 "Thou knowest the commandments,	20 "Thou knowest the commandments,	
18 He saith unto him, "Which?" Jesus said,[e] " 'Thou shalt do no murder, 'Thou shalt not commit adultery, 'Thou shalt not steal, 'Thou shalt not bear false witness,' 19 'Honour thy father and *thy* mother:' and, 'Thou shalt love thy neighbour as thyself.'"	'Do not commit adultery,' 'Do not kill,' 'Do not steal,' 'Do not bear false witness,' 'Defraud not,' 'Honour thy father and mother.'"	'Do not commit adultery,' 'Do not kill,' 'Do not steal,' 'Do not bear false witness,' 'Honour thy father and thy mother.'"	
Law keeping cannot give peace of mind	*Law keeping cannot give peace of mind*	*Law keeping cannot give peace of mind*	
20 The young man saith unto him, "All these things have I kept from my youth up:[f] what lack I yet?"	20 And he answered and said unto him, "Master, all these have I observed from my youth."[f]	21 And he said, "All these have I kept from my youth up."[f]	
Repent of your hindrance	*Repent of your hindrance*	*Repent of your hindrance*	
21 Jesus said unto him, "If thou wilt be perfect, go *and* sell	21 Then Jesus beholding him loved him, and said unto him, "One thing thou lackest: go thy way, sell	22 Now when Jesus heard these things, he said unto him, "Yet lackest thou one thing: sell	

Matt. 19:21-27	Mk. 10:21-28	Lk. 18:22-28	John
that thou hast, and give to the poor, and thou shalt have treasure in heaven: and come *and* follow me."(g)	whatsoever thou hast, and give to the poor, and thou shalt have treasure in heaven: and come, take up the cross, and follow me."(g)	all that thou hast, and distribute unto the poor, and thou shalt have treasure in heaven: and come, follow me."(g)	
22 But when the young man heard that saying, he went away sorrowful: for he had great possessions.(h)	**22** And he was sad at that saying, and went away grieved: for he had great possessions.(h)	**23** And when he heard this, he was very sorrowful: for he was very rich.(h)	
Warning against riches	*Warning against riches*	*Warning against riches*	
23 Then said Jesus unto his disciples, "Verily I say unto you, That a rich man shall hardly enter into the kingdom of heaven.◄	**23** And Jesus looked round about, and saith unto his disciples, "How hardly shall they that have riches enter into the kingdom of God!"◄	**24** And when Jesus saw that he was very sorrowful, he said, "How hardly shall they that have riches enter into the kingdom of God!" ◄	
►*Again, we note that what Matthew called "the kingdom of heaven," Mark and Luke called "the kingdom of God." They are the same. In verse 24, Matthew now calls it the kingdom of God.*	**24** And the disciples were astonished(i) at his words. But Jesus answereth again, and saith unto them, "Children, how hard is it for them that trust in riches to enter into the kingdom of God!		
24 "And again I say unto you, It is easier for a camel to go through the eye of a needle,(j) than for a rich man to enter into the kingdom of God."	**25** "It is easier for a camel to go through the eye of a needle,(j) than for a rich man to enter into the kingdom of God."	**25** "For it is easier for a camel to go through a needle's eye,(j) than for a rich man to enter into the kingdom of God."	
The disciples' question	*The disciples' question*	*The disciples' question*	
25 When his disciples heard *it,* they were exceedingly amazed, saying, "Who then can be saved?"(k)	**26** And they were astonished out of measure, saying among themselves, "Who then can be saved?"(k)	**26** And they that heard *it* said, "Who then can be saved?"(k)	
26 But Jesus beheld *them,* and said unto them, "With men this is impossible; but with God all things are possible."	**27** And Jesus looking upon them saith, "With men *it is* impossible, but not with God: for with God all things are possible."	**27** And he said, "The things which are impossible with men are possible with God."	
Peter's question	*Peter's question*	*Peter's question*	
27 Then answered Peter and said unto him, "Behold we	**28** Then Peter began to say unto him, "Lo, we	**28** Then Peter said, "Lo, we	

Matt. 19:27-30	Mk. 10:28-31	Lk. 18:28-30	John
have forsaken all, and followed thee;[l] what shall we have therefore?”	have left all, and have followed thee.”[l]	have left all, and followed thee.”[l]	
Difficult texts	*Difficult texts*	*Difficult texts*	
28 And Jesus said unto them,[m] “Verily I say unto you, That ye which have followed me, in the regeneration when the Son of man shall sit in the throne of his glory, ye also shall sit upon twelve thrones, judging the twelve tribes of Israel.	29 And Jesus answered and said,[m] “Verily I say unto you,	29 And he said unto them,[m] “Verily I say unto you,	
29 “And every one that hath forsaken houses, or brethren, or sisters, or father, or mother, or wife, or children, or lands, for my name’s sake, shall	There is no man that hath left house, or brethren, or sisters, or father, or mother, or wife, or children, or lands, for my sake, and the gospel’s,	There is no man that hath left house, or parents, or brethren, or wife, or children, for the kingdom of God’s sake,	
	30 “But he shall	30 “Who shall not	
receive[n] an hundredfold,	receive[n] an hundredfold now in this time, houses, and brethren, and sisters, and mothers, and children, and lands, with persecutions; and in the world to come eternal life [o]”	receive manifold[n] more in this present time, and in the world to come life everlasting.’[o] (Verse 31 cont. in Section 141.)	
and shall inherit everlasting life.[o]			
30 “But many *that are* first shall be last; and the last *shall be* first.’[p] (Next chap., Matt. 20:1 cont. in Section 140.)	31 “But many *that are* first shall be last; and the last first.’[p] (Verse 32 cont. in Section 141.)		

Footnotes–Commentary

(a) We note several things: he was a *young* man, a *ruler* either of the synagogue or in some capacity as a civil magistrate, and that he came *running* to the Lord Jesus in a sense of urgency. He *knelt* before the Messiah, a common act of paying respect to a great teacher in Israel. Lastly, Dr. Luke informs Theophilus, the original recipient of his letter, that this ruler was *very* rich (Lk. 18:23).

(b) **“Good master”** was a standard address used among the Jews to show honor and esteem to famed rabbis and important persons. It had nothing to do with the moral character of Jesus (which was perfect) but rather to His standing as an excellent and highly respected rabbi among the wiser Jews.

(c) O that this inquiry would burn in the heart of every man! Matthew records him as saying, “have eternal life” while Mark and Luke use the words “inherit eternal life,” both meaning the same thing. This ruler was ignorant of the fact that man can do nothing to “inherit” or “have” life everlasting. All Jews except the Sadducees believed in the after-life, revealing this youth was not a member of this group. His confusion was in that he sought to obtain this highest of prizes (eternal life) by obedience to the Law of Moses, and especially their oral traditions, which contained thousands of rules, regulations, and often useless commands. Every pious Jew struggled day and night to meet the demands as laid before them by their religious leaders hoping to gain everlasting life in the world to come. See Section 30, footnotes a, and b, for the classic example of Nicodemus, who *also* did not understand how to receive eternal life, though he was a famed teacher in Israel.

2p-Certain dispensationalists teach that this young man knew Jesus was offering the Jews a kingdom and Himself as the King have again mishandled God's Word. *For readers who are interested in what the Lord Jesus did offer this man, please peruse the chart located at the end of footnote g in Section 39. It absolutely was not an earthly kingdom or Himself as Israel's King. Such a proposal would have been absurd for a man who was unsaved.*

3p-The event of this young man and Jesus fills our minds with curious wonderment since many Jews were saved by grace while living under the Mosaic Law. However, their salvation was not acquired by strict obedience to the letter of the law, be they positive or negative commands, or the oral traditions. Those who lived during the Old Testament saw Christ (yet to come) pictured in the law, trusted Him, and were saved as surely as Paul was on Damascus road. Refer to Section 10, footnote b, and Section 144, footnote i for explanation of salvation across the Old Testament. The subject of "eternal life" was common among the people as reflected in the question of this rich young man. It is mentioned in the following Talmudic passages of Jewish literature, tractates, Berachoth 48b; Shabbath 10a; and Sanhedrin 105.

(d) "None good but God." This curious response of the Lord Jesus has caused tremendous wondering among believers. What did He mean by correcting the young man for calling Him "Good master," then declaring that only God was good? Jesus did not deny that He was "good," for He was perfect in both His human and divine natures. Religious infidels have seized upon this statement to "prove" that Jesus denied His perfect equality with God, and therefore, was not God. The answer to this enigma is in the *reasoning behind* the question that he put to Jesus. This Jewish ruler looked upon Christ as a man, but One who was a most extraordinary teacher and miracle worker. Upon the basis of his trust in Christ as a good teacher and man, he asked his question. It was established theology and a firm social custom that among the rabbis and devout Jews, that only God and the Torah Law were to be addressed as "good." No others were worthy of this unique appellative. Certainly, this is to be understood of God and the other members of the Holy Trinity in an exclusive sense about all things. However, in Scripture others were also called "good." It is noted that this is said of Joseph of Arimathaea (Lk. 23:50), and of Barnabas (Acts 11:24). A thousand years prior, David wrote of a "good man" whose steps are ordered of God (Ps. 37:23). The Chinese proverb that "There are but two good men; one is dead and the other not yet born," failed to consider the Savior. No man apart from Jesus Christ can be described as being *truly* good before God. Thus, on this occasion, our Lord was trying to correct the man in his hasty but incorrect public greetings. See fuller explanation in next paragraph below. To assert that the Savior was denying His deity and saying in effect, "Young man you have got this all wrong. Only God is good, not Me or anyone else," is wrong. This claim demonstrates the "straw grabbing" efforts of desperate men who reject what the Bible says about the deity of Jesus Christ.

2p-This youthful ruler addresses Jesus as "good master." *This was a public verbal blunder of serious nature that must not be committed by one in his position.* He counted Christ a wonderful rabbi but gave to Him the title belonging (in the Jewish mind) solely to God! It was highly improper and seriously offensive to misapply divine titles in this manner. As said above, the Savior did not deny that He was good or God, rather He sought to correct the serious error of the young man according to the teaching of that day. Christ was saying to this youth "Why do you address Me by the title that belongs to God, and yet consider me only a good man and teacher? Don't you know the offence this will cause among the Jews, who do not yet understand and believe the truth about Me?" On previous occasions, the Savior had publicly claimed equality with God and to believe that He would now deny this is ill thinking. Our Lord was trying to help this young man.

(e) "If you want to have eternal life you must keep the commandments." This was the essence of our Lord's reply. Only Matthew records these Words of Christ. In response to the man's question "Which?" [commandment should I keep], Jesus quotes selected parts from the Decalogue in Ex. 20:12-16 as in footnote d above, this statement, too, has become the object of fierce debate. If men can be saved from sin and hell by law keeping, then why did Jesus die on the cross? Years later, Paul made it abundantly clear that no man is *justified* and made *righteous* by the works of the law, but only by simple faith in the finished work of Christ (Rom. 3:20, 27-28). Further, he wrote that those who seek to be saved by the law are under a perpetual curse if they do not keep all of its commands (Gal. 3:10 with James 2:10-11), and all true believers are like father Abraham, saved by faith in the gospel apart from the code of Moses (Gal. 3:6-9). Therefore, our Lord was not telling the ruler that if he kept the law, he would be saved, for later in the conversation, he confessed that though he had done this very thing, even from childhood days, he was still without hope. See this in Matt. 19:20, footnote f. What then did Christ mean?

2p-Jesus answered him according to his present religious state. He was a man who had lived all his life under the yoke of a perfect law that could not save his soul and satisfy his heart. Moreover, to this fact he openly confessed. The Lord Jesus knowing that he was *depending* on his obedience to the law for salvation said, "Keep your law and see if that will satisfy the longing of your heart." The ruler cried out, "Which, Lord must I keep?" Jesus responded by citing five commands from the Decalogue. Then He quoted in free style from Lev. 19:18, which was later described as the "second greatest commandment" (Matt. 22:36-40). It is of interest that our Lord did not quote *one word* from the oral law or the tradition of elders. The reason is that God at Sinai gave none of these traditions. Nor could they point so wonderfully to the Messiah and Savior of Israel and mankind as did the great Torah Law. In this part of the conversation, Christ proved to His inquirer that observing, keeping, doing, and obeying the Law of Moses with the strictest of intentions does not save the human soul and give peace to the troubled heart of any Jew.

(f) **"What lack I yet?"** What a pitiful confession! Millions entangled in Christless religions secretly carry the same lament in their hearts. This Hebrew youth confessed that he had kept both the positive and negative commands of the Torah Law—*yet he was without peace*. All who seek forgiveness of sins and eternal life by the Law of Moses, and the oral traditions should ponder this man's honest question. What he did not have was earth's poverty; and what he needed was heaven's riches, and a heart that trusted the lowly Nazarene as his Lord and Savior instead of his wealth. Pitifully, he gazed into the black pit of what he lacked, but failed to gaze up into the face of Jesus the Messiah, whom he sorely needed. From childhood (Lk. 18:21), he had walked in the Torah Law with a sincere heart. Now, grown, full of the prospects of life and youth, he cries out that his soul is poor, barren, unconverted, and lost. If this does not prove that men cannot be saved by keeping the Decalogue or any other part of Moses' laws, then nothing will. See all of footnote h below for more on this thought.

2p-Churches and religious bodies of a thousand sorts have within their shadows, those who cry out these pitiful words "I have done it all and yet am lost without peace of conscience and mind." Reader, some of you have tried everything religion has to offer; you have worked to keep the law, but all has failed. Why do you not come to the Son of God? Call upon His Name and trust Him as personal Lord and Savior—NOW. See Rev. 3:20. It strikes us that Jesus did not say to him "Son *after* you are saved then you should live by the law that could not save you!" For details on the myth of living under or by the Jewish law after salvation, see Section 45, footnote b with its relevant subheadings.

(g) In response to his question "What lack I yet?" our Lord's answer fell upon his ears like a sentence of death! Never had any rabbi in Israel told him such things, for the Pharisees counted wealth as a token of blessing and God's favor. And it comes from the lips of Him at whose dusty feet he kneels. Selling his possessions and giving the income secured from this to the poor was a painful and new teaching. Though the Jews put great merit in alms giving, this command of the Savior was overwhelming. No rabbi had ever required such extremes in the service of Jehovah God. Mk. 10:21 adds Christ's Words "come, take up the cross and follow me." For an earlier mention made by the Lord Jesus on "cross carrying," and its horrible implications to the people of that day, refer to Section 128, Lk. 14:27, footnote d. The mention of carrying a cross must have shaken the very soul of this young fellow, for being a dedicated Jew, he understood the horror of Jesus' Words. *In essence, he was told to repent of that which stood between him and the Savior, and then he was instructed to "follow Jesus."* The greatest enterprise of all human endeavors is to pursue the Son of God through this life and into heaven at last.

(h) **"He had great possessions."** This ruler did not possess the greatest treasure, which is eternal life and the forgiveness of sins. Our Lord's admonition sounds strange to the western ear, "If thou wilt be perfect." Jesus was *not* saying that "perfection" (maturity) would be found in alms giving, as if this was meritorious to salvation. Rather, he was using a teaching of the Pharisees in these words, which may suggest this young man was of this infamous number. It was stoutly held among the religionists of Israel, that "he who gives alms lays up treasure for himself, and he will be made perfect in the world to come." The Lord Jesus informs him of the exact opposite: "give your earthly goods for others and perfection [maturity] will begin its sweet work in your life." How strange these words must have fallen into the hearing of this confused patron and servant of the law. We wonder if he had really kept any of the commandments, for his idol was money and possessions. What does the commandment teach in Ex. 20:3 about idolatry? It is noteworthy that Christ did *not* quote this verse to him. With hands full but heart and soul empty, he rises to his feet and walks away. Originally, he ran to Christ, but he walks in leaving. Something dreadful happened between arrival and departure: *he had made the fatal choice!* He would never arrive to the "perfection" of Israel's God, for He had rejected their Messiah and Savior. For the meaning of "perfection," note Section 45, Matt. 5:48, footnote q. Those who want eternal life tagged onto a powerfully rich, luxurious, and Christ rejecting lifestyle will end up in hell at the end of their journey. As stated previously in this work, it is alright to have money but money must not have us.

2p-**"Beholding him loved him."** In Mk. 10:21 this reaction of the Lord Jesus touches us deeply. Every Word out of His mouth came from His pure love and concern for the tender youth that bowed before Him. Christ knowing the heart, with but a few words instantly revealed the source of his problem. The Master required repentance, or turning from that which stood between man and God. For the meaning of repentance, see Section 50, Matt. 9:13, footnote h. Though the ruler had affirmed that he kept the Law of Moses from youth, now we see him cringe at the commandment he had not obeyed! Number ten in God's Decalogue reads, "Thou shalt not covet" (Ex. 20:17). James the half-brother of Jesus warned that to keep *all the* commandments and break one is as though every one of them (613 in total) had been broken (James 2:10-11). The rich man's "great possessions" barred his soul from eternal life in this world and heaven in the world to come, because they prevented Him from trusting Christ. His love for the goods of this world held him back from faithful obedience to the Words of Messiah. *The "Good Master" was too good for him!*

3p-What He did not say. Christ is not teaching that it is *always* necessary for persons to part with every earthly possession before they can be saved. It was, however, required of this man, as money was his god. The command of Christ for this person is not intended for all men. No medical doctor demands that all his patients take the same medicine. The communal, socialistic infected religionists, and political crackpots that teach total abandonment of all goods, and properties are controlled by paranoid minds. They usually see themselves as being a Messiah of some kind, or a figure of the past. They often point to this verse at footnote g as justification for their "Christian Marxism." David Koresh and his disciples at Waco, Texas, stand as a more recent example of this horrid teaching, and what it produces in those who are wooed into it. These things *always* have their origin in demon spirits and often result in deaths or mass suicides. This, guarantees all unsaved souls a sure home in hell.

(i) **"Astonished at his words."** He trusted his riches instead of Jesus. As the young man walked down the road, the Lord Jesus took occasion of the entire event to make some observations for the benefit of His disciples. They had listened to the whole conversation. Jesus' statement about the rich finding it very difficult to enter His new kingdom disturbed them. In 2006, Steven K. Scott published an excellent little book, *The Richest Man who ever Lived; King Solomon's Secrets to success, wealth, and happiness.* Scott traces his thesis through the book of Proverbs and seemingly proves his case. However, he failed to show his readers the last days and end of "the richest man who ever lived." In the book of 1 Kings 11:1-43 we read the slow decline and final decadent state of the happy billionaire. His heart turned from Jehovah, the only true and living God. Solomon went into the demonic temples of Devil worship and bowed before Ashtorech and Milcom or Molech the gods of the heathens. He built altars for Chemosh and Molec the idols in which infants were burnt to death as sacrifices! These abominations brought the wrath of God upon him. There have been some men who could handle great riches but very few. The rich young ruler in the encounter with Jesus, is but another example of the billions in history who could not handle money, rather it handled them. Not even King Solomon, the man who wrote several books of the Bible is an example. Nevertheless, chapter 9 of Scott's work is a brief classic on the subject of "resolving conflicts" from Scripture, and should be read by every Christian.

2p-Again, we must remember the teaching of the scribes and Pharisees that wealth and riches signaled that one was in good favor with God and a part of His spiritual kingdom or church. This was ingrained into their minds. Repeatedly, their Lord had taught the opposite. No wonder they were "astonished at his words" (Mk. 10:24).

(j) **The eye of a needle."** This common expression of the camel and needle was used among the Jews and other ancients. The Arabs spoke of an elephant walking through the eye of a needle. I have heard black Africans use the identical expression. It reflects a great difficulty or impossibility. Built into some of the larger city gates were small narrow ones, located at the bottom of the structure. They were called the "needle's eye." Through this, a camel might enter if stripped of its entire load and passed through on its knees. *A Dictionary of the Bible,* page 505, edited by James Hastings in 1900 denies this. *The International Standard Bible Encyclopedia,* (1987 version) vol. iii, page 510, in an article by J. J. Hughes tries to mitigate the Words of Jesus to make them "less harsh." Hughes continues by saying the small gate in the larger gate "lacks supporting evidence." Many years ago, there was one such gate displayed in the ruins of the ancient city of Joppa. The author saw an old black-and-white photograph of this in a book printed in the late 1899. The objection that there is no archaeological evidence for the "eye of the needle" means nothing. Those who think it necessary to dig up an ancient artifact before they will believe the Word of God are of all men most foolish. One can read examples of the needle in Jewish literature. Such may be found in the Talmud tractates, Baba Metzia 38b; Erubin 53a and b; and Berachoth 55b. Like all the metaphors used by the ancients this one also carried a variety of meanings depending on the culture and location of those who used it. The disciples knew exactly what their Lord was saying, "A rich man may go to heaven, but he must be stripped (or repent) of everything that he trusts, except me." Again, they were amazed at their Lord's teaching, for so much of it contradicted the message of their rabbis! Refer to footnote i above for further explanation on this subject.

2p-Jesus' Words here are not a universal command for His people to "go and dispose of all earthly goods." Rather, they were a sharp warning about the danger of riches hindering one from entering into the kingdom of God. This had just been manifested in the rich young ruler as he walked away.

3p-It should be noted in the parallels here that the "kingdom of heaven" in Matt. 19:23, becomes the "kingdom of God" in Mk. 10:23 and Lk. 18:24, which (again) reveals they are the same. Mark and Luke only used the term "kingdom of God." See the diagram drawn across Matthew's version of this event at the end of Section 39. *It unequivocally demonstrates that the kingdom of heaven, kingdom of God, eternal life and salvation all mean the same thing.* Extreme dispensationalists have butchered this teaching in God's Word and created a completely new eschatology that is foreign to the New Testament. For more on this, see Section 138, number 3, under footnote b.

(k) **"Who then can be saved?"** This puzzling question from the disciples again reveals how little they understood their Master's message, even at this late period in His life. "If Jewish rich men cannot enter the kingdom, then who can?" was their real query. They were examples of the partly twisted theology of the rabbis and Pharisees, who taught that riches and worldly honor were a prerequisite for all Jews to gain entrance into God's earthly, political kingdom. See footnote i above. In Matt. 19:26, Christ informs them that the impossible rules laid down by the religious Jews for salvation are negated by God, who saves all that believe on Him.

(l) Upon hearing the Words of his Lord, Peter was suddenly alarmed. Thinking upon his financial condition and that of his fellow apostles ("we have forsaken all"), he puts this question to Jesus. Their forsaking probably consisted of fishing boats, nets, little cottages and a few earthly goods. Later, we hear Peter confess that he had neither silver nor gold (Acts 3:6). Some thirty years afterward, he wrote about "an inheritance incorruptible, and undefiled, and that fadeth not away, reserved in heaven" (1 Peter 1:4). Time and experience often greatly change our minds about the material and temporal things of this short life.

(m) Seemingly, Peter was saying to Jesus that they had done for Him what the young rich man had refused to do: forsaken all to follow. In Matt. 19:28-30 we note our Lord's answer to Peter's inquiry. It is candidly admitted that there are both mystery and difficulty contained in the answer of Jesus. Whenever this occurs, the problem is always in our inability to understand the true meaning of such texts. Hasty or forced exegesis is not the answer to these things. Some speculations regarding our Lord's Words are as follows:

1. **Verse 28a.** This speaks of "the regeneration" that shall be upon earth when Christ sits on the throne of glory. Some see in this "regeneration," the new birth or salvation in which all believers share. This word occurs but one other place in the New Testament in Titus 3:5. Here, it means "new birth." See *Vines Expository Dictionary of New Testament Words*, page 267. Christ could *not* have been speaking of conversion from sin, and that His disciples had followed Him in this experience. Jesus Christ being sinless did not need salvation. He may have been speaking of the final restoration of all things to their former state: the time when the entire universe will be born again or completely made new. The ancient rabbis spoke of a literal renewing of the created earth that would occur after a long period of reigning by the Messiah. See the Talmud tractate, Sanhedrin 97b. They said the prophets forecast this in Isa. 34:4, 51:6 and 65:17. Various other Jewish writings speak of the same idea along with several New Testament verses (Acts 3:21; Rom. 8:19-21; 2 Peter 3:13; and Rev. 21:1). For the wildly exaggerated rabbinical meanings of time, see Section 82, footnote d, and Section 95, footnote k. Some of the above things were believed more or less in the days of Christ on earth, and no doubt held in varying degrees by his apostles.

2. **Verse 28b.** The twelve apostles sitting on thrones judging the twelve tribes of the nation of Israel. Jesus' Words have their origin in Dan. 7:9, 13-14 which speaks of "thrones" and the "Ancient of days" or Messiah in a judgment context. Some old rabbis held that this had reference to Messiah's judgment rule, and the thrones (plural) were reserved for the "great men of Israel" who would share this time with Him. *Together* they judge the twelve tribes of Israel. See *Jesus and the Kingdom of God*, pages 275-276 by G. R. Beasley-Murray. This work is exhaustive but ruined by its overly academic scrutiny and disbelief in the inspiration of all Scriptures. Christ made a later reference to these thrones in Section 169, Lk. 22:30, footnote f. In this text, the Lord also speaks of eating and drinking in His kingdom. How the redeemed will eat and drink in that future kingdom will not be the same kind of human consumption as known on this earth. There will be no cold food, sour vegetables, strong drink, ulcers, and upset stomachs medicated with Tums or Nexium. All joys will be experienced in a glorified body free from the infirmities of the functions of our present sinful human anatomy. Could it be that perfect eating and drinking as experienced by Adam and Eve before the fall into sin? *In time, we will know, now we do not!*

3. Some hold that the twelve symbolize the church ruling over its enemies. There is no merit in such *super spiritualized* interpretations. Others see in this figure the twelve apostles literally resurrected and actually reigning co-jointly with Christ over the world. However, Scripture teaches that "the saints" (not just the twelve) will in some way (not explained) also share the rule and judgment work of Christ at the end (1 Cor. 6:2; 2 Tim. 2:12; Rev. 5:10; and 20:4). Regardless, Christ is the supreme Judge of all men (John 5:22). It seems right that the original apostles should have a special distinction during Christ's great honor, for they were endowed with unique power and special gifts as the forerunners in establishing His kingdom-church. Likewise, the eternal preservation of the *saved* members of the nation of Israel is clear in Scripture. Such verses as Ezek. 34:11-13; 36:22-28; and 37:15-28 are a few samples of this truth. To spiritualize the twelve tribes into becoming the church is to do violence to Scripture. Could it be that Jesus withheld the *finer details* of this wonderful New Age that is surely coming and the apostles' full part in it, lest they should have been swept up into a dream-like euphoria of Jewish kingdom glory? Under such, they would forget the future of suffering and death that awaited Him at Jerusalem and most of them later. When Christ spoke these strange things, the shadow of the cross would soon become substance: these men needed facts not dreams to brace them for what was ahead. The prudent expositor will not inject private assumptions and "feelings" into such mysterious words, since our Lord Himself refrained from a precise surgical-like explanation of their meaning. One should never build absolute

conclusions on personal assumptions, regardless of how reasonable they seem. Whatever all this *finally* means and will become in the plan of God for earth and the redeemed of all ages, the twelve would understand later. *After all, God is not hard to get along with; we are!*

4. There are expositors that see in our Lord's Words, the twelve apostles *physically* ruling over fellow Jews during the millennium time. This interpretation seems far-fetched. Who can imagine twelve men sitting on thrones for a thousand years pronouncing various judgments over millions of fellow Jews? Did our Lord speak in allegorical terms as in John 6:53 and 10:9? Like the sheep-goat scenario of Matt. 25:31-46, this statement of our Savior is difficult to rightly divide and more difficult to place chronologically in the plan of God for earth and men. On a millennium of misery and human suffering, see Section 39, tenth paragraph of footnote a, and Section 171, fourth and fifth paragraphs of footnote b. In God's time, it will happen just as Jesus said and then we will understand the meaning.

(n) **"Shall receive a hundred fold" of what?** Jesus promised that the workers in His new kingdom would have their needs met. This has been proven a million times and more over the past two thousand years of Christian history. *Often, our needs supplied by the loving hand of God are vastly different from what we supposed* (Phil. 4:19). That best of missionaries needed a "thorn in his flesh" for the power of God to rest upon his life and ministry (2 Cor. 12:7-9). The author of this work, as an eighteen-year-old lad, needed his legs paralyzed in a high school football accident, and God supplied that need! It was the most wonderful tragedy and lighted darkness to fall into his life. Some, Christians upon the call of God, have forsaken hearth and home for the distant mission fields of the world. *There* they found new brothers, sisters, fathers, mothers, many children, and lands abundant. Again, the author and his wife have literally experienced this for over fifty years as they followed Christ in the footsteps of faith around the world. Paul said that in the life of faith, we are like people "having nothing, and yet possessing all things "(2 Cor. 6:10). The rich young man walked away from life's most *enduring* wealth. One muses in deep melancholy what became of this fellow and how did he die? Since his encounter and rejection of Jesus, millions of others have walked into eternal riches upon receiving Him as personal Lord and Savior. Right direction in the Christian journey is seriously important, especially as the end of life approaches. Years ago, I read these words inscribed in an old book, in the Johannesburg Public Library. "O the joy that seeketh me through sorrow, O the peace that teacheth me through pain, O the hope that findeth me through heartache, by it all Christ is my gain."

(o) **"Shall inherit eternal life."** This eternal life is both the present and future possession of every born again believer in the Lord Jesus Christ. Its *full* benefits will be eternally realized in that wonderful place called heaven.

(p) **God's way of doing things.** There is something sadly joyful about the words of Matt. 19:30. This was a common term used among the Jews and understood by all. The Savior says that even though every need will be supplied for all who follow Him, still within this grand company some that are first will be last. Among the children of God, there are those who are *faithful,* work hard day and night but always seem to be behind. In the world to come, these "last ones" will be first in God's new order of things. There is also a strong possibility that this was originally addressed to Peter, who seemed to express a sense of high anxiousness over his financial situation in Matt. 19:27 and parallel texts. It could also have been a rebuke to his persistent quest for authority and rank among the twelve. Such is the order of grace as it sees the heart and rewards all accordingly.

2p-In using the term, about the first becoming last, the Lord Jesus was referring to the rich young ruler as he disappeared down the road. He was a great Jew first, and highly esteemed among his countrymen; but wrong choices had placed him last for the remainder of life, and dreadfully so in eternity to come. Contrary wise, publicans and sinners, who were held as the lowest and last by Jewish religion, had received Jesus the Messiah and were now first in the new kingdom of Christ. The curious ways of God are explained further in the following paragraph.

3p-Example of God slowly doing things. The strange yet glorious actions of God are seen in the following illustration. When we went to Australia in 1961, God clearly directed us through some little children playing on a beach to go and plant a church, in a small town called Gladstone, in Queensland. Within one year, over eighty people had been saved, and the whole village knew of what was happening. As the missionary involved in this I, felt quite satisfied that I was doing a good work! In 1963, I was invited to Brisbane to attend a prayer meeting in the old Temperance Hotel, no longer standing. There were some fifty men present, for this three-day prayer effort. On the second night, as I entered the large room where the men were gathered, an elderly white headed man beckoned me to sit by him. His name I do not remember, but I cannot forget what said. With joy in his face, he inquired about the work in Gladstone. In my evil pride, I told him what I was doing. Then came the shock. Leaning over he placed a hand on my mine and said, "Young man, forty years ago the Holy Spirit led me to go to Gladstone, rent a hotel room and spend one week in prayer and fasting, asking God to send spiritual awakening to that godless place." (I was not even born when this old saint was pleading in prayer.) His face beamed as he exclaimed, "How wonderful that He answered my prayers, through you!" Stunned, my pride in what was taking place in Gladstone, mocked me, and the sovereignty of God in prayer stood high and mighty. Who can explain why the Lord of heaven waited forty years to answer a week of fasting and prayer? *"As for* God his way is perfect" (Ps. 18:30). For another example of the Lord waiting four decades to save a lost Tennessee farmer, see Section 135, sixth paragraph of footnote e.

Jesus continues to answer Peter's question* with the Parable of the Vineyard Laborers. He explains that the first may be last and the last first in His work. Humility, loyalty, and trust are required in the service of His new kingdom.

* For this heart touching enquiry by Simon Peter, see Section 139, Matt. 19:27, footnote l.

Matt. 20:1-16—*Peraea*	Mk.	Lk.	John
First workers hired			
1 "For the kingdom of heaven(a) is like unto a man *that is* an householder,(b) [land owner or land lord, verse 11] which went out early in the morning to hire labourers into his vineyard.			
2 "And when he had agreed with the labourers for a penny a day, [about 17 cents] he sent them into his vineyard.(c)			
Second workers hired			
3 "And he went out about the third hour,(d) [9:00 a.m.] and saw others standing idle in the marketplace,			
4 "And said unto them; 'Go ye also into the vineyard, and whatsoever is right I will give you.' And they went their way.			
Third workers hired			
5 "Again he went out about the sixth [12:00 noon] and ninth hour,(e) [3:00 p.m.] and did likewise.			
Fourth workers hired			
6 "And about the eleventh hour(f) [5:00 p.m.] he went out, and found others standing idle, and saith unto them, 'Why stand ye here all the day idle?'			
7 "They say unto him, 'Because no man hath hired us.' He saith unto them, 'Go ye also into the vineyard; and whatsoever is right, *that* shall ye receive.'			
Payday is coming someday			
8 "So when even was come, the lord of the vineyard saith unto his steward, [administrator] 'Call the labourers, and give them *their* hire,(g) [wages] beginning from the last unto the first.'			
9 "And when they came that *were hired* about the eleventh hour, [5:00 p.m.] they received every man a penny.(h) (about 15 to 17 cents*)			
10 "But when the first came, they supposed that they should have received more; and they likewise received every man a penny.*			
11 "And when they had received *it*, they murmured against the goodman [land owner or land lord, verse 1] of the house,			
12 "Saying, 'These last have wrought *but* one hour, and thou hast made them equal unto us, which have borne the burden and heat of the day.'			
13 "But he answered one of them, and said, 'Friend, I do thee no wrong: didst not thou agree with me for a penny?*			
14 'Take *that* [which] thine *is*, and go thy way: I will give unto this last, even as unto thee.			
15 'Is it not lawful for me to do what I will with mine own? Is thine 'eye evil,'(i) because I am good?'			
The final meaning of the parable			
16 "So the last shall be first, and the first last: for many be called, but few chosen."(j) (Verse 17 cont. in Section 141.)			

Footnotes-Commentary

(a) As in the previous Section, the lesson here also pictures activities in the new kingdom that He was building. This parable was drawn from a literal event that had occurred somewhere in the land and from it Jesus drew His message. The previous Section 139, Matt. 19:30, concludes with Christ warning His disciples, *especially Peter*, that many of those who are first now, will be last in the future, and many of the last will be first. In this Section, Jesus explained what these curious words meant in the Parable of the Laborers in the Vineyard. See footnote j below. Here, Jesus commences with the Parable of the Laborers: it shows the attitudes and ranks of workers within Christ's kingdom. The lesson here is only understood by connecting it with the last verse of the proceeding chapter and Peter's anxious question "What shall we have?" Jesus answered his inquiry by explaining how laborers-workers will be paid (rewarded) in His kingdom; how the first (in some cases) will be last and the last first; and what their attitude towards the Master's payment plan should *not* be. We can believe that Simon Peter finally understood and got the lesson his Lord was teaching. This seems obvious upon reading his words in 1 Peter 5:5, written about three decades later, "Yea, all *of you* be subject one to another, and be clothed with humility: for God resisteth the proud, and giveth grace to the humble."

2p-"Householder." He is the "goodman" in verse 11. For more on this person, and other places where this term is used, see Section 71, footnote p, footnote b below.

(b) **Hiring laborers at the first hour 6:00 a. m. or sunrise.** Land owners ("householders") would hire temporary workers during harvest seasons for short periods of time. These land owners were also called "goodman" in verse 11. *Gill's Commentary*, vol. 7, pages 221-222 lists examples of this, confirming that the time of hiring as mentioned in Jesus' parable here, agrees with ancient practice. Jewish history mentions those hired to work all day, and those for a few hours often received the same pay. Christ used the customs and terms of the day, and His audience understood it. Work always began at sunrise or about 6:00 a.m. before the heat became hot overbearing, and normally ended at sundown. It was something of a twelve hour a day job. Though the men hired first went early into the field, the task was too great for them; more help was needed. The goodman got busy looking for others to hire and recruited more laborers at the sixth, ninth and eleventh hours.

(c) Christ tells His audience that the householder is God; the vineyard is the world, and the laborers are those who are called into divine work, whether they serve with genuine or feigned loyalty. He is the steward or overseer of God's house (Heb. 3:6). The first batch of laborers went to work at sunrise for the wage of one penny each. This was approximately 15 to 17 cents a day. Jewish writings abound with mention of workers being hired for the denarius or penny a day. Perhaps these earliest recruits point to the first laborers and prophets over the Old Testament era. They were the original servants in Gods' work. We could say it started from the sunrise of antiquity with Abel, Enoch, Noah, Abraham, and their successors who were the first to labor in the early vineyard for the Lord. In Lk. 1:70, we read of God's witnesses from the beginning of human time.

(d) **The third hour or 9:00 a.m.** Later, in the progress of human history, God, the *true* householder, called others to labor in His vineyard. Perhaps these are the successors of those first or earliest workers: Moses, Joshua, David and the like. The householder promises to pay them what was "right."

(e) **The sixth hour or 12:00 noon, and ninth or 3:00 p.m.** More workers were recruited to labor in the vineyard. The task became overwhelming to the early laborers. More help was urgently needed. It is notable that no fixed amount was agreed upon for these late comers. Can one find here the latter prophets giving themselves in desperate efforts to bring the people of Israel back to God? Possibly, these may represent Isaiah, Jeremiah, Daniel, and the later prophets down to Malachi.

(f) **The eleventh hour or 5:00 p.m.** Sundown and darkness would shortly move over the vast vineyard and yet there is much to be done. The great householder sees "others standing idle" and employs them to hurry into service. They have spent most of the day in small talk and vain chatter. How true of many Christians in this present era. Every born again believer has been given some level of service, which may change over the passing years. Nevertheless, we always have a work to do. These works differ and vary. None is counted small and others great. Genuine service for our Lord emanates from the heart and its attitude. *It is here that everything stands or falls.* For more on this see footnote i below.

(g) Pay time arrived for the long hard day was over. The Torah Law required that laborers be paid at the end of each day (Deut. 24:14-15). The lord or householder ordered the "steward" to settle with each of the workers. For explanation of the meaning of "steward," see Section 130, footnote b. In this present parable, however, Christ Himself is the steward of His Father's House. See footnote c above.

(h) **"Every man a penny" or denarius. Verses 8-15.** The content of these eight verses falls odd onto the western mind, not understanding ancient customs that prevailed across the Middle East. Various cities and towns differed in their methods of hiring and paying wages. Probably, the custom mentioned by the Lord Jesus in this lesson was one employed by the citizens of the place where He was teaching. Thus, all who heard would have instantly understood it. These eastern customs are reflected in the parable outlined below. Western minds need not make some mysterious lesson of dark apocalyptic nature or some outlandish typology from what Jesus said at the end of Section 139, Mk. 10:31, footnote p. The lesson in this Section explains what Jesus said. It was clear, simple, and instantly understood by all those who listened. Note the following points regarding this Parable of the Vineyard Laborers. He commenced by paying first those who were hired *last,* and therefore, had labored the shortest time. Then he ended by paying *last* those that were hired *first.* Thus, we see how the first become last and the last become first when men are finally rewarded for Christian service. The ancients often paid hired laborers in this fashion. Each one received a penny. See footnotes c and f above. We have no report of what was said when those hired at the third, sixth and ninth hours received their wages. Apparently, they had no complaint and went away happy:

1. **Verses 10-12.** The title "goodman" may have been taken from Prov. 7:19. Lastly, in the pay-line stood those who had been hired *first* and had served all day long, working ever so hard in their lord's vineyard. (Now, we see the first becoming last.) They too were given one penny each as originally agreed upon at the time of hiring (verse 2). Looking at the coin in hand, they broke out into murmuring and complaining over their pay. They objected that the lord or steward had counted the last workers, who had toiled so short a time, equal with them. Had they not born the burden and heat of the day? Therefore, they had toiled longer and harder than the late comers had. Again, eastern customs come to the fore. Continually, hired workers would *automatically* complain if they felt there was the slightest possibility of getting more out of their employer than originally agreed. This is what these laborers did.

2. **Verses 13-14.** The steward justified his actions on the basis that he had been true to their original agreement and had paid what was promised. It was not the length of time served but the verbal contract that gave validity to the steward's response. Both had agreed to this.

3. **Verse 15.** The steward reveals that the problem was in the "eye" of the complainers. Their "eyes" had seen only the outside and not the heart's motive. His actions were "good" because he had evaluated, then judged correctly their motives and paid each one accordingly. In God's service, some have toiled their lifetime, with no recognition, praise or public fame. Position and recognition in the service of Christ are matters of heavenly choice; woe be the church where men decide these things. Many are the insignificant, unseen servants in the Master's world vineyard who have labored a lifetime. Others enter the fields late in the day, even at the eleventh hour, ere sundown. For reasons unknown to the weary ones, these are often extolled and lauded above all other workers. It is not good when all are leaders! In a war, some plan while others fight. The general gets the praise while the foot soldiers, have done the fighting and dying. In this parable, the Lord Jesus explained to Peter how the last will be counted first and the first be last in His kingdom. *It has to do with the heart's motive as seen by God.* See footnote j below for the conclusion.

(i) **"The evil eye."** The steward quoted these words from Prov. 28:22 which seems to confirm he was Jewish and had knowledge of the Old Testament. In this application, it means an "evil [stingy] eye" and reveals that the steward was rebuking his workers for being tight-fisted. The complainers had a grudging eye while the steward had a liberal or generous eye toward others. They were offended because he was greathearted and had rebuked them for murmuring over his goodness to those who had *not* worked as long as they had. The wise steward had judged the stream by the fountain. He knew well that a small quantity of work done in the right spirit, and motive was of greater value than a large quantity performed from resentful intents. The "first" are those in God's Church, who serve out of necessity. Often, many of these are secretly angry, boiling with resentment, doing their work, and then becoming furious because there is little or no recognition.

2p-The *two classes* of workers in the parable are treated differently for they were of opposite character and motive. For the grumbling vineyard employees to be dismissed with this "evil [stingy] eye" charge laid upon them was a very humiliating experience. According to the custom of that day, friends and neighbors would shame them, because the Jews taught that God owned all things and was the greatest benefactor, giving freely to all Israelites. Pious Jews should emulate this example. For an earlier mention of the "evil eye" during the Sermon on the Mount, see Section 46, Matt. 6:22-23, footnote k.

(j) Our Lord had spoken similar words in the previous Section 139, Matt. 19:30, footnote p. *This specific statement was addressed first to Simon Peter and in this instance had nothing to do with the divine call to salvation; instead, it refers to one's call to serve in the work of God.* Later, we notice that Christ seems to have used it in reference to unsaved Israel as explained in Section 154, Matt. 22:14, footnote j. Nevertheless, no man is saved by serving, but rather he is saved to serve. Moreover, this service must issue out of a heart of love and thankfulness because he has been saved. This same expression about the "last" and "first" had been previously used by the Lord Jesus in Lk. 13:30. Simon Peter, who prompted the explanation, should have been the first one to understand. See footnote a above. After all, one's work does not rest wholly on the amount of time spent on it. A. T. Robertson quotes an ancient Hebrew saying, "Even so hath Rabbi Bun bar Chija in twenty-eight years wrought more than many studious scholars in a hundred years." See *Word Pictures in the New Testament*, vol. 1, page 161. This maxim given by Robertson well describes the events recorded in these passages.

2p-Faithful service, not success. Lastly, Christ speaks these words to *all* servants in His kingdom. Regardless of how long they have labored, the abundance of work, or the difficulties attached to each duty, unless they have served from a heart of true love and humility, it is nothing. Like a fly in the ointment, their years of "Christian service" are spoiled (Eccles. 10:1). At the Judgment Seat of Christ, all falsely motivated labor will be counted as loss (1 Cor. 3:11-15). Our Lord's admonition that "many" of the first shall be last, stand as a ten-fold beacon to warn those who labor in His church or new kingdom. Servants of God, who read these lines, should carefully examine their motives for Christian labor. *We are all where we are in life and Christian service solely by the grace of God.* Thoughtful and serious contemplation of this fact should greatly assist us in throwing off all silly complaints. The brevity of life hangs over each of us: serve Christ with a glad heart, doing, giving, going, and sharing with all who would stop to hear the gospel. Reader, if you cannot be the first best for Christ; be the second. Both the swift rabbit and slow turtle reach their destinations in time. *Crawl like a turtle or run like a rabbit, God is equally pleased with both!* We do not escape the responsibilities of tomorrow by evading them today. Because you cannot do everything don't do nothing! Simply do what you can. Some fifty years ago, I met an elderly retired F.B.I agent. Inquiring of his conversion, he related the following. While hurrying down a busy street in New York City, the wind blew a piece of paper across his face. A bed-ridden aged woman, living in a small high-rise apartment lay near an open window. Each day she took gospel tracts, scribbled on them her name and address, prayed, and gradually tossed them out of the window. Several months later, the seed sown some two hundred feet up, blew into the face of this young man. This tract was used of the Holy Spirit and finally led him to Christ! His wrinkled countenance glowed with the joy of Christ as he related his testimony. We must also remember that not all tract distribution is this dramatic. The fact that God's ways are beyond us is surely for our good. Ours is to labor in faith and leave the results in His hands.

3p-Jewish rejection. Embedded in this statement of Christ in verse 16 is a strong warning to the Jews. His original followers consisted entirety of converts from the nation of Israel. Now, the suggestion is that they will be outstripped in decades to come by those they hated the most. The predominantly Gentile church, which was yet to be born, and the Gentile world languishing in awful darkness, may point to those standing idle in the marketplace (verse 6). When the gospel of grace triumphed in their lives, they would outrun the Jews in His kingdom service. It was written by the prophet, "Sing, O barren, thou *that* didst not bear; break forth into singing, and cry aloud, thou *that* didst not travail with child: for more *are* the children of the desolate than the children of the married wife, saith the LORD" (Isa. 54:1). Who would deny that this has not been done? The Jews were enraged and provoked into great jealousy at the conversion of Gentiles, into the spiritual kingdom of Christ. Nevertheless, this did not cause a serious self-examination and their return to the Messiah.

4p-Gentile acceptance. On the other hand, barren, unsaved, and held in the deadly coils of demonic idolatry, countless millions of heathens upon hearing the gospel, gradually welcomed the Messiah as their Lord and Savior. Rescued by the grace of God they have to this day marched forward in kingdom service. Adamant and fierce rejection of Jesus the Son of God carries with it an awful curse! As previously discussed in this work, before the foundation of the world, God decreed to "elect" into salvation all who would believe on His Son. His elect are those who trust Christ as Savior. For further comments regarding "the elect" see Section 1, Part 3, first paragraph of footnote h, and Section 135, all of footnote e. Paul wrote that the Jews of his time were blinded while the elect or believing Gentiles "obtained it" or were saved (Rom. 11:7). Like the metaphor of the olive tree employed by Paul, it is written, "because of unbelief they [the Jews] were broken off" (Rom. 11:20). After the rejection and blasphemy of their Messiah, Israel crashed as a nation. She was possessed with the demons of slumber, spiritually blind eyes, had deaf ears, stumbled, and fell into a snare and a trap. Her back was bent, stooping beneath the burden of sin and rejection (Rom. 11:8-10). *Later, a few days before the cross, Jesus warned the Jews that the kingdom would be taken from them and given to the Gentiles, who would bring forth fruits to the glory of God. Refer to this, in Section 153, Matt. 21:43, footnote k.* For two thousand years, this prediction of the Savior has been operative. By comparison, over the centuries only a small number of Jews have come to the saving knowledge of "Yeshua ha' Mashiach," or Jesus the Messiah. This does not signal that God is forever finished with Israel (Rom. 11:1-6)

5p-Where God dwells today. The redeemed of all ages are "builded together for an habitation of God through the Spirit" (Eph. 2:22). This habitation or dwelling place is manifested first in individual saved Christians, and second in *true* local assemblies around the world. Paul called them "God's husbandry, [and] . . . Gods' building" (1 Cor. 3:9). Peter described this as "Ye also, as lively stones, are built up a spiritual house, an holy priesthood, to offer up spiritual sacrifices, acceptable to God by Jesus Christ" (1 Peter 2:5). Neither Paul nor Peter had in mind a two million dollar "sanctuary" in downtown Boston or New York! God does not dwell in material buildings, but in souls redeemed by the precious blood of Jesus (John 14:17 with Eph. 3:17). Biblical truth is often smothered by the fuss and fume of American Christians concerning their "new church," "house of worship," or "educational building that everyone must come and see!" This is not to degrade or decry a clean place for corporate worship, but it is intended to help bring important things into proper focus. The Lord of heaven is just as pleased with a handful of Iraqi or Chinese Christians, meeting in secret, with no Bible, pastor, or building, as He is with those enchanted by colorful robed choirs, stained-glass windows, resounding pipe organs, and "comforting sermons."

The Lord Jesus crosses westward over Jordan's forge and moves toward Jerusalem,* He speaks again of His crucifixion and resurrection. None of the twelve apostles understood those awful words at that time.**

*See verse 17 below which suggest that He had now entered Judaea by the words "going up to Jerusalem." **For the disciples not comprehending their Lord's death at this time, see Sections 104-105, and 107.*

Crossing the Jordan River into Judaea

Matt. 20:17–19	Mk. 10:32–34	Lk. 18:31–34	John
Heading for Jerusalem: His disciples are terrified **17** And Jesus going up to Jerusalem took the twelve disciples apart [aside] in the way, and said unto them,	***Heading for Jerusalem: His disciples are terrified*** **32** And they were in the way going up to Jerusalem; and Jesus went before them: and they were amazed; [perplexed] and as they followed, they were afraid. And he took again the twelve, and began to tell them what things should happen unto him,	 ***Heading for Jerusalem: His disciples are terrified*** **31** Then he took *unto him* the twelve, and said unto them,	
Terrible news again: "I am going to die"[a] **18** "Behold, we go up to Jerusalem;	***Terrible news again: "I am going to die"***[a] **33** *Saying*, "Behold, we go up to Jerusalem;	***Terrible news again: "I am gong to die"***[a] "Behold, we go up to Jerusalem, **and all things that are written by the prophets concerning the Son of man shall be accomplished.**	
and the Son of man shall be betrayed unto the chief priests and unto the scribes, and they shall condemn him to death,	and the Son of man shall be delivered unto the chief priests, and unto the scribes; and they shall condemn him to death,		
19 "And shall deliver him to the Gentiles**[b] **to mock, and** **to scourge,** **and to crucify** *him*: **and the third day he shall rise again."**[c] (For third day, see *Appendix One.* (Verse 20 cont. in Section 142.)	**and shall deliver him to the Gentiles:**[b] **34 "And they shall mock him, and** **shall scourge him, and shall spit upon him,** **and shall kill him: and the third day he shall rise again."**[c] (Verse 35 cont. in Section 142.) ► *Refer to Section 196, John 20:9 for more on this.*	**32** "For he shall be **delivered unto the Gentiles,**[b] **and shall be mocked, and spitefully entreated, and spitted on:** **33** "And they shall scourge *him*, **and put him to death: and the third day he shall shall rise again."**[c] ***They fail to comprehend his death on the cross*** **34** And they [the ◄apostles] understood[d] none of these things: and	

Matt.	Mk.	Lk. 18:34	John
		this saying [about His death and resurrection] was hid[e] from them, neither knew they the things[f] which were spoken. (Verse 35 cont. in Section 143.)	

Footnotes-Commentary

[a] Here, Christ gives in Lk. 18:31-33 with their parallel verses a summary review of various predictions from several Old Testament prophets about the death, burial, and resurrection of Christ. Hence, they are highlighted in gray. This is a general selection of various words from these Scriptures. See footnote c below for further explanation. It is noted that He, specifically names the "chief priests and scribes" as ringleaders in His decease (Mk. 10:33). Matthew wrote that the Lord Jesus "took the twelve disciples apart [aside] in the way." He withdrew them into some isolated place and instructed them in depth about His death: Mark records (verse 32) that the twelve were "amazed," (confused or perplexed) and "afraid," as they followed their Master. The meaning is that these men had heard Jesus speak of His death so many times, and at this point, they were literally terrified as they drew closer to Jerusalem wondering what this meant and what fate waited for them.

2p-Mark's words about "going up to Jerusalem" are geographically correct as the city sits on several hills with their general height being some 2,500 feet above sea level. As it was near the Passover all roads leading into Jerusalem, especially the one from Jericho, were packed with thousands of pilgrims making their way to the temple. The Words of Jesus "shall be betrayed," are a second hint that one of the twelve, Judas Iscariot would turn on Him. See Section 95, footnote x for our Lord's first mention of him being the traitor. Section 180 gives the story of the betrayal and Section 183 for Judas' death. Who could describe the feelings, fears and questioning of the twelve as they followed behind their Master amid the crowds toward the holy city?

3p-**Verses 31–33** and their parallels are highlighted for they speak in general terms of various Old Testament predictions of the suffering, death, and resurrection of Messiah.

[b] This was predicted a thousand years before in Ps. 2:1-4. It was fulfilled in Christ according to Acts 4:28. Matthew and Mark include the "Gentiles" as partakers in Jesus' death. This predication had reference to the Roman officials and soldiery who were involved in the scourging, the mockery and carried out the actual crucifixion of our Lord. See footnote a above, and c below for details, and the main heading of Section 186.

2p-**Matt. 20:19.** In strict Jewish chronology, the expression "the third day" meant any part of three days regardless of how long or short these parts were. *Never* were they confined to a literal twenty-four-hour day-period as we force them to mean in the western world. It is interesting that Jewish teachers accepted the witness of one's death as being valid, only after a three-day period had passed regardless of how many hours it ran over into the fourth day. The non Christian writer Gustaf Dalman (died 1941), in his work *Jesus-Jeshua: Studies in the Gospels*, page 188, mentions this curious custom practiced among the Jewish people.

[c] The verses highlighted in gray are a selection of various words from different Old Testament passages all of which Jesus blended into one quote. As such, they reveal something of His sufferings, death, and resurrection. For a detailed discussion regarding these three days and nights, see *Appendix One*.

2p-Even though all of Christ's disciples and apostles had heard these predictions read hundreds of times in the synagogue and temple, yet they could not relate them to their Master the Lord Jesus. So close to His death, yet the apostles were still chained to the rabbinical notion of a literal kingdom with an all-powerful, superman Messiah ruling the world. Jesus' use of the word "crucify" filled them with horror! It is no wonder, they were "afraid" as they moved closer to Jerusalem. They all well understood what death by crucifixion meant!

[d] **They did not understand.** Again, we are informed that the closest men to Christ did *not* yet understand His death and resurrection from the dead. At this point, in the life of our Lord, His death on the cross and resurrection was only a few days away. Some teach that the apostles had "forgotten" about His death on the cross, or that it was not first place in their lives! Whoever invented this myth was surely unfamiliar with the synagogue background of these men, how they had been taught incorrectly about Israel's coming Messiah, and His *first work* of personal salvation.

[e] **"Hid from them."** This term has the idea that their minds could not (yet) comprehend what Jesus was saying. *It does not mean that God deliberately withheld this information from the apostles.* Their religious thinking was so cluttered with rabbinical literalism and Jewish nationalism that only by the coming of the Holy Spirit in full power at Pentecost did they receive complete enlightenment of all Jesus had previously taught them. Refer to footnote d above. Concerning their inability to understand this, see Section 26, footnote f; Section 27, footnote n;

Section 29, footnote j; and Section 39, footnotes a and g. How people were saved in this time, though they did not yet know of Jesus' death on the cross, is explained in Section 10, footnote b, and Section 30, footnote h. Refer also to Section 144, footnote i for more on this subject that puzzles so many Christians. .

(f) **They did not know these things.** This has reference to the apostles not understanding what Christ was saying about His upcoming death at Jerusalem. Refer to footnotes d and e above for more on this curious subject. Nothing in the life and ministry of our Lord has been so missed by expositors and commentators as this fact. Until it is understood that the death, burial, and resurrection of Jesus were almost completely unknown to His disciples and foes alike, they will be handicapped in rightly dividing Scripture. Joseph, Nicodemus, and the women seeking to complete the burial ritual for His body reveals that none of them knew of His resurrection. His continual appearing, trying to persuade them that He had really risen from the dead is further evidence of this.

2p-**Matthew Henry's comments.** The great English Presbyterian minister and staunch Calvinist, Henry (died 1714) penned the following helpful comments about Jesus' death and the disciples not understanding the cross and His resurrection. His words are an example of the beautiful old English style of saying things. "The confusion that the disciples were hereby put into. This [His death] was so contrary to the notions they had had of the Messiah and his kingdom, such a balk to their expectations from their Master, and such a breaking of all their measures, that "they understood none of these things (v. 34). Their prejudices were so strong that they *would not* understand them literally, and they *could not* understand them otherwise, so that they did not understand them at all. It was a mystery, it was a riddle to them, it must be so; but they think it impossible to be reconciled with the glory and honour of the Messiah, and the design of setting up his kingdom. This saying was hidden from them. It was apocrypha [hidden] to them, they could not receive it: for their parts, they had read the Old Testament many a time, but they could never see anything in it that would be *accomplished* in the disgrace and death of this Messiah. They were so intent upon those prophecies that spoke of his glory that they overlooked those that spoke of his sufferings, which the scribes and doctors of the law should have directed them to take notice of, and should have brought into their creeds and catechisms ..." See *Matthew Henry's Commentary,* vol. 5, page 629-630. The common notion among present day Christians that everyone in town knew of Jesus' upcoming death, and were thankful for it, is sorely wrong. This thankfulness came with the fullness of the Holy Spirit at Pentecost (John 14:26). Missing this truth about the Savior creates a great handicap in rightly dividing God's Word to understand His life and why the Jews rejected Him.

3p-**The apostle John's confession.** John's statement, looking back some years after Jesus' resurrection, concerning his and Peter's personal ignorance of this miracle is astounding! This is especially true when we remember that they had just spent at least the last two years of their lives following the Lord Jesus and listening to Him teach. See his confession in Section 196, John 20:9 and comments attached by the symbols ◄ and ◻. The apostles and others not understanding the death and resurrection of the Savior, is discussed more fully in Sections 104-105, 107, and 141. As stated many times in this work, "It was all made clear on the day of Pentecost with the coming of the Holy Spirit in His glorious fullness."

Inspired by their ambitious mother, Salome, James, and John make a foolish request of Jesus. The other apostles become angry with the two brothers. The Savior gives all of them another lesson on humility and serving others in His new kingdom.

Near Jericho?

Matt. 20:20–27	Mk. 10:35–44	Lk.	John
The family plot and their question **20** Then came to him the mother[a] of Zebedee's children with her sons, worshipping *him,* and desiring a certain thing of him.	*The family plot and their question* **35** And James and John,[a] the sons of Zebedee, come unto him, saying, "Master, we would that thou shouldest do for us whatsoever we shall desire."		
21 And he said unto her, "What wilt thou?"[b] She saith unto him, "Grant that these my two sons may sit, the one on thy right hand, and the other on the left, in thy kingdom."	**36** And he said unto them, "What would ye that I should do for you?"[b] **37** They said unto him, "Grant unto us that we may sit, one on thy right hand, and the other on thy left hand, in thy glory."		
Jesus' response **22** But Jesus answered and said,[c] "Ye know not what ye ask. Are ye able to drink of the cup that I shall drink of, and to be baptized with the baptism that I am baptized with?" They say unto him, "We are able."	*Jesus' response* **38** But Jesus said[c] unto them, "Ye know not what ye ask: can ye drink of the cup that I drink of? and be baptized with the baptism that I am baptized with?" **39** And they said unto him, "We can."		
23 And he saith unto them, "Ye shall drink indeed of my cup, and be baptized with the baptism that I am baptized with: but to sit on my right hand, and on my left, is not mine to give, but *it shall be given to them* for whom it is prepared[d] of my Father."	And Jesus said unto them, "Ye shall indeed drink of the cup that I drink of; and with the baptism that I am baptized withal shall ye be baptized: **40** "But to sit on my right hand and on my left hand is not mine to give; but *it shall be given to them* for whom it is prepared."[d]		
The other apostles are angered **24** And when the ten[e] heard *it,* they were moved with indignation against the two brethren.	*The other apostles are angered* **41** And when the ten[e] heard *it,* they began to be much displeased with James and John.		
Jesus' response **25** But Jesus called them *unto him,* and said, "Ye know that the princes of the Gentiles[f] exercise dominion over them, and they that are great exercise authority upon them.	*Jesus' response* **42** But Jesus called them *to him,* and saith unto them, "Ye know that they which are accounted to rule over the Gentiles[f] exercise lordship over them; and their great ones exercise authority upon them.		
26 "But it shall not be so among you: but whosoever will be great among you, let him be your minister; **27** "And whosoever will be	**43** "But so shall it not be among you: but whosoever will be great among you, shall be your minister: **44** "And whosoever of you will be		

651

Matt. 20: 27–28	Mk. 10:44–45	Lk.	John
chief among you, let him be your servant:(g) *"Learn from Me: become a servant to all"* **28** "Even as the Son of man came not to be ministered unto, but to minister,(h) and to give his life a ransom(i) for many." (Verse 29 cont. in Section 143.)	the chiefest, shall be servant of all.(g) *"Learn from Me: become a servant to all"* **45** "For even the Son of man came not to be ministered unto, but to minister,(h) and to give his life a ransom(i) for many." (Verse 46 cont. in Section 143.)		

Footnotes–Commentary

(a) **Mother and sons make a request.** This woman's name is *assumed* to be Salome. See Section 192, Matt. 27:56 with Mk. 15:40, footnote e, and Section 196, number 3 under footnote b for comments on this. We met Zebedee and his two sons some three years before, busy mending nets at the beginning of Jesus' ministry. Refer to Section 39, Matt. 4:21-22, footnote g. It is now about three years since that first call for the brothers to leave their fishing and follow Him on a temporary basis. One can believe that a close relationship had grown between the Messiah and Zebedee's family, yet we note that they bowed in His presence and "worshipped him," or showed Him high respect. The meaning of these two texts as given by Matthew and Mark is that James and John used their mother to make intercession for them. Here, is a classic example of family conniving and power struggling for religious prominence. This wretched business is seen in so many local churches today. For the historical meaning of "right and left" see, Section 205, second paragraph of footnote e.

(b) **Verse 21a and parallel. "What can I do for you?"** Matthew records the mother's request and Mark that of the two sons. No doubt, both were said. The request given here reveals that the apostles of Christ were still captives to the Jewish aspirations for earthly glory and honor in a literal Hebrew kingdom. This problem had risen a few weeks prior when they had inquired of their Master, "Who is the greatest in the kingdom of heaven?" See main heading Section 109, Matt. 18:1. It is scarcely necessary to prove that among the Jews, it was firmly held that in their literal, material kingdom, there would be distinctions of authority and rank. Further, it must be noted that this ambitious request was made about one week before the death of Christ on Calvary's cross, and none of His apostles understood yet His death by crucifixion! This is reaffirmed in Section 104, 105, 107, and 141. They wanted the highest and most exalted positions in the kingdom of Christ, still thinking it was (somehow) the same kingdom as that of the scribes and rabbis. In this petition, neither Salome nor her sons had yet understood that Christ's kingdom consisted of that which He was presently building. They cleverly schemed to secure their high places in a material, literal dominion that was *not* the kingdom of Christ *at this time* in His ministry.

2p-Drawing closer to Jerusalem, they also (like the crowds) believed that the kingdom of God was about to appear, and this aspiring mother wanted one son on Jesus' right hand, and the other on His left! See this in Section 145, Lk. 19:11 with footnotes b and c for the high expectation of the soon coming kingdom. These two seats sought by Salome were reckoned as the highest positions of honor among the Jews. In the Sanhedrin, the prince of the court sat at the chief position above all others with a seat on each side, which was reserved for the closest persons to the prince. There can be little doubt that this was the exalted honor that Salome sought for her sons. This event reveals that Salome was also a victim of the rabbinical hopes for an earthly Jewish kingdom at this time.

3p-Verse 21b and parallel. The ignorant request. Few mothers pray "Lord, thy will be done for my children." Parents seem to relish informing God as to what they want their children to do and be. There can be little doubt the (selfish) request made here was instigated because of the Messiah's earlier address about the "twelve sitting on thrones judging the tribes of Israel." This was given in Section 139, Matt. 19:28, footnote m. Just prior to giving this illustration, Christ had laid before them a clear lesson on humility in Section 138 by using small children as an example. Even so, *again,* they failed to understand the teaching of their Master. While ten of the apostles were looking forward to their special places in the material kingdom of Israel, James and John schemed with their mother and postured for the highest places in Israel's earthly kingdom (or so they thought). These two excited brothers previously requested to call fire down from heaven and kill a village of Samaritans. Their foolish request is found in Section 112, Lk. 9:54. Someone said, *"Oh, what a tangled web we weave, when first we practice to deceive."*

(c) **"Ye know not what ye ask."** Our Lord's response to their request reveals that they were still ignorant of the *nature* of the spiritual kingdom He was building, which was not of this world. If these brothers had given serious thought to what Jesus had spoken in Section 141 (about His sufferings, mockery, and death at Jerusalem), they may not have rushed forward with their selfish plot. Just before that, He had given them a unique lesson in Section 140 on humility, which they seem to have also forgotten. It touches us deeply to read how Jesus bore gently with their selfishness and error. They were asking in ignorance for two unique positions in His kingdom. Not many days afterwards, they were to see these two places occupied in shame and anguish by the two thieves. These brigandines were the first to be placed on the right and left hand of King Jesus. And they did so as He shed His blood to give eternal foundation to His blessed kingdom. Twelve literal thrones captured their carnal imagination. Meanwhile, the Savior's thoughts were of three crosses and salvation for mankind. Typical products of rabbinical theology, these men and their mother dreamt of Hebrew earthly power and glory; their Lord saw a cup of bitter suffering and shame. Instantly, Christ switched over into spiritual language as He tries to drag them out of their stubborn Jewish literalness. He informs them that He has a bitter cup to drink and a terrible baptism just ahead. These were common terms often employed by the rabbis to express the awfulness of a pending situation or dangerous service to be performed. The *bitter cup* of His betrayal, mocking, scourging, shame, and death by terrible crucifixion was near, and He must drink its full contents. There is no doubt the bitterest part of it all as His temporary separation from the Father. Christ asks James and John, "Can you drink of this cup with me?" They respond out of ignorance and their presumptuous dreams of a literal Jewish kingdom, "we are able." The brothers wanted places of high honor and exerted their grasp for such in this encounter with the Messiah. Little did they know what they were saying to the Son of God. Vain confidence possessed these two men and their excited mother. This ill-planted flower would fade in a few days as Calvary's shadow fell over them all.

2p-Verse 22. Here, Jesus employed another metaphor and puts it before the two brothers "Are you able to follow me in my baptism?" This could not have reference to his baptism in water, which had occurred over three years before. Refer to the main heading in Section 22.

3p-Shortly, Messiah would be plunged into a sea of darkness and sorrow like no other man. (Who can imagine this means sprinkling?) Bearing the sins of the world, He went down (as it were) into the terrible fury of God's judgment on evil, suffering the full punishment for the sins of all Adam's race. Doubtless, He was speaking of His soon fulfillment of Ps. 22 and Isa. 53. The rabbis used such verses as Ps. 69:1-2, and Lam. 3:54 to express thoughts of sorrow and pain. In reply to His query concerning them being able to share in this, they answered, "We are able." Again, presumption speaks before the head thinks. How strange the blindness of good men who cannot discern the will of God. This quick affirmative came out of their groundless confidence and materialistic mindedness preached and promoted by the rabbis in every synagogue across Israel. Their enabling would come later, after Pentecost, when they were endued with the full power of the Holy Spirit to serve their Lord unto physical death. In time, these brothers *did* drink their cups. James was the *first* martyr recorded in Scripture to die by Herod's sword. Later, Emperor Domitian banished John to the island of Patmos (Acts 12:1-2 with Rev. 1:9). Stephen died earlier at the hands of the Sanhedrin. We question what mother Salome thought (if she was living) about Christ's statement when her sons drank their cups? Christ had earlier spoken of His death as "baptism" Section 71, Lk. 12:50.

(d) In the latter part of verse 23, He assured them that God alone would select the places of distinction and honor for His servants; this honor was illustrated by the ancient example of the honored one sitting on a throne. No better understood metaphor could have been used for the eastern mind. It is noted that Christ did not *deny* that these seats of special honor would be given to certain ones in His kingdom, but simply that His Father had already decided this issue; and therefore, it was settled. Some spiritualize the thrones of the twelve as symbols of honor and high esteem in the church, while others see them as literal entities in the earthly kingdom rule of Christ. For explanation of the kingdom, see Section 39, footnotes a and g.

(e) Ten angry preachers. The other apostles had been listening to this conversation and were moved with heated indignation at James and John for such trickery. No doubt, they revealed their wrath with looks, gestures, and words. *However, the same ambitious spirit was in them as well!* At this point, in the life of Christ, so close to the cross, the twelve were still blatantly ignorant of precisely what His spiritual church-kingdom was and its purpose among mankind. Seeking positions of religious lordship over others is one of the great causes of murmuring and strife in churches around the world.

2p-Killing your enemies. False churches and satanic religions have employed the sword of the state to kill thousands who did not agree with their theology. The classical example of this is the Roman Catholic Church during its bloody inquisitions, the Reformed Church under the leadership of John Calvin with his death squads in Geneva, and later across Europe. Anglicans, Presbyterians, Independents, and split off sects from the Anabaptist all share the same guilt. Religious tyrants have always been sure that they did God a service. In 1871, Alexander B. Bruce, a Scottish minister penned these words, "It is the very nature of zealotry to make the man of whom it has taken possession believe that the Almighty not only approves, but shares his fierce passion, and fancy himself intrusted (sic) with a carte blanche to launch the thunders of the Most High against all not approved by his tyrannic conscience." See *The Training of the Twelve*, by Alexander B. Bruce, pages 245-246. Atheistic and pagan governments have also butchered Christians, who would not bow to their godless commands. The twelve apostles, by their joisting for power and position provided Jesus with the occasion for speaking such sublime and heavenly words about true child-like humility and servitude in His new kingdom or church. These good virtues were missing in the lives of the "Christian" killers mentioned above, though some of them marched under the "banner of the cross" while bathing their hands in the blood of the innocent. Men and women who participated in these horrific deeds were serving Satan not God. Worse are those "experts in church history," who cover up, mitigate, or deny these facts. I once heard a Bible Presbyterian pastor, the late Dr. Fred Stroud, call these people "Christian liars." *It remains a solid fact of history that church and state must always remain separate entities.*

(f) Drawing examples from pagan Gentile practices, the Lord Jesus sought to humble His men with this stinging rebuke. He was saying that heathen rulers who do not know the true and living God, nor Me the Savior, exercise lordship over their subjects. They set their favorites into places of honor while crushing those in disfavor. In sharp contrast, Christ tells them that His kingdom will never operate on such demeaning principles. The government of the kingdom or church is vastly different from that of heathen societies. All of His children are on the same level. All are equally loved and cared for. Those who walk in humility, caring first for the good, and welfare of others will be given prominent places before God and men in eternity. The leaders in His great work are to be most humble above all. Never had the twelve men heard such things! This was completely contrary to the theology of the scribes and Pharisees and their political, materialistic Jewish kingdom ruling the world. For brief comments on the substance of Christ's rule on earth, see Section 169, first through sixth paragraphs under footnote f.

(g) **Verses 26-27. "The greatest and chiefs are to be servants."** Again, the twelve were astounded! Now, their Lord informs them that whosoever is the greatest among them was to be the minister (servant) of all. The Greek word for "minister" in this sentence is the same term for "deacon," with *one* of its meanings being "one who serves by giving himself." The religious leaders of Israel had never exercised such conduct before the Hebrew people, the apostles, or anyone else. The haughty scribes, Pharisees, Sadducees and their followers were, for the most part, arrogant and self-exalted above the common people. They pretended a humility that was obnoxious before God and good men. For their hypocrisy in fasting, see Section 46, Matt. 6:16, footnote i. The word for "servant" in verse 27, is "doulos," meaning "bond slave." In this passage, the Savior inverted the role of master with slave! Such a thing was unheard of in antiquity. The twelve understood what their Lord had said and were astounded. For them to become "bond-slave-servants" in His new kingdom was incomprehensible.

2p-This word from Christ must have touched the two brothers in both heart and conscious. *Had they not just sought to acquire the highest positions in their Master's kingdom by use of their mother?* See footnotes a and b above. He tells them that whoever is "chief among you" will be the servant of others. (Did they hasten to withdraw their petition after hearing this?) The way to be first in the kingdom of Christ is to be last among men. See Section 140, Matt. 20:16, second paragraph of footnote j, for more on the thought of humility among the twelve. This principle was foreign to the rabbis and the understanding of the normal religious Jew.

(h) **"But to minister."** Deeply embarrassed, the twelve listened as Christ presented Himself the model of true servant hood that they should pursue. For meaning of the word "minister," see footnote g above. They knew by daily observation that He was unique in the heavenly virtue of ministering to others. His days were spent in reaching out to the crowds in a thousand ways. His flawless example of love and humility shamed them to no end. They were a bickering band of would-be preachers filled with awful contention, debate, and ever quarreling among themselves over who would be first and the greatest in their Master's service. Even at this late hour in the ministry of Christ, the twelve were exceedingly ignorant of Old Testament truth regarding the nature of Christ's kingdom, they were narrow-minded men, full of their Jewish prejudices and hatred for all Gentiles. We note that after following Jesus several years they still had not *unlearned* very much! The night before the morning of the cross, we hear the twelve arguing with each other as to who was the greatest. Note the main heading under Section 170 for this awful deed.

(i) **"Ransom.** The Greek word here is "lutron." It was used by the ancients for the price paid to set a slave free. For numerous pungent illustrations of its usage, see the work by the German liberal, Adolf Deissmann's, *Light from the Ancient East*, pages 327-328. With this, the Lord Jesus makes direct reference to His atoning death on the cross by which the slaves of sin and Satan are set free. Again, the apostles were hearing of His death as they had on numerous times. Jesus' usage of "many" speaks of the many that receive Him by repentance and faith and are saved. However, in contrast to this, "more" will not receive Him than the "many" who do. These "more" in time become the "many" that travel the "broad way" which leads to destruction. Refer to Section 47, Matt. 7:13, footnote f.

2p-"Scholars" who deny that the Savior was speaking of His substitutionary death for sinners, on the grounds that the word "lutron" is used *only here,* and in Mark's corresponding passage, demonstrate their spiritual sickness. They are as uncircumcised Philistines, enemies within the camp of God fighting against the atonement of Christ's precious blood, of which they are ignorant. Why not argue that since Gen. 1:1 and John 3:16 are only found once in Scripture, they too cannot be genuine? Why not call them "interpolations" or "later additions" to the text?

3p-If one applied the academic rule of exegesis across the Bible, as used by the unsaved critics, only utter chaos would result. It is never how many times God says something in the Scripture, but rather the fact that he said it once. Because it was recorded in an earlier portion of Holy Scripture hardly gives grounds for "translators" to drop it from another text or relegate it to an ambiguous footnote at its next mention in God's Book. It is the old problem of unconverted men of "great learning" that never experienced the new birth by faith. The Bible is another piece of historical literature to be scrutinized, analyzed, and finally laid aside as unworthy of divine origin and assignment. Worse, are those "saved translators" who handle Holy Scripture as the skeptic infidels do.

Two blind men are healed. They applied Israel's title for Messiah, "the son of David" to Jesus. The amazed multitudes break out into spontaneous praises to God.

Jericho

Matt. 20:29-32	Mk. 10:46-51	Lk. 18:35-41	John
	One blind man	*One blind man*	
	46 And they came to Jericho: and as he went out of Jericho[a] with his disciples and a great number of people,	35 And it came to pass, that as he was come nigh unto Jericho,[a] a certain	
Both blind men 29 And as they departed from Jericho,[a] a great multitude followed him.			
30 And, behold, two[b] blind men	blind Bartimaeus,[b] the son of Timaeus,	blind man[b]	
sitting by the way side,	sat by the highway side begging.	sat by the way side begging:	
		36 And hearing the multitude pass by, he asked what it meant.[c]	
They call upon Messiah when they heard that Jesus passed by, cried out, saying, "Have mercy on us, O Lord, *thou* son of David."[d]	*He calls upon Messiah* 47 And when he heard that it was Jesus of Nazareth, he began to cry out, and say, "Jesus, *thou* son of David,[d] have mercy on me."	*He calls upon Messiah* 37 And they told him, that "Jesus of Nazareth passeth by." 38 And he cried, saying, "Jesus, *thou* son of David,[d] have mercy on me."	
31 And the multitude rebuked them, because they should hold[e] their peace: but they cried the more, saying, "Have mercy on us, O Lord, *thou* son of David."	48 And many charged him that he should hold[e] his peace: but he cried the more a great deal, "*Thou* son of David, have mercy on me."	39 And they which went before rebuked him, that he should hold[e] his peace: but he cried so much the more, "*Thou* son of David, have mercy on me."	
Jesus the Messiah stops 32 And Jesus stood[f] still, and called them,	*Jesus the Messiah stops* 49 And Jesus stood[f] still, and commanded him to be called. And they call the blind man, saying unto him, "Be of good comfort, rise; he calleth thee." 50 And he, casting away his garment, rose, and came to Jesus. 51 And Jesus answered and said unto him, "What wilt thou that I should do unto thee?"[g]	*Jesus the Messiah stops* 40 And Jesus stood,[f] and commanded him to be brought unto him: and when he was come near, he asked him, 41 Saying, "What wilt thou that I shall do unto thee?"[g]	
and said, "What will ye that I shall do unto you?"[g]			

Matt. 20:33-34	Mk. 10:51-52	Lk. 18:41-43	John
33 They say unto him, "Lord, that our eyes may be opened."[h] 34 So Jesus had compassion[i] *on them*, and touched their eyes:	The blind man said unto him, "Lord, that I might receive my sight."[h]	And he said, "Lord, that I may receive my sight."[h]	
	52 And Jesus said unto him, "Go thy way; thy faith[j] hath made thee whole."	42 And Jesus said unto him, "Receive thy sight: thy faith[j] hath saved thee."	
Instantly healed and immediately their eyes received sight, and they followed him.[k] (Next chap., Matt. 21:1 cont. in Section 148.)	*Instantly healed* And immediately he received his sight, and followed Jesus[k] in the way. (Next chap., Mk. 11:1 cont. in Section 148.)	*Instantly healed and crowd reaction* 43 And immediately he received his sight, and followed him,[k] glorifying God: and all the people, when they saw *it*, gave praise unto God.[l] (Next chap., Lk. 19:1 cont. in Section 144.)	

Footnotes-Commentary

(a) With these words, all three writers confirm that Christ was *now* in Judaea. We note that vast multitudes still followed Him. Jericho was one of the wealthiest cities in all of Judaea and was heavily populated with some twelve thousand priests living there. See the story Christ told of a man who had walked this road *alone* in Section 116, footnotes g and h. Because of its wealth the approximate eighteen miles of winding road between Jericho and Jerusalem was a haven for bandits and robbers. Most people traveling this way went in large groups or companies. This created a formidable deterrent to the murdering gangs of bandits and thieves. Matthew and Mark reported that Jesus was leaving the city (verse 29 and 46), while Luke places the event as they were near Jericho (verse 35). Unsaved critics continually point to this as another "contradiction in the Bible." There were two places that bore the name Jericho during this time: one was the *old city* of Jewish origin, which is still inhabited today. The other was a newer city standing about a mile away that had been built by the Romans. *Christ simply moved from one Jericho into the other.*

(b) Matthew wrote that **"two blind men"** met Jesus. Even though these men were sightless, in some glorious way, they could see things better than those with eyesight could. Please note that Mark and Luke mention but one. As in the case of the two demon-possessed maniacs of Gadara, here also Matthew was inspired to write that there were two of them. See Section 88, Matt. 8:28, footnote b. For whatever reason one was more prominent or in some way different from the other; thus Mark and Luke single him out while Matthew *combines* the actions and words of both into one drama. It has been mentioned in footnote a above; due to its wealth, Jericho had become a favorite haunt of beggars and unfortunate people. Mark alone gives his original readers the name of this special blind man. "Bar," meaning "son of," combined with "Timaeus," his father. In the name, we discover that he was a thorough Jew. It was known that Jericho had many Gentile visitors and business people seeking to cash in on the good fortune of the place. Each beggar had his private spot from which to seek alms of those who passed by.

(c) Hearing the rush of the scuffling crowds, the shouts, and excited voices, the wild stirring in the main street of the city, Bartimaeus inquired from out of his darkness "What's this noise about?" Someone shouted back "Jesus of Nazareth passeth by." This late in the ministry of Christ, He was still popularly known by this title. The heart of these two blind men must have "skipped a beat" when they heard mention of Jesus walking by. They, like every other person, had heard much of this great Jew and the miracles He was performing across the land of Israel.

(d) **"Son of David."** See Section 66, Matt. 12:23, footnote b, and Section 90, Matt. 9:27, footnote b, for other usages of this Messianic identification. *The Jewish Encyclopedia*, page 481, reads, "That the Messiah will be a descendent of King David." For the two blind beggars to address the Lord Jesus by this supreme title informs us that they had prior knowledge of this great Man and had heard the numerous reports of His power to heal the blind. Refer to footnote h below for further comments on what Messiah would do when He came. They knew that the

Messiah would perform this miracle among the people of Israel. By faith, they saw Him out of their darkness and knew He could open their eyes to behold the light of earth's day; they loudly petitioned Him for this favor.

(e) **"Be quiet!"** All three evangelists recorded that among the excited crowds were those who sought to silence the cries of these two men. It was a now or never situation with both: they refused to be denied. Christian soldiers of long standing confess quickly that when souls are near the kingdom, Satan is present to hinder or prevent their salvation and deliverance from sin's awful darkness. *Why* these detractors chided the blind men is not clear. Were they opponents of Christ? Were they companions of the scribes and Pharisees, who hated this holy title being placed upon the carpenter from despised Nazareth? Alternatively, were they simply the ignorant bystanders who are always present to "see the show" but never buy a ticket? Regardless, we read that one of them, Bartimaeus "cried so much the more." He would not be denied help from Jesus!

(f) **The Savior stood still!** Here is a fantastic manifestation of the arresting power of simple faith, and the persuasion of a sincere supplication to our Lord. He was "stopped in His tracks" as the cries of the needy touched Him in pitiful compassion. Amid the clatter of the silly crowds, the Master *only* hears the pleas of those who sit in darkness. He "commanded" the beggars to be brought to Him. Some ready persons stepped forward and taking the arms and hands of the two blind men, direct them into the presence of the Son of God. Here, is reflected the duty of every true believer in Christ. It is the work of all believers to lead those in darkness to the Light of the world. How touching the words of Mark who wrote that Bartimaeus "cast away his garment, rose and came to Jesus" (verse 50). Some worthy expositors see in this a picture of men repenting (turning) from their sins, leaving them behind, and being led by the grace of God to Christ. Such allegorizing as this does not press typology into the realm of absurdity.

(g) **"What can I do for you?"** It is noted, that this was the same reply Christ had just given to Salome and her two sons in the previous Section 142, Mk. 10:36. In our manner of speech today, the Lord would have said, "What do you want?" This was not said out of ignorance or lack of intelligence but to offer His willingness to help them in their need. Hearing the voice of Christ their faith leaped out of darkness and into His marvelous light and hope. Our Lord's question to the blind men is similar to the one He put to the crippled man months before, "Wilt thou be made whole?" For comments on this strange question, see Section 52, footnote f.

(h) These men would have been familiar with the Old Testament prediction that Messiah would open the eyes of the blind (Isa. 35:5-6). See Section 38, Lk. 4:17-18, footnote d where Christ had earlier proposed to be the Messiah with healing powers. Had they not just addressed Jesus as "the son of David," the supreme title for Israel's Messiah? See footnote d above. Luke is careful to write that Jesus not only affirmed their healing but the salvation of their souls during this single moment of faith in Him the wonderful Messiah (verse 42).

(i) **"Jesus had compassion."** Repeatedly, the Lord Jesus was moved by compassion on humanity as they came before Him, devastated by sin and Satan. Note in this verse that Matthew records "he touched their eyes." There was something extraordinary about His touch. See Section 41, Matt. 8:15, footnote b, and Section 48, Mk. 1:41 footnote c, for more on His marvelous touches. The human nature of the Son of God felt their sorrows and woes; He deeply pitied their distressed condition and longed to help all who would trust Him.

(j) **"Faith"** was the channel *through* which their healing was received and their souls saved but not the *cause*. Realizing the strange voice heard in their darkness was that of the Messiah, and upon hearing His question addressed to them (footnote g above), they instantly believed in Him. Through faith in Christ, *both* men simultaneously received physical healing (Mk. 10:52) and spiritual salvation (Lk. 18:42). Later, another man (Zacchaeus) and his family were also saved by faith in Christ the Messiah. However, in their case, there is no mention of physical healing involved. See Section 144, Lk. 19:9 footnote i.

(k) **"They followed him."** One can picture these two men, shouting praises to God, leaping and dancing about the street amid the motley crowds; both elevated into heavenly joy. Now their eyes can see and their sins are forgiven! As with every miracle of Jesus, the people were stunned into wonderment upon realizing what had happened. The joy of Christ is contagious.

(l) What a marvelous benediction to this grand event. Holy Scripture reads that all the people "gave praise to God" (Lk. 18:43). This means the two *former* blind men joined the crowds journeying with Jesus as He made His way westward to the house of Simon the leper at Bethany, and finally Jerusalem for His last Passover. It is *conjectured* that Jesus arrived in Bethany the next day, if He spent the night with Zacchaeus after going home with him. For our Lord being a "guest" of this "sinner," refer ahead to Section 144, Lk. 19:7, footnote g. For His arrival at Bethany, see Section 146.

He arrives at Jericho. Zacchaeus, a chief among tax collectors is saved sitting in a tree. Christ announces that salvation* has now come into this man's life and family. The Lord Jesus goes home with Zacchaeus.

*The crowds pressing near the Savior heard Him tell Zacchaeus that salvation had come to his house. Misinterpreting what He said, they thought He was publicly proclaiming to the people that Israel's earthly kingdom was about to appear. Word of what Jesus had said spread rapidly along the road from Jericho to Jerusalem. The anxious Jews believed that Messiah upon nearing the city and entering its Eastern Gate would suddenly set up a literal, physical kingdom for the nation of Israel. See next Section 145, Lk. 19:11, footnotes a, b and c for a detailed explanation of these things.

Matt.	Mk.	Lk. 19:1-10—Jericho	John
		A tax official climbs a tree to see Jesus 1 And *Jesus* entered and passed through Jericho.[a] 2 And, behold, *there was* a man named Zacchaeus, which was the chief among the publicans, [tax collectors] and he was rich.[b] 3 And he sought to see Jesus[c] who he was; and could not for the press, [multitude] because he was little of stature. 4 And he ran before, and climbed up into a sycomore tree to see him: for he was to pass that *way*. *Jesus invites Himself home with a publican: crowd reaction* 5 And when Jesus came to the place,[d] he looked up, and saw him, and said unto him, "Zacchaeus, make haste, and come down; for to day I must abide at thy house."[e] 6 And he made haste, and came down, and received him joyfully.[f] 7 And when they [the religious leaders] saw *it*, they all murmured, saying, "That he was gone to be guest with a man that is a sinner."[g] 8 And Zacchaeus stood, and said unto the Lord; "Behold, Lord, the half of my goods I give to the poor; and if I have taken any thing from any man by false accusation, I restore *him* fourfold."[h] *The divine results of the tree meeting* 9 And Jesus said unto him, "This day is salvation come to this house,[i] forsomuch as he also is a son of Abraham. 10 "For the Son of man is come to seek and to save that which was lost."[j] (Verse 11 cont. in Section 145.)	

Footnotes-Commentary

[a] Luke, in writing about the life of Christ, pens here another event that occurred in Jericho that neither Matthew nor Mark recorded.

[b] **"Zacchaeus"** meaning "pure," was a standard Jewish name widely used. It is listed as "Zaccai" among the exiles returning from Babylonian captivity in 536 B.C. (Ezra 2:9). The Talmud mentions this name seven times in a single tractate. See tractate, Rosh HaShana 29b. For details on publicans and their despised work, see Section 50, footnote d. Jericho being a rich city, the Romans were omnipresent, bleeding taxes out of every person who passed that way. In the Talmud tractate, Nedarim 27b, the Jews hated publicans so badly that they were classified with "murderers and robbers."

2p-**"Chief among the publicans."** This *cannot* mean any less than what it states. Zacchaeus presided over *all* tax collectors in the Jericho district. His work was to receive their payments and transmit them to the Roman government. In today's terms, he would be called the General Manager of taxes for the city of Jericho and surrounding area. He was a rich, powerful, and a very important man serving well in the pagan Roman system. When the Messiah entered his city, Zacchaeus' entire life was gloriously changed; things became different. To think that he had never heard of Christ until this event took place is impossible. See second paragraph of footnote f below for more on this thought.

[c] **Why did he want to see Jesus?** As the two blind men just healed on the wayside, he also had heard about this wonderful Person. See the previous Section 143, Matt. 20:30, footnote b, for more on the two blind men. Every mortal in Jericho at one time or another had received word about Jesus of Nazareth. They had heard His Name, and

when He entered their city, everyone wanted to see Him. Being directed by the divine curiosity that grace produces in the human heart, Zacchaeus was determined to see the Man, who professed to be Israel's Messiah. His curiosity led to his conversion. Two special persons in the four gospels "desired" to see Jesus. These were Herod Antipas, in Lk. 9:9, and Zacchaeus, the hated tax boss at Jericho. Heart's motive is the all-important factor and catches the eye of God in heaven. Wretched Antipas, filled with superstition and self-interest wanted to see a miracle; while Zacchaeus wanted to see the Man, who did the miracles, being already convinced that He was Israel's Messiah.

2p-"**Little of stature.**" Recorded in *The Works of Nathaniel Lardner*, vol. 1, page 453 is an ancient testimony (not tradition) which affirms, "Zacchaeus was a dwarf." One can picture a midget size Jew dashing in and out of the crowds, standing on tiptoes, jumping up and down, and peeking around others. Since he was a publican, the crowds would curse him and push him aside. Suddenly, he remembered; some distance ahead, there was a large tree that would afford him a position from which he could see Jesus of Nazareth. The text reads, "He ran before." Here is a rising faith that blossomed into unusual works—even tree climbing! "Sycomore" is a large Egyptian fig tree often growing wild and also under cultivated conditions. Its fruit was almost identical to the standard fig tree of the land of Israel. This sycomore was different from the sycamine tree in Section 132, Lk. 17:6, footnote h. The wood was used in constructing costly furniture, houses, and coffins. Solomon, in building Jerusalem and the temple, had thousands planted over the land (1 Kings 10:27). Some Egyptian coffins made of sycomore wood have been found dating over three thousand years old and in a perfect state of preservation. This tree was planted along roadsides because of its abundant shade and had branches with "some touching the ground" growing from its trunk. Hence, the easy access for our little man scurrying about to see Jesus. The teaching that this was an "unclean tree" seems unfeasible in light of the above facts.

(d) **What a shock!** The Master walks under Zacchaeus' limb-perch, stops, looks up, calls him by name, and then invites Himself home with the most cursed man in the city! Note, under main heading Section 50, where Jesus had previously caused a terrible upset among the religious leaders by attending a supper in the home of another taxman named Matthew-Levi. Everyone standing in earshot was dumbfounded at His Words. See footnote e below. *No respectable Jew would ever visit in the home of a publican.* We wonder what the apostles were thinking as they tagged along behind their Master going to the house of a hated man. Did they recall the several days they had spent with Jesus, some three years prior, living in a cursed Samaritan village? Refer to this event in Section 35, footnote j.

(e) "**Today I must abide at thy house.**" Our Lord's announcement rattled everyone listening. This great rabbi and prophet, who professed Messiah, goes to be the guest of the chief publican and notorious sinner who had robbed everybody in the city by exorbitant tax collections. The Savior still desires entrance into the house and heart of all who seek Him as Lord and Savior, regardless of their past. He pardons and saves all who receive Him (John 1:12).

(f) "**Received him joyfully.**" Thousands stood, pushed, and shoved trying to get near this blessed scene. The Messiah did not look about upon the milling crowds, but rather up to the small man sitting on a tree limb and called him down. Such power of the Holy Spirit accompanied the Words of Christ that they hit Zacchaeus' heart like a dart. His conscience was instantly awakened, his faith was loosed, and he believed in that Man looking up into his face. It is written in Ps. 18:28, "For thou wilt light my candle." This happened to the little Jew of Jericho! Beaming with joy, the former tax collector making "haste" slid down the tree and hit the dust with a thud. Jesus was going home with him! Of the thousands in Jericho, the Savior picked the house of the most notorious person in the city and district. Jesus will enter his home to "abide" with him. What blessed words penned by Luke when he wrote that Zacchaeus "received him joyfully." This was another way of saying that he was now a child of God by *simple faith* in Christ as the Messiah. He received the Savior both physically and spiritually.

2p-For such a simple and instant conversion, we must believe that this little man carried in his heart many questions about Jesus. He had pondered them thousands of times: now he has the opportunity to meet this wonderful Person, who loves all men. Had Zacchaeus heard the news about Jesus and Matthew's conversion? Surely, he had, for they were in the same business together. Had he been present at the big party Matthew threw for his newfound Messiah several years past? Refer to this previous event at Matthew's house as explained in Section 50, footnote g below. Note others saved, even without baptism, in Section 203, number 4, under footnote c.

(g) "**Going to be guest with a sinner.**" As usual, Satan's detractors were present to complain and grumble. One can readily believe that this objection came from the scribes, Pharisees, and their associates in hypocrisy. In his work *Jesus the Messiah*, page 261, Donald Guthrie wrote that the crowds condemned Jesus based on "guilt by association." Had the Messiah not demonstrated many times that lost sinners were his goal, His harvest to be reaped, His converts to be saved, and gathered into His new kingdom? Almost two years prior, He had entered the home of Matthew the publican and witnessed of God to the wild crowds attending his supper given for Jesus. Now, a few days before the cross, the Savior continues to seek tirelessly the souls of men who are not being turned aside by the opinions of the religious hypocrites. The comment of the crowds was and still is correct. Jesus remains the friend of sinners! The Jewish religion as taught by the scribes and Pharisees strictly forbade any association with sinners. This is explained in Section 50, Matt. 9:10, footnote c. The amazement at Him going home with a low-down publican was beyond their understanding. False religion still poisons men towards the *true* needs of others.

(h) **"Restore him fourfold."** Far more transpired here than the text reveals. Zacchaeus had previously heard about Jesus of Nazareth, the Messiah, and His great miracles. One can believe that he had also heard of Matthew's conversion some two years before. Was he a friend of Matthew? It is difficult to believe that he was not being in the same high position, as Matthew had been when he became a follower of Jesus. For a renegade Jew who had forsaken his nation, the Torah Law, and people, to serve the pagan Romans, to make this confession, he either was saved or had lost his mind! Clearly, his deeds as seen here are the fruits of genuine repentance; he shows outside that he is changed inside. It is interesting that the amount of "fourfold" (four times as much) was that which was required in the Jewish Law in repayment for those convicted of sheep stealing (Ex. 22:1). His spontaneous unsolicited restitution went far beyond the law, which required fourfold or (in some cases) fivefold restitution, but *only* if the beasts were slaughtered and sold. Every informed Jew in the crowd knew exactly what he was saying, and they were amazed. The ancient rabbis continually stressed, "The repentance of shepherds and tax collectors is very difficult." See Talmud tractate, Baba Kama 94b. In this *public confession,* heard by hundreds, Zacchaeus was showing the genuineness of his faith in Christ. Refer to Section 21, Part 3, footnote l, for John the Baptist's requirements that men show their repentance outwardly before he would baptize them. If the rugged old Baptist had been present at this confession, he would have granted baptism immediately to this converted ex-publican for he glowed with the beautiful fruits of repentance.

(i) **"Salvation comes to this house."** The Master meant one thing by this statement, but the earthly kingdom incensed Jews instantly understood something different. Salvation coming to a publican in their thinking signified that God's kingdom was ready to "come" on the scene or suddenly appear. Hearing this, the crowds went wild believing He was about to produce their literal, political rule on earth. However, Jesus meant that His spiritual kingdom had arrived in the heart of Zacchaeus. He was not only a Jew outwardly but was now one inwardly: one of the spiritual seeds of Abraham (Gal. 3:29). "Salvation" had entered his house, not a building of stones and mortar, but the hearts of the entire family of this little Jew. This proves that men were saved before Christ died on the cross, even before they *fully understood* the meaning of His death. Their faith in Him was counted by God as faith in all He would yet do; even the greatest of works, shedding His blood for the atonement of mankind's sin and rising from the grave to save and give new life. The faith of all men across the whole of Old Testament history and during the earthly ministry of Christ moved forward to the cross of Christ and His empty tomb; *here,* that faith met and grasped eternal redemption. A few moments previously, Christ had physically healed and spiritually saved two blind men along the Jericho road. Refer to Section 143, footnote j for comments.

2p-In Section 30, second paragraph of footnote h we viewed salvation in the Old Testament. *Radical* dispensationalists vehemently deny this. The esteemed Dr. Lewis S. Chafer, founder of the Dallas Theological Seminary, wrote that men were saved in the Old Testament by law keeping and sacrifices! See his Systematic Theology, vol. 4, pages 215-216. Clearly, C. I. Scofield, Charles Ryrie, Arno C. Gaebelein, Dwight Pentecost, and many others borrowed this error from Chafer's blurred view of God's saving grace across the Old Testament. Charles Ryrie went so far as to write, "Those who died before Christ's first advent" are not among the "dead in Christ." See Ryrie's *Dispensationalism Today,* page 136. What shocking words from such a great man! As already stated in this work, one perusal of the long list of names from Abel to Samuel, and hundreds unnamed, covering some three thousand years, demonstrates to any kindergarten student how men were saved from the beginning. See Heb. 11 in its entirety for this lesson. Peter made it clear to the first church council in Jerusalem that people under the Old Testament were "saved by grace" (Acts 15:11). Paul also made it clear that souls are saved the same way today (Eph. 2:8). For more on these matters, see Section 11, second paragraph of footnote q.

(j) Christ makes it clear that the *supreme* intent of His work on earth was to seek and save those who are lost; not to build a material physical empire. Had He not just sought out and found Zacchaeus sitting in the fig tree? The more rigid Jews believed that if one deserted Israel to work for the pagan Romans, he was no longer a Jew. Christ corrects this error and identifies him as a "son of Abraham." Now he was a true Jew inwardly, and his circumcision was that of the heart. Had Messiah not just forgiven his sin by speaking the words of grace and pardon? See an earlier example of one who was also saved by faith in the Words of Christ in Section 64, Lk. 7:47-50, footnotes j and k.

2p-**The kingdom is coming now!** Among the multitudes following Jesus through Jericho going to Bethany and Jerusalem, were Jewish kingdom fanatics. Upon hearing His Words about saving the lost, they related this to the rabbinical teaching that Messiah would save Israel, restore her former glory, and gather her in as lost sheep. This is the contextual meaning of these passages, for instantly in the next Section 145, we read in Lk. 19:11 that when the Jews "heard these things ... they thought the kingdom of God should immediately appear." Luke wrote that the Jews based their false expectation on a misinterpretation of the Words Jesus had spoken to Zacchaeus. In Lk. 19:12-27, Christ explained in the Parable of the Pounds that there would be no literal kingdom (at that time) with Israel bossing the world. Instead, His new kingdom was already there in embryo form. Each member would answer for himself regarding his service. The Jews who rejected Him, as their true nobleman would be destroyed in A.D. 70. Refer to Section 163 for our Lord's prediction of this terrible event about forty years in advance.

The excited crowds expected the literal kingdom to appear suddenly. The Savior corrects their error of setting dates by the Parable of the Pounds.* Traveling to Simon the leper's house at Bethany, near Jerusalem, there was a popular surge of wild enthusiasm. He explains true kingdom service and its rewards.

*There is a similarity between this lesson given by the Savior and the Parable of the Talents spoken two days before His death in Section 165, Matt. 25:14-30. Some historians think that Jesus based the Parable of the Pounds on several problems that had occurred in the Herodian family, with which every Jew in the land would have been familiar. The story is that the Jews sent a large deputation to far-away Rome to protest the cruelties of King Herod's half-crazy son, Archelaus. Emperor Augustus dispatched a representative to access the trouble and judge the guilty. Much of the uproar stemmed from the fact that Archelaus had constructed a large palace at the city of Jericho, which seriously offended the Jews. It is noted that Jesus gave this parable as He was leaving Jericho and moving to Bethany; it would have been instantly understood by everyone in His audience.

Matt.	Mk.	Lk. 19:11-22—*From Jericho to Bethany near Jerusalem*	John
		The reason for the parable **11** And as they heard these things,[(a)] he added and spake a parable, because he was nigh to Jerusalem, and because they [the Jews] thought[(b)] that the kingdom of God should immediately appear.[(c)] ***The nobleman assigns duties and leaves*** **12** He said therefore, "A certain nobleman [wealthy ruler] went into a far country to receive for himself a kingdom, and to return.[(d)] **13** "And he called his ten servants, and delivered them ten pounds, [each pound about $20.00] and said unto them, 'Occupy [engage in business] till I come.' ***The nobleman is rejected by his people*** **14** "But his citizens hated him, and sent a message after him, saying, 'We will not have this *man* to reign over us.' ***The nobleman returns: the servants give account*** **15** "And it came to pass, that when he was returned, having received the kingdom, then he commanded these servants to be called unto him, to whom he had given the money, that he might know how much every man had gained by trading. ***First servant*** **16** "Then came the first, saying, 'Lord, thy pound [$20.00]hath gained ten pounds.' ($200.00) **17** "And he said unto him, 'Well, thou good servant: because thou hast been faithful in a very little, have thou authority over ten cities.' ***Second servant*** **18** "And the second came, saying, 'Lord, thy pound [$20.00] hath gained five pounds.'($100.00) **19** "And he said likewise to him, 'Be thou also over five cities.' ***Third servant*** **20** "And another came, saying, 'Lord, behold, *here is* thy pound, [$20.00] which I have kept laid up in a napkin:'(cloth similar to a handkerchief) **21** 'For I feared thee, because thou art an austere [hard and severe] man: thou takest up that thou layedst not down, and reapest that thou didst not sow.' **22** "And he [the nobleman] saith unto him, 'Out of thine own mouth will I judge thee, *thou* wicked servant. Thou knewest that I was an austere [hard and severe] man, taking up that I laid not down, and	

Matt.	Mk.	Lk. 19:22 -27— *Jericho and near Jerusalem*	John
		reaping that I did not sow:	
		23 'Wherefore then gavest not thou my money into the bank, that at my coming I might have required mine own with usury?' (interest)	
		24 "And he[(e)] [the nobleman or wealthy ruler] said unto them [servants] that stood by, 'Take from him the pound, [$20.00] and give *it* to him that hath ten pounds.' ($200.00)	
		25 ("And they [the servants] said unto him, [the nobleman] 'Lord, he hath ten pounds.') ($200.00)	
		The parable interpreted and applied	
		26 "For I [Jesus] say unto you, That unto every one which hath [used his talents] shall be given; and from him that hath not, [used his talents] even that he hath shall be taken away from him.[(f)]	
		27 'But those mine enemies, [said the angry nobleman] which would not that I should reign over them, bring hither, and slay[(g)] *them* before me.'"	
		(Verse 28 cont. in Section 148.)	

Footnotes-Commentary

(a) **"They heard these things."** These "things" or words that had stirred the crowds into following Jesus, now changed into the feverish political notion that God's Jewish Kingdom was about to visibly appear. They instantly caught what Jesus said to Zacchaeus, that "salvation had come to his house," and that He (the Lord Jesus) "had come to seek and save that which was lost." The rabbis, to describe the work of Messiah when He would gather Israel into their national land used the terms "salvation today," and "seeking the lost in Israel." (At this time in Jewish thinking, these terms had nothing to do with *personal* redemption from sin. That came later.) The crowds seized upon Christ's words. They thought He meant the literal kingdom was ready to appear! For the materialistic minded Jews, "salvation" was a physical experience in which Messiah would destroy the Romans and rule as King saving them from their enemies. We see later, in Acts 1:6 that Christ's own apostles were still looking for this kind of kingdom forty days after Jesus' resurrection and just before His ascension.

2p-When this furor about the kingdom broke out, the Jews were walking with Jesus to Simon the leper's house located at Bethany, about two miles east of Jerusalem. See main heading next Section 146 for His arrival at this village. The people knew that He was going from Bethany, to Jerusalem and the temple to observe Passover. The elated crowds recalled what the rabbis had taught them: Messiah would set up His earthly reign when He entered the Eastern Gate of their city and temple on the eve of a Passover. They based this on Ezek. 43:2. The Talmud expresses similar things in tractate, Pesachim 54a. Those following Jesus believed that upon His arrival at Jerusalem, He would assume the appearance of a prince and proclaim Himself King of Israel. His kingdom would be so glorious that weeping would vanish forever, and peace would come to Israel. See Talmud tractate, Chagigah 5b for more on this interesting subject. However, the Jews, the followers of Christ, and even His own apostles, did not at this point understand the spiritual manifestation of their Lord's new kingdom, later known as the church. For detailed explanation of this subject, see Section 39, footnotes a and g.

(b) For an earlier mention by the Pharisees, a few days prior to this belief in the *sudden* appearing of the kingdom, and our Lord's correction of this error, see Section 134, Lk. 17:20-21 footnotes a, and b.

(c) **"That the kingdom should instantly appear."** In an effort to correct this erroneous hope (that He would suddenly set up a material kingdom), Jesus gave them the Parable of the Pounds. Verse 11 states explicitly that Jesus spoke this "because they (the Jews) thought the kingdom of God should immediately appear." The Master tried to explain to them that His kingdom would not appear in some physical, material form at that time as they thought. *Here, again, the myth that He offered the Jews their political kingdom and Himself as their King is exploded.* To write that Jesus presented Himself as their King on this occasion, and they rejected Him is ridiculous. Our Lord could have instantly collected a following of thousands. The reason He did not was that He was not offering anybody a kingdom. A short while later, when He rode into Jerusalem, with tears running down his face, to die on the cross for the sins of all mankind, He did not say, "Look I am your King; receive me now and we will inaugurate Israel's earthly kingdom today." For His entry into the city, refer to Section 148.

2p-Verse 12. He must (like the "certain nobleman') go away into a "far country" (heaven) for a long time. Later, He would return and receive His kingdom. During this *long period,* His kingdom workers on earth need to be faithful and productive. Upon His return, He will judge His servants and "receive" His kingdom in which they had been serving. The point of this parable was to warn His disciples, "Stop looking for a physical kingdom; instead, get busy and serve in my spiritual kingdom now while you can and use what you have been given for my glory." The new kingdom of Christ was already present at this time, albeit in its infantile stage; it was within the hearts of all who had trusted Him as Messiah and Savior. For the location of His kingdom, see Section 134, footnote d. For more on the proposed physical kingdom of the Jews, of which the Lord Jesus would have no part during His earthly ministry, see Section 200, the first paragraph of footnote f.

(d) The Jews were again astounded: they had *never* heard the rabbis speak of such a kingdom as Jesus preached. It was totally different from their aspired Jewish rule of the earth under the authority of their political King and Messiah. In this parable, the Savior presented several lessons. Those who slice this parable up and see in every verse a specific type of just about anything they wish to see, do the Holy Scriptures an injustice. Only portions of it point to Jesus and His church, while other parts clearly do not. See number 5 below for this warning. Verses 12 and 13 have been temporarily rearranged (with verse 13 before 12) only for harmonizing this lesson. Note the following about this parable:

1. **Verses 13.** The nobleman or ruler assigned His workers specific duties, each represented in fixed amounts (pounds) or money. Christ is teaching about the financial responsibilities of those who serve Him. See Section 130, for an earlier lesson to His disciples on the subject of being financially dependable persons in His kingdom. One pound was about a hundred day's wages or $20.00 in our currency. They were ordered to "occupy" until their lord returned. This meant they were to take what God had given them and expand it by increasing the original worth into something larger. "Occupy," signifies "get engaged in my work," or "get busy and start using what I have given you."

2. **Verse 12.** After dispensing one pound to each of his ten servants the nobleman went away for a long time, expecting them to work faithfully and increase their allotment by useful service. His purpose in going to the far country (heaven) was to wait for His kingdom to develop and mature. The idea is that when His kingdom on earth was ready, he would return and take it for himself. This speaks of Christ returning for His church.

3. **Verse 14.** Shortly after his departure for the "far country," his own citizens rebelled and rejected his reign as their sole lord and ruler. Here, Jesus depicts the Jewish rejection of Him as their Messiah, Lord, and King. The Hebrews would not have Christ to reign over them. The words are clear when the text reads, "they hated him." This pointed to Jesus of Nazareth, their Messiah, and how they finally rejected Him as their Savior and ruler.

4. **Verse 15.** The nobleman finally returned after a long absence and received the kingdom that his servants had labored to prepare in view of His coming back again. Presently, it has been almost two thousand years since our Lord ascended back to heaven and the Father. Over the centuries, Christians have waited for His return, not knowing when it would be. They do not set dates, they watch and wait. As the earthly nobleman called each servant forward for reckoning concerning how he had used the gift left with them, so all believers shall give an account at the judgment seat of Christ (Rom. 14:10 with 1 Cor. 3:9-15). Though there were originally ten servants, Jesus only described the reckoning experiences of three of them. These three generally represent everyone who has labored in the kingdom of Christ, the church. Note the following points about these three servants in numbers 5 through 7 below.

5. **Verses 16-17. The first servant** had worked diligently and gained ten pounds ($200.00) from the one given to him. He was rewarded by being given rulership or supervision over ten cities belonging to his master. This too, was a frequent custom. Lords would often give to faithful workers who had unusual administrative skills greater levels of service and a wider ranger of authority. If the lord's kingdom were large, the most talented would be appointed ruler over certain districts, regions, or even entire cities. *This has nothing to do with "Christians ruling over cities during the millennial reign of Christ." It was simply an illustration the Lord Jesus employed, which was taken from the standard practices of noblemen or rulers of that day.* Everyone in His audience understood exactly what He was saying. For other comments on the distorted subject of Christians in the millennial rule of Christ, see Section 165, second paragraph of footnote i. Today, some two thousand years later, the ancient custom (of delegating ruler ship over certain cities) has been twisted out of its original meaning by *hyper* dispensationalists who seem to be clueless regarding ancient customs and the historical background meaning of various Scriptures. Because of this, bizarre interpretations have been injected into God's Word. In time, these are embraced as though they were fundamental doctrines of the Christian faith. Mixing trash with truth is hardly honoring to the cause of Christ and will never strengthen or edify the Church of God.

6. **Verses 18-19. The second servant** had gained five pounds ($100.00) for His master. He was commissioned to rule over five cities. It seems the nobleman granted one city for each pound gained. See number 5 above for explanation of what this meant in ancient Bible background history.

7. **Verse 20. The third servant** handed back the original one pound ($20.00) given to him by his ruler. He instantly broke out with excuses for his slothfulness. His entrusted pound was kept in a folded "napkin" or "sweat cloth," like our modern day handkerchief. The servant's *frank description* of his lord reveals the sheer cruelty of ancient rulers. This blunt revelation of the nobleman's character (cannot at this point

in the parable) represent the blessed Lord Jesus. It reflects the callousness of various ancient rulers, their ruthlessness in business practices, and oppressive treatment of workers who failed to meet their every demand.

8. **Verse 21.** These words out of his mouth will condemn him. He is sternly informed that if he knew this in advance about his lord, he should have deposited the money into a bank, and it would have acquired some sort of usury or interest. Banks and money lenders were replete during this time. Even powerful rulers borrowed money when needed! Josephus wrote in *Antiquities*, Book 18:6. 3, lines 157–160, of Herod Agrippa borrowing vast sums of money. Here, the servant described the lord's hard treatment of workers and tough business practices. Knowing in advance the stern methods of the master, this servant still made no effort to serve him. He was guilty by chosen neglect. Those who *know* the will of God and do it not shall be beaten with many stripes. Our Lord mentioned this earlier in Section 71, Lk. 12:47, footnote u. However, what form this correction or chastisement of God takes in their lives we may not know.

9. **Verses 22-23.** These are the words of the returned nobleman and *not* of the Savior. He showed no pity on the careless servant who was instructed along with the other nine about their duties during his absence. The nobleman's words about putting his money in the bank and gaining interest may also point to Christ, who instructed the Jews and His apostles to take what they had and increase it in the service of God.

(e) **Verse 24.** These are not the Word's of Christ, but rather of the nobleman. Jesus explained to his audience what he did to his slothful servant. The one pound was taken from him and given to the first worker (see number 5 above), whose diligence commended him for greater reward at the master's hand. It was a common practice among ancient kings and rulers to take from the slothful what they had and give it in turn to the servant who was most prudent and productive in the work of his lord.

2p-**Verses 25.** We read the words of the servants ("they") regarding their master giving an extra pound to the one who already had ten pounds. This was something of a *guarded* complaint on their part.

(f) **Christ interprets His parable.** In verse 26, the nobleman responds to his servant's inquiry. He declares the principles by which he chose to distribute the rewards to those who had served well during the time His kingdom was being prepared. In the new kingdom of Christ shadowed in the visible local church are those who have worked (with the right heart's motive) long and hard. They will be given double rewards and more. Those who have failed to use their talent(s) will find that their prospective rewards are placed to the credit of others. The Lord Jesus was warning the Jews, who originally had all talents given to them but would soon have them taken away and given to the Gentiles. These converted former pagans would use and greatly multiply their talents to the glory of their Lord. This truth of our Savior has been manifested so clearly over the past two thousand years of church history.

(g) **Verse 27.** Richard C. Trench wrote the following of this passage, "When the king had thus distributed praise and blame, rewards and penalties, to those who stand in the more immediate relations of servants to him, to those of his own household, he proceeds to execute vengeance on his enemies, and all who openly cast off allegiance to him. See Trench's, *Notes on the Parables of our Lord*, vol. 2, page 512.

2p-**"Slay them before me."** The death sentence was pronounced. In quoting these words of the nobleman, Christ referred to the custom of ancient kings who publicly put their enemies to death before the eyes of many onlookers and servants as well (Jer. 52:10). Without doubt, Jesus applied the words of the angry nobleman to the Jews, who hated Him as their Messiah and would have none of His rule. *They* were the wicked servants who despised their talents and gifts and hid them because of their hatred for the Savior. Their judgment and destruction came first in A.D. 70. In these concluding Words, the Lord Jesus pronounced another sentence of doom upon the scribes, Pharisees and all Jews, who scorned Him as their Messiah. Among the thousands who heard Him teach, some of them and their children were slaughtered when the sword of Rome fell in awful judgment upon the nation of Israel, Jerusalem, and the temple. See asterisk under main heading of Section 68, for more on the predicted judgments coming upon the Jews, and Section 134, footnotes i and n.

3p-*Again,* these stubborn Jews missed this parable of warning from their Messiah. They were blinded by their belief in the literal kingdom suddenly coming to Israel, their firm obedience to the oral law, and tradition of the elders. The lowly carpenter from Nazareth who stood before them and attested to be Messiah was their target of scorn, ridicule, and their bitterest hatred.

Arriving at Bethany, six days before His final Passover, He attends a supper.* Mary, Martha, and the newly resurrected Lazarus are present! Foreseeing His death and resurrection, Mary anoints Him. Led by Judas all the apostles objected. Jesus rebukes them and gives Mary a lasting prominent place in gospel history.

*It is conjecture that this supper at Bethany occurred Saturday before Jesus rode into Jerusalem on the next day, which was Palm Sunday. This would place the actual Passover observance six days later. The meal here is not the one recorded in Section 117, where Martha called for her sister to help in serving.

Simon the leper's house at Bethany or the house of Lazarus?

Matt. 26:6-7	Mk. 14:3	Lk.	John 11:55-57 (12:1-3)
			His fourth and final Passover as Israel's Messiah. For third, see Section 93, John 6:4
			55 And the Jews' passover[a] was nigh at hand: and many went out of the country up to Jerusalem before the passover, to purify themselves. 56 Then sought they for Jesus, and spake among themselves, as they stood in the temple, "What think ye, that he will not come to the feast?"[b]
			Orders given to take Jesus 57 Now both the chief priests and the Pharisees had given a commandment, that, if any man knew where he were, he should shew *it*, that they might take him.[c]
			Supper at Simon's house
			John 12:1-3
			1 Then Jesus six days before the passover came to Bethany, where Lazarus was which had been dead, whom he raised from the dead. 2 There [at Bethany] they made him a supper;[d] and Martha served: but Lazarus was one of them that sat at the table with him.
Supper at Simon's house 6 Now when Jesus was in Bethany, in the house of Simon the the leper,[d]	*Supper at Simon's house* 3 And being in Bethany in the house of Simon the leper, as he sat at meat,[d]		
The Savior anointed 7 There came unto him a woman[e] [Mary] having an alabaster box of very	*The Savior anointed* there came a woman[e] [Mary] having an alabaster box of		*The Savior anointed* 3 Then took Mary[e] a pound [fourteen ounces weight in Israel] of

665

Matt. 26:7-12	Mk. 14:3-8	Lk.	John 12:3-8
precious ointment, and poured it on his head, as he sat *at* *meat*.	ointment of spikenard very precious; and she brake the box, and poured *it* on his head.		ointment of spikenard, very costly, and anointed the feet of Jesus, and wiped his feet with her hair: and the house was filled with the odour [smell] of the ointment.
Judas and the apostles object **8** But when his disciples[(f)] saw *it*, they had indignation, [became angry] saying, "To what purpose *is* this waste?[(g)] **9** "For this ointment might have been sold for much, and given to the poor."[(h)]	***Judas and the apostles object*** **4** And there were some[(f)] that had indignation [became angry] within themselves, and said, "Why was this waste[(g)] of the ointment made? **5** "For it might have been sold for more than three hundred pence, [a year's wages] and have been given to the poor."[(h)] And they murmured against her.		***Judas and the apostles object*** **4** Then saith one[(f)] of his disciples, Judas Iscariot, Simon's *son*, which should betray him, **5** "Why was not this ointment sold for three hundred pence, [a year's wages] and given to the poor?"[(h)] **6** This he said, not that he cared for the poor; but because he was a thief, and had the bag, and bare what was put therein.
Jesus defends Mary **10** When Jesus understood *it*, he said[(i)] unto them, "Why trouble ye the woman? for she hath wrought a good work[(j)] upon me. **11** "For ye have the poor[(k)] always with you; but me ye have not always.	***Jesus defends Mary*** **6** And Jesus said,[(i)] "Let her alone; why trouble ye her? she hath wrought a good work[(j)] on me. **7** "For ye have the poor[(k)] with you always, and whensoever ye will ye may do them good: but me ye have not always.		***Jesus defends Mary*** **7** Then said Jesus,[(i)] "Let her alone: against [in view of] the day of my burying[(j)] hath she kept this. **8** For the poor[(k)] always ye have with you; but me ye have not always."
A lasting tribute to Mary **12** "For in that she hath poured this ointment on my body, she did *it* for my	***A lasting tribute to Mary*** **8** "She hath done what she could: she is come aforehand to anoint my		

Matt. 26:12-13	Mk. 14:8-9	Lk.	John 12:9-11
burial.◄ **13** "Verily I say unto you, Wheresoever this gospel shall be preached in the whole world, *there* shall also this, that this woman hath done, be told for a memorial[(l)] of her." (Verse 14 cont. in Section 147.)	body to the burying.◄ **9** "Verily I say unto you, Wheresoever this gospel shall be preached throughout the whole world, *this* also that she hath done shall be spoken of for a memorial[(l)] of her." (Verse 10 cont. in Section 147.)		◄*Matthew and Mark place the mention of His burial in these verses, while John pens it in verse 7 above.* ***Curious Jews desire to see Lazarus: the religious leaders plot to kill him also*** **9** Much people[(m)] of the Jews therefore knew that he was there: [at the supper] and they came not for Jesus sake only, but that they might see Lazarus also, whom he had raised from the dead. ***They attempt to stop men from believing on Christ*** **10** But the chief priests consulted that they might put Lazarus also to death;[(n)] **11** Because that by reason of him many of the Jews went away, and believed[(o)] on Jesus. (Verse 12 cont. in Section 148.)

Footnotes-Commentary

[(a)] This verse stating the Passover was near has no chronological connection with the preceding verse of John 11:45. Details on this passage are found in Section 124, second paragraph of footnote x. For the first Passover Jesus attended at the beginning of His ministry and an explanation of this event, see Section 29, John 2:13, footnote a.

2p-"Purify themselves." The rabbis made a great fuss about purification before the annual feasts of Israel according to their law in Num. 9:10-13. Various levels of purification were in vogue; some requiring longer time than others to accomplish their purpose. The Talmud tractate, Shabbath 19a required thirty days before Passover. The fact that the Passover is mentioned over two thousands times in the Talmud reveals the rabbinical respect for this celebration. See tractates, Rosh Hashana 16b and Berachoth 22b for examples of instructions for purification. By the time of Christ, about four weeks were required for preoperational cleansing, meaning that the pilgrims traveling from abroad had to arrive extra early to make ready for the grand Passover. Some sources state that the time required was only two weeks. For an old review of these things, see *The Jewish Nation: Containing An Account Of Their Manners And Customs, Rites And Worship, Laws and Polity,* by Daniel Parish Kidder, pages, 252-254, 306-308, originally printed in 1850.

3p-John's use of the word "many" is of interest. It does not mean several hundred as the critics assume. Josephus who served as a priest in the temple computed that the number attending the celebration in the year A.D. 65 (five years before the fall of the city) was some 2,700,000. See *Wars of the Jews,* Book 2:14, 3, footnote b, and Book 6:9. 3, footnotes b and c. If one reduces this figure to 1,000,000 it still staggers the imagination to comprehend such a vast gathering. The city and surrounding countryside would have been literally packed with thousands of Hebrew pilgrims, proselytes, and curious visitors from all over the known world. Tents and makeshift dwellings were erected as far as the eye could see. Villages within walking distance of the temple would accommodate all pilgrims with open arms and love. It is remarkable that no foreign power came upon Jerusalem during any of their annual feasts from the days of Moses (fifteen hundred years) until now. However, their sin and apostasy had reached its full; judgment was next for Israel for they had scorned and rejected their Messiah and Savior. And came it did in A.D. 70 at the hands of the pagan Romans. This awful judgment for Israel is explained in Section 163.

(b) **"Will he come to the feast?"** Some six months prior, the Jews had put this same question regarding His presence at the Feast of Tabernacles in Section 119, John 7:11, footnote a. *The Name of Jesus of Nazareth was on the lips of every person at Jerusalem.* Whispering secretly among themselves for fear of the Sanhedrin, the countless thousands present mused, "Will He attend the Passover?" This reveals that many of the Jews from over the known world of that day had heard of the Lord Jesus and His Messianic claims. Upon their arrival at Jerusalem, He was the topic of secret conversation. Little did they know that He would be the *final* Passover Lamb offered for the nation of Israel and the sins of the world.

(c) Having continually clashed with the scribes, Pharisees, Sadducees and Sanhedrin, orders had been issued that any person knowing the whereabouts of Jesus must report to them. He was to be taken into custody! Such an ultimatum would only heighten curiosity and interest in the Savior from the thousands of pilgrims coming to Jerusalem from far off countries of the world. He was the talk of the Passover; this further infuriated the religious leaders and their sympathizers. When one understands that several million visitors were in Jerusalem for the Passover, it becomes clear as to why it was so difficult for the religionists to find Him among this sea of humanity. See third second paragraph of footnote a, above for the numbers that attended this annual celebration.

2p-Verse 1. "Six days before the passover." For explanation of this, see number 1, under footnote d below.

(d) It was common for great suppers to be given in the honor of special persons, especially teachers and religious leaders. For information on Simon the leper, see number 3 below. Present and reclining at the table was Lazarus, a trophy of the Messiah's power and authority over death and the grave. *Both* he and Jesus were the honored persons and objects of a thousand gazing eyes, some filled with hostile intent. How many questions did people asked Lazarus about the time he had spent in eternity? This event and Mary's actions have been subjected to all sorts of exegesis and religious fantasies. *Six different Mary's are mentioned in the New Testament.* They are listed in Section 9, footnote c. Note the following points of interest regarding this occasion:

1. **The time of this anointing.** John wrote that Jesus came to Bethany where Lazarus was (or lived) "six days before the passover." For more on Bethany, see Section 117, footnote a. John does not mention the particular house in which the anointing occurred, only that He arrived at the village six days before Passover time. It would be natural for him to mention Lazarus, since he was the single gospel writer who recorded the story of his resurrection from the dead. Matthew and Mark were inspired to name the village and the exact location where the event took place, "in the house of Simon the leper" (Matt. 26:6 with Mk. 14:3). Some hold that John's "six days" had reference only to the time when Christ arrived at Bethany, not the time when the supper and anointing occurred. It seems more sensible that John was counting backward from the starting day of Passover and was saying, "Jesus arrived at Bethany six days before the *first* or starting day of the actual celebration." The apostle John does not date the *time* when the supper took place, rather the time when Christ entered Bethany, which was "six days" prior to the first day of the Passover Feast. The author of this work *conjectures* that this is the better chronology and was actually a Saturday night meal, after Sabbath ended, and before the next day, which was Palm Sunday. It is correct that the Jews had blended the one-day Passover event into the Feast of Unleavened Bread, which lasted for seven days.

2. **The Sanhedrin was busy.** Reading *all* of Mark's comments in Section 147, Mk. 14:10-11, we note that the Sanhedrin had been plotting the murder of Christ while He was at the supper being anointed by Mary for His soon to be death, burial, and resurrection. Judas knew of this meeting of the religious leaders, for upon leaving the supper and anointing by Mary, he went to Jerusalem and began bartering with them over the "going price" for the Son of God. Note footnotes f and g below for more on Judas' actions.

3. **"Simon the leper."** Who Simon was, we cannot know for Scripture is silent. It is sure that he was *not* infected with leprosy at this time, for no devout Jew would have been in his presence due to the uncleanness (supposedly) transmitted by all lepers. Apparently, this was something of a "nickname" attached to him, being previously healed of his former malady. We may easily believe that Jesus had healed him because the malady was incurable, and no one in Israel had ever healed another of this dreadful disease. Only Messiah could perform this miracle. Calling him "Simon the leper" was similar to John writing of Lazarus "whom he had raised from the dead" or "a woman of Samaria." It must be remembered that John wrote some years after this all happened and was looking back on the sacred history about which he was inspired to write.

4. **In whose house?** This is precisely stated in the narratives as being the house of Simon. This could have also been another name for the house of Lazarus, Mary, and Martha, and by the time Matthew and Mark wrote, it was known as the "the house of Simon the leper." All the fuss the rationalists and unbelieving critics make of this "house' simply reflects their unbelief in the inspiration of Scripture. They are saying in so many words, "If we can't figure it out then its wrong."

(e) **"Mary having an alabaster box."** Three times, we read of this Mary in the gospels. Each time she is at Jesus' feet! Martha served tables while Jesus served Mary and the others (John 12:2). This difference was noted earlier in Section 117, where the two sisters were contrasted. John alone records the name of the woman who anointed the Savior. It was Mary, the sister of Lazarus and Martha. The historian Herodotus (circa 485 B.C.) wrote that these bottles of oil were used as presents for kings (*Herodotus* iii, 20). (For more on alabaster, refer to Section 64, Lk. 7:37, footnote f.) "Spikenard" came from a "bearded grass" that grew in far-away India. It was a rare, costly import. From this was extracted a powerfully fragrant oil greatly used in the east. John 12:3 mentions "fourteen ounces." Mk. 14:5, lists the monetary value at more than "three hundred pence." Footnote h below gives the present day value of the substance. This amount was considered the "life's savings" of Mary. It was a common social practice to anoint feet with oil but to do so with aromatic ointment of this nature was a rare thing indeed! Mark's words that "she brake the box," had reference to the wax seal or putty that was affixed to the opening of the small vase. She simply pushed or punched it open allowing the oil to flow freely.

2p-After prying loose the wax seal, Mary joyfully poured it upon her wonderful Lord. What a good way to live; the best was given to Jesus! It is ever true that we keep only what we give away and lose what we keep. Putting the three records together, we learn that Mary anointed (or "poured down") on the head and feet of the Lord Jesus the costly oil. A "pound" as used here was approximately fourteen ounces. It was customary at these events to anoint the heads of guests with pleasant smelling oil and provide water for their feet to be washed, but such an expensive ointment as this was never used at these occasions. *However, this event was extraordinary and deserved only the best.* A thousand years prior, David wrote that God had anointed his head with oil (Ps. 23:5). Now, a thousand years later, God in the Person of Christ has His head anointed! This has reference to the wax seal or putty that was affixed to the opening of the small vase. She pushed or punched it open allowing the oil to flow freely.

3p-Pious Jews fiercely resented a woman uncovering her head and letting her hair down in public. It was looked upon as an act of surrender and submission to the one before whom it was done! This was based on Num. 5:18 where the priest ministered the bitter water test and uncovered the suspected female's hair in order to shame her. John adds a beautiful annotation that she "wiped his feet with her hair." Mary, in this posture goes far beyond the social custom of that day. *She knew that the Person before Whom she bowed, would in two days die for her sins.* This is explained in footnote j below. For someone else who may have understood Jesus' death, see Section 168, second paragraph of footnote b. Earlier, Jesus was anointed by an evil woman in Section 64, Lk. 7:37-38, footnote g. The Mary in this story is not the sinful woman of Section 64, or the Mary Magdalene of Section 65. Six women in the New Testament are named Mary; see Section 9, footnote c.

(f) Angry with Mary. Two of the evangelists inform us that the Savior's disciples were angry or "had indignation" as Mary anointed the Messiah. John is explicit to write that the ringleader in the vocal objection was Judas Iscariot, the arch-traitor. He directly influenced the other eleven to voice their objections, and they did. See footnote i below for the Savior's rebuke of His crumbling preachers.

(g) Instantly, Judas became vocal and vehemently expressed his objection to the actions of Mary. It was normal for men to rebuke women in public events and Judas takes advantage of this eastern custom. Some of the other eleven apostles, out of ignorance joined refrain with him in a "thief's chorus" of unbelief. Mark wrote that "some" of them objected (verse 4). The basis for Judas' objection was financial, which would enhance the position and service of any treasurer (John 12:6), and make him appear a wise, careful spender of God's money. See footnote h below, along with Section 95, footnote x for more on Judas, the cunning one whom Jesus called "a devil."

2p-The power of influence. Jack Holcomb (died 1968) was a powerful gospel singer. Standing in his bedroom he heard his little son talking with several playmates just outside, near the window. They were discussing, whom of importance did their fathers know. One lad said, "My dad knows the police chief." Another responded, "My dad knows the bank boss." Holcome, stood in awe waiting for his son to reply. The child said, "My dad knows God!" O the power of influence before watching eyes and hearing ears. Note a classical example in Acts 4:13.

(h) "Given to the poor." His pretense of charity served as the cloak for his covetousness. The market for this particular oil was always at its peak. It would sell quickly, and Judas knew this. He even knew its probable value in the words "sold for more than three hundred pence and given to the poor" (Mk. 14:5). This is approximately one-year's wages or about $50.00 U.S. They described Mary's expression of love and worship to the Lord Jesus a "waste" (Matt. 26:8). Some waste! A thousand years prior, David had written of Judas, a terrible pre-eulogy in Ps. 109:6-19. He wrote that the extortionists would catch all that he had (after his suicide). Ten days before Pentecost, Peter interpreted these verses in Ps. 109, as applying strictly to Judas Iscariot (Acts 1:15-26). They are deeply instructive regarding Judas, for they speak of his vile vocabulary, wife, children, mother, and the sins of his parents. His name and posterity were blotted out from among human kind. David wrote these words about Judas, a thousand years before he was born. A careful perusal of them reveals that he was truly "a devil."

2p-John looking back on history can now explain to his readers the true character of Judas, the son of Simon. We are amazed that two days before the cross our Lord's apostles did not know that Judas was a thief. He served as the prototype for all con men that would slip into the local churches over the centuries to come. "Bag" is from the Greek word "glossokomon." Among other things, it had reference to a leather case or bag in which was kept the mouthpieces for various musical wind instruments. Here, it was Judas' cash box. It is also used in Section 172, John

13:29. At this verse, see the first paragraph of footnote j. The word "bare" (John 12:6) actually signifies that Judas *took out* the money and the "glossokomon" or collection bag was "bare" of its contents. See A. T. Robertson's, *Word Pictures of the New Testament*, vol. v. pages 216-217 for explanation. Today, it would be tantamount to stealing from the church collection plates. For more details on Judas, see Section 57, and Explanation Box at the end of the footnotes.

(i) **"Let her alone."** The Lord Jesus instantly responded and defended Mary against the onslaught launched by Judas and the other apostles. See footnote g above. What a stern admonition! It was uncustomary if not unheard of for a man to defend a woman, especially in a public debate. Mary was now the center of observation from everyone present. The Son of God takes her side. Judas and the others were offended at Jesus' rebuke of them and His defense of Mary. Meanwhile, a secret, dark fire blazed in the base heart of Judas the pretended welfare villain. Note Section 147, footnote b where the traitor hurriedly returned to Jerusalem and arranged to betray the Lord Jesus.

(j) **"She hath wrought a good work."** The Lord Jesus is saying here "Let her alone for she has done this in view of my burial." The Talmud speaks of anointing the dead in tractate, K'rithhoth 6b. He knew Mary's heart was fixed on His approaching death and its aftermath. He read her thoughts and instantly spoke out in her defense against His disciples who harangued her for pouring out the ointment. John informs us that Christ saw that she had (to use a modern day term) "prepped" His body in view of His death, burial, and resurrection. The Savior's Words "against [in view of] the day of my burying hath she kept [done] this," are clear. Mary *knew* that her Master would soon die. Jesus vindicated her bold deed, and it was to become a lasting worldwide memorial to her. The amazing confession of tribute to this woman was never said of any other mortal! For the blasphemous Mormon interpretation of Mary, Martha and Jesus, see Section 27, footnote a.

2p-Verse 3. "The house was filled with the odour of the ointment." The hundreds present stopped the feasting and begin to sniff the air and inquire, "What is that beautiful smell?" Thus, it is with the saving gospel of Christ: it wafts a fragrance so exotic and elegant that men over the centuries have paused to ask about its wonder. The ministration of the glorious message of Jesus as it has been carried around the world is emblematically mirrored in the sweet savor emanating from the costly perfume. Its charming attraction arrested the attention of those present. Some among the people believed on Messiah, while others breathing in the same fascinating aroma, rejected Him, went back to Jerusalem, and reported to the Pharisees their vindictive observations.

(k) It is written in the Talmud tractate, Shabbath 63a that "The poor will never cease out of the land." Apparently, this was a popular expression in the days of Christ, and He reiterates it in different words with approval. Several hundred years later, it was included in the Babylonian Talmud. The Pharisees made a great thing out of helping the poor and needy in Israel, yet they devoured the houses of Israel's widows (Mk. 12:40). In response to the self-righteous words of Judas about helping the poor, the Lord Jesus informed everyone at the supper that His presence was only for a few more days; therefore, they should hasten to bestow upon Him every honor possible. They could minister to the needy as long as they lived, but not to Him for He would soon return to the Father in heaven. Mary had employed great wisdom in anointing the feet and head of her Lord. We only keep what we give to Jesus! It has been pointed out repeatedly in this harmony commentary that none of our Lord's apostles yet understood His death on the cross. A few days before Calvary, this woman understood history's most dramatic event and tried to tell everyone present by anointing His head and feet. For more on the mystery of His death in the minds of the apostles, see Section 104, footnote a with its cross-references to other footnotes. This problem was solved on Pentecost with the coming of the Holy Spirit in His fullness (John 16:12-14).

2p-"Me ye have not always. How painful to memory are lost opportunities. They do not bid our convenience. When gone, few ever return. Jesus would not be with them in a bodily presence much longer. They must heed His Words and determine to do His biding. Who among us has not let that precious opportunity slip by, that open door close, that neighbor or friend perish without sharing the gospel? Even in this dispensation of time, the Savior will not always be present. He passes by in youth when conscience is tender and affections are unengaged, when the Spirit is silently striving, when some peculiar providence has awakened our souls to contemplate eternal things. Now, is the time to turn to Christ; today is the day of salvation. Rare are the occasions when men can grasp eternity in earth's time. Jacob did and would not let go (Gen. 32:24-30). In this life only we can prepare to meet God. Scripture warns, "if the tree fall toward the south, or toward the north, in the place where the tree falleth, there it shall be" (Eccles. 11:3). Death is so final! In the afterlife, there is "a great gulf fixed" that cannot be crossed (Lk. 16:26). Men make their "calling and election sure" by trusting Christ as personal Lord and savior (2 Peter 1:10). How ironic that many ancient Jews in building their houses would leave a room unfinished. This was to remind them that death was coming; they must complete God's work for their lives.

(l) **"A memorial" for Mary.** Matthew and Mark alone record this extraordinary command spoken by the Lord Jesus. It was intended as a duty for all people of all times who carry the saving message of Christ to others. Wherever the death, burial, and resurrection (the gospel) of Christ will be heralded, the preacher or teacher is here commanded to salute Mary for anointing His body for burial. She is to be habitually and perpetually memorialized. Why? Such a time-long and worldwide salute to any mortal has never been commanded anywhere in the pages of

Holy Scripture! Repeatedly, in this harmony commentary, we have stressed that almost no one understood the supreme purpose of Messiah coming into this world. This lack of knowledge has been explained numerous times. For example, see Section 26, footnote f; Section 27 footnote n; Section 29, footnote j; and Section 39 footnote a. His death on a Roman cross for the sins of Adam's race was impossible; the Jews believed only in a human all conquering, political Messiah, who would establish their earthly kingdom or rule. *A few days before Calvary, Mary knew the truth about Jesus!* She had sat at His feet and listened intently to His teachings; now she understands that her Lord will die for her sins. We have previously noted Mary sitting at Jesus' feet, learning who He was, and why He came in Section 117, Lk. 10:38-39. She takes her very expensive possession, all her costly treasure contained in that little flask, and poured it on His head and feet, for these were soon to be crowned with thorns and pierced with nails. By faith, Mary knew the great secret and tries to tell her Lord that she understands!

2p-One rarely or *never* hears a pastor, Bible teacher, professor of theology, missionary or the everyday Christian, salute Mary as Jesus instructed. Her story is to be told as long as the gospel is preached for a memorial to her insight into the death of Jesus. It is ironic that the super twelve complained of the very act that shadowed our Lord's death on the cross, while cringing Mary quietly demonstrated that she knew it was coming soon. This charge made by Christ about her spiritual understating has a universal touch. Here, was her glory as she saw Calvary's awfulness vanish in the dawn of resurrection morning. *Every* future generation is to know of her unique insight into God's plan of redemption; she knew that Jesus was heading for the cross and empty tomb and attempted in this quiet act to show the hundreds present at the great supper. One can well imagine the discussions of the apostles, years later as they looked back with both joy and shame on this occasion in the house of Simon the leper.

(m) John 12:9-10. "Much people" does not signify a few dozen. Across the gospels, it has reference to thousands. The thousands of Jews at Jerusalem who had gathered to attend the Passover, when they heard that Christ was at Bethany (about two miles east of the city), came to see Him and Lazarus fresh from the dead! It shows that news of this miracle had traveled across Jerusalem and further abroad. Who could describe the talk, gossip, and wild rumors that had developed around this wonderful Messianic deed? Continually, news spread everywhere that Jesus had performed another miracle; one of those only the true Messiah of Israel could perform. See Section 124, John 11:53, second paragraph of footnote w, for the reason the Jews were so greatly upset with the raising of Lazarus. Thousands flocked to Bethany, anxious to see *both* the Messiah and the man He had called from eternity.

(n) After seeing Jesus and the resurrected Lazarus, hundreds of the Jews returned to Jerusalem, convinced believers that Jesus was their Messiah. This fact precludes any possibility of faking his death; it is clear that these Jews new Lazarus and knew that he had died. Note Section 124, John 11:19, where "many of the Jews" were present to comfort the bereaved sisters after his burial. Now, they know He has risen from death, for they have seen and talked with Him. It takes no little imagination to realize that the curious Jews conversed with Lazarus about his experience. However, it must be remembered that miracles performed, for the most part, will not bring men to a saving knowledge of Christ. No cities had seen such miracles as had Chorazin, Bethsaida, and Capernaum. Yet, they were doomed because of their deliberate rejection of Jesus the Messiah. Note Section 63, Matt. 11:20-24 for the awful details. Those who busy themselves praying for a great resurgence of signs, miracles, and wonders should start praying for the Holy Spirit to fall on men, convicting them of their sin and its eternal consequences in hell, and their need for Christ as personal Savior. *This is the only way anyone has ever been saved.* How people were saved before Jesus' death, see Section 10, footnote b; Section 64, footnote k; and Section 144, footnote i. Filled with rancor, the Jews plotted to kill Jesus and Lazarus. As long as Lazarus lived, he would tell others about Jesus. This would be incontestable proof that He was Israel's Messiah.

(o) Jews who trust Christ are still persecuted. The Jewish religionists and their sympathizers could not bear hearing of any more Israelites being persuaded that Jesus was the Messiah. He must be stopped! Among *some* Orthodox Jews of today, it is the same. They hate the Man Jesus Christ vehemently, deny that He is Messiah, and castigate in the most shocking manner any fellow Hebrews, who dare trust Him as Lord and Savior. For an outstanding volume on the subject of unsaved Jews persecuting fellow Jews, who have come to know Christ as Savior and Messiah, see *Famous Hebrew Christians,* by Jacob Gartenhaus. It contains the true-life stories of thirty-five Jews (some of whom were rabbis) who were saved, and the price they paid for their faith in Jesus Christ. Many have been forced to leave their homes, family, friends, and jobs. Saved Jews are scornfully called "meshumadim" or "traitors" by their fellows. Over the centuries, their persecution at the hands of Christ hating Jews has been horrific. It reminds one of the treatment radical Muslims give those among their ranks who are saved by the grace of God.

2p-Historian Ruth A. Tucker, published in 1999, *Not Ashamed. The Story of Jews for Jesus.* This is a helpful work. On pages 290-291, Professor Tucker briefly and carefully answers the question, "Should Jews who believe in Jesus behave like other Christians?" Her explanation that Hebrew holidays have their origin in God, not paganism, as do so many Christian celebrations is refreshing. For other comments on the persecution of Jews who come to know Messiah-Christ as personal Lord and Savior, refer to Section 130, second paragraph of footnote o. For the amazing difference concerning the ancient Hebrew opinion of Jesus Christ of Nazareth, against that of present day Jews, see Section 14, all of footnote f. It is indeed a surprising story!

Leaving Simon the leper's house at Bethany, Judas goes to Jerusalem and bargains with the Sanhedrin to betray the Lord Jesus. The selling price is thirty pieces of silver. He seemingly became angry at our Lord's rebuke of his objection to Mary anointing Him, and his false proposal to sell the ointment for the poor failed.

Somewhere in Jerusalem: probably the high priest's palace

Matt. 26:14–16	Mk. 14:10–11	Lk. 22:3–6	John
Betrayal and stealth	*Betrayal and stealth*	*Betrayal and stealth*	
14 Then one of the twelve, called Judas[a] Iscariot, went	10 And Judas[a] Iscariot, one of the twelve, went unto	3 Then entered[a] Satan into Judas surnamed Iscariot, being of the number of the twelve. 4 And he went his way, and communed with the chief priests[b] and captains, [temple police] how he might betray him unto them.	
unto the chief priests,[b]	the chief priests,[b] to betray him unto them.		
15 And said *unto them*, "What will ye give me,[c] and I will deliver him unto you?"			
The Savior's going price	*The Savior's going price*	*The Saviors' going price*	
And they covenanted[d] with him for thirty pieces of silver. [about $19.00]	11 And when they heard *it*, they were glad, and promised[d] to give him money.	5 And they were glad, and covenanted[d] to give him money.	
Judas waits for the time	*Judas waits for the time*	*Judas waits for the time*	
16 And from that time he sought opportunity to betray[e] him. (Verse 17 cont. in Section 168.)	And he sought how he might conveniently betray[e] him. (Verse 12 cont. in Section 168.)	6 And he promised, and sought opportunity to betray[e] him unto them in the absence of the multitude. (Verse 7 cont. in Section 168.)	

Footnotes–Commentary

(a) Judas played a leading role in the death of Christ. For prophetic details of this and information regarding his life, family, children, and wealth, refer to Section 172, all under footnote e. The verse of Lk. 22:3 gives us a shudder when it reads, "Satan entered him." With this, he became something of a "devil Man," and was directed in his course by the Prince of darkness. Later, we read of another satanic entrance into the soul of this wretch, the night before the morning of the cross in Section 172, John 13:27, footnote i. These verses confirm that Satan had free access into his body and moved in and out at his choice. This devilish entrance and exit is also seen in the main heading of Section 68 where the reference is to the demonized religious leaders of Israel. For comments on the selection of Judas with the twelve, refer to Section 57, and the Information Box at the end of the footnotes.

(b) **"Went unto the chief priests.** Leaving the supper at Bethany, Judas made his way back to Jerusalem and contacted the Jewish authorities; no doubt, he was fuming mad over Jesus' rebuke of him at the supper in front of all the guests. This was because of his hypocritical plea to sell the oil and give the proceeds to the poor. See previous Section 146, footnote h for details on this. Harmonizing all three of the inspired writers, we safely conclude that he met with the Sanhedrin or a representative body of these men. *The normal place for such meetings was the palace of the high priest.* Their fierce hatred for Christ has been recorded many times in this work. They gladly welcomed Judas and listened intently to his proposal to betray the Son of God into their hands. It is noteworthy that Luke states that "captains" (verse 4) were consulted in the plot. These men were the officers in charge of the temple police force and were called by the Jews the "captains of the temple." For details on this subject, see Section 119, John 7:32, footnote m.

(c) **"What will ye give me?"** These infamous words reveal the heart of this human monster. Money can buy his Messiah if the price is right. One senses that Judas was also angered over Mary freely giving her most valuable treasure to the Savior. *What a contrast between Mary and Judas.* She gave all to her Lord while Judas bargained to sell Him to death! Both Mark and Luke inform us that this body of men was "glad" when they heard the traitor's financial proposal. At last, their hated enemy, who had so embarrassed and silenced them, will be delivered into their hands for destruction, or so they believed.

(d) **"Covenanted."** The word also means, "weighed." The meaning is that the Jews took scales or balances and precisely measured out the coinage price of their Messiah. How curious that wicked men often choose to do iniquitous things in the most precise manner. *However, every sin has its own awful torment that afterwards emerges in the conscience of the committer.* Some five hundred years prior, the prophet Zechariah had predicted this selling price for Israel's Messiah in the Old Testament (Zech. 11:12-13). The contextual and historical lesson portrayed in Zechariah's prediction was that of a shepherd asking for his pay for tending sheep over a long period. He was given thirty pieces of silver. This amount reflected that the owner of the flock counted the shepherd's service as worthless and not deserving of salary. His lengthy attendance of the sheep was counted no more than the price of a dead slave (Ex. 21:31-32). The dejected and mistreated shepherd was directed by God to "throw the money into the potter's house" which was a public expression for contemptuous treatment. This act pointed far into the future when the betrayer of God's Son (Judas), later returned his blood money to the Jews in the temple. Apparently, there was a potter who served full time in the temple or nearby and had his workshop established there. The objection that potters were banned from the temple and city because of the smoke from their furnaces being unclean seems ludicrous in view of the continual stream of smoke powering up from the giant altar of sacrifice. Refer to Section 183, Matt. 27:3-10, for Judas returning the money and the sarcastic attitude of his former co-partners in the sin of betraying and selling the Messiah.

2p-As stated above in the Torah Law (Ex. 21:31-32) thirty pieces of silver was the price paid for a dead slave! In time, it became an emblem of infamy. Contempt for Jesus was uppermost in the minds of these men as they agreed on this price. The rich would send thirty pieces of silver to their most detested and hated enemies to show they were counted as a dead slave. Thirty pieces tallies out to approximately $18.00 in present day American currency. F. W. Farrar in his *Life of Christ* pages 591-592 described the stamp or image imposed upon this particular piece of silver, of which one was discovered in Jerusalem in 1874. Ironically on one side was the Jewish olive branch symbolizing peace in Israel. On the reverse was that of a temple censer, the great emblem of prayer offered to God! With gloating eyes and both fists filled with blood money, the Devil incarnate walked out of the presence of Israel's religious leaders with his prize. He had procured a bargain! It is striking that on silver coins of this denomination were stamped the words "Jerusalem the holy." Who among normal men can phantom the awful abyss of a heart and mind that had spent some two years with the Lord from heaven, and now walks back to join the apostolic band as though nothing had happened? From henceforth, he secretly sought opportunity to betray his Master. The name "Judas Iscariot" has gone down in the pages of history and remains as both infamous and scurrilous to this day. The author once knew a pastor in Houston, Texas, who named his *treacherous* dog, Judas!

3p-Over sixteen hundred-year prior, Joseph was sold by his brothers into Egypt for twenty pieces of silver (Gen. 37:28). He is one of the most beautiful type-pictures of Christ found anywhere in the Old Testament. Many of the things that happened to Joseph in some odd way similarly happened to the Savior many centuries later.

(e) **"Opportunity to betray him."** Section 167, footnote c contains more on this move of stealth to betray and capture the Lord Jesus without creating a disturbance among the people during the sacred Passover Feast. The religious leaders counted it a high abomination to have any disturbance during their holy Passover celebration, yet they arrested, tried and had Jesus put to death during this occasion! O the depths of human hearts corrupted by sin and employed by the Devil to accomplish his vile purpose. The Jews believed that many opportunities would occur, either at Jerusalem or elsewhere, when the great Passover was over, and the city had lapsed into its ordinary calm. This "opportunity" to deliver Christ presented itself a short time later during His lonely prayer vigil in the Garden of Gethsemane. For details on this scene of holy prayer, and the subsequent arrest of the Savior, refer to the main heading of Section 179. The actions of a man often betray his secret intentions.

2p-Over the course of my life and ministry as a missionary, I have heard and seen the Devil or demon spirits speaking and performing through the actions and words of certain people. The covert work of Judas exemplifies this. An Australian truck driver angered over the conversion of his wife shook his fist toward heaven, daring God to strike him dead! A powerful little verse of Scripture often overlooked is 1 Sam. 2:3, "and by him (God) actions are weighed." For a vivid illustration of Satan reacting through his servants against the gospel, read the true story recorded in Section 106, third paragraph of footnote k. "Learned religious specialists" and "highly trained Christians" who deny the reality of the Devil and his demons serve them well.

CHAPTER 14

PALM SUNDAY.* RIDING INTO JERUSALEM UPON A DONKEY, JESUS IS HAILED AS MESSIAH BY THE EXCITED CROWDS. HIS ACTIVITIES UNTIL ENTERING THE UPPER ROOM. AN ARGUMENT BREAKS OUT AMONG THE APOSTLES. HE WASHES THEIR FEET DEMONSTRATING HUMILITY.

Upon arriving at the east gate of Jerusalem, the waiting multitudes go wild thinking He would instantly set up a political kingdom for Israel to rule the world. Instead, He returned to Bethany.

Time: Palm Sunday, the first day of the crucifixion week.

This name appeared later in church history. According to the Biblical, Theological, and Ecclesiastical Cyclopaedia, vol. vii, pages 599-600, by M'Clintock & Strong it surfaced in the Greek churches of the fourth century, then spread into others. The confused church fathers were "blessing palm branches" and burning them into ashes to be used on their Ash Wednesday. These ashes were "blessed" by the priests and placed on the foreheads of people to remind them that they are but ashes and dust, and that they should be very humble when they come to do penance! It is true that the popular palm branch was a symbol used for centuries by pagans in the worship of their heathen gods. The International Standard Bible Encyclopedia, (1987) vol. 3 page 649 carries a picture of pagan gods collecting sap from palm trees. The Roman Catholic system turned it into something of mystical if not an occultist nature. The Passover crowds greeting Jesus as He rode to Jerusalem, used palm branches because thousands of palm trees grew along the roads that led into Jerusalem. It was a matter of convenience for the people; nothing evil was intended as these Jews were all pagan haters. The text seems to suggest that the people also cut limbs from other "trees" to place before Messiah (Matt. 21:8). Only John mentions palm trees (verse 13).

From Mount of Olives, to Shushan Gate, into the temple, and back to Bethany

Matt. 21:1-2	Mk. 11:1-2	Lk. 19:28-30	John 12:12
			The word spreads
			12 On the next day much people that were come to the [Passover] feast, when they heard that Jesus was coming to Jerusalem,
Jesus' strange orders	***Jesus' strange orders***	***Jesus' strange orders***	
1 And when they drew nigh	**1** And when they came nigh to	**28** And when he had thus spoken, he went before, ascending up to Jerusalem.	
unto Jerusalem, and	Jerusalem,	**29** And it came to pass, when he was come nigh	
were come to Bethphage, unto	unto Bethphage and Bethany, at	to Bethphage and Bethany, at the mount	
the mount of Olives,(a) then sent Jesus two disciples,	the mount of Olives,(a) he sendeth forth two of his disciples,	called *the mount* of Olives(a) he sent two of his disciples,	
"Bring me a donkey"	***"Bring me a donkey"***	***"Bring me a donkey"***	
2 Saying unto them, "Go into the village over against you, and	**2** And saith unto them, "Go your way into the village over against you: and as	**30** Saying, "Go ye into the village over against *you*; in	

Matt. 21:2–7	Mk. 11:2–7	Lk. 19: 30–35	John 12
straightway ye shall find an ass tied, and a colt with her: loose *them,* and bring[(b)] *them* unto me. **3** "And if any *man* say ought unto you, ye shall say, 'The Lord hath need of them;'[(c)] and straightway he will send them." **4** All this was done, that it might be fulfilled which was spoken by the prophet, saying, ▶ **5 "Tell ye the daughter of Sion, 'Behold, thy King cometh unto thee, meek, and sitting upon an ass, and a colt the foal of an ass.' "**[(d)]	soon as ye be entered into it, ye shall find a colt tied, whereon never man sat; loose him, and bring[(b)] *him* . **3** "And if any man say unto you, 'Why do ye this?' say ye that 'the Lord hath need of him;'[(c)] and straightway he will send them hither." ◀ *John's record of this prophecy is placed in John 12:14-15 below.*	the which at your entering ye shall find a colt tied, whereon yet never man sat: loose him, and bring [(b)] *him hither.* **31** "And if any man ask you, 'Why do ye loose *him?*' thus shall ye say unto him, 'Because the Lord hath need of him.' "[(c)]	
Made ready for Jesus **6** And the disciples went, and did as Jesus commanded them,	*Made ready for Jesus* **4** And they went their way, and found the colt tied by the door without in a place where two ways met; and they loose him. **5** And certain of them that stood there said unto them, "What do ye, loosing the colt?" **6** And they said unto them even as Jesus had commanded: and they let them go.	*Made ready for Jesus* **32** And they that were sent went their way, and found even as he had said unto them. **33** And as they were loosing the colt, the owners thereof said unto them, " Why loose ye the colt?" **34** And they said, "The Lord hath need of him."	
7 And brought the ass, and the colt, and put	**7** And they brought the colt to Jesus, and cast	**35** And they brought him to Jesus: and they cast	

675

Matt. 21:7–9	Mk. 11:7–10	Lk. 19:35–38	John 12:13–15
on them their clothes, and they set▶ *him* thereon.	their garments on him; and he sat▶ upon him.	their garments upon the colt, and they set▶Jesus thereon.	◀*John puts this event in verse 14 below.*
The crowds go wild **8** And a very great multitude spread their garments in the way; others cut down branches from the trees, and strawed *them* in the way.[(e)]	***The crowds go wild*** **8** And many spread their garments in the way: and others cut down branches off the trees, and strawed *them* in the way.[(e)]	***The crowds go wild*** **36** And as he went, they spread their clothes in the way.[(e)]	**13** Took branches of palm trees, and went forth to meet him,
		A Messianic Psalm **37** And when he was come nigh, even now at the descent of the mount of Olives, the whole multitude of the disciples began to rejoice and praise God with a loud voice for all the mighty works that they had seen;	and cried,
A Messianic Psalm **9** And the multitudes that went before, and that followed, cried, saying, **"Hosanna**[(f)] **to the son of David: 'Blessed *is* he that cometh in the name of the Lord;'** **Hosanna in the highest."**	***A Messianic Psalm*** **9** And they that went before, and they that followed, cried, saying, **"Hosanna;**[(f)] **'Blessed *is* he that cometh in the name of the Lord:'** **10 Blessed *be* the kingdom of our father David, that cometh in the name of the Lord: Hosanna in the highest."**	**38** Saying, **" ' Blessed *be* the King that cometh in the name of the Lord:' peace in heaven, and glory in the highest."**	**"Hosanna:**[(f)] **'Blessed *is* the King of Israel that cometh in the name of the Lord.' "**
		▶ *Matthew puts this in verse 7. Mark in verse 7 and Luke in verse 35.* ▶ *Matthew records this prophecy in verses 4 and 5 above. Mark and Luke do not mention this. See footnote d for more on this prediction.*	**14** ◀And Jesus, when he had found a young ass, sat thereon; as it is ◀written, **15 "Fear not, daughter of Sion: behold, thy King cometh, sitting on an ass's colt."**

Matt. 21:10	Mk. 11:11	Lk. 19:39-44	John 12
		The Pharisees object **39** And some of the Pharisees[g] from among the multitude said unto him, "Master, rebuke thy disciples." **40** And he answered and said unto them, "I tell you that, if these should hold their peace, the stones would immediately cry out." ***He predicts the destruction of A.D. 70*** **41** And when he was come near, he beheld the city, and wept over it, **42** Saying,[h] "If thou hadst known, even thou, at least in this thy day, the things *which belong* unto thy peace! but now they are hid from thine eyes. **43** "For the days shall come upon thee, that thine enemies shall cast a trench about thee, and compass[i] thee round, and keep thee in on every side, **44** "And shall lay thee even with the ground, and thy children within thee; and they shall not leave in thee one stone upon another; because thou knewest not the time of thy visitation." (Verse 45 cont. Section 150.)	
He enters the city **10** And when he as come into Jeru-salem, all the city was	***He enters the city*** **11** And Jesus entered into Jeru-salem,		

Matt. 21:10–11	Mk. 11: 11	Lk.	John 12: 16–19
moved,[j] saying, "Who is this?" **11** And the multitude said, "This is Jesus the prophet of Nazareth of Galilee." (Verse 12 cont. in Section 150.)	***He surveys the temple*** and into the temple: and when he had looked round about upon all things,[k] ***He returns to Bethany*** and now the eventide [of Sunday] was come, he went out unto Bethany[l] with the twelve. (Verse 12 cont. in Section 149.)	▶ *Again, the disciples of our Lord did not comprehend the truth of His work, leading up to His death on the cross and resurrection. It was only after He rose from the grave and appeared to them with many infallible proofs that He was alive, that they understood and fully believed. See Section 196, John 20:9 and attached notes. Also, see Section 207, Acts 1:3 and notes on the forty days of proofs. It should be noted that John penned his words, looking back some years after Jesus' ascension. He included himself among those who did not understand at that time.*	***Remembering later*** ◀**16** These things understood not his disciples at the first: but when Jesus was glorified, then remembered they that **these things were written of him,**[m] and *that* they had done these things unto him. ***Word was spread*** **17** The people therefore that was with him when he called Lazarus out of his grave,[n] and raised him from the dead, bare record. **18** For this cause the people also met him, for that they heard that he had done this miracle. ***Religious Jews upset over the masses*** **19** The Pharisees therefore said among themselves, Perceive ye how ye prevail

678

Matt.	Mk.	Lk.	John 12:19
			nothing? behold, the world is gone after him."(o) (Verse 20 cont. in Section 161.)

Footnotes-Commentary

(a) **Did Jesus enter Jerusalem on a Sunday?** He was at the house of Simon the leper, according to Section 146, John 11:1. From here, he walked to Jerusalem about two miles west, secured the donkey, and entered the city. The day before this Sunday entrance into Jerusalem was the Hebrew Sabbath. Jews allowed for traveling limited distances on this day. This was called "a sabbath day's journey" in Acts 1:12. This reference deals with walking a limited number of steps on the Sabbath day as regulated in the oral law. For exceptions to the Sabbath rules, see Section 52, footnote l, Section 54, footnote d, and Section 119, footnote h. On the Jews hypocritical eating habits, see Section 23, footnote b. There is no problem with Jesus making this trip during the Saturday or Sabbath afternoon, or after it ended at sundown. It seems historically true that He did ride into Jerusalem on a Sunday, later dubbed "Palm Sunday." The chronology in the Detailed Table of Contents, Sections 150 through Section 187 outlines this in chronological order up to Him being delivered to die by Pilate. The Papal Church and other Orthodox groups have turned Palm Sunday and the week following into something almost sacred. Observing certain days has been a human custom from the beginning of time. However, doing this to secure one's salvation is a plot of the Devil. Only faith in Jesus Christ saves from sin, not keeping a special day, ritual, ceremony, or event. Across the so-called world of "Christendom," Palm Sunday and the week following is observed in hundreds of different ways ranging from the sublime to the ridiculous! For a brief history of the term "Palm Sunday," see asterisk under the main heading at the beginning of this Section. The Savior had determined with calm deliberation of what was involved for Him to enter publicly the city of Jerusalem, thus openly demonstrating for thousands to witness that He was Messiah! News had spread by early Sunday morning that sometime during that day He would appear in the Holy City. Jews, who had visited Bethany on the previous evening, after the sunset had ended the Sabbath, also carried word that Jesus was coming. Across Jerusalem, the message spread that Messiah was moving toward the Eastern Gate. His band of preachers, accompanied by great crowds followed Him. Soon, the Savior would change His mode of transport and enter the Eastern Gate. He would be riding on a donkey! *Every scripturally informed Jew knew what this signaled.* For explanation of the donkey, see footnote d below. Why Christ came to the Eastern Gate, is explained in the second paragraph of footnote j below.

2p-The Mount of Olives (or Olivet) is on the eastern side of the city with the sprawling Valley of Kedron nestling between it and Jerusalem. It was named from the thousands of olive trees that grew there. Kedron is called "the king's dale" in Gen. 14:17 and 2 Sam. 18:18. It is actually a range of hills about two miles in length with several summits, all of which are just less than three thousand feet in height. The middle summit, known as the Mount of Ascension, is situated on a lofty elevation directly east of the temple. It was from here that Christ gave His great eschatological discourse. This is recorded in Sections 163 through 166. It is held that Christ ascended back to heaven from this site, which was in some unknown way associated with Bethany, perhaps the entire district being called by this name (Section 207, Acts 1:9-11 with Lk. 24:50-51). This is the Bethany where Lazarus was raised from the dead, where Mary and Martha lived (Section 124), and where Mary had anointed Him with the costly oil (Section 146).

3p-Both Bethphage and Bethany were geographically connected to the Mount of Olives. Bethphage, was on the western side of the mount, and Bethany on the eastern as one approached from Jericho. Mark and Luke both wrote that He came ("near") to these villages. Bethphage, meaning "house of figs" was about one mile from Bethany, situated near Jerusalem. Bethany means "house of dates" and was about two miles in an easterly direction from the city. There were two *main* roads from Jerusalem to Bethany; one passing the southern end of the Mount of Olives and the other going over the summit of the mount itself. This was the shorter of the routes but the more difficult one to transverse. Apparently, the Lord Jesus came to Bethany first and probably spent the night there. In the morning, He sent two unnamed disciples over part of the mount to the adjacent town of Bethphage to secure His animal transportation to the Eastern Gate of Jerusalem.

(b) **"Bring to me."** Some commentators have questioned this command Jesus gave to His disciples. See footnote c below for comments. Mark and Luke wrote that Jesus told them they would find the colt tied. They mentioned only the colt, for it was upon this animal that the Messiah rode. Matthew wrote of both an ass and a colt. Putting the story together, it seems our Lord rode part of the way on one animal and on the other the remainder of the trip (Matt. 21: 5 with John 12:14-15). The colt had to be of some maturity to carry the Savior. It is a common sight in Israel today, to see an Arab riding a donkey with his sandals often dragging the ground! Asses or donkeys, camels and mules were abundant in the land. Horses used mostly for war were not so plentiful. Riding on a mule or donkey was often looked upon as an emblem of peace as seen at the inauguration of King Solomon (1 Kings 1:33). The Jews well understood this historical custom, and it was both right and appropriate that the Son of God, the King of Israel, should appear at the gate of his capital, the city of Jerusalem, in this manner. Further, it had been predicted in the Old Testament that Israel's Messiah would appear before the city in this fashion. See footnote d below. Hitherto, He had always entered the Holy city on foot; this day, however, He would do so as the Son of David, even as the judge of Israel riding on a special animal designated for that purpose. In Jewish thinking, this act was nationalistic. Had not Moses led his wife into Egypt seated on a donkey. Did not judges ride on white donkeys as they entered a village or city for court? The rabbis had taught pious Jews, that "Messiah would enter Jerusalem from the east, riding on an ass," and they pointed to Holy Scripture as proof (Matt. 21:4-5). Now, it was about to happen before their very eyes! For other interesting comments on this, see *The Life and Works of Christ,* pages 660-661, by Cunningham Geike.

(c) **"The Lord hath need of him."** Matthew wrote of two animals while Mark and Luke mentioned only one. The owners of the mother and her colt would naturally inquire as to why the two disciples were untying the animals from their hitches. Various Antichrist liberals have intimated that Christ "stole the animals." This reveals their bias, ignorance, and hatred for inspired Scriptures and the sinless Son of God. Whoever the owners were when they heard the response, "The Lord hath need of him," understood instantly the identification, "The Lord." Being acquainted with the Messiah, they "straightway" and joyfully relinquished the animals into the hands of the two disciples for Jesus to use. Seemingly, the owners also knew the disciples who came to collect the animals at the behest of their Lord. One thing is sure, they instantly understood who "the Lord" was that had need of their beasts. Their response was instant. On the other hand, Christ has the right to call for anything we have, whatever, He wants to use. He has the right to call for our time, money, family, health, earthly possessions—anything! It is all His more than it is ours. The title deeds to all of earth's goods and treasures are in His omnipotent hands. Everything we have has been temporarily loaned to us for life's little while. *Alas! How have we used these things?*

2p-Various Jewish writings speak of an animal on which their Messiah would ride. Typical of rabbinical exaggeration and perversion of truth, some held that the animal on which their Messiah would enter Jerusalem was the one Abraham used in the offering of his son Isaac some two thousand years prior (Gen. 22:3). Others held that it would be a white horse, some a Zebra with a hundred stripes. For more on this rabbinical perversion, see the Talmud tractate, Sanhedrin 98a, and F. W. Farrar's, *Life of Christ,* footnote number 5, page 532 for the interesting but absurd details. Apart from this scribal error, it is interesting that the ancient rabbis commenting on Ezek. 11:23, which spoke of their Messiah, said that He would retire from Jerusalem, and move to the Mount of Olives. From here, he would call for three years with a human voice for Israel to repent of her sins.

(d) **Quoted from Zech. 9:9**. Shaded in gray signifying a prophecy. Matthew quoted this from the Jewish Old Testament for the benefit of his Hebrew readers. It was a general blending of words selected from two verses, Isa. 62:11, and the remainder from Zech. 9:9. All informed Jewish readers of Matthew's book understood that these two passages spoke of their Messiah, and that Jesus of Nazareth had fulfilled them. John also records this same prediction in verse 15 of his gospel.

2p-**"Daughter of Zion."** Cities are often referred to as daughters in Scripture. Babylon is thus in Isa. 47:1, and Tyre in Ps. 45:12. The gospel writers use the words "ass" and "colt" interchangeably. Matthew states that they put their clothes on both in verse 7. The Talmud carries an interesting comment about the Jewish Messiah riding on the beast of burden in tractate, Sanhedrin 98a. It speaks of Daniel 7:13, where He comes in the clouds of heaven and ties this to Zech. 9:9, where He is on the back of a donkey. The rabbis attempted to explain the difference by saying that "if Israel is good he will be high and in the heavens," and if not "Messiah will be on the back of the donkey." If this rabbinical interpretation was correct, then its meaning was *literally fulfilled* in Jesus of Nazareth riding up to the Eastern Gate of the city. At that time, the nation of Israel, especially its religious leadership was anything but "good." Perhaps our Lord's humility is reflected in this act as He stood in the shadow of the cross. This ride on the lowly colt may be contrasted with His future coming with overwhelming power in the clouds of heaven (Rev. 1:7). Another return of Jesus, riding on a white horse is portrayed in which He is victorious over the world and all foes (Rev. 19:11-16.) It seems so wrong to spiritualize these verses into meaning something less than their *natural reading* states.

(e) **Verses 7-8. A road paved with clothing.** This literally happened. The wild crowds made a tapestry of clothing and paved the dusty road to welcome the Messiah as He moved along the way to Jerusalem. No doubt, some of His disciples were leading the donkey. It was a custom often practiced among the Jews in time of high celebration and triumph to spread clothing for the heroes to march over while entering their cities. Several hundred years prior, when Simon Maccabeus had cleansed a battle tower in Jerusalem (after its occupation by pagans), the Jews re-entered it with great joy and spread branches and boughs along the way (1 Maccabees. 13:51 with 2 Maccabees 10:6-7). The excited crowds that were present to observe the Passover, upon hearing of the arrival of Jesus, removed a part of their outer garments and threw them over the back of both animals and along the roadside leading up to the city gate. Eastern crowds to this day still practice the same thing amid weddings and celebrated events of joy and high expectation. Such is the enduring nature of the habits of these people. Branches were cut from nearby trees and strewn along Messiah's way but not on the path of the animal carrying Him. Most men carried

680

swords at their sides for protection, and these were used to collect the branches. It is noteworthy that in the Torah Law the branches of palm and other trees were to be used in times of great joy (Lev. 23:40) during the Feast of Tabernacles. The actions of the people indicate that they thought their literal King, and His kingdom had arrived, and they were busy building booths or huts to celebrate this occasion. See Section 119, footnote a, for a review of the Feast of Tabernacles observance. The last mention of Palms in Scripture is in Rev. 7:9 where countless millions who have been redeemed are seen standing before God and His Son, dressed in white robes, with palms in their hands singing eternal praises. Those who suggest that Jesus prearranged all this in order to deceive the people into thinking He was Messiah, again, reflect their hatred for the Son of God and blatant ignorance of His Word. These people argue so professionally for their own damnation.

2p-**Lk. 19: 37. "The descent of the mount of Olives."** The soon to be crucified Messiah of Israel rides over the very ground where some forty years later the tenth Roman legion would be encamped as part of the mighty besieging force destined to lay all the splendor of Jerusalem into ash heaps. Now, the materialistic minded Orthodox Jews, anxious for their literal political kingdom to appear, fill the air with a thousand shouts of praise. A generation later, some ten thousand legionaries stormed up this same Mount Moriah, screaming out their shouts of vengeance, death, and destruction for these very people and their city.

(f) **Vain excitement.** Believing their material kingdom had come, the crowds went wild. The people were singing a Jewish hallel. This term "Hosanna," and following words were cited from Ps. 118:25-26. This was one of the most famed Messianic Psalms known to Israel. Thousands of local Jews and pilgrims from over the known world were present for the Passover. Many of them ran before the Lord as he rode near the city. This was a procession of lowly pomp; and yet beside it, the grandest triumphs of all wars and aggressive conquests vanish in shame and disgrace. Several Old Testament Messianic predictions are blended together in this cry. It was also a term used by lowly people begging help or redress from their kings or superiors. This word was well known as it was used during the Feast of Tabernacles celebration. *Gill's Commentary* gives a clear and documented explanation of this in vol. 7, pages 234-235. However, the salvation they expected from Messiah was of earthly and material nature. It would throw off the Roman yoke, and the physical kingdom of Israel would be established at Jerusalem. Here, it did not refer to the salvation of the soul from sin and hell.

2p-**Verse 10. "The kingdom of our father."** *They expected Him to establish instantly their political earthly kingdom.* For explanation of the kingdom in its two different aspects see Section 39, footnotes a and g. The connection of "Hosanna," ("save, we pray") with the words "Son of David," reveal the crowds took Jesus for their Messiah. See Section 5, footnote a, for more on the "Son of David." They proclaimed Him as Messiah, and He let them do so without restraint. This acclamation may have been originally located in Ps. 148:1. Their united voices of praise remind one of the words of heaven's angelic host at the birth of Jesus in Section 14, Lk. 2:14, first paragraph of footnote f. We note that Ps. 113–118 was sung regularly during the Passover time, and thus it would be fresh in the minds of the Jews. These Psalms were purely Messianic and held dearly in the memory of every pious Hebrew. Two days later, Christ cited the Messianic prediction in Ps. 118:22, and applied it to Himself (Matt. 21:42). At this time, the people accepted Him as Messiah with all joyfulness, triumph, and affection of heart. Clearly, they saw Him as the promised One of Israel, and they had no other way of expressing their joy than by reciting one of their Old Testament promises. They expected great things from Him, but He did not fulfill their expectations, as a cross, not a crown (except one of thorns) was just ahead. Rabbis taught the Jews, that when Messiah came to the gate of Jerusalem, He was to be welcomed with the chant or hallel, "Blessed is he that cometh in the name of the Lord." However, these cheering crowds would shortly call for the crucifixion of the very Man they now praised, for He did not produce their earthly kingdom. In John 12:13 it affirms that some among the crowds called Him the "King of Israel." A few days later during His trial, the same Jews shouted that Caesar was their king (John 19:15).

(g) **The envious religious leaders.** Standing among the thousands at the Eastern or Shushan Gate of Jerusalem and along the roadway were the angry Pharisees. They instantly understood that the crowds were calling for the crowing of Jesus, and requested the Savior to calm them down. Our Lord's answer was one often employed by the ancients in expressing the impossible. In Lk. 19:40 our Lord says, that if the people stopped shouting and singing the eternal truth that He was the Son of David, the Messiah of Israel, then the "stones would immediately cry out" in objection to such truth being silenced. The words about the stones crying out seem to be an allusion to Hab. 2:11. To hinder or prevent this wave of Messianic praise would be intolerable; so much so, that all nature and the objects of geology would complain. For more on the burning envy of the religious Jews, see footnote o below.

2p-**John 12:15.** This quotation is taken from Zech. 9:9. John in writing his account of this event placed it here, while Matthew placed it earlier in Matt. 21:5. Both citations contain the basics of the prediction as written by Zechariah the prophet some five hundred years before.

(h) **Jesus wails over Jerusalem.** The road from Bethany to Jerusalem was about two miles long. It rises by natural ascent to a crest at the top of the Mount of Olives. Once at this crest, the traveler looks ahead and downward: there stands the city of God and the magnificent temple. The rays of the morning sun reflect off the gold plated walls, gilded roofs and marble pinnacles creating a fiery, snowy splendor that took one's breath! Thousands of Jews and Gentiles had stood upon this crest awed beyond measure at the sight before them. When we contemplate that this gorgeous structure would be brought to ashes and the Church of Jesus Christ would forever take its place, one is left breathless at the counsels and works of God.

2p-Luke informs us that *before* the Savior had entered the city, He stopped somewhere (probably on the summit of Mount Olivet), and beholding Jerusalem wept over it (verse 41). The dramatic language in this verse informs us that He broke out and wept loudly, not a sob as at the tomb of Lazarus. (One wonders what the shouting crowds and nearby apostles thought of their Lord audibly weeping.) A. T. Robertson translated it as "burst into tears" in *Word Pictures of the New Testament*, page 246. As Nehemiah had wept over the fallen stones and material ruins (Neh. 1:3-4), now some four hundred years later, Messiah weeps over the ruined spiritual state of Israel and its religious leaders. Like Jeremiah or other prophets, He too lamented over the Hebrew people (Jer. 6:26, 9:1). In our Lord's reaction over Jerusalem, we understand the meaning of Lam. 3:51, "Mine eye affecteth mine heart." Months earlier He had bewailed the fate of Jerusalem while still north in Galilee as seen in Section 126, Lk. 13:34, footnote k. Oddly, at that former occasion, He quoted the same verse (Ps. 118:26) that the crowds had just shouted as He entered the city on this occasion. A few hours later, our Lord again lamented over the Jewish people, their city, and dreadful fate. Note this in Section 159, Matt. 23:37-39. He cites Ps. 118:26. In each case, He was confirming to the people that He was indeed the Messiah according to their Holy Scriptures. He was not offering anyone a kingdom. To hold that our Lord was predicting the sufferings of Jews during the future tribulation time is a reprehensible form of exegesis and is without warrant in the best of commentaries. Thus, we have two records of Christ weeping over Jerusalem in Scripture, here and as mentioned above, in Lk. 13:34. There is a vast difference in the two.

(i) **Verse 42. "Had known thy peace."** The multitudes look on in amazement as Messiah weeps over Jerusalem and the nation. The Jews did not know their peace when He came to them, for they had hated and rejected the peace of God found in their Messiah. Now, it was hidden from their eyes: Israel had crossed the line; judgment was next for their city, temple, and people. In some forty years, the ground on which they stood would be literally covered with thousands of Roman soldiers.

2p-**Verse 43. Trapped by the trench.** Here, is a direct reference to the tenth Roman legion that dug a battle trench around the entire city during its siege in A.D. 70, some four decades hence. It sealed in the Jews for their final doom. Many escaped but thousands were captured and crucified on the hills surrounding the city. *This has nothing to do with the Antichrist's armies surrounding Jerusalem over two thousand years later.* Such a statement would have meant nothing to those listening to Jesus speak; indeed, it would have only further confused their thinking. Forty years later when the soldiery of Rome did this very thing, many of the Jews, who had heard Jesus speak these Words, surely remembered His warning, but too late. For a lengthy discussion of Jerusalem being surrounded by the Roman army, see Section 163, Lk. 21:20, all of footnote g. John Lightfoot, in *Commentary on the New Testament . . .* pages 77-78 gives a detailed description of this trench taken from a much older source. It carefully explains the directions in which the Romans dug this trap to keep the Jews shut within the city.

3p-**Verse 44. "The time of thy visitation."** This passage is explicit that the reason for the destruction of the city, temple, and millions of Jews was they did not know "the time of their visitation," that is, the gracious offer of mercy God gave to them in the ministry and message of His blessed Son. The Jews, especially the leaders of religion, deliberately refused to open their eyes to the light of the Messiah, who had shone so brilliantly among them. This began with the preaching of John the Baptist and ended with the coming of Roman armies. It was truly the time of divine visitation for Israel. The terrible announcement of not "one stone left upon another" was repeated a few hours afterward in Section 163, Matt. 24:1-2 with parallel verses. Even to this day certain Jews pretend that the cause for the doom of their city and temple was "idolatry" or "failing to keep the Sabbaths" or other ills. Holy Scripture is clear; it was because they rejected Jesus of Nazareth as their Messiah and Savior. The horrible visitation came in A.D. 70 and had nothing to do with the tribulation period thousands of years later. Refer to the first paragraph of footnote i above for more on this.

(j) **"All the city was moved."** The word "moved" also carries the idea of an earthquake suddenly hitting. Even though Jerusalem was chained in religious formalism and the hypocrisy of the scribes and Pharisees, this sudden wave of popular enthusiasm for the Man on the donkey struck like an earthquake! The Lord Jesus had entered this gate hundreds of times during his life and public ministry, but never had the reception been like this one. Pious Jews had a deep reverence for the great Shushan Gate or Eastern Gate, where Jesus alighted from the animal. The Talmud in tractate, Berachoth 54a reads, "One should avoid showing disrespect to the Eastern Gate because it is in direct line with the Holy of Holies."

2p-**Messiah at the gate.** Their rabbis taught that Messiah would come from the east to this very gate (Ezek. 43:2). One can picture the Jews, shouting, running, waving their hands and enraptured in the high excitement of the moment, for they believed their kingdom had come. Talk spread over the city that Messiah had arrived at the gate. Many people standing nearby put the question, "Who is this?" These were the Jews, who had traveled to the city for Passover and had never seen Jesus. Matthew points out to his Jewish readers that "the multitude" answered the question with, "This is Jesus the prophet of Nazareth of Galilee" (verse 11). This public exclamation reveals that they knew well of Him, even His hometown and province. About five days later, they were shouting "Away with him!" "Crucify him!" "Crucify him!" It is most curious how men can declare the truth of God one moment, and the next be at absolute variance with what they had just proclaimed. "O Ephraim, what shall I do unto thee? O Judah, what shall I do unto thee? For your goodness *is* as a morning cloud, and as the early dew it goeth away" (Hosea 6:4). As a baby, the Savior stirred Jerusalem when the wise men rode into the city looking for a Jewish King. Refer to Section 17, Matt. 2:3-3, footnotes d, e, and f for the details.

3p-Muslim cemetery at the gate. The "prophetic teaching" based in Eze. 44:1-4, that Jesus will *again* enter Jerusalem via the Eastern Gate is wrong. Muslims hearing of this supposed prophecy created a large cemetery filled with many bodies, knowing Jews counted such a place as unclean. They did this to prevent any possibility of the Lord Jesus entering Jerusalem as King at future date. Both over enthusiastic Christians and ignorant Muslims do not understand that the Eastern Gate of Jerusalem today, is not that of the Old Testament or the time of Jesus. The ashes of the original gate in Jesus' day were buried some eighty feet down after the Romans destroyed the city in A.D. 70.

4p-Matt, 21:11. At this late moment in the life of Christ, He was popularly known as "Jesus of Nazareth." This reflects that the whole story of our Lord's life is not recorded within the pages of the four gospels, but only what God wanted men to have.

(k) "His last look." The Lord of the temple enters into the temple of the Lord and looks upon all things. God's house of prayer was covered with a veil of false religion, merchandising of holy things, fraudulent exchanges at the money tables, and ecclesiastical employment secured by flattery and bribery; on all sides were damnable profanities and sin. It was a seething pot of evil and doomed to the fire and sword some forty years later at the hands of the fierce heathen Romans. Now, its doom was sealed. The Son of God surveyed this place for the final time. Its judgment was both just and justified because those in charge of its sacred functions had rejected Him as Messiah and Savior, and beyond cure had polluted this place of worship. A haunting tenor may be heard in these words of Mark, an echo of dreadful finality that reverberates down to us in this present day. They remind us that mercy and saving grace will not always tarry. Hurry O soul without Christ; He stands and knocks at the door of your heart and life (Rev. 3:20). Let Him in, for soon the awful night of eternal darkness will fall on all who know Him not.

(l) Back to Bethany. At the setting of the sun, Jesus with His twelve apostles retired to Bethany. This first day of the week, later named "Palm Sunday" was over. See footnote a above for details regarding Bethany located some two miles east of Jerusalem. A dreaded sadness and sense of rejection fell over the whole day of glad triumph. It was not safe for the Messiah and His preachers to spend the night in Jerusalem. The dark shadow of Judas fell over the Master and His preachers. The man of Kerioth had chosen the road of betrayal, and assisted by the Devil, he followed it to the end. For the Savior's return to Jerusalem the next morning, which would have been our Monday, see Section 149, Matt. 21:18, footnote a.

(m) Highlighted in gray because "these things" were recorded in the Old Testament. After Christ was glorified (raised and ascended to the Father) the apostles remembered these predictions. This is another clear statement that His closest disciples and apostles, even at this late point in His life, still did not understand His soon death, burial, and resurrection. For more on their failure to comprehend this, see Sections 104-105, 107, and 141 footnotes d and e. John writes looking back on history. He is saying that *after* our Lord's resurrection and ascension, and with the coming of the Holy Spirit in full power on Pentecost, *then* the disciples understood the meaning of the Old Testament Scriptures. Now, they could understand the full truth of their Messiah's death on the cross and resurrection. All the difficult things the Savior had taught them made sense! See *Appendix Three* for a listing of many Old Testament predictions that were fulfilled by the Lord Jesus during His life and ministry.

(n) Verse 17. Among those following Jesus into Jerusalem at this time, some had been present at the resurrection of Lazarus. Section 124 carries the story of his resurrection from the dead. They had so testified (or "bare record") of this fact that His popularity again spread over the land with thousands hearing of Him. Jerusalem and the surrounding countryside were packed with hundreds of thousands of pilgrims present to attend the upcoming Passover celebration. In Section 146, John 11:55-56, the Lord Jesus attending this Passover was the (secret) hot topic among the Jews from near and afar. Many of these were amid the crowds waiting at Jerusalem's Eastern Gate on this occasion as Jesus rode in on the back of a donkey. A few days later, they would be shouting for His death! See footnote o below.

(o) "The world is gone after him." This was an exaggeration, unless they meant the world of the Jews, represented at the Passover. Still this cannot mean just a few people. All the high excitement about Jesus entering the city as Messiah greatly upset the Pharisees. It was bitter indeed, when they saw the thousands of Jews dancing, screaming, shouting about Jesus, and proclaiming Him as Messiah! See footnote g above where the religious leaders called on Christ to stop the praises and accolades being showered upon Him, and His answer to their fierce envy. These evil men were wild with fury and boiling with hatred for Jesus of Nazareth. It was clear for this moment that He was their Messiah, but they refused to accept Him as such. Section 163 carries the horrible story of their judgment that fell some four decades later at the hands of the mighty Romans in A.D. 70.

Monday. Spending Sunday night at Bethany, Jesus returns to the temple the next morning. A hypocritical fig tree is cursed along the way. Matthew placed the cleansing of the temple before the fig tree. Mark* placed it after the tree was cursed. Neither Luke nor John mentions this event. The apostles heard Him denounce the tree. The next day on Tuesday morning** as they returned to Jerusalem, Peter noticed the tree was withered from the roots upward. The apostles were amazed at the sight. The Savior used the occasion to give them a powerful lesson on "faith in God." Monday's events are continued in Section 150.

Time: Monday after Palm Sunday and before the cross on Friday.

*This harmony commentary accepts that Matthew's gospel was written before Mark's and thus attempts to follow Matthew's chronology in reporting the life of Christ. However, in this case Mark's placement is preferred. **This was as they returned to Jerusalem from the night spent at Bethany. The ● dot below marks where both Matthew and Mark were inspired to divert from their story. They reported in advance that the fig tree was found dead early morning of the next day, which would have been on Tuesday morning our time, as Christ, and His men returned to Jerusalem. See His departure from the city in Section 150, at Matt. 21:17.

Between Bethany and Jerusalem

Matt. 21:18-20	Mk. 11:12-14. Mk. 11:20-21	Luke	John
The hypocrite tree: leaves no fruit **18** Now in the morning[(a)] [Monday] as he returned into the city, he hungered. **19** And when he saw a fig tree in the way, he came to it, and found nothing thereon, but leaves[(b)] only, and said unto it, "Let no fruit grow on thee henceforward forever." And presently[(c)] [overnight] the fig tree withered away. *(Chronologically the temple cleansing fits at the end of Matt. 21:12 in Section 150.)*	*The hypocrite tree: leaves no fruit* **12** And on the morrow,[(a)] [Monday] when they were come from Bethany, he was hungry: **13** And seeing a fig tree afar off having leaves, he came, if haply he might find any thing thereon: and when he came to it, he found nothing but leaves;[(b)] for the time of figs was not *yet*. **14** And Jesus answered and said unto it, "No man eat fruit of thee hereafter forever." And his disciples heard *it.* (Verse 15 cont. in Section 150.)		
●*At this place Matthew moves ahead from Monday to Tuesday morning in verses 20-22 below. He then reports the death of the fig tree and repeats Jesus' lesson to the apostles on faith. See next Section. Note Mark's words in verse 20, "in the morning."*	●*At this place Mark moves ahead from Monday to Tuesday morning in verses 20-26 below. He then reports the death of the tree and repeats Jesus' lesson to the apostles on faith. See next Section. Note Mark's words below in verse 20, "in the morning."*		
The only thing Jesus killed: a hypocritical fig tree **20** And when the disciples [on Tuesday morning] saw[(d)] *it,* [the dead tree] they marvelled, saying, "How soon is the fig tree	Mk. 11:20-21 *The only thing Jesus killed: a hypocritical fig tree* **20** And in the morning, [Tuesday] as they passed by, they saw[(d)] the fig tree dried up from the roots. **21** And Peter[(e)] calling to remembrance saith unto him, "Master, behold, the fig tree which		

Matt. 21:20-22	Mk. 11:21-26	Luke	John
withered away!"	thou cursedst is withered away."		
Have faith in God	***Have faith in God***		
21 Jesus answered[f] and said unto them,	**22** And Jesus answering[f] saith unto them,		
	"Have faith in God.		
"Verily I say unto you,	**23** "For verily I say unto you, That whosoever		
If ye have faith, and doubt not, ye shall not only do this *which is done* to the fig tree, but also if ye			
shall say unto this mountain, 'Be thou removed, and be thou cast into the sea;'	shall say unto this mountain, 'Be thou removed, and be thou cast into the sea;' and shall not doubt in his heart, but shall believe that those things which he saith shall come to pass; he shall have whatsoever he saith. (or asks)		
it shall be done.			
22 "And all things,[g] whatsoever ye shall ask in prayer, believing, ye shall receive." (Verse 23 cont. in Section 151.)	**24** "Therefore I say unto you, What things[g] soever ye desire, when ye pray, believe that ye receive *them*, and ye shall have *them*.		
	You must forgive one another		
	25 "And when ye stand[h] praying, forgive, if ye have ought against any: that your Father also which is in heaven may forgive you your trespasses.		
	26 "But if ye do not forgive, neither will your Father which is in heaven forgive your trespasses."[i] (Verse 27 cont. in Section 151.)		

Footnotes–Commentary

(a) Christ and His twelve had departed from Jerusalem at the close of "Palm Sunday" and went to Bethany for the night, probably at the house of Lazarus. Often, our Lord found solace and peace in this home of trusted friends. It seems that He walked back and forth from Bethany or the Mount of Olives to the city and the temple in which He taught. In Matt 21:18 above, He was returning to Jerusalem on Monday morning after the night at Bethany. Following the examination and cursing of the fig tree on the road early that morning (Matt. 21:18-19a and Mk. 11:12-14), He entered the temple and drove out the merchants, healed many, and accepted the praise of children and infants as seen in Section 150, Matt. 21:12-16 with Mark's parallel. (At this point both Matthew and Mark move ahead into the events of Tuesday and report the apostle's comments about the dead fig tree as seen in Matt. 21:19b-22 and Mk. 11:20-26.) At the conclusion of this Monday and the confrontation with the religious leaders, He returns to peace and quiet at Bethany and spends Monday night (Matt. 21:17).

2p-Rising early Tuesday, He walks two miles westward back to the temple for another day of conflict with the Jews and Sanhedrin. This is recorded in Section 151, Matt. 21:23 with Mk. 11:27. We have no record of what occurred that Tuesday night or where He went.

(b) **"Leaves only."** The critics of God and Christ have rallied their infidelity about another historical event in the life of our Lord. Some assert that Jesus out of anger killed the tree because He was hungry, and it had no fruit! Others affirm that He destroyed a valuable fruit tree belonging to someone else. Therefore, the little noises of Lucifer's crowd continue to echo over the centuries to this present moment as they continually struggle to discredit the glorious Son of God. His looking for food early in the morning signaled His humanity. As a man, He hungered and sought food to satisfy that hunger.

2p-There were thousands of fig trees growing in this district. This particular one caught His attention due to its large profusion of leaves. Because of this "he came" (as Mark writes), "if haply he might find anything thereon" (verse 13). Early leaves were a sign the tree was filled with fruit; but after sacred inspection, it proved not so! Some wise expositors have seen in this barren but leafy tree a picture of the Jewish people, especially its religious leaders. All outward show and noise but inwardly barren and cursed.

(c) **"Tree, die!"** Suddenly, He spoke to the tree by the power of the indwelling Holy Spirit. He commanded it to die for not having fruit. One cannot but wonder what the twelve thought as they heard their Master talking to a fig tree! Here is another place where the critics have their little playtime with the Word of God. The criticisms upon this miracle are singularly idle and irreverent, because they are based upon ignorance or malice toward the Savior. The notion that Christ did wrong in killing the tree is foolish. A. T. Robertson explains the fig tree at this season (Passover time) of the year. "The early figs start in the spring before the leaves and develop after the leaves." See *Word Pictures in the New Testament*, vol. 1, page 169. For a detailed explanation, see Lightfoot's *Commentary on the New Testament . . . ,* vol. 2, pages 277-282. A fig tree covered with leaves would have an abundance of fruit beneath its thick foliage. Full foliage of leaves signaled fresh tender fruit to all observers. Here, is a powerful object lesson on hypocrisy for the twelve and all men to consider. This was a hypocrite tree; it pretended one thing but had another! No wonder that it caught the attention of Messiah. It said one thing on the outside with its many leaves, but did not have the corresponding fruit on the inside. In Mk. 11: 13 it states that the "time of figs was not yet." This puts the tree in jeopardy, for it was out of step with nature. Figs did not ripen until some fifty days later, yet this particular tree showed all the outward signs of maturity and development. We only feel disgust for this horticultural pretender. When examined by the Son of God, it proved to be false: one thing outside but nothing inside. It reminds one of so many present day church members!

2p-Many are in churches who flaunt their spirituality with outward sounds and noises, waving their talents and skills profusely for all to see and hear; but inside, they are barren in soul and without the *genuine fruit* of the Spirit. These are "clouds without water, trees without fruit, twice dead, plucked up by the roots" (Jude 12). Unless they repent and are saved, all such imposters are destined to be eternally cursed.

3p-Could this tree picture the Jewish religionists in the days of Christ? They were the pretenders of high-class society, always filled with the leaves of self, false religion, and their oral law, but deathly void of the fruit that was acceptable to Jehovah God. For explanation of the oral law, refer to Section 52, footnote h; Section 89, footnote c; and Section 96, footnote d. This tree depicted the true moral and spiritual condition of Israel at this time in history. Review Section 67, fourth paragraph of footnote b, and Section 100 footnote d, for a survey of Israel's sins. Matthew Henry wrote that the first Jewish priesthood was ratified by the dry rod that blossomed in one night (Num. 17:7-8), while this contrary miracle of the fig tree dying in one night points to the punishment of the Hebrew priests that abused it. See Henry's *Commentary*, vol. 5, page 427.

(d) The writer Matthew did not distinguish between the two mornings in his history as Mark did. Mark records more fully, what Matthew was inspired to write in brief. In Matt. 21:20 it states that the "disciples saw it" (the withered tree). Then, we note that Mk. 11:12 reads, "And on the morrow." This must speak of the Monday morning while walking back to Jerusalem when Jesus cursed the hypocritical tree. Yet Mk. 11:20-21 describes the *next* morning when Peter saw it was dead and mentioned this to Jesus. They had heard the Lord pronounce doom upon the fig tree on Monday morning, and saw it was dead the next morning (Tuesday) as they traveled from Bethany back to the temple. These differences again demonstrate that both men wrote as God inspired them, that there was no copying from each other; both were honest men not conspiring to deceive their readers. Mark used the word "cursed" in reference to the tree (verse 21). Cursed as used here has nothing to do with anger or foul language. It was a verbal judgment pronounced upon that which was false and deceiving. The ancients did this continually. The difference being with the Lord Jesus: what He said visibly happened.

(e) **"Master behold."** As explained in the footnote above, Peter said this, the morning after the original curse was placed upon the tree, as they were returning to Jerusalem. Note, how Matt. 21:20 reveals that "the disciples" inquired about the wonder, but Mark singles out Peter, being the "mouth" or "spokesman" for the apostolic band.

(f) **The blessed answer.** Our Lord's response was understood by His disciples. To "have faith in God" was a common expression used among the Jews. The rabbis often spoke of Jewish teachers whose lessons were so powerful that they were compared to a "rooter up [or remover] of mountains." See an example of this term in the Talmud tractate, Baba Berachoth 62a. Here, the Savior, heaven's true Rabbi gives a lesson of similar import to His apostles. It is noted that Jesus called attention to a specific mountain in His Words "this" recorded by both evangelists. This was a reference to one of the summits making up the mountain range east of Jerusalem, seemingly the Mount of Olives. The sea was probably the Sea of Galilee, with which all were familiar, especially those among Jesus' group that fished its waters for livelihood. See Section 148, footnote a, for details on the mountain ranges east of Jerusalem. Peter in his usual impetuosity sought for a detailed explanation of how the tree died "from the roots." Herein is a sterling lesson we must not overlook. Often in the Christian life, one is curious to inquire of God and ask, "Why this" or "why that" has happened. All such endeavors are vain pursuits. Rarely, will the Almighty let mortal man enter the counsel of His sovereign reasons for most of life's experiences. As with Peter, we are called upon to "have faith in God." Nothing so pleases the heart of our heavenly Father, as when we trust Him when life's calamities seem senseless and even wrong (Heb. 11:6).

(g) **"Whatsoever ye shall ask in prayer."** Extremists have abused this text for years. The healthy-wealthy cults impose their mythology upon this statement affirming, "Here is a blank check that we can fill out for whatever we want." Where is the man or woman over the course of church history that has literally and geologically uprooted a mountain and then cast it into the sea? Such people are where they have always been, they do not exist. Every promise dealing with prayer in the whole Bible presupposes that the answer is based upon the "will of God" as written in 1 John 5:14-15. This divine safeguard for prayer has been changed, altered, and explained away by the charlatans who use the Lord of heaven as their bank account.

2p-For comments on wealth and health as the highest mark of spirituality, see Section 58, footnote o. In the mystery of God's sovereign will for His children, some are delivered and spared according to Heb. 11:32-35. Others prayed sincerely yet they passed into destitution, affliction, physical torments, and were put to death (Heb. 11:36-37). The long list of sufferings that Paul passed through reveal that God does not always put "pie in the sky" for His children (2 Cor. 11:18-31). The great missionary wrote that he was often "hungry, thirsty, and naked" (1 Cor. 4:11). Clearly, these things were the will of God for His servant at different times. We question why Paul did not "name it and claim it," and thus be delivered from the sorrows and calamities experienced while in the service of God. Where was his "seed faith" that we hear about so much on national television? This nonsense has wrecked the lives of thousands of ignorant but good Christians who have embrace these vicious untruths.

3p-**"And all things."** Jesus' unlimited promise of unique power was *exclusively* for the apostles. It pertained to their service in His new kingdom or church as described in the book of Acts. Many believers have "claimed" this only to discover that it did not work. The great Presbyterian minister, Albert Barnes (died 1870) rightly says of this promise in *Notes on the New Testament*, page 223, that to the apostles "it was true, but it is manifest that we have no right to apply this promise to ourselves." See the main heading under Section 110, for more on other exclusive privileges given to the apostles of Christ, and never intended for all Christians. Prayer is not a matter of what God can do, but rather what He wills to do in the lives of His individual children. Often, this is as varied as the patterns of the snowflakes. Seasoned saints praise God that not all of their prayers were answered! The "all things" of verse 22 are the "all things" God wills for his children, not what the vain flesh desires (1 John 5:14).

4p-**Confusing a promise with a principle, Prov. 22:6.** *How frustrating when Christians confuse a biblical promise with a biblical principle.* No single verse in the Bible has been abused like Prov. 22:6. Millions of believing parents have mistakenly claimed this as a sure-fire promise for their children. However, this is a principle. In Scripture, some of God's promises have requirements before fulfillment while others do not. On the other hand, a biblical principle is an admonition to do a certain thing, but does not carry with it a sure benefit from God as some promises do. Christians with children need to learn early that Prov. 22:6 is not a guarantee that if they do right, then their children will be saved and live for Christ. Nowhere, does the Bible teach this. Each mentally normal person is self-responsible and has a will to accept or reject. As the individual is enlightened by the Word of God and the Holy Spirit, God's grace allows him or her the freedom to choose or refuse. This divine order makes God the giver and man the receiver. No one is forced into faith. For Martin Luther's "Bondage of the Will," in which he toys with the folly of Calvinism, see Section 201, third paragraph of footnote n.

5p-Later, the night before the morning of the cross, Jesus mentioned more of the Holy Spirit's work. See Sections 173 through 177 for the story.

(h) **"And when ye stand praying, forgive."** What a beautiful Hebraism the Savior employed in this sentence. The ancient Jews taught, "The world stands because men pray." Thus, it became the usual (but not the only) posture for them in making supplications to Jehovah God. Later, the early Christians adopted kneeling as a sign of their humility before the Lord. It is not the geographical or physical position that counts when in prayer; rather, the condition of the heart. "Forgiveness" is the hinge on which the door of prayer swings; faith is the key that unlocks it. It is a prerequisite to approach God. For the rabbinical rule concerning forgiveness, see Section 110, footnote h. All the apostles had been taught this error by the rabbis from their earliest days. They must have been shaken at the teaching of their Lord on this subject.

2p-**Make a statue of prayer.** Viewing the various postures adopted by men as they speak to God, history has a marvelous lesson. Bertal Thorwaldsen, was a famed Danish sculpture. On one occasion, he was ordered by his King of Denmark to make a statue that revealed how men may best see the Savior. One year later, the brilliant Thorwaldsen had placed before his majesty a statue of Jesus that could only be seen on one's knees! He died in 1884, and his works are housed in a museum at Copenhagen, Denmark. What a message left in stone by a Christian sculpture pointing to the very soul of holy prayer. *The Lord Jesus Christ is best seen when one is on his knees.*

(i) Our Savior had earlier used this saying in the Sermon on the Mount. Note Section 46, Matt. 6:15, footnote h, for explanation. Again, here is another of the many examples of Christ repeating Himself.

Monday continued. Events from the previous Section 149 are resumed. Hundreds of merchants filled Solomon's porch selling their wares at Passover. For a second time, Christ exerts His authority as "Lord of the temple" and drives them out, purging God's house.* Many infirmed people came forward to be healed. Infants and small children recognizing Him, break out in loud praises to God. The enraged Jews seek to kill Messiah. Afterwards, He returns to Bethany and spends the night.**

Time: Still Monday following His triumphal entry on Palm Sunday.

*For the first cleansing of the temple in the early months of Jesus' ministry, refer to Section 29, footnote c. **Matthew 21:17 below reveals that our Savior spent the night at Bethany about two miles east of Jerusalem. The main heading of Section 149, speaks of Matthew and Mark moving ahead to record the death of the fig tree. In Section 148, Mk. 11:11 the Lord Jesus returned to Bethany in the evening after Palm Sunday and spent Sunday night. It seems clear from Matt. 21:18 and its parallel in Mark, that Jesus returned to the temple the next morning (our Monday) after the fig tree miracle along the road. Upon arrival, He purged God's house of the merchants, healed the infirmed, blessed infants and children as explained below. When His work on this Monday was over, He went back to Bethany again as stated in Matt. 21:17 and spent the night. On Tuesday morning, he returned to the temple where He instantly fell into conflict with the religious leaders who challenged His authority as Messiah. This is found in Section 151, Matt. 21:23 and Mk. 11:27. The Savior then gave them three parabolic warnings, each one reflecting the doom of the Jewish state, and the destruction of Jerusalem and the temple; these are contained in Sections 152 through 154. The Jews responded by putting three difficult questions to Him. These are recorded in Sections 155 through 157. Lastly, in Section 158 Messiah puts His great request to the religious leaders regarding "whose son Christ was." Unable to answer they were put to shameful silence. Regarding the words, "six days before the Passover" in John 12:1, read comments in Section 146, by the asterisk under main heading.*

In the temple court

Matt. 21:12–13	Mk. 11:15–17	Lk. 19:45–46	John
●At this place Matthew moves back to Monday. See previous Section 149	●At this place Mark moves back to Monday. See previous Section 149.		
The second temple purge	***The second temple purge***	***The second temple purge***	
12 And Jesus went into the temple of God, [Monday morning] and cast out all them that sold and bought ⁽ᵃ⁾ in the temple, and overthrew the tables of the moneychangers, and the seats of them that sold doves,	**15** And they come to Jerusalem: and Jesus went into the temple, [Monday morning] and began to cast out them that sold and bought⁽ᵃ⁾ in the temple, and overthrew the tables of the moneychangers, and the seats of them that sold doves; **16** And would not suffer [allow] that any man should carry *any* vessel through the temple.	**45** And he went into the temple, [Monday morning] and began to cast out them that sold therein, and them that bought;⁽ᵃ⁾	
First, the temple is the house of prayer for all nations	***First, the temple is the house of prayer for all nations***	***First, the temple is the house of prayer for all nations***	
13 And said unto them, "It is written,⁽ᵇ⁾ 'My house shall be called the house of prayer;' "but ye have	**17** And he taught, saying unto them, "Is it not written,⁽ᵇ⁾ 'My house shall be called of all nations the house of prayer?' "but ye have	**46** Saying unto them, "It is written,⁽ᵇ⁾ 'My house is the house of prayer:' "but ye have	

Matt. 21:13-17	Mk. 11:17-19	Lk. 19:46-48	John
made it 'a den of thieves.'"	made it 'a den of thieves.'"	made it 'a den of thieves.'"	
He heals in the temple **14** And the blind and the lame came to him in the temple; and he healed them.[c]			
		He teaches in the temple **47** And he taught daily in the temple.	
The Jews are infuriated **15** And when the chief priests and scribes saw[d] ◄ the wonderful things that he did, and the children crying in the temple, and saying,[e] **"Hosanna to the son of David;"** they were sore displeased, **16** And said unto him, "Hearest thou what these say?" And Jesus saith unto them, "Yea; have ye never read,[f] **'Out of the mouth of babes and sucklings thou hast perfected praise?'"**	*The Jews are infuriated* **18** And the scribes and chief priests heard[d] it, ► *The religious leaders "saw" and "heard" the joyous and happy commotion created by the deeds and Words of Jesus. They were both furious and fearful.*	*The Jews are infuriated* But the chief priests and the scribes and the chief of the people	
	and sought how they might destroy him:[g] for *Listening with astonishment* they feared him, because all the people was astonished[h] at his doctrine.	sought to destroy him,[g] *Listening with carefulness* **48** And could not find what they might do: for all the people were very attentive[h] to hear him. (Next chap., Lk. 20:1 cont. in Section 151.)	
Back to Bethany **17** And he left them, and went out[i] of the city [Jerusalem] into Bethany; and he lodged there. (Monday night) (Verse 18 cont. in Section 149.)	*Back to Bethany* **19** And when even was come, he went out[i] of the city. (Jerusalem) (Verse 20 cont. in Section 149.)		

Footnotes-Commentary

(a) Though He had entered the temple hundreds of times, this entrance was different. Only yesterday, He rode to the Eastern Shushan Gate amid thousands of shouts affirming that He was the Messiah of Israel, the Son of David (Section 148). Hundreds tramped behind Him expecting any moment Israel's earthly, physical kingdom to appear miraculously. Over three years before in the early months of His ministry, He had suddenly appeared at the temple during another Passover and violently purged the house of God. Now, at the close of His ministry, for a second and final time, He again cleans out His Father's house, revealing again that He was indeed the Messiah. Refer to next paragraph below for a rabbinical prophecy that foretold Messiah would purge the temple when He came to Israel. For a description of the grand Passover event, see both main headings under Section 29, footnotes a, and b. Jewish pilgrims from across the world of that era, converged upon the city for this happy occasion in the nation of Israel.

2p-"Money changers." It is known that the Jewish high priest actually sold tickets for business privileges in the temple during this celebration! Refer to Section 29, footnote b for more on this. There is a curious prophecy in Zech. 14:21, which according to the rabbis, foretold of the cleansing of the temple in the days of Messiah. It reads that in that day (of Messiah) there would "be no more the Canaanite [meaning merchants] in the house of the LORD of hosts." The Lord Jesus fulfilled this final prediction of the prophet Zechariah on this very occasion, as He drove out the merchants, who were Jews and not pagan Canaanites. Pious Jews referred to the crooked money changers as "Canaanites." It is noted that to refer to a Hebrew as a Gentile as did the prophet Zechariah was a high insult!

3p-"Vessels through the temple." Mark's words (verse 16), that Jesus would not let any man carry a vessel through the temple, must have reference *only* to the wide variety of articles being sold by the Jewish merchants. Hundreds of vessels were used daily in the function of the temple and were all dedicated to God. These were not included in His expulsion of unwarranted goods, and objects being sold. The temple had laundries, bakeries, butcher shops, sleeping quarters, and even hot water bathing facilities for the priests in its large basement area. We note that Zech. 11:13, informs us that a potter's shop was located in the house of God. The rich often deposited their fortunes at the temple for safekeeping. Jerusalem and the temple influenced national commerce in two ways. They drew much trade from the known world and met the insatiable Hebrew demand for luxury in clothing, exquisite foods, and jewelry. There was a constant need for "sacred wood to burn," wine, oil, grain, expensive incense, precious stones, linen, and other items. Material for the high priest vestments came from far away India! The quantities of sacrificial animals, bulls, calves, sheep, goats, and doves were overwhelming.

(b) From a "House of prayer" to a "a den of thieves." Jesus selected various words from Isa. 56:7 and Jer. 7:11. From these He built these two quotations. It is of interest that the *first purpose* of the magnificent and glorious temple was not for sacrifice, but prayer! However, now the Savior described it as a "den of thieves." Some expositors think this was an allusion to the dens and caves used by killers and robbers along the road to Jericho, and well known to all the people. If so, it would have been a high insult to the scribes and Pharisees. Some forty years later, in A.D. 70, the Words of Christ were literally fulfilled when the murderous factions began fighting and killing each other within the temple. This occurred after the Romans had encircled Jerusalem and cut off the city from all outside help. The bloody men who led the civil factions within Jerusalem at this time were known as the 'sicarii." This name comes from a special type of curved dagger hidden under one's skirts. The temple sanctuary had become a refuge, and a shop of tyranny among the Jews. Wounded fighters were brought into the sanctuary, and their blood defiled the sacred floors. The blood of the dead and wounded was so thick on the marble floors that the Roman soldiers wearing spiked shoes and boots would slip, slide, and fall while pursuing their enemies over the temple precincts. After the fall of the city, soldiers plundered and stole everything of value and carried it away. We wonder if this was also part of what our Lord had reference to when He declared that God's house was now a "den of thieves." *During this horrible time no passion of the Jews was as entirely lost among them as that of showing mercy. In their madness for food and water, they fought, killed, and plundered one another.* In the early months of His ministry when Jesus had *first* purged the temple, He then described it as being a "house of merchandise." Refer to this in Section 29, John 2:15-16, footnote c. Over the next three years, there was a regression in the titles Jesus used to describe this house of God. The degradation in business practices from honesty to thievery moved Christ to rename it now "a den of thieves." The decline was from praying to stealing! Note that John 2:16, footnote c, explains how God's temple became a place for Jewish merchants and thieves.

2p-"Called of all nations." Though countless thousands of sacrifices, offerings, and services of many sorts were performed within this magnificent edifice, it was looked upon by heathen nations as a "house of prayer." This most profound statement made by the Savior sheds new light on the Jerusalem temple. Above all sacrifices and divinely appointed functions, prayer was first in this place. See Section 136, where the Lord Jesus describes a temple prayer meeting of a Pharisee and publican.

(c) The suffering and afflicted to come Jesus. *How beautiful!* After driving out the unscrupulous merchants and crooks from God's house, a tidal wave of suffering humanity poured in seeking the Messiah. Here, He shows the real purpose of this holy site: it is the house of prayer where infirmed and afflicted mortals may find help, hope, healing, and salvation. Sufferers came to him and He healed them. Listeners by the hundreds thronged around Him. They were astonished at His doctrine and hung upon His Words in great awe waiting for the next sentence. Here, we see Messiah at His best, saving, blessing, healing, teaching, and rebuking the religious hypocrites of Israel. The blind were led, and the lame were carried into His holy presence. Verse 14 explicitly states, "He healed them." We learn from Matt. 21:15 and 16 that "children" and "nursing infants" ("sucklings") were brought to the Savior on this occasion. For the amazing reaction of these little ones, see footnote f below. A church where men cannot find Christ waiting with open arms is not worth attending.

(d) The leaders of religion were infuriated at the sight and sounds emanating from "their" temple. They could, without sting of conscience, profane God's house with false merchandising and corrupted business enterprises, but shouts of praise from souls healed and lives changed were intolerable. At this time in history, it is true that non-Jews could enter the temple to a limited access, and the Court of the Gentiles allowed further admission to all non-

Israelites. In the Torah Law, priests who were blind or lame were not permitted in the sanctuary (Lev. 21:18 and 21). Later, a ruling of the Sanhedrin stated that the blind and lame were not required to attend the various feasts. Suddenly, the place is filled with both! Word quickly spread that Messiah was present in the temple and hundreds rushed forward to reach Him. It was a stampede of broken, hurting humanity that crowded their way to Christ. The scribes, Pharisees, and Sadducees stood aghast at the sight and were helpless to do anything about it.

(e) **"Hosanna to the son of David."** Another pure Messianic title being applied to Jesus of Nazareth. This greatly agitated the religious leaders. They had heard this chant a thousand times and were horrified at its implications. The crowds, which included children, were openly acknowledging Jesus as the Messiah of Israel in the heat of this moment. Refer to Section 148, Matt. 21:9 footnote f for the crowds shouting the same acclamation a short time prior, as He rode up to the Eastern or Shushan Gate on the donkey, early on Palm Sunday.

(f) **The miracle of infants praising the Savior.** This was a marvelous thing! In response to the fierce objections of the Jewish religious leaders, and the wave of praises for the Savior, our Lord quoted from Ps. 8:2, which they identified as pointing to their Messiah. We ask the question, "How could nursing infants ["sucklings"] recognize Jesus as Messiah and praise Him?" *This is a most stupendous statement!* Not only were small children shouting praises to the Savior, but also infants suddenly ceased their nursing; lifting tiny hands and raising their trembling little heads they cooed and kicked with an innate joy, somehow knowing who this noble man was that stood before them and their parents. The entire scene was as if all natural goodness sang an anthem of praise to the Son of God. If "The ox knoweth his owner and the ass his master's crib" (Isa. 1:3), could not helpless babes that had never committed sin have unique insight into Jesus' deity? For notes on Jewish beliefs about the unborn, see Section 121, footnote b. For an earlier meeting of Jesus with little children, refer to Section 138, Matt. 19:13 and 15, footnotes a, and d. *Innocent* children knew the Messiah while the leaders of the nation despised Him. By divine genetic compulsion, this flock of little ones in the temple instantly recognized who Jesus of Nazareth was! They did this because inherent sin had not at this stage corrupted them into resentment and hatred of the Messiah as it had the religious leaders of Israel. Calvinists struggling to bring infants into their covenant theology, invented germinal faith, which "waits in the bosom of all elect babies." And babies not of the elect are damned for hell, so the lie goes.

2p-**"Baby faith?"** Infants born in sin but not yet sinners. The Reformed doctrine of "baby faith" or "slumbering salvation in the soul of elect infants" is foreign to Scripture. Over the course of church history, various persons have propagated this myth in a struggle to justify their erroneous predestination philosophy. Infants do not enter potential saving grace because their parents are saved. *Salvation is an individual matter, not a corporate or genetic process passed from parents to children.* Calvin in his *Institutes*, 4:23, wrote, "Infants . . . possess faith with adults . . . in baptizing infants we are obeying the Lord's will." Theodore Beza (died 1605) and Abraham Kuyper (died 1920), along with others spread the false doctrine of "baby faith." These people never understood that even though all infants are born *in* sin and *with* sin, they are not yet sinners by action, volition, and practice. In Rom. 9:11, it is clear that the "unborn" have not, indeed cannot, do "good or evil." The same truth is given in Deut. 1:39. In Jonah 4:11 it speaks of thousands of infants within the gigantic city of Nineveh that could not "discern between their right hand and their left hand." This was an ancient expression used to signify innocence. It was employed here in direct reference to the children in the city of Nineveh, who were not yet accountable to God for their actions. Paul made it clear how faith comes into one's heart to be saved, "by hearing the Word of God" (Rom. 10:17). This instantly rules out the joke of "baby faith." The Roman Church incorporated infant baptism to *remit sin* from the church fathers and unconverted pagans within Constantine's state religion. Later, the Reformers brought it out of Romanism and into their churches. They attempted to tone it down in their various Confessions of Faith. Gradually, it spread over Europe, England, and was brought later into Colonial America. For cheerful comments on the thousands of saved people in Reformed Churches, who are not on the lunatic fringe over this issue, see Section 203, the fifth paragraph, footnote d.

(g) **The religious leaders seek to kill Jesus.** Repeatedly, in this work, we have noted how the spiritual leaders tried to kill the Lord Jesus. Certain Messianic Jews, who try to paint the scribes and Pharisees as mostly good men have the milk giving the cow. *It was the exact opposite.* See Section 52, footnote l, Section 55, footnote a; and Section 123, John 10:31, footnote f. This text reveals their cowardliness in view of the crowds that were so attentive to His teaching. They dared not interfere at this time. In Section 159, the Savior announces their awful doom.

(h) **The people were astonished!** Numerous times this is said of the Lord Jesus. The comment was often heard, "No man ever spoke like Him." At the conclusion of His majestic Sermon on the Mount, this was the verdict of the people. Read their words in Section 47, Matt. 7:28-29, footnotes m and n.

(i) After these Monday events in the temple, He returns to Bethany for another night's lodging. See Section 149, footnote a for the details. The good shepherd with His little flock sought rest from the labor and turmoil of that day. There is something disconcerting about this scene, for the shadow of the traitor fell over it all. We cannot help but wonder how well Judas slept that night. He had chosen his road and was left alone, except for the presence of Satan to follow it to the end. At sunrise on Tuesday morning, the Lord Jesus returned to Jerusalem and the temple. He immediately fell into fierce conflict again with the Jews. This is the clash is recorded in Section 151.

Tuesday. He returns to the temple after another night at Bethany.* The Jews challenge His claim to be Israel's Messiah. Christ answers their question with a question. Being put to shame, they are unable to respond. He proceeds to give them three parables that forecast their coming doom.**

It is *conjectured* that the various activities of Jesus recorded in this Section through Section 166, occurred on Tuesday. The events of the final "two days" (Matt. 26:1-2) which were Wednesday and Thursday before Passover commenced at sunset Thursday, are recorded in Section 167 through 180. The crowds had praised Him as their Messiah-hero upon His triumphal entry into Jerusalem. They mistakenly thought He had ridden into their city to establish an earthly political kingdom and rule the world. See the single asterisk below for His activities at this time. The ancient Jews calculated time differently from our western methods. Each new day began at sundown and ended with sunset the following day. We have not slavishly followed the Hebrew method of chronology in the upcoming Sections though it is referred to in several places. Where our Lord spent Wednesday night following the many activities of Tuesday is unknown. Did He go to Mount Olivet for accessibility to the city in view of the approaching Passover or did He return to Bethany? During this time, thousands of pilgrims were camped everywhere about Jerusalem.

Time: Tuesday after Palm Sunday before His death on Friday mid-afternoon.

*For the Monday night at Bethany, after Palm Sunday, see the previous Section 150, Matt. 21:17, footnote i. Below, Matt. 21:23, and Mk. 11:27 states that He and those with him returned again to Jerusalem's temple: this would have been on Tuesday morning. All of His teaching, preaching, debates, miracles, and other events occurred during this same day. **His three parables are located in Sections 152-154. Each carried a message that signaled the doom of the Jews, Jerusalem, the temple, and the transfer of God's kingdom to the Gentiles. This series of warnings culminated with His blistering words about the religious leaders in Section 159 and the terrible announcement of their coming judgment in Section 163. This came in A.D. 70.

In the temple court

Matt. 21:23-24	Mk. 11:27-29	Lk. 20:1-3	John
Sanhedrin's question	*Sanhedrin's question*	*Sanhedrin's question*	
23 And when he was come into the temple, [Tuesday] the chief priests and the elders of the people came unto him as he was teaching, and said, "By what authority doest thou these things? and who gave thee this authority?"(a)	27 And they come again to Jerusalem: and as he was walking in the temple, [Tuesday] there come to him the chief priests, and the scribes, and the elders, 28 And say unto him, "By what authority doest thou these things? and who gave thee this authority(a) to do these things?"	1 And it came to pass, *that* on one of those days, as he taught the people in the temple, [Tuesday] and preached the gospel, the chief priests and the scribes came upon *him* with the elders, 2 And spake unto him, saying, "Tell us, by what authority doest thou these things? or who is he that gave thee this authority?"(a)	
Christ's question	*Christ's question*	*Christ's question*	
24 And Jesus answered and said unto them, "I also will ask you one thing, which if ye tell me, I in like wise will tell you by what authority I do these things.	29 And Jesus answered and said unto them, "I will also ask of you one question, and answer me, and I will tell you by what authority I do these things.	3 And he answered and said unto them, "I will also ask you one thing; and answer me:	

692

Section 151: The countdown to the cross continues. More conflict with the Jews.

Matt. 21:25-27	Mk. 11:30-33	Lk. 20:4-8	John
25 "The baptism of John, whence was it? from heaven, or of men?"[b]	**30** "The baptism of John, was *it* from heaven, or of men?[b] answer me."	**4** "The baptism of John, was it from heaven, or of men?"[b]	
The Jews cannot answer	***The Jews cannot answer***	***The Jews cannot answer***	
And they reasoned with themselves, saying, "If we shall say, 'From heaven;' he will say unto us, 'Why did ye not then believe him?'[c]	**31** And they reasoned with themselves, saying, "If we shall say, 'From heaven;' he will say, 'Why then did ye not believe him?'[c]	**5** And they reasoned with themselves, saying, "If we shall say, 'From heaven;' he will say, 'Why then believed ye him not?'[c]	
26 "But if we shall say, 'Of men;' we fear the people; for all hold John[d] as a prophet."	**32** "But if we shall say, 'Of men;' they feared the people: for all *men* counted John,[d] that he was a prophet indeed."	**6** "But and if we say, 'Of men;' all the people will stone us: for they be persuaded that John[d] was a prophet."	
Messiah will not answer	***Messiah will not answer***	***Messiah will not answer***	
27 And they answered Jesus, and said, "We cannot tell."	**33** And they answered and said unto Jesus, "We cannot tell."	**7** And they answered, that they could not tell whence *it was.*	
And he said unto them, "Neither tell I you by what authority I do these things."[e] (Verse 28 cont. in Section 152.)	And Jesus answering saith unto them, "Neither do I tell you by what authority I do these things."[e] (Next chap., Mk. 12:1 cont. in Section 153.)	**8** And Jesus said unto them, "Neither tell I you by what authority I do these things."[e] (Verse 9 cont. in Section 153.)	

Footnotes–Commentary

[a] According to Mk. 11:27, He is back again at Jerusalem after the night in Bethany. For more on this, see Section 150, Matt. 21:17, footnote i. Outraged over His purging of the temple, the praises of the people, and the healing of the infirmed, the Jewish spiritual leaders (or Sanhedrin) swooped upon Him demanding to know the source of His authority for such deeds. *Only the religious prelates had the right to issue authority for varying activities within the temple precincts.* This permission Christ did not have. The word "authority" in this text means "laying on of hands," which among the Jews was traced back to Moses laying hands on Joshua and the seventy elders of Israel, and thus conferring upon them their God–given power (Num. 11:16-17, 24-25 with 27:18-23). Christ was being asked when did the Jewish authorities lay hands on Him and thereby delegate this special right to function as a rabbi and prophet, and for riding into Jerusalem as the Messiah of Israel. They had asked a similar question some three years prior when he cleansed the house of God the first time. Only then, they requested a Messianic sign to confirm His Messianic authority. On this occasion, they dared not ask for a sign, for He had given them hundreds that authenticated His mission and work. Note Section 29, John 2:18, footnote e for details. The Savior instantly put them on the defensive when they came to Him with an offensive question.

2p-Earlier, the Sanhedrin had put the same question to John the Baptist in different words when they sent a delegation to inquire of his credentials permitting him to baptize. Refer to this in Section 24, John 1:19, footnote a, for details. For the source of John's baptism, see footnote b below.

3p-In the next several chapters, we see an example of the standard methods of debate and rebuttal employed by the ancients. We have a series of various questions, counter questions, answers, and cunning responses. All the Jews were struggling to entrap the Lord Jesus in what He said. It continually backfired in their faces.

[b] **"The source of John's baptism."** The Lord Jesus answered their inquiry with His own question. Christ asked them if John's baptism was from heaven or of men. In essence, He said, "You answer me and then I will answer you." In Section 24, footnote e, we noted the Sanhedrin rule that there could be no (proselyte) baptisms in Israel without the presence of three magistrates or doctors of the Torah Law. John did not have permission, and the scribes and Pharisees knew this. Here, Christ throws them into a terrible dilemma: these evil men knew that many of

693

the Jews had accepted John as God's prophet, and they looked upon His ministry and message as being divine. If they do not say, "It was from heaven" (an expression signifying that he acted under God's authority), then they would lose more favor with the people. If they had answered the Messiah by saying, "It was from men," they risked the possibility of the people hearing this as blasphemy! The Jewish prelates at this point were terrified for they knew the boiling impetuousness of the milling, excited crowds might lead to their being suddenly stoned. Verse 26 is clear that all of them revered John as a prophet and held him long after his death in the highest respect. Josephus informs us in *Antiquities,* Book 18:5, 2, lines 116–117, that to defy John the Baptist was tantamount to endangering one's personal safety before God. No wonder the men of religion were in such a straight. Evil cunningly takes its victims into self-entrapment a thousand times or more as demonstrated here. *How horribly true it is that each sin carries its own peculiar torment.*

(c) **"They reasoned within themselves."** Only the Holy Spirit could have revealed to the three evangelists the thoughts of these wicked men. This truth is more profound when we realize that all of them wrote their respective books, individually some years after it had all happened and were looking back on history. It is another proof of the heavenly inspiration of Scripture.

(d) **John the Baptist, a prophet**. The religious men of Israel (for the most part) over the past three years engaged their lives in denying, decrying, and denouncing their Lord Jesus, their blessed Messiah. Here, the Jews knew the people counted John a true prophet, and they were afraid of a popular uprising. Men of all times who busy themselves to oppose Divine truth are abandoned to the demonic spirit of falsity. They are persons without holy scruples, pretending to know everything while they know nothing of eternal worth. The brilliant agricultural scientist, Dr. Henry Burton Sharmon, was saved in a Methodist revival that swept parts of America in 1884. Later, he wrote, *Studies in the Life of Christ*. On page 167, he penned these terse words concerning religious hypocrites. "To tell the proud, self-satisfied zealots for [legal] righteousness that the moral scum of society was nearer the kingdom of God than they, was to offer them a mortal and unpardonable insult." It is one of those strange but sure rules of authentic Christian living: that God often hides from the humanly wise and worldly, what He then reveals to His babes and little children of simple faith.

(e) **"We cannot tell."** What a lie! Better, the truth would have been "We will not tell." Christ had taken their loaded question regarding His authority and so turned it around that these men of religion, (contrary to their office and work) must now lie to save their skins. Since they would not answer His original inquiry (verse 24), according to the rules of public debate, He therefore, was not required to respond to their question (verse 23). John and Christ had preached and baptized without their permission (John 4:2). Despite this, many among the crowds knew God was with both. This fact, the Sanhedrin, and their friends fearfully understood. The religious Jews dared not take the conversation any further. Standing all about and holding their breath were hundreds of listening people sympathetic with Jesus and John, but terrified at the power of their religious leaders. Regarding whom men should fear, note Section 59, footnote o, where the Savior had spoken earlier on these things.

2p-**The right religion and fearing the wrong things.** As with those Christ hating religious leaders in the four gospels, it is not much different today. Men who slavishly engage themselves against divine truth become abandoned to a spirit of falsity. All of us have been wrong on many things. However, there is one place where we dare not trifle; the salvation of our souls and preparation for eternity. The great question looming over a thinking man is, "Which religion is right?" *Refer to Section 175, sixth paragraph of footnote e for the absolute and final answer.* The Pharisees and scribes were "double dealing" with the Lord from heaven. They pretended to be shepherds of the people, and by this office were obliged to be cognizance of divine things and ready to help and answer their needs. Now their mouths are shut; they will not answer. Centuries before, Malachi had written of Israel's spiritual guides, "The priest's lips should keep knowledge, and they [the people] should seek the law at his [the priest's] mouth . . ." (Mal. 2:7). It strikes one deeply that the Jewish religionists lied because of the crowds standing about. How curious that the common Hebrew people were deathly afraid of their religious peers; now these evil men of are afraid of the common people! Matthew Henry in his *Commentary,* vol. 5, page 246 penned the following remarkable words of wisdom; "As the fear of the fear of man may bring good people into a snare (Prov. 29:25), so sometimes it may keep bad people from being overmuch wicked, lest they should die before their time (Eccle. 7:17)."

3p-**Debating for hell!** One is astounded at the plausible and learned arguments so many put forth for the damnation of their souls! It is as though they preferred hell to heaven, torment to bliss, and misery to joy. For extended comments on this appalling subject, see Section 58, second paragraph of footnote w. Men today are paralyzed by the fear of wrong things not right things. Thus, they become prisoners to mental illusions and false imaginations (Prov. 1:7 with Job. 28:28). The godless, unsaved world accuses *true* Christians, who warn others about hell, and how to avoid this place of "using fear as a tool" to frighten men into believing in God. One of the healthiest tokens of any nation or human society is the fear of God, for by it men depart from evil (Prov. 16:6). For more on the stupidity of atheism as they "debate for hell," see Section 12, twelfth paragraph of footnote k.

FIRST WARNING: THE PARABLE OF THE TWO SONS.

The Savior gives three sharp warnings to the hostile Jews. His first parable is a response to the question of the Sanhedrin in which they challenged His authority as Messiah.* He informs them that loathsome sinners will be saved before the religious, self-righteous chief priests, Pharisees, Sadducees, and elders of Israel.

Time: Tuesday after Palm Sunday before His death on Friday mid–afternoon.

*See Section 151, Matt. 21:23, footnote a for this challenge put to the Lord Jesus.

Matt. 21:28-32—*In the temple court*	Mk.	Lk.	John
The Parable **28** "But what think ye? A *certain* man had two sons;(a) and he came to the first,(b) and said, 'Son, go work to day in my vineyard.' **29** "He answered and said, 'I will not:' but afterward he repented, and went. **30** "And he came to the second,(c) and said likewise. And he answered and said, 'I *go*, sir:' and went not. ***The meaning: two kinds of persons represented here. Some prove better than they promise and others promise better than they prove*** **31** "Whether of them [the] twain [two] did the will of *his* father?" They say unto him, "The first."(d) Jesus saith unto them, "Verily I say unto you, That the publicans [tax collectors] and the harlots go into the kingdom of God before you.(e) **32** "For John came unto you in the way of righteousness, and ye believed him not: but the publicans [tax collectors] and the harlots believed him: and ye, when ye had seen *it*, repented not afterward, that ye might believe him."(f) (Verse 33 cont. in Section 153.)			

Footnotes–Commentary

(a) "But what think ye?" This was an ancient way of speaking designed to direct attention to what was being said. By these two sons, the Lord Jesus clearly contrasted the false and hypocritical attitude of the Jews against the sincere but sinful attitude of the publicans and other sinners. The blatant hypocrisy of the scribes and Pharisees was reflected as they pretended to do the works of righteousness, yet they rejected the ministry and message of John, who introduced them to their Messiah. Men of high religious standing who are unsaved, yet sincere in their errors and evil are more dangerous than they are pitiful. They remind one of the old proverb, "The cobbler's children have the worst shoes," and "The mechanic's car hardly runs." Israel's professional religionists consisted of mostly wicked men, filled with evil, despising any who would slightly disagree with them. Their disciples were the cobbler's children and the mechanic's car, which, according to Matt. 23:15 were guaranteed a home in hell. See third paragraph of footnote f below. Read the Savior's awful doom pronounced on them in Sections 159 and 163.

(b) **The first son**. He was called by the father to work in the vineyard. His blunt answer was, "I will not." However, afterwards he repented (was sorry and changed his mind) then went and served in obedience to his father's command.

2p-"I will not." Apparently, this had been the language of publicans at the beginning of Jesus' ministry. However, with the conversion of Matthew-Levi and the aftermath of the great supper given in honor of his Savior, things quickly changed. Refer to this event in Section 50, and see with this footnote e below. They refused Jesus at first and were not willing to go with Him. Talk spread among the notorious publican community about what had happened to Matthew. He had found a true Hebrew, one that loved the outcasts of Israel, and offered them forgiveness, new life, and hope.

(c) **The second son**. He promised his father "I will go" but he did not. This is a picture of the conduct of the religionists of Israel. They continually and loudly professed to obey God but fiercely opposed His Son and the demands laid down by Him as their Messiah.

(d) After giving the parable, the Savior inquired of the religious leaders, "Which of the two did the will of the father?" Being unable to lie themselves out of the clarity of our Lord's parable, they responded that it was the "first son" who obeyed his father. The concluding commentary of Christ on His lesson was intended to show the Jews their eternal estate before God, resulting from their disobedience to the preaching of John and their rejection of God's Son. What a sharp rebuke for these men of big religion. They were warned that notorious sinners such as the cursed publicans would get into the kingdom before them! It is a most difficult task to bring a self righteous man to the Lord Jesus, as he is held captive by his religious goodness and finds it near impossible to believe that all such is as "filthy rags" apart from Christ, in the sight of God (Isa 64:6). Often hardened sinners (who are honest) have no argument about their sinfulness. Many of them, upon hearing that Christ loves them and died for their sins, are simply overwhelmed. The author of this work has seen men literally run over benches and chairs in their rush to be saved! On one occasion amid a Sunday morning service in 1958, a woman jumped to her feet amid the congregation and called loudly, "Stop Mr. Pike, please stop. I want to be saved, now." The sermon ended and Mrs. Davies was led to Christ. Self-righteous people rarely come to Christ and are usually filled with resentment at the things mentioned above. Such happenings in today's church assemblies would produce fear, frustration, and even anger among "the saints of God." For more on spiritual awaking, see Section 56, second paragraph, footnote d.

(e) Sinners would enter His kingdom: the Jewish hypocrites would not. The Messiah points out to the Jews the solemn meaning of their own answer. It was the "publicans and harlots," despite their shamelessness in sin and disobedience, who were actually showing the religious elite of Israel the way into God's kingdom. The scribes, Pharisees, and Sadducees bitterly hated these outcasts within their nation. They had nothing to do with them. Yet, these very dregs of Hebrew society and culture were streaming to the Door of hope, which the religionists had rejected and shut! Earlier in Section 50, Matt. 9:10, footnote d, we saw how "many publicans and sinners" came to the Lord Jesus at Matthew's supper. See second paragraph of footnote b above. They had no self-righteous rules or oral law to wrangle over; they were the despised outcasts of Israel, frowned upon by the pious scribes, and shunned by the caretakers of the Jewish religion. They were sinners and these are the only people Jesus Christ saves (1 Tim. 1:15).

(f) Contemplating the message from the fiery Baptist, who came to these outcasts "in the way of righteousness," coupled with Messiah's teaching, many of these people instantly "repented" and entered into the loving care and salvation of Christ. They were among the hundreds that believed John's preaching and turned to the Lord Jesus. Thus, they are described in the parable as going to work in His vineyard.

2p-The stubborn Jews saw and heard both John and Christ. They gave a short-lived nod of agreement; but after a second thought, bitterly refused to repent of their sins and trust the Lord Jesus as their Messiah-Savior. Therefore, they did not work in His vineyard. See footnote d above. We may be sure that those standing about our Lord understood His message. Publicans and notorious sinners heard and believed the message of John and Jesus. Thus, they were made righteous before God through faith in Christ. The angry Jews rejected the gospel of hope, remained lost in sin and doomed.

3p-Matthew Henry in his *Commentary,* vol. 5, page 248 wrote the following words. "The scribes and Pharisees, the chief priests and elders, indeed the Jewish nation in general was like the other son that gave good words." John explained that when God's kingdom was set before them in the preaching of Jesus and himself, they turned their backs upon it. Henry goes on to say, "Hypocrites are harder to convince and convert than gross sinners." The haughty religious leaders were infuriated that such people of low morals, and base character should be part of God's kingdom. To them, it was strictly a Jewish thing, and Gentiles could only gain access as proselytes. Even after seeing the publicans and harlots enter the kingdom, they would not repent and believe. The social rejects who believed were fit representatives of the Gentile world. The publicans and harlots were like the first son, who later repented and went to work in the vineyard. They got the job done. From the Jews, John and Christ expected nothing. Many of the common people upon hearing the message of the Baptist and Jesus were converted to true righteousness and holy living; something the Hebrew religious elite knew nothing about. This fruit of John's ministry proves that he came in the "way of righteousness." His proclamation, "Behold the Lamb of God, which taketh away the sin of the world" remains valid to this day.

SECOND WARNING: THE PARABLE OF THE VINEYARD WORKERS.

Below is the second response of the Lord Jesus to the Sanhedrin, who challenged His authority as Messiah.* His parable illustrates that the responsibility for the propagation of the gospel will be taken from the Jews and given to the Gentiles. For over two thousand years, Gentiles have come to Christ by the millions, thus, gradually fulfilling our Lord's Words spoken below. The religious leaders understood the meaning of His message and sought to kill Him but were fearful of the people who held Him in popular support for a short time.

Time: Tuesday after Palm Sunday before His death on Friday mid-afternoon.

*See main heading, Section 150 for details concerning His earlier clash with the Jewish leaders of religion. The Messiah was in a continual state of war with the Sanhedrin and religious authorities of the nation of Israel.

In the temple court.

Matt. 21:33–36	Mk. 12:1-4	Lk. 20:9-11	John
	He begins the parable	*He begins the parable*	
	1 And he began to speak unto them by parables.[a]	**9** Then began he to speak to the people this parable;[a]	
He begins the parable			
33 "Hear another parable:[a] There was a certain householder, [owner-lord] which planted a vineyard,[b] and hedged it round about, and digged a winepress in it, and built a tower, and let it out to husbandmen, [workers*] and went into a far country:	"A *certain* man [owner-lord] planted a vineyard,[b] and set an hedge about *it*, and digged *a place for* the winefat, and built a tower, and let it out to husbandmen, [workers*] and went into a far country.	"A certain man [owner-lord] planted a vineyard,[b] and let it forth to husbandmen, [workers*] and went into a far country for a long time.	
Servants mistreated	*Servants mistreated*	*Servants mistreated*	
34 "And when the time of the fruit drew near, he sent[c] his servants to the husbandmen,* that they might receive the fruits of it.	**2** "And at the season he sent[c] to the husbandmen* a servant, that he might receive from the husbandmen* of the fruit of the vineyard.	**10** "And at the season he sent[c] a servant to the husbandmen,* that they should give him of the fruit of the vineyard: but the husbandmen* beat him, and sent *him* away empty[d]	
35 "And the husbandmen* took his servants, and beat one, and killed● another, and stoned another.	**3** "And they* caught *him*, and beat him, and sent *him* away empty.[d]		
Second group mistreated	*Second group mistreated*	*Second group mistreated*	
36 "Again, he sent other servants more than the first: and they did unto them likewise.	**4** "And again he sent unto them another servant; and at him they cast stones, and wounded *him* in the head, and sent *him* away shamefully handled.	**11** "And again he sent another servant: and they beat him also, and entreated *him* shamefully, and sent *him* away empty.	

697

Matt. 21:37–42	Mk. 12:5–10	Lk. 20:12–17	John
	Third group mistreated 5 "And again he sent another; and him they killed,● and many others; beating some, and killing some.	**Third group mistreated** 12 "And again he sent a third: and they wounded him also, and cast *him* out.	
●*Matthew wrote of the killings in verse 35 above and Mark here. Luke did not mention this.*		**The only son is sent** 13 "Then said the lord [owner] of the vineyard, 'What shall I do?	
The only son is sent 37 "But last of all	**The only son is sent** 6 "Having yet therefore one son, his well beloved,		
he sent unto them his son, saying, 'They will reverence my son.'(e)	he sent him also last unto them, saying, 'They will reverence my son.'(e)	I will send my beloved son: it may be they will reverence *him* when they see him.'(e)	
The only son is murdered 38 "But when the husbandmen [workers*] saw the son, they said among themselves, 'This is the heir; come, let us kill him, and let us seize on his inheritance.'	**The only son is murdered** 7 But those husbandmen [workers*] said among themselves, 'This is the heir; come, let us kill him, and the inheritance shall be ours.'	**The only son is murdered** 14 "But when the husbandmen [workers*] saw him, they reasoned among themselves, saying, 'This is the heir: come, let us kill him, that the inheritance may be ours.'	
39 "And they* caught him, and cast *him* out of the vineyard, **and slew(f) *him*.**	8 "And they* took him, **and killed(f) *him*,** and cast *him* out of the vineyard.	15 "So they* cast him out of the vineyard, **and killed(f) *him*.**	
Jesus asks a question 40 "When the lord therefore of the vineyard cometh, what will he do unto those husbandmen? (workers)	**Jesus asks a question** 9 "What shall therefore the lord of the vineyard do? (to the workers)	**Jesus asks a question** What therefore shall the lord of the vineyard do unto them? (the workers)	
The crowd's response 41 "They say unto him, 'He will miserably destroy(g) those wicked men, and will let out *his* vineyard unto other(h) husbandmen, which shall render him the fruits in their seasons.'"	**Jesus answers His question** he will come and destroy(g) the husband-men, and will give the vineyard unto others."(h)	**Jesus answers His question** 16 "He shall come and destroy(g) these husband-men, and shall give the vineyard to others."(h)	
		The crowd's response And when they heard *it*, they said, "God forbid."	
Ignorant of Scripture 42 Jesus saith unto them, "Did ye never read in the scriptures,(i) **'The stone**	**Ignorant of Scripture** 10 "And have ye not read this scripture;(i) **"The stone**	**Ignorant of Scripture** 17 And he beheld them, and said, "What is this then that is written,(i) **'The stone**	

698

Matt. 21:42-46	Mk. 12:10-12	Lk. 20:17-19	John
which the builders rejected, the same is become the head of the corner:[j] this is the Lord's doing, and it is marvellous in our eyes?""	which the builders rejected is become the head of the corner;"[j] **11** 'This was the Lord's doing, and it is marvellous in our eyes?'"	which the builders rejected, the same is become the head of the corner?'"[j]	
43 "Therefore say I unto you, The kingdom of God shall be taken▶ from you, [Jews] and given to a nation [Gentiles] bringing forth the fruits thereof.[k]	◀*It can be no clearer that the Jews had the kingdom taken from them and given to the Gentiles. This could not have been a literal physical kingdom. It can only speak of the church or Christ's new kingdom, which the Jews relinquished by rejecting Jesus their Messiah-Savior. Israel did not reject the kingdom, rather the King.*		
The results of believing or rejecting Christ		*The results of believing in or rejecting Christ*	
44 "And whosoever shall fall on this stone shall be broken: but on whomsoever it shall fall, it will grind him to powder."[l]		**18** "And whosoever shall fall on this stone shall be broken: but on whomsoever it shall fall, it will grind him to powder."[l]	
45 And when the chief priests and Pharisees	**12** And they [the religious leaders] sought to lay hold on him, but feared◀ the people: for	**19** And the chief priests and the scribes the same hour sought to lay hands on him; and they feared◀ the people: for	
The Jews understood	*The Jews understood*	*The Jews understood*	
had heard his parables, they perceived that he spake of them.[m]	they knew that he had spoken the parable against them:[m] and they left him, and went their way. (Verse 13 cont. in Section 155.)	they perceived that he had spoken this parable against them.[m] (Verse 20 cont. in Section 155.)	
Fearful of the people			
46 But when they sought to lay hands on him, they feared▶ the multitude,[n] because they took him for a prophet.[o] (Next chap., Matt. 22:1 cont. in Section 154.)	◀*Mark and Luke place this same text in verses 12 and 19 just above.*		

Footnotes-Commentary

(a) **Israel crossing the deadline.** Christ drew this lesson from some actual event that had occurred in the past. Though Luke wrote that this was spoken to the people (verse 9), clearly the religious leaders were its main object. Matthew 21:45 reads, that "the chief priests and Pharisees perceived that he spake [this parable] of them." See footnote n below for their violent reactions at the conclusion of this message. It was another appeal to the Jews offering them time to repent of their rejection and hatred of Him. They rejected this act of mercy from Jehovah. With this God's work was gradually placed into the hands of saved Gentiles and has continued so up to this present time. Almost thirty years after Jesus had spoken this warning to the religious leaders of Israel, Paul under house arrest in Rome, Italy, again warned his Jewish visitors that they were fulfilling the words of the prophet Isaiah in refusing Jesus as their Savior and Messiah. See Acts 28:16-28 for the intriguing story. For other comments on this subject, see the Information Box under Section 60, and Section 140, third and fourth paragraphs of footnote j.

(b) The "householder," "landowner" or "lord" in a general sense pictures the Lord of Hosts and His efforts to build up the nation of Israel, chosen by God, cultivated with great care and favored above all nations of the earth. In these Words, our Lord alludes to the Old Testament where Israel is said to be a vineyard raised up by God (Isa. 5:1-2). The Jews frequently referred to Israel as "God's vineyard." The winepress was standard for all vineyards for it was here the fresh blood of the grape was pressed for human consumption and joy (not drunkenness). For comments on wine, see Section 27, footnote k and l. The tower or "watch house," as the Jews called it, was a booth erected in the middle of the growing area. It was of different heights with guards posted therein who guarded the precious vineyard from ravaging animals and thieves. These "watch houses" are mentioned in Isa. 1:8 ("lodge"), and 5:2. The "landowner" departing for a far country could well point to God in heaven observing the affairs of all mankind, but especially the conduct of Israel as they abused and rejected His Son, their Messiah.

2p-"A long time." Prophecy experts would do well to ponder these words. How long a "long time" is no man knows; likewise, no man knows the time of our Lord's return. At this typing, it has been two thousand years! See *Appendix Eight* for more on this subject.

(c) **"He sent his servants."** From time to time God sent His prophets and seers to His vineyard or Israel to gather their fruits for His glory. It is noted that Matt. 21:34 employs the plural "servants," while Mk .12: 2 and Lk. 20:10, is in the singular. Both are true.

(d) No honest exegete can deny that this reflects the treatment Israel meted to the prophets across Old Testament history. After settling in Canaan, God's Hebrew preachers were sorely mistreated. Jeremiah was beaten by Pashur (Jer. 20:1-2), Micaiah was smitten by Zedekiah (2 Chron. 18:23), Zechariah was murdered (2 Chron. 24:20-21), and so the story goes. Wave after wave of fearless men stood to represent Jehovah before the vineyard of a wicked Israel, who would not listen. The author of 2 Chron. 36:13-17 reveals the nation's dastardly treatment of holy prophets just before the beginning of the three Babylonian invasions in 606 B.C. Finally, Heb. 11:32-39 condenses the awful story of how His choice servants were treated.

(e) **"My beloved son."** Luke penned these words in 20:13. In the fullness of time (Gal. 4:4), God, the great "householder," after all the prophets and sagas had spent their course and completed their work, sent to Israel His blessed and only begotten Son. Matthew wrote these words of heaven's most majestic Person, "they will reverence my son" (verse 37). This has reference to a landowner contemplating his situation. The religious leadership of Israel did not reverence the Son of God, their promised Messiah. See this gradual rejection of Jesus the Messiah in the main headings under Sections 66 through 68. John in the opening sentences of his gospel informs his original readers of the greatest sin of Israel in the rejecting of their Messiah. Note Section 1, Part 3, John 1:11-12, footnote g. For the *human* emotion and hurt of the Savior over Israel's vicious rejection of Him, see Section 159, Matt. 23:37-38 and relative footnotes.

(f) **Who killed Jesus?** The killing of the son as given in this story reflected the Jews and Gentiles killing the Messiah. It is highlighted in gray, though not a direct Old Testament prophecy. This has reference to the Jews putting Christ to death. It should be remembered that others besides the Jews took part in the death of the Lord from heaven. This is illustrated below. After persecuting and killing many of God's earlier prophets, they crucified His Son and their Messiah on the tree of the cross. "Casting him out of the vineyard" (Heb. 13:12), refers to the city of Jerusalem from where they led Him to Mount Calvary outside the northern gate for His death by Roman crucifixion (Acts 2:23 with 7:51-52). *All the fuss about "Who killed Christ?" is answered in Holy Scripture.* In the sovereign plan of God for the salvation of mankind, a number of individuals and groups played *willing* parts in His death on the cross. Note the following points on this subject:

1. God killed Jesus as stated in John 3:16 with 1 John 4:10.
2. Satan killed Him as seen in Heb. 2:14.
3. Pilate, Herod Antipas, and the Roman soldiers killed the Son of God. See John 19:18 with Matt. 27:35, and Acts 4:27.
4. Christ killed Himself. He freely laid down His life according to John 10:10-18.
5. The Sanhedrin and Jews killed their Messiah. See Acts 3:13-14.
6. *We all killed him.* Christ died for "the sins of the whole world" according to 1 John 2:2, and 1 Tim. 2:6. This sixth and highest reason for the death of our Lord embraces total humanity. We all stand guilty of this crime. Those who blame the "dirty Jews" for His death or the "pagan Romans" have totally missed the reason for His coming into this world. Christ came first to take upon Himself our sins. In dying for all of them, He paid their consequences that we might not have to die for them. Before the foundation of the world, the Holy Trinity laid down this plan. To read 1 John 2:2 as stating that Christ "died only for the sins of the elect of the whole world" is a travesty unspeakable. Later, in one John 5:19, we read, "The whole world lieth in wickedness" or "the wicked one." *Both* "whole worlds" mean the same. Both were the objects of Christ's atoning death for both are under the rule of the Devil. How absurd to force these

verses to read, "Christ died for the elect but everyone else is under the power of Satan." *We all killed the Son of God on the cross because He died for the sins of all Adam's fallen race.* For other comments the theological cancers of Calvinism and Arminianism, see Section 50, fifth paragraph of footnote h.

(g) "He will miserably destroy." Again, the Savior predicts the doom of Jerusalem, the temple, and Jewish state. This literally took place in A.D. 70 at the hands of Titus and the Roman armies. This historical calamity has been mentioned repeatedly in this harmony commentary of the four gospels. See the main headings of Sections 63, 134, 163-165 for other comments and details.

(h) "Other husbandmen." This has reference to Gentiles. They have over the past two thousand years of church history demonstrated their respective seasons of life and service for Christ. It should be noted that Lk. 20:16 seems to be the response of some of Jesus' audience. Some of them clearly understood what He meant and cried, "God forbid." See footnote k below.

(i) What a question! These purveyors of the Jewish religion prided themselves in knowing their Old Testament better than anyone in the nation. Now, the Man they hate most rebukes them for not knowing what they boasted so much to know. Refer to Section 52, footnote y, for more on the Jews reading their Scriptures in hope of gaining eternal life and Jesus' comments.

(j) The rejected corner stone. Cited from Ps. 118:22-23. The Jewish builders, the priests, Levites, scribes, Pharisees and Sadducees, for the most part, hated Him and rejected His claims to be Messiah and Savior. To their shame, He quoted a prime verse from the Passover hallel, which all of them knew was a direct reference to their Messiah. He knew the Scriptures, and they did not! It pointed to the Lord Jesus and His rejection by the Jews. A few hours later, they would be singing this very Psalm during their Passover celebration.

2p-He was the "cornerstone" they had rejected, but God made Him to be the "head of the corner" for a new temple, His kingdom, later called the church. About thirty years afterward, Peter quoted this very passage and applied it as being realized in the Savior, who was the foundation of God's church (1 Peter 2:4-10). At this time in history "cornerstone" had reference to the *largest and first stone* laid, and the one upon which the weight of the entire structure was to have lain. Some called this the foundation, while others considered the foundation as being built out from this giant stone. Either way, Christ is viewed as *both* in Scripture (1 Cor. 3:11 with Eph. 2:20). The Talmud contains an interesting note in tractate, K'rithoth 28b, when it reads that Jewish rabbis or teachers "were the builders of the world." Here, our Lord shows from their Scriptures, who is the true builder of mankind. How could the Jews remain builders any longer, when the whole focus of their workmanship had been purposely overruled and rejected?

3p-Did not their Messianic predictions imply that God would call other builders to the work of His spiritual temple, kingdom, or church? Refer to footnote k below for more on this fact. They stumbled because they rejected Jesus of Nazareth. About forty years later in A.D. 70 the chief corner stone they had despised would "grind them to powder" (Dan. 2:34-44). See footnote g above for more on this thought.

4p-Mk. 12:11. "Marvellous in our eyes." The word means to be "astonished." Psalm 118:22-23 was written about one thousand years before the coming of Christ. The writer was "astonished" when he foresaw the coming Messiah, his rejection by Israel, and acceptance by Gentiles. It was "marvellous" in the eyes of the Old Testament sages, who according to the text "saw with their eyes" the deeds of Christ yet to come. Continue this thought in footnote k below.

(k) Verse 43. "Kingdom of God taken from you [Jews]." The words in verse 43 conclusively affirm that there is a spiritual side to the kingdom of God. It cannot mean that a literal, physical, political Jewish kingdom was first offered to the Jews and then given to Gentile believers. Such a proposal is hilarious. For explanation of *both* manifestations of the kingdom, refer to Section 39, footnotes a and g. The only sensible meaning is that the kingdom taken from Israel (because they rejected their Messiah) and given to converted heathens was a spiritual one, even His church. In "bringing forth fruit thereof" and "giving the vineyard to others," Jesus was speaking of the believing Gentiles, who became productive in His new kingdom. They would bring forth fruit to the glory of God, by their love and obedience to the Messiah-Savior in carrying His saving gospel around the earth thousands of times. It is true that some saved Jews have also shared in this glorious task as well, but it has been predominantly the work of Gentiles, who have been called out of darkness into His marvelous light. In our Lord's new kingdom or church, each member is a priest, offering up "spiritual sacrifices, acceptable to God by Jesus Christ" (1 Peter 2:5). Saved Christians are called "a chosen generation, a royal priesthood, an holy nation, a peculiar people" (1 Peter 2:9). This is the final and only holy temple in which the Lord will dwell (Eph. 2:21-22). There will be no other! Now, the individual believer is God's house or temple because His Holy Spirit dwells within their born again, saved souls (Eph. 3:16).

2p-Regarding the myth of a rebuilt Hebrew temple at Jerusalem, animal sacrifices, a restored Levitical priesthood, and God being *acceptably* worshiped again in this manner, see Section 134, all under footnote d. Also note footnote m below for other thoughts on this subject.

3p-In verse 43 above, Matthew's record is clear. Messiah said that His kingdom was taken from Israel and given to saved Gentiles. For over two thousand years, the Gentiles have done with God's kingdom what ancient Israel failed to do by their rejection of Jesus the Messiah. In Matt. 21:45 with Lk. 20:19 it is profoundly clear that the Jewish leaders listening to Him speak understood clearly the meaning of His Words. They knew He was predicting that they would kill Him, the Son of heaven's great landowner. Had they not recently conspired with the traitor, Judas Iscariot to bring about this very deed? See main heading of Section 147 for the deal they had previously struck with Judas, the shady Devil-man from Kerioth.

(l) This is a general quotation from Isa. 8:14-15, with selected words and thoughts being added to the quotation from Dan. 2:34 and Isa. 28:16. The destruction of the Jewish state is mentioned in footnote g above. Here, Christ speaks another warning of this coming judgment. If ever the Hebrew nation was "ground to powder," it occurred during and after that awful holocaust of A.D. 70. Since that dreadful period in history, the Jews have never suffered such devastation and ruin, not even under the Inquisitions of the Papal Church, the pogroms of the Russian Czars, or the scourge of that mad man Adolf Hitler. For more on the satanic hatred of the Jews, from so-called "Christian heroes of the faith", see footnote f, under Section 14.

2p-In these verses, the Jews were highly offended at His claim to be the foundation of God for mankind. He had just alluded to Himself as a stone in verse 42. He is the stone (the symbol of strength and security) that saves all who trust Him but will crush in judgment all who reject Him. His verbal doom was directed at the religious leaders of Israel. However, there is a blessed reversal of this scenario. Those who fall upon Christ (surrender themselves to Him without reserve) will be broken or thoroughly ashamed of their sins, find forgiveness, new life, and hope in Him the rock or foundation and security of salvation. It is sure that the same sun that melts butter also hardens clay. And this is how the Son of God affected the nation of Israel.

(m) **"The chief priests and Pharisees perceived."** This statement, recorded by all three evangelists interprets the parable. Their "perception" of what Jesus said was correct! The Jewish authorities knew that it was they of whom the Lord Jesus spoke. However, it was too late. They had crossed the deadline of mercy and grace. Their minds were reprobate, their hearts obstinate, their fate sealed. The material, political kingdom as they looked for would never be: it was now a spiritual thing and placed into the hands of Gentile believers. This kingdom is Christ's Church and has been operative for over two millenniums. Almost thirty years after Matthew had written the words in verse 45, while under house arrest and waiting trial in Rome, Italy, Paul warned the stubborn Jews, "Be it know therefore unto you, that the salvation of God is sent unto the Gentiles, and *that* they will hear it" (Acts 28:28). For some two thousand years, millions of Gentiles have received this salvation; while only a few Jews believe. For more on this, see footnote k above. In the early days of Christ's ministry, the leadership of Israel had sinned grievously in their treatment of Messiah. This is seen in Sections 66 through Section 68, where they blasphemed Him and the Holy Spirit, would be condemned in judgment by the people of Nineveh and the Queen of Sheba, and were demonized seven times in the sins. In Section 163, the Savior announced the awful doom that would come upon them in A.D. 70.

(n) Their rage was so intense upon understanding that His message was directed at them, they looked about seeking an opportunity to seize Him. The presence of great crowds to observe the upcoming Passover deterred their madness. The fear of the people standing about restrained the Jewish hierarchy from trying to kill Him during these days. Several times, we meet this statement, which suggests that many among the crowds were aligned with Christ in their sympathies. However, on the day of His crucifixion, all of this dramatically changed as the crowds, being inflamed by the religious leaders, screamed for His death. For more on this awful but glorious event, see main heading of Section 188. The rabbis taught that God would judge one who touched His prophets for harm; it was based on 1 Chron. 16:22. They used this verse as a shield for their hypocrisy, and now it backfires in their faces! Refer to Section 159, for eight terrible woes the Savior places on the religious leaders of Israel.

2p-Anyone who has witnessed an eastern or oriental mob go wild over some emotional issue will have no problem understanding the fear of the religious Jews. These people snap on the spur of a moment and kill indiscriminately anyone suspected of not being in sympathy with their cause. Television newscasts depict millions of *radical* Muslims in the streets shouting, screaming, shooting off guns, tearing apart buildings in their bloodthirsty rampage. Because of the imminent possibility of public anarchy, the Jews did not take the Lord Jesus by force on this occasion.

(o) Over the course of Hebrew history, many of the extraordinary deeds performed was put down to the work of a prophet of God. This had it roots in the fact that out of ancient Israel came the greatest *genuine* prophets in human history. Abraham the federal head of these great people is the first person after the Noah's flood to be called a prophet (Gen. 20:7). After him, there is a long stream of mighty Jewish prophets beginning especially with Moses. Hence, many in the crowds following Jesus attested that He also was a prophet. This is vividly noted in the words of the two men on the Emmaus road, in Section 200, Lk. 24:19. For the number of prophets found across the entire Old Testament, see Section 105, first paragraph of footnote i. For the rejection of many of these prophets of God's Word, see footnote d above.

THIRD WARNING: THE PARABLE OF THE KING'S SON.

Below is the last of three parables the Lord Jesus gave to the religious leaders after they had challenged His Messianic claims.* He ends this series of lessons by telling the Jews that He has called many of them (the whole nation) but only those few who believe in Him will be chosen. They, like the fellow without the wedding garment in His parable, will be shut out of God's kingdom into a terrible abyss of darkness, weeping, and pain.

Time: Tuesday after Palm Sunday before His death on Friday mid-afternoon.

*Refer back to the main heading of Section 151 for the details regarding this earlier event in His ministry.

Matt. 22:1-14—*In the temple court*	Mk.	Lk.	John
He begins the parable			
1 And Jesus answered and spake unto them again by parables, and said,			
2 "The kingdom of heaven[a] is like unto a certain king, which made a marriage for his son,[b]			
3 "And sent forth his servants to call them that were bidden to the wedding: and they would not come.[c]			
4 "Again, he sent forth other servants, saying, 'Tell them which are bidden, "Behold, I have prepared my dinner: my oxen and *my* fatlings *are* killed, and all things *are* ready: come unto the marriage." '			
The king's invitation is scorned			
5 "But they made light of *it*, and went their ways, one to his farm, another to his merchandise:			
6 And the remnant took his servants, and entreated *them* spitefully, and slew *them*.[d]			
The angry king: "go everywhere and find guests"			
7 "But when the king heard *thereof*, he was wroth: and he sent forth his armies, and destroyed those murderers, and burned up their city.[e]			
8 "Then saith he to his servants, 'The wedding is ready, but they which were bidden were not worthy.'			
9 'Go[f] ye therefore into the highways, and as many as ye shall find, bid to the marriage.'			
10 "So those servants went out into the highways, and gathered together all as many as they found, both bad and good: and the wedding was furnished with guests.			
The unprepared are cast out			
11 "And when the king came in to see the guests, he saw there a man which had not on a wedding garment:[g]			
12 "And he saith unto him, 'Friend, how camest thou in hither not having a wedding garment?' And he was speechless.[h]			
The horrible judgment for all who are unprepared			
13 "Then said the king to the servants, 'Bind him hand and foot, and take him away, and cast *him* into outer darkness; there shall be weeping and gnashing of teeth.'[i]			
14 "For many are called, but few *are* chosen."[j] (Verse 15 cont. in Section 155.)			

Footnotes-Commentary

(a) In the previous Section 153, Matt. 21:43, footnote k, the Lord Jesus used the term "kingdom of God." A few moments later, He continues His teaching and issues the third warning to the Jews. This time He speaks of it as the "kingdom of heaven." *Obviously, they are both the same.* See Section 39, footnotes a and g for explanation of the two. Our Lord's message here is an answer to the Pharisees, who flew into a rage over His Parable of the Vineyard and the kingdom being taken from them and given to Gentiles.

(b) His illustration was understood by all listening. The idea here is that God deals with man in His kingdom or church similarly, as to how a certain king dealt with the people invited to his son's wedding feast. The king's son is to be married, and hundreds have been called to share in the happy occasion but reject the invitation. Likewise, over the centuries, the Holy Spirit has called millions to the marriage supper of the Lamb (Rev. 19:9). Some have accepted, and others spurned the invitation. Men accepting God's call to salvation has nothing to do with human works or merit, nor is it forced down their throats. They do not (sort of) wake up the next morning and discover they have been saved *and then* decide to repent of their sins! In the sovereign plan of God, men may accept or reject eternal life in Christ.

2p-As previously stated, men do not go to hell because they reject Jesus Christ the Son of God. (If this is so, then we should immediately stop sharing the gospel with pagans.) Men go to hell because their sins have not been perfectly and totally atoned. The only atonement acceptable to God is that of His Son on the cross and in His resurrection. Heathens held in the chains of pagan darkness are without the true knowledge of Christ; therefore, they cannot reject someone they never knew. Their plight is to die in their sins (John 8:21). Millions of others knowing of Christ choose to die in their unforgiven sins. Either way, it is hell at the end of the road. For a review of how the first and early churches carried the gospel to the world of their day, refer to Section 163, third paragraph of number 16, footnote f. Regarding the subject "Are the heathen lost?" refer to Section 1, Part 2, second through fourth paragraphs under footnote f for a discussion. Those who object so strongly to the above statements have little or no understanding of the Holiness of God and how it is offended by man's sin. Only the atoning death of Christ and His resurrection appease God's angered holiness and satisfy His justice to punish evil. When men receive Jesus Christ by faith, they are instantly pardoned, forgiven, and justified before the Almighty. Thus the need of the educated academic at Oxford and the savage in the Amazon jungles of Brazil. Without Christ, both are lost and doomed.

(c) Ancient wedding feasts were large events. The rich and powerful would invite the whole village, city, or district to attend. This open call to all men brought in hundreds or thousands of guests. Jewish celebrations of this nature usually lasted for seven days or longer and the guests were expected to remain for the entire event. Such a commitment required great sacrifice on behalf of the poorer classes in view of work time being lost. However, to refuse the invite of the king was no light thing and could bring his wrath! It was a custom for servants to go to the houses of those previously invited, remind them of the exact time of the wedding, and present them with a special wedding garment provided by the king. See footnote g below for explanation. This act is strange to the western mind but was the normal procedure in the East and among the ancient Jews. The double invitation is mentioned in Esther 5:8 with 6:14. This perhaps speaks *first* of the prophets of the Old Testament, who gave God's invitation to the Jewish people during that era of history, but they spurned it. All who accepted their call received a robe of righteousness, tailor-made for every saved soul! See Rom, 4:6-8, where David, who lived a thousand years before Christ, wrote of this perfect righteousness given to all who believe. Recipients were called "blessed" (Ps. 32:1-2).

(d) It should be noted in verse 3 that those who had been called twice to attend the dinner "would not." The king dispatches another body of servants: they go out and invite others to the great feast. With this second invitation, he would send a wedding garment (or white robe) that guests were to wear for the special occasion. If some of those invited lived in poverty, they would be furnished with complete wardrobes fitting them to stand in the presence of their lord. This last appeal was urgent. The servants stressed the good news that "All things are now ready. Come with haste unto the marriage." See footnote g below.

2p-Verse 5. To ridicule such an invitation was rare indeed and considered an act of the highest insult to the one sending out the appeals to attend the wedding. Here, we perhaps may see a picture of the Jews during the ministry of John the Baptist, the Lord Jesus and His twelve apostles. No one of sound mind can debate the shameful treatment the Jews (especially the religious leaders) meted out to their Messiah, Jesus of Nazareth. Verse 6 reveals again the hatred of the Jews to God's *true* preachers and prophets, whom they abused and killed.

(e) Symbolized in these who were first invited, then called a second time to the great occasion, we see the Jews and their rejection of God's loving offer for them to believe on His Son. This parable is an altered repetition of the lesson in Section 153, but stated here in different terminology. As the Jews abused, mistreated, and killed God's early prophets who called them to repent of their sin, it is the same lesson in this Section. The religious leaders were doing the same to Christ and His preachers.

2p-Verse 7. "Burned up their city." Jesus affirmed that the angry king destroyed their city. Here, the Savior again predicts the doom of Jerusalem, which was burned to ashes by the Romans. Millions of Jews perished in this terrible judgment. See Section 163 for a comprehensive description of this awful calamity as given by the Lord Jesus to four of His apostles from a summit on the Mount of Olives. In A.D. 70, the Roman armies literally "burned up" the city of Jerusalem and the temple just as the Savior stated in this lesson.

(f) **"Go."** This pictures the Lord Jesus dispatching His early and infantile church under the banner of the Great Commission to take the gospel to every creature. The book of Acts carries the glorious history of this story. For an

704

explanation of the Great Commission given by our Lord five different times, see the main headings in Sections 201, 203, 204, 205 and 206. During their obedience to King Jesus, many of these servants found themselves also hated for the cause of Christ and suffering as their forbearers of God's truth had done.

2p-Verse 10. This is a viable and glorious testimony to their service as they invited both "bad and good" to the grand occasion! Every man is a prospect to heaven! Time eventually tells the truth on all. How wonderful that the grace of God reaches to every class and offers salvation to every man. "For the grace of God that bringeth salvation hath appeared to all men" (Titus 2:11). What many of them do with this grand invitation of grace is another story. See footnote j below and b above for more on this thought.

(g) **"Wedding garment"** Footnote d above explains that this garment was an absolute necessity for this occasion. These expensive articles of clothing were given freely by the king for each guest to wear at the wedding feast. They were long white robes constructed of the finest linen. With this, we may peek into the local church. Amid the millions are those who are clothed inwardly with the righteousness of Christ, washed white in the blood of the lamb. God alone views this vesture of the soul and purified inward condition; men cannot see such divine wonders. Some seven hundred years before the birth of Christ, Isaiah the prophet spoke of these marvelous things. "I will greatly rejoice in the LORD, my soul shall be joyful in my God; for he hath clothed me with the garments of salvation, he hath covered me with the robe of righteousness …" (Isa. 61:10). In Rom. 3:21, we read that the prophets witnessed of this righteousness. It is the holiness of God in Christ and imputed (given freely) to all who receive Him as personal Lord and Savior. In 1 Cor. 1:30 we read that the Lord Jesus "is made unto us . . . .righteousness." Later, the Savior in giving the Parable of the Ten Virgins spoke of being ready. See Section 164, second paragraph of footnote i for further explanation of this custom.

(h) **"He was speechless."** Dumbfounded, the unprepared intruder into the king's palace was caught. Paul said of these people that their "damnation is just" (Rom. 3:8). Jesus' prime lesson here is that the Jews, who have rejected Him as Messiah and Savior will be shut out of God's eternal home. In 1963, the author knocked on a door in the coastal town of Gladstone, Queensland, Australia. A middle age woman responded to my knock and was surprised that someone was visiting the neighborhood in such scorching temperatures. She inquired of my business to which I replied, "I am a Baptist missionary visiting in the community; I want people to be ready for the judgment of God by receiving Christ as their Lord and Savior." To my amazement, she responded, "O, I've always talked my way out of everything, and I'll talk my way out of God's judgment too!" Later, while reflecting back on that event, I remembered this passage, "He was speechless" when standing before the king. Some three years prior in His Sermon on the Mount, Jesus said that at the judgment, some will (apparently?) debate with Him over their status and plead various deeds of religious goodness to avoid eternal damnation. See this amazing fact in Section 47, Matt. 7:21-23, footnotes j and k.

(i) First, it will be Israel weeping and wailing in hell over their rejection of Jesus the Messiah. See footnote j below. Second, when the spiritual and highly symbolic marriage of God's Son with the church at last takes place (as dimly pictured in this parable), those in the local churches who have pretended to know Him but do not wear the *inward apparel* of saving righteousness will be doomed. What a terrible place hell must be to consist of "outer darkness, there shall be weeping and gnashing of teeth." The Jews frequently used this common expression. See examples of this in Section 60, Matt. 8:12, and Section 165, Matt. 25:30. Refer to Section 82, footnote g, for an explanation of these horrible words and their origin. For twenty-one things the Bible says about hell-lake of fire, see Section 103, number 8, under footnote g. Without the necessary garment, he was shamed. This may point to the religious hypocrites such as the scribes, Pharisees and their associates in opposing and rejecting Messiah. The self-righteousness of Israel was called "filthy rags" some seven hundred years before (Isa. 64:6). It is no different now.

(j) **"Many called, but few *are* chosen."** As stated above under the main heading, the Savior declares here that many members of the house of Israel were called to God and saving grace during the ministry of John the Baptist and Himself. However, only those who repent and receive Jesus as the Messiah-Savior were chosen to be the children of God. It works precisely the same today! Christ had used this saying earlier in Section 140, Matt. 20:16, footnote j with another arrangement of the wording. The teaching that God chose so many for heaven and consigned the rest to hell, regardless, is heresy. When great men embrace this heresy, it possesses them. It tarnishes their greatness and cauterizes the faith of the thousands who believe what they teach and preach. Many of these people profess a unique insight into Scripture that others (who reject their heresy) do not have. However, inwardly is the secret tormenting fear that dear loved ones may be among the pre-damned, appointed to this fate by the "sovereign good pleasure of God." Years ago in South Africa, a Dutch Reform minister confessed to me that he worried himself sick, wondering if God had reprobated his children to hell. Some five hundreds years before the birth of Christ, Jehovah warned the Jews, "As I live, saith the Lord God, I have no pleasure in the death of the wicked; but that the wicked turn from his way and live: turn ye, turn ye from your evil ways; for why will ye die, O house of Israel?" (Ezek. 33:11). God has not predestinated anyone to hell. Contrary wise, He has no pleasure in the death of the wicked.

FIRST QUESTION:* SHOULD THEY PAY TRIBUTE TO CAESAR? THE JEW'S RESPOND TO JESUS WITH THREE* TRICK INTERROGATIVES.

They were furious over the three parables He had just given because each one pictured their doom. In vengeance, the Pharisees united with the Herodians to entangle Him with a question about paying tribute to their Roman conquerors. He instantly confounded their scheme to make Him guilty of supporting tax evasion against the Roman Empire.***

Time: Tuesday after Palm Sunday before His death on Friday mid-afternoon.

*Their second question is in the next Section. **It was noted on a previous occasion that the Pharisees joined hands with their enemies the Herodians in another attempt to destroy the Lord Jesus. Refer to Section 54, Mk. 3:6, footnotes g and h. ***Earlier in His ministry, the Jews again tried to entangle Him into conflict over the question of paying taxes. On this first occasion, it had to do with temple taxes and not the Roman government, as was the case here. Section 108 gives the story of how the Lord Jesus and Peter paid their dues. It is conjectured above that it was still Tuesday. Matthew and Mark wrote of this new union between the Pharisees and Herodians, which reveals their intense opposition and hatred of the Lord Jesus. They sought to catch Him in some doctrinal or political error.*

In the temple court

Matt. 22:15–18	Mk. 12:13–15	Lk. 20:20–23	John
His enemies scheme **15** Then went the Pharisees, and took counsel how they might entangle him in *his* talk.[a]	*His enemies scheme* **13** And they send unto him certain of the Pharisees and of the Herodians, to catch him in *his* words.[a]	*His enemies scheme* **20** And they watched *him*, and sent forth spies, which should feign themselves just men, that they might take hold of his words,[a] that so they might deliver him unto the power and authority of the governor.	
16 And they sent out unto him their disciples with the Herodians, saying,	**14** And when they were come, they say unto him,	**21** And they asked him, saying,	
Tax evasion "Master, we know that thou art true, and teachest the way of God in truth, neither carest thou for any *man*: for thou regardest not the person of men.[b]	*Tax evasion* "Master, we know that thou art true, and carest for no man: for thou regardest not the person of men,[b] but teachest the way of God in truth:	*Tax evasion* "Master, we know that thou sayest and teachest rightly, neither acceptest thou the person *of any*,[b] but teachest the way of God truly:	
Their wicked conniving **17** "Tell us therefore, What thinkest thou? Is it lawful to give tribute unto Caesar, or not?"[c]	*Their wicked conniving* Is it lawful to give tribute to Caesar, or not?[c] **15** "Shall we give, or shall we not give?"	*Their wicked conniving* **22** "Is it lawful for us to give tribute unto Caesar, or no?"[c]	
His profound answer **18** But Jesus perceived their wickedness, and said, "Why tempt ye me, *ye* hypocrites?[d]	*His profound answer* But he, knowing their hypocrisy, said unto them, "Why tempt ye me?	*His profound answer* **23** But he perceived their craftiness, and said unto them, "Why tempt ye me?	

Matt. 22:19-22	Mk. 12:15-17	Lk. 20:24-26	John
19 "Shew me the tribute money." And they brought unto him a penny."(e)	bring me a penny, that I may see *it*." 16 And they brought *it*.(e)	24 "Shew me a penny.	
Image of a pagan ruler 20 And he saith unto them, "Whose *is* this image and superscription?"(f) (name)	*Image of a pagan ruler* And he saith unto them, "Whose *is* this image and superscription?"(f) (name)	*Image of a pagan ruler* Whose image and superscription(f) [name] hath it?"	
21 They say unto him, "Caesar's." Then saith he unto them, "Render therefore unto Caesar the things which are Caesar's; and unto God the things that are God's."(g)	And they said unto him, "Caesar's." 17 And Jesus answering said unto them, "Render to Caesar the things that are Caesar's, and to God the things that are God's."(g)	They answered and said, "Caesar's." 25 And he said unto them, "Render therefore unto Caesar the things which be Caesar's, and unto God the things which be God's."(g)	
Stunned into silence 22 When they had heard *these words*, they marvelled, and left him, and went their way.(h) (Verse 23 cont. in Section 156.)	*Stunned into silence* And they marvelled at him. (Verse 18 cont. in Section 156.)	*Stunned into silence* 26 And they could not take hold of his words before the people: and they marvelled at his answer, and held their peace. (Verse 27 cont. in Section 156.)	

Footnotes-Commentary

(a) **"Then went the Pharisees."** *When* did they go? After hearing the three parables of Christ, each one containing a unique lesson in which they saw themselves illustrated. These parables are given in the previous three Sections. The desperation of the religious leaders flashes from the three parallel passages above as recorded by the evangelists. Lk. 20:20 informs us that the Pharisees sent spies among the crowds, pretending to be good men and sympathetic with our Lord. In verse 13, Mark wrote that the Herodians were included in this plot. Their mission was to find some political fault in the Words of Christ and then report Him to Governor Pilate, thus bringing Him into conflict with the mighty Roman Empire. Their question had to do with paying taxes to Rome! See footnote c below.

2p-**Verse 20. "Deliver him to the governor,"** Pontius Pilate. A short time later, they took Him to Pilate as seen in the main heading of Section 183. This time, however, it was to demand His death by crucifixion.

3p-**Verse 16. "Herodians."** Several years earlier, we noted the Pharisees in their frustration and anger had previously joined hands with their old enemies the Herodians in an attempt to trap the Savior. This is mentioned in the sub heading above. Note this in Section 54, Mk. 3:6, footnote h, for explanation on this political group.

(b) False piety is among the most disgusting things on earth. Another name for it is "hypocrisy." These religious animals approached the Savior with mouths full of sour cream. Verse 18 reveals that He instantly detected their plot.

(c) **"Tribute."** This taxing was imposed upon the Jews by force and paid to the Roman government. It was the old story of tax evasion in which the Pharisees and Herodians attempted to entangle Christ. For an earlier mention of a Roman taxation that led to the good of all mankind, see Section 13, footnote c. After the death of Julius Caesar in 44 B.C., all succeeding rulers adopted the title "Caesar." It supposedly means "the hairy one." There was a *tradition* that Julius was the first person born by caesarian surgery—hence his name. Caesar Tiberius ruled at this time. He was distinguished for the most horrific vices, especially with small children. For a brief review of Tiberius, refer to Section 21, Part 1, and number 1 under footnote b. He was ruling when Christ was crucified.

(d) **"Ye hypocrites."** The Lord exposed their united wickedness. Again, he labels them as "hypocrites" and strips away their self-righteous pretension and flattering words with His piercing question, "Why tempt ye me?"

(e) He asked them to show Him the coin with which taxes were to be paid, and they had one! If this was the Roman denarius, it was worth about seven cents. All foreign coins bore the image of a god, goddess or pagan rulers and were highly offensive to the Jews. They were forbidden to be brought into the temple, hence the omni present moneychangers were ready to swap them into the Jewish coinage void of all such heathen images. For details on the money changers in the temple, see Section 29, footnote b. The Herodians did not object in paying taxes to the pagan Romans or the Herods, while the scribes, Pharisees, Sadducees and Sanhedrin did. The Herodians were political pals of Herod Antipas. This explains their support of the Jews paying taxes to that scoundrel. See footnote g below.

(f) **"Image and superscription."** This was a Roman coin. The Jews loathed currency with images and pagan motifs engraved in them. They were banned from the temple of God. Thousands of coins have been found bearing the image of Tiberius, with his name inscribed in Latin and the title "Pontifex Maximus." He was emperor when this event took place. "Superscription" means the name or title of the particular emperor was struck on the coins. Pious Jews refused to take oaths of allegiance to Caesar. Amazingly, they carry in hand a coin with his image when trying to trap the Savior in a tax scandal. No lie can wear the golden robe of truth. *What image do we bear as Christians?*

(g) **Caesar or God?** In His response, the Savior apparently agrees with the Herodians in paying taxes to pagans! See footnote e above. This reveals a flash of divine wisdom as He throws these two groups into conflict with each other. If our Lord had told them to "give it to Caesar," all the Jews would have turned upon Him. If He had said, "Don't give to Caesar," then the spies present would have carried this as a suggestion of treason to Pilate. It is somewhat humorous that the Jews had a coin bearing a pagan image, and yet they fiercely opposed all such things! Where did they obtained the "cursed" piece of pagan money? Some think from the tables of the nearby moneychangers. He corrects their question "Is it lawful to give" with the profound reply "Render [give back] therefore to Caesar the things which are Caesar's; and unto God the things that are God's." It was firmly held by the rabbis that to accept the coinage of any king was to acknowledge his supremacy. Thus by accepting the coin, they were openly declaring that Caesar was their sovereign! Jesus responds with far weightier Words, "and to God the things that are God's." Here, our Lord clearly affirms that believers are to render tribute, custom, fear, and honor to whom it is due. Later, during the trial of Jesus, we hear these professional hypocrites shouting to Governor Pilate that Jesus was "forbidding to give tribute to Caesar" (Lk. 23:2). It was a misrepresentation of what He had said.

2p-Adam Clarke has given us a good interpretation of Christ's Words in his *Commentary* vol. 5. page 212. Regarding Christ's response, he wrote, "You [Jews] acknowledge this to be Caesar's coin; this coin is current, in your land; the currency of this coin shows the country to be under the Roman government; and you acknowledge that it is Caesar's, proves you have submitted. Don't, therefore, be unjust; but render to Caesar the things which you acknowledge to be his; at the same time, be not impious, but render unto God the things which belong to God." The Savior affirmed that God, and Caesar would retain what was theirs. He recognized both levels of divinely appointed authority in His response to these tricksters. First, God Almighty is supreme above all. The second authority is that of a legally constituted civil authority (Rom. 13:1-7). See the fourth paragraph below.

3p-To highly esteem the office of authority, be it council member, magistrates, member of the Senate or Congress. Government authority, military, local security, or police are both proper and honorable. Such acts are not inconsistent with our *highest reverence* and respect to God Almighty, His blessed Son, the Holy Spirit and the Scriptures, nor is subjection to civil magistrates sinful, wrong or idolatrous (Rom. 13:6-7 with 1 Peter 2:11-17). Christians are not commanded to honor a scoundrel who abuses any position of authority but to honor that office.

4p-**Laws and injustice.** Those who teach civil disobedience against duly appointed authorities should be publicly exposed and prosecuted. For more on this see Section 21, Part 2, fifth paragraph of footnote i. However, when any authority forbids men to worship God, serve Christ, love His Word, and correctly share this love to others, it is at this *single and exclusive* point they are to be disobeyed (Acts 5:17-18, 27-29). Communism has killed millions for the crime of loving God and His Son. Today, radical Islam wields a bloody sword of oppression, murder, and genocide upon all who will not confess, "Allah and Mohammed his prophet." Laws are passed that forbid the *free and orderly* exercise of the Christian faith. Mark Levin has exposed the abuse of judicial power in, *Men in Black: How the Supreme Court is Destroying America.* Meanwhile, sodomite judges strike down laws that forbid same sex marriage and assure us they are not prejudiced!

5p-**America's first whiskey distillery. America a Christian nation? Masonic emblems.** Among those who migrated here were people of many religious and political persuasions. There were freethinkers, atheists, infidels, agnostics, pantheists, humanists, deists, and a few Christians. *Paramount among the abominations of infant America was that of human slavery.* George Washington, the "father of our country," was a "Worshipful Master Mason." He built America's first whiskey distillery. Once, while addressing his troops, he encouraged them to "drink moderately." Masons planned the architecture of Washington D.C. according to their symbols. This does not make them bad men, but it does qualify them for a blue ribbon of ignorance. Regarding satanic symbols used by the lodge, see *Transcendental Magic: Its Doctrine and Ritual,* by Eliphas Levi and Arthur E. Waite. John Ankerberg and John Weldon provide a shocking look into the Masons in, *The Secret Teachings of the Masonic Lodge.* Thomas Jefferson, who drafted the Declaration of Independence, said the book of Revelation was "the ravings of a maniac," and that the "teachings of Jesus were full of imposture and stupidity." Benjamin Franklin, a sex manic, renounced the gospel as untrue. Jefferson, James Madison, and John Adams denied the deity of Christ, His virgin birth, and reliably of Scripture. Many of America's founding fathers were brilliant strategists and built the greatest political systems ever known. Sadly, most were without the saving knowledge of Christ. This did not hinder them from laying down guidelines for honorable government, but it failed them in death (John 15:5). The Constitution does not state that this country was founded on the Christian faith. It does not mention, "Jesus Christ, Bible, salvation, or God" except in the *"exclusionary"* conditions. The religious sentiments of its framers are recorded in Article, 6, section 3. It reads, "No religious test shall ever be required to any office or public trust under the United States." This offered equal citizenship to anyone, regardless of creed, color, or religion. *Wisely, the framers wanted to make sure that no religion could become the official state church as had occurred in Old England and Europe. This had resulted in the slaughter of thousands! They refused to go forward into the cruel past.* Acting under this Article 6, section 3 in 1782, Congress, in a gesture of good will had the Bible printed for use in schools and the legislature. Such an act today would bring a thousands lawsuits! The Great Awakenings of early America spanning loosely from 1734 through 1880, brought the salvation of many. It began with a Presbyterian minister Gilbert Tennant. Other believers became involved. Preacher Jonathan Edwards challenged the Puritans ruthless magisterial treatment of persons not of their persuasion. See sixth paragraph below. From Britain, George Whitefield appeared and through him, God spread awakening across the colonies. *From these people, not political cleverness came America's greatness.* "Righteousness exalteth a nation: but sin is a reproach to any people" (Prov. 14:34). Today, across America, wickedness, often protected by the court systems traduces divine things, proper constraints, and scorns the Bible. Godless politicians legislate, and godless teachers educate this country into legal immorality, and the grossest abominations of human evil. Gunshots ring out in church buildings, class rooms, and public forums while millions of babies are murdered by abortion (Prov. 6:17). See *"The majority vote flops"* discussed in Section 101, fifth paragraph of footnote b. Refer also to Section 129, second paragraph of footnote h for more on these thoughts.

6p-Not all Puritans were pure. The despised Baptists. In early America, Puritan *leaders* enforced their doctrinal views by coercion or death! For more on this, note Section 1, Part 3, second paragraph under footnote i. They brought this "convert them or kill them" demon spirit out of the Roman Catholic Church and the Reformers back in England and Europe. In 1660, they publicly hanged Mary Dyer in Boston, who objected to their ruthless policies. Fierce persecution fell especially on those wearing the name "Baptist." Earlier, Roger Williams had established America's first Baptist Church in Rhode Island in 1639. Baptist groups existed in Holland and England. They were fined, imprisoned, beaten, pelted, banished, burnt, and tormented in early America until religious freedom was legislated. Persecution of Baptists and other non-conformists came from the Calvinistic infected Puritans and Anglicans. It was enforced via the judicial systems, controlled by men who were members of the persecuting churches. The Baptists and their sympathizers championed the fight that resulted in religious freedom. In time, the "good old Puritans" and Anglicans killing their religious enemies (according to Moses' law!) succumbed, and sheathed their bloody swords. Many Calvinistic historians are oddly silent about these facts!

7p-Maryland Tolerance Act. In 1649, the Toleration Act (or Act Concerning Religious freedom) became law. Due to the growing number of Puritans, their political power, and barbarity in destroying those who would not subscribe to their beliefs, this Act afforded new (but not full) protection from these religious zealots. An extract from *Browne's Archives of Maryland,* I, 244-247 records this law and reads, "And whereas the enforcing of the conscience in matters of Religion hath frequently fallen out to be of dangerous consequence in those commonwealthes (sic) where it hath been practiced . . ." Because of the "dangerous consequence" of not bowing to heresy of the ruling churches, *The Toleration Act"* was finally passed by the assembly of the Province of Maryland. It gave freedom of worship for Christians in Maryland, who were not in sympathy with Puritan beliefs, but it sentenced to death anyone who denied the divinity of Christ! Men, who profess belief in the deity of Christ under the threat of death, do not believe in His deity. Perry G. E. Miller in, *Church History,* vol. 4, no. 1, pages 45-48, printed in 1935, records the details. Thomas O. Hanley in, *Their Rights and Liberties: The Beginnings of Religious and Political Freedom in Maryland,* covers this subject. *Croscup's United States History,* by George E. Croscup, pages 55-70, printed in 1911 also has very helpful information on *"The Tolerance Act."*

(h) "And went their way." Foiled again, these enemies of Christ walked away shamed at His reply to their chicanery. The plot to embarrass the Son of God recoiled upon their heads. Sullenly, they retire in total confusion. In Lk. 20:26 we read that "the people," or His audience present at this encounter with the Jews and Herodians marveled at His answer. The Messiah had just answered one of the most perplexing questions that had troubled pious Jews for years, "Should we pay taxes to foreign powers?" To their shock, He said "Yes."

2p-No fun in hell. Men of all ranks and learning contend with divine truth. In Isa. 50:8, God inquires, "Who will contend with me?" Meanwhile, national television shows vomit out ridicule and mockery of the Savior, while the crowds cheer and bark their approval like Pavlovian dogs. Relishing the filth of the average "late night talk- show," millions clap their way into hell. Five minutes with Jerry Springer reflects the dirt depravity of many Americans. To rebuke this trash publicly is a "hate crime," yet their vulgarity, filth, and blasphemy are acceptable. There is no cheering, dancing, and partying in hell. They "weary themselves to commit iniquity" (Jer. 9:5).

SECOND QUESTION:* WHAT ABOUT MARRIAGE IN HEAVEN?

In the previous Section, the Pharisees and Herodians were dumbfounded in their failed attempt to trap the Lord Jesus. Next, the Sadducees approach Him with their questions also seeking to lead Him into a contradiction. An honest scribe agrees with the Savior. Hearing His answer, the factious Jews are stunned into silence, fearful of debate with the Messiah any further.

Time: Tuesday after Palm Sunday before His death on Friday mid-afternoon.

Their third inquiry to entrap Him is located in the next Section 157. The first attempt is found in Section 155.

In the temple court

Matt. 22:23–28	Mk. 12:18–23	Lk. 20:27–33	John
Enter thou Sadducees	*Enter thou Sadducees*	*Enter thou Sadducees*	
23 The same day came to him the Sadducees, which say that there is no resurrection,(a) and asked him, 24 Saying,	18 Then come unto him the Sadducees, which say there is no resurrection;(a) and they asked him, saying,	27 Then came to *him* certain of the Sadducees, which deny that there is any resurrection;(a) and they asked him, 28 Saying,	
Their perfidious question	*Their perfidious question*	*Their perfidious question*	
"Master, Moses said,(b) 'If a man die, having no children, his brother shall marry his wife, and raise up seed unto his brother.'	19 "Master, Moses wrote unto us,(b) 'If a man's brother die, and leave *his* wife *behind him*, and leave no children, that his brother should take his wife, and raise up seed unto his brother.'	"Master, Moses wrote unto us,(b) 'If any man's brother die, having a wife, and he die without children, that his brother should take his wife, and raise up seed unto his brother.'	
25 "Now there were with us seven brethren: and the first, when he had married a wife, deceased, and, having no issue, left his wife unto his brother:	20 "Now there were seven brethren: and the first took a wife, and dying left no seed.	29 "There were therefore seven brethren: and the first took a wife, and died without children.	
26 "Likewise the second also, and the third, unto the seventh. 27 "And	21 "And the second took her, and died, neither left he any seed: and the third likewise. 22 "And the seven had her, and left no seed:	30 "And the second took her to wife, and he died childless. 31 "And the third took her; and in like manner the seven also: and they left no children, and died.	
last of all the woman died(c) also.	last of all the woman died(c) also.	32 "Last of all the woman died(c) also.	
Their ignorance of Scripture	*Their ignorance of Scripture*	*Their ignorance of Scripture*	
28 "Therefore in the resurrection(d) whose wife shall she be of the	23 In the resurrection(d) therefore, when they shall rise, whose wife shall she be of	33 "Therefore in the resurrection(d) whose wife of them is she?	

710

Matt. 22:28-33	Mk. 12:23-27	Lk. 20:33-40	John
seven? for they all had her."[(e)]	them? for the seven had her to wife."[(e)]	for seven had her to wife."[(e)]	
29 Jesus answered and said unto them,[(f)] "Ye do err, not knowing the scriptures, nor the power of God.	**24** And Jesus answering said unto them,[(f)] "Do ye not therefore err, because ye know not the scriptures, neither the power of God?	**34** And Jesus answering said unto them,[(f)]	
		His astounding answer "The children of this world marry, and are given in marriage:	
His astounding answer **30** "For	***His astounding answer*** **25** "For when they shall	**35** "But they which shall be accounted worthy to obtain that world, and the resurrection from the dead,	
in the resurrection they neither marry, nor are given in marriage,	rise from the dead, they neither marry, nor are given in marriage;	neither marry, nor are given in marriage: **36** "Neither can they die any more: for they are	
but are as the angels[(g)] of God in heaven.	but are as the angels[(g)] which are in heaven.	equal unto the angels;[(g)] and are the children of God, being the children of the resurrection.	
31 "But as touching the resurrection of the dead, have ye not read that which was spoken unto you by God, saying,[(h)]	**26** "And as touching the dead, that they rise: have ye not read in the book of Moses, how in the bush God spake unto him, saying,[(h)]	**37** "Now that the dead are raised, even Moses shewed at the bush, when he calleth the Lord[(h)]	
32 '**I *am* the God of Abraham, and the God of Isaac, and the God of Jacob?**' God is not the God of the dead, but of the living."[(i)]	'**I *am* the God of Abraham, and the God of Isaac, and the God of Jacob?**' **27** "He is not the God of the dead, but the God of the living:[(i)] ye therefore do greatly err." (Verse 28 cont. in Section 157.)	'**the God of Abraham, and the God of Isaac, and the God of Jacob.**' **38** "For he is not a God of the dead, but of the living:[(i)] for all live unto him."	
The audience amazed **33** And when the multitude heard *this*, they were astonished at his doctrine.[(j)] (Verse 34 cont. in Section 157.)			
		An honest scribe responds **39** Then certain of the scribes answering said, "Master, thou hast well said." **40** And after that they durst not ask him any *question at all*.[(k)] (Verse 41 cont. Section 158.)	

Footnotes-Commentary

(a) **"The same day."** Meaning the day when the Jews came and put to Him the question about paying tribute to Caesar. See this in Section 155. Matthew is careful to inform his readers that this next event he is reporting occurred "the same day" as did the previous encounters of Messiah with the Jews. No sooner had the defeated Pharisees, and Herodians walked off the verbal battlefield, then this group steps forward to engage Jesus in discussion. Here, the Sadducees return with another question for the Savior. For information on this group, see Section 100, second paragraph of footnote a, and Section 101, Matt. 16:6, number 2 under footnote b. All three evangelists state that the Sadducees did not believe in the resurrection. The heresy and doctrinal untruths of the Sadducees lives on today in the Jehovah's Witness and Seventh Day Adventist cults; both deny the separation of the soul from the body at death and the eternal conscious suffering of the damned in the afterlife. The Pharisees believed in life after death and taught that in the resurrection, the woman would be the wife of her first husband. One can feel that the Sadducees brought this question to Christ in order to throw Him into doctrinal conflict with the Pharisees.

(b) Their quotation comes from the Torah Law in Deut. 25:5. The meaning of this odd passage is that children produced by this kind of marriage were to be reckoned in the genealogy of the deceased brother and were to enjoy the benefits of his estate left at death. This kind of union was commonly known as a "levirate" marriage. This term comes from the Latin term "levir," meaning "a brother-in-law." Joachim Jeremias, in *Jerusalem in the Time of Jesus*, pages 92-94, 371-376, documents these and other marriage practices among the Jews at this time in history. He shows that polygamy was practiced among the wealthier Jews and generally explains the state of women in this era. His history is excellent; his theology is a disaster being void of Jesus Christ the Savior. In modern day Israel, if a wife cannot bear children or is mentally ill, the rabbis give the husband the right to marry another woman without divorcing the first one. This seems to be a revised version of the old levirate marriage.

(c) Among the thousands of Jewish legends, there was the story of a woman named Sarah, who had been married to a succession of seven brothers. Edersheim in *Life and Times of Jesus the Messiah*, pages 750-751, briefly discusses this story. He wrote that such a thing might "have really happened." The rabbis had decreed that if a woman had two husbands in this life, she would only have the first one in the life to come. See F. W. Farrar's, *Life of Christ*, page 561 for more interesting background and details.

(d) **"In the resurrection." Marriage in heaven.** They vehemently denied there would be such an event! Josephus wrote in *Antiquities,* Book 18:1. 4, lines 16-17 that the Sadducees held the soul died with the physical body, and that there was no such thing as the punishment of those in hell. The question put to Jesus was ludicrous and impossible according to their theology. It was an interrogative of evil intent.

(e) The men of wealth and high position in the temple priesthood, the powerful Sadducees, felt they had presented the unanswerable question to Jesus of Nazareth. The rabbis taught that if a woman had two husbands in this life, she would have the first only in the life to come. Christ corrects their ignorance from Holy Scripture.

(f) **"Ye do err, not knowing the Scriptures, nor the power of God."** *What a stinging rebuke!* The Savior responded to their arrogant and conceited dilemma with a devastating reply: one that put them into a corner with their own confusion. The Sadducees prided themselves as being better informed in the Torah Scriptures than anyone in Israel. Messiah's response opens the gates of paradise and gives honest hearts a brief glimpse of the conditions of eternity. Childish questions from men of religion have always emanated from their ignorance of Holy Scripture. The Sadducees erred "not knowing the scriptures, [Old Testament] nor the power of God." We are challenged by these Words of Christ to return to the Bible and the divine power that is beyond the works of human flesh.

2p-How interesting it is to note that our Lord appealed to the Scripture as the final authority in questions of life, death, and eternity. His answer was from God's Word in the Old Testament. In His opinion, that settled the matter. Today, "men of religion" have greatly departed from this divine source and thus mislead those who inquire for heavenly direction. After His resurrection, the Savior continued to adhere to the Scripture as His authority. See Section 201, Lk. 24:44, and attached side note indicated by the ◄ symbol. It is noticed that the Son of God found the basis for the resurrection in the Old Testament, while many present day "Bible scholars" deny this truth. During His temptation, at the beginning of His public ministry, the Lord Jesus used only the Word of God and the Holy Spirit to thwart the devices of Satan. The best of flesh and blood (if such ever existed) could not handle this!

(g) **"Are as the angels of God in heaven."** These Words of Christ afford all men (who are interested) a peek into the intriguing mystery of the world to come. It is noted that He spoke of a single "resurrection to come," not plural as of several resurrections, however, Dr. Luke seems to distinguish for us that there will be more than one resurrection. In Lk. 20:35 he wrote, "But they which shall be accounted worthy to obtain that world, and the resurrection from the dead ..." This cannot mean that those unworthy will not be resurrected! Hence, we have here the confirmation of a different resurrection for the saved and lost. The ignorance of the Sadducees is seen in their supposing that if there were a resurrection, then men and women must afterwards marry as they do in this life. The things of human life cannot measure the things of eternity. *Only a speck of eternity's story has been given.*

2p-Christ uses "equal" or "as angels," to inform men that those in the first resurrection (of the righteous) shall be as angels *in the sense* that they will be elevated above the conditions of human mortality like the holy angels. In the declaration "neither do they die," we learn that physical death is not a part of that heavenly spiritual world. Therefore, the propagation of the human race is unnecessary through the divinely appointed means of earthly marriage. Amid the everlasting eons of eternity, the saved of all ages will be immortal and free from all human passions of earth's flesh. In that glorious heaven (where pure love remains) beyond death and the grave, all the brief earthliness of the human experience is superseded. All things over there are transfigured into the glory of God Himself! The failing frailty of all human relationships will be transfigured into such ineffable majesty, that it is against the divine law to talk about them (2 Cor. 12:4). Some enjoy asking, "Where does the Bible say we have an immortal soul?" It states in 1 Tim. 1:17 that God is "immortal." However, His exclusive immortality dwells in a light that no earthly human can approach or see (1 Tim. 6:16). Whatever the soul of man is, it is that inward part, that carries the imagery of God in eternal substance and being. While the outward body perishes the inward man lives on; thus, we look at the invisible which endures forever (2 Cor. 4:16-18). Abraham had been dead some two thousand years, yet he was alive in eternity according to the teaching of Jesus (Lk. 16:22-25). Whatever heaven is, it will be wonderful because Jesus is there, and we will be *like Him* (Phil. 3:20-21; Ps. 16:11; and 1 John 3:2). For continued comments on heaven, see Section 38, third paragraph of footnote o. All the fuss from end time experts about the differences in our bodies and lives in the millennium and eternity are more guessing speculations.

(h) A quote from Ex. 3:6. The Sadducees held that only the five books of Moses called the Torah Law was the Word of God. Jesus answers them from their own source instead of other Old Testament verses proving the resurrection, such as Job 19:26 and Dan. 12:2. He charges them with ignorance of what they swore to believe!

(i) The grave and soul sleep. Messiah interprets His quotation from Scripture for the unbelieving Sadducees. He affirms that Moses' experience at the burning bush, some fifteen hundred years prior, reveals that when men die, they do not cease to exist. Only their physical bodies die. God speaking to Moses from the bush declared that He was the God of Abraham, Isaac, and Jacob. At the time, He spoke these Words the three patriarchs had been dead hundreds of years; yet, God affirms that He was still their God! The Eternal One would not introduce Himself as the God of dust, annihilated souls, or the long ago decayed bodies of these three men. God is the God of the living; therefore, Abraham, Isaac, and Jacob were dead only in their physical bodies, which had returned to dust. They continued to live in eternity, and God was their Lord. Jesus refutes the heresy of the Sadducees, the lies of annihilation, and soul sleep after death. This may explain the Talmud saying in tractate, Bereachoth 4a, "The righteous in their death exist in the land of the living." In 1855, Thomas B. Thayer, a chief promoter of the doctrine of no endless retribution for sins, wrote *The Origin and History of the Doctrine of Endless Punishment.* In Section I and II of this heretical work, he affirmed that nowhere in the Old Testament did Moses or anyone else mention life after death. Thayer missed God's Word to Abraham. It reads, "and thou shalt go to thy fathers in peace" (Gen. 15:15). When Abraham died, Moses wrote, "and [he] was gathered to his people" (Gen. 25:8). This cannot mean burial of a corpse with deceased family members in a common grave. Abraham's family ancestors were interred in a distant foreign country. His father was buried in Haran (Gen. 11:32) over three hundred miles northeast. Other family members were buried in Ur of Babylon (Josh. 24:2) Therefore, this means something more than burial of a dead body in a grave. It has reference to a common gathering place for the departed dead, and it was not the grave. Jacob lamented, "I will go down into the grave [sheol] unto my son [Joseph] mourning" (Gen. 37:35). He believed wild beasts had devoured his son (Gen. 37:29-33). He could not have meant a common grave for burial of the dead. The famed Bishop William Warburton (died 1779) and his predecessors were seriously wrong when they wrote that the Scriptures do not speak of a future abode for the soul of man after death. Men of the Old Testament believed in a life after death as well as those of the New Testament. For more on this, see Section 89, footnote p. Soul sleep is a doctrine of demons (1 Tim. 4:1). It began among pagans, and then crept into churches through the church fathers, the radical Anabaptist, and others. Paul's words to "die is gain" (Phil. 1:21) are hardly compatible with soul sleep.

(j) "Not the God of the dead." See footnote i above for the meaning of this statement. Repeatedly, the Savior astonished the crowds by His supreme exegesis of their Old Testament. The Sadducees were so put to shame that they dared not approach the Lord Jesus any more with their loaded questions. Yet, the stubborn Pharisees were not deterred. In the following Section, they send one of their Torah specialists to the Savior with another trick question seeking to entangle Him in some doctrinal or moral contradiction. On this attempt, the trickster was convinced that Jesus spoke the truth and agreed with Him!

(k) No more questions. This has reference to the Sadducees. Only the Son of God could have silenced these evil men, and He did so by quoting to them from the very Scripture they boasted in knowing better than all other Jews. After the citation, He gave Ex. 3:6, with its correct interpretation and application. The Sadducees were dumbfounded at His skillful handling of God's Word. They quickly withdrew from a further debate on the subject of the resurrection. This does not mean that the Sadducees put no further questions to Jesus, for later, during His trial, numerous questions were asked. Caiaphas, the high priest who directed the interrogation of Christ was also a member of the Sadducees. His first question to Jesus is in Section 181, Matt. 26:63, "Are you the Messiah?"

THIRD QUESTION: WHAT IS THE GREATEST COMMANDMENT?

A Pharisee who was a scribe of the Torah Law questions the Savior. Christ answers, and surprisingly, he agrees. Whoever this man was, our Lord said that he was near to entering* God's kingdom or being saved.

Time: Tuesday after Palm Sunday before His death on Friday mid-afternoon.

*Only the credulous could believe that this man was ready to enter into a literal, political, and physical Jewish kingdom existing on earth at that time or would exist thousands of years in the future. See footnote g below.

In the temple court

Matt. 22:34–40	Mk. 12:28–33	Lk.	John
The religious leaders regroup **34** But when the Pharisees had heard that he had put the Sadducees to silence, they were gathered together. *Another trick question* **35** Then one of them, *which was* a lawyer,[(a)] (or scribe) asked *him a question,* tempting him, and saying, **36** "Master, which *is* the great commandment in the law?"[(b)] *The Savior's response* **37** Jesus said unto him,[(c)] **"Thou shalt love the Lord thy God with all thy heart, and with all thy soul, and with all thy mind.'** **38** "This is the first and great commandment. **39** "And the second *is* like unto it,[(d)] **'Thou shalt love thy neighbour as thyself.'** **40** "On these two commandments hang all the law and the prophets."[(e)] (Verse 41 cont. in Section 158.)	*Another trick question* **28** And one of the scribes[(a)] came, and having heard them reasoning together, and perceiving that he had answered them well, asked him, "Which is the first commandment of all?"[(b)] *The Savior's response* **29** And Jesus answered him, "The first of all the commandments *is,*[(c)] **'Hear, O Israel; The Lord our God is one Lord:** **30** **'And thou shalt love the Lord thy God with all thy heart, and with all thy soul, and with all thy mind, and with all thy strength:'** this *is* the first commandment. **31** "And the second *is* like, *namely* this,[(d)] **Thou shalt love thy neighbour as thyself.'** There is none other commandment greater than these."[(e)] *The inquiring scribe approves Jesus' response* **32** And the scribe said unto him, "Well, Master, thou hast said[(f)] the truth: for there is one God; and there is none other but he: **33** "And to love him with all the heart, and with all the under- standing, and with all the soul, and with all the strength, and to love *his* neighbour as himself, is more than		

Matt.	Mk. 12:33-34	Lk.	John
It is impossible that the Savior was▶ *speaking of His glorified rule over two thousand years in the future. His spiritual kingdom was then and there, not future. This Pharisee doctor of the Torah Law was close to salvation and thus becoming a member in Christ's spiritual kingdom.*	all whole burnt offerings and sacrifices." ***The scribe almost persuaded.*** ***The Jews are silenced for the time being*** **34** And when Jesus saw that he answered discreetly, he said unto him, "Thou art not far from the kingdom of God."(g) And no man after that durst ask him *any question.* (h) (Verse 35 cont. in Section 158.)		

Footnotes-Commentary

(a) **The lawyer's question.** Whoever this fellow was, he had listened to Christ's response to the Sadducees' question regarding the resurrection and knew the Savior had spoken the irrefutable truth to these men (Mk. 12:28). Seemingly, his *original* inquiry contained ill intentions. However, after hearing our Lord's answer, he reflected another side of his character. It is noted that Matthew called him "a lawyer" while Mark describes him as "one of the scribes." *They were both the same.* In verse 32, after hearing Christ's response, he suddenly agreed that the right answer had been given.

2p-*Clarke's Commentary,* vol. 5, page 214, quotes from Dr. William Wotton (died in 1726), who demonstrated in one of his works that this man was a member of a unique Jewish sect known as the Karaites that existed among the Pharisees in the days of Jesus. As teachers of the law, they were also called scribes. Like the Sadducees, they fiercely rejected the oral law or tradition of the elders, defending only the written Word and were often called "letter men." (The Sadducees did not do the latter.) Being thus, they held more strongly to the literal meaning of the Torah and the prophets. Karaites believed in a broad and more *practical* application of Scripture: rather, a "do the truth," instead of "talk about it." In addition, this very point is clearly reflected in his response to Jesus' message as recorded in Mk. 12:32-34. See footnote f below for other comments on this Jewish authority. For a helpful article on the Karaites, see the *Biblical, Theological, and Ecclesiastical Cyclopaedia,* vol. v, pages 17-18, by M'Clintock and Strong.

(b) **The greatest commandment.** It has been pointed out in this harmony commentary that the rabbinical schools had divided the Torah Law into various divisions. Refer to Section 52, footnote h, Section 89, footnote c, and Section 96, footnote d for further explanation. They went so far as to name some commandments as being "heavy" (or binding) and others "light" (not so binding). The religious leaders at this time put the greater stress on the oral law to the demise and degrading of the Torah given by God on Mt. Sinai. This man's question dealt with the "great" or "first commandment" of the Torah and reflects typical Jewish divisions of the law. It was this scribal chopping up and dividing of the Torah Law of God that Jesus opposed. For more on this, see footnote c below.

(c) Quoted from Deut. 6:5. The Lord Jesus repeated to him the beloved "Shema," which every Jew was compelled to repeat in his devotions and, which was to be always on his lips and in his heart. It was a deep expression of his faith in the God of Israel. Every synagogue in the nation began by the recitation of "Hear, O Israel; the Lord our God is one Lord." It is noteworthy that Jesus refrained from the rabbinical approach by using such terms as the "smaller," "heavier," or "lighter" parts of the law. Correctly speaking, there were no such divisions according to James 2:10-11. The Torah was one complete unit and to break one of its 613 commandments was as though all had been broken! However, He does place things in priority order by the words "first and great commandment." The Jews were continually toying with the Torah Law. The rabbinical schools, in their meddling, carnal, superficial spirit of word weaving, and letter-worship, had created large accumulations of worthless subtlety over the Mosaic code. Among other things, they attempted to count, classify, weigh, and measure all separate commandments of the ceremonial and moral law. They failed to see Him to whom all the law and prophets gave witness, Jesus of Nazareth, their promised Messiah (John 5:45-47 with Acts 10:43).

(d) Regarding the number one command of God, our Lord hinges it onto Lev. 19:18 translated here, "Thou shalt love thy neighbor as thyself." Every pious Hebrew was familiar with this text but had been taught that his neighbor was another Hebrew *only*, never a Gentile. The ancient Jews held God as the first cause of everything in their daily lives. To love God with all the faculties of soul and body as stated above in Matt. 22:37 and Mk. 12:30, is to please His great Heart. A human life that springs from pure love lives forever: it is like an eternity without end. Even better than this nice Jewish philosophy, is a soul saved by grace, filled with the indwelling Spirit and bearing His first fruit (Gal. 5:22). One thoughtful reading of 1 Cor. 13 stabs our hearts with conviction. All the preaching today about "obedience" is upside down. *Men continually obey God without loving Him, but they cannot love him without obeying.* The night before the morning of the cross, our Lord gave His eleven apostles a "new commandment" that is similar to this one. Refer to Section 172, John 13:35, second paragraph of footnote o.

(e) **"All the law and prophets."** This was a well-known Jewish expression. Christ was not teaching that some commandments were of greater importance and others lesser (as did the rabbis). Rather, He taught that the entire Torah flowed from these two: first, love for God, and second, love for our neighbor. Any devout Jew seeking to follow God by following the Torah Law would soon discover that its precepts and commands pointed them to the coming Messiah and Savior of Israel (John 5:46 with Acts 10:43). The moral beauty of the Mosaic code faded into insignificance when standing before the superior ethical teachings of Christ's new kingdom. Every noble command it carried called for all readers to "look ahead for Messiah is coming with instructions higher and holier than those of the law." See main heading under Section 45, for six examples of this truth. Some ten years after Jesus said this, James quoted part of Jesus' Words about loving one's neighbor (James 2:8-11). He then proceeded to tell believers within the twelve tribes scattered abroad that if they try to keep the "Royal" Hebrew law and break only one point, they are guilty of breaking it all! In other words, James was saying to his legally entangled readers about the code of Moses, "It is all or nothing at all." Rabbis called their law "Royal." The numerous law cults operating as Christians, keeping the Sabbath, observing the seven feasts of Israel, have unwittingly laid upon themselves the burden of fulfilling all the 613 parts of the Torah Law. These people step over this by dividing the law into three different sections, then selecting the division they think they should live by! These three parts are the moral, civil, and ceremonial laws. All law cult prisoners boast that they live by the moral code of Moses' Law, but (oddly) disregard the punishment for breaking any of them. For a review of this subject, refer to Section 45, footnote b.

(f) So heavenly was our Lord's answer to this scribe, for a moment, he swayed toward truth and eternal life. For a professional lawyer or scribe to confess that the love of God and man was more than "all whole burnt offerings and sacrifices" signaled his entire mind set had gone through some great change. *However, as stated, it is well to remember that in rabbinic theology, the only neighbor of a Jew was another Jew, never a Gentile.* Ancient Hebrew writings reflected their hatred of Gentiles. Several examples are as follows. The Talmud tractate, Sanhedrin 57a reads, "When a Jew murders a Gentile [Cuthean], there is no death penalty." Sanhedrin 58b declares, "If a heathen [Gentile] hits a Jew, he is worthy of death." For more on other shocking statements found in the Hebrew Talmud, see Section 6, the third paragraph of footnote d.

2p-One cannot but wonder what became of this honest scribe who companioned among such religious hypocrites and yet was so close to the kingdom of God. It would be wonderful to meet him in heaven some day! See footnote a above for more on this honest Jewish theologian.

(g) **"Not far from the kingdom."** What touching Words from our Lord! He who came to seek and save the lost, and befriended all willing sinners, now, speaks a Word of hope to one from the camp of His most hateful enemies. See Section 84, third paragraph of footnote b for Jerusalem's "Lost and found stone." This fellow was "not far from the kingdom of God." As stated under the main heading above, who could believe that Jesus was speaking of a literal kingdom to come over two thousand years later and that this man was not far from it! Such a proposal is absurd. For explanation of the kingdom in its different aspects, see Section 39, footnotes a and g. Christ's new kingdom or church was *then and there*, a present entity though in its infant stages. A few hours earlier, He had spoken similar Words regarding publicans and harlots being near His kingdom in Section 152, Matt. 21:32, third paragraph of footnote f. The kingdom Jesus spoke of was a present reality into which men could enter by faith.

2p-**The willing Savior.** Observe how readily the Savior received this man from corrupted Jewish religion. He did not fall into debate and argument. (See His later rebuke of the Hebrew hypocrites in Section 159.) Here, was a soul, lost, and without eternal hope, yet he was honest when confronted with truth (Mk. 12:34). These are the kind of people Jesus came to save (Lk. 19:10 with 1 Tim. 1:15). *True* Christians must stand like strong trees reaching out with many branches to those who are lost without Christ. It is our work to help all we can, even our enemies when the opportunity affords itself (Matt. 5:43-48). Religion without the Son of God has created more problems than could be written in the skies above. On the other hand, churches that claim the Son of God as their Savior, but dishonor His name, live like pious devils, and bring reproach on God's work, are also enemies of the gospel. They must be exposed for what they are; poor unconverted, hell bound church members, void of God's true saving grace. For more on the curse of church hypocrites, especially among liberal Baptists, see Section 32, the third paragraph of footnote b. The Lord needs no man to help Him, but in mercy has chosen to use us as we make ourselves restfully available for His service.

(h) This means that Jesus had no more questions put to Him at this particular time. Again, He foiled the stratagems of these religious hypocrites. It does not mean that they never questioned Him again. Later, we read that the Sanhedrin fiercely interrogated Christ during His several trials before the crucifixion. An example of this is in Section 182, Lk. 22:66-71.

JESUS QUESTIONS THE PHARISEES ABOUT MESSIANIC PROPHECY.

If the religious leaders had correctly answered this inquiry, it would have demonstrated from their Old Testament Scriptures that Jesus was the Messiah.* They did not respond to His question realizing they would have trapped themselves.

Time: Tuesday after Palm Sunday before His death on Friday mid-afternoon.

*It is conjecture from Matt. 22:46 that in this Section, the Lord Jesus concluded His debate with the religious leaders over the questions regarding His Messiahship and deity. The syntax and tenor of the next Section reveals that He turned full attention to the people that were present listening to His debates and preaching. In Section 159, He pronounces terrible judgments upon the religious Jews, their city, temple, and state. See Matt. 23:1 with Lk. 20:45-47, and note the words "multitude," "all the people," and "his disciples," who were present to hear His shocking Words of doom. Standing there listening to His stinging denunciations were the scribes, Pharisees, and their companions in hatred of Jesus of Nazareth, the Son of God. Soon, they would be screaming for His death.

In the temple court

Matt. 22:41–46	Mk. 12:35–37	Lk. 20:41–44	John
He questions the Jews[a] **41** While the Pharisees were gathered together, Jesus asked them, **42** Saying,[b] "What think ye of Christ? [Messiah] whose son is he?" They say unto him, "*The son of David.*" **43** He saith unto them, "How then doth David[c] in ▶**S**pirit call him 'Lord,' saying, **44** 'The LORD said unto my Lord, "Sit thou on my right hand, till I make thine enemies thy footstool?" ' **45** "If David then call him 'Lord,' how is he His son?"[e] ***The Jews cannot answer*** **46** And no man was able to answer him a word, neither durst any *man* from that day forth ask him any more questions.[f] (Next chap., Matt. 23:1 cont. in Section 159.)	 ***He questions the Jews***[a] **35** And Jesus answered and said,[b] while he taught in the temple, "How say the scribes that Christ [Messiah] is the son of David? **36** "For David himself said[d] by the Holy Ghost, 'The LORD said to my Lord, "Sit thou on my right hand, till I make thine enemies thy footstool." ' **37** "David therefore himself calleth him 'Lord;' and whence is he *then* his son?"[e] ***Ordinary people heard Him*** And the common people heard him gladly.[g] (Verse 38 cont. in Section 159.)	***He questions the Jews***[a] **41** And he said unto them,[b] "How say they that Christ [Messiah] is David's son? **42** "And David himself saith[d] in the book of Psalms, "The LORD said unto my Lord, "Sit thou on my right hand, **43** 'Till I make thine enemies thy footstool." ' **44** "David therefore calleth him 'Lord,' how is he then his son?"[e] (Verse 45 cont. in Section 159.) ▶*Above in Matt. 22:43, the underlined letter "S" has been changed into uppercase. It is speaking of the Holy Spirit as seen in Mark verse 36. This was a typesetter's or proof reader's error and has nothing to do with divine inspiration. It is also lowercase in the original version of the KJV 1611 Bible.*	

Footnotes-Commentary

(a) As the Pharisees regrouped, the Lord Jesus takes occasion of this gathering of His greatest enemies and puts to them several questions of His own. Skeptics have smiled at the idea of hundreds gathering anywhere in the temple to hear the Lord Jesus preach and teach. Josephus said that some of the temple courts alone could hold up to six thousand people at any given time. See, F. W. Farrar's *The Life of Christ*, footnote 1, page 569. The gigantic Solomon's porch could accommodate innumerable crowds at any given time.

(b) **"What are your views about the Messiah?"** This is what Jesus was asking. The small difference in the wording of this first question means nothing. Each writer was inspired to put down what he put down. Here, was one of the most important and familiar subjects in all Jewish theology: the Person, and descent of their Messiah. Amid the many diversities of rabbinical opinion, it was agreed that Messiah would enter the world through the line of Abraham, federal head of their nation, and King David their most popular king. This subject has been profusely discussed in chapter 3. For details, refer to Section 5, under the various footnotes in the vertical left hand column. Our Lord's questions and their answers revealed they knew their Messiah would descend from David's family line. Among Orthodox Jews, this was clearly acknowledged as seen in Section 119, John 7:42. Hence, the reason He is often spoken of as the "Son of David" during His ministry. For an example of this, refer to Section 66, Matt. 12:23, footnote b. Their answer was orderly and according to their Scriptures, yet they were blind to the meaning. Jesus of Nazareth was the "son of David," but was more than just a natural or physical seed. Since David called Him "Lord," that means, He is God-equal or God Himself. *Jews when referring to spiritual matters would only call Jehovah their Lord and no one else.* See footnote d and e below for more on this thought.

2p-What most men think of Jesus. In the ordinary experiences of mankind, objects nearby attract the affections most strongly. To the human imagination, distant things often lend to enchantment, especially if they are partly cloaked in mystery. However, the truest and deepest affections of the heart fix their strongest hold on those with whom we are near and converse most familiarly. How true was this with the Lord Jesus as He moved among human society. In the simple narratives of His life as recorded in the four gospels, we stand near Him. We trace His daily course among men of every rank, going about, doing good, and healing all oppressed of the Devil. His Words are true; His character so noble and lofty that we bare and bow our heads in shame to know that He came to rescue and save us sinful mortals. We see Him as the affectionate brother and friend, weeping for others, even His foes. Bearing the awful title, "a man of sorrows and acquainted with grief," He reached out to every concerned human in His path of service. All of His heartaches were ours; His tears were for others. Amid the unspeakable pain of the crucifixion, He prays for His tormentors, pardons a thief, and requests a disciple to care for His broken mother. Long meditation upon this unparallel scene of filial love, moves us to many tears, and prolonged weeping. Who among normal men can contemplate the life, death, and resurrection of Jesus Christ without falling on his face and pleading for divine pardon. The heavens have taken Him out of human sight, but His presence in the Holy Spirit is with us forever. This is but a "grain of sand description" of what we think of Christ. If, like the unsaved critics, we should remove from the gospels any mention of Jesus, we would have committed a most unholy abomination.

(c) **Verse 43. "David . . . call him Lord."** Christ inquires of the Jews how this belief of theirs was consistent with what David wrote in Ps. 110, where he called the Messiah "My [his] Lord" and did this in the power of the Holy Spirit. How could Messiah be David's Son and Lord? Could Abraham have called Isaac, Jacob, or any of his descendants near or remote, his lord? If not, how could David do this? There was one answer: that Son would be divine, not just human only. Thus, He was David's Lord, the promised Messiah, who came into the world through the family line of King David. It was deity and divinity that David recognized, not humanity. Refer to the second paragraph of footnote d below for more on this thought.

(d) **"Spirit."** The Spirit of God should always be in uppercase as it has reference to supreme deity. Verse 36 confirms that the "Spirit" David was "in," was the Holy Ghost. This needed grammatical correction has nothing to do with inspiration, but is rather a typesetters or proofreaders oversight. In verse 44 and parallels, our Lord cites from Ps. 110:1. This is the most frequently quoted Old Testament passage in the entire New Testament. Why do the inspired writers use it so much? One thousand years before the birth of Jesus, David inspired by God looked into the future and saw His Messiah-Savior stepping into His Father's presence after His earthly work was completed at His ascension. God the Father greets the Son with these Words of triumph "Sit thou on my right hand, till I make thine enemies thy footstool." In the temple at Jerusalem, the priests could not sit for their work was never ended. David (by the Holy Spirit) looked into the distant future, saw Christ enter heaven, and sit at God's right hand, thus signaling that His work of atonement for the sins of the world was completed forever. We read that there "remaineth no more sacrifice for sins" (Heb. 10:26). The sweet psalmist of Israel saw His Messiah enter "once into the holy place, having obtained eternal redemption for us" (Heb. 9:12). Further, David heard and recorded the Father's "welcome home" to the Son. Being instructed to sit at His right hand, signals Jesus has satisfactorily completed what God appointed Him to do on earth. Now, He has been given the highest position of honor thus taking up His *eternal priesthood*. For more on this, note Section 207, footnote b.

2p-The rabbis considered the entirety of Ps. 110 as Messianic. In verse 1, we note that the first LORD has His Name spelt in uppercase letters, while the second Lord is lowercase. This reveals great diligence in translating God's Word. The capital LORD speaks of Jehovah, while the lowercase Lord speaks of His divine Son or Adonai. Most new translations of the Bible have dropped out this inspired distinction. In Mk. 12:36 Jesus said that David had this glorious vision "by the Holy Ghost." *Thus, we see all three Persons of the divine Trinity presented in these verses.*

(e) Messiah. David's Lord, (Savior), and Son." In Ps. 110, David (a descendent of Abraham) acknowledged that the second Lord about whom he wrote was also his Lord. Thus, Christ inquired of the Jews "How could he do this?" Their greatest of all kings would never call anyone Lord, unless it was Jehovah God. *Matthew Henry's Commentary,* vol. 5, page 264 carries a profound note on this. It reads, "He did not thereby design to ensnare them, as they did him, but to instruct them in a truth, they were loath to believe—that the expected Messiah is God." The fact that Jesus was to descend to men on earth through David's family line making Him a "son of David" from the genealogical and human point of view pales into insignificance. Greater is the truth that He is David's God and David called Him this in the Psalm. In a lesser sense, He is David's Son because He came into the world through Mary, who was of the house of David (Section 9, Lk. 1:26-33). David knew Messiah was both Lord and God and worshiped Him as such, even though he entered the world via his family tree. Refer to footnote c above for more on this subject. *Upon hearing the response of Jesus, the Pharisees suddenly realized the trap into which they had fallen. They refused to answer the Savior.*

2p-In a unique sense, Mary, Jesus' mother experienced similar things with Christ being both her son and Savior. Note her words in Section 10, Lk. 1:47, where "God is her Saviour." Our Jewish friends, who only regard Messiah as the son of the line of David, are regarding the lesser part, which is the conception of His human frame. O, how they should consider the Person that dwelt within that mortal house of clay! He is their Messiah. This, the Pharisees and their colleagues in religion refused to do, and they writhe in hell at this present moment.

(f) With this, the persistent "question attacks" upon the Lord Jesus by the hostile Pharisees are ended. (It is noted that the Savior had earlier silenced the Sadducees, in Section 156, Lk. 20:40, footnote k.)

2p-If these religious leaders had answered His question in verse 45 (as He had answered theirs), they would have confessed that He was indeed the promised Messiah and Savior of Israel. It is clear in Ps. 110 that the One who reigns over God's great kingdom, setting at His right hand, was David's Lord and not merely a person of royal descent. Therefore, this reigning One would be greater than David would, and to this, the psalmist joyfully gave acquiesces. Several weeks later, Peter quoted this very Psalm while preaching to the crowds at Pentecost. *In Acts 2:29-36, he dogmatically affirmed that Jesus of Nazareth was the Lord of David's Psalm, and that He is now seated at God's right hand as "both Lord and Christ [Messiah]" (verse 36). Add to this the words of Ps. 110:4, which affirms that He is also our eternal high priest, after the order of Melchizedek.* Thus, according to Peter, Jesus upon return to the Father's house was given the honored seat at God's right hand. From here, He is *both* our spiritual King and spiritual eternal high priest forever. This does not cancel the fact that in time to come, He will rule in some glorified way over the redeemed of Israel as *both* their spiritual and literal King. Such promises to Israel as those recorded in Ezek. 37:21-28 can in no way be spiritualized and applied to the church. The author of this harmony commentary does not profess to know all the fine details of this mystery but believes this is taught in Holy Scripture. For more on the subject of Christ and the redeemed of Israel at the consummation of the ages, see Section 207, footnote b.

3p-In 1990, the Messianic Jew, Dr. Renald E. Showers, of The Friends of Israel Gospel Ministry Inc. produced an excellent book giving a brief history of the various eschatological views. It is titled, *There Really is a Difference!* He briefly traces dispensationalism from the radical church father, Clement of Alexander (died A.D. 220) to the heretic Augustine (died A.D. 430). Showers is to be saluted for his outright honesty when he wrote on page 27 this truth, "It must be said, however, that these Church leaders did not develop these recognized principles into a system of thought. They were not Dispensational Theologians." In places, his work is off balance by his over-literal dispensationalism. Nevertheless, it is a helpful book in tracing the growth of so-called covenant theology. Further, on pages 27-29, Showers gives an excellent but concise history to the early rise and growth of dispensationalism up to John Darby, C. I. Scofield, and the Presbyterian minister who espoused it so strongly, Dr. James H. Brookes of St. Louis, Missouri.

(g) Over the course of Christian history, it has always been the same. The everyday, normal individual is usually the one who *first* gladly hears the good news of Jesus Christ. Rarely does one hear of kings, heads of state, presidents, or the rich and famous praising the Savior. The reason for their silence is obvious. These people are unsaved and thus dwelling in darkness regarding things of eternal value. For the stirring testimony of a rich and famous person coming to the saving knowledge of Christ, see the book *To Hell and Back,* by the well-known heart surgeon, Dr. Maurice S. Rawlings.

Publicly, Jesus warns the people about their religious leaders. He pronounces upon them eight terrible woes. They are hypocrites and cursed of God. He laments Jerusalem's fate, and the desolation of her magnificent temple.

Jesus delivers a public denunciation of the hypocritical religious leaders. Such a scathing rebuke of Israel's spiritual peers was unheard of. His Words in Matthew verses 13–38 came to pass in A.D. 70. Section 162 carries His last warning to Israel. Her fate is described in Section 163.

Time: Tuesday after Palm Sunday before His death on Friday mid–afternoon.

In the temple court

Matt. 23:1-6	Mk. 12:38-39	Lk. 20:45-46	John
Marks of hypocrisy **1** Then spake[(a)] Jesus to the multitude, and to his disciples, **2** Saying, "The scribes and the Pharisees sit in Moses' seat:[(b)] **3** "All therefore whatsoever they bid you observe,[(c)] *that* observe and do; but do not ye after their works: for they say, and do not. **4** "For they bind heavy burdens[(d)] and grievous to be borne, and lay *them* on men's shoulders; but they *themselves* will not move them with one of their fingers. **5** "But all their works[(e)] they do for to be seen of men: they make broad their phylacteries, and enlarge the borders of their garments,	*Marks of hypocrisy* **38** And he said[(a)] unto them in his doctrine, "Beware of the scribes,	*Marks of hypocrisy* **45** Then in the audience of all the people he said[(a)] unto his disciples, **46** Beware of the scribes,	
6 "And love the ►uppermost rooms [places] at feasts, and the chief seats◄ in the synagogues, ►*Matthew places the "uppermost rooms" before the chief seats. Mark and Luke reverse the order.*	which love to go in long clothing, and *love* salutations in the marketplaces, **39** "And the chief seats◄ in the synagogues, and the uppermost rooms [places] at feasts:	which desire to walk in long robes, and love greetings in the markets, and the highest seats◄ in the synagogues, and the chief rooms [places] at feasts;	

Matt. 23:7–15	Mk. 12:40	Lk. 20:47	John
7 "And greetings in the markets, and to be called of men, 'Rabbi, Rabbi.'			
Disdain high titles			
8 "But be not ye called Rabbi: for one is your Master, *even* Christ; and all ye are brethren.			
9 "And call no *man* your father(f) upon the earth: for one is your Father, which is in heaven.			
10 "Neither be ye called masters:(g) for one is your Master, *even* Christ.			
The greatest servant			
11 "But he that is greatest among you shall be your servant.(h)			
12 "And whosoever shall exalt himself shall be abased; and he that shall humble himself shall be exalted.			
Woe one			
13 "But woe unto you, scribes and Pharisees, hypocrites! for ye shut up the kingdom of heaven against men:(i) for ye neither go in *yourselves*, neither suffer [let] ye them that are entering to go in.			
Woe two	***Woe two***	***Woe two***	
14 "Woe unto you, scribes and Pharisees, hypocrites! for ye devour widows' houses,(j) and for a pretence make long prayer: therefore ye shall receive the greater damnation.(k)	**40** Which devour widows' houses,(j) and for a pretence make long prayers: these shall receive greater damnation.(k) (Verse 41 cont. in Section 160.)	**47** Which devour widows' houses,(j) and for a shew make long prayers: the same shall receive greater damnation.(k) (Next chap., Lk. 21:1 cont. in Section 160.)	
Woe three			
15 "Woe unto you, scribes and Pharisees, hypocrites! for ye compass sea and land to make one proselyte,(l) and when he is made, ye make			

Matt. 23:15-34—*In the temple court*	Mk.	Lk.	John

him twofold more the child of hell than yourselves.

Woe four

16 Woe unto you, *ye* blind guides, which say, 'Whosoever shall swear by the temple, it is nothing; but whosoever shall swear by the gold of the temple, he is a debtor!'(m)

17 "*Ye* fools and blind: for whether is greater, the gold, or the temple that sanctifieth the gold?(n)

18 "And, 'Whosoever shall swear by the altar, it is nothing; but whosoever sweareth by the gift that is upon it, he is guilty.'(o)

19 "*Ye* fools and blind: for whether *is* greater, the gift, or the altar that sanctifieth the gift?(p)

20 "Whoso therefore shall swear by the altar, sweareth by it, and by all things thereon.

21 "And whoso shall swear by the temple, sweareth by it, and by him that dwelleth therein.

22 "And he that shall swear by heaven, sweareth by the throne of God, and by him that sitteth thereon.(q)

Woe five

23 "Woe unto you, scribes and Pharisees, hypocrites! for ye pay tithe(r) of mint and anise and cummin, and have omitted the weightier *matters* of the law, **judgment, mercy, and faith:** these ought ye to have done, and not to leave the other undone.

24 *Ye* blind guides, which strain at a gnat, and swallow a camel.

Woe six

25 "Woe unto you, scribes and Pharisees, hypocrites! for ye make clean the outside of the cup and of the platter, but within they are full of extortion and excess.

26 "*Thou* blind Pharisee, cleanse first that *which is* within the cup and platter, that the outside of them may be clean also.(s)

Woe seven

27 "Woe unto you, scribes and Pharisees, hypocrites! for ye are like unto whited sepulchres, which indeed appear beautiful outward, but are within full of dead *men's* bones, and of all uncleanness.

28 "Even so ye also outwardly appear righteous unto men, but within ye are full of hypocrisy and iniquity.

Woe eight

29 "Woe unto you, scribes and Pharisees, hypocrites! because ye build the tombs of the prophets, and garnish the sepulchres of the righteous,

30 "And say, 'If we had been in the days of our fathers, we would not have been partakers with them in the blood of the prophets.'

31 "Wherefore ye be witnesses unto yourselves, that ye are the child-dren(t) of them which killed the prophets.

32 "Fill ye up then the measure of your fathers.

Their sure fate

33 "*Ye* serpents, *ye* generation of vipers, how can ye escape the damnation of hell?(u)

Their continued killing of God's servants

34 "Wherefore, behold, I send unto you prophets, and wise men, and

Matt. 23:34-39—*In the temple court*	Mk.	Lk.	John
scribes: and *some* of them ye shall kill and crucify; and *some* of them shall ye scourge in your synagogues, and persecute *them* from city to city:(v) ***Their collective guilt*** **35** "That upon you may come all the righteous blood shed upon the earth, from the blood of righteous Abel unto the blood of Zacharias son of Barachias, whom ye slew between the temple and the altar. ***Their generation doomed*** **36** "Verily I say unto you, All these things shall come upon this generation.(w) ***Their city rejected Jesus the Messiah*** **37** "O Jerusalem, Jerusalem, *thou* that killest the prophets, and stonest them which are sent unto thee, how often would I have gathered thy children together, even as a hen gathereth her chickens under *her* wings, and ye would not!(x) ***Their temple will be destroyed*** **38** "Behold, your house [temple] is left unto you desolate.(y) ***A Messianic confession spoken by the Jews several months later*** (z) **39** "For I say unto you, Ye shall not see me henceforth, [again] till ye shall say, 'Blessed *is* he that cometh in the name of the Lord.'" (Next chap., Matt. 24:1 cont. in Section 163.)			

Footnotes-Commentary

(a) **Attack the problem not the person?** The ancient proverb, "A wise man picks his enemies before his friends," is demonstrated here. Vast crowds had gathered about Christ in the temple and listened to His verbal devastation of the Jewish authorities. Standing nearby and aghast at the whole affair were His twelve apostles and other disciples. The meek and lowly Jesus suddenly speaks like another person; now with a dreadful voice of awful judgment. He puts upon the heads of the religious leaders one doom after another. We hear words of moral anger like awful thunderclaps, and hot lightening bolts of condemnation crashing upon the scene. It was as though vengeance had leaped upon the stage and shot her deadly arrows into the hearts of Messiah's implacable enemies. *They were the problem, and he attacked them with truth!* This was another divine death sentence for these pretentious hypocrites of Israel, their city, and beloved temple. Their horrible fact is described in Section 163.

(b) **"Moses seat."** He was the great lawgiver for the nation of Israel. The work of expounding the law among the Hebrews was the responsibility of the scribes and Pharisees. In synagogues, the Jewish lawyers or teachers stood to read the Torah, but sat while explaining it. They believed that Moses sat in something of a magistrate's chair made especially for him. From this posture, he explained the law to Israel. After the resurrection of Christ, the Jews actually placed a "Moses chair" in their synagogues and from this, the rabbis taught the law. One of these is pictured in the *Biblical Archaeological Review*, pages 32-35, 1987 edition, followed by a most fascinating article. The Words of Christ in verse 2, probably meant that the authority to teach both the oral and Torah Law likened the scribe to Moses as he sat and taught the people of Israel. It was another pretentious act of the religious leaders of the nation.

(c) **"Bid and observe."** Messianic Jews often point to this as proof that believers *today* are under the Law of Moses, because Jesus said to obey the law as it was taught. However, common sense dictates that these Words of our Lord are restricted only to things that were in harmony with the Torah Law. The subject here is not the Torah but rather the oral commands of the Jews. This is clear from verse 4, footnote d. The religious leaders had taken their thousands of oral traditions and superimposed them upon the Torah, thus making God's Word of no effect. See Section 96 and relative footnotes where the Lord Jesus corrected the Jews for their subversion of the Torah in favor of their oral laws and traditions. The first mark of a religious hypocrite is that he preaches one thing and does another. Messiah was *not teaching* His Jewish listeners to disobey the Law of Moses, but rather to continue in its teachings until the remainder of written revelation was vouchsafed to the church. All the Torah Law had the high design of pointing men to Him as their Lord and Savior (John 5:46-47 with Acts 10:43). After the day of Pentecost, when the Spirit came in fullness and the complete revelation of God was given to believers, this contained the total of inspired instructions regarding scriptural guidelines for the church. These directives are found mostly in the letters of Paul and are embraced in the closed canon of the New Testament.

(d) "**They bind heavy burdens.**" This has exclusive reference to the thousands of "fences" or the killing rules and regulations of their oral traditions. Refer to Section 96, footnote d; Section 89, footnote c; and Section 52, footnote h for an explanation of these man-made rules that so weighted down the average pious Jew, putting them in terrible bondage. The scribes for generations had added hundreds of glosses, fables, and myths that were repugnant to God's Word in the Old Testament. Those Messianic Jews who defend the Pharisees and dilly with truth trying to present them as mostly a group of "good ole boys" have seriously erred. They tell us that the fierce language used by Jesus in this chapter was spoken in a "family context" and that this was common for debate among the Hebrews, then and today as well. Regarding the spiritual *family origin* of the scribes, Pharisees, and their kind, our Lord declared they were "of their father, the devil" and they did his works (John 8:44). Toning this awful truth down by soft-soaping these wicked men is to white wash Satan's children and their evil works. The talk about Jesus not taking these men to task for being Pharisees is sheer wrong and diverts from the real problem. He took them to task because they hated Him, the Messiah, and loved their self righteous, do-it-yourself-religion.

2p-Honest readers of the four gospels will concede that the policy of the Pharisees was hatred and death for the carpenter from Nazareth. There were a few exceptions to this rule. He flew in the face of their false religious practices, misuse, and corruption of the great Torah Law. With but few exceptions, the entire organization was rotten and hated the Son of God with demonic passion. (The classic example of an honest Pharisee is that of Nicodemus in Section 30, footnote a.) *Not one time in any Scripture of the four gospels does our Lord make the distinction between the "good Pharisees" and their party name, or does He ever compliment these hypocritical murderers for their exemplarily religious lives.* It would be tantamount to a Jew attacking Himmler for murdering millions of his countrymen because he was a German, but not because he belonged to the SS or Gestapo. We ask, "Did those Nazi organizations have anything to do with it? Was it their policy or was it an individual choice of Heinrich Himmler and his companions in genocide?" Those who struggle to exonerate the Pharisees as a religious body with only a few bad members are wrong. No *honest* informed soul could believe and defend that thesis. As far back as 1925, the Jewish writer Moses Gaster penned this untruth: "The few allusions to the Pharisees in the New Testament are misleading." This ridiculous statement is in Gaster's work, *The Samaritans: Their History, Doctrines and Literature*, page 53. See footnote e below for more on this thought.

3p-Some three decades *after* the conversion of Paul, he referred to himself as a Pharisee in the present tense (Acts 23:6 with Phil. 3:5). Does this prove that he was still a Pharisee three decades after being saved, and that they were good people after all? His Words were merely a reflection on something in the past, explained in the present tense. Luke described Joseph of Arimathaea as *still* being a member of the Sanhedrin long after the ascension of Jesus in Section 193, Lk. 23:50. Are we to understand that this honorable man maintained his membership in that body of hypocrites years after he withdrew from being a secret disciple of Christ?

4p-Was the Jew, Paul, speaking in a "family context" when he called the false prophet at Paphos "thou child of the devil, thou enemy of all righteousness" (Acts 13:10). Was he speaking in a "family context" of debate and disagreement when he wrote the Corinthians that the "god of this world hath blinded the minds of them which believe not, lest the light of the glorious gospel of Christ should shine unto them" (2 Cor. 4:4). Perhaps John the Jew was using this "Jewish method of criticism" when he said that "the Son of God was manifested, that he might destroy the works of the devil" (1 John 3:8). Did he really mean Satan or not? Will some of our Jewish friends' adventure to explain the meaning of Matt. 25:41 and Rev. 20:10 within the framework of their "family discussion" customs? No candid reader could ever believe that the eight horrific woes Christ pronounced upon these wicked men (starting at footnote i below), were a courteous way of expressing one's self in the standard Hebrew style of social debate. Such a proposal when applied to our Lord on this stern occasion is woefully incorrect.

(e) "**All their works.**" Christ did not say, "some of their works." He knew that the *majority* of these men were evil and relished their wicked hypocrisy. Their prayers, alms deeds, and fasting, were done in a public show that men might applaud them. Jesus commenced to name several obvious places where the hypocrisy of the Pharisees shined like a herring in the moonlight and smelled just as bad. They are as follows.

2p-"**Phylacteries.**" This word means "observatories," or "outposts. It put the Jews in mind of always watching their law. Some think it also means to "keep" or "guard." There were four different parts of the law written on parchments folded up in the skin of a clean beast, placed in a small box, and then tied to the head and hand. The citations from the law were in the following scrambled order, Deut. 11:13-22, with Deut. 6:4-9; Ex. 13:11-16 with Ex. 13:1-10. They also served as amulets or charms. Some of the more deeply superstitious Jews looked upon them to defend the wearer from evil spirits and diseases of the body. The physical usage of these things came from the rabbis over literal interpretation of Ex. 13:16 long before the Pharisees appeared on the scene. Orthodox Jews continue to wear these today. One small box was attached to the head near the middle of the eyes and the other tied to the left hand. Christ rebukes the Pharisees because they had enlarged them, to the extent that they became the object of public attention. Some believe the Lord Jesus may have worn these objects. However, this is doubtful, since He knew the meaning of Ex. 13:16, and was not given to *overly excessive literal interpretation* of the Torah Law as the scribes and Pharisees were. For earlier comments on this, see Section 20, second paragraph of footnote c.

3p-"Borders of garments." This speaks of the fringes the Jews sewed upon the borders of their garments. These were by law to have a strip of blue cloth attached to them, which distinguished the Hebrews from other nations. This blue color closely resembled a blend of purple. It signaled that they kept the commandments of their God (Num. 15:38-40 with Deut. 22:12). The religious leaders made their fringes much wider than other Jews to show their respect for the law. Lightfoot's *Commentary on the New Testament . . . ,* vol. 3, pages 88-91 carries a good discussion on the subject of Jewish clothing drawing his material from ancient sources. The Pharisees in another show of their religious hypocrisy deliberately wore extra long robes to distinguish themselves from the common people of Israel. For the border on Jesus' garment being touched for healing, see Section 89, Matt. 9:20-21, second paragraph of footnote g.

4p-"Uppermost rooms." Today, we would say they chose the front seats in the synagogues or the front row at every special celebration where many people were assembled. The corrupt religious leaders loved positions of distinction and honor among men. Christ had rebuked them earlier for this jostling of exalted places in public occasions. Refer to Section 127, Lk. 14:7-11, footnotes f, and g for details.

5p-"Greetings in the markets." Here, the Son of God publicly exposes another dark side of these religious monsters. "Rabbi," most assuredly means "my great one" or "my master" or "teacher." There were three clerical titles used among the Jews. There were "rab," "rabbi," and "rabban." Each one denoted different degrees of Torah learning and ability as a teacher. Custodians of the Jewish religion would stroll about the markets, public streets, and places of human concourse seeking to hear the praise of men. Upon sight of these devils of Israel, men would "bow their knees," "uncover their heads," or "stretch out the hands." Alfred Edersheim in *The Life and Times of Jesus the Messiah*, pages 755-757 gives a good coverage of the rabbis in ancient Israel. They often presented themselves as having the faces of angels, light emanating from their countenance, and with the power to pronounce awful curses upon all who did not obey their commands! For example, this is recorded in the Talmud tractate, Sanhedrin 90b. They were said to be able to produce all kinds of amazing miracles. Their arrogant blasphemy is reflected in the shocking statements of the Talmud that place them on par with or even higher than God. The true servants of Messiah were never to use these haughty titles as they went out preaching the saving gospel.

6p-It should be cautiously held that not *all rabbis* (like the Pharisees) were of such extraordinary and shameless depravity. However, the majority were of this ilk. Hence, in view of all this, we instantly understand our Lord's admonition to the twelve not to be called by such vain titles, but to remember they were "brethren" banded together in the service of their Savior. Does this declaration from the Messiah also forbid Messianic (saved) Jews from calling their spiritual leaders by the term rabbi? For a look into the origin of the usage of rabbi as a high title, see Lightfoot's *Commentary on the New Testament . . . ,* vol. 2. pages 289-295.

(f) Verse 9. "Call no *man* your father." Christ is not teaching that believers abandon all titles of filial connections, respect, and civil distinction. Nor is he teaching that children must not call their parents by proper titles or names. Fellow Jews called the Pharisees "father" or "abba," and these men of religion loved it! Jewish writings as found in the Talmud abound with the usage of "abba" as a rabbinical distinction. See tractates, Berachoth; Yevamoth; and Kethuboth. (This has nothing to do with the Roman Catholic Church, calling their priests "father," as this false religion did not exist until some four hundred years later.) Christ warns his preachers to avoid all rabbinical self-glorification, lest they purvey feelings and sentiments of superiority, thus exalting one above the other. The scribes and rabbis were famed for their pretentious self-glorification. In the Talmud, there is the shocking story about heaven, which was represented as a school of rabbis! During one of the discussions, God disagrees with all the angels on a particular question regarding lepers. The hard question is referred to the decision of Rabbi Ben Nachman, who agrees with God, and the Lord of heaven is much pleased! See tractate, Babba Mezia 86a for this rabbinical foolishness.

(g) "Neither be ye called masters." The term "masters," means "guides" or "leaders." Here was another title, which was self-conferred upon the rabbis as they claimed to be the only "leaders" for the nation of Israel. Every one of Christ's disciples had used these titles in referring to their rabbis, but now the Messiah forbids it! Again, our Lord is not condemning appropriate tiles being applied to those who lead us in civil and spiritual life. Contextually, Christ forbids His disciples to be like the wicked rabbis, who thought *they alone* could guide the people to God.

(h) The greatest is the slave. What humbling sentiments. "The greatest among you shall be the servant." The word "servant" is the same term used for the famous seven in Acts 6:3 who were happy slaves of that first church and community in need. By using this stout term our Savior forbids *every kind* of personal lordship and spiritual domination among the members of His church. This awful domination is seen in the Roman Catholic Church as she rules the souls of men in error and damning untruth. On the other hand, this does not teach that God's flock has been left without authority and divinely appointed leadership. The church has its men who have led us according to the teachings of the Scripture. See this in such places as Acts 20:28; 1 Cor. 9:14; 1 Tim. 3:1-15; Heb. 13:7, 17, 24; with 1 Peter 5:1-4. Rarely today do we see the "greatest" being the "servant" of all. See Section 170, where the Son of God washed the feet of His bickering disciples, showing them genuine servant hood and leadership meekness.

2p-Verse 12. God, in His own time will lift high the Christian, who purposely takes the low place among fellow believers. The Lord Jesus had a continual problem with His preachers over pride of position and power. This is introduced in the main headings of Sections 109, 138 and 142. A few hours before the cross, we note that the apostles fell into bickering among themselves over who was the greatest. Refer to the main heading of Section 170 for the quarrel between the apostles, and Jesus' efforts to correct this by the example of washing their feet.

(i) Eight woes. Verse 13. First woe. Hindering the salvation of men. Albert Barnes in his *Notes On the New Testament*, page 243, may best summarize the eight woes with these chilling words, "This most eloquent, most appalling, and most terrible of all discourses ever delivered to mortals was pronounced in the temple, in the presence of multitudes. Never was there a more faithful dealing, more reproof, more profound knowledge of the working of hypocrisy, or more skill in detecting the concealments of sin than [are] recorded here. This was the Savior's final public discourse. It is a most impressive summary of all that he said, or that he had to say, of a wicked and hypocritical generation." To damn one's soul is one thing but to work for the damnation of fellow men is a most horrible charge! By their false teachings, adherence to the oral law or traditions, and rejection of Messiah and the counsel of God, they doomed themselves to hell and all who believed them. Again, we note that the "kingdom of heaven" here cannot have reference to some literal Jewish rule over the world more than two thousand years in the future. Such an interpretation would have confounded even the wicked Pharisees.

(j) Verse 14. Second woe. Stealing from widows in Israel. *Not only were the Pharisees famed for their hypocrisy, but they were thieves as well!* What a condemnation upon men of religion who continually taught about the welfare of widows. It is of interest that the word "houses" denotes possession of any kind. Our Lord charges them with taking away the property of the widows who had no one to instruct and guide them after the decease of their husbands. A fine example of their thievery is seen in the charge of Christ in Section 96, footnotes e and f, where they were guilty of lying and stealing from their own parents. Was this also a regular problem among these vile men?

(k) Verse 14 "Greater damnation." This was waiting for these hypocrites hiding under the cloak of Israel's unique religion. They laid terrible burdens on the innocent and would not help bear them; their dress and public appearance exalted them before men; they loved to hear their names and titles spoken by the common people. Messiah called them "fools, blind, hypocrites, destined for double damnation, robbers of widows, full of false, vulgar and vain oaths and swearing, shutting men out of heaven and not going themselves." They seriously attended the small things of religion, while caring not for that, which affects men for eternity. They were foul with hatred and sin within, outwardly looking good, but inside filled with hell itself, like freshly painted tombstones outside but rotten in their hearts. This was Jesus' description of the scribes and Pharisees of His day.

2p-In the Savior's Words, "greater damnation" we meet the doctrine of degrees of punishment. The pagan doctrine of soul sleep or annihilation cannot be fitted into the Word's of Christ. Over the ages of time, men have embraced whatever religion, and then lived lives that denounce all they affirm. Hypocrites of whatever "faith" have front seats reserved in hell. At the very least, "greater damnation" means that the torments of some will be more intense than that of others, namely hypocrites! *Beware of men who pray long wordy prayers, especially in open assemblies and meetings of the saints.* Could this mean that they are catching up in public on what they have failed to do in private? The Jews were infamous for making lengthy public prayers spoken loudly to catch the attention of others. Earlier in the Sermon on the Mount, the Lord Jesus rebuked them for this foul practice. Refer to Section 46 footnote d. Prayer is the highest divine art in *true* Christianity. Handling God's Word is next. It is not the arithmetic, poetry, or piousness of prayer that moves God, but the motive of the supplicant's heart. One praying heart is worth more than a thousand talking tongues. Men cannot speak with power and effectiveness, unless they have lingered long in the secret closet of holy conversation with Heaven. In *true* prayer, we kiss the face of our Father in heaven. O Saint, be careful when you bow in His majestic presence! Better that you learn to pray, and touch His heart, then being able to read Hebrew, Greek, and Latin. For more on these things, see Section 46, second paragraph of footnote e. Better to utter a few halting words from a clean heart than many for a dirty tongue.

(l) Verse 15. Third woe. Proselytes or converting sinners to hell. The word "proselyte" gives us a brief glimpse into the long time synagogue missionary program and means "one who comes over." For several hundred years before the birth of Christ, whenever possible, the Jews had made a concerted effort to bring their pagan Gentile neighbors into the Hebrew religion. They compassed sea and land. The Jews had a small pamphlet called the "*Sibylline Oracles.*" It was purported to be the testimony of an ex pagan female who converted to Judaism and wrote her testimony for the purpose of converting other heathens to their religion. Thousands of Gentiles came into Judaism: men, women, and entire families. The process leading one into the synagogue was long and tedious. It required intense study of the Torah Law, a denunciation of one's entire past, shaving of hair, trimming of nails, circumcision for all men, changing of names, and finally, water baptism by immersion in total nakedness. Afterward, they offered a sacrifice and then this person was a Jew, described as being "born again." He was given a "white robe of fine linen," and a "white stone with a new Jewish name written thereon (Rev. 2:17). The Roman historian, Tacitus (died A.D.12), gives a beautiful description of the Jews and their proselytes in his *Histories* 5.5. In Hebrew literature there were two kinds of Gentile proselytes:

1. There was "the proselyte at the gate." This had reference to a Gentile, who lived in any of the Jewish towns or cities and was interested in the religion of Judaism.
2. Next was "a proselyte of righteousness." This spoke of a man who had been circumcised and passed through all the stringent requirements for entrance into Israel. Proselytes are mentioned several times in Scripture, especially the book of Acts as Paul encountered them in the synagogues during his missionary work. They are found in such verses as Acts 2:10; 6:5; and 13:**43**.

2p-Here, the Lord Jesus renounces their missionary outreach and informs them that the more converted they are, the more perverted they become. The Pharisees who boasted to be "children of the kingdom" (Section 60, Matt. 8:12), are pointedly told by the Messiah that not only they, but also their converts are moving into hell. How sad that the very doorkeepers of the kingdom were outside the door themselves and prevented others from entering. It is amazing how certain Messianic Jews try to play down this terrible condemnation of Messiah and struggle to portray the Pharisees as good men with a *few* bad members in their organization. Our Lord said the exact opposite. See all of footnote d above for more on this.

(m) Verses 16-19. Fourth woe. Making false vows. Again, the Savior renounces the vanity of the Pharisees. Being immersed in swearing, the Jews of this era would make verbal oaths by the temple and then break them without any feeling of guilt. See Section 45, Matt. 5:33-34, footnote j for an earlier rebuke of the awful habit of swearing among the Hebrews. It meant nothing to cancel their affirmations of oath and bond if they had sworn by the temple building itself. If one swore by the gold plates attached to portions of the temple walls, he was bound to keep the oath, or he would be counted a "debtor" or "guilty." Some, however, believe that the mention of gold in this text has reference to the gold of Corban or gifts offered at the temple. See reference in footnote j above for explanation of this term used among the Jews and their plundering the houses of widows. To find binding religious reverence in the metallic substance of gold, yet find none in the house of God was a reflection of the depth of the hypocrisy of the religious leaders at this time. Gold was more to be revered than God!

(n) In these words our Lord attempts to correct their perverted view of the temple. That grand structure should have been considered by the Jews greater than all the gold of the world. It was the seat of divine Majesty, the only place singularly appointed by Jehovah where He could be acceptably worshiped. In every pen and peg, its entire function pointed in some way to the coming Messiah and His finished work of redemption, ascension, and intercession. God sanctified the temple, and the gold attached to it was only made pleasing by this divine act. Therefore, it was foolish for the Jews to think their gifts were sanctified by gold and not God. This mirrors their blindness into eternal things. All this fuss about their temple and yet the older rabbis had decreed that God, and the Holy Spirit had departed from this house with the death of Malachi and several of the latter prophets. For more on this, note Section 25, footnote c, and Section 66, footnote g. Lightfoot's *Commentary on the New Testament . . .* , vol. 3, page 242 has a short paragraph on this subject.

(o) "Swearing." Again, the Lord Jesus reveals the false practices and words of the religious leaders. They would continually swear by the vast altar of sacrifice that stood in the temple court of the Priests. As with the gold and building itself, here also they have it backwards! It was God's altar of sacrifice that gave meaning and acceptance to whatever was laid upon it, not the offering itself. This reflected how far the Jews were from religious reality in the worship of Almighty God. The Lord Jesus had earlier rebuked the Jews for their reckless vanity in swearing. Refer also to Section 45, Matt. 5:34, footnote j. F. W. Farrar in, *The Life of Christ*, footnote 1, page 570 documents how the heathen about Israel ridiculed the Jews of this era for their pernicious vain oaths and swearing.

(p) "Fools and blind." Amazingly, the meek and mild Jesus calls the scribes and Pharisees "fools and blind." We cannot believe this was a "family expression" used among the Jews when debating with each other. See paragraph four of footnote d above for explanation. Either Christ meant this or He did not! *They were "fools and blind," or they were not!* The Master tries again to explain to the Jews that it was God's anointed altar that gave meaning and acceptance to whatever was placed on it, not the reverse. Earlier, our Lord called Herod Antipas by the scurrilous term "that fox" (Lk. 13:32). When dealing with hypocrisy the Savior described things as they were. This divine art is missing today from many pulpits, while preachers mince their words to "keep peace" in the assembly.

(q) Verses 20-21. This does not mean that Jesus approved the profane swearing habits practiced by the Jews at this time in history. For He clearly forbid it in other places as in Section 45, Matt. 5:34, footnote j. (Swearing here does not mean the invoking of foul and evil language, but rather it refers to binding one to something by uttering profound words in the presence and hearing of God or others.) He was informing the Jews that regardless of what they swore by, it was still an oath of affirmation, and Jehovah would hold them responsible for its proper fulfillment: they would be accountable regardless.

2p-Verse 21. "Him that dwelleth therein." This has reference to God. He was supposed to be the chief entity and glory of the temple. However, at this time in history, the Jews believed that His glory had vacated their house over four hundred years before. *Possibly, the Lord Jesus was, instead, speaking of Himself!*

3p-Verse 22. Jews continually swore by heaven. Christ informs them that to do so was to invoke both God and His holy throne to behold their actions or commitments. What a fearful thing to which the foolish scribes and Pharisees were blind. The meaning is that to swear by something that has any relation or connection with The Almighty is the same as swearing by Him! It implicitly calls God into the matter and is absolutely binding on the one hearing it spoken. No wonder Eccles. 5:1-2 reads, "Keep thy foot when thou goest to the house of God, and be more ready to hear, than to give the sacrifice of fools: for they consider not that they do evil. Be not rash with thy mouth, and let not thine heart be hasty to utter *any* thing before God: for God *is* in heaven, and thou upon the earth: therefore let they words be few."

(r) Verses 23-24. Fifth woe. Guilty of an outward show in tithing. Majoring on minors and minoring on majors is the lesson here. Quick to pay their various tithes according to the law, even of the smallest plants or herbs, they were oblivious to the more important precepts of the great Torah Law. The scribes often spoke of the "heavier things of the law and the lighter." Jesus may be using their synagogue terminology at this time to get across His lesson. Our Lord had earlier mentioned the matter of tithing small plants in Section 70, Lk. 11:42, footnote g. See this reference for a detailed explanation of what these mean. The law commanded that all Jews should give tithes of the fruit of the earth in Deut. 14:22. These men of religion counted the smallest product as part of this category. Christ does *not* condemn their tithing of tiny earth plants, rather, He approves it! Some grab at this to prove He did not condemn their oral law or traditions. This is incorrect in view of Section 96 where He blasted the Jews for their dedication to the traditions, and rejection of the Torah teachings. Regardless, their old problem emerges again. So fanatical were the Hebrews that they questioned whether they should pay tithes of the anise flower only, or also of the seed and the stalk! They would meticulously tithe, and then live like Satan. This was unacceptable! In the higher matters of judgment, mercy, and faith, they were ignorant and stone blind. Jesus may have alluded to Micah 6:8 in these words. Hence, they are shaded in gray as probably coming from the Old Testament:

1. **Verse 23. "Judgment."** This seems to have reference to the judicial practices in the courts of Israel. These men stole from widows, lied about Corban, and then prayed long prayers in public ears! For meaning of "Corban," see Section 96, second paragraph of footnote f.

2. **Verse 23. "Mercy."** The word embraces acts of compassion toward the distressed, less fortunate, helpless, and those abandoned without others to assist or support. These cruel, hard-hearted men believed and taught that mercy was to be shown only to fellow Jews, never to the cursed Gentiles. The Savior had previously exploded this rabbinical myth in His Parable of the Good Samaritan in response to one of the Torah lawyers of Israel. See Section 116, main heading, and footnote m for details.

3. **Verse 23. "Faith."** Earlier, in Luke's record, while speaking of similar things to the Jews, it is noted that he mentioned "love" as one of the requirements of Christ but did not mention mercy. Our Lord spoke of all these things. His instruction for the scribes and Pharisees to have faith, must point directly to Himself. They did not; indeed, they refused to believe that He was their Messiah and Savior. Men may have faith in a thousand things, but if they fail to have faith in the Son of God, better had they never been born. This was the fatal mistake of many of the religious leaders of ancient and present day Israel. Jesus said the scribes, and Pharisees were blind. They were leading the nation away from their Messiah and hope. Being so sensitive and meticulous, they tithed the smallest herbs, yet they neglected the most important subject of the Jewish religion, their Messiah and Savior, Jesus of Nazareth.

4. **Verse 24. "Blind guides."** No better illustration of the leaders of false religion can be given.

5. **Verse 24. Gnat swallowing.** The Jews were such self-righteous fanatics that they literally filtered their water through linen to avoid swallowing any unclean insects, based on Lev. 11:41-43. This ritual had nothing to do with hygiene or personal cleanness, but was looked upon as gaining favor with God and showing off before men. It was all an outward show of purity, while their hearts were rotten in sin and hatred for the Messiah. See the second paragraph of footnote s below. Oddly, the Jews made a fuss over gnats! They are mentioned in the Talmud some ten times. An example of rabbinical absurdity is read in the tractate, Adovah Zarah 26b which states that, "If one eats a flea or a gnat he is an apostate" (in Israel). When Jesus spoke of straining a gnat, they understood His reference. He reverses the maxim and informs the religious leaders that they were the real gnat eaters in Israel!

(s) Verses 25-26. Sixth woe. Cleaning the wrong things. Decked out in large phylacteries and brown robes with extra wide borders, and basking in the praises of the people, the Pharisees' real inward condition is revealed by the Lord. Again, He restates that they are blind to spiritual realities, filthy, and corrupt inside. They are warned to seek inside purity that did not come by the washings of pot, cups, pans, or vessels and the hundreds of rules and restrictions of their oral tradition. The *outside cleanliness* had reference to their ever working to obey the traditions as found in the Talmud. These men picture the thousands that fill local churches today: nice and well perfumed outwardly but filled with sin and evil on the inside. Only Jesus Christ can clean a man's heart of its trash.

2p-Verses 27-28. Seventh woe. White outside, rotten inside. In these passages, the Lord compares them to white washed tombs externally, but filled with putrid corruption internally. A month before Passover, all burial sites were whitewashed lest some Jew unwittingly touched one of them, thus disqualifying him from observing the feast. This is the figure Jesus used and was understood by those listening. The Son of God came to change men's hearts and give them new life. These religious men of Israel could only become clean inwardly by trusting Him as the Messiah-Savior, and this most of them did not. It is to be noted that Jesus did not say, "Some of you are like this, but most scribes and Pharisees are not." So it is today. The church has men appearing clean outwardly but rotten inwardly.

[t] **Verses 29-31. Eighth woe. Boasting, self conceited children of murderers**. Jesus said that they had built elaborate tombs over the prophets of God, which their fathers had slain. They were liars to say they would have disapproved of the deeds of their ancestors, for they had plotted to kill Him, the Prince of Peace, and Messiah. Their garnishing the graves of God's prophets testified that they were as wicked as their murderous fathers were.

2p-Verse 32. "A full measure." Several days later, when these men slew the Lord of heaven they filled up the measuring cup of God's wrath by their rejection of Him. With that, their terrible doom was sealed. Our Lord affirmed that the fury of God would fall on the Jews, their city and temple. It came some forty years afterward when God's wrath was poured out upon Jerusalem and the Hebrew people in A.D. 70. See footnotes x and y of this Section for more on this fact.

[u] **Verse 33. "The damnation of hell" is not the grave.** Was this friendly "family talk" among Jewish men, or did the Son of God determinately mean these awful Words? Did the scribes and Pharisees die in their sins and go into a burning hell or not? Those who would have us to believe otherwise are kidding themselves! See footnote d above, for more on the effort of certain people to whitewash the wicked scribes and Pharisees. For a detailed review of hells various names and titles, see Section 103, all of number 8 under footnote g. Cultists struggle with such verses in their hopeless quest to make hell the grave and the grave hell. One ponders what kind of "damnation" is in the common grave where dead bodies are buried? For further comments on this subject, see Section 59, footnote o.

[v] **Verse 34. "Persecution coming."** In these words, our Lord referred to the apostles, early believers, and missionaries of the church. He told the scribes and Pharisees that they would kill some of them and scourge others, and persecute them from city to city. The Lord Jesus warned His disciples of this coming persecution several times during the latter part of His ministry. While walking to the Garden of Gethsemane, the night before the morning of His cross, He again reminded them of what was coming. Refer to this in Section 177, John 16:1-4, footnotes a and b. A survey of earlier chapters of Acts and the missionary journeys of Paul reveals this happened exactly as predicted.

2p-Verse 35. Abel to Zacharias. Though it is not a direct quotation, yet these events literally happened and are recorded in Gen. 4:8 and 2 Chron. 24:20-21. Hence, they are shaded in gray as coming from the Old Testament. Refer to Section 70, Lk. 11:50-51, numbers 7 and 8 under footnote h for explanation of Zacharias.

[w] **Verse 36. "This generation."** A similar statement had been made earlier by the Lord with different wording. *His Words "this generation" meant that "generation" living then and there.* They were standing and sitting before Him. There is no way our Lord's Words can be interpreted to mean that He was speaking of Jews over two thousand years in the future going through a tribulation period. To trace the usage of the word "generation" by Christ, refer to Section 67, footnote b, and all under the asterisk in main heading of Section 68. "All these things" came upon them and their city in A.D. 70, just as their Messiah had predicted. This is explained in Section 163.

[x] **What a lament!** Here is the Savior's last heart rendering plea to Israel. He had spoken similar Words a few weeks earlier while north in Galilee (Section 126, Lk. 13:34, footnote k). For more on this see footnote y and z below. Jerusalem was the metropolis of Judea, the seat of great kings, and the place of divine worship of the true and living God. The city once called "the joy of the whole earth" is now cursed beyond recovery! The *human* Christ breaks out through these moving Words and reminds those standing about in the temple how many times He wanted to save them and their children—but they "would not." Messiah sought to gather all of Israel, the Sanhedrin, the scribes, Pharisees, Sadducees, all of them into His love. Ancient rabbis referred to God's glory or Shekinah as "the holy bird," with Israel resting under her wings. The protection of Jehovah is mentioned in Ps. 57:1, 61:4 and 91:4. There is an expression similar to the Words of Christ as used here found in the old apocryphal book of 2 Esdras 1:20. It reads, "I gathered you as a hen gathered her chickens under her wings." Regardless of the date when this *spurious book* was written, it confirms the familiar historical use of this term spoken here by the Lord Jesus.

[y] **"Your house left desolate."** Shaded in gray because this was a paraphrase taken from Jer. 22:5. Some also see this prediction of Jesus as the fulfillment of Isa. 6:11-12. "House," meant the vast and gorgeous temple in which Christ was giving one of His last ultimatums to the religious leaders of Israel. See Section 126, Lk. 13:35 for similar Words spoken earlier by the Messiah while still in Galilee, and footnote z below. Pious Jews called the temple, "Beit HaMikdash," meaning The "House of the Holy." It was anything but that. For more on the wickedness of the Jews and utter corruption of this place, see Section 176, footnote t. In about forty years, it would be desolate in two ways:

1. His holy presence as their Messiah would be forever gone, and these Jews would not see and hear Him any longer. His teaching and miracles performed in their temple would cease. Nor did they see Him throughout their centuries of hard and bitter captivity up to this present time. Israel without salvation will never again see their Messiah in His glory unless they, as individuals, hear the gospel, are convicted of their sin, repent and trust Him as personal Lord and Savior!

2. The Romans destroyed the temple in A.D. 70. *Some* Messianic Jews deny this is the meaning of Christ's Words and reapply them to the nation of Israel instead of the temple at Jerusalem. This fanciful exegesis smacks more of the infamous Rabbi Rashi and his juggling of Holy Scripture. For explanation of this, refer to Section 6, the seventh paragraph of footnote d.

(z) He quotes again from Ps. 118:26. With this Old Testament citation, Messiah concludes His denunciation of the religious leaders of Israel and those in His audience who hated Him. Some months earlier, while in Galilee, He cited this same verse from the Psalms; there also it was in the context of His first lengthy lament over Jerusalem, the temple and the Jewish people. Refer to this moving event in Section 126, Lk. 13:34-35. Note also in this same Section, footnote l where He informed the Jews the next time they saw Him, it would be as He rode into Jerusalem and the crowds hailed Him as Messiah, the King. Later, in Matt. 21:9 (and parallel verses) this is exactly what these people did. The Jews, whom He said would not see Him again until this event, *now saw Him* as He had predicted, and some of them shouted out this verse! Thus, His first usage of this Messianic Psalm was later fulfilled exactly as He stated. However, this occurred some weeks following the above prediction given in Galilee. Here, our Lord employed this same passage for a second time, and it was several days before the cross. On this occasion, Jesus told the scribes and Pharisees, "Ye shall not see me henceforth." This cannot mean that they never saw Him again. After this discourse, they saw Jesus in the Garden of Gethsemane, the palace of the high priest, at the residence of Pilate, and hanging on the cross. He was telling them that *they* would see Him no more as their merciful Messiah, sitting in their presence, performing miracles, teaching, and offering His new kingdom and eternal life to all who trust Him. He seems to be saying, that now their fate had been sealed by their rejection of Him, and they were doomed. However, Israel would not always be without hope. Christ's Words at this time strictly applied to *that* wicked generation to whom He was speaking. They were destroyed in A.D. 70. See Section 163 for coverage of this. When Jews anywhere on earth, confess Him through repentance and faith as their Messiah-Redeemer (which Ps. 118:26 clearly states), He will then become their Lord and Savior. This is not a Hebrew thing only; it is for whosoever will of Adam's fallen race. Neo Calvinists, desperate to save their faces, now tell us that those who preach, "a whosoever will gospel" are propagating universalism! Alas! The low ignominy *some* go to in order to defend a theological lie. *Unsaved* Jews, Gentiles, Calvinist, and Arminians, all need the grace of God to cure their doctrinal distempers.

2p-Some expositors see in the above quotation of Jesus from Ps. 118:26, the prediction of Paul in Rom. 11:1-2, 24-27. He wrote in these verses that in a time yet to come "all Israel shall be saved" (meaning all who repent of their sins and trust Jesus of Nazareth as their Messiah-Savior). *The idea of every Jew on earth suddenly being saved is foreign to this text.* The "corporate salvation of physical Israel" is a stranger to the plan of redemption as laid down in the Bible. Those who write about the "national conversion of the entire nation of Israel" apparently do not know that God saves *individuals* within earth's nations but not entire nations. For a discussion of the myth that the literal nation of Israel will be saved in a day when they see the scars in Jesus' hands, refer to Section 193, number 2, under footnote d. Paul made it clear that "For they *are* not all Israel, which are of Israel" (Rom. 9:6). This pungently speaks of God's spiritual Israel, Abraham's seed, which has reference to all the saved of all times (Rom. 2:28-29 with Gal. 3:29). Among this number are millions of Gentiles saved by the grace of God.

3p-Romans 11: 23 states that saved Hebrews will be "grafted" into salvation by belief, [or faith] as "they were broken off" because of their unbelief in Messiah (verse 20). This grand event has not yet been fully accomplished, but the time is coming when many believing Jews within national Israel will hail Jesus as the Messiah-Savior and receive Him whom their forefathers slew. Of this chapter in Romans, Philip Mauro wrote in *The Hope of Israel*, pages 151-152 These clear words, "It contains a strong intimation that it lay in the purpose of God, at some time in the near future, to extend special mercy to the Jews." Those who make this a mystic spiritual event have missed the meaning of the text. See this curious interpretation in *The Millennium Bible*, page 326, by W. E. Biederwolf. For further comments on Israel, see Section 9, footnote g, along with Section 39, footnotes a and g.

4p-An incorrect interpretation of Ps. 118:26. Some wrongly hold that Jesus was telling the Jews that during the devastation of Jerusalem in A.D. 70, those who audibly confessed this Messianic Psalm would be saved. A reading of verses 35-37 and footnote x above belies this false notion. Men are only saved through faith in Christ, not reciting a Psalm or anything else. After this, the Savior goes into the Women's Court or Treasury and sits down.

5p-Scriptures often says the same things in different words. We are saved by grace through faith (Eph. 2:8). Then, Titus 3:5 affirms that it was His mercy that saved us. Which was it, grace, or mercy? Then, according to Rom. 8:24, we are saved by hope. The great verse in Acts 16:31 tells us to "believe on the Lord Jesus Christ' to be saved. According to Rom. 10:13, we may "call upon the name of the Lord" and be saved. Which is it; hope, believing, or calling on His Name? We are justified freely by His grace in Rom. 3:24. Yet, Rom. 3:28 affirms that we are justified by faith, while James 2:24 declares that works are involved in justification! In Gal. 3:13, it is Christ who has redeemed us, however in 1 Peter 1:19, we read that it is His precious blood that has redeemed us. All of these seeming differences mean the same thing. They must be rightly divided to be understood, and then one will see they all blend into united truths. This unique literary style of stating facts in different ways is another mark of divine inspiration of the Scriptures. God did not write the Bible as man would. For more on this curious manner in which Scripture says the same thing in differing ways, see Section 203, the second paragraph of footnote d.

Leaving the angry Jews, Jesus passes through the temple and stops in the Women's Court or treasury.* Sitting with His apostles, they note the people dropping their offerings into the huge chests. He points out a certain woman and teaches them a lesson on how and what she gave to God.**

Time: Tuesday after Palm Sunday before His death on Friday mid-afternoon.

*On the north side in the Court of Women were receptacles wherein the Jews dropped their dues and offerings. This interesting place is explained in footnote a below. It was daily crowded with hundreds of Jews bringing gifts to God. **When men today give to the cause of Christ and to the needs of others, these beautiful acts of kindness and charity are counted as though they gave to the Lord of heaven. True Christian love is an act not a feeling.

In the temple Women's Court or treasury

Matt.	Mk. 12:41-44	Lk. 21:1-4	John
	Watching the people **41** And Jesus sat over against the treasury, and beheld how the people cast money into the treasury:[(a)] and many that were rich cast in much.	*Watching the people* **1** And he looked up, and saw the rich men casting their gifts into the treasury.[(a)]	
	A poverty stricken widow **42** And there came a certain poor widow, and she threw in two mites, which make a farthing.[(b)] (A mite was the smallest coin in use.) ▶	*A poverty stricken widow* **2** And he saw also a certain poor widow casting in thither two mites.[(b)] (A mite was the smallest coin, about 1/8 of 1 cent.)	
	The Savior comments **43** And he called *unto him* his disciples, and saith[(c)] unto them, "Verily I say unto you, That this poor widow hath cast more in, than all they which have cast into the treasury: **44** "For all *they* did cast in of their abundance; but she of her want did cast in all that she had, *even* all her living."[(d)] (Next chap., Mk. 13:1 cont. in Section 163.)	*The Savior comments* **3** And he said,[(c)] "Of a truth I say unto you, that this poor widow hath cast in more than they all: **4** "For all these have of their abundance cast in unto the offerings of God: but she of her penury [poverty] hath cast in all the living that she had."[(d)] (Verse 5 cont. in Section 163.)	

Footnotes-Commentary

[(a)] **"Treasury."** This vast area could accommodate some fifteen thousand people at any given time. At the northern edge of the treasury under the cover of beautiful ornate colonnades, stood thirteen large horn-shaped alms chests, each shaped like a trumpet, broadening downward from the aperture, each adorned with various inscriptions. The Jews called them "shopharoth." Into these collection boxes were cast benevolent contributions, which helped to furnish the temple with its splendid wealth. The names of the twelve tribes of Israel were inscribed on these receptacles. It was while sitting in this open room that he called the attention of His preachers to the poor widow moving in the line to bring her offerings to God. For more on these gift receptacles, see Section 46, footnote b. Hundreds of benches were there. Here the people sat, rested, and talked. It was on one of these that our Lord postured Himself while speaking to His disciples about the poor widow. For further details on this vast open room and other events that took place there, see Section 119, sixth paragraph of footnote a.

2p-Alfred Edersheim wrote the following of the beautiful temple treasury. "Along these colonnades [in the treasury] were the thirteen trumpet-shaped boxes . . . for gifts to be distributed in secret to the children of the pious poor, and that where votive vessels were [also] deposited." See *Life and Times of Jesus the Messiah,* page 741. These votive containers seem to have been different from the original twelve marked by the names of Israel's sons. The money received was used for the maintenance of the temple building, purchase of wood, buying sacrifices, incense, and many other things. Jews counted it a sacred duty to contribute to these things. It was the work of the priests to attend to this business and administer the money received.

3p-Mark stated that our Lord "sat" in the treasury. Doubtless, He was bone weary after hours of debating and wrangling with the scribes, Pharisees, and their supporters. Hundreds of people were present. Long lines of Jews moved slowly through as they stepped forward and dropped their offerings into the huge trumpet-like chests. These offerings amounted annually to several million pounds in English sterling. This place may also have reference to the "secret chambers" that Jesus spoke of in under Section 163, Matt. 24:26, fourth paragraph under footnote k. The rabbis believed that Messiah would meet with chosen men of Israel in these rooms.

(b) "Farthing." *It is impossible to compute the exact value of New Testament coinage in currant day values.* Opinions vary regarding the word "farthing." However, we can be sure farthings were not pagan coins. All such forms of currency were prohibited within the temple. It probably means "two lepta," and had reference to the smallest coin used among the Hebrews at this time. It was made of brass. The Jews called this piece "prutah" or "pertah." The translators of the *King James Version* used the Word "mites" which is a perfect rendering. Our English word "mite" has its origin in the French term "miete," signifying the smallest crumb from a piece of bread. These two brass coins amounted to about 1/8 of .01 cent. The rabbis had decreed that it was unlawful to contribute *less* than this amount and that all gifts should be supervised by a priest. Anything given by Gentiles was considered sinful, unless it was first purified. If the proposed gift carried the image of a pagan god, goddess, or ruler they were considered beyond purification and rejected. See the Talmud tractate, Baba Bathra 10b for the curious and confusing details of rabbinical rules regarding gifts and charity. For more on heathen coinage, see Section 155, footnote f. See the fine rules laid down by the Sanhedrin for worshipers to follow while in the temple. Some of these are listed in Section 59, second paragraph of footnote d. It is noted that the Pharisees were the first to break their own rules.

(c) Ever alert to the need for instructing His preachers, Jesus called their attention to this poor widow as she deposited her offering. With no husband to provide for her, nevertheless she was present at the house of God during this Passover celebration and brought her offering to the God of Israel. Women were not required to attend this celebration. Today, in so many churches, men applaud those who contribute vast amounts. Their names are set in the stained glass windows or attached at the end of the pew on a brass plate. Regardless, God sees the heart's intent and His blessing of approval is thus bestowed.

(d) To His little band of special men, Christ drops an eternal principle into their listening ears. As the rich Jews poured their vast contributions into the chests, having still just as much at home, she gave all her living that she had. Will some Christians never learn that we keep only what we give and ultimately surrender what we keep? Our earthly possessions are sanctified as we give the *right* portion to God and others. Then, His blessing will rest on that which remains. It should be remembered that this little woman in giving her total living does not teach that *every child of God* is to abandon all possession and step into the world as a beggar or hobo. Whoever she was, she was the exception and Christ knowing this used her for a glorious example of unselfishness. What a beautiful trust she had in divine providence to perform this special act in giving. This deed clearly reflected her past fellowship and walk with the Lord. Would to God we were all as this daughter in Israel, unknown to men in what we give but hailed by the Lord of heaven and earth. O thou poor saint who may read these lines, hold it in your heart that God sees every penny you possess and watches how you lay it out. He, who counts the hairs of your head, also counts the pennies in your purse. *Few "Christian millionaires" have ever given as much as the widow in Israel did.*

2p-The other side to this story is that the poor, unnamed widow never knew that Messiah selected her quiet actions for an object lesson from which millions have learned to this present moment. Ah, the wonders and eternal endurance of saving grace. The God of heaven is pleased with two mites, she offered more than a talent of gold because the heart's motive was right in giving. Humble curiosity leaves us wondering of her life after this grand deed. Where did she live and how did she die? Her act of love and trust lives fresh today in the heart's of God's people all over the world. How marvelous it will be to meet her in sweet heaven when the rigors of this world and life are forever past. Reader, what lesson are you leaving behind for those who follow in your train?

3p-Regarding the meaning of Jesus' instructions for a young rich man to dispose of all earthly goods and give to the poor, see Section 139, Matt. 19:21, third paragraph of footnote h.

Greek proselytes attending the Passover celebration want to see Jesus. They approach Philip asking for help. During Jesus' conversation with these men and others standing about listening, God suddenly speaks audibly to His Son from heaven for the third time. The crowds are stunned!

Time: Tuesday after Palm Sunday before His death on Friday mid-afternoon.

Matt.	Mk.	Lk.	John 12:20-36 *At Jerusalem amid the Passover crowds*
			They inquire of Philip
			20 And there were certain Greeks[a] among them that came up to worship at the feast:
			21 The same came therefore to Philip,[b] which was of Bethsaida of Galilee, and desired him, saying, "Sir, we would see Jesus."[c]
			22 Philip cometh and telleth Andrew: and again Andrew and Philip tell Jesus.[d]
			Jesus' odd answer
			23 And Jesus answered[e] them, saying, "The hour is come, that the Son of man should be glorified.
			24 "Verily, verily, I say unto you, Except a corn of wheat fall into the ground and die, it abideth alone: but if it die, it bringeth forth much fruit.
			25 "He that loveth his life shall lose it; and he that hateth his life in this world shall keep it unto life eternal.
			26 "If any man serve me, let him follow me; and where I am, there shall also my servant be: if any man serve me, him will *my* Father honour.
			The Father speaks from heaven
			27 "Now is my soul troubled; and what shall I say? 'Father, save me from this hour:' but for this cause came I unto this hour."
			28 "Father,[f] glorify thy name." Then came there a voice from heaven, *saying,* "I have both glorified it, and will glorify it again."[g]
			29 The people therefore, that stood by, and heard *it*, said that it thundered: others said, "An angel spake to him."[h]
			30 Jesus answered and said, "This voice came not because of me, but for your sakes.[i]
			31 "Now is the judgment of this world: now shall the prince of this world be cast out.[j]
			He predicts His death on the cross
			32 "And I, if I be lifted up from the earth, will draw all *men* unto me."
			33 This he said, signifying what death he should die.[k]
			34 The people answered him, "We have heard out of the law that Christ [Messiah] abideth for ever: and how sayest thou, 'The Son of man must be lifted up?' who is this Son of man?"[l]
			After warning of light and darkness, He hides from the people
			35 Then Jesus said[m] unto them, "Yet a little while is the light with you. Walk while ye have the light, lest darkness come upon you: for he that walketh in darkness knoweth not whither he goeth."
			36 "While ye have light, believe[n] in the light, that ye may be the child-ren of light." These things spake Jesus, and departed, and did hide himself from them.[o] (Verse 37 cont. in Section 162.)

Footnotes-Commentary

(a) **"Greeks."** This is what the Holy Spirit called these men through the writing of John. It means real Greeks from that far off country and not Greek speaking Jews, who were called Hellenists. Apparently, they had (converted) to the Jewish religion. For details on Gentile proselytes to Judaism, see Section 159, footnote l. One is surprised at the statements various commentators make regarding these men. Some postulate that they could not have been Gentiles born abroad and visiting Jerusalem for the Passover feast. The text reads that their purpose was to "worship" during this grand occasion. They would take their lamb to the temple for killing and then eat the Passover meal as other Jews did during this one-day event. A similar case was that of the politician from Ethiopia in Acts 8:26-40, who attended a celebration at the temple. One can almost believe that these Greeks were some new arrivals on the scene, and had not yet learned of the plot of the Jews to kill the Lord Jesus, hence their public openness in seeking out Messiah. It is obvious that they had previously heard much of Him, in their home country. Some commentators think that these men were among the people who witnessed Jesus' triumphant entry on the donkey as given in Section 148. If so, is this what raised their curiosity level and inspired them to search for the Savior?

2p-Baptist perversion of Scripture. The Lord's supper debacle. Various Gentiles sent gifts and sacrifices to the temple, from time to time, but especially during various annual celebrations. After being cleansed by the priests, these gifts were received. However, an uncircumcised Gentile could not offer a sacrifice; hence, the riot that developed about Trophimus being brought by Paul into the Jewish house of God (Acts 21:29). The Talmud contains the story of a Syrian who was killed for offering sacrifices in the temple. Refer to this in tractate, Pesachin 3b. The Jews based the killing of Gentiles for committing such religious offensives on Ex. 12:43. This passage from Exodus has been greatly abused by certain separatist Baptist ministers, teaching that only Baptists can administer and partake of the Lord's Supper. They point to the words, "There shall no stranger eat thereof" in verse 43 above. Contextually, this had strict reference to banning Gentiles from eating the Hebrew Passover meal. The Savior in the upper room (the night before the cross) did not institute the Lord's Supper until some fifteen-hundred years after Moses wrote the book of Exodus! Ultra Landmark Baptists do not know that the Passover is not the Lord's Supper, and the Lord's Supper is not the Passover. Law and grace will not mix. Christ instituted the Lord's Supper *after* the Passover meal, not during it. In the late 1800s, a sect rose up within Baptist ranks teaching "Jesus was a Baptist," and the "bride of Christ is the Baptist Church." Therefore, only their ministers can administer correct baptism and officiate in the serving of communion. Loosely known as "Baptist briders," or "Baptist Landmarkism," these people make a big noise out of the word "authority," assuring us that *they alone* have God's authority to do these things. Roman Catholicism and other cults make the same false claim. For a concise explanation of this error, see Section 21, Part 4, third paragraph of footnote n and Section 168, footnote h. The bread and cups used in the Jewish Passover are briefly explained in Section 174, footnotes a, b, and d. It should be remembered that *some* of the greatest Christians to appear on the stage of extant church history were not Baptists.

(b) Why did they approach Philip with their inquiry? Had someone in the crowds pointed him out as a disciple of this wonderful Man? According to A. T. Robertson in *Word Pictures in the News Testament*, vol. 5, page 224, their request was not a demand "but perfectly polite." Perhaps they went to Philip because his name was a common Greek one and used by thousands. The text is clear that Philip "was of Bethsaida of Galilee," which at that time in history had a large Greek population. This was the man who earlier had brought his friend Nathanael to Jesus (John 1:45). The name "Philip" curiously means "lover of horses." This is not the Philip in Acts 6:5, 8:5, 26, and 21:8.

(c) **"Sir, we would see Jesus."** It is wonderful how genuine goodness often draws to itself the troubled, outcasts, and hurting. This request alone reveals that news of Christ had spread to far away Greece. No man has lived until through the eyes of faith, he has seen the Lord Jesus Christ! His unique human life left astounding results across the face of the earth and in the hearts of humanity. His greatness is singularly different, modest, and quiet: never repelling honest beholders. It has attracted and invited many to the warmth of his great heart. *There never lived a more harmless being on earth than Jesus Christ of Nazareth.* He injured nobody, spoke not one improper word, and committed not one wrong action. Even His enemies were forced to concede that He did all things well (Mk. 7:37). Our Lord was assaulted by His own Hebrew people, hounded by devils, by pain, family, a man of sorrows, terrible vexations, even by His bickering apostles. Popular Hebrew religion branded Him as, "a glutton and winebibber," and on one awful occasion "Beelzebub." He was poor, suffered hunger, fatigue and had no permanent place to lay His head. Beasts and fowls had resting places while Jesus did not. He shed tears at the grave of a friend and wept over His fierce enemies. The world taught Him nothing and continues to this day to hate Him for what He taught them. Lastly, after suffering indignities and shame unspeakable, He was tied and nailed on a cross of pain and terror for sins He had not committed. This is the Christ of God, the Messiah, and Savior of mankind. Men and women, who live life without seeing Him, by simple faith; better had they never been born.

(d) How prudent that Philip dared not attempt to fulfill such a request without the wise consultation and the advice of a fellow apostle. We can believe that hundreds pushed, shoved, and jostled to "see" this great man. Did Philip select Andrew because he was more amiable or senior of the twelve? How many major endeavors of the church and Christians as individuals have come to naught due to lack of sound advice and wise "in put" from (especially) the older and more experienced members of God's family. "Without counsel purposes are disappointed: but in the multitude of counsellors they are established" (Prov. 15:22).

(e) Verses 23-27. Unsaved textual critics point to the answer of Christ as further proof that the Scriptures are disjointed, filled with interpolations, and have later additions being inserted into the original written text. Their wicked unbelief slaps their own faces to shame. The Greeks wanted to see the human Christ; his frame, looks, expressions, sound of His voice; no doubt even a miracle would have been appreciated since this was one of the hallmarks of Messiah. Our Lord knowing their intentions speaks a profound answer. His response was directly indirect. *He candidly tells them the only way men must see Him.* All other views are vain and empty. Note the following Words of Jesus to these curious inquirers:

1. **Verse 23. "See, My greatest hour."** Christ is saying, "You desire to see me? However, you have selected the wrong time. See Me on the cross when My hour of glorification will begin. It will be at the nine o'clock hour when I am lifted up to die for the sins of the world (Mk. 15:25). If men do not see Me first on the cross, they will never see Me aright and in my eternal glory."

2. **Verse 24. "See My greatest work."** Again, our Lord was saying, "Like the corn [grain] of wheat that falls into the ground, so I will die soon. Herein is My greatest work." In this drama of atonement, millions of Gentiles would be brought into His church or new kingdom. Here, the Master reflects that it will be only in His death that He would be glorified in the salvation of men. Such a profound thought is found later in Heb. 2:9 with Phil. 2:8-9. By His death, the debt of sin was paid and the kingdom of God was opened to all Jews and Gentiles alike who would repent of their sins and believe in Him. Even Greeks are invited!

3. **Verse 25. "See your greatest joy."** Jesus was saying something like this, "Disdaining human life, with its perplexities, sorrows, and sins, losing it in Me and My cause is how you will find true life forever." He had previously employed this old maxim in Matt. 10:39. Here, again, the Savior repeated Himself.

4. **Verse 26. "See your greatest service."** This is following Me as a servant does his master and knowing the intimate joy of My presence. Finally, where I am in heaven, there your life of dedicated and honorable service will end—with my Father's honor and Me.

5. **Verse 27. "See Me yielded to God's will; the death of the cross."** Affirming that the plan of salvation for mankind was not an after thought, our Lord tells the Greeks that His final and ultimate reason for coming to earth was to fulfill this hour of death on the cross. We may see in the Words of Jesus at this place a faint picture of the human and divine sides of our Savior: the human cries one thing, the divine another. With this, we note faith and sight suddenly joined in glorious unity. The struggle is resolved as the Son prays, "Father, glorify thy name" (verse 28).

2p-They must see this Christ! If they desire to follow Him, they must in their own strange way share in His calamities and sorrows. Any other picture of Him is false, exaggerated, deceiving, and deathly in error. What did these men from pagan Greece think as they heard the Son of God speak these strange words. Shortly they would see Him aright, hanging between two thieves, and dying for the sins of mankind! Alas, did they then understand?

(f) "Father." After speaking these astounding words to the curious Greeks, He breaks out into spontaneous audible prayer to His Father. He is requesting that the Father's Name be glorified as never before in the approaching agonies of Gethsemane and the unspeakable horror of Calvary. That His willingness to bear whatever, that God may be honored in all things. See more of Jesus' use of the word "Father," in His high priestly prayer, the night before the morning of the cross in Section 178, footnote t.

(g) Highlighted in red font for it is the voice of God speaking audibly. What an answer! For the third and final time, the voice of God spoke audibly to the Son from heaven. The crowds standing about heard it without understanding. For an explanation of these three events, refer to Section 22, footnote g. God had glorified His Name in the life, and ministry of the Son, but come Friday, He will glorify it again, as never before! For then He will die as the atonement for the sins of humankind and the curse upon all creation. His great plan, which was laid from the foundation of the world, will be realized. Salvation, hope, and reunion with the Creator are now possible for whosoever will. "I will glorify *it* again." And this He did in the death, burial, and resurrection of His Son.

(h) "Did it thunder?" As it was then, so it is today. We still struggle to discern the Word of God speaking to our hearts by the Holy Spirit. The crowds standing nearby heard His prayer. They were shaken to no end when God spoke an audible response. It was a popular opinion among the Jews, that God rarely spoke audibly to men, but rather His angels would speak on His behalf. This explains the meaning of the comments from the excited crowds standing about. Some thought an angel had spoken to Him in a voice like powerful heavenly rumblings (verse 29).

(i) "But for your sakes." The meaning is that God's voice hit like a thunderclap. This heavenly phenomenon was designed first for them. By now they should know that He was the Messiah, for here was another extraordinary miracle; even God speaking to Him. See footnote g above for more about God speaking to His Son on two previous occasions.

(j) **"The prince of the world cast out."** Later, when Jesus died and rose from the grave, a unique judgment would be accomplished within the unseen spiritual world. It cannot mean that mankind stood at the bar of divine reckoning when He died on the cross. That is future. This act directly involves the "prince of this world," which was a popular term among the Jews, usually having reference to an angel of death or Satan. There was a myth that when God divided the nations (Deut. 32:8), that seventy of these nations were committed to the care of specific angels. Then, over these nations, He appointed one foul angel, named Samael, the angel of death. This was the Devil or Satan. Hence, the origin of the name "the prince of the world." It is interesting that our Lord used the very title that the rabbis did in His statement when referring to Satan. The name "Samael" is found in the Talmud tractate, Yevamoth 16b. Jesus also later used the term, "the prince of the world," in John 14:30, and John 16:11. Satan is referred to under similar titles in 2 Cor. 4:4; Eph. 2:2 with 6:12. The thought is, that Satan, who had control over the bodies and souls of men through their sin would lose that control when Christ bore man's sins, paid their full penalty on the cross, and rose from the bondage of death. Thus, the power of sin was canceled or negated for all who trust Christ as Lord and Savior. Now, Satan's chains can be loosed from any man who knows Christ. At Calvary, Satan's control of mankind through sin was spoiled (stripped away); the Lord Jesus made a public show of his defeat on the cross. He triumphed over sin and all evil in His death (Col. 2:15) and resurrection (Rev. 1:18). Now, the Lord of glory imputes this victory to His children. Victory over the Devil is theirs! It was provided by God's grace and must be appropriated daily by faith, obedience, and self-discipline. This is not to keep one saved, but because he is saved. The sins of the world were laid on Christ. He suffered their punishment or wages, thus paying their debt. In this, He has conquered every sin of mankind. On the cross, Christ bore the judgment of God for all the world's sins of all times. However, only those who are saved are benefactors of this pardon and atonement. Lastly, in His victorious resurrection, He secured the final and ultimate fate and eternal doom of Satan, who is the father of sin. This awful fate is emphatically declared in Matt. 25:41 with Rev. 20:10.

(k) **Verse 32. "Lifted up"** was a standard expression having direct reference to the dreaded wood and nails of the cross or death by crucifixion. Earlier Jesus had spoken similar words to Nicodemus in John 3:14. Verse 33 below explains the meaning of verse 32.

2p-**Verse 33.** John wrote looking back on history. From this perspective he understood the story of redemption for mankind. He explains to his readers the exact meaning of Jesus' Words about being "lifted up," thus drawing *all men* unto Himself (verse 32). What an interesting claim in the words, "all men." Like John 1:9, which states that He "lighteth every man that cometh into the world," and Titus 2:11, "the grace of God that bringeth salvation hath appeared to all men," the invitation is for all. To read these verses as meaning "all the preordained elect" is preposterous. It is true that most men refuse, reject, spurn, or simply neglect the "effectual call" of grace upon their lives. "Few there be that find it" (Matt. 7:14). To the religious leaders of Israel, the Lord Jesus announced, "And ye will not come to me that ye might have life" (John 5:40). They chose not to receive Jesus as their Messiah and Savior. God forces or compels no one to believe or not believe. For Israel being Jehovah's elect, see Section 163, third paragraph under footnote k. Note also Section 1, Part 3, the first three paragraph of footnote h.

(l) **"We have heard out of the law that Christ [Messiah] abideth for ever."** Here was a response from the people standing about. By this time in Jewish history, their entire Old Testament was called "the law," not just the first five books of Moses. Hence, they confess their Scripture affirms that Messiah lives without end, even forever. However, where are such things written in the Jewish Old Testament or Tanakh? In Ps. 110:4, we read of the perpetuity of His priesthood, as David's Lord, who, after being raised from the dead would sit at the right hand of God forever. In Isa. 9:6-7, and Ezek. 37:25. In Ps. 89:4, Messiah's throne is forever. Again, He is "the Ancient of days" whose kingdom is everlasting in Dan. 2:44, 7:13-14, 27. The sages and Hebrew teachers saw in all these passages their Messiah. This is how the people standing about Christ had "heard out of the law" that their Messiah abides forever. The final book of the Bible *seals* this claim in Rev. 1:18.

2p-**Messiah's life span.** Those familiar with rabbinical teachings during this era know something of their opinions of Messiah's life span. It varied from the sublime to the ridiculous. Some of them held that there would be two different Messiah's in Jewish eschatology. For details on this, see Section 6, sixth paragraph of footnote d, and next paragraph below. Some taught Messiah would live thirty years, some forty, some a hundred, others a thousand and so on! *So what can this mean?* Simply, that *after* Messiah's earthly work was over, eternity would follow, and their Messiah would live forever. This is more rabbinical error. Jesus of Nazareth, the Messiah of Israel had no beginning or ending: He has been forever and will be. The only interlude in His eternality was His appearing among men in human flesh for a short time. For a review of old Hebrew traditions, myths, and beliefs about the life, deeds, and chronology of Messiah, see Section 82, footnote d. For the modern day Jewish opinion of the Lord Jesus Christ, contrasted with that of the ancient Jewish people, note Section 14, footnote f.

3p-**"Be lifted up" and the two Messiahs.** The audience understood that Jesus was speaking of death by crucifixion when He used the expression "lifted up." See footnote k above. They had learned about Messiah out of their Scriptures, and that Messiah son of David, would live forever. These same Jews noted in their Scriptures the predictions of Messiah's death as seen in Ps. 22 with Isa. 53. The rabbis had (for the most part) seriously misinterpreted these prophecies. During the Talmudic period (A.D. 250-500), Jewish scribes invented a Messiah called "the son of Joseph," also known by some as "the son of Ephraim," and the "son of Manasseh." This *imaginary* Messiah would be killed in a future war with Gog and Magog. Such rabbinical plotting was designed to remove Jesus of Nazareth from Isa. 53, thus proving He was not the true Messiah. Christians had used Isaiah's predictions to great advantage, proving repeatedly that Christ fulfilled these. The Christ hating rabbis invented their own Messiah, the "son of Joseph," and declared that he would fulfill the predictions of Isaiah and other Old Testament passages at a future time. In our present century the alleged "son of Joseph" Messiah is mostly unknown by the Jewish people. "Messiah son of David" is the one familiar to most informed Orthodox Jews. Along with this mythical "son of Joseph," they affirm that their *true* Messiah, the "son of David," will come and establish His literal kingdom for Israel. Among rabbinical opinions, some held he was born in A.D. 70 at the destruction of Jerusalem and remains hidden until the time is right for his appearing. Their ideas regarding this literal kingdom an Messiah are often wild and reckless. For more on these things, see Section 4, footnote d.

4p-Over the centuries, unsaved Jewish apologists have been intimidated by the predictions of Isa. 53 and Ps. 22. They struggle to reinterpret or explain them away. About the year A.D. 1100, a famed Jewish teacher, Rabbi Solomon Yazchaki, better known as "Rabbi Rashi," wrote a classic but novel interpretation of Isa. 53. *He stated that the pronouns in this chapter spoke exclusively of the nation of Israel and her sufferings, not the sufferings of Jesus of Nazareth.* Since it was the nation of Israel that was suffering it could not have reference to the Jesus of Christianity, Israel's true Messiah (Prov. 4:19). The discerning mind can see this whole scenario was designed by Satan to keep the great Hebrew people from coming to know Jesus as the Messiah and Savior. For more on this, see Section 6, third and sixth paragraphs under footnote e. *Appendix Three* carries a list of many prophecies given hundreds and thousands of years in advance that pointed to the birth, life and work of the Lord Jesus. These demonstrate that the Messiah of the Jewish Tanakh or Old Testament is Christ of the New Testament.

5p-**"Who is this son of man?"** Apparently, in verse 34 some of the Jews were confused that Jesus had referred to Himself as "the Son of man" back in verse 23. This reflects again their ignorance of their Scriptures. In Dan. 7:13 we read the prophecy of Israel's Messiah being called "the Son of man." This spoke of His humanity as a man and sharing in the Adamic experience. Our Lord first used it of Himself in the very early stages of His ministry in John 1:51. Here, it was in connection with the miraculous. Later, during His religious trial, He employed the term "Son of man," as also meaning "the Son of God" (Matt. 26:63-64 with Mk. 14:61-62). It is clear from the reaction of the high priest at His trial that he understood exactly what the Lord Jesus was saying and flew into a rage. For more on the title "Son of man," refer to Section 103, footnote b. One of the outstanding treatises in the English language on this subject is, *The Doctrine of the Manifestations of the Son of God under the Economy of the Old Testament,* by George B. Kidd, printed in 1852. This old work is a forgotten classic in the field of Christian apologetics. We bow our heads in thankful reverence that the Son of God became a Son of men that we might become the sons of God!

(m) The Savior did not reply to their question about the Son of man. He detected that they were offended by the suggestion that their Messiah would be lifted up on a cross. "Walk while ye have light" was His direct invitation to the Greeks and Jews standing about. They were called upon to trust Him immediately as Messiah and Savior. Groping in their awful darkness of rejection, the Lord Jesus pleads with them to enter His saving light. In the words "Yet a little while," He warns them that the time was short, and that they must act quickly.

(n) **"Hurry and believe in me."** This is the jest of His Words as He pleads with the Jews to believe in Him while He is present with them. Because He was there in the flesh, spiritual light was both near and present; they must hurry and accept every ray of His divine light. Those without His illumination walk in awful darkness and do not see hell waiting at the end of earth's short tenure. His admonition was something like this, "Walk in my light while it is here, for soon I will return to my Father in heaven. Your city and temple will be destroyed, and your nation scattered across the world."

(o) **"Jesus departed and hid himself from them."** One detects a dirge of finality in these words. They were among His last admonitions to Jews, who were drawn to Him with the curious Greeks. We do not know *where* our Lord "hid" Himself from the infuriated religionists or for how long. Apparently, it was only long enough for their wrath to subside. In Section 162, John 12:37-43, John continuing, wrote a summary of the Jew's rejection of Jesus' miracles (which reflected that He was Messiah), and that many of the chief rulers believed in Him. He penned this concluding summary some years later as he reflected back on the events that happened in the temple at that time. Writing *after* the fullness of the Spirit at Pentecost, he then perfectly understood the whole story. The basis of the Spirit coming in His glorious totality was the death, burial, and resurrection of Christ. This is stated in John 7:39, 12:16 and 23, with John 17:1. Note Section 206, fifth paragraph of footnote e for other comments on this subject.

2p-Later, in John 12:44, we note that Jesus had withdrawn from hiding and was back among the crowds again, pleading with them to believe on Him. It is noteworthy that this was His *final* appeal to the unbelieving Jews. The teaching of Christ contained in Section 163 through the end of 166 predicted the fall of Jerusalem, demise of the Jewish state, and destruction of the temple in A.D. 70. This was given to four of His apostles, not the blasphemous religious leaders, and their companions who hated Him.

THE SAVIOR'S FINAL WARNING TO ISRAEL.*

John looked back and wrote of Jewish unbelief at that time. It was predicted in Old Testament prophecy. By divine inspiration, he recalls the final Words that Christ directed at those who had rejected Him. Below, in seven verses are Messiah's warnings to His people. Still, many secret believers remained among the crowds. His Words end with the grim finality of, "so I speak."

Time: Tuesday after Palm Sunday before His death on Friday mid–afternoon.

It is conjecture that He left the temple at the end of this Section and retired to the Mount of Olives with four of His apostles. There, He gave the lengthy and successive discourses found in Sections 163 through 166.

Matt.	Mk.	Lk.	John 12:37–50 *At Jerusalem amid the Passover crowds*
			John's personal comments and Isaiah's prophecy
			37 But though he had done so many miracles[a] before them, [the Jews] yet they believed not on him:
			38 That the saying of Esaias [Isaiah] the prophet might be fulfilled, which he spake,[b] **"Lord, who hath believed our report? and to whom hath the arm of the Lord been revealed?"**
			39 Therefore they could not believe, because that Esaias [Isaiah] said again,[c]
			40 **"He hath blinded their eyes, and hardened their heart; that they should not see with their eyes, nor understand with their heart, and be converted, and I should heal them."**
			41 These things said Esaias, [Isaiah] when he saw his glory, and spake of him.[d]
			Secret believers
			42 Nevertheless among the chief rulers also many believed on him; but because of the Pharisees they did not confess *him*, lest they should be put out of the synagogue:[e]
			43 For they loved the praise of men more than the praise of God.[f]
			What faith in Christ is
			44 Jesus cried and said,[g] "He that believeth on me, believeth not on me, but on him that sent me.
			45 "And he that seeth me seeth him that sent me.[h]
			46 "I am come a light[i] into the world, that whosoever believeth on me should not abide in darkness.
			What rejection of Christ is
			47 "And if any man hear my words, and believe not, I judge him not: for I came not to judge the world, but to save the world.[j]
			48 "He that rejecteth me, and receiveth not my words, hath one that judgeth him: the word that I have spoken, the same shall judge him in the last day.
			49 "For I have not spoken[k] of myself; but the Father which sent me, he gave me a commandment, what I should say, and what I should speak. [l]
			50 "And I know that his commandment is life everlasting: **whatsoever I speak therefore, even as the Father said unto me, so I speak."**[m]
			(Next chap., John 13:1 cont. in Section 170.)

Footnotes-Commentary

[a] **"So many miracles."** One sure proof that Jesus was Israel's Messiah was the astounding signs and wonders He performed over the course of His ministry. See all by the asterisk under main heading Section 48 for explanation regarding Christ and His Messianic signs. John wrote that even this did not convince the Jews. Most of them refused

to believe in Him. However, according to verse 42, He had numerous covert believers among the people for it reads, "many believed on him." This was kept secret due to the awful consequences of being associated with Christ. Expulsion from the synagogue was the worst fate for any pious Jew. See footnote e below.

(b) From Isa. 53:1. **"Who hath believed our report?"** John explains to his original readers the meaning of what he had just written in verse 37. In this Old Testament quotation, the prophet Isaiah was greatly confounded because the people to whom he preached in that day refused to believe his words. His experience with the stubborn Jews was similarly the experience of Messiah over seven hundred years later. As Isaiah's message was despised by the nation so was the message of Christ. *Among the Jews few, by comparison, had believed the Son of God and the Old Testament report concerning Him.* "The arm of the Lord" was an expression that signified that God's "power" had been shown to Israel through Jesus of Nazareth like no other time in its history. However, it was rejected. This does not mean that the Jews mostly rejected Christ that the prediction of Isaiah might be fulfilled. Rather, that it was fulfilled in their self-chosen, continual, and final rejection of Him. John penned these words some years after these events happened. Now, he looks back and clearly understands Isaiah's prediction.

(c) John quotes this from Isa. 6:9-10. These citations reveal his familiarity with the Jewish Old Testament. The prophet here states that it was God, who had blinded the Jews' eyes and hardened their hearts so that they would not be converted. For explanation of these strange words, see Section 74, footnote e, where our Lord much earlier quoted this prediction. Those who cite this text to prove that God was unwilling for the Jews to turn to Him, or to save them speak unmitigated heresy. They make our Savior into an ignorant preacher who wasted His time and life on a people that He could not help to begin with. This is not an example of the "determinate counsel and foreknowledge of God" as ignorance often states (Acts 2:23). God has never forced, decreed, or ordained any person *not* to believe in His blessed Son. This error springs from the wretched philosophy of John Calvin, plagiarized from that forerunner of Popery, the erratic Catholic, preacher-lawyer-philosopher, Saint Augustine. Will Durant, the agnostic, but perfidious historian penned these words in, *The Story of Civilization,* vol. 6, page 465. "It is remarkable how much of Roman Catholic tradition and theory survived in Calvin's theology. He owed something to Stoicism, especially to Seneca, and something to his studies of law; but his chief reliance was on St. Augustine . . ."

2p-Calvin, lover of wine. His genius lay not in conceiving new ideas but in developing the thoughts of his predecessors to ruinously logical conclusions, especially those of Augustine. He also had a unique genius for wine. The Geneva City Council freely afforded him "some two hundred and fifty gallons of wine annually for his household." In *Calvin and the Reformation,* edited by William Park Armstrong, pages 48-50, are numerous quotes from the Reformer about drinking. Such things as, "the gaiety and pleasure which we get from wine may not disturb our worship of God," and believers "may receive new strength [from wine] for the fulfillment of our vocation." *True* Christians work in the power of the Holy Spirit not high proof alcohol. Calvin is described as "a man who loves banquet, to make good cheer, and to drink a few glasses of wine with friends." Lastly, the "greatest theologian in history" said a "man who cannot carry three glasses of wine without being overcome and then drinks indiscreetly, is he not a hog?" The philosophy, "A man should be able to hold his drink, and then he can serve God with strength, joy, and pleasure," borders on insanity. This is the man of whom Dr. McFetridge wrote, "Next to Paul, John Calvin has done most for the world." See *Calvinism in History,* by Nathaniel. S. McFetridge, page 68. We are sure that Calvin's breath did not smell like that of Paul. His joy was in Christ not a flagon of wine (Phil. 4:4). We wonder where the Savior fits into McFetridge's equation. The Baptist, Augustus H. Strong wrote, "Calvinists have been the most strenuous advocates of civil liberties" in his *Systematic Theology,* page 368-369. Strong, McFetridge, and their kind, never experienced the imprisonments, beatings, tortures, or being burnt to death by these famed "defenders of civil liberties." If so, they would have written differently.

(d) **"Saw Messiah's glory."** Isaiah, some seven hundred years before Jesus was born of Mary at Bethlehem, "saw" the glory of Jesus the Messiah. How out of touch are those "academicians" who tell us that Old Testament people knew very little, if anything of Christ-Messiah, the blessed Son of God.

(e) **"Put out of the synagogue."** John pens this surprising editorial comment informing his original readers that though most of Israel rejected Jesus as their Messiah, yet among the "chief rulers many believed on him." What a fantastic statement! We know of only two by name, Nicodemus and Joseph of Arimathea. Earlier in our Lord's ministry, the Pharisees inquired of the temple police, "Have any of the rulers or of the Pharisees believed on him" (John 7:48)? Some years later, John reported, "many believed." The greatest threat that the Sanhedrin held over their fellows, and the common people was, "You will be put out of the synagogue." For the horrors of being excommunicated, note Section 121, footnote j.

(f) This sad commentary has at various times fit very well upon most of our backs! However, in this text it has direct reference to the scribes and Pharisees, who were given wholly to the praise and applause of men.

(g) **Verses 44-50.** *These are our Lord's final words to the Jews, who had so hounded His life and work.* In verse 44, He informs them that when men believe in Him, it is counted as if they had believed in God! Have we not heard such equal terms, in "He that hath seen me hath seen the Father," or "he who honors the Son honors the Father" and so forth? Jesus, in these words, again asserted His Oneness and full equality with the Father. All the Hebrew prattle about the "one God," and, "there is no God beside the God of Israel;" their recitations of the beautiful Shema from Deut. 6:4-5 were pious prattle for they had rejected the only way to this true and living God. In a few hours, these same people would be screaming for His blood! The conclusion of verse 44 is simply, "He who believes in me, has already believed in God." Men cannot have One without the Other, or the Other without the One. All the religious and political prattle about believing in God but rejecting His Son, Jesus Christ, is another lie of Satan designed to damn the souls of those who embrace it. For continued comments on this apostate and liberal ecumenical approach to the Bible and the doctrine of Christ, see Section 175, the fourth through sixth paragraphs of footnote e.

(h) **Verse 45.** This enigma puzzled Philip. A while later in the upper room, the night before the morning of the cross, we hear him asking about it in John 14:8. For comments on Christ, the only Person who came to reveal and make known the true and living God, see Section 1, Part 4, John 1:18, footnote l.

(i) **Verse 46.** The rabbis taught that Messiah was the light of the world. This is discussed in Section 1, Part 1, John 1:4, second paragraph of footnotes e and f. Every informed Hebrew knew exactly what He was purporting by this claim—*that He was Messiah!* His invitation was for them to believe on Him and be saved out of the spiritual darkness in which they lived. However, they preferred their blindness and refused to repent and confess Him as Messiah and Savior. They sought to kill Jesus and refused His light to shine illumination into their dark hearts. As far as the religious leaders representing *legitimate* divine authority, Jesus bade His hearers to respect that representation, but warned them never to mime their falsity, hypocrisy, love for preeminence, fondness of public titles and arrogance. See Section 159 for Jesus' denunciation of these men spoken under eight fearful woes.

(j) **Verse 47. "Save the world."** The meaning is that He will save those who repent of their sins and believe on Him. According to Calvinism He should have said that He "Came to save the elect of the world." Among the Jews, many heard Him speak hundreds of times, but chose not to believe His message of life and hope (John 5:40). In such cases, the Son does not need to judge His haters. The very living and eternal Words of God that He had preached and taught among them would rise up in judgment and condemn their deliberate unbelief. This statement from our Lord shows the everlasting existence and infallibility of what He has spoken. A guilty conscious needs no accuser but with the Jews and all Christ rejecters, there will be something far worse—the Word of God; the voice that lives and abides for ever. The religious leaders were the chief culprits in rejecting Him, their blessed and faithful Messiah. Their physical doom, as predicted by the Savior in Section 163, came in A.D. 70.

2p-**"But to save the world."** Obviously, those who repent and believe on the Lord Jesus Christ are those who are saved in this world. There is no universalism or Unitarianism found here.

3p-**Verse 48. "The last day."** Refer to Section 124, footnote j for an explanation and various cross–references to this term and its meaning in the four gospels.

(k) **Verse 49.** Jesus declares that He has not preached His own self-interest to the people, but only what God had commanded Him to say. He had not attempted to derive any form of gain or otherwise from the Jews. He absolutely affirms that His message was the truth of the God they claim to worship, and that as His envoy and messenger, He had spoken to them only truth. How God instructed Jesus what to say during His earthly ministry is found in Section 19, footnote c, footnote l below.

2p-**"What I should speak."** This does not have reference to a common conversation, but it refers to the doctrines of God that He had taught. Also, how He responded to the needs of others.

(l) Highlighted in gray as having reference to a paraphrase from the Old Testament (Isa. 50:4). This verse reveals how God instructed Jesus what to speak. The expression "his commandment" means "God's commission for Him." It has nothing to do with the Torah Law. God sent or commissioned His Son, Jesus Christ-Messiah, to come into the world. The Son was the only Savior of Jew or Gentile. He informs the Jews in this final sentence that every Word of His was accredited and verified by Jehovah; that those who believe would find peace with God and self. In spite of their trickery, lies, slanders, blasphemy and many threats of death, Christ faithfully proclaimed His Father's message to them. *By choice, they had sealed their own fate.* What a testimony to our Lord's faithfulness to His Father's will, and Word. See footnote k above for more on God instructing Jesus what to say and teach.

(m) **Verse 50. "So speak I."** This calamitous warning is highlighted in red. See footnote l above for the divine origin of our Lord's Words. These utterances are weighted with grim finality directed at the stubborn Jews. It means, "Hear Me or be doomed." Jesus the Messiah had spoken only God's Word to them. They intentionally rejected Him, thus sealing their fate. Christ briefly describes Israel's terrible judgment in the following page and the next Section.

2p-**Goodbye temple.** With the last three words of verse 50, *the public ministry* of the Savior was finished. He departed from the Jerusalem temple never to preach within its walls again. A short time later, He walked through this mighty structure with the eleven apostles on His way to Gethsemane where He was arrested. Lastly, He was led back through this building to the high priest's house on the western side of the city after being taken prisoner. Then, to the quarters of Governor Pilate on the northeast side of Jerusalem near the temple. Refer to Section 180 through 188 for the story. Exiting the house of God, He led four of His apostles to Mount Olivet. There He spent several hours in private instructions regarding the fate of their city, nation, and temple. This is recorded in Sections 163 through 166 with an introduction to this on the next page.

INTRODUCTION TO SECTION 163 AND THE HORRORS OF A.D. 70.

Immense interpretative difficulties are embedded in the discourse contained in Matt. 24 and its parallels. This manifests the divine inspiration of Scripture and the natural inability of mortals to grasp their *absolute* meaning. Over the years, men have written thousands of treatises to remove these problems; no one has succeeded. This Introduction makes no such attempt. The frequent metaphorical language in which this message is clothed and the intentional obscurity in which God has always embraced the details of the future are obvious. Christians who read these verses out of idle curiosity find themselves paralyzed trying to make it *all* fit into a previously held eschatological framework. Some force it to fit. The entire lesson given by our Lord in the following verses was recorded by divine direction, not human genius. *However, it is given to us in a condensed form with only the basic substances recorded.* This clearly admits of verbal, but not incorrect divergences. The divine object of prophecy over all ages has been first a moral warning instead of a chronological meter to fix dates and times for future events to occur. The practitioners of date setting have always produced disappointments and frustrations for the weak and unlearned who follow them.

By harmonizing the separate accounts of Matthew, Mark, and Luke as closely as possible, we discover that they often throw mutual light upon each other. John was not inspired to write of A.D. 70. The Lord Jesus turned the thoughts of His four apostles into two different horizons; one near, and the other very far off. At times, He takes them from the terrible events in that present epoch of world history into another, far away in the distant future. Christ was first speaking partly, and second, primarily of the forty years that led up to the fall of the Jewish polity and dispensation. Then partly and secondarily of the end of the world, and He did this by an interchange back and forth of thought and speech. Such speaking was natural for our Lord because His whole being moved first in the sphere of eternity and not of earth's time. He gave this discourse in deep solemnity and with a serious countenance never before seen by His troubled apostles, Peter, James, John, and Andrew, who sat before Him (Mk. 13:3).

Christ's terrible warning, "Behold, your house is left unto you desolate," hung like an ominous storm cloud soon to burst upon Israel, and the city which had "become a harlot," and that house of prayer now "a den of thieves." The historian Josephus, who died about A.D. 100, witnessed it all. He wrote, "I cannot but think that it was because God had doomed this city to destruction as a polluted city, and was resolved to purge His sanctuary by fire, that he cut off these their great defenders and well wishers; while those that had before worn the sacred garments and presided over the public worship, and had been esteemed venerable by those that dwelt in the whole habitable earth, were cast out naked, and seen to be food of dogs and wild beasts." Again, Josephus wrote, "The blood of all sorts of dead carcasses, priests, and strangers profane, [all] standing in lakes [of blood] in the holy courts. The corpses lying in piles and mounds on the very altar slopes; fires feeding on cedar work overlaid with gold, friend and foe trampled to death on the gleaming mosaics in terrible carnage. The beautiful House of God was a heap of ghastly ruin, where the burning embers were half-slaked in pools of gore." He ended this chilling eulogy over Jerusalem and Israel with these doleful words, "Nor did any age breed a generation more fruitful in wickedness than this was, since the beginning of the world." See Josephus' *Wars of the Jews,* Books 5 through 7 for the horrible details. How odd that Jesus had spoken similar things to Josephus in Matt. 24:21. He affirmed that all the righteous blood shed upon the earth since Abel would be required of that generation of Jews, who perished in the flames of their dying Jerusalem and temple.

Never in the annuals of human events has there been a narrative more full of horrors, frenzies, unspeakable degradations, and overwhelming miseries than the history of the siege and destruction of a single city, Jerusalem. The famed Presbyterian missionary to Syria, Dr. William H. Thomson (died 1894), in his classic work, *The Land and the Book,* pages 692 and 696, wrote that there were, "1,200, 000 [Jews] shut up in Jerusalem by Titus," and that the length of the siege was "four months and twenty-five days–from April 11, A.D. 70, to the 7 of September." Never was a mass of prophecy more closely and terribly, fulfilled than the things predicted by Christ in this Olivet Discourse.

The shuddering denunciations and fearful predictions spoken by the Son of God in this message reveal a permanent break had taken place. It was "too late." The "door of hope" was shut. Israel, Jerusalem, and the brilliant temple were sentenced to destruction. Over the next four decades, the Word's of Christ were gradually fulfilled and culminated into "The doom of A.D. 70." With this, all heaven broke open in fierce judgment upon these stubborn people and their city. The record of our Lord's prophecies and commentaries on His Words and their partial fulfillment are contained in the next Section.

THE GREAT OLIVET DISCOURSE.

Christ rebuked the Pharisees in Section 159, commented on the widow's mites in Section 160, spoke to the Greeks in Section 161, and made a final plea to the Jews in Section 162. Departing from the temple, He moved down the eastern slope of Mount Moriah. Crossing the brook Cedron, He walked up to the summit of Mount Olivet and sat down. With Jerusalem and the temple in full view, He answers the four apostle's questions by giving this prophetic discourse on the destruction of the city, its temple, and the collapse of the Jewish state in A.D. 70.* Christ blends into these lessons pictures of His far off second advent when He will return for His children and to judge all mankind.

Jesus gave this message "two days" before His death. For explanation of this, see number 6 in the Information Box before footnotes in Section 164. This discourse began in Matt. 24:1 and concluded at Matt. 25:46, a total of ninety-seven verses. Not counting Mark and Luke's parallel verses, this is the second longest recorded message Jesus gave. The first is, The Sermon on the Mount, in Sections 44 through 47, and consists of a hundred and eleven verses. Following His warnings on last things as given below, He concluded with two successive parables on readiness in Sections 164 and 165. The Olivet Discourse ends in Section 166 with a lesson on the final judgment depicted by sheep and goats. The lesson in Matt. 24 is different from the message given earlier in Section 134, but there are similarities. The Savior repeated Himself here as on other occasions. In the message below, He added dozens of new details not found in the message previously given in Section 134. This discourse about Jerusalem could be called, "the New Testament book of Lamentations."

Time: Sometime Tuesday after Palm Sunday.

Parts of this discourse make up some of the most difficult portions of Scripture to rightly divide. Thousands of books have been written about Matt. 24. The Millennium Bible, by William E. Biederwolf, pages 326–339 lists Christian conservatives who disagree regarding portions of Christ's teachings in this chapter. Some of the thoughts below are the conjectures of the author who firmly disdains making this message a Jewish thing only. Important points are often highlighted in gray, such as the apostles three question, which appear as headings in gray boxes.

On the western side of the Mount of Olives

Matt. 24:1-3	Mk. 13:1-3	Lk. 21:5-7	John
The disciples show Him the temple architecture **1** And Jesus went out,[a] and departed from the temple: and his disciples[b] came to *him* for to shew him the buildings of the temple.	***The disciples show Him the temple architecture*** **1** And as he went out[a] of the temple, one of his disciples[b] saith unto him, "Master, see what manner of stones and what buildings *are here!*"		
		The disciples show Him the temple architecture **5** And as some spake[b] of the temple, how it was adorned with goodly stones and gifts,	
His answer disturbs them: they are shocked **2** And Jesus said unto them, "See ye not all these things? verily I say unto you, There shall not be left here one stone upon another, that shall not be thrown down."[c]	***His answer disturbs them: they are shocked*** **2** And Jesus answering said unto him, "Seest thou these great buildings? there shall not be left one stone upon another, that shall not be thrown down."[c]	***His answer disturbs them: they are shocked*** he said, **6** "As for these things which ye behold, the days will come, in the which there shall not be left one stone upon another, that shall not be thrown down."[c]	
The disciples' questions **3** And as he sat[d] upon the mount of Olives, the disciples came	***The disciples' questions*** **3** And as he sat[d] upon the mount of Olives over against [overlooking] the temple, Peter and James and	***The disciples' questions*** **7** And they	

Matt. 24:3–9	Mk. 13:3–9	Lk. 21:7–12	John
unto him privately, saying,(e) "Tell us, when shall these things [temple destroyed] be? and what *shall be* the sign of thy coming, and of the end of the world?" [age]	John and Andrew asked(e) him privately, 4 "Tell us, when shall these things [temple destroyed] be? and what *shall be* the sign when all these things shall be fulfilled?"	asked(e) him, saying, "Master, but when shall these things [temple destroyed] be? and what sign *will there be* when these things shall come to pass?"	
Jesus begins to answer their questions 4 And Jesus answered(f) and said unto them, "Take heed that no man deceive you.	***Jesus begins to answer their questions*** 5 And Jesus answering(f) them began to say, "Take heed lest any *man* deceive you:	***Jesus begins to answer their questions*** 8 And he [answering](f) said, "Take heed that ye be not deceived:	
5 "For many shall come in my name, saying, 'I am Christ;' [Messiah] and shall deceive many.	6 "For many shall come in my name, saying, 'I am *Christ;*' [Messiah] and shall deceive many.	for many shall come in my name, saying, 'I am *Christ;*'[Messiah] and 'the time draweth near:' go ye not therefore after them.	
6 "And ye shall hear of wars and rumours of wars: see that ye be not troubled: for all *these things* must come to pass, but the end is not yet.	7 "And when ye shall hear of wars and rumours of wars, be ye not troubled: for *such things* must needs be; but the end *shall* not *be* yet.	9 "But when ye shall hear of wars and commotions, be not terrified: for these things must first come to pass; but the end *is* not by and by.	
Before Jerusalem falls many signs will occur 7 "For nation shall rise against nation, and kingdom against kingdom: and there shall be famines, and pestilences, and earthquakes, in divers places. ▲*Matthew puts the famines before the earth-quakes. Mark verse 8 and Luke verse 11 place them after.*	***Before Jerusalem falls many signs will occur*** 8 "For nation shall rise against nation, and kingdom against kingdom: and there shall be ▶earthquakes in divers places, and there shall be famines and troubles:	***Before Jerusalem falls many signs will occur*** 10 Then said he unto them, "Nation shall rise against nation, and kingdom against kingdom: 11 "And great ▶earthquakes shall be in divers places, and famines, and pestilences; and fearful sights and great signs shall there be from heaven.	
8 "All these *are* the beginning of sorrows.	these *are* the beginnings of sorrows.	12 "But before all these,	
9 "Then shall they deliver you up to	9 "But take heed to yourselves: for they shall deliver you up to councils; [the Sanhedrin]	they shall lay their hands on you, and persecute *you*, delivering *you* up to the	

Matt. 24:9–14	Mk. 13:9–12	Lk. 21:12–16	John
be afflicted, and shall kill you: and ye shall be hated◄ of all nations for my name's sake.	and in the synagogues ye shall be beaten: and ye shall be brought before rulers and kings for my sake,	synagogues, and into prisons, being brought before kings and rulers for my name's sake.	

be afflicted, and shall kill
you:
and ye shall be hated◄ of
all nations for my name's
sake.

▲ *Mark and Luke wrote of this hatred in
verses 13 and 17 below.*

Offences, hatred, betrayals, and false prophets

10 "And then shall many be offended, and shall betray one another, and shall hate one another.

11 "And many false prophets shall rise, and shall deceive many.

12 "And because iniquity shall abound, the love of many shall wax cold.

13 "But he that shall endure► unto the end, the same shall be saved.

The gospel to all nations of that day

14 "And this gospel of the ▼kingdom shall be preached in all the world for a witness unto all nations; and then shall the end come.

▲ *This is not a unique tribulation gospel
designed only for the Jews. There is no
such thing, neither has there ever been.
Regardless of the age, Jews or anyone else
are saved only by the gospel of Christ. It
is the same gospel that God preached to
Abraham (Gal. 3:8), and to the millions
of stubborn Jews in the wilderness (Heb.
3:17-18, 4:1-2). Paul called it the "our
gospel," "the gospel of God," and "the
gospel of Christ"(1 Thess. 1:5, 2:1, and
3:2). Above in verse 14 it is called the
"gospel of the kingdom." It alone saves
(Rom. 1:16). The gospel was known
from the beginning (Lk. 1:69-70 with
Acts 3:21). Those who change or pervert
it are under a divine curse (Gal. 1:6-11).
Regarding the nature of this kingdom, see
Section 39, footnotes a and g.*

---

and in the synagogues ye
shall be beaten: and ye shall
be brought before rulers and
kings for my
sake,

for a testimony against them.

◄*Several of the warnings spoken in
this discourse were previously given
when Jesus sent out the twelve across
Galilee, some two years earlier. They are
Mk. 13:9 above, with Matt. 10:17.
Then Mk. 13:11-12 below, with Matt.
10:18-21.*

► *See comments at Mk. 13:13 below
on the word "endure."*

The gospel to all nations of that day

10 "And the gospel must first be published among all nations.

Anointed to answer by the indwelling Holy Spirit

11 "But when they shall lead *you*, and deliver you up, take no thought beforehand what ye shall speak, neither do ye premeditate: but whatsoever shall be given you in that hour, that speak ye: for it is not ye that speak, but the Holy Ghost.

Sinister betrayals

12 "Now the brother shall betray the brother to death, and the father the son; and children shall rise up against *their* parents, and

---

synagogues, and into
prisons, being
brought before
kings and rulers for my
name's sake.

13 "And it shall turn to you for a testimony.

Anointed to answer by the indwelling Holy Spirit

14 "Settle *it* therefore in your hearts, not to meditate before what ye shall answer:

15 "For I will give you a mouth and wisdom, which all your adversaries shall not be able to gainsay nor resist.

Sinister betrayals

16 "And ye shall be betrayed both

by parents,
and brethren, and
kinsfolks, and friends; and

Matt. 24:15–18	Mk. 13:12–16	Lk. 21:16–21	John
Matthew wrote of this hatred in▶ *verse 9 above.* ▶ *"Endure" and "saved." The believers of that time endured and were saved from the slaughter of A.D. 70 by escaping to the city of Pella. See third paragraph of number 16, footnote f below in Footnotes-Commentary section.*	shall cause them to be put to death. ◀13 "And ye shall be hated of all *men* for my name's sake: but he that ◀shall endure● unto the end, [of Jerusalem's fall] the same shall be saved. ●*Salvation of the soul is not acquired by "enduring" but by faith in Jesus Christ. This speaks of being saved from physical death during the destruction of Jerusalem.*	*some* of you shall they cause to be put to death. 17 "And ye shall be hated of all *men* for my name's sake. 18 "But there shall not an hair of your head perish. 19 "In your patience possess ye your souls.	
Jerusalem surrounded by Roman armies 15 "When ye therefore shall see[(g)] the 'abomination of desolation,'[(h)] spoken of by Daniel the prophet, stand in the holy place," (whoso readeth, let him understand:)	***Jerusalem surrounded by Roman armies*** 14 But when ye shall see[(g)] the 'abomination of desolation,'[(h)] spoken of by Daniel the prophet, standing where it ought not," (let him that readeth understand,)	***Jerusalem surrounded by Roman armies*** 20 "And when ye shall see[(g)] Jerusalem compassed with armies, then know that the 'desolation'[(h)] thereof is nigh.	
Believers flee quickly: go into the mountains 16 "Then let them which be in Judaea flee into the mountains:	***Believers flee quickly: go into the mountains*** "then let them that be in Judaea flee to the mountains:	***Believers flee quickly: go into the mountains*** 21 "Then let them which are in Judaea flee to the mountains; and let them which are in the midst of it depart out; and let not them that are in the countries enter thereinto. (Judaea) ◀*This cannot speak of the removal of the church. See the ninth paragraph under footnote h below for why this is true.*	
Don't turn back to gather earthly possessions 17 "Let him which is on the housetop not come down to take any thing out of his house: 18 "Neither let him which is in the field return back to [the city] take his clothes.	***Don't turn back to gather earthly possessions*** 15 "And let him that is on the housetop not go down into the house, neither enter *therein*, to take any thing out of his house: 16 "And let him that is in the field not turn back again [to the city] for to take up his garment.		

745

Matt. 24:19–23	Mk. 13:17–21	Lk. 21:22–24	John
		Vengeance upon the people of Israel	
	These "days of vengeance" are ▶ *the same as "great tribulation," "affliction," and "great distress" in verses 21, 19 and 23 below. This all occurred in A.D. 70. It is not future.*	**22** "For these be the days of vengeance,[(i)] [upon Israel] that all things which are **written may be fulfilled.**	
Maternal woes and fleeing	***Maternal woes and fleeing***	***Maternal woes***	
19 "And woe unto them that are with child, and to them that give suck [nurse] in those days!	**17** "But woe to them that are with child, and to them that give suck [nurse] in those days!	**23** "But woe unto them that are with child, and to them that give suck, [nurse] in those days!	
20 "But pray ye that your flight [from the Romans] be not in the winter, neither on the sabbath day:	**18** "And pray ye that your flight [from the Romans] be not in the winter.		
Tribulation upon the people of Israel in A.D. 70.	***Affliction upon the people of Israel in A.D. 70.***	***Distress and wrath upon the people in A.D. 70.***	
21 "For then shall be great tribulation,[(i)] [upon Israel] such as was not since the beginning of the world to this time, no, nor ever shall be.	**19** "For *in* those days shall be affliction,[(i)] [upon Israel] such as was not from the beginning of the creation which God created unto this time, neither shall be.	for there shall be great distress[(i)] in the land, [of Israel] and wrath upon this people.(the Jews)	
		Jerusalem falls: Jews led captive: times of the Gentiles begin	
		24 "And they [the Jews] shall fall by the edge of the sword, and shall be led away captive into all nations: and Jerusalem shall be trodden down of the Gentiles, until the times of the Gentiles be fulfilled.	
A.D. 70 shortened	***A.D. 70 shortened***		
22 "And except those days should be shortened,[(j)] there should no flesh [those in the city] be saved: but for the elect's sake, [believer's] those days shall be shortened.	**20** "And except that the Lord had shortened[(j)] those days, no flesh [those in the city] should be saved: but for the elect's sake, [believer's] whom he hath chosen, he hath shortened the days.		
False Messiahs: chaos	***False Messiahs: chaos***		
23 "Then if any man shall say unto you, 'Lo, here *is* Christ,' [Messiah] or 'there;' believe *it* not.[(k)]	**21** "And then if any man shall say to you, 'Lo, here *is* Christ;' [Messiah] or, 'lo, *he is* there;' believe *him* not:[(k)]		

Matt. 24:24–29	Mk. 13:22–25	Lk. 21:25–26	John
24 "For there shall arise false Christs, [Messiahs] and false prophets, and shall shew great signs and wonders; insomuch that, if *it were* possible, they shall deceive the very elect.	**22** "For false Christs [Messiahs] and false prophets shall rise, and shall shew signs and wonders, to seduce, if *it were* possible, even the elect.		
You have been warned: now prepare	***You have been warned: now prepare***		
25 "Behold, I have told you before.	**23** "But take ye heed: behold, I have foretold you all things.		
26 "Wherefore if they shall say unto you, 'Behold, he [the Messiah] is in the desert;' go not forth: 'behold, *he is* in the secret chambers;' believe *it* not.	◄ *For the meaning of this curious place, see the fourth paragraph of footnote k below in the Footnotes-Commentary section.*		
27 "For as the lightning cometh out of the east, and shineth even unto the west; so shall also the coming of the Son of man be.[(l)]			
Roman eagles gathering			
28 "For wheresoever the carcase is, there will the eagles[(m)] be gathered together.			
The signs of A.D. 70 similar to second advent	***The signs of A.D. 70 similar to second advent***	***The signs of A.D. 70 similar to second advent***	
29 "Immediately after[(n)] the tribulation of those days shall the sun be darkened, and the moon shall not give her light, and the stars shall fall[(o)] from heaven,	**24** "But in those days, after[(n)] that tribulation, the sun shall be darkened, and the moon shall not give her light, **25** "And the stars of heaven shall fall,[(o)]	**25** "And there shall be [after that tribulation][(n)] signs in the sun, and in the moon, and in the stars; and upon the earth distress of nations, with perplexity; the sea and the waves roaring;[(o)]	
		Horrible phenomena occurs	
		26 "Men's hearts failing them for fear, and for looking after those things which are coming on the earth: for the powers of	
and the powers of the heavens shall be shaken.	and the powers that are in heaven shall be shaken.	heaven shall be shaken.	

Matt. 24:30–34	Mk. 13:26–30	Lk. 21:27–32	John
The sign and sight of Jesus returning	*The sight of Jesus returning*	*The sight of Jesus returning*	
30 "And then shall appear the sign of the Son(p) of man in heaven: and then shall all tribes of the earth mourn, and they shall see the Son(p) of man coming in the clouds▶ of heaven with power and great glory.	26 "And then shall they see the Son(p) of man coming in the clouds▶ with great power and glory.	27 "And then shall they see the Son(p) of man coming in a cloud◀ with power and great glory. ▲*Matthew and Mark use the plural "clouds." While Luke uses the singular. It means both. See Acts 1:9-11.* 28 "And when these things begin to come to pass, then look up, and lift up your heads; for your redemption draweth nigh."(r)	
31 "And he shall send his angels with a great sound of a trumpet, and they shall gather together his elect(q) [believers] from the four winds, from one end of heaven to the other.	27 "And then shall he send his angels, and shall gather together his elect(q) [believers] from the four winds, from the uttermost part of the earth to the uttermost part of heaven.		
The fig tree sign	*The fig tree sign*	*The fig tree and all trees are a sign*	
32 "Now learn a parable of the fig tree;(s) When his branch is yet tender, and putteth forth leaves, ye know that summer *is* nigh:	28 "Now learn a parable of the fig tree;(s) When her branch is yet tender, and putteth forth leaves, ye know that summer is near:	29 And he spake to them a parable; "Behold the fig tree, and all(s) the trees; 30 "When they now shoot forth, ye see and know of your own selves that summer is now nigh at hand.	
33 "So likewise ye, when ye shall see all these things, know that it(t) [the kingdom of God] is near, *even* at the doors.	29 "So ye in like manner, when ye shall see these things come to pass, know that it(t) [the kingdom of God] is nigh, *even* at the doors.	31 "So likewise ye, when ye see these things come to pass, know ye that the kingdom(t) of God is nigh at hand.	
The generation living then will see these things	*The generation living then will see these things*	*The generation living then will see these things*	
34 "Verily I say unto you,	30 "Verily I say unto you,	32 "Verily I say unto you,	

Matt. 24:34–42	Mk. 13:30–33	Lk. 21:32–34	John
This generation shall not pass, till all these things be fulfilled.	that this generation shall not pass, till all these things be done.	This generation shall not pass away, till all be fulfilled.	
The surety of these things	*The surety of these things*	*The surety of these things*	
35 "Heaven and earth shall pass away, but my words shall not pass away.(u)	31 "Heaven and earth shall pass away: but my words shall not pass away.(u)	33 "Heaven and earth shall pass away: but my words shall not pass away.(u)	
Exact hour unknown at this time: therefore, be ready	*Exact hour unknown at this time: therefore, be ready*		
36 "But of that day and hour knoweth no *man*, no, not the angels of heaven,(v) but my Father only.	32 "But of *that* day and that hour knoweth no man, no, not the angels which are in heaven, neither the Son,(v) but the Father.		
Signs of A.D. 70 similar to those of Noah's days			
37 "But as the days of Noe(w) [Noah] *were*, so shall also the coming of the Son of man be.			
38 "For as in the days that were before the flood they were eating and drinking, marrying and giving in marriage, until the day that Noe [Noah] entered into the ark,			
39 "And knew not until the flood came, and took them all away; so shall also the coming of the Son of man be.			
40 "Then shall two be in the field; the one shall be taken, and the other left.			
41 "Two *women shall be* grinding at the mill; the one shall be taken, and the other left.			
Exact hour unknown: watch	*Exact hour unknown: heed, watch and pray*	*Be aware of life's troubles: they will destroy you*	
42 "Watch therefore: for ye know not what hour your Lord doth come.	33 "Take ye heed, watch and pray: for ye know not when the time is.	34 "And take heed to yourselves, lest at any time your hearts be over charged with surfeiting, [a giddy sickness from	

Matt. 24:43–44	Mk. 13:34–37	Lk. 21:34–36	John
		excessive wine] and drunkenness, and cares of this life, and *so* that day come upon you unawares.	
		Exact hour unknown: therefore pray for mercy	
		35 "For as a snare shall it come on all them that dwell on the face of the whole earth.	
		36 "Watch ye therefore, and pray always, that ye may be accounted worthy to escape all these things that shall come to pass, and to stand before the Son of man."	
	"May be accounted worthy ► *to escape all these things." This can only be speaking of the apostles and other believers of that time. If it referred to believers over two thousand years in the future, surely the Lord would have said "they" and not "ye." It seems senseless to call prayer for those who would be living over two millenniums away. It was the apostles who were admonished to "watch and pray," not the "tribulation saints." John wrote the Revelation some thirty years after Jesus spoke these words.*		
Parable of Goodman: watch[(x)]	***Parable of Traveling Man: watch***[(x)]		
43 "But know this, that if the goodman [lord or owner]of the house had known in what watch the thief would come, he would have watched, and would not have suffered his house to be broken up.	**34** "*For the Son of man is* as a man taking a far journey, who left his house, and gave authority to his servants, and to every man his work, and commanded the porter to watch.		
	35 Watch ye therefore: for ye know not when the master of the house cometh, at even, or at midnight, or at the cockcrowing, or in the morning:		
	36 Lest coming suddenly he find you sleeping.		
	37 And what I say unto you I say unto all, Watch." (Next chap., Mk. 14:1 con t. in Section 167.)		
Reason for watching[(y)]			
44 "Therefore be ye also			

Matt. 24:44–51	Mk. 13	Lk. 21:37–38	John
ready: for in such an hour as ye think not the Son of man cometh.			

Matt. 24:44–51

ready: for in such an hour as ye think not the Son of man cometh.

Parable of Two Servants(z)

1. Faithful servant rewarded

45 "Who then is a faithful and wise servant, whom his lord hath made ruler over his household, to give them meat [food] in due season?

46 "Blessed *is* that servant, whom his lord when he cometh shall find so doing.

47 "Verily I say unto you, That he shall make him ruler over all his goods.

2. Evil servant doomed

48 "But and if that evil servant shall say in his heart, 'My lord delayeth his coming;'

49 "And shall begin to smite *his* fellowservants, and to eat and drink with the drunken;

50 "The lord of that servant shall come in a day when he looketh not for *him,* and in an hour that he is not aware of,

51 "And shall cut him asunder, and appoint *him* his portion with the hypocrites: there shall be weeping and gnashing of teeth." (Next chap., Matt. 25:1 cont. in Section 164.)

Mk. 13

Jerusalem stood behind several▶ massive walls. The temple's four main gates and lesser ones were shut and barred at sundown, with guards posted. They were opened at sunrise each morning. In the eastern wall stood the famed Shushan gate. The Persian King Darius II, son of Queen Esther gave the Jews permission to rebuild the second Temple. As an act of appreciation, the Jews placed a carving of Shushan, the capital of Persia above the gate.

Lk. 21:37–38

Summary of His final days about Jerusalem

37 And in the day time he was teaching in the temple; and at night he went out, and abode in the mount that is called *the mount* of Olives.

38 And all the people came early in the morning to him in the temple, for to hear him. (Next chap., Lk. 22:1 cont. in Section 167.)

751

Footnotes–Commentary

(a) **"And Jesus went out."** What solemn words! *The Lord of the temple has departed from the temple of the Lord.* At His first visit to this house, He was forty days old and carried in the arms of His mother. On that occasion, He was welcomed with joy by praying Simeon and wise old Anna (Section 16). Now, two days before the end of His human life, He departs from the temple forever as a place of preaching and teaching. Most of the religious leaders of His nation have rejected Him. Chillingly, we hear Messiah's final and fatal denunciation of Jerusalem, the Jewish state, and the abuse of the holy temple. In the words, "Jesus went out," it was, as if He had shaken the dust off His sandals against it all. He has quit this house. There will be no more heart piercing lessons and pleadings from Messiah. The sound of that different but familiar voice articulating those stirring, powerful Words would cease to reverberate within the walls of that awesome structure. His dreadful warning, "Behold, your house is left unto you desolate" (Matt. 23:38), and "so I speak" (John 12:50), are the concluding verdicts upon Israel from the lips of heaven's Supreme Judge. For the final time, they had rejected Messiah and sealed their fate. For a thorough study into the fall of Jerusalem, see *A History of the Jewish People in the Time of Jesus Christ*, vol. II, pages 207–256, by Emil Schurer. Josephus, the Hebrew historian wrote an eyewitness account of the fall of the city. His works are heavily drawn from in this present Section and other parts of this harmony commentary as well. A sketch of his life is given in the second paragraph of footnote c below.

(b) While exiting the temple via the Eastern Gate, the disciples "came to *him*" desiring to show their Lord the architectural wonders of that dazzling structure. They had just heard Him warn the Jews that all these things would be destroyed (Section 159, Matt. 23:33-38 and main heading of Section 162). In their thinking, this was impossible because of the massiveness and security of that wonderful place where they had often sought the God of heaven in sacrifices and prayers. Shocked by His stern denunciations of it all they could not comprehend what He meant. Their three questions starting with footnote e below are boxed in and highlighted in gray. This will serve as an easy guide for the reader to the Savior's amazing answers to their inquiries.

(c) **"Not one stone upon another, that shall not be thrown down."** Meaning the stones in the specific place pointed out by the four apostles. This did not mean *every* stone in the entire building. Knowing Jesus was not given to verbal trifles, they were dumbfounded at His reply to their comments about the stones in the temple walls and building. To grasp the emotion of this occasion, one must understand what history said regarding this place. We have the extant writings of an actual eyewitness to it all. This is explained in the following paragraph.

2p-Flavius Josephus. Numerous comments in this Section 163 come from the works of Josephus, the non-Christian Jewish historian. Steve Mason, in his *Josephus and the New Testament*, pages 1-3 wrote that he was born in A.D. 37, a few years after the resurrection of Christ and the conversion of Paul. He grew up in Jerusalem. Becoming an active Pharisee and a priest, he was intimately acquainted with the temple structure and the functions of priestly services. His history mentions New Testament characters such as King Herod and his sons, Pilate, the Pharisees, Sadducees, John the Baptist, and James the half-brother of Jesus. In one sentence, he wrote of Christ, though the liberal critics decry this as a later addition to his work. His mention of our Savior is in *Antiquities,* Book 18:3. 3. The Sanhedrin appointed him governor and military commander of Galilee during the Jewish wars (A.D. 67-70). Captured by the Romans, he defected believing God had doomed Jerusalem and the Hebrew nation.

3p-While a prisoner in Galilee, Josephus predicted before Commander Vespasian, his elevation to the throne of the Roman Empire. Shortly afterwards this occurred! The amazed Vespasian left his son, Titus, in command of the war and hastened off to Rome to claim his throne. Josephus supervised much of the fall of Jerusalem from the tent of General Titus. After the city fell, he accompanied Titus back to Rome. Due to his services to Titus, the Roman Senate awarded him an annual pension. It was during these years of retirement that he wrote his famous work the *Antiquities of the Jews.* This work contains great amounts of biblical and non-biblical information. It is the most significant extra biblical source of that entire century. Critics have attacked his writings from every angle trying to discredit him. In such a large, uninspired, and definitive history, it is impossible that there be no mistakes, doublets, and anachronisms. His history is invaluable in New Testament studies. Christians unfamiliar with it are handicapped, especially in studying the fall of Jerusalem, the temple, and the demise of the Hebrew state. A recent publication, *Jerusalem's Traitor: Josephus, Masada, and the Fall of Judea,* by Desmond Seward, is a view of Josephus in which he attempts to exonerate him of continual Jewish condemnation.

4p-Josephus' wise caution. Being a former military commander, he wrote his history with great caution. Josephus knew many of the Roman soldiery that fought at Jerusalem were still alive and would read his work with biased scrutiny. He penned nothing that would jeopardize his standing with the emperor, the powerful Senate, or the aristocratic class of the Roman people. *No Jewish favoritism was in his history.* He died about A.D. 100. Some historians think he was one of the "few men" predicted in Ezek. 12:16. Work on the temple in which he served is briefly mentioned in the Talmud tractate, Sukkah 51b, with possibly a cross-reference to Josephus. The following footnotes contain excerpts from his history. He described the greatness of the temple, its amazing functions, and the horror of its doom. All this causes us to understand why the four apostles of Christ were stunned when their Lord spoke of the destruction of it all. To them this was impossible. In an uncanny way, the doom uttered upon Jerusalem by the exiled prophet Ezekiel (5:5-13), and the pitiful cries of Lamentations which happened in 586 B.C. were re-fulfilled in A.D. 70. Now, it was by the hands of the Gentile Romans from the West instead of the Gentile Babylonians from the East.

5p-Background of the temple. About 20 B.C., King Herod the Great began rebuilding the Jerusalem temple. He kept ten thousand workers busy for eight successive years. The Talmud in tractate, Baba Bathra 4a, records an old story (probably a fable) of a rabbi named Bava Ben Buta consulting with King Herod about the project. The story ends with these words, "He that never saw the temple never saw a beautiful building." Some of its stones were ninety-four feet long, ten feet high, and thirteen feet wide! Thousands of them were of yellow, red, and white marble, laid in alternate positions. Standing today is one of its stones weighing four hundred and eighty five tons! Some of these were laid so close that a piece of paper cannot be pushed between them. Lightfoot records in his *Commentary on the New Testament . . . ,* vol. 2, pages 308–309, that rare and costly "spotted marble stones" were laid in different places within this mega structure. The Jews called the temple, "the light of the world."

6p-Temple size. Josephus gives a good description of the temple, including various measurements in *Antiquities,* Book 15, all of chapter 11. In the Talmud, the temple and temple mount are mentioned almost four thousand times! It had one hundred and sixty-two marble columns, each was fifty-two feet high and held up the porches. Columns were also used in building the wall at the southeastern end. Thousands of pieces of that gigantic masonry remain to this day. Some of the smaller ones are still visible in the famed Jewish Wailing Wall. The Talmud in tractate, Sukkoth 51b speaks of the "dream of rabbis" to cover all the temple walls with gold. However, they chose rather to cover some of her walls with variegated marble instead, which at a distance resembled the waves of the sea in motion as the sun beams bounced off its substance in early morning and late evening hours. Its flooring was of yellow, green, and black-and-white marble. These were likely some of the stones the disciples pointed our Lord to as they gloated over their grand building. Storerooms within this structure contained billions of dollars worth of luxurious gifts lavished upon this place by various kings and rulers. All sorts of golden articles and costly gifts were hung from the pillars or on the inside walls. There was the gigantic altar of sacrifice with its road-like ramp, the large golden vines, furniture in the Holy Place, or its breathtaking curtains of dazzling colors, and the four golden candelabras in the Women's Court. For comments on the candelabras, see Section 119, eighth paragraph of footnote a. No grander edifice stood anywhere in the world at that time. Satellite photography has determined that the ground area for the entire temple precinct was *at least* thirty-four square acres but probably larger. To hear Jesus say all this would be destroyed seemed impossible to the four apostles. That gorgeous building at Jerusalem was like the city dump in comparison to the true Church of Christ, redeemed by His precious blood, which is forever the temple of the living God. Refer to the ninth paragraph under footnote n below for more on this thought.

7p-His solemn warning. Christ's Words about "no stones standing," left the four apostles aghast. His prediction of the destruction furnishes us with the most profound evidence for the veracity of the Scriptures and the Words of our Lord. Everything Jesus predicted about the doom of this place happened some forty years later. Despite the *chosen* self-limits of His humanity regarding the exact hour of this calamity, He foresaw it all and warned His disciples (and through them, all other believers) of that time to be ready. Serious Christians continually watched for the fulfillment of His predictions.

8p-The apostles did not understand what Jesus was saying. It is incorrect that they understood His warning about the doom of their city, and temple. They had no "prior knowledge of certain Old Testament" verses pointing to this disaster. The rabbis had not *correctly* understood or expounded such passages as Zech. 14:4 that spoke of Messiah coming to establish His kingdom. Nor did the disciples believe that Zech.12:1-3; 13:8-9; and 14:1-3, warned that Jerusalem would be destroyed and its people slaughtered. *The only prediction the rabbis understood that foretold the doom of the city was Daniel 9:26.* Not until it was all over did they look back and understand that Daniel spoke of A.D. 70, and the "prince that destroyed the city and sanctuary" was Titus. The apostles and other disciples had no clear understanding (at that time) of their future as it was revealed in the Words they heard Jesus speak on that occasion. They were *all* equally ignorant regarding the subversion and collapse of their nation soon to occur. Rabbinical and Jewish eschatology of those days was as bizarre as the opinions of many Baptists, Pentecostals, and postmillennialists about the return of Christ. *The apostles' eschatology was that of the rabbis who had taught them.* At that time, they knew only of a literal, physical, political kingdom with Israel led by Messiah ruling the world. In their wildest imaginations, they had no idea that the kingdom Jesus had been building and preaching was at that time a spiritual entity. Jesus had earlier warned that it would be given to Gentiles. See this in Section 153, Matt. 21:43-45, footnote k in the Parable of the Vineyard Workers. In time, it would be called "the church." As mentioned so often across this work, up to this point they had *never* heard of the "rapture of the church, the *biblical* Antichrist, and the beast out of the sea." Their literal kingdom did not include the things Paul and John wrote about years later. They did not understand eschatology and the church supplanting their physical-material kingdom for a time. These things had not yet been revealed to them. Christ's announcement about the temple and Jerusalem threw them into shock. It is incorrect that they understood what Jesus said and arrived at "certain conclusions" based on their prior knowledge of Old Testament Scripture. Their earlier knowledge was as wrong as that of their rabbis. Hearing the Savior's Words, they sank into bewildered frustration. For the rabbinical understanding of their political Messiah and the Antichrist, see Section 103, footnote d, and the second subheading under *Appendix Eight*.

9p-No cross and resurrection. It has been stressed repeatedly in this harmony commentary that the first apostles-disciples of our Lord did not know of or understand His death on the cross and resurrection. This is dealt with in Sections, 104-105, 107, and Section 141. This is the major factor in trying to interpret rightly Christ's message given on this occasion just two days before the cross (Matt. 26:1-2). Near the end of His physical life, they still did not comprehend His cross, resurrection, and the rest of the story. The four apostles could not have inquired about the "signs of His return," when at this place they were ignorant of His death and resurrection from the dead! *Commentators continually overlook this critical point.* Shortly after this troubling message, they were with their Lord in the upper room. Here, He began to explain what would happen at Pentecost with the coming of the Holy Spirit. Not until then would they clearly understand the puzzling things that He had taught them. See Section 175, John 14:26, footnote n for details.

(d) The apostles had questions. Walking the road that led down the side of Mount Moriah, from the Eastern Gate, and across the brook Cedron was the quickest way from Jerusalem to Olivet and Gethsemane. Due to the Passover crowds, the bridge over the Valley of Kidron would have been packed with human traffic. Sensibly, Jesus with His apostles took the alternative route as they departed from the temple for Gethsemane. Seating Himself on the western side of the Mount of Olives, or as Mark wrote, "over against [in full view of] the temple," four of the apostles, Peter, James, John and Andrew (Mk. 13:3-4), sought clarification of His alarming words. Lightfoot wrote in his *Commentary on the New Testament . . . ,* vol. 1, page 88, "The Jews believe the Messias shall converse [teach] very much in the mountain" (of Olives). He further wrote on pages 87-88 of the same volume that there was a bridge built from the east gate of the temple across the valley below and jutted into a lower western level of the Mount of Olives. It was especially designed for the priest who brought the blood of the red heifer to sprinkle on the mount. We never read in the New Testament of this bridge. This does not mean it did not exist. An illustration of this crossover structure is found in the *Thompson Chain Reference Bible,* page 90, Fourth Revised Edition. Dr. Cunningham Geike in *The Life and Works of Christ*, page 663, mentioned, "the bridge over [C]Kedron." Christ did not use it to reach the summit of Mount Olivet. John wrote that He crossed the brook Cedron to enter the garden (John 18:1). Cedron flowed underneath this overhead walkway.

2p-Matt. 24:3. "Privately." This reveals that four of the apostles came to Jesus apart from the others and the crowds that were always standing about. The shocking things they learned from Christ on that occasion were shared with the entire Christian community over the next forty years. In time, believers across the land of Israel and over the world of that era became familiar with the predictions of doom spoken by their Lord on this occasion.

(e) Three questions. Matthew wrote that three inquiries were put to the Savior by the four apostles, while Mark and Luke were inspired to record only two. These are discussed below. For quick identification, each question is boxed and shaded in gray. Christ answered their inquiries, though *at the time* they failed to comprehend what He said. Afterward, they looked back in the knowledge given by the Holy Spirit at Pentecost and understood the meaning of *every* difficult statement He had spoken. Forty years later when these calamities occurred, they were ready, fled Jerusalem and the land of Israel, before judgment engulfed the entire walled city and countryside.

The first question is in Matt. 24:3a. "Tell us, when shall these things be?"

(f) Christ responded to their first question regarding "when" the destruction of the temple would take place. He had spoken of similar things a few days prior in Section 134. What He said then, as now, seemed impossible. His explanation reveals that they were *totally unfamiliar* with the succession of calamities and disasters (accompanied by signs and phenomena) that would occur over the next four decades. These troubles gradually signaled the coming fall of Jerusalem and the horrific atrocities that followed. The author *conjectures* that the eleven verses of Matt. 24:4-14 with their parallel texts in Mark and Luke, answered the apostles' first question. A lengthy discussion of this follows on the next page beginning with numbers 1 through 16.

2p-Jacob's trouble and a Jewish thing? Dwight Pentecost, in *The Words & Works of Jesus Christ*, page 399, wrote that Matt. 24:4-8 describes the seven-year tribulation; it is "the time of Jacob's trouble" (Jer. 30:7). This interpretation of the Jeremiah text was unheard of two hundred years ago in *traditional* eschatology. It was invented by John Darby, popularized by Blackstone, Scofield, Larkin, and accepted by dispensationalists as sound doctrine. How odd that this interpretation of "Jacob's trouble," was unknown prior to Darby, who was born in 1800! Pentecost makes all of Matt. 24 a Jewish thing only. He applies it to the nation of Israel during the tribulation period, because "the church is not mentioned anywhere in this discourse." Note the error of this reasoning. The entire books of Mark, Luke, and John do not mention the church either. Are they also strictly "Jewish things?" Nor is the word church mentioned in any miracle or parable that Christ performed and spoke. Are they "Jewish things too?" This bad hermeneutic is necessary to make Matt. 24 fit with a prior incorrect exegesis of Dan. 9:27, and portions of the book of Revelation. Ironically, this (Jewish only) approach was also unknown two hundred years ago in the early history of *established* Christian doctrine. It is relatively a new teaching. Worse, top dispensationalists are divided among themselves as to *where* the "tribulation" fits into Matt. 24. If you ask ten of them, you may get twelve different answers. It is an exegetical nightmare. Scofield finds it in Matt. 24:15-28; Lewis S. Chafer found it in Matt. 24:9-26; Arno C. Gaebebelin saw it in Matt. 24:4-16; while Schuyler English has placed it in Matt. 24:4-28. The list is much longer. Those who reject any kind of rapture or tribulation, have as many divisions as the dispensationalists. Technical hair-splitting opinions divide all of them. Few would admit that something is wrong with their conflicting eschatological beliefs. Contrary to the "Jew only" thing error, Christ's church or new kingdom is mentioned in Matt. 24:14 and Lk. 21:31. See Section 39, footnotes a and g for an explanation of both manifestations of the kingdom of our Lord. For more on the origin of the church, refer to Section 103, number 6 under footnote g.

3p-Verses 4-14. Jesus answered them. The Savior described specific events, local, countrywide, and national, including portions of the known world of that era. All of these events systematically led up to A.D. 70. The "gospel preached to the world" (Matt. 24:14 and Mk. 13:10) is explained in the third paragraph of number 16 below. The things Jesus predicted progressively occurred and climaxed in the final overthrow and burning of the city and temple. The apostles' question, "When shall these things be" was briefly answered like this, "Men, when you see the following things gradually come to pass, know that the time is near for your city to fall and the temple to be desolate." Believers, especially those living in Judaea, witnessed over the coming decades their Lord's predictions slowly happening, until Jerusalem was destroyed. And they were ready when it came (Prov. 22:3).

4p-The following seventeen numeric headings are a view of Matthew 24:4-14 with parallel verses in Mark and Luke. Not every passage in Matthew has a parallel in the other two gospels and vice versa. Regardless, this is not a "Jewish thing only," that will occur during the tribulation period. Yet there are notable illusions of the second advent of Christ, couched in some of our Savior's Words. To project *everything* Jesus said in this discourse into the future, over two thousand years later is absurd. Not one of His apostles or any other believer at that time would or could have understood such a projection. Below is a short review of the Savior's answers:

1. **Matt. 24:4-6. "Take heed . . . deceive you" and "ye shall hear."** Jesus' remarks were addressed to "them," "you," and "ye" (verses 4-6). This can *only* mean the four apostles sitting in front of Him. In verse 6, He told His preachers, "And ye shall hear of wars." *Was this addressed to them or Jews living thousands of years later?* Were the apostles to "hear" these rumors or were they not? Our Savior did not speak this of a Jewish remnant in "the last days of the tribulation," over twenty centuries into the future. This is plain linguistic and contextual horse sense. The "ye," and "you," were grammatically the four apostles who heard these things in response to their questions. The apostles living in Judaea and Jerusalem lived to see many of the things Jesus warned them about in verses 4-14. The only exception was James the brother of John, who was killed in Acts 12:2, about thirty years before A.D. 70.

   2p-The restricted use of the personal pronouns "ye" and "you," as explained above is not a concrete rule across the entire Bible. There are many contextual exceptions. When Jesus told Nicodemus, "Ye must be born again" (John 3:7), clearly this is applicable to all men of all ages, and not just Nicodemus. The immediate or distant context usually decides the person or persons addressed in a particular verse. In verses 4-6 it is obvious *to whom* the Lord Jesus directed His Words. Unless this grammatical fact is understood, the reader will be handicapped in trying to rightly divide the Words of Christ on this and other occasions. It is foul grammar to take these *direct and specific* instructions spoken to Peter, James, John, and Andrew, and apply them over two millenniums later to Israel in the tribulation, which at this time (2011) has not yet occurred.

2. **Matt. 24:5. False Messiahs. "Many come saying 'I am Christ'" (Messiah).** See footnote k below for more on these false Messiahs. Continually, this prediction is misread and therefore, misinterpreted. The Lord Jesus spoke of "false Christs" (plural) meaning "false Messiahs," that would appear during the time between His ascension and A.D. 70. (For the meaning of Christ-Messiah, see Section 5, footnote a, in left hand vertical column.) This proclamation about false Christ's appearing has nothing to do with the numerous cults that have risen under the umbrella of Bible Christianity over the past two thousand years. Our Lord was warning His preachers regarding the tidal wave of pseudo "Messiahs" and prophets that would appear within the nation of Israel prior to A.D. 70. Some claiming to be the promised Messiah of Israel acquired large followings. This literally happened in the days of the apostles and was not intended for fulfillment several thousand years later. The Savior described their specific message. They would proclaim, "I am Christ [or Messiah]." The results of their lying proclamations were that they would "deceive many." *Never* have Jehovah's Witnesses, Mormons or any cult representative announced at the front door "I am Messiah!" Such a proclamation appealed only to Jews, who were looking for this unique Person promised in their Scriptures. They had rejected their true Messiah, Jesus of Nazareth.

3. Historians have vouchsafed that the above occurred over the next several decades just as Jesus said. Near the end of Pilate's rule in A.D. 36 a false prophet appeared in Samaria claiming to be "the Messiah" and led thousands to their death. After Pilate, Governor Fadus faired no better dealing with pretended Messiahs. In A.D. 45, more false Messiahs appeared only to be crushed by Roman might. During the rule of Felix from A.D. 53-60, Josephus wrote, "The country was again filled with robbers and imposters, who deluded the multitude." Note *Antiquities,* Book 20:8. 5, lines 160-178 for a description of these

things. He also mentioned, "a great number of false prophets" that rose up and deceived the Jews into following them. They too were killed by the Romans. See *Wars of the Jews*, Book 5: all 13 chapters.

4. The counterfeit Messiahs whom Jesus spoke of appeared between His ascension and the fall of Jerusalem. The book *Bandits, Prophets and Messiahs*, by R. A. Horsley and J. S. Hanson, gives a history of this subject. See especially pages 118-126 for the period from A.D. 66-70. *The Millennium Bible,* by William E. Biederwolf, pages 329-330 lists several specialists who claimed that no false Christ-Messiahs appeared during the forty years. Today, the "end-time experts" face a mountain of history stating they are wrong. Regardless, the Words of Christ were fulfilled whether any historian wrote of them or not.

5. **False religions and rethinking certain verses.** The Savior was not speaking of the thousands of false religionists that would appear over the centuries of future church history. What He predicted here happened in the forty years leading up to A.D. 70. In the previously mentioned *Works of Nathaniel Lardner*, printed in 1724, vol. 6, pages 421- 424, there is an excellent coverage of the rise of false Messiahs and prophets during this period. Lardner was an English Presbyterian minister whose writings are unequalled in the field of Christian apologetics. Some expositors hold that 1 and 2 John were written before the fall of Jerusalem. If so, then John's warnings about a plurality of "antichrists" (1 John 2:18-19), and "false prophets" (2 John 7-11), who are connected with "the last time" (the doom of the Jewish state and city) are clear. He wrote that "the last time [hour]" (verse 18) was already present in his day. Stretching John's "last time" to cover two thousand years of history is impossible. This did not have reference to the "soon return" of Christ for His church. It has now been two millennial periods since the apostle John penned these words. The expression "you see the day approaching" in Heb. 10:25 cannot have reference to Christ's return. That *visible* "day approaching," would hardly take two thousand years to arrive. The words in Heb. 13:14, "For here we have no continuing city" seems to be a poetic and forceful allusion to the destruction of Jerusalem. Paul's words, "the night is far spent, the day is at hand" may carry the same meaning (Rom. 13:12). "At hand" does not intelligently mean twenty centuries later! Here, as in Heb. 10:25 mentioned just above, it cannot refer to the return of our Lord for His church. John's words "It is the last time," and how believers had "heard that antichrist shall come" (1 John 2:18), more sensibly points to the warnings of Jesus about false Christ- Messiahs, who would appear. Could 1 Peter 4:7, and 1 Cor. 7:29 also have reference to the fall of Jerusalem? The expression "the coming of the Lord draweth nigh" (James 5:8), is more appropriate for A.D. 70, instead of present day events. It does not take our Lord two thousand years to "draw nigh." Some believe it refers to Christ coming in a spiritual sense to judge Jerusalem and the Jews. Whatever the correct meaning, it cannot speak of the "rapture of the church" which is as sure as the throne of God.

2p-In Acts 2:16-21, Peter cited from Joel 2:28-32 about "the last days," and "the day of the Lord." He expressly identified this as occurring at Pentecost! The words of Joel can only refer to the last days of the Jewish age for that time and not the end of the world. The catastrophe for Israel and Jerusalem were imminent. Why do certain men encumber this prediction with suppositions, double references, and ulterior fulfillments? Nothing fits the predictions of Joel except that to which they alone refer. This hermeneutic makes sense of these verses. Those who struggle to explain this within a ridged dispensationalist's framework contradict what Peter said. Better to stay with Peter than John Darby on this point. These comments do not deny great sorrows and suffering before the real return of our Lord, or the fact of a real Antichrist appearing on the stage of world history at a time yet to come.

6. **Matt. 24:6a. "Ye shall hear of wars and rumors of wars."** Again, we inquire, to whom was the Savior speaking when He said, "Ye shall hear." He addressed His four apostles setting in front of Him. Jesus stated that *they* ("Ye") would hear these rumors. Regularly, pastors warn their flocks, "The increase of wars is a sure sign of Jesus' soon return." In using this verse, they have taken something that was fulfilled two millenniums ago and misapplied it in today's history. The forty-year period from the time Christ spoke these Words until Jerusalem's destruction were filled with continued increasing violence, wars, and civil unrest. This originated among the Jews in the land of Israel and spread into distant parts of the world. The following are examples of what secular and religious history said regarding this era.

2p-Josephus records in *Antiquities,* Book 18, all of chapters 8 and 9, many of the troubles of Israel in those days. Other sources tell us that in Caesarea, some 20,000 Jews were killed; at Scythopolis 13,000, at Ptolemais 2,000. At Alexander, Egypt, pagans and Jews fought awful wars in which some 50,000 lost their lives. At Damascus, 10,000 died in violent uprisings. Josephus wrote that the slaughter of Jews over the land was so bad that farmers had to leave off tilling certain areas. This resulted in famine and starvation. During this period, four successive Roman emperors died by violent means from A.D. 54-69: the empire fell into instability. See *Clarke's Commentary,* vol. 5. pages 226-227. Coneybear and Howson, in their classic work, *Life and Epistles of St. Paul,* chapter iv, wrote that in the reign of Emperor Caligula from A.D. 37–41, he sought to place his statue in the temple at Jerusalem. Thousands of Jews perished in the bloodshed that followed. Many earthquakes occurred during Caligula's rule.

Numerous insurrections and seditions occurred in Jerusalem. Thousands died in these fierce conflicts. Awful calamities fell upon Israel for their blasphemous wickedness and rejection of Messiah. They are history, not future, and occurred just as our Lord predicted.

7. **Matt. 24:6b. "But the end is not yet."** We inquire, "What end?" This reveals that these predictions did not point to something many centuries in the future, because none of the apostles lived long enough to see these things. The only "end" Christ can be speaking of is the destruction or end of the temple, and city. The reason He said, "not yet" is that these things did not finalize until A.D. 70, which was about forty years ahead. The Savior cannot be speaking of an "end" over two thousand years away. Messiah warned His preachers not to be alarmed at these coming things. They were to remember that many signs and tragedies would yet fall upon the land of Israel and its people. He told them that the end of the Jewish state, its city, and temple would not be until all the remaining disasters had occurred.

8. **Matt. 24:7a. "Nation shall rise against nation."** Not only were the Jews continually engaged in wars with their pagan neighbors but also in far away countries, there would be great turmoil. Italy fell into a civil war over the selection of new emperors. One reading of Michael Grant's excellent book, *The Twelve Caesars*, pages 177-196 gives numerous details of the "civil wars" of Rome that ripped the empire apart. The infidel historian Edward Gibbon's work, *The Decline and Fall of the Roman Empire* meticulously details this, along with Will Durant's *The Story of Civilization*. See indexes passim in both works for many references. These things happened during the forty years from Jesus' ascension up to A.D. 70. Those who lift these predictions about the nations from their historical context and make them as a "sure sign that Jesus is coming soon," or apply them to the Jews in the tribulation time are mistaken. *Christ will only return when the time is right, wars or no wars, and not until then.*

9. **Matt. 24:7b. "There shall be famines."** End-time "specialists" unceasingly remind us that famines occurring in modern day Africa, Asia, China, and India fulfill this prediction. These people have been preaching this for over a thousand years! Their pulpits, books, TV programs, and radio broadcasts continually blare this out. *How can it be when these things were to happen during the lives of the apostles?* There is a famine mentioned in Acts 11:28 that came "throughout the [known] world . . . in the days of [Emperor] Claudius Caesar" (died A.D. 54). This famine was so severe in Jerusalem that thousands perished from lack of food. In 1982, Hal Lindsey wrote in *The Promise*, page 198 the following, "Jesus predicted a great outbreak of worldwide famine on a scale never before known to men. Today, the headlines of *Time, Newsweek,* and the daily newspapers scream out the devastating facts that millions are dying of starvation right at this moment." Lindsey, like thousands of other red-hot prophecy experts fired another blank. He transferred the famines that occurred during the forty years from Jesus' ascension up to the fall of Jerusalem and transported them into the twentieth and twenty-first centuries. His statement, that newspapers and magazines prove these things are happening in our days, and that this is another "sign of the soon coming of Christ" is sheer fiddle faddle. Beware of those who determine the last days by reading newspaper headlines. Their prognostications shame the cause of Christ and give many occasions for infidels to mock the great doctrine of our Lord's return.

10. **Others guessers.** Hal Lindsey is not alone in his guessing. Cult bodies such as the Seventh Day Adventist, Jehovah's Witness, and the Worldwide Church of God (with its many splinter groups) often teach the identical signs absurdities. In an Adventist book printed in 1976, entitled *Good-bye, Planet Earth,* the author Robert H. Pierson promotes this same false sensationalism on pages 8, 15, 19-21, 23, 48-49. Jehovah's Witnesses in their January 15, 1973 edition of *Watch Tower* made an appeal to famines as proof of the Lord's soon return. That was over thirty years ago. This is not to deny that great sorrows will befall humanity before our Lord returns, but it dogmatically affirms that the predictions of Christ, given in Matt. 24:7b were fulfilled two thousand years ago. It is right that famines have killed millions over the centuries. What is not right is that famines are a *distinctive* sign in any period of history that Jesus will return soon or at any moment. The "famine signs" error travels the highway of gullibility.

11. **Matt. 24:7b–c. "Pestilences in divers [different] places and earthquakes."** Deadly epidemic diseases follow on the heels of natural famines. The bubonic plague and infamous Black Death of Europe in the 1300s are classic examples. Hal Lindsey wrote in *The Promise,* pages 198-199, of plagues or pestilences these words, "Jesus said that plagues would sweep the world prior to his return." If this interpretation is true, then it means that there should have been a dramatic increase in world pestilences this past century. It did not happen. The pestilences Christ predicted in this text happened after His ascension and culminated in the fall of Jerusalem. History confirms that awful disasters also occurred in the years following A.D. 70. Horrible judgment befell the Jews living in Babylon in A.D. 40. Thousands died. The pagan writer Tacitus, told of a killing plague across Italy, in A.D. 66, in his work *Tacitus* Book 16: 13. He also wrote of Jerusalem's demise in his *Annals*, Book 5. 13-14. He mentioned a pestilence that came to Rome in the days of Emperor Nero (died A.D. 68). Tacitus said, "Within the space of one autumn there died no less than 30,000 persons." For more on this, see *What the Bible says about the Great*

Tribulation, pages 29–32 by William R. Kimball. When considering ancient calamities, we should remember that most of them were not recorded by the historians of those days. (It would reflect the disfavor of their gods!) The recent hurricanes that pounded Florida and the southern coasts of America, the war in Iraq, and Russia's temporary invasion of Georgia, have become some of the latest "proofs" of the "soon return of Christ." Recently, several "T. V. prophetic experts" named Dubai on the coast of the Persian Gulf as the rebuilt city of Babylon (Rev. 17)! This large tourist resort of over one million people has the world's tallest building. Authorities of end-time doctrine have dubbed this, "the rebuilt Tower of Babel." Such "guessing" scenarios are a form of "Bible believing" heresy.

2p-Hal Lindsey wrote in *The Late Great Planet Earth,* pages 52–53, that earthquakes are a chief sign marking the time of Christ's return to set up His kingdom. Again, we note that the major cults parrot the same line basing it on our Lord's Words in verse 7. The recent earthquake killing over 200,000 in Haiti is hailed as a sure sign that Jesus is coming soon! The Messiah was speaking to His four apostles of things that would happen during their lifetime. He was *not* forecasting an unprecedented upheaval in world seismology over two thousand years in the future! Numerous "earthquakes, in divers places" struck over the next four decades after Christ spoke these things. Some are documented in the history of that period. Thomas Newton in his *Dissertations on Prophecies,* written in 1754, pages 377–379 stated that earthquakes occurred at Crete, Smyrna, Miletus, Chios, Asmos, Rome, Hierapolos, and Colosse, during the reign of Emperor Nero. *Clarke's Commentary,* vol. 5. page 227 has listed some thirteen different places where earthquakes struck in the decades before Jerusalem fell.

3p-Every time, an earthquake hits Japan, China, India, Pakistan, or some foreign country, a Baptist preacher leaps into his pulpit and informs his congregation, "This is another sign the coming of Christ is near." A famed evangelist warned his radio audience that they had "better get earthquake insurance" for this was a prime sign of the end. *We may have a thousand more quakes before our Lord returns, but earthquakes are not a sure sign of His near coming.* Jesus spoke this warning to His apostles and the believers of that time: it was never intended as a proof that He is returning any day now. How strange that every generation of believers think their days are unique; that their times are worse than all others are and that these things positively point to the soon coming of Christ. People do not consider that what appears momentous to one generation is not so to the next. If the history of eschatology has any lesson for us, it is the foolishness of date setting the return or *near* return of Christ. In September 1984, editor Noel Mason put it this way in the *Good News Unlimited* magazine, page 4, "The history of Jewish and Christian 'date-setters' with all its bitter disappointments, and disillusionment has not curbed the desire of many Christians to calculate the end." On the desk before me is a book where the publisher wrote that the author has covered all the Old Testament prophecies and shows that "Jesus is coming soon." It was written over fifty years ago! Do these people know the meaning of the word "soon" or not? Such eschatological pot shots have misled weaker Christians for centuries and played havoc in churches.

4p-A recent advertisement from a signs crazed organization read, "Bank failures, stock market crashes, business bailouts, foreclosure threat, unemployment up, terrorism, Syria, Iran's nuclear bomb, factories closing are all in prophecy!" We ask them one question, "Where?" During the Great Depression from 1929 to 1939, that rocked America, prophecy enthusiasts parroted similar "signs" and went wild assuring their adherents that it was the last days. It is now 2011! The "experts" were wrong again!

12. **Lk. 21:11b** adds, **"And fearful sights and great signs shall there be from heaven."** This has no parallels in Mathew or Mark. Fierce earthquakes shook Judea. Dreadful tempest, violent winds, vehement rains, with continual lightning and thunders, led many to believe that these things portended some uncommon calamity would accompany it. Josephus wrote that one Judaean quake brought death to some ten thousand men and cattle in *Antiquities,* Book 15:5. 2, lines 121-124. Similarly, *Gill's Commentary,* vol. 7, page 700 carries the story regarding "fearful sights and great signs from heaven." It affirms that terrible things both heard and seen occurred during this time. Mysteriously, the doors of the temple's Eastern Gate opened of themselves. Each gate required twenty men to open and close! Comets "hanging over Jerusalem" terrified the Jews. Other phenomena such as "a star resembling a sword" appeared, "a bright light over the temple and altar," the frightful sight of "chariots and soldiers running among the clouds and [over] all the cities of the land" were seen. There was the strange story of the priest leading a heifer to the altar for sacrifice when she suddenly gave birth to a lamb! Could these things have been some of the "fearful sights and great signs from heaven" our Savior mentioned? Those who teach that this same phenomenon will happen over two thousand years later in the tribulation period are wrong. Contextually, Christ spoke this first to His apostles. It took place during their lifetimes. To take Christ's Words, gallop off to the book of Daniel or Revelation, and seek their fulfillment in the terrible plagues and judgments of future days, is erroneous exegesis. This does not belie that horrible things will take place before our Lord returns; they will, whenever that time arrives. At this typing (February 2011), with

earth reeling under, floods, fire, quakes, devastating tsunamis, and popular uprisings, this is *not a positive sign* that Jesus' return is near. It is rather a sign that all creation is cursed by sin (Rom. 8:22).

13. **Matt. 24:8 and Mk. 13:8. "All these *are* the beginnings of sorrows."** What did Jesus mean when He said this to His four preachers on the Mount of Olives? Simply, that the things He had just spoken were only the start; more was to follow *before* the destruction of the city and collapse of the Jewish state. How infantile to transfer what He had spoken into the far-distant future, millenniums away. The "beginnings of sorrows" here are not the sufferings of the tribulation or "Jacobs's trouble," but exclusively the sorrows of the nation of Israel (especially its religious leaders) during the coming decades. They culminated in the bloody conquest of Israel's city, temple, and land.

    2p-Josephus relates in *Wars of the Jews,* Book 6:5, 3, lines 300-309, the ghastly story of a man named "Jesus, the son of Ananus." He suddenly appeared in the streets of Jerusalem wailing among other things, "Woe be to this city, the temple, and the people." *He did this for seven years.* He was almost beaten to death by fellow Jews, but incessantly continued this fearful lament of doom. When the Romans began their final siege, he climbed the wall facing their forces and shouted at them his doleful refrain. No sooner did the words leave his mouth, when a tone from a Roman catapult ripped his head off! How odd that his name was Jesus, and his own Jewish people hated him!

14. **Matt. 24:9 with parallels in Mk. 13:9 and Lk. 21:12. "Sorrows, deliver you up, afflicted, killed, hated of all nations, beaten, and brought before rulers and kings."** Who are the "you" (people) to suffer these things? They cannot be a Jewish remnant over two millennia away. One of the men listening to the Savior was James. He was killed some ten years later in Acts 12:1-2. Luke wrote that Jesus said some of them would be brought into the synagogues to be beaten: where is this happening today? *This was to be a Jew on Jew thing.* It did happen to the apostles and early Christians. Such things are not even slightly intimated anywhere in the book of Revelation. In the latter part of Matt. 24:9, we read of the early believers being "hated of all nations." They could not be hated in all places where they had never been. This has reference to the nations where they went preaching, and who rejected their testimony of Jesus Christ. Though their sufferings would be great, Luke records Jesus' promise that "not a hair of your head shall perish" (Lk. 21:18). The physical body may be beaten to pulp and burnt to ashes, but the redeemed soul is forever secure in the hand of God (Matt. 10:28).

    2p-Mk. 13:9. "Councils." This word has exclusive reference to the Jewish Sanhedrin court. Check its meaning in any concordance or lexicon. *Where across the world are Christians being made to stand before the Sanhedrin in these "end-times?"* Only the most naive could believe this will happen during the awful earth shaking tribulation. After the fall of Jerusalem, the Sanhedrin limped along and finally collapsed in A.D. 425. In Israel, certain Jews have revived a model of the original body. However, this group of elderly men will never reconstruct the ancient Sanhedrin of Israel, nor will it be restored in the tribulation. For more on this new Sanhedrin, see Section 134, number three, under firth paragraph of footnote d. Jesus directed His Words about suffering to His apostles and other believers of that time. Subsequent history demonstrates that this is precisely what happened to them and the early Jewish believers. The book of Acts relates a small part of this story. The Sanhedrin imprisoned Peter and John in Acts 4:3. Herod in Acts 12:2 murdered James. Paul and Silas were beaten and thrown in jail in Acts 16:24. Paul stood before Gallio, the famed Roman teacher-politician in Acts 18:12, before Felix in Acts 24:24, King Agrippa in Acts 25:23, and Caesar Nero in Acts 27:24. Refer to his catalogue of suffering in 2 Cor. 11:16-33. The Sanhedrin stoned Stephen to death as recorded in Acts 7.

    3p-In an old book, *The Parousia,* by J. Stuart Russell, printed in 1878, on page 70, we read, "How exactly all this was verified in the personal experiences of the disciples we may read in the Acts of the Apostles and in the Epistles of St. Paul." The liberal ecumenical church historian Phillip Schaff, in his *History of the Christian Church,* vol. 1, wrote on pages 381-382 of the horrors and unspeakable deaths that thousands of Christians passed through from A.D. 64-68. The earliest believers fulfilled Jesus' Words before A.D. 70. It is emphatic in Mk. 13:12 that this church-wide suffering in those years past was "for His name's sake." Some five weeks after this warning given by Christ, the Sanhedrin or Supreme Court of Israel commanded the apostles not to speak in Jesus' Name (Acts 5:40). This persecution of believers continued long after A.D. 70. Dr. C. E. Haines, in his work, *Heathen Contact with Christianity During its First Century and a Half,* page 3, wrote how the Jews accused Christians of "child murder and incest." This brought great suffering for decades on the believers of that era.

15. **Matt. 24:10-12. "Offended, betrayed, deceived, love turning cold."** Some of the experiences of the apostles and early Christians are recorded in Scripture. *Most are not.* Countless calamities fell upon believers during the next forty years. If every experience in the lives of all the first and early Christians were recorded in the Bible, we would have thousands of volumes. God in His wisdom has only given us a few of them in Scripture, and these are sufficient.

16. **Matt. 24:13. "Endure to the end, shall be saved, no hair shall perish, have patience."** This is repeated by different words in Mk. 13:13 and Lk. 21:18-19. What great consolation this gave believers at that time. Some assume to find in these words basis for the false doctrine of Arminianism, salvation by good works and losing salvation by bad works. They point to this passage as proof that we must add something to, or hold onto our salvation in order to be "finally saved." This belief comes from ignorance of the historical and chronological background of these texts, and from a misunderstanding of the totality of Christ's atonement. The "end" as mentioned here by our Lord is not death. The context forbids this thought. *Christ referred to the "end" of this period of time (forty years) that resulted in the destruction of Jerusalem.* "Saved" as used here cannot speak of salvation from sin or eternal life in Christ. The four apostles had already been saved. "End" had reference to believers being physically "saved" from the catastrophic doom that destroyed the city and temple. The subject of human life being saved occurs also in Matt. 24:22 in the words "there should no flesh be saved." Again, the emphasis here is saving physical life [flesh] not the soul. The soul is saved in this life and the body at the resurrection.

2p-After the ascension of Jesus, believers knew something dreadful was pending for the land of Israel, the Jews, the temple, and Jerusalem. Over the next four decades, Christians in the land looked for and saw the warning signs gradually unfold as Christ had said. *They diligently discussed these things among themselves and fervently watched with patience each prediction transpire.* We need no passage from the Bible to prove common sense! A few verses later in Matt. 24:22 and Mk. 13:20, footnote j, Christ said these days (of judgment) would be shortened for the "elect's [or believer's] sake." There were thousands of Christians living at Jerusalem, over Judaea and in the surrounding areas. The mother church was there. Luke recorded Messiah's Words of comfort spoken to the apostles, "But there shall not an hair of your head perish," and "patience" would sustain them in this time. Though the Roman commander, Cestius Gallus had surrounded the city, to the amazement of all, he suddenly lifted the siege, and withdrew his legions. It was during this withdrawal that believers (remembering the Words of Jesus) fled to safety in a distant city of Pella. In this, we note the sovereign control of God over human affairs. As mentioned in Section 134, footnote m, later, Emperor Constantine's liberal historian, Eusebius, recorded the brief story of this escape in his *The Ecclesiastical History,* III, 5. Edward Gibbon, in *The Decline and Fall of the Roman Empire,* vol. 1, pages 389-391 gives more regarding the Christians at Pella and their disastrous efforts to return to the ruins of Jerusalem after the Roman conquest. However, Gibbon missed the mark by centralizing all Christians at Pella and Rome during this era of church history. Albert H. Newman, in *A Manuel of Church History,* vol. 1, page 119 records other details on this subject. It happened just as Jesus predicted. Not a hair of any believer's head perished in the unspeakable terror and death that fell upon the Jewish people at this time.

3p-Matt. 24:14 with Mk. 13:10. "This gospel of the kingdom preached to all the world" or "among all nations." There is one gospel, not many (1 Cor. 15:1-3 with Rom. 1:16). Scripture teaches one way of forgiveness and salvation. There is one saving faith, not many (Eph. 4:5). The distinction between the "gospel of grace" and a "gospel of the kingdom" is a myth. Jesus instructed the church to go into the world, teach and preach the gospel, and baptize believers. There is not a gospel for this age and an entirely different gospel for the Jews in the tribulation period (Rev. 14:6). Dr. C.I. Scofield invented this fable. *Prior to his birth in 1800, it was unheard of.* The "gospel of the kingdom," in the above text went through gradual name changes over time. Yet it remained the same old-fashioned news that Jesus saves sinners by His atonement on the cross. (For the gospel and salvation in the Old Testament, see Section 30, second paragraph under footnote h. Refer to Section 39, footnotes a and g for an explanation of the two sides of Christ's kingdom.) From the sunrise of antiquity, men have been saved only one way. Salvation becomes efficacious by the grace of God through repentance and faith in Jesus Christ. As Old Testament people looked ahead to the cross and empty tomb, so those of the New Testament and afterward look back to the same cross and resurrection. *It is stressed again that Holy Scripture does not teach several methods of salvation.* Jesus' Words above, about the gospel being preached everywhere before A.D. 70, has caused much wonderment. He was still addressing *His disciples,* not some far distant group of Jews centuries away. He said that the fall of Jerusalem, the temple, and Jewish society would not occur until this gospel dissemination was accomplished. The early church did this! Fifty days after the resurrection of Christ, on Pentecost, Simon Peter preached the gospel, to "devout men out of every nation under heaven" (Acts 2:5). "Every nation under heaven," means "every nation under heaven." These countless thousands of men carried Peter's message home with them across the habitable world of that era. At the end of his third and (probably) final missionary journey, Paul was at Corinth (Rom. 16:23). From here, he penned the Roman letter. Part way through this he makes an amazing statement. In the context of Romans 10, he wrote about men being sent to preach: they were so special that their feet were beautiful because they carried the gospel of salvation (verses 14-15). In Rom. 10:18, he declared that the "sound" (or voice) of these messengers "went into all the earth," and "their words [the gospel] unto the ends of the world." Paul ended the Roman letter with a similar word in Rom. 16:25-26. Here, he taught that the "gospel, and preaching of Jesus Christ … is made manifest" [or] "known to all nations for [their] obedience to the faith." Note the words "all nations." In the previous chapter, Paul stated, "he had no more place in these parts [Greece and surrounding areas] to preach" (Rom. 15:23).

4p-A fair estimate for the writing of the Roman letter is about A.D. 59, some ten years before A.D. 70. By this date, the early and first Christians had already taken the gospel to "all the earth" of that era, and to "all nations" of their day. About three years later, Paul was under house arrest for two full years at Rome (Acts 28:30-31). From here, he wrote the Colossian letter and stated the same thing, but was more emphatic. In Col. 1:5, he wrote about "the truth of the gospel." Then to our modern day shock in verse 6, he declared that this gospel had not only gone to the Colossians but "in all the world," and that it had brought forth fruit. In amazement, we move forward to Col. 1:23, where our missionary mentioned the "hope of the gospel," which he declared, "was preached to every creature which is under heaven." This is the same man who a few years later wrote to Titus, "The grace of God that bringeth salvation hath appeared to all men" (Titus 2:11). Grace appearing to "all men" rings of "whosoever will may come."

5p-Commentators have wrestled with Matt. 24:14 and Mk. 13:10. *We are not told how the first churches, their missionaries, and workers accomplished this amazing feat; but we are told they did.* The first generation of believers took the Great Commission to heart and fulfilled it in their days. They did the job just as their Savior had commanded prior to His ascension and reached their generation with the saving gospel of Christ. It has been estimated that 95% of early Christian history has never been penned. Within these unwritten volumes is the history of how this was done.

6p-This bright picture is darkened by the fact that succeeding generations of Christians failed in this task. Christ's statement that the "gospel must first be published among all nations," before the fall of Jerusalem in A.D. 70, was realized by about A.D. 59. As stated above, Paul wrote these things some ten years before A.D. 70. At no time in history will any church or missionary society ever share the gospel with *every* individual on the face of this earth. The Great Commission does not teach this. Evangelizing the world does not mean that Christians workers must give to *each* person, individually, the gospel of Christ. Nor does it mean that every person on earth will be brought to Christ. *Most will not.* To illustrate this, in the work of foreign missions a single missionary gives the gospel to a pagan tribe in the highlands of New Guinea. Several in his audience take the message and share it with hundreds or thousand of others. Jonah did not preach individually to *every* one of the two million people living at Nineveh. That would have taken years and been physically impossible. He preached to some and they spread the word over the length and breadth of that vast walled city even into the king's palace. This explains the meaning of Acts 19:10, "All they which dwelt in Asia heard the word of the Lord Jesus," and Mk. 16:15, "the gospel to every creature." Missionary work is the same today. One Bible page snatched from a book burning in communist China, in time, resulted in dozens of small underground churches coming into existence. This reveals the power of God's Word.

7p-In light of the above, we better understand Acts 19:20, "So mightily grew the Word of God and prevailed." Christ said that the temple would not be destroyed until the gospel was spread over the world (of that era). This massive missionary endeavor was completed *before* A.D. 70. From that time to the present, the church has failed in the task of world evangelization. The famed Baptist minister, John A. Broadus (died 1895), in his book, *An American Commentary on the New Testament,* page 485 wrote that theorizers should restrain "from insisting that the second coming of Christ cannot take place until this [the gospel to every creature] has been fulfilled with literal completeness." It was first fulfilled over two thousand years ago. Then, shortly afterward, Christ came in a unique mystic sense to judge the wickedness of the Jewish people in A.D. 70. *This historical fact does not negate the reality of His return for the church and the events that will follow.* These events are descried in the book of Revelation. The problem here is that so many different interpretations abound regarding this book. The author of this work holds to a moderate form of premillennialism void of extreme dispensationalism. He refuses to condemn fellow Christians, who hold different but non-radical interpretations of eschatology. *If Matt. 24:14 means Jesus will not return for the church until the gospel is preached to every person on earth, then He will never return!* Every year the church gets further behind and the world gets bigger.

17. **Mk. 13:11 with Lk. 21:13-15** (no parallel in Matthew). **"What ye shall speak," "you for a testimony," "a mouth and wisdom."** This applied to the apostles and early believers who were filled with the Holy Spirit and extraordinary power in witnessing for Christ. Mark is clear on this in Mk. 13:11 by recording our Lord's Words about the Holy Ghost. (There is not one thread of evidence that Jesus was speaking of "144,000 Jews witnessing during the tribulation." Certain "experts" lift this imagined scenario from the book of Revelation and force into it Jesus' Words spoken here.) Several examples of anointed preaching are Stephen before the Sanhedrin in Acts 7, Peter and John in Acts 4:13, and Paul and Barnabas in Acts 14:1. The indwelling Spirit gave these men divine wisdom. They answered their enemies with irresistible

eloquence. When the Holy Spirit came on Pentecost, this began the fulfillment of Jesus' promise about their supernatural abilities to teach, preach, and answer their enemies. Christ's Words in this text are not for *all* Christians of all ages. Across church history, there have been rare exceptions to this rule, especially believers suffering under paganism, communism, and radical Islam.

Second question in Matt. 24:3b; Mk 13:4; and Lk. 21:7. "And what shall be the sign of thy coming?"

5p-This question came out of the Jewish belief that Israel's triumphant Messiah would appear, after certain signs and events, overturn the giant stones of the old temple, and then rebuild a new one for the nation. The rabbis taught that many amazing things would occur *before* this took place. For more on Jewish and rabbinical eschatology, see number 3 below. The four apostles were inquiring about what their rabbis had taught regarding Israel's coming Messiah. They asked Christ for a sign to prove this. Note the following things about their request.

1. **The sign they could not have asked for.** The apostles could not have inquired about a sign or signs pertaining to the return of Christ for the church. *At this time, they were ignorant of His death on the cross, burial, resurrection, ascension, and much later, His return for the church.* In view of this, they could not have known of His future coming for believers. It has been pointed out repeatedly in this work that none of Jesus' closest disciples-apostles understood, at this time, His death on the cross, though He had often spoken of it. Refer to Sections 104, 105, 107, 141, and 148 for this. To seize upon the word "sign" in this text, and then *assume* the apostles were inquiring about signs that would appear over two thousand years later is ridiculous! At this time these men had never heard of the "rapture of the church" and ensuing events as recorded later by Paul and John in their inspired letters. A few days prior, they had been shaken at Jesus' teaching that Gentiles would be given God's kingdom, and the Jews would be shut out. Refer to this in Section 153, Matt. 21:31-44, footnotes h and k, and Section 154, the Parable of the King's Son. Never had they heard such incredible things! Like all synagogue indoctrinated Jews they were looking *only* for a political, material kingdom ruled by a human Messiah. As a conquering Prince, He would subdue the Gentiles and bring *physical salvation* to Israel. Then, He would rule the world as Messiah-King. This was the basics of Jewish eschatology known by Christ's disciples at this time.

    2p-Therefore, the word "sign" in Matt. 24:3 cannot have reference to the "rapture, first resurrection, bema judgment, tribulation period, seals, and trumpets, beast out of the sea, a woman clothed in scarlet, and tribulation saints." Never, had these four men heard of such things. Later, they would understand these various eschatological entities, but at this moment, they did not. Hence, it was impossible that they inquired for signs pointing to the "rapture of the church," and associated events. This is what they could not and did not inquire about of the Savior. *Their hope in the return of Christ really began in Acts 1:11.*

2. **The "sign" they asked for pertained to rabbinical predictions for Israel's coming Messiah.** The ancient rabbis had invented many signs that pointed to the coming of their political Messiah to rule the world. In Jewish sources, all sorts of fantastic imaginary things were supposed to occur before, and then accompany His appearing and earthly kingdom. It was held by many Jews, that after years of moving in and out of Israel, Messiah would suddenly appear from the east for a final time in great splendor

3. **Rabbinical eschatology.** It was a conglomeration of Old Testament Scripture, superstition, and myths. *After the ascension of Jesus, it was blended with a distorted version of New Testament teaching.* Jewish eschatology began to appear in a rough written form in the seventh century A.D. Prior to that it was mostly verbal. Briefly, it stated there would be a terrible future war in which Israel, led by Messiah, would clash with Gog and Magog. In rabbinical thinking, Gog and Magog represented all world resistance against Jehovah and Israel. They were not two separate nations such as Russia and China! Jewish eschatological literature speaks of a hostile figure called "Armilius" (Antichrist). He would deceive the Gentiles and gather a formidable army to attack the Holy Land. Some Jewish myths taught that Armilius would come from a pregnant stone statue in Rome! (A rabbinical distortion of the virgin birth of Jesus.) His armies would attack Jerusalem three times. In the third and final battle, Gog, Magog (representing many Gentile nations), and Armilius were to be destroyed *along with Jerusalem and the temple.* (Some sources say that Messiah would abolish the temple and city.) After this war, Messiah would rebuild a New Jerusalem and temple and reside there as King of Israel. The Hebrew writer, Raphael Patai, in *The Messiah Texts*, page 157, quotes an ancient Jewish verse that reads, "Messiah . . . would build the temple." It would be the capital of a New World Order of lasting peace. Patai has produced a comprehensive compilation of Jewish texts about Messiah. There is a broader discussion of Armilius-Antichrist, see *Appendix Eight.* For the diversity of rabbinical eschatology, see *The Life and Times of Jesus the Messiah*, pages 775-778, by Alfred Edersheim.

4. **The sign.** The only "sign" the four apostles could have inquired about was what they had been taught by their rabbis. Jesus' Words that the temple would be destroyed terrified them. They thought He was saying that this calamity was imminent and asked Him for the sign when it would happen. He did not attempt to correct twisted rabbinical eschatology regarding His coming. He told them about signs that signaled the

real destruction of their city and temple by the Romans in a few more decades. For more eschatological signs invented by the rabbis, see Section 95, footnote g; Section 100, third and fourth paragraphs under footnote a. Shortly after the ascension, Stephen spoke of Jesus and the temple being destroyed in Acts 6:14. This demonstrates that Christ's warnings were already common knowledge among believers.

Third and final question of the four apostles is found in Matt. 24:3c. "End of the world" (age).

6p-The third inquiry in Matt 24:3c had to do with "the end of the world" (or age) as the Jews calculated time. This New Testament term is frequently misunderstood. It was a common Hebrew expression used by teachers, scholars, masters, and disciples alike. "World" or "age" had no reference to the total end of time and cessation of all human activities. Jewish teaching about age and ages, or the end of time is what Christ responded to so that His apostles would understand. He was speaking of the end of a fixed period of time, which afterward, other events would follow. "End of the age" cannot mean the end of our age that we live in now. Scripture declares that Jesus came to speak to men in "the last days" (Heb. 1:1-2). Our Lord died at "the end of the [world] age" (Heb. 9:26). His death was over two thousand years ago. The writer of Hebrews employed the ancient Jewish meaning of the expression for the benefit of his original Hebrew readers. For explanation of the word "world," see Section 82, all of footnote d. Unless this is understood, only chaos will result in interpreting biblical eschatology.

7p-Christ told His apostles that the Jewish age (*as they knew it*) would end with the destruction of Jerusalem, temple, and dispersion of their nation. In Lk. 21:24, He informed them that these catastrophic events would commence the "times of the Gentiles." This would mass launch God's plan for the salvation of the heathen, which had slowly started during the ministry of Christ. At the time our Lord said this, none of His preachers yet understood God's design in history for saved Gentiles and mankind in general. Complete understanding came later at Pentecost. Again, see under main heading of Section 153 with Matt. 21:33-46, footnotes h and k for more on the kingdom of God being taken from the Jews and given to believing Gentiles. Refer also to Section 154, the Parable of the King's Son, for continued explanation of the "times of the Gentiles."

(g)Matt. 24:15a with parallels in Mk. 13:14a and Lk. 21:20a. "When ye see the abomination of desolation," and "Jerusalem compassed." Highlighted in gray, not being an Old Testament quotation, but to emphasize to whom Christ spoke this statement, and for easy parallel harmonization. *Again, we ask, "who are the 'ye' in this text?"* This plural pronoun can only have reference to the apostles, and other believers who would learn about Christ's instructions given here. See number 1 under footnote f above for explanation of "ye" as used by the Savior in this message. The Lord Jesus said *they* would "see" this awful sight, not the tribulation saints. For more on "the abomination" being the Roman forces which Jewish Christians *saw*, note footnote h below. He was not speaking of an Antichrist (Beast) over two thousand years away with his armies about Jerusalem.

2p-Upon seeing the Roman army surround Jerusalem the first time (from which they were temporarily withdrawn but later returned), the Christians knew this was the divine signal to flee. Josephus described the mysterious withdrawal of the Roman commander, Cestius Gallus, "But it was, I suppose, owing to the aversion God had already [sent] at the city and the sanctuary . . ." See *Wars of the Jews,* Book 2:19. 6, lines 538-545, with footnote b. This sudden retreat provided time for Christians within Jerusalem and those hiding in the countryside to escape. The sealing mote was dug about the city after some six weeks of conflict. Refer to Section 148, the second paragraph of footnote i for more on this trench. As often mentioned, believers fled to Pella, a Gentile city located some eighty miles northeast of Jerusalem near the Jordan River. For a brief explanation of their flight after the Roman withdrawal, see *What the Bible says about the Great Tribulation*, pages 78-80 by William R. Kimball.

3p-What would have happened to the thousands of believers in Jerusalem and surrounding countryside had they not heeded the instructions of Christ to flee? In verse 16, our Lord begins to give directions for the escape of His followers after the Roman forces mysteriously retreated from the walls. These directions are contained in Matt. 24:16-28; Mk. 13:14-23; and Lk. 21:21-23. This was for His disciples and not some remote body of Jews yet unborn and millenniums in the future. It all happened in A.D. 70 and has nothing to do with the book of Revelation.

(h) "The abomination of desolation." Christ told His apostles that *they would see* this abomination. Daniel had predicted this some six hundred years prior. Is this abomination a human Antichrist setting in a "rebuilt Hebrew temple showing himself as God" over twenty centuries later (2 Thess. 2:4)? Will he be a Pope of the Catholic system, which came out of the state church of Emperor Constantine? *Common sense dictates that none of the apostles or early Christians lived to see any of these things.* Up to Matt. 24:15 the Savior had been telling His apostles of the various phenomena, signs, and events that would gradually take place, all of them leading to the final attack on the city. Here, He moves from the signs to the immediate cause of Jerusalem's destruction; the Roman armies. If we read Matthew's verse as harmonized above, into Mk. 13:14, then Lk. 21:20, we discover that Luke explained that this abomination would be the Roman military. Harmonizing Luke's account with Matthew and Mark, undisputedly demonstrates that all three evangelists wrote of the same event. The *Scofield Reference Bible*, page 1106, footnote 1, turns this siege into two separate sieges occurring several thousand years apart!

2p-Luke identifies the abomination. What Christ called "the abomination of desolation," in Matt. 24:15, Mark called it the same in 13:14. Luke went further; in verse 20, he was inspired to explain the meaning of this term.

In short, "the abomination of desolation," that had been predicted by Daniel in 9:27, pointed to the Roman armies, which would encircle Jerusalem and finally invade the holy temple site. (This cannot be a revived Roman empire over two thousand years later: none of the apostles lived that long to see such things.) "Abomination" was a common word among Jews. They knew a *previous* abomination had been "spoken [written] of by Daniel the prophet," centuries before. He predicted a terrible judgment would befall Israel in the future. It did in 168-167 B.C. This was a Syrian king named Antiochus Epiphanes. He captured Jerusalem and the temple, slew a pig, and burnt the carcass on the sacred altar, then sprinkled the place with its blood. The historical non-canonical book 1 Maccabees 1: 54 says of this event, "Now in the fifteenth day of the month of Casleu, [December] in the hundred forty and fifth year, [168 B.C.] they set up the abomination of desolation upon the altar, and builded idol altars throughout the cities of Juda on every side." The author of 1 Maccabees also called it "the abomination of desolation." In *Antiquities*, Book 12:7. 6, line 320, Josephus wrote that the Jews understood this "desolation" to have reference to Antiochus. Jews familiar with the history of their nation celebrate annually the Feast of Dedication in remembrance of their victory over King Antiochus. See Section 123, John 10:22, footnote a, for explanation of this event. Christ, now tells his preachers that a *similar event* but much in greater magnitude to what Daniel predicted would occur when the Romans take Jerusalem. They would be the "desolation." Luke's passage defines what the abomination would be. "And when ye shall see Jerusalem compassed with armies, then know that the desolation thereof is nigh." In other words, the second "desolation" was the coming destruction of the city, the defilement of the temple and the Holy of Holies. A formidable force of over 80,000 men threw up mounds and dug trenches about Jerusalem. It was Passover and pilgrims from over the known world were trapped behind those death walls. Josephus recorded that "three million Jews" were present during these celebrations. He described this encirclement and doom of the city in *Wars of the Jews,* Book 5. Yet, some managed to escape before the total lock down.

3p-Non-Christian Hebrew writers confirm the story of Antiochus and the abomination of which Daniel wrote. See Solomon Grayzel's work, *A History of the Jews,* pages 55-56, and Max Margolis with Alexander Marx in their *A History of the Jewish People,* pages 137-138. Grayzel described the "abomination of desolation" in his work on pages 171-172. He wrote that Titus went to the Holy Place of the temple with dozens of soldiers. "His sacrilegious act so offended the Jews, that they placed him forever alongside Nebuchadnezzar, Haman, and Antiochus in the gallery of their enemies. Among the Jews, he has been known as 'Titus the wicked.'" For a horrifying account of these unspeakable days and the slaughter of Jews, see F. W. Farrar's, *The Early Days of Christianity*, pages 486-490. Josephus also wrote that Titus went into the "Holy Place" (or what was left of it) in *Wars of the Jews,* Book 6:4. 7, line 260. After the battle for Jerusalem was over, Christ's preachers and other Christians heard of these things, looked back and understood His Words. We are sure that they had gotten the precise details of the horror story! Despite the obvious meaning of the "abomination of desolation," Scofield in his *Reference Bible* page 915, footnote 3 wrote, "The expression ["desolation"] occurs three times in Daniel." He then said that these have reference "to the "Beast," the "man of sin," also known as the Antichrist (2 Thess. 2:3-4). He continues his interpretation on page 1033 with footnote 1. Finally, on page 1272, footnote 1, we read that this "Beast" is also the "lawless one" or the Antichrist. He is supposed to sit in a rebuilt Jewish temple at Jerusalem and show himself as God. Scofield, apparently based his deduction on a statement from the heretical church father, Hippolytus (died in A.D. 235). He produced, *Treatise on Christ and Antichrist.* For a brief but good review of the eschatology of Hippolytus, see *The Man of Sin,* pages 135-138, by Dr. Kim Riddlebarger.

4p-A Gentile Abomination. The Jews called Romans and all heathen societies "abominations." Anything associated with idolatry or paganism was tagged by this word (Deut. 18:9; 1 Kings 11:7, with Ezek. 5:9). This is also written in the Talmud tractates, Shabbath 56b and 75a. Weeks before the city fell, squads of soldiers fighting the Jews moved in and out of the temple precincts and compound. With their presence, it became polluted as pagans treaded on holy ground. Josephus wrote of the heathen images, idols, emblems, insignias, motifs, some of which the soldiers brought into the temple and attached to its walls and tied onto the gates. Then the Roman soldiery offered animal sacrifices to these satanic emblems. In Mk. 14:14, Mark adds an editorial note that informs his readers that this uncircumcised pagan army was "standing where it ought not" (to be). This had reference to the inside precincts of the temple and later in the Holy of Holies itself. After five months of intermittent fighting had ended, the Romans plundered, looted, and razed the city. Interpreting Jesus' statement to mean the Antichrist sitting in a *rebuilt* Jewish temple over two thousand years later or the Pope in the Ecumenical Church is "too late" eschatology.

5p-The Antichrist problem. It is popularly taught that the Antichrist will appear on the scene immediately after the rapture. If so, he must be born some twenty-seven years prior, for as the imitator of Christ, he should be about thirty-four years old when he begins his work to rule the world. If he is born at the time of the rapture, then he will be a seven-year-old boy when the seven years of tribulation are completed. These figures present monstrous problems for the experts. *The author is not denying the fact of the Antichrist but pointing out some of the wrong teaching regarding this inhuman, human monster.* One questions how the apostles and early Christians (who have been dead two thousand years) witness these things, when, they are still future? They would need to outlive old brother Methuselah (Gen. 5:27). One *ultra* wild dispensationalist preaching on a local radio station said, "They will see them from heaven during the tribulation period!" These steamed up people believe that heaven will be watching the slaughterhouse, blood, and gore of that awful time in human history. With the present war raging in Iraq and Afghanistan, certain "prophecy buffs" picked George Bush as the *real* Antichrist. And they have a website to prove it! Now that Bush is out of office, and Obama is the president, we wonder how either of these men (who are not Jews) would fair "sitting in a rebuilt Jewish temple at Jerusalem showing the world that they are God."

6p-Certain "professional Reformed theologians," (like the Baptist *ultra* dispensationalists) are also up to their necks in the mire of guess-naming Antichrist. They have selected persons and events over church history to fit with particular verses of Scripture. These "scholars" tell us that it was not only the pagan Roman armies and Titus that polluted the temple at Jerusalem, but this also points ahead to the Papal church that captured and polluted the Christian Church. The teaching that the Antichrist in the form of the Roman Catholic system and its Popes rule over the Church of God belies the promise of Christ in Matt. 16:18. During the height of Catholic supremacy in Europe and the Middle Ages, thousands of believers were never part of this religious monster. *They were not in that dark system and therefore, could not come out of it.* Selecting Wycliffe, Huss, Luther, and John Calvin with his Reformers as the fulfillment of prophecy is more eschatological garble. These guessers so artfully exhibiting their "vast learning of history and eschatology," apparently do not know that over the past fifteen hundred years there have been more than one thousand different candidates for the Antichrist (not to mention the mark of the beast). And all of them have flopped! This has become a religious lottery with millions of tickets being bought by the gullible Christian public. *None of them can win, for no man knows who the Antichrist will be until he appears.*

7p-"**Readers will understand." Matt. 24:15b and parallel in Mk. 13:14b.** The double admonition, "Whoso readeth, let him understand" are the human writers' inspired comments. These are the words of Matthew and Mark, not the Savior. This proves that at the time of their writing, Jerusalem had not yet been destroyed! Their purpose in these words was to direct the reader's attention to the correct meaning of Daniel's prediction in order that they might understand the soon coming doom and escape. Both books were written before A.D. 70, and read by people dwelling in or near the land of Israel. Dr. H. W. House and Dr. Thomas Ice collaborated in 1988 and produced a timely and needed book entitled, *Dominion Theology: Blessing or Curse.* Part of this book is an *extreme* dispensationalist's view. On page 287 regarding Matt. 24:15 they affirm, "One major reason Matthew 24 could not have been fulfilled in A.D. 70 is that 'abomination of desolation' was not accomplished in the destruction of Jerusalem." They make this statement by affirming that Matt. 24:15 and Lk. 21:20 are "two separate events." If these two verses are left to stand as they read, then clearly both refer to the identical event. Those who compare these three parallel passages in the harmony presented above will instantly see they all speak of the same thing. This "disconnect a verse exegesis," used by some, demonstrates a struggle to prove an impossible point. On the other hand, it seems clear that the words of Peter, in 2 Peter 3:10-12, were not fulfilled in A.D. 70. Contextually, they speak of the *real* second coming of Christ and briefly about several of the ensuing events to occur at that time. Comments on Zech. 14 are found in Section 169, fifth and sixth paragraphs under footnote f.

8p-**Matt. 24:16-18 with parallels in Mk. 13:14b-16 and Lk. 21:21. "Flee Judaea," and "don't turn back."** About four decades after Jesus gave this warning, believers, seeing the Roman army approaching, fled Judaea for protection in the hills and mountain areas. Later, the believers inside Jerusalem escaped to the distant city of Pella on the northeastern side of the River Jordan in Peraea. (See second paragraph of footnote g above for more on this.) At sight of the awful Romans, those on their housetops, raced down the outside stairwell in great haste. Farmers and servants alike working fields were warned not to return to the houses for any earthly possessions, not even for a single garment (Mk. 13:16). The risk would be too great. As previously mentioned, Jesus had earlier spoken similar words of warning in Section 134, Lk. 17:31, footnote k. For more on their escape, see footnote f above, the third paragraph under number 16. The Savior's Words recorded by Matthew and Luke had nothing to do with, "Jews fleeing from the persecution of the Antichrist" (Rev. 12:6-17). Such a rendering neglects the background of these verses, the geographical and historical setting, who was speaking, and to whom He addressed His comments. There is nothing here about Jews in the future tribulation period.

9p-**Not the "rapture of the church."** Interpreting these verses as having reference to the removal of the church does not agree with our Lord's admonition about "turning back." The departure of the church will be an *instantaneous* event. The warning in these passages *cannot* be applied to the rapture at the return of Christ. That blessed event will be sudden and fast. It is described as occurring "in a moment" and the "twinkling of an eye" in 1 Cor. 15:51-52, and "quickly" in Rev. 22:12. Not one Christian anywhere on earth will be running home to collect their earthly treasures when the trumpet sounds! Though continually used as referring to the catching out of the saints, this is exegetically an impossible interpretation. The things Christ spoke of occurred as the Roman armies suddenly appeared on the horizon across the land and settled in their various campsites. It is ironic that Titus camped near the Mount of Olives, the very site from which Jesus gave this discourse of judgment! Hundreds of Christian Jews and Gentiles recalled the Words of Christ, and fled at this overwhelming sight of the terrible Roman legions. The Lord Jesus warned them against returning to their houses, villages, or Jerusalem to gather up their personal belongings. This would entrap them. They must quickly flee. And flee, they did, some forty years later just as their Lord commanded. *There is no rapture here.* It must be forced into the context. It was Paul, who *later* explained briefly in his letters the removal of the church (1 Thess. 2:19-20; 3:13; and 4:13-18).

10p-Lk. 21:22. "Things written may be fulfilled." Earlier, the Savior had pronounced a curse upon *that* generation of Jews. The blood of God's servants they had persecuted and slain would be required of their hands. Refer to this in Section 70, Lk. 11:50-51, number 9 under footnote h. Various Old Testament passages had predicted the doom of Jerusalem and temple centuries before the birth of Jesus. Some writers see Israel's judgment as a continuing thing at the hands of both the Babylons (586 B.C.), and the Romans (A.D. 70) as it was predicted in Deut. 28:20-68; 32:22-26; Isa. 6:10-12; Jer. 46:10; Hosea 9:7; and Dan. 9:26-27. In verse 26 of Daniel, the "prince" that destroyed Jerusalem was General Titus. Luke's words in 21:23 about "great distress in the land, and wrath upon this people," are a direct reference to the Jews and the land of Israel. It was to these and other Old Testament verses that Christ made an appeal when He said that the "things written must be fulfilled." Though written centuries before in the Old Testament, they had reference to a future time in Israel's history. That time came in A.D. 70.

11p-Matt. 24:19-20 with parallels in Mk. 13:17-18 and Lk. 21:23. Maternal sufferings, wintertime, and fleeing Jewish women. Some years ago, the author heard an evangelist preach that, "Unsaved women carrying children at the time of the rapture would have their babies ripped from their wombs and taken to heaven!" This is a prime example of radical and irresponsible dispensationalism. The warning here had nothing to do with the church today. They relate to first century Jewish females who were pregnant at the time of the Roman invasion. The Messiah knew that women in this condition are unable to run; neither could they bear the pain, suffering, and terror that would attend fleeing from the cruel Romans. He announced a future "woe" (warning) upon all women who would be trapped in this plight. A few days after sharing these horrible details with His four apostles, the Savior was led over the streets of Jerusalem to the cross. Suddenly, He stopped and warned the women of that city who were following Him about the coming horrors of A.D. 70. See this dreadful lament in Section 188, Lk. 23:28-31. It is erroneous exegesis to take His Words and fit them into the tribulation period, which has not yet occurred. These women have been dead for two thousand years and they did experience the doom spoken of by the Savior.

12p-Matt. 24:20 with the admonition about winter and Sabbath day traveling is pertinent. During winter in the land of Israel, the days are short and back roads were difficult and often impossible to travel. No fleeing person would traverse the paved main roads due to the presence of thousands of soldiers. On the Sabbath, the Hebrews kept their doors shut and the gates to all cities barred. If they fled on that sacred day, they should not expect admission and protection anywhere. Their oral law limited all Sabbath travel to just under one mile (Acts 1:12 with Ex. 16:29).

13p-During the siege horrible things happened to both women and children who were trapped in the city. Houses filled with mothers and little ones perished in the robbery, killing, fires, mayhem, and awful famine that raged behind the walls of Jerusalem. One event concerns a woman of high social rank named Maria (Mary) who was the daughter of Eliezar, a powerful rich man. She was stripped, abused by the soldiers and robbed of her few possessions. Near starvation, she killed and then secretly boiled her nursing baby before her shocking deed was discovered. See *Wars of the Jews*, Book 6:3. 4, lines 201 through 211 for details of this sickening story. Similar deeds were done during the earlier destruction of the city and temple in 586 B.C. See Jer. 19:9 for the story.

(i) Matt. 24:21a with parallels in Mk. 13:19a, and Lk. 21:22-23. "Great tribulation, affliction, vengeance, and distress." Matthew wrote, "For then shall be;" while Mark wrote, "For in those days." We inquire, "*When* was Matthew's 'then,' and *when* would Mark's 'those days' be?'" Jesus referred to the things He had just said, and "when" those things occurred it would be the time of great tribulation for Jerusalem and its inhabitants. *There is no other grammatical sense to these statements*. It is this "great tribulation," "affliction," or "distress," coming upon the city that He uses as the reason for their speedy flight to shelter in the mountains. To lift Matthew's verse out of its context and transport it over two thousand years into the future is erroneous. This style of biblical interpretation has produced every cult, sect, and weird doctrine flaunting itself under the guise of Bible Christianity. *The "great tribulation" as here stated by the Savior, was directly connected with the fall of Jerusalem, and Jerusalem's fall with the "great tribulation."* Luke makes this evident when he explained the calamities that would attend this "great tribulation," would begin at Jerusalem. He wrote in verse 24, "And they [Jews] shall fall by the edge of the [Roman] sword, and shall be led away captive into all nations: and Jerusalem shall be trodden down of the Gentiles, until the times of the Gentiles be fulfilled." The "they" of Luke's text can only mean the Hebrew people, and the "they" that lived after the massacres were taken prisoners and led into captivity. Irrefutable history has shown that this is what happened to millions of Jews in A.D. 70. And it is all in the past. The "great tribulation" of Matt. 24:21 is over, and it will not occur again. (This does not deny a horrible time yet coming upon this world.) Swords were the weapons of centuries ago and a chief piece of fighting equipment for the Roman army. They are no longer used in warfare but are collector's items and museum pieces. Refer to Lk. 21:24 in the eleventh paragraph below for more on the usage of the Roman sword. "End time specialists" have written many books "proving" how the sword will be reinstituted again in modern day warfare, thus demonstrating that these verses speak of a future event!

2p-More than one "great tribulation." In Rev. 2:22, the Savior warned the Thyatira Church that He would "cast her . . . into great tribulation." The "great tribulation" of Rev. 7:14 is not the one recorded by Matthew, and Matthew's tribulation cannot be the one of Rev. 2:22. The verse in Rev. 2:22 can only speak of a time of suffering that occurred over two thousand years ago to the church at Thyatira, yet it is called "great tribulation." *Thus, we have two "great tribulations" in the book of Revelation, and they are vastly different!* This reflects the elasticity of the term.

3p-Israel's greatest historical calamity was in A.D. 70. Matthew's concluding words, that *this* tribulation was unparalled in world history, meant that there had never been anything like it from the beginning of the world, nor would there ever be again for Israel. That the Lord Jesus had in view the horrors which were to befall the Jewish nation, and not the tribulation period several thousand years away, is clear from His closing words in this verse, "no, nor ever shall be." The three words, "ever shall be" meant from that calamity forward, Israel will never again pass through anything like this, even to the end of the world. *Therefore, the future tribulation could not be worse in its effect on Israel!* Both secular and religious writers describe in graphic language the destruction of Jerusalem during these months, and especially the final days of the war. The past centuries of awful afflictions in Egypt, the captivity in Babylon, oppressions under successive foreign powers, the wars of the Maccabees, the hatred of Gentile tyrants for Israel, pale into insignificance for nothing so horrible as A.D. 70 ever befell that nation. Josephus wrote in *Wars of the Jews*, Book. 5:11. 1, line 451 that so many Jews were crucified that there was no room to hang others! Christ's Words here do not have reference to a future tribulation for Israel. That is something entirely different from A.D. 70. Eusebius wrote, "The cities could be seen full of unburied corpses, the dead bodies of the aged flung down along side those of infants, women without a rag to conceal their nakedness, and the whole province [was] full of indescribable horror. See *The History of the Christian Church*, pages 105-106, by Esuebius Pamphilus.

4p-With the fall of Jerusalem, millions of Jews died, were enslaved, or sold to perish in the Roman gladiatorial theaters. However, the *greatest of all woes,* their beautiful temple, and house of the true and living God was reduced to a pile of stones and smoldering ashes. It was sacked, and every piece of gorgeous exotic wood, burned. So intense was the heat that tons of gold melted and ran between the gigantic stones. Nothing like this had befallen Israel since the final Babylonian attack and captivity in 586 B.C. This disaster was far greater than the one of old. Titus, awed by the magnificence of the temple architecture and its dazzling beauty issued orders "not to destroy it." (Some sources say this was not true.) During a night incursion, a Roman soldier standing on the shoulders of a fellow legionnaire accidentally dropped a flaming torch through a storeroom lattice window. It fell into a barrel of olive oil, exploded, and fire gradually engulfed the temple. Soon the entire structure was ablaze.

5p-General Titus attempted to stop the enraged assault of his men across the city. They were driven by demonic impulse, fierce rancor, and unbridled hatred for the Jews. It is a historical fact that Titus wanted to save the temple. Some pagan writers deny this, probably because of their hatred for the Jews. Behind all this was a Sovereign act of Almighty God in destroying the earthly temple to make way for His spiritual house, the church, or the new kingdom of Jesus Christ. In this spiritual house, men can worship God anywhere on earth (John 4:23), and offer sacrifices that are more glorious (Rom. 12:1; Heb. 13:15; and Eph. 2:18-22). Every believer in this spiritual temple is a priest of royal descent (1 Peter 2:9). If the Jews build another temple in the future, it is certain that Jehovah will have nothing to do with it. Christ's death on the cross forever abolished all the sacrifices and rituals of the Torah Law. *To reconstitute these in any form is awful of sacrilege in view of Christ' perfect death on the cross.* Refer to Section 134, third paragraph of footnote d for comments on a supposed "rebuilt Hebrew temple."

6p-During the final weeks of the siege, a great slaughter followed. Ernest R. the celebrated French infidel and religious blasphemer, wrote in *Renan's Antichrist*, page 254 these words, "From this time forth, hunger, rage, despair, and madness dwelt in Jerusalem. It was a cage of furious maniacs, a city resounding with howling and inhabited by cannibals, a very hell. Titus, for his part, was atrociously vindictive; every day five hundred unfortunates were crucified in the sight of the city with hateful refinements of cruelty . . ." Some three hundred years after A.D. 70, a historian named Sulpitius Severus, wrote of this horrible great tribulation, "The Pharisees for a time maintained their ground most boldly in defense of the Temple, and at length . . . committed [they threw] themselves to the flames" rather than surrender. See *The Nicene and Post-Nicene Fathers*, 2nd series, vol. 11, page 111, for the grizzly details. The Jews fought to keep the pagan Romans out of the Holy of Holies but succumbed to the superior force of the fierce legionnaires. At the end of it all, Jerusalem, the city of God, the beauty of all the earth, and her glorious house lay in ghastly ruins. Thus, the warnings Christ had given the religious leaders and Jewish people were fulfilled. To review these, see the main headings in Sections 68, 126, 154, and 159.

7p-As mentioned several times, because it was during the annual Passover that the Roman armies appeared about the city, several million Jews from over the known world were trapped behind the walls. The enormity of the situation becomes incomprehensible. After sealing off the city, three major factions paired against each other within Jerusalem. Men going about dressed as women, murdered and killed without discrimination. Josephus also wrote of these factions led by Eleazer, John, and Simon, all power insane, merciless killers. Concerning this, Spurgeon, in *The Treasury of the New Testament,* vol. 1, page 343 recorded these apt words, "Before the Romans attacked Jerusalem, the inhabitants had begun to kill one another. Various factions divided the city. They took possession of three sections and fought against one another, night and day. Meanwhile, the fierce Romans waited for their time outside the city walls. Among ungodly men filled with evil, manhood breaks loose against itself. Starvation and looting raged . . ." The stench of thousands of rotting corpses stacked in piles about the temple altar, and blood running like thick water over the once highly polished floor was the general tenor in this judgment nightmare.

8p-Years later, looking back on the scene, Josephus penned these words in *Wars of the Jews*, Book 4:5, 2, line 323, "I cannot but think that it was because God had doomed this city to destruction as a polluted city, and was resolved to purge his sanctuary by fire." All of this and more was the "great tribulation" Jesus warned about in Matt. 24:21. Every word came to pass. So much bloodshed occurred that the Talmud in tractate, Gittin 57a reads in satirical language these doleful words, "For seven years did the nations [Gentiles] of the world cultivate their vineyards with no other manure than the blood of Israel." After the battle, a captain in the Roman army, Terenitius Rufus, plowed with a team of oxen over the exposed earth surface areas of the temple. This was a fulfillment of Micah 3:12 written some seven hundred years prior. In 1805, George Peter Holford wrote an invaluable work dealing with this subject. Its lengthy title is *The Destruction of Jerusalem. An Absolute and Irresistible Proof of the Divine Origin of Christianity: Including a Narrative of the Calamities which befell the Jews, so far as they tend to verify our Lord's Predictions Relative to that Event.* Holford's book has excellent material. Mistakenly, he held that all of Matt. 24 was fulfilled when the city and temple were destroyed in A.D. 70. Rigid postmillennialists believe the same. *Radical* dispensational premillennialists tell us that all of it is yet to be fulfilled. The sobering question is, "How will all of us answer to God for these conflicting doctrines?" Someone is partly or totally wrong!

9p-Matt. 24:21b and parallel in Mk. 13:19b. "Not since the beginning of the world." In over five thousand years of Israel's history, these people have never suffered such loss, destruction, and death as in A.D. 70. In 586 B.C. when Babylonian soldiers killed thousands, destroyed the city, and took Israel captive, it was not comparable with the slaughter at the hands of the Romans. The barbaric holocaust under Adolf Hitler was not like the horrible slaughter of the Romans in A.D. 70. Large temple archives filled with genealogies where Jews could trace their ancestries back to Abraham were burnt. In Jewish thinking, their greatest losses were the magnificent temple, cessation of rituals, and sacrifices, and the devastation of the Hebrew state. Some forty years prior, Jesus Christ had provided the final and everlasting sacrifice for the sins of mankind on the cross; there would never be another (Heb. 10:12-14). Israel was physically punished, especially its religious leaders for their sins. Somehow, this occurred in a mystic but awful manner; both the Father in heaven and His rejected Son, directed, and implemented the entire disaster. The Messiah, hated, scorned, and His Spirit blasphemed by His own Hebrew people was vindicated. Whoever reads Josephus' description of their evil in *Wars of the Jews*, Books 6 and 7, will be convinced of his words, "Never did any city suffer such things, nor was there ever any generation that more abounded in malice or wickedness." Refer to Dr. William Nast's chilling description of Israel's decadence in Section 100, first paragraph of footnote d. The "great tribulation" of Matt 24:21 was accomplished over two thousand years ago during the period from April to September A.D. 70. This does not negate an awful judgment yet to come upon Israel. Whenever this happens, Jews, who believe on the Messiah-Savior will be saved (Rom. 11:25-32).

10p-Lk. 21:22. "Things that are written." We inquire, "Written where?" Obviously, in the Hebrew Old Testament or Tanakh. For some of the verses forecasting Israel's doom, see the tenth paragraph under footnote h above. This declaration from the lips of Jesus proves His total familiarity with the Hebrew Scriptures.

11p-Lk. 21:24. No parallel. "Fall by the sword" and "the times of the Gentiles." Who are the "they," to fall by the sword and be taken captive by Gentiles? It is sure they are not Jews during the future tribulation. The "Gentiles" referred to in Luke's text can only be the Romans. No other hermeneutic makes sense. The weapon used is the "sword" and not nuclear warheads, guided missiles, or atomic bombs, the war tools of today. These "times of the Gentiles," began with the Roman invasion and conquest of Jerusalem. Over the past two thousand years, Jerusalem has been trodden down by wave after wave of Gentiles; Arabs, Turks, infidels, Muslims, murderers, false religions, and armies. A mosque of Islam erected in A.D. 691 now stands over portions of the temple site, and their pagan crescent banner flies in the air. Scofield wrote in his *Reference Bible*, page 1106, that the "times of the Gentiles" began with the captivity of Judah under Nebuchadnezzar (2 Chron. 36:1-21), since which time Jerusalem has been under Gentile over-lordship." Yet, Christ said that the "times of the Gentiles" began with Roman destruction and occupation of the city. (This is something different from "the fulness of the Gentiles" in Romans 11:25, the latter having to do with the conversion of non-Jewish people.) Gentile domination and "treading down" of Jerusalem and the land of Israel began in A.D. 70. It continues to this moment, although *limited* parts of the land and city are now in Israel's control since 1948. See more on this in the fifth paragraph of footnote s below.

12p-With A.D. 70, God was not finished with the Hebrew nation. William Cox in, *Biblical Studies in Final Things*, page 103, mistakenly wrote, "We know that the great tribulation of A.D. 70 brought the Jewish state to its complete and final end." It has been a long end, but it is not final. Jehovah is not through with Israel. Originally, they were His "chosen" people (Deut. 7:6-9 with Amos 3:1-2), selected to bring His Son into the world through Mary (Lk. 1:34-38). Saved Jews were united with saved Gentiles at Pentecost (Eph. 2:16-19). This union continues today in the body of Christ. According to Rom. 11:1-2, God has a future plan for Jews, who repent and believe the gospel. This will be realized after the olive tree (bringing in all saved Jews and Gentiles) has reached its full growth, or the church is complete. *There is not a different plan of salvation or gospel for the Jews.*

(j) Matt. 24:22 and parallel in Mk. 13:20. "Days shortened" and "no flesh be saved." From sealing off the city to the victory of the Romans in the temple lasted several months. This sealing cut off all supplies of food and water to Jerusalem. Had the siege continued into several years, not one person or ("no flesh") would have survived. Internal faction fighting, slaughter, and famine raged within the city. It is the saving of physical life that is the subject here, not the salvation of the soul. This statement, if left in its historical context has nothing to do with God cutting short the tribulation period of Revelation in order to spare the Jews. This is more extreme dispensationalist patchwork. The apostles would have never understood such things at this time in their lives. Lifted out of their context, Bible verses are used to prove just about anything, especially future events, since they are unknown.

2p-Elect's sake. God cut short the destruction because thousands of His "elect" or "believers" lived in the land of Israel. The mother church was also located at Jerusalem. Otherwise, they would have been slaughtered in the bloodbath that followed. The number of Christians that escaped to Pella before the *final encirclement* of Jerusalem, we have no way of knowing. Were some unbelievers among their number? Many of the older Jews who were killed during this time had heard Christ preach years before in this very temple. Some commentators wonder if any of these old men called upon God for mercy. However, the Words of our Savior spoken previously suggest that they had crossed the divine deadline (Matt. 23:37). Very early in His ministry, Christ solemnly warned the Jews that they had gone too far: they had blasphemed the Holy Spirit, the sin that is unforgivable. Refer to Section 66 for the story.

(k) Matt. 24:23-24a with parallel in Mk. 13:21-22a. False Messiahs and false miraculous wonders. The Lord Jesus re-emphasized what He had just previously said in Matt. 24:4-5. See number 2 under footnote f above for explanation. This warning had reference to those religiously insane Jews, who presented themselves as Messiahs to their fellow Hebrews. They were not men who were misrepresenting Christianity. Rather, they misrepresented Messiah to Judaism. The seriousness of this warning to the apostles is stressed by this repetition. The Jews at this point in their history, especially those of Jerusalem, were buoyed up with false hopes by grand imposters who infested the land and lied to the people. Josephus wrote of these charlatans, "There were at this time many prophets suborned by the tyrants to delude the [Jewish] people, by bidding them wait for help from God, in order that there might be fewer desertions, and that those who were above fear and control might be encouraged by hope." He concluded, "Thus it was that the imposters and pretended messengers of heaven at that time beguiled the wretched people." He described his own people, trapped behind the walls as "wretched." See *Wars of the Jews,* all thirteen chapters of Book 5 for the numerous and horrific scattered details. It reads like a description of Hitler's death camps.

2p-Matt. 24:24b with parallel in Mk. 13:22b. "Great signs and wonders. As the judgment of Jerusalem and Israel drew near, numerous false Messiahs and prophets appeared in Judaea both before and afterward. Their portents of great wonders dazzled many benighted followers. The *Biblical, Theological, and Ecclesiastical Cyclopaedia,* vol. vi, pages 141-144, by M'Clintock and Strong, carries a comprehensive article on False Messiahs covering this subject into 1850. Christ's predictions were literally fulfilled while elements of these religious "quacks" continued long after A.D. 70. They claimed to their credit much of the eerie phenomena that occurred during the period shortly before the city fell. This does not negate the fact that over the course of church history, countless religious "crackpots" calling themselves "Messiah," and claiming supernatural powers will yet appear. The warning from the Lord Jesus *spoken here* has nothing to do with the Antichrist in a future tribulation period showing great and deceiving wonders to his followers. Whatever the grizzly horrors of Rev. 13 all mean for a future generation, they are different events from those spoken of by our Lord on *this* occasion. They will happen in the future just as Christ's predictions upon Israel for A.D. 70 did in the past.

3p-"Deceiving the very elect." The rabbis taught that Israel was the *elect nation* of God. All others (Gentiles) were cursed or non-elect (Isa. 45:4). This Hebrew election had nothing to do with salvation; rather, it was strictly a nationalistic and geographical thing. The Talmud uses the term "elect" in tractate, Magilah 9a in reference to the Hebrew nation. However, here the Lord Jesus Christ spoke of Jews, who were saved. The idea in the passage is that the false Messiahs and prophets would perform demonic wonders that would deceive many, but not the saved elect because the Lord Jesus had pre-warned them of these things. "The elect" had reference to Jewish believers (and Gentiles as well) who were in Jerusalem and the regions about when the Roman forces appeared. They were forewarned to be ready. Regarding the word "elect," God determined from the foundation of the world to save any person who will repent of their sins and believe on the Lord Jesus Christ. This is how one enters into "the election of grace." Out of His "Sovereign good pleasure," He established the pre-conditions of repentance and faith, not man. New Testament believers are often referred to as "elect" (Rom. 8:33; Col. 3:12; and 1 Peter 1:2).

4p-Matt. 24:25-26. No parallels. "Behold, *he is* in the secret chambers." In the temple were two secluded rooms called the "chambers of secret." Some of the older rabbis taught that when Messiah came, He would frequent these places to pray and choose certain Jews to meet Him here at various times. Apparently, this is the meaning of our Lord's words. Since He gave no explanation, we can believe that His apostles understood what He meant. Jesus was clearly denying the validity of this claim that will be made by the false prophets, charming and deceiving the Jews before the doom of A.D. 70. He said, "Believe *it* not." In this, He corrected another rabbinical myth held by the Jews. See Section 160, third paragraph of footnote a for more on these "secret chambers."

(l) Matt. 24:27a. "As lightning." No parallels. Our Lord had previously spoken a similar thing in Lk. 17:24. Some expositors hold that Jesus spoke here of coming in a *mystic* way to unleash judgment and that this occurred in the form of the savage Roman legions, thus decimating the Jewish people. It would all be engineered and supervised by Israel's hated Messiah, Jesus of Nazareth. However, this does not cancel His return for the church. The origin of A.D. 70 was in heaven. Its results struck Judea and Jerusalem like a lightning bolt from the hand of Jehovah. How *incorrect* for commentators to write that this expression about lightning "refers to the final aspect of Jesus' return," and the battle of Armageddon. The old fable that Christ will return from the east is also based on Matt. 24:27. A stroll through older cemeteries, especially in the southern United States reveals that many Christians were buried facing the east, believing their Savior would return from that direction. The truth is that when our Lord returns, He will come from *all* directions, everywhere at the same time! With some "end time experts, Titus 2:13 and 1 Thess. 4:16-17 become one-way streets leading to America only. However, they embrace the whole world at the same time.

2p-Matt. 24:27b. "So shall also the coming of the Son of man be." Visible or invisible? That is, when Christ comes in vengeance against the Jews and Jerusalem, it will be swift and deadly as lightning striking the earth. *It is incorrect that the word "coming" when used in reference to Jesus, always speaks of His visible return.* Those who teach this use Acts 1:11 as proof, where a visible appearing of Christ is the meaning. However, every reference to His return does not speak of a visible, literal event. Some do and some do not. In the book of Revelation, five of the seven churches are threatened with the Lord's "coming" to chastise them! To the lukewarm congregation at Ephesus He warned, "I will come to thee and I will remove thy candlestick" (Rev. 2:5). To the church at Pergamos, the Lord Jesus declared, "Repent, or else I will come unto thee quickly" (Rev. 2:16). Similar words were spoken to Thyatira (Rev. 2:25), Philadelphia (Rev. 3:11), and to Laodicea (Rev. 3:20). In each of these, Jesus warned that He was "coming" to these churches. Who would hold that these five "comings" of Christ refer to literal, visible returns? Christ can come to something or someone, and it be an invisible event. When the Savior told His apostles, "I will not leave you comfortless: I will come to you" (John 14:18), it was an invisible coming in the Person of the Holy Spirit. The previous verses reveal that the "coming" of our Lord can be both literal and figurative, both visible and invisible. Therefore, to make *all* the comings of Christ mentioned in this Olivet Discourse, to speak only of His *literal* return is unjustified. The context and historical background often helps us to understand the meaning. When a text is unclear, a forced interpretation imposed upon it should be rejected.

3p-We believe that in the above text of Matt. 24:27a and b, the Savior was speaking of His coming in a mystical way to judge Jerusalem and the Jews through the Roman army. Its results were like deadly lightning. How ironic that General Titus and His fierce tenth legion camped at the *eastern* side of the city on the Mount of Olives, and moved into battle from that location which was the east. After months of fighting, this war ended at the *western* wall of Jerusalem. The fierce Roman soldiery moved the battle from "east to west" just as the Savior predicted.

(m) Matt. 24:28. "The eagles." No parallels. Jesus had used a similar expression earlier. Refer to Section 134, Lk. 17:37, footnote p. for more on "the eagles." This statement also has nothing to do with Christ coming for His church. It was fulfilled at the destruction of Jerusalem. Sincere pastors, busy preaching on the topic "Watch for the Eagle coming for the church" project a beautiful idea but the illustration is several millenniums too late. The "eagles" (plural) Jesus spoke about in verse 28, swooped into Jerusalem about two thousand years ago; they were not wearing feathers but armor, and there were some eighty thousand of them. They carried thousands of military ensigns, which were "eagle gods" attached to the top of a pole or a flag signal carrier. From 195 B.C. forward, each Roman legion used an aquila (eagle) as a fighting banner or standard. An official called the "aquilifer" carried this standard. Its loss or capture was considered an act of the gods and could lead to the disbanding of the entire legion. In *Gallic War*, Book IV, paragraph 25, Julius Caesar wrote that during the Roman invasion of Britain in 55 B.C., his soldiers feared to leave their ship due to the savage Britons. Seeing this, the aquilifer of the tenth legion leaped overboard and carried the eagle standard into the face of the enemy. This so infused the cowering soldiers with courage that they too jumped from the ships and flew into battle. The eagle standard was a terrifying sight to the enemies of Rome. Finding the "rapture of the church" in these Words of Jesus requires one to scrap the historical background and contextual setting in which they were spoken. To restrict the introduction of Roman eagles into Jerusalem to Pilate (long before A.D 70), is a misinterpretation of Josephus, in *Antiquities of the Jews*, 18:3, 1, line 1. Pilate was the first governor to do this, but it was not the first time it had been done nor was it the last time.

2p-A vulture type fowl called the "kite," dwelling in the land of Israel lived from rotted carrion. They were known to follow marching armies and circle in the heavens until the fighting was over. Tearing large pieces of flesh from the living and the dead, animals, or humans, these were taken to their nests to feed the young or themselves. Job 39:30 speaks of these hideous creatures in the words, "Her young ones also suck up blood: and where the slain *are*, there *is* she." The author saw many varieties of these repulsive and menacing creatures while serving in Africa. Our Lord referred to this in His statement, and all four of His apostles understood. The removal of the church must be *forced* into these Words of Christ, for it cannot be found here.

(n) Matt. 24:29a, with parallels in Mk. 13:24a, and Lk. 21:25a. "Immediately after the tribulation of those days" or after the fall of Jerusalem. Up to this point, we have attempted to trace the Words spoken by the Lord Jesus in Matt. 24:4-28 with their parallel texts of Mark and Luke, as having reference to the physical destruction of Jerusalem. Now, we meet Matt. 24:29a, "Immediately after the tribulation of those days [in A.D. 70] shall the sun be darkened, and the moon shall not give her light." According to the chronology of John in Revelation, the convulsions of heavenly bodies will occur at the *beginning* of the real tribulation and continue spasmodically through parts of it, but not afterwards (Rev. 6:12-14, 8:10, 9:4 and passim.) *"The tribulation," mentioned here by Jesus had reference to events following the destruction of Jerusalem not something two thousand years later.*

2p-Did everything happen in A.D. 70? It is historically valid that awful phenomena continued for decades after the city had fallen. Several interpretations of the Savior's Words are briefly discussed in this paragraph and paragraphs 3p- through 10p- below. For example, over a hundred years ago, J. Russell Stuart wrote *The Parousia*. On page 77 he stated, "Here also the phraseology absolutely forbids the idea of any transition from the subject in hand to another." Stuart is saying that it is impossible to see *another event,* such as the second coming of Christ foreshadowed in Jerusalem's doom. Milton S. Terry espoused the same belief in his classic book, *Biblical Hermeneutics*, pages 443-444. Both men held that *everything* spoken by the Lord Jesus, on this occasion happened in A.D. 70. This includes, "the Son of man coming in a cloud with power and great glory" (Mk. 13:26 with Lk. 21:27); "the stars falling and heaven being shaken" (Matt. 24:29b with Mk. 13:25); and the angels, trumpet call and the elect being gathered from all of earth (Matt. 24:31 with Mk. 13:27). Older expositors like Terry and Stuart refuse to allow a "shadow meaning" in any of these passages, such as a dim outline of the far off events that will accompany the literal return of Christ. Despite the opinions of these great men, it seems wrong to hold that all of these terse words were only *poetical terms,* employed by the Messiah to express the awfulness of A.D. 70. If they are all poetic Hebrew imagery then such language transports what Jesus said into the realm of "say much but mean little." *Sorting out what words are pictorial and what are not is the problem.*

3p-Symbolic words. Old Testament Scriptures often speak of great disasters or tribulations in *symbolic* language. An example is the destruction of Edom recorded in Isa. 34:4-5 where it speaks of "the heaven being rolled together." We read of mountains and hills that "skipped" in Ps. 114:4-5. Scripture talks of hills singing and the trees clapping their hands in Isa. 55:12. Clearly, this is symbolic language, for these things did not literally occur, but the horrific judgments they often pointed to, did. Some hold that the *entirety* of the Matt. 24 discourse is strictly figurative, using various emblems to point to unnatural upheavals to momentous and earth shaking times. It seems naive to assert that Jesus intended *all* of His predictions to have only reference to spiritual phenomena; that none of them literally occurred. It seems that some were symbolic and others were not. We have previously noted that the signs of Matt. 24:4-14 were not symbolic. They actually took place. Since most everything up to Matt. 24:29 is taken as literally happening, then what can Matt. 24:29a and its parallels mean?

4p-The author's conjectures. Possible answers to the events occurring *after* the great tribulation or fall of Jerusalem. If we take Luke's account in verse 24 and blend it into Matthew's, and let the "those days" of Matthew's verse 29, embrace Luke's "times of the Gentiles" (during which Jerusalem is trodden down), then, we have a possible solution to this enigma. In favor of this, seems to be the record of Mk. 13:24, "But in those days after the tribulation . . ." This could extend Matthew's "immediately" into many more days instead of a short time period. *Again, it is stressed that this is strictly the author's assumption.* Various expositors struggling with this hold that the word "immediately," grammatically belongs to the end of verse 28. It would thus read, "There will the eagles be gathered together immediately." Because no punctuation marks were in the Greek manuscripts, this could be allowable. I see no problem in the words "Immediately after the tribulation of those days [of Jerusalem's fall]" speaking of the historical phenomena that occurred in the days and years that followed. To assert that these "after tribulation" cataclysmic events speak of the power that will accompany Christ when He returns to set up His earthly kingdom at the end of the tribulation is chronologically too late. These events occurred in the years that followed the collapse of the Jewish state and burning of the temple. They do not fit into the story over two thousands years later.

5p-Continued troubles. Wars and awful signs continued in the years *after* the fall of Jerusalem. It took the Roman army decades to mop up the last vestiges of individual and Jewish group resistance. Not only was there a Jerusalem aboveground, but there was one underground as well. It burrowed itself beneath the upper or northern part of Jerusalem. The vast size of these large subterranean tunnels and rooms is an established fact. Masses of Jews hid in these, trying to flee from the Romans. This underground resistance continued for several years. Some two thousand dead bodies were found in these underground rooms when all resistance was quelled.

6p-Masada. Roman armies continued to battle against a Jewish remnant for several centuries after they had crushed the Hebrew political state and destroyed their city and temple. Large and small conflicts occurred intermediately in Judaea, and spread over the countryside and abroad. About one thousand Jews escaped Jerusalem and fled to Masada, the mountain top fortress of Herod near the southwest coast of the Dead Sea. The mountain fortress of Masada was breached after two years and finally taken in A.D. 72. The occupying Jews had committed mass suicide. They chose to die by their own hands rather than to become captives of the pagan Romans.

7p-False Messiah. During the first hundred years or so *after* the destruction of the temple, there was a high expectation among the Jews, that they would reclaim their land and rebuild their temple. Many of them lived in small villages over the country and served as caretakers by Roman permission. Restoration hopes flared again among this subjected remnant. Emperor Hadrian (died A.D. 138) hearing of this potential uprising crushed their expectations by plowing over the ruins of the old city and renaming it "Colony of Rome." This prompted a rebellion and resulted in large-scale slaughter of Jews at Caesarea and other communities. Over half a million died. In A.D. 132, a Jewish rebel Bar Kochba, ("son of the star") claiming to be a Messiah, attempted to rebuild the temple! News spread that he had fully liberated Jerusalem and Judea, but time proved this a deadly fallacy. Some three years later, the Roman army marched against Bar Kochba, slaughtering him and his followers. Because so many Roman soldiers were killed in this conflict, Emperor Hadrian refused to let the Jews of return to the temple site under pain of death. Circumcision and reading the Torah were banned. Hebrew scholars were put to death. Jews who professed Christianity were included in these restrictions. The infuriated emperor erected a pagan shrine to Jupiter on temple grounds and a statue of himself on horseback. The next Roman Emperor, Antonius Pius (A.D. 138–161) also placed his image on temple grounds. This led to more deaths. Wars and bloodshed continued long after A.D. 70.

8p-**No rebuilt temple.** Several centuries later, a Roman Emperor came to power known as "Julian the apostate." He ruled from A.D. 331 to 363. To acquire political favor, he pretended tolerance for Christianity. Shortly afterward, Julian went mad, restored the pagan religions, and schemed to rebuild the Jewish temple at Jerusalem. By this, he sought to prove Christianity false. Julian allowed thousands of Jews to return to Judaea. A British minister, and an outspoken annihilationist, Rev. William Warburton, (died 1779) wrote a description of Emperor Julian's insanity. It is titled *Julian, or a Discourse Concerning the Earthquake and Fiery Eruption which Defeated that Emperor's Attempt to Rebuild the Temple at Jerusalem.* The 286 pages of this old English writing are a treasure chest of information. It deals with the insane emperor and how he supported the Jews in their attempt to erect another temple. Awful but miraculous interpositions of divine providence defeated his every scheme. The infidel skeptic historian Edward Gibbon wrote of this in his popular, *Decline and Fall of the Roman Empire,* vol. 4, page 107. Streams of fire shooting upward from the ditches burned the workers to death; the collapsing of wooden structures and scaffolding continued day and night; sudden and untimely accidents killing numerous laborers all led to the abandoning of the project. It was as if God's hand stopped the emperor's project. The deranged Julian was "taken in his own craftiness," as God frustrated his schemes. Julius H. Greenstone, in, his popular work, *The Messiah Idea in Jewish History,* plays down the miraculous stopping of temple construction. On pages 107–109, he credits this to a lack of interest among the Jews and not the work of God. Greenstone rejected Jesus as the Messiah.

9p-**God's new temple.** Jerusalem's temple was destroyed in A.D. 70. It will never be rebuilt, as something that will bring God glory by resuming animal sacrifices. This would be sacrilege. *Whatever unbelieving Israel does apart from God and Jesus Christ the Messiah may be a different story.* Since the resurrection of Christ, God's new and eternal temple is beautifully described in Eph. 2:20-22 with 1 Peter 2:5. He no longer dwells in temples of material and earthly grandeur. He lives "through the Spirit" in the soul or inner man of *every* born again believer (Eph. 3:16; 1 Cor. 6:19:20; and 2 Cor. 6:16-18). This is God's final temple, known as the church. It is an everlasting spiritual entity not one of brick, mortar, and timber. See Section 153, first paragraph of footnote k for more on this.

10p-**"Immediately after."** As stated, in footnote n above, meaning "immediately after" A.D. 70, weird phenomena would commence. Footnote o below gives a description of some of these events that continued for centuries after the fall of the city, and end of the temple. *Hyper* dispensationalists do no better with this text than their opponents, teaching that the terrible judgments Jesus spoke of will have been completed by the end of the last three and one-half years of the tribulation. This is sheer speculation. Both postmillennialism and amillennialism fall just as short. However, in Matt 24:29, other terrible astral judgments would continue "immediately" *after* the tribulation period of A.D. 70 was over. Those who introduce the atomic bomb or nuclear warfare into these words are too late. The "time of Jacob's trouble" (the supposed tribulation period), is over. A popular "end-time expert" on a recent television program, clearly struggling with this problem, said that "God may extend the tribulation beyond seven years to accommodate these remaining events." This is *radical* dispensationalism in action.

(o) **Matt. 24:29b with parallels in Mk. 13:24b-25 and Lk. 21:25. "Stars fall and powers of the heavens shaken, distress and sea roaring."** Great and terrible phenomena occurred before and after A.D. 70. The sun darkening, the moon not reflecting her light, celestial and terrestrial powers being shaken, the sea and waves reacting, distress of nations, men's hearts failing for fear and perplexities, the sign of the Son of man in heaven, all earth's tribes mourning, are either real, or they are not. The author *conjectured* that a time gap may exist between words "Immediately after," in Matt. 24:29, and the "the sun be darkened." If Matthew's "Immediately" is blended into Mk. 13:24, where he interprets it into "those days after the tribulation," this seems to modify the seeming immediacy of Matthew's words. If so, these events move from the present tense into a future time span called by Mark "those days." No one would expect all the events listed by the three evangelists at this place to happen within a few days or even months. Various writers *conjecture* the possibility of a "time period" of some years at this point forward. Matthew, Mark, and Luke were not inspired to record the details of these aftermath events. This is a compelling thought. One look at the comparative harmony of this discourse proves that not everything said by the Lord Jesus on this occasion has been recorded. Jesus only gave to his apostles (and us) a concise summary of this horrible history of the Jewish people and the years that followed. Filling in the gaps inspired by the Holy Spirit is an eschatological noose that has a strangle hold on many of the "experts."

2p-It seems credulous to relegate all of these after-math wonders of A.D. 70 into the realm of allegorical or symbolic. Some affirm that Matt. 24:30 speaks only of Jesus coming invisibly. If this is so, we wonder when all the tribes of the earth were in a state of mourning since they could not have seen the invisible coming Savior. Others tell us that whatever these verses may have meant for the "after-doom years of Jerusalem," they also point centuries ahead to His *real* coming, and things that will accompany that blessed event before and after. This may be the most sensible solution. The postmillennialists spiritualize everything in these passages. The Presbyterian minister, Dr. Nigel Lee in his booklet "excerpted from a large work still in preparation" entitled *The Olivet Discourse and The Destruction of Jerusalem in Prophecy*, page 12, employs the same extremes as the *radical* dispensationalists do with their literalizing. Lee conjectures that, "The stars of heaven [which] fall in Mark 13:25– are world leaders, who shall also politically yet come to worship the Lord Jesus as a result of the success of the universal Great Commission." This postulation agrees with neither the background, contextual flow, nor the Words spoken by the Savior. It is foreign to all Jesus had just said and is a fine example of postmillennial super spiritualizing. Hal Lindsey wrote in, *There's a New World Coming*, page 110, that the falling stars are Russian missiles streaking to earth! Other *radical* dispensationalists make just as big a mess in their interpretation of these stars, finding here biological, chemical, and nuclear warfare! Older dispensationalists such as Walter Scott, Harry A. Ironside, and Arno C. Gaebelein saw the stars falling from heaven as being literal human events. Whatever is intended by these words, they portray awful things that occurred "after the tribulation" or fall of Jerusalem. Christ did not give the meaning of the falling stars. Neither should we. The calamities of A.D. 70 were a "church picnic" in comparison to what is yet coming upon this world prior to the *real* return of our Savior.

(p) Matt. 24:30a with parallels in Mk. 13: 26 and Lk. 21:27. "The sign of the Son of man in heaven," and "see the Son of man coming in the clouds." Highlighted in gray as being a general quotation from Dan. 7:13. It is noted that Dr. Sigmund Mowinckel in, *He that cometh. The Messiah Concept in the Old Testament & Later Judaism,* page 357, footnote 4, quotes an ancient Jewish text, which calls Messiah "The cloud man." Church fathers such as Cyril of Jerusalem, Hilary, Chrysostom, Augustine, Jerome, and others believed clouds were the "sign of the cross." Erasmus, the basic giver of the Textus Receptus also held this opinion. Some think this sign is "the Son of man [Christ] coming in the clouds of heaven" or "in a cloud" (Mk. 13:26 with Lk. 21:27). Hal Lindsey wrote in *The Late Great Planet Earth,* page 173, "Perhaps this 'sign of the Son of man' will be a gigantic celestial image of Jesus flashed upon the heavens for all to see." Others make a distinction, saying that the "sign" and "seeing" Christ are separate events. Contextually, there may be a difference in the two. Some have suggested that the Savior appeared visibly to the Jews and religious leaders during the doom of Jerusalem. If this means that Jesus came *visibly* in the "clouds of heaven with power and great glory" at this time, and He was only seen by the doomed Israelites, then this text is clear. If this *conjecture* is correct, still this is not His return as propounded in other New Testament books. Acts 1:10-11 with Rev. 1:7 affirm that He will come visibly. This cannot have reference to the fall of Jerusalem. In 1 Thess. 3:13 He will come "with all his saints," while 1 Thess. 4:13–17 lists numerous things that will occur at this time. It seems creditable to suggest that these Words of Jesus may have had some single portent for the Jews at the fall of their city. However, they cannot end with this. In some way, they also mirror a future time or even the day of His *real* return, which has not yet occurred. If He did come to Jerusalem in a mystic visible manner, which was exclusively for the wicked Jews to behold, still, this is not His *real* return for the church, which is yet future.

2p-Matt. 24:30b. "All the tribes of the earth mourn." If this audibly happened over the entire world in A.D. 70, we have no record of it. Surely, millions did mourn in Jerusalem and Judaea, but not *all* of earth's tribes. The emphasis in these words seems universal instead of local. In Zech. 12:11-14 there is a future mourning, but contextually it is confined to Israel and Jerusalem, not the world. Many expositors make a play on "ge," the Greek word for "earth," and translate it to mean "land." This is a legitimate rendering. It seems that the most sensible reading is that this passage refers to all the tribes in the land (earth) of Judaea and surrounding areas. It was noted in footnote n above, starting with the fourth paragraph, that there were continual wars spreading over the known world of that era, and centuries of mourning continued long after Jerusalem and Israel fell.

3p-Matt. 24:30c. "See the Son of man coming." See first paragraph of footnote p above for a possible explanation of this statement.

(q) Matt. 24:31a with parallel in Mk. 13:27a. "Send forth his angels." Saved Jews were not gathered from the four winds in A.D. 70. As explained, they fled Jerusalem and surrounding countryside going to Pella for refuge. For an explanation of their escape, refer to footnote f above, the second paragraph under number 16.

2p-Matt. 24:31b. "With a great sound of a trumpet." The word trumpet signifies the Hebrew ram's horn or "shofar." The only sensible explanation is that these words speak of a literal sound. This was not a silent sound! What Christ said in the two parallel verses of Matt. 24:31 and Mk. 13:27 did not happen in A.D. 70 at Jerusalem or anywhere else in the world. If it did happen in some unknown way and was not recorded, there is still another overriding lesson. It must have reference to His coming for the church, which will be a universal event. There are those who hold that this happened *silently and invisibly* during the doom of Jerusalem; that only some of the Jewish believers heard the sound and were taken up to meet Christ. Such an interpretation is unacceptable to common sense. A silent trumpet call reminds one of the old silent dog whistles of years gone by. This "great sound of a trumpet" will not be for calling in the dogs. Nor is the trumpet ("shofar") in 1 Thess. 4:16 a dog whistle!

3p-Matt. 24:31c with parallel in Mk. 13:27b. "Gather together His elect." For explanation of what "elect," *meant in Jewish thinking* at this time, see third paragraph under footnote k above. During the Jewish–Roman wars, holy angels did not gather all believers from earth to the utter most part of heaven (Mk. 13:27). In fact, at the time of the war, Paul had not yet written the wonderful rapture texts of 1 Thess. 4:13-17. He penned these about three decades later! It is futile to explain this statement as an invisible event. It is certain that if all of God's elect (children) vanished from the earth at the fall of Jerusalem, there would have been extant records of this universal phenomena. John Gill in his *Commentary, v*ol. 7, page 295 offers an odd Calvinistic infected interpretation. He affirms that these are "men-angels or messengers, the ministers and preachers of the gospel, whom Christ would . . . send forth to preach the gospel" like a trumpet sounding to the Gentiles. Ministers are referred to as angels when addressing the seven churches of Asia in Rev. 2 and 3. If this conjecture is true, then Matt. 24:31c and Mk. 13:27b move us into the decades after A.D. 70, when the church scattered by persecution reached untold thousands for the Savior. Gill's interpretation does not blend with the contextual flow of the Savior's Words. It departs abruptly from His immediate line of thought and leaps too many centuries into the future. To understand these angel preachers out "bringing in God's elect" over church history seems far fetched. Matthew mentions angels nineteen times in his book. They always mean real heavenly beings, not men preaching the gospel.

(r) **Lk. 21:28. No parallels. "Your redemption draweth nigh."** Again, Jesus used the pronoun "your," which was directed to His apostles and other believers in the Christian community. "Your redemption" could not have been a reference to their soul's salvation, for the apostles had been saved decades before A.D. 70. The word "redemption," as used in this verse speaks of a physical deliverance out of Jerusalem and the countryside round about before the bloody Roman-Jewish war fully erupted. Seemingly, our Master was speaking of one of the *results* of their previous soul's redemption, which was being saved from the doom that was coming. For comments on the popular Jewish idea of political redemption enjoyed in a material earthly kingdom, and how it was used at this time, see Section 16, Lk. 2:38, footnote l, and Section 193, second paragraph of footnote f.

(s) **Matt. 24:32-33 with parallels in Mk. 13:28-29 and Lk. 21:29-31. The Parable of the Fig Tree.** Highlighted in gray because of its importance. As mentioned in number 1, footnote f above, again Jesus uses the pronouns "ye" and "you." This could only be His apostles and fellow believers. His message was given on the Mount of Olives, which was covered with thousands of olive and fig trees. It was Passover time, and the fig trees were budding profusely. Many were already with foliage of fresh green leaves. Christ's lesson here must not be transferred into the future some two thousand years later. He unequivocally told His four-man audience that *they* would "see these things," and when they took place, they would know His kingdom was near. This kingdom suddenly becoming "nigh at hand" and what it did to the Jews, and their city is explained in the second paragraph of footnote t below. Since His disciples would *see* this judgment work of His kingdom upon Jerusalem, it could not have reference to some far away future judgment. They all would be long dead and could not have seen anything. Christ declared that the signs He had given them would be infallible proof that "it is near, even at the doors." Mark states the same. Luke explains to Theophilus what the mysterious "it" is. He interprets the "it" (which was close to the doors) as being "the kingdom of God [which] is nigh at hand" (verse 31). Further confirmation that Christ was speaking of events that would occur during that specific period are in Matt. 24:33-34 with parallels in Mark and Luke. Some hold that He was speaking of the judgment that God's kingdom would bring upon the wicked and hypocritical Jews and religious leaders of Israel, their city, and temple.

2p-**The World War I debacle.** This war began in 1914, and was hailed by prophecy preachers as "the budding of the fig tree," and proof that "the kingdom of God was at hand." Documentation for this is found in the old publication *The King's Business*, vol. XI, October 1920, page 947, and in vol. XIII, and November 1922, page 1137. After the First World War, the great Methodist preacher, Dr. William E. Blackstone in his popular book, *Jesus is Coming*, wrote that Zionism (which began in 1897 at Basel, Switzerland) was a sure sign of the budding of the fig tree (*Armageddon Now!* page 34, by Dwight Wilson). In chapter 21, Blackstone's book reeks with scores of "signs" proving the soon return of Christ. In early 1904, he had hundreds of Hebrew Bibles carefully wrapped and hidden over Petra, an ancient city in Jordan. These were supposed to be read by Jews fleeing from the Antichrist during the tribulation! Blackstone set the following dates for our Lord's return, 1915, 1916, 1926, and 1927. He died in 1935. This good man stands as a classic example of someone who went overboard regarding the return of Christ. Looking back some seventy years later, we should learn a stern lesson about zeal without right knowledge and sincerity without truth. Cults such as Jehovah's Witness, Seventh Day Adventist, Mormonism, Armstrongism, and certain present day "authorities" have been doing this for decades. *Can the past teach us nothing about the present?*

3p-**The 1948 debacle.** Hundreds of "prophecy specialists" tell us the "budding of the fig tree" (verse 32) was fulfilled or had prophetic links to the re-establishment of Jewish statehood. This claim was based on the Savior's Words in verse 34, "this generation shall not pass till all these things be fulfilled." This supposedly meant that Christ would return within the generation *after* Israel became an independent state in May 1948. A biblical generation is about forty years long. From 1948 (when Israel again became a nation), forty years later calculates to 1988, and Christ did not return as the "experts" said. Date setting Christ's return is the only multi million-dollar industry in the world that is always wrong but stays in business. This reflects the ignorance of many Christians about this subject.

4p-The World War II debacle. Harry A. Ironsides wrote in 1938 in *The King's Business*, XXIX, page 9 regarding the pending war, "Lift up your head. Your redemption draweth nigh." That was some seventy years ago, which is a long time to keep one's head "lifted up." Nevertheless, the "experts" were *sure* that this war would lead to Armageddon and the end. Hitler's invasion of Poland in 1939, and later murder of millions of Jews highly fueled the expectations of America's "end timers." Japan and China's involvement gave further credence to the "yellow hoard's' of Rev. 16:12. Louise Bauman (like others) saw in the Fascist Benito Mussolini a possible candidate for Antichrist, so stated *The King's Business*, vol. XXXVI. page 239. Dwight Wilson wrote in *Armageddon Now!* page 120, that two Belgian premillennialists interviewed Mussolini, (early in the war) pointing out that he may be the fulfillment of prophecy. This list goes on. Hundreds of prophetic enthusiasts lined up during this war and pitched their guesses into the end-time hat. Over sixty years later, we look back, and see they were all wrong. It was another misfire from good men, who went overboard in trying to figure out something that God forbids. Their successors are with us today, and they continue to play their games of eschatological "pot luck" with ill-informed Christians.

5p-The fig tree debacle. Over the centuries, the guesses about what the budding of the fig tree means have ranged from popes, kings, princes, Catholic Church, communism, various world wars, Charlemagne, and literally hundreds of other persons, things, and events. All have been wrong because the Lord Jesus said it was a signal that Jerusalem's doom was near at hand. This occurred in A.D. 70. This fig tree budded some two thousand years ago. Regardless, budding trees have nothing to do with Christ returning for His people. Thomas Ice in *Pre-Tribulation Perspectives*, page 3 wrote, "The fact that ethnic Israel has been reestablished as a nation and now controls Jerusalem is a strong indicator that we are near the end of the church age." As stated above, Israel's reestablishment occurred in 1948. One questions how far these "strong indicators" can stretch themselves without breaking before Christ returns? Can they go fifty, sixty, a hundred, five hundred, or perhaps even a thousand years? Despite Dr. Ice's words, not all Jerusalem is under the control of Israel. What now stands on the sacred temple site? A former Prime Minister of the nation (Ariel Sharon) gave Israeli land to the phony (Islamic) "Palestinian State." Could this be a reversed indicator or sign proving that Christ is not coming soon since a Jew has given Israeli land to their fierce Muslim enemies? For further comments on the "Palestinian State," see Section 18, second paragraph of footnote e.

6p-A doomed nation. In Section 149, Matt. 21:18-20, we read of the Savior killing the barren, hypocritical fig tree as He traveled from Bethany into Jerusalem. This tree pictured fruitless Israel, showing many leaves, but having no fruit underneath. Earlier in His ministry, Jesus gave another Parable of the Fig Tree in Section 72, Lk. 13:6-9, footnote j. This also pointed to Israel with whom God ran out of patience and ordered her doom. Thus, the fig tree does symbolize Israel in several places. However, this is not an established doctrine. Historically, the vine is the accepted emblem for this nation, not the fig tree (Isa. 5:7). Other things have symbolized the Hebrew nation apart from vines and fig trees. For example, a tile, razor, hair, and baggage are also pictured as Israel in Ezek. 4-12.

7p-The "and all the trees" debacle. Christians zealous about the "fig tree" should reread Lk. 21:29. Luke recorded the rest of Jesus' Words. He says that our Lord also included "all the trees" in His statement. This is highlighted in gray. Thus, instead of "fig tree" specialists, we also need the "oak tree," or the "maple tree" seers. Surely, this is allowable according to the Words of Christ. The fig tree is not an *exclusive* international emblem of Israel. Some of the biggest dispensationalists in the business agree with this fact. Finis J. Dake who was an *extreme* dispensationalist, wrote in *Annotated Reference Bible*, page 27, this about the Jewish fig tree sign. "The fig tree is universally interpreted to mean the Jewish nation, but this could not possibly be the meaning." H. L. Ellison in *The New Laymen's Bible Commentary*, page 1213 wrote, "It is not permissible to [always] equate the fig tree with the Jews." A budding tree informed its observers that summer was nigh, not that it had already come. Christ was telling His preachers that doom was at the door. His predictions would be fulfilled before that generation passed away.

(t) Matt. 24:33a. "When ye see all these things." This was an appeal to human observation. When they (His disciples-apostles and the other believers living at that time) saw the fig trees as well as other trees budding, they knew that summer was coming soon. Likewise, when they saw the signs occurring (that He had warned them about, such as the false Messiahs, celestial, and terrestrial wonders and so forth) they would know that the end of Jerusalem, and the temple was approaching. This is the only sensible meaning to His Words. To interpret the fig tree as Israel returning to their homeland in 1948 is rationally and biblically unacceptable. Refer to the third paragraph under footnote s above for more on the Jews reclaiming part of their ancestral promised land.

2p-Matt. 24:33b with parallels in Mk. 13:29 and Lk. 21:31. "The kingdom of God is near, *even* at the doors." In the doom of A.D. 70, believers saw and heard an extraordinary display of Messiah's kingdom in the judgment of its chief enemies, the Christ hating religious Hebrews. Their rejected Messiah sent this doom upon them. In a mystic way, the kingdom of God and Christ was at Israel's doors and smashed them down. This passage cannot mean that Christ's kingdom had its *first appearing* or began at that time. Its spiritual manifestation had occurred over three years prior to Jesus making this prediction. His kingdom was introduced during the ministry of John the Baptist. One of the clearest verses that the kingdom was a *present entity* in the days of Christ (decades before A.D. 70) is in Section 66, Matt. 12:28, footnote g. In the context of this verse, our Savior informed the Pharisees, "But if I cast out devils by the Spirit of God, the kingdom of God is come unto you." Did Christ cast out devils? This self-answering question confirms that the kingdom was there because He cast out demons. He had told the Pharisees that His kingdom was within believers (Section 134, Lk. 17:20-21, footnotes a through d). The statement by Jesus in Lk. 21:31 that "the kingdom of God is nigh at hand," cannot speak of something yet to be, such as a literal kingdom two thousand years in the future. That future manifestation of the kingdom is a different story and has not arrived at this present moment. The expressions "at hand," and "at the doors," refer to nearness of God's judgment on Jerusalem. Scripture presents the kingdom as being a past, present and future reality. *Each of these kingdom manifestations must be carefully distinguished and placed in correct chronologies.* Edersheim believed Christ came *into* his kingdom at the destruction of Jerusalem and the completion of His return will be His literal appearing at the end of the age. See *Prophecy and History in Relation to the Messiah*, pages 132-133).

3p-Matt. 24:34 with parallels Mk. 13:30 and Lk. 21:32. "This generation." The consummation of these things was to occur within the confines of that existing generation. However, the *precise hour* when the stroke of doom would fall, had not, at that time been revealed to any man, or angel. In using the word, "generation," the Lord Jesus was speaking of a contemporary expectation set in a fixed time frame called "this generation." He said, "This generation would not pass, till all these things are fulfilled." For more on the word "generation," refer to Section 67, Matt. 12:39 footnote b, and Section 68, comments by the asterisk under the main heading. For a review of every place where Matthew used the word, see Section 106, Matt. 17:17, footnote c. In His earlier condemnation of the scribes and Pharisees, Jesus again used the word "generation." Refer to Section 159, Matt. 23:36, footnote w.

4p-Messiah declared in response to His apostles' three questions these words, "Verily I say unto you, This generation shall not pass, till all these things be fulfilled" (Matt. 24:34 and parallel texts in Mk. 13:30 and Lk. 21:32). Without controversy, our Savior in using the pronoun "this," was speaking to that *present living* generation of Jews. Perhaps He took the ugly colors of A.D. 70 to paint a dim portrait of His far distant future coming in glory and judgment. He was first making reference to that body of Jews living at that time. In the old *Meyer's Commentary on the New Testament,* printed in 1852, vol. 1, page 420, there is a long list of the numerous (and humorous) explanations that have been given to the word "generation," as used here by our Savior. Meyer gathered these from the eschatological experts of earlier days. Thomas Scott in, *Commentary on the New Testament,* printed in 1817, vol. 1, pages 32-34 wrote that the "Primary interpretation of the prophecy of the destruction of Jerusalem . . . took place within forty years," or it occurred to that generation. How pitiful to read of certain men trying to persuade their adherents that "generation" here means "a race of people or age of time," and then they apply this to the Jews over two thousand years later! Historically, this cannot mean "race." There has never been a Hebrew or Jewish race, only a nation. This is affirmed in the *Encyclopedia Judaica Jerusalem,* 1971, vol. 3, page 50. True to style, Hal Lindsey in, *The Late Great Planet Earth,* pages 53-54 penned these words, "What generation? In the context, it was the generation that would see the signs; the chief among them was the rebirth of Israel." Lindsey concluded that this happened in 1948. Christ disagreed with "Mr. End-Time," for He said His apostles would "see" these things, which they did. None of them lived until A.D. 1948. Lindsey's date setting goes like this: First, he picked 1948+40=1988, the time when Jesus would return. That flopped. Next, it was 1967+40=2007. Again, no rapture. Having changed a "generation" to mean 60-80 years, now he has picked the dates of 2040 and 2047. Nothing like playing it safe when you do not know what you are talking about.

(u) Matt. 24:35 with parallels in Mk. 13:31 and Lk. 21:33. "My Word shall not pass away." As if to banish all doubt regarding His shocking discourse, the Lord Jesus now reaffirms everything He has said up to this point. God's creation of heaven and earth would cease to exist before His prediction about Jerusalem, the destruction of the Jewish state, and pointers to His future second advent would fail. It is an infallible peak of history that A.D. 70 took place. And it is just as sure that Christ will appear someday and take His church away. No man knows when this will occur. It could be tomorrow, next month, next year, or hundreds of years from now.

(v) Matt. 24:36a with parallel in Mk. 13:32a. "No man knows that day and hour." We ask, "What day and hour?" Though He had given numerous signs to watch for that pointed to the general destruction of their city, here the Savior gets acutely specific. No one sign would reveal to the apostles the *exact* day and hour when the attack on Jerusalem would commence or end. The apostles and other believers had general knowledge but did not know that *fatal and final hour.* As a bolt of lightning, suddenly thousands of Roman troops emerged on the scene. Hordes of men in fearful battle dress with their endless entourage of wagon trains, herds of cattle, horses, and large flocks of sheep for food, tents, and hundreds of wagons loaded with baggage and equipment. There were gigantic catapults for throwing stones, battering rams, hundreds of auxiliaries, blacksmiths, cooks, medical teams, mechanics, technicians, and supply trains all making up the Roman army. Unannounced, they topped the horizons and pitched their thousands of tents about Jerusalem. Peering over the walls, the Jews were terrified at the overwhelming sight!

2p-The Kedron valley and Mount of Olives on the eastern side of Jerusalem held the largest contingent of troops. Here, and on Mount Scopus a few miles north of Jerusalem, Titus and his legions pitched camp. Several months later, his military sealed off the city. *Sealing off the city assured its doom.* Yet thousands did escape as seen above in footnote n, the sixth paragraph, with many of them fleeing to the fortress of Masada. Jesus referred to the sealing off in Lk. 21:20, in the words, "Jerusalem compassed with armies." It happened on a set hour of a specific day. However, none of his disciples would know the *exact* time. Jesus called it, "That day and hour." Their escape is mentioned in the second paragraph of footnote g and eighth paragraph of footnote h of this Section.

3p-Matt. 24:36b with parallel in Mk. 13:32b. Why Christ did not know the exact day or the hour. Matthew reported only part of these words. He wrote that Jesus said, "no man, not angels, but my Father only" will know this. It was Mark who penned the puzzling statement about Jesus not knowing. Religious and secular infidels have pointed to this statement for centuries trying to discredit the deity of our Lord. Among "evangelicals," we note those who stumble about trying to explain our Savior's strange words under the banner of "kenotic or kenosis theories." For earlier comments on the "kenotic theory," refer to Section 52, footnote t. *At no point during His earthly life did Jesus Christ lay aside any part of His total equality with God.* However, at times He chose not to use certain of His God-equal attributes. This was one of those times, when as a *human,* Christ, for reasons unknown (unless He was sharing the feelings and infirmities of His disciples), chose not to know the exact "day and hour" when the Romans would shut off Jerusalem. After His resurrection and before the ascension, Peter confessed that Jesus "knew all things" (Section 205, John 21:17 footnote l). Note also Section 52, John 5:19, footnote n for other comments on this. Regarding His physical growth and mental development, refer to Section 19, Lk. 2:40, footnote c.

4p-He was not speaking of His return for the church. The Savior said that He (at that time) did not know the precise hour when Jerusalem would be attacked. *He was not talking about His second coming.* After resurrection in a glorified body, He resumed omniscient equality with God and no longer used self-imposed human limitations. For over two millenniums, He has been seated at God's right hand in the heavenly realm, with all power in His hands. The chosen limitations of *human* flesh are no more. He is forever the Son of God and God the Son in total omniscience. For more on this refer to Section 206, Acts 1:6-7, footnotes c and d. As just said above, the statement about Jesus, "not knowing" has nothing to do with His future return, the blessed hope. Rather, it had reference to the *specific time* of the final doom of A.D. 70. The finer details of Jesus choosing to know or not know are a divine mystery hidden in the unfathomable councils of God. *The wise Christian will stay out of this forbidden territory.*

(w) Matt. 24:37-39. No parallels. "The days of Noe." (Another spelling for Noah still in use today.) Highlighted in gray because the prevalent sins in the days prior to the worldwide flood (Gen. 6-8), would reoccur within the next forty years among the Jews. This becomes a prophetic expression. We note a similarity between the Words spoken by Jesus here, two days before His death, and those spoken several months much earlier while still in Samaria or Galilee. The verbal resemblance affirms that these were repetitive statements. In both places, He spoke of the sins of Noah's days and the resulting doom of the global deluge. The willful disobedience of those who lived in that era was an abomination before God. Because of this, it also became a stern warning to men of every age who love sin and give no care about their eternal destiny. Those who heeded God's Word were saved in Noah's time. Likewise, only those who heeded Christ's warnings were saved from the deadly sword of Rome in A.D. 70.

2p-The wickedness, which will prevail before Christ returns for His own (whenever that occurs), will make the people of Noah's days blush by comparison. Most sins have always been the same but their fierceness, velocity, and magnitude will be overwhelming in the genuine last days of time.

3p-Matt. 24:40-41. No parallels. "One taken and the other left." Refer to Section 134, Lk. 17:31, footnote k, for Christ's Words about "he that is in the field," and verse 35, for the "two women grinding at the mill." Jewish writings speak much about women grinding, sifting, and winnowing. The subject is mentioned seventy-nine times in the Talmud. Jesus is saying that men and women in the land of Israel would be about their business of husbandry, plowing, merchandising, sowing some crops, while reaping others. The children of Jacob would be occupied with city or rural enterprises when suddenly the fierce Roman army would appear! The "One taken" represented the thousands captured, and taken away by the Romans during the awful months leading up to the fall of Jerusalem. Jesus' teaching about "other[s] left" (verse 41) has reference to those thousands that remained but were crucified outside the city walls, tortured or sold into slavery. The number "one" cannot mean only "one" numerically. It is a single digit but literally speaks of tens of thousands of Jews slain by the Roman soldiery. No sensible mind can believe that the Romans would take only "one" person as a prisoner. As mentioned already, the Savior had spoken earlier of these same things in Section 134, Lk. 17:34-36. Now, He repeats Himself. No "snatch rapture" is found in these Words. There will be nothing secret about the international shock when Jesus returns to take His redeemed home. The truth about the catching out of the church was recorded some twenty years after our Lord spoke these words. It is primarily found in the letters of Paul (1 Thess. 4:13-18 and 1 Cor. 15:51-52). The *real* taking out of the redeemed is described as, "shall be caught up," and in 1 Cor. 15:52 as, "In a moment, in the twinkling of an eye."

4p-Matt. 24:42 with parallels in Mk. 13:33 and Lk. 21:34-36. The Savior tells His four apostles to watch, take heed, and be ready for the *exact time* of His mystic coming in the form of the merciless Roman army to judge Israel, is unknown. Both dispensational premillennialists and postmillennialists are in notable confusion with these words, "Watch therefore: for ye know not what hour your Lord doth come;" "Therefore, be ye also ready;" and "Watch for ye know neither the day nor the hour wherein the Son of man cometh." They struggle to make them compatible with what is now a delay of more than two thousand years! He told the four apostles, "watch," it therefore, had first application to them during their lifetimes. To shift this instruction millenniums into the future is wrong. *They* were to "watch" for the signs Jesus had warned them about that led to the doom of A.D. 70.

5p-Some hold that this means to "watch," for Christ comes at physical death to take us to heaven. Death is to be "absent from the body and present with the Lord" (2 Cor. 5:8). Physical death is not the return of Christ. "Watch and be ready" had both immediate and future short-term meanings. He was not instructing His apostles to "watch for the rapture." At this writing, they have been dead some two thousand years, and He has not yet returned.

Christ gives His apostles four successive warnings about being watchful and ready for A.D. 70.

6p-Matt. 24:43. **(1) The Parable of the Watching Goodman. No parallel in Mark or Luke.** *A first warning to be watchful and ready.* His continual warnings are reemphasized in using a metaphor understood by the four apostles. The lord of the house, "goodman or owner" watched through the long night for thieves to prevent the loss of his goods. Of whom was Christ speaking? Was it a Jewish remnant preaching in the tribulation period over two thousand years later? Sensibly, it could only have been those who were listening to His message. Had He not just explained why they should be looking? Not knowing the exact day or hour, they must "watch" in view of what was coming. The apostles were to be watching for the signs pointing to A.D. 70.

(x) Mk. 13:34-37. **(2) The Parable of the Traveling Man. No parallel in Matthew or Luke.** *A second warning to be watchful and ready.* This illustration came from the custom of a landowner issuing instructions to his servants, leaving home, and commanding his porter (chief servant) to watch, for he did not know the exact hour of his master's return. In this, Jesus states that the coming catastrophe would take men by surprise. Here, the surprise return of the lord to his house is equated to the shock of Jerusalem's doom. Mark concludes his record of the Olivet Discourse with Jesus' warning, "Watch."

(y) Matt. 24:44. **(3) The Savior pleads, "Be ye also ready." No parallel in Mark or Luke.** *It is a third warning to be watchful and ready.* Again, our Lord employed the word "ye." This plural pronoun had strict reference to the four men listening to Him speak. (For explanation of Jesus' use of "ye" and "you," see number 1, under footnote f above.) The "Son of man" in this text seems to point foremost to His mystical coming to judge the Jews, their city, and to destroy their temple through the armies of Titus. See the fourth paragraph under footnote w above for other comments on this. Couched in this stern warning to His own, the Lord Jesus also reflected centuries forward to that grand time when He shall take His church out of this world to meet Him in the air.

2p-A few hours before going to Mount Olivet, Jesus gave the Jews in the temple the Parable of the King's Son. He warned that they would be shut out of God's kingdom and later cast into hell. In this parable, the king was furious over the response from his citizens to attend his son's wedding. Some were killed. The king illustrates God sending the Romans to burn Jerusalem and destroy the Jews. Refer to Section 154, footnotes i, and j for the story.

(z) Matt. 24:45-50. **(4) The Parable of the Two Servants. No parallel in Mark or Luke.** *A fourth and final warning to be ready.* Jesus had spoken a similar parable much earlier in Section 71, Lk. 12:41-48. In these verses, see footnotes s and t for explanation and application to this present discourse. The entire thrust of this concluding parable of warning was for His disciples and all believers of that time to be ready. It spoke of the ancient custom of a returning lord rewarding his faithful servant who was prepared when he appeared. It does not teach (as often heard) "Brother so-and-so will be given rule over his city or home town during the millennial reign of Christ." For more on this myth, note Section 145, Lk. 19:17, number 5, under footnote d. Servants who worked well were rewarded well. Jesus also speaks of those who were full of indifference, doubt, and revelry. Sin succumbed many into negligence and judgment was pronounced upon them. This reveals that among the followers of Christ, there were those who were insincere, indifferent, and unsaved. Their fate was physical death in the fall of the city and eternal hell afterwards (Matt. 24:50-51). Jesus used "weeping and gnashing of teeth" earlier while at Capernaum (Matt. 8:12). It was a common Hebrew expression denoting the fate of the pagan Gentiles. Now, Messiah reverses the meaning and lays it upon the Jews. He employed it again at the end of this discourse in Section 165, Matt. 25:30.

2p-Verse 51. **"Weeping and gnashing of teeth."** False cults such as the Jehovah's Witness, Seventh Day Adventists, Christadelphians, Universalists, and others call this symbolic language. The author recently was sharing Christ with an electrical technician. This young man replied, "I'm a Jehovah's Witness, and I have learned there is no hell, so I am safe." One wonders how decaying bodies in the grave "weep and gnash their teeth." For twenty-one things the Bible says about suffering in hell-lake of fire, see Section 103, all of number 8, under footnote g.

3p-Lk. 21:37-38. **A brief review of the Savior's last days among the people.** Luke concludes his version of the Olivet discourse with a summary of Jesus' final days before the cross, and the reactions of the people. His pulpit in the daytime was the vast temple compound, and His bed at night was probably somewhere on the Mount just east of Jerusalem, or in the village of Bethany about two miles east of the city. Luke takes up his story of Christ about two days later at the final Passover in Section 167, Lk. 22:1-2. His record of the events, predicted for A.D. 70, was written about twenty-five years *after* Jesus had spoken these things, and shortly *before* they occurred. Infidel critics have attacked just about everything Luke wrote. These people come and go, live and die, while Luke's two books remain and have blessed millions over the centuries. We read in 1 Peter 1:23, that "the word of God . . . liveth and abideth for ever." Time is the graveyard of all antichrist unbelief and hell its everlasting tormenter.

THE PARABLE OF THE TEN VIRGINS.*

The lesson below continues the Savior's warning to be ready and watchful along with those just given in Matt. 24:42, 44, 46, and 50. First, it alerted His disciples of that terrible day in A.D. 70. Second, it carries a timeless lesson for believers of all ages admonishing them to readiness, for no man knows when God's judgment may fall on the wicked or Christ will return for His church. The Lord Jesus built this lesson from a standard Hebrew wedding with which His four apostles were familiar. Unless this is understood, His message here will be missed or radically changed.

Time: Late Tuesday after Palm Sunday.

---

*There is nothing in this parable about the "rapture of the church", Israel, split rapture, tribulation period, being filled with the Holy Spirit, or oil representing the Spirit of God and so on. The teaching that five of the virgins represent Jews saved in the tribulation, and the other five represent those not saved is false. Such absurdities must be forced into this lesson. It does not have one shred of contextual evidence, neither immediate nor distant. The apostles, Peter, James, John, and Andrew (Mk. 13:3) listening to Christ give this stirring discourse, had up to this point, never heard of a seven years tribulation and Jews being saved during this time. The rabbis and scribes of this era in Jewish history did not interpret Dan. 9:24-27 as the "specialists" do today. Much of the present exegesis on this topic is the work of carnal imaginations, coupled with the handicap of trying to make everything fit into a previously adopted frame of eschatology. What strange doctrines emerge when expositors force every parable, event, or lesson in Scripture to have a hidden type or shadow and give us their explanations of these mysteries. It is amazing how the over literalists often spiritualize, and then suddenly they will literalize to make things fit their spiritualizing. For the early origin of this erroneous method of hermeneutics, see Section 1, Part 1, footnote c. The overwhelming lesson was for readiness on the part of His followers. This was urgent in view of what was coming for the nation of Israel, Jerusalem, and the temple in a few more decades during A.D. 70.

Matt. 25:1-13 —*On the western side of the Mount of Olives*	Mk.	Lk.	John
Waiting for the bridegroom			
1 "Then[a] shall the kingdom of heaven[b] be likened unto ten virgins, which took their lamps, and went forth to meet the bridegroom.[c]			
Both wise and foolish were present for the occasion			
2 "And five of them were wise, and five *were* foolish.[d]			
3 "They that *were* foolish took their lamps, and took no oil with them:			
4 "But the wise took oil in their vessels with their lamps.[e]			
5 "While the bridegroom tarried, they all slumbered and slept.[f]			
6 "And at midnight there was a cry[g] made, 'Behold, the bridegroom cometh; go ye out to meet him.'			
7 "Then all those virgins arose, and trimmed their lamps.[h]			
Out of oil: give us some of yours			
8 "And the foolish said unto the wise, 'Give us of your oil; for our lamps are gone out.'			
We cannot give: go and buy for yourselves			
9 "But the wise answered, saying, '*Not so*; lest there be not enough for us and you: but go ye rather to them that sell, and buy for yourselves.'[i]			
The foolish miss the parade and are locked out of the wedding			
10 "And while they went to buy, the bridegroom came; and they that were ready went in with him to the marriage: and the door was shut.[j]			
11 "Afterward came also the other virgins, saying, Lord, Lord, open to us.'[k]			
12 "But he [the groom's father] answered and said, 'Verily I say unto you, I know you not.'[l]			
The great lesson: always be ready			
13 "Watch therefore, for ye[m] know neither the day nor the hour wherein the Son of man cometh.'"[n] (Verse 14 cont. in Section 165.)			

Section 164: Messiah pleads by use of a parable for His people to be prepared for what is coming.

Be ready and watch: As written in the main heading of Section 163, this great eschatological discourse from a summit on the Mount of Olives, embraced all of Matthew 24 through the end of Matthew 25:1–46. Across these verses, the Lord Jesus used some six different illustrations in an effort to stress the need for watchful readiness among His disciples in view of the coming doom of Jerusalem, the temple, and Jewish state. The meaning is obvious: not all will be ready, watching and serving (occupying) when the end of these things comes in A.D. 70. The word for "watch" used here also means "to keep awake." Firstly, to make this entire discourse exclusively a "Jewish thing" speaking of the tribulation period is incorrect. It is a neglect of the syntax, the historical, cultural, and the (then) *immediate* meaning of Jesus' Words to the four apostles. Secondly, this message also carries lesser but succinct admonitions for believers of all succeeding ages to be ready always, for the time of Christ's return for His church is unknown. His six illustrations regarding watchful readiness are as follows:

1. **The watching goodman often called "lord" or "land-owner".** In Section 163, Matt. 24:43–44.
2. **The two servants.** In Section 163, Matt. 24:45–51. One was ready for his lord's return and the other was not.
3. **The traveling man going into a far country.** In Section 163, Mk. 13:34–37. He commanded his porter to watch for his return. (This is not the same lesson as in number 1 above.)
4. **Two kinds of virgins.** In Section 164, Matt 25:1–13. Five prepared and watched in readiness for the bridegroom to appear and lead them to the wedding at the house of the groom's father. Five did not prepare.
5. **Three kinds of talent holders.** In Section 165, Matt. 25:14–30. Two watched, worked, and were ready when their lord returned for reckoning. One did not.
6. **Two judgments.** In Section 166 Matt. 25:31–46. Two different groups of people symbolically represented by the sheep and goats. The sheep were watching, working, and ready for Christ's return and judgment. The goats were not. The Lord Jesus gave this address "two days" before the Passover celebration of Israel at which time He died on the cross (Matt. 26:1–2).

Footnotes-Commentary

(a) **"Then."** With this word, the Lord Jesus did not discontinue the subject with which He was formally occupied throughout the whole of Matt. 24. No new theme is introduced by this present lesson; rather, it is the connecting link between the (supposed) conclusions of Matt. 24:51 and Matt. 25:1. The first word "then," grammatically demonstrates that His former discourse is continued in this new parable. The lesson of this parable of ten virgins is basically the same as that of the goodman of the house, and the faithful servant at the ending of the previous chapter in Matthew. The warning, "watch therefore" in Matt. 24:42 joins hands with the final verse of the virgin's lesson with "watch therefore" (Matt. 25:13). The message given here by our Lord is still the subject of which He was previously occupied; the destruction of Jerusalem, temple and Jewish state. What five of these young women did, Christ somberly warns that none of His disciples must do. They failed to prepare. See footnote m below.

(b) Jesus said in the first verse that **"the kingdom of heaven shall be likened to,"** or its adherents shall do things that resemble the actions of the ten virgins. And did they ever! He spoke of His church and shows that some are ready and others are not. This is reflected in thousands of *local churches* over the world. In Section 39, footnotes a and g, the kingdom has two aspects; one the spiritual side introduced by the ministry of John the Baptist and continued by Christ, His preachers and all succeeding generations of believers up to this moment. The other aspect is yet to come. It will be some type of glorified literal kingdom established by God but hardly the exaggerated conglomeration so often taught by the *ultra* dispensationalists. The then existing new kingdom of Christ was partly reflected by conduct of these girls getting ready for the big wedding. There are commentators who find something mystic, hidden, shadowed, and typified in almost every word of this lesson. This sort of exegesis is hardly a mark of high spiritually but more the product of a rubber band imagination. There were ten real girls waiting to attend a real wedding and watching for a real bridegroom coming with his bride. The Jews delighted in the number ten. At normal weddings, there were ten bridesmaids, though in most rich marriages the number could be as high as seven groups of ten, thus seventy. A synagogue could be built if ten "able men" were available. Bands of ten men were professional mourners in Israel. As far back as the book of Ruth, we note that ten elders of the city were witnesses when Boaz took Ruth to wife (Ruth 4:2, 9–10). Jesus employed a numeric with which His apostles would have been familiar. He is not saying that only ten guests attended this wedding. Our Lord was using a number that signified understanding and acceptance in the minds of His apostles. It was a number they instantly understood. Hundreds normally attended these highly celebrated occasions.

(c) **Bride and Bridegroom.** Weddings were high social events over the land of Israel. Christ had attended the wedding at Cana during the early months of His ministry and there performed His first miracle. This is recorded in Section 27, John 2:1–11. Verse 1 reads, "they [the ten virgins] went forth," meaning from their respective homes to wait for the bridegroom along the roadside. He would be dressed in his most costly attire usually covered with various colorful ornaments (Isa. 61:10). The bride was also decked with costly and elaborate clothing. Fred H. Wight in his fine work, *Manners and Customs of Bible Lands*, pages 130-134 described the bride to be in these words, "Every effort was put forth to make her complexion glossy and shining with a luster like unto marble (Ps. 144:12). The locks of her hair were braided with gold and pearls. She was weighted down with precious stones and

780

jewels that her family had inherited (Jer. 2:32 with Ezek. 16:11-12)." These ten virgins were simply friends of the bride, or bridegroom or both, and followed them to the wedding (Ps. 45:14). *They were not the bridegroom's bride!* Not do not picture or represent the kingdom of Christ or His true church in any fashion.

2p-As the bridegroom did not marry five women, so the five women who went into the wedding celebration cannot depict Christ's bride or the church. Another well-known term used to describe them was "children of the bride chamber," and is found in the Talmud tractate, Baba Bathra 145b. In today's terminology, we could call them the "invited guests," but as stated above, Christ may have purposely selected the number ten in order to have even halves in His lesson. *It is sure that more than this number attended such grand social events.* By no stretch of the imagination does this mean that half the world will be saved and the other half lost as some teach. This is forcing typology into a biblical text and making Scripture say something it had never said. Every false cult operating under the guise of Christianity employs this method of interpretation to prove their heresies. It has spilt over into the ranks of those who classify themselves as "militant, Bible believing fundamentalists, defending the faith." The hermeneutics emanating from some of these is as preposterous as that from the radical sects. For example, a new theological straw emerging within certain ranks teaches, "Adam and Eve may have lived hundreds or thousands of years before they had children." Despite the verse that states, "And Adam lived an hundred and thirty years, and begat . . . Seth" (Gen. 5:3). Cain and Abel were born long before Seth! Such statements about Adam and his children mesmerize "deep spiritual minds" who seem to find secret meanings in everything.

(d) "Five *were* foolish." Weddings commenced with the sight of the evening star at early sunset. At this sighting, the bridegroom would go forth to get his bride waiting at her parent's house. Then, he would escort her back to his father's house for the wedding and festivities that followed. On *odd occasions,* the process was reversed. The reasons for this are unknown. In case of bad weather and the stars were not visible, sundown was the time for the bridegroom to begin his journey. Along the roadside traveled by the bridegroom, going to fetch his bride, and then returning, were hundreds of friends and relatives. They would fall in behind the happy pair and formed a grand procession all the way back to the father's house. In Jer. 7:34 it speaks of a time when the "voice of the bride, and the voice of the bridegroom" would cease from the streets of Jerusalem. The crowds were singing, shouting, and dancing while making all sorts of noises on drums and curious musical devises. A clear explanation of these things is found in Edmond Stapfer's work, *Palestine in the Time of Christ.* As most streets were dark, it was necessary for each person to carry an oil-burning lamp attached to the end of a long pole. Due to the smallness of the lamp's fuel tank, it was customary for the owner to carry a container with extra oil in case of emergency. However, in this crowd of excited spectators and guests, five girls were foolish, and for whatever reasons they did not secure that extra provision. In other words, they failed to heed normal practice of making themselves ready. Jesus gave this lesson first, to His four apostles with Him on the Mount of Olives (Mk. 13:3). The main thrust was, "Be ready for what is coming in A.D. 70, I have forewarned you."

(e) Extra oil. Jesus told His disciples that of these ten women who went out to meet their friend and enjoy the wedding, five took vessels containing another supply of oil. They were esteemed as being wise for they were ready should the unexpected occur and the bridegroom be delayed. *Oil here does not symbolize the Holy Spirit.* Some with oil and some without only meant five of them had fuel for their pole lamps and the others ran out. *Whoever heard of someone running out of the Holy Spirit!*

(f) "While the bridegroom tarried." This has nothing to do with the present dispensation or period of time. It does not speak of the era from the ascension of Christ until His return. It simply meant that the bridegroom was delayed for a great length of time for reasons unknown. Meanwhile, growing weary of waiting, all ten of the young women fell into sleep along the roadway. It is noted that *both* the wise and unwise took a nap! Such conduct was considered highly rude or even an insult to the bridegroom and his company soon to pass that way. Sleeping would suggest they were not genuinely interested in the wedding soon to occur. See Paul's words in Rom. 13:11-12 that may have reference to sleeping on such occasions.

(g) "At midnight." After waiting for hours, the entire party of ten virgins dropped into weary slumber. Suddenly, at "midnight" persons traveling ahead of the coming bridegroom were heard shouting, "Behold, the bridegroom cometh; go ye out to meet him." The work of this forerunner or herald was to have the guests ready to follow the bridegroom as he passed by going to fetch his bride, or as he returned. This does not point to Christ coming for His people. Nor will a "split rapture" figure into the lesson. *The ten virgins do not point to the bride of Christ, because none of them were the young man's bride.* They were only friends. He was going to his bride's house where she lived under the authority of her father to claim her as his own. There is no great eschatological lesson in the word "midnight," though some extremists have seen it as the hour of Christ's return. This is hardly sensible since midnight on one part of the earth means high noon on the other. In countries such as Finland and the Arctic where they have weeks of total sunlight, this prophetic forecast would mean that Christ must wait until the earth's rotation before the sunlight again brought midnight darkness to those parts of the world. This is an example of extreme biblical typology. What is worse, many Christians are quick to accept such sensational teaching. It makes them feel deeply informed and greatly wise in the things of God! Correctly, it is a form of self-delusion concerning the rightly divided Scriptures in this lesson as given by the Lord Jesus. And this is because they do not understand the ancient Jewish wedding and the events surrounding it from which the Savior drew His lesson.

(h) Trimming lamps was the standard procedure. It was done by removing all excess carbon from the wick in order to have better light, which in turn consumed much more fuel. Some lamps had polished brass reflectors attached to them, which gave a great profusion of illumination to the bearer. We have no way of knowing for sure what type of portable lamps these women used.

2p- "Our lamps are gone out." Upon discovering their lamps were burning out, the foolish called upon the wise; they wanted to use their supply of extra oil carried in separate vessels. They knew that without burning lamps they would not be admitted into the house to share in the wedding and its happy festivities. Therefore, they refused to share their extra oil. Dr. John A. Broadus clearly explained this old Jewish custom in his *Commentary on the Gospel of Matthew*, vol. I., page 498. These women do not depict "unsaved Jews during the tribulation." Such an interpretation is wild imagination at its worst and must be forced into the story. Again, it is the fruit of *radical dispensationalism.*

(i) "Go and buy for yourselves." They advised the other five to go to the oil merchants. All oil merchants were required to be prepared to sell their product at any hour of the night and could refuse no one. One is amazed at the popular preaching, which identifies the oil as being typical of the Holy Spirit in the life of a believer! Again, we ask who ever heard of "running out" of the Spirit of God or going to a merchant and buying a vessel filled with the Spirit? Such exegesis reflects the same thoughtlessness as found in the unwise virgins. Some Calvinists call this "the oil of grace" given to the believer. Another shocker. Do these people who profess to have such unique insight to the deep counsels of the Almighty, to have discovered truths yet unrevealed to the average believer, not know that grace is always sufficient? It cannot burn out or be purchased at the shop of a Hebrew merchant. Grace is God's unique eternal gift bringing salvation and all efficiency and sufficiency to every real believer.

2p-"They that were ready went in." The necessary wedding garment. Every guest that attended was required to wear a (previously furnished) white wedding garment. It was carefully delivered to all who had been invited several weeks before the occasion. If, for some reason, they could not attend, the garment was refused upon delivery. Without this gown and the burning lamp, (if it was after sundown) no one was granted admission. This was a firmly established social custom and would not be violated. Our Lord had mentioned this wedding garment earlier in His Parable of the King's Son. Refer to Section 154, Matt. 22:11, footnote g for the story.

(j) "And while they went to buy." Good advice is often heeded too late. While going to the merchants these young women missed the grand event, for which they had waited. As the bride and groom came by, the crowds followed them to the father's house. After entering, the door was shut, barred, guards posted, and further entrance forbidden. The most important moment of the entire marriage festivity was that in which the bride entered her new home; something everyone wanted to see. The grand event is reflected in Ps. 45:14-15, "They shall enter into the king's palace." After all those present were granted entrance into the house, every entrance was shut. Guards stood by for fear of robbery because of the abundance of gold, silver, and precious stones present on these occasions. Refer to footnote c above for more on this thought. Because most of these events usually took at least seven days, this created even a greater vulnerability for robbery and theft. In ancient Jewish weddings, there was no religious ceremony of any fashion. Instead, friends and relatives pronounced numerous benedictions upon the couple. This corresponds to our western "toasting" or "well wishing" the bride and groom. A grand feast was always part of this event. Wine (like our tea or coffee) was used as an accepted social drink. It was not *always* intoxicating. However, at times, it was and some weddings (like today) became drunken parties. Morally pious Jews frowned on drinking as seen in Prov. 31:4-5. Regarding strong drink being given those who were perishing, see Section 188, Matt. 27:34, footnote f. For Jesus turning the water to wine at the Cana wedding, note Section 27, footnotes k and l.

(k) "Open to us." As explained above, when all the guests were gathered into the wedding house then all entrances were closed and guards posted at each one. It was after this that the foolish virgins approached the location having made their trip to the oil merchant. They called in vain to the lord of the wedding; their pleas for entrance were denied. This was standard social practice; the five foolish girls would have been familiar with this custom. Nevertheless, despite knowing this requirement they attempted to gain entrance! For their rejection of admittance into the wedding festivities, see footnote l below.

(l) "I know you not." The lord of the wedding (the groom's father) refused the pleas of the foolish virgins standing outside. His stern reply, "I know you not," was because they had not prepared themselves for the occasion. It was customary for the master of ceremonies or lord of the event to shout loudly, "I know you not," to all who sought late admission after the doors were shut. *They were rejected because they were not ready when the bridegroom came!* This was the main thrust of Christ's parable given to His four apostle's setting on the Mount of Olives. Clearly, He was warning them to be ready for what was coming in a few more decades. And came it did!

2p-Barred from the reign? The teaching that the five foolish girls being excluded from the wedding, points to those who will not be permitted entrance into the thousand year millennial reign is preposterous. Such interpretative calumny must be forced into this parable, for nothing of the sort is warranted in these verses. This spurious teaching was unknown in Christian eschatology until it was invented by *extreme* premillennialists in 1800. The Presbyterian minister, Dr. Lewis S. Chafer in his *Systematic Theology,* vol. IV, page 396, attempts to make a distinction between the marriage supper in heaven and the marriage feast, which (he says) will be held on earth. One is dumbfounded that such a great man as Chafer (died 1952) would then point to the story of the ten virgins as proof of this. Of all people, here a Reformed Presbyterian took radical dispensationalism to the wildest extreme! Further, these five girls barred from a Jewish wedding do not represent persons shut out of the millennial reign. Such radical typology does violence to the Word of God and should be rejected. They were forbidden entrance into the bridegroom's house and the celebration that followed because they were not prepared. Forcing the millennium into this event is wrong. Nor does this celebration teach that heaven will be a place of eternal food, fun, and fellowship. For comments on eating in heaven, see Section 171, third and fourth paragraphs of footnote b. The popular preaching that heaven will be one never-ending party for the saved of all ages is more eschatological sour cream. It will be what God wants it to be and that will be forever and endlessly perfect! For other thoughts on heaven, see Section 38, the third paragraph of footnote o.

3p-Again, *radical* dispensationalism forces the Word of God to say something not found in the immediate context or relevant Scriptures. Various expositors over the years have tried to force from God's Word, every minute detail about our Lord's return, when the Scriptures do not give these things. The wise man will leave the blank places alone and not press them into his eschatological fancies. Our personal *conjectures* about end-times are "junk theology" if presented as established basic truths that must be embraced by all Christians. However, there are particular doctrines of the Christian faith that men had better received, or they will die damned. The supreme example of this is the everlasting atonement of Christ. *Wicked men hate the singular exclusiveness of God's Son.*

(m) "Watch . . . ye." Christ used the pronoun "ye" in ending this lesson. Again, we ask, "Who were those He called "ye" (you) in this passage? Contextually, they were His four apostles. Refer to Section 163, number 1 under footnote f, for explanation. Obviously, our Lord was telling *them* to "watch." Therefore, how can this apply to all believers of succeeding centuries? If He spoke this *first,* foremost, and meaningfully to the four apostles, then what was He telling them to "watch" for? Surely, it was not his return for the church! As previously stated they have been dead for two thousand years, and Christ still has not returned. This cannot be the *prime and sole meaning* of His words. It seems, but mockery that He was admonishing them to "watch" and be "ready" for that event, when He knew they would be dead long before it would occur. Alternatively, was He warning them to "watch" for all the signs He had given, that pointed to the coming of the Romans and the destruction of their city and nation in A.D. 70? *If* this is correct, then it meant that He came in some mystic way amid the judgment and destruction of the city: thus, this mystical coming of the Son of man has been fulfilled. Though this is probably true, however, more is intended in these words than their fulfillment when Jerusalem lay in smoldering ashes with several million Jews dead. Jesus also used the literal events of that epochal destruction of A.D. 70, and from them pointed all future readers of Matthew's book to a time when He returns for His own. For a review of the ways, that Christ may come to individuals or congregations, see Section 163, second paragraph of footnote l. Thus all the "comings" of Christ to persons, events, churches, and so forth, are not always literal events as is popularly taught. The Son of God can come invisibly or literally as He may choose.

2p-Matt. 25:13. First, this verse *when left in its historical context,* speaks of something that occurred over two thousand years past in A.D. 70, when Christ came in the judgment of Jerusalem. However, when considered *by itself, apart from the context,* it points future readers and hearers of Matthew's work to that time when the real, visible, and Personal Son of God will "descend from heaven with a shout, with the voice of the archangel, and the trump of God" (1 Thess. 4:16). Christ was first warning His preachers, and next men of all succeeding ages to be ready for at a future date He will come again. If this does not happen in our lifetime, then death will beckon us out of the world. Either way, the warning is "Be ready." Regarding Jesus coming both visibly and invisibly, see Section 163, second paragraph of footnote l.

3p-In using *again* the word "watch," Jesus was repeating what was just said a few breaths before in Matt. 24:42-43. He was stressing that they were to "watch," be ready and not unprepared as were five of the young women. It was no accident that Christ concluded His parable with the watch-warning in verse 13. Everything said in this message terminates into the word "watch." He warned, "As these foolish virgins were shut out of the wedding, because they were not prepared, be sure you are ready when the fall of your city and temple comes. Do not be excluded from God's protection by procrastinating; *be prepared by heeding my words.*" It is preposterous to teach that this points to Jews during the tribulation period watching for the signs of Jesus' second advent.

(n) It is noticed that our Lord did not finish the story of the bride and bridegroom entering the father's house, the happy festivities, and the consummation of the holy event. Why? Could it be that the *real Bridegroom* has not yet come for His church, for only then will the story be completed? The long-range emphasis of this discourse for present day Christians is to "watch, watch, watch," and thus be ready for no one knows the exact time when the bridegroom will arrive to claim His people or death will sweep them away. For a survey of the speculations of thousands of people over the centuries regarding the signs of Jesus' return, see *Appendix Eight.*

THE PARABLE OF THE TALENTS.

This follows the previous admonition to watch in Matt. 25:13. Below, our Lord warns about service in His new kingdom while watching for His sudden return. There is also a message here for future believers of all succeeding ages. It reveals diligence is required in exercising of our God-given gifts and talents. True Christian service is the most serious work in life, and it will be judged. Some will be rewarded for their genuine works as believers. Others, who are mixed in with Christianity among various churches, but have never been saved, will be doomed when Christ returns.

Time: Late Tuesday after Palm Sunday.

Matt. 25:14-26—*On the western side of the Mount of Olives*	Mk.	Lk.	John
A departing lord assigns responsibilities[a] 14 "For *the kingdom of heaven*[b] *is* as a man travelling into a far country, *who* called his own servants, and delivered unto them his goods.[c] 15 "And unto one[d] he gave five talents, [if gold, each talent about $1,000*] to another two, and to another one; to every man according to his several ability; and straightway took his journey. 16 "Then he that had received the five talents* went and traded with the same, and made *them* other five[e] talents.* 17 "And likewise he that *had received* two, he also gained other two.[f] 18 "But he that had received one went and digged in the earth, and hid his lord's money.[g] *The lord returns: he reckons with His servants* 19 "After a long time[h] the lord of those servants cometh, and reckoneth with them.[i] *The five talents* 20 "And so he that had received five talents* came and brought other five talents,* saying, 'Lord, thou deliveredst unto me five talents:* behold, I have gained beside them five talents* more.' 21 "His lord said unto him, 'Well done, *thou* good and faithful servant: thou hast been faithful over a few things, I will make thee ruler over many things: enter thou into the joy of thy lord.' *The two talents* 22 "He also that had received two talents*[j] came and said, 'Lord, thou deliveredst unto me two talents: behold, I have gained two other talents* beside them.' 23 "His lord said unto him, 'Well done, good and faithful servant; thou hast been faithful over a few things, I will make thee ruler over many things: enter thou into the joy of thy lord.' *The one talent* 24 "Then he which had received the one talent*[k] came and said, 'Lord, I knew thee that thou art an hard man, reaping where thou hast not sown, and gathering where thou has not strawed:' (sown seed) 25 'And I was afraid, and went and hid thy talent [if gold, each talent about $1,000*] in the earth: lo, *there* thou hast *that is* thine.' *The terrible response* 26 "His lord answered[l] and said unto him, '*Thou* wicked and slothful servant, thou knewest that I reap where I sowed not, and gather where I have not strawed: (sown seed)			

Matt. 25:27-30—*On the western side of the Mount of Olives*	Mk.	Lk.	John
27 'Thou oughtest therefore to have put my money to the exchangers, and *then* at my coming I should have received mine own with usury. (interest) **28** 'Take[m] therefore the talent* from him, and give *it* unto him which hath ten talents.'* **29** 'For unto every one that hath shall be given, and he shall have abundance: but from him that hath not shall be taken away even that which he hath.' ***The awful fate*** **30** 'And cast ye the unprofitable servant into[n] outer darkness: there shall be weeping and gnashing of teeth.' " (Verse 31 cont. in Section 166.)			

Footnotes-Commentary

[a] Nowhere within this lesson did the Lord Jesus use the pronoun "ye" or "your," which, as we have seen, referred exclusively to His apostles who were with Him on the Mount of Olives. See Section 163, number 1 under footnote f for explanation. This absence of personal pronouns frees the lesson given here to fly across the spans of all earthly time and light upon the hearts of all who work in the spiritual kingdom of God or the church. Its purpose is to pre-inform them of other things that will be part of their judgment at the end of life's little while. *With this parable, we no longer hear the Lord Jesus pressing hard upon His apostles about the coming disaster of A.D. 70.* They had been given sufficient warning of this pending calamity.

[b] **"Kingdom of heaven."** For explanation of this, see Section 39, footnotes a and g, and Section 164, footnote b. In the previous Parable of the Ten Virgins, our Lord's message was *first* to the four apostles. They were to "be ready" for the mystical judgment coming of Christ in A.D. 70, and second, for the saved of all future ages to be ready for the *real return* of their Lord in the sky for His own. Nevertheless, it is obvious that the lesson above is a continuation of the Olivet Discourse started in Section 163, Matt. 24:3. Here, a different aspect of the same subject is set into this Parable of the Talents. The writer J. Stuart Russell penned these words of discernment in *The Parousia*, published in 1878, page 100, "The moral of the preceding parable [of the ten virgins] was vigilance; that of the present [parable] is diligence." On the other hand, perhaps we could say the former calls for *readiness,* while this message of the talents calls for *thoughtful diligence* in God's service before judgment comes.

[c] **"Delivered his goods."** Before this wealthy lord departed into a far country, he gave each servant specific work to perform during his absence, and placed the means whereby to accomplish this work into the hands of each one. Considering the vast amounts the lord gave, he was indeed a powerful and very rich man. See all under footnote d below for the large sums distributed to his servants. God calls men into His holy service and enables them to accomplish their assignments. Grace saves us, mercy spares us, and peace comforts us amid the duties of a lifetime of Christian service (2 Tim. 1:2 with Titus 1:4).

[d] **"Five talents"** presumably of gold worth about $5,000.00. The word talent as used here has reference to weighing something and thus denotes a large sum. In this verse, it is used to signify the various gifts or endowments that God's grace bestows upon men. The first servant was a person of extraordinary abilities and genius because he was entrusted with five of his master's talents.

2p-**"Two talents"** if gold, it amounted to about $2,000.00. This servant received a lesser amount of gifts or abilities; however, his master, nonetheless, loved him.

3p-**"One talent"** if gold, this was about $1,000.00. The services that God calls upon men to perform in His great church are all suited to their situations and the talents they receive. No man has ever been called of God to do that, which was impossible for him to do. The "one talent Christian" is not esteemed below the "five talent" one, "For there is no respect of persons with God" (Rom. 2:11). The text says that the lord dealt "to every man according to his several ability." This selected bestowment is seen in the natural world. A hare is swift and outruns the slow tortoise: God is pleased as each travels to the best of its ability. A lion roars while the mouse squeaks. God expects each Christian to strive to improve and enlarge the gift of grace that he has received. The servants or slaves in Jesus' message had nothing. It was an act of mercy that moved their tough and mean lord to lay into their hands these talents. As illustrated above, God's gifts are diverse, not all receiving the same; some get more, others less. Each one is granted what he needs according to heaven's wisdom. God does the choosing. Over the course of the Christian life, we often fail in the battle, but at last, we win the war, for suffering and loss are the schools of character building for true Christians. Sadly, this divine institution has many dropouts as well as the faithful remnant that will remain true to the end. God has arranged the earthly life of a true Christian where both His grace and our sanctified self-discipline hold hands. Together, we get the job done. David wrote, "I was also upright before him, and I kept myself from mine iniquity" (Ps. 18:23). Someone remarked, "If you say you can or you can't, both are right!" Paul exclaimed, "I can do all things through Christ, which strengtheneth me" (Phil. 4:13). This has reference to all things that God wills for any particular life. Reader, in which category are you? The can or the can't?

(e) This fellow reflected in his actions that he was wise and used his lord's gifts to double the amount.

(f) Likewise, this slave accomplished good things with his original two talents. He had also doubled them.

(g) **"Hid his lord's money."** Here may be a picture of those under the umbrella of Christianity who willfully and foolishly neglect the abilities given them. *Could it be they were never saved?* They cannot teach a Bible class, play an instrument, or chair a meeting, so they refuse to sweep the floor, clean the restrooms, pick up the paper, dust the furniture, mow the lawn, and help in the nursery and so on. As this servant dug a literal hole in the earth and buried his lord's gift, so slothful professors of the faith dig holes by their irresponsible reaction to the opportunities of service in the cause of Christ. It was an act of mercy that moved the tough lord to lay into their hands these talents.

2p-The one talent "oil man." Years ago, there lived in East Nashville, Tennessee, a little old man who was a courteous and kind Christian gentleman. He carried a small oil can in his pocket. Pastor W. W. Miles of the Fatherland Street Baptist Church often mentioned how he had seen this fellow oiling a squeaky gate, door hinges, or bike wheels for children playing on the sidewalks. The people of the community loved him. He was dubbed, "The oil man." When he died, hundreds packed the church for his funeral, because "he had been a blessing to them with his oil can." Alas! How the churches need hundreds of "oil men," doing their jobs, quietly and unassumingly blessing others and honoring God. This "one talent servant," used his small gift of an oil can for the blessing of countless men, women, and children. God said to Moses, "What *is* that in thine hand?" (Ex. 4:2). The Shepherd's rod in his hand was transformed into many things when once Moses released it! Later, God used it to part the Red Sea (Ex. 14:16)! As an eighteen-year-old youth, the author of this work was knocked unconscious in a high school football game. Many months later, he was sent home from Vanderbilt University Hospital in Nashville, Tennessee, as a paraplegic with steel braces on both legs! How hopeless the future seemed at that time. Now, sixty years later, looking back across life, these braces have been a gift from God. This bitter–sweet talent-gift has kept me broken, dependent, needing help, trusting God's Word, and the Savior, instead of human strength. Ugly caterpillars still become beautiful butterflies, in time! Romans 8:28 has more meaning as we look back on it and not so much looking forward tying to make it fit our situation.

(h) **"After a long time."** This "long time" has now become two thousand years! As sure as the foundations of heaven and earth stand, it is certain that some day, our Lord will return to judge His servants. No man knows the time when this will occur. Readers, are you ready to stand before Almighty God?

(i) **"And reckoneth with them." "Five talents," and an Australian missionary named Arnold Long.** See footnote d above for value. The lord or master had suddenly returned! He calls forward the first servant to whom he had dealt five talents many years ago. What a happy man! He stood before his master with a clear conscience and placed a double return into his hand. As a missionary serving in the Gibson Desert of Australia, in 1966 I met a famed Christian, the elderly Arnold Long. What a man! Upon our arrival at Alice Springs, Northern Territory, he visited our little dusty home. Missionary Long had already spent thirty-eight years living in a shack on the banks of the dry Todd River, trying ever so hard to reach the difficult Aboriginal people with the saving gospel of Christ. Holding his weather–beaten, worn out hat in a trembling hand, he bowed his white head and said, "Mr. Pike, I don't have anything to show for these years, but I've tried to be faithful to God and my calling." Later, we learned that he had led a young Aboriginal youth to Christ. About two decades later, during a return trip to Australia in 1996, I learned that this same youth was now a professor of Aboriginal history at a New South Wales university. He became a powerful witness of Christ among his students. Mr. Long's tough tenure of service in that hot, fly infested desert is still paying dividends. Missionary Arnold Long went to be with Christ many years ago. One-talent readers, learn from this and use what you have for the glory of God and good of men. Your will stand before your Lord some future day and give account of the service you have rendered. For further comments on faithful Christian service and a lasting illustration of this, see Section 140, second paragraph of footnote f.

2p-"Ruler over many things." This has nothing to do with the millennial reign of Christ and individual believers ruling over towns, cities, and districts. Dwight Pentecost makes this mistake in his popular work, *Things to Come*, page 501, under part E. He missed the local color and ancient meaning of these verses about ruling. Pentecost said that believers would hold positions of authority and rule for Christ over various things. One thing is sure; this is not the *original* meaning of these verses according to custom and practice of those ancient times. Concerning the apostles sitting on thrones and judging (not ruling) the twelve tribes of Israel, see Section 139, Matt. 19:28, number 2, under footnote m. The delegating of authority, mentioned in verse 21 by the returned lord was an ancient custom practiced by rich and powerful rulers as a means of honoring those who had served faithfully. Those men listening to Jesus speak, clearly understood what He was saying, as they were familiar with their customs. The average Christian is abysmally uninformed about the curious ancient customs practiced in Bible lands. Because of this, they often make serious mistakes in interpreting Scripture. This results in bizarre exegesis. Our Lord was giving a lesson on faithfulness and drew it from the ancient practice of a ruler rewarding his servants for being responsible with what they had been entrusted. He was not teaching that certain believers would rule over various parts of the earth during the glorious millennial reign. This was added some eighteen-hundred years later by *radical* dispensationalists who missed the cultural background of these things. Lifting these old social customs from the history of the ancients and applying them in today's life styles has resulted in dreadful perversions of Holy Scripture. If this is done long enough, by popular preachers and teachers, it soon becomes "established Bible doctrine." And all the king's horses and all the king's men cannot remove it from the church! For more on this misuse of Scripture, see Section 145, number 5, under footnote d. As stated numerous times, this does not deny or discredit a glorified reign of Christ on a new earth, but it does reject the wild radicalism and carnal nonsense of so many "end time experts" of today.

(j) **"Two talents."** See second paragraph of footnote d above for value. Basically, the same remarks apply to this servant as the one described under footnote i above. It is noted that the first two servants were invited to enter the joy of their lord. This has contextual and historical reference to ancient slaves partaking of their master's wealth because of their faithful service performed during his long absence. It may also shadows redeemed believers who have worked so hard in God's service being eternally blessed at the end of their earthly tenure. See the illustration of the Australian missionary, Arnold Long in the first paragraph of footnote i above.

(k) **"One talent."** See third paragraph of footnote d above for the value of one talent. The lesson here demonstrates that no one is excused for neglecting his duty in the service of God, be it ever so small. God will require of each person according to his ability. One must be cautious to leave this part of the parable in its ancient and historical context. The lazy slave spoke of his lord these words, "I knew thee that thou art an hard man, reaping where thou hast not strawed" (or scattered seed). There is no form of proper exegesis that can apply these words to the Lord of heaven and earth. The servant tells his master that because he was so cruel, that he was afraid of losing the one talent and hid it. (We ponder why the first two servants did not register a similar complaint?)

(l) **"His lord answered."** The fierceness of the lord vibrates in this reply. He agrees with the slave's assessment of his business practices. Now, the servants words condemn him! The angry lord roars back, "Thou knewest that I reap where I sowed not, and gather where I have not strawed." Knowing this in advance, the slave had no excuse. He should have taken the one talent, put it into the moneylenders, and derived at least the interest for his master.

(m) **"Take."** It was an ancient practice to take from the unsuccessful what they had failed to use and give it into the hands of the most successful. Those who were indolent and shiftless would have taken from them what little they possessed. Again, our Lord used the customs of the time in His teaching, and His apostles understood it.

(n) **"Cast into outer darkness."** *A proverbial term used several ways.* Originally, spoke of being shut out of the house, or punishing servants who did not please their masters. See next paragraph below for more explanation.

2p-Verse 30. **"Weeping and gnashing of teeth."** Jesus, first used this expression in Section 60, Matt. 8:12. Here, see the second and third paragraphs under footnote h for more on this subject. *Clarke's Commentary*, vol. 5 page 102, carries an interesting note on this subject. He relates that those who were shut out of banquets, weddings and various night celebrations were counted as being removed from the light (of the banquet hall) to the darkness on the outside of the house! Hence, the origin of the term "outer darkness." Gradually this became associated with the outer darkness in eternity, the city of the damned, where men gnash their teeth, cursing their fate forever. For twenty-one things the Bible says about suffering in hell-lake of fire, see Section 103, number 8, under footnote g.

3p-A hell made of ice? Ancient pagan tribes that once lived in what we now call Scandinavia, had a myth (which was a demonic distortion of hell) about the wicked being cast into freezing cold waters where they would suffer endlessly in some kind of unspeakable frigid, icy agony. This heathen fable could have only been derived from valid original teaching on the subject. Another example of these tales of demons is found in Section 174, the second paragraph of footnote b. The first sentence of footnote 4p below gives further information regarding these awful perversions of truth. Regardless, the Son of God said that hell is a place where, "The worm dieth not and the fire is not quenched" (Mk. 9:44, 46, and 48). For a vivid picture of the suffering of the dammed given by the Savior, refer to Section 131.

4p-A summary review of ancient pagan religions corrupting original history and divine doctrines is given in Section 1, Part 4, the third paragraph of footnote j. The records of suffering and punishment of those servants who did not please their masters or lords are replete in the annals of history. There are thousands of examples of exacting horrible tortures, throwing, and chaining the guilty into dark wet pits or dungeons. Egyptians took sharp razors and cut off all body parts before their gods. Trained dogs and monkeys were loosed upon the enclosed victims to punish for various crimes, especially those of a financial nature. Babylon, Persia, Greece, Rome, across Africa, over into the west and early America, men were merciless in exacting punishment for whatever ill was committed. Christ was not exaggerating when He used such terms as described in verse 30 above.

5p-The ruthless lord mentioned in Jesus' lesson (verses 26–30) was a mere mortal. He could not have had his worthless slave chained in the fires of hell's basement. This is beyond any man's authority. However, an overture from this story hits us powerfully. We conjure up in the long halls of human imagination the awful scenes of a real hell of the blackness of darkness forever, where men are confined without any hope of parole. Only God could do this.

A SHORT REVIEW OF THE HISTORY AND PROGRESS OF CHRISTIAN DOCTRINE, ESPECIALLY ESCHATOLOGY.

Were the doctrinal beliefs of the earliest Christians like those of true conservative or orthodox believers of today? "Yes," a little and sometimes "no," a lot! The only Scriptures of those first followers of Christ were the books of the Tanakh or Hebrew Old Testament. Receiving the fullness of the Spirit at Pentecost, the twelve apostles thoroughly understood all truth that Jesus had previously taught them from the Old Testament. This body of beliefs became known as "the apostles' doctrine." In Acts 2:42 we read, "And they [the first believers] continued steadfastly in the apostles' doctrine." Paul's letters did not exist at this time. They were written later between A.D. 50 and 68. *Appendix Seven* discusses the possibility that the four gospels, or part of them were in circulation in the days of Paul. The original Christians went forth armed with the fullness of the Spirit and the "apostles' doctrine." (Later, the instructions of Paul and others written by divine inspiration were added to the "apostles' doctrine" and became known as the New Testament.) The Sanhedrin charged that the apostles had filled Jerusalem with their doctrine (Acts 5:28). This reveals they had fulfilled the first part of the Great Commission as recorded in Acts 1:8. They had covered Jerusalem first. Despite this miraculous teamwork achievement in so short a time it was true that *some* Christians in the early churches did not always exegete Scripture in total agreement. At times, there was diversity among the believers in understanding various teachings. This is nowhere more evident as when speaking of the return of Christ or living under the Jewish law. (It remains just the same today.) Doctrinal conflicts are clearly reflected in Paul's letters to the Thessalonians, and single verses such as 1 Cor. 11:19 and 2 Tim. 2:18. Freedom from the Torah Law was the major issue until the destruction of the temple in A.D. 70. Then we hear the blasphemy of Gnosticism as seen in 1 John. Refer to Section 1, Part 1, footnote b for a brief explanation of Gnostic philosophy. Over the following centuries, "end-time events" took the front and center stage in the conflicts among ancient believers. Eschatology has experienced continual highs and lows on the stage of church history to the present moment.

What did the "apostles' doctrine" that was spread over Jerusalem by those early New Testament believers consist of? Primarily, it was the message that Jesus of Nazareth was the promised Messiah of Israel; that He came, began to establish His spiritual kingdom or the church, died for the sins of the world, rose again, ascended to heaven, and will return. A perusal across the book of Acts (which covers at least the first thirty years of church history) gives us some forty-seven examples of preaching, teaching, and witnessing. These examples reveal that the death, burial, and resurrection of Jesus, the promised Messiah was the major theme of all they said. First, the emphasis was for men to believe on the Lord Jesus Christ and thus be saved. Other important doctrines relevant to this, written by inspired men gradually fell into place. Sharing the gospel and it's "after salvation requirements" soon became paramount for early believers. This is predominant, especially in Paul's letters to churches and individuals.

Nothing was as urgent as the good news of personal salvation through the finished work of Christ. However, what was their understanding of the return of Jesus, the millennial rule, judgments, and related issues? It is clear from the New Testament that early believers were taught to look for the return of Jesus but not to set the date. Some of them, like many today, expected it to occur in their life span. *Time proved them wrong.* The same scenario still exists. This has nothing to do with inspiration of Scripture, but rather the longings and expectations of those early believers down through the ages and many today.

A literal interpretation of Rev. 20:1-6, and fierce persecutions led some of the early Christians to distinguish between a first and second resurrection, and look for an intervening real millennial kingdom. Some went to extremes as they meditated on this millennial hope. They conjured up all sorts of weird ideas of a future age, where materialism would be at its highest and human ambitions fulfilled. Others were not so extravagant. Later, this physical reign on earth necessitated several returns of Christ and judgments instead of one. It is untrue that the teaching of the thousand year's earthly rule of Christ was pre-eminently the doctrine of the first three centuries. It was known in a fragmented form and embraced by some, but not by the multitudes. The majority never receives the truth of God, regardless. They are always wrong on serious spiritual matters and at times become enemies to the truth, persecuting those who hold to it, often putting them to death. This martyrs bloodline runs throughout most of extant church history. It is glaring today in the lands where extreme Islam and paganism rules.

As the centuries slowly passed, Christ did not appear, and persecutions generally eased for a time, many among the non-conformists became thoroughly "grounded" in their convictions or understanding of Holy Scriptures. Thousands of *individuals* not associated with any particular "body of believers" did the same. Though their teaching on personal salvation was rock solid, the eschatology of these groups and individuals was a mixed bag and often taken to radical extremes. It is the same today.

During the Middle Ages, (circa. A.D. 500 to 1500) millenarianism, called "chiliasm," was mostly counted as heresy by the state installed and protected churches. Some small groups not associated with the emperor's church (which later became the full-fledged Papal system), embraced chiliasm. The emerging Roman Catholic Church opposed millenarianism and sought to execute those who would not subscribe to their teachings. During the Reformation of the sixteenth century, the so-called "Protestants" (those who came out of the Roman Church) also renounced this teaching. Luther and Calvin fiercely rejected millenarianism, yet both retained their infant Papal baptisms without renouncing its falsity and untruth. How odd that these men, who so fiercely renounced this system of religion would die this way. Various separate groups, which had *never* been part of the "Protestant Reformation," held to certain points of chiliastic teaching. One group, in particular, was the Anabaptists. Their religious enemies laid this name on them because they opposed infant baptism. Out of this movement came splinter bodies, and varying fanatical sects unworthy of mention. These radical factions were as ruthless and savage as the Catholic Church was during the Inquisition, and the Reformers at Geneva. On the other hand, thousands of Anabaptists became noble Christians, who died for not compromising the *major doctrines* of the Christian faith. Three of these were baptism by immersion for believer's only, a simple communion observance strictly for those who had been saved, and the separation of church and state. True Anabaptists held that the first two ordinances pointed back to salvation already experienced by the participants, but they did not provide it. Leonard Verduin's outstanding work *The Reformers and their Stepchildren* describes the horrific persecutions the Reformers unleashed upon those who would not subscribe to their baptism of infants (often for salvation), corruption of the Lord's Supper, eschatology, and use of the sword of the state to enforce their doctrines and destroy opponents. As stated earlier, Rabid Calvinists hate Verduin's work. They have tried every trick in the Devil's handbook to discredit his writings. It throws too much light on their religious ancestors of the past, bringing shame, ignominy, infamy, and disgrace upon their history. Like the mentally deranged Anabaptists at Münster, Germany, and the Papal inquisitions across Europe and Spain, these people also stand knee-deep in the blood of those their predecessors murdered in the Name of God and truth! *True Christianity does not work this way! A counterfeit, false, and Devil inspired version does.*

Later, during the eighteenth and nineteenth centuries the doctrine of the millennium flourished and was embraced by thousands. It spread over parts of England and America. Unhappily, among some of those who adopted versions of this teaching were the newly formed sects and cults. Two examples are the Jehovah's Witness and Seventh Day Adventist. The objection submitted against millennial teaching, that none of the major Reformed Church Confessions approved it, means a lot of nothing. Some of these same confessions also teach or intimate salvation by infant baptism and often approve a Roman Catholic flavoring of communion observance and church polity. On these two subjects alone, they have disqualified themselves as *true* Church Confessions of the Christian faith. It is notable how certain "theologians" refer to their Confessions like the Adventists refer to Ellen G. White, and the Mormons point to Brigham Young or Joseph Smith. Among premillenarians, there is a wide diversity as to the order of final events and the nature of things during the thousand years. This is nothing new for extreme variations in the finer points of eschatology are found within *every* school of thought. Both postmillennialism and amillennialism have as many conflicting voices, as do the schools of *historic* premillennialism, and *dispensational* premillennialism. Someone said, "They are all more or less tarred with the same brush." Those who claim they have sorted it out and have the total truth are people who enjoy hearing the sound of their voice or reading their own books.

For a systematic study on early church doctrine, including eschatology and its fragmented historical progress over the centuries, see *Early Christian Doctrines,* by J. N. D. Kelly. This famed church historian, draws much from the church fathers and little from the New Testament to demonstrate his thesis. Continually quoting from any of the fathers is like drawing from the Jewish Talmud; both have some truths but are well mixed with effective forms of soul poison. For a look into the heresy of the fathers, see Section 12, sixth paragraph under footnote k. An older and more comprehensive work on original Christian beliefs is, *Introduction to the Early History of Christian Doctrine*, by J. F. Bethune-Baker. Louis Berkhof's, *The History of Christian Doctrines,* covers the subject in a shorter form, but is weakened by his paranoid infatuation with covenant theology. Jaroslav Pelikan in his five volumes, *The Christian Tradition,* gives a wealth of documented information on the subject. He also draws heavily from the church fathers and seeks to confirm various Christian doctrines by what they wrote. Such a task is impossible due to their vacillating heretical and apostate approach to Holy Scripture, especially the doctrine of the Lord's Supper and water baptism.

No man knows *all* the answers (much less the questions) about the vastness of Bible eschatology. It takes more than academic superiority and expertise in the original languages, to penetrate the frequent mysteries of Holy Writ. Those who depend on mental gifts *only,* become cold, professional religionists who know everything about nothing. Popular figures of the past and present who have written for years about eschatology (and all of us, for that matter) could be seriously wrong on certain points. Along with this obvious fact, there continually looms another tough problem already touched upon in this harmony commentary. For almost two thousand years, armies of professional "seers" who have assured their adherents that they are right have done great damage to the church and untaught believers. These people purport to show flashes of unique insight into the mysteries of Scripture, and in time acquire a significant following. This scenario adds to the already existing confusion. As world conditions change these "experts" fade away only to have a new army of "prophecy authorities" to take their place.

On the other hand, there are clear Bible doctrines that we must be positive about and uphold them with absolute dogmatism (Titus 2:7 with Jude 3). The cardinal one is soteriology, the doctrine of salvation. Those who disagree with instant salvation or the new birth through repentance and faith in Christ the Son of God, are wrong. There is no further room for discussion with these people *if* they choose to remain adamant in their error regarding this fact. Nevertheless, some doctrinal issues are not as clear and concrete as soteriology. With such things, we must walk softly, reassuring fellow Christians and ourselves that we have more to learn about other Bible doctrines, especially eschatology.

The following Section mirrors some of the attendant problems that are part of the great doctrine of Christ's return, related subjects, and ensuing events. Over the past five or six decade's, interest in biblical eschatology has reached a new high. World events, book sales, and hundreds of churches, preaching and believing anything that sounds good, are springing up on all sides. The explosion of prime-time TV preachers and Bible teachers has helped increase the "end-time fever." Among some fundamentalist groups, if one dares to reject certain footnotes of the *Scofield Reference Bible,* he is ostracized as an apostate from the faith. (Not all of Scofield's comments and notes are of this nature.) Whatever a believer thinks about Scofield's footnotes, a dark problem looms over his interpretation of the Parable of the Sheep and Goats. He wrote of a Jewish remnant preaching in the tribulation and Gentile nations of the world being judged, based on how they treated the Jews during this time. Scofield's interpretation of this parable was unknown the first seventeen hundred years of church history. He apparently borrowed it (with certain alterations) from John Nelson Darby, born 1800, in London, England. Later, Darby was associated with the founding of the Plymouth Brethren, among whom have been some great Christians over the decades.

The general judgment doctrine presents interpretative problems for those who do not hold to it. On the other hand, the words of Paul, "Caught up to meet the Lord in the air" (1 Thess. 4:17), present just as many difficulties for believers who work so hard defending a general judgment. The book of Revelation is the final battleground for all schools; how they interpret it determines their eschatological stance. Each school of thought works hard to prove that their eschatology is right. Woe be the person who will not bow to the *extreme* teachings of the *radical* dispensationalists, or the idealism of postmillennialists working to create a better world through the gospel. Standing out front are the date setting *radical* dispensationalists reading all the signs and assuring us the Lord will return just any day or tomorrow at the latest. They prove this from newspaper and magazine headlines! Thinking non-Christians watching this eschatological sideshow back off as they ponder the obvious contradictions, conflict, and confusion it generates.

Who knows how many Christians have had their faith wounded or destroyed by the "prophecy specialists" who have it all figured out? One of the greatest friends of the author was an elderly man (now in heaven) who became an authority on Christ's return. A young evangelist and his wife visited this friend. They had inherited some money and sought advice about purchasing a house. My friend advised them not to waste their money, for Christ was coming soon! That was over fifty years ago. They spent the inheritance, and now, old, worn, and bitter, they have no roof over their heads! *It is stressed again, that not all of these men are charlatans preying on the ignorant and innocent.* Many are sincere but overheated enthusiasts who have gone too far into a forbidden zone. The looming problem is that when they have continually proven themselves wrong, they are unashamed and unabated in their eschatological failures. A fresh return to the instructions of Acts 1:6-7 with 2 Peter 3:16 would be good for all of us.

COMMENTS ON THE SHEEP-GOAT JUDGMENT AND RELATED SUBJECTS.

Christ's predictions of doom upon Jerusalem, the temple, and the Jewish state in Section 163 (blended with reflections of His far distant future advent) were followed by three more warnings. First, is the Parable of the Ten Virgins in Section 164, which calls for watchfulness. Second, is the Parable of the Talents in Section 165, which teaches responsibility in His kingdom with individual accountability. Third, He concluded His series with the Sheep-Goat Judgment parable in Section 166. This reveals His glorious coming as King to judge the nations of the world, and mete out rewards and punishments accordingly. All four of these messages followed on the heels of each other. There was no break in continuity between any of these. The sheep and goat discourse has become something of an "eschatological battlefield," with each interpreter struggling to make it fit what he thinks is right. Jesus used a series of two's while giving the Olivet Discourse. In Section 163, Matt. 24:44-51 we have two kinds of servants, one was watching, one was not. In Section 164, Matt. 25:1-13, there are two kinds of virgins, one group was ready and watching, and the other was not. In Section 165, Matt. 25:14-30 we note two kinds of talent holders, one ready, watching, and the other not. Lastly, in this present Section 166, Matt. 25:31-46, Christ spoke of two classes of people (nations) being judged; the sheep group was prepared and ready while the goat group was not. These admonitions to watchfulness and their systematic order are the natural conclusion to what He had just taught in Sections 163 through Section 165 about the coming doom of A.D. 70.

Those who reject a general judgment are confounded by the sheep-goat parable. To remove this, their only alternative is to resort to the *Scofield* and *Ryrie Bible* footnotes. As explained, those who hold to a general judgment find that the removal of the church (rapture), also presents them with insurmountable difficulties. Commentators are sharply divided by trying to interpret (or reinterpret) the Scriptures that speak of these things. Augustus Strong in *Systematic Theology*, pages 1004-1014 defends the spiritualizing hermeneutic, while Henry Thiessen in *Lectures in Systematic Theology*, pages 496-513 moves in the opposite direction defending the literal interpretation of the rapture and the thousand years followed by the judgment of the unsaved. Which is right? There are five primary schools of thought regarding the return of Christ, judgments, the millennial and other points. Within each of these, the variety of thought and interpretation is bewildering. A British clergyman, Ethelbert Bullinger (died 1913), popularized *ultra radical* dispensationalism. He seems to have gotten it from Pierre Poiret (died 1719) a French philosopher. Later, John Darby and C. I. Scofield became its chief promoters with certain revisions. Then, Darby's new teaching influenced a Presbyterian minister, J. H. Brookes, of Saint Louis, Missouri. Apparently, Darby had read the *Coming of Messiah in Glory and Majesty* by a Jesuit priest, Emmanuel Lacunza published in 1827. Lacunza (died 1801) seems to have borrowed his eschatology from another priest, Francisco Ribera (died 1591). From two Spanish Catholics the "secret rapture" seems to have originated! Yes, the church will be taken out but not in secret. For more on this, see Section 134, footnotes j and all of k. These topics became Darby's battle cry and are looked upon today by certain people as established Bible doctrine. Historically, this is incorrect. Below is a brief review of the five major systems of eschatology. Each has numerous breakaway groups:

First: Postmillennialism. Called "preterists," their teaching seems to have originated in England, with a Unitarian, named Daniel Whitby (died 1726). They believe the gospel will gradually convert most of the world to Christ, while He is presently reigning spiritually from heaven. The majority of men will be saved through fulfilling the Great Commission. Then, Christ will return and set up His Kingdom. The promises of God for future Israel are spiritualized and given to the church. This hermeneutic is partly right. In *some* of the Old Testament, God's promises to Israel do fit the church; however, others do not. Spiritualizing the book of Revelation is a task of exceeding difficult proportions. The Presbyterian minister, Kenneth L. Gentry, Jr. attempted this in, *Before Jerusalem Fell*. Within the postmillennial camp, one finds both liberals and conservatives with various interpretations of eschatology. Calvinism rules among preterists. How this system reconciles world conversions with Christ's Words regarding eternal life, "Few there be that find it," (Matt. 7:14), we question. Neither dominion or reconstruction theology as propagated by the Torah Law imprisoned Rushdonnyites, can convert the world to Christ.

Second: Amillennialism. Known as the "historicists" school, it does not agree with postmillennialism that things must get better and then Christ will return. They mostly believe that Jesus rules the world now from the throne of God in heaven. Both evil and good will continue to the end. Like postmillennialism, they spiritualize *all* the Scripture promises to Israel by transferring these to the church. This is often called "replacement theology." To them, the kingdom and millennium of Rev. 20 are spiritual things. The Holy Spirit and Word of God are now accomplishing both in the church on earth, as the victorious Christ rules His people from heaven's throne. Satan is (supposedly) chained by faith and/or by the deceased martyrs with Christ in heaven. Christ will return and there will be one resurrection and one judgment. The embryo of this teaching originated with the brilliant but unstable Augustine (died A.D. 430), who held that unbaptized babies went to hell! The philosophy of amillennialism was basically laid down in his work, *The City of God*, Book XX, chap. 9, pages 725-726. He was the "father" who founded some of the most monstrous doctrines of the Papal system. Augustine is listed as a "Doctor of the Roman Catholic Church." Like Thomas Aquinas, both believed in killing opponents of their church! Refer to Section 14, number 2 under footnote f for more information on Augustine. He was supposedly a "converted African lawyer," noted most for continually changing his mind about Scripture, doctrine, and practice. Like the other church fathers, he cannot be trusted for anything of *basic* doctrinal value. *Honest* amillennialists trace their roots to Augustinian eschatology. One finds many theological liberals with a few conservatives in the amillennial frame of reference. As previously mentioned, a conservative Reformed minister, Dr. Kim Riddlebarger, published an excellent work on *The Man of Sin,* from the amillennial viewpoint. It is loaded with invaluable ancient documentation and written in the spirit of high Christian candor and grace.

Third: Dispensational premillennialism. Those who hold this are called "futurists." Briefly, they see the world getting worse with wickedness abounding. The older school originally held that after many observable signs were fulfilled the Lord Jesus would return, take out His church, judge her, and then a tribulation period would commence. Several decades ago, however, many of these people changed their minds and transferred their signs over into the tribulation period! Now Christ will *secretly* rapture out the church, then the seven-year tribulation will commence with many signs occurring. There will be some three and one half years of world peace under the direction of the Antichrist through a one-world church. This will end in three and a half years of horrific worldwide suffering. At the conclusion of the tribulation, King Jesus will return, there will be the sheep-goat judgment followed by a literal thousand year's reign on earth. Then, will follow the great white throne judgment. Afterward, the eternal age will commence. Among those who embrace this form of dispensationalism, one finds an overwhelming variety of interpretations on end time subjects. Great divisions exist among these people regarding the rapture. Some have it before the tribulation, some mid way through, and others afterwards. They all have verses to prove their point! As in the church at Corinth, "every one hath an interpretation" (1 Cor. 14:26). These Christians miss the fact that God did not give us full details regarding biblical eschatology. Bible truth has always been recorded in this fashion. Awful problems arise when men pry beyond the divine limits established in Scripture. Every false cult in church history came out of this forbidden trespass.

There are difficult questions regarding all end-time topics; the same is true of the incarnation, the oneness of God and the Son, and other eternal truths. As said earlier, "Difficulties do not negate divine truth, nor do they constitute contradictions." In the Bible, God has laid down limited specifics concerning doctrine and history. In none of these did He give to us every minute detail. As repeated in this work, all biblical truth was divinely transmitted this way. Regardless, it would be a rarity to find a theological liberal within the dispensationalist camp. One will often encounter ruthless church dictators with little or no respect for the *honest* questions and opinions of their congregations or other Christians.

In 1960, Clarence B. Bass released, *Backgrounds to Dispensationalism* in which he indisputably documents that the dispensationalism of today was formulated in the nineteenth century. Prior to that, dispensational teaching was known but not as an *established defined* doctrine over the course of church history. *The extreme dispensationalism of today is foreign to that of decades past.* Staunch dispensationalists such as Dr. John Walvoord (now in heaven), often described as "the greatest student on prophecy in American history," admitted the same. As far back as 1957, he wrote in *The Rapture Question* pages 5 and 15-16 these amazing words, "This teaching [dispensationalism] was espoused by Darby, the Plymouth Brethren movement, and popularized by the famous *Scofield Reference Bible*." Darby (born 1800), was an Irish Calvinistic theologian, lawyer, and Anglican. Thinking Christians are confounded as to why someone would spend their lives supporting a teaching that was *unknown* in the first eighteen hundreds years of church history! The famed Samuel P. Tregelles, one of the early Plymouth Brethren, wrote that Darby's interpretation was the "height of speculative nonsense." Quoted from Bass' *Background to Dispensationalism*, page 21. For a devastating critique of extreme Darbyism, see *A Dispensational Premillennial Analysis of the Eschatology of the Post Apostolic Fathers.* This is a Thesis in the library of Dallas Theological Seminary, by Alan Patrick Boyde, written in 1977.

In several early writings of the church fathers, one finds scraps of *unsystematic* dispensationalism. Papias (died A.D. 165) mentioned the literal reign of Christ on earth, as did a few others. This hardly proves that the first churches held to what is today called "premillennial dispensationalism." For an older look at this, see *The Lord's Return,* printed in 1914, by J. F. Silver. Paul wrote about, "the dispensation of the grace of God" (Eph. 3:2). How did Darby miss "the dispensation of the fullness of time" in Eph. 1:10? Where does this fit in with the other seven dispensations? It is absent in the eschatology of Darby, Clarence Larkin, and other famed dispensationalists. No informed Christian should object to the fact that God has chosen over the course of human history to work with nations and persons in various ways. This is vastly different from Scofield's shocker that no one was saved by grace until Christ rose from the dead in about A.D. 30! As previously mentioned, he wrote that prior to this, men were saved by "legal obedience" to the Jewish law. See Scofield's *Reference Bible,* footnote 2 at John 1:17, page 1115. We ask, "What became of the billions who lived and died before Moses received the Torah Law, fifteen hundred years before Christ was born?" (Gal. 3:17). "No saving grace until the cross" is a heresy of unspeakable proportions. Some five thousand years *before* Calvary, old man Noah "found grace in the eyes of the LORD." (Gen. 6: 8). God's grace is found only in one place (2 Tim. 2:1). Regarding how people were saved before the death and resurrection of Christ, see Section 10, footnote b, and Section 144, footnote i. Hebrews chapter 11 reveals how men were saved from the beginning of the human race starting with Abel. The two important words across this chapter are "by faith."

Extreme dispensationalism has egg on its face because of the bizarre eschatological proclamations made by so many of it proponents. Their shots in the dark about the time of Jesus' return for His people, *who* and *where* the Antichrist is, are no longer humorous; they are disgusting. One of the most infamous date setters was Edgar Whisenant. It is in his book, *On Borrowed time; and 88 Reasons Why the Rapture Could be in 1988.* Whisenant (died 2001) was not alone in his erroneous forecasts. Hal Lindsey, Charles Taylor, Jack van Impe, Salem Kirban, and the Southwest Radio Church all stand in the long line. A few of the dates chosen over the centuries are, 1033, 1420, 1650, 1666, 1809, 1914, 1970, and hundreds of others! In 1981, Mary Stewart Relfe published her book, *When Your Money Fails. The "666 System" is Here.* This was one of the biggest flops in decades. She even found the mark of the beast on the J. C. Penney credit card! Colin Deal, the "end time expert" who authored *Christ Returns by 1988: 101 Reasons Why,* greatly applauded her work. There have been thousands of guessers. Apart from the omnipresent "eschatological crackpots," these are good people went into the forbidden realm. They were teaching things God had not said and misleading thousands. Herein is the great danger for untaught Christians.

John Nelson Darby said that a dispensation is a period of time during which man is tested in respect of obedience to some specific revelation of the will of God. The word "dispensation" does not mean "a period of time." In the Greek language, it *always* signified "the management of household duties." It is another word for "stewardship." Our English noun "economy" comes from this word. The London lawyer invented seven of these time periods. They are like concrete and cannot commingle. One does not reach over into the other. Each dispensation is radically different. What God does in one He will not do in the others! Zealous dispensationalists have also created several other gospels, resurrections, double and triple fulfillment of troublesome Scriptures to prove their claims. Meanwhile, "specialists" who were "led of God" have invented several extra dispensations apart from Darby's original seven! Worse, there presently exists among these people four different views about the rapture of the church. *Extreme* dispensationalism is loaded with secret plots lurking in the shadows. Conspiracies have always been part of their history, but beware of those "prophecy specialists" who discover one in every old and new global organization. That den of international America haters and political gangsters, the United Nations, is pointed to as a prime example of world conspiracy. As a world body, the UN is excellent for earthquake relief and humanitarian aid during the worst of natural calamities. In the field of honest politics and true religious faith the UN is a pawn of the Devil and will always be, while American tax dollars foot their bills. For a fair review of the conspiracy theories rampant among *radical* dispensationalists and others, see *Selling Fear,* pages 169-191, by Gregory S. Camp.

Fourth: Historical premillennialism. This eschatological system does not hold to the seven dispensations (mentioned above) during which God is supposed to deal with men in different ways. It rejects the steel wall separation between Israel and the church as taught by Darby and popularized by Scofield' footnotes. The eminent George E. Ladd (died 1982) rejected the dispensational approach to Scripture. In his book, *The Blessed Hope,* page 31, he vigorously affirms the anti-dispensational feature of historic premillennialism. Briefly, main line historical premillennialism holds that the church is the fulfillment of a spiritual Israel and believes that the saved of all ages are part of one group. They place the return of Christ and the resurrection of the redeemed just before the millennium and after the great apostasy of the tribulation. According to this, the Savior's return is not an imminent event from God's viewpoint. It can only take place *after* the rise of the Beast and False Prophet in Rev. 13. The duration of the millennial kingdom is unsure; on this point, historical premillennialists have reached no consensus.

As already stated, long before the birth of Christ and Christianity, the ancient Jews had gradually developed the concept of an earthly kingdom with their human Messiah ruling the world. The rabbis due to their ultra literal interpretation of various Old Testament Scriptures distorted this. Jewish apocalyptic literature written *before* the birth of Christ, and after the close of the Hebrew canon, speaks of this coming physical kingdom. Such ancient books as 1 Enoch and 4 Ezra mention a political Hebrew monarchy. Like all apocryphal works, these bristle with ridiculous exaggerations.

Some among the historic school hold that during the millennial, Israel will again worship God in a rebuilt temple and offer animal sacrifices. After the millennium, Satan will be loosed; Gog and Magog will oppose God's kingdom and be defeated. Lastly, is the final resurrection and judgment. Obviously, in this scheme there are two resurrections, the righteous before the millennial and the wicked afterwards. Most historical premillennialists hold that the Antichrist will be a real person and not a system. In short, they believe that one can be a balanced chiliast without resorting to the novel artifices and exegetical stratagems of *extreme* dispensational premillennialism. They reject the supposed "Christian world" imagined by postmillennialism and the excessive spiritualizing of amillennialism.

Some eschatologists believe things will improve morally, while others wait for human society to totally corrupt, then collapse before the Savior returns. This reminds one of the Presbyterian pastor who knew things were getting better because his local church was growing beyond expectations. On the other hand, the Baptist Chaplain of the nearby state prison was sure that wickedness was at an all time high because his congregation was also rapidly increasing. Both were right from the observation of their individual situations, but were wrong when they were viewed together. For a presentation of the historic school of thought, see Craig L. Blomberg and Sung W. Chung's, *A Case for Historic Premillennialism*.

Fifth: Progressive dispensationalism: The major difference between progressive dispensationalists and premillennial dispensationalism is God's promise that the throne of David would always be occupied. The progressives teach that Christ is presently reigning in heaven from the Father's right hand, although He is not yet actually sitting on David's literal throne. He is phasing the church into the already inaugurated (activated) covenant of King David. When Christ has fulfilled all the promises that God made to David, He will return to this world. The church is looked upon as the spiritual kingdom today, which is already in action. Nevertheless, God will at a future date establish a glorified literal kingdom when Christ returns. This will be realized during the open-ended, literal thousand-year reign of our Lord. *Specific details* about this reestablishment are missing by divine inspiration. Imagining what these are and then adding them to the story is distorting the truth and adding more end-time foolishness to the Scripture.

Progressive dispensationalists have renamed the dispensations to fit their eschatology. They have the Patriarchal, Mosaic, Ecclesial, and Zionic categories. Not much of substantive nature can be given about this relatively new eschatology. At this writing, it is not yet twenty years old. One can be sure that with the passing of time it will take on new and probably surprising features as all the others have done.

Similarities and yet differences in interpretation are in all five groups, as previously mentioned above. Postmillennialism transfers many of God's promises to Israel into the lap of the church. Some of these fit this application but not all. For example, Paul takes two Old Testament Jewish promises and applies them to the church (Hosea. 1:10 in Rom. 9:26, and Hosea. 2:23 in Rom. 9:25). God is not through with Israel; even though the church is called the spiritual seed of Abraham, and he is called the "father of those who believe" (Rom. 4:11, 16; Gal. 3:7, 29). Peter's statement on Pentecost (Acts 2:28-36) declares that Christ is now reigning as co-regent from a (spiritual) throne of David in heaven. This does not negate some kind of literal reign over the saved people of Israel forever (Lk. 1:30–33 with Isa. 9:6-7). For two-thousand years, the Lord Jesus has been executing His eternal and divinely appointed office as "a priest for ever after the order of Melchisedec." See Section 207, footnote b for explanation of this priestly order.

James' quotation from Amos 9:11-12, recorded in Acts 15:13-18, that God will "rebuild the tabernacle of David," contextually, historically, and exegetically must be applied to the church. Nevertheless, this hardly signals that God is finished with Israel (Rom. 11:1-2). Paul described the church as "the Israel of God" (Gal. 6:16 with Rom. 9:6). He did not say that Jehovah was no longer the national

God of Israel (Isa. 26:13 with Jer. 46:28.) After the ascension of Christ, Peter stated before the Sanhedrin that God was "the God of our [Jewish] fathers" (Acts 5:30).

Despite their disagreements, the above schools of eschatology all firmly believe that Jesus is coming again. Wide differences exist because of the *inspired* gaps and finer details in the doctrine of His return that God has not explained. Often, theological malice exists among commentators. Some are hostile and mean in affirming their positions regarding this subject. *These differences will not be resolved in this life.* Someone is wrong; how will we all fair at the judgment seat of Christ when confronted with these things?

The general judgment is the catalyst in eschatology. The next Section presents a general judgment scene in the sheep-goat lesson. *Radical* dispensationalists have a shock answer for this problem. It is found (again) in Scofield's footnotes. This ex-jail bird, drunkard, southern lawyer, and veteran of the Civil War was gloriously saved in 1879. With his rigidly trained legal mind, he invented a novel interpretation of the sheep nations. They had assisted the Jews during the tribulation period! Several things are noted about sheep in the life of Christ. During His ministry, the Savior called His people "sheep." He said that He had "one fold," and that He was the "one shepherd" (John 10:16). The sheep (called "his" in John 10:3) are the church or kingdom in its spiritual manifestation. To our surprise we now discover that the Great Shepherd has two flocks instead of one: His church and the "Gentile sheep nations" seen at this judgment in Matt. 25. Can this mean that the sheep church is the same as the sheep nations at His right hand? The verses state that Christ "as a shepherd divided *his* sheep from the goats" (Matt. 25:32). Does our Lord have a "church flock" saved by grace, and a "Gentile nations flock," with the latter proving they are saved by being good to Jews during the tribulation?

Some understand the sheep-goat discourse teaches that the bema judgment of believers will be included within this event under the emblem of sheep, but they will be *separately* judged for their works in God's service. Afterwards, the goats (unsaved) will also be *separately* gathered at the great white throne for their judgment and doom. The millennial will occur between the two. This presents a vast time interval between the two judgments, even though Christ placed them together in this lesson. It has been described as one judgment divided into two different sessions. Could the "gathering out of his kingdom all things that offend" be the same (Section 82, Matt. 13:40-42)? The Parable of the Dragnet in Section 85, Matt. 13:48-51 also carries this meaning of separation. In both the "good" are separated from the "bad." Christ's Words in Matt. 25:34, "Come ye blessed of my Father, inherit the kingdom prepared for you from the foundation of the world," have more reference to eternal heaven than a limited thousand years millennial. To restrict this to Gentiles, who were kind to the Jews during the tribulation is wrong. *This "do good to the Jews eschatology" was unknown until Scofield popularized it in his Bible, originally published in 1909. Where was it for the first nineteen hundred years of church history?*

Scripture is clear that believers will *never* be judged or condemned for their sins; this was done on the cross, where Christ bore the full condemnation and judgment for all sins (John 5:24 with 2 Cor. 5:21). Nevertheless, Christian service will be called into accountability at the judgment seat of Christ, regardless of when and where this takes place. There is so much debate about the "when's" and "where's" of the bema judgment, that the *reason* for it has slipped into the background. Judgment for believers is to examine their original heart's motive in every act of Christian service to determine its worth of reward or not. The bema judgment occurs after the resurrection of believers, which occurs at the removal of the church. This calling out of the dead (bodies) asleep in Christ is expressly called in Lk. 14:14, "the resurrection of the just." In John 5:29, it is described as "the resurrection of life." Paul wrote that upon the return of our Lord, the sleeping physical bodies of "the dead in Christ shall rise first" (1 Thess. 4:16). At this return He will also bring with Him the souls who had lived in those bodies and went to Him when they died (1 Thess. 3:13). If the dead in Christ rise first, then the dead *not* in Christ will rise second. Some extremists have added to this a third and fourth raising of the dead! In the passage of 1 Thess. 4:16, the "first resurrection" would occur when "the Lord himself descends from heaven with a shout."

After the first resurrection and the glorious transformation of the physical bodies of those who are living (1 Cor. 15:51-53), these countless millions will be caught up to meet the Lord in the air and be judged. Romans 14:10 reads, "We [believers] shall all stand before the judgment seat [bema] of Christ." It states in 1 Cor. 3:11-15 that at the bema, the works of individual saints will be judged to determine reception or loss of rewards. However, fitting all this into a general judgment is like trying to unring a bell. Fitting a general judgment into the rapture is worse. In Rev. 20:5-6, we note a "first resurrection" taking place *after* the thousand-year reign, yet Paul wrote that it takes place when Christ descends from heaven. Both are called "first." It is here that some expositors think they find a basis for one resurrection of the saved divided into two parts and separated by a period of one thousand years. Some spiritualize the thousand years believing they occurred in centuries past. Some think they are happening now. Dispensationalists affirm that they are literal and future. It is the old story of spiritualizing some verses and literalizing others. And each group is always right!

Because the sheep-goat parable presents such difficulties, many interpretations have been developed. Each one is designed to make it fit into a previously adopted eschatological system. It is an impasse for those who reject a general resurrection with judgment following. On the other hand, the "rapture and bema judgment of believers" present just as big a problem to the sheep-goat discourse, if it is left to stand as one event occurring at the same time. Spiritualizing the book of Revelation and the millennial is the best, but the *worse* way out of this difficulty. The author believes God has purposely given us some things this way to keep men from knowing more than they should. It is still true, "For *as* the heavens are higher than the earth, so are my ways higher than your ways, and my thoughts than your thoughts" (Isa. 55:9). *Thus we may know only a little about God's ways.* Too much "knowledge" still "puffs up" (1 Cor. 8:1). A trademark of many (but not all) "end-time specialists" is their arrogant cult-like attitude. They are *always* right and the slightest deviation from their infallible eschatological knowledge is branded as apostasy.

No one will be doomed to hell because he mistreated Jews during the tribulation. Nor will anyone be ushered into the joys of life eternal because he helped them. *This is the height of doctrinal absurdity.* Whatever our Lord's Words to the sheep nations finally mean, they do not mean this. The editors of *The Life Application Bible*, pages 1620-1621 do not attempt to explain these things. On the other hand, the editors of *The King James Study Bible*, page 1475 agree with Scofield in their comments. Frustrated men trying to figure everything out invented this new method of salvation by a system of "do-good-to-the-Jews" works theology. The sheep and goats message does not teach salvation by works. Nor does it assert that helping the Jews during the tribulation proves their prior salvation and ushers them into the millennial kingdom. Note the following illustrations regarding this ill founded proposal.

When my family and I arrived in Queensland, Australia in 1961, to begin pioneer missionary work, our *atheistic* Greek neighbors were a tremendous help to us. Openly confessing their atheism, they did much to assist us with settling into our rented house. We were never able to really witness to them of Christ; they simply would not listen. Their good deeds to strangers hardly proved their salvation. What the local newspaper called "a religious war" broke out in this same town some two years after we began our work. One of my close friends during this hard time was the local tailor, a gambler and horse race bookmaker. When visiting his shop, he encouraged me, "Not to back down under the pressure." Bob came to know Christ as personal Lord and Savior many years later. His words of good cheer to an embattled missionary while engaged in a *very* hot public debate hardly reflected his salvation.

It is not true that the Gentile nations will aid the Jews in the tribulation and the Jews will win millions to Christ. Not one straw of evidence can be found anywhere in the Bible for this alien eschatology. Presently, (2011) there are a hundred and ninety three different nations on earth making up almost seven billion people. (Every Arab nation and their compatriots in *radical* Islam fiercely hate Israel, America, and Christianity.) During the tribulation, everyone on earth will need help just as much as the Jews will. To infer that men are saved or demonstrate their previous salvation by charitable acts toward Jews, "who have preached the gospel during the tribulation" is wrong. See the *Scofield Reference Bible*, page 1036, footnote 1 for this error. This fable has been adopted and propagated without research. The reason, "It must be true because it's in the *Scofield Reference Bible* footnotes." *The Ryrie Study Bible*, in a footnote on page 1387, reflects that he slightly revised Scofield's comments on the same subject and added them to his Bible. He wrote that this is a judgment of the Gentiles "whose heart relationship to God is evidenced by their treatment of the Jews" during the tribulation. More second hand eschatology.

That certain things are seen at the white throne judgment which are not mentioned in the sheep-goat event and vice versa means nothing. There is not one event recorded in Scripture where the *entire* story is given with *every* minute detail. God did not write the Bible that way. If He had, we would have thousands of books to read and study instead of sixty-six. An example of this is seen in the eighteen silent years in the life of Christ. The time blanks in the missionary work of Paul would fill volumes, but they have not been given. The mention of "books" and "the book of life," at the great white throne and not at the sheep-goat event does not necessarily prove that they were different events. Obviously, every event recorded in Scripture, be it a judgment or whatever, gives only part of the story, just a thin sketch of details but never all of them. It is written, "we know in part" (1 Cor. 13:12). The sheep-goat and great white throne judgments were written in this inspired biblical style. *Where God stopped, we had better stop!*

One thing is sure; someone is seriously out of step because we all cannot be right. Truth and error are found in all sides of this debate. Sorting it out is a job that only God can handle. For over fifty years, the author of this harmony commentary has heard the "end-time specialists," "signs authorities," and "I believe the Antichrist is alive today" teachers proclaim their eschatological highs. Jesus is coming but no man knows when. The Bible does not give a "prophetic clock" whereby we may set the date.

When Israel became an independent state in May 1948, prophecy buffs around the world went wild. They assured us that "the end is near, Jesus is coming soon." That was sixty years ago! What is their definition of "soon?" Does it mean "soon," or does it mean a year, two years, sixty years, or hundreds? If it does, we wish they would define their teaching on this point. One will rarely hear these people make this clarifying statement. To them "soon" means "soon," possibly "even today." It cannot mean decades or centuries ahead, even though that is how their predictions turn out, continually wrong, decades and centuries later. If we allow years of "soons" for them to juggle, still their predictions fail. The wise man says, "The Lord is coming, but I don't know when." Today, sober thinking Christians along with Paul in Titus 2:13 are looking for His return but the time is unknown. Prudent men will circumspectly leave off the "soon" or "maybe today" prognostications. All of imagined dates or *near* dates are conjectured from "reading the signs." And they always miss. An elderly Alabama farmer who had lived through sixty years of this irresponsible teaching said, "These people need to get their eyes checked. They can't read right."

For centuries, the *radical* experts have pointed us to hundreds of major events, persons, and signs in world history as "proof that Jesus is coming soon." (The words *"radical"* and *"ultra,"* are mostly in italics across this work when attached to the word dispensationalists to make a clear distinction, because not all dispensationalists are of this stripe.) Their signs include, Halley's Comet, the Russian–Japanese War, the Civil War, First and Second World Wars, the *Protocols of the Learned Elders of Zion*, and the various Antichrists of Nostradamus. Add to this the Pyramids, Palestine Wars, chip implants, Adam Weishaupt's Illuminati, Federal Reserve, the Suez Crisis, Iraqi, oil, the June War, the Six Days War, Adolf Hitler, Andrew Carnegie, King Jan Carlos of Spain, the Popes, Lyndon B. Johnson, Anwar Sadat, Saddam Hussein, George Bush, and countless other Antichrist candidates and signs. Other last day selections have been the alignment of the planets, Y2K, Desert Storm, war in Iraq, almost every major international event, earthquakes, hurricanes, plagues, and famines. Russia's invasion of Georgia (August– September 2008) was hailed as proof of the near end. Now "global warming" is a sure sign of the end. One reading of Gen. 8:22 Corrects this anti-biblical rhetoric. These guesses and "I feel it's this way," shots in the dark, when tested by history and foundational Bible truth, are "spiritual filth" (2 Cor. 7:1).

At the height of World War II in 1942, it was popularly preached in certain evangelical circles across America, "Hitler was the Antichrist and Mussolini the false prophet" of Rev. chapter 13. Paperback books written to this end became best sellers. That was over sixty years ago. The two witnesses of Rev. 11:3 are still being guessed after two thousand years. Some specialists have "studied so deeply" that they know their names! The kings of the east in Rev. 16:12 have been identified as being (almost) everything but Italian pizza. Prophecy barons assure us that their prognostications are right even though they are always proven wrong. What they have learned from end-time prophecy is that they have learned nothing.

For years many of us thought that Communist Russia (USSR), and China were the big bears with whom we would have to deal at the end of the church age. *Time proved us wrong.* Communism has backed off the stage in Russia, while China is rising as the greatest military and economic giant on earth, even to the demise of the USA. Around the world radical Islam, inspired by a million demons of hate defies Christianity, western society, and Israel. Because of these things, some tell us they can predict the near time of Christ's return from the feet and toes of iron and clay (Dan. 2:41-44), or the beast with ten horns and a little horn (Dan. 7:7-8). Just before His ascension, Jesus warned the apostles, "It is not for you to know the times or the seasons, which the Father hath put in his own power" (Acts 1:7). It is amazing that Jesus (as a man in His humanity) *chose* not to know the hour of His mystic return in the destruction of Jerusalem in A.D. 70. See Section 163, Mk. 13:32, footnote v for explanation of this statement. Oddly, today's "experts" know the time or "near time" of His return for the church. Paul told the Thessalonians that they did not need to know "the times and the seasons" (1 Thess. 5:1). For Sir Robert Anderson's faulty calculations about the "seventieth week," refer to Section 123, third paragraph of footnote c. The "revived Roman Empire" of Daniel (the supposed EU) is discussed in *Appendix Eight*.

Most end-timers resent being told they are wrong. Prudent believers who object to their "pin the tail on the donkey" predictions are, "carnal," or "ignorant of God's Word." Over forty years ago in a "Prophecy Conference" at Johannesburg, South Africa, a Christian Jew spoke. He was advertised as a "brilliant authority on the subject of Messiah's soon return." During question time a woman inquired, "Where can I see signs of Jesus' soon return?" He curtly responded, "You need to read the newspapers."

The shame of this eschatological burlesque is that satanic groups operating under the umbrella of Christianity often teach what "Bible believing Christians" propagate. *Both* set dates or near dates for Christ's return from reading "the signs." They are busy naming the Antichrist, identifying the beast, the false prophet, and so forth using their sophisticated charts and eschatological time-lines. The sermons, books, and writings of Seventh Day Adventists, Worldwide Church of God, Jehovah's Witness, and other sects bristle with their (false) "proofs." This prophetic ballyhooing reminds one of the herring in the moonlight: shining brilliantly, but smelling badly. Among these people are voices calling for less sensationalism. A documented examination of this awful problem is, *Armageddon NOW!* by Dwight Wilson. It deals with "date setting" and "signs reading" of Jesus' return over the past one hundred years.

The author heard it preached in 1945, that when Christ returns *every* saved person on earth would be taken out to meet Him in the air. Now, over sixty years later this has changed! We read books and watch movies about backslidden Christians "Left Behind," "great worldwide revivals" with "millions being converted to Christ," *after* the rapture and during the tribulation. Scofield wrote in his Bible that the great tribulation is "a period of salvation," (page 1337, second paragraph of footnote 1). We are told that 144,000 Jews will win millions to Christ, preaching a new kind of gospel in the tribulation. Where do these "missionaries" come from since *all believers* will be removed from earth at the rapture? Not one saved person will be left behind. These Jews cannot be unsaved "itinerate preachers traveling across the world." Where did they come from? Who won them to Messiah-Christ? If they were saved, they would have been taken out with the church of which they were part. Did Christ split His church and leave 144,000 born again Hebrews behind? One can read Rev. 7:1-8 until he is blue in the face and find no answers to these questions. Some run amuck trying to fill in these gaps. Charles C. Ryrie's *Basic Theology,* page 572, states that one can consider these 144,000 Jews as unconverted people! Beyond this joke, when did these Israelites learn *all* the languages of the world in order to accomplish this astounding feat? Presently there are some 6,809 known languages. About four thousand of these have never been put into print! With the "planet convulsing under the wrath of Antichrist," we are told these "Jewish missionaries" will travel to all the Gentile nations and tribes of earth; the jungles of South America, Africa, the sands of the Gobi desert, the mountains of Tibet and Afghanistan, the islands of the seas, and the frozen arctic poles. (Of course, one could always pull a miracle out of the bag!) The teaching that these 144,000 Jews will "bring millions to Christ out of all nations" is wrong. It is another hangover from radical dispensationalism. *Nowhere is it written in Scripture that these "tribulation saints" owe their conversion to thousands of Jewish missionaries.* The word "tribulation" is found four other times in Rev. 1:9, 2:9, 10, and 22. These have reference to suffering Christians in churches almost two thousand years ago. In Rev. 14:1-5, the 144,000 Jewish-Christians are called "firstfruits" believers meaning that they were among the first saved in *early* church history. Because they are the "firstfruits," they cannot be saved during the *future* tribulation, which is yet to occur. Whatever "tribulation they came out of" it cannot be, that future nightmare recorded in the book of Revelation. God did not tell us when these people were saved. Paul wrote of "tribulation" (singular) eight times in his letters; all had reference to sufferings being experienced at the time he wrote. None of these points us to a future tribulation period.

The author cannot reconcile the sheep-goat parable with the rapture of the church. Christians armed with Darby-Bullinger-Scofield-Blackstone-Larkin-Ironside-Walvoord-Ryrie-Pentecost eschatology think they have. What would these men have believed had this material been nonexistent? Postmillennialists, saving the world so Christ can return, have only further muddied the waters. Christ's response to the inquisitive apostles just before His ascension in Act. 1;6-7, has the answer for all of us!

Matthew in penning the sheep-goat lesson wrote only what the Holy Spirit directed. The absence of precise explanations keeps honest people in check; they do not know how it all fits together. Some refuse to force things into the inspired blanks. The Bible does not contain the *totality* of eschatology. What we have is overwhelming! How every piece of this puzzle fits into place, I do not know; nor do I wish to know. What we understand carries with it an overwhelming responsibility. Oddly, it is the dark side of a mirror that gives reflection. We grasp what is understandable, use it to honor our Lord, win the lost, and comfort fellow men. Those segments of life and Scripture we cannot comprehend should be left for later consideration. How comforting to know our God can write on a crooked wall as well as a straight line! The next Section contains the Parable of the Sheep and Goats given by Jesus two days before His death, while sitting with four of His apostles on Mount Olivet (Matt. 25:1-2 with Mk. 13:3-4).

THE PARABLE* OF KING JESUS COMING TO JUDGE ALL NATIONS.

This judgment is expressly associated with His coming as the Son of man in glory (verse 31) and flows out of it. Contextually, it is tied to the preceding two lessons on readiness in Section 165 and 164, and moves from them into the natural conclusion, which is that of final judgment. The time span between the two previous messages and Christ's coming to judge the nations (as seen in this Section) has been at this point in history almost two thousand years: we are still waiting for the latter. The doctrine found here manifestly declares the eternal destinies of the righteous and the wicked that are both called nations. They are symbolically depicted as sheep and goats being individually separated by King Jesus, the Great Shepherd, and appointed their everlasting future.**

Time: Late Tuesday after Palm Sunday. His death was on Friday mid-afternoon.

*Some worthy expositors understand that this is not a parable, rather a message with illustrations. **The statements in the Footnotes below are a straightforward commentary on this Section. Questions regarding the rapture of the church and the judgment seat of Christ, in connection with this parable are only slightly mentioned. The reason for this is that the author is unsure regarding parts of this parable, and the chronological placement of some of its events. It is difficult at the best to be dogmatic about each event in this lesson of our Savior. See the Information Box at symbol ▶ near the top of next page for more on this question of chronology.*

Matt. 25:31-44—*On the western side of the Mount of Olives*	Mk.	Lk.	John
His return to judge			
31 "When **the Son of man shall come**[(a)] **in his glory,**[(b)] and all the holy angels with him, then shall he sit upon the throne of his glory:			
32 "And before him shall be gathered all nations:[(c)] and he shall separate them one from another, as a shepherd divideth *his* sheep from the goats:			
Those symbolized as sheep			
33 "And he shall set the sheep on his right hand, but the goats on the left.[(d)]			
34 "Then shall the King[(e)] say unto them on his right hand, 'Come, ye blessed of my Father, inherit the kingdom prepared for you from the foundation of the world:			
35 'For I was an hungred, and ye gave me meat: I was thirsty, and ye gave me drink: I was a stranger, and ye took me in:			
36 'Naked, and ye clothed me: I was sick, and ye visited me: I was in prison, and ye came unto me.'			
37 "Then shall the righteous answer him, saying, 'Lord, when saw we thee an hungred, and fed *thee*? or thirsty, and gave *thee* drink?[(f)]			
38 'When saw we thee a stranger, and took *thee* in? or naked, and clothed *thee*?			
39 'Or when saw we thee sick, or in prison, and came unto thee?'			
40 "And the King shall answer and say unto them, 'Verily I say unto you, Inasmuch as ye have done *it* unto one of the least of these my brethren,[(g)] ye have done *it* unto me.'			
Those symbolized as goats			
41 "Then shall he say also unto them on the left hand, 'Depart from me, ye cursed,[(h)] into everlasting fire, prepared for the devil and his angels:			
42 "For I was and hungred, and ye gave me no meat: I was thirsty, and ye gave me no drink:			
43 'I was a stranger, and ye took me not in: naked, and ye clothed me not: sick, and in prison, and ye visited me not.'			
44 "Then shall they also answer him, saying, 'Lord, when saw we thee			

Matt. 25:44-46—*On the western side of the Mount of Olives*	Mk.	Lk.	John
an hungered, or athirst, or a stranger, or naked, or sick, or in prison, and did not minister unto thee?' 45 "Then shall he answer them, saying, 'Verily I say unto you, Inasmuch as ye did *it* not to one of the least of these, ye did *it* not to me.'[i] *Two destinies: both are eternal* 46 "And these shall go away into everlasting punishment: but the righteous into life eternal."[j] (Next chap., Matt. 26:1 cont. in Section 167.)			

►The author has made no serious effort to reconcile the two judgments in this Section with any system of eschatology. He has listed some of the opinions given by believers but has no satisfactory solutions for the differences. All problems that exist are first in the mind of the reader, not inspired Scripture. *Extreme* dispensationalism (not yet three hundred years old) parroting C. I. Scofield, assures us that this judgment is to determine who enters the millennium and who is excluded. However, the context reveals the impossibility of this claim. It explicitly declares that the "righteous go away [from this judgment] into eternal life and the wicked into eternal punishment." According to dispensationalists, the entrance into the blessing of "eternal life" is not at the beginning of the millennium (which is limited to a thousand years) but afterwards in "the age to come." This answer puts their eschatological cart before the horse. Others believe that this "entrance" is for both the millennium and the eternal world to follow. Many believe it has nothing to do with the millennium. The famed Milton S. Terry, wrote that this judgment has been operative over all the ages of church history! This is a desperation interpretation from the heart of postmillennialism. See his popular work published in 1883, *Biblical Hermeneutics*, pages 449-450. Because someone wrongly interprets or corrupts a Scripture does not make that passage any less the infallible Word of God. The anvil is not afraid of the hammer. The message as given here by the Savior is but a *small part* of the whole story regarding the sheep-goat judgment. As is the case with all Bible events, only a brief explanation of this time is recorded in the Bible. This curious brevity of finer details missing is another mark of divine inspiration. The problems begin when over-anxious enthusiasts try to fill in the inspired blanks with their personal conjectures, and then persuade themselves to believe that these are established Bible doctrines since the days of the first church.

Footnotes-Commentary

(a) **"When the Son of man shall come."** A partial quotation by selecting specific words from Dan. 7:13, thus shaded in gray. This "coming," as stated here has nothing to do with A.D. 70. Rather, it speaks of our Lord's return to judge all mankind, called "all nations." Up to this point, we have found the Olivet Discourse, to be one almost unbroken message with many of its verses pointing to the great catastrophe which was to take place (and did) at the destruction of Jerusalem and the temple in A.D. 70. *With the present parable, this changes.*

2p-Christ's message in this Section has become another eschatological debating theatre where expositors have differed over the centuries about its meaning. The brutal truth is that postmillennialists, amillennialists, dispensational premillennialists, and historical premillennialists, all struggle to make it compatible with their prior views. These four groups work hard to keep from being wrong in their eschatology. Within *each* school, there is a wide diversity of opinion. A "wiser than Solomon" could not sort it out. It is reiterated that some of the comments in this present Section are the *conjectures* of the author and other commentators. Below, are several of the most popular interpretations offered to explain our Savior's Words:

1. One group believes that this parable has reference first to the final judgment of professing Christians. Yet, goats (or unbelievers out of the nations) are also being judged at this time. This would make it a general judgment of all mankind, but with each group being judged in its order. See number 3 below.

2. Similarly, to the above, another school affirms that this parable is the final judgment of *both* saved and lost at the end of earth's time but not in different settings. Those who hold this reject any idea of a literal millennium. This would make it a *general judgment* of all humanity. It is the same as the great white throne judgment in Rev. 20. The saved are not mentioned as being present in the Revelation passages, they are, nevertheless, there. Those who hold this view have a struggle fitting the words of 1 Thess. 4:13-17 into this scheme. Just as those who hold to the 1 Thessalonian verses have a struggle fitting the sheep and goat event into their eschatology. Something of a new twist to this has emerged over the past twenty years. This different approach affirms that Christ will remove His people, then return to earth and commence separate judgments of both the church (sheep believers), and goats (unbelievers). Next, will follow the millennial period. The problem with this theory is that the great white throne judgment does not occur in the book of Revelation until *after* the thousand years. They usually get around this objection

by stating that those judged at the white throne were the millions born during the thousand years millennial. This curious response to the problem requires several different judgments for the unsaved.

3. Some believe that this is a judgment of living nations at the beginning of the millennium, which comes after the tribulation. This post tribulation judgment was gradually introduced into the eschatological arena about two hundred years ago. Before this, it was unknown in the first seventeen hundred years of church history. One can check any of the hundreds of commentaries written prior to A.D. 1800, and this theory will not be found in relation to Matt. 25:31-46. It was hatched by John Darby and popularized by C. I. Scofield. Then it was presented to the Christian public as *established* Bible doctrine. It is impossible to believe that the church was without this "truth" for almost two thousand years! Only the most naive would embrace a teaching unknown for the first seventeen hundred years of Christian history. This is the approach to Scripture of every cult working under the guise of Christianity.

4. This is something of a blurred revision of number 3 above. It states that Christ will return at the conclusion of the seven-year tribulation and "sit upon the throne of His glory." Then, all the Gentile nations of the world that were good to the Hebrew remnant (who preached the gospel during the tribulation) will be granted admission into the thousand-year reign. Those who were not benevolent to the "Jewish tribulation missionaries," are the "goats" and will be cast into hell. As explained in number 3 above, this novel eschatology was basically invented by John Darby and then popularized by C. I. Scofield, through the footnotes of his Bible. As previously stated, it is the height of absurdity to teach that these sheep-men are qualified for entrance into the millennial period for assisting Jews, while the goats are cast into hell for not helping these people. Men are only saved by what Christ accomplished on the cross. On salvation *before* the cross, refer to Section 144, footnote i.

5. Though hard to believe, some understand this to speak of the judgment of those among the world's Gentile nations who have never heard the saving gospel of Christ. They are judged based on how they have treated believers in Christ. A truth mostly overlooked is that men go to hell not because they reject Christ, but because they are natural and inherent sinners. Unless this sin is atoned for and pardoned, they will die doomed. Thousands have never heard of Jesus in *truth* to reject or receive Him. If rejecting Him brings damnation, then we must not take the gospel to them. Therefore, they cannot reject Him and be lost. By withholding the gospel from these pagans, we can assure that they cannot refuse the Son of God, and thus have secured themselves a home in heaven! All such reasoning is erroneous. For heathens knowing *fragments* of the saving gospel, see Section 1, Part 2, third paragraph of footnote f.

6. A final hypothesis is that Christ in concluding His Olivet Discourse, simply took the church (which is called sheep in John 10:11), and on this occasion placed them into the same time frame as the judgment of the goats. He did this so His four apostles would understand. However, in reality, it cannot be this way for there will be a lengthy chronology between the sheep and goat judgments. Honest people familiar with Scripture can instantly see conflict in this proposed system. A reading of, *The Rapture: Pre,-Mid-or Post–Tribulation,* by Archer, Jr., Feinberg, Moo and Reiter, demonstrate the scope of the diversity among men concerning eschatological matters. The differences regarding this subject will never be resolved. Woe be the Christians, in certain circles, who only slightly disagree with the "experts" on some infinitesimal point. In some churches, he will be doomed! There are genuine Christians, who walk with Christ and yet embrace a wide and odd variety of beliefs about eschatology. For a review of the vast difference among believers regarding end time subjects and their finer points, see *Appendix Eight.*

(b) As stated in footnote a above, the Lord Jesus begins this parable (if indeed it is that) by a general quotation from Dan. 7:13-14, which in the context speaks of the final judgment of the world, and the establishing of Messiah's kingdom. He interprets Himself to be the Son of man that Daniel had written about some five hundred years prior. The Savior had earlier cited this same Old Testament quotation in Matt. 16:27-28. With each of these quotes, the Savior adjusted the Scripture wording to apply to the particular points that were being stressed.

2p-The opening statement of Christ in this final lesson of the Olivet Discourse is a declaration of His return. He will be accompanied by "holy angels," called "King," and will "sit upon the throne of his glory." The angels will act as witnesses and executors of His will. Our Lord said something almost identical much earlier in Matt. 19:28 and Mk. 8:38. *It must be remembered that these verses do not speak of the destruction of Jerusalem in A.D. 70.* There are some seven different passages in the New Testament, which state that when the Lord comes again, angels will accompany Him. With several doublets, these are Matt. 13:41, 49; 16:27; 24:31; 25:31; Mk. 8:38; with parallel in Lk. 9:26; Mk. 13:27; and 2 Thess. 1:7. Whatever exegesis one places upon these passages, they all affirm that Jesus will return to this world escorted by holy angels. Those who see numerous comings of our Lord, and then attempt to fit the difficult verses into these (to solve the mystery) are playing games with Scripture. The author has counted at least *eight* different returns of Christ, invented by the present day "experts." They are the rapture, revelation, visible, invisible, first, second, intermediate, and immediate. Several of these also are doublets. In addition, they have created a series of extra resurrections. Clearly, somebody has gone too far in trying to figure out all the pinpoint details of our Lord's return and subsequent events. There looms the fact that God, in His wisdom, has not intended for little man to know *all* finer and deeply technical points about the coming of His Son. Those who cross this line and remain, fall into fragmented forms of exaggerated and extra-biblical doctrine. Evidence of this is abundant on every hand. Another gap in final events without explanation is found in Paul's words to the Corinthians, "we [believers] shall judge angels" (1 Cor. 6:3). At what point will this occur? Could it be at the judgment seat or white throne and yet not mentioned in Scripture as occurring at these places? Guesswork does not answer these questions.

(c) **Verse 32. "All nations."** This judgment of "all nations" is linked to the coming of the Son of man in verse 31, and it must include Israel, for there has never been a nation like her in world history! To read, "all nations," and then exclude Israel is incorrect. This would make "all," not mean "all," but only part of "all nations." Expositors that make this a mystic, invisible, event occurring when Jerusalem fell are wrong. In the doom of A.D. 70, all nations did not appear before King Christ on His throne for the separation between the righteous and wicked. At this writing in 2011, there are a hundred and ninety three nations on earth with some seven billion people. It is overwhelming to imagine this ocean of humanity standing before Christ in judgment. Zechariah 14:9 speaks of a time when "the LORD shall be king over all the earth." To make this an invisible spiritual kingship seems senseless. For other comments on this, see Section 169, fourth through sixth paragraph, footnote f.

2p-The common sight of an eastern shepherd dividing sheep from the goats *one at a time*, explains the procedure of this judgment. Christ had earlier spoken of other negative and positive mixtures being separated at the end by judgment. We have the wheat and tares (Matt. 13:25), and the good and bad fish (Matt. 13:48). Now, two days before the cross He gives a similar lesson in the separation of sheep and goats. Nowhere in the New Testament can one find the slightest hint that these Gentile nations "came out of the tribulation period." To take the nations of Rev. 7:9 and 14 and make them become the nations of Matt. 25:32 is unwarranted when contextually *nothing* of the sort is slightly inferred. *It must be forced to read this way.* This approach was invented by anxious expositors trying to put the whole picture together when inspiration did not. Often Joel 3:2-21 is forced to refer to this national judgment. Historically, and contextually, Joel's predictions happened with the return of Israel from Babylonian captivity hundreds of years before the birth of Christ.

3p-As stated, "end-time specialists" teach that the sheep or Gentile nations of the world will be judged based on their works as they helped the preaching missionary Jews during the tribulation. And this Jewish remnant of 144,000 missionaries won these Gentiles to Jesus during this terrible time of world history. Arno C. Gaebelein, in his book, *The Gospel According to Matthew*, II, page 247, teaches this. Dwight Pentecost in, *Things to Come*, pages 415–422, pulls selected verses from the Old Testament and makes them fit into a "Jewish, tribulation, Gentile" scenario without historical or contextual basis. Nowhere in Scripture does it intimate that these sheep-people were saved through the preaching of 144,000 Hebrew evangelists. This conjecture is without one shred of evidence. The natural feel of the sheep and goat story is that these are individual people, saved and made righteous from all nations of the earth, and are judged by King Jesus. Sheep-nations here represent billions of redeemed individuals while goat-nations symbolize billions of unsaved individuals. Never, has any *entire* nation been converted to Jesus Christ and never will there be. *Matthew was speaking of single persons among earth's billions while using "nations" as a collective form of speech.* Revelation 21:24 speaks of millions of saved Gentiles from their former lands that were described collectively as "nations." This may have been predicted seven hundreds years earlier in Isa. 60:3-5.

4p-**Bless the Jews and God will bless you!** *Ultra* dispensationalism teaches that America and Britain have been superabundantly blessed because various political administrations have shown goodness to Israel. This is based on God's statement to Abraham in Gen. 12:1-3. The *prime reason* for God's mercy on America is not her aid to Israel or anyone else. It is because there has always been a remnant of saved believers, who have honored His Word and Son. As a rule, Israel is opposed to the message of Jesus the Messiah. God favors no one who hates His blessed Son and curses at the mention of His Name. It is incorrect to teach that we will be kept, protected, and blessed as long as we are kind to our friend Israel. It is "Righteousness [that] exalteth a nation," not being good to Israel or any other ethnic group (Prov. 14:34). The sheep spoken of by Christ were saved believers wherever they came from.

(d) **"Sheep on the right, goats on the left."** Shepherds continually did just this in separating their flocks. Sheep were economically more valuable than goats, hence they were always sent to the right side. The ancient Jews had many curious sayings. They held that with Jehovah, there was a right and a left side. It was held that if the officiating priest handling the sin offering should sprinkle the blood with his left hand, he was instantly disqualified. This is written in the Talmud tractate, Zevachim 24a. So sensitive was the subject of "left hand and right hand," that they are mentioned in the Talmud four hundred and twenty-one times! During Sanhedrin Court sessions, a scribe stood on the right and left sides of the court. The one on the right wrote the sentence for acquittal, while the one on the left penned the condemnation. Possibly, our Lord alluded to this well-known custom in this parable. Somehow, the symbolism of right and left represented good and bad, acceptance and rejection. This distinction has been carried over into the political realm as well. Men speak of those on the "left" and on the "right." Christ's four apostles understood His usage of these terms. Today, the western mind struggles with such things. For Jesus' instructions to fish "on the right side," and the history of the "right" and "left," see Section 205, second paragraph of footnote e.

(e) Verse 34. "The King." Here, for the first and only time the Lord Jesus *gave Himself* this title. Prior, in the context of this same message He was "the Son of man" (verse 31). Now, He is King. Some see in this title proof that this begins His rule on earth, and that He has just been crowned King of Kings. The background of His life reveals that He was *already* King when he came with His angels. He was born King according to Matt. 2:2. Days before, when He rode into Jerusalem, He was hailed by the people for fulfilling the Old Testament prediction of being Israel's King (Zech. 9:9 with Matt. 21:4-5). Nathanael had called Jesus "the king of Israel" in John 2:49, at the beginning of His ministry. At the end of His ministry, Governor Pilate inquired of our Lord, "Art thou the King of the Jews?" (Matt. 27:11). It should be noted that Jesus answered his question in the affirmative. The apostle Paul wrote that Christ was King long before this, even before John penned the book of Revelation. He stated this in 1 Tim. 1:17 with 6:15. In the book of Hebrews, Christ was made *both* priest and King, "after the order of" (or like) Melchisedec (Heb. 5:6, 10) when he ascended back to heaven. *The point is that our Lord had been King for thousands of years before His return for the sheep-goat judgment.* That He will be suddenly be crowned, preparatory for the coming millennium is centuries too late. Jesus' depiction in Rev. 14:14, as "the Son of man" with a golden crown reflects something that had been true for thousands of years. His return to earth with "many crowns on his head" (Rev. 19:12), is the result of these crowns being previously given to Him by the twenty-four elders who represent millions of believers (Rev. 4:10). He has always been the King of the Jews and all humanity though mostly unaccepted. Using verse 34 as proof that Christ has now become King and will enter the millennium is locking the barn door after the horse has been stolen.

2p-At the beginning of His message, Christ projects into the future for His preachers and declares that He will (in time) descend to earth in glory, as King, with the holy angels. (It has been explained that His disciples at this time did not understand His death, resurrection, and ascension, much less his second coming for the church.) We learn from other verses that all the heavenly members of His spiritual kingdom who went to be with Him at physical death (1 Thess. 3:13, 4:14) will accompany him. Those living at this kingly coming of Christ will be judged individually; some are typified as sheep others as goats. Entire single nations consisting of millions of people will not be judged in one lump sum. How this fits into the great white throne judgment of Rev. 20, we do not know, or how the great white throne fits into the sheep-goat judgment is also a mystery. (There is the possibility that they do not fit!) Postmillennialists make both judgments the same and escape the facts of Revelation by spiritualizing them into the past. Neither the over literalizing of *hyper* premillennialists, nor the super spiritualizing of the postmillennialists harmonizes the sheep-goat judgment with the white throne judgment. The first school turns molehills into mountains, while the second turns mountains into molehills.

3p-A truth previously stated is that no major event recorded anywhere in the Bible has the *whole* story or every detail given. Only the parts are recorded that God wanted us to have. The fact that the white throne judgment does not mention certain things, and the sheep and goat lesson does not mention particular things means nothing. Scofield made this mistake when he wrote on page 1036, footnote 1 These words, "This judgment is to be distinguished from the great white throne. Here, there is no resurrection; the persons judged are living nations; no books are opened; three classes are present, sheep, goats, and brethren; the time is at the return of Christ (verse 31); and the scene is on earth." Ryrie follows the same line in *Basic Theology*, pages 576-577. Silence is a poor foundation on which to build. Is not the book of Revelation silent about the sheep-goat judgment? Only Matthew wrote about this event. The *whole* story about eschatology and final judgments is not given in Scripture. If every detail of both judgments were recorded, we would have dozens of books to study instead of the condensed records of Matthew and John. We are to believe what is written, without a word-for-word exhaustive explanation of each detail. This, many expositors refuse to do. Some of them fill in the missing parts and this is where the trouble begins.

4p-Verse 34. "Come ye [sheep] blessed of my Father." This cannot mean the billions that make up earth's Gentile nations were saved. It speaks of individual persons or sheep within these nations. *Entire* nations are not saved, nor have they ever been. Such is foreign to Christian history. God redeems individuals in the nations of the world but (as explained) never has an entire nation of millions been converted to Christ. The Bible says nothing about God saving corporate nationalities at one time. Jesus uses the plural word "nations" as a euphemism for individuals. Each one is symbolically illustrated in one sheep or goat at a time. The word "nation" in singular and plural is found sixty-three times in the New Testament. Not one of them speaks of an entire nationality being saved. Individual sheep saints are invited to enter the future blessings of His kingdom. They had previously entered the spiritual kingdom of God at the new birth (John 3:3). Looking into eternity ahead, Christ invites them to inherit the everlasting spiritual benefits of this glorious kingdom. All of this takes place at the return of King Jesus.

5p-"Inherit the kingdom prepared for you from the foundation of the world." Only imagination can make this a *singular* Jewish thing, planned from the beginning of time. A material kingdom consisting of bricks, mortar, garbage pick up, earth, and temporal substance, human flesh, running hot and cold water, toilets, sewerage, electricity, and other necessities is not intended here. It will not be the imaginary kingdom cooked up by end-time specialists, who speak of babies being born, people dying, some having glorified bodies while others do not. Nor will Israel as a nation function in a rebuilt temple, offering again blood sacrifices to Jehovah. Human flesh and blood cannot be part of God's Kingdom (1 Cor. 15:50), and sin is banished from its domain (Gal. 5:21). Christ had earlier promised His disciples, "Fear not, little flock; for it is your Father's good pleasure to give you the kingdom" (Lk. 12:32). God has chosen "the poor of this world rich in faith, and heirs of the kingdom which he hath promised to them that love him" (James 2:5). This kingdom "is not meat and drink; but righteousness, and peace, and joy in the Holy Ghost" (Rom. 14:17). The kingdom prepared from the foundation of the world will be everlastingly perfect. And as stated above it is entered by the new birth (John 3:3). The *spiritual manifestation* of Christ's Church had been a reality since the days of John the Baptist, who introduced it. The inheritance given here has reference to future blessings and not those received during human life on earth. This does not negate a *future* kingdom consisting of the redeemed of Israel in a perfect and glorified condition as members of the body of Christ. In eternity there will not be saved Jews living on one side of the fence and saved Gentiles on the other!

6p-Scofield wrote that this sheep-goat judgment takes place just *before* the millennial begins; that it points to saved nations and the church, ruling over millions of unsaved people. A 144,000 Jewish missionary evangelists supposedly won these nations to Christ during the tribulation. An examination of the word "nations" in the book of Revelation is helpful. Revelation 7:9-14 reveals masses that came out of "great tribulation" from among all nations. It does not tell us what "great tribulation" they came out of and when. *These people were with God and the Lamb before the horrors of the real tribulation began in the following chapters.* This is not a judgment scene but one of consolation. Later, during the real tribulation, we read in Rev. 11:18, that the nations are angry with God because of His wrath upon them. In Rev. 13:7 and 14:8, a person called "the beast" overcomes nations. In Rev. 14:8 with 18:3, all nations are influenced (made drunk) by the intoxicating wine from a city called Babylon. Revelation 15:4 reveals that all nations will subjectively worship God. The verses in Rev. 17:1 and 15, depict the Gentile nations as troubled waters yielding to the authority of the great harlot. Revelation 18:23 states that the nations had been deceived by satanic sorceries. Lastly, Rev. 20:3 states that Satan deceived the nations. Nowhere in the Bible does it say that these nations assisted thousands of Jewish evangelists *during the real tribulation*. This was added to the story by Scofield. Revelation 12:5 and 19:15, reveals that Christ will destroy the wicked nations by treading them in the winepress of divine wrath; then He will rule the world. Christians will in some way share in this blissful rule according to Rev. 2:26-27 with 2 Tim. 2:12. This kingdom yet to come will not be a knock-down-drag-out-affair with the toughest man ruling! Peace will reign "as the waters that cover the sea" (Isa. 11:9). For more on this time of real peace, see fifth paragraph of footnote e above. In God's time, King Jesus will reign over a glorified earth, and all believers will somehow share in this glorious time. The minute details are not given in Scripture. When a subject is not fully clear in Scripture, it is because God has put it that way. Wise Christians refrain from the wild speculations regarding the reign of Christ. For timely comments on this reign, see Section 171, fourth and fifth paragraphs of footnote b.

7p-**Verses 35-37**. Charitable deeds were standard practice in Jewish ethics of this time among themselves but were not ensued among the Gentiles. The individual sheep deeds seem to reflect that they were benevolent towards others. The ancient Jews made a big noise about assisting the needy, clothing the naked, feeding those hungry, but especially visiting the sick. So important was the latter that it was allowed on the Sabbath day according to the Talmud tractates, Shabbath 12a and 127b. In these texts, it is described as "a loving deed." The sheep were called "righteous" (verse 37), because the imputed righteousness of Christ was freely received at the time of salvation.

8p-The teaching that these Gentile "sheep nations" consisting of billions are won to Christ by Jewish preachers amid the earth-shattering time known as the tribulation period is ludicrous. We have wondered how *all* the Gentile nations of the world (presently in 2011, there are one hundred ninety three of them) can visit Hebrews in prison, take them food, water and clothing amid the horrors of worldwide devastation, wars and disaster? For example, how will the Gentiles, who make up Sweden and Denmark travel thousands of miles from Scandinavia to the Holy Land to aid suffering Jews? It would take years for millions of Swedes and Danes to enter all the prisons, the hospitals in their part of the world, and visit hurting Jews during these terrible times. This does not take into consideration the remaining Gentile nations of the entire world doing the same thing! A hundred and ninety-three Gentile nations traveling over the globe assisting Jews, who were naked, hungry, incarcerated, or hospitalized is a myth. Even worse, amid all this, we are told that one-third of the human race will be killed during this time!

(f) *To be humble and not know it is one of the greatest jewels set in a believer's life.* Giving to others, while genuinely expecting nothing in return is the way of Christ. This had been the testimony of the sheep believers now standing before the Chief Shepherd of the flock, the King of Kings and Lord of Lords. Blessed is the man who can give without remembering and receive without forgetting. So amazed were they at what He said that their question came spontaneously "When did we do these things, Lord?" This inquiry comes from the innocence void of covert thoughts of good being returned. To teach that "hungered," "thirsty," "stranger," "naked," "sick," and "in prison," speak only of the tribulation is wrong. Men have been in these straights since the beginning and will be to the end. It is impossible that *every person* of the billions of these "sheep nations" were "good to Jews in the tribulation."

(g) Verse 40. Who are "My brethren." How amazing that the majestic King, amid the rigors of an awful judgment would hold conversation with those being judged, even answering the questions of His sheep people (verses 37-39). The King's reply is puzzling. Present at that judgment scene was a third group called "my brethren." There is great debate about the identity of Christ's "brethren" who were the benefactors of the charitable work of the sheep believers. During His public ministry, the Savior identified "His brethren," as those who do the will of God. Refer to Section 69, Matt. 12:46-50, footnote d for explanation. He called His disciples "brethren" in Matt. 28:10. Some think these "brethren" were those millions among God's sheep, who have struggled through life, having nothing, hurting, and burdened down with the trials of human time. If so, here the Son of God recognizes them with honor. Whoever they are, they were saved people who had lived lives of suffering. It is exegetical desperation to assert that these "brethren" will be Jews, who passed through the tribulation. The *Ryrie Study Bible*, footnote on page 1387 states, "This is a judgment of those Gentiles, who survive the tribulation and whose heart relationship to God is evidenced by their treatment of the Jews, especially during that time." Ryrie makes a grand guess when he concludes, "Surviving Jews will also be judged at this time." This Plaster of Paris hermeneutics used to fill the inspired vacancies in eschatology. Ryrie's assumption is nowhere intimated in this message given by Christ. Dwight Pentecost presents the same line in *The Words & Works of Jesus Christ,* pages 409-410. The teaching that Jesus' brethren means saved Jews, who suffered (sick, hungry, and naked) during the tribulation and were supported by Gentile nations is without a shred of support. We dare not guess our way through any difficult Bible verse.

2p-Honesty dictates that there are no "Jewish, great tribulation, or Gentile distinction" found here. Never did the Savior use the word "brethren" to denote *singly* the nation of Israel. Of all redeemed Jews and Gentiles, it is written that Jesus, "Is not ashamed to call them brethren" (Heb. 2:11). Brotherhood with Christ is not based on genetics, but a spiritual relationship acquired by faith in His finished work of redemption.

3p-Verse 40. "Ye have done *it* unto me." Christ knows no difference between Himself and His little flock or body of believers, "For we are members of his body, of his flesh, and of his bones" (Eph 5:30). This mystical union between the Lord Jesus and His children is the highest of spiritual things. To feed a fellow believer in great straits, to put a blanket over a cold trembling body, a cup of milk to that starving child is as though it were done to the Son of God, the King! A *fable* in early church history relates that a Roman soldier named Felix, who was a Christian, entered a village one freezing night. A cold, shivering, and ragged old man begging for help met him. Having nothing to give, Felix removed his coat and handed it to the stranger. That night Felix had a dream. He saw heaven, and all the angelic hosts gathered. Suddenly, the Lord Jesus appeared, wearing a ragged Roman soldier's coat. Gabriel inquired, "Master, why are you wearing that old worn out garment?" The Savior answered softly, "Felix gave it to me last night!" This ancient fable explains the meaning of Matt. 25:40 and Heb. 13:2.

4p-While serving as principal of a small Bible school in Queensland, Australia, during the late 1960s, I noticed one of my students frequently vanished on Thursday afternoons during off time. Later, I learned that he drove some 25 kilometers (one way) up the coast to a nearby fishing village and mowed the grass of a poor widow, Molly Bowman. Molly is now in heaven, and Kevin is a tottering old man. He and his wife Dawn, were used of God many years in Christian service. This example illustrates what Jesus said in the Words, "Ye have done *it* unto me." Today, the Savior requires a benevolence that reflects the heart of God in receiving its enemies with the holy embrace of Christian love. Our Lord had earlier spoken of this in Section 45, Matt. 5:44-48.

(h) Verse 41. "Depart from me, ye cursed." The goat people were not nations coming out of the tribulation. They reflected outwardly their emptiness inwardly and represent millions over the ages who have hated the Lord Jesus, despised the Bible, persecuted, and even murdered the sheep of God. Among these goats are the courteous "thank you, no thank you" masses, who think, a God of love does not punish unforgiven sin.

2p-"Everlasting fire." Those who deny the eternal *conscious suffering* of the damned struggle with this passage. The Seventh Day Adventists affirm that damnation was only "prepared for the devil and his angels," therefore, it is not for men! They hold that all sinners will be annihilated into ashes at the last judgment. This is a satanic-demonic lie. Christ the Judge says that the "goats" are going into "everlasting punishment" (verse 46). The punishment of the wicked is unalterable (Rev. 14:11). No eternal ash pile is intended here. Walter T. Rea gives a devastating examination of the mentally deranged co-founder of the Adventist law cult, in *The White Lie.* For twenty-one things the Bible says about hell, see Section 103, number 8, under footnote g. In Matt. 8:29, even demons confess their dread of torment. Cults should learn from these evil spirits!

(i) Verse 45. "Ye did *it* not to me." See third paragraph of footnote g above for our Lord's opposite verdict pronounced on the sheep people. The sheep were saved children of God. Putting this strictly into the horrors of the tribulation is beyond imagination: It is going on now around the world! No one is sentenced to eternal hell for not visiting those in prison, or the sick, clothing the naked, and so forth. These goats represented millions who were unsaved. God's estimate of earth's nations is recorded in Isa. 40:15-17.

(j) Summary review of both verdicts. "Fire" is the punishment of the goat people, while "life" denotes the blessing of the sheep saints. The adjective "everlasting" describes the duration of both sentences. No form of annihilation can be described as carrying "everlasting punishment." *Cults tell us it is unconscious suffering!* The destiny of the sheep and goats is a knowing, wakened consciousness in heaven or hell. The sheep are described as "the righteous," it is obvious that the goats are not. How men are made righteous before heaven's King is found in Rom. 3:22-23. The goat's absence of divine righteousness was the source of their doom. This absence was due to their unsaved condition before the King on His throne.

JESUS INFORMS THE APOSTLES THAT PASSOVER IS TWO DAYS* OFF.

He speaks of His betrayal and soon death. The Sanhedrin conspires to capture Him without drawing public attention. They fear the crowds gathered for Passover will be drawn into a massive public uproar.

The Savior's lengthy Olivet Discourse contained in Sections 163 through 166 is now ended. He turns His attention to the little band of distraught apostles struggling to understand His Words about dying, and the destruction of their beloved Jerusalem and temple. The predictions in Mal. 4:5 are considered as occurring at the crucifixion of Christ in A.D. 30, and the fall of Jerusalem in A.D. 70. See Section 134, fourth paragraph of footnote k for more on this.

Time: Late Tuesday our time or into Wednesday Jewish time.
---

*This harmony commentary has conjectured that all the biblically recorded activities of Jesus from Section 151, through Section 166 possibly occurred over Tuesday after the Palm Sunday ride into Jerusalem. This is only a thought for it is also possible that part of these events would have occurred over into Wednesday as well. Mystery greatly shrouds most of our Savior's activities during these "two days" before Passover as mentioned in verse 2 below. We only have brief information about the meeting of the religious leaders to apprehend Him. In Section 168, the Savior sends Peter and John to purchase the lamb for the Passover meal. (The animal had to be taken to the temple for slaughtering by the officiating priest and then to the upper room for cooking.) Lastly, we note an argument among the twelve apostles before the actual Passover commences and Jesus washing their feet in the upper room (Sections 169-170).

In or near the city of Jerusalem

Matt. 26:1-5	Mk. 14:1-2	Lk. 22:1-2	John
Two days to the cross **1** And it came to pass, when Jesus had finished all these sayings, [in Matt. 24-25] he said unto his disciples, **2** "Ye know that after two days is *the feast*[a] of the passover, and the Son of man is betrayed to be crucified."	◄ *Verses 1 and 2 reveal that Jesus finished His Olivet warnings on Tuesday before Passover at sunset Thursday.* **1** After two days was *the feast*[a] *of the* passover, and of unleavened bread:	**1** Now the feast[a] of unleavened bread drew nigh, which is called the Passover. ◄ *In the original 1611, KJV Bible, Passover is printed in the uppercase in Matthew and Mark as well. It is spelled "Passeouer" in the 1611 version.*	
The Jews plot to kill Him **3** Then assembled together the chief priests,[b] and the scribes, and the elders of the people, unto the palace of the high priest, [at Jerusalem] who was called Caiaphas, **4** And consulted that they might take Jesus by subtilty,[c] and kill *him*. **5** But they said, "Not on the feast *day*, lest there be an uproar[d] among the people." (Verse 6 cont. in Section 146.)	***The Jews plot to kill him*** and the chief priests[b] and the scribes sought how they might take him by craft,[c] and put *him* to death. **2** But they said, "Not on the feast *day*, lest there be an uproar[d] of the people." (Verse 3 cont. in Section 146.)	***The Jews plot to kill Him*** **2** And the chief priests[b] and scribes sought how they might kill him;[c] for they feared[d] the people. (Verse 3 cont. in Section 147.)	

Footnotes-Commentary

(a) **"After two days the Passover."** This passage dates for us when the Lord Jesus finished His Olivet Discourse. It was two days before the Passover. For a general timetable of the events that led up to this statement, see Section 150, the two asterisks under main heading. After completing His lengthy warnings, in Sections 163 through 166, he concluded with a final notice about His betrayal and crucifixion as seen above. It has been pointed out repeatedly that His closest apostles did not yet understand about the cross, His death, burial, and resurrection.

2p-**Passover and Unleavened Bread were blended.** Because the Feast of Unleavened Bread followed immediately on the heels of the one-day Passover celebration, the Jews over time blended the two together as seen above in Mk. 14:1, where both are called the same. Refer also to the next Section 168, Mk. 14:12, footnote a where they are again counted as the same, though, in fact, they were not. The older Jews would not confuse the two celebrations, while the younger generation freely blended them together as being one. This answers the question as to why they are spoken of as different in some verses and the same in others. The inspired Scriptures described these things as they were. Today, men wrangling with these matters often point their fingers at God and mutter questionable things about the record of Scripture. In the book, *Chronological and Background Charts of the New Testament*, page 81, by H. Wayne House, a drawing purports to show that the Galileans reckoned the Passover time differently from the people of Judaea. However, this is fraught with conjecture. To believe that a sect of Jews in Galilee or anywhere else would observe Passover by a totally different time scale other than that decreed by the Sanhedrin and the Torah Law seems absurd. Yet, Israel was riddled with religious factions. Sectarian groups were everywhere within Judaism. However, mainstream Judaism accepted no one who did not adhere tenaciously to the finest jots and tittles of the great Torah Law. The hypocritical religious leaders adjusted their laws to fit their carnal self-interests. This double standard is explained in Section 96. It was noted in Section 9, footnote b that Jews from Galilee were looked upon as being ignorant country bumpkins by those who resided in Judaea, near Jerusalem, and the temple. Because a statement in Scripture is not clear to us does not mean that it is wrong. Rather, it means we do not have all the facts about that statement. Pointing a finger at God's Word because something is difficult to comprehend by modern day standards is hardly a mark of "academic excellence." Rather, it is childish immaturity at its worst. Real maturity is when you can see with your heart, not your eyes.

(b) This was probably a meeting of the Sanhedrin in Caiaphas' palace located at the western side of Jerusalem on the hill called Mount Zion. Concerning the academic objection of the Sanhedrin meeting anywhere other than their temple, refer to Section 182, Matt. 27:1, footnote a. The Lord Jesus, by preaching truth, healing thousands, and blessing suffering humanity, had caused the Sanhedrin to call many emergency sessions! He was their great nemesis, and they feverishly sought to destroy Him. Matthew identifies the high priest for his Hebrew readers, which suggests that some of them were not familiar with that part of their history. This may have been for the benefit of the younger Jews, who read his letter after these events were history and not well known to them.

(c) **"Take him by craft."** This reflects the utter abandon and sheer wickedness of the Jewish religious leaders. It is *conjectured* that Judas was also present at this meeting. We have harmonized the traitor as abruptly leaving Mary's house a few days earlier and going to Jerusalem to bargain with the Jews, following Christ's rebuke of him. This is explained in the main heading of Section 147.

(d) **"But they said."** This was the consensus of the Sanhedrin. With all their plotting and scheming there was a nagging feeling that something might go amuck and the thousands present for the feast be drawn into this conflict. Their hypocrisy flares as they worry about desecrating the Passover, yet plot, and kill the Son of God on that holy occasion. The looming danger of a mob uprising during the annual feast would have instantly brought hundreds of Roman soldiers into the temple precincts and thus rendered the whole occasion unclean and invalid in Jewish thinking. Such would have been a national calamity for Israel. Refer to Acts 21:27-36 for an example of the pagan army of Rome breaking up a temple riot about twenty-five years after the events described in this Section. Israel's religious leaders had bitter memories of their temple being defiled. On one occasion, the hated Samaritans had slipped into the temple at midnight during the Feast of Unleavened Bread, and scattered the bones of dead men in the cloisters seeking to stop the seven-day celebration. Pursuant to this act of religious sabotage all Samaritans were summarily banned from the temple and guards were posted to enforce this command. See Section 133, footnote e for the story of a Samaritan being healed by Jesus but could not go to the temple at Jerusalem to give thanks, and what he did. This banning did not include Samaritans, who were proselytes to the Jewish religion.

2p-The following Sections 168 through 207, introduce us to the night before the morning of the cross and events leading up to Jesus' ascension. These include His curious instructions to Peter and John to prepare for the Passover observance. We see the washing of feet, the Passover meal, and the establishment of the communion or Lord's Supper, His notice of the coming Holy Spirit in fullness, the betrayal of Judas, His arrest, and Peter's denial. Lastly, there remained at the end of His human journey the mock trials at the hands of false religion and corrupt politics, His cross of shame and suffering, and that glorious morning of eternal resurrection. His final hours on earth after resurrection were designed to convince them that He had arisen from the grave. Next, He issued instructions about His work for all succeeding ages and returned to the Father in heaven.

Peter and John receive curious instructions to prepare for Passover in an upper room at Jerusalem. Our Lord explains His longing to have this meal with His apostles. It will be their final, earthly Passover with the Savior.*

Time: Thursday, before His death on Friday mid-afternoon.

*For Jesus' first Passover as Messiah and those following that led up to this final one, see Section 29, and italicized note attached to John 2:13, footnote a.

On the road from Bethany and in the city of Jerusalem

Matt. 26:17–18	Mk. 14:12–15	Lk. 22:7–12	John
Go and prepare	*Go and prepare*	*Go and prepare*	
17 Now the first *day* of the *feast of* unleavened bread[(a)]	**12 And the first day of unleavened bread,**[(a)] **when they killed the passover,**	**7 Then came the day of unleavened bread,**[(a)] **when the passover must be killed.**	
the disciples came to Jesus, saying unto him, "Where wilt thou that we prepare for thee to eat the passover?"	his disciples said unto him, "Where wilt thou that we go and prepare that thou mayest eat the passover?"		
	13 And he sendeth forth two of his disciples, and saith unto them, "Go ye into the city,	**8** And he sent Peter and John, saying, "Go and prepare us the passover, that we may eat."	
18 And he said, "Go into the city			
	▶ *Luke places their question after Jesus' command. Matthew and Mark place it before as seen in verses 17 and 12 above.*	**9** ◄And they said unto him, "Where wilt thou that we prepare?"	
		Follow a man with a pitcher	
		10 And he said unto them, "Behold, when ye are entered into the city, there shall	
Follow a man with a pitcher	*Follow a man with a pitcher*		
to such a man,[(b)]	and there shall meet you a man[(b)] bearing a pitcher of water: follow him.	a man[(b)] meet you, bearing a pitcher of water; follow him into the house where he entereth in	
	14 "And wheresoever he shall go in, say ye to		
and say unto him, 'The Master saith, "My time is at hand; I will keep the passover at thy house with my disciples." '	the goodman [lord or owner] of the house, 'The Master saith, "Where is the guestchamber, where I shall eat the passover with my disciples?" '	**11** "And ye shall say unto the goodman [lord or owner] of the house, 'The Master saith unto thee, "Where is the guestchamber, where I shall eat the passover with my disciples?" '	
	15 "And he will shew you a large upper room furnished[(c)] *and* prepared:	**12** "And he shall shew you a large upper room furnished:[(c)]	

Matt. 26:19–20	Mk. 14:15–17	Lk. 22:12–16	John
His Word was true **19** And the disciples did as Jesus had appointed them; and they made ready^(d) the passover. **20** Now when the even was come,^(e) he sat down with the twelve. (Verse 21 cont. in Section 172.)	there make ready for us." *His Word was true* **16** And his disciples went forth, and came into the city, and found as he had said unto them: and they made ready^(d) the passover. **17** And in the evening he cometh^(e) with the twelve. (Verse 18 cont. in Section 172.)	there make ready." *His Word was true* **13** And they went, and found as he had said unto them: and they made ready^(d) the passover. **14** And when the hour was come,^(e) he sat down, and the twelve apostles with him. *Introduction to the last Passover begins* **15** And he said unto them, "With desire^(f) I have desired to eat this passover with you before I suffer: **16** "For I say unto you, I will not any more eat thereof, until it^(g) be fulfilled in the kingdom of God."^(h) (Verse 17 cont. in Section 171.)	

Footnotes-Commentary

(a) Passover and Unleavened. Highlighted in gray, as these verses help in determining the approximate length of Jesus' ministry. By this time in Jewish history, Passover and the Feast of Unleavened Bread were blended together as though they were the same. As seen in Lk. 22:7, these terms were used interchangeably. Note, that "the first day of the Unleavened Bread" celebration is now called the time "they killed the Passover." Thus, the Unleavened Bread event was viewed as being part of the Passover Feast. According to the Torah Law, the unleavened period did not begin until the day *after* the Passover. See this in Lev. 23:5-6, under words "the fourteenth day and fifteenth day." *This reflects how technically un-technical the Jews had become in keeping their law.* Overlapping of the two separate or distinct feasts resulted in them also being called "eight days." See the previous Section 167, second paragraph of footnote a, for further explanation.

(b) Our Lord had probably camped somewhere outside the city. Every road leading into Jerusalem would have been packed with thousands of Jews going to the temple to keep holy Passover. There is a fascinating article by Joachim Jeremias in his book *Jerusalem in the Time of Jesus,* pages 77-84 about the number of pilgrims attending these occasions, measurements of the temple, the number of lambs slaughtered, and other details. The instructions of Jesus to two apostles reflect His foreknowledge. Upon entering the Jerusalem, John, and Peter would meet a man (servant) carrying a pitcher of water gathered for evening use from one of the fountains. They were to follow him to his master's house. Arriving at the designated place, they spoke the Words of Christ to the "goodman" or "keeper" with whom Jesus was apparently acquainted. They had been instructed to tell this unnamed person that Jesus' time was "at hand" (Matt. 26:18), and then to make ready the guest chamber (or dining room) for Him and His apostles to observe Passover.

2p-Verse 14 with parallel in Lk. 22:11. "Goodman" speaks of the owner of a house. For the extended meaning of this old English word, see the *Expository Dictionary of New Testament Words,* page 166 by W. E. Vine. Whoever this "goodman" was, he seems to have been a disciple of Christ because he understood the meaning of the statement, "My time is at hand." Perhaps this expression was Christ's way of saying that it was near the time for Him to partake of the Passover meal with His disciples. Perhaps it seems more sensible that He was referring to His death on the cross. If so, does this mean that the "goodman" understood this when our Lord's disciples did not? For the first person to understand Jesus' death, and how she exhibited her belief in this, see Section 146, footnote e.

(c) **"Large upper room furnished."** Each guest room for Passover observance was furnished with several tables, reclining couches, bowls of water for washing hands and feet and towels for drying. Pegs protruded from the walls on which various items could be hung. It was customary to eat the roasted lamb only after the setting of the sun, which would begin the fifteenth day of Nisan. This eating was to take place within the walls of Jerusalem if possible. Every Passover table must have at least ten participants present, or it was invalid. See third paragraph of footnote d below for further details. Edersheim in his, *Life and Times of Jesus the Messiah* page 815 has a diagram illustrating the type of tables used for these occasions. See all of Section 29 and the lengthy footnote a, for an explanation of this event. Just as the sun set in the west, a loud blast resounded from silver trumpets on the temple mount. This signaled for several miles about, that the sacred Passover had begun. Little did those present know, it would be the final *true Passover* for their sin cursed nation. A few decades later millions would die in Jerusalem!

(d) **Peter and John, "made ready the Passover."** After checking out the table in the upper room, John and Peter made their way to the sheep market or some nearby lamb vendor to purchase the animal for their Passover. Next, they made their way through the thick crowds to the temple. Standing in one of the three groups or companies of "not less than thirty persons" with each man holding his lamb, they moved forward to the waiting priest. A loud threefold blast from the silver trumpets signaled the work of sacrifice was to begin. The lamb was to be killed on the fourteenth day of Nisan, which is our March or April (Ex. 12:6). This was the month in which God delivered ancient Israel out of the land of Egypt (Lev. 23:5 with Num. 28:16). Either Peter or John killed the lamb after laying their hands on its head. The priest in a silver bowel collected the blood. Then he poured and sprinkled it at the base of the altar. Refer to Section 119, sixth paragraph of footnote a for explanation of the drainage system connected to the base of the altar. The remainder of the carcass was flayed, gutted, and washed, all in "one minute." Because of the thousands waiting for their turn to slaughter their lambs, the killing began early in order to accommodate the great crowds. (One must distinguish between the actual killing of the lamb, and the eating of the carcass that night after sundown, which was the beginning of a new day.) The skin went to the officiating priest for service payment, or it was given to the host in whose house the feast might be held. Passover lambs were always slain in the temple, never in private homes because the blood of the lamb was used ceremonially at the altar (2 Chron. 35:10-11).

2p-In the book, *The Life and Words of Christ*, page 151, by Dr. Cunningham Geikie, we read this interesting note, "The tail . . . often weighs many pounds and the fat was handed to the nearest priest . . . to be burned as an offering to God." Fred H. Wight has a short article with two illustrations about the famous "fat-tailed sheep," in his work entitled, *Manners and Customs of Bible Lands,* pages 147-148. Years ago while preaching across the Holy Land, the author saw a sheep whose tail was so large that it was carried in a small wagon-like device with two slides for wheels! This apparatus was strapped across the back and under the stomach of the animal. My Arab Christian friend said it was a common thing.

3p-After slaughtering, the carcass was carried on shoulder poles to the "goodmen" (see second paragraph of footnote b above) of the upper room. He would roast the flesh and prepare the table with all necessary items for Passover. The roasted lamb for the Passover was to serve not fewer than ten but not more than twenty people. Women were allowed to join their households, but it was not required that they actually eat of the meal. Boys from the age of fourteen, even slaves and foreigners could partake if they were circumcised. Everything was done in a highly organized rush so that the lamb could be eaten within the specified hours, which are still the subject of debate. The Talmud tractate Pesachim has hundred of guidelines for Passover preparations and celebration. Passover is mentioned in the Hebrew Talmud over two thousand times! For other details on this Jewish celebration, see Section 29, second through the fourth paragraphs of footnote a.

4p-The ancient meal also included three pieces of unleavened bread, bitter herbs, a thick dipping sauce, dish vinegar, and four cups of red wine. The wine was mixed with one-fourth part water to alleviate its ultra strong sweetness. The first cup was supped at the commencement of the feast, the second about mid-way through, while the remaining two were used during the final moments of the Passover occasion. For mention of the last cup, see Section 174, footnote b. The Jews gave four reasons for the number of cups being used. They pointed to the deliverance of Israel out of Egypt, when God spoke of four things, He would do for them. **First,** "I will bring forth," **second,** "I will deliver," **third,** "I will redeem," and **forth,** "I will take" (Ex. 6:6-7). Hence, each of these acts performed by Jehovah was represented in the four cups employed in observing Passover. Later, only three cups were used. These were described as being, one "for the priests," "one for the Levites" and "one for Israel." This changed the original practice from four cups to three. Today, Ashkenazi Jews will not eat lamb at Passover, for there is no temple in which to slaughter the animal. For the three basic geographical divisions of the Hebrew people, see Section 30, second paragraph under number 7 of footnote e.

5p-**No wine.** In the original instructions Jehovah God gave for Passover (Ex. 12:1-28), there was no mention of wine being used. The Jews added this about a thousand years later, *after* the Babylonian captivity had ended in 536 B.C. For the countless confusing rituals invented and required by the rabbis, see Lightfoot's *Commentary on the New Testament . . .*, vol. 2, pages 350-351. *(We have no way of knowing all the details of the original Hebrew Passover celebration.)* Amid all the fanfare and excitement, there was the loud and joyful singing of Jewish "hallels" or songs of praise from different parts of Ps. 113-136. These were sung by the temple choirs, in homes, or at private gatherings like the one with Jesus and His apostles in the upper room at Jerusalem the night before the morning of the cross (Matt. 26:30). Today's Christian Jews singing their hallels, and truly observing the *final meaning* of Passover will thrill the heart of any child of God, who is in fellowship with his Savior.

(e) **"When the even was come."** The celebration of Passover could only commence after sunset or when "even was come." Luke describes it as, "when the hour was come."

2p-**"Sat down with the twelve."** The first or original Passover was eaten in Egypt, while standing with loins girded (Ex. 12:11). "Sat down" means that they lay in reclining horizontal positions on couches as was customary for meals. The verse in Lk. 22:14 is careful to state that the "twelve apostles were with him." This included Judas Iscariot, who had already made his deal with the Sanhedrin to sell Jesus. See Section 147 where the price was agreed upon, and Section 167 where the plan was decided, and then enacted with great caution because of vast multitudes present at Passover. In Section 180, Judas arrives in the garden to betray the Savior.

(f) **"Desire"** meaning "intensely wanting something." Why was the Son of God so anxious to *get through* this final Passover? He knew that on the other side of this meal stood Gethsemane and His cross. This event was the Preface to victory and eternal life for mankind. It was the will of the Father for Him to celebrate with His preachers this final Passover, then later walk to Calvary's hill. He rejoiced to do the Father's will. He would be the final Passover Lamb dying for the sins of Adam's descendents, but more personally "for us" (1 Cor. 5:7). As the first Passover in dark Egypt was a memorial to deliverance from death and freedom from bondage, so the last one provides salvation from sin's bondage and hell's eternal death. Here, the Master says to the twelve something of this nature. "I have longed for this hour in which I shall finish this Passover, for tomorrow, I will offer up myself as the final and eternal Passover for the salvation of mankind; this is the prime purpose of my coming into the world."

2p-**Another mention of His soon death.** We ponder what the apostles thought of His words, "before I suffer." At this point, they still did not understand the cross, His death, burial, and resurrection. For more on this curious truth, see Sections 104-105, 107, and 141. On Jesus' resurrection, see Section 196, John 20:9 with associated comments by the symbols ◀ and ◻.

(g) **"It."** This pronoun can *only* have reference to the actual Passover meal and not the communion meal, which (at this time) had not yet been instituted. The ordinance or memorial meal best known as "The Lord's Supper," or "communion" was instituted about an hour later at the conclusion of the Passover. This is recorded in Section 174. *Communion was not the Jewish Passover, but it came out of the Passover.*

(h) **"Fulfilled in the kingdom of God."** Everything the Passover prefigured or symbolized (which was the atonement for sin) was *fulfilled* in God's spiritual kingdom when Christ died on the cross and rose from the dead. It is true that the Jews at this time had myths about some outlandish banquet with their Messiah when he had established his political, material rule of Israel over all nations. Christ is not referring to these fables. Nevertheless, the church retains the hope of a future heavenly banquet (of whatever sort) with her Lord and Savior (Rev. 19:9). For a brief *conjectural* explanation of the kind of kingdom there will be in eternity, see Section 169, fourth through sixth paragraphs under footnote f. Some see in Rev. 3:20, the fulfillment of our Lord eating and drinking or fellowshipping with those who have been brought into His church as they responded to His knock on the door of their lives. This could be the meaning of His Words "fulfilled in the kingdom of God." Today, the observance of communion that Jesus introduced at the *conclusion* of this final Passover points back to His death and resurrection and forward to His return. It was intended to be a humble observance that reminds those already saved of what Christ did for them in His atonement and what He will do when He returns again (1 Cor. 11:26).

2p-**The simplicity of the supper.** Communion as instituted by the Savior in the upper room had nothing to do with salvation. It does not, nor was it ever intended to give eternal life to those who participate. This wonderful ordinance of the church should only be observed by those who have been saved and are in fellowship with God (1 Cor. 11:28-34). The corruption and horrific abuse of the Lord's Supper is reflected in the names applied to it by churches infected with Romanism. They call it "Holy Eucharist." The word "Eucharist" means "favor or grace." *All* the favor and grace of God are found only in His blessed Son, the Lord Jesus Christ, and not the humble emblems of Christian Communion (2 Tim. 2:1). One is placed into divine favor by faith in the finished work of Christ and not by "eating His flesh and drinking His blood at a church altar." Nor is it ever called "the sacred host," or "Holy Communion." The emblems are not "holy" in the sense that they impart some kind of favor, mercy, or salvation. No priest or religious cleric has the power to change the bread or contents of the cup into anything. For earlier comments regarding the command about "eating of Jesus' flesh and drinking His blood," note Section 95, footnote r.

3p-**The abuse of the supper.** On the church fathers and their corrupting the original meaning of the Lord's Supper and baptism, see Section 12, sixth and seventh paragraphs of footnote k. The changing of the *meaning and purpose* of the communion meal and water baptism in early church history by the so-called "fathers" and their successors was one of the greatest calamites every suffered by Christianity. Millions have been deceived into trusting the bread and cup or water baptism for eternal life instead of Christ and Him alone. Regarding which religion is right, see Section 175, sixth paragraph of footnote e and Section 151, second paragraph of footnote e.

An argument* breaks out among the twelve. It was just before the Passover meal, which formerly commenced at sunset. They shamelessly quarrel over who among them was considered "the greatest."**

Time: Late Thursday, just before the Jewish Friday at sunset and the day of the cross.

*This power struggle and personal bickering had been previously noted among the apostles. Christ continually attempted to put down their quarrelsome spirit and teach them humility. One may trace this faction within their ranks starting at the main heading of Section 109 and moving into Sections 138, 142 and 170. Of all times, to fall into quibbling with each other the evening before His death on the cross was the worst. **This carnal, if not satanic spirit of self-exaltation and personal honor seeking runs rampant today among churches, ministers, missionaries, and so-called spiritual leaders of God's work. "Jealously is [still] as cruel as the grave" (Song of Sol. 8:6).

Matt.	Mk.	Lk. 22:24-30—*The upper room in Jerusalem just prior to Passover*	John
		The apostle's quest for vain glory: Christ's response 24 And there was also a strife[a] among them, which of them should be accounted the greatest. 25 And he said[b] unto them, "The kings of the Gentiles exercise lordship over them; and they that exercise authority upon them are called 'benefactors.' 26 "But ye *shall* not *be* so: but he that is greatest among you, let him be as the younger; and he that is chief, as he that doth serve. 27 "For whether *is* greater, he that sitteth at meat, or he that serveth? *is* not he that sitteth at meat? but I am among you as he that serveth.[c] 28 "Ye are they which have continued[d] with me in my temptations. *"All of you will share in my kingdom: stop auguring"* 29 "And I appoint[e] unto you a kingdom, as my Father hath appointed unto me; 30 "That ye may eat and drink at my table in my kingdom, and sit on thrones judging the twelve tribes of Israel."[f] (Verse 31 cont. in Section 173.)	

Footnotes-Commentary

[a] **"Strife among them."** Again, we see rising up within the apostolic twelve the foul spirit of pride and self-supremacy. Quibbling among the choice servants of God has been a problem from the start. In pained silence, Messiah listened to their murmured jealousies as they were taking their places about the Passover table. See all by the asterisk under main heading above. *Among preachers, there is nothing more abhorrent than proud humility!*

[b] Their Master informs them (to their shame) that they were acting as the pagan Gentiles do! What a stern rebuke to these Hebrews who prided themselves of not being like the heathen Gentiles. "Benefactors" as used here has reference to persons who gracefully bestowed favor upon others. Slaves would apply it to their masters and court officials to kings (in flattery) to curry favor, mercy, and secure various material benefits.

[c] **What a lesson!** Never had they heard anything like this from their haughty rabbis. The Lord Jesus said, "Whoever is the greatest among you let him be as a young person learning, and he that is chief shall be the servant (slave) of the others." This admonition was an attempt to explain to His preachers the lowly nature and inside workings of His spiritual kingdom or church. In the next few moments, He physically demonstrated what He had just said. Did He not state here that He was among them as a slave? Soon, He would perform the duty of the most menial slave in Israel. See main heading of Section 170, where Christ washed their feet.

[d] O the grace of God! With this rebuke comes hope and promise to the weary and little flock. He had chosen these twelve as apostles from the thousands of disciples that followed him. This had been some two and half-years before and is mentioned in Section 57. They had stumbled along behind their great Master, and did not understand much of what He said and did. At times, they were terrified at the wrath of the Sanhedrin while at the same time they were continually astounded at His Words and works. The whispers of assassination plots against the Lord Jesus had shocked them to no end, but they stayed with their Messiah. They had witnessed His sorrows, the attempts to stone Him, the reproach, and scorn of the religious hypocrites, and more. Yet the marvel of it all was, "They had continued with Him." If these haggard men, who two days before His death were fussing among themselves about who was the greatest, could stay with the Savior, what about us?

(e) **"And I appoint you."** The sense here is that the Lord Jesus had assigned each of the apostles (except the traitor) a place in His new kingdom or church. The Savior could do this because God had appointed Him as Head of it all. Now, they can share the divine glory and the highest honor of human life as ministers of the new covenant and the saving gospel. For explanation of this new covenant, see Section 95, second paragraph of footnote u.

(f) **Verse 30. "Eat and drink."** For more on this curious expression, see Section 171, third paragraph of footnote b, and Section 174, footnote d. In the new kingdom of Christ, when it has finally unfolded into its eternal manifestation, His servants will "eat and drink at His table." *Could this be something of a euphemism for everlasting fellowship and joy?* It cannot be one pointing to *continual* eating and drinking in a human body throughout all eternity! There will be no super markets, grocery buying, vast shopping centers, hospitals, drug stores, police stations, emergency ambulances or rest rooms in the eternal home of the saved. Sickness, sorrow, suffering, and the ills of this human life will not be part of this kingdom. Of it, God has said, "Behold, I make all things new" (Rev. 21:5). With this verse we meet a statement of similar nature to the one made earlier by the Savior in Matt. 19:28. Refer to Section 139, number 2 under footnote m, for another possible explanation of these terms.

2p-The words about literal eating and drinking may be better understood if they refer to a glorified experience rather than a spiritualized non-material thing. Christ could also be referring to a new physical condition of which we are presently unaware and of which Scripture is silent. Those who seize on these words and create a worldwide reign of Christ, with various fundamentalist preachers ruling different parts of the world are having religious hallucinations. Nor does it have reference to the interpretations of the critics who reject God's Word, kick Israel out of His eternal plan, and spiritualize everything except their shoes!

3p-Regardless of our inability to understand or describe in detail the rule of Christ among men, we would do well to remember that our Lord's kingdom would function differently from those of all earthly domains, empires, and kingdoms. The statement in verse 30, no doubt refers to the great restoration of divine order to the entire universe. There, sin's curse will be forever abolished and all things eternally new. Such is beyond our comprehension or ability to understand, much less describe.

4p-The predictions recorded in Ezek. 37:21-28, seem to reveal that our Lord will reign with inexpressible glory over Israel at a future time. To make these prophecies applicable only to the church in a spiritual significance does violence to the context of Ezekiel's vision, especially the sign of two sticks (verses 15-20 of the same chapter). As in other Scriptures, God has chosen to leave out the finer details and *exact* chronology of events. Problems are created when men invent their own timetables and force them into the blank sections of God's Word. The sins of the religious leaders and the Jews in general, which the apostles witnessed during their Lord's public ministry, would be corporately punished. This happened in A.D. 70, at the destruction of the temple, and scattering of the nation of Israel. Millions died in this carnage of national destruction. See Section 163 for part of the horrific story.

5p-In Zechariah chapter 14, we note several verses in which some think they see the millennial reign of Christ in operation. Others make all of this a spiritual thing with the Lord Jesus ruling as king over the earth from His throne in heaven (verse 9). Originally, the millennial rule was to be a time of "peace on earth" and great blessing. Even the animal world would be changed (Isa. 11:6-9.) The "experts" changed this. In this chapter of Zechariah, we note God punishing Gentile nations for not coming to Jerusalem to worship (verses 16-19). To read that the heathen who does not observe the Feast of Tabernacles will be judged of God is astounding (verse 18)! How can this be literal when all pagans were barred from God's house and every religious or national celebration of Israel.

6p- **Verse 20. Horses with inscribed bells.** This cannot fit into the future rule of King Jesus and His people. The ancients attached bells to horses and camels to amuse and spur them on in their work. *Men will not revert to animal labor in the millennial reign of Christ!* The mention of "no more Canaanite in the house of the LORD of hosts" (verse 21), hardly fits into the future of Israel. Canaanites vanished from the earth almost two thousand years ago! For the fulfillment of this verse in the ministry of Christ, see Section 150, second paragraph of footnote a. A look into twenty-five conservative commentaries, all dating back of 1880 reveals that none of the authors understood this chapter as referring to a literal future thousand years of peace on earth. All of them held that the things described in Zechariah chapter 14 speak of past events that occurred in ancient Israel. The hermeneutic that applies these passages to a restored Hebrew people in their land, the Jewish priesthood functioning, temple worship, and animal sacrifices restored is wrong. Refer to Section 134, paragraphs two through four of footnote d for more on this subject. At the judgment bema of Christ, it may be interesting to learn how wrong we have been in certain areas of Christian eschatology. When Christ rules the world, it will be perfect and sublime beyond the wildest speculations of any red-hot Baptist preacher. No one will be bossing anyone else; Jesus will be King of Kings and Lord of Lords! He will wonderfully cover everything, "as the waters that cover the sea" (Isa. 11:9). For continued comments on these thoughts, see Section 171, third and fourth paragraphs of footnote b.

7p-**"Judging the twelve tribes."** The apostles judging the twelve tribes must surely speak of a future time when these very men will join God in pronouncing eternal doom on the Messiah rejecters within the nation. It seems so incorrect to spiritualize this statement. Once this is done, we wonder what does it mean?

Teaching them true greatness, He washes their feet, demonstrating genuine humility and the glorious grace of preferring one above the other. This was in response to their argument as they debated* which among them was the greatest.** He mentions the traitor to the eleven to increase their faith in Scripture.

The Savior temporarily delayed the Passover meal in order to give His apostles a lesson on humility. The exchanges below between Jesus and His preachers are continued through Section 175 and John 14:31. At this place, they leave the upper room for the temple and the Garden of Gethsemane on the eastern side of the city.

Time: Late Thursday, just before the Jewish Friday commenced at sunset and the day of the cross.

*This spirit of rivalry, self-exaltation, pride, and debate is discussed in Section 169 and relative footnotes. **John was not inspired to write details about the actual Passover meal or the Lord's Supper being established as Matthew, Mark and Luke were. He was directed by the Holy Spirit to pen the story of Judas, the traitor, and his leaving the room to gather the mob and later arrest Jesus in the garden. All the fuss about John's record here is because men do not believe in the divine inspiration of Holy Scripture. Therefore, they have no option but to devise their own academic and intellectual methods of "filling in," and "patching together" God's Word. This has always resulted in a perversion of what is being stated.

Matt.	Mk.	Lk.	John 13:1-12—*The upper room in Jerusalem just prior to Passover*
			John's after thoughts as he looks back
			1 Now before the feast[a] of the passover, [began] when Jesus knew that his hour was come that he should depart out of this world unto the Father, having loved his own which were in the world, he loved them unto the end.
			2 And [the preparations for the] supper being ended,[b] the devil having now put into the heart of Judas Iscariot, Simon's *son*, to betray him;[c]
			3 Jesus knowing that the Father had given all things into his hands, and that he was come from God, and went to God;[d]
			The Savior's strange actions
			4 He riseth from supper, and laid aside his garments; and took a towel, and girded himself.[e]
			5 After that he poureth water into a bason, and began to wash the disciples' feet, and to wipe *them* with the towel wherewith he was girded.
			Peter's question
			6 Then cometh he to Simon Peter: and Peter saith unto him, "Lord, dost thou wash my feet?"[f]
			7 Jesus answered[g] and said unto him, "What I do thou knowest not now; but thou shalt know hereafter."
			Peter's objection
			8 Peter saith unto him, "Thou shalt never wash my feet."[h] Jesus answered him, "If I wash thee not, thou hast no part with me."
			Peter's willingness
			9 Simon Peter saith unto him, "Lord, not my feet only, but also *my* hands and *my* head."[i]
			10 Jesus saith to him, "He that is washed needeth not save to wash *his* feet, but is clean every whit: and ye are clean, but not all."
			11 For he knew who should betray him; therefore said he, "Ye are not all clean."[j]
			Jesus' question
			12 So after he had washed their feet, and had taken his garments, and was set down again, he said unto them, "Know ye what I have done

Matt.	Mk.	Lk.	John 13:12-20—*The upper room in Jerusalem just prior to Passover*
			to you?
			13 "Ye call me Master and Lord: and ye say well; for *so* I am.
			14 "If I then, *your* Lord and Master, have washed your feet; ye also ought to wash one another's feet.
			His supreme example they should follow
			15 "For I have given you an example, that ye should do as I have done to you.[k]
			16 "Verily, verily, I say unto you, The servant is not greater than his lord; neither he that is sent greater than he that sent him.
			17 "If ye know these things, happy are ye if ye do them.
			The traitor is at the table eating with the Savior
			18 "I speak not of you all: I know whom I have chosen: but that the Scripture may be fulfilled,[l] **'He that eateth bread with me hath lifted up his heel against me.'**
			19 "Now I tell you before it come, that, when it is come to pass, ye may believe that I am *he*.
			20 "Verily, verily, I say unto you, He that receiveth whomsoever I send receiveth me; and he that receiveth me receiveth him that sent me."[m]
			(Verse 21 cont. in Section 172.)

Footnotes-Commentary

[a] Here, is another inspired editorial comment by John as he wrote looking back upon the history he had shared with Christ and the other apostles. The former fisherman reflects with fond memories as he recalls *again* that his Lord had loved all of them to the very end of His human life. *Now,* John understood that Jesus did these things because He knew His hour of death on the cross had arrived. It would be tomorrow, He would depart from this life by physical death. He reiterates this again in verse 3.

2p-Was this the Passover meal? "Academicians" have debated for centuries, whether this was the actual Passover meal or some kind of supper before that grand event. They are thrown off balance because John was not inspired to give various details about the Passover meal and establishment of communion as did Matthew, Mark, and Luke. He was led by the Holy Spirit to pen other major details, which occurred that night, especially the foot washing and the actions of Judas. Matthew, Mark, and Luke did not mention any of these; they dealt more with the actual communion meal than associated events.

3p-Trying to patch together an unbroken chronology for the entire Passover night through the Lord's Supper is something God will not allow, for He did not inspire the story to be written that way. One can partially harmonize John with Matthew, Mark, Luke, and vice versa. What God has given is sufficient. The prudent man will leave it there. The book, *Last Supper and the Lord's Supper,* by I. Howard Marshall, has many quotations by "academicians," and "scholars" who all agree that the biblical record cannot be trusted. Their grand conclusion regarding the Lord's Supper is "your guess is good as ours." This is because they do not believe in a Bible that is inspired and therefore, is untrustworthy. God had His Word written the way He wanted it written; this the "greatly learned scholars" cannot stomach. They call into question His record and write their tripe about Matthew, Mark, and Luke being wrong or Jesus not knowing what He was saying. Men and women who discredit the Scriptures are assistants of Satan regardless of how sincere they are.

4p-Ministers, theological professors, lecturers, Sunday school teachers, pastors, and missionaries who disdain a Bible that is thoroughly trustworthy, and from God, should resign or be fired from their work of poisoning the minds of others. An honest day's hard, sweaty labor in the godless, secular work-world would do all of them good. Reading their books, one feels they believe the Bible has more lies than the *New York Times*.

5p-It will be pointed out in Section 171, Lk. 22:17, footnote a that the Master *officially began* the Passover by lifting the "cup of thanksgiving" or "blessing" and pronouncing the formal Jewish prayer over it. (This act had nothing to do with the Lord's Supper, which was instituted at the *end* of the Passover meal.) After sipping from the cup, the next step in the ceremony was for the head of the company (or master of ceremonies) to go to a table and wash his hands. John alone records that Jesus rose from the supper (verse 4). He bypasses Christ washing his hands and picks up the story with foot washing. Our Lord departed from standard tradition. He took a towel and basin, knelt to the floor, and began to wash their feet. Such actions were never part of the official Jewish Passover. This unusual deed is given prominence by John in his book. The Savior attempted to show His bickering preachers the supreme example of servant-hood and humility. It occurred immediately after the first cup and Jesus washing His hands. Edersheim reports that there were *two washings* at the Passover meal. The first, which Jesus converted into the foot washing, and a second when the participants cleaned their hands just before eating the roasted lamb. See his *Life and Times of Jesus the Messiah,* pages 817-818 for details. Though there is no biblical record of the twelve washing their hands, it is obvious they did. One must believe that considerable elasticity and liberty existed during this greatest of Israel's celebrations, while tenaciously following the traditional rules. Refer to footnote e below for further explanation of what Jesus did on this occasion.

(b) **"The supper being ended."** This means that all the preparations for the Passover meal had "ended," or were completed. It does not have reference to the actual meal. The furnished U shaped eating table, couches aligned, water tables, copper basins, water jars, and towels were all in place. This custom may have been borrowed from the Sanhedrin, who during meals would often lounge about a horseshoe style or half moon shaped table. It *cannot* mean that the meal, which required about one hour to complete, had ended. After John's words about "the supper being ended," we read in verse 5 of the washing, which as explained above occurred *before* the meal commenced. In Section 172, John 13:26 we read of Christ giving a sop to Judas. This act was a prime part of the Pascal observance and given as the meal ended. The person in command of the feast customarily gave sops to various guests during the meal. At the conclusion, he would break off a final piece of bread and dip it into the sauce. Then it was handed to the one in whom he had a special interest and loved dearly. *Jesus gave this to the traitor, Judas Iscariot!*

2p-Some commentators hold that this supper was the meal at Bethany, in the house of Simon the leper given in Section 146. It seems unfeasible that part of the story was given in the first eleven verses of John 12, suddenly stopped, only to resume the event many verses later in John chapter 13.

(c) **"The devil put into his heart."** This is not the first time Satan had gotten together with Judas. These words mean that the evil one had originally prompted the idea, thus tempting him to betray his Messiah and Lord. He willfully responded to the suggestion! Judas' trouble with Satan began earlier. See this in Section 147, Lk. 22:3, footnotes a and b. Here, the text states explicitly that he "entered into" the traitor. A few weeks later, we discover the Devil again intimating his lies into the minds of those who lend an ear, but do not consider the awful consequences that follow (Acts 5:3-11). Near the end of this Passover meal, we read of Satan's presence in the upper room, and that he actually entered *a second time* into the physical body of the traitor (John 13:27). The terrible meaning is that Satan went in and out of Judas' human frame as he chose. During the first year of Jesus' ministry, He spoke of demons moving in and out of a man (who represented the religious leaders and Israel in general). Refer to Section 68, Matt. 12:43-45, footnotes e, f, and g for this story.

(d) The Lord Jesus saw the end of His work. He knew every upcoming event was "in his hands," or under His control. John introduces the foot washing by saying that Christ was fully conscious of His origin from the Father, and that He had all sovereign power; yet, He was willing to condescend to the slave's work of foot washing. In view of the apostles' bickering for position and authority, they needed an impregnable lesson that would hang in their memories throughout life. With this in mind, He prepared to leave them this undying picture: the Son of God from heaven washing the feet of mortal men!

(e) Our Lord officially commenced the Passover in the next Section 171. He did this by speaking the "blessing" over the first cup. See fifth paragraph of footnote a above. Immediately afterward, it was customary for the one in command to move to the table of water, scrub both hands, and dry them with a large towel. To the amazement of the twelve apostles, their Lord does something out of order. Messiah removed his gown or outer garment along with the sash girded about His waist. The towel about the waist was the mark of the foot washing slave! *Now, He, the Lord of heaven, wears it!* Probably, he tied the long flowing towel about His waist in place of the girdle laying with his garment on one of the tables. Pouring water from a container into one of the "basons," Christ dropped to His knees and silently began to wash their feet, moving slowly along the floor from one to the other. This was the duty of the lowest of slaves. Such persons were the objects of ridicule and mockery among all other slaves within a household. No respectable Jew would ever attempt such a thing! Here, we can better understand the shock of the apostles as in a stunned reverential awe, they watch their Master. None dared to ask, "Why," and none attempted to stop Him, until He came to Simon Peter! For an earlier washing of Jesus' feet with tears, refer to Section 64, Lk. 7:38 footnote g.

(f) **"Wash my feet?"** Many times Peter had noted the humility of Messiah. Never had he witnessed anything like this! Out of confusion and probably resentment (that his Messiah would do such a low deed) he inquired, "Lord, are you going to wash my feet too?" The rough tough former fisherman was dumfounded.

(g) In essence, our Lord replied to Peter's verbal protest something like this, "Let me do this now, and I will shortly explain to you why I have performed this curious action and my motives, in so doing."

(h) **"You will never wash my feet!"** Upon hearing the explanation of Jesus, impetuous Peter exploded. One must understand the nature of this man. We can believe that his intentions were honorable, but his tongue spoke before his brain went into gear! *Had he and the others not just engaged in a verbal war about which of them was the greatest?* Refer to the main heading under Section 170 for more on this sad event. Peter sees the greatest Person in his life, crawling along the floor of the upper room, quietly doing this shameful work. The boisterous man from Galilee did not so quickly understand Christ's reply. Yet, His Words struck Peter's troubled heart like a dart!

Whatever all this meant, Peter, wanted more than life, a part with this good Man, Whom he had confessed as Messiah and Savior (Section 103, Matt. 16:16). We see again that our Lord requires total *trust* in what He does in our lives. At times, this seems ridiculous, inappropriate, harsh, and even cruel. He was saying to Peter and us, "My followers must accept my will when it cannot be understood." Alas! Someday, we will kiss the hand that has wounded us. All things are working for good (Rom. 8:28), and even for our sakes (2 Cor. 4:15). Regardless of what Jesus was doing, Peter wanted his "part" in being one to serve Messiah. How compelling when we read Peter's words, written some thirty years later, where he identifies himself as "a servant" ["doulos" slave] of Jesus Christ" (2 Peter 1:1). Time and God's grace taught the fisherman from Galilee, as they will also teach us *if* we are willing.

(i) **"Wash me clean."** Being suddenly convinced by the Savior's reply, Peter understood his terrible mistake in resisting the Lord Jesus. In usual form, he moves from one *sincere* extreme to another. How quickly his mind was changed. The awful thought of no longer having any "part" with his dear Lord was more than he could bear. He broke out with, "wash my hands and my head." The rabbis laid special emphasis on these parts of the human anatomy. Hands represented one's deeds. The head was the origin of man's thoughts. Phylacteries were worn on the head and hand, which (supposedly) demonstrated the wearer both knew and obeyed the Torah Law. See this in Section 159, Matt. 23:5, second paragraph under footnote e. Peter was possibly trying to say, "Wash me Lord, where I will both *know* and *do* thy will."

(j) This speaks of Judas, who was to betray Him. See footnote l below for more on the traitor. Here, John makes another editorial comment on an event long past as he now looks back. Years later, he understood the Words of his Savior. Jesus knew who would betray Him from the beginning. For more on this, note Section 95, John 6:70–71, footnote x. Often we hear the question, "What would have happened if Judas had repented?" To which we respond, "Why do you call to question a thing long ago settled by personal choice of the man involved?" Man always acts freely, failing mostly to contemplate the consequences, which at the end they are all his. God foresaw that Judas would act as he did: thus, he became the victim of his own decisions and ate bitter fruit from the tree he planted. There is no predestination here, no assigning of a man into sin in this life, and hell in the afterlife. As we sow, so we will reap! One is amazed at the Words of Christ, when he announced to the apostles, "Ye are clean every whit: but not all" (having reference to the traitor). He was saying something like this, "Eleven of you are believers in Me, the Messiah and Savior. You are counted wholly clean within by the Father, all except the traitor." This unique statement reflects something of how God sees and counts all who are in Christ, complete, whole, and saved forever.

(k) **"For I have given you an example."** Washing and drying the dusty feet of twelve grown men, (Judas included) must have taken considerable time and effort. Returning to the eating couch, the Savior puts the question of verse 12 to all of them "Know ye what I have done?" No one replies! Jesus answered His question for them something like this, "What I have done is to be an example for all of you. Now, practice upon one another what you have seen me do." One of the highest glories of a Christian is that of simple humility. O that we would work at emulating the example of our Savior in this story. Many years ago, while serving as missionaries in South Africa, I saw an aged black woman, wrinkled, and worn, bow and kiss the feet of my wife! We learned in time that this was a revered custom among older Zulu people of showing humility and the deepest respect to others. The Lord Jesus repeated in a general sense verse 16, during His lesson on the true vine in John 15:20.

2p-Verse 17. This may be the untapped river of true happiness so obviously absent in the conduct and demeanor of many believers. Some have hung this lesson in the long hallways of human memory but so few of us practice it. For the biblical meaning of "happiness," refer to Section 44, first paragraph of footnote f.

(l) With a quotation from Ps. 41:9, the Lord Jesus suddenly spoke pointedly to His preachers. He informs them that he had not been deceived in choosing Judas. He knew perfectly everything from the beginning, and that He had not made the wrong choice. In a few moments, He would hand to Judas the very piece of bread (or sop) that was predicted in the Psalm written a thousand years prior. These things have occurred in order that divine prophecy in the Old Testament may be completed. This does not mean that Judas was forced or driven by a decree of God into his evil course and fellowship with Satan. Rather, it shows that this passage from Ps. 41:9 was fulfilled in his self-chosen actions and free willed determined decisions. He was giving His apostles a prediction of what would transpire within the next few days. Then, they would understand anew that He was God and foresaw the future deeds of all men.

(m) *It is now two days before the cross.* In these Words, Christ gives a pre-notice to the apostles. Those who would receive their message would receive Him, and to receive Him was equal to receiving God. The Savior had said a similar thing in Section 59, Matt. 10:40 when He had earlier sent out these same men on their first missionary effort across Galilee. That was almost three years ago. With this, again we note our Lord repeating Himself. Over the course of church history, repetition has been a chief vehicle for perpetuating the truth. Divine preservation has safeguarded this truth to ensure its authority and power to save and bless. All the academic talk about the Bible not being inspired but a "good book," is more folly. Are we born again of the Holy Spirit and God's Word or from "good books?" Note James 1:18 with 1 Peter 1:23. On being "born of water," see Section 30 footnote f.

CHAPTER 15
SUNSET AND HIS LAST PASSOVER WITH THE TWELVE APOSTLES.*

It commences with Christ offering the traditional Jewish "cup of thanks." Shortly, He would become the final Passover Lamb for the sins of all mankind. At this time, His apostles-disciples did not yet understand His death on the cross. At the end of the meal, He established the Lord's Supper.

Time: Thursday ends. The Jewish Friday, the day of the cross has commenced at sunset.

*To trace the four Passovers that occurred during the earthly ministry of our Lord, see Section 29, John 2:13 and relative footnotes. This is crucial in determining the approximate length of His public ministry. As explained in the next Section 172, John 13:30, footnote k, Judas Iscariot, the traitor, left the room near the conclusion of the Passover. Thus, only eleven of our Lord's apostles remained and partook of the first communion that He established on that occasion. At that time, none of them understood what He said or did. Full enlightenment came on the Day of Pentecost and with this, an absolute understanding of all the strange things their Lord had taught them.

Matt.	Mk.	Lk. 22:17-18— *In the upper room at Jerusalem, during Passover*	John
		The last Passover begins 17 And he took the [first] cup, and gave thanks,[(a)] and said, "Take this, and divide *it* among yourselves: 18 "For I say unto you, I will not drink of the fruit of the vine, until the kingdom of God shall come."[(b)] **(Verse 19 cont. in Section 174.)**	

Footnotes-Commentary

(a) **"He took the [first] cup, and gave thanks."** This was a preliminary introduction. It was always used to *begin* the Passover meal and had nothing whatsoever to do with the Lord's Supper. The person officiating lifted it and pronounced a blessing known as "Kiddush" upon those present and the cup's contents. The words of that ancient blessing have remained the same for centuries. It begins with, "Blessed art thou, Jehovah our God, who has created the fruit of the vine." These were the Words spoken by our Lord on that occasion. According to some Jewish texts, four cups of red wine were placed upon the table. For details on this custom, see Section 168, fourth and fifth paragraphs under footnote d. These cups were mixed with one fourth part water not to lessen any alcohol content, but rather to reduce the extreme sweet taste of the liquid which otherwise would prove repulsive to the drinker. This mixing of water into the cup of blessing or thanksgiving is mentioned in the Talmud tractate, Baba Bathra 97b. After the invocation, the cup was passed about the table and all present supped of it, ("divide it among yourselves"). This was standard ancient Passover procedure and (as stated above) had nothing at this point to do with the Lord's Supper which came later. Over the centuries, highly pious Jews have changed or added several things to the original Passover meal. One of these additions is mentioned in the second paragraph below.

2p-**"Drink of the fruit of the vine."** The vine produces its fruit called "grapes." According to Prov. 3:9-10, pressed grapes produce their fruit called "new wine" (not old). It is written in Isa. 65:8, "Thus saith the LORD, 'As the new wine is found in the cluster ...'" How "unscholarly" it is (according to the experts) for God to call the fresh liquid of unmashed grapes, "new wine." The product of pressed vintage is also called "the pure blood of grapes" (Deut. 32:14). The mockers on the day of Pentecost, ridiculing the Spirit filled believers, taunted them with these words, "These men are full of new wine" (Acts 2:13). It was as impossible to get drunk on "new wine" as it was on a cup of tea! "New wine" or "the pure blood of the grape" is only turned into intoxicating beverage when additives are placed into its substance. Man makes it alcoholic, destructive, and deadly by what he does to it, not God. Ironically, ancient drunkards would often consume *fresh grape pressings* (new wine) in an effort to mitigate their state of inebriation, check their vomiting, and sober them up (Joel 1:5). And it worked!

3p-**The Torah Law did not enjoin the use of wine at Passover.** The word "wine" cannot be found in any of the Old Testament instructions regarding the Passover celebration. It was not a part of the *original* Passover established in Ex. 12. Drinking wine was not added to this grand occasion until after the Babylonian captivity which ended in 536 B.C. Centuries after the first Passover, the Talmud informs us that the rabbis began to lay down meticulous rules for serving wine during the feast; how many cups, and their mixture with warm water to dilute the powerful sweet taste, and make it go further. After the addition of wine to this event, the Talmud in tractate, Gittin 31b speaks of it being sold "shortly before the Passover" for the occasion. Christ's usage of the cups again shows that He took the traditions of the Jews, *whenever they pointed to Him as Messiah and Savior,* and drew valuable lessons from them. He rejected all other man-made Hebrew traditions such as the oral law and its thousands of burdensome regulations. This is noted in Section 96, where He sharply berated the religious leaders for abandoning

God's Word for their traditions and verbal rules. As mentioned above, the Jews had also changed the original custom of standing with "staff in hand" (Ex. 12:11) while observing the Passover, to that of reclining.

4p-What kind of wine? Concerning the use of *alcoholic* wine for this occasion, we can be sure that many Jews did employ intoxicating liquid for Passover just as many of them do today. However, not all Jews were drinkers or drunkards because of potent wine. An ancient rabbi named Meir, wrote these words about intoxicating drink, "When the wine enters the system of a person, out goes sense, wherever there is wine, there is no understanding." Cited from an English translation of an old commentary on the Midrash, marked by Rabbah Nosso 10. For a very enlightening discussion of the rabbis debating the subject of wine, alcoholic and other wise, see *The Temperance Bible-Commentary,* pages 28, 281-286. This classic work was printed in London in 1923, and has been mostly overlooked or neglected when dealing with the subject of intoxicating drink. In Lk. 22:18 it reads that the cups contained "the fruit of the vine," not the juice of grapes mixed with additives to make it become fermented or alcoholic. In Gen. 40:11, it is abundantly clear what "fruit of the vine means." This text graphically explains what Pharaoh's butler put in his drinking cup, "And Pharaoh's cup was in my hand: and I took the grapes, and pressed [squeezed] them into Pharaoh's cup, and I gave the cup into Pharaoh's hand." The king of Egypt could have never gotten "tipsy" drinking this fresh squeezed liquid! Fermented wine with its poison content is not a symbol of the precious blood of Jesus, shed for our sins. Conversely, the fresh and pure blood of the grape makes the perfect emblem. In 1 Peter 1:18-19 it is clear that the blood of Jesus was incorruptible. Making all wine in the Bible alcoholic is a serious error. For Jesus turning the water into wine, refer to Section 27, footnote k.

(b) "I will not drink until." Our Lord informs His apostles that He will never partake of the Passover observance again in this ceremonial and legal way, because of what it pointed to He would soon fulfill as Messiah on the cross and in the kingdom of God. "Until the kingdom of God shall come" must have reference to its complete and final consummation. It has been pointed out that the kingdom had *already come* and was a present spiritual entity at the time Jesus spoke these words, albeit in infant form. See Section 39, footnote a, and Section 134, footnote d for explanation. Therefore, He was speaking of the coming of His kingdom in another manifestation apart from its then present form. Opinions vary and are many in answer to this statement. Matthew Henry, in his *Commentary,* vol. 5, page 562, understands this as having reference to the Holy Spirit being poured out at Pentecost and then the disciples partaking of the Lord's Supper in a more glorious manner. The first "cup" used here had *nothing* to do with communion but only the Passover as explained in footnote a above.

2p-A marriage? Some see in the words "drink of the fruit of the vine," the marriage of the Lamb in Rev. 19:7-8. They think the Passover cup will be used of on that occasion. This seems wrong. There is no exegetical application of the Passover cup whatsoever in this future marriage. Why will this Pascal tool (the first cup of wine) be used at that glorious event? Some think they find here a statement that was anticipatory of a heavenly festival, a sublime and divine feast in which all God's children will share. This seems different from the marriage supper of the Lamb and is supposed to be the same event as "sitting down with Abraham, Isaac, and Jacob in the kingdom." The Savior had spoken of this earlier in Matt. 8:11. Nor, can this be the twelve sitting on thrones judging the twelve tribes of Israel. There is the opinion that Christ is speaking here of His literal kingdom coming, and it will be part of that eternal bliss. Even if this were so, one still ponders what place the cup of thanksgiving, used by the Jews to commence the ancient Jewish Passover, will have in that endless age of joy and blessing? Where and how this occurs is expressed in the text; Christ will "drink" with His own in that glorified phase of His kingdom. For a more sensible interpretation of eating and drinking in the eternal kingdom, see Section 139, number 2, under footnote m.

3p-Banqueting in heaven? The mystery of saints with glorified bodies, eating and drinking in heaven or on earth is not explained in the Scripture. *Therefore, men should not attempt to explain it!* Those who do so make a mess out of another unrevealed mystery of divine truth. One thing is sure; they will not eat and drink because of hunger or thirst pangs. Whatever it means it will be well, for God our Father, Christ our Savior, and the Spirit our Comforter will all be present at the holy festivities. See the fourth and fifth paragraphs below.

4p-Millennium dining. In Rom. 6:5, it is stated that we shall be in the likeness of His resurrection. Then, 1 John 3:2 affirms, "We shall be like Him." Paul wrote that there is a spiritual body (1 Cor. 15:44). We note that our Lord ate fish and honeycomb after His resurrection (Lk. 24:42). Our glorified spiritual bodies, whatever they finally are, will be like that of Christ. Amid the wonder of God's best for His children, there will be no acid reflux, purple pills, Tums, or indigestion in the millennium! No earthly feast of whatever proportions or joy can be compared with what God has planned for those that are saved. All efforts of expositors to blend the best of legitimate human pleasures with heaven's eternal bliss fall miserably short of what God has in store. This is because sin has spoiled everything! *Rational boundaries in eschatology are required or carnal radicalism will sweep our imaginations away!* Refer to Section 174, footnote d for other comments on eating and drinking in eternity and related thoughts.

5p-A millennium of suffering? The ruckus about dining in heaven, a millennial of *enforced* peace, with prisons, jails, hospitals, women suffering the pangs of childbirth, deaths, and so forth is more nonsense. Isaiah 9:6-7 and 65:25 gives a brief explanation of the peace and tranquility during this time, and how long it will last. A fallen world cannot be whitewashed for a thousand years with sinful human nature still present. For further comments on these things, see Section 104, number 1 under footnote i and Section 169, all paragraphs under footnote f.

Judas Iscariot is exposed as the Passover ends. Jesus gives him the final sop. With this, Satan enters his body, and he leaves the room.* Amazingly, the remaining eleven apostles did not yet realize that He was the great traitor.

Time: Amid the Passover, the night before the Friday morning of the cross.

It is important to remember that Judas departed from the upper room at this time. Thus, he was not present when our Savior established the first Lord's Supper or to hear the final instructions given to the eleven.

In the upper room at Jerusalem, near the end of the Passover meal

Matt. 26:21-24	Mk. 14:18-21	Lk. 22:21-23	John 13:21-22
The traitor is here	*The traitor is here*		
21 And as they did eat,(a) he	18 And as they sat and did eat,(a) Jesus		*The traitor is here*
			21 When Jesus had thus
said,	said,		said, he was troubled in spirit, and testified,
		The traitor is here	and said,
"Verily I say unto you(b) that one of you shall betray me."	"Verily I say unto you,(b) One of you which eateth with me shall betray me."	21 "But, behold, the hand of him that betrayeth me *is* with me on the table.	"Verily, verily, I say unto you,(b) that one of you shall betray me."
	The word "One" above should be in lower case as it is in the first edition of the 1611 version. As stated, this has nothing to do with inspiration.	22 "And truly the Son of man goeth, as it was determined: but woe unto that man by whom he is betrayed!"	
The troubled apostles	*The troubled apostles*	*The troubled apostles*	*The troubled apostles*
22 And they were exceeding sorrowful,(c) and began every one of them to say unto him, "Lord, is it I?"	19 And they began to be sorrowful,(c) and to say unto him one by one, "Is it I?" and another *said,* "Is it I?"	23 And they began to enquire among themselves,(c) which of them it was that should do this thing. (Verse 24 cont. in Section 169.)	22 Then the disciples looked one on another,(c) doubting of whom he spake.
The awful warning	*The awful warning*		
23 And he answered and said,(d)	20 And he answered and said(d) unto them, "It is one of the twelve, that dippeth with me in the dish.		
"He that dippeth *his* hand with me in the dish, the same shall betray me.			
24 "The Son of man goeth as it is written of him: but woe unto that man by whom the Son of man is betrayed! it had been	21 "The Son of man indeed goeth, as it is written of him: but woe to that man by whom the Son of man is betrayed!		

Matt. 26:24-25	Mk. 14:21	Lk.	John 13:23-35
good for that man if he had ▶not been born."(e)	good were it for that man if he had ▶never been born."(e)	◀*All the quibbling about whether or not Judas was a saved man is answered in this awful statement. See verse 27 below with the comments at footnote i for more on Judas.*	
The traitor speaks	(Verse 22 cont. in Section 174.)		
25 Then Judas, which betrayed him, answered and said, "Master, is it I?" He said unto him, "Thou hast said."(f) (Verse 26 cont. in Section 174.)			

23 Now there was leaning on Jesus' bosom(g) one of his disciples, whom Jesus loved.

24 Simon Peter therefore beckoned to him, that he should ask who it should be of whom he spake.

John's question: Jesus' answer and the final sop

25 He then lying on Jesus' breast saith unto him, "Lord, who is it?"

26 Jesus answered, "He it is, to whom I shall give a sop,(h) when I have dipped *it*." And when he had dipped the sop, he gave *it* to Judas Iscariot, *the son* of Simon.

The devil incarnates himself into the body of Judas Iscariot

27 And after the sop Satan entered(i) into him. Then said Jesus unto him, "That thou doest, do quickly."

28 Now no man at the table knew for what intent he spake this unto him.

29 For some *of them* thought, because Judas had the bag,(j) that Jesus had said unto him, "Buy *those things* that we have need of against [for] the feast; or, that he should give something to the poor."

Judas departs: it is night in his soul: the eleven are now "little children"

30 He then having received the sop went immediately out: and it was night.(k)

31 Therefore, when he was gone out, Jesus said, "Now is the Son of man glorified, and God is glorified in him.(l)

32 "If God be glorified in him, God shall also glorify him in himself, and shall straightway glorify him.

33 "Little children,(m) yet a little while I am with you. Ye shall seek me: and as I said unto the Jews, Whither I go, ye cannot come; so now I say to you.

The wonderful new commandment

34 "A new commandment(n) I give unto you, That ye love one another; as I have loved you, that ye also love one another.

35 "By this shall all *men* know that ye are my disciples, if ye have love one to another."(o) (Verse 36 cont. in Section 173.)

Footnotes-Commentary

(a) **"Shall betray me."** Jesus and His apostles engaged in cross conversation with one another while eating the Passover meal. Again, He brings up the subject of a traitor in their midst. Luke records that He was "troubled in spirit" (moved inwardly) and thus prompted to speak openly of this awful matter. "One of you shall betray me." These words sent shock waves across the room.

(b) Highlighted in gray as having reference to the Old Testament prediction of Judas. At Jewish meals, it was customary to eat from a common dish with the fingers. In response to their question about the identity of the traitor, the Lord Jesus answered their inquiries twice; here, and then shortly afterwards in John 13: 25-26.

(c) Hearing His sober declaration, the apostles suddenly detected the deep sorrow of their Lord. They became grieved by His grief. Casting glances at each other across the table they begin to enquire "who" it was among them that would betray Him? They had forgotten their quarrel over greatness and were suddenly sobered into a serious mood as they beheld the sorrow of their dear Lord, and were eager to know who the traitor was and prevent this treachery. We are astounded at the careful deceit engineered by Judas. Having been with Christ for over two years, yet he remained undetected by the eleven. Paul later wrote, "And no marvel; for Satan himself is transformed into an angel of light. Therefore, *it is* no great thing if his ministers also be transformed as the ministers of righteousness; whose end shall be according to their works" (2 Cor. 11:14-15). Even to this moment, men and women of the same satanic disposition are mixed among the true people of God. For an earlier lesson given the by Savior on these things, see His Parable of the Wheat and Tares in Section 82, especially Matt. 13:40, footnote e.

(d) Highlighted in gray because it is prophecy pointing to Judas' eating bread with Jesus at the final Passover. This was written a thousand years prior and is recorded in Ps. 41:9. Since all of them dipped their hands into the dish it was unclear which one was the culprit. The ancients did not eat with plates, spoons, knives, and forks as we of the West do. They ate with their fingers out of single dishes. See footnote b above. Refer to footnote h below for more on this special final dip or sop given to the covert traitor.

(e) **"Better to have never been born."** *What terrible words!* Though not an Old Testament prediction, yet it speaks specifically of Judas. When we remember that this chilling statement came from the purest lips of love that ever spoke, we shudder at its meaning. Is the Lord of heaven referring to annihilation after death? Is "soul sleep" intended here? The inference is clear that some kind of conscious knowing exists and waits for the dark traitor in the endlessness of eternity. It was a common expression among the Jews to say of those who had greatly transgressed the law, "It would have been better for him had he never been born." There is a quotation in the Talmud tractate, Kiddushin 40a that rings similar to this. It reads "He who is careless of his Master's honor, it were well for him had he not come into the world." The internet is loaded with cult websites (denying the reality of hell) telling us that Judas was a saved man and is now in heaven. *Annihilation of the wicked stands as a lie before these Words of Jesus!*

2p-History of Judas Iscariot. The apostles understood what Jesus said for it was a normal Hebrew expression. However, today we fail to grasp the meaning of this immeasurable woe. Couched here is something awful, exceedingly dreadful, as though a black gulf of damnation yawned before his soul. The enormity of Judas' crime was so dark and deep that finite minds cannot hold to it. A thousand years prior, David under the inspiration of the Holy Spirit penned a review of the life, deeds, and family of the man from Kerioth in Ps. 109:6-20. These greatly overlooked passages speak of Judas; for so Peter interpreted and applied them in Acts 1:16-20, shortly after the ascension of Christ. From these verses, found only in the Old Testament, we see terrible glimpses of this human monster. Note the following twelve points:

1. **Ps. 109:6.** He was the wicked man set over or among the apostles of the Lord Jesus.
2. **Ps. 109:7.** His remorse and regret were too late. Matt. 27:3-10.
3. **Ps. 109:8.** His life was shortened by his sin and Matthias took his place among the apostles (Acts 1:26).
4. **Ps. 109:9.** Judas was a married man with children. They became fatherless and his wife a widow.
5. **Ps. 109:10.** His children were reduced to begging or scrapping for pieces of bread to exist.
6. **Ps. 109:11.** Thieves and strangers stole his wealth.
7. **Ps. 109:12.** In his last hours, he found no mercy or help from men. This probably referred to the chief priest and elders of the Jews when he attempted to return the blood money. Matt. 27:3-4.
8. **Ps. 109:13.** His name and family descendents vanished from the records of Jewish genealogy.
9. **Ps. 109:14-15.** His fathers were notorious men, and his mother was stained by some infamous but unnamed iniquity that loomed before the Lord of heaven.
10. **Ps. 109:16.** He showed no mercy to the helpless and poor.
11. **Ps. 109:17-19.** He was a man wholly given to cursing and foul language. His violent articulations became his bread in the eternal existence of hell. One is amazed that the other eleven apostles did not notice Judas' foul mouth. Apparently, he was the perfect con man. Peter also had trouble with bad language according to Matt. 26:74. Years later, he wrote about a mouth without guile (1 Peter 2:21-22).
12. **Ps. 109:20.** All the above was the traitor's reward from the hand of the Lord.

3p-For more information on Judas Iscariot, refer to Section 57, and number 12 in the Information Box under footnote m. One cannot but wonder what Judas thought as he looked down and saw the Son of God, with head bowed, washing his soiled feet, and carefully drying them! For him, there had been no cleansing inside the chambers of his dark heart. Christ's Words "Ye are clean but not all" met their terminus with him. Oddly, at this point none of the other apostles understood the meaning of their Lord's sober statement. This was because of the esteemed place of prominence Judas held among the little band of preachers. Unseen by mortal eye there suddenly stood in the upper room an invisible and uninvited guest. Satan, the prince of darkness appeared on the scene, waiting for his moment to enter again the heart of this fellow (verse 27). For an earlier penetration of Satan into the soul of Judas, see Section 147, Lk. 22:3, footnote a. Following this incarnation of the wicked one, Judas hurried to Jerusalem and arranged with the Jews to betray Messiah for thirty pieces of silver. For more on this refer to footnote i below.

(f) Knowing in his heart that he had already betrayed his Lord, and the price had been agreed upon, from a soul filled with vile impudence, Judas puts the same question to Jesus in Matt. 26:25. We are amazed at his brazen self-confidence, even his audacity! Apparently, Judas whispered his inquiry to Jesus, and the Master replied in tones of a divine whisper, "Thou hast said." It seems as though none of the others overheard this conversation.

(g) "Leaning on Jesus' breast." The western mind has difficulty with this statement not understanding eastern customs. The posture of Jews at a table was to recline on their left side across a couch. The Talmud mentions this in tractate, Berachoth 48a. This does not mean that he was actually physically leaning on or lying in the bosom of Christ. Such an act would have been highly irreverent on the part of John. It means that he occupied the couch next to Jesus at the table. From his leaning position, he was partly on the couch occupied by the Savior. To recline *next to one* who was greatly loved and held in high regard was spoken of as "Leaning on his bosom." There is a Persian fable of an earthen pot that fell upon a rose; its perfume passed into the vessel and remained for years. Thus, it was with John. For Christ in the bosom of the Father, see Section 1, Part 4, John 1:18, third paragraph of footnote l. The writers of the four gospels were rarely inspired to mention their names. They sought no self-glory as the human authors of the life of Christ. This is another mark of inspiration. In this case, the joy of reclining beside the Savior was more important than the name of the one experiencing such blessing.

2p-Peter, seeing John reclining closest to his Lord beckoned him to enquire of the Messiah, who it was that would betray him. John 13:25 reveals that John leaned over and whispered his question into the ear of Jesus. In the process, he actually had his head on the Lord's shoulder. "Breast" and "shoulder" were counted the same among Jewish males. Even today among Gentiles, the shoulder is still a place of repose in time of sadness or great sorrow.

(h) "Give a sop, when I have dipped it." It is of interest that the word "dip" in this text means to immerse and is the same word translated baptize in the New Testament. This act of Christ affirmed that the Passover meal had been in progress and was now nearing its end. According to Edersheim, this was the time when "the sop" was dipped into the sauce. For Jesus to hand it directly to Judas reveals that he occupied a place within reach of Christ. *There was a final sop at the Passover meal. It was given to the person in whom the master of ceremonies had a special interest!* It was this piece of bread that Jesus handed to Judas. Seemingly, the Savior had whispered His reply to John the beloved as He had to Judas in footnote f above. Hence, it was unheard by the other eleven men, and they did not understand the sop as John did. The other apostles looked at the act from their traditional understanding of what it meant. The one to whom Christ gave a sop (piece of broken bread) was the culprit among the apostles, but they did not understand this or the actions of their Master. Close at hand, yet invisible to human eyes, Lucifer knew very well what this gesture signified and instantly moved into the physical body of Judas. See footnote i below.

(i) "Satan entered into him." This literally happened. Lurking and ready, Satan waited, for the moment, to reenter the soul of this man. Pitiful indeed are those "professional theologians" who down play these things into "figures of speech," or "mythical pagan expressions," as they struggle to explain away the meaning of evil. Christ knowing that Judas was now the Devil incarnate suddenly commanded him, "That thou doest, do quickly." In modern day language, the Lord Jesus was saying to Judas, "I know what thou art contriving against me; what thou doest, therefore, do it quickly so that I may hurry to the cross of redemption to save others from the wiles of the Devil, whom you have invited into your heart." The Jews had a saying that no one commits wickedness until a spirit of madness enters them. Refer to Talmud tractate, Sota 3a for this proverbial expression. This was manifested in the actions of Judas after Satan entered his physical body. For an ancient pagan imitation of the above events with Judas and Satan, refer to Section 174, second and third paragraphs under footnote b.

2p-Verses 28. The other men hearing Christ's instructions to Judas still did not understand. They assumed that Judas had been instructed to go and buy more supplies to finish their meal or give something to the poor. It was customary for the Jews to share and give to the less fortunate during the Passover Feast. It was looked upon as a time of reaching out and blessing others. Another point worth consideration is that on the day *after* Passover, all shops and merchants shut down during the Feast of Unleavened Bread that followed. Thus, some of the apostles probably understood Jesus to be telling Judas, the treasurer to go and buy supplies for them before the shops close! There is an interesting note in Lightfoot's *Commentary on the New Testament . . .* , concerning Jewish butchers when closing their shops on special occasions and feast days. In vol. 1. page 76, he wrote that after closing shop, they "laid the key in the window which was above the door." This allowed entrance to all customers. They would take what they wanted and leave money for payment in a box sitting on a short table! These actions, without the owner being present, were not considered unlawful or infringing any of the rules governing their annual feasts!

(j) "The bag." Being the treasurer for the apostolic band, Judas carried this. As mentioned, the word for bag had reference to a small case in which a wind instrument was stored. See Section 146, second paragraph, footnote h. Apparently, Judas used it as a moneybox. There is an old *legend* that Judas was a musician. Leonardo da Vinci's famous painting from the 1400s entitled, "The Last Supper," showing Judas holding a leather bag with strings tied at the top is incorrect. So are his depictions of Jesus and the apostles sitting with knees under a western style table.

2p-"Buy *those things* we have need of." During Passover, the Jews would purchase all sorts of items, such as extra meats, bread, clothing, sandals, household goods, and gifts of benevolence to be given to the poor or used for themselves. Some of the men at the Passover table thought this was what Jesus was saying to Judas. They still did not understand he was the traitor. See second paragraph of footnote i above for more on this puzzling enigma.

(k) *It had been night for several hours!* The reference here is to the satanic darkness that shrouded the soul of this wretched individual as the Devil stepped into his body. Stealing through the night, he went on a still darker errand to the religious leaders of Israel. Satanically, he moved under the cover of earth's sunless shadows.

(l) **"Now is the Son of man glorified."** As Judas departed from the upper room, the atmosphere changed for Satan went out with him and in him. The despot was gone, and the Son of God turned to His eleven and spoke to them as a Father would farewell his beloved children. See footnote m below. Suddenly, He breaks out with a voice of blessing and this holy praise to God. "Now is the Son of man glorified," for the last deed has been done to secure His death on the cross. In His death, burial, and resurrection, God was glorified as never before, and He was glorified in God. At the cross, the Two met. Together, they provided atonement and eternal life for mankind. The Lord of heaven was magnified in the life and death of His Son. In addition, for over two thousand years God has honored His Son and given a million and more attestations to the triumph of Calvary and the empty tomb.

(m) **"Little children."** We have heard Him use such titles as "little ones" (Matt. 10:42), and "little flock" (Lk. 12:32) but now it is "little children." One could almost believe that Isa. 8:18 is intended here, "Behold I and the children whom the LORD hath given me." This title of endearment dropped into the heart of John and remained there. Years later, he wrote the epistle known as 1 John and used it some nine times, as though it was his very own. See 1 John 2:1, 12, 13, 18, 28; 3:7, 18; 4:4; and 5:21. Preparing them for what is next; He hinted that He must depart from them by death on the morrow. Again, they were dumbfounded at another reference of Him leaving them.

(n) **Verse 34. "A new commandment."** Not even the glorious Ten Commandments were like this one! In what sense were the apostles to understand this as a new commandment? Their Torah Law commanded, "Thou shalt love thy neighbor as thyself" (Lev. 19:18). *However, by rabbinical interpretation one's neighbor was only a fellow Jew, never a Gentile.* They had witnessed with amazement His unselfish love, without partiality toward all men. He received everyone, regardless of class or race. They were stunned as He touched lepers, received pagan Gentiles, healed cursed Samaritans, and even wept over the wicked religious leaders of Israel. Now, He commands them to love each other after the same model. In view of their quarreling for superiority, this commandment hit like a bomb.

(o) **Verse 35. The badge of universal recognition.** The scribes and Pharisee were identified by their flowing brown robes, broad bands on the fringes, extra large phylacteries, long public prayers, slamming their gifts into the metal horns at the Women's Court in order to make loud noises, painful adherence to the oral law, and scrupulously tithing of the smallest herb. The Savior forbids any such conduct among the members of His new kingdom. Religious men of today glory in securing public recognition. They dress in gorgeous robes; wear traditional beards, collars of various designs, gold chains about the neck, red scarves, crimson, purple, miters on their heads and long sticks in their hands. Swinging pots of smoking incense and chanting all sorts of weird invocations and benedictions are an outward show of the flesh and have nothing to do with the Spirit of God. Nowhere in Holy Scripture is there warrant for such religious pomp. (The garments of the Jewish high priests in Ex. 28 all typified in some way the coming Savior.) Historically, it is a reflection of pagan ceremonies. Magnificent processions and external splendor mirror the evil spirits of heathen religions still imbued in these rituals. Humility and shamefacedness are the hallmarks of God's men; not religious noise and outward show. Wise Christians flees these antics and refuses to be enchanted by their vain displays. The eleven apostles who heard their Lord give this "new commandment" were familiar with the Ten Commandments. Now, Jesus gives them one that exceeds anything they have ever heard from a rabbi. It was "new" in that it excelled the Torah Law and tradition of the elders.

2p-False honor. In particular circles today, if one subscribes to a certain creed, attends the "fellowship meetings," always supports the program, and submits to every infinitesimal regulation (that have nothing to do with Holy Scripture) he is accepted. By these actions, he is "faithful brother," and "solid Bible preacher." If one stays at this long enough, he will dress in a black gown, march over a stage, and be given an honorary doctorate, amid thunderous applause. This statement is not to be negatively misunderstood for God teaches us, to give honor to whom honor is due (Rom. 13:7). Man's recognition is not the high mark of service, though it is appreciated. "Love" is the royal public badge Christ commanded us to wear. Bearing this, we imitate Jesus at His highest and obey His commands (Matt. 5:43-48). *Again, Christians must not forget that love is an action not a feeling.*

3p-The little boy at the door. Years ago while home on furlough from Africa, I was sitting on the top step leading down into my study, one morning when the doorbell rang. A tiny voice said to my wife, "Is Mr. Pike here?" Looking up I saw a child about ten year's old. He smiled and said, "Mr. Pike would you pray with me; I'm not as close to the Lord as I should be." I did not recognize the lad. Sitting down on the step, I put my arm around his tiny shoulder and prayed. When the prayer was over, I inquired, "Son, have I met you before?" His response shook me, "Sure Mr. Pike, when you were here about four years ago, I was walking up the road, and you came out, gave me a piece of candy, a big hug, and said you loved me. I never forgot that and when I saw you were home again, I knew you could help me. My mother said to ask for your prayers." Five years later, while on another furlough I was preaching at a church in Greenville South Carolina. A young man in his teens walked up, shook my hand, and said, "Mr. Pike, I'm the little boy you prayed for that day on the step. I wanted to tell you that I live for Jesus and go to church here." *Love is the highest way!*

824

Reclining at the Passover table, Jesus predicts Peter's denial, and their scattering in the garden. His Words, at this late hour upset the apostles. Over anxious they inform Him that they have two swords and are ready to fight.

Time: Amid the Passover, the night before the Friday morning of the cross.

In the upper room at Jerusalem, after the Passover meal

Matt. 26:31-33	Mk. 14:27-29	Lk. 22:31-33	John 13:36-37
			Peter's question
			36 Simon Peter said unto him, "Lord, whither goest[a] thou?" Jesus answered him, "Whither I go, thou canst not follow me now; but thou shalt follow me afterwards."
		Simon and Satan: Jesus' warning	
		31 And the Lord said, "Simon, Simon,[b] behold, Satan hath desired *to have* you, that he may sift *you* as wheat:	
		32 "But I have prayed for thee, that thy faith fail not: and when thou art converted, strengthen thy brethren."	
A shock announcement	*A shock announcement*		
31 Then saith Jesus unto them, "All ye shall be offended because of me this night: for it is written,[c] 'I will smite the shepherd, and the sheep of the flock shall be scattered abroad.'	**27** And Jesus saith unto them, "All ye shall be offended because of me this night: for it is written,[c] 'I will smite the shepherd, and the sheep shall be scattered.'		
32 "But after I am risen again, I will go before you into Galilee."[d]	**28** "But after that I am risen, I will go before you into Galilee."[d]		
Peter's boast	*Peter's boast*	*Peter's boast*	*Peter's boast*
33 Peter answered and said[e] unto him,	**29** But Peter said[e] unto him,	**33** And he [Peter] said[e] unto him, "Lord, I am ready to go with thee, both	**37** Peter said[e] unto him, "Lord, why cannot I follow thee now? I

Matt. 26:33–35	Mk. 14:29–31	Lk. 22:33–37	John 13:37–38
		into prison, and to death."	will lay down my life for thy sake."
"Though all *men* shall be offended because of thee, *yet* will I never be offended."	"Although all shall be offended, yet *will* not I."		
A rooster will crow **34** Jesus said unto him,	***A rooster will crow*** **30** And Jesus saith unto him,	***A rooster will crow*** **34** And he said,	***A rooster will crow*** **38** Jesus answered him, "Wilt thou lay down thy life for my sake? Verily, verily, I say unto thee,
"Verily I say unto thee, That this night, before the cock crow,**(f)** [twice]	"Verily I say unto thee, That this day, *even* in this night, before the cock crow**(f)** twice,	"I tell thee, Peter,	
thou shalt deny me thrice."	thou shalt deny me thrice."	the cock shall not crow**(f)** [twice] this day, before that thou shalt thrice deny that thou knowest me."	The cock shall not crow,**(f)** [twice] till thou hast denied me thrice." (Next chap., John 14:1 cont. in Section 175.)
They all object **35** Peter said unto him,	***They all object*** **31** But he spake the more vehemently,		
"Though I should die with thee, yet will I not deny thee." Likewise also said all the disciples.**(g)** (Verse 36 cont. in Section 179.)	"If I should die with thee, I will not deny thee in any wise." Likewise also said they all.**(g)** (Verse 32 cont. in Section 179.)		
		Prepare for conflict **35** And he said unto them, "When I sent**(h)** you without purse, and scrip, and shoes, lacked ye any thing?" And they said, "Nothing." **36** Then said he unto them,**(i)** "But now, he that hath a purse, let him take *it*, and likewise *his* scrip: and he that hath no sword, let him sell his garment, and buy one. **37** "For I say unto you, that this that is written must yet be accomplished in me,**(j)** 'And he was	

Matt.	Mk.	Lk. 22:37-38	John
		reckoned among the transgressors:' for the things concerning me have an end." (fulfillment) **38** And they said, "Lord, behold, here *are* two swords." *"Stop this idle talk! You do not yet understand"* And he said unto them, "It is enough."(k) (Verse 39 cont. in Section 179.)	

Footnotes-Commentary

(a) **"Lord, where are you going?"** Previously, in John 13:33, Jesus had mentioned His soon leaving the eleven apostles. Peter quickly caught his Master's Words and was alarmed by the intimidation he felt in them. He was tormented with uncertainty and sorely grieved at the thought of being separated from Jesus. Being forward and quick to speak, he immediately puts a question regarding "where" his Lord was going. Christ's answer baffled him as well as the others. "He cannot go with Him now, but he can follow later." What did these strange words mean?

(b) **Lk. 22:31-32. "Simon, Simon."** For a review of Satan and his devices, see Section 23, all under footnote c. Jews held that to call one's name twice was to show the greatest of love and personal concern. They would point to such examples in the Old Testament as God calling "Abraham, Abraham" (Gen. 22:11), or "Moses, Moses" (Ex. 3:4). As Judas left the upper room with Satan in his body, we are introduced to another machination of the wicked one. He seeks to move from the traitor to the fisherman! Christ foreseeing that Peter would soon deny Him issued a warning trying to bring him to high alert. Was this interest of Lucifer in Peter the source of his frequent outbursts and rashness? We have no written record of where the Lord Jesus had special prayer for Peter nor do we need one. If the Son of God saw it right to pray for His weaker sheep, especially those given to pride and arrogance, struggling and arguing for preeminence, how much more should we pray for ourselves and the brethren? Our Lord prayed for Simon that "his faith fail not." We note a short time later that his faith did temporarily fail. Herein is a grand lesson for all who pray. Peter had to exercise common sense and self-discipline in this matter. He knew what was right, but refused to do so. Again, we note the high lesson that God forces the will of no man into doing His will. Peter succumbed to Satan's devices, even to denying his Lord, but not totally. He went dangerously far away but not into apostasy. We read earlier, "God heard Jesus always" (John 11:42), and the problem with Peter was no exception. He lived through the trauma of denying Christ. He was not kept from being tempted but from being destroyed. This came by the grace of God, provided through the prayers of the Lord Jesus.

2p-Regarding Simon's hassle with Satan, in 1889, Albert H. Newman, wrote in *A Manual of Church History*, vol. one, page 18, this truth. "To know how large a proportion of those that have professed Christianity have lived in sin and dishonored the name of Christ will tend to put us on our guard against a similar failure, and to prevent us from despairing when we see how imperfectly many of those around us fulfill their Christian duties."

3p-**"When thou art converted, strengthen thy brethren."** This shows that Christ knew in advance of Peter's recovery. The "prayer of faith" prevails. "Converted," carries the meaning of being restored to good sense and clear understanding, not of salvation. Sin will dull the senses of the sharpest saint. Those who spend time bickering for position and power (as did Peter) will lose the practical use of Christian wisdom. Today, the Devil has most husbands and wives in a state of habitual conflict, families divided, children hating parents, rebellious teen-agers scorning the wise advice of their elderly peers. As stated, two things are infinite; God and human stupidity.

(c) **"All eleven apostles offended in their Messiah!"** This is an interpretation of the prediction written in Zech. 13:7. His arrest, trial, beatings, unjust treatment, and finally death by crucifixion would be too much for them! The great Shepherd would be smitten, and the little flock of eleven sheep would flee. Christ took this Old Testament prediction and saw its fulfillment in Himself a short time ahead in the Garden of Gethsemane. Immediately, after His reply to Peter's inquiry, the Lord Jesus tries to forewarn the eleven about the ensuing events of that awful night. Not only will Peter run away, but all of them will flee their Master, leaving Him alone. This happened some hours later as seen in Section 180, Mk. 14:50, footnote m. Fear can freeze every ounce of courage in men. One would think the eleven would be bold as a raging bull when their Master seemed to be in peril. *It remains painfully so, that the truer a believer remains to Christ, greater is the possibility that he will find himself slipping into intellectual and spiritual arrogance.* Brokenness and suffering are the pathways into humble service for the Savior.

(d) He speaks *again* of rising from the dead! How mysterious and puzzling were these words to His preachers. His first mention of death on the cross was spoken during the early months of His ministry as He fell into conflict with the religious leaders at the Passover (John 2:19-21). Could it be possible that their Lord was going to die? Was this to be the end for their wonderful Messiah? He makes an appointment to meet them in Galilee *after* His resurrection. In using the words "I will go before you," we see an allusion of a shepherd leading his flock. This appointment was kept later after His resurrection as seen in Section 195, Matt. 28:7 with Mk. 16:7, footnote j.

(e) **"Peter said unto him."** Amazing indeed! The Lord of glory and King of Israel had just spoken a direct warning to Peter and look at his double response! *First*, "If everyone is offended because of you, I will never be." *Second*, "Why, don't you know Lord, I am ready for prison and death for your cause." We believe that these rash words were, nevertheless, sincere, coming from the heart of this rough, tough fisherman. That Peter meant them with his entire being, we cannot doubt. Later in Peter's life, he did go to prison for Christ (Acts 4:3, and 12:5). *Often, we see more in the school of darkness than the school of light (Micah 7:8).*

2p-Crucified up side down. Jesus met the arrogance of Peter, by telling him that he should not so confidently assume what he would do. In a few hours, he denounced his Lord thrice. Refer to Section 181, for the history of Peter's denial of Messiah and the outcome of this impulsive calamity. Several ancient writers affirm that as a feeble old man he died by crucifixion up side down lest he should emulate the death of his Lord. Refer to John 21:19 with 2 Peter 1:13-15 for more on this. Also, see articles on this in *The New Unger's Bible Dictionary,* page 993; and *Halley's Bible Handbook,* page 662. The Roman Catholic Church has distorted Peter's life and death to enhance their system of religious falsehood. Refer to Section 41, third paragraph of footnote a for more on this.

3p-Infallible in nothing. The Papal Church has an admirable record of building hospitals, children's homes, and ministering to the poor and needy. The author has spent many days in Catholic hospitals; their service was impeccable. In witnessing to the nuns and priests who visited nightly, he found that *none* of them knew they would go to heaven when life ended. In over fifty years of witnessing for Christ, I have never met a Catholic priest or nun who knew they were saved. Claiming to be the infallible church, with the Pope as God's voice (Vicar) on earth, and her priests having authority to forgive sins, yet Catholics do not know where they will go at death! How can they presume to instruct others in this most serious issue when they are unsure themselves? Sincere religious deceit concerning heaven and hell is the greatest calamity among mankind. Its consequences are eternal. The best of Catholics are in the dark regarding their destiny in the after life, yet they are taught that outside *their church,* there is no salvation. What a blatant contradiction! Attending confessional, partaking of mass, has never given anyone the positive assurance of eternal life. A church that leaves its adherents without sure hope regarding death, and the afterlife is not infallible, it is false. *God is big enough to save us, and we will know it.* The blessed assurance of sins forgiven, and a home in heaven comes by simple faith in the finished work of Christ on the cross and His resurrection. If a person is seeking the salvation of his soul, he had better flee the Roman Catholic religion. It cannot help him! It teaches the untruth that we are saved through baptism, the "sacraments," and then increase our hold on grace and forgiveness by our righteous deeds. This religious system is infallible in nothing. See also, Section 103, number 2, under footnote g for other thoughts on this disturbing subject.

(f) **Peter and the rooster problem.** Peter is always addressed as Simon, except in this verse. Jesus spoke these words to him in the evening, *at the end* of the Passover meal. It must have been at least 9:00 p.m. Matthew wrote, "before the cock crow," while Mark was inspired to add the words "before the cock crow twice." Asian Roosters *normally* crow two times during night hours, once at about midnight and the other at daybreak. However, this often changes depending on the time of the year and weather conditions. Both Matthew and Mark wrote, "this night" while Luke penned the words "this day." Being after sundown, thus it was the day according to Jewish reckoning of time. The final call of this particular fowl, just before sunrise, was known in the east, as the "cock crowing." Mark also wrote of a second crowing, meaning the same time. Before Peter could utter his final swear word and his third denial, from the darkness of that last Passover night came the old familiar cock-a-doodle–do. The "rooster problem" discovered by the critics of Holy Scripture flies away! Peter would deny his Lord at least thrice. Christ informed Peter that within the time and space of the *different* cockcrowing, he would deny Him three times.

2p-Another point frequently missed is that the Jewish doctors of the law divided the cockcrowing into the first, second, and third sessions, a custom that was apparently not known among other nations of antiquity. This odd belief is mentioned in the Talmud tractate, Yoma 21a without explanation. When "learned scholars" attack the Scriptures as wrong concerning the rooster crowing, they would do well to consider the social customs of the people involved before announcing their infidel judgments. Benjamin Davies, *Harmony of the Gospels,* footnote w on page 154 carries an excellent comment on this matter of the crowing cock. He reveals how Mark was more specific. He related the rooster crowed twice, while the other evangelists were inspired to write in more general terms.

(g) **"Likewise, said they all."** It is sometimes overlooked that Christ spoke this warning not to Peter only but to all the apostles. Matthew being one of those present at this time, wrote that all of the disciples (including himself) boasted along with Peter that they would not deny their Master.

(h) Here, the Savior refers to first sending out the twelve on their evangelistic trip across Galilee. Section 57 is the record of where they were chosen. Then, they were sent out in Section 59. He wants them to recall God's provisions in service after He is gone. This will help them to trust Him for future work in His new kingdom-church.

(i) The former assignment to preach across Galilee was limited. There was no extended preparation necessary for that short adventure. Tomorrow, He will die on the cross. Redemption's plan for the salvation of men will be totally realized and finished. After His resurrection, their new missionary assignment would be the whole world of their day. They will move among strangers and dangers previously unknown. He is telling them to be wise, think, pray, and make every practical arrangement necessary for their work of carrying the gospel to every creature. The Lord Jesus gave them the Great Commission five different times. See these in Sections 201, 203, 204, 205, and 206.

2p-"Purse." Here the meaning is that it took money to get God's work done then, as it does today. Even backslidden Jonah had to buy his ticket to get aboard that doomed ship (Jonah 1:3). Every time Paul boarded a boat to sail away and carry the gospel afar, he had to pay the fare. Dr. Tenny Frank, in his amazing six-volume work, *An Economic Survey of Ancient Rome* goes to great length explaining the costs of living in the Roman world during the days of Christ and Paul. As it was then, so it is today. Money was needed for everything, especially Roman taxes. Christ tells his preachers "You better take some money when you go." (Young missionaries going to the field would be wise to heed this injunction from Christ.) How different from that earlier and first sending of the twelve on the limited commission to the nation of Israel, in Matt. 10:1 and 6. At that occasion, He instructed them not to take a purse for it was a limited effort, and many extra things would not be needed. That was almost three years prior. For the charlatans within the church and on television, see Section 207, second and third paragraphs of footnote i.

3p-"Script." This was a leather or cloth bag used by travelers to carry provisions. For an earlier mention of this, see Section 59, Matt. 10:10, footnote d.

4p-"Sword." The Savior admonished His apostles, "Buy a sword if you don't have one." With these words, the so-called "Christian pacifists" have a terrible struggle. Matthew Henry wrote, "The Galileans generally wore swords" in his *Commentary,* vol. 5, page 656. Josephus, who lived in Galilee for some years, also wrote of the Galileans carrying swords. Contemporary history informs us that the countryside was infested with bandits and robbers. Swords were as common as air! Christ is teaching His servants the need for practical sense and self-protection. He was telling His preachers, in essence "If you don't have a sword, sell your coat (or outer garment, mantel), and buy one." Pacifism is not taught in Holy Scripture, nor is aggressive war with the intent to steal the lands and goods of others. Self-protection and defending our own, is both honorable and upright. Among the eleven apostles, reclining about the Passover table, someone reported that there were two swords in their company. We wonder to which of the apostles they belonged. Apparently, Peter was one of them! See footnote k below for more on these two swords and what the Lord Jesus said about their "warlike" big talk.

(j) **"Reckoned among transgressors."** Jesus quotes this from Isa. 53:12, which is strictly Messianic and applied it to Himself. He was telling His preachers that His work is about finished, has an end or fulfillment, but theirs is just beginning. Tomorrow, He will be hung between two thieves and thus fulfill the prediction of the prophet in this passage. The Savior was "reckoned [or placed] with the transgressors," yet, He was not one. In His death on the cross, He bore the sins and transgressions of all men, thus making forgiveness and eternal life possible for those who repent and believe. The eleven apostles must have been dizzy at this barrage of instructions and warnings. None of them knew that on the coming morrow, their Lord would be nailed to a Roman cross. In the latter portion of verse 37, the Savior was telling His preachers, "My work is about done; yours is just beginning."

(k) **"Stop this talk. It is enough."** The entire conversation at this time was integrated with confusion and uncertainty. Peter reflected this as he boasted of going to prison or death for his Lord. Jesus cited from Isa. 53:12, and considered Himself as being counted with "transgressors" or evil men. Not really understanding what He said, the apostles thought it was time to "get ready for the big fight," that was pending with the Jews and religious leaders.

2p-For more on "Sword," see the fourth paragraph of footnote i above. They replied that among them were two swords. Jesus' response has been often misunderstood. His rebuke "It is enough," meant, "Enough of such war talk, don't speak these things anymore." He was not telling them that "two swords" were sufficient to battle the crowds; rather, their carnal language had gone far enough. They were not to fight for His deliverance upon being arrested at the garden. Later, during the actual skirmish in the garden, He instructed Peter to put up his sword after he had wildly made an attack on one of Jesus' arrestors. Refer to Section 180, Matt. 26:51-52 for this event. Simon Peter seems to have forgotten his Master's orders about "leave your swords out of this."

3p-A point frequently overlooked is that the Sanhedrin made it a punishable offence for anyone to carry a weapon in Jerusalem on any of the feast days. However, this did not apply to the temple police. Did our Lord have this in mind when He tried to calm His apostles, who apparently thought they were ready to take on the angry Jews with two swords.

As the meal ends, He establishes communion. Judas had previously left the room as seen in Section 172. The eleven apostles are amazed at their Lord's actions. Again, they failed to understand what He did and said.*

Time: The Passover has ended. It is the night before the Friday morning of the cross.

Not only did the eleven apostles fail to understand the meaning of this first Lord's Supper, but the great apostle Paul wrote almost thirty years later, that he only understood its meaning after a revelation from the Lord (1 Cor. 11:23-25). As explained, with the coming of the Spirit in fullness at Pentecost, the preachers of Christ were given total understanding of these previously unrevealed divine mysteries. See note by the symbol ◙ below.

In the upper room at Jerusalem: He does something new

Matt. 26:26-29	Mk. 14:22-25	Lk. 22:19-20	John
A new meaning given to the bread	*A new meaning given to the bread*	*A new meaning given to the bread*	
26 And as they were eating,[(a)] Jesus took bread, and blessed *it*, and brake *it*, and gave *it* to the disciples, and said, "Take, eat; this is my body."	22 And as they did eat,[(a)] Jesus took bread, and blessed, and brake *it*, and gave to them, and said, "Take, eat: this is my body."	19 And he took bread,[(a)] and gave thanks, and brake *it*, and gave unto them, saying, "This is my body which is given for you: this do in remembrance of me."	
A new meaning given to the cup	*A new meaning given to the cup*	*A new meaning given to the cup*	
27 And he took the [last] cup,[(b)] and gave thanks, and gave *it* to them, saying, "Drink ye all of it;"	23 And he took the [last] cup,[(b)] and when he had given thanks, he gave *it* to them: and they all drank of it. 24 And he said unto them,	20 Likewise also the [last] cup[(b)] after supper, saying, "This cup *is*	
28 "For this is my blood of the new testament,[(c)] which is shed for many for the remission of sins.	"This is my blood of the new testament,[(c)] which is shed for many.	the new testament[(c)] in my blood, which is shed for you." (Verse 21 cont. in Section 172.)	
29 "But I say unto you, I will not drink henceforth[(d)] of this fruit of the vine, until that day when I drink it new with you in my Father's kingdom." (Verse 30 cont. in Section 175, at the end of the Scripture harmonization.)	25 "Verily I say unto you, I will drink no more[(d)] of the fruit of the vine, until that day that I drink it new in the kingdom of God." (Verse 26 cont. in Section 175, at the end of the Scripture harmonization.)	◙ *After Passover, Jesus and the apostles did not eat the meal of "chagigah," often observed by pious Jews. See Section 183, fourth paragraph of footnote c for more on this after Passover meal.*	

Footnotes-Commentary

(a) **"Eating."** This speaks of the end of the Passover. If any remnants of the lamb and bread were still in the dishes and not eaten it was to be burned according to Ex. 12:10. No doubt, Jesus let the meal continue amid the conversations that took place between Him and the apostles. From out of this ancient celebration of Israel, the Son of God will now constitute the Lord's Supper. For explanation of the cups of red wine used in the Passover, see Section 171, Lk. 22:17, footnote a. Three cups of wine had been consumed during the meal. A fourth cup was waiting at the close of the Passover supper and several Psalms were sung amid prayers being said. A blessing in prayer was announced over this. Hence, Paul's words years later as he wrote to the Corinthians of the "cup of blessing" in 1 Cor. 10:16. For the number of cups used during Passover, and their original meaning, see Section 168, fourth and fifth paragraphs under footnote d. It was at the close of the Passover meal that Jesus took bread and explained to His apostles that it represented His body. Filled with Satan, Judas received the final sop and left the upper room. See Section 172, John 13:25-29, footnotes h, i, and j. *He did not partake of this first communion.*

2p-A strange ending. At this time, none of the apostles understood Jesus' death the next morning. What He was going to do now would be meaningless. Later, with the coming of the Holy Spirit at Pentecost, in His fullness, they understood everything He did and taught them. To their surprise, the Master suddenly departs from the traditional Pascal conclusion. The middle cake of the three was hidden before the meal started. This was known as "yahats." Half of it was broken off, and this was called "afikoman." Jesus takes this broken part and holds it up before the apostles, breaks it again and announces, "Take, eat, this is [represents] my body, which is broken for you." Never, had they heard a Passover end with these words! Christ was telling them that this piece of bread pictured His body that was broken tomorrow as He was nailed to the cross. It is preposterous to hold that Christ was instructing them to eat His literal flesh. *He was there dwelling in that flesh as he spoke!* Luke wrote that He instructed them to eat this bread in "remembrance of him" (verse 19). For the error of "eating Jesus' flesh" in the Roman Catholic mass, or any other church, see Section 95, first through the fourth paragraphs under footnote r.

(b) "He took the cup." Luke also wrote that it was "after supper" in verse 20. This was the final cup. The one in Lk. 22:17, footnote a, was the first. As mentioned above, for the number of cups used during Passover, see Section 168, fourth and fifth paragraphs under footnote d. With this, He gave a prayer of thanks. Luke records Him as saying that "This cup is the new testament in my blood, which is shed for you" (verse 20). Mark wrote that His blood was "shed for many" (verse 24). Both Matthew in verse 28, and Mark in verse 24, wrote that His blood provides for "many" (all who believe) the remission of their sins. Christ shed His blood for all men everywhere. However, only those who are saved constitute the "many" of these two passages. (His precious blood was not actually shed until the next day as He hung on the cross. The liquid in the cup only symbolized it.) These words must have dumbfounded His preachers. What did their Lord mean? Never had they heard anything like this during their sacred Passover. Later, they would come into full understanding of Jesus' statement.

2p-Ancient demonic imitations of communion. Centuries before the birth of Messiah there existed a pagan belief known as Mithraism. The roots of this demonic cult are traced a thousand years prior to the birth of Christ. In Mithraism, a heathen priest officiated over a cup of water or blood, and a piece of bread, which was set before the participants. These elements were supposed to give life and forgiveness to the participants. (Romanism teaches the same pagan myth.) The Mithra priests taught that the blood of a slain bull could purify the earth. Atheistic "scholars" have worked overtime trying to prove that the early Christian believers borrowed the ordinance of communion from this heathen practice, and that Christ did not *originally* establish it on the Passover evening. Charles Panati, in his book, *Extraordinary Origins of Everyday Things*, pages 12-13 reveals how Norse mythology in the pre-Christian era had similar fables. There was a banquet for Valhalla (a pagan god), to which twelve gods were invited. A foul spirit named "Loki" entered the banquet and this raised the number present to thirteen. This represented the presence of Satan. A riot broke out and Balder the favorite of all gods was killed. Unsaved "academicians" view this Norse legend as prefiguring the Last Supper. It is the opposite. Rather, it reveals the hatred and fear of the Devil for the atonement of Jesus Christ, and how he has imitated and mocked this for centuries in heathen rituals long before our Lord's incarnation and earthly life. For more on Dr. Charles Panati, and his blasphemies of God, the Bible, and Christ, see to Section 1, Part 4, and the fourth paragraph of footnote j.

3p-Heathen religious blood washings. The right religion. Certain pagan religions required that each initiate to be literally "washed in the blood of the lamb." They were placed in a hole with a metal grid over the top. A lamb was slain, and its blood dripped onto those below. Mithraism used a bull, which symbolized strength and power. Eating its flesh gave new life. This was a satanic imitation of the statement in Rev. 7:14, (and similar texts) that speak of salvation by the blood of Christ. Practically, every major doctrine and many minor ones of the New Testament appeared within the vast labyrinth of heathenism centuries before the coming of Christ. Satanic forces worked over the millenniums to discredit the salvation God provided through His Son Jesus Christ. This truth has been greatly stressed across this work. These historical facts manifest which religion is right! Again, it is stated that the service of communion or the Lord's Supper was never established by Jesus to bring forgiveness and salvation to anyone. It points back to salvation *already received* in the soul of those who participate. For an example of the pagan practice of blood washings, practiced in South Africa, see Section 95, the sixth paragraph of footnote r.

4p-Academic infidelity. Dr. Bart D. Ehrman, in his book, *Lost Christianities: The Battle for Scripture and the Faiths We Never Knew,* gives us a classic example of academic arrogance and ignorance. The "learned professor" demonstrates that he too is a servant of the Devil, whom he so "scholarly" denies. The internet also vibrates with shocking affronts and brazen statements slamming everything pertaining to Bible Christianity. An example of this is Alfred Reynolds' disgusting work published in 1988, *Jesus Versus Christians.* Reynolds scandalized the Holy Scripture and Jesus Christ, its central theme. Dr. Timothy Jones answers these critics in, *Misquoting Truth.* There are two places where everyone is a believer; heaven and hell. Some of these are too late!

(c) "My blood of the new testament." Obviously, our Lord was saying that the liquid in the cup symbolized or pointed to His blood to be shed tomorrow on the cross. Matthew wrote that Jesus said, "many," and Mark used the same word. Calvinists, spiritually sterilized by their "limited atonement," think they see in this proof of their dogma. Why not take their exegesis to Luke, who wrote that Jesus said His blood was shed "for you." According to their interpretation, this would prove that Christ died just for the eleven apostles and no one else. We read in 1 John 2:2, that Christ's atoning death propitiates for the sin of the "whole world." However, only those under conviction of the Holy Spirit through the Word of God, who repent and believe on Christ, are saved. In Heb. 8:6-13, it affirms that Christ is the "mediator of a better covenant, which was established upon better promises." This means "better" than those promises found in the Torah Law of Israel. In this passage, Jesus makes a clear connection with Ex. 24:8, where it speaks of "the blood of the covenant" at Mount Sinai.

2p-His blood for the remission of sin, Lev. 17:11. "The life of the flesh *is* in the blood: and I have given it to you upon the altar to make atonement for your souls." Hebrews 10:4, "For *it is* not possible that the blood of bulls and goats should take away sins." Again, Hebrews 9:12 reads, "By his own blood he entered in once into the holy place, [heaven] having obtained eternal redemption for us." Colossians 1:20, "And having made peace through the blood of his cross." In 1 John 1:7, it states, "The blood of Jesus Christ his [God's] Son cleanseth us from all sins." Simon Peter wrote in 1 Peter 1:18-19, "Forasmuch as ye know that ye were not redeemed with corruptible things as silver and gold . . . But with the precious blood of Christ, as of a lamb without blemish and without spot." John declared in Rev. 1:5, "Unto him that loved us and washed us from our sins in his own blood." Hebrews 12:24, affirms, "And to Jesus the mediator of the new covenant, and to the blood of sprinkling, that speaketh better things than *that of* Abel." Finally, Rev. 5:9, "And they [the saints in heaven] sung a new song, saying, . . . thou wast slain, and hast redeemed us to God by thy blood out of every kindred, and tongue, and people, and nation."

3p-Those who wrangle about being in or under the Law of Moses, or living by the positive portions of the Jewish oral traditions, should note Heb. 13:20-21. "Now the God of peace, that brought again from the dead our Lord Jesus, that great shepherd of the sheep, through the blood of the everlasting covenant, Make you perfect in every good work to do his will, working in you that which is well pleasing in his sight, through Jesus Christ; to whom *be* glory forever and ever. Amen." All we have in Christ comes by "the blood of His everlasting covenant." Beware of those who add or take from this. See Section 95, second paragraph of footnote u for more on this.

4p-The Hebrew Law is not the everlasting covenant but pointed men to that new and perfect covenant established by Christ. He did this in His death, burial, resurrection, and ascension. The *first and foundational* purpose of Christ shedding His blood was to atone for and take away the sins of those who trust him by simple faith (Heb. 9:22). From God's viewpoint, this forgiveness is eternal. Many untaught Christians not understanding this truth and live in the "misery of doubt" regarding their forgiven sins. They struggle ever so hard trying to make secure God's forgiveness when it has been eternally settled (Ps. 103:10-14 with Heb. 10:10). All tormenting anxiety over personal salvation finds its origin in the lie of Arminianism. *The sins of every genuinely saved person are where last winter's snow is—forever gone!* Who among humankind can find last year's snow?

5p-The Mormon Church, the blood of Christ, and the Mountain Meadows Massacre. The doctrine of this church teaches that there are certain sins that the blood of Christ will not remit. In 1979, Thelma Greer, whose great-grandfather was the adopted son of Brigham Young, published, *Mormonism, Mama & Me!* Chapter Nine documents the historical fact that Mormons have murdered other Mormons for committing certain sins; "sins the blood of our Lord did not atone for." Members of this satanic group, with the help of Indians, engineered the infamous Mountain Meadows Massacre of 1857. Together they slaughtered a hundred settlers, including women and children, who were traveling to California. Today, Mormonism works hard to present itself as a Christian body. For more on this deceiving, massive, and powerful cult, see Section 27, footnote a.

(d) "I will not drink henceforth." Jesus was saying that He would never partake of another Jewish Passover like this one and drink the fruit of an earthly vine. This was the final time He partook in the Jewish Pascal Feast in this manner. In His words, "until the day when I drink it new with you in my Father's kingdom" (Mark uses the words "kingdom of God"), He reflects into the eternal future; and again we note that both kingdom terms mean the same. He is referring to the consummation of His kingdom and the reception of all things in heaven, when human life was over. For explanation of the kingdom in its two different manifestations, see Section 39, footnotes a and g. The Savior is not speaking of rotted intoxicating *literal* wine, but rather what the *true* blood of the grape points to His precious blood. The word "new" seems to be the key in understanding this statement of Christ. Refer to Section 171, Lk. 22:18, footnote b for further explanation on this passage. The teaching about eating, drinking, childbirth, and so forth, in the millennial is not explained in Scripture. Radical literalists have tried to figure this out but always fail. Whatever it all means it is certainly not "eating and drinking" and other things as known in this life with the human anatomy and the results that follows. Nor can it refer to physical hunger that drives one to food and drink, something with which we are acquainted. When *glorified* human bodies "eat and drink" in eternity, it is different from those of this present life. *Nor will the food be as it is now.* Speculation is wrong, for God has not given us the details of these mysteries. Lastly, the teaching that Christ's presence mystically reappears in the bread and cup of the Lord's Supper, and that we are saved by eating and drinking these is a vicious untruth. *No one is saved from sin and hell via the digestive tract!* For an explanation concerning "eating Jesus' flesh" in the mass of the Roman Catholic Church, or any other church, see Section 95, third and fourth paragraphs under footnote r.

CHAPTER 16
FROM PASSOVER TO THE GARDEN OF PRAYER AND JUDAS.

Time: The night before the Friday morning of the cross.

Jesus' farewell instructions to the eleven. He answers their questions. They were shaken to hear that He was leaving. He promises to send the Holy Spirit, Who will comfort them. Leaving* the upper room, they walk eastward through the crowded city to the temple, and then to Gethsemane near the foot of Mount Olivet.

*It is important that we note His departure from the upper room at this point as recorded in John 14:31. According to the restrictions of the Sanhedrin, most Jewish businesses were located at the western side of Jerusalem where He used the upper room. From here to the garden located at the foot of Mount Olivet, was a lengthy walk. Because the streets of Jerusalem were packed with pilgrims who had come from over the known world for Passover, it would have taken well over an hour to reach Gethsemane. It was during this time that Judas gathered the armed men from the high priest, and a detachment of soldiers from Pilate. Next, they moved to Gethsemane where Christ was arrested. His Words in John chapters 15 through 17 were spoken as He led His apostles to the temple and then the garden. Their arrival at Gethsemane is recorded in Section 179, John 18:1.

Matt.	Mk.	Lk.	John 14:1-14 (Matt. 26:30 & Mk. 14:26)—*Still in the upper room*
			Comforting the apostle's troubled hearts **1** "Let not your heart be troubled:[a] ye believe in God, believe also in me. **2** "In my Father's house are many mansions:[b] if *it were* not *so*, I would have told you. I go to prepare a place for you. **3** "And if I go and prepare a place for you, I will come again, and receive you unto myself; that where I am, *there* ye may be also. **4** "And whither I go ye know, and the way ye know."[c] *Thomas' question* **5** Thomas saith[d] unto him, "Lord, we know not whither thou goest; and how can we know the way?" *The Savior's answer* **6** Jesus saith[e] unto him, "I am the way, the truth, and the life: no man cometh unto the Father, but by me. **7** "If ye had known me,[f] ye should have known my Father also: and from henceforth ye know him, and have seen him." *Philip's request* **8** Philip saith unto him, "Lord, show us the Father, and it sufficeth us." *The Savior's answer* **9** Jesus saith unto him, "Have I been so long time with you, and yet hast thou not known me, Philip? he that hath seen me hath seen the Father;[g] and how sayest thou *then*, 'Show us the Father'? **10** "Believest thou not that I am in the Father, and the Father in me? the words that I speak unto you I speak not of myself: but the Father that dwelleth in me, he doeth the works. **11** "Believe me that I *am* in the Father, and the Father in me: or else believe me for the very works' sake. **12** "Verily, verily, I say unto you, He that believeth on me, the works that I do shall he do also; and greater *works* than these shall he do; because I go unto my Father.[h] **13** "And whatsoever ye shall ask in my name, that will I do, that the Father may be glorified in the Son. **14** "If ye shall ask any thing in my name, I will do *it*.

Matt.	Mk.	Lk.	John 14:15-31 (Matt. 26:30 & Mk. 14:26)—*Departing the upper room*

15 "If ye love me, keep my commandments.[i]

Help is coming from the Father in heaven

16 "And I will pray the Father, and he shall give you another Comforter,[j] that he may abide with you for ever;

17 "*Even* the Spirit of truth; whom the world cannot receive, because it seeth him not, neither knoweth him: but ye know him; for he dwelleth with you, and shall be in you.

18 "I will not leave you comfortless: I will come to you.

19 "Yet a little while,[k] and the world seeth me no more; but ye see me: because I live, ye shall live also.

Soon you shall know and understand our spiritual indwelling

20 "At that day ye shall know that I *am* in my Father, and ye in me, and I in you.

21 "He that hath my commandments, and keepeth them, he it is that loveth me: and he that loveth me shall be loved of my Father, and I will love him, and will manifest myself to him."

Judas' question

22 Judas saith[l] unto him, not Iscariot, "Lord, how is it that thou wilt manifest thyself unto us, and not unto the world?"

The Savior's answer "Fellowship with the Father and Me"

23 Jesus answered[m] and said unto him, "If a man love me, he will keep my words: and my Father will love him, and we will come unto him, and make our abode with him.

24 "He that loveth me not keepeth not my sayings: and the word which ye hear is not mine, but the Father's which sent me.

25 "These things have I spoken unto you, being *yet* present with you.

New teacher, new peace: love me and rejoice

26 "But the Comforter, *which is* the Holy Ghost, whom the Father will send in my name, he shall teach you all things,[n] and bring all things to your remembrance, whatsoever I have said unto you.

27 "Peace I leave with you, my peace I give unto you: not as the world giveth, give I unto you. Let not your heart be troubled, neither let it be afraid.

28 "Ye have heard how I said unto you, 'I go away, and come *again* unto you.' If ye loved me,[o] ye would rejoice, because I said, 'I go unto the Father:' for my Father is greater than I.[p]

29 "And now I have told you before it come to pass, that, when it is come to pass, ye might believe.[q]

The prince of this world can make no claim on Christ:
He is the sinless Son of God

30 "Hereafter I will not talk much with you: for the prince of this world [Satan] cometh, and hath nothing[r] in me.

They leave the upper room

31 "But that the world may know that I love the Father; and as the Father gave me commandment, even so I do. **Arise, let us go hence.**"[s] (Next chap., John 15:1 cont. in Section 176.) *With the last five words above, we mark the departure of Jesus and the eleven apostles from the upper room. Between the end of chapter 14 and the beginning of 15 they move eastward over the city and into the temple. Later, in Gethsemane He was arrested. This is explained in Section 180.*

Matt. 26:30	Mk. 14:26	Lk.	John
Leaving the upper room **30** And when they had sung an hymn, they went out[t] into the mount of Olives. (Verse 31 cont. in Section 173.)	*Leaving the upper room* **26** And when they had sung an hymn, they went out[t] into the mount of Olives. (Verse 27 cont. in Section 173.)		

Footnotes-Commentary

[a] **"Troubled hearts."** With Passover finished and the memorial supper of communion now established (which they would only understand later) the Messiah turns full attention to His eleven still reclining on their couches about the table. The words about His death had burdened them unmercifully. The thought of Him dying, or leaving was too much for their already breaking souls. They were in a night of sorrow and not one solitary star was shining to alleviate its awful gloom. To these eleven men, He begins to speak fresh words of hope and good cheer. For more on this, refer to footnote g below.

2p-**Believe in Me as you believe in God.** They ought to believe equally in Him as they believe in Jehovah God. In so doing, Christ again affirmed that He is equal with God: for to believe in the God of Israel was the same as believing in Him. Earlier, the Savior had declared, "I and *my* Father are one" (John 10:30), and "the Father *is* in me, and I in him" (John 10:38). The Lord Jesus is making the same claim in these words (John 14:10-11).

[b] **"My Father's house."** Did the Lord Jesus speak these Words in an effort to draw their hearts away from the rabbinical notion of an earthly, secular kingdom? By using the term, "Father's house," He was addressing something in heaven and not on earth. Christ had employed these exact Words at the beginning of His ministry when He purged the temple and called it "my Father's house" (John 2:16). The Jews believed that God dwelt in their temple at Jerusalem, though they held that, His glory had departed with the close of their Old Testament some four hundred years prior. It is erroneous to hold that Christ was going to build mansions in the Jerusalem temple, which was destroyed in A.D. 70. He was clearly transferring the meaning of the Father's house to a higher hill than earthly Mount Moriah. The teachers of the Torah Law often spoke of "mansions" or "seven mansions," which suggested perfection in heaven. Edersheim explains in his *Life and Times of Jesus the Messiah*, pages 829-830, how the Jews believed that saints in heaven occupied abodes that corresponded with their ranks. The word "mansions" conjures up palaces of gold and silver, with dozens of bedrooms, beautiful gardens, and lawns. *However, God's heaven cannot be measured by earth's best yardstick.* Mansions meant, "Dwelling places." It is found later in verse 23 of this same chapter where it is translated as "abode." Whatever heaven is, it will be just what every child of God needs!

2p-**"If *it* were not *so.*"** We ask, "If *what* were not so?" And what does the word *"it"* mean? Is there intimation here that some of the eleven did not really believe this, or had rumors been spread that Jesus' doctrine of heaven was false? Regardless, the Lord assures them that "if it were not so" He would have told them.

3p-**Verse 3. "And if I go."** Some expositors see in these words the verbal commitment of a young Hebrew man after his formal engagement to a woman. He would affirm that he was going to prepare a place for her and come again to take her into his father's house on the occasion of their wedding. If the apostles did relate these Words of Jesus to this custom, they were, nevertheless, hard to understand. At this time they did not, indeed could not understand what He was saying. His coming again as mentioned here seemingly had *first* reference to His coming at death to receive each of the eleven and take them to their "mansion" or "abiding places" in His Father's house. Christ's use of the pronoun "you," must be applied, first to the apostles to whom He was speaking. There is a higher and grander application to these words. They reflect far ahead to that blessed hope of His second advent.

[c] At this time, they did not know where He was going! Why did He make this statement? It was designed to draw out the question from Thomas, who was aghast in shock at His Lord's Words about leaving them.

[d] **"Lord, how can we know the way?"** Thomas asked this question. He becomes a spokesman for the apostles and tells Jesus that none of them knew what He was talking about; that being so, how could they possibly understand what He meant about them knowing the way to the Father's house? As Jews, they believed and held to the rabbinical teaching about their Messiah, though Christ had shaken them to no end regarding much of this. The rabbis had taught that Messiah would be an earthly King and a mighty warrior. He would appear and disappear many times amid His work, and then reappear for a final time, destroy Gog and Magog, (Gentile opposition) their evil leader Armilius, Jerusalem, and the temple and rebuild all of it in such splendor, and dimensions that staggered the wildest imagination. For a review of these rabbinical teachings and exaggerations, see *Life and Times of Jesus the Messiah*, pages 774-778, by Alfred Edersheim. *The New Schaff-Herzog Encyclopedia of Religious Knowledge*, vol. II, pages 323-329 explains various Jewish ideas about Messiah's origin, work, kingdom, and accomplishments.

[e] **The narrowness of Christ's teachings. God is the way to Himself!** Here, the Lord Jesus was refuting another Hebrew idiom or popular saying. The scribes taught that the Torah Law and tradition of the elders were the

"way, the truth and the life." This is reflected in the Talmud tractate, Baba Batha 74a, which reads, "Moses and his law are truth." It is noted that earlier John had written these pungent words that may reflect this Talmudic error when he stated, "The law was given by Moses, *but* grace and truth came by Jesus Christ" (Section 1, Part 4, John 1:17). The Savior had been instructing them about His departure from their presence, the place He was going to, and what He would do when He arrived there. Here, He responds to the question of Thomas, who had just inquired, "How can we know the way?" The answer of Jesus is one of the most momentous declarations recorded in the entire Bible! All men of *true* faith dearly love and defend this single passage. The world and its thousands of religions fiercely hate it. The Supreme Court and Congress of the United States disdain these Words of the Savior. Secular and much of religious education struggles to reinterpret what they so exclusively and obviously declare; for if they are left to stand as they are, they spell doom for all who do not come to God via His Son. Earlier, Christ called Himself "the light of the world" (John 8:12), "the door" into God's sheepfold (John 10:9), and "the resurrection and the [source of eternal] life" (John 11:25). A while later He informed these same men that He was "the true vine" (John 15:1), and not the nation of Israel as they had been taught. Note the following things about John 14:6:

1. **He is the way to God.** *Sensible men know that without the way, there is no going.* The word "way" was a popular Hebrew idiom. It was used in traveling the roads of Israel. See Section 47, Matt. 7:13, footnote f for an explanation. Therefore, any who do not travel this exclusive "Jesus way" will not arrive to God. Without Christ, there is no home in eternity to come; hell is the only alternative.

2. **He is the truth of God.** *Without the truth of the gospel, there is no knowing the joy of sins forgiven and eternal life.* No apostle could say, "I am the truth," though all could say, "I speak the truth." All who claim they are the truth are, in reality, false. The gospel of Jesus Christ stands singularly opposed to all other gospels. Herein is the dignity of true education, that to know the truth is to know God. Over the course of Christian history, Satan has raised up countless thousands of false religionists. Rev. Moon, Charles Taze Russell, Brigham Young, Joseph Smith, Ellen G. White, Father Divine, Scientology's Ron Hubbard, and Buddha, are a few historical examples. The Lordship of Christ is the mainspring of human society; those who know Him, as personal Lord and Savior possess the truth, those who do not are damned. This is viciously hated by unsaved society. As quoted above, "The law was given by Moses, *but* grace and truth came by Jesus Christ" (John 1:17). Secular society and false religions despise this fact. The Bible declares emphatically "He that hath the Son hath life; *and* he that hath not the Son of God hath not life" (1 John 5:12). The Lord Jesus declared, "For without me ye can do nothing" (John 15:5).

3. **He is the life of God**. *Without life, there is no living.* Jesus of Nazareth is the promised Messiah of Israel, the Savior of mankind. He alone came down from heaven "and giveth life unto the world" (John 6:33). In Him, men have life and "have it more abundantly" (John 10:10). In John 5:26, the Father is said to have given life to the Son. This has reference to His physical life only. Jesus' eternality has always been.

2p-In the above, there is no place for syncretism or the blending of all faiths into one common belief for all mankind. This dark philosophy has captured most of the civilized religious world. Every effort is being made to ban the Name of Jesus from public prayers, schools, the halls of business concourse, and institutions of learning. It has become a crime to display the *convicting authority* of the Ten Commandments in public halls. Men marry men, and women marry women. We see radical Muslims defy organized social decency and rebellious students burn the American flag, but to call the Name of Jesus Christ at the invocation of a public event is to flirt with lawsuits, fines, or prison. The reason Bible Christianity is so viciously hated is because it is the one and only true faith for Adam's fallen race. The millions who work tirelessly to blot it out are, in reality, fighting against God Almighty. Moreover, they, in time will learn this terrible lesson, too late. *Jesus is not the better way, or the best way, He is the only way.*

3p-Churches gone wild. Over the past thirty years or so, America has witnessed a profusion of "Christian" churches, religious movements, groups, organizations, bodies, sects, and cults suddenly appearing. Much of this phenomena slithered out of the *hyper* charismatic movements or the smooth talking, liberal ecumenical "ministers and pastors." Within this religious circus, one often sees shadows of occult demonism in operation. Dark music, accompanied by high-pitched emotional jargon, dancing wildly, swinging, crawling over the floor, jumping amazing heights into the air, barking like dogs, and growling like animals, frequently accompanies these gymnastics. As with Pavlov's dogs, certain musical beats induce a state of hypnotic passivity. The victim can then be manipulated into doing whatever "the spirit" or "an open mind" dictates. Men honestly seeking God often but unwittingly embrace this appealing darkness. Christless religions continually use His name, sing their songs, and give nice little "lessons" about life. The innocent newcomers are taught, "The Bible does not lay down infallible rules for Christian living." Everyone does what he or she "feels" is right. In these "churches," "assemblies," and "groups," one rarely hears about sin and its horrible wages, the damnation of hell, or the inscrutable holiness of Jehovah God. The Roman cross with a bloody, dying Savior, nailed there paying our sin debt is taboo. Personal know-so salvation by the shed blood of Christ on the cross is reinterpreted into individual preferences and choices. We hear that every religion is right as long as they are sincere. No bigger lie has ever been believed than this one! For explanation and demonstration of this vicious deception, embraced by millions of well meaning people, see Section 95, sixth paragraph of footnote r. The paragraph below is a classic illustration of this in the American ecumenical church scene. On the other side of this religious circus, we see the hard-bitten, Bible thumping, "non compromising fundamentalists." Many of these people have convinced themselves that they have saved God's work by their firm stance! Without them, there would be no voice for Christ in the world. However, amid their ranks, chaos often reigns and secret sins surface. With a *King James Bible* in hand, and a thousand killing legal rules to live by, some of these "Christians" have been caught in adultery, molestation, cheating on the wives and husbands, lying, breaking up homes, stealing money, arrested for child pornography, and a thousand other evils. It is time "for judgment to begin at the house of God" (1 Peter 4:17). Cheap confessions and *false repentance* of church people (during "the revival meeting") has crippled the church, and angered God. Israel of old went this way. Finally, Jehovah declared, "For though thou wash with nitre, and take thee much soap, *yet* thine iniquity is marked before me, saith the Lord GOD" (Jer. 2:22). In heaven, some awful marks have been put down against hypocritical, phony Christians, regardless of their church affiliations, playing like angels, while secretly living like the Devil. See also, Section 76, the second paragraph of footnote f, for more on the mess many churches are in and why,

4p-Robert Schuller. Satan is too clever to put all of his eggs into one basket. Miles apart from the wild charismatic groups with their heresies of "seed faith," "word of knowledge," "positive thinking," "name it, claim it," and "healthy wealthy promises," stands the dignified *liberal* mega church with thousands in attendance. They are orderly, and calm, well dressed men of wealth, power, and prestige. Nevertheless, they are deceived just as much as the clamoring, noise making, and money grabbing people on the other side of the apostate spectrum. No better example of this is found than in the popular Dr. Robert Schuller, now retired. His church touches millions weekly via a worldwide ministry and mailing list of over one million. He has become the epitome of religious apostasy.

5p-Schuller wrote in, *My Journey*, page 502, "I met once more with the Grand Mufti (Muslim), truly one of the Christ-honoring leaders of faith . . ." He continued, "That leaders of the major faiths will rise above doctrinal idiosyncrasies, choosing not to focus on disagreements, but rather to transcend divisive dogmas to work together to bring peace and prosperity and hope to the world . . ." Earlier, on page 501, this ecumenical fox said, " Standing before a crowd of devout Muslims, with the Grand Mufti, I know that we're all doing God's work together." Does Schuller know that Islam hates the deity, death, and resurrection of Christ? How ignorant and blind he is.

6p-Which religion is right? Ecumenical pluralism states that all religions finally lead to God. A companion to this lie is "Postmortem Evangelism." It teaches that men will have the opportunity to believe in Christ after physical death! The Bible declares in 2 Tim. 1:1 that "God's promise of life" is found in Christ. Eternal life and forgiveness are not the property of Baptists, Methodists, Presbyterians, Lutherans, Roman Catholics, Church of Christ, Church of God, Pentecostal, or whatever. *The church that Christ died for (Eph. 5:25) consists of every soul genuinely saved by the grace of God, regardless of what they belonged to on earth.* Salvation from hell is the sole prerogative of Christ (Rom. 6:23). A man can belong to every religion or church on earth and die damned if he expires without being saved. In eternity, God will gather all His people together as one, forever (Eph. 1:10). The hallmark of every false cult is their claim to be right while declaring all others are wrong. Adam Clarke wrote that the Church of England was "purest and nearest to the apostolical model in doctrine . . ." See Clarke's Commentary, vol. 5, page 724. What nonsense from such a great man! He should have written that Jesus Christ alone is right, not his church. All else is deceiving, and leads to hell. Those who present Him as the absolute truth are right; those who do not are wrong. No church, religion, or individual has a patent on the Son of God. *His arms are open to all.* Faith in His death for our sins and resurrection brings complete forgiveness and acceptance by God. Millions believe in Him as a good man, great teacher, and wise philosopher, but not to know Him as Lord and Savior is eternally fatal.

(f) Christ is not saying that His eleven apostles were not true disciples, rather, that at this point in their lives, they had not yet acquired complete and accurate knowledge about Him and His Father. Later, they knew the whole truth. They understood that when they looked upon Christ, they were looking upon God in human flesh, for He alone revealed the Father. With the coming of the Holy Spirit in fullness on Pentecost, these men were instantly understood the truth about Messiah and the Father. His Words, "from henceforth ye know him," have reference to their complete understanding received with the fullness of the Spirit. Refer to footnote j below for more on this.

(g) Hast thou not known me?" This question was not from a sense of frustration but rather of hopeful and helpful interrogation. A measure of false religious darkness had veiled the minds of the apostles, who had been weaned on the oral traditions of the scribes and Pharisees and wrong interpretations of the great Torah Law. They acknowledged Jesus as Messiah, but being "brainwashed" by the teaching of a literal, physical, material kingdom with Messiah ruling the world, Christ reclining before them did not measure up to rabbinical standards.

2p-Verse 8. "Lord, show us the Father." This was Philip's request. He wanted the Jesus to show them God or suddenly make God appear! In verses 10-11, Christ pled with Philip to "believe." After Pentecost, he not only believed but also *understood* what the Lord had told him in the upper room. Christ's statement here does not contradict John 1:18 where we read, "No man hath seen God at any time." John could only have been speaking of God in His totality apart from being veiled in human flesh, as He was in the Person of Jesus Christ.

3p-To see Christ was to see God. Men saw God manifested through the physical body of Christ, but have never seen Him in the fullness of His Majesty and power. Mortal eyes could not bear such a glorious sight!

(h) **"Greater *works* than these."** Christ changes the conversation to the subject of divine works, ascension, and answered prayer. This promise of greater works being done seems to have a peculiar reference to the eleven apostles, the apostle Paul, and others unnamed in sacred history. It cannot be understood as occurring in the life of *every* believer over the past two thousand years. No one has ever done greater works than Christ has. When we note the countless thousands that those early believers reached for Christ in their missionary efforts, the fantastic things they did, and how their original endeavors have marched over the past two thousand years to this present hour, then our Lord's Words are better understood. Some think Jesus meant greater in *quantity* but not in *quality*. In quality of works it was said of Christ, "He hath done all things well" (Mk. 7:37). Of no Christian at any time in history can this be said. The book of Acts covers about the first thirty years of church history, but only carries a *few* of the events that occurred among the early Christians during this time. If it were all recorded, we would have thousands of books to study filled with the most amazing things. The works of the first believers were not confined to healings alone. For more on this refer, to Section 207, second paragraph of footnote i.

2p-Verse 12. He speaks of going to the Father. Because of His place at the right hand of God, ever making intercession, prayer takes on a new dimension and outreach. Now, we may talk to Him in prayer about anything or "whatsoever" as the verse reads. The One representing the eleven then, and us today, before the Father was tempted in all points as we are, yet emerged victorious over it all! He had stepped (as it were) into our shoes and felt our sorrows and pains. He is now the merciful and faithful high priest; He understands our pain for it had raged in His human frame long before it did in ours. See Section 207, for Christ enthroned as priest-king at the right hand of God.

3p-Verse 13. Get anything we want? Extremists so abundant in the church today, point to these words as proof that God will give us anything we ask for in prayer, as long as we believe. However, verse 13 is qualified by the words, "that the Father may be gloried in the Son." *In other words, if the answering of our prayers does not glorify Christ in God, they will not be answered!* All prayer, for whatever reason, must be first funneled through 1 John 5:14-15. For more on this subject, note Section 149, Matt. 21:22, second paragraph of footnote g.

(i) Our Lord was instructing the apostles to keep what He had just commanded them regarding prayer and God's will. This statement has nothing to do with keeping the Ten Commandments as the law cults and *some* Messianic Jews are so quick to point out. A few breaths later, He said a similar thing in verse 21, then in verse 24, summed it all up as "my sayings." See number l under footnote m below. Note John 15:10, where the Lord Jesus said something like this about keeping His commandments or His Word. This is not the Ten Commandments.

(j) **Another Comforter forever.** Among the many names and titles, the ancient Jews gave Messiah was "Menahem" or "Comforter." This is found in the Talmud tractate, Sanhedrin 98b. In using the word "another," our Lord is confirming this rabbinical teaching. He had been their sole Comforter. He had just stated that He was equal with God, was going to prepare a place for them, that He was the way, the truth, and life in all things regarding the Father. Therefore, that if they wanted to know what God was like, look at Him. He assured them that answered prayer was guaranteed, if it glorified the Father. He would ask the Father to send someone to take His place among the little flock of eleven apostles. And that would be the Holy Spirit. The priceless gift of the Son was followed up by the gift of the Holy Spirit. We must not think less of the Spirit, as though He came in second place! We cannot honor the Savior by giving to the Holy Spirit a disproportionate place. We grieve Him when we neglect Him. Christ's prayer for the Spirit does not mean that He had not previously been a part of their lives. Almost two years earlier, when He sent them across Galilee they preached by the power of the Spirit *in* them (Matt. 10:20). We read, "If any man have not the Spirit of Christ, he is none of his" (Rom. 8:9). See Section 10, Lk. 1:41, footnote b, for a survey of the Holy Spirit across Old Testament history. Now, He would come in absolute fullness and power, something obviously unknown to them. The coming fullness of the Spirit depended on the death and resurrection or glorification of Jesus. This is stated in John 7:39, with 12:`16 and 23.

2p-Verse 17. "*Even* the Spirit of truth." At this time, the whole world lay in the chains of religious falsehood, error, through the dark thralls of paganism. The entire Gentile world was bound by the demons of delusion; the Jews were mostly cheats, imposters, and hypocrites having rejected their Messiah. Amid this horror, the Spirit of truth comes, to enlighten, direct, lead, and show men salvation and genuine hope. As Christ was the truth, so now they will have the bonus of the Spirit of this truth dwelling *with* and *in* them (Eph. 3:16). The unsaved world cannot comprehend this fact. Earlier, the Savior said that this world hated Him (John 7:7 with 8:23).

3p-Verse 18. "I will not leave you comfortless." Repeatedly, our Lord tries to console the troubled hearts of His eleven apostles over His leaving them. He also came after His resurrection and appeared various times, working to convince them that He had risen from the dead. This is explained beginning with Section 195. He did "come to them" at Pentecost in the Person of the Holy Spirit. See the first paragraph of this footnote j above.

(k) **"Yet a little while."** That is, for the next few hours of that night and during the morning watch, He would be seen by the unbelievers. After His death, they would see Him no more. "But ye [apostles] see me." We note in Acts 1:3, there is an introduction of His several post resurrection appearances during forty days and nights in which the risen Christ revealed Himself to His disciples *only* (Acts 10:40-43). For details, see Section 207.

2p-Verse 20. During those forty days and nights, they would begin to understand that He was God, as stated in verse 10 of this upper room lesson.

3p-Verse 21. This is simply an addition to what He had just said in verse 15. Here, see footnote i above for explanation of this statement.

(l) **"Lord, how is it . . . ?**" Thomas put his question in verse 5 and Philip spoke his request in verse 8. Here, Judas (not the traitor) speaks up with his own inquiry. This question reveals that Judas had listened intently to Christ's Words in verse 21, that He would "manifest" himself to them. Judas wants to know how this will be done.

(m) The answer of Christ is unique. He informs Judas and the others "how" both, He and the Father will make themselves known to them. Note the following:

1. **Verse 23.** Those who love Christ will keep His Words or instructions. Honoring Christ by loving obedience to His Word will bring the love of God upon one's life, and both Christ and God will dwell with this kind of believer. The instructions, commandments, or teachings of Christ are recorded in the New Testament, especially the four gospels. In verse 24 our Lord makes it clear that His Words were not invented or thought up by Himself, rather they are what God told Him to teach those who are in His new kingdom-church. See footnote i above.

2. **Verse 24.** It is the exact opposite with the unsaved of this world. They do not, indeed cannot rightly love God until their hearts have been changed by the miracle of the new birth. With this, the Holy Spirit comes and dwells or lives in their inner being or soul (Eph. 3:16) and defuses true love in their hearts (Rom. 5:5). Hence, the reason they cannot hear God's Word, much less keep it. How pitiful to see unsaved men and women struggling to obey Holy Scripture when they have never been changed inside by genuine conversion to Christ. A worm cannot fly like the bird because it is a worm!

3. **Verse 25.** I am here with you, and you have heard Me say these things. However, men are prone to forget divine truth or let it slip. The Spirit would make up what is lacking in their lives when Jesus was gone.

(n) **"Bring all things to your remembrance."** This is often misinterpreted and thus misapplied. *The promise of infinite and total divine knowledge was first, foremost, and exclusively for the apostles.* It was not intended for Christians in general over-all church history. We hear it abused to justify the most absurd claims. The gift of the Spirit is the earnest of all born again believers, but the supreme knowledge of the things of God and Christ are not. The deranged David Koresh of Waco, Texas, pointed his deceived followers to John 14:26 as his source of "special insight and infallible understanding of Scriptures." Hundreds followed this mad man (daring not to question anything) into a burning inferno that slammed them into eternity! We have noted numerous times in this harmony commentary how the apostles were continually baffled and confused at the teachings of Christ. He taught them hundreds of choice truths that would pertain to the future of His church. A while later in His high priestly prayer, the Savior said that He had given His men all that the Father had given Him (John 17:8). This is a most profound statement! With the coming of the Spirit at Pentecost in full power, they were instantly enlightened and immediately understood *everything* Jesus had taught them; it all made sense then. Briefly, this is the meaning of verse 26. From Pentecost forward, the indwelling Holy Spirit taught them "all things" needed, and brought every Word of Jesus fresh into their minds. This was solely an apostolic gift. See main heading under Section 110, where Jesus had earlier promised the apostles exclusive authority to be used in the service of His early church or new kingdom.

2p-*This is not to decry that the Spirit will fill, guide, teach, and instruct God's children, but it is to state that this all-embracing promise of doctrinal infallibility was vouchsafed only to the apostles.* Later, we read in 1 John 2:27 that the same Holy Spirit will anoint and then "teach" believers "all things" that they need to know in God's service. Only the Spirit can bring us into fellowship with God, Christ, and Himself. He does this unspeakable work through the written Word of God and a yielded heart. There is a difference in the filling of the Spirit and His anointing in the life of a believer. The former is an event that occurs from within where the Holy Spirit dwells, and then works outwardly. Anointing is intermediate and gives unique strength for powerful Christian service. Certain TV evangelists and phony healers have scandalized the third Person of the Trinity. Many claim His power to perform "signs and wonders," then spend ten minutes begging for money or selling junk. Many thinking people have turned from *true* Christianity as they watch these charlatans masquerading with a Bible or "prayer cloth" in their hand. The push today (borrowed from Oral Roberts) is the "seed faith" hoax. "Give God a thousand dollars, and He will double it back to you!" And they (mis)quote Scriptures to prove it.

3p-Verse 27. "Peace I leave with you." Soon to die on the cross, the Savior reads (as it were) His last will and testament to the eleven. He has bequeathed to them peace in a world of war! The first application of this promise was to the fearful apostles. They were devastated at the thought of Jesus leaving them. Reaching forth to console their anxiety, He promises them "peace." They received that peace with the fullness of the Spirit at Pentecost. Then, they understood His death, burial, resurrection and going away. Today, this peace is not changed by what we see, hear, have, or where we go. God put it in us. It is from Him; its Name is Jesus Christ (Eph. 2:14). And it came by "the blood of his cross" (Col. 1:20). *We change, He does not.* Note the following about divine peace:

1. There is "peace *with* God' over sin, and its awful guilt. This is given when one receives Jesus as personal Lord and Savior, at which moment, they are counted justified before God (Rom. 5:1).

2. There is the life of having the "peace *of* God" in one's heart. This comes by daily walking in fellowship with Him and seeking to do His will, as one best understands it in the spirit of praise and thanksgiving. Missionary Paul explained it so well in Phil 4:6-7. One can find themselves amid the most disastrous situations and sorrows of life and yet still have the peace of God reigning in their aching hearts.

(o) This does not mean that none of the eleven truly loved Him. He was saying that after they came into the full understanding of what He had taught, they would rejoice over his going away. For then they would know of His intercessory work for them and all believers. Today, men say, "God is so good to me," If we never receive another blessing, He is still good and worthy of all we have, when we look afresh at Calvary and the cross!

(p) **"Greater than I." Christ's human subordination.** False cults denying the deity of Christ have seized upon these words for centuries. In this profound statement, the Savior does *not* compare His divine nature or eternal being with the Father's, for they were the same in every aspect. He was speaking of His *place there and then as a man,* in His human frame and the *choice* for Him to obey the Father's will for His earthly life and ministry. It was in this sense that He said, "My Father is greater than I." *The word "greater" as used here refers to position not a* person. No blasphemous Arianism or Unitarianism, denying the deity of Christ, is to be found here! This is concrete proof that Christ was God in human flesh. He came as such and rejoiced at the end of His course praying, "I have finished the work which thou gavest me to do" (John 17:4). In this same prayer, He looked forward to that ineffable reunion with the Father in the incomprehensible perfect oneness, and eternal glory they shared forever (John 17:5, 24).

2p-Scripture recognizes the *human subordination* of Christ to the Father. It was one of order, office, and operation, not of divine equality. At incarnation, Christ preannounced that He was taking on flesh "to do God's will" (Heb. 10:5-7). He "took upon him the form of a servant, and was made in the likeness of men." (Phil. 2:7). As a "man" and "servant" on earth, He lived under, and did the will of God. This was human subordination. From eternity past to the creation, Christ was ineffably equal with the Father. From creation to incarnation, He maintained the rank of absoluteness with God. At birth in human flesh, (incarnation) He became voluntarily subordinate to the Father's perfect will for His work and atonement with no distinction of His deity being lessened. *Only One who is God can reconcile us to God!* Thus, the meaning of "My Father is greater than I." This explains John 5:19, 22, 23, 26-27, 30; 6:38; 7:16; and Mk. 14:36. For more on this, see Section 123, John 10:30-31, footnote f. The Oneness of the Trinity had no beginning; it has been forever. Three are totally God. and God is totally One, in three Persons.

(q) He was saying, "When it all happens you will remember that I told you. Your faith will be strengthened by understanding my divine foreknowledge of these events, and that I told you of them well in advance."

(r) **"The prince of this world cometh."** A testimony to the sinless purity of Christ. In Him, we have One in whom the wicked one has nothing! Holy, spotless, and forever pure is Jesus, Savior of men. For the origin of the Jewish term, "prince of the world," see Section 161, footnote j. For his work among men, note Section 23, footnote c. Satan is not an omnipresent spirit person. He seeks to be this through the universal activities of his millions of demons or fallen angels. About an hour previous, he had entered Judas while the traitor was in the upper room observing Passover. He went with Judas to collect Roman soldiers, and the temple police to arrest Jesus in the garden. Now, he will continue his work through Judas. Christ looks ahead and sees the wicked one performing in Gethsemane, as he inspires the Jews and Gentiles to bind Him. He was saying that the Devil was coming inside Judas to Gethsemane. Knowing this, Jesus triumphantly declares, "He has nothing in me." Only the pure Son of God could make such a profound claim! The Devil has something in all of us unless we have been forgiven,.

2p-Verse 31. **The world will know**. The unsaved world will eventually know at the judgment of God that Christ obeyed every commandment given Him from His Father, and that he obeyed even unto the death of the cross in order to provide forgiveness and salvation for mankind.

(s) **"Arise, let us go hence."** At this point, Jesus and His apostles leave the upper room. Between end of chapter 14 and the beginning of chapter 15, they walked eastward through the crowded streets of Jerusalem to the temple. This must have taken some considerable time, due to the thousands of people present for the Passover observance.

(t) **"They sung an hymn."** Just before departing the upper room, at the Passover conclusion, Jesus and His men followed Jewish tradition. They all stood, sipped from a fourth cup, and sang the remaining portion of the hallel (or praise) hymn of Ps. 115-118. The rabbis looked at Ps. 118 as being Messianic. Earlier, the crowds at the Eastern Gate had used parts of the same Psalm as Jesus road the donkey into Jerusalem. See Section 148, Mk. 11:9-10, footnote f. The first part of hallel was sung at the beginning of Passover. It was near the midnight hour as they departed from the upper room. All pious Jews would seek a solitary place to pray at the end of the Pascal supper. *How deeply it touches us when we read that the last thing Jesus did before marching off to Gethsemane, His arrest, trials, and the terrible cross, was to sing a Jewish Messianic psalm-hymn of praise to God.* This explains a little more the meaning of Heb. 12:2. The "joy that was before Him" was His exclusive authority to save all who would believe on Him. O, how all heaven seemed to yearn for the redemption of humanity. And Jesus Christ He Son of God made it possible.

Jesus and the eleven walk eastward and cross the illuminated Bridge of Zion over the rocky Tyropoeon* Valley. This lead into Solomon's porch on the west end of the temple. Hundreds of oil lamps with reflective brass mirrors brilliantly lighted all the area. The gigantic candelabra** in the Women's Court shot their beams everywhere. After entering the temple, He tells the eleven that He is the true vine, the source of eternal life and fruitfulness, and of the Holy Spirit coming in fullness.

Time: The night before the Friday morning of the cross.

**The word seems to signify "the valley of cheese mongers" Its cold rocks provided an ancient form of refrigeration.* ***For temple lighting system and the golden oil candelabra lights, see Section 119, eighth paragraph of footnote a.*

Matt.	Mk.	Lk.	John 15:1-16—*In the streets of Jerusalem and the temple*
			The illustrated relationship of believers to Christ **1** "I am the true vine,**(a)** and my Father is the husbandman. **2** "Every branch in me that beareth not fruit he taketh away:**(b)** and every *branch* that beareth fruit, he purgeth**(c)** it, that it may bring forth more fruit. **3** "Now ye are clean through the word which I have spoken unto you. **(d)** **4** "Abide in me, and I in you. As the branch cannot bear fruit of itself, except it abide in the vine; no more can ye, except ye abide in me. **(e)** **5** "I am the vine, ye *are* the branches. He that abideth in me, and I in him, the same bringeth forth much fruit: for without me ye can do nothing. **(f)** **6** "If a man abide not in me, he is cast forth as a branch, and is withered; and men gather them, and cast *them* into the fire, and they are burned. **(g)** **7** "If ye abide in me, and my words abide in you, ye shall ask what ye will, and it shall be done unto you. **(h)** **8** "Herein is my Father glorified, that ye bear much fruit; so shall ye be my disciples. **(i)** **9** "As the Father hath loved me, so have I loved you: continue ye in my love. **(j)** **10** "If ye keep my commandments, **(k)** ye shall abide in my love; even as I have kept my Father's commandments, and abide in his love. **11** "These things have I spoken unto you, that my joy might remain in you, and *that* your joy might be full. ***Relationship of believers to one another*** **12** "This is my commandment, That ye love one another, as I have loved you. **13** "Greater love hath no man than this, that a man lay down his life for his friends. **(l)** **14** "Ye are my friends, if ye do whatsoever I command you. **15** "Henceforth I call you not servants; for the servant knoweth not what his lord doeth: but I have called you friends; for all things that I have heard of my Father I have made known unto you. **16** "Ye have not chosen**(m)** me, but I have chosen you, and ordained you, that ye should go and bring forth fruit, and *that* your fruit should remain: that whatsoever ye shall ask of the Father in my name, he may give it you.

Matt.	Mk.	Lk.	John 15:17-27—*In the streets of Jerusalem and the temple*
			17 "These things I command you, that ye love one another.[n]
			Relationship of believers to the world
			18 "If the world hate you, ye know that it hated me before *it hated* you.[o]
			19 "If ye were of the world, the world would love his own: but because ye are not of the world, but I have chosen you out of the world, therefore the world hateth you.
			20 "Remember[p] the word that I said unto you, 'The servant is not greater than his lord.' If they have persecuted me, they will also persecute you;[q] if they have kept my saying, they will keep yours also.
			21 "But all these things will they do unto you for my name's sake, because they know not him that sent me.
			22 "If I had not come and spoken unto them, they had not had sin: but now they have no cloak for their sin.[r]
			23 "He that hateth me hateth my Father also.[s]
			24 "If I had not done among them the works which none other man did, they had not had sin: but now have they both seen and hated both me and my Father.
			25 "But *this cometh to pass*, that the word might be fulfilled that is written in their law, **'They hated me without a cause.'**"[t]
			The Holy Spirit is coming in fulness: His first great work
			26 "But when the Comforter is come, whom I will send unto you from the Father, *even* the Spirit of truth, which proceedeth from the Father, he shall testify of me:[u]
			27 "And ye also shall bear witness, because ye have been with me from the beginning."[v] (Next chap. John 16:1 cont. in Section 177.)

Footnotes-Commentary

[a] **"I am the true vine."** Among later Jewish doctors of the law, a mystic separatist group called the Cabalists interpreted "the choice vine" in Gen. 49:11, as having reference to Messiah. Their writings are found in a book called the Zohar, which is attributed to Rabbi Simon Ben Yochai. The Zohar was prepared in the thirteenth century. Here, our Lord claimed to be the "true vine" before the apostles. In Berachoth 57a, there is a curious saying from a rabbi, "He who sees a choice vine may look forward to seeing the Messiah." In His Words "I am," Jesus presented Himself (again) as the supreme and preeminent One, even the God of the burning bush. For our Lord's previous usages of the title "I am," refer to Section 95, footnote i. *God be praised that the bush still burns today!*

2p-The common grapevine is mentioned in Scripture from the time of Noah (Gen. 9:20). Christ passed over the Bridge of Zion into the temple's vast southern porch, as He moved from the upper room toward Gethsemane. This was the most direct and shortest route to His Gethsemane destination. Any other route would have taken several hours more amid the crowds present. Upon entering the temple precincts, Jesus stopped and called the attention of His apostles to the gigantic network of golden vines, which hung at various places on the temple structure. Powerful oil lights with large reflectors illuminated almost every square foot of this vast building. The four tall candelabras in the Women's Court caused every bright object to glisten under its beams, especially the golden vines. The largest vine was placed above the entrance to the Holy Place; another stood on props over the Beautiful Gate leading into the temple area. On this particular vine, people would hang gold pieces that had been shaped into leaves, grapes, or floral clusters. More golden vines were seen over various temple doors. Some were attached to the walls as well as the top outward face of the colonnades that ran the entire length of Solomon's porch. These numerous objects of gold glistened under the powerful lights of the four candelabras. The crowds moving about in the temple were filled with wonder at the size of these objects and the rich gifts that were hung on them. The large golden grape clusters were as tall as a man was. The inward door of the porch also had vines attached to it having similar golden clusters. The Talmud mentions the temple vines in the tractate, Chullin 90b.

3p-Rabbis taught that the vine symbolized several things, including Israel and their Messiah (Gen. 49:11, Ps. 80:8-11, and Isa. 5:1-7). For a Hebrew to dwell under his vine and fig tree was an emblem of prosperity, civil and domestic tranquility across the nation (1 Kings 4:25 with Micah 4:4). The rabbis taught that Israel was the vine that gave life to the world and that "the vine is Jerusalem and the Torah." See Talmud tractate, Chullin 92b. With this in mind, we hear the Lord Jesus say to His eleven apostles, "I am the true vine." The word "true" is used as a comparative term, meaning that *all* other vines were false in comparison to Him, even the nation of Israel. Who can imagine the reaction of the apostles to this profound comparison of Himself to the beautiful vines in the temple? Had He not just two days prior predicted the destruction of this very building?

(b) **"Every branch in me."** Men must be planted by faith in Christ and not the Jewish religion, which had been degraded into a system of oral traditions, self-righteousness, and works. With this came hatred for all other men, especially the Gentiles and less fortunate Jews of Israel. For salvation under the Old Testament system, see Section 10, all under footnote b, and Section 30, second paragraph, footnote h. Pointing to the golden vines, Christ informs His preachers that men must be in Him to have life as the branch is in the vine. At the moment of salvation one is put into Christ by the work of the Holy Spirit (1 Cor. 12:13). Perhaps, there is also an allusion here in which our Lord is saying that the apostles will no more be planted in the dead Jewish religion, but in Him, their Messiah, Lord and Savior. The lesson is that the vine and branches picture Christ and His own, but they do not reflect the whole story. Every type is restricted by its contents and never carries the full picture. In fact, portions of it may point to nothing of divine nature or truth while other parts do. No better example of this is found than in the husband-wife relationship being a picture of Christ and His church (Eph. 5:21-25). We know this is true, but realize it has strict limitations. For example, all marriages will eventually end in death. Thinking Christians would never take the marriage picture of Christ and His church into this realm. No type, shadow, or illustration *totally* portrays every detail of that to which it points. It is imperfect. Only the original item or object is perfect. Across Old Testament Scripture, many things pointed to the coming Savior. However, they only portrayed a limited picture of Him. Nevertheless, He fulfilled and filled full their every demand and gave meaning to what they pointed too.

2p-**"He taketh away." Purging dead branches.** The vinedresser has one goal in mind, more grapes. And pruning is the single most important technique to ensure this end. The tool bringing about an abundant harvest is the sharp pruning knife. The quality of the fruit produced was safeguarded by pruning. Someone said that because of the grape's tendency to grow vigorously, much wood must be cut away each year. Grapevines can become so dense that the sun cannot reach into the area where fruit forms. If left to itself, a vine will always favor new growth over more grapes. In other words, there is plenty of wood, but little fruit. We have seen many who affirm that they "are growing in grace," but oddly, there is no corresponding fruit. Proper growth comes from correct pruning, and only this produces fruit, more fruit, and much fruit. From His own apostolic band, heaven's Master Vinedresser had to prune or cut away a false branch. In saying, "He taketh away." Christ was explaining to His apostles, *what* had just taken place in the upper room. There was a bad or dead branch among the original twelve apostles; his name was Judas Iscariot. Refer to footnote d below for more on this. As the vinedresser cuts off the dead branch and throws it into the fire so will be the fate of this wicked person. God, the great caretaker and vinedresser had just cut Judas off through the Words of Christ (John 13:26-30). This verse does not teach or even remotely suggest that Christians may be lost after salvation. Contextually, it *first* refers to the calamity of the traitor among the eleven faithful ones, and Judas being purged by the hand of God from the true eleven, because from the beginning, he was never part of them (John 6:70-71). Judas was like many in the local church today who appear to be growing outwardly, but are obviously void of the fruit of the Spirit (Gal. 5:22-23). See second paragraph of footnote c below for an explanation of the bad branches and their fate.

3p-Some make the vine and branches a symbol or type of Christ and the church, and then point to the bad branches as those who forfeit their salvation for whatever reasons. This is an erroneous interpretation in view of the fact that Christ did not employ this type of exegesis in giving this lesson to the eleven apostles. At this time, they hardly understood the church and were ignorant of His soon death, burial, and resurrection. He kept this lesson in a Jewish context for the admonition of the eleven. Some expositors struggling with this passage see in it Christians losing all their works at the judgment seat of Christ. This is based on Rom. 14:10 with 1 Cor. 3:12-15, but such an interpretation seems more of a desperation response instead of sound Bible exegesis. A safe rule of hermeneutics is that one must not build a doctrine on any type or shadow, but the type or shadow may point to a *previously established,* valid biblical doctrine. Whatever these dead branches represent, they cannot speak of saved believers, becoming unsaved and unborn again. *The wretched doctrine of Arminianism is not taught here.*

(c) Conversely, in the latter part of verse 2, the Master tells His eleven that they will be purged, the purpose was to produce "more fruit" for the glory of their owner, the Father. There is also a broader lesson in these Words of Messiah. First, it was all applicable to the eleven; secondly, it surely points ahead, into the local churches yet to be established. For the past two millenniums of church history, there have been thousands of "dead branches" in the local churches, feigning their profession without having possession. As Judas became the grand example of a dead branch and was extracted, so shall all branches that do not *ultimately* bring forth fruit, be finally cut off, and cast into the eternal fire. Refer to the second paragraph of footnote b above.

2p-A vine with fruitless branches. There was a curious type of vine that grew in the Middle East, which always had fruitless branches. It grew naturally beside the fruitful ones! Every vinedresser automatically cut these away. They were not pruned in hopes of bearing fruit, but recognized by their outward appearance as foreign to the life and purpose of the real vine. After being severed from the true vine in which they were intertwined, they were burned. The Lord Jesus was pointing out to His preachers that among His own there are those who are unsaved, but in time will be cut away from the true children of God. As stated, the cut off branches pointed to Judas the traitor and his kind. This lesson was part of what Jesus was teaching. Later, His apostles understood this illustration.

3p-The difference between pruning and discipline. The dead branches (as explained in the 2p- above) were cut away and put into the fire. The natural vines loaded with their branches were pruned. The Bible teaches that divine discipline for the child of God is about unconfessed sin in their lives (Heb. 12:5-11). This is different from pruning! It is true that both hurt, but one is to produce greater fruit bearing, and the other is to shed off or repent of sin. It is a curious fact of horticulture that the vine can only produce richer fruit if it is pruned annually; if not, it becomes worthless to the owner.

(d) During the footwashing, Christ told the apostles that they were not all clean (John 13:10-11). *This was spoken of Judas, who was present during this occasion.* Shortly after hearing this, Satan entered his soul, and he left the room. Following the footwashing, Jesus announced that they were all (the eleven) clean. This does not mean that they were perfect, for they had been in the process of purification and cleansing by the Word of God that He had been teaching them for over two years. It signified that up to that point, they were being drastically affected by His doctrines and examples; that God's Word was slowly cutting from their lives those things that hindered fruit bearing. In using the word "clean," the Lord Jesus was probably referring to the Torah Law in Lev. 19:23-25 where God commanded Jewish farmers that they could not eat any new fruit of a tree or vine until the fifth year, for it was accounted uncircumcised or *unclean.* As the apostles had been with their Lord for several years, they were becoming "clean by the word" He had spoken to them. This process was later called "growing in grace" (2 Peter 3:18). See footnote e below.

(e) **"Abiding faith."** *This is not "saving faith" which is called the "one faith" in Eph. 4:5.* Another descriptive term for "abiding faith" could be "fellowship with the Father and his Son Jesus Christ" (1 John 1:3). Peter called it "growing in grace and in the knowledge of our Lord and Saviour, Jesus Christ" (2 Peter 3:18). Many have been saved, but most fail to grow in God, not living in this blessed "abiding faith." That indivisible union in the closet of prayer, the wonder of His Word, the awe of worship, the joy of service; this and more attaches to our souls and lives in a mystical, but *realistic* bond to the true vine. The natural branch upon being severed from the vine dies. The spiritual branch of the redeemed soul, abiding in the true vine, receives from the parent stock everything needed to bear fruit, more fruit, and much fruit. Contextually we may see Christ warning the eleven about apostasy, or turning back to the ways of hypocritical Judaism. O reader, have you through carelessness, indifference, sorrow, or suffering cut yourself off from the sap of continuing hope and power? Are you no longer living in this "abiding faith?" *If so, return to your Lord now!*

(f) **"Ye are the branches."** Who are the "ye" to whom our Lord addressed these words? Obviously, it was first spoken to His eleven apostles walking with Him to the garden. God was the husbandman (or vinedresser), His Son was the true vine, and the branches were His disciples. Then, the saved of all ages limitedly picture the branches in this living true vine.

2p-"Without me ye can do nothing." What strange words. *They are either arrogant or divine!* No head of state, military commander, prudent man, saint, prophet, missionary, preacher, or anyone in a position of leadership would dare say such to those under their charge. It would be the height of pomp and credulous arrogance. There is something different, exclusive, totally narrow, and single in these Divine Words. We hear in this charge the voice of deity, even the echo of God Himself, for only God could say such, and it be valid. The world despises these words for they reveal who is Lord of all. It refuses to acknowledge that Jesus of Nazareth is the Son of God and their only hope for forgiveness of sin. To hear that without Him, all their works and deeds of wonder are but trash, infuriates their dark souls into anger and resentment. *Christ's narrowness is a firm New Testament teaching.* Refer to Section 128, Lk. 14:27, footnote e, and Section 175, John 14:6, footnote e for more on this subject. See footnote s below.

(g) The first part of this passage is the reverse of verse 4. As Judas did not abide in the Messiah and would be cast into the eternal fire, so shall all be who do not find their place in Christ. Dead branches were gathered for fuel. The allusion here seems to point to this custom.

(h) **"If ye abide in me."** This refers to those whose understandings are in Christ, who daily seek to walk in fellowship with their Lord and work to honor His Holy Name. All this is accomplished by simple faith activated by a disciplined will (Prov. 16:32 with 25:28). Who among us has ever seen a "worried branch." They do not know how to fret and be dismayed! Branches simply abide in the mother vine. This pictures a resting and abiding faith quietly placed daily in the Savior. Even when the branch fails its duty, the mother vine remains faithful.

2p-"Ye shall ask what ye will." We note here that another evidence of "abiding faith in Christ" is found in the realm of prayer. The apostles are the "ye" in this text. See verse 16 for a second mention of prayer in this discourse. Christ informs them that His Words must be in them as mentioned in footnote d above. Here, we notice a new thing: His Words must abide in us as well! On God giving Christians "whatever, they ask" in prayer, see Section 175, John 14:13, third paragraph of footnote h. This is not a blank check to be filled out by believers to get whatever they want from God. *The Bible teaches no such thing.*

(i) Here is the chief aim in living life, glorifying God our heavenly Father, and being a true disciple of Christ, His son. Doing this is another way to demonstrate that we today, as the apostles back then, are His disciples. Earlier, while in the upper room He made known another way in which His followers can show to all honest observers what true Christianity is. See Section 172, John 13:34-35, footnote n. *See the second paragraph of footnote v, below.*

(j) God's love for His only begotten Son is the highest and the noblest love we can think of. To read that our Lord loves us as His Father loved Him is beyond mortal comprehension. And this is our promise as His children! What a charge to both the eleven and to us! We hear of continuing education, continuing science and technology, continuing medical advances but when have we heard of continuing the love of our Lord. That would be a different kind of course in most Bible schools or theological seminaries.

(k) This has nothing to do with the Ten Commandments. Contextually, it can only have reference to what He had taught them, especially at that time. In John 15:12, He explicitly stated what one of these commandments was that He had been teaching them.

2p-Verse 11. "These things." This has reference to what He was teaching them. When understood they would expel the sorrow and despondence so heavy in their hearts upon knowing that He was leaving them.

3p-Verse 12. See footnote n below where He repeated this same command.

(l) We can do no better at this verse than did Albert Barnes. He wrote the following in 1832 in *Barnes Notes,* on *The Gospels,* page 340, "No higher expression of love could be given. Life is the most valuable earthly object we possess apart from our souls; and when a man is willing to give that for his friends or his country, it shows the utmost extent of love." It has been said that no man can carry his love for a friend farther than this. Perhaps the example of Jonathan and David are a prime Old Testament illustration of this high truth. See 1 Sam. 18 for the beautiful story. We are dumbfounded that Christ died for us when we were his enemies (Rom. 5:6-8).

2p-Verse 14. Christ tells His preachers then and us today these wonderful Words. As Abraham was the friend of God (James 2:23) we have a greater prospect than the old patriarch did. We can be the friends of Jesus. There may be an allusion here to the blessing that the ministering priests in the temple would pronounce upon their fellow priests at the end of their service each Sabbath day. They would chant something along these lines, "Let him who dwells in this house plant among yourselves brotherhood, love, peace and friendship." It was not by accident that the Savior used several of these words in His blessing upon the eleven apostles. See Lightfoot's *Commentary on the New Testament . . . ,* vol. 3, page 404 for reference on the above quotation.

(m) **"I have chosen you."** It was a custom among the Jews, that the disciple should choose his own master or teacher. Here, Jesus refers to this accepted social practice; however, He has now reversed the order. He chooses His own. Using this verse to prove that God has chosen certain men to be saved while reprobating all others to eternal hell is foul exegesis. *Contextually the subject here has nothing to do with salvation;* rather Christ speaks of the apostles who were already believers and had been chosen "out of the world" to bear fruit that will forever remain. See verse 19 below where this very thing is stated by the Savior. On the first mention of prayer in this particular discourse, see second paragraph of footnote h above.

2p-Calvin, in his *Institutes,* III, xxi, 1, wrote, "It is unreasonable that man should scrutinize with impunity those things which the Lord has determined to be hidden in Himself." Yet, the Geneva tyrant broke his own rule. He professed to know why God arbitrarily chose to purposely damn millions, while saving other millions. His chilling words that hinge on blasphemy were "to promote our admiration of His glory" by this display of His great power. He concluded this cruel accolade by writing, "It was appointed by His [God's] own decree." See his *Institutes,* III, xxiii, 7 and IV, i, 10 for more of this theological poison. God's ineffable glory was promoted beyond human and angelic expression in the death, burial, and resurrection of His son for the sins of *all* mankind. He is not glorified in deliberately withholding all hope from sinners, then casting them into the horror of eternal hell. This barbaric act is supposed to result in "our admiration of His [God's] glory." Such talk rattles like the babblings of a mad man. The words in Ps. 59:6 describe Calvin and his supporters, "They make a noise like a dog, and go round about the city."

(n) Jews were taught in their Torah Law (Lev. 19:18) to love their neighbor. However, it was only fellow Jews and *never* Gentiles. By the time of Christ on earth, Jewish decadence had succumbed to such teaching as Matt. 5:43 "Thou shalt love thy neighbor, and hate thine enemy." See Section 45, footnote n. Things are in bad condition when the apostles of Messiah have to be commanded to "love one another." Were they not given to wrangling with each other over earthly trifles? Note this in the main heading of Section 170. Paul had not yet written the golden words of 1 Cor. 13:4-5 "Charity suffereth long, and is kind, charity envieth not; charity vaunteth not itself, is not puffed up," and "Doth not behave itself unseemly." ("Charity" is love in action.) Earlier during the footwashing event, He explained that the commandment to "love one another" was "new," meaning it was unknown to them (John 13:34-35). He had mentioned this earlier in verse 12. The grace of God teaches things unknown to the Torah Law of Israel.

(o) This *real world* has always hated true believers and will never be the friend of grace. Their malignancy stems originally from their hatred for the Son of God, the standards He taught, the doctrine He preached, and the requirements He laid down for men to be saved. In short, the sinless, perfect, Son of God, and His righteous moral laws condemn a vicious world. They cannot stand hearing these things in their bedeviled ears. Months earlier the Lord Jesus stated that, He had testified that the works of the world system were evil, and it hated Him for speaking this truth (John 7:7). For more the world's hatred of Christ, see Section 21, Part 2, fifth paragraph of footnote i.

(p) He asked if they remembered what He told them a few minutes prior. This statement, "the servant is not greater than his lord," was also said during the footwashing (John 13:16). Did they did remember this, or was the Lord stressing again this truth?

(q) Walking to the garden, with His arrest, and death in a few more hours, the Savior is trying to ready His little band of apostles for the task ahead. Each of these men knew how the religious leaders had persecuted their Lord. Now, He assures them that as this was so with Him, it will be with them. In verses 20-22, Jesus employed the plural pronoun "they" some eight times. He made direct reference to the Jews and especially their religious leaders.

(r) **"No cloak for sin."** These Jews were without excuse. Jesus had demonstrated hundreds of times in words and works that He was Messiah, yet they deliberately rejected Him. This was the heart of their hideous sin for which they had no cloke or cover. Our Lord said this very thing of them in verse 24.

(s) **They hate God and Me.** One of the most profound theological statements ever made! All the religious chatter from "good men" about the God they love and serve, and how others need to know Him is but blasphemy when these same people reject His Son, deny His virgin birth and holy deity, play down His miracles, and denigrate His blood atonement for sin. Low rating Christ to the level of the world's famous founders and leaders of the various religions is a mockery that God will not forget! *Those who hate Christ, in fact, hate God, for they are both the same.* See second paragraph of footnote f above. Hell waits for all who hate the Lord Jesus, regardless!

(t) Their hatred had been foretold by God in Ps. 69:4 over a thousand years prior. It is noted that here our Lord calls the book of Psalms "law." For more on this, see Section 89, number 1 under footnote c. The eleven apostles would have been familiar with this prophecy from their Hebrew Scriptures. The rabbis cited it as pointing to their Messiah. There is a curious, if not condemning passage in the Talmud tractate, Yoma 9b. A rabbi who lived *after* the destruction of Jerusalem in A.D. 70, looking back on "why" the city was destroyed asked this question, "Why was the second sanctuary [temple] destroyed?" The rabbi then answered His own question with these words, "Because in it [the temple] prevailed hatred without a cause." Does this refer to the Jew's hatred of their Messiah? In Sections 148 through 159, we traced our Lord's final messages to the Jews, delivered in the temple just after Palm Sunday. In *every* message without exception, He fell into fierce conflict with the religious leaders because of the opposition they had for His preaching, teaching, and Messianic claims.

(u) **He shall testify of Christ.** We last heard Him speak of the coming Holy Spirit in John 14:26. With that lesson fresh on their minds, He completes the discourse on the true vine, and then returns them to this urgent subject. Jesus assures His preachers that the Spirit will have *one supreme purpose* as He works through their lives; to testify of Him. We live in a time of great preaching, with thrilling and colorful pulpit orations, as the voices of a thousand "Christian philosophers" are heard. Yet, where is the Holy Spirit? Few men any longer see their sin, understand its curse and doom, and are divinely enlightened by the Spirit pointing them to Christ, the only Savior. If men do not see Christ through the eyes of repentance and faith, all is vain. Even the church business meetings should be conducted in a pure evangelical atmosphere where Christ is foremost. For an illustration of this, see next paragraph.

2p-Many years ago, I attended a church business meeting of several dozen Russian Christian leaders in Adelaide, Australia. Sitting in a circle, I noticed an empty chair in the middle of the room. Inquiring of my interpreter regarding this seat, he replied, "That is the seat for Jesus where he watches how we do His business." I was struck with the serious solemnity in which the two-hour meeting was conducted. After it was over, I asked a Polish Christian for further information. He answered in simplicity and power, "The Holy Spirit seeks first to testify of and glorify Jesus in our midst; even in a business meeting."

(v) These Words spoken by our Lord reveal that we have part with the Holy Spirit in witnessing for Christ. In His Words, "And ye [the apostles] shall also bear witness," and "He shall testify of me," reveals the joint effort of believers with the Holy Spirit in telling men of Christ. There is no such thing as a passive witness of the gospel. God has always used some channel through which to accomplish His purposes. These are often diverse and numerous. It is not that He needs men to get His work done; rather, it is that He has chosen men to share in it with Him.

2p-**Lifestyle evangelism?** This new approach to witnessing for Christ has possessed many Christian young people. Now, we hear that one should not verbally speak so much about Jesus, but just live upright and that will bring men to salvation. Here, balance is needed. *Believers must be equal in both their talk and walk for the Savior.* Too much of one without the other is like a sun that cannot shine or bird that cannot fly. In Ps. 107:2 we read, "Let the redeemed of the LORD say *so* . . ." The Sanhedrin noted of Peter and John, "that they had been with Jesus" (Acts 4:13). The unsaved word must both see and hear the true gospel of Christ in action. See footnote i above.

Moving through the Passover crowds in the temple, He warns the eleven apostles of persecutions they must endure, expulsion from the synagogues, of His death, and the Holy Spirit coming in His fullness. They should now make all prayer in His Name. Shortly, in the Garden of Gethsemane they will forsake their Lord and flee.

Time: The night before the Friday morning of the cross.

Matt.	Mk.	Lk.	John 16:1-18—*In the streets of Jerusalem and the temple*
			Warning of persecution: expulsion from synagogue
			1 "These things[a] have I spoken unto you, that ye should not be offended.
			2 "They shall put you out of the synagogues:[b] yea, the time cometh, that whosoever killeth you will think that he doeth God service.
			3 "And these things will they do unto you, because they have not known the Father, nor me.
			4 "But these things have I told you, that when the time shall come, ye may remember that I told you of them. And these things I said not unto you at the beginning,[c] because I was with you.
			5 "But now I go my way to him that sent me; and none of you asketh me, 'Whither goes thou?'[d]
			6 "But because I have said these things unto you, sorrow hath filled your heart.[e]
			"I go and then the Spirit will come"
			7 "Nevertheless I tell you the truth; It is expedient for you that I go away: for if I go not away, the Comforter will not come unto you; but if I depart, I will send him unto you.[f]
			8 "And when he is come,[g] he will reprove [convict] the world of sin, and of righteousness, and of judgment:
			9 "Of sin, because they believe not on me;
			10 "Of righteousness, because I go to my Father, and ye see me no more;
			"The prince of the world"
			11 "Of judgment, because the prince of this world is judged.
			12 "I have yet many things to say unto you, but ye cannot bear them now.[h]
			13 "Howbeit when he, the Spirit of truth, is come, he will guide you into all truth: for he shall not speak of himself; but whatsoever he shall hear, *that* shall he speak: and he will shew you things to come.[i]
			14 "He shall glorify me:[j] for he shall receive of mine, and shall shew *it* unto you.
			15 "All things that the Father hath are mine: therefore said I, that he shall take of mine, and shall shew *it* unto you.[k]
			His death and resurrection again foretold
			16 "A little while, and ye shall not see me: and again, a little while,[l] and ye shall see me, because I go to the Father."
			17 Then said *some* of his disciples among themselves,[m] "What is this that he saith unto us, 'A little while, and ye shall not see me: and again, a little while, and ye shall see:' and, 'Because I go to the Father?'"
			18 They said therefore, "What is this that he saith, 'A little while?'

Matt.	Mk.	Lk.	John 16:18-33—*In the streets of Jerusalem and the temple*
			we cannot tell what he saith."

19 Now Jesus knew that they were desirous to ask him, and said unto them,(n) "Do ye enquire among yourselves of that I said, 'A little while, and ye shall not see me: and again, a little while, and ye shall see me?'

"Your sorrow will vanish: we will meet again"

20 "Verily, verily, I say unto you,(o) That ye shall weep and lament, but the world shall rejoice: and ye shall be sorrowful, but your sorrow shall be turned into joy.

21 "A woman(p) when she is in travail hath sorrow, because her hour is come: but as soon as she is delivered of the child, she remembereth no more the anguish, for joy that a man is born into the world.

22 "And ye now therefore have sorrow:(q) but I will see you again, and your heart shall rejoice, and your joy no man taketh from you.

Solace in prayer: a new thing, you can now ask in my name

23 "And in that day ye shall ask me nothing. Verily, verily, I say unto you, Whatsoever ye shall ask the Father in my name, he will give *it* you. (r)

24 "Hitherto have ye asked nothing in my name:(s) ask, and ye shall receive, that your joy may be full.

25 "These things have I spoken unto you in proverbs:(t) but the time cometh, when I shall no more speak unto you in proverbs, but I shall shew you plainly of the Father.

26 "At that day ye shall ask in my name: and I say not unto you, that I will pray the Father for you:(u)

27 "For the Father himself loveth you, because ye have loved me, and have believed that I came out from God.

"I am returning to the Father"

28 "I came forth from the Father, and am come into the world: again, I leave the world, and go to the Father."(v)

29 His disciples said unto him, "Lo, now speakest thou plainly, and speakest no proverb.

30 "Now are we sure that thou knowest all things, and needest not that any man should ask thee: by this we believe that thou camest forth from God."(w)

31 Jesus answered them, "Do ye now believe?(x)

A warning of their defection and coming tribulations

32 "Behold, the hour cometh, yea, is now come, that ye shall be scattered, every man to his own, and shall leave me alone:(y) and yet I am not alone, because the Father is with me.

33 "These things I have spoken unto you, that in me ye might have peace. In the world ye shall have tribulation: but be of good cheer; I have overcome the world."(z) (Next chap. John 17:1 cont. in Section 178.)

Footnotes-Commentary

(a) Contextually, there is no break between John 15:27 and John 16:1. Verse 1 is a continuation of verse 27 at the end of chapter 15. For chapter and verse divisions of Scripture, see Section 53, footnote a. He informs the apostles that He has been sharing with them "these things" (in the previous chapter) concerning the world's hatred, persecution, and the comfort of the Holy Spirit. Now, when these things happen, they can recall His warnings and not be offended. For more on chapter and verse division in the Bible, and what it means, see Section 3, footnote a.

(b) "They shall put you out." This awful sentence fell like a crash of thunder into their ears. The Master warns them of what to expect after He has gone. "Killing you will be a favor for God." Early Christian history is replete with examples of the countless thousands murdered. *Radical* Islam is now the world's classic example of butchering those who do not subscribe to its religious philosophy. Centuries ago, the Roman Catholic Church held this infamy during the horrible inquisition. For a description of horror that was involved in expulsion from the Jewish synagogue, refer to Section 121, John 9:22, footnote j. There is an old story recorded in the Talmud tractate, Sanhedrin 107b which records that Jesus had been excommunicated from the synagogue by a rabbi named Joshua ben Perachiah with the blast of four hundred trumpets. The validity of this story is dubious, but that He was *finally* put out of the synagogue at Nazareth, cannot be doubted. This probably occurred near the end of His ministry.

2p-Verse 3. With these Words, the Lord Jesus reveals the true source of their unmitigated hatred and furious zeal to destroy Him and (later) His apostles and servants. *All of this sprang from the fact that these leaders of Jewish religion did not know God!* Like millions today, they boasted about God, talked daily about God, prayed to God, taught God in their synagogues, and academies, yet they knew not the Lord God of Israel, the only true and living God of mankind. The reason they did not know God, was because they had rejected His Son, the Lord Jesus as their Savior and Messiah. Many ask why over the course of church history some of its "famed heroes" have been ruthless tyrants and murderers as were the leaders of Israel's religion. This is because these men were never saved. They missed the mark and put faith in infant baptism and communion for salvation.

(c) These words reveal that the Lord Jesus taught many things to the twelve that were not recorded in the four gospels. During much of His ministry, He did not speak of the severe persecution coming on the apostles, for His presence was with them, and they were not ready for this truth. Now, on the eve of His death and soon departure to heaven, He begins to share these things with them.

(d) Again, He brings up the painful subject of His departure from them. In this discourse, the Savior is requesting that from this moment forward none of the eleven should ask Him where He was going, as Peter had in John 13:36. Over the next few weeks, they would gradually understand the whole story.

(e) Knowing the deep sorrow that raged in their hearts and the questionings in their minds, He admonishes them with fresh hope by saying, "The Holy Spirit will comfort you."

(f) Verse 7. "I will send him to you." This affirms that if Christ did not return to the Father, the Holy Spirit would not come to them in His fullness at Pentecost and do the things He had promised. In John 14:16, Christ said the Father would send the Spirit. Now, the Son will send Him! Both collaborated in sending the Holy Spirit at Pentecost in a manner and power, as He had never demonstrated before over all Old Testament history.

2p-He took the place of Jesus. His Words to the apostles must not be understood to mean that the Holy Spirit was something new to them. Nor does it mean that these men did not have the Spirit, for it is written, "If any man have not the Spirit of Christ, he is none of his" (Rom. 8:9). As true believers in the Savior, they were born again men. Only by the Holy Spirit and Word of God is one begotten into heaven's family (John 3:5 with 1 Peter 1:23 and James 1:18). The Spirit coming to take the place of Jesus was an entirely new thing for the third Person of the Trinity. He had not previously worked among man in this capacity. This was the way our Lord spoke of His coming at Pentecost. Jesus did not mean that He was a new Person, or something unknown in previous history. For a survey of how people were saved during the Old Testament dispensation, and the work of the Holy Spirit, see Section 30, first through third paragraphs footnote h. There has never been a time when the Spirit was not; being everything God is and therefore, God, He has ever been omnipresent but not always omni active in the affairs of men everywhere. Prior to the worldwide flood in Noah's time, He moved among men through the preaching of God's Word (Gen. 6:3 with 2 Peter 2:5). For a review of the Spirit's work across Bible history, refer to Section 10, footnote b.

3p-Abusing the Holy Spirit. There is need to guard the doctrine of the Holy Spirit from mysticism. Among certain Baptists, charismatic groups and others, everyone claims to be "led by the Spirit." The sheer chaos that often results from the lives and deeds of these super elites, reveal they were led by a spirit that was not Holy. Our spiritual emotions, when they become exceedingly wild may be justified by appealing to the "leadership of the Holy Spirit." Cult leaders and satanic religions plead this to justify their demands and deeds. For examples of this, see Section 21, Part 1, fifth paragraph of footnote i. *True Christians must walk softly with the Spirit!*

(g) Verses 8-11. Here, the Savior outlines the *major* work of the Spirit in the lost world. Note the following three things the Holy Spirit does among men who are unsaved:

1. **"He will reprove the world of sin."** The Greek verb used here is "elencho." Among several things, it means to "expose" or "bring to shame." It is no small thing that the *first* work of the Spirit is to "expose" to the world their sin! Until a man realizes that his problems stem from his inward fallen sinful state, all is vain. The Spirit *alone* can enlighten the sinner's darkened mind into understanding his awful ill before God and the resulting doom of it. Men are thus, by birth and nature. Only Christ can save them from their sins (verse 9). The knowledge that one has never believed in Christ to eternal life is not received by eloquent sermons, beautiful oratory, learned expositions, and worldly-wise debate. Only the work of the Sovereign Spirit of God can affect such divine enlightenment. He will demonstrate these things so

849

clearly, leaving no doubt in the minds of the unconverted as to their doomed estate and need for Christ. Great preaching, pulpit oratory, and wordy expositions *alone* will never get the job done. Possibly, our Lord had *first in mind* the sin of the Jews in rejecting Him as Messiah and Savior. The Holy Spirit did this, as Jesus was going back to heaven. His would no longer be present to convince men of their sin.

2. **"He will reprove [convict and convince] the world of righteousness."** The second major work of the Holy Spirit is to show mankind that they are unapproved before God; that all must have the perfect acceptance before Him, which is known as righteousness. The human race stands corrupt in its sin and void of holiness. This is because they have not trusted and received the Lord Jesus, who will save every repenting believing sinner and instantly account or give to them the perfect righteousness that is absent in their lives. The wonder of this transaction is that we receive the very righteousness or holiness of God. This is a gift of love given freely by grace. It is written, "Even the righteousness of God *which is* by faith of Jesus Christ unto all and upon all them that believe" (Rom. 3:22). With such a blessed miracle (the gift of divine righteousness now clothing the saved soul), man's foul and unholy condition vanishes before the all-holy God. This glorious transaction of sinners being made righteous is granted because Christ went back to the Father and sits at His right hand to save and justify all who believe Him (John 16:10). Even Abraham, who lived some two thousand years before the birth of Christ, was counted, saved, and made righteous when he believed the gospel (Gal. 3:6-9). Again, Jesus warns the apostles that they will "see him no more," as they were seeing Him at that time. They did see him after the resurrection for some forty days and nights (Acts 1:3). Our Lord speaks here of His return to the Father some weeks later. See the story of Christ's ascension back to heaven in Section 207.

3. **"He will [convict and convince] the world of judgment."** The word "judgment" in this text is the word for "crisis," and is linked to the condemnation and overthrow of the Devil. Satan is described as "the prince of this world." This title reflected his former rule through sin over the entire human race. For Jewish history on the origin of this title for Satan, see Section 161, footnote j. On the cross, God laid the sins of all humanity, of all times, on His beloved Son. Then He condemned the Son (because of our sins), judged Him guilty, and put Him to death for our sins and in our place. Christ bore the world's sins, took the punishment justly due to all humankind, and willingly died under that penalty. In this supreme act of love, He provided salvation from sin and freedom from satanic bondage strapped on humankind by the prince of evil. No longer could Satan hold men in their chains of sin. The Lord Jesus snapped every iron and shattered every fetter for all who would trust Him as Lord and Savior.

4. **Prince of evil, is judged.** Jesus spoke as though the cross was already past. He counts His atonement and resurrection a finished work, something already done! The prince of this world was torn from his throne, and lost his authority over mankind through what Christ did at Calvary, and the resurrection. However, this victory is not hereditary, spontaneous or naturally received at physical birth; it is only acquired by those who put faith in the Lord Jesus Christ. With this, all He accomplished in His death becomes theirs as a gift of God. Thus, in verses 8-11 we see the process that leads to forgiveness and eternal life. We are convicted or convinced of our sinfulness of not believing in Christ, made fearfully aware that our goodness is not acceptable, and that we need God to make us righteous. *The work of genuine conviction that leads to repentance and faith in Christ is the work of the Holy Spirit alone.* Without this, no man can ever be saved. Lastly, our former slave master and cruel lord, the Devil was judged, condemned and beaten on the cross. His fetters of sin no longer shackle our lives. We are free in Christ. After genuine conversion to the Lord Jesus, the believer must *daily* implement and appropriate this victory; not to keep saved but because he is saved. In Eph. 6:10-18 this is called "putting on the whole armour of God." In 2 Peter 1:5-10, this is called "adding to your faith" so that you "never fall." Woe be those who ridicule these things, make light of walking in the Spirit and fail or neglect to maintain daily fellowship with the Father and the Son (1 John 1:3).

(h) **"Ye cannot bear them now."** As they moved through the crowded temple area toward Gethsemane, their heads were spinning as they hung onto every Word from the mouth of Jesus. *Never had they heard such teachings as this!* In trying to explain the major work of the Holy Spirit, He laid upon their minds doctrines unknown to them at that time. The "many things" that He later taught them clarified the brief instructions given in the upper room and along the way to the garden.

(i) **"Into all truth and shew you" is not for every Christian.** This profound and all comprehensive promise was *originally* intended for the apostles and not all believers in general over the history of the church. Being the prime leaders of the first and earliest churches, these men were given extraordinary powers and authority: here Christ promised them that the Holy Spirit will "guide them into all truth" and will "shew them things to come" (or future events). It is amusing to hear evangelists and radio preachers cite this verse and then assure their audience that their vast knowledge of God, and His Word is rooted in this promise. We have wondered when they came into the knowledge of "all truth," and were shown "all truth about things to come." Listening to some of them preach, one cannot help but muse what kind of spirit it was that gave them their great revelation! Also, there are those who boasts they have "never used any book except the Bible." *Only God taught them, not man!* It is curious how these people end up in heresies, cults, and radical doctrinal extremes. For more on the apostle's *exclusive* power with God and the Holy Spirit, which were never intended for all believers, see the main heading in Section 110, and especially the second paragraph of footnote e. Jesus had earlier mentioned these same things to His eleven before leaving the upper room. Note this in Section 175, John 14:26, footnote n.

(j) **"He shall glorify me."** The chief purpose of all the Holy Spirit came to do is to glorify and honor Christ among those who are saved. See His three major works among the lost in footnote g above. Previously, in John 15:26 our Lord said, "He shall testify of me." Here see footnotes, u, and v. In this passage Christ affirms, "He shall glorify me." *True* Spirit filled ministers of the gospel may be quickly detected among the clamoring crowds and bright stage lights; they are ever busy testifying and seeking to honor the Son of God. Anything less is unacceptable.

(k) He had previously said this in verse 14. See footnote i above for explanation.

(l) **"A little while."** Here, is the first "little while." This refers to His death tomorrow. After that, they will not see Him for three days and nights. The second "little while" of time when they would see Him pointed to the various post resurrection appearances He made during the forty days and nights of Acts 1:3. "Because I go to my Father" apparently speaks of their beholding His ascension that occurred some weeks later as recorded in Section 207, Acts 1:9-11. See footnote q below for more on this thought.

(m) **"What is this that he saith?"** Verses 17-18. At this point, a discussion broke out between some of the apostles. This explains that they did not yet understand. When we remember that John, the human author of this book was one of them, then this passage is his inspired effort to explain to his readers their ultra confusion at that time. His readers, looking back could now understand what he wrote.

(n) Knowing the thoughts of their hearts the Savior quotes what they were thinking!

(o) **Verse 20.** Here, the Lord Jesus explains their various reactions to His crucifixion on the morrow. The apostles and the true followers of Jesus would "weep and lament," while the world, the Jews, and others who opposed Him would "rejoice." Forty days after His resurrection, when He had convinced them that He was alive, *then* their sorrow would become joy. See their rejoicing after His ascension in Section 207, Lk. 24:53, footnote h.

(p) **"A woman."** Their sorrow and dismay would be short lived. As a woman enters labor during the pains of childbirth—in time it will end. The joy over having her baby boy will suppress and surpass the physical anguish of bringing him into the world. It would be similar with them during the days ahead. They would have awful pain and sorrow, but it would be short lived in comparison to eternity. See footnote q below.

(q) **"You now have sorrow."** What can these odd words mean? Was the sorrow and pain of Christ leaving them comparable to that of childbirth? Apparently, it was! However, three days and nights later, when Christ rose victorious over death, their joy would be greater than the woman who pained deeply for her child to be brought into the world. His resurrection and infallible deeds that followed, exhibited to them His Messianic power that they would not again doubt what He said. See footnote l above for more on these thoughts.

(r) This has reference to His resurrection, ascension, and coming of the Holy Spirit, for after that their questionings forever vanished; then they understood it all. Note this in Section 207, Mk. 16:20, footnote i, which explains the wonderfully drastic change in their outlook after Pentecost.

2p-"Whatsoever ye shall ask." Answered prayer *within the will of God* is assured because Christ ascended to heaven and now represents His children at the throne of grace. On the heresy of God answering all prayers regardless, and Christians getting whatever they want, refer to Section 175, second paragraph of footnote n, and Section 176, John 15:7, footnote h.

(s) **"Ask in my name."** *Jews have never prayed in the name of any person!* In prayer, they appealed to the Name of God but never through the name of any of their religious personalities or individuals (1 Kings 18:24 with Ps. 18:49). Ancient Jews and those of today pray something like this, "O God of Abraham, Isaac and Jacob, hear us, we pray." Again, what difficult words these must have been to the eleven as they walked to the garden. A thousand times and more they had heard some rabbi give instructions from Jewish traditions in the name of a previous rabbi. Now, Jesus instructs them to call on God in His Name! Up to this time, none of these men had ever prayed to Jehovah in this manner. After the resurrection and ascension of Christ, God honored Him and gave Him a Name, which is above every name. In all creation, time, and eternity, no one has been exalted like Jesus Christ. *His station is the highest of all.* See Matt. 1:21; 28:18; Lk. 10:17; Acts 4:12; with Phil 2:9-11. Because of this God is pleased to give quick attention to the faintest cry or supplication whispered in the blessed Name of Jesus, His eternal Son.

(t) **"In proverbs."** Christ reveals that He understands their frustrations over His teaching. It sounded like ancient proverbs, so difficult to understand, or even as old maxims that wise men spun among themselves. The time of clear, absolute, and complete understanding came at the day of Pentecost with the fullness of the Spirit.

(u) **"At that day."** As in footnote t above He speaks of the time when they will know the full truth and understand everything He had taught them. "I will no longer pray for you." The meaning is that once the Holy Spirit has taken up total dwelling in their souls, *and is with them as never before*, they will have absolute knowledge. They will not need Christ to explain difficult doctrines, for He will intercede on their behalf regarding these things.

2p-Verse 27. Our Lord seems to be saying something like this, "When that day of fullness at Pentecost has come, God my Father will direct all things, and will love you with unspeakable love because you loved me and know that I came from Him to earth."

(v) "And go to the Father." This is the greatest space travel ever known by man! The journey began as a babe in a manger and ended with His ascension back to the place from where it started. The most glorious round trip ever made in all history. For other details, see Section 207. Even the godless world loves the manger and the little babe, who slept there, (good for business and sales), but hates the old rugged cross on which He died to save us from hell.

(w) Verses 29-30. This does not mean that they *suddenly understood* all Jesus had told them. Rather, it reflects the over anxiousness of the eleven; their speaking too quickly, their aching hearts and confused minds, but still desperately reaching out to understand what their Messiah was saying. Footnote x below explains that this was the case with these eleven men.

(x) "Do you now believe?" Sensing their frustration, and knowing their poor hearts, the Savior gently rebukes them with something like this, "Are you sure you understand and believe the things I have just expounded?" At this time, they did not, for in the following passage, He warns them of a soon coming desertion on their part.

(y) "You will forsake me." The hour of their forsaking Him in Gethsemane was near. He had warned them of this during the Passover in Section 173, Matt. 26:31. Now, they were issued another warning of what would happen. Still, they did not understand what this meant. *Despite their defection, the Father was with Him!*

(z) "In the world ye shall have tribulation." This word is as sure as the throne of God. As then, so it is today: the highway to heaven is paved with blood, sweat, and tears, but our proven and trusted Conductor overcame every evil along this way. Therefore, at its end He will land us safely on that beautiful shore of heaven. In 1 John 4:4 we find revealed the secret of this truth. "Ye are of God, little children, and have overcome them: because greater is he that is in you, than he that is in the world." And who is in us? *All three Persons of the Holy Trinity!* In John 14:17 and 23 Jesus affirmed that the Spirit, He, and the Father would make their abode with believers!

2p-"I have overcome the world." At that *present* hour, the apostles were greatly perplexed over His troubling Words about leaving them. Later, they came into divine understanding of all He taught. See footnote u above. He will be nailed to a Roman cross in the morning; He will die among thieves the death of infamy. Yet, He tells them He had overcome it all! How contradictory this all sounded later. Often, our Lord spoke of the future as though it was present and accomplished. This is illustrated in Section 178, John 17:11, footnote l. Thus, when future tribulations came, they would take it in "good cheer." These men remembered that He in whom they trusted had conquered Satan, the hateful world, overcame sin, paid its penalty, beat the grave, and lived forever more! *In every conquest of Christ, He makes His people to share the victory because they have trusted Him as Lord and Savior.* We read in 1 John 5:5, this pointed question, "Who is he that overcometh the world, but he that believeth that Jesus is the Son of God?" True faith or belief is never alone; it is always accompanied by helpful virtues given from the hand of God. It was the triumph of Christ over the world and all its sin that we fully trust and through this faith, God sends forgiveness and pardon into our lives. It has been faithfully repeated in this work that the world system is not a friend of God or His saving grace. Its course is straight to hell (Eph 2:2), its god is Satan (2 Cor. 4:4), and its evil has always been a deceiving allurement to Christians (1 John 2:15-17). It is not the duty of believers in Christ to make the world a better place. (This does not justify believers neglecting their social and community duties.) As the leper cannot change his spots, so men without Christ cannot create a perfect planet for future generations. The author knew of an African politician who was trained at Oxford in England. Returning to his native country, he became a highly respected leader and was a "people's favorite." However, in time, the depravity of his sinful humanity came out. During certain nights, he returned to his pagan tribe, joined in their shocking rituals, drank blood, and cut parts from dead bodies to make "muti," or witch doctor medicine. The Devil is too clever to take all men in this direction. Others, he keeps clean, well-dressed, moral, sincere, and upright, but blinds their minds to God, Jesus Christ, and the Holy Bible. Either way, he is the winner for it is eternal hell for both at the end of human life. *On sincerity in religion without the truth , see Section 95, sixth paragraph of footnote r.*

3p-Some of our duties. On the other hand, *true* Christians should strive to live according to civil law, honor their fellow men as they can, and seek peace and tranquility among others. There are things in this world that are good and blessed and others that are satanic and damming. It is written, the Devil "deceiveth the whole world" (Rev. 12:9). Christians work day and night to bring lost souls to the saving knowledge of Christ, knowing that eternity waits for every man. Often, they are scorned, ridiculed, mocked, and degraded. In other lands to bear the Name of Christ is to court torture, prison, and death. False religions and political movements of hate and vengeance connive to destroy all not of their persuasion. To fight the Christ of the Bible is to fight against Almighty God and lose! In view of all this, it is no marvel that the Savior admonished the eleven apostles and us of today, "Be of good cheer, I have overcome the world." For other comments along these lines, see Section 79, third paragraph of footnote e.

Before exiting the temple, Christ gives the great high priestly prayer.* He offers thanks to the Father, that His will has been done. This begins His work as heaven's only High Priest interceding for His apostles and all future believers. Here, was our Lord's final prayer among the eleven before His death.

Time: The night before the Friday morning of the cross.

---

*All debate over where the Messiah made this prayer is senseless. Had He not a few days earlier purged this very temple and declared that His Father's house was a house of prayer? See this dramatic event recorded in Section 150, Mk. 11:17. It is ironic that the Jewish high priest offered a prayer in the temple for Israel on the Passover evening. Now, the only true High Priest for all of mankind supplicates to God. The milling crowds shied away from the prayer area of the temple: the Jews designated it as "holy ground." John, looking back on this event years later could only have written the exact Words of Jesus' prayer by divine inspiration. For more on prayers being made in the temple, especially how the pious elderly resorted there to seek God, refer to Section 16, second paragraph of footnote k. For the Pharisee and publican praying in the temple, note Section 136.

Matt.	Mk.	Lk.	John 17:1-14—*In the temple*
			He prays for Himself[a]
			1 These words[b] spake Jesus, and lifted up his eyes to heaven, and said,[c] "Father, the hour[d] is come; glorify thy Son, that thy Son also may glorify thee:
			2 "As thou hast given him power over all flesh, that he should give eternal life to as many as thou hast given him.[e]
			3 "And this is life eternal, that they might know thee the only true God, and Jesus Christ, whom thou hast sent.
			4 "I have glorified thee on the earth: I have finished[f] the work which thou gavest me to do.
			5 "And now, O Father, glorify thou me with thine own self with the glory which I had with thee before the world was.[g]
			He prays for His disciples
			6 "I have manifested thy name unto the men which thou gavest me out of the world: thine they were, and thou gavest them me;[h] and they have kept thy word.
			7 "Now they have known[i] that all things whatsoever thou hast given me are of thee.
			8 "For I have given unto them the words which thou gavest me; and they have received *them*, and have known surely that I came out from thee, and they have believed that thou didst send me.
			9 "I pray for them:[j] I pray not for the world, but for them which thou hast given me; for they are thine.
			10 "And all mine are thine, and thine are mine;[k] and I am glorified in them.
			11 "And now I am no more in the world,[l] but these are in the world, and I come to thee. Holy Father, keep through thine own name those whom thou hast given me, that they may be one, as we *are*.
			12 "While I was with them in the world, I kept them in thy name: those that thou gavest me I have kept, and none of them is lost, but the son of perdition;[m] that the scripture might be fulfilled.
			13 "And now come I to thee; and these things I speak in the world, that they might have my joy fulfilled in themselves.
			14 "I have given[n] them thy word; and the world hath hated them, because they are not of the world, even as I am not of the world.

Matt.	Mk.	Lk.	John 17:15-26—In the temple
			15 "I pray not that thou shouldest take them out of the world, but that thou shouldest keep them from the evil.[o]
			16 "They are not of the world, even as I am not of the world.
			17 "Sanctify them through thy truth: thy word is truth.[p]
			18 "As thou hast sent me into the world, even so have I also sent them into the world.
			19 "And for their sakes I sanctify myself,[q] that they also might be sanctified through the truth.
			He prays for all believers
			20 "Neither pray I for these alone, but for them[r] also which shall believe on me through their word;
			21 "That they all may be one;[s] as thou, Father, *art* in me, and I in thee, that they also may be one in us: that the world may believe that thou hast sent me.
			22 "And the glory which thou gavest me I have given them; that they may be one, even as we are one:
			23 "I in them, and thou in me, that they may be made perfect in one; and that the world may know that thou hast sent me, and hast loved them, as thou hast loved me.
			24 "Father, I will that they also, whom thou hast given me, be with me where I am; that they may behold my glory, which thou hast given me: for thou lovedst me before the foundation of the world.
			The world does not know God
			25 "O righteous Father,[t] the world hath not known thee: but I have known thee, and these have known that thou hast sent me.
			Your love and Me in them
			26 "And I have[u] declared unto them thy name, and will declare *it*: that the love wherewith thou hast loved me may be in them,[v] and I in them."[w] (Next chap., John 18:1 cont. in Section 179.)

Footnotes-Commentary

[a] **"These words,"** refer to His lessons, discourses, commandments, statements of comfort, hope, direction and instruction, that He had given the eleven apostles in the three preceding chapters. These things were spoken as they moved eastward through the city streets and temple area heading for the garden. See all by the asterisk under main heading above for discussion of where this final prayer of the Master with His eleven apostles occurred.

2p-*This is the longest prayer of Jesus found in the New Testament.* It has been objected that He could not have made this prayer at the temple because its gates were closed this late at night. However, during Passover, the gates were only closed for emergencies: at midnight of the Passover, there was a special closing and opening of the gates as a symbol of inviting Messiah to come in. When He had finished instructing the eleven, He stood with hands lifted, face upwards to heaven, and prayed these words as mankind's great High Priest.

3p-**"Lifted up His eyes to heaven."** That is toward the seat of Holy Majesty, even the throne of His Father. Jews often employed this beautiful facial gesture as they made prayer. Sarcastic critics berate Christians for looking upward toward the abode of God Almighty. They say, "A man on the north pole looks in a totally opposite direction from a man at the South Pole. Which one looks toward God?" Poor men without Christ argue ever so eloquently for their own damnation. "Behold, the heaven and heaven of heavens cannot contain thee" (1 Kings 8:27). God is everywhere except in the heart of the unsaved.

[b] Edersheim in *Life and Times of Jesus the Messiah*, page 839, puts this holy scene into words that bring tears of joy to our dim eyes. Listen to this late Jewish Christian of over one hundred years ago. "We now enter most reverently what may be called the innermost Sanctuary (John 17). For the first time, we are allowed to listen to what was really 'the Lord's Prayer,' and as we hear, we humbly worship. This prayer was the preparation for his great agony, cross, and passion." Reading this exquisite prologue we cannot help but write this burst of spontaneous praise to Him who redeemed us, "Hallelujah what a Savior!"

(c) This prayer is briefly discussed under three separate divisions below with comments attached.

He prays for Himself—Verses 1-5

(d) **"The hour is come."** This was the hour of atonement, which had been planned in the dateless past of eternity. Now, it has arrived. Christ will die on the cross for the sins of mankind. He first spoke of this at the wedding in Cana about three years before. See Section 27, John 2:4, footnote f for the details on this expression used by the Lord Jesus.

(e) **"Power over all flesh."** Though dwelling in a human frame, yet He had power over all flesh, meaning Jews and Gentiles alike. Learned, unlearned, sophisticated or rustic, rich or poor, high or low, the Son of God is supreme above all men; thus, His sovereign power to give salvation to each one the Father gives Him to save. And whom does the Father "give" to the Son? Every convicted, repenting sinner who will believe on Christ is given, and He instantly saves them. This is true because He "has power over all flesh." He can subdue all things unto Himself, and at no place is this so wonderfully seen as in the salvation of lost men from every nation and race across the world. God gives to Jesus all who repent of their sins and trust His death, burial, and resurrection for forgiveness and salvation. The apostles' clear understanding of these things came into total view on the day of Pentecost. In verse 6 the Lord Jesus again speaks of "the men" that God gave him. Over the centuries, God has been giving millions to His Son because they have put faith in Him as Lord and Savior. According to Rom. 10:17, this faith develops in the heart out of hearing the gospel and God's Word. It is clear in John 3:36, that those who exercise this faith are saved and those who do not are doomed.

2p-**"Give eternal life."** *Scofield Reference Bible*, page 1139, carries an excellent footnote at this passage. It reads, "Seven times Jesus speaks of believers as given to Him by the Father (verses 2 and 6 [twice], 9, 11, 12, 24)." He continues with "Jesus Christ is God's love-gift to the world (John 3:16), and believers are the Father's love-gift to Jesus Christ. Christ commits the believers to the Father for safekeeping. The believer's security rests upon the Father's faithfulness to His Son, Jesus Christ."

3p-**Verse 3. "This is life eternal."** He joyfully reiterates to the Father the origin and way into salvation for mankind, "Knowing both God and Christ aright" brings salvation to any soul. This means to know them in the pardon of sins by faith in the finished work of Christ on the cross. See 1 John 5:20 for more on this thought.

(f) He had finished the Father's work up to that time. Tomorrow, heaven's capstone will be placed on the building of His holy service. He will finalize all He has done and said by His atoning death on the cross, His glorious resurrection, and ascension to follow.

(g) **"Before the world was."** These few words afford us a glimpse into eternity past. Before the world was, there was Christ with God the Father, sharing His oneness. For readers interested in the ineffable glory, co-equally shared between all persons of the Holy Trinity, refer to Isa. 6:1-4. We have the words of the apostle recorded in John 12:41, that Isaiah the prophet actually "saw the glory" of Jesus Christ as he penned his profound description of heaven's dazzling glory. It touches us that the seraphim's continually fly above the throne crying out the divine anthem, "Holy, holy, holy," (Isa. 6:2-3).

He prays for His disciples—Verses 6-19

(h) **The men you gave me.** Messiah knows that He has not removed the difficulties and dispelled all gloom, questionings, and doubts from the minds of His eleven apostles. He understands that they are weak, confused, still bickering, and failing to comprehend what He had taught them. Faithfully, He has loved them to the end of His earthly ministry. In saving grace and long running mercy, He jealously claims them as belonging to the Father and Himself. We are amazed to read this line in His prayer "they have kept thy Word." This is explained in verse 8, where the Lord says that they had kept the Word of God that He had given them. At this late moment in the ministry of Jesus, His preachers believed all He had taught them, but understood precious little. See footnote n below.

(i) **Verses 7-8.** Again, He speaks of the future as though it were an accomplished present fact. In the days ahead, they will understand all the mysteries heard from His lips, His every word would shine as diamonds in the sun; they will be seen, loved, and shared. Then the apostles will comprehend how He "came out from the Father" and will believe that the Father sent Him. All this was realized and understood on the day of Pentecost with the outpouring of the Holy Spirit in His fulness.

(j) **"I pray for them."** He prays for the eleven. How touching. In view of the hazards that awaited them, Christ knew that prayer would support them through the rigors ahead. If the Son of God prayed for His preachers, how much ought we to seek God on behalf of others? We heard Him earlier admonishing Peter that He had prayed for Him that his faith would not fail (Lk. 22:32). Now, all of them are the attention of this High Priestly prayer. Our Lord's Words that He did not pray for the world in this supplication have troubled some.

2p-**"I pray not for the world."** The meaning is that *in this prayer,* He was not including the entire world, at that time, but rather His apostles whose work would be to take the gospel to that very world. Later, Paul made it clear that we are to "Pray for all men, including kings, those in authority" and that this "is good and acceptable in the sight of God." (1 Tim. 2:1-3). In this prayer, the Lord Jesus requested the Father to attach His special care upon those men, for in their hands lay the fortunes of infantile Christianity. He prays for them as a dying mother would her children. They are the first fruit of His labors; and must be kept, as He will soon leave them. They are God's as well as His.

(k) Here is another claim to perfect equality with God. For more on this, see footnote g above. Any believer can say that "all mine are thine," but only the Lord Jesus can say, "All thine are mine."

(l) "I am no more in the world." Christ looks upon His work as an accomplished fact already completed. He speaks as though it was finished, and He had ascended to the Father. However, the work of His preachers had just started. They would be left in the world and needed the Father's keeping. Jesus prays for unity among His apostles, without which the work of God would suffer. We have previously noted there was constant bickering and arguing among these men. See all by the single asterisk in italics under main heading of Section 170. For a short chronology of their bickering, see Section 104, 105, 107, and 141.

(m) "Son of perdition," is highlighted as having reference to Judas, because he was spoken of in Old Testament prophecy. See Section 172, second paragraph of footnote e. After commending the apostles to the Father, the Lord Jesus then gives an account of His stewardship as their Master. He had kept them all except the traitor. On Judas fulfilling Scripture, see Section 172, all under footnote e. Some expositors have seized upon these words and forced into them alien meanings totally unsuited to their historical context. "Son of perdition" was a common Jewish expression for any "worthless individual of base character." It was similar to the popular but much older Jewish term "belial," meaning one who was "worthless" and was applied to both men and women (Deut. 13:13; 1 Sam. 1:16; and 1 Kings 21:10). There were thousands that fit this description in Israel; but Judas was the chief of them all. He was not "the," but rather "a son of evil." Years later, Paul wrote to one of his churches about "that man of sin the son of perdition" (2 Thess. 2:3). Over anxious students of prophecy are quick to link Judas to this same person and now preach that the Antichrist will be Judas Iscariot reincarnated! The famed Calvinist preacher, Author Pink (died 1954) wrote a book "proving" that Judas was Antichrist! Thousands have guessed the identity of this evil person over the centuries and all of them have been proven wrong. It is best to let God handle such things. The question of whether or not the traitor was saved is answered below. Only wild exegesis can connect Isa. 28:15 to Judas and Judas to the Antichrist. On "the day of the Lord," see section 134, fourth paragraph of footnote k.

2p-Judas was lost. This should settle the debate regarding the salvation of Judas. His suicide occurred after Jesus was arrested. He was not born a son of perdition. He became such because of his willful malice, rejection of the Messiah, His grace, mercy, and message of salvation. The scribes and Pharisees and many other Jews did exactly the same thing with their Messiah. In Judas' case, he was evil personified. Even the prince of darkness found lodging in this man's soul. For Satan entering Judas, see Section 147, Lk. 22:3, footnote a, and references. In the Talmud tractate, Ta'anith 5a we read about the doom of men in perdition, which here has reference to a place (gehenna) rather than a person. See *Appendix Eight* for a historical review of the Antichrist.

3p-Expositors that see Judas as the beast coming out of the bottomless pit of hell in Rev. 17:8, have gone into the extreme. This sort of exegesis plays to sensationalism instead of rightly dividing the Word of God.

(n) "Given them thy word." No greater treasure could be placed into the minds and hearts of mankind than the Word of God. This Christ did for His preachers. However, much of what He had given them, they did not understand at this time. It would all be made clear at the day of Pentecost not very far away.

2p-"The world hath hated them." At this point, they were totally confused and bewildered beyond measure about this Word (doctrine) that He had instilled into their hearts. Refer to footnote h above for more on this thought. Later, it came into fruition, and they fully understood every doctrine He had taught them. See footnote i above for explanation. The world did hate them, especially the Jewish leaders and their Sanhedrin. After all is said and done, this harsh statement remains true. The Christ rejecting world still hates the Son of God and His Word to this very hour and will continue to do so. Saved Christians are not of this world, but only in it for a short tour. Theirs is a pilgrim journey, a passing through. Woe be those thousands in the church who madly love this world system, who know more about Hollywood than the holiness, who fiercely cling to the passing things of time and have no treasure laid up in heaven. Many "believers" in the west are more interested in a "tummy tuck," "face lift," "implants," "impressing their friends," than in touching the great heart of God in prayer and helping to win lost souls to the Lord Jesus. While the "sipping saints," are busy blowing cigarette smoke in one another's faces, driving the most exquisite cars in town, jockeying for prominence in the country club, their sons, daughters, and family members are dropping into eternal hell. "Believers" who are so blindly in love with this world, and its system are walking in spiritual darkness and know not where they go. *It remains true that the world still hates the things of God and Jesus Christ.* For more on the general mess of the average church body, refer to Section 184, fourth paragraph of footnote f, and Section 206, fourth paragraph of footnote e. Nevertheless, God does have exceptions to this calamity.

(o) "Keep them from the evil." Jesus does not pray for them to seclude themselves in deserts, caves, convents, cloisters and monasteries. Rather that they would be kept from the wiles and devices of Satan and his emissaries. Again, we detect in these Words of our Lord the secret power of prayer on behalf of others. Nor did He pray for them to withdraw from the unsaved world. They were to mix among mankind, live as witnesses of Christ, and thus bring others to a saving knowledge of their Lord. Amid this service, Jesus prayed for His workers to be kept from "the evil," another expression for Satan. We are under the same directives today. With this in mind note Rom. 12:21.

(p) **"Sanctify them."** Alexander B. Bruce (died 1899) wrote in *The Training of the Twelve*, page 458, "Yet, notwithstanding their sincerity, the eleven still needed not only keeping, but *perfecting*; and therefore, their Master went on to pray for their sanctification in the truth." The word "sanctify" means to "set apart" from the profane and vile to sacred use. At this point, in history, "God's Word" consisted of the Old Testament, along with the many things Christ had taught them. The Bible of the early church and churches was the Old Testament only. With this, the apostles and first missionaries turned the world upside down. As they obeyed these inspired Words, the inherit power of Holy Scripture, working in their beings set them apart for divine service. On apostolic miracles, see Section 207, fourth paragraph of footnote i. *The Word of God is a stream in which the lambs may wade and elephants swim!* The divine process of sanctification is explained in numbers 1–3, under 2p below.

2p-Today, we have the closed canon of Holy Scripture consisting of sixty–six books. The author of this work believes the *Authorized* or *King James Version* is the Word of God; that all Scriptures were inspired one time at their *original writing,* and the sovereign providence of God has maintained this surety over the ages to the present hour. Difficulties in understanding, problems with background and ancient culture, or translating an adjective by a verb have nothing to do with the infused and inherent infallibility of Holy Scripture. It should be remembered that the Old Testament of the apostles was a copy, of a copy, of a copy reproduced over the centuries. However, Paul assured Timothy that the copy of Scripture, he possessed, and had known from childhood was given "by inspiration," and able to "furnish" God's man "unto all good works" (2 Tim. 3:14-17). The sanctifying power of God's Word is what our Lord prayed to change the lives of His preachers. It was obtainable because it was rooted in the pages of Scripture by the work of Holy Spirit. The effect of the Bible on men is both amazing and astounding. The author knew of a British professional boxer who came to the saving knowledge of Christ. His life was profoundly changed! One morning while reading the Bible, he noted the verse in 1 Tim. 3:3 which states that a bishop must be no "striker." Thinking this meant that a Christian should not strike or hit another with his fist, he immediately renounced his boxing career and became a preacher of the gospel! After hearing him speak at a Brethren Assembly in Butrams, near Johannesburg, it was apparent that he made the right decision. We are amazed at the curious and often unorthodox way the Holy Spirit so freely uses God's word in the lives of men. This is another proof of divine inspiration and demonstrates that God will use what He chooses to accomplish what He pleases. Three stages of sanctification are taught in Scripture. They are as follows:

1. **Present sanctification, complete.** Received upon conversion to Christ. Our redeemed souls are counted before God as being clothed in His perfect righteousness, received by faith from the Lord Jesus at conversion. When a man is saved, he is, in the eyes of God, sanctified forever, perfected in divine holiness, and beyond the possibility of being lost again. This is how heaven looks upon the born again child of the King. Thus, Scripture announces, "ye are complete in him" (Col. 2:10).

2. **Progressive sanctification, gradual.** This speaks of growing in grace and towards maturity in the faith as we live out life in these physical bodies. The Scriptures, blessed by the Holy Spirit, along with Christian service, and suffering are the chief instruments through which this is accomplished. In the process of this, believers become "a vessel unto honor, sanctified, and meet for the master's use" (2 Tim. 2:21). See also the first paragraph of footnote p above.

3. **Perfect sanctification, future and total.** When we arrive in heaven with a glorified body to compliment our saved souls, we will be completely perfect at last! It is written, "We shall be like him" (1 John 3:2).

3p-Verse 18. **"As thou hast sent me into the world."** On the Sunday night of the Resurrection Day, we hear the Savior saying a similar thing to the eleven as He gives them The Great Commission for the first time. Refer to this in Section 201, Lk. 24:47-49.

(q) Christ had no sin to be sanctified from; He was perfect. The idea here is that He had separated or set Himself apart to do the will of God during His earthly life as a human. Every believer should follow this same plan and in steel-like disciplined faith, determinately make themselves *restfully available* for God's divine use.

He prays for all believers of all times—verses 20-26

(r) **"For them which shall believe."** This request of the Lord Jesus has extended itself over the past two thousand years and reaches out to embrace every saved soul that has trusted Him. This is as valid now as it was the time He prayed it in the temple long ago. *All* saved people of God who read these lines should rejoice to know that Christ prayed for them, and that prayer remains as sure as the throne of God!

(s) **"They may be one."** This is not an ecumenical oneness of blending all faiths into a universal system as taught by the World Council of Churches and many national church councils. Scripture teaches no such thing. Until Christ returns disagreements will exist on points of doctrine and practice. Our saved friends in the Reformed Churches will continue to baptize their babies, teach various forms of Calvinism, and covenant theology. On the other side, Arminians are busy losing their salvation! Believers in *extreme* charismatic churches will continue with their emotional circus of imaginary "dreams, healings, visions, and words of knowledge." Each, more or less evangelical group will do as they have always done, including the Baptists. *The major point where we refuse to disagree agreeably is on how men are saved!* Jesus prayed for unity among His servants some five times in this prayer. Verses 21-23 reveal that the unity, love, and eternal glory of that blessed day, which will be experienced by all the redeemed is comparable to that between the Father and Son. This part of His prayer is yet to be answered! Only in heaven will true Christians of all ages be one. The Bible doctrine denying ecumenical movement, working for universal unity is not of God. For more on this, see Section 120, second paragraph of footnote m.

2p-"The glory . . . I have given them." What a profound thing our Lord prayed in verse 22. And He spoke this in the past tense. This was a singular thing designed and designated for the apostles only. It cannot mean the majestic glory of His deity, for that would have elevated them to a place no mortal can go. These eleven men had heard words and seen sights hitherto unknown in history. A few days hence, Matthias filled the office left vacant by Judas (Acts 1:23-26). As forerunners of the spiritual kingdom, they were crowned with unique heavenly honor. So vivid was God's presence upon them that their enemies knew they had been with Jesus (Acts 4:13).

(t) Verse 1. "Father." Our Lord's use of this noun is most instructive. It is found the second time in verse 5, and now becomes **"O Father."** In verse 11, it is **"Holy Father."** Lastly, in verse 21, He returned to how He started with **"Father."** This prayer concludes in verse 25, **"O righteous Father."** John records in his book a hundred and twelve times where the Lord Jesus used this endearing Name "Father," when speaking of God. It was true then and remains so today that "the world does not know" God, just as the Lord Jesus stated in this prayer. For further comments on our Lord's use of the word **"Father,"** refer to Section 115, footnote b.

(u) Jesus used the Words, "I have," ten times in the prayer of John 17. They all speak of particular works He had accomplished during His earthly ministry:

1. **"I have glorified** thee on the earth" (verse 4).
2. **"I have finished** the work" (verse 4).
3. **"I have manifested** thy name" (verse 6).
4. **"I have given them** thy Words" (verse 8).
5. **"I have kept them"** (verse 12).
6. **"I have given them** thy word" (verse 14).
7. **"I have sent them** into the world" (verse 18).
8. **"I have given them** thy glory" (verse 22).
9. **"I have known** thee" (verse 25).
10. **"I have declared** thy name unto them" (verse 26).

(v) They move to the garden. This beautiful prayer concludes with a whisper that God's love and His holy presence will be in the hearts of His preachers, for soon they will step forward and take up His torch. After prayer, Jesus and the eleven immediately departed the temple compound through the vast Shushan Gate, walked down the side of Mount Moriah, and approached the brook Kidron or Cedron ready to cross over into the garden. Kidron was something of a small creek about seven feet wide at the bottom of a deep ravine. This walk must have taken fifteen minutes being downhill to the brook in the valley below. The actual garden entrance was about two-mile distance from the Shushan Gate. All roads and paths leading into the city were filled with pilgrims present for Passover, making down hill walking even more difficult.

2p-Though it was night, during Passover celebration the entire area surrounding Jerusalem and its thoroughfares were well illuminated by torches and reflective oil lights. The four vast candelabras, standing in the Women's Court, sent waves of light across the entire temple area. However, none of these luminaries could drive off the ugly shadows of Gethsemane. Being Passover, the full moon shown upon that soon sorrowful scene. See next Section for continuation. The Lord Jesus traveled this route because it was the shortest way from the city to the Garden of Gethsemane. Any other road from the southern or northern side of Jerusalem would have taken more than an hour to travel being packed with thousands of Jews. Our Lord did not transverse the great bridge that spanned the valley between the Shushan Gate and Gethsemane. For this, see Section 179, footnote a for some of the details.

(w) "I in them." Unitarians and their friends hate this statement. It terrifies them in their spiritual darkness. For an irrefutable defense of the deity of Christ, see *The Jehovah's Witness New Testament,* by Dr. Robert H. Countess. This outstanding apologetic work will aid anyone seeking to win cult members to the Lord Jesus. Years ago, in Alice Springs, Australia, a member of the Witnesses' cult scornfully said, "O, so you have a full-grown man living in your body." Her statement revealed her ignorance of personal salvation by the miracle of God's grace. Paul wrote, "That Christ may dwell in your hearts by faith" (Eph. 3:17). To the Colossian Christians, he wrote, "Christ in you, the hope of glory" (Col. 1:27). We rejoice over the Father, Son, and Spirit dwelling in our born again, redeemed souls (John 14:23). This blessing is not promised to a group of special persons to the predetermined exclusion of all others. It is for whosoever will.

Arriving in the garden late at night, He prays three times. Burdened with great sorrow, the Son of God agonized and struggled in lonely supplications to the Father. His choice apostles fell asleep and missed history's greatest prayer drama.

Time: Late night or the early hours on the Friday morning of the cross.

In the Garden of Gethsemane

Matt. 26:36-39	Mk. 14:32-36	Lk. 22:39-42	John 18:1
			In the garden
			1 When Jesus had spoken these words,
In the garden	*In the garden*	*In the garden*	
36 Then cometh[(a)] Jesus with them unto a place called	**32** And they came[(a)] to a place which was named	**39** And he came[(a)] out, and went, as he was wont, to the mount of Olives;	he went forth[(a)] with his disciples over the brook Cedron, where
Gethsemane,	Gethsemane:		was a garden, into the which he entered,
		and his disciples also followed him.	and his disciples. (Verse 2 cont. in Section 180.)
and	and he	**40** And when he was at the place, he	
saith unto the disciples, "Sit ye here, while I go and pray yonder."	saith to his disciples, "Sit ye here, while I shall pray."	said unto them, "Pray that ye enter not into temptation."	
37 And he took[(b)] with him Peter and the two sons of Zebedee, and began to be sorrowful and very heavy.	**33** And he taketh[(b)] with him Peter and James and John, and began to be sore amazed, and to be very heavy;		
38 Then saith he unto them,[(c)] "My soul is exceeding sorrowful, even unto death: tarry ye here, and watch with me."	**34** And saith unto them,[(c)] "My soul is exceeding sorrowful unto death: tarry ye here, and watch."		
His first prayer	*His first prayer*	*His first prayer*	
39 And he went a little farther,	**35** And he went forward a little, and	**41** And he was withdrawn from them about a stone's cast, [some fifty feet]	
and fell on his face,[(d)] and prayed,	fell on the ground,[(d)] and prayed that, if it were possible, the hour might pass from him.	and kneeled[(d)] down, and prayed,	
His greatest anguish	*His greatest anguish*	*His greatest anguish*	
saying,[(e)]	**36** And he said,[(e)]	**42** Saying,[(e)]	
"O my Father, if it be	"Abba, Father, all	"Father, if thou be willing,	

859

Matt. 26:39-42	Mk. 14:36-39	Lk. 22:42-46	John
possible, let this cup pass from me: nevertheless not as I will, but as thou *wilt*."	things *are* possible unto thee; take away this cup from me: nevertheless not what I will, but what thou wilt."	remove this cup from me: nevertheless not my will, but thine, be done."	
		An angel appears **43** And there appeared an angel unto him from heaven, strengthening him. **44** And being in an agony he prayed more earnestly: and his sweat was as it were great drops of blood falling down to the ground.	
40 And he cometh[(f)] unto the disciples, and findeth them asleep, and saith unto Peter, "What, could ye not watch with me one hour?	**37** And he cometh,[(f)] and findeth them sleeping, and saith unto Peter, "Simon, sleepest thou? couldest not thou watch one hour?	**45** And when he rose up from prayer, and was come[(f)] to his disciples, he found them sleeping for sorrow, **46** And said unto them, "Why sleep ye?	
A forgotten warning **41** "Watch and pray,[(g)] that ye enter not into temptation: the Spirit◄ indeed *is* willing, but the flesh *is* weak."	***A forgotten warning*** **38** "Watch ye and pray,[(g)] lest ye enter into temptation. The Spirit◄ truly *is* ready, but the flesh *is* weak."	***A forgotten warning*** rise and pray,[(g)] lest ye enter into temptation."(Verse 47 cont. in Section 180.) ◄*The author holds that this has reference to the Holy Spirit who is "ready" and not the foul and depraved spirit of man. It is incapable of doing anything of eternal value unless revived and changed by the power of God. Scripture states, "every man at his best state is altogether vanity" (Ps. 39:5).*	
His second prayer **42** He went away again the second time, and prayed, saying,[(h)] "O my Father, if this cup may not pass away from me, except	***His second prayer*** **39** And again he went away, and prayed, and spake[(h)] the same words.		

Matt. 26:42-46	Mk. 14:40-42	Lk.	John
I drink it, thy will be done."			
43 And he came and found them asleep again:[i] for their eyes were heavy.	**40** And when he returned, he found them asleep again,[i] (for their eyes were heavy,) neither wist they what to answer him.		
His third prayer			
44 And he left them, and went away again, and prayed the third [j] time, saying the same words.	*His third prayer* **41** And he cometh the third[j] time,		
Rise up the hour has come			
45 Then cometh he to his disciples, and saith unto them, "Sleep on now, and take *your* rest: behold, the hour is at hand, and the Son of man is **betrayed into the hands of sinners.**[k]	*Rise up the hour has come* and saith unto them, "Sleep on now, and take *your* rest: it is enough, the hour is come; behold, the Son of man is **betrayed into the hands of sinners.**[k]		
46 "Rise, let us be going: behold, he is at hand that doth betray me."[l] (Verse 47 cont. in Section 180.)	**42** "Rise up, let us go; lo, he that betrayeth me is at hand."[l] (Verse 43 cont. in Section 180.)		

Footnotes-Commentary

(a) **"His disciples followed him."** The picture here is that of a shepherd leading his sheep. They had now reached the entrance to Gethsemane, meaning "olive or oil press." John wrote that they crossed over the brook Cedron; the garden being on the yonder side. This seems to vindicate that Christ did not cross the bridge built over the valley as it spanned the brook below. He could not have crossed Cedron had He been walking on the bridge.

2p-Many ancient nations living behind the walls of their cities for protection had dozens of beautiful gardens of flowers, fruit, and vegetables planted outside those walls for the pleasure of its citizens. The Mount of Olives was separated from Jerusalem by a long narrow valley. The Garden of Gethsemane lay at the mount's base with a stream flowing nearby. When King David was driven from Jerusalem by his son Absalom, he and his men waded through this stream in flight (2 Sam. 15:23). Probably, the name Cedron is derived from the word "Kadar" which means "black" or "dung." This is an allusion to the waters being colored by the blood from the temple sacrifices as it traveled down hill in an underground pipeline into the stream. It was something of a sewer receptacle for the temple. Here, "blood merchants" sold the substance in a dried form to farmers and gardeners for fertilizer. Since the blood of the sacrifices had been dedicated to God, the merchants sold it at a very high price! Lightfoot's *Commentary on the New Testament . . .*, vol. 3, pages 413-414, gives some of the interesting details about this place.

3p-The insightful Reformed preacher, Friedrich W. Krummacher (died in 1848), penned these touching words that give rise to a mixture of tears of joy and the terrors of hell into our hearts. In describing the walk of Jesus to the garden he wrote, "He proceeds upon His path, and O, how much is laid upon Him! The guilt of thousands of years, the world's future-the salvation of millions! Alas! Whither should we have been going had He not traversed this path for us? Our future fate would have been in unquenchable fire. He knew this. He apprehended [understood]

Himself as being sent by the Father to close the chasm which sin had caused between God and the creature, between heaven and earth." See Krummacher's work, *The Suffering Saviour*, pages 79-80.

(b) **Peter, James, and John.** These three had received special training from their Lord. They had witnessed the raising of Jairus' daughter in Section 89, and shared in the glory of the Mount of Transfiguration experience in Section 105. In their hearing, Jesus had just concluded the lofty priestly prayer in the temple as recorded in Section 178. Our Lord had been a man of sorrows all His earthly days and acquainted with grief; but now a new scene of sorrows unfolds upon Him as He again prays. Now the loving Father lays upon Him the iniquity of us all. Upon reaching the garden of agony, His heart was burdened so greatly that His countenance changed. Being under deep sorrow and agony, His natural vigor and demeanor were altered. The words "exceeding sorrowful," signify one being overwhelmed with anguish, like a man drowning in water. It is noted, Luke wrote that Jesus "went as he was wont to the Mount of Olives," that is, as it was His custom to go to this place (verse 39).

2p-A few hours later the Lord of glory would be nailed to a Roman cross and crucified. The thoughts of it all pressed hard upon the human nature of Jesus, but there was one aspect of this that became unbearable. Like a threatening ugly storm cloud, it loomed over the Savior; He would be separated from the Father. Apparently, our Lord said several different things to His three men. He told them of the pain of His soul and the sorrow that was so heavy that it pushed Him near the hands of death (Matt. 26:38 with Mk. 14:34). In concern for His three preachers, He admonished them, "Pray that ye enter not into temptation" (Lk. 22:40). *Most believers are tempted every day of their mortal lives.* Therefore, the Lord Jesus was speaking of something different in these words. Perhaps, He was saying to His own, "If you cannot endure human fatigue and must sleep when there is no real suffering, how will you endure when the great trial of faith falls upon you?" History confirms that later most of His apostles died as martyrs for His cause. Thus, they learned to obey the willingness of the Holy Spirit in their lives, even unto death.

(c) The prediction of Isa. 53:3 was again being fulfilled in the sorrows of Christ. John mentioned nothing of the agony of Christ in Gethsemane. He continues his story with Jesus' arrest and related details in Section 180. Selecting Peter, James, and John to be with Him, He instructs the remaining apostles to sit at a selected place. This was probably the garden's entrance through a stonewall. His first meeting with these three men had been over three years prior as related in Section 26. He now selects them *to watch the world's greatest prayer drama unfold.* Below are the records of three different sessions of prayer the Savior passed through that late night hour before the cross.

His first prayer—Matt. 26:39-41

(d) What follows were not the experiences of ordinary prayer. The perfect Man struggling in the moonlight of that hour was being crushed by the weight of His sorrow. He knew that the terrible hour of His humiliation had come; all that the human anatomy can tolerate was heaped upon His weary frame. One wonders what the three apostles thought as they saw their Lord staggering forward and falling on His face to the ground! Luke says, He walked about "a stones cast" (fifty feet) and kneeled down. Both were true in different moments of time. He went ahead of them, dropped to His knees, and bent forward with His face on the ground of Gethsemane. *Heaven's pure olive was being pressed!* However, one awful thing remained before the horror of the cross: He must "tread the winepress alone" (Isa. 63:3). Refer to third paragraph, footnote e below for more on this thought.

(e) **How could Christ call God His Father?** The only way Jesus was not equal with God His Father was in His physical nature, earthly position as a servant, and doer of the divine will among men. *It was strictly within this realm that He called God His Father.* Never in spiritual and eternal being or consistence was He ever unequal with God. Refer to Section 175, footnote p, Section 191, third paragraph of footnote c and Section 197, footnote i for more on this sublime truth. Section 1, Part 1, footnotes a and b carry a discussion of the equality of Jesus and God.

2p-**"If thou be willing, remove this cup from me."** Strange are these Words from the mouth of our Lord. "What cup," we inquire? Across ancient history and in Scripture as well, we discover a "cup" was used to symbolize one taking in great sorrow, fury, trembling, suffering, and fierce judgment (Ps. 75:8 with Ezek. 23:33). Thus is it employed here. He prayed, "If it were possible" to let it not be. One can believe that the Savior also wrestled with a raging Devil hosted by myriads of evil spirits.

3p-**Praying to avoid the cross?** The teaching that Christ begged God to divert Him from the cross is too ridiculous to mention. His death on Calvary for our sins was prearranged, even before the foundation of the world. The cup that He dreaded above the nails, shame, and agony of crucifixion was that dark hour when His Father would forsake Him amid death. And it comes on the morrow. Nothing would be so painful as losing that sweet, intimate, fellowship with Him. He had walked in the sunlight of this pure joy all of His human life. Now, it will cease for a time. *This was the horror of Gethsemane.* It brought bloody sweat from His sacred brow. Pleading from His humanity, He begs God to take *only* this part of tomorrow away. He can endure the cross, despise the shame. He will take the sins of Adam's race into His body, and "taste death for every man" (Heb. 2:9), but He cannot bear the absence of His Father. O this terrible cup, He begs that it be taken away. However, it cannot be! His suffering for our sins must be total and comprehensive with none of Satan's devices bypassed. As sin separates men from God, He too must feel the agony of that in some kind of human experience; He must drink every dreg of our sins, know our experience, and the horrors of being cut off from the Father. In this He will be the understanding and compassionate redeemer (Heb. 4:15-16). See footnote d above for Christ dying alone.

4p-Lk. 22:43. "There appeared an angel." More is here than meets the casual eye. Not only were devils watching this holy conflict, but also it was necessary for the Father to send an angel to sustain the physical anatomy of His beloved Son. The lesson is that His human *frame* would have collapsed or died, had assistance not come! The great burdens upon His soul pressed His humanity to the dying point. This was the *man,* Jesus Christ suffering. That entire garden seemed haunted by a dual presence of divine good and vicious evil struggling in a terrible, but silent contest for the eternal victory. We dare not intrude too closely into this amazing scene. Over it all looms a halo of holy mystery into which no human footstep or curiosity must attempt to enter.

5p-The night silence was disturbed by the "strong crying and tears" from the soul of the most harmless man that ever lived. Approximately three and a half years earlier in His ministry, we noted angels ministering to the Savior following His forty days and nights of war with Satan. Note this in Section 23, Mk. 1:13, footnote a and n. *Exactly how these angels assisted the Lord at the beginning and the end of His earthly work, we are not told.* It is striking that He began His ministry in conflict with Satan, and concluded it in a similar manner.

6p-Lk. 22:44. "And being in an agony." These terrible words declare that He repeated this same supplication; this time in the deepest of agony, so intense that blood streamed through the pours of His face. The Greek word used here for blood is found in ancient medical writings. It speaks of blood clots. It was here that Heb. 5:7 occurred. His blood and sweat fell to the ground in clots. What a sight that must have been! In this sacred time of pleading with the Father, we find our Lord praying without comparison, without companions, and without comfort.

(f) "Sleeping from sorrow." Rising from that first prayer battle, He returned to His three preachers and found them sleeping because of their great sorrow. Even Simon Peter, after all his impetuous and noisy promises lay in sleep, for his eyes too were heavy. Often in the work of God, we have seen men and women so loaded down with the heartaches of life that they fall into bed and drop instantly into deep sleep. Their sorrow had weakened them into total exhaustion. Elijah fell asleep amid much sorrow and fear (1 Kings 19:4-5), and Jonah did the same (Jonah 1:5). We wonder what the three apostles thought as through dim eyes and half-awake, they watched in full moonlight and saw those memorial scenes. How strange it all was. Their Messiah is so different now! Before, He but spoke a calm Word and demons fled, the dead rose, Galilee's wind lay quiet. Now things have changed. It is that same distinct voice, but He was wailing in broken agony, sobbing, and crying as though He was no longer the supreme Lord of all. *O what our sins did to the Son of God!* Refer to footnote i below for more on the sleeping preachers.

(g) "Watch and pray." Both Matthew and Mark record that He returned to the three apostles with this plea. Wakening Peter, He spoke to him something like this, "Why don't you watch and pray with Me, Peter; don't you know your flesh is weak, but the Spirit is willing?" The word "watch" was well known among the Jews. It had reference to the temple police on guard duty. In the Talmud, it is recorded that, "The officer of the temple mount used to go round to every [station] with lighted torches before him, and if any guard did not rise [at his approaching] and say to him, 'Peace be to thee, supervisor of the temple mount,' it was obvious that he was asleep." The supervisor would then beat him with a stick, and often set his clothing alight with a torch! This poor fellow was considered naked if his top garment burnt away. There can be no doubt this is the message embedded in Rev. 16:15.

2p-What is this willing Spirit? This cannot speak of the human spirit, for it is fouled by sin, unable and unwilling to rise up in the holy art of prayer. It is of interest that Christ spoke of the Holy Spirit as One presently available and ready to help these men. They surely had the Holy Spirit at this time, but not in His fullness as would occur a few weeks later at Pentecost. No other interpretation makes sense to this statement of Jesus. Romans 8:9 is emphatic: "Now if any man have not the Spirit of Christ, he is none of his." And what did our Lord desire these men to "watch?" Some think they were to act as sentinels and watch for Judas, soon to come with the mob to arrest Him. See footnote k below. This seems incorrect in view of the fact they could have done nothing about that regardless. Contextually, He wanted them to watch Him struggle in prayer, with his humanity, with Satan and demons, in bloody sweat as He prepared Himself for Calvary a few hours away. He had accepted the Father's will, even that terrible separation from Him that loomed as a storm cloud.

3p-The Savior called first for His preachers to "watch," then "pray." The wise children of God should watch in all things. Do not our actions, words, and thoughts need to be scrutinized and daily viewed with great carefulness? *Men who fail to watch themselves are men who do not influence others for God and men who cannot pray.* Woe be the congregation that has a minister who preaches so good but lives so bad. When in the pulpit, one wishes he would never get out; when out of the pulpit, one wishes he would never get in. Four of the highest abominations in civilized society are a quack doctor, crooked cop, corrupt politician, and an immoral preacher. Someone quipped, "God has front seats in hell reserved for all four." However, salvation in Christ and His forgiveness are preferable!

His second prayer—Matt. 26:42-43

(h) This second surge of holy prayer reveals that He still struggled with the pain of lost fellowship with His Father in heaven. Refer to footnote e above for more on this awful thought. There were two wills in Christ, one divine and the other human. In this event, we see they are different, but *not contrary* with each other. Our Lord's will was always that of His Father in heaven. His human will, though differing as on this occasion, yielded itself to God after sincere prayer and supplication. Thus is should finally be with God's children.

(i) **"Asleep again."** Though He had awakened Peter and the others, they lapsed back into the weary slumber of sorrow and fear. Note the words "for their eyes were heavy." *O the honesty of God with mortal man!* This reveals the total exhaustion of these men, worn out by the events of the past night and days. Not understanding, and terrified for their lives, they resorted to sleep as an escape. See the first paragraph of footnote f above for other comments on their sleeping during this most critical time.

His third prayer—Matt. 26:44-46

(j) Returning to His place of prayer in the sands of Gethsemane, Jesus called on the Father a third time, then returns to His weary preachers. In this third prayer struggle, He speaks the same words, adding, "The hour [of betrayal and death] is at hand." For other comments on "the hour," see Section 178, John 17:1, footnote d. Years later, the apostle Paul also prayed three times regarding his painful thorn in the flesh (2 Cor. 12:8). These three supplications of Jesus, repeating the same words, reflect deep anguish of His spirit. Which of God's true servants has not experienced times of trouble, laboring hard in prayer for the souls of men and the needs of others and self? The shallowness of prayer is obvious today. Men continually articulate pious expressions amid a congregation of disinterested or spiritually half-dead saints. For more on the scourge of prayerlessness, see Section 76, second paragraph of footnote f. Those who speak long about prayer, and have read the latest books on the subject but rarely pray are people that talk pious but act poorly. On the other hand, beware of men who relegate prayer solely to the realm of human emotion, and then dump their practical duties onto God's sovereignty. We must not avoid our physical actions of seeking and waiting on God. It is written, "The LORD *is* good to them that wait for him, to the soul *that* seeketh him" (Lam. 3:25). When prayer less leadership guides the church, she goes astray. Like Philistines in the Christian camp, these people cannot lead sheep. They must not be counted as an enemy but admonished as brothers (2 Thess. 3:15). Regarding the abuse of divine sovereignty and the neglect of obvious human responsibility, see Section 29, third paragraph of footnote j.

(k) Apparently, this was something of a paraphrase of an Old Testament prediction. It spoke of Judas, who betrayed the Lord Jesus when He was arrested by the mob (Ps. 41:9). It reveals our Lord's foreknowledge of future events. Further, this demonstrates that He did not leave His apostles to watch for Judas and the soldiers as commonly thought. See the first paragraph of footnote g above.

(l) Though not an actual prediction, yet it spoke of Judas, the traitor, who was a special subject of Old Testament prophecy. The meaning is that Christ called on His weary preachers to join Him as He went forward to meet the gang converging upon the garden. Somewhere in between the lines of this story, He had vouchsafed the victory and accepted the terrible cup of tomorrow's separation on the cross from His Father. A few moments later, we hear Him declare in joyful triumph, "The cup which my Father hath given me, shall I not drink it?" And that He did! See this unique statement of yielding to God's will in Section 180, John 18:11. Our Savior had foretasted a worse bitterness than the agony of physical death. He had, as it were, in advance, drank already the full cup, and in the power of the Holy Spirit was ready for Calvary, and that dark abyss of separation from His Father. This was because He loved us unto death, even the death of the cross (Heb. 12:1-3).

2p-Like little David of old, his descending Messiah, Jesus of Nazareth, also goes forth to meet the Goliaths of Satan, demons, sin, the Roman cross, and the grave. Israel's greatest Son, the Champion, and Captain of salvation, storms the stronghold of death's darkness. At the thought of it all, our soul is overwhelmed; Calvary's horrible cross of pain and shame will be transformed into the emblem of redemption for mankind. No longer could it be called "the awful wood." The best Man ever to grace a sin cursed world was nailed there for us. He is our salvation, and freely gives that wonderful transformation of new life and eternal hope to all who believe. In contemplation of this, we bow our heads in shameful humility, and raise glad voices of many hallelujahs. The cross worked two ways. It brought death to sin and life to those who believe. With the resurrection of Jesus, the grave surrendered its holding power! It could not keep the Son of God. He broke it bars and rose. Years later to John on Patmos He proclaimed, "*I am* he that liveth and was dead; and, behold, I am alive for evermore, Amen; and have the keys of hell and of death" (Rev. 1:18). In the shadows of Gethsemane's sorrows, this glorious drama, all began.

3p-A thousand years before the birth of Christ, King Solomon, in poetic language may have written of Christ's resurrection and return for the redeemed. His words were, "The voice of my beloved! behold, he cometh leaping upon the mountains, skipping upon the hills. My beloved is like a roe or a young hart: behold, he standeth behind our wall, he looketh forth at the windows, shewing himself through the lattice. My beloved spake, and said unto me, 'Rise up, my love, my fair one, and come away' " (Song of Solomon 2:8-11). O weary believer in Christ, somewhere down the road He will return, "Skipping upon the mountains" calling for His own. It may be soon or hundreds of years away, no man knows. All born again believers of all languages, places, and times, will understand the universal heavenly summons. It will somehow be a repeat fulfillment of the beautiful Old Testament song above. Again, our Savior will command, "Come away," and away we will go (1 Thess. 4:16-17)!

Judas and the mob appear. Jesus is kissed and arrested. Peter, swinging a sword tries to defend his Lord and wounds a servant of the high priest. Jesus heals him instantly. All the apostles flee. Arrested, the Savior is led from the garden, up the hill to the city, through the Shushan Gate, and escorted first to the house of Annas.

Time: Late night or an early hour on the Friday morning of the cross.

In the Garden of Gethsemane and back to Jerusalem

Matt. 26:47	Mk. 14:43	Lk. 22:47	John 18:2-6
			Judas knew the place 2 And Judas also, which betrayed him, knew the place: for Jesus ofttimes resorted thither with his disciples.
Judas and the crowd 47 And while he yet spake, lo,	*Judas and the crowd* 43 And immediately, while he yet spake, cometh	*Judas and the crowd* 47 And while he yet spake,	
Judas, one of the twelve, came, and with him a great multitude[a] with swords and staves, from the chief priests and elders of the people.	Judas, one of the twelve, and with him a great multitude[a] with swords and staves, from the chief priests and the scribes and the elders.	behold a multitude,[a] and he that was called Judas, one of the twelve,	*Judas and the crowd* 3 Judas then, having received a band[a] of men and officers from the chief priests and Pharisees, cometh thither with lanterns and torches and weapons.
			His foreknowledge 4 Jesus therefore, knowing all things that should come upon him, went forth, and said unto them, "Whom seek ye?"[b]
			His powerful Words 5 They answered him, "Jesus of Nazareth." Jesus saith unto them, "I am *he*." And Judas also, which betrayed him, stood with them. 6 As soon then as he had said unto them, "I am *he*," they went backward, and fell to the ground.

865

Matt. 26:48-51	Mk. 14:44-47	Lk. 22:47-50	John 18:7-10
			7 Then asked he them again, "Whom seek ye?" And they said, "Jesus of Nazareth." **8** Jesus answered, "I have told you that I am *he*: if therefore ye seek me, let these go their way:" **9** That the saying might be fulfilled, which he spake, "Of them which thou gavest me have I lost none."[c]
This signal given	*The signal given*		
48 Now he that betrayed him gave them a sign, saying,[d] "Whomsoever I shall kiss, that same is he: hold him fast."	**44** And he that betrayed him had given them a token, saying,[d] "Whomsoever I shall kiss, that same is he; take him, and lead *him* away safely."		
49 And forthwith he came to Jesus, and said, "Hail, master;" and kissed him.	**45** And as soon as he was come, he goeth straightway to him, and saith, "Master, master;" and kissed him.	went before them, and drew near unto Jesus to kiss him.	
50 And Jesus said unto him, "Friend,[e] wherefore art thou come?"			
		48 But Jesus said unto him, "Judas,[e] betrayest thou the Son of man with a kiss?"	
		◀*John records the arrest in 18:12 below.*	
The arrest is made	*The arrest is made*	*A question of alarm*	
Then came they,▶ and laid hands on Jesus, and took him.[f]	**46** And they▶ laid their hands on him, and took him.[f]	**49** When they which were about him saw what would follow, they said unto him, "Lord, shall we smite with the sword?"	
Peter and his sword	*Peter and his sword*	*Peter and his sword*	*Peter and his sword*
51 And, behold, one	**47** And one	**50** And one	**10** Then Simon Peter

Matt. 26:51-55	Mk. 14:47-49	Lk. 22:50-53	John 18:10-11
of them which were with Jesus stretched out *his* hand, and drew his sword,[g] and struck a servant of the high priest's, and smote off his ear.	of them that stood by drew a sword,[g] and smote a servant of the high priest, and cut off his ear.	of them smote the servant of the high priest, and cut off his right ear.	having a sword[g] drew it, and smote the high priest's servant, and cut off his right ear. The servant's name was Malchus.
Jesus intervenes 52 Then said Jesus unto him,[h] "Put up again thy sword into his place: for all they that take the sword shall perish with the sword. 53 "Thinkest thou that I cannot now pray to my Father, and he shall presently give me more than twelve legions of angels?[i] 54 "But how then shall the scriptures be fulfilled, that thus it must be?"[j]			***Jesus intervenes*** 11 Then said Jesus unto Peter,[h] "Put up thy sword into the sheath:
			the cup which my Father hath given me, shall I not drink it?"
		Jesus' last healing 51 And Jesus answered and said, "Suffer [let them go] ye thus far." And he touched his ear, and healed[k] him.	
55 In that same hour said Jesus to the multitudes,	48 And Jesus answered and said unto them,	52 Then Jesus said unto the chief priests, and captains of the temple, and the elders, which were come to him, "Be ye come out as against a thief,[l] with swords and staves?	
"Are ye come out as against a thief[l] with swords and staves for to take me?	"Are ye come out, as against a thief,[l] with swords and *with* staves to take me?		

867

Matt. 26:55–56	Mk. 14:49–52	Lk. 22:53	John 18:12–13
I sat daily with you teaching in the temple, and ye laid no hold on me."	49 "I was daily with you in the temple teaching, and ye took me not:	53 "When I was daily with you in the temple, ye stretched forth no hands against me: but this is your hour, and the power of darkness."[m] (Verse 54 cont. in Section 181.)	
56 "But all this was done, that the scriptures of the prophets might be fulfilled."	but the scriptures must be fulfilled."		
		▶ *Matthew records the arrest in verse 50 and Mark in verse 46 above.*	***Binding the Savior*** 12 ◀Then the band and the captain and officers of the Jews took Jesus, and bound him,
Jesus is deserted **Then all the disciples forsook him, and fled.**[n] (Verse 57 cont. in Section 181.)	***Jesus is deserted*** **50 And they all forsook him, and fled.**[o] ***The mystery youth*** 51 And there followed him [Jesus] a certain young[o] man, having a linen cloth cast about *his* naked *body*; and the young men laid hold on him: 52 And he left the linen cloth, and fled from them naked. (Verse 53 cont. in Section 181.)		
			To Annas first 13 And led him away to Annas[p] first; for he was father in law to Caiaphas, which was the high priest that same year.[q] (Verse 14 cont. in Section 181.)

Footnotes–Commentary

[a] **"A great multitude." Judas and the armed mob.** Highlighted in gray because it has reference to the traitor who was spoken of in the Old Testament. All four evangelists record the account of Judas' betrayal of Christ. Hundreds came to arrest the lowly Nazarene. They had been commissioned and sent by our Lord's enemies "the chief priests, scribes and elders of the people." Judas led them to the lonely spot, knowing the Messiah would be there. Among the group was a detachment from the temple police, plus several hundred Roman soldiers. For the mystery group of youth among this mob, see footnote o below.

2p-Just north of the temple wall stood the formidable Castle of Antonia connecting itself to the temple by two stairways. Josephus wrote of this in *Wars of the Jews,* Book 5:5, 8, lines 238–247. Present at the temple during all

868

Jewish feasts was a powerfully armed cohort, which consisted of some four hundred to six hundred men. A legion was always stationed there as "peace keepers." Their presence served as a deterrent to any tumult that might arise among the several million present for the Passover. It reads in John 18:3, "Judas received a band of men" which had reference to the Roman military among the crowds going to apprehend the Savior. They approached the moon lit garden armed with swords, sticks, and other weapons of warfare. Jesus, hearing the tumult, and the scuffling footsteps, seeing the bobbing lights, and hearing the clank of swords surely called His preachers to awake: they must witness this scene. It was an electric hour when Messiah faced Judas and the wild gang intent on "bringing Him in."

(b) **Verse 4. "Knowing all things."** This statement demonstrates that Christ was God, for only God could do this. "Whom seek ye?" To the shock of all, Christ instantly stepped forth into the light of the torches, and raised lamps and inquired for whom they sought. Someone in the mob replied that it was "Jesus of Nazareth." In this title, we note that He was, at this late hour in His human life, still known as the man from "Nazareth." Matthew's statement made so many years prior that He would be "called a Nazarene" is again proven true. Refer to this in Section 18, Matt. 2:23.

2p-**Verse 6. "They fell to the ground."** Note His powerful response and the awesome results. "I am *he*," answered the Lord Jesus. For a final time and in the most peculiar of circumstances we hear the Messiah attest His deity in the terms, "I am." For a detailed explanation of this, see Section 95, footnote i. This affirmation to equality with God was so powerful (with inherit authority) that hundreds of men were sent sprawling backward over the sand and grass of Gethsemane. What a noise that must have made! What did the eleven apostles think of this knock down as well as Judas, who apparently was also laid out with them?

3p-**Verses 7–8.** This scenario is repeated as the mob of arrestors got up from the ground and put their question to Jesus again. It is noted that they did not drop to the earth at our Lord's second response. Christ repeated His answer and with it adds a request for the eleven to be left out of the skirmish, and let go free.

(c) **Verse 9.** This is not a quotation from the Old Testament. The Lord had previously spoken this in His high priestly prayer a short time before (John 17:12). John looking back on the event, now understands what his Savior meant in the prayer, which he and the other apostles had heard Him pray in the temple just before leaving for Gethsemane. Some hold it was a paraphrase from John 6:37, but this seems untenable.

(d) **Verse 48. The traitor's sign.** This is a reference to Judas. Quickly getting up from the ground and regrouping, the crowd moved in. It is obvious to the careful reader that Judas impetuously rushed forward. Alarm ran high after their being knocked down by the power of God's spoken Word. What a lesson we may learn here. Judas, who had only a few hours before, reclined at the Passover meal with Jesus and His apostles, has now changed sides! He led the band of rogues and rascals to the place of prayer where he knew the Lord would be. Judas had previously arranged a signal whereby the arresting officers would identify the Savior—a kiss! To the western mind, this is hard to understand. Kissing between men of one or both sides of the face is fervently practiced today in eastern culture. It is tantamount to our handshake. Both Matthew and Mark record the last words Judas spoke (loudly) to the Savior, "Hail, master" (or "rabbi"), then he kissed Him. On use of the term, "hail," see Section 9, Lk. 1:28, footnote d. The construction of this word signifies that Judas kissed him several times. This act was designed to show high honor and respect for one's teacher, master, or rabbi. The masters would kiss their disciples, but rarely would it be the other way around as done by Judas! The verse in Mk. 14:45 reveals that Judas repeated the esteemed title several times saying, "rabbi, rabbi." Herein is the origin of the infamous expression, "the Judas kiss."

2p-**Why did they not recognize Jesus?** One would think that as well known as Jesus was He could have been quickly identified in the garden that night. This demonstrates that our Savior did not dress in a long white flowing gown or robe as portrayed in "Christian art." Nor did He carry a pagan halo about His head. Centuries earlier the prophet had predicted of Messiah that in youth He was "as a tender plant." In manhood "as a root out of dry ground." Isaiah wrote, "*there* is no beauty that we should desire him" (Isa. 53:1-2). As explained, there were hundreds gathered at that scene. Even with the full moon light, torches, and lanterns, amid the skirmish all Jewish men looked basically alike as they dressed in a common fashion. In order to expedite the capture of Jesus from among the milling crowds, and not create an uproar, Judas hit on the idea of kissing the Savior thus pointing Him out to the soldiers and temple police. See footnote o below for more on the crowds and action of that night.

(e) **Verse 50. "Friend."** The response of Christ to His enemy is most touching, "Friend, wherefore art thou come?" and, "betrayest thou the Son of man with a kiss?" We are amazed at Him referring to Judas as a "friend." No better picture is there of grace still being offered to a sinner on the brink of his doom than this act of our Lord. Christ's question was not out of ignorance of the situation, but rather intended to pierce the traitor's heart, and penetrate his consciousness with the guilt of his deed.

(f) **John 18:12. "Took Jesus."** Meaning His hands were bound behind His back. However, there was a divinity upon Him that they could neither seize nor bind. As a human, He let common ropes restrain him; as God, He was Lord of the scene. Amid the clamor of the whole event, suddenly, the apostles remembered that they had two swords, and called out, "Lord, shall we smite with the sword" (Lk. 22:49)? Several hours earlier, while in the upper room, Christ had approved carrying swords for protection. See Section 173, Lk. 22:35-38, fourth paragraph of footnote i for more details on this.

(g) **An ear is cut off.** Peter whipped out a sword and sliced off the ear of Malcus, the servant of Caiaphas the high priest. Luke and John are careful to note that it was his "right ear" (verses 50 and 10). One is not surprised at Peter's actions. In addition to his strong headlong zeal, we feel sure that he would have been the first to misunderstand Jesus' Words about carrying a sword, spoken while in the upper room (Lk. 22:36, 38). Jewish law made it a punishable offence to carry a weapon on a feast day such as this Passover celebration. The serious situation that had risen because of the hatred of the Sanhedrin and their friends toward the Lord Jesus, must have given rise to Peter knowingly breaking this prohibition. The word for sword ("machaira") signified a weapon used by the Roman soldiers and also a sacrificial knife employed by the priests serving in the temple. Whether Peter was wielding a Roman type sword or a razor sharp long knife like those employed by the priest in killing and flaying, is unclear. Anyone who has been accosted by an angry knife-wielding person can relate to the tenseness of this frightening situation. It is noted that John alone names this servant and Luke tells of his healing (verse 51). This is the only record of Christ healing a fresh wound, open, raw, and bleeding. See footnote k below as it describes this *final healing* of Jesus before His death on the cross.

(h) Rebuking Peter, Christ commands him to put the sword in its place. The Son of God is warning that those who live by the sword (meaning violence, killing and mayhem), will perish by these same actions. It has proven true thousands of times across human history. This statement condemns aggressive war in view of conquering other nations, and expanding one's territory beyond its legitimate borders. There is nothing here about "Christian passivism" and "non violent resistance." In the face of robbery, rape, rapine, looting, and savage intrusion into the lives of innocent people and nations, resistive and defensive action is right and honorable.

(i) **Matt. 26:53. "Twelve legions of angels."** Our Lord said that He could easily meet human opposition by the intervention of angels. One had just ministered to Him minutes before, during the great prayer struggle (Lk. 22:43). It is noted that He said, "twelve legions of angels" which had reference to a Roman army structure of soldiers. Estimates slightly differ about the size of legions but if this means six thousand per legion, then we have some seventy-two thousand angels that God would dispatch to His Son. With the cross of redemption looming just ahead, the Savior declined the help of armies from heaven, for He must tread the winepress of sin's wrath alone! This event reminds one of Elisha at Dothan and the presence of angelic beings to protect him as God' prophet (2 Kings 6:17). See the second paragraph of footnote k below for other comments on holy angels.

(j) **The Scriptures must be fulfilled.** Earlier Jesus had made a similar statement in Section 123, John 10:35, footnote i. The life and ministry of Christ was according to the Old Testament Scriptures. He lived by them, fulfilled them, and was acutely aware of their every prediction. We should not fail to note the priceless worth of Scripture in the estimation of our Savior. The fulfillment of many prophecies fell due that night and the next morning; our blessed Lord meticulously saw to it that they were not broken. This testified that the Son of God held them as trustworthy and inspired in the minutest detail. In this specific utterance, He referred to His separation from God when He became "sin for us" and the sufferings as seen in the parallel verse of John 18:11, under the metaphor of drinking the cup the Father had given Him. See second paragraph of footnote k below. See *Appendix Three* for numerous Old Testament passages fulfilled by Christ over the course of His life on earth.

(k) **Malcus' ear. The final miracle of Christ before Calvary**. What a marvelous attestation of our Lord's sure mercies as we see here in His healing a hateful enemy, who rushed forward to apprehend Him. We have wondered about this miracle. Did Christ place the ear back on his head, and it reattached itself? Did He produce a new one or what? What did the mob present think when they witnessed this divine wonder? It is noted that only Luke reports that Christ healed the wound, and John alone gave his name as well as informing us that it was Peter, who did the sword act that terrible night (John 18:10). The name Malchus, means "king" and was common among both pagans and Jews. It is mentioned in the list of names recorded in Neh. 10:4 where it is spelled "Malluch." This man had quite a story to tell when he returned home late that night! Refer to footnote g above for more on this miracle.

2p-Though He could have called ten thousand angels to destroy the world and set Him free, He would not. God's Word across the Old Testament predicted that the death of Christ for the sins of mankind must be fulfilled. This reveals that Jesus was tied to the Scriptures, and that He would end His human life in their completion. He is the central theme of the entire Old Testament, with the Torah Law pointing to Him and His work with dozens of shining fingers. Refer to footnote j above for more on this wonderful thought.

(l) **"The chief priests and captains of the temple, and the elders."** Christ's remarks were addressed to these men according to the record of Luke in verse 52. It was something of a reverse rebuke to the leaders of religion. Thieves and robbers were forbidden entrance into the heart of the temple. Yet, they let Christ teach in this holy place for several years. How is it that they can now treat Him as one banned from God's house? Now, they abuse Him to shame, as though He were a thug, and bind Him as a common criminal. In a few hours, they will crucify Him between two thieves and murderers.

(m) Lk. 22:53. "Your hour and the power of darkness." What awful words! The Devil had returned with Judas in whose heart he had found a home several hours prior in the upper room. Just before departing from the room, Christ told the apostles that He saw the prince of this world coming upon the scene. Refer to Section 175, John 14:30, footnote r. This monster from outer space, hoary with antiquity, history's first murderer, and liar had arrived with his human imps. He was housed in the soul of Judas. Satan had possessed the religious men of Israel and their companions in sin. They were ready to kill the Lord Jesus, their Messiah, the Prince of Peace, and Savior of the world. The powers of darkness directed their lives as they attacked the Savior; yet God in holy sovereignty overruled the whole debacle to fulfill His will. Year's later, Paul testified that he had spent his life as a Christian, turning men from darkness to light (Acts 26:18 with Col. 1:13).

2p-"Darkness." The rabbis had a peculiar interpretation of Gen. 1:2, "and darkness was upon the face of the deep." They held that this darkness was the presence of the Devil, the angel of death, who blinded the eyes of men (especially the Gentiles) to prevent the light of Jehovah from shining into their souls. Jesus' Words in this verse seem to echo something of that belief. On the other hand, in typical extreme, the rabbis also affirmed, "The angel of death [Satan] could not approach one who was studying the Torah." Refer to the Talmud tractate, Shabbath 30b. These men were immersed in studying the Torah, yet here they are seeking to kill the very Messiah mentioned so many times in their Scriptures. Reading and studying the Torah hardly made them Devil proof. For the later Jewish opinion of Jesus, see the alarming statements contained in parts of the Talmud. Several of these are found in Section 6, footnotes d and e. Hatred for the Son of God has continued to this very hour by all men who are gripped by the "power of darkness."

(n) "They forsook him, and fled." Highlighted in gray as this was the fulfillment of prophecy recorded in Zech. 13:7. In this Old Testament verse, the prophet wrote of a shepherd who was smitten, and His flock scattered. However, this was not a quotation from an Old Testament passage, but was something of a paraphrase or brief summation of what it stated. It should be noted that here is a final editorial comment on this event given by Matthew. Mark does the same in verse 50. Others hold that this was their way of condensing the prophecies that pointed to His arrest at Gethsemane and the fleeing of the apostles. It has been set in a gray background showing it was an Old Testament citation. This comment was given by Matthew and Mark, the human authors. Christ had foretold the apostles of their desertion while eating the Passover meal a few hours earlier in the upper room. See this warning in Section 173, Matt. 26:31, footnote c. It happened and the eleven fled like fearful sheep in the presence of the wolf. Their glorious Shepherd was bound and led away like a criminal.

(o) Mk. 14:51-52. "A certain young man fled." This is the curious story of an unknown youth fleeing the garden scene. It suggests that more people were standing nearby than these verses reveal. Seemingly, among these were other followers of Christ. It reveals that a group of "young men" mingled among the mob that came for Jesus. As the situation exploded into chaos, they attacked the other young persons who were seemingly sympathetic with Jesus. The scene became violent. Then, someone ripped the outer garment from the body of one of the fleeing youths. Without this garment, men were considered as being naked. For details, see Section 205, John 21:7, and the third paragraph of footnote e. We have no way of knowing who he was, though over the centuries many have submitted their guesses. The gist of this curious little story gives us deeper insight into the satanic darkness that prevailed that night. It spilled over into the lives of young people both good and bad. Here, a verse from the Torah Law takes meaning, "Thou shalt not follow a multitude to do evil" (Ex. 23:2). For other details on the mob that came to arrest the Savior, see footnote a above. Refer also to second paragraph of footnote d above for more on this night of betrayal.

(p) Christ was taken first to Annas. He lived at the western side of Jerusalem, which was a long walk from Gethsemane. Probably, Jesus was taken first to him because it was required that Annas be present at the temple for the morning sacrifice (at sunrise) and to ensure all things were in order. Priestly supervision such as this at the temple is prescribed in the Talmud tractate, Yoma 28a. He departed for the temple immediately after the mob left his home. Then Jesus was taken to his son-in-law Caiaphas. This was done because Annas had no actual judicial authority, as his wretched son-in-law was the appointed high priest for this time. His authority was of defacto nature.

2p-For more about the political abuse of the Jewish priesthood by Annas and his son-in-law, see Section 21, Part 1, numbers 6 and 7 under footnote b. Annas served as the high priest from A.D. 6–14 or 15. The Roman procurator (governor) Valerius Gratus, for financial corruption and overstepping his delegated authority had deposed Annas from office. Prior to his dismissal, he had leased portions of the temple compound for merchants to sell their wares. From his corrupt dealings, he had become powerfully rich. Annas was a Sadducee of imminence. Later, five of his sons, a son-in-law, and grandson filled the office. He was ruling when the Lord Jesus was in His late teen years. Now, as an old man, he is still meddling in the affairs of the nation and had a leading part in seeking the death of Messiah. How ironic that the word the word "annas" (in lower case) was later used in the Talmud and Jewish writings as a synonym for thievery! See tractates, Baba Kama 67a and 114a.

(q) "That same year." The wording used here by John reflects that he wrote this letter some years after the events recorded were established history.

CHAPTER 17

HIS NIGHT TRIALS BEFORE THE JEWS AND ROMANS. PETER'S THREE DENIALS. GOVERNOR PILATE'S FIVE INNOCENT VERDICTS OF THE SAVIOR. GUILT STRICKEN, THE LEADERS OF THE HEBREW RELIGION HURRY OFF TO PILATE FOR HELP.

Time: Very early morning of the crucifixion day on Friday.

Jesus is taken to Annas' house,* then to Caiaphas' palace where the Sanhedrin interrogated Him late at night. He is beaten and abused. Peter's rooster problem and his three denials.

**The mysterious trip to Annas is briefly mentioned in the previous Section 180, John 18:13, footnote p. There are no details as to what occurred during this meeting between Jesus and elderly Annas.*

To Annas and Caiaphas in Jerusalem. He is questioned, beaten, mocked, and sentenced.

Matt. 26:57-58	Mk. 14:53-54	Lk. 22:54-55	John 18:14-15
			The chief culprit **14** Now Caiaphas[(a)] was he, which gave counsel to the Jews, that it was expedient that one man should die for the people.
He is led away to Caiaphas **57** And they that had laid hold on Jesus led[(b)] *him* away to Caiaphas the high priest, where the scribes and the elders were assembled.[(c)]	*He is led away to Caiaphas* **53** And they led[(b)] Jesus away to [Caiaphas] the high priest: and with him were assembled[(c)] all the chief priests and the elders and the scribes.	*He is led away to Caiaphas* **54** Then took they him, and led[(b)] *him,* and brought him into the high priest's house.	
Peter follows at a great distance **58** But Peter followed[(d)] him afar off	*Peter follows at a great distance* **54** And Peter followed[(d)] him afar off,	*Peter follows at a great distance* And Peter followed[(d)] afar off.	*John also follows the Savior* **15** And Simon Peter followed[(d)] Jesus, and *so did* another disciple: that disciple was known unto the high priest, and went in with Jesus
unto the high priest's palace, and went in,	even into the palace of the high priest:		into the palace of the high priest.
and	and	**55** And when they had kindled a fire in the midst of the hall, and were set down together, Peter sat down among them.	
sat with the servants, to see the end.	he sat with the servants, and warmed himself at the		

Matt. 26:59–63	Mk. 14:54–61	Lk. 22:	John 18:
	fire.		
The Jews connive	*The Jews connive*		
59 Now the chief priests, and elders, and all the council, [Sanhedrin] sought **false witness against Jesus,**(e) to put him to death;	**55** And the chief priests and all the council [Sanhedrin] sought for **witness against Jesus**(e) to put him to death; and found none.		
60 But found none: yea, though many false witnesses came, *yet* found they none.	**56** For many bare false witness against him, but their witness agreed not together.		
Accused of sacrilege	*Accused of sacrilege*		
At the last came two false witnesses, **61** And said, "This *fellow* said, I am able to destroy the temple of God, and to build it in three days."	**57** And there arose certain, and bare false witness against him, saying, **58** "We heard him say, I will destroy this temple that is made with hands, and within three days I will build another made without hands." **59** But neither so did their witness agree together.		
62 And the high priest arose, and said unto him, "Answerest thou nothing? what *is it which* these witness against thee?"	**60** And the high priest stood up in the midst, and asked Jesus, saying, "Answerest thou nothing? what *is it which* these witness against thee?"		
63 But Jesus held his peace,(f)	**61 But he held his peace,**(f) **and answered nothing.**		
The greatest question: Jesus is put under oath	*The greatest question: Jesus is put under oath*		
And the high priest answered and said unto him, "I adjure(g) thee by the living God, that thou tell us whether thou	Again the high priest asked him, and said unto him,		

873

Matt. 26:63-69	Mk. 14:61-66	Lk. 22:	John 18:16
be the Christ, [Messiah] the Son of God."▶	"Art thou the Christ, [Messiah] the Son of the Blessed?"▶	◀A short time later they again put this same troubling question to Him, twice. See Section 182, Lk. 22:67, 70. Was He Israel's Messiah? Yes!	
64 Jesus saith(h) unto him, "Thou hast said: nevertheless I say unto you, Hereafter shall ye see the Son of man(i) 'sitting on the right hand of power,' and 'coming in the clouds of heaven.'"	62 And Jesus said,(h) "I am: and ye shall see the Son of man(i) 'sitting on the right hand of power,' and 'coming in the clouds of heaven.'"		
65 Then the high priest rent(j) his clothes, saying, "He hath spoken blasphemy; what further need have we of witnesses? behold, now ye have heard his blasphemy.	63 Then the high priest rent(j) his clothes, and saith, "What need we any further witnesses?		
66 "What think ye?" They answered and said, "He is guilty of death."	64 "Ye have heard the blasphemy: what think ye?" And they all condemned him to be guilty of death.		
He is beaten and mocked	*He is beaten and mocked*		
67 Then did they▶ Spit in his face, and buffeted him; and others smote *him* with the palms of their hands,	65 And some▶ began to spit on him, and to cover his face, and to buffet him,	▶What a travesty of justice as the Supreme Court of Israel breaks out into shame and chaos. They are beating the accused! Even the servants present joined in the mayhem, smiting the Savior (Mk. 14:65). See Appendix Five for an explanation of the Sanhedrin and how they conducted trials.	
68 Saying, "Prophesy unto us, thou Christ, Who is he that smote(k) thee?"	and to say unto him, "Prophesy:" and the servants did strike▶ (k) him with the palms of their hands.	◀Luke mentions a blindfolding and beating in verses 63-65 below.	
69 Now Peter sat without in the palace:	66 And as Peter was beneath in the palace,		16 But Peter stood at the door without. Then went out that other disciple, which was

874

Matt. 26:69–71	Mk. 14:66–68	Lk. 22:56–57	John 18:16–25
			known unto the high priest, and spake unto her that kept the door, and brought in Peter.
Peter's accusers begin	*Peter accusers begin*	*Peter's accusers begin*	
and a damsel came	there cometh one of the maids of the high priest: **67** And when she saw Peter warming himself,▶	**56** But a certain maid beheld him as he sat by the fire,	
		◀*John puts this warming in verse 18 below.*	
unto him, saying,	she looked upon him, and said,	and earnestly looked upon him, and said,	*Peter's accusers begin* **17** Then saith the damsel that kept the door unto Peter,
"Thou also wast with Jesus of Galilee."	"And thou also wast with Jesus of Nazareth."	"This man was also with him."	"Art not thou also *one* of this man's disciples?"
Peter's first denial[1]	**Peter's first denial**[1]	**Peter's first denial**[1]	**Peter's first denial**[1]
70 But he denied before *them* all, saying, "I know not what thou sayest."	**68** But he denied, saying, "I know not, neither understand I what thou sayest."	**57** And he denied him, saying, "Woman, I know him not."	He saith, "I am not."

18 And the servants and officer stood there, who had made a fire of coals; for it was cold:[m] and they warmed themselves: and Peter stood with them, and warmed himself.

Jesus is interrogated and responds

19 The high priest then asked Jesus of his disciples, and of his doctrine.

20 Jesus answered him, "I spake openly to the world; I ever taught in the synagogue, and in the temple, whither the Jews always resort; and in secret have I said nothing.

21 "Why askest thou me? ask them which heard me, what I have said unto them: behold, they know what I said."

Jesus is slapped and responds

22 And when he had thus spoken, one of the officers which stood by struck Jesus with the palm of his hand, saying, "Answerest thou the high priest so?"

23 Jesus answered him, "If I have spoken evil, bear witness of the evil: but if well, why smitest thou me?"

24 Now Annas had sent him bound unto Caiaphas the high priest.

Matt. 26:69–71	Mk. 14:66–68	Lk. 22:56–57	John 18:16–25
Peter leaves the room: a rooster crows	*Peter leaves the room: a rooster crows*		
71 And when he was gone out into the porch,	And he went out into the porch; and the cock crew.		*Peter outside standing by the fire* **25** And Simon Peter stood and warmed himself.

Matt. 26:71–75	Mk. 14:69–72	Lk. 22:58–61	John 18:25–27
Peter's second denial(n) another *maid* saw him, and said unto them that were there, "This *fellow* was also with Jesus of Nazareth." **72** And again he denied with an oath, "I do not know the man."	**Peter's second denial**(n) **69** And a maid saw him again, and began to say to them that stood by, "This is *one* of them." **70** And he denied it again.	**Peter's second denial**(n) **58** And after a little while another saw him, and said, "Thou art also of them." And Peter said, "Man, I am not."	**Peter's second denial**(n) They [the maid and others] said therefore unto him, [Peter] "Art not thou also *one* of his disciples?" He denied *it*, and said, "I am not."
Peter's third denial(o) **73** And after a while came unto *him* they [the crowds] that stood by, and said to Peter, "Surely thou also art *one* of them; for thy speech bewrayeth thee." **74** Then began he to curse and to swear, *saying,* "I know not the man."	**Peter's third denial**(o) And a little after, they [the crowds] that stood by said again to Peter, "Surely thou art *one* of them: for thou art a Galilaean, and thy speech agreeth *thereto.*" **71** But he began to curse and to swear, *saying,* "I know not this man of whom ye speak."	**Peter's third denial**(o) **59** And about the space of one hour after another confidently affirmed, saying, "Of a truth this *fellow* also was with him: for he is a Galilaean." **60** And Peter said, Man, I know not what thou sayest."	**Peter's third denial**(o) **26** One of the servants of the high priest, being *his* kinsman whose ear Peter cut off, saith, "Did not I see thee in the garden with him?" **27** Peter then denied again:
Rooster conviction(p) And immediately the cock crew.	***Rooster conviction***(p) **72** And the second time the cock crew.	***Rooster conviction***(p) And immediately, while he yet spake, the cock crew.	***Rooster conviction***(p) and immediately the cock crew. (Verse 28 cont. in Section 183)
Bad memories **75** And Peter remembered the word of Jesus, which said unto him, "Before the cock crow, [twice] thou shalt deny me thrice."	***Bad memories*** And Peter called to mind the word that Jesus said unto him, "Before the cock crow twice, thou shalt deny me thrice."	***Bad memories*** **61** And the Lord turned, and looked upon Peter. And Peter remembered the word of the Lord, how he had said unto him, "Before the cock crow, [twice] thou shalt deny me thrice."	

Matt. 26:75	Mk. 14:72	Lk. 22:62-65	John
Broken and weeping And he went out, and wept bitterly.(q) (Next chap., Matt. 27:1 cont. in Section 182.)	*Broken and weeping* And when he thought thereon, he wept.(q) (Next chap., Mk. 15:1a cont. in Section 182.)	*Broken and weeping* 62 And Peter went out, and wept bitterly.(q) *The Savior is mocked and abused again* 63 And the men that held Jesus mocked him, and smote *him.*(r) 64 And when they had blindfolded(s) him, they(t) **struck him on the face,** and asked him, saying, "Prophesy, who is it that smote thee?" 65 And many other things blasphemously spake they against him. (u) (Verse 66 cont. in Section 182.)	
	Too awful to be ▶ recorded were the things spoken of our Savior. It is the same today!		◀*Matthew mentions a beating in verse 67 and Mark in verse 65 above,* ◀*For the soldier's separate beating and mocking of the Savior, which occurred a short time later, refer to Section 186, Matt. 27:27, footnote a.*

Footnotes-Commentary

(a) This passage in not an interpolation (later addition) as the skeptics affirm. John was inspired to pen this editorial comment for the benefit of his original readers to show them that there was no hope for Jesus to have a fair trial at the hands of the Jews. Cynical critics of Scripture have pondered for years why John did not write about the *actual trial* of Jesus before Caiaphas and the Sanhedrin, as did the other three evangelists. Hundreds of books and thousands of pages have come from the pens of men, with each one trying to solve this "mystery." We can expect no better of men and women who do not believe in the total inspiration of God's Word. They, along with many others will never understand that each writer of the four gospels put down strictly what the Holy Spirit inspired them to write. John left out of his narratives and put into it only what was divinely dictated. However, this hardly pleases these poor souls for they cannot conceive that God has given to mankind His infallible Word. The Bible must be written as they think it should have been, not as God gave it to us. Because this is true, they scorn or smile at the very mention of a Bible that is dependable and trustworthy in every line, even with its hard sayings, problems, and difficulties.

2p-Returning to John's report, we notice that several weeks *prior,* Caiaphas had already pronounced the death sentence upon Christ before the Sanhedrin, because of the resurrection of Lazarus (John 11:50). It was unlawful for any member of the Sanhedrin to issue the death sentence until three days after the guilty verdict was announced. This was especially so for the high priest, who in the case of Jesus had already given his verdict even before His trial had taken place. Such an act was an infraction of the honorable standards of Jewish judicial proceedings and the revered Sanhedrin Court. Refer to all of footnote c below for more on the Sanhedrin.

(b) It has been noted that the mob took their prisoner first to Annas. See Section 180, John 18:13, footnote p. What transpired at his house we cannot know. For detailed information on the crooked, conniving high priest, Annas, see Section 21, Part 1, numbers 6 and 7, under footnote b.

2p-**Jesus the revolutionary fighter?** Over the years, evil men have laid many charges upon the Son of God. Dr. Samuel G. F. Brandon (died 1971) in his masterpiece of religious trash, *Jesus and the Zealots: A Study of the Political Factor in Primitive Christianity,* presented Christ as a political activist opposing the Roman occupation of Israel! He was supposed to have been influenced by the terrorist group called Zealots. Such ignorant audacity reflects what the human heart and mind may conjure up, when they step into the sacred realm of true faith without knowing Jesus Christ as Lord and Savior. When men of Brandon's caliber take the Bible into hand and purport to

877

explain it, the disaster is beyond all imaginations. A head packed with learning and a heart locked in satanic darkness makes a deadly combination. The "church" is cursed with these wolves in sheep's clothing.

(c) **Before the Sanhedrin.** For a further explanation of Jesus' trials, those who partook in them, and how the Sanhedrin broke their own judicial rules, see *Appendix Five*. After Annas had finished with the Lord Jesus, He was led off to a prearranged meeting at the house of Caiaphas, who served as the high priest of Israel at this time. He was also a member of the sect of the Sadducees. Caiaphas was not adorned in the gorgeous and colorful garments worn only by the high priest. Between the years 6 and A.D. 37, the Romans in the Castle of Antonio held the priestly vestments in safekeeping. They were only given back for the rituals and functions of Israel's special feast days. These sacred priestly garments were received from the Romans seven days before their usage in order to sanctify them from heathen uncleanness. Josephus gave an interesting description of the high priest's ornaments in *Antiquities*, Book 3:7 lines 151 through 187. They were only worn during the actual ceremonies and rituals.

2p-The entire religious leadership of the nation assembled waiting for Christ to be brought before them. The Sanhedrin, Pilate, and Judas the traitor had prearranged it all. Present at this gathering were two older men, Joseph of Arimathaea and Nicodemus of Jerusalem, with deep misgivings about the trial of Jesus. Joseph was a "secret disciple" of Christ and Nicodemus a sympathizer or perhaps a covert believer too. The next afternoon, immediately after the crucifixion, both men abandoned their secrecy and openly acknowledged Jesus as their Messiah. Refer to the main heading of Section 193, where Joseph and Nicodemus secured permission from Pilate to take the body of Jesus and properly bury it. Also, see footnote k below, for more on these two noble men who had been members of the great Sanhedrin Court of Israel. Regarding the Sanhedrin not meeting at night, see Section 182, footnote a.

(d) **"Peter followed afar off."** Thousands today follow their Savior at the same distance! After the episode in the garden of cutting off the servant's ear, and fleeing in terror, we are surprised to find Peter anywhere in the city! This reveals the true man. Peter loved his Lord, and despite everything, he wanted to be with Him even in the worst of times. John informs us that Peter did not actually go into the high priest's palace with the crowds. "Another disciple" has reference to John, who was granted instant access into this exclusive residence. This could have only been done because he was well known to the doorkeepers, servants, and guards in attendance at this time.

2p-**Verses 15-16**. John also followed behind, but arrived ahead of Peter for he was already in the house and had the maid to let Peter in upon arrival. The text is explicit, that "he [John] went in with Jesus."

(e) This was predicted a thousand years prior in Ps. 35:11. Matthew 26:59-62 with parallel texts, reflects the wild fanaticism blended with terrible hatred for the Son of God. False witnesses came by the dozens, but their stories conflicted. Someone in the crowd remembered His statement spoken over three years before about rebuilding the temple. Matthew's record of one false witness in verse 61 should be compared with Mark's in verses 58-59. The witnesses contradict each other! What a difference in their stories.

2p-**Matt. 26:61. "Build it in three days."** For what Jesus spoke on this occasion, note Section 29, John 2:19-21, footnote f.

(f) **Isa. 53:7.** It was predicted about seven hundred years in advance that He would be as "a lamb to the slaughter, and as a sheep before her shearers is dumb, so he openeth not his mouth." False witnessing is not worthy of a rebuttal when men stand before God. The silence of Christ *at this moment* troubled, thwarted, confounded, and maddened them. Before His calm and serenity, they felt as if they were the culprits. Divine silence can be deafening.

(g) **"I adjure thee by the living God."** Oddly, the only other usage of this expression in the gospels was by a demon speaking through the mouth of Legion. Refer to Section 88, Mk. 5:7. Was it the same evil spirit in both? The word "adjure" meant that the high priest put Christ under oath before God in heaven. This was standard Jewish court procedure. The high priest's question to our Lord reveals the anxiety of every pious Jew in the nation that had heard of Jesus of Nazareth. *"Is this man our promised Messiah?"* Mark records the remainder of Caiaphas' question, "Art thou the Christ [Messiah] the Son of the Blessed?" This question was asked again a few hours later in the morning of His death. See Section 182, Lk. 22:67-70, footnotes b, c, and d. Note that here the high priest confessed that Messiah was also called "the Son" of God. The religious leaders knew that this title was strictly Messianic and used it this way. Earlier in the ministry of Jesus, Simon Peter had confessed the same in Matt. 16:16 and later in John 6:69. All the apostles in holy unison called Him "the Son of God" in Matt. 14:33, after He had stilled the tumultuous waters of Galilee and walked on them! This has reference to Ps. 2:7 where Jehovah had called Messiah His Son, a thousand years earlier. The Hebrew people during Jesus' earthly days had a different opinion of Him from what Orthodox Hebrews have today. He was looked upon as "the Son of God," as stated here by the high priest. Today, most Jews vehemently deny this mark of deity and fiercely oppose such a thing. They are not along in this error; every false cult feigning to be Christian takes the same stance and opposes the Son of God's *eternal* credentials.

2p-**No one confessed Jesus as the Son of God.** The debate was not whether God's Messiah was also His Son, (clearly He was), but whether or not Jesus of Nazareth was that unique Person. For the most part, the leaders of Israel bitterly rejected Jesus as being God's Son, their Messiah. This rejection was because He had condemned their subjection of the Torah Law to the oral tradition of the elders, and that He did not seek to overthrow the Romans and establish an earthly political kingdom for Israel. For more on the oral law, see Section 52, footnote h; Section 89, footnote c; and Section 96, footnote d. For a detailed explanation of the opinion of various modern day Jews about Christ compared to that of the religious leaders while He was on earth, see Section 14, footnote f.

3p-In 1956, Professor Sigmund Mowinckel, of Norway, famed as one of the "premier biblical scholars of the twentieth century" revealed his scholarly unbelief in God's Word. He wrote in, *He that Cometh,* page 293 this shocker, "It is, however, most improbable that the Jews ever called Messiah the 'son of God . . .'" The late professor should have given some time to explaining (or explaining away) such verses as Matt. 14:33, 16:16, 26:63; John 9:35, 10:36, 11:4, 27. Demons had earlier confessed the deity of Christ (Matt. 8:29 with Mk. 3:11). A few months after the resurrection of our Savior, a government politician from Ethiopia publicly made this confession and was then baptized (Acts 8:36–38). Saul of Tarsus, *after* his conversion preached that Jesus Christ is the Son of God in the synagogues of Damascus (Acts 9:20–22). Paul's message "confounded the Jews which dwelt at Damascus." Interestingly enough he proved his claim from Old Testament Scriptures. "Son of God" was one of the ancient Hebrew titles for the Messiah despite the distorted theology of the rabbis before and after our Lord's life, ministry, and ascension. For a discussion of the "two Messiahs" and other Jewish opinions of their promised One, see Section 6, sixth paragraph of footnote d.

(h) "Thou hast said." How did the carpenter from Nazareth respond to the serious question of the high priest when He was put under oath? *He confessed He was the Messiah!* In verse 62 of Mark, His Words were, "I am." If this does not mean that Jesus Christ is the Messiah of Israel then nothing makes sense anymore. Refer to Section 119, John 7:26 footnote i for more on Jesus, Israel's Messiah. Also, see Section 41, footnote g, where demons confessed Him as the Messiah, while the Jews refused to do so. Flying into a wild rage, Caiaphas leaps to his feet and taking his top garment by the thin edge seam rips it downward. Dr. Joseph Lightfoot informs us that in cases of blasphemy, the Jews were not allowed to sew up their garments again. See his *Commentary on the New Testament . . . ,* vol. 2, pages 358–359. Blasphemy was considered a sin that was unpardonable and worthy of the death sentence (Lev. 24:16). Thus, we read their *hasty* verdict in verse 66 of Matthew's record. This was another fracturing of their rules. In previous trials, the Sanhedrin traditionally would not issue the death sentence immediately at the conclusion of the matter; they would wait for several days and nights, spend much time in fasting and prayer, and then give their verdict. *How different things often become when Jesus Christ, the Son of God, is involved!* See footnote j below for another breaking of their rules governing court procedures.

(i) Verse 64. A difficult passage. We have here a combination of *two* separate prophecies about Messiah. The first part is a general citation from Ps. 110:1; the second part is from Dan. 7:13. The Lord Jesus had spoken similar Words months earlier in Matt. 16:28. Some hold that Christ was telling these particular Jews that they would, later, from their home in hell actually see Him coming at His second advent. Others think this occurred in a spiritual sense in A.D. 70 at the doom of Jerusalem. The author has no opinion on this difficult verse. Surely, it could be either or something totally different that we have all missed. Whatever it means it did or will yet happen as Jesus stated.

(j) "He rent his clothes." This action was contrary to the Torah Law. It is forbidden in Lev. 10:6 and 21:10 for the high priest to rend [the edges] of his garments. It was a public way of expressing grief among the ancients and is found numerous times in Scripture (Gen. 37:29 with Job 1:20). It is still practiced today by various tribes in Africa. However, it was strictly forbidden for the high priest of Israel to do such a thing. Here, the leader of Israel breaks their glorious law and apparently, no one said anything.

2p-Verse 67. "They spit in his face." This record of His mistreatment and its parallel in Mk. 14:65 are the fulfillment of the prophecy in Isa. 50:6. In that long-ago history, the religious leaders spat in the face of Christ. At a time yet future, we read the awesome words of Rev. 20:11, "And I saw a great white throne, and him that sat on it, from whose face, the earth and the heaven fled away." In a day to come the Savior, who bore the shame of evil men, will sit upon a throne to judge the world (John 5:22 and Matt. 25:31). At no time during this fierce mockery was there a flinch of anger, indignation, or wrath from the Master. Jesus' patience, gentleness, His compassion, and mercy overwhelmed those evil men of false religion. Jews and Gentiles alike were confounded. Spitting in the face of the Savior did not cease with the Sanhedrin. Secular and public authorities who brazenly deny His deity, virgin birth, substitutionary death for our sins, His glorious resurrection, ascension, and return; continue to slander Him. To this infamy should be added those hypocrites *within* the church who oppose the doctrine of hell, the final authority of Holy Scripture, the need for the new birth, and reduce the saving gospel to an emotional nursery rhyme. The "god" of these bleeding heart religionists is the "the old man downstairs," the devil. With this read Ps. 50:22.

(k) "Who smote thee?" The great illegal trial. The demonic fury of the religious leaders of Israel is now fully released upon Jesus. Beating, pounding, punching, slapping, and spitting in their madness until "his visage was so marred more than any man, and his form more than the sons of men" (Isa 52:14). The Christian Jew, Dr. Arnold Frucktenbaum, informs us in his writings and tape-recorded lectures that everything the Sanhedrin did during their trials of Jesus was illegal. To beat a prisoner in court was a high insult to Jewish custom. Three levels of fines were attached to the maltreatment of prisoners. For more on this, see *Appendix Five,* sub heading *"Modes of trial . . . and several forms of punishment."* Note the following rules governing the abuse of those being tried:

1. **Fist.** To strike a man with the fist carried the fine of four denari or four days salary.

2. **Slap.** Slapping with the palm was two hundred denari or two hundred days wages.

3. **Spitting.** Worse, to spit upon one during a legal proceeding was punishable by four hundred denari. This was equal to four hundred–days wages.

2p-The Sanhedrin, which made such noble laws as these, and now breaks them out of their hatred for the Savior. We are sure that both Joseph of Arimathaea, and Nicodemus had no part in this foul treatment of the Messiah. See footnote c above for more on these secret disciples who were members of the Sanhedrin Court.

3p-We should note that John 18:15 tells us that John was apparently well acquainted with Caiaphas and actually had instant entrance into the hall where a large fire was burning due to the cold of the night. In verse 16, John spoke to the door keeper and secured permission for Peter to enter the room. Matthew notes that Peter "sat with the servants" of the high priest. Where was Malchus, whose ear, he had just cut off and Christ instantly healed? Refer to this event in Section 180, John 18:10, footnote g. We are amazed that John had such freedom and authority in the house of Jesus' enemies. There is much more to this story than we have been given.

(l) Peter's first denial. A damsel or maidservant of the high priest suddenly accuses Peter of being an accomplice of the prisoner now under interrogation. Instantly, Peter denied her charge, with "I am not." Putting the gospel records together, apparently Peter expressed his denials several different ways. See footnote n an o below.

(m) "It was cold." For more on Jesus and bad weather, note Section 123, John 10:22, footnote b. At this point in the trial, John was led to digress from the trouble of his friend and companion Peter, and give his readers a brief review of the actual trial scene. Verses 19–24 are something of a parenthetical picture of what the other evangelist had already written. They are discussed below. See footnotes h through k for a review of Matthew, Mark, and Luke's account of *this part* of Jesus' trial.

2p-Verse 18. Their spies had been omnipresent in an attempt to catch Jesus in some contradictory word or statement. They knew what He had taught and warned the people about, especially the hypocrisy of the religious leaders and their sure damnation. This grated them to the core!

3p-Verse 19. "His doctrine." Jesus Christ was and is the very embodiment of divine truth. His Word will never pass away. Kings and kingdoms come and go; but Christ remains forever. If the mathematical truth that two plus two equals four should suddenly vanish from all living memory, that calculation would still remain, it cannot be changed. It cannot be reinterpreted or revised. A million years ago, it was true; a million years henceforth, it will still be true. Thus, it is with Jesus the Son of God. "His doctrine" is eternal! For more on our Lord's teaching, see Section 119, John 7:46, footnote u. For how He was instructed by God as a child, refer to Section 19, third paragraph of footnote c. According to Section 162, John 12:49, footnotes k and l, Jesus only spoke what God commanded Him to say.

4p-Verses 20–21. His answer shut their mouths! He shifts the answer to their question to the very Jews standing in front of Him!

5p-Verse 22. Highlighted in gray for this act fulfilled another prophecy in Isa. 50:6. Who can imagine slapping God in the face! O, the wretchedness of Adam's fallen race.

6p-Verse 23. It was a slap without a reason, therefore, the Master asked them, "why?" For slapping, a prisoner during a trial, see number 2, under footnote k above. Could they prove where He has spoken evil among the people? In the book of Luke, we read what Christ did through His human body while on earth among men: in Acts, we learn what He did through His spiritual body, the church, for thirty some years after His ascension.

(n) Peter's second denial. With the dozens staring at him after his first skirmish with the maid, Peter moves away onto a porch to escape their sharp glares. There was a fire here as well. To his horror, just as he enters the porch, a rooster crows from somewhere in the night! Standing and warming himself, suddenly another maidservant speaks out, "This fellow was also with Jesus of Nazareth." She accused him of the same guilt in various words as seen in the parallel verses of Mark, Luke, and John. For the second time poor Peter vehemently denied his Lord.

(o) Peter's third denial. What Matthew and Mark describe as a little while later, John pinpoints as being about one hour. One can believe that after an hour Peter was feeling relieved that the pressure was off. Our sins will never go away until they see the grace of God and the blood of Christ coming for them. Then they flee. Standing amid this great crowd of people was one particular man who had eyed Peter for some time. Whoever this fellow was, he was related to Malchus, whose ear Peter had removed with his sword. No doubt, Malchus had explained the whole thing to this kinsman and perhaps given some description of the man who had attacked him. We note the text in John affirms that this man was also with the multitude that came to arrest Jesus. Now, he claims to have seen Peter in the garden. In great compassion, the Lord Jesus had healed the wounded ear of His hateful enemy.

2p-Upon hearing this, Peter responded. Instantly, they caught his thick Galilean accent; others joined in the clamor. Soon, many were charging the bewildered fisherman with being a follower of Jesus. This was too much! Exploding in shame, fear, and rage, Peter bursts into vile language, even cursing and swearing. Some writers have tried hard to play on the Greek words here and tell us that it does not really mean foul language. This again is faulty exegesis. While raging in a pitiful effort to persuade the wild crowd that he had no part with Messiah, suddenly out of yonder night comes the crowing of another rooster. His heart sank; he was smitten to his soul by a simple cock-a–

doodle-do. He instantly remembered Christ's Words to him hours before in the upper room. See this in Section 173, John 13:38, footnote f.

3p-It is a wonder what God uses in the lives of His children. For Moses, it was a rod; Rahab, a scarlet cord; Samson used a jawbone; Jonah, a gourd; and for the tough fisherman from Galilee, it was a lonely rooster crowing in the night. We read in a Psalm of "Fire, and hail; snow, and vapour; stormy wind fulfilling his Word" (Ps. 148:8). Perhaps thinking about his foul mouth, and wicked language, years later Peter wrote of his Lord these beautiful words, "Who did no sin, neither was guile found in his mouth;" (1 Peter 2:22). It is a fact of Christian counseling that men look for their secret sins in the lives of their leaders, and if not found, they are filled with deep respect for these guiltless ones and will usually trust them explicitly.

(p) A rooster problem. Critics of Scripture have pounded on this old rooster and Peter's denials of Christ for centuries in their futile effort to show contradictions in the Bible. Several explanations have been put forward that satisfy the wordings of these texts. It is normally overlooked that "cock crowing" was a time or "watch period" in the Jewish night. Christ could have been pointing out to Peter that he would deny Him before this specific watch was over. Some hold that there were six denials; three before the first rooster crowed, and three more before another one crowed. Since God chose not to give us the specific details or a "crow-by-crow" explanation of this sad story, wisdom dictates that we leave it there. Regardless of the hostile objections of the skeptics, one thing is sure: God used an old rooster to smite the heart of a pig-headed preacher and bring him to repentance and good sense. *Reader, what rooster will God cause to crow in your life in order to bring you back to Himself?*

2p-The Levites working in the temple would not sweep the ashes from about the giant altar until they heard the cock crowing, which was just before sunrise. The crowing of the rooster was a common sound echoing across the temple area and over various parts of Jerusalem. Peter would have been familiar with this, being a signal for the altar in God's house to be purged, scrubbed, and cleaned, ready for a new day of service and sacrifice. We wonder if he felt that it was now time for him to purge the altar of his heart and make ready for genuine service for his Lord. This cleaning of the altar ashes is recorded in the Talmud tractate, Yoma 20a. Some Jewish texts interpret the cock crowing as being a priest or ruler calling forth the first admonition for preparations to be made in the service of God for that new day. However, this is a dubious argument of the rabbis, trying to transfer credit to themselves from the old rooster! Lightfoot reports in *Commentary on the New Testament . . .* , vol. 2, page 357, the odd story of the Sanhedrin having a fowl stoned for pecking a small child to death! Apparently, Peter was not the only Jew, who had a rooster problem!

(q) Peter wept bitterly. The tears of repentance are sweeter than honey in the comb. They wash the eyes to see, cleanse the heart to think, and raise the soul to heights of new joy. The fall of Simon Peter leaps upon us with a lesson for all believers. It warns those who, without wise counsel and prolonged prayer, may enter realms of service beyond their ability and mortal strength. An old tradition relates that for the remainder of Peter's life, whenever he heard a cock crowing, he would break down and weep. Somehow, even in strange legends one may sometimes detect a fragment of personal truth that stirs the heart for God.

(r) Mocking the Son of God from heaven! Verse 63-65. *What troublesome words.* See footnote u below for more on this awful thought. Various Old Testament predictions were completed during the session of mistreating the Messiah. Some seven hundred years prior the prophet wrote of Christ, "I gave my back to the smiters, and my cheeks to them that plucked off the hair: I hid not my face from shame and spitting" (Isa. 50:6).

(s) "Blind-folded him." With this, we are introduced to a game as old as mankind, "blind man's bluff." The Egyptians, Persians, Romans, and others would blindfold or veil the face of their enemy, slap, beat, and hit the victim over the head and facial area, then inquire, "Guess, who hit you?" This ancient pastime was now played upon the Lord Jesus. From the sunrise of antiquity, evil men have enacted mocking sport upon their enemies. Samson felt the pain of this as the Philistines mocked him before their pagan god (Judges 16:25). This awful scene presents an impeccable example of the utter depravity and total degeneracy of humanity at large. *All men are born originals but die dirty, worn-out copies if they are without Christ!* How clearly the soldier's actions demonstrate to fair and honest minds the need for a supernatural change in man's heart, without which he can become no more than an educated animal. These mockers had heard the crowds refer to our Lord as a prophet, and now they lay this affront upon Him in terrible scorn.

(t) It was during this tyrannical rage that His face was beaten to a pulp as predicted in Isa. 52:14, and the beard was ripped from His face (Isa. 50:6). For beating prisoners, note the fines in first paragraph, footnote k above.

(u) "Many other things." The Jews, especially their religious leaders, had followed Christ over the country continually slandering Him, and His good deeds, and miracles. They described Him as being demon possessed, a mean man, wicked person, profane sinner, glutton and "winebibber, Sabbath breaker, lawbreaker, a companion of Beelzebub, seditious, tax evader," and other things. We are appalled to imagine what else would be included in the "many other things they blasphemously" called Him. Earlier, our Lord had rebuked the Jews regarding the false charges and evil words they had spoken against Him (Matt. 12:31-37).

Friday. It is early the next morning,* the Sanhedrin holds a brief council meeting at Caiaphas' house to question the Lord Jesus again. Twice, the chief priests inquired if He is the "Messiah, the Son of God." He responded in the affirmative, and they instantly called for His death. Afterward, they go to Pilate** seeking permission to crucify the Savior.

Time: Very early morning of the crucifixion day on Friday.

---

*Where was the Lord Jesus during the remaining hours of that early morning before He was led away to stand before Governor Pilate? About seven hundred years prior, the prophet Isaiah foretold where Messiah would be in the words, "He was taken from prison" (Isa. 53:8). He was in restraint during these few hours. Was this where He met the two thieves and one learned of His kingdom, and requested to be remembered by the Messiah as He died (Section 190, Lk. 23:39-43)? **Jesus was taken to Caiaphas late at night after a mysterious visit to the house of Annas. At sunrise, He was led to Governor Pilate for judgment (Section 183 John 18: 28).

From night prison back to the Sanhedrin Court where He is condemned

Matt. 27:1	Mk. 15:1a	Lk. 22:66–71	John
Sunrise of that awful but wonderful day	*Sunrise of that awful but wonderful day*	*Sunrise of that awful but wonderful day*	
1 When the morning[(a)] was come, all the chief priests and elders of the people took counsel◄	**1a** And straightway in the morning[(a)] the chief priests held a consultation with the elders and scribes and the whole council,◄ [Sanhedrin] (Verse 1b and 2 cont. in Section 183.)	**66** And as soon as it was day,[(a)] the elders of the people and the chief priests and the scribes came together, and led him into their council,◄ [Sanhedrin] saying,	
against Jesus to put him to death: (Verse 2 cont. in Section 183.) ▲ *Matthew's word above has been translated that they took "counsel." Mark and Luke used "council." They did both. The word "council" has reference to the Sanhedrin court.* "Counsel" *was a deliberative session of the "council" regarding the fate of the Lord Jesus.*	*The Sanhedrin and Jewish► religious leaders hated Him for claiming to be the Messiah and only Savior of Israel. They ask Him twice of His Messiahship in verses 67 and 70. Earlier in our Savior's trial, He was interrogated over this same question. See Section 181, Matt. 26: 63, 64 and Mk. 14:61.*	*The great question* **67** "Art thou the Christ?[(b)] [Messiah] tell us." And he said unto them, "If I tell you, ye will not believe: **68** "And if I also ask *you,* ye will not answer me, nor let *me* go. **69** "Hereafter shall the Son of man sit on the right hand of the power of God."[(c)] *The same question again* **70** Then said they all, "Art thou then the Son of God?"[(d)] (Messiah) *The same answer again* And he said unto them, "Ye say that I am." *The Sanhedrin understood* **71** And they said, "What need we any further witness? for we ourselves have heard of his own mouth."[(e)] (Next chap., Lk. 23:1 cont. in Section 183.)	

Footnotes-Commentary

(a) **"When morning was come."** This meant the crack of dawn. After His arrest in the garden, He was led back to Jerusalem and taken to the house of Annas. From here, He went to Caiaphas for something of a night trial or hearing. Amid this confusion came the denials of Peter. Only a few hours remained before He was taken to Pilate, early next morning. See comments by the single asterisk under main heading above to see where Jesus spent the remaining time that morning before being taken to Pilate. The parallel texts reveal that three bodies of men were present at His early morning judicial proceeding. They were the chief priests, scribes, and elders. The objections by "authorities" and unbelieving Jews about the Sanhedrin never meeting at night, and their citations from the Talmud to prove this, are incorrect. The Talmud has both lies and truth! *Hatred blinds men and often turns them into lawbreaking animals.* Skeptics argue so eloquently that the Jews would have never called a meeting of the Sanhedrin outside the temple precincts. In their passion to kill the Lord Jesus, they broke many of their own court rulings. Refer to *Appendix Five* and the last subheading entitled, *"Sanhedrin Court procedures,"* for a list of their rules broken by this body of lawmakers, out of rage against the Savior. At sunrise, they scurry about to question Jesus regarding His Messianic assertions. For their verdict on this second hearing, see footnote e below.

(b) **"Art thou the Christ?"** See footnote d below. Why did this so trouble these men of religion? This was their biggest worry; it haunted them day and night. They had deliberately rejected Jesus' claims to be their Messiah, although His Words and works proved who He was. These Jews had put this same question to Christ a short time earlier during His first hearing or trial appearance before the Sanhedrin in Section 181, Matt. 26:63, footnote g.

(c) This is a reference to the prediction of Ps. 110:1 written by David over a thousand years before. It was a Messianic prophecy stating that Messiah would be seated at God's right hand. Some writers also see in these words a foreshadow of Dan. 7:13-14. Jesus used a similar statement about Himself during the early part of His first appearing before the Jews, their leaders and Supreme Court. See Section 181, Matt. 26:64 footnote i. Those listening knew very well that He was purporting to be the Messiah of Israel in citing this passage. Hence, again, they repeat their all-important question in the next verse.

(d) **"Art thou the Son of God?"** See footnote b above and relative references where the exact same question was put to Him in different words. Luke is explicit to write that "all" questioned Him. How interesting that the Hebrew leaders of religion knew God had a Son and said so in this passage. They identified Him as Messiah or Christ! For the ancient and present Jewish opinion of Jesus, see Section 14, first three paragraphs under footnote f. The judgment of the New Testament Jews about Jesus Christ and those of Orthodox Israelites today are vastly different. Unbelieving Jews and "liberal Christians" argue that there were many claiming to be Israel's Messiah, and that Jesus of Nazareth was another one of these aspiring seers! We are to believe that He meant nothing of divine purpose by His direct answer in the affirmative. See footnote e below for our Lord's response. For a pitiful discussion of Jesus being the Messiah, and His kingdom, see *Jewish-Christian Debates: God, Kingdom, Messiah,* by Jacob Neusner and Bruce Chilton. For one of the timeless classics on this subject, see *The Life and Times of Jesus the Messiah,* by Alfred Edersheim.

(e) **Out of his own mouth.** How could it be plainer? Our Lord's enemies clearly understood Him to confess He was Israel's Messiah. Unsaved skeptics debate He was not that Messianic Person. Had He not proven this over the past three years of public ministry? These men had reached the same verdict earlier that night and said almost the exact words. Note this in Section 181, Matt. 26:65-66. After double-checking, they are convinced that Jesus is a fraud and blasphemer worthy of death. *Alternatively, were they convinced that He was a fraud?* In the early 1990s, a band of "eminent and learned theological expert scholars" met at Princeton for the First Princeton Symposium on Judaism and Christian Origins. Their findings were printed by Fortress Press in 1992 in a book called *The Messiah.* This is a classic example of academic unbelief in God's Word, its inspiration, and trustworthiness. Not one mention is made of the personal salvation of any of these "great scholars." No word of thanks and praise for His death on the cross for our sins and glorious resurrection from the dead. Theological scholarship without the life-changing new birth is a tool of Satan. It blinds, deceives, and finally damns those who are its victims. Refer to Section 6, the ninth paragraph of footnote d for other comments on Jesus the Messiah, and the vain pursuit of unbelieving scholars to find Him in extra biblical literature instead of Holy Scripture. For a classic on scholarly unbelief, see *The Sceptre and the Star,* by John J. Collins. It reeks with doubt, unbelief, and heresy regarding Jesus the Messiah.

2p-The author has spoken to many Jews about Jesus of Nazareth being their Messiah. Some of them fly into fits of rage, red faced, shaking their fists, and cursing when "Yeshua ha'Hamashiach" is mentioned. Similar fierce reaction comes from certain Muslims, especially when one speaks of His death, burial, and resurrection. Why this, if He was the imposter they presented Him to be?

3p-Where the thousands that He had healed, blessed, fed, clothed, and saved? Their absence reveals the absolute terror with which the religious leaders ruled Israel. To challenge or defy them could result in excommunication from the Jewish community or death. For the horrible consequences of being put out of the synagogue, refer to Section 121, third paragraph of footnote j. The threat of this hung like a death sword over the heads of the Hebrew people, especially the poorer class.

PILATE'S FIRST VERDICT

The Sanhedrin seeks the Roman Governor's permission to kill Jesus. He is led across the city to the Castle of Antonio where Pilate is residing. Judas, seeing Christ condemned to die, repents, returns his silver, and commits suicide. Pilate rejects the Jew's charges against the Lord Jesus and publicly gives his first verdict.

Time: Early morning of the crucifixion day on Friday.

From the Sanhedrin to Pilate's quarters at the Castle of Antonio

Matt. 27:2–10	Mk. 15:1b	Lk. 23:1	John 18:28–30
Led as a lamb 2 And when they had bound him, they led *him* away, and delivered him to Pontius Pilate[a] the governor.	*Led as a lamb* and bound Jesus, and carried *him* away, and delivered *him* to Pilate.[a]	*Led as a lamb* 1 And the whole multitude of them arose, and led him unto Pilate.[a]	*Led as a lamb* 28 Then led they Jesus from Caiaphas unto the hall of judgment: and it was early; [morning] and they themselves went not into the judgment hall,[b] lest they should be defiled;[c] but that they might eat the passover. 29 Pilate then went out[d] unto them, and said, "What accusation bring ye against this man?" 30 They answered and. said unto him, "If he were not a malefactor, [criminal] we would not have delivered him up unto thee."[e]
Judas repents too late: his money used to buy a cemetery for the poor			

3 Then Judas, which had betrayed him, when he saw that he was condemned, repented himself, and brought[f] again the thirty pieces of silver to the chief priests and elders,

4 Saying, "I have sinned in that I have betrayed the innocent blood."[g] And they said, "What *is that* to us? See thou *to that*."(or that's your problem)

5 And he cast down[h] the pieces of silver in the temple, and departed, and went and hanged himself.[i]

6 And the chief priests took the silver pieces, and said, "It is not lawful for to put them into the treasury, because it is the price of blood."

7 And they took counsel, and bought with them the potter's field, to bury strangers in.[j]

8 Wherefore that field was called, "The field of blood, unto this day."[k]

9 Then was fulfilled that which was spoken by Jeremy [Jeremiah] the prophet, saying,[l] **"And they took the thirty pieces of silver, the price of him that was valued, whom they of the children of Israel did value;"**

10 And gave them for the potter's field, as the Lord appointed me.

Matt. 27:11	Mk. 15:2	Lk. 23:2-3	John 18:31-36
		Many false accusations 2 And they began to accuse him, saying, "We found this *fellow* perverting the nation, and forbidding to give tribute to Caesar, saying that he himself is Christ a King."	
			31 Then said Pilate unto them, "Take ye him, and judge him according to your law."[m] The Jews therefore said unto him, "It is not lawful for us to put any man to death:"[n] 32 That the saying of Jesus might be fulfilled, which he spake, signifying what death he should die.
Jesus before Pilate 11 And Jesus stood before the governor: and the governor asked him, saying, "Art thou the King of the Jews?" And Jesus said unto him, "Thou sayest."	*Jesus before Pilate* 2 And Pilate asked him, "Art thou the King of the Jews?" And he answering said unto him, "Thou sayest *it*."	*Jesus before Pilate* 3 And Pilate asked him, saying, "Art thou the King of the Jews?" And he answered him and said, "Thou sayest *it*."	*Jesus before Pilate* 33 Then Pilate entered[o] into the judgment hall again, and called Jesus, and said unto him, "Art thou the King of the Jews?" 34 Jesus answered him, "Sayest thou this thing of thyself, or did others tell it thee of me?" 35 Pilate answered, "Am I a Jew? Thine own nation and the chief priests have delivered thee unto me: what hast thou done?"[p] 36 Jesus answered, "My kingdom is not of this world:[q] if my kingdom were of this world, then would my servants fight, that I

Matt. 27:12	Mk. 15:3	Lk. 23:4	John 18:36-40
			should not be delivered to the Jews: but now is my kingdom not from hence."
			37 Pilate therefore said unto him, "Art thou a king then?"[(r)] Jesus answered, "Thou sayest that I am a king. To this end was I born, and for this cause came I into the world, that I should bear witness unto the truth. Every one that is of the truth heareth my voice."
			Pilate's great question
			38 Pilate saith unto him, "What is truth?"[(s)] And when he had said this, he went out again unto the Jews, and saith unto
		4 Then said Pilate to the chief priests and *to* the people,	them,
		Pilate's first verdict	**Pilate's first verdict**
	See Information Box at▶ *the end of the next page for a harmony of Pilate's five verdicts concerning the Lord Jesus.*	**"I find no fault in this man."**	**"I find in him no fault *at all.*"**
			Pilate's hopeful alternative
			39 "But ye have a custom, that I should release ◀[(t)] unto you one at the passover: will ye therefore that I release unto you the King of the Jews?"
		▶*Matthew placed the story of this release in 27:20-21, Mark in 15:11, and Luke in 23:17-19.*	*"Give us the criminal"*
			40 Then cried they all again, saying, "Not this man, but Barabbas." Now Barabbas was a robber. (Next chap., John 19:1 cont. in Section 185.)
Silence speaks loudly	*Silence speaks loudly*		
12 And when he was accused of the chief priests and elders, **he answered nothing.**[(u)]	**3** And the chief priests accused him of many things: but **he answered nothing.**[(u)]		

Matt. 27:13-14	Mk. 15:4-5	Lk. 23:5	John
13 Then said Pilate unto him, "Hearest thou not how many things they witness against thee?" *Innocence needs no defense* 14 And he answered him to never a word; insomuch that the governor marvelled greatly. (Verse 15 cont. in Section 185.)	4 And Pilate asked him again, saying, "Answerest thou nothing? behold how many things they witness against thee." *Innocence needs no defense* 5 But Jesus yet answered nothing; so that Pilate marvelled. (Verse 6 cont. in Section 185.)	*"He is a Galilean"* 5 And they were the more fierce, saying, "He stirreth up the people, teaching throughout all Jewry,(v) beginning from Galilee to this place." (Verse 6 cont. in Section 184.)	

Pilate's five verdicts harmonized. During our Lord's trials before the Roman Governor (which must have lasted at least an hour), Pilate gave his official judgment of Christ five different times. Each one declared the Son of God was innocent. A Roman judge was required to give his verdict only once. Pilate's announcements are listed below:
1. Section 183, Lk. 23:4 with parallel text in John 18:38.
2. Section 185, Lk. 23:14, with no parallel text.
3. Section 185, Lk. 23:22, with no parallel text.
4. Section 187, John 19:4, with no parallel text.
5. Section 187, John 19:6, with no parallel text.

Footnotes-Commentary

(a) **"Pontius Pilate the governor."** The title "Pontius" was conferred upon him because of an outstanding military victory over the pagan tribes dwelling in the region known as Pontus, meaning "sea." Jews were present at Pentecost from this area (Acts 2:9). It was the birthplace of Paul's friend, Aquila (Acts 18:2), and Peter addressed his first epistle to believers dwelling in Pontus (1 Peter 1:1).

2p-The Jews' brief examination of Jesus regarding His Messianic claims is over. It is recorded in Section 182, Lk. 22:67-71. Nothing so disturbed them as the possibility that He might have been that Messianic Person predicted in their Scripture, whom they had condemned. *Again* binding His hands, they leave the residence of Caiaphas. See Section 180, John 18:12, for Him being bound in the garden prior to the walk back to Jerusalem. Their destination is the residence of the Roman governor Pilate, who was temporarily holding up in the Castle of Antonio during the Passover occasion. This giant structure was located at the northeast corner of Jerusalem, near the temple walls. *This meeting with the governor had to have been prearranged by the Jews.* This is obvious when we note that it was in the wee hours of the morning and that Pilate was in the judgment hall waiting for them. Refer to previous Section 182, Matt. 27:1, footnote a, for further details and information by the asterisk under main heading.

(b) **Verse 28. "Judgment hall."** This building had direct reference to the Roman "pretorium." There was a designated seat where the governor would hear and decide the cases brought before him in this large room. This same word is translated "common hall" (Matt. 27:27), which reveals it was also a large room. It was often referred to as a "council chamber." The Sanhedrin had already condemned the Lord Jesus and pronounced their death sentence on Him in Matt. 26:66. Due to Roman Law (at this time), the Jews could not put Him to death. They besought Pilate to do this for them. The whole scenario was supervised by God in heaven (Acts 15:18).

(c) **"Lest they should be defiled."** Pious Jews considered the touch of a Gentile to be thoroughly defiling, thus disqualifying them from eating the Passover. When these particular men ate of this meal is not clear. Refusing to enter the dwelling of a pagan, they sent the soldiers in and out to communicate with the governor. We again see a mark of true religious hypocrites: always attending to the outside with great care, but void and corrupt within. The Savior had rebuked them regarding this about two days before. He said that they made "clean the outside of the cup and platter," (their physical bodies) but were filled with rottenness within (Matt. 23:25). They would not defile their feet and garments in the house of a cursed Gentile, but wanted to kill their sinless Messiah, Jesus of Nazareth, during the Passover celebration. Permission for His execution had to be obtained from the ruling governor.

2p-**"They might eat the passover."** This is a difficult text because it states these religious leaders had *not* yet eaten the Passover meal. John wrote looking back on history. We have noted that Christ and His apostles had eaten it after sunset (with the rest of Jerusalem) on the previous night, which was the accepted time. The story for this is found in the main heading of Section 170. There is no intimation here Christ had fulfilled the feast at the wrong time, or that He had chosen a different time as the critics affirm. We ask, "Why had these Jews not yet eaten of the meal?" A sensible answer is that they were forced to postpone it due to their involvement in making the tedious arrangements for the arrest, trials, and murder of Jesus. This involved securing the temple police and guards, servants from the high priest, and obtaining the soldiers from Pilate to assist in His arrest. *Above all, they sought to avoid the crowds, many of whom were sympathetic with Jesus.* Their rendezvous with Judas, the long walk to the garden and back to the city took them well past the midnight hour. When we remember that, the streets of Jerusalem were thronged with thousands of pilgrims at this time it makes more sense. It is an indisputable fact that the Sanhedrin broke *many* of their established laws during the trial of Jesus.

3p-**The "extra meal" after Passover.** We can easily believe that the Jews would violate the set time for eating Passover in their madness to destroy the Lord Jesus. When and where they ate it, we are not told in Scripture. Another point is that the term "eat the Passover" embraced not only consuming the lamb and other trimmings, but a custom called "Passover chagigah." This was eaten *after* the actual Passover meal was finished. It was also called the "Pascal festival," and included the seven days of unleavened bread. Any of these could be the meaning of this verse. Again, we refer to Lightfoot's *Commentary on the New Testament . . . ,* vol. 3, pages 420-423. He makes it abundantly clear that there were separate herds of oxen used for the chagigah meal (as there were lambs for Passover) and that these were eaten at a period after the Passover had ended. It was during the eating of this flesh that the Jews fulfilled Deut. 16:14 and "rejoiced in the [Passover] feast." John wrote this about the religious leaders of Israel. It could not have referred to a custom that followed their Passover celebration. Any factual and historical-based answer would be acceptable. Though we may not be able to determine, which is the correct one at least we know it is there. With these possibilities, any of which would solve this "problem text," why do the critics and heathen expositors rage against what God has written? Could it be that some of them are looking for contradictions in Scripture, which they secretly resent or hate in their unsaved souls? This is a "problem text" because the critics want a problem with God's Word. For other feasible conjectures regarding this matter, see *Gill's Commentary*, vol. 8. pages 101-102. *Davies' Harmony of the Gospels,* pages 134, 137 has an excellent article on this subject.

4p-After the Savior partook of the Passover in Section 174, there is no mention of the "after meal" called "chagigah," being observed by Him and the apostles. *It was not a compulsory obligation ordered in the Torah Law of Israel.* Read 3p- above for explanation of the "chagigah" meal.

(d) For the reason "why" the governor had to go to the Jews waiting outside his residence, see the first paragraph of footnote c above. Being a strict Roman, Pilate follows the judicial protocol with his question. His first words were those spoken by all presiding judges, "What accusation bring ye against this man?"

(e) The Jews replied to Pilate's question with the charge that He was a "malefactor," meaning both criminal and lawbreaker. It is not a mere assumption that Pilate had heard many things about Jesus, just as Herod Antipas had. The governor surely had his intelligence services busy watching the Man, who had turned the country upside down. He had willingly given a legion of military to bring Him in for the Jews to try. Being pre-informed, Pilate had been waiting in the early hours of that morning for the Sanhedrin to bring Jesus to his judgment seat. However, it was more than he bargained for! Things were different from what he had planned.

2p-**Verse 3. Judas saw that "he [the Lord Jesus] was condemned."** This clearly means that *Judas did not expect Christ to be condemned;* rather, the traitor thought that He would work some miracle or had devised a plan to affect His deliverance from the wrath of the Sanhedrin. When he saw that Christ was condemned to die, and did not deliver Himself, Judas panicked! Satan dwelling in his soul suggested suicide as the way out (verse 5.) He was quick to obey his master's command!

(f) **Judas returns the blood money**. He fulfilled prophecy in bringing back the silver. See footnote g below. We saw the traitor earlier debating with the Jews over the going price for Jesus, in Section 147, footnote c, d, and e. Judas was not, nor had he ever been a saved man. Christ made this clear in His high priestly prayer in John 17:12.

His repentance reveals that he did not think that his deed would result in such a monstrous thing. Many are the opinions of the word "repentance" used here of Judas. The author has no special comment on that. *However, he would dogmatically affirm that true repentance and faith in Christ resulting in salvation would not lead one to go and commit suicide!* Judas sought to return the silver to its original source, "the chief priests and elders" of Jewish religion. This adventure was casting pearls before swine. Now, they turn and rend the man from Kerioth! For further information on Judas, see Section 95, footnote x, and Section 146, footnote h.

(g) **"Betrayed innocent blood"** was a Hebraism referring to one who was put to death in their innocence. This expression is found in the Talmud at least fourteen times. For examples, see tractates, Baba Kama 119a and Sotah 46a. Judas applied it to the Messiah, which signified that he knew Jesus was a perfect Man! Had he not just spent something over two years with Christ, hearing, seeing, and feeling the impact of this wonderful Person? Here, we have a true confession but false repentance. The Jews made a big noise about shedding innocent blood in Israel. This is documented in Section 185, Matt. 27:25, footnote n. The scornful reply of these religious men into the face of Judas reveals their callousness toward one of their kind. They tell him, in essence "You made the deal, and we got the goods: look after your own guilt." Numbers 32:23 reads, "Be sure your sin will find you out." "And sin when it is finished bringeth forth death" (James 1:15). Only a few moments later Pilate said a similar thing about the innocence of Jesus in Section 185, Matt. 27:24, footnote m.

2p-**"What *is that* to us?"** This response of the religious leaders of Israel reflects their heartlessness toward a "pawn" they had previously used. Now, they are finished with him! Judas served their maligned purpose; they throw him out like a dirty rag. This deed explains Prov. 12:10b, "the tender mercies of the wicked *are* cruel."

(h) **Returned the money.** Where in the temple, Judas slammed down the silver pieces is not clear. His actions allude back to Zech. 11:13. Probably, it was in the Women's Court, also called the treasury. No doubt, it caused quite a stir with thousands of people always present. Surely great questions and whisperings were flying about regarding this erratic man who threw a handful of silver upon the floor of God's house. Many of them knew he was a "disciple" of Jesus. See footnote j below for more on this question.

(i) **"Hanged himself."** This means just what it says. The theological questioning of this awful act is wrong. Some forty days later, Peter, speaking of the traitor's death, said that Judas "purchased a field with the reward of iniquity; and falling headlong, he burst asunder in the midst, and all his bowels gushed out" (Acts 1:18). He hanged himself at some considerable height, and the rope or its attachment broke beneath the weight. His body fell into a ravine below, split open, and was disemboweled upon impact. It is of note that Peter stated his suicide was known unto "all dwellers at Jerusalem" (Acts 1:19). Word spread like wild fire of this event across the entire city filled with thousands of pilgrims present for Passover. See footnote f above.

2p-**"Not lawful."** See Deut. 23:18. The motto of the State of Virginia consists of the words of Brutus as he drove a knife into Caesar. In some way, these words describe Judas, the man who killed himself. Brutus shouted as his dagger pierced the wretched emperor, "Sic simper tyrannis" ("Thus always to tyrants"). Over the long, bloody course of human history, this motto remains valid. In God's time, all tyrants known and unknown will have a knife, in the hand of divine Justice, driven into their souls, though it seems she has forgotten their crimes. If the world should last ten million years, God's day of reckoning is coming for all men. *Reader, are you ready?*

(j) As a small lad, the author of this work vividly remembers strolling through an old cemetery with his father just east of Nashville, Tennessee. Upon seeing an area overgrown with weeds and clearly neglected, he inquired "Dad, who's buried in that place?" His response was, "Son, that's potter's field where the unwanted are buried." Various older cemeteries across the southern United States had a potter's field used to inter those who had no one to bury them. It is known from history that the place purchased with the blood money was located outside the southwestern wall of Jerusalem, near Mount Zion and was later used to bury Armenian Christians. See *Barnes' Commentary*, page 310. He quoted from an older publication known as the *Missionary Herald*, page 66, dated 1824.

2p-The Talmud in tractate Baba Bathra 25a, required Jews to bury their dead not under fifty cubits (75 feet) but usually much further from any town or village. This was done because of the smell and defilement. Dry and rocky places were selected for grave sites. If buried in the earth, all graves must be a foot and a half apart. It was counted dishonorable for one to walk over a burial plot. Roses and other flowers were *planted* on graves. In Jerusalem, all criminals and executed persons were buried in special places. Edersheim informs us in *Life and Times of Jesus the Messiah,* page 693-694, that among the various requirements for a fully organized community one is surprised to find nothing written about a cemetery. The list called for a law court, provision for the poor, a synagogue, a public bath, a doctor, a surgeon, a scribe, a butcher, and a schoolmaster. Jews called their cemeteries such names as "house of the dead," "house of silence," "house of stone," "the couch," and "the resting place." In time, they ruled against earth burials because of the pagan practice of cremation. Apparently, children not a month old were buried without a coffin and probably in a separate place. As in the case of Judas Iscariot, suicides, and criminals were not accorded the honors of those who died natural deaths. Unless family or friends collected their bodies, they were thrown on the city dump of Jerusalem. In some cases they were left to rot where they had died.

The dump was also known as gehenna. The Lord Jesus used it to picture the eternal home of the damned. For more on this, see Section 59, Matt. 10:28, footnote o.

(k) **"To this day."** Matthew wrote that the place to bury the unfortunate was called, "The field of blood, unto this day." This pungent declaration has reference to the "day" when Matthew penned his book to fellow Jews. The stories about Judas and what his silver had purchased were well known years afterwards. This is another indication that Matthew wrote his book a few years after its events. There is also a statement regarding the date of the book in Matt. 28:15. He wrote before the doom of A.D. 70. See *Appendix Seven*, for when the four gospels were written.

(l) This was a general quotation gathered from several Old Testament verses or words spoken by several prophets. The main thrust of the citation comes from Zech. 11:13 in words altered to suit the thought being presented. In Jer. 18:1-3, the weeping prophet visits the potter's house, and in Jer. 32:6-7 he buys a field. However, it is in Zechariah that the thirty pieces of silver are mentioned. God inspired Matthew to take certain words out from the verses of both writers and then blend them together to make this passage. *The gist is simply that Jeremiah said something, but Zechariah wrote it down years later.* Frequently, New Testament speakers and writers alike were inspired to use this method of writing. In Section 18, footnote h this subject is further discussed.

2p-Lk. 23:2. "Tribute to Caesar." This occurred earlier in the life of Christ when the Jews attempted to throw Him into conflict with the Roman authorities. This event is recorded in Section 155.

(m) **"Take and judge him according to your law."** Instantly, Pilate snaps back with this resolve. The Jews were dismayed at this sudden and unexpected response. It was customary for the Sanhedrin to obtain permission from their ruling governors to execute capital cases without many problems. Now, they had one! *Later, in Section 185, Matt. 27:18, we read that Pilate knew the Jews had delivered Jesus to them out of envy!* No doubt, this was the reason for his curt words and sudden change of attitude.

(n) **"Not lawful for us."** Reliable commentators have wrestled with this confession of the Jews. At this time, the Roman Senate did not permit Jewish courts, even the mighty Sanhedrin to implement the death penalty except in unusual situations: one of these being if a Gentile intruded into the innermost part of the temple. As seen in Paul's missionary work, the Romans flogged whomever they would (Acts 16:22-23; 2 Cor. 11:25). Rome's means of exacting death for its foes was usually crucifixion and decapitation. Some believe the Jewish courts had this right until A.D. 70, and others think it was withdrawn after A.D. 30. Whatever the truth is, it is sure that the Jews (in the case of Jesus) had to secure permission for His death. Regardless of the political reasons for this statement of the Jews, it was another of their lies to appear as "good citizens who were quick to obey the law" before Governor Pilate. (They hated Rome, and everything associated with it.)

2p-Verse 32. Here, is the prophetic reason as to why the Jews could not take Christ and kill Him. Old Testament Scripture had been written in which it was predicted that the Gentiles, and their rulers would share in His death. The classic example of this is Ps. 2:1-4 with Acts 4:25-28. However, the chief reason for this was to fulfill the teaching of Jesus over the past few years concerning His death. *Across the four gospels, our Lord spoke of His death and then His going away at least forty-two times!*

(o) **Verse 33.** At this point, Pilate walked back into his judgment chamber, sat upon the bema seat, and "called" Jesus to enter and stand before him. *We wonder what language they spoke.* For details of this ancient judge's bench, see Section 187, footnote h. This passage reads that he "called Jesus" (to himself) after entering into the judgment hall again. Pilate put his question to Jesus without any prompting from the milling crowds outside.

2p-Verse 11. Pilate's question. "Art thou the king of the Jews?" He had heard it whispered over his domains of Idumea, Judea, and Samaria that "Many people think this new prophet is the King of the Jews." This would have instantly been considered as a threat to Roman rule in the land. John gives the more comprehensive response of Christ to the governor's question. Jesus replied something like this, "Are you asking this question of your own initiative, or have others told you this thing?" According to Matthew, Mark, and Luke's record, our Lord then said, "Thou sayest," or "It is just as you said, I am the King of the Jews." Pilate asked the question and Christ answered, "You are right!" For more on the King of the Jews, see Section 25, number 19 under footnote a.

(p) The governor said, "I'm not a Jew and will not be influenced by Jewish religious politics against any person. Now, tell me what have you done to cause such hatred from your own people?" This honest question would be asked by any Roman judge seeking to resolve a dangerous situation.

(q) **"My kingdom is not of this world."** This response of the Lord Jesus requires no interpretation but rather acceptance. Radical dispensationalists run amuck here, terrified that these words may suggest that there will be no future for Israel in the divine plan of God for the ages! Nevertheless, their fears are in vain. It is foolish to hurry off to the Greek wording in this text and attempt to prove that it means something different from what it says. Christ affirms that He is the King of the Jews, and that one of the reasons for Him coming into the world was to fulfill this role. However, His kingdom at this time (later called the church) was not of that physical, material world, the only kind with which Pilate was acquainted. As a former Roman military officer, he understood a kingdom in which men fight, kill, and destroy the rule of others. *He had no concept of any rule or kingship other than those based on armed force. An unearthly royalty of divine nature from the hand of God in heaven was unheard of.* It is the same with world rulers today. There is a spiritual kingship, a world unseen by mortal eye over which the Son of God reigns. Its people live in holiness and loving self-sacrifice and are ever reaching out to bring others into its citizenship by the new birth. In response to Pilate, Jesus affirmed that His *present* kingdom was not of material substance, a literal, political kingdom. Pilate could not understand. Confused, he retorts back the question in footnote r below.

2p-What kind of kingdom? There is an ancient testimony (not tradition) emerging from history that suggests the nature of our Lord's kingdom. Doctor Lardner in *The Works of Nathanael Lardner*, vol. 1, pp. 154-155 informs us that Emperor Domitian, who ruled from A.D. 81-96, heard of Christ's kingdom and became fearful of what this implied. He had brought before him the grandsons of Jude, Jesus' half-brother, and interrogated them about this kingdom. Quoting an earlier writer Hegesippus, who was a Jew and supposedly converted to Christ, Lardner wrote, "At that time [shortly before A.D. 100] there was, yet remaining of the kindred of Christ, the grandsons of Jude, who was called [Jesus'] brother according to the flesh. Domitian asked Jude's grandsons what kind of kingdom Christ had and when it should appear. They answered that it was not worldly, nor terrestrial, but heavenly and angelic. It would be manifested in the end of the world." This is precisely what our Lord told Governor Pilate in verse 36 above. For an explanation of *both* manifestations of Christ's kingdom, the present spiritual one and the future glorified material one, refer to Section 39, footnotes a and g. See also, Section 171, paragraphs three through five of footnote b for the nature of His kingdom.

(r) Verse 37. "Are you a king or not?" Again, Pilate puts the provocative question to Jesus. The Savior agreed with his interrogator and affirmed that He was exactly that. His strange Words "everyone that is of the truth heareth my voice," were confusing to the governor. Being an astute Roman, he was acquainted with the philosophers of that day, each proclaiming their ideals as truth, and gathering disciples to follow them. The Greeks had left this legacy to the Romans, who quickly adopted it into their culture. Pilate must have mused, "Is this Jesus of Nazareth another of the thousands of philosophers of the day?" Over thirty years later, Paul reflecting on his knowledge of Jesus' trial wrote that Christ gave a good confession before Pilate (1 Tim. 6:13). *What an enlightening brief commentary this is on the trial of our Lord!* It reveals that Paul, who at that time was unsaved, yet was deeply familiar with the whole proceeding and knew what Jesus told the governor.

2p-Truth heareth my voice. This truism remains valid forever; it will not and cannot change. Men may know the truth about the sciences, and have profound knowledge in philosophy, history, and the arts. However, if they do not know Christ as personal Savior, they are among the most ignorant and unlearned persons on earth when it comes to eternal matters. Death will make this truth known to them; but often it will then be too late.

(s) Verse 38. "What is truth?" A pitiful question from a man of such worldly position and power! Christ had just affirmed that men of truth, wherever they were would, in time, hear His words. He came into the world to speak the truth that all men needed to hear. Those who will not hear are not the children of truth. Here, stands a *true Roman* with a trained, disciplined mind and will, steeled by years of service in the empire. He did have some insight into human nature, but sadly from the viewpoint of a darkened pagan, void of any genuine spiritual enlightenment. Strangely, he sensed deep in his heart that this Jew, torn, ragged, beaten, and bloody, standing before him was different. He was infinitely nobler than that screaming mob of sanctimonious accusers who stood before him.

2p-After asking the question, "What is truth?," he led Christ outside to face the Jews. Would things have been different had he waited for an answer? (Footnote o above explains when he first took Christ away from the screaming Jews into his judgment hall.) Again, outside and standing on the raised stone porch, Pilate lifted his right hand and spoke. A deep silence fell over the restless multitude as he said, "I find no fault in him at all." Pilate used a language they all understood. Was it Hebrew, Greek, or the Devil's language, Latin?

3p-"I find no fault in him." What a confession! No *honest* man has ever found any fault in Jesus Christ. Those who give Jesus a smile, then deny His deity, sinless life, death on the cross for our sins, and glorious resurrection are His greatest enemies. For more on this, see Section 52, footnote q.

(t) This peculiar amnesty of a criminal during Passover is explained in Section 185, Matt. 27:15, footnote d. It was here that Pilate first mentioned Barabbas, and then spoke of him up again a short time later. This reveals the governor knew exactly what was going on and followed the correct judicial procedures of Roman law.

(u) Verse 12. "Answered nothing." Upon the shock announcement of Pilate, the Jews went wild screaming in mad fury. Their Messiah stood in innocent quietness. The same thing is repeated in verse 14 below and its parallel. This was another fulfillment of Isa. 53:7. Pilate's proposed acquittal kindled their fury into hotter and fiercer flames.

2p-Verse 14. Hearing their shouts, Pilate takes Christ and returns to the judgment room within his quarters. Again, he questions our Lord. To his amazement, Jesus became silent! "He is brought as a lamb to the slaughter, and as a sheep before her shearers is dumb, so he openeth not his mouth" (Isa. 53:7).

(v) "Throughout all Jewry." For one time during this trial, the Jews now told the truth about Jesus. However, their words were in the form of fierce objections; they were incensed with rage. Pilate's ear suddenly heard someone shouting the word, "Galilee." With a stroke of genius (or so it seemed at the time), eager for any chance to get this Man off his hands he hit on a master plan to defuse the explosive situation. See next Section 184 for details of Pilate sending the Lord Jesus to Herod Antipas, another Roman ruler visiting Jerusalem at that time.

Attempting to rid himself of Jesus, Pilate sends Him to Herod Antipas who was present to observe the Passover.* Christ remained silent before the "fox" from Galilee. After being fiercely mocked by Herod's military, He is returned to Pilate. From this exchange, Herod Antipas and Governor Pilate became mutual friends after a long and bitter disagreement.

Time: Early morning of the crucifixion day on Friday.

*Herod was reported to be a proselyte to the Jewish religion, hence his presence on this annual occasion. For details regarding his life, see Section 21, Part 1, number 3 under footnote b, and Section 92, footnotes a, and e. The footnotes in this particular Section will provide more information into the life of this wicked man.

Matt.	Mk.	Lk. 23:6–12—*From Pilate's quarters to Herod, then back to Pilate*	John
		Pilate sends Jesus to Herod Antipas 6 When Pilate heard of Galilee, he asked whether the man were a Galilean. (a) 7 And as soon as he knew that he belonged unto Herod's jurisdiction, he sent him to Herod, who himself also was at Jerusalem at that time.(b) 8 And when Herod saw Jesus, he was exceeding glad: for he was desirous to see him of a long *season*, because he had heard many things of him; and he hoped to have seen some miracle done by him.(c) 9 Then he questioned with him in many words; but **he answered him nothing.**(d) 10 And the chief priests and scribes stood and vehemently accused him. ***He is mocked, ridiculed and returned to Pilate*** 11 And Herod with his men of war **set him at nought, and mocked him,**(e) and arrayed him in a gorgeous robe, and sent him again to Pilate. ***The innocent Savior makes enemies to become friends*** 12 And the same day Pilate and Herod were made friends together: for before they were at enmity between themselves.(f) (Verse 13 cont. in Section 185.)	

Footnotes-Commentary

(a) Though born in Judaea the Lord Jesus was considered a Galilean, having spent most of His life and ministry in that part of the land. Pilate asked the crowds if Jesus were a Galilean. Someone shouted back the affirmative answer.

(b) **Herod at Jerusalem.** With the response that Jesus was from Galilee, Pilate saw his way out of a serious problem, or so he thought. He had been at odds for several years with Herod Antipas who ruled to the north over all Galilee. See footnote f below for details. *We have the record of only one contemptuous expression used by our Lord, which was when He referred to Antipas as "that fox"* (Lk. 13:32). This was the Herod, who had murdered John the Baptist. He was a weakling ruled by a woman, his former sister-in-law, he had stolen from his half-brother Philip. He stands as a despicable figure, wretched, dissolute, drowned in his debauchery and the blood of his many victims. Friedrich W. Krummacher in his classic work *The Suffering Saviour* page 243, wrote of Herod these startling words: "A Sadducee according to his mental bias, more heathen than an Israelite, and entirely devoted to licentiousness, he was, nevertheless, as is often the case of such characters, not disinclined to base acts of violence and capable of the most refined cruelties."

2p-What was he doing in Jerusalem amid the several million Jewish pilgrims who had packed the city to observe Passover? Antipas was considered a Jew by birth, the son of a proselyte. At this time, he was the ruler over thousand of Jews across Galilee. He was currying political favor with the people while observing the Passover at the same time. When visiting Jerusalem, he and his great entourage stayed at an old palace-fortress built by the Maccabees located across the city almost against its west wall. This musty fort had been constructed over a century prior and remodeled. Joachim Jeremias in *Jerusalem in the Time of Jesus*, page 60, states that all members of the Herodian family when visiting the city had permanent lodging in this place.

(c) **Herod wanted to see Him.** The distance from Pilate's residence at the fortress just north of the temple to that of Herod's palace was about half the length of Jerusalem. Being escorted by a detachment of soldiers, members of the temple police, and according to verse 10, the chief priests, and scribes, Christ was led through the streets of Jerusalem again. This scene must have created something of a furor amid the thousands of pilgrims and the citywide stir that erupted over Him being arrested and tried by the Sanhedrin. Being pre-informed that Jesus was being sent to him, Herod Antipas waited anxiously to see the Man of whom he had heard so much. Many rumors filtered into his palace at Tiberias, as his servants and domestic workers all spoke of this wonderful Man. Amazingly, one of Herod's palace employees "Chuza," had a wife (Joanna) who was a follower of Jesus. See this recorded in Section 65, Lk. 8:3, second paragraph of footnote f. "Heard many things" must have included news about His miracles, great deeds and conflict with the religious leaders. This demonstrates that word concerning Jesus of Nazareth had covered the country and went everywhere, even into the palaces of the rulers. Though the Lord Jesus had been reared in Herod's jurisdiction, had preached across the land of Galilee and done many wonders there. It seems that Herod had never seen the Savior. Luke wrote that he wanted Jesus to perform a miracle. His wish was not granted!

(d) **"He answered him nothing."** The silent Sheep is now before His shearers. He fulfills again the prediction made some seven hundred years prior in Isa. 53:7. Our Lord remained silent several times during His trial. Refer to this in Section 183, Matt. 27:12 and 14, footnote u. He fulfilled more than once the prediction of Isaiah. Shocked by the passive attitude of Jesus, Herod Antipas launched a barrage of questions, no doubt regarding His work, John the Baptist preaching throughout the land and the many stories he had heard of Him. The silence of Christ infuriated Herod even further. Donald Guthrie in his work, *Jesus the Messiah*, page 337, makes this terse comment regarding Antipas, "He probably had never been confronted with such silent strength." The quieter Christ became, the louder were the charges from the chief priests and scribes also present (verse 10). They went along, being fearful, that Herod might let Him go. Luke wrote that they "vehemently accused him" (verse 10). The Son of God refused to indulge in the curiosity of this tyrant ruler or his ruthless military. He answered Herod in neither word nor deed. One can believe that Herod was both amazed and astounded at the meek and quiet conduct of this carpenter from Galilee, of whom he had heard so much.

2p-Silence of Christ. It was of patience, not of indifference, of courage, and not of cowardice. He was not silent when it was necessary for truth to be spoken or defended. A sterling example was His confession that He was Israel's Messiah, as seen in Section 181, Matt. 26:63-64, footnotes h and i. Another of His profound silences came a short time later before Pilate in John 19:9. Then suddenly He broke His own verbal moratorium and explained to the Roman Governor the true source of power and authority (John 19:10-11).

3p-Silence or sound? It is written in Eccles. 3:7, "There is a time for silence and a time to speak." Silence can be both golden and treacherous! When it is time to speak God's truth men must speak, regardless! Jesus demonstrated this in the above. The author knew a Christian Jew, living in a communist land, who taught the Bible for eleven hours taking only an hour's break for food and short trips to the toilet. The entire congregation sat on the floor with their eyes riveted on the preacher. How different today. The average congregation cannot bear thirty minutes of *true* Bible preaching. On one particular Sunday, in Africa, the author preached ten times to different groups scattered over a fifty mile radius. The last congregation plead with him to "stay a longer and tell us more." Paul spoke "from morning to evening" to those who came into his rented house in Rome, Italy (Acts 28:23).

(e) Highlighted in gray, for a thousand years earlier it was written in prophecy that Christ would be the object of scorn and ridicule in Ps. 22:7. The soldiers were a company of personal bodyguards that traveled with Antipas. The text is clear that *both* Herod and his men mocked the Lord Jesus. When men of this vile caliber are frustrated, then the most savage vulgarity pours out; they are ruthless in their cruelty. The exact type of mockery is not stated, yet it must have revolved around His being the King of the Jews. Throwing a "gorgeous robe" over His shoulders and mocking Him as King, they sent Him back across the city to Pilate. The word "gorgeous" means "brilliant and shining." It was a stark contrast to the modest dress of our Lord. History records occasions of men assigned to die who were often dressed in bright robes called "a fools coat." A while later, Pilate's soldiers would also afford the Lord similar treatment prior to His crucifixion (Section 186, Matt. 27:28, footnote b). What were the reactions of the crowds along the streets as they led the Savior back to the castle and governor Pilate?

(f) **Two killers are now "friends together."** There had been serious trouble between Herod and Pilate for years. In Lk. 13:1, we read of the time when Pilate, in a rage actually killed some Galileans and mixed their blood with the sacrifices they had brought to offer in the temple. It should be remembered that all Galileans were Herod's subjects and not Pilates. Both legally and technically, he was out of order in killing these people. This would have greatly offended Herod Antipas. See next paragraph for more on this subject.

2p-History records what the problem *real* was between these two men. Herod was a long time ruler in the land of Israel (from 4 B. C to A.D. 39) in comparison to the newcomer, Pilate, the fifth governor in the land (from 26 to A.D. 36). Being greatly unfamiliar with Hebrew customs, when Pilate entered into Jerusalem to assume his governorship, he made a deathly mistake! His soldiers carried flags, banners, and golden plated shields having the figure of the pagan emperor, and idolatrous images on them. They marched to the castle of Antonio and hung their shields on the walls. (One account says they were also hung on the outside of the temple wall and on the gates.) Being painted with pagan gods and emblems, the Jews flew into a rage and demanded they be immediately taken down from their temple. In a wild fit of anger, Pilate refused, and a bloody battle ensued with hundreds killed and wounded by Pilate's superior forces. This is what created the rift between these two rulers. Jesus, that wonderful Man, so meek and quiet, who was such an enigma to both Pilate and Antipas, restored their friendship. How amazing are the ways of Jesus Christ even among the godless.

3p-Herod sharply reproved Pilate for his actions. It became so bad that some fifty Jewish dignitaries made an appeal to Emperor Tiberius at Rome. Pilate, realizing this could cost him his job or head, ordered the shields to be removed, and at the instructions of the emperor, they were transferred to the temple of Augustus, located at Caesarea. For the details, see, *Herod Antipas. A Contemporary of Jesus Christ*, pages 176-180 by Harold W. Hoehner, and *A History of the Jewish People in the Time of Jesus Christ*, vol. II, pages 82-84, by Emil Schurer. Now, however, the old wound was to be healed. Herod was greatly pleased that Pilate had openly acknowledged his authority by sending one under his jurisdiction to him for legal determination. How beautiful it is that Jesus the peacemaker mended the rift between two of history's biggest political tyrants. Men pray that God would somehow bring together the leaders of world nations into a bond of lasting peace. All such reasoning is vain, for most of the political leaders of this present world and those to come will have none of Jesus Christ. His holy Name may be covertly invoked, for personal advantage, in a word, speech, or private prayer, but who He is and what He demands of mankind they resent with fierce passion. The Name "Jesus Christ" is abused, blasphemed, and employed in the grossest of profanity in Washington D. C., all political circles, and the public domain in general. However, to mention it publicly in sacred prayer or deep reverence is to bring scorn and risk of litigation. This is how twisted American society has become. The Bible says, "Woe unto them that call evil good, and good evil: that put darkness for light, and light for darkness; that put bitter for sweet, and sweet for bitter" (Isa. 5:20). *God meant that!*

4p-Christian stupidity and the original meaning of atheist. If the Savior could mend the break between Pilate and Herod, both being godless men, what has happened among those "Christians" who hate one another and carry their grudges to the grave or hell? Eloquent robed clerics standing in perfect posture give soupy sermons from two-thousand dollar pulpits every Sunday, while their congregations sink deeper into sin, despair, and damnation. Jesus Christ is not real to these people, and many of them do not want Him to be real! Years ago, I visited the local Presbyterian pastor. During our little chat, I asked to hear his testimony of conversion of Christ. This elderly, white-headed man, leaped to his feet, and with a red face, and raging voice ordered me out of his house. (Not all Presbyterian ministers are like this, just those who serve the Devil.) The finger of God writes on the wall about our sins, but blind eyes cannot read the message. That is real "Christian stupidity!" President Calvin Coolidge (died 1933) was a man of few words. When returning from church one Sunday, his wife inquired, "What did the pastor preach about?" He grunted, "About sin." She asked again, "And what did he say, Calvin?" Coolidge replied, "He's against it!" God is also against sin; so much that He sent His Son to die on the cross for sinners (Rom. 5:6-8). The attitude of President Coolidge should be the attitude of every, truly saved Christian, whether we understand it all or not. The Russian writer, Feodor Dostoevski (died 1881) summed up when he wrote, "Every one of us is guilty of everything before everyone." The Bible puts it this way, "For all have sinned, and come short of the glory of God" (Rom. 3:23). For further explanation of the spiritual state of men, see Section 48, the second and third paragraphs of footnote h, Section 76, second and third paragraphs of footnote f, and Section 178, second paragraph of footnote n. The devastating words of Isa. 1:5-6 reveal the state of all men without Jesus Christ as their *real* personal Lord and Savior. *For the other side of this bizarre story, called "atheistic stupidity" see Section 12, twelfth paragraph of footnote k.* It is indeed an interesting fact that the word "atheist," originally was given to the first Christians who refused to worship the multiple pagan gods and goddesses of the Roman Empire. They dubbed were "atheist" because they believed in the only true and living God and not the inventions of demon-possessed pagans.

5p-Something is wrong. *Every religion confesses that something is broken with mankind.* Only rightly divided Scripture reveals the problem and its answer. As stated in the 4p- above, Adam's race has been devastated by sin! All mortals are victims of this curse that has separated us from God. Its wages, unless canceled are eternal death (Matt. 25:41 with Rom. 6:23). Our sins have offended God's holiness and insulted His justice. They must be forgiven or judged. The very God, who is angered over our wickedness, has provided the means for their total remission and our full reconciliation back into His loving favor. Jesus Christ is the final solution for lost humanity. In His death on the cross, He bore sin's punishment for us and provided the only atonement that pleases the Almighty. Men can only partake of this blessing by faith in Christ. In the case of Herod Antipas and Governor Pilate, even there the Son of God influenced the godless into a renewed human friendship (Lk. 23:12). The apostles and early Christians linked Pilate and Herod to the death of Christ in Acts 4:27. Some nine years later, both rulers were expelled from their positions by the emperor and died infamous deaths in banishment. What a curious twist in history: Jesus standing before Herod, "that fox," was silent amid terrible humiliation, but ironically, He reconciled two of history's biggest scoundrels. For a brief but helpful and documented discussion of this and related subjects, see *Chronological Aspects of the Life of Christ*, pages 109-111, by Harold W. Hoehner. You who read these lines will meet *both* Pilate and Herod someday in the judgment of God! Will you stand as a Christ rejecter as they did? Our sins and guilt are abolished in Christ when He died for all of them on the cross. Note p4- above and avoid being another "stupid Christian."

PILATE'S SECOND AND THIRD VERDICTS

Events that occurred before the Roman Governor and the enraged Jews. Frustrated, Pilate seeks to free the Lord Jesus. * Fiercely objecting, the Jews prefer a criminal-murderer instead of Christ to be released. Pilate's wife sends an urgent message to her distraught husband. Jesus is scourged and delivered to die.

Time: Early morning of the crucifixion day on Friday.

*Several weeks after His death, resurrection and ascension, Peter addressing the Jews in the temple said of Pilate, that "he was determined to let him [Jesus] go" (Acts 3:13). Pilate's intentions were well known but he failed.

At Pilate's quarters in the Castle of Antonio just north of the temple area

Matt. 27:15	Mk. 15:6	Lk. 23:13-18	(John 19:1)
		The Jews with Pilate **13** And Pilate, when he had called together the chief priests and the rulers and the people,	
	For the chronology of ▶ *Pilate's judgments of our Lord, see the Information Box at the end of Section 183 marked by the symbol* ◉ *at Mk. 15:5.*	***Pilate's second verdict*** **14** Said[a] unto them, "Ye have brought this man unto me, as one that perverteth the people: and, **behold, I, having examined** *him* **before you, have found no fault in this man touching those things whereof ye accuse him:**[b]	
		Wicked Herod found him innocent **15** "**No, nor yet Herod: for I sent you to him;**[c] **and, lo, nothing worthy of death is done unto him.** **16** "I will therefore chastise him, and release *him*."	
A prisoner release is enacted **15** Now at *that* feast the governor was wont to release unto the people a prisoner,[d] whom they would.	***A prisoner release is enacted*** **6** Now at *that* feast he released unto them one prisoner,[d] whomsoever they desired.	***A prisoner release is enacted*** **17** (For of necessity he must release one unto them at the feast.) **18** And they cried out all at once, saying, "Away with this *man*, and release unto us	◄*Luke records the objection of the crowds here. Mark puts in in verse 8 below.*

Matt. 27:16–21	Mk. 15: 7–11	Lk. 23:18–20	(John 19:1)
16 And they had then a notable▶ prisoner, called Barabbas.(e)	**7** And there was one▶ named Barabbas,(e) *which lay* bound with them that had made insurrection with him, who had committed murder in the insurrection.	Barabbas:" ◀*For more on this man, see right vertical column at Luke 23:25 below.* **19** (Who for a certain sedition made in the city, and for murder, was cast into prison.)	
17 Therefore when they were gathered together, Pilate said unto them, "Whom will ye that I release unto you? Barabbas, or Jesus which is called Christ?" (Messiah)	**8** And the multitude crying aloud began to desire *him to do* as he had ever done unto them. **9** But Pilate answered them, saying, "Will ye that I release unto you the King of the Jews?"		
18 For he knew that for envy(f) they had delivered him.	**10** For he knew that the chief priests had delivered him for envy.(f)		
Mrs. Pilate's message **19** When he was set down on the judgment seat, his wife(g) sent unto him, saying, "Have thou nothing to do with that just man: for I have suffered many things this day in a dream because of him."			
20 But the chief priests and elders persuaded the multitude that they should ask Barabbas,(h) and destroy Jesus.	**11** But the chief priests moved the people, that he should rather release Barabbas(h) unto them.		
Pilate pleads again **21** The governor(i)		*Pilate pleads again* **20** Pilate(i) therefore, willing to release Jesus,	

Matt. 27:21-24	Mk. 15:12-14	Lk. 23:20-23	(John 19:1)
answered and said unto them, "Whether of the twain will ye that I release unto you?" They said, "Barabbas."	▶ *The word "again" in Lk. 20:20 reveals that Pilate tried a second time to get Jesus acquitted.*	spake again ◀ to them.	
Life's most serious question	*Life's most serious question*		
22 Pilate saith unto them, "What shall I do then with Jesus which is called Christ?"**(j)** *They* all say unto him, "Let him be crucified."**(k)**	**12** And Pilate answered and said again unto them, "What will ye then that I shall do *unto him* whom ye call the King of the Jews?"**(j)** **13** And they cried out again, "Crucify**(k)** him."	**21** But they cried, saying, "Crucify**(k)** *him*, crucify him." ▶**Pilate's third verdict**	
23 And the governor said, "Why, what evil hath he done?"**(l)**	**14** Then Pilate said unto them, "Why, what evil hath he done?**(l)**	**22** And he said unto them the third time, "Why, what evil hath he done?**(l)** **I have found no cause of death in him: I will therefore chastise him, and let him go."**	◀*For the chronology of Pilate's judgments of Jesus, see the symbol ◉ in Section 183, at Mk. 15:5..*
The Jews fiercely respond But they cried out the more, saying, "Let him be crucified."	*The Jews fiercely respond* And they cried out the more exceedingly, "Crucify him."	*The Jews fiercely respond* **23** And they were instant with loud voices, requiring that he might be crucified. And the voices of them and of the chief priests prevailed.	
Pilate's infamous hand washing **24** When Pilate saw that he could prevail nothing, but *that* rather a tumult was made, he took water, and washed**(m)** *his* hands before the multitude, saying, "I am innocent of the blood of this just			

897

Matt. 27:24-26	Mk. 15:15	Lk. 25:24-25	John 19:1
person: see ye *to it.*"			
The Jews self imposed a terrible curse			
25 Then answered all the people, and said, "His blood *be* on us, and on our children."[(n)]			
The murderer freed	***The murderer freed***	***The murderer freed***	
26 Then	**15** And *so* Pilate, willing to content the people,	**24** And Pilate gave sentence that it should be as they required.	
released[(o)] he Barabbas unto them: and	released[(o)] Barabbas unto them,	**25** And he released[(o)] unto them him▶ that for sedition and murder was cast into prison, whom they had desired; but he delivered Jesus to their will. (Verse 26 cont. in Section 188.)	◀*Barabbas. In verse 16, Matthew calls him "notable." In verse 7, Mark calls him a political fighter guilty of murder and bound in prison. Luke in verses 19 and 25 described Barabbas as being guilty of "murder" and "sedition" somewhere in Jerusalem. John 18:40 says he was a "robber." See footnote e below for more.*
	and delivered Jesus,		
			John 19:1
			1 Then Pilate therefore took Jesus, and scourged[(p)] him. (Verse 2 cont. in Section 186.)
when he had scourged[(p)] Jesus, he delivered [to the soldiers] *him* to be crucified.[(q)] (Verse 27 cont. in Section 186.)	when he had scourged[(p)] *him*, to [the soldiers to] be crucified.[(q)] (Verse 16 cont. in Section 186.)		
▶ *Matthew places the scourging of Jesus before being delivered to the soldiers, while Mark places it afterward. John only mentions the beating.*			

Footnotes–Commentary

[(a)] Again, Pilate finds himself in a great dilemma. By transferring the proceedings to Herod Antipas, he hoped to have escaped a painful situation and the angry Jews. Sorely disappointed, the governor is informed that Jesus is being returned to him for judgment. To the shock of the screaming Jews, Pilate stands on the porch of the Castle of Antonio, raises his hands, and legally absolves Christ from all criminalities. He shouted loudly so that the wild mob could hear his verdict. He affirms the innocence of the Savior for the second time! Up to this point, he had fairly judged the circumstances, rightly evaluated the situation, and spoke the truth regarding Jesus. See footnote f below.

[(b)] Nothing of which they accused Him was justified. Their charges were all groundless and false. This was the second verdict given by the presiding judge.

(c) **"I sent you to him."** It is noted here that Pilate had ordered the Jews to go with Jesus to Herod's palace and stand in on the trial by Antipas and his ruthless military. See Section 184, footnote c for more on this action of Pilate. *Pilate affirmed that even Herod Antipas could find no fault in the Lord Jesus.*

(d) **Release a prisoner.** Unsaved critics of Holy Scripture have pounced upon this custom. They point out that it is not mentioned in ancient history, especially in the writings of Josephus. Therefore, this biblical statement is wrong! (As if these critics had access to all the annals of history during this time or any other.) As far back as 1949, the skeptic Pierre van Passen in his book, *Why Jesus Died*, page 171 wrote, "this custom had never existed except in the imagination of the evangelists." In these words, this late religious infidel demonstrated his ignorance. History reveals a Roman celebration called "Lectisternium" meaning "couches." It was observed during times of public grief and great calamity. Gods and goddesses were removed from their pedestals and laid on couches. Enemies forgot their hatred, and all prisoners were liberated. However, some think it had its origin in the emperor's birthday when prisoners were freed. For an earlier mention of this "academic" approach to denying the authority of Scripture, note Section 18, Matt. 2:16, footnote d. Nowhere in the Torah Law is it suggested that a criminal, murderer, and robber be set free as a token of Jewish good will on the Passover, or any other feast. *This custom originated with the Romans, not the Hebrews.* It was designed to show mercy before their demonic gods and hope to secure their favor.

2p-Dr. Josef Blinzer in *The Trial of Jesus,* pages 207-208, explains, "Two forms of amnesty existed in Roman Law, the *abolitio,* or the acquittal of a prisoner not yet condemned, and the *indulgentia,* or pardoning of one already condemned." Blinzer concludes that it was the first form of amnesty that Pilate intended to use for Jesus. More importantly, we note that the Jews chose the murderer to go free, an act that signified that they had absolved Barabbas from all charges. In Matt 27:25 it is "all the people" who shouted for a curse upon themselves and their children, in order to kill Jesus. How could it be that the people who, only a few days prior on Palm Sunday, had welcomed Jesus into Jerusalem with shouts of loud praises, now scream for His death? Their shouts changed from "Hosanna to the son of David," to "crucify Jesus." Some weeks later, Peter berated the people of Jerusalem with sharp words for this choice (Acts 3:13). It was the sovereign purpose of God, established before the foundation of the world, and was accomplished without arm twisting or forcing any free will. Man chooses, and God disposes.

(e) **"Barabbas."** Pilate's words in Matt. 27:16-17 reveal that he was familiar with who was in prison at Jerusalem. Whoever Barabbas was, he is described in Scripture as being guilty of both insurrection and sedition or political overthrow. In the process some innocent persons had been murdered. When this particular insurrection occurred, we do not know. Barabbas is described by Matthew as a "notable prisoner." This meant that there was public notoriety attached to him. Note the following about this man:

1. "Barabbas" meant "the son of the father."
2. Jesus our Lord is heaven's unique "Barabbas" or "the Son of the Father." Thus, we have two men bearing the same name or title. Why did Pilate select this infamous prisoner with a title exactly like that of Christ, as the alternative to the Savior? It seems that the politically astute and clever governor would have chosen one of the two thieves who were then sitting in prison, and later crucified with Him.
3. Men today face the same choice. They too must choose between "Jesus the Son of God" and "Barabbas the son of an unknown earthly father?" Reader, which have you chosen? How odd that all the good and mercy contained in the blessed redeemer seemed worthless in the eyes of His haters whom He loved and came first to save. They preferred a guilty killer with blood on his hands to the sinless Son of God.

2p-Verse 17. Even Pilate knew Jesus was called "Christ" or "Messiah." News that He was the Messiah had reached his ears as well as those of every informed person in the land. He said the same thing again of our Lord in Matt. 27:22. Twice he called Jesus the Messiah.

(f) **"For envy they had delivered him."** Pilate well knew that out of envy they had brought Jesus to him. What pertinent words! This shows that he understood the hatred of the religious leaders for Jesus of Nazareth. The heathen procurator, former sailor in the Roman navy, cavalry officer, and politician, sees through the pernicious schemes to have Jesus put to death. A raw pagan had more insight than the religious men of Israel did. It is to be remembered that God in His sovereignty overruled and used the actions of men and history to provided salvation by the death of His Son. The plan of eternal life was established in eternity before the foundation of the world (Acts 15:18 with 1 Peter 1:19-20). It became a historical reality in time, by the death, burial, and resurrection of Christ.

(g) **Pilate's wife.** Matthew wrote that Pilate seated himself on the judgment bench or bema usually called "the chair of state." It was from this posture that he officially announced judgment in all cases tried. Suddenly, a servant rushed forward and thrusts into his hand a note scribbled in Latin. It was unheard of for the wife of any Roman dignitary to interfere in judicial proceedings. In an old apocryphal writing known as the *Gospel of Nicodemus,* her name is given as Claudia Porcula. Several sources read that she was (of all things) a proselyte to the Jewish religion! See *The Life of Christ,* pages 673-674, by F. W. Farrar. Joseph Blinzler, in his work, mentioned above, *The Trial of Jesus,* page 217 has an instructive footnote in which he documents various sources that affirm how many Roman women of rank became proselytes to the Jewish religion; even "Poppaea, wife of Emperor Nero," was one of them! In Ethiopian literature, Pilate's wife was named "Abrokla." As it was still very early in the morning hours, she had spent a troubled night, with dreams about this just Man, Jesus of Nazareth. Stirred by that dream, she did a most unheard of thing. A servant was sent to intrude into Pilate's hearing of Jesus, and place the warning note into her husband's hand.

2p-We quickly forget most dreams. A few we think are remarkable, and only now and then is one impressed upon us for years. This one engrained itself into the very soul of Pilate's wife. She must warn her husband (the judge!) to dismiss this Jesus. More is here than the sacred text records. In some inexplicable way, a wife stands between her husband, and history's most hideous crime, yet the providence of Jehovah rides the waves in this raging sea. When we recall that, the Romans had a strong superstition that "morning dreams would come true," the whole drama takes on a cloak of divine mystery. Pilate had climbed out of bed early that morning to meet the Jews with Jesus, and left her to sleep. Sleep's sweet rest fled as dreams of Jesus pierced her soul. She must warn her husband!

3p-Ironically, there had been a similar dream by the wife of another famed Roman, Julius Caesar. In 44 B.C., Calpurnia had warned her husband Julius not to go to the senate house on a particular day for she had dreamed he would be assassinated. Not heeding the word of a woman, Caesar was stabbed to death by the hands of Brutus and Cassias. The Roman writer Suetonius (born circa. A.D. 75), has left specific details about Julius' murder in his work *Suetonius,* vol. I, Book 1, pages 107-109. Walter M. Chandler in his book *The Trial of Jesus*, vol. 2, page 24 quotes from the apocryphal gospel mentioned above. He gives alleged contents of Mrs. Pilate's benighted letter. Though only a tradition, there is something uncanny about the last sentence of her appeal. "O Pilate, evil waits thee if thou wilt not listen to the prayer of thy wife." *Assuming* that our Lord was put to death in about A.D. 30, about six years later Pontius Pilate was removed from his glory by the Roman Senate in A.D. 36-37 and died in infamy. For alleged details of his death, see Section 21, Part 1, number 2, under footnote b.

4p-All the objections about Roman rulers not being allowed to take their wives with them while on foreign duty is a favorite sport for Bible critics. It was not a fixed rule. However, after the death of Augustus in A.D. 14, the new emperor, Tiberius, did not maintain this prohibition. The ancient historian Tacitus wrote of Roman officials having their wives with them while on foreign duty. See Tacitus, *Annals,* Book 3. 33-34.

(h) Release Barabbas. The place reverberated with their united shout. The erring Jewish people reeling under the results of their rejection of Jesus the Messiah scream out of the blindness of their awful sin that they prefer a murderer to the sinless Son of God.

(i) "Pilate, willing to release Jesus." Apparently moved by his wife's warning note, he again affirmed the innocence of Christ before the blood thirsty crowds.

(j) "What shall I do then with Jesus which is called 'Christ?'" Upon hearing their cries, Pilate asked of these blackguards the greatest of human questions. As if it were choursed from the regions of the damned, with a single voice, they all screamed in furious unison, "Crucify him." This question from the Gentile heathen, Pilate, is most instructive. Where did he learn that Jesus of Nazareth was popularly called "Christ" or Messiah? Even from the mouth of a Roman who worshiped demonic idols of many sorts, comes the truth that Jesus was the "Messiah." This impregnable fact of the Scriptures and history remains just as valid now as when Pilate asked his question to the incensed Jews over two thousand years ago.

(k) "Crucify him." Only when one has heard an eastern mob screaming for blood will they understand the absolute horror of scenes and sounds such as this. The entire crowd agreed to kill Jesus, having been instigated by the priests and elders. Behind this awful scene and terrible clamor, the sovereignty of God Almighty overruled and directed every move to His glory and the salvation of lost mankind (Acts 2:23). "A man's heart deviseth his way: but the LORD directeth his steps" (Prov. 16:9). "Surely the wrath of man shall praise thee" (Ps. 76:10).

(l) "Why, what evil hath he done?" "I find no cause of death in him." The governor knew more about Jesus than he could say. Here, Pilate gave his third judgment of Christ. *Innocent again!* With this, the chief priests and elders incited the Jews into mob hysteria. Standing in front of the judgment hall at the Castle of Antonio, they urged the crowds to request the release of Barabbas, and demanded death for Christ. The place reverberated with their united shout. The Jewish people reeling under the results of their rejection of the Messiah scream out that they preferred a murderer to the sinless Son of God.

(m) Verse 24. Pilate washes his hands. Pilate's hand washing ritual was a well-known symbolism used by both Jews and Gentiles. It is mentioned in the Torah Law in Deut. 21:6-7. See also Ps. 26:6. The Talmud speaks of it in tractate, Sotah 45b. Pilate performed this washing as a gesture before the incensed Jews demonstrating that he was guiltless of killing an innocent man! Clearly, the thousands of onlookers would have understood his actions. The governor was conforming to a well-known Jewish custom. The Jews comprehended this and responded with a roar, that Jesus' blood should be placed on them and their children. A few years prior, there was an occasion when pagan Greeks sacrificed doves in front of a Jewish synagogue at Caesarea, and then washed their hands. This was to mock the Hebrews as being filthily leprous people who were supposed to use doves in their ritual dealing with leprosy. The traitor Judas did a similar thing regarding the blood of Jesus, when he attempted to return the guilt money to the religious leaders. For the meaning of "innocent blood," see Section 183, Matt. 27:4, footnote g. Both Jews and Gentiles who read these lines need to know that it is the heart that first need washing, not the hands!

(n) **"His blood *be* on us, and on our children."** What a horrible imprecation! The ancients in their hot passion for vengeance would shout rash oaths. They were saying, "The guilt in putting Jesus to death should be laid us and our children." So sensitive were the rabbis about killing the guiltless that the Talmud in tractate, Sotah 46a reads, "Innocent blood cannot remain in the land of Israel." One shudders at such an affirmation from the incensed crowds. How noticeable that only a few months later these very Jews were trying to stop the apostles' preaching the gospel of Christ on the basis, "you have filled Jerusalem with your doctrine, and intend to bring this man's [Jesus] blood upon us" (Acts 5:28). About forty years later, this self-imposed curse hit their city, temple, and children. Millions were slaughtered. So great was the number put to death on Roman crosses outside the walls of Jerusalem, that no more trees or wood could be found about the city for several miles. Some five hundred Jews died each day upon the cruel tree of the cross. During the siege and destruction of the city, thousands perished by famine, suicide, fire, arrows, and stones flung through the air from powerful catapults. Hebrew blood ran in the streets and temple compound like thick muddy water. They had despised and rejected the Son of God their Messiah. Now, their own curse fell upon them. The thousands spared in the massacre were taken to Rome and forced to march in the triumphal entry of the conquering legions. Others, especially young people, were sold into slavery. Jacob's sons were sown as chaff into the four winds and became the scorn of the world. Some twenty years before the doom of Jerusalem, Paul, knowing of their fate, wrote of his own Jewish people, "The wrath [of God] is come upon them to the uttermost" (1 Thess. 2:15-16). Their request for blood to be on them and their children was granted four decades later. Section 163, describes the massacre of the Hebrew people and the horrors that come upon them in A.D. 70. *This calamity had nothing to do with a real tribulation period that would fall over two thousand years later.*

2p-A short time later Jesus made His way to Calvary. He stopped and warned the women who followed and bewailed His fate of the coming doom at the hands of the Romans (Lk. 23:27-31).Those who lift these words from their context and apply them to Israel over two thousand years later in a tribulation period have *seriously* misapplied Scripture. Not even the famed "secondary application" will fit the setting, historical context, and background of our Savior's Words on this occasion. Christians who take this statement concerning the Jews as justification for the history long persecution and slaughter of these people by tyrants are seriously wrong. Millions hate the nation of Israel. Satan, who seeks vengeance on the people that gave us our Savior, fosters this hatred.

(o) **"Released Barabbas."** A first reading of verse 26 indicates that Barabbas was present as Pilate spoke the command for his freedom before the multitude. Seated on the tribunal or bema, he reluctantly announced death upon Christ to satisfy the Jews. These men, who decried the death of any person on their beloved Passover Feast, again break their laws. Hatred and envy often make exceptions to the rigid rules of religious zealots.

(p) **"Pilate scourged Jesus."** This fulfilled Ps. 129:3, "The plowers plowed upon my back: they made long their furrows." All four evangelists record the scourging of Jesus, but are inspired to give different, yet true details. It was customary (but not compulsory) among Romans for the officiating judge to whip or beat a slave who had been sentenced to death by crucifixion. Normally, a soldier did the beating though it was ascribed to the political official. Possibly, Pilate did the beating in order to save his skin from the furious Jews, who had just accused him of a death-serious crime against the emperor. The ancient writer, Suetonius, informs us in his work, *Caligula 26*, that in the provinces of the empire, it was the work of the soldiers to scourge the condemned. John's words in 19:1 that Pilate "took Jesus," could mean that he removed the Savior from the judgment porch and placed Him into the hands of the soldiery, to implement the scourging. History mentions these beatings being so severe that some died before their crucifixion. The Lord Jesus is treated as a criminal and receives their pre-death treatment. Crucifixion was a Roman mode of inflicting the capital sentence. The Anglican F. W. Farrar in *The Life of Christ,* pages 675-677 gives a detailed description of the magisterial whipping of the condemned. "The unhappy sufferer was publicly stripped, was tied by the hands in a bent position to a pillar, [in front of the judgment hall] the tense quivering nerves of the naked back, [then] the blows were inflicted with leathern thongs, weighted with jagged edges of bone and lead ... the blows [sometime] fell with terrible barbarity on the face and eyes." Farrar continues, "And this awful cruelty, on which we dare not dwell—this cruelty, which makes the heart shudder, was followed by the third bitterest derision—the derision of Christ as King." Cunningham Geikie gives a horrible picture, in colorful words of this cruel event in *The Life and Words of Christ,* pages 768-769. This acceleration of His passion carries us into a dark abyss. His sufferings become torture, His disgrace, infamy. Isaiah wrote, "He is despised and rejected of men; a man of sorrows and acquainted with grief: and we hid as it were our faces from him," (Isa. 53:3), are being fulfilled.

2p-A few moments later, Pilate pronounced a fourth and fifth judgment upon Christ. Shouting to the maddened crowds, again he said that he *found no fault in the King of the Jews*. See Section 187, John 19: 4-6 with appropriate highlighted headings for these two final verdicts. Note Section 185, Matt. 27:26 which reads, Pilate "delivered him [to the soldiers] to be crucified." Note next Section 186, Matt. 27:27-30, footnotes a through d, for the treatment afforded Christ by the soldiers before leading Him to Mount Calvary.

(q) **"To be crucified."** Crucifixion was the most infamous death in human history. Often pagan historians and writers decried this awful means of executing men and women. Many of them called for its abolition from history and human memory. For an explanation of this horrible death, see Section 189, footnotes a and b.

Pilate yields to the Jew's demand to have Jesus the Messiah crucified. Following custom, the Savior is scourged with a short whip. He was then taken into the "common hall." Roman soldiers* taunt, beat, mock, and torment the Son of God.

Time: Early morning of the crucifixion day on Friday.

It touches us with grace and mercy that several of these very soldiers, if not all, later confessed Jesus as the Son of God and a righteous man. Note this amazing confession in Section 192, Matt. 27:54 and relative footnotes.

Somewhere in the Castle of Antonio, just north of the temple

Matt. 27:27-30	Mk. 15:16-19	Lk.	John 19:2-3
Jesus in the hands of the Roman soldiers	*Jesus in the hands of the Roman soldiers*		*Jesus in the hands of the Roman soldiers*
27 Then the soldiers(a) of the governor took Jesus into the common hall,	16 And the soldiers(a) led him away into the hall, called Praetorium;		2 And the soldiers(a)
and gathered unto him the whole band *of soldiers*.	and they call together the whole band.		
28 And they stripped him, and put on him a scarlet robe(b)	17 And they clothed him with purple,(b)		
29 And when they had platted a crown◄ of thorns, they put *it* upon his head,	and platted a crown◄ of thorns, and put it about his *head,*		◄platted a crown of thorns, and put *it* on his head, and they put on him a purple robe,(b)
			▲ *John is inspired to reverse the order of the robe and crown. This reveals that he wrote independently of Matthew and Mark.*
and a reed in his right hand: and they bowed the knee before him, and mocked him, saying, "Hail, King of the Jews!"(c)	18 And began to salute him, "Hail, King of the Jews!"(c)		3 And said, "Hail, King of the Jews!"(c)
	19 And they smote him on the head with a reed,		
30 And they spit upon him,(d)	and did spit upon▶ him,(d) and bowing *their* knees worshipped him. (Verse 20 cont. in Section 188.)		▶ *This beating of the Savior was the work of the Roman soldiers and should be distinguished from the mobs in Section 181, Lk. 22:63-65.*
and took the reed, and smote(e) him on the head. (Verse 31 cont. in Section 188.)			and they smote(f) him with their hands. (Verse 4 cont. in Section 187.)

Footnotes-Commentary

(a) **"Then the soldiers of the governor took Jesus into the common hall."** They led Him from the "pavement" where Pilate's judgment bench was into a room within the gigantic stone castle. It was here the Son of God received His pagan coronation as the King of the Jews. Mark called this room, "Praetorian." It was used as a staging point just before victims were led away to be executed. Paul used the term in Phil. 1:13, where it is translated "palace" and had reference to the quarters of the emperor's elite Praetorian Guard in Rome, Italy. Pilate is now free from the problem of Jesus King of the Jews, or so he thought. See Section 185, Matt. 27:26, footnotes p and q for his relinquishing Christ into the hands of the military for crucifixion. Being at Gentile quarters, the Jews refused to enter least they become defiled on the holy Passover for the Unleavened Bread, which followed immediately. It was well known that the Roman soldiery often laid severe and deadly treatment upon their victims, especially the detested Jewish people among whom they were stationed.

(b) **The King is robed.** Heathen soldiery went wild in their madness to torment the condemned, now they had Jesus the King of the Jews to themselves! Someone in the crowd sent word to the entire cohort of some four to six hundred men present within the soldier's quarters, at the vast Castle of Antonio. Understanding that the Roman army consisted of persons from many pagan lands, we see in the hundreds of men gathered about the Lord Jesus, David's prediction being fulfilled, "For dogs have compassed me: the assembly of the wicked have enclosed me" (Ps. 22:16). It was common sport among hard-bitten men of war to scorn their prisoners before putting them to death. Earlier, that night Herod's military had enjoyed their "play time" with the Son of God. See Section 184, Lk. 23:11, footnote e for details. They stripped Him naked and threw about His bloody and lacerated back a scarlet robe. The word here actually signifies a short kind of cloak worn by soldiers, military officers, magistrates and others of high rank. Mark and John describe it as being purple. Critics see here another "contradiction in Scripture," or so they say. However, their "contradiction" vanishes when we note that the ancients gave the name purple to any color that had a mixture of red in it. Thus, both were often called by the same name. The two colors being nearly identical reflect the cultural understanding of the writers of Scripture at that time. In *The Illustrated Bible Dictionary*, Part 1, pages 306-307 there is an excellent article explaining colors in the Bible.

2p-Apparently, the Lord Jesus was still wearing what was left of the "white robe" with which Herod's soldiers had earlier decked Him in ridicule. When the soldiers had finished their beating of the Savior, His garment was torn, shredded, and blood soaked.

3p-**The King is crowned.** Jesus' crown of thorns has been used by writers, poets, expositors, and taken from sublime to ridiculous extremes. One of the soldiers hit on the idea of crowning the King of the Jews. Seemingly, this was intended as a tool for torture and a crown for the mocked King. Whoever this man was he had to go and secure the needed green growth from which to build his crown of mockery for the coronation of Jesus. The *common* thorn growing in this area was known as "acantus" or "bear's foot." It consisted of narrow spikes up to six and seven inches in length. The "bear's foot" was a flexible short branch that could be easily woven into any desired shape due to its prickly or almost adhesive type leaves. Its needles were about one inch or less in length. This was intended as mimicry of the emperor's laurel, and now it crowned the sacred head of our Lord. Only a few days prior, our Savior had ridden into Jerusalem amid the excited shouts, "Blessed *is* the King of Israel that cometh in the name of the Lord." Refer to Section 148, John 12:13, footnote f. On this occasion "all the city was moved" over the presence of Jesus. The King of Israel is scorned by pagans and rejected *again* by His own Hebrew people.

4p-The original curse God placed on man is the source of earth's thorns and thistles (Gen. 3:17-19). Now, it is placed upon Christ. He died to banish this curse from the labors of men. Someday, in God's new heaven and earth, this deed of Christ in wearing the crown of thorns will be realized by the saved of all ages. In that wonderful and everlasting age, the unspeakable curse of sin manifested even in the soil of earth will be unknown.

5p-Gideon taught the men of Succoth with thorns, a lesson they *sorely* did not soon forget (Judges 8:16). So we may be taught by the thorns that adorned the head of our Savior. Each one, piercing, and hurting that noble Man may signal the pain and poison of our sins; shouting to us that He gladly bore them all for our salvation. Today, we may crown Him too! Make, O Christian reader, a chaplet of praise and thanks; place it upon His head and worship The King. The doctrine of the crown and cross are foolishness to the unsaved man who perishes in his blind arrogance; to those redeemed by the blood of the Lamb, it remains the power of God unto salvation. How bizarre that the foundational truths of God and Christ become absurdities to obstinate unconverted men and women of earth. Yet this demonstrates the reality of Satan, demons, and finally hell.

6p-**Many crowns**. In Rev. 19:12, our Lord is depicted returning to this world and on His head are "many crowns." This reflects that He is the final Sovereign of all creation. The platted thorns of the Roman soldiers no longer pierce his sacred brow. For other thoughts about His crowns, see Section 166, first paragraph of footnote e.

(c) **The King's salute. "Hail, King of the Jews."** Pasquier Quesnel, who died in 1719, was saved and became a renegade from the Roman Catholic Church, fleeing for his life from its apostasy. Being accused of heresy and sedition within that dark system, he went into hiding. Once when contemplating the crown of Jesus, he wrote these most eloquent and touching words, "Let the crown of thorns make those Christians blush who throw away so much time, pains, and money, in beautifying and adorning a sinful head and face. Let the world do what it will to render the royalty and mysteries of Christ contemptible, it is my glory to serve a King thus debased; my salvation, to adore that which the world despises; and my redemption, to go unto God through the merits of Him who was crowned with thorns." See *Clarke's Commentary*, vol. 5, page 272 for further details. In shouting out to the thorn crowned Christ "Hail, king of the Jews," they were making Him a laughing stock to the thousands of onlookers.

2p-**Verse 19. The King's sceptre.** In His right hand was the mock sceptre forced by a soldier upon the despised Jewish King (Matt. 27:29). Reeds grew in wet marshy locations, especially along the banks of the Jordan River. *The taller ones were firm with razor-sharp edges and points. Their needle-like points were often used in short* *arrows to bring down birds and small game.* The smaller variety of water reeds were predominately used by craftsmen in basket and mat making due to their endurance and weaving elasticity when green.

3p-Kings and Potentates would often carry a short sceptre made of gold or ivory as a symbol of their authority. This mock sceptre was thrust into Jesus' hand to ridicule His dignity as King of Israel, and to deride His claim to that honor. With sneering irreverence, they did a devilish homage to Him. Earlier, Matthew had associated Messiah with an Old Testament prophecy about a bruised reed. Refer to Section 55, Matt. 12:20 and second paragraph of footnote h for details about the reeds of the Jordan River. According to Heb. 1:8, His is a sceptre of righteousness, not of a wilting river reed. For an explanation of the ancient Jewish belief regarding their Messiah, and conversely, the world's hatred of the Jews over the centuries, see Section 14, and all of lengthy footnote f.

(d) Highlighted in gray because the Old Testament predicted some seven hundred years prior that Messiah would not "hide his face from shame and spitting" (Isa. 50:6). With feigned reverence, the soldiers buckled their knees and bowed to Jesus in shameless mockery. Snatching the reed out of His hand, one of them repeatedly whipped Him over the head with this emblem of broken sinners that He came to save. See third 3p- above for more on this. John wrote that they also "smote him with their hands." In all these infamous shames, He was bearing the consequences of humanity's sins. Here, we see what sin compels men to do to their fellows. For God laid on Him the iniquity of us all (Isa. 53:6). The spit from the cursing mouths of the incensed soldiers, the terrible mockery, and blasphemy of it all—was a clear and awful picture of *our* depravity, *our* darkness, *our* caviling with Satan and sin. This demanded swift judgment. Shortly, God sent that judgment upon our sins as they lay on His innocent Son.

(e) They repeatedly beat Him over the head with a hand-made reed sceptre. Note the comments about the "razor sharp" taller type reeds given under the second paragraph of footnote c above. For specific details and the different fines attached to the maltreatment of prisoners, see Section 181, footnote k. In verse 30 above, He was beaten by the Romans (Matt. 27:30; Mk. 15:19; and John 19:3), while in the earlier references of Section 181, Matt. 26:67-68, the Savior was beaten by the religious leaders, whose actions were against their own laws.

(f) The bruised Savior. Behold, the King stands holding a mock scepter. Next, came the fierce pounding and slapping of many hands and fists upon His noble head. A continual smiting of the face leaves one dizzy, disoriented, and faintish. How is it that the best man who ever lived received such treatment? "Why," millions have inquired, "was it this way?" It was for us, for Adam's fallen race that Jesus of Nazareth became sin by taking our sin and sorrows upon Himself. In some inexplicable way, the Lord of heaven laid on Christ the iniquities of us all. This awful but glorious drama moved into the painful culmination of a Roman cross. After six indescribable hours, His thorn crowned head bowed, and He cried, "It is finished" (John 19:30). "What was finished?" ask the unsaved men of this world. Since the fall of Adam, God's holiness had been offended by our sins. Evil demands correct punishment. God laid our sins on Christ and then punished Christ for those sins. The Savior became the final vicarious and everlasting substitutionary atonement for humanity. This is what was "finished" on the cross. Our pardon is as sure as the throne of God. Forgiveness and salvation wait for "whosoever will," because "he is the propitiation for . . . *the sins of* the whole world" (1 John 2:2). Some inquire, "Who believes that God punishes the same sin twice; first, His Son, and then the sinner?" Does the word whosoever teach this? Chafer wrote that whosoever, and its equivalents are "used at least 110 times in the New Testament, and always with the unrestricted meaning." See his *Systematic Theology*, Vol. II, p. 78. Someone said, "The Calvinistic efforts to limit this word to "all the elect constitutes one of the saddest chapters in exegesis." It reads like, "The father's have eaten sour grapes, and the children's teeth are set on edge" (Ezek. 18:2). That God only loves the elect, and punished their sins on the cross is heresy. It flies in the face of what Jesus Christ taught in Matt. 5:44-46. Christian love is to be "without dissimulation" (Rom. 12:9). This is the standard for believers. Thus, can the standard for God be lower?

2p-What He did for you. The grave does not end it all. Jesus Christ stands singularly apart from the founders of all earth's religions. They have died, or will die, and remain dead. However, this is not so with the Son of God. Three days and nights after His crucifixion, in the sovereign power of the Holy Spirit, He rose from the grave, never to die again! Sin, Satan, and the grim reaper are conquered. God has decreed that all who turn to this living Savior, believing that He paid for their sins will be saved. Churches, sects, religions, whoever or whatever, that adds to this divine plan of salvation are the enemies of divine truth and insult the Almighty. Many "learned academics" busy themselves "proving" that Christ did not really die for the sins of mankind. Read the blasphemy of certain "religious men" regarding the death of our Lord, in Section 131, the second paragraph of footnote d. Liberation theology makes Jesus a political fighter and the Romans nailed Him to a cross. And they are sure that He did not rise from the dead! History channel presents Christ as a revolutionary figure with a small following, out to overthrow Rome. Wise men will flee the dubious philosophies of "greatly learned" unsaved religious infidels. They will abandon all else except the Son of God. It is written, "Believe on the Lord Jesus Christ, and thou shalt be saved, and thy house" (Acts 16:31). Earlier, Christ told the angry religious Jews, "If you believe not that I am *he*, [the Messiah-Savior] ye shall die in your sins: [and] whither I go, [to heaven] ye cannot come" (John 8:21). If they could not go to Him in heaven, then they went to hell. Only dishonest or weak minds can believe He was speaking of unconscious annihilation in the grave.

904

PILATE'S FOURTH AND FIFTH VERDICTS

Jesus is taken from the soldier's "common hall" back to the governor. Pilate is terrified as the Jews accuse him of treason to Emperor Tiberius. He announces his two final verdicts of "no fault," and then delivers Christ* to die.

Time: Early morning of the crucifixion day on Friday.

*Just before he handed Christ over to the Jews, Pilate had already "delivered Jesus to them to be crucified" (Matt. 27:26). Seemingly, the governor had not issued the word of command to kill Him until verse 16 below. This would be in the term "delivered he him." Luke's earlier statement that Pilate gave "sentence that it should be as they required" had reference to the release of Barabbas, not the death of our Savior (Lk. 23:24-2.)

Matt.	Mk.	Lk.	John 19:4-16—*In the Castle of Antonio, north of the temple area*
			Pilate's fourth verdict 4 Pilate therefore went forth again,(a) and saith unto them, **"Behold, I bring him forth to you, that ye may know that I find no fault in him."** 5 Then came Jesus forth, wearing the crown of thorns, and the purple robe. And *Pilate* saith unto them, "Behold the man!"(b) **Pilate's fifth verdict** 6 When the chief priests therefore and officers saw him, they cried out, saying, "Crucify *him*, crucify *him*." Pilate saith unto them, **"Take ye him, and crucify *him*: for I find no fault in him."**(c) 7 The Jews answered him, "We have a law, and by our law he ought to die, because he made himself the Son of God."(d) 8 When Pilate therefore heard that saying, he was the more afraid; 9 And went again(e) into the judgment hall, and saith unto Jesus, "Whence art thou?" **But Jesus gave him no answer.** 10 Then saith Pilate unto him, "Speakest thou not unto me? knowest thou not that I have power to crucify thee, and have power to release thee?" 11 Jesus answered, "Thou couldest have no power *at all* against me, except it were given thee from above:(f) therefore he that delivered me unto thee hath the greater sin." ***The Jew's terrifying words, "Not Caesar's friend"*** 12 And from thenceforth Pilate sought to release him: but the Jews cried out, saying, "If thou let this man go, thou art not Caesar's friend: whosoever maketh himself a king speaketh against Caesar."(g) 13 When Pilate therefore heard that saying, he brought Jesus forth, and sat down in the judgment seat(h) in a place that is called the 'Pavement,' but in the Hebrew, 'Gabbatha.' 14 And it was the preparation of the passover, and about the sixth hour:(i) and he saith unto the Jews, "Behold your King!" ***"Kill your King?"*** 15 But they cried out, "Away with *him*, away with *him*, crucify him." Pilate saith unto them, "Shall I crucify your King?" The chief priests answered, "We have no king but Caesar."(j) ***Pilate yields the Lord Jesus to die*** 16 Then delivered he him therefore unto them to be crucified. And they took Jesus, **and led *him* away.**(k) (Verse 17 cont. in Section 188.)

▶For a chronological list of Pilate's judgments of the Savior, see the Information Box at the end of Luke 23:5 in Section 183. His words about the Lord Jesus were another fulfillment of the prediction, "Surely the wrath of man shall praise thee: the remainder of wrath shalt thou restrain" (Ps. 76:10).

Footnotes-Commentary

(a) Pilate had been moving in and out of his quarters to confer with the Jews, who were waiting out front. All his conversations with the religious leaders occurred somewhere outside (probably on a large front porch) of the Castle of Antonio. These Hebrew hypocrites believed they would become unclean or defiled if they entered the dwelling of a pagan Gentile. Read what the Lord Jesus had earlier said about their defilement in Section 96, first paragraph of footnotes l and m.

(b) **"Ecce homo," or "Behold the man"** shouted the governor in Latin. We would do well to obey Pilate's words and learn more of our glorious Savior. In this awful hour of shame and suffering, with blood-splattered robe, red stained reed in hand, crown of thorns beaten down into his brow, and beard torn from His face, Pilate presented Him to the Jews. Now, we may behold the majesty of meekness and sublime patience that shames our miserable impatience. Though trembling from exhaustion, bent due to physical weakness, the Lord Jesus displayed a lofty grandeur of holy calm that somehow mastered the screaming crowds and threw them into fits of deeper rage. Hated, yet showing love, wronged, yet He speaks no word of retaliation. Pure white snow with scummy filth will not mix. A lie can never wear the golden robe of truth! Some commentators believe that Pilate presented Jesus in this pitiful manner in order to elicit from the maddened Jews an ounce of sorrow for their King. Little did the perplexed Roman governor realize that he was calling attention to the greatest figure of all human history. A few moments later (verse 14) Pilate exclaimed, "Behold your king," instead of "behold the man." O reader, "Behold the Man!"

(c) **"I find no fault in him."** As the appointed provincial governor, Pilate had full authority to issue the death sentence. For all five of his verdicts regarding the Lord Jesus chronologically arranged, see the comment box just before the footnotes in Section 183.

(d) **"He made himself the Son of God" or their Messiah.** Note how truth slips out! This is the core of their hatred for Jesus of Nazareth; although He had always been the Son of God and was Israel's promised Messiah, He did not perform, as they believed their Messiah should. Challenging their corruption of the Hebrew religion, their distortion of the great Torah Law, and madness for the tradition of the elders, their love for money, power, and hypocrisy, He became their most hated enemy. Refer to Section 181, Matt. 26:63, footnote g, for further comments on the glorious term the "Son of God."

2p-**Verse 8. The governor was filled with fear!** What a strange thing. With legions of men at his disposal, he could have put down the angry Jews with one command. This reveals the sheer horror that a wild mob could turn any given situation into all-out war. Pilate knew this very well and was terrified that these incensed and maddened Jews would cause a bloodbath that would capture the attention of Rome. On the other hand, there is something here deeper than meets the eye. Why was Pilate so frightened when he heard that Jesus made himself to be the Son of God? Did this political pagan have some prior knowledge of this fact? Alternatively, was he confusing this declaration of Christ with the myths of Roman gods, and their sons and daughters supposedly coming to earth and performing miracles among men? For more on this, see Section 1, Part 4, third paragraph of footnote j.

(e) See footnote a above for comments on Pilate having to move in and out to speak to the Jews. Being a pagan, the governor knew little or nothing of the Hebrew faith in its original pure form. He was ignorant of their peculiar history, famed patriarchs, Holy Scriptures, and the promise of God that the Savior of mankind would enter the world through the nation of Israel. See Section 183, John 18:38, footnote s, for further comments on this thought.

2p-**"No answer."** Highlighted in gray for this was predicted of the Lord Jesus in Isa. 53:7. This silence of the Savior occurred several times during His trials before the Jews and Gentiles. For example, He answered Herod Antipas not a word (Lk. 23:9). He fulfilled the single prophecy written by Isaiah several times, not just once.

3p-Pilate's pagan background was replete with the standard fables and myths of idolatry. Many "sons of gods" walked the earth in a human form according to heathen fables. They could not be distinguished from normal men. Pagan priests and priestesses had all sorts of miracles and wonders credited to them. These heathen fables surely swept through the governor's mind as he glared at the Lord Jesus. "Is this man one of our gods?" was a thought he may have pondered. Filled with fear, superstition, and dread of the raging Jews he called Jesus aside and put to Him the question, "Whence [or where] art thou [from]?" *Again,* our Lord fulfills prophecy and "gave him no answer" (Isa. 53:7). For other details on the fantasies of pagans about their gods walking the earth, see Section 1, Part 4, third paragraph of footnote j. For a good review of Greek-Roman paganism at this period in history, see *The Trial of Jesus*, vol. two, Part II, pages 95–137, by Walter M. Chandler. This is an excellent work, yet Chandler fails to explain the *purpose* of all idolatry, which is Devil worship, via demons often resident within the millions of idols and images. As the heathen worshipers brought innumerable sacrifices, (which were sometimes humans and infants), and offered these to the gods and goddesses, demons transferred this service to Satan. *Hence, all idolatry is worship of Satan.* Because this is the exact and singular purpose of idolatry, we understand why God Almighty, in the Torah Law, called for the death of all who commit such heinous acts (Ex. 34:12-17 with Deut. 12:29-31). Pilate too was held by demonic grip in awful heathen religious darkness. What men sow, in time they will reap. The Roman Emperor banished him six years after the death of Christ. His expulsion and exile from office occurred in A.D. 36. For more on Pilate's fears and political troubles, see all under footnote g below. An ancient tradition states that he committed suicide a few years after Jesus' resurrection. Refer to Section 21, Part 1, number 2, under footnote b for some of the details.

4p-Verse 10. "I have power to crucify thee." Suddenly, Pilate became angry with Jesus. Resenting His thundering silence, he looked upon Him with scorn and contempt. The governor shouts, "Speakest thou not unto me?" Note the pronoun "me" in his outburst. Up to this point Pilate had declared the Lord Jesus innocent of the charges laid against Him by the crazed Jews. See verse 6 above for his fifth judgment. Now, he boasts of his own power and threatens with his authority to punish the Son of God.

(f) Genuine authority is from above. In great intrepidity and boldness, not being dismayed at Pilate's threats, the Savior affirms to him that his authority comes from the councils of God above. Few of earth's finite creatures with their little hands full of high authority, realize the sovereign source of their being and existence. Over history, we have seen an insane mustachio Austrian wallpaper hanger strut his power amid a million "Heil Hitler's." Later, he blasted his brains out in a sealed underground room with his partner in adultery. A stumped off Italian, Benito Mussolini, famed for arrogance and cruelty, was hung upside down and murdered with his mistress by those he had persecuted. Who could forget the African tyrant, Idi Amin? He fed his unpleasing wives to crocodiles. Amin died in 2003 while in exile under the protection of King Faisal of Saudi Arabia. It was the truth of man's dependency upon God for existence that inspired Paul to preach to the pagan crowds and nine judges on Mar's Hill. His nocturnal words were, "Seeing he [the true God] giveth to all life, and breath, and all things" (Acts 17:25). Pilate's ears were dull to the warning of Christ when He said, "Thou couldest have no power *at all* against me, except it were given thee from above." *God is always in control, whether we understand it or not. Usually, we don't.*

2p-"The greater sin." Here, our Lord was saying, "You did not create the authority you have, and though you too are guilty, yet the Jews, who delivered Me to thee bear the greatest condemnation." The word "he" does not speak of Judas for he did not take Jesus to Pilate. The Jews and Sanhedrin did. Our Lord considers them as *one* in their machinations against Him and thus used the pronoun "he." This statement also reveals that not all sins are of the same magnitude and that not all of them are equal. The circumstances of events that led up to certain crimes often make a mitigating difference in the verdict. The courts of the land are supposed to allow for the same circumstances today.

(g) "Pilate sought to release him." As if the schizophrenic Pilate suddenly becomes a normal man and now sides openly with Jesus. What all is involved in John's words stating that the governor "sought to release him," we do not know. Whatever it was, the crowds exploded and shouted many accusations at the troubled governor.

2p-"Not Caesar's friend." Raging in their fury, the Jews screamed back at Pilate these words that sent a chill down his spine, "You are not Caesar's friend" if you let Jesus go free. The reigning emperor at this time was Caesar Tiberius. All succeeding rulers from the death of Julius Caesar (44 B.C.) bore the title, "Caesar," (meaning "the hairy one") which was similar to "king" or whatever title was used by a supreme ruler. *Every* Roman emperor was a monster of sub human proportions: ruthless, cunning, and guilty of the most heinous sins.

3p-Pilate's fears were justified. Back at Rome, someone had uncovered an assassination plot against Emperor Tiberius. One of those implicated was a wealthy Roman, and commander of the famed Praetorian Guard, named Sejanus. He was also a close friend of Pilate and had helped secure his position as governor in the land of Israel. News of Sejanus' implications in a secret plot to overthrow the emperor cast shadows on his accomplices and friends across the empire. *This naturally implicated Pilate.* To have the Jews inform Rome, "Pilate was not a friend of Caesar," would at this critical time surely spell his doom! About a year after, the plot became public knowledge and Emperor Tiberius in a letter to the Senate ordered his execution. Some details of this conspiracy are given in *Suetonius*, vol. I, section LXV, pages 385–386. Sejanus' corpse was dragged through the streets of Rome. This reveals to us the fearful anxiousness of Pilate when he heard the Jews shout that he was not a friend of Caesar. *Upon hearing this, his defense of Christ vanished. He was panic-stricken and surrendered whatever scruples he had into the hands of the howling Jews.* One cannot but wonder if a certain solemn line in the Law of Twelve Tables of the Roman Empire may have flashed into his mind and haunted him. He had sworn to keep and abide by them as a ruler of the empire. The line reads, "The empty cries of the people must not be regarded when they call for the release of the guilty, or the doom of the innocent." See *The Life of Christ*, page 683, by F. W. Farrar, for the details.

(h) "Sat down." This text seems to suggest that the judgment seat or bema of Pilate had now been moved to the outside of the building. This judge's bench was portable for transporting to various locations. There was a specific place for the bench called "the Pavement," or in Hebrew "Gabbatha." Edersheim wrote in *Life and Times of Jesus the Messiah,* page 874, that this place "overlooked the city." A. T. Robertson wrote that the grammatical construction of the word points to "a mosaic or tessellated pavement spread over the stones." See, *Word Pictures in the New Testament,* vol. 5, page 299. It "overlooking the city" was because of the towering prominence of the Castle of Antonio that loomed at the northeast wall of Jerusalem. On the front porch (called Gabbatha) at the entrance of

Pilate's quarters; postured in a judgment seat, he gave legal determinations on all cases brought before him. Messiah stands at Gabbatha and a heathen governor sentences Him. How ironic and odd! Next, are the unmitigated sorrows of Gethsemane, and finally, the agony of Golgotha as He dies for the sins of mankind.

(i) **"Preparation of the passover."** This entire passage caused some to ponder what John meant. The one-day event of Passover (as far as eating the supper) was already over at this time, and it is early morning on the first day of the Unleavened Bread celebration. The Jews continued to do good deeds to the poor and needy, not only during the actual Passover day, but also before, and for seven days afterwards. All these activities plus many other things the Jews included in the meaning of "preparation."

2p-*Originally,* "preparation" had reference only to the Jews purging all leaven from their dwellings in view of the Feast of Unleavened Bread that followed on the heels of the Passover. By the time of Christ, many other things were added to "preparation," and it overlapped the Passover as well as the Unleavened Feast and was often called by that name. This is seen in Section 168, Lk. 22:7, footnote a. We note in Lk. 23:54, that both events are joined together. *Gill's Commentary,* vol. 8, pages 109-110 gives a detailed explanation of the "preparation" verses dealing with the "'Passover." His vast research into these matters is helpful, yet he often employs as many as two entire pages for *one* sentence with no paragraphs! Obviously, this makes for extremely difficult reading. His helpful commentaries were published in 1809 but are thrown off balance regarding the atonement of Christ by his *radically extreme* Calvinistic views.

3p-**"The sixth hour."** Infidel critics make a big noise out of this statement. They will not accept that here, John used Roman time, not Jewish. It would therefore, be about 6:00 a.m. John was inspired to use Roman chronology *at this place* because the crucifixion was scheduled by Roman time. He used Jewish time every other place in his book. These are located in John 1:39, the tenth hour or 4:00 p.m.; John 4:6, the noon hour or 12:00; and lastly, John 4:52, the seventh hour or 1:00 p.m. The Hebrew day was divided into twelve hours as seen in John 11:9. These twelve hours were divided into four parts. Each division consisted of three hours being called individually the third, sixth and ninth hours of their day. In Jewish reckoning of time all the space from nine o'clock until twelve was called the third hour! Then the time from twelve noon until three in the afternoon was known as the sixth hour. In *such cases,* where time was thus reckoned it is impossible to pinpoint the *exact* hour of a particular event. Jesus was nailed to the cross at the third hour or nine a.m. (Mk. 15:25). From Roman time given in this passage of six a.m., it took several hours to get Him to Calvary, located somewhere north of the city of Jerusalem outside her walls. The wild crowds, physical weakness of Jesus, and events along the way took up the time as they walked to the death site.

(j) **Only Caesar.** At this time, Emperor Tiberius ruled the empire. He held power from A.D. 14 to 37. See second paragraph of footnote g above. He was a murderous tyrant who dealt ruthlessly with all opposition. Suddenly, the religious Jews went savage at the possibility that Christ might be freed. Pilate had, a few moments earlier, exclaimed of Christ, "Behold the man!" Now, he shouts to the Jews, "Behold your king!" The bloodthirsty mob screams back, "We have no king but Caesar." What hypocrisy amid their religious madness! These very men cursed the Romans and their emperor; they taught their children to hate all Gentiles, especially those who treaded on the "holy soil" of the land of Israel. Suddenly, they claim a monstrous pagan, Caesar Tiberius, as their sovereign. With this Judaism was guilty of the denial of God, blasphemy, and absolute apostasy. The late Christian Jew, Alfred Edersheim wrote these words of Israel, "They committed suicide; and, ever since, has its dead body been carried in show from land to land, and from century to century; to be dead, and to remain dead, till He [Jesus] comes a second time, who is the Resurrection and the Life." From *Life and Times of Jesus the Messiah,* page 874.

2p-Here, we learn that even the powerful governor with all his troops at hand was no match for the wild Jews when their religious zeal was aroused and united in their hatred for Jesus, their Messiah. They demand the blood of the Nazarene and threaten to bring Pilate's downfall by accusing him to Caesar! Three times in terrible unison, they had shouted "Crucify him," "Crucify him," "Crucify him." Anyone who but casually reads the court proceedings of Jesus Christ feels that things were irregular, out of order, and lacking the elements that made up normal trials of this era in both Roman and Jewish history. *Standing over it all was the Lord of heaven and earth, Jehovah God, bringing about His plan for the final and eternal atonement of sin and the salvation of all who would believe in His Son.*

(k) **"Led *him* away."** Highlighted in gray because this was another prediction of the death of Christ. Some seven hundreds years before, the prophet of God had written these words about Jesus' trip to Calvary, "He is brought [led] as a lamb to the slaughter" (Isa. 53:7). Leading the parade of death were the *four Roman soldiers,* which were specialists in the work of crucifixion. An officer of the rank of a centurion commanded this death squad. For details on the rank of centurions, see Section 60, footnote c. Craig S. Keener in his work, *The IVP Bible Background Commentary: New Testament,* page 313, gives a good, but concise explanation of the basic units of soldiers in the Roman army. This group walked from Pilate's quarters across the city to its northern gate. They were accompanied by the mob of crazy Jews and curious spectators who had heard that a crucifixion was about to take place. Again, we must hold in mind that during Passover, the city was packed with hundreds of thousands of Jewish pilgrims from over the known world of that era. From among those present to keep Passover, thousands fell into the train and followed the Jews and soldiers to the place of death.

THE AWFUL GLORY OF ALL WORLD HISTORY: HE IS LED AWAY TO DIE.

How astounding that the four gospel writers penned the story of Jesus'
death without one bad word for those who brought such suffering on their
Lord. The only exception is Judas, called "the traitor" in Lk. 6:16.

Jesus Christ, the sinless Son of God from heaven, is taken by wicked men to be crucified.* A stranger from North Africa is compelled to carry the "horizontal part** of His cross." Many women followed bewailing His fate. He predicts again the doom of Jerusalem and its people in A.D. 70. At the death site, He refused a narcotic to dull the awful pain of death by Roman crucifixion.

Time: Approaching 9:00 a.m. the hour of His crucifixion.

*It is amazing that men are among us to this day who vehemently deny the death of Christ on the cross as a historical fact. The pagan historian Tacitus (born circa. A.D. 56) in his Annals, Book 15. 44, wrote of, "Christus, the founder of the name, had undergone the death penalty in the reign of Tiberius, by the sentence of the procurator Pontius Pilate." Tacitus was not a friend of Christianity. Justin Martyr in A.D. 150 wrote in Apology I, 35, that Pilate sent Emperor Tiberius a report of the trial and death of Jesus with an account of the miraculous signs that attended it. For a sweeping review of Jesus' death alluded to or mentioned by early writers, see Heathen Contact with Christianity during the First Century and a Half, by C. R. Haines. This is the book that many Antichrist infidels manage to overlook or reinterpret. **See footnote b below for explanation of "horizontal part of His cross."

From Pilate's quarters to a hill called Golgotha outside Jerusalem's northern gate

Matt. 27:31-32	Mk. 15:20-21	Lk. 23:26-28	(John 19:17)
Simon and the cross **31** And after that they had mocked him, they took the robe off from him, and put his own raiment on him, and led[a] him away to crucify *him*. **32** And as they came out, they found a man of Cyrene, Simon by name: him they compelled to bear his cross.[b]	***Simon and the cross*** **20** And when they had mocked him, they took off the purple from him, and put his own clothes on him, and led[a] him out to crucify him. **21** And they compel one Simon a Cyrenian, who passed by, coming out of the country, the father of Alexander and Rufus, to bear his cross.[b]	 ***Simon and the cross*** **26** And as they led[a] him away, they laid hold upon one Simon, a Cyrenian, coming out of the country, and on him they laid the cross, that he might bear[b] *it* after Jesus. ***Many women follow*** **27** And there followed him a great company of people,[c] and of women, which also bewailed and lamented him. ***Prediction of A.D. 70*** **28** But Jesus turning unto them said, "Daughters of Jerusalem, weep not for me,	

Matt. 27:33–34	Mk. 15:22–23	Lk. 23:28–31	John 19:17
		me, but weep for your-selves, and for your children. **29** "For, behold, the days are coming, in the which they shall say, 'Blessed *are* the barren, and the wombs that never bare, and the paps [breasts] which never gave suck.'(were nursed) **30** "Then shall they begin to say to the mountains, "Fall on us;" and to the hills, 'Cover us.' " (d) **31** "For if they do these things in a green tree, what shall be done in the dry?" (Verse 32 cont. in Section 189.)	
The skull and drugs **33** And when they were come unto a place called Golgotha,▶ that is to say, "a place of a skull,"(e)	*The skull and drugs* **22** And they bring him unto the place Golgotha,▶ which is, being interpreted, "The place of a skull."(e)	◀*Matthew and Mark are inspired to place the name Golgotha before giving the meaning of the word. John does the opposite. This is another mark of inspiration of the Holy Spirit as these men freely wrote their narratives independent of each other.*	*The skull* **17** And he bearing his cross went forth into a place called "*the place* of a skull,"(e) which is called in the Hebrew "Golgotha:"◀ (Verse 18 cont. in Section 189.)
34 They gave him vinegar to drink mingled with gall:(f) and when he had tasted *thereof*, he would not drink. (Verse 35 cont. in Section 189.)	**23 And they gave him to drink wine mingled with myrrh:**(f) but he received *it* not. (Verse 24 cont. in Section 189.)		

Footnotes–Commentary

(a) **Led him and the two thieves away.** Though their trial is not mentioned, immediately after the sentencing and removal of Jesus from the scene, Pilate proceeded to "try" the thieves and sentence them to execution on the cross. Their death walk to Calvary followed not far behind that of our Lord. This journey terminated on top of the skull (verse 17).

2p-For other comments regarding the Lamb of God being led to the slaughter, see previous Section 187, John 19:16, footnote k. After our Lord had endured the farce of His trial, again, He was unrobed, the blood soaked cape of kingly mockery ripped off and His own clothes put on Him. At normal trials by the Sanhedrin, if one was sentenced to death, there was a judicial process meticulously followed by the Jews. It went something like this:

3p-As the guilty was being led to death one went before him on a black horse and cried to the people standing along the way. He shouted that if any had other proof that might save the life of the condemned, they were to come forward at once. Other accounts state that one stood with a linen cloth in hand and cried for new evidence. If someone responded that he had fresh testimony to give, the person would wave the linen or the rider on the black horse would stop and turn back to the judgment hall. After a retrial, if the evidence was sufficient, the condemned was freed and the matter concluded. If not, the execution was ensured as quickly as possible. Some of the details are found in the Talmud tractate, Sanhedrin 45a. This judicial process was not followed in the death of Jesus. The Jews later recorded in their Talmud the myth that forty days before Jesus was hanged (crucified) on the Passover, a crier went over the city and found no one who would speak a good word in His favor. See Sanhedrin 43a for the fable. *This is their admission of putting Him to death with the help of the Gentiles. All these proceedings were controlled by the sovereignty of God according to His foreknowledge, as the plan of redemption for mankind was being unfolded. He forced no one to do anything sinful but simply used the wicked devices of men as they planned them and then deliberately acted in putting His Son to death on the Roman cross (Acts 2:23, 3:14 with 4:26-28).* It is written, "Known unto God are all his works from the beginning of the world" (Acts 15:18).

4p-At the bark of Pilate's order, "Go soldier, get the cross ready!" the terrible procession began. We read the dirge, "And led him away to crucify him." (The two thieves also walked in this death parade to Calvary, and carried the top bar of their crosses.) As explained, four soldiers were detailed to do the ghastly work of crucifying the condemned. They were under the superintendence of a centurion who would at times lead the way to the death site. A *tradition* states that the soldier who led Jesus to His death and pierced His side was named Longinus. History confirms those appointed to the cross were stripped and paraded off to the death site. Cassius and Lupus, the murderers of Emperor Caligula in A.D. 41, were naked as they walked to the place of execution. The pious talk about "the Jews would have never so shamed Jesus" is an abysmal error in view of their fierce hatred for Him.

5p-Mk. 15:21. "Alexander and Rufus." Mark wrote that he was the father of Alexander and Rufus, which must have carried some special significance to his original readers. It reveals that they knew these two men for Mark gave no further explanation. Paul mentioned a Rufus in Rom. 16:13 of which we cannot know if they were the same.

6p-The origin of crucifixion and female idolatry. Crucifixion was known long before the Roman era. It had been in vogue from the sunrise of antiquity. Legend accredits it to Semeramis, the wanton wife of King Nimrod at the tower of Babel. The Talmud, in tractates Eiruvin 53a and Pesachim 94b, both state that Nimrod was the king of Babylon. Upon being scattered from the Tower of Babel (Gen. 11), the idea of death by crucifixion was carried into the nations of antiquity; hence, its origin and usage among them. It was practiced in ancient India and Japan. This was centuries before the Roman Empire came into existence. The fifth-century B.C. Greek historian, Herodotus, wrote of crucifixion some four hundred years before the birth of Christ. See *Herodotus* 1:128.2; 3:125, 3; and 3:159, 1. For a thoroughly researched article on crucifixion, see the *Biblical, Theological, and Ecclesiastical Cyclopaedia*, vol. II, pages 588-592, by M'Clintock and Strong. Semeramis was defied as a goddess. Her name changed according to the language of each people-group as her infamy spread over the pagan ancient world. In Babylon, she was the "virgin Queen of heaven (Ishtar). The Roman Catholic Church has used this title for centuries! She was Astarte for the Greeks, Venus and Juno for the Romans. The Zidonians called her Ashtoreth. Her worship was slowly "Christianized," and received into many of the early churches. The church fathers and the Papal system committed this heinous crime. See Section 13, fifth paragraph of footnote f for more on this horrific story.

(b) Simon carries His cross. The death procession must have taken extra time due to the vast crowds, the weakness of Christ, and the general tenor of the horrible affair. Somewhere along the way, He was unable to continue with the cross patibulum beam over His shoulders. From the horrified onlookers, one of the soldiers pulled a man named Simon, from the country of Cyrene (today Libya in North Africa), and ordered him to take the cross beam from Christ and carry it. History tells us that many Jews lived in Cyrene. We read about some of them fifty-three days later in attendance at the Day of Pentecost (Acts 2:10). Cyrenian Jews were so plenteous in Jerusalem that they had built a synagogue with their name attached to it (Acts 6:9).

2p-No one in his right mind would volunteer to carry the cross of a condemned man, lest he implicate himself with the guilty person. The horizontal beam called in Latin "patibulum," was always carried by the condemned. The vertical post was affixed solidly in the ground waiting its victim. It was tall enough so that the feet of the condemned were about one yard or meter from the ground. The posters, drawings, movies, and paintings of Christ carrying the entire cross (both pieces affixed in place) are incorrect and contradict well-documented history. They have come down to us from mostly Roman Catholic artists, who reveal their shallow knowledge of both history and Scripture. Our Lord carried the cross bar but a short distance, and then Simon took it to the death site. What a memory this man had the rest of his life!

(c) Verses 27-29. "And there followed him a great company." This means *hundreds* of people fell into the human train following behind the Savior. Among these were women, which "bewailed and lamented him." We saw earlier that during his Galilean ministry, many women supported His work. Refer to Section 65, Lk. 8:2-3, footnote e for more of the interesting details. It is still an eastern custom for hundreds of women to amass, weep, shout, howl, toss dust into the air, and tear their garments during times of awful loss and human sorrow. There are no words that could describe the emotion amid this "great company" of brokenhearted women. Earlier in Section 148, at footnote h the Lord Jesus had lamented the fate of Jerusalem and its citizens.

2p-Verse 30. Highlighted in gray because it was a prediction from the Old Testament. This is a general quotation from Hosea 10:8. It speaks of the time when the Assyrians pulverized the Jews in the northern kingdom in 721 B.C. Christ informs these women that a similar terror will fall upon them and their children at the hands of the fierce Romans. This came some forty years later in A.D. 70. Our Lord paused to reaffirm to those that followed in His death procession, that they had better transfer their weeping onto themselves and their little ones. In about forty years, the forces of Rome would decimate them, their city, and nation. His statement of doom was addressed to the unbelieving females within this vast company. Jesus had previously given a similar warning during the great Olivet Discourse a few days earlier in Section 163, Matt. 24:19. After His death, numerous believing women assisted in His burial not realizing His resurrection was next! Several of their names and efforts are noted in Section 195, Lk. 24:1 with Section 192, Matt. 27:55-56. He had refused their pity and tears as He shortly would refuse their narcotic, designed to mitigate His sufferings on the cross. For more on this interesting story, see footnote f below.

3p-Drug makers of Jerusalem. Women of high rank in larger cities would voluntarily take on the task of making a narcotic to be administered to those condemned to death by crucifixion. They did this at their own expense. No doubt, some among this multitude following Jesus, were drug makers, and probably professional mourners practicing their art along the way. Others were true believers in Christ. It was to the unbelievers in that vast company of women that He spoke the curse of verses 28-31, and explained in footnote d below. *Dake's Annotated Reference Bible,* page 89, left vertical column, note g of the New Testament, carries a pertinent comment regarding some of these women. "These of the same sex that first sinned now stayed truer to the Savior than those of the sex which chose to sin without being deceived" (1 Tim. 2:13-14).

(d) "Fall on us, cover us." This expression commonly used among the Jews to express the horror of judgment. It is also found in Rev. 6:16. *Christ was not speaking of a far away tribulation period as recorded in the book of Revelation.* His Words about the Jews praying to the mountains and hills to cover them are a general quotation from Hosea 10:8 and highlighted in gray. No doubt, many women cried out such things in the doom and slaughter of their city that came a few decades later, as millions perished under the wrath of God.

2p-Verse 31. "A green and dry tree." This too was a familiar proverb or Jesus would not have used it in this critical hour. Something similar is written in Ezek. 20:47-48, which was looked upon by rabbis as speaking of Messiah! Being a Messianic prediction, it is colored in gray. Some commentators think our Lord was referring to this Old Testament passage, which spoke of the destruction of Jerusalem by the Babylonians in 586 B.C. The rabbis stated, "Prohibition [pardon] applies to a green tree but not a dry one." See Talmud tractate, Eiruvin 100b. Augustus Neander in *The Life of Jesus Christ,* page 463, footnote i thinks our Lord was saying to these women, "If the Holy One, entering among sinful men, is so entreated, what must happen to those whose sufferings will be the just penalty of their own accumulated guilt?" The Lord Jesus was saying something like this, "If you destroy me, heaven's green tree of life and hope, what will God do to the dead trees of your corrupted religion, which have caused many to reject Me?" We know what God later brought upon them, their glorious temple, city, and Jewish state in A.D. 70. Alfred Edersheim in his *Life and Times of Jesus the Messiah,* page 879, put it succinctly, "For, if Israel had put such flame to its 'green tree' [Messiah], how terrible would divine judgment burn among the dry wood of an apostate and rebellious people." This came at the hands of the Romans. Jesus spoke of the Jews praying for the mountains and hills to cover them. As mentioned in paragraph 2 above, this was a general quotation from Hosea. 10:8. It had become a common expression among Jews for relating the terror of trouble falling upon a people. It is noted that similar prayers will also be made during the future horrors of Rev. 6:16.

3p-Verse 17. "And he bearing his cross." In Jesus' death on the cross the believer finds the strongest motives for holy living. Viewing its awful scene, we resolve to live for Him who died for us. At the cross, sin becomes infinitely hateful and evil. If there was such a thing as "holy cursing," we could use it to describe ravages sin! As He bore His cross, so we bear ours with hearts full of joy and praise!

(e) "Golgotha" is translated by John as meaning "place of a skull." Those "defenders of the faith" who so fiercely object to retranslating (not mistranslating) certain words in the Scripture for clarity should debate their case with John the inspired apostle. He did the same in John 1:38, 41, 42, and 9:7. For the root meanings of particular medical words, used by Dr. Luke, and set in their social and historical context, see Section 4, the first paragraph under main heading.

2p-Many traditions and legends abound regarding this curious name, "Golgotha." Some say that Adam's skull was found on this hill; others that it being the commonplace for crucifixion, numerous bones of those put to death were scattered over the place. Some hold that it signifies a mount shaped like a skull. The *present* site for our Lord's death is on a high hill north of Jerusalem. Jesus was not put to death within the city as no capital punishments were allowed within Jerusalem's precincts (Num. 15:35). It is true that the exposed face-rock of this present site resembles the eyes, nose, and mouth of a human skull. However, these geological features were etched into the hillside by miners drilling in the strata over seventy years ago. This has nothing to do with Bible prophecy, unless God in His providence arranged it this way! In Lk. 23:33, the site is called "Calvary." This word is derived from the old Latin term "cranium," later "calvaria," meaning "skull." As stated elsewhere, our Savior's death for our sins is not against man's intellect but above it. Years ago, in South Africa, the author worked with a professional chemist trying to win him to Christ. On one occasion, I read the simple text of John 3:16. Silent for a moment he suddenly replied, "I cannot accept that statement, unless it is properly analyzed." I responded, "Peter, when you sat down in that desk chair you did not analyze it; God requires the same trust in His gospel." This young academic represents millions who have been cauterized in their minds to the things of God by the secular educational systems. The unsaved world is spiritually astray, lost from the truth, and wandering in a dark forest of non-reality. Being dead to life's true values, certain women think it is right to murder the baby they carry in their wombs, but lay down in front of a bulldozer to save trees for spotted owls to roost in at night. This false sentimentality seized America. People are *true value* sick. Beautiful femininity with its wonder, shyness, charm, and glory is vanishing. Many women today resemble tattooed circus clowns or professional wrestlers. Course, rough, puffy faced, blowing smoke and sipping beer, they can out curse a drunken sailor, outfight a wild cat, and wallow in adultery and fornication every night without a sting of conscience. In some cases, one cannot distinguish if they are male or female. Some of the public "big mamas" are so tough and bawdy they could kick-start a 747. Boasting loudly and shamelessly of their adventures in sin and wickedness they are blind as dirt to true happiness in this life, and that which is coming. God described these people as having a "conscience sheared with a hot iron" (1 Tim. 4:2).

3p-Among the *reprobate godless* of society there are those from whom the Almighty has withdrawn His mercy. Removing the leash of divine constraint, God has had enough of their sin and turned them loose in their mad rush to hell. Their mental and moral state and ultimate fate is described in Rom. 1:26-32. It reads as follows: "For this cause God gave them up unto vile affection: for even their women did change the natural use into that which is against nature: And likewise, the men, leaving the natural use of the woman, burned in their lust one toward another; men with men working that which is unseemly, and receiving in themselves that recompense of their error which was meet. And even as they did not like to retain God in *their* knowledge, God gave them over to a reprobate mind, to do those things, which are not convenient; Being filled with all unrighteousness, fornication, wickedness, covetousness, maliciousness; full of envy, murder, debate, deceit, malignity; whisperers, Backbiters, haters of God, despiteful, proud boasters, inventors of evil things, disobedient to parents, Without understanding, covenant breakers, without natural affection, implacable, unmerciful: Who knowing the judgment of God, that they which commit such things are worthy of death, not only do the same, but have pleasure in them that do them." The only cure for spiritually sick people is the salvation of Christ provided on the cross. However, this is rejected and trodden under foot. Doctor Benjamin Spock of decades past, and Dr. Phil of the present, cannot help. God's gospel still radically changes the lives of men who surrender to its demands and not twist it to surrender to theirs. True Christians *must love these people, look beyond their offensive and vile conduct, and do their best to bring them to Christ.* The same man who wrote the severe things above, also wrote that he wept over men because they were "enemies of the cross of Christ" and its offer of forgiveness and new life (Phil 3:17-19).

(f) "And they gave him to drink." Another Old Testament prediction pertaining to the death of Christ fulfilling Ps. 69:21. Refer to the third paragraph of footnote c above for information on the female drug makers in Jerusalem. The Talmud speaks of this in tractate, Sanhedrin 43a, and reads, "When a person is led out to be executed, he is given a glass of wine containing a grain of frankincense, in order to numb his senses." The Jews based this act of mercy on Prov. 31:6, "Give strong drink unto him that is ready to perish."

2p-There is disagreement among commentators about the actual procedure here. Matthew wrote that they gave Jesus "vinegar mingled with gall." Mark put it down as "Wine mingled with myrrh." Mark's record is supposed to have referred to the custom of the nation in giving this as a sedative to the condemned person. This would be the drug made by the honorable women of the city. *However, some worthy expositors believe that Matthew wrote about what they actually did despite their moral custom.* He affirmed that vinegar, and gall was given to Christ. These were supposed to have no sedative element (which is incorrect). They are fiercely bitter, carrying a sickening sense of rancor that creates an overwhelming nausea, and urge to vomit. John Lightfoot in his *Commentary on the New Testament . . . ,* vol. 2. page 366 believes that this was a trick of the religious leaders to further heap upon Christ, "all kinds of ignominy and vexation." Others hold that Christ was given the four different substances at the same time, or a mixture of vinegar, gall, wine, and myrrh. The ancients frequently referred to vinegar as wine and wine as vinegar.

3p-Holding to the inspired text, the author of this work understands that the Lord Jesus was offered a mixture of all four at the same time. Regardless of our human *conjectures* on this point, the verses are clear that Jesus refused the first offer of narcotic liquid. This was in order that He might suffer the full penalty for our sins, being sober and in a right mind and frame of thought. For a discussion of the "two different drinks" theory, see *Clarke's Commentary,* vol. v, pages 273-274. Several hours later, as Messiah neared death, He called for a drink. The soldiers gave Him vinegar or "posca" from a nearby vessel; He received it and died. This was a standard liquid used by the Roman military to quench thirst. It is explained in Section 191, John 19:28-29, footnote e.

HIS FIRST THREE HOURS ON THE CROSS COMMENCE.

Behold, God at His best and man at his worst. The crucifixion* of Jesus, the Messiah of Israel, and Savior of mankind. At the third hour or 9:00 a.m., He was hung between two thieves. The conquering Lion becomes the suffering Lamb. His first Words from the pulpit of the cross are a prayer for His executioners. Pilate refuses to change his written confession of who Jesus was. The chief priests object. At the cross, God kissed the world with the greatest token of His divine love.

Time: The beginning of His crucifixion.

*Over the centuries, every device known to men and devils has been employed to change, mitigate, alter, reface, reword, embellish, and reinterpret the death, burial, and resurrection of Jesus Christ. Infidel and atheistic professional theologians, religious historians, and certain academicians have struggled with the atonement of Christ. This again demonstrates that in the Son of God is found humanity's only hope for forgiveness of sins and eternal life. The unsaved world inspired by the Devil fiercely hates Jesus Christ and His unique claims.

Outside the northern gate of Jerusalem on Golgotha or Mount Calvary

Matt. 27:35	Mk. 15:24-25	Lk. 23:32-34	John 19:18
		32 And there were also two other, malefactors, [criminals]► led with him to be put to death. **33** And when they were come to the place, which is called Calvary,	◄*Luke wrote of the two thieves at this place. Matthew records it in verse 38, below and Mark in verses 27-28, below.*
Between two thieves **35** And they crucified[(a)] him,	***Between two thieves*** **24** And when they had crucified[(a)] him,	***Between two thieves*** there they crucified[(a)] him, and the malefactors, [criminals] one on the right hand, and the other on the left.	***Between two thieves*** **18** Where they crucified[(a)] him, and two other with him, on either side one, and Jesus in the midst.
		His first Words spoken from the cross **34** Then said Jesus, "Father, forgive► them; for they know not what they do."[(b)] And	*Below is a chronology of His cries from the cross:*
and parted his garments, casting lots:	they parted his garments, casting lots upon them, what every man should take.	they parted his raiment, and cast lots.	*1. Here in Luke 23:34.* *2. Section 190, Luke 23:43.* *3. Section 190, John 19:26-27.* *4. Section 191, Matthew 27:46 with Mark. 15:34.* *5. Section 191, John 19:28.* *6. Section 191, John 19:30.* *7. Section 191, Luke 23:46.*
that it might be fulfilled which was spoken by the prophet,► "They parted my garments among them, and upon my vesture did they cast lots."	◄*This same prediction is placed by John in verse 24 below.*		
	25 And it was the		

Matt. 27:36–37	Mk. 15:25–26	Lk. 23:35–38	John 19:19–22
	third hour, [9 a.m.] and they crucified him.	◄ *Measured from the first hour beginning at sunrise.*	
36 And sitting down they [the soldiers] watched[c] him there;		**35** And the people stood beholding.[c] And the rulers also with them derided *him*, saying, "He saved others; let him save himself, if he be Christ, [Messiah] the chosen of God." **36** And the soldiers also mocked him, coming to him, and offering him vinegar,[d] **37** And saying, "If thou be the king of the Jews, save thyself."	
The great truth **37** And set up over his head his accusation written,[e]	*The great truth* **26** And the superscription of his accusation was written[e] over,	*The great truth* **38** And a superscription also was written[e] over him in letters of Greek, and Latin, and Hebrew,●	*The great truth* **19** And Pilate[e] wrote a title, and put *it* on the cross. And the writing was
►**"THIS IS JESUS**		**"THIS IS**	**"JESUS OF NAZARETH**
THE KING OF THE JEWS." ▲ *Each inspired writer mentioned the sign over the cross, penning only what the Holy Spirit directed them to write. See the second paragraph of footnote e below for an explanation of the sum total of what was written.*	**"THE KING OF THE JEWS."**	**THE KING OF THE JEWS."** (Verse 39 cont. in Section 190.)	**THE KING OF THE JEWS." 20** This title then read many of the Jews: for the place where Jesus was crucified was nigh to the city: and it was written in Hebrew, *and* Greek, *and* Latin.●
		●*Luke in verse 38, above and John in verse 20, to the right place the three languages in different order. This again reveals that the evangelist did not copy from one another.*	***The Jews object and Pilate's response* 21** Then said the chief priests of the Jews to Pilate, "Write not, 'The King of the Jews;' but that 'he said, "I am King of the Jews." ' "[f] **22** Pilate answered,

915

Matt. 27:38	Mk. 15:27–28	Lk.	John 19:22–24
38 Then were there two thieves▶ crucified with him, one on the right hand, and another on the left. (Verse 39 cont. in Section 190.)	**27** And with him they crucify two thieves;▶ the one on his right hand, and the other on his left. **28** And the scripture was fulfilled, which saith, **(g)** "**And he was numbered with the transgressors.**" (Verse 29 cont. in Section 190.)	◀ *Matthew and Mark mention the two thieves at this place, while Luke recorded it earlier in verses 32-33 above. These different placements are the choice of the Holy Spirit not the human authors.*	"What I have written I have written."
			Lottery at the cross
			23 Then the soldiers, when they had crucified Jesus, took his garments, **(h)** and made four parts, to every soldier a part; and also *his* coat: now the coat was without seam, woven from the top throughout.
			24 They said therefore among themselves, "Let us not rend it, but cast lots for it, whose it shall be:" that the scripture might be fulfilled, which saith, **(i)** ◀ "**They parted my raiment among them, and for my vesture they did cast lots.**" These things therefore the soldiers did. **(j)** (Verse 25 cont. in Section 190.)
		▶ *Matthew placed this prediction in verse 35 above.*	

Footnotes–Commentary

(a) "And they crucified him." He treads the winepress of sin alone (Isa. 63:3). Perhaps we should subtitle this, "And *we* crucified Him." The cross of Christ is our only hope of life everlasting. God laid on Him our iniquities, and from His wounds flowed the precious blood that cleanses from all sin. In the wonders of creation, wicked men may see the fingerprints of God, but in the cross, the maturing born again believer beholds the wisdom and power of God. We are smitten to contemplate that our sins murdered Him. We waste no time with religious infidels, trying to prove the cross had a divine origin. This is demonstrated in its power to save and sanctify the corrupt human heart, and bring crooked men, filled with mischief and evil into willful and joyful subjection to Him. In the cross of Jesus, all divine perfections are gloriously and harmoniously displayed. The heavens declare the glory of God above; but the cross of earth's Calvary below outshines the wonders of the skies above. Once we become *deeply acquainted* with the cross, the world ceases to allure and charm us; soon, we learn why it hates Him, and us who love and serve Him. It is not an occult charm worn about the neck, waist, wrist, or ankle, *nor is it a tattoo*. It stands erected on the highest hill of the redeemed soul. Upon its contemplation, we slowly learn to be somewhat like the Man, who died there. In the presence of this old rugged cross, the saved Christian senses, the omnipotent grace of God that captured his heart and brought him into eternal life. Pilate confessed there was no blame in Him. Alas! He was then hanged from the tree of Calvary, drooping on the cross like a bruised flower, creation showed its funeral grief at the holy sight. All natural substances paid a salute of honor to this sad but Highest Majesty of pure innocence. Heaven had deposited upon Him the crown of glory divine and unequaled. Consult Section 120, footnote o for more on the cross.

2p-Ancient crucifixion. For the origin of death by crucifixion, see Section 188, sixth paragraph of footnote a. It was the most wretched form of death known to men. The nations of antiquity and the Romans used it to punish thieves, murderers, political fighters, slaves, military deserters, state infractions, anarchists, high treason, and other crimes. Even women were put to this shameful demise. Ancient crucifixions employed different forms of the cross. Some used the **T**. It was called "crux commissa." Others the **X**, or "cross decussate." "Crux simplex," or the **I** type was used mostly for impaling. The **II** configuration seems to have had no special name in Latin. Lastly, was the † cross or "crux immissa," known throughout antiquity and used by heathen nations thousands of years *before* Christ was born. In this latter style of crucifixion, the upper cross bar or "patibulim" was used. See the third paragraph of footnote b below for other details on this. Not only were various configurations of the cross employed, the Romans were known to have attached their enemies to city gates, walls, living tree trucks, large rocks, and stone mountain sides. At times, special victims were tied to a high cross overlooking a city and left for the carnivorous fouls to pick away their flesh until death ensued. The pain of lingering crucifixion produced excruciating suffering. It was the most scandalous death known; the highest mark of public infamy. In His death, the sinless Son of God became sin for us, by (somehow) taking our sins in His human body, then receiving God's judgment for those sins (1 Peter 2:24). In the innocent Jesus, hanging on the cursed cross, God demonstrated His holy repugnance for sin and judged it. He provided the perfect and eternal atonement for all who trust Jesus as personal Savior. No religion in all history offers such love, hope, total forgiveness, and peace. Thus, the reason *true* Christianity is so bitterly hated.

3p-Lk. 23:33. "One on the right hand, the other on the left." Not many days prior, James, and John (assisted by their mother) had attempted to secure from Jesus a word of assurance that they would sit one on each side of Him in His political kingdom, which they believed, was soon to appear. Now, as He dies to vouchsafe the spiritual kingdom, the church, His right and left hand positions are taken by two thieves, as they die with Him on their crosses. One wonders if these two apostles and their mother thought of this as they watched their Messiah experiencing such an ignominious death by Roman crucifixion. Like Joseph of old, in prison between two malefactors, one was delivered the other hanged (Gen. 40). Here, at the cross, one was saved the other was damned.

4p-For a comprehensive but Roman Catholic tainted look at the cross, see *The Cross In Tradition, History and Art*, by Rev. William W. W. Seymour, published in 1898. Jewish methods of capital punishment were by beheading, strangling, burning, and stoning. The Torah Law had *no place* for crucifixion, though the Jews might hang up the bodies of their victims after they had died (Josh. 10:26). They also spoke of death by crucifixion as being "hung on a tree" (Acts 5:30, 10:39; and 13:29; with 1 Peter 2:24). However, all dead bodies were removed before sundown (Deut. 21:22-23). Hebrew capital punishment was ensued in the following ways, though in the days of Christ, the Jews had mostly neglected and forsaken these practices:

1. **Beheading.** This was considered a most horrific way of dying by the Jews. It was the penalty for deliberate murder and communal apostasy from Judaism to idolatry. Tied to a post, the culprit's head was severed with one swift blow.

2. **Strangling.** This was accomplished by burying the guilty up to his waist in soft mud, and then tightening a cord wrapped in a cloth about his neck, until suffocation ensued. This was the punishment for adultery, kidnapping, false prophecy, bruising one's father or mother, and prophesying in the name of pagan gods and deities. In some cases, it was enforced for the corrupt administration of Gods' work.

3. **Burning.** This does not mean the consuming of the victim in flames of hot fire as John Calvin did his opponents at Geneva, and the Papal Church did in Spain. Refer to Section 14 and all of footnote f for details on this subject. The term "burning" actually seems to be the wrong word to describe this method of death. In this form of the death sentence, the individual was stood up in a pit dug in the ground. Loose dirt was thrown in and tamped down up to his neck. A soft rope was placed about his neck, and then two strong men would pull it tight until his lower jaw dropped which signaled death. Quickly, a lighted lamp wick was thrown into his sagging mouth. In some cases, molten lead seems to have been thrust into his mouth. Burning was for sex offenders guilty of various forms of incest within the family circles.

4. **Stoning.** The condemned was taken to the top of a sharp hill or a scaffold. If a man, he was stripped naked, then dropped downward upon his head. The intent was to break his neck. If he did not die from the planned fall, he was, then stoned to death from those standing above him. Those who had witnessed against him had to cast the first stones! With this, see Section 120, John 8:7, footnote g. This was given for such crimes as practicing magic, idolatry, blasphemy, pythonism (an occult practice involving snakes), pederasty, necromancy, cursing a parent, violating the Sabbath, and bestiality practiced by a man. For a sound work dealing with the crucifixion of Jesus, the Sanhedrin, Talmud, and the Jewish forms of punishment, see *The Trial of Jesus*, by Walter M. Chandler.

(b) **His first Words from the cross. "Father, forgive them; for they know not what they do."** The Savior prayed for the Jews and Romans, who were physically putting Him to death. *What did the milling crowd, and the two thieves think as they heard this prayer from a Man dying on the terrible cross?* It was not a prayer for the whole world. The question is asked, "Did the Father answer this supplication of His beloved Son?" God forces no man into His will. Some of the persons at this awful scene trusted the Man in the middle and were forgiven. This was the thief, and several, if not all the Roman soldiers responsible for the gory crucifixion. See comments on the soldiers in Section 192, Matt. 27:54, footnote b for their public confession about the Lord Jesus. Christ's prayer for His tormentors demonstrates the unspeakable depths of God's councils! In His plan for earth and humanity, often things seem so wrong, lop sided, even contrary to the existence of the Almighty. Sin and evil rampage, right goes down and wrong rises up. A million prayers seem unanswered. "Where is God?" we secretly ponder. As noble as the human intellect can be, it is ruined by sin and apostasy. If the stars fall from heaven tonight and the sun never shines again, God is too good to do wrong. Knowing His death before the foundation of the world, Jesus prayed in loving compassion for His crucifiers. We too must keep this cross in our hearts and pray from its bar as our Lord did.

2p-Verse 35. "They parted his garment." Matthew wrote of this prediction made a thousand years prior in Ps. 22:18. John's mention of the casting of the lots and parting of Jesus' clothing was recorded later in his history, while Matthew recorded it earlier. These late and early entries are explained in vertical columns and marked by the symbol ▶. See comments regarding John's record under the first paragraph of footnote i below.

3p-"The actual crucifixion." At the crucifixion site, our Lord was stripped of His clothing, and laid face upward on the ground, His hands were extended outward, tied, and then nailed to the cross bar or "patibulim" under His shoulders. See Section 188, second paragraph of footnote b for further explanation. Cunningham Geikie wrote of the tying and nailing of victims in his work, *The Life and Words of Christ*, page 779. It was a standard practice that the victim's clothing was divided among his crucifiers. Hence, the garments of Jesus were gambled over by the soldiers, thus fulfilling Ps. 22:18. See footnote h and i below. The patibulim was hoisted over the top of the upright post by rope and pulley until the victim's feet were some distance off the ground below.

4p-The patibulum cross beam was affixed to the upright post and the victim's feet were criss-crossed and nailed through both sides. Often, a peg-seat was insetted to protrude from the upright stake on which the victim could painfully rest! It is *untrue* that persons being put to death by this measure were actually nailed through the wrists to prevent the body weight from pulling them down. There have been documented cases where some were nailed *several or many times* and in different ways to the cursed wood of the fatal tree. Martin Hengel in his amazing little book *Crucifixion,* page 24 affirms that the victims were not only nailed, but also tied or bound to their crosses at the same time. The height of the cross of death varied often to the whim of the crucifier! The short-lived Roman emperor, Galba had an enemy fastened to a cross painted white that was described as being "very high." Other cases are given where men were hoisted until they could overlook the city beneath them. *Nothing in human history was as awful as death by crucifixion.* See the first paragraph of footnote a above for more on this subject.

(c) **Watching Jesus die.** In verse 36 Matthew wrote this of the soldiers. Observing the Savior die, and hearing Him speak from the cross, no doubt played a great part in the later confession of these men. Mark. 15:25 states it was the third hour or nine o'clock a.m. Thousands present for the Passover and Feast of Unleavened Bread that followed gathered there and were curious to see another man crucified. Some sat on the ground, while others stood to watch the death of Jesus and the thieves. The time of the morning sacrifice in the temple was the same time in which the Son of God was lifted up to die for our sins on the cross. See Section 120, footnote o for more on this.

(d) **"Offering him vinegar."** For a discussion of the drink offered the Lord Jesus, see Section 188, Matt. 27:34, footnote f. It was a standard practice for Roman soldiers while on duty to have a pot of sour wine vinegar near. It was not of intoxicating content, as this might impair their duties and alertness. It was called "posca" and made from sour vinegar and herbs. See Section 191, John 19:28-30, footnote e where near the end of His life, one of the soldiers offered Him a drink after His cry, "I thirst." He received it, and died.

(e) **The languages over His head.** Pilate, the heathen governor, placed these three languages *above* the head of Jesus. *Many scholars do the same today!* They are tools to assist us in Scripture study, not the saving gospel of the Scripture. All Hebrew, Greek, and Latin must be laid at the foot of the cross, not above it. It was the common practice of the Romans for the presiding judge to write the crimes of the convicted on a board or wooden plaque and for one to carry this held high for the public and curious spectators to read. This custom was widely used by the Chinese communists during the blood purges of the regime of Mao Tse Tung, which ended in 1959. John informs us that Pilate wrote the inscription on the board and put it on the cross. Amid the explosive atmosphere, Pilate did not walk the distance to Calvary pushing his way through the wild mob to write the royal titles of Jesus. This was a way of saying that someone else did it for him, no doubt one of his military.

2p-Each of the four evangelists wrote, as they were inspired. Putting the trilingual inscription together from their individual letters, we see that the *entire* wording was, "THIS IS JESUS OF NAZARETH THE KING OF THE JEWS." Matthew recorded that it was "set up over his head" (verse 37), which may give credence to the type of cross on which He was crucified. See footnote a above. All the fuss about the order of the three languages used is another useless "academic" exercise. The order as listed by Luke (verse 38) differs from that given by John (verse 20). This signals that God was not concerned in linguistic priority but rather in the message itself. Hebrew, Greek, and Latin were the three major tongues of that era. Later in history, Latin was called "The Devil's language." Jews and others from over the known world were present, observed the death of Christ, and read God's truth about Jesus, written by order of the pagan ruler, Pilate. Dr. Josef Blinzler in *The Trial of Jesus*, pages 254-255 wrote that in the neighborhood of Rome, ancient gravestones with inscriptions in the three languages of the cross are still standing. This demonstrates the truth of Scripture. *Yet, God's Word is true whether secular evidence corroborates it or not.*

3p-Verse 20. John wrote that Jesus was crucified near Jerusalem. It was Passover and Unleavened Bread time. Thousands of people from over the known world would have seen this awful event take place. Curious spectators gathered in large numbers to watch another crucifixion.

(f) "King of the Jews." Christ had said this to Pilate in Matt. 27:11. We note from John 19:21 that the chief priests wanted the title to be changed. Word of their request was hurried back to Pilate, who (in seeming revenge) refused to do so. It is striking that this eternal truth about Jesus of Nazareth being 'THE KING OF THE JEWS" was written in the three most widely known languages of that era. Over thirty years earlier, wise men from the east came to Jerusalem searching for the King of the Jews. Refer to Section 17, Matt. 2:2, footnote d. Those gathered about the cross read this message that Jesus was the king of the Jews, and carried the story back to their respective countries and homes (John 19:20). "The Word of God is not bound" (2 Tim. 2:9).

(g) Seven hundred years prior, the prophet Isaiah predicted that Messiah would die among transgressors or thieves (Isa. 53:12). We cannot help but feel that He may have been placed between the two thieves as if to show that He was the worst felon of the three. Behold all men of earth: here hanging with a scoundrel on either side is the only Man to keep and totally fulfill the six hundred and thirteen precepts of the Torah Law; the most harmless Person who ever lived! He, never did wrong to any creature; the sinless Son of God dies for the sins of all mankind. Upon His mortal frame, God laid the sins of the two thieves between whom He hung. Alas! How sin distorts human reasoning regarding true virtue and goodness. Where was Barabbas, the one who was traded for Jesus? Did he watch this scene? Refer to Section 185, Matt. 27:16, footnote e, and f, for the story of this shady figure.

(h) "They took his garments." Before tying and then nailing His hands to the horizontal cross bar, He and the two thieves were stripped naked. All the pious talk from sensitive commentators about the "moral code of the Jews" is a joke in view of their vitriolic hatred for Jesus their Messiah. The Sanhedrin has already broken many of its own laws governing a fair trial. It was customary to divide the victims clothing and personal articles (if there were any) among the four soldiers assigned to a crucifixion. The death of Christ was at the demand of the Jews, ordered by Governor Pilate, and performed by a quaternion or four soldiers. The *five pieces* of clothing normally worn by the Jews were the head covering, sandals, girdle, coat, and costly undergarment called a tunic. Exactly, what our Lord had on at this point we cannot know. The Roman Catholic Church invented the myth that His mother sewed this tunic (translated coat) for our Lord. Other writers have called attention to the fact that the high priests of Israel also wore similar vesture made without seam (Ex. 39:22), and that it was forbidden for them to tear it (Lev. 21:10). We cannot accept that the pagan Romans refused to rend this tunic based on an Old Testament text. This would have meant nothing to them. Others see in this garment a picture of our Lord's deity, without break and perfect.

2p-Among the Jews, a *tradition* existed that Moses also ministered in a garment without seam. It was believed that his vesture was pure white, and all made of one thread! This is another example of the ridiculous superstition that was rampant among the Hebrews at this time in their history.

(i) "Cast lots." John mentioned this later in his narrative, while Matthew recorded it earlier. How did John know what the soldiers said among themselves? Was he standing close enough to hear them or did the Holy Spirit reveal this to him years later? We also note that he understood the language they spoke. He later connected their actions with the fulfillment of Scripture as written in verse 24.

2p-Little did these hard-bitten soldiers realize that their decision fulfilled another Old Testament prediction about the death of the Lord Jesus. David penned this prophecy a thousand years earlier in Ps. 22:18. See second paragraph of footnote b above where the prediction was mentioned earlier in Matt. 27:35. Whatever one sees here, it must be noted that the soldiers would not tear our Lord's tunic into four parts. As there were five pieces of clothing and four soldiers, hence they cast lots to determine the owner of the odd piece. Tearing it into four parts would have rendered it worthless. See footnote h above for more on this coat of Christ. All the learned speculation about its color being sky blue or pitch black is useless guesswork. We care nothing of its color, texture, or origin; but we are passionate about the Person, who wore it.

3p-John's emphatic last sentence reveals that he actually witnessed the history he was inspired to write several years later. This is confirmed in John 19:26, where he stated that he was "standing by" with Jesus' mother and others as the Lord died. He physically heard Christ speak to him specific orders regarding His mother and her care. The teaching that the "elect lady" to whom John wrote in 2 John 1 is Mary, is incorrect.

(j) These are the words of an eyewitness to the crucifixion. He was John the former fisherman, brother of James, and son of Zebedee. He was inspired to write five of the New Testament books.

HIS FIRST THREE HOURS ON THE CROSS CONTINUE.

Jesus is ridiculed by the Jews for claiming to be the Son of God, their Messiah. The reaction of the two thieves. His second Words were spoken to the penitent thief who trusted Him as Savior and Messiah. Our Lord's third Words were uttered to Mary, His mother, and the apostle John.

Time: From 9:00 a.m. until 12:00 noon (Mk. 15:25 with 15:33).

Outside the northern gate of Jerusalem on Golgotha or Mount Calvary

Matt. 27:39-43	Mk. 15:29-32	(Lk. 23:39-43)	(John 19:25-27)
Mocking the Messiah as He hung on the cross	*Mocking the Messiah as He hung on the cross*		
39 And they that passed by reviled him, wagging their heads,	**29** And they that passed by railed on him, wagging their heads,		
40 And saying, "Thou that destroyest the temple, and buildest *it* in three days,	and saying, "Ah, thou that destroyest the temple, and buildest *it* in three days,		
save thyself. If thou be the Son of God, come down from the cross."[a]	**30** "Save thyself, and come down from the cross."[a]		
Chief priests and scribes of Israel	*Chief priests and scribes of Israel*		
41 Likewise also the chief priests mocking *him*,	**31** Likewise also the chief priests mocking said among themselves with the scribes,		
with the scribes and elders, said,			
42 "He saved others; himself he cannot save.	"He saved others; himself he cannot save.		
The hated King	*The hated King*		
If he be the King of Israel, let him now	**32** "Let Christ the King of Israel		
come down	descend now		
from the cross,	from the cross, that		
and we will believe him.[b]	we may see and believe."[b]		
43 "He trusted in God; let him deliver him now, if he will have him: for he said, 'I am the Son of God.'"[c]			
Both thieves rail on Him at first	*Both thieves rail on Him at first*		

920

Matt. 27:44	Mk. 15:32	Lk. 23:39-43	John 19:25-26
44 The thieves also, which were crucified with him, cast the same in his teeth. **(d)** (Verse 45 cont. in Section 191.)	And they that were crucified with him reviled**(d)** him. (Verse 33 cont. in Section 191.)	*One thief trusts Him* **39** And one**(e)** of the malefactors [criminals] which were hanged railed on him, saying, "If thou be Christ, save thyself and us." **40** But the other answering rebuked him, saying, "Dost not thou fear God, seeing thou art in the same condemnation?**(f)** **41** "And we indeed justly; for we receive the due reward of our deeds: but this man hath done nothing amiss"**(g)** **42** And he said unto Jesus, "Lord, remember me**(h)** when thou comest into thy kingdom." **His second Words spoken from the cross** **43** And Jesus said unto him, "Verily I say unto thee, Today shalt thou be with me in paradise."**(i)** (Verse 44 cont. in Section 191.) *For our Lord's fourth Words from the cross, see Section 191, Matt 27:45-46.*	◄*For the chronology of His cries from the cross, see Section 189, Luke 23:34.* *Standing by the cross His mother and friends* **25** Now there stood by the cross of Jesus his mother, and his mother's sister, Mary**(j)** the *wife* of Cleophas, and Mary Magdalene. ◄**His third Words spoken from the cross** **26** When Jesus therefore saw his mother,**(k)**

Matt.	Mk.	Lk.	John 19:26–27
		The Lord Jesus spoke▶ twice at this moment. First, to His mother, Mary (verse 26), and second to the apostle John (verse 27). Because His Words were simultaneous, they are held as one continuing statement. See page 1690 topic 4308-h, fifth edition of the Thompson Chain Reference Bible, for a drawing that explains this.	and the disciple standing by, whom he loved, he saith unto his mother, **"Woman, behold thy son!"**[l] 27 Then saith he to the disciple, **"Behold thy mother!"**[m] And from that hour[n] that disciple [John] took her unto his own *home.* (Verse 28 cont. in Section 191.)

Footnotes-Commentary

(a) **Verses 39–40.** Marching about the three crosses, the Jews, and their partners in wickedness taunted the Messiah. "Wagging" or shaking their heads back and forth was a common mode of expressing contempt and mockery for one's enemies.

2p-"Destroy the temple." *Again,* we hear them repeat the Words Christ had spoken in the early months of His ministry to the Jews at the temple during His first manifestation as Israel's Messiah. Although this was about three years ago, they vividly remembered what He had said, and it greatly troubled them. See Section 29, John 2:19, for His first mention of these words. The Jews also had brought it up during His trial that past night (Matt. 26:61). On this occasion, it was distorted from the original wording. *Lastly,* they used this on Pilate in order to obtain a military guard to watch over His borrowed tomb. These conscious stricken men tried every means possible to remove the awful guilt that tormented their minds. Self torture is the greatest of inflicted mental pain.

3p-"If thou be the Son of God - save thyself and come down." What awful mockery from the mouths of the Jews. It echoes of Satan's sneering at the beginning of His ministry during the great temptation. See Section 23, the third paragraph of footnote c. All informed Jews knew that the title, "Son of God" (as used in Prov. 30:4 with Ps. 2:7-12) was purely Messianic. By its misuse here, they were showing their contempt for Him. Only by dying for their sins and those of all mankind could He be the absolute Savior of mankind (1 John 2:2). Had Christ come down from that cross, the world would be without hope in this life and that, which is to come.

4p-"Son of God." This expression occurs first in its plural form in Gen. 6:2 and Job 1:6. In this usage, it speaks of a certain class or classes of God's creatures prior to it being used as a distinctive appellation of the One to whom it belongs in a sense altogether unique and peculiar. From the beginning of His physical life to the very end, Jesus of Nazareth was called "the Son of God." Before His earthly sojourn, He was known by this blessed and holy title from the sunrise of antiquity and even in the dateless past. During our Lord's trial, the high priest in a rage of anger put Jesus under oath and asked Him if he was the Son of God. His answer in the affirmative threw them into a fit of rage as they called for His death (Section 181, Matt. 26:63-66 with its parallels).

(b) Another prophecy fulfilled from Ps. 22:8. Their own words betray their thoughts. Were they worried that He may have been "the King of Israel," and "Christ" their "Messiah?" If not, we wonder why these words?

(c) **"For he said, I am the Son of God."** Here, it comes again! See the references in second and third paragraphs under footnote a above for "the Son of God." Note also Section 7, for many Names and titles of Jesus.

(d) **"Cast the same in his teeth."** An old expression used to describe symbolically vicious ridicule being thrown at an innocent person. Mark used the word "reviled" (verse 32). The text is clear that in the *early hours* of the crucifixion, *both* thieves taunted Christ. Apparently, they too were Jews and employed the same taunt as used by the religious leaders of Israel in Matt. 27:43. See footnote e and g below for more on this.

(e) Suddenly, amid their mockery, one of the thieves shouted that if Jesus were the Messiah, He should save Himself and them. Surely, this reveals that they were Jews and understood the work of their Messiah in rescuing fellow Jews from pagan deaths. In Lk. 23:40 the second malefactor spoke out. His statement and confession reveals that he sought more than deliverance from death by crucifixion. See next footnote for affirmation of this.

(f) **"The same condemnation."** Amid the unspeakable agony of crucifixion, *one* of these men suddenly contemplated the welfare of his soul as he faced sure death. From the horror of it all, he was struck with the divine patience and forbearance of Jesus. (He knew more about Christ than the text reveals.) In great pain he rebuked his fellow thief for the foolish remark, he had just made to the Messiah. Despite the sentimental preaching that men should not fear God, it is still one of the healthiest traits found in the life of Christians. This was the first step forward to forgiveness that kept this man's soul out of hell. He feared death without Christ and eternity without God.

(g) "Nothing amiss." *How did he know Christ was sinless or had done nothing amiss, and that He had a kingdom?* Surely, he had heard the truth regarding this Man at some time in the past. He confessed his wickedness and deserving of doom. They had both been professional thugs and highwaymen, robbing, stealing, and plundering the innocent. In the face of death, men often rethink their lives and need for God.

(h) "Lord remember me." What a call for mercy! No man can say Jesus is "Lord" but by the Holy Ghost (1 Cor. 12:3). "Remember me." The faintest, weakest, most pitiful of calls, such as this one caused all heaven to snap into instant attention! A sinner pleads for mercy and saving grace, and he gets it. We cannot bring ourselves to believe that this poor soul was asking admittance into a literal kingdom, yet over two thousand years in the future. *He knew Christ had a kingdom,* and requested entrance before he died. Where had he learned this great truth? Sinners have always been saved the same way, by repentance and faith in the Son of God. Salvation is an *instantaneous gift,* received through the channel of faith in Jesus Christ. God saves no one on the "installment plan." Usually, there is a process of hearing the gospel, thinking on its claims, waiting, but ultimately, at the moment of faith in Christ, that person is saved instantly and forever.

(i) Christ's second Words from the cross. Spoken to a believing thief, the dying Savior promised, "Today shalt thou be with me." *Here is the first trophy of grace that the cross secured!* A penitent thief had requested mercy in the future; Christ granted it in the present. Some commentators see in this second cry of Christ, the first fulfillment on the literal cross of Ps. 68:18. With this in mind, it is highlighted in red. Those who are so daring as to assert that Jesus' Words should be grammatically punctuated as an interrogative or question, instead of a concrete and absolute promise are playing childish games to justify a previous false doctrine. To teach that the Son of God asked a dying man if he wanted to go to heaven is totally credulous; especially because this same dying man had just asked for the Savior's mercy and confessed his sinfulness. Demonic cults and religious men denying salvation was provided before the death and resurrection of Christ, or proclaiming baptism is necessary for eternal life, argue that the thief on the cross fits into "a different dispensation." Apart from this theological prattle, this man was saved without baptism and is in heaven now. *This does not signify that men should not be baptized after they are saved by the grace of God.* For more on others who were saved without water baptism, see Section 203, third paragraph of footnote d. At the least, the baptismal cults must agree that here was one man saved without water baptism. Millions died under the Old Testament system. They were saved without any form of baptism, immersion, or sprinkling!

2p-"In Paradise." Having its origin in antiquity, "paradise" pointed to a place in the after life of peace and eternal happiness, in some cases with walls. Being about six hours before the Jewish day ended at sundown, Jesus made this promise near high noon. He assured a place with Messiah in "paradise" that day. Jesus died before the thieves. Therefore, He arrived in paradise *before* the believing ex-thief. Where will the wretched doctrine of soul sleep or unconsciousness be found here? Will the annihilationist, Universalist, Adventist, or Unitarian respond to the Son of God's Words? Jewish writings contrast paradise with gehenna; one being a place of fiery punishment and the other of peace and beauty. This is noted in the Talmud tractates, Eiruvin 19a, and Sotah 22a. Christ told this man that he would join Him in paradise after his death, and he did. For an explanation of the abode of the damned and the saved after death, and before the resurrection of Christ, see Section 59, footnote o, and Section 131, footnote f. That former thief is *now* in the presence of God enjoying the indescribable bliss of heaven-paradise. The paradise this new believer went into and joined the Messiah after physical death was *first* located in the lower parts of the earth in the rest-comfort division of sheol-hades. Christ at some period after His death and before His ascension transferred the souls of the saved from this place to be with God in heaven (Eph. 4:8-11). Years later, during the missionary work of Paul, God took him into paradise, call the "third heaven.." There he heard and saw things that are beyond the laws of goodness and love to talk about because they were so glorious (2 Cor. 12:1-4). In Rev. 2:7, the Lord Jesus affirmed that the "tree of life" is in the midst of the paradise of God. Thus, paradise-heaven is now where God and the souls of all who have died saved are. Whatever distortions the rabbis and pagans placed upon the meaning of paradise and gehenna (and there were many), hardly negates the fact of their existence. They rather prove it. *They are both real places.* For several other names for heaven that are often overlooked, see Heb. 12:22-24.

(j) "There stood by the cross." *What a place to stand!* Being this near the awful wood, they could audibly communicate with their Lord as He died. In Mk. 15:40, we read of some who "stood afar off" from the cross. Would to God that we, so many centuries later, might also by faith stand and live by the old rugged cross.

2p-Mary, His mother. O the unspeakable pain that cut through the heart of Mary, the mother of Jesus, as she beheld her Son dying on a cursed cross of Gentile heathendom. Crosses had been pagan emblems for thousands of years, and now heaven's best is nailed to this awful tree. Was the prediction of elderly Simeon, spoken so long ago ("a sword would pierce her soul") again fulfilled? This forecast was spoken almost thirty-four years prior (Lk. 2:34-35). It is touching that three women, all named Mary, stood near the cross of Christ as He died, and two of them were sisters. This reflects the influence He *finally* had among some of His human family members, though many of them had rejected Him earlier in His ministry. Read of their early opposition to Jesus and His work in Section 66,

Mk. 3:21, footnote a, and later opposition in John 7:5. Only John wrote of Jesus' mother being present at this ugly scene. The other three evangelists were not inspired to give this part of the story. For the six women named Mary, mentioned in the New Testament, see Section 9, footnote c.

3p-Verse 25a. "Mary, the wife of Cleophas." She was also a sister of Jesus' mother or His auntie. This reveals that members of our Lord's immediate earthly family had become followers of His kingdom and stood by Him even at the cross. Cleophas mentioned here, must not be confused with the later Emmaus road disciple "Cleopas" of Section 200, Lk. 24:18. Many are the traditions about this person. There is a note in the work of Eusebius, who in turn quotes from another ancient source close to the time of Jesus. This was a writer named Hegesippus who said, "Cleophas was a brother of Joseph," the husband and foster-father of Jesus! This is documented by Eusebius, in *Ecclesiastical History* III: 11 and IV: 22. He died in A.D. 340. It seems safe to hold that the Cleophas in the above text (verse 25) was a different person from the Cleopas in Luke's gospel. Edersheim in *Life and Times of Jesus the Messiah,* pages 888–889, attempts to untangle the relationship of these persons.

4p-Verse 25b. "Mary Magdalene." See Section 65, Lk. 8:2, footnote e for details on her. She and another Mary (along with others) were first at the tomb of Jesus on resurrection morning, Section 195, Mk. 16:1, footnote b. A short time later, she met Him, and He called her by name. See Section 197, John 20:11-18, footnotes f and g.

5p-The missing Mary of Bethany. How touching to find Mary, the sister of Martha, who had anointed the Savior for his death and resurrection was absent! She foresaw the cross and the resurrection of her Savior, and did not attend this scene of His crucifixion, knowing in advance the outcome. Here, a beautiful story is recorded in Section 146, and the perpetual salute of honor that Christ commanded to be given her over the ages of earthly time.

(k) These words mean just what they say. Again, the Papal Church has perverted Scripture at this point. *Christ was not calling his mother's attention to Himself dying on the cross.* Rather, he was telling Mary to behold or look at John, for now he will become her son and take care of her in old age. This implies that Christ had been tending well to His mother, but now because of His death, John will acquire this duty. Amid the agony of the crucifixion, Jesus obeys the Torah Law of Ex. 20:12 by honoring His mother even in death. Where was Joseph, husband of Mary and foster-father of Jesus? Where were Jesus' four half-brothers and two half sisters (Matt. 13:55)? Why did they not take their mother? *We do not know because God did not tell us.* For more on these thoughts, see footnote m below.

2p-Commentators and writers who continually refer to Mary as the "virgin mother" astound us. The myth of perpetual virginity was a nightmare invented by the radical church fathers and later embellished by the Romanish Church. It is foreign to Scripture; even to the Catholic Bible, and was not held in the Catholic system of religion until A.D. 998. The Bible is clear that Mary had at least six children by Joseph, and that Christ was "her firstborn." Nowhere does it say He was her "only born." For more on this, see Section 91, Matt. 13:55-56, footnotes d and e.

(l) The third Words of Christ from the cross. "Woman, behold thy son!" *The statement here and those in footnote m below were both spoken at the same time and considered as one.* Now, our Lord called Mary's attention to John; then He informed John that Mary will become a mother to him and John will become (as it were) her son. The real mother of John (Salome) was still living at this time, and present at the cross (Mk. 15:40), and later at the empty tomb (Mk. 16:1). About six months earlier, we noted her intrepid method of trying to secure a special favor for her sons from the Lord Jesus. See the main heading of Section 142, footnote a for the story.

(m) The third statement of Jesus concluded. "Behold thy mother!" See footnote l above. Whatever the commentators of today see in these Words of Jesus, at least John understood them for the text concludes by informing us that "from that hour," or time, he took Mary into his own house. See footnote n below. This means more than the house he was staying in during the Passover at Jerusalem, but his own house somewhere up north near the Sea of Galilee. Her whereabouts after that is lost in the romantic and silly religious traditions.

2p-As mentioned in footnote k above, all this begs the question of where Joseph the foster-father of Jesus was. Common sense dictates that he was not alive, for if so, he would have taken care of Mary, his wife. She was obviously a widow, as she stood at the cross. There are many myths and fables regarding the death of Joseph as well as Mary. *We have previously noted that he was alive some twelve months prior to this, as seen in John 6:42.* In this passage, the Jews spoke of *presently* knowing Jesus' father and mother. Surely, Joseph the quiet carpenter, the man who never said one word in Holy Scripture, was not alive at this time. No greater service of love could have been performed than this act of the apostle John, in taking the mother Jesus into his home. On Joseph being called "the father of Jesus," see Section 38, footnote h.

(n) "From that hour." A pungent term meaning that John received Mary as a loving ward, even as his own mother, and cared for her from the moment Jesus spoke this request. How contrary that the great apostles, continually arguing for prominence, have fled (all except John). Only four women, weak and of the timorous sex stood by their Savior as He died! No doubt, John, in love, led Mary away from that awful scene. One is disturbed to read of such men as Alfred Edersheim, referring to Mary as the "blessed virgin." This term smacks of pagan Romanism and is used by men who do not think upon these things. False religious traditions are as hard to remove from the heart as tattoos are from the skin. For more on Mary, see Section 13, fifth and sixth paragraph of footnote f.

HIS LAST THREE HOURS ON THE CROSS CONCLUDED.

At 12:00 mid-day, an eerie darkness covers the land until 3:00 mid-afternoon. Jesus speaks a fourth time. The pain of the Father turning away because He became sin for sinners breaks His great heart. As a suffering human, He asks, "why?" Near death, He speaks for the fifth time calling for a drink. A Roman soldier standing nearby honors the request. He cries a sixth time from the cross declaring His work of redemption is finished. Lastly, His seventh saying is a prayer as He commits His spirit into the hands of God. With this, His physical body expires. Atonement is accomplished, perfect, and complete for Adam's fallen race. His soon resurrection guarantees it is so.

Time: From 12:00 noon until 3:00 p.m. See Mk. 15:25 with 15:33-34, and Matt. 27:46.

Outside the northern gate of Jerusalem on Golgotha or Mount Calvary

Matt. 27:45-47	Mk. 15:33-35	Lk. 23:44-45	John 19:28-29
Darkness falls	*Darkness falls*	*Darkness falls*	
45 Now from the sixth hour[a] [12 noon.] there was **darkness over all the land**[b] unto the ninth hour. (3 p.m.)	**33** And when the sixth hour[a] [12 noon] was come, there was **darkness over the whole land**[b] until the ninth hour. (3 p.m.)	**44** And it was about the sixth hour,[a] [12 noon] and there was a **darkness over all the earth**[b] until the ninth hour. (3 p.m.)	
His fourth Words spoken from the cross	**His fourth Words spoken from the cross**	◄ *His third words from the cross are in Section 190, John 19:26. The fifth is in verse 28 below.*	
46 And about the ninth hour [3 p.m.] Jesus cried with a loud voice, saying,[c] **"Eli, Eli, lama sabachthani?"** that is to say, **"My God, my God, why hast thou forsaken me?"**	**34** And at the ninth hour [3 p.m.] Jesus cried with a loud voice, saying,[c] **"Eloi, Eloi, lama sabachthani?"** which is, being interpreted, **"My God, my God, why hast thou forsaken me?"**	◄ *Both writers were inspired to interpret Jesus' saying for readers not familiar with this language. This confirms that Gentiles also read Matthew's original book. The spelling difference is the translator's choice of letters.*	
47 Some of them that stood there, when they heard *that*, said, "This *man* calleth for Elias." (Elijah)	**35** And some of them that stood by, when they heard *it*, said, "Behold, he calleth Elias." (Elijah) *Luke wrote of the sun►and veil here in verse 45. Matthew and Mark pen this at different places. See Section 192, Matt. 27:51 with Mk. 15:38. Some think Luke wrote of a second eclipse of the sun and veil tearing, different from that by Matthew and Mark. The full details of our Lord's death would fill many volumes.*	**45** And the sun was darkened, and the veil of the temple was rent in the midst.	*His sixth and seventh words are on the next page.* ▼ **His fifth Words spoken from the cross** **28** After this, Jesus knowing that all things were now accomplished, that the scripture might be fulfilled, saith,[d] **"I thirst."** **29** Now there was set

Matt. 27:48-50	Mk. 15:36-37	Lk. 23:46	John 19:29-30
48 And straightway one of them ran, and took a spunge, and filled *it* with vinegar, and put *it* on a reed,[f] **and gave him to drink.** **49** The rest said, "Let be, let us see whether Elias [Elijah] will come to save him."	**36** And one ran and filled a spunge full of vinegar, and put *it* on a reed,[f] **and gave him to drink,** saying, "Let alone; let us see whether Elias [Elijah] will come to take him down."	◄ *Note the old English spelling of the word spunge. Today it is sponge. However, both mean the same.*	a vessel[e] full of vinegar: and they filled a spunge with vinegar, and put *it* upon hyssop,[f] **and put *it* to his mouth.** **His sixth Words spoken from the cross** **30** When Jesus therefore had received the vinegar, he said,[g] **"It is finished:"** and he bowed his head,
50 Jesus, when he had cried again with a loud voice,[h]	**37** And Jesus cried with a loud voice,[h]	**His seventh Words spoken from the cross** **46** And when Jesus had cried with a loud voice, he said,[h] **"Father, into thy hands I commend my spirit:"**	◄ *For the chronology of His cries from the cross, see Section 189, Luke 23:34.*
The Savior dies yielded up the ghost.[i] (Verse 51 cont. in Section 192.)	***The Savior dies*** and gave up the ghost.[i] (Verse 38 cont. in Section 192.)	***The Savior dies*** and having said thus, he gave up the ghost.[i] (Verse 47 cont. in Section 192.)	***The Savior dies*** and gave up the ghost.[i] (Verse 31 cont. in Section 193.)

Footnotes-Commentary

(a) It was the noontime ("sixth hour") or twelve o'clock.

(b) **Darkness falls.** Shaded in gray being an Old Testament prediction. It was written some seven hundred years prior in Amos 8:9. Of the four gospel writers, John alone was not inspired to write about this darkness. A terrible thing fell over the "whole land" or "earth" and lasted until three o'clock ("ninth hour") that afternoon. The chief light of creation blushed out in shame and sorrow as its Maker died for sinful man. *The Son eclipsed the sun!* When we remember how the Pharisees clamored for Jesus to show them a sign from heaven (Matt. 16:1), now their request is granted. It is accompanied with terror and awe. Secular ancient writers have confirmed this darkness. They were pagans and had no sympathy with Christianity. Josh McDowell and Bill Wilson in their work, *He Walked Among Us,* pages 35-37, lay down impressive demonstrations of this fact. However, the faith of God's Word is never based upon any secular evidence whatsoever. God's truth stands alone on divine inspiration. If secular history agrees with Scripture, it is correct; if it disagrees with Holy Scripture, then it is wrong. Charles Spurgeon comments on the darkness with these pungent words, "Never forget that this miracle of the closing of the eye of day at high noon was performed by our Lord in His weakness . . . He has come to His lowest, the fever is on Him, He is faint and thirsty . . . yet He has power to darken the sun at noon. He is still very God of very God." From *The Treasury of the New Testament,* vol. 1, page 392. This sudden darkness sent fear and wonderment upon all present. One can believe that across Jerusalem and other parts of the earth men rushed to their houses, retrieved and lit candles, and oil lamps. To be cloaked in awful darkness at mid afternoon was a terrible omen of divine origin. One ponders over the fear and confusion that prevailed amid the priests and Levites in the temple a few miles from the mount of crucifixion.

2p-Verse 45. "The sixth hour." Three o'clock mid afternoon was when the "between afternoon" sacrifice was slain in the temple. It was here that God laid the sins of all mankind upon His beloved Son. With this, see Isa. 53:6; 2 Cor. 5:21; and 1 Peter 2:24. When Christ became sin for sinners, it was then God judged, condemned, and punished our sins on Him and Him for our sins. He bore the judgment for all of our sins, as though He had committed them. Therefore, those who have received Him as personal Lord and Savior are beyond condemnation. Because Christ has redeemed them, there is no condemnation to all who are in Him (John 5:24). Saved Christians may lift their voices and shout to the world, "Who shall lay anything to the charge of God's elect?" (Rom. 8:33).

(c) His fourth cry from the cross. The difference in the spelling between Matthew and Mark is normal. See for example, the spelling difference of the name "Nahor" in Gen. 11:27, against that in Lk. 3:34 spelled "Nachor." The Nahor in Gen. 11:27 is a brother of Abraham. The Nachor in Lk. 3:34 is Abraham's grandfather. He is spoken of in Gen. 11:22-25. There are numerous examples of this in the Bible. This spelling difference is frequently seen in the standard literature of today. See seventh paragraph below for more on these thoughts.

2p-"My God, my God, why hast thou forsaken me?" God is estranged from God! Jesus drinks the awful cup of (temporary) separation from the Father and wails in agony! In this, He fulfills another prophecy. It was recorded in Ps. 22:1, a thousand years prior. What is it like to be totally forsaken by God? Even in hell, men remember Him as they remember their past and realize their horrible future. He has promised His children, "I will never leave thee, nor forsake thee" (Heb. 13:5), yet He forsook Jesus on the cross! In view of this deep, dark thing, we inquire, "O God, what is sin to do such things to thy Son?" At the beginning of His ministry, the Father attested to Christ the Words, "In whom I am well pleased" (Matt. 3:17). Now, at the end of His work, the Father turns from Him being the greatest of all sorrows to the Man of sorrows. Nothing so wounded Him as the cup He drank. Bearing the sinner's sins, He was treated as a sinner by the Father. God judged Jesus by His perfect justice on the cross.

3p-How could Jesus call God His God? Anti-Trinitarians point to this and tell us that since Jesus had a God over Him; therefore, He cannot be God. Entering the world, wrapped in human flesh, He was subordinate, or submissive to God's will for His earthly life. *It was only within the realm of this submission that He claimed God as His God and prayed for His will to be done.* From His subordinate level as a human He said, "I ascend to my Father, and your Father; and *to* my God, and your God" (John 20:17). As a man on earth doing the will of heaven, He was dependent upon God the Father, His perfect co-equal in heaven. In the prayers of Jesus to the Father, blasphemers taunt Scripture and mock, "O, your Jesus is praying to himself; why does He even pray if He is God?" These poor people are mute to the fact that in His human subordination and earthly state, He was giving to us the high example of how our relationship with the Father should also be. Jesus never executed His duties, independent of God. On occasion, He chose not to use certain divine attributes. However, He never laid them aside. As a man, He always sought His Father-God, as we should. The Fatherhood of God to Jesus is different from all earthly fatherhoods, in that they (and the Holy Spirit) were perfectly co-equal from all eternity. The incarnation *temporarily* brought a new dimension into these mysteries while the blessed Son lived among men as a Man.

4p-Did God forsake Jesus? There is strange talk today that God did not actually forsake His Son. At a moment in time, upon the cross, God laid the total sins of all mankind upon the Lord Jesus. It is written that God "made him to be sin for us" (2 Cor. 5:21). He was the sinless One, who now became the guilty sinner for all sinners! The words in Isa. 59:2 have reference to the sins of Israel and is not a prediction of the dying Savior. Israel deliberately chose to sin against Jehovah and thereby separated themselves from Him. On the cross, the perfect One became sin by taking the sins of others. It is written of God in Hab. 1:13, *"Thou art* of purer eyes than to behold evil, and canst not look on iniquity: wherefore lookest thou upon them that deal treacherously?"* In Prov. 15:3 we read, "The eyes of the LORD *are* in every place, beholding the evil and the good." The old wives' tale that "God cannot look upon sin" is just that! He beholds a sin maddened world every human hour of its existence. Those who argue that God did not forsake Christ (because of our sins that were laid upon Him) base their error upon John 9:31. In this text, a former blind man said to the Pharisees "Now we know that God heareth not sinners." He took this statement from popular rabbinical teaching of that era, heard in the synagogues every Sabbath. The scribes propounded that all Gentiles were sinners, and God would never hear them until they became proselytes to Israel. If God does not hear sinners then all of us are doomed, for we came to Christ as repenting, believing sinners, and he heard us (Rom. 10:13). Did he hear the thief on the cross? Our Savior on the cross became sin without being a sinner!

5p-Jesus physically "bare our sins in his own body on the tree" (1 Peter 2:24). In some way, God laid them on Him (Isa. 53:6). He literally "gave himself for us an offering and a sacrifice to God" as the atonement for those sins (Eph. 5:2). God refused to hear Him, not because He had been or was a sinner, rather, because he became our sin with all its sickening and horrible consequences. Therefore, our sins laid upon Him answer the question, "Why hast thou forsaken me?" We are the villains, the culprits, and the guilty. On the cross, He took our place. God punished Him, as though He had committed our sins. In theology this is called the "vicarious suffering" of Christ. There is no inconsistency in the predictions of Ps. 22. Every Word of God is pure (Prov. 30:5). Inconsistencies and contradictions lurk in the minds of those who think they have discovered some hidden truth that the Christian community has missed for over two thousand years. On the cross as a *human,* our Lord did despair, and as a *human,* He cried out, "Why hast thou forsaken me?" As a *human* in Gethsemane, He agonized to the shedding of great drops of blood. As a *human,* He was "a man of sorrows and acquainted with grief" (Is. 53:3). As a *human,* Satan tempted Him (Matt. 4:1). As a *human,* He wept over wicked Jerusalem (Lk. 19:41), though He had known all these things before the foundation of the world. "Forasmuch then as the children [of Adam] are partakers of flesh and blood, he also himself, likewise, took part of the same" (Heb. 2:14). This does not reflect an attitude of faithless resignation to the Father's will; rather, it portrays the true Christ from heaven: Perfect Man and Perfect God. Both natures responded exactly as they should. Technical definitions, and explanations of this are beyond mortal man. Like numerous other things, it is to be believed and not defined.

6p-One is amazed that the hundreds of Jews and religious leaders standing about the cross did not connect His various quotes from the Old Testament with their Messiah, or did they? At this point, He slowly drinks the cup that so troubled His soul in the shadows of Gethsemane's awful sorrows the night before. Seemingly, it was here that the Father (temporarily) forsook the Son. For more explanation of this, see Section 179, Matt. 26:39, footnote e.

7p-Verse 47. "Calleth for Elijah." Pious Jews of this time believed that (Elias) Elijah never died. They held that he would appear on special errands among the people of Israel and even assist those Jews, who died hard and painful deaths. Apparently, the religious leaders standing by the cross assumed that Jesus was calling on the old prophet to assist Him in this terrible hour. We note in Matt. 27:49 that some of the Jews wanted to see if Elijah would appear to help Him, which validates the belief of his appearing. They did not know that Jesus and Elijah had earlier discussed his death on the Mount of Transfiguration. See Section 105, Lk. 9:30-31. The difference in the spelling of the name Elijah is normal. This is common in the translation of historical documents. For more on variant names spellings in Scripture, see Section 6, second paragraph of footnote a.

(d) His fifth cry from the cross. John alone records Jesus' call for water in verse 28. At this moment, the human body of our Lord screamed for moisture. See footnote e below for more on this. Out of His dying humanity, He called, "I thirst." Two Old Testament predictions were fulfilled in this statement. They are Ps. 22:15 with Ps. 69:21. For comments on the various drinks offered the Savior, see Section 188, Matt. 27:34, footnote f.

(e) "Vessel full of vinegar." Probably, the drink offered Jesus at this final moment was taken from the soldier's drinking pot sitting nearby. This container was the standard practice among the Roman military and used to refresh men on duty. This particular vinegar was *strictly* no intoxicating, as it might interfere with their ability to perform duties under a command and amid dangerous situations. This liquid was known as "posca" (with variations in spelling) among the Roman soldiery. Shortly before physical death, the Lord Jesus received a sip of "posca," from the hand of one of the soldiers. *We wonder if this was the same centurion who, with his companion's only moments later, confessed that He was the Son of God* . Refer to Section 192, Matt. 27:54 for his words.

(f) This act fulfilled the prediction of Ps. 69:21. Reeds growing out of the hyssop were about four feet in length and grew in abundance, especially in marshy areas of the Jordan River. Critics who make a big noise about the difference between the reed, and hyssop should stop playing their infantile games with God's Word. Their problem lies in an unconverted heart not in a reed or hyssop with a sponge stuck on the end of it. These plants were used for numerous purposes: basket making, building, fire, small weapons, and decorations. Jews used hyssop in connection with certain sacrifices as seen in Ex. 12:22, and Lev. 14:4–7.

(g) "It is finished." His sixth cry from the cross. Some see this as referring to Gen. 2:1, when Christ the creator (Eph. 3:9 with Heb. 1:3), had "finished" all things. We have highlighted it in gray with this possibility in mind that it could have been a prophetic cry. Atonement was accomplished; redemption was vouchsafed for all who would believe in The Son of God. It was secured, realized, and sin had been dealt with to the satisfaction of God, the Judge of all the earth. Divine justice was appeased, and His holiness satisfied. God's will for the atonement of man's sin was done. *The millions since Adam, who had put their faith forward into the coming Savior of mankind rejoiced; now, at last full redemption was accomplished. No more sacrifices or burnt offerings; they had met their final terminus as the Lamb on Calvary swallowed them up.* The great Torah Law with its standards of perfection bowed at His feet and surrendered to Messiah. It shadowed Him many times; now He had fulfilled its every demand. *What the law could not do but pointed to, grace had done.* The curse of Adam's sin was now cursed and broken for all who repent and believe on the Savior. Every type or shadow, every sacrifice and offering, all things in the old covenant vanished in the new covenant. Satan, the prince of darkness, was stripped of his control over mankind through their sin. This victory is appropriated in the soul of everyone who receives Christ. For the origin of the Devil's title "prince of the world," see Section 161, footnote j. The new kingdom-church is open for whosoever will! Messiah *willingly* gave His human life, paying for our sins with the perfect sacrifice of His sinless physical body (Heb. 10:10). There is a strange prediction in Isa. 53:10. It states, our Savior made His soul and offering for sin! Somehow, both His body and soul suffered on the awful cross. *Who among rational men would dare comment very far on this!*

(h) "Father, into thy hands …" His seventh and final cry from the pulpit of the cross. Christ died with the words of Ps. 31:5 on His lips. This Psalm reads, "Father, into thine hand I commit my spirit." Physical death moves toward all of us. God grant that every believer can utter this prayer with firm confidence and sure hope. *Reader, into whose hands will you commit your spirit at the moment of death?* The change from singular "hand," to plural "hands," between Ps. 31:5 and Lk. 23:46, signify that men are as safe in one of God's hands as they are in both.

(i) "Gave up the ghost." This old English saying beautifully expresses what happens to men at death. In this case, the physical body of the Lord Jesus expired and the real Person dwelling inside moved out. The word "ghost" is another translation of the word "spirit" or life within the human frame. When we die, the life in a physical body goes back to God, who gave it (Eccles. 12:7 with James 2:26). The real us on the inside (the soul) moves out into eternity. The physical body surrenders the soul upon its death. (James 2:26). See also 2 Cor. 4:16 and Eph 3:16. Peter makes clear the distinction between the human body and soul in 1 Peter 2:11. The Old Testament teaches the same in Gen. 35:17-19 with 1 Kings 17:17-22. The ancients associated both body and soul with death and the grave. Elihu spoke of his "soul drawing near to the grave" (Job 33:22). He was using a common expression meaning death and the grave were close. At death, his inward being would exit his physical body as "God took away his soul" (Job 27:8). In Matt. 27:52, it is clear that *only* "bodies" sleep in death not souls. Paul's trip to the third heaven, "in or out of the body," reveals the difference between the body and spiritual soul (2 Cor. 12:1-4).

2p-In this act of "giving up the ghost" the work of eternal atonement was done! Before this, humankind labored under the load of sin. No one could rescue us from this plight. Christ, the perfect, pure, and innocent Son of Man, and Son of God came into the world to take all of our sins and die for them. No longer do we entertain a thousand reminiscences of past transgressions that crowd about and shout terrible accusations into our poor souls. Prophecy was fulfilled, as the ancient covenant of the Torah Law bowed out and the new covenant of grace stepped forward. It forever raised a holy standard. The Reformed preacher, F. W. Krummacher, wrote over a century ago in his opus, *The Suffering Saviour*, page 343, these words, "Let us congratulate ourselves, therefore, on the incomparable inheritance left us by Him who expired on the cross." To this, we add: not only congratulate ourselves but also praise the God of heaven for this act of unspeakable grace. Christ's death forever provided redemption. The reception, application, and benefits of this inheritance are guaranteed by His resurrection. Men partake of them by faith. For explanation of the new covenant as mentioned above, see Section 95, second paragraph of footnote u.

3p-No human mind fathoms the depths of God's government and *total* plan for this world. It remains a sealed mystery how the all-loving God sees men born whose course of life will terminate in the abyss of eternal damnation. We fail to comprehend the omnipotent love that goes hand in hand with justice. Jehovah loves differently from men who cannot understand divine ways (Isa. 55:7-9). On the other side, what would liberty be if the Almighty forced or constrained men into blind obedience? If (as some teach) that before the foundation of the world, He chose certain persons to be saved and reprobated all else, to be damned, then we are victims of fate, some to its good side, and others to the bad. How dreadful the thought, that God should put aside justice to avoid punishing sin or wink at mercy to execute justice. His entire throne would come down in shame and infamy. All these paradoxes meet in the cross, as Christ dies for the sin of all men of all times. We rest in the truth, "Shall not the Judge of all the earth do right" (Gen. 18:25)? *With some things, it is wise to remain content in ignorance.*

4p-Did Jesus die twice on the cross? There is a heretical teaching, which says the Lord Jesus died twice on the cross! Pastor R. B. Thieme Jr., in his booklet, *The Blood of Christ,* page 34 penned these words, "Our Lord died twice on the cross. His first death is called 'the blood of Christ,' and only after the compilations of this, His spiritual death, did He die physically." This is more philosophical error trying to dissect the death of Christ for mankind. The continual message of Scripture is that "Christ died for our sins." Not that He "dies" for them. In death, His blood was shed, and in shedding his blood, He died. The two are inseparable. Jesus, by providing the complete blood atonement, perfected every born again child of God forever. The Savior did not die twice! Hebrews chapters 9 and 10 positively affirm the one time, forever death of Christ for our sins.

5p-"Revisionist theology." This perversion of truth changes, reinterprets, and plays down many of the fundamental doctrines of Holy Scripture. Among their grossest distortions are those concerning the atoning blood of Christ. They make learned distinctions between the literal blood of Christ flowing from His veins, and His physical body dying. See the 4p- above. Another lie is their justification of homosexuality by pretentious exegesis of Scripture, which is practiced by every false cult. Ignorant, gullible Christians often embrace and defend "Revisionists theology because it sounds good or offers them a way to continue in their sins. Nobler and stronger believers should drive from their pulpits men who preach and teach these hideous untruths. Wordy philosophical verbiage is typical of religious wolves in sheep's clothing. Men who have more brains than heart, more Greek than God, and more syntax than the Savior are dangerous. They fain to know Hebrew but deny heaven and hell. Their expertise in conjugating a verb is amazing while their failure to win a lost soul to Jesus is appalling. One will never hear a Revisionist theologian dealing biblically with sin, its judgment, and doom in hell. The reason is obvious.

6p-The national anthem of heaven will be about the blood of Christ (Rev. 5:8-12). Those who play down this supreme fact, cast evil inferences on it, and cleverly explain it away are the human devils mentioned in 2 Peter 2:1-3. From the counsel halls of the dateless past, the Holy Trinity planned redemption for fallen men through the death and blood being shed of the innocent. The millions of sacrifices offered during the Old Testament rituals all pointed ahead to the final supreme sacrifice (1 Peter 1:18-20). Under the Torah Law of Israel, God announced that it was the blood that made atonement for the soul (Lev. 17:11). Without this there was no remission or moving sin ahead to the next sacrifice (Heb. 10:1-4). When Christ came onto the scene, God had given Him a body, on which the sins of all ages past were laid (Isa. 53:6 with 1 Peter 2:24). *This became the final and absolute offering for all sins forever (Heb. 10:5, 10).* Christ willingly gave Himself to die on the cross for our sins as the supreme ransom for the "many" or the masses of all mankind (Heb. 9:22 with Matt. 26:28). God accepted what Christ did as the perfect atonement. Based on that, He forgives all repenting believing sinners "for Christ's sake" (Eph 4:32). This is His beloved Son in whom He is "well pleased" (Matt. 3:17). The above is a *tiny* sketch of divine grace in action (Eph. 2:8).

THE AWFUL AFTERMATH OF HIS DEATH.

Dramatic, supernatural phenomenon occurred as Christ died. Family members, friends, and hundreds of others gathered to watch. Awful convulsions of nature struck terror into the hearts of everyone present. Suddenly, hundreds of graves yawned opened when Jesus died! Three days and nights later, *after* His resurrection, recognizable bodies of Old Testament saints came out of these resting places and appeared before many across the city Jerusalem.

Time: Immediately after His death at 3:00 p.m.

Outside the northern gate of Jerusalem on Golgotha or Mount Calvary

Matt. 27:51-55	Mk. 15:38-40	Lk. 23:47-49	John
Terrible phenomena	*Terrible phenomena*		
51 And, behold, the veil[a] of the temple was rent in twain from the top to the bottom; and the earth did quake, and the rocks rent;	38 And the veil[a] of the temple was rent in twain from the top to the bottom.	◄ *Luke's account of the veil is found in the previous Section 191, Lk. 23:45. Note comments at this place.*	
52 And the graves were opened; and many bodies of the saints which slept arose, 53 And came out of the graves after his resurrection, and went into the holy city, and appeared unto many.	◄ *Here, briefly recorded is one of the most phenomenal events that accompanied the resurrection of Jesus Christ. It is dealt with at number 3, under footnote a below.*		
The soldiers' confession	*The soldiers' confession*	*The soldiers' confession*	
54 Now when the centurion, and they that were with him, watching Jesus, saw the earthquake, and those things that were done, they feared greatly, saying, "Truly this was the Son of God."[b] ▲ *"They." All the soldiers made this confession.*	39 And when the centurion, which stood over against him, saw that he so cried out, and gave up the ghost, he said, "Truly this man was the Son of God."[b]	47 Now when the centurion saw what was done, he glorified God, saying, "Certainly this was a righteous man."[b] 48 And all the people that came together to that sight, beholding the things which were done, smote their breasts,[c] and returned.	
Devout women present	*Devout women present*	*Devout women present*	
55 And many women[d] were there beholding afar off, which followed Jesus from Galilee, ministering unto	40 There were also women[d] looking on afar off:	49 And all his acquaintance,[d] and the women that followed him from Galilee, stood afar off, beholding these things. (Verse 50 cont. in Section 193.)	

Matt. 27:55-56	Mk. 15:40-41	Lk.	John
him: **56** Among which was Mary Magdalene, and Mary the mother of James and Joses, and the mother[e] of Zebedee's children. (Verse 57 cont. in Section 193.)	Among whom was Mary Magdalene, and Mary the mother of James the less and of Joses, and Salome;[e] **41** (Who also, when he was in Galilee,▶ followed him, and ministered unto him;) and many[f] other women which came up with him unto Jerusalem.[g] (Verse 42 cont. in Section 193.)	◀*How touching are the words of the evangelist that Jesus was supported by godly women from Galilee and other places. Standing like a flock of frightened sheep, they watched their shepherd die on a Roman cross! At this point, none of them yet realized He would soon rise from the tomb, ever victorious over death, hell, and the grave. For more on this, see Section 196, and the symbol ◀ at John 20:9.*	

Footnotes-Commentary

(a) The divine sciences of astronomy and geology fell into fits of convulsion upon the death of Christ their Creator. Nature was terrified. Heaven and earth shout their objections to His death! One cannot but feel sheer disgust as the "learned men of theology" call into question these and other passages. They line up like spoiled children, each one casting his wicked opinion as to why this or that cannot be true; always calling into question what the inspired authors penned. Spurgeon, in *The Treasury of the New Testament,* vol. 1, page 404, wrote the following, "The death of our Lord Jesus Christ was fitly surrounded by miracles; yet it is itself so much greater a wonder than all beside, that it as far exceeds them as the sun outshines the planets which surround it." We note below some of the fearful phenomena mentioned in verse 51 that fell as the Son of God expired on the cross.

1. **Mk. 15:33 in the previous Section. Darkness.** An abnormal and terrifying darkness fell over the land from high noon until three o'clock, mid-afternoon. This could not have been a darkness of natural causes, for during Passover, there was always a full moon even though it might have been clouded. The blazing noonday sun suddenly shrouded itself with an unnatural eclipse. For details on this black out, see the previous Section 191, Matt. 27:45-46, footnote b. An Old Testament prophet seems to have predicted this solar phenomenon some seven hundred years prior in Amos 8:9.

2. **Verse 51. Veil.** This was torn in half by an act of God. This showed that figurative worship was ended and that the true religion was established. According to the Talmud tractates, Yoma 54a and Kethuboth 106a there were some thirteen different veils hung in various places about the temple. Two other veils were also hung, one at the entrance of the Holy Place, and the other between this and the Holy of Holies. Behind the second veil entered the high priest once a year to procure temporary atonement for the sins of Israel (Heb. 9:2-9). These two veils were some sixty feet long and thirty feet high, being the thickness of a man's palm. They were made of some seventy-two different squares neatly sewn together with purple and gold, and were iridescent with brilliance. Some one hundred priests were needed to raise this curtain to its hanging position. It weighed over a thousand pounds! It could not have torn or rent from top to bottom, unless its upper lintel (holding bar) had broken and fallen. It was an act performed by God. This last veil also typified the sinless human body of Jesus (Heb. 10:5, 20). When He died for our sins, His physical anatomy was shattered and torn as it suffered under the judgment of God upon mankind's iniquities (Isa. 53:3-5). Paul wrote in Gal. 1:4 that He "gave himself for our sins." John penned in 1 John 2:2 that "He is the propitiation for our sins: and not for ours only, but also for *the sins* of the whole world." In His death and atonement, He became the Lamb of God that takes away the sin of the world for those who trust him as personal Savior (John 1:29).

   Suddenly, the Holy of Holies in Jerusalem's temple that separated men from God became forever obsolete; the eternal atonement of Christ was accepted by Jehovah. No sign was needed to prove this glorious fact. The great veil crashed to the floor never to be hung again. This awesome curtain that stood as a steel impasse between men and God was now abolished! The way into the Holiest of all, the one in yonder heaven, was open for whosoever will. Any man may now draw near to the heart of God, with humble boldness (Heb. 10:19-21). Among the thirteen veils that hung in the temple this was the inner curtain that shut off the Holy of Holies from human gaze and presence.

History mentions the temple veil. The pagan writer Tacticus mentioned the temple veil in *Histories*, vol. 3. *It split from the top down to the floor, thus demonstrating that God made the access into His presence for all men.* These terrifying phenomena occurred just as Israel's Messiah gave up the ghost on Mount Calvary, outside the northern wall of the city. Every worker in the temple compound must have been terrified at the crashing sound booming from within the holy place. Horrified priests looking into this room suddenly were gazing into the forbidden Holy of Holies! The rendering of the main veil also pointed out that the separation between Jews and Gentiles was forever abolished; that the exclusive privilege of the high priest to enter God's presence was now available to all believers in Christ. All saved Christians regardless of race or rank have free access to the throne of grace (Eph. 2:11-21; 1 Peter 2:9- 10; and Heb. 10:20-21).

There was a story among the Jews, that several decades before the temple was destroyed, that its doors and curtains would mysteriously open of themselves. See Talmud tractate, Yoma 39a. In this same tractate, there is a curious legend. It says that on the Day of Atonement, the priest tied a piece of scarlet cloth between the horns of the bull to be sacrificed (Lev. 16:14). If it turned white, this signaled that God had forgiven Israel of their sins. This was based on Isa. 1:18. The remainder of tractate, Yoma 39a and 39b tells that for the forty years *before* the temple was destroyed in A.D. 70, "the scarlet cloth never turned white." How eerie this is in view of Israel's rejection of their Messiah and the doom of the city four decades later! The destruction of Jerusalem and the temple is discussed in Section 163.

3. **Verse 52. The graves opened and the dead were raised.** A fearful demonstration that death was conquered and all men would rise someday for eternal judgment. They were called *"saints,"* meaning believers. This passage makes it clear that it is the human body alone that sleeps in the grave, not the soul. Many expositors have misread this by not connecting it with the following verse 53. None of these resurrected bodies came out of their graves until *after* Christ had risen. The idea is that when Jesus expired physically on the cross, there were violent earthquakes: with this, the graves of hundreds or thousands of Old Testament saints opened around the city of Jerusalem and probably further out. However, their dead bodies did not come out until *after* the resurrection of Christ. (As open graves were forbidden by the Jews, one can imagine the stir this caused for three days and nights!) Many read that this resurrection occurred the *moment* Jesus died. Not so, for Christ was the first fruits of those who slept (1 Cor. 15:23). With these seismological upheavals graves or cavern sepulchers, and the cave tombs of the Jews yawned opened and stayed that way for some three days and nights! Their bodies did not reunite into a recognizable, solid form and rise from their resting places until He had risen first. No dead body was buried behind the walls of Jerusalem, but outside the city in locations previously designated by the Sanhedrin. When we recall that this occurred during the Passover celebration time, thousands of Jews knew of this fearful event, and talk of it spread over the city and across the land. Surely, with thousands of open burying sites everywhere, the whole city and Jewry were horrified. It was in the middle of the Feast of Unleavened Bread and this would have defiled the entire land. This is one of the extraordinary miracles that occurred with the death of Christ that is recorded in only a few words. The brief details of this phenomenon reveal the inspiration of Scripture. When the Passover pilgrims returned to their homes over the known world of that day, what stories they had to tell!

As explained several times, the soul departs from the human body at death and goes into eternity (Gen. 35:17-18; 1 Kings 17:21-22; Job 27:8; and 2 Cor. 5:8). Before our Lord's resurrection, the souls of the saved at death went into the rest area or side of sheol-hades. There they waited for Messiah to come and announce His perfect atonement was accomplished. Victory over death and the grave was His. He then led these millions out of their "half way house" and ushered them into the presence of God (Eph. 4:8-11). For more on this fascinating subject, see Section 190, Lk. 23:43, second paragraph of footnote i.

These deceased saints returning from the shades of death caused great turmoil among the inhabitants of Jerusalem, as they "appeared unto many." Matthew's words fuel the imagination! Some ancient expositors held that this had reference to all that had died from Adam to that time. Did a Jew on the morning of Christ's resurrection look out his window and see Job, David, or Daniel standing nearby? Alternatively, as the women went early to draw water did they suddenly confront Moses, Joel, or Abraham? The text suggests that those to whom these risen saints appeared instantly knew who they were! We cannot accept that these were formerly dead bodies, now resurrected without their respective souls within them. Some believe this fulfilled Isa. 26:19. Here, were physical bodies raised in a perfect condition with the saved soul reunited in its former but now immortal, incorruptible house. If this were not the case, then these resurrected saints had to die physically again. They were among the millions that

Christ led to heaven into the presence of God as mentioned in the paragraphs just above. This brief and haunting passage so full of mystery, demonstrates that God does not minister to our curiosity.

Glorious wonder is embedded in verses 52 and 53. Matthew wrote nothing as to *why* this occurred. Was it another heavenly effort to convince the Jews that Jesus was Messiah? Some see in this army of resurrected Old Testament saints, a unique resurrection. Certain *radical* dispensationalists use this as justification to invent another resurrection to prop up their exaggerated eschatology. God has not given to us the *finer details* of this wonder; therefore, prudence dictates that we do not press the subject. Why we have no more information on this miracle is the choice of God. Matthew's brevity in writing of this affirms that he was led of the Holy Spirit, for human curiosity would have penned many lines to hold the attention of readers. God gives us what we need in His inspired Word.

4. **Verses 51–54. Violent earthquakes and geological upheavals.** The crowds "feared greatly." No wonder! Those who have passed through an earthquake or geological shock waves understand this fear. The author lived in Johannesburg, South Africa, for many years and has both felt and seen the horror that often accompanies these convulsions of nature occurring in sunken mine shafts. The geology of earth gave terrible testimony to the innocence of the dying Christ, showing she feared to open her mouth and swallow His blood. The quake waves shook Mount Calvary and surrounding parts of the earth so violently that the rocks split asunder. To what distance these fierce seismological vibrations hit land and sea, we have some written evidence. *Gill's Commentary,* vol. 7, page 365 quotes from ancient writers who spoke of such events in their day, even to "the destruction of twelve different cities in Asia." Regardless, the several million people present at Jerusalem and surrounding areas at this Passover and Unleavened Feast, knew something dreadful had befallen the land. It is of note that the earth convulsed at both the death and then the resurrection of our Lord. Refer to the "great" resurrection earthquake in Section 195, Matt. 28:2. Nature quivered at His death, and trembled again at His glorious resurrection!

(b) The centurion's confession. Matthew changes to the plural by use of the pronoun "they," twice in verse 54 when writing about the "greatly fearful" reaction of the soldiers. These men were battle hardened and fearless. Now, something divine was taking place! He states that all the soldiers "watching him" made some kind of simultaneous confession about Christ on the cross. Matthew's emphasis is on all four of these men. Mark and Luke wrote of the officer in charge, called a "centurion." Looking at the three parallel texts, we get the full statement of these men of the Roman military: Christ was "the Son of God," and "a righteous man." Had not Nathanael much earlier made a similar statement in John 1:49, and Peter in Matt. 16:16? This officer was apparently the centurion or the one in command over the soldiers who had mocked Christ in Pilate's hall. It reads in Section 189, Matt. 27:36 that the soldiers sat down and watched Jesus die. This particular officer saw something in the dying Messiah that he had never seen in any victim on the cross. He had just witnessed, in terror, the miracles of nature that struck as Jesus died. Some discredit this confession due to his pagan background. Pagans had little knowledge of Israel's Messiah: they were polytheistic and worshiped Satan in the form of idolatry. However, countries near Israel had received news about this marvelous Person. Thousands had heard of Him, even in the mighty Roman military.

2p-For the *first soldier saved* in the ministry of Christ, see the italicized main heading of Section 60 for details. It is true that the term "son of God" in *pagan thinking* signified any eminent or divine person within their satanic religions. To hold that these men were referring to some pagan deity is wrong. We are sure that they heard Jesus pray for their forgiveness as they crucified Him (Lk. 23:34). Did the earthquake, darkness, wailing women, conversations between Christ and the thief, or John and Mary touch their hearts? Did they read the words on the board above the head of Jesus and receive the faith that comes by the Word of God (Rom. 10:17)? Surely, all the soldiers heard the thief's plea for mercy and the response of Christ. How wonderful it would be to meet these men responsible for Jesus' crucifixion in heaven, when our earthly tenure is completed. For other interesting details concerning the soldier that pierced Jesus' side with a spear, see John 19:34, footnote c.

(c) "Smote their breasts." Still today, this is an oriental way of expressing deep grief. The author has seen Africans in dire distress and sorrow dancing about violently, beating on their chests, while throwing dust into the air. Being Passover time and the city packed with pilgrims from over the known world, thousands had gathered to watch another crucifixion. Many were the implacable enemies of Christ, others uncommitted, some curious, but many believers were also present. When these multitudes saw the skies darken, and felt under their feet the convulsions of nature they were horrified. No doubt, they feared some terrible judgment from heaven might befall them. The suggestion in this wording is that some of them fell prostrate upon their faces in sheer horror of what was happening. Jews who beat upon their breasts in deep lamentation usually did so while on their knees in a posture of broken humility. The book of Lamentations is the Bible's best example of the antics and words of Jews in overwhelming grief. Loud and sorrowful emotions during the Passover celebration were forbidden.

2p-Verse 49. "All his acquaintance." It is wrong to retranslate these words into not meaning what they say. Who these family members were, we do not know. See d and e below for several names in this company.

(d) **"Many women."** This cannot mean a few dozen! Matthew used "many" some thirty-seven times in his book. Contextually it always referred to large numbers. Here, we meet again those faithful women from Galilee, who greatly loved their Lord. For more about these female disciples, see Section 65, Lk. 8:2, footnote e. To their everlasting honor, this band of women evidenced more love and courage for their Lord and Messiah than most of His special apostles. Where was Peter, who had solemnly promised to die with Him? Out of the apostolic company, only John stood near the awful cross of death. The statement that they "stood afar off," or "looking on from afar off," is not in conflict with the earlier words of John 19:25-27. In these passages, John wrote that *some* of these women were so near to Christ that He conversed with them, while others were not. As His hour of death drew near, the women retreated to some further distance, knowing that the soldiers would break the legs of the condemned; hence, they stood away from this awful scene. Mary, his mother stood near to John amid the horror. Surely, the terror of nature's reactions must have struck their hearts with fear. One can only hope that the terrified other ten apostles were with them. John led Mary from that crushing sight. Mark gives the names of three women, Mary Magdalene, Mary the mother of James and Joses, and the mother of Zebedee's children, also named Salome (Mk. 15:40). It has been noted that *three women* named "Mary" were at the crucifixion. Refer to Section 190, footnote j.

(e) **Salome the mother of Zebedee's children.** One ponders what Salome thought a while later as she beheld Jesus dying on a Roman cross? Several weeks earlier, she approached Him with a scheme to secure for her two sons top positions in His earthly kingdom. Refer to Section 142 for the story. *Now, He is crucified!* The sight of their Messiah dying on a cross devastated all of them. Salome was shaken! The grandeur dreams of a material political kingdom vanished in front of her eyes: their King was being crucified! At this place, neither Salome, nor the others understood the correct plan of God for Israel, the cross and resurrection. After Pentecost, it was understood. For the apostles' material kingdom and Jesus correcting them, see Section 206, Acts 1:6-8, footnotes c, and d.

(f) **"Many other women."** The syntax of these parallel verses gives the impression that a *great* number (hundreds) of women had become supporters of the ministry of Jesus and His apostles. Only a few of them are named here. Luke described some of this group as "all his [Jesus'] acquaintance" (verse 49). "All" was surely a large number. Matthew does not write of the anguish of heart experienced by these pious women. He drops the curtain on that sad scene, while Dr. Luke *briefly* wrote of their sorrow in the words "beholding these things." Some among this company of female disciples fell into such agony at the sight of their Lord dying that they "smote their breasts and returned" to their houses, unable to bear it any longer. How striking that Mary of Bethany, sister of Martha who had previously anointed Him for His death and resurrection is not named among these women. *She alone foresaw His resurrection.* Refer to this marvelous woman in Section 146, John 12:3, footnote e.

2p-The wording, "came up with him unto Jerusalem," signifies that many of them were from other parts of the country. They traveled with Messiah as He made His journey to Jerusalem to die. Prudent men who study soon detect that some things are said in Scripture that are not in print! Such unrecorded but obvious facts were expressed by the framers of the Declaration of Independence as "self evident." Mark. 15:41, is also "self evident" that thousands followed Jesus and have no mention in Scripture. For those at the cross, see footnote c and d above.

(g) Here is evidence that many people followed Christ as he made His last journey to Jerusalem for Passover observance. None of them understood *at this point,* that He would be the final Passover Lamb and die for the sins of the world. This passage, with others, refutes the "unbelieving academic" consensus that Jesus of Nazareth, was a lone itinerant preacher trying to act like Israel's promised Messiah. The blasphemy of "liberation theology" popularized during the Vietnam era, presented Him as a liberator from racism, political bondage, poverty, and sexism. Liberation theology was another invention of unsaved men who know nothing of God's saving grace.

2p-**Human needs and the saving gospel.** Christians must not wink at obvious injustices but do all within their means to rectify these crimes. God's Word teaches believers to produce works of benevolence toward all men possible (Gal. 6:10 with 1 Thess. 5:15). It is said of Jesus that He "went about doing good" (Acts 10:38). Paul ordered that those who have believed in God must "maintain good works" (Titus 3:1-8). Yet, these deeds are not the gospel of Scripture. Christ's death for our sins, burial to conquer the grave, and resurrection to give eternal life constitutes the gospel. Good works bless the human body; the glorious gospel saves the soul. *Both* must be balanced and operative in the lives of *true* Christian. One without the other is like a bird trying to fly with one wing.

3p-**Decisional evangelism.** In the early years of American evangelism, thousands were saved. The word "decision" was used in the context of correct gospel meaning. *This changed as a new definition slowly emerged.* Now, in churches the people are being called upon to "decide for Christ." This is done after a soupy invitation, and hands being raised. A *mental decision* to "bow your heads," "let Jesus into your heart," is deceiving, unless the individual is ruthlessly condemned by the Holy Spirit and God's gospel that he is lost in sin, headed for eternal hell, and only Jesus can save him. At this point, through repentance from sin and simple faith in Christ the individual instantly receives salvation; thus, a true decision. Men must be confronted with the gospel and its exclusive, strict demands. Refer to Section 32, third paragraph of footnote b, for further explanation of "decisional evangelisms" and its curse. For other comments on the demise of *basic* doctrine in churches, refer to Section 63, second and third paragraphs of footnote h.

THE WEDNESDAY CRUCIFIXION MYTH.

Appendix One at the conclusion of this work lays out a detailed explanation as to why the Lord Jesus was put to death on Friday and not Wednesday. It also deals with the so-called Good Friday ritual invented by the Roman Catholic Church. Below is a list of the reasons from Scripture that demonstrate the Friday death of our Savior. A perusal of these verses arranged in systematic and chronological order will help the reader to understand better this issue. Strong conflict over this only began about one hundred and fifty years ago with the rise of European theological liberalism, the profusion of the law cults, and a new emergence of Islam defying the whole world, especially biblical Christianity.

1. In Section 148, the Savior rode into Jerusalem on what was later named "Palm Sunday." Mark. 11:11 states that when "the eventide [of that Sunday] was come; he went unto Bethany with the twelve." Matthew. 21:17 says the same thing. Thus, he spent what we call Sunday night in this village about two miles east of Jerusalem. See the explanatory note regarding Palm Sunday under the asterisk in Section 148.

2. In Section 149, Matt. 21:18, the Lord Jesus returns to Jerusalem on Monday morning and has the incident with the fig tree along the way. He returns to Bethany for this Monday night.

3. In Section 151, Matt. 21:23 with Mk. 11:27, the Savior returns to Jerusalem on Tuesday morning of the next day. Where He spent this Tuesday night is not clear, unless Lk. 21:37-38 answers the question. It reads that He often went to the Mount of Olives for the night.

4. If Christ was put to death on Wednesday, then, He had only Tuesday to do the many things recorded in Sections 151 through Section 166. This is a sheer impossibility, as a perusal of these sixteen Sections will show. Check each of these in the Detailed Table of Contents.

5. The probability of the above proposal, Jesus dying on Wednesday, is beyond acceptable reasoning. Section 167, Matt. 26:1-2 makes it clear that at the end of the Olivet Discourse it was still "two days" *before* the Passover Feast began. This surely means "two days." How could it mean anything else? Further, it is impossible to take the time from Tuesday morning (number 3 above) to the next day, Wednesday morning (which is the time often selected for the death of Christ), and then squeeze into this period the numerous events in the life of Christ *before* His death. These events are recorded in Sections 168 through 180. A Wednesday morning crucifixion at 9 a. m. requires too much to be done and no time in which to do it. Among other things, it must include the Passover meal which was observed on Tuesday night after sundown, the establishing of the Lord's Supper, the upper room discourse, and the long walk from the eastern side of Jerusalem to Gethsemane. This includes His lessons given to the eleven apostles, prayer offered in the temple, departing the temple through the Eastern Gate, and walk down Mount Moriah to the garden. Then, we have His agony in prayer at Gethsemane, arrest, and return trip to the western side of the city where the mock trials began. This listing does not include Pilate and Herod's trials of Jesus. When one remembers that the inspired records of these events given by Matthew, Mark, Luke, and John, are only *condensed versions* of the whole story; it is obvious there was not enough time for all these things to occur, as well as those things that are not recorded. Jesus was not crucified on Wednesday. This is a myth invented by people trying to *save* the Bible from error. God's Word is eternally inherent with divine life, and He will keep it that way forever (Ps. 119:89 with 1 Peter 1:23). It is our duty to uphold it when necessary, and God's duty to *preserve* it. This, He has done!

6. The transactions listed above in numbers 3, 4 and 5, must have taken place mostly on Tuesday and a few hours of Wednesday morning before the cross. As stated above, the Passover was eaten *after* sunset on Thursday, which (as stated above), was early into the Jewish Friday. Jesus was crucified that Friday morning at 9 a.m. (Mk. 15:25). He died the same Friday afternoon at 3 p.m. (Mk. 15:34-37). Joseph and Nicodemus buried His body in great haste, late that afternoon as the Sabbath was fast approaching and would begin at sundown (Lk. 23:54). It was considered the highest of sins for a dead body to be unburied on the Sabbath.

SATURDAY OR SABBATH. HIS HURRIED BURIAL BEFORE SUNSET.

Joseph obtains permission from Pilate to bury Jesus' body. It is quickly removed from the cross, partly prepared for interment, and placed in Joseph's new tomb. Certain women sitting nearby observe His burial.*

Time: After His death at 3:00 p.m. and before sundown Friday.

Due to the nearness of the Jewish Sabbath, our Lord's body was not completely readied for burial as is seen later in Lk. 24: l, with the women returning after the Sabbath with the embalming spices. How wonderful that the powders and anointments prepared for the body of Jesus were not needed. He had risen!

Outside the northern gate of Jerusalem at the tomb

Matt. 27:57	Mk. 15:42-43	Lk. 23:50	John 19:31-38
	–		***Hypocrites worry about their Sabbath*** **31** The Jews therefore, because it was the preparation,(a) that the bodies should not remain upon the cross on the sabbath day, (for that sabbath day was an high day,)(b) besought Pilate that their legs might be broken, and *that* they might be taken away.

The thieves' legs are broken: Jesus' side is pierced

32 Then came the soldiers, and brake the legs of the first, and of the other which was crucified with him.

33 But when they came to Jesus, and saw that he was dead already, they brake not his legs:

34 But one of the soldiers with a **spear pierced his side,**(c) and forthwith came there out blood and water.(d)

35 And he that saw *it* bare record, and his record is true: and he knoweth that [what] he saith [is] true, that ye might believe.

36 For these things were done, that the Scripture should be fulfilled, **"A bone of him shall not be broken."**

37 And again another scripture saith, **"They shall look on him whom they pierced."**

Matt. 27:57	Mk. 15:42-43	Lk. 23:50	John 19:31-38
The Sabbath is near Joseph must hurry **57** When the even was come,	***The Sabbath is near Joseph must hurry*** **42** And now when the even was come, because it was the preparation,(e) that is, the day before the sabbath,		
No longer a secret there came a **rich man**(f) of Arimathaea, named Joseph,	***No longer a secret*** **43** Joseph(f) of Arimathaea, an honourable	***No longer a secret*** **50** And, behold, *there was* a man named Joseph,(f)	***No longer a secret*** **38** And after this Joseph(f) of Arimathaea,

Matt. 27:57–58	Mk. 15:43–45	Lk. 23:50–52	John 19:38–39
who also himself was Jesus' disciple:	counsellor, [member of the Sanhedrin]	a counsellor; [member of the Sanhedrin] *and he was* a good man, and a just:	being a disciple of Jesus, but secretly for fear of the Jews,
		51 (The same had not consented[g] to the counsel and deed of them;) [the Sanhedrin] *he was* of Arimathaea, a city of the Jews: who also himself waited for the kingdom of God.	
	which also waited for the kingdom of God, came, and		
Joseph before Pilate 58 He went to Pilate, and begged the	***Joseph before Pilate*** went in boldly unto Pilate, and craved the	***Joseph before Pilate*** 52 This *man* went unto Pilate, and begged the	***Joseph before Pilate*** besought Pilate that he might take away the body of Jesus:[h]
body of Jesus.[h]	body of Jesus.[h]	body of Jesus.[h]	
	44 And Pilate marvelled if he were already dead: and calling *unto him* the centurion, he asked him whether he had been any while dead.		
Joseph and Nicodemus take the body of Jesus Then Pilate commanded the	***Joseph and Nicodemus take the body of Jesus*** 45 And when he knew *it* of the centurion,		
body to be delivered.	he gave the body to Joseph.		and Pilate gave *him* leave. ***Joseph and Nicodemus take the body of Jesus*** He came therefore, and took the body of Jesus. 39 And there came also Nicodemus,[i] which at the first came to Jesus by night, and brought a mixture of myrrh and aloes, about an hundred pound *weight*. (an old eastern

Matt. 27:59–61	Mk. 15:46–47	Lk. 23:53–56	John 19:39–42
			measure, of about 75 pounds)
Joseph and Nicodemus bury Him	*Joseph and Nicodemus bury Him*	*Joseph and Nicodemus bury Him*	*Joseph and Nicodemus bury Him*
59 And when Joseph had taken the body, he wrapped it in a clean linen[(j)] cloth,	**46** And he bought fine linen, and took him down, and wrapped him in the linen,[(j)]	**53** And he took it down, and wrapped it in linen,[(j)]	**40** Then took they the body of Jesus, and wound it in linen[(j)] clothes with the spices, as the manner of the Jews is to bury. **41** Now in the place where he was crucified there was a garden;[(k)] and in the garden
60 And laid it in his own new tomb, which he had hewn out in the rock:	and laid him in a sepulcher which was hewn out of a rock,	and laid it in a sepulchre that was hewn in stone, wherein never man before was laid.	a new sepulchre, wherein was never man yet laid. **42** There laid they Jesus
Sealed with a stone and he rolled a great stone[(l)] to the door of the sepulchre, and departed.	*Sealed with a stone* and rolled a stone[(l)] unto the door of the sepulchre.	**54** And that day was the preparation, and the sabbath drew on.	therefore because of the Jews' preparation *day*; for the sepulchre was nigh at hand. (Next chap., John 20:1 cont. in Section 195.)
Devout women present **61** And there was Mary Magdalene, and the other Mary, sitting[(m)] over against the sepulchre. (Verse 62 cont. in Section 194.)	*Devout women present* **47** And Mary Magdalene and Mary *the mother* of Joses beheld[(m)] where he was laid. (Next chap., Mk. 16:1 cont. in Section 195.)	*Devout women present* **55** And the women also, which came with him from Galilee, followed after, and beheld[(m)] the sepulchre, and how his body was laid. *They will complete His burial after Sabbath* **56** And they [the women] returned, [to the city] and prepared spices and ointments; and rested the sabbath day according to the commandment.[(n)] (Next chap., Lk. 24:1 cont. in Section 195	◄ *This verse demonstrates that these women did not yet understand or believe in His resurrection from the dead. For more on this, see Section 195, and the note at Lk. 24:7-8, with Section 196, and the note attached to John 20:9.*

Footnotes-Commentary

(a) **Lk. 23:54 with John 19:42. "Preparation."** According to Josephus in *Antiquities*, Book 16:6, 2, line 163 with footnote b, every Sabbath day had a preparation time before it began. Technically, this started at the ninth hour or three o'clock mid afternoon before Sabbath commencement at sundown. Pious Jews, often commenced this time weeks before. Many of these were carried over into "Queen Sabbath " as in John 19:31 above. Some six hundred years before the birth of Christ, in the days of King Hezekiah, we read of the Jews, who had not purified or cleansed themselves, asking for pardon of their sins (2 Chron. 30:18). Different lengths of time were required in this cleansing process according to the defilement incurred. Those who touched a dead body were required one full week, though attending to the dead was permitted. Other purifying acts were shorter. Some of the cleansing rituals required shaving, washing clothes, sprinkling ashes, and other things. By the time of Christ, the Jews had distorted the ritual of purification and preparation into complicated, impossible duties by blending it with their overbearing oral laws or traditions. For a brief review, see *Gills Commentary*, vol. 8, pages 33-35, and Lightfoot's *Commentary on the New Testament . . .* , vol. 3, page 373. The Talmud, Seder Tohoroth, has twelve tractates (sections) with hundreds of pages explaining the cleansings to be observed by the Hebrew people before, during, and after their Passover. See next paragraph for further details. All pious Jews light candles to welcome the Sabbath.

2p-Verse 31. This "preparation" has nothing to do with a so-called "double Sabbath" or a "Wednesday crucifixion" and other extremes. It is simply stating that the Jewish people would begin at this mid afternoon hour getting ready for their Sabbath commencing at sundown that day. Dead bodies must not be present on the Sabbath; hence, the hurry to remove Jesus' corpse and the thieves from their crosses. The Jews in their stern approach to these national celebrations fell into the habit of beginning the "preparation" many days before the designated time. "Preparation" meant they were preparing themselves, food, especially baking, lodging for pilgrims, and many other duties before the start of "Queen Sabbath," at sunset. As noted, the more liberal Jews blended preparation, Passover, and the Feast of Unleavened Bread together. The Unleavened Feast should have started immediately at the end of the Passover. This overlapping is clear in Mk. 14:12. For more on the "preparation," refer to Section 194, Matt. 27:62, footnote a.

(b) **Verse 31. The approaching Sabbath was called a "high day."** This was the celebrated name for the Sabbath occurring at Passover time with the Feast of Unleavened Bread immediately afterwards. It was considered a special day of splendor and glory, thus called a "high day." The Jews hurried to light sabbatical candles just as darkness fell over the land. These were to welcome Messiah, should He appear at this time. During this time, the people presented themselves in the temple according to the command of God (Ex. 23:17). The Jewish religious leaders urged Pilate to hurry and break the legs of the victims (the customary thing) so that they might remove the bodies from hanging positions before the Sabbath began a few hours later at sundown. The Torah Law strictly forbid bodies of the dead to be left exposed after sunset (Deut. 21:22-23). Such a spectacle would profane their Sabbath. Who took charge of the body of Judas the traitor? His corpse was given a quick burial in view of the approaching Sabbath. For more on the annual Hebrew feasts, see Section 167, Lk. 22:1, footnote a.

2p-The communal meal in Sections 171 and 172 is the Passover meal at its conclusion. *Out of this,* the Savior instituted the Lord's Supper and presented it to His apostles in Section 173. For a lengthy discussion of the time relating to these matters, see *Handbook of Biblical Chronology*, pages 353-368, by Jack Finegan. This work is helpful but marred by Finegan's absence of faith in the total inspiration of Scripture.

3p-"Their legs might be broken." It was standard custom to break the legs of the living victims as they hung on the cross. This was done near the end. The Jews who requested this of Pilate were ignorant of their own Scripture. In Ex. 12:46 and Num. 9:12 it commands that no bone of the Passover lamb was to be broken. Christ was the ultimate Passover Lamb, that millions of others pointed to; they all met their terminus in Him. He was the grand culmination of every Passover sacrifice. Therefore, not one of His bones was broken. Again, the very sovereignty of God overrules the traditions of evil men; they spared Christ from this leg smashing, pagan ritual. See verses 32 and 33 above. Instead, the soldiers did something that fulfilled yet another prophecy of Jesus. See number 1 under footnote d below for further details.

(c) **"A spear pierced his side."** This act fulfilled the prophecy of Zech. 12:10. After breaking the leg bones of both thieves, the soldiers upon discovering that Christ was dead, did not smash His legs, instead they thrust a spear into His side. As mentioned in Section 188, fourth paragraph, footnote a, an ancient *tradition* states this soldier's name was Longinus. This became the name for the lengthy spear he drove into the Savior's side. It has been assumed by medical writers that the flow of blood mixed with water reveals that the spear went through the pericardium and then the physical heart of Jesus. The water flowed from the former and the blood from His wounded heart. This may be so, as the human heart leans to the left side within the body. What, however, should be noticed is the *order* of the liquids that flowed from our Lord. *It was the blood first and the water second!* Only when one has placed saving faith in Christ's atonement and saved by His precious blood, then is he ready and qualified for the water—that is believer's baptism by immersion. Commentators have found all sorts of types in these words. I will leave this to them and stick with the order as given above: salvation by the blood and water baptism for those saved through the blood.

2p-There is in Jewish literature an interesting legend that may point us to the punctured side of the Lord Jesus. In Num. 20:11, when Moses struck the rock twice, some of the ancients held that first blood came out, and second water! This is documented in Lightfoot's *Commentary on the New Testament . . .* , vol. 3. page 440. The thought here points us to Christ of which a similar thing is stated in John 19:34 above. The Jews said that when Moses smote the rock, blood and water came out. The New Testament affirms that when the Roman solider pierced Christ's side, blood, and water came out. Later, the Jew, Paul, wrote in 1 Cor. 10:4 that "this Rock [Moses smote] was Christ." It is provocative that some of the Hebrew teachers saw in the smitten rock a prototype of their coming Messiah. There is a curious story in Hebrew literature, which says that this rock was actually a "rolling well," that followed Israel throughout their wilderness journey pouring out water for their needs to be met. David Stern mentions this in his *Jewish New Testament Commentary,* page 469. We are struck with the words of Paul in 1 Cor. 10:4, where he wrote, "The Rock that followed them was Christ." What did he mean by "followed them?" A large, heavy, stationary rock cannot follow anyone, unless it was the work of God.

(d) Verse 34. "Pierced his side." This recalls one of John's later statements in 1 John 5:6. Writing of Christ, he said, "This is he that came by water and blood, *even* Jesus Christ." Refer to the first paragraph of footnote c above for other comments. Whether it was His right or left side the Holy Spirit has not revealed this.

2p-Verse 35. "He that saw it." Here is another proof that John witnessed the crucifixion. See John 19:26 for another evidence that John was there, and Jesus spoke to Him from the cross. In great modesty, John is allowed by the Holy Spirit to conceal his name as the physical author of this book. At this time several prophecies were fulfilled that pointed to Messiah's death. They were:

1. **Verse 36. "A bone not broken."** Quoted from a blending of selected words in Ex. 12:46, Num. 9:12 with Ps. 34:20. These predicted that not one of Messiah's bones would be broken during His death. It was customary for the executioners to break the legs of their victims during the latter stages of the crucifixion. However, there is something much deeper in this. The Jews held that if anyone breaks a bone of the Passover lamb, he must receive forty stripes. So reads the Talmud in tractate, Pesachim 86a. We wonder how many devout Jews noticed that the soldiers did not break Messiah's leg bones, and what message this conveyed to them in view of their belief about the bones of the Passover lambs.

2. **Verse 37. "Look on him."** This second prediction was from Zech. 12:10. Some teach that this will be fulfilled at the coming of Christ to establish His earthly kingdom. However, John told his original readers that it was fulfilled at the death of Christ on the cross. *I prefer the exegesis of John.* The "they" of Zechariah's prediction spoke first of the Roman soldiers and then all others who saw the body of Christ hanging from the cross, after it had been pierced with a spear. It has nothing whatsoever to do with Jews looking at the scars of Messiah over two thousand years later and suddenly believing in Him. There are millions of Jews, who know nothing about the scars in Jesus' body. To believe that the *entire* nation of Israel will suddenly be saved this way is seriously incorrect. Paul's words, "And so all Israel shall be saved" (Rom. 11:26) can only have reference to Hebrews, who trust Christ the Messiah, as Lord and Savior. When anyone is awakened by the Holy Spirit and the gospel, he is saved the instant, he puts faith in Christ as personal Lord and Savior. No one has ever or will ever be redeemed my looking at the scares in Jesus' hands or side. This is *radical* dispensationalism gone wild. In the contextual setting of Zechariah's predictions, the key thought is that of a "fountain being opened for sin and uncleanness" to Israel (Zech. 13:1). This fountain was opened on the cross and was found in their Messiah dying before their eyes. This is not to decry that many Jews will yet be saved in the plan of God for these people. For more on this, see Section 95, second paragraph of footnote u.

(e) Again, we meet the term "preparation." See footnote a above for explanation.

(f) "Joseph of Arimathaea." Shaded in gray and found in Isa. 53:9. It predicted that Christ's death would be associated with a wealthy person. Suddenly, Joseph, a rich man appears, hitherto unheard of in the life of Messiah.

2p-Verse 43. "An honourable counselor." *Gill's Commentary,* vol. 7, page 491 described Joseph this way: "A man of good aspect, well dressed, and that behaved . . . honorably in his office, as a counselor: he seems to have been a priest, and one of the bench of priests that sat in the high priest's chamber, which is called 'the chamber of the counselors.'" He was a person of lofty character and impeccable standards for Luke describes him as "good," and "just." Lk. 23:51 reads, "That he waited for the kingdom of God." This means that he was expecting the *literal* kingdom of God to appear soon in a physical, material form. (Joseph was wrong!) Arimathaea, his hometown, was about twenty miles north-west of Jerusalem. He had stood among the wild crowds and witnessed His Lord put to death like a common criminal. That was enough cowardliness for him! See first paragraph of footnote i below for more on this.

3p- The validity of the many traditions regarding him, we have no way of knowing. As a member of the Sanhedrin, Joseph had to be in his mid sixties or older and rich. Jerusalem was razed forty years later making Joseph about one hundred years of age if he was still living. There is a *worthless* tradition, which tells that he went to England after A.D. 70, and died there a martyr for preaching Christ among the pagans.

4p-John 19:38. "Secretly for fear of the Jews." John wrote his book some years after it was all over. He informs his readers that Joseph had been a covert disciple of Messiah. This was because of the threats of the religious leaders and the Sanhedrin. It touches us deeply that in looking back on these events he did not scold or speak disparagingly of Joseph for being a secret believer in the Lord Jesus. How easy to condemn a man who does not do and act as we do in every step of the way.

5p-Hurry, the Sabbath enters at sundown. Joseph could lose no time if sacred homage was to be paid to the body of his Lord. Shortly, the sun would set, and "Queen Sabbath" would be ushered in by a trumpet blast from a rabbi at the temple in Jerusalem. He must complete his work before sundown.

(g) Doctor Luke was careful to inform Theophilus that Joseph, though a member of the Sanhedrin, had not voted to kill Christ (verse 51). Who among the seventy-one members of the Sanhedrin cast their votes to kill the Lord Jesus? This was surely a topic of wide discussion among the Jews after it was all over. How interesting that Luke had learned that Joseph was not among that number, and he is inspired to write this fact for his friend, Theophilus. We wonder how the aged Luke learned of this. Did Joseph later tell him the whole story or was it given by revelation of the Holy Spirit? Divine inspiration could do this either way.

(h) **Begging for Jesus' body.** The idea here is that of urgency. John in verse 31, states that the Jews asked Pilate to remove the bodies from their crosses, lest their Sabbath be defiled! Little did they realize that one of their own, a member of the Sanhedrin would fulfill their request. Making his way quickly from the crucifixion site, Joseph hurries back to Jerusalem to Pilate's quarters, located on the northeastern side of the city. He obtains an audience with the pagan governor and begs for the corpse of his dead Messiah. As it was after hours for the governor, Joseph must have been a person of great prominence to secure this hearing. In this contact with the pagan Romans, he now became ritually unclean in the eyes of the religionists who had killed Jesus. Pilate was shocked that Jesus had died so soon, but the centurion in command of the crucifixion affirmed that it was so. He then grants permission for Joseph to take the body away. Joseph knew that victims of a crucifixion were often left on their crosses for ravens, eagles, and other carnivorous fouls to devour, or until they rotted and fell to the ground, limb from limb. With this, they quickly became food for wild dogs and jackals. Some were removed and thrown onto the city dump, south of Jerusalem in a place called gehenna or the Valley of Hinnom. Here, the fire, beasts, dogs, and fowls devoured the crucified corpses. The Jews held that the "guilty" could not be buried with the just.

2p-The nearness of the Sabbath (within a few hours) pressed the two men into urgent action. Returning to the hill of death (with many people milling about) they disconnect Jesus' feet from the vertical post, lowered the patibulum horizontal crossbeam and placed it on the ground. Cutting the ropes that help to bind him to the beam, we cannot help but *reverently wonder* how they extracted the cruel iron nails from His now stiff hands. Pry bars, hammers, and heavy metals tools had to be used for this awful task. (Paul referred to the removal of Jesus' body over twenty years later in Acts 13:29). Refer to Section 189, footnote a, for details on how crucifixion was enacted. If the wood on which the victim was crucified was thin enough the nails were driven completely through and clinched on the hinder side. *The Illustrated Bible Dictionary,* Part 1, page 344, carries the photograph of the petrified anklebones of a man who was crucified. A clinched nail is clearly visible in this old black-and-white illustration. The bloody, beaten corpse was laid on a makeshift carrier and taken to the garden burial site. What did the spectators and curious watchers think as they witnessed two members of the famed Sanhedrin take the body of Jesus from the cross and carry it away to the nearby garden? (All Sanhedrin members wore distinguishing long brown garments.) Refer to footnote j below for the preparation of a corpse, and footnote k below for more on this garden that was located near Calvary's hill of death.

3p-Verse 44. Pilate's report to Emperor Tiberius. Roman law mandated that Pilate send a full report of the death of Jesus to his emperor. We need no Scripture for this, rather common sense. Justin Martyr in his work *Apology* 1: 35, 9, records that such a report was lodged in the imperial archives at Rome. The heretic Tertullian, another ancient writer, stated the same in his book, *Apology* 5:2, 21. 20.

(i) Suddenly, John introduces Nicodemus into the event. He is seen as a partner of Joseph. Matthew, Mark, and Luke wrote mostly of Joseph's side of the event while John alone was inspired to write about Nicodemus. This elderly Hebrew was also a member of the powerful Sanhedrin. For details on Nicodemus, his background, place in the Sanhedrin, and several possible mentions of him in the Talmud, refer to Section 30, John 3:1 and all of footnotes a and b. Regarding his conversion, see Section 30, second paragraph of footnote k. The *previously* shy Sanhedrinist, who came to Jesus by night, unashamedly comes forward in broad daylight, with hundreds watching, and assisted in unnailing the corpse from the cross and its burial. A glorious change had occurred in his life. Now, he demonstrates a fearless love and devotion toward the man hated most by his colleagues. At last, he came to understand the Words of Jesus spoken to him some three years before, at night in Jerusalem, "Ye must be born again" (John 3:3).

2p-The price of Jesus' funeral. "An hundred pound weight." The word here is "litra" which was a measure of twelve ounces each; thus, the total weight was about seventy-five pounds! *This was enough to cover* *approximately two hundred bodies for burial.* It reflected Nicodemus' boundless love and devotion for Messiah. The value in present day currency is about $2,500.00. The purpose for such a tremendous amount of aromatics was to perfume the body of Jesus. Embalming, as we know it in the west, was unheard of by the Jews and ancients. Refer to John 19:38-42 above and relative footnotes for more on this thought. (The Egyptians alone seemed to have had peculiar methods of burying their dead to remain in a state of preservation.) Costly burials such as Joseph gave the Savior were only afforded by the wealthiest of persons. When Herod the Great died, servants went to his burial each one carrying large measures of expensive spices. See *Antiquities,* Book 17:8, lines 188-205 for some of the details.

[j] **Preburial preparations.** As mentioned in footnote i above, we note again that Matthew, Mark, and Luke give Joseph's side of the story, while John gives that of Nicodemus. "And he [Joseph] bought the fine linen." It is noticed that Joseph purchased the very *costly* cloth for Jesus' burial. One cannot but wonder what the price was! Washing the body of our Lord, which was beaten and bruised from the agonies of crucifixion, and thoroughly blood stained was tenderly done with many sad tears of remembrance. Over the corpse, they sprinkled a thick coating of myrrh, aloes, and other burial powders; hurriedly, it was wrapped in clean linen. Placing the head cloth or napkin over His face, it was tied under the chin. He was laid to rest in a large niche tomb hewn out of new rock. *Their carefulness in securing Jesus' body and partial burial preparations proves that neither of these men understood that Jesus would rise again.* Oddly, not one of Christ's apostles seemed to have shared in His burial! We cannot but wonder, "Where were they?" Due to the approaching Sabbath, Joseph and Nicodemus were not able to complete the burial necessities for His body. Later, after the Sabbath, a band of devout women made their way to the interment site to complete the work. This is discussed in Section 195. Like the men, not one of them knew of or comprehended His resurrection, though He had told them many times during His ministry. *All of them failed to understand Messiah's death, burial, and resurrection.* For examples of their wrong understanding of Messiah's work, see the main headings of Section 104, 105, 107, and 141. See also footnote m below for other comments on His burial. In the *Works of Nathaniel Lardner,* vol. 10, pages 283-297 there is a coverage of the ancient methods of Jewish burials and embalming. These pages carry helpful information that is not found in most books that cover this subject.

[k] **"There was a garden."** How wonderfully odd that a beautiful garden would be located near the ghastly site of human crucifixion! Yet, is it not true that we move from death to life and from ashes to beauty in the Christian journey through this world? Soon, our daily cross dying will give way to the eternal paradise of heaven.

[l] **"A great stone."** These large door stones were set in roll-troughs angled slightly downward, which made it easy to push them across the opening of the burial room. (Getting the great stone moved upward from its resting position was another story!) Nicodemus, being a rich man, we can be assured this was one of the finest burial plots anywhere in the area. Only the most wealthy had burial sites carved into stonewalls. Where in history did a man ever use a grave plot, then give it back to the original owner three days and nights after his death?

[m] **Mk. 15:47. Sitting nearby and watching.** A band of faithful women beheld as the two men laid Jesus' body in the burial place. These same female believers had stood and watched Him die as recorded in Section 192, Mk. 15:40-41, footnotes d and e. They wanted to see "where" and "how" their Lord's body was laid to rest. Due to the approaching Sabbath at sundown, the burial preparation for Jesus was not completed. However, they planned after the Sabbath to return and show full burial reverence to His body. See Section 195, Matt. 28:1 and parallel text for their return early on the Sunday morning of the Resurrection Day. Again, we note that Mary of Bethany, who had anointed Jesus for His death and resurrection, is never named among these women. She knew her Lord would rise from the dead. Refer to Section 146, John 12:3-8 for her story and the history-long commendation given her by Jesus. This is one of the most forgotten women in the New Testament in light of what she did.

2p-The body of Jesus was buried just *before* sunset Friday; a full sunset hailed the entrance of "Queen Sabbath" for all pious Hebrews. See *Appendix One* for a detailed explanation of the "three days and nights" Joseph, Nicodemus, and their helpers made sure that Jesus' body was interred before the Hebrew Sabbath day began. It is interesting to note that those appointed by the Sanhedrin to reap the sheaf of firstfruits, also began their work just before sundown! (There are accounts of this being carried over into the Sabbath, with the approval of the Sanhedrin.) Thus, both Christ's entombment and the reaping of the firstfruits (to be waved in the temple at sunrise Sunday morning) took place simultaneously. Paul made it clear in 1 Cor. 15:20, that this firstfruit sheave, waved before God on the morning of the first day of the week symbolized the resurrection of Christ

[n] Law cults point to this verse as proof that these faithful followers of Christ "kept the Sabbath day." Those who seek to bring Christians under this (or any) part of the Torah Law should know that *at this time* in history all these Jews were under the law, and none of them knew that Jesus would rise from the dead. They were all devout Hebrews trying to obey the Torah, along with the thousand of oral traditions strapped upon their lives. Not one of them *at this point* understood Jesus' resurrection, the church, believer's baptism, the meaning of the Lord's Supper, and dozens of other things, much less that they would be free from the law. With the coming of the Holy Spirit at Pentecost, some fifty days after this sad moment, and the revelations of Paul written in his letters, these truths gradually dawned upon the first and early Christian churches. They are held precious to this present moment. For a brief discussion of Christians under the Torah Law, see Section 45, paragraphs one through four, footnote b.

Smitten in conscience, the Jewish religious leaders hurry to Governor Pilate for help. They request a detachment of soldiers to guard Jesus' tomb. He commands a watch to be posted at the burial site. He orders his official seal to be impressed upon the moveable stone that covered the entrance of Christ's grave.

Time: The late afternoon of His burial.

Matt. 27:62-66—*Pilate's quarters and the burial site*	Mk.	Lk.	John
A haunting remembrance **62** Now the next day,[a] that followed [or after] the day of the preparation, the chief priests and Pharisees came together unto Pilate, **63** Saying, "Sir, we remember[b] that that deceiver said, while he was yet alive, 'After three days I will rise again.' *(For "three days" see Appendix One)* **64** "Command therefore that the sepulchre be made sure until the third day, lest his disciples come by night, and steal him away, and say unto the people, He is risen from the dead: so the last error shall be worse than the first."[c] *"As sure as ye can"* **65** Pilate said unto them, "Ye have a watch: go your way, make *it* as sure as ye can."[d] **66** So they went, and made the sepulchre sure, sealing[e] the stone, and setting a watch. (Next chap., Matt. 28:1 cont. in Section 195.)			

Footnotes-Commentary

(a) **"The next day."** This text states that the Jews in their anxiety about Jesus rising from the dead went to Pilate at some point during their Sabbath day, which was "the next day." These religious hypocrites break their rules, again! To set foot on the premises of a pagan Gentile was considered defiling. No pious Hebrew would dare to approach a burying place of the dead on the Sabbath. Believing this, they assumed the body of Jesus would not be touched during this time. Some, however, understand this to mean that they went to Pilate just after sunset Saturday, thus not breaking their Sabbath rules. Regardless, they secured Pilate's favor, and he assigned a detachment of soldiers to guard the tomb to guarantee that nothing happened. Clearly, the disciples *could not* have stolen His body during broad daylight hours, but rather would have attempted this under cover of darkness. Such an attempt would have proven disastrous in the daytime. At night, they could never have gotten past the guards. The Sanhedrin greatly troubled worked to be sure nothing went amiss and that the body of Jesus was not stolen away by His friends.

2p-**Verse 62. "The day of preparation."** For explanation of this important term mentioned at least six times in the four gospels, see Section 193, footnotes a, and b.

(b) **"Sir, we remember."** *Surely, they did!* The Words Jesus had spoken concerning His resurrection some three years prior, still haunted their memories. Alas! The unspeakable torment of a troubled memory drives some to madness. In hell, men are tortured as much by their memories as they are by the flames of suffering. O the agony of lost hope, gone forever. The religious leaders had thrown the same taunt into His face as He suffered on the cross some hours before. See Section 190, Matt. 27:40, second paragraph of footnote a, for comments. Oddly, they are back at Pilate's place in the Castle of Antonio on the northeast side of Jerusalem. Adam Clarke, in his *Commentary,* vol. 5, page 280 has penned this most fitting comment, "While these wicked men are fulfilling their own vicious counsels, they were sub serving the great cause of Christianity. Everything depended on the resurrection of Christ; if it did not occur then the whole Christian system is false, and no atonement was made. It was necessary that the chief priests should use every precaution to prevent an imposture, that the resurrection of Christ might have the fullest evidence to support it." In their evil attempts to hold down divine truth, we see that the tormenting misgivings of guilty consciences continued on, even after their chief enemy was dead! Did they *also* remember His statement about the "sign of the prophet Jonah" (Matt. 12:40)? How true the old proverb that "Bad men are tormented by bad memories." *We are amazed to know that the wicked religionists remembered His promise to rise from the dead, but His own apostles did not.* It has been said that good memories are a sign of grace. This cannot be true for evil persons often have good memories, and good men have bad ones. The most sacred of thoughts are those centered on the blessed Lord Jesus, the service of God, and reaching out to our fellow men with the gospel and sure hope.

(c) They described Messiah's statement about His resurrection as being the "first error." If his disciples should come and by stealth take away His body, then this would be the "second error." These religious leaders of Israel had committed the greatest error of mankind; the rejection of Jesus of Nazareth as their Messiah and Savior. They are suffering in hell today for this "error."

(d) Making the grave stone sure. Securing permission from the governor, they went immediately from his residence to the garden tomb. Accompanying these Jews was a detachment of four soldiers who would guard the tomb where the body of Jesus the Messiah lay. A few hours later, these men of the Roman military were in for the biggest shock of their careers. The crucified man returned to life again! After fainting, they regained their mobility and fled, terrified at the sight! One cannot but wonder with whom they shared this shocking news in the years ahead.

2p-Still trying to "make it sure." Over the centuries, men and devils have labored to keep the tomb of Jesus "sure." The thought of Him rising haunts them for it spells their doom. They must prove He did not rise from the dead. The defunct Anglican preacher, Charles Darwin (died 1881), postulated his *Origin of the Species,* and with this made "sure." Karl Marx (died 1882), the baptized Lutheran, added his *Communist Manifesto* to the scrap pile. Vladimir Lenin (died 1924), heard an Orthodox priest order his father to "beat him back into the church." Ripping the cross from his neck in anger, he embraced atheism. Joseph Stalin (died 1953), studying in a theological seminary for the Russian Orthodox ministry, read Marx's work, renounced God, and became a mass murderer. They tried to make the "stone sure." For more on these men, see Section 12, twelfth paragraph of footnote k. Millions have marched in this parade of fools over the centuries. Education, philosophy, science, evolution, sophistry, wisdom, debate, wealth, and "supreme knowledge" has not kept Jesus in His borrowed grave. Among these "arts and sciences" are the infamous Jesus Seminar religious infidels. They busy themselves denying the deity, atoning death, and bodily resurrection of Christ. Working with the broken tools of blind intellectualism they have tried to make "sure" the Hebrew preacher from Galilee was a phony. John D. Crossan, a Roman Catholic priest and professor at DePaul University, was a co-founder of the Jesus Seminar snake pit. Along with his colleagues in unbelief, they have "searched for the historical Jesus." They do not know that He is only found in the joy of the new birth as revealed in Holy Scriptures. Crossan and his kind are in churches, educational systems, and the media, glorying in their academic shame, articulating their blasphemy and "learned" heresy. Puny men pit their superior education against God's Word. Paul, warned the nine judges of Athens Supreme Court, "And the times of this ignorance God winked at; but now commandeth all men everywhere to repent" (Acts 17:30). And why this command? "Because he hath appointed a day, in the which he will judge the world in righteousness by *that* man whom he hath ordained; *whereof,* he hath given assurance unto all *men,* in that he hath raised him from the dead" (Acts 17:31). This warning remains valid. The "Jesus Seminar" theological trash comes from the hearts of men and women who do not believe in an inspired, trustworthy Bible, and who are void of a personal saving knowledge of Jesus Christ. This assessment is the results of "fruit inspection" as recommended by the Savior (Matt. 7:15-20), and not personal judgment. Refer to Section 159, for our Lord's public condemnation of the religious hypocrites of His day who rejected Him. Some religionists were so full of blasphemy that Paul turned them over to the Devil (1 Tim. 1:20 with Ps. 50:22). *Christ said that men who do not honor Him do not honor God (John 5:23 with 1 John 2:23). Those who want God without Christ will discover that they have neither at the end of life. The world and all false religions hate this truth.*

(e) Sealing the stone. The debate about whose seal this was is useless. In Matt. 28:12, it is stated that the bribe money was given to the "soldiers" that guarded the tomb. No seal of the Sanhedrin or Jews would have been attached to a dead man's grave. It would have rendered the applicator personally unclean! It could only have been the seal of Governor Pilate, the official voice for the Roman Senate in Judaea, Samaria, and Idumea. Therefore, an appointed soldier affixed it to the rolling stone of the tomb. The death sentence was certain for anyone who tampered with or broke this wax imprint. And these soldiers knew this! With the resurrection of Christ, their lives were at stake because it had been broken, hence their terrified panic. The Roman seal was (in this case) attached by driving two metal spikes into the stones; one into the wall face and the other into the rolling door. A strong cord was affixed between these two spikes, and hot wax was poured over the cord, as it lay taut over the heavy door. The wax was then impressed by a portable hand instrument, which bore the official insignia of the governor. *The soldiers dared not use this instrument without permission from Pilate.* It is noted that the cave into which Daniel was cast some six hundred years before, had been secured in a similar manner by the king's signet (Dan. 6:17). The *Biblical, Theological, and Ecclesiastical Cyclopaedia,* vol. ix, page 492-493, by M'Clintock and Strong carries a brief but helpful article on ancient seals with nine illustrations, of how they looked.

2p-We see in these meticulous arrangements of the Jews, sealing and making secure, the sovereign wisdom of God overriding the foolishness of men to achieve His purposes. All of their clever devices to keep the tomb sealed, only served to eliminate any possibility of fraud or deception. The Jews in their madness against Messiah actually assisted God in assuring the world that He rose from the dead. The securely locked the door and the soldiers on guard, are infallible proofs that men did not break in and steal His body away. All the efforts of sinister men to frustrate the purposes of God are described thus, "He that diggeth a pit shall fall into it; and whoso breaketh an hedge, a serpent shall bite him" (Eccles. 10:8). This, the Jews did. How applicable is the passage that God makes the wrath of man to praise Him (Ps. 76:10). Paul wrote that the "princes of this world come to nought" (1 Cor. 2:6). The king's heart is still in the hand of the LORD and He turns it according to His divine will (Prov. 21:1).

CHAPTER 18
SUNDAY MORNING. DEATH IS CONQUERED, LOVE HAS WON! JESUS IS ALIVE AND APPEARS TO HIS DISCIPLES SHOWING THEM MANY INFALLIBLE PROOFS OF HIS RESURRECTION. PETER AND JOHN RACE TO THE TOMB. THE TERRIFIED ROMAN GUARDS SEEK HELP FROM THE JEWS. EVERYONE IS IN A STATE OF SHOCK AND AWE!

A group of women leaves Jerusalem as the gates are opened at sunrise ◙. Going to the tomb, they carry a heavy load of spices to complete His burial that was cut short by the approaching Sabbath. Mary Magdalene, Mary the mother of James, Salome, and Joanna go ahead of the others. They are frightened at the presence of holy angels appearing as two young men. Hearing that He had risen from the dead Mary Magdalene, and Mary the mother of James with several others* leave the women with the spices and run back into the city to tell the disciples.

Time: His Sunday morning resurrection, early on the first day of the week.

The history recorded below reveals that these women did not believe in the resurrection of Jesus. If so, why were they going to complete the embalming of His body? They were in for the biggest shock of their lives! For other comments on this subject, see Section 196, and the symbols ◄ and ◘ by John 20:9. Also, note the comment attached to the end of Luke 24:7 below. *See Lk. 24:9-10, and parallel passages for the story of those loyal women who tried to complete the burial of Jesus, discovered He was gone, and their hurried report to the other disciples. The fact of Christ's resurrection proves that death is not our final destiny because His life is now ours forever.

Dawn of the first day of the week at the burial site near Jerusalem

Matt. 28:1	Mk. 16:1–2	Lk. 24:1	John 20:1
Jewish Sabbath is past. **1** In the end[(a)] of the sabbath,	***Jewish Sabbath is past*** **1** And when the sabbath was past,[(a)] Mary Magdalene, and Mary the *mother* of James, and Salome, had bought sweet ◄spices, that they might come and anoint him.		"At sunrise" ◙. *When did Mary and the other women come to the tomb? In Matthew 28:1 it reads, "as it began to dawn toward the first day of the week." Then, Mark 16:2 states, "at the rising of the sun." In Luke 24:1, we note, "very early in the morning they came." John wrote that it was, "early when it was yet dark." All four writers said the same thing in different ways. See footnote b.*
Mark mentions the spices here, while Luke left off the women's names and wrote of the spices later at the end of verse 1. All these differences are tokens of inspiration.			
Never a first day like this one! as it began to dawn◙ toward the first *day* of the week,	***Never a first day like this one!*** **2** And very early in the morning◙ the first *day* of the week, they[(b)]	***Never a first day like this one!*** **1** Now upon the first *day* of the week, very early in the morning,◙ they[(b)]	***Never a first day like this one!*** **1** The first *day* of the week
came Mary Magdalene[(b)]◄ and the other Mary to see the sepulchre. ▲*Mathew Mark, and John mention Magdalene here. Luke mentioned her later in Lk. 24:10.*	came unto the sepulchre at the rising of the sun.◙	came unto the sepulchre, bringing the spices which they had prepared, and certain *others* with them.	cometh Mary Magdalene[(b)]◄ early, when it was yet dark, ◙ unto the sepulchre,

Matt. 28:2–5	Mk. 16:3–6	Lk. 24:2–5	John 20:1
	The big question already answered		
	3 And they said among themselves, "Who shall roll us away the stone from the door of the sepulchre?"(c)		
Before the women arrived an angel had opened the door			
2 And, behold, there was a great earthquake: for the angel of the Lord descended from heaven, and came and rolled back(d) the stone from the door, and sat upon it.	◀ *There were two angels. One rolled back the stone and sat upon it. Then the other went inside and sat on the right side of Jesus' tomb. John was not inspired to write of these amazing wonders.*		
3 His countenance was like lightning, and his raiment white as snow: **4** And for fear of him the keepers did shake, and became as dead men.			
	They enter the tomb	***They enter the tomb***	***They enter the tomb***
	4 And when they looked, they saw that the stone was rolled away:(e) for it was very great. **5** And entering into the sepulchre,	**2** And they found the stone rolled away(e) from the sepulchre. **3** And they entered in, and found not the body of the Lord Jesus. **4** And it came to pass, as they were much perplexed(f) thereabout, behold, two men stood by them in shining garments:	and seeth the stone taken away(e) from the sepulchre. (Verse 2 cont. in Section 196.)
Who can adequately ▶ *describe what holy angels look like? Matthew and Mark wrote of one, while Luke mentioned two. John also wrote of two in 20:12.*	they saw a young man sitting on the right side, clothed in a long white garment;		
	A good kind of fear	***A good kind of fear***	
	and they were affrighted.	**5** And as they were afraid, and bowed down *their* faces to the earth, they said unto them,	
5 And the angel answered and said unto the women,	**6** And he saith unto them, "Be not		

Matt. 28:5-7	Mk. 16:6-7	Lk. 24:5-8	John
"Fear not ye: for I know that ye seek Jesus, which was crucified.[(g)]	affrighted: Ye seek Jesus of Nazareth, which was crucified:[(g)]	"Why seek ye the living among the dead?	
The greatest news of all world history **6** "He is not here: for he is risen, as he said. 'Come, see the place where the Lord lay.'[(h)]	***The greatest news of all world history*** he is risen; he is not here: behold the place where they laid him.[(h)]	***The greatest news of all world history*** **6** "He is not here, but is risen: remember how he spake unto you when he was yet in Galilee,[(i)] **7** "Saying, 'The Son of man must be delivered into the hands of sinful men, and be crucified, and the third day rise again.'" *(For the "third day" see, Appendix One.)*	
"Meet Me in Galilee" **7** "And go quickly, and tell his disciples that he is risen from the dead; and, behold, he goeth before you into Galilee;[(j)] there shall ye see him: lo, I have told you." (Verse 8 cont. in Section 196.)	***"Meet Me in Galilee"*** **7** "But go your way, tell his disciples and Peter that he goeth before you into Galilee:[(j)] there shall ye see him, as he said unto you." (Verse 8 cont. in Section 196.)	***Remembering, they still do not yet understand*** **8** And they remembered his words. (Verse 9 cont. in Section 196.)	◀ *We are continually amazed that His own disciples did not know of His death, burial, and resurrection. Refer to the symbol ◀ by Section 196, John 20:9 for the apostle John's later admission of this. If these women had known and believed in His resurrection from the dead, their act of bringing spices to complete the embalming was senseless.*

Footnotes–Commentary

(a) Matthew 28:1, was a unique prophetic declaration! It reads, "In the end of the sabbath, as it began to dawn toward the first *day* of the week . . ." Why did Matthew-Levi being a Jew so pointedly specify that the Sabbath had ended, when he knew the Sabbath could only end at sunset Sunday not dawn? *No Sabbath could end at the dawn of any day!* Looking back, years later, as he wrote, Matthew now understood that *all* Hebrew Sabbaths were a thing of the past for believers in Yeshua ha'Mashiach (Jesus the Messiah). They stepped off the stage forever on that early

Sunday morning of the first day of that week, not that evening. Mark understood the same. He wrote, "The Sabbath was past" (Mk. 16:1). The resurrection of Jesus occurred early Sunday morning and with this, the Sabbath concluded. Jews called the ending of their holy day "the goings out of the Sabbath." In a *deeper sense* than words can convey, the Sabbath of the Torah Law with all its 613 commands had forever gone out some twelve hours earlier on that Sunday morning. The cross and resurrection obliterated them (Col. 2:14). This was the "day break" of the greatest era in all human history. Old man Sabbath limped off the scene. No day like this had dawned upon God's creation and mankind, nor would one ever rise. By inspiration Matthew, call this "the first day of the week" excluding the remaining Sabbath hours. When he wrote these words some years after Christ rose, the resurrection day was already, officially "the first day of the week" in a grand and special way. The Torah Sabbath was history. It took the early *hard-line Jewish* converts to Christ, decades to grasp this truth, and that law keeping and circumcisions were not necessary for salvation. The first church council was an attempt to settle this issue (Acts 15). Paul wrote the book of Galatians trying to stamp out this problem that had crept into his churches. For saved Jews and law cultists who try to live by selected commandments from the Torah, including the Sabbath day, see Section 45, the third paragraph of footnote b. Some of these cults are so fanatic teaching that men must worship God on the Sabbath to be saved. Obedience to a day does not save us from hell; only faith in the finished work of Christ does.

2p-Christ's resurrection is the centerpiece of eternal life. It occurred on "the first day of the week." (In Jewish chronology, it was the Sabbath day after the night.) The Sabbaths with their bondage are ceased. Over twenty years later, Paul instructed the Corinthian believers, that "Upon the first *day* of the week let every one of you lay by him in store, as *God* hath prospered him, that there be no gatherings when I come" (1 Cor. 16:2). By this time in church history, it was a naturally known fact that this was the accepted day for collective worship, even in far off Corinth. The gifts for the poor saints in Jerusalem were brought in on this day (Rom 15:25-28). Under heathen rule, there were no "days off" for cessation of human toil. Hence, believers in Christ met mostly at night or on pagan holidays. These meetings were normally held in the homes of fellow believers, or rented halls (Acts 2:46; 8:3, 19:9, Rom. 16:5; 1 Cor. 16:19; Col. 4:15; and Phile. 2). In the Hebrew letter, there was also a plurality of spiritual leaders over the Jewish Christians (Heb. 13:7, 17, 24). This is the reason that in Paul's letters, he addressed a plurality of bishops or pastors for the individual church bodies, for it took many men to shepherd such large groups meeting in dozens of homes (Phil. 1:1). However, when we read Christ's words addressed to the leadership of the seven churches in Asia, now it was singular with the pastor being called "angel." The chief rabbis of Jewish synagogues were called "angels" (messengers), "chazan," "bishop," or overseer." This may signal that these seven churches were more Hebrew in nature than Gentile. Roman Law forbid Christians permission to erect public buildings for worship until the year A.D. 222. Even this was short lived, as succeeding emperors were unfavorable to the cause of Christ. Various law cults operating under the guise of Christianity are so bold to state that it is either the Sabbath or hell. The Adventist cult affirms that Sunday worship will in the future become the mark of the beast. (Some of them deny this.) Men are not barred from heaven because they worship on a certain day or do not worship on that day. They are shut out of heaven because the blood of Jesus Christ, God's perfect sacrifice for all mankind has not atoned for their sins. And this atonement is received by faith, not by Sabbath or Sunday keeping. Paul told the Christians in the Colossian Church to let no man judge them regarding Sabbaths, which were only a shadow of things to come (Col. 2:16-17). The law cults should learn from this apostolic instruction.

3p-**Easter Sunday?** The resurrection of Jesus Christ had nothing to do with pagan religions and worship of the female goddess Astarte. This was an ancient heathen festival called "Easter." These dark customs were brought into the state church during the reign of Emperor Constantine, (A.D. 306-337) and spread widely after his death. Out of his ecumenical barnyard, came the Roman Catholic system, which is loaded with pagan customs and rituals. Because of this, many believers fled the emperor's state church and it corruptions. "Christianized paganism" slowly infiltrated churches all over the world and became part of their rituals and so-called worship. Dave Hunt in his work, *A Woman Rides the Beast,* page 392, wrote these accurate words, "We have noted that for centuries before the Reformation, simple Christian fellowships existed outside the Catholic Church. These believers abhorred the heresies and hypocrisy of Rome and refused to honor the pope. For this they were hounded to terrible deaths by the hundreds of thousands." For a brief review of paganism in the Papal Church, see *A Summary of Christian History,* pages 36-40, by Robert A. Baker. Two old volumes dealing with this awful subject are *Sex Worship and Symbolism* (1922) by Sanger Brown II., and *Sex Worship: an Exposition of the Phallic Origin of Religion,* (1909) by Clifford Howard. Both books expose the horrific religious rites of demon-possessed pagans. The authors were unbelievers who wrote from an honest but spiritually blind viewpoint. Their books have historical value, but are worthless for spiritual instruction. For more on this neglected side of Christian history, see Section 1, Part 4, third paragraph of footnote j. See also Section 98, third through the fifth paragraphs under footnote c. Regarding believer's taking *genuine demonic objects* into their homes, refer to Section 20, third through the fifth paragraphs of footnote l.

(b) **The women at the tomb.** The terrible night had passed. Before the faint streaks of dawn tinged with bright silver the darkness of that resurrection morning, the love of these women, who lingered last by the cross, compelled them to be first at the tomb. The gates of Jerusalem were opened at the early rays of sunlight. The two Mary's were seemingly foremost in the resurrection event. After them came Salome, Joanna, and the others who are unnamed.

Reading the four parallel verses given by the authors, they show that each reported a *different aspect* of the women's walk to the tomb that morning. They were all correct in what they reported. For an excellent harmony of the women, Peter and John's trips back and forth to the tomb, see the *Scofield Reference Bible*, page 1043, footnote 1. *Mary (of Bethany) who had anointed Christ in view of His resurrection was not present among the group.* Critics have fiercely attacked this part of Scripture. Being unsaved, these people cannot understand that God did not inspire the four evangelists to put down a systematic, chronological, word-for-word report of the resurrection narrative. (This is true of most events recorded in Scripture and is one of the peculiar marks of inspiration.) However, He did superintend them to write what was necessary for our faith to rest on an unshakable solid foundation.

2p-The disciples did not know or understand. Mary, was the exception. We wonder what thoughts assailed the minds of Joseph, Nicodemus, the eleven, and others who had trusted the carpenter from Nazareth as Messiah. He was dead; they saw Him die or heard it from others. They did not know that He would rise from the grave; all except one person, a woman named Mary, who lived at Bethany some two miles east of Jerusalem. See main heading of Section 146, for details on Mary, and John 12:3 of this Section with relative footnotes for her beautiful story. Where was the lonely woman who had anointed her Lord for His burial? She was conspicuously missing from the cross scene. *We can easily believe that Mary was not present because she knew and believed in His resurrection to follow.* Had the rest of His disciples expected Him to rise, there would have been no formal burial or costly anointing the body with many pounds of spices, no deep sorrow, and disappointment over His decease; however, these dark clouds overshadowed the whole event. Looking back on the death of Jesus as he wrote, John explained it this way, "For as yet they knew not the Scripture, that he must rise again from the dead" (John 20:9). This reveals the ignorance of the apostles regarding their understanding of the Old Testament predictions of the death of Messiah for their sins and His resurrection. It amazes us in view of the fact that Jesus mentioned these things to them many times over the course of His ministry and teaching. See the second paragraph under footnote e below for more on the disciples not understanding their Lord's death and resurrection.

3p-It was because none of them knew of His resurrection that we read of the women going to His tomb to finalize their Lord's burial. *Had they known of this, there would have been no such endeavor on their part.* The earliest streaks of dawn appeared in the eastern skies as the women, who had previously marked where He was laid (Mk. 15:47), made their way to the tomb of Joseph. John mentioned *only* Mary Magdalene in his account while Matthew, Mark, and Luke listed several others by name. He informs us that she and those with her, came when it was "yet dark." The idea is that they left their residence somewhere in Jerusalem before sunrise and moved to the northern gates waiting for them to be opened. As the Sabbath ended (with the first rays of dawn), a loud trumpet blast sounded from the temple tower, and the gates of Jerusalem were opened. The first day of the week dawned. Upon hearing this, the band of women carrying the very heavy load of spices to finish embalming the dead body of Jesus, hastened to the garden tomb some distance away. *They were in for the biggest surprise of their lives!*

[(c)] **"Who will move the stone?"** Making their way to the burial site, the women began to discuss the *large stone* that was rolled over the entrance. In Mk. 16: 4, we read that, "It was very great." They did not know that the tomb had been under watch by Roman soldiers and sealed by the signet of Governor Pilate, or they would not have made this trip. Getting past either would be an impossible task for this group of females loaded down with the spices. For more on the official Roman seal and guards, refer to Section 194, Matt. 27:65-66, footnotes d, and e.

[(d)] **The stone had been moved.** The problem of the vast stone covering the doorway to Jesus' burial site was instantly solved as an angel from heaven with wonderfully awful countenance appeared. Suddenly, an earthquake struck, and he rolled the stone *upward* in the slide trough into a fixed position! There had been an earlier earthquake at the moment of Jesus' death (Matt. 27:51). In Lk. 24:4-6 it states there were actually two angels, both of which spoke first to the women. Later, they affirmed His ascension in Section 207, Acts 1:10. Reading that the face of one was like lightning and his clothing white as snow, we understand the holy terror that fell upon the women and knocked the Roman soldiers into paralyzed fear. At what exact time these men fled the site, we are not informed. One can believe that they spent some time trying to collect their wits for their lives would be forfeited, because the Roman seal had been broken and the dead man, they were to secure was gone! See Section 199, where later in the scheme of these events they went first to the Jewish religious leaders after fleeing the tomb, begging for help.

2p-Verse 3. "Raiment white as snow." It was a commonly held notion among the Hebrews that the good angels of God were clothed in white, and the angels of the Devil in black. (Paul disproves this in 2 Cor. 11:13-15.) The Talmud has several curious passages that seem to reflect this belief. They are Yoma 39b and Menachoth 109b. The rabbis based this idea on Ezek. 9:2. It is not by accident that genuine Satanists, and those who think themselves so, take pride in wearing *only* black apparel, with fingernails and lips painted black, makeup, eyeshade, shoes, hose, and so forth. There is a strange inexpressible evil connection in all this with the prince of darkness. *Not everyone who wears black is connected with these dark things.*

3p-Verse 4. "Became as dead men." These soldiers were veterans of the famed Roman army. They were men of long experience, battle hardened, filled with extraordinary courage in the face of all fear. Yet, in the presence of heavenly beings, they were seized with awful trepidation and anxiety. Every muscle froze; they were paralyzed in terror at the sight of holy angels sent from God. Falling to the ground they seemed lifeless. If these were the same men who superintended the crucifixion, then we can believe they felt that divine judgment had now befallen them. As they lay prostrate upon the earth, did they hear the conversation that followed between the women and the angels in white? If so, these men heard that Jesus had risen and was alive! Such an experience never left their minds. They carried the thoughts of this the rest of their lives. One wonders whom they later told of this amazing thing. For the Sanhedrin bribing the soldiers to lie about their shocking experience, see Section 199 and relative footnotes.

(e) Their concern about who would roll the weighty stone door back was answered from heaven. See footnote c above. Upon arrival, the tomb was open, the seal broken, and the soldiers (after regaining their senses) had fled into the city. Luke wrote, "They entered in, and found not the body of the Lord Jesus" (verse 3). This was a shock as great as that of the angels appearing, and one of them sitting upon the rolled back stone door (Matt. 28:2-3).

2p-Luke 24:3. "And found not the body." Therefore, it must be, for the Jewish Old Testament (Tanakh) had predicted that Messiah would rise from the dead. Refer to Lev. 23:10-11; Ps. 16:10; Isa. 53:9-12: Acts 2:24-32; and 1 Cor. 15:20. The women and apostles who came to the tomb, including Joseph and Nicodemus who buried the Savior's body, did not know the meaning of these predictions at that time. For more on this, see the second paragraph under footnote b above. John himself stated this fact as he wrote his account of Jesus' death and resurrection some years later. Note this straight forward and honest confession in Section 196, John 20:9, with footnote i.

3p-"The Lord Jesus." This is the first occurrence of this full title found hereafter forty times in the epistles. Now, because of His resurrection, He is Lord even of death!

(f) **"Perplexed" as "two men stood by."** It is conjecture that these two angels were the cherubims over the ark of the covenant (Ex. 25:20-21). Later, 1 Kings 8:7 tells us that these cherubims had wings. Messiah's body had vanished, and two holy beings from another world announced amazing news into their ears. See second paragraph of footnote b above. As the life of Christ on earth began with the miracle of His virgin birth, so it ended with one even greater: *His resurrection from the dead.* In the dateless eons of eternity past, the Son of God reposed in the bosom of His Father. Within the frame of earth's time, He lay in the arms of a human mother. At the outset of His ministry, He went under the water's of Jordan in baptism to reflect how His life would end a few years hence. At the end of His work, He was placed in a rich man's borrowed tomb, but returned it after a few days and nights. This fulfilled the prophets words "And he made grave with the wicked, and with the rich in his death" (Isa. 53:9).

2p-Men and devils have hated, opposed, blasphemed, and bitterly denied this final miracle of Jesus the Nazarene. Today, as in days of yore, many seminaries and schools of theological learning have relegated the atoning death of Christ and His resurrection into the realm of myth. One is appalled at the sophisticated academic arguments put forward by God rejecters. They, so cleverly, and with high-sounding oratory, debate for their own damnation. Arrogantly, they lock themselves into hell, and throw the key away! No religion on the face of planet earth today so hates, opposes, and denies the death, burial, and resurrection of God's Son like that of *radical* Islam. Mohammed, the founder knew that he could not exalt himself as the final and true prophet, unless he demoted the Lord Jesus Christ, God's only begotten Son, and humanity's exclusive Savior. Therefore, the rabid followers of his religion continue the dark legacy of their "prophet." There is not a Muslim on the face of the earth, be they radical or non-radical (and there are thousand of these), who has in his heart the sure hope of sins forgiven and eternal life. This is because they deny God's only begotten Son, His death in which He paid for their sins, and His resurrection by which the grave was conquered for all who trust Him alone as supreme Lord and Savior. Any religion that teaches the murder of its enemies by self-martyrdom has its origin in Satan and its end in hell.

(g) **"Ye seek Jesus which was crucified: he is risen; he is not here"** Either the angel from heaven spoke this as truth, or he was confused, or lied. As stated in the last paragraph of footnote f above, Satan has employed every scheme in his bag of dirty tricks to denounce or explain away the death of Christ for the sins of the world and His resurrection from the dead. In 1965, Hugh Schonfield's blasphemous book *The Passover Plot,* conjured up and revamped the ancient myth that "Jesus swooned or fainted on the cross," was taken down, placed in the cool rock tomb, revived and slipped out: hence, His resurrection! With these satanic yarns, every devil in town climbed onto this bandwagon and began to beat their drums. Religious infidels such as Rudolf Bultmann, Albert Schweitzer, David Strauss. G. A. Wells, and others have postulated many fables in their struggle to rob God's Son of His uniqueness and deity. For more on these men, see Section 2, third paragraph of footnote g.

2p-For a sound response to the writings of these Antichrist theologians, historians, and their present day contemporaries, see *Ancient Evidence For the Life of Jesus*, by Gary R. Habermas, and the 10-volume opus, *The Works of Nathaniel Lardner.* The latter collection was written in the early 1700s, before the lie of higher criticism was invented, and Satan's "learned" proponents rose on the stage of religious skepticism to embrace this poison. In the providence of God, Lardner's works were something of an advanced warning and response to a future attack on Holy Scripture, especially the record of the life of Christ. *There are thousands of men who are truly "greatly learned theologians," and they defended the veracity of Holy Scripture.* For more on this subject, refer to Section

87, footnote j. Several testimonies of dying unsaved men, are in Section 115, third paragraph of footnote e. For the misplaced sentiments of many Christians today, see the third paragraphs of footnote h below.

3p-Luke 24:5. "The living among the dead." This was a common parable employed among the Jews. Having heard this many times they instantly understood what the angel was saying. It had reference to people doing foolish things and involved in impossible tasks. Regardless, what a question! In other words, they were in the wrong place looking for the right Person. The living Christ would not be found in the graveyard. He had returned His borrowed tomb to Joseph, the original owner. Living men do not need a grave!

(h) "As he said." There is some debate over who said these words. Contextually, all three personal pronouns "he" reflect a direct antecedent to the Lord Jesus. *Our Savior said thousands of things that are not recorded in the four gospels.* Some expositors hold that this was the angel's condensed version of our Lord's former predictions of His death and resurrection. Regardless, they are highlighted in the harmony commentary in red as being *originally* spoken by Jesus of Nazareth in whatever context. They are similar to the angel's words where he again quotes Christ in Lk. 24:5-8. We do not know when He said this for the reason God has not put it in Scripture. What an invitation! How many men over the course of world history have borrowed a tomb to be buried in, and then several days after their death, returned it to the original owner! The grave clothes were folded and in order, while the head cloth was in a place by itself (John 20:6-7). As mentioned, this required a miracle; coming out of the burial clothes without disturbing them! The angels said, "go quickly and tell his disciples that he is risen from the dead" (Matt. 28:7).

2p-The empty unvisited tomb. After the apostles and disciples were convinced of their Lord's resurrection from the dead, we are struck that never again in Scripture do we read of anyone visiting the empty tomb! Not even Paul, when passing through Jerusalem at the end of several missionary journeys went to look upon this place (Acts 18:22 with 21:17-18). Not one of the eight writers of the twenty-seven books of the New Testament (which span a time period of about thirty-five to forty years) mentions seeing or visiting the empty tomb of Christ. Over the past decades, literally millions have filed past the *supposed* burial places of Jesus and looked into them. The Church of the Holy Sepulcher in the old section of Jerusalem, and Gordon's tomb are the two of the conjectured locations.

3p-Looking at the wrong thing? Many present day Christians put so much stock in peering into a hollowed out rock just outside the city of Jerusalem? Should we not look rather into Holy Scripture and read of those devout women, Peter, John and the others that found the tomb empty? We must consider the startling announcement of the angels, the terrified soldiers, and the scramble of the Sanhedrin to cover it up. This is our infallible surety, our witnesses. No others are needed. Those who find comfort in filing past a cave, looking inside, and then weeping with joy, have missed the mark. What would these people do if an earthquake destroyed this revered burial site? What then would be their surety? Historically, no man knows if this is the right place or not. It is absurd to walk through Colonel Gordon's tomb location, and "because it's empty" feel reassured that Jesus rose from the dead. Rather, let all readers try moving through God's Bible. It emphatically affirms that Christ lives. Our Lord's empty tomb as portrayed in Scripture etches into our minds the truth of this fact, while the living Savior abides in our hearts by faith (Eph. 3:17). This is so because God's Word attests to it and has vouchsafed for all who believe its veracity. Reader, if you were walking a road and found a fork with two men there, one dead and the other alive, from which would you ask directions? With David of old we say, "I hope in thy word" (Ps. 119:81), or like Jeremiah who declared, "Thy word was unto me the joy and rejoicing of mine heart" (Jer. 15:16). What more could a child of God ask for? Believers are more secure here than gazing into a hewn out stone. Better is the view yonder at God's right hand! *How interesting that men never speak of "the late Jesus Christ." Why? Is it because He is not late!*

(i) "The third day." See *Appendix One* for the meaning of this term. This angel reminded them of what Jesus had said over a year before. At least twice, while north in Galilee, our Lord had spoken to His disciples of His death and resurrection after three days. The original mention is found in Lk. 9:22. The second is recorded in Matt. 17:22-23, which was a few weeks after the first one and was given in Galilee. In each of these cases, Christ spoke of His upcoming death at Jerusalem. His disciples at that time did not understand what He was saying. Even on resurrection morning, they still did not comprehend His death, burial, and resurrection. Refer to Section 196, footnote i for others details on this confounding problem.

2p-Verse 8. "They remembered his words." Yet they did not understand. This understanding would come shortly, and then they put the whole picture together. These women had been with Jesus in Galilee, but are now at the tomb near Jerusalem. Mark in 16:1 lists some of the names of this company. Refer also to the first paragraph of footnote d. In shock, they heard the angel's announcement. *The body they came to embalm was gone!*

(j) "Meet Me in Galilee." After establishing the Communion Supper with the eleven, He spoke of the Galilean meeting for the first time (Matt. 26:32). To keep this prearranged engagement, we should remember that the disciples had to walk some ninety miles north (a three-day trip one way) to get there! They were at Jerusalem at the empty tomb when the angel gave them this reminder. A few moments later, Christ Himself appeared to these women and reminded them *again* to tell the other disciples of this meeting (up north) in Galilee. See Section 198, Matt. 28:10, footnote b. About a week afterward they kept this important rendezvous with their risen Savior and Messiah on some unknown mountain in Galilee. Refer to Section 204, Matt. 28:16, footnote a for the dramatic story.

951

Mary Magdalene and the other women leave the tomb and report to the apostles, and "all the rest"* who were in Jerusalem. They spoke of meeting angels. Peter and John raced to the burial site and John outruns Peter. Peering in, they see empty burial cloths and a head covering in another place. Jesus was not there!

Time: His Sunday morning resurrection, early on the first day of the week.

*"And all the rest." This comment by Luke informs us that not only were the eleven apostles gathered together, but also others were with them at this time.

At the burial site and in Jerusalem

Matt. 28:8	Mk. 16:8	Lk. 24:9-12	John 20:2-4
Running with news	*Running with news*	*Running with news*	
8 And they departed quickly from the sepulchre	8 And they went out quickly, and fled from the sepulchre; for they trembled and were amazed: neither said they any thing to any *man*; for they were afraid. (Verse 9 cont. in Section 197.)	9 And returned from the sepulchre,	
with fear and great joy;			*Running with news*
			2 Then she runneth, and cometh to Simon Peter, and to the other disciple, whom Jesus loved, and saith unto them, "They have taken away the Lord out of the sepulchre, and we know not where they have laid him."
and did run to bring his disciples word.[a] (Verse 9 cont. in Section 198.)		and told all these things unto the eleven, and to all the rest.[a]	
		Who told the apostles	
		10 It was Mary Magdalene, and Joanna, and Mary *the mother* of James, and other *women*[b] *that were* with them, which told these things unto the apostles.	
		11 And their words seemed to them as idle tales, and they believed them not.[c]	
		Peter and John race	*Peter and John race*
		12 Then arose Peter,[d]	3 Peter[d] therefore went forth, and that other disciple, and came to the sepulchre.
		John outruns Peter	*John outruns Peter*
		and ran unto the	4 So they ran both

Matt.	Mk.	Lk. 24:12	John 20:4-10
		sepulchre;	together: and the other disciple did outrun Peter, and came first[e] to the sepulchre. **5** And he stooping[f] down, *and looking in,* saw the linen clothes lying; yet went he not in.
		and [Peter] stooping down, [to get in] he beheld the linen clothes laid by themselves,	***Peter arrived last*** **6** Then cometh Simon Peter following him, and went into the sepulchre, and seeth the linen clothes lie, **7** And the napkin, that was about his head, not lying with the linen clothes, but wrapped together [folded] in a place by itself.[g]
		Peter leaves amazed: ***John remains there*** and departed, wonder-ring in himself at that which was come to pass. (Verse 13 cont. in Section 200.)	***John believed what?*** **8** Then went in also that other disciple, which came first to the sepulchre, and he saw, and believed.[h] ***They did not know***
		What a statement! It was resurrection morning and neither Peter or John knew the Old Testament verses that predicted His resurrection, nor did they understand. John, the writer of this verse was one of them! Earlier in Section 29, John 2:22, we read that the disciples recalled a verse about His resurrection. When this recalling occurred we are not told. Surely it was after verse 9 above. See also Section 148, John 12:16, and attached notes.	**9** ◄**For as yet they [Peter and John] knew not the scripture,(i) that he must rise again from the dead.** *(See this symbol ▫ below.)* **10** Then the disciples went away again unto their own home.[j] (Verse 11 cont. in Section 197.) ▫ *After the day of Pentecost the great requirement of Rom. 10:9 is demanded of all men. See Section 2, third paragraph of footnote g.*

Footnotes-Commentary

(a) Upon entering the sepulchre the women found not His body. Mark wrote, that they "fled from the sepulcher" (verse 8). Matthew explains that their minds were filled with "fear and great joy" (verse 8). *Only those who have experienced this strange combination will understand Matthew's statement.* He knew what was in their minds by divine inspiration, since he wrote his history some years after it was over. Meeting dozens of people along the way back to Jerusalem, they were so terrified that they dared not say anything about that morning in the garden. Luke is careful to write that these running women returned to the *eleven apostles* and others ("all the rest") who were with them, staying somewhere in the city. Apparently, this was a gathering of many of Jesus' followers. The bewildered women raced in upon them and blurted out the amazing news of what had just happened at the tomb of Jesus. Everyone present fell into a state of holy fear! Who among us today could even imagine the thoughts storming the minds of this band of believers? They saw Him die on a cross; now He is alive again!

(b) **How many women went to the tomb and when?** John was inspired to give Mary Magdalene's side of the story; thus, he wrote about her as if the others were not involved, though they were. He did not deny they were present, but dealt exclusively with Magdalene. The events of this time were as follows: Several women (with unnamed "others" helping to carry the heavy spices Lk. 24:1) went first to the tomb very early in the morning. These included the following names:

1. **Mary Magdalene** (Matt. 28:1).
2. **Mary the mother of James the less and Joses or Mark** (Matt. 28:1 with Mk. 16:1).
3. **Salome** (feminine form of Salmon) who is the mother of the apostles and former fishermen James and John (Mk. 16:1; Matt. 27:56; with Mk. 15:40). Their father was Zebedee (Matt. 4:21). On Salome's plot to exalt her sons in Christ's kingdom, see main heading under Section 142. Mark mentioned Salome at the cross (Mk. 15:40) and in the resurrection narrative (Mk. 16:1).
4. **Joanna the wife of Chuza**, Herod Antipas' steward. For her history, see Section 65, Lk. 8:3, footnote f. Only Luke wrote of her being among the women coming early to the tomb (24:10). She and other believing women had followed Christ from Galilee down to Jerusalem and watched Him die on the cross as explained in Section 192, Lk. 23:48-49, footnote d, and parallel verses. Three days and nights later, they were the first to the tomb. Note Section 195, footnote b for comments on the sunrise venture. See footnote b above. Here, John only wrote about Mary Magdalene's trip to the burial site and did not mention any of the other women who also came. This selection is another mark of divine inspiration.

(c) **"Idle."** This is from a Greek medical word that speaks of a "delirium" or "confused mental condition." They thought the women were having hallucinations as they told their amazing story.

2p-**"Believed them not."** Repeatedly, in this harmony commentary it has been pointed out how none of our Lord's disciples or apostles knew of His death on the cross and subsequent resurrection from the dead. The grand news of the excited women was a joke (at that time) to the future leaders of the infant church. The Lord Jesus spent forty days and nights after His resurrection and before His ascension, during which He finally convinced them that He had risen from the grave and was alive forevermore. Their problem is explained in John 20:9 footnote i below. For other details on this problem, the disciples had with Jesus' death, note Section 104, footnote a.

(d) **"Run Peter, run!"** Luke gives Peter's side of the story, while John wrote about both going to the tomb. Upon hearing Mary's story and after recovering from his "idle tale" first impression, Peter detected the ring of sincerity and truth in her report. John was of the same mind. Suddenly, both leaped to their feet and raced out the door, across Jerusalem, through the northern gate, and to the garden tomb. It was early morning, and the streets of the city were packed with pilgrims and thousands of Jews from over the known world of that era. Technically, this very morning began the Feast of Unleavened Bread, though it was counted as starting before the Passover and overlapping it. For further explanation on this curious fact, see Section 168, Lk. 22:7, footnote a.

(e) **John was first**. Many conjectures have been postulated as to why John outran Peter. Perhaps age or a head start may have had something to do with John winning their footrace to the empty tomb of Jesus.

(f) **"Stooping down beheld."** Meaning "bending over" to look. This is said of Peter in Lk. 24:12, and of Mary Magdalene in John 20:11. Apparently, the actual tomb door opening was extremely low. In order to avoid one hitting their head on the top stone lintel, it was necessary to bend over, bow, or stoop to gain entrance. John bent over and looked into the tomb chamber, which was illuminated by the early morning sunlight. About that time, Peter came on the scene. Stooping, he quickly slipped through the opening and stepped downward into the burial room. Behind him came John, motivated by Peter's forward example, who probably beckoned him to enter also.

(g) **Everything in order.** There were no signs of grave robbery, haste, or pillage. The linen wrappings were neatly positioned each in its proper place and had the appearance as though the body had slipped out of them without disturbing their circular folds. This alone was a miraculous thing! We are struck with awe upon reading of the "napkin" or "head covering" for the dead, being wrapped or folded over in a place by itself. This cloth was also about the head of Lazarus (John 11:44). It was wrapped about the head and held the jaw from sagging downward

954

after the person had expired. Could this be a picture of Christ, the head of the church, now in heaven (a place by itself) tarrying until the final member of His body (the church) be wrapped in the fine linen of His perfect righteousness? When this is completed, He will return for her whenever that may be.

2p-The folded napkin. Some see in this a reflection of an ancient Jewish mealtime custom. When the master had completed his meal, he would wipe his hands, mouth and beard, then toss the wadded napkin on the table. It was a signal to the attending servant that he had finished eating. However, if he neatly folded the napkin and laid it at his place of reclining, it meant he was not finished; he would return to complete what he had started. Was this the sign left by the resurrected Son of God? Was He saying that He would return and finish His work?

3p-Verse 12. Peter wondered. Peter knew that neither friend, nor foe would have left the burial garments in such order had they stolen the body of Jesus. They would not have taken the time required to unwrap the corpse. At this point, he did not understand or believe in the resurrection of Christ. See footnote i below on the apostle's ignorance of their Scripture at this time. Dumbfounded, Peter returns to his place of lodging somewhere in the city.

(h) John believed? This passage is not saying that John, at this point believed in the resurrection of His Lord because the Scriptures predicted it. Rather, it states that he believed the words of Mary (verse 2) that someone had taken away or stolen Jesus' body. See all of footnote j below for further explanation of this.

(i) "They [Peter and John] knew not the Scripture." To know Scripture is one thing, to practice it daily is another. Later, John looking back wrote these words of both himself, and his companion in the gospel, Simon Peter. It is a frank explanation of their spiritual condition at *that* time. Their ignorance of Scripture was mentioned later by the Savior in Section 200, Lk. 24:25, footnote h. Neither of them understood the death, burial, and resurrection of Messiah as it was laid down in their Old Testament. This is a profound reflection upon the rabbis, scribes, and what they had been teaching the men of Israel. Christ had mentioned this to them on numerous occasions, but they continually failed to understand. A few hours later, He gave two of them a complete course on how the Old Testament pointed to Him in hundreds of ways, but they missed that too (Lk. 24:44-46). They were looking for a literal, material kingdom to be established. Instead, their Messiah had been put to death! Refer to the second paragraph of footnote j below for more on His death and their reaction.

2p-The fact these men saw their resurrected Lord on several occasions and still could not believe, means just what it says. Never in all human history had a dead man returned from the grave and tried to convince his loved ones he was alive again, back from the dead. *We would have been just as confounded and fearful as they were; no doubt asking ourselves, "Am I dreaming?"* This explains their dilemma to all honest men, except the "highly trained critics." Perhaps they would have taken a forensic DNA sample and checked it before believing in the risen Son of God! After all, scientific evidence is necessary before "educated men" should believe anything!

3p-The belief in a self-existent personal God is in harmony with all the facts of our mental and moral nature, as well as the phenomena of the material world displayed all about us. *Not to believe in God is so unnatural. It keeps a man from becoming what he should be and from being what he could be, and damns his soul at the end of it all.* In general, historians have attempted to classify the belief systems of men. The atheist flaunts that there is no God. Agnostics affirm that we cannot know if the Supreme Person exists, while pantheists declare that all finite things are part of an Eternal One. Polytheists have millions of gods and goddesses. It has been shown in this work that all idolatry is Devil worship. Dualism teaches there are two distinct substances or co-eternal things. One is good (God) and the other evil (Satan). Satan is not eternal. He is a created spirit being and ever subject to the Almighty. The Deist view sees God's power present in nature. This philosophy denies special revelation, divine miracles, the deity of Jesus Christ, and states that the Bible is only a book on the principles of natural religion. This teaching is the brother of Natural Theology, another popular heresy embraced by many of America's founding fathers. See Section 1, Part, 4, the fourth paragraph of footnote m for explanation of this error. Like the others just listed, Deists have no atonement for sins or personal salvation. Anything that keeps men from the saving knowledge of Jesus Christ is false regardless of how "learned, authoritative, and academic" it sounds. For a review of the Scriptural-historical reliability of the death, burial, and resurrection of Jesus Christ, see Section 207, under the heading, *"An explanation of the forty days."* It is marked by the symbol ◙ just before the commentary portion.

(j) "Their own home." The means that Peter and John returned to their temporary lodging in Jerusalem among friends or family members. Thousands of Jews from different parts of the known world of that era did this while observing Passover and Unleavened celebrations. Both these men physically made their homes near Lake Galilee, some ninety miles north of Jerusalem. They left the tomb confounded about what had happened to the body of their Lord. We read that John "saw, and believed." (John 20:8). The meaning of his belief at this time is explained in footnote h above.

2p-Upon entering the tomb, they found everything in such neat order that grave robbery was out of the question, as explained in footnote g above. Not knowing the Old Testament verses that spoke of the death, burial, and resurrection of their Messiah, they were at a loss as to what had happened. Stealing a dead body would be the highest of abominations among pious Jews! For more on the ignorance of the eleven apostles regarding the death of Messiah for their sins, see footnote i above, with Sections 104, 105, 107, and 141.

Peter and John leave the tomb. Mary Magdalene returns to weep over her missing Lord. The angels asked her a question. As she departs, suddenly, Christ appeared and calls her name! Mary hurries back into the city and tells the disciples her experience. Still, they did not believe* that He had risen.

Time: His Sunday morning resurrection on the first day of the week.

*For an explanation of this continuing unbelief among the apostles and disciples, even though they had seen the risen Savior, see Section 196, second paragraph of footnote i. The critical abuse of Mark 16:9-20, which asserts that these twelve verses should be dropped out of the text, is repugnant. Primarily, this is based on an old book type manuscript, known as Codex Sinaiticus compiled in the fourth century. Because these twelve verses are missing in this ancient writing and several lesser ones, we are to believe that they must be left out of all subsequent translations. Yet, they were quoted by the wild Irenaeus (died in A.D. 192), and Hippolytus (died A.D. 235), many years before Sinaiticus was written! A German infidel critic, Johann Griesbach, (died 1812) laid the foundation for "modern textual critics" by leaving various passages out of his second edition of the New Testament printed in 1806. After this, "great scholars," possessed with the lie that there was no such thing as divine inspiration of Scripture, across Europe, England, and America followed the lead of Dr. Griesbach. See all by the asterisk under main heading Section 120 for further explanation of the myths invented by liberal critics who take it on themselves to remove all the "errors" from the Bible, which they do not believe in the first place. James White, in his popular book, The King James Only Controversy, pages 255-257, generally agrees they should be there, and then lists a string of "problems," why they should not! The author of this harmony commentary has preached these passages many times and seen lost souls come to the saving knowledge of Christ. "Authorities" expunge these twelve verses from Mark in their translations, because they are missing in the questionable Codex Sinaiticus and Vaticanus. Oddly, however, they still bring men to the Savior. This alone demonstrates the seriousness of toying with Holy Scripture. See Author's Introduction for a broader discussion of this subject.

At the burial site and in Jerusalem

Matt.	Mk. 16:9	Lk.	John 20:11-15
	Mary Magdalene meets Jesus **9** Now when *Jesus* was risen early the first *day* of the week, he appeared first(a) to Mary Magdalene, out of whom he had cast seven devils.		◄*Most modern translations have unjustly deleted or dropped to a footnote verses 9-20 from Mark chapter 16.* ***Mary Magdalene meets two angels*** **11** But Mary(a) stood without at the sepulchre weeping: and as she wept, she stooped down, *and looked* into the sepulchre, **12** And seeth two angels in white sitting, the one at the head, and the other at the feet, where the body of Jesus had lain. **13** And they say unto her, "Woman, why weepest thou?" She saith unto them, "Because they have taken away my Lord, and I know not where they have laid him."(b) ***Mary Magdalene meets Jesus*** **14** And when she had thus said, she turned herself back, and saw Jesus standing,(c) and knew not that it was Jesus. **15** Jesus saith unto her, "Woman, why weepest thou? whom seekest thou?"(d) She, supposing him to be the

Matt.	Mk. 16: 10–11	Lk.	John 20:15–18
			gardener, saith unto him, "Sir, if thou have borne him hence, tell me where thou hast laid him, and I will take him away."(e)
			16 Jesus saith unto her,(f) "Mary." She turned herself, and saith unto him, "Rabboni;" which is to say, "Master."(g)
			17 Jesus saith unto her, "Touch me not;(h) for I am not yet ascended to my Father: but go to my brethren, and say unto them, I ascend unto my Father, and your Father; and *to* my God, and your God."(i)
	Mary reports seeing the Savior		*Mary reports seeing the Savior*
	10 *And* she went and told(j) them that had been with him, as they mourned and wept.		**18** Mary Magdalene came and told(j) the disciples that she had seen the Lord, and *that* he had spoken these things unto her. (Verse 19 cont. in Section 201.)
	They do not believe her story		
	11 And they, when they had heard that he was alive, and had been seen of her, believed not.(k) (Verse 12 cont. in Section 200.)		

Footnotes–Commentary

(a) **"First to Mary Magdalene."** She is shocked at the sight of two angels postured on either end of the cavity tomb where Jesus' body had been interred by Joseph and Nicodemus. Luke refers to them as "men," for they had the semblance of human male forms but wore shining garments (Lk. 24:4.) The Jews spoke of good angels appearing in white clothing and wicked ones dressed in black. This is recorded in the Talmud tractate, Yoma 39b, when upon the death of a Rabbi Simon "an old man [evil angel] appeared to him dressed in black." These angels inquired about Mary's weeping. Amazingly, she holds a conversation with these two creatures from the other world. Still thinking that someone had stolen Christ's body, she turns to leave the scene. Something wonderful was about to happen!

(b) Peter and John had raced to the tomb and left Mary at their place of residence in Jerusalem. See Section 196, footnote d. Now the two men depart from the tomb and return to the city. As they leave, she returned to the garden site perhaps by a different route from that being used by the two men. Mary, also, "stoops" and peers into the tomb chamber. Refer to Section 196, footnote f for meaning of "stooping down."

(c) Suddenly, she saw a man standing in front of her. He was dressed in ordinary clothing similar to what the hired gardener would have worn. Adam was the world's first gardener, the second Adam (Christ) was mistaken for one (Gen. 2:15 with 1 Cor. 15:45).

(d) **"Whom seekest thou" and "why weepest thou?"** Twice, this question was put to poor Mary in verses 13 and 15. Are heavenly beings troubled when they see us mortals weeping over things that are without cause or justification? They seem to be saying to this distraught and broken woman, "Stop this, for your Lord lives!" Her response is most touching as seen in footnote g below.

(e) **"I will take him away."** What heavenly love could motivate a little woman to inquire where a corpse was so that she might retrieve it for proper burial? Mary thought the figure before her was the gardener. Does this signal that she knew this person previously? "They" have taken Him away. We do not know who the "they" are in this sentence. Could she have meant the disciples of Jesus or His friends? The *seeming* absence of Christ is always the cause of great distress among pious souls saved by the grace of God. According to the promise in Heb. 13:5, our Lord is never so near as when He seems so painfully absent.

(f) **"Mary."** It was commonly believed among the ancients that death washed from the mind all memories of human acquaintances and things in this earthly life. Apparently, Mary had turned from the "gardener" and started down the path leaving the garden. "Mary," the stranger called! She had heard that sweet voice speak her name on other occasions; no other was as precious as that. He spoke to her in a tone that caused her poor heart to swell with fearful joy and wondrous amazement, as she turned about. With this, see Isa. 43:1, "I have called *thee* by thy name."

(g) **"Rabboni."** The word means "Master" or "my teacher." Great people often say little in great moments. The sheep know the shepherd's voice. (John 10:4). Instantly, she spun about and fell at His feet responding to these words of endearment. The meaning could also be, "My great One." David Stern in, *Jewish New Testament Commentary*, page 212, wrote, "As a title *'rabban'* was conferred only on the heads of the central academy and of the Sanhedrin." Now it is conferred upon the greatest rabbi who ever lived, Jesus of Nazareth, Israel's Messiah, and Savior of men. Mary had heard that voice a thousand times or more. No one was as precious as Messiah was. He had saved her from the torments of seven devils dwelling in her physical body (verse 9).

(h) **"Touch me not."** This does not mean that His body was of spirit substance or some mystic nature. His prohibition for her not to touch Him shows the exact opposite, for fingers of flesh could not touch a spirit. Our Lord's reason for forbidding her touch of worship was, "I am not yet ascended to my Father." Some think Jesus was saying that He had not yet taken those millions of souls from the rest side of sheol-hades into the presence of God in heaven. Other expositors believe that the sleeping bodies of dead Old Testament saints, which rose *after* His resurrection, were those bodies that belonged to the souls in paradise. After being reunited again, the Lord Jesus led them into heaven's eternal abode. Refer to Section 192, Matt. 27:51-53, number 3, under footnote a, for dead or sleeping bodies coming out of their graves. For comments on the heavenly paradise, see Section 190, Lk. 23:43, footnote i. Some think that this restriction was exclusively for Mary. It was intended to show her that the previous personal fellowship with Him by sight, sound, and touch no longer exists; that the ultimate state of glory had not yet begun. Our Lord's statement "for I am not yet ascended to my Father" gives this indication. Jesus seems to be saying to Mary, "Now your visible, audible fellowship with me has ended. Life through this world for you and my servants will be that of 'walking by faith.'" We can easily believe that Mary carried in her heart this glorious picture of her risen Lord calling her name! She became the first person to see the resurrected Son of God and was instructed to go and tell the others. Those who employ this story to justify women becoming pastors and ministers of the gospel have strained at a gnat and swallowed a camel. One could equally argue that persons must literally see the Lord Jesus as Mary did, before they qualify for the ministry.

2p-Evidence that this "touch me not" was *strictly* an experience for Mary is found in that Christ permitted the other band of women leaving the tomb to hold His feet. Note this in Section 198, Matt. 28:9, footnote a. A few days later, He also invited Thomas to touch His glorified body in Section 202, John 20:27.

(i) **"My God, and your God."** Some are troubled by this statement. In what sense can God be both the Father, and God of the Lord Jesus? Similar things were written by Paul in Rom. 15:6, "God, even the Father of our Lord Jesus Christ," thus demonstrating that this term was commonly known. From the cross of His agony, the Son shouted, "My God, my God, why hast thou forsaken me?" (Mk. 15:34). What is the meaning here? First, it is the great consolation of all true believers that the God of the Lord Jesus is their God also. Our trust is pointedly centered exactly where His trust and hope were during the days of His humanity. During our days of earthly flesh, we too have God (supreme and almighty) as Jesus did, and also as our Father, loving, caring, and providing. Our Savior experienced the same. God was the God of Christ *while on earth,* because He decidedly did God's work and will in His life. A few hours before the cross He rejoiced in prayer because He had "finished the work" God had given him to do (John 17:4). There is a question in Heb. 10:5, taken from a quotation from Ps. 40:6-7. It tells us what Jesus said to God a thousand years before His birth, "a body hast thou [God] prepared me." The humanity of Christ had its *visible, tangible* beginning at Bethlehem's manger though predicted centuries prior. God begat Jesus' physical body in the womb of Mary by the Holy Spirit (Lk. 1:34-35). The words of Ps. 2:7, quoted in Heb. 1:5, that God had "begotten" Jesus on a specific "day," spoke of his physical birth, not His creation. His Sonship with God, called His Father, had forever been without beginning or ending. God is the eternal Father of Christ, and Christ is the eternal Son of God by a declared statement of Holy Scripture (Isa. 9:6). The Bible affirms this but does not explain it. For more on Christ's equality with God, see Section 1, Part 1, second and third paragraphs, footnote a.

2p-Nothing concerning Christ is more hated by false religions, wicked men, and devils. than that of His perfect equality with God or deity. *At the birth of Jesus, God came down to men. In His death and resurrection, men may come up to God.* Thus, the God and Father of Christ, now in a unique sense is our God and Father as well.

(j) **"Told them."** After Peter and John left the tomb, she returned to the abode of the other disciples and shared with them what had happened. She told them that she had seen and spoken to the Savior! He was alive!

(k) **"Believed not."** This is often repeated. The apostles and even His closest companions did not understand His death on the cross at this time. They were looking for a political Messiah, who would set up an earthly kingdom and destroy Gentile opposition. Learned critics who have written much about the resurrection being staged by His disciples to fool the world, are themselves the biggest fools in the world. Christ's closest friends and confidants disputed, debated, and refused to believe in His resurrection. *Finally, after forty days and nights, He had convinced them.* From that time, they went forth fearlessly proclaiming the saving gospel, even the face of beatings and death. To hold that these men gave up all and that most of them were finally martyred for a dead man is more nonsense.

ANOTHER POST RESURRECTION APPEARANCE TO A GROUP OF WOMEN. SLOWLY, THE UNBELIEVING BELIEVERS ARE BECOMING GENUINE BELIEVERS IN THE RESURRECTION OF CHRIST!

Now, the Lord Jesus made Himself known to another company of women after His appearance to Mary Magdalene in the previous Section. They were carrying* a load of heavy spices * to the tomb to complete His burial. Thus, they were last to arrive at the burial site. Several of the women ** walking with them raced ahead and met two angels who announced that Christ was risen. Amazed and stunned, they ran back to the city to tell the disciples. To their shock, they suddenly met the Lord Jesus, and He gives them special instructions.

Time: His Sunday morning resurrection early on the first day of the week.

*We learn from John 19:39 that the weight of these spices and ointments was about seventy-five pounds. Therefore, the women carrying this load moved slowly to the garden tomb and arrived after the earlier events in Sections 195-197 had taken place. The Scofield Reference Bible has an excellent note regarding the order of these events on page 1043, footnote 1.
**Refer to the second paragraph under the main heading of Section 195, for some of the names of those who rushed ahead to the tomb of Jesus, and upon arrival were met by an earthquake; the stone was rolled back and holy angels greeted them!

Matt. 28:9-10—*Somewhere near the sepulcher of Jesus*	Mk.	Lk.	John
"All hail the risen Son of God" **9** And as they went to tell his disciples, behold, Jesus met them, saying, "All hail."◄ And they came and held him by the feet,(a) and worshipped him. **10** Then said Jesus unto them, "Be not afraid:(b) go tell my brethren that they go into Galilee, and there(c) shall they see me." (Verse 11 cont. in Section 199.)			

►**"All hail" or "rejoice."** Though proclaimed two thousand years ago this majestic announcement sends waves of glory over our hearts! "All hail," was a unique term of honor used by the rabbis to express the highest greetings to the most respected persons. It is illustrated in the Talmud tractate, Berachoth 55b. Someday, the whole world and men of all times, ages, and places will bow, giving reverence and respect to the Son of God (Phil. 2:9-11). Every tongue will say, "All hail." It may be centuries away, or it may be next year; no man knows, but that hour is coming! We are born, and we die; over birth and death, we have no control. For what we do between the two, we are responsible to God. This is of eternal consequence. The prudent person will be ready.

Footnotes-Commentary

(a) **"As they went."** This was the band of women that Mary Magdalene had left at the tomb. Matthew takes up the story with them as they also returned to Jerusalem to tell the other disciples the message of the angels, which they had just heard at the burial site. However, Mary had already beaten them to the job! She had raced ahead and told of her meeting and talking with the risen Messiah. As they run wildly back to the city, somewhere along the way, suddenly Jesus stands before them! His glorious Words, "All hail" sounded in their ears!

2p-**"Held him by the feet."** Mary Magdalene had been forbidden to do this, as seen in the previous Section 197, John 20:17. At that time, it was a unique prohibition just for her. The Jews would grasp the feet of great men and kiss them out of deep respect and love. See an earlier example of this act in 2 Kings 4:27. The author has seen this done in Africa while serving as a missionary. It is a common and accepted form of reverence, respect, and honor. The western mind has great difficulty with these ancient customs still in practice in some countries. It is wrong to spiritualize such things and change their literal meaning. This passage means just what it says about these women.

3p-**"And worshipped him."** If Jesus of Nazareth was not God, He was therefore, unworthy of worship. Consequently, He committed a great sin in accepting, that which was deserving of the Almighty alone.

(b) **"Be not afraid."** This expression and its equivalents contains a beautiful lesson for the fearful child of God. It is explained in Section 71, footnote j.

(c) For comments on the special Galilee meeting of Christ and His disciples, after His resurrection, see Section 195, Matt. 28:7, footnote j.

The terrified Roman guards at Jesus' tomb flee the garden and report to the authorities what had happened. The religious leaders of Israel bribe them to lie about the resurrection of Christ.* News of this surely came to Pilate. How the Jews talked him out of executing these guards we do not know.

Time: Sunday morning of the first day of the week.

---

*For the terrifying experience of these Roman soldiers, see Section 195, Matt. 28:3-4, footnote d.

Matt. 28:11-15—*From the garden tomb to the Jews in Jerusalem*	Mk.	Lk.	John
11 Now when they were going, behold, some of the watch came into the city, and shewed unto the chief priests all the things that were done.^(a) **12** And when they were assembled with the elders, and had taken counsel, they gave large money unto the soldiers,^(b) **13** Saying, "Say ye, His disciples came by night, and stole him *away* while we slept. **14** And if this come to the governor's ears, we will persuade him, and secure you."^(c) **15** So they took the money, and did as they were taught: and this saying is commonly reported among the Jews until this day.^(d) (Verse 16 cont. in Section 204.)			

Footnotes–Commentary

^(a) Quickly rising from before the Lord Jesus, these women fled the garden and raced back to the disciples anxiously waiting in the city. As they left, the terrified Roman soldiers slowly regained their composure and strength. The text reads that "some" of them went to the Jewish Sanhedrin for help. We wonder what happened to the others of their terrified company. They were doomed men, because the seal of Pilate had been broken and the dead man, they guarded was gone! No battlefield encounter had ever been like this one for these men of the mighty Roman military!

^(b) **"Large money."** No doubt a great deal more than what they gave to Judas, as there were four of these men. The Sanhedrin paid Judas to betray the Lord Jesus. Now, these hypocritical leaders of the Jewish religion convened a special meeting. They heard the terrified guards report what had taken place. This report must have included the awful earthquake, and the appearing of an angel from heaven whose raiment shined above the brightness of the sun. Did they mention hearing the angels talk with the women? One can imagine the sheer horror that filled the hearts of the evil men as they listened to the soldier's story. The Sanhedrin hit on the plan to bribe them with *large* sums of money for their distortion of the truth about what had happened. *This is the only miracle in the ministry of Christ that men were paid to lie about.* Why? Because if Jesus did rise from the dead, then He is God (Rom. 1:1-4). This would be the death kneel for the chief priests, scribes, and their companions.

^(c) **"We will secure you."** The soldiers plead with the Jews to keep these things away from the governor, or he would have them summarily executed! See an example of this in Acts 12:19. How the Jews managed to accomplish this is not stated. According to verse 15 above, the Sanhedrin "taught" or "instructed" them on what to say to Pilate, and apparently, he accepted their story. Dr. Dwight Pentecost made a very pertinent comment regarding these Roman soldiers. He wrote in, *The Words & Works of Jesus Christ*, page 502 this terse statement, "It is significant that while the disciples disbelieved the report of the resurrection and sought confirmation of it, the Sanhedrin believed the report and sought an explanation to deny it."

^(d) **"Until this day."** Matthew informs the original Jewish readers of his book that the rumor of this pay off was still well known among them as he finished his writing. He wrote his book to fellow Hebrews, not many years after the ascension of Jesus. By this time Pilate had been removed from power (in A.D. 36) and sent to exile probably in Switzerland, where a *tradition* says that he later committed suicide by throwing himself off a cliff into a lake. For more on Pilate's death, see Section 21, Part 1, number 2 under footnote b. Though it was late in the story, the Jews still talked about these things and continued to wonder about Jesus of Nazareth and His resurrection from the dead. The big question remained, "Was He our promised Messiah?"

2p-Matthew wanted his Jewish readers to know the truth of the events about which he had just written. It is clear that many of them were generally familiar with the story of Christ. Now, in the inspired book of Matthew, they have the truth as to what really happened on that early morning. Every pious, sincere Jew who read Matthew's words must have been deeply stirred over this record penned by one who had been an eyewitness to many of the events of which he had written. Refer to *Appendix Seven* for the question of when the four gospels were written.

About mid afternoon of the Resurrection day, two disciples walk the road from Jerusalem to Emmaus. A Wonderful Stranger joins them.

Time: Sunday afternoon of the resurrection day.

On their way to a village called Emmaus

Matt.	Mk. 16:12	Lk. 24:13-29	John
	His appearing on a country road **12** After that he appeared in another form[a] unto two of them, as they walked, and went into the country. (Verse 13 cont. in Section 201.)	*His appearing on a country road* **13** And, behold, two of them went that same day[b] to a village called Emmaus, which was from Jerusalem *about* threescore	

Furlongs. (approximately eight miles.)

14 And they talked together of all these things which had happened. *(Jesus' death and reported resurrection verses 18-24.)*

15 And it came to pass, that, while they communed *together* and reasoned, Jesus himself drew near, and went with them.

16 But their eyes were holden [prevented from seeing who He was] that they should not know him.[c]

"Why are you so sorrowful?"

17 And he said unto them, "What manner of communications *are* these that ye have one to another, as ye walk, and are sad?"

18 And the one of them, whose name was Cleopas,[d] answering said unto him, "Art thou only a stranger in Jerusalem, and hast not known the things which are come to pass there in these days?"

19 And he said unto them, "What things?" And they said unto him, "Concerning Jesus of Nazareth, which was a prophet mighty in deed and word before God and all the people:[e]

20 "And how the chief priests and our rulers delivered him to be condemned to death, and have crucified him.

"We thought He was our [political] Messiah"

21 "But we trusted that it had been he which should have redeemed Israel:[f] and beside all this, to day is the third day since these things were done. *(For "third day," see Appendix One.)*

22 "Yea, and certain women also of our company made us astonished, which were early at the sepulchre;[g]

23 "And when they found not his body, they came, saying, that they had also seen a vision of angels, which said that he was alive.

24 "And certain of them which were with us went to the sepulchre, and found *it* even so as the women had said: but him they saw not."

"Too slow to believe your Scriptures"

25 Then he said unto them, "O fools,[h] and slow [hesitant] of heart to believe all that the prophets have spoken:

26 "Ought not Christ to have suffered these things, and to enter into his glory?"

27 And beginning at Moses and all the prophets, he expounded unto them in all the scriptures the things concerning himself.[i]

28 And they drew nigh unto the village, whither they went: and he made as though he would have gone further.[j]

"Spend the night with us." He suddenly vanishes

29 But they constrained him, saying, "Abide with us: for it is toward

961

Matt.	Luke 24:29-32—*On the way to a village called Emmaus*	John
	evening, and the day is far spent." And he went in to tarry with them.[k] **30** And it came to pass, as he sat at meat[l] with them, he took bread, and blessed *it*, and brake, and gave to them. **31** And their eyes were opened,[m] and they knew him; and he vanished out of their sight. *The effect of God's Word when understood* **32** And they said one to another, "Did not our heart burn within us, while he talked with us by the way, and while he opened to us the scriptures?"[n] (Verse 33 cont. in Section 201.)	

Footnotes-Commentary

[a] Mark writes briefly of the Emmaus road wonder. He is careful to show that Jesus appeared at this time in another form or manner different from the other appearances he had mentioned.

[b] **"That same day."** According to these words, this event occurred on the Sunday afternoon of the Resurrection Day. We learn later in this story that one of these men was Cleopas, while the other is unnamed (verse 18). See footnote d below for more on this unknown person. The named is spelled as Cleophas in John 19:25. In Section 190, see the third paragraph of footnote j, where we note that he married the sister of Jesus' mother. It was not uncommon for several children in the same family to bear like first names. We practice similar customs in the west but attach Jr. at the end of the name. He was an uncle to Christ by marriage. For those who have nervous breakdowns over differences in name spellings in Scripture, see Section 6, second paragraph of footnote a. "Three score furlongs" equal about eight miles. Emmaus was located northeast of Jerusalem and could be walked at a fast pace in about two and a half hours. The road would have been packed with pilgrims returning to their homes from the Passover celebration at Jerusalem. Josephus seemingly wrote of Emmaus in *Antiquities*, Book 18:2. 3, lines 36–37, and *Wars of the Jews,* Book 7:6. 6, line 217 with footnote d. He informs us that "warm baths" were located here and that people in great numbers came to visit because of this luxury. For a good historical review of Emmaus, see the *Biblical, Theological, and Ecclesiastical Cyclopaedia,* vol. III, pages 178–179, by M'Clintock and Strong. Like everything else in the Bible, this too is disputed by the "greatly learned authorities."

[c] **"Their eyes were holden."** Despite the bizarre explanations given for this statement, it means just what it says. No medical explanation is given. Christ would not let them understand who He really was; He needed to explain some things in order to lead them into the correct knowledge that He had risen from the dead. See footnote m below for the lifting of this restraint. There are no religious metaphysics, "Silva Christ consciousness" mind control, or occult "suggestion arts" found here. It was a miracle performed by the eternal Son of God. Those who imagine they see in this the Savior using a form of "white magic," are wrong. All forms of occult mind control, thought seduction, paranormal experiences, and magic of whatever sort are forbidden to the Christian. For detailed information on various occult practices and satanic inroads into the lives of innocent and gullible people, see Section 20, second through fifth paragraphs, footnote l.

2p-**Christianed sins. Occult sanctioned in the Bible?** Section 23, Matt. 4:5-6 reveals that Satan quotes Scripture with intentions to deceive and destroy. He has continued this practice up to the present moment. The Internet reeks with websites that struggle to portray occult-demonism in its various forms as being sanctioned in God's Word. Joseph's cup is hailed as an occult device borrowed from the pagans of Egypt (Gen. 44:2). Whatever Joseph learned from his cup it was of God, not from the occult. Even the pagan Pharaoh of the land confessed that Joseph was "a man in whom the Spirit of God" dwelt (Gen. 41:38). This was the source of his discernment. Like the Urim and Thummim, given to the high priest by Jehovah, at times it would reveal His will, and other times it would not (Ex. 28:30 with 1 Sam. 28:6). The "bitter water test" was ordained of God to detect adultery, and had nothing to do with the demonic occult (Num. 5:12-31). The same is true of "casting lots" as recorded in Num. 26:55 and Prov. 18:18. When the eleven apostles cast lots to select one to fill the vacancy left by Judas Iscariot, they prayed for Divine direction before taking action (Acts 1:23-26). It is noted after the Holy Spirit came in His fullness on Pentecost that this method was no longer used for decision making by believers (Acts 6:1-7). Direction today, in the lives of believers is *first* sought from God's Word and the Holy Spirit, with this blended in prayer and waiting. If God should choose to use an event, circumstance, or some other happening, along with His Word and Spirit that would be His business. *Scripture condemns the occult in its totality. There is no such thing as the "Christian occult."* For further details regarding the intrusions of "Christianized sins" within the church and among untaught believers, refer to Section 50, second paragraph of footnote g. Previously mentioned in the early portions of this commentary is the documented work, *Christian Counseling and Occultism,* by Kurt E. Koch. This book is an invaluable guide if one has a genuine reason for investigating these things.

(d) Only Cleopas is named. Refer to Section 190, John 19:25, third paragraph of footnote j for earlier information on this person, who was an uncle of Jesus. See also footnote b above. (Some expositors believe the tradition that Luke, the author of this book, was the second man in the Emmaus road event. All sorts of guesses have been made, but we cannot know for sure who this second unnamed traveler was.) Some have held that the other unknown traveler was Simon Peter. This error is explained in Section 201, footnote c.

2p-The question asked by Cleopas reveals that the news of Jesus' death had spread over the length and breadth of the land, and that every listening ear heard it. Word of public executions by the Romans was widely spread and even more so at this time during the conclusion of the Passover and commencement of the Feast of Unleavened Bread. At that time, several million extra Jewish pilgrims were present at Jerusalem and that region. Writers who state that the death of Christ was only "local news" and not known abroad are sadly missing the mark.

(e) Our Lord "played dumb" in order to draw out His uncle and friend on this matter. The answer of Cleopas was a typical Jewish response. He described Jesus as being "mighty in Word and deed." This was the accepted profile of their promised Messiah. It is explained by the asterisk under main heading of Section 48. As a thorough Hebrew, he knew these were the two distinguishing factors that would identify Israel's Messiah.

(f) "We trusted that it had been he." There is no better passage in the entire New Testament proving that, even on the afternoon of His Resurrection Day, the Jews still did not understand why their Messiah came. The statement of this traveler mirrors the abysmal confusion among the best of Jews regarding their Christ. Clearly, neither Cleopas nor his companion could connect the death of Christ on the cross with their idea of political redemption! Like all informed Jews, Cleopas was looking for a physical, material salvation, not one by blood atonement of Christ on the cross. This would be clearly understood with the coming of the Spirit at Pentecost. Dr. Sigmund Mowinckel wrote in *He that Cometh. The Messiah Concept in the Old Testament & Later Judaism,* the following words on page 7, "The Messiah [in ancient Jewish understanding] is he who shall restore Israel as a people, free her from her enemies, rule over her as king, and bring other nations under her political and religious sway." In other words, Messiah was only a human who would bring about a literal, physical kingdom for the Hebrew people: a kind of human salvation for the nation. Redemption by the blood of Christ, and the joy of salvation by faith as realized in the New Testament did not figure into the material, earthly kingdom of Israel. This does not mean that no one was saved in this historical era of the nation. For salvation by grace *before* the cross and resurrection of Christ, see Section 10, all of footnote b; Section 64, footnote k; and Section 144, footnote i.

2p-Verse 21. The third day observation in Hebrew history. Cleopas' use of these words reveals that he had been taught by the rabbis. The Jews made a great fuss over this expression. They taught that "Abraham lifted up his eyes the third day" (Gen. 22:4); "After two days God will revive Israel" (Hosea 6:2); the importance of Joseph's interpretation of the three baskets as "three days" (Gen. 40:18); "The spies hid themselves for three days" (Josh. 2:16); "The law as declared on the third day" (Ex. 19:16); "Jonah was three days in the belly of the whale" (Jonah 1:17); "The Jews that came up from captivity, abode in tents for three days" (Ezra 8:15); and "Esther put on her royal apparel on the third day" (Esther 5:1). Three days marked a point of departure from something that had passed into some wonderfully new and eternally present. This is how Cleopas, used a timely synagogue expression.

(g) These two men were among the group who was stormed by the women (earlier that morning) coming from the tomb with the news that they had seen Jesus. However, at that time, no one believed what they said. See Section 198, Matt. 28:9-10 with footnotes a and b for details of this event.

(h) "Fools and slow to believe." The disciple's ignorance of their own Scriptures was mentioned earlier in Section 196, John 20:9, footnote i and the symbols ◄ and ◘. It strikes us that Christ described those who do not believe the Scripture as "fools" and "slow of heart." These words from the "stranger" must have shaken them to no end. The Lord Jesus instantly called attention to the cause of their problem; they had not understood or believed the passages in their Jewish Old Testament that spoke of the coming Messiah of Israel. See reference in footnote f above. It is exactly the same problem today: men are untaught or negligent of God's Word and thus live in abysmal ignorance of the most important issues of mortal life. This is more painfully true among men who are "leaders of the church" and live in a mental blackout to the basic teaching of Holy Scripture. The ancient Sadducees were an example of this. Christ pungently rebuked them for their ignorance of what God had said about the resurrection of the dead. See this event in Section 156, Matt. 22:29, footnote f for details.

2p-Verse 26. It was necessary for Christ to go this way in order to enter the eternal glory of being the only Savior of mankind and hope of the world. Refer to Heb. 12:2 for more on this thought and Section 178, John 17:5, footnote g for earlier comments on the glory of Christ.

(i) *The Lord Jesus saw Himself mentioned in the Old Testament Scriptures and pointed these out. This is something that many modern day "scholars" are unable to do.* It must have taken several hours for this discussion as they strolled along the road to Emmaus with Jesus joining them at the beginning of their journey. This was a sweeping exposition of every passage in the works of Moses, all the prophets, and the Psalms that pointed in any way to "the things concerning himself." There are hundreds of such verses, the majority of, which are not cited in the closed canon of the New Testament. See *Appendix Three* for many different prophecies fulfilled by Christ during His life, ministry, death, and resurrection. Never had these two men heard anything like this in their lives. They were utterly amazed. This alone shows that the major theme of the Old Testament was "Christ, the Jewish Messiah coming to die for our sins." For more on this subject, see Section 52, John 5: 45-47, footnotes y and z.

(j) Arriving at their place of stay or residence, just as the sun was setting, again the Lord Jesus "played along with them" in order to write an indelible lesson in their hearts. It was standard accepted courtesy for a person to first refuse such an invitation and then afterward accept it. *There was nothing hypocritical about this Jewish custom.* We of the western world do the same thing a thousand times or more and think nothing of it. He spoke as if He should move on in order to draw out their heart feelings about Him after that stirring Bible lesson on eternal redemption.

(k) **"They constrained him."** Stopping at their destination, the two men planned to spend the night. Little did they realize what was coming next! Not yet knowing that it was their risen Lord, they pressed upon Him to come in and spend the night. O that we might press hard upon our Lord to spend every hour of earth's dark night with us! The Savior did this in order to show the true feelings of their hearts toward Him. Years ago in Kimberly, South Africa, I read a plaque attached to the front door of a Dutch minister's house. It read, "Dear Lord Jesus. Please enter my home with me, until I enter thine with thee."

(l) **"He took bread and gave to them."** After going into the upper room, washing their hands and feet, a table already prepared stood before them. It was standard hospitality to offer bread to visitors, before retiring, regardless of the night hour. "Meat" was a euphemism for different kinds of food. According to social custom, one of the men requested their visitor to say the Jewish thanks over their loaf of bread. See Section 93, Mk. 6:41, footnote m for an earlier example of the Savior offering thanks over bread and fish and the standard Jewish prayer that was offered. After the blessing, the one who prayed would then break the bread in pieces and pass it to those reclining at the table. The text reveals that as Jesus handed them the bread, "their eyes opened" (verse 31). *As they took the piece of bread out of His hand, did they suddenly see the nail scars in His palms?* When by faith one views the stigmas (marks) of our Lord's crucifixion for their sins, their eyes are opened to spiritual realities as never before.

(m) **"Their eyes were opened."** As their eyes had been "holden" in verse 16 with footnote c above, now the restraint is lifted, and they instantly recognize this curious stranger as their Lord and Messiah. This means these men had known Him previously. The Jews believed that angels would appear to men in various disguises and then suddenly disappear when their mission was complete (Heb. 13:2).

2p-"He vanished." This means just what it says. The resurrected Son of God in His glorified body literally disappeared out of their sight! It was not subject to the laws of physics; distance, and material limitations. They leaped from the table, rushed back the eight miles to Jerusalem to the other disciples. To their shock, the Lord Jesus was also there and appeared to the collective group (Lk. 24:33-37). Still not understanding His resurrection, they were "terrified" at this new appearing of their Lord. Today, we would have done no better! If a deceased loved one suddenly appeared to us, our reactions would have been the same or far worse.

(n) Now, they understood why their hearts were aflame as this wonderful stranger took them through the Jewish Scriptures and explained every passage that referred to Himself, the promised Messiah. This statement reveals the divine power of God's Word upon the hearts of willing men. Happily, this type of heartburn is not confined to these men alone. We of today like John Wesley of old, have also felt our hearts "strangely warmed" under the anointed exposition of Holy Scripture from God's true servants. In such times, we have a unique communication with our Lord. This also reveals that good men may be blind to the simplest doctrines of the faith until they are correctly explained. These men had heard the Scriptures expounded thousands of times by their rabbis but did not understand. Churches today are filled with this kind of people. Philip had to explain to the powerful political figure from Ethiopia the meaning of Isa. 53 before he could understand the death of Christ for his sins and be saved (Acts 8:27-35). Paul had to expound the Word of God to the jailer and his family before they could "believe on the Lord Jesus Christ" and be saved (Acts 16:25-34).

2p-The simplicity of salvation. In 1973, my wife met a woman eighty-seven years old in a nursing home at Kensington, a suburb near Johannesburg, South Africa. She went and spent an hour, explaining over and over God's great plan of salvation. Suddenly, Mrs. Gilbert slightly rose up on her deathbed and said, "This is the most beautiful story I have ever heard. Mrs. Pike, I want to receive Christ as my Savior." A few months later, this lovely person met her Maker. When the gospel is explained in the power of the Holy Spirit, men are divinely enlightened to consider eternal things. They will either receive or reject this great salvation. With some, this halting between two opinions may continue for years. Others, like the woman above are saved the moment, they hear the gospel, understand its claims, and believe. *This process subjects men to God and not God to men.* God has ordained that His "effectual call" becomes *actively* "effective" the moment men repent of their sins and exercise their divinely given faith in His Son the Lord Jesus Christ. The fable of "free agency" invented by radical Calvinists, pitted against "free will" is another example of desperation exegesis to prop up prior false teaching. The dear woman mentioned above heard the gospel explained, the Holy Spirit illuminated its truth to her mind, and she instantly exercised the faith from God's Word that was in her heart, and believed it. Thus, the simplicity of instant salvation by the grace of God.

CHAPTER 19

FIRST MENTION OF THE GREAT COMMISSION.

(Given five different times in five different places. For a chronology of the
Commission, see Section 201, the symbol ● by Lk. 24:47 below.)

Having made Himself known to the Emmaus road travelers, He vanished. Both men hurried the eight miles back to Jerusalem where the eleven apostles and others were gathered that night. Amid the furor of explaining that they had seen Jesus, He suddenly appeared and gave the first version of the Great Commission. Thomas apparently left the room just before Jesus appeared. His absence is noted again in Section 202, John 20:24. The version of the Commission in Lk. 24:46-49 is blended with that in John 20:19-23 as being the same event. They are harmonized below for the reader to consider their sameness. This is a conjecture and not presented established biblical chronology.

Time: Early Sunday night of the Resurrection Day.

Regarding the validity of Mk. 16:9-20, see the Author's Introduction and all by the symbol ▶ in the italicized paragraph under the main heading of Section 197. Most modern versions of the Bible leave these twelve verses out, or drop them to a questionable footnote or into a center reference column. The similarity between the words and instructions in John 20:19-23 compels the author to speculate that this is the same event as recorded in Lk. 24:33-38. Thus, they are harmonized below for the reader to consider their sameness. This is only a conjecture.

From Emmaus back to a room somewhere in Jerusalem

Matt.	Mk. 16:13	Lk. 24:33–39	John 20:19
	Back to Jerusalem **13** And they went and told *it* unto the residue: (the others)[a]	*Back to Jerusalem* **33** And they rose up the same hour, and returned to Jerusalem, and found the eleven gathered together,[a] and them that were with them, **34** [The eleven were] Saying, "The Lord is risen indeed, and hath appeared to Simon." [c] **35** And they [the two men from Emmaus] told what things *were done* in the way, and how he was known of them in breaking of bread.[d] *Jesus appears again* **36** And as they thus spake, Jesus himself stood in the midst[e] of them, and saith unto them, "Peace *be* unto you." [f] **37** But they were terrified[g] and affrighted, and supposed that they had seen a spirit. **38** And he said unto them, "Why are ye troubled? and why do thoughts arise in your hearts?[h] **39** "Behold my hands and	*Back at Jerusalem* **19** Then the same day at evening, being the first *day* of the week, when the doors were shut where the disciples[a] were assembled for fear of the Jews,[b] ▲ *"The same day" means the day of resurrection as seen in the previous verses 1-18.* *Jesus appears again* came Jesus and stood in the midst,[e] and saith unto them, "Peace *be* unto you." [f] ▲ *In reference to these Jewish greetings, see note by the symbol ◀ at the left side of John 20:21 below in this column.*

Matt.	Mk. 16:13	Lk. 24:39-49	John 20:20
		my feet, that it is I myself: handle me, and see; for a spirit hath not flesh and bones, as ye see me have."	
		40 And when he had thus spoken, he shewed them *his* hands and *his* feet.[i]	**20** And when he had so said, he shewed unto them *his* hands and his side.[i]
	neither believed they them. (Verse 14 cont. in Section 203.)	**41** And while they yet believed not for joy,[j] and wondered, he said unto them, "Have ye here any meat?"	Then were the disciples glad,[j] when they saw the Lord.
		42 And they gave him a piece of a broiled fish, and of an honeycomb.	
		43 And he took *it*, and did eat before them.[k]	
		Prophecy must be fulfilled	
		44 And he said unto them, "These *are* the words which I spake unto you, while I was yet with you, that all things must be fulfilled, ◄which were written[l] in the law of Moses, and *in* the prophets, and *in* the psalms, concerning me."	
	Our Lord again affirmed the veracity of the Old Testament. He fulfilled every prediction that pointed to His life and work. Note verse 46 below, where He explained the specific prophecies He had recently fulfilled. Appendix Three lists many forecasts that Jesus brought to completion. Such provides us with impeccable evidence of divine inspiration. For continued comments on the Mosaic authorship of various portions of the Old Testament, see Section 52, John 5: 45-47, footnotes y and z.	***A miracle in their minds***	
		45 Then opened he their understanding,[m] that they might understand the Scriptures,	
		46 And said unto them, "Thus it is written, and thus it behoved Christ to suffer, and to rise from the dead the third day:	◄*The Savior states that His death and resurrection had been predicted in the Jewish Tanakh or Old Testament. Refer to Section 196, and side note attached to John 20:9 for more on this. Also, see comments to the left of verse 44 above by symbol* ◄.
		Great Commission given the first time[n]	
	●*Here is a chronology of the Great Commission as given five different times by the Lord Jesus.* *1. Here, in Lk. 24:47-49.* *2. Section 203, Mk. 16:15-18.* *3. Section 204, Matt. 28:18-20.* *4. Section 205, John 21:22.* *5. Section 206, Acts 1:8.*	●**47** "And that repentance and remission of sins should be preached in his name among all nations, beginning at Jerusalem.	
		48 "And ye are witnesses[o] of these things.	
		49 "And behold, I send the promise of my Father upon	

Matt.	Mk.	Lk. 24:49	John 20:21-23
		you: but tarry ye in the city of Jerusalem, until ye be endued with power[p] from on high." (Verse 50 cont. in Section 207.) ▶ *Verse 21 reveals that Jesus repeats this Jewish greeting "Peace be unto you," for a second time. Clearly, the word "again" affirms this. He had used it first in Lk. 24:36 above with the parallel in John 20:19.*	21 Then said Jesus to them again, "Peace *be* unto you:[q] as *my* Father hath sent me,[r] even so send I you." 22 And when he had said this, he breathed[s] on *them*, and saith unto them, "Receive ye the Holy Ghost: ***Results of believing or rejecting the gospel***[t] 23 "Whose soever sins ye remit, [by people believing the gospel] they are remitted unto them; *and* whose soever *sins* ye retain, [not remitted by them rejecting the gospel] they are retained." (unforgiven)[u] (Verse 24 cont. in Section 202.)

Footnotes-Commentary

[a] **"Found the eleven gathered together."** This occurred on what we now call Sunday night. These words demonstrate that Peter (one of the eleven) was present in the room upon the arrival of the two men from Emmaus. Therefore, he could not have been the unnamed partner of Cleopas. Refer to Section 200, Lk. 24:18, footnote d for more on this error. Words cannot be found in human vocabulary to describe the confusion and feelings of these two men. Surely, they thought of the women who earlier that morning reported to them that Jesus was alive and how they had refused to believe their excited report about angels speaking to them. Now, they had seen Him for themselves. Whatever business they had walked to Emmaus for, vanished! Jumping from their table-couches, in a state of shock and deeply stunned, they race down the road to Jerusalem, bearing the greatest news they had ever carried. The dangers of night travel and the distance to Jerusalem became nothing; their Messiah was alive! Glad, yet horrified, they must share their amazing experience with fellow believers at Jerusalem.

2p-John 20:19-23. "The same day at evening." What "same day?" The context is clear that this "same day" was the day our Lord rose from the grave. Therefore, these events recorded by John occurred sometime later during the night of the Resurrection Day. This is why they are harmonized with Luke's version of the events when the two men rushed in from Emmaus in the early hours of the night. For more on this, see footnote n below. Cleopas and his friend returning from Emmaus knew where the eleven apostles were and "those that were with them." The plural pronoun "them" has reference to many other believers still together mourning the death of their Lord. *However, their darkest night ever encountered was about to turn into their brightest day.*

3p-John, writing his book was seemingly unaware of Matthew's letter written to the Jews. He was addressing an entirely different group of readers living outside the land of Israel and gave details regarding this account not recorded by the other three gospel writers. Refer to Section 1, Part 1 and all in italics under main heading for more on the original recipients of John's book. He used Jewish time reckoning in verse 19. Sunday, by Hebrew time, would have started at sundown Saturday and continued all through that night until sunset the next day. It was as John wrote, "at evening, being the first day of the week."

(b) **"For fear of the Jews."** Hiding now, in a few more days they would receive the fullness of the Holy Spirit on the Day of Pentecost, and then step publicly before the Jews and all men to proclaim Jesus as Lord and Savior (Acts 4:13). For others who were fearful of the Jews, see John 7:13; 9:22; 12:42; and 19:38. The term "afraid of the Jews" had reference to the Sanhedrin Court. Most of these men fiercely hated Christ and His followers and sought to destroy them. For explanation of the Sanhedrin, see *Appendix Five*.

(c) **The mysterious appearing of Jesus to Peter.** It was surely near or after the midnight hour when they arrived at Jerusalem. Pounding on the locked door (see John 20:19 above) they were granted entrance. Bursting into the room, wide-eyed, overly excited, and waving their hands, they entered and the apostles said to them, "The Lord is risen indeed, and hath appeared to Simon." *Verse 34 does not convey the words of the two men from Emmaus but of the eleven.* When this appearing to Peter occurred, we are not told by any of the four evangelists. Paul mentioned this about twenty years later in 1 Cor. 15:5. Simon Peter may have alluded to it while preaching to Cornelius in Acts 10:40-42. Regardless of when it occurred, the chief lesson is that this special appearing was divine proof of love and favor to Peter after his awful denial of the Savior. It reveals the depth of Christ's forgiveness to one who had so bitterly denied him a few days prior. It was on the evening of the Resurrection Day, after Peter went into our Lord's tomb, saw it empty, and then returned to the city. This is explained in Section 196, John 20:3-10. However, even with this, Peter (like his apostolic companions) still could not at that time bring himself to understand and believe that Christ had risen from the dead. It is helpful to remember that most of the biblical records are only condensed (but still inspired) versions of the story. Peter was present among "the eleven" as they heard the news from Emmaus and would have been the first to agree with their report. Even the most sober-thinking men would find it impossible to believe that a dead friend had arisen and was again among the living. *It is believed that Thomas had left this group just before the Lord Jesus appeared to them.* See the main heading of next Section 202, footnote a, where it is written that he was not present for this event.

(d) This makes it clear that Cleopas and his friend reviewed their entire experience with everyone present in that room. They all listened with rapt attention!

(e) **"Jesus stood in the midst."** The shock of His body vanishing out of the tomb, the terror of the Sanhedrin and religious leaders wanting to kill them for being associated with this "false Messiah," lingered painfully in their minds. Thus, they kept the doors locked. Even after seeing the Lord, a week later the following Sunday, they still kept the doors shut. Note this in Section 202, John 20:26, footnote d. Amid their excited talking among each other, suddenly, Jesus appeared before His little flock of terrified sheep! See footnote g below.

(f) **"Peace be unto you."** The normal greeting "shalom aleikhem." This was the standard and accepted form of Jewish social greetings to everyone. Jesus used these Words three times on this one occasion (Lk. 24:36, with John 20:19 and 21). The terrified believers should have known that a ghost or evil apparition would never have used this method of salutation. He spoke it a week later at another Sunday night gathering of the disciples and apostles in Section 202, John 20:26, footnote e.

(g) **"They were terrified."** Oddly, the Jews distinguished between angels, spirits, and demons. This verse is clear that they were greatly alarmed at the sight of their Lord. Most of them believed they had seen some kind of spirit apparition or materialization and were terrified. The twelve apostles earlier experienced something of this nature in Jesus walking on the water. See Section 94, Matt. 14:25-26, footnote f, for the record of this event.

(h) No persons on earth had more cause for rejoicing and blessing God than these distraught men. However, human frailty and weakness of the flesh again dominated the hour. Is this not true with all of us?

(i) **"Hands, feet, and side."** Messiah did this in an effort to dispel their fears of some demonic apparition working to deceive them about His resurrection. John adds that He showed them His "side" also. With this demonstration, the tide of terror and doubt started to subside among the little flock of terrified believers. For the soldier piercing His side, see Section 193, John 19:34.

(j) **"Believed not for joy."** Luke's words have puzzled some. The idea here is that though they had been given confirmations of His resurrection, by the women, by Simon Peter, by the two men from Emmaus, and now they had seen Him for themselves; yet, it was too good to be true! They believed what they had seen but were held in reserve, wondering, "Is this a dream." *Their heads were convinced, but their hearts had not yet experienced the joy of that glorious miracle.* In so many words, they were saying, "We're so happy to see you, but don't believe it's true!"

(k) Christ understood their frustration. They needed yet further proof that was infallible. Jews believed that spirits could not eat. By taking the fish and honeycomb and eating it, He instantly convinced them, He was really there, and it was not a spirit from another world. Still, they could not handle the shock and wonder of it all. Over eight years later, Peter, while preaching to the house of Cornelius, recalled, "eating and drinking" with Jesus after His resurrection and before His ascension (Acts 10:40-41).

(l) **Hebrew Scriptures.** We have no record in the four gospels where Christ said these *exact* Words, nor do we need one. This is another of the thousands of unrecorded statements of our Savior. Among this company were many who had followed the Lord Jesus during His ministry. He reminds them of His previous lessons about Himself that

968

were predicted and pictured in their Old Testament Scriptures. While journeying with the two men on the road to Emmaus, He had given thorough and exhaustive instructions about Himself from Moses and the prophets. (These two men were also present on this occasion as well and were about to receive the second installment in Old Testament prophecy.) Here the Lord Jesus makes direct reference to the Hebrew canon of Holy Scriptures. These are called Tanakh or Mikra (reading) by modern day Jews. The word **T**-a-**N**-a-**K**-h is a clever acrostic with the letters **T**, **N**, and **K**, representing the first alphabetical character of the three divisions of their Scripture as given below:

1. **The Torah or Law.** This included Genesis, Exodus, Leviticus, Numbers, and Deuteronomy.
2. **The Nevi'im or prophets.** These were divided into Former and Latter Prophets. The Former contained Joshua, Judges, the two books of Samuel, and the two of Kings. Next, were the Latter Prophets, which contained Isaiah, Jeremiah, Ezekiel, Hosea, Joel, Amos, Obadiah, Jonah, Micah, Nahum, Habakkuk, Zephaniah, Haggai, Zechariah, and Malachi.
3. **The Ketuvim or Psalms–Writings.** Embraced in this category are Psalms, Proverbs, Job, Song of Solomon, Ruth, and Lamentations, which was joined to Jeremiah. Next were Ecclesiastes, Esther, Daniel, Ezra, Nehemiah, and the two books of Chronicles. The Jewish Bible had only twenty-two books, which was achieved by joining various books together. Apparently, the scribes made this arrangement to correspond with the twenty-two letters of their Hebrew alphabet. The academic fuss about some sources claiming twenty-four books in the Hebrew Bible means a lot of nothing because certain books were counted as one in the Jewish Tanakh.

(m) "Opened their understanding." See Ps. 119:18 for David's prayer to understand the Torah Law a thousand years earlier. At the highest of learning, the wisest of men cannot *finally* understand the message of Holy Scripture, unless they have divine assistance. This does not negate the need for practical help. For more on this, see the *Author's Introduction.* It is untrue a believer must be inspired, as were the holy men of old, before he can comprehend the Word of God. However, it is to affirm, "The natural man receiveth not the things of the Spirit of God" (1 Cor. 2:14). Worldly wise men have found beautiful lessons in Scripture regarding good works, humanitarian deeds, love of neighbor and so forth, but many of them remain blind to their need for the new birth. Later they die in their sins, and awake amid the eternal torments of the damned. For more on these thoughts, see footnote p below. Here, we meet the horrendous problem of unsaved "scholars" feigning to interpret and teach Scripture. In doing so, they have wounded, crippled, and destroyed the young and tender faith of thousands.

2p-Verse 46. "And [Jesus] said unto them." Shaded in gray because it speaks of the Old Testament Scriptures that foretold of the death, burial, and resurrection of Jesus the Messiah of Israel. Because this is true, the orders to take this message to all men are laid down in verses 47 and 48.

(n) At this place Jesus gave the first version of the Great Commission. *Each of these is printed in a heavy red font for quick identification.* The verses in Section 201, Lk. 24:47–48 are harmonized with Jesus' Words and actions in John 20:21-23 in this Section as occurring at the same time. This happened in Jerusalem to the eleven and others present. It was Sunday night after the Resurrection Day, in the wee hours of the morning. See second paragraph of footnote a above for more on this. For Christ giving the Great Commission the second time, see Section 203.

2p-Verse 47. "Repentance should be preached." *Here is the great summation of the gospel ministry.* The popular cry resounding from certain persons that repentance is not required prior to salvation is exposed for what it is in this statement. Rank Calvinists with their amputation of the Bible truth about repentance invented this myth. (A gospel without repentance is like washing without soap.) They affirm that repentance is a human work, and therefore, cannot be prerequisite to the new birth; that God grants men the ability to repent after they have been saved! Peter Toon, an Anglican priest, reflects this error in his book *Born Again.* On page 63, he wrote these amazing words, "The question whether the new birth or repentance comes first cannot be definitively answered." Toon wrote this because he is a prisoner to the heresy of hyper Calvinism. When Paul, reflecting over his missionary work said that he had gone from house to house, testifying to one and all "repentance toward God, and faith toward our Lord Jesus," he definitively answered this imaginary problem invented by men who have perverted the gospel (Acts 20:20-21). The order was "repentance" then "faith." John the Baptist preached, "Repent ye, and believe the gospel" (Mk. 1:15). This was "definitive." For further comments related to the command to repent, see Section 72, Lk. 13:5, footnote f. In verse 47 above, the Son of God *commanded* that repentance should be preached "among all nations." Note again Paul's words concerning repentance while speaking on Mars Hill in Acts 17:29-31. In Rev. 9:20-21, men were judged with terrible plagues, because "they repented not of the [evil] works of their hands."

3p-Bondage of the will. In 1525, Martin Luther published *Bondage of the Will.* This was his reply to the nonsense of Erasmus about man's *moral or natural ability* to respond to the message of salvation. Informed Calvinists love Luther's work for they believe it bolsters their soteriological errors, especially when and how one is saved. The gospel united with the Holy Spirit enlightens the bondage of the human will to understand the need for repentance and faith in Christ. Through this heavenly illumination, a man is given divine enablement to turn from his sins (repent) or to stay in them. God's grace appearing to all men (Titus 2:11) results in a temporary freeing of the human will from bondage. At this point, of divine enlightenment, God grants salvation to all who repent and believe in the Lord Jesus Christ. This is so because the Eternal all wise God of heaven has arranged it this way. It does not embarrass, minimize, or take from His sovereign grace, nor does it lessen the awful bondage of sin in a man's mind and soul. It gives the needed illumination and opens the door for deliverance of the imprisoned will to respond. When thus enacted it results in the salvation of the lost soul. This stupendous event is so wonderful that it causes rejoicing in the presence of heaven's angels (Lk. 15:7 and 10).

4p-Those who overly meddle into the hidden things of God often end in philosophical and doctrinal perversions. At times, these distortions become doctrines of demons and seize the mind with a steel-like grip, so strong that it is rarely freed (1 Tim. 4:1-2). For a classical example of what poison doctrine will do to the mind of a man, see Section 1, Part 3, third paragraph of footnote i. For comments on "Martin Luther's will" still in bondage of Romanism after leaving the Papal Church, see Section 203, eight paragraph of footnote d. His statement after leaving the Catholic Church, that communion and infant baptism saves from sin, reveals that he was blinded regarding how men come to the personal saving knowledge of Christ.

5p-Living dead men and dead living men. Scripture teaches we are spiritually "dead in trespasses and sins" (Eph. 2:1, 5 with Col. 2:13). The doctrine of absolute sinful depravity is foundational. This is not outward physical deadness, rather, it is spiritual, being strictly an inward condition. Reformed doctrine states that man is so dead that he is unable to comprehend rightly anything about God. The rich man in Lk. 16:22-31 deceased and his body was buried. When his outward body died physically he was also dead inwardly in his trespasses and sins! However, in eternity this changed, for his soul, though still dead in sin was alive and suddenly knew everything! Over there he was living as never before. In eternity, he recalled that his five brothers back on earth were lost, their need for repentance, felt the torments of hell, and remembered the past on earth. Amazingly, he even recognized Abraham, who had died hundreds of years before he was born! On the other hand, here on earth we read in Scripture that a saved person is "dead to sin," but at the same time is "alive to God." (Rom. 6:2 and 11). Thus, believers are both alive and dead at the same time. Sort of living dead men and dead living men. We understand so little about the effects of sin on the entire man especially his inward being.

6p-How dead is dead? Can saved people who are "dead to sin," sin again, since they are dead to sin? The Scriptures say, "yes." Take Peter, for example, in Lk. 22:31-34. How did he manage such wicked conduct and vile language when he was dead to sin? We are taught that a dead person can do nothing because he is dead. Does this mean that those dead inwardly are so totally dead that they cannot think, remember, feel, sin, and respond anymore? The unsaved rich man in hell was "dead in trespasses and sin," yet he was very much alive! There is a strange anomaly between a physical corpse and a soul dead in sin. The soul of a dead man is alive with unlimited conscious memory, and feeling in eternity, while the body back on earth knows nothing in the grave where it decays.

7p-Different kinds of Grace? Paragraph three above explains that in the operation of grace, man's will though held fast in sin's bondage is offered freedom. The "natural [human] man" apart from heavenly enabling of grace, "Receiveth not the things of the Spirit of God" (1 Cor. 2:14). His best choices without Christ are death (Prov. 16:25). He must be enlightened by the Holy Spirit, the Word of God, and drawn to Christ (John 6:44). Amid this process, one can reject the gospel (Acts 7:54), purposely call for a delay or openly mock (Acts 17:32, 34 with 24:25), or believe in the Lord Jesus Christ and be saved (Acts 8:35-38, 16:27-33, and 18:8.). God's call or drawing of one who is dead in trespasses and sins is God enabling (not forcing) that person to respond. Those who respond to this effectual enabling are those who are saved. To justify their errors, Calvinists have invented different kinds of grace! There is "common grace" revealing God's mercy and goodness to lost men, but it cannot save them. Next, there is "prevenient grace" which makes salvation possible but does not save! Lastly, there is "free or sovereign grace" that kidnaps and saves sinners. These people sort of wake up the next day and realize they have been saved! This could be called "post mortem salvation." Calvinists tell us, "Being saved this way does not subject God to man's approval." Finding a Scripture to confirm the above "different kinds of grace," and the "wake up next morning repentance" is a job the angels would run from! It is an invention like the seven frozen time periods used by the *radical* dispensationalists to justify prior eschatological errors. Each group seems to have invented its own set of rules to prove what they believe. Calvinist created their "covenant of redemption," "covenant of works," "and covenant of grace," and convinced themselves they were historical biblical doctrines. The *radical* dispensationalists embracing Darby's seven time periods have done exactly the same thing. Is this grace or grease in operation?

8p-The aftermath of any foul doctrine is church splitting, ill feelings, and separating long-time friends. Those who embrace *major* false teachings soon discover that they must backtrack, undo, and then redo their former doctrinal beliefs. Pastors ensnared in this error work overtime trying to persuade the church body to believe and accept that which was formerly rejected. Only Satan could devise such chaos through "newly enlightened" Christians concerning the sovereign grace of God, eschatology, and other *major* doctrinal issues.

(o) "Witnesses." This word has its origin in martyrs who gave their lives for Christ. Not only were those early believers to witness of Christ, but all men who are saved have the same commission. While home on furlough in 1979, the author of this work stopped at a gas station on White Horse Road in Greenville, South Carolina, to enquire for directions from a shaking old man. Just before driving off I enquired, "Sir, please tell me do you know Jesus Christ as your personal Lord and Savior." Instantly, he flew into a wild cursing rage demanding to know where I got the authority to ask him such a question. I replied, "From the Bible." He retorted, "I've read the Bible through many times and never found where it said that." I quoted the words of our Lord in Lk. 24:48, thanked him, and drove off. Those who oppose Christians calling for men to repent are wrong. *They preach a defective gospel that will not result in sinners being saved.* It is stressed in this book that God does not save men in their sins, but from them.

(p) **Their need for divine power.** As was said of those attempting to understand Scripture in footnote m above, a *similar lesson* emerges here. The eleven who were present on this occasion (verse 33) had heard Jesus speak of the promise of the Father the night before the morning of His cross, while with them in the upper room. This is recorded in Section 175, John 14:16, footnote j. Now, after His resurrection, He again reaffirms that His servants can only effectively do His work in the power and anointing of the Holy Spirit. He would come to them at Pentecost in the power they needed to be true servants of Christ.

(q) **"Peace."** See footnote f above for the meaning of this common Jewish expression of greetings. The Lord Jesus said these Words three times on this occasion (verses 36, 19, and 21). Christ spoke this again to them a week later in Section 202, John 20:26, footnote e.

(r) **"As me, so you."** In addition, how did the Father send His Son into the ministry? In the fullness and power of the Holy Spirit being a man of sorrows and acquainted with grief. After His battle with Satan, amid fierce temptations, the Bible says of our Lord that He "returned in the power of the Spirit into Galilee," where He began his work (Lk. 4:14). There is a peculiar and *unexplainable* similarity between what the Father sent the Son to suffer and do, and what He may send us to suffer and do in obeying the Great Comission. Those who have given their lives without reserve in the Master's cause or have spent years in His work understand by experience, what is said here.

(s) **"He breathed on them."** Among the ancients, the act of breathing over or upon a person signaled their readiness for some great event soon to follow. The Jews based this upon God breathing into Adam the breath of life, and he lived (Gen. 2:7 with Job 33:4). The error of many expositors is to teach that *here* these disciples received the fullness of the Holy Spirit and then received it *again* at Pentecost. Christ's breathing upon them may have an allusion back to Adam at his creation, but it must not remain there (Gen. 2:7). He revealed by this act what He had just said, "They will soon be endued with power to be His witnesses." *They did not receive the fullness of the Spirit here.* This was the first token for them to prepare for the great event that would soon happen at Pentecost. Confirmation that they did not receive the fullness of the Spirit at this time is seen later in Section 206, Acts 1:4–8, where it was ten days *before* the Spirit came. At this time, Christ commanded His disciples to wait at Jerusalem until they had received this power, and then they may commence witnessing for Him. *In other words, wait here until He empowers you.* After breathing over them, Jesus was saying in so many words, "You will receive the Holy Spirit in full power at Pentecost." When this occurred, the apostles were ready to do the things mentioned in verse 23. He had explained the coming of the Spirit the night before the cross in the upper room. Refer to Section 175.

2p-The Roman Catholic Church has taken this breathing action of Christ and with great impudence; the priests seek to imitate it during their (so-called) baptism of infants and others. This awful pretense of imparting to helpless infants the Holy Spirit by the breath of a priest mocks the actions and Word's of Jesus Christ.

(t) **God alone can forgive or remit sins.** In John 20:23, Christ makes known the two-sided effect of the saving gospel. It remits the sins of those who believe it or retains the sins of those who reject it. Because Jesus of Nazareth is His Son and perfect coequal, He fully shares the Father's exclusive prerogative to forgive men of their sins. *He never communicated such power to any of His apostles or any other mortal.* The Catholic Church with its priests claiming authority to absolve men of their sins is a vicious untruth. Some of the heretical church fathers boasted to have the same authority. Refer to Section 12, sixth, seventh and eighth paragraphs of footnote k for their pseudo claims. For the sham of Papal priests forgiving sins, see Section 13, third and fourth paragraphs of footnote f.

(u) The apostles and others who heard His Words, and on whom He breathed the token of power, would soon understand *how* they remitted or retained the sins of men. By sharing the saving gospel of Christ, all who repent and believe it have their sins instantly remitted or forgiven. All who finally reject it and die in this condition have their sins forever retained in hell. In Acts 10:43, it is clear that "all who believe in him shall receive remission of sins."

2p-**We are commanded to forgive.** Our glad forgiveness does not secure the actual absolution sins against us. *We do the forgiving; God does the pardoning.* This is briefly discussed in Section 46, Matt. 6:14–15, footnote h. God's forgiveness is based on the atonement of Christ, when He died for the sins of all mankind, once and forever. Those who receive Him as personal Lord and Savior have their sins *instantly* remitted, never to be remembered against them again! Every false religion teaches the error of salvation and forgiveness by man's good works. Because of this, many staunch conservatives have overreacted and almost condemned good works in the life of a believer. One error is as serious as the other. Good works and charitable deeds are the fruits of the new birth but not the cause of it. The millions of "born again" people who have lived without any of the fruits of salvation manifested in their lives do not know Christ as personal Lord and Savior. The old proverb says, "People, who live like hell are not going to heaven." On God's chastisement of erring believers who return to their old ways and sins, see Section 46, the eleventh paragraph of footnote g. Living the *true* Christian life is the most serious thing in the world.

Eight days later, Christ appears and speaks to Thomas, who was absent at the previous Sunday* night of the resurrection day, when He gave His disciples the Great Commission the first time. **Thomas had apparently left the room just before our Lord appeared on this occasion. Below, he is present on the following Sunday. He had earlier refused to believe that his fellow apostles had seen the Savior. The Great Commission was not mentioned at this time as Jesus gave full attention to rescuing Thomas from the pain and frustration of his unbelief.

Time: Eight days after the Sunday morning resurrection.

---

*This is what we call it in the western world. Law cults operating under the umbrella of Christianity struggle to prove that Jesus rose on the Sabbath, in order to justify their heresies. For explanation of this, see Section 195, the first paragraph of footnote a. Unsaved Jews chained to the Torah Law call this day the Sabbath. Saved Christians, believing God's Word, call it the first day of the week or Sunday night. **The number of apostles in the room on the night of the Resurrection Day, after the men returned from Emmaus, is stated in Lk. 24:33 as being "eleven" and "them that were with them." See footnote a below for explanation. It was on this occasion that the Savior gave the Great Commission for the first time. In the verses below, He appeared again but made no mention of the Commission. Jesus gave the Great Commission for the second time somewhere in Jerusalem to the eleven apostles as they ate. This is recorded in Section 203. For a chronology of the Commission, see ● by Lk. 24:47.

Matt.	Mk.	Lk.	John 20:24-31— *Somewhere at Jerusalem in a locked room*
			Thomas absent
			24 But Thomas, one of the twelve, called Didymus, was not with them when Jesus came.(a)
			25 The other disciples therefore said unto him, "We have seen the Lord." But he said unto them, "Except I shall see in his hands the print of the nails, and put my finger into the print of the nails, and thrust my hand into his side, I will not believe."(b)
			A week later: Thomas is present: his doubt vanishes
			26 And after eight days(c) again his disciples were within, and Thomas with them: *then* came Jesus, the doors being shut,(d) [locked] and stood in the midst, and said, "Peace *be* unto you."(e)
			27 Then saith he to Thomas, "Reach hither thy finger, and behold my hands; and reach hither thy hand, and thrust *it* into my side: and be not faithless, but believing."(f)
			28 And Thomas answered and said unto him, "My Lord and my God."(g)
			The blessedness of true believers of all ages
			29 Jesus saith unto him, "Thomas, because thou hast seen me, thou hast believed: blessed *are* they that have not seen, and *yet* have believed."(h)
			Why John wrote this book
			30 And many other signs(i) truly did Jesus in the presence of his disciples, which are not written in this book:
			31 But these are written, that ye might believe that Jesus is the Christ, the Son of God; and that believing ye might have life through his name.
			(j) (Next chap., John 21:1 cont. in Section 205.)

Footnotes-Commentary

(a) **Thomas missing.** He was present among the other ten apostles but for some reason, had left the room just before the Lord Jesus made His dramatic appearing and gave the Great Commission for the first time. This appearing of Christ is recorded in Section 201, Lk. 24:33, footnote a where it reads, "The eleven gathered together." We note in verse 24 above that he was not with the other ten when Jesus came. The name "Didymus" means "twin." It is used of Thomas here and in John 11:16 and 21:2. We have no record of his twin, who he or she was, or where they were. It is of interest that the term "the twelve" was still used of the apostles after Judas was dead and in his place (Acts 6:2). Later, after the ascension of Christ and about ten days before Pentecost, Matthias was chosen to replace the traitor Judas (Acts 1:23-26). With this, the number twelve was complete again.

(b) Seeing is believing! When the disciples who had seen the Lord Jesus, met Thomas later, they swamped him with the wonderful news that their Messiah was alive, and that they had seen him. The reactions of the disciples again demonstrate the power and influence of Jewish theology on their minds. Thomas was but another product of rabbinical teaching regarding their Messiah. There was no material, literal kingdom for them at that time. The Romans were still rulers with the sword in hand and sin reigned on every side. Why should Thomas believe since he was but another brain-washed victim of the Hebrew eschatological *over literalistic* untruths? Did it not take the Lord Jesus much effort to convince those who now failed to convince Thomas?

(c) "After eight days again." That is, the eighth day after the last meeting of believers on the previous first day of the week. In Hebrew counting of time, the first and last days are always included. This means on the following Sunday, that the disciples were within their enclosed room. We have no record of where they went or what they did from that first memorial Sunday of Jesus' resurrection, until this, the next Sunday. It can be safely assumed that they were still in Jerusalem or thereabout. Some see here the establishment of a weekly meeting of the followers of Christ on the day of His resurrection. However, we note that after Pentecost, they were in daily gatherings (Acts 2:46).

2p-The law sects argue that all early believers met on Saturday night for worship and fellowship. In Hebrew time reckoning, *instantly* after sundown Saturday, the next day began, which was the first day of the week or Sunday, which also ended at sundown. The Roman Empire dominated the known world of that era. There was no such thing as "a day off to go to church," for those employed by Gentiles or Romans. Sinners and saints alike labored at their earthly occupations seven days a week. The only holidays afforded were those associated with pagan gods and goddesses. During Roman rule, Gentile believers gathered before sunrise Sunday morning for united worship. At the first streaks of dawn, they went to work! Jewish however, still bound in conscience to the Torah Law, held to Saturday. Most Roman authorities allowed them freedom on their seventh day Sabbath. Not to do so usually resulted in violence, war, and bloodshed! With the destruction of the temple, Sabbath worship declined among believing Hebrews. The church gradually became predominately a Gentile body, and soon they were meeting on the day (Sunday) their Lord rose from the dead. Today, if certain Christians desire to meet and worship on Saturday, the Jewish Sabbath let them do so. They create the problem by demanding that all Christians the world over must also meet on Saturday. Then, they condemn those who do not. *It is because of these things that the "Sabbath day keepers" of whatever variety smack of heresy and rank cultism.*

(d) "Doors being shut" or barred. This means just what it says. No doubt, the same room as used the week prior. Though they had seen their Lord and knew beyond any doubt that He was alive, they exercised practical common sense and remained behind closed and locked doors. At this point, they did not yet understand the whole story; they were confused and confounded at what has taken place over the past few days. Their theological world has crashed about them! It has been noted that all doors were also shut at the previous Sunday meeting in Section 201, John 20:19, footnote a. In addition, why were the doors secured? There can be no doubt that they were terrified at the thought of the Sanhedrin swooping down upon them at any moment! After all, they were the publicly known followers of the Man, the Jews had just put to death! Here, would be an example of "condemnation by association."

(e) "Peace be unto you." Jesus used this common Jewish greeting four times. See Section 201, John 20:21, at the symbol ◄ and footnote q for meaning of the word. In doing so, He was trying to convince the disciples that it was really Him, their Lord. It was believed that evil spirits never used the word "peace," as their mission was always to create fear and distrust in God.

(f) "Be not faithless." He had used this same method on the previous Sunday to convince the other ten apostles and those with them that He was alive from the dead. Had not the other ten apostles, likewise, refused to believe the report of the women that Jesus had risen? Instead of "doubting Thomas," maybe we should say the "doubting eleven." See Section 197, Mk. 16:11, footnote k for their collective unbelief. The method He used to persuade the others, He now offers to Thomas. These words with Heb. 11:6 tell us that nothing so pleases the heart of our God and Savior as when we simply "believe them."

(g) These words mean what they say. This was not a mere exclamation. It is one of the most irresistible and plainest testimonies of the deity of Christ. Here, was the same fellow (Thomas), who a few days prior in the upper room, asked Christ the way to the Father's house. See this in Section 175, John 14:5, footnote d. In addition, Jesus answered his inquiry. Now, we hear him speaking again. He expressly gives the Name of God to Christ, even in His presence. *The Savior did not correct Thomas for this supposed theological error!* This was not an excited articulation from a frightened man, as those who deny the deity of Jesus would have us believe. Rather, it is a confession of one doubting apostle who suddenly and shockingly realized that only God could beat death by crucifixion and rise again. If Jesus Christ is not divine and perfectly co-equal with God, and therefore, perfect God, then He was dishonest in not correcting Thomas for blasphemy. Thomas' words reconfirm the unfathomable depths of what is written in Section 1, Part 1, footnote a and b of this harmony commentary; that Jesus is God! "Doubting Thomas," as he has been dubbed, was the first person in the New Testament to outright call Jesus Christ "God."

Adam Clarke in his *Commentary,* vol. v. page 659 penned this terse statement, "It is worthy of remark, that from this time forward the whole of the disciples treated our Lord with the most supreme respect, never using that familiarity towards him which they had often used before." The famed Daniel Webster (died 1852) attended a meeting of America's intellectuals. He spoke openly of his faith in the atonement of Christ. A learned professor put this question to him, "Mr. Webster, how can you comprehend that Jesus was both God and man?" "No" he responded, "I can't. If I could, He would be no better than I am. I need a Savior, who is supernatural, and I have that in Jesus the Son of the living God." The subject of Him being equal with God, and therefore, God, was brought up earlier by the angry Jews. Refer to this in Section 123, John 10:31-33, footnote g.

(h) **The sweet consolation of believing.** It is marvelous to note that no special blessing is pronounced on those who have seen Christ, over those who have not. We have not seen, but we believe with all our poor hearts that Christ died for our sins, was buried and rose the third day. Thus, because He lives, we live also. What a joy to carry this approval of our Savior, that we are "blessed by believing." The world says, "Show me, and I will believe." God says, "Believe, and in time I will show you." The author of this work has passed into eighty years of human life. He can testify that the most blessed, sweet, and peaceful people he has met are those who have rested saving faith in Christ and kept immovable trust in the Holy Bible. Woe be those who have that infidel academic bend, who must first run God, Jesus Christ, and Scripture through their mental test tubes and check them out by their superior learning before they believe. Contrary wise, it is blessed to remember that not all academicians have an evil mind towards eternal things. *This latter company is the only religious authority that one can trust.*

2p-There is another lesson in this benediction of Christ over all of His future children. When a Gentile proselyte was fully accepted into the Jewish religion, the rabbis would pronounce over him a benediction very similar to these Words Jesus used! The proselyte had not seen Moses or stood with the nation before Sinai. They had not seen the wonders of God's works with Israel, yet they believed it all. Millions of people have not seen the life of Christ on earth, His wonders, and works—yet we have believed and are numbered with the blessed in Jesus' prayer.

(i) **"Many other signs."** Because the Lord Jesus did thousands of deeds not recorded in divine Scripture, the writers of the phony apocryphal gospels produced their ridiculous writings that are worthless regarding sound Bible doctrine. *These two verses are not John prematurely closing his book.* Rather, they are an early benediction to what he had just written about his Lord and a preface to the marvelous event and miracle of the next and final chapter of his book. As a typical Jew, he informed all Hebrew readers that the man of whom he has written did countless signs, wonders, and miracles that he had not recorded. A scan of his work reveals that John recorded *seven unique sign miracles* Jesus had performed. Thousands of others were not mentioned. The seven listed below show that Christ is the Lord of life. They present Him as:

1. **The Creator of Life.** In John 2:1-10, He turned the water into wine, thus creating life.
2. **The Sustainer of Life.** In John 4:46-54, He healed the nobleman's son, thus sustaining existing life.
3. **The Empowerer of Life.** In John 5:1-16, He healed the impotent man at Bethesda and thereby empowered his helpless body with fresh life.
4. **The Provider of Life.** In John 6:1-14, He fed the five thousand by providing life from bread and fish.
5. **The Protector of Life.** In John 6:15-20, in the storm on Lake Galilee, he protected life from destruction.
6. **The Illuminator of Life.** In John 9:1-41, the man born blind can now see! Jesus is the illuminator of life.
7. **The Recreator of Life.** In John 11:1-45, the Savior raised Lazarus, four days deceased. In this, He created new life for the dead body of Lazarus.

(j) **"May have life through his name."** Here, Jesus of Nazareth is presented as the Lord of everlasting life. The Holy Spirit impressed upon John's heart the greatest of all reasons to write his book. That many of its readers will understand and believe that Jesus is the Christ or Messiah, the Son of God, and by this have eternal life through His Name. Later, 1 John 5:1 explains how men are saved. The first purpose of his book was to bring men to the saving knowledge of our Lord. Hence, the reason why critics and unsaved scholars have assailed this work.

2p-Skeptics have taken it upon themselves to point out that John ended his work with these final two passages. Thus, they affirm that the following chapter 21 was added much later by Christians to give it something of a miraculous boost to future readers. Men reason this way because they are unsaved and do not believe in the trustworthiness and total inspiration of the preserved Word of God. One ponders what these people will do on the deathbed? To what will they resort? Into whose hands will they entrust their souls? Many spend their lives denying the Scriptures, discrediting the Son of God, shooting holes in its infallible declarations about sin, salvation, the new birth, heaven, and hell. Alas! What is the destiny of these benighted people as they take their awful leap into that dark, terrible unknown? Will academic superiority, mental prowess, their reputation at Princeton, Yale, or Harvard, their fame and learned achievements give comfort at the end? Can they embrace the cold hand of atheism, materialism, socialism, or skepticism and find sure comfort in the final seconds of human life? It is far wiser to heed the simple words of the ex-fisherman from Galilee, "These things were written that you might believe." *O unknown reader, receive God's Word and trust His Son as your Savior now!*

SECOND MENTION OF THE GREAT COMMISSION.

(For a chronology of the Commission, see Section 201, the symbol ● by Lk. 24:47.)

The event below occurred after Jesus had confronted Thomas and showed him His wounds. It took place as the eleven "sat at meat." There is no mention of others being present. He rebukes them for their "unbelief and hardness of heart," and gives the second version of the Great Commission.

Time: An undisclosed night after the eighth day of Thomas in Section 202, John 20:26.

Matt.	Mk. 16:14-18—*Somewhere in Jerusalem with the eleven*	Lk.	John
	He appears again to the eleven and rebukes them **14** Afterward[(a)] he appeared unto the eleven as they sat at meat, and upbraided them with their unbelief and hardness of heart,[(b)] because they believed not them which had seen him after he was risen. *Second giving of Great Commission* **15** And he said unto them,[(c)] **"Go ye into all the world, and preach the gospel to every creature.** **16** **"He that believeth and is baptized[(d)] shall be saved; but he that believeth not shall be damned.** *Divine attestation upon the work of early believers* **17** **"And these signs[(e)] shall follow them that believe; In my name shall they cast out devils; they shall speak with new tongues;** **18** **"They shall take up serpents; and if they drink any deadly thing, it shall not hurt them; they shall lay hands on the sick, and they shall recover."** (Verse 19 cont. in Section 207.)		

Footnotes-Commentary

[(a)] **"Afterward."** This word points in two directions. First, the event in the previous verse 13 had now past. Second, it takes us into an entirely new thing starting with verse 14, which occurred while the eleven were eating and the Savior appeared to them *again*. This appearing apparently took place at the night meal.

[(b)] We learn from the words "hardness of heart," that to doubt, reject, or make light of the message of the risen Christ affects the hearts of men. Exactly, when this appearing of Jesus occurred is difficult to say. We *conjecture* that this transpired after the Savior had shown Himself to Thomas (John 20:26-29). If this is near correct then it was into the second week of the resurrection of our Lord. Could this hardness explain their odd condition of believing without joy? This difficult question is discussed in Section 201, Lk. 24:41, footnote j.

[(c)] **Compare and contrast. "Go."** Richard Wurmband, in *Little Notes Which Like Each Other*, page 106, relates the following story. A ship at sea received an S-O-S from a sinking vessel. The captain ordered his pilot to head into the fearful storm in aid to the stricken boat. A youth aboard plead with the captain, "We may never come back, we must not go out there. " The old man retorted, "We have been ordered to go, not come back." Here, in Mk. 16:15-16 we also are ordered to "go." This was spoken to the eleven while in shock and doubt. Their hearts were hardened by refusing to believe the *first* reports of His resurrection given to them by the women returning early that morning from the tomb (Mk. 16:13.) It is *conjectured* that the meeting above took place shortly after the eighth day encounter with Thomas (John 20:26). A brief comparison-contrast of the Great Commission is given below:

1. **Luke** wrote of preaching repentance and the remission (forgiveness) of sins in Jesus' Name. This was to begin at Jerusalem (Lk. 24:47). Mark mentions none of these things, including Jerusalem. Surely, his readers understood they were naturally included in the preaching of the gospel.

2. **Mark** wrote that Jesus said to, "Go ye into all the world, and preach the gospel to every creature." The words "every creature," prove Calvinism is a hoax. Luke penned a similar term used by Christ, "all nations" (Lk. 24:47). They mean the same. The apostles are now commanded to go to the pagan Gentiles.

3. **Luke** wrote nothing about baptism of converts while Mark did.

4. **Mark** wrote that Jesus said only believers were to be baptized. He joined baptism immediately *after* salvation in order to show that the former demonstrated the latter. Those who do not believe (baptized or not) will be damned. It is unpardoned sin that brings damnation, not the failure to be baptized. This does not teach salvation by baptism, but it does teach that salvation should result in *believer's* baptism. A short time later, Philip would not baptize the Ethiopian eunuch, unless he first believed with all his heart that "Jesus was the Son of God" (Acts 8:36-38). (Who can imagine a baby doing this?) We also read of

Simon the sorcerer in Acts 8:13, who "believed and was baptized." His faith was false because it did not result in a change of heart as Peter stated in verse 21. Simon went to hell *with* baptism, while the thief on the cross went to heaven *without* it. Peter warned Simon that his money would *perish* with him (verse 20). Jaroslav Pelikan in his work, *The Christian Tradition. A History of the Development of Doctrine,* vol. 1, page 23, quotes from ancient sources, which state that this same "Simon from Samaria" became known as the "inventor of heresy." Earlier in the ministry of Christ, a wicked woman was saved without baptism when anointing His feet. While recently passing through Jericho, salvation came to the house and heart of Zacchaeus as he sat perched in a tree. See Section 144, Lk. 19:9-10, footnotes i and j for details of this miracle. A crucified thief was saved while hanging from a cross (Lk. 23:43). To excuse these examples of salvation without baptism as "another dispensation" is defending heresy. The paralytic man was saved without baptism in Matt. 9:1-2. The thousands in Heb. 11 were saved without the baptism. Circumcision under the Torah Law answers to baptism as salt does to sugar. They will not mix!

5. **Luke** wrote that they were all to become "witnesses" of Christ's death, burial, and resurrection (Lk. 24:46 and 48). Mark did not use the word "witness" in his inspired record.

6. **Mark** wrote that various signs would follow those who believed (verses 17-18). These included casting out demons, speaking with new tongues, being serpent and poison proof, and having gifts to heal the sick. (Genuine demonic exorcism is not a gift but a work performed by the grace of God.) *Everything that Christ mentioned here occurred in the lives of these people over the coming years.* This was the holy confirmation of their work, as promised, by the Lord Jesus. It is seriously wrong to take all the events that happened in the experiences of the earliest Christians and claim that they are to occur today in the service of believers, just as they did two thousand years ago. We have no biblical record that several of these things ever happened to those first believers as Christ said they would. We do not have a *complete history* of all that occurred in their lifetime of service. Later, we read of Paul being bitten by a deadly serpent in Acts 28:3-5 and feeling no harm. He also "laid his hands on" a sick native chief, and the man was instantly healed (Acts 28:8). There is no biblical history of saints being poisoned by their enemies. There is evidence of the sick being healed by the thousands (Acts 3:1-8, 5:16, and 8:6-8). Years later, Paul had to leave a fellow worker sick at the seaport city of Miletum (2 Tim. 4:20). The phony "faith healers" are quick to say, "Trophimus was not healed because he did not have faith." Refer to Section 41, second paragraph of footnote h for more on the subject of divine healing.

7. **Luke** wrote that He commanded them to wait in Jerusalem for spiritual empowerment (Lk. 24:49).

8. **Mark** made no record of this command given by Luke about the fullness of the Spirit. Mark wrote almost nothing about the coming of the Spirit at Pentecost in comparison to the other evangelists. The final command for their waiting for Pentecost is in Section 206, Acts 1:4. One writer was inspired to give a certain detail, while another something different. This is a mark of inspiration.

2p-Verse 15. "Into all the world." What did this little band of preachers think as they heard these astounding words? At that time, they were terrified of the Sanhedrin, fearful of their lives, not knowing what to do. The Holy Spirit corrected this at Pentecost. Afterward, they went into the world of that day with the gospel.

(d) Verse 16. "Baptized and be saved." Here, is a figurative connection between the remission of sins and the ordinance of believer's baptism. Our sins are washed away in baptism in the same sense in which we eat the body and drink the blood of Christ in the Lord's Supper. Figures must not be confused with the things they represent! *Only in symbolic language does water baptism washes sins away.* Biblically, "The blood of Jesus Christ cleanses from all sin" (Matt. 26:28 with 1 John 1:7). This was the meaning of Paul's words before the angry Jews in Acts 22:16. How fatal when one relies on the figure instead of the reality to which it points. Faith brings us His atonement not baptism. The latter depicts what was received through the former. In ancient Judaism, water and blood illustrated cleansing. *After* personal salvation total water immersion outwardly illustrates the washing of the blood inwardly. The figure (baptism) is only for those who have previously received the thing (salvation) to which it points.

2p-Does Baptism or faith bring remission of sins? Peter's message at Pentecost mentions, repentance, baptism, and the remission of sins. *There is not mention of faith!* Does baptism remit or wash away our sins? Yes, if we take only part of the truth, and no, if we take all that Scripture states on this subject. In Acts 2:38, Peter told his inquirers to "be baptized . . . for the remission of sins," then they would receive the gift of the Holy Ghost. This was part of the story but not all of it. Some eight years later, Peter preached at the house of Cornelius. Hundreds were saved, filled with the Spirit, then baptized (Acts 10:44-48)! Peter concluded his address with, "To him [Christ] give all the prophets witness, that through His Name whosoever believeth in him shall receive remission of sins" (Acts 10:43). Note, "*all* the Old Testament prophets" witnessed that faith in Christ secured remission of sins. None said baptism did. This is the correct blending of Acts 2:38 with Acts 10:43. *Baptism is nowhere called "sinner's baptism" or "unbeliever's baptism."* Baptism and remission are cousins, but the former follows the latter. Hebrews 11 mentions thousands who were saved through faith, lived, and died without baptism. Excusing this as "another dispensation" is child's play. On salvation in the Old Testament, see Section 30, third paragraph of footnote h.

3p-Reformation without regeneration. Saved without baptism. Jesus announced to the woman weeping at

His feet, "Thy faith hath saved thee; go in peace" (Lk. 7:50). Similarly, He informed the grumbling crowds regarding the publican Zaccheaus, "This day is salvation come to this [Zaccheaus'] house" (Lk. 19:9). Christ assured the dying thief, "Verily I say unto thee, today shalt thou be with me in paradise" (Lk. 23:43). These were saved without water baptism. The belief that "Baptism puts one into the blood of Christ, then he receives remission of sins," is quasi-pagan teaching. The church fathers brought this sacramental conception of Christianity into the church. It was incorporated into their theological dogma after A.D. 200, following the death of the last apostle, John. The church fathers and Rome borrowing from heathen religions believed that water had magical efficacy, which would remit sins. Though the Reformers left the Catholic Church, they were contaminated by this error. It spread into much of Christianity through Calvin and his partners. With the rise of Martin Luther, and his false views of baptism and communion, the dye was cast. See eighth paragraph below. These errors spread over Europe, into England, Ireland, Scotland, and later Colonial America. It remains in many churches today. Such antics as inordinate affection of a cross, the pomp of exotic colors, with elaborate clerical dress, "bishops" and clergymen marching in embroidered gowns and vestments, impresses man's vanity. Folded hands, caps, hats, flashing frock-like garments, amid curious rituals, and unintelligible mumbling "at the altar" are not marks of true Bible Christianity. Sprinkling water on helpless infants or adults for salvation, and a perverted version of the Lord's Supper has nothing to do with Jesus Christ. Portions of Christian hymnology also reflect the influence of Catholicism. In 1866, Samuel J. Stone (died 1633) an Anglican, published the hymn, *The Church's One Foundation*. His words that we are God's new creation "by water and the blood" reveal this fact. Baptismal regeneration was carried from the Papal Church into the Anglican community. Men do not become new creatures in Christ by water of any quantity, sort, or application. The divine order is salvation first, water baptism second. The great Anglican hymn writer August M. Toplady (died 1778) penned *Rock of Ages*. Verse 1 reads that God created His church by "water and blood." Salvation is by grace through faith in the finished work of Christ. In John 19:34 the blood is *first* and water second. The Catholic-Anglican distortion of baptism is clear in the hymns of Stone and Toplady. This does not make them bad men, but reflects their confusion of Scripture. Section 76, fourth paragraph of footnote f has more on this. *Much of the Reformation was an outward thing void of divine inward change. Hence, the ruthless conduct of many of it leaders.*

4p-Distortion of the word "sprinkling" in the Bible. The radical advocates of baptism by sprinkling have gone to bizarre extremes. Some teach that Adam and Eve were the first church; that when God killed the animals for their covering, He then sprinkled them with water. The rain falling on Noah's ark pictures infant baptism! Every mention of water sprinkling across the Torah Law and the history of Israel symbolize the same. Naaman, the captain of Syria's army, was actually "sprinkled in the Jordan River," not self-immersed! Even though the text states that he was to "Wash, and be clean" (2 Kings 5:13-14). Job's friends sprinkling dust on their heads portrays infant baptism (Job 2:12). The verse that reads, "So shall he [God] sprinkle many nations," points to the heathen being brought to Christ by sprinkling them with water at baptism (Isa. 52:15). God told Israel, "Then will I sprinkle clean water upon you, and ye shall be clean: from all your filthiness, and from all your idols, will I cleanse you" (Ezek. 36:25). We are assured this pictures salvation by sprinkling. King Nebuchadnezzar running in the fields like an animal, with "dew falling on him prefigured baptism by sprinkling" (Dan. 4:25-37). Amazing, is the sheer ignorance of some men!

5p-Many great Christians from other camps. The author of this work defends believer's baptism by immersion and is a staunch opponent of *both* Calvinism and Arminianism. However, he knows that thousands of true believers came from the *better* Reformed and Arminian churches. Among these were Matthew Henry, Albert Barnes, Mel Trotter, J, Wilber Chapman, and Billy Sunday, who were Presbyterians. The Arminian John Wesley won thousands to Christ. The Anglican, J. C. Ryle was a noble man who led many souls to Jesus. Andrew Murray of South Africa and Dr. Martin Loyde-Jones of England were powerful Reformed preachers. From such ranks, we have received some of the finest apologetic literature and Christian hymnology. Frances R. Havergal, famed British hymn writer and witness for Christ came from the Episcopalian Church. *True* Christians are not waiting for the "sovereign God to bring in His elect." Instead, they are in the highways and hedges leading men to Christ. They are unlike the super Calvinist Dr. Jay Adams, who wrote sheer nonsense about winning men to Christ. Refer to Section 1 Part 3, third paragraph of footnote i for his remarks. All *honest* Reformed Christians abhor the deeds of the psychopaths John Calvin, William Farel, and the magisterial Reformers, burning Michael Servetus, witches, and others to death, while using green wood to prolong their sufferings. A twelve-year-old girl was beheaded for "breaking the Sabbath" under Calvin's Geneva dictatorship. See Shaff's *History of the Christian Church*, Vol. 111, pages 489-493 for the horrific stories. Splitting churches with the "doctrine of five point Calvinism" is sin. Calvinist preachers have a two-faced cross. The side they cannot preach offers salvation to all men. The other side consigns billions of "non-elect" men, women, boys, girls, and infants to hell, with no hope of forgiveness. The lie of "limited atonement" shames God's grace and has resulted in unspeakable suffering. *There are thousand of Calvinists, who profess this untruth in theory but do not practice it in evangelism. These are our dear friends and companions in the gospel.*

6p-America's early Puritans and the Salem witch trials. The "good old Puritans" in Colonial America had their religious enemies hanged, imprisoned, banished, tortured, and crushed to death. Their celebrated history is stained by many ruthless deeds. At Salem Village, Massachusetts, Puritan ignorance of the Scriptures they boasted to obey violently emerged. Aligned with the courts and magistrates they murdered some fourteen people accused of witchcraft in 1692. *And it was all done in the name of God and the Bible.* This has always been the dogmatic of religious fanatics. Binding an eighty-year-old farmer, Giles Cory, they pressed him to death under tons of weight. Benjamin F. Morris, in his book *The Christian Life and Character,* presented all the Civil Institutions and Puritans of early America as bands of holy angels doing the will of God. On page 81 of his old work reprinted in 2007, Morris wrote of the Puritans, ". . . if they breathe not the genuine spirit of Christianity, if they speak not high approaches towards moral perfection . . . then indeed have I illy [wrongly] read the human heart; then indeed have I strangely mistaken the inspiration of religion." Looking back, Morris indeed misread the hearts of the Puritans. How troubling to peruse the history of this era written by "Christian conservatives" and hear the noisy silence of the Calvinistic poisoned Puritan's murderous deeds. *Honest* Christian historians will not deny the hand of God moving over the early colonies. However, to give the Puritans the credit for this is ludicrous. Not all of them were pure! They persecuted and killed their opponents as their predecessors did in the Old Country. Refer to Section 1, Part 3, second paragraph of footnote i for the Puritans in Old England, and their laws to execute all who dissented from their religious views. In Colonial America, they banished, imprisoned, whipped, or put to death, especially the Baptists, and others that would not bow to their dictates. This was called "sovereign grace." The book by Douglas F. Kelly, *The Emergence of Liberty in the Modern World. The Influence of Calvin on Five Governments from the 16th through the 18th Centuries,* is the joke of the decade! Kelly, a Reformed professor whitewashes the Puritans and their tyrannical rule in early America. On page 25, he penned Calvin's words, "Christ . . . comes down in the sacraments [to] give us the proper clue to understanding his view of ministerial authority in the church . . ." This is a revised version of the Roman mass. Calvin and friends practiced their own brand of Catholic tyranny in Geneva and across Europe. *True* Reformed Christians will not cover this up! America became what it did not because of "Calvinism," "Arminianism," or any other "ism." It only was by the mercy and grace of God.

7p–Anabaptist. Like the Puritans mentioned above, other "Christians" have disgraced the cause of Christ by heresies and killing their opponents. *Honest* Baptists make no apologies for the lunatic fringe Anabaptists, who bloodied their history at Münster, Germany. Religious savages such as Thomas Munzer, Balthasar Heubmaier, Melchior Hofmann, Jan Mattys, Jan van Leyden, and their army of lunatics were involved in apostasy, polygamy, communal living, murder, and pillage. In 1533-1535, they established "the New Jerusalem," and announced the Lord's soon return! Later, they were killed, scattered, and Münster restored to normality. The flowers of saving grace blossom in a believer's life without him seeking to silence or kill all who disagree with him. Many "heroes of the faith" never learned this lesson. See Section 14, fourth paragraph of footnote f for good advice on these things.

8p–Large and Small catechism. Was Luther a great reformer? Yes, but shipwrecked when dealing with baptism and the Lord's Supper. He was a German Catholic priest who daringly inspired the "Protestant Reformation" against the evil practices of the Papal Church. On October 31, 1531, he nailed on a church door in Wittenberg, Germany his ninety-five objections to Papal indulgence. Preachers continually quote Luther's battle cry "justified by faith alone." His writings betray this claim. In 1529, he wrote a *Small Catechism* aimed at children. In 1530-31, Luther produced his *Large Catechism* for adults, ministers, and those of his church. Both works contain "the essentials of the faith." In *The Large Catechism,* translated by Robert Fischer, Luther wrote, "Moreover it is solemnly and strictly commanded that we must be baptized or we shall not be saved" (pages 80-81). He continued, "Thus faith clings to the water and believes it to be baptism in which is sheer salvation and life" (page 84). What strange words from a man who spoke so much about grace! Luther wrote both of his *Catechisms* before he defied the Roman system in October 1531. This remains in the *Lutheran Catechism* to this day. Coming out of Catholicism, he would not have all these issues right. On matters of lesser importance, we agree. However, on the *greatest* of all issues, "How can I be saved from my sins and miss hell" we cannot. Luther held to a version of baptismal regeneration that he brought out of Catholicism. He even called it "saving, divine water." In the *Moody Handbook of Theology,* we read how he taught that although infants are unable to exercise faith in Christ, God through his prevenient grace, works faith in the unconscious child (pages 452–453). In 1855, August J. C. Hare (died 1902) an English author wrote *A Vindication of Luther.* On page 177 he pens these words spoken by the great reformer, "Take thy stand on thy baptism . . . Therein thou wast received by him to be his child." Will Durant in *The Story of Civilization,* vol. 6. page 851, quotes Luther from an older source, "I would have no compassion on . . . witches. I would burn them all." Like Calvin, he was stained by the Papal system and carried it throughout his life.

9p–Luther did no better with the Lord's Supper or communion. In his *Large Catechism,* he wrote that communion "conveys God's grace and Spirit with all his gifts, protection, defense, and power against death and the devil and all evils" (page 98). The emblems of the Lord's Supper convey nothing. There is no grace, salvation, protection from Satan, or innate mercy in these emblems. Martin Luther of yesterday, like millions today, believed in, propagated, and clung to a sacramental gospel, which is foreign to the New Testament. *The above is not a mean condemnation of Luther but points out the seriousness of trusting the wrong things for salvation.*

10p–The Augsburg Confession. At a deliberative meeting (called "Diet") in 1530, Philip Melancthon presented the Lutheran "Confession of Faith" to His Imperial Majesty Charles V. It was approved and accepted. This document reflects the stains that the Roman system left on those who departed from its dark ranks. Article IX on baptism reads, "Baptism is necessary to salvation, and that through Baptism is offered the grace of God, and that children are to be baptized who, being offered to God through Baptism are received into God's grace." Article X speaks of the Lord's Supper. It affirms, "That the Body and Blood of Christ are truly present, and are distributed to those who eat the Supper of the Lord; and they reject those who teach otherwise." Article IV of the Augsburg Confession reads that men are justified by faith alone in the finished work of Christ! Then it requires baptism and communion to be saved from sin and hell. We ask, "Which is it?" Are we justified by faith and faith alone, or do we add baptism and the Lord's Supper to faith? This official Lutheran Confession reeks with the stench of Papal infant baptism and the mass for salvation. Augustine's heresy also lived with the early Reformers; so much so, they later incorporated part of it, though slightly revised, in their Westminster Confession (1643-1747). It declared, "elect infants dying in infancy" are saved. Conversely, they are stating that "non-elect infants" are lost.

11p-Are infants damned? Those who teach that "non-elect babies" are pre-damned, lie. The Holy Scriptures say nothing in respect to the *future condition* of those who die in infancy. Silence concludes the subject and refutes this blasphemy regarding "non-elect infants." The Holy Spirit imposed it. No man of God, prophet, seer, apostle, mother, or father ever expresses sorrow or grief for those who died before they could discern good and evil. There are no prayers recorded for those taken away in infancy. Nowhere does Jesus or any of the eight writers of the New Testament teach that they are lost. Therefore, we confidently believe that they are made *safe* from sin's awful wages by the precious blood of Christ. King David ceased to fast and weep when his child died. He said, "I shall go to him, but he shall not return to me" (2 Sam. 12:23). He was not speaking of a joyful reunion in the grave with his infant son. Concerning when children are responsible for their sin, see Section 150, second paragraph of footnote f.

(e) "Signs" following. Everything Jesus said here literally happened over the coming decades. Most of the signs and miracles that early believers performed were not recorded. That these things did occur is clear in Heb. 2:3-4. *In 2 Cor. 12:12 it may suggest that this was mostly and apostolic gift.* Winning lost souls to Christ should never be overshadowed by any other accomplishment of God's people. Note also number 6 under footnote c above.

2p-Verse 17-18. "Devils, new tongues, serpents, and deadly things." These two passages along with Lk. 10:19 are distorted into the grossest of perversions. Below is a brief look into some of these extremes.

3p-Exorcising evil spirits is not a game. It must be of God or disastrous consequences will follow. Not all Christians, especially those of a flippant nature, should venture into this realm. It is untrue that this was exclusively an apostolic gift, and therefore, cannot be employed today. Exorcism is not a "gift of the Holy Spirit." It is a tool that *sometimes* must be used in the spiritual warfare believers may find themselves facing.

4p-"New tongues." This may have reference to a vocabulary changed at conversion. The author knew a Rhodesian army officer who was saved. His language so radically changed that the men under his command thought he had mental problems! Under John Wesley's preaching hundreds of tough Welsh miners came to Christ. They instantly ceased cursing the mules that pulled the coal wagons. Because of this, the dumb animals stopped doing their work, for the miners were no longer cursing them! Others think the "new tongues" to be a reproduction of Pentecost in Acts 2. On the Day of Pentecost, they spoke foreign languages not previously learned. "New tongues" are not the incoherent gibberish of extreme charismatic movements. In the early church, when men spoke in a genuine unknown tongue or language, an interpreter gave the meaning, or it was forbidden (1 Cor. 14:10-28).

5p-"Take up serpents." Charles W. Hensley of Cleveland, Tennessee (died 1955) is credited for starting the first holiness movement church in the 1920s that practiced snake handling. This pagan craft was transported from the Appalachian Mountains across the south. It then was taken into Canada. In 2004, snake-handling cults were located in Alberta and British Columbia, Canada. Later, one James Miller claimed he had a revelation from God, about snake handling based on Mk. 16:18. He brought this to Sand Mountain, Alabama. From here, it spread into the various radical churches and the wilder Pentecostal movements. (Later, both groups banned the practice from their churches.) In the 1940s, Raymond Harris and Tom Harden, started the Dolly Pond Church of God in the hills of East Tennessee. "Snake handling, proved faith and secured salvation." There were outbreaks of tongues, deafening music, screaming, dancing, fainting, and "healings." Barelegged pastors stood in boxes of poisonous snakes and "preached the Word." Some died from bites before state governments banned this satanic circus.

6p-Pagan religions and snakes. In India, Burma, South America, and many parts of Africa, pagans practice similar rites, as do the American snake handlers. They kiss, caress, sleep with, and worship deadly serpents. For a study of snake handling in America, see *Serpent Handling Believers* by Tom Burton and *Salvation on Sand Mountain: Snake Handling and Redemption in Southern Appalachia* by Dennis Covington. God has no part in this.

7p-"Drink any deadly thing" (poison). We have no biblical record of where these things occurred. However, they did for our Lord said it would be. His Words regarding taking up deadly creatures or drinking poison were never intended to be a public spectacle of men, women, and youth, "demonstrating their faith." Backward, ignorant people, assisted by the Devil, created this demonic practice and call it "faith." Refer to Section 207, Mk. 16:20 footnote i for more regarding genuine wonders accompanying the work of God in the early church and during her first missionary efforts. For other thoughts on divine healing, refer to Section 41, all under footnote h.

8p-"The sick shall recover." Over the centuries, this has occurred. It is not the sideshow seen on national television. Paul did this in the latter days of his work (Acts 28:1-10). When these healings take place, it is always "according to God's will" (Heb. 2:4). See Section 41, the first three paragraphs of footnote h for more on this.

THIRD MENTION OF THE GREAT COMMISSION.*

(For a chronology of the Commission, see Section 201, the symbol ● by Lk. 24:47.)

Below is Matthew's version of the mountain top meeting and the third* giving of the Commission. This is placed before that of John's record of a meeting on the shores of Galilee in Section 205. The Savior had previously instructed His apostles to **meet Him in Galilee _after_ His death and resurrection. Because the province of Galilee was north of Jerusalem, the apostles and other disciples had to walk this distance of three days journey one way to meet Him. Thus, the two commissions given in Galilee cannot be the same as the previous two He had given down south in Jerusalem. It is ***_conjectured_ that the apostles went fishing after their appointment with Christ on the designated but unnamed mountain somewhere in Galilee.

Time: Several weeks after His resurrection in the Province of Galilee.

**_The first mention of this appointment is recorded in Section 173, Matt. 26:32. The second and third mentions are found in Section 195, Matt. 28:7, and Section 198, Matt. 28:10. There seems to be a sense of extreme importance attached to this occasion. However, inspired Scripture only gives us a snippet of what was said at that monumental event._ *******_The author realizes this conjecture may be wrong. If so, we can simply swap the events and place Matthew's mountain meeting second and John's Lake Galilee fishing trip first. Since the Holy Spirit did not give us an established correct order, we therefore, recognize the possibility of error in our placements of these two events and list them as only conjectures. This has nothing to do with divine inspiration of the Scriptures._

Matt. 28:16-20—_A mountain in Galilee ninety miles north of Jerusalem_	Mk.	Lk.	John
The Galilee meeting			
16 Then the eleven disciples went away into Galilee, into a mountain where Jesus had appointed them.[a]			
17 And when they saw him, they worshipped him: but some doubted.[b]			
Third giving of the Great Commission			
18 And Jesus came and spake unto them, saying, **"All power is given unto me in heaven and in earth.**[c]			
19 **"Go**[d] **ye therefore, and teach all nations, baptizing them in the name of the Father, and of the Son, and of the Holy Ghost:**			
20 **"Teaching them to observe all things whatsoever I have commanded you: and, lo, I am with**[e] **you alway,** _even_ **unto the end of the world."**[f] **Amen.**[g]			

Footnotes-Commentary

[a] Suddenly, Matthew moves his readers from Jerusalem and the undesignated residence where believers had gathered after the crucifixion, to a distance of some ninety miles north on a mountaintop in Galilee. It was a three-day walk one-way from Jerusalem, north to the Lake of Galilee. Sometime _after_ their Jerusalem experiences in seeing the resurrected Savior, the disciples made this trip to keep their mountain top appointment with Messiah. For more on this, as mentioned above, see Section 195, Matt. 28:7, footnote j. _Some conjecture that it was on this occasion, that "he was seen of above five hundred brethren at once"_ (1 Cor. 15:6). However, this hypothesis is fraught with uncertainty. Five hundred people gathered together would have surely caught the attention of the Jews, who hated both Christ and His disciples. And it was during this waiting period when the Holy Spirit had not yet come in full power; thus, they were fearful, meeting behind barred doors as noted in Section 202, John 20:26, footnote d. Regardless, the text in Matt. 28:10 says that Jesus had made a previous appointment with the eleven. Nothing was said about hundreds of other believers, though it must be granted that they could have been there.

[b] They had now made the long walk northward from Jerusalem to Galilee and assembled on that unnamed mountain to meet their Lord. Again, we are amazed at the reading of this text. _Some of them (the eleven) worshipped Him, yet others doubted!_ Jesus demonstrated before their eyes that He had risen and was alive, yet some of His own still doubted! Living in an ongoing state of shock about His death and resurrection, doubt was the continual enemy of Christ's first disciples. Surely, we of today would have done no better. For more on this, see Section 203, Mk. 16:14, footnote b. If Jesus had been an invention of men, the ones who invented Him would never have written in their gospels that they themselves had doubts about Him! _The gospels are the only religious books in the world, which express the truth together with doubts about this same truth. Therefore, they are true!_

[c] **"All power is given unto me."** Knowing the painful and fearful questions that rose in their hearts, Christ makes this reassuring statement. He was saying that He now had all power restored to Him as the Son. He had been

eternally equal with the Father before coming to earth in a human form. As a man, He chose at times to limitHis humanity and not use the totality of His Godhead power. With His earthly work finished, and having risen from the dead, the Son reverted to His sovereign equality with God, no longer needing to employ limited might and authority. There is no final and greater power in eternity and time like that of the risen Messiah. The Father honored Him with this unique prerogative. In these Words of Jesus, we see an allusion to the Messiah predicted in Dan. 7:14.

(d) Most expositors think this was the first time Jesus gave the Great Commission to His disciples. However, above in Matt. 28:18-20 the Lord gave His third edition of the Great Commission. This was not at Jerusalem, but far north on a mountaintop in Galilee. Some of those who saw and heard Him speak were still troubled with unbelief. The fourth and *shortest* version of the Commission is found in Section 205.

2p-See Section 203 and all under footnote c where we have compared Luke's record of the first edition of the Great Commission with the second version as given by Mark. Matthew's record of the third version is as follows:

1. **"Go."** Matthew used the action word just as Mark did. Luke did not use this word. Our Lord informs His disciples with something like this: "In view of my authority as the risen Lord who has conquered Satan, sin, death, and the grave, I hereby commission you to continue the work that I have started and take the gospel message of salvation to all men everywhere in your generation." Regarding how the *first* Christians literally fulfilled this original Great Commission during their lifetime, see Section 163, third paragraph under number 16, footnote f.

2. **"Teach."** Jesus ordered that His preachers, teachers, missionaries, or disciples were to "teach" or make disciples and learners of believing individuals in all nations. Neither Mark nor Luke used the word teach. Luke wrote that Jesus said to witness," while Mark said, "preach," and Matthew said, "teach." These three words cover the entire range of gospel witnessing. The commission calls for "disciples" to be baptized. Fitting helpless infants into the "disciple category" is an impossible task.

3. **"All nations."** Matthew used these words spoken by the Lord Jesus. All nations mean all nations. **"Every creature"** was Mark's designation for those to hear the gospel. The lesson is clear: *Whether individuals or collective groups such as nations, all are to have the gospel taken to them.* In world history, never has any entire nation been saved, but individuals out of nations have. The words in Rev. 21:24 have reference to the saved out of all nations walking in the light of heaven's splendor. At this writing there are a hundred and ninety three different nations on planet earth.

4. **"Baptizing them in the name of."** Luke wrote nothing about baptism. Mark did. However, Matthew gave the entire formula by which baptism was to be performed: the Holy Trinity. When our Lord began His public ministry by baptism, we observed that the Trinity also shared in that event. All converts to Christ, who have been saved and properly taught, are then to be immersed under water, one time, in the Name of the Father, and of the Son, and of the Holy Ghost. (Note it is not "Names" plural, but rather "Name" singular, revealing their oneness as expressed in 1 John 5:7.) Saved persons *who have been taught* the elementals of the faith are baptized one time. This is in the Name of the Father because He sent His Son; in the Name of the Son because he died for our sins; and lastly, in the Name of the Holy Spirit for He enlightened us to the need of personal salvation and drew us to the Savior, who graciously saved our souls. It is correct that we baptize converts in this manner because the Trinity working together provided salvation. Triune immersion as practiced by various sects and the infant immersion of the Greek Orthodox Church are unfounded in Scripture. Infants cannot be *first* "taught" before baptism, as instructed by the Lord Jesus in this verse. Some cultists ask, "What is the Name of the Father, the Son, and the Holy Spirit?" *Here*, God is Named "Father," Christ is named, "Son" and the Spirit is the "Holy Spirit." Jews did not baptize in the name of anyone, singular or plural. This command of Christ must have boggled the minds of His disciples. They had never heard of such things! With the coming of the Spirit in His fullness at Pentecost *all this* was understood. Jesus had previously explained these things to them in the upper room. Refer to Section 175, John 14:26, footnote n for the story.

2p-**"Jesus Only" baptizers.** Sabellius was a third century heretic. He denied the equality and oneness of the Trinity. In early 1913, the Sabellianism heresy was reborn at a Pentecostal camp meeting near Los Angeles, California. A Canadian preacher, R. E. McAlister declared that the apostles only baptized in the Name of Jesus; they never used the Trinitarian formula. With this, the "Jesus Only" or "Oneness Pentecostal" curse was born! These people point out that nowhere across the book of Acts do we read of anyone being baptized in these three Names, but only in the Name of Jesus. We inquire, "Does this prove they were not? We respond that nowhere across the thirty-year history of Acts do we find the names of the apostles after Acts 1:1. Does this affirm they did not exist after this verse? The reason for this early form of baptism is that among the Jews, the controversy was about the true Messiah; among the Gentiles, it was about the true God. It was therefore, proper among the Jews to baptize in the Name of Jesus that he might be vindicated as the true Messiah; and among the Gentiles, in the Name of the Father, and the Son, and the Holy Ghost, that they might hereby be instructed in the doctrine of the true God. The adherents of this "Jesus Only" cult teach that the new birth is achieved by 'faith, repentance, water baptism, and the baptism of the Holy Ghost." They teach Arminianism, which states that one may lose his salvation! Concerning the "Jesus Only" cult and its various factions, see *Origins and Development of the Theology of "Oneness" Pentecostalism in the United States,* by David A. Reed.

5. Polycarp. Later, the church fathers twisted the true meaning of believer's baptism by immersion and the Lord's Supper as a simple ordinance for believers, into tools of coercion and control. The famed Polycarp, a disciple of John, was instructed by the heretical church father Ignatius who said, "Let your baptism be your shield." See *Vincent Word Studies of the New Testament,* vol. iii, page 407. This reflects their ignorance of Holy Scripture. Paul wrote in Eph. 6:16 that faith is the shield for believers. In time, these perversions of New Testament doctrine emerged full-blown in the Roman Catholic Church, which was born out of the state church of Emperor Constantine. Later, the Reformers coming out of the Papal Church brought many other doctrinal errors and practices with them. John Calvin and Martin Luther are glaring examples of this. They *retained* their Catholic baptisms received while babes at the hands of Roman priests and died with these. They were never correctly baptized after leaving that unholy religious system. Apologists for these men and their religious ideologies have consigned this subject to the realms of silence! How many of the *better* Reformed churches today (and there are plenty of them) would have a man ministering in their pulpits or teaching catechisms who held to a baptism administered by a Papal priest? *True* Reformed ministers would never do this. Yet, their theological heroes of the past did. See Section 203, eighth and ninth paragraphs of footnote d for Luther's words about baptism

6. Calvin and his Reformers put to death believers who had been baptized by immersion *after* personal salvation. The Roman Church out of which they came did the same thing. The only difference was on which side of the religious fence the killing of Christians was done: the Papal side or the Reformers. Either way, could we perhaps call this "Christian murder" and it be acceptable? Their barbaric deeds carry the reflections men without the saving knowledge of Christ and understanding of New Testament Scripture. Only human Devils lurking in "the church," beat, hate, murder, burn, torture, and persecute those who disagree with them. History is bent over by these wolves in sheep's clothing. Few "great church historians" dare deal with this horrific subject! Others, carefully cover it up or justify it.

7. It is noteworthy that Matthew mentioned both "teach" and "teaching." These words carry the idea of enrolling as a learner. First, we are to "teach" men the gospel. Not every person can understand the western style of Bible preaching, especially as we hear some of it in the southern United States! As a missionary serving in Africa, in 1972, a friend and I met an old African on a mountain trail near Zululand. He had *never* heard the words "Jesus," "God," "Holy Spirit," or "Bible." (One wonders how some American "know-it-all" preachers would have handled this one?) Our starting place with this old native was to point him to the wonders of creation in heaven and earth then ask, "Who made all this?" Paul used this exact method with the pagans in the districts of Lycaonia (Acts 14:11-18). There is a tribe in the Highlands of New Guineas among which missionaries worked for over three years before a breakthrough came, and dozens were saved. These pagans were slowly taught, each step of the way to God. The patient missionaries started with creation and three years later ended with Christ! A thousand years before Christ, David contemplated the wonders of heaven and saw the handiwork of Jehovah. The lessons regarding this are in Ps. 19:1-6. On the impossibility of Natural Theology alone bringing men to the saving knowledge of Christ, refer to Section 1, Part 4, fourth and fifth paragraphs of footnote m.

8. In Matthew's version of the Great Commission, the Savor said to "teach" the saved and newly baptized converts to observe all of His instructions. Again, we ask, how can infants meet these requirements? For the meaning of "teaching," see number 7 above. After salvation, comes the life-long process of "growing in grace and knowledge of our Lord and Savior Jesus Christ" (2 Peter 3:18). It is "growing in grace," not "growing *into* grace." Fulfilling the Great Commission does not mean to give unsaved people communion, sprinkle water on their heads, "teach them to speak in tongues," or to "seek the gifts of the Spirit," then tell them they are saved. These deceptive tactics only produce counterfeit believers, who have never experienced the new birth. Thousands of pseudo converts are in churches today; full of religion, but without Christ as Lord and Savior. Read Jesus' shock announcement to these people at judgment. See Section 47, Matt. 7:21-23 with relevant footnotes.

(e) **"I am with you."** This promise of Christ for those early believers on that unknown mountaintop in Galilee is valid to this present moment. It is the same as Heb. 13:5-6. Sufficient grace to live or die for the Savior is available in plentiful supply. It is, however, given at the time when needed.

(f) **"World."** The Greek word used here is "aion." It does not mean the end of earth or humankind, but rather the end of a specific period of history. A good Reference Bible will have this footnoted. See Section 82, Matt. 13:39, footnote d for an explanation of "world" and the Jewish usages of chronology during this era of history.

(g) For information regarding the shocking abuse of this benediction of Scripture, see Section 46, Matt. 6:13, the seventh paragraph of footnote g.

FOURTH AND INDIVIDUAL VERSION OF THE GREAT COMMISSION.*

(For a chronology of the Commission, see Section 201, the symbol ● by Lk. 24:47.)

The mountaintop meeting in the previous Section is over. At Peter's behest, seven of the apostles return to the Sea of Galilee to fish. Toiling all night, they catch nothing. Early morning, Christ appears on the shore and gives fishing instructions. With nets full, He beckons them to land. Peter gets personal instructions from the Savior. Rumors spread regarding the death of the apostle John.

Time: After the meeting on the mountain in Galilee in Section 204.

*For explanation of this concise version of our Lord's instructions for His disciples (especially Peter) and their successors to continue carrying the saving gospel to all men, see footnote q below in the commentary.

Matt.	Mk.	Lk.	John 21:1-14—*On the Sea of Galilee or Tiberias*
			John explains another appearing of Christ
			1 After these things[a] Jesus shewed himself again to the disciples at the sea of Tiberias; and on this wise shewed he *himself.*
			2 There were together[b] Simon Peter, and Thomas called Didymus, and Nathanael of Cana in Galilee, and the *sons* of Zebedee, and two other of his disciples.
			Fishing that catches nothing: Jesus appears unrecognized
			3 Simon Peter saith unto them, "I go a fishing."[c] They say unto him, "We also go with thee." They went forth, and entered into a ship immediately; and that night they caught nothing.[d]
			4 But when the morning was now come, Jesus stood on the shore: but the disciples knew not that it was Jesus.
			5 Then Jesus saith[e] unto them, "Children, have ye any meat?" They answered him, "No."
			Fishing that catches hundreds
			6 And he said unto them, "Cast the net on the right side of the ship, and ye shall find." They cast therefore, and now they were not able to draw it for the multitude of fishes.
			John recognizes His Lord
			7 Therefore that disciple whom Jesus loved saith unto Peter, "It is the Lord." Now when Simon Peter heard that it was the Lord, he girt *his* fisher's coat *unto him,* (for he was naked,) and did cast himself into the sea.
			8 And the other disciples came in a little ship; (for they were not far from land, but as it were two hundred cubits,) [about 100 yards] dragging the net with fishes.
			9 As soon then as they were come to land, they saw a fire of coals there, and fish laid thereon, and bread.
			10 Jesus saith unto them, "Bring of the fish which ye have now caught."[f]
			11 Simon Peter went up, and drew the net to land full of great fishes, an hundred and fifty and three: and for all there were so many, yet was not the net broken.
			The Savior serves breakfast
			12 Jesus saith unto them, "Come *and* dine." And none of the disciples durst ask him, "Who art thou?" knowing that it was the Lord.[g]
			13 Jesus then cometh, and taketh bread, and giveth them, and fish likewise.
			14 This is now the third time[h] that Jesus shewed himself to his

Matt.	Mk.	Lk.	John 21:14-25—On the Sea of Galilee or Tiberias
			disciples, after that he was risen from the dead.

Peter is questioned three times

15 So when they had dined, Jesus saith to Simon Peter,[i] "Simon, *son of* Jonas, lovest thou me more than these?" He saith unto him, "Yea, Lord; thou knowest that I love thee." He saith unto him, "Feed my lambs."

16 He saith to him again the second[j] time, "Simon, *son of* Jonas, lovest thou me?" He saith unto him, "Yea, Lord; thou knowest that I love thee." He saith unto him, "Feed my sheep."

17 He saith unto him the third time,[k] "Simon, *son of* Jonas, lovest thou me?" Peter was grieved because he said unto him the third time, "Lovest thou me?" And he said unto him, "Lord, thou knowest all things;[l] thou knowest that I love thee." Jesus saith unto him, "Feed my sheep.

18 "Verily, verily, I say unto thee, When thou wast young, thou girdest thyself, and walkedst whither thou wouldest: but when thou shalt be old, thou shalt stretch forth thy hands, and another shall gird thee, and carry *thee* whither thou wouldest not."[m]

19 This spake he, signifying by what death he should glorify God.[n] And when he had spoken this, he saith unto him, "Follow me."[o]

Jesus leaves: John follows: Peter's inappropriate question

20 Then Peter, turning about, seeth the disciple whom Jesus loved following; which also leaned on his breast at supper, and said, "Lord, which is he that betrayeth thee?"

21 Peter seeing him saith to Jesus, "Lord, and what *shall* this man *do*?"[p]

Fourth and briefest version of the Great Commission
spoken first to Simon Peter

22 Jesus saith unto him, "If I will that he tarry till I come, what *is that* to thee? **follow thou me.**"[q]

A rumor is spread about John

23 Then went this saying abroad among the brethren, that that disciple should not die: yet Jesus said not unto him, "He shall not die; but, If I will that he tarry till I come, what *is that* to thee?"[r]

24 This is the disciple which testifieth of these things, and wrote these things: and we know that his testimony is true.[s]

Too much to be written in books

25 And there are also many other things which Jesus did, the which, if they should be written every one, I suppose that even the world itself could not contain the books that should be written.[t] **Amen.**[u]

Footnotes-Commentary

[a] **"After these things."** John was inspired to add one other miraculous appearing of Christ with which he ended his book. Being a professional fisherman, this final word is most appropriate, for it was at this sea that the Savior first called him and his brother James to service. Refer to Section 39, Matt. 4:21-22, footnote g for this event. It was obvious that he was still fishing, but now it was for men! None of the other evangelists recorded the story above. It is the seventh appearing of Christ to His disciples after the Sunday morning resurrection. *Numerically, however, this is the third appearing as they were listed in John's book.* See footnote h below.

2p-**"The Sea of Tiberias."** Distinction must be made between this sea spelled "Tiberias" and the Roman Emperor Tiberius Caesar, who ruled from A.D. 14-37. The first is the name of a city and a sea. The second is that of the man who ruled the known world during most of the life of Christ. For information on Emperor Tiberius, refer to Section 21, Part 1, number 1 under footnote b.

3p-"Two other disciples." We have no way of knowing who these other two men were. Their names being left out of the list is another curious choice of divine inspiration. Human genius would have naturally included them. God does not write as man do. For a lengthy discussion of biblical inspiration, see the *Author's Introduction*.

(b) It is noted in Section 204 that our Lord was in Galilee and had met with His disciples and the eleven on a mountaintop. Even though they all saw Him, yet some continued to doubt. This present Section makes it clear that He was still in Galilee with part of His apostles, for we read of them going fishing in the lake.

(c) "I go a fishing." Peter and six fellow apostles are together. Peter informs them that he is going fishing. All sorts of speculations have risen over these words. Some commentators hold that his association with Christ had ended all financial income. Other writers are of the opinion that he was in a backslidden condition, greatly confused, not knowing what to do. This hardly makes sense as Jesus had previously appeared to Peter and the others; He had given them their orders and told them to wait for the coming Holy Spirit. Seemingly, on this occasion, Peter and his friends probably went fishing in need of financial income.

(d) "Caught nothing." These words strike us with meaning. It had been over two years ago, that in this body of water that several of these men had spent the night fishing and had the same results. This event is recorded in Section 43, Lk. 5:1-11, footnote e. On that previous occasion, Christ appeared, preached from a boat, and called Peter and his work companions to follow Him into full-time service. Note that Lk. 5:11 of Section 43 reads, "They forsook all, and followed him." How time *does not* change some things! Here, we read that they are back at it again, fishing and catching nothing.

(e) "Then Jesus saith unto them." Amid the frustration of weariness and fishless work, Christ suddenly appeared on the shoreline and inquired of their success. Then, He instructed them to cast their nets "on the right side" of the ship. On that first occasion, His orders were "Launch out into the deep, and let down your nets for a draught" (Lk. 5:4). What a lesson is here! Christ knows exactly *where* we should work and that the methods of yesterday may not necessarily get the job done today. Obedience brought the results they desired; a multitude of extra large fish filled the net. When they let the Savior instruct their fishing, they made a great catch.

2p-Verse 6. "The right side." In mystical Jewish thinking, "The right side" was the place of judgment, pardon, or clemency. In heaven, it is the position of God's favor designated for His Son (Rom. 8:34; Col. 3:1; and Heb. 1:3). It was noted earlier that the elderly priest Zacharias was struck with terror upon seeing an angel standing at the right side of the altar. See Section 8, footnotes e and f for this event. For a brief review of this ancient belief, see Section 166, footnote d. Over the centuries, "the right" has come to mean the conservatives in politics and religion, while "the left" usually signifies the liberals and those seemingly void of traditional moral values. However, this is not a hard set rule as we often see a small spill over from one side into the other. Historically, the terms "Right" and "Left" appeared during the French Revolution of 1789 when members of the national assembly divided into supporters of the king to the right hand of the president. Those who supported the revolution sat to the left. Traditionally, the Left includes the progressives, social liberals, social democrats, socialists, communist, Christ denying religionists and so forth. The Right includes the conservatives, reactionaries, capitalists, monarchists, nationalists and at times the fascists. This division between good and bad has been handed down to the present day and has become part of religious terminology. It is not by accident that the Bible states, "A wise man's heart *is* at his right hand; but a fool's heart at his left" (Eccles. 10:2).

3p-Verses 7-9. "It is the Lord." Peter without his clothes. John instantly recognized the stranger calling to them from the shore: it was Christ. Peter, without his top garment, was shamed and leaped into the water along the shoreline. (He was still covered with his undergarment or tunic.) This sensitivity of nakedness, among men and women is gradually vanishing in American society. "Bare is better," cries the unsaved world and its clothing fashions reflect the same. In the Torah Law of Israel, written some fifteen years before Christ was born, God laid down specific rules regarding the sanctity of the human body. The entirety of Lev. 18 speaks on these matters. Verse 30 concludes the chapter by warning the Israelites that openly displaying human nakedness was an abomination practiced by the pagans into whose land they were moving. Those who did this defiled themselves before God. If this was the rule of Jewish law, what would grace say today? Nevertheless, churning in the water, the net filled with fish was apparently tied to another ship, while Peter and John went in a separate boat to land. Because the net was so heavy, they were unable to pull it aboard and had to drag or tow it to shore being about "two hundred cubits" or some three hundred and fifty feet away. To their delight, the Messiah had breakfast ready for the weary men, bread and fish were on the menu that morning. This was a common meal among fishermen.

(f) "Bring the fish." Simon Peter was quick to obey his Master. No doubt with the help of the others he pulled the net, packed with flopping, struggling, gigantic size fish onto the sand along the shore. They counted the exact number for verse 11 states it was one hundred and fifty three. This was a miraculous catch in view of the size of the fish, and the fact that the net was not broken. There is something curious about this divinely ordered catch. Fishing in the Lake of Galilee was a huge industry, but the smaller type fish were prized. They were caught annually by the millions, then dried, smoked, salted, or precooked and consumed by the locals or shipped to countries near and far. Every fisher worked to catch the smaller variety called "opscarion" due to its delicious taste and price. The fish Jesus had cooked and made ready was probably of this kind. Why did our Lord fill their net with the larger variety? Perhaps this was His way of saying, "Men, your lake fishing is over. Your last catch is your best! Now, you shall move across the land and catch the souls of men in the gospel net."

2p-The *Biblical, Theological, and Ecclesiastical Cyclopaedia,* vol. III pages 574–580, by M'Clintock and Strong, carries an exhaustive article on fish. It contains ancient engravings, pyramid drawings, and pictorial woodcuts reproduced showing the sizes of fish in those times. The larger ones could be up to four feet in length, while the smaller are the size of a human leg. This gives some idea of the meaning of the words "great fish." One wonders what they did with this overwhelming catch now that their fishing days had ended.

(g) "Come and dine." A glorious invitation that remains valid to this day. He prepares for His servants regardless of where they are. What a sight: the Son of God, chief cook and servant and His little band of seven preachers being served. As pointed out in footnote b above, Christ had revealed Himself to these men on several occasions in which He demonstrated beyond doubt that He was alive from the dead. One can feel that these seven men were embarrassed, ashamed, and fearful to make any comment in His holy presence; that is, all except Simon Peter! Jesus initiated the conversation *after* they had dined by first addressing Peter (verse 15). This causes us to wonder if they ate in silence.

(h) "The third time Jesus shewed Himself." John is saying that this is the third time Jesus appeared to His disciples in the order as laid out in his book. The first was in John 20:19, the second in John 20:26, and the third, here on the shore of Lake Galilee (John 21:1). See footnote a above. There is the possibility that He may be saying that this is the third time He appeared to the majority of them. Technically, and chronologically, this is the seventh appearing since His resurrection.

(i) The first time Jesus spoke to Peter. Did they eat in silence being in frightful awe at the presence of their Master? See footnote g above for more on this thought. When breakfast was over the Lord Jesus addressed Peter. The object of our Lord's inquiry to Peter was not the fishing boats, nets, and fish. He is questioning Simon if he loved Him more than the other six apostles loved Him. In the upper room when Jesus (again) announced His departure, Peter was most upset. He boasted that he would die for Messiah. See Section 173, John 13:36-38, footnote e. A few hours later in the garden, he whipped out the sword (or sacrificial knife) and attacked Malchus the servant of Caiaphas, the high priest. See Section 180, John 18:10-11 with footnotes g and h. Apparently, Peter had assumed that his love and devotion of Messiah was greater than that of the other apostles. And it may very well have been! There are many who love with all their hearts but (as strange as it sounds) they are not able to show or express this in eloquent words and great deeds.

2p-Simon's response to the Savior was sensible and clear. "Yea, Lord; thou knowest that I love thee." Peter was so conscious of his love for Christ that he fearlessly asks Him to judge or answer His own question. Without responding to Peter's request, He orders, "Feed my lambs" or the weaker among my followers, who need the support and aid of those who are stronger and more experienced. This alone would have thrilled the tough heart of this fisherman. Now, his Messiah gives him work, responsibility, and a serious duty to perform; he is to feed God's little ones. We do not put much stock in the play made on the two Greek words for love, "agapao," and "phileo," in this history, believing this has been taken to the extreme. For a brief, but clear explanation of this, see David Stern's *Jewish New Testament Commentary,* pages 213-214. The command of Christ spoken here has nothing to do with the Popes of the Roman Church claiming to have descended from Peter and tending to God's children. That is a gross myth invented by perverse minds and believed by millions. Refer to Section 12, sixth through tenth paragraphs under footnote k for other comments regarding the dark history of the Papal system and some of its Popes.

(j) The second time Jesus spoke to Peter. It is the same scenario. Christ must draw him out. Peter must understand kingdom service is not accomplished by fits of anger, rage, temper, cursing, swinging swords, and then running away. It is born from above, energized by the Holy Spirit, and motivated by pure love. To love Christ is the highest of all gifts. It is the bright star that illuminates the darkest night, the patience that forgives the worst of transgressions all of life through. However, there is a unique lesson from the first instruction to the second given to Simon Peter. Christ shifts His instruction to Peter from lambs to sheep. Adults like him need help, support, and guidance. Peter, the most unlikely of all the apostles was given this task. Did he fulfill it? A cursory reading of 1 and 2 Peter reflects that he has been feeding God's people for almost two thousand years through the inspired words and instructions of these two letters. What a lesson in Peter's final words to the Christian community as given in 2 Peter 3:18. He tells all who would read them, "To grow in grace, and *in* the knowledge of our Lord and Saviour Jesus Christ." If this advice were followed, the Church of God would be virtually free from internal strife and problems.

(k) The third time Jesus spoke to Peter. Had he not denied Christ three times amid profane oaths and foul language? One can sense that third question recalled to Peter's mind his past performance at the fire of the Devil's crowd in the palace of the high priest. This was the tender way to reprove a stubborn believer, and surely, he got the message. Our Lord is saying between the lines, "Peter is thy love really strong, hearty, and what you know it should be?" The root of Messiah's questions to Peter is simply that only those who are saved and love Him and His service are fitted to feed God's flock, be it lambs, sheep, or both. All others are imposters amid God's flock.

2p-We dare not miss the Lord's three-fold statement, "Feed, feed, feed." Now, we can understand how he wrote almost thirty years later these words to the younger elders of God's church, "Feed the flock of God which is among you" (1 Peter 5:1-2). Only a preacher, who has spent his life feeding others, can instruct others to feed.

(l) "Thou knowest all things." The hope of a genuine believer hangs upon these words. To think that there was something in our lives that God did not know would be a hell on earth! How fresh and wonderful to say with the psalmist of old "Thou knowest my down sitting and mine uprising, thou understandest my thought afar off" (Ps. 139:2). *O the joy of knowing that God knows us as His children!* To Israel, He said, "For I know the things that come into your mind, *every one of* them" (Ezek. 11:5). Blundering Peter was trying to tell Jesus that he knew there was nothing hidden from Him. Upon hearing his reply, Jesus again responded, "Feed my sheep." See second paragraph of footnote k above. Concerning Simon's words that Jesus knew all things, however, we note earlier He did not know the *exact* time of Jerusalem's destruction in A.D. 70. See Section 163, Mk. 13:32, footnote v for details. It should be remembered that Peter was among those who heard Jesus say this a few days prior!

(m) From youth to old age. In these Words, Christ takes Peter back to earlier years when as a young man he was healthy and agile, who could dress himself and go wherever he chose with freedom. The Savior reflects about thirty-five years into Simon's future, when things will be changed. Then, as an old preacher filled with the service of God, having fed the lambs and sheep of Christ's flock, others will take you up and carry you where men dare not tread. Peter's love for Christ grew into such glory that it was at last crowned with martyrdom. Years later, as an old man he was led out of the city of Rome to be crucified as His Lord had been. Tradition has it that he pled with his executioners to hang him upside down for he was unworthy to die as His Lord had. See *The New Unger's Bible Dictionary*, pages 992-993 for a concise but clear article on Peter's decease. It is untrue that the Roman Catholic Church created this story about Peter's death. It is true, however, that many years after Peter's death, the hierarchy of this church took it from history, distorted, and exploited it for their glory and economic profit.

(n) John looking back on history as he wrote, now fully understood the meaning of Christ's Words to his fellow apostle. *This also means that John may have written his book after the death of Peter.*

(o) Verse 19. "Follow me." With this, the Lord Jesus rose and walked away from the cooking fire. As He did so, He spoke to Peter the command, "Follow me." Upon hearing this, John instantly leaped to his feet and fell in behind his Lord.

2p-Verse 20. Seeing John go off with the Savior, Peter was disturbed. Was someone going to get ahead of him? His overwhelming anxiety seems to have started in the upper room. Refer to John 13:36-38 for this.

(p) Peter still in a sitting posture turned and saw John following behind Jesus (footnote o above) and called out to his Lord this question, "What *shall* this man [John] *do*?" Alternatively, "What is John going to do seeing he is following after you?" His question seems rather curt if not impertinent. We wonder if he inquired out of jealously, genuine concern, or plain old rashness. How could we forget that the Lord Jesus had committed His elderly mother into the keeping of John, as He hung, dying on the cross. We ponder, where was she while John was fishing again? For this heart-touching story, see Section 190, John 19:27, footnote m.

(q) "Thou" also means every *true* Christian. Set in heavy font, we see in John 21:22 above a fourth mention of the Great Commission, be it ever so small. He had given it the third time in Section 204 on an unknown mountaintop in Galilee. On this occasion, Jesus makes it an *individual* duty for all believers when He spoke this command to Peter, by the shores of Lake Galilee. We cannot determine which of these two events came first. The order given by the author of the third and fourth mentions of the Great Commission is strictly a conjecture and may be reversed without violence being done to the inspired text. The fifth giving of the Great Commission is discussed in Section 206. It is recorded in Acts 1:8. Note, especially footnote e at this verse. This Scripture contains the last recorded Words of the Lord Jesus in the gospels. It is most fitting that this final instruction was not to Peter alone. In the word "Thou," all saved believers are included. Though most do not obey this, it is, nevertheless, the duty of every child of God to take some part in getting the saving gospel out to fellow men and women. Christians can go with their money and their prayers, as others go by going! Reader, "Thou" means you and yours! Get going with the gospel. When you pay your bills put a tract in the envelope. The next time you pump gas tuck a salvation tract under the handle. Whoever follows you at that pump is sure to find it. Read Christ's lesson on the sower, in Section 73 and its meaning in Section 75. In Section 90, second paragraph of footnote d there is the story about old Jim Doss of Houston Texas in 1961. It is worth reading and heart warming for all Christians, who faithfully distribute God's Word. In Section 140, second paragraph of footnote j, carries the record of a young F.B.I agent who eventually came into the saving knowledge of Jesus Christ because a gospel tract blew into his face on a windy New York street.

2p–"If John tarries [lives] till I come." In today's talk, the Lord said, "Simon, if I choose for John to live until I return that is none of your business. Your job is to get up and follow me, as he is doing." Jesus' Words "till I return" have confounded the greatest minds over the ages. Some honorable men see in this a reference to His coming invisibly in A.D. 70 to bring the destruction of Jerusalem. This could be the meaning, as the apostle John lived many years after the doom that fell upon Israel. Some of the seven disciples listening at that time conjectured that it meant John would never die! Some expositors hold that it spoke of Jesus coming for John at his physical death. Some believe that Messiah was referring to His return for the church; however, this is ludicrous, as it would mean that John would still be alive today and over two-thousand years old! It is obvious that the Lord Jesus has not yet returned for His church. For other comments on this subject regarding the death of John, see Section 104, number 4, under footnote i.

3p-"Follow thou me." This command was addressed first to Simon Peter. Nevertheless, it embraces our personal and individual place in the Great Commission. *It is not by accident that this is the final command spoken by the Lord Jesus in the four gospels.* What a way to conclude the story of His life! This directive confronts every dedicated, upright Christian on earth! All of us serve under this command; it often reflects the proverb, "at times less is better." This is the Great Commission, in a nutshell, embraced in the little word "thou" which includes every individual believer. The apostles' knowledge of their Lord's ascension, the church age, and so forth were almost unknown *at that time.* They were staggered with the mystery of His death and resurrection. *There was a meaning in what He said that was only understood by Him and them.* However, there is no mystery in the Savior's command, "Follow thou me." It is ours now, just as well as it was Peter's some two thousand years ago.

(r) The other six men sitting about the fire heard the conversation between Peter and the Lord Jesus; it was through them that the word of what He said was spread over the Christian community. As normal, it was altered from its original form and content. Soon, a wave of whispering swept through the churches of that day. Many of them believed that Jesus promised John he would not die until He had visibly returned to the world. See second paragraph of footnote q above for possible explanations of what this may have meant. It is no different today; things are altered from their original form into all sorts of exaggerations and perversions "among the brethren" over the passing of time. *This is one of the prime reasons that God led men to pen an inspired, trustworthy, and totally reliable record of His Word.*

(s) "We Know." These are the words of an outside witness (or several of them) who gave personal attestation to the truthfulness of this final chapter and all before it that John had written. Who this was is not stated. However, clearly, he or they were familiar with the ministry and works of the Lord Jesus. In ancient courts, the testimony of one that was an eye and ear witness, as John was of what he wrote, was held true and without question. Noticeably, this is seen in the pronoun "we." Other witnesses accompanied whoever added these two final verses for the line reads "we know that his [John's] testimony is true." Thus, here is the testimony of other believers to the trustworthiness of the history recorded in this book. This raises another question, "Why was this confirmation needed?" Was it because a tidal wave of forged letters bearing the names of the apostles of Christ had swept across the Christian community at this time?

(t) All the books about Jesus. If the *entire* life, Words, and works of Christ, were in printed from the number would be so voluminous that our minds would sink into dismay at any attempt to read them! The expression "many other things" embraced hundreds of thousands of deeds performed and Words spoken by our Lord that have not been written in Holy Scripture. John's statement may be understood as a large figure of speech so often heard among men today. However, it points to an undeniable historical reality.

2p-John's words about the world itself not being able to contain everything written in a book about Christ is an expression of greatness beyond human imagination. The ancients (as well as we today) continually use this method of verbal extremes in speaking of things outside the realm of mental comprehension. Did not our Lord say of Capernaum that it was "exalted unto heaven" (Matt. 11:23)? Only the most naive would think that the vast city was actually lifted up and went into the heavens or skies above. The human author of Hebrews wrote that the descendents of Abraham would be in a number as the "sand which is by the sea shore" (Heb. 11:12). We mortals have no other method to articulate greatness of incomprehensible proportions except by such extreme expressions. They are acceptable when kept within the bounds of propriety.

3p-*Gill's Commentary,* vol. 8, page 137 carries a fitting and helpful quotation from an ancient Jewish source known as Sir ha-shirim Rabba, 4:2. In this quotation, a rabbi is explaining the endless beauties and lessons found in the Torah Law. It reads, "If all the seas were ink, and the bulrushes pens, and the heavens and earth volumes, and all the children of men scribes, they [all] would not be sufficient to write the law which I have learned." Admittedly, this sounds faintly similar to the confession of John about the many things Jesus did and said. Did the ex-fisherman borrow this old rabbinical expression as he concluded his book to explain the greatness of his Savior's life and deeds? It has been noticed that the above ancient Jewish quotation is also similar to part of the third verse in the beautiful Christian hymn written in 1917 by Frederick M. Lehman, *"The Love of God."*

(u) "Amen." For information regarding the shocking abuse of this beautiful benediction, see Section 46, Matt. 6:13, the seventh paragraph of footnote g.

988

FIFTH AND FINAL MENTION OF THE GREAT COMMISSION.

(For a chronology of the Commission, refer to Section 201, the symbol ● by Lk. 24:47.)

This Section contains the last instructions of the Savior to His apostles on the day of His ascension. These verses add a few more ascension details found only in Acts that are not recorded by Matthew, Mark, or John. Luke wrote an earlier, but brief version of the departure of Christ and the subsequent actions of the disciples in Section 207, Lk. 24:50-53. Between the fourth and fifth version of the Commission, the apostles-disciples had to walk the ninety miles south back to Jerusalem. As previously explained, this journey one way took about three days.

Time: Forty days after Jesus' resurrection and just before His ascension to heaven (Acts 1:1-3).

Some six years later, Peter made a brief reference to the Great Commission in Acts 10:42, while preaching to the household of the Roman officer Cornelius, and his men stationed at Caesarea. In this present Section, we move our harmonization out of the four gospels and into the book of Acts. This is because the story of His ascension is continued and concluded here with further details, recorded below and in Section 207. Refer to the second paragraph of footnote a below for more on this thought.

Matt.	Mk.	Lk.	John	Acts 1:4-8—*Near the Mount of Olives in the Bethany area*
				"Stay in Jerusalem until" 4 And, being assembled[a] together with *them,* commanded them that they should not depart from Jerusalem, but wait for the promise of the Father, "which," *saith he,* "ye have heard of me. 5 "For John truly baptized with water; but ye shall be baptized[b] with the Holy Ghost not many days hence." 6 When they therefore were come together, they asked of him, saying, "Lord, wilt thou at this time restore again the kingdom to Israel?"[c] 7 And he said unto them, "It is not for you to know the times or the seasons, which the Father hath put in his own power.[d] ***Great Commission given the fifth time***[e] **8 "But ye shall receive power, after that the Holy Ghost is come upon you: and ye shall be witnesses unto me both in Jerusalem, and in all Judaea, and in Samaria, and unto the uttermost part of the earth."[f]** (Verse 9 cont. in Section 207.)

Footnotes-Commentary

(a) **"Being assembled."** Luke dates *the time* when this gathering occurred in Acts 1:3, as being "after his [Jesus'] passion" or suffering on the cross. This same verse also states that it was during a period of "forty days" after His death and resurrection. Luke's record above reveals that it is now the end of this forty-day span. Jesus assembled with His apostles for the final time and admonished them to stay in Jerusalem until the promised Holy Spirit came upon them. The Savior had also explained this great event of Pentecost in length, while in the upper room. For comments on His earlier instructions about the Spirit coming in His fulness, given in the upper room the night before His death, see Section 175, John 14:16-31, footnote j. Regarding the Holy Spirit during the Old Testament era, refer to Section 10, footnote b.

2p-**First sixty years of church history; joining Luke with Acts.** If one will take the book of Luke (which begins about nine months before the birth of Christ and ends with His ascension), and connects it with the first chapter of the book of Acts (which begins with His ascension and ends about thirty years later), he will have an outline of the first sixty years of church history. The entire record, though brief, is inspired and trustworthy in every detail. Learned critics relish finding "disconnections," "anachronisms," "human revelation," and "spurious additions," in the Bible. They object that there is no straightforward chronology of the life of Christ and the early church. As explained above, Luke's two letters to his friend Theophilus give us this chronology. In Luke, we learn what Jesus did through His human body while on earth. In Acts, we read what He did through His mystic body, the church, or spiritual kingdom. The second was made possible because of the first. If we had records of everything that happened to the first Christians across the six decades of Luke and Acts, we would have thousands of books to read instead of two! *As with everything recorded in the Bible, God in mercy has given us condensed versions.* Men who will not believe the Scripture would not be persuaded if one rose from the dead and tried to convince them (Lk.

16:31). Christ called these people "fools and slow of heart" in Lk. 24: 25. Surely, the Son of God was not "name calling" when He said this. Men today, who refuse to believe God's Word are also fools, according to Jesus Christ.

(b) **"But ye shall be baptized."** The lesson here is that there was a baptism different from that which was witnessed-administered by John Baptist. A perusal of what John preached reveals that he understood and foresaw the coming fullness of the Spirit at Pentecost. This is clear by his words in Matt. 3:11. Our Lord first *intimated* to His disciples the coming of the Spirit in *fullness* over two years ago as seen in Section 118, Lk. 11:13, footnote h. About six months before His death, He again spoke briefly of this at the Feast of Tabernacles in Section 119, John 7:37-39, footnotes q and r. His detailed exposition on the coming Spirit to His apostles was given in the upper room the night before the morning of the cross. This is in Sections 175, 176 and 177. On the Sunday night after His resurrection, He also mentioned it to the ten apostles (Thomas not being present). Now, it is ten days before Pentecost, the day when the Holy Spirit came, and Christ still impresses upon the minds of His disciples their need to be "baptized with the Holy Ghost" (Acts 1:5). We should not overlook the fact that the "baptism of the Spirit" in verse 5, was also called being "filled with the Spirit" after it occurred in Acts 2:4. *Even though this is true, later there was a clear distinction made between the baptizing and filling of the Spirit.* This is found in the letters of Paul. Refer to second paragraph of footnote e below.

2p-**"Not many days hence."** This refers to the ten days from the end of the "forty days" (Acts 1:3), until the day of Pentecost, which came exactly ten days later. The Torah Law had fixed a period of fifty days from the "morning after the Sabbath when the sheaf was waved before the Lord" (which pointed to the resurrection of Jesus) until the day of Pentecost (Lev. 23:15-16). See footnote c below for more on this thought. The Jews celebrated the Feast of Pentecost to commemorate Moses receiving the law on Mount Sinai. During this event, the people and religious leaders read the book of Ruth. It was a *compulsory* one day celebration (Deut. 16:16). Devout Jews from all over the known world of that era were present by the hundreds of thousands. This great attendance is reflected in Luke's words, "out of every nation under heaven" (Acts 2:5).

(c) **The old question again: Israel and the literal kingdom.** It is now ten days before the coming of the Spirit in His fullness at Pentecost. Christ has risen, and they have all seen many infallible proofs of this over the past forty days and nights. Yet, the apostles are still looking for Israel's literal, material, and political kingdom headed up by Messiah! Numerous times in this harmony commentary, we have pointed out how this became the major problem with all pious Jews in accepting Jesus as their Messiah. Their big question was *"Why doesn't He establish our Jewish kingdom and rule the world?"* Like the scribes, Pharisees, and other religious rulers, the Savior's eleven apostles (Judas was dead at this time) and other disciples did not yet understand the spiritual manifestation of His kingdom or the church. Christ affirms that the time for His future kingdom to be is hidden in the counsels of God. *It should be stressed that it remains there to this day.* Dates and date setting are both foolish and often destructive to the cause of our Lord. Continued comments on this deceiving mania are found in footnote d below. For Christ's explanation before Governor Pilate of what His kingdom was, see Section 183, John 18:36, footnote q.

(d) **"It is not for you to know."** This conclusive statement should be memorized by those who continually call our attention to the "signs that point to the soon coming of Christ." An example of this is the recent book *10 Reasons Why Jesus Is Coming Soon,* compiled by John Van Diest. The author would have been wise to leave off the word "soon," for neither, he nor any man on earth knows how soon our Lord will return for His people. End-time specialists "reading the signs" have existed for almost two thousand years. Without exception, their calculations have been wrong every time. How striking that even at this point the eleven apostles still did not understand God's plan for His spiritual kingdom, which was the church. They were sure the literal kingdom would be established immediately. When God sees the time is right to "restore the kingdom to Israel," it will not be revealed to some "end-time fanatic," who is drunk on signs, which he sees through rose-colored glasses of eschatological illusions. *Surely, if there were no divine plan for the kingdom to be restored to Israel, the Lord Jesus would have corrected such a gross error before returning to heaven.* The context here is clear that He did no such thing. However, on the other side of the fence, we may be sure that this kingdom, restored again to the saved people of Israel, will be very different from the wild interpretations given to it by certain "signs specialists." Our Lord's Words remain true after some two thousand years that "It is not for you to know." They remain hidden in the mind of God, and the prudent man dares not venture into this forbidden realm. How helpful it would be to the cause of Christ if some of these people would surrender to the words of David when he confessed, "*Such* knowledge *is* too wonderful for me; it is high, I cannot *attain* unto it" (Ps. 139:6). See Section 171, second through fifth paragraphs of footnote b for comments on the kind of kingdom it will *not* be!

2p-Considering further the apostles' inquiry, we must remember that the Jews associated the coming of the Holy Spirit with the restoration of their kingdom. The rabbis based this on Ezekiel's vision of dry bones, where God promised the scattered nation that He would put His Spirit or breath in them, and they would live again in their land (Ezek. 37:6,12-14). Contextually, since Christ had commanded them to wait for the coming Spirit, they may have made this connection with these verses in Ezekiel, hence the reason for their question. The rabbis taught that the Spirit departed from Israel with the completion of the book of Malachi, and that He would return with the appearing of their Messiah. This is explained in Section 25, footnote c. Again, we note that at this late hour, just before their Lord ascended to heaven, they were still looking for their physical political kingdom with Israel ruling the world. This reveals that they had failed up to this time to understand what their Lord had taught them regarding this subject. For details on the kingdom and its several manifestations, see Section 39, footnotes a and g. On the day of Pentecost, with the coming of the Spirit, the apostles, *then* and continually afterward, understood everything Christ had previously said. With the fullness of the Holy Spirit, it all came into bright and perfect focus. This is exactly what He had promised them in the upper room, as recorded in Section 175, John 14:26, footnote n. For more on the *exclusive* powers of the apostles, see the main heading under Section 110 and relative footnotes.

(e) In verse 8, we have the fifth and final mention of the Great Commission spoken by the Lord Jesus to His disciples just before His ascension. It was given forty days *after* His resurrection and ten days *before* Pentecost. The original command for witnessing as embodied in the Great Commissions was first given by Messiah on the night of the Resurrection Day. See the main heading of Section 201. The second giving of the Commission is recorded in Section 203, the third in 204, and the fourth in Section 205. Thus, it is recorded in Scripture. See asterisk under main heading above for a later mention of the Great Commission spoken by Peter at the house of Cornelius.

2p-Here again, the Savior emphasized the necessity for His preachers and missionaries to be Spirit-filled servants. Like the proverb, "The ax head does the cutting but the handle provides the power." One without the other creates a hopeless situation. The filling of the Holy Spirit does not involve obscenities, vulgar anatomical postures, falling to the floor, crawling and barking like dogs, covering naked legs and thighs with blankets, leaping in the air, or speaking gibberish with "interpretations" following. God's work has never been accomplished in the might of man's wisdom or the weird abilities of the flesh. For the very inappropriate slang term so popular today, "drunk in the Spirit," see Section 27, footnote k. *Scripture teaches there are many fillings of the Spirit for believers, but only one baptism, which puts them into the body or church (Eph. 4:5; 1 Cor. 12:13).* Thousands of believers existed prior to Pentecost in the form of the saved Old Testament saints. At Pentecost, all believers were put into the "household of God" and made "fellow citizens" with the already existing saints (Eph. 2:12-22). As stated elsewhere in this work, from this time forward, the saved were often referred to as the kingdom of God and Christ. This is seen in ten following passages: Acts 8:12, 14:22, 19:8, 20:25, 28:23, 30-31; Rom. 14:17; 1 Cor. 6:9; Col. 1:13, and 4:11. Slowly, the noun "church" gradually became the predominate term used to describe believers in Christ.

3p-It is a heinous error to teach that water baptism by immersion, sprinkling, pouring, infusion, or whatever puts one into the true body of Christ, His church or spiritual kingdom. If this is so, millions of unsaved rouges (including Karl Marx and Adolf Hitler, sprinkled as Lutherans, and Joseph Stalin as Russian Orthodox) are in heaven! Admittance into the select and elected company of God's redeemed is the sovereign work of the Holy Spirit performed through repentance of sin and faith in the Lord Jesus Christ as personal Savior. It is open to whosoever will. There is no other way given among men whereby one may be saved (Acts 4:12). Sick preaching-teaching produces sick saints, who toy with sin, live carnal lives, court the evil of the world, do not walk in the fear of God, and cannot effectively witness for Christ. In the workplaces of life, they stand for nothing and fall for everything.

4p-**Dead pulpits.** These have emptied houses of worship and Sunday school rooms across America. It is no wonder that so many children and young people hate the church. They are bored stiff amid its dead formalism and colorful but empty pageantry of religion *without* Christ. Mega churches springing up over the land, where men do not hear the Word of God in its totality, are producing "sickly saints" whose lives are not much different from the unsaved world. Spirit filled pastors and evangelists of yesteryear, who cracked down on sin, and laid out God's requirements for practical holiness are vanishing from the scene. Now, everyone must be "happy" and "feel good about themselves." The groans and wailings of men, *lost in sin*, dangling over eternal hell, calling on the Name of the Lord have become coldly silent. These echoes from centuries past have been gradually replaced by a "sing out," "clap out," "dance out," "wiggle out," and big time upbeat to the tune of the "young people's band" amid a "praise service." The shadowy spirit of a worldly "night club presentation" often oozes out of the actions of the *extreme* contemporary movements. The blessed Son of God is courted with a troublesome familiarity that reveals the congregation is ignorant of who He is. Jesus Christ is not "our buddy." Rather, He is the God of heaven manifested in human flesh to become *both* our Lord and Savior. *In short, it is "the Christ of God or hell."* A pending disaster hangs over America because of these things enacted in the Name of Jesus, while the religious stoics continue in their sin. Worship practices are being built on *feelings* instead of *needs* as revealed in the pages of Scripture. On the other side, among the "Bible believing churches," their program of three hymns, one choir number, announcements, prayer, take up the offering, then a special, followed by a well-planned sermon is not changing people's lives. They exit as they entered, having learned something new but unable or unwilling to ingest it into their daily lives as professing Christians. *(This is not to decry order in the service of God.)*

5p-**After He comes upon you.** This cannot mean that these men did not have the Spirit of God (Rom. 8:9). Rather, it has reference to His *fullness* coming into their lives at Pentecost. When the Holy Ghost sent down from heaven, again superintends the work of God, things will wonderfully change and the humdrum of another hour of religious boredom will vanish. This was the dynamic of the first and early churches. The anointing of the Spirit in which God's work must be done is so conspicuously absent that it paves the way for the death of many local assemblies. When Zechariah inquired as to how God's temple would be built amid the sin and devastation of that era, the answer then is the same now, "Not by might, nor by power, but by my Spirit, saith the LORD of hosts" (Zech. 4:6).

6p-"Witnesses unto me." The word "witnesses" is from "martyrdom." Christ warns His little flock that they will be martyrs in His service. There is evidence from history that all of His apostles died by martyrdom, except the apostle John. Here, a new missionary work-plan was laid out by the Savior, which revealed the geographical areas where the first missionaries were to start and move through, as they carried the gospel to the known world of their generation. It was as follows:

1. **"In Jerusalem."** Chapter 1 through 7 of Acts reveals they completed this part of the task.
2. **"And in all Judaea and Samaria."** Acts 8 through 12 briefly explains how they covered these areas.
3. **"And unto the uttermost part of the earth**." Acts 13 through 28 reflects that the first church and churches fulfilled this part of the Great Commission in their age. See the story of the first and early Christians carrying the saving gospel to their generations before the fatal doom of A.D. 70. This wonder is explained in Section 163, third paragraph of number 16, under footnote f.

7p-Regarding the gospel being *originally* known to all of humanity, and the perversion of it over the centuries after the Tower of Babel, see Section 1, Part 2, and all of footnote f for the details. Because the gospel is "the power of God unto salvation to everyone that believes" (Rom. 1:16), it has been attacked, changed, altered, revised, added to, taken from, reworked, mitigated, revamped, refaced, defaced, and distorted in general by Satan and his crowd. Nevertheless, it remains valid and still saves all who repent of their sins and believe it (Mk. 1: 15).

8p-God does not save men in their sins, and they continue in them, but saves them from sin. Millions have been taught, "Just believe in Jesus and everything will be all right." Hence, local assemblies are loaded with men, women, young people, and even children who have never been saved. A "belief" in the Son of God that does not result in a changed and then gradually changing life is a false belief or faith. This newness or change will vary between older men and children, or younger persons at conversion to Christ; nevertheless, it will be there in whatever appropriate degree (Lk. 7:47). This does not discount the fact that some may (through toying with sin) gradually drift out of fellowship (not relationship) with God and their Savior. However, if they were originally saved God will pursue a *variety* of methods to bring them back to Himself, either in life or through death. For further details on this overlooked or neglected subject, see Section 46, eleventh paragraph, footnote g.

9p-The easy believism of today, where people walk the isle, shake a deacons hand, fill out a card, and they are hailed as "Christians" is satanic deceit. The Son of God told the factious, quarrelsome, hate filled Jews, "Except ye repent, ye shall all likewise perish" (Lk. 13:3, 5). He affirmed to a chief leader of religion in the nation of Israel, "Except a man be born again, he cannot see the kingdom of God" (John 3:3). John the revelator wrote this horrifying statement, "And whosoever was not found written in the book of life was cast into the lake of fire" (Rev. 20:15). Some seven hundred years before Christ, the prophet Isaiah put this question to the wicked people of his day, "Who among us shall dwell with the devouring fire? Who among us shall dwell with everlasting burnings?" (Isa. 33:14)? At a terrible universal reckoning yet to come the Judge and King of all men will judicature this terrible sentence, "Depart from me, ye cursed, into everlasting fire, prepared for the devil and his angels" (Matt. 25:41).

10p-It is not true that all godless men die begging for mercy. The Devil is too clever for that one! However, it is true that men, be they good or bad who die in their sins without the Lord Jesus Christ, die damned (John 8:21). Only those who names are written in the "Lamb's book of life" will enter heaven after death (Rev. 21:27).

(f) Great Commission in the Twenty–First Century. The world of the apostles and early church is not the world of today. The first Christians were humble fundamentalists in the *correct* meaning of the word. They went, worked, and built churches of redeemed men and women. It was not with bricks, mortar, and a bank debt of two million dollars hanging over their heads! The culture, legal, economic, religious, and political systems in which they lived and died would destroy most believers today. Now, the Great Commission is subjected to electronics, jets, personal media players, cell phones, smart phones, power point presentations, currency exchanges, passports, visas, language school, computer software, retirement funds, hospitalization insurance, bank transfers, and the rest. *Technology has exceeded our humanity!* The first missionaries never forgot that it was only by the power of the Holy Spirit and the gospel of Christ that men were genuinely saved from hell. Among the many things that have changed in today's world, Christians may justifiably change with *some* of them but not all. Some things that have not changed are lost souls, Satan, sin, the authority of God's Word, man's utter depravity, and the old rugged cross. Brains alone will not get the job done; devotion, love, full self-sacrifice to Christ and fellow men will.

2p-Often, young men and women graduating from college or seminary, armed with their masters or doctorate, believe they are ready to take on the world. Sadly, the world often takes them on! Never have academics, oratory, great learning, and worldly-wise tactics brought men to the new birth in Christ. *This does not decry the need for proper education, order, necessary training, and arrangement in the Master's service.* Nevertheless, the first warning priority was penned by the prophet of old, "Cursed *be* the man that trusteth in man, and maketh flesh his arm, and whose heart departeth from the LORD" (Jer. 17:5). This admonition remains valid today. The Great Commission of the Twenty-First Century clashes head on with certain unalterable facts of changing human history.

CHAPTER 20

THE LORD JESUS ASCENDS TO HEAVEN.

His earthly work completed, Christ returns to the Father and takes up His exalted offices as the only eternal High Priest and King for the saved of Adam's race.

Time: His ascension forty days after the resurrection.

Near the Mount of Olives in the Bethany area

Matt.	Mk. 16:19	Lk. 24:50–52	Acts 1:3 and 9–12
		▶ *Some six years later in the house of Cornelius, Peter made it clear that the Savior appeared only to the chosen apostles, not all the people (Acts 10:40-43).* *The "forty days" are explained on the next page marked by the symbol* ◉.	3 To whom ◀ [the apostles] also he shewed himself alive after his passion [suffering and death] by many infallible proofs, being seen of them ◀ forty days . . .
			Acts 1:9–12
	Farewell little flock 19 So then after the Lord had spoken unto them,	*Farewell little flock* 50 And he led them out as far as to Bethany,(a) and he lifted up his hands, and blessed them. 51 And it came to pass, while he blessed them, he was parted(b) from them, and carried up into heaven.	*Farewell little flock* 9 And when he had spoken these things, while they beheld,
	he was received up(b) into heaven,		he was taken up;(b) and a cloud received him out of their sight.
	and sat on the right hand of God.		*The promise of angels:* *"He will come again"* 10 And while they looked stedfastly toward heaven as he went up, behold, two men stood by them in white apparel; 11 Which also said, "Ye men of Galilee,(c) why stand ye gazing up into heaven? this same Jesus, which is taken up from you into heaven, shall so come in like manner as ye have seen him go into heaven.
		Back to Jerusalem 52 And they worshipped him, and returned to Jerusalem with great joy:	*Back to Jerusalem* 12 Then returned they unto Jerusalem from the mount called Olivet, which is

993

Matt.	Mk. 16:20		Lk. 24:53	Acts 1:12–14
				from Jerusalem a Sabbath day's journey.[(d)]
				United in holy prayer the eleven wait on God
				13 And when they were come in, [to the city] they went up into an upper room, where abode both Peter,[(e)] and James, and John, and Andrew, Philip, and Thomas, Bartholomew, and Matthew, James *the son* of Alphaeus, and Simon Zelotes, and Judas *the brother* of James.[(f)]
				Last picture in Scripture of Jesus' mother and half-brothers together
			Before Pentecost	**14** These all continued with one accord in prayer and supplication, with the women, and Mary the mother of Jesus, and with his brethren.[(g)]
	After Pentecost		**53** And were continually in the temple,[(h)] praising and blessing God. **Amen.**[(j)]	
	20 And they went forth, and preached every where, the Lord working with *them*, and confirming the word with signs following.[(i)] **Amen.**[(j)]			

◉ **An explanation of the "forty days."** If one considers the history surrounding the death and post resurrection events in the life of Christ, the "forty days" of Acts 1:3 constitute profound demonstrations that He rose from the grave. Christ's human body was crucified on a Roman cross and expired some six hours later. A centurion pierced His side with a spear "and forthwith came there out blood and water." Joseph and Nicodemus un-nailed His corpse from the cross and only partially buried it. Certain women came to complete the process of Jewish burial but were cut short by the approaching Sabbath at sundown. Roman soldiers sealed and guarded His tomb. The women returned after the Sabbath, early Sunday morning to complete their task. Not one of His chosen apostles knew that He would die on a cross, though He had foretold them of this many times. Their subsequent actions reveal they did not understand He would rise again. During His ministry, He raised others from the dead; not one of these had to convince his friends that he had returned from eternity! All who saw those that Christ raised had no doubt of their resurrections. Second opinions were not required. Neither the widow's son at Nain, Jairus' daughter, nor Lazarus had to shew [prove] themselves alive." However, the Lord Jesus did. He appeared first to Mary Magdalene, to the men on Emmaus road, to the ten with Thomas being absent, and then to the eleven with Thomas being present. After that, He came to the eleven on a mountain in Galilee. Then, He appeared to over five hundred brethren at once, which seemingly occurred on a mountain. With all this, they still doubted! Afterward, the seven who returned to fishing in Lake Tiberius or Galilee also saw Jesus. He also appeared to James alone (1 Cor. 15:7). Lastly, all the eleven visibly witnessed His ascension back to the Father in heaven. There were at *least* eleven post resurrection appearances of Christ to His disciples and the eleven apostles. (Some expositors believe there were twelve.) He had eaten in their presence; showed them His glorified wounds of redemption; they had touched Him in order to remove all possibilities that it was a spirit or phantom apparition. Being "seen of them forty days," does not mean He was with them continually over this period, but rather, that He appeared intermittently. During these times, He spoke to them of His kingdom and its affairs. This cannot mean a millennial kingdom over two thousand years later! "Many infallible proofs" given *after* His resurrection are far more than the eleven listed in the four gospels.

The number forty is a remarkable numeric across Scripture. It is the number of probation. The world-wide flood was forty days (Gen. 7:17); Moses was alone with God on the terrible mount forty days (Ex. 24:18); the Hebrew nation tramped through the wilderness for forty years being proven of God (Deut. 8:2); the spies searched out Canaan forty days (Num. 13:25), and Goliath presented himself to mock God and Israel's armies for forty days (1 Sam. 17:16). Elijah had his forty days of super strength from one meal (1 Kings 19:8); Ezekiel bore the iniquity of the house of Judah for forty days (Ezek. 4:6); Nineveh had forty days to repent (Jonah 3:4); and Jesus was tempted as a human forty days and nights in the wilderness (Lk. 4:2). It is no accident that He walked among His followers for forty days in the post resurrection period. About forty years after His ascension came the doom of A.D. 70, which was the destruction of Jerusalem, the magnificent temple and demise of the Jewish state.

Several hundred years after the death of Christ, unbelieving Jews penned a lie about His crucifixion in their Talmud tractate, Sanhedrin 43a. It reads, "On the even of the Passover Yeshu [a blasphemous and deliberate misspelling of the Name Jesus] was hanged [on a cross]. For forty days before the execution took place, a herald went forth and cried, 'He is going to be stoned because he practiced sorcery and enticed Israel to go to apostasy. Anyone who can say anything in his favor let him come forward and plead on his behalf.' But since nothing was brought forward in his favor, he was hanged [crucified] on the even of the Passover." This was the standard procedure followed before any person was executed by the decision of the Sanhedrin. In the case of Jesus, there was no herald calling for someone to defend the Savior or speak in His favor. The compilers of the Talmud added this untruth to mitigate the Sanhedrin's guilt in participating in the death of Jesus the Messiah. An explanation of the Sanhedrin and how it worked is given in *Appendix Five*. Regarding who killed Jesus, see Section 153, footnote f.

For details on the Talmud slandering Jesus and Christianity, see Section 6, second and third paragraphs of footnote d. The fact that Jesus spent forty days proving to His disciples that He had risen constitutes irrefutable evidence that He did! Was this God's way of divinely heralding over the world and to all ages that His Son's resurrection from the dead literally occurred? Evil men and devils fiercely hate this truth; it spells their doom someday at the judgment bar of God and reveals that Christianity is the world's only true religion. Which other of history's millions of religions has the Savior, who conquered sin, defeated death, the grave, and hell, and lives victorious, forever more? Where is the prophet, guru, or founder of any religion that can say, "Fear not; I am the first and the last. *I am* he that liveth, and was dead; and, behold, I am alive for evermore, Amen; and have the keys of [authority over] hell and of death" (Rev. 1:17-18)? Only the Son of God can make this claim. He alone is the supreme Lord and Savior of humankind. *Never do men speak of, "The late Jesus Christ, who lived centuries ago!"*

Footnotes-Commentary

(a) **"As far as Bethany"** which, according to John 11:18 was about "fifteen furlongs" (two miles) east of Jerusalem. He was then "received up," "carried up," and "taken up." The ascension was the proper conclusion to the resurrection. The Son of God literally went up! This is not a word picture, myth, fable, or Hebrew imagination. It is reality. His high priestly prayer of John 17 was answered. After forty days and nights of convincing them that He was alive from the dead, the Savior returned to the Father in heaven. Following Pentecost, this living Redeemer was preached across the thirty-year history of Acts and believed in by thousands. His glorious resurrection became the sure pledge, guaranteeing that all who know Him as personal Lord and Savior are forgiven and become the children of God. The basis of the spiritual life of born again Christians is the life of Christ, which is forever. Because He lives, we live also (John 14:19).

2p-**"Lifted up his hands."** This was an ancient way of pronouncing blessing upon people or an object (1 Kings 8:22). Rabbis did this continually in the synagogue services and practice the same today over their congregations. Many Gentile Christians also lift their hands toward God in heaven for various reasons.

(b) **"He was taken up."** This means what it says. See footnote a above. As the Son of God entered human life through the womb of a virgin mother, with all the glory and mystery attached to that miracle, so at the end of His work, His return to the Father in heaven was enshrouded with wonder and ineffable glory. Gravity stepped back, and He went up! We are awe struck to read the first words the Father spoke to the Son upon His arrival back home again. A thousand years *before* Christ, David, in the Holy Spirit, heard in advance this welcome-home greeting to the Son. The psalmist wrote that God said to the Lord Jesus, "Sit thou at my right hand, until I make thine enemies thy footstool" (Ps. 110:1 with Mk. 12:36). We read in Heb. 10:12-13, "This man, after he had offered one sacrifice for sins for ever, sat down on the right hand of God." Paul wrote in Eph. 1:20 that God "raised him from the dead and set *him* at his own right hand in the heavenly *places*." With this, Ps. 24:9-10 were fulfilled when the "King of Glory came in." When the time is right, the Almighty will present before the world Jesus Christ, as the "blessed and only Potentate, the King of kings, and Lord of lords" (1 Tim. 6:15). It is then that "every knee should bow, of *things* in heaven, and *things* in earth, and *things* under the earth; and *that* every tongue should confess that Jesus Christ *is* Lord, to the glory of God the Father" (Phil. 2:10-11). Though unrecognized by the world now, He is nevertheless, "the King eternal" (1 Tim. 1:17). Quoting a prediction by Isaiah, Paul wrote that the reign of Christ is now operative in the lives of saved Gentiles (Isa. 11: 1, 11 with Rom. 15:12). The kingship-reign of Christ is not limited to the future, during a divine millennium. It has been for two thousand years and will extend through eternity (2 Tim. 2:2; Rev. 5:10, 11:15). In God's future, there is a unique, *glorified* kingly reign with redeemed Jews and Gentiles.

2p-In the Psalm's passage quoted above, God inducted His Son into the *eternal office* as heaven's exclusive high priest after the order (or similar to that) of ancient Melchizedek (Gen. 14:17-24). It is not by coincidence that Ps. 110:1 is the most quoted Old Testament verse found in the New Testament. It should be! It was the Father's "welcome home" to His Son, who had finished the work of man's eternal redemption. The verse regarding Christ's priesthood being modeled after that of Melchizedek is quoted *seven times* in the book of Hebrews. See Heb. 5:6, 10, 6:20, 7:11, 15, 17, and 21. Note Section 178 for our Lord's Prayer made at the temple the night before His death. In this supplication, He spoke of His place with the Father before the world was (John 17:5 and 24).

3p-**Verse 10. "Two men."** This literally, visibly happened. Perhaps these same men appeared at the empty tomb and announced to the women His resurrection. If so, they now affirm His ascension. Refer to Section 195, Lk. 24:4 for the two angels at the tomb early in the morning on that glorious first day of the week.

(c) "Ye men of Galilee." All of Christ's apostles were from the "cursed, ignorant, and backward state of Galilee," except the traitor Judas Iscariot. For explanation of this stigma cast on the citizens of Galilee, see Section 9, Lk. 1:26, footnote b. On Peter's Galilean accent getting him into serious trouble, see Section 181, Mk. 14:70, second paragraph of footnote o. The religious leaders of Jerusalem ridiculed men born in Galilee, yet angels from heaven gladly identify them as such. This demonstrates the difference between false religion and heavenly reality.

2p-**Pagan mythology.** As explained, it was replete with stories of "hero gods" ascending to some kind of heaven. These myths were inspired by demons in the minds of heathen priests and taught to the worshipers in their temples and shrines over the world. They were satanic counterfeits of the real ascension of Jesus Christ that was to come. For more on this lie that has poisoned human history, see Section 1, Part, 4, the third paragraph of footnote j.

3p-**"Shall so come."** Two holy angels promised that our Lord would return. Refer to verse 10 under footnote b above for the possible identity of these two men. Though it has been over two thousands years, since they spoke these words of hope, the Son of God will come again when the time is right. Few truths of Scripture have been abused as much as this one. Regardless, at a future time known only to the Holy Trinity, Jesus Christ will return. Note the words of Peter regarding those who mock and scorn the coming again of Christ (2 Peter 3:1-14).

(d) "A sabbath day's journey." What does this mean? The group departed Bethany and walked along the road westward to the near by Mount of Olives. Luke used the oral law measurement to explain the distance from here back to Jerusalem. No such thing as "a sabbath day's journey" is mentioned in the Torah Law. Again, we are introduced to another of those infamous oral traditions of the Jewish elders. After Israel's return from the Babylonian captivity of seventy years, in 536 B.C., the scribes added literally thousands of extra laws, rules, and commandments to their Torah Law. These were called "fences," or "hedges," and were built about the original commandments, their purpose being to prevent each succeeding generation of Jewish young people from getting to the actual Torah Laws and breaking them. One of these oral laws regulated how many steps a pious Jew could walk on the Sabbath and no more! A Sabbath day's journey was not to exceed 2,000 yards. The Pharisees based this self-made rule on a twisted interpretation of Ex. 16:9 and 21:13. Oddly, these verses have nothing to do with the Sabbath! They not only made thousands of rules but also invented ways to get around those they had made!

2p-**Hebrew hypocrisy.** Dr. F. W. Farrar in his work, *The Life of Christ*, pp. 748-750 gives an excellent review of the double standards employed by the Pharisees and their companions in breaking their own oral laws. In 1882, he wrote, "It was the custom of the Pharisees to join in "sysitia," or daily banquets, which they subjected to the most stringent conditions, and which they assimilate in all respects to priestly meals. However, their homes were often more than 2,000 yards from the place of meeting, and as the bearing of burdens on the Sabbath was strictly forbidden they would, without a little ingenuity, have been prevented from dining in common on the very day [Sabbath] on which they mostly desire it. On the evening before the Sabbath, they deposited food a distance of 2,000 feet from their houses, thus creating a fictitious home: from this they could go 2,000 yards farther to the place of meeting, thus giving them double the real distance!" On page 749, Farrar gives other examples of Jewish hypocrisy used to hedge their own traditions and oral rules. "If a Jew's ox is dying, he may kill it on a holy day, provided, he eats a piece of the meat as big as an olive, to make believe that it was killed for a necessary meal. If a Jew wants to buy something, which is sold by weight or measure on a holy day, he may do so, if he pays the next day, and does not mention the name, weight, or measure. He may buy from a butcher on a holy day, only he must not say, 'give me meat for money,' but only 'Give me a portion, or half a portion.'" It was all a wicked and ingenious farce! For further explanation of these mythical traditions and rules that have *nothing* to do with the great Torah Law of God, see Section 52, footnote h, Section 89, footnote c, and Section 96, footnote d. Christ fiercely condemned these rules.

Many Orthodox Jews today still attempt to live by these endless and impossible traditions. For an older but comprehensive view of Jewish fictions, see *Kitto's Bible Cyclopedia*, vol. iii, pages 722-723.

3p-Messiah disrupts and unites. Despite the Jew's professions of reverence for Scripture, many of their interpretations were designed to alter meanings, which they disliked or hated, especially if they spoke of the Messiah. In view of this, one is amazed at the attempt of certain historians and Messianic Jews to deny Farrar's list of impeccable facts of history concerning Jesus of Nazareth in paragraph two above. To shield the Christ hating Pharisees and their friends is tantamount to blasphemy. Refer to Section 159, for our Lord's personal evaluation of these men. There were a few exceptions such as Nicodemus and Joseph of Arimathaea. A few weeks after our Lord's resurrection, "a great company of priests were obedient to the faith" (Acts 6:7). This disrupted the day-by-day functions of the temple services. With the gigantic veil falling at the death of Christ, things dropped into a state of perpetual confusion. This only grew worse until the destruction of the city, temple, and Jewish state in A.D. 70.

(e) We last noted Peter and his companions up north on a mount in Galilee meeting with Jesus and afterwards back at Lake Galilee trying to fish again. See this in Sections 204 and 205. Now, they have again made the long trip south to Jerusalem. They are reunited with their Lord as He bids them farewell and returns to the Father.

(f) For details on the twelve apostles, see Section 57, footnotes g, k, l, and m.

(g) Upper room of prayer. These words paint a beautiful portrait. Some one hundred and twenty believers were now gathered in the holy art of prayer, immediately after their Lord returned to the Father. In this, they found solace and comfort. We are touched with deep pathos to read that Mary, the mother of Jesus, who is now under the care of John, was present along with her (former) Christ rejecting four sons. There is no mention of Jesus' half-sisters in this passage. This may signal that they were not present on this occasion, but we hardly think it means they were unbelievers in Messiah, who was their physical half-brother. For more on Jesus' human family, see Section 91, Matt. 13:55-57, footnote d and e for details. For the earlier sarcastic opposition of His four half-brothers during the Feast of Tabernacles, six months before the cross, refer to Section 111, John 7:5, footnotes b, c, and d. In the sacred and divine science of prayer, they all found peace and comfort amid their frustrations and fears.

(h) "Continually in the temple." *After* His ascension and the Feast of Pentecost ten days later, they are found in the Jerusalem temple giving thanks to God that their Messiah and Savior is alive forever more! The word "continually" means they were frequenting the temple location. During the ten days before Pentecost, they were hidden from the wrath of the Sanhedrin and sought God in prayer. "Praising and blessing God" had not been an experience during their final few weeks with Jesus. However, after Pentecost, it all changed and at last, they all understood the truth about Messiah. He died for their sins, rose, and has gone back to the Father. The questions they had in the upper room weeks ago are now being answered: they must praise God. Joy filled their hearts as Jesus had promised (John 16:20). At Pentecost, they were released into the highest level of happy service for Jesus their Messiah. Christ. *By the fullness of the Holy Spirit, they remembered and understood all the Savior had said to them.*

(i) "They went forth." "They" points to the early believers and apostles. *After* the Feast of Pentecost (which was ten days after His ascension) and their endowment with spiritual power, they moved forward preaching Christ. God confirmed or approved their message with the miraculous signs and wonders following as Christ had said in Mk. 16:17-18. With these verses, see also Heb. 2:3-4. Mark explains that the apostles began to fulfill the Great Commission that Jesus had given them. It was mentioned the final time in Section 206, Acts 1:8, just before His ascension. The prophet Isaiah had foretold some seven hundred years earlier that during the Messianic era many wonderful things would take place. This included healing the sick, mute tongues would speak anew, and the blind would see (Isa. 35:5-6). All this occurred during the ministry of Christ and His apostles, as well as some of the early disciples. These marvelous wonders were the fulfillment of Isaiah's predictions.

2p-"Signs following." For more details on this, see Section 203, number 6, under footnote c. Luke penned Acts of the Apostles about thirty years after the ascension of Christ. He wrote looking back on history and confirmed that, "many wonders and signs were done by the apostles" (Acts 2:43 with 4:29-30). It happened just as Jesus said, "And by the hands of the apostles were many signs and wonders wrought among the people . . ." (Acts 5:12). Various TV Prime Time preachers tell us that they do the same things in their work. In 2007, a famed German evangelist claimed on national television, "Over three million people were saved in my African campaigns." The author of this work, having lived in Africa for years, knows that if this many of the African people had been saved, the entire nation would have been turned upside down! *This was more exaggerated charismatic rhetoric.* These people assure us that they are "healing the sick, curing the blind, filling teeth, raising the dead, making the lame to walk, amid signs and wonders." Realistically, they seem unfamiliar to the effects of sin, human suffering, sickness, disease, and misery. They cannot do what Jesus and His apostles did while on earth. Their claims are phony, false, and fake. Sincerity apart from the truth is one of the most dangerous things on earth. See this illustrated in Section 95, sixth paragraph of footnote r. If God did heal some suffering person, it was in spite of their preaching, not because of it, for they do not preach the *whole truth* on these issues. Their credulous statements bring reproach on the cause of Christ and give the wicked occasion to blaspheme the work of God. One wishes they would send a team of "faith healers" to Saint Jude's Children's Hospital in Memphis, Tennessee, and demonstrate their supernatural gifts. Like American politicians who make big noises about starving children, they too live in million dollar mansions, fly over the country in private jets, and bask in their wealth. The Savior they fain to represent had no place to lay His head (Matt. 8:20). For Christ bearing our sicknesses, refer to Section 41, Matt. 8:17, footnote h.

3p-"We do the works of Jesus and His apostles." This flamboyant claim is pompous verbiage in the light of God's Word and the facts of church history. Each of us may do what God gives strength and grace to do. *He has never intended for all men to perform the same duties in His service.* "For as we have many members in one body and all members have not the same office" (Rom. 12:4). "For the body [of Christ] is not one member, but many" (1 Cor. 12:14). Whether it is a gifted preacher, a missionary on the foreign field, a widow shut away in her room, a busy housewife, hard toiling husband, little child, or a teenager in prayer, all of us can serve Christ where we are. It is not how much we give that counts, but *what* we give; even spending our lives for Christ and the needs of others. This is the final and grand goal of Christian human existence. The ancient historian Eusebius (died A.D. 340) in *Ecclesiastical History*, V: 7 wrote that various signs and miracles were still seen "in some of the churches" during the life of Irenaeus (died A.D. 220). In 1918, the Reformed minister, Benjamin B. Warfield foresaw, the rise in certain churches, of those claiming miraculous gifts, the ability to perform miracles, and supernatural wonders. These people teach that the unique gifts of the Holy Spirit are operative today for everyone. Warfield's book *Counterfeit Miracles* gives an excellent coverage of this subject. The section on Faith Healing, pages 157-196 is a classic response to the naivety that dominates these groups. Warfield's *Miracles Yesterday and Today* is also helpful. In some places, he goes too far with his assessment, denying that any miracles occurred after the decease of the apostles. In 2009, Andrew Dauton-Fear published *Healing in the Early Church: The Church's Ministry of Healing and Exorcising from the First to the Fifth Century.* He shows how various supernatural things intermittently occurred among Christians for some five centuries after the apostles. These fluctuated over the years and slowly vanished. In this present era, divine miracles are the *rare* exceptions and not the rule. The approximate twenty-six gifts of the Spirit as listed in Mk. 16:17-18: Rom. l2:6-8: Eph. 4:8-12; and 1 Cor. 12:4-11 are not all operative today. Regarding the healing and tongues groups involved in snake handling, see Section 203, all of footnote e. All "supernatural" things are of God. Some have their origin in the Devil (Matt. 7:21-23 with Rev. 13:13).

4p-Miracles? The astounding miracles performed by the apostles served to help establish the first church and churches, but were not necessary for its permanent maintenance. Christ's miracles were not for *all believers* to perform over the ages and continue doing so to this day. It has been explained across these pages that His astounding deeds were intended as demonstrable and irrefutable proof that He was the true Messiah of Israel. For explanation of this, see Section 5, footnotes a and d, and Section 48, italicized paragraph under main heading.

(j) "The abuse of Amen." Regarding the abuse of this blessed benediction of verbal affirmation used so much by Christians, over the world, see Section 46, Matt. 6:13, the seventh paragraph of footnote g.

Conclusion

This final Section 207 concludes with our Lord's return to the Father in heaven and Eight Appendices to follow. Between His visible presence and us, a cloud still hangs. However, the sure eye of faith pierces it. The incense of prayer penetrates its substance, showering the dews of many blessings upon our lives, bringing good cheer to weary hearts. Even better, God has given us the indwelling Holy Spirit. He provides a nearer sense of His presence, a closer enfolding in the arms of His tenderness, than we could have enjoyed had we lived with Him in the home at Nazareth or walked with Him over the roads of Galilee. Still dearer, we touch His pierced feet and sense the warmth of His great heart when we kneel in pilgrim prayer before heaven's throne of grace.

The noises of a sin-maddened world and the dull hearing of many lost souls press hard upon us. Thankfully, the Savior's gentle call, "Come unto me all *ye* that labour and are heavy laden, and I will give you rest" (Matt. 11:28) still captures wanting, willing hearts. Across the whole of "Christian America" and the western world, the dark insolence and blasphemy of scoffing tongues defy the God of heaven, ridicule His Son, and scorn the Bible. A billion times daily, their Holy Names are abused in profanity, cursing, and shame. O the unfathomable depth of man's ingratitude, the mastery of sin, and depravity of the human heart. Only the miracle of the new birth by the grace of God can correct humankind's wretched ills. While men curse their way into hell the union of the humanity and deity of Christ remain indissoluble and eternal! He is forever "Lord of all." To Him, all mortals will answer.

Soon life will be over. Now, is the time to prepare for death and eternity. To those who read these final words, I plead, if you are unsaved trust Jesus the Messiah as your personal Lord and Savior. God has given you a clear invitation in the Bible, "For whosoever shall call upon the name of the Lord shall be saved" (Rom. 10:13). *Stop, now, call upon His Name, and by faith receive Jesus Christ as your personal Lord and Savior.* With this, God receives you into the blessed number of whom it is written, "He that hath the Son hath life; *and* he that hath not the Son of God hath not life" (1 John 5:12). Then, spend the remaining days of earth's little while serving Him. How beautiful is the life that has been a harmony commentary of the four gospels, pointing others to the Son of God and bringing wherever possible, help, hope, and good cheer to those in need. This is true Christianity.

SELAH! "THINK OF THAT."

The author: Missionary Henry R. Pike.

APPENDICES

APPENDIX ONE

HOW LONG WAS JESUS' BODY IN THE TOMB?

The Hebrew methods of dividing days and nights

The numerous repetitions in this Appendix are intentional. Their design is to imbed this lesson into the mind of the amiable but serious reader. When the Savior said that His physical body would be, "Three days and nights in the heart of the earth" (Matt. 12:40), what did He mean? This first Appendix is an attempt to reasonably answer this question. The ancient Jews reckoned time differently from how we of the western world do two thousand years later. With them, a new day always started at sundown, even though there was darkness, it was still called the beginning of a new day. This day ended at the next sundown. Their basis for this was Gen. 1:5, "The evening and the morning were the first day." With the setting of the sun, regardless of what season of the year it was, a new day began. As stated, this new day lasted until sunset the following day. Hence, the Savior's Words, "Are there not twelve hours in the day? If any man walks in the day, he stumbleth not, because he seeth the light [sun] of this world" (John 11:9). Jews divided daytime into four periods of three hours each, totaling twelve hours:

The first period was counted from sunup at 6 a.m. until the third hour at 9 a.m.

The second was from 9 a.m. until noon.

The third period was from noon until 3 p.m.

Fourth, there was the span from 3 p.m. until 6 o'clock sundown. These four periods calculate into a total of twelve hours just as our Lord stated above in John 11:9.

Similarly, the Jewish night time starting at sundown, was also divided into four equal parts called "watches." These four parts amounted to twelve hours as demonstrated below.

The first watch began at sunset and lasted until 9 p.m.

The second was from 9 p.m. until midnight.

The third watch, which was from midnight until 3 a.m.

The fourth period was from 3 a.m. until sunrise or about 6 a.m. in the morning. The time of sunrise and sunset varied somewhat depending on the seasons of the year. However, Jewish time measurements remained the same.

The Jews had a twelve-hour night and a twelve-hour day, both totaling more or less a period of twenty-four hours. (Pious Orthodox Jews still attempt to maintain this time schedule.) They counted the shortest part of a day as being the whole day; this included the night before as well. For example, if a king took his throne on the last day of December of whatever year, later, when his royal history was written it was stated that he had ruled all that year, while, in fact, he had ruled only one day. *They just did things that way!* Another example of this is found in the Parable of The Laborers and how their wages were paid (Section 140, Matt. 20:1-16). Those who worked only a few hours were paid the same as those who had toiled all the day (verses 8-15). A few hours labor was counted as all day by the landowner. He even said his actions were "lawful" (verse 15). Whether our western minds can accept this or not, changes nothing; this is how the ancient Israelis reckoned time.

To understand the chronology of how long Jesus' body lay in the tomb, Jewish time must be first comprehended and applied to the event or otherwise an error will result and the computation will be incorrect. Simply put; use their time and we will find the answer to the question above.

Three Old Testament examples of Jewish time calculating

First, in 2 Chron. 10:5 and 12, the Hebrew method of counting time is depicted. The event described here took place about nine hundred years before the birth of Christ. In the context, Jeroboam and all Israel served an ultimatum to young King Rehoboam. They wanted to know what kind of rule he would place upon them as his prospective subjects. He answered, "Come again unto me after three days" (verse 5). It was "*after*" a three daytime period that Israel was ordered to return for their new king's verdict. We read in verse 12, "So Jeroboam, and all the people came to Rehoboam on the third day." It is sure they did not come to the king after sundown, which would have been into the fourth day. (Each Jewish day started at this time.) The text reads they appeared before their king "on the third day." However, according to verse 5, the king had specifically commanded that they were to return to him "after three days." Either the people did not obey their king, or they did. Surely, they did, for "after three days" also meant in their understanding the same as *on* the third day.

Second, in Esther 4:16 with 5:1, a similar scenario is recorded. These two verses could not make it any plainer. Again, we can now see how the "fourth day" also went back into the "third day" and was counted as part of it although technically it was not. In addition, at times the "third day" could move forward into the "fourth day" and be calculated as part of it when, in fact, it was not.

Third, Jer. 28:1 is an illustration of how this time calculation works. It too deals with a king ruling over the Jewish people. We read in this verse, "in the beginning of the reign of Zedekiah king of Judah, in the fourth year, and in the fifth month . . ." Technically, he did not commence his rule until almost half way through the fourth year; for the text reads "in the fourth year, and in the fifth month." How then could it be stated that he ruled the fourth year when it was only a little over half of it? The text says, "in the fifth month" of that fourth year. Later, Jer. 52:1 affirms that Zedekiah "reigned eleven years in Jerusalem," while we note by a precise count that it was not a full eleven years to the day. However, this is how they reckoned time, by counting a part of a year as the whole. We do the same thing today. For example, John says, "I lived in Texas last year." While mathematically speaking, he lived there for nine months and three days. He simply counted part of his last year there as a whole year. This was not a misrepresentation but simply a way of expressing one's self in calculating time. Is it wrong to apply the same common-sense method of Jewish time counting to the period that our Lord's body lay in a borrowed tomb? How can it be incorrect since this was the system used in those days and observed by our Savior?

The length of time Jesus was on the cross

The Son of God was nailed to the cross on Friday, mid-morning Jewish time near to 9 a.m. (Mk. 15:25). He died on that same day (Friday) at 3 p.m. near mid-afternoon Jewish time (Mk. 15:33-34). He did not die until 3 p.m. that afternoon, and therefore, was not dead all day Friday. Though late in the day that Friday was counted as an entire day, and it automatically reached back and included the previous night, which started at sundown Thursday. Thus, we have the first full night before His death, and the (day) Friday when He was crucified. This makes one night and one day, or the first night and first day during which His body lay in the tomb. Technically speaking, His body was not in the tomb all day Friday, but only a few hours at the most. Again, the ancients counted a part of this day as the whole day, including the previous night. Our Lord's body was hurriedly buried a few hours before sunset Friday. This was because the Sabbath began immediately after sundown and was introduced by six trumpet blasts. Nicodemus and Joseph buried Jesus' body before these were sounded across Jerusalem.

At sundown Friday, we move over into the beginning of the second night. His body lay in the tomb that night and the next daylight period, which was Saturday or the Jewish Sabbath. This gives us the second night and second day, which ended at sundown Saturday. At sundown Saturday, the Sabbath ended and a new day commenced at sunset. Our Lord rose early (sunrise) on Sunday morning, which was the *first day* or beginning of a new week. Therefore, we have the previous night, which began at sundown Saturday and ended at sunrise the next morning. Jews counted each new daylight period as starting at sunrise. This was the time when our Lord rose from the grave. With Saturday night now past and early Sunday morning sun rising, we have the third night and day. All three days and three nights are thus accounted for by using the Jews' time system not ours. Those who use our western time system have been forced to invent extra days and Sabbaths in order to squeeze out the needed hours for *exactly* three days and nights. The big noise about a Wednesday or Thursday crucifixion is erroneous.

The Scriptures when interpreted in their traditional and historical context are final on this issue. It happened exactly as our Lord said it would, within the Jewish period (not American) of three days and nights. Therefore, we should "let God be true." Who dares contradict Him (Rom. 3:4)? Many good people do this without knowing it. One thing this passage does (among others) is to classify every person who denies that Jesus was three days and nights in the heart of the earth, as Scripture states. It may also include those who try to *prove* what God said in the Scripture instead of believing it (Heb. 11:6). There is a difference.

Because an original statement cannot be understood at first reading, does not signify that it is wrong. Scripture states, "He that believeth shall not make haste" (Isa. 28:16). The world says, "Show us, and we will believe." God has said, "Believe and [in time] I will show you" (John 11:40). The choice is ours to make because God in His wisdom has arranged it this way.

The wise man will keep faith in God's Word even when he does not understand certain statements it makes. Often, we are like the eunuch who was riding along reading from the book of Isaiah and humbly confessed that he did not understand and needed help (Acts 8:27-38).

Christian myths and inventions

Christians (trying to defend the Bible!) have invented various myths about the time Christ's body was buried or lay in Joseph's borrowed tomb. These include extra Sabbaths, Passovers, Tuesday, and Wednesday crucifixions. Not letting ancient Jewish custom and culture of Bible times speak regarding this matter, they have forced upon Christ's burial a western or American time system. These determined zealots believe that they must have an *exact* twenty-four-hour day for three straight days. According to the Hebrew method of reckoning time, Jesus' body was three days and three nights in the tomb. *This does not mean a literal or exactly measured seventy-two hours.* Neither God, nor the ancient Jews had a stopwatch or used American Central, Standard, or Pacific Time.

Some Christians feel intimidated because they cannot milk out of the Bible a fixed seventy-two hours for the three days and nights. Let the Muslims and liberal ecumenists howl in protest to the teaching of God's Word: their howling is at the moon, not truth. In desperation over this, many have gone so far as to invent a Thursday Sabbath, trying to get in all the time they need for three literal twenty-four-hour periods. This sort of Scripture wrangling is wrong. Using the time methodology of the ancient Jews (as illustrated on the first page of this Appendix), when Jesus died and was buried, we understand the meaning of Scripture, and the mystery vanishes from the event. It is held that when Christ spoke about His death and resurrection, He used the Jewish time system of His day; not that of the (unknown) western world. Common sense dictates this is true. Can we imagine our Lord saying, "Now, people, I want you to understand that I am speaking of 'daylight saving time' as will be used in America some two thousand years from now!" We must correctly interpret the Words of our Savior as He spoke on this matter. We are assisted in this task by putting them into their proper historical-cultural context.

A "fourth day" resurrection?

As stated above, God's Son died around mid-afternoon on Friday (Mk. 15:33-34). He rose from death in the early sunrays of that first day of the new week (Matt. 28:1-6), later named Sunday by the pagan Romans in honor of the sun god, just as they also named Saturday after the planet Saturn which was the name for the pagan god of agriculture. The ancients counted from Friday mid-afternoon when He died, and the night before this afternoon as the first day and night. The following Saturday night, and the coming new day, make the second day and night. The next night and early Sunday morning made a period of three days and nights. For those who debate for an exact over-the-counter total seventy-two-hour period, we invite them to explain the Words of Jesus in Mk. 8:31. On this occasion, He was at Caesarea Philippi with His apostles and the crowds of people who followed Him. They were discussing public opinion concerning "who" He was (Matt. 16:13-19). Mark records that on this occasion Jesus said, He would *"after* three days rise again" (Mk. 8:31). (Italics added to the text.) Would someone define what day it is *"after* the third day?" Could it possibly be the fourth? According to our western time system *"after* three days" means the fourth day. Alas! Here, the Savior said that He would rise from the grave on the fourth day. Is this what He meant? Did Christ rise from the grave on the fourth day?

Using American chronology, "after three days" has reference to the day following which could only have been the fourth day. Those who demand a literal or precise seventy-two hours for Christ's body to lie in the tomb, hit a steel wall with this passage in Mark. Let them now carry their concrete literalism over into Mk. 8:31. It should be remembered that it was our Savior, who spoke these Words. He was not given to extremes, jesting, or guesswork preaching. He was a Jew using the terminology of His people. We are sure they all understood what He meant on this occasion.

In Mk. 8:31, Jesus told His disciples and those present that He would suffer many things, be despised of the religious leaders, killed, and *"after* three days rise again." Remember, Christ said *"after* three days." If we hold to strict western time measurements, we must now push our Lord's resurrection over into the fourth day. Hard literalism sets the concrete. However, no reasonable person will do that, for everything now stops with this "fourth day" statement. As explained above, the Jewish fourth day would be counted as part of the previous day, and as seen in this passage from Mark, the third day could spill over into the fourth. If the text had read, "rise on the third day," or "rise after the third day," (which it does as shown below●), they both would mean the same. This is because one day spilt over into the next or the next spilt back into the former. That is how Jewish people calculated time over two thousand years ago.

On one occasion, the religious leaders of Israel demonstrated the above point. They were among those who had heard Christ make His earlier words about "the fourth day." After His death, the anxious

Jews went to Governor Pilate and said, "Sir, we remember that deceiver said, while he was yet alive, after• three days I will rise again" (Matt 27:63). (Emphasis again added to the text.) Note, they also used the word "after" just as Jesus had. If these men had understood this as literally *after* three days, then the Roman soldiers would not have been sent to the tomb that same Friday afternoon or early evening. Clearly, these religious hypocrites understood Jesus' use of the word "after" as having reference to a general period fitting within a time frame of three days and nights. It makes no other sense whatsoever. Whether our Lord said He would rise the third day or the fourth day it also makes no difference, for He did just what He said. Both days lapped over into each other.

Those who debate for hours, minutes, and seconds play silly games. Men who try to save the Bible from being wrong are like the flea who tried to save the lion; he was scratched off!

The Good Friday debacle

The former Roman Catholic practice of abstaining from meats on Friday (to remember the death of Christ on that day) has no basis in the Bible, not even in the Catholic Bible. The Papal Church did not invent this myth until the year A.D. 998. This was a long time after the resurrection of Christ! The date for the origin of "Good Friday" is documented in the work, *The Secrets of Romanism,* page 210, by the ex-priest Joseph Zacchello. Therefore, we cannot (as so many do), teach that a Friday crucifixion was the exclusive invention of the Papal Church system. It was not, for they did not teach their untruth of Good Friday, until some eight hundred years *after* the death and resurrection of our Lord. Those who argue, "The Roman Church invented the Friday crucifixion," have gravely erred, being unfamiliar with Catholic Church history and the false declarations of various Popes.

Belief in Jesus' death on Friday mid-afternoon was the established historical and biblical criteria for some eighteen hundred years of church history. Next, various satanic religions and apostate law cults appeared on the stage of Christianity and began to call this into question. They distorted the day Christ rose and made it a legal Jewish Sabbath to agree with their heresy. Refer to Section 195, the first paragraph of footnote a for explanation of this.

Ill-informed Christians joined in the parade of disinformation adding their miscalculated chronological opinions of this issue. Further, they attempted to make Jesus' death agree with their misunderstanding of the time system used by the ancient Jews. Confused believers had to get seventy-two hours out of His time in the tomb to prove the Bible was right. The whole scenario was one grand debacle invented by men who were unfamiliar with the chronology of the ancients. The mother of this problem is easy to identify. Certain Christians found themselves afraid to trust God's Word for what it says! Next, they rushed forward to *prove* that Holy Scripture was true. It is at this point of high unbelief that Satan steps into the picture. Amid the lack of correct historical background information, or just plain ignorance among God's people, Satan and evil spirits have a field day, promoting unbelief in what the Bible states. The Devil's inquiry put to Mother Eve in the garden is the same today. To her, he sneered, "Yea, hath God said . . . ?" (Gen. 3:1). He continually uses the same counter-argument. From all directions, men repeat Satan's question, "How do we know the Bible is true?" or "Did God really say that?"

When the conflict started

Debate about "how long Jesus' body lay in the tomb" surfaced on the theological scene about one hundred and fifty years ago. Prior to this, it was not a matter of concern. It started when "scholars" such as B.F. Westcott, the numerous Sabbath day law cults, Muslims, and religious skeptics began to assert that Jesus' body could not have been in the grave a *literal* three days and nights, or seventy-two hours. This could not be reconciled because He died on Friday. (The religion of Islam vehemently denies that Christ even died on the cross.) Voices were heard declaring, "Here is a serious mistake in the Scripture." When this unbelief and rank ignorance became public, many Christians began to calculate the time and were horrified to discover they could not get the needed seventy-two hours if Jesus died on Friday. Being unfamiliar with ancient Jewish methods of reckoning chronology, they went to work and *invented* their own Sabbath days and time scales for the crucifixion and burial of the Savior. Seventy-two hours were needed in order to prove the Bible right! The most infamous one was a mid-week Sabbath. (It is true that the Jews had various Sabbaths apart from the seventh day one.) Rallying to the front line of battle, with swords drawn, thousands of believers were ready to fight for the defense of Scripture (so they thought). Defending the Bible is like defending a fierce African elephant; a most ridiculous undertaking.

Historically, and scripturally there was nothing to fight for or defend. It had been a settled fact for two thousand years. The big noise, made by well-meaning Christians, terrified that the Bible may be wrong, only added greater frustration to the issue. It served to assist the heresies of the Jewish Law keepers who were trying to act like Bible believing Christians. The calumny of this calamity is that many saints have attempted to put the Words of Jesus into an American time clock and punch them out! They needed an exact, to-the-split-second, seventy-two-hour time scale to prove God's Word was true. All the juggling of days, Passovers, high Sabbaths, Wednesdays, Thursdays, and Fridays are useless in view of the culturally chronological statements made by Christ about His death and the time of His resurrection.

Those who heard the Son of God speak on this subject understood. Several thousand years later, many who read His Words do not understand. *Again*, this is because they are unfamiliar with the customs of the people from whom the events of Scripture come to us. These social customs are often referred to as "local color." The table below is designed to make this as clear as possible. It begins in the top left column with the burial of Jesus' body on late Friday afternoon, and lays out the Jewish pattern of the three days and nights associated with the burial of our Lord. This is the Hebrew time system, not the American, British, French, Australian, or anyone else! As explained, Gentile time systems are different.

The three days and nights in Joseph's tomb illustrated

Friday death † and burial	Saturday in the tomb	Sunday and resurrection
Died and then buried late Friday afternoon by Joseph and Nicodemus	This included the previous Friday night plus all day Saturday	The Sabbath ended at sunset Saturday. He arose early Sunday morning the first day of the week.
First day and night	**Second day and night**	**Third day and night**

Hundreds of priests working in the temple killed thousands of Passover lambs during the day Thursday. After being slaughtered they carried it to the owner of the upper room who prepared for them the Passover meal (Mk. 14:12-16). Jesus and the twelve apostles commenced eathing it just after sundown on Thursday. Technically, this would have fallen over into the first hours of Friday the next day. They partook of the Passover, in a room located on the West side of Jerusalem. Judas Iscariot left the room as the Passover meal *ended* and *before* the Savior instituted communion or the Lord's Supper (John 13:30)

At the conclusion of this meal, Jesus introduced the Lord's Supper. Following this, He and His eleven apostles departed from the upper room and made their way eastward across Jerusalem to the temple. Passing through selected areas and Solomon's porch, they walked down the side of Mount Moriah and entered the Garden of Gethsemane. Here, He was arrested and taken back to the city. (It is stressed again, that each new day on the Jewish calendar began immediately at sundown and ended on the next day at sunset. The western world does not use this method of reckoning time.)

The end of the Sabbath on a Sunday morning?

Matthew 28:1 reads, "In the end of the sabbath, as it began to dawn toward the first *day* of the week . . ." Why did Matthew-Levi being a Jew so pointedly specify that the Sabbath had ended at dawn, when he knew it could only end at sundown. *No Sabbath ever ended at the dawn of any day, but only at its end!* Looking back, years later, he understood that *all* Hebrew Sabbaths were then a thing of the past for believers in Yeshua ha'Mashiach (Jesus the Messiah). They ceased forever on that resurrection morning of the first day of that week (Sunday), not that evening. Mark understood the same when he wrote, "The Sabbath was past" (Mk. 16:1). Their words were prophetic. The resurrection of Jesus occurred early Sunday morning and with it, all Sabbaths ended. Jews called the ending of their holy day "the goings out of the Sabbath." In a *deeper sense* than words can convey, the Sabbath of the Torah Law and all of its 613 commands were gone out forever. The cross blotted them out (Col. 2:14). The old Hebrew day expired on that Sunday morning at dawn; it never saw the sunset of its normal ending. Then came the "dawn," or "day break" of the greatest era in human history. No day like this had risen upon God's creation, nor would one ever rise again. Christ had risen from the dead! By divine inspiration Matthew, called this, "the first day of the week." By the time he wrote these words, some twenty years after Christ rose, the resurrection was held to be on "the first day of the week." Though the Sabbath was finished, it took the early hard-line Jewish converts to Christ, decades to grasp the truth that law keeping, the Sabbath, and circumcisions were not necessary for salvation. The first church council was a united attempt to settle this issue (Acts 15). Paul wrote the book of Galatians trying to stamp out this problem that had caused such discord in his churches. *Sunday worship by the early Christians was in vogue several hundred years before the mad man Constantine supposedly decreed it by law.* He tried to enforce something already settled. Others say the Pope changed it! For more on this and its impact on Christians of that era, see Section 202, second paragraph of footnote c. In early churches, there was no such thing as Sunday school, training union, regular Sunday evening services, Wednesday night prayer meetings, as we know today. All these functions and much more came centuries later. In time, certain activities of the organized church became established Bible doctrine. Most are not, but are necessary for fellowship and growth of believers. To shun these is to court disaster in the Christian life.

Fanaticism is rife today among the law cults. They teach that we can only worship God acceptably on the Jewish Sabbath. These people do not see that the Scripture affirms that the Sabbath was finished. Christ's resurrection is now the centerpiece of eternal life, and it occurred on "the first day of the week." *If one is keeping Hebrew law, it occurred the morning after the Sabbath night.* It is the event, not the day that is critical. Neither Sabbath nor Sunday keeping redeems us from hell. Christ alone is the savior.

Over twenty years later, Paul instructed the Corinthian believers that "upon the first *day* of the week let every one of you lay by him in store, as *God* hath prospered him, that there be no gatherings when I come" (1 Cor. 16:2). By this time in church history, it was an established fact that this was the accepted day of collective worship for believers even in far off Corinth! The Corinthian saints brought their gifts to be later taken to the Hebrew Christians at Jerusalem. And they did this on the first day of the week (Rom 15:25-28). It was a matter of convenience as this was the time when they came together. Under pagan rule, there were no "days off" for cessation of human toil. Hence, believers in Christ met mostly at night. In some cases, they assembled on pagan holidays to worship the true and living God. These meetings were normally held in the homes of fellow Christians, or if possible in rented halls (Acts 2:46, 8:3, 19:9; Rom. 16:5; 1 Cor. 16:19; Col. 4:15; and Phile. 2). Later, they met in secret due to fierce persecution. In the book of Hebrews, there was a plurality of spiritual leaders over the Jewish Christians (Heb. 13:7, 17, 24). This is the reason that Paul addressed a plurality of bishops or pastors for the individual church bodies. It took many pastors and shepherds to oversee such large groups meeting in dozens of homes and other locations (Phil. 1:1). This was true, especially in the larger cities. Later, we read Christ's words addressed to the leadership of the seven churches in Asia. Here, it was singular with the pastor being called "angel." Oddly, the chief rabbis of the synagogues were frequently called "angels" (messengers), "chazan," "bishop," or "overseer." This may signal that these seven churches were more Jewish in nature than Gentile. Roman Law forbid Christians to erect public buildings for worship until the year A.D. 222. Even then, this was short lived. Succeeding emperors were unfavorable to Christianity and abolished this freedom. Afterwards, believers resorted again to covert methods of worship.

Torah-entangled law cults teach that it is "either the Sabbath or destruction." The Seventh Day Adventist sect affirms that Sunday worship will, in the future, be the mark of the beast. (Some of the more clever ones deny this.) Men are not barred from heaven because they worship on a certain day or do not worship on that day. This is heresy! They are shut out of heaven because the blood of Jesus Christ, God's perfect sacrifice for all mankind, has not redeemed their souls. This atonement is received by repentance from sin and by faith; not by Sabbath or Sunday keeping or "knowing the mark of the beast." Teaching that men are saved by grace, then *kept* saved by keeping parts of the law, notably the Sabbath, contradicts the grace of God (Rom. 11:6). It is a mixture of grace and works. They will not mix. How these people calculate their Sabbath in the Polar Regions where there are continued months of darkness is strange indeed. Paul told the Christians at Colosse to let no man judge them regarding Sabbaths, which were only a shadow of things to come (Col. 2:16-17). Cultists respond by saying this means the ceremonial Sabbaths, which were different from the weekly ones. This is false. The Greek word "sabbata" is used only once in the New Testament when speaking of more than a single day. In Acts 17:2, the plurality of its meaning is demonstrated by the use of the numeric "three." Zealots debating for weekly Sabbath keeping are shadow boxing. There are no winners in this contest, for their opponents are imaginary.

A summary conclusion of this *Appendix One* is as follows. After death on the cross, the body of Jesus was taken down and partially embalmed. Next, it was *quickly* entombed by Joseph and Nicodemus, *before* sundown Friday when the Hebrew Sabbath began. (We read in Mk. 16:1 and Lk. 24:1 of the women coming early on Sunday morning to complete his embalming or anointing.) The Friday afternoon crucifixion death which occurred at 3 p. m. (Mk. 15:33), and the previous night was counted as the first night and day. His body lay in the grave for a short time Friday afternoon, that night, and all day Saturday. Here, we have the second night and day. Lastly, Jesus' body lay entombed all Saturday night and rose with the beginning of the next morning, which was Sunday. The Jewish Sabbath began at sundown on Friday a few hours after Jesus' burial; it ended at sundown on Saturday evening. The early beams of daylight Sunday morning signaled the beginning of the *first day* of the new week. Jesus rose at dawn on that first day of the week. Later, among the pagan Gentiles this first day named "Sunday" (from the heathen sun god) and remains so to this hour. "Sabbath day saints" object that Sunday was named after the pagan sun god. We remind them that every day of the week bears a heathen name as well as the twelve months of our year! Even their prized Sabbath or Saturday, was named after Saturn the Roman god of agriculture. Adventists charge Christians of worshiping on Sunday, the day of the sun god. This is countered by reminding them that they worship on Saturday, the day of the pagan agriculture god!

As seen in the above we have the three days and nights, our Lord's body lay in Joseph's borrowed tomb. God's Word is true. Every problem that men think they see in Scripture has its origin in their minds, not in the sacred inspired text. This should be the first rule of biblical hermeneutics. It is from this stance that we approach all *assumed* Scripture contradictions. Those who practice this will discover where the problems have their origin. God may choose to resolve difficulties, or He may not. Either way, "Shall not the Judge of all the earth do right?" (Gen. 18:25). *Sometimes, God solves problems by leaving us in them!* It was the flames burnt the ropes off the three Hebrew children and set them free (Dan. 3:19-25).

Who has ever borrowed a tomb, used it for three days and nights, and returned it to the original owner? World religions have their founders who were born, lived, worked, and died. They have remained dead; none resurrected triumphant over death, and the grave, except one Man. That was Jesus Christ, the Son of God. This demonstrates that He is God, for only God could beat death, hell, and the grave (Rev. 1:18). Some day, humankind will give an account to this Person. That awful reckoning may be centuries away, but it is coming and all will be present. Those who trust in their denomination, church, religion, spiritual leaders, confirmation, catechism, baptism, ceremonies, rituals, paganism, gods, goddesses, nationality, race, idols, charms, infidelity, atheism, materialism, agnosticism, philosophy, works, academic achievements, evolution, human merits, and not the Son of God will be damned. It is written, "He that hath the Son hath life; *and* he that hath not the Son of God hath not life" (1 John 5:12). Jesus Christ atoned for the sins of all mankind in His death, burial, and resurrection. In this only, God is pleased and will forgive and save those who trust what His Son did. All other means or methods that promise forgiveness and salvation are false, contrary to the Bible, be they ever so beautiful. Any religious leader, church, denomination, organization, or group, who teaches that they are right and all others wrong are, fools. *Only the Jesus Christ is right,* and what He did on the cross, and in His resurrection will one find true forgiveness of sins! Those who know Him as personal Lord and Savior are going to heaven; those who do not, go to hell. This is a fact fiercely hated by the unsaved world and all false religions.

On all sides, we hear men, women, and youth, cursing, swearing, and blaspheming the sacred Names "Jesus Christ," and "God." With this profanity are attached the awful words "hell" and "damn" (Rom. 3:13-14). Why are these the most popular words in the vocabularies of wicked men? Behind this unceasing verbal barrage is Satan working to cheapen and vulgarize eternal truths about Christ, God, heaven, and hell. This is how the unsaved world thinks. At death, they are in for a *long* surprise.

On the night of April 14, 1912 when the Titanic sank, the grim reaper did his work. Men and women who had no time for God madly scrambled for their lives! John Astor, the richest man in the world, sneaked into a lifeboat (reserved for women and children) and was stopped! Daniel Buckley, disguised himself as a woman and attempted to board another lifeboat. Rosa Abbott, the only woman to go down with the ship and survive, afterwards told of a man who tried to climb on her back to save his life. There is a legend that just before the Titanic titled and sank, the band began playing, *Nearer my God to Thee.* (Wicked men often do strange things in the face of sure death!) However, it was no legend that prior to hitting the iceberg they were making the music of revelry, jazz, ragtime, dancing, course jesting, cursing, swearing, wild partying, gambling, and drunkenness. Amid the terror of it all, a Baptist minister, John Harper, gave his life jacket to a banker and his pet dog. A survivor testified he heard Harper pleading with a young man to trust Christ as his Lord and Savior. Pastor Harper paddled in the icy waters amid the piteous cries for help shouting loudly, "Believe on the Lord Jesus Christ and thou shalt be saved." Suddenly, his voice silenced! He had preached his last sermon. Later, in Hamilton, Canada, a man who had held to a floating board and was rescued testified, "I was John Harper's last convert to Christ."

The risen Christ was Pastor John Harper's joy in life and peace in death. Christ remains humanity's only eternal hope, Savior, and redeemer. His resurrection distinguished Him and Christianity as the world's *exclusive* religion and summarily condemns all others as false. Herein lies the reason for the universal hatred of *true* Christianity. Agnostic, skeptic, and atheistic websites rail this subject. The founders of all earth's religions have died and remain dead. Because the Lord Jesus was raised from the grave early on the third day, is exalted at God's right hand, and is triumphant over all things, wise men trust Him and Him alone for eternal life and heaven. Reader, are you trusting a dead man or a living Man for your salvation? *Think and act!*

APPENDIX TWO

Some of the quotes of James took from his half-brother Jesus

James, the son of Mary by Joseph and half brother of Jesus, was inspired to draw a number of citations that apparently came from the Sermon on the Mount. Being directed by the Holy Spirit, James incorporated them into his book, The General Epistle of James. This reveals that he was greatly familiar with Jesus' message given on that occasion or that Matthew's book was already written and in circulation when James wrote. The other possibility is that the Holy Spirit gave these similar or comparative verses to James, the son of Joseph by direct revelation. The seven comparisons demonstrate that James quoted from the Sermon on the Mount as given by the Lord Jesus.

Regardless of how James knew these various quotes, God inspired him to pen them as he wrote his little epistle. At the time Jesus gave the Sermon on the Mount, during the early part of His ministry, none of His half-brothers believed His Messianic claims. Their rejection continued up until about six months before His death on the cross. The Savior's half-brothers are named in Section 91, Matt. 13:55-56. For the final mention of Jesus' family in the Bible, see Section 207, Acts 1:14, footnote g. Regardless, James could have only written his epistles *after* the Lord Jesus had given this great discourse and His rejection in John chapter 7.

It has been fairly established that James was martyred about A.D. 62. Therefore, his letter was written before that date. Josephus made mention of his death in *Antiquities*, Book 20:9. 1, line 200. Some historians hold his work as the earliest New Testament book written. It has been dated as far back as A.D. 42. This was before the Church Council in Acts 15. It is a thoroughly Jewish flavored epistle, written to believers among "the twelve tribes scattered abroad" (1:1). One is struck that the Lord Jesus is mentioned only twice in this letter (1:1 and 2:1). Yet, portions of our Lord's instructions spoken years before in the Sermon on the Mount continued to live in the heart of His half-brother. Listed below are several of the words and thoughts from that masterpiece of divine instruction given by the Messiah. The Sermon on the Mount is in Section 44 through Section 47.

The seven quotes below are not in order with the flow of the sermon as recorded by Matthew. This reveals that the Holy Spirit gave them to James in this fashion as he penned his epistle or recalled them to his memory. It is clear he was led of God to adjust and rework these quotations to fit the different lines of thought being presented in his letter. James' quotations contain in direct word or substance some of the very words used by Christ. See Section 19, footnote b for more on this standard method of verse quoting as used by the ancients. In the one hundred and eight verses of this book, James quotes or alludes to at least fifteen Old Testament books. These include Genesis, Exodus, Leviticus, Joshua, 1 Kings, Job, Proverbs, and Isaiah. The half-brother of Jesus reflected general familiarity with the Jewish Old Testament by quoting or alluding to some twenty verses from its various scrolls.

His mother, Mary, was equally familiar with the Hebrew Tanakh or Old Testament. Refer to Section 10 footnote f where she quotes from many Old Testament writings in her audible song of praise to God her Savior. Like all pious Jews, they received this knowledge of sacred Hebrew Scriptures from home training (Deut. 6:4-9) and synagogue teaching. Often, parts of the synagogue instructions were distorted and then adjusted to fit the wild perversions of the rabbis. The foundation of the New Testament is the Old Testament. Thus, the Old Testament Scriptures must be correctly understood before moving into the New Testament. There are enough direct quotes, intimations, allusions, or mentions of Old Testament persons, places, events, and things in the New to make a book almost the size of Matthew's gospel.

The citations below suggest that Matthew's book was extant early in the piece and that James drew quotes from it as the Holy Spirit inspired him to write his work. For a more thorough look into the question of when the four gospels were written, see *Appendix Seven*.

Verses used by James that seem to have their origin in the book of Matthew

1. Matt. 5:4 with James 4:9.
2. Matt. 5:7 with James 2:13.
3. Matt. 5:9 with James 3:18.
4. Matt. 5:12 with James 5:10.
5. Matt. 5: 34-37 with James 5:12.
6. Matt. 6:19 with James 5:2.
7. Matt. 7:7 with James 1:5-6.

APPENDIX THREE

Forty-two predictions of the birth, life, death, and resurrection of Jesus

Prophecy is the department of theology that deals with predictive statements in the Bible. The verses listed below demonstrate that the Old Testament contains many ancient predictions. Next, we note their fulfillment recorded centuries later in the New Testament. The ancient forecasts listed below were given hundreds or thousands of years prior to the birth and ministry of Jesus of Nazareth the Messiah of Israel. They were realized in Him before and during the period of His earthly life, which was about thirty-four years in length. Only God could have given such forecasts, which were later fulfilled in exact details in the life of Christ. No mortal could foresee the future of Messiah and then record with accuracy these facts. This shows that God inspired the Bible. "For the prophecy came not in old time by the will of man: but holy men of God spake *as they were* moved by the Holy Ghost" (2 Peter 1:21). *True* Christians know that the Bible is the infallible and preserved Word of God. All dates below attached to the various prophecies are approximate but close enough to be honestly realistic.

This list of Old Testament predictions is not exhaustive. There are several hundred others not given. For further details of the background, history, and family tree of the Savior not covered in these prophecies, see Sections 3 through 7.

The Jewish Bible or "Tanakh," which is our Old Testament, contains scores of verses pointing to various aspects of Israel's coming King. These were literally fulfilled centuries later, by "Yeshua ha'Mashiach" or "Jesus the Messiah." For example, Dan. 9:24 predicted that He would "make reconciliation [atonement] for [the] iniquity" of humanity. Dan. 9:26 foretold that He [Christ] would "be cut off [killed] but not for himself." He was that innocent One put to death to atone for our sins. His decease on the cross was for all humankind. Jesus literally fulfilled these verses recorded in Daniel. See (f) under number 38 below for more on Daniel's predictions.

Theological skeptics and humanistic philosophers claim Bible predictions were written *after* the events they describe, and that there is no such thing as valid prophecy. They do this to escape the obvious fact of divine inspiration. The forty-two forecasts below point to that unique and exclusive Person, Jesus Christ, the Son of God. Sadly, the objections of the "learned critics" are aimed at the very God, who loves them and gave His Son to die for their sins. Education without Christ still makes men clever devils. The prophecies below irrefutably point to Israel's promised Messiah. They were fulfilled prior to His birth, and during His life, death, burial, resurrection, and ascension.

1. **Messiah the seed of the woman. ("Seed" means "child.")**
   Prophecy: "And I will put enmity between thee [Satan] and the woman, and between thy seed and her seed; it [Christ] shall bruise thy head, and thou shalt bruise his heel" (Gen. 3:15). Note that the "it" of this passage becomes "his" at the end of the sentence.
   Time: given shortly after Adam's fall into sin, which was at *least* 7000 years ago.
   Fulfillment: Lk. 1:30-31; Gal. 4:4; Heb. 10:5-7; Col. 2:15; with 1 Cor. 15:25.

2. **Messiah the seed of Abraham.**
   Prophecy: "And in thy [Abraham's] seed [which was Christ] shall all the nations of the earth be blessed" (Gen. 22:18).
   Time: about 2000 B.C.
   Fulfillment: Matt. 1:1; Gal. 3:16; Acts 3:25; with Heb. 2:16.

3. **Messiah the seed of Isaac.**
   Prophecy: "And God said, 'Sarah thy wife shall bear thee [Abraham] a son indeed; and thou shalt call his name Isaac: and I will establish my covenant [of salvation in Christ] with him for an everlasting covenant, *and* with his seed after him'" (Gen. 17:19).
   Time: about 1950 B.C. This prophecy was given some years before the one in number 2 above but is listed this way because Abraham lived before Isaac.
   Fulfillment: Matt. 1:2; Lk. 3:34; with Rom. 9:7.

4. **Messiah the seed and star of Jacob or Israel.**
   Prophecy: **(a)** Seed. "And in thee and in thy [Jacob's] seed [Messiah] shall all families of the earth be blessed" (Gen. 28:14).
   Time: about 1900 B.C.

Fulfillment: Matt. 1:1-2. Jacob in Jesus' family line.

Prophecy: **(b)** Star. "There shall come a Star out of Jacob, and a Sceptre shall rise out of Israel" (Num. 24:17).

Time: about 1500 B.C.

Fulfillment: Isa. 60:1-3; Matt. 2:2; with Rev. 22:16.

5. **Messiah from the tribe of Judah and little Bethlehem.**

Prophecy: **(a)** "The sceptre [of a Gentile ruler] shall not depart from [the land of] Judah . . . until Shiloh [Messiah] come" (Gen. 49:10).

Time: about 1500 B.C. With the death of Herod the Great in 4 B.C., his son Archelaus was appointed ruler of Edom, Samaria, and Judea. Due to his raging violence, the Emperor Augustus banished him to Vienna in Gaul, which at that time included Italy, France, and Belgium. The above prediction said that when "Shiloh" or Messiah came, the Gentile ruler of the land of Judea would be removed. With the dethronement of Archelaus, A.D. 6, the last pagan *king* reigned over the little area called Judea. It went under the authority of a succession of Roman governors with Pilate being the fifth. The new and rightful King had come, albeit He was only a small Child named Jesus. In God's time, this Person will yet be King of all. Note (c) under number 6 below for more on His kingship.

Fulfillment: Lk. 3:33; Matt. 1:2; 2:19-23; Heb. 7:14; with Rev. 5:5.

Prophecy: **(b)** "But thou, Bethlehem Ephratah, *though* thou be little among the thousands of Judah, *yet* out of thee shall he [Messiah] come forth unto me *that is* to be ruler in Israel; whose goings forth *have been* from of old, from everlasting" (Micah 5:2).

Time: 710 B.C. See Section 7 for the family line of Messiah from Abraham to Mary His mother.

Fulfillment: Matt. 2:1-6. Refer to number 9 below for more on this.

6. **Messiah is the seed or Son of David.***

Prophecy: **(a)** "And when thy [David's] days be fulfilled, and thou shalt sleep with thy fathers, I will set up thy seed [Christ] after thee" (2 Sam 7:12). Speaking first of Solomon and in a lesser sense of the coming Messiah-Savior (see (b) below).

Time: about 1070 B.C.

Fulfillment: Matt. 1:1; 21:9; 22:42; Rom. 1:3; and 2 Tim. 2:8.

Prophecy: **(b)** "I have made a covenant with my chosen, I [God] have sworn unto David my servant . . . thy seed [Christ] will I establish for ever . . ." (Ps. 89:3-4).

Time: about 1000 B.C.

Fulfillment: Acts 13:22-23.

Prophecy: **(c)** "Behold, the days come, saith the LORD, that I will raise unto David a righteous Branch, and a King shall reign and prosper, and shall execute judgment and justice in the earth . . ." Then the text reads, ". . . and this *is* his name whereby he [Messiah] shall be called, 'THE LORD OUR RIGHTEOUSNESS' " (Jer. 23:5-6).

Time: Jeremiah's forecast was approximately 610 B.C.

Fulfillment: Lk. 1:30-33. With this, see also Ps. 89:3-4; 132:10-11. This prediction of universal kingship has not yet been totally fulfilled.

*On one occasion Jesus questioned the religious leaders thus, "What think ye of Christ? Whose son is he?" They replied, "*The son* of David" (Matt. 22:42). This confirms they knew Messiah would come from David's family line. Such knowledge came from reading their Old Testament Scriptures. This was a regular theme of synagogue teaching by the rabbis. Ascendancy of Messiah from Abraham, Isaac, Jacob, Judah, and King David was a serious matter among learned Jews. This is seen in a statement recorded in John 7:42. Review chapter 3 in this harmony commentary for a comprehensive view of the human family line of Christ from five different angles. Other details are also given in Section 5, Matt. 1:1, footnote a.

Orthodox Jews to this day believe that Messiah must be of the family line of David. This firm requirement must not be overlooked in studying the life of Christ. For further comments on this and the early rabbinical teaching of two different Messiahs and the roles they were *supposed* to play in Jewish eschatology, refer to Section 6, sixth paragraph of footnote d

7. **Messiah born of a virgin.**

Prophecy: "Therefore the Lord himself shall give you a sign; Behold a virgin shall conceive, and bear a son, [Jesus] and shall call his name Immanuel" (Isa. 7:14).

Time: about 700 B.C.

Fulfillment: Matt. 1: 21-23; Lk. 1:26-38; 2:7; Gal. 4:4; Heb. 1:5; and 10:5.

Much debate has raged about the meaning of the Hebrew word translated "virgin" in Isa. 7:14. Skeptics and conservatives have written thousands of pages to prove their arguments. The useless controversy vanishes when men believe Matthew's interpretation and application of the verse. Being a Jew and living at that time in history, surely, he was better informed than today's "experts" are on this subject. It is the same old problem of not holding to the total inspiration of all Scriptures. In the context of Isa. 7:14, God instructed Isaiah to go and meet King Ahaz and take his little son, "Shearjashub" (Isa. 7:3). This was the child of verse 15-16. The one of verse 14 was born some seven hundred years later and was the Son of God. For the virgin birth, Mary, and other matters associated with her, see Section 12, Matt. 1:22-23, footnotes f and g. Jews and Muslims fiercely object, "How could Jesus be divine and yet born of a woman?" Is such a miracle beyond the power of Almighty God? See Jer. 32:27. The Holy Spirit created the human body in which Christ lived. Mary carried that embryo until its full development and birth.

8. **Messiah heir to the throne of King David.**

   Prophecy: "Of the increase of *his* [Christ's] government and peace *there shall be* no end, upon the throne of David, and upon His kingdom, to order it, and to establish it with judgment and with justice from henceforth even for ever" (Isa. 9:7). Peter on the day of Pentecost said that Christ at His ascension went into heaven and sat down on the throne of David at God's right hand (Acts 2: 29-35). This is the rule of Christ over His spiritual kingdom the church. This heavenly reign dimly shadows the *glorified literal* reign of Christ with His saints, which is yet to be (Rev. 5:10). See Section 39, footnotes a and g for an explanation of both manifestations of the kingdom.

   Time: about 700 B.C.

   Fulfillment: Lk. 1:32-33 with Acts 2:29-35 tell of King Messiah's birth, ascension and place at God's throne. See number 42 below for more on Jesus seated at God's right hand in heaven.

9. **Messiah born in Bethlehem.**

   Prophecy: "But thou, Bethlehem Ephratah, *though* thou be little among the thousands of Judah, *yet* out of thee shall he [Messiah] come forth unto me *that is* to be ruler in Israel; whose goings forth *have been* from of old, from everlasting" (Micah 5:2).

   Time: about 710 B.C.

   Fulfillment: Matt. 2:1-6; Lk. 2:1-20; with John 7:42. Refer to number 5 above for more on this.

10. **Messiah's life endangered as King Herod murders the innocent children.**

    Prophecy: "A voice was heard in Ramah, [Bethlehem] lamentation, *and* bitter weeping; Rahel [Rachel] weeping for her children refused to be comforted for her children, because they *were* not" (Jer. 31:15).

    Time: this Old Testament prophecy was given about 600 B.C.

    Fulfillment: Matt. 2:16-18.

11. **Messiah with His mother taken into Egypt as a little Child.**

    Prophecy: "When Israel was a child, [immature] then I loved him, and called my son [both the nation of Israel and Jesus] out of Egypt" (Hosea 11:1).

    Time: about 710 B.C.

    Fulfillment: Ex. 4:22 where Israel is called "God's son" with Matt. 2:14-15.

For Joseph taking Mary and the Christ Child and fleeing into the land of Egypt, see Section 18, Matt. 2:13-15. He stayed there for a short time until God sent Word by an angel in a dream that King Herod the Great was dead. With this, he returned to the land of Israel. See number 12 below.

12. **Messiah returns to Nazareth in Galilee, after an unknown short time in Egypt.**

    Prophecy: "And he came and dwelt in a city called Nazareth: that it might be fulfilled which was spoken by the prophets, 'He shall be called a Nazarene.'" (Matt. 2:23). Matthew, in typical Jewish fashion selected various words from a number of Old Testament verses and then builds this quotation. This was the standard practice among the rabbis and teachers for years. He drew his selected words from Isa. 11:1; Jer. 23:5; 33:15; Zech. 3:8; and 6:12. For a further explanation of this, see Section 18, Matt. 2:23, footnote h.

    Time: for writing the verses in Isa. Jer. and Zech. ranges from about 700 to 515 B.C.

    Fulfillment: Matt. 2:23; Lk. 2:51; and 4:16. *For comments on the length of little Messiah's stay in Egypt, refer to Section 18, footnote f.

13. **Messiah's growth and glorious development.**

Prophecy: "And there shall come forth a rod out of the stem of Jesse, and a Branch shall grow out of his roots: And the spirit of the LORD shall rest upon him, the spirit of wisdom and understanding, the spirit of counsel and might, the spirit of knowledge and of the fear of the LORD." (Isa. 11:1-2).
Time: about 700 B C.
Fulfillment: "And the child grew, and waxed strong in spirit, filled with wisdom: and the grace of God was upon him. And all that heard him were astonished at his understanding . . ." (Lk. 2:40, 47).

14. **Messiah's entrance into His ministry was prepared by John the Baptist, His forerunner.**
   Prophecy: "Behold, I will send my messenger, and he shall prepare the way before me: and the Lord, [Messiah] whom ye seek, shall suddenly come to his temple, even the messenger of the covenant, whom ye delight in: behold, he shall come, saith the LORD of hosts" (Mal. 3:1).
   Time: about 425 B.C.
   Fulfillment: Mk. 1:1-3; John 1:6-8; with Lk. 7:24-27.

15. **Messiah's kingdom and appearing to Israel was preached by John the Baptist.**
   Prophecy: "The voice of him that crieth in the wilderness, 'Prepare ye the way of the LORD, make straight in the desert a highway for our God'" (Isa. 40:3).
   Time: about 700 B.C.
   Fulfillment: Matt. 3:1-3; Mk. 1:6-8; Lk. 3:16-18; with John 1:19-28.
   It is noted that Christ is called both "LORD" and "God" in this prediction quoted above and recorded by Isaiah in 40:3. This means what it says for Jesus of Nazareth is *both*! When "LORD" is found in the uppercase, it speaks exclusively of "Jehovah" the eternal, self-existent God of Israel.

The Lord Jesus did not "offer Israel a kingdom," but rather Himself as their Messiah and Savior. The Jews did not refuse a "kingdom offer." Extreme dispensationalists invented the "kingdom offer" myth. Instead, the Jews, for the most part, hated and rejected Him as their promised Messiah-Savior and King.

For an exhaustive review of what John the Baptist preached and did, see Section 21, Part 4, footnote q. John 1:11 is explicit that the Lord Jesus came first to His own Jewish people. After six months of a public ministry, they began to scorn and reject our Savior. Refer to number 19 below for more on this. Several days before the cross, Jesus gave the Jewish leaders the Parable of the Vineyard Workers in which he said that His kingdom would be taken from the Jews and given to the Gentiles. This was not a literal kingdom. Gentile Christians today do not serve in a kingdom of flesh and blood and material substance. The present kingdom of Jesus Christ is spiritual according to Rom. 14:17. It is entered by the new birth (John 3:3). In this heavenly birth, all recipients are washed and justified from their sins, and delivered from the power of darkness (1 Cor. 6:9-11 with Col. 1:13). For the *two* manifestations of the kingdom, the present *spiritual one* and the future *glorified material one*, see Section 39, footnotes a and g.

16. **Messiah declared to be the Son of God.**
   Prophecy: "I will declare the decree: the LORD hath said unto me, 'Thou *art* my Son; this day have I begotten thee'" (Ps. 2:7).
   Time: about 1000 B.C. This verse is cited three times in the New Testament and interpreted each time as speaking of a different work of Christ.
   (a) In Heb. 1:5, the writer applied it to the physical birth of the Lord Jesus, the first to be born of a virgin.
   (b) In Acts 13:33, where Paul applied it to the resurrection of Christ, the first begotten from the dead never to die again (Rom. 6:9 with Rev. 1:18).
   (c) In Heb. 5:5-6, where it is applied to the Melchisedec priesthood of Christ, who was the first to ascend into heaven and be given the exalted seat at God's right hand as the eternal high priest, and King for all who know Him as Lord and Savior. These three usages of a single Old Testament prophecy demonstrate how the Holy Spirit directed the writers of the New Testament to interpret and apply God's Word to different events in the life of Christ as well as other persons.
   Fulfillment: God declared Christ-Messiah as His Son in Ps. 2:7 a thousand years before his physical birth. In the four gospels, He audibly said Jesus was His Son: first at His baptism when He spoke from heaven the words of Matt. 3:17. The second declaration was given mid-way through His ministry on the Mount of Transfiguration in Section 105, Matt. 17:5. God's third audible confirmation that Christ was indeed that divine Person is recorded in Section 161, John 12:28 a short time before the cross. Later, Paul wrote that our Lord Jesus was "declared to be the Son of God by the resurrection from the dead" (Rom. 1:4). Conquering death was the ultimate demonstration that Jesus of Nazareth was indeed the promised Messiah, the Son of God from heaven and the only Savior of mankind.

17. **Messiah came after Elijah's (or John the Baptist's) preaching had turned many to humility, repentance, and faith thus preparing them for Him.**
    Prophecy: "Behold, I will send you Elijah the prophet before the coming of the great and dreadful day of the LORD: And he shall turn the heart of the fathers to the children, and the heart of the children to their fathers" (Mal. 4:5-6). For more on the "day of the Lord," see Section 134, fourth paragraph, of footnote k.
    Time: about 425 B.C.
    Fulfillment: Matt. 11:13-14 and Lk. 1:16-17.

The "coming great day" in Malachi's verse was a prediction of the triumphant death, burial, and resurrection of Christ. The "coming dreadful day of the LORD" was that unprecedented calamity of the fall of Jerusalem, destruction of the temple, the death, and enslavement of millions of Jews, and scattering of Israel over the known world. This "dreadful day" was totally realized in A.D. 70. It is not the tribulation period of over two thousand of years later. *That time will be even worse than A.D. 70!*

18. **Messiah would be like Moses.**
    Prophecy: Moses said, "The LORD thy God will raise up unto thee a Prophet from the midst of thee, of thy brethren, like unto me; unto him ye shall hearken" (Deut. 18:15).
    Time: about 1500 B.C.
    Fulfillment: John 6:14; 7:40; and Acts 3:20-24.

19. **Messiah hated by the Jews and the world without a cause.**
    Prophecy: "They that hate me without a cause are more than the hairs of mine head" (Ps. 69:4).
    Time: about 1000 B.C.
    Fulfillment: John 1:11; 7:7; 15:18; and 22-25.

20. **Messiah rejected by the Jewish religious leaders, friends, and family members.**
    Prophecy: **(a)** "The stone *which* the [Jewish] builders refused is become the head *stone* of the corner" (Ps. 118:22).
    Time: about 1000 B.C.
    Fulfilled: Matt. 21:42 with Acts 4:8-12.
    Prophecy: **(b)** "He is despised and rejected of men" (Isa. 53:3).
    Time: about 700 B.C.
    Fulfilled: Matt. 27:39; Mk. 15:32; John 1:11-12; with 12:37-38.
    Prophecy: **(c)** "I am become a stranger to my brethren, and an alien unto my mother's children" (Ps. 69:8).
    Time: about 1000 B.C.
    Fulfilled: Mk. 3:21, 6:4 with John 7:2-5.

21. **Messiah betrayed by Judas, one of His apostles.**
    Prophecy: **(a)** "Yea, mine own familiar friend, [Judas] in whom I trusted, which did eat of my bread, hath lifted up *his* heel against me" (Ps. 41:9). David wrote this prediction and *first* spoke of a trusted friend who had betrayed him. This does not mean that the Lord Jesus trusted Judas as a true believer. It does reveal that the traitor feigned close friendship with the Savior during their time together.
    Time: about 1000 B.C.
    Fulfillment: Matt. 26:14-16; Mk. 14:10; John 13:21, 26; with Matt. 26:47-50.
    Prophecy: **(b)** "For *it was* not an enemy *that* reproached me . . . But *it was* thou, a man of mine equal, my guide, and mine acquaintance." (Ps. 55:12a, 13).
    Time: about 1000 B.C.
    Fulfillment: These verses speak of the traitor Judas Iscariot (Matt. 10:4).

22. **Messiah sold by Judas for thirty pieces of silver.**
    Prophecy: "So they [the Sanhedrin] weighed for my [Jesus'] price thirty *pieces* of silver" (Zech. 11:12).
    Time: about 515 B.C.
    Fulfillment: Matt. 26:14-15.

23. **Messiah's selling price was returned to the Jews and used to buy a potter's field.**
    Prophecy: "And the LORD said unto me, [Zechariah playing the part of Judas Iscariot] 'Cast it unto the potter . . .' And I took the thirty *pieces* of silver, and cast them to the potter in the house of the LORD" (Zech. 11:13).
    Time: about 515 B.C.

Fulfillment: Matt. 27:3-10.

24. **Messiah's entry into Jerusalem on a donkey.**
   Prophecy: "Rejoice greatly, O daughter of Zion; shout, O daughter of Jerusalem: behold, thy King cometh unto thee: he is just, and having salvation; lowly, and riding upon an ass, and upon a colt the foal of an ass" (Zech. 9:9).
   Time: about 515 B.C.
   Fulfillment: Matt. 21:1-11; Mk. 11:1-11; Lk. 19:28-41; with John 12:12-16.

25. **Messiah purges the temple for a second and final time.**
   Prophecy: "Even them [believers] will I bring to my holy mountain, and make them joyful in my house of prayer: their burnt offerings and their sacrifices [Rom. 12:1 and Heb. 13:15] *shall be* accepted upon mine altar; for mine house shall be called an house of prayer for all people" (Isa. 56: 7).
   Time: about 700 B.C.
   Fulfillment: Matt. 21:12-13; Mk. 11:15-19; and Lk. 19:45-46. (For his *first* cleaning of the temple, see Section 29, John 2:13-17).

26. **Messiah is miraculously recognized and adored by infants and small children in the temple.**
   Prophecy: "Out of the mouth of babes and sucklings [nursing infants] hast thou ordained strength [praise] because of thine enemies, that thou mightest still [silence] the enemy [the religious leaders] and the avenger [Satan]" (Ps. 8:2).
   Time: approximately, 1000 B.C.
   Fulfillment: Matt. 21:15-16.

The fulfillment of the above predictions concerning the little ones constitutes one of the most outstanding and amazing events pertaining to innocent and helpless children as recorded in the New Testament. It reveals their unique insight into who Jesus Christ was and how they broke out into joyful, infantile praise to the Son of God as He stood in the temple. This wonderful event occurred a few days before His death. For details on this extraordinary prophecy, see Section 150, footnote f. This miracle has nothing to do with the Calvinistic myth of "baby faith slumbering in the bosom of elect children."

27. **Messiah is forsaken by His apostles in the Garden of Gethsemane and arrested.**
   Prophecy: "Awake, O sword, against my shepherd, and against the man *that is* my fellow, saith the LORD of hosts: smite the shepherd, [Messiah] and the sheep [apostles] shall be scattered" (Zech. 13:7). *Time:* of this prediction about 515 B.C.
   Fulfillment: Matt. 26:31, 55-56; and John 16:32.

28. **28. Messiah is accused by false witnesses during His trial.**
   Prophecy: "False witnesses are risen up against me, and such as breathe out cruelty" (Ps. 27:12). "False witnesses did rise up; they laid to my charge *things* that I knew not" (Ps. 35:11).
   Time: about 1000 B.C. for both predictions.
   Fulfillment: Matt. 26:59-61 with Mk. 14:53-61.

29. **Messiah was bound, smitten, spat upon, mocked, taunted, and severely beaten at His trial.**
   Prophecy: **(a)** "They shall smite the judge of Israel with a rod upon the cheek" (Micah 5:1).
   Time: about 710 B.C.
   Fulfillment: John 18:12; Matt. 27:30; Mk. 15:19; with Lk. 22:63-65.
   Prophecy: **(b)** "I gave my back to the smiters, and my cheeks to them that plucked off the hair: I hid not my face from shame and spitting" (Isa. 50:6).
   Time: 700 B.C.
   Fulfillment: Mk. 14:65; 15:19; Lk. 22:63-65; and 23: 8-11.
   Prophecy: **(c)** "The plowers plowed upon my back: they made long their furrows." (Ps. 129:3).
   Time: 1000 B.C.
   Fulfillment: John 19:1.
   Prophecy: **(d)** "All they that see me laugh me to scorn: they shoot out the lip, they shake the head *saying,* He trusted on the LORD *that* he would deliver him: let him deliver him, seeing he delighted in him" (Ps. 22:7-8). There is a possible allusion to this in Ps. 109:25.
   Time: about 1000 B.C.
   Fulfillment: Matt. 27:39-44 with Mk. 15:29.

30. **Messiah's clothing gambled for by the Roman soldiers.**
   Prophecy: "They part my garments among them, and cast lots upon my vesture" (Ps 22:18).
   Time: about 1000 B.C.
   Fulfillment: Matt. 27:35; Lk. 23:34; with John 19:23-24.

31. **Messiah nailed to the cross.**
   Prophecy: **(a)** ". . . they pierced my hands and my feet." (Ps. 22:16).
   Time: about 1000 B.C.
   Fulfillment: Thomas said unto them, "Except I shall see in his hands the print of the nails" (John 20:25). "Then saith he unto Thomas, 'Reach hither thy finger, and behold my hands.'" (John 20:27).
   Time: about 1000 B.C.
   Prophecy: **(b)** "And *one* shall say unto him, 'What *are* these wounds in thine hands?' Then he shall answer, '*Those* with which I was wounded *in* the house of my friends.'" (Zech. 13:6).
   Time: about 515 B.C.
   Fulfillment: "And it was the third hour and they crucified him" (Mk. 15:25).

32. **Messiah prayed for His enemies after He was fixed on the cross.**
   Prophecy: **(a)** "He . . . [Messiah] made intercession for the transgressors" (Isa. 53:12).
   Time: about 700 B.C.
   Fulfillment: Lk. 23:34.
   Prophecy: **(b)** "For my love they are my adversaries: but I *give myself unto* prayer" (Ps. 109:4).
   Time: about 1000 B.C.
   Fulfillment: In the Garden of Gethsemane, Matt. 26:36-46, and on the cross in Lk. 23:34.

33. **Messiah suffered between two thieves.**
   Prophecy: "He was numbered with the transgressors" (Isa. 53:12).
   Time: about 700 B.C.
   Fulfillment: Matt. 27:38; Mk. 15:27-28; Lk. 23:32-34; with John 19:18.

34. **Messiah forsaken by God on the cross.**
   Prophecy: "My God, my God, why hast thou forsaken me?" (Ps. 22:1 and possibly alluded to in Ps. 88:14).
   Time: about 1000 B.C.
   Fulfillment: Matt. 27:46 with Mk. 15:34.

For a discussion of the popular fallacy that God did not really turn His back on Christ, see Section 191, the fourth paragraph of footnote c. This form of hermeneutic reflects the modern-day trend to extract from biblical words their plain sense and then insert into them meanings that are foreign to the natural thought of the text. This method of biblical interpretation has been used by every false cult operating under the cover of Bible Christianity. God's people should reject such foul parlance of Holy Scripture. It is a mark of ignorance, not spiritual insight. See an example of this word game in the last paragraph under number 38 below. Note here, how the word "whosoever" is toyed with by a "good old Puritan authority."

35. **Messiah given gall and vinegar to drink.**
   Prophecy: "They gave me [Messiah] also gall for my meat; and in my thirst they gave me vinegar to drink" (Ps. 69:21).
   Time: about 1000 B.C.
   Fulfillment: Matt. 27:34 with John 19:28-30.

36. **Messiah died by crucifixion.**
   Prophecy: "I am poured out like water, and all my bones are out of joint: my heart is like wax; it is melted in the midst of my bowels. For dogs have compassed me: the assembly of the wicked have inclosed me: they pierced my hands and my feet" (Ps. 22:14, 16).
   Time: about 1000 B.C.
   Fulfillment: Matt. 27:35; Mk. 15:20; Lk. 23:33; with John 19:18.

37. **Messiah's side pierced by a spear as He hung on the cross.**
   Prophecy: "And they shall look upon me whom they have pierced"* (Zech. 12:10).
   Time: about 515 B.C.
   Fulfillment: John 19:34-37.

*By direction of the Holy Spirit, John said that this prediction was fulfilled at the death of Christ on the cross. The erroneous teaching that this speaks of Israel being converted at the revelation of Christ is more eschatological error. We prefer to believe John.

38. **Messiah died as the supreme and final sacrifice for the sins of the world.**
   Prophecy: **(a)** "But he *was* wounded for our transgressions, *he was* bruised for our iniquities: the chastisement of our peace *was* upon him; and with his stripes we are healed" (Isa. 53:5).
   Fulfillment: John 1:29, 11:49-50.
   Prophecy: **(b)** "The LORD hath laid on him the iniquity of us all" (Isa. 53:6).
   Fulfillment: 2 Cor. 5:14, 21; 1 Tim. 2:6; and 1 John 2:2.
   Prophecy: **(c)** "For the transgression of my people was he stricken" (Isa. 53:8).
   Fulfillment: Rom. 5:8; 1 Cor. 15:3 with Eph. 5:2.
   Prophecy: **(d)** "Thou [God] shalt make his soul an offering for sin" (Isa. 53:10).
   Fulfillment: John 10:11; Gal. 1:4; Heb. 10:12.
   Prophecy: **(e)** "For he shall bear their iniquities" (Isa. 53:11).
   Fulfillment: 1 Peter 2:24.
   Prophecy: **(f)** "He [Messiah] shall cause the [animal] sacrifice and the oblation [grain offering] to cease" (Dan. 9:27). The pronoun "He" above does not have reference to a coming Antichrist. First, it spoke of Antiochus Epiphanes, who invaded the temple and stopped all sacrifices and offerings in 163 B.C. Josephus informs us that pagan Egyptians started a rumor that Epiphanes found an "ass' head" made of much gold and postured in the holy place: this was worshiped by the Jews! See Josephus' *Against Apion,* Book 2: lines 80 and 81 for the story. Regardless, Daniel's prediction lastly pointed to Jesus Christ, who *forever* abolished all acceptable temple rituals by His atoning death on the cross.
   Fulfillment: "It is finished" (John 19:30)). "In burnt offerings and *sacrifices* for sin thou [God] hast had no pleasure" (Heb. 10:6). "There remaineth no more sacrifice for sin" (Heb. 10:26). This classic verse speaks of *every* temple sacrifice and offering made from the time Jesus died, up to its writing in about A.D. 60. Because the rent veil could not be restored, all temple functions were greatly impaired. Worse, Jehovah accepted none of them. Finally, He destroyed their temple, city, and Jewish state in A.D. 70. This was predicted by Christ and is discussed in Section 163.
   Time: All of the above prophecies were given about 700 B.C. except that of Daniel. He was carried to Babylon in the first deportation of 606 B.C. His prediction would have been reasonably after this date.

The supreme sacrifice of Christ in number 38 above calls out, "and whosoever will, let him take the water of life freely" (Rev. 22:17). Surely, "whosoever" means "whosoever?" To read into this, "Whosoever will of the elect," is theologically idiotic. The Holy Spirit and the bride [redeemed] of Christ spoke this final invitation of Scripture. It is the enduring hope of every soul winner and the chief work of the Holy Spirit to bring to the Son of God "whosoever will." If certain people were chosen before the foundation of the world to eternal life, and all others appointed to damnation, then this passage mocks the work of the Spirit and genuine Christian evangelism. The Puritan John Owen (died 1683) in his infamous book, *The Death of Death in the Death of Christ* attempted every trick in the art of distortion to reinterpret the fact that God provided salvation for all men, everywhere. His handling of John 3:16 and Rev. 22:17 is shameful. That God loves the world, but has pre-damned millions in the world never to be saved is theological claptrap. (Among the wilder Calvinists is a group that teaches, God does not love the world, only the world of the elect!) The talk about "denying the sovereign right of choice to God" is answered in Gen. 18:25, "Shall not the Judge of all the earth do right?" Who could deny God anything? No greater right has been manifested in world history than in the death of Christ for all men. Owen's conclusions regarding God's elect and the scope of Christ's atonement are heretical if not blasphemous. The doctrine of Arminianism regarding redemption and how one becomes a recipient of eternal life is just as corrupt and false. As previously stated, both are radical departures from main line biblical truths.

39. **Messiah, the final Passover Lamb had no bones broken during or after His crucifixion.**
   Prophecy: "He keepeth all his bones: not one of them is broken" (Ex. 12:46 with Ps. 34:20).
   Time: The Psalm quotation was given in approximately 1000 B.C. Exodus was written in about 1500 B.C. *Fulfillment:* John 19:32-36.

40. **Messiah buried in the borrowed tomb of Joseph a rich man.***
   Prophecy: "And he made his grave with the . . . rich" (Isa. 53:9).
   Time: about 700 B.C.

Fulfillment: Matt. 27:57-60; Mk. 15:42-46; Lk. 23:50-55; with John 19:38-42.

*For a discussion of the vast amount of money used by the wealthy Joseph and Nicodemus in burying the body of our Lord, see Section 193, footnotes i and j. Their risks, work, and expense demonstrated that they neither knew of nor understood the resurrection of Christ, though He had mentioned this many times over the length of His earthly ministry. If this had been understood, they would have never gone through the trouble and great costs to prepare His body and entomb it. Nor would the women have gone there early morning on that first day of the week to complete His embalming. Later, it was a joyful shock to them and other believers that He had risen from the dead.

41. **Messiah was to rise from the dead after three days and nights in the grave.**
    Prophecy: **(a)** "For thou wilt not leave my soul in hell; [the rest part of sheol-hades] neither wilt thou suffer thine Holy One to see corruption," or Jesus' body to decay in the tomb. (Ps. 16:10).
    Time: about 1000 B.C.
    Fulfillment: Matt. 28:1-6; Mk. 16:1-8; Lk. 24:1-12; with John 20:1-10.
    Prophecy: **(b)** "Now the LORD had prepared a great fish to swallow up Jonah. And Jonah was in the belly of the fish three days and three nights" (Jonah 1:17).
    Time: predicted about 760 B.C.
    Fulfillment: Matt. 12:38-40; Matt. 16:21; Mk. 8:31; 9:31-32; Lk. 18:33; and John 2:19. On the "three days and nights" Jesus' body lay in Joseph's tomb, see *Appendix One* for detailed explanation.

42. **Messiah ascended to God's right hand in heaven.**
    Prophecy: "The LORD [God] said to my [David's] Lord, [Christ] 'Sit thou at my right hand, until I make thine enemies thy footstool' " (Ps. 110:1).
    Time: predicted about 1000 B.C. See number 8 above for an explanation of the Lord Jesus seated in heaven and what this signifies today.
    Fulfillment: Mk. 16:19; Lk. 24:51; Acts 2:33-36; 7:55-56; Eph. 1:20; Col. 3:1; Heb. 7:24-26; 10:12-13; and Rev. 3:21.

Conclusion

The numerous prophecies just given demonstrate that God wrote the Holy Bible. The greatest human intellect could not have foreseen the future and predicted the specific events and details recorded in the above verses of Scripture. Biblical archaeology often gives credence to various portions of God's Word. However, the greatest evidence of the divine origin of Scripture is first, personal experience by the new birth, and second, fulfilled prophecy. The born again Christian walking in fellowship with his Lord needs no archaeological discoveries (though they are respected and often referred to) to bolster his faith. It stands on the immutability of inspired Scripture. See *Author's Introduction* for a survey of this subject. Perhaps the greater story behind Christianity is what we cannot see, instead of what we do see.

While serving as principal of a small Bible school in Queensland, Australia, in the late 1960s, one of the students had previously worked for a large British bank as a counterfeit detection expert. I asked him how he could so easily find a false note among hundreds of genuine bills. He replied, "We study the original for one year and learn everything about it. Because we thoroughly know the real product, we can quickly detect the false." This rule should be carried over into every level of *established* Christian doctrine. Those who know the original, in time can detect the counterfeit.

The sweet lie that regardless of what one believes, teaches, or practices it is acceptable to God if he is deeply sincere, is wrong. *If what we believe contradicts rightly divided Scripture, we are wrong.* Paul continually struggled with false doctrines and religious practices within his churches as reflected in the books of Galatians and Colossians. For continued comments on the subject of sincerity in a false religion, and the horrors resulting from it, even to sleeping with snakes and eating dead human flesh, see Section 95, sixth paragraph of footnote r. There are especially two stages of life where clowns, fools, hypocrites, and knaves perform their best. These are *false* religion and *corrupt* politics. While false religion dooms the soul, *corrupt* politics is the art of the impossible and usurps the God given authority of the state and national leaders. As rotten as these things are, we can only get along with them by going along with them. Sensitive Christians find this a most difficult task. A poisoned pulpit and poisoned politicians are the arch enemies of God and civilized men. For continued comments on this calamity, see under sub heading *"The majority vote flop"* in Section 101, fifth paragraph of footnote b.

APPENDIX FOUR

What the ancient Jews taught about the coming of Elijah

Centuries before Christ was born, Jewish teachers instructed their people that the prophet Elijah must appear on earth *before* Messiah came. This was the same Elijah of the Old Testament, who left earth in a whirlwind and chariot of fire about seven hundred years prior (II Kings 2). It was taught that his appearing would literally occur. Elijah's work was to prepare the way for the soon coming Messiah. Our Lord's disciples had embraced (at least) parts of this doctrine. It comes out clearly in their question to the Savior in Matt. 17:10, "Why then say the scribes?" The ancient rabbis based their teaching on a literal interpretation of Mal. 3:1-5; 4:5-6; and Isa. 40:1-9. This was why the delegation was sent from the Sanhedrin in Jerusalem to John, who was baptizing in Jordan. To him, they put the big question, "Are you Elijah?" (John 1:19-21). John answered in the negative (John 1:21). In his response, he affirmed that he was not the Elijah they were looking for (the real one from the Old Testament times). Later, Christ made it clear that John the Baptist was the Elijah, who was to prepare the way for Him. Jesus spoke of him in a figurative sense, yet He was making strict reference to the *real* John the Baptist not the great prophet of the Old Testament. Christ's Words to His disciples regarding this are recorded in Matt. 17:10-13 and Mk. 9:11-13.

In the immediate context of Matt. 17:1-9, several of the apostles had just seen Elijah appear on the Mount of Transfiguration. Because the scribes had taught them, "That Elias [Elijah] must come first" (verse 10), or before Messiah came, they naturally thought (since they had just seen him) that he had arrived. They could not reconcile why Messiah (or Jesus) was with them, but Elijah had appeared afterward. In their thinking, it was all happening backwards! Christ answered their dilemma by telling them that John the Baptist was the promised Elijah of the Old Testament, and that he had already come (Matt. 17:11-12). The apostles knew that John had previously appeared within Israel and ended his ministry by martyrdom at the hands of Herod Antipas (Mk. 6:16). Suddenly, it clicked in their minds! We read, "Then the disciples understood that he spake unto them of John the Baptist" (Matt. 17:13). Many play games with these passages in their struggle to prove that Christ did not mean what He said. "Make it fit" exegesis is unnecessary for those who believe in the *true* premillennial return of Christ and reject the wild and distorted interpretations continually applied to this doctrine. Giving names to unnamed persons, countries, cities, lands, and events in Bible prophecy is risky business. The sensational preaching about the "Second coming of Elijah" is a myth built on someone's personal conjecture. Nowhere in the book of Revelation is the name Elijah found; it is imagined being there by association and comparison. This is a poor foundation on which to build such an amazing doctrine. The wise man will leave it to God as to exactly *who* these prophets are that shall appear in the future tribulation period (Rev. 11:3).

Zacharias, the physical father of John the Baptist, understood that his son would be the second Elijah, only in the sense of Elijah's "spirit," or "likeness." This referred to his outward appearance and actions. John mirrored the great prophet in dress, habits, and powerful preaching. Refer to this in Lk. 1:11-17, and note especially verse 17. The old priest knew very well that his son would not be the real flesh and blood Elijah from Old Testament days. Mark interpreted Mal. 3:1 and Isaiah 40:3 as having reference to John the Baptist in Mk. 1:1-6. The ancient Christ-hating scribes and modern day, newspaper-headline-based *hyper-dispensationalists* do the exact opposite of Zacharias and Mark. They tell us that the physical Elijah of the Old Testament will literally reappear some day, "During the latter part of the great tribulation period." Despite these claims, no one knows for sure who the two "witnesses" are in Rev. 11:3. Scripture does not tell us. Can we presume to do better? Drawing solid conclusions from personal assumptions is the best shortcut to error. Every false cult within Christianity does this.

What Elijah would do when he appeared in Israel?

According to the ancient Jews, Elijah was to perform the following list of amazing deeds. These reflect some of the ridiculous beliefs of the Hebrews before and during the days of Christ on earth. Various Orthodox Jews still hold to fragments of these teachings. They show a strange exegesis blended with the conjectures of religious Jews, who looked for only a literal, material kingdom. It is noted that salvation from sin was not included in these Hebrew ideals for their coming Messiah.

The points below were gathered from a variety of ancient Jewish writings. In Hebrew literature, there are hundreds of dark and even blasphemous statements. Some of these are mentioned in Section 6, under footnote d. Several of the research sources from which some of this material was taken are given at the conclusion of this Appendix. This is to help those who may do further research into this subject. Below are eight of Elijah's most important accomplishments, according to the hallucinations of ancient rabbis and various Jewish philosophers. Not a one of these is based on any Scripture of their (Tanakh) Old Testament.

1. Elijah would appear three days before the Messiah comes.
2. He would stand on a high mountain in the land of Israel and bewail the nation's sins before the whole world. His voice would be heard around the earth as he proclaimed for three days the following three things:
   a. "Peace cometh to all the world." This will be proclaimed on the first day.
   b. "Good cometh to the world." This will be declared on the second day.
   c. "Salvation cometh to the world. Zion thy King cometh." To be spoken on the third day.
3. After the above, Elijah would move over the land of Israel solving all problems, answering all questions about how to offer correct sacrifices, making peace between all rival groups within Israel, and so on. In short, he would bring the people to repentance and peace among themselves, thus preparing the way for the soon coming Messiah.
4. Elijah would restore to the nation of Israel three things:
   a. The golden pot of manna (see Ex. 16:33).
   b. The oil vessel for anointing used by the priests (Ex. 29:7 and Ps. 133:2).
   c. Aaron's rod that budded (Num. 17:1-8).
5. Many Jews held that Elijah would raise the dead, appear, and then disappear several times. He would assist Messiah in fighting the war with Gog and Magog.
6. Elijah would bring true repentance to Israel. (With this, note John's message of repentance to the nation in Matt. 3:2).
7. When Messiah finally came, Elijah will "anoint Him" (Ps. 45:7 and Mal. 3:1). At the baptism of Jesus the Holy Spirit came upon Him (Matt. 3:16).
8. Lastly, it was taught that many of the Old Testament prophets would appear and assist Elijah in his work. In Matt. 17:10, "first" had reference to Elijah being the "first" of the other prophets to appear. Next, it spoke of Elijah coming on the scene "first" or before Messiah. The prophet of Deut. 18:18 was not Elijah. Just after the day of Pentecost, Peter interpreted this "prophet" as meaning the Savior (Acts 3:22-26).

Some of these teachings were believed before, during, and after the days of Christ on earth. As pointed out in the first paragraph of this Appendix, our Lord's own apostles were also victims of certain erroneous rabbinical teaching. Exactly, how many of these myths were believed by the apostles and other Jewish converts to Christ, we cannot know.

On occasion, Jesus and others spoke of the long expected days of Messiah on earth; how saints, prophets, kings, and others had looked for them. Refer to this in Matt. 13:16-17; Lk. 10:24; John 8:56; with John 12:41. When Christ came, what He did was so different from what the rabbis had taught their Messiah would do that the Jews were shocked at His life and ministry. He did not appear with a sword in hand, assisted by Elijah, destroying the conquering pagan Romans. Instead, He took a cross beam on His back, went to Calvary and died for the sins of the world. This was not the Messiah of ancient Judaism.

Despite the numerous Old Testament prophecies that spoke of Christ's birth, life, death, resurrection, and ascension, the Jews rejected or deliberately reinterpreted these. (Many of these prophecies are listed in *Appendix Three.*) The Savior denounced their tradition of the elders or oral laws, did not perform as they believed, and was crucified at the demand of the Sanhedrin by the command of Governor Pontius Pilate. However, supervising the whole scenario was the sovereignty of God, preparing salvation for the souls of all who would believe in His Son, Jesus Christ. He forced the hand of no man to commit sin or contrive wickedness, but foresaw all thoughts and actions, then overruled, and employed these to accomplish His divine intentions. Others He "gave up" to accomplish their own destruction.

For extended information on Elijah's supposed appearing among the Jews, see Alfred Edersheim's, *Life and Times of Jesus the Messiah*, Appendix VIII, and Emil Schurer's, *A History of the Jewish People in the Time of Jesus Christ*, II Division, vol. II, pages 156-158. One of the greatest sources of information about ancient Israel are the works of Johannes Buxtorf (died 1629). Sadly, most of his writings are not translated into English. Joachim Jeremias' *Jerusalem in the Time of Jesus* is a classic on culture, history, and background, but terrible on theology. *Gill's Commentary on the New Testament,* volume VII, under "The Introduction," also carries excellent information on Jewish life and culture.

APPENDIX FIVE

The Great Sanhedrin Court of Israel

There were two basic judiciary bodies in ancient Israel during the earthly life of Christ. These were the Great Sanhedrin and the Lesser Sanhedrin Courts. The Lesser Sanhedrin consisted of twenty-three members. It was found in every city in the land of Israel where there were not less than a hundred and twenty households. The Great Sanhedrin was called "Beth-Din" or "House of Judgment." It was the highest religious and civil tribunal in the nation and was allowed to function under the watchful eye of the Romans. This august body was established at Jerusalem after the Babylonian captivity. Jewish tradition states that it was modeled after the famous council of seventy elders instituted by Moses in the wilderness (Num. 11:16, 24). The word "Sanhedrin" seems to signify in etymology an assembly of men in a sitting posture.

How to find the Sanhedrin in the New Testament

Because "council" is the English word translated from "Sanhedrin" in the New Testament, the normal reader thinks "council" has reference to a meeting for whatever reason. There are twenty-two places in the New Testament where "council" actually means the Great Sanhedrin, not a general assembly of religious, social, or political bodies. They are: Matt. 5:22; 10:17; 26:59; Mk. 13:9; 14:55; 15:1; Lk. 22:66; John 11:47; Acts 4:15, 5:21, 27, 34, 41, 6:12, 15, 22:30, 23:1, 6, 15, 20, 28 and 24:20. In Acts 22:5, the Sanhedrin is called "estate of the elders." There are two verses where the word "council" does not mean Sanhedrin: Matt. 12:14 and Acts 25:12. Here, it has reference to a called meeting to discuss some issue or problem and was not a convening of the Jewish Supreme Court.

Number of members

As previously mentioned, the Great Sanhedrin consisted of seventy-one members. The ancient rabbis proved this by referring to Num. 11:16 where God instructed Moses, "Gather unto me seventy men of the elders of Israel." These same rabbis concluded, "Seventy men plus Moses makes seventy-one." As with everything else in Scripture, the "learned critics" deny the membership of seventy-one in this judicial system of the Hebrew people. They apparently know more than the ancients who formed this body.

Structure of the Sanhedrin

This body of legal specialists for the nation of Israel consisted of the following:

1. **Twenty-four chief priests, all of whom were Sadducees.** See, for example, 1 Chron. 24:4; Acts 4:1, and 5:17. For a sweeping coverage of the Sadducees, see *Smith's Dictionary of the Bible*, vol. IV, pages 2777-2784. In the front of his work, The Life of Flavius Josephus, part 12, Josephus wrote of seeking permission from the Sanhedrin regarding a problem. The Sadducees were the nobility of Israel, powerful men of wealth and means, and considered the theological liberals of the nation of Israel.

2. **Twenty-four elders, all were Pharisees.** See Matt. 16:21; 26:3, 47, 57; with Mk. 8:31. Again, Josephus wrote many lines about this religious body of which he was a member. See "Pharisees" under Index in *The Works of Josephus*. For a short review of the Pharisees, refer to Section 30, footnote a.

3. **Twenty-two scribes, all were Pharisees.** See Matt. 7:29; 26:3, 57; with Mk. 8:31. *The New Unger's Bible Dictionary*, pages 1141-1143 carries a good review of the Jewish scribes.

4. **The high priest, who was usually a Sadducee.** He was counted as number seventy-one. A person known as the president or prince (Nasi), and a vice-president (Father of the house or tribunal) were chosen out of the seventy-one men. Both had places of honor and were seated on thrones at the extremity of the hall, having their helpers at their sides sitting in the form of a semi-circle. In Israel, only the oldest, wisest, and richest men were selected for membership in this court system. It was the most revered judicial body in the nation.

5. **The chamber of high priests.** During the time of Christ on earth, an assembly of priests was a natural thing for the Jews. Yet, how could there be a group of men called "high priests" when according to the Torah Law, there could only be one high priest at a time whose office was tenable for life? Decades before the birth of Christ, detestable abuse prevailed within this honorable office. It had become a position of commercial gain and pompous arrogance. This

collection of elderly men consisted of those retired from the office and others being appointed by the Roman governor. The sacred office was often given to the one who offered the most money for it! Certain Jewish mothers, anxious for their sons to acquire this position of dignity, wrangled among themselves to secure this appointment for their own. By the time of Christ, religion was so corrupt that money was the god of many Jews.

Qualification for membership

1. Morally and physically blameless.
2. At least sixty years, but preferably older. Must be especially tall and handsome. Those feebly old were forbidden membership.
3. Must be among the richest men in the nation of Israel.
4. Greatly learned in the sciences, especially medicine, mathematics, astronomy, and magic to be able to discern any evil that may appear during court sessions. Must be totally familiar with idolatry and all of its attendant evils. Must have a keen business mind and be deeply refined in Jewish culture and history.
5. Must know several foreign languages to understand foreigners in court sessions.
6. Must be married with children, so they can sympathize and have compassion.
7. Be able to prove their pure Hebrew descent from the genealogical files in the temple archives.
8. Could not play dice, loan money for interest, fly pigeons to attract others, or deal in produce on the Sabbath day. (Apparently, pigeon flying was a form of gambling.)
9. Have previously served as a judge in a Smaller Court in his hometown or district.
10. Must be transferred by his Smaller Court colleagues to the Sanhedrin in Jerusalem.
11. Must have a trade, profession, or occupation. Members were not paid salaries.
12. Had previously been inducted a judge in his native town or city. This could be done after the Sanhedrin Nasi (also called) president had given permission. There was no putting on of hands upon induction into any Hebrew judicial office at this time, the Sanhedrin or otherwise. The imposition of hands upon any person was strictly a religious function.

Place of meeting

About a hundred years before the birth of Christ, a Jewish builder, Simon ben-Shetach, constructed a place named "Gazith" or "The Hall of Hewn Stones." Seemingly, it was located within the temple area on the southern side, though some writers place it at the western end of the city. This became the regular meeting place for the Sanhedrin. It was considered illegal to meet in the house of the high priest for any type of judicial occasion. During the early part of Jesus' ministry, history seems to affirm that the Sanhedrin moved outside the temple precincts to the west side of Jerusalem. If this is true, the reason for such a move is unknown.

Times when the Sanhedrin met and those present

They met every day from mid-morning to mid-afternoon, except on the Sabbath and during the feast days of Israel. The president (Nasi) sat on a raised platform with the vice president (Father of the House) at his right hand. Present was one called the "referee." A "referee" was often stationed at the entrance to the larger synagogues in Israel. He was seated or reclined to the left side of the vice-president or Father of the House. His work was to serve as something of a bodyguard or peace keeper! The remaining members sat with legs crossed on cushions in a half-circle formation. They were always positioned according to age and learning. Each member could clearly see all the others. Twenty-three of the actual seventy-one were required for a quorum. Less than twenty-three present would make any meeting invalid.

The jurisdiction of the Sanhedrin

This body of elderly and august men watched over every aspect of Jewish life and society. They controlled everything from religious, to civil, political, and social conduct. All pious, God-fearing Hebrews considered their decisions as coming direct from Jehovah. Hundreds of committees were formed by the Sanhedrin to supervise everything from sweeping the streets of Jerusalem to investigating movements or persons claiming to be Israel's Messiah. They granted permission to build villages or cities, and managed water regulations, security, hygiene, sanitation, and care of the poor and elderly. The local police force fell under their supervision. In some larger villages, street paving with salt was a priority before the rainy seasons. The Sanhedrin served as a "Chamber of Commerce" for Jewish businesses and even controlled fishing in Lake Galilee. A curious twist to their history is that the "official jurisdiction" of this court body was restricted in the time of Christ to the eleven districts into which Judea was then divided. Hence, they had no legal authority over the Lord Jesus, who was from Galilee. When He entered Judea, this limitation seemed to have been not applicable. Despite whatever limitations, it is sure that Jews over the known world feared the power and control of the august group of men. Practically and mentally, their influence and reputation dominated Israel regardless of who ruled the land.

No proselyte baptisms could be performed without permission being granted by the Sanhedrin or their appointed agents. These were mostly doctors of the Torah Law or local magistrates. Baptisms were strictly forbidden unless at least two of these officials were present. This practice helps us understand why the Jews sent a deputation from Jerusalem to question John regarding his baptizing (John 1:19-25).

Apparently, for a time under Roman rule, the Sanhedrin had the authority to execute offenders after clearance was secured from the governor. Hence, the Jews led Jesus off to Pilate to obtain permission to have Him crucified. The governor's orders automatically meant that his soldiery would carry out the sentence given. In the case of Stephen, there is no record of the Jews seeking official permission to kill him. However, this could have been done, and Luke was not inspired to write about it. On the other hand, it could have been a defiance of Roman rule inflamed by their mad passion to have Stephen silenced. Some twenty-three years before the trial of our Lord, the Sanhedrin lost the power of passing the death sentence. This occurred with the deposition of Archelaus (A.D. 6), son and successor of Herod the Great. Upon removal of insane Archelaus, Judea became a Roman province with a governor who administered justice in the name of the emperor. With this, the Sanhedrin was stripped of its right to execute those considered worthy of death. This authority was now in the hands of the duly appointed governor. In the case of our Savior, this was Pontius Pilate, who ruled from A.D. 26-36 and was banished.

The Sanhedrin after A.D. 70

What became of the Supreme Court of Israel? James Drummond, in the *Jewish Messiah*, pages 165-166, gives a curious and brief history of this body of men. He tells of one Rabbi Yochanan ben Zakkai, who escaped the doom of Jerusalem in A.D. 70 by being secretly conveyed out of the city in a coffin. Later, when hostilities subsided, he gathered a group of disciples in the city of Jamnia and attempted to reconstitute the Sanhedrin. Despite this brave effort, within two centuries, Zakkai's plans for a revived and operative Supreme Court for Israel died along the way and the Sanhedrin became extinct.

Two converts from the Sanhedrin

At least two members of this judicial body came to a saving knowledge of Jesus the Messiah. First, there was Nicodemus, a "ruler of the Jews" (John 3:1). Second, was Joseph of Arimathaea, who is described as being "a counsellor" or member of the Sanhedrin (Lk. 23:50). Joseph is called a "rich man" (Matt. 27:57-60). Nicodemus was also a wealthy person. This is reflected in the "hundred pound[s] weight" of myrrh and aloes used to bury the Lord Jesus (John 19:39). This was enough to embalm some two hundred bodies and cost a small fortune! See qualification number 3 on previous page.

The following information gives an overall picture of the operational methods used by the Sanhedrin. These historical facts are given, and then applied to the trials of Christ and His treatment at the hands of this revered body of Israel's greatest leaders. Portions of this are repeated several times in this harmony commentary. Clearly, their treatment of the Messiah was among the greatest travesties of justice in Israel's excellent judicial history.

Mode of trials, various rules, and several forms of punishment

Few courts over time have shown such compassion for humanity as did the ancient Hebrew Sanhedrin. (This was not true when a Gentile was tried.) Every trial was bathed in patience, mercy, long-suffering, and even anxiety on the part of the judges, working together to acquit the accused, especially in cases of capital crimes. It was said of the Great Sanhedrin, "They worked to save life not destroy it." Yet, when it came to the trial of Christ, they broke their own laws, abandoned their sterling reputation, and forever tarnished their beautiful name. The trial of Stephen in Acts 6:12-15, and 7:1-60, was not much different from that of Jesus in its injustice, lying, and outright abandonment of their brilliant judicial guidelines.

Below are some of the directives by which this court conducted their proceedings, explaining their system of voting or giving individual verdicts:

1. Voting commenced with the youngest, moving up to the eldest. This prevented the men who were younger from being influenced by the older members of the court.
2. In the death sentence, a majority of at least two votes was needed to condemn the accused.
3. If found guilty, the verdict of death could only be given the next day.
4. The judges who voted for death had to fast and pray all day before giving their verdict.
5. No trial could be held at night.
6. While the condemned person was moved away to execution, a man led him on a black horse loudly shouting, "This one is found guilty to die. If anyone has further evidence let him come forth to save the condemned." If someone stepped forward and offered to present new evidence, the rider on the black horse would suddenly turn and give a signal to another man standing on a high platform and watching from the open door of the courtroom (Hall of Hewn Stones). The procession stopped and returned to the court building for further evidence to be heard. The condemned person was led with a rope about his neck. Jesus carried the cross beam or patibulum over His shoulders. For more on this, see the third paragraph in "The forty days" sub heading of Section 207.
7. Strong narcotics were given to stupefy or knock the victim out before execution. This is the meaning of Prov. 31:6. The ancient Jews practiced the historical meaning of Prov. 31:6. Jesus was offered this drink in Matt. 27:34 and John 19:29-30.
8. There were four modes of capital punishment:
   a. Stoning.
   b. Burning.
   c. Beheading.
   d. Strangling.
9. In the days of Jesus on earth, the Romans allowed the Sanhedrin to exercise the death sentence only after the appointed governor, ruling at that time, granted permission. The case of Stephen may be an exception to this rule, but there is no reason why the clever Sanhedrin could not have already secured permission to have him stoned and it not be recorded in Scripture. The Sanhedrin was finally dissolved years after the fall of Jerusalem and destruction of the temple in A.D. 70.
10. To strike the accused during a trial was the highest insult among the ancient Jews and was punishable by their law. The following fines were levied for this crime:
    a. Striking with the fist-4 denari (four days' wages).
    b. Smiting with the open palm-200 denari (two hundred days' wages).
    c. Spitting on the accused-400 denari (four hundred days' wages).

In view of the above harsh fines, note the treatment of Jesus during His trial as recorded in Matt. 26:67. No one was fined for striking, smiting, and spitting upon the Lord of Glory. *Hatred* changes unsaved religious men into animals. The Sanhedrin decreed that eleven votes were needed for acquittal; thirteen votes were required for conviction. A majority was two votes instead of the one, as is used in our present day ballot or voting system.

Sanhedrin court procedures. These were all broken during Jesus' trial.

Below are some of the guidelines established by the Supreme Court of the Jewish nation. Several of their directives for court proceedings were based on Old Testament Torah Laws. These are seen in numbers 1, 9, and 11 below. The remainder became their personal rules designed to show compassionate concern for the accused. The fifth division of the Talmud, known as Seder Nezikin (damage), contains a tractate (section) called Sanhedrin. This has some eleven chapters explaining the functions of the ancient Hebrew court systems, especially the Sanhedrin.

In the trials of our Savior, the twenty-two laws listed below were all broken. Their hatred for Jesus of Nazareth, who claimed to be the promised Messiah, was astounding. Read the following passages in dark font to locate in Scripture the different laws broken by these men during Jesus' trial:
1. No arrest by religious authorities that involved a bribe. **Ex. 23:8 with Matt. 26:14-16.**
2. There were to be no steps of criminal proceedings after sunset. **John 18:1-3.**
3. Judges or Sanhedrin members were not allowed to participate in the arrest. **John 18:3.**
4. There were to be no trials before the morning sacrifice. **Matt. 27:1.**
5. There were to be no secret trials, only public. **Matt. 26:57 with Mk. 14:53.**
6. Trials were only conducted in the Hall of Judgment. **Lk. 22:54 with John 18:12-13.**

7. The procedure was as follows. First, the defense of the one charged followed by the accusation. **Matt. 26:58-64.**

8. All may argue in favor of acquittal. They may not all argue in favor of conviction. **Matt. 26:59-66 with Mk. 14:64.**

9. There were two or three witnesses, their testimony had to agree in every detail. **Deut. 19:15 with Mk. 14:55-56.**

10. There was no allowance for the accused to testify against himself. **Matt. 26:59-63.**

11. The High Priest could not rend his garments. **Lev. 21:10 with Matt. 26:62, 65.**

12. Charges could not originate with any of the judges; they could only investigate charges brought before them by others. **Matt. 26:65.**

13. Accusation of blasphemy was valid only if the name of God was pronounced. **Matt. 26:65.**

14. A person could not be condemned based on his words alone. **Matt. 26:65.**

15. The verdict could not be announced at night, only in the daytime. **Matt. 26:66.** See number 19 below, for more on sentence announcements.

16. In cases of capital punishment, trial and guilty verdict could not occur at the same time. They must be separated by at least twenty-four hours. **Matt. 26:66.**

17. Voting for the death penalty was done by individual members. It began with the youngest so that they would not be influenced by elders. **Mk. 14:64-65.**

18. Unanimous decision for guilt showed innocence, since it is impossible for twenty-three (a quorum) to seventy-one men to agree without plotting. **Mk. 14:64.**

19. The sentence could only be announced three days after the guilty verdict. **Mk. 14:64.** For more on this, see number 15 above.

20. Judges were to be humane and kind to all persons being tried. **Mk. 14:65.**

21. A person condemned to death could not be scourged or beaten beforehand. **Mk. 14:65.**

22. No trials were held on the eve of the Sabbath, or on a feast day after sundown. **Lk. 22:1, 15.**

For an excellent, but old coverage of the Jewish Sanhedrin, see the work *Jesus Before the Sanhedrin,* translated from French by Julius Magath, dated 1911. In a careful and judiciary manner, this book demonstrates at least twenty-seven serious irregularities committed by the members of this body during the trial of Jesus. It confirms the above twenty-two different points and adds several others not mentioned. As previously touched on, in the Talmud tractate, Sanhedrin 67a, the Jews wrote that Jesus was hanged on "the day before the Passover." This is an obvious attempt to rewrite their history and cover up the facts concerning the death of Jesus Christ, the Messiah.

The Jewish priesthood and the trials of our Lord. The Hebrew high priests

The Jewish priesthood was divided into three groups. Lev. 8-9 outlines some of their duties. The following two pages give a brief look into the work and duties of these ancient people.

1. The high priest
2. The chief priests
3. The Levites.

These groups of religious functionaries all descended from Jacob's son, Levi (Gen. 49:1, 5). See blocks in Section 7. All priests were Levites, but not all Levites were priests. There were several thousand of these men on duty within the large temple structure. It is noted that before Christ's death, we read, "among the chief rulers also many believed on him" (John 12:42). A few weeks after His ascension, we read these profound words, "and a great company of the priests were obedient to the faith" (Acts 6:7).

The high priests

The term "high priest" is recorded some eighty-two times in Scripture. Only twenty-one of these are in the Old Testament, while it is mentioned almost three times as often in the New Testament. This is because of their opposition to the Savior, apostles, and early Jewish believers. This term appears some twenty-four times in the record of the trial of Jesus! The corrupted combination of Annas, and his son-in-law Caiaphas led the Jews in the fierce opposition of Christ, clamoring for His death. Refer to the fifth paragraph below for details. *Dake's Annotated Reference Bible,* page 236, carries a list of the eighty-six high priests named in the recorded history of Israel. Alfred Edersheim in *Life and Times of Jesus the Messiah,* page 972, gives a list of the high priests from the accession of King Herod the Great to the destruction of Jerusalem in A.D. 70. It has been noted that the wretched Caiaphas also called "Joseph" is number thirteen on the list!

The high priest stood at the head of the Jewish religious hierarchy in that he alone could enter the Holy of Holies once a year, on the Day of Atonement (Lev. 16), to offer sacrifice for the nation. It was his single high privilege to take part at any time in any of the offerings and sacrifices, regardless of what they were! He also served as president (Nasi) of the Great Sanhedrin.

The colorful robes of the high priest were kept by the Romans until needed on the Day of Atonement. See Index in *The Works of Josephus,* under the headings, *"priests, high priest"* for references. Joachim Jeremias in his classic work, *Jerusalem in the Time of Jesus,* pages 147-159, gives a sweeping coverage of the duties of these men of the Jewish clergy. During Roman rule over the land of Israel (as the Jews had no king to represent them), the high priest served as the main "go-between" for them and the pagan Romans. In New Testament times, the famed priesthood lost its hereditary character. It was no longer strictly a father-to-son inherited affair. Rome deposed and appointed whom it chose into the sacred office. With this, the hereditary nature of the high priests' office ceased. Rome filled the office as a matter of political convenience, or to curry favor of certain factions among the Hebrew people.

The chief priests

This term is found in the New Testament about sixty-four times. Because it is in the plural, it has reference to the special temple officers, possibly the captain of the temple police, those in command of various oversights, and the treasurers of the temple income. Basically, they held "administrative" duties and were the "brains" behind the smooth functioning of the vast temple complex and its untold services, rituals, and operations. Today, this task would be comparable to running the gigantic Ford Motor Company in Detroit, Michigan.

The Levites

Apparently, these were the ordinary priests at the Jerusalem temple. Probably, they include the famed twenty-four courses that worked in the temple twice each year (1 Chron. 24). Zechariah, the father of John the Baptist, served in this capacity (Lk. 1:5-10). A part of this group had the duty of attending to the temple music and all services connected with it. Out of this number, the temple police force was built who was responsible for keeping law and order about the temple complex. They attempted the arrest of Jesus (John 7:32, 45-48, and John 18:3, 12), and later arrested the apostles (Acts 4:1; 5:17, 18, 22, 26). This body of special security guards consisted of two hundred and forty Levites, with thirty priests; two hundred and seventy men continually on duty by shifts throughout the vast temple area.

The high priests and the trials of Christ

Two high priests figured prominently in the trials of Jesus. They were "Annas" and "Caiaphas" (John 18:12-13). These verses inform us that Annas "was father in law to Caiaphas." Here, we meet a corrupt setup of two high priests in office at the same time and both in the same family! (This reflects the utter decadence into which this holy office had plunged.) Annas ruled from approximately A.D. 7 to 14. The (then) Roman governor, Valaris Gratis, deposed him for financial corruption and incompetence. Nevertheless, Annas' powerful influence remained. He had four sons, his son-in-law (Caiaphas), and later, a grandson, who were all appointed to the honorable office.

Annas and his family turned the temple compound into a commercial adventure by leasing space for the moneychangers, sellers of livestock, and pigeons. Jesus demolished this business at both the beginning and ending of His ministry (John 2:13-17 and Mk. 11:15-18). Hence, the reason for Annas' fierce hatred of the Savior. His son-in-law, Caiaphas, ruled (part time) co-jointly with his father-in-law, which was illegal according to Jewish tradition and law. Caiaphas' total rule as the high priest was from A.D. 25 to 36. Afterwards, he committed suicide in A.D. 38. Annas, the clever one of the two, was later murdered in a riot caused by one of his sons. As president (Nasi) of the Sanhedrin and as the high priest, he presided at the hearings and trials of Jesus and the apostles, Stephen, and Paul. He had heard the saving gospel many times and rejected it. For other details regarding these religious prelates and their wickedness enacted in the Name of Jehovah God and Israel, see Section 21, Part 1, numbers 6 and 7, under footnote b. These things illustrate again that religion without Christ often turns men and women into clever devils who will stoop to the lowest levels of sin.

APPENDIX SIX

Comments on the life of King James 1 of England and associated events

James Charles Stuart was the only child of Mary I, Queen of Scots, by her second husband, Henry Stuart, known as Lord Darnley. James was born on June 19, 1566 at Edinburgh Castle, Scotland. The marriage of Mary and Henry was tumultuous, filled with fighting, strife, and harassments from Protestants, who bitterly opposed them for being Roman Catholics. Shortly after her imprisonment in 1568, James' mother, Queen Mary 1, escaped prison and led a popular revolt against the ruling powers. She was rearrested and years later beheaded for the crime of trying to put herself on the throne as Queen of England. James' father was murdered on February 10, 1567 in Edinburgh, Scotland, before James was one-year-old. Some three months later, his mother remarried James Hepburn, who was involved in the murder plot of the Duke of Albany. This created a malicious scandal that resulted in an uprising. with the Protestants arresting Mary and throwing her into prison. She was forced to abdicate the throne on July 24, 1567. Her son was crowned five days later as James VI, King of Scotland, at the age of thirteen months!

Like most monarchs, James was reared without father or mother. He was placed in the care of men associated with the national Church of Scotland and given a thorough education by teachers with staunch Presbyterian sympathies. They were all Scottish "lords" and "famed tutors." His education was superior and his mind sharp. "James was given Greek before breakfast." He became fluent in Latin, French, English, Italian, and Spanish. He enjoyed riding, writing, and hunting. He was weak in frame, had a very pointed chin, thin rickety legs, and due to a thick tongue, spoke with a slur and drank liquids with a slurping sound. His abiding physical weakness often required someone to support him when walking. He was noted for a giving, as well as a receiving spirit. His hygiene was terribly lacking. James was intelligent, enjoyed theological debates, and was feared for his "raging temper." When loosed, it resulted in devastating havoc. During his "growing up years," control of his kingdom was in the hands of a series of men called "regents."

At the age of nineteen, James began to rule his native Scotland. Later, he wedded "by proxy" Anne, the fifteen-year-old Protestant daughter of Frederick II, ruler of Denmark and Norway. This marriage took place in 1589. Afterward, King James traveled by ship to Denmark to consummate and celebrate the union. The King and Queen had eight living children and one stillborn. Only three survived infancy: Henry, Prince of Wales, who died of typhoid in 1612 at the age of 19, Charles, who succeeded his father to the throne as Charles 1, and Elizabeth, later, to become Queen of Bohemia, today the Czech Republic.

Queen Elizabeth 1 of England died in 1603. After much political conniving, Scotland and England were finally made a new single state, called the "Kingdom of Great Britain," with King James 1 as the sovereign of both. When he ascended to the English throne in 1603, at the death of Queen Elizabeth, James had already been King of Scotland for thirty-six years! He was now known as "King James VI of Scotland and 1 of England." Upon his arrival in London as supreme ruler of both lands, he found himself plunged into a cesspool of religious and political war, hatred, murder, witchcraft, sodomy, plots, slandering, drunkenness, adultery and the lot. As a Scotsman ruling over the English, the king endured a life long deluge of racism and hatred, especially from the powerful English Lords and Ladies, who were gradually replaced by James' Scottish countrymen. Almost miraculously, he succeeded in uniting Scotland and England into what we call today, Great Britain. In January 1604, James met with certain church dignitaries. The meeting set in motion plans for the *Authorized Version of the Bible* to be produced. In 1605, the Papal Church attempted to kill King James and his political leaders at the opening of Parliament, in a subversive move historically named the "Gunpowder Plot." Some writers believe this was an attempt to stop God's Word from being put into the hands of English-reading people. Knowing the murderous record of the Roman system at this time in history, these suspicions were probably correct.

Anthony Weldon had been knighted by James, but was dismissed from the king's court and became his bitter enemy. Over twenty years *after* his death in 1625, Weldon charged that he was involved in homosexuality. The defenders of the king struggled to absolve him of this heinous sin. Historians had written of his unsavory deeds with "younger men" years *before* Weldon had entered the royal court. Those who make this accusation and use Weldon as their *only* source-reference, have not read enough history. Otto Scott, in his classic work, *James 1: The Fool as King,* vol. 1 page 467, under the heading *"Homosexuality of James,"* lists eight different source-references for this charge. Not one of them mentions the name Weldon. Checking the indexes of twenty different history books about King James 1, his name is not to be found, yet the blot continually emerges. Those who seek to exonerate him as innocent and Weldon guilty, spend too much time on one man. This awful charge had been made long *before* Weldon entered the king's domain. Anthony Weldon, who despised the king, is not a good reference source for anything pertaining to the crown. His writings reek with hatred for the Scottish people and vengeance on the king. Neutral documentation dealing with King James I *before* Weldon came on the scene is more reliable than the words of Anthony Weldon alone. The rebuttal that "formal charges were never laid against the king" is childish. Who ever heard of "formal charges" being laid against the man who could have your head chopped off at the flick of a finger?

The serious issues that harassed King James 1 are swept away by twisting history. Hundreds of historians have written of these. *There are over 5,000 articles about King James I on the internet alone!* This does not include the thousands of books in British and American Universities and public libraries. The older works are coldly void of the pious claims certain writers poured upon the king. He was hardly the "greatest Christian in British royal history." The only faith he defended was that of his Presbyterian Church while struggling to pacify the powerful Anglican community. Those who write that he was a "fearless defender of Bible truth" have read with their eyes closed. William Roughhead, on page 6 in *The Rebel Earl and Other Studies*, gives an example of the king's highly acclaimed valor. He wrote about an intense argument that broke out between two of his attendants, and they drew swords. King James 1, watching the fierce conflict was terrified, fled into a nearby guardhouse, and "fouled his breeches in fear." Translated into modern day English it meant, "The Most High and Mighty Prince, Defender of the Faith" was so frightened that he wet his royal pants.

More serious works dealing with King James 1 are W. L. Mc Elwee's, *The Wisest Fool in Christendom;* David Matthew's, *James I;* Robert Chambers, 2 vols. *The Life of King James the First;* Eric Linkletter's, *The Royal House;* John F. H. News, *Anglican and Puritan: the Basis of their Opposition,* and Charles Williams work, *James I.* The effort by Sir Ralph Winwood in 1972, *Memorials of Affairs of State in the Reigns of Queen Elizabeth & King James 1* is a revelation. Historians such as Sir Edmund Coke, Anthony Wood of James' time, Robert Chambers, and Peter Heylyn portrayed him as a good, upright, moral man. Over history, men have written at great length in the defense of both devils and saints. King James I is another example of this literary conflict that rages to this present moment.

Because James was humanly responsible for launching the *Authorized Version* of the Bible, a psychological myth developed: that this act made him one of the greatest Christians in British history. It is the old story that a bad man could not have given the English world its best Bible. Over history, evil men have given us good things and vice versa. John Chrysostom (died A.D. 407), called "the golden mouthed one," made men weep when he preached. His writings earned him the title "the greatest of Christian expositors." Yet they thunder with vitriolic hatred for the Hebrew people and were used by Hitler to help justify the holocaust! The same was true for some of Martin Luther's works in which he expressed hatred for Jews. Certain *KJV* defenders puzzlingly address the long-time dead monarch as "His Majesty!" These "historians" should know that calling a foreign sovereign "His Majesty" (in the era of King James) was treasonous to one's own country and ruler. Many *KJV* Baptists (and others) are brick blind to the fact that had they lived under James' rule they would have been fined, imprisoned, exiled, or put to death for most of their beliefs. Chief among these were believer's baptism by immersion, separation of church and state, and communion as a simple meal for believers. These facts are dismissed by parroting, "He was an evangelical Christian and would have never done such things." Historical naivety of this sort makes it difficult for honest and fair people who uphold the *KJV Bible.* Refusing to shuffle the facts is the best way to defend them. Those who twist the truth cripple their defense of truth.

Several decades before James was born, the Reformed Church had legalized religious murder at the Diet [council] of Speyer in 1529. Their law read, "All Anabaptist and rebaptized persons, male or female, of mature age, shall be judged and brought from their natural life to death, by fire, or swords or otherwise, as may befit the person." See *A Short History of the Baptists,* page 104, by Henry C. Vedder, 1907 edition. It was at this council that the name "Protestant" was given to all who opposed these Reformed tyrants. A bloody pogrom against Baptists, both true and false, continued into the rule of James 1 and for decades afterwards. The above Reformed edict of hate reflects that they carried the poison of the Papal Church out of which they came. For example, during the Inquisition, Pope Gregory VIII (died 1121) ordered, "A heretic merits the pains of fire. By the gospel, the canons, Civil law, and the custom, heretics must be burned." From *Directory for Inquisitors,* pages 148, 169, by the Cardinal's Inquisitor General. Refer to Appendix I of David Cloud's remarkable work, *Rome and the Bible: Tracing the History of the Roman Catholic Church and Its Persecution of the Bible and of Bible Believers.*

King James I was a scoundrel and political conniver, plagued with intermittent drinking problems and a "lover of Scottish ale." Once while on a hunting trip, he wrapped himself in the bloody skin of a freshly killed deer to "ward off evil spirits." This was a druid occult practice brought into England from Europe: the design was to drive away demonic beings. To his credit, he introduced eating with forks, instead of fingers, and banned tobacco. In 1604, he wrote a scathing booklet against it entitled *Counterblast to Tobacco.* Later, Lord Cecil, the king's secretary, pointed out how badly the tax revenue from imported tobacco was needed to support the kingdom. The king lifted his ban. Sir Walter Raleigh, an enemy of the king, and one of the three men who brought tobacco and potatoes into England, was imprisoned. Raleigh was beheaded by royal command in 1618 at London Tower after two stays of sentence. How strange that the "evangelical Bible believing king" ordered his opponent's head chopped off.

King James' psychotic behavior is reflected in a treatise he wrote in 1597, defending the fact that witches exist, yet severely punished and tortured to death his subjects for believing in them! He launched a "witch hunt" in the late 1500s, which resulted in women and several young girls being put to death. While returning home to England from Denmark with his fifteen-year-old wife, Queen Anne, of Denmark, a horrific storm fell upon the ship. Later, two women (deemed witches) were held "responsible" and burned at a public stake by his command. Will Durant wrote that, "James moderated his fanaticism . . . [and later] insisted on fair trials of the accused." See *The Story of Civilization,* vol. 7, pages 162-163. After this sudden change of mind, the king is credited with saving the lives of five women who had been accused by a mentally deranged boy of practicing witchcraft. Nevertheless, many were tortured to make confessions and others put to death by his orders, during this era of royal madness.

In time, the "good old Puritans" busy leaving England, brought their Calvinistic "kill–the–witches" religious insanity into America. This was seen during the infamous Salem Witch Trials from 1692-1693. The famed Puritan, Cotton Mather, minister of Boston's Old North Church, shared in the murder of fourteen women and five men accused of being or assisting witches. Later, but too late for those hanged, Mather attempted to revise his position on the belief in supernatural entities such as devils and witchcraft. The religious fanatics in old England, Europe, and America based their authority to destroy witches on the *false use* of a passage from the Law of Moses, in Lev. 20:27. (This reflected their permanent entanglement in the Jewish law.) Satan quoted Scripture to Jesus (Matt. 4:5-6) to prove his point. So did King James I, many of the Puritans, the lunatic fringe of the Anabaptists, and others. They all cited the Torah Law to vindicate their barbaric actions. The book by J. I. Packer, *A Quest for Godliness: The Puritan Vision of the Christian Life,* is amazingly silent regarding the bloody deeds of Puritan leadership, as they ruthlessly murdered their opponents and those accused of witchcraft. For earlier comments on the people, called "Puritans," see Section 203, sixth paragraph of footnote d. King James I and the Puritans were continually at enmity fighting with each other.

 Gary North, in his interesting booklet *Puritan Economic Experiments,* attempts to show that everything the Puritans did in America was "inherited [by] intellectual tradition" or brought here from the old country (pages 1-2, 57-58). The murdering of their religious enemies was also imported from the old country! The king and the church in power set the example. Thinking men are confounded why these deeply religious persons did not read and practice what Jesus said about one's enemies in the New Testament. The Reformers and Puritans famed battle cry "Sola Scriptura" ("Scripture Alone") and "Sola Gratia" ("Grace Alone") strangely vanished as they executed men, women, and children with the support of their civil rulers. In 1871, the Scottish Christian, Alexander B. Bruce wrote in *The Training of the Twelve,* pages 245-246 these stirring words, "It is the very nature of zealotry to make men of whom it has taken possession believe that the Almighty not only approves, but shares his fierce passion, and fancies himself instructed with carte blanche to launch the thunders of the Most High against all in whom his small peering inhuman eye can discern aught not approved by his tyrannical conscience."

For comments concerning Reformed Christians not in sympathy with the heinous deeds of those religious marauders both in Europe, England, and early America, refer to Section 203, the fifth paragraph under footnote d. The demons of imprisonment, torture, banishment, and killing your opponents prevailed in the reign of James 1. Apparently, nothing was wrong with James' intelligence. His character was twisted. History demonstrates that men with brilliant minds often have stupid hearts. He revealed this in 1612 by having two men burned at the stake for doubting the deity of Christ. After reading the Scriptures to them then, he then signed the order for their execution. Such deeds reflect the mentality of a religious psychopath. The *Biblical, Theological, and Ecclesiastical Cyclopaedia* of 1872, vol. IV, pages 752-764, by M'Clintock & Strong, carries a devastating article regarding his character. Previously mentioned is a study of numerous persons contemporary with King James 1, found in Will Durant's, *The Story of Civilization*, vol. 7, pages 58, 135-141. Durant was a Roman Catholic agnostic. However, he gives a fair, documented, but shocking look into the conduct, dress, language, and drinking habits of the king. The exhaustive index in volumes 6 and 7 of Durant's books, lists hundreds of persons, places, and events during this period in English history, with page numbers for quick reference. *The Life of James the First,* two volumes, by Robert Chambers is helpful. This work was published in 1830 long before the controversy over the *KJV Bible* erupted. It contains none of the present day biases.

His Majesty the King suffered from fiercely erratic mood swings. They went from peaceful humility to uncontrolled fits of anger. On one occasion, His Majesty flew into moods of wild rage, kicked and pounded on a Court Attendant, John Gib, who had lost a valuable document. Later, when the paper was found, the King fell on his knees before the humiliated aide and begged his forgiveness. During a session of Commons (meeting of politicians), the King exploded into a violent outburst, ripped a page from the official records, and had four of the parliamentary leaders thrown into prison for disagreeing with him. See index of vol. 7 in Durant's, *The Story of Civilization*, pages 58, 158-159 for the details.

For the covert attempt of James to marry his only living son, Prince Charles, (after the death of the eldest, Prince Henry, heir to the throne) to the infanta (daughter) of the Spanish Roman Catholic king in 1623, refer again to Durant, vol. 7, pages 159-161. It was a plan designed to bring peace between Catholics and Protestants in England. This plan does not make James a covert Catholic, but it does classify him as a fool. Love and diplomacy are treacherous bedfellows. A howl of protest that erupted from the British people instantly squashed the plan. This was two years before his death. Historian Durant labeled him the "peaceful dogmatist," because he sought peace at any price. James was a voluminous writer, producing books, poems, advice to rulers, and many religious proclamations regarding Jesus Christ, God, Scripture, and family values. This was standard public rhetoric for the British crown. James' religious accolades, as read in his 1599 work, *Basilicon Doron* (Kingly Gift), written for his oldest son Prince Henry, are quoted to prove he was a sound Christian. In these pages, he blasted effeminacy, sodomy, wild dress, and loose living styles. Some hold that he used English law to crack down on various sins, as a cover for his own wickedness. The *On Line Wikipedia* pages 7-10, notes that his religious writings (such as *Basilicon Doron*) did not appear until *after* the scurrilous and inflammatory gossip of his sordid and shameful conduct became public knowledge. Then "His Majesty" condemned the very sins of which he was guilty. Using James' words as a defense of his character was like stepping into water to test its depth! It is the old story of, "Polish the Devil's boots and no one will know who's wearing them."

Millions have said wonderful things concerning God and Christ, yet their hearts are alien to both. As with King James 1, hundreds of years ago, so it is now. Prelates of the Anglican Church (especially when a new queen or king takes the throne or a royal marriage) speak swelling words of religion. Hundreds of times, I heard their "royal proclamations" over the wireless (radio) while working in Australia. On many occasions, I stood at attention and sang with the Australians their stirring original national anthem, "God Save the Queen." (The anthem has since been changed to "Advance Australia Fair.") These religious semantics are traditional, public-relation actions, sprinkled with biblical truths. *Gullible* American Christians, not understanding other cultures, swallow almost anything they read or hear, especially if it mentions the Bible or Jesus Christ. This base naivety disseminates false information in churches and among *uninformed* believers, creating many religious myths like those regarding the character of King James I. A primary reason James had the Bible translated for English-reading people was that he became terrified that some of his subjects would return to the Roman Catholic Church! However, God turned this into His eternal glory. The prime translator on the king's various committees was the high Anglican churchman, Dean Burgon. He fiercely opposed anyone not of his church, especially Baptists. "He felt their inclusion would lead to the dissolution of the orthodoxy and exclusive authority of his Anglican Church." Burgon said, "I candidly avow that it was a serious breach of Church orders that, on engaging in so solemn an undertaking as the Revision of the Authorized Version, a body of divines [Anglicans] . . . [should] associate with themselves Ministers of various denominations—Baptist, Congregationalists, Wesleyan, Methodists, Independents, and the like: and especially that a successor of the Apostles [the head of Anglican Church!] should have presided over . . . this assemblage of Separatists." Here the Papal travesty of apostolic succession and infallibility (still a part of the Anglican Church today) emerges. For Burgon's exact words, see *The Revision Revised,* by J. W. Burgon, pages 504-505, 1883 edition, printed in London. He was a fierce defender of biblical inspiration. However, unless one was in his Anglican

Church, he was an enemy to the cause of Christ. Independent Baptists, Southern Methodists, Bible Presbyterians, and others who enjoy using Burgon's name in their defense of the *KJV* should note who his enemies were. If living today, he would not be found dead with anyone belonging to these groups! Burgon was not a true fundamentalist. He was a bigoted, exclusive Anglican, who held to infant baptism for salvation; nevertheless, he believed in the inspiration of Holy Scripture, and fiercely defended the Received Text, but strongly resisted *all* Christians outside of his church. Infant baptism for salvation was a lie passed down from the church fathers into the Roman Catholic system. Burgon's claim to be on the equal with Paul, borders on religious insanity. The Reformers reworked infant baptism, tied it to circumcision, and made it acceptable to the ignorant. Those who opposed this were put to death by the church in power and the likes of His Majesty, King James I.

Because the Catholics looked upon Sunday as a holiday, and the Puritans as a day of rest, James attempted to appease both. He published the *Book of Sports,* in which he advised his subjects that Sunday could also be used for games and good times if they went to church first! Priests were permitted to re-enter the country and say mass in private homes. Romanism growth became alarming. Anglican and Presbyterian pressure moved the king to reverse his policy and re-enforce the original anti-Catholic laws.

What about the king's translators? We hear it preached that they were "All great Bible believing, soul winning evangelicals." Those who teach this have either misread or altered history to prove their point. Such claims reflect blatant ignorance of the Anglican Church's theological dogma of soteriology, the tyranny of the British Crown, and its cruel, ruthless treatment of those not in agreement with its religious decrees. Sketchy details about some of the king's forty-seven translators, their backgrounds, lives and morals are found in *The Men Behind the KJV King James Version*, by Gustavus S. Paine, and an older work, first published in 1858, *Translators Revived*, by Alexander McClure. Paine documents how two of the king's translators Andrewes, and Abbot, shared in the burning at the stake of Bartholomew Legate for not believing in the deity of Christ. Paine wrote these words about two of the king's "great Christian translators" on page 142 of his work, "In Smithfield Market on March 18, 1611, at the urging of Andrewes, Abbot, and other irate divines, the king's agents burned Bartholomew Legate at the stake." Oddly, Legate's murder took place in 1611, the very year the *Authorized Version* was completed! In April, another Arian, named Whiteman was also burnt to death. See *Systemic Theology,* page 329, by Augustus Strong. Those, who present the king's translators as *all* being "saintly, angel-like clergymen," should ponder Gustavas S. Paine's chilling words. On pages 40, 69, he mentioned Richard Thomson, a translator who "drank" daily. Equally wrong are those "hard bitten defenders" of the *Authorized Version,* who viciously degrade, slander, smear, and denigrate all who do not embrace their *every* view. One must accept their alterations of history, name calling, mud slinging, and their frequent rejection of historical facts. All who disagree with them are branded "apostates." Such religious apologetics prove the validity of ignorance. However, not all who love and hold to the *Authorized Version* are of this base ilk.

During the seven years of translating, a constant war of white-hot words continued between the Anglicans and Puritans. Meanwhile, the Separatists, Anabaptists, and others stood on the sidelines taking their share of pot shots at each other. This conflict is mentioned in the "Dedication to King James." It reads, "we [the translators] shall be traduced by Popish Persons at home or abroad, who therefore will malign us . . . [on the other hand] "we shall be maligned by self conceited Brethren, who run their own ways, and give liking unto nothing, but what is framed by themselves, and hammered on their anvil." Such confusion proves that God can write on a crooked wall as well as a straight line. The *original* Dedicatory or Preface in the *1611 KJV Bible* is a classic example of the regal, religious double talk always used when presenting documents to royalty. Historically, it was probably Dr. Miles Smith, who drew up the "Preface" or "Dedication." It was not the work of the body corporate of translators. Miles Smith's Preface is a sterling example of "royal boot licking" and "currying favor with His Majesty." Pointing to this Dedication as proof that all the translators were strong Christians in loving fellowship, is like pointing to the Pope as the greatest defender of the virgin birth. Any half-informed person knows that the so-called "Pontiff" and his church has distorted, twisted, and perverted the truth about Mary, and her virgin-born Son. Nevertheless, it is strongly affirmed that some of the king's translators were saved Christians, who labored under the providence of God to give us the greatest of Bibles. To make *all* of them "godly men" because they gave us the *1611 KJV Bible* is credulity in the spotlight.

Nonconformists at this time in church history, including "Baptists" (both good and bad) were singled out, persecuted, imprisoned, and often executed by the crown. Anglicans, Catholics, Puritans, and Reformers, all shared in this religious genocide. Radical Anabaptists ruthlessly killed their opponents.

The hatred demonstrated by early Reformed leaders against *all* not of their "persuasion" is documented history. In the Middle Ages, those not of the Reformed or Lutheran movements were labeled as "Manichees," a name for heretics. This word had reference to a dualistic, oriental religion mixed with fragments of Christian doctrine and heathen philosophies. Various Reformed writers stress the horrific sins of these heretical, breakaway elements among Baptists, then judge *all* Baptists "guilty." All Anabaptists are "Münsterites" or "Manichees," so they write. Research on Anabaptists has been tainted by their enemies in attempts to slander them, and friends to vindicate them. The difference between the larger and quieter body of Baptists in that era and the fragmented lunatics, pretending to represent all others, is overlooked or misconstrued. On the other hand, the silence of Reformed writers regarding the atrocities of John Calvin and his crazed followers at Geneva (even the beheading of a twelve-year-old child), booms likes thunder. These "sola gratia" ("grace alone") Reformers used green wood to ensure a slow, painful death of their foes at fiery stakes. What kind of "sovereign grace" was this?

Historian E. H. Broadbent, in *The Pilgrim Church,* traces the story of those who hated certain baptistic doctrines and distinctive truths embraced by early Christians. They were murdered for their beliefs. Broadbent incorrectly refers to such groups as the Waldenses-Vaudois, Albigenses-Cathars, and Bogomils, as people who believed the Bible. Among these sects were true believers who had to "stomach" the doctrinal poison amid which they lived. No *single* group among these nonconformists (such as those mentioned above) was thoroughly "fundamentalist" in their understanding and practice of Scripture. However, thousands of *individuals* were. Ancient believers who defended and preserved certain major teachings of the faith could be called "baptistic" in doctrine, but not a Baptist Church. Their eschatology was a mixed bag, just as it is among Baptists today.

The Cathars and Albigenses went on a rampage against the ruling Catholic Church. They killed the official representative of the Pope in 1208. Like the pagan Gnostics of old, they held that all matter was evil, which led them to reject the incarnation and resurrection of Christ. This travesty was a fragment of Plato's dualism. In 1209, Pope Innocent III had secured the French army to destroy both groups. Thousands were slaughtered during these purges. In the French town of Beziers, the Pope's orders were to "kill all, kill all, for God knows his own." Since Catholics were forbidden (at that time) to use the sword, they took clubs and beat to death men, women, and children alike. This gave birth to the bloody Catholic inquisitions that later swept across Spain and Europe. It was "dog eat dog" war as one false religion sought to destroy the other false religions. The whole murderous affair was supervised by Satan!

Johannes Warns (died 1937) was a German by birth. Confirmed in the Lutheran Church, he studied for the ministry. The saving grace of God changed his life in 1896. Warns was invited by a simple washerwoman to attend a meeting of the Salvation Army, in Berlin. At this meeting, he found what he had failed to obtain in his church and academic career: a personal saving knowledge of the Lord Jesus Christ. Later, he penned a classic work regarding the Reformation and its leaders. On page 237, of his book, *Baptism,* he wrote, "It is a sad testimony to the superficial and imperfect character of the Reformation that it effected so little change in the spirit of its leaders. Their mind was altered on various vital matters, such [as] salvation by grace and justification by faith, but their spirit frequently remained hard and cruel. Calvin approved the burning of Servetus; Melancthon led Baptists to execution and attribute their constancy to a Satan-infused obstinacy; Ulrich Zwingli endorsed severe penal measure against Baptists at Zurich." Warns continued, "Sometimes it was not otherwise with Nonconformists when they attained to civil power. In the middle of century seventeen, the Presbyterians were as intolerant and fierce as Papist and Episcopalians. These men suffered bitterly to gain religious liberty for themselves and then ruthlessly deny it to others." The evil that directed the barbaric deeds of certain "Reformation heroes" was omni-present before, during, and after the reign of King James 1. He was born into a climate of religious repression and murder. His psychotic behavior suggests that these things affected him. Oddly, James often worked to "compel uniformity" among the religions of his time (Broadbent, page 256).

Neither King James I, the Reformers, Puritans, Presbyterians, Separatists, Independents, Anglicans, Baptists, nor Lutherans were all holy angels. Each group had tyrants within their ranks, especially in leadership positions. Many of these "great Christians" tortured, murdered, and drove out of their walled cities those who would not agree with their doctrines and practices. In past religious history, whenever the clergy joined hands with the civil authorities, persecution and slaughter followed. Among the subjects of James I and the Reformers were thousands who held no sympathies with their barbaric deeds. All *secret dissenters* kept life within their human frames by maintaining a code of strict silence. Most Reformation leaders displayed an abysmal lack of Scripture knowledge and its daily *practice* in their efforts to achieve unity through intimidation, torture, and death. The Reformer's boast, of using only Scripture to direct their work, is a classical example of maddened religious tyranny. Over the course of church history, every fanatic believes God is on his side and points to the Bible to justify his insanity. Standing in the shadows of this dark scenario is Satan, seeking to discredit Holy Scripture and the little community of *true* Christians, who have always been, despite the ravages of history and religious mad men.

On March 27, 1625, King James 1 became seriously ill and called for Archbishop Abbot to give him "extreme unction" or "the sacraments of the Church of England." This reflects the Papal practice of "Last Rites" (still used in both the Roman and Anglican rituals) administered only to terminally ill persons, which "gives them dying grace." God's grace is found only in Jesus Christ, not the wafer or bread of the Lord's Supper (2 Tim. 2:1). James died shortly after "extreme unction." His body was buried in Westminster Abbey. The grandest achievement of his unbalanced rule was providing the English-reading world with the greatest of all books, the *Authorized KJV Bible*. It has been used of the Holy Spirit to bring untold millions to the saving knowledge of Jesus Christ. God Almighty took the reigns of British history, overruled the wrath of man, used the old rascal King James 1, and his translators (good and bad), to give us this Bible. Never in English literary history has there been anything like it, not even the works of Shakespeare. This is not to state that the world did not have the inspired Scripture until the *KJV Version*. What God had written earlier, He preserved and brought to fruition in this greatest of English Bibles.

Religious history before, during, and after the reign of James 1, was a boiling caldron in England, Scotland, Ireland, and across Europe. The divisions between Protestants (whoever they were!) and Catholics mushroomed. Anglicans, Presbyterians, Lutherans, Puritans (already divided into many splinter groups), Quakers, and Baptists, all had their private agendas and exclusive *unbiblical* religious beliefs. As then, so today, a group of extremists called the Fifth Monarchy Men, or Millenarians, believed that Jesus would appear in their lifetime and set up His earthly kingdom. John van Leyden, the deranged Anabaptist, who went to Münster, Germany, in 1533, and declared that he was Enoch. He established a city of murder, torture, rape, and anarchy and called it "the millennium." Hotheaded Baptists split from the other Baptists and created their "Separatist Baptist Groups." Out of these divisions came the General Baptist and the Particular Baptists. This religious wrangling and killing of opponents led many unsaved observers to conclude, "There is no God," and "The Bible is false." Publicly, others daringly denied the reality of heaven and hell, while calling the deity of Christ into question. Free Thinkers, agnostics, and atheists became temporary kings on the mountains. Amid this satanic turmoil, God had His people quietly serving Him, while trying to avoid the wrath of the crown and the organized church. Men trembled at the thought of the torture chambers of the Papal system, as well as the state churches. Confessing Christ at the point of a sword, threats of drowning, flaying, or a fiery stake, does not bring salvation. No one is intimidated into heaven. Worse, the Pope had forbidden the laity (people) to read and translate the Bible!

Weary of persecution, terror, and executions by church-state religions, scores of believers set sail for far-away America and the hope of something better. Streaming into this new land was a tidal wave of religious, as well as anti-God men and women of every persuasion. Over the past four centuries, this has developed into a seedbed for everything secular and religious. Minds are so imprisoned by the intellectual trash of today that few are able to free themselves and think responsibly. Now, both God and Satan are worshiped in America! Governments legislate out proper social restraints, time honored customs, Jesus Christ, and legislate in evil. "Freedom and human rights" become licenses for wickedness. For Colonial America's struggles with mixed religions, see Section 203, sixth paragraph of footnote d.

Advocates for a supreme religious Episcopacy, ruling all Christianity to prevent the terrible mixture mentioned above, are proponents of the "one world ecumenical church" beast. The balance between *true* religious authority and individual freedom is dangerously delicate. Two thousand years of church history demonstrates that it has not been reached. As one religious body apostasies from the faith, out of it comes a minority of true believers. In future decades, some of these drifted from the moorings of biblical truth. Again, true believers withdrew themselves from these heretical church bodies. Some call this "spiritual evolution." It is God's sovereign method of preserving the truth of His Word for future generations.

Amid the darkness of religious insanity in old England and across Europe, God hung out lights of hope for the English-reading world. One of these was the *Authorized Version* of the Bible. After many editions and updates, its impact remains unparalleled in all English literary history. And the wonder of it all is that He used the erratic King James 1 and his quibbling translators to produce this miracle. It is written, "The king's heart *is* in the hand of the LORD, *as* the rivers of water; he turneth it whithersoever he will" (Prov. 21:1).

APPENDIX SEVEN
When were the four gospels written?

The author of this work understands that all four evangelists wrote their books *before* the fall of Jerusalem in A.D. 70. There is no date in Hebrew history as significant. It was the year that Christ predicted for the complete destruction of this great city as recorded by Matthew, Mark, and Luke. See Section 163 for details. Our Lord uttered these terrible words two days before His death. Not one of the four gospels slightly intimates the doom of the city, the temple, and collapse of institutional Judaism as being an accomplished fact. Many have attempted to explain away this loud silence, but ended up only making a little noise. The reason seems clear; all four evangelists wrote *before* this greatest catastrophic epoch in the history of Israel had occurred. We would expect that such a disaster would have left a permanent dent in the literature of that era; it did not, save for the *Works of Josephus,* which were written afterward. This eerie silence is like the omnipotent hand of God forbidding any more to be said than what His Son predicted forty years before it occurred. Because the nation of Israel, and especially its religious leaders, refused to believe this warning from their Messiah, why spend further time with them?

Certain biblical verses indicate that the four gospels had been written and were in circulation among Christians shortly after Jesus' ascension. Matthew's statement about the "potter's field," was still known in his day, and the story of the soldiers being bribed by the Sanhedrin was common knowledge (Matt. 27:7-8 with 28:15). Matthew's editorial comment "whoso readeth, [in the book of Daniel] let him understand," (about the fall of the city) also reveals this fact. If Matthew wrote *after* the city fell then his comment is senseless. Thus, Matt. 24:15 suggests that this book was written *before* the fall of Jerusalem.

Paul sent his first letter to the Corinthian Church about A.D. 54. In 1 Cor. 13:2, he used the term "remove mountains." Prior, both Matthew and Mark had penned similar expressions in Matt. 21:21 and Mk. 11:23. Did Paul paraphrase from one of these two, or was it a well-known expression? Perhaps it was both. Some think they see fragments of Mk. 12:26-27 reflected in Rom. 14:8-9.

The apostle wrote of the Lord Jesus, "That he was buried, and that he rose again the third day according to the Scriptures" (1 Cor. 15:4). We naturally assume that he was speaking of the Old Testament Scriptures. However, there is no place in Old Testament Messianic predictions, which read explicitly that Jesus "rose again the third day." This was the symbolic meaning of Jonah's stay in the fish as recorded in Jonah 1:17 with Matt. 12:40. The "third day" was also the fulfillment of the sheaf of firstfruits waved before Jehovah on the "morrow after the Sabbath [Sunday]" (Lev. 23:9-11 with 1 Cor. 15:20). Could Paul have possibly read this "rose again the third day" (or a similar wording) from one of the four gospels? Were they at this early stage already considered as "Scriptures?" Peter, before his death, classified Paul's letters as "Scriptures" in 2 Peter 3:15-16. The word "Scripture" had reference to the closed canon of the Old Testament. The expression "rose the third day" is recorded in the four gospels in Matt. 20:19; Mk. 9:31; 10:34; Lk. 9:22; 18:33; 24:7, 46; and John 2:19-22. We can easily believe that the term "rose again the third day," and its equivalents had become popular terminology by this time (A.D. 54) among Christians in general. It was the regular language used in speaking of their Lord's death and resurrection. Did the apostle place "standard language" on par with the Holy Scriptures of the Hebrew Bible when he used these words? The weight of this falls in favor of Paul referring to one of the four gospels. Christ's Words in Lk. 24:44-46 reveal that the expression "rise from the dead the third day," came from Old Testament Scripture. Perhaps our Savior was speaking of an interpretation of particular verses meaning this. Note the apostle's words spoken later to King Agrippa (Acts 26:22-23).

Writing to the church at Thessalonica, Paul said his knowledge of the removal of the church was given to him "by the word of the Lord" (1 Thess. 4:15). His words in verses 15-17, cannot be found anywhere in the Old Testament. So where did he obtain this information? It was by divine revelation (2 Cor. 12:1). It was on this surety that he based his specific statements about Christ's return for His own. (Lev. 23:9-11 with 1 Cor. 15:20). Could Paul have possibly read this "rose again the third day" (or a similar wording) from one of the four gospels? Were they at this early stage already considered as "Scriptures?" Peter, before his death, classified Paul's letters as "Scriptures" in 2 Peter 3:15-16. The word "Scripture" had reference to the closed canon of the Old Testament. The expression "rose the third day" is recorded in the four gospels in Matt. 20:19; Mk. 9:31; 10:34; Lk. 9:22; 18:33; 24:7, 46; and John 2:19-22. We can easily believe that the term "rose again the third day," and its equivalents had become popular terminology by this time (A.D. 54) among Christians in general. It was the regular language used in speaking of their Lord's death and resurrection. Did the apostle place "standard language" on par with the

Holy Scriptures of the Hebrew Bible when he used these words? The weight of this falls in favor of Paul referring to one of the four gospels. Christ's Words in Lk. 24:44-46 reveal that the expression "rise from the dead the third day," came from Old Testament Scripture. Note the apostle's words spoken later to King Agrippa (Acts 26:22-23).

At the end of his third missionary journey Paul wrote to the church at Rome, "Bless them which persecute you: bless, and curse not" (Rom. 12:14). Part of this command rings in harmony with Matt. 5:44 where the Savior said, "Love your enemies, bless them that curse you, do good to them that hate you." Is the apostle paraphrasing from the passage in Matthew? If so, then Matthew's book was known this late in Paul's life and quoted as truth. Some think Paul was quoting from John 8:34 in Rom 6:17 and 20. Again, if so, then the book of John was in use at this time and cited as divine authority.

While under house arrest in Rome (Acts 28:30-31), Paul also wrote to the Colossian Christians in approximately A.D. 60. In Col. 3:16, he makes an arresting statement, "Let the Word of Christ dwell in you richly in all wisdom." Where could the believers in this church find the "Word of Christ?" We know His Words were not found in the writings of Moses and the prophets, even though these pointed to Him in many ways. Thus, in what form did the Colossian saints have access to the Words spoken by our Savior? Can this suggest that the gospels or at least part of them were in circulation among believers, even in far away Colosse? We cannot appeal to the perpetuation of frail human memory as the wellspring for the sayings of Jesus. There had to be a common source, established and known to these believers. From this, they were able to ingest the Words of Christ into their lives. What was this mysterious source?

In Paul's first letter to Timothy, written about A.D. 63, he appears to be quoting from either the book of Matthew or Luke in 1 Timothy 5:18b. He wrote, "The labourer is worthy of his reward." Years prior Dr. Luke, in recording the instructions of the Lord Jesus to the seventy, sent ahead of His upcoming trip to Judea, wrote that Christ told them " . . . for the labourer is worthy of his hire" (Lk. 10:7). Did Paul cite this from Luke's letter, or again was it a common colloquialism? It is noted that Matt. 10:11 used a similar but modified form of this expression in the words "who . . . is worthy." If Paul cited this from Matthew or Luke, then the source had to be extant at that time and in circulation. Further, in this same letter to Timothy, a statement seems to affirm overwhelmingly that some, if not all the four gospels were in use, over the known Christian world of that era. This seems to have been established knowledge among Christians even in far away Ephesus. Paul wrote, "If any man teach otherwise, and consent not to wholesome words, *even* the Words of our Lord Jesus Christ, and to the doctrine which is according to godliness" (1 Tim. 6:3). This letter was sent to Timothy, who was presumably the bishop or minister of the church at Ephesus, which was hundreds of miles from the land of Israel. Question: Where or to what source could men resort to read the wholesome Words of the Lord Jesus? And where were these Words of our Savior recorded? There is one answer. (Paul could not have been advising fellow believers to search out the hundreds of extra-biblical books about Christ.) The Words of Christ that God gave for mankind to read and study are recorded *only* in the four gospels. Where did Paul gain the knowledge that Jesus had "witnessed a good confession" before Governor Pilate (1 Tim. 6:13)? Such information is found only in the four gospels. Can this signal that some of these four were popularly known and available for believers to read at this time? During this period in history, pagan government considered these Christian writings conspiratorial. Believers would keep them in secret. Such covert practices helped preserve the four gospel writings as well as the other New Testament books. Apart from human genius, God's providence secured the preservation of His Word. Luke's letters to Theophilus demonstrate this truth. For these two writings to have been kept by Theophilus, guarded, copied, and recopied, and handed down with reverence over the decades to those who would protect them, had to be of God. Centuries later, their divenly preserved messages were still in existence and finally canonized! This applies to every letter in the New Testament. As God worked by the Holy Spirit through men to write them, He also used men to keep them.

Practical reasoning is a compelling voice that says the gospels had been written in Paul's lifetime, and their accessibility presented no problem. This conclusion constitutes evidence that some, if not of all of the inspired records of the life of Christ, were available, widely known throughout first-century Israel, and further abroad. The four gospels were not documents written decades later, as taught by German rationalists such as David Strauss (died 1874). The clamor from those who deny biblical inspiration about the "quest for the historical Jesus," are the word's of the Devil. One finds the "historical Jesus" in the four gospels. Only men who deny the inspiration of Holy Scripture talk this tripe. Believing this, they must reject the Messiah or Christ as presented in the gospels, stripping Him of His deity, miracles, and divine claims. Having no authoritative source they created their own Jesus Christ, one foreign to the four gospels, and historical Christianity; an ignorant, helpless Jew, struggling to make a religious name for Himself. Infidel religionists rejecting a trustworthy Bible invented these fables. For a summary review of "higher biblical criticism," its proponents, and devastating results, see the *Author's Introduction*.

John 5:2, reads, "Now there is at Jerusalem by the sheep *market* a pool . . ." The obvious overture is that Jerusalem and its temple were standing, intact, and operative when John wrote this. These words if taken at face value were penned before the fall of the city in A.D. 70. Hostile critics famed for their late dating of everything, struggle with this verse because it affirms that the temple operations were functioning when John penned his gospel. This flies in the face of their infidelity. Therefore, they must date John's letter (regardless to whom it was originally written) long after A.D. 70. However, the "learned theologians" will turn heaven and earth upside down to prove that it does not mean what it says. Luke had informed Theophilus at the beginning of his letter that "many others have taken in hand" to write about the Lord Jesus (Lk. 1:1). "Many others" cannot mean a few, or even the four gospels. Hundreds, if not thousands, of writings were in circulation about the Savior as Luke dipped his pen into ink to write to Theophilus. The objection that these thousands of other writings have not been found is ridiculous! Why will not these "experts" apply the same argument to the documents of Roman political history? For example, how many copies of government proclamations made by any of the Caesars do they have? According to the "scholars," because we do not have a copy of Governor Pilate's official report to Emperor Tiberius' about the death of Christ, He did not die! Such reasoning is sheer academic folly.

Near the end of his missionary activities, Paul addressed the elders of the church at a seacoast city named Miletus (Acts 20:17-18). This was about A.D. 59. At the close of his message, he makes a startling statement in Acts 20:35. The aged missionary recites some of the *unrecorded* Words of the Savior. These are not found in the four gospels. He called on his audience to "remember the words of the Lord Jesus, how he said, 'It is more blessed to give than to receive.'" This affirms that a body of oral words uttered by the Lord Jesus were in vogue and remembered among believers, even in the far away pagan city of Miletus. A few verses down in Acts 20:32, Paul reminded them of "the word of his [Jesus'] grace which was able to build them up." Where did they find this word of Christ's grace? Can this have reference to any of the four gospels? Surely, he was not speaking of the Old Testament by using the personal pronoun "his." The ascension of our Lord had taken place some twenty-five years earlier. It is impossible that the elders to whom Paul spoke could have remembered these things, unless some of those in his audience previously knew them. The Words and works of Jesus were recorded, collected together, while others were stored in the nomenclature of human memory, and these were well known across the Christian world of that day. It is not much different today.

Though not directly relevant to subject of this Appendix, there is also evidence that Jerusalem was standing when the book of Revelation was written. How odd that the apostle would have been commanded to measure the ruins of a temple long since destroyed (Rev. 11:1). It is noted that there is no temple in heaven (Rev. 21:22). These actions make no sense, unless the city and temple were intact when John received his revelation from God. To spiritualize the commands given by the angel is to beg the question. If these things are true, surely this serves to bolster the proposal that the four gospels along with the book of Revelation had been written much earlier. With this, see *Appendix Two* and the time James wrote his epistle in which he quoted from Jesus' Sermon on the Mount. John penned the book of Revelation before the temple was destroyed or the angel was playing games with him. It is impossible that a book of this nature would fail to mention the destruction of the city and demise of the Jewish nation. The reason this is missing is that John wrote the Apocalypse *before* the doom of A.D. 70 occurred.

The question arises, why did Paul, Peter, John, and the other writers of New Testament not quote from the four gospels if they were in circulation? The *final* answer to this we do not know. However, it can be stated that thousands were living for the next fifty years after Christ's ascension, who saw and heard Him preach and teach. They became public witnesses to His life and message. Books about Christ's life were hardly needed during these years with so many audible witnesses present. As the early believers died out, persecutions arose, and heresies appeared (degrading the Person and work of Christ), God inspired the four evangelists, Matthew, Mark, Luke, and John, to pen the infallible records of the life of His Son. They are the absolute surety that our Lord is who He claimed to be.

Peter admonished those of "like precious faith" to "grow in grace, and in the knowledge of our Lord" (2 Peter 3:18). What was their source for this knowledge by which they could grow? Surely, it was some written document. In 1978, David Estrada and William White Jr. published an astounding little book called *The First New Testament*. It proves that attempts were made to write about the life of Christ, if not during his ministry, then shortly afterwards. As would be expected their work was attacked, slammed, ridiculed, and lambasted by the "learned scholars and higher critics" of the day. This reveals that here was another truth that their infidelity could not bear. It is no wonder that such a book was a failure in the sales of Christian literature. It proved miserably wrong the majority of "scholarly opinions" on when the gospels were written. For continued comments on the canonization of the New Testament Scriptures, see Section 2, second and third paragraphs under footnote g.

Men and women who sit in the church pews, pay the bills, and keep things running in general should rise up against every vestige of academic religious atheism that shows its ugly face in their midst. It has cursed their pulpits and benighted the minds of their children. It attacks Jesus from all sides. The final aim of biblical skepticism is to demote the blessed Son of God, the Savior of men, by calling into question the record of His life, redemption on the cross, and resurrection. Poor and miserable is that believer who struggles under the sophistry of religious toil without knowing Christ as personal Lord and Savior. He does not know that where God is, Satan cannot stay long, and where the Holy Spirit does not rule, all work is of the flesh and therefore, fruitless. No *true* worship is ever performed where the Lord Jesus is scorned, degraded, or courteously reduced to a mere man, though a good one. Failure to discern this is to fail in the service, adoration, and worship of God Almighty. With unsaved men running the church, singing hymns, directing the programs, teaching and preaching, the Holy Spirit is offended. The Bible in the pastor's hand may "contain" the Word of God; he is not sure. Calling Jesus "Lord" within the "the sanctuary," then denying Him and His Word in private and public life is the Judas kiss of betrayal.

The towering figure of "contemporary critical theology" with a debauched retranslated four gospels is the work of a religious Goliath, defying the Lord of heaven and His people. The death stone from a little David's sling is long overdue for this monster, which casts its hideous shadow over the lives of millions. Christians sitting in this unholy atmosphere must rise up against the satanic invasion and cast this Devil out of the house of worship. The struggle to retain the purity of the gospels is a struggle of *unbelieving* academic learning against the shocking ignorance of ordinary, born-again Christians sitting in the pews. They know things are wrong but are fearful to challenge and correct the source of evil. In this battle, we dare not elevate the problem above the solution. The solution is in the hands of Christian men and women who are helpless. They are so weak in prayer and God's Word that the problem rules them with awful intimidation. Like the little sparrow with a broken wing, they cannot fly with the remedy.

God has vouchsafed for humanity the four gospels, which are the only and *totally* true records of the earthly life of His Son. Religious men and women who give no confession of personal salvation by faith in Christ, and therefore, do not believe the Bible is God's inspired Word are the greatest enemies of mankind. Academic qualifications only support their spiritual darkness. No one is qualified to write anything of value concerning Jesus Christ, unless they know Him as personal Lord and Savior. When they do, it is always the religious falsity of academic darkness mixed with microscopic fragments of truth. To these people, Christ never knew if He was just a carpenter from Nazareth or the Son of God and Savior of men. He wandered over the land of Israel trying to get a religious following. His virgin birth, sinless life, and miracles can be explained by the natural, never the supernatural. Worse, His death on the cross and resurrection were either faked or can be explained in political terms.

The malignant teaching that Paul wrote his letters fifteen to twenty years *before* Mark has its origin in French and German rationalism. They tell us that Paul was ill informed, or at best uninformed on the life of Jesus. We are to believe that Mark was an ignoramus who could not figure out if Jesus was the Son of God or not. And that Matthew and Luke plagiarized from Mark in order to pad their gospels.

Years ago, I spoke on the death and resurrection of Christ from the book of Matthew, at an African college in Natal, South Africa. Afterward, a teenage Zulu boy came to me and said, "Thank you sir, for the Word of God. I have received Jesus Christ as my Lord and Savior. Please tell all Africans that there are no round trip tickets to hell!" This young man was saved in the morning meeting while standing in the school courtyard for almost two hours under the scorching sun. A week later, he drowned in a pond near his village (kraal). Better to be as that heathen lad who was instantly redeemed from his sin than among the army of brainy supermen, who have many degrees but no heat, and blazingly pit their spiritual ignorance against the Word of God and the God of the Word. The four gospels were written early in Christian history and remain the only infallible witness of the life of Christ. Their message still saves those who believe, and will finally serve as a witness in judgment against those who do not (John 12:48).

APPENDIX EIGHT

A brief historical survey of the Antichrist and end time guessing game

This final Appendix examines the Antichrist in a *brief* general manner void of the standard dogmatism on the more difficult passages. Innumerable speculations regarding this person, his work, and companions, increase each year. Fascination with the Antichrist has existed over the course of Jewish and church history with its highs and lows. During the past centuries untold thousands claimed to have discovered his identity. In Christian eschatology, he has come to mean many things. To some, the Antichrist is a real person who will appear in the "end-times" to rule the world. For others, he could be an image or spirit of heresy. One theory says he is dead, in hell, and will rise from that place at a future date. Some have considered the Antichrist as being such calamities as the Black Death, diseases, and censures by kings, rulers, government oppression, natural disasters, and ethnic pogroms. Many hold that the name points to a political or religious institution, possibly a nation. Over the past two millennia, the meaning of Antichrist has acquired multiple definitions. Amid every extraordinary social, political, economic, religious, and human calamity, someone, somewhere, believes he has found the Antichrist. Time has proven all of them wrong without exception. Their proposed Antichrists gradually changed forms, retired from politics, while others were executed, banished, died of old age, or simply disappeared from human activity. This sensational, lucrative, and ill based guessing game continues to this day.

Antichrist in Jewish mythology

Jewish tradition and mythology are rich and ridiculous with legends regarding this theme. Rabbinical writings belonging to the post-Christian era and onwards refer to an Antichrist, who was called (among other things) "Armilius." This word is probably derived from Isa. 11:4, being a euphemism for someone in the text called "the wicked." The story of the Jewish Antichrist's birth from a virgin statue of stone at Rome, smacks of a distortion of Jesus' birth by Mary in Bethlehem. The ancient rabbis affirmed that there would be various signs prior to the appearing of Armilius-Antichrist. These signs or religious phenomena were more or less, built around the activities of Jewish history and nations with whom they were associated. Amid numerous tumultuous historical events, Armilius would appear. For a review of the absurd signs claimed by ancient Jewish rabbis, see Section 100, the third and fourth paragraph of footnote a. Below is a short review of these signs and events associated with this evil person. They have been gathered from various rabbinical exaggerations and fables.

1. Three false kings would appear, all pretending to be God.
2. An unbearable rise in the sun's heat.
3. A dew of blood would cover earth.
4. Dew from heaven that would heal the pious.
5. Darkness would cover the sun.
6. Rome would have universal power to rule for nine months by the hand of their great leader. At the end of these months a Messiah would appear, known as "Messiah Ben [son of] Joseph." (This is the first of two different Jewish Messiahs.) He would slay this Roman authority. Further details concerning these "two Messiahs" allegedly to rise in the Hebrew traditions of eschatology are found in Section 6, sixth and seventh paragraphs under footnote d.
7. Suddenly, "Armilius" would appear. He is the one whom Gentiles and Christians call "Antichrist." He will be born from a marble statue in Rome being impregnated by Satan. Then (to our amazement) we read that the Romans will receive him as their Messiah. Afterward, the entire world will fall subject to this powerful figure. Suddenly, and without warning, he would reject the Torah Law and demand worship of himself. War and destruction will follow with the first Messiah called "Ben [son of] Joseph" being killed.
8. Michael the archangel will blow a trumpet three times. At the first blast, Israel's *true* Messiah, Ben [son of] David, and Elijah would appear. He would raise a great army of Christians, and lead them to conquer Jerusalem. Lastly, God will rain fire and brimstone from heaven (Ezek. 38:22) resulting in the destruction of the armies of the evil one.
9. At a second trumpet blast, all graves shall open and "Messiah Ben [son of] Joseph" will rise from the dead. See number 7 above.

10. With the third trumpet sounding, the ten lost tribes will be led to paradise and celebrate the wedding of their Messiah called "Ben [son of] David." One can detect *fragments* of New Testament teaching concerning the Antichrist in these ancient Hebrew traditions and legends.

Parts of the above reveal that the *later* rabbis borrowed from early Christian doctrine and the existing New Testament books to embellish their fables and myths. This plagiarizing is also detected in portions of the Talmud. The ten signs above are colored with standard rabbinical exaggerations, and traditions. Often, one detects in their juggling of history an attempt to explain (away) certain events in the life of Christ, especially His resurrection. For the modern day Jewish understanding of Jesus, which was not that of the ancient Hebrews, see Section 14, footnote f.

Antichrist in Islamic eschatology

Islamic teaching about the Antichrist was partly plagiarized from the Bible and Jewish tradition. It has been grossly distorted to fit their religious superstitions. Muslim eschatology abounds with signs, which signal the end of time. They are classified as "greater" and "lesser." The foolishness of this is seen in the following examples: "The sun will rise from the west. A beast will appear from the earth some eighty feet (24 meters) high. This creature will carry the staff of Moses and Solomon's kingly seal. The word 'unbeliever' is to be stamped on the face of all who have not converted to Islam."

In *early* Islamic history, after Muslim Turks captured Constantinople in A.D. 1453, suddenly the Antichrist was to have appeared using his older name "Al Dajjal," ("imposter-liar"). He would be blind in one eye, deaf in one ear and have "unbeliever," written on his forehead. This will be the same person that the rabbis named "Messiah Ben [son of] David." He was to enter Mecca and Medina then set up his kingdom. Suddenly, Jesus would appear in Jerusalem riding on a donkey and kill him at the gate of the city. (Obviously none of these things happened.) Sunni, the largest branch of modern day Islam teaches that a "great Imam" is coming to earth; he will destroy western democracy, Christianity, America, and Israel. This Muslim Messiah will induct sharia law, and the religion of Islam will rule the world. He will be a "divinely guided" person (Messiah), the twelfth Imam and final Caliph of universal Islamic rule. Jesus will embrace their religion, marry a wife, and have children after reigning in peace for forty years! Some older Muslim writers identified Paul the apostle as the Antichrist!

In 2006, Joel Richardson published *Antichrist: Islam's Awaited Messiah*. This helpful book has more speculations than facts about final events. *God's War on Terror—Islam, Prophecy and the Bible*, by Walid Shoebat, former PLO terrorist, who found Jesus as Lord and Savior, gives a rare inside look at Islam the "religion of peace." For classic works on Islam and Muhammad its founder, see *Answering Islam*, by Normal L. Geisler and Abdul Saleeb. Robert Spencer's opus, *The Truth about Muhammad* is a brief masterpiece on the subject of Islam's founder. Islamic eschatology (like that of the Jews already mentioned) is an example of plagiarizing from earlier historical documents, then blending them with pagan mythology. All this is a distortion of biblical truth about the real Antichrist that is yet to appear. For an excellent review of Antichrist in early Islamic teachings, see the *Biblical, Theological, and Ecclesiastical Cyclopaedia,* vol. I, pages 253-260, by M'Clintock and Strong. The entire religion of Islam is Antichrist in the sense that it denies Jesus Christ's deity, death for our sins, and glorified bodily resurrection. The savage hatred of *radical* Muslims for America, Israel, and Christianity has its origin in Satan and demon spirits.

Antichrist in Old Testament history

Nimrod, Pharaoh, Balaam, Edom, the Philistines, Assyrians, Nebuchadnezzar, Cyrus, Arabians, Korah, Ahab, Alexander the Great, Julius Caesar, and many others are a dim caricature of the evil one according to various writers. To some, the well-known term "Belial" reflects the Antichrist (Judges 19:22 with 2 Cor. 6:15). Certain Old Testament commentators believe they have found dozens of names in Scripture for this villain. Thus, Old Testament characters, persons, and nations mirror him. In Dan. 7:7-12, we read about "the little horn." He has "a mouth speaking great things" (verse 8). Historically, this had *first* reference to the Syrian ruler Antiochus Epiphanes, who desecrated the Hebrew temple in 167 B.C. However, his wickedness seems to reach ahead even into the real end of things. For then, the Ancient of Days, the Lord Christ, at His coming (2 Thess. 2:8) will destroy him. Therefore, he cannot be totally relegated to past events for Jesus has not returned, nor did this happen in A.D. 70. Daniel is history and prophecy written for persecuted Jews, but it contains future predictions. Unsaved critics deny this, believing that the Bible is another poorly written history book.

Later, in Daniel, we meet the "king of fierce countenance" (Dan. 8:23-25). This also seems to have reference to Epiphanes the Syrian lunatic who is often considered a prototype of the Antichrist yet to appear. In Dan 9:26-27, we read of one called "the prince that shall come," who would set up the "abomination of desolation." Historically, this had fulfillment in Titus, who destroyed Jerusalem in A.D. 70 and desecrated the temple. Many expositors see in this prince a shadow of the future Antichrist. Some make the "abomination" of Daniel the same as Paul's "man of sin" (2 Thess. 2:3-4). Daniel 11:21-45 tells of a "willful king" who would appear on the scene and defy both man and God amid his blasphemous prosperity and awful authority (verse 36). In this terrible person of the past, there may be a precursor of the future Antichrist. Within this eschatological labyrinth, expositors jockey hard to prove their interpretation. One thing remains sure; not all of them can be right.

It is surely incorrect to relegate all the above persons and forecasts *totally* into the past. Historically, various wicked men committing horrible acts have risen over the course of time. Beyond the infamous figures of ancient history, some of these monsters propel us forward, and dimly portray for the world and a generation yet to come, a human Devil, the *real* Antichrist, who will finally appear.

Antichrist and a revived Roman Empire

The words of Rev. 13:1 and 17:10 are used to prove that the above superman will rise on the scene of world politics from within a revived Roman Empire. Verse 10 reveals that "there are seven kings: five are fallen, and one is, *and* the other is not yet come; and when he cometh, he must continue a short space." History impeccably vindicates that the five kings (rulers) or kingdoms referred to in this statement, which had fallen, were Egypt, Assyria, Babylon, Medo-Persia, and Greece. The power ruling when John penned these words was Rome, which disintegrated from within and collapsed about A.D. 500. He wrote that the final world power had not yet risen up in his time. Thousands hold that this last global authority will be the ten toes of Dan. 2:41-44. The specialists tell us that this conglomeration of ten nations will constitute a revived Roman Empire during the final years of this dispensation. The Antichrist is to be the chief figure within this global economic-political body. The name given the mega body is (EU) or European Union, (referred to as ECM or the European Common Market), which is slated by "prophetic specialists" to become the revived Roman Empire. To the dismay of many, the EU or European Union presently (2011) has a membership of twenty-seven different countries. This is seventeen too many for the ten toes of Daniel chapter 2. Ten of the member nations have what is known as "separate status" full membership. The remaining nations, which joined after the original ten, have only "associate membership." Again, certain "specialists" taught that these *original ten nations*, which came together in the 1960's, fulfilled the predictions of Daniel's ten toes. Clearly, here is another pragmatic guess, for we find nothing, not even an infinitesimal suggestion of "associate membership" or "separate status" in these biblical predictions. As it stands today, Daniel's statue has too many toes to qualify for Bible prophecy! The EU theory at its best is riding in a spiritual wheelchair. It suffers from lack of *sound* historical and biblical support. The "experts" assure us that these toes will become a united world power. This is a blind guess! Those who believe they have the *right answer* should be honest and admit it is only brainy conjecture. For some this is difficult being a prisoner of the eschatological pride and cannot handle the embarrassment of being wrong, again.

Over the centuries, "end-time specialists" have kneaded into biblical eschatology a bewildering assortment of interpretative identifications. These include China with nukes, America's decline, Islamic Tehran, Jewish efforts to reconstitute the Sanhedrin, world money lords setting up offices in Jerusalem, Johannesburg, New York, and Sydney; deadly viruses, Israel ("God's time piece"), oil, Iran, Iraq, swine flu, Russia's nuclear missiles, apostate Christianity, and other things. We hear that the Antichrist, and his associates will ultimately supervise all global events. Some believe he will sign a peace treaty with Israel. Later, he will break this and then sit in a rebuilt Hebrew temple at Jerusalem, with the world worshiping him through one ecumenical religion. Many think that this religion is the woman of Revelation chapter 17. Others interpret the scarlet female as a declining America, others as Islam. Apart from the intrigue, there is a tremor of uncertainty attached to these guesses. However, it remains true that parts of this end-time scenario are surely right. Other interpretations are too young to qualify as historically established Bible doctrine. (A 144,000 Jewish missionaries preaching in the tribulation is an example of this.) Forcing extraordinary historical events and people into prophecy is forbidden. *Rarely does the Bible justify putting the name of a person, city, or country on prophetic passages.* Many preachers have no problem doing this, even though time has proven them wrong for almost two thousand years.

God has *not* recorded the whole story of eschatology, only pieces of it. Filling in the gaps that He has purposely written with guesses is daring business! In time, these traditionally filled-in-gaps gradually become accepted as basic doctrines of the Christian faith. Conservative churches across America are cursed with this error. One should not put traditions, ideas, and assumptions of great men on par with God's inspired Word. This error has caused dissension and division among millions of Christians, especially when dealing with the return of Christ. It is wrong; it is sin!

There may be a revived form of the old Roman Empire or there may not. *Perhaps, there will be something far worse; something that no one has yet understood.* It is curious how things change, disappear, and then reappear in another form over time. The biggest surprise (that God has *not* recorded in Holy Scripture) may yet come! We see through a glass darkly when dealing with and attempting to interpret the courses of *entire* world history. There is more to this than we Christians understand.

Over history, various world bodies were formed causing certain events to transpire. Many of these were marked as the "tool of Antichrist." Already mentioned is the European Union (EU) supposedly laying the groundwork for a global economic organization, the emergence of Antichrist, and a one-world government. Among the thousands on the prophetic scrap pile of time are, the old League of Nations, Nazi Germany, Imperial Japan, Mussolini's fascist Italy, the Soviet Union, Communist China, Russia, and scores of others. The predictions of Daniel and John are seized upon during crisis times and turned into proofs that the "rapture is near." The First World War alarmed "the end-timers" and provided them cannon fodder for their infamous predictions. Prophecy specialists such as James M. Gray, Isaac M. Haldeman, A. B. Simpson, R. A. Torry, Arno C. Gaebelein, William E. Blackstone, W. W. Fereday, A. E. Thompson, and others set dates or near dates for Christ to return. They had "read the signs." Yet World War I ended in 1918, and Jesus did not return. The same was true of World War II. During the height of this war, a famed southern evangelist persuaded himself that Hitler was the Antichrist and Mussolini the false prophet! This good man's books "proving" this sold by the thousands. That was well over fifty years ago. Another guesser "bit the dust."

No one knows the exact chronology of when *genuine* final events will end and Jesus will return, much less the names of the actors in this drama of hell. The world's largest false cults started mostly in America in the 1800s. A few began in England and Europe. They all began with a common denominator which "Spirit filled and gifted" date setters was purporting to know the time of Jesus' appearing. They were wrong just like the "Bible believing conservatives" are today. It is another miserable chapter in the disgusting book of human speculations about when our Savior will return for His church.

Part of the Antichrist end time guessing list since the ascension of Jesus

Two thousand years ago, various Roman Caesars were candidates. Included were Caligula, Nero, Vespasian, Titus, Domitian, Diocletian, Julian, and especially Constantine. Following the death of Emperor Constantine (A.D. 337) and the rise of the so-called Holy Roman Empire, whatever attacked the Roman Catholic Church was "Antichrist." Ancient cults such as the Gnostics, Ebionites, Nicolaitans, Nestorians, Cerinthians, and those now on the stage of Christianity join the number of Antichrist guessers. For some, the entire Roman Empire was the Antichrist. Within this mangled maze, we have the Popes, Protestantism, various Roman Catholic cardinals and bishops, Charlemagne, Martin Luther, John Calvin, Zwingli, Melancthon, Beza, the Orthodox Church Patriarch Nikon, the Russian madman Rasputin, a German "philosopher" Friedrich Nietzsche, Charles Darwin, Clarence Darrow, the Rockefellers, Rothschilds, and Henry Ford. Hundreds more could be added to this list. In past decades the Illuminati, Masonic Lodge, Nazism, Marxism, Leninism, Stalinism, socialism, Proctor and Gamble, highways numbered 666, the ACLU, international bankers, numerous movies, the Muslim terrorist organization Hamas, the Freedom from Religion Foundation (FFRF), and capitalism ranked high among the nominees for the Antichrist title or mark. The madness does not end here.

Other personality identifications have been Adolf Hitler, Mussolini, Franklin Roosevelt, Joseph Stalin, Heinrich Himmler, Nelson Rockefeller, Muammar Gaddafi, Mikhail Gorbachev, Kofi Annan, Henry Kissinger, Ian Paisley, David Koresh, Jim Jones, Jimmy Carter, Elvis Presley, Ted Kennedy, Prince William of England, and Vladimir Putin. Recent candidates are Bill Gates, Tony Blair, Bill Clinton, George Bush, and Barack Obama. A cult called "Share International" founded by Benjamin Crème, says the Antichrist is "an energy released." Over the past two millenniums, unrestrained religious enthusiasts have marked countless thousands of things, movements, spirits, individuals, or even themselves as being that wicked person the Antichrist. All have been wrong!

Clarke's Commentary, vol. vi, page 999 bluntly states, "Even Protestantism may have its Antichrist as well as Popery." The Seventh Day Adventist cult and much of Reformed theology have appointed the Popes as this person. Among fragments of Reformed scholarship, the guesses about who or what this person will be are as bizarre as those invented by certain Baptists and Pentecostal preachers. The latter are notorious for finding Antichrists in every extraordinary event of world history, especially if they occurred in or near the land of Israel. What is more alarming than the fact that they have been wrong for over a hundred years, is that they persist in this time-proven false eschatology! When theological error becomes tradition, and tradition becomes "truth," most of those who embrace it are enslaved for a lifetime.

Apocalypticism on the rampage. Men have continually picked thousands of dates over the centuries, guessed the Antichrist, and the time of Jesus' appearing. All have failed.

The champions of the "it's near" movement continually parrot the worn out cliché, "All the signs are in place; I believe Christ is coming soon." The author has heard this hundreds of times over six decades and read it in scores of books; several of these writings were over a thousand years old. Research demonstrates this prediction has been in vogue for almost two millenniums. We wonder what the word "soon" means to these people. Like rubber band it can be stretched over several thousand years without breaking! Carl E. Armerding and W. Ward Gasque's work, *Hand of Biblical Prophecy*, gives a short history of end time date setters. A brief historical review of the guessing game reveals the following:

In the time of Paul, these guessers had greatly troubled the Thessalonian Christians (2 Thess. 2:1-3). Hippolytus (died A.D. 236), wrote that Christ would return several centuries after his death. Hundreds postulated their guesses over the next eight centuries as convulsions of nature in the form of earthquakes, floods, storms, hurricanes, typhoons, plagues, wars, famines, volcanic eruptions, droughts, epidemics, eclipses, and other phenomena fell upon mankind. However, our Lord did not return! Millions trembled as the year A.D. 1000 approached. These "shaking saints" had calculated that the one thousand years in Rev. 20:7-8 had expired and that Jesus would appear in judgment. When this did not happen, they reset the date counting from His ascension to A.D. 1033. The bubonic plague of A.D. 1348 was another sign of the end. Mother Shipman was a British seer (or hoax) who died in 1561. Her prediction that the world would end in 1881, caused a great stir across old England and parts of colonial America.

The British "rapture authority," Arthur E. Ware set dates for Jesus to return in 1933, 1953, 1963, and 1970. He died in 1978. Ware was part of the company of thousands who had special revelations and knowledge of Christ's return. They all met their end before the *real* end came.

Nostradamus (died 1566), a French Jewish physician, occultist, and stargazer wrote in his *Centuries,* quatrains (stanza of four lines) 23 and 81 that Antichrist would appear between 2008 and 2012.

Christopher Columbus believed Christ would return in 1672. He died in 1506.

Martin Luther, predicted Jesus would return three hundred years after his death, which occurred in 1546. For more on Luther's strange statements, see *The Familiar Discourses of Dr. Martin Luther*, pages 5-10, translated by H. Bell in 1818, and revised by J. Kerby. Refer to Section 14, number 5 under footnote f, and Section 203, eighth paragraph of footnote d for another shocker from the great German Reformer.

In 1593, the brilliant but erratic German mathematician, John Napier, published his book *A Plain Discovery of the Whole Revelation of St. John*. He based his work on personal calculations from dates found in Daniel and Revelation. This eschatological fluke was "dedicated to Prince James VI, King of Scottes." Napier set the "day of judgment at A.D. 1700." In 1830, Adam Clarke, wrote of Baron Napier's revelations these words of truth. "We who have lived to . . . see the fallacy of these predictive calculations; and with such an example before us of the miscarriage of the first mathematician in Europe, in his endeavors to solve the prophetical periods marked in the most obscure book, we should proceed in such researches with humility and caution, nor presume to ascertain the times and the season which the Father has reserved in his own power." See *Clarke's Commentary*, vol. 1, pages 23-24.

The popular Baptist preacher, Benjamin Keach said that the Savior would return in the years 1689.

Jonathan Edwards, one time President of Princeton College, looked for the return of Jesus and the Antichrist in his day. Edwards died in 1758. This great man missed it well over two hundred years!

The Shakers cult, which began in England in 1747, was led by "Mother Ann who represented the divine female." She calculated the date of 1792 for the return of Christ. Her diluted followers believed it!

In 1820, a fourteen-year-old boy, Joseph Smith, fell into a demonic trance in Palmyra Forest, New York, and received a "divine revelation." This led to the birth of the Mormon cult. They have set dates, perverted Scripture, committed mass murder, and gained notoriety for polygamy, adultery, fornication, and covert political intrigue. According to the Mormon publication, *Ensign,* April 1992, page 12-13, counterfeit spiritual phenomena has also been a part of this false religion. We read that in March 1836 during the dedication of a temple at Kirtland that there was an outbreak of tongues as angels entered the windows and Jesus appeared to many! Shortly after Smith, appeared William Miller, a defunct Baptist minister. He started in the 1830s what eventually became the Seventh Day Adventist Church. From incorrect calculations in the book of Daniel, Baptist William Miller picked the date of March 21, 1843 for the end and revised it to 1844 and 1850. Thousands sold their farms, houses, livestock, personal goods, and did not plant crops. Hundreds dressed in white bed sheets, climbed to housetops, up in trees, and on high elevations waiting for the Lord Jesus. Then, Ellen G. White became the chief seer and solidified the Adventist cult acquiring Miller's mantle of leadership. She said that the Civil War was a sign of the soon coming of Christ. She picked the date of 1856. When White died in 1915, the Savior had not returned.

Other date setters were Charles Taze Russell (died 1916) who started the Jehovah's Witnesses false cult. Its leaders set the dates of 1874, 1878, 1881, 1910, 1914, 1925, and 1975 for the coming of Christ. H. Grattan Guinness (died 1910) the powerhouse evangelist who shook England, Ireland, and Wales with his preaching, selected the year 1923. The Scotsman, Edward Irving (died 1834), a purveyor of the tongues and faith healing movement and founder of the Catholic Apostolic Church, picked the dates of 1835, 1838, 1864, and 1866. The hymn writer, Leila N. Morris (died 1929) penned the beautiful hymn, *What If It Were Today*. Her words in verse 3 are, "signs of his coming multiply." That was almost eighty years ago. (What would she have said of 2011?) In 1978, Chuck Smith, of Calvary Chapel in Costa Mesa, California, wrote on the back cover of *End Times, a Report on Future Survival*, this warning, "prepare for the breath-taking events about to happen in your lifetime!" That was thirty years ago. The anti-Trinitarian "evangelist" William Branham (died 1965) predicted 1977 as the end. One of the outstanding religious crackpots of the past century was Herbert Armstrong. This incestuous, anti-Trinitarian, whiskey imbued "prophet" selected Hitler as the beast, who would fight with Christ, and Mussolini as the false prophet. Armstrong set many dates for the return of Christ. These included 1936, 1937, 1972, and 1979. He died in 1986. In 1957, the British "prophet," Adam Rutherford, published four volumes proving from the Great Pyramid of Egypt that Jesus will return in 1978 or 1979. Another dud on the massive prophetic scrap pile.

In 1980, written on the back cover of Hal Lindsey's *Countdown to Armageddon*, is this shocker, "We are the generation that will see the end time . . . and the return of Jesus." That was thirty years ago. Lindsey has picked so many dates or "near dates" for our Lord's return that one cannot keep up with them. This demonstrates that he is an incapable preacher, unable to minister God's truth in the field of Bible eschatology. However, suckers keep buying his books, so he keeps writing them.

In 1986, a horrific nuclear explosion occurred in Chernobyl, Ukraine. Thousands died from this. Because "Chernobyl" may mean "wormwood," and this word is found in Rev. 8:11, here was another "proof," submitted by the "authorities" that the end was near. That was twenty-five years ago.

Preacher John Hinkle of Los Angeles said that June 9, 1994 was the date. Paul Crouch of Trinity Broadcasting defended this prophetic vanity. Lester Sumrall (died 1993) chose A.D. 2000. Harold Camping chose May 21, 2011. Bloodthirsty pagan Myans of ancient Mexico made a stone calendar with the future date of December 2012 as the end of a certain age, which was known, only to them. Thousands could be added to the "flop list" of those who "discovered the time or near time of Jesus' return."

America is not alone with its countless sects and sick religions finding the Messiah, second guessing prophecy, deceiving the gullible and setting dates for the return of Christ. They are everywhere. Semi pagan natives, called "Rastafarians" living mostly in Jamaica believed that the Emperor of Ethiopia, Halle Selassie was God incarnate! They taught that he would come to power as the Messiah and take them to an African paradise. These people think that they are the lost ten tribes of Israel (which have never been lost), and that Ethiopia is the promise land and heaven on earth! Thousands are presently starving to death in this great promise land! Unhappily, for this cult, their god, Halle Selassie, died in 1975.

One of the latest "prophets sent from God to the people of the world" is a Church of God law cult preacher, Ronald Weinland. He considers himself on par with John, the writer of Revelation. Weinland says that God explained to him the meaning of the seven thunders in Rev. 10:4. In his book *2008-God's Final Witness*, this "God sent end-time prophet" predicts that very *soon*, the whole world will be plunged into war, and billions will die! This will slowly begin in 2008. He predicted that by the year 2009 America will "be down the tubes." According to Weinland, Jesus will be here by the fall of 2011. As with thousands of others, time has shown that Weinland is another false visionary misleading thousands. The Latter Rain, prophet, J. Preston Eby, and law cultist David C. Pack are part of this infamous body. A South African, Kim Clement, even predicted an attempt on the life of President Obama in the middle of 2010! The "knock 'em out" charismatic evangelist, Benny Hinn, said Jesus was coming in 1993. Petticoat Pentecostal preacher, Marilyn Agee, set three different dates in 1999 for our Lord to return. Another miss!

Date picking is not an exclusive feature of religious crackpots. Sadly, great men of God such as John Wesley, Oswald J. Smith, John Walvoord, and many others all aimed at nothing and hit it in selecting dates or near dates. (Later, to his credit, Dr. Walvoord renounced date setting.) On a TV program some years ago, Jack van Impe said, "Everything would wind up with the next ten years." When 1994 came, he changed his prognostications to 2001, then 2002. It is presently 2011. Impe has set about as many dates or near dates as Hal Lindsey for the secret rapture. Men who presume to know what God has not revealed are trespassers into a forbidden territory. This is epidemic among certain *extreme* Fundamentalist Baptists and conservative writers. The books by John MacArthur, *Because the Time is Near,* and Ron Rhodes, *The Coming Oil Storm,* are typical of the end time signs game. David Jeremiah's *The Coming Economic Armageddon* has found the global economy in prophecy. Sherman Smith partly answers him in *Exploding the Doomsday Money Myth.* Time will prove these good men wrong. They reflect a presumptuous understanding of Holy Scripture, especially prophecy. Putting names on persons, places, and things that are not found in the Bible is shooting in the dark. To our regret, we have all done this on various issues. The problem is the poor people who have unwittingly believed our arrogant errors!

There is not one sign in Scripture or to be seen anywhere on earth that gives credence on *dating* the time or near time of Jesus' return. It is a lucrative industry based on speculative sensationalism blended with abysmal naivety. Each claimant asserts accuracy. *Never* have I heard one of them apologize for their false prognostications. Hal Lindsey once said if he was wrong people could call him a "Bum." Well, "Bum Lindsey" has been wrong repeatedly. In time, the works of "the best selling prophecy expert," Mark Hitchcock will also prove themselves greatly erroneous for we cannot speculate our way into understanding prophecy. Among these people are some great Christians, but they slowly undermine their credibility and increase further skepticism toward God's Word. Amid all the eschatological thunder and lightening, no one seems to have assigned this title to a female Antichrist. Who knows? This may be next on the prophetic agenda of some "authority." At least, it would make a best seller for gullible believers who have for two thousand tired to find the date of our Lord's return. God be praised that Jesus is coming, but further praised that no one knows when not even the "experts."

For an older look into pagan mythology and the Antichrist, see the work by the German writer, Wilhem Bousset, *The Antichrist Legend: A Chapter in Christian and Jewish Folklore,* published in 1896 and translated by A. H. Keane. Bousset (died 1920) was a leftist infidel theologian who denied the deity of Christ and inspiration of Scripture. His work has historical research value but is deadly poison in spiritual matters. Thousands of books have been written about the Antichrist, Jesus' return. Those that set dates and name the Antichrist will always be wrong. When men invade a realm of truth that has been forbidden by God, error and disaster are always the results.

The internet vibrates with hundreds of books, ads, messages, lessons, studies, sermons, blogs, and testimonies assuring us that they know when Jesus is coming. Clearly, some of these people are "religious nuts." Others have sincere intentions. Nevertheless, one thing is certain; they do not know what they are saying. Worse, they are propagating falsehoods regarding the time of Lord's return.

Some sixty years have passed since the popular Pentecostal publication *Evangel,* May 21, 1949, page 2, brazenly stated, "Atomic war will start on, before, or at least by January 1953." This predicted "Atomic war" is over fifty years late. Presently, we are hearing about "Russia developing new mystery nuclear missiles," "China teaming up with Russia," "new technologies," "the rise of Islam," "mondex bio-chips," "microchip implants," a "New World Order," "universal bar code," "social security numbers," "DNA," "eye-scanner," "cashless payments," "smart cards," and "oil," as the latest proofs that Antichrist is near and the "rapture is imminent." None of these are conclusive evidence of the soon end. Things could be a thousand times worse ten years from now. This is called "deceiving, and being deceived" (2 Tim. 3:13).

All of this is another pitiful chapter in the time long saga of prophecy guessing among zealous over enthusiastic good Christians, charlatans, crackpots, and religious lunatics. We are loaded down with speculations from those trying to "prove the Bible is right." *God's Word is right whether we find signs or not.* It is right, true, correct, and infallible because He wrote it. The problem is not God's Word but man's interpretation of it. Notably, all the "end-time specialists" claim to be "led by the Holy Spirit." How comforting to read, "God is not *the author* of confusion, but of peace, as in all churches of the saints" (1 Cor. 14:33). The highly lucrative but always wrong signs racket is not from God. Where is it from?

Antichrist in the New Testament

Matthew and Mark: In Section 163, Matt. 24:24 with its parallel in Mk. 13:22, Jesus spoke of a time when Israel would be flooded with men claiming to be Christ (Messiah) and other false prophets.

This prediction was literally fulfilled in the forty years before the fall of Jerusalem in A.D. 70. The Antichrists our Lord spoke of in these passages during the Olivet Discourse belong to the past not the future. This does not belie the fact that the present and future will be full Satan's servants and deceivers of men. It affirms that what Jesus predicted for Israel and Jerusalem in the past happened just as He stated. Apart from the two verses above, neither Matthew nor Mark, make any *clear* mention of this future world dictator. A wild and undisciplined imagination is capable of finding whatever it wants to find.

Luke: His Words in Lk. 21:8, regarding the flood of Antichrists prior to A.D. 70, are part of the harmonized record of Matthew and Mark found in Section 163, footnote k.

John: "If another come." Mid-way through His ministry, the Savior tangled with the Sanhedrin at Jerusalem after healing a man on the Sabbath. In John 5:43b, He replied to their charges of desecrating the Sabbath with the words, "If another shall come in his own name, him ye will receive." Amazingly, some hold that this "another" is the Antichrist, whom the Jews will welcome over two thousand years later! Jesus had just shown His authority in healing the man at the Pool of Bethesda (verse 2-9). This miracle revealed his Lordship over their sacred Sabbath day. The Savior was telling the Jews that others would come, having no genuine authority as He did, unable to do His works, and they would welcome them. In the decade before the fall of their city and temple, dozens of false teachers and prophets appeared, claiming to be Messiah. The Jews went after these with open arms to their doom. It is the way of God that those who reject the truth (as taught by Jesus the Messiah) eventually become prisoners to the worst of lies. Christ was not speaking of the real Antichrist yet to appear over two millenniums later when He used the Word "another." This erroneous interpretation of John 5:43b was popularized by the *Scofield Reference Bible* page 975, footnote 4, and page 1121, center column, footnote t.

John 17:12: During the Savior's high priestly prayer, the night before the morning of the cross, He spoke of "the son of perdition" who was "lost." This was an obvious reference to the traitor, Judas Iscariot. Some expositors have pointed to this and attempted to prove that Judas will resurrect from the dead and become the end-time Antichrist! Refer to Section 178, John 17:12, footnote m for explanation of this myth with the origin and usage of the term "son of perdition." Judas and the Antichrist are not related, apart from the fact that both were destined to hell by their choices. Such irresponsible handling of God's Word gives the *rightly divided doctrine* of premillennialism a bitter taste among sober thinking Christians. No man knows who the Antichrist will be. Judas Iscariot does not qualify.

2 Thessalonians: During his second missionary journey, Paul wrote several letters back to the church he founded at Thessalonica. In 2 Thess. 2:3-4 he speaks of a "falling away," and a lawless person who "opposeth and exalteth himself above all that is called God, or that is worshipped; so that he as God sitteth in the temple of God, shewing himself that he is God." This dreadful person may have ties with the terror figure mentioned by Daniel in the pages above. Because the calamity of A.D. 70 occurred about twenty years after Paul penned these words, it seems incorrect to make this mystery figure have reference to that event. Over the centuries, the exegesis applied to Paul's words has been as varied as the patterns in snowflakes. J. Vernon McGee and others said the falling away was the secret rapture. In the same chapter to the Thessalonians, Paul wrote of something "withholding" or preventing this person from appearing in that time (verse 6). As with all the finer points of the end-times, there have been literally thousands of guesses as to who or what this "withholder" refers. The author does not know and refuses to cast his opinions as established Bible doctrine regarding this question.

Various church fathers, whose beliefs about salvation were like "muddy water," also had their Antichrist candidates. Irenaeus, penned something called *Against Heresies*. In this book, he thought the Antichrist would be a Jew. He wrote that as Christ was incarnated so will be this coming deceiver. Hippolytus (died A.D. 235) compiled a treatise titled, *On Antichrist*. He stated that Babylon would be the birthplace for this monster who would be a Jew from the tribe of Dan. He would also rebuild the temple in Jerusalem. (John Darby probably borrowed part of his eschatology from Hippolytus.) The Puritans said the Antichrist was popery, while the Popes pointed to the Puritans. In Paul's writings to the Thessalonian Christians, "the man of sin" [Antichrist] is singular, never plural; therefore, this cannot refer to a series of persons or an institution. "Man of sin" or "lawlessness," strictly singles out one person. He will be *eternally* destroyed at the coming of Christ (Rev. 20:10). Thus, he will be on the scene when our Lord returns. One should not relegate this "man of sin" and his empire to history. These verses in 2 Thessalonians speak of future realities. They do not have exclusive reference to the Church of Rome. One cannot deny the Antichrist practices of this religious system since its beginning with Emperor Constantine. However, spiritual darkness is not a sole feature of the Papal Church. Many so-called

"Protestants," churches, and individuals march in this ecumenical parade of religious apostasy. The evidence seems clear that Paul's "man of sin" is yet to appear on the stage of world events. For over a hundred years, many American Christians have been obsessed by locating and naming the Antichrist. For an investigation into this subject, see Dr. Robert C. Fuller's work, *Naming the Antichrist: the History of an American Obsession*, published in 1995.

1 and 2 John: The English word "Antichrist" is derived from a Greek word "antichristos," meaning "instead of" or "against Christ." This definition constitutes the entire doctrine and purpose of this evil person. It is an undue linguistic refinement of words to affirm that it means *only* "false Christ." In the Bible, the word appears in 1 John 2:18, 22; 4:3; 2 John 7, and nowhere else. Contrary to the popular belief, it is not mentioned in the book of Revelation. Dr. Raymond Brown in the *Anchor Bible*, states on page 33, "The term *Antichrist* refers to a false thing (anti) taking the place of a real thing with great antagonism between the substitute and the real Christ and an arch-foe." Historically, and chronologically, John originally wrote to people living *before* the fall of Jerusalem in A.D. 70. He was informing them that many Antichrists had already appeared. They were immediately present. He used the plural "antichrists." In verse 18 John seems to make a distinction between "antichrist" (singular) and "antichrists" (plural). It is pertly noted in 1 John 2:19 that he wrote, "They went out from us." These apostates or "antichrists" had left the Christian assembly where John was serving; they were individuals.

John's terminology, "it is the last time," and "we know that it is the last time," seems to have reference to the doom of A.D. 70. "Last time," cannot mean (as it stands now) over two thousand years later! He explained in 2 John 7 what these false religionists would *not* confess, "For many deceivers are entered into the world, who confess not that Jesus Christ is come in the flesh. This is a deceiver and an antichrist." "Many antichrists" had appeared and were present when John wrote his letters. "Many" cannot mean one. Antichrists must not be relegated *only* to the last days. They were present in John's era and denied that Jesus was God in the flesh. This is the great fatal doctrinal error. By inspiration, John made this point clear to his original readers. Some think his description of these people was connected with what he had heard the Lord Jesus say years before in the Olivet Discourse. Refer to Section 163, Matt. 24:24 with Mk. 13:22. On that occasion, Jesus warned Peter, James, John, and Andrew (Mk. 13:3-4) of a soon coming tidal wave of Antichrists that would sweep the land of Israel. This evil phenomenon occurred in their lifetime. In view of the appearing and false teaching of many Antichrists in the past, it is odd that some teach that no Antichrist will appear until the tribulation. This is a mistaken viewpoint. Various Antichrists appeared before A.D. 70, then afterward, and have continued up to the present with highs and lows. However, the *super Antichrist* of them all is yet to be revealed. Jude takes the words of "the apostles of our Lord Jesus Christ" about "mockers in the last time" (Jude 17-18), and related them to his present day. He wrote about five years before the fall of Jerusalem. Some think Paul meant this in 1 Tim. 4:1 and 2 Tim. 3:1-9 by using the words "the latter times" and "perilous times." He wrote that the folly of these men would be "manifest [exposed] unto all" (verse 9). Did this happen in A.D. 70? If true, none of this negates the *genuine signs* that will appear before the return of our Lord for His people.

A popular teaching exists that we are now in the "end of time period," but the climax may yet be centuries ahead! That is a very long "end." In John's epistles, Antichrist was not an individual, rather *many* individuals who were in his time propagating their blasphemy. Later, in Revelation, he described a unique and exclusive future person in more detail who seems to be the final Antichrist. However, this title is never applied to him in the book. A faint relation seems to exist between John's Antichrists and that single wicked figure yet to appear. Differences between the various Antichrists of 1 and 2 John and the one in the Revelation are enormous.

Revelation: Identifying the ancient symbolism used in Ezekiel, Daniel, and Revelation with modern day persons, nations, and events is like finding the right hair in a barbershop. Even when believers "compare Scripture with Scripture," the answer is usually one that fits their prior eschatological thinking. (This is not necessarily wrong.) Where Scripture does the identifying, as in Rev. 12:9, the answer is explicit and exact. Oddly, in interpreting these things everyone's guess seems to become authentic. The Presbyterian, Kenneth L. Gentry in, *The Beast of Revelation* attempts to identify the Antichrist and explain the mysteries of John's revelation. He went into history and found a person, place, or event that explains the difficult symbols and emblems that fill Revelation. On page 217, he sees the red color of the beast in Revelation as "an identifier" of Nero's red beard! (Even the most radical dispensationalist does not go that far.) One is amused to read on the back cover, "He [Dr. Gentry] has constructed an iron-clad case." Gentry is confident that he has accomplished what myriads of others failed to do for the past two millenniums. Nevertheless, he is not alone in this self-imbued delusion. Over church history, thousands imagined that they had solved all the ominous mysteries of Revelation. In this last book of the Bible, Antichrist (the beast out of the sea) has been subjected to every form of hermeneutic known to humanity as well as some that are unknown. Revelation chapter 13 reveals in *symbolic form* three distinct foes of Christ and mankind who are yet to appear on the stage of human history. Correctly interpreting these symbols is the big problem. They are as follows:

1. The "beast out of the sea" (verse 1). Waters represent the billions of humanity (Rev. 17:15).
2. The "dragon which gave power to the beast" (verse 4).
3. Lastly, "another beast rising from the earth with two horns like a lamb" (verse 11).

These are often referred to as "The satanic trinity." Below is a *brief* survey of this malignant triad.

A red dragon gives his power to the beast: This symbolic figure is indisputably identified as "the devil and Satan" (Rev. 12:9). His earthly history began in the Garden of Eden (Gen. 3:1-3 with 2 Cor. 11:3). It ends in the lake of fire (Matt. 25:41 with Rev. 20:10). Many expositors recognize this character as Satan but then identify the following two persons listed below as something in history, long ago. This interpretation detaches the first from the latter, as if no collaboration existed between them. The context of this chapter teaches the opposite. The red dragon (Satan) has two chief associates working with him during this time in earth's history. These partners in wickedness are as follows:

A beast rising out of the sea: Whoever this monster is, he will be the arch-villain of human history, the incarnation and epitome of evil. Verses 2 and 4 state that he was given power from Satan the red dragon. This beast will be a unique military genius, so brilliant that the inhabitants of the earth applaud him. Verses 5-6 reflect his articulate international blasphemy for forty and two months. With awful brazenness, he daringly defies God in heaven. Verses 7-8 is staggering in its scope as he "overcomes the saints," and controls the world. The difficulties and implications of these claims are overwhelming. Great differences of opinion emerge as to the meaning of "the saints he overcomes." Some see these as believers of centuries past, others as future. The idea that "saints" refers *only* to a Jewish remnant is speculative guesswork. Paul employed this term about forty times in his letters and embraced all believers in its usage. John uses it thirteen times in Revelation in a strictly non-nationalistic manner. Extreme dispensationalists force it to mean, "Thousands of Jews and others saved during the tribulation."

Some hold that certain features in John's sea beast correlate him with Paul's "man of sin" (2 Thess. 2:3). Whoever this beast is, he will be a real human figure, earth's greatest and *final* Antichrist. On the other hand, many have relegated him to something or someone of the past, an already accomplished fact. This seems so incorrect. *When his true identity is revealed all men will be astounded!*

Ultra dispensationalists assure us that Antichrist will "sign a peace treaty with Israel" to restore temple sacrifices. Suddenly, he will break the agreement mid-way through. This interpretation of Dan. 9:26-27, is shaky, being built on one word, "cease." Any Bible doctrine hinged on a single verb is not an established historical doctrine. Postmillennial defenders of the "traditional interpretation" of these two verses admit they also have problems trying to figure it out. See *Prophecy & The Church,* page 114-115, Oswald T. Allis. All of us will be stunned when we learn the full meaning of these predictions. For more on Daniel's prophecy and the seventy weeks, see Section 123, third paragraph of footnote c.

Next, we have Daniel's vision of a metallic-earthen colossus (Dan. 2:31-49). History affirms that Babylon, Persia, Greece, were the upper torso, and Rome the two legs of this image. It is not so clear regarding the ten toes consisting of a mixture of iron and clay. As the upper parts and legs represented real nations, so also must the ten toes. One idea discussed earlier in this Appendix is that the toes point to a Revived Roman Empire, now branded as the European Union (EU). Thousands of speculations, conjectures, and multitudes of interpretations, reinterpretations, and assumptions have stepped on these ten toes for centuries. Non-dispensationalists have just as much trouble with Daniel's toes as their eschatological opponents. It is a matter of grab-bag dogmatism. Each grabber assures us he is right.

A beast rising from the earth: His "two horns like a lamb" seem to indicate some religious dignitary ("prophet") serving the Antichrist or beast (verse 11). Speaking "as a dragon" may reflect his verbal power source from Satan. In several verses, his title is "the false prophet." This reflects a show of religiosity (Rev. 16:13; 19:20; and 20:10). Demonically endowed, he will perform extraordinary wonders and miracles. A point, greatly overlooked is that this human monster will succeed in bringing about some form of *universal* Devil worship (verse 12). Verse 14 affirms this is accomplished because he "deceiveth them that dwell on the earth" by producing demonic signs and wonders. This statement reveals that not all miraculous things are from God. Genuine satanic forces via demons also produce *deceiving* signs, wonders, and miracles. The dynamic power of the beast is noted in verse 15, where he causes an "image" of [his superior] "the beast out of the sea" to literally "speak." (In a curious reversal, some identify the beast from the earth as the real Antichrist, not the beast out of the sea.) Global executions, economic control of buying and selling will be introduced. This monster establishes some kind of one world marketing system (verse 16-17). Speculations about his mark are beyond counting. Decades ago, when the United States Postal Department introduced zip codes a famous radio preacher in Colorado strongly asserted that this was the "mark of the beast." Assigning a numerical value to letters in the alphabet is called "gematria." Thousands have tried to discover the mark of the beast via "gematria" and have failed. Within the Torah-Law-entangled Seventh Day Adventist cult, many hold the mark is "going to church on Sunday." Among some early Christians, Caesar Nero was a prime candidate for the mark. However, when he committed suicide in A.D. 68, they changed their views! Over church history, more than one thousand interpretations of the Antichrist, mark of the beast, the great whore, and so on have been given. Time has proved them wrong. *Whenever all these things happen, everyone will be surprised!*

Some see the Antichrist in Zech. 11:17. It reads, "His right eye shall be utterly darkened." From this statement, certain eschatologists assume that Antichrist will be a one-eyed person! Years ago the famed Israeli military genius Moshe Dyan was pointed to as the fulfillment of this prediction. Dyan, had only a single functional eye, the left one. He wore a black patch over the other. In 1971, while on the foreign field, I heard a fellow missionary say, "The Antichrist is here," referring to Dyan. However, the Jewish Antichrist, General Dyan, died in 1981. If the Antichrist is to duplicate Jesus, the true Christ-Messiah, we wonder when our Savior had His right eye out, and His arm withered. Sensational exegesis of this nature will not fit the bill; instead, it turns thinking people away. Over twenty years ago, Dave Hunt wrote in 1990, "Somewhere, at this very moment, on planet Earth, the Antichrist is certainly alive—biding his time, awaiting his cue." See *Global Peace and the Rise of Antichrist.* Review page 55-65, 87-99 passim to get the background of Hunt's thoughts on this. Date setters, like Salem Kirban, have been pointing to newspaper headlines and world events for centuries assuring us that Antichrist is at the door, and the "rapture may be tomorrow." In 1977, he wrote on the back cover of *The Rise of the Antichrist,* "We are living in the age of Antichrist! The world is on the threshold of catastrophe." That was over thirty years ago. Kirban's Antichrist had better hurry, or he will end up in an old age home.

Changing eschatology. Rome, Mecca, or who? For over five centuries, true evangelicals have mostly interpreted the harlot in Rev. 17 as the Roman Catholic Church. With the rise of Islam, new hermeneutics are emerging. Among some of the "authorities," this woman no longer points to the Papal Church but Islam! Those who embrace this new interpretation use ancient geography, emblems, and etymology to "prove" their guesses. Those who made her Rome did the same thing. Others now see the unnamed eighth nation in Rev. 17:10-11, as being Islam! This is another eschatological "shot in the dark." Some think that they have found the absolute truth on these *unexplained* verses. Many prophecy teachers "after years of careful research" make themselves believe what they think is right. To build eternal truth on personal assumption has been the modus operandi of every false cult specializing in prophecy and end time events. This Appendix bristles with a mountain of facts that demonstrate this truth. These writers should *clearly* state that, their postulations on these matters are conjectures and not established historical Bible doctrine. Now, we hear that "democracy is invading Islam" and it will receive the Antichrist!

In future decades, something far worse than Roman Catholicism or Islam could appear and shake the world. Who is wise enough to say this will not happen on the stage of changing human events? Good men, who have gone too far into a forbidden zone, write books to prove their eschatological guesses, while passing time always proves them wrong. There have been countless thousand of these people over the course of church history. No one positively knows what the woman of Rev. 17 or any other *unidentified* emblem or metaphor in Scripture represents. Nor have they discovered in Holy Scripture the final role of antichrist Islam in the end times. The reason is that God has not written it there. This being unarguably so, Christians "who love his appearing," need facts and less fiction. (The book market is flooded with "Christian fiction" and less Bible doctrine.) True Christianity is discredited by the latest experts with their "unique insights," and "years of research." These people are sure the "Lord is at the door." While the godless world mocks and ridicules their false predictions, they, nevertheless, continue with their eschatological charades. *One thing is as sure as God's throne: whenever the Lord Jesus appears, all of us will all be shocked, stunned, and amazed at some of the things we have believed!*

As this present age ends its course (whenever that will be), the real beast-Antichrist out of the sea is depicted leading "The kings of the earth and their armies," attempting to war against Christ and the hosts of heaven (Rev. 16:14 with Rev. 19:14, 19). Some understand this is the same conflict as seen in Ezek. 38-39. Whatever opinion one holds of this battle, the statements in Ezek. 37:21-28 clearly point to a time of lasting peace for Israel in her land. Messiah (referred to as "David my servant" in verse 24) will be King. The amazing conditions mentioned here are for a redeemed Israel in the future. It is exegetically and sensibly impossible to transfer such promises as found in these verses to the church. Nor do they fit Israel at any historical period *after* her return from Babylonian captivity (536 B.C.). In Dan. 2:34, we read of a "stone [that] was cut out without hands" (the virgin birth) which smashes world powers. The application of this to our Lord founding His church is impossible. Christ did not destroy all world powers during His ministry when He began to build His church or new kingdom. After grinding His then present enemies to powder (complete destruction) the stone "became a great mountain that filled the whole earth" (verse 35). This can only be Messiah putting down all opposition to the final and eternal consummation of His kingdom. Those who make this to be a carnal, earth-dirt kingdom of blood, sweat, and tears, with sin rampant and law enforcement over worked are wrong. This hyper literalizing Scripture is another attempt to fill in the blanks that have been purposely left by divine inspiration. Near the close of Revelation, Christ's *true kingdom* is inaugurated. His opponents, the beast and false prophet are "cast alive" into the eternal lake of fire (Rev. 19:20-21). Satan is chained (divinely restrained) for a thousand years. In this time, earth will experience a period of unique peace (Rev. 20:1-3). With the climax of the millennium of peace on earth (with all its unanswered questions), the Devil is released from restraint. From somewhere he gathers a great army and joins in battle for the city of Jerusalem. *Where* Satan's armies come from is a difficult question, since they were all "ground to powder" a thousand years prior. Many answers are submitted to solve this query. These include, people "living to be one thousand years old," "millions of babies born during the reign of peace," "clones," to "aliens from outer space." The war for Jerusalem ends with Christ and His people the victors. Later, all whose names are not in the book of life will, after judgment, share with Satan in the eternal fire (Matt. 25:41; Rev. 20:10; and 20:15).

Apparently, the "beast out of the sea" is the *real* Antichrist. He will be empowered by Satan and assisted by a charming, persuasive religionist who speaks with overwhelming authority. This director of world religion, "the false prophet," will be history's greatest ecumenist. The interpretation that these things have already occurred is historically unacceptable. The author's little opinion is that this beast-Antichrist will be a real person, not a church, institution, spirit, philosophy, or world event. This will be fulfilled when God's sees it is right. Perhaps, *George Orwell's 1984* will yet be realized in the future!

Summary

Innumerable interpretations have existed over the past two thousand years of church history regarding final world events. In unclear and difficult areas of eschatology, believers should refrain from concrete dogmatism and confess they use conjectures. For centuries, some of the greatest saints have held differing positions in this field. Mass condemnation of fellow believers because of the *uncertain finer points* in eschatology is wrong. Christians should beware of the "experts who have sifted through all the evidence" and can tell you anything about Antichrist you want to know, except perhaps, what brand of toothpaste he will use. Avoid those who dote to know everything about anything pertaining to Bible prophecy. Simon Peter, as an old man facing death still found some of the things in Paul's inspired letters "hard to understand" (2 Peter 1:14-15 with 3:16). It has not changed that much today. Some things about prophecy are still "hard to understand." This is not because God does not want us to know, but rather, because He wants us to comprehend correctly what He has written on this subject. Guesswork teaching regarding end-time events is not acceptable. Nevertheless, the parade of eschatological vanity marches on as millions of Christians keep cadence to its dull drumbeat, and ears tuned to its many centuries of predictive failures. Jesus is coming, but not when the date setters teach. Toward His return, all history slowly moves and will reach its consummation. Meanwhile, mankind's dying carcass struggles on the roadside of life, while the vultures of time watch with eager anticipation for its demise. Only in the living Son of God can we mortals find forgiveness of our sins, the joy of life everlasting, and genuine peace about eternity to come. I beg all readers to heed His invitation now, "Come unto me, all *ye* that labour and are heavy laden, and I will give you rest" (Matt. 11:28).

With the Bible's final prayer, which is now two thousand years old, this work is concluded. This prayer will be answered in God's time and way, whenever that may be. It reads as follows:

"Even so, come, Lord Jesus" (Rev. 22:20).

SELAH! "Think of that."

GENERAL SUBJECT INDEX

Persons mentioned in the Scriptures of the four gospels are not recorded in this Index. Because the gospels greatly repeat one another, this would result in hundreds of unneeded entries. Selected references found in the 207 Section headings, Introductions, vertical page columns, Information Boxes, Footnotes-Commentary, and Appendices are given below. Some of the organizations, individuals, and events of social, political, moral, and religious impact that have affected Christianity, the Bible, true freedom, and the gospel of Christ are also mentioned. Some of the entries below are cross-referenced connected to similar subjects in other places of this Index. These are printed in italics for quick identification. The asterisk * indicates that this entry is mention more than one time on that particular page. To find a specific Scripture, refer to *Verse Finder, page xvi.* This easily locates every passage in the four gospels.

Calvin, John. *(Too many to list.)*

Calvin, lover of wine, 739.

Calvinism, 9*, 110*, 135, 165, 220, 233*, 292, 294, 399*, 425, 472, 527, 594*, 620*, 621, 687, 701, 739, 740, 791, 857, 969, 975, 977*, 978. *(See Covenant theology and T-U-L-I-P.)*

Camping, Harold, 1041.

Can we do the things Jesus did?, 274.

Capernaum. *(Too many to list. See Verse Finder, page xvi.)*

Capitalist(ism), 985, 1039.

Carrying part of Jesus' cross, 911.

Castle of Antonio, 124, 546, 868, 878, 884, 887, 893, 895, 898, 900, 902*, 903, 905, 906, 907, 943.

Castle of Machaerus, 81, 235, 286, 287, 289, 290*, 291*, 400, 404*–405*.

Catholic Church, xx, xxv, xxvi, xxvii, 21*, 27, 35*, 47, 48, 50*, 53, 54, 57*, 58*, 67, 134, 136, 139, 141*, 169*, 189, 201, 253, 317*, 331, 351, 426, 427, 428, 453, 464*, 465, 472*, 509*, 530, 587, 602, 628*, 634, 653, 709, 725*, 775, 789*, 792, 828, 832, 849, 903, 911, 919, 935, 948, 970, 971*, 977, 978, 982, 987, 1003, 1027, 1028, 1030, 1039, 1046. *(See Roman Catholic Church or Papal Church.)*

Celsus, 46, 626.

Centurion, 122*, 124, 280*, 281*, 282, 283*, 284, 290, 301, 442*, 908*, 911, 928, 933*, 941, 994.

Chafer, Lewis S., 162, 660*, 754, 783*, 904.

Change must occur inwardly, 437.

Changing eschatology, Rome or Mecca, 1046.

Changing the message of the Bible, 113.

Chernobyl, Ukraine, 1040.

Child abuse and Inquisition, 50*, 331.

Children made holy?, 633–634.

Chiliasm, 789*, 794.

Chorazin and Bethsaida, 294–295.

Christ laid aside none of His equality with God, 243–244. *(See Kenosis.)*

Christ opposed false traditions, 237.

Christ taking our sicknesses, 171.

Christ's human subordination, "Greater than I," 840.

Christ's new kingdom or church and four of its different names, 164.

Christiadelphian(s), 4, 612.

Christian Science, 4.

Christian socialism, 329*.

Christian stupidity, 894*. *(See Atheistic stupidity.)*

Christian tyrants, 57, 58, 509–510.

Christianity is hated, 456.

Christianized Gnostic spirit, 2.

Christianized idolatry, Mary worship, 49, 53.

Christianized paganism, 53*, 948*. *(See Easter.)*

Christianized prostitution and other sins, 232*, 962.

Christians must remember, 11.

Chrysostom, John, 58*, 773, 1026.

Church fathers, 4*, 14, 48, 49*, 50, 55, 57*, 96, 97, 134, 141, 427, 440, 453, 464, 467*, 468*, 538, 620*, 633*, 634, 674,

691, 713, 773, 789*, 790, 792*, 811, 911, 924, 971, 977*, 982, 1029, 1043.

Church fathers and their heretical radicalism, 49*.

Church of Christ, 93, 138, 139, 189, 268, 371, 427, 634, 753, 837.

Church of God, 268, 353, 384, 436, 453, 465, 500, 663, 757, 765, 798, 979, 986, 1041.

Church of Jesus Christ of Latter Day Saints, 113, 249, 354, 505, 515. *(See Mormons.)*

Church sign that spoke to a man's heart, 555*.

Church steeple, meaning of the, 445*.

Churches gone wild, 259, 836–837.

Churchill, Winston, 329, 520.

Chuza, 152*, 301*, 302*, 402*, 893.

Circumcision, *(Too many to list. See Verse Finder, page xvi.)*

Cities in Galilee, 174–175.

City on a hill, 184, 190.

Clement, 4*, 48, 49, 791.

Clement, Kim. 1041.

Clemons, Bill, 621*.

Cleopas, 924*, 962*, 963*, 967*–968.

Cleopatra, 367, 404–405*.

Cleophas, 35, 924*, 962.

Cloak and coat, 267–268.

Cloud, David, 1027.

Colbert, Stephen, 554.

Colonial America, 594*, 620, 628, 691, 709, 977*, 978*, 1031, 1040.

Columbus, Christopher, 1040.

Communion, xxvii, xxviii, xxix, 8, 14, 49*, 58*, 75, 213, 268*, 426*, 427, 428*, 445, 500, 612*, 613*, 620, 674, 734, 789*, 807, 811*, 815*, 818, 819, 830, 831*, 835, 849, 951, 970, 977, 978*, 979, 982, 1004, 1026. *(See the Lord's Supper.)*

Communion or the Lord's Supper, *(Too many to list. See Verse Finder, page xvi.)*

Communion, a demonic pagan imitation of, 831.

Communism, 110, 187, 189, 222, 232, 351, 359, 377, 383, 452, 473, 507, 520, 587, 622, 708, 762, 775, 797.

Comparison and contrast of the five different versions of the Great Commission, 975–976.

Confirmation and the Holy Spirit, 530.

Confirmation as practiced by Paul, 530.

Confusing a promise with a principle, 687.

Congregationalists, 350, 427*, 1028.

Conspiracies, xxiv, xxv*, xxx*, 1, 84*, 150, 793*, 907, 1033.

Construction of the Hebrew Scriptures, 968–969.

Contemporary Christianity, 473*, 991,

Corban or Korban, 435*, 727, 728*.

Corn field, Jesus in the, 247*.

Cost of discipleship, 75, 587–588.

Council of Nicaea, 5, 14*, 57.

Council of Trent, 201, 628.

Covenant theology, 36*, 634, 691, 719, 789, 857–858. *(See Calvinism and T-U-L-I-P.)*

Cramer, Thomas, xxix.

Cross. *(Too many to list. See Verse Finder, page xvi.)*

Crouch, Paul, 1041.

Crucifixion, Jesus, 909–934.

Crucifixion, methods, 917.

Crucifixion, origin of, 911.

Crucify and crucified. *(Too many to list. See Verse Finder, page xvi.)*

Crumpton, James, 448.

Crusaders, 50, 58*, 189, 207, 253, 427*.

Cults seek acceptance, 249.

Cybele, queen of heaven, 53, 428*. *(See Mary queen of heaven,)*

Cyril, of Alexandria, 48.

Cyril, of Jerusalem, 468, 620, 773.

-D-

Damnation of hell, 729.

Dance of Lights, 404, 526, 534, 563. *(See Feast of Tabernacles.)*

Daniel's seventy weeks, 564*, 1045.

Daniel's ten-toed image, 797, 1038*, 1045*.

Darby(ism), John Nelson, 162*, 191, 564*, 612, 719, 754*, 756, 790*, 791*, 792*, 793*, 798, 801*, 970, 1043.

Darby's definition of a dispensation, 793.

Darwin(ism), Charles, 4, 944, 1039.

Daughter of Abraham, 577.

Daughter of Zion, 680.

Day of atonement, 235, 285, 517, 623, 932, 1024*.

Day of the LORD, 476, 616*, 617, 677, 756, 856, 1012*.

Dead pulpits, 991.

Dead Sea, 28, 81, 287, 289, 404, 461, 771.

Debating in a room full of drinking gamblers, 232.

Decapolis, the meaning of, 175.

December in Jerusalem, 562, 563*, 564–566*.

Decisional evangelism, 934*. *(See Easy believism, Baptist bloopers, and Winds of change.)*

Deficit religions of the world, 244.

Degrees of punishment, 295, 331*, 332, 726.

Degrees of satanic bondage, 317.

Demon of insanity. *(See Tazazith.)*

Demon-possessed boy, 484–486.

Demon-possessed girl, 263.

Demon-possessed masses, 170.

Demon-possessed nurse in South Africa, 489.

Demon-possessed person, blind and dumb, 303–305.

Demon-possessed wild man, 378–480.

Demon-possessed woman with crooked back, 575–577.

Demons or evil spirits. *(Too many to list. See Verse Finder, page xvi.)*

Demons, exorcising, *(Too many to list. See Verse Finder, page xvi.)*

Depravity. 101, 116, 223, 370, 413, 437*, 438, 446, 455, 499, 602*, 612, 618, 627, 725, 852, 881, 904, 970, 992, 998.

Devil. *(Too many to list. See Lucifer and Verse Finder, page xvi.)*

Devil worship, 3, 6, 102, 103*, 118*, 144, 427, 641, 906, 955, 1045. *(See idolatry.)*

Did Jesus die twice on the cross?, 929.

Did the Holy Spirit indwell Old Testament believers?, 39.

Diet (council) of Speyer, 1026.

Different kinds of grace?, 970.

Discovery channel, 71.

Dispensational premillennialism, 768, 777, 789, 792*, 794, 800. *(See Futurists.)*

Dispensationalists. *(Too many to list. See Verse Finder, page xvi.)*

Distance healing, 152, 283*.

Distortions of the word sprinkling, 977.

Divorce. *(Too many to list. See Divorce, Jewish style.)*

Divorce, Jewish style, 45, 46, 204*. *(See Divorce.)*

Do animals have souls?, 474. *(See Soul of man different from the physical body.)*

Does baptism or faith bring remission of sins?, 976.

Dog(s), 58, 80, 136, 178, 214*, 217*, 237, 242, 252, 293, 296*, 315, 317, 377*, 441*, 453, 459, 465, 473, 509*, 580, 585, 601*, 673, 691, 709, 741, 773*, 787, 836*, 845, 903, 941*, 991, 1006, 1014, 1030.

Doss, Jim, the traveling tract man, 396*.

Drink any deadly thing, 979.

Dry places, demons and, 314*.

Dumb spirit, 486.

Dyan, General Moshe, 557, 1046*.

-E-

Early healing movements, 538.

Easter, 57, 67*, 146, 445*, 472*, 948*, *(See Christianized paganism.)*

Eastern Gate of Jerusalem, 78, 475, 537, 580, 581, 658, 662, 679*, 680, 682*, 683, 752, 754, 758, 764, 840, 935. *(See Shushan Gate.)*

Easy believism, 139, 992. *(See Decisional evangelism and the Emerging Church.)*

Eating grain on the Sabbath, 246, 247, 248–249.

Eby, J. Preston, 1041.

Ecumenical, xxi*, xxx, 4*, 5, 11*, 21*, 57, 58, 103, 141*, 191, 196, 232, 369*, 370*, 391, 427, 428, 464, 500*, 509, 559, 560, 587*, 602, 617, 740, 759, 764, 836*, 837*, 857, 858, 941, 948, 1002, 1031, 1038, 1044, 1047.

Edwards, Jonathan, 110, 220, 427, 594*, 1040*.

Efforts to discredit Christ, 79–80.

Eichorn, Johann, xxvii.

Eight woes on the religious leaders of Israel, 728, 729.

Elijah, the coming of, 86*, 106, 107, 364, 483*, 1017–1018.

Elizabeth I, Queen, xxix, 1025*–1026.

Elizabeth, mother of John the Baptist, 202, 291.

Eliziver family, xxix.

Elohim, 1*, 46, 243, 307, 566.

King of the Jews, 31*, 59, 66, 67*, 68*, 69, 72, 73, 102, 108, 109, 414, 417*, 438, 471, 573, 803*, 890*, 893, 901, 902, 903*, 918-919*.

Kingdom instantly to appear?, 662-663.

Kingdom of God and kingdom of heaven the same, 141, 170, 162, 163, 357, 476, 635, 641.

Kingdom offer to the Jews, 18*, 93, 107, 128, 144, 162*, 175, 187*, 365, 417*, 611, 612, 682, 1011*.

Kirban, Salem, 793, 1046*.

Kissing Peter's toe, 53.

Kissinger, Henry, 452*, 1039.

Koran, xxix, 27*, 437*, 464.

Korban, (See Corban.)

Koresh, David, 88, 237, 641, 839, 1039.

Krishna, Hare, 48*, 53, 253, 456, 559.

Kuyper, Abraham, 36, 691.

-L-

Lacunza, Emmanuel, 791*.

Lake of fire, xxiv, 93, 158, 167, 200, 218, 219, 269, 276, 277*, 282, 331, 364, 370, 382, 438, 466*, 475, 499*, 515, 517, 548, 579, 601, 602, 603, 705, 778*, 787, 1045, 1047.

Lake of Galilee, 373, 980, 985. (See Sea of Galilee and Sea of Tiberias.)

Large Catechism, Martin Luther's, 978*.

Larkin, Clarence, 162, 359, 564, 612, 754, 793, 798.

Last rites, King James, 1031.

Law (and the) prophets, 94, 156, 198, 199, 218, 291, 481*, 523, 598-599.

Law cults, 64, 198*, 202, 249*, 372, 481, 522, 554*, 716, 838, 935, 942, 948*, 972, 973, 1003*, 1004-1005*.

Lazarus (and the) rich man, 600-604.

Lazarus raised, 567-574.

Leaning on Jesus' breast, 823.

Leaven, 124*, 328*, 336*, 349, 357, 359*, 360*, 362*, 366, 367, 455*, 456*, 457, 467, 577*, 908.

Left Behind Series, 615-616.

Lenin, Vladimir, 50, 473, 944, 1039.

Leper. (Too many to list. See Leprosy.)

Leprosy, 197, 222*, 223*, 224, 608*, 668, 900. (See Leper.)

Lesbian(ism), 232, 368*, 427, 627, 631.

Lewis, C. S., 602*.

Liberation theology, 75, 904, 934.

Lifestyle evangelism?, 846.

Light of the world, 5*, 63*, 190*, 313*, 356, 394*, 395*, 424*, 426, 545*, 551, 563, 558, 657, 740, 836.

Lilith, Jewish queen of demons, 171.

Limbaugh, Rush, 237.

Limited commission abused by radicals, 274.

Limited or restricted commission, 270*, 273*, 275, 276, 301, 406*, 514*, 516, 609, 829.

Lindsey, Hal, 162, 310, 417, 757*, 758, 773*, 776*, 793, 1041*-1042*.

Linneman, Eta, xxi*.

Little children preaching, 489.

Living dead men and dead living men, 970.

Living under or by the Jewish Law?, 194.

Loftus, John W, 176*.

Logos, a name for Christ, 1, 2*, 3*, 11*, 446.

Long, Australian missionary Arnold, 786*, 787.

Looking at the wrong thing, 951.

Lord's prayer, 211, 854, 996.

Lord's Supper, (Too many too list. See Verse Finder, page xvi. See also Communion.)

Loyde-Jones, Dr. Martin, 602, 977.

Lucifer, 100, 101, 118, 217, 219, 255, 256, 348, 350, 353, 430, 487, 516, 517*, 685, 823, 828. (See Devil and Satan.)

Lunatic(k) or moonstruck, 175, 486.

Luther believed that infant baptism and communion saved, 978, 979.

Luther, Martin, 7, 8*, 21, 58*, 75*, 96, 97, 110, 133*, 141, 201*, 399, 428, 587, 602*, 620, 687, 713, 765, 789, 969*, 970, 977, 978*, 982*, 1026, 1039-1040*.

Lying love, 302.

-M-

Maccabees(aeus), xxv, 201, 563*, 680*, 764*, 767, 892, 904.

Madagascar, Queen Ranavalona of, 413*.

Magdalene, Mary, 35, 117*, 298, 301*, 302, 351, 669, 924, 934, 945*, 949, 952, 954*, 956, 957, 959*, 994.

Maimed are healed, 170, 210, 443*, 446*, 488.

Maimonides, Rabbi Rambam, 194, 199, 389.

Majority vote failure, 456.

Making the grave stone sure, 944.

Mammon, 213*, 214, 597*-598*.

Man of sin, 557, 764*, 792, 856, 1038, 1043*, 1044-1045.

Manichees, 1030*.

Many called, but few are chosen, 705.

Many great Christians from other camps, 977.

Mao, 50, 253*, 437, 918,

Marian and pagan shrines, 9, 54*, 771, 996.

Mark of the beast, 197, 249*, 363, 452, 505, 765, 793, 948, 1005*, 1046*.

Marriage in heaven, 710-712.

Mary, bringing men to Jesus, 48-49.

Mary, mediator for Jesus?, 49, 53. (See Cybele queen of heaven.)

Mary, Queen of heaven?, 49, 53*, 428, 911.

Mary, six in the New Testament named, 35.

Mary, the wife of Cleophas. 924.

Maryland Tolerance Act, 709. (See Act of Tolerance.)

Masada, 752, 771*, 777.

Masonic Lodge, 28, 708*, 709*, 1039.

Masonic oath, 437.

Mass, Roman Catholic, xxv, xxvi, xxviii, 49*, 54, 117, 351, 372, 426, 427*, 428*, 828, 832, 978, 979*, 1029. (See Holy Eucharist, Holy Communion, and Sacred Host.)

Mather, Cotton, 1027*.

May 1948, Israel an Independent State in, 310*, 768, 774*, 775*, 776*, 797.

Mayan calendar, 1041.

McGee, J. Vernon, 1043.

Mecca, 1037, 1046.

Medina, 1037.

Mega churches, 259, 351*, 837, 991.

Melancthon, Philip, 978, 1030, 1039.

Melchisedec, 97, 135, 794, 803, 1011*.

Memorial for Mary of Bethany, 670, 671.

Memra, 1, 3*, 11*, 48, 446.

Men as trees walking, 458.

Menahem, the Jewish comforter named, 838.

Mental abuse, 205, 630.

Messiah. (Too many to list. See Verse Finder, page xvi.)

Messiah, David's Lord, (Savior), and Son, 719.

Messiah in Daniel, 564.

Messiah in the clouds, 476, 773.

Messiahs, two different Jewish, 28*, 364*, 736, 737*, 879, 1036.

Messianic Jews, 130, 195*, 196*, 249, 307, 435, 523, 535, 547, 563, 599, 691, 723, 724, 727, 729, 730, 838, 997.

Messianic signs, 127, 303, 311*, 450, 451, 452*, 738.

Methodist churches and people, 202, 259, 310, 350, 453, 459, 594, 634, 694, 774, 837, 1028-1029.

Mikvah immersion, 91*.

Miller, William, 249, 505*, 1041*.

Millstone, 499*, 605.

Mithra(ism), the cult of, 426*, 427*, 831*.

Mixing clay with spittle, 552.

Modern day paganism, 313.

Moderate or controlled drinking, 117, 118-119.

Mohammed, 253, 277, 437, 456, 559, 708, 950.

Moloch, 200, 276.

Money changers, 125*, 126, 492*, 690*, 708.

Montefiore, Claude Joseph, 182-183.

More tradition than Scripture?, 197.

Morgan, G. Campbell, 616.

Mormon Church and the blood of Christ, 832.

Mormon sex god and sex heaven, 116.

Mormon(s)(ism), xxvii*, 50, 88, 116*, 172, 217, 237, 249*, 352, 354*, 505, 515*, 602, 670, 755, 774, 789, 798, 832*, 1040*. (See Church of Jesus Christ of Latter Day Saints.)

Mormons, Jesus the polygamist and, 115*-116.

Mormons, Mountain Meadows massacre and, 832.

Moses. (Too many to list. See Verse Finder, page xvi.)

Moses' seat, 723.

Mote, 217*, 606.

Mother Ann, 1040.

Mount Hermon, 103, 461*, 464, 474, 480.

Mount Moriah, 681, 742, 754, 835, 858, 935, 1004.

Mourners, professional, 285, 393*, 394, 572, 780, 912, 933.

Müller, George, 616.

Münster(ites), 223, 317, 509, 978*, 1030-1031*.

Murray, Andrew, 292, 499*, 977.

Muslim cemetery at Jerusalem's Eastern Gate, 683.

Muslim(s), xxix, 4, 27, 72*, 144, 172, 176, 182, 189, 195, 228, 249, 253*, 277, 292*, 322, 427, 437*, 548, 613, 671, 683, 702, 768, 775, 836, 837*, 883, 950, 1002, 1003, 1010, 1037*, 1039. (See Islam.)

Mussolini, Benito, 775, 797, 907, 1039*, 1041.

-N-

Name cults, 187, 212.

Napier, John, 1040*.

National Geographic channel, vi, xxii, 413.

Natural Theology, 12*, 295, 520, 982.

Nazareth, (Too many to list. See Verse Finder, page xvi.)

Nazarite(s), 33*, 293, 483*.

Nazi war criminals, Catholic Church and 58*.

Neander, Augustus, 52*, 96*, 134, 462, 912.

Negatives are a part of Christianity, 141.

Nero, Emperor, 757, 758, 759, 899, 1039, 1046.

Nero's red beard, 1044.

Neutral society, 368.

Neutral text, xxvii*.

New Age cult, 116, 253*, 642.

New birth. (Too many to list. See Verse Finder, page xvi.)

New birth in the Old Testament, 134-135. (See Salvation in the Old Testament.)

New cloth onto an old garment, 236.

New covenant, 59, 196, 203*, 231, 429*, 434, 598, 599, 813*, 929*. (See Everlasting covenant.)

New tongues, 979.

New wine, 119, 236*, 237*, 377, 818*.

New World Order, xxx, 762, 1042.

Nicanor Gate, 62, 63, 223, 534, 608.

Nicene, Creed, 5.

Nichols, W. P., 292.

Nicodemus. (Too many to list. See Verse Finder, page xvi.)

Nimrod, 587, 911, 1037.

No fun in hell, 709.

No doctors and no medicine needed?, 255.

Noah's flood, 6, 26, 109, 143, 296, 345, 434, 587, 615, 616, 618, 626, 645, 702, 777*, 793, 842, 849, 977, 995.

Nonconformist, 1029-1030*.

None good but God, 639.

Nostradamus, 797, 1040.

Not all New Testaments commandments were from the Torah Law, 198, 199.

Nuns, Roman Catholic, 428, 631*, 828.

-O-

O'Reilly, Bill, 237, 554.

Obama, President Barack, 228, 370, 765, 1039, 1041.

Occult(ish)(ist), xxv*, xxvi, 6, 67, 68*, 69*, 71, 80*, 118, 171, 218*, 237, 259, 372*, 453, 471, 561, 602, 621, 674, 709*, 836, 916, 917, 962*, 1027, 1040.

Odessa Plot, the, 58.

Olbermann, Keith, 237, 554.

Old African man on a mountain trail, 982.

Old wine of right and left wing politics and religion, 237.

Old woman singing in a communist slave labor camp, 377.

Olive tree, 279, 282, 335, 647, 679, 768.

Olivet Discourse, 71, 127, 449, 741, 742*, 770, 773, 778*, 785, 791, 800, 801*, 806*, 807, 912, 935, 1042, 1044.

On a street in Madrid, Spain, 471, 472.

One as bad as the other, 233.

Oral law. (Too many to list. See Tradition of the elders and Verse Finder, page xvi.)

Ordained, 261.

Origen, 4*, 48, 49*, 57, 631.

Origin of the first Pope, 53.

Original Hebrew and Greek will not totally explain Scripture, 392.

Original meaning of atheist, 894.

Orr, James, 5, 60.

Outer darkness, 88*, 282, 585, 705, 787*.

-P-

Pack, David C., 1041.

Packer, J. I., 1027*.

Pagan gods. Their supposed sons and daughters, 10, 81, 462, 465, 563, 732, 831, 881, 893, 917, 996.

Pagan myth of heaven and hell, 312.

Paganism. (Too many to list. See Verse Finder, page xvi.)

Palestinian State, the pseudo, 72. (See also, Who owns the land of Israel?)

Palm Sunday, the triumphal entry on, 674*, 683.

Panati, Charles, 10*, 11, 213, 404, 831*.

Panthera, a Roman solider named, 46, 626.

Papal Church, xxv, xxix*, 9, 48*, 49, 53, 58, 97, 116, 117, 201, 207, 301, 427, 428*, 444, 463, 464*, 467, 472, 509, 530, 587, 620, 628, 631, 633, 702, 765, 828, 917, 924*, 948, 970, 977, 982, 1003*, 1025-1026, 1043, 1046. (See Roman Catholic Church.)

Paradise, 44, 212, 300, 319, 466, 354, 601, 603*, 627, 712, 923*, 942, 958*, 977, 1037, 1044.

Paralyzed by prayerlessness, 224.

Passivism, 319, 870.

Passover. (Too many to list. See Verse Finder, page xvi.)

Passover and Unleavened Bread blended together in name, 807.

Paul quoting heathen writers, xxv.

Peace of Jerusalem, pray for the, 162.

Pedobaptist, 91, 633.

Pentecost, Dwight, 131, 162, 163*, 198*, 417, 429, 612*, 626, 660, 754, 786, 802, 805.

Pericopes, xxix.

Permission to baptize from the Sanhedrin, 107, 140.

Peter a married man, 169.

Peter and John not knowing the Scriptures of Christ's resurrection, 955.

Peter and John prepare for Passover, 810-811.

Peter crucified up side down, 828.

Peter goes fishing, 985-986.

Peter the rock, 464. (See Petra and Petros.)

Peter's denials, 872-881*, 883, 968.

Peter's rooster problem, 828*, 872, 881*.

Petra, 463. (See Peter the rock.)

Petros, 463. (See Peter the rock.)

Pharisees, (Too many to list. See Verse Finder, page xvi.)

Pharisees, four different kinds of, 130.

Philo, 2.

Phylacteries, 77, 389, 522, 724, 728, 817, 824.

Piercing of Jesus' body, 939, 940, 968.

Pilate, Governor Pontius, (Too many to list. See Verse finder, page xvi.)

Pilate and Herod become friends, 893.

Pilate washes his hands, 900.

Pilate whips the Lord Jesus, 901.

Pilate's five verdicts of Jesus, 872, 887.

Pilate's wife, 899-900.

Pink, A. W., 98, 620*.

Plato and the soul of man, 474. (See Do animals have souls?)

Plato(nism), xx, 2*, 3, 4* 182*, 474*, 1030.

Pliny the Elder, 5, 175.

Pliny the Younger, 267.

Plowing or ploughing, 255, 339*, 340*, 341, 459*, 510*, 607, 768, 771, 777, 901*, 1013.

Plymouth Brethren, 790, 792*.

Polycarp and baptism, 983.

Pool of Bethesda, 241*, 251, 535*, 545, 555, 974, 1043.

Popoff, Peter, 255*.

Popov, Harlan, 290, 377.

Pope water, Catholic Church selling, 464.

Pope's attire, 463.

Postmillennialism, 310, 358, 359, 612, 753, 768, 772* 773, 777, 789, 790, 791*, 794* 798, 800, 803*, 1045. (Also called "preterists.")

Potter, Harry, 253.

Praying for the peace of Jerusalem. (See Peace of Jerusalem.)

Predestinated to reject Messiah?, 292, 633, 691, 705, 817.

Predestination, 7, 8, 9, 110, 117, 292, 293, 345, 355, 561, 634, 692, 706, 818.

Premillennialism, 162, 245, 310, 417, 761, 768, 775, 777, 789*, 790, 792*, 793*-794*, 800*, 803, 1017, 1043. (Also called "futurists.")

Presbyterian churches and people, xxii, xxvii, 7, 54, 80, 92, 110*, 139, 259, 306, 350, 509*, 525, 571, 633*, 650, 654, 687, 719, 756, 772, 783*, 791*, 794, 837, 894*, 978, 1025, 1026, 1029, 1030*, 1031*, 1044.

Price of Jesus' funeral, 941, 942.

Prime time preachers, 274, 559, 790, 997.

Prince of darkness, 100, 102, 103, 672, 822, 856, 928, 949.

Prince of evil, 850.

Prince of hell, 306. (See Asmodeus.)

Prince of Peace, 47, 56, 59, 219, 729, 871.

Prince of the power of the air, 101.

Prince of this world, 103, 255, 514, 736, 840*, 850*, 871.

Procula, Claudia, supposed wife of Pilate, 83.

Progressive dispensationalism, 794*.

Proselyte(s)(ed), 8, 21, 83, 88, 91*, 92, 93, 96, 107*, 132*, 133, 135*, 136, 195, 207, 259, 281, 355, 425, 445, 492, 535, 580, 609, 667, 693, 696, 726*, 727, 733, 734*, 807, 892*, 899, 927, 974*, 1021.

Protestants, 50*, 176*, 301, 350, 351, 370, 428, 445, 464, 789*, 978, 1025*, 1026, 1028, 1031, 1039*, 1044.

Pseudepigrapha, 106.

Publicans and sinners, 230.

Purgatory, 49, 53*, 136*, 201*, 332, 364, 428*, 475, 538, 602*.

Puritan(s), 9*, 50, 445, 453*, 465, 594*, 709*, 977*, 978*, 1014, 1015, 1026, 1027*, 1029*, 1030, 1031, 1043*.

Put out of the synagogue, 553-554.

-Q-

Quaker(s), 9, 12, 1031. (See Shaker's cult.)

Queen of Sheba, 312*, 313, 702.

Queen Sabbath, 196, 243, 251, 939*, 941-942.

-R-

Raleigh, Sir Walter, 3, 1027*.

Ram's horn, 210, 284, 533, 773. (See Shofar.)

Rapture, 36, 452, 564, 616*, 617*, 618*, 682, 753, 755, 756, 762*, 764*, 765*, 766, 770, 776, 777*, 778*, 779*, 781, 791*, 792*, 793*, 795*, 796, 798*, 799, 801*, 1039, 1040, 1042, 1043.

Rapture, no secret, 616*, 617*, 777, 791, 792, 1042, 1043, 1046.

Rashi, Rabbi, 28*, 47, 730, 737.

Rationalist(ic)(ism), xx*, xxii, xxvi, xxix, 16, 50, 56, 171, 183, 493, 668, 1033, 1035.

Rawlings, Dr. Maurice S., 377, 719.

Red heifer, 613*, 754.

Redemptive suffering, 471, 472.

Reformation, 97, 141, 628, 739, 789, 948, 977*, 978, 1030*.

Reformation without regeneration, 976, 977.

Reformed Church, 504, 554, 628, 633, 653, 691, 789, 857, 977, 982, 1026.

Reincarnated, 551, 856.

Religious and ecumenical pluralism, 369*, 370*, 399, 837.

Religious radicals, 255.

Renan, Ernest, 14, 377, 617*, 767*.

Repentance, no longer required?, 233.

Repentance, repent, repenting, repented. (Too many to list. See Verse finder, page xvi.)

Repentance, the handmaid of faith, 399.

Resurrection of damnation, 244.

Resurrection of Jesus, 945-964*.

Revisionist theology, 456, 929*.

Revived Roman Empire. 764, 797, 1038*, 1039*, 1045.

Revolution, French, 985.

Rhodes, Ron, 1041.

Ribera, Emmanuel, 791.

Riddlebarger, Kim, 764, 792.

Ridley, Nicholas, xxviii.

Right and left in politics and religion, 237, 473.

Roberts, Oral, the seed faith hoax of, 839.

Roman army officer believes, 279, 280, 282.

Roman Catholic Church. (Too many to list. See Papal Church or system.)

Roman Law or Lex Romana, 200, 201.

Roman military legions, 334*, 335, 557, 615, 617, 618*, 681, 682, 760, 765, 769, 770*, 776, 869, 870*, 888, 901, 906.

Rome, Italy, (Too many to list. See Verse Finder, page xvi.)

Rossing, Barbara R., 616*.

Rufus, Roman solider Terenitius, 768.

Russell, Charles Taze, 191, 249*, 286, 836, 1041.

Ryle, Bishop J. C., 977.

Ryrie, Charles, 417*, 612*, 660*, 791, 796, 798*, 803, 805*.

-S-

Sabbath day's journey, 996.

Sabbath fanaticism, 242, 249.

Saccas, Ammonius, 3-4*.

Sacred Host, 811. (See Mass, Roman Catholic; Holy Eucharist; and Holy Communion,)

Sacredotalism, 49*, 53, 613.

Sacrifice and offerings are forever over, 612, 614.

Sadducees. (Too many to list. See Verse Finder, page xvi.)

Saint Bartholomew's Day Massacre, 464.

Saint Francis of Assisi, 351.

Salem village, Reformer's witch trials at, 594, 978.

Salome, dancing girl, 84, 289, 403, 404*, 405*.

Salome, mother of James, John, and their plot for kingdom prominence, 651, 652-653.

Salt, 89*, 184, 190*, 302, 464, 499*, 500*, 588*, 617, 619, 976, 1021.

Salvation in the Old Testament, 8, 11, 32, 134, 135, 480, 611, 660, 760. (See New birth in the Old Testament.)

Samaritan Pentateuch, 26, 145.

Samaritan woman, 108, 116, 117, 140, 144, 145, 146, 157, 300, 384, 402, 507, 538, 609.

Same sex marriage, vii, 88, 113, 167, 368, 427, 455, 456*, 457, 627, 708*, 912.

Sanhedrin, structure of the, 1019, 1020-1021, 1023. (See Appendix Five.)

Sanhedrin, two converts from the, 1024.

Satan. (Too many to list. See Lucifer and Verse Finder, page xvi.)

Satanic literature and objects, 80, 118, 383.

Satanists infiltrating churches, 118, 383.

Schuller, Robert, 49, 50*, 837*

Schweitzer, Albert, 14, 950.

Scofield's footnotes, xxix, 5, 15, 162*, 163*, 166, 167, 186*, 187*, 191, 359, 365*, 382, 429, 483, 564, 612, 616*, 660, 719, 754, 760, 763, 764*, 768, 790*, 791, 793*, 795, 796*, 798*, 800, 801, 803, 804, 855, 948, 959, 1043.

Scripture's absolute divine authority, 566.

Sea of Galilee, 83, 103, 154, 156, 161, 163, 178, 179, 254, 337, 370, 373, 374, 377, 381, 402, 410*, 413, 419, 443, 448, 454, 686, 924, 983. (See Lake of Galilee and Sea of Tiberias.)

Sea of Tiberias, 983. (See Sea of Galilee and Lake of Galilee.)

Second miracle of Jesus, 153.

Second purging of the temple, 688, 690. (See First purging of the temple.)

Seed faith, 840.

Seed of Abraham and Abraham's seed, 23-24, 44, 101, 730, 794, 1008.

Selassie, Halle, 1041*.

Semeramis, 911*.

Septuagint Version, 20, 25*-26.

Sermon on the Mount. (Too many to list. See Verse Finder, page xvi.)

Serpent and dove, 275.

Servetus, Michael, 977, 1030.

Seven cries from the cross, 914.

Seventy Weeks problem, 564*.

Shakers cult, 1040. (See Quaker(s).)

Share International, 1039.

Shari'a law, 253.

Sharing the guilt, 50.

Shedd, W. G. T., 633*.

Sheep and Goat judgment, 799-805.

Sheep herding frowned upon, 55, 557.

Sheep in wolves' clothing, 218.

Sheep market by the pool, 125, 558, 810, 1033.

Sheep that are wolves, 505.

Shema prayer, 166, 522*, 523*, 560, 715, 740.

Shipman, Mother, 1040.

Shofar, 210, 533, 773*. (See also Ram's horn.)

Shriners', oath of the, 437.

Shushan Gate, 543, 674, 681, 682, 689, 691, 858*, 865. (See Eastern Gate of Jerusalem.)

Sick people need a doctor, 231.

Signs. (Too many to list. See Messianic signs.)

Signs following, 979, 997.

Silence of Christ, 893.

Silence or sound, 893.

Siloam's pool, 241, 334, 534*, 537*, 552*.

Simeon and baby Jesus, 37, 51, 63*, 64*, 68, 78*, 85, 91, 106, 752, 923.

Simeon of Cyrene, 206.

Simon the leper, 574, 579, 657, 661, 662, 665, 668*, 671, 672, 816.

Sinaitic Codex, 47, 540*, 956*.

Sit down with Abraham, 282.

Small Catechism, Martin Luther's, 978*.

Smith, Chuck, 1041.

Smith, Joseph, 115*, 116, 237, 286, 559, 789, 836, 1040.

Smith, Oswald J,. 616, 1041.

Smith, Sherman, 1041.

Smoking flax, 256*, 299, 354.

Snake handling cults, 979*, 998.

So great faith in Israel, 280.

Socialism(ist), 329*, 338, 385, 457*, 520, 974, 985, 1039.

Socrates, 2*, 3, 186.

Sodom and Gomorrah, 113, 275*, 368.

Sodom(y)(ites), 2, 27, 113, 117, 167, 237, 275*, 281*, 295*, 331, 368, 383*, 427, 456, 457*, 515, 615*, 617, 627, 629, 631, 1025, 1028.

Solomon's porch, 564*, 688, 718, 842, 1004.

Something is wrong, 294.

Son of Abraham, 24, 29, 660. (See Seed of Abraham.)

Son of man. (Too many to list. See Verse Finder, page xvi.)

Son or seed of David, 20*, 21, 28, 35, 73*, 101, 109, 127, 248, 306*, 307, 395*, 440, 441, 491, 655, 656, 679, 681*, 689, 691, 718*, 719, 736, 737*, 899, 1009*.

Soteriology(ical), xxi, 9, 19, 97, 110, 135, 186, 191, 369, 616, 620, 790, 969, 1029.

Soul and body in gehenna, 276.

Soul of man different from his physical body, 276, 277, 474. (See Do animals have souls?)

Southwest Radio Church, 793.

Spelling differences in Scripture, 26*, 48.

Spock, Dr. Benjamin, 88, 437*, 913.

Springer, Jerry, 224, 384, 709.

Sproul, R. C., 110.

Spurgeon, Charles H., 119*, 620*, 621, 767, 926, 931.

Stalin, Joseph, 50, 253, 255, 315, 437, 944, 991.

Standing by the cross, 923-924.

Stanley, Dean Arthur, xxviii*.

Stephanas, Robert, xxix.

Still trying to "make it sure," 944.

Stoddard(ism), 427*.

Stoning, 45, 548, 551, 565*, 630, 917*, 1022.

Strange changes in churches, 350, 473.

Strauss, David, xxix, 14, 176, 950, 1033.

Strife among the apostles, 109, 632, 651, 653, 811, 817.

Strobel, Lee, 176, 626*. Stoic(ism), 4, 739, 991.

Strong, Augustus, 5, 134, 244, 633, 634, 791.

Sublapsarianism, 7*.

Succoth, 903. (See Sukkoth.)

Sukkoth, 533, 534, 537, 753. (See Succoth.)

Sully, Henry, 612*.

Sumrall, Lester, 1041.

Sunday, Billy, 292.

Sunday worship the mark of the beast?, 249, 948, 1005.

Supralapsarianism, 7*.

Supreme Court, 8, 944.

SELECTED BIBLIOGRAPHY

Part of the subject matter in this book came from libraries in America, South Africa, Australia, and the internet. The overseas material was collected from 1980 through 1996. American sources were mostly gathered after 1996. Records of some of the quotes drawn from overseas sources and other personal effects were stolen while in ocean transit from South Africa to Australia. Newspaper articles, magazines, recordings, and periodicals are not listed in this Bibliography.

Abanes, Richard, *The Truth Behind the de Vinci Code*. (Eugene, OR. Harvest House Publishers, 2004.)

_____. *One Nation Under gods: a History of the Mormon Church*. (NY. Four Walls Eight Windows, 2002.)

Abbot, Ezra, & Hackett, H. B. Reviser & editor. *Smith's Dictionary of the Bible*. (Grand Rapids, MI. Baker Book House, 1981.)

Adams, Jay. *Competent to Counsel*. (Phillipsburg, NJ. Presbyterian and Reformed Publishing Co., 1977.)

Adams, Moody. *The Titanic's Last Hero: a Story of Courageous Heroism & Unshakable Faith*. (Belfast, Ambassador, 1998.)

_____. *Jesus Never Spoke in Tongues*. (Baker, LA. Moody Adams Evangelist Association, 1974.)

Adler, Cyrus and Singer, Isidore. Editors. *The Jewish Encyclopedia*. Twelve Volumes. (NY. Ktav Publishing House, 1964.)

Alcorn, Randy. *Heaven*. (Wheaton, IL. Tyndale House Publishers, 2004.)

Allis, Oswald T. *The Five Books of Moses*. (Phillipsburg, N.J. Presbyterian and Reformed Publishing Company, 1949.)

_____. *Prophecy & The Church*. (Phillipsburg, NJ. Presbyterian and Reformed Publishing Company, 1947.)

Alnor, William M. *Soothsayers of the Second Advent*. (Old Tappen, NJ. Power Books, 1989.)

Anderson, Einar. *I Was a Mormon*. (Grand Rapids, MI. Zondervan Publishing House, 1964.)

Anderson, Robert T., Giles, Terry. *Tradition Kept: the Literature of the Samaritans*. (Peabody, MA. Hendrickson Publishers, 2005.)

Anderson, Sir Robert. *The Coming Prince* . . . (Grand Rapids, MI. Kregal Publications, 1975.)

_____. *Spirit Manifestations and "The Gift of Tongues."* (London. Evangelical Alliance and Marshall, 1909.)

Ankerberg, John & Weldon John. *The Secret Teachings of the Masonic Lodge. A Christian Perspective*. (Chicago, IL. Moody Press, 1990.)

Archer, Gleason L.; Feinberg, Paul D.; Moo, Douglas J.; & Reiter, Richard R. *The Rapture. Pre-Mid, or Post-Tribulation?* (Grand Rapids, MI. Zondervan Publishing House, 1984.)

Armitage, Thomas. *A History of the Baptist: traced by Their Vital Principles and Practices. From the Time of Our Lord and Savior Jesus Christ to the Present*. (Watertown, WI. Maranatha Baptist Press, 1976.)

Armstrong, William Parks. Editor. *Calvinism and the Reformation*. (Grand Rapids, MI. Baker Book House, 1909.)

Arthur, Anthony. *The Tailor-King; The Rise and Fall of the Anabaptist Kingdom of Münster*. (NY. Thomas Dunne Books, 1999.)

Augustine, Saint. *The City of God*. (NY. Modern Library, 1950.)

_____. *Saint Augustine's Conversion*. (NY. Viking, 2004.)

_____. *Enchiridion or Manual to Laurentius concerning Faith, Hope, and Charity*. (London, S.P.C.K., 1953.)

Baar, Marius. *The Unholy War*. (Nashville, TN. Thomas Nelson Publishers, 1980.)

Bailey, Albert Edward. *The Gospel in Hymns*. (NY. Charles Scribner's Sons, 1950.)

Baker, Robert A. *A Summary of Christian History*. (Nashville, TN. Broadman Press, 1959.)

Banerjee, Pompa. *Burning Women: Widows, Witches, and Early Modern European Travelers in India*. (NY. Palgrave, 2003.)

Banks, William A. *Three Days & Three Nights: The Case for a Wednesday Crucifixion*. (Conshohocken, PA. Infinity, 2005.)

Banvard, Joseph. *Protestant Persecution of Baptists in Early America: A Historical Account of the Brutal Punishment Inflicted upon Elder Obadiah Holmes and Other Baptist Brethren*. (Ashland, KY. Baptist Examiner Bookshop, 19?? (Date unclear.)

Barclay, William. *Educational Ideals in the Ancient World*. (Grand Rapids, MI. Baker Book House, reprint 1974.)

Barnes, Albert. *Barnes' Notes on the New Testament*. Fourteen volumes. (Grand Rapids, MI. Baker Book House. Reprint from the 1884–1885 edition, n. d.)

Barnett, Paul. *Messiah: Jesus-The Evidence of History*. (Nottingham, England, Methuen, 1929.)

Barth, Karl, Skyes, S. W. *Karl Barth Centenary Essays*. (NY. Cambridge University Press, 1989.)

Bass, Clarence B. *Backgrounds to Dispensationalism*. (Grand Rapids, MI. Eerdmans, 1960.)

Bateman, Herbert H., Bock, Darrell L., & Johnston, Gordon H. *Jesus the Messiah* (Grand Rapids, MI. Kregel Publications, 2011.)

Bauer, Rick. *Toxic Christianity: the International Churches of Christ*. (Bowie, MD. Freedom House Ministries, 1994.)

Beasley-Murray, George R. *Jesus and the Last Days. The Interpretation of the Olivet Discourse*. (Peabody, MA. Hendrickson House Publishers, 1993.)

Bennett, Richard & Buckingham, Martin. *Far from Rome, Near to God: the Testimonies of Fifty Converted Catholic Priests.* (Edinburgh, Scotland. Banner of Truth Trust, 1997.)

Berkhof, Louis. *The History of Christian Doctrines.* (London. The Banner of Truth Trust, 1937.)

Bernis, Jonathan. *A Rabbi Looks as Jesus of Nazareth.* (Minneapolis, MN. Bethany House Publishers, 2010.)

Berry, George Ricker. *The Interlinear Literal Translation of the Greek New Testament.* (Chicago, IL. Wilcox & Follett Company, 1954.)

Bethune-Baker, J. F. *The Influence of Christianity on War.* (Cambridge, 1888.)

_____ . *An Introduction of the Early History of Christian Doctrine.* (London. Methune & Company Ltd., 1933.)

Biedermann, Hans. *Dictionary of Symbolism.* Translated from German by James Hulbert. (Oxford, England. Facts on File, 1992.)

Biederwolf, William Edward. *The Millennium Bible.* (Grand Rapids, MI. Baker Book House, 1964.)

Bird, Michael F. *Jewish Missionary Activity in the Second Temple. Crossing Over Sea and Land.* (Peabody, MA. Hendrickson House Publishers, 2010.)

Bivin, David & Blizzard, Jr., Roy. *Understanding the Difficult Words of Jesus. New Insights from a Hebraic Perspective.* (Shippensburg, PA. Destiny Image Publishers, 1994.)

Blomberg, Craig L. *The Historical Reliability of the Gospels.* (Leicester; Downer Grove, IL. Intervarsity Press, 1987.)

Bock, Darrell L., Wallace, Daniel B. *Dethroning Jesus: exposing Popular Culture's Quest to Unseat the Biblical Christ.* (Nashville, TN. Thomas Nelson Publishers, 2007.)

Boettner, Loraine. *The Millennium.* (Philadelphia, PA. The Presbyterian and Reformed Publishing Company, 1969.)

_____ . *The Reformed Doctrine of Predestination.* (Grand Rapids, MI. Eerdmans, 1932.)

_____ . *Roman Catholicism.* (Philadelphia PA. Presbyterian and Reformed Publishing Company, 1962.)

Bonhoeffer, Dietrich; Kelly, B. Geffrey; Nelson, F. Burton. *A Testimony to Freedom: The Essential Writings of Dietrich Bonhoeffer.* (San Francisco, CA. Harper Publishers, 1990.)

_____ . *Creation and Fall: A Theological Interpretation of Genesis 1-3.* (The Macmillan Company, NY. 1959.)

_____ . *No Rusty Swords.* (NY. Harper & Row, 1956.)

Bonner, Hypatic B. *The Christian Hell: From the First to the Twelfth Century.* (Whitefish, MT. Kissinger Publications, 2007.)

Book of Common Prayer. (Cambridge University Press, n. d.)

Bousset, William. *The Antichrist Legend: A Chapter in Jewish and Christian Folklore.* Translated by A. H. Keane. (London. Hutchinson, 1896.)

Boyde, Alan Patrick. *A Dispensational Premillennial Analysis of the Eschatology of the Post-Apostolic Fathers (until the death of Justin Martyr.)* A thesis to the faculty of the Department of Historical Theology, Dallas Theological Seminary, 1977.)

Boyer, Paul, and Nissenbaum, Stephen. Editors. *The Salem Witchcraft Papers in Three Volumes.* (NY. Da Capo Press, 1977.)

Brandon, Samuel G. F. *Jesus and the Zealots: a Study of the Political Factor in Primitive Christianity.* (NY. Scribner's Sons, 1967.)

Bray, John L. *Matthew 24 Fulfilled.* (Lakeland, FL. Self published by John L. Bray, 1996.)

Briscoe, John Thomas. *Calvinism: Arminianism: either? Neither? or Both?* (London. Baptist Tract Society, 1882.)

Broadbent, E. H. *The Pilgrim Church.* (London, Marshall Pickering, 1981.)

Broadus, John A. & Robertson, A.T. *A Harmony of the Gospels for Students of the Life of Christ.* (NY. Harper & Brothers, 1950.)

Bromiley, G. W. *(GE) The International Standard Bible Encyclopedia.* Four volumes. (Grand Rapids, MI. Eerdmans, 1982.)

Brown, Michael L. *Our Hands Are Stained with Blood: The Tragic Story of the "Church" and the Jewish People.* (Shippensburg, PA. Destiny Image, 1992.)

Brown, Raymond E. *The Death of the Messiah from Gethsemane to the Grave: A Commentary on the Passion Narratives in the Four Gospels.* (NY. Doubleday, 1994.)

Brown, Sanger. *Sex Worship and Symbolism.* (NY. AMS Press, 1975.)

Bruce, A. B. *The Training of the Twelve.* (Grand Rapids, MI. Kregel Publications, 1971.)

Brumbelow, David R. *Ancient Wine & The Bible . . .* (Carrelton, GA. Free Church Press, 2011.)

Brunner, Borgna. Editor. *Information Please Almanac.* (Boston, MA. Inso Corporation, 1998.)

Bubeck, Mark I. *Overcoming the Adversary. Warfare Praying Against Demonic Activity.* (Chicago, IL. Moody Press, 1984.)

_____ . *The Adversary: the Christian Versus Demon Activity.* (Chicago, IL. Moody Press, 1975.)

_____ . *Preparing for Battle: a Spiritual Warfare Workbook.* (Chicago, ILL. Moody Press, 1999.)

Buechler, A. *Studies in Sin and Atonement in the Rabbinic Literature of the First Century.* (NY. Ktav Publishing House, 1967.)

Bullinger, Ethelbert. *The Companion Bible. The Authorized Version of 1611.* (Grand Rapids, MI. Kregal Publications, 1990.)

Burgon, John W. *The Revised Revised.* (Fort Worth, TX. A. G. Hobbs Publication, 1991.)

_____ . *The Causes of the Corruption of the Traditional Text of the Holy Gospels.* Edited by Edward Miller. (London. Published by George Bell & Sons, 1896.)

Burkett, Elinor, Bruni, Frank. *A Gospel of Shame: Children, Sexual Abuse and the Catholic Church.* (NY. Viking Press, 1993.)

Burton, Thomas, G. *Serpent-Handling Believers.* (Knoxville, TN. University of Tennessee Press, 1993.)

Bushnell, Horace. *The Character of Jesus: Forbidding His Possible Classification With Men.* (NY. Charles Scribner's Sons, 1917.)

Buxtorf, Johannes. Synagoga Judaica. *The Jewish Synagogue, or an Historical Narration of the State of the Jewes.* (London, T. Roycroft for H. R. and T. Young, 1657.)

Calvin Jean. *Institutes of the Christian Religion.* (Grand Rapids, MI. Eerdmans, 1953.) Translated from Latin by Henry Beveridge.

Camp, Gregory S. *Selling Fear. Conspiracy Theories and End—Paranoia.* (Grand Rapids, MI. Baker Books, 1997.)

Campbell, Ron. *Free from Freemasonry. Understanding "the Craft" and How It Affects Those You love.* (Ventura, CA. Regal Books, 1999.)

Canright, D. M. *Seventh-Day Adventism Renounced.* (Nashville, TN. Gospel Advocate Company, 1961.)

Carr, John D. *The Hem of His Garment. Touching the Power in God's Word.* (Atlanta, GA. Restoration Foundation, 2000.)

Carroll, James. *Constantine's Sword: The Church and the Jews: A History.* (Boston, MA. Houghton Mifflin, 2001.)

Carroll, Michael P. *The Cult of the Virgin Mary.* (NJ. Princeton University Press, 1986.)

Cavert, Samuel McCrea. *The American Churches in the Ecumenical Movement, 1900-1968.* (NY. Association Press, 1968.)

Chafer, Lewis S. *Systematic Theology.* Eight volumes. (Dallas, TX, Dallas Seminary Press, 1948.)

Chandler, Walter M. *The Trial of Jesus.* (Norcross, GA. The Harrison Company Publishers, 1976.)

Charlesworth, Charles. Editor. *The Messiah. The First Princeton Symposium on Judaism and Christian Origins.* (Minneapolis, MN. Fortress Press, 1992.)

Child, Heather, Colles, Dorothy. *Christian Symbols, Ancient and Modern.* (NY. Charles Scribner's Sons, 1971.)

Chilton, David. *Paradise Restored: A Biblical Theology.* (Tyler, TV. Reconstruction Press, 1985.)

Clark, Gordon H. *Logical Criticism of Textual Criticisms.* (Jefferson, MD. The Trinity Foundation, 1987.)

Clarke, Adam. *Adam Clarke's Commentary on the Bible.* Six volumes. (Nashville, TN. Abington Press, n. d.)

Clarke, John. *Ill Newes From New-England; or A Narrative of New-England Persecution. Where in is Declared that While Old England is Becoming New, New-England is becoming Old.* London. Printed by Henry Hills, 1652.)

Clay, Albert T. *Light on the Old Testament from Babel.* (Philadelphia, PA. The Sunday School Times Company, 1907.)

Coffey, John. *Persecution and Toleration in Protestant England, 1558-1689.* (Harlow, England; NY. Longman, 2000.)

Cohn, Norman. *Warrant for Genocide. The Myth of the Jewish World - Conspiracy and the Protocols of the Elders of Zion.* (London. Eyre & Spottiswoode, 1967.)

Cohn, Sherbok. *The Jewish Doctrine of Hell.* (Lancaster, England. University of Lancaster, 1978.)

Collins, Larry & Dominique, Lapierre. *O Jerusalem* .(NY. Simon & Schuster. 1972.)

Comsky, William. *Hebrew. The Eternal Language.* (Philadelphia, PA. Jewish Publication Society of America, 1957.)

Coneybear, W. J. and Howson, J. S. *The Life and Epistles of Saint Paul.* (London. Longman, Green, Longman and Roberts, 1862.)

Cornell, James C. *The Great International Disaster Book.* (NY. Pocket Books, 1979.)

Cotton, Paul. *From Sabbath to Sunday.* (Bethlehem, PA. Times Publishing Company, 1933.)

Countess, Robert H. *The Jehovah Witnesses' New Testament.* (Phillipsburg, N.J. Presbyterian & Reformed Publishing Co., 1982.)

Croscup, George E. *Historical Charts of the Life and Ministry of Christ.* (London. The Sunday School Times, 1912.)

Cross, F. L. & Livingstone, E. A. *The Oxford Dictionary of the Christian Church.* (NY. Oxford University Press, Second edition, 1974.)

Crutchfield, Larry V. *The Origins of Dispensationalism: the Darby Factor.* (Lanham, MD. University Press of America, 1992.)

Curtiss, George L. *Arminianism in History: or, The Revolt From Predestinationism.* (Cincinnati, OH. Cranston & Curtiss, 1894.)

Custer, Stewart. *The Truth About the King James Controversy.* (Greenville, SC. Bob Jones University Press, 1981.)

Dagg, J. L. *Manual of Theology.* (Harrison, VA. Gano Books, 1982.)

Dake, Finis J. *Dake's Annotated Reference Bible.* (Atlanta, GA. Published by F. J. Dake, 1965.)

Dalman, Gustav. *Jesus Christ in the Talmud, Midrash, Zohar and the Liturgy of the Synagogue.* (NY. Arno Press, 1973.)

Darby, John N. & William Kelly. *The Works of John Nelson Darby.* (London. George Morrish, date printed unclear.

Darby, John N. *Letters of J.N.D.* Three volumes. (London, George Morrish, 1898.)

Daube, David. *The New Testament and Rabbinic Judaism.* (Peabody, MA. Hendrickson House Publishers, 1956.)

Daunton-Fear, Andrew. Healing in the Early Church . . . (Colorado Springs, CO. Paternoster, 2009.)

Davies, Benjamin. *Harmony of the Gospels.* (Greenville, SC. Bob Jones University Press, 1978.)

Davies, W. D. *Paul and Rabbinic Judaism.* (London. S. P. C. K., 1958.)

Davis, John J. *Biblical Numerology.* (Grand Rapids, MI. Baker Book House, 1968.)

Decker, Ed & Hunt, David. *The God Makers.* (Eugene, OR. Harvest House Publishers, 1984.)

Demos, John. *Entertaining Satan: witchcraft and the Culture of Early New England.* (NY. Oxford University Press, 1983.)

Dickason, C. Fred. *Demon Possession and the Christian.* (Chicago, IL. Moody Press, 1987.)

Dillow, Joseph. *Speaking in Tongues: Seven Crucial Questions.* (Grand Rapids, MI. Zondervan Publishing House 1975.)

Dosick, Wayne. *Living Judaism.* (San Francisco, CA. Harper Collins Publishers, 1995.)

Doughty, Norman F. *The Case of D.M. Canright.* (Grand Rapids, MI. Baker Book House, 1964.)

Dowley, Timothy E. *The History of the English Baptist During the Great Persecution, 1660-1688.* (A thesis to the Department of Historical Theology, Florida State University of Manchester 1976.)

Doyl, Thomas P, Sipe, A. W. Richard, Wall, Patrick J. *Sex, Priests, and Secret Codes: The Catholic Church's 2000-year Paper Trail of Sexual Abuse.* (Los Angeles, CA. Volt Press, 2006.)

Driver, Samuel & Neubauer, Adolf. *The Suffering Servant of Isaiah.* Translated from German. (Eugene, OR. Wipf and Stock Publishers, 1999.)

Duncan, Homer. *The King is Coming. Ninety-Seven Scriptural Signs that Indicate the Imminent Return of the Lord Jesus Christ.* Lubbock, TX. Missionary Crusader, 1977.)

Durant, Will. *The Story of Civilization.* Eleven volumes. (NY. Published by MJF Books, 1950.)

Durso, Keith E. *No Armor For the Back: Baptist Prison Writings, 1600s-1700s.* (Macon, GA. Mercer University Press, Atlanta, GA. Baptist History & Heritage Society, 2007.)

Duty, Guy. *Divorce & Remarriage.* (Minneapolis, MN. Bethany House Publishers, 1967.)

Edersheim, Alfred. *Prophecy and History in Relation to the Messiah.* (London. Longmans, Green and Company. n. d. Approximately 1886.)

_____. *Life and Times of Jesus the Messiah.* (Peabody. MA. Hendrickson House Publisher, 1993.)

_____. *Sketches of Jewish Social Life in the Days of Christ.* (London: James Clarke & Company, 1961.)

_____. *The Temple. Its Ministry and Services.* (London: James Clarke and Co. Ltd., 1959.)

Ehrman, Bart D. *God's Problem: How the Bible Fails to Answer Our Most Important Question-Why we Suffer.* (NY. HarperOne, 2008.)

_____. *Jesus, Interrupted: Revealing the Hidden Contradictions in the Bible and Why We Don't Know About Them.* (NY Harper-One, 2009.)

Ellerbe, Helen. *The Dark Side of Christianity.* (San Rafael, CA. Morning Star Books, 1995.)

Enns, Paul P. *The Moody Handbook of Theology.* (Chicago, IL. Moody Press, 1989.)

Enroth, Ronald M., *Churches that Abuse.* (Grand Rapids, MI. Zondervan, 1992).

Ephraim, Emerton. *Desiderius Erasmus of Rotterdam.* (N.Y. G. P. Putnam's Sons, 1899.)

Estep, William R. *The Anabaptist Story.* (Grand Rapids, MI. Eerdmans, 1975.)

Estrada, David, and White, William. *The First New Testament.* (NY. Thomas Nelson Publishers, 1978.)

Eusebius, Pamphilus. *The Ecclesiastical History of Eusebius Pamphilus.* (Grand Rapids, MI. Baker Book House, 1958.)

Farrar, F.W. *The Life of Christ.* (London. Cassell and Company, LTD., 1903.)

Finegan, Jack. *Myth & Mystery: An Introduction to the Pagan Religions of the Biblical World.* (Grand Rapids, MI. Baker Book House, 1989.)

_____. *Handbook of Biblical Chronology: principles of Time Reckoning in the Ancient World and Problems of Chronology in the Bible.* (Princeton, NJ. Princeton University Press, 1964.)

Fisher, George P. *History of the Christian Church.* (NY. Charles Scribner's Sons, 1888.)

Fisk, Samuel. *Calvinistic Paths Retraced.* (Murfreesboro, TN. Biblical Evangelism Press, 1985.)

_____. *Divine Sovereignty and Human Freedom.* ((Neptune, NJ. Loizeaux Brothers, 1986.)

Foote, G. W. Wheeler, J. M. *Crimes of Christianity.* (London. Progressive Publishing Company, 1887.)

Fox, John. *Fox's Book of Martyrs.* Edited by William B. Forbush. (Grand Rapids, MI. Zondervan Publishing House, 1967.)

Frank, Tenny. *An Economic Survey of Ancient Rome.* Six volumes. (Paterson, NJ. Pageant Books, 1959.)

Frazier, Gary. *7 signs of the Second Coming of Christ.* (Greenville, TX. Casscom Media, 2006.)

Fredriksen, Paula. *Augustine and the Jews: a Christian Defense of Jews and Judaism.* (NY. Doubleday, 2008.)

Friesen, James G. *Uncovering the Mystery of MPD.* (San Bernardino, CA. Here's Life Publishers, 1991.)

Fruchtenbaum, Arnold G. *Jesus Was a Jew.* (Nashville, TN. Broadman Press, 1974.)

Fuller, Robert. *Naming the Antichrist: The History of an American Obsession.* (NY. Oxford University Press, 1995.)

Gaebelein, Arno Clemens. *The Conflict of the Ages. The Mystery of Lawlessness: Its Origins, Historic Development and Coming Defeat.* (No place or publisher listed, 1968.)

Gale, Theophilus. *The Court of the Gentiles.* (London. Printed by F. Macock for Thomas Gilbert, 1676.)

Gartenhaus, Jacob. *Famous Hebrew Christians.* (Hixson, TN. International Board of Jewish Missions, Inc., 1998.)

Gaster, Moses. *The Samaritans. Their History, Doctrines and Literature.* (England. Oxford University Press, 1925.)

Gaussen, L. *The Inspiration of the Holy Scriptures.* (Chicago. Moody Press, n. d.)

Geike, Cunningham. *The Life and Words of Christ.* (NY. D. Appleton and Co., 1880.)

Geisler, Norman L. *Chosen but Free*. (Minneapolis, MN. Bethany House Publishers, 1999.)

_____. Betancourt, Joshua M. *Is Rome the True Church: a Consideration of the Roman Catholic Claim*. (Wheaton, IL. Crossway Books, 2008.)

Gentry, Kenneth L. *Before Jerusalem Fell*. (Tyler, TX. Institute for Christian Economics, 1989.)

Gerstner, John H. *The Theology of the Major Sects*. (Grand Rapids, MI. Baker Book House, 1960.)

_____. *Wrongly Dividing the Word of Truth*. (Brentwood, TN. Wolgemuth & Hyatt, Publisher, Inc., 1991.)

Gibbon, Edward. *The Decline and Fall of the Roman Empire*. Two volumes. (NY. Random House, n.d.)

Gibson, Larry A. *The Return of Christ in 29 Years*. (Victoria, B.C. Trafford, 2006.)

Gill, John. *Exposition of the Old and New Testaments*. Nine volumes. (Paris, Arkansas. Baptist Standard Bearer Inc., 1989.)

Godley, A. D., Translator. *Herodotus I*. Four volumes. (Cambridge, MS. Harvard University Press, MCMLXXXI.)

Goetz, William R. *The Economy to Come in Prophetic Context. What Will Happen When Your Money Fails?* (Camp Hill, PA. Horizon Books Publishers, 1988.)

Goldstein, Morris. *Jesus in the Jewish Tradition*. (NY. The Macmillan Company, 1950.)

Goni, Uki. *The Real Odessa*. (London/NY. Granta, 2002.)

Graham, Billy. *Just As I Am; The Autobiography of Billy Graham*. (Grand Rapids, MI. 1997.)

Grant, Michael. *History of Ancient Israel*. (NY. Charles Scribner's Sons, 1984.)

Gratus, Jack. *The False Messiahs*. (London. Victor Gollancz, 1975.)

Graves, J. R. *John's Baptism*. (Texarkana, AR. Baptist Sunday School Committee, 1939.)

Green, J.P. Sr. Editor. Volume 1. *Unholy Hands on the Bible. Including the Complete Works of John W. Burgon, Dean of Chichester*. (Lafayette, IN. Sovereign Grace Trust fund, 1990.)

_____. *The Gnostics, the New Versions and the Deity of Christ*. (Lafayette, IN. Sovereign Grace Publishers, 1994.)

Greenleaf, Simon. *The Testimony of the Evangelists, Examined by the Rules of Evidence Administered in Courts of Justice*. (Grand Rapids, MI. Reprint of 1874 edition. Baker Book House, 1984.)

Greenstone, H. Julius. *The Messianic Idea in Jewish History*. (Westport, CT. Greenwood Publishers, 1906.)

Greer, Thelma. *Mormonism, Mama & Me*. (Tucson, AZ. Published by Calvary Missionary Press, 1980.)

Gribbin, John R. & Plagemann, Stephen H. *The Jupiter Effect*. (NY. Vintage Books, 1982.)

Gromacki, Robert G. *The Modern Tongues Movement*. (Grand Rapids, MI. Baker Book House, 1967.)

Gundry, Robert H. *The Church and the Tribulation*. (Grand Rapids, MI. Zondervan Publishing House, 1973.)

Gurganus, Gene. *Islam and the End Times*. (Greenville, SC. Truth Publishers, 2010.)

Habermas, Gary Robert. *The Resurrection of Christ: Fact or Fiction*. (Kansas City, MO. Midwestern Baptist Seminary, 2007.)

Haines, Charles R. *Heathen Contact With Christianity During its First Century and a Half*. (Cambridge. Deighton, Bell and Company, 1923.)

Haley, Mike. 101 *Frequently Asked Questions About Homosexuality*. (Eugene, OR. Harvest House Publishers, 2004.)

Halley, Henry C. *Halley's Bible Handbook*. (London. Oliphants, 1965.)

Hammond. Peter. *Slavery, Terrorism and Islam: the Historical Roots and contemporary Threat*. (Cape Town, South Africa. Christian Library Books, 2002.)

Hanegraaff, Hank. *Counterfeit Revival*. (Dallas, TX. Word Publishers, 1997.)

Hanson, J. S. & Horsley, R. A. *Bandits, Prophets and Messiahs: Popular Movements in the Time of Jesus*. (Philadelphia, PA. Winston Press. 1985.)

Harrison, A. W. *Arminianism*. (London. Duckworth, 1937.)

Hasler, August. *How the Pope Became Infallible*. (NY. Doubleday & Company, 1981.)

Haude, Sigrun. *In the Shadow of "Savage Wolves." Anabaptist Münster and the German Reformation During the 1530s*. (Boston, MA. Humanities Press, 2000.)

Haught, James A. *Honest Doubt: essays on Atheism in a Believing Society*. (Amherst, NY. Prometheus Books, 2007.)

_____. *Holy Horrors: An Illustrated History of Religious Murder and Madness*. (Buffalo, NY. Prometheus Books, 1990.)

Haynes, Carlyle B. *Twelve Great Signs of the Return of Jesus*. (Takoma Park, MD. Review and Herald, 1925.)

Hazlitt, William, & Chalmers, Alexander. *The Table Talk of Martin Luther*. (London. Published by G. Bell, 1902.)

Hengel, Martin. *Crucifixion*. Translated by John Bowden. (Philadelphia, PA. Fortress Press, 1977.)

Matthew Henry's Commentary. Six volumes. (Peabody, MA. Hendrickson House Publishers, second edition, 1992.)

Henstenberg, E. W. *Christology of the Old Testament*. (Grand Rapids, MI. Kregel Publications, 1970.)

Herbert, A. S. *Historical Catalogue of Printed Editions of the English Bible 1525-1961*. (London. The British and Foreign Bible Society, NY. The American Bible Society, 1968.)

Herzig, Steve. *Jewish Culture & Customs: A Sampler of Jewish Life*. (Bellmawr, NJ. The Friends of Israel Gospel Ministry, Inc., 1997.)

Hessy, James Augustus. *Sunday. Its Origin, History, and Present Obligation*. (London. Published by John Murray, 1860.)

Hislop, Alexander. *The Two Babylons*. (NY. Loizeaux Brothers, 1943.)

Hoad, Jack. *The Baptist.* (London. Grace Publications Trust, 1980.)

Hoehner, Harold. *Chronological Aspects of the life of Christ.* ((Grand Rapids, MI. Zondervan Publishing house, 1977.)

Holford, Peter. *The Destruction of Jerusalem: An Absolute and Irresistible Proof of the Divine Origin of Christianity.* (Nacogdoches, TX. Reprint of 1830 edition. Covenant Media Press, 2001.)

Holmes, Obadiah, Gaustad, Edwin S. *The Last Will & Testament of Obadiah Holmes.* (Grand Rapids, MI. Christian University Press, 1978.)

Hughes, Jeremy. *Secrets of the Times: Myth and History in Biblical Chronology.* (Sheffield. Sheffield Academic Press 2009.)

Hunt, Dave. *A Woman Rides the Beast.* (Eugene, OR. Harvest House Publishers, 1994.)

_____. *Global Peace and the Rise of the Antichrist.* (Eugene, OR. Harvest House Publisher, 1990.)

_____. *What Love is This?* (Sisters, OR. Loyal Publishing, Inc., 2002.)

Hobart, William K. *The Medical Language of St. Luke.* (Dublin. Hodges, Figgs u.a. 1882.)

Hoehner, Harold W. *Herod Antipas: A contemporary of Jesus Christ.* (Grand Rapids, MI. Zondervan Publishing House, 1972.)

Hoekema, Anthony A. *The Four Major Cults.* Grand Rapids, MI. Eerdmans publishing, 1963.)

Hoffman, Joseph R. *The Secret Gospels: A Harmony of Apocryphal Jesus Traditions.* (Amherst, NY. Prometheus Books, 1996.)

Holy Bible Edition of 1611, King James Version. (Nashville, TN. Thomas Nelson Publishers, 1982.)

Holy Bible. Revised Standard Version. (NY. Thomas Nelson & Sons, 1952.)

Hoover, Peter. *History of the Baptist Church in Colonial America.* A thesis to the faculty of the Department of Church History of the Wesleyan University, Middletown, CT., 1983.

Horn, W. V. & Schafer, Peter. *Jewophobia. Attitude Toward the Jews in the Ancient World.* (London. Times Newspaper Ltd., 1998.)

Hort, Arthur Fenton. *Life and Letters of Fenton John Anthony Hort.* Two volumes. (London/NY. The Macmillan Company Ltd., 1896.)

Horton, Michael S. Editor. *The Agony of Deceit.* (Chicago, IL. Moody Press, 1990.)

_____. *Christless Christianity: the Alternative Gospel of the American Church.* (Grand Rapids, MI. Baker Books, 2008.)

House, H. Wayne. *Chronological and Background Charts of the New Testament.* (Grand Rapids, MI. Zondervan Academie Books, 1981.)

Howard, Kevin, Rosenthal, Marvin J. *The Feasts of the LORD.* (Orlando, FL. Thomas Nelson Publishers, 1997.)

Hurlbut, Jesse L. *A Bible Atlas.* (NY. Rand McNally & Company, 1954.)

Ingram, M.V. *Authenticated History of the Bell Witch, and Other Stories of the World's Greatest Unexplained Phenomenon.* (Nashville, TN. Rare Book Reprints, 1961.)

Inman, Thomas. *Ancient Pagan and Modern Christian Symbolism.* (NY. Peter Eckler Publishing Company, 1922.)

Jacoby, Susan. *Freethinkers: a History of American Secularism.* (NY. Metropolitan Books, 2004.)

Jakob, Jocz. *The Jewish People and Jesus Christ.* (London. S. P. C. K. Publishers, 1954.)

Jenkins, Jerry B, LaHaye, Tim. *The Rise of False Messiahs.* (Wheaton, ILL. Tyndale Kids, 2004.)

Jenks, Gregory C. *The Origins and Early Development of the Antichrist Myth.* (NY. Walter De Grayters, 1991.)

Jeremias, Joachim. *Infant Baptism in the First Four Centuries.* (Bristol, England. SCM Press Ltd., 1960.)

_____. *Jerusalem in the Time of Jesus.* Translated from German by F.H. Cave and C. H. Cave. Based on an earlier work by M. E. Dahl. (Philadelphia, PA. Fortress Press, 1969.)

Jonsson, Lewis S. *The Old Testament in the New.* (Grand Rapids, MI. Zondervan Publishing House, 1980.)

Johsson, Carl Olof, & Herbst, Wolfgang. *The Sign of the Last Days. When?* (Atlanta, GA. Commentary Press, 1987.)

Jones, Timothy Paul. *Conspiracies and the Cross.* (Lake Mary, FL. Frontline Publishers, 2008.)

_____. *Misquoting Truth: a Guide to the Fallacies of Bart Ehrman's "Misquoting Jesus."* (Downers Grove, IL. IVP Books, 2007.)

Josephus, Flavius. *The Works of Josephus.* (Complete and Unabridged. Peabody, MA. 1992. Hendrickson House Publishers, 1992.)

Joslin, Barry C. *Hebrews, Christ, and the Law: the Theology of the Mosaic Law in Hebrews 7:1-10:18.* (Colorado Springs, CO. Milton Keynes, Publisher, Paternoster, 2008.)

Krakauer, Jon. *Under the Banner of Heaven.* (NY. Doubleday, 2003.)

Kang, G. H., and Nelson, Ethel R. *The Discovery of Genesis. How the Truths of Genesis were Found Hidden in the Chinese Language.* (St Louis, MO. Concordia Publishing House, 1979.)

Kauffman, Donald T. *The Dictionary of Religious Terms.* (Westwood, N.J. Fleming Revell Company, 1967.)

Keener, Craig S. *And Marries Another.* (Peabody, MA. Hendrickson House, 1991.)

_____. *The Spirit in the Gospels and Acts.* (Peabody, MA. Hendrickson House, 1997.)

Keil, C. F., Delitzsch, F. *Biblical Commentary on the Old Testament.* (Grand Rapids, MI. Eerdmans, 1950-1956.)

Kelly, Douglas F. *The Emergence of Liberty in the Modern World: The Influence of Calvin on Five Governments from the 16th Through the 18th Centuries.* (Phillipsburg, NJ. P & R Publishing, 1992.)

Kelly, J. N. D. *Early Christian Doctrines.* (San Francisco, CA. Harper Collins Publishers, 1978.)

Kennedy, D. James. *The Real Meaning of the Zodiac.* (Ft. Lauderdale, FL. TCRM Publishing, 1997.)

Kertzer, David I. *The Popes Against the Jews: The Vatican's Role in the Rise of Modern Anti-Semitism.* (NY. Alfred A. Knopf, 2001.)

Kick, Russ. Editor. *Everything you Know About God is Wrong.* NY. Disinformation, 2007.)

Kidd, George B. *The Doctrine of the Manifestation of the Son of God Under the Economy of the Old Testament.* (London. Ward & Company, 1852.)

Kidder, Daniel Parish. *The Jewish Nation: Containing An Account Of Their Manners And Customs, Rites And Worship, Laws And Polity.* (NY. Lane & Scott Publishers, 1850.)

Kimball, William R. *The Rapture.* (Grand Rapids, MI. Baker Book House, 1985.)

Kirban, Salem. *The Plain Truth About the Plain Truth.* (Huntington Valley, PA. Salem Kirban, Inc., 1970.)

Klausner, Joseph. *The Messianic Idea in Israel From its Beginning to the Completion of the Mishnah.* (NY. The Macmillan Company, 1955.)

Knight, William. *The Arch of Titus and the Spoils of the Temple.* (London. Religious Tract Society. 1896.)

Koch, Kurt. *Between Christ and Satan.* (Western Germany. Evangelization Publisher, n. d.)

_____. *Demonology Past and Present.* (Grand Rapids, MI. Kregel Publication, 1973.)

_____. *Christian Counseling and Occultism.* (Grand Rapids, MI. Kregel Publications, 1965.)

Krummacher, Friedrich. W. *The Suffering Saviour.* (Chicago, IL. The Moody Bible Institute, 1947.)

Kung, Hans. *Justification: the Doctrine of Karl Barth and a Catholic Reflection* (Philadelphia, PA. Westminster Press, 1981.)

Kupelian, David. *The Marketing of Evil; How Radicals, Elitists, and Pseudo-Experts Sell us Corruption Disguised as Freedom.* (Nashville, TN. WND Books, 2005.)

Kyle, Richard. *The Last Days Are Here Again. A History of the End Times.* (Grand Rapids, MI, 1998.)

Ladd, George E. *The Presence of the Future.* (Grand Rapids. MI. Eerdmans, 1981.)

LaHaye, Tim F., Jenkins, Jerry B. *Desecration: Antichrist Takes the Throne.* (Wheaton, IL. Tyndale House, 2001.)

_____. *Are We Living in the End times?* (Wheaton, IL. Tyndale House Publishers, 1999.)

Lardner, Nathanel. *The Works of Nathaniel Lardner.* Ten volumes. (London. W. Ball, 1838.)

Lecky, W. E. H. *History of European Morals.* Two volumes. (London. Longmans, Green & Company, 1869.)

Lees, Frederic R., and Burns, Dawson. *Temperance Bible Commentary: Giving at One View, Version, Criticism, and Exposition, in Regard to all Passages of Holy Writ Bearing on 'Wine' and 'Strong Drink' or Illustrating the Principles of the Temperance Reformation.* Twelve volumes. (NY. Sheldon & Company, 1870.)

Leon, Harry J. *The Jews of Ancient Rome.* (Peabody, MA. Hendrickson House Publishers, 1995.)

Letis, Theodore P. *The Revival of the Ecclesiastical Text and the Claims of the Anabaptists.* (Fort Wayne, IN. The Institute for Reformation Biblical Studies, 1992.)

Levi, Eliphas & Arthur E. Waite. *Transcendental Magic: its Doctrine and Ritual.* (London. Rider, 1923.)

Levin, Lee I. *The Ancient Synagogue: The First Thousand Years.* (London. Yale University Press, 2005.)

Levin, Mark R. *Men Black; how the Supreme Court is Destroying America.* (Washington D.C. Regnery Publishers, Inc. 2005.)

Lewis, C. S. *Mere Christianity.* (NY. Walker and Company, 1987.)

_____. *The Screwtape Letters.* (London. Geoffery Bles, 1942.)

Lewis, W. G. *The Trades and Industrial Occupations of the Bible.* (London. RTS, n. d.)

LeMann, M. M. *Jesus Before the Sanhedrin.* (Nashville, TN. Methodist Episcopal Church of the South, 1886.)

Life Application Bible. (Wheaton, IL. Tyndale House Publishers, 1986.)

Lightfoot, John. *A Commentary on the New Testament from the Talmud and Hebraica.* Four volumes. (Peabody, MA. Hendrickson House, 1989.)

Lightner, Robert P. *Angel, Satan, and Demons: Invisible Beings that Inhabit the Spiritual World.* (Nashville, TN. Word Publishing, 2006.)

_____. *The Death Christ Died.* (Des Plaines, IL. Regular Baptist Press, 1967.)

Lightner, Paul. *The God of the Bible and Other Gods: [Is the Christian God Unique Among World Religions?]* (Paris AK. Baptist Standard Bearer, 2009.)

Lindsell, Harold. *The Battle for the Bible.* (Grand Rapids, MI. Zondervan Publishing House, 1976.)

Lindsey, Hal. *Facing Millennial Midnight: The 2K Crisis Confronting America and the World.* (Beverly Hills, CA. Western Front, 1998.)

_____. *The Late Great Planet Earth.* (Grand Rapids, MI. Zondervan Publishing House, 1970.)

Linnemann, Eta. *Historical Criticism.* (Grand Rapids, MI. Baker Book House, 1992.)

_____. *Is There a Synoptic Problem? Rethinking the Literary Dependence of the Firs Three Gospels.* (Grand Rapids, MI. Baker Book House, 1992.)

Little, Lewis Peyton. *Imprisoned Preachers and Religious Liberty in Virginia. A Narrative Drawn Largely from the Official Records of Virginia Counties, Unpublished Manuscripts, Letters, and other Original Sources.* (Lynchburg, VA. J. P. Bell Company, 1938.)

Lockyer, Herbert. *All the Messianic Prophecies of the Bible.* (Grand Rapids, MI. Zondervan Publishing House, 1988.)

_____. *All the Men of the Bible: All the Women of the Bible*. (Grand Rapids, MI. Zondervan Publishing House, 1996.)

Lofus, John W. *Why I Became an Atheist. A former Preacher Rejects Christianity*. (Amherst, NY. Prometheus Books, 2008.)

Ludwig, Charles. *Ludwig's Handbook of Old Testament Rulers & Cities*. (Denver, CO. Accent Books, 1984.)

_____. *Rulers of the New Testament Times*. (Denver, CO. Accent Books, 1976.)

Luther, Martin, & Packer, J. I., Jackson, O. R. *Bondage of the Will*. (Old Tappen, NJ. Revell, 1957.)

Luther, Martin. *The Large Catechism*. (Minneapolis, MN. Augsburg Publishing House, 1936.)

_____. *Martin Luther's Large & Small Catechism*. (Publisher [S.I]. NuVision Publications, 2007.)

_____. *Luther's Small Catechism with Explanation*. (Saint Louis, MO. Published by CPH, 1991.)

Lutzer, Erwin. *Christ Among Other Gods*. (Chicago, IL. Moody Press, 1994.)

_____. *Getting to NØ: How to Break a Stubborn Habit*. (Colorado Springs, CO. David C. Cook, 2007.)

M'Clintock John, & Strong, James. *Cyclopaedia of Biblical, Theological, and Ecclesiastical Literature*. Ten volumes. (NY. Harper Brothers, 1867-1881.)

McClure, Alexander Wilson. *The Translators Revived: A Biographical Memoir of the Authors of the English Version of the Holy Bible*. (NY. Charles Scribner' Sons, 1853.)

MacArthur, John. *Because the Time is Near*. (Chicago, IL. Moody Publishers, 2007.)

McDowell, Josh. *The New Evidence that Demands a Verdict*. (Nashville, TN. Thomas Nelson Publishers, 1999.)

Machen, J. Gresham. *The Virgin Birth of Christ*. (NY. Harper, 1930.)

Marcel, Pierre C. *The Biblical Doctrine of Infant Baptism*. Translated from French by Philip E. Hughes. (London, James Clarke & Co., Publishers, 1959.)

Marshall, Alfred. *The Interlinear Greek-English New Testament*. (London, Samuel Bagster and Sons Ltd., 1964.)

Marshall, I. Howard. *Last Supper and Lord's Supper*. (Grand Rapids, MI. Eerdmans, 1980.)

Martin, James. *The Reliability of the Gospels*. (London. Hodder & Stoughton, 1959.)

Martin, Walter. Ravi Zacharias, general editor. *The Kingdom of the Cults*. (Minneapolis, MN. Bethany House Publishers, 2003.)

Mason, Steve. *Josephus and the New Testament*. (Peabody, MA. Hendrickson House Publishers, 1992.)

Masters, Peter. *Should Christians Drink? The Case for Total Abstinence*. (London. The Wakeman Trust, 2003.)

Mather, George A, & Nichols, Larry A. *Dictionary of Cults, Sects, Religions and the Occult*. (Grand Rapids, MI. Zondervan Publishing House, 1993.)

Mauro, Philip. *The Gospel of the Kingdom with an Examination of Dispensationalism*. (Boston, MA. Hamilton Bros. Scripture Truth Depot, 1928.)

_____. *The Number of Man: the Climax of Civilization*. (NY. Fleming H. Revell Company, 1909.)

_____. *The Wonders of Bible Chronology*. (First printing 1922. Swengel, PA. Reiner Publications, 1977.)

Mayhue, Richard. *Divine Healing Today*. (Chicago. Moody Press, 1983.)

McConnell, D. R. *A Different Gospel*. (Peabody, MA. Hendrickson House Publishers, 1988.)

McDowell, Josh. *Evidence that Demands a Verdict: Historical Evidence for the Christian Faith*. (Arrow Springs, CA. Campus Crusade for Christ, 1971.)

McElveen, Floyd C. *The Mormon Illusion*. Venture, CA. Gospel Light Publishing, 1979.)

McFetridge, Nathaniel S. *Calvinism and History*. (Philadelphia, PA. Presbyterian Board of Publication, 1882.)

McGee, J. Vernon, *Thru the Bible*. Five volumes. (Nashville, TN. Thomas Nelson Publishers, 1994.)

McGarvey, J.W. & Pendleton, Philip Y. *The Fourfold Gospel: A Harmony of the Four Gospels*. (Cincinnati, OH. The Standard Publishing Company, 1914.)

McGoldrick, James Edward. *Baptist Successionism: A Crucial Question in Baptist History*. (Lanham, MD. The Scarecrow Press, 1994.)

McIntire, Carl. *Testimony to Christ and a Witness for Freedom*. (Collingswood, NJ. Twentieth Century Reformation Hour, 1962.)

McManners, John. *The Oxford Illustrated History of Christianity*. (NY. Oxford University Press, 1990.)

McNamara, Martin. *Targum and Testament. Aramaic Paraphrases of the Hebrew Bible: A Light on the New Testament*. (Grand Rapids, MI. Eerdmans, 1972.)

_____. *The New Testament and the Palestinian Targum of the Pentateuch*. (Rome. Pontifical Biblical Institute, 1966.)

McQuaid, Elwood. *The Zion Connection*. (Eugene, OR. Harvest House Publishers, 1996.)

Miller, Andrew. *Miller's Church History*. (Addison, IL. Bible Truth Publishers, 1980.)

Miller, H. S. *General Biblical Introduction*. (Houghton, NY. The Word-Bearer Press, 1960.)

Montefiore, Claude J. *Rabbinic Literature and Gospel Teachings*. (NY. KTAV Publishing, House, 1970)

Montgomery, John W. *Evidence for the Faith: Deciding the God Question* (Probe Books, Dallas, TX. 1991.)

Moore, George F. *Judaism in the First Centuries of the Christian Era; the Age of the Tanniaim*. Two volumes. (Cambridge, MA. Harvard University Press, 1927.)

Moorman, Jack. *Early Church Fathers and the Authorized Version: A Demonstration!* (Collingswood, NJ. Bible for Today, 1985.)

_____. *Forever Settled: a Survey of the Documents and History of the Bible.* (Collingswood, NJ. The Dean Burgon Society Press, 1999.)

_____. *Bible Chronology: The Two Great Divides.* (Collingswood, NJ. Bible for Today Press, 1999.)

Morris, Henry M. *The Defender's Study Bible.* (Grand Rapids, MI. World Publishing, 995.)

Morris, Henry M, and John C. Whitcomb. *The Genesis Flood: The Biblical Record and its Scientific Implications.* (Philadelphia, PA. Presbyterian and Reformed Publishing Company, 1961.)

Mowinckel, Sigmund. *He that cometh. The Messiah Concept in the Old Testament & Later Judaism.* (Grand Rapids, MI. Eerdmans, 2005.)

Murphy, Ed. *The Handbook for Spiritual Warfare.* (Nashville, TN. Thomas Nelson Publishers, 1992.)

Murray, George L. *Millennial Studies: A Search for Truth.* (Grand Rapids. MI. Baker Book House, 1960.)

Nast, William. *The Gospel Records: Their Genuineness, Authenticity, Historic, Verity, and Inspiration.* (Cincinnati, OH. Published by Cranston & Curts, 1866.)

Neander, Augustus. *The Life of Christ in its Historical Connection and Development.* (NY. Harper & Row, 1858.)

Nee, Watchman, *The Salvation of the Soul.* (NY. Christian Fellowship Publishers, 1978.)

Nelson, Byron C., *The Deluge Story in Stone.* (Minneapolis, MN. Bethany Fellowship, 1968.)

Neusner, Jacob. Translator. *Tosefta.* Six Volumes. (Peabody, MA. Hendrickson House Publishers, 2002.)

Newman, Albert H. *A Manual of Church History.* Two volumes. (Chicago, IL. The American Baptist Publication Society, 1931.)

Nichols, James, and Nichols, William. Translators. *The Works of James Arminius.* Three volumes. (Grand Rapids, MI. Baker Book House reprint, 1991.)

Nicholls, William. *Christian Antisemitism: a History of Hate.* (Northvale, NJ. Jason Aronson, 1993.)

Nolan, Frederick. *An Inquiry into the Integrity of the Greek Vulgate, or Received Text of the New Testament.* (London. F.C. & J. Rivington Publishers, 1815.)

Odeberg, Hugo. *The Fourth Gospel.* (Chicago, IL. Argonault, Inc., Publishers, 1929.)

Oesterreich, T. K. *Possession Demonical & Other, Among Primitive Races, in Antiquity, the Middle Ages, and Modern Times.* (NY. University Books, 1966.)

Ogg, G. A. *The Chronology of the Public Ministry of Jesus.* (London. Longmans, Green & Company, 1931.)

Orchard, Stephen, and Briggs, John H. Editors. *The Sunday School Movement: studies in the Growth and Decline of Sunday Schools.* (Waynesboro, GA. Paternoster, 2007.)

Oropeza, Brisco Javier. *99 Reasons Why No One Knows When Christ Will Return.* (Downers Grove, IL. IVP, 1994.)

Orr, James. *The Problem of the Old Testament.* (NY. Charles Scribner's Sons, 1906.)

Osbeck, Kenneth W. *Singing With Understanding. Including 101 Favorite Hymn Backgrounds.* (Grand Rapids, MI. Kregel Publications 1979.)

Owen, John. *The Death of Death in the Death of Christ.* (London. The Banner of Truth Trust, 1963.)

Packer, J. I. *Evangelicals and Catholics Together.* (NY. Institute on Religion & Public Relations, 1990.)

Paine, Gustavus S. *The Men Behind the King James Version.* (Grand Rapids, MI. Baker Book House Publisher, 1959.) Originally published as *The Learned Men,* by Thomas Y. Corwell Company, 1959.)

Panati, Charles. *Extraordinary Origins of Every -day Things.* (NY. Harper & Row, 1987.)

_____. Sacred *Origin of Profound Things.* (NY. Penguin Books, 1996.)

Parker, Gary. *Creation Facts of Life.* (Colorado Springs, CO. Master Books, 1994.)

Partee, Charles, *The Theology of John Calvin.* (Louisville, KY. Westminster Press, 2008.)

Patai, Raphael. *The Messiah Texts.* (NY. Avon Books, 1979.)

Patton, Francis L. *A Summary of Christian Doctrine.* Philadelphia, PA. The Westminster Press, 1911.)

Pelikan, Jaroslav. *The Christian Tradition: A History of the Development of Doctrine.* Five volumes. (Chicago, IL. The University of Chicago Press, 1989.)

Pentecost, J. Dwight. *Things to Come.* (Grand Rapids, MI. Dunham Publishing Company, 1966.)

_____. *The Words and Works of Jesus Christ.* (Dallas, TX. Dallas Theological Seminary, 1986.)

Peters, Edward. Editor. *Heresy and Authority in Medieval Europe.* (London. Scolar Press, 1980.)

Peterson, Robert A., and Williams, Michael G. *Why I Am Not an Arminian.* (Downers Grove, IL. Intervarsity Press, 2004.)

Pfeiffer, Charles F. *Between the Testaments.* (Grand Rapids, MI. Baker Book House, 1961.)

_____. *The Patriarchal Age.* (London, Pickering & Inglis Ltd., 1961.)

Phillips, J. B. *Ring of Truth.* (NY. The MacMillan Company. 1967.)

Pickering, Wilbur N. *The Identity of the New Testament Text.* (Nashville, TN. Thomas Nelson Publishers, 1980.)

Pieper, Donald. *Luther's Large Catechism Part 1-2: The Creed, Lord's Prayer, Baptism, Lord's Supper.* (Milwaukee, WI. Northwestern Publishing House, 1998.)

Pirkle, Estus. *The 1611 King James Bible.* (Southhaven, MA. The King's Press, 1994.)

Porter, Stanley. Editor. *The Messiah in the Old and New Testaments.* (Grand Rapids, MI. Eerdmans, 2007.)

Poythress, Vern S. *Understanding Dispensationalists.* (Grand Rapids, MI. Zondervan Publishing House, 1987.)

Price, Randall. *The Coming Last Days Temple.* (Eugene, OR. Harvest House Publishers, 1999.)

Rabow, Jerry. *50 Jewish Messiahs: the Untold Life Stories of 50 Jewish Messiahs Since Jesus . . .* (Jerusalem, NY. Gefen Publishing House, 2002.)

Rawls, John. *A Theory of Justice.* (Oxford University Press, 1985.)

Rea, Walter T. *The White Lie.* (Turlock, CA. M & R Publications, 1982.)

Reese, Edward. *The Reese Chronological Bible.* (Minneapolis, MN. Bethany House Publishers, 1980.)

Relfe, Mary Stewart. *When Your Money Fails. The "666 System" is Here.* (Montgomery, Al. Ministries, 1981.)

Renan, Joseph-Ernest. *Antichrist.* Translated by W. C. Hutchinson. (London, Walter Scott, 1899.)

Rhodes, Ron. *The Coming Oil Storm.* (Eugene, OR. Harvest House Publishers, 2010.)

Rhodes, Erroll F., & Lupas, Liana, Editors. *The Translators to the Reader: The Original Preface of the KING JAMES VERSION of 1611 Revisited.* (NY. American Bible Society, 1997.)

Richardson, Don. *Eternity in Their Hearts.* (Ventura, CA. Regal Books, 1984.)

Ridley, Mark. *Evolution.* (NY. Oxford University Press, 1997.)

Riddlebarger, Kim. *The Man of Sin. Uncovering the Truth About the Antichrist.* (Grand Rapids, MI. Baker Book House, 2006.)

Ridenour, Fritz. *So What's the Difference?* (Ventura, CA. Regal Books, 2001.)

Roberts, Alexander, and Donaldson, James. Editors. *The Ante-Nicene Fathers,* volumes 1 through 7. (Grand Rapids, MI. Eerdmans, 1989.)

Roberts, R. Philip. *Mormonism Unmasked: Confronting the Contradictions Between Mormon Beliefs and True Christianity.* (Broadman & Holman Publishers, 1998.)

Robertson, A. T. *Luke the Historian in the Light of Research.* (NY. Charles Scribner's Sons, 1920.)

_____. *Word Pictures of the New Testament.* Six volumes. (Nashville, TN. Broadman Press, 1991.)

Rocco, Sha. *The Masculine Cross and Ancient Sex Worship.* (NY. Commonwealth Co., 1904.)

Rodwell, J. M. *The Koran.* Translated by the Rev. J. M. Rodwell. (NY. J. M. Dent & Sons Publishers, 1909.)

Rordorf, Willy. *SUNDAY. The History of the Day of Rest and Worship in the Earliest Centuries of the Christian Church.* (Philadelphia, PA. The Westminister Press, 1968.)

Rosenberg, Joel C. *Epicenter.* (Carol Stream ILL. Harvest House Publishers, 2008.)

Rosenthal, Marvin J. *The Pre-Wrath Rapture of the Church.* (Nashville, TN. Thomas Nelson Publishers, 1990.)

Rossetti, Stephen J., *Slayer of the Soul: child Sexual Abuse and the Catholic Church.* (Mystic, CT. Twenty-Third Publications, 1990.)

Rowe, Dewey. *Serpent Handling as a Cultural Phenomenon in Southern Appalachia.* (NY. Carlton Press, 1986.)

Rummel, Erika. *Erasmus' Annotations on the New Testament.* (Toronto. University of Toronto Press, 1986.)

Rushdoony, Rousas J. *The "Atheism" of the Early Church.* (Blackheath, N.S.W. Australia. The Logos Foundation, 1983.)

Russell, J. Stuart. *The Parousia.* (Grand Rapids, MI. Baker Book House, Reprinted from the 1883 edition, 1983.)

Ryle, J. C. *The Cross; a Call to the Fundamentals of Religion.* (NY. Depository 683 Broadway, 1852.)

Ryrie, Charles C. *Ryrie Study Bible, King James Version.* (Chicago, IL. Moody Press, 1976.)

_____. *Dispensationalism Today.* (Chicago, IL. Moody Press, 1965.)

Schaeffer, Edith. *Christianity is Jewish.* (Wheaton IL. Tyndale House Publishers, 1975.)

Schaff, Philip. *The Creeds of Christendom.* (NY. Harper & Row, 1905.)

_____. *History of the Christian Church.* Eight volumes. (Grand Rapids, MI. Eerdmans, 1910.)

Schafer, Peter. *Jesus in the Talmud.* (Princeton, NJ. Princeton University Press, 2007.)

Schurer, Emil. *A History of the Jewish People in the Time of Jesus Christ.* Five volumes. (Peabody, MA. Hendrickson House Publishers, 1994.)

Scofield, C. I. *The Scofield Reference Bible.* (NY. Oxford University Press, 1945.)

Scott, Julius J. *Customs and Controversies: Intertestamental Jewish Backgrounds of the New Testament.* (Grand Rapids, MI. Baker Book House, 1995.)

Scott, Otto. *James 1: The Fool as King.* Two volumes. (Vallectio, CA. Ross House Books, 1986.)

Scott, Steven K. *The Richest Man Who Ever Lived; King Solomon's Secrets to Success, Wealth, and Happiness.* (NY, A Currency Book, Doubleday, 2006.)

Scott, Thomas. *The New Testament; according to the Authorized Version . . .* (Philadelphia, PA. J. B. Lippincott, 1857.)

Scrivener, Frederick. *The Authorized Edition of the English Bible (1611), Its Subsequent Reprints and Modern Representatives.* (London. Cambridge University Press, 1884.)

Scroggie, W. *A Guide to the Gospels.* (London. Pickering & Inglis, 1948.)

Seutonius. *The Twelve Caesars.* (Baltimore, MD. Penguin Books, 1951.)

Shaw, S. B. *The Dying Testimonies of Saved and Unsaved . . .* (Cincinnati OH. Walter, 1898.)

Shedd, William G. T. *Dogmatic Theology.* Three volumes. (NY. Charles Scribner's Sons, 1889.)

Sidwell, Mark. *Faith of our Fathers: Scenes from Church History.* (Greenville, SC. Bob Jones University Press, 1980.)

Shortt, David A. *Calvinism or Arminianism.* (Bloomington, IN., 2004.)

Showers, Renald. E. *There Really is a Difference!* (Bellmawr, NJ. The Friends of Israel Gospel Ministry, Inc., 1990.)

Silver, J. F. *The Lord's Return.* (NY. Fleming H. Revell Company, 1914.)

Skolfield, Ellis H. *Demons in the Church.* (Fort Myers, FL. Fish House Publishers, 1993.)

Skolnick, Fred, and Berenbaum, Michael. Editors. / *Encyclopedia Judaica.* (Detroit, MI. Macmillan Reference USA in association with the Keter Publications House, 2007.)

Smail, Raymond C. *The Crusaders in Syria and the Holy Land.* (London. Thames and Hudson, 1973.)

Smith, Arthur E. *Studies in Leviticus.* (Waynesboro, Ga. Christian Missions Press, Inc., 1968.)

Smith, Gerald D. *The Time is at Hand.* (Brisbane, Australia, G. D. Smith, self- published, 1922.)

Smith, Simeon O. *The Wednesday Crucifixion of Christ.* (San Antonio, TX. Christian Jew Hour, 1966.)

Smith, William. *Smith's Dictionary of the Bible.* Four volumes. (Grand Rapids, MI. Baker Book House, 1981.)

Snowden, J. H. *The Coming of the Lord: Will it be Premillennial?* (NY. The Macmillan Company, 1919.)

Snyder, James. Editor. *Tozer: Fellowship of the Burning Heart.* (Orlando, FL. Bridge Logos, 2006.)

Spencer, Robert. *The Truth About Muhammad.* (Washington, D.C. Regnery Publishing, Inc., 2006.)

Spittler, Russell P. *Cults and Isms.* Grand Rapids, MI. Baker Book House, 1962.)

Stanton, V. H. *The Jewish and the Christian Messiah.* (Edinburgh, Scotland. T. & T. Clark, 1886.)

Steele, David N. & Thomas, Curtis C. *The Five Points of Calvinism.* (Phillipsburg, NJ. Presbyterian and Reformed Publishing Company, 1963.)

Stein, Robert H. *The Method and Message of Jesus' Teachings.* (Philadelphia, PA. The Westminister Press, 1978.)

Steinfels, Robert. *A People Adrift: The Crisis of the Roman Catholic Church in America.* (NY. Simeon & Schuster, 2003.)

Stern, David C. *Jewish New Testament Commentary.* (Clarksville, MD. Jewish New Testament Publishers, Inc., 1995.)

Strachan, Gordan. *The Pentecostal Theology of Edward Irving.* (Peabody, MA. Hendrickson House Publishers, 1973.)

Strobel, Lee. *The Case for the Real Jesus: a Journalist Investigates Currant Attacks on the Identity of Christ.* (Grand Rapids, MI. Zondervan Publishing House, 2007.)

_____. *The Case for Christ: A Journalist's Personal Investigation of the Evidence of Jesus.* (Santa Monica, CA. Lionsgate, 2007.)

Strong, Augustus. *Systematic Theology.* (Valley Forge, PA. Judson Press, 1976.)

Sue, Eugene. *The Wandering Jew.* (NY. The Modern Library, 1940.)

Sumner, Robert L. *Herbert W. Armstrong: A False Prophet.* (Murfreesboro, TN. Sword of the Lord Foundation, 1981.)

Sutton, Ray. *Second Chance. Biblical Blueprints for Divorce and Remarriage.* (Fort Worth, TX. Dominion Press, 1988.)

Swanson, Reuben J. *The Horizontal Line Synopsis of the Gospels.* (Dillsboro, NC. Western North Carolina Press, Inc., 1975.)

Sweet, William W. *The Story of Religion in America.* (NY. Harper & Row, 1950.)

Talmud, The Soncino. CD Rom from the Judaic Classics Library. (Chicago, IL. Davka Corporation, 1991-1995.)

Taticus II. Moore, C. H. Translator. (Cambridge, MS. Harvard University Press, MCMLXXX.)

Terry, Milton S. *Biblical Hermeneutics.* (NY. Philips and Hunt, reprint, 1883.)

Thayer, Joseph Henry. *A Greek-English Lexicon of the New Testament.* Grand Rapids, MI. Zondervan Publishing House, 1973.)

Thayer, Thomas, B. *The Origin and History of the Doctrine of Endless Punishment.* (Boston, J. M. Usher, 1856.)

Thiessen, Henry C. *Lectures in Systematic Theology.* (Grand Rapids, MI. Eerdmans, 1977.)

Thomson, William M. *The Land and the Book. . .* (NY. Harper & Brothers, 1880.)

Torbet, Robert G. *A History of the Baptist.* (London. The Carey Kingsgate Press Limited, 1965.)

Torrance, Thomas F. & Walker, Robert T. *Incarnation: the Person and Life of Christ.* Downers Grove, IL. IVP Academic, 2008.)

Toynbee, J. M. C. *Death and Burial in the Roman World.* (Ithaca, NY. Cornell University Press, 1971.)

Tozer, A. W. *A Treasury of A. W. Tozer: A Collection of Tozer Favorites.* (Grand Rapids, MI. Baker Book House, 1980.)

Trulin, Paul G. *The Pursued Generation: the Generation That Will Give Birth to the Return of Christ.* (Champlain, NY. Moriah Publications, 2007.)

Unger, Merrill F. *The New Unger's Bible Dictionary.* (Chicago, IL. Moody Press, 1988.)

Ussher, James. *The Annals of the World.* Revised and updated by Larry and Marion Pierce. (Original printing 1658. USA. Master Books, 2003.)

Van der Waal, *Hal Lindsey and Biblical Prophecy.* (Neerlandia, Atlanta, GA. 1991.)

Van Scott, Miriam. *Encyclopedia of Hell.* (NY. St. Martin's Press, 1998.)

Van Voorst, Robert E. *Jesus Outside the New Testament. An Introduction to the Ancient Evidence.* (Grand Rapids, MI. Eerdmans, 2000.)

Vance, Laurence M. *A Brief History of English Bible Translations.* (Pensacola, FL. Vance Publications, 1993.)

_____. *The Other Side of Calvinism.* (Pensacola, FL. Vance Publications, 1999.)

Vedder, Henry C. *A Short History of the Baptists.* (Valley Forge, PA. Judson Press, 1907.)

Verduin, Leonard. *The Reformers and Their Stepchildren.* (Grand Rapids, MI. Eerdmans, 1964.)

Vine, W. E. *An Expository Dictionary of New Testament Words.* (Oliphants Ltd., Edinburgh, 1959.)

Walmsley, Luke S. *Fighters and Martyrs for the Freedom of Faith.* (London. James Clarke & Company, 1912.)

Walvoord, John F. *Daniel: The Key to Prophetic Revelation.* (Chicago, IL. Moody Press, 1971.)

————. *The Millennial Kingdom.* (Grand Rapids, MI. Zondervan Publishing House, 1959.)

Warburton, William. *Julian or a Discourse Concerning the Earthquake and Fiery Eruption, which Defeated that Emperor's Attempt to Rebuild the temple.* (Printed for J. and P. Knapton, 1650.)

Ward, J. S. M. *Who Was Hiram Abiff?* (London. The Baskerville Press Ltd. n.d,)

Warfield, B. B. *Counterfeit Miracles.* (Carlisle, PA. Banner of Truth Trust, 1983.)

Warner, Marina. *Alone of All Her Sex: the Myth and the Cult of the Virgin Mary.* (London. Quartet books, 1978.)

Warns, Johannes. *Baptism.* (Grand Rapids, MI. Kregel Publications, 1962.)

Washington, Sandra Y. *Eschatology: the Signs of the Times of Jesus Christ's Soon Return: His Coming is Closer Than You Think.* (Bloomington, IL. Questar, 2010.)

Watson, Alan. *Rome of the XII Tables. Persons and Property.* (Princeton, NJ. Princeton University Press, 1975.)

Water, Mark. *Encyclopedia of World Religions, Cults & the Occult.* (Chattanooga, TN. AMG Publishers, 2006.)

Webb, James. *The Occult Underground.* (La Salle, IL. Open Court Publishing Company. 1974.)

Weldon, John. *Decoding the Bible Code: Can We Trust the Message?* (Eugene, OR. Harvest House Publishers, 1998.)

Wells, David F. *No Place for Truth or Whatever Happened to Evangelical Theology.* (Grand Rapids, MI. Eerdmans, 1993.)

Wells, Jerry L. and Dongell, Joseph R. *Why I am not a Calvinist.* (Downers Grove ILL. Intervarsity Press, 2004.)

Westcott, Arthur. *Life and Letters of Brooke Foss Westcott.* Two volumes. (London. Macmillan & Company, 1903.)

Westcott, B. F. *The Epistles of St. John.* (Grand Rapids, MI. Eerdmans, 1949.)

Whisenant, Edgar C. *On Borrowed Time: and 88 Reasons Why the Rapture Could Be in 1988 . . .* (Nashville, TN. World Bible Society, 1988.)

White, Ellen Gould. *The Great Controversy.* (Nampi, ID. Pacific Press, 2002.)

White, James R. *The King James Only Controversy. Can you Trust the Modern Versions?* (Minneapolis, MN. Bethany House Publishers, 1995.)

Wight, Fred H. *Manners and Customs of Bible Lands.* (Chicago, IL. Moody Press, 1953.)

Wiker, Benjamin. *The Darwin Myth: the life and lies of Charles Darwin.* (Washington, D.C. Regnery Publishing Inc., 2009.)

Wilkinson, John. *Israel My Glory.* (London. Milday Mission to the Jews, 1894.)

Williams, Alesia T. *Mark of the Beast.* (Lake Mary, FL. Creation House, 2010.)

Wilson, Dwight. *Armageddon NOW!* (Tyler, TX. Institute for Christian Economics, 1991.)

Wilson, Robert Dick. *Is Higher Criticism Scholarly?* Philadelphia, PA. The Sunday School Times, 1922.

Wolf, Miroslav. *Body Counts- The Dark Side of Christian History.* (Chicago, IL. Christian Century Company, 1902.)

Woodrow, Ralph. *The Babylon Connection.* (Palm Springs, CA. Self published, 1999.)

Worth, Richard. *Heinrich Himmler: murderous Architect of the Holocaust.* Berkeley Heights, NJ. Enslow Publishers, 2005.)

Wright, Christopher J. H. *Knowing the Holy Spirit Through the Old Testament.* (Downers Grove, IL. Intervarsity Press, 2006.)

Wurmbrand, Richard. *Christ on the Jewish Road.* (London. Hodder and Stoughton, 1970.)

————. *Little Notes Which Like Each Other.* (London. Hodder & Stoughton, 1974.)

Yallop, David A., *Beyond Belief: the Catholic Church and the Child Abuse Scandal.* (London. Constable Publishers, 2010.)

Yonge, C. D. Translator. *The Works of Philo.* Complete and Unabridged. (Peabody, MA. Hendrickson House Publishers, 1993.)

Zacchello, Joseph. *Secrets of Romanism.* (NY. Loizeaux Brothers, 1955.)

Zetterholm, Magnus. Editor. *The Messiah: In Early Judaism and Christianity.* (Minneapolis, MN. Fortress Press, 2007.)

Zuck, Roy B. *The Speaker's Quote Book.* (Grand Rapids, MI. Kregel Publications, 1997.)